1 MONTH OF
FREE
READING

at
www.ForgottenBooks.com

By purchasing this book you are eligible for one month membership to ForgottenBooks.com, giving you unlimited access to our entire collection of over 1,000,000 titles via our web site and mobile apps.

To claim your free month visit:
www.forgottenbooks.com/free1118689

ISBN 978-0-331-40149-3
PIBN 11118689

A TREATISE

ON THE

LAW OF MORTGAGES

OF

REAL PROPERTY

BY

LEONARD A. JONES, A. B., LL. B. [HARV.]

AUTHOR OF LEGAL TREATISES AND LATE JUDGE OF THE COURT OF LAND REGISTRATION OF
MASSACHUSETTS

SEVENTH EDITION
IN WHICH THE ORIGINAL TEXT IS THOROUGHLY REVISED BY
THE PUBLISHERS' EDITORIAL STAFF

IN THREE VOLUMES
VOLUME I

INDIANAPOLIS
THE BOBBS-MERRILL COMPANY
PUBLISHERS

PREFACE TO THE SEVENTH EDITION

THE treatise of Judge Leonard A. Jones on the law of real estate mortgages, in its various editions, has been used and relied upon as authority by the bench and bar of this country for nearly forty years.

The favor with which the profession has received former editions of this work may be attributed largely to the fact that Judge Jones has discussed, with the skill of a master, those subtle and perplexing questions upon which courts so often are inclined to disagree. Wherever he has found discord among the authorities on a given proposition he has endeavored to find the fundamental principle by which these differences may be harmonized, or failing in this, he has stated what he considers to be the correct rule. Many of these opinions thus stated by him have come to be the acknowledged rule of law by their subsequent acceptance and adoption by the courts.

Sufficient reason for this new edition is found in the growth of the subject in the nearly twelve years that have elapsed since the publication of the sixth edition. In this enlarged edition of the work we have retained the original text, except in a few instances where the rules have been changed to conform to modern conditions.

We have added considerable to the text by way of explanatory illustrations, so as to enable the reader to see the true use which is made of the rules, and wherever the importance of the principle under discussion is sufficient to warrant it, that part of the language of the court pertinent to the point being considered is stated. This enables us to verify our conclusions, and is an aid to the busy lawyer. Other text that we have added embodies many new and important phases of the law not found in the original work. This has resulted in the addition of hundreds of new sections, which have been added and placed in their proper positions with reference to the other treatment of the subject.

We have inquired into all the statutory regulations, and brought the citations thereto down to date. All the important late cases have been cited either in support of the original text or in support of the added new text.

The law of corporate bonds and mortgages is the subject of a separate treatment by the author and is not included in this work.

FROM THE PREFACE TO THE FIRST EDITION

THE Law of Mortgages is a subject which can not be treated altogether with reference to general principles. At the present time, two opposite theories of the nature of a mortgage hold about equal sway in this country, and this difference of view at the foundation of the subject has naturally led to many divergences in the details of it. It is a subject, too, which legislation, directly and indirectly, largely controls. All that part of it which relates to remedies is closely connected with the systems of Civil Procedure in the several States, which are quite dissimilar. The author has endeavored to follow a natural order of arrangement in this treatise; and while presenting not merely the common law of the subject, but as well the modifications of that law made through statutory enactments and judicial decisions, in order to avoid confusion of statement, and to enable one who consults the book to turn with as little trouble as possible to the statement of the law upon any part of the subject for any State in the Union, he has stated in detail for each State the law upon some of the more important divisions of the subject, in which there is a want of harmony. In this way, at the same time, a fuller presentation of the law and of the authorities upon these topics has been made than would otherwise have been practicable.

TABLE OF CONTENTS
VOLUME ONE

CHAPTER I

NATURE OF A MORTGAGE

I. *History of the Development of the Law,* §§ 1–16
II. *The Nature of a Mortgage in the Different States,* §§ 17–59

I. *History of the Development of the Law*

II. *The Nature of a Mortgage in the Different States*

CHAPTER II

FORM AND REQUISITES OF A MORTGAGE

I. *The Form Generally,* §§ 60–62

II. *The Formal Parts of the Deed,* §§ 63–68a

III. *The Condition,* §§ 69–78a

IV. *Special Stipulations,* §§ 79–80

V. *Execution and Delivery,* §§ 81–89

VI. *Filling Blanks, Making Alterations and Reforming,* §§ 90–101a

I. *The Form Generally*

II. *The Formal Parts of the Deed*

III. *The Condition*

IV. *Special Stipulations*

V. *Execution and Delivery*

VI. *Filling Blanks, Making Alterations, and Reforming*

CHAPTER III

THE PARTIES TO A MORTGAGE

PART I

WHO MAY GIVE A MORTGAGE

PART II

WHO MAY TAKE A MORTGAGE

I. *Introductory*

II. *Disability of Insanity*

III. *Disability of Infancy*

IV. *Married Women*

CHAPTER IV

WHAT MAY BE THE SUBJECT OF A MORTGAGE

I. *Existing Interests in Real Property*, §§ 136–148
II. *Accessions to the Mortgaged Property*, §§ 149–161a

I. *Existing Interests in Real Property*

II. *Accessions to the Mortgaged Property*

CHAPTER V

EQUITABLE MORTGAGES

I. *By Agreements and Informal Mortgages*, §§ 162–171
II. *By Assignments of Contracts of Purchase*, §§ 172–178
III. *By Deposit of Title Deeds*, §§ 179–188

I. *By Agreements and Informal Mortgages*

CHAPTER VI

VENDOR'S LIEN BY CONTRACT OR RESERVATION

CHAPTER VII

ABSOLUTE DEED AND AGREEMENT TO RECONVEY

I. *When They Constitute a Mortgage in Law*, §§ 241–255

II. *When They Constitute a Sale or a Conditional Sale*, §§ 256–281

I. *When They Constitute a Mortgage in Law*

II. *When They Constitute a Sale or Conditional Sale*

CHAPTER VIII

PAROL EVIDENCE TO PROVE AN ABSOLUTE DEED A MORTGAGE

I. *The Grounds Upon Which it is Admitted,* §§ 282-323
II. *What Facts are Considered,* §§ 323a-342d

I. *The Grounds Upon Which it is Admitted*

II. *What Facts are Considered*

CHAPTER IX

DEBT SECURED

I. *Description of the Debt,* §§ 343–363
II. *Future Advances,* §§ 364–378
III. *Mortgage of Indemnity,* §§ 379–387
IV. *Mortgages for Support,* §§ 388–395

I. *Description of the Debt*

II. *Future Advances*

III. *Mortgage of Indemnity*

IV. *Mortgages for Support*

CHAPTER X

INSURANCE

I. *Insurable Interests of Mortgagor and Mortgagee*

II. *Insurance by the Mortgagor for the Benefit of the Mortgagee*

III. *Insurance by the Mortgagee*

IV. *A Mortgage is not an Alienation*

CHAPTER XI

FIXTURES

I. *Rules for Determining What Fixtures a Mortgage Covers,* §§ 428–443

II. *Machinery in Mills,* §§ 444–451

III. *Rolling Stock of Railways,* §§ 452–452a

IV. *Remedies for Removal of Fixtures,* §§ 453–455

I. *Rules for Determining What Fixtures a Mortgage Covers*

CHAPTER XII

RECORDING AS AFFECTING PRIORITY

I. *Nature and Application of Registry Acts*

II. *Requisites as to Execution and Acknowledgment*

III. *Requisites as to the Time and Manner of Recording*

IV. *Errors in the Record*

V. *The Effect of a Record Duly Made*

VI. *Torrens System of Registration*

CHAPTER XIII

NOTICE AS AFFECTING PRIORITY

I. *Notice as Affecting Priority under the Registry Acts,* §§ 538–542

II. *Actual Notice,* §§ 543–559

III. *Implied Notice,* §§ 560–570

IV. *Constructive Notice,* §§ 571–582

V. *Lis Pendens,* §§ 583–585

VI. *Possession as Notice,* §§ 586–601

VII. *Fraud as Affecting Priority,* §§ 602–603

VIII. *Negligence and Miscellaneous Matters Affecting Priority,* §§ 604–609

I. *Notice as Affecting Priority under the Registry Acts*

II. *Actual Notice*

III. *Implied Notice*

IV. *Constructive Notice*

V. *Lis Pendens*

VI. *Possession as Notice*

VII. *Fraud Affecting Priority*

CHAPTER XIV

VOID AND USURIOUS MORTGAGES

I. *Void Mortgages,* §§ 609a–632

II. *Usury,* §§ 633–663

I. *Void Mortgages*

II. *Usury*

VOLUME TWO

CHAPTER XV

A MORTGAGOR'S RIGHTS AND LIABILITIES

I. *As to Third Persons*

II. *As to the Mortgagee*

III. *His Personal Liability to the Mortgagee*

IV. *After-acquired Titles and Improvements*

V. *Waste by Mortgagor*

CHAPTER XVI

MORTGAGEE'S RIGHTS AND LIABILITIES

I. *The Nature of His Estate or Interest, §§ 699–706a*

II. *His Rights Against the Mortgagor, §§ 707–721*

III. *His Liability to Third Persons, §§ 722–734*

I. *The Nature of His Estate or Interest*

II. *His Rights Against the Mortgagor*

CHAPTER XVII

PURCHASER'S RIGHTS AND LIABILITIES

I. *Purchase Subject to a Mortgage*

II. *Assumption of Mortgage by Purchaser*

CHAPTER XIX

ASSIGNMENT OF MORTGAGES

I. *Formal Assignment*

II. *Compelling Assignment*

III. *Who May Make an Assignment*

IV. *What Constitutes an Assignment*

V. *Equitable Assignments*

VI. *Construction and Effect of Assignments*

VII. *Whether an Assignee Takes Subject to Equities*

CHAPTER XXI

PAYMENT AND DISCHARGE

I. *Tender Before and After Default*

CHAPTER XXII

REDEMPTION OF A MORTGAGE

I. *Redemption a Necessary Incident of a Mortgage*

II. *Circumstances Affecting Redemption*

III. *When Redemption May Be Made*

IV. *Who May Redeem*

V. *The Sum Payable to Effect Redemption*

CHAPTER XXIII

MORTGAGEE'S ACCOUNT

I. *Liability to Account*

II. *What the Mortgagee Is Chargeable With*

III. *Allowances for Repairs and Improvements.*

IV. *Allowance for Compensation*

V. *Allowances for Disbursements*

VI. *Annual Rests*

CHAPTER XXIV

WHEN THE RIGHT TO REDEEM IS BARRED

I. *The Statute of Limitations Applies by Analogy*

II. *When the Statute Begins to Run*

III. *What Prevents the Running of the Statute*

CHAPTER XXV

WHEN THE RIGHT TO ENFORCE A MORTGAGE ACCRUES

CHAPTER XXVI

WHEN THE RIGHT TO FORECLOSE IS BARRED

CHAPTER XXVII

REMEDIES FOR ENFORCING A MORTGAGE

I. *Are Concurrent*

II. *Personal Remedy Before Foreclosure*

III. *Personal Remedy After Foreclosure*

CHAPTER XXVIII

FORECLOSURE BY ENTRY AND POSSESSION

I. *Nature of the Remedy*

II. *Statutory Provisions*

III. *The Entry*

IV. *The Possession*

V. *The Certificate of Witnesses*

VI. *The Certificate of the Mortgagor*

VII. *When the Limitation Commences*

VIII. *Record of the Certificate*

IX. *Effect of the Foreclosure Upon the Mortgage Debt*

X. *Waiver of Entry and Foreclosure*

CHAPTER XXIX

FORECLOSURE BY WRIT OF ENTRY

I. *Nature of and Where Used*

II. *Who May Maintain*

III. *Against Whom the Action May Be Brought*

IV. *The Pleadings and Evidence*

V. *The Defenses*

VI. *The Conditional Judgment*

CHAPTER XXX

STATUTORY PROVISIONS RELATING TO FORECLOSURE AND REDEMPTION

CHAPTER XXXI

PARTIES TO AN EQUITABLE SUIT FOR FORECLOSURE

I. *Who Are the Proper Parties Plaintiff*

II. *Who Are the Necessary or Proper Parties Defendant*

III. *Intervention, New Parties and Process*

VOLUME THREE

CHAPTER XXXII

FORECLOSURE BY EQUITABLE SUIT

I. *Jurisdiction, and the Object of the Suit*

II. *The Bill of Complaint*

III. *The Answer and Defense*

CHAPTER XXXIII

APPOINTMENT OF A RECEIVER

I. *When a Receiver will be Appointed*

II. *Duties and Powers of a Receiver*

CHAPTER XXXIV

DECREE OF STRICT FORECLOSURE

I. *Nature and Use of the Remedy*

II. *In What States It Is Used*

III. *Pleadings and Practice*

IV. *Setting Aside and Opening the Foreclosure*

CHAPTER XXXV

DECREE OF SALE

I. *A Substitute for Foreclosure*

II. *Form and Requisites of the Decree*

III. *The Conclusiveness of the Decree*

IV. *The Amount of the Decree*

V. *Costs*

CHAPTER XXXVI

FORECLOSURE SALES UNDER DECREE OF COURT

I. *Mode and Terms of Sale*

II. *Sale in Parcels*

III. *Order of Sale*

CHAPTER XXXVII

APPLICATION OF PROCEEDS OF SALE

I. *Payment of the Mortgage Debt*

II. *Disposition of the Surplus*

CHAPTER XXXVIII

JUDGMENT IN AN EQUITABLE SUIT FOR A DEFICIENCY

CHAPTER XXXIX

STATUTORY PROVISIONS RELATING TO POWER OF SALE MORTGAGES AND TRUST DEEDS

I. *Introductory*

1722. Necessity of power of sale in English mortgages.

II. *Statutory Provisions in the Several States*

CHAPTER XL

POWER OF SALE MORTGAGES AND TRUST DEEDS

I. *The Nature and Use of Powers of Sale*

SECTION
1764. In general.
1765. Validity of power.
1766. Scope of powers in mortgages used in England.
1767. When power of sale mortgages first used in United States.
1768. How far a power of sale a necessary incident of a mortgage.
1769. Deeds of trust distinguished from mortgages with power to sell.
1770. Why deed of trust preferred to mortgage.
1771. Trustee the agent of both parties.
1771a. Effect of trustee's irregular sale and conveyance.
1772. Where trustee claims debt secured.

II. *Power of Sale a Cumulative Remedy*

SECTION
1773. Power of sale a cumulative remedy.
1774. New trustee.
1774a. What laws govern enforcement of deeds of trust.
1775. Sale is by power and not by decree where court enforces power.
1776. When debt is unliquidated.

III. *Formalities in Creation of Power*

SECTION
1777. Form of power.
1777a. Power conferred by married women.
1777b. Stipulating when power may be exercised.
1777c. Payment of taxes a condition.
1777d. Consent of grantor to exercise power.
1778. Form of power authorizing sale.
1779. What is a sufficient power.
1780. Acceptance of trust.
1781. Obvious error on face of power.
1782. Entry and possession under power.
1783. Foreclosure by mortgagee after he has taken rents and profits.
1784. Necessity for record of mortgage or power of sale.
1785. Who may exercise power.
1786. When power may be executed by executor or administrator of mortgagee.
1787. Effect of assignment of mortgage with power of sale.

XV. *Costs and Expenses*

XVI. *The Surplus*

THE LAW OF MORTGAGES
OF REAL PROPERTY

CHAPTER I

NATURE OF A MORTGAGE

I. *History of the Development of the Law,* §§ 1–16

II. *The Nature of a Mortgage in the Different States,* §§ 17–59

I. *History of the Development of the Law*

§ 1. Antiquity of mortgages.—Mortgages owe their origin more to the necessities of men in civilized life than to the creative genius of any particular individual, age, or nation. They were in no sense a subject of invention, but followed as a necessity in the wake of civilization. The necessity of credit, and the consequent sudden demand for money in a moment of business or commercial embarrassment would naturally suggest the idea of a mortgage as the quickest method of raising it, and at the same time affording to the lender a perfect security, easy of transfer, which may itself in turn render to such lender the same service that it did to the original mortgagor.

1

That mortgages, or pledges in the nature of mortgages, were not unknown to the nations of antiquity may be inferred from the following Scriptural language: "Some also there were that said, We have mortgaged our lands, vineyards and houses, that we may buy corn, because of the dearth."[1] It is certain that mortgages of some nature were known among the ancient Jews, and it is believed by some writers that the practice of mortgaging lands had its origin with them.[2] By the Jewish law, land could not be aliened beyond the next jubilee, which occurred every fifty years, and the original owner could redeem at any time during the fifty years on payment of the value to be computed from the date of redemption to the next jubilee. When the day of jubilee arrived the land reverted to the original owner discharged of the debt by operation of the law. From the Jews the idea of a mortgage seems to have passed to the Greeks and Romans. But the Romans were the first to make a distinction between things pledged and things mortgaged. They recognized two sorts of transfer of property as security for debts, namely, the pignus and the hypotheca. The pignus or pledge was where anything was pledged as a security for a debt, and the possession of the thing pledged passed to the creditor upon the condition that he would return it to the debtor when the debt was paid. The hypotheca was where the thing pledged was not delivered to the creditor, but remained in the possession of the debtor.[3]

The civil law made little distinction between mortgages of real and mortgages of personal property, whether pledged or hypothecated; but the term pledge became more commonly used in reference to a chattel, so the term pignus came to signify in strictness a pledge of movable, and the word hypotheca of immovable property. The Roman hypotheca closely corresponds with our present idea of a mortgage.[4] The historians are at variance as to whether the idea of pledging or mortgaging real property was borrowed from the Romans by the English. No less an authority than Littleton contends that mortgages were introduced in England less upon the model of the Roman pignus or hypotheca, than upon the common law of conditions,[5] an observation which can not at least apply to the equity of redemption. It is nevertheless true that the law of feuds and tenures was decidedly opposed to mortgages; but it is not altogether improbable that, during

---

[1] Nehemiah, Chap. V, 3.
[2] See Cunaeus, pp. 11–14; Ancient Universal History, pp. 130, 131.
[3] Story's Eq. Jur. § 1005.
[4] Story's Eq. Jur. § 1006.
[5] Litt. § 332.

the long period of Roman possession, some of the civil law principles were engrafted upon the common law of England.

§ 1a. Mortgages used by the Anglo-Saxons.—Very little is known concerning the nature of Anglo-Saxon real property law on the continent. It seems to be admitted, however, that a right of free alienation of property existed, which implied the right of mortgage or conditional sale. When they invaded England they found there Roman law and Roman authority. There can be no doubt, therefore, that the Anglo-Saxon law was most sensibly affected by Roman influence. However this may be, it is reasonably certain that mortgages, or at least pledges of land in the nature of mortgages, were not unknown to the Anglo-Saxons in England before the Norman conquest.

In at least two ancient charters the transactions are clearly enough defined to show that land was given as security for the payment of money, though as to the manner and form of the transfer, and the rights of the parties under it, very little can be made out. The most important of these cases is quoted below.[a] It appears from this that

---

[a] The translation is taken from a collection of essays of much interest published in 1876, entitled Essays in Anglo-Saxon Law. Appendix, Case No. 18, p. 342. See also the Essay on Anglo-Saxon Land Law, p. 106. As a coincidence it may be mentioned that the present chapter with the following quotation had been written before the same charter had appeared, as illustrating Anglo-Saxon mortgages, in the third edition of Mr. Fisher's excellent treatise on Mortgages. It is to be observed that Eadgifu mentioned in this document was queen of Edward the Elder, whose reign was from A. D. 901 to 925.

"Eadgifu makes known to the archbishop and the community of Christ's Church how her land at Cooling came [to her]; that is, that her father left her land and charter as he rightfully got, and his parents left them to him. It happened that her father borrowed thirty pounds of Goda, and assigned him the land in pledge for the money, and he held it seven years. Then it happened about that time that all Kentish men were summoned to Holme on military service; so Sighelm, her father, was unwilling to go to the war with any man's money unpaid, and gave thirty pounds to Goda, and bequeathed his land to Eadgifu, his daughter, and gave her the charter. When he had fallen in war, then Goda denied the return of the money, and refused to give up the land till some time in the sixth year. Then [her kinsman] Byrhsige Dyrineg firmly pressed her claim, until the Witan, who then were, adjudged to Eadgifu that she should cleanse her father's hand by [an oath of] as much value [namely, thirty pounds]. And she took oath to this effect at Aylesford, on the witness of all the people, and there cleansed her father in regard to the return of the money, with an oath of thirty pounds. Even then she was not allowed to enjoy the land until her friends obtained of King Edward that he forbade him [Goda] the land, if he wished to enjoy any [that he held from the king]; and he so let it go. Then it happened, in course of time, that the king brought so serious charges against Goda, that he was adjudged to lose charters and land, all that he held [from the king, and his life to be in the king's hands]. The king then gave him and all his property, char-

the mortgagee was in the possession of the land, and that he doubtless had the use of the land in return for the use of the money loaned by him. Upon the payment of the loan it was his duty to render back the land to the mortgagor, and his failure to do so in this case was the occasion of litigation, commencing in the reign of Edward the Elder, extending through the reigns of Æthelstan, Edmund, Eldred, and Edwy, and finally ending in the reign of Edgar. The tribunal was the Witan, or national assembly, which was also the highest court of law in the kingdom.

From another charter in which refer nce is made to a mortgage, it seems that the title to the mortgaged land, at some time and in some way not revealed, became vested absolutely in the mortgagee, who conveyed away the land. Slight as the knowledge is which these charters give us in respect to the law of the Anglo-Saxon mortgage of real property, it is of interest; for, while we find the elements of our present system of the law of real property in the customary laws of the period preceding the Norman Conquest, we may well expect to find in this source as well the beginnings of the law of mortgage as a part of that system.

§ 2. **Vivum vadium.**—At a later period, as is apparent from the Domesday, pledges of land were frequent. Later still, in the time of Glanville, pledges of land had taken two distinct forms, the

ters, and lands to Eadgifu, to dispose of as she would. Then said she that she durst not, for [fear of] God, make such a return to him as he had merited from her, and gave up to him all his lands except two hides at Osterland, but would not give up the charters before she knew how truly he would hold them in regard to the lands. Then king Edward died, and Æthelstan took the throne. When it seemed to Goda seasonable, he went to King Æthelstan, and prayed him to intercede with Eadgifu for the return of his charters; and the king then did so, and she returned him all except the charter of Osterland; and he relinquished the charter voluntarily to her, and thanked her with humility for the others. And, further, he, with eleven others, gave an oath to her, for born and unborn, that the matter in dispute was forever settled; and this was done in the witness of King Æthelstan and his Witan, at Hamme, near Lewes. And Eadgifu held the land, with the charters, during the days of the two kings, her sons [Æthelstan and Eadmund]. Then Eadred died, and Eadgifu was deprived of all her property; and two sons of Goda (Leofstan and Leofric) took from Eadgifu the two before-mentioned lands at Cooling and Osterland, and said to the child Edwy, who was then chosen king, that they were more rightly theirs than hers. This then remained so until Edgar obtained power; and he and his Witan adjudged that they had been guilty of wicked spoliation, and they adjudged and restored to her her property. Then by the king's leave and witness, and that of all his bishops [and chief men], Eadgifu took the charters, and made a gift of the land to Christ's Church, [and] with her own hands laid them upon the altar, as the property of the community forever."

vivum vadium and the mortuum vadium. The former denoted a pledge of land when the creditor took possession of the land under the conveyance, and held it for a certain period, during which the rents and profits received by him went toward the payment of the debt. Upon payment of the debt the debtor was entitled to have his lands back again, and might recover them by suit if not voluntarily restored. This was apparently the form of the mortgage referred to in the Anglo-Saxon charter of the tenth century already quoted; and the mortgages mentioned in Domesday seem to imply that possession of the property was in the mortgagee; and also, in the time of Glanville, the possession seems usually to have followed the security.[7]

The vivum vadium and also the mortuum vadium, as at first known, were determinable or base fees, with a right of reverter in the feoffor and his heirs, on the payment of a designated sum; but they differed in that the former gave the feoffor a continuing right to redeem, while under the latter the title to the estate and all interest in it became vested in the feoffee, in case the conditions were not punctually performed. The distinguishing characteristics of a vivum vadium were that there was no proviso in the instrument that the conveyance was to be void on payment of the debt, and there was no covenant, express or implied, for such payment.[8]

§ 3. **Vivum vadium and Welsh mortgage distinguished.**—This form of mortgage is like the Welsh mortgage of a later period, in so far that it contains no condition that the conveyance is to be void upon payment of the debt, as is the case with the common mortgage, but the mortgagee had the possession of the property assured to him, and received the rents and profits either in lieu of interest, or in discharge of both principal and interest. Under this form of mortgage the mortgagee had no remedy whatever. He could not sue for the debt. There was no covenant for payment, either express or implied.[9] He could neither compel the mortgagor to redeem, nor cut off his right

---

[7] See also Cortwright v. Cady, 21 N. Y. 343, 344, 78 Am. Dec. 145.

[8] O'Neill v. Gray, 39 Hun (N. Y.) 566.

[9] Lawley v. Hooper, 3 Atk. 280; O'Connell v. Cummins, 2 Ir. Eq. 251; Jortin v. Southeastern R. Co., 6 DeG. M. & G. 270, 3 Eq. Rep. 281, 1 Jur. (N. S.) 433, 24 L. J. ch. 343. Howell v. Price, 1 P. Wms. 291; Longuet v. Scawen, 1 Ves. Sen. 402.

A mortgage which secures a bond, note, or other personal obligation of the mortgagor, and is conditional to become void on payment, is not a Welsh mortgage, or a mortgage in the nature of such a mortgage, though it provides that the mortgagee may collect the rent of the mortgaged premises, and apply the same on account of the mortgage debt. O'Neill v. Gray, 39 Hun (N. Y.) 566.

of redemption by foreclosure. In this respect the transaction was like a conditional sale. The mortgagor could redeem at his option, and could enforce his right either at law or in equity. After full payment of the debt from the rents and profits, the mortgagor's right to redeem would be barred, finally, by the lapse of the statutory period of limitation. This form of security is the same as one form of the Welsh mortgage, or of a mortgage in the nature of a Welsh mortgage, where the property is conveyed to the mortgagee and his heirs, to hold until out of the rents and profits he shall have received both principal and interest.[10] The principal distinction between the ancient vivum vadium and the modern Welsh mortgage seems to be that, while in the former the rents were applied in satisfaction of the principal, in the latter they were received in satisfaction of the interest, the principal generally remaining undisturbed.

§ 4. **Mortuum vadium.**—The mortuum vadium was the designation of a pledge of land of which the mortgagee did not necessarily receive the possession, or have the rents and profits in reduction of the demand. In the time of Glanville this form of security was looked upon with much disfavor as a species of usury. That the creditor was liable to the penalties of usury if he received money for the use of the loan, and was considered dishonest as well, is a sufficient reason why this kind of security, though not prohibited, was then seldom used. The mortuum vadium spoken of by Littleton is the common-law mortgage. It had then become a conditional estate; the condition being that upon payment of the debt at a fixed time the grantor might re-enter, but upon breach of the condition the conveyance became absolute.[11] It was at a later day that the equitable right of redemption after forfeiture became an incident of the mortgage. The nature of the transaction as a mere

---

[10] Coote on Mtg. 208; Rankert v. Clow, 16 Tex. 9; Angier v. Masterson, 6 Cal. 61. See also O'Neill v. Gray, 39 Hun (N. Y.) 566; Howell v. Price, Prec. Ch. 423, 477, 24 Eng. Reprint 189, 214, 1 P. Wms. 291, 2 Vern. Ch. 701, 23 Eng. Reprint 1055.

[11] Littleton's Tenures, lib. iii. ch. 5, § 332. "(Of Estates upon Condition.) item: If a feoffment be made upon such condition that if the feoffor pays to the feoffee, at a certain day, forty pounds of money, that then the feoffor may re-enter; in this case the feoffee is called tenant in mortgage, which is as much to say in French as mortgage, and in Latin mortuum vadium. And it seemeth that the cause why it is called mortgage is, for that it is doubtful whether the feoffor will pay at the day limited such sum or not; and, if he doth not pay, then the land which is put in pledge upon condition for the payment of the money is taken from him forever, and so dead to him upon condition. And if he doth pay the money, then the pledge is dead as to the tenant."

security for a debt was not then regarded, but the rules applicable to other estates upon condition were enforced with all their strictness. This is illustrated in the statement of Littleton, that if the condition was that the debtor should pay a certain sum of money to the mortgagee, no definite time being fixed for the payment, if the debtor died before making payment, a tender of payment by his heir was void, because the time within which the payment should be made was past, the condition that the debtor should pay being as much as to say that he should pay during his lifetime. But if the condition was that the payment should be made by a day certain, then, if the debtor died before that day, his heir or executor might, as his representative, tender the money within the time limited.[12]

By the application of the severe rules of the common law to this form of mortgages, great injustice was done to the debtor. If the conditions of the mortgage were not punctually kept, the title passed absolutely and forever from the debtor. He had no redress whatsoever, until the courts of chancery began to engraft the enlightened and equitable principles of the civil law of mortgages upon the harsh rules of the common law. These courts established the rule, that "once a mortgage, always a mortgage," and that no mortgage could be enforced without a decree of the chancellors. Finally the equity of redemption became a fixed right in every mortgagor.

§ 5. **Mortgages suspended under feudalism.**—The introduction of the feudal system into England by William of Normandy, was a memorable epoch in the history of the English law. Such restraints upon the free alienation of lands were imposed after the Norman Conquest under the feudal system then established that

---

[12] Littleton's Tenures, lib. iii. ch. 5, § 337. "Also, if a feoffment be made upon condition that if the feoffor pay a certain sum of money to the feoffee, then it shall be lawful to the feoffor and his heirs to enter; in this case if the feoffor die before the payment made, and the heir will tender to the feoffee the money, such tender is void, because the time within which this ought to be done is past. For when the condition is, that if the feoffor pay the money to the feoffee, this is as much to say as if the feoffor during his life pay the money to the feoffee; and when the feoffor dieth then the time of the tender is past. But otherwise it is where a day of payment is limited, and the feoffor die before the day; then may the heir tender the money as is aforesaid, for that the time of the tender was not past by the death of the feoffor. Also it seemeth that in such case, where the feoffor dieth before the day of payment, if the executors of the feoffor tender the money to the feoffee at the day of payment, this tender is good enough; and if the feoffee refuse it, the heirs of the feoffor may enter. And the reason is, for that the executors represent the person of their testator." Followed in Alsop v. Hall, 1 Root (Conn.) 346.

it is probable that mortgages were almost unknown in England for the next two hundred years.[13] That military institution, the nature of which was such as to exclude any idea of a mortgage, soon absorbed all the real property of the kingdom. By the restrictions placed upon alienation of lands, mortgages were practically extinguished.

At length the statute of quia emptores restored freedom of alienation to all except the immediate tenants of the crown, and not long afterward questions relating to the nature of mortgages and the respective rights of the parties began to receive the attention of the courts and of Parliament.[14]

§ 6. **Growth of the doctrine of an equity of redemption.**—In the latter part of the reign of Elizabeth it seems to have been an unsettled question whether an absolute forfeiture of the estate had not been incurred by a nonpayment of the debt at the day named in the condition.[15] But the right of the mortgagor to redeem after forfeiture seems to have been a recognized right in the reign of Charles I;[16] although at the close of the reign of Charles II an equity of redemption was declared to be a mere right to recover the estate in equity after breach of the condition, and not such an estate as was entailable within the statute de donis.[17] In this case Chief Justice Hale made the often quoted remark, "By the growth of equity on equity, the heart of the common law is eaten out, and legal settlements are destroyed." He thought the mortgagor's equity of redemption

---

[13] Coote on Mtg. 5. "In the twentieth year of William's reign, and on the completion of Domesday Book, he summoned a meeting of all the principal landholders in London and Salisbury, and accepted from them a surrender of their lands, and regranted them on performance of homage and the oath of fealty. The mesne lords, on their subinfeudations, also demanded homage and fealty, and it was held the bond of allegiance was mutual, each being bound to defend and protect the other. From this flowed the doctrine that the tenant could not transfer his feud without his lord's consent, nor the lord his seigniory without his tenant's consent, although the tenants, even of the crown, it would seem, might grant subinfeudations (i. e. to hold of themselves, without license). It was further held, the tenant could not subject his lands to his debts by execution of law, for, if he could, he might have effected that circuitously which he could not by direct means have accomplished. Nor, if the lands came to him by descent, could he aliene them without the consent of the next collateral heir."

[14] 18 Edw. I. (A. D. 1325).

[15] Goodall's case, 5 Rep. 96; Wade's case, 5 Rep. 115.

[16] See 2 Min. Insts. 335; Co. Litt., Butler's note, 204b; 2 Story Eq. Jur. § 1014.

Emanuel College v. Evans, 1 Rep. in Ch. 18. In this case, although the money was not paid at the day but afterward, it was held that the mortgage term ought to be void, just as it would have been at law on a payment according to the condition.

[17] Roscarrick v. Barton, 1 Ca. in Ch. 217.

had already been carried too far, saying: "In 14 Richard II the Parliament would not admit of redemption; but now there is another settled course; as far as the line is given, man will go; and if a hundred years are given, man will go so far, and we know not whither we shall go. An equity of redemption is transferable from one to another now, and yet at common law, if he that had the equity made a feoffment or levied a fine, he had extinguished his equity in law; and it hath gone far enough already, and we will go no further than precedents in the matter of equity of redemption, which hath too much favor already."

Even so late as 1737 it was strenuously argued before the High Court of Chancery that an equity of redemption was not an estate in land of which a husband was entitled to be a tenant by the curtesy. It was insisted that the equity of redemption was no actual estate or interest in the wife, but only a power in her to reduce the estate into her possession again by paying off the mortgage; it was compared to the case of a proviso for a re-entry in a conveyance when no entry had ever been made, and to a condition broken when no advantage had ever been taken thereof; that the wife was never seised in fee in law, because the legal estate was out of her by virtue of the mortgage, but had only a bare possession, and was in receipt of the rents and profits; so that the mortgagor had merely a right of action or a suit in a court of equity, in order that the estate might be reconveyed to her upon complying with the terms in the mortgage. But Lord Hardwicke declared that an equity of redemption is an estate in the land, for it may be devised, granted, or entailed with remainders, and such entail and remainders may be barred by a fine and recovery, and therefore can not be considered as a mere right only, but such an estate whereof there may be a seisin; the person, therefore, entitled to the equity of redemption is considered as the owner of the land, and a mortgage in fee is considered as personal assets.[18]

§ 7. When the doctrine was first established.—The doctrine of the right of redemption had its origin in the great fountainhead of equitable doctrines—the Roman or civil law. But it is not clearly ascertained when this doctrine was first allowed in England. Equitable interposition is attributed to the courts of equity; but the doctrine of redemption was probably adopted long prior to the establishment of distinct chancery courts.

Courts of equity had become fully established in their authority in

---

[18] Casborne v. Scarfe, 1 Atk. 603.

the reign of James I, and although many equitable principles now recognized in the doctrine of mortgages were not fully established till long afterward, it is probable that at this time the subject of mortgages was so far within their jurisdiction as to enable them to relieve the mortgagor from the forfeiture of his rights through failure to pay according to the condition, and to establish the doctrine of the equity of redemption.[19] "No sooner, however, was this equitable principle established than the cupidity of creditors induced them to attempt its invasion, and it was a bold but necessary decision of equity that the debtor could not, even by the most solemn engagements entered into at the time of the loan, preclude himself from his right to redeem; for in every other instance, probably, the rule of law, Modus et conventio vincunt legem, is allowed to prevail. In truth it required all the firmness and wisdom of the eminent judges who successively presided in the courts of equity to prevent this equitable jurisdiction being nullified by the artifice of the parties."[20]

Accordingly, "Once a mortgage always a mortgage," became one of the most important maxims in this branch of the law; and a strict adherence to it has at all times been enforced. The parties have not been allowed to provide that the deed creating the mortgage shall at any time, or upon the happening of any event, cease to be a mortgage, and become an absolute conveyance.[21] An agreement or stipulation cutting off the right of redemption has always been held to be utterly void.[22] Even a subsequent release of this right by the mortgagor has always been looked upon with suspicion, and sustained only when made for a proper consideration and without oppression on the part of the mortgagee.[23]

This doctrine is deemed essential to the protection of the debtor, who, under pressing circumstances, will often submit to ruinous conditions, expecting or hoping to be able to pay the debt at maturity and thus prevent the condition from being enforced and his property sacrificed.

§ 8. **Mortgage at law distinguished from mortgage in equity.**— A mortgage at law differs much in its nature from a mortgage in

[19] Coote on Mtg. 21.

[20] Coote on Mtg. 21. See also Price v. Perrie, 2 Freem. 258; Willett v. Winnell, 1 Vern. 488; Bowen v. Edwards, 1 Rep. in Ch. 222.

[21] Newcomb v. Bonham, 1 Vern. 7; Coote on Mtg. 22; 2 Story Eq. Jur. § 1019.

[22] Quartermous v. Kennedy, 29 Ark. 544; Lee v. Evans, 8 Cal. 424. See also Bearss v. Ford, 108 Ill. 16; Johnson v. Prosperity Loan &c. Assn., 94 Ill. App. 260.

[23] Pritchard v. Elton, 38 Conn. 434. See also Carpenter v. Carpenter, 70 Ill. 457; Haggerty v. Brower, 105 Iowa 395, 75 N. W. 321; Richmond v. Richmond, 20 Fed. Cas. No. 11, 801. See post §§ 1038–1046.

equity. A mortgage being a qualified conveyance of property, whereby the owner parts with it so far as to make it a security to his creditor, and his creditor holds it in such a way that the owner may, by equitably fulfilling his obligation, have his own again, the question, what are the respective rights and titles of each, is one that lies at the foundation of the law upon this subject. Originally an estate upon condition at law, equity assumed jurisdiction to relieve the mortgagor against an absolute forfeiture upon his default in performing the condition subsequent; and for two hundred years and more a mortgage has been one thing at law and quite another thing in equity, although the equitable view of the subject has largely encroached upon, and sometimes quite superseded, the legal, even in courts of law.[24] For a number of years both law and equity courts exercised concurrent jurisdiction over mortgages, resulting in great confusion, more especially while the courts of the common law continued to be presided over by men whose early training had led them to regard the interference of the courts of equity as an offensive innovation. But in course of time the justness of the decrees of the chancellors gradually came to be recognized by the common-law courts and were acquiesced in by them.

Courts of equity could not alter the legal effect of the forfeiture which followed a breach of the condition, and did not attempt to do so; but they regarded it as in the nature of a penalty which ought to be relieved against. They recognized the purpose of the mortgage as merely a pledge to secure a debt, and declared it unreasonable that the mortgagee should, by the failure of the debtor to meet his obligation at the day appointed, be entitled to keep as his own what was intended as a pledge.[25] At law the legal right of the mortgagor to have his estate again was forfeited; but in equity he was allowed still to reclaim it upon payment of his debt with interest.

---

[24] "The case of mortgages," says Chancellor Kent, "is one of the most splendid instances in the history of our jurisprudence of the triumph of equitable principles over technical rules, and the homage which those principles have received by their adoption in the courts of law." 4 Kent Com. 138. "It is difficult to conceive," says Mr. Coote, "had the courts of the law been so inclined (which it does seem they were), on what principle they would have proceeded in giving the debtor relief. The forfeiture was complete; the mortgagee, by the default of the mortgagor, had become the absolute owner of the estate; it could not be divested from him without a reconveyance, and there remained no remedy, short of an actual legislative enactment, without disturbing the settled landmarks of property " Coote on Mtg. 17.

[25] Coote on Mtg. 19.

This is the equity of redemption. From the combined influence of these rules of law and principles of equity has come the present law of mortgages.

The equitable view of a mortgage, as merely a security for the payment of a debt or the performance of some duty, is that which is at the present day so constantly presented, both in theory and practice, that it is difficult to realize that the rules of the common law in respect to it remain for the most part unaltered; that the transaction is still a conveyance conditional upon the nonpayment of the debt on a day certain, and that upon a breach of the condition the mortgagor at law is without right or remedy. The whole legal estate upon the default passes irrevocably to the mortgagee. But at this point a court of equity allows and enforces the right of redemption; and the jurisdiction of courts of equity to give this remedy is fully recognized in courts of law.

§ 9. Statute of 7 Geo. II, ch. 20.—In courts of law the rigor of the doctrine, in respect to the conditional character of the mortgage, was not at all abated in England until the enactment of the statute of 7 George II, ch. 20,[26] which permitted a mortgagor, when an action was brought on the bond, or ejectment on the mortgage, pending the suit, to pay to the mortgagee the mortgage money, interest, and all costs expended in any suit at law or in equity; or, in case of a refusal to accept the same, to bring such money into court where such action was pending, and the moneys so paid or brought into court were declared to be a satisfaction and discharge of the mortgage, and the court was required, by rule of court, to compel the mortgagee to assign, surrender, or reconvey the mortgaged premises to the mortgagor, or to such other person as he should for that purpose nominate and appoint. "In cases strictly within the terms of this statute, the English courts of law have exercised an equitable jurisdiction to enforce redemption on payment of the mortgage debt, after default in payment according to the condition, by compelling a reconveyance. Except in cases within this statute, the doctrine of the English courts is in accordance with the ancient common law, that at law a failure to pay at the day prescribed forfeits the estate of the mortgagor under the condition, leaving him only an equity of redemption, which chancery

[26] Re-enacted in New Jersey, December 3, 1794, Nix. Dig. (4th ed.) 608. See also Virginia Code 1904, §§ 2742, 2743; Davis v. Teays, 3 Grat. (Va.) 283; Connecticut Gen. Stat. (1875), p. 47

will lay hold of and give effect to by compelling a reconveyance on equitable terms."[27]

The object of this statute was to relieve the mortgagor from the delay and expense of a suit in equity for redemption, and to lessen the rights of the mortgagee. It was only applicable where the mortgagee was not in possession and no exercise of power of sale was attempted by him.[28] The statute is strictly construed, and is not applicable in any case in which the mortgagor is himself the actor. It is applicable only in the cases mentioned in the preamble and introductory words of the statute, and was not intended to supplant bills for redemption which afford a more complete remedy.[29]

§ 10. **Trust arising through relationship of mortgagor and mortgagee.**—The respective claims of mortgagor and mortgagee in courts of common law and of equity afford a notable instance of the rise of a trust through the mere existence of another legal relationship.[30] "In a court of common law, a mortgage is an ordinary conveyance following upon a contract for a sale or for a lease. The mortgagee takes the place of the mortgagor as owner of the land, and the mortgagor that of the mortgagee as owner of the money borrowed, the subsequent repayment of the money and reconveyance of the land being regulated by what is in fact nothing else than a subsidiary contract. In a court of equity the mortgagee is recognized as having nothing more than the sort of security for his debt which is provided by a conditional power of sale, and, whether he be in possession of the land or not, is treated as the mere trustee of the land for the benefit of the mortgagor and his heir. The money lent descends, on the death of either of the parties, as a debt due from the one, or his executors, to the other, or his executors."

§ 11. **The modern common-law doctrine of mortgages.**—At common law the legal estate vested in the mortgagee and was forfeited upon default. Equity established the right of redemption after default. From these principles is derived the doctrine of mortgages as it exists at the present day, in England and in a large part of our own country. The legal title passes to the mortgagee by the

[27] Per Mr. Justice Depue, in Shields v. Lozear, 34 N. J. L. 496, 3 Am. Rep. 256.
[28] Sutton v. Rawlings, 3 Exch. 407; Dowle v. Neale, 10 W. R. 627.
[29] Shields v. Lozear, 34 N. J. L. 496, 3 Am. Rep. 256; Good-title v. No-title, 11 Moore 491; Hurst v. Clifton, 4 Ad. & E. 809.
[30] Mr. Sheldon Ames, in the Science of Jurisprudence, p. 269.

deed, but the mortgagor has after default a right to redeem, which he may enforce in equity. A mortgage is one thing at law and another in equity; in the one court it is an estate, and in the other a security only. The mortgagee has certain legal remedies and the mortgagor certain equitable remedies. These have been so adjusted that a perfectly defined system is the result. Courts of law and courts of equity mutually recognize the jurisdiction of each other over this subject. Courts of law have so far adopted the principles of equity that they allow the legal title of the holder of the mortgage to be used only for the purpose of securing his equitable rights under it. Courts of equity allow the mortgagee, for the purpose of protecting and enforcing his lien against the mortgagor, the remedies of an owner; he may enter into and hold possession, and take the rents and profits in payment of his mortgage debt, and may have his action of ejectment to recover such possession, and hence is sometimes called the owner.[31] The mortgagee has something more than a mere lien; he has a transfer of the property itself and a legal estate in it, giving him a standing at law as well as in equity.[32] His interest can be called a lien only in a loose and general sense, in contradistinction to an absolute and indefeasible estate.[33]

In equity a mortgage of land is regarded as a mere security for a debt or obligation, which is considered as the principal thing, and the mortgage only as the accessory.[34] The mortgagor continues to be the owner of the fee until after foreclosure. His equity of redemption is subject to grant or devise, and may be taken in execution; and is regarded as the real and beneficial estate tantamount to the fee at law.[35] The legal title vests in the mortgagee merely for the protection

[31] Clark v. Reyburn, 1 Kans. 281; Code Civ. Proc. (N. Y.) § 1498. See also Barron v. San Angelo Nat. Bank (Tex. Civ. App.), 138 S. W. 142; Ackland v. Gravener, 31 Beav. 484; Berney v. Sewell, 1 Jac. & W. 648; Silver v. Bishop of Norwich, 3 Swanst. 113n. The action of ejectment against a mortgagor has been abolished in New York. 5 Wait Pr. (N. Y.) 190.

[32] Willamette Woolen Mfg. Co. v. British Columbia Bank, 119 U. S. 191, 30 L. ed. 384, 7 Sup. Ct. 187; Weeks v. Baker, 152 Mass. 20, 24 N. E. 905; Barnard v. Eaton, 2 Cush. (Mass.) 294, 304; Poarch v. Duncan, 41 Tex. Civ. App. 275, 91 S. W. 1110. See also Datesman's Appeal, 127 Pa. St. 348, 17 Atl. 1086.

[33] In re Tobin's Estate, 139 Wis. 494, 121 N. W. 144; Conard v. Atlantic Ins. Co., 1 Pet. (U. S.) 386, 441; Evans v. Merriken, 8 Gill & J. (Md.) 39. Compare Farr v. Semmler, 24 S. Dak. 290, 123 N. W. 835.

[34] Timms v. Shannon, 19 Md. 296, 81 Am. Dec. 632.

[35] Hannah v. Carrington, 18 Ark. 85; Hannah v. Vensel, 19 Idaho 796, 116 Pac. 115; Schumann v. Sprague, 189 Ill. 425, 59 N. E. 945; Barrett v. Hinckley, 124 Ill. 32, 14 N. E. 863, 7 Am. St. 331; Ætna L. Ins. Co. v. Broecker, 166 Ind. 576, 77 N. E. 1092; Hussey v. Fisher, 94 Maine 301, 47 Atl. 525; Timms v. Shannon, 19 Md. 296, 81 Am. Dec. 632; Watkins v. Vrooman, 51 Hun 175, 5 N. Y. S. 172; Killebrew v. Hines, 104 N. Car.

of his interest, and in order to give him the full benefit of the security; but for other purposes the mortgage is a mere security for the debt.[36] A recital in a mortgage that the note secured is collateral to the mortgage does not change the character of the instruments or their relation to each other under the general rule as to principal and incident; and the fact that the note is indorsed by a third person makes no difference.[37]

As to all persons except the mortgagee and those claiming under him, it is everywhere the established modern doctrine that a mortgagor in possession is at law, both before and after breach of the condition, the legal owner.[38] This is the rule not merely in courts of equity, but in courts of law as well. Lord Mansfield, by his decisions upon the subject of mortgages, did much to naturalize these equitable doctrines in courts of law. In a case before the King's Bench, he said: "It is an affront to common sense to say the mortgagor is not the real owner;" and therefore he held that a mortgagor in possession gains a settlement, because the mortgagee, notwithstanding the form, has but a chattel, and the mortgage is only a security.[39]

Again, in construing a will, he held that whatever words were sufficient to carry the money due on a mortgage would carry the interest in the land along with it, saying,[40] "that a mortgage is a charge upon the land; and whatever would give the money will carry the estate in the land along with it, to every purpose. The estate in the land is the same thing as the money due upon it. It will be liable to debts; it will go to executors; it will pass by a will not made and executed with the solemnities required by the statute of frauds. The assignment of the debt, or forgiving it, will draw the land after it, as a consequence; nay, it would do it, though the debt were forgiven only by parol, for the right to the land would follow, notwithstanding the statute of frauds."

§ 12. **Lord Mansfield's views.**—It is true that some opinions expressed by Lord Mansfield would seem to lead to the conclusion that he regarded a mortgage even at law as merely a security for a debt,

---

182, 10 S. E. 159, 17 Am. St. 672; Craft v. Webster, 4 Rawle (Pa.) 242; Williams v. Beard. 1 S. Car. 309; Johnson v. Robinson, 68 Tex. 399, 4 S. W. 625; Hale v. Horne, 21 Grat. (Va.) 112.
[36] Gabbert v. Schwartz, 69 Ind. 450; Glass v. Ellison, 9 N. H. 69.

[37] Catlin v. Henton, 9 Wis. 476.
[38] See post §§ 667, 702.
[39] The King v. St. Michael's, Doug. 630.
[40] Martin v. Mowlin, 2 Burr. 969, decided in 1760.

and not a legal conveyance.[41] "Lord Mansfield, indeed," says Mr. Coventry,[42] "appears to have entertained mistaken conceptions on this and other subjects connected with the law of mortgages. His chief error seems to have been in mixing rules of equity with rules of law, and applying the former in cases where the latter only ought to have prevailed." An unqualified adoption of some of the expressions of Lord Mansfield is inconsistent with a legal view of the nature of mortgages; it would lead to the conclusion that a mortgage is merely a security and not an estate in the land. The English courts by universal consent have refused to adopt this conclusion; but in this country his lead has been followed in about half of the states; and the adoption of equitable principles by courts of law has been followed by legislative enactments taking from the mortgagee the right of possession, so that in these states it is the established doctrine that a mortgage confers no title or estate upon the mortgagee, but only a security. The legal theory of a mortgage has wholly given place to the equitable, according to which a mortgage is nothing more than a mere lien or security for a debt, passing no title or estate to the mortgagee, and giving him no right or claim to the possession of the property.

§ 13. **Change from legal to equitable theory in United States.**— The courts of New York at an early day took the lead in this direction. The first important step was to deny the legal character of the mortgagee's title prior to a breach of the condition and a taking of possession by the mortgagee in consequence.[43] Before default he was not allowed to take possession; on the contrary, the mortgagor in possession could maintain trespass against him.[44] But after a breach of

---

[41] See also Ren v. Bulkeley, Doug. 292; Eaton v. Jacques, 2 Doug. 455.

[42] In note to Powell on Mtg. 267, n. Lord Redesdale in Shannon v. Bradstreet, 1 Sch. & Lef. 52, speaking of Lord Mansfield's tendency to give courts of law the power of courts of equity, said: "Lord Mansfield had on his mind prejudices derived from his familiarity with the Scotch law, where law and equity are administered in the same courts, and where the distinction between them which subsists with us is not known; and there are many things in his decisions which show that his mind had received a tinge on that subject not quite consistent with the Constitution of England and Ireland in the administration of justice. It is a most important part of that constitution that the jurisdictions of the courts of law and equity should be kept perfectly distinct; nothing contributes more to the due administration of justice; and, though they act in a great degree by the same rules, yet they act in a different manner, and their modes of affording relief are different."

[43] Phyfe v. Riley, 15 Wend. (N. Y.). 248, 30 Am. Dec. 55.

[44] Bryan v. Butts, 27 Barb. (N. Y.) 503; Runyan v. Mersereau, 11 Johns. (N. Y.) 534, 6 Am. Dec. 393. See also Kortright v. Cady, 21 N. Y. 343, 78 Am. Dec. 145; Kents' Com. p. *155.

the condition and possession taken by the mortgagee, he was regarded as invested with the legal estate.[45] The right to take possession, even upon a breach of the condition, was finally taken away by statute,[46] and thereafter it was held that the legal title to the mortgaged premises remained in the mortgagor, and that title was not affected by default in payment, or by surrender of possession to, or the taking of possession by, the mortgagee.[47] This enactment was regarded as completing the change in the nature of mortgages, and removing from them the last remaining common-law attribute.

And yet an examination of the cases in New York in which questions in regard to the nature of mortgages are involved and discussed shows considerable conflict and contradiction of views. This is especially the case with the decisions prior to the statute taking from the mortgagee the right to recover possession of the mortgaged property; and even since that statute, although in theory the legal title remains in the mortgagor until foreclosure, it has been frequently admitted by judges and legal writers, that for some purposes and in some cases his interest must be treated and regarded as a title for the purpose of protecting his equitable rights.[48] Where the mortgagor's interest is regarded as the legal estate in the land, it is undoubtedly a misnomer to call it an equity of redemption either before or after default.[49] But although the term has ceased to be an accurate description of his right in the land, it has an established place among legal terms, and doubtless will continue to be used to describe his interest even in states which have by statute changed his actual rights. But the equity of redemption must not be confounded with a right of redemption. A mortgagor has an equity of redemption until the sale, and not afterward. After sale he has a right of redemption, if the statute gives it.[50]

§ 14. Incongruities in both the common-law and equitable theories. —There are some incongruities in both theories. Many attempts have been made to state a perfectly harmonious and consistent system of law in regard to mortgages, but complete success has

---

[45] Bolton v. Brewster, 32 Barb. (N. Y.) 289.

[46] 2 Rev. Stat. 312, § 57, enacted 1828. See also Becker v. McCrea, 193 N. Y. 423, 86 N. E. 463, 23 L. R. A. (N. S.) 754; Packer v. Rochester &c. R. Co., 17 N. Y. 283.

[47] Trim v. Marsh, 54 N. Y. 599, 13 Am. Rep. 623.

[48] Thomas on Mtg. 16; White v. Rittenmyer, 30 Iowa 268; Hubbell v. Moulson, 53 N. Y. 225, 13 Am. Rep. 519.

[49] Per Earl, C., in Trimm v. Marsh, 54 N. Y. 599; Chick v. Willetts, 2 Kans. 384, per Crozier, C. J.

[50] See Mayer v. Farmers' Bank, 44 Iowa 212.

ιever attended them. On the one hand, the modern common-law view of mortgages, by which the mortgagee is regarded as the owner of the legal estate for the purpose of protecting and enforcing his rights, and the mortgagor is regarded as the legal owner as against every other person, is objected to as presenting the incongruous position that one person may be the legal owner for one purpose, and at the same time another person may be the legal owner for another purpose; that in one court the mortgagee is the legal owner, and in another the mortgagor is the legal owner; that after the legal title has passed to the mortgagee by a legal conveyance, it may be defeated by the act of the mortgagor from whom the title has passed merely by payment before forfeiture.[51]

On the other hand, it has been thought that by regarding a mortgage both at law and in equity as a mere security, a more harmonious and consistent doctrine regarding this instrument would be secured. It is admitted that this doctrine is anomalous. That a legal conveyance does not pass a legal title is not in accordance with legal principles.[52] Moreover, it has been found that in order to secure the equitable rights of parties, the mortgagee's interest must in some cases be treated and regarded as a title. This is admitted by Mr. Justice Andrews in a comparatively recent case before the Court of Appeals of New York;[53] and he mentions instances in the decisions of that state where the mortgagee's interest has been so treated and regarded, notwithstanding the doctrine that he has a lien only. It is claimed, however, that no title in a strict sense vests in him, but only that his interest for some purposes is in the nature of a legal title. He is treated as if he had a legal title, by being protected in his possession, when he has once acquired it, until the debt is fully paid.[54] The only remedy for recovering possession from him in such case is by a bill in equity to redeem,[55] as is the case where the mortgagee is regarded as holding the legal estate.

In other ways also the mortgagee is treated as holding an estate. He is deemed a purchaser to the extent of his interest, and is protected in his rights in the same way and to the same extent as a

[51] White v. Rittenmyer, 30 Iowa 268.

[52] White v. Rittenmyer, 30 Iowa 268.

[53] Hubbell v. Moulson, 53 N. Y. 225, 13 Am. Rep. 519.

[54] Mickles v. Townsend, 18 N. Y. 575. See also Bussey v. Page, 14 Maine 132; Pace v. Chadderdon, 4 Minn. 499; Henry v. Confidence Gold &c. Min. Co., 1 Nev. 619; Pettengill v. Evans, 5 N. H. 54; Den v. Wright, 7 N. J. L. 175, 11 Am. Dec. 543; Chase v. Peck, 21 N. Y. 581; Harris v. Haynes, 34 Vt. 220; Hennesy v. Farrell, 20 Wis. 42. See post § 715.

[55] Hubbell v. Moulson, 53 N. Y. 225, 13 Am. Rep. 519.

purchaser of an absolute estate.[56] As an estate in him, his interest is protected against a claim of dower by the wife of the mortgagor when she has released this right in the mortgage, although she may be entitled to it in the equity of redemption.[57] And so also a title acquired by the mortgagor after making the mortgage inures, by force of the covenant of warranty contained in it, to the benefit of the mortgagee.[58]

§ 15. **Mortgage as a legal estate and as a personal lien distinguished.**—What, then, are the practical distinctions between a mortgage regarded as a legal estate in the mortgagee, and a mortgage regarded as a mere personal lien? In what respect are the rights of both the mortgagor and the mortgagee, where the one view prevails, the same as they are where the other prevails; and in what respect are their rights different under the one doctrine from what they are under the other?

In the first place, wherein are the two doctrines in harmony as regards the rights and interests of the mortgagor? Everywhere the mortgagor's interest in the land may be sold upon execution; his widow is entitled to dower in it; it passes as real estate by devise; it descends to his heirs at his death as real estate; it gives him a right of settlement as an owner of real estate; he is a freeholder; he may maintain a real action for the land against a stranger, and the mortgage can not be set up as a defense.

In the second place, wherein are the rights and interests of the

[56] See also Woodruff v. Adair, 131 Ala. 530, 32 So. 515; Turman v. Bell, 54 Ark. 273, 15 S. W. 886, 26 Am. St. 35; Bush v. Golden, 17 Conn. 594; Scott v. Atlas Sav. &c. Assn., 114 Ga. 134, 39 S. E. 942; Erwin v. Hall, 18 Ill. App. 315; Lehman v. Hawks, 121 Ind. 541, 23 N. E. 670; Koon v. Tramel, 71 Iowa 132, 32 N. W. 243; Straeffer v. Rodman, 146 Ky. 1, 141 S. W. 742, Ann. Cas. 1913 C, 549; Thompson v. Whitbeck, 47 La. Ann. 49, 16 So. 570; Pierce v. Faunce, 47 Maine 507; Fair v. Howard, 6 Nev. 304; Frisbey v. Thayer, 25 Wend. (N. Y.) 396; James v. Johnson, 6 Johns. Ch. (N. Y.) 417, 2 Cow. (N. Y.) 246; Ledyard v. Butler, 9 Paige (N. Y.) 132, 37 Am. Dec. 379.

[57] Van Dyne v. Thayre, 19 Wend. (N. Y.) 162. See also Lidster v. Poole, 122 Ill. App. 227; Mark v.

Murphy, 76 Ind. 543; Morgan v. Wickliffe, 24 Ky. L. 2104, 72 S. W. 1122; Johnson v. Hines, 61 Md. 122; Burrall v. Clark, 61 Mich. 624, 28 N. W. 739; McLean v. Ragsdale, 31 Miss. 701; Miller v. Farmers' Bank, 49 S. Car. 427, 27 S. E. 514, 61 Am. St. 821; Thomson v. Thomson, 37 Nova Scotia 242.

[58] Vary v. Smith, 162 Ala. 457, 50 So. 187; Howze v. Dew, 90 Ala. 178, 7 So. 239, 24 Am. St. 783; Yerkes v. Hadley, 5 Dak. 324, 40 N. W. 340, 2 L. R. A. 363; Watkins v. Houck, 44 Kans. 502, 24 Pac. 361; Caple v. Switzer, 122 Mich. 636, 81 N. W. 560; Parsons v. Little, 66 N. H. 339, 20 Atl. 958; Dearing v. Jordan (Tex. Civ. App.), 130 S. W. 876; Trust &c. Co. v. Ruttan, 1 Can. S. Ct. 564. Compare Newell v. Banking Co. (Ky.), 118 S. W. 267.

mortgagee the same, whether regarded under the one theory or the other? Everywhere it is held that he has no such estate as can be sold on execution; his widow has no right of dower in it; upon his death the mortgage passes to his personal representatives as personal estate; and it passes by his will as personal property.

The practical distinctions between these views are these: Under the common-law view, as we may term the former, the mortgagee is entitled to immediate possession of the mortgaged property as an incident to the title when not restrained by the terms of the mortgage; and upon default he is always entitled to the possession, and may recover it by action at law; whereas, under the equitable view, the mortgagor is entitled to possession, until foreclosure, unless perhaps he may by express contract give this right to the mortgagee. This is the great difference resulting from these different theories. In large degree resulting from these different ways of viewing the interest of the parties follow the further distinctions: that while generally, under the former view of the law, a tender or payment to defeat the mortgagee's title must be made at or before the law day, as the day of payment is termed, under the latter view a payment at any time, though after default, revests the interest in the mortgagor; and while under the former view it is generally held that a transfer of the mortgage interest can only be made by an assignment or deed duly executed as conveyance, under the latter view it is held that a mere transfer of the mortgage note by indorsement or delivery passes the interest in the land as an incident of the debt. These two distinctions do not, however, necessarily and inevitably attend the different theories.

In strict conformity with the theory that the mortgagee has no estate in the land, but a mere lien as security for his debt, it has been held that a conveyance by the mortgagee before foreclosure, without an assignment of the debt, is in law a nullity.[59] But this view seems to be inconsistent with the whole current of decisions supporting the doctrine that if a person sui juris, having the legal title to land, intentionally delivers to another a deed therefor, containing apt words of conveyance, the title at law, at least, will pass to the grantee; but for what purposes or uses the grantee will hold it, or to what extent he will be able to enforce it, will depend upon circumstances. If the mortgagee conveys the land without assigning the debt to the grantee,

[59] Delano v. Bennett, 90 Ill. 533; Wilson v. Troup, 2 Cow. (N. Y.) 231; Jackson v. Curtis, 19 Johns. (N. Y.) 325.

the latter would hold the legal title as trustee for the holder of the mortgage debt.[60]

§ 16. **Present day mortgage defined.**—How, then, may a mortgage at the present day be defined? Baron Parke, speaking of the mortgagor, said: "He can be described only by saying he is a mortgagor."[61] In the same way it may be said that the most accurate and comprehensive definition of a mortgage is that it is a mortgage. As remarked by Lord Denman, "It is very dangerous to attempt to define the precise relation in which mortgagor and mortgagee stand to each other, in any other terms than those very words."[62] A definition given by Kent, and one which has been quoted, adopted, or approved in a great many cases, is that, "A mortgage is the conveyance of an estate by way of pledge for the security of a debt, and to become void on payment of it."[63] A definition broad enough to cover any view of the transaction, and any form of it, can only be that it is a conveyance of land as security.[64] This embraces the two things essential to constitute a mortgage. If more be attempted, it results in a description of some one of the many forms which a mortgage may take. In a note are given references to definitions and descriptions of mortgages by several eminent authors and judges. But to define the different kinds of mortgages, and the many different rights under them, is the service attempted by a treatise on the subject.[65]

[60] Barrett v. Hinckley, 124 Ill. 32, 14 N. E. 863, 7 Am. St. 331; Barnard v. Eaton, 2 Cush. (Mass.) 304; Sanger v. Bancroft, 12 Gray (Mass.) 367; Jackson v. Willard, 4 Johns. (N. Y.) 40.
[61] Litchfield v. Ready, 20 L. J. Ex. 51.
[62] Higginbotham v. Barton, 11 Ad. & El. 307.
[63] 4 Kent Comm. 133. See also Williams v. Davis, 154 Ala. 422, 45 So. 908; Priddy v. Smith, 106 Ark. 79, 152 S. W. 1028, 44 L. R. A. (N. S.) 285; Ansonia Nat. Bank's Appeal, 58 Conn. 257, 18 Atl. 1030, 20 Atl. 394; Everett v. Buchanan, 2 Dak. 249, 6 N. W. 439, 8 N. W. 31; Brown v. Bryan, 5 Idaho 145, 151, 51 Pac. 995; Eldridge v. Pierce, 90 Ill. 474, 483; Babcock v. Hoey, 11 Iowa 375, 385; Goddard v. Coe, 55 Maine 385, 388; Gothard v. Flynn, 25 Miss. 58; Murray v. Walker, 31 N. Y. 399; Cheatham v. Jones, 68 N. Car. 153; Helfenstein's Estate, 135 Pa. St. 293, 20 Atl. 151; Poarch v. Duncan, 42 Tex. Civ. App. 275, 91 S. W. 1110; Wing v. Cooper, 37 Vt. 169; Sandusky v. Faris, 49 W. Va. 150, 38 S. E. 563; Parkinson v. Higgins, 40 U. C. Q. B. 274.
[64] Williams v. Davis, 154 Ala. 422, 45 So. 908; Gassert v. Bogk, 7 Mont. 585, 19 Pac. 281 (quoting text); Helfenstein's Estate, 135 Pa. St. 293, 20 Atl. 151; Wilson v. Fisher, 148 N. Car. 535, 62 S. E. 622.
[65] Washburn's Real Prop. ch. 16, § 1; Fisher on Mtg. (3d ed.) p. 2; Coventry, in Powell on Mtg. p. 4; Cruise, 1 Dig. of Law of Real Prop. (Am. ed.) tit. xv. ch. I. § 11; Coote on Mtg. p. 1; Erskine v. Townsend, 2 Mass. 493, 3 Am. Dec. 71; Carter v. Taylor, 3 Head (Tenn.) 30; Briggs v. Fish, 2 D. Chip (Vt.) 100; Montgomery v. Bruere, 4 N. J. L. 260; Lund v. Lund, 1 N. H. 39, 8 Am. Dec. 29; Mitchell v. Burnham, 44 Maine

II. *The Nature of a Mortgage in the Different States*

§ 17. Generally.—While the common-law doctrine of mortgages prevails in some of the states, with more or less of modification by equitable principles, in a majority, however, partly by force of statutes, and partly by judicial decisions, the common-law doctrine has been abrogated, and has given place to the purely equitable theory.

The conflicting views of the nature of mortgages entertained at law and in equity have resulted in the just and harmonious system which is now administered in the courts of England and in most of the courts of the older states of America. In these courts a mortgage is regarded as a conveyance in fee, and this construction is thought best adapted to give to the creditor full protection in preserving and enforcing his securities, while at the same time the debtor is secured in his right to redeem. In other states, however, this system has been changed, for the most part by statute, so that a mortgage is regarded

---

286; Wing v. Cooper, 37 Vt. 169; Gen. Stat. of New Hampshire, 1867, ch. 122, § 1.

By the Code of California, a mortgage is defined to be "a contract, by which specific property is hypothecated for the performance of an act, without the necessity of a change of possession." Civil Code, § 2920; adopted also by Civil Code of Dakota 1871, § 1608. In Florida it is provided that all conveyances securing the payment of money shall be deemed mortgages. Gen. Stat. 1906, § 2495.

as merely a pledge, and the rights and remedies under it are wholly equitable. There are also a few modifications of each.

In examining the various questions that arise under the law of mortgages, it is often important to distinguish between the opinions of courts acting under these different views of the nature of a mortgage. On several topics frequent reference will be made to the distinguishing features of the two systems. On these topics authorities of several states having the same system will be harmonious, but will differ from those of several states in which the other system prevails. It is therefore thought best to give briefly, under the name of each state, the law there in force upon this fundamental matter of the nature of the conveyance in mortgage, as announced by the courts or enacted by statute.

§ 18. **Alabama.**—In Alabama a mortgage passes to the mortgagee, as between him and the mortgagor, the estate in the land. It confers something more than a mere security for a debt: it confers a title under which the mortgagee may take immediate possession, unless it appears by express stipulation, or necessary implication, that the mortgagor may remain in possession until default.[1] After the law day, the legal estate is absolutely vested in the mortgagee, who may forthwith maintain ejectment, and the mortgagor has nothing left but an equity of redemption.[2] A conveyance by the mortgagee will pass the legal title, though the debt be not assigned.[3] Nothing but payment, or a release of the mortgage, or a reconveyance, can operate in a court of law to revest the title in the mortgagor; and it is questioned whether payment alone after the law day is sufficient.[4] But the payment of a mortgage debt ipso facto revests the legal title in the owner of the equity of redemption.[5] It is held that a partial payment after default and after the law day does not operate to divest the mort-

[1] Stephens v. Head, 138 Ala. 455, 35 So. 565; Toomer v. Randolph, 60 Ala. 356; Knox v. Easton, 38 Ala. 345; Welsh v. Phillips, 54 Ala. 309, 25 Am. Rep. 679. See also Holman v. Ketchum, 153 Ala. 360, 45 So. 206; Marks v. Robinson, 82 Ala. 69, 2 So. 292.

[2] High v. Hoffman, 129 Ala. 359, 29 So. 658; New England Mtg. Sec. Co. v. Clayton, 119 Ala. 361, 24 So. 562; Fields v. Clayton, 117 Ala. 538, 23 So. 530, 67 Am. St. 189; Lomb v. Pioneer Sav. &c. Co., 106 Ala. 591, 17 So. 670; Downing v. Blair, 75 Ala. 216; Barker v. Bell, 37 Ala. 354;

Paulling v. Barron, 32 Ala. 9. See also Foster v. Carlisle, 148 Ala. 259, 42 So. 441.

[3] Toomer v. Randolph, 60 Ala. 356; Welsh v. Phillips, 54 Ala. 309, 25 Am. Rep. 679.

[4] Henderson v. Murphree, 124 Ala. 223, 27 So. 405; Lomb v. Pioneer Sav. &c. Co., 106 Ala. 591, 17 So. 670; Barker v. Bell, 37 Ala. 354; Powell v. Williams, 14 Ala. 476, 48 Am. Dec. 105. But see Union Naval Stores Co. v. Pugh, 156 Ala. 369, 47 So. 48.

[5] Denman v. Payne, 152 Ala. 342, 44 So. 635. Code 1896, § 1067.

gagee's title. A more formal conveyance or grant seems to be required.[6] But as against all persons other than the mortgagee and his assigns, the mortgagor is regarded as the owner of the fee, and is entitled to the possession.[7]

After the legal title has vested in the mortgagee by reason of the condition being broken, he may convey the premises to another, even though not in possession. The mortgagor still has an equity of redemption which the courts of law will not notice, but which may be asserted and protected in equity until duly foreclosed.[8]

§ 19. **Arkansas.**—In Arkansas the mortgagee was, in an early case, considered as having the legal estate after condition broken, following in this respect some of the earlier cases in New York.[9] In later cases, it is said that the legal title passes, at law, directly to the mortgagee, subject to be defeated by the performance of the conditions of the mortgage; and that the right of possession follows the legal title, unless it be expressly provided in the deed, or clearly appears to be the intention of the parties, that the mortgagor shall remain in possession until default.[10] As between mortgagor and mortgagee, the legal estate is in the mortgagee; but as to all others, it is in the mortgagor, and may be conveyed by him subject to the mortgage.[11] Whenever the mortgagee is entitled to possession, he may acquire it by an action of ejectment. He may upon default pursue any or all of his remedies; may bring actions for the debt, for possession, and to foreclose the equity of redemption and sell the land.[12] A mortgagee

[6] Foster v. Carlisle, 148 Ala. 259, 42 So. 441.

[7] Hamilton v. Griffin, 123 Ala. 600, 26 So. 243; Turner Coal Co. v. Glover, 101 Ala. 289, 13 So. 478; Cotton v. Carlisle, 85 Ala. 175, 4 So. 670, 7 Am. St. 29; Allen v. Kellam, 69 Ala. 442; Scott v. Ware, 65 Ala. 174; Denby v. Mellgrew, 58 Ala. 147; Knox v. Easton, 38 Ala. 345; Mansony v. United States Bank, 4 Ala. 733.

[8] Hayes v. Banks, 132 Ala. 354, 31 So. 464; High v. Hoffman, 129 Ala. 359, 29 So. 658; Fields v. Clayton, 117 Ala. 538, 23 So. 530, 67 Am. St. 189; Lomb v. Pioneer Sav. &c. Co., 106 Ala. 591, 17 So. 670; Downing v. Blair, 75 Ala. 216; Scott v. Ware, 65 Ala. 174; Toomer v. Randolph, 60 Ala. 356; Denby v. Mellgrew, 58 Ala. 147; Welsh v. Phillips, 54 Ala. 309, 25 Am. Rep. 679; Barker v. Bell, 37

Ala. 354; Paulling v. Barron, 32 Ala. 9.

[9] Reynolds v. Canal &c. Co., 30 Ark. 520; Fitzgerald v. Beebe, 7 Ark. 310, 46 Am. Dec. 285; Phyfe v. Riley, 15 Wend. (N. Y.) 248; Perry County Bank v. Rankin, 73 Ark. 589, 84 S. W. 725; Danenhauer v. Dawson, 65 Ark. 129, 46 S. W. 131, 44 L. R. A. 193; Whittington v. Flint, 43 Ark. 504, 51 Am. Rep. 572.

[10] Terry v. Rosell, 32 Ark. 478; Turner v. Watkins, 31 Ark. 429; Kannady v. McCarron, 18 Ark. 166.

[11] Terry v. Rosell, 32 Ark. 478.

[12] Vaughan v. Walton, 66 Ark. 572, 52 S. W. 437; Danenhauer v. Dawson, 65 Ark. 129, 46 S. W. 131; Whittington v. Flint, 43 Ark. 504; Reynolds v. Canal &c. Co., 30 Ark. 520; Gilchrist v. Patterson, 18 Ark. 575; Fitzgerald v. Beebe, 7 Ark. 310, 46 Am. Dec. 285.

in possession under the mortgage can not be ousted by the mortgagor in a suit for possession until the debt is paid.[13]

§ 20. **California.**—In California a mortgage does not convey the legal title for any purpose, either before or after condition broken. It is a mere security for the payment of money, and passes no estate in the land. This is the declaration of the code.[14] "It was from a consideration of the character of the instrument," says Chief Justice Field,[15] "as settled by these decisions and the modern cases generally, that we were induced to adopt the equitable doctrine as the true doctrine; and it was from a consideration of the provisions of the statute which led us to go beyond these cases, and carry the doctrine to its legitimate and logical result, and regard the mortgage as a security under all circumstances, both at law and in equity. Mortgages, therefore, executed before the statute, can only be treated as conveyances when that character is essential to protect the just rights of the mortgagee; mortgages since the statute are regarded at all times as mere securities, creating only a lien or incumbrance, and not passing any estate in the premises."[16]

It is fully settled that a mortgage does not convey the title, but only creates a lien on the property, the title remaining in the mortgagor subject to the lien.[17] It is provided by statute that the mortgagee shall not be entitled to possession unless authorized by the express terms of the mortgage.[18] Whatever the terms of the instrument, it will not be deemed a conveyance so as to entitle the mortgagee

---

[13] Daniel v. Garner, 71 Ark. 484.

[14] Civil Code Cal. 1885, § 2927; Mack v. Wetzlar, 39 Cal. 247; Kidd v. Teeple, 22 Cal. 255; Dutton v. Warschauer, 21 Cal. 609, 82 Am. Dec. 765; Goodenow v. Ewer, 16 Cal. 461, 76 Am. Dec. 540; McMillan v. Richards, 9 Cal. 365, 70 Am. Dec. 655, where Mr. Justice Field examines the subject at great length. See also Booker v. Castillo, 154 Cal. 672, 98 Pac. 1067; Hall v. Arnott, 80 Cal. 348, 22 Pac. 200; Smith v. Smith, 80 Cal. 323, 21 Pac. 4, 22 Pac. 186, 549; Raynor v. Drew, 72 Cal. 307, 13 Pac. 866; Healey v. O'Brien, 66 Cal. 517, 6 Pac. 386; Frink v. Le Roy, 49 Cal. 314; Harp v. Calahan, 46 Cal. 222.

[15] Dutton v. Warschauer, 21 Cal. 609, 82 Am. Dec. 765.

[16] Stat. 1851, § 260, declared a mortgage shall not be deemed a conveyance, whatever its terms, so as to enable the owner of the mortgage to recover possession, without a foreclosure and sale. But prior to this statute a mortgage was not a conditional estate which became absolute on a breach of condition, as at common law. Skinner v. Buck, 29 Cal. 253.

[17] Harp v. Calahan, 46 Cal. 222; Carpentier v. Brenham, 40 Cal. 221; Mack v. Wetzlar, 39 Cal. 247; Jackson v. Lodge, 36 Cal. 28; Bludworth v. Lake, 33 Cal. 255; Fogarty v. Sawyer, 17 Cal. 589; Boggs v. Hargrave, 16 Cal. 559; Haffley v. Maier, 13 Cal. 13. See also Booker v. Castillo, 154 Cal. 672, 98 Pac. 1067.

[18] Civil Code, § 2927. The owner may make an independent contract for the mortgagee's possession. Fogarty v. Sawyer, 17 Cal. 589.

to obtain possession otherwise than by foreclosure and sale.[19] Entry and possession by the mortgagee do not affect the nature of his interest. They can neither abridge nor enlarge that interest, nor convert what was previously a security into a seisin of the freehold.[20] But if the mortgagee, after condition broken, take possession by consent of the mortgagor, it is presumed, in the absence of clear proof to the contrary, that he is to receive the rents and profits, and apply them to the debts secured, and that he is to hold possession until the debt is paid.[21] This possessory right may be transferred by express terms, though it does not pass by an ordinary assignment.[22] Even an absolute deed without any defeasance, if in fact made to secure a debt, so that in equity it is a mortgage, passes no title to the grantee.[23] Of course, under this view of the nature of a mortgage, payment after default operates to discharge the lien equally with payment at the maturity of the debt.[24] Under such a deed the grantee is entitled to recover the premises in ejectment, unless the defendant in answer sets up his equities, with an offer to pay the amount of the mortgage lien, and prays that the conveyance be decreed a mortgage.[25]

But a deed of trust to secure a debt is not a mortgage requiring judicial foreclosure, but a conveyance of the legal title; and being such a conveyance, and not merely a lien or charge upon the property, it is not affected by the statute of limitations, which operates equally to bar the debt and a mortgage given to secure it; but the trustee under such deed may, after such periods of general limitation, proceed to sell the land.[26]

§ 21. **Colorado.**—In Colorado a mortgage is considered a security only, and does not before foreclosure confer any right of entry on the mortgagee.[27] A legal title is recognized in the mortgagee only for the

[19] Booker v. Castillo, 154 Cal. 672, 98 Pac. 1067; Skinner v. Buck, 29 Cal. 253; Kidd v. Teeple, 22 Cal. 255.
[20] Nagle v. Macy, 9 Cal. 426. See also Keller v. Berry, 62 Cal. 488.
[21] Frink v. Le Roy, 49 Cal. 314; Dutton v. Warschauer, 21 Cal. 609, 82 Am. Dec. 765. See also Cummings v. Cummings, 75 Cal. 434, 17 Pac. 442.
[22] Dutton v. Warschauer, 21 Cal. 609, 82 Am. Dec. 765.
[23] Jackson v. Lodge, 36 Cal. 28. Though the grantee be put in possession. Murdock v. Clarke, 90 Cal. 427, 27 Pac. 275. See also Todd v. Todd, 164 Cal. 255, 128 Pac. 413;

Beckman v. Waters, 161 Cal. 581, 119 Pac. 922; Couts v. Winston, 153 Cal. 686, 96 Pac. 357; Adams v. Hopkins (Cal.), 69 Pac. 228; Ahern v. McCarthy, 107 Cal. 382, 40 Pac. 482; Locke v. Moulton, 96 Cal. 21, 30 Pac. 957; Moisant v. McPhee, 92 Cal. 76, 28 Pac. 46; Boughton v. Vasquez, 73 Cal. 325, 11 Pac. 806, 14 Pac. 885.
[24] Johnson v. Sherman, 15 Cal. 287, 76 Am. Dec. 481. See also Dutton v. Warschauer, 21 Cal. 609, 82 Am. Dec. 765.
[25] Pico v. Gallardo, 52 Cal. 206.
[26] Grant v. Burr, 54 Cal. 298.
[27] Drake v. Root, 2 Colo. 685, per Hallett, C. J.; Fehringer v. Martin,

benefit of the holder of the mortgage debt. As against all other persons the mortgagor has the legal estate.[28] But it seems that a mortgagee who has acquired possession may retain it; and that he may recover the property by ejectment against third persons not holding under the mortgagor.[29] The code now provides that a mortgage of real property shall not be deemed a conveyance, whatever its terms, so as to enable the owner of the mortgage to recover possession of the property without foreclosure and sale; but this provision does not apply to trust deeds and mortgages with powers of sale.[30] The right of possession remains in the mortgagor until a valid sale is made.[31]

§ 22. **Connecticut.**—In Connecticut a mortgage passes the legal estate subject to be defeated by performance of the condition, and the mortgagee may maintain ejectment; but the mortgagor is to be regarded as the owner of the property, subject to the rights of the mortgagee to enforce payment of his debt by means of his title.[32]

In form, and in legal theory, a mortgage in fee is a conveyance of the fee to the mortgagee. It is an estate in the land upon condition, to become absolute upon nonperformance of the condition. The mortgagee is the owner of the land, while the mortgagor has no legal estate therein until he performs the conditions. If he fails to do so all his right to the land is gone. In substance and effect, however, and except for a very limited purpose, the mortgage is regarded as a mere security for the performance of the duty described in the mortgage; and the mortgagor is for most purposes regarded as the sole owner of the land, as well after forfeiture as before the execution of the deed; and the mortgagee has rather a power than an interest, the use of which is strictly limited to the collection of the debt, or en-

---

22 Cal. App. 634, 126 Pac. 1131; Pueblo &c. R. Co. v. Beshoar, 8 Colo. 32, 5 Pac. 639; Longan v. Carpenter, 1 Colo. 205.
[28] Ranch &c. Co. v. Howell, 22 Colo. App. 584, 126 Pac. 1096.
[29] Eyster v. Gaff, 2 Colo. 228.
[30] Code of Civil Procedure, 1887, § 261 in Laws 1887, p. 174. Trust deeds given as security and mortgages containing a power of sale vest the legal title in the trustee. The equity of redemption or equitable title remains in the mortgagor or the owner. The legal title of the trustee is supplemented by a power which authorizes him, upon default

in payment of the mortgage debt, to advertise and sell the property; the right to exercise this power being dependent upon his possession of such legal title. Stephens v. Clay, 17 Colo. 489, 30 Pac. 43.
[31] Lewis v. Hamilton, 26 Colo. 263, 58 Pac. 196; Bent-Otero Imp. Co. v. Whitehead, 25 Colo. 354, 54 Pac. 1023; Belmont M. &c. Co. v. Costigan, 21 Colo. 471, 42 Pac. 647.
[32] McKelvey v. Creevey, 72 Conn. 464; Middletown Sav. Bank v. Bates, 11 Conn. 519; Chamberlain v. Thompson, 10 Conn. 243, 26 Am. Dec. 390; Beach v. Clark, 6 Conn. 354; Rockwell v. Bradley, 2 Conn. 5.

forcement of the duty, which the mortgage was intended to secure.[33]

In this view of the matter the equity of redemption is regarded as the land, and its owner as the owner of the land, for most purposes; while the estate in fee of the mortgagee is, except for a limited purpose, regarded as personal estate and mere security.[34]

In accordance with this view it has been held that the estate of the mortgagor is subject to dower, descends to heirs, may be attached and set off on execution, may as real estate confer rights of settlement, is divisible and taxable as real estate, and is based upon a title sufficient to maintain ejectment; while to the estate of the mortgagee none of these incidents attach, save the right to maintain ejectment.[35]

When the debt is satisfied after forfeiture, if the legal title be permitted to remain vested in the mortgagee, he holds it in trust for the mortgagor.[36] The mortgage when paid is no longer an incumbrance, though it may be a cloud on the title.[37]

Courts of law have adopted equitable principles as to the effect of a mortgage, holding that it is a conveyance merely by way of pledge for the debt, and that the mortgagee holds the title solely for this purpose, aside from preserving and enforcing his security.[38] The mortgagor is the owner of the mortgaged land as against every one but the mortgagee. His equity of redemption may be devised, granted, levied upon, and set off in execution. The wife of a mortgagor is entitled to dower, and the husband of a mortgagor to curtesy. A mortgagor in possession may acquire a settlement, may maintain trespass against his mortgagee, and may take the emblements, without being liable to account; and although the mortgagee has only a chattel interest,—a mere pledge for the payment of the debt,—yet the legal title vests in him upon the execution of the mortgage, subject to be defeated only on performance of the condition; and after condition broken the only relief for the mortgagor is in equity.[39]

[33] New Haven Sav. Bank &c. Assn. v. McPartlan, 40 Conn. 90; Clinton v. Westbrook, 38 Conn. 9; Porter v. Seeley, 13 Conn. 564. See also McKelvey v. Creevey, 72 Conn. 464; Cook v. Bartholomew, 60 Conn. 24, 22 Atl. 444, 13 L. R. A. 4521.

[34] McKelvey v. Creevey, 72 Conn. 464; Downing v. Sullivan, 64 Conn. 1; Waterbury Savings Bank v. Lawler, 46 Conn. 243.

[35] McKelvey v. Creevey, 72 Conn. 464; Savage v. Dooley, 28 Conn. 411, 73 Am. Dec. 680; Swift v. Edson, 5 Conn. 531; Roath v. Smith, 5 Conn. 133; Huntington v. Smith, 4 Conn.

235; Barkhamsted v. Farmington, 2 Conn. 600; Fish v. Fish, 1 Conn. 559.

[36] Cross v. Robinson, 21 Conn. 379, 387; Dudley v. Cadwell, 19 Conn. 218; Phelps v. Sage, 2 Day (Conn.) 151.

[37] New Haven Savings Bank v. McPartlan, 40 Conn. 90; Clinton v. Westbrook, 38 Conn. 9; Doton v. Russell, 17 Conn. 146; Griswold v. Mather, 5 Conn. 435.

[38] Bates v. Coe, 10 Conn. 280. See also Lacon v. Davenport, 16 Conn. 331.

[39] Downing v. Sullivan, 64 Conn. 1; Smith v. Vincent, 15 Conn. 1, 38

§ 23. Delaware.—In Delaware a mortgage, as between the mortgagor and mortgagee, is only a security for the payment of the debt, and, so long as the mortgagor continues in possession, does not convey the legal title to the mortgagee;[40] but in the meantime it is a lien of so high a nature that it is not divested by a sale of the premises on a judgment subsequently obtained against the mortgagor. Yet after breach of the condition and possession obtained by the mortgagee, the legal title is in the mortgagee, and it is no longer in the power of the mortgagor, or any one claiming under him, to recover possession by ejectment.[41] As against every one but the mortgagee, the mortgagor in possession before foreclosure is regarded as the owner and freeholder, with the civil and political rights belonging to that character.[42] The mortgagee may, upon breach of the condition, use at the same time all the remedies the law affords against the person and the property; and he can not, without some special equity in favor of the debtor, be restrained from proceeding at his election upon either or both his remedies.[43]

What is termed the equity of redemption is, in this state, the title to the mortgaged land, with the right to redeem it from the incumbrance of the mortgage. The mortgagee takes by the mortgage no title to the land, but merely a lien upon it, which, upon his dying intestate, passes not to his heirs at law, but to his personal representative. A mortgage no more divests the title of the mortgagor in the mortgaged premises than does a general judgment divest the title of the defendant in land bound by the lien of such judgment.[44]

§ 24. Florida.—In Florida a mortgage is not deemed a conveyance so as to entitle the mortgagee to recover possession without a foreclosure.[45] It does not pass an estate in fee. It is a specific lien upon the property, and the mortgagor is divested of the title only by for-

---

Am. Dec. 52; Chamberlain v. Thompson, 10 Conn. 243, 26 Am. Dec. 390; Wakeman v. Banks, 2 Conn. 445.

[40] Fox v. Wharton, 5 Del. Ch. 200; Malsberger v. Parsons, 24 Del. 254, 75 Atl. 698.

[41] Hall v. Tunnell, 1 Houst. (Del.) 320; Malsberger v. Parsons, 24 Del. 254, 75 Atl. 698.

[42] Cooch v. Gerry, 3 Harr. (Del.) 280; Cornog v. Cornog, 3 Del. Ch. 407, 416; Walker v. Farmers' Bank (Del.), 14 Atl. 819, 10 Atl. 94, 100, per Salisbury, Ch.

[43] Newbold v. Newbold, 1 Del. Ch. 310.

[44] Cornog v. Cornog, 3 Del. Ch. 407; Fox v. Wharton, 5 Del. Ch. 200, 225; Grant v. Jackson &c. Co., 5 Del. Ch. 404; Cooch v. Gerry, 3 Harr. (Del.) 280; Robinson v. Harris, 3 Harr. (Del.) 283, note "a"; Hall v. Tunnell, 1 Houst. (Del.) 320; Walker v. Farmers' Bank, 8 Houst. (Del.) 259, 10 Atl. 94, 14 Atl. 819; Seals v. Chadwick, 2 Pennew. (Del.) 381, 45 Atl. 718; Ellison v. Dolbey, 3 Pennew. (Del.) 45, 49 Atl. 178; Malsberger v. Parsons, 24 Del. 254, 75 Atl. 698.

[45] Gen. Stat. 1906, § 2495, p. 985; Coe v. Finlayson, 41 Fla. 169, 26 So.

feiture of the condition and a foreclosure sale.[46] A mere failure to comply with the conditions of the mortgage does not divest the mortgagor of the legal title, nor vest it in the mortgagee.[47] It is held, however, that a deed of trust conveying land to trustees, with power to sell and convey it in fee and apply the proceeds to the payment of certain liabilities of the grantor, is not a mortgage, but is a conveyance which vests the legal title in the trustees.[48]

§ 25. Georgia.—In Georgia a mortgage is a mere security for a debt, and the mortgagee can neither enter nor maintain ejectment.[49] All he can do is to foreclose and sell, and make his money out of the sale; and the rents and profits belong to the mortgagor until the sale, for the reason that the title remains in him until the sheriff sells him out, and puts another in his place.[50] No title passes by the mortgage: it is only by foreclosure that the title is changed.[51] It is now declared in the code that a mortgage is only a security for a debt, and passes no title.[52]

But an absolute deed with a bond to reconvey passes the legal title.[53] The deed and bond do not, separately or together, indicate the creation of a mere lien, but the purpose indicated is, to divest the grantor of title, and to vest title in the grantee, until the debt be paid.[54] A provision that the deed shall be surrendered to the grantor and canceled if the grantor shall pay a specified sum to the grantee by a designated time does not convert the instrument into a mortgage, if it was originally framed so as to pass title, and especially if the payment by the grantor is optional and not obligatory.[55]

704; Jordan v. Sayre, 24 Fla. 1, 3 So. 329.

[46] Connor v. Connor, 59 Fla. 467, 52 So. 727; Coe v. Finlayson, 41 Fla. 169, 26 So. 704; Seedhouse v. Broward, 34 Fla. 509, 16 So. 425; Jordan v. Sayre, 29 Fla. 100, 10 So. 823; Berlack v. Halle, 22 Fla. 236, 1 Am. St. 185; McMahon v. Russell, 17 Fla. 698.

[47] Berlack v. Halle, 22 Fla. 236, 1 Am. St. 185; McMahon v. Russell, 17 Fla. 698; Pasco v. Gamble, 15 Fla. 698.

[48] Soutter v. Miller, 15 Fla. 625.

[49] Phillips v. Bond, 132 Ga. 413, 64 S. E. 456; Thomas v. Morrisett, 76 Ga. 384; Carter v. Gunn, 64 Ga. 651; Carter v. Hough, 60 Ga. 588; Vason v. Ball, 56 Ga. 268; United States v. Athens Armory, 35 Ga. 344; Elfe v. Cole, 26 Ga. 197; Ragland v. Justices, 10 Ga. 65; Davis v. Anderson, 1 Ga. 176; Seals v. Cashin, 2 Ga. Dec. 76.

[50] Vason v. Ball, 56 Ga. 268, per Jackson, J.

[51] Burnside v. Terry, 45 Ga. 621; Jackson v. Carswell, 34 Ga. 279.

[52] Code, 1911, § 3256.

[53] Groves v. Williams, 69 Ga. 614; Phinizy v. Clark, 62 Ga. 623; Allen v. Frost, 62 Ga. 659; Broach v. Barfield, 57 Ga. 601. See post, § 292.

[54] Gibson v. Hough, 60 Ga. 588; West v. Bennett, 59 Ga. 507.

[55] Pirkle v. Equitable Mtg. Co., 99 Ga. 524, 28 S. E. 34; McLaren v. Clark, 80 Ga. 423, 7 S. E. 230; Jay v. Welchel, 78 Ga. 786, 3 S. E. 906.

§ 26. **Idaho.**—In Idaho, it is provided by statute that a mortgage of real property shall not be deemed. a conveyance, whatever its terms, so as to enable the owner of a mortgage to recover possession of the premises, without a foreclosure and sale.[56] A deed of real property, made by a debtor to his creditor, accompanied by a contemporaneous agreement between the parties for a reconveyance of the property upon payment of the debt, constitutes a mortgage.[57]

§ 27. **Illinois.**—In Illinois it was at first held, in accordance with the rulings of the English courts of common-law jurisdiction, that, as an incident to the ownership in fee by the mortgagee, he can enter before condition broken or bring ejectment, unless the mortgage provides that the mortgagor shall retain possession.[58]

But it is now the settled rule that the right of a mortgagee to maintain ejectment against the mortgagor is confined to cases where the conditions of the mortgage have been broken, or there has been default in the payment of principal or interest.[59] The legal title remains in the mortgagor, and the mortgagee has a lien only on the premises as a security for the mortgage debt.[60]

It is held that the title of a mortgagee in fee in courts of law is regarded in the nature of a base or determinable fee.[61] While the mortgagor is the legal owner of the mortgaged premises against all persons except the mortgagee,[62] the mortgagee, as against the mortgagor, is held to be the owner of the fee, and entitled to all the rights and remedies which the law gives to such owner.[63]

The right of the mortgagor to hold possession may be implied. The permission granted to the mortgagor to hold possession until default may be implied from the terms of the mortgage, even though there is no express provision to that effect.[64] The right of the maker of a

[56] Rev. Stat. § 4523; Kelley v. Leachman, 2 Idaho 1112, 29 Pac. 849.

[57] Kelley v. Leachman, 2 Idaho 1112, 29 Pac. 849; Pritchard v. Butler, 4 Idaho 518, 43 Pac. 73.

[58] Lightcap v. Bradley, 186 Ill. 510, 58 N. E. 221; Ortengren v. Rice, 104 Ill. App. 428.

[59] Kranz v. Uedelhofen, 193 Ill. 477, 62 N. E. 239; Esker v. Heffernan, 159 Ill. 38, 41 N. E. 1113; Davis v. Dale, 150 Ill. 239, 37 N. E. 215; Taylor v. Adams, 115 Ill. 570, 4 N. E. 837; Anderson v. Strauss, 98 Ill. 485; Mester v. Hauser, 94 Ill. 433; Oldham v. Pfleger, 84 Ill. 102; Kilgour v. Gockley, 83 Ill. 109; Vansant v. Allmon, 23 Ill. 30.

[60] Ortengren v. Rice, 104 Ill. App. 428.

[61] Ladd v. Ladd, 252 Ill. 43, 96 N. E. 561; McFall v. Kirkpatrick, 236 Ill. 281, 86 N. E. 139; Ware v. Schintz, 190 Ill. 189, 60 N. E. 67; Lightcap v. Bradley, 186 Ill. 510, 58 N. E. 221; Barrett v. Hinkley, 124 Ill. 32, 14 N. E. 863, 7 Am. St. 331.

[62] Seaman v. Bisbee, 163 Ill. 91, 45 N. E. 208.

[63] Bradley v. Lightcap, 195 U. S. 1, 49 L. ed. 65, 24 Sup. Ct. 748; Esker v. Heffernan, 159 Ill. 38, 41 N. E. 1113; Oldham v. Pfleger, 84 Ill. 102.

[64] Kranz v. Uedelhofen, 193 Ill. 477, 62 N. E. 239; Carroll v. Ballance, 26 Ill. 9; Hobart v. Sanborn, 13 N. H.

trust deed to retain possession and collect the rents and profits is implied where the trust deed provides that upon breach of condition the maker waives all right to possession and to the income and rents of the premises.[65]

Upon breach of the condition, the mortgagee has the legal title,[66] and may bring his action without giving the party in possession any notice to quit.[67] The condition is broken when one or more instalments are due and unpaid; because, the condition being an entirety, it is invisible, and a failure to pay any part of the debt is a breach of the condition.[68] The mortgagee may pursue all his remedies at the same time: he may proceed against the debtor personally; against the property by bill in chancery for a strict foreclosure, or for a foreclosure and sale; or, when the debt is all due, by scire facias; and he may bring ejectment for the possession, or make peaceable entry.[69] But even after condition broken, a mortgage is not an absolute outstanding title of which a stranger can take advantage to defeat a recovery, in ejectment by the mortgagor.[70] Except as against the mortgagee, the mortgagor is regarded for all beneficial purposes as the owner of the land.[71] Moreover the mortgagor or a purchaser from him is the legal owner of the mortgaged estate as against all persons except the mortgagee or his assigns, who are the legal owners for one purpose only, namely, the enforcement of the debt secured.[72]

§ 28. **Indiana.**—In Indiana the common-law doctrine, that the legal estate vests in the mortgagee, was adhered to many years, as appears by the earlier cases; but it no longer prevails. The settled doctrine in this state is that a mortgage is but a lien on the land as a security for the debt, and that the legal title remains in the mortgagor, subject to the lien of the mortgage.[73] It is merely an

226; Jamieson v. Bruce, 6 Gill & J. (Md.) 74.

[65] Kranz v. Uedelhofen, 193 Ill. 477, 62 N. E. 239.

[66] Walker v. Warner, 179 Ill. 16, 53 N. E. 594, 70 Am. St. 185.

[67] Lightcap v. Bradley, 186 Ill. 510, 58 N. E. 221; Barrett v. Hinckley, 124 Ill. 32, 14 N. E. 863; Delano v. Bennett, 90 Ill. 533; Harper v. Ely, 70 Ill. 581; Gibson v. Rees, 50 Ill. 383; Pollock v. Maison, 41 Ill. 516; Jackson v. Warren, 32 Ill. 331; Nelson v. Pinegar, 30 Ill. 473; Carroll v. Ballance, 26 Ill. 9, 79 Am. Dec. 354; Vansant v. Allmon, 23 Ill. 30, 33; Delahay v. Clement, 4 Ill. 201.

[68] Kranz v. Uedelhofen, 193 Ill. 477, 62 N. E. 239.

[69] Karnes v. Lloyd, 52 Ill. 113; Erickson v. Rafferty, 79 Ill. 209.

[70] Oldham v. Pfleger, 84 Ill. 102; Hall v. Lance, 25 Ill. 277.

[71] Barrett v. Hinckley, 124 Ill. 32, 14 N. E. 863, 7 Am. St. 331; Vallette v. Bennett, 69 Ill. 632; Fitch v. Pinckard, 5 Ill. 69.

[72] Lightcap v. Bradley, 186 Ill. 510, 58 N. E. 221; Barrett v. Hinckley, 124 Ill. 32, 14 N. E. 863; Delano v. Bennett, 90 Ill. 533; Emory v. Keighan, 88 Ill. 482; Gibson v. Rees, 50 Ill. 383.

[73] Fletcher v. Holmes, 32 Ind. 497,

incumbrance or security for a debt, and does not transfer the legal estate.[74] It is provided by statute that, in the absence of stipulations to the contrary, the mortgagor, until foreclosure, may retain possession of the mortgaged estate.[75] His equity of redemption may be granted, devised, or taken in execution; and it is therefore regarded as the real and beneficial estate tantamount to the fee at law.[76]

§ 29. **Iowa.**—The interest of the mortgagee is regarded as a lien upon the land for the debt, which may, by certain proceedings, ripen into a title, or rather may divest the title of the mortgagor. Some act of the mortgagee is necessary, that he may acquire an indefeasible title which the mortgagor will not be able to defeat by redemption. The interest of the mortgagor is an estate of inheritance, which is in no way affected by the mortgage before entry and foreclosure, except by the lien created. The fact that a mortgage confers upon the mortgagee a right of entry upon breach of the condition gives him no additional right, inasmuch as the right exists under the law, without such provision.[77] It is now provided by statute that, in the absence of stipulations to the contrary, the mortgagor retains the legal title and the right of possession.[78]

This statute applies to a conveyance absolute in terms to secure the payment of a debt.[79] An absolute deed made as security for a debt conveys the legal title.[80] But it has been held that where a husband and wife join in deeds conveying lands to the wife, and the grantee at the time executes a defeasance in which it is recited that he holds the husband's obligation for a certain sum, and that upon payment of the same he will reconvey the land, the transaction constitutes a

513; Grable v. McCulloh, 27 Ind. 472; Morton v. Noble, 22 Ind. 160, 11 Am. Rep. 7; Franci˙ v. Porter, 7 Ind. 213; Reasoner v. Edmundson, 5 Ind. 393; Baldwin v. Moroney, 173 Ind. 574, 91 N. E. 3, 30 L. R. A. (N. S.) 761; Sinclair v. Gunzenhauser, 179 Ind. 78, 98 N. E. 37.

[74] Fletcher v. Holmes, 32 Ind. 497; Grable v. McCulloh, 27 Ind. 472; Morton v. Noble, 22 Ind. 160; Francis v. Porter, 7 Ind. 213.

[75] See Reed v. Ward, 51 Ind. 215; Jones v. Thomas, 8 Blackf. (Ind.) 428; Grimes v. Doe, 8 Blackf. (Ind.) 371.

G. & H. Stat. p. 335. Prior to 1843, when this statute was passed, the mortgagee could recover possession at any time unless restrained by the terms of the mortgage.

[76] Ætna L. Ins. Co. v. Broecker, 166 Ind. 576, 77 N. E. 1092.

[77] White v. Rittenmyer, 30 Iowa 268; Courtney v. Carr, 6 Iowa 238; Hall v. Savill, 3 G. Greene (Iowa) 37, 54 Am. Dec. 485; Fitzgerald v. Flannagan (Iowa), 125 N. W. 995.

[78] Code, Iowa, § 2922; Whitley v. Barnett, 151 Iowa 487, 131 N. W. 704.

[79] Harrington v. Foley, 108 Iowa 287, 79 N. W. 64. As to discussions prior to this statute, see Richards v. Crawford, 50 Iowa 494; Burdick v. Wentworth, 42 Iowa 440; Farley v. Goocher, 11 Iowa 570.

[80] Haggerty v. Brower, 105 Iowa 395, 75 N. W. 321; In re Snyder, 138 Iowa 553, 114 N. W. 615, 19 L. R. A. (N. S.) 206.

mortgage, differing, however, from the ordinary mortgage in that the fee in the land passes to the grantee.[81]

§ 30. Kansas.—In Kansas the legal estate remains in the mortgagor after making a mortgage, and it is provided by statute that, in the absence of stipulations to the contrary, he may retain possession of the mortgaged estate.[82] "Some of the states still adhere to the common-law view, more or less modified by the real nature of the transaction; but in most of them, practically, all that remains of the old theories is their nomenclature. In this state a clear sweep has been made by statute. The common-law attributes of mortgages have been wholly set aside; the ancient theories have been demolished; and if we could consign to oblivion the terms and phrases—without meaning except in reference to those theories—with which our reflections are still embarrassed, the legal profession, on the bench and at the bar, would more readily understand and fully realize the new condition of things."[83]

A trust deed, being merely a mortgage, is regarded as conveying no estate or title in the land, but as creating merely a lien.[84] "Where a deed of trust is executed with the understanding between the parties that the title is to be transferred forever from the grantor to the grantee and his heirs or grantees, then such deed of trust is not a mortgage. But where the deed of trust is executed with the understanding between the parties that it is a mere security for a debt, and that when the debt is paid the title shall be again placed in the grantor, such deed of trust is a mere mortgage."[85]

§ 31. Kentucky.—In Kentucky, since the adoption of the Civil Code, a mortgage is regarded as a mere security for debt, and substantially, both at law and in equity, the mortgagor is the real owner of the mortgaged property until foreclosure.[86] The mortgagee only

[81] Collier v. Smaltz, 149 Iowa 230, 128 N. W. 396, Ann. Cas. 1912 C, 1007; Haggerty v. Brower, 105 Iowa 395, 75 N. W. 321; Richards v. Crawford, 50 Iowa 494; Lomax v. Smyth, 50 Iowa 223; Burdick v. Wentworth, 42 Iowa 440.

[82] Gen. Stat. 1909, § 5194; Beckman v. Sikes, 35 Kans. 120, 10 Pac. 592; Seckler v. Delfs, 25 Kans. 159; Robbins v. Sackett, 23 Kans. 301; Watterson v. Devoe, 18 Kans. 223; Lenox v. Reed, 12 Kans. 223; Chick v. Willetts, 2 Kans. 384.

[83] Chick v. Willetts, 2 Kans. 384. See also Southern Kans. R. Co. v. Sharpless, 62 Kans. 841, 62 Pac. 662; Hunt v. Bowman, 62 Kans. 448, 63 Pac. 747; Waterson v. Devoe, 18 Kans. 223; Chicago K. & W. R. Co. v. Need, 2 Kans. App. 492, 496, 43 Pac. 997.

[84] Lenox v. Reed, 12 Kans. 223; Robbins v. Sackett, 23 Kans. 301.

[85] McDonald v. Kellogg, 30 Kans. 170, 2 Pac. 507.

[86] Taliaferro v. Gay, 78 Ky. 496; Woolley v. Holt, 14 Bush (Ky.)

has a lien for his debt, and a deed of mortgage is not a conveyance of title.[87] The rents and profits of the mortgaged premises belong to the mortgagor until he is divested of the title, unless there is a specific pledge of them in the mortgage.[88] A mortgagee in possession can not be ousted until the debt secured thereby be paid and the mortgage satisfied.[89]

An agreement to bid in the land of a debtor at a judicial sale and to hold it subject to his redemption is held to constitute a mortgage, and the purchaser a mere holder of the land to secure the price bid until redemption is effected.[90]

§ 32. **Louisiana.**—In Louisiana a mortgage is a species of alienation, but not a sale. It is an alienation of a right on the property, not of the property itself. The title, as well as the possession, remains in the owner.[91] Default in the payment of the debt secured does not give the creditor an absolute title to the property, but only a right to have it sold and the proceeds applied to the satisfaction of his claim.[92]

The civil code of this state defines a mortgage as "a right granted to the creditor over the property of the debtor for the security of his debt, and gives him the power of having the property seized and sold in default of payment. Mortgage is a species of pledge, the thing mortgaged being bound for the payment of the debt, or fulfilment of the obligation. The conventional mortgage is a contract, by which a person binds the whole of his property, or a portion of it only, in favor of another, to secure the execution of some engagement, but without divesting himself of the possession."[93] A conventional

788; Douglass v. Cline, 12 Bush (Ky.) 608. See also Bullock v. Grinstead, 95 Ky. 261, 24 S. W. 867, 15 Ky. L. 663; Mercantile Trust Co. v. South Park Residence Co,. 94 Ky. 271, 22 S. W. 314, 15 Ky. L. 70; Sheffield v. Day, 28 Ky. L. 754, 90 S. W. 545; Alderson v. Casky, 15 Ky. L. 589, 24 S. W. 629, 29 S. W. 976; Gossman v. Gossman, 13 Ky. L. 243, 15 S. W. 1057; Edrington v. Harper, 3 J. J. Marsh. (Ky.) 354, 20 Am. Dec. 145.

[87] Rissberger v. Louisville (Ky.), 118 S. W. 319; Board of Council v. Fidelity T. &c. Co., 111 Ky. 676, 64 S. W. 470; Mercantile Trust Co. v. Southern Park Residence Co., 94 Ky. 276, 22 S. W. 314; Clore v. Lambert, 78 Ky. 228; Douglass v. Cline, 12 Bush (Ky.) 608; Woolley v. Holt, 14 Bush (Ky.) 788; Guill v. Co-

rinth Deposit Bank, 24 Ky. L. 482, 68 S. W. 870; Parks v. Parks, 9 Ky. L. 347.

[88] Taliaferro v. Gay, 78 Ky. 496; McElroy v. Barbee, 4 Ky. Opin. 165.

[89] McMichael v. McMichael, 3 Ky. Opin. 608.

[90] Nichols v. Marquess, 141 Ky. 642, 133 S. W. 562.

[91] Miller v. Shotwell, 38 La. Ann. 890; Duclaud v. Rousseau, 2 La. Ann. 168. See also Conrad v. Prieur, 5 Rob. (La.) 49; Marbury v. Colbert, 105 La. 467, 29 So. 871; Randolph v. Stark, 51 La. Ann. 1121, 26 So. 59.

[92] Duclaud v. Rousseau, 2 La. Ann. 168.

[93] Merrick's Rev. Civ. Code, § 3278; Benjamin Succession of, 39 La. Ann. 612, 2 So. 187; Gates v. Gaither, 46 La. Ann. 286, 15 So. 50.

mortgage is one founded upon the covenants of the parties in contradistinction to a legal mortgage.[94]

§ 33. **Maine.**—In Maine a mortgage vests the mortgagee with the legal estate conditionally,[95] and it is provided by statute that he may enter before breach of the condition, when there is no agreement to the contrary. The mortgagor,[96] as to every one but the mortgagee, is considered as having the legal estate, and the power of conveying it or incumbering it subject to the lien of the mortgage.[97]

As between the mortgagor and the mortgagee, the mortgagee holds the legal estate in the mortgaged premises with all the incidents of ownership in fee, while the mortgagor retains an equitable right under a condition subsequent in the deed.[98]

It is held that so long as the right of redemption exists the title can not become absolute in the mortgagee, nor can he appropriate it in the payment of his debts; and until his title is perfected the law will not so appropriate it.[99]

§ 34. **Maryland.**—The mortgagee has the legal estate, and is entitled to possession immediately upon the execution of the mortgage, unless there be some agreement of the parties to the contrary.[1] Ordinarily he may pursue all his remedies at the same time.[2] He may, even before breach of condition, maintain ejectment and oust the mortgagor, unless he has waived this right by a stipulation in the mortgage.[3] As to all other persons, the mortgagor is deemed the owner. He may, therefore, when the mortgage allows him to remain in possession until default, maintain ejectment against a third party

---

[94] See Walmsley v. Resweber, 105 La. 522, 30 So. 5.

[95] Allen Co. v. Emerton, 108 Maine 221, 79 Atl. 905; Brastow v. Barrett, 82 Maine 456, 19 Atl. 916; Anderson v. Robbins, 82 Maine 422, 19 Atl. 910, 8 L. R. A. 568; Jones v. Smith, 79 Maine 446, 10 Atl. 254; Bragdon v. Hatch, 77 Maine 433, 1 Atl. 140; Howard v. Houghton, 64 Maine 445; Mitchell v. Burnham, 44 Maine 286; Blaney v. Bearce, 2 Maine 132. See post § 702.

[96] Rev. Stat. 1903, ch. 92, § 2; Hussey v. Fisher, 94 Maine 301, 47 Atl. 525.

[97] Wilkins v. French, 20 Maine 111.

[98] Allen Co. v. Emerton, 108 Maine 221, 79 Atl. 905; Gilman v. Wills, 66

Maine 273; Howard v. Houghton, 64 Maine 445.

[99] Covell v. Dolloff, 31 Maine 104.

[1] Chelton v. Green, 65 Md. 272, 4 Atl. 271; Baltimore City Appeal Tax Ct. v. Rice, 50 Md. 302; Annapolis &c. R. Co. v. Gantt, 39 Md. 115; Sumwalt v. Tucker, 34 Md. 89; McKim v. Mason, 3 Md. Ch. 186; Brown v. Stewart, 1 Md. Ch. 87; Leighton v. Preston, 9 Gill (Md.) 201; Jamieson v. Bruce, 6 Gill & J. (Md.) 72, 26 Am. Dec. 557, per Archer, J.

[2] Wilhelm v. Lee, 2 Md. Ch. 322; Brown v. Stewart, 1 Md. Ch. 87.

[3] Commercial Bldg. &c. Assn. v. Robinson, 90 Md. 615, 45 Atl. 449; Hagerstown v. Groh, 101 Md. 560, 60 Atl. 467; Brown v. Stewart, 1 Md. Ch. 87.

who rests his defense entirely on possession and an outstanding title in the mortgagee.[4] Moreover, being the substantial owner, he is entitled to sue for damages done the estate by a third person.[5]

§ 35. **Massachusetts.**—In Massachusetts the English characteristics of a mortgage are retained. It confers upon the mortgagee a legal estate and the right of possession. "The first great object of a mortgage," says Chief Justice Shaw,[6] "is, in the form of a conveyance in fee, to give to the mortgagee an effectual security, by the pledge or hypothecation of real estate, for the payment of a debt, or the performance of some other obligation. The next is to leave to the mortgagor, and to purchasers, creditors, and all others claiming derivatively through him, the full and entire control, disposition and ownership of the estate, subject only to the first purpose, that of securing the mortgagee. Hence it is that, as between mortgagor and mortgagee, the mortgage is to be regarded as a conveyance in fee; because that construction best secures him in his remedy and his ultimate right to the estate, and to its incidents, the rents and profits. But in all other respects, until foreclosure, when the mortgagee becomes the absolute owner, the mortgage is deemed to be a lien or charge, subject to which the estate may be conveyed, attached, and in all other respects dealt with as the estate of the mortgagor. And all the statutes upon the subject are to be so construed; and all rules of law, whether administered in law or in equity, are to be so applied as to carry these objects into effect." And in another case the same eminent jurist says:[7] "Mortgaging is not such a conveying away of the estate as divests the entire title of the owner. It is a charge or incumbrance created out of that estate, and may amount to a small part only of its value. Although, as between mortgagor and mortgagee, it is a transmission of the fee, which gives the mortgagee a remedy in the form of a real action, and constitutes a legal seisin, yet to most other purposes a mortgage, before the entry of the mortgagee, is but a pledge and real lien, leaving the mortgagor to most purposes the owner."[8]

---

[4] George's Creek Coal &c. Co. v. Detmold, 1 Md. 225, 237. See also Ann. Code, art. 75, § 72, p. 1667. Morgan v. Davis, 2 Har. & M. (Md.) 9.

[5] Annapolis & Elkridge R. Co. v. Gantt, 39 Md. 115.

[6] Ewer v. Hobbs, 5 Met. (Mass.) 1.

[7] Howard v. Robinson, 4 Cush. (Mass.) 119.

[8] Norcross v. Norcross, 105 Mass. 265; Erskine v. Townsend, 2 Mass. 493, 3 Am. Dec. 71; Steel v. Steel, 4 Allen (Mass.) 417; Sparhawk v. Bagg, 16 Gray (Mass.) 583; Silloway v. Brown, 12 Gray (Mass.) 30; Hapgood v. Blood, 11 Gray (Mass.) 400; Bradley v. Fuller, 23 Pick. (Mass.) 1. See also post § 702.

As between the parties, the mortgage is regarded as a conveyance of the fee for the protection of the rights of the mortgagee, and entitles him to immediate possession. But in all other respects, the mortgage is considered as a mere lien or security, subject to which the estate may be conveyed, attached or dealt with as the estate of the mortgagor.[9] The mortgagee may, even before breach of condition, maintain ejectment and oust the mortgagor.[10]

§ 36. **Michigan.**—In Michigan no action of ejectment can be maintained by a mortgagee, or his assigns or representatives, for the recovery of the mortgaged premises, until the title shall have become absolute upon a foreclosure of the mortgage.[11] Not being allowed as mortgagee to bring an ejectment suit, he is not allowed to maintain a bill for foreclosure as a proceeding auxiliary to the ejectment suit. Nor can he convert a bill in aid of ejectment proceedings into a foreclosure bill by merely substituting the ordinary prayer for foreclosure in place of the prayer originally made.[12] The mortgagee has no legal title in the land mortgaged, but only a lien for the security of the mortgage debt.[13] A mortgage in common-law form, executed prior to the statute which deprived mortgagees of the right of possession, gave the mortgagee or his assigns the right to go into the enjoyment of the lands and hold them until redeemed.[14] Under the existing statute a mortgagor is entitled to recover possession from his mortgagee at any time before his rights have been foreclosed.[15]

A conveyance in trust to secure an indebtedness is only a mortgage, and does not preclude the mortgagor from claiming the title in

---

[9] Norcross v. Norcross, 105 Mass. 265. See also Gray v. McClellan, 214 Mass. 92, 100 N. E. 1093; Kinney v. Treasurer, 207 Mass. 368, 93 N. E. 586, 35 L. R. A. (N. S.) 784, Ann. Cas. 1912 A, 902; Delano v. Smith, 206 Mass. 365, 92 N. E. 500, 30 L. R. A. (N. S.) 474.

[10] Lackey v. Holbrook, 11 Metc. (Mass.) 458; Fay v. Cheney, 14 Pick. (Mass.) 399.

[11] Howell's Stat., § 13206; Bowen v. Brogan, 119 Mich. 218, 77 N. W. 942, 75 Am. St. 387; Michigan Trust Co. v. Lansing Lumber Co., 103 Mich. 392, 61 N. W. 668; Cook v. Knowles, 38 Mich. 316; Wagar v. Stone, 36 Mich. 364; Hoffman v. Harrington, 33 Mich. 392; Newton v. McKay, 30 Mich. 380.

[12] Livingston v. Hayes, 43 Mich. 129, 5 N. W. 78.

[13] Dawson v. Peter, 119 Mich. 274, 77 N. W. 997; Detroit v. Detroit Bd. of Assessors, 91 Mich. 78, 51 N. W. 787, 16 L. R. A. 59; Taggart v. Sanilac County, 71 Mich. 16, 38 N. W. 639; Byers v. Byers, 65 Mich. 598, 32 N. W. 831; Morse v. Byam, 55 Mich. 594, 22 N. W. 54; Lee v. Clary, 38 Mich. 223; Wagar v. Stone, 36 Mich. 364; Gorham v. Arnold, 22 Mich. 247; Caruthers v. Humphrey, 12 Mich. 270.

[14] Hoffman v. Harrington, 33 Mich. 392; Mundy v. Munroe, 1 Mich. 68; Schwarz v. Sears, Walk. Ch. (Mich.) 170; Stevens v. Brown, Walk. Ch. (Mich.) 41.

[15] Humphrey v. Hurd, 29 Mich. 44.

fee.[16] A deed of conveyance, absolute and unconditional on its face, but intended and understood by the parties to be merely a security for a debt or obligation, is regarded in equity as a mortgage, giving to the parties the relative rights of mortgagor and mortgagee.[17]

§ 37. **Minnesota.**—In Minnesota it is declared by statute that a mortgage of real property shall not be deemed a conveyance, so as to enable the owner of the mortgage to recover possession of it without a foreclosure.[18] Referring to this statute, Chief Justice Emmet says:[19] "This, it appears to me, deprives the mortgagee of the only material advantage which remained to him from being considered the owner of the fee; and although, out of deference to the past, we may still regard him as the legal owner, he is such in theory only, having no right to interfere with the possession save by consent of the mortgagor. The effect of the change just referred to is to dissipate whatever of title he may formerly have had beyond that of a mere lien or security. And although the mortgagee may, by obtaining a strict foreclosure, eventually secure possession, and thus complete his title under the mortgage, yet, as the courts may, and in practice generally do, direct the property to be sold, even when a strict foreclosure is asked for, he is by no means certain of ever perfecting that title which the mortgage purports to convey. And if the property, by direction of the court or otherwise, be sold to satisfy the mortgage, the purchaser, when he receives his deed, takes not the title of the mortgagee, for that is extinguished by the application of the proceeds of the sale; nor does he take simply the title of the mortgagor at the time of the sale, for that is incomplete; but he takes the title which was in the mortgagor at the time the mortgage was given, which is equivalent to both."

One who is in reality a mortgagee, although the conveyance to him is in the form of an absolute deed, has no greater rights than a mortgagee under a mortgage in the usual form, and therefore is not entitled

---

[16] Flint & Pere Marquette R. Co. v. Auditor General, 41 Mich. 635, 2 N. W. 835.

[17] Ferry v. Miller, 164 Mich. 429, 129 N. W. 721; Schmidt v. Barclay, 161 Mich. 1, 125 N. W. 729; Ruch v. Ruch, 159 Mich. 231, 124 N. W. 52; Flynn v. Holmes, 145 Mich. 606, 108 N. W. 685, 11 L. R. A. (N. S.) 209; Darling v. Darling, 123 Mich. 307, 82 N. W. 48. But see Jeffery v. Hursh, 42 Mich. 563, 4 N. W. 303.

[18] Gen. Stat. 1913, § 8077.

[19] Geib v. Reynolds, 35 Minn. 331, 28 N. W. 923; Busse v. Page, 32 Minn. 111, 19 N. W. 736, 20 N. W. 95; Adams v. Corriston, 7 Minn. 456. See also Rice v. St. Paul & Pac. R. Co., 24 Minn. 464; Berthold v. Fox, 13 Minn. 501, 97 Am. Dec. 243; Berthold v. Holman, 12 Minn. 335, 93 Am. Dec. 233; Donnelly v. Simonton, 7 Minn. 167.

to possession of the premises if not voluntarily surrendered to him by the grantor.[20]

§ 38. **Mississippi.**—In Mississippi, upon a breach of the condition of a mortgage, the legal title becomes absolute in the mortgagee, who thereupon becomes entitled to the possession of the property as an incident to the title.[21] The code now provides that before a sale under a mortgage, or deed of trust, the mortgagor or grantor shall be deemed the owner of the legal title of the property conveyed, except as against the mortgagee and his assigns, or the trustee, after breach of the condition of the mortgage or deed.[22]

But with reference to the dual nature of a mortgage, and the rights of the mortgagee after default, the modified common-law doctrine prevails in this state also.[23] The debt is considered as the principal, and the mortgage as an incident only. The mortgagee, notwithstanding the form of the conveyance, has but a security. The principles long established in chancery have, under the code, become naturalized in the courts of common law, so that until foreclosure the mortgagee is regarded as having a chattel interest only. Even after the mortgagee has taken possession, the mortgaged estate is regarded as a pledge only.[24]

As respects third persons, and the mortgagee also until after forfeiture, the mortgagor is the owner of the legal real estate, and the mortgagee has only a security for the debt. "The legal title," says Chief Justice Simrall,[25] "may be asserted by the mortgagee, but only for the protection of his debt, and to make the security available for its payment."

§ 39. **Missouri.**—In Missouri a mortgage is only a security for a debt, and remains so even after a condition broken; but upon default in the payment of the debt the mortgagee may maintain ejectment,

---

[20] Meighen v. King, 31 Minn. 115, 16 N. W. 702.

[21] Hill v. Robertson, 24 Miss. 368; Harmon v. Short, 8 Sm. & M. (Miss.) 433; Buck v. Payne, 52 Miss. 271.

[22] Miss. Code, 1906, § 2779; Carpenter v. Bowen, 42 Miss. 28.

[23] Buck v. Payne, 52 Miss. 271; Buckley v. Daley, 45 Miss. 338; Carpenter v. Bowen, 42 Miss. 28; Heard v. Baird, 40 Miss. 793; Hill v. Robertson, 24 Miss. 368.

[24] Buckley v. Daley, 45 Miss. 338, 345. "The relation of debtor and creditor exists," says Chief Justice Peyton, "and the equity of redemption is unimpaired. Although the mortgagee has a chattel interest only, yet in order to render his pledge available, and give him the intended benefit of his security, it is considered as real property to enable him to maintain ejectment for the recovery of the possession of the land mortgaged; when contemplated in every other point of view, it is personal property." To same effect is Carpenter v. Bowen, 42 Miss. 28, 49.

[25] Buck v. Payne, 52 Miss. 271.

because he is then in law regarded as the owner of the estate; but the legal title vests in him only for the purpose of protecting his debt.[26] By a mortgage, or a deed of trust in the nature of a mortgage, the legal title, after condition broken, passes to the mortgagee or trustee.[27] The addition of a power to sell, without judicial proceedings to fore-close, can not avoid the legal effect of the grant.[28]

Where a mortgage debt is payable by instalments, the condition is broken by nonpayment of any one of them, and the mortgagee may thereupon enter or bring ejectment, and it is no defense to such a suit that all the instalments are not due. The authorization contained in a mortgage, to sell only in event that "the said notes should not be well and truly paid," should be construed to mean in case they should not be paid as they respectively become due. The mortgagee is not by such condition compelled to wait till the last note is dishonored before applying his remedy.[29] But although a mortgage is a conveyance in fee upon condition, it is, even after the condition is broken and the legal title has passed to the mortgagee, merely a security for the debt, and is extinguished, and the title revested, whenever the debt is paid.[30] The trustee, after dishonor of the notes secured, may enter, and without sale or foreclosure may maintain his possession for the use of the beneficiary, not only against all outsiders, but against the maker of the deed himself, until the payment of the debt. It has long been established in this state that after condition broken the mortgagee may maintain ejectment.[31]

§ 39a. Montana.—A mortgage of real property is not deemed a conveyance, whatever its terms, so as to enable the owner of the mortgage to recover possession of the real property without fore-closure and sale.[32] A mortgagee in possession of the mortgaged prem-

[26] Bailey v. Winn, 101 Mo. 649, 12 S. W. 1045. See also Jackson v. Johnson, 248 Mo. 680, 154 S W. 759; Siemers v. Schrader, 88 Mo. 20; Barnett v. Timberlake, 57 Mo. 499; Leather Co. v. Ins. Co., 131 Mo. App. 701, 111 S. W. 631.

[27] Meyer v. Campbell, 12 Mo. 603.

[28] Johnson v. Houston, 47 Mo. 227; Woods v. Hilderbrand, 46 Mo. 284, 2 Am. Rep. 513; Kennett v. Plummer, 28 Mo. 142.

[29] Reddick v. Gressman, 49 Mo. 389.

[30] Pease v. Pilot Knob Iron Co., 49 Mo. 124.

[31] Bailey v. Winn, 101 Mo. 649, 12 S. W. 1045; Reddick v. Gressman, 49 Mo. 389; Sutton v. Mason, 38 Mo. 120; Walcop v. McKinney, 10 Mo. 229.

[32] Mont. Codes Ann., § 3816; Mueller v. Renkes, 31 Mont. 100, 77 Pac. 512; Wilson v. Pickering, 28 Mont. 435, 72 Pac. 821; Muth v. Goddard, 28 Mont. 237, 72 Pac. 621, 98 Am. St. 553; Holland v. Commissioners, 15 Mont. 460, 39 Pac. 575; First Nat. Bank v. Bell S. &c. Min. Co., 8 Mont. 32, 19 Pac. 403; Fee v. Swingly, 6 Mont. 596, 13 Pac. 375; Gallatin Co. v. Beattie, 3 Mont. 173.

ises, after condition broken, and with the consent of the mortgagor is entitled to the possession until the debt is paid.[33]

§ **40. Nebraska.**—The doctrine is established that the mortgagee is not seised of the freehold, either at law or in equity, either before or after condition broken.[34] The mortgage vests no title either before or after default, but merely creates a lien.[35] It is a mere security in the form of a conditional conveyance, and the interest which it vests in the mortgage is not essentially different from that created by a purchaser's lien or an ordinary judgment.[36] It is provided by statute that the mortgagor, in the absence of stipulations to the contrary, retains the legal title and right of possession,[37] until confirmation of a foreclosure sale. A deed of trust to secure the payment of a debt, being in effect a mortgage, is held, in accordance with the general rule that a mortgage does not pass the legal title, not to vest a legal estate in the trustee.[38]

§ **41. Nevada.**—In Nevada the courts seem to hold the title does not pass from the mortgagor before breach of the condition.[39] It is provided by statute that a mortgage of real property shall not be deemed a conveyance, whatever its terms, so as to enable the owner of the mortgage to recover possession of the land, without a foreclosure and sale.[40] It seems that even a deed absolute in form amounts only to an equitable lien, and does not vest the legal title in the grantee.[41]

§ **42. New Hampshire.**—The seisin, or possession, as well as the title, passes directly to the mortgagee unless he is restrained by the provisions of the deed; and upon a breach of the condition he is in

[33] Fee v. Swingly, 6 Mont. 596, 13 Pac. 375.
[34] Morrill v. Skinner, 57 Nebr. 164, 77 N. W. 375; Barber v. Crowell, 55 Nebr. 571, 75 N. W. 1109; McHugh v. Smiley, 17 Nebr. 626, 20 N. W. 296; Union Mut. Life Ins. Co. v. Lovitt, 10 Nebr. 301, 4 N. W. 986; Hurley v. Estes, 6 Nebr. 386; Kyger v. Ryley, 2 Nebr. 20.
[35] Morrill v. Skinner, 57 Nebr. 164, 77 N. W. 375; Orr v. Broad, 52 Nebr. 497, 72 N. W. 850; Davidson v. Cox, 11 Nebr. 252, 9 N. W. 95.
[36] Barber v. Crowell, 55 Nebr. 571, 75 N. W. 1109.
[37] Cobbey's Ann. Stat., § 10855; Clark v. Missouri K. &c. Trust Co., 59 Nebr. 53, 80 N. W. 257; Orr v.

Broad, 52 Nebr. 490, 72 N. W. 850; Connolly v. Giddings, 24 Nebr. 131, 37 N. W. 939.
[38] Hurley v. Estes, 6 Nebr. 386; Webb v. Hoselton, 4 Nebr. 308, 19 Am. Rep. 638; Kyger v. Ryley, 2 Nebr. 20.
[39] Whitmore v. Shiverick, 3 Nev. 288; Hyman v. Kelly, 1 Nev. 179.
[40] Gen. Stat. 1885, Civ. Proc. § 3284; Orr v. Ulyatt, 23 Nev. 134, 43 Pac. 916; Winnemucca First Nat. Bank v. Kreig, 21 Nev. 404, 32 Pac. 641.
[41] First Nat. Bank v. Kreig, 21 Nev. 404, 32 Pac. 641. But see Brophy Min. Co. v. Brophy & Dale Gold and Silver Min. Co., 15 Nev. 101; Bingham v. Thompson, 4 Nev. 224.

any case entitled to the possession. The mortgagor retains, as against the mortgagee, nothing more than a mere power to regain the fee upon the performance of a condition, and this condition is strictly a condition precedent.[42] As against all other persons the mortgagor is regarded as the owner, and may maintain a real action to recover possession. The mortgagee has the legal title merely so far as is necessary, in order to enable him to obtain the full benefit of the security, and prevent any violation of his rights under the mortgage.[43]

Whenever the mortgagee is entitled to possession he may doubtless treat the possession of the mortgagor as a disseisin, at his election, and may at once maintain a writ of entry for the recovery of possession, without notice to quit; but until such election the possession of the mortgagor can not be regarded as a disseisin, but as permissive, and bearing in many respects a close analogy to strict tenancy at will or at sufferance. Until this power of election is exercised, the mortgagor is in with the privity and assent of the mortgagee, and in subordination to his title; and it is therefore held, upon the ground of such presumed assent, that the mortgagor is not liable to the mortgagee for the rents and profits while so in possession.[44]

It has been held that where a mortgage to secure purchase-money was void, for the reason that there was only one subscribing witness, the mortgagee could not maintain a writ of entry to recover the land from his grantee.[45]

§ 43. **New Jersey.**—In New Jersey the nature of the mortgage as a conveyance of an estate to the mortgagee in fee simple, subject to be defeated by the performance of the condition, remains as it was at common law, with the modification that the mortgagee can not enter immediately as at common law, but only upon breach of the condition.[46] A mortgage is merely auxiliary to the debt, and the estate of the mort-

---

[42] Morse v. Whitcher, 64 N. H. 591, 15 Atl. 207; Perkins v. Eaton, 64 N. H. 359, 10 Atl. 704; Fletcher v. Chamberlin, 61 N. H. 438; Tripe v. Marcy, 39 N. H. 439; Hobart v. Sanborn, 13 N. H. 226, 38 Am. Dec. 483; Southerin v. Mendum, 5 N. H. 420; M'Murphy v. Minot, 4 N. H. 251; Brown v. Cram, 1 N. H. 169.

[43] Whittemore v. Gibbs, 24 N. H. 484; Great Falls Co. v. Worster, 15 N. H. 412; Ellison v. Daniels, 11 N. H. 274; Parish v. Gilmanton, 11 N. H. 293.

[44] Furbush v. Goodwin, 29 N. H. 321; Chellis v. Stearns, 22 N. H. 312.
[45] Rundlett v. Hodgman, 16 N. H. 239.
[46] Wilbur v. Jones, 8 N. J. Eq. 520, 86 Atl. 769; Devlin v. Collier, 53 N. J. L. 422, 22 Atl. 201; Jersey City v. Kiernan, 50 N. J. L. 246, 13 Atl. 170; Woodside v. Adams, 40 N. J. L. 417; Kircher v. Schalk, 39 N. J. L. 335; Shields v. Lozear, 34 N. J. L. 496; 3 Am. Rep. 256, per Depue, J.; Sanderson v. Price, 21 N. J. L. 637.

gage is annihilated by the extinguishment of the debt secured by it, even after the day of payment named in the condition. In fact, the latter conclusion will necessarily follow whenever the mortgage is regarded, not as a common-law conveyance on condition, but as a security for the debt, the legal estate being considered as subsisting only for that purpose.[47] Yet the generally received aspect in which a mortgage is regarded is as a mere security for the debt and not an alienation.[48] The land conveyed by way of mortgage subsists as an estate only to the extent that it is subservient to such purpose.[49]

In a general way it may be said that a mortgage in New Jersey has a dual character—first, it is a covenant to pay a sum of money upon an expressed consideration, and second, it is a conveyance of land to secure the debt. The first is an executory contract, and the second an executed conveyance with a defeasance, and liable to be defeated if at any time it is sought to be enforced there is nothing due upon the executory contract it was given to secure.[50]

[47] Schalk v. Kingsley, 42 N. J. L. 32; Wade v. Miller, 32 N. J. L. 296.

[48] Shields v. Lozear, 34 N. J. L. 496, 3 Am. Rep. 256, per Depue, J., citing Osborne v. Tunis, 25 N. J. L. 633; Montgomery v. Bruere, 4 N. J. L. 260, per Southard, J., whose dissenting opinion was adopted in the Court of Errors, 5 N. J. L. 865; Verner v. Betz, 46 N. J. Eq. 256, 19 Atl. 206; McMahon v. Schoonmaker, 51 N. J. Eq. 95, 25 Atl. 946; Marshall v. Hadley, 50 N. J. Eq. 547, 25 Atl. 325.

The case of Sanderson v. Price, 21 N. J. L. 637, 646, note, is referred to by Depue, J., in Woodside v. Adams, 40 N. J. L. 417, 422, where he says that "this decision, though perhaps not satisfactory to the profession when it was promulgated, has come to be regarded as settled law; and it may now be considered the established doctrine of the courts of this state that a mortgage of lands is not a common-law conveyance on condition, but a mere security for the mortgage debt, the legal estate being considered as subsisting in the mortgagee only for that purpose. The consequence of these decisions is the separation, in legal contemplation, of the estate of the mort-gagor from that of the mortgagee, and the recognition of an actual and distinct legal estate in each. The legal estate of the mortgagee, after breach of condition, has all the incidents of common-law title, for the purposes of an action of ejectment; but its existence is, nevertheless, regarded as compatible with a legal estate at the same time in the mortgagor. This legal estate of the mortgagor is capable of conveyance, mortgage, or a sale under execution against him, at any time before his estate is divested by foreclosure. The cases clearly recognize the equity of redemption of a mortgagor as a legal estate, and as such it must subsist until extinguished in the manner in which legal estates are by law extinguishable. Entry on the mortgaged premises does not work an extinguishment. It merely operates to transfer the possession to the mortgagee with all the rights that actual possession confers, leaving the ultimate rights of the parties unaffected."

[49] Devlin v. Collier, 53 N. J. L. 422, 22 Atl. 201, per Beasley, C. J.

[50] Wilbur v. Jones, 8 N. J. Eq. 520, 86 Atl. 769; Perkins v. Trinity Realty Co., 69 N. J. Eq. 723, 727.

§ 43a. **New Mexico.**—In New Mexico, a mortgage is not an interest in land, but merely a security for the payment of a debt.[51] As between the mortgagor and mortgagee it does not convey the legal title to the mortgagee.[52]

In the absence of a stipulation to the contrary, the mortgagor of real property has the right of possession thereof.[53] The mortgagee has no interest in the land mortgaged until default in the terms of the mortgage. He can not take possession, nor interfere in its management or control, unless his security is in danger of being diminished.[54]

A conveyance absolute on its face, though intended merely as a security for a debt, will be treated in equity as a mortgage.[55]

§ 44. **New York.**—Following the views of Lord Mansfield, the courts of New York from the first regarded a mortgage as merely a security of a personal nature upon the land of the mortgagor, who retained the legal title, at least until possession taken.[56] But prior to the Revised Statutes of 1828, the title of the mortgagee must in fact have been something not very different from the legal estate, for, unless prevented by the terms of the mortgage, he had the right to recover possession of the property by ejectment, and after default he could so recover it at any time.[57] This right was taken away then, and, so far as possession before foreclosure is concerned, his only right is to retain possession when he has once obtained it by the mortgagor's consent or without force.[58] But after default in payment of the debt secured or other breach of condition, he is entitled to possession, and

---

[51] Alexander v. Cleland, 13 N. Mex. 524, 86 Pac. 425; Palmer v. Albuquerque (N. Mex.), 142 Pac. 929.
[52] Stearns-Roger Mfg. Co. v. Aztec Gold Min. &c. Co., 14 N. Mex. 300, 327, 93 Pac. 706; Comp. Laws 1897, §§ 2220, 2226.
[53] Comp. Laws 1884, § 1593.
[54] Stearns-Roger Mfg. Co. v. Aztec Gold. Min. &c. Co., 14 N. Mex. 300, 93 Pac. 706.
[55] Palmer v. Albuquerque (N. Mex.), 142 Pac. 929.
[56] In re Kellogg, 113 Fed. 120; Becker v. McCrea, 193 N. Y. 423, 86 N. E. 463, 23 L. R. A. (N. S.) 754; Barson v. Mulligan, 191 N. Y. 306, 84 N. E. 75, 16 L. R. A. (N. S.) 151; Lynch v. Pfeiffer, 110 N. Y. 33, 17 N. E. 402; Barry v. Hamburg-Bremen F. Ins. Co., 110 N. Y. 1, 17 N. E. 405; Shriver v. Shriver, 86 N. Y. 575; Union College v. Wheeler, 61 N. Y. 88; Trimm v. Marsh, 54 N. Y. 599, 13 Am. Rep. 623; Merritt v. Bartholick, 36 N. Y. 44; Power v. Lester, 23 N. Y. 527; Kartright v. Cady 21 N. Y. 343; Packer v. Rochester &c. R. Co., 17 N. Y. 283; Bryan v. Butts, 27 Barb. (N. Y.) 503; Calkins v. Calkins, 3 Barb. (N. Y.) 305; Waters v. Stewart, 1 Caines Cas. (N. Y.) 47, per Kent, J.; Jackson v. Bronson, 19 Johns. (N. Y.) 325; Stanard v. Eldridge, 16 Johns. (N. Y.) 254; Runyan v. Mersereau, 11 Johns. (N. Y.) 534, 6 Am. Dec. 393; Jackson v. Willard, 4 Johns. (N. Y.) 41; Bell v. Mayor, 10 Paige (N. Y.) 49; Astor v. Hoyt, 5 Wend. (N. Y.) 603, 2 Paige (N. Y.) 68; In re Krupper, 141 App. Div. 54, 125 N. Y. S. 878.
[57] Jackson v. Dubois, 4 Johns. (N. Y.) 216.
[58] 2 Rev. Stat. 312, § 57; Waring

may enter peaceably or by means of a judgment in ejectment.[59] It is said that he does not, however, acquire any estate from his possession.[60]

§ 45. North Carolina.—In North Carolina upon the execution of a mortgage the mortgagor becomes the equitable, and the mortgagee the legal, owner, and this relative situation remains until the mortgage is redeemed or foreclosed.[61] Until the day of redemption is passed, the mortgagor has no special equity, but he may pay the money according to the proviso, and avoid the conveyance at law; and this privilege is termed his legal right of redemption.[62]

After the special day of payment has passed, the mortgagor still has an equity of redemption until there is a foreclosure, and this right is regarded as a continuance of the old estate; and so long as he is permitted to remain in possession, he is considered to hold by virtue of his ownership, and is not accountable for the rents and profits of the mortgaged lands. If the mortgagor be allowed to remain in possession for a long period by the acquiescence and implied approval of the mortgagee, he is not a trespasser; and although he may not be a tenant, he is a permissive occupant, and as such is entitled to a reasonable demand to terminate the implied license before an action can be brought to recover possession.[63] The mortgagee, after forfeiture, may recover the land in an action at law by virtue of his title as mortgagee.[64]

§ 45a. North Dakota.—In North Dakota a mortgage does not entitle the mortgagee to the possession, but the mortgagor may agree to

v. Smyth, 2 Barb. Ch. (N. Y.) 119, 47 Am. Dec. 299; Phyfe v. Riley, 15 Wend. (N. Y.) 248; Shriver v. Shriver, 86 N. Y. 575. The mortgagee can not maintain an action to recover the mortgaged premises. Code of Civ. Procedure 1880, § 1498.

[59] Randall v. Raab, 2 Abb. Pr. (N. Y.) 307; Bolton v. Brewster, 32 Barb. (N. Y.) 389; Phyfe v. Riley, 15 Wend. (N. Y.) 248, 30 Am. Dec. 55.

[60] Parker v. Rochester &c. R. Co., 17 N. Y. 283. See ante § 13.

[61] Watson v. Ins. Co., 159 N. Car. 638, 75 S. E. 1105; Cauley v. Sutton, 150 N. Car. 327, 64 S. E. 3; James v. Western &c. R. Co., 121 N. Car. 523, 28 S. E. 537, 46 L. R. A. 306;

Kiser v. Combs, 114 N. Car. 640, 19 S. E. 664; Coor v. Smith, 101 N. Car. 261, 7 S. E. 669.

[62] Hemphill v. Ross, 66 N. Car. 477. See also Kiser v. Combs, 114 N. Car. 640, 12 S. E. 664; Ellis v. Hussey, 66 N. Car. 501. A mortgagor in possession is a freeholder within the meaning of an act relating to jurors. He has not any legal estate, but the act does not provide that he shall be a legal freeholder; that he is an equitable freeholder is sufficient. State v. Ragland, 75 N. Car. 12.

[63] Hemphill v. Ross, 66 N. Car. 477.

[64] Wittkowski v. Watkins, 84 N. Car. 456; Kiser v. Combs, 114 N. Car. 640, 19 S. E. 664.

such change of possession upon a new consideration.[65] The mortgage is a mere lien given as security for a debt, and confers no right of possession before or after default. Possession can not be taken until there has been a valid foreclosure.[66]

§ 46. Ohio.—In Ohio a mortgagee is regarded as holding the legal title to the estate during the continuance of the mortgage, but neither in a court of law nor of equity is he permitted to use this legal title except for the purpose of making effectual the security.[67] The legal title as between the parties is held to be in the mortgagee. As to all the world beside, it is in the mortgagor. After condition broken, the mortgagee may recover possession by an action of ejectment.[68]

§ 46a. Oklahoma.—A mortgage creates only a lien on real estate until after foreclosure and sale, and even where a deed is taken as security for a debt, the grantee must foreclose before he becomes the owner of the title.[69] The mortgage does not give the mortgagee either a legal or an equitable title,[70] nor does it give him a right to the possession of the mortgaged premises.[71] He is not entitled to possession even though the mortgage purports on its face to be a deed absolute.[72]

§ 47. Oregon.—In Oregon a mortgage does not convey a title, but only creates a lien.[73] By statute a mortgagor can not against his will be divested of possession of the mortgaged premises, even upon default, without a foreclosure and sale.[74] He retains the right of possession

[65] Rev. Code 1905, § 6164; Roberts v. Parker, 14 S. Dak. 323, 85 N. W. 591; Shimerda v. Wohlford, 13 S. Dak. 155, 82 N. W. 393; Comp. Laws, § 4358; Yankton Bldg. &c. Assn. v. Dowling, 10 S. Dak. 535, 74 N. W. 436.

[66] McClory v. Ricks, 11 N. Dak. 38, 88 N. W. 1043.

[67] Harkrader v. Leiby, 4 Ohio St. 602. "But it is incorrect to say that a mortgage does no more than to create a mere lien upon the property." Per Ranney, J. See also Brown v. National Bank, 44 Ohio St. 269, 6 N. E. 648; Home Bldg. &c. Assn. v. Clark, 43 Ohio St. 427, 2 N. E. 846; Martin v. Alter, 42 Ohio St. 94; Allen v. Everly, 24 Ohio St. 97; McArthur v. Franklin, 16 Ohio St. 193.

[68] Ely v. McGuire, 2 Ohio 223; Allen v. Everly, 24 Ohio St. 97; Rands v. Kendall, 15 Ohio 671.

[69] Balduff v. Griswold, 9 Okla. 438, 60 Pac. 223.

[70] Stat. 1893, § 3198; Gilette v. Roming, 17 Okla. 324, 87 Pac. 325; Jones v. Black, 18 Okla. 344, 88 Pac. 1052, 90 Pac. 422.

[71] Jones v. Black, 18 Okla. 344, 88 Pac. 1052, 90 Pac. 422.

[72] Yingling v. Redwine, 12 Okla. 64, 69 Pac. 810.

[73] Bailey v. Frazier, 62 Ore. 142, 124 Pac. 643; Kinney v. Smith, 58 Ore. 158, 113 Pac. 854; Kaston v. Storey, 47 Ore. 150, 80 Pac. 217, 114 Am. St. 912; Adair v. Adair, 22 Ore. 115, 29 Pac. 193; Thompson v. Marshall, 21 Ore. 171, 27 Pac. 957; Sellwood v. Gray, 11 Ore. 534, 5 Pac. 196.

[74] Bellinger & Cotton's Codes & Stat., § 336; Besser v. Hawthorn, 3 Ore. 129; Anderson v. Baxter, 4 Ore. 110; Semple v. Bank of British Columbia, 5 Sawy. (U. S.) 88, 394;

and the legal title.[75] But if a mortgagor choose, he can give possession to the mortgagee, or the mortgagee may obtain possession in any lawful or peaceable mode; and when this is done, and the duration of the mortgagee's possession is not limited by agreement, the latter may retain possession until the debt is paid; and until it be paid, the mortgagor can not recover possession by an action of ejectment.[76] But a mortgagee in possession by virtue of a foreclosure and sheriff's deed, is not in the position of one in possession with the consent of the mortgagor until the debt is paid.[77]

§ 48. **Pennsylvania.**—In Pennsylvania a mortgage passes to the mortgagee the title and right of possession to hold till payment be made. He may enter at pleasure, and take actual possession. His estate is conditional, and ceases upon payment of the debt; but until the condition is performed, both his title and his right of possession are as substantial and real as though they were absolute.[78] As between the parties, the mortgage transmits the legal title to the mortgagee, and leaves the mortgagor only a right to redeem. As to all others, the mortgage is a lien merely and not an estate. This is the view taken both in courts of equity and courts of law.[79] It is well settled that a mortgagee or his assignee may maintain ejectment and recover possession of the mortgaged property before the condition is broken, unless there be a stipulation in the instrument to the contrary.[80] "For some purposes a mortgage is something more than a mere security

Witherell v. Wiberg, 4 Sawy. (U. S.) 232.

[75] Besser v. Hawthorn, 3 Ore. 129.

[76] Cooke v. Cooper, 18 Ore. 142, 22 Pac. 945, 17 Am. St. 709; Roberts v. Sutherlin, 4 Ore. 219.

[77] De Lashmutt v. Sellwood, 10 Ore. 319.

[78] "Thus we perceive," says Chief Justice Agnew, "an interest or estate in the land itself, capable of enjoyment, and enabling the mortgagee to grasp and hold it actually, and not a mere lien or potentiality, to follow it by legal process and condemn it for payment. The land passes to the mortgagee by the act of the party himself, and needs no legal remedy to enforce the right. But a lien vests no estate and is a mere incident of the debt, to be enforced by a remedy at law, which may be limited. It is true, if the mortgagee be held out,

he may have to resort to ejectment, but this is to avoid a conflict and the statutory penalties for forcible entry, for otherwise he may take peaceable possession, and is not liable as a trespasser." Tryon v. Munson, 77 Pa. St. 250; and see numerous cases in that state cited by the learned judge in support, and in illustration, of this doctrine.

[79] Brobst v. Brock, 10 Wall. (U. S.) 519, 19 L. ed. 1002; Bonstein v. Schweyer, 212 Pa. 19, 61 Atl. 447; McIntyre v. Velte, 153 Pa. St. 350, 25 Atl. 739; Lance's Appeal, 112 Pa. St. 456, 4 Atl. 375; Tryon v. Munson, 77 Pa. St. 250; Soper v. Guernsey, 71 Pa. St. 219; Youngman v. Elmira &c. R. Co., 65 Pa. St. 278; Horstman v. Gerker, 49 Pa. St. 282, 88 Am. Dec. 501.

[80] Youngman v. Elmira &c. R. Co., 65 Pa. St. 278, and cases cited.

for a debt. It is a pledge of a specific property. It gives to the creditor the exceptional remedy of ejectment."[81]

§ 49. **Rhode Island.**—The common-law doctrine of the nature of mortgages prevails in this state. The mortgagee may recover possession by suit at law. Upon any breach of the condition, such as the nonpayment of interest, the mortgagee may maintain ejectment, though the principal sum be not due.[82] The mortgagee's remedy for waste done by the mortgagor, when a writ of estrepement will not lie, is usually to be sought in equity; but it is a wrong at law also, and therefore a mortgagee may maintain against a mortgagor an action of replevin for wood and timber cut on the land in waste of the same.[83]

§ 50. **South Carolina.**—Since the act of 1791 a mortgage has not been a conveyance of any estate, but simply a lien to secure the payment of a debt.[84] It is provided that the mortgagee shall not be entitled to maintain any possessory action for the mortgaged estate even after the mortgage is due, but that the mortgagor shall still be deemed the owner of the land and the mortgagee the owner of the money lent or due.[85] A release of the equity of redemption operates as a conveyance of the land.[86]

[81] Twitchell v. McMurtrie, 1 Wkly. Notes Cas. 407.

[82] Carpenter v. Carpenter, 6 R. I. 542; Waterman v. Matteson, 4 R. I. 539. 'Formerly," says Chief Justice Ames, "the right of the mortgagor was, upon breach of the condition of the mortgage, wholly gone at law; and his equity to redeem was recognized only by the tribunal able to enforce such a right. It is true that in modern times the courts of law have, for many purposes, treated the mortgagor in possession as the real owner of the estate, looking upon a mortgage in the same light that a court of equity does, as a mere security for the mortgage debt; but we can see no reason why such courts would recognize in a mortgagor in possession under a forfeited mortgage greater rights over the mortgaged estate than courts of equity do." See also Reynolds v. Hennessy, 15 R. I. 212, 2 Atl. 701.

[83] Waterman v. Matteson, 4 R. I. 539. See post § 688.

[84] McDaniel v. Stroud, 106 Fed. 486; Wallace v. Langston, 52 S. Car. 133, 29 S. E. 552; Patterson v. Rabb, 38 S. Car. 138, 17 S. E. 463, 19 L. R. A. 831; Hardin v. Hardin, 34 S. Car. 77, 12 S. E. 936; Bredenberg v. Landrum, 32 S. Car. 215, 10 S. E. 956; Navassa Guano Co. v. Richardson, 26 S. Car. 401, 2 S. E. 307; Warren v. Raymond, 12 S. Car. 9, 17 S. Car. 181; Simons v. Bryce, 10 S. Car. 354.

[85] Code of Laws, 1912, § 3460, p. 953; Hughes v. Edwards, 9 Wheat. (U. S.) 489; In re Bennett, 2 Hughes (U. S.) 156, 158; Hardin v. Hardin, 34 S. Car. 77, 12 S. E. 936, 27 Am. St. 786; Williams v. Beard, 1 S. Car. 309; Thayer v. Cramer, 1 McCord Ch. (S. Car.) 395; Nixon v. Bynum, 1 Bailey (S. Car.) 148.

[86] Mitchell v. Bogan, 11 Rich. (S. Car.) 704; Simons v. Bryce, 10 S. Car. 354; Navassa Guano Co. v. Richardson, 26 S. Car. 401, 2 S. E. 307; Tant v. Guess, 37 S. Car. 489, 16 S. E. 477.

§ 50a. South Dakota.—In South Dakota a statute provides that a mortgage does not entitle the mortgagee to the possession of the property unless authorized by the express terms of the mortgage.[87] Under the statute of this state a mortgage upon the real estate is not a conveyance of title, but only a lien upon the land as security for a debt. After the foreclosure sale the certificate still remains a lien only, until the time for redemption has expired, and no title is transferred until the sheriff's deed has been duly issued.[88]

It is held that an instrument designated by the parties as a trust deed, in which it is expressly stipulated that upon failure to perform certain specific acts by the obligor the obligee may enforce his rights in the manner prescribed for the foreclosure of mortgages, such writing is a mortgage, and is governed by the rules of law applicable to mortgages.[89]

§ 51. Tennessee.—In Tennessee the legal title vests in the mortgagee, who is entitled to immediate possession, unless the mortgage otherwise provides. He may recover possession without first giving notice to quit.[90] Upon satisfaction of the mortgage debt the legal title immediately revests in the mortgagor or after his death in his heirs.[91] A trust deed is nothing more than a mortgage with power of sale added.[92] The mortgagee's interest in the mortgaged land is only a security for the debt—the debt being the principal thing and the land only an incident thereto.[93]

§ 52. Texas.—A mortgage is but a security, and the title remains in the mortgagor, subject to be divested by foreclosure. In this respect a deed of trust is held not to differ from a mortgage; the legal title and right of possession remain with the grantor.[94] And since the

[87] Rev. Codes 1903, § 2054, p. 827. This applies to an absolute deed given as security. Shimerda v. Wohlford, 13 S. Dak. 155, 82 N. W. 393; Roberts v. Parker, 14 S. Dak. 323, 85 N. W. 591.

[88] Farr v. Semmler, 24 S. Dak. 290, 123 N. W. 835; West v. Middlesex Banking Co. (S. Dak.), 146 N. W. 598.

[89] Langmaack v. Keith (S. Dak.), 103 N. W. 210.

[90] Henshaw v. Wells, 3 Humph. (Tenn.) 568; Vance v. Johnson, 10 Humph. (Tenn.) 214; Carter v. Taylor, 3 Head (Tenn.) 30; Lincoln Sav. Bank v. Ewing, 12 Lea (Tenn.) 598.

[91] Vaughn v. Vaughn, 100 Tenn. 282, 45 S. W. 677.

[92] Robinson v. Owens, 103 Tenn. 91, 52 S. W. 870; Bennett v. Union Bank, 5 Humph. (Tenn.) 612; Carter v. Taylor, 3 Head (Tenn.) 30.

[93] McGan v. Marshall, 7 Humph. (Tenn.) 121.

[94] Wright v. Henderson, 12 Tex. 43; Mann v. Falcon, 25 Tex. 271; Holland v. Frock, 2 Posey Un. Rep. Cas. 566; Walker v. Johnson, 37 Tex. 127; Stitzle v. Evans, 74 Tex. 596, 12 S. W. 326; McCammant v. Roberts, 87 Tex. 241, 27 S. W. 86; Kerr v. Galloway, 94 Tex. 641, 64 S. W. 858; Parker v. Benner, 1 Tex. Civ. App. 64; Denison &c. Suburban

mortgagor remains the real owner of the land and is entitled to the possession, after as well as before breach of condition, the mortgagee can not dispossess him by an action of trespass to try title.[95]

§ 53. **Utah.**—It is provided that a mortgage shall not be deemed a conveyance, so as to entitle the mortgagee to recover possession without foreclosure.[96] The mortgagor may convey the title subject to the lien of the mortgage, to a third person; but such third party can acquire no greater rights than those possessed by his immediate grantor.[97]

§ 54. **Vermont.**—In Vermont the mortgagor's right of possession is by statute continued as against the mortgagee until condition broken, unless otherwise stipulated in the mortgage.[98] Upon the happening of that event the interest of the mortgagor becomes absolutely vested in the mortgagee, and he has a right to the immediate possession of the estate.[99] He may assert this right by entering peaceably by his own act, or may bring an action of ejectment without previous notice to quit. Until he asserts this right, the mortgagor in possession is regarded as the owner of the land, and may use and occupy it without accounting to the mortgagee.[1] The mortgage passes the legal title to the mortgagee.[2]

A deed, absolute on its face, but intended merely as security for existing and future liabilities, will be treated as a mortgage in Vermont.[3]

§ 55. **Virginia.**—At law, the mortgagee has the legal estate, and the immediate right of possession, unless there be some stipulation in the mortgage deed to the contrary. Upon a breach of the condition, the mortgagee may enter, or recover possession by action without previous notice. He is then, to all intents and purposes, the legal owner

---

R. Co. v. Smith, 19 Tex. Civ. App. 114, 47 S. W. 278; Ferguson v. Dickinson (Tex. Civ. App.), 138 S. W. 221.

[95] Mann v. Falcon, 25 Tex. 271.

[96] Comp. Laws 1907, § 3517; Sidney Stevens Imp. Co. v. South Ogden Bldg. &c. Co., 20 Utah 267, 58 Pac. 843; Dupee v. Rose, 10 Utah 305, 37 Pac. 567; Neslin v. Wells, 104 U. S. 428, 26 L. ed. 802.

[97] Azzalia v. St. Claire, 23 Utah 401, 64 Pac. 1106.

[98] Pub. Stat. 1906, § 1853; Brunswick Co. v. Herrick, 63 Vt. 286, 21 Atl. 918.

[99] Hagar v. Brainerd, 44 Vt. 294; Lull v. Matthews, 19 Vt. 322; Wright v. Lake, 30 Vt. 206; Walker v. King, 44 Vt. 601; Fuller v. Eddy, 49 Vt. 11; Brunswick-Balke-Collender Co. v. Herrick, 63 Vt. 286, 21 Atl. 918.

[1] Hooper v. Wilson, 12 Vt. 695; Wilson v. Hooper, 13 Vt. 653, 66 Am. Dec. 366; Walker v. King, 44 Vt. 601.

[2] Pierce v. Brown, 24 Vt. 165.

[3] Gibson v. Seymour, 4 Vt. 518; Bigelow v. Topliff, 25 Vt. 273, 60 Am. Dec. 264; Rich v. Doan, 35 Vt. 125.

of the land, and vested with full legal title. The mortgagor is then regarded as a tenant at sufferance, and is not entitled to the emblements. In equity, however, the mortgagor may redeem, and the mortgagee in possession is regarded as merely a trustee of the property, with liability to account.[4] Trust deeds are used almost exclusively in place of mortgages, and the legal title vests in the grantee in such deeds.[5]

Any instrument pledging land for the payment of a debt is an equitable mortgage, without regard to its form.[6] Also a deed, absolute on its face, but given merely as a security for a debt, will, in equity, be considered a mortgage.[7]

§ 55a. **Washington.**—In Washington a mortgage is nothing more than a mere lien or security for a debt, passing no estate to the mortgagee, and giving him no right or claim to the possession of the property.[8] A mortgage of real property is not deemed a conveyance so as to enable the owner of the mortgage to recover possession of the real property without a foreclosure and sale according to law in the absence of an agreement giving the mortgagee the right of possession.[9]

§ 56. **West Virginia.**—Trust deeds are used in place of mortgages. The law in regard to mortgages is that which prevailed in Virginia before the separation.[10] Here, as elsewhere generally, a deed absolute on its face, but given merely as security for a debt or obligation, will, in equity, be considered a mortgage.[11]

§ 57. **Wisconsin.**—In Wisconsin the fee of the premises does not vest in the mortgagee, except upon foreclosure sale.[12] It is provided by statute that no action shall be maintained by the mortgagee for the

[4] Code 1904, § 472; Faulkner v. Brockenbrough, 4 Rand. (Va.) 245; Bank v. Beard, 100 Va. 687, 42 S. E. 694.

[5] Faulkner v. Brockenbrough, 4 Rand. (Va.) 245.

[6] Wayt v. Carwithen, 21 W. Va. 516.

[7] Chowning v. Cox, 1 Rand. (Va.) 306, 10 Am. Dec. 530.

[8] Codes & Stat. 1910, § 8750; Snyder v. Parker, 19 Wash. 276, 53 Pac. 59, 67 Am. St. 726; Brundage v. Home Sav. &c. Assn., 11 Wash. 277, 39 Pac. 666; Norfor v. Busby, 19 Wash. 450, 53 Pac. 715; State v. Kittitas County Superior Ct., 21 Wash. 564, 58 Pac. 1065.

[9] State v. Superior Court, 21 Wash. 564, 58 Pac. 1065.

[10] Childs v. Hurd, 32 W. Va. 66, 9 S. E. 362; Grant v. Cumberland Val. Cement Co., 58 W. Va. 162, 52 S. E. 36.

[11] Klinck v. Price, 4 W. Va. 4, 6 Am. Rep. 268; Zane v. Fink, 18 W. Va. 693; Hoffman v. Ryan, 21 W. Va. 415.

[12] Wood v. Trask, 7 Wis. 566, 76 Am. Dec. 230; Schreiber v. Carey, 48 Wis. 208, 4 N. W. 124; Wolf v. Thresa Village Mut. F. Ins. Co., 115 Wis. 402, 91 N. W. 1014; Gerhart v. Ellis, 134 Wis. 191, 114 N. W. 495; Tobin v. Tobin, 139 Wis. 494, 121 N. W. 144.

recovery of possession of the mortgaged premises until the equity of redemption shall have expired.[13]　The statute in effect preserves the fee in the mortgagor until foreclosure,[14] when it vests in the purchaser at the sale.　When, however, the mortgagee has, after default, gone into peaceable possession, he can not be ejected by the mortgagor while the mortgage remains unsatisfied.　The only remedy of the mortgagor is by bill to redeem, under which he must pay whatever is due upon the mortgage debt.[15]

A deed absolute in form, shown by testimony to be given to secure a debt, with an oral agreement by the grantee to execute a defeasance, is construed a mortgage by the courts of Wisconsin.[16]

§ 58.　Summary of legal and equitable theories in the different states.—As a summary of this examination it will be found that in Alabama, Arkansas, Connecticut, Illinois, Maine, Maryland, Massachusetts, New Hampshire, New Jersey, North Carolina, Ohio, Pennsylvania, Rhode Island, Tennessee, Vermont, Virginia, and West Virginia, the courts have adhered to the doctrines of the common law as regards the nature of the mortgage interest and the respective rights of the parties.　They regard the mortgage deed as passing at once the legal title to the mortgagee, subject to defeasance, as a condition subsequent which divests or defeats the estate on performance of it.　The right of possession follows the title so that the mortgagee may enter into possession of the mortgaged property immediately unless restrained by express provision, or necessary implication, of the mortgage; and in any case upon breach of the condition he becomes entitled to the possession and may recover it by action.　The legal title is in the mortgagee, only for the protection and enforcement of his interests.　The mortgagee's title is in the nature of a base or determinable fee, which continues only so long as the debt continues.[17]

[13] Wis. Stat. 1913, § 3095.
[14] Wood v. Trask, 7 Wis. 566, 76 Am. Dec. 230.
[15] Hennesy v. Farrell, 20 Wis. 42; Tallman v. Ely, 6 Wis. 244; Gillett v. Eaton, 6 Wis. 30; Fladland v. Delaplaine, 19 Wis. 459; Avery v. Judd, 21 Wis. 262; Stark v. Brown, 12 Wis. 572, 78 Am. Dec. 762; Roche v. Knight, 21 Wis. 324; Schreiber v. Carey, 48 Wis. 208, 214, 48 N. W. 124; Wisconsin Cent. R. Co. v. Wisconsin River Land Co., 71 Wis. 94, 36 N. W. 837, 839.
[16] McCormick v. Herndon, 86 Wis. 449.

[17] Lightcap v. Bradley, 186 Ill. 510, 519, 58 N. E. 221; Gibson v. Rees, 50 Ill. 383; Pollock v. Maison, 41 Ill. 516; Delano v. Bennett, 90 Ill. 533. See also Welsh v. Phillips, 54 Ala. 309, 25 Am. Rep. 679; Chamberlain v. Thompson, 10 Conn. 243, 26 Am. Dec. 390; Blaney v. Bearce, 2 Maine 132; Jamieson v. Bruce, 6 Gill & J. (Md.) 72, 26 Am. Dec. 557; Ewer v. Hobbs, 5 Metc. (Mass.) 1; Hobart v. Sanborn, 13 N. H. 226, 38 Am. Dec. 483; Tryon v. Munson, 77 Pa. St. 250; Simmons v. Brown, 7 R. I. 427, 84 Am. Dec. 569.

In Delaware, Mississippi, and Missouri the common-law doctrine is so far modified, that until breach of the condition and possession taken, the mortgagor is regarded as the owner of the legal estate, not only as against third persons, but as against the mortgagee himself. But upon forfeiture and entry of the mortgagee, he is regarded as having the legal title for the purpose of obtaining satisfaction out of the property.[18]

In other states the common-law doctrine upon this subject has been wholly abrogated by statute, and both at law and in equity, and both before and after a breach of the condition, a mortgage is regarded as merely a lien upon the property. It passes no title or estate in it to the mortgagee, and gives him no right of possession before foreclosure. This is the doctrine of mortgages in California, Colorado, Florida, Georgia, Idaho, Indiana, Iowa, Kansas, Kentucky, Louisiana, Michigan, Minnesota, Montana, Nebraska, Nevada, New Mexico, New York, North Dakota, Oklahoma, Oregon, South Carolina, South Dakota, Texas, Utah, Washington, and Wisconsin. In Iowa, Kansas, and Nevada the statutes imply that the parties may by express stipulation give the right of possession to the mortgagee.[19]

§ 59. Doctrine in different sections of the United States.—Grouping the states geographically, it will be noticed that the English doctrine of the nature of mortgages, with slight modifications, prevails east of the Mississippi river in a large majority of the states; while west of the Mississippi, except only in the states of Missouri and Arkansas, the doctrine everywhere prevails that a mortgage passes no legal estate or right of possession.[20]

This change from the common-law rule may be traced to two sources: to the views of the early jurists of New York, who adopted and carried to logical conclusions the opinions of Lord Mansfield;

[18] Cooch v. Gerry, 3 Harr. (Del.) 280; Doe v. Tunnell, 1 Houst. (Del.) 320; Walker v. Farmers' Bank, 8 Houst. (Del.) 258; Hill v. Robertson, 24 Miss. 368; Buck v. Payne, 52 Miss. 271; Woods v. Hilderbrand, 46 Mo. 284, 2 Am. Rep. 513; Johnson v. Houston, 47 Mo. 227; Reddick v. Gressman, 49 Mo. 389.

[19] See McMillan v. Richards, 9 Cal. 365, 70 Am. Dec. 655; Dutton v. Warschauer, 21 Cal. 609, 82 Am. Dec. 765; Drake v. Rood, 2 Colo. 685; McMahon v. Russell, 17 Fla.

698; Burnside v. Terry, 45 Ga. 621; Grable v. McCulloh, 27 Ind. 472; Chick v. Willetts, 2 Kans. 384; Taliaferro v. Gay, 78 Ky. 496; Caruthers v. Humphrey, 12 Mich. 270; Adams v. Corriston, 7 Minn. 456; Rogers v. Benton, 39 Minn. 39, 12 Am. St. 613; Webb v. Hoselton, 4 Nebr. 308, 19 Am. Rep. 638; Phyfe v. Riley, 15 Wend. (N. Y.) 248, 30 Am. Dec. 55; Hubbell v. Landrum, 32 S. Car. 215; Wright v. Henderson, 12 Tex. 43.

[20] Bredenberg v. Landrum, 32 S. Car. 215, 10 S. E. 956 (quoting text).

and to the civil law[21] established in Louisiana, under which a mortgage is merely a pledge, giving no right of possession. The influence of the civil law is seen in the codes of a few states; but the most potent influence in bringing about this change in the nature of mortgages in the new states has come from their adoption to a large extent of the code and judicial authorities of the state of New York. As to the nature of a mortgage, the civil law doctrine, and what may be called the equitable doctrine adopted in New York and the other states mentioned, are practically and essentially the same.

[21] "In the Roman law there were two sorts of transfers of property, as security passed to the creditor, upon the condition of returning it to the owner when the debt was paid. The hypotheca was when the thing pledged was not delivered to the creditor, but remained in the possession of the debtor. * * * It seems that the word pignus was often used indiscriminately to describe both species of securities, whether applied to movables or immovables, * * * so that it answered very nearly to the corresponding term pledge in the common law, for debts; namely, the pignus and the hypotheca. The pignus, or pledge, was when anything was pledged as a security for money lent and the possession thereof was which, although sometimes used in a general sense to include mortgages of land, is, in the stricter sense, confined to the pawn and deposit of personal property. In the Roman law, however, there was generally no substantial difference, in the. nature and extent of the rights and remedies of the parties, between movables and immovables, whether pledged or hypothecated." 2 Story Eq. Jur., §§ 1005, 1006.

CHAPTER II

I. *The Form Generally*, §§ 60–62
II. *The Formal Parts of the Deed*, §§ 63–68a
III. *The Condition*, §§ 69–78a
IV. *Special Stipulations*, §§ 79–80
V. *Execution and Delivery*, §§ 81–89
VI. *Filling Blanks, Making Alterations and Reforming*, §§ 90–101a

I. *The Form Generally*

§ 60. Formal requisites generally.—No particular form is necessary to constitute a mortgage.[1] It must be in writing,[2] and must clearly indicate the creation of a lien, specify the debt to secure which it is given, and the property upon which it is to take effect.[3] "An

[1] Woodworth v. Guzman, 1 Cal. 203; De Leon v. Higuera, 15 Cal. 483; Burnside v. Terry, 45 Ga. 621; Cross v. Weare Commission Co., 153 Ill. 499, 38 N. E. 1038, 46 Am. St. 902; Bray v. Ellison, 26 Ky. L. 1039, 83 S. W. 96; Baldwin v. Jenkins, 23 Miss. 206; Mason v. Moody, 26 Miss. 184; Iodence v. Peters, 64 Nebr. 425, 89 N. W. 1041; quoted with approval in Harris v. Jones, 83 N. Car. 317; Williamson v. Bitting, 159 N. Car. 321, 74 S. E. 808; Bredenberg v. Landrum, 32 S. Car. 215, 10 S. E. 956; Beebe v. Wisconsin Mtg. &c. Co., 117 Wis. 328, 93 N. W. 1103; Scheiber v. Le Clair, 66 Wis. 579, 29 N. W. 570, 889. A mortgage of real property written on a form intended for a chattel mortgage and acknowledged as such is nevertheless valid. Lindley v. Ross, 200 Fed. 733, 119 C. C. A. 177; Cross v. Weare Commission Co., 153 Ill. 499,

38 N. E. 1038, 46 Am. St. 902; Williamson v. Bitting (N. Car.), 74 S. E. 808.

[2] Eikelman v. Perdew, 140 Cal. 687, 74 Pac. 291; Porter v. Muller, 53 Cal. 677; Georgia So. &c. R. Co. v. Thompson, 111 Ga. 731, 36 S. E. 945; Duke v. Culpepper, 72 Ga. 845; Roberts' Trustee v. Terry (Ky.), 170 S. W. 965. Under a statutory provision that deeds, which include mortgages, shall be signed by the party to be bound, a valid mortgage must be in writing. American Savings Bank &c. Co. v. Helgesen, 64 Wash. 54, 116 Pac. 837, Ann. Cas. 1913 A, 390. A mortgage is valid although not all written on the same sheet of paper, where the completeness of the instrument is not destroyed by the separation. Norman v. Shephard, 38 Ohio St. 320.

[3] New Orleans Nat. Banking Assn. v. Adams, 109 U. S. 211, 3 Sup. Ct.

instrument must be deemed and held a mortgage, whatever may be its form, if, taken alone or in connection with the surrounding facts and attendant circumstances, it appears to have been given for the purpose or with the intention of securing the payment of money, and the mere absence of terms of defeasance can not determine whether it is a mortgage or not."[4] Fulfilling these conditions, it is immaterial that the mortgage should be embraced in one instrument. As will be elsewhere noticed, a mortgage is frequently made by an absolute deed with a separate defeasance executed by the grantee; and an absolute deed with a defeasance resting in parol may be a mortgage also. In this chapter, however, it is proposed to treat of the form and requisites of a formal legal mortgage, or deed of trust.

The term "mortgage" has a technical signification at law, and is descriptive of an instrument having all the requisites necessary to establish it in a court of law, as distinguished from that which may be so regarded in a court of equity.[5] It is very clear that a verbal agreement to mortgage realty does not attain the dignity of a mortgage where the statutes of the state require mortgages to be in writing and subscribed by the mortgagor.[6] A mortgage which only a court of equity will recognize is properly designated an "equitable mortgage."

A formal mortgage differs from a warranty deed in a condition added, that if the grantor pay a certain sum of money, or perform other obligations named, then it shall be void. Other things besides the payment of the principal sum of money are usually made part of the condition, as for instance the payment of interest, of taxes upon the premises, of insurance upon any buildings there may be upon the land, together with a covenant against making or suffering waste.

A mortgage in some states usually contains also a power authorizing the mortgagee to sell upon the happening of any breach of the condition; but this is not an essential requisite of a mortgage, and will be treated elsewhere.

§ 61. **Statutory forms.**—The form of the granting part of the deed as well as the condition differs much in different parts of the country. In some states statutes have been enacted by which deeds and mortgages are reduced to the shortest possible forms; and stat-

161, 27 L. ed. 910; National Bank v. Tenn. Coal &c. R. Co., 62 Ohio St. 564, 57 N. E. 450.

[4] Connor v. Connor, 59 Fla. 467, 52 So. 727. See post §§ 162, 168, 264.

[5] Walton v. Cody, 1 Wis. 420.

[6] Williams v. Davis, 154 Ala. 422, 45 So. 908.

utory forms are given in some states, which are declared to be good and effectual.[7] All that is requisite to a good deed or mortgage may be expressed in a very few words. It was remarked by Coke, that if a deed of feoffment be without premises, habendum, tenendum, reddendum, clause of warranty, etc., it is still a good deed. "For if a man by deed give land to another and to his heirs without more saying, this is good, if he put his seal to the deed, deliver it, and make livery accordingly."[8]

By statute the legal tenor and effect of the different covenants may be, and in some states are, obtained simply by naming them without repeating the covenants themselves. In like manner the full effect of a power of sale may be had by simple reference in the mortgage to a statutory power,[9] instead of cumbering the record with the elaborate powers now in use. Attempts by legislation to bring about simplicity and brevity in legal forms have not always been successful;

---

[7] California: 2 Civ. Code 1907, § 2948.
Illinois: Ann. Stat. 1885, ch. 30, § 12, Rev. Stat. 1908, ch. 30, § 11.
Indiana: Burns' Rev. Stat. 1914, § 3961.
Iowa: Ann. Code 1897, § 2958.
Kansas: Gen. Stat. 1905, § 4482.
Maryland: Pub. G. L. 1904, art. 21, §§ 54–61.
Michigan: 3 Comp. Laws 1897, § 8960.
Mississippi: Ann. Code 1906, § 2820.
Missouri: 4 Ann. Stat. 1906, pp. 4998, 5000.
Montana: Rev. Civ. Code 1907, § 5748.
New York: 3 Rev. Stat. 1901, Birdseye, p. 3057; Laws 1897, ch. 277.
North Carolina: Pub. Laws 1907, ch. 337.
North Dakota: Rev. Code 1905, § 6174.
Oklahoma: Rev. Stat. 1908, § 5486.
South Dakota: Comp. Laws 1908, § 2063.
Tennessee: Code 1896, § 3680.
Utah: Rev. Stat. 1898, § 1983; Comp. Laws 1907, § 1983.
Virginia: Code 1904, § 2441.
West Virginia: Code 1906, ch. 72, § 3052.
Wisconsin: Ann. Stat. 1898, § 2209.

Wyoming: Rev. Stat. 1899, §§ 2774, 2775, 2796.

[8] Chancellor Kent gives a very brief form of a deed, and observes: "But persons usually attach so much importance to the solemnity of forms, which bespeak care and reflection, and they feel such deep solicitude, in matters that concern their valuable interests, to make 'assurance double sure,' that generally, in important cases, the purchaser would rather be at the expense of exchanging a paper of such insignificance of appearance for a conveyance surrounded by the usual outworks, and securing respect and checking attacks by the formality of its manner, the prolixity of its provisions, and the usual redundancy of its language." 4 Kent Com. 461. He further says: "I apprehend that a deed would be perfectly competent, in any part of the United States, to convey the fee, if it was to be the following effect: I, A B, in consideration of one dollar to me paid by C D, do bargain and sell (or, in New York, grant) to C D and his heirs (in New York, Virginia, &c., the words, 'and his heirs,' may be omitted) the lot of land [describe it]. Witness my hand and seal," &c.

[9] See post, §§ 1722, 1761.

but much has been accomplished in this direction in some of the American states, making a practical return through this means to the simplicity of the ancient Saxons, who "in their deeds observed no set form, but used honest and perspicuous words to express the things intended with all brevity, yet not wanting the essential parts of the deed, as the names of the donor and donee; the consideration; the certainty of the thing given; the limitation of the estate; the reservation, and the names of the witnesses.'[10]'

§ **62. Trust deeds.**—A deed of trust to secure a debt is in legal effect a mortgage.[11] It is a conveyance made to a person other than the creditor, conditioned to be void if the debt be paid at a certain time, but if not paid that the grantee may sell the land and apply the proceeds to the extinguishment of the debt, paying over the surplus to the grantor.[12] It is in legal effect a mortgage with a power of sale,[13] but the addition of the power of sale does not change the character of the instrument any more than it does when contained

[10] Sir Henry Spellman's Works, by Bishop Gibson, p. 234.

[11] Union Nat. Bank v. Bank, 136 U. S. 223, 34 L. ed. 341, 10 Sup. Ct. 1013; Shillaber v. Robinson, 97 U. S. 68, 24 L. ed. 967; In re Anderson, 23 Fed. 482; Means v. Montgomery, 23 Fed. 421; Stafford Nat. Bank v. Sprague, 17 Fed. 784; Connecticut Mut. L. Ins. Co. v. Jones, 8 Fed. 303; Turner v. Watkins, 31 Ark. 429; Empire Ranch &c. Co. v. Howell, 22 Colo. App. 584, 126 Pac. 1096; Barth v. Deuel, 11 Colo. 494, 19 Pac. 471; Pershing v. Wolfe, 6 Colo. App. 410, 416, 40 Pac. 856; De Wolf v. Sprague Mfg. Co., 49 Conn. 283; Wood v. Grayson, 22 App. D. C. 432; Middleton v. Parke, 3 App. D. C. 149; Ware v. Schintz, 190 Ill. 189, 60 N. E. 67; Brantley v. Wood, 97 Ga. 755, 25 S. E. 499; McGuire v. Barker, 61 Ga. 339; Brown v. Bryan, 6 Idaho 1, 5 Idaho 145, 51 Pac. 995; Union Mut. L. Ins. Co. v. White, 106 Ill. 67; Smith v. Sheldon, 65 Ill. 219; Sargent v. Howe, 21 Ill. 148; Newman v. Samuels, 17 Iowa 528; Lenox v. Reed, 12 Kans. 223; Chaffee v. Fourth Nat. Bank, 71 Maine 514, 36 Am. Rep. 345; Harriman v. Woburn Electric Light Co., 163 Mass. 85, 39 N. E. 1004; Eaton v. Whiting, 3 Pick. (Mass.) 484; Flint &c. R. Co. v. Auditor General, 41 Mich. 635, 2 N. W. 835; Mills v. Williams, 31 Mo. App. 447; Fiske v. Mayhew, 90 Nebr. 196, 133 N. W. 195; Webb v. Hoselton, 4 Nebr. 308; Hurley v. Estes, 6 Nebr. 386; Stearns-Roger Mfg. Co. v. Aztec Gold Min. &c. Co., 14 N. Mex. 300, 328, 93 Pac. 706; Lawrence v. Farmers' Loan &c. Co., 13 N. Y. 200; Palmer v. Gurnsey, 7 Wend. (N. Y.) 248; Wright v. Fort, 126 N. Car. 615, 36 S. E. 113; Forester v. Van Auken, 12 N. Dak. 175, 96 N. W. 301; National Bank v. Tenn. Coal &c. R. Co., 62 Ohio St. 564, 57 N. E. 450; Kemper v. Campbell, 44 Ohio St. 210, 6 N. E. 566; Martin v. Alter, 42 Ohio St. 94; Woodruff v. Robb, 19 Ohio 212; Hoffman v. Mackall, 5 Ohio St. 124, 64 Am. Dec. 637; Thompson v. Marshall, 21 Ore. 171, 27 Pac. 957; Union Co. v. Sprague, 14 R. I. 452; Austin v. Sprague Mfg. Co., 14 R. I. 464; Aggs v. County, 85 Tex. 145, 19 S. W. 1085; McLane v. Paschal, 47 Tex. 365; Dupee v. Rose, 10 Utah 305, 37 Pac. 567; New York Central Trust Co. v. Burton, 74 Wis. 329, 43 N. W. 141. See post § 1769.

[12] Huene v. Cribb, 9 Cal. App. 141, 98 Pac. 78; Austin v. Sprague Mfg. Co., 49 Conn. 283; State Bank v. Chapelle, 40 Mich. 447.

[13] Connecticut Mut. L. Ins. Co. v. Jones, 8 Fed. 303; Aggs v. Shackel-

in a mortgage.[14] Such a deed has all the essential elements of a mortgage; it is a conveyance of land as security for a debt. It passes the legal title just as a mortgage does,[15] except in those states where the natural effect of a conveyance is controlled by statute;[16] and in states where a mortgage is considered merely as a security, and not a conveyance, a trust deed is apt to be regarded in this respect just like a mortgage.[17] Both instruments convey a defeasible title only; the mortgagee's or trustee's title in fee being in the nature of a base or determinable fee;[18] and the right to redeem is the same in one case as it is in the other

The only important difference between them is, that in the one case the conveyance is directly to the creditor, while in the other it is to a third person for his benefit. Another practical difference is that the deed of trust with power of sale may be foreclosed according to its terms by the trustee without authority of court, whereas a simple mortgage can be foreclosed only under decree of court.[19] The instru-

ford County, 85 Tex. 145, 19 S. W. 1085.

[14] De Wolf v. Sprague Mfg. Co., 49 Conn. 283; Newman v. Samuels, 17 Iowa 528; Eaton v. Whiting, 3 Pick. (Mass.) 484.

[15] Ware v. Schintz, 190 Ill. 189, 60 N. E. 67; Esker v. Heffernan, 159 Ill. 38, 41 N. E. 1113; Fountain v. Bookstaver, 141 Ill. 461, 31 N. E. 17; Oldham v. Pfleger, 84 Ill. 102.

[16] Turner v. Watkins, 31 Ark 427; National Bank v. Tennessee Coal &c. R. Co., 62 Ohio St. 564, 57 N. E. 450.

[17] As in Kansas: Lenox v. Reed, 12 Kans. 223; in Nebraska: ante, § 40. See however ante, § 25, as to Florida.

[18] Ware v. Schintz, 190 Ill. 189, 60 N. E. 67; Lightcap v. Bradley, 186 Ill. 510, 58 N. E. 221.

[19] Cornell v. Conine-Eaton Lumber Co., 9 Colo. App. 225, 47 Pac. 912; Axman v. Smith, 156 Mo. 286, 57 S. W. 105. See also Southern Bldg. &c. Assn. v. McCants, 120 Ala. 616, 25 So. 8; Koch v. Briggs, 14 Cal. 257, 71 Am. Dec. 651. "There is a manifest and well-settled distinction between an unconditional deed of trust and a mortgage, or deed of trust in the nature of a mortgage. The former is an absolute and indefeasible conveyance of the subject-matter thereof for the purpose expressed; whereas the latter is conditional and defeasible. A mortgage is the conveyance of an estate, or pledge of property, as security for the payment of money, or the performance of some other act, and conditioned to become void upon such payment or performance. A deed of trust in the nature of a mortgage is a conveyance in trust by way of security, subject to a condition of defeasance, or redeemable at any time before the sale of the property. A deed conveying land to a trustee as mere collateral security for the payment of a debt, with the condition that it shall become void on the payment of the debt when due, and with power to the trustee to sell the land and pay the debt in case of default on the part of the debtor, is a deed of trust in the nature of a mortgage. By an absolute deed of trust, the grantor parts absolutely with the title, which rests in the grantee unconditionally for the purpose of the trust. The latter is a conveyance to a trustee for the purpose of raising a fund to pay debts, while the former is a conveyance in trust for the purpose of securing a debt, subject to a condition of defeasance." Hoffman v. Mackall, 5 Ohio St. 124, 64 Am. Dec. 637.

ment evidences a contract between the debtor and a creditor, and it is not binding upon any one until accepted by the beneficiary.[20]

Statutes abolishing uses and trusts in real property, except for certain purposes, have no application to trust deeds in the nature of mortgages, where these do not convey a title. It does not matter that such deeds or mortgages contain a trust clause declaring the conveyance to be in trust for the benefit of persons named or the holders of certain bonds.[21] Formerly, in Wisconsin, it was held that a deed to a trustee conditioned that if the grantor does not pay a debt due from him to a third party, then the trustee shall advertise and sell the lands, pay the debt, and return the surplus money to the grantor, did not constitute a mortgage, but a trust which is prohibited by the statute.[22] But this decision has since been overruled.[23]

There is a well-settled distinction between a deed of trust and a deed of trust in the nature of a mortgage; the one being for the trust purposes unconditional and indefeasible, while the other is conditioned and defeasible, in the same way that a mortgage is.[24] The term "deed of trust," however, as used in this treatise, has reference always to a conveyance in the nature of a mortgage. "A deed conveying land to a trustee as mere collateral security for the payment of a debt, with the condition that it shall become void on the payment of the debt when due, and with power to the trustee to sell the land and pay the debt in case of default on the part of the debtor, is a deed of trust in the nature of a mortgage. By an absolute deed of trust, the grantor parts absolutely with the title, which rests in the grantee unconditionally, for the purpose of the trust. The latter is a conveyance to a trustee for the purpose of raising a fund to pay debts; while the former is a conveyance in trust for the purpose of securing a debt, subject to condition of defeasance."[25]

[20] Byrd v. Perry, 7 Tex. Civ. App. 378, 26 S. W. 749.

[21] Carpenter v. Black Hawk Min. Co., 65 N. Y. 43; Curtis v. Leavitt, 15 N. Y. 9, 207; King v. Merchants' Exch. Co., 5 N. Y. 547.

[22] Goodrich v. Milwaukee, 24 Wis. 422. Active trusts, lawful before the statute, may still be created.

[23] Marvin v. Titsworth, 10 Wis. 320.

[24] Fox v. Fraser, 92 Ind. 265; Hoffman v. Mackall, 5 Ohio St. 124, 64 Am. Dec. 637; Union Co. v. Sprague, 14 R. I. 452. In Texas it is said that a deed of trust conveying property to trustees, made to secure particular creditors, though expressed in terms sufficient to pass title if made for creditors generally, is a mortgage with some of the qualities of an assignment superadded. Baldwin v. Peet, 22 Tex. 718, 75 Am. Dec. 806; Jackson v. Hardy, 65 Tex. 710. In this state the legal title remains in the mortgagor. See ante, § 52.

[25] Per Bartley, J., in Hoffman v. Mackall, 5 Ohio St. 124, 64 Am. Dec. 637.

II. *The Formal Parts of the Deed*

§ 63. Parties described.—It is important that the names of the parties to a deed should be given accurately and fully in the granting part of the instrument.[1] Persons accustomed chiefly to commercial transactions and forms sometimes neglect to observe this requirement, and use the initial only of the given name, and thereby needlessly introduce a new element of confusion and uncertainty into the record title. Parol evidence is admissible to show who was really intended as the grantee in a deed when the name is claimed to be erroneous, and there is a person of the name used in the deed.[2] It is not absolutely essential to the validity of a mortgage that a mortgagee be described by name, if there be such other description as will distinguish the person intended from all others,[3] as for instance when the mortgage is made to the heirs at law of a person named who was deceased;[4] but it would be void if made to the heirs of a person living, because it is then uncertain who are intended to have the benefit of the mortgage.[5] A mortgage "to the trustees" of an unincorporated association or society is good, although the trustees be not named.[6] It is sufficient if they are so clearly described as to distinguish them from all others, so that there can be no uncertainty in the grant.

[1] Davidson v. Alabama Iron &c. Co., 109 Ala. 383, 19 So. 390; Berrigan v. Fleming, 70 Tenn. 271. See also Sheldon v. Carter, 90 Ala. 380, 8 So. 63. Mistake as to initial of wife does not invalidate mortgage as to her. Gaddie v. Hodges, 5 Ky. L. 241. Not fatal to the validity of a mortgage given by husband and wife, that the husband's name only appears as a signer. Hadley v. Clark, 8 Idaho 497, 69 Pac. 319.

[2] Thus a deed to "Hiram Gowing" was shown in this way to be intended for "Hiram G. Gowing," and not for his son, whose name was "Hiram Gowing." Peabody v. Brown, 10 Gray. (Mass.) 45. See also Scanlan v. Wright, 13 Pick. (Mass.) 523, 25 Am. Dec. 344; Fisher v. Milmine, 94 Ill. 328; Swan v. Vogel, 31 La. Ann. 38; Menage v. Burke, 43 Minn. 211, 45 N. W. 155, 19 Am. St. 235. As to the name of the grantor or mortgagor, his signature fixes the actual identity of the person.

[3] Madden v. Floyd, 69 Ala. 221; Frederick v. Wilcox, 119 Ala. 355, 24 So. 582, 72 Am. St. 925; Beaver v. Slanker, 94 Ill. 177; Richey v. Sinclair, 167 Ill. 184, 47 N. E. 364; Bay v. Posner, 78 Md. 42, 24 Atl. 1084.

[4] Shaw v. Loud, 12 Mass. 447. See also Thomas v. Marshfield, 10 Pick. (Mass.) 364, 367.

[5] Hall v. Leonard, 1 Pick. (Mass.) 27.

[6] Sleeper v. Iselin, 62 Iowa 583, 17 N. W. 922; Lawrence v. Fletcher, 8 Metc. (Mass.) 153.

A mortgage made under an assumed name by the owner of land is binding, the identity of the mortgagor as the owner being proved.[7] Likewise a mortgage made to a third person, consenting thereto, instead of to the mortgagee direct, is valid, as in the case of a trust deed.

It is quite desirable that the name and description of the mortgagor should be fully stated at the beginning of the instrument; but a duly signed mortgage which recites that the undersigned is indebted to another in a certain sum and for the purpose of securing the same he conveys to him certain land described and concludes the instrument with the words "witness my hand and seal," is valid.[8] A mortgage to a partnership in its firm name only is valid.[9]

The omission of the mortgagee's name from the granting clause will not invalidate a mortgage, if the person intended to be secured is identified by other parts of the instrument, as where the mortgage recites that the party of the first part is indebted to the party of the second part in a certain sum for which a promissory note of even date is made to the order of a person named and secured by the mortgage.[10]

A trust deed to a certain party "or his successors in trust" is not void for uncertainty of grantee. A mortgage to a corporation, by a name to which it was contemplated at the time to change the existing name of the company, is valid, if made to the corporation intended and it was then existing. In a proceeding upon the mortgage it should be averred that the mortgage was made to the company by the name used, it being then known by that name, as well as by the name it was legally entitled to.[11] But a mortgage to secure an indebtedness to the corporation is not rendered unenforcible by the corporation by reason of the fact that it runs to the manager of the corporation instead of to the corporation itself.[12] A deed to a public trustee

[7] Scanlan v. Grimmer, 71 Minn. 351, 74 N. W. 146, 70 Am. St. 326; Newton Sav. Bank v. Howerton (Iowa), 145 N. W. 292.

[8] Frederick v. Wilcox, 119 Ala. 355, 24 So. 582, 72 Am. St. 925.

[9] Lumber Co. v. Ashworth, 26 Kans. 212; Foster v. Johnson, 39 Minn. 380, 40 N. W. 255; Menage v. Burke, 43 Minn. 211, 45 N. W. 155, 19 Am. St. 235; Barber v. Crowell, 55 Nebr. 571, 75 N. W. 1109. In Arkansas, a mortgage to a partnership in the firm name is valid and enforcible in equity but not at law. Carpenter v. Zarbuck, 74 Ark. 474, 86 S. W. 299.

[10] Beaver v. Slanker, 94 Ill. 175; Richey v. Sinclair, 167 Ill. 184, 47 N. E. 364; Ray v. Power, 78 Md. 42. The designation of a successor in trust to the trustee in a trust deed as the "acting sheriff" was sufficient since it referred to the sheriff of a particular county and state. Killgore v. Cranmer, 35 Colo. 485, 84 Pac. 70; Empire Ranch &c. Co. v. Stratton, 22 Colo. App. 577, 126 Pac. 1094.

[11] City Bank v. McClellan, 21 Wis. 112.

[12] Anglo-Californian Bank v. Cerf, 147 Cal. 384, 81 Pac. 1077.

should name him in person adding his official title, but where he is designated as the "public trustee" of a particular county the omission of his name is usually held immaterial.[18]

The designation of "junior" or "second" is no part of a man's name, and although convenient and desirable for the purpose of distinguishing the party from another person of the same name, it is not essential, and the person intended may be shown in some other way.[14] The description of a person by his occupation is an addition of the same character, though of less importance, because the terms used to describe the occupation are so general that they are of but little aid in identifying the person.

When a party to the mortgage is a woman, it is important, if she be married, to give her husband's name, and, if she be not married, to state that she is a "spinster" or a "widow." Neat conveyancing would seem to require that a man not married should be described as a "bachelor" or a "widower." The terms "single" and "unmarried" are ambiguous, and are sometimes used to describe a divorced person.[15]

It is usual and desirable to state the place of residence of the parties by naming not merely the town or city of such residence, but the county and state as well.

§ **64. Recital of consideration.**[16]—Generally, the consideration named in a mortgage is the actual amount of the debt secured by it. In case the amount be not otherwise described, it may be presumed that the consideration named is the amount of the debt secured.[17] But it is not essential that this should be so. A nominal consideration named is sufficient, and in fact it is not essential that any consideration at all should be expressed.[18] The recital is never conclusive as to the real consideration.[19] The real consideration is the debt or obligation which the mortgage is given to secure, and upon that depends

---

[13] Healey v. Zobel, 45 Colo. 294, 101 Pac. 56.

[14] Kincaid v. Howe, 10 Mass. 203; Cobb v. Lucas, 15 Pick. (Mass.) 7.

[15] "The original and usual meaning of the word 'unmarried' is never having been married, but circumstances may show that it is used in the sense of not having a husband or wife living at the time of death." Peters v. Balke, 170 Ill. 304, 48 N. E. 1012. See also Reg v. Wymondham, 2 Ad. & E. (N. S.) 541.

[16] For consideration generally see post § 610 et seq.

[17] Burnett v. Wright, 135 N. Y. 543, 32 N. E. 253; Rowell v. Williams, 54 Wis. 636, 12 N. W. 86.

[18] Robinson v. Williams, 22 N. Y. 380. In re Farmers' Supply Co., 170 Fed. 502.

[19] Shoemaker v. Smith, 80 Iowa 655, 45 N. W. 744; McAteer v. McAteer, 31 S. Car. 313, 9 S. E. 966; Keyes v. Bump, 59 Vt. 391, 9 Atl. 598.

the validity of the mortgage, so far as the consideration is concerned. The seal implies a consideration.[20] The amount of the debt secured is in no way fixed or controlled by the nominal consideration.[21] The condition of the mortgage describes the debt and fixes the amount of it either specifically or in general terms.[22] A mortgage to indemnify against a liability, or to secure future advances, is generally of the latter description, but even in these cases the nominal consideration is immaterial.

§ 65. **Description of premises.**—An accurate description of the premises is of great importance as affecting the value of the security, and oftentimes affecting as well the interest of the mortgagor and of persons holding title under him. But a description, however general and indefinite it may be, if by extrinsic evidence it can be made practically certain what property it was intended to cover, will be sufficient to sustain the lien.[23]

A description by reference to other deeds is sufficient.[24] If a deed

---

[20] See post § 613.

[21] Gray v. Bennett (Iowa), 105 N. W. 377.

[22] Miller v. Lockwood, 32 N. Y. 293; Caston v. McCord, 130 Ala. 318, 30 So. 431.

[23] O'Neil v. Seixas, 85 Ala. 80, 4 So. 745; Began v. O'Reilly, 32 Cal. 11; Hancock v. Watson, 18 Cal. 137; De Leon v. Higuera, 15 Cal. 483; Whitney v. Buckman, 13 Cal. 536; Broach v. O'Neal, 94 Ga. 474, 20 S. E. 113; Patterson v. Evans, 91 Ga. 799, 18 S. E. 31; Richey v. Sinclair, 167 Ill. 184, 47 N. E. 364; Mason v. Merrill, 129 Ill. 503, 21 N. E. 799; Casler v. Byers, 129 Ill. 657, affg. 28 Ill. App. 128; Bybee v. Hageman, 66 Ill. 519; Works v. State, 120 Ind. 119, 22 N. E. 127; Thomson v. Madison Bldg. &c. Assn., 103 Ind. 279, 2 N. E. 735; Rucker v. Steelman, 73 Ind. 396; Blakemore v. Taber, 22 Ind. 466; English v. Roche, 6 Ind. 62; Godfrey v. White, 32 Ind. App. 265, 69 N. E. 688; Frazer v. Taliaferro, 6 Ky. L. 744; Roberts v. Bauer, 35 La. Ann. 453; Coogan v. Burling Mills; 124 Mass. 390; Tucker v. Field, 51 Miss. 191; Bollinger Co. v. McDowell, 99 Mo. 632, 13 S. W. 100; Morse v. Dewey, 3 N. H. 535; Boon v. Pierpont, 28 N. J. Eq. 7; Redfields v. Redfields (N. J.), 13 Atl. 600; People v. Storms, 97 N. Y.

364; Anderson v. Casey-Swasey Co. (Tex. Civ. App.), 120 S. W. 918. See also Baker v. Bank of La., 2 La. Ann. 371. "The part of a deed which describes the premises conveyed or mortgaged should be construed with the utmost liberality, and the deed should not be held void for uncertainty; if by any reasonable construction it can be made available. It is the office of the description to furnish the means of identification, and if the intent of the parties can, by any possibility, be gathered from the language used, it will be effectuated." Hannon v. Hilliard, 101 Ind. 310.

In Connecticut it is declared to be the policy of the law with regard to mortgages that they shall give definite information as to the property mortgaged; and it is intimated that a description which would be sufficient in an absolute deed might not be sufficient in a mortgage. Herman v. Deming, 44 Conn. 124; North v. Belden, 13 Conn. 376, 35 Am. Dec. 83; De Wolf v. Sprague Mfg. Co., 49 Conn. 282, 316. It is doubtful if these cases would be law anywhere else.

See post §§ 489, 1642.

[24] Wallace v. Furber, 62 Ind. 103; Willard v. Moulton, 4 Maine 14. See also Berry v. Derwart, 55 Md. 66;

describe lands by metes and bounds, a reference for further description to other deeds recorded will convey additional land described in the deeds referred to, unless otherwise controlled.[25] Although the first call in a description by boundaries be uncertain and ambiguous, other calls which are definite and certain and can be located will govern.

A description by boundaries prevails as against a description by reference to other deeds.[26] A description by metes and bounds prevails over a general description of the land as being "all" of a certain tract of which a person named died seised.[27] If a mortgage describes a definite quantity of land, another considerable tract of land, the title to which was derived from another source, is not covered by the mortgage, although the description concludes with a general reference to a deed which conveyed both tracts.[28] If the mortgage clearly and unequivocally describes more land than is embraced in the deeds referred to, although the premises described are mentioned as "the same estate" mentioned in the deeds, the conveyance is not restricted by such reference to the premises described in the deeds referred to, but will also embrace the land described by metes and bounds.[29] The lines of ascertained boundaries generally control, rather than a description of the quantity of land, unless it appears that the averment or covenant of quantity was intended to control.[30] A reference to the "same premises" may enlarge the terms of a specific description.[31]

A mortgage may be sustained though a portion of the description is plainly erroneous where after the rejection of the erroneous portion the remaining description is sufficiently definite to render the location of the premises susceptible of ready ascertainment by any one acquainted with the locality, or by a competent surveyor.[32] A mortgage describing the lands as all the lands of the mortgagor in a named county will pass all the land owned by him in such county.[33] And in like manner a mortgage of all the lots the mortgagor then owned in a

Edmonston v. Carter, 180 Mo. 515, 79 S. W. 459.

[25] Coogan v. Burling Mills, 124 Mass. 390; Bell v. Leggett, 175 Ala. 443, 57 So. 836.

[26] Steele v. Williams (Ky.), 15 S. W. 49.

[27] Spiller v. Scribner, 36 Vt. 245; Cummings v. Black, 65 Vt. 76, 25 Atl. 906.

[28] Holmes v. Abrahams, 31 N. J. Eq. 415.

[29] Auburn Congregational Church v. Walker, 124 Mass. 69.

[30] Maguire v. Bissell, 119 Ind. 345, 21 N. E. 326; Doyle v. Mellen, 15 R. I. 523, 8 Atl. 709.

[31] Patterson v. Harlan, 124 Pa. St. 67, 16 Atl. 496.

[32] Carpenter Paper Co. v. Wilcox, 50 Nebr. 659, 70 N. W. 228.

[33] Vanmeter v. Vanmeter, 3 Grat. (Va.) 148.

certain town, whether he had the legal or equitable title thereto, conveys all the lots which can be identified as belonging to him by either title.[34] But a mortgage of all the lands the mortgagor owns in a certain town does not include lands held by him in mortgage, though by absolute deed with a separate defeasance not recorded.[35] A mortgage "of all my estate," or "of all my lands wherever situated," or "of all my property," is not invalid by reason of the generality of the description.[36] A mortgage of "all the real estate" the mortgagor owns in certain towns, "of whatsoever name or nature," includes his rights as tenant in common of undivided land.[37] But such a mortgage could not be made to apply to after-acquired lands.[38] A mortgage of all the land owned by the mortgagor in a certain town does not include certain lots previously sold by him, the deeds of which had not been recorded at the time the mortgage was recorded.[39] A mortgage by an heir of his undivided interest in an estate inherited by him includes all interest which he owns, whether in possession, reversion or remainder.[40]

When the objection is merely to the indefiniteness of description, it does not lie with the mortgagor to say that he conveyed the property by a description so loose or indefinite that no title could pass upon a foreclosure sale of the property.[41] If nothing passes, it is the misfortune of the mortgagee, but the mortgagor is not hurt; if anything does pass, the mortgagee is entitled to the benefit of the mortgage as it stands.[42] When, however, the description is such that property may pass or be sold under the mortgage which the mort-

[34] Starling v. Blair, 4 Bibb (Ky.) 288. See also Easter v. Severin, 64 Ind. 375; City Nat. Bank v. Barrow, 21 La. Ann. 396; Strouse v. Cohen, 113 N. Car. 349, 18 S. E. 323.

[35] Mills v. Shepard, 30 Conn. 98.
A mortgage of all "unappropriated" lands in a certain place may not cover lands which the mortgagor had previously conveyed, though the conveyance had not been recorded at the time of the mortgage. Crawford v. Bonner, 53 Tex. 194.

[36] Wilson v. Boyce, 92 U. S. 320, 23 L. ed. 608; Usina v. Wilder, 58 Ga. 178; Leslie v. Merrick, 99 Ind. 180; City Nat. Bank v. Barrow, 21 La. Ann. 396; Drew v. Carroll, 154 Mass. 181, 28 N. E. 148; Fitzgerald v. Libby, 142 Mass. 235, 7 N. E. 917; Woodman v. Lane, 7 N. H. 241; Har-

key v. Cain, 69 Tex. 146, 6 S. W. 637. See also Albertson v. Prewitt, 20 Ky. L. 1309, 49 S. W. 196; Jackson v. De Lancey, 13 Johns. (N. Y.) 537, 7 Am. Dec. 403; Strouse v. Cohen, 113 N. Car. 349, 18 S. E. 323; Florence v. Morien, 98 Va. 26, 34 S. E. 890.

[37] Drew v. Carroll, 154 Mass. 181, 28 N. E. 148.

[38] Calhoun v. Memphis &c. R. Co., 2 Flip. (U. S.) 442.

[39] Fitzgerald v. Libby, 142 Mass. 235, 7 N. E. 917.

[40] Carter v. McDaniel, 94 Ky. 564, 23 S. W. 507. See also McPherson v. Snowden, 19 Md. 197; Anderson v. Casey-Swasey Co. (Tex. Civ. App.), 120 S. W. 918.

[41] Whitney v. Buckman, 13 Cal. 536.

[42] Tryon v. Sutton, 13 Cal. 490.

gagor did not include, or intend to include, it is proper that he should ask to have it reformed. Very strong proof is required to support an allegation that by mistake a mortgage was made to embrace lands that ought not to have been put in; and the testimony of the mortgagor that he did not intend the mortgage should cover a portion of the premises described, which were in a condition to be mortgaged, and were deliberately included, is wholly insufficient to exclude such portion.[43]

A practical location of boundaries which has been acquiesced in for a long series of years will not be disturbed. If the owner of a lot makes a practical location of its side boundaries, by erecting a building which covers its entire width as described in his deed, and thereafter executes a mortgage with covenants, intended to cover the entire lot, but which for some unexplained reason describes it as a few inches narrower, such practical location, and the covenants in the mortgage, may be successfully invoked, as against the original owner and mortgagor and his heirs, to extend to the entire original lot a title acquired through a foreclosure sale, after the practical location has been acquiesced in for between thirty and forty years.[44] If the description of the property in the granting part of a mortgage be inconsistent with a provision contained in the condition, the latter must give way.[45]

§ 65a. **Descriptions held sufficient.**—Among others the following descriptions have been held sufficient and capable of ascertainment, as against the contention of uncertainty: "A certain tract or parcel of land known as the A. H. Draughn farm on left hand fork of Troublesome creek;"[46] all the lands the mortgagor holds "on the Dry Fork of Otter creek;"[47] "the Zacariah Emerson place" and "the Thomas Bazemore place," in a specified county;[48] "the Noel Mill property, situated in the Seventeenth Civil district of Franklin county;"[49] grantor's undivided third interest in "Wanalaw plantation in Holmes county;"[50] "one hundred acres of land No. 173, known as the Jones place, in the Fifth district of Wilcox county;"[51] "one acre of land off of the north-

[43] Shepard v. Shepard, 36 Mich. 173.

[44] Katz v. Kaiser, 154 N. Y. 294, 48 N. E. 532.

[45] Donnan v. Intelligencer Printing &c. Co., 70 Mo. 168.

[46] Watts v. Parks, 25 Ky. L. 1908, 78 S. W. 1125.

[47] Albertson v. Prewitt, 20 Ky. L. 1309, 49 S. W. 196.

[48] Johnson v. McKay, 119 Ga. 196, 45 S. E. 992.

[49] Grace v. Noel Mill Co. (Tenn.), 63 S. W. 246.

[50] Eggleston v. Watson, 53 Miss. 339. See also Fields v. Fish, 26 Ky. L. 659, 82 S. W. 376.

[51] Jones v. McKinney, 135 Ga. 60, 68 S. E. 788, 31 L. R. A. (N. S.) 900.

west corner of block 27 of South Lawn," a platted subdivision, which the court construed as one square acre;[52] "seventy acres in the southwest corner of the southwest quarter section of section 14," which was construed as seventy acres in the form of a square;[53] "one hundred acres in the southeast corner of lot No. 307 in the Seventh district of North county, Georgia," where it was clear from the instrument that the land conveyed should be in the form of a square;[54] "one tract or parcel of land lying in Jefferson county, Georgia, in the Seventy-ninth district, containing one hundred acres and bounded on the north by my own land, east by land of K. Walden, on south by W. L. Phillips, on west by Sarah and Emily Walden;"[55] "a tract of land in a specified county adjoining the lands of Patrick Lynch and R. N. Bowden situate on the east side of the road leading from Jerusalem church to Patrick Lynch's, it being a portion of the G. R. P. tract, and containing fifty acres;"[56] parts of specified lots in a designated district and county, "it being land purchased by J. L. Henson from J. E. Derrick;"[57] "seventy acres in McCracken county, on which E resides, formerly owned by H," in a specified section;[58] "a part of Broad Ripple Float, section No. 1, being the tract deeded to John H. Brown, by E. Kitch, trustee;"[59] "three hundred and twenty acres of land known as the Middlebrooks place, where the said Hurston lived last year, and where Henry Tally now lives;"[60] "My entire undivided one-tenth interest in about two hundred and sixty-five acres of land," in a specified county;[61] "thirty acres" in a certain quarter section, where the only property owned by the mortgagor in the section contained about thirty acres lying south of a creek;[62] "a lot of land near Florence, north of the fair grounds, containing thirty-five acres," where grantor owned but one such lot;[63] "lots 8, 13, and 14, in block 17, and lot 5 in block 18, and the stock in the paper mill on said premises," where the mortgagor never owned any other lot on which there was a paper mill;[64] "sixty acres lying on Mill Pond road" and being the same

[52] Richey v. Sinclair, 167 Ill. 184, 47 N. E. 364.

[53] Walsh v. Ringer, 2 Ohio 327, 15 Am. Dec. 555. See also Scott v. Gordon, 109 Mo. App. 695, 83 S. W. 550.

[54] Payton v. McPhaul, 128 Ga. 510, 58 S. E. 50.

[55] Walden v. Walden, 128 Ga. 126, 57 S. E. 323.

[56] Edwards v. Bowden, 99 N. Car. 80, 5 S. E. 283, 6 Am. St. 487.

[57] Derrick v. Sams, 98 Ga. 397, 25 S. E. 509, 58 Am. St. 309.

[58] Eby v. Lovelace, 4 Ky. L. 449.

[59] Wilson v. Brown, 82 Ind. 471.

[60] Tranum v. Wilkinson, 81 Ala. 408, 1 So. 201.

[61] Fields v. Fish, 26 Ky. L. 659, 82 S. W. 376.

[62] Vanvalkenberg v. American Land Mtg. Co., 87 Fed. 617, 31 C. C. A. 145.

[63] O'Neal v. Seixas, 85 Ala. 80, 4 So. 745.

[64] Bowden v. Wood, 35 Ind. 268.

set over to the grantor in the division of his father's land, where partition proceedings disclosed that a certain platted lot 3 was awarded the grantor;[65] "section 21, less one and one-half acres in the northeast corner of the west half of southeast fourth of said section 21," the exception if anything being void;[66] "seventy-two acres of land situate near Hamlin, bought of the Land Company, also twelve and one-half acres of land situate near Hamlin, conveyed to B. F. Curry by James T. Carroll, also three acres situate near Hamlin, and known as the old church lot, also my storehouse and lot and livery stable and lot in Hamlin;"[67] "lot 36, in the town of Webb," where the trust deed was dated at Webb, Mississippi;[68] land lying "in the village of Raysville," without naming state or county, where grantors described themselves as of "Raysville, Henry county, Indiana."[69]

§ 66. **Insufficient description.**—The description may be so uncertain that no title will vest in the mortgagee by the deed unless it be reformed,[70] or even so uncertain that it can not be reformed.[71] A mortgage describing land by township and range, without stating in what county or state the land was situated, has been held void;[72] but the courts take judicial notice of government surveys and legal subdivisions, and, when the state and county are not named, will generally presume that the land is situated in the state where the parties reside.[73]

A mortgage describing land as parts of different sections, without stating the township or range, is void.[74] But an error in the number of the range, or in the omission of it, will not affect the validity of a mortgage, if the property be otherwise described with such certainty as to clearly identify it.[75] An error in giving the number of a block

---

[65] Hinton v. Moore, 139 N. Car. 44, 51 S. E. 787.

[66] Claraday v. Abraham, 174 Ala. 130, 56 So. 720.

[67] Holley v. Curry, 58 W. Va. 70, 51 S. E. 135, 112 Am. St. 944.

[68] Wilkerson v. Webb, 75 Miss. 403, 23 So. 180.

[69] Parker v. Teas, 79 Ind. 235.

[70] Osborne v. Rice, 107 Ga. 281, 33 S. E. 54; White v. Hyatt, 40 Ind. 385; Swatts v. Bowen, 141 Ind. 322, 40 N. E. 1057; Keiffer v. Starn, 27 La. Ann. 282; Peck v. Mallams, 10 N. Y. 509.

[71] Freed v. Brown, 41 Ark. 495; Lewis v. Owen, 64 Ind. 446; Merchants' Bldg. Assn. v. Scanlan, 144 Ind. 11, 42 N E. 1003.

[72] Barron v. Barron, 122 Ala. 194, 25 So. 55; Murphy v. Hendricks, 57 Ind. 593; Cochran v. Utt, 42 Ind. 267.

[73] Smith v. Green, 41 Fed. 455; Bybee v. Hageman, 66 Ill. 519; Burton v. Ferguson, 69 Ind. 486; Russell v. Sweezey, 22 Mich. 236; Quinn v. Champagne, 38 Minn. 322, 37 N. W. 451.

[74] Boyd v. Ellis, 11 Iowa 97; Wilson v. Calder, 8 Kans. App. 856, 55 Pac. 552; Martin v. Kitchen, 195 Mo. 477, 93 S. W. 780. See post § 66a.

[75] White v. Hermann, 51 Ill. 243, 99 Am. Dec. 543; Kile v. Yellowhead, 80 Ill. 208; Thornhill v. Burthe, 29 La. Ann. 639; Gerald v.

is immaterial when the description is otherwise accurate and could apply only to the lot intended, and the names of the streets upon which the land is situated are correctly given.[76]

An erroneous description of real estate in a mortgage that is full and consistently complete within itself, and clearly and correctly identifies a tract of land, will not be reformed to embrace an entirely different tract, to the prejudice of a subsequent mortgagee who accepted his mortgage of the latter in ignorance of the mistake and in bona fide reliance upon the appearance of the public record.[77]

A mortgage of all the property of a mining company, particularly described as "located at and near the mouth of Alder Gulch, in section 10" of a certain township, does not cover property of said company located in other sections of that township; and a decree authorizing the sale of property proved to be owned by the company in other sections is a nullity as regards such property. The only property that could be sold is that located in section 10.[78]

A mortgage of fifty acres of land by description, the same being part of the large farm, or the next and adjoining fifty acres that is unincumbered, provided the first be incumbered, is not void for uncertainty as to either tract. The whole farm in such case is subject to the mortgage, which is to be satisfied out of any unincumbered tract nearest to that first described; but the mortgage is not defeated although the whole farm be incumbered.[79] A mortgage of five hundred acres of land out of a larger tract described, "beginning at the west boundary, and extending east sufficiently far to embrace five hundred acres," has been held valid as containing a sufficient description.[80] A mortgage of a certain number of acres out of a large tract, the portion mortgaged not being described or located, has been held to pass such an undivided joint interest in the whole tract as the quantity mortgaged bears to the quantity contained in the whole tract.[81] A

Gerald, 31 S. Car. 171, 9 S. E. 792. As to whether the meridian or county controls, see Sickmon v. Wood, 69 Ill. 329. As to definiteness of description of portions of sections, see Mettart v. Allen, 139 Ind. 644, 39 N. E. 239; Collins v. Dresser, 133 Ind. 290, 32 N. E. 883; Cook v. Gilchrist, 82 Iowa 277, 48 N. W. 84.

[76] Sharp v. Thompson, 100 Ill. 447, 39 Am. Rep. 61; Rhodes v. Outcalt, 48 Mo. 367; Baker v. Bartlett, 18

Mont. 446, 45 Pac. 1084; Cake v. Cake, 127 Pa. St. 400, 17 Atl. 984.

[77] Pence v. Armstrong, 95 Ind. 191; Rhinehardt v. Reifers, 158 Ind. 675, 64 N. E. 459.

[78] Largey v. Sedman, 3 Mont. 472.

[79] Lee v. Woodworth, 3 N. J. Eq. 36. See also Kruse v. Scripps, 11 Ill. 98; Gray v. Stiver, 24 Ind. 174.

[80] Westmoreland v. Carson, 76 Tex. 619, 13 S. W. 553.

[81] Brown v. Maury, 85 Tenn. 358, 3 S. W. 175.

description is fatally defective which describes the land as the north part of a described quarter section.[82]

A mortgage which does not name the town, county, or state in which the land is situated may nevertheless be rendered certain in the description of the premises by a reference to another deed, which contains a full and accurate description,[83] or to the land of the adjacent owners,[84] or by extrinsic evidence.[85] A deed which omits to name the state and county in which the land is situated, but purports to have been executed in a certain county and state between parties residing therein, is presumed to be of land situated in such county and state.[86] A mistake in the number of a lot may be rendered immaterial by the boundaries, which will control when fixed and certain, as for instance when they are public streets.[87]

§ 66a. **Insufficient description—Illustrations.**—The following descriptions of mortgaged premises have been held insufficient, and too indefinite to pass title: "A portion of the northeast quarter of section 22, in township 6, range 20, containing twenty acres;"[88] "the west part of lot 8 in block G;"[89] "the south part of" certain premises;[90] "a farm owned by me in townships 65 and 66 of Worth county, etc., south of Grant City, one and one-half miles," without designating section or range;[91] "the east half of the southeast fourth of section 13, township 13, range 4 east," without naming the state or county;[92] "the northwest quarter of section 7, north of Castor river," in a certain county, without reference to township or range, where the northwest quarter of section 7 of more than one township were north of the Castor river;[93] "all the west half of the northwest quarter of section 8, township 6, range 7," the county or state not being named;[94] "all that tract lying in the county aforesaid, on the waters of the

[82] Hill v. Hite, 86 Fed. 268.

[83] Harding v. Strong, 42 Ill. 148, 89 Am. Dec. 415; Robinson v. Brennan, 115 Mass. 582; Slater v. Breese, 36 Mich. 77; Boon v. Pierpont, 32 N. J. Eq. 217.

[84] Ells v. Sims, 2 La. Ann. 251.

[85] Slater v. Breese, 36 Mich. 77.

[86] Dutch v. Boyd, 81 Ind. 146; Mann v. State, 116 Ind. 383, 19 N. E. 181.

[87] Cooper v. Bigly, 13 Mich. 463.

[88] Freed v. Brown, 41 Ark. 495.

[89] Merchants &c. Assn. v. Scanlan, 144 Ind. 11, 42 N. E. 1008.

[90] Hickox v. Lowe, 10 Cal. 197; Armstrong v. Short, 95 Ind. 326; Hodgdon v. Shannon, 44 N. H. 572; South Sea Co. v. Duncomb, 2 Stra. 919. See post § 364.

[91] Carter v. Holman, 60 Mo. 498.

[92] Barron v. Barron, 122 Ala. 194, 25 So. 55.

[93] Martin v. Kitchen, 195 Mo. 477, 93 S. W. 780. See also Boyd v. Ellis, 11 Iowa 97; Keiffer v. Starn, 27 La. Ann. 282.

[94] Cochran v. Utt, 42 Ind. 267. See also Murphy v. Hendricks, 57 Ind. 593.

South Beaverdam creek, adjoining the lands of Peter Rice and Sarah A. Rice, to be run off the lower end of my tract of land formerly owned by Robert Steel, containing ten acres, all the remainder to be upland, in all twenty acres;"[95] "all that certain tract of land adjoining the lands of John Summerville on the east, Peter Spence on the south, and Hiram Allen on the north, being a portion of the north end of the upper half of the lower half of the upper section of Conner's reservation, said to contain one hundred and fourteen acres;"[96] "a certain piece or tract of land, grist mill and storehouse, adjoining the lands of Anderson Breedlove, J. C. Usry and Dora Harris, containing three acres," which were not otherwise designated out of a forty-acre tract owned by the mortgagor.[97]

§ 67. **Habendum.**—The office of the habendum is to define the estate conveyed; to explain how long the grantee is to hold it, and whether in an absolute or qualified manner.[98] To create an absolute and unqualified estate in the grantee, the habendum must be to him and his heirs. A mortgage to one, "his executors, administrators, and assigns," without naming his heirs,[99] or a mortgage to an individual, "his successors and assigns forever," without the word "heirs,"[1] con-

[95] Osborne v. Rice, 107 Ga. 281, 33 S. E. 54.

[96] Swatts v. Bowen, 141 Ind. 322, 40 N. E. 1057.

[97] Harris v. Woodard, 130 N. Car. 580, 41 S. E. 790.

[98] New York Indians v. United States, 170 U. S. 1, 18 Sup. Ct. 531, 42 L. ed. 927; Sumner v. Williams, 8 Mass. 162, 5 Am. Dec. 83; Hart v. Gardner, 74 Miss. 153, 20 So. 877; Redstrake v. Townsend, 39 N. J. L. 372; Clapp v. Byrnes, 3 App. Div. 284, 38 N. Y. S. 1063; Hafner v. Irwin, 20 N. Car. 570, 34 Am. Dec. 390; Miller v. Graham, 47 S. Car. 288, 25 S. E. 165; Horn v. Broyles (Tenn. Ch.), 62 S. W. 297. The habendum of a mortgage, containing a power of sale in the mortgagee, passing "all the right, title, interest, claim, demand, and equity" of the mortgagors, in the premises, included whatever interes the mortgagors had and carried their equity of redemption. Strother v. Law, 54 Ill. 413.

[99] Clearwater v. Rose, 1 Blackf. (Ind.) 137. Where a mortgage is not a conveyance but a lien merely, the word "heirs" is not necessary to create a lien on the fee simple estate of the mortgagor.

[1] Sedgwick v. Laflin, 10 Allen (Mass.) 430; Allendorff v. Gaugengigl, 146 Mass. 542, 16 N. E. 283; Bredenberg v. Landrum, 32 S. Car. 215, 10 S. E. 956; Kidd v. Teeple, 22 Cal. 255; Purser v. Eagle Lake Land &c. Co., 111 Cal. 139, 43 Pac. 523. In the latter case a married woman in a mortgage of her separate estate joined her husband in releasing her estate to the "grantee," though in the dower and homestead clause she released to the grantee and "his heirs and assigns" all right to dower and homestead in the premises. It was held the mortgage conveyed her general title to the grantee for life only; the word "grantee" not including "heirs and assigns," and these words, used in the relinquishment of dower and homestead, not relating back so as to include, in the relinquishment of her general title to the grantee, his heirs and assigns.

A colonial statute of 1651 provided that all deeds, in order to pass an estate of inheritance, should contain a habendum to the grantee, his

veys only a life estate; and the executor of the mortgagee can not maintain a writ of entry to foreclose the mortgage because it terminated with the mortgagee's life. A power of sale in such a mortgage, authorizing the mortgagee upon default to sell the land and execute a conveyance in fee simple, if not executed does not operate to enlarge the estate. But a fee simple may be created without the use of the word "heirs" where the intention to create such an estate is clear.[2] Thus where a mortgage was executed in Indiana upon lands in Ohio, according to a form authorized by statute in the former state, whereby the words "mortgage and warrant" are declared to pass an estate in fee simple, it was held in the latter state that the mortgage passed the entire estate of the mortgagor, and upon foreclosure the purchaser acquired an estate in fee simple.[3]

But a mortgage made to a treasurer of a corporation named, with habendum "unto him the said treasurer and his successors in office, to his and their use and behoof forever," the condition of the mortgage being that the mortgagor should "pay to the said treasurer, or his successors in office," a certain sum, is held to pass an estate in fee, on the ground that these expressions in the deed showed that the grantee took the conveyance simply as trustee for the corporation, and that the nature of the trust required that a fee should pass by the deed.[4] The estate of the trustee must be commensurate with the equitable estate of the cestui que trust. A mortgage to trustees for bondholders, from which words of inheritance have been inadvertently omitted, but the provisions of which require that the trustees should have an estate in fee simple in order to execute them, will be construed as a conveyance in fee simple, and may be reformed as against subsequent purchasers with notice; and the record of the mortgage would be notice that the instrument was intended to pass a fee.[5] But a mortgage to executors, "their successors and assigns," containing the usual clause conveying all the mortgagor's estate, right, and title, when duly recorded, is notice to subsequent purchasers, mortgagees, and judgment creditors that such mortgage was intended to convey the fee.[6]

heirs and assigns. This provision has been continued in each successive revision of the statute of the state.

[2] Gould v. Lamb, 11 Metc. (Mass.) 84, 45 Am. Dec. 187.

[3] De Leon v. Higuera, 15 Cal. 483; Brown v. National Bank, 44 Ohio St. 269, 6 N. E. 506.

[4] Brooks v. Jones, 11 Metc. (Mass.) 191.

[5] Randolph v. N. J. West Line R. Co., 28 N. J. Eq. 49; Coe v. N. J. Midland R. Co., 31 N. J. Eq. 105.

[6] Bunker v. Anderson, 32 N. J. Eq. 35.

A mortgage giving the mortgagee a life estate only will not be reformed to convey a fee, as against the rights of a bona fide purchaser of the premises, without notice of any claim on his part of a greater estate than the mortgage as recorded purports to convey.[7] Although mortgages of real estate are usually in fee, constructive notice merely of the existence of a mortgage, with no notice as to the estate conveyed, is not notice that the mortgage is in fee, when in terms a life estate only is expressed.

In a mortgage or other conveyance to a corporation it is usual to make the habendum to it and its "successors and assigns;" but neither of these words is necessary to give the corporation all the estate it can take in the land conveyed. There is an implied condition, in every conveyance to a corporation, that upon the civil death of the corporation while retaining the land it shall revert to the original grantor and his heirs.[8]

Clerical errors in the habendum clause may be disregarded as surplusage, as where, for example, the draftsman has erroneously inserted the names of the grantors in the habendum, and as covenantees in the covenants.[9]

§ 68. Covenants.—The covenants of a mortgage are usually those of a warranty deed, and have the same effect and construction. If, however, a mortgage with covenants be given for purchase-money of land conveyed to the mortgagor by a deed having like covenants, and the mortgagor is evicted, he may recover damages in an action for breach of the covenant, and the vendor who holds the mortgage is not allowed to set up the covenants in the mortgage deed as a defense by way of rebutter, especially when he holds the plaintiff's promissory notes secured by the mortgage.[10] "Various cases might be readily supposed," says Mr. Justice Dewey, "when such a defense ought not to prevail; as in cases of large payments advanced toward the purchase-

---

[7] Wilson v. King, 27 N. J. Eq. 374.

[8] 2 Kent Com. 282, 307. The chancellor, in taking a mortgage under order of court, is regarded as acting in the capacity of a corporation; Chancellor v. Hoxley, 41 N. J. L. 217; and the word "successors" having been omitted, if it be regarded as material, the mortgage may be reformed. Chancellor v. Bell, 45 N. J. Eq. 538, 17 Atl. 684.

[9] Perley v. Woodbury, 76 N. H. 23, 78 Atl. 1073.

[10] Hubbard v. Norton, 10 Conn. 422; Smith v. Cannell, 32 Maine 123; Sumner v. Barnard, 12 Metc. (Mass.) 459; Haynes v. Stevens, 11 N. H. 28. Covenants of title and warranty expressed in a mortgage or implied by statute, have the same effect as in an absolute deed. Lockwood v. Sturdevant, 6 Conn. 373; Blanchard v. Haseltine, 79 Mo. App. 248; Weed v. Covill, 14 Barb. (N. Y.) 242.

money, and a mortgage to secure only a small residue, and that, by the terms of the contract, to be paid at some remote future day. The rights of the defendant may be protected by postponing entry of judgment to await the set-off upon the mortgage debt."[11] In other words, the covenants in the mortgage do not estop the mortgagee to recover upon those in his vendor's deed to him. As between these parties, the mortgagor for purchase-money really pledges nothing but the interest which he obtained under his vendor's deed, and is answerable to him for no imperfection in the title existing before the conveyance. If the mortgage be redeemed, that is the end of it; and if it be foreclosed, the title which the grantor parted with is restored to him by foreclosure, or he gets the full benefit of it. One having the mortgagee's right after foreclosure is not allowed to recover damages for a breach of the covenant which existed at the time of the conveyance by the mortgagee; for the effect of such recovery would be to obtain all that he parted with in the conveyance, and the value of the incumbrance, which he is relieved from removing by the foreclosure.[12]

If upon the foreclosure of a mortgage not for purchase-money the mortgagee purchase the property for the amount of the mortgage debt, he can not afterward maintain an action upon the covenants of warranty contained in the mortgage, without first having the sale and satisfaction of the judgment set aside.[13]

The covenants of warranty in a mortgage are often of importance where the mortgagor has no title, or an imperfect one at the time of making the mortgage, but afterward acquires one; they then operate by way of estoppel or rebutter, so that the after-acquired title inures to the benefit of the holder of the mortgage. Except in this way the ordinary covenants are of little use in a mortgage, because the damages for a breach of them would only entitle the holder of the mortgage to recover the amount due him on the mortgage, and this he can more readily recover by suit for the mortgage debt upon the note or bond, or upon the covenant for the payment of it sometimes contained in the mortgage.[14]

[11] Sumner v. Barnard, 12 Metc. (Mass.) 459.

[12] Hardy v. Nelson, 27 Maine 525; Brown v. Staples, 28 Maine 497, 48 Am. Dec. 504; Smith v. Cannell, 32 Maine 123; Geyer v. Girard, 22 Mo. 159; Connor v. Eddy, 25 Mo. 72; Lot v. Thomas, 2 N. J. L. 407, 2 Am. Dec. 354. See also Hancock v. Carlton, 6 Gray (Mass.) 39, 61; Cross v. Robinson, 21 Conn. 379; Kellogg v. Wood, 4 Paige (N. Y.) 578.

[13] Todd v. Johnson, 51 Iowa 192, 1 N. W. 498.

[14] Quoted with approval in Todd v. Johnson, 51 Iowa 192, 1 N. W. 498.

§ **68a. Continuing covenants.**—A mortgage may, however, contain covenants which do not cease to exist upon its discharge. Thus, where a mortgage securing a debt payable in five years contained covenants by the mortgagor with the grantee and his heirs and assigns that no building nor part of a building should be erected upon the granted premises for five years from the date of the mortgage, and that no building nor part of a building erected thereafter upon the granted premises should be more than two stories in height, and that these covenants should be binding upon and available to heirs and assigns and run with the land for the benefit of the adjoining land of the grantee, and in the condition it is further provided that, upon payment and other performance by the grantor the deed, with the exception of the covenants above recited should be void; an intention is clearly manifested that the operation of the covenants should not cease with the discharge of the mortgage, and the covenant that the land should not be used for buildings of over a certain height is in effect the grant of an easement in favor of the adjoining premises the violation of which may be restrained.[15]

III. *The Condition*

§ **69. Form and essentials of condition.**—The usual words of the proviso are, that upon the payment of the debt or performance of the duty named, "then this deed shall be void." But any equivalent expression may be used,[1] and in fact, if it appear from the whole instrument that it was intended as a security, although there be no express provision that upon the fulfilment of the condition the deed shall be void, it is a mortgage.[2] The substance and not the form of expression is chiefly to be regarded; and an enlarged and liberal view is to be taken

---

[15] Brown v. O'Brien, 168 Mass. 484, 47 N. E. 195.

[1] Bernstein v. Humes, 71 Ala. 260; Adams v. Stevens, 49 Maine 362; Cowles v. Marble, 37 Mich. 158;

Pearce v. Wilson, 111 Pa. St. 14, 56 Am. Rep. 243; Wisconsin Cent. R. Co. v. Wisconsin &c. Land Co., 71 Wis. 94, 36 N. W. 837.

[2] Snyder v. Bunnell, 64 Ind. 403.

of the instrument in order to ascertain and carry into effect the intention of the parties.[3]

It is not necessary that the condition of the mortgage should be so certain as to preclude the necessity of extraneous inquiry as to what it really is, and whether it has been performed,[4] as in the case of a mortgage to secure future advances or to indemnify a surety. But unless it appears upon what event the deed is to become void, or that it is to become void in some event, it is not in itself a mortgage.[5] If the defeasance clause leaves blank the amount of the debt intended to be secured, the defect may be supplied by parol evidence.[6] Even a deed absolute on its face may in equity be shown by extrinsic evidence to have been intended as a mortgage. But a deed in the form of a mortgage, and complete except in the omission to state the amount of the debt secured, is upon its face prima facie a mortgage.[7]

§ 70. **Description of the debt secured.**[8]—To constitute a mortgage, there must necessarily be a debt which is the subject of the security. But it is not necessary that there should be any personal liability for the payment of the debt; as, in the case of a mortgage to secure advances to be made subsequently, the parties may agree that the mortgagee shall advance the money, and rely solely for his security upon the pledge of the real estate. Formerly mortgages were frequently given for the security of existing debts without mentioning any note, bond, or other personal obligation. There can be no question as to their validity, not only as against the mortgagor, but against all claiming subsequently. Whether there can be any action against the mortgagor personally may depend upon the particular circumstances of different cases. Where there is a contract, express or implied, for

[3] Steel v. Steel, 4 Allen (Mass.) 417; Lanfair v. Lanfair, 18 Pick. (Mass.) 299; Burnett v. Wright, 135 N. Y. 543, 32 N. E. 253 (quoting text); Skinner v. Cox, 4 Dev. L. (N. Car.) 59. "As a mortgage in this state conveys no estate, but merely creates a lien, an instrument properly executed, describing the parties, the land, and the debt, and evidencing an intention to charge the debt as a lien upon the land, is sufficient to constitute a mortgage. Words of conveyance, being inoperative, are unnecessary." Morrill v. Skinner, 57 Nebr. 164, 77 N. W. 375.

[4] Youngs v. Wilson, 27 N. Y. 351.

[5] Goddard v. Coe, 55 Maine 385; Adams v. Stevens, 49 Maine 262; Freeman's Bank v. Vose, 23 Maine 98.

[6] Burnett v. Wright, 135 N. Y. 543, 32 N. E. 253. But see Heburn v. Reynolds, 73 Misc. 73, 132 N. Y. S. 460.

[7] Burnett v. Wright, 135 N. Y. 543, 32 N. E. 253.

[8] See post §§ 343-395; South Sea Co. v. Duncomb, 2 Stra. 919; Hickox v. Lowe, 10 Cal. 197; Hodgdon v. Shannon, 44 N. H. 572.

the payment of the debt, this is not merged in the security created by the mortgage, and the creditor may maintain assumpsit.[9]

The mortgage must identify the indebtedness it is intended to secure.[10] But a literal exactness in this respect is not required; it is sufficient if the description be correct so far as it goes, and full enough to direct attention to the sources of correct and full information in regard to it, and the language used is not liable to deceive or mislead as to the nature or amount of it.[11] Thus, the condition of a mortgage specified that the mortgagee was an accommodation indorser and signer for the mortgagors on sundry notes, drafts, and bills of exchange then maturing to the amount of $50,000, a particular description of which could not be given. The mortgagors were in a failing condition, and at the time the mortgages were given it was necessary to give the security before a more accurate description could be made; but this description was held to be sufficient.[12]

The mortgage itself need not necessarily state the amount of the debt secured. The amount may be ascertained by reference to some other instrument, like a note or a bond.[13] Even a mortgage to secure all existing debts of the mortgagor to the mortgagee is not invalid for want of certainty in the amount secured.[14] So, the description of the note may omit the names of the makers, and it will suffice, if it sets out the date, the amount, the time of payment and the interest on the note.[15] In the absence of fraud a mortgage to secure against future liabilities or advances described with reasonable certainty is valid.[16]

The condition of the mortgage must give reasonable notice of the incumbrance on the land mortgaged in order to affect the creditors

[9] Yates v. Aston, 4 Ad. & El. (N. S.) 182.

[10] Chilbrooks v. McEwen, 29 Ind. 347; Brick v. Scott, 47 Ind. 299; In re Hawks, 204 Fed. 309.

[11] Curtis v. Flinn, 46 Ark. 70; Ricketson v. Richardson, 19 Cal. 330; Stoughton v. Pasco, 5 Conn. 442, 13 Am. Dec. 72; Booth v. Barnum, 9 Conn. 286, 23 Am. Dec. 339; Bacon v. Brown, 19 Conn. 29; Gardner v. Cohn, 191 Ill. 553, 61 N. E. 492; Ogden v. Ogden, 79 Ill. App. 488; New v. Sailors, 114 Ind. 407, 5 Am. St. 632; Bowen v. Ratcliff, 140 Ind. 393, 39 N. E. 860, 49 Am. St. 203 (citing this section); Morris v. Murray, 82 Ky. 36 (quoting text); Morris v. Murray, 5 Ky. L. 774; Curtis v. Flinn, 46 Maine 362; Williams v. Moniteau Nat. Bank, 72 Mo. 292;

Gilman v. Moody, 43 N. H. 239; Sheafe v. Gerry, 18 N. H. 245; Hurd v. Robinson, 11 Ohio St. 232; Gill v. Pinney, 12 Ohio St. 38.

[13] Lewis v. De Forest, 20 Conn. 427; In re Hawks, 204 Fed. 309. But see post § 515.

[12] Pike v. Collins, 33 Maine 38; Hurd v. Robinson, 11 Ohio St. 232.

[14] Machette v. Wanless, 1 Colo. 225; Michigan Ins. Co. v. Brown, 11 Mich. 265.

[15] Ogborn v. Eliason, 77 Ind. 393. See also Security Loan &c. Co. v. Mattern, 131 Cal. 326, 63 Pac. 482.

[16] Tulley v. Harloe, 35 Cal. 302, 95 Am. Dec. 102; Hubbard v. Savage, 8 Conn. 214; Brooks v. Lester, 36 Md. 65; Summers v. Roos, 42 Miss. 749, 2 Am. Rep. 653; Blackmar v. Sharp, 23 R. I. 412, 50 Atl. 852.

of the mortgagor who have no notice of the real incumbrance.[17] It need not be so complete as to preclude extraneous inquiry concerning the liens on the property; but it must with reasonable certainty show what is the subject-matter of the mortgage, and must so define the incumbrance that a fraudulent mortgagor may not substitute other debts and shield himself from the demands of his creditors.[18]

A mortgage which does not purport to secure an indebtedness but merely the payment of a certain note can not be foreclosed as drawn, so as to cut off intervening rights of third parties, even though an indebtedness existed, where the note was not executed with the mortgage, but after such intervening rights had attached.[19]

§ 71. Construction of note and mortgage as one instrument.—

The note and mortgage are construed together as if they were parts of one instrument, when they were made at the same time, and in relation to the same subject, as parts of one transaction constituting one contract.[20] They explain each other so far as the indebtedness is

[17] Bacon v. Brown, 19 Conn. 33; Merrills v. Swift, 18 Conn. 257, 46 Am. Dec. 315; Stoughton v. Pasco, 5 Conn. 442, 446, 13 Am. Dec. 72.

[18] Bramhall v. Flood, 41 Conn. 68; Booth v. Barnum, 9 Conn. 286, 23 Am. Dec. 339; Hubbard v. Savage, 8 Conn. 215; Crane v. Deming, 7 Conn. 387; Stoughton v. Pasco, 5 Conn. 442, 13 Am. Dec. 72; Pettibone v. Griswold, 4 Conn. 158, 10 Am. Dec. 106. The Connecticut cases are exceptionally strict in this matter, and are not followed elsewhere. See Jones on Chattel Mortgages, § 85. Where a mortgage described the debt as a note of $1,000, which was never given, but the mortgagor was indebted to the mortgagee for goods to the amount of $756, and the latter had agreed to furnish additional goods up to the sum of $1,000, the mortgage so given as security for the whole was held void against an attaching creditor. The indebtedness actually existing could not be substituted for the indebtedness described. Bramhall v. Flood, 41 Conn. 68. But this is an extreme case, and is not to be relied upon. This statement is quoted with apparent approval in Clark v. Hyman, 55 Iowa 14, 26, 7 N. W. 386, 39 Am. Rep. 160.

[19] Ogden v. Ogden, 180 Ill. 543, 54

N. E. 750, affg. Ogden v. Ogden, 79 Ill. App. 488.

[20] Farnsworth v. Hoover, 66 Ark. 367, 50 S. W. 865; Phelps v. Mayers, 126 Cal. 549, 58 Pac. 1048; Meyer v. Weber, 133 Cal. 681, 65 Pac. 1110; Trinity County Bank v. Haas, 151 Cal. 553, 91 Pac. 385; San Gabriel Valley Bank v. Lake View Town Co. (Cal. App.), 86 Pac. 727; Graham v. Fitts (Fla.), 43 So. 512; Clark v. Paddock, 24 Idaho 142, 132 Pac. 795, 46 L. R. A. (N. S.) 475; First Nat. Bank v. Peck, 8 Kans. 660; Spesard v. Spesard (Kans.), 88 Pac. 576; Round v. Donnel, 5 Kans. 54; Chick v. Willetts, 2 Kans. 384; Loan &c. Co. v. Gill, 2 Kans. App. 488, 43 Pac. 991; Waldron v. Moore (Maine), 91 Atl. 178; Phelps v. Lowell Institution (Mass.), 83 N. E. 939; Bartels v. Davis, 34 Mont. 285, 85 Pac. 1027; Fletcher v. Daugherty, 13 Nebr. 224, 13 N. W. 207; Consterdine v. Moore, 65 Nebr. 291, 96 N. W. 1021, 101 Am. St. 620; Flesher v. Hubbard, 37 Okla. 587, 132 Pac. 1080; Bastin v. Schafer, 15 Okla. 607, 85 Pac. 349; Green v. Frick (S. Dak.), 126 N. W. 579; Vinson v. Carter (Tex. Civ. App.), 161 S. W. 49; Bell v. Engvolsen, 64 Wash. 33, 116 Pac. 456. A mortgage executed long after the note which it was in-

concerned.[21] The mortgage usually describes the note, stating the date, amount, the makers of it, and the time when it is payable. Such description serves to identify the note.[22] The mortgage may describe the debt as well, and thus may qualify the terms of the note. For instance, where a note was given payable in five years from date, with interest at ten per cent., and at the same time a mortgage was given to secure the payment of the note, in which it was stipulated that the interest should be "payable annually," the agreement was held to be that interest at ten per cent. should be payable annually, and that foreclosure might be had for the nonpayment of interest.[23] And so where the mortgage contained a stipulation that a general execution should not issue upon it, although a note accompanied the mortgage, it was held that the mortgagee could not recover a general judgment on the note, his remedy being limited to the property.[24]

Except in this way, the mortgage notes constitute no part of the mortgage. They are not essential to its validity.[25] They need not be produced in evidence, in order to establish the mortgage title and right to possession. The mortgage itself is a conveyance of the estate, and the recital in the condition of the notes secured is an admission of their existence, and of the existence of the debt. For the purpose of establishing the title or right of possession, the mortgage alone without the notes is evidence of title and of the mortgage debt.[26] An indorsement upon a note of a provision contained in the mortgage securing it, neither adds to nor detracts from the rights of the parties.

But upon the foreclosure of a mortgage it is necessary to produce the note if there be one; and if the note produced corresponds with the description in the mortgage as to date, amount, parties, rate of interest, and maturity, such correspondence, coupled with the possession of the note by the holder of the mortgage, raises a presump-

tended to secure will become a part of the contract, the same as if both instruments had been executed together. Spesard v. Spesard (Kans.), 88 Pac. 576. See post § 351.

[21] McDonald v. Second Nat. Bank, 106 Iowa 517, 76 N. W. 1011; Evans v. Baker, 5 Kans. App. 68, 47 Pac. 314; Crafts v. Crafts, 13 Gray (Mass.) 360; Somersworth Savings Bank v. Roberts, 38 N. H. 22; Boody v. Davis, 20 N. H. 140, 51 Am. Dec. 210; Bassett v. Bassett, 10 N. H. 64.

[22] Webb v. Stone, 24 N. H. 282;

Sheafe v. Gerry, 18 N. H. 245; Robertson v. Stark, 15 N. H. 109.

[23] Meyer v. Graeber, 19 Kans. 165; Muzzy v. Knight, 8 Kans. 456; American Mortg. Co. v. Woodward, 83 S. Car. 521, 65 S. E. 739; Irion v. Yell (Tex. Civ. App.), 132 S. W. 69; Bell v. Engvolsen, 64 Wash. 33, 116 Pac. 456.

[24] Kennion v. Kelsey, 10 Iowa 443.

[25] O'Conner v. Nadel, 117 Ala. 595, 23 So. 532.

[26] Mathews v. Light, 40 Maine 394; Morse v. Stafford, 95 Maine 31, 49 Atl. 45; Powers v. Patten, 71 Maine

tion of identity, and throws upon the mortgagor the burden of showing another note of like description.[27]

A provision in the mortgage making the principal due for nonpayment of interest is effectual, although not contained in the note.[28] Where the provisions of a note, concerning the debt or payment thereof, vary from the terms of the mortgage securing it, the provisions of the note or bond control.[29] Parol evidence is admissible to identify the note intended to be secured.[30] When no note or bond accompanies the mortgage, a recital of indebtedness in the mortgage is sufficient evidence of the debt in a suit to foreclose it.[31]

Two mortgages from the same mortgagor to the same mortgagee on the same property, executed the same day are not construed together as one instrument, but each is a separate contract.[31a]

§ 72. Covenant to pay debt.—Although it is essential that a mortgage should secure the payment of some debt or the performance of some duty, yet it is not essential that it should contain any covenant to that effect,[32] and it is not necessary that there should be any collateral or personal security for the debt secured, such as a note or bond.[33] In such case, of course, the remedy of the mortgagee is confined to the land alone.[34] If the mortgage contains a recital of an indebtedness, that is sufficient.[35] "The want of an express agreement," says the Supreme Court of Indiana, "in the mortgage, and in a valid writing thereby secured, to pay the debt, will prevent a personal judgment against the mortgagor; but if the mortgage sufficiently describes and identifies the indebtedness, it may be foreclosed as to the prop-

583; Smith v. Johns, 3 Gray (Mass.) 517; Matt v. Matt, 156 Iowa 503, 137 N. W. 489.

[27] Jones v. Elliott, 4 La. Ann. 303.

[28] Trinity County Bank v. Haas, 151 Cal. 553, 91 Pac. 385; Clayton v. Whitaker, 68 Iowa 412, 27 N. W. 296. But see Indiana &c. R. Co. v. Sprague, 103 U. S. 756, 26 L. ed. 554.

[29] Tipton v. Ellsworth (Idaho), 109 Pac. 134; Keys v. Lardner, 55 Kans. 331, 40 Pac. 644; New England Mtg. Co. v. Casebier, 3 Kans. App. 741, 45 Pac. 452; Ferris v. Johnson, 136 Mich. 227, 98 N. W. 1014; Fletcher v. Daugherty, 13 Nebr. 224, 13 N. W. 207; Consterdine v. Moore, 65 Nebr. 291, 96 N. W. 1021, 101 Am. St. 620; Rothschild v. Rio Grande R. Co., 84 Hun 103, 32 N. Y. S. 37; Bastin v. Schafer, 15 Okla. 607, 85 Pac. 349.

[30] Prescott v. Hayes, 43 N. H. 593;

Melvin v. Fellows, 33 N. H. 401. See post § 352.

[31] Whitney v. Buckman, 13 Cal. 536. See also Eyster v. Gaff, 2 Coll. 228.

[31a] Dahlstrom v. Unknown Claimants, 156 Iowa 187, 135 N. W. 567.

[32] Hickox v. Lowe, 10 Cal. 197; Evans v. Holman, 244 Ill. 596, 91 N. E. 723; Dougherty v. McColgan, 6 Gill & J. (Md.) 275; Heburn v. Reynolds, 73 Misc. 73, 132 N. Y. S. 460. See post §§ 343, 678, 1225.

[33] Mitchell v. Burnham, 44 Maine 286; Smith v. People's Bank, 24 Maine 185; Brookings v. White, 49 Maine 479.

[34] Weed v. Covill, 14 Barb. (N. Y.) 242.

[35] O'Connor v. Nadel, 117 Ala. 595, 23 So. 532.

erty, although there be no express covenant to pay the debt, either in the mortgage or in any collateral instrument."[36]

The mortgages commonly used in this country refer to the debt only in the condition, and there merely by way of recital of the event upon which the deed is to be void. It is seldom that any express promise is made by the debtor in the mortgage to pay the debt; and no promise can be implied from the recital in the condition. It is provided by statute in several states that no such promise shall be implied in the mortgage.[37]

When there is an express covenant in the mortgage for the payment of the debt, the mortgagee may maintain an action at law upon it, and the mortgagor is personally liable, although he gave no note, bond or other separate evidence of the debt. He is not confined to his remedy by foreclosure suit.[38] "It seems to be generally admitted in the books," says Chancellor Kent, "that the mortgagee may proceed at law on his bond or covenant at the same time that he is prosecuting on his mortgage in chancery."[39] Instead of pursuing both the remedy against the person and that against the thing, he may elect to pursue either one, and afterward, if he has not obtained satisfaction, may follow the other.[40]

§ 73. Interest.—Interest is the primary object for which the mortgage is made, when it secures a loan of money, and the rate and time of payment should be stated with care.[41] Interest coupons are sometimes executed, payable at the times when interest will be due upon

---

[36] Layman v. Shultz, 60 Ind. 541; Gregory v. Van Voorst, 85 Ind. 108.

[37] See post § 678. O'Haver v. Shidler, 26 Ind. 278; Brown v. Cascaden, 43 Iowa 103; Conger v. Lancaster, 6 Yerg. (Tenn.) 477; Newby v. Forsyth, 3 Grat. (Va.) 308; Frank v. Pickle, 2 Wash. Ter. 55, 3 Pac. 584.

[38] In Brown v. Cascaden, 43 Iowa 103, the covenant was as follows: "And the said party of the first part (the mortgagor) covenants with the said party of the third part (the mortgagee), that he will pay the said mortgage money and interest on the days and times aforesaid." The court say that such a covenant is no part of the condition of the instrument, and in no way pertains to the conveyance of the land. "It is not a covenant securing the mortgagee against the failure of the title, or warranting possession or enjoy-

ment of the land. It is simply an obligation binding the mortgagor to pay the money. We know of no rule of law which will invalidate such a covenant, when found in a mortgage." In Newbury v. Rutter, 38 Iowa 179, the mortgagors recited that "we are justly indebted" in a sum named, and "if from any cause said debt, interest, and charges, we covenant and agree to pay the deficiency;" and there being no note for the debt, an action at law, without first foreclosing the mortgage, was sustained. See post § 1225.

[39] Dunkley v. Van Buren, 3 Johns. Ch. (N. Y.) 330. See post § 1215.

[40] Vansant v. Allmon, 23 Ill. 30; Lichty v. McMartin, 11 Kans. 565. See post § 1215 et seq.

[41] For the rates of interest allowed in the several states, see post § 633.

the mortgage by its terms during the whole period it has to run. These are usually negotiable in form, and though detached from the mortgage note or bond are still secured by the mortgage.[42] Interest is usually payable annually or semi-annually from the date of the mortgage. A provision for the payment of "interest annually on the first day of April in each year" makes the first interest due on the first day of April following the date of the mortgage, though its date be much later in the year.[43] A provision concerning interest on the mortgage may supplement a stipulation in the note.[44]

§ 74. Rate of interest—Conflict of laws—Rates before and after maturity.—A mortgage debt made payable with interest, without naming the rate, bears interest at the rate fixed by law at the place of performance;[45] and the law in force at the date of the instrument governs.[46] As a general rule the law of the state where the contract is to be performed, controls the rate of interest thereon.[47]

If the times when the interest shall be paid are not specified, but the language is such that some periodical payment is intended, it may be proved by parol evidence that the payments were to be made yearly, for instance, even as against a purchaser.[48] The terms of the mortgage can not be changed as against a purchaser, but he is subject to the agreement contained in the mortgage, and to such construction as may be required of what is ambiguous. The proof of the periods at which the interest is payable does not alter the instrument, but merely supplies what was omitted, and is necessary to its proper interpretation.

When the time of payment of the mortgage debt is definitely fixed, and the amount of it as well, interest is allowed from the date of the default, although not stipulated for in the mortgage or the note accompanying it. Interest follows in such case as an invariable legal in-

---

[42] For the law relating to the construction of coupons, their negotiability, their order of payment, overdue coupons, and suits upon coupons, see Jones on Corporate Bonds and Mortgages, §§ 235-267.

[43] Cook v. Clark, 3 Hun (N. Y.) 247, 5 Thomp. & C. (N. Y.) 493, 68 N. Y. 178.

[44] American Mtg. Co. v. Woodward, 83 S. Car. 521, 65 S. E. 739; Irion v. Yell (Tex. Civ. App.), 132 S. W. 69; Bell v. Engvolsen, 64 Wash. 33, 116 Pac. 456.

[45] Hayes v. Southern Home Bldg. &c. Assn., 124 Ala. 663, 26 So. 527.

For statutory rate in the several states see post § 633.

[46] Ackens v. Winston, 22 N. J. Eq. 444.

[47] Clarke v. Taylor, 69 Ark. 612, 65 S. W. 110; Barstow v. Thatcher, 3 Houst. (Del.) 32; Ayer v. Tilden, 81 Mass. 184, 77 Am. Dec. 355; French v. French, 126 Mass. 360; Faison v. Grandy, 128 N. Car. 438, 38 S. E. 897, 83 Am. St. 693. But see Eccles v. Herrick, 15 Colo. App. 359, 62 Pac 1040.

[48] Ackens v. Winston, 22 N. J. Eq. 444. The language was, "within sixty days from the time it be-

cident of the principal debt.[49] But when the time of payment is uncertain, as for instance in case of a mortgage debt made payable at the decease of a third person, interest can be recovered only from the date of a demand for payment.[50]

The statutes of several states prescribe a rate of interest for contracts in which the parties have not agreed upon a rate, and for cases in which interest is given by law, but allow the parties to agree in writing for any rate of interest.[51] Under such a provision the rate of interest agreed upon by the parties continues the same after the maturity of the obligation down to the time of rendering judgment upon it.[52] The interest both before and after maturity is recoverable by virtue of the contract, as an incident or part of the debt.[53] But although the weight of authority seems to favor this view, there are numerous authorities which hold that where the parties have not by special agreement fixed the rate at which the interest shall run after maturity, the rate fixed for cases where the parties have not agreed upon a rate prevails.[54] The interest after maturity is regarded as recoverable not upon the contract but upon the provisions of the statute.[55] Accordingly where the contract does not fix the rate of interest to be paid after the maturity of the debt, the debt will thereafter carry the legal rate, whether more or less than the contract rate.[56]

There is a general agreement in the authorities that a valid contract

comes due, at any time during the ten years." This is sufficient to put a purchaser upon inquiry as to the periods of payment.

[49] Spencer v. Pierce, 5 R. I. 63.

[50] Gardiner v. Woodmansee, 2 R. I. 558.

[51] Old Colony T. Co. v. Allentown &c. Rapid Transit Co., 192 Pa. St. 596, 44 Atl. 319. See post § 633.

[52] Casey v. Gibbons, 136 Cal. 368, 68 Pac. 1032.

[53] Cromwell v. County of Sac, 96 U. S. 51, 24 L. ed. 681; Kohler v. Smith, 2 Cal. 597, 56 Am. Dec. 369; Beckwith v. Hartford &c. R. Co., 29 Conn. 268, 76 Am. Dec. 599; Etnyre v. McDaniel, 28 Ill. 201; Hand v. Armstrong, 18 Iowa 324; Brannon v. Hursell, 112 Mass. 63; McLane v. Abrams, 2 Nev. 199; Marietta Iron Works v. Lottimer, 25 Ohio St. 621; Hopkins v. Crittenden, 10 Tex. 189; Pruyn v. Milwaukee, 18 Wis. 367. For English cases see Gordillo v. Weguelin, L. R. 5 Ch. D. 287; Morgan v. Jones, 8 Ex. 620; Price v.

Great Western R. Co., 16 M. & W. 244.

[54] Cook v. Clark, 3 Hun (N. Y.) 247, 5 Thomp. & C. 493, affd. 68 N. Y. 178.

[55] Brewster v. Wakefield, 22 How. (U. S.) 118, 16 L. ed. 301; Johnson v. Downing, 76 Ark. 128, 88 S. W. 825; Searle v. Adams, 3 Kans. 515, 89 Am. Dec. 598; Rilling v. Thompson, 12 Bush (Ky.) 310; Eaton v. Boissonnault, 67 Maine 540, 24 Am. Rep. 52; Lash v. Lambert, 15 Minn. 416, 2 Am. Rep. 142; Pearce v. Hennessy, 10 R. I. 223; Langston v. South Carolina R. Co., 2 S. Car. 248; Virginia v. Canal Co., 32 Md. 501. See, for discussion of some of these cases, Jones on Corporate Bonds and Mortgages, §§ 235-237.

[56] Toler v. Keiher, 81 Ind. 383; Robinson v. Kinney, 2 Kans. 184; Evans v. Chapel, 13 Bush (Ky.) 121; Wright v. Hanna, 210 Pa. 349, 59 Atl. 1097; Angel v. Miller, 90 Tex. 505, 39 S. W. 916. But see Pierce v. Boston Five Cent Sav.

may be made, however, for a lawful rate of interest from date to maturity, and for a higher, but lawful, rate after maturity. Such a provision is not regarded as a penalty but as a contract to pay a higher rate on a contingency.[57] "The fact that the creditor is content with a lower rate before maturity," says the Supreme Court of North Carolina, "does not affect his right to demand under a special agreement a higher rate, not exceeding the limit fixed by law, after maturity."[58]

But it has been held that when the mortgage note provided for the payment of a certain rate of interest from date until paid, and the mortgage provides that in default of the payment of any part of the sum secured when due, a higher rate of interest shall be paid from the date of the note, the note governs and the rate of interest is limited to that therein recited.[59]

§ 75. **Time of payment.**—The time of payment of the debt secured should be fixed, so that it may be known with certainty when a default occurs. If no time of payment be named, the debt is due immediately and payable upon demand, and suit may be brought to enforce both the debt and the mortgage immediately. The time of payment may be made to depend upon the happening of some event or contingency, without specifying any exact date.[60] When the time of payment is fixed by the mortgage, or the note secured by it, the mortgagor is not entitled to any notice of it.[61] Grace is to be allowed in computing the time of payment of a mortgage note, or of any instalment of it, payable at a day certain, in the same manner as upon a note not secured by mortgage.[62] It is allowed also upon an instalment of interest falling

Bank, 129 Mass. 425, 37 Am. Rep. 371; Evans v. Rice, 96 Va. 50, 30 S. E. 463.

[57] Vermont Loan &c. Co. v. Dygert, 89 Fed. 123; Linton v. National Life Ins. Co., 104 Fed. 584; Finger v. McCaughey, 114 Cal. 64, 45 Pac. 1004; McKay v. Belknap Sav. Bank, 27 Colo. 50, 59 Pac. 745; Hubbard v. Callahan, 42 Conn. 524, 19 Am. Rep. 564; Holmes v. Dewey,.66 Kans. 441, 71 Pac. 836; Capen v. Crowell, 66 Maine 282; Havermeyer v. Paul, 45 Nebr. 373, 63 N. W. 932; Home Fire Ins. Co. v. Fitch, 52 Nebr. 88, 71 N. W. 940; Sanfcrd v. Lichtenberger, 62 Nebr. 501, 87 N. W. 305; Close v. Riddle, 40 Ore. 592, 67 Pac. 932, 91 Am. St. 580; Draper v. Horton, 22 R. I. 592, 48 Atl. 945.

[58] Pass v. Shine, 113 N. Car. 284, 18 S. E. 251.

[59] Mortgage Security Co. v. Casebier, 3 Kans. App. 741, 45 Pac. 452; Wright v. Shumway, 30 Fed. Cas. No. 18093, 1 Biss. (U. S.) 23; Carnall v. Duval, 22 Ark. 136; Sullivan v. Corn Exch. Bank, 154 App. Div. 292, 139 N. Y. S. 97; Castelli v. Burns, 156 App. Div. 200, 140 N. Y: S. 1057; Balfe v. Lord, 1 C. & L. 519. 2 Dru. & War. 480, 4 Ir. Eq. 468.

[60] Fetrow v. Merriwether, 53 Ill. 275; Bank v. Price, 8 Ohio St. 299; Board of Church Erection Fund v. First Presby..Church, 19 Wash. 455, 53 Pac. 671. See also Iberia Cypress Co. v. Christen, 112 La. 451, 36 So. 491.

[61] Ing v. Cromwell, 4 Md. 31.

[62] Coffin v. Loring, 5 Allen (Mass.) 153.

due at the same time with the principal or any instalment of the principal. But on an instalment of interest alone, falling due when no part of the principal becomes due, the debtor is not entitled to days of grace.[63]

The usual form of power of sale mortgage in use in Massachusetts and other New England states provides,[64] that upon a sale under the power the mortgagee may, out of the money arising from the sale, "retain all sums then secured by this deed, whether then or thereafter payable." This provision in effect makes the whole mortgage payable upon any default which authorizes the exercise of the power of sale, if he in fact does exercise the power; and in the form in common use the condition is for the payment of the principal, instalments, and interest at the times named, as also the taxes and insurance, and upon any breach of the condition the mortgagee may proceed to foreclose. Of course in such case the right to receive payment of sums not due arises only upon a sale. When a trustee in a trust deed is empowered to sell the property when the first instalment falls due, and all the indebtedness is to be considered as matured upon the first default, for the purpose of the application of the trust fund, the indebtedness not then due can not be considered as matured, so that a personal judgment can be rendered for it.[65]

§ 76. **Stipulations concerning default—Acceleration of maturity.** —A stipulation that the whole sum shall become due and payable upon any default in the payment of the principal or interest is universally held to be legal and valid. It is not objectionable as being in the nature of a penalty or forfeiture.[66]

---

[63] National Bank v. Kirby, 108 Mass. 497; Macloon v. Smith, 49 Wis. 200, 5 N. W. 336.

[64] See post § 1778.

[65] Mason v. Barnard, 36 Mo. 384.

[66] Copper Belle Min. Co. v. Costello, 12 Ariz. 318, 100 Pac. 807; Ottawa Northern Plank Road Co. v. Murray, 15 Ill. 336; Curran v. Houston, 201 Ill. 442, 66 N. E. 228; Perry v. Fisher, 30 Ind. App. 261, 65 N. E. 935; Kramer v. Rebman, 9 Iowa 114; Stanclift v. Norton, 11 Kans. 218; First Nat. Bank v. Peck, 8 Kans. 660; Union Trust &c. Co. v. Marshall, 130 Ky. 206, 113 S. W. 73; Mobray v. Leckie, 42 Md. 474; Schooley v. Romain, 31 Md. 574, 100 Am. Dec. 87; Hawkinson v. Banaghan, 203 Mass. 591, 89 N. E. 1054; Caldwell v. Kimbrough, 91 Miss. 877, 45 So. 7; McCarthy v. Benedict, 89 Nebr. 293, 131 N. W. 598 (in Nebraska stipulation considered as permissive and default must be declared by commencing foreclosure proceedings); Hale v. Gouverneur, 4 Edw. (N. Y.) 207; Noyes v. Clark, 7 Paige (N. Y.) 179, 32 Am. Dec. 620; Valentine v. Van Wagner, 37 Barb. (N. Y.) 60; Ferris v. Ferris, 28 Barb. (N. Y.) 29; Crane v. Ward, Clarke (N. Y.) 393; Rubens v. Prindle, 44 Barb. (N. Y.) 336; Smith v. Lamb, 59 Misc. 568, 111 N. Y. S. 455; Robinson v. Loomis, 51 Pa. St. 78; First Nat. Bank v. Citizens' State Bank (Wyo.), 70 Pac. 726;

In some states such a provision is so usual that authority to an agent to execute a mortgage, the terms and conditions of which are not specified, would authorize him to insert this provision; while in other states special authority to use this provision is necessary. His general authority only authorizes the use of the terms and provisions ordinarily inserted, and therefore implied by the term "mortgage." But the unauthorized use of this provision would not invalidate the mortgage in other respects.[67]

If the provision be that the mortgagee may upon default, or after the default has continued a certain time, elect that the whole amount of the debt shall become payable, the mortgagee, after the happening of this contingency, can not be compelled to accept the interest or instalment due, and yield his claim for the whole amount.[68] In such case courts of equity have no power to relieve against the default and its consequences.[69] It is no ground for such relief that the mortgagor was unable to find the holder of the mortgage until the time of payment had passed.[70] It is not required that a formal demand should be made for interest due on a mortgage which authorizes foreclosure on default in interest payments. It is enough that the mortgagee give the maker of the note an opportunity to pay the interest when due.[71] Of course there would be relief if the payment was prevented by fraud on the part of the mortgage creditor.

It is not essential that the interest clause, or option clause, as it is sometimes called, should be contained in the note or bond as well as the mortgage, to make it effectual, inasmuch as both instruments are to be construed together.[72] The stipulation making the whole debt due on default in the payment of the interest may be enforced though contained in the note and not in the mortgage. The note and mortgage are construed as one contract.[73]

Steel v. Bradfield, 4 Taunt. 227; James v. Thomas, 5 B. & Ad. 40. See post §§ 1176-1181.

[67] Pershing v. Wolfe, 6 Colo. App. 410, 40 Pac. 856; Jesup v. City Bank, 14 Wis. 331.

[68] For construction of interest clauses, see post §§ 1179-1186.

[69] Malcolm v. Allen, 49 N. Y. 448; Bennett v. Stevenson, 53 N. Y. 508; Rubens v. Prindle, 44 Barb. (N. Y.) 336; Hale v. Gouverneur, 4 Edw. (N. Y.) 207; Broderick v. Smith, 26 Barb. (N. Y.) 539, 15 How. Pr. 434;

Ferris v. Ferris, 28 Barb. (N. Y.) 29, 16 How. Pr. 102; Valentine v. Van Wagner, 37 Barb. (N. Y.) 60, 23 How. Pr. 400.

[70] Dwight v. Webster, 32 Barb. (N. Y.) 47, 19 How. Pr. 349. But see Isaacs v. Baldwin, 105 N. Y. S. 38.

[71] James v. Brainard, 64 Wash. 175, 116 Pac. 633.

[72] ch   m   v. Taylor, 14 Wis. 313.S   oon   aker

[73] San Gabriel Valley Bank v. Lake View Town Co., 4 Cal. App. 630, 89 Pac. 360.

§ 77. Payment of taxes.[74]—The mortgage usually provides by way of covenant or condition that the mortgagor shall pay all taxes and assessments levied upon the premises.[75] The payment of the taxes thus becomes as obligatory upon the debtor as the payment of the mortgage debt; and upon his failure to pay them, the mortgagee may pay them, and have the amount included in any judgment that he may afterward obtain upon the mortgage. Sometimes the mortgage provides that such taxes, when paid by the mortgagee, shall become a part of the mortgage debt; but without such provision, the amount so paid in fact becomes a lien under the mortgage.[76] In like manner if the mortgagee redeems the mortgaged land from a tax sale, the mortgagee is entitled to have the amount paid by him to redeem the land treated as part of the mortgage debt.[77]

A provision that the mortgagee may retain from the proceeds of a sale under the mortgage all charges and expenses incurred by reason of any failure of the mortgagor to perform the condition and covenants of the mortgage, includes payments for taxes and the like. A stipulation in a mortgage that, upon a failure to pay the taxes levied upon the premises, the principal debt shall become immediately due and payable, is valid.[78] It is similar to the provision very common in mortgages, and generally sustained, that the principal shall become due on a failure to pay the interest promptly.[79]

This covenant can not be enforced after the debt is discharged. It expires with the mortgage. The effect upon the covenant is the

[74] See post §§ 358, 636, 1134, 1175, 1597.

[75] It is provided by statute in Maryland that there may be such a covenant. Ann. Code Md. 1911, art. 66, § 5, p. 1520.

[76] Stanclift v. Norton, 11 Kans. 218. This decision had reference to a statute then in force declaring that taxes so paid should be a lien on the land; but the court declare that without the statute the mortgagee would probably have this right, in order to keep his security perfect. See also Sharp v. Barker, 11 Kans. 381; Jackson v. Relf, 26 Fla. 465, 8 So. 184; Wright v. Langley, 36 Ill. 381; Barthell v. Syverson, 54 Iowa 160, 6 N. W. 178; Williams v. Hilton, 35 Maine 547, 55 Am. Dec. 729; Spencer v. Levering, 8 Minn. 461; Johnson v. Payne, 11 Nebr. 269, 9 N. W. 81; Stoning-ton Sav. Bank v. Davis, 14 N. J. Eq. 286; Burr v. Veeder, 3 Wend. (N. Y.) 412. See post §§ 358, 636, 1134, 1597.

[77] Windett v. Union M. L. Ins. Co., 144 U. S. 581, 36 L. ed. 551, 12 S. Ct. 751; Worcester v. Boston, 179 Mass. 41, 60 N. E. 410; Skilton v. Roberts, 129 Mass. 306.

[78] Spesard v. Spesard, 75 Kans. 87, 88 Pac. 576; Hockett v. Burns, 90 Nebr. 1, 132 N. W. 718; Germania Life Ins. Co. v. Potter, 57 Misc. 204, 107 N. Y. S. 912; Booth v. Wolff Process Leather Co., 224 Pa. 583, 73 Atl. 959; Clark v. Elmendorf (Tex. Civ. App.), 78 S. W. 538. See also Bradley v. Glenmary Co., 64 N. J. Eq. 77, 53 Atl. 49; Germania Life Ins. Co. v. Potter, 124 App. Div. 814, 109 N. Y. S. 435. See post 1175.

[79] Stanclift v. Norton, 11 Kans. 218.

same whether the mortgagor voluntarily pays the mortgage debt, or whether it is paid by the mortgagee's buying in the mortgaged premises at a foreclosure sale. If, therefore, the mortgagee purchase at the sale for less than the debt, and the deficiency be paid by the mortgagor, he can not afterward be compelled to pay to the mortgagee the amount the latter has been obliged to pay to redeem the premises from sales for taxes assessed while the mortgage was in force. The covenant to pay taxes, being part and parcel of the mortgage, expires with it.[80]

§ 78. Insurance.—It is usually a condition of the mortgage, also, that the mortgagor shall keep the buildings upon the mortgaged premises insured against fire in a certain sum for the benefit of the mortgagee, at such insurance office as he may approve.[81] A breach of this condition, or of the condition to pay taxes assessed upon the premises, is as effectual in giving the mortgagee a right to enforce his mortgage as is a breach of the condition to pay an instalment of interest or principal, or the whole principal debt.[82] The provision authorizing the mortgagee to pay insurance and charge the lands with the amounts so paid does not authorize payments beyond the time of the payment of the mortgage debt.[83]

§ 78a. Attorneys' fees.—In most jurisdictions a promise by a mortgagor to pay a stipulated attorney's fee in case of foreclosure is valid when the sum stipulated for is reasonable and not unjust or oppressive.[84] In some jurisdictions, however, these stipulations are expressly prohibited by statute and in other jurisdictions they are

---

[80] Hitchcock v. Merrick, 18 Wis. 357. See also Worcester v. Boston, 179 Mass. 41, 60 N. E. 410.

[81] See chapter X on Insurance, post §§ 396-427.

[82] Mix v. Hotchkiss, 14 Conn. 32; Wedelhofen v. Mason, 201 Ill. 465, 66 N. E. 364; Barthell v. Syverson, 54 Iowa 160, 6 N. W. 178; Moore v. Crandall, 146 Iowa 25, 124 N. W. 812, 140 Am. St. 276; Leland v. Collver, 34 Mich. 418; Neale v. Albertson, 39 N. J. Eq. 382; Garza v. Western Mtg. &c. Co. (Tex. Civ. App.), 27 S. W. 1090.

[83] Garza v. Western Mtg. &c. Co. (Tex. Civ. App.), 27 S. W. 1090.

[84] Burns v. Scoggin, 16 Fed. 734; Bailey v. Butler, 138 Ala. 153, 35 So. 111; Hovey v. Edmison, 3 Dak.

449, 22 N. W. 594; Durham v. Stephenson, 41 Fla. 112, 25 So. 284; Broadbent v. Brumback, 2 Idaho 336, 16 Pac. 555; Barnett v. Davenport, 40 Ill. App. 57; Salomon v. Stoddard, 107 Ill. App. 227; Jones v. Schulmeyer, 39 Ind. 119; Nelson v. Everett, 29 Iowa 184; Weatherby v. Smith, 30 Iowa 131, 6 Am. Rep. 663; Tholen v. Duffy, 7 Kans. 405; Maus v. McKellip, 38 Md. 231; Griswold v. Taylor, 8 Minn. 342; McLane v. Abrams, 2 Nev. 199; Armijo v. Henry, 14 N. Mex. 181, 89 Pac. 305, 25 L. R. A. (N. S.) 275; McAllister's Appeal, 59 Pa. St. 204; Branyan v. Kay, 33 S. Car. 283, 11 S. E. 970; Boyd v. Summers, 10 Wis. 179; Hitchcock v. Merrick, 15 Wis. 522.

held to violate public policy unless authorized by statute.[85] Where the laws authorize an attorney's fee it becomes a part of the mortgage debt on default though stipulated for in the note alone and not in the mortgage.[86]

IV. *Special Stipulations*

Section	Section
79. Stipulations for partial payment and release.	80. Mortgagor's possession.

§ 79. **Stipulations for partial payment and release.**[1]—Special provisions of various kinds, to suit the convenience of the parties, may be inserted in the mortgage. Among those most frequently used is a provision that upon making certain payments the mortgagor shall be entitled to have certain portions of the mortgaged premises released from the operation of the mortgage;[2] or a provision that the mortgagor may pay the whole or a part of the debt, at his option, before the time fixed for the payment of it. A provision in a mortgage, reserving to the mortgagor "the right to pay all or any part of said indebtedness, at any time during the present year, in current paper funds," does not restrict him to a single payment of the entire amount due, but authorizes partial payments at different times during the year.[3]

A stipulation for partial releases of lots embraced in the mortgage upon the payment of stipulated sums, "provided that the covenants and conditions of said mortgage shall be faithfully kept and performed" by the mortgagor, can be enforced only upon strict performance of the conditions, and making all payments of principal and interest as they become due. Whether such a covenant running only to the mortgagor, without mention of his assigns, is personal in character, and can not be enforced by a purchaser from him, is a question upon which the authorities are not agreed, but the better view is that such a covenant runs with the land.[4] A stipulation that in case the mortgagor should be able to sell the premises or mortgage them

---

[85] Thomasson v. Townsend, 10 Bush (Ky.) 114; Vosburgh v. Lay, 45 Mich. 455; Kittermaster v. Brossard, 105 Mich. 219, 63 N. W. 75, 55 Am. St. 437; Security Co. v. Eyer, 36 Nebr. 507, 54 N. W. 838, 38 Am. St. 735; Leavans v. Ohio Nat. Bank, 50 Ohio St. 591, 34 N. E. 1089; Balfour v. Davis, 14 Ore. 47.

[86] Bailey v. Butler, 138 Ala. 153, 35 So. 111; Durham v. Stephenson, 41 Fla. 112, 25 So. 234.

[1] See post §§ 981-982.

[2] Ontario Land &c. Co. v. Bedford, 90 Cal. 181, 27 Pac. 39. See post § 981.

[3] Stalworth v. Blum, 41 Ala. 319.

[4] That it is personal, Pierce v. Kneeland, 16 Wis. 672, 84 Am. Dec. 726. That it runs with the land, Vawter v. Crafts, 41 Minn. 14, 42 N. W. 483.

to another, so as to pay off the mortgage debt, the mortgagee should reconvey to him, so as to enable him to carry out the transaction, does not confer upon him a power of sale, for he had that already, but operates as a covenant to reconvey for the purpose named.[5] A reservation by a mortgagor of "the privilege of selling said land at any time, and to appropriate the proceeds first to the payment of the mortgage debt," enables him to contract for a sale of the land, and to compel the mortgagee to credit the proceeds upon the debt. But while the mortgagor has no power either to convey the land, or to receive the proceeds of a sale of it, the mortgagee is bound to make the proper conveyance, and to receive and credit the proceeds.[6]

An agreement to release any parcel of the mortgaged land, upon payment at any time of a sum equal to the value of such parcel, must be construed as referring to the value of the parcel at the time of the release, and not at the date of the agreement.[7]

The provision for the release of portions of the land on the payment of stated amounts must correctly describe the portions to be released. In one of the cases a provision for the release of one acre for every six hundred dollars paid was held void for indefiniteness of description of the part to be released.[8]

§ 80.—**Mortgagor's possession.**[9]—The provision, now almost universally inserted in mortgages, that, until default in the performance of the condition of the deed, the mortgagor may hold the premises, was formerly exceptional.[10] In 1819, Chief Justice Parker said that such a provision was seldom seen in Massachusetts.[11] In another case in this state the same year, the court say that, although parties intend that the mortgagor shall remain in possession, yet they go on making mortgages without any covenant respecting the possession.[12]

For construction of other provisions for release of portions of the property, see Brigham v. Avery, 48 Vt. 602.

[5] Coffing v. Taylor, 16 Ill. 457.

[6] Frierson v. Blanton, 1 Baxt. (Tenn.) 272.

[7] People's Sav. Bank v. Nebel, 92 Mich. 348, 52 N. W. 727.

[8] McCormick v. Parsons, 195 Mo. 91, 92 S. W. 1162.

[9] See post §§ 389, 667, 668, 702.

[10] In Louisiana, where the civil law prevails, it is held that it is not the essence of a mortgage that the mortgagor should remain in possession. Moore v. Boagin, 111 La. 490, 35 So. 716.

[11] Smith v. Dyer, 16 Mass. 18, 24.

[12] Colman v. Packard, 16 Mass. 39, 40.

In Massachusetts it is provided that the statutes relating to foreclosure shall not prevent the mortgagee's entering on the premises or recovering possession before breach of the condition, when there is no agreement to the contrary, but in such case he must account for the rents and profits. Rev. Laws Mass. 1902, ch. 187, § 9, p. 1642.

Evidence of the intention of the parties, or of their agreement, at the time of making the mortgage, that the mortgagor should continue in possession until he should fail to perform the condition, can not be received to control the settled rule of law, that without such provision the mortgagee is entitled to immediate possession.[13]

But although the mortgagor's right of possession be not expressly provided for, he is entitled to it if the condition of the mortgage be such as to imply his possession for the purpose of performing it.[14] When the mortgagor's right of possession is provided for, or necessarily implied, the mortgagee can not enter until default, and can not, until he has made actual entry, or brought suit for possession, give any one else the right to occupy, and exclude the owner of the equity.[15] In many of the states the rule now is that, the mortgagee has no right of possession of the mortgaged premises prior to foreclosure and sale, in the absence of a stipulation in the mortgage to that effect,[16] and this is true though the mortgage purports on its face to be an absolute deed.[17]

V. *Execution and Delivery*

§ 81. Seals.[1]—In most of the eastern states sealing is a formality still essential to the conveyance of real estate, but a scroll or scrawl, or generally the printed word "Seal" or "L. S." is sufficient. The New England states, Maine, New Hampshire, Vermont and Massachusetts, still require a formal seal by an impression upon wax, paper

---

[13] Hagerstown v. Groh, 101 Md. 560, 61 Atl. 467.

[14] Wales v. Mellen, 1 Gray (Mass.) 512, and cases cited; Clay v. Wren, 34 Maine 187; Ferris v. Wilcox, 51 Mich. 105, 16 N. W. 252, 47 Am. Rep. 551. See post §§ 389, 668, 702.

[15] Silloway v. Brown, 12 Allen (Mass.) 30; Reading v. Waterman, 46 Mich. 107, 8 N. W. 691.

[16] Harrington v. Foley, 108 Iowa 287, 79 N. W. 64; State v. Superior Court, 21 Wash. 564, 58 Pac. 1065.

[17] Yingling v. Redwine, 12 Okla.

64, 69 Pac. 810; Yankton Bldg. &c. Assn. v. Dowling, 10 S. Dak. 535, 74 N. W. 436.

[1] For seal of corporation, see post § 128; seal as consideration, § 613; seal as requisite to record, § 492. At law a mortgage of realty requires a seal, unless otherwise provided by statute. Butler v. Meyer, 49 Ill. App. 176; Portwood v. Outton, 3 B. Mon. (Ky.) 247; Hebron v. Centre-Harbor, 11 N. H. 571; McFarland v. Cornwell, 151 N. Car. 428, 66 S. E. 454; Duke v. Mark-

or some adhesive substance.[2]   Private seals have been abolished either
by statutory enactment or judicial decision in most of the states, including Alabama, Georgia, Indiana, Kentucky, Michigan, Mississippi,
and in all of the states west of the Mississippi river, except Oregon.
Recent cases in New York and Georgia hold that a seal is unnecessary
to the validity of a mortgage.[3]   The decided tendency of modern decisions is to minimize the old distinctions between sealed and unsealed instruments, where they have not been entirely abrogated by
legislation.[4]   All mortgages by corporations should be executed under
the official seal of the corporation, which is customarily an impression
upon the paper.   In New York and the New England states, it is
preferable and in some cases has been held necessary that the impression of the corporate seal should be upon wax or other adhesive substance, which must be attached to the instrument.[5]

A mortgage executed without a seal, in the states where it is required, is not a legal mortgage.   In equity it amounts to a compact
for a mortgage, and as such creates no lien as against purchasers from
the mortgagor, or as against his creditors, or even against an assignee
under a general assignment for the benefit of creditors.[6]

§ 81a.   **Signatures.**—Signing is the act which imparts life to the
deed.   Although the most essential thing of all in the execution of the
deed, it is a matter so much of course that it hardly need be mentioned

ham, 105 N. Car. 131, 10 S. E. 1017, 18 Am. St. 889; Erwin v. Shuey, 8 Ohio St. 509; Bloom v. Noggle, 4 Ohio St. 45; White v. Denham, 16 Ohio 59; Arthur v. Screven, 39 S. Car. 77, 17 S. E. 640; Shattuck v. Knight, 25 W. Va. 590; Pratt v. Clemens, 4 W. Va. 443. See also Martin v. Nixon, 92 Mo. 26, 4 S. W. 503.

[2] There was formerly much prejudice against the use of a scroll as
a seal, which still exists in a few
of the eastern states.

Chancellor Kent says: "Whether
land should be conveyed by writing
signed by the grantor only, or by
writing signed, sealed, and delivered by the grantor, may be a
proper subject for municipal regu-
lation; but to abolish the use of
seals by the substitute of the flourish of a pen, and yet continue to
call the instrument which has such
a substitute a deed or writing sealed

and delivered, within the purview
of the common or the statute law
of the land, seems to be a misnomer, and is of much more questionable import." 4 Com. 453.

[3] Heburn v. Reynolds, 73 Misc. 73,
132 N. Y. S. 460; Hawes v. Glover,
126 Ga. 305, 55 S. E. 62; Vizard v.
Moody, 119 Ga. 918, 47 S. E. 348.
See also Ames v. Holderbaum, 44
Fed. 224; Woods v. Wallace, 22 Pa.
St. 171.

[4] Rockwell v. Capital Trac. Co., 25
App. D. C. 98.

[5] Bank of Little Rock v. McCarthy,
55 Ark. 473, 18 S. W. 759, 29 Am. St.
60; Farmers' &c. Bank v. Haight, 3
Hill (N. Y.) 493.

[6] McFarland v. Cornwell, 151 N.
Car. 428, 66 S. E. 454; Erwin v.
Shuey, 8 Ohio St. 509; Bloom v.
Noggle, 4 Ohio St. 45. See J. S.
Gabel Lbr. Co. v. West (Nebr.), 145
N. W. 849. For signature as pre-
requisite to record, see post § 491.

among the requisites. The signature of the grantor in a mortgage should be in precisely the same form as in the deed by which he received title, whether or not the latter contained his full name or initials only; and careful conveyancers always refer to the former deed or abstract for the exact name of the grantor in a mortgage or trust deed. Obviously the name in the granting clause and acknowledgment should be in the same form as in the signature.

A mortgagor is bound by a signature of his name made by another person in his presence and by his direction. If his name be subscribed by another in his absence, he may adopt the signature as his own.[7] His acknowledgment of the deed is a sufficient recognition of it.[8] Execution of a mortgage may be proved by the admission of the grantor or by testimony of any one who saw him execute it.[9]

A forged signature of a mortgagor can be ratified by him only by executing a new mortgage though he be willing to acquiesce in its enforcement; and no ratification by him can affect intervening parties.[10]

A mortgage executed by the owner of land in the name of a fictitious person to whom he has made a fictitious conveyance is valid between mortgagor and mortgagee.[11]

Under a statute providing that deeds, which include mortgages, shall be signed by the party to be bound, it is not necessary that a mortgage be subscribed as distinguished from signed.[12]

§ 82. **Witnesses.**—The statutes of several states provide that mortgages and other conveyances of real estate shall be attested by witnesses, two being required in some states, one in others, and in still others none at all;[13] but this requirement, like that for the acknowledgment of deeds, has reference chiefly to the recording of them, and does not affect the validity of the instruments as between the parties.[14]

---

[7] Fouch v. Wilson, 59 Ind. 93. As to what is sufficient signing, see Zann v. Haller, 71 Ind. 136, 36 Am. Rep. 193; Gotthelf v. Shapiro, 136 App. Div. 1, 120 N. Y. S. 210.

[8] Ward v. Ward, 144 Fed. 308; O'Neal v. Judsonia State Bank (Ark.), 164 S. W. 295; Kepcha v. Lowman, 249 Ill. 118, 94 N. E. 102; Bartlett v. Drake, 100 Mass. 174, 97 Am. Dec. 92, 1 Am. Rep. 101. But see Dietrich v. Deavitt, 81 Vt. 160, 69 Atl. 661; American Savings Bank &c. Co. v. Helgesen, 67 Wash. 572, 122 Pac. 26.

[9] Ross v. Harney, 139 Ill. App. 513.

[10] Finley v. Babb, 144 Mo. 403, 46 S. W. 165; Rothschild v. Title Guarantee &c. Co., 139 App. Div. 672, 124 N. Y. S. 441.

[11] Blackman v. Henderson, 116 Iowa 578, 87 N. W. 655.

[12] American Savings Bank &c. Co., v. Helgesen, 64 Wash. 54, 116 Pac. 837, Ann. Cas. 1913 A, 390.

[13] See post § 494.

[14] Gardner v. Moore, 51 Ga. 268; Marable v. Mayer, 78 Ga. 60; Benton v. Baxley, 90 Ga. 296, 15 S. E. 820; Pulliam v. Hudson, 117 Ga. 127, 43 S. E. 407; Hawes v. Glover, 126 Ga. 305, 55 S. E. 62; Carrico v.

Although a mortgage defectively executed in this respect is not a legal mortgage, it may be enforced in equity.[15]

An agent or stockholder of a corporation, who has no personal interest in the transaction, is competent as an attesting witness to a mortgage executed in favor of the corporation.[16] A general counsel and stockholder of a mortgagee corporation is not incompetent as a witness to the signature of the mortgagor, though incompetent to act as notary.[17] The grantee is held incompetent to attest the mortgage.[18] Stockholders of a corporation mortgagee may, however, attest the signature of the mortgagor.[19] Attestation by a justice's signature does not affect the validity of a mortgage, where no attestation was required.[20] A void acknowledgment of a mortgage operates as an attestation by the officer taking it.[21]

§ 83. **Acknowledgment.**—An acknowledgment is essential in order to admit a deed to record, but is not necessary as between the parties.[22] This subject is fully treated elsewhere,[23] and is introduced here solely with reference to the necessity of complete execution of the mortgage otherwise, before acknowledgment. The acknowledgment is the final act before the delivery of the deed, and must be made of a completed deed. There can be no valid acknowledgment of a mortgage until all material parts of the instrument are written in, such for instance as

Farmers' &c. Nat. Bank, 33 Md. 235; Baker v. Clark, 52 Mich. 22, 17 N. W. 225; Holmes v. Hull, 50 Nebr. 656, 70 N. W. 241; Prout v. Burke, 51 Nebr. 24, 70 N. W. 512; Jubb v. Thorpe, 1 Wyo. 356; Conradt v. Lepper, 13 Wyo. 473, 81 Pac. 307. Otherwise in Alabama, Dugger v. Collins, 69 Ala. 324.

[15] Lake v. Doud, 10 Ohio 415; Stelts v. Martin, 90 S. Car. 14, 72 S. E. 550.

[16] Stimpson Computing Scale Co. v. Holmes-Hartsfield Co., 6 Ga. App. 569, 65 S. E. 358; Read v. Toledo Loan Co., 68 Ohio St. 280, 67 N. E. 729, 62 L. R. A. 790, 96 Am. St. 663. See also Gilbert v. Garber, 69 Nebr. 419, 95 N. W. 1030.

[17] Maddox v. Wood, 151 Ala. 157, 43 So. 968.

[18] Amick v. Woodworth, 58 Ohio St. 86, 50 N. E. 437.

[19] Read v. Toledo Loan Co., 68 Ohio St. 280, 67 N. E. 729, 62 L. R. A. 790, 96 Am. St. 663.

[20] Wilson v. Kirkland, 172 Ala. 72, 55 So. 174.

[21] Maddox v. Wood, 151 Ala. 157, 43 So. 968.

[22] Johnson v. Graham Bros. Co., 98 Ark. 274, 135 S. W. 853; West v. Mears, 17 Cal. App. 718, 121 Pac. 700; Ross v. Harney, 139 Ill. App. 513; Gray v. Ulrich, 8 Kans. 122; Arn v. Matthews, 39 Kans. 272, 18 Pac. 65; Munger v. Baldridge, 41 Kans. 236, 21 Pac. 159, 13 Am. St. 273; Straeffer v. Rodman, 146 Ky. 1, 141 S. W. 742, Ann. Cas. 1913 C, 549; Wilson v. Kimmel, 109 Mo. 260, 19 S. W. 24; Hannah v. Davis, 112 Mo. 599, 20 S. W. 686; Hess v. Trigg, 8 Okla. 286, 57 Pac. 159; Lynch v. Cade, 41 Wash. 216, 83 Pac. 118; American Savings Bank &c. Co. v. Helgesen, 64 Wash. 54, 116 Pac. 837, Ann. Cas. 1913 A, 390. See also Colonial Trust Co. v. Foster, 234 Pa. 152, 82 Atl. 1128.

[23] See post § 495.

the name of the grantee, and the amount of the lien.[24] The want of an acknowledgment does not affect its validity as between the parties.[25]

This rule applies with particular force to acknowledgments made by married women, where the law protects them by requiring a separate examination by the magistrate who takes the acknowledgment.[26] In a case where a wife so acknowledged an instrument intended to be a mortgage of her separate lands, while there were blanks for the insertion of the mortgagee's name and the sum borrowed, it was urged that she should be estopped from denying that she had signed and acknowledged the mortgage. But Mr. Justice Nelson said: "The answer to this is, that to permit an estoppel to operate against her would be a virtual repeal of the statute that extends to her this protection, and also a denial of the disability of the common law that forbids the conveyance of her real estate by procuration. It would introduce into the law an entirely new system of conveyances of the real property of feme coverts. Instead of the transaction being a real one in conformity with established law, conveyances by signing and acknowledging blank sheets of paper would be the only formalities requisite. * * *   The difficulty here is not in the form of the acknowledgment, but that it applied to a nonenity, and was, therefore, nugatory. The truth is, that the acknowledgment in this case might as well have been taken and made on a separate piece of paper, and at some subsequent period attached by the officer, or some other person, to a deed that had never been before the feme covert."[27]

The mortgage will be valid between the parties, though the notary taking the acknowledgment may be disqualified to take the particular acknowledgment.[28]

§ 83a. Release of homestead.—A homestead right can be barred only by complying strictly with the statute prescribing the mode of alienation; but a mortgage of it duly executed is valid.[1] If the statute

---

[24] Drury v. Foster, 2 Wall. (U. S.) 24, 17 L. ed. 780.

[25] Johnson v. Graham Bros. Co., 98 Ark. 274, 135 S. W. 853; Ross v. Harney, 139 Ill. App. 513; Gray v. Ulrich, 8 Kans. 122; Arn v. Matthews, 39 Kans. 272, 18 Pac. 65; Munger v. Baldridge, 41 Kans. 236, 21 Pac. 159; Straeffer v. Rodman, 146 Ky. 1, 141 S. W. 742; Wilson v. Kimmel, 109 Mo. 260, 19 S. W. 24; Hannah v. Davis, 112 Mo. 599, 20 S. W. 686; Hess v. Trigg, 8 Okla. 286, 57 Pac. 159; Lynch v. Cade, 41 Wash. 216, 83 Pac. 118; American Savings Bank &c. Co. v. Helgesen, 64 Wash. 54, 116 Pac. 837.

[26] Drury v. Foster, 2 Wall. (U. S.) 24, 17 L. ed. 780; followed in McQuie v. Peay, 58 Mo. 56.

[27] Drury v. Foster, 2 Wall. (U. S.) 24, 17 L. ed. 780.

[28] Southwestern   Mfg.   Co.   v. Hughes, 24 Tex. Civ. App. 637, 60 S. W. 684.

[1] New England Mtg. Sec. Co. v. Payne, 107 Ala. 578, 18 So. 164; Morris v. Sargent, 18 Iowa 90; Whitlock

provides that the homestead release shall be made by the joint deed of the husband and wife, a deed or mortgage executed by the husband alone is void, and it does not become valid by reason that the homestead is afterward abandoned.[2] Neither can the wife afterward re-

v. Gosson, 35 Nebr. 829, 53 N. W. 980; McCreery v. Schaffer, 26 Nebr. 173. 41 N. W. 996; Bonorden v. Kriz, 13 Nebr. 121, 12 N. W. 831; Fleming v. Graham, 110 N. Car. 374, 14 S. E. 922; Hughes v. Hodges, 102 N. Car. 236, 9 S. E. 437; Nielson v. Peterson, 30 Utah 391, 85 Pac. 429 (necessary that homestead should be declared).

A sale of a homestead under a power of sale in a mortgage is not a forced sale under a constitution exempting homesteads from forced sales. Karcher v. Gans, 13 S. Dak. 383, 83 N. W. 431; Moran v. Clark, 30 W. Va. 358, 4 S. E. 303.

Under statutes providing for the filing or recording of a claim or declaration of homestead by the wife in order to acquire the right, until such filing or recording the husband may mortgage the homestead without the wife's joining.

Missouri: Rev. Stat. Mo. 1909, § 6704. Tucker v. Wells, 111 Mo. 399, 20 S. W. 114.

California: Civ. Code Cal. 1903, § 1241; First Nat. Bank v. Bruce, 94 Cal. 77, 29 Pac. 488.

Texas: The Constitution of Texas, art. 16, § 50, provides that no mortgage of a homestead shall be valid except for purchase-money or improvements, whether executed by the husband alone or together with his wife, and that all pretended sales of the homestead involving any condition of defeasance shall be void. Under this provision any transaction, though purporting to be for cash, which is only a means to secure a loan to the husband is void. O'Shaughnessy v. Moore, 73 Tex. 108, 11 S. W. 153. But this provision does not apply where there is only an intention to create a homestead which has not been consummated by the use of the property as such. Kempner v. Comer, 73 Tex. 196, 11 S. W. 194.

An unmarried man may execute a valid mortgage of his homestead. Lacy v. Rollins, 74 Tex. 566, 12 S.

W. 314; Smith v. Von Hutton, 75 Tex. 625, 13 S. W. 18. And a surviving husband may mortgage his homestead, though it is community property, to secure payment of a debt against such property. Watts v. Miller, 76 Tex. 13, 13 S. W. 16; Hensel v. Loan Assn. (Tex.), 20 S. W. 116.

A husband may incumber the homestead for the payment of purchase-money in the acquisition of it. McCarty v. Brackenridge (Tex.), 20 S. W. 997. He can renew the incumbrance or change it, at his discretion, so long as he does not add other indebtedness to it. Morris v. Geisecke, 60 Tex. 633; Clements v. Lacy, 51 Tex. 150; Gillum v. Collier, 53 Tex. 592; De Bruhl v. Maas, 54 Tex. 464. He may make such purchase-money mortgage in pursuance of a parol agreement made at the time of the purchase, in case the agreement is supported by a valuable consideration, for such agreement is itself treated in equity as a mortgage. McCarty v. Brackenridge (Tex.), 20 S. W. 997.

A mortgage of a homestead, executed by both husband and wife, to pay off a subsisting vendor's lien against the property, is valid to extent of the lien so paid off. Hensel v. Int. Bldg. &c. Assn., 85 Tex. 215, 20 S. W. 116.

A trust deed for borrowed money given on land actually occupied by the borrower and his family as a homestead is invalid. Texas Land Co. v. Blalock, 76 Tex. 85, 13 S. W. 12; Chamberlain v. Trammell (Tex. Civ. App.), 131 S. W. 227.

Conveyance of subject of homestead right by a husband alone is not void but voidable only at the instance of one having a right to have it pronounced void. Reid v. Allen (Ala.), 62 So. 801.

[2] Gleason v. Spray, 81 Cal. 217, 22 Pac. 551, 15 Am. St. 47; Barber v. Babel, 36 Cal. 11; Iowa Ann. Code 1897, § 2974; Harsh v. Griffin, 72 Iowa 608, 34 N. W. 441; Bruner v.

lease her homestead right by her separate deed.[3] If the statute provides that the wife shall acknowledge her deed releasing her homestead rights, a mortgage without her acknowledgment creates no lien upon the homestead.[4] Under a statute which provides that the homestead release shall be by joint consent of husband and wife, if the husband executes a mortgage and signs his wife's name to it, and procures a fraudulent acknowledgment of it in her name, the wife can not subsequently ratify the mortgage by executing a separate release.[5]

The mere signature of a married woman to a mortgage by her husband is no evidence of a release or waiver by either him or her of the homestead exemption, unless it is affirmatively and substantially stated in the body of the instrument that she is a party to and unites in the conveyance.[6] But it is sufficient that the wife joins in the husband's deed, wherein it is recited that she "hereby waives right of homestead and dower in and to the real estate mentioned in this mortgage," though her name does not appear in the granting clause.[7] The fact that the wife is not named at all in the deed is not material in case she describes herself as "one of the undersigned mortgagors," and signs and acknowledges the deed, for by such a deed she conveys all the interest she has, and is thereby as certainly identified, and as

Bateman, 66 Iowa 488, 24 N. W. 9; Ott v. Sprague, 27 Kans. 620; Stafford v. Tarter, 29 Ky. L. 1184, 96 S. W. 1127; Shoemaker v. Collins, 49 Mich. 597, 14 N. W. 559; Murphy v. Renner, 99 Minn. 348, 109 N. W. 593, 8 L. R. A. (N. S.) 565, 116 Am. St. 418; American Sav. &c. Assn. v. Burghardt, 19 Mont. 323, 48 Pac. 391; Waterson v. Bonner, 19 Mont. 554, 48 Pac. 1108; Kimmerly v. Mc-Michael, 83 Nebr. 789, 120 N. W. 487; Justice v. Souder, 19 N. Dak. 613, 125 N. W. 1029; Compl. Laws Okla. 1909, § 1187-1189. Hall v. Powell, 8 Okla. 276, 57 Pac. 168. The rule is the same where the mortgage is executed by the wife alone, or where the husband is insane. Hathaway v. Cook, 258 Ill. 92, 101 N. E. 227.

[3] Poole v. Gerrard, 6 Cal. 71, 65 Am. Dec. 481; Wilson v. Mills, 66 N. H. 315, 22 Atl. 455; Dickinson v. McLane, 57 N. H. 31; Ott v. Sprague, 27 Kans. 620. In the latter case it was said that it might be that a husband and wife, by two separate instruments could alienate the homestead when it was intended by both that such instruments should operate together as a single instrument.

[4] Park v. Park, 71 Ark. 283, 72 S. W. 993; American Sav. &c. Assn., 19 Mont. 323, 48 Pac. 391; Montana Nat. Bank v. Schmidt, 6 Mont. 610, 13 Pac. 382; Phillips v. Bishop, 31 Nebr. 853, 48 N. W. 1106.

[5] Howell v. McCrie, 36 Kans. 636, 14 Pac. 257, 59 Am. Rep. 584. A mortgage by a husband and signed by him in his individual capacity and as guardian of his insane wife was held void under the statute concerning release of homestead, prior to an act authorizing such mortgages. Curry v. Wilson, 45 Wash. 19, 87 Pac. 1065.

[6] Hawkins v. Pugh (Ky.), 16 S. W. 277, per Lewis, J. But see Sledge &c. Co. v. Craig, 87 Ark. 371, 112 S. W. 892; Ward v. Stark, 91 Ark. 268, 121 S. W. 382; Long v. Branham, 30 Ky. L. 552, 99 S. W. 271.

[7] Davis v. Jenkins, 93 Ky. 353, 20 S. W. 283.

fully bound, by the stipulations contained in the deed, as if she had been formally mentioned by name in the caption.[8] After the husband's death all the rights in the homestead land which before were vested in the husband and wife pass by a devise by the husband to his wife, so that a mortgage made by her while occupying the land with her children is a valid incumbrance. The consent of the children is never required for the purpose of alienating the homestead.[9] A mortgage given to secure the purchase-price of a homestead need be signed only by the person taking title to the homestead.[10]

§ 83b. **Mortgage by tenants in common.**—A tenant in common has no power to mortgage the interest of his cotenant,[11] and a mortgage given by him will operate only on his own interest in the premises.[12] So, a mortgage by a husband and wife of property owned by them as tenants in common, in which the wife is not mentioned except as releasing and conveying her rights of dower and homestead in the premises conveyed, is not operative to convey her undivided interest in the land, although signed and acknowledged by both.[13] It is the holding of one of the cases that the mortgage of an interest of a tenant in common pending a suit for partition, though invalid as against a purchaser at the partition sale creates a valid lien on such mortgagor's interest in the premises.[14]

§ 84. **Delivery and acceptance.**—A delivery and acceptance of the mortgage are essential to its validity.[15] If not delivered directly to

[8] Hawkins v. Pugh (Ky.), 16 S. W. 277.

[9] Shepard v. Brewer, 65 Ill. 383; Allen v. Holtzman, 63 Kans. 40, 64 Pac. 966; Vining v. Willis, 40 Kans. 609, 20 Pac. 232.

[10] Jarvis v. Armstrong, 94 Miss. 145, 48 So. 1; Irwin v. Gay, 3 Nebr. (Unof.) 153, 91 N. W. 197; Prout v. Burke, 51 Nebr. 24, 70 N. W. 512.

[11] Metzger v. Huntington, 139 Ind. 501, 37 N. E. 501; Leavell v. Carter (Ky.), 112 S. W. 1118; Barber v. Toomey (Ore.), 136 Pac. 343. See also Burge v. Chestnut (Ky.), 121 S. W. 989.

[12] Huffman v. Darling, 153 Ind. 22, 53 N. E. 939; Barry v. Baker, 29 Ky. L. 573, 93 S. W. 1061; Janney v. Lillard, 35 La. Ann. 1198; Manti City Sav. Bank v. Peterson, 33 Utah 209, 93 Pac. 566, 126 Am. St. 817.

[13] Penny v. British &c. Mtg. Co.,

132 Ala. 357, 31 So. 96; Burrows v. Pickens, 129 Ala. 648, 29 So. 694; Fite v. Kennamer, 90 Ala. 470, 7 So. 920; Thompson v. Sheppard, 85 Ala. 611, 5 So. 334; Long v. Mostyn, 65 Ala. 543.

[14] Huffman v. Darling, 153 Ind. 22, 53 N. E. 939.

[15] Freeman v. Peay, 23 Ark. 439; Edwards v. Thom, 25 Fla. 222, 5 So. 707; Honfes v. Schultze, 2 Bradw. (Ill.) 196; Fitch v. Miller, 200 Ill. 170, 65 N. E. 650; Johnson v. Prosperity Loan &c. Assn., 94 Ill. App. 260; Woodbury v. Fisher, 20 Ind. 387, 83 Am. Dec. 325; Hoadley v. Hadley, 48 Ind. 452; Goodwin v. Owen, 55 Ind. 243; Henry v. Carson, 96 Ind. 412; Fitzgerald v. Goff, 99 Ind. 28; John Shillito Co. v. McConnell, 130 Ind. 41, 26 N. E. 832; J. S. Gabel Lbr. Co. v. West (Nebr.), 145 N. W. 849; Hoagland v. Green, 54

the mortgagee or his agent, but to a third person not authorized to act for him, it is essential to show the subsequent acceptance of it by the mortgagee, or else to show notice to him of the existence of the mortgage, and such additional circumstances as will afford a reasonable presumption of his acceptance of it.[16]

Such presumption, as against others who may acquire an interest in the property, does not arise merely from the fact that the mortgage would be beneficial to him.[17] Until there be something more to show the grantee's acceptance, the presumption of it only exists for his benefit as against the grantor, his heirs, devisees, and ordinary creditors.[18] The possession of the deed by the mortgagee is presumptive evidence of his acceptance of it.[19] Proceedings by him to enforce the title, or his release of it, are conclusive of his acceptance.[20]

Without delivery there is no mortgage.[21] It takes effect only from the time of its delivery.[22] That a mortgage has been recorded raises a presumption of its delivery to the mortgagee but this is not conclusive against his denial of it. An actual delivery is not necessary, but there must be some act which in legal contemplation is equivalent

Nebr. 164, 74 N. W. 424; Gadsden v. Thrush, 56 Nebr. 565, 76 N. W. 1060; Yeomans v. Petty, 40 N. J. Eq. 495, 4 Atl. 631 (undelivered memorandum ineffective as equitable mortgage); Durfee v. Knowles, 50 Hun 601, 2 N. Y. S. 466; Shirley v. Burch, 16 Ore. 83, 18 Pac. 351; Gorham v. Meacham, 63 Vt. 231, 22 Atl. 572; Ault v. Blackman, 8 Wash. 624, 36 Pac. 694; Garner v. Martin (W. Va.), 80 S. E. 495; Croft v. Bunster, 9 Wis. 503. Delivery is included in the "execution" of a mortgage, required by statute. Van Valkenburgh v. Oldham, 12 Cal. App. 572, 108 Pac. 42. See post §§ 501, 539.

[16] Bailey v. Gilliland, 2 Kans. App. 558, 44 Pac. 747. See also Knapstein v. Tinnette, 156 Ill. 322, 40 N. E. 947; Maxwell v. Hewey, 111 Maine 62, 88 Atl. 88. When a mortgage to a married woman was delivered to her husband, her acceptance was presumed. Rhea v. Planters' Mut. Ins. Assn., 77 Ark. 57, 90 S. W. 850.

[17] Ruckman v. Ruckman, 6 Fed. 225; Freeman v. Peay, 23 Ark. 439; Evans v. White, 53 Ind. 1; Moody v. Dryden, 72 Iowa 461, 34 N. W. 210; Bell v. Farmers' Bank, 11 Bush (Ky.) 34, 21 Am. Rep. 205; Tuttle v. Turner, 28 Tex. 759. But see Merrills v. Swift, 18 Conn. 257, 46 Am. Dec. 315; In re Immanuel Pres. Church, 112 La. 348, 36 So. 408.

[18] Bell v. Farmers' Bank, 11 Bush (Ky.) 34.

[19] Ray v. Hallenbeck, 42 Fed. 381; Van Valkenburgh v. Oldham, 12 Cal. App. 572, 108 Pac. 42; Wolverton v. Collins, 34 Iowa 238; Chandler v. Temple, 4 Cush. (Mass.) 285.

[20] Ely v. Stannard, 44 Conn. 528; Crocker v. Lowenthal, 83 Ill. 579; Huber v. Jennings-Heywood Oil Syndicate, 111 La. 747, 35 So. 889.

[21] Freeman v. Peay, 33 Ark. 439; Van Valkenburgh v. Oldham, 12 Cal. App. 572, 108 Pac. 42; Honfes v. Schultze, 2 Bradw. (Ill.) 196; Fitch v. Miller, 200 Ill. 170, 65 N. E. 650; Hoadley v. Hadley, 48 Ind. 452; Hoagland v. Green, 54 Nebr. 164, 74 N. W. 424; Gadsden v. Thrush, 56 Nebr. 565, 76 N. W. 1060; Shirley v. Burch, 16 Ore. 83, 18 Pac. 351, 8 Am. St. 273; Gorham v. Meacham, 63 Vt. 231, 22 Atl. 572, 13 L. R. A. 676; Croft v. Bunster, 9 Wis. 503. See post § 539.

[22] Milliken v. Ham, 36 Ind. 166.

to this.[23] The actual receipt and recording of an instrument of defeasance is a complete acceptance thereof, notwithstanding prior objection to its terms.[24] A subsequent attempt by the mortgagee to enforce the mortgage may be relied upon to show an acceptance as between the parties.[25]

Delivery may be made to an agent.[26] Delivery to a third person who subsequently delivered it to the mortgagee, though after the mortgagor's death, has been held sufficient.[27] An unconditional delivery by a husband, as agent for his wife, though unauthorized, is binding upon her.[28] When the mortgage is to a corporation, a delivery to any officer or attorney who customarily acts for it in such matters is sufficient.[29] An agent authorized to sell land is authorized to accept delivery of a mortgage in part payment of the purchase-money, unless it clearly appears that it was delivered to him for some other purpose.[30] Where the mortgage is to secure debts for which another is surety, the surety may accept the mortgage for his principals.[31] A delivery of a trust deed to the cestui que trust is a sufficient delivery to the trustee. His acting under the trust by advertising the property for sale is an acceptance of the trust by him, although he may not have had possession of the deed.[32] A delivery of a mortgage running to several creditors to one of them is a delivery to all, unless there is some reason to the contrary, such as repudiation of it by some. A separate delivery to each mortgagee is not necessary.[33]

The fact of delivery may be shown by other writings of the parties or their privies, in which reference is made to the mortgage as an existing security; or by their subsequent acts with reference to it.[34]

If it appear that a note and mortgage have been executed and left

[23] Foley v. Howard, 8 Iowa 56; Preston v. Albee, 120 App. Div. 89, 105 N. Y. S. 33; Goodwynne v. Bellerby, 116 Ga. 901, 43 S. E. 275.

[24] Moore v. Hopkins, 84 Kans. 469, 114 Pac. 1066. See also Immanuel Presbyterian Church, 112 La. 348, 36 So. 408.

[25] Aldrich v. Willis, 55 Cal. 81.

[26] Lydia Pinkham Med. Co. v. Gibbs, 108 Ga. 138, 33 S. E. 945; Lampkin v. First Nat. Bank, 96 Ga. 487, 23 S. E. 390; Rushing v. Citizens' Nat. Bank (Tex. Civ. App.), 162 S. W. 460; Greene v. Conant, 151 Mass. 223, 24 N. E. 44. A justice of the peace who goes for the mortgagee to obtain the execution and acknowledgment of the mort-

gage is the mortgagee's agent to accept a delivery of the instrument.

[27] Booker v. Booker, 119 App. Div. 482, 104 N. Y. S. 21.

[28] Alexander v. Welcker, 141 Cal. 302, 74 Pac. 845.

[29] Patterson v. Ball, 19 Wis. 243.

[30] Akerly v. Vilas, 21 Wis. 88. See post §§ 501, 539.

[31] McLaughlin v. Carter, 13 Tex. Civ. App. 694, 37 S. W. 666.

[32] Crocker v. Lowenthal, 83 Ill. 579.

[33] Sheldon v. Erskine, 78 Mich. 627, 44 N. W. 146.

[34] Renken v. Bellmer, 55 Cal. 466; Dodsworth v. Sullivan, 95 Minn. 39, 103 N. W. 719; Truman v. McCollum, 20 Wis. 360.

where the mortgagee could readily obtain wrongful possession of them and negotiate them, the maker's negligence might prevent his setting up the defense that they have no legal existence.[35] If a mortgage be so disposed of as to evince clearly the intention of the parties that it should take effect as such, there is a sufficient delivery.[36]

The fact that the mortgage and note are in the hands of the mortgagee is sufficient, in the absence of any evidence to the contrary, to warrant a finding by the court that the same had been delivered by the mortgagor.[37] Where a mortgage has been duly delivered, the delivery is unaffected by the fact that the grantee suffers it to remain in the custody of the grantor,[38] or returns it to the grantor's attorney for recording, and it is mislaid after being recorded.[39] But where a mortgage was not produced in evidence or recorded or otherwise accounted for the proof of execution and delivery was insufficient.[40]

§ 85. Subsequent acceptance—Intervening rights.—A subsequent acceptance by the mortgagee of a mortgage delivered to the recording officer, or to an unauthorized third person, gives effect to it from the time of the first delivery, as between the parties to it; but as to persons who have acquired title to the property, or an interest in it, or lien upon it, through or under the mortgagor, before the time of the actual acceptance of the deed by the mortgagee, the subsequent acceptance gives effect to the deed only from the time of acceptance.[41] In the meantime an attachment of the property as belonging to the grantor,[42] or a judgment lien upon his property, will prevail.[43] The acceptance can not relate back so as to defeat the intervening lien.[44]

---

[35] Tisher v. Beckwith, 30 Wis. 55, 11 Am. Rep. 546.

[36] Nazro v. Ware, 38 Minn. 443, 38 N. W. 359; Herman v. Clark (Tenn.), 39 S. W. 873.

[37] Van Valkenburgh v. Oldham, 12 Cal. App. 572, 108 Pac. 42; Schallehn v. Hibbard, 64 Kans. 601, 68 Pac. 61. A mortgage duly executed and acknowledged and admitted in evidence in a suit to foreclose is sufficiently proved, without further proof of delivery and acceptance, under the New York Code. Preston v. Albee, 120 App. Div. 89, 105 N. Y. S. 33. Possession by the receiver of a building association of a mortgage executed by a member is presumptive evidence of delivery. Preston v. Albee, 120 App. Div. 89, 105 N. Y. S. 33.

[38] Clymer v. Groff, 220 Pa. 580, 69 Atl. 1119.

[39] In re Goldville Mfg. Co., 118 Fed. 892.

[40] Diamond v. Dennison, 102 Minn. 302, 113 N. W. 696.

[41] Parmelee v. Simpson, 5 Wall. (U. S.) 81, 18 L. ed. 542; Clark v. Bank, 66 Fed. 404, 13 C. C. A. 545; Hibberd v. Smith, 67 Cal. 547, 4 Pac. 473, 8 Pac. 46, 56 Am. Rep. 726; Moody v. Dryden, 72 Iowa 461, 34 N. W. 210. See post §§ 502, 540, 541.

[42] Bell v. Farmers' Bank, 11 Bush (Ky.) 34.

[43] Woodbury v. Fisher, 20 Ind. 387, 83 Am. Dec. 325.

[44] Goodsell v. Stinson, 7 Blackf. (Ind.) 437.

When a mortgage has been executed and tendered in compliance with an agreement of a debtor to make a mortgage, and the creditor refuses to accept the mortgage as a compliance with the agreement, and directs his agent to procure a mortgage that will meet the terms of the agreement, the creditor can not afterward accept the mortgage without the debtor's consent.[45]

It is sufficient proof of the delivery of a mortgage that it was filed for record by the mortgagor, and was afterward found in the mortgagee's possession.[46] The subsequent acceptance of it ratifies the act and gives it effect from the time it was filed for record.[47]

§ 86. **Delivery for sale and assignment.**—A mortgage made for the purpose of being sold is not a lien in the mortgagee's hands as against subsequent purchasers or lien creditors, except from the time the advances are actually made upon it, either by the mortgagee or his assignee.[48] An engagement on the part of the mortgagee, or another, to advance the money in the future, would be a consideration for the making of it sufficient to support it against other liens from the time of its delivery and record.[49] An assignee with notice that the mortgage was originally given without consideration, for the purpose of raising money by a subsequent sale, is put upon inquiry as to whether there were any liens intervening between its date and his purchase. The fact that the mortgagor negotiates the sale of the mortgage is a circumstance that should put the purchaser upon inquiry.[50]

Where a mortgage is made for the purpose of raising money for the mortgagor, and is recorded without any delivery to the nominal mortgagee, and, before it is assigned and delivered to one who subsequently buys it, another person acquires a lien upon the mortgaged premises, the latter has priority. The mortgage in such case has life and validity only from the time of its assignment and delivery to the assignee for value; and it can have no retroactive operation so as to prejudice others who have acquired rights in the meantime. It is immaterial in this respect that the assignee, before taking the assignment, required and obtained from the mortgagor an affidavit that the mortgagee advanced the whole sum of principal secured by

[45] Adams v. Johnson, 41 Miss. 258.
[46] Haskill v. Sevier, 25 Ark. 152; Carnall v. Duval, 22 Ark. 136; Sessions v. Sherwood, 78 Mich. 234, 44 N. W. 263.
[47] Carnall v. Duval, 22 Ark. 136.

[48] Bailey v. Gilliland, 2 Kans. App. 558, 44 Pac. 747.
[49] Fox v. Gray, 105 Iowa 433, 75 N. W. 339.
[50] Mullison's Estate, 68 Pa. St. 212

the mortgage without abatement, and that there was no offset or defense to it.[51]

A mortgage made to a person who is entirely ignorant of the transaction, and never ratified it or claimed any interest in it, the money being advanced by a person who at the time had no authority to act for the nominal mortgagee, is fictitious and void in law, and equity will not decree a foreclosure of it though the person who advanced the money acted in good faith.[52]

Where a corporation executes a mortgage to secure its bonds issued to a trustee, to be delivered by him to its creditors in payment of their claims, neither the bonds nor the mortgage have any vitality until they are so delivered; and a creditor who has not demanded or received bonds before the dissolution of the corporation and appointment of a receiver has no right to demand them on the ground that this debt existed when the mortgage was executed; nor has he a lien under the mortgage.[53]

§ 87. **Delivery in escrow.**—A delivery in escrow is sufficient, and the fact that the depositary was at the time an agent of the mortgagee, or, where the mortgagee is a corporation, the fact that he was then a director of it, does not prevent his holding in escrow.[54]

A mortgage and note placed in the hands of a third person, to be delivered to the mortgagee upon the happening of a certain event, and delivered by him without authority, without waiting for such event, are invalid, and can not be enforced even by a bona fide holder for value.[55] There is in such case no delivery of the note and mort-

---

[51] Schafer v. Reilly, 50 N. Y. 61.

[52] Shirley v. Burch, 16 Ore. 83, 18 Pac. 351, 8 Am. St. 273.

[53] Hubbell v. Syracuse Iron Works, 14 N. Y. S. 345. As was said in Lord v. Fuel Gas Co., 99 N. Y. 547, 2 N. E. 909: "Where a bond of this description, having no previous vitality, is delivered to a creditor of the company to pay or secure his debt, the delivery of the bond is the act by which his debt becomes secured. The security to the creditor then for the first time comes into being, and is as effectual as if the mortgage were executed at the same time with the delivery of the bond. The effect is the same if the bond is sold to provide means to pay a debt existing at the time of the sale, and the proceeds are paid to the creditor."

[54] Andrews v. Thayer, 30 Wis. 228. A reconveyance by way of defeasance to a grantor, who had given an absolute deed to secure a loan, may be placed in escrow, and such deed becomes void when the time of payment expires. Fitch v. Miller, 200 Ill. 170, 65 N. E. 650.

[55] Chipman v. Tucker, 38 Wis. 43, and cases cited, 20 Am. Rep. 1. A mortgage release delivered as an escrow is a nullity if delivered by the depositary, or obtained from him without full compliance with the condition specified, and the registration thereof will be enjoined. Matteson v. Smith, 61 Nebr. 761, 86 N. W. 472. Where a mortgagor fraudulently obtained possession of a release, deposited in escrow for delivery on payment of the debt, and recorded it without payment,

gage, and they have never had a legal existence. A promissory note, although negotiable, can have no legal inception without a delivery, and the rules of commercial paper do not apply; these can operate only after the paper has a valid existence. As in the case of a forged note, or of one purloined from the maker, the inquiry goes back of all considerations of negotiability, and the effect of that, to the existence of the paper as a legal obligation. A mortgage without consideration, deposited to await the performance of conditions which would make a consideration for it, is not made operative by a fraudulent delivery before the performance of the conditions, and without the mortgagor's consent. The mortgage in such case never becomes operative at all. It is void from the beginning.[56]

But the mortgagor may waive the provisions of an escrow agreement and ratify an unauthorized delivery of a mortgage.[57]

Where the note and mortgage of a husband and wife are delivered in escrow, and the condition performed by the mortgagee, the depositary is bound to deliver the instruments to him, notwithstanding the intervening death of the husband.[58]

Where a note and mortgage are delivered in escrow, with the understanding that upon delivery to the mortgagee, the times of payment of interest and principal should be computed from the date of its delivery to the depositary, such intention should control.[59]

§ 88. **Acceptance of cestui que trust presumed.**—A trust deed is a contract between the parties and acceptance by the beneficiary is essential to its validity,[60] but it is not necessary that the cestui que trust should sign it, or in any way assent to it in writing;[61] the law will presume an assent from circumstances that will raise such an implication.[62] As a general rule the deed passes the legal title as

---

the release was ineffective, both against the original parties and subsequent bona fide purchasers. Franklin v. Killilea, 126 Wis. 88, 104 N. W. 993.

[56] Powell v. Conant, 33 Mich. 396. See also Burson v. Huntington, 21 Mich. 415, 4 Am. Rep. 497; Fitch v. Miller, 200 Ill. 170, 65 N. E. 650; Andrews v. Thayer, 30 Wis. 228. As to right of the mortgagor to withdraw a deed left as an escrow, before acceptance by the mortgagee, see McDonald v. Huff, 77 Cal. 279, 18 Pac. 243.

As to evidence of the performance of the conditions, see Mudd v. Green (Ky.), 12 S. W. 139.

[57] Dooley v. Potter, 146 Mass. 148, 15 N. E. 499.

[58] Davis v. Clark, 58 Kans. 100, 48 Pac. 563.

[59] Bither v. Christensen, 1 Cal. App. 90, 81 Pac. 670.

[60] Byrd v. Perry, 7 Tex. Civ. App. 378, 26 S. W. 749.

[61] Skipwith v. Cunningham, 8 Leigh (Va.) 271, 31 Am. Dec. 642.

[62] Wiswall v. Ross, 4 Port. (Ala.) 321.

soon as it is executed by the grantor and trustee, and can be avoided only by the dissent, express or implied, of the creditor.[63]

§ 89. The date.—A mortgage is not invalid although it is not dated, or has a false date, or an impossible one, as, for instance, February 30th, provided the real day of its date or delivery can be proved. The date, being no part of the substance of the deed, may be contradicted. The true date or time of execution may be shown by parol evidence in contradiction of the date as it appears by the deed or by record.[64]

It is said that there is a presumption that a mortgage was executed and delivered on the day of its date, arising from the due execution, acknowledgment, and record of it.[65] It is elsewhere said that, "The absence of a date from the mortgage does not invalidate the mortgage. The fact that the record of the mortgage shows no date is therefore immaterial, as the validity of the mortgage does not depend upon its being dated, but it becomes effective by delivery."[66] The date of the acknowledgment, together with other circumstances appearing upon the face of the deed, may be sufficient to rebut this inference.[67] If the date of the mortgage be later than that of the acknowledgment, it may be shown that the date of the acknowledgment is erroneous, and that the mortgage was not acknowledged until after it was executed.[68] The date may be implied from the date of the note secured.[69]

[63] Field v. Arrowsmith, 3 Humph. (Tenn.) 442, 39 Am. Dec. 185. That the trustee need not give an express assent, see Martin v. Paxson, 66 Mo. 260.

[64] McFall v. Murray, 4 Kans. App. 554, 45 Pac. 1100; Grove v. Great Northern Loan Co., 17 N. Dak. 352, 116 N. W. 345, 138 Am. St. 707 (absence of date); Parke v. Neeley, 90 Pa. St. 52. If material at all, the date is only necessary to fix the time of payment of the debt secured. Woolsey v. Jones, 84 Ala. 88, 4 So. 190. Although post-dated, the mortgage becomes operative upon delivery, creating a present charge upon the property, and its record is at once effective against subsequent purchasers. Jacobs v. Denison, 141 Mass. 117, 5 N. E. 526.

[65] Lyon v. McIlvaine, 24 Iowa 9; Savery v. Browning, 18 Iowa 246; Parke v. Neeley, 90 Pa. St. 52.

[66] Grove v. Great Northern Loan Co., 17 N. Dak. 352, 116 N. W. 345, 138 Am. St. 707.

[67] Parke v. Neeley, 90 Pa. St. 52.

[68] Hoit v. Russell, 56 N. H. 559.

[69] Woolsey v. Jones, 84 Ala. 88, 4 So. 190.

VI. *Filling Blanks, Making Alterations, and Reforming*

§ 90. Execution in blank.—A blank form of mortgage signed and acknowledged, and afterward filled up in the signer's absence by another person without written authority, so as to make it a mortgage on land owned by the person signing the paper, is not a deed in writing valid to pass an estate in land under the statute of frauds.[1]

The ancient doctrine of the common law, as stated in Sheppard's Touchstone,[2] is, that "every deed well made must be written; i. e. the agreement must be all written before the sealing and delivery of it; for if a man seal and deliver an empty piece of paper or parchment, albeit he do therewithal give commandment that an obligation or other matter shall be written in it, and this be done accordingly, yet this is no good deed." This remains the law in England,[3] and is generally supported by the authorities in this country.[4]

[1] Ayres v. Probasco, 14 Kans. 175, and cases cited; Vermont Accident Ins. Co. v. Fletcher (Vt.), 89 Atl. 480.

[2] Page 54.

[3] Hibblewhite v. M'Morine, 6 M. & W. 200; Davidson v. Cooper, 11 M. & W. 778, 793. These cases distinctly overrule Texira v. Evans, cited and stated by Wilson, J., in Master v. Miller, 1 Anstr. 225, as follows: Evans wanted to borrow £400, or so much of it as his credit should be able to raise; for this purpose he executed a bond, with blanks for the name and sum, and sent an agent to raise money on the bond; Texira lent £200 on it, and the agent accordingly filled up the blanks with that sum and Texira's name, and delivered the bond to him. On non est factum Lord Mansfield held it a good deed.

[4] The doctrine that written authority is requisite for the filling up of material blanks in a deed after execution is declared in Cross v. State Bank, 5 Ark. 525; Upton v. Archer, 41 Cal. 85, 10 Am. Rep. 266; Ingram v. Little, 14 Ga. 173, 58 Am. Dec. 549; Whitaker v. Miller, 83 Ill. 381; McNab v. Young, 81 Ill. 11; Wilson v. South Park Commissioners, 70 Ill. 46; Chase v. Palmer, 29 Ill. 306; People v. Organ, 27 Ill. 27, 79 Am. Dec. 391; Richmond Mfg. Co. v. Davis, 7 Blackf. (Ind.) 412; Ayres v. Probasco, 14 Kans. 175; Cummins v. Cassily, 5 B. Mon. (Ky.) 74; South Berwick v. Huntress, 53 Maine 89, 87 Am. Dec. 535; Byers v. McClanahan, 6 Gill & J. (Md.) 250; Burns v. Lynde, 6 Allen (Mass.) 305; Parker v. Parker, 17 Mass. 370 (time of payment left blank); Stebbins v. Watson, 71 Mich. 467, 39 N. W. 721; Williams v. Crutcher, 5 How. (Miss.) 71, 35 Am. Dec. 422; Graham v. Holt, 3 Ired. L. (N. Car.) 300, 40 Am. Dec. 408; Ayres v. Harness, 1 Ohio 368, 13 Am. Dec. 629; Shirley v. Burch, 16 Ore. 83, 18 Pac. 351, 8 Am. St. 273; Pennsylvania Ins. Co. v.

"The filling of the blanks," said Mr. Justice Chapman in a case in which this rule of the common law was asserted by the Supreme Court of Massachusetts,[5] "created the substantial parts of the instrument itself; as much so as the signing and sealing. If such an act can be done under a parol agreement, in the absence of the grantor, its effect must be to overthrow the doctrine that an authority to make a deed must be given by deed. We do not think such a change of the ancient common law has been made in this commonwealth, or that the policy of our legislation favors it, or that sound policy would dictate such a change. Our statutes, which provide

Dovey, 64 Pa. St. 260; Gilbert v. Anthony, 1 Yerg. (Tenn.) 69, 24 Am. Dec. 439; Mosby v. Arkansas, 4 Sneed (Tenn.) 324; Preston v. Hull, 23 Grat. (Va.) 600, 14 Am. Rep. 153.

But the authority of Texira v. Evans has been adopted by some authorities in this country: Ex parte Kerwin, 8 Cow. (N. Y.) 118; Chauncey v. Arnold, 24 N. Y. 330, where the earlier cases in New York are cited; and although the doctrine of Texira v. Evans is spoken of by Mr. Justice Smith as the settled doctrine in that state, yet Mr. Justice Denio speaks with apparent approval of the English cases overruling the "looser doctrine" of that case. In the case before the court, the question whether the mortgagee's name could be filled in by one acting for the mortgagor under parol authority was left undecided, for in that case the name of the lender was not filled in at all; and it was held that the mortgage was ineffectual as security in the hands of one who had advanced money upon it in that condition. See also Campbell v. Smith, 8 Hun 6, 71 N. Y. 26, 27 Am. Rep. 5.

The authority of Texira v. Evans has also been followed in South Carolina: Duncan v. Hodges, 4 McCord (S. Car.) 239, 17 Am. Dec. 734; Gourdin v. Commander, 6 Rich. (S. Car.) 497.

It was followed in the earlier cases in Pennsylvania: Wiley v. Moor, 17 Serg. & R. (Pa.) 438, 17 Am. Dec. 696; but in Wallace v. Harmstad, 15 Pa. St. 462, 53 Am. Dec. 603, Chief Justice Gibson said that Texira v. Evans could only be

sustained on the ground that the obligor had estopped himself by an act in pais; which is in effect to wholly discard the doctrine of the case.

There is a dictum by Mr. Justice Nelson of the Supreme Court of the United States, followed by Wagner, J., in Missouri, that a person competent to convey real estate may sign a deed in blank and authorize an agent to fill it up; but it was held in both cases that a married woman could not make such a conveyance of her separate estate, having no authority to delegate such powers. Drury v. Foster, 2 Wall. (U. S.) 24, 17 L. ed. 780; McQuie v. Peay, 58 Mo. 56.

It is followed, also, in Wisconsin: Van Etta v. Evanson, 28 Wis. 33, 9 Am. Rep. 486; Vliet v. Camp, 13 Wis. 198; Nelson v. McDonald, 80 Wis. 605, 50 N. W. 893. In Van Etta v. Evanson, 28 Wis. 33, where it was held that the name of the mortgagee might be filled in by an agent after the execution of the mortgage, the ground was taken that the fact of the delivery of the paper to the agent sufficiently showed the intention that he should supply the name of the person who might take the mortgage.

It is held in Missouri that the delivery of an instrument with blanks creates an agency in the receiver to fill the blanks in the way contemplated by the maker; and this principle is applicable to the blanks for a description in a mortgage. Roe v. Town Mut. Fire Ins. Co., 78 Mo. App. 452.

[5] Burns v. Lynde, 6 Allen (Mass.) 305.

for the conveyance of real estate by deed acknowledged and recorded, and for the acknowledgment and recording of powers of attorney for making deeds, are evidently based on the ancient doctrines of the common law respecting the execution of deeds; and a valuable and important purpose which these doctrines still serve is, to guard against mistakes which are likely to arise out of verbal arrangements, from misunderstanding and defect of memory, even where there is no fraud. * * * If this method of executing deeds is sanctioned, it will follow that, though the defendant has a regularly executed deed, yet it remains to be settled by parol evidence whether he ought to have been the grantee, what land should have been described, whether the deed should have been absolute or conditional, and, if conditional, what the terms of the condition should have been. To leave titles to real estate subject to such disputes would subject them to great and needless insecurity."

A mortgage will not be declared void because it contained no description of the property when it was created, unless it be shown by a preponderance of the evidence that such was the fact. If the instrument appears upon its face to have been regularly executed, there is a presumption that it has not been altered since its execution; and if the evidence is conflicting and evenly balanced as regards such alteration, the instrument will not be held void.[6]

§ 91. **Authority to fill in blanks.**—Written authority is essential for filling any blank which materially affects the meaning and operation of a deed. If any such blank be filled after execution by another person having only verbal authority, unless the instrument be redelivered and acknowledged anew, it is void. Such authority to another to fill up an instrument or any material part of it after its execution is sufficient in a case of a simple contract, but not for filling up a sealed instrument. The stream can never rise higher than its source. Authority to make an instrument under seal, or to affix a seal to it, must be given by an instrument of equal authority.[7] The name of

---

[6] Des Moines Nat. Bank v. Harding, 86 Iowa 153, 53 N. W. 99; Harding v. Bank, 81 Iowa 499, 46 N. W. 1071; Pennsylvania Ins. Co. v. Dovey, 64 Pa. St. 260.

[7] Upton v. Archer, 41 Cal. 85, 10 Am. Rep. 266.

In a case before the Court of Appeals in Virginia (Preston v. Hull, 23 Grat. (Va.) 600, 14 Am. Rep. 153), where the filling in of the name of an obligee in a bond, after the execution of it, was held to render it invalid, the doctrine of the text was fully declared. Upon the point under consideration Mr. Justice Staples said: "If the name of the obligee may be inserted, why may not the sum also? And if these may be supplied, why not the more formal parts of the deed? If we once depart from the

the grantee or mortgagee can not be properly filled in after execution of the instrument. Such name may, however, be filled in by the officer taking the acknowledgment of the deed, before the delivery of it to the grantee.[8]

Where the mortgagor, after the execution of the deed by his wife, without her knowledge inserts the description of additional property, the mortgage is a valid lien upon the property originally covered by it; and though it would ordinarily be valid as to the additional property against the husband, it is not so when the additional property is a homestead, for the conveyance of which it is necessary that the husband and wife should join.[9]

But in a few states it is held that the authority to fill material blanks may be given by parol; and it is even held that if the agent exceeds his instructions in filling the blanks, and negotiates the instrument with innocent third persons, the principal will be bound by the acts of his agent, although unauthorized.[10]

§ 92. Irregular execution—Estoppel.—The mortgagor may be estopped from taking advantage of the irregular execution, through the filling of blanks by some one not authorized in writing, by his acts in relation to the transaction.[11] Thus where a deed was so filled up and delivered to the grantee, who was ignorant of any

rule, how is the line to be drawn consistently with the preservation of any rule at all? If we say that the name or sum may be inserted by the agent, will it not lead us inevitably to the doctrine that the entire deed may be executed by the agent also? We shall be carried on step by step, if we mean to be consistent, until we have destroyed all the well-settled distinctions between sealed and unsealed instruments."

In Iowa, however, it is held that a deed executed in blank as to the grantee confers authority on a real or intended grantee to fill in his own name. Logan v. Miller, 106 Iowa 511, 76 N. W. 1005; McClain v. McClain, 52 Iowa 272, 3 N. W. 60; Montgomery v. Dresher, 90 Nebr. 633, 134 N. W. 251; Roe v. Town Mut. Fire Ins. Co., 78 Mo. App. 452. The latter case held that delivery of a contract with blanks, constituting a mortgage, created an agency in the receiver to fill the blanks in the manner contemplated by the maker.

[8] McNab v. Young, 81 Ill. 11.

[9] Van Horn v. Bell, 11 Iowa 465, 79 Am. Dec. 506. See also White v. Owen, 30 Grat. (Va.) 43; Jenkins v. Simmons, 37 Kans. 496, 15 Pac. 522.

[10] Nelson v. McDonald, 80 Wis. 605, 50 N. W. 893. In this case a wife signed a note with her husband, and signed a mortgage securing it, the description of the property being blank. The purchaser advanced the money thereon, and had no notice of the fraud on the wife. It was held that the wife was bound by the acts of her husband. Johnston Harvester Co. v. McLean, 57 Wis. 258, 15 N. W. 177. See also Langhorst v. Shutteldryer, 2 W. L. B. 125.

[11] Carr v. McColgan, 100 Md. 462, 60 Atl. 606; Lockwood v. Bassett, 49 Mich. 546, 14 N. W. 492; Hemmenway v. Mulock, 56 How. Pr. (N. Y.) 38.

irregularity in the execution of it, and the grantors, being fully advised of the delivery of the deed, permitted the grantee to enter into possession and make improvements, and became his tenants and paid him rent, they were not allowed to claim that the deed was void by reason of such irregularity.[12] But the mere fact that the mortgagor has enjoyed the benefit of the money loaned, or a portion of the money, is not by itself a sufficient ground upon which to found an equitable estoppel. Objection that a deed was executed in blank, and the name of the grantee inserted after delivery, can only be taken by the grantor, or by some one claiming through him, or in his right.[13]

§ 93. **Essentials of estoppel.**—A mortgagee invoking the aid of estoppel must show that he has been vigilant and careful in the protection of his own rights and interests. No protection will be given him against his own negligence and folly.[14] To avail himself of the acts and admissions of the mortgagor, he must have been ignorant of the irregularity in the execution of the mortgage, and must have taken it with good reason to suppose it was properly executed.

Moreover, the subsequent acts of the mortgagor are no admission or ratification of the giving of the mortgage, unless the facts of the transaction be known to him.[15] He can not ratify a thing that he does not know the existence of, and can not be estopped by acts he never performed. An estoppel may arise from acquiescence. Thus a mortgagee who took from a prior mortgagee a relinquishment waiving priority was held estopped thereafter to allege that the prior mortgage was fraudulent.[16]

---

[12] Knaggs v. Mastin, 9 Kans. 532.
[13] McNab v. Young, 81 Ill. 11.
[14] Ayres v. Probasco, 14 Kans. 175, 190, Mr. Justice Valentine said: "Where a person negligently or knowingly puts it within the power of some other person to swindle and defraud him, and he is thereby swindled and defrauded, he is generally allowed to suffer the consequences of his own negligence and folly." In the case before the court, the mortgagee, through his agent, knew that the mortgage was executed in blank and afterward filled up in the absence of the wife, whose land it was intended to mortgage, inasmuch as the deed was filled up in the agent's presence. When the mortgage so executed was offered to him he should have said: "I know that mortgage is void as a mortgage of Mrs. Ayres; I will, therefore, not receive it. You must furnish me a better mortgage if you want the money."

[15] In the same case, in illustration of this point, the same justice said: "There is no evidence showing that Mrs. Ayres ever beforehand authorized said mortgage to be filled up as it was in fact filled up, or ever afterward knew that the same was so filled up, or ever knew that it was delivered to Probasco as the mortgagee, or ever performed an act which could be construed into a ratification of the instrument."

[16] Parker v. Parker, 52 S. Car. 382, 29 S. E. 805.

§ 94. **Material alteration.**—A material alteration of a mortgage made without the consent of the mortgagor by the holder of it, or by any one after delivery, and while in the possession or custody of the rightful owner of it, has the effect of destroying and annulling the instrument as between the parties to it.[17] A material alteration of an instrument is any alteration which causes it to speak a language different in legal effect from that which it originally spoke.[18] An alteration by a mere stranger without the knowledge or consent of the holder, and while it is out of his custody, does not have this effect.[19]

A material alteration of a promissory note secured by a mortgage cancels the debt and discharges the mortgage. The note is not merely vitiated, but the debt is discharged, and with the discharge of the debt goes a discharge of the mortgage.[20] This principle was applied to making void a mortgage altered under the following circumstances: A married woman, being the owner of a house and lot, known as lot H, executed a mortgage to secure her husband's debt, in consideration of the extension of the time of payment. The mortgage, however, did not describe her property, but described a lot known as lot 26. After the delivery of the deed the error was discovered, and the mortgagee's attorney took the mortgage to the husband and his attorney for correction. The words, "being the same property conveyed to the party

[17] Russell v. Reed, 36 Minn. 376, 31 N. W. 452; Merchants' &c Bank v. Dent, 102 Miss. 455, 59 So. 805 (fraudulent alteration of description in trust deed); Kime v. Jesse, 52 Nebr. 606, 72 N. W. 1050; Meyer v. Huneke, 55 N. Y. 412; Marcy v. Dunlap, 5 Lans. (N. Y.) 365; Waring v. Smyth, 2 Barb. Ch. (N. Y.) 119, 47 Am. Dec. 299; Pigot's Case, 11 Coke 26b. The insertion of the word "gold" before "dollars" is a material alteration. Foxworthy v. Colby, 64 Nebr. 216, 89 N. W. 800, 62 L. R. A. 393. A deed of trust altered by the beneficiary, to secure other notes than those intended, is void. Powell v. Banks, 146 Mo. 620, 48 S. W. 664. Such is the effect of an alteration by a mortgagee after delivery of the mortgage, by inserting a clause to the effect that scire facias may issue in case of twenty days' default in payment. McIntyre v. Velte (Pa.), 25 Atl. 739. The restoration of an instrument to its original form after an unauthorized

material alteration will not avail to revive the instrument and give it force. Snell v. Davis, 149 Ill. App. 391.
[18] Murray v. Klinzing, 64 Conn. 78, 29 Atl. 244; Wheelock v. Freeman, 13 Pick. (Mass.) 168, 23 Am. Dec. 674; Bridges v. Winters, 42 Miss. 135, 97 Am. Dec. 443; Foxworthy v. Colby, 64 Nebr. 216, 89 N. W. 800, 62 L. R. A. 393.
[19] Marcy v. Dunlap, 5 Lans. (N. Y.) 365, per Johnson, J., and cases cited; Fry v. Jenkins, 173 Ill. App. 486; Smith v. Chadsey, 1 Thomp. & C. (N. Y.) addenda 7. Delivery and acknowledgment of a mortgage, after alteration of the date, constitutes a ratification of the alteration. Styles v. Scotland, 22 N. Dak. 469, 134 N. W. 708.
[20] King v. Bellamy, 82 Kans. 301, 108 Pac. 117; Warder v. Willyard, 46 Minn. 531, 49 N. W. 300, 24 Am. St. 250; Whitmer v. Frye, 10 Mo. 349; Walton Plow Co. v. Campbell, 35 Nebr. 173, 52 N. W. 883; Smith

of the first part," etc., describing the deed to the mortgagor of lot H, were added to the description contained in the mortgage, by the husband's attorney, in the presence of the attorney of the mortgagee, without consulting the wife in regard to the alteration, and she had no knowledge of the change until suit was brought to reform and foreclose the mortgage. It was held that the suit could not be maintained for either purpose.[21]

The unauthorized insertion of the word "gold" before the word "dollars" in a mortgage after its execution and delivery has been held a material alteration.[22]

An indorsement on a mortgage note by a purchaser of the equity of redemption, agreeing to pay a higher rate of interest, made without the knowledge or consent of the maker of the note, is not an alteration of the note, for the alteration did not bind the maker, but only the purchaser of the equity of redemption. The original note and the maker's obligation remained intact.[23]

But the former rule, rendering void an instrument altered while in the custody of the rightful holder, has in many courts given place to the more equitable rule that the instrument is not rendered void if the alteration was made by mistake, or without any fraudulent intent.[24] Thus an alteration of the description in a mortgage by the husband of the mortgagor, with the mortgagee's consent, in good faith, in an honest effort to correct a mistake, and to make it conform to the intention of the parties at the time of its execution, does not render the mortgage void, but it is operative as to the land actually described in the original deed.[25] The alteration is, of course, void, but the title granted by the instrument is not divested.[26]

Where an alteration or erasure is apparent upon the face of the instrument, the presumption of law is that it was made prior to its

v. Mace, 44 N. H. 553; Martendale v. Follett, 1 N. H. 95; Bigelow v. Stilphen, 35 Vt. 521; Newell v. Mayberry, 3 Leigh (Va.) 250. A marginal notation of the name of a subsequent purchaser is not an alteration available to the mortgagors. Schafer v. Jackson, 155 Iowa 108, 135 N. W. 622.

[21] Marcy v. Dunlap, 5 Lans. (N. Y.) 365.

[22] Foxworthy v. Colby, 64 Nebr. 216, 89 N. W. 800, 62 L. R. A. 393.

[23] Boutelle v. Carpenter, 182 Mass. 417. See also Stone v. White, 8 Gray (Mass.) 589.

[24] Mathias v. Leathers, 99 Iowa 18, 68 N. W. 449; Gunter v. Addy, 58 S. Car. 178, 36 S. E. 553; McClure v. Little, 15 Utah 379, 49 Pac. 298, 62 Am. St. 938.

[25] Harding v. Des Moines Nat. Bank, 81 Iowa 499, 46 N. W. 1071; Nichols v. Rosenfeld, 181 Mass. 525, 63 N. E. 1063; Kime v. Jesse, 52 Nebr. 606, 72 N. W. 1050.

[26] Burgess v. Blake, 128 Ala. 105, 28 So. 963; Alabama State Land Co. v. Thompson, 104 Ala. 570, 16 So. 440; Burnett v. McCluey, 78 Mo. 676.

execution, and the burden is upon the maker to show that it was altered after delivery. The question when an alteration was made, by whom it was made, and with what intent, is one of fact, to be submitted to the jury upon the whole evidence, intrinsic and extrinsic.[27] If the evidence in regard to the fact of an alteration is conflicting and evenly balanced, the presumption that the mortgage had not been altered must prevail.[28]

§ 95. Immaterial alteration.—An alteration of an instrument which does not change its legal effect does not in law amount to an alteration, and of course does not invalidate it either at law or in equity.[29] The alteration of numbers upon a series of negotiable state bonds is an immaterial alteration, where the law does not require the bonds to be numbered, and the presence or absence of the number does not affect in substance or form the written contract or proof thereof.[30] An alteration which does change the legal effect of the deed may at any time be made by consent of both parties to it;[31] thus it has been held that authority given in a mortgage to the recorder to insert a portion of the description omitted, when it could be obtained, is equivalent to a power of attorney to make such addi-

---

[27] Wilson v. Hayes, 40 Minn. 531, 42 N. W. 467, 12 Am. St. 754; Rodriguez v. Haynes, 76 Tex. 225, 13 S. W. 296.

[28] Vogel v. Ripper, 34 Ill. 100; Foote v. Hambrick, 70 Miss. 157, 11 So. 567; State Savings Bank v. Shaffer, 9 Nebr. 1, 1 N. W. 980.

[29] Hart v. Sharpton, 124 Ala. 638, 27 So. 450; Fry v. Jenkins, 173 Ill. App. 486 (alteration of date); Bayse v. McKinney, 43 Ind. App. 422, 87 N. E. 693; Goodenow v. Curtis, 33 Mich. 505; Styles v. Scotland, 22 N. Dak. 469, 134 N. W. 708 (alteration of date). The immaterial alteration of a note secured by a mortgage, by adding the name of the wife of the mortgagor does not invalidate the mortgage. Souza v. Lucas (Cal. App.), 100 Pac. 115.

As to burden of proof to show whether an interlineation was made before or after execution, see Cox v. Palmer, 1 McCrary (U. S.) 341, where McCrary, J., said: "If the interlineation is in itself suspicious, as, if it appears to be contrary to the probable meaning of the instrument as it stood before the insertion of the interlined words; or if it is in a handwriting different from the body of the instrument, or it appears to have been written with different ink—in all such cases, if the court considers the interlineation suspicious on its face, the presumption will be that it was an unauthorized alteration after execution. On the other hand, if the interlineation appears in the same handwriting with the original instrument, and bears no evidence on its face of having been made subsequent to the execution of the instrument, and especially if it only makes clear what was the evident intention of the parties, the law will presume that it was made in good faith, and before execution." See also Hart v. Sharpton, supra. As to burden of proof, see Hill v. Nelms, 86 Ala. 442, 5 So. 796; Montgomery v. Crossthwait, 90 Ala. 553, 8 So. 498.

[30] Commonwealth v. Emigrant Industrial Sav. Bank, 98 Mass. 12, 93 Am. Dec. 126.

[31] Gunter v. Addy, 58 S. Car. 178, 36 S. E. 553.

tion, and that a subsequent incumbrancer could not object to the exercise of this power.[32] It would seem, nevertheless, that the description given in the mortgage to warrant such a filling up must be sufficient to indicate the property with such certainty that the lien upon it would exist without further description.

A mortgage is not rendered invalid by the grantee's fraudulently adding the name of the mortgagor's wife in release of dower.[33] It is valid as against the husband without the wife's signature. The title to the property passes and vests in the grantee by the execution of the deed, and the subsequent alteration or destruction of the instrument does not affect this title.

§ 96. **Alteration by parol.**—The terms of a mortgage can not be varied by any verbal agreement or understanding of the parties anterior to the execution of it. It can not rest partly in writing and partly in parol. No evidence of the acts or conversation of the parties prior to the execution of the mortgage, or at the time of it, can be admitted to contradict or vary the instrument where its terms are unambiguous.[34] "The true meaning of the terms of a mortgage, like the meaning of the terms in other written instruments, must be gathered from the writing itself where it is plain and unambiguous. It can not be added to or varied by showing extrinsic matters, or a prior or contemporaneous parol agreement."[35] It may not be shown by parol that a mortgage securing advances made was also to cover future advances.[36]

The fact that a mortgagor, before the signing of the mortgage, objected to the terms of it, and desired to reserve a certain portion of the property included in it, can not be received to vary the effect of

[32] Harshey v. Blackmarr, 20 Iowa 161, 89 Am. Dec. 520. The description was as follows:
"We, J. L. Blackmarr and Belinda (his wife), sell and convey unto John Harshey, etc., the following described premises, in Marshall county, Iowa, to wit: eighty acres of land, bought of Rev. James M. Holland, lying ten miles southward from Marshalltown, in Marshall county, Iowa; and so soon as the numbers of the above land are obtained, we agree that they shall be inserted in this deed, as our own voluntary act, and the recorder of Marshall county is instructed to do the same for us."
[33] Kendall v. Kendall, 12 Allen (Mass.) 92.

[34] Hanchey v. Powell, 171 Ala. 597, 55 So. 97; Cox v. Smith, 99 Ark. 218, 138 S. W. 978; Quartermous v. Kennedy, 29 Ark. 544; Fowler v. Pendleton, 121 Md. 297, 88 Atl. 124; Kirkbride &c. Oil Co. v. Satterlee, 32 Okla. 22, 121 Pac. 635; Smith v. Texas &c. R. Co. (Tex. Civ. App.), 105 S. W. 528. The rule forbidding the varying of written contracts by parol applies to a mortgage executed in Porto Rico before that island became territory of the United States. Veve v. Sanchez, 226 U. S. 234, 33 Sup. Ct. 36.
[35] Bartlett Estate Co. v. Fairhaven Land Co., 49 Wash. 58, 94 Pac. 900, 15 L. R. A. (N. S.) 590.
[36] Barnhart v. Edwards, 115 Cal 17, 47 Pac. 251.

it.[37] Even an agreement of the parties at the time of the execution of the mortgage, that it should not be a lien upon certain portions of the property included in it, would have no effect against the terms of it.

The terms of the mortgage may, however, be varied by a written agreement executed at the time of the mortgage. Such an agreement then becomes in fact a part of the mortgage, and the two instruments must be construed together.[38]

Parol evidence is sometimes admissible to show the real object of a mortgage and that it was given for a purpose not disclosed in the condition.[39] The rule against the varying of written instruments, including mortgages, applies solely to the parties to the instrument and not to third parties.[40]

§ 97. Reformation.—Whenever there has been a material omission or mistake in the deed, so that it fails to express what the parties intended, a court of equity may, as between the parties, reform and correct it in accordance with the transaction as it was actually agreed upon.[41]

The mortgage may be reformed in the matter of a mistake of description to conform to the intentions of the parties.[42] So, when part of the lands agreed to be mortgaged were omitted in the mortgage deed, it may be so reformed as to include them.[43] And so, on the other hand, if by mistake it include land not belonging to the grantor,[44] or other land of his not intended to be included, the description may be reformed. A material mistake in any part of the

[37] Patterson v. Taylor, 15 Fla. 336.

[38] Pitzer v. Burns, 7 W. Va. 63.

[39] Campbell v. Perth Amboy Shipbuilding &c. Co., 70 N. J. Eq. 40, 62 Atl. 319; Boren v. Boren, 29 Tex. Civ. App. 221, 68 S. W. 184; Lippincott v. Lawrie, 119 Wis. 573, 97 N. W. 179. See also Brouillard v. Stimpson, 201 Mass. 236, 87 N. E. 493.

[40] Aleshire v. Lee County Sav. Bank, 105 Ill. App. 32; Livingston v. Heck, 122 Iowa 74, 94 N. W. 1098; Wilson v. Mulloney, 185 Mass. 430, 70 N. E. 448.

[41] Bright v. Buckman, 39 Fed. 243; Kerchner v. Frazier, 106 Ga. 437, 32 S. E. 351; Phillips v. Roquemore, 96 Ga. 719, 23 S. E. 855; Loomis v. Hudson, 18 Iowa 416; Lear v. Prather, 89 Ky. 501, 12 S. W. 946; Men-

denhall v. Steckel, 47 Md. 453, 28 Am. Rep. 481; Godwin v. Da Conturbia, 115 Md. 488, 80 Atl. 1016; Anderson v. Baughman, 7 Mich. 69, 74 Am. Dec. 699; McMillan v. N. Y. Water Proof Paper Co., 29 N. J. Eq. 610; Dietrich v. Hutchinson, 73 Vt. 134. See post § 1464.

[42] Manogue v. Bryant, 15 App. D. C. 245; Keys v. Lardner, 59 Kans. 545, 53 Pac. 758; Silliman v. Taylor, 35 Tex. Civ. App. 490, 80 S. W. 651; Jenkins v. Jenkins University, 17 Wash. 160, 49 Pac. 247. But see Adams v. Baker, 24 Nev. 162, 51 Pac. 252, 77 Am. St. 799.

[43] Keister v. Myers, 115 Ind. 312, 17 N. E. 161; Hunt v. Hunt, 38 Mich. 161; Blodgett v. Hobart, 18 Vt. 414.

[44] Ruhling v. Hackett, 1 Nev. 360.

deed, as for instance the description of the land,[45] in the condition,[46] or in the estate conveyed, the word *successors* having been used instead of *heirs,* may be reformed.[47] But the court will not correct a mere error of statement as to the origin of the mortgagor's title, when the deed is effectual as it stands.[48] A mortgage will be reformed and enforced which was intended by the parties to convey the fee, but which by mistake or ignorance only conveyed the life estate.[49] The mortgage may be corrected so as to include land omitted through mutual mistake.[50] Reformation will generally be allowed for mutual mistake in the absence of waiver or estoppel,[51] but a void mortgage is incapable of reformation.[52] A mortgage may be reformed by inserting the name of the mortgagee when this has been omitted by mistake, and it appears upon the face of the mortgage that the consideration moved from the complainant, that it was given to secure a debt due to him, and that the omission of the name was a mere oversight.[53]

When a mistake is clearly shown, a claim by the adverse party of misapprehension on his part will not be regarded.[54] But the fact of mistake must be shown beyond a reasonable doubt;[55] as also what the parties really intended.[56] "The proof of mistake must be clear and certain before an instrument can be reformed; as the object of the reformation of an instrument is to make it express what the minds of the parties to it had met upon, and what they intended to express, and supposed they had expressed, in the writing. Unless this meeting of minds, and mistake in expressing it, is made quite clear and certain by evidence, the court should it undertake to reform, might,

---

[45] Craig v. Pendleton, 89 Ark. 259, 116. S. W. 209; Fisher v. Villamil, 62 Fla. 472, 56 So. 559, 39 L. R. A. (N. S.) 90, Ann. Cas. 1913 D, 1003; Adams v. Davis, 63 Fla. 324, 58 So. 837; Snell v. Snell, 123 Ill. 403, 14 N. E. 684; Tichenor v. Yankey, 89 Ky. 508, 12 S. W. 947; Harper v. Combs, 61 W. Va. 561, 56 S. E. 902.

[46] Wooden v. Haviland, 18 Conn. 101; Manatt v. Starr, 72 Iowa 677, 34 N. W. 784.

[47] McMillan v. N. Y. Water Proof Paper Co., 29 N. J. Eq. 610; Fish v. N. Y. Water Proof Paper Co., 29 N. J. Eq. 16.

[48] Hathaway v. Juneau, 15 Wis. 262.

[49] Lardner v. Williams, 98 Wis. 514, 74 N. W. 346.

[50] First Nat. Bank v. Wentworth, 28 Kans. 183; Martin v. Nixon, 92 Mo. 26, 4 S. W. 503; Land Mortgage Co. v. Nicholson, 24 Wash. 258, 64 Pac. 156.

[51] Rowell v. Smith, 123 Wis. 512, 102 N. W. 1.

[52] Day v. Shiver, 137 Ala. 185, 33 So. 831; Montgomery v. Perryman, 147 Ala. 207, 41 So. 838, 119 Am. St. 61.

[53] Parlin v. Stone, 1 McCrary (U. S.) 443.

[54] Wooden v. Haviland, 18 Conn. 101.

[55] Hervey v. Savery, 48 Iowa 313; Bodwell v. Heaton, 40 Kans. 36, 18 Pac. 901.

[56] Turner v. Hart, 1 Fed. 295.

under color of reformation, make a contract for the parties which both never assented to, or intended to make.'[57]

A mortgage may be reformed to express the mutual intention of the parties that the principal of a senior mortgage should be excepted from the operation of its covenants, where this failure of the mortgage in this respect was due to a scrivener's mistake.[58] The mistake, to be the subject of reformation, must be not merely the oversight of one of the parties, but such that the deed fails to express what was intended and agreed upon by both parties.[59] The court will not reform a deed so as to add to it a new condition not contemplated by one of the parties in the execution of it;[60] it will not make it include what was intended by one party, unless it appear that the other party at the time had the same intention;[61] or unless the other party fraudulently induced him to believe the mortgage contained what he asks to have it made to include; as where the mortgagor by false and fraudulent representations induced the mortgagee to believe, when he loaned the money and accepted the mortgage, that it covered more and other land and buildings than it did, the mortgage was reformed, and enforced against the lands fraudulently omitted.[62]

In case part of the mortgage contract is contained in a will executed by the mortgagee at the same time with the mortgage, the mortgagor need not seek for reformation of the mortgage for the purpose of incorporating in the mortgage such part of the contract. Thus, where the mortgagor testified that the debt was to be paid in ten years after the mortgagee's death by annual instalments, and this was confirmed by the mortgagee's will executed at the same time, it was held that such will and mortgage would be construed together as one contract, and the testator could not, by a later will, deprive the mortgagor of his right of redemption by annual payments within the time named.[63] The right to have a deed reformed may be lost by laches.[64]

---

[57] Per Johnson, J., in Marcy v. Dunlap, 5 Lans. (N. Y.) 365. See also Alexander v. Caldwell, 55 Ala. 517.

[58] Allis v. Hall, 76 Conn. 322, 56 Atl. 637.

[59] Bernheim v. Talbot, 54 Ore. 30, 100 Pac. 1107; Barker v. Harlan, 3 Lea (Tenn.) 505.

[60] Hart v. Hart, 23 Iowa 599, where the court refused to reform a mortgage for support, so as to require the mortgagee to live at a particular place.

[61] Fry v. Jenkins, 173 Ill. App. 486.

[62] De Peyster v. Hasbrouck, 11 N. Y. 582. See also Rider v. Powell, 28 N. Y. 310.

[63] Keagle v. Pessell, 91 Mich. 618, 52 N. W. 58.

[64] Paulison v. Van Iderstine, 29 N. J. Eq. 594. See also First Nat. Bank v. Gough, 61 Ind. 147. In the following cases the delay was held insufficient, under the circumstances, to constitute laches: Travelli v. Bowman, 150 Cal. 587, 89 Pac. 347 (failure of plaintiff's attorney to

Any consideration that will support a mortgage is sufficient to entitle the mortgagee to maintain an action to correct a mutual mistake in the same against the mortgagor and those holding under him as purchasers with notice.[65]

§ 98. **Who may obtain reformation.**—A mortgagee who has sold the note and mortgage, and afterward bought them back again, has the same right to have a mistake corrected as he had before he made the transfer, if he indorsed the note at the time of the sale.[66] He may have the mistake corrected upon its discovery for the first time after he has purchased the land under a foreclosure sale, and taken possession as purchaser.[67] But equity will not, ordinarily, reform a mortgage at the instance of one who is a mere volunteer, and not a party to the instrument.[68] Accordingly the court will not reform a description in a mortgage deed at the suit of another who has become purchaser at a sale by the mortgagee.[69] If, however, a sheriff in making a deed of land sold by him under a foreclosure sale inserts a wrong description, he has an interest, both as an individual and as trustee, to prevent an injury to himself and the grantor in the mortgage because of the mistake, and is a proper party to bring suit in equity to reform the deed.[70]

The party desiring a reformation of a deed should bring a bill in equity for the purpose. A mortgagor can not ask for this relief in answer to a bill to foreclose, but he may file a cross-bill.[71] The mortgagee may ask for a reformation of the mortgage in a bill to foreclose it.[72] Before a trustee in a trust deed can maintain a suit to reform it so as to include other lands, he must show that the debt has not been paid.[73] A mortgagee who has assigned his mortgage is not a necessary or proper party to a suit by the assignee for its reformation.[74]

discover the trust deed among his papers); Kelsey v. Agricultural Ins. Co., 78 N. J. Eq. 378, 79 Atl. 539 (reformation by second mortgage after four years); Arnstein v. Bernstein, 127 App. Div. 550, 111 N. Y. S. 987 (reformation upon foreclosure, in reference to assumption clause).
[65] Citizens' Nat. Bank v. Judy, 146 Ind. 322, 43 N. E. 259.
[66] Kennard v. George, 44 N. H. 440.
[67] Davenport v. Sovil, 6 Ohio St. 459. See also First Nat. Bank v. Gough, 61 Ind. 147.
[68] Gould v. Glass, 120 Ga. 50, 47 S. E. 505.

[69] Haley v. Bagley, 37 Mo. 363. See also Jackson v. Lucas, 157 Ala. 51, 47 So. 224, 131 Am. St. 17. But see Greer v. Watson, 170 Ala. 334, 54 So. 487; Goulding Fertilizer Co. v. Blanchard, 178 Ala. 298, 59 So. 485.
[70] Dodson v. Lomax (Mo.), 21 S. W. 25.
[71] French v. Griffin, 18 N. J. Eq. 279.
[72] Alexander v. Rea, 50 Ala. 450; Miller v. Kolb, 47 Ind. 220. See post § 1464.
[73] Dessart v. Bonynge, 10 Ariz. 37, 85 Pac. 723.
[74] Keister v. Meyers, 115 Ind. 312, 17 N. E. 161.

§ 99. Against whom reformation may be had.—A mistake in the description of the land may be corrected as between the parties, or as against the heirs of either,[75] or judgment creditors of the mortgagor,[76] or purchasers with notice,[77] but courts of equity can grant no relief as against one who has purchased the property in good faith and for a valuable consideration without notice of the mistake; and consequently a bill which seeks to do this is defective when it fails to allege that the purchaser took the land with notice of the mistake.[78] It is obvious, however, that a purchaser with notice stands in no better position than the mortgagor himself.[79] As against a purchaser at an execution sale, notice of mistake before or at the sale is sufficient.[80] It is the holding of one of the cases that where a mortgage upon real estate does not contain a correct description of any land, but the description therein contained is sufficient to indicate to any person familiar with such matters what was intended thereby, and the correct description is further indicated by a plat contained in the application for the loan,—it was proper to decree reformation though the land was then owned by a subsequent purchaser.[81]

A voluntary grantee also stands in the same position as the mortgagor, and a conveyance for less than the real value is held to be voluntary so far as the value exceeds the consideration paid.[82] The mort-

[75] Brinson v. Berry (Miss.), 7 So. 322; Gates v. Union Naval Stores Co., 92 Miss. 227, 45 So. 979; Mississippi Val. Trust Co. v. McDonald, 146 Mo. 467, 48 S. W. 483; Straman v. Rechtine, 58 Ohio St. 443, 51 N. E. 44; Jenkins v. Jenkins University, 17 Wash. 160, 49 Pac. 247.

[76] Citizens' Nat. Bank v. Judy, 146 Ind. 322, 43 N. E. 259.

[77] Citizens' Nat. Bank v. Judy, 146 Ind. 322, 43 N. E. 259; Doom v. Holmes, 9 Kans. App. 520, 60 Pac. 1096; Carpenter Paper Co. v. Wilcox, 50 Nebr. 659, 70 N. W. 228; Peters v. Fell, 15 S. Dak. 391, 89 N. W. 1014.

[78] Reeves v. Vinacke, 1 McCrary (U. S.) 213; Bright v. Buckman, 39 Fed. 243; Munford v. Miller, 7 Bradw. (Ill.) 62; Sickmon v. Wood, 69 Ill. 329; Easter v. Severin, 64 Ind. 375; Ford v. Daniels, 71 Mich. 77, 38 N. W. 708; Farmers' &c. Bank v. Citizens' Nat. Bank, 25 S. Dak. 91, 125 N. W. 642; McLouth v. Hurt, 51 Tex. 115; Fitch v. Boyer, 51 Tex. 336; Reid v. Rhodes, 106 Va. 701, 56 S. E. 722.

[79] Bright v. Buckman, 39 Fed. 243; Fielder v. Varner, 45 Ala. 428. See also Goodman v. Randall, 44 Conn. 321; Craig v. Pendleton, 89 Ark. 259, 116 S. W. 209; Manogue v. Bryant, 15 App. D. C. 245; Manatt v. Starr, 72 Iowa 677, 34 N. W. 784; Hunt v. Hunt, 38 Mich. 161; Toll v. Davinport, 74 Mich. 386, 42 N. W. 63; Gale v. Morris, 29 N. J. Eq. 222; Rutgers v. Kingsland, 7 N. J. Eq. 178, 658; Ruhling v. Hackett, 1 Nev. 360; Strang v. Beach, 11 Ohio St. 283, 78 Am. Dec. 308.

[80] Williams v. Hatch, 38 Ala. 338.

[81] Doom v. Holmes, 9 Kans. App. 520, 60 Pac. 1096.

[82] Snyder v. Partridge, 138 Ill. 173, 29 N. E. 851; Keeder v. Murphy, 43 Iowa 413; Strong v. Lawrence, 58 Iowa 55, 12 N. W. 74; Worthington v. Bullitt, 6 Md. 172; Norton v. Norton, 5 Cush. (Mass.) 524; Robinson v. Stewart, 10 N. Y. 189; and citing Boyd v. Dunlap, 1 Johns. Ch. (N. Y.) 58, 478; Church v. Chapin, 35 Vt. 223.

gagor's assignee in bankruptcy is not in the position of a purchaser for value without notice, and therefore the mortgage may be reformed as against him.[83]

The reformation of a mortgage relates back to the date of its execution, as against the mortgagor's wife, who became such after the making of the mortgage.[84] A mortgage can not be reformed as against a prior judgmen: creditor; but if, having notice of the proceeding, and of a decree for the sale of the property free of incumbrances, he omits to protect his rights, and the property is sold under such decree, he can not afterward assert his rights as against the purchaser.[85] A mistake in the mortgage of a married woman in a matter of description merely may be reformed.[86] A homestead waiver is not affected by a reformation of the description of the land.[87]

A mortgage may be reformed as against a junior mortgagee whose mortgage was taken, without notice of such a mistake, as security for an antecedent debt, without the surrender of any old security, and without any new consideration moving from him,[88] in a state where such a purchaser is not considered a purchaser for value.[89] The mistake may be corrected, too, against a subsequent judgment creditor;[90] but not against a purchaser of a subsequent judgment, who has invested his money in the purchase of the judgment upon the faith of the apparent lien upon the land.[91] The equity of the mortgagee is regarded as stronger than that of the judgment creditor, who has not, probably, parted with his money on the faith of the apparent facts. But when the judgment has been sold and assigned to one ignorant of the mistake in the mortgage, and who has expended his money upon the faith of the rights of the parties as they appear in

[83] Schulze v. Bolting, 8 Biss. (U. S.) 174.

[84] Hawkins v. Pearson, 96 Ala. 369, 11 So. 304. She is, however, a proper party to the suit, since she would be entitled to dower and homestead if complainant fails on his proof to correct the description of the mortgaged property, and hence she is entitled to her day in court to contest that issue. Per McLellan, J.

[85] Fowler v. Hart, 13 How. (U. S.) 373.

[86] Carper v. Munger, 62 Ind. 481; Hamar v. Medsker, 60 Ind. 413. But see Petesch v. Hambach, 48 Wis. 443, 4 N. W. 565.

[87] Snell v. Snell, 123 Ill. 403, 14 N. E. 684.

[88] Busenbarke v. Ramey, 53 Ind. 499. See also Herring v. Fitts, 43 Fla. 54, 30 So. 804, 99 Am. St. 108; First Nat. Bank v. Wentworth, 28 Kans. 183.

[89] See post § 458.

[90] Brewster v. Clamfit, 33 Ark. 72; Ft. Smith Mill. Co. v. Mikles, 61 Ark. 123, 32 S. W. 493; Sample v. Rowe, 24 Ind. 208; White v. Wilson, 6 Blackf. (Ind.) 448, 39 Am. Dec. 437; Wainwright v. Flanders, 64 Ind. 306.

[91] Flanders v. O'Brien, 46 Ind. 284; Wainwright v. Flanders, 64 Ind. 306; Rutgers v. Kingsland, 7 N. J. Eq. 658.

the respective securities, it is not considered that there is any superior equity in the mortgagee.[92]

A mortgage as between the parties to it may be reformed by affixing a seal to it; but such reformation would give no validity to a sale made by virtue of a power contained in it. The sale would be a nullity for want of any authority in the mortgagee to make it, and the reformation could give no validity to a transaction originally void.[93]

If a reformation be resisted when there is really no defense, the defect being a mistake of both parties, the defendant should pay costs.[94]

§ 100. **Lost mortgage deeds—Equitable relief.**—On proof of the loss of a mortgage deed without record of it having been made, the court may, under ordinary circumstances, decree the making of a new mortgage.[95] This may be the only adequate remedy, and without it the mortgagee may be exposed to the total loss of his security. The loss of deeds is a familiar ground of equitable relief. As a general rule a lost mortgage may not be foreclosed unless its execution is as clearly established as though the bill had been filed primarily to establish it as a lost instrument.[96]

§ 101. **Construction—Intention—Extrinsic evidence.**—A principle of construction applicable to mortgages is, that inasmuch as the mortgagor is supposed to make his own selection of words and terms in drawing the deed, whenever the language is equivocal or ambiguous it is construed most strongly against him, and in such manner as to make it a valid and binding security for the mortgagee.[97] "Courts of equity have ever taken a broad and humane view of the obligations of a mortgagor, and have leaned against the harsh remedies which are often invoked against him, and are inclined to protect him so long as they can justly do so without impairing the obligation of his contract with the mortgagee."[98]

[92] Flanders v. O'Brien, 46 Ind. 284. The rule is otherwise, however, in Ohio. Van Thorniley v. Peters, 26 Ohio St. 471; White v. Denman, 1 Ohio St. 110, 16 Ohio 59; Hood v. Brown, 2 Ohio 266.

[93] Springfield Sav. Bank v. Springfield Cong. Soc., 127 Mass. 516.

[94] Meserole v. Leary (N. J.), 23 Atl. 1074.

[95] Lawrence v. Lawrence, 42 N. H.

109, and cases cited. See also Embree v. Embree, 37 Ind. App. 16, 74 N. E. 44.

[96] Union Baptist Church v. Roper (Ala.), 61 So. 288.

[97] Jerome v. Hopkins, 2 Mich. 96; Stuart v. Worden, 42 Mich. 154, 3 N. W. 876.

[98] Duncan v. Home Co-op. Co., 221 Mo. 315, 120 S. W. 733.

Another principle of construction is, that the intention of the parties as gathered from the instrument is to govern, if the intention be such that it may be legally enforced.[99] The intention of the parties is to be ascertained in accordance with the rules applicable to other contracts.[1] "There is no doubt that the intention is the object to be sought for in construction. And to get at that, the situation of the parties, and the nature and object of their transactions, may be looked at. But it must be borne in mind that it is not the business of construction to look outside of the instrument to get at the intention of the parties, and then carry out that intention whether the instrument contains language sufficient to express it or not; but the sole duty of construction is to find out what was meant by the language of the instrument."[2]

The construction which the parties themselves have placed upon a mortgage has force in case of ambiguity, but prior negotiations in writing leading up to the execution can not affect the instrument finally executed.

The whole document should be construed together, by a fair consideration of all its terms and provisions. It is improper to isolate phrases from their context and examine them separately.[3] Where property is exchanged by deeds, and one grantee gives a mortgage upon that which he receives, to secure the difference in value, the deeds and mortgage may be read together and with reference to the circumstances, in construing the intention of the parties; and their manifest intent is not to be derogated from by adhering to the literal terms of the papers. Equity regards substance rather than form, and enforces the actual intent if lawful and just.[4]

A mortgage is subject to and is construed in the light of all existing laws of the state where executed. If such laws affect the rights

[99] Walker v. Bement (Ind. App.), 94 N. E. 339; Weinstein v. Sinel, 133 App. Div. 441, 117 N. Y. S. 346.

[1] Clark v. Brenneman, 86 Ill. App. 416; Houston v. Curran, 101 Ill. App. 203; Northern Central R. Co. v. Hering, 93 Md. 164, 48 Atl. 461.

[2] Paine, J., in Farmers' Loan &c. Co. v. Commercial Bank, 15 Wis. 424, 82 Am. Dec. 689. Intention of the parties will be determined by a fair construction of all the terms and provisions of the instrument; it is improper to detach isolated phrases from their context and examine them by themselves. Harnickell v. Omaha Water Co., 146 App. Div. 603, 131 N. Y. S. 489. In re Howard, 207 Fed. 402; Matt v. Matt, 156 Iowa 503, 137 N. W. 489.

[3] Harnickell v. Omaha Water Co., 146 App. Div. 693, 131 N. Y. S. 489.

[4] Stuart v. Worden, 42 Mich. 154, 3 N. W. 876. A mortgage executed after the passage of a law relating to the opening of streets is subject to the act. Jackson v. Pittsburg, 36 Pa. Super. Ct. 274.

of a party to the mortgage, they enter into and become a part of the contract.[5]

The rights of the mortgagee are not affected by statements made by the mortgagor in an unrecorded application for another loan on other lands.[6]

§ 101a. Construction—What law governs.—In determining what law governs the construction of a mortgage, several elements must be considered; first and perhaps most important, the place where the real property lies; second, the place of execution; third, the place of performance, and fourth, the residence of the parties. The rule most in accord with the construction of conveyances generally, seems to be that the law of the state where the mortgaged land lies, determines the construction.[7] Where this is the rule of construction the parties may not vary it by stipulations in the mortgage that the note "is understood to be made with reference to and under the laws" of another state.[8]

There is some authority, however, that the place of execution and of payment controls, though different from the place where the land lies.[9] In some jurisdictions all the foregoing elements are considered and the question is determined by the intention of the parties.[10]

The law in force at the time of the execution of a mortgage governs its execution and performance.[11]

[6] Crippen v. Comstock, 17 Colo. App. 89, 66 Pac. 1074.
[7] In re Kellog, 121 Fed. 333, 57 C. C. A. 547; Ashurst v. Ashurst, 119 Ala. 219, 24 So. 760; Hannah v. Vensel, 19 Idaho 796, 116 Pac. 115; Sinclair v. Gunzenhauser, 179 Ind. 78, 98 N. E. 37; Manton v. Seiberling, 107 Iowa 534, 78 N. W. 194; Gault v. Equitable Trust Co., 100 Ky. 578, 38 S. W. 1065; Bramblet v. Commonwealth &c. Co., 27 Ky. 156, 84 S. W. 545; Miller v. Shotnell, 38 La. Ann. 890; People's Bldg. &c. Assn. v. Parish, 1 Nebr. (unoff.) 505, 96 N. W. 243; Hutchinson v. Ward, 192 N. Y. 375, 85 N. E. 390, 127 Am. St. 909; Bowdle v. Jencks, 18 S. Dak. 80, 99 N. W. 98; Klinck v. Price, 4 W. Va. 4, 6 Am. Rep. 268. An express provision in a mortgage that the note secured be governed by the law of the state where the premises are situated is effective though the note was executed and was payable else-where. Girard Trust Co. v. Paddock, 88 Nebr. 359, 129 N. W. 550.
[8] Building &c. Assn. v. Bilan, 59 Nebr. 458, 81 N. W. 308.
[9] Lamkin v. Lovell, 176 Ala. 334, 58 So. 258; Varick v. Crane, 4 N. J. Eq. 128. The place of residence and of execution control in the following: Caldwell v. Edwards, 5 Stew. & P. (Ala.) 312; Cubbedge v. Napier, 62 Ala. 518.
[10] The question of lex loci is one of intention, to be decided by all the facts of the case, among which may be the residence of the parties, the place of payment, and the location of the land mortgaged. Newman v. Kershaw, 10 Wis. 333. The element of intention was also recognized in Chappell v. Jardine, 51 Conn. 64, where a mortgage upon land supposed to be in New York, but actually in Connecticut, was construed under the New York law.
[11] Purcell v. Barnett, 30 Okla. 605, 121 Pac. 231.

CHAPTER III

THE PARTIES TO A MORTGAGE

PART I

WHO MAY GIVE A MORTGAGE

I. *Introductory,* §§ 101b–102c
II. *Disability of Insanity,* §§ 103, 103a
III. *Disability of Infancy,* §§ 103b–105
IV. *Married Women,* §§ 106–118a
V. *Tenants in Common of Partnership Real Estate,* §§ 119–123
VI. *Corporations,* §§ 124–128
VII. *Power to Mortgage,* §§ 129–130a

PART II

WHO MAY TAKE A MORTGAGE

Parties in Various Relations, §§ 131–135a

I. *Introductory*

SECTION	SECTION
101b. In general.	102b. Capacity of guardian to mortgage.
102. Legal capacity to mortgage.	
102a. Capacity of executors and devisees to mortgage.	102c. Generally of disabilities.

§ **101b. In general.**—It is essential to the validity of a mortgage that there be proper contracting parties, a party to make the mortgage and a party to accept it. A person can not make a mortgage to himself, though he claims to make it in one capacity and to accept it in another. Thus, where an administrator, for the purpose of securing an indebtedness to the estate under his administration, executed a mortgage and note to himself as administrator to secure such indebtedness, and after his death they were found among his papers, the mortgage not recorded, it was held that the mortgage was invalid for want of contracting parties. The mortgagor and mortgagee were one and the same person. The addition of the word "administrator" to the mortgagee's name does not change the legal effect of the grant, which is by the mortgagor in his individual capacity to himself as mortgagee in his individual capacity.[1]

---

[1] Gorham v. Meacham, 63 Vt. 231, 22 Atl. 572. But see Lyon v. Lyon, 67 N. Y. 250.

A mortgage executed in the name of a fictitious person, to whom the real owner had made a fictitious conveyance, is valid as between the mortgagor and the mortgagee.[2] Likewise title is passed by a mortgage to a person under an assumed name.[3]

§ 102. **Legal capacity to mortgage.**—In general, any person who has a legal capacity to act for himself may make a mortgage of his property, or may authorize any one else to do this in his behalf. By statutory provisions in many states, guardians or others acting for infants, insane or other persons without legal capacity to act for themselves, may be authorized, upon application to court showing sufficient cause, to convey in mortgage the real estate of their wards. Like authority is sometimes given to trustees, executors, or administrators, although not having title to the property themselves, but only authority over it for certain purposes, and acting in a representative capacity in respect to it, to mortgage it for the benefit of the parties in interest.[4]

The jurisdiction of a court to order the mortgaging of a decedent's real estate can only be exercised in the manner and by the procedure prescribed by the statute.[5] A mortgage made by an executor or administrator without the authority of a statute and license by a court of competent jurisdiction is void, and the heirs in whom is vested the estate are not estopped to plead the invalidity of the mortgage by reason of the benefit resulting to them from the money obtained upon it.[6] Such mortgages depend upon the particular provisions authorizing them, which are too various to be given here. It may be remarked, however, that this statutory power must be exercised strictly for the purposes for which it is given, and all the requirements of the statutes in regard to obtaining and exercising the authority must be strictly followed.[7] But when the power to mortgage has been granted by a

[2] Blackman v. Henderson, 116 Iowa 578, 87 N. W. 655.
[3] Wilson v. White, 84 Cal. 239, 24 Pac. 114.
[4] Ames v. Holderbaum, 44 Fed. 224; Camden Safe Deposit &c. Co. v. Lord, 67 N. J. Eq. 489, 58 Atl. 607.
[5] Duryea v. Mackey, 151 N. Y. 204, 45 N. E. 458. Minor irregularities, however, in an order of court to the administrator do not invalidate the mortgage. The failure to direct him, as provided by statute, to execute a promissory note, which he did in connection therewith, is immaterial. Fast v. Steele, 127 Cal. 202, 59 Pac. 585. Nor do mere ir-

regularities in the mortgage invalidate it. Smith v. Eels, 27 Ind. App. 321, 61 N. E. 200; Griffin v. Johnson, 37 Mich. 87.
[6] Kirkbride v. Kelly, 167 Ala. 570, 52 So. 660; Black v. Dressell, 20 Kans. 153; Shrigley v. Black, 59 Kans. 487, 53 Pac. 477.
[7] Merritt v. Simpson, 41 Ill. 391; Wetherill v. Harris, 67 Ind. 452; Smith v. Eels, 27 Ind. App. 321, 61 N. E. 200; Edwards v. Taliafero, 34 Mich. 13; Smithwick v. Kelly, 79 Tex. 564, 15 S. W. 486. For circumstances authorizing an order to mortgage, see In re Morris, 18 N. Y. S. 680.

court of competent jurisdiction, the parties to the mortgage are protected by the license without investigating the truth of the facts upon which it was granted; their truth can not be questioned in any collateral proceeding.[8] Such mortgage must show that it was executed in pursuance of the power granted, and not in a personal capacity.[9]

An administrator or executor who without authority undertakes to bind the estate of a decedent may make himself personally liable, although he adds to his own name the designation of his office.[10] Devisees who execute a mortgage upon the land devised to them bind their interests in the land, and this is the result, though some of them execute the mortgage in their capacity as executors.[11]

A corporation, if capable of holding real estate, has, like a person, the power of conveying it in mortgage, unless it is under some disability imposed by statute or implied from its duties to the public. But while a person capable of making a grant may, if he choose, employ another to act for him, a corporation must always act by an agent.[12]

§ 102a.   **Capacity of executors and devisees to mortgage.**—A testator may provide by his will that his executor may mortgage his real estate, or some specific portion of it, for the purpose of raising money for the payment of his debts. A mortgage made by virtue of such authority is valid unless the making of it under such authority is in conflict with statutory provisions. But the mortgage of an executor must be strictly within the terms of the power granted in the will.[13] A power given to the executor to sell does not confer on him the power to mortgage.[14] The statutory provisions by which the court may order the sale of property for the payment of debts in no way con-

[8] Griffin v. Johnson, 37 Mich. 87. See also United States Trust Co. v. Roche, 116 N. Y. 120, 22 N. E. 265.
[9] Thomas v. Parker, 97 Cal. 456, 32 Pac. 562.
[10] Black v. Dressell, 20 Kans. 153; Shrigley v. Black, 59 Kans. 487, 53 Pac. 477; Hellier v. Lord, 55 N. J. L. 367, 26 Atl. 986. See also De Coudres v. Union Trust Co., 25 Ind. App. 271, 58 N. E. 90, 81 Am. St. 95.
[11] Shrigley v. Black, 59 Kans. 487, 53 Pac. 477.
[12] See post § 124 et seq.
[13] Smith v. Peyrot, 201 N. Y. 210, 94 N. E. 662.
[14] Webb v. Winter, 135 Cal. 455, 67 Pac. 691; Parkhurst v. Trumbull,

130 Mich. 408, 90 N. W. 25; Stokes v. Payne, 58 Miss. 614, 38 Am. Rep. 340; Dubois v. Van Valem, 61 N. J. Eq. 331, 48 Atl. 241; Columbia Ave. Sav. &c. Co. v. Lewis, 190 Pa. St. 558, 42 Atl. 1094. But power to mortgage has been held given under clause of will which authorized the executor "to sell, exchange and dispose" of testator's property. Faulk v. Dashiell, 62 Tex. 642, 50 Am. Rep. 542. Where the will gives the executor power to raise in such way as it seems best to him a sufficient amount of money to pay the debts of the testator, the executor may borrow money to pay on the debts and secure the loan by mort-

fliet with the authority of a testator to prescribe that the property may be sold with or without such a necessity. Such a mortgage may have the sanction of a statute;[15] and if it has, the testator's creditors can have no valid ground of objection to it. Their claims are not liens upon the real estate having priority of such a mortgage. Claims merely proved against the estate are not in any proper sense liens upon the real estate. But even if such claims could be considered liens upon the real estate in general, a mortgage made by authority of the testator's will to pay debts would be a lien superior to such claims. "The mortgage incumbrance is one created by the administration, and is a means of raising money to aid in settling the estate. It is a means provided by the law whereby the real estate is used in the settlement."[16] There being nothing originally to show that the manner prescribed by the will for settlement of the estate was prejudicial to creditors, the fact that in the end it proved to be so is immaterial. The power of the executor to mortgage any particular tract is not exhausted by a single exercise of such power on such tract.

An executor authorized by will to borrow money in such way as it seems best to him for the purpose of paying the testator's debts has authority to execute a mortgage upon the testator's land to secure a loan for this purpose.[17] Although not expressly authorized by the will, an executor may under general discretionary power to dispose of the property and settle an estate, make a valid mortgage and borrow money to pay the debts of the estate, and neither judgment creditors nor residuary legatees are entitled to object to the validity of the mortgage.[18] Where a principal legatee, with priority of interest,

gage. Fletcher v. American Trust &c. Co., 111 Ga. 300, 36 S. E. 767, 78 Am. St. 164.

[15] Smith v. Eels, 27 Ind. App. 321, 61 N. E. 200; Iowa Loan &c. Co. v. Holderbaum, 86 Iowa 1, 52 N. W. 550; Brown v. Morrill, 45 Minn. 483, 48 N. W. 328.

[16] Ames v. Holderbaum, 44 Fed. 224. Iowa Loan &c. Co. v. Holderbaum, 86 Iowa 1, 52 N. W. 550. Granger, J., delivering the opinion, said: "In a very significant sense it may be said that the real estate, to the extent of the incumbrance, has been exhausted, and the proceeds used in payment of debts. We may aid the thought by the supposition that the loan secured by the mortgage is the entire value of the land—all that it could be sold for

under the order of the court. With such a state of facts, the real estate would as clearly be exhausted as if sold in the usual way, reserving by the transaction an equity of redemption. If incumbered for but a fraction of its value, it is for the same reason partly exhausted, and the remainder, the equity of redemption, remains to be sold, if needed and the court should so order. To our minds, there are no considerations leading to a conclusion that claims against the estate are liens superior to such a mortgage."

[17] Fletcher v. American Trust &c. Co., 111 Ga. 300, 36 S. E. 767.

[18] Thomas v. Provident Life &c. Co., 138 Fed. 348, 70 C. C. A. 448; Taliaferro v. Thornton, 26 Ky. L. 183,

joins with the executor in a mortgage to pay debts, it is immaterial to the rights of other beneficiaries whether the mortgage was authorized by the will, for if any one was injured by the transaction it was such legatee.[19]

A provision in a will giving a devisee the power to sell and convey land does not of itself authorize a mortgage thereof.[20] But a testamentary power to sell, amplified by other words of more general meaning may be construed to include the power to mortgage under certain circumstances.[21]

A mortgage by the devisees of a decedent, some of whom are executors, and sign as such, but have no authority to do so, is binding upon them in their individual capacity.[22] After the testator's creditors have for several years acquiesced in the executor's management of the estate under a provision in the will allowing him to mortgage the real estate for the payment of debts, they can not question the validity of the mortgages executed by him under such authority.[23].

If a married woman joins in the application for an order authorizing a mortgage of trust property in which she is interested, and acquiesces in the making of such a mortgage, she is estopped from denying that her interest is liable for the debt intended to be secured.[24]

A provision in a devise of land in fee, that the devisee shall never mortgage it is void as a restraint on alienation.[25]

§ 102b. Capacity of guardian to mortgage.—A guardian may mortgage the property of his ward when licensed by the proper

---

80 S. W. 1097; Dewein v. Hooss, 237 Mo. 23, 139 S. W. 195. Under a limited discretion concerning division of the property an executor can not authorize a mortgage of an undivided interest of one of the heirs. Garman v. Hawley, 132 Mich. 321, 93 N. W. 871. An executor can not mortgage property of the estate to a partnership of which he is a member, or for any purpose other than to benefit the estate. Camden Safe Deposit &c. Co. v. Lord, 67 N. J. Eq. 489, 58 Atl. 607.

[19] Taliaferro v. Thornton, 26 Ky. L. 183, 80 S. W. 1097.

[20] O'Brien v. Flint, 74 Conn. 502, 51 Atl. 547. A devise with "the right to sell, devise, or exchange" confers no power to mortgage. Quisenberry v. Watkins Land-Mtg. Co., 92 Tex. 247, 47 S. W. 708.

[21] "The power to sell, transfer and dispose of" real estate devised, for the support of the devisee for life, gives the right to mortgage for the purpose specified. Hamilton v. Hamilton, 149 Iowa 321, 128 N. W. 380. A power in a will authorizing a wife to sell and dispose of her life estate as she may deem best to support her family and carry on the testator's business, gives the wife power to mortgage the estate for such purpose. Lardner v. Williams, 98 Wis. 514, 74 N. W. 346.

[22] Shrigley v. Black, 59 Kans. 487, 53 Pac. 477.

[23] m v. Holderbaum, 44 Fed. 224.A es

[24] Carrigan v. Drake, 36 S. Car. 354, 15 S. E. 339.

[25] Freeman v. Phillips, 113 Ga. 589, 38 S. E. 943; Jones v. Port Huron &c. Co., 171 Ill. 502, 49 N. E. 700.

court under statutory authority;[26] he has no inherent power to mortgage his ward's estate.[27] The license must be strictly followed.[28] Such mortgage passes the title of the ward; but if the ward has no title, none passes by the mortgage. Thus, under a will by which the testator provided that land "be reserved for his children, and be equally divided among them when the youngest attains the age of twenty-one years," and devised the land to his executors in trust during the minority of his children, no title vests in the children until the youngest becomes twenty-one years old; and a mortgage made by the children's guardian under an order of court, during their minority, passes no title.[29]

A mortgage upon an infant's real estate obtained through the forms of law in pursuance of a collusive agreement between the infant's guardian, and the guardian's own creditor, the result of which is to make the infant's property security for the guardian's debt, is properly set aside by a suit in equity by the infant, attacking the proceeding by which leave to mortgage was obtained from the court.[30]

The fact that the guardian had not given a bond at the time of his appointment as required by statute does not invalidate his mortgage executed in the manner provided by statute.[31] Since a guardian is entirely without authority to mortgage his ward's property, without an order of court, it is proper to charge him with the debt where he executes a mortgage not so authorized.[32]

The power in any court to direct a mortgage of the real estate of an infant is purely statutory. There is no such power inherent in a court of equity.[33] A statute prescribing specific purposes for which

[26] United States Mtg. Co. v. Sperry, 138 U. S. 313, 34 L. ed. 969, 11 Sup. Ct. 321; Ankeny v. Richardson, 187 Fed. 550, 109 C. C. A. 316.

[27] Tyson v. Latrobe, 42 Md. 325; Sample v. Lane, 45 Miss. 556.

[28] Merritt v. Simpson, 41 Ill. 391; McMannis v. Rice, 48 Iowa 361.

[29] Kingman v. Harmon, 131 Ill. 171, 23 N. E. 430.

[30] Warren v. Union Bank, 157 N. Y. 259, 51 N. E. 1036, 68 Am. St. 777.

[31] Hunt v. Insley, 56 Kans. 213, 42 Pac. 709.

[32] Bell v. Dingwell, 91 Nebr. 699, 136 N. W. 1128.

[33] Losey v. Stanley, 147 N. Y. 560, 42 N. E. 8; Jenkins v. Fahey, 73 N. Y. 355; Horton v. McCoy, 47 N. Y. 21; Forman v. Marsh, 11 N. Y. 544; Baker v. Lorillard, 4 N. Y. 257;

Rogers v. Dill, 6 Hill (N. Y.) 415. In Losey v. Stanley, supra, Andrews, C. J., said: "The origin of the jurisdiction of the Court of Chancery in England over the persons and estates of infants is involved in some obscurity. The better opinion seems to be that it grew out of the transfer by the Crown to the Chancellor of the supervision theretofore exercised by the king as parens patriæ over persons who, by reason of nonage, were incapable of action for themselves."

Lord Hardwicke in Taylor v. Philips, 1 Ves. Sr. 229, said: "There is no instance in this court binding the inheritance of an infant by any discretionary act of the court. As to personal things, as in the composition of debts, it has been

a guardian may mortgage his ward's land, for example, education and maintenance, does not authorize a mortgage to discharge a pre-existing incumbrance, or for any other purpose.[34] Authority to mortgage gives the guardian the right to mortgage the ward's reversionary interest in real estate.[35]

§ 102c. **Generally of disabilities.**—Disabilities are either natural, as in the case of insane persons, or legal, as in the case of married women and corporations, while the disability of infancy is either the one or the other, according to the circumstances of the case.

II. *Disability of Insanity*

Section	Section
103. Capacity of insane persons.	103a. Capacity of intoxicated persons.

§ 103. **Capacity of insane persons.**—In general, the mortgage of an insane person is invalid as against the mortgagor, his heirs or assigns,[1] unless it be confirmed by him when of sound mind, or by his legally constituted guardian, or by his heirs or devisees. It may be disaffirmed without returning the consideration money to the mortgagee.[2] A mortgage made by one who was insane at intervals both before and after the execution of it, as to its validity, depends upon the question whether he was sane at the time; and the fact of his sanity must in such case be established by clear and satisfactory evidence.[3]

If the mortgagor at the time he executed the mortgage comprehended what he was doing, and the consequences of his acts, it will be held valid, if it be fair and no undue advan-

done; but never as to the inheritance; for that would be taking on the court a legislative authority, doing that which is properly the subject of a private bill." Andrew, C. J., in Losey v. Stanley, above cited, said: "The question of the inherent power of a court of equity to order a sale of an infant's real property, upon the theory of a supposed benefit to him, is quite distinct from its acknowledged power in the enforcement and protection of trusts and from the power of courts in the exercise of their ordinary jurisdiction to establish or enforce rights of property between parties to a litigation, whether infants or adults. . . . The legislature possesses whatever power as parens patriæ was in England lodged in the sovereign over the estates of infants, consistent with constitutional limitations."

[34] Gapen v. Garrison, 193 Mo. 335, 92 S. W. 368, 5 L. R. A. (N. S.) 838.
[35] Foster v. Young, 35 Iowa 27.
[1] Bowman v. Wade, 54 Ore. 347, 103 Pac. 72.
[2] Brigham v. Fayerweather, 144 Mass. 48, 10 N. E. 735; Valpey v. Rea, 130 Mass. 384; Chandler v. Simmons, 97 Mass. 508, 93 Am. Dec. 117. But see Wiser v. Clinton, 82 Conn. 148, 72 Atl. 928, 135 Am. St. 264.
[3] Holmes v. Martin, 123 Mich. 155, 81 N. W. 1072; Ripley v. Babcock, 13 Wis. 425.

tage has been taken of him, although it may appear probable that there were times, previous to the execution of the mortgage, when he might not have had sufficient capacity, on account of a disease which would not be uniform in its influence on his mind.[4] This test of mental capacity is employed for grantors in deeds generally. Ability of the grantor to comprehend the nature and consequences of his act determines the validity of the deed.[5] Another test frequently employed is his knowledge of the extent and value of his property, and his ability to transact ordinary business.[6]

Sanity is presumed, as it is the normal condition of the human mind, and therefore the burden is upon a mortgagor, who seeks to avoid his mortgage on the ground of his mental disability, to prove such disability.[7]

A mortgage made by one who had had periodical recurrences of insanity, and was insane at the time he gave the mortgage, was set aside, though he had all along managed his own affairs with average correctness, and had been treated by his neighbors as competent to do business even while they considered him of unsound mind, and though he was not so manifestly insane as to make the conduct of the mortgagee fraudulent in making the bargain which it was meant to secure, notwithstanding the latter had been given sufficient warning to put him on his guard.[8]

Mere weakness of mind will not enable one to avoid a mortgage, unless it appears that his memory or reasoning faculties were seriously impaired.[9] A mortgage will not be set aside on account of the weakness

[4] Howell v. Griffiths (N. J.), 22 Atl. 928; Day v. Seely, 17 Vt. 542. So held in construing and applying a statute. Jacks v. Deering, 150 Cal. 272, 88 Pac. 909. Where a mortgagor is so demented that he is unable to understand the nature of the instrument, the mortgage is void. Farmers' Bank v. Normand, 3 Nebr. (unoff.) 643, 92 N. W. 723.

[5] Frederic v. Wilkins (Ala.), 62 So. 518; Jacks v. Estee, 139 Cal. 507, 73 Pac. 247; Dunn v. Evans, 139 Ga. 741, 78 S. E. 122; De Nieff v. Howell, 138 Ga. 248, 75 S. E. 202; Kelly v. Nusbaum, 244 Ill. 158, 91 N. E. 72; Beaty v. Hood, 229 Ill. 562, 82 N. E. 350; Coody v. Coody, 39 Okla. 719, 136 Pac. 754; Mansfield v. Hill, 56 Ore. 400, 107 Pac. 471; Du Bose v. Kell, 90 S. Car. 196, 71 S. E. 371; Caddell v. Caddell (Tex. Civ. App.), 131 S. W. 432;

Wampler v. Harrell, 112 Va. 635, 72 S. E. 135.

[6] Greene v. Maxwell, 251 Ill. 335, 96 N. E. 227; Altig v. Altig, 137 Iowa 420, 114 N. W. 1056; Terry v. Terry, 170 Mich. 330, 136 N. W. 448; Brugman v. Brugman, 93 Nebr. 408, 140 N. W. 781; Hacker v. Hoover, 89 Nebr. 317, 131 N. W. 734; Krings v. Krings, 43 Pa. Super. Ct. 590; Farmers' State Bank v. Farmer (Tex. Civ. App.), 157 S. W. 283; Cox v. Combs, 51 Tex. Civ. App. 346, 111 S. W. 1069.

[7] Brown v. Cory, 9 Kans. App. 702, 59 Pac. 1097.

[8] Curtis v. Brownell, 42 Mich. 165, 3 N. W. 936.

[9] Chancellor v. Donnell, 95 Ala. 342, 10 So. 910; White v. Farley, 81 Ala. 563, 8 So. 215; In re Carmichael, 36 Ala. 514; Stubbs v. Honston, 33 Ala. 555; Rawdon v. Raw-

of the mortgagor's intellect, unless advantage has been taken of such weakness in procuring the mortgage. This is the rule applicable to the execution of any deed.[10] The rule is the same in cases of impaired memory or advanced age.[11]

Allegations of undue influence in obtaining a mortgage from an aged and infirm debtor are not sufficient to warrant the setting aside of the mortgage, when it is not alleged that any fraud or deception was practiced upon him.[12]

In some cases parties dealing in good faith with insane persons, without knowledge of their insanity, will be protected in equity to the extent of the consideration paid, and a few cases have permitted foreclosure;[13] but a mortgage made by an insane person without any consideration is absolutely void,[14] and will not be upheld even in favor of an assignee of the mortgage who takes it relying upon the record, without knowledge of the mortgagor's insanity.[15] A mortgage or other conveyance of an insane person not under guardianship, is ordinarily held voidable and not absolutely void, and when made to one acting in good faith and without knowledge of the incompetency can only be avoided upon return of the consideration.[16]

§ 103a. Capacity of intoxicated persons.—One may lack the mental capacity to execute a mortgage where he is in such a state of intoxi-

don, 28 Ala. 565; Pidcock v. Potter, 68 Pa. St. 342, 8 Am. Rep. 181. An actual understanding of the effect of a mortgage or trust deed is not essential to its validity. McDaniels v. Sammons, 75 Ark. 139, 86 S. W. 997.

[10] Oxford v. Hopson, 73 Ark. 170, 83 S. W. 942; Jones v. Bolling, 101 Ark. 611, 141 S. W. 1168; Clarke v. Hartt, 56 Fla. 775, 47 So. 819; Johnson v. Coleman, 134 Ga. 696, 68 S. E. 480; McLaughlin v. McLaughlin, 241 Ill. 366, 89 N. E. 645; Thulin v. Anderson, 154 Ill. App. 41; Marmon v. Marmon, 47 Iowa 121; Paulus v. Reed, 121 Iowa 224, 96 N. W. 757; Altig v. Altig, 137 Iowa 420, 114 N. W. 1056; Slaughter v. McManigal, 138 Iowa 643, 116 N. W. 726; Tichy v. Simicek, 4 Nebr. (unoff.) 597, 95 N. W. 629; Kime v. Addlesperger, 24 Ohio Cir. Ct. 397; Woodville v. Woodville, 63 W. Va. 286, 60 S. E. 140; Black v. Post, 67 W. Va. 253, 67 S. E. 1072.

[11] Broaddus v. James, 13 Cal. App. 464, 110 Pac. 158; Bretthauer v. Fo-

ley, 15 Cal. App. 19, 113 Pac. 356; Sears v. Vaughan, 230 Ill. 572, 82 N. E. 881; Riordan v. Murray, 249 Ill. 517, 94 N. E. 947; Crosby v. Dorward, 248 Ill. 471, 94 N. E. 78; Howard v. Howard, 112 Va. 566, 72 S. E. 133.

[12] Reeves v. Lampley, 125 Ala. 449, 27 So. 840; Holt v. Agnew, 67 Ala. 360; Waddell v. Lanier, 62 Ala. 347; Lacy v. Rollins, 74 Tex. 566, 12 S. W. 314.

[13] Wiser v. Clinton, 82 Conn. 148, 72 Atl. 928; McCracken v. Levi, 24 Ohio Cir. Ct. 584; National Metal Edge Box Co. v. Vanderveer, 85 Vt. 488, 82 Atl. 837, 42 L. R. A. (N. S.) 343.

[14] D. M. Smith's Committee v. Forsythe, 28 Ky. L. 1034, 90 S. W. 1075; Bowman v. Wade, 54 Ore. 347, 103 Pac. 72; Tatum v. Tatum, 101 Va. 77, 43 S. E. 184.

[15] Hull v. Louth, 109 Ind. 315, 10 N. E. 270, 58 Am. Rep. 405.

[16] Coburn v. Raymond, 76 Conn. 484, 57 Atl. 116, 100 Am. St. 1000, citing numerous cases.

cation at the time of its execution as to be deprived of capacity to render an intelligent assent to the contract.[17]   The instrument is generally held void where executed by a drunkard under guardianship.[18]   Where it is sought to set aside such a mortgage it must be shown affirmatively that the transaction was fraudulent, or that undue influence was taken of the intoxicated vendor, or that such intoxication was produced or procured by the other party, or that he had notice of the vendor's intoxicated condition at the time of the execution of the mortgage.[19]   A mortgage will not, ordinarily, be set aside on the ground that the mind of the mortgagor was diseased by drink, where it is shown that his business dealings were conducted with skill, ability, shrewdness and memory and it furthermore appears that the mortgage was executed in conformity with an agreement made at a time when his sanity was unquestioned.[20]

An injunction to prevent a sale by a mortgagee was made perpetual, where it appeared that the mortgagor was in a condition verging upon insanity through habitual drunkenness, and the mortgagee, who had complete power over him, could not show that he had given any consideration for the mortgage.[21]

III. *Disability of Infancy*

SECTION
103b. Infants—Mortgage to relieve incumbrances.
104. Infants—Purchase-money mortgage — Avoidance — Necessaries.

SECTION
105. Ratification or disaffirmance of infant's mortgage.

§ 103b. Infants—Mortgage to relieve incumbrances.—If an infant purchases land subject to liens, of which he assumes the payment, and to pay these executes a mortgage, he can not upon coming of age retain the land and disaffirm the mortgage.[1]   Where the owner of a farm incumbered by mortgages and liens for half its value, entered into an agreement with his son, a minor, to convey the farm to him

---

[17] Hale v. Stery, 7 Colo. App. 165, 42 Pac. 598; Reinskopf v. Rogge, 37 Ind. 207; Youn v. Lamont, 56 Minn. 216, 57 N. W. 478; Tatum v. Tatum, 101 Va. 77, 43 S. E. 184.
[18] Cockrill v. Cockrill, 92 Fed. 811.
[19] Youn v. Lamont, 56 Minn. 216, 57 N. W. 478.
[20] Parker v. Marco, 76 Fed. 510.
[21] Van Horn v. Keenan, 28 Ill. 445. United States Mtg. Co. v. Sperry, 138 U. S. 313, 34 L. ed. 969, 11 Sup. Ct.

321, an able decision as to a guardian's power to mortgage in Illinois, written by Mr. Justice Harlan; Kingsbury v. Powers, 131 Ill. 182, 22 N. E. 479; Kingsbury v. Sperry, 119 Ill. 279, 10 N. E. 8; Bond v. Lockwood, 33 Ill. 213.
[1] MacGreal v. Taylor, 167 U. S. 688, 42 L. ed. 326, 17 Sup. Ct. 961; Langdon v. Clayson, 75 Mich. 204, 42 N. W. 805.

in consideration of the son's executing a mortgage to pay off these incumbrances and accordingly conveyed the farm to his son, who executed a mortgage, the proceeds of which were used to free the farm from incumbrances, the father representing to the mortgagee in the presence of his son that the latter was of legal age, it was held that the son upon arriving of age could not retain the land and disaffirm the mortgage.[2]

§ 104. **Infants—Purchase-money mortgage—Avoidance—Necessaries.**—An infant who has purchased land, and given back a mortgage for the purchase-money or a part of it, may, upon coming of age, avoid the transaction;[3] he may relinquish the property and reclaim the money paid on account of it.[4] But if he seeks to avoid the debt and mortgage, he must surrender and reconvey the property. If he continue to hold the estate and to apply it to his own uses, he affirms the mortgage and makes himself legally liable for its payment.[5]

The contract being voidable only, if he wishes to disaffirm it he must do so promptly upon coming of age.[6] A tender of a deed of reconveyance is generally held a sufficient disaffirmance to avoid a purchase-money mortgage given by the purchaser during infancy.[7] Where, however, he ratifies the conveyance to himself, he ratifies his mortgage for the purchase-money. They constitute one transaction,

[2] MacGreal v. Taylor, 167 U. S. 688, 42 L. ed. 326, 17 Sup. Ct. 961; United States Investment Co. v. Ulrickson, 84 Minn. 14, 86 N. W. 613; Johnson v. Northwest Mut. L. Ins. Co., 56 Minn. 365, 57 N. W. 934, 59 N. W. 992.

[3] Myers v. Knabe, 51 Kans. 720, 33 Pac. 602; Leavitt v. Files, 38 Kans. 26, 15 Pac. 891; Gribben v. Maxwell, 34 Kans. 8, 7 Pac. 584; Kane v. Kane, 13 App. Div. 544, 43 N. Y. S. 662. See also Pedro v. Pedro, 71 Misc. 296, 127 N. Y. S. 997; Hetterick v. Porter, 20 Ohio Cir. Ct. 110, 11 O. C. D. 145.

[4] Willis v. Twambly, 13 Mass. 204. By statute in Ohio a woman of the age of eighteen years may execute a valid conveyance. Rev. Stat. 1905, § 4836.

[5] Hubbard v. Cummins, 1 Maine 11; Badger v. Phinney, 15 Mass. 359, 8 Am. Dec. 105; Ready v. Pinkham, 181 Mass. 351, 63 N. E. 887; Young v. McKee, 13 Mich. 552; Roberts v.

Wiggin, 1 N. H. 73, 8 Am. Dec. 38; Robbins v. Eaton, 10 N. H. 561; Henry v. Root, 33 N. Y. 526, 553; Lynde v. Budd, 2 Paige (N. Y.) 191, 21 Am. Dec. 84; Kitchen v. Lee, 11 Paige (N. Y.) 107, 42 Am. Dec. 101; Coutant v. Servoss, 3 Barb. (N. Y.) 128; Bigelow v. Kinney, 3 Vt. 353, 21 Am. Dec. 589; Callis v. Day, 38 Wis. 643; Grace v. Whitehead, 7 Grant (U. C.) Ch. 591. If, however, the infant mortgagor spends the money borrowed before reaching majority, he may disaffirm without returning the money. Kane v. Kane, 13 App. Div. 544, 43 N. Y. S. 662.

[6] Pedro v. Pedro, 71 Misc. 296, 127 N. Y. S. 997; Loomer v. Wheelwright, 3 Sandf. Ch. (N. Y.) 135; Featherston v. McDonell, 15 U. C. C. P. 162.

[7] And such reconveyance is sufficient disaffirmance though the grantee's name is left blank. Kane v. Kane, 13 App. Div. 544, 43 N. Y. S. 662.

and he can not enjoy the one without being bound by the other.[8]   The infant is not allowed, after coming of age, to try his chances of gaining something by the transaction, and then, upon finding that he can not, to plead his disability.   If an action to foreclose the mortgage be brought after his coming of age, and he allows a decree of sale to be entered, he can not then, upon finding there is a deficiency instead of a surplus, escape liability for it by setting up his disability.[9]

The rule is the same in case a guardian purchases land for minor children and takes a deed to himself and them, and gives a mortgage for the purchase-money; the mortgage is good in equity against the minors who do not disclaim the title to the land vested in them.[10]

An infant's mortgage for necessaries is neither void nor voidable, and the services of an attorney in defending him in a criminal action are regarded as necessary, and the infant's mortgage to secure them is valid, but the recovery upon it may be reduced to the reasonable value of the services.   Though an infant's naked power of sale is void, the rule is different when the power of sale is coupled with an interest, as in a power of sale given in such a mortgage.   Such a power is voidable only, and is ratified by the infant's failure to pay or tender the reasonable value of the services within a reasonable time after reaching his majority.[11]

Whenever money has been received from the sale of lands or other sources by one who is the custodian of an infant, and the money applied to his use and benefit, the infant is estopped to assert the invalidity of the mortgage unless the purchaser can be put in statu quo, or the infant has made some offer of restoration, which, if accepted, would leave the mortgagee unharmed.[12]

An infant's mortgage being invalid, a power of sale in such mortgage is invalid, an infant being incapable of appointing an attorney. Upon a bill setting out the invalidity of a sale under the power, the infant, although he may have satisfied the mortgage, would be entitled to redeem.[13]

---

[8] Dana v. Coombs, 6 Maine 89, 19 Am. Dec. 194; Robbins v. Eaton, 10 N. H. 561; Heath v. West, 28 N. H. 101.

[9] Terry v. McClintock, 41 Mich. 492, 2 N. W. 787; Flynn v. Powers, 35 How. Pr. (N. Y.) 279.

[10] Peers v. McLaughlin, 88 Cal. 294, 26 Pac. 119, 22 Am. St. 306.

[11] Askey v. Williams, 74 Tex. 294, 11 S. W. 1101.

[12] Goodman v. Winter, 64 Ala. 410; Robertson v. Bradford, 73 Ala. 116; Pershing v. Wolfe, 6 Colo. App. 410, 40 Pac. 856; McClanahan v. West, 100 Mo. 309; Commonwealth v. Shuman, 18 Pa. St. 343.

[13] Rocks v. Cornell, 21 R. I. 532, 45 Atl. 552.

§ 105. Ratification or disaffirmance of infant's mortgage.—A mortgage given by an infant, being as a general rule voidable only and not void, he may, on coming of age, ratify it. This he may do in various ways. His payment of interest on the mortgage debt after coming of age is a ratification of the mortgage.[14] The mere retaining possession of land, for which he has given a mortgage for the purchase-money, is a ratification of the whole transaction, and makes him liable upon the mortgage.[15] So he may, on coming of age, make any other mortgage for his benefit good and effectual by recognizing or confirming it. His conveyance of the same land, after attaining his majority, subject to the mortgage, is a sufficient confirmation of it.[16] If he sells the land after reaching majority such sale will be considered a ratification of the mortgage.[17] A mortgage ratified after majority is superior to a deed made during minority and ratified subsequently to the mortgage.[18] A subsequent execution of a deed to a third person, which does not refer to the mortgage, does not necessarily amount to a repudiation of the mortgage.[19] And so a will made by one after coming of age, whereby he directed the payment of "all his just debts," is, upon his death, a sufficient confirmation of a mortgage and bond executed during his infancy to secure the payment of borrowed money.[20] An infant's mortgage being voidable merely, must be disaffirmed within a reasonable time after majority is attained.[21]

An infant's right to avoid his mortgage is a personal privilege of the infant only, and can not be availed of by others. Thus his assignee in insolvency is not permitted to disaffirm a mortgage made by the insolvent while under age, and not ratified or affirmed by him after attaining his majority.[22] The right to rescind his contract is for the protection of the infant, and he alone, or his heirs or representatives, can exercise it. A subsequent purchaser or lien-holder, or other person standing in the place of the infant, can not take advantage of

[14] American Mtg. Co. v. Wright, 101 Ala. 658, 14 So. 399.
[15] Callis v. Day, 38 Wis. 643, and cases cited.
[16] Phillips v. Green, 5 Mon. (Ky.) 355; Boston Bank v. Chamberlin, 15 Mass. 220; Keegan v. Cox, 116 Mass. 289; Allen v. Poole, 54 Miss. 323 (ratification by part payment); Lynde v. Budd, 2 Paige (N. Y.) 191, 21 Am. Dec. 84; Story v. Johnson, 2 Y. & C. Exch. 607.
[17] Hubbard v. Cummings, 1 Maine 11; Langdon v. Clayson, 75 Mich.

204, 42 N. W. 805; Uecker v. Koehn, 21 Nebr. 559, 32 N. W. 583, 90 Am. Rep. 849; Callis v. Day, 38 Wis. 643.
[18] Tolar v. Marion County Lumber Co., 93 S. Car. 274, 75 S. E. 545.
[19] Palmer v. Miller, 25 Barb. (N. Y.) 399.
[20] Merchants' Fire Ins. Co. v. Grant, 2 Edw. Ch. (N. Y.) 544.
[21] Lawder v. Larkin (Tex. Civ. App.), 94 S. W. 171.
[22] Mansfield v. Gordon, 144 Mass. 168, 10 N. E. 773.

this defense.[23] A mortgagee can not compel a present exercise by or for the infant of his right to affirm or disaffirm.[24]

Notice by a mortgagor, given at a foreclosure sale shortly after his removal of disability of nonage, that his interest would not pass under the sale, and the execution of a warranty deed of the same land shortly after such disability is removed has been held to constitute a disaffirmance of the mortgage.[25] An infant's trust deed may be disaffirmed by the execution of a mortgage upon the same premises shortly after his attaining majority.[26]

The subsequent ratification in all cases relates back to the original execution of the mortgage as against all persons except purchasers for a new and valuable consideration.[27]

It has been held, however, that a mortgage by an infant which was not in any way for his benefit, as, for instance, one made as surety for another, is not merely voidable, but void, and therefore not subject to ratification. Thus a mortgage given by an infant feme covert, to secure the debt of her husband, is held to be absolutely void, and incapable of confirmation.[28]

Coverture of a female infant does not remove the disability of minority. If she has given a mortgage of her land during her minority, her husband joining in it, she may repudiate it on coming of age, and she is not bound to return the consideration received unless she still has the proceeds of it in her hands specifically.[29] This disability of an infant feme covert is removed by statute in some states.[30] An infant feme covert can not relinquish her dower by joining with her husband in a mortgage, but the same is void as to her.[31]

---

[23] Baldwin v. Rosier, 48 Fed. 810.
[24] Watson v. Ruderman, 79 Conn. 687, 66 Atl. 515.
[25] Scott v. Brown, 106 Ala. 604, 17 So. 731.
[26] Phillips v. Hoskins, 33 Ky. L. 378, 108 S. W. 283.
[27] Palmer v. Miller, 25 Barb. (N. Y.) 399.
[28] Cronise v. Clark, 4 Md. Ch. 403; Chandler v. McKinney, 6 Mich. 217, 74 Am. Dec. 686.

[29] See Walsh v. Young, 110 Mass. 396, and cases cited; Dill v. Bowen, 54 Ind. 204; Losey v. Bond, 94 Ind. 67; Bradshaw v. Van Valkenburg, 97 Tenn. 316, 37 S. W. 88.
[30] Knight v. Coleman, 117 Ala. 266, 22 So. 974. See Jones on Real Property, § 37, Code of Alabama 1907, § 4499.
[31] Glenn v. Clark, 53 Md. 580.

IV. *Married Women* .

§ 106. Common-law disabilities—Statutes.—At common law a married woman could not make a mortgage even to secure the payment of the purchase-money of real estate conveyed to her. Both the mortgage and the note were void.[1] She had no power to make contracts.[2]

In equity, however, she has long occupied quite a different position in regard to her own property, and her power to contract in relation to it. In England the courts of equity have extended her rights over her separate estate and her liability for her contracts, until it is now the settled doctrine that her property is holden in equity for her engagements, whether in writing or not. Yet at law they can not be enforced. Her obligations are not strictly debts. She is not personally holden for them; but her separate estate is subjected to their payment. The proceeding to enforce them, therefore, is in the nature of a proceeding in rem.

In this country the common-law rights and liabilities of married women have been greatly changed by statute. Liberal provision is generally made in all the states for the holding of separate property by married women, and for their contracting in relation to it; but they have not generally gone to the extent of declaring that her entire .separate estate shall be liable for her pecuniary engagements. Under these statutes, as a rule, she is generally authorized to contract with reference to her separate property as if she were sole, and she is not

---

[1] Corinth Bank &c. Co. v. King (Ala.), 62 So. 704; Savage v. Holyoke, 59 Maine 345; Newbegin v. Langley, 39 Maine 200, 63 Am. Dec. 612; Heburn v. Warner, 112 Mass. 271, 17 Am. Rep. 86; Owens v. Johnson, 8 Baxt. (Tenn.) 265.

[2] Pickens v. Kniseley, 36 W. Va. 794, 15 S. E. 997.

allowed to impair her husband's tenancy by the curtesy, except with the concurrence of her husband.[3] Her deed made without such consent or authority is invalid, and can not be enforced even in equity.[4] Even when given to secure the purchase-money of the land, it does not amount to a declaration of trust in favor of the vendor.[5] Therefore a deed by her in the name she bore before marriage, and not disclosing this, although made with the fraudulent purpose of imposing upon the grantee, does not estop her from setting up title to the land as against the grantee.[6] Her sole deed is absolutely void at common law.[7]

§ 107. **Equity doctrine.**—The equity doctrine in England, adopted also in some of our states, is that the separate property of a married woman is answerable for her debts and engagements to the full extent to which it is subject to her disposal. At a very early period in England it was held that a married woman, although incompetent at law to make a valid contract, would be regarded in equity as a feme sole in respect to her separate estate.[8] "And the rule seems to have been universally recognized, where a married woman made an express

[3] As, for instance, in Massachusetts. See Rev. Laws 1902, ch. 153, p. 1; Weed Sewing Machine Co. v. Emerson, 115 Mass. 554; Concord Bank v. Bellis, 10 Cush. (Mass.) 276. But now, under Stat. 1874, ch. 184, a married woman may contract "as if she were sole," and therefore the consideration of her contracts need not inure to her own benefit. Major v. Holmes, 124 Mass. 108.

To pass any interest in her property she must be a party to the granting part of the deed. A mortgage which purports on its face to be that of her husband merely does not bind her estate, though she signs and acknowledges it. Berrigan v. Fleming, 2 Lea (Tenn.) 271. See also Equitable Bldg. &c. Assn. v. King, 48 Fla. 252, 37 So. 181.

[4] Elder v. Jones, 85 Ill. 384; Herdman v. Pace, 85 Ill. 345.

[5] Morrison v. Brown, 83 Ill. 562; Lewis v. Graves, 84 Ill. 205.

[6] Lowell v. Daniels, 2 Gray (Mass.) 161, 61 Am. Dec. 448.

[7] Warner v. Crouch, 14 Allen (Mass.) 163; Perrine v. Newell, 49 N. J. Eq. 57, 23 Atl. 492; Rake v. Lawshee, 24 N. J. L. 613; Moore v. Rake, 26 N. J. L. 574. In Perrine v. Newell, it was held, however, that the bond or note given by a married woman with her invalid mortgage is an acknowledgment of a debt due by her for the benefit of her separate estate. "Although the mortgage is not valid as such, it will nevertheless operate in equity as an appointment of the property described in it for the payment of that debt; and equity will decree that the debt be a charge upon the property so appointed, and that the property shall be sold to pay it. The debt is not a lien upon the estate until made so by the decree of this court. The lien is in virtue of the decree of this court, not in virtue of the mortgage." Citing Pentz v. Simonson, 13 N. J. Eq. 232; Wilson v. Brown, 13 N. J. Eq. 277; Harrison v. Stewart, 18 N. J. Eq. 451; Cutler v. Tuttle, 19 N. J. Eq. 549; Armstrong v. Ross, 20 N. J. Eq. 109; Perkins v. Elliott, 22 N. J. Eq. 127; on appeal, 23 N. J. Eq. 526; Homœopathic M. L. Ins. Co. v. Marshall, 32 N. J. Eq. 103, 2 Story Eq. Jur. § 1399.

[8] Grigby v. Cox, 1 Ves. Sen. 517; Peacock v. Monk, 2 Ves. Sen. 190.

contract respecting such an estate, of which she was entitled to the beneficial use, that she and the party with whom she contracted might have the aid of a court of equity to make the contract effectual."[9] Lord Thurlow[10] carried the doctrine further, and declared he had "no doubt about this principle, that if a court of equity says a feme covert may have a separate estate, the court will bind her to the whole extent, as to making that estate liable to her own engagement; as, for instance, for the payment of debts." This subject and the English authorities upon it were fully examined by Lord Brougham, who arrives at the same result.[11]

[9] Per Hoar, J., in Willard v. Eastham, 15 Gray (Mass.) 328, 77 Am. Dec. 366.

[10] Hulme v. Tenant, 1 Bro. C. C. 16; and see same case in White & Tudor's Lead. Cas. in Eq. (Am. ed.), 324, and the authorities there collected.

[11] In Murray v. Barlee, 3 Myl. & K. 209. "In all these cases," he says, "I take the foundation of the doctrine to be this: The wife has a separate estate, subject to her own control and exempt from all other interference or authority. If she can not affect it, no one can; and the very object of the settlement which vests it in her exclusively is to enable her to deal with it as if she were discovert. The power to affect it being unquestionable, the only doubt that can arise is whether or not she has validly incumbered it. At first the court seems to have supposed that nothing could touch it but some real charge, as a mortgage, or an instrument amounting to an execution of a power, where that view was supported by the nature of the settlement. But afterward her intention was more regarded, and the court only required to be satisfied that she intended to deal with her separate property. When she appeared to have done so, the court held her to have charged it, and made the trustees answer the demand thus created against it. A good deal of the nicety that attends the doctrine of powers thus came to be imparted to this consideration of the subject. If the wife did any act directly charging the separate estate no doubt could exist; just as an instrument expressing to be in execution of a power was always of course considered as made in execution of it. But so, if by any reference to the estate it could be gathered that such was her intent, the same conclusion followed. Thus, if she only executed a bond, or made a note, or accepted a bill, because those acts would have been nugatory if done by a feme covert, without any reference to her separate estate, it was held, in the cases I have above cited, that she must have intended to have designed a charge on that estate, since in no other way could the instrument thus made by her have any validity or operation; in the same manner as an instrument, which can mean nothing if it means not to execute a power, has been held to be made in execution of that power, though no direct reference is made to the power. Such is the principle. But doubts have been in one or two instances expressed as to the effect of any dealing whereby a general engagement only is raised, that is, where she becomes indebted without executing any written instrument at all. I own I can perceive no reason for drawing any such distinction. If, in respect of her separate estate, the wife is in equity taken as a feme sole, and can charge it by instruments absolutely void at law, can there be any reason for holding that her liability, or more properly her power of affecting the separate estate, shall only be exercised by a written instrument? Are we entitled to invent a rule, to add a new chapter to the statute of frauds, and to require writing where that

§ 108. Debts charged to separate property.—Equity enforces her contract on her separate property, because, her contract not being a personal liability, there is no remedy at law. Lord Cottenham,[21] agreeing in the doctrine established, was of opinion that in the reason of it there is nothing which has any resemblance to the execution of a power. "What it is, it is not easy to define. It has sometimes been treated as a disposing of the particular estate; but the contract is silent as to the particular estate, for a promissory note is merely a contract to pay, not saying out of what it is to be paid, or by what means it is to be paid; and it is not correct, according to legal principles, to say that a contract to pay is to be construed into a contract to pay out of a particular property, so as to constitute a lien on that property. Equity lays hold of the separate property, but not by virtue of anything expressed in the contract; and it is not very consistent with correct principles to add to the contract that which the party has not thought fit to introduce into it. The view taken of the matter by Lord Thurlow in Hulme v. Tenant is more logical. According to that view, the separate property of a married woman being a creature of equity, it follows that if she has a power to deal with it, she has the other power incident to property in general, namely, the power of contracting debts to be paid out of it; and inasmuch as her creditors have not the means at law of compelling payment of those debts, a court of equity takes upon itself to give effect to them, not as personal liabilities, but by laying hold of the separate property, as the only means by which they can be satisfied."

§ 109. American rule.—The American courts do not carry the doctrine to this extent, but as a general rule hold that her separate estate is not chargeable with her debts or obligations not relating to her separate estate, unless she specially makes them a charge upon it by some instrument in writing. Her contracts, which do not concern her separate estate and are not made upon its credit, remain void as they were at common law.[13] The statutes of the several states differ considerably in their effect upon her power to make

act requires none? Is there any equity, reaching written dealings with the property, which extends not also to dealing in other ways, as by sale and delivery of goods? Shall necessary supplies for her maintenance not touch the estate, and yet money furnished to squander away at play be a charge on it, if fortified by a scrap of writing? No such distinction can be taken upon any conceivable principle."

[12] Owens v. Dickenson, Cr. & Phil. 48.

[13] Pickens v. Kniseley, 36 W. Va. 794, 997. Except as to her separate estate, such obligation is void in equity as well as at law.

contracts, and to charge herself and her real estate with them; but, as a general rule, equity, while holding it not to be answerable for any implied undertaking of hers, will enforce upon it her mortgage or other express contract, although it be not made for her benefit, but for the sole benefit of another.[14] In a case in the Supreme Court of Massachusetts,[15] Mr. Justice Hoar, after a careful review of the authorities, said: "Our conclusion is, that when by the contract the debt is made expressly a charge upon the separate estate, or is expressly contracted upon its credit, or when the consideration goes to the benefit of such estate, or to enhance its value, then equity will decree that it shall be paid from such estate or its income, to the extent to which the power of disposal by the married woman may go. But when she is a mere surety, or makes the contract for the accommodation of another, without consideration received by her, the contract being void at law, equity will not enforce it against her estate, unless an express instrument makes the debt a charge upon it."

§ 110. **Reference to separate property—Notes and mortgages.**—
A married woman can bind herself personally only by such obligations as have reference to her separate property. She is not generally bound, therefore, by a note given by her alone or jointly with her hus-

---

[14] Young v. Graff, 28 Ill. 20; Heburn v. Warner, 112 Mass. 271, 17 Am. Rep. 86; Willard v. Eastham, 15 Gray (Mass.) 328, 77 Am. Dec. 366; Rogers v. Ward, 8 Allen (Mass.) 387, 85 Am. Dec. 710; Dyett v. Central Trust Co., 140 N. Y. 54, 35 N. E. 341; Yale v. Dederer, 18 N. Y. 265, 22 N. Y. 450, 72 Am. Dec. 503, 78 Am. Dec. 216; Owen v. Cawley, 36 N. Y. 600; Knowles v. McCamly, 10 Paige (N. Y.) 342; Gardner v. Gardner, 7 Paige (N. Y.) 112; Jaques v. Methodist Epis. Ch., 17 Johns. (N. Y.) 548; Curtis v. Engel, 2 Sandf. (N. Y.) 287; Cruger v. Cruger, 5 Barb. (N. Y.) 225; Ballin v. Dillaye, 37 N. Y. 35; White v. McNett, 33 N. Y. 371; White v. Story, 43 Barb. (N. Y.) 124; Ledlie v. Vrooman, 41 Barb. (N. Y.) 109.

The earlier cases in New York approximate to the English rule, but the case of Yale v. Dederer took the ground stated in the text, and has been followed since. See post § 111.

Special attention is called to the case of Yale v. Dederer for a full and careful examination of the subject; also to Corn Exchange Ins. Co. v. Babcock, 42 N. Y. 613, 1 Am. Rep. 601, where the English and American cases are reviewed.

[15] Willard v. Eastham, 15 Gray (Mass.) 328, 335, 77 Am. Dec. 366. Taylor v. Barker, 30 S. Car. 238, 9 S. E. 115. In this case a note had been given by a married woman to her brother to establish him in business; but no mortgage or other charge upon her separate estate was given. Upon a bill in equity to charge it upon her estate, it was held that she was not liable, and the bill was dismissed. But in the later case of Heburn v. Warner, 112 Mass. 271, where a married woman, to enable her son to borrow money, gave her note, secured by mortgage of her separate estate, it was held that, while she was not liable upon the note, and the mortgage was void at law, yet in equity the mortgage should be enforced. See also Nourse v. Henshaw, 123 Mass. 96.

band for a debt of the husband.[16] The fact that the note is secured by a mortgage on her real estate does not make the note such an obligation respecting her separate estate as to render her liable upon it,[17] although the mortgage itself be in equity a valid and binding lien upon her separate property.[18]

In some of the states a married woman may incumber her separate estate without her husband joining in the conveyance.[19] In states which require the joinder of the husband in mortgages of the wife's separate estate a mortgage of the separate estate of the wife in which he does not join is generally held invalid at law,[20] but equity may be invoked to enforce the lien against her estate.[21]

Where a wife gives her husband an absolute deed to be used as a mortgage in procuring a loan, renewal loans, made in reliance upon the security of the deed after the death of the wife, are valid liens upon the land.[22]

Where the wife joins in the deed of the husband, to relinquish her dower and effectuate a valid alienation of the homestead, she is not a covenantor in the covenants of seisin, warranty of title and against incumbrances contained in the deed. The joinder of a wife in a

---

[16] Stafford Sav. Bank v. Underwood, 54 Conn. 2, 4 Atl. 248; Rowell v. Jewett, 69 Maine 293; Brookings v. White, 49 Maine 479; Nourse v. Henshaw, 123 Mass. 96; Heburn v. Warner, 112 Mass. 271; Athol Machine Co. v. Fuller, 107 Mass. 437; Willard v. Eastham, 15 Gray (Mass.) 328, 77 Am. Dec. 366; Burns v. Lynde, 6 Allen (Mass.) 305; Graham v. Myers, 67 Mich. 277, 34 N. W. 710; Northwestern Mutual Life Ins. Co. v. Mallory, 93 Nebr. 579, 141 N. W. 190; Wilson v. Mills, 66 N. H. 315, 22 Atl. 455; Conway v. Wilson, 44 N. J. Eq. 457, 11 Atl. 607; White v. McNett, 33 N..Y. 371; Yale v. Dederer, 18 N. Y. 265; Ledlie v. Vrooman, 41 Barb. (N. Y.) 109. In Rhode Island a mortgage given by a husband and wife to secure the husband's note is valid though the wife is not bound on the note. Thacker v. Medbury, 33 R. I. 37, 80 Atl. 186.

[17] Williams v. Hayward, 117 Mass. 532.

[18] Thacher v. Churchill, 118 Mass. 108; Thacker v. Medbury, 33 R. I. 37, 80 Atl. 186; Dearing v. Jordan (Tex. Civ. App.), 130 S. W. 876.

[19] Stacey v. Walter, 125 Ala. 291, 28 So. 89, 82 Am. St. 235; Williamson v. Yager, 91 Ky. 282, 15 S. W. 660, 34 Am. St. 184; Turner v. Shaw, 96 Mo. 22, 8 S. W. 897, 9 Am. St. 319; Richardson v. De Giverville 107 Mo. 422, 17 S. W. 974, 28 Am St. 426; Farmers' Exchange Bank v. Hageluken, 165 Mo. 443, 65 S W. 728, 88 Am. St. 434. A mortgage by a married woman of property in which her husband has a freehold interest is void if his name does not appear therein as grantor; though he signs and acknowledges it. Dietrich v. Hutchinson, 73 Vt. 134, 50 Atl. 810, 87 Am. St. 698.

[20] Starkey v. Starkey, 166 Ind. 140, 76 N. E. 876; Bogie v. Nelson, 151 Ky. 443, 152 S. W. 250; Densch v. Questa, 116 Ky. 474, 25 Ky. L. 707, 76 S. W. 329; Realty Title &c. Co. v. Schaaf, 81 N. J. Eq. 115, 85 Atl. 602. Where a husband is a nonresident his joinder in wife's mortgage is unnecessary, Collier v. Doe, 142 Ala. 422, 38 So. 244.

[21] Realty Title &c. Co. v. Schaaf, 81 N. J. Eq. 115, 85 Atl. 602.

[22] Strong v. Gambier, 155 App. Div. 294, 140 N. Y. S. 410.

mortgage by her husband, of land conveyed to him by a deed expressly reserving to the wife a lien for prior advances by her to the grantor operates simply as a relinquishment of her dower therein, and of the homestead.[23]

Where a married woman is empowered by statute to bargain, sell, and convey her real estate or personal property, and enter into contracts in reference to it, she may deal with the property itself, by sale or otherwise, and assume obligations in connection therewith, as, for instance, for buildings upon her land; and she may bind herself to pay money for property purchased, as the property will become hers by the purchase, and the obligation to pay is in reference to her separate property.[24] But this is the limit of her power. She can not contract as surety for her husband or for any one else. The character of a note or other contract made by her is not affected as a contract applying to her separate property by reason that it is secured by a mortgage on her land. The mortgage is collateral to the note; the one is the principal, the other the incident; when the note is void the mortgage is void also, and can not be foreclosed at law.[25] "In an action brought by a mortgagee against his mortgagor, on a mortgage given to secure the payment of a note, the defendant may show the same matters of defense which he might show in defense of an action on the note,"[26] excepting only that he can not plead the statute of limitations.[27]

In foreclosure, the burden is upon defendant to prove coverture of the mortgagor, and execution of the mortgage by her as surety, together with knowledge of such facts by the mortgagee.[28]

But a married woman may, with the proper assent of her husband, convey her separate real estate; and if there be a valid consideration for the conveyance, it is as effectual as it would be if she were not married. She may, therefore, convey her real estate in mortgage to secure a valid debt, as, for instance, a valid note of her husband. Her mortgage is then binding, because it is a contract entered into by her in relation to her separate property, and to secure a valid and existing

---

[23] Curry v. American Freehold Land Mtg. Co., 107 Ala. 429, 18 So. 328.

[24] Heburn v. Warner, 112 Mass. 271, 17 Am. Rep. 86, and cases cited.

[25] Brigham v. Potter, 14 Gray (Mass.) 522; Denny v. Dana, 2 Cush. (Mass.) 160, 48 Am. Dec. 655. But see McGee v. Cunningham, 69 S. Car. 470, 48 S. E. 473.

[26] Mr. Justice Metcalf, in Winton v. King, 4 Allen (Mass.) 562.

[27] Thayer v. Mann, 19 Pick. (Mass.) 535.

[28] Webb v. John Hancock Mut. Life Ins. Co., 162 Ind. 616, 69 N. E. 1006, 66 L. R. A. 632.

debt.[29] A statutory provision that the separate property of a married woman shall not be liable for the debts of the husband does not affect her power to mortgage her land to secure the payment of her husband's debt.[30]

It does not matter that she has also signed her husband's note as surety. To a suggestion in such a case that the mortgage was void, because it was made to secure a note signed by the married woman as surety, Chief Justice Bigelow said:[31] "This might be a very sound argument if the note was signed by the married woman alone. In such case, the note being void, the demandant would not be entitled to judgment for possession. But the note is not void. It is a valid contract binding on the other promisors. It is, therefore, the ordinary case of the conveyance of real estate by a valid deed to secure the payment of debt due to the grantee." But when her mortgage is made to secure her own note given for the accommodation of her husband or any one else, the note being void, the security incident to it is void also. She can make the defense of invalidity in the same way that any mortgagor may defend on the ground of want of consideration, or of duress. Her defense at law to the note extends to the mortgage.

§ 111. **Deficiency upon foreclosure.**—The foregoing examination of the question, how far a married woman can bind herself individually by her contracts, is applicable to the question of her liability for a deficiency[32] arising upon the foreclosure of a mortgage upon her estate. It has been noticed that, while in equity the lien upon her estate may be valid, her note or other personal obligation secured may be wholly void.[33] Of course in such case, when the remedy has been exhausted against the mortgaged estate, there is no further remedy against her.[34] If, for instance, she borrow money upon a mort-

---

[29] Newhart v. Peters, 80 N. Car. 166. In North Carolina a conveyance by a married woman not a "free trader" is not valid unless executed by her and her husband, with a privy examination before the magistrate. Her recital in her mortgage that she is a "free trader" does not make her such if she has not filed the prescribed writing in the registry of deeds. Williams v. Walker, 111 N. Car. 604, 16 S. E. 706. Code, §§ 1827, 1834. See post § 113.

[30] Hitz v. Jenks, 123 U. S. 297, 31 L. ed. 156, 8 Sup. Ct. 143.

[31] Bartlett v. Bartlett, 4 Allen (Mass.) 440.

[32] See post § 1718.

[33] Heburn v. Warner, 112 Mass. 271.

[34] Adams v. Fry, 29 Fla. 318, 10 So. 559; Nourse v. Henshaw, 123 Mass. 96; Kidd v. Conway, 65 Barb. (N. Y.) 158.

Prior to the Stat. of 1860, ch. 90, it was held in New York that a married woman could not bind herself personally for the price of real estate bought by her and conveyed to her; Knapp v. Smith, 27 N. Y. 277; nor for the rent re-

gage of her real estate for the accommodation of her husband, and it is paid to him, she is under no liability for any deficiency after the application of the property to the repayment of the loan.[35]

A married woman is not liable for a deficiency, where the consideration for the note and mortgage, given by herself and husband, does not inure to her private use or benefit her separate property.[36] A married woman may bind herself personally for a loan made to her upon her mortgage of her real estate, if the loan be for the benefit of her separate estate.[37] That the loan is for the benefit of her separate estate may appear by the mortgage, or may be shown by evidence.[38] The burden of proving the loan a benefit to the wife's separate estate is upon the mortgagee.[39] Where part of the loan is used for the wife's benefit and the balance for the debt of the husband, the wife may repudiate the mortgage, except as to the part used for her benefit.[40]

§ 112. **Separate estate in equity—Power to contract under statutes.**—In some states a wife's separate property is in equity held

served upon a lease to her, though the lease itself was otherwise valid, and the lessor might re-enter. So a mortgage for the price of real estate conveyed to her was valid in equity, though the note or bond given in connection with it was not. Since the above statute, she can bind herself for any matter pertaining to her separate estate.

[35] White v. McNett, 33 N. Y. 371; Payne v. Burnham, 62 N. Y. 69; Manhattan Brass &c. Co. v. Thompson, 58 N. Y. 80.

In New York, by Laws 1882, ch. 172, § 7, it was provided that a married woman might be sued in any court, and a judgment recorded against her may be enforced against her sole and separate estate in the same manner as if she were sole. The effect of this statute is to give a legal remedy against her property generally for her debts, and not merely a remedy in equity against her estate expressly charged with the payment of a debt for which she was not personally liable. Corn Exchange Ins. Co. v. Babcock, 42 N. Y. 613; First Nat. Bank v. Garlinghouse, 53 Barb. (N. Y.) 615; Andrews v. Monilaws, 8 Hun (N. Y.) 65.

[36] Loizeaux v. Fremder, 123 Wis. 193, 101 N. W. 423.

[37] Booth Mercantile Co. v. Murphy, 14 Idaho 212, 93 Pac. 777; Payne v. Burnham, 62 N. Y. 69; Littler v. Dielmann, 48 Tex. Civ. App. 392, 106 S. W. 1137. Otherwise in Pennsylvania. Sawtelle's Appeal, 84 Pa. St. 306. A decree of foreclosure against husband and wife is conclusive as to the liability of the wife in proceedings for a deficiency. Christian v. Soderberg, 124 Mich. 54, 82 N. W. 819. Under the constitution and statutes of Florida a married woman may mortgage her separate statutory estate in order to carry on mercantile business on the premises. Mercantile Exch. Bank v. Taylor, 51 Fla. 473, 41 So. 22.

Where a married woman borrowed money ostensibly for her own use and benefit, a bona fide holder of the note and mortgage is protected although the money was used by the husband. Josephson v. Powers, 123 La. 5, 48 So. 564. See also American Mtg. Co. v. Woodward, 83 S. Car. 521, 65 S. E. 739.

[38] Corn Exch. Ins. Co. v. Babcock, 42 N. Y. 613.

[39] Opelousas Nat. Bank v. Fahey, 129 La. 225, 55 So. 772, Ann Cas. 1913 B, 687.

[40] Wredman v. Falls City Sav. &c. Assn., 40 Ind. App. 478, 82 N. E. 476.

liable generally for her debts.[41] As to her separate property she is regarded as a feme sole, and is allowed to make any contract in relation to it she may choose; and if she executes a note secured by a mortgage upon her separate property, her promise to pay is construed as relating not only to the mortgaged premises, but to her separate property generally.[42] It is regarded as right that her property should pay her pecuniary engagements, whether they are made for her own benefit or not, and whether they are charged upon particular property or not. Neither does it matter whether her engagements be express or implied; whether they be in writing or by parol merely. Having the power to contract debts, and to bind her separate property for their payment, she is regarded as intending that her obligations shall be enforced according to their purport.

In other states the capacity of married women to make contracts has been enlarged by statute, so that in effect she is enabled to bind herself and her property as if she were sole.[43] In such states her

[41] Alexander v. Bouton, 55 Cal. 15; Cummings v. Sharpe, 21 Ind. 331; Deering v. Boyle, 8 Kans. 525, 12 Am. Rep. 480 (where the cases are fully examined); Smith v. Wilson, 2 Metc. (Ky.) 235; Johnston v. Ferguson, 2 Metc. (Ky.) 503; Sharp v. Proctor, 5 Bush (Ky.) 396; Hobson v. Hobson, 8 Bush (Ky.) 665; Webb v. Hoselton, 4 Nebr. 308, 19 Am. Rep. 638; Johnson v. Cummins, 16 N. J. Eq. 97, 84 Am. Dec. 142; Wheaton v. Phillips, 12 N. J. Eq. 221; Pentz v. Simonson, 13 N. J. Eq. 232; Glass v. Warwick, 40 Pa. St. 140, 80 Am. Dec. 566; Goll v. Fehr, 131 Wis. 141, 111 N. W. 235; Todd v. Lee, 15 Wis. 365; Heath v. Van Cott, 9 Wis. 516; 1 Bishop on Mar. Women, § 873; Schouler's Dom. Relations, 230.

[42] Alexander v. Bouton, 55 Cal. 15; Marlow v. Barlew, 53 Cal. 456.

[43] California: Civil Code 1903, §§ 158, 162. Property acquired after marriage by either husband or wife, or by both, is community property, of which the husband has the management and control with absolute power of disposition, except by will. Property conveyed to a married woman by an instrument in writing is presumed to vest in her as her separate property. Civil Code 1903, §§ 164, 172. See Rosenberg v. Ford, 85 Cal. 610, 24 Pac. 779. If real

estate be purchased with such property, and the title be taken in the name of the wife, a mortgage of it by her creates no lien. Yet if the husband dies, and the wife inherits the property, the mortgage becomes a lien on her interest. Parry v. Kelley, 52 Cal. 334. The fact that a note and mortgage were given by a wife while living apart from her husband does not of itself prove that the lands mortgaged were her separate property. McComb v. Spangler, 71 Cal. 418, 12 Pac. 347.

Georgia: Act of 1866; Code 1911, §§ 2993, 3007, 3011; Hawkins v. Taylor, 61 Ga. 171; Tift v. Mayo, 61 Ga. 246; Harrold v. Westbrook, 78 Ga. 5, 2 S. E. 695. But the Const. of 1877, § 3, art. 9, prohibits the mortgaging of a homestead. Planters' Loan &c. Bank v. Dickinson, 83 Ga. 711, 10 S. E. 446. Code 1895, § 2488, declares that "the wife is a feme sole as to her separate estate, unless controlled by the settlement. But, while a wife may contract, she can not bind her separate estate by any contract of suretyship, nor by any assumption of the debts of her husband." But a mortgage under a settlement to secure the debt of the husband is valid. Ætna Ins. Co. v. Brodinax, 48 Fed. 892, 9 Sup. Ct. 61.

Indiana: Burns' Ann. Stat. 1914, § 7853; provided her husband joined

mortgage of her separate real estate is effectual, whether executed by her alone or jointly with her husband.

§ 113. Debts of husband.—In some states a married woman may make a valid mortgage of her separate property to secure the payment of the debt of her husband or of any other person, in the same manner as if she were unmarried.[44] Any consideration which would be suffi-

with her. Layman v. Schultz, 60 Ind. 541; Brick v. Scott, 47 Ind. 299.

Kentucky: See Woods v. Davis, 153 Ky. 99, 154 S. W. 905.

Louisiana: A married woman can not mortgage her estate without judicial authority. Stuffier v. Puckett, 30 La. Ann. 811.

Massachusetts: P. S. 1882, ch. 147, § 1; Rev. Laws 1902, ch. 153, § 1, p. 1359; Nourse v. Henshaw, 123 Mass. 96; Frickee v. Donner, 35 Mich. 151.

Minnesota: Gen. Stat. 1913, ch. 72, §§ 7143-4; Northwestern Mut. Life Ins. Co. v. Allis, 23 Minn. 337; Sandwich Mfg. Co. v. Zellmer, 48 Minn. 408, 51 N. W. 379.

[44] Stephen v. Beall, 22 Wall. (U. S.) 329, 22 L. ed. 786; Parsons v. Denis, 2 McCrary (U. S.) 359; De Roux v. Girard, 105 Fed. 798, 112 F'ed. 89. Harper v. McGoogan (Ark.), 154 S. W. 187; Collins v. Wassell, 34 Ark. 17, 33; Johnson v. Graham Bros. Co., 98 Ark. 274, 135 S. W. 853; Goodrum v. Merchants' &c. Bank of England, 102 Ark. 326, 144 S. W. 198; Marlow v. Barlew, 53 Cal. 456; Stafford Sav. Bank v. Underwood, 54 Conn. 2, 4 Atl. 248; Lynch v. Moser, 72 Conn. 714, 46 Atl. 153; Dzialynski v. Bank, 23 Fla. 346, 2 So. 696.

In Alabama, the statute in effect inhibits the mortgaging of the wife's property as security for her husband's debt. But the joinder of a wife in a mortgage with her husband without expressly limiting her execution to a release of dower, does not raise a presumption that the mortgage embraces her separate property. Burgess v. Blake, 128 Ala. 105, 28 So. 963. For Alabama cases see post § 117. Josephson v. Powers, 123 La. 5, 48 So. 564; Comegys v. Clarke, 44 Md. 108; Plummer v. Jarman, 44 Md. 632; Mich. Ann. Stat. 1913, § 11545

note; Marx v. Bellel, 114 Mich. 631; Watson v. Thurber, 11 Mich. 457; Smith v. Osborn, 33 Mich. 410; Just v. State Sav. Bank, 132 Mich. 600, 94 N. W. 200; Kieldsen v. Blodgett, 113 Mich. 655 (consideration of husband's debt sufficient); Sandwich Mfg. Co. v. Zellmer, 48 Minn. 408, 51 N. W. 379; Insurance Co. v. Allis, 23 Minn. 337; Campbell v. Tompkins, 32 N. J. Eq. 170; Conover v. Grover, 31 N. J. Eq. 539; Tooker v. Sloan, 30 N. J. Eq. 394; Robbins v. Abrahams, 5 N. J. Eq. 465; Conway v. Wilson, 44 N. J. Eq. 457, 11 Atl. 607; Hallowell v. Daly (N. J. Eq.), 56 Atl. 234; Pape v. Ludeman (N. J. Eq.), 59 Atl. 9; Demarest v. Wynkoop, 3 Johns. Ch. (N. Y.) 129, 144, 8 Am. Dec. 467; Foreman's Ins. Co. v. Bay, 4 Barb. (N. Y.) 407; Newhart v. Peters, 80 N. Car. 166; Moore v. Fuller, 6 Ore. 272, 25 Am. Rep. 524; Gable's Appeal (Pa.), 7 Atl. 52; Kuhn v. Ogilvie, 178 Pa. St. 303, 35 Atl. 957; Siebert v. Bank, 186 Pa. St. 233, 40 Atl. 472; Righter v. Livingston, 214 Pa. 28, 63 Atl. 195.

In Indiana, under Acts 1879, p. 160, Rev. Stat. 1881, § 5119, which provided that a married woman should not mortgage her separate property acquired by descent, devise, or gift, as security for the debt of any other person, a mortgage executed by her to secure her husband's debt on land acquired by purchase, was not void or voidable. Gardner v. Case, 111 Ind. 494, 13 N. E. 36. A mortgage properly executed by a married woman upon her separate real estate is a valid and binding security, unless it constitutes a contract of suretyship. Johnson v. Jouchert, 124 Ind. 105, 24 N. E. 580. Such mortgage by her of her land to secure a loan, the proceeds of which are partly used to purchase land, the title to which is taken in her name, is valid to the extent so used;

cient to support the obligation if made by any one else, as, for instance, the granting of the original loan, or a subsequent extension of

Johnson v. Jouchert, 124 Ind. 105, 24 N. E. 580; Jouchert v. Johnson, 108 Ind. 436, 9 N. E. 413; Vogel v. Leichner, 102 Ind. 55, 1 N. E. 554; Noland v. State, 115 Ind. 529, 18 N. E. 26; Morgan v. Street, 28 Ind. App. 131; though invalid to the extent the proceeds are for the husband's benefit.' The burden of proving that a wife's mortgage securing her own note is invalid under this statute is upon the party who contests its validity. Field v. Noblett, 154 Ind. 357; Crisman v. Leonard, 126 Ind. 202, 25 N. E. 1101; Miller v. Shields, 124 Ind. 166, 24 N. E. 670. Otherwise when the note is by husband and wife. Crisman v. Leonard, 126 Ind. 202, 25 N. E. 1101; Cupp v. Campbell, 103 Ind. 213, 2 N. E. 565; Vogel v. Leichner, 102 Ind. 55, 1 N. E. 554. A mortgage is not within the prohibition of the statute when the consideration upon which it was executed inured to the benefit of the married woman, or to the benefit of her estate. Badger v. Hoover, 120 Ind. 193, 21 N. E. 888. If the mortgage is upon the joint property of both husband and wife, and is made to secure a loan obtained upon their joint application, the burden is upon them to show that the consideration was not obtained and used for the benefit of their joint estate. Security Co. v. Arbuckle, 119 Ind. 69, 21 N. E. 469; Jenne v. Burt, 121 Ind. 275, 22 N. E. 256. Such a mortgage made to secure the husband's note, or debt, though given in payment for the land, is void as to the wife. Stewart v. Babbs, 120 Ind. 568, 22 N. E. 770; State v. Kennett, 114 Ind. 160, 16 N. E. 173; Jones v. Ewing, 107 Ind. 313, 6 N. E. 819; Pritchett v. McGaughey, 151 Ind. 638, 52 N. E. 397; Shaw v. Jones, 156 Ind. 60, 59 N. E. 166. The provision against a married woman becoming a surety was intended for her protection alone, and the defense of coverture can not be made solely for the benefit of a third person. A stranger can not set up this defense. Johnson v. Jouchert, 124 Ind. 105, 24 N. E. 580. As is in

effect said in Sutton v. Aiken, 62 Ga. 733, 741, the purpose of the statute is economical, not moral; and its policy is in favor of a class, and not of the public at large.

Under this statute a mortgage by a married woman upon her separate real estate, owned by herself and husband by entireties, is voidable by her. McCormick Harvesting Machine Co. v. Scovell, 111 Ind. 551, 13 N. E. 58; Dodge v. Kinzy, 101 Ind. 102; Crooks v. Kennett, 111 Ind. 347, 12 N. E. 715; Bridges v. Blake, 106 Ind. 332, 6 N. E. 833; Fawkner v. Scottish-American Mtg. Co., 107 Ind. 555, 8 N. E. 689; Vogel v. Leichner, 102 Ind. 55, 1 N. E. 554; McLead v. Ætna L. Ins. Co., 107 Ind. 394, 8 N. E. 230.

Under this act a married woman may convey her land to her husband to enable him to secure a loan by mortgage. Long v. Crossman, 119 Ind. 3, 21 N. E. 450; Trimble v. State, 145 Ind. 154, 44 N. E. 260; Grzesk v. Hibberd, 149 Ind. 354, 48 N. E. 361; Wilson v. Logue, 131 Ind. 191, 30 N. E. 1079. Whether husband's mortgage of land which belonged to husband and wife as tenants by entireties, and was conveyed to him through a third person is void, see Government Bldg. &c. Inst. v. Denny, 154 Ind. 261, 55 N. E. 757. If conveyance to a third person was without consideration, the mortgage is voidable both as to wife and as to husband. Abicht v. Searls, 154 Ind. 594, 57 N. E. 246. See Burns' Ind. Ann. Stat. 1914, § 7852.

But where one in good faith, and without notice, advances money on a mortgage executed by a married woman and her husband, on the faith of the representations of the mortgagors that the money is for the sole benefit of the wife, he is not affected by a secret agreement between the husband and the wife that the money should be used by the husband in his business. Ward v. Berkshire Life Ins. Co., 108 Ind. 301, 9 N. E. 361.

Iowa Code, § 2506; Low v. Anderson, 41 Iowa 476.

the time of payment of the debt, is sufficient to support her undertaking.[45] Her mortgage, given to secure the payment of the bond of her husband, will not be regarded as having no validity or binding effect simply because the consideration of the bond is an obligation merely moral, and not enforcible at law or in equity.[46] Whatever conflict there may be in the authorities as to the ability of a wife to charge herself personally for any debts not contracted for her own benefit, there is a general unanimity in holding that a mortgage upon her property may be enforced against that, whether made for her benefit or not.[47]

In Kentucky, a married woman may mortgage her separate estate to pay her own debt created for her own benefit; Hounshell v. Insurance Co., 81 Ky. 304; but she can not make such a mortgage to secure a debt of her husband. Merchants' &c. Loan &c. Assn. v. Jarvis, 92 Ky. 566, 18 S. W. 454; Lane v. Traders' Deposit Bank (Ky.), 21 S. W. 756; Miller v. Sanders, 98 Ky. 535, 33 S. W. 621.

In Missouri she may mortgage her property not held to her separate use for any purpose. Rev. Stat. 1889, § 2396; Meads v. Hutchinson, 111 Mo. 620, 19 S. W. 1111; Ferguson v. Soden, 111 Mo. 208, 19 S. W. 727; Rosenheim v. Hartsock, 90 Mo. 357, 2 S. W. 473; Wilcox v. Todd, 64 Mo. 388; Thornton v. Bank, 71 Mo. 221; Hagerman v. Sutton, 91 Mo. 519, 4 S. W. 73; Rines v. Mansfield, 96 Mo. 394, 9 S. W. 798. The mortgage is valid though the debt is evidenced by the wife's void note, the debt being a valid one. Meads v. Hutchinson, 111 Mo. 620, 19 S. W. 1111; Bell v. Bell, 133 Mo. App. 570, 113 S. W. 667.

In South Carolina, a mortgage by a married woman of her separate estate, which shows on its face that it was given to secure a debt of her husband, was till recently void under the constitution and statutes of the state. Aultman v. Rush, 26 S. Car. 517, 2 S. E. 402; Habenicht v. Rawls, 24 S. Car. 461, 58 Am. Rep. 268; Harris v. McCaslan, 31 S. Car. 420, 10 S. E. 104; Carrigan v. Drake, 36 S. Car. 354, 15 S. E. 339. Her mortgage for the benefit of her husband was void, provided the lender had knowledge of such intended use. Bates v. Am. Mtg. Co., 37 S. Car. 88, 16 S. E. 883; Tribble v. Poore, 30 S. Car. 97, 8 S. E. 541; Gwynn v. Gwynn, 31 S. Car. 482, 10 S. E. 221; Greig v. Smith, 29 S. Car. 426, 7 S. E. 610; Goodgion v. Vaughn, 32 S. Car. 499, 11 S. E. 351; Salinas v. Turner, 33 S. Car. 231, 11 S. E. 702; Chambers v. Bookman, 32 S. Car. 455, 11 S. E. 349. The amount of the husband's debt included in the mortgage was, upon foreclosure, deducted in computing the amount due. Brown v. Prevost, 28 S. Car. 123, 5 S. E. 274; Erwin v. Lowry, 31 S. Car. 330, 9 S. E. 961. But now, by Act 1887, p. 819, any mortgage affecting her separate estate, executed by a married woman, is made a charge on her separate estate, whenever the intention to do so is declared in such mortgage. When such intention is declared by a married woman she is bound thereby, though in fact the mortgage was given to secure her husband's debt, and the mortgagee had knowledge of the fact. Scottish-American Mtg. Co. v. Mixson, 38 S. Car. 432, 17 S. E. 244; Ellis v. American Mtg. Co., 36 S. Car. 45, 15 S. E. 267; Reid v. Stevens, 38 S. Car. 519, 17 S. E. 358.

Eaton v. Dewey, 79 Wis. 251, 48 N. W. 523, where it was held that the husband might make a mortgage of his wife's land partly for his own benefit, there being no evidence of collusion between the husband and the mortgagee. See anté §§ 109, 110.

[45] Short v. Battle, 52 Ala. 456; Low v. Anderson, 41 Iowa 476.

[46] Campbell v. Tompkins, 32 N. J. Eq. 170.

[47] A married woman may mort-

The mortgage of a married woman upon her property, given to secure a debt of her husband, but taken by the mortgagee in good faith, and without fraud on his part, will seldom, if ever be set aside, even on proof that her husband procured her execution of it by fraudulent representations.[48] A wife having executed a paper at the request of her husband, without reading it or inquiring as to the contents of it, although it was a mortgage of her property, the mortgagee having no knowledge of this fact, was not allowed to restrain the delivery of it, on the ground that it was procured by fraud or deceit.[49] But the court will refuse to enforce a mortgage, the execution of which by the wife was procured by harshness and threats on the part of the husband so excessive as to subjugate and control the freedom of her will;[50] or one procured by the husband as agent for his creditor upon a false representation that the consideration of it was merchandise to be shipped to her for her use in her separate business.[51] The plea of coverture is a personal privilege, and a mere creditor of a married woman will not, ordinarily, be allowed to attack her mortgage on the ground that it was given to secure her husband's debt.[2]

It is provided by statute in many of the states that a married woman shall not mortgage nor enter into a contract to mortgage her separate real estate, unless her husband join in such mortgage.[53]

§ 113a. Consideration for wife's mortgage.—The mortgage of a married woman is not valid unless made for a valid consideration.[54]

gage her land to raise money to pay a debt of her husband, although the mortgagee had knowledge of the purpose of the mortgage, if this is not made directly to the husband's creditor. Chastain v. Peak, 111 Ga. 889, 36 S. E. 967; Nelms v. Keller, 103 Ga. 745, 30 S. E. 572.

[48] Spurgin v. Traub, 65 Ill. 170. Text quoted with approval in Collins v. Wassell, 34 Ark. 17, 33.

[49] Comegys v. Clarke, 44 Md. 108. See also Mersman v. Werges, 112 U. S. 139, 28 L. ed. 641, 5 Sup. Ct. 65; Freeman v. Wilson, 51 Miss. 329.

[50] Central Bank v. Copeland, 18 Md. 305, 81 Am. Dec. 597. But where the payee of the mortgage had no notice of threats or duress of the husband, a finding in his favor is proper. Johnson v. A. Leffler Co., 122 Ga. 670, 50 S. E. 488.

[51] Haskit v. Elliott, 58 Ind. 493.
[52] Hawes v. Glover, 126 Ga. 305, 55 S. E. 62.
[53] Interstate Bldg. &c. Assn. v. Agricola, 124 Ala. 474, 27 So. 247; Burns' Ind. Ann. Stat. 1914, § 7853; McLead v. Ætna Co., 107 Ind. 394, 8 N. E. 230; Starkey v. Starkey, 166 Ind. 140, 76 N. E. 876; Field v. Campbell, 164 Ind. 389, 72 N. E. 260, 108 Am. St. 301; Deusch v. Questa, 116 Ky. 474; 76 S. W. 329; Weber v. Tanner, 23 Ky. L. 1107, 64 S. W. 741; Dietrich v. Hutchinson, 73 Vt. 134, 50 Atl. 810, 87 Am. St. 698.
[54] The consideration to the wife may be certain contractual rights contemporaneously acquired, such as an agreement to relieve her from a prior mortgage, or a contemporaneous conveyance of property to her, and the payment of her husband's

Thus, where a married woman executed a mortgage, without her husband's concurrence, to her mother, to secure, as was claimed, advances made to her by her father long before, and the evidence showed that the advances were intended by her father as a gift, and that the real object in executing the mortgage was to protect the property from her husband, it was held that the mortgage was not valid, and that a court of equity could not declare the loan to be a lien on the wife's separate property.[55] So, a mortgage of the separate property of a wife to her husband and another as partners, when she owes them nothing, is without consideration and void, although her husband was credited on the firm books.[56]

It is essential to a consideration that there should be some benefit to the wife or a detriment to the mortgagee. Where a past consideration is void, a mortgage of a wife to secure a pre-existing debt of the husband is invalid.[57]

A mortgage given by a wife to indemnify a surety on her husband's bond and save him from arrest has been held supported by a sufficient consideration. The arrest "would entail loss of support and disgrace, not only upon her husband, but upon herself and family. No true wife would, under such circumstances, refuse to execute a mortgage upon her home, and we do not think a court will ever be found to hold that a mortgage so executed is without consideration."[58]

In jurisdictions which do not forbid a wife to become surety for her husband a mortgage by a wife of her separate property to secure her husband's note is made for a sufficient consideration if there was a sufficient consideration for his note.[59]

§ 114. **Wife in position of a surety—Exoneration.**—A wife who has mortgaged her separate property for her husband's debt is in the position of a surety.[60] She is entitled to all the rights of a surety, and her liability and the mortgage lien are discharged by the extension

debt. Hamilton v. Hamilton, 162 Ind. 430, 70 N. E. 535.

[55] Heller v. Groves (N. J.), 8 Atl. 652.

[56] Bliss v. Cronk, 68 N. J. Eq. 655, 60 Atl. 1133.

[57] Bell v. Bell, 133 Mo. App. 570, 113 S. W. 667.

[58] Bode v. Jussen, 93 Nebr. 482, 140 N. W. 768.

[59] Post v. First Nat. Bank, 138 Ill. 559, 28 N. E. 978; Sigel Campion Live Stock Com. Co. v. Haston, 68 Kans. 749, 75 Pac. 1028; Eaton v. Dewey, 79 Wis. 251, 48 N. W. 523.

[60] Cross v. Allen, 141 U. S. 528, 35 L. ed. 843, 12 Sup. Ct. 67; Spear v. Ward, 20 Cal. 659; Bull v. Coe, 77 Cal. 54, 18 Pac. 808, 11 Am. St. 235; Young v. Graff, 28 Ill. 20; Post v. Losey, 111 Ind. 74, 12 N. E. 121, 60 Am. Dec. 677; Philbrooks v. McEwen, 29 Ind. 347; Ellis v. Kenyon, 25 Ind. 134; Kinney v. Heuring, 44 Ind. App. 590, 87 N. E. 1053; Indianapolis Brew. Co. v. Behnke, 41 Ind.

of the time of payment without her consent,[61] if the extension be a binding obligation upon the mortgagee,[62] or by anything that would discharge a surety who is personally bound.[63] Her rights in this respect are the same as if she were sole.

Where a husband and wife execute a mortgage upon the homestead, the title to which is in the husband, to secure the debt of the husband, the wife's relation to the debt is not that of a surety, so that payments made by the husband upon the debt have the effect of continuing the debt in force.[64]

Many jurisdictions, however, deny a married woman the right to become a surety for her husband and this without regard to the use that is made of the money realized on the note and mortgage.[65] The mortgage in these jurisdictions is generally held merely voidable but not absolutely void.[66] The wife's right or interest in the homestead rests upon the marital relation and the husband's ownership in fee. Her right is a possessory right merely and when she joins her husband in making a mortgage of the homestead she conveys no title of her own but merely waives her possessory right to the property upon a default in the conditions of the mortgage.[67] But the husband can

App. 288, 81 N. E. 119; Green v. Scranage, 19 Iowa 461, 87 Am. Dec. 447; Hubbard v. Ogden, 22 Kans. 363; Eaton v. Nason, 47 Maine 132; Bartlett v. Bartlett, 4 Allen (Mass.) 440; Carley v. Fox, 38 Mich. 387; Watson v. Thurber, 11 Mich. 457; White v. Smith, 174 Mo. 186, 73 S. W. 610; Wilcox v. Todd, 64 Mo. 388; Northwestern Mut. L. Ins. Co. v. Mallory, 93 Nebr. 579, 141 N. W. 190; Smith v. Townsend, 25 N. Y. 479; Purdy v. Huntington, 42 N. Y. 334; Hawley v. Bradford, 9 Paige (N. Y.) 200, 37 Am. Dec. 390; Demarest v. Wynkoop, 3 Johns. Ch. (N. Y.) 129, 8 Am. Dec. 467; Vartie v. Underwood, 18 Barb. (N. Y.) 561; McGowan v. Davenport, 134 N. Car. 526, 47 S. E. 27; Insurance Co. v. Miller, 24 Ohio Cir. Ct. 667; Red River Nat. Bank v. Bray (Tex. Civ. App.), 132 S. W. 968. But see Hamilton v. Hamilton, 162 Ind. 430, 70 N. E. 535.

[61] Spear v. Ward, 20 Cal. 659; Post v. Losey, 111 Ind. 74, 60 Am. Dec. 677; Newman v. Kling, 73 Miss. 312, 18 So. 685; White & Tudor Lead. Cas. in Eq. (4th ed.), 1922 and cases cited; Barrett v. Davis (Mo.), 15

S. W. 1010; Bank of Albion v. Burns, 46 N. Y. 170; Coleman v. Van Rensselaer, 44 How. Pr. (N. Y.) 368; Smith v. Townsend, 25 N. Y. 479.

[62] Frickee v. Donner, 35 Mich. 151.

[63] Cross v. Allen, 141 U. S. 528, 35 L. ed. 843, 12 Sup. Ct. 67, per Lamar, J.

[64] Roberts v. Roberts, 10 N. Dak. 531. The case of People's State Bank v. Francis, 8 N. Dak. 369, 79 N. W. 853, not followed.

[65] Richardson v. Stephens, 114 Ala. 238, 21 So. 949; Continental Nat. Bank v. Clarke, 117 Ala. 292, 22 So. 988; Wright v. Parvis &c. Co., 1 Marv. (Del.) 325, 40 Atl. 1123; Lewis v. Howell, 98 Ga. 428, 25 S. E. 504; Lowenstein v. Meyer, 114 Ga. 709, 40 S. E. 726; Gross v. Whiteley, 128 Ga. 79, 57 S. E. 94; Burns' Ind. Ann. Stat. 1914, § 7855; Voreis v. Nussbaum, 131 Ind. 267, 31 N. E. 70, 16 L. R. A. 45; Indianapolis Brew. Co. v. Behnke, 41 Ind. App. 288, 81 N. E. 119.

[66] Field v. Campbell (Ind. App.), 68 N. E. 911.

[67] Jenness v. Cutler, 12 Kans. 500; Smith v. Scherck, 60 Miss. 491; Kuhnert v. Conrad, 6 N. Dak. 215,

not create a new incumbrance upon the homestead without the wife's consent.[68] The rule is otherwise in states where a married woman is held to bind her separate property generally by her contract in relation to any part of such property. Where this is the case, she is bound as principal when she makes a mortgage to secure her husband's debt, and her liability is not affected by any understanding she may have with her husband, or by the giving of additional security as collateral to the mortgage.[69] As between the husband's homestead exemption and the wife's dower interest, the homestead exemption must first be applied to the mortgage, and his property must be wholly exhausted before resorting to hers.[70]

Generally she is entitled to have her estate exonerated out of the estate of her husband, if this be practicable.[71] When he has mortgaged or pledged his own property for the same debt, his property should in the first instance be applied to satisfy the mortgage.[72] The creditor having security upon the husband's property for the payment of the same debt, by releasing this discharges the wife's estate.[73] The husband being the principal debtor, if he acquire the mortgage it will be discharged.[74] Although the right of redemption be limited to him, she may nevertheless redeem, unless it appear from the instrument itself, or from extraneous evidence, that she intended to make a gift of the property to her husband, and that the conveyance, therefore, should be absolute.[75]

A married woman who has joined her husband in a mortgage of his land is, according to some authorities, entitled to have a payment made by a sale of personal property belonging to her husband, mortgaged to secure the same debt, applied in exoneration of her inchoate dower interest, in preference to an application of the same to a debt

69 N. W. 185; Roberts v. Roberts, 10 N. Dak. 531, 88 N. W. 289.

[68] Barber v. Babel, 36 Cal. 11; Bank v. Burns, 46 N. Y. 170; Spencer v. Fredenhall, 15 Wis. 666.

[69] Alexander v. Bouton, 55 Cal. 15. See also Hassey v. Wilke, 55 Cal. 525.

[70] Stoehr v. Moerlein Brew. Co., 27 Ohio Cir. Ct. 330.

[71] Browne v. Bixby, 190 Mass. 69, 76 N. E. 454; Wilcox v. Todd, 64 Mo. 388; Shinn v. Smith, 79 N. Car. 310; Harrington v. Rawls, 136 N. Car. 65, 48 S. E. 571; Huntingdon v. Huntingdon, 2 Bro. P. C. 1.

[72] Johns v. Reardon, 11 Md. 465;

Knight v. Whitehead, 26 Miss. 245; Wilcox v. Todd, 64 Mo. 388; Wright v. Austin, 56 Barb. (N. Y.) 13; Gahn v. Neimcewicz, 3 Paige (N. Y.) 614, 11 Wend. 312; Loomer v. Wheelwright, 3 Sandf. Ch. (N. Y.) 135; Sheidle v. Weishlee, 16 Pa. St. 134; Weeks v. Haas, 3 Watts & S. (Pa.) 520, 39 Am. Dec. 39.

[73] Ayres v. Husted, 15 Conn. 504; Johns v. Reardon, 11 Md. 465.

[74] Fitch v. Cotheal, 2 Sandf. Ch. (N. Y.) 29.

[75] Demarest v. Wynkoop, 3 Johns. Ch. (N. Y.) 129, 8 Am. Dec. 467; Duffy v. Insurance Co., 8 Watts & S. (Pa.) 413, 433.

to the mortgagee secured by a second mortgage made by the husband alone.[76]

To make the mortgagee chargeable with the equitable rights of the wife, as surety for her husband, it must appear that he had notice of this relation.[77]   Such notice can not be inferred merely from the fact that the money was paid to the husband, because he may have acted as his wife's agent in the transaction.   But if the mortgage be made to secure a pre-existing debt of the husband's, the creditor is affected with notice of the wife's equity as surety, and in his dealings with the husband is bound by this knowledge.[78]

§ 115.   Husband's authority over wife's mortgage—Extension— Litigation.—A husband has no presumptive authority to consent to an extension of a mortgage given by his wife to secure his debt.   The holder of such a mortgage is chargeable with notice of her ownership, and that she stands in the relation of surety to the husband.   The lien is therefore discharged by an extension of the time of payment without her concurrence.[79]   A renewal note has the same effect as an extension.[80]

In a case where a wife's mortgage covered not only her land, but also property of her husband, it was held that his release of his own property without her consent operated as a release of her land.[81]

A husband has no implied authority to employ counsel to represent his wife, and to bind her in litigation respecting her separate estate.[82]

---

[76] Gore v. Townsend, 105 N. Car. 228, 11 S. E. 160. See post § 1694.

[77] Von Hemert v. Taylor, 73 Minn. 339, 76 N. W. 42; Benedict v. Olson, 37 Minn. 431, 35 N. W. 10; Agnew v. Merritt, 10 Minn. 308.

[78] Knight v. Whitehead, 26 Miss. 245; Loomer v. Wheelright, 3 Sandf. Ch. (N. Y.) 135; Gahn v. Neimce- wicz, 3 Paige (N. Y.) 614. As to Kentucky, see Hobson v. Hobson, 8 Bush (Ky.) 665.

[79] White v. Smith, 174 Mo. 186, 73 S. W. 610; Bank of Albion v. Burns, 2 Lans. (N. Y.) 52; Smith v. Town- send, 25 N. Y. 479; De Barrera v. Frost, 39 Tex. Civ. App. 544, 88 S. W. 476; Red River Nat. Bank v. Bray (Tex. Civ. App.), 132 S. W. 968. See also Johnson v. Franklin Bank, 173 Mo. 171, 73 S. W. 191. The husband's insolvency does not affect the rule that his extension alone discharges the wife's property.

De Barrera v. Frost, 39 Tex. Civ. App. 544, 88 S. W. 476. A material alteration in a note secured by the trust deed of a married woman dis- charges the land. Higgins v. Deer- ing Harvester Co., 181 Mo. 300, 79 S. W. 959. But see Dearing v. Jor- dan (Tex. Civ. App.), 130 S. W. 876. Where the legal title to the mort- gaged premises is in the husband, his extension without her knowl- edge or consent does not release her property, though she subsequently claims it under an antenuptial agreement. Creighton v. Crane, 73 Nebr. 650, 103 N. W. 284.

[80] Johnson v. Franklin Bank, 173 Mo. 171, 73 S. W. 191; Westbrook v. Belton Nat. Bank (Tex. Civ. App.), 75 S. W. 842.

[81] Schneider v. Sellers (Tex.), 81 S. W. 126.

[82] Mason v. Johnson, 47 Md. 347.

§ 115a. Debts of third persons.—Where the law of the particular jurisdiction limits the liability of the separate estate of a married woman, she may not, as a general rule, mortgage her separate estate as security for the debt of a third person.[83] But a married woman will not be permitted to avoid a mortgage given by her to secure the debt of a third party, when the mortgage was made at the time she took title to the mortgaged premises, and as a part of the transaction by which she became vested with title thereto. Such a transaction "is very different from the one where a married woman, without any consideration whatever, executes a mortgage upon her separate estate to secure the debt of a third party."[84]

§ 116. Assumption of mortgage by married woman.—A married woman may make a valid contract to assume a mortgage in a conveyance to her of lands so incumbered, and may render herself liable for a deficiency.[85] Such a contract is not an undertaking to pay the debt of another, but to pay her own debt for the benefit of her own estate. Having the capacity to make contracts for the acquisition of land, she must have the capacity of binding herself for the payment of the price of it. It is as much within her capacity to make an agreement to assume the payment of an existing mortgage as it is to give a new mortgage and note for a part of the purchase-money. She is bound by a vendor's implied lien for the purchase-money of land conveyed to her,[86] and by a vendor's lien reserved in his deed or by contract.[87]

A mortgage given by her in part payment of the purchase-price of land at the time of the conveyance to her, although it imposes no personal liability upon her, is nevertheless valid, and may be enforced

[83] Webb v. John Hancock Life Ins. Co., 162 Ind. 616, 69 N. E. 1006, 66 L. R. A. 632; Heburn v. Warner, 112 Mass. 271, 17 Am. Rep. 86; Conkling v. Levie, 66 Nebr. 132, 94 N. W. 988. But see Shipman v. Lord, 58 N. J. Eq. 380, 44 Atl. 215; Kuhn v. Ogilvie, 178 Pa. St. 303, 35 Atl. 957.

[84] Conkling v. Levie, 66 Nebr. 132, 94 N. W. 987.

[85] Carpenter v. Mitchell, 54 Ill. 126; Ballin v. Dillaye, 35 How. Pr. (N. Y.) 216, 37 N. Y. 35; Flynn v. Powers, 35 How. Pr. (N. Y.) 279, 36 How. Pr. (N. Y.) 289; Vrooman v. Turner, 8 Hun (N. Y.) 78, 69 N. Y. 280, 25 Am. Rep. 195; Huyler v. Atwood, 26 N. J. Eq. 504; Perkins v.

Elliott, 23 N. J. Eq. 526; Indiana Yearly Meeting v. Haines, 47 Ohio St. 423, 25 N. E. 119.

An earlier case in the Supreme Court of New York held that a married woman was not liable in such case, because a purchase which turned out so poorly—the property not being worth the amount of the mortgage covenant—could not be for the benefit of her separate estate. Brown v. Hermann, 14 Abb. Pr. (N. Y.) 394. See post § 753.

[86] Thompson v. Scott, 1 Bradw. (Ill.) 641; Haskell v. Scott, 56 Ind. 564; Cox v. Wood, 20 Ind. 54. See post § 193.

[87] See post § 231.

in equity upon the land by foreclosure sale.[88]   The conveyance and mortgage, read together as parts of one instrument, in legal effect create in the grantee an estate upon condition; and, without reference to statutes removing the wife's common-law disabilities, a court of equity would treat her as the trustee of the grantor, and would subject the land to the payment of the purchase-money.[89]   If the husband assented to the transaction, a court of equity would compel him and the wife to execute a valid mortgage to secure the payment of the purchase-money.[90]

§ 116a.   **Execution of mortgage by attorney in fact for married woman.**—In states where a married woman is given the power of a feme sole as to the incumbrance of her separate property she may mortgage her real estate by or through her attorney in fact.[91]

§ 117.   **Alabama rule.**—In Alabama a married woman can not bind either herself or her statutory separate estate by a mortgage made to secure debts contracted by her husband.[92]   But the burden is upon

[88] Marks v. Cowles, 53 Ala. 499, overruling Cowles v. Marks, 47 Ala. 612, and in part Hapgood v. Marlowe, 51 Ala. 478. See also Kieser v. Baldwin, 62 Ala. 526; Prout v. Hoge, 57 Ala. 28; Smith v. Carson, 56 Ala. 456; Strong v. Waddell, 57 Ala. 471; Johnson v. Ward, 82 Ala. 486, 2 So. 524.

[89] Patterson v. Robinson, 25 Pa. St. 81; Ramborger v. Ingraham, 38 Pa. St. 146.

[90] Leach v. Noyes, 45 N. H. 364. The statute of Alabama does not diminish the capacity of the wife to take and receive property as recognized at common law. The statute relates to her common-law incapacity to hold and transmit property, and partly removes this. At common law the right to disaffirm a conveyance to herself during coverture did not pertain to her, for the same reason that power to contract was denied her. Disaffirmance during coverture was within the power of the husband only, and not within his power after he had once assented to the transaction. In Marks v. Cowles, 53 Ala. 499, the husband having assented to the purchase, the court decide that the husband, as trustee of the wife, having under the statute power

to invest, with her concurrence, the proceeds of her statutory estate in the purchase of lands, the investment being a judicious one and such as a court of equity might have directed, the transaction of which the mortgage was a part should be sustained. For present statute see post § 117, note.

[91] Linton v. National Life Ins. Co., 104 Fed. 584.

[92] Osborne v. Cooper, 113 Ala. 405, 21 So. 320; Richardson v. Stephens, 122 Ala. 301, 25 So. 39, qualifying 114 Ala. 238, 21 So. 949; McNeil v. Davis, 105 Ala. 657, 17 So. 101; Hawkins v. Ross, 100 Ala. 459, 14 So. 278; Davidson v. Lanier, 51 Ala. 318; Wilkinson v. Cheatham, 45 Ala. 337; Cowles v. Marks, 47 Ala. 612; Northington v. Faber, 52 Ala. 45; Fry v. Hammer, 50 Ala. 52; Riley v. Pierce, 50 Ala. 93; Coleman v. Smith, 55 Ala. 368; Lansden v. Bone, 90 Ala. 446, 8 So. 65; Clement v. Draper, 108 Ala. 211, 19 So. 25; Elston v. Comer, 108 Ala. 76, 19 So. 324; Henderson v. Brunson, 141 Ala. 674, 37 So. 549; Campbell v. Hughes, 155 Ala. 591, 47 So. 45; Evans v. Faircloth-Byrd Mercantile Co., 165 Ala. 176, 51 So. 785; Hanchey v. Powell, 171 Ala. 597, 55 So. 97; Lamkin v. Lovell, 176 Ala. 334, 58 So.

her to prove that the debt secured was the separate debt of the husband and not her own.[93]

Formerly she was incapable of incumbering such estate even to secure her own debt, although her husband joined in the conveyance. Her mortgage was an absolute nullity.[94] The statutes creating the wife's statutory separate estate define the debts to which it may be subjected, and the remedy by which the liability for such debts may be enforced; consequently, even a mortgage given by husband and wife, to secure the payment of any such debt, could not be enforced.[95]

A mortgage of a married woman's statutory separate estate, executed by herself and husband to secure the payment of their joint

258. See Code Ala. 1907, § 4497. But see Short v. Battle, 52 Ala. 456.

In case the land has been paid for by money drawn from the husband's firm, a mortgage by her of the land to secure a debt of the firm will not be set aside. Mathews v. Sheldon, 53 Ala. 136.

A mortgage on a wife's property is void only pro tanto where part of the debt secured is the husband's. Mills v. Hudmon, 175 Ala. 448, 57 So. 739.

The fact that the money borrowed on a mortgage of the separate property of a married woman, securing the husband's note on which she was a surety, was used by the husband to improve and cultivate the land mortgaged, does not make the note and mortgage valid. Richardson v. Stephens, 114 Ala. 238, 21 So. 949; Hawkins v. Ross, 100 Ala. 459, 14 So. 278; McNeil v. Davis, 105 Ala. 657, 17 So. 101; Lansden v. Bone, 90 Ala. 446, 8 So. 65; Dudley v. Collier, 87 Ala. 431, 6 So. 304; Robertson v. Hayes, 83 Ala. 290, 3 So. 674; Heard v. Hicks, 82 Ala. 484, 1 So. 639.

If a married woman purchases land and gives a mortgage for a part of the purchase-money without the assent in writing of her husband, her coverture and disability not relieved by such assent are no defense to a bill to foreclose the mortgage which seeks no personal decree against the purchaser. Joseph v. Decatur Land Imp. &c. Co., 102 Ala. 346, 14 So. 739; Bogan v. Hamilton, 90 Ala. 454, 8 So. 186;

Crampton v. Prince, 83 Ala. 246, 3 So. 519; Wadsworth v. Hodge, 88 Ala. 500, 7 So. 194.

Where she is regularly invested by the court, with the right to buy, sell and mortgage her property, she may exercise each of these powers in her own discretion, just as if she were a feme sole. Robinson v. Walker, 81 Ala. 404, 1 So. 347. If the decree intended to relieve a married woman of her disabilities is void for insufficiency of the petition (Powell v. Security Co., 87 Ala. 602, 6 So. 339), a mortgage executed under such void decree is itself void, and can not be ratified so as to be made valid without a new consideration, after the Act of February 28, 1887, giving a married woman the rights of a feme sole.

[93] Mohr v. Griffin, 137 Ala. 456, 34 So. 378; Sample v. Guver, 143 Ala. 613, 42 So. 106; Gibson v. Wallace, 147 Ala. 322, 41 So. 960; Lamkin v. Lovell, 176 Ala. 334, 58 So. 258; Interstate Bank v. Wesley, 178 Ala. 186, 59 So. 621.

[94] Curry v. American Freehold Land Mtg. Co., 107 Ala. 429, 18 So. 328; Conner v. Williams, 57 Ala. 131; Chapman v. Abrahams, 61 Ala. 108; McDonald v. Mobile Life Ins. Co., 56 Ala. 468; Gans v. Williams, 62 Ala. 41; Thames v. Rembert, 63 Ala. 561. But she could make a conditional sale. Vincent v. Walker, 86 Ala. 333, 5 So. 465.

[95] Gilbert v. Dupree, 63 Ala. 331; Harper v. T. N. Hays Co., 149 Ala. 174, 43 So. 360.

promissory note, is not binding upon her or her estate. The consideration of the note may be shown by parol to have been the indebtedness of the husband.[96] But if the contract of purchase was made by the husband alone, though the conveyance was taken in the name of his wife, and the vendor had no notice of the wife's claim to the money, his equity under the mortgage is regarded as superior to hers.[97]

A distinction is taken between the statutory real estate of a married woman and that which is her equitable separate estate; and such an equitable separate estate may be created when the gift or devise, or conveyance to her, clearly and certainly shows an intent to exclude the marital rights of the husband under the statute. Such separate estate not affected by the statute she can mortgage for her own debt or the debt of her husband, or of any one else, as if she were a feme sole.[98]

§ 117a. **Georgia and Louisiana.**—Georgia and Louisiana have code provisions similar to that of Alabama, and a wife can not bind her

---

[96] Stribling v. Bank of Kentucky, 48 Ala. 451.

[97] Haygood v. Marlowe, 51 Ala. 478.

[98] Short v. Battle, 52 Ala. 456; Helmetag v. Frank, 61 Ala. 67; Burrus v. Dawson, 66 Ala. 476; Allen v. Terry, 73 Ala. 123; Hooks v. Brown, 62 Ala. 258; Smythe v. Fitzsimmons, 97 Ala. 451, 12 So. 48.

Under Code 1867, §§ 2371, 2372, 2376, all property of the wife, held by her previous to the marriage, or which she may become entitled to after the marriage, in any manner, is the separate estate of the wife, and is not subject to the liabilities of the husband. This provision is continued by Code 1886, § 2341. The earlier Code provided that property thus belonging to the wife vests in the husband as her trustee, who has the right to manage and control the same, and is not required to account with the wife, her heirs, or legal representatives, for the rents, income, and profits thereof. The Code of 1886, §§ 2346, 2348, 2349, and Code of 1896, §§ 2528, 2529, however, declare that the wife has full legal capacity to contract in writing as if she were sole, with the assent or concurrence of the husband expressed in writing; but she can not directly or indirectly become a surety for her husband. Clement v. Draper, 108 Ala. 211, 19 So. 25; Hawkins v. Ross, 100 Ala. 459, 14 So. 278; Lansden v. Bone, 90 Ala. 446, 8 So. 65; McNeil v. Davis, 105 Ala. 657, 17 So. 101.

The wife, joining in her husband's deed to release dower, etc., is not bound by a covenant of warranty. Threefoot v. Hillman, 130 Ala. 244, 30 So. 513. The wife, except in certain cases specified, can not alienate her land without the concurrence of her husband. For construction of the earlier statute, see Marks v. Cowles, 53 Ala. 499; Smith v. Carson, 56 Ala. 456; Strong v. Waddell, 56 Ala. 471; Ravisies v. Stoddart, 32 Ala. 599; O'Connor v. Chamberlain, 59 Ala. 431; Gilbert v. Dupree, 63 Ala. 331.

But while a married woman can not mortgage her land to secure or pay the debt of her husband she can convey it for that purpose. Giddens v. Powell, 108 Ala. 621, 19 So. 21.

A mortgage executed by a married woman, her husband not joining, is void; but where the mortgage does not show on its face that

separate estate for the debts of her husband.[99]   Although a wife may
not bind her separate estate by assumption of the debts of her husband,
or by way of suretyship, she may voluntarily borrow money and give
her note and mortgage therefor, although the lender knows she intends
to use the money to pay her husband's debts.[1]

The code provision does not affect the power of a widow to contract
as to the debts of her deceased husband.[2]

A note and mortgage by a wife to repay a third person for discharging her husband's fine were held an original undertaking of the
wife, and not security for a debt due by the husband.[3]

§ 118. **Mississippi.**—In Mississippi a married woman can make
contracts binding her separate property only for certain purposes.
In general, it may be said that she has no power to borrow money by
mortgaging her real estate; but if the lender can show that the money
was actually applied to discharge a debt for which her separate estate
was already bound, or to make purchases for which she might charge
her estate, then the lender may recover upon the property mortgaged.[4]
She can not bind the corpus of her property to pay her husband's
debt;[5] it being provided by statute that "no conveyance or incumbrance for the separate debts of the husband shall be binding on the
wife beyond the amount of her income."[6]   Although such a mortgage
may be operative on her estate to that extent, it ceases to be operative
upon it in any way upon her death.[7]   But during her lifetime the
mortgagee, when entitled to possession after default, may maintain
ejectment.   She may maintain a bill to redeem, or for an account
against the mortgagee in possession.[8]

the mortgagor is a married woman,
the mortgage is not void on its face,
and its invalidity rests upon proof
aliunde that she was married. Such
a mortgage is a cloud upon the title
for removal of which a bill to quiet
title may be maintained. Interstate Loan &c. Assn. v. Stocks, 124
Ala. 109, 27 So. 506; Lansden v.
Bone, 90 Ala. 446, 8 So. 65.

[99] Keating v. Wilbert, 119 La. 461,
44 So. 265 (construing La. Rev. Civ.
Code 1899, art. 2398).

[1] Johnson v. A. Leffler Co,. 122 Ga.
670, 50 S. E. 488.

[2] Walker v. Walker, 139 Ga. 547,
77 S. E. 795.

[3] Hall v. Coleman, 138 Ga. 734, 75
S. E. 1132.

[4] Allen v. Lenoir, 53 Miss. 321;
Harmon v. Magee, 57 Miss. 410.

[5] Klein v. McNamara, 54 Miss. 90;
Viser v. Scruggs, 49 Miss. 705; Freeman v. Wilson, 51 Miss. 329.   See
also Dibrell v. Carlisle, 51 Miss.
785; Erwin v. Hill, 47 Miss. 675;
Cross v. Hedrick, 66 Miss. 61, 7 So.
496.

[6] Sevier v. Minnis, 71 Miss. 473, 15
So. 234.   Code 1871, § 1778.

[7] Reed v. Coleman, 51 Miss. 835.

[8] Stephenson v. Miller, 57 Miss. 48.
See Miss. Code 1880, § 1167; Code
1906, § 2517, completely emancipat-
ing married women.   See also Bell
v. Clark, under this statute, 71 Miss.
603, 14 So. 318.

§ **118a. What law governs capacity.**—The law of the state where the land is situated governs as to the capacity of a married woman to execute a mortgage, though it be executed in another state. Thus, if a married woman should execute a mortgage without her husband joining her, in a state where such a mortgage would be valid, conveying land in another state where the law required the husband to join with her in her conveyance, the mortgage would have no effect in the latter state, and could not be enforced.[9]

V. Tenants in Common of Partnership Real Estate

§ **119. Generally.**—Land conveyed to members of a copartnership as tenants in common, but purchased with copartnership funds and used for copartnership purposes, is treated in equity as copartnership personal property.[1] The creditors of the copartnership are in such case entitled to priority of payment out of it in preference to the

[9] Swank v. Hufnagle, 71 Ind. 53, 12 N. E. 303, 13 N. E. 105; Brown v. Bank, 44 Ohio St. 269, 6 N. E. 648. See post § 823.

[1] Thompson v. Bowman, 6 Wall. (U. S.) 316, 18 L. ed. 736; Ames v. Ames, 37 Fed. 30; Hatchett v. Blanton, 72 Ala. 423; Chapman v. Hughes, 104 Cal. 302, 37 Pac. 1048, 38 Pac. 109; Robertson v. Baker, 11 Fla. 192; Hartnett v. Stillwell, 121 Ga. 386, 49 S. E. 276, 104 Am. St. 151; Jackson v. Stanford, 19 Ga. 14; Pepper v. Pepper, 24 Ill. App. 316; Morgan v. Olvey, 53 Ind. 6; Paige v. Paige, 71 Iowa 318, 32 N. W. 360, 60 Am. Rep. 799; Pepper v. Thomas, 85 Ky. 539, 9 Ky. L. 122, 4 S. W. 297; Spalding v. Wilson, 80 Ky. 589, 4 Ky. L. 575; Galbraith v. Cedge, 16 B. Mon. (Ky.) 631; May v. New Orleans, 44 La. Ann. 444, 10 So. 769; Buffum v. Buffum, 49 Maine 108, 77 Am. Dec. 249; Fall River Whaling Co. v. Borden, 10 Cush. (Mass.) 458; Burnside v. Merrick, 4 Metc. (Mass.) 537; Dyer v. Clark, 5 Metc. (Mass.) 562, 39 Am. Dec. 697; Goodwin v. Richardson, 11 Mass. 469; Willet v. Brown, 65 Mo. 138, 27 Am. Rep. 265; Matthews v. Hunter, 67 Mo. 293; Quinn v. Quinn, 22 Mont. 403, 56 Pac. 824; Whitmore v. Shiverick, 3 Nev. 288; Cilley v. Huse, 40 N. H. 358; Harney v. Jersey City &c. Bank, 52 N. J. Eq. 697, 29 Atl. 221; Matlack v. James, 13 N. J. Eq. 126; Hiscock v. Phelps, 49 N. Y. 97; Leary v. Boggs, 1 N. Y. St. 571; Smith v. Tarlton, 2 Barb. Ch. (N. Y.) 336; Haynes v. Brooks, 8 Civ. Proc. (N. Y.) 106; Struthers v. Pearce, 51 N. Y. 357; Ross v. Henderson, 77 N. Car. 170; Miller v. Proctor, 20 Ohio St. 442; Page v. Thomas, 43 Ohio St. 38, 1 N. E. 79, 54 Am. Rep. 788; Abbott's Appeal, 50 Pa. St. 234; Hayes v. Treat, 178 Pa. St. 310, 35 Atl. 987; Tillinghast v. Champlin, 4 R. I. 173, 67 Am. Dec. 510; Lime Rock Bank v. Chetteplace, 8 R. I. 56; Wilson v. Wilson, 74 S. Car. 30, 54 S. E. 227; Boyce v. Coster, 4 Strob. Eq. (S. Car.) 25; Winslow v. Chiffelle, Harp. Eq. (S. Car.) 25; Willis v.

creditors of individual members of the firm.[2] But if one member of the copartnership mortgages his apparent interest as tenant in common of such land for a consideration paid him at the time, as, for instance, for a loan of money, the mortgagee having no notice of the character of the property in equity as copartnership property, he is entitled to hold it under his mortgage. He may rely upon the legal effect of the conveyance to his mortgagor, and upon his apparent title upon record. A person taking a mortgage without notice that it covers partnership property is a purchaser, and is subject to no equity in favor of the partnership or of its creditors.[3]

Whether real property is partnership assets depends upon the intention or agreement of the partners. Such intention may be express or implied. In the absence of an express agreement, parol evidence may be resorted to for the determination of the question. The manner in which the members of the firm have treated and used the property always goes far in determining its character.[4]

If the property has been purchased by the individual partners with their own funds, each taking a conveyance of an undivided interest, the fact that the property has for a time been used for the partnership business is not generally sufficient to impress it with an equitable lien for the payment of partnership debts as against a mortgage of one partner's interest to secure his individual debt.[5]

§ 120. Mortgage of partnership property by one partner—Notice of partnership equities.—A mortgage made by a partner of his in-

Freeman, 35 Vt. 44, 82 Am. Dec. 619; Forde v. Herron, 4 Munf. (Va.) 316; Jones v. Neale, 2 Pat. & H. (Va.) 339; Cunningham v. Ward, 30 W. Va. 572, 5 S. E. 646. But see Taber-Prang Art Co. v. Durant, 189 Mass. 173, 75 N. E. 221; Gordon v. Gordon, 49 Mich. 501, 13 N. W. 834; Frey v. Eisenhardt, 116 Mich. 160, 74 N. W. 501; Dexter v. Dexter, 43 App. Div. 268, 60 N. Y. S. 371.

[2] Matlock v. Matlock, 5 Ind. 403; Hewitt v. Rankin, 41 Iowa 35; Messer v. Messer, 58 N. H. 375; Everett v. Shepmoes, 6 Hun (N. Y.) 479; Buchan v. Sumner, 2 Barb. Ch. (N. Y.) 165, 47 Am. Dec. 305; Hogle v. Lowe, 12 Nev. 286; Tarbel v. Bradley, 7 Abb. (N. Cas.) (N. Y.) 273; Meily v. Wood, 71 Pa. St. 488, 10 Am. Rep. 719; Pollock's Dig. of Law

of Partnership, ch. 6; Story on Partnership, §§ 92, 93.

[3] Reeves v. Ayres, 38 Ill. 418; Robinson Bank v. Miller, 153 Ill. 244, 38 N. E. 1078, 27 L. R. A. 449, 46 Am. St. 883; Hewitt v. Rankin, 41 Iowa 35; quoted with approval in Seeley v. Mitchell, 85 Ky. 508, 4 S. W. 190; Hiscock v. Phelps, 49 N. Y. 97; Richmond v. Voorhees, 10 Wash. 316, 38 Pac. 1014.

[4] Jenkins v. Jenkins, 81 Ark. 68, 98 S. W. 685; Brown v. Morrill, 45 Minn. 483, 48 N. W. 328; Deming v. Moss, 40 Utah 501, 121 Pac. 971; Bosworth v. Hopkins, 85 Wis. 50, 55 N. W. 424; Riedeburg v. Schmitt, 71 Wis. 644, 38 N. W. 336. See also Richtman v. Watson, 150 Wis. 385, 136 N. W. 797.

[5] Wilhite v. Boulware, 88 Ky. 169, 10 S. W. 629.

terest in partnership real estate, to one who knows it to be such, is not a mortgage of the partner's undivided interest in such real estate, but of his interest in the portion mortgaged after the payment of the firm debts upon a settlement of the partnership accounts. The mortgage is not available until the partnership debts have been paid and the partnership accounts have been discharged, if the other partner chooses to assert his equity, or if subsequent partnership mortgagees assert their priority;[6] or if creditors of the partnership attach the property or levy an execution upon it as belonging to the partnership.[7] There would in such case be no distinction between debts incurred prior to the mortgage and those incurred subsequently.[8] Upon the bankruptcy of the firm, the assignee, in behalf of the creditors, would be entitled to the property in preference.

If one partner, upon retiring from the partnership, conveys his interest in the partnership real estate to another person, who then comes in and forms a new firm, and this new partner executes a mortgage of such real estate to secure the purchase-money, in the absence of any evidence that the mortgage was intended to be a mortgage of this partner's interest in the new firm, it is proper to regard it as a mortgage of the same partnership interest in the old firm which was conveyed to the new partner, and not of his interest in the new firm. Such a mortgage is subject to the payment of the debts of the old firm, but not to the payment of the debts of the new firm.[9] But the mortgagee must be in the position of a bona fide purchaser for value; he must have parted with money or goods, or something valuable, in reliance upon the security. If he has simply taken the mortgage to secure an existing debt, or has knowledge of the facts which make the property in equity assets of the firm, then his mortgage will be postponed to the equities of those who have a right to have the property applied as assets of the copartnership.[10] But a recital in a deed to three persons that the conveyance was in the proportion of an undivided half to one of them, and an undivided fourth to each of the others, "this being the proportional undivided interest of each of the above partners in the firm and lands" of the partnership, was held not necessarily to impart

[6] Goldthwaite v. Janney, 102 Ala. 431, 15 So. 560, 48 Am. St. 56; Beecher v. Stevens, 43 Conn. 587; quoted with approval in Seeley v. Mitchell, 85 Ky. 508, 4 S. W. 190; Rockefeller v. Dellinger, 22 Mont. 418, 56 Pac. 822; Page v. Thomas, 43 Ohio St. 38, 1 N. E. 79, 54 Am. Rep. 788.

[7] Fargo v. Ames, 45 Iowa 491; Seaman v. Huffaker, 21 Kans. 254; Lovejoy v. Bowers, 11 N. H. 404; French v. Lovejoy, 12 N. H. 458.
[8] Lovejoy v. Bowers, 11 N. H. 404.
[9] Beecher v. Stevens, 43 Conn. 587. See also Phelps v. McNeely, 66 Mo. 554, 27 Am. Rep. 378.
[10] Hiscock v. Phelps, 49 N. Y. 97.

notice to a mortgagee of the interest of one of the grantees of the equitable rights of the others as representing the creditors of the firm.[11]

A mortgage by one partner of his interest in a mill and machinery in the continued use and occupation of the partnership, to secure such partner's individual debt, passes only what interest such partner may have after paying the debts of the copartnership.[12] The continued use of such property by the partnership is notice of the equitable rights of the partnership in the property.

If the description of the property in the mortgage itself shows that the property is that of a partnership, as where it is described as all the right, title, and interest of a partner individually, and as a member of a certain firm in all the real estate and other property of the firm, the mortgagee necessarily has notice of the partnership equities. The existence of such a mortgage can not prevent the copartners from disposing of the real estate for the legitimate purposes of the copartnership, such as adjusting its affairs with creditors, or with each other. The recording of such mortgage is without effect upon the other members of the copartnership, or upon any one taking a conveyance made for partnership purposes.[13]

§ 121. Mortgage of partnership property by one partner—Assent of other partner.—A valid mortgage of partnership property to secure a partnership debt, may be made by one partner[14] with the express or implied assent of the other partner.[15] Under some authorities

[11] Van Slyck v. Skinner, 41 Mich. 186, 1 N. W. 971. But the decision in this case seems not to be quite in harmony with other authorities.

[12] Mechanics' Bank v. Godwin, 5 N. J. Eq. 334.

[13] Tarbel v. Bradley, 7 Abb. N. Cas. (N. Y.) 273. See note to this case for decisions relating to partnership realty.

[14] Long v. Slade, 121 Ala. 267, 26 So. 31; Breen v. Richardson, 6 Colo. 605 (given to prevent sacrifice of partnership realty); Citizens' Nat. Bank v. Johnson, 79 Iowa 290, 44 N. W. 551; Horton v. Bloedorn, 37 Nebr. 666, 56 N. W. 321 (in absence of copartner, firm being insolvent); Weeks v. Mascoma Rake Co., 58 N. H. 101; Neer v. Oakley, 2 N. Y. S. 482 (without consulting copartner); Baldwin v. Richardson, 33 Tex. 16; Schwab Clothing Co. v. Claunch (Tex. Civ. App.), 29 S. W. 922 (with consent of copartner). Under Georgia Civ. Code 1910, § 3172, each partner has power to contract or otherwise bind the firm and execute any writing in the course of the business.

[15] McGahan v. Rondout Bank, 156 U. S. 218, 39 L. ed. 403, 15 Sup. Ct. 347; Greer v. Ferguson, 56 Ark. 324, 19 S. W. 966 (in presence of copartner with consent); Greer v. Ferguson, 58 Ark. 324, 19 S. W. 966 (in presence of copartner); Sutlive v. Jones, 61 Ga. 676; Printup v. Turner, 65 Ga. 71; Cottle v. Harrold, 72 Ga. 830; Ely v. Hair, 55 Ky. 230 (with knowledge and assent of copartner); Ely v. Hair, 16 B. Mon. (Ky.) 230; Kahn v. Becnel, 108 La. 296, 32 So. 444 (power to mortgage not implied from power to secure advances); Baker v. Lee, 49 La. Ann. 874, 21 So. 588; Chittenden v. German-Amer. Bank, 27 Minn. 143,

such a mortgage, made without authority of the other partner, is held to bind only the interest of the partner executing it.[16]

Where a copartnership carried on business in a store built by the firm upon land, the legal title of which was in A, and one of his copartners, to secure a copartnership debt, executed a mortgage of the land with the consent of his copartners, and in the firm name of A. & Co., and acknowledged the execution of it "as his free act and deed in behalf of said firm," it was held valid as against a person who, with actual notice of this, took a subsequent mortgage of the same property executed by A.[17] Such a mortgage is valid, too, as against creditors of the firm whose lien attached afterward.[18]

An exception to the general rule, that an authority to bind another by an instrument under seal must itself be created by a like instrument, seems to have been established in the case of partners; they may give each other authority by parol to bind each other by instruments under seal.[19] Some of the cases cited do not refer to conveyances of real estate. But if authority to execute a personal contract under seal may be implied from this relation, the same authority may as well extend to conveyances of real property. Lord Kenyon said that, if the relation of partnership gave this authority in the one case, it "would extend to the case of mortgages."[20]

An unauthorized mortgage of partnership property made by one partner using the name of his copartner may be ratified by the latter by parol, or by any act showing his recognition of the mortgage. A mortgage of such real estate by one partner to secure a copartnership

---

6 N. W. 773; Jones v. Davis (N. J. Eq.), 25 Atl. 370; Hardin v. Dolge, 46 App. Div. 416, 61 N. Y. S. 753; Tarbell v. West, 7 Abb. N. Cas. (N. Y.) 273, affd. 86 N. Y. 280; Lance v. Butler, 135 N. Car. 419, 47 S. E. 488; McNeal Pipe &c. Co. v. Woltman, 114 N. Car. 178, 19 S. E. 109; Napier v. Catron, 2 Humph. (Tenn.) 534; Wier Plow Co. v. Evans (Tex. Civ. App.), 24 S. W. 38; Schwab Clothing Co. v. Claunch (Tex. Civ. App.), 29 S. W. 922; Caviness v. Black (Tex. Civ. App.), 33 S. W. 712; Byrd v. Perry, 7 Tex. Civ. App. 378, 26 S. W. 749 (mortgage by one partner procured by other); Wilson v. Hunter, 14 Wis. 683, 80 Am. Dec. 795. But see Beckman v. Noble, 115 Mich. 523, 73 N. W. 803;

Cohen v. Miller, 46 Misc. 106, 91 N. Y. S. 345.

[16] Sutlive v. Jones, 61 Ga. 676; Printup v. Turner, 65 Ga. 71; Cottle v. Harrold, 72 Ga. 830; Baker v. Lee, 49 La. Ann. 874, 21 So. 588; Weeks v. Mascoma Rake Co., 58 N. H. 101.

[17] Wilson v. Hunter, 14 Wis. 683, 80 Am. Dec. 795.

[18] Citizens' Nat. Bank. v. Johnson, 79 Iowa 290, 44 N. W. 551.

[19] Cady v. Shepherd, 11 Pick. (Mass.) 400, 22 Am. Dec. 379; Swan v. Stedman, 4 Metc. (Mass.) 548; Smith v. Kerr, 3 N. Y. 144. See also Wilson v. Hunter, 14 Wis. 683, 80 Am. Dec. 795.

[20] Harrison v. Jackson, 7 T. R. 203.

debt is valid;[21] but it is not valid if made in opposition to the will of another partner with the knowledge of the creditor.[22]

§ 122. **Mortgage of a partner's separate property to secure partnership debt.**—On the other hand, if a partner mortgage his separate property to secure a partnership debt, he becomes a surety for the firm, and his separate creditors, upon his bankruptcy or insolvency, have a right to insist that the partnership property be first applied to the payment of the debt so secured.[23]

§ 122a. **Mortgage to pay individual debt of partner.**—One partner has no right to mortgage the corporate property for the payment of his individual debt without the assent, express or implied, of the other partners, and it makes no difference in the application of this principle that the separate creditor had no knowledge at the time of the fact of the property being partnership property.[24]

Justice Story of the United States Supreme Court says: "The implied authority of each partner to dispose of the partnership funds strictly and rightfully extends only to the business and transactions of the partnership itself; and any disposition of those funds, by any partner, beyond such purposes, is an excess of his authority as partner, and a misappropriation of those funds, for which the partner is responsible to the partnership; though in the case of bona fide purchasers, without notice, for a valuable consideration, the partnership may be bound by such acts. Whatever acts, therefore, are done by any partner, in regard to partnership property or contracts beyond the scope and objects of the partnership, must, in general, in order to bind the partnership, be derived from some further authority, express or implied, conferred upon such partner, beyond that resulting from his character as partner. Such is the general principle; and in our judgment, it is founded in good sense and reason. One man ought not to be permitted to dispose of the

---

[21] Cooley v. Hobart, 8 Iowa 358; Holbrook v. Chamberlin, 116 Mass. 155, 17 Am. Rep. 146. Harvey v. Ford, 83 Mich. 506, 47 N. W. 242. But see Baker v. Lee, 49 La. Ann. 874, 21 So. 588 (ratification by parol insufficient).

[22] H. Y. McCord Co. v. Callaway, 109 Ga. 796, 35 S. E. 171; Fidelity Banking &c. Co. v. Kangara Val. &c. Co., 95 Ga. 172, 22 S. E. 50; Bull v. Harris, 18 B. Mon. (Ky.) 195.

[23] Averill v. Loucks, 6 Barb. (N. Y.) 470.

[24] Rogers v. Batchelor, 12 Pet. (U. S.) 229, 9 L. ed. 1063; H. Y. McCord Co. v. Callaway, 109 Ga. 796, 35 S. E. 171; Rainey v. Nance, 54 Ill. 29; Deeter v. Sellers, 102 Ind. 458, 1 N. E. 854; Livingston v. Roosevelt, 4 Johns. (N. Y.) 251, 4 Am. Dec. 273; Lance v. Butler, 135 N. Car. 419, 47 S. E. 488.

property, or to bind the rights of another, unless the latter has authorized the act. In the case of a partner paying his own separate debt out of the partnership funds, it is manifest that it is a violation of his duty and of the rights of his partners, unless they have assented to it. The act is an illegal conversion of the funds; and the separate creditor can have no better title to the funds than the partner himself had."[25]

Such a mortgage may, however, be given with the assent of copartners.[26] The mortgage will also be valid in cases where the property covered is setoff to the mortgagor on a division of the assets of the firm.[27]

§ 123. Disposition of partner's separate property upon death.—

Upon the death of a partner holding such an interest in partnership real estate, his share descends to his heirs, but equity converts the legal title into a trust, to be devoted to the payment of partnership obligations, before it can be taken as a part of his separate estate.[28] As against the partnership creditors there can be no dower in such land. But when such real estate is not required for the payment of the partnership debts or the adjustment of accounts between the partners, it is to be treated as realty in the settlement of the estate, and is subject to dower. It is then treated in every way as real estate, and does not go to the personal representatives of the deceased. It is to be regarded as real estate, and subject to all the rules applicable to real estate.[29] The conversion of such real estate into personalty for the purpose of the settlement of the partnership affairs, is a device of equity; and as soon as the reason of the rule ceases, by the closing of the partnership affairs without calling upon the real estate, the rule itself no longer applies.[30] This equitable interference is not extended so as to convert all real estate into personalty for the purpose of a division.

A mortgage by an individual partner of such real estate is relieved of all equities in favor of the partnership so soon as the business of the partnership is closed, without requiring the application of it to the firm debts.[31]

[25] Rogers v. Batchelor, 12 Pet. (U. S.) 229, 9 L. ed. 1063.
[26] Huiskamp v. Moline Wagon Co., 121 U. S. 310, 30 L. ed. 971, 7 Sup. Ct. 899.
[27] Smith v. Andrews, 49 Ill. 28.
[28] Piatt v. Oliver, 3 McLean (U. S.) 27; Wilcox v. Wilcox, 13 Allen (Mass.) 252; Burnside v. Merrick, 4 Metc. (Mass.) 537; Dyer v. Clark, 5 Metc. (Mass.) 562, 39 Am. Dec.

697; Howard v. Priest, 5 Mass. 582.
[29] Hewitt v. Rankin, 41 Iowa 35, and cases cited; Wilcox v. Wilcox, 13 Allen (Mass.) 252; Foster's Appeal, 74 Pa. St. 391, 15 Am. Rep. 553.
[30] Judge Story says, in his work on Partnership, § 93, that this is an open question. But the authorities now seem decisive of the law as stated in the text.
[31] Hewitt v. Rankin, 41 Iowa 35.

VI. *Corporations*

§ 124. Implied power of corporations to mortgage.—A corporation has the power to mortgage its real estate as an incident to the power to acquire and hold it, and to make contracts in regard to it, when the power is not expressly denied, and is not inconsistent with the public obligations of the corporation.[1] A general power conferred upon a corporation to sell, or otherwise dispose of its property, includes the power to mortgage.[2] But the lack of the power to sell or alienate the property does not necessarily amount to an inhibition on the power to mortgage.[3]

The general powers of a corporation "to sell and convey its property, and to borrow money, and make contracts" imply the power to mort-

---

See also Shearer v. Shearer, 98 Mass. 107, for an able opinion by Mr. Justice Wells.

[1] Jones v. Guaranty &c. Co., 101 U. S. 622, 25 L. ed. 1030; Aurora Agr. &c. Soc. v. Paddock, 80 Ill. 263; Thompson v. Lambert, 44 Iowa 239; State v. Topeka Water Co., 61 Kans. 547, 60 Pac. 337; Fitch v. Lewiston Steam-Mill Co., 80 Maine 34, 12 Atl. 732; Leggett v. New Jersey Mfg. &c. Co., 1 N. J. Eq. 541, 23 Am. Dec. 728; Curtis v. Leavitt, 15 N. Y. 9; Fisher's Appeal (Pa.), 14 Atl. 225; Hunt v. Memphis Gaslight Co., 95 Tenn. 136, 31 S. W. 1006; Pumphrey v. Threadgill, 87 Tex. 573, 30 S. W. 356. As to mortgages by corporations, see Jones on Corporate Bonds and Mortgages, § 5.

[2] Williamette Woolen Mfg. Co. v. Bank of B. C., 119 U. S. 191, 30 L. ed. 384, 7 Sup. Ct. 187; Susquehanna Bridge &c. Co. v. General Ins. Co., 3 Md. 305, 56 Am. Dec. 740; Liggett v. New Jersey Mfg. &c. Co., 1 N. J. Eq. 541, 23 Am. Dec. 728; Gordon v. Preston, 1 Watts (Pa.) 385, 26 Am. Dec. 75; Watts' Appeal, 78 Pa. St. 370. See also Booth v. Robinson, 55 Md. 419; McAllister v. Plant, 54 Miss. 106.

[3] Dubuque v. Miller, 11 Iowa 583; Middleton Sav. Bank v. Dubuque, 15 Iowa 394; Krider v. Western College, 31 Iowa 547. "This principle was illustrated in an early Iowa case where a statute gave a city council full power as to the city's real estate; but provided that the council should not have the power to sell any such real estate, except in a specified manner. The court concluded that but for the proviso the city council would clearly have had the power to make either a mortgage or an absolute conveyance. The inquiry was then resolved into the proposition of the power to mortgage where there could be no absolute conveyance; in other words, whether a mortgage was an alienation within the meaning of such provision. The inhibition was said to have reference to transactions which would result in parting with the title and vesting it permanently and entirely in another. The

gage its property.[4] The corporate power to borrow money implies the power to execute a mortgage to secure the loan when such power is not expressly denied.[5]

The power to mortgage for proper corporate purposes has been implied in the case of banking corporations,[6] trading corporations,[7] building corporations,[8] navigation companies,[9] power companies,[10] water companies,[11] and gaslight[12] and heating companies.[13] A municipal corporation has also the power to mortgage its real estate.[14]

In general, it may be said, that the jus disponendi of private corpo-

sale contemplated in the restriction referred to an alienation and not to a mere incumbrance. In that state the mortgage was but a lien upon the land to secure the payment of the debt. The conclusion was that the proviso applied to alienation and not to the execution of a mortgage." Thompson Corp. (2d ed.), § 2538.

[4] Packets Despatch Line v. Bellamy Mfg. Co., 12 N. H. 205, 37 Am. Dec. 203; Flint v. Clinton Co., 12 N. H. 430; Pierce v. Emery, 32 N. H. 484; Richards v. Merrimack &c. R. Co., 44 N. H. 127; De Ruyter v. St. Peter's Church, 3 Barb. Ch. (N. Y.) 119, 3 N. Y. 238; Haxtun v. Bishop, 3 Wend. (N. Y.) 13; Jackson v. Brown, 5 Wend. (N. Y.) 590; Gordon v. Preston, 1 Watts (Pa.) 385, 26 Am. Dec. 75.

[5] Jones v. Guaranty &c. Co., 101 U. S. 622, 25 L. ed. 1030; Cleveland Sav. &c. Co. v. Bear Val. Irr. Co., 112 Fed. 693; Memphis &c. R. Co. v. Dow, 19 Fed. 388; Gaytes v. Lewis, Fed. Cas. No. 5288, 2 Biss. (U. S.) 136; Taylor v. Agricultural Assn., 68 Ala. 229; Savannah &c. R. Co. v. Lancaster, 62 Ala. 555; Kelly v. Alabama &c. R. Co., 58 Ala. 489; Mobile &c. R. Co. v. Talman, 15 Ala. 472; Union Water Co. v. Murphy's Flat Fluming Co., 22 Cal. 620; Wood v. Whelen, 93 Ill. 153; West v. Madison County Agricultural Board, 82 Ill. 205; Wright v. Hughes, 119 Ind. 324, 21 N. E. 907, 12 Am. St. 412; Thompson v. Lambert, 44 Iowa 239; Warfield v. Marshall Canning Co., 72 Iowa 666, 34 N. W. 467, 2 Am. St. 263; Bardstown & L. R. Co. v. Metcalfe, 4 Metc. (Ky.) 199, 81 Am. Dec. 541; In re Mechanics' Soc., 31 La. Ann. 627; Swift v. Smith, 65 Md. 428, 5 Atl. 534, 57 Am. Rep. 336; Booth v. Robinson, 55 Md. 429; Burrill v. Bank, 2 Metc. (Mass.) 163, 35 Am. Dec. 395; Wood v. Meyer (Miss.), 7 So. 359; Thompson v. Water &c. Co., 68 Miss. 423, 9 So. 821; Richards v. Merrimack &c. R. Co., 44 N. H. 127; Central Gold Min. Co. v. Platt. 3 Daly (N. Y.) 263; Nelson v. Eaton, 26 N. Y. 410; Preston v. Loughran, 58 Hun 210, 12 N. Y. S. 313; Osborn v. Park, 89 Hun 167, 35 N. Y. S. 610; Moses v. Soule, 63 Misc. 203, 118 N. Y. S. 410; Hays v. Light &c. Co., 29 Ohio St. 330. In Pennsylvania corporations are expressly empowered by statute to borrow money on mortgages and bonds. Purdon's Pa. Digest 1903, Corp., § 140, p. 812; Miller v. Montgomery R. Co., 36 Vt. 452; Endres v. Board of Works, 1 Grat. (Va.) 364; Lehigh Valley Coal Co. v. West Depere &c. Works, 63 Wis. 45, 22 N. W. 831.

[6] Leggett v. New Jersey Mfg. Co., 1 N. J. Eq. 541, 23 Am. Dec. 728; Jackson v. Brown, 5 Wend. (N. Y.) 590.

[7] Wood v. Meyer (Miss.), 7 So. 359.

[8] Barry v. Merchants' Exchange Co., 1 Sandf. Ch. (N. Y.) 280.

[9] Australian &c. Clipper Co. v. Mounsey, 4 K. & J. 733.

[10] American Loan &c. Co. v. General Elec. Co., 71 N. H. 192, 51 Atl. 660.

[11] Hackensack Water Co. v. De Kay, 36 N. J. Eq. 548.

[12] Detroit v. Mutual Gaslight Co., 43 Mich. 594, 5 N. W. 1039.

[13] Evans v. Boston Heating Co., 157 Mass. 37, 31 N. E. 698.

[14] Vanarsdall v. Watson, 65 Ind. 176.

rations is at common law unlimited. This right may of course be circumscribed by statute,[15] or by the charters under which corporations are organized; and it is the case generally that corporations, to which are given large powers and valuable privileges, from the exercise of which it is expected the public will derive advantage, are impliedly restrained in their power of alienation.

§ 124a. **Power to mortgage all or part of the corporate property.**—The power to acquire or sell includes by necessary implication the power to mortgage. From this it follows that corporations possess, ordinarily, without any express grant, the power to mortgage all their property, to the same extent as a natural person may.[16]

A general power to mortgage the whole of any property necessarily carries with it the power to mortgage a part of such property, provided the property is of such a nature as to be divisible without detriment to the public interest. Thus, under an authority to mortgage the whole of a turnpike road, the company was held to have power to mortgage any specific part, upon which separate tolls could lawfully be collected.[17] So, the power conferred by directors upon the president of a turnpike corporation to mortgage its entire road, was held to authorize him to mortgage a part of the road.[18]

The same general principle has been applied to a railroad company.[19] But this doctrine has been doubted.[20] But if, however, the statutory

[15] One, for instance, requiring the written assent of a majority; Mass. Stat. of 1870, ch. 224, § 15; or of two-thirds of the stockholders. 2 Rev. Stat. of N. Y., p. 499, § 18. Such a statute is for their protection against the improvident acts of the officers, and is not exacted because mortgaging corporate property is improper in itself. Therefore a defect in the assent to invalidate the mortgage must be material. Greenpoint Sugar Co. v. Whitin, 69 N. Y. 328. See also Carpenter v. Blackhawk Gold Min. Co., 65 N. Y. 43; Moran v. Strauss, 6 Ben. (U. S.) 249.

[16] Allen v. Montgomery R. Co., 11 Ala. 437; Mobile &c. R. Co. v. Talman, 15 Ala. 472; Aurora Agri. &c. Soc. v. Paddock, 80 Ill. 263; Thompson v. Lambert, 44 Iowa 239; Bardstown &c. R. Co. v. Metcalfe, 4 Metc. (Ky.) 199, 81 Am. Dec. 541; Susquehanna Bridge &c. Co. v. General

Ins. Co., 3 Md. 305, 56 Am. Dec. 740; Richards v. Merrimack &c. R. Co., 44 N. H. 127; Jackson v. Brown, 5 Wend. (N. Y.) 590; Barry v. Merchants' Exch. Co., 1 Sandf. Ch. (N. Y.) 280; Burt v. Rattle, 31 Ohio St. 116; Watts' Appeal, 78 Pa. St. 370; Gordon v. Preston, 1 Watts (Pa.) 385, 26 Am. Dec. 75.

[17] Joy v. Jackson &c. Plank Rd. Co., 11 Mich. 155. See also Snell v. Chicago, 133 Ill. 413, 24 N. E. 532, 8 L. R. A. 858; Chartiers R. Co. v. Hodgens, 85 Pa. St. 501.

[18] Greensburgh &c. Co. v. McCormick, 45 Ind. 239.

[19] Pullam v. Cincinnati &c. R. Co., 4 Biss. (U. S.) 35, 20 Fed. Cas. 11461; Bickford v. Grand Junction R. Co., 1 Can. Sup. Ct. 696.

[20] East Boston &c. R. Co. v. Hubbard, 10 Allen (Mass.) 459; East Boston &c. R. Co. v. Eastern R. Co., 13 Allen (Mass.) 422.

authority to mortgage clearly indicates that any mortgage must embrace the entire property, then, under familiar rules, a part of the property can not be mortgaged. Thus, where a statute authorized a railroad company to mortgage or pledge its lands, tolls, revenues and other property for the purpose of completing, maintaining and working its road, this was held to prohibit by implication the authority to mortgage a part.[21] Where a railroad company mortgaged the part of its road which was completed, and the mortgage was subsequently foreclosed, it was held that the purchaser at the foreclosure sale could not be required to complete the road.[22]

Railroad companies can not mortgage their franchises or property essential to the continued operation of the roads[23] except with legislative authority.[24] Such a mortgage, directly prohibited by statute, is void in toto.[25] But an unauthorized mortgage, or one defectively executed, or securing bonds not properly drawn, may be subsequently confirmed by the legislature.[26] Statutory power to mortgage a railroad ordinarily

[21] Grand Junction R. Co. v. Bickford, 23 Grant Ch. U. C. 302. See also Bickford v. Grand Junction R. Co., 1 Can. Sup. Ct. 696.

[22] Chartiers R. Co. v. Hodgens, 85 Pa. St. 501.

[23] Thomas v. West Jersey R. Co., 101 U. S. 71, 25 L. ed. 950; State v. Mexican Gulf R. Co., 3 Rob. (La.) 513; Commonwealth v. Smith, 10 Allen (Mass.) 448, 87 Am. Dec. 672; Atkinson v. Marietta &c. R. Co., 15 Ohio St. 21; Coe v. Columbus, Piqua &c. R. Co., 10 Ohio St. 372, 75 Am. Dec. 518; Frazier v. East Tennessee &c. R. Co., 88 Tenn. 138, 12 S. W. 537. Contra Savannah &c. R. Co. v. Lancaster, 62 Ala. 555; Allen v. Montgomery R. Co., 11 Ala. 347; Mobile &c. R. Co. v. Talman, 15 Ala. 472; Kelly v. Alabama &c. R. Co., 58 Ala. 489; Miller v. Rutland R. Co., 36 Vt. 452.

The power of such companies to mortgage their property was regarded as necessarily implied in Kelly v. Alabama &c. R. Co., 58 Ala. 489.

This subject is barely mentioned in this treatise, because it is fully treated in the author's work on Corporate Bonds and Mortgages.

A general mortgage covering the railroad, its franchise, and all its property is void. Richardson v. Sibley, 11 Allen (Mass.) 65, 87 Am. Dec. 700.

[24] Compton v. Jesup, 68 Fed. 263, 15 C. C. A. 397; Bishop v. McKillican, 124 Cal. 321, 57 Pac. 76, 71 Am. St. 68; State v. Florida Central R. Co., 15 Fla. 690; Georgia &c. R. Co. v. Barton, 101 Ga. 466, 28 S. E. 482; Palmer v. Forbes, 23 Ill. 301; State v. Morgan, 28 La. Ann. 482; Baker v. Guaranty Trust &c. Co. (N. J.), 31 Atl. 174; Platt v. New York &c. R. Co., 9 App. Div. 87, 41 N. Y. S. 42; Gloninger v. Pittsburgh R. Co., 139 Pa. St. 13, 21 Atl. 211; Frazier v. East Tenn. &c. Co., 88 Tenn. 138, 12 S. W. 537; Galveston R. Co. v. Fontaine, 23 Tex. Civ. App. 519, 57 S. W. 872. The power may be implied from legislative act. Parker v. New Orleans &c. R. Co., 33 Fed. 693; Electric Lighting Co. v. Rust, 117 Ala. 680, 23 So. 751; Bardstown &c. R. Co. v. Metcalfe, 4 Metc. (Ky.) 199, 81 Am. Dec. 541; East Boston &c. R. Co. v. Eastern R. Co., 13 Allen (Mass.) 422; Miller v. Ratterman, 10 Ohio Dec. (reprint) 555; Coe v. Columbus R. Co., 10 Ohio St. 372, 75 Am. Dec. 518; Pierce v. Milwaukee &c. R. Co., 24 Wis. 551, 1 Am. Rep. 203.

[25] Richardson v. Sibley, 11 Allen (Mass.) 65, 87 Am. Dec. 700.

[26] Chapin v. Vermont &c. R. Co., 8 Gray (Mass.) 575; Shaw v. Norfolk County R. Co., 5 Mass. 162.

covers all of the property owned by the company and necessary to the operation of the road.[27]

A mortgage by a corporation de facto is good until the state has interposed and declared its exercise of corporate powers a usurpation. Until this is done, it is assumed that the corporation de facto rightfully possessed and exercised corporate powers.[28]

The right of a railroad company to construct a road being given because of the benefit to the public arising from the use of the road, a power conferred upon it to mortgage its property is construed to confer upon the mortgagee, or a purchaser under the mortgage in possession, all needful authority to use the road in a proper and beneficial manner, but no authority to take up and sell the material of which the road is made.[29]

A mortgage made by a solvent corporation to one who is at the time a director and stockholder, to secure a loan made by him, is not invalid on account of the relation between the parties.[30]

§ 124b. **Whether express power to mortgage is exhausted by single exercise of power.**—Whether express power to a railroad company to mortgage its property is exhausted after it is once exercised, seems to depend first on the terms of the authority; and second on the uses or purposes for which the mortgage is made. Under a charter which authorized a railroad company to increase its capital stock to a sum sufficient to complete the road, and to stock it with everything necessary to give it full operation and effect, either by selling new stock, or by borrowing money on the credit of the company or by mortgage of its charter and works, it was held that when this charter power to mortgage was once exercised it was then exhausted, and that in respect

[27] Dunham v. Earl, Fed. Cas. No. 4149; Phillips v. Winslow, 18 B. Mon. (Ky.) 431, 68 Am. Dec. 729; Ludlow v. Hurd, 1 Disn. (Ohio) 552, 12 Ohio Dec. (reprint) 791; Coe v. Columbus &c. R. Co., 10 Ohio St. 372, 75 Am. Dec. 518.

[28] Duggan v. Colorado Mtg. &c. Co., 11 Colo. 113, 17 Pac. 105; Collins v. Rea, 127 Mich. 273, 86 N. W. 811.

In Pennsylvania a limited partnership, organized under the Act of June 2, 1874, which has apparently complied with the provisions of the act by filing its articles of association and complying with other formalities, becomes a quasi corporation de facto, and a mortgage executed by the chairman and secretary with the partnership seal, as provided by the act, is valid. Briar Hill Coal &c. Co. v. Atlas Works, 146 Pa. St. 290, 23 Atl. 326; Eliot v. Himrod, 108 Pa. St. 569.

[29] Palmer v. Forbes, 23 Ill. 237.

[30] Mullanphy Bank v. Schott, 135 Ill. 655, 26 N. E. 640; Roseboom v. Whittaker, 132 Ill. 81, 23 N. E. 339, Beach v. Miller, 130 Ill. 162, 22 N. E. 464.

to further contracts and rights it was as though it had never been granted.[31]

But in another case, where it appeared that under the authority of congress a mortgage had been given by a railroad company for the purpose of raising funds with which to construct its road, it was held that after the mortgage was executed pursuant to such power, the purchaser at foreclosure sale and successor to the rights of the original corporation could again mortgage the road for the purpose of raising funds to complete it. In the course of the opinion the court said: "Upon this branch of the controversy the contention for the plaintiff is that the joint resolution of congress was a privilege to the original corporation only, and did not pass to the present corporation upon the reorganization, and that, further, in any event, it only permitted a single mortgage to be created, and the power was spent upon the creation of the first mortgage. This seems to be an astute rather than a reasonable interpretation of the language of the joint resolution. The purpose of including the right to mortgage the franchises of the corporation in the consent of congress was palpably in order that a purchaser under a foreclosure might succeed to all the rights and privileges of the original corporation. As there was no restriction in that consent respecting the amount for which a mortgage might be created by the corporation, or relating to the scope or character of the mortgage, the implication seems not only fair, but irresistible, that congress intended to leave all this to the discretion of the corporation itself, to be exercised in view of the exigencies of the undertaking. Obviously, congress was quite indifferent whether the mortgage should be a large one or a small one, whether it should cover the whole or a part of the property of the company, or whether all the bonds to be secured should be issued at one time or in one series or class. The power conferred is limited only by the purpose expressed, that the bonds are to be issued to aid in the construction and equipment of the road, and are to be secured by mortgage.[32]

§ 125. **Lands not necessary for the business of a railroad.**[33]—But this limitation of the power of a railroad corporation to mortgage its real estate does not apply to lands not required to enable it to carry on the business which it was chartered to do for the benefit of the public, and not needed or used for that purpose. The alienation of such lands

---

[31] East Tennessee &c. R. Co. v. Frazier, 139 U. S. 288, 35 L. ed. 196, 11 Sup. Ct. 517.
[33] Du Pont v. Northern Pac. R. Co.,
18 Fed. 467. See also Mead v. New York &c. R. Co., 45 Conn. 199.
[33] See Jones on Corporate Bonds and Mortgages, § 12.

in no wise impairs or affects the usefulness of the company as a railroad corporation, or its ability to exercise any of its corporate franchises. Mr. Justice Foster, of Massachusetts,[34] in a case involving this point, said: "The recent cases in which railroad mortgages have been adjudged invalid by this court do not countenance any doubt of the power of a railroad company to sell and convey whatever property it may hold, not acquired under the delegated right of eminent domain, or so connected with the franchise to operate and maintain a railroad that the alienation would tend to disable the corporation from performing the public duties imposed upon it, in consideration of which its chartered privileges have been conferred." If a mortgage by a railroad company includes lands which it can mortgage without distinct legislative authority, and also lands which it can not convey without such authority, the mortgage will be upheld as to the former, but will be inoperative and void as to the latter.[35]

§ **125a. Foreign corporations.**—Foreign corporations have the same power to mortgage their property as domestic corporations,[36] except as restricted by charter or statute.[37] A corporation, organized under the laws of one state, which acquires property and carries on business in another state, may mortgage its property there, unless prohibited by statute; and such corporation is estopped from questioning the validity of a mortgage described in a deed which it accepted.[38]

§ **126. Religious corporations.**[39]—A religious corporation has in general, under our laws, the same right to mortgage and create liens upon its real estate that any corporation has. Having the power to hold and enjoy real estate, unless there be an express prohibition, it has the power to mortgage it.[40] The trustees of such a corporation are

---

[34] Hendee v. Pinkerton, 14 Allen (Mass.) 381.

[35] Hendee v. Pinkerton, 14 Allen (Mass.) 381; Jones on Railroad Securities, § 12.

[36] American Water Works Co. v. Farmers' Loan &c. Co., 73 Fed. 956, 20 C. C. A. 133; Saltmarsh v. Spaulding, 147 Mass. 227, 17 N. E. 316; Union Nat. Bank v. State Nat. Bank, 155 Mo. 95, 55 S. W. 989, 78 Am. St. 560; Bassett v. Monte Christo Gold &c. Min. Co., 15 Nev. 293; Talmadge v. North American Coal &c. Co., 3 Head (Tenn.) 337.

[37] Union Nat. Bank v. State Nat. Bank, 155 Mo. 95, 55 S. W. 989, 78

Am. St. 560; Talmadge v. North American Coal &c. Co., 3 Head (Tenn.) 337.

[38] American Water Works Co. v. Farmers' Loan &c. Co., 73 Fed. 956, 20 C. C. A. 133.

[39] See Jones on Corporate Bonds and Mortgages, §§ 5a and 6, for mortgages by and to religious corporations.

[40] Methodist Epis. Church v. Shulze, 61 Ind. 511; Madison Av. Ch. v. Oliver St. Ch., 9 Jones & S. (N. Y.) 369; Walrath v. Campbell, 28 Mich. 111. "It was usual in England to restrain both the power of acquisition and the power of sale of

presumed to have power to mortgage the church property.[41] Such power may be conferred by statute,[42] by by-laws, articles of incorporation or special resolution.[43] An unauthorized mortgage of the trustees may be accepted and ratified by the members of a religious society, and long acquiescence will be treated as a ratification.[44] In some states authority of court is necessary for a religious corporation to mortgage its real estate.[45]

§ 126a. **Limitations as to amount of mortgage.**—A corporation may be limited as to the amount of a mortgage upon the corporate property; the restriction may be that the mortgages shall not exceed the amount of the capital stock; or two-thirds of the value of the property. Where such a limitation was imposed it was held that the corporation could not execute a mortgage to secure an issue of bonds in excess of such limit, although the excess was to be issued at some future date and then upon the required consent of the stockholders.[46] But it has been held that a mortgage securing a debt in excess of the statutory amount, or in excess of its capital stock, was binding on the corporation as well as its subsequent creditors.[47] So, a corporation mortgage securing bonds in excess of half of its corporate property is not void, but only renders the directors liable for any damages by

ecclesiastical corporations, and a similar policy has been adopted in some of the American states in reference to the real estate of such corporations; and certain restrictions of this kind will be found in our own statutes." Per Christiancy, J. In Missouri, church corporations have power to mortgage their real estate by virtue of a statutory provision "that every corporation as such has power * * * to hold, purchase, mortgage or otherwise convey such real and personal estate as the purposes of the corporation may require." Keith &c. Coal Co. v. Bingham, 97 Mo. 196, 10 S. W. 32.

[41] Zion Church v. Mensch, 178 Ill. 225, 52 N. E. 858, affg. 74 Ill. App. 115; Page v. Church, 78 N. J. Eq. 114, 78 Atl. 246.

[42] Zion Church v. Mensch, 178 Ill. 225, 52 N. E. 858; Methodist Episcopal Church v. Shulze, 61 Ind. 511; Scott v. First Methodist Church, 50 Mich. 528, 15 N. W. 891.

[43] Zion Church v. Mensch, 178 Ill. 225, 52 N. E. 858.

[44] Scott v. First Methodist Church, 50 Mich. 528, 15 N. W. 891; McCallister v. Ross, 155 Mo. 87, 55 S. W. 1027; Page v. Church, 78 N. J. Eq. 114, 78 Atl. 246; Rountree v. Blount, 129 N. Car. 25, 39 S. E. 631.

[45] In re Church of Messiah, 25 Abb. N. Cas. 354, 12 N. Y. S. 489.

[46] Flynn v. Coney Island &c. R. Co., 26 App. Div. 416, 50 N. Y. S. 74.

[47] Sioux City Terminal R. &c. Co. v. Trust Co., 173 U. S. 99, 43 L. ed. 628, 19 Sup. Ct. 341, affg. 82 Fed. 124, 27 C. C. A. 73; Central Trust Co. v. Columbus &c. R. Co., 87 Fed. 815; Farmers' Loan &c. Co. v. Toledo &c. R. Co., 67 Fed. 49; Allis v. Jones, 45 Fed. 148; Smith v. Ferries &c. R. Co. (Cal.), 51 Pac. 710; Warfield v. Marshall &c. Co., 72 Iowa 666, 34 N. W. 467, 2 Am. St. 263; Des Moines Gas Co. v. West, 50 Iowa 16; International Trust Co. v. Davis &c. Mfg. Co., 70 N. H. 118, 46 Atl. 1054; Hackensack Water Co. v. De Kay, 36 N. J. Eq. 548; New Britain Nat. Bank v. Cleveland Co., 91 Hun 447, 36 N. Y. S. 387, affd. without opinion 158

reason thereof.[48] In Kentucky it was held that a mortgage by a corporation in excess of the limit of indebtedness fixed by the articles of association is void.[49] The execution and delivery by a corporation of a mortgage on its real estate, to secure bonds, was held to be a transfer of real estate securities under a statute providing that corporations should fix a maximum of indebtedness, but the provision was not to apply where the corporate bonds were issued and secured by an actual transfer of real estate securities.[50]

§ 126b. **Mortgages by corporations to secure purchase-money.**— The proposition has been asserted that the power to mortgage may be implied from other powers, and that the general power to purchase and sell implies the power to mortgage. It therefore follows that where a corporation is authorized to purchase property, express power is not required to the validity of a mortgage securing the purchase-money. If a corporation could legitimately purchase, in order to attain its legitimate objects, it may deal precisely as an individual. "No precedent has been found," said a federal judge, "denying to a corporation the power to execute a mortgage of everything it acquires by a purchase, when the mortgage is a condition of making the purchase; and there seems to be no reason, in a case like the present, for denying the power when the purchase of the mortgagor includes the franchise and the whole property of the corporation."[51]

Where the vendor refused to receive a purchase-money mortgage executed by a corporation, and the corporation thereupon used the bonds secured by such mortgage, it was held that the vendor lost his lien.[52] In New York it was held that a corporation could give a mortgage securing the purchase-money of property without the assent of the stockholders.[53] Where a conveyance was made to a corporation which bound the grantee to pay and discharge certain mortgages, it was held that acceptance of the deed would be presumed and that the corporation would

N. Y. 722, 53 N. E. 1128; Fidelity &c. Co. v. West Pennsylvania &c. R. Co., 138 Pa. St. 494, 21 Atl. 21, 21 Am. St. 911; Union Trust Co. v. Mercantile Library &c. Co., 189 Pa. St. 263, 42 Atl. 129. But see Fountaine v. Carmarthen R. Co., L. R. 5 Eq. 316; Pittsburgh &c. R. Co.'s Appeal (Pa. St.), 4 Atl. 385.

[48] Beebe v. Richmond Light &c. Co., 13 Misc. 737, 35 N. Y. S. 1.

[49] Bell &c. Co. v. Kentucky &c. Co., 20 Ky. L. 1089, 48 S. W. 440.
[50] First Nat. Bank v. Sioux City Terminal R. &c. Co., 69 Fed. 441.
[51] Memphis &c. R. Co. v. Dow, 19 Fed. 388; Memphis &c. R. Co. v. Dow, 120 U. S. 287, 30 L. ed. 595, 7 Sup. Ct. 482.
[52] Rice's Appeal, 79 Pa. St. 168.
[53] Farmers' Loan &c. Co. v. Equity Gaslight Co., 84 Hun 373, 32 N. Y. S. 385.

be bound by the covenant to pay the mortgages.[54] So, in Massachusetts, it was held that a purchase-money mortgage, by which the vendor was to be paid a certain sum, or was to have the option of taking certain shares of stock, might be included in the deed.[55] And in Alabama it was held that the purchase-money mortgage included in the deed required the vendee to complete the construction of a railroad and issue certain stock to the vendor.[56] The power to purchase real estate includes the power to purchase real estate that is incumbered, and the power to purchase incumbered real estate implies the power to assume the incumbrance.[57]

§ 126c. **Mortgage of fixtures.**—The rights of a corporation with reference to fixtures are the same as those of individuals; and corporate mortgages of realty cover fixtures as distinguished from personal property. So, fixtures, whether attached before or after the execution of a general mortgage of the real estate of a corporation, are held to be subject to the lien of such mortgage.[58]

The rule is stated by the Massachusetts court thus: "Whatever is placed in a building subject to a mortgage, by a mortgagor or those claiming under him, to carry out the purpose for which it was erected, and permanently to increase its value for occupation or use, although it may be removed without injury to itself or the building, becomes part of the realty, as between mortgagor and mortgagee, and can not be removed or otherwise disposed of while the mortgage is in force.[59] The rule as to the lien of a mortgage on fixtures in a factory has been stated thus: "A mortgage of a factory, eo nomine includes ex vi termini, all the machinery and other articles essential to the factory."[60]

A trust deed of corporate property and covering the "machinery"

[54] Stokes v. Detrick, 75 Md. 256, 23 Atl. 846.

[55] Pinch v. Anthony, 8 Allen (Mass.) 536.

[56] Tennessee &c. R. Co. v. East Alabama R. Co., 73 Ala. 426.

[57] Woods Inv. Co. v. Palmer, 8 Colo. App. 132, 45 Pac. 237.

[58] Porter v. Pittsburg &c. Steel Co., 122 U. S. 267, 30 L. ed. 1210, 7 Sup. Ct. 1206; Southbridge Sav. Bank v. Mason, 147 Mass. 500, 18 N. E. 406, 1 L. R. A. 350; McConnell v. Blood, 123 Mass. 47, 25 Am. Rep. 12; McLaughlin v. Nash, 14 Allen (Mass.) 136, 92 Am. Dec. 741; Shepard v. Blossom, 66 Minn. 421, 69 N. W. 221, 61 Am. St. 431; Delaware &c. R. Co. v. Oxford Iron Co., 36 N. J. Eq. 452; McRea v. Central Nat. Bank, 66 N. Y. 489; McFadden v. Allen, 134 N. Y. 489, 32 N. E. 21, 19 L. R. A. 446; Vail v. Weaver, 132 Pa. St. 363, 19 Atl. 138, 19 Am. St. 598; Morotock Ins. Co. v. Rodefer, 92 Va. 747, 24 S. E. 393, 53 Am. St. 846; Kendall Mfg. Co. v. Rundle, 78 Wis. 150, 47 N. W. 364; Homestead &c. Co. v. Becker, 96 Wis. 206, 71 N. W. 117; Gunderson v. Swarthout, 104 Wis. 186, 80 N. W. 465, 76 Am. St. 860.

[59] Smith Paper Co. v. Servin, 130 Mass. 511.

[60] Potts v. New Jersey Arms &c. Co., 17 N. J. Eq. 395; Delaware &c. R. Co. v. Oxford Iron Co., 36 N. J. Eq. 452; Voorhis v. Freeman, 2

belonging to a cotton print works company was held to include certain copper rolls on which the designs to be printed on the cloth were engraved, but which were not a part of the printing presses, but were purchased in the market separate from the presses, and were unavailable for use except in the presses.[61] So, a mortgage on the real estate was held to include a dynamo and appurtenant machinery screwed to timbers spiked to the floor of the building and operated by belts from shafting firmly attached to the floor of the building.[62] So, ponderous machinery resting by its own weight on a platform supported by posts, was held to be covered by a mortgage.[63] But where finished machines were set up in a factory and required no particular adaptation for use, or any alteration in the factory itself, and which could be removed without injury, either to themselves or to the building, they were held not to be covered by a mortgage of the real estate which included the factory as well as "the steam engines, boilers, shafting, belting, gearing, and all other machinery appertaining to said premises, now upon said premises, or that shall hereafter be placed or erected thereon."[64] And the wires of one telegraph company placed on the poles of another under a contract that certain rent should be paid for the privilege, were held not to be covered by a mortgage made by the company owning the poles.[65]

The rule is perhaps more strict in its application to railroad property; and generally all articles which are used by or which become affixed to the railway system are regarded as fixtures subject to the lien of a general mortgage.[66] Thus, both new and old rails intended for use, or which have been used, have been held to be fixtures.[67]

Watts & S. (Pa.) 116, 37 Am. Dec. 490; Pyle v. Pennock, 2 Watts & S. (Pa.) 390, 37 Am. Dec. 517.

[61] Doty v. Oriental Print Works Co., 28 R. I. 372, 67 Atl. 586.

[62] Vail v. Weaver, 132 Pa. St. 363, 19 Atl. 138, 19 Am. St. 598; Gunderson v. Swarthout, 104 Wis. 186, 80 N. W. 465, 76 Am. St. 860.

[63] Shepard v. Blossom, 66 Minn. 421, 69 N. W. 221, 61 Am. St. 431.

[64] Rogers v. Prattville Mfg. Co., 81 Ala. 483, 1 So. 643, 60 Am. Rep. 171; Penn Mut. &c. Ins. Co. v. Semple, 38 N. J. Eq. 575; Knickerbocker Trust Co. v. Penn Cordage Co., 62 N. J. Eq. 624, 50 Atl. 459.

[65] United States v. New Orleans R. Co., 12 Wall. (U. S.) 362, 20 L. ed. 434; Porter v. Pittsburg &c. Steel Co., 122 U. S. 267, 30 L. ed. 1210, 7 Sup. Ct. 1206; Tifft v. Horton, 53

N. Y. 377, 13 Am. Rep. 537; Union College v. Wheeler, 61 N. Y. 88; American Union Tel. Co. v. Middleton, 80 N. Y. 408; New York &c. R. Co. v. Western Union Tel. Co., 36 Hun (N. Y.) 205; Farnsworth v. Western Union Tel. Co., 6 N. Y. S. 735, 25 N. Y. St. 393.

[66] Porter v. Pittsburg &c. Steel Co., 122 U. S. 267, 30 L. ed. 1210, 7 Sup. Ct. 1206; Fosdick v. Schall, 99 U. S. 235, 25 L. ed. 339; Dillon v. Barnard, 21 Wall. (U. S.) 430, 22 L. ed. 673; United States v. New Orleans R. Co., 12 Wall. (U. S.) 362, 20 L. ed. 434; Galveston R. Co. v. Cowdrey, 11 Wall. (U. S.) 459, 20 L. ed. 199; Dunham v. Cincinnati &c. R. Co., 1 Wall. (U. S.) 254, 17 L. ed. 584.

[67] Palmer v. Forbes, 23 Ill. 237; Lehigh Coal &c. Co. v. Central R.

§ 127. Powers of stockholders and directors.—The power to mortgage resides primarily in the body corporate, or, in other words, in the stockholders. They may authorize the execution of the deed by any agents they may by special vote, or general by-law, constitute for that purpose. The directors of a corporation, without authority either expressly or impliedly derived from the stockholders, have no right to execute a mortgage or to authorize any one to do so.[68] But even if the directors exceed their authority in borrowing money for the corporation and executing a mortgage to secure the repayment of it, the corporation can not, after enjoying the benefit of the loan, and acquiescing in the transaction, question their authority. The stockholders may restrain the directors, or other officers, in any attempt to transcend their powers; but if they remain silent, permitting them to execute mortgages upon their property, and receiving the benefits of the loan, they are estopped to say that the officers were not authorized to do these acts.[69] A corporation ratifies a mortgage made by its directors by issuing bonds under it, and paying interest upon them.[70] The ratification may be through any acts which show that the corporation accepts the acts of its officers or agents;[71] such as receiving and using the proceeds of such mortgage.[72]

A statute or a by-law of a corporation, providing that in the management of its affairs the directors shall have all the powers which the corporation itself possesses, invests them with power to borrow money, issue bonds, and convey in mortgage the lands of the corporation as security.[73] Whether the directors of a corporation, in the absence of

---

Co., 35 N. J. Eq. 379; Weetjen v. St. Paul &c. R. Co., 4 Hun (N. Y.) 529; First Nat. Bank v. Anderson, 75 Va. 250.

[68] Campbell v. Mining Co., 51 Fed. 1; Graves v. Mono Lake Hydraulic M. Co., 81 Cal. 303, 22 Pac. 665; Long v. Powell, 120 Ga. 621, 48 S. E. 185; McElroy v. Nucleus Assn., 131 Pa. St. 393, 18 Atl. 1063. Directors have no authority to execute a mortgage except by resolution regularly adopted at a board meeting. State v. Manhattan Rubber Mfg. Co., 149 Mo. 181, 50 S. W. 321.

[69] Hotel Co. v. Wade, 97 U. S. 13, 24 L. ed. 917; Aurora Agr. &c. Soc. v. Paddock, 80 Ill. 263; Bradley v. Ballard, 55 Ill. 413, 7 Am. Rep. 656; Ottawa Northern Plank Poad Co. v. Murray, 15 Ill. 336; Beach v. Wakefield, 107 Iowa 567, 59, 76 N. W.

688, 78 N. W. 197; McCurdy's Appeal, 65 Pa. St. 290.

[70] Campbell v. Min. Co., 51 Fed. 1; McCurdy's Appeal, 65 Pa. St. 290.

[71] Holbrook v. Chamberlin, 116 Mass. 155, 17 Am. Rep. 146, and cases cited.

[72] Cooke v. Watson, 30 N. J. Eq. 345.

[73] Hendee v. Pinkerton, 14 Allen (Mass.) 381; Saltmarsh v. Spaulding, 147 Mass. 224, 17 N. E. 316. Under a provision requiring the written assent of a majority of the stockholders owning at least two-thirds of the capital stock to be filed in the office of the county clerk, the assent may be given by those representing two-thirds of the stock actually issued, and it does not matter that some of the shares represented in the assent have not been paid for

any restriction by charter or by-law, may, without further authority in behalf of the corporation, mortgage its property to secure debts they are authorized to incur, is left uncertain by the authorities; though in general the directors are regarded as having by implication all the power of the corporation in this regard.[74] Where the authority to mortgage is vested in the directors, it is doubtful whether the owner of the entire stock, though a director, could execute a mortgage without the consent of the other directors, who are nominal stockholders.[75]

It is, of course, essential that the stockholders or the directors of the corporation, whichever body is authorized to act, should be legally convened by notice given in accordance with the statute of the state or by-laws of the corporation, and a mortgage authorized at a meeting held without due notice is void.[76] A statute prescribing a certain vote of shareholders, and due notice of the meeting, does not apply to mortgages given for unpaid purchase-money delivered upon receipt of the conveyance.[77]

If the directors have power to execute a mortgage of corporate property, neither the president nor any other officer can execute a mortgage without a resolution of the board of directors duly assembled,[78] but such resolution need not be evidenced by an instrument under seal of the corporation, nor need it be recorded with the deed, since it is not a power of attorney.[79]

in full. The Lyceum v. Ellis, 30 N. Y. St. 242, 8 N. Y. S. 867.

[74] Jones on Corp. Bonds & Mtg. § 45; Bell &c. Co. v. Kentucky Glass-Works Co., 20 Ky. L. 1089, 48 S. W. 440; Augusta Bank v. Hamblet, 35 Maine 491; Hendee v. Pinkerton, 14 Allen (Mass.) 381, per Foster, J.; Sargent v. Webster, 13 Metc. (Mass.) 497, 503, 46 Am. Dec. 743; Burrill v. Nahant Bank, 2 Metc. (Mass.) 163, 35 Am. Dec. 395; Hoyt v. Thompson, 19 N. Y. 207; Bank of Middlebury v. Rutland &c. R. Co., 30 Vt. 159; Miller v. Rutland &c. R. Co., 36 Vt. 452. See also Forbes v. San Rafael Turnpike Co., 50 Cal. 340, where the power of the directors was limited.

A statute requiring a vote of the stockholders of a corporation to authorize a conveyance of its real estate, does not apply to a conveyance made by a foreign corporation. Saltmarsh v. Spaulding, 147 Mass. 224, 17 N. E. 316.

[75] Union Nat. Bank v. State Nat. Bank, 155 Mo. 95, 55 S. W. 989, 78 Am. St. 560.

[76] Southern Building &c. Assn. v. Casa Grande Stable Co., 128 Ala. 624, 29 So. 654; Bank of Little Rock v. McCarthy, 55 Ark. 473, 18 S. W. 759.

[77] Farmers' Loan &c. Co. v. Equity Gaslight Co., 84 Hun 373, 65 N. Y. St. 591, 32 N. Y. S. 385. See also McMurray v. St. Louis Oil Mfg. Co., 33 Mo. 377; McComb v. Barcelona Apart. Assn., 134 N. Y. 598, 31 N. E. 613, 45 N. Y. St. 784.

[78] Alta Silver M. Co. v. Mining Co., 78 Cal. 629, 21 Pac. 373; Mason &c. Co. v. Metcalfe Mfg. Co., 19 Ky. L. 1864, 44 S. W. 629; Leggett v. New Jersey Mfg. &c. Co., 1 N. J. Eq. 541, 23 Am. Dec. 728; Jennie Clarkson Home v. Missouri &c. R. Co., 182 N. Y. 47, 74 N. E. 571, 70 L. R. A. 787.

[79] Beckwith v. Windsor Mfg. Co., 14 Conn. 594.

Where it was part of the arrangement under which land was conveyed to a corporation that it should give a mortgage to secure future advances for improvements thereon, such mortgage, being made contemporaneously with the deed, is not within a statute requiring corporations to obtain the assent of two-thirds of the owners of the capital stock as a condition precedent to the giving of a mortgage to secure a debt contracted by it in the course of its business.[80]

§ 128. **Use of corporate seal.**—In states where seals have not been abolished a corporation can not make a valid mortgage of its real estate except by an instrument under its corporate seal.[81] But an impression of the seal of a corporation indented into the substance of the paper upon which the instrument is written is a good seal, although no wax, wafer, or other adhesive substance be used.[82] This is so held in states where the distinction between sealed and unsealed instruments is inflexibly preserved. But where a scroll is not treated as a seal, a facsimile of the seal of a corporation printed with ink on the paper is not a valid seal.[83] "No definition of a seal has ever been made," says

[80] McComb v. Barcelona Apartment Assn., 10 N. Y. S. 546.

[81] Koehler v. Black River Falls Iron Co., 2 Black (U. S.) 715; In re St. Helen Mill Co., 3 Sawyer (U. S.) 88, Fed. Cas. No. 12222; Danville Seminary v. Mott, 136 Ill. 289, 28 N. E. 54 (deed); Duke v. Markham, 105 N. Car. 131, 10 S. E. 1017, 18 Am. St. 889; Eagle Woollen Mills Co. v. Monteith, 2 Ore. 277; Thayer v. Nehalem Mill Co., 31 Ore. 437, 51 Pac. 202; McElroy v. Nucleus Assn., 131 Pa. St. 393, 18 Atl. 1063; Texas Consol. &c. Assn. v. Dublin Compress &c. Co. (Tex. Civ. App.), 38 S. W. 404 (deed). In Tennessee, only the private seals of individuals are abolished. Garrett v. Belmont Land Co., 94 Tenn. 459, 29 S. W. 726.

[82] Pillow v. Roberts, 13 How. (U. S.) 472, 14 L. ed. 228; Follett v. Rose, 3 McLean (U. S.) 332, Fed. Cas. No. 4900; Orr v. Lacey, 6 McLean (U. S.) 243, Fed. Cas. No. 10589; Connolly v. Goodwin, 5 Cal. 220; Woodman v. York &c. R. Co., 50 Maine 549; Carter v. Burley, 9 N. H. 558; Allen v. Sullivan R. Co., 32 N. H. 446; Corrigan v. Trenton &c. Co., 5 N. J. Eq. 52; Curtis v. Leavitt, 15 N. Y. 90, 17 Barb. 309.

Hendee v. Pinkerton, 14 Allen (Mass.) 381. "After our own courts have allowed wafers instead of wax, and paper with gum or mucilage instead of wafers, there seems little reason why we should hesitate also to allow the sufficiency of an impression of a corporate seal on the paper itself. The extent to which this practice has prevailed among corporations; the fact that the seals of all our own courts have been from an early period of the same description; the sanction of numerous decisions in other states and in the federal courts; the convenience and unobjectionable character of the usage,—are arguments in its favor too powerful to be resisted, in the absence of any decisive authority to the contrary." Per Foster, J. See also article, 1 Am. Law Rev. 638, by Geo. S. Hale, Esq.

A corporate seal by impression in the paper has been legalized in many states including: Connecticut, Georgia, Massachusetts, Minnesota, New Hampshire, New York, Ohio, Oregon and West Virginia.

[83] Bates v. Boston &c. R. Co., 10 Allen (Mass.) 251.

Mr. Justice Foster,[84] "and none can be suggested, liberal enough to include the method adopted in that case, which would not destroy the distinction uniformly adhered to in the usage and judicial decisions of this state. If we should pronounce every scroll a seal, we should speedily be called upon to take the next step of pronouncing every flourish to be a scroll, and nothing would remain of the ancient formality of sealing."

The form now required for a corporate seal is less exacting. Various devices are held valid, including a scrawl or scroll,[85] and a bit of paper attached opposite the signatures.[86]

Where an instrument purports to be sealed with the corporate seal, and is shown to have been signed by the proper officers of the corporation, a presumption arises that the seal was affixed by the proper authority, and the instrument will be held valid until its invalidity is shown.[87]

VII. *Power to Mortgage*

<table>
<tr><td>SECTION</td><td>SECTION</td></tr>
<tr><td>129. Power of attorney — Implied power to mortgage.</td><td>130. Mode of exercising the power.
130a. Joint mortgagors.</td></tr>
</table>

§ 129. Power of attorney—Implied power to mortgage.—An agent or attorney may be authorized to mortgage the property of his principal,[1] but his authority must be in writing,[2] and executed with the same formalities required in the instrument it authorizes. Where cor-

---

[84] Hendee v. Pinkerton, 14 Allen (Mass.) 381; Rauch v. Oil Co., 8 W. Va. 36, a deed of trust reciting a corporation as the grantor, but having the following attestation: "Witness the signature and seal of William Scott, president of said Blennerhassett Oil Co., and who is legally authorized by the board of directors of said company to make this grant, this date aforewritten. William Scott (seal);" the corporate seal not being used, was held not to be the deed of the corporation.

[85] Johnson v. Crawley, 25 Ga. 316, 71 Am. Dec. 173 (mortgage); Reynolds v. Glasgow, 6 Dana (Ky.) 37 (deed). A scrawl or scroll is permitted by statute in many states including: Georgia, Illinois, Minnesota, Mississippi, Missouri, New Jersey, Ohio and Oregon; but seals of corporations are excepted from such statutes in Connecticut, Michigan, Virginia and Wisconsin.

[86] Gashwiler v. Willis, 33 Cal. 11, 91 Am. Dec. 607 (deed); Mill Dam Foundry v. Hovey, 21 Pick. (Mass.) 417; Stebbins v. Merritt, 64 Mass. 27 (mortgage); Tenny v. East Warren Lbr. Co., 43 N. H. 343; St. Phillips Church v. Zion Pres. Ch., 23 S. Car. 297.

[87] Mullanphy Bank v. Schott, 135 Ill. 655, 26 N. E. 640; Wood v. Whelen, 93 Ill. 153; Fidelity Ins. Co. v. Shenandoah Val. R. Co. 32 W. Va. 244, 9 So. 180.

[1] Alta Silver Min. Co. v. Alta Placer Min. Co. 78 Cal. 629, 21 Pac. 373; Seawell v. Payne, 5 La. Ann. 255; Eaton v. Dewey, 79 Wis. 251, 48 N. W. 523.

[2] Alta Silver Min. Co. v. Alta Placer Min. Co., 78 Cal. 629, 21 Pac. 373.

porate property is controlled by the directors, a mortgage executed by the president and secretary, and ratified by the stockholders, is void.[3] By a power of attorney duly executed, a wife may constitute her husband and other named persons her agents to convey and mortgage her property.[4]

A power to sell and convey real estate does not, as a general rule, confer a power to mortgage, and a mortgage executed under a power of attorney, authorizing the attorney to sell and convey only, is void.[5]

A devise of so much of the testator's estate as may be sufficient for the maintenance of the devisee during his life, "he having full power to sell and convey any and all of my real estate, at any time, if necessary to secure such maintenance," does not give to the devisee the right to mortgage the estate in fee.[6] The power should expressly declare the

[3] Alta Silver Min. Co. v. Alta Placer Min. Co., 78 Cal. 629, 21 Pac. 373.

[4] Eaton v. Dewey, 79 Wis. 251, 48 N. W. 523.

[5] Colesbury v. Dart, 61 Ga. 620; Salem Nat. Bank v. White, 159 Ill. 136, 42 N. E. 312; Reed v. Kimsey, 98 Ill. App. 364; Switzer v. Wilvers, 24 Kans. 384; Wood v. Goodridge, 6 Cush. (Mass.) 117, 52 Am. Dec. 771; Jeffrey v. Hursh, 49 Mich. 31, 12 N. W. 898; Morris v. Watson, 15 Minn. 212; Kinney v. Mathews, 69 Mo. 520; Bloomer v. Waldron, 3 Hill (N. Y.) 361; Morris v. Ewing, 8 N. Dak. 99, 76 N. W. 1047.

De Bouchout v. Goldsmid, 5 Ves. 211; Australian &c. Co. v. Mounsey, 4 K. & J. 733; Huldenby v. Spofforth, 1 Beav. 390; Stronghill v. Anstey, 1 De G., M. & G. 635.

Otherwise in Pennsylvania: Lancaster v. Dolan, 1 Rawle (Pa.) 231, 18 Am. Dec. 625; Zane v. Kennedy, 73 Pa. St. 182; Presbyterian Corporation v. Wallace, 3 Rawle (Pa.) 109; Gordon v. Preston, 1 Watts (Pa.) 385, 26 Am. Dec. 75; Duval's Appeal, 38 Pa. St. 112; Penn. Life Ins. Co. v. Austin, 42 Pa. St. 257.

In Georgia: Allen v. Lindsey, 113 Ga. 521, 38 S. E. 975; Henderson v. Williams, 97 Ga. 709, 25 S. E. 395; Miller v. Redwine, 75 Ga. 130; Adams v. Rome, 59 Ga. 765. When, by the terms of a will, real and personal property is given to the wife for life with the remainder to the children of the testator, a power

conferred on the executrix, who was the wife of the testator, to sell any or all of the property devised and reinvest the proceeds, expressed in language which plainly and unequivocally limits the purpose for which any sale can be made to that of reinvestment only, does not, notwithstanding the will may contain broad and liberal provisions as to the manner in which this power may be exercised, empower the executrix to mortgage the property devised, nor to convey the title of such property, as security for a debt created by her. McMillan v. Cox, 109 Ga. 42, 34 S. E. 341.

But a mortgage made under such a power for a greater sum than is actually loaned may be repudiated by the principal. Cleveland Ins. Co. v. Reed, 1 Biss. (U. S.) 180.

[6] Hoyt v. Jaques, 129 Mass. 286, per Morton, J. "The two transactions of a sale and a mortgage are essentially different. A power to sell implies that the attorney is to receive for the benefit of the principal a fair and adequate price for the land; a power to mortgage involves a right in the attorney to convey the land for a less sum, so that the whole estate may be taken on a foreclosure for only a part of its value. So, under a will, a trust with a power to sell prima facie imports a power to sell 'out and out,' and will not authorize a mortgage, unless there is something in the will to show that a mortgage

intention that the agent should have authority to mortgage the property. A general power may be sufficient if it appears that the principal intended his agent should have authority to raise money on mortgage, and the nature of the business intrusted to him is such as to make it proper for him to exercise this power.[7] A power to lease or mortgage real estate for the purpose of procuring money thereon, in case the attorney can not sell the property, gives him the option to mortgage it, in the event he can not sell at a reasonable price.[8] A power to sell for the expressed purpose of raising money is held to imply a power to give a mortgage which is only a conditional sale.[9] A power, by will or otherwise, to raise a sum of money upon certain land, authorizes either an absolute sale or a mortgage, as may be deemed expedient.[10]

A power to mortgage may be created by reservation in a deed by the owner of land; as where the owner of a farm conveys it to a relative "saving and reserving the right to occupy the premises with the full power to mortgage said premises to raise money for my own personal benefit, at any time I may desire for and during my natural life." It was held that the power was not limited to making a mortgage of the life estate so created, but included the power to mortgage the fee of the premises; and that the reservation was not repugnant to the deed.[11]

A power to mortgage given in general terms, without specifying the provisions the deed shall contain, includes the power to make it in the form and with the provisions customarily used in the state or country where the land is situated.[12] Thus such a power to mortgage given in England, or in some American states, would authorize the giving of a mortgage with a power of sale;[13] while, in states in which such a power is not in general use, a power inserted without special authority would be void. And in regard to any other provision, as, for instance, that forfeiting credit on the mortgage upon any default in the payment of interest, and giving the mortgagee the option thereupon to consider the

---

was within the intention of the testator." The rule that the greater includes the less may, in a charter, make a power to sell include a power to mortgage. Williamette Mfg. Co. v. Bank of British Columbia, 119 U. S. 191, 30 L. ed. 384, 7 Sup. Ct. 187. See also O'Brien v. Flint, 74 Conn. 502, 51 Atl. 547.

[7] See Coutant v. Servoss, 3 Barb. (N. Y.) 128.

[8] Mylius v. Copes, 23 Kans. 617.

[9] Powell on Mort. ch. 4; Mills v. Banks, 3 P. Wms. 1; Ball v. Harris, 4 Myl. & C. 267; Page v. Cooper, 16 Beav. 396; Oxford v. Albermarle, 17 L. J. (N. S.) Ch. 396; Devaynes v. Robinson, 24 Beav. 86.

[10] Wareham v. Brown, 2 Vern. 153.

[11] Bouton v. Doty, 69 Conn. 531, 37 Atl. 1064.

[12] Monroe Mercantile Co. v. Arnold, 108 Ga. 449, 34 S. E. 176.

[13] Wilson v. Troup, 7 Johns. Ch. (N. Y.) 25, 2 Cow. (N. Y.) 195, 14 Am. Dec. 458; see post §§ 1764–1768.

whole sum due, a general power to mortgage would authorize its use in some states, while the same power would not authorize it in others.[14]

A power to execute a mortgage, though it does not in express terms limit the right of the agent to the execution of a mortgage for the benefit of the principal only, does not warrant the agent in making a mortgage for the benefit of himself or any other person, and such a mortgage is ineffectual.[15]

§ 130. **Mode of exercising the power.**—It is a rule of conveyancing that a deed by an attorney must be executed in the name of the principal.[16] It should be signed in the name of the principal with the agent's name below, preceded by the word "by" and followed by the word "agent."

In Combe's case,[17] "it was resolved that when any has authority, as attorney, to do any act, he ought to do it in his name who gives the authority; for he appoints the attorney to be in his place, and to represent his person; and therefore the attorney can not do it in his own name, nor as his proper act, but in the name, and as the act, of him who gives the authority."

A mortgage by a corporation must be executed in its name by the agent or officer authorized to act for it. Although it may purport to be the mortgage of a corporation, yet, if executed by its attorney or officer in his individual name, it is not the legal mortgage of the corporation, and does not bind it except in equity.[18] But a mortgage executed in behalf of a corporation and formal in every other respect is not vitiated, as between the parties, by any informality in the certificate of acknowledgment whereby the treasurer acknowledges the instrument to be his own free act and deed.[19] Although not bound by the act of an agent in giving a mortgage, the principal may ratify it by taking the benefit of it, or may otherwise so act with reference to the exercise of the power as to preclude himself from attempting to invalidate the security.[20]

---

[14] Bolles v. Munnerlyn, 83 Ga. 727, 10 S. E. 365; Jesup v. City Bank of Racine, 14 Wis. 331. See ante § 76.

[15] Hubback v. Ross, 96 Cal. 426, 31 Pac. 353; Nippel v. Hammond, 4 Colo. 211.

[16] State v. Jennings, 10 Ark. 428; Copeland v. Mercantile Ins. Co., 6 Pick. (Mass.) 198; Elwell v. Shaw, 16 Mass. 42, 8 Am. Dec. 126.

[17] 9 Coke 75.

[18] Taylor v. West Ala. Agl. &c. Assn., 68 Ala. 229; Love v. Sierra

Nevada &c. Min. Co., 32 Cal. 639, 91 Am. Dec. 602. See also Brinley v. Mann, 2 Cush. (Mass.) 337, 48 Am. Dec. 669; Sargent v. Webster, 13 Metc. (Mass.) 497, 46 Am. Dec. 743.

[19] Fitch v. Lewiston Steam-Mill Co., 80 Maine 34, 12 Atl. 732.

[20] Mechanics' &c. Bank v. Harris Lumber Co., 103 Ark. 283, 146 S. W. 508, Ann. Cas. 1914 B, 713; Fitch v. Lewiston Steam-Mill Co., 80 Maine 34, 12 Atl. 732; McAdow v. Black, 4

§ 130a. Joint mortgagors.—Owners of separate lands may join in a mortgage, and joint owners may mortgage their entire interest.[21] If the joint mortgagors are tenants in common the entire property is liable for the debt.[22] But where two persons mortgage their separate lands for one debt, each is presumed to be liable for half the debt, and his land is chargeable accordingly.[28]

PART II

WHO MAY TAKE A MORTGAGE

Parties in Various Relations

§ 131. Capacity of mortgagees in general.—In general any one capable of holding real estate may be a mortgagee. The disabilities which prevent the making of a valid mortgage in no case prevent the taking of a mortgage, which is for the benefit of the mortgagee. An infant may take a mortgage. He is bound by the conditions of the deed, which must be wholly good or void altogether.[1]

A director, stockholder or officer of a private corporation is not debarred by his relation to the corporation from loaning money to it, and taking a mortgage from it for security; but he must act fairly and in good faith.[2] A receiver, however, is debarred upon grounds of public policy from taking a mortgage upon property which he holds as re-

---

Mont. 475, 1 Pac. 751; Perry v. Holl, 2 Gif. 138, 2 De G., F. & J. 38. Ratification of invalid corporate mortgages: Aurora Agl. &c. Soc. v. Paddock, 80 Ill. 263 (approval of minutes authorizing the mortgage); Middleton v. Arastraville Min. Co., 146 Cal. 219, 79 Pac. 889; Browning v. Mullins, 12 Ky. L. 41, 13 S. W. 427 (acquiescence until loan is expended). See also Nevada Nickel Synd. v. National Nickel Co., 90 Fed. 133; Alta Silver Min. Co. v. Alta Placer Min. Co., 78 Cal. 629, 21 Pac. 373 (assessment of shareholders to pay the loan, not a ratification); Chicago v. Cameron, 120 Ill. 447, 11 N. E. 899 (long delay not a ratification).

[21] Bowen v. May, 12 Cal. 348; Pres-ton v. Compton, 30 Ohio St. 299; Stroud v. Casey, 27 Pa. St. 471.

[22] Schoenewald v. Dieden, 8 Ill. App. 389.

[23] Cumming v. Williamson, 1 Sandf. Ch. (N. Y.) 17; Hoyt v. Doughty, 4 Sandf. (N. Y.) 462.

[1] Parker v. Lincoln, 12 Mass. 16.

[2] St. Joe &c. Min. Co. v. First Nat. Bank, 10 Colo. App. 339, 50 Pac. 1055; Harts v. Brown, 77 Ill. 226; Farmers' Loan &c. Co. v. New York &c. R. Co., 150 N. Y. 410, 44 N. E. 1043, 34 L. R. A. 76, 55 Am. St. 689; First Nat. Bank v. Commercial Travelers' Home Assn., 108 App. Div. 78, 95 N. Y. S. 454; In re Mechanics' Bldg. &c. Assn., 202 Pa. 589, 52 Atl. 58.

ceiver, to secure a loan or advances made by him to the owner of the property. He is not allowed to deal in respect to the property which he holds in trust.[3]

§ 132. Aliens.—In the United States aliens are generally empowered to hold real estate. But aside from any statutory privilege, a mortgage being regarded as a personal interest, the debt the principal thing, and the land merely an incident, an alien is entitled to hold and enforce a mortgage.[4] "The alienage of a mortgagee if he be a friend, can, upon no principle of law or equity, be urged against him."[5]

§ 133. Married women.—A married woman may at common law be a mortgagee; but she can not enforce a foreclosure of a mortgage of which the equity of redemption is held by her husband, either by suit at law or in equity, or by entry to foreclose in the presence of two witnesses. Though her title as mortgagee still continues, she is debarred from all proceedings to foreclose the mortgage during the continuance of the marriage relation.[6] Conversely, the same rule applies in case the husband holds a mortgage made by the wife.[7] But there are decisions that a mortgage or other conveyance, made directly from a husband to his wife, to secure his debt to her, is in equity valid and may be enforced.[8]

A mortgage given by the husband and wife in trust for the wife, to secure money loaned out of her separate estate is valid, but is a lien subsequent to a junior mortgage by the same parties.[9]

A statute forbidding contracts between husband and wife relative to real estate of either invalidates a mortgage from the husband to the wife, and this though the mortgage is made after separation.[10]

---

[3] Thompson v. Holladay, 15 Ore. 34, 14 Pac. 725.

[4] Hughes v. Edwards, 9 Wheat. (U. S.) 489; Richmond v. Milne, 17 La. 312; Silver Lake Bank v. North, 4 Johns. Ch. (N. Y.) 370.

[5] Craig v. Radford, 3 Wheat. (U. S.) 594, 4 L. ed. 467.

[6] Tucker v. Fenno, 110 Mass. 311. See also Campbell v. Galbreath, 12 Bush (Ky.) 459. See post § 850.

[7] Butler v. Ives, 139 Mass. 202, 29 N. E. 654.

[8] Wochoska v. Wochoska, 45 Wis. 423; Putnam v. Bicknell, 18 Wis. 333. In the former case the wife enforced her rights after a divorce, and in the latter case after the death of her husband. Northington v. Faber, 52 Ala. 45; Coleman v. Smith, 55 Ala. 368. "A married woman could acquire a mortgage on her husband's lands, and against him, just as freely as she could buy or take any other security already existing, and the fact that she had joined in the mortgage to release her dower could not affect her right to hold it, as it was not her own obligation." Youmans v. Loxley, 56 Mich. 197, 22 N. W. 282.

[9] McFarland v. Gilchrist, 25 N. J. Eq. 487.

[10] Phillips v. Blaker, 68 Minn. 152, 70 N. W. 1082.

§ 134. Corporations.—A corporation, whether private[11] or municipal,[12] though not expressly authorized by its charter or by statute to take a mortgage, if not prohibited may do so, provided only it be in furtherance of the objects for which it was created. A railroad company, when not forbidden to take anything but money in payment for its stock, may take mortgages of real estate securing notes or bonds given for the stock.[13]

Building and loan associations have implied power to take mortgages to secure their loans.[14] A loan association which, under its charter, or under the law by which it was organized, has no power to acquire and hold real estate except such as has been mortgaged to it or in which it has an interest can not acquire other land and assume the payment of a mortgage thereon, and upon the foreclosure of the mortgage no decree for a deficiency can be rendered against the association.[15]

A corporation de facto, though defectively organized, may take a mortgage, and a junior mortgagee can not defeat it by showing such defective organization.[16]

A bank organized under the national banking act[17] is authorized to take and hold a mortgage of real estate by way of security for debts previously contracted,[18] but not to take such a mortgage as security

---

[11] Jackson v. Brown, 5 Wend. (N. Y.) 590; Gordon v. Preston, 1 Watts (Pa.) 385, 26 Am. Dec. 75; Madison &c. Plank Road Co. v. Watertown &c. Plank Road Co., 5 Wis. 173.

[12] Alexander v. Knox, 6 Sawyer (U. S.) 54; Vanarsdall v. Watson, 65 Ind. 176; State Bank v. Chapelle, 40 Mich. 447.

[13] Massey v. Citizens' Bldg. Assn., 22 Kans. 624; National Trust Co. v. Murphy, 30 N. J. Eq. 408; Lyon v. Ewings, 17 Wis. 61; Andrews v. Hart, 17 Wis. 297; Western Bank v. Tallman, 17 Wis. 530; Clark v. Farrington, 11 Wis. 306; Blunt v. Walker, 11 Wis. 334, 78 Am. Dec. 709; Cornell v. Hichens, 11 Wis. 353.

[14] Massey v. Citizens' Bldg. Assn., 22 Kans. 624; Victoria Bldg. Assn. v. Arbeiter Bund, 6 Ohio Dec. (reprint) 1108, 10 Am. L. Rec. 485. See also Juergens v. Cobe, 99 Ill. App. 156.

[15] National Home Bldg. &c. Assn. v. Home Sav. Bank, 181 Ill. 35, 54 N. E. 619, revg. 79 Ill. App. 303; Bldg. &c. Assn. v. Barrett, 160 Mo. App.

164, 141 S. W. 723; Vos v. Cedar Grove Land &c. Assn., 8 Ohio Dec. (reprint) 682; Faulkner's Appeal, 11 Wkly. N. Cas. (Pa.) 48. See also Cahall v. Citizens' Mut. Bldg. Assn., 61 Ala. 232.

[16] Williamson v. Kokomo Building Assn., 89 Ind. 389. See also Mechanics' Bldg. Assn. v. Stevens, 5 Duer (N. Y.) 676.

[17] June 3, 1864, §§ 8, 28.

[18] Genesee Nat. Bank v. Whitney, 103 U. S. 99, 26 L. ed. 443; Penn v. Borman, 102 Ill. 523; Mapés v. Scott, 94 Ill. 379; Warner v. DeWitt County Nat. Bank, 4 Ill. App. 305; Turner v. Madison First Nat. Bank, 115 Ind. 341, 17 N. E. 612; Waterloo First Nat. Bank v. Elmore, 52 Iowa 541, 3 N. W. 547; Heath v. Second Nat. Bank, 70 Ind. 106; Matthews v. Skinner, 62 Mo. 329, 21 Am. Rep. 425; Thornton v. National Exchange Bank, 71 Mo. 221; Wherry v. Hale, 77 Mo. 20; Scofield v. State Nat. Bank, 9 Nebr. 316, 2 N. W. 888, 31 Am. Rep. 412; Graham v. New York Nat. Bank, 42 N. J. Eq. 804;

for a debt contracted at the time or for future advances. Such a mortgage was formerly regarded as invalid.[19] Therefore, a mortgage made to a national bank by a customer, as collateral security for the payment of all notes then discounted and held by the bank, "or for any other indebtedness now due, or that may hereafter become due," was regarded a valid security only for the indebtedness existing when it was given; and upon the payment of such indebtedness, and the surrender of the specific notes constituting such indebtedness, the mortgage was discharged.[20] The Supreme Court has, however, established a different and more reasonable construction of the prohibition in the national banking act of a loan made upon real estate security, declaring that, although such a loan is prohibited, it is not void. A mortgage taken in violation of the prohibition is valid between the parties and may be enforced. The remedy for the violation is a forfeiture of the bank's charter.[21] The statute authorizes banks to hold real estate in mortgage for debts previously contracted. It does not in terms, but only by implication, prohibit a loan on real estate. It does not declare such a security void. It is silent upon the subject. If congress so meant, it would have been easy to say so, and it is hardly to be believed that this would not have been done, instead of leaving the question to be settled by the uncertain results of litigation and judicial de-

Simmons v. Union Springs First Nat. Bank, 93 N. Y. 269; Walden Nat. Bank v. Birch, 130 N. Y. 221, 29 N. E. 127, 14 L. R. A. 211, 41 N. Y. St. 275; Buffalo Ger. Ins. Co. v. Buffalo Third Nat. Bank, 10 Misc. 564, 43 N. Y. S. 550; Oldham v. Wilmington First Nat. Bank, 85 N. Car. 240; Allen v. First Nat. Bank, 23 Ohio St. 97; Winton v. Little, 94 Pa. St. 64; Wroten v. Armat, 31 Grat. (Va.) 228.

[19] Kansas Val. Nat. Bank v. Rowell, 2 Dill. (U. S.) 371, Fed. Cas. No. 7611; Ripley v. Harris, 3 Biss. (U. S.) 199; Chicago Merch. Nat. Bank v. Mears, 8 Biss. (U. S.) 158, Fed. Cas. No. 9450; Fridley v. Bowen, 87 Ill. 151; Spafford v. Tama City First Nat. Bank, 37 Iowa 181, 18 Am. Rep. 6; First Nat. Bank v. Maxfield, 83 Maine 576, 22 Atl. 479; Kentucky Bank v. Clark, 4 Mo. 59, 28 Am. Dec. 345; Crocker v. Whitney, 71 N. Y. 161; Fowler v. Scully, 72 Pa. St. 456, 13 Am. Rep. 699; Woods v. People's Nat. Bank, 83 Pa. St. 57. See also Barron v. McKinnon, 196 Fed. 933; Magoffin v. Bank, 24 Ky. L. 585, 69 S. W. 702.

[20] Crocker v. Whitney, 71 N. Y. 161; Woods v. People's Nat. Bank, 83 Pa. St. 57.

[21] National Bank v. Matthews, 98 U. S. 621, 19 Alb. L. J. 132, 8 Cent. L. J. 131; National Bank v. Whitney, 103 U. S. 99, 26 L. ed. 443; Kesner v. Trigg, 98 U. S. 50, 25 L. ed. 83; Camp v. Land, 122 Cal. 167, 54 Pac. 839; First Nat. Bank v. Elmore, 52 Iowa 541, 3 N. W. 547. Contra: Skowhegan First Nat. Bank v. Maxfield, 83 Maine 576, 22 Atl. 479; Butterworth v. Kritzer Milling Co., 115 Mich. 1, 72 N. W. 990; Fifth Nat. Bank v. Pierce, 117 Mich. 376, 75 N. W. 1058; Thornton v. Nat. Exchange Bank, 71 Mo. 221; George v. Somerville, 153 Mo. 7, 54 S. W. 491; Graham v. New York Nat. Bank, 32 N. J. Eq. 804; Myers v. Campbell, 64 N. J. L. 186, 44 Atl. 863; Winton v. Little, 94 Pa. St. 64; Wroten v. Armat, 31 Grat. (Va.) 228.

cision. In other instances contracts are not void where they are not in terms made so. Thus, where a corporation is made incompetent by its charter to take a title to real estate, a conveyance to it is not void, but only voidable, and the sovereign alone can object. It is valid until assailed in a direct proceeding instituted for that purpose. In conclusion, Judge Swayne, delivering the opinion of the court, said: "We can not believe it was meant that stockholders, and perhaps depositors and other creditors, should be punished and the borrower rewarded by giving success to this defense whenever the offensive fact shall occur. The impending danger of a judgment of ouster and dissolution was, we think, the check, and none other, contemplated by congress. That has been always the punishment prescribed for the wanton violation of a charter, and it may be made to follow whenever the public authority shall see fit to invoke its application. A private person can not directly or indirectly usurp this function of government."[22] Where a bank already holds a mortgage upon land and for its own protection pays the amount of a prior lien, and then takes a mortgage for this sum, the transaction does not come within the prohibition of the statute as to taking mortgages for debts concurrently created.[23]

There is sometimes a limitation that the mortgage to a state bank shall be for debts previously contracted. In a case where a charter contained this provision "it was adjudged by Chancellor Kent, that, if the loan and mortgage were concurrent acts, and intended so to be, it was not a case within the reason and spirit of the restraining clause of the statute, which only meant to prohibit the banking company from investing their capital in real property and engaging in land speculations; 'a mortgage taken to secure a loan, advanced bona fide as a loan, in the course, and according to the usage, of banking operations, was not surely,' says he, 'within the prohibition.' "[24]

When a state bank was authorized to hold mortgages, but it was provided by statute that all conveyances of real estate should be made to the president of the bank, it was held that a mortgage directly to the bank was valid notwithstanding;[25] for it was considered that the

[22] Supporting this view, see Silver Lake Bank v. North, 4 Johns. Ch. (N. Y.) 370; Graham v. National Bank of N. Y., 32 N. J. Eq. 804; Baird v. Bank of Washington, 11 Serg. & R. (Pa.) 411.
[23] Ornn v. Merchants' Nat. Bank, 16 Kans. 341.
[24] Morse on Banks and Bkg. (4th ed.), § 74; Silver Lake Bank v. North, 4 Johns. Ch. (N. Y.) 370. A statute providing that banks shall not own real estate more than sufficient for the conduct of their business, unless taken in payment of debts does not prevent the taking of real estate as security for loans. Alexander v. Brummett (Tenn. Ch.), 42 S. W. 63.
[25] Kennedy v. Knight, 21 Wis. 340 94 Am. Dec. 543. See also Wis. Stat 1913, §§ 2024-35.

object was not to prohibit the bank from taking title, but merely to facilitate business by permitting conveyances to be made for the benefit of the bank to an officer of it.

§ **134a. Foreign corporations.**—In the absence of statutory prohibition, foreign corporations, created under laws of other states, may take mortgages of domestic real estate.[26] A few cases have held that only the state can set up a want of power of a foreign corporation to take a mortgage.[27] It has also been held that the mortgagor was estopped to deny the power of a foreign corporation to make a domestic loan after accepting its benefits, and that the defense of ultra vires was unavailable. The doctrine is that "a party to a contract is estopped from urging his discharge from liability on it, by reason of the other's want of authority to make it."[28]

The validity of mortgages taken on domestic property by foreign corporations, including mortgage companies and building and loan associations, may depend on whether the foreign corporation has complied with the domestic statutes imposing certain duties as a condition to doing business in the state.[29] A constitutional or statutory provision

---

[26] Dry Dock v. Hicks, 5 McLean (U. S.) 111, Fed. Cas. No. 10204; Farmers &c. Co. v. McKinney, 6 McLean (U. S.) 1, Fed. Cas. No. 4667; Caesar v. Cappell, 83 Fed. 403; Boatmen's Bank v. Fritzlen, 175 Fed. 183; Christian v. American Freehold Land &c. Co., 89 Ala. 198, 7 So. 427; Stevens v. Pratt, 101 Ill. 206; Commercial &c. Co. v. Scammon, 102 Ill. 46; Pancoast v. Travelers' Ins. Co., 79 Ind. 172; Lathrop v. Commercial Bank, 8 Dana (Ky.) 114, 33 Am. Dec. 481; Frazier v. Wilcox, 4 Rob. (La.) 517; American &c. Ins. Co. v. Owen, 15 Gray (Mass.) 491; Lebanon Sav. Bank v. Hollenbeck, 29 Minn. 322, 13 N. W. 145; Williams v. Creswell, 51 Miss. 817; Connecticut &c. Ins. Co. v. Albert, 39 Mo. 181; Long v. Long, 79 Mo. 644; Ferguson v. Soden, 111 Mo. 208, 19 S. W. 727, 33 Am. St. 512; Carlow v. Aultman, 28 Nebr. 672, 44 N. W. 873; National Trust Co. v. Murphy, 30 N. J. Eq. 408 (mortgage valid as additional security, though not authorized upon the original investment); Bard v. Poole, 12 N. Y. 495; Silver Lake Bank v. North, 4 Johns. Ch. (N. Y.) 370; Leasure v.

Union &c. Ins. Co., 91 Pa. St. 491; Pioneer Savings &c. Co. v. Cannon, 96 Tenn. 599, 36 S. W. 386, 33 L. R. A. 112, 54 Am. St. 858; Charter Oak Life Ins. Co. v. Sawyer, 44 Wis. 387.

[27] St. Louis Union Nat. Bank v. Matthews, 98 U. S. 621, 25 L. ed. 188; Carlow v. Aultman, 28 Nebr. 672, 44 N. W. 873.

[28] St. Louis Nat. Bank v. Matthews, 98 U. S. 621, 25 L. ed. 188; Pancoast v. Travelers' Ins. Co., 79 Ind. 172; Silver Lake Bank v. North, 4 Johns. Ch. (N. Y.) 370.

[29] Semple v. British Columbia Bank, 5 Sawy. (U. S.) 88, Fed. Cas. No. 12659; Farrior v. New England Mtg. &c. Co., 88 Ala. 275, 7 So. 200; Mullens v. American &c. Mtg. Co., 88 Ala. 280, 7 So. 201; Christian v. American &c. Land Co., 89 Ala. 198, 7 So. 427; Hanchey v. Southern Home Bldg. Assn., 140 Ala. 245, 37 So. 272; Hoskins v. Rochester Sav. Assn., 133 Mich. 505, 95 N. W. 566; Henni v. Fidelity Bldg. &c. Assn., 61 Nebr. 744, 86 N. W. 475, 87 Am. St. 519; Pioneer Sav. Assn. v. Eyer, 62 Nebr. 810, 87 N. W. 1058; New York Nat. Bldg. Assn. v. Cannon,

that no foreign corporation shall do "any business" in a state without having at least one known place of business, and an authorized agent therein, is violated by a single act of making one loan of money, and taking a mortgage to secure it, by a foreign corporation engaged in the business of loaning money on mortgages, when it has no place of business or agent in the state. In such case the promise of the mortgagor to pay is void, and a bill to foreclose the mortgage can not be maintained.[30] In a suit under such a provision to foreclose a corporate mortgage, the complaint must aver that the corporation was authorized to do business in the state at the time the mortgage was executed and delivered. A complaint which states that complainant has complied with the laws of the state which authorize a foreign corporation to do business in the state, and that the mortgage sued on was executed and delivered in the state, is not sufficient.[31] But though a mortgage was originally invalid by reason of the failure of the mortgagee, a foreign corporation, to comply with such laws, after the contract evidenced by the mortgage has been fully executed by a sale and conveyance under the mortgage, the mortgagor can not thereafter avail himself of the objection.[32]

In a few states foreign corporations have at different times been prohibited from making loans and taking security upon real estate therefor. A mortgage within such a prohibition is invalid from its delivery, and consequently a sale and conveyance under it is nugatory, and does not divest the owner of his interest in the mortgaged premises.[33] But if the mortgagor comes into a court of equity to obtain a

99 Tenn. 344, 41 S. W. 1054; Gilmer v. United States Savings &c. Co., 103 Tenn. 272, 52 S. W. 851.

[30] Farrior v. Security Co., 92 Ala. 176, 7 So. 200; Dudley v. Collier, 87 Ala. 431, 6 So. 304. See also Miller v. Gates, 22 Mont. 305, where decree of foreclosure was had before objection was taken, the mortgage being not void, but only voidable. Black v. Caldwell, 83 Fed. 880.

[31] Mullens v. Mortgage Co., 88 Ala. 280, 7 So. 201.

[32] Electric Lighting Co. v. Rust, 117 Ala. 680, 23 So. 751; Kindred v. New England Mtg. Sec. Co., 116 Ala. 192, 23 So. 56; Diefenbach v. Vaughan, 116 Ala. 150, 23 So. 88; Shahan v. Tethero, 114 Ala. 404, 21 So. 951; Thornhill v. O'Rear, 108 Ala. 299, 19 So. 382; Gamble v. Caldwell, 98 Ala. 578, 12 So. 424; Long

v. Georgia Pac. R. Co., 91 Ala. 519, 8 So. 706; Dudley v. Collier, 87 Ala. 431, 6 So. 304.

[33] Such was the statute in Illinois prior to the Act of 1875 (Laws of 1875, p. 65), repealing the former statute, and confirming and validating prior loans made in contravention of it. Scammon v. Commercial Union Assurance Co., 6 Bradw. (Ill.) 551; United States Mtg. Co. v. Gross, 93 Ill. 483. See also Hards v. Conn. Mut. L. Ins. Co., 8 Biss. (U. S.) 234. The subsequent act of May 26, 1897, providing that a foreign corporation failing to file a copy of its charter with the secretary of state, etc., shall not maintain any suit, etc., does not apply to mortgages taken before this statute was enacted. Richardson v. United States Mtg. Co., 194 Ill. 259, 62 N. E. 606. See Rev. Stat. Ill., p. 538, §§ 67, 67a.

cancelation of such a mortgage on the ground that the mortgagee had not complied with the requirements of the statute as to the right to do business in the state, he must offer to repay the money received with interest.[34] In an earlier decision the court said: "We can not assent to the proposition that a person can obtain another's money upon the faith and assurance of a mortgage security, and the next moment after he receives and appropriates it, go into a court of conscience, where the maxim that he who seeks equity must do equity has ever been vigorously upheld and applied, and ask that court to cancel the security as a cloud on his title, still retaining the money and making no offer to return or repay it."[35]

§ 135. Joint mortgagees.—A mortgage given to secure a joint debt creates a joint estate in the mortgagees.[36] Payment to either satisfies the mortgage.[37] In case of the death of one of such mortgagees, an action to recover the debt or to enforce the mortgage may be maintained in the name of the survivor.[38]

A mortgage may be made to several persons jointly to secure separate debts.[39] Such a mortgage given to two or more persons to secure their separate debts is several and not joint; each mortgagee has a right to enforce his claim under the mortgage, in a form adapted

In Pennsylvania a foreign corporation may enforce a mortgage upon lands in that state. Leasure v. Union Mut. Life Ins. Co., 91 Pa. St. 491. Const. Ala., § 4, art. 14; New England Mtg. Co. v. Powell, 94 Ala. 423, 10 So. 324.

[34] George v. New England Mtg. Security Co., 109 Ala. 548, 20 So. 331; Ross v. New Eng. Mtg. Sec. Co., 101 Ala. 362, 13 So. 564; Hartly v. Matthews, 96 Ala. 224, 11 So. 452.

[35] Grider v. American Freehold Land Mtg. Co., 99 Ala. 281, 12 So. 775.

[36] Appleton v. Boyd, 7 Mass. 131. In Massachusetts mortgages are expressly excepted from the provision of statute that conveyances made to two or more persons shall be construed to create estates in common. Rev. Laws 1902, ch. 134, p. 1268, § 6. It leaves the nature of the estate open to inquiry. In Maine a mortgage to two or more persons is considered as constituting a joint tenancy unless otherwise expressed. Acts 1881, ch. 46; Rev. Stat. 1903, ch. 75, p. 659, § 16.

In Minnesota it is provided that all mortgages heretofore made of any real property, or of any interest therein, to any partnership or firm, in their partnership or firm name, which mortgages have been foreclosed by advertisement pursuant to the statute relating to foreclosure by advertisement, in the name of the said partnership or firm, and the same are, together with all proceedings had in such foreclosure, hereby legalized and confirmed so far as relates to any question of defect by reason of the mortgagees' names being stated in said mortgages by their partnership or firm name instead of the individual names of said partnership or firm. Laws 1881, ch. 140.

[37] Wright v. Ware, 58 Ga. 150.

[38] Blake v. Sanborn, 8 Gray (Mass.) 154; Webster v. Vandeventer, 6 Mass. 428; Mutual L. Ins. Co. v. Sturges, 32 N. J. Eq. 678.

[39] Adams v. Nieman, 46 Mich. 135, 8 N. W. 719; Scarlett v. Nattress, 23 Ont. App. 297.

to the case, and of course the surviving mortgagee can not maintain an action on the mortgage to enforce payment of the debt due the deceased mortgagee.[40] Such mortgagees are tenants in common, each having an undivided interest; and the fact that the mortgage is void as to one of the mortgagees will not affect its validity as to the other.[41] A round sum named as the debt may be divided by the mortgage into specific items payable to each of several creditors. In such case the mortgage secures each of such creditors for a fixed and definite sum, and may be enforced by such of them as bring suit for foreclosure without awaiting the bringing in of all the parties secured.[42] The mortgage is presumed to be for the benefit of the mortgagees pro rata to the debts secured;[43] though, if the amount of the debts be not fixed, the mortgage might be presumed to be for their benefit equally. Such a mortgage does not constitute the mortgagees trustees one for the other, at least before the law day.[44] But whether the debt secured be joint or several, after foreclosure the mortgagees become tenants in common of the land.[45]

A mortgage to husband and wife upon the death of the husband vests in the wife.[46]

A mortgage and note payable in the alternative to one or the other of two named payees is valid.[47]

Under statutes which make grants to two or more persons tenancies in common, unless there are words which clearly show an intention to create a joint tenancy, the mere fact that the conveyance is in mortgage affords no implication controlling the statute and making the mortgagees joint tenants.[48]

A mortgagee of an undivided half of a parcel of land does not become a tenant in common with the owner of the other half until his title has become absolute by a completed foreclosure. Before that

[40] Brown v. Bates, 55 Maine 520, 92 Am. Dec. 613; Gilson v. Gilson, 2 Allen (Mass.) 115, 117; Burnett v. Pratt, 22 Pick. (Mass.) 556.

[41] Bates v. Coe, 10 Conn. 280; Gilson v. Gilson, 2 Allen (Mass.) 115; Burnett v. Pratt, 22 Pick. (Mass.) 556; Roberts v. McWilliams, 2 Ohio Dec. (Reprint) 152; Farwell v. Warren, 76 Wis. 527, 45 N. W. 217.

[42] Shelden v. Erskine, 78 Mich. 627, 44 N. W. 146.

[43] Seedhouse v. Broward, 34 Fla. 509, 16 So. 425; Adams v. Robertson, 37 Ill. 45; Willis v. Caldwell, 10 B. Mon. (Ky.) 199. See also Jones on Chattel Mortgages, § 84.

[44] Bates v. Coe, 10 Conn. 280.

[45] Randall v. Phillips, 3 Mason (U. S.) 378; Goodwin v. Richardson, 11 Mass. 469; Donnels v. Edwards, 2 Pick. (Mass.) 617; Burnett v. Pratt, 22 Pick. (Mass.) 556.

[46] Draper v. Jackson, 16 Mass. 480.

[47] Seedhouse v. Broward, 34 Fla. 509, 16 So. 425.

[48] Randall v. Phillips, 3 Mason (U. S.) 378.

time the mortgage is only a lien, and the estate is to be dealt with as belonging to the mortgagor.[49]

§ 135a.   **Partnerships—Firm name—Beneficiaries in trust deed.**— A mortgage to a partnership in its firm name, without naming the individual members of the firm, though irregular and informal, may be enforced by the partnership. The partnership name, containing the name of one or more of the partners, sufficiently identifies the partners named so that the title will vest in them. For stronger reasons, this is the rule in states in which a mortgage is regarded as merely a lien and not a title; for there is no question that a lien may accrue to a partnership in its firm name.[50] But a mortgage of real estate to "D. B. Dorman & Co." which was a partnership composed of D. B. Dorman and another conveys only to Dorman, whose name appears in the partnership name.[51]

A mortgage to "The People's Bank," under which name an individual contracts business, vests the legal title in the individual.[52]

In a trust deed, the legal title is conveyed to a trustee for the benefit of third persons named or described. It is not essential, however, that the beneficiaries shall be named; it is sufficient if they are so described or designated that they may be ascertained. Thus, where a deed of trust was given by a dairyman to a trustee to secure all persons who might furnish milk to be made into butter and cheese and sold by the grantor on their account, but he failed to state the names of the beneficiaries to be secured, the deed was held valid, for the beneficiaries were those who should thereafter furnish to the grantor milk to be manufactured by him into butter and cheese. The deed of trust was a continuing offer by the grantor to secure all persons who might patronize him.[53]

[49] Norcross v. Norcross, 105 Mass. 265, and cases cited.

[50] Woodward v. McAdam, 101 Cal. 438, 35 Pac. 1016; Foster v. Johnson, 39 Minn. 378, 40 N. W. 255; Schupert v. Dillard, 55 Miss. 348.

[51] Gille v. Hunt, 35 Minn. 357, 29 N. W. 2.

[52] Carlisle v. People's Bank, 122 Ala. 446, 26 So. 115.

[53] First Nat. Bank v. Schween, 127 Ill. 573, 20 N. E. 681, 11 Am. St. 174.

CHAPTER IV

I. *Existing Interests in Real Property*

§ **136. Interest subject to sale and assignment.**—Every kind of interest in real estate may be mortgaged if it be subject to sale and assignment.[1] It does not matter that it is a right in remainder or reversion, a contingent interest, or a possibility coupled with an interest, if it be an interest in the land itself.[2] But an interest in the

---

[1] 2 Story Eq. Jur., § 1021; 4 Kent's Comm. 144; Massey v. Papin, 24 How. (U. S.) 362, 16 L. ed. 174; Brodrick v. Kilpatrick, 82 Fed. 138; McLeod v. Barnum, 131 Cal. 605, 63 Pac. 924; Hardy v. Ruggles, 1 Hawaii 457; Miller v. Tipton, 6 Blackf. (Ind.) 238; Dorsey v. Hall, 7 Nebr. 460; Neligh v. Michenor, 11 N. J. Eq. 539; Mendenhall v. West Chester &c. R. Co., 36 Pa. St. 145; Bourn v. Robinson, 49 Tex. Civ. App. 157, 107 S. W. 873; Clark v. Altizer (Tex. Civ. App.), 145 S. W. 104; Scott v. Farnam (Wash.), 104 Pac. 639; Mor-

tenson v. Morse, 153 Wis. 389, 141 N. W. 273.

[2] Wilson v. Russ, 17 Fla. 691; Curtis v. Root, 20 Ill. 518; Spalding v. Wayne (Ky.), 45 S. W. 517; Smith v. Provin, 4 Allen (Mass.) 516; Bacot v. Varnado, 91 Miss. 825, 47 So. 113; Flanders v. Greely, 64 N. H. 357, 10 Atl. 686; Neligh v. Michenor, 11 N. J. Eq. 539; Wilson v. Wilson, 32 Barb. (N. Y.) 328; In re John & Cherry Streets, 19 Wend. (N. Y.) 659; E. A. Beall Co. v. Weston, 83 S. Car. 491, 65 S. E. 823; Lipscomb v. Hammett, 56 S. Car.

proceeds of land ordered to be sold and distributed among legatees is not a subject of mortgage.[3] The interest of a cestui que trust may be mortgaged and sold in foreclosure proceedings.[4] A mere personal right or interest, as, for instance, a right of pre-emption of public lands, is of course not susceptible of mortgage;[5] yet the land subject to pre-emption may be mortgaged,[6] and so may be a mining claim located upon public land.[7] If one entitled to redeem from a foreclosure sale assigns such right as security for a debt, the assignee is a mortgagee.[8]

The Code of California states the general rule of law upon this subject in the provision that any interest in real property which is capable of being transferred may be mortgaged.[9]

Such, for instance, is the interest of one who holds an agreement or bond for title;[10] the interest of a grantee in possession under a deed held in escrow until the performance of certain conditions;[11] the interest of the one in possession under a parol contract to purchase;[12] or the interest of the holder of school land certificates until forfeited by

---

549, 35 S. E. 194; People's Loan &c. Bank v. Garlington, 54 S. Car. 413, 32 S. E. 513, 71 Am. St. 800; Bourn v. Robinson, 49 Tex. Civ. App. 157, 107 S. W. 873; Barnes v. Dow, 59 Vt. 530, 10 Atl. 258; Trent v. Hunt, 9 Exch. 14.

[3] Gray v. Smith, 3 Watts (Pa.) 289; Wood v. Reeves, 23 S. Car. 382.

[4] Christian v. American Freehold Land Mtg. Co., 92 Ala. 130, 9 So. 219.

[5] Whitney v. Buckman, 13 Cal. 536; Reasoner v. Markley, 25 Kans. 635; Penn v. Ott, 12 La. Ann. 233; Gilbert v. Penn, 12 La. Ann. 235; Broussard v. Dugas, 5 La. Ann. 585. See post § 177. Bush v. Marshall, 6 How. (U. S.) 284, 12 L. ed. 684; Warren v. Van Brunt, 19 Wall. (U. S.) 646, 22 L. ed. 219.

A court of equity will not set aside a mortgage made by a pre-emptor, for the reason that the statute prohibits him from perfecting his pre-emption after he has executed a mortgage, and that he gave the mortgage in ignorance of the law. Douglas v. Gould, 52 Cal. 656.

[6] Bush v. Marshall, 6 How. (U. S.) 284, 12 L. ed. 684; Whitney v. Buckman, 13 Cal. 536.

[7] Alexander v. Sherman (Ariz.),

16 Pac. 45; United States Mtg. &c. Co. v. Eastern Iron Co., 120 App. Div. 679, 105 N. Y. S. 291.

[8] San Jose Safe-Deposit Bank v. Bank of Madeira, 121 Cal. 539, 54 Pac. 83; Grant v. Cumberland Val. Cement Co., 58 W. Va. 162, 52 S. E. 36.

[9] Civil Code 1903, enacted March 21, 1872, § 2947.

[10] Davis v. Davis, 88 Ala. 523, 6 So. 908; Houghton v. Allen, 75 Cal. 102, 16 Pac. 532, 14 Cal. 641; Baker v. Bishop Hill Colony, 45 Ill. 264; McCauley v. Coe, 51 Ill. App. 284; Laughlin v. Braley, 25 Kans. 147; Perkins v. Robinson (Ky.), 124 S. W. 310; McPherson v. Hayward, 81 Maine 329, 17 Atl. 164; Crane v. Turner, 7 Hun (N. Y.) 357, 67 N. Y. 437; Farmers' Loan &c. Co. v. Curtis, 7 N. Y. 466; Titcomb v. Fonda, J. &c. R. Co., 38 Misc. 630, 78 N. Y. S. 226; Simonson v. Wenzel (N. Dak.), 147 N. W. 804; Scott v. Farnam, 55 Wash. 336, 104 Pac. 639; Smith v. Patton, 12 W. Va. 541.

[11] Masters v. Clark, 89 Ark. 191, 116 S. W. 186.

[12] Sinclair v. Armitage, 12 N. J. Eq. 174; Hagar v. Brainerd, 44 Vt. 294; Bull v. Sykes, 7 Wis. 449.

nonfulfilment of the conditions of sale;[13] or of a certificate of stock in an unincorporated company representing an interest in real estate.[14]

An easement appurtenant to the land described, and all rights, privileges and easements subsequently acquired, which are essential to the full enjoyment of the property, pass by the mortgage, though not specifically mentioned.[15] Thus a contract which the mortgagor has for the purchase of a strip of land adjoining the land described and necessary for the support of the building on the mortgagor's lot passes by his mortgage, though the contract was subsequent to the mortgage.[16]

A contract for an option to purchase land at an agreed price within a time limited, based upon a sufficient consideration, is an interest in real estate that may be sold or assigned, and therefore may be mortgaged.[17]

A widow who has an unassigned right of dower in land can make a mortgage of such land which will cover her interest in it. But though at the same time she has a power under her husband's will to mortgage such land, a mortgage executed by her, without referring to the power, will be deemed a mortgage of her dower right, and not an execution of the power.[18]

A devisee who has a vested interest in the land devised may mortgage that interest.[19]

A mere possibility or expectancy, not coupled with any interest in

[13] Jarvis v. Dutcher, 16 Wis. 307; Mowry v. Wood, 12 Wis. 413; Dodge v. Silverthorn, 12 Wis. 644.

[14] Durkee v. Stringham, 8 Wis. 1.

[15] Hyde Park Thomson-Houston Light Co. v. Brown, 172 Ill. 329, 50 N. E. 127; Swedish-Am. Nat. Bank v. Conn. Mut. L. Ins. Co., 83 Minn. 377, 86 N. W. 420; Putnam v. Putnam, 77 App. Div. 554, 78 N. Y. S. 987; Maupai v. Jackson, 64 Misc. 407, 118 N. Y. S. 513; Latta v. Catawba Electric &c. Co., 146 N. Car. 285, 59 S. E. 1028.

[16] Barnard v. Wilson, 74 Cal. 512, 16 Pac. 307; Swedish-Am. Nat. Bank v. Conn. Mut. L. Ins. Co., 83 Minn. 377, 86 N. W. 420; In re Bull, 15 R. I. 534, 10 Atl. 484.

[17] Bank of Louisville v. Baumeister, 87 Ky. 6, 7 S. W. 170.

[18] Penny v. Weems, 139 Ala. 270, 35 So. 883; Mutual L. Ins. Co. v. Shipman, 119 N. Y. 324, 24 N. E. 177. In Rhode Island it is held that a dowress can mortgage her unassigned dower interest to the terre-tenants only and that her mortgage of such interest to a stranger conveys no title. Ritt v. Dooge, 20 R. I. 133, 37 Atl. 810; Maxon v. Gray, 14 R. I. 641; Weaver v. Sturtevant, 12 R. I. 537.

[19] Drake v. Paige, 127 N. Y. 562, 28 N. E. 407. A will devised the residue of the testator's estate to four persons, share and share alike. A subsequent clause empowered the executors to sell a portion or all of the land for the payment of debts in case the personalty should prove insufficient, and also authorized them to partition the land among the four devisees after the payment of all such debts and expenses. It was held that the land vested in the devisees, subject to the execution of the power by the executors, and that consequently a mortgage executed by one of the devisees, before partition, on his undivided one-fourth interest, was valid. See also Davis v. Willson, 115 Ky. 639, 74 S. W. 696.

or growing out of the property, can not be made the subject of a mortgage.[20] A mere expectancy of acquiring property, without a present interest in it, is not a subject of sale, and therefore not of mortgage. "The next cast of a fisherman's net" has long been used as an illustration of a mere expectancy, not the subject of grant. In a Massachusetts case it was sought to substantiate such a sale, and the court were obliged to adjudge that a man has no salable interest in halibut in the sea. There is a possibility, they say, the man may catch halibut, but he has no actual or potential interest in the fish until he has caught them.[21]

§ 137. **Vested, contingent and future interests.**—All kinds of vested, contingent, and future interests may be mortgaged. An estate tail may be mortgaged by the life tenant. Such tenant can not prejudice the rights of the remaindermen, but can convey whatever interest he has.[22] But it has been held that where a widow, to whom real estate is devised for her own use and benefit during her natural life, with remainder of whatever may remain, may execute a binding mortgage on the premises for moneys used in making improvements thereon by means of which she secured her support from the property.[23] A vested interest in remainder may be conveyed in mortgage.[24] A contingent or possible interest may also be the subject of a mortgage,[25] upon breach of which the mortgagee may sell whatever interest the mortgagor may have in the property, without waiting until the happening of the condition on which the remainder would become vested.[26] Reversions and remainders, being capable of assignment, may be the

---

[20] Skipper v. Stokes, 42 Ala. 255, 94 Am. Dec. 646; Purcell v. Mather, 35 Ala. 570; Low v. Pew, 108 Mass. 347, 11 Am. Rep. 357. See also Hoff v. Burd, 17 N. J. Eq. 201.

[21] Low v. Pew, 108 Mass. 347, 11 Am. Rep. 357. The other maxim '(not of the law) is applicable: "First catch your fish," etc. In Miles v. Miles, 78 Miss. 904, it was held that a deed by a son to his brother of his interest in particular land of their father during his life, but not disclosing this fact, with a reservation of a lien for the purchase-money is not void, but may be enforced after the father's death, the father having in confirmation of the deed made a conveyance of this land to the grantee above.

[22] Hosmer v. Carter, 68 Ill. 98. The limitation was to "her body heirs." Lehndorf v. Cope, 122 Ill. 317, 13 N. E. 505. See also New South Bldg. &c. Assn. v. Gann, 101 Ga. 678, 29 S. E. 15; Beall Co. v. Weston, 83 S. Car. 491, 65 S. E. 823.

[23] Swarthout v. Ranier, 143 N. Y. 499, 38 N. E. 726; In re Jenks, 21 R. I. 390, 43 Atl. 871.

[24] Flanders v. Greely, 64 N. H. 357, 10 Atl. 686.

[25] Wilson v. Wilson, 32 Barb. (N. Y.) 328; E. A. Beall Co. v. Weston, 83 S. Car. 491, 65 S. E. 823.

[26] People's Loan &c. Bank v. Garlington, 54 S. Car. 413, 32 S. E. 513, 71 Am. St. 800. See also Davis v. Willson, 115 Ky. 639, 74 S. W. 696.

subject of a mortgage.[27] A reversionary interest in land subject to homestead rights may be mortgaged.[28] When the estate mortgaged is a contingent remainder, the mortgage, of course, becomes void upon the happening of the contingency which divests the mortgagor.[29]

§ 138. Interests passed by mortgage.—A mortgage passes the interest of the mortgagor whatever it may be.[30] When a mortgage is made of an estate or interest already incumbered in any manner, the mortgage of course attaches only to the interest then remaining in the mortgagor. Upon the discharge of any prior incumbrance, the mortgage interest has the full advantage of the discharge. If the mortgagor acquires any title after making the mortgage, that, as a general rule, accrues to the benefit of the mortgage title.

Although the mortgage purports to convey a title in fee simple, when the mortgagor has only an equitable title, it is effectual to pass such equitable title, and the record of it is notice to subsequent purchasers of the mortgagor's interest.[31]

But a mortgage of the fee given by one who only had a life estate, though he had held the property under a will for thirty years supposing he took a fee simple, is a mortgage of a life interest only, and a foreclosure of it after the death of the mortgagor passes no title to the purchaser.[32] And one to whom a life estate in land is conveyed can not bind the remaindermen by a mortgage given for the purchase-price, they not being parties to the mortgage.[33]

A mortgage on a leasehold interest conveys no interest beyond the term of the lease, and a mortgagee in possession thereunder can

[27] 2 Story Eq. Jur. § 1021; Curtis v. Root, 20 Ill. 518; Spalding v. Wayne (Ky.), 45 S. W. 517; Coomes v. Frey, 141 Ky. 740, 133 S. W. 758; Neligh v. Michenor, 11 N. J. Eq. 539; Barnes v. Dow, 59 Vt. 530, 10 Atl. 258; Trent v. Hunt, 9 Exch. 14.

[28] Smith v. Provin, 4 Allen (Mass.) 516.

[29] L'Etourneau v. Henquenet, 89 Mich. 428, 50 N. W. 1077.

[30] Brockschmidt v. Archer, 64 Ohio St. 502, 60 N. E. 623. Such, for instance, as an undivided interest in common with others. Baker v. Shephard, 30 Ga. 706. A lessee may mortgage his leasehold interest in the building which he has erected upon the land of another. Knapp v. Jones, 143 Ill. 375, 32 N. E. 382; Cross v. Weare Commission Co., 153 Ill. 499, 38 N. E. 1038, 46 Am. St. 902; Miller v. Michoud, 11 Rob. (La.) 225; French v. Prescott, 61 N. H. 27; Hagar v. Brainerd, 44 Vt. 294. See also Clark v. Lyster, 155 Fed. 513, 84 C. C. A. 27; Holmquist v. Gilbert, 41 Colo. 113, 92 Pac. 232; Re Carroll, 11 Ont. W. R. 179.

[31] Christian v. American Freehold Land Mtg. Co., 92 Ala. 130, 9 So. 219; Laughlin v. Braley, 25 Kans. 147; Lovering v. Fogg, 18 Pick. (Mass.) 540; Lincoln Bldg. &c. Assn. v. Hass, 10 Nebr. 581, 7 N. W. 327.

[32] Mixter v. Woodcock, 154 Mass. 535, 28 N. E. 907. See also New South Bldg. &c. Assn. v. Gann, 101 Ga. 678, 29 S. E. 15.

[33] McDonald v. Woodward, 58 S. Car. 554, 36 S. E. 918.

acquire no greater right by virtue of his possession than the lessee had.[34]

Unless the conveyance in mortgage be limited in its operation, it passes all the interest of the mortgagor in the property described. It passes any reversionary interest he has; for instance, a mortgage of land subject to a homestead right conveys the reversionary interest after the expiration of the homestead estate, although the wife did not join in it.[35] If there be an outstanding contract of sale of which notice is imparted by the record or by the vendee's possession, the mortgage is subject to the vendee's right to purchase; and upon a foreclosure and sale the purchaser takes the property subject to the same right.[36]

A mortgage may be made of any imperfect title which the mortgagor has, as, for instance, an imperfect Spanish title which was subject to sale and assignment.[37]

A clause in a mortgage, "excepting therefrom so much of said tracts as have been conveyed by the mortgagor by deed to different individuals," does not reserve from its operation a portion of the premises covered by a prior unrecorded mortgage.[38]

A mortgage of several lots of land described by numbers on a plat, and by courses and distances, will pass all the title the mortgagor has in the lots, although he has only a mortgage title to one of them.[39] But where a mortgagor became the husband of the mortgagee, and the two joined in a second mortgage of the premises to secure a prior debt of the husband, it was held that the wife's interest under the first mortgage was not thereby affected. She had not joined in the mortgage to assign her own mortgage, but to effectually pass the equity of redemption.[40] So a mortgage of all the land and right to land which the grantor has in a certain town does not include land to which he has only a possibility of a reversion on the nonperformance of a condition subsequent.[41] But a mortgage of land by a vendor, who holds notes for the purchase-money of the same land and a vendor's lien,

---

[34] Miller v. Warren, 182 N. Y. 539, 75 N. E. 1131.

[35] McGuire v. Van Pelt, 55 Ala. 344; Smith v. Provin, 4 Allen (Mass.) 516.

[36] Laverty v. Moore, 33 N. Y. 658. See also Masters v. Clark, 89 Ark. 191, 116 S. W. 186; Morley v. Quimby, 132 Mich. 140, 92 N. W. 943.

[37] Massey v. Papin, 24 How. (U. S.) 362, 16 L. ed. 174.

[38] Eaton v. White, 18 Wis. 517.

[39] Murdock v. Chapman, 9 Gray (Mass.) 156.

[40] Power v. Lester, 23 N. Y. 527.

[41] Richardson v. Cambridge, 2 Allen (Mass.) 118, 79 Am. Dec. 767.

does not transfer the notes in the absence of an express mention of them.[42]

§ 138a. **Homestead subject of mortgage.**—Constitutional and statutory provisions establishing homestead exemptions do not necessarily deprive the owner of land of his right to execute a valid mortgage thereof.[43] But in some states the mortgage of a homestead is prohibited altogether.[44]

In other states, homesteads may be mortgaged for specific purposes; such as, for instance, to secure payment of money loaned for improvements on the land.[45] In a majority of the states permitting mortgages of homesteads such mortgages are effectual only when there has been a special release and waiver of the homestead right;[46] while in all the states, the free and voluntary assent of the mortgagor's wife, if he be a married man, is a condition precedent to the vesting of the lien.[47] But a husband may execute a valid mortgage upon a community homestead in his own name and as his wife's attorney in fact, she having given him a general power of attorney to convey or otherwise dispose of their community property.[48] It has been held that an unmarried woman may mortgage her homestead, although she is the head of a family of minor children.[49]

§ 138b. **When owner estopped to deny mortgage made by a third person.**—By way of estoppel in pais, an owner of land may be bound by a mortgage of it made by a third person. Thus, a person having title to real estate, who represents another as the owner, and thereby

[42] Bell v. Blair, 65 Miss. 191, 30 So. 373.

[43] New England Mtg. Sec. Co. v. Payne, 107 Ala. 578, 18 So. 164; Morris v. Sergent, 18 Iowa 90; Fruge v. Fulton, 120 La. 750, 45 So. 595; Adkinson &c. Co. v. Varnado (Miss.), 47 So. 113; McCreery v. Schaffer, 26 Nebr. 173, 41 N. W. 996; Bonorden v. Kriz, 13 Nebr. 121, 12 N. W. 831; Fleming v. Garham, 110 N. Car. 374, 14 S. E. 922; Hughes v. Hodges, 112 N. Car. 236, 9 S. E. 437.

[44] Planters' &c. Bank v. Dickinson, 83 Ga. 711, 10 S. E. 446; Van Wickle v. Laundry, 29 La. Ann. 330; Texas Land &c. Co. v. Blalock, 76 Tex. 85, 13 S. W. 12; Smith v. Von Hutton, 75 Tex. 625, 13 S. W. 18; Hall v. Jennings (Tex. Civ. App.), 19 Tex. Ct. 602, 104 S. W. 489; Dignowity v. Lindheim (Tex. Civ. App.), 109 S. W. 966.

[45] Hicks v. Texas Loan &c. Co., 51 Tex. Civ. App. 298, 111 S. W. 784.

[46] Balkum v. Wood, 58 Ala. 642; Browning v. Harriss, 99 Ill. 456; Trustees v. Beale, 98 Ill. 248.

[47] Long v. Mostyn, 65 Ala. 543; Anderson v. Culbert, 55 Iowa 233, 7 N. W. 508; Chambers v. Cox, 27 Kans. 393; Griffin v. Proctor, 14 Bush (Ky.) 571; Sherrid v. Southwick, 43 Mich. 515, 5 N. W. 1027; Justice v. Souder, 19 N. Dak. 613, 125 N. W. 1029.

[48] Oregon Mtg. Co. v. Hersner, 14 Wash. 515, 45 Pac. 40.

[49] McGee v. Tinner (Tex. Civ. App.), 129 S. W. 866.

induces a third party to accept from that other a mortgage for a valuable consideration, is in equity bound by such mortgage, and is not permitted to set up his own title against it.[50] Also where a stranger to the title, or one having only a limited interest in a tract of land, conveys the property by mortgage, and the owner receives the benefit of any part of the proceeds derived from the mortgage, knowing the facts, he is estopped to deny that the mortgage conveys a good title. And likewise, if the owner, though ignorant of the facts when he receives the proceeds, afterward learns the truth, his retention of the proceeds thereafter estops him from disputing the validity and effect of the mortgage.[51] Furthermore, if the owner, knowingly and without disclosing his title, stands by and permits his property to be mortgaged by another to one who is, to the owner's knowledge, relying on the apparent ownership of the person executing the mortgage, such conduct, irrespective of who benefits by the transaction, will estop the owner from asserting his title against the mortgagee.[52]

§ 139. **Mortgage of a mortgage interest.**—There may be a mortgage of a mortgage. One may mortgage an interest in real estate which he himself holds in mortgage.[53] He conveys all the interest he has; and if he afterward acquire an absolute title, the second mortgagee by foreclosing his mortgage acquires an absolute estate.[54] Where the mortgagee conveys the estate by way of a mortgage, his mortgagee takes it subject to the original mortgagor's right to redeem; but in such a case notice to such mortgagor of the second mortgage by his mortgagee would require such original mortgagor to make payment to the sub-mortgagee, so that he might protect his interests against the

---

[50] Parlin v. Stone, 48 Fed. 808; Rice v. Bunce, 49 Mo. 231; Sweaney v. Mallory, 62 Mo. 485; Hart v. Giles, 67 Mo. 175; Story Eq. Jur. § 385.

[51] Kahn v. Peter, 104 Ala. 523, 16 So. 524; Ansonia v. Cooper, 66 Conn. 184, 33 Atl. 905; Brewster v. Baker, 16 Barb. (N. Y.) 613; Gaddes v. Pawtucket Inst. for Savings, 33 R. I. 177, 80 Atl. 415, Ann. Cas. 1913 B, 407; East Greenwich Sav. Inst. v. Kenyon, 20 R. I. 110, 37 Atl. 632; Robinson v. Bailey, 19 R. I. 464, 36 Atl. 1126; Brewer v. Nash, 16 R. I. 458, 17 Atl. 857, 27 Am. St. 749.

[52] Bryan v. Ramirez, 8 Cal. 461, 68 Am. Dec. 340; Thompson v. Sanborn, 11 N. H. 201, 35 Am. Dec. 490; Craw-

ford v. Bertholf, 1 N. J. Eq. 458, 471; Brewster v. Baker, 16 Barb. (N. Y.) 613; Gaddes v. Pawtucket Inst. for Savings, 33 R. I. 177, 80 Atl. 415, Ann. Cas. 1913 B, 407; East Greenwich Sav. Inst. v. Kenyon, 20 R. I. 110, 37 Atl. 632.

[53] Cutts v. York Mfg. Co., 18 Maine 190. This point was not before the court. See also Cutts v. York Mfg. Co., 18 Maine 201; Graydon v. Church, 7 Mich. 36; Slee v. Manhattan Co., 1 Paige (N. Y.) 48; Henry v. Davis, 7 Johns. Ch. (N. Y.) 40. But see Hudson City Sav. Inst. v. McArthur, 8 N. Y. W. Dig. 63.

[54] Murdock v. Chapman, 9 Gray (Mass.) 156. See also Power v. Lester, 23 N. Y. 527.

mortgage.[55] If a married woman having a mortgage upon her husband's land unites with him in the granting part of the deed and in the covenants, she conveys her mortgage interest;[56] but if, having such a mortgage, she join her husband in a subsequent mortgage merely to release her dower and homestead, she does not thereby subject her mortgage interest to the lien of the latter mortgage.[57]

§ 140. **Mortgage of rents and profits.**—The rents, income, and profits arising out of real estate are just as much property as the estate out of which they arise, and as such are equally the subject of mortgage.[58]

A mortgage may be made of rents due under a lease, and, although a right of entry be given to the mortgagee, the mortgage is a mere security, like any other mortgage of real estate, and the mortgagor remains the real owner until foreclosure and sale.[59] A mortgage may be made of a ditch for mining purposes, the grantee having authority to collect the rents and profits of it.[60] Where a mortgage of the realty includes the rents and profits as an additional pledge or security for the debt, this does not interfere with the equity of redemption. The court will give the rents and profits as well as the real estate to the mortgagee as a fund to be applied to the extinguishment of the debt.[61]

§ 141. **Mortgage by one part owner or tenant in common.**—A mortgage given by one part owner of land upon purchasing the remaining portion, which describes the whole parcel, is construed to embrace the entire interest, and not merely the undivided interest conveyed by the mortgagee.[62]

The owner of certain land, having conveyed an undivided half of

[55] Hidden v. Kretschmar, 37 Fed. 465; Coffin v. Loring; 9 Allen (Mass.) 154; Brown v. Tyler, 8 Gray (Mass.) 135; Murdock v. Chapman, 9 Gray (Mass.) 156; Murray v. Porter, 29 Nebr. 288, 41 N. W. 1111; Slee v. Manhattan Co., 1 Paige (N. Y.) 48; Henry v. Davis, 7 Johns. Ch. (N. Y.) 40; Johnson v. Blydenburgh, 31 N. Y. 432; Harrison v. Burlingame, 48 Hun (N. Y.) 212; Solomon v. Wilson, 1 Whart. (Pa.) 241.

[56] Gregory v. Gregory, 16 Ohio St. 560.

[57] Kitchell v. Mudgett, 37 Mich. 81.

[58] 4 Kent's Comm. 144; Wright v. Shumway, 1 Biss. (U. S.) 23; Farmers' Loan &c. Co. v. American Water-works Co., 107 Fed. 23; Barroilhet v. Battelle, 7 Cal. 450; Bagley v. Illinois Trust &c. Bank, 199 Ill. 76, 64 N. E. 1085; Owsley v. Neeves, 179 Ill. App. 61; Townsend v. Wilson, 155 Ill. App. 303; Schaeppi v. Bartholomae, 118 Ill. App. 316; Neligh v. Michenor, 11 N. J. Eq. 539; Van Rensselaer v. Dennison, 35 N. Y. 393.

[59] Potts v. Blanchard, 19 La. Ann. 167.

[60] Carpenter v. Millard, 38 Vt. 9.

[61] Ortengren v. Rice, 104 Ill. App. 428.

[62] Shirras v. Caig, 7 Cranch (U. S.) 34, 3 L. ed. 447.

it by a deed fully describing it, afterward conveyed the remaining un-divided half to the same grantee, and received from him at the same time a mortgage conveying "the following real estate in Stamford: viz., the same and all the real estate described in the deed of the said grantor to me dated November 18, 1847," the first-named deed. The mortgage was construed to cover the whole title and interest acquired by the mortgagor by the two deeds, and not merely the undivided half conveyed to him by the former deed.[63]

A mortgage by a tenant in common of a moiety of land passes only his interest, although he at the time holds a power from the owner of the other moiety, and the mortgage purports to be of the whole estate, if it does not purport to be made by virtue of his power from the other owner, as well as in his own right.[64] One tenant in common may mortgage his interest in the common property to secure his in-dividual indebtedness, but such transaction will not affect the rights of his cotenants.[65] In a case where four of eight tenants in common conveyed their interest in the common property to the remaining four tenants, and three of the latter executed a mortgage covering the entire property to secure a portion of the purchase-price, it was held that the mortgage lien did not cover the interest of the grantee who did not join in the mortgage.[66]

§ 142. **Effect of mortgage of building to include land.**—The mort-gage of a building carries with it the land on which it stands which is essential to its use, if such appears to have been the intention of the parties.[67] Thus a mortgage, made to secure advances to enable the mortgagor to erect a building on leased land, of "all his right, title, and interest which he now has in the foundation or stone-work of said building, and which he may have in and unto said building, during its erection and completion, and after it is completed," passes the land on which the building stands.[68] The right which the grantor has in the foundation, stone-work, and building is not merely or mostly a right to the materials of which they are composed, but the right of having

[63] Van Rensselaer v. Dennison, 35 N. Y. 393.

[64] Kidd v. Teeple, 22 Cal. 255; First Nat. Bank v. Illinois Steel Co., 174 Ill. 140, 51 N. E. 200 (quoting text).

[65] Foltz v. Wert, 103 Ind. 404, 2 N. E. 950; Peck v. Williams, 113 Ind. 256, 15 N. E. 270; Beck v. Kall-meyer, 42 Mo. App. 563.

[66] Shreve v. Harvey, 74 N. J. Eq. 336, 70 Atl. 671.

[67] Wilson v. Hunter, 14 Wis. 683. See also Humphreys v. McKissock, 140 U. S. 304, 35 L. ed. 473; Whitney v. Olney, 3 Mason (U. S.) 280; Dike-man v. Taylor, 24 Conn. 219; Esty v. Baker, 48 Maine 495; Doyle v. Lord, 64 N. Y. 433, 21 Am. Rep. 629.

[68] Greenwood v. Murdock, 9 Gray (Mass.) 20, 69 Am. Dec. 272.

them on the land as part of a structure, with the right to use and occupy them for a long period of time. It is a grant of his right to use
and occupy the land under the lease.

As a general rule, a building erected upon the land of another becomes a part of the realty, and it is only by an express agreement that
one can have a separate property in such a building as a chattel, with
a right to remove it. If one having a contract for the purchase of a
lot of land erects a house upon it, in pursuance of an agreement that
he will do so, and that on receiving a deed of the land he will mortgage it to the owner to secure the purchase-money, he can not, before
receiving a deed of the land, mortgage the house as personal property
to another. This agreement, instead of being an agreement that the
house may be held separate from the land, is in effect an agreement
that the building and land shall be united and held together.[69]

Buildings erected under an agreement with the owner of land to
convey it to the builder upon his paying a certain sum within a limited
time are not strictly personal property; but they are fixtures and constitute a part of the realty. The builder has an equitable interest in
the realty, and not a pure ownership of the buildings as chattels; and
therefore a mortgage by him of the buildings should be recorded as a
mortgage of real estate, and not as a chattel mortgage.[70]

§ 143. **House moved from the land.**—A mortgage was made of a
lot of land upon which was a dwelling-house. Subsequently, and without the knowledge or consent of the mortgagee, the mortgagor removed
the house from the lot upon which it stood, and placed it upon an
adjoining lot. It was held that the mortgagee retained his lien upon
the dwelling-house, and that the house might be sold after first applying the lot covered by the mortgage toward satisfying it. The adjoining lot was owned by the wife of the mortgagor, and the removal was
with her knowledge.[71] A mortgagor in possession of the mortgaged
premises can not, without the mortgagee's consent, authorize a third
person to erect buildings on the mortgaged property and remove

[69] Milton v. Colby, 5 Metc. (Mass.)
78. Or the mortgage might maintain
trespass. Smith v. Goodwin, 2 Maine
173. See post § 687; and Jones on
Chattel Mortgages, § 123.

[70] Eastman v. Foster, 8 Metc.
(Mass.) 19; Holt Co. Bank v. Tootle,
25 Nebr. 408, 41 N. W. 291.

[71] Hamlin v. Parsons, 12 Minn. 108,
90 Am. Dec. 284. See also Hutchins v. King, 1 Wall. (U. S.) 53, 17
L. ed. 544; Betz v. Muench (N. J.),
13 Atl. 622; Betz v. Verner, 46 N. J.
Eq. 256, 19 Atl. 206. In Kansas it is
unlawful to remove a building from
mortgaged land without the consent
of the mortgagee. As to the indictment or prosecution, see State v.
Decker, 52 Kans. 193, 34 Pac. 780.
See post §§ 453, 688.

them.[72] By agreement, express or implied, between the owner of real estate and the owner of buildings, the latter may annex the buildings to the realty without their becoming part of it. So, in the case stated, the house did not necessarily become a part of the lot upon which it was placed by the removal. Under such circumstances there is no reason why the mortgagee should not have the benefit of the security for which he contracted. No question arises in this case as to the effect of substantial alterations in the building, which might sometimes affect or change the title to property altered from its original form. Such was the case where a mortgagor removed a dwelling-house from the mortgaged premises, and used the materials in the construction of a house upon another lot of land, and afterward sold the house and lot. The materials having thus become a part of the freehold, the right of property therein vested in the grantee of the land; and therefore the mortgagee could not maintain trover against the purchaser, either for the new house or for the old materials used in its construction.[73]

§ 144. **Legal effect of removal of fixtures from mortgaged premises.**—Whether fixtures severed from the realty become personal property, and when taken away from the realty are freed from the lien of

[72] Ekstrom v. Hall, 90 Maine 186, 38 Atl. 106.

[73] Pierce v. Goddard, 22 Pick. (Mass.) 559, 33 Am. Dec. 764. "The general rule is," says Mr. Justice Wilde, "that the owner of property, whether the property be movable or immovable, has the right to that which is united to it by accession or adjunction. But by the law of England as well as by the civil law, a trespasser who wilfully takes the property of another can acquire no right in it on the principle of accession, but the owner may reclaim it, whatever alteration of form it may have undergone, unless it be changed into a different species and be incapable of being restored to its former state; and even then the trespasser, by the civil law, could acquire no right by the accession, unless the materials had been taken away in ignorance of their being the property of another. But there are exceptions to the general rule. It is laid down by Molloy as a settled principle of law, that if a man cuts down trees of another, or takes timber or plank prepared for the erecting or repairing of a dwelling-house, nay, though some of them are for shipping, and builds a ship, property follows, not the owners, but the builders. Mol. De Jure Mar. lib. 2, ch. 1, § 7. * * * In the present case it can not be questioned that the newly erected dwelling-house was a part of the freehold, and was the property of the mortgagor. The materials used in its construction ceased to be personal property, and the owner's property in them was divested as effectually as though they had been destroyed. It is clear, therefore, that the plaintiff could not maintain an action, even against the mortgagor, for the conversion of the new house. And it is equally clear that he can not maintain the present action for the conversion of the materials taken from the old house. The taking down of that house and using the materials in the construction of the

the mortgage, is a question upon which the authorities are divided.[74]

It has been held that when buildings are severed from the mortgaged premises and become part of another freehold, they become freed from the mortgage lien.[75] Also where property affixed to mortgaged land is severed and sold to a bona fide purchaser, it can not be followed and reclaimed.[76]

A house having been floated off the lot covered by the mortgage into an adjacent street by a flood was sold by the owner to a person who had notice of all the circumstances. An action was brought to foreclose the mortgage upon the land and the house, then standing in the street. The court held that the house was effectually removed from the operation of the mortgage lien; and that, so far as the legal effect of the removal was concerned, it was immaterial whether the severance was by the act of God, as in this case, or the act of man.[77] But in a case before the Supreme Court of the United States,[78] Mr. Justice Field declared that the mortgage covers the timber after it is cut and removed from the land as well as before; that the sale of it by the mortgagors does not divest the mortgage lien; that the purchaser of the timber takes it subject to this paramount lien; and that the holders of the mortgage can follow it and take possession of it, and hold it until the amount due upon the mortgage is paid. But what the effect of the severance of fixtures is depends very largely upon the view taken

new building was the tortious act of the mortgagor, for which he alone is responsible."

[74] Hill v. Gwin, 51 Cal. 47; Gardner v. Finley, 19 Barb. (N. Y.) 317, hold that the lien is lost. See also Clark v. Reyburn, 1 Kans. 281; Harris v. Bannon, 78 Ky. 568; Citizens' Bank v. Knapp, 22 La. Ann. 117; Woehler v. Endter, 46 Wis. 301, 1 N. W. 329. But contra, see Hutchins v. King, 1 Wall. (U. S.) 53, 59, 17 L. ed. 544, per Field, J., cited below; Dorr v. Dudderar, 88 Ill. 107. See post § 688.

[75] Harris v. Bannon, 78 Ky. 568.

[76] Hutchins v. King, 1 Wall. (U. S.) 53, 17 L. ed. 544; Cooper v. Davis, 15 Conn. 556; Clark v. Reyburn, 1 Kans. 281; Citizens' Bank v. Knapp, 22 La. Ann. 117; Gore v. Jenness, 19 Maine 53; Byrom v. Chapin, 113 Mass. 308; Gowding v. Shea, 103 Mass. 360, 4 Am. St. 563; Kircher v. Schalk, 39 N. J. L. 335; Van Pelt v. McGraw, 4 N. Y. 110; Wilson v. Maltby, 59 N. Y. 126; Gardner v. Heartt, 3 Denio (N. Y.)

232; Lane v. Hitchcock, 14 Johns. (N. Y.) 213; Kimball v. Darling, 32 Wis. 684.

[77] Buckout v. Swift, 27 Cal. 433, 87 Am. Dec. 90. Mr. Justice Shafter, delivering the opinion of the court, said: "A building, severed and removed from mortgaged lands, of which lands it formed a part when the mortgage was given, is disincumbered of the lien, substantially on the same principle that a building, erected upon the lands after the giving of the mortgage, is subject to the lien. In the first case the building is withdrawn from the operation of the mortgage, for the reason that it has ceased to be a thing real; in the other, mere materials are brought under the lien, for the reason that they have become a structure by combination, and the structure has become a thing real by position."

[78] Hutchins v. King, 1 Wall. (U. S.) 53, 59, 17 L. ed. 544. See also Gore v. Jenness, 19 Maine 53.

as to the nature and effect of a mortgage; whether it be regarded as a conveyance of the legal title to the property, giving the mortgagee also the right of possession, or whether it be regarded merely as a lien, and the mortgagor is protected in his possession until foreclosure. On the one hand the mortgagee's legal ownership or his actual or constructive possession enable him to follow and recover the property severed; but on the other hand he has merely a right to restrain the removal of the property by injunction, or after the removal at most only a right to recover damages for wrongfully impairing his security.[79]

§ 145. Severed and growing wood subjects of mortgages.—A mortgage of wood not standing on the land of the mortgagor is a mortgage of personal property, and a record of it as a mortgage of real estate is ineffectual.[80] Also a mortgage of trees to be cut and severed from the soil is a mortgage of personalty, and is to be recorded as a chattel mortgage.[81] But growing wood or timber is a portion of the realty, and is embraced in a mortgage of the land.[82]

§ 146. Mortgage of improvements.—A mortgage of improvements conveys no title to the land itself. It passes only a right to the improvements placed upon the land by the mortgagor, or an equitable right to compensation for them in case the owner of the land should take possession. A subsequent acquisition of the title to the land by the mortgagor does not in such case inure to the benefit of the mortgagee.[83] A mortgage of a building erected on leased land under an agreement that the lessee might remove it, or the lessor should pay for it at its appraised value, is a mortgage of realty falling within the designation of a chattel real at common law,[84] and should be recorded as a mortgage of real estate, and not as a chattel mortgage.[85]

Where a building has been erected by a tenant whose lease gives him the right of removal at the expiration of the lease, this right must be exercised within a reasonable time; and one who has taken from him

[79] Verner v. Betz, 46 N. J. Eq. 256, 19 Atl. 206. See post § 453.

[80] Douglas v. Shumway, 13 Gray (Mass.) 498.

[81] Erskine v. Plummer, 7 Maine 447, 22 Am. Dec. 216; Nelson v. Nelson, 72 Mass. 385; Cook v. Stearns, 11 Mass. 533; First Nat. Bank v. Weed, 89 Mich. 357, 5 N. W. 864; Cudworth v. Scott, 41 N. H. 456; Wood v. Lester, 29 Barb. (N. Y.) 145; Boykin v. Rosenfield, 69 Tex. 115, 9 S. W. 318.

[82] See Green v. Armstrong, 1 Denio (N. Y.) 550; Wintermute v. Light, 46 Barb. (N. Y.) 278; Kimball v. Sattley, 55 Vt. 285, 45 Am. Rep. 614; Crosby v. Wadsworth, 6 East 602; Carrington v. Roots, 2 M. & W. 248.

[83] Mitchell v. Black, 64 Maine 48.

[84] Griffin v. Marine Co., 52 Ill. 130.

[85] Eastman v. Foster, 8 Metc. (Mass.) 19; Holt Co. Bank v. Tootle, 25 Nebr. 408, 41 N. W. 291.

a mortgage upon the building acquires no better right than the tenant had, and can not remove the building after the tenant's right of removal has expired.[86] Where the provisions of a lease show that the parties to it intended that the improvements which it was contemplated the lessee would erect on the premises should not be removed therefrom until the rent was paid, the mortgagee of such improvements has no right to remove same unless and until all the rent in arrears has been paid.[87]

§ 147. **When realty mortgage covers improvements subsequently made.**—The lien of a mortgage extends to all improvements and repairs subsequently made upon the mortgaged premises, whether made by the mortgagor or by a purchaser from him without actual notice of the existence of the mortgage.[88] Thus a mortgage of a ditch or flume in process of construction includes, without any special mention, all improvements or fixtures then on the line located for the flume, as well as those which may afterward be put thereon.[89]

The improvements which the mortgagor, remaining in possession and enjoyment of the mortgaged premises, makes upon them, in contemplation of law he makes for himself, and to enhance the general value of the freehold. Such improvements go, of course, to the benefit and security of the mortgagee, by increasing the value of the pledge.[90]

§ 148. **When abstract of title part of security.**—An abstract of title delivered by the owner of land to the mortgagee's attorney, for the purpose of decreasing the expenses of searching the title, may be regarded as part of the security for the loan; and accordingly it has been held that the mortgagor is not entitled to the possession of it until the mortgage is paid. In case of a sale of the mortgage, or of a

[86] Smith v. Park, 31 Minn. 70, 16 N. W. 490.
[87] In re Potee Brick Co., 179 Fed. 525. See also Simpson Brick Press Co. v. Wormley, 61 Ill. App. 460; O'Brien v. Mueller, 96 Md. 137, 53 Atl. 663.
[88] Martin v. Beatty, 54 Ill. 100; Mutual Ben. L. Ins. Co. v. Huntington, 57 Kans. 744, 48 Pac. 19; Rice v. Dewey, 54 Barb. (N. Y.) 455; Gibson v. Am. Loan &c. Co., 58 Hun 443, 12 N. Y. S. 444; Wharton v. Moore, 84 N. Car. 479, 37 Am. Rep. 627; Grosvenor v. Bethell, 93 Tenn. 577, 28 S. W. 1096.

[89] Union Water Co. v. Murphy's Flat Fluming Co., 22 Cal. 620.
[90] Hamilton v. Huntley, 78 Ind. 521, 41 Am. Rep. 593; Bass Foundry v. Gallentine, 99 Ind. 525; Ekstrom v. Hall, 90 Maine 186, 38 Atl. 106; Meagher v. Hayes, 152 Mass. 228, 25 N. E. 105, 23 Am. St. 819; Thompson v. Vinton, 121 Mass. 139; Roddy v. Brick, 42 N. J. Eq. 218, 6 Atl. 806; Great Western Mfg. Co. v. Bathgate, 15 Okla. 87, 79 Pac. 903; McGrillis v. Cole, 25 R. I. 156, 55 Atl. 196, 105 Am. St. 875.

foreclosure, it would be necessary that the mortgagee should have it, or that another should be made.[91]

II. *Accessions to the Mortgaged Property*

§ 149. Legal and equitable view concerning after-acquired property.—At common law, nothing can be mortgaged that does not belong to the mortgagor at the time the mortgage is made.[1] "It is a common learning in the law, that a man can not grant or charge that which he hath not."[2] He must have a present property, either actual or potential, in the thing sold or mortgaged.[3] Therefore at law, although a mortgage in terms is made to cover after-acquired property, yet, after such property is acquired, an execution levied upon it as the property of the mortgagor or a sale by him will prevail over the mortgage.[4]

But a different rule prevails in equity.[5] Equity will give effect to

---

[91] Holm v. Wust, 11 Abb. Pr. (N. S.) (N. Y.) 113. See also Equitable Trust Co. v. Burley, 110 Ill. App. 538.

[1] Jones on Chattel Mortgages, § 138; Moody v. Wright, 13 Metc. (Mass.) 17, 46 Am. Dec. 706; Jones v. Richardson, 10 Mass. 481; Ross v. Wilson, 7 Bush (Ky.) 29; Amonett v. Amis, 16 La. Ann. 225; Pierce v. Emery, 32 N. H. 484. See also Maxwell v. Wilmington Dental Mfg. Co,. 77 Fed. 938; Sillers v. Lester, 48 Miss. 513; Everman v. Robb, 52 Miss. 653, 24 Am. Rep. 682; Hickson Lumber Co. v. Gay Lumber Co., 150 N. Car. 281, 63 S. E. 1045; Coe v. Columbus, Piqua &c. R. Co., 10 Ohio St. 372, 391, 75 Am. Dec. 518; Lunn v. Thornton, 1 Com.

B. 379; Lunn v. Thornton, 1 C. B. 383, 50 E. C. L. 383; Tapfield v. Hillman, 6 M. & G. 245, 46 E. C. L. 245.

[2] Perkins tit. Grant § 65.

[3] Looker v. Peckwell, 38 N. J. L. 253; Smithurst v. Edmunds, 14 N. J. Eq. 408; Benjamin on Sales, §§ 78-84. See also Ross v. Wilson, 7 Bush (Ky.) 29.

[4] Looker v. Peckwell, 38 N. J. L. 253 and cases cited.

[5] Little Rock &c. R. Co. v. Page, 35 Ark. 304; Frank v. Hicks, 4 Wyo. 502, 35 Pac. 475; Langton v. Horton, 1 Hare 549.

In a Kentucky case, however, it is said that if such a mortgage is enforcible in equity at all, it can only be enforced as a right under

a mortgage embracing future-acquired realty,[6] and will enforce it against the mortgagor and all other persons except purchasers for value and without notice.[7]

Judge Story, after an elaborate examination of the question, in stating the result of it, says: "It seems to me the clear result of all the authorities, that wherever the parties by their contract intended to create a positive lien or charge, either upon real or personal property, whether then owned by the assignor or not, or, if personal property, whether it is then in esse or not, it attaches in equity as a lien or charge upon the particular property as soon as the assignor or contractor acquires a title thereto against the latter, and all persons asserting a claim thereto under him, either voluntarily or with notice, or in bankruptcy."[8]

§ 150. **Products of the soil.**—Upon this principle a valid mortgage may be made by an owner or lessee in possession of land of a crop to be raised by him the coming season, or of crops to be grown within a certain period.[9] But such a mortgage does not attach until the crops come into existence and are acquired by the mortgagor.[10]

It is a general rule that a thing which has a potential existence may be mortgaged. "Land is the mother and root of all fruits," says Lord

---

the contract, and not as a trust attached to the property. Ross v. Wilson, 7 Bush (Ky.) 29.

[6] Hickson Lumber Co. v. Gay Lumber Co., 150 N. Car. 281, 63 S. E. 1045.

[7] Toledo &c. R. Co. v. Hamilton, 134 U. S. 296, 33 L. ed. 905; Maxwell v. Wilmington Dental Mfg. Co., 77 Fed. 938; Burns v. Campbell, 71 Ala. 271; Christy v. Dana, 34 Cal. 548; Rice v. Kelso, 57 Iowa 115, 7 N. W. 3, 10 N. W. 335; Phillips v. Winslow, 18 B. Mon. (Ky.) 431; Hollingsworth v. Chaffe, 33 La. Ann. 547; Morrill v. Noyes, 56 Maine 458, 96 Am. Dec. 486; Howe v. Freeman, 14 Gray (Mass.) 566; Sillers v. Lester, 48 Miss. 513; Pierce v. Emery, 32 N. H. 484; Stevens v. Watson, 4 Abb. App. Dec. (N. Y.) 302; Coopers v. Wolf, 15 Ohio St. 523; Bailey v. Allegheny Nat. Bank, 104 Pa. St. 425; Sweetzer v. Jones, 35 Vt. 317, 82 Am. Dec. 639.

[8] Mitchell v. Winslow, 2 Story (U. S.) 630; Jarvis v. State Bank, 22 Colo. 309, 45 Pac. 505. See also Smithurst v. Edmunds, 14 N. J. Eq. 403.

[9] Booker v. Jones, 55 Ala. 266; Jones v. Webster, 48 Ala. 109; Lehman v. Marshall, 47 Ala. 362; Hutchinson v. Ford, 9 Bush (Ky.) 318, 15 Am. Rep. 711; Arques v. Wasson, 51 Cal. 620, 21 Am. Rep. 718; Jones on Chattel Mortgages, § 142; Barnard v. Eaton, 2 Cush. (Mass.) 294, per Shaw, C. J. See also Wilkerson v. Thorp, 128 Cal. 221, 60 Pac. 697; Van Hoozer v. Cory, 34 Barb. (N. Y.) 9; Stover v. Eycleshimer, 3 Keyes (N. Y.) 620. See contra at law, Milliman v. Neher, 20 Barb. (N. Y.) 37; Schweinber v. Great Western Elev. Co., 9 N. Dak. 113, 81 N. W. 35; Comstock v. Scales, 7 Wis. 159. But see Tomlinson v. Greenfield, 31 Ark. 557; Redd v. Burrus, 58 Ga. 574; Gittings v. Nelson, 86 Ill. 591.

[10] McMaster v. Emerson, 109 Iowa 284, 80 N. W. 389.

Hobart.[11] "Therefore he that hath it may grant all fruits that may arise from it after, and the property shall pass as soon as the fruits are extant."

A landlord has no such interest in, or title to, crops grown on the rented lands as can be made the subject of a valid mortgage.[12]

A mortgage of grain "now standing and growing" in the field does not cover, as against an attaching creditor, grain which had at the time of the execution of the mortgage been cut.[13]

Under a mortgage of a greenhouse and nursery, together with the shrubs and plants belonging to the same, new plants and shrubs, the growth of cuttings from those growing at the time of the mortgage, pass to the mortgagee by accession.[14]

In some jurisdictions, however, it has been held that a mortgage of annual crops, which have not been planted at the time the mortgage was executed, is invalid, especially as against attaching creditors, since such crops can not be regarded as having even a potential existence, they being distinguished in this respect from the spontaneous product of the earth, or the increase of that which is already in existence.[15] *

§ **151. Crops not sown.**—A valid mortgage of a crop before it is raised may be made by an owner or lessee of land.[16] And although the

[11] Grantham v. Hawley, Hobart 132. He further remarks that "a person may grant all the tithe wool that he shall have in such a year; yet perhaps he shall have none; but a man can not grant all the wool that shall grow upon his sheep that he shall buy hereafter; for there he hath it neither actually nor potentially." See also Jones v. Webster, 48 Ala. 109; Arques v. Wasson, 51 Cal. 620, 21 Am. Rep. 718; Everman v. Robb, 52 Miss. 653, 24 Am. Rep. 682; Cotten v. Willoughby, 83 N. Car. 75, 35 Am. St. 564; Moore v. Byrum, 10 Rich. (S. Car.) 452, 30 Am. Rep. 58.

[12] Broughton v. Powell, 52 Ala. 123.

[13] Ford v. Sutherlin, 2 Mon. (Ky.) 440.

[14] Bryant v. Pennell, 61 Maine 108, 14 Am. Rep. 550. The plaintiff attached so much of the stock of plants and shrubs as were not covered by the mortgage. His counsel claimed that the maxim, "Partus sequitur ventrem," did not apply; that it might as well be contended that trees raised from the seed of apples picked from a mortgaged tree passed under the mortgage, as to say the cuttings did.

[15] Gittings v. Nelson, 86 Ill. 591; Long v. Hines, 40 Kans. 220, 19 Pac. 796, 10 Am. St. 189; Hutchinson v. Ford, 9 Bush (Ky.) 318, 15 Am. Rep. 711; Rochester Distilling Co. v. Rasey, 142 N. Y. 570, 37 N. E. 632, 40 Am. St. 635. But see Butt v. Ellett, 19 Wall. (U. S.) 544, 22 L. ed. 183; Arques v. Wasson, 51 Cal. 620, 21 Am. Rep. 718; Wheeler v. Becker, 68 Iowa 723, 28 N. W. 40.

[16] Jones on Chattel Mortgages, § 143; Ellett v. Butt, 1 Woods (U. S.) 214; Robinson v. Mauldin, 11 Ala. 977; Grand Forks Nat. Bank v. Minneapolis &c. Elev. Co., 6 Dak. 357, 43 N. E. 806; Everman v. Robb, 52 Miss. 653, 24 Am. Rep. 682. See also Woods v. Rose, 135 Ala. 297, 33 So. 41; Cobb v. Daniel, 105 Ala. 335, 16 So. 882; Robinson v. Kruse, 29 Ark. 575; Wilkerson v. Thorp, 128 Cal. 221, 60 Pac. 679; Hall v. Glass, 123 Cal. 500, 56 Pac. 336, 69·

seed of it has not been sown or planted.[17] In such case the lien attaches, in equity, as soon as the crop is gathered, and may be enforced against purchasers with record notice.[18] A person having the right by parol agreement to sow certain land with wheat upon shares with the owner of the land may, after sowing the wheat, make a valid mortgage of his interest in the crop, which will cover the interest of the mortgagor in the land.[19] But a tenant's mortgage of ungrown crops passes no title to his mortgagee, where, under his contract with his landlord it is stipulated that the ownership and possession of the crops are to remain in the latter, who is entitled to hold them as security for and have a deduction of all indebtedness due him for advances before division, and the tenant fails subsequently to request any division of the crop.[20]

A mortgage of crops by one who is cultivating a farm upon shares covers only his share.[21] The owner of the land can not mortgage a

Am. St. 77; Stephens v. Tucker, 55 Ga, 543, 58 Ga. 391; Hall v. State, 2 Ga. App. 739, 59 S. E. 26; Headrick v. Brattain, 63 Ind. 438; Pennington v. Jones, 57 Iowa 37, 10 N. W. 274; Ambuehl v. Matthews, 41 Minn. 537, 43 N. W. 477; First Nat. Bank v. Rogers, 24 Okla. 357, 103 Pac. 582; Moore v. Byrum, 10 S. Car. 452, 30 Am. Rep. 58; Cook v. Steel, 42 Tex. 53; Smith v. Atkins, 18 Vt. 461; Kimball v. Sattley, 55 Vt. 285, 45 Am. Rep. 614. But see Cole v. Kerr, 19 Nebr. 553, 26 N. W. 598; Rochester Dist. Co. v. Rasey, 142 N. Y. 570, 37 N. E. 632, 40 Am. St. 635, 20 N. Y. S. 583. See ante § 150.

[17] Butt v. Ellett, 19 Wall. (U. S.) 544, 22 L. ed. 183; Woods v. Rose, 135 Ala. 297, 33 So. 41; Shows v. Brantley, 127 Ala. 352, 28 So. 716; Apperson v. Moore, 30 Ark. 56, 21 Am. Rep. 170; Comstock v. Scales, 7 Wis. 159.

Ellett v. Butt, 1 Woods (U. S.) 214. In Mississippi mortgages and deeds of trust may be made to cover growing crops, or crops to be grown within fifteen months from the making of such mortgage or deed, which are valid on the interest of the mortgagor or grantor in such crop, but are subject to any lien in favor of the landlord for the rent of the property. Such mortgages must be recorded in a separate book, entitled a chattel deed book. Laws 1876, pp. 100, 113.

In Arkansas mortgages may be made of crops already planted, or to be planted, and are binding upon such crops and their products. And a laborer may mortgage his interest in a crop for supplies furnished to him. Acts 1875, p. 230; Dig. of Stat. 1884, § 4747.

The statute of Mississippi, providing that mortgages may be made on cotton crops to be produced within fifteen months, is merely declaratory of the law, with a limitation as to the time within which the crop must be produced. Act February 18, 1867; Sillers v. Lester, 48 Miss. 513.

[18] Butt v. Ellett, 19 Wall. (U. S.) 544, 22 L. ed. 183; Hudmon v. DuBose, 85 Ala. 449, 5 So. 162; Varnum v. State, 78 Ala. 28; Jarratt v. McDaniel, 32 Ark. 598; White v. Thomas, 52 Miss. 49. See also McMaster v. Emerson, 109 Iowa 284, 80 N. W. 389; Kelley v. Goodwin, 95 Maine 538, 50 Atl. 711.

[19] Shuart v. Taylor, 7 How. Pr. (N. Y.) 251.

[20] Savings Bank v. Canfield, 12 S. Dak. 330, 81 N. W. 630.

[21] McGee v. Fitzer, 37 Tex. 27.

future crop to be raised thereon as against a tenant raising the crop on the shares under a lease prior to the mortgage.[22]

Possession by prior mortgagee of a crop is notice of his rights to subsequent purchasers.[23] The mortgage in equity attaches as soon as the crop comes into existence.[24] The crop is a chattel merely after it is gathered, and a mortgage of it, to take effect when it is gathered, should be recorded as a chattel mortgage; but a growing crop attached to the soil may be an interest in the real estate; so that a mortgage of a present interest should, under some circumstances, be recorded as a mortgage of real estate.[25] When properly recorded, one who purchases and removes the crop, without the knowledge of the mortgagee, takes it subject to the rights of the mortgagee, who may recover the property if it can be identified, and if not, he may recover the value of it from such purchaser.[26] The mortgagee is entitled to the possession of the crop when it is matured and gathered, and may then maintain an action to recover it or its value.[27] Such a mortgage passes a mere equitable interest while the crop is growing, but after severance the equitable interest ripens into a legal title.[28] If the crop be severed and sold without the consent of the mortgagee, he may recover the value of it from a purchaser, although he has purchased it in the usual course of trade, and without actual notice. The record is constructive notice. The removal of the crop is not such a change in the property as will divest the title of the mortgagee.[29]

The doctrine of the federal courts is that, although an instrument which purports to mortgage a crop, the seed of which has not yet been sown, can not at the time operate as a mortgage of the crop, yet when the seed of the crop intended to be mortgaged has been sown and the crop grows, a lien attaches.[30]

§ 152. Railroad mortgage covering after-acquired property binding in equity.—A mortgage by a railroad company specifically covering after-acquired property is binding in equity upon real estate and

---

[22] Knaebel v. Wilson, 92 Iowa 536, 61 N. W. 178.

[23] Grimes v. Rose, 24 Mich. 416.

[24] Butt v. Ellett, 19 Wall. (U. S.) 544, 22 L. ed. 183; Lehman v. Marshall, 47 Ala. 362; Apperson v. Moore, 30 Ark. 56, 21 Am. Rep. 170. See also McMaster v. Emerson, 109 Iowa 284, 80 N. W. 389.

[25] Butler v. Hill, 57 Tenn. 375.

[26] Duke v. Strickland, 43 Ind. 494.

See also Meyer v. Davenport Elev. Co., 12 S. Dak. 172, 80 N. W. 189.

[27] Lehman v. Marshall, 47 Ala. 362; Robinson v. Mauldin, 11 Ala. 977; Adams v. Tanner, 5 Ala. 740.

[28] Mauldin v. Armistead, 14 Ala. 702, 18 Ala. 500.

[29] Duke v. Strickland, 43 Ind. 494.

[30] Butt v. Ellett, 19 Wall. (U. S.) 544, 22 L. ed. 183; Senter v. Mitchell, 5 McCrary (U. S.) 147, 16 Fed. 206.

personal property afterward purchased for the use of the road, as against the mortgagors and all persons claiming under them, except purchasers for value and without notice; and especially will it bind such property as against claimants under a junior mortgage, which by its terms is subject to the prior mortgage.[31]

That a contract by way of mortgage intended by the parties to create a positive lien or charge either upon real or personal property, whether owned by the mortgagor or not, or, if personal property, whether it is then in being or not, attaches in equity as a lien or charge upon the particular property as soon as the mortgagor acquires title thereto, is a proposition that is almost universally supported by the authorities.[32] The substance of the authorities is to the effect that, when the mortgage is intended to cover after-acquired property, either express terms should be used to that end, or else it must clearly appear from the language of the instrument that such was the manifest intention of the parties.[33]

If the mortgage in distinct terms covers after-acquired property, the record of the mortgage is sufficient notice of the lien. "Whenever a mortgage is made by a railroad company to secure bonds, and the mortgage declares that it shall include all present and after-acquired property, as soon as the property is acquired the mortgage operates upon it. In other words, it seizes the property or operates upon it by way of estoppel as soon as it comes into existence and is in possession of the mortgagor; and the mortgagees, under such circumstances, have a prior equity to the claims of creditors obtaining judgments and executions after the property is thus acquired and placed in possession of the mortgagor."[34] Such is the settled law of the federal courts,[35] and

[31] Calhoun v. Memphis &c. R. Co., 2 Flip. (U. S.) 442; Stevens v. Watson, 4 Abb. App. Dec. (N. Y.) 302; Thompson v. White Water &c. R. Co., 132 U. S. 68, 33 L. ed. 256, 10 Sup. Ct. 29; Central Trust Co. v. Kneeland, 138 U. S. 414, 34 L. ed. 1014, 11 Sup. Ct. 357; Parker v. New Orleans &c. R. Co., 33 Fed. 693; Frost v. Galesburg E. &c. R. Co., 167 Ill. 161, 47 N. E. 357. See Jones on Corporate Bonds and Mortgages, §§ 91–120; Beach v. Wakefield, 107 Iowa 567, 76 N. W. 688, 78 N. W. 197; Omaha &c. R. Co. v. Wabash, St. L. &c. R. Co., 108 Mo. 298, 18 S. W. 1101.

[32] Central Trust Co. v. Kneeland, 138 U. S. 414, 34 L. ed. 1014; Bar-

nard v. Norwich &c. R. Co., 4 Cliff. (U. S.) 351, 14 N. Bank. Reg. 469; Parker v. New Orleans &c. R. Co., 33 Fed. 693; Williamson v. New Jersey &c. R. Co., 29 N. J. Eq. 311, 15 Am. R. Cas. 572.

[33] Toledo D. &c. R. Co. v. Hamilton, 134 U. S. 296, 33 L. ed. 905, 10 Sup. Ct. 546; Parker v. New Orleans B. R. &c. R. Co,. 33 Fed. 693.

[34] Wood v. Holly Mfg. Co., 100 Ala. 326, 13 So. 948; per Drummond, J., in Scott v. Clinton &c. R. Co., 8 Chicago Legal News 210.

[35] Pennock v. Coe, 23 How. (U. S.) 117, 16 L. ed. 472; Galveston R. Co. v. Cowdrey, 11 Wall. (U. S.) 459, 481, 20 L. ed. 199; Dunham v. Cincinnati, Peru &c. R. Co., 1 Wall.

generally of the state courts as well.[36] The rule is applied equally to real estate and personal property; to mortgages by individuals as well as those made by corporations.[37] In Louisiana, however, a mortgage does not extend to property acquired after the date of it.[38]

§ 153. Rule as to after-acquired property generally.—A conveyance of what does not exist does not operate as a present transfer in equity any more than it does in law. The difference is merely that at law the conveyance, having nothing to operate upon, is void; while in equity what is in form a conveyance operates, by way of present contract, to take effect and attach to the subject of it as soon as it comes into being; the agreement to convey then ripens into an actual transfer.[39]

(U. S.) 254, 17 L. ed. 584; Mitchell v. Winslow, 2 Story (U. S.) 630. See also McGourkey v. Toledo &c. R. Co., 146 U. S. 536, 36 L. ed. 1079, 13 Sup. Ct. 170; Campbell v. Texas &c. R. Co., 2 Woods (U. S.) 271; Central Trust Co. v. Chattanooga &c. R. Co., 94 Fed. 275.

[36] Mitchell v. Amador C. &c. Co., 75 Cal. 464, 17 Pac. 246; Phillips v. Winslow, 18 B. Mon. (Ky.) 431, 68 Am. Dec. 729; Morrill v. Noyes, 56 Maine 458; Howe v. Freeman, 14 Gray (Mass.) 566; Sillers v. Lester, 48 Miss. 513; Hoyle v. Plattsburgh &c. R. Co., 51 Barb. (N. Y.) 45; Seymour v. Canandaigua &c. R. Co., 25 Barb. (N. Y.) 284; Benjamin v. Elmira, Jeff. &c. R. Co., 49 Barb. (N. Y.) 441, 54 N. Y. 675; Coopers v. Wolf, 15 Ohio St. 523; Philadelphia, Wil. &c. R. Co. v. Woelpper, 64 Pa. St. 366, 3 Am. Rep. 596; Pierce v. Milwaukee &c. R. Co., 24 Wis. 551, 1 Am. Rep. 203. See also People's Trust Co. v. Schenck, 195 N. Y. 398, 88 N. E. 647, 133 Am. St. 807.

[37] Holroyd v. Marshall, 10 H. L. Cas. 191; overruling dictum of Baron Parke in Mogg v. Baker, 3 M. & W. 195. The latter case was followed by the Supreme Court of Massachusetts in Moody v. Wright, 13 Metc. (Mass.) 17, holding that property not in existence at the time of making the mortgage is incapable of being conveyed by it. In the District Court of Massachusetts the doctrine of the state courts was dissented from in Brett v. Car-

ter, 2 Lowell (U. S.) 458, where it was held that a mortgage of after-acquired chattels is valid against the assignee in bankruptcy of the mortgagor. See same case in 3 Cent. L. J. 286, and an article upon it in the same volume, p. 359. See also in same volume, p. 608, decision of Judge Clifford, in the case of Barnard v. Norwich &c. R. Co., before the Circuit Court of the United States, reported also in 14 N. Bank. R. 469.

See Jones on Chattel Mortgages, §§ 138-175, for a full discussion of the subject of mortgages of future personal property both at law and in equity.

[38] State v. Mexican &c. R. Co., 3 Rob. (La.) 231, 513; State v. New Orleans &c. R. Co., 4 Rob. (La.) 231.

[39] Mitchell v. Winslow, 2 Story (U. S.) 630, where the cases are reviewed; Rust v. Electric Lighting Co., 124 Ala. 202, 27 So. 263; Wood v. Holly Mfg. Co., 100 Ala. 326, 342, 13 So. 948; Christy v. Dana, 34 Cal. 548; Hubbard v. Mulligan, 13 Colo. App. 116, 57 Pac. 738; Moore v. Jaeger, 2 MacAr. (D. C.) 465; Amonett v. Amis, 16 La. Ann. 225; Emerson v. European &c. R. Co, 67 Maine 387, 24 Am. Rep. 39; Brady v. Johnson, 75 Md. 445, 26 Atl. 49, 20 L. R. A. 737.

In Georgia the Civ. Code, § 2723, limits the subject-matter upon which a mortgage can operate, to "property in possession or to which the mortgagor has a right of pos-

Courts of equity hold such conveyances operative as executory agreements binding on the property when acquired; the mortgagor holding the property and equity enforcing the trust, and in some of the decisions the adjudications rest upon the ground of equitable lien.[40] Equity considers as done that which the mortgagor has distinctly agreed to do, and is in consequence bound to do. Upon every acquisition of property within the description contained in the mortgage, a decree might be obtained that the mortgagor should execute a mortgage of such property; but instead of actually following out this troublesome process, equity treats the mortgage as already attaching to the newly acquired property as it comes into the mortgagor's possession, or, in other words, considers that, of every article of property as acquired, there was an actual mortgage then executed in fulfilment of the mortgagor's contract.[41]

A mortgage purporting to convey all after-acquired lands in a certain county, but covenanting for further conveyance and assurance of property afterward acquired for the business of the mortgagor, covers the latter only.[42] The chief question, therefore, is, whether the parties to the mortgage intended that the after-acquired property, which is in any case the subject of litigation, should be subject to the lien of the mortgage; and it will be noticed that in the recent cases the contention is generally upon this question.[43]

The mortgage lien upon after-acquired property only attaches from the time of the acquisition thereof by the mortgagor, and is subject to all pre-existing liens.[44] The mortgage only attaches to such interest as the mortgagor acquires.[45]

---

session at the time." Durant v. D'Auxy, 107 Ga. 456, 33 S. E. 478. See also Holt v. Henley, 193 Fed. 1020; In re Williamsburg Knitting Mill, 190 Fed. 871; People's Trust Co. v. Schenck, 195 N. Y. 398, 88 N. E. 647, 133 Am. St. 807; People's Trust Co. v. Schenck, 121 App. Div. 604, 106 N. Y. S. 782; Hickson Lumber Co. v. Gay Lumber Co., 150 N. Car. 281, 63 S. E. 1045; McClung v. Quincy Carriage &c. Co. (Tenn.), 196 S. W. 960.

[40] National Sav. &c. Bank v. Small, 7 Fed. 837; Griffith v. Douglass, 73 Maine 532, 40 Am. Rep. 395; Cayce v. Stovall, 50 Miss. 396; Sillers v. Lester, 48 Miss. 513; Keating v. Hannenkamp, 100 Mo. 161, 13 S. W. 89.

[41] Deshautel v. Parkins, 1 Mart. (N. S.) (La.) 547; Semple v. Scarborough, 44 La. Ann. 257, 10 So. 860; Stevens v. Watson, 45 How. Pr. (N. Y.) 104.

[42] Grape Creek Coal Co. v. Farmers' Loan &c. Co., 63 Fed. 891, 12 C. C. A. 350.

[43] Omaha &c. R. Co. v. Wabash, St. L. &c. R. Co., 108 Mo. 298, 18 S. W. 1101. See also Hickson Lumber Co. v. Gay Lumber Co., 150 N. Car. 281, 63 S. E. 1045.

[44] Brady v. Johnson, 75 Md. 445, 26 Atl. 49, 20 L. R. A. 737; Monmouth County Electric Co. v. McKenna, 68 N. J. Eq. 160, 60 Atl. 32.

[45] Williamson v. New Jersey &c. R. Co., 28 N. J. Eq. 277, 29 N. J. Eq. 311.

§ 154. Applied to railroad companies.—Unquestionably a railroad company having power to borrow money and secure it by mortgage on its property may, by express terms, mortgage property to be acquired subsequently.[46] This doctrine has been held to apply to a de facto corporation.[47]

A mortgage which by its terms covers property which a railroad company may afterward acquire, adapted to its use, though given before any part of the road is built, covers after-acquired property contemplated by the mortgage.[48] It attaches to the property as it comes into existence.[49] As against the railroad company and its privies, the after-acquired property feeds the estoppel created by the deed. Even against a contractor who has at his own expense finished a railroad under contract that he shall keep possession until he has been paid, a mortgage in such terms will pass the road afterward built and acquired.[50] A mortgage of its line of road, its tolls and revenues, covers

[46] Dunham v. Cincinnati &c. R. Co., 1 Wall. (U. S.) 254, 17 L. ed. 584; Parker v. New Orleans &c. R. Co., 33 Fed. 693; Kelly v. Alabama &c. R. Co., 58 Ala. 489; Buck v. Seymour, 46 Conn. 156; Bell v. Chicago &c. R. Co., 34 La. Ann. 785; Hamlin v. European &c. R. Co., 72 Maine 83; Omaha &c. R. Co. v. Wabash &c. R. Co., 108 Mo. 298, 18 S. W. 1101; Baker v. Guarantee &c. Co. (N. J. Eq.), 31 Atl. 174; Coopers v. Wolf, 15 Ohio St. 523; Ludlow v. Hurd, 1 Dis. (Ohio) 552; Philadelphia &c. R. Co. v. Woelpper, 64 Pa. St. 366, 3 Am. Rep. 596; Covey v. Pittsburg &c. R. Co., 3 Phila. (Pa.) 173; In re General South American Co., L. R. 2 Ch. Div. 337; In re Panama &c. Mail Co., L. R. 5 Ch. 318. See also Guaranty Trust Co. v. Atlantic Coast Electric R. Co., 138 Fed. 517, 71 C. C. A. 41; People's Trust Co. v. Schenck, 121 App. Div. 604, 106 N. Y. S. 782.

[47] McTighe v. Macon Const. Co., 94 Ga. 306, 21 S. E. 711, 32 L. R. A. 208, 47 Am. St. 153; Detroit &c. R. Co. v. Campbell, 140 Mich. 384, 103 N. W. 856.

[48] Galveston R. Co. v. Cowdrey, 11 Wall. (U. S.) 459, 20 L. ed. 199; Calhoun v. Memphis &c. R. Co., 2 Flip. (U. S.) 442; Parker v. New Orleans R. Co., 33 Fed. 693; California Title Ins. &c. Co. v. Pauly, 111 Cal. 122, 43 Pac. 586; Jones on Corporate Bonds and Mortgages, § 93; Hawkins v. Mercantile Trust &c. Co., 96 Ga. 580, 23 S. E. 408; Frost v. Galesburgh E. &c. R. Co., 167 Ill. 161, 47 N. E. 357; Bell v. Chicago &c. R. Co., 34 La. Ann. 785; Willink v. Morris Canal &c. Co., 4 N. J. Eq. 377, 402.

In Iowa the Code 1894, § 1931, provides that "where a deed purports to convey a greater interest than the grantor was at the time possessed of, any after-acquired interest of such grantor, to the extent of that which the deed purports to convey, inures to the benefit of the grantee." But under this provision a mortgage, which by mistake, includes land to which the mortgagor had no title at the time of its execution does not pass any title to such land when he subsequently acquires the title thereto, it appearing that he did not intend to mortgage any property which he did not own at the time he made the mortgage. Cook v. Prindle, 97 Iowa 464, 66 N. W. 781, 59 Am. St. 424.

In Louisiana a future property can never be the subject of conventional mortgage. Rev. Civ. Code, art. 3308; New Orleans &c. R. Co. v. Union Trust Co., 41 Fed. 717.

[49] Boston Safe Dep. &c. Co. v. Bankers' &c. Tel. Co., 36 Fed. 288.

[50] Dunham v. Cincinnati, Peru &c. R. Co., 1 Wall. (U. S.) 254, 17 L.

all the rolling stock and fixtures, whether movable or immovable, essential to the production of tolls and revenues.[51] A mortgage by a railroad company of "all the present and future to be acquired property of the company, including the right of way and land occupied, and all rails and other materials used therein or procured therefor," includes the rolling stock of the road.[52] A mortgage on a road with its engines, depots, and shops then owned by the company, or which it might thereafter acquire, "with the superstructure, rails, and other materials used thereon," is construed to embrace wood provided for the use of the road from time to time.[53]

The lien attaches to the property as soon as it is acquired;[54] and is superior to that of a subsequent mortgage or of a judgment.[55] But it generally attaches to the property in the condition in which it comes to the mortgagor and does not displace existing liens.[56]

§ 155. **After-acquired property passing as an incident to the franchise.**—After-acquired property may pass as an incident to the franchise, and as an accession to the subject of the mortgage.[57]

Where the franchise and property of the company are regarded as an indivisible entity the after-acquired property will pass by the mortgage even in the absence of express words of futurity.[58]

ed. 584; Bear Lake &c. R. Co. v. Garland, 164 U. S. 1, 41 L. ed. 327, 17 Sup. Ct. 7.
[51] State v. Northern Central R. Co., 18 Md. 193.
[52] Pullan v. Cincinnati &c. R. Co., 4 Biss. (U. S.) 35. See also Hoyle v. Plattsburg &c. R. Co., 51 Barb. (N. Y.) 45.
[53] Coe v. McBrown, 22 Ind. 252. See also Bath v. Miller, 53 Maine 308.
[54] Parker v. New Orleans &c. R. Co,. 33 Fed. 693; Frost v. Galesburg, 167 Ill. 161, 47 N. E. 357; Brady v. Johnson, 75 Md. 445, 26 Atl. 49, 20 L. R. A. 737; Seymour v. Canandaigua &c. R. Co., 25 Barb. (N. Y.) 284. But see New Orleans Pac. R. Co. v. Parker, 143 U. S. 42, 36 L. ed. 66, 12 Sup. Ct. 364.
[55] Bear Lake &c. Co. v. Garland, 164 U. S. 1, 15, 41 L. ed. 327, 17 Sup. Ct. 7; McGourkey v. Toledo &c. R. Co., 146 U. S. 536, 36 L. ed. 1079, 13 Sup. Ct. 170; Dunham v. Cincinnati &c. R. Co., 1 Wall. (U. S.) 254, 17 L. ed. 584; Pennock v. Coe, 23 How. (U. S.) 117, 16 L. ed.

436; Scott v. Clinton &c. R. Co., 6 Biss. (U. S.) 529; Nichols v. Mase, 94 N. Y. 160.
[56] Bear Lake &c. Co. v. Garland, 164 U. S. 1, 16, 41 L. ed. 327, 17 Sup. Ct. 7; Williamson v. New Jersey &c. R. Co., 28 N. J. Eq. 277, 29 N. J. Eq. 311. Compare Porter v. Pittsburg &c. Co., 122 U. S. 267, 30 L. ed. 1210, 7 Sup. Ct. 1206.
[57] Stevens v. Buffalo, Corning &c. R. Co., 45 How. Pr. (N. Y.) 104. The decision was not, however, based upon this proposition. See also Electric Lighting Co. v. Rust, 117 Ala. 680, 23 So. 751; Rowan v. Sharps' Rifle Mfg. Co., 29 Conn. 282; McClain's Iowa Code, §§ 1965, 1966; Beach v. Wakefield, 107 Iowa 567, 76 N. W. 688; Pierce v. Emery, 32 N. H. 484; Chew v. Barnet, 11 Serg. & R. Pa. 489.
[58] Parker v. New Orleans &c. R. Co., 33 Fed. 693; Willink v. Morris Canal &c. Co., 4 N. J. Eq. 377; Davidson v. Westchester Gaslight Co., 99 N. Y. 558, 2 N. E. 892; Shamokin &c. R. Co. v. Livermore, 47 Pa. St. 465, 85 Am. Dec. 552.

The suggestion that a mortgage by a railroad company made in pursuance of its charter, or of a law authorizing it, attaches to subsequently acquired property, for the reason that the franchise by virtue of which the property was acquired itself passed by the mortgage, was noticed by the Supreme Court of Wisconsin. The court, however, while questioning the reason so assigned, held that, when a mortgage by express terms covers lands that may be subsequently acquired for the uses of the company, the lien will attach to such lands the moment the company acquires an interest in them, although this interest be only a contract of purchase. The mortgagee may compel a conveyance under such a contract, and the company can not impair the lien by a sale without the mortgagee's consent.[59] But in a case before the Court of Appeals of Kentucky the power of a corporation to pass by its mortgage after-acquired property was placed altogether upon this ground, the court saying that the power to pledge the franchises and rights of the corporation implies, as incident thereto, the power to pledge everything that may be necessary to the enjoyment of the franchise, and upon which its real value depends. When a railroad mortgage is made which is to continue for many years, new cars and engines and materials of different kinds will become necessary from time to time, and the road would be of little value without them; therefore if included in a mortgage they are effectually covered by it.[60]

On the principle of accession it has been held that, without particular mention of the property afterward acquired, a mortgage by a railroad company of all its property and rights of property will pass property afterward acquired and essential to its use, even as against other creditors who claim by later mortgages. Such a mortgage is regarded as in substance a conveyance of the road and franchise as an entire thing, and the subsequently acquired property as becoming a part of it by accession, and as incident to the franchise; and therefore a cargo of railroad iron, after it is delivered to the railroad company, becomes subject to the lien of such a mortgage.[61]

This doctrine rests upon the authority of a few cases, and is not generally supported. Mortgages of after-acquired property, although made by corporations, are made to rest upon the broad equitable principles applicable to such mortgages in general. Ordinarily such prop-

---

[59] Farmers' Loan &c. Co. v. Fisher, 17 Wis. 114; Hill v. La Crosse &c. R. Co., 11 Wis. 214; Farmers' Loan &c. Co. v. Commercial Bank of Racine, 11 Wis. 207, 15 Wis. 424, 82 Am. Dec. 689.

[60] Phillips v. Winslow, 18 B. Mon. (Ky.) 431, 68 Am. Dec. 729.

[61] Pierce v. Emery, 32 N. H. 484.

erty is not covered unless apt words are used to confer the right, or unless the instrument shows that the parties clearly intended that it should pass.[62]

§ 156. **What property included by implication in a railroad mortgage.**—A mortgage of all the property of a railroad company, including its franchises, etc., contemplates property owned both at the time of the mortgage and that to be subsequently acquired.[63] But a mortgage by a railroad company does not by implication cover property not essential to its business, unless it is specifically described by the terms of the mortgage. Thus a mortgage by a railroad company of its real estate, road, bridges, ferries, locomotives, engines, cars, and all other personal property belonging to it, does not include canal boats run in connection with the road beyond its terminus.[64] And a mortgage on property "thereafter acquired for railroad purposes" was held not to cover an undivided interest in land subsequently acquired, since there was no purpose to which the railroad could put such undivided interest.[65]

Town lots, held by a railroad company, do not pass by a sheriff's sale, under a mortgage of the road, "with its corporate privileges and appurtenances," when they are not directly appurtenant to the railroad and indispensably necessary to the enjoyment of its franchises.[66] Thus, it has been held not to extend to property adjacent to a depot which the company leases for a store and other purposes foreign to the operation of the road.[67]

But a mortgage of an entire road, "as said railroad now is or may be hereafter constructed, maintained, operated or acquired, together with all the privileges, rights, franchises, real estate, right of way, depots, depot grounds, side tracks, water tanks, engines, cars, and other appurtenances thereto belonging," has been held to include real

[62] Thompson v. White &c. R. Co., 132 U. S. 68, 33 L. ed. 256, 10 Sup. Ct. 29; Maxwell v. Wilmington Dental Mfg. Co., 77 Fed. 938.

[63] Pennock v. Coe, 64 U. S. 23, 16 L. ed. 436; Quincy v. Chicago, B. &c. R. Co., 94 Ill. 537; Coe v. McBrown, 22 Ind. 252; Howe v. Freeman, 14 Gray (Mass.) 566; Pierce v. Emery, 32 N. H. 484. See also Pere Marquette R. Co. v. Graham, 136 Mich. 444, 99 N. W. 408.

[64] Parish v. Wheeler, 22 N. Y. 494.

[65] Chicago &c. R. Co. v. Tice, 232 Ill. 232, 83 N. E. 818.

[66] Shamokin Val. R. Co. v. Livermore, 47 Pa. St. 465, 86 Am. Dec. 552. See also Calhoun v. Memphis &c. R. Co., 2 Flip. (U. S.) 442; Morgan v. Donovan, 58 Ala. 241; Mississippi Val. Co. v. Chicago &c. R. Co., 58 Miss. 896, 38 Am. Rep. 348; Millard v. Burley, 13 Nebr. 259, 13 N. W. 278; Seymour v. Canandaigua &c. R. Co., 25 Barb. (N. Y.) 284; Walsh v. Barton, 24 Ohio St. 28; Brainard v. Peck, 34 Vt. 496; Farmers' Loan &c. Co. v. Commercial Bank, 11 Wis. 207.

[67] Chicago &c. R. Co. v. McGuire, 31 Ind. App. 110, 65 N. E. 932, 99 Am. St. 249.

estate separated from the right of way by a street, but of easy access to the station and side tracks, which real estate had been subsequently purchased by the company and upon which it had built a restaurant for the accommodation of its employes and passengers.[68]

A mortgage by a railroad company of its road and real estate then owned by it, or which it might afterward acquire, is considered an equitable mortgage as to the property subsequently acquired for the purposes of its road, and is a valid lien upon after-acquired land so taken and used.[69] A mortgage of the stock, materials, and every other kind of personal property which shall be used for operating a railroad, does not profess to cover railroad chairs afterward bought by the company, but which were never used by it.[70] A mortgage which does not purport to cover materials subsequently acquired is not made valid as to such materials from any consideration of the nature and object of the mortgage, as, for instance, that it was made for the purpose of raising money to complete the road.[71] A mechanic's lien upon such property is subsequent to the lien of such mortgage; if this was recorded before the materials and labor were furnished.[72] Any property connected with the use of its franchise, whether real or personal, either already or subsequently acquired, may be effectually mortgaged.[73] Upon foreclosure of such a mortgage, the property and rights of the corporation as they exist at the time of the foreclosure pass to the mortgagees or to the purchasers.[74]

§ 157. **Rule as to after-acquired land.**—While at law nothing can be mortgaged not in existence and not owned by the mortgagor at the time the mortgage is executed, yet equity will give effect to a mortgage embracing land to be afterward acquired.[75]

---

[68] See Central Trust Co. v. Kneeland, 138 U. S. 414, 34 L. ed. 1014, 11 Sup. Ct. 357; Omaha &c. R. Co. v. Wabash &c. R. Co., 108 Mo. 298, 18 S. W. 1101.

[69] Benjamin v. Elmira, Jefferson &c. R. Co., 49 Barb. (N. Y.) 441, 54 N. Y. 675; Seymour v. Canadaigua &c. R. Co., 25 Barb. (N. Y.) 284.

[70] Farmers' Loan &c. Co. v. Commercial Bank, 11 Wis. 207.

[71] Farmers' Loan &c. Co. v. Commercial Bank, 15 Wis. 424, 82 Am. Dec. 689.

[72] Reed v. Ginsburg, 64 Ohio St. 11, 59 N. E. 738.

[73] Raymond v. Clark, 46 Conn. 129; Coe v. Peacock, 14 Ohio St. 187.

[74] Miller v. Rutland &c. R. Co., 36 Vt. 452.

[75] Bear Lake &c. Waterworks &c. Co. v. Garland, 164 U. S. 15, 41 L. ed. 333, 17 Sup. Ct. 7; National Waterworks Co. v. Kansas City, 78 Fed. 428; New England Waterworks Co. v. Farmers' Loan &c. Co., 136 Fed. 521, 69 C. C. A. 297; Washington Trust Co. v. Morse Iron Works &c. Co., 106 App. Div. 195, 94 N. Y. S. 495; Hickson Lumber Co. v. Gay Lumber Co., 150 N. Car. 281, 63 S. E. 1045; Cummings v. Consolidated Mineral Water Co., 27 R. I. 195, 61 Atl. 353; Frank v. Hicks, 4 Wyo. 502, 35 Pac. 495, 1025.

After-acquired land not within the terms of the mortgage is not covered by it. Thus a mortgage of a one-fourth interest in certain land which the mortgagor had inherited, does not embrace additional interests in the same land which the mortgagor subsequently purchased at an administrator's sale.[76] A mortgage by a railroad company of its road and appurtenances, and of lands after acquired for stations, shops, and the like uses, does not create any lien upon a tract of woodland afterward acquired, situate seven miles from its road, although purchased and used by the company for the purpose of supplying the road with timber and wood; for such a mortgage contains no apt words to embrace land remote from the road, and which can not be used for any of the specific purposes mentioned.[77]

The lien will not extend to lands situated outside of the "layout" of the road, even though such lands were taken over by the company in securing their right of way, but will be confined to such lands as are actually necessary and convenient for the construction and operation of the road, including the right of way, lands for shops, depots, stations, turnouts for fuel or water, or for other legitimate purposes.[78]

The authority of a company to bind its future acquisitions by mortgage is limited to such property as it has the power by law to acquire; and therefore it has been held that a railroad company having at the time of making a mortgage no power by its charter or by general law to accept a land grant from the United States, its mortgage, though broad enough in terms to cover such a grant, would not embrace a land grant subsequently made, and which the company was by special act afterward empowered to accept.[79] But a railroad company having the authority to accept a land grant may undoubtedly mortgage it before it has fulfilled the conditions upon which the grant is to be

[76] Wheeler v. Aycock, 109 Ala. 146, 19 So. 497.

[77] Dinsmore v. Racine &c. R. Co., 12 Wis. 649. See also Pardee v. Aldridge, 189 U. S. 429, 47 L. ed. 883, 23 Sup. Ct. 514; Boston &c. R. Co. v. Coffin, 50 Conn. 150; Walsh v. Barton, 24 Ohio St. 28; Shirley v. Waco Tap. R. Co., 78 Tex. 131, 10 S. W. 543; Aldridge v. Pardee, 24 Tex. Civ. App. 254, 60 S. W. 789.

[78] See New Orleans Pac. R. Co. v. Parker, 143 U. S. 42, 36 L. ed. 66, 12 Sup. Ct. 364; Humphreys v. McKissock, 140 U. S. 307, 35 L. ed. 595, 11 Sup. Ct. 1022; Boston &c. R. Co.

v. Coffin, 50 Conn. 150; Chicago, I. &c. R. Co. v. McGuire, 31 Ind. App. 110, 65 N. E. 932, 99 Am. St. 249; Mississippi Val. R. Co. v. Chicago, St. L. &c. R. Co., 58 Miss. 896, 38 Am. Rep. 348; Seymour v. Canandaigna &c. R. Co., 25 Barb. (N. Y.) 284; People's Trust Co. v. Schenck, 121 App. Div. 604, 106 N. Y. S. 782; Shirley v. Waco Tap. R. Co., 78 Tex. 131, 10 S. W. 543; Eldridge v. Smith, 34 Vt. 484; Farmers' Loan &c. Co. v. Commercial Bank, 11 Wis. 207.

[79] Meyer v. Johnston, 53 Ala. 237, 331.

made.[80] A mortgage by a railroad company in its terms embracing all property which it may subsequently acquire includes a lease it afterward takes of another railroad.[81]

§ 158. Prior liens on after-acquired property.—The mortgage is subject to any liens there may be upon the property when acquired. The mortgage attaches to the property in the condition in which it comes into the mortgagor's hands. If it be at that time already subject to mortgages or other liens, the general mortgage does not displace them, though they may be junior to it in point of time.[82] It is subject to a vendor's lien for unpaid purchase-money on realty, the mortgagee not being considered a purchaser for value.[83]

"It only attaches to such interest as the mortgagor acquires; and if he purchase property and give a mortgage for the purchase-money, the deed which he receives, and the mortgage which he gives, are regarded as one transaction, and no general lien impending over him, whether in the shape of a general mortgage or judgment or recognizance, can displace such mortgage for purchase-money. And in such cases a failure to register the mortgage for purchase-money makes no difference. It does not come within the reason of the registry laws. These laws are intended for the protection of subsequent, not prior, purchasers and creditors."[84] The fact that the mortgage was given to secure purchase-money may be shown by parol evidence.[85] Thus a

[80] See Campbell v. Texas &c. R. Co., 2 Woods (U. S.) 263.

[81] Barnard v. Norwich &c. R. Co., 2 Lowell (U. S.) 608, 14 N. Bank. 469, 3 Cent. L. J. 608. See also Columbia Finance &c. Co. v. Kentucky &c. R. Co., 60 Fed. 794; Buck v. Seymour, 46 Conn. 156; Hamlin v. European &c. R. Co., 72 Maine 83.

[82] Bear Lake &c. Irr. Co. v. Garland, 164 U. S. 1, 41 L. ed. 327, 17 Sup. Ct. 1; Fosdick .v. Schall, 99 U. S. 235, 25 L. ed. 339; General Elec. Co. v. Transit. Equip. Co., 57 N. J. Eq. 460, 42 Atl. 101. See also Myer v. Car Co., 102 U. S. 1, 26 L. ed. 59; Branch v. Jesup, 106 U. S. 468, 27 L. ed. 279, 1 Sup. Ct. 495; Dunham v. Cincinnati &c. R. Co., 1 Wall. (U. S.) 254, 17 L. ed. 584; Galveston R. Co. v. Cowdry, 11 Wall. (U. S.) 459, 20 L. ed. 199; United States v. N. O. R., 12 Wall. (U. S.) 362, 20 L. ed. 434; Branch v. Atlantic &c. R. Co., 3 Woods (U. S.) 481; Western Union Tel. Co. v. Burlington &c. R. Co., 3 McCrary (U. S.) 130; Boston Safe Deposit &c. Co. v. Bankers' &c. Co., 36 Fed. 288; Lake Erie &c. R. Co. v. Priest, 131 Ind. 413, 31 N. E. 77; Haven v. Emery, 33 N. H. 66; Williamson v. New Jersey Southern R. Co., 28 N. J. Eq. 277, 29 N. J. Eq. 311.

[83] Loomis v. Davenport &c. R. Co,. 17 Fed. 301; Pierce v. Milwaukee &c. R. Co., 24 Wis. 551, 1 Am. Rep. 203.

[84] United States v. New Orleans Railroad, 12 Wall. (U. S.) 362–365, 20 L. ed. 434, per Bradley, J.; Wood v. Holly Mfg. Co., 100 Ala. 326, 13 So. 948; Continental Ins. &c. Soc. v. Wood, 168 Ill. 421, 48 N. E. 221; Willink v. Morris Canal &c. Co., 4 N. J. Eq. 377; Daly v. New York, G. &c. R. Co., 55 N. J. Eq. 595, 38 Atl. 202.

[85] Bisbee v. Carey, 17 Wash. 224, 49 Pac. 220.

mechanic's lien for work done and materials furnished on such after-acquired property takes precedence of the mortgage.[86]   Property acquired under a conditional sale comes under the mortgage subject to the terms of such sale.[87]   Property afterward acquired through fraud is not affected by an existing mortgage.[88]

In Massachusetts it is held that a mortgage of after-acquired property is not effectual as against the attacking creditors or assignees in insolvency of the mortgagor, unless the mortgagee takes possession of the property.[89]

§ 159. **Mortgage of choses in action.**—It would seem that corporations usually possess power to mortgage their choses in action; and a federal court, deeming a contract to pay money for stock to be a chose in action, has held that it is negotiable by delivery and passes by voluntary assignment.[90]   But choses in action will not pass by sale under a mortgage unless there is a specific description and a certain designation so that bidders may know what they are about to purchase;[91] in other words, they must be described with such particularity that they can be identified.[92]

It seems clear that a general futurity clause will not include calls for unpaid subscriptions to the capital stock.[93]   Thus, a railroad mortgage on its property, present and prospective, was held to give no right to purchasers under foreclosure sale to county bonds issued in payment of a subscription.[94]

§ 160. **Mortgage of future net earnings of railroad company.**—A mortgage may be made of the future net earnings of a railroad company to secure the payment of interest upon its construction bonds.[95]

---

[86] Jarvis v. State Bank, 22 Colo. 309, 45 Pac. 505; Williamson v. New Jersey Southern R. Co., 28 N. J. Eq. 277, 29 N. J. Eq. 311.

[87] Haven v. Emery, 33 N. H. 66; Taylor v. Burlington, Cedar Rapids &c. R. Co., 11 West. Jur. 337.

[88] Williamson v. N. J. Southern R. Co., 28 N. J. Eq. 277, 298.   See also Frazier v. Frederick, 24 N. J. L. 162; Field v. Post, 38 N. J. L. 346.

[89] Harriman v. Woburn Elec. Light Co., 163 Mass. 85, 39 N. E. 1004.

[90] Coler v. Grainger Co., 74 Fed. 16, 20 C. C. A. 267.

[91] Milwaukee &c. R. Co. v. Milwaukee &c. R. Co., 20 Wis. 174, 88 Am.

Dec. 740.   See also Merchants' Bank v. Petersburg R. Co., 12 Phila. (Pa.) 482; Bennett v. Keehn, 57 Wis. 582, 15 N. W. 776.

[92] General Elec. Co. v. Wightman, 3 App. Div. 118, 39 N. Y. S. 420.

[93] Dean v. Biggs, 25 Hun (N. Y.) 122; Gardner v. London &c. R. Co., L. R. 2 Ch. 201; King v. Marshall, 33 Beav. 565; Moor v. Anglo-Italian Bank, 10 Ch. D. 681.

[94] Morgan Co. v. Allen, 103 U. S. 498, 26 L. ed. 498; Smith v. McCullough, 104 U. S. 25, 26 L. ed. 637; Morgan Co. v. Thomas, 76 Ill. 120.

[95] See Jones on Corporate Bonds and Mortgages, § 87; Jessup v. Bridge, 11 Iowa 572, 79 Am. Dec.

A mortgage by a railroad company of "after-acquired" property has been held to include future net earnings of the road.[96]

Even a mortgage of a railroad and its present and subsequently acquired property is a prior lien upon the net earnings of the road while the mortgagor retains possession.[97] A mortgage of tolls and revenues covers only the net income after the payment of all expenses.[98] But until the mortgagee takes possession, the earnings belong wholly to the railroad company, and are subject to its control.[99] Even after the road has passed into the possession of a receiver appointed by the court in the interest of the bondholders, the net earnings may be applied by the receiver to the payment of claims having equities superior to those of the bondholders.[1] The net earnings may be mortgaged, but so long as they are retained by the mortgagor they are subject to trustee process in favor of the general creditors of the railroad company.[2]

In a comparatively recent case, a railroad company had leased its unfinished road to a company operating a connecting line and mortgaged its property, rights and franchises to secure certain bonds which were to be disposed of by the lessee, and the latter, in order to insure the prompt payment of interest and a ready sale of the bonds, being advised that it had no power to guarantee them, mortgaged to the lessor for that purpose all the net earnings of its own line which might accrue to it "by reason of business coming to it from or over" the lines of the lessor. It was held that this included not only the profits of the business which came literally from off the lessor's road into the lessee's road, but, also, the net earnings or business which came to the latter from both directions by reason of the fact that the leased road was an important feeder and brought new business to the lessee's road by opening up new markets and giving increased facilities. The court also held that, as there was nothing in the mortgage prescribing the

513; Dunham v. Isett, 15 Iowa 284; Farmers' Loan &c. Co. v. Cary, 13 Wis. 110.

[96] Tompkins v. Little Rock &c. R. Co., 15 Fed. 6; Addison v. Lewis, 75 Va. 701. Contra, Emerson v. European &c. R. Co., 67 Maine 387, 24 Am. Rep. 39; DeGraff v. Thompson, 24 Minn. 452.

[97] Hale v. Frost, 99 U. S. 389, 25 L. ed. 419.

[98] Jones on Corporate Bonds and Mortgages, §§ 80–90; Parkhurst v. Northern Cent. R. Co., 19 Md. 472, 81 Am. Dec. 648.

[99] Fosdick v. Schall, 99 U. S. 235, 25 L. ed. 339.

[1] Hale v. Frost, 99 U. S. 389, 25 L. ed. 419.

[2] Gilman v. Illinois &c. R. Co., 91 U. S. 603, 23 L. ed. 405; Galveston R. Co. v. Cowdery, 11 Wall. (U. S.) 459, 20 L. ed. 199; Mississippi &c. R. v. United States Exp. Co., 81 Ill. 534; Galena &c. R. Co. v. Menzies, 26 Ill. 121; Dunham v. Isett, 15 Iowa 284; Emerson v. European &c. R. Co., 67 Maine 387, 24 Am. Rep. 39; Noyes v. Rich, 52 Maine 115; Bath v. Miller, 51 Maine 341; Smith v. Eastern R. Co., 124 Mass. 154; Ellis v. Boston &c. R. Co,. 107 Mass. 1; Clay v. East Tenn. &c. R. Co., 6 Heisk. (Tenn.) 421.

method of ascertaining the net earnings, they must be determined in the usual way, that is, from the gross receipts must be deducted the cost of producing them, and that it knew of "no way to arrive at all this, save, approximately, by a proportion distributing the total operating expense over the whole business," thus treating the business of the entire system as a unit.[3]

§ 161. Whether mortgage conveys primary corporate franchise.— A mortgage by a railroad company of its road and franchise, as security for debt, is held not to convey its corporate existence, or its general corporate powers, but only the franchise necessary to make the conveyance beneficial to the grantees, and to enable them to maintain and manage the road, and receive the profits to their own use.[4]

A mortgage of corporate property therefore does not cover the franchise to be a corporation—that is, the primary franchise—unless the power to incumber is clearly conferred.[5] It is another statement of the principle to say that a mortgage conveying the corporate property and appurtenances and also its corporate franchises, incumbers only the franchise necessary to make the conveyance productive and beneficial to the grantees,—namely the franchise to maintain, manage and operate the corporation and receive the income and profits thereof for its own benefit, and not the franchise to be a corporation or the general corporate powers.[6] It follows that the purchaser of the property and franchises of a corporation at a foreclosure sale,[7] or a sale by an assignee in bankruptcy,[8] will not acquire thereby any corporate ca-

[3] Schmidt v. Louisville &c. R. Co., 95 Ky. 289, 25 S. W. 494, 26 S. W. 547, 61 Am. & Eng. R. Cas. 680. See also United States v. Kansas Pac. R. Co,. 99 U. S. 455, 25 L. ed. 289; St. John v. Erie R. Co., 22 Wall. (U. S.) 136, 22 L. ed. 743; Pullan v. Railroad Co., 5 Biss. (U. S.) 237.

[4] Meyer v. Johnston, 53 Ala. 237, 325; Eldridge v. Smith, 34 Vt. 484; Miller v. Rutland &c. R. Co., 36 Vt. 452, 498. See article 19, American Law Rev. 440. See also Wilmington R. Co. v. Reid, 13 Wall. (U. S.) 264, 20 L. ed. 568; Pullan v. Cincinnati &c. R. Co., 4 Biss. (U. S.) 35; Bradstown &c. R. Co. v. Metcalfe, 61 Ky. 199, 81 Am. Dec. 541; McAllister v. Plant, 54 Miss. 106.

[5] Willamette &c. Mfg. Co. v. Bank, 119 U. S. 191, 30 L. ed. 384; New Orleans &c. R. Co. v. Delamore, 114 U. S. 501, 29 L. ed. 244, 5 Sup. Ct.

1009; Memphis &c. R. Co. v. Railroad Comrs., 112 U. S. 609, 28 L. ed. 837, 5 Sup. Ct. 299; City Water Co. v. State, 88 Tex. 600, 32 S. W. 1033.

[6] Branch v. Atlantic &c. R. Co., 3 Woods (U. S.) 481; Pullan v. Cincinnati &c. R. Co., 4 Biss. (U. S.) 35; Meyer v. Johnston, 53 Ala. 237; New Orleans &c. R. Co. v. Delamore, 34 La. Ann. 1225; Joy v. Jackson &c. Plank Rd. Co., 11 Mich. 155; Beebe v. Richmond &c. Power Co., 13 Misc. 737, 35 N. Y. S. 1; City Water Co. v. State, 88 Tex. 600, 32 S. W. 1033; Eldridge v. Smith, 34 Vt. 484.

[7] Atkinson v. Marietta &c. R. Co., 15 Ohio St. 21.

[8] Metz v. Buffalo &c. R. Co., 58 N. Y. 61, 17 Am. Rep. 201; Commonwealth v. Central Pass. R. Co., 52 Pa. St. 506.

pacity whatever. It has been pointed out that "If it were held that all the corporate franchises, including the power of corporate existence, were conveyed by the mortgage, the conclusion would seem to be logical, that, on breach and foreclosure, the mortgagees would step into the shoes of the company and merely succeed to their rights in the property, and also to their corporate liabilities—a result by no means favorable to their interest."[9] So authority to mortgage "the entire road, fixtures ,and equipments, with all the appurtenances, income and resources thereof," does not include the right to mortgage the franchise to be a corporation, but does include the right to mortgage the franchise to maintain a railroad and take compensation as a carrier.[10] But the fact that the mortgage does profess to include the primary franchise will not for that reason render the instrument entirely void. A rule in other cases of contracts is applicable here, and the instrument will be valid to convey the secondary franchises subject to alienation, and will be void only so far as it undertakes to convey the primary franchise.[11]

§ 161a. Mortgage of primary franchise under legislative authority.

—The franchise to be a corporation may be incumbered by the corporation when authorized by the legislature to do so. The legislature having the power to create the corporation may, without doubt, unless prevented by the constitution, clothe the corporation with the power to transfer its primary franchise. But even these cases require positive provisions in the statutes as to the methods of making the transfer.[12]

---

[9] Eldridge v. Smith, 34 Vt. 484.
[10] Coe v. Columbus &c. R. Co., 10 Ohio St. 372, 75 Am. Dec. 518.
[11] Fietsam v. Hay, 122 Ill. 293, 13 N. E. 501, 3 Am. St. 492; Butler v. Rahm, 46 Md. 541.
[12] Mahaska Co. R. Co. v. Des Moines &c. R. Co., 28 Iowa 437; Daniels v. Hart, 118 Mass. 543; Richardson v. Sibley, 11 Allen (Mass.) 65, 87 Am. Dec. 700; East Boston &c. R. Co. v. Eastern R. Co., 13 Allen (Mass.) 422; Hendee v. Pinkerton, 14 Allen (Mass.) 381; St. Paul &c. R. Co. v. Parcher, 14 Minn. 297; McAllister v. Plant, 54 Miss. 106; Stewart v. Jones, 40 Mo. 140; Pierce v. Emery, 32 N. H. 484; Black v. Delaware &c. Canal Co., 22 N. J. Eq. 130; Carpenter v. Black Hawk &c. Min. Co., 65 N. Y. 43; Troy &c. R. Co. v. Kerr, 17 Barb. (N. Y.) 581; Woodruff v. Erie R. Co., 25 Hun (N. Y.) 246; State v. Richmond &c. R. Co., 72 N. Car. 634; State v. Sherman, 22 Ohio St. 411; Coe v. Columbus &c. R. Co., 10 Ohio St. 372, 75 Am. Dec. 518; Steiner's Appeal, 27 Pa. St. 313; Lauman v. Lebanon Val. R. Co., 30 Pa. St. 42. See also Vicksburg v. Vicksburg Waterworks Co,. 202 U. S. 453, 50 L. ed. 1102, 26 Sup. Ct. 660; Memphis &c. R. Co. v. Railroad Comrs., 112 U. S. 609, 28 L. ed. 837, 5 Sup. Ct. 299; Branch v. Jesup, 106 U. S. 468, 24 L. ed. 279, 1 Sup. Ct. 495; Pullan v. Cincinnati &c. R. Co., 4 Biss. (U. S.) 35; Frazier v. East Tennessee &c. R. Co., 88 Tenn. 138, 12 S. W. 537; Threadgill v. Pumphrey, 87 Tex. 573, 30 S. W. 356; Pierce v. Milwaukee &c. R. Co., 24 Wis. 551, 1 Am. Rep. 203.

The power to sell or mortgage the primary franchise will not be implied from authority in a statute to sell or mortgage "the property and franchises of a corporation";[13] nor from authority to mortgage its "road, income, and other property."[14]

[13] Cook v. Detroit &c. R. Co., 43 Mich. 349, 5 N. W. 390; Pierce v. Emery, 32 N. H. 484; Coe v. Columbus &c. R. Co., 10 Ohio St. 372, 75 Am. Dec. 518; Eldridge v. Smith, 34 Vt. 484.

[14] Pullan v. Cincinnati &c. R. Co., 4 Biss. (U. S.) 35.

CHAPTER V

EQUITABLE MORTGAGES

I. *By Agreements and Informal Mortgages*, §§ 162–171
II. *By Assignments of Contracts of Purchase*, §§ 172–178
III. *By Deposit of Title Deeds*, §§ 179–188

I. *By Agreements and Informal Mortgages*

§ 162. Introductory.—It has been noticed that a conveyance, accompanied by a condition contained either in the deed itself or in a separate instrument executed at the same time, constitutes a legal mortgage, or a mortgage at common law. In addition to these formal instruments which are properly entitled to the designation of mortgages, deeds and contracts which are wanting in one or both of these characteristics of a common-law mortgage are often used by parties for the purpose of pledging real property, or some interest in it, as security for a debt or obligation, and with the intention that they shall have effect as mortgages. Equity comes to the aid of the parties in such cases, and gives effect to their intentions. Mortgages of this kind are therefore called equitable mortgages.[1]

---

[1] Quoted with approval by Harlan, J., in Ketchum v. St. Louis, 101 U. S. 306, 25 L. ed. 999; Alexander v. Mortgage Co., 47 Fed. 135 (quoting text); Hall v. Mobile &c. R. Co., 58 Ala. 10; Gesner v. Palmateer, 89 Cal. 89, 24 Pac. 6C8, 26 Pac. 789, 13 L. R. A. 187. See also Brown v. Brown, 103 Ind. 23, 2 N. E. 233; Cummings v. Jackson, 55 N. J. Eq. 805, 38 Atl. 763; New Vienna Bank v. Johnson, 47 Ohio St. 306, 24 N. E. 503 (quoting text); Wayt v. Carwithen, 21 W. Va. 516; Hoile v. Bailey, 58 Wis. 434, 17 N. W. 322.

An equitable mortgage may be broadly defined as a transaction which has the intent, but not the form, of a mortgage, and which a court of equity will enforce to the same extent as a mortgage.[2] There are many kinds of equitable mortgages—as many as there are varieties of ways in which parties may contract for security by pledging some interest in lands.[3] "An agreement in writing to give a mortgage, or a mortgage defectively executed, or an imperfect attempt to create a mortgage or to appropriate specific property to the discharge of a particular debt, will create an equitable mortgage, or a specific lien on the property intended to be mortgaged."[4] So, an equitable mortgage will result from different forms of transactions, in which there is present an intent of the parties to make a mortgage, to which intent, for some reason, legal expression is not given in the form of an effective mortgage; but in all such cases the intent to create a mortgage is the essential feature of the transaction.[5]

Whatever the form of the contract may be, if it is intended thereby to create a security, it is an equitable mortgage.[6] The intent to create an equitable mortgage, or security for the payment of a debt must be manifest, as distinguished from an intent to apply to the payment of the debt the proceeds from the sale of the property.[7] It

[2] Davidson v. Fox, 65 App. Div. 262, 73 N. Y. S. 533.

[3] Donald v. Hewitt, 33 Ala. 534, 73 Am. Dec. 431; Newlin v. McAfee, 64 Ala. 357; Clarke v. Sibley, 13 Metc. (Mass.) 210; Payne v. Wilson, 74 N. Y. 348.

[4] Baltimore &c. R. Co. v. Berkeley Springs &c. R. Co., 168 Fed. 770; Higgins v. Manson, 126 Cal. 467, 77 Am. St. 192; Racouillat v. Sansevain, 32 Cal. 376; Daggett v. Rankin, 31 Cal. 231; Martin v. Nixon, 92 Mo. 26; McQuie v. Peay, 58 Mo. 56, 1 Am. Lead. Eq. Cas. 510.

[5] Western Nat. Bank v. National Union Bank, 91 Md. 613, 46 Atl. 960.

[6] Flagg v. Mann, 2 Sumn. (U. S.) 486, Fed. Cas. No. 4847; Gest v. Packwood, 39 Fed. 525; quoted with approval in Edwards v. Scruggs, 155 Ala. 568, 46 So. 850; Woodruff v. Adair, 131 Ala. 530, 32 So. 515 (quoting text); Ross v. Perry, 105 Ala. 533, 16 So. 915; Wood v. Holly M. Co., 100 Ala. 326, 13 So. 948; Newlin v. McAfee, 64 Ala. 364; Hall v. Mobile &c. R. Co., 58 Ala. 10; Higgins v. Manson, 126 Cal. 467, 77 Am.

St. 192; Reitze v. Humphreys, 53 Colo. 177, 125 Pac. 518; Fort v. Colby (Iowa), 144 N. W. 393; Charpie v. Stout, 88 Kans. 318, 128 Pac. 396; Reed v. Lansdale, Hard. (Ky.) 6; Carter v. Holman, 60 Mo. 498; Arnold v. Fraser, 43 Mont. 540, 117 Pac. 1064; Archer v. Archer, 147 App. Div. 44, 131 N. Y. S. 601; New Vienna Bank v. Johnson, 47 Ohio St. 306, 24 N. E. 503 (quoting text); Barber v. Toomey (Ore.), 136 Pac. 343; Marquam v. Ross, 47 Ore. 374, 83 Pac. 852; Armstrong v. Burkitt (Tex. Civ. App.), 34 S. W. 759; Wayt v. Carwithen, 21 W. Va. 516; Hoile v. Bailey, 58 Wis. 434; Harrigan v. Gilchrist, 121 Wis. 127, 99 N. W. 909, 981, citing numerous cases, and Jones on Corporate Bonds and Mortgages, §§ 33-38, also Jones on Mortgages, §§ 163-168. This principle is chiefly illustrated in the case of absolute deeds intended merely as security. This subject is fully treated in chaps. VII and VIII, § 241 et seq.

[7] Smith v. Rainey, 9 Ariz. 362, 83 Pac. 463.

is not necessary that the contract should be in express terms a security,[8] for equity will often imply this from the nature of the transactions between the parties. For instance, a contract for security is, in England and in some states of America, implied from a deposit of title deeds.

As in case of a legal mortgage there must be some debt, liability or obligation secured.[9] But the debt secured by an equitable mortgage need not be evidenced by notes, bonds, or other written obligation.[10]

The statutes of a state relating to the execution and recording of mortgages are limited in their application to these particulars. They do not go beyond what they require as to the signing, acknowledgment, and recording of the instrument. "They prescribe no requisites as to the contents of the instrument, as to how lands shall be charged as a security, or the intent manifested. The character of the instrument in this regard, and its effect, are left to be determined by the application of the general principles of law and equity on the subject. So that any instrument that would, by the application of these principles, be regarded as constituting a lien on land as against third persons with notice, will have the same effect, under our recording statutes, where it has been duly executed and recorded."[11]

A bona fide purchaser for value of property subject to an equitable mortgage, without notice of such mortgage, takes the property free of the equitable mortgage.[12] But if part of the purchase-money remains unpaid at the time when the purchaser receives notice of the equitable mortgage, the lien of the equitable mortgage holds to the extent of the purchase-money so remaining unpaid.[13] It has been noticed in the preceding chapter that rights and interests in realty which are only equitable are often the subject of mortgage; that in equity formal mortgages are often made to embrace property which at common law would not be covered at all; as, for instance, property acquired after the execution of the mortgage. But the term "equitable mortgage" is used more properly with reference solely to the kind of instrument or contract by which equity establishes a lien.

[8] Bradley v. Merrill, 88 Maine 319, 34 Atl. 160.

[9] McLaren v. Clark, 80 Ga. 423, 7 S. E. 230; Mix v. White, 36 Ill. 484.

[10] Bradley v. Merrill, 88 Maine 319, 34 Atl. 160.

[11] New Vienna Bank v. Johnson, 47 Ohio St. 306, 24 N. E. 503, per Minshall, C. J., citing Strang v. Beach, 11 Ohio St. 283; Hurd v. Robinson, 11 Ohio St. 232; Dodd v. Bartholomew, 44 Ohio St. 171, 5 N. E. 866.

[12] Watkins v. Reynolds, 123 N. Y. 211, 25 N. E. 322; Watkins v. Vrooman, 51 Hun 175, 5 N. Y. S. 172.

[13] Watkins v. Vrooman, 51 Hun 175, 5 N. Y. S. 172.

It is the equitable form of the transaction, rather than the equitable nature of the property, to which this chapter has reference. There are some kinds of equitable mortgages so common and so important that they will be treated of at length farther on; as, for instance, absolute conveyances without any defeasance except by parol, and liens of vendors under written contracts or reservations. In this chapter, therefore, the less important transactions which in equity are recognized as creating securities will be considered.

§ 163. **Agreement to mortgage.**—An agreement to give a mortgage or security on certain property, not objectionable for want of consideration, is treated in equity as a mortgage, upon the principle that equity will treat that as done which by agreement is to be done. This doctrine has been asserted frequently, both in this country and in England.[14] "An executory agreement in writing, stipulating for the execution in future of a mortgage or deed of trust, is of common occurrence, and is valid, and will be specifically enforced as an equi-

---

[14] White &c. Canal Co. v. Vallette, 21 How. (U. S.) 414, 16 L. ed. 154; Biebinger v. Continental Bank, 99 U. S. 143, 25 L. ed. 271; Baltimore &c. R. Co. v. Berkeley &c. R. Co., 168 Fed. 770; Bridgeport Elec. &c. Co. v. Meader, 72 Fed. 115; Central Trust Co. v. Bridges, 57 Fed. 753; Gest v. Packwood, 39 Fed. 525; Hester v. Hunnicutt, 104 Ala. 282, 16 So. 162; O'Neal v. Sexias, 85 Ala. 80, 4 So. 745; Morrow v. Turney, 35 Ala. 131; Richardson v. Wren, 11 Ariz. 395, 95 Pac. 124, 16 L. R. A. (N. S.) 190; Richardson v. Hamlett, 33 Ark. 237; Earle v. Sunnyside Land Co., 150 Cal. 214, 88 Pac. 920; Remington v. Higgins, 54 Cal. 620; Racouillat v. Sansevain, 32 Cal. 377; Daggett v. Rankin, 31 Cal. 321; Hall v. Hall, 50 Conn. 104; Hamilton v. Hamilton, 162 Ind. 430, 70 N. E. 535; Textor v. Orr, 86 Md. 398, 38 Atl. 939; Osgood v. Osgood, 78 Mich. 290, 44 N. W. 325; Adams v. Johnson, 41 Miss. 258; Petrie v. Wright, 6 Sm. & M. (Miss.) 647; Carter v. Holman, 60 Mo. 498; McQuie v. Peay, 58 Mo. 56; English v. Rainear (N. J.), 55 Atl. 41; Oliva v. Bunaforza, 31 N. J. Eq. 395; Hamilton Trust Co. v. Clemes, 163 N. Y. 423, 57 N. E. 614; Perry v. Board of Missions, 102 N. Y. 99, 6 N. E. 116; Husted v. Ingraham, 75 N. Y. 251; Payne v. Wilson, 74 N. Y. 348; Hale v. Omaha Nat. Bank, 64 N. Y. 550; Chase v. Peck, 21 N. Y. 581; In re Howe, 1 Paige (N. Y.) 125, 19 Am. Dec. 395; Burdick v. Jackson, 7 Hun (N. Y.) 448; Cotterell v. Long, 20 Ohio 464; Bank of Muskingum v. Carpenter, 7 Ohio 21, 28 Am. Dec. 616; Delaire v. Keenan, 3 Desaus. (S. Car.) 74, 4 Am. Dec. 604; Boehl v. Wadgymar, 54 Tex. 589; Ott v. King, 8 Grat. (Va.) 224; Alexander v. Newton, 2 Grat. (Va.) 266; Poland v. Lamoille Val. R. Co., 52 Vt. 144; Atkinson v. Miller, 34 W. Va. 115, 11 S. E. 1007; Starks v. Redfield, 52 Wis. 349; Harrigan v. Gilchrist, 121 Wis. 127, 99 N. W. 909, 981 (citing text and numerous cases); Russel v. Russel, 1 Bro. C. C. 269; Finch v. Winchelsea, 1 P. Wms. 283; Ex parte Heathcoat, 2 Mont. D. & D. 711, 6 Jur. 1001; Burn v. Burn, 3 Ves. Jr. 582; Shakei v. Marlborough, 4 Madd. 463. But see Humphreys v. Snyder, Morris (Iowa) 263. Equity will not recognize as a mortgage an agreement to execute mortgage in presenti, the execution of which fails through inadvertence. Price v. Cutts, 29 Ga. 142, 74 Am. Dec. 52.

table mortgage."[15] It is of frequent application under the bankrupt laws, where it operates to make valid a mortgage given to a creditor shortly before the filing of a petition in bankruptcy by the mortgagor, when this is done in pursuance of an agreement made at a time when the giving of the mortgage would not have been a fraudulent preference.[16]

An agreement to make a conveyance of land, when intended as security for a debt, is in the same manner a mortgage. But all such agreements to give mortgages or other conveyances by way of security are ineffectual when no particular property is specified on which the security is to be given.[17] An agreement to give a mortgage on "sufficient property" is not effectual.[18] Such agreement can of course bind only the maker of it and his heirs, and persons having notice. It is not of any force as against his subsequent judgment creditors.[19]

The meaning of the maxim, that equity looks upon things agreed to be done as actually performed, is that equity will treat the matter, as to collateral consequences and incidents, in the same manner as if the final acts contemplated by the parties had been executed exactly as they ought to have been.[20]

Among other things, an equitable mortgage has been held to result from a written contract to secure a debt, in which the intention is expressed to create a lien by way of mortgage upon particular real estate, upon breach of certain conditions;[21] from a written agreement by a mortgagor owning an equity of redemption, to execute a new mortgage to his creditor, upon the latter's discontinuing foreclosure;[22] and from an agreement to hold property recovered in litigation, as security for advances.[23] But it has been held that an agreement to secure a loan by mortgage on certain land, upon obtaining an interest

---

[15] Atkinson v. Miller, 34 W. Va. 115, 11 S. E. 1007, 9 L. R. A. 544.

[16] Burdick v. Jackson, 7 Hun (N. Y.) 488; Harrigan v. Gilchrist, 121 Wis. 127, 99 N. W. 909, 981 (quoting text).

[17] Langley v. Vaughn, 10 Heisk. (Tenn.) 553.

[18] Goldthwaite v. Ellison, 99 Ala. 497, 12 So. 812; Adams v. Johnson, 41 Miss. 258.

[19] Racouillat v. Sansevain, 32 Cal. 376; Price v. Cutts, 29 Ga. 142, 74 Am. Dec. 52. But in England an equitable mortgage has priority of a subsequent judgment. Whitworth v. Gaugain, 3 Hare 416; Abbott v. Stratten, 3 Jo. & Lat. 603.

[20] Daggett v. Rankin, 31 Cal. 321, per Currey, C. J.; Wayt v. Carwithen, 21 W. Va. 516.

[21] Donald v. Hewitt, 33 Ala. 534, 73 Am. Dec. 431; Richardson v. Wren, 11 Ariz. 395, 95 Pac. 124, 16 L. R. A. (N. S.) 190; Cummings v. Jackson, 55 N. J. Eq. 805, 38 Atl. 763; In re Dimond, 14 Pa. St. 323. See also Clarke v. Sibley, 13 Metc. (Mass.) 210.

[22] Matthew v. Damainville, 43 Misc. 546, 89 N. Y. S. 493.

[23] Jackson v. Carswell, 34 Ga. 279; Potter v. Kimball, 186 Mass. 120, 71 N. E. 308 (agreement binding on heirs of equitable mortgagee).

in such land, does not operate as an equitable mortgage upon the acquisition of an equitable interest therein.[24] And it has been held that a mere executory contract to give a mortgage on the happening of a contingent future event, although executed in writing and recorded, is not an equitable mortgage.[25]

§ 164. **Parol agreements.**—There must be some kind of an agreement between the parties in interest,[26] but it is not necessary that the agreement should in all cases be in writing. Although a parol agreement in respect to lands while it remains altogether executory is not enforcible,[27] yet, when there has been a part performance of it, it can not in equity be avoided.[28] The parol agreement, though partly performed, must be sufficiently clear and definite for the court to enforce the understanding of the parties.[29] When such parol agreement has been performed by a delivery of a formal mortgage, all objection to the validity of the agreement is removed, and it becomes as effectual for all purposes as if it had been reduced to writing originally.[30] In this way a mortgage made a few days before the bankruptcy of the mortgagor, but in pursuance of a parol agreement made fifteen months before, and based upon a good consideration, is good against the assignee in bankruptcy, and is not open to the objection that it is void as a fraudulent preference.[31]

[24] Dudley v. Nickerson, 214 Mass. 274, 101 N. E. 465.

[25] Mathews v. Damainville, 100 App. Div. 311, 91 N. Y. S. 524.

[26] Levy v. McDonnell, 92 Ark. 324, 122 S. W. 1002, 135 Am. St. 183; Cotten v. Blocker, 6 Fla. 1; Iowa State Sav. Bank v. Coonrod, 97 Iowa 106, 66 N. W. 78; Barber v. Toomey (Ore.), 136 Pac. 343.

[27] Smith v. Smith, 153 Ala. 504, 45 So. 168; Washington Brewery Co. v. Carry (Md.), 24 Atl. 151; Clabaugh v. Byerly, 7 Gill (Md.) 354, 48 Am. Dec. 575; Bennett v. Harrison, 115 Minn. 342, 132 N. W. 309, 37 L. R. A. (N. S.) 521; Meixel v. Meixel, 146 N. Y. S. 587; Mathews v. Damainville, 100 App. Div. 311, 91 N. Y. S. 524.

[28] Coster v. Georgia Bank, 24 Ala. 37; King v. Williams, 66 Ark. 333, 50 S. W. 695; Foster Lumber Co. v. Harlan County Bank, 71 Kans. 158, 80 Pac. 49, 114 Am. St. 470; Cole v. Cole, 41 Md. 301; Hicks v. Turck, 72 Mich. 311, 40 N. W. 339; Wenzel v. Weigand, 92 Minn. 152, 99 N. W. 633; Irvine v. Armstrong, 31 Minn. 216, 17 N. W. 343; Dean v. Anderson, 34 N. J. Eq. 496; Sprague v. Cochran, 144 N. Y. 104; Smith v. Smith, 125 N. Y. 228; Freeman v. Freeman, 43 N. Y. 34, 3 Am. Rep. 657; Stoddard v. Hart, 23 N. Y. 556; Burdick v. Jackson, 7 Hun (N. Y.) 488; Baker v. Baker, 2 S. Dak. 261, 49 N. W. 1064; McCarty v. Brackenridge, 1 Tex. Civ. App. 170, 20 S. W. 997.

[29] Girault v. Adams, 61 Md. 1; McClintock v. Laing, 22 Mich. 212 (clear and satisfactory proof required).

[30] Dodge v. Wellman, 1 Abb. App. (N. Y.) 512; Carr v. Carr, 4 Lans. (N. Y.) 314; Burdick v. Jackson, 7 Hun (N. Y.) 104; McBurney v. Wellman, 42 Barb. (N. Y.) 390; Petrie v. Wright, 6 Smed. & M. (Miss.) 647 (merger of equitable into legal mortgage).

[31] Burdick v. Jackson, 7 Hun (N. Y.) 488.

The agreement must show an intention to create a lien on some particular property, sufficiently designated.[32] An agreement to give a mortgage on one of several houses to be built on certain land has been held sufficient, however, although the particular house was not designated.[33]

In jurisdictions where a mortgage actually conveys an interest in land, even courts of equity, in the light of the statute of frauds will not give effect to a parol agreement to execute a mortgage, as an equitable mortgage.[34]

§ 164a. Agreement by purchaser at judicial sale.—A purchase at a judicial sale for the benefit of the debtor in accordance with a verbal or written agreement with him will be regarded as an equitable mortgage to him.[35] So, an equitable mortgage is created by an assignment of a sheriff's deed or certificate of purchase to a stranger advancing money for redemption of lands from judicial sale, under an agreement to reconvey to the debtor on repayment.[36] The case is the same where a junior mortgagee buys in plaintiff's land at foreclosure sale under a

[32] Seymour v. Canandaigua &c. Co., 25 Barb. (N. Y.) 284.

[33] Kendall v. Niebuhr, 13 Jones & S. (N. Y.) 542; Payne v. Wilson, 74 N. Y. 348.

[34] Alexander v. Pardue, 30 Ark. 359; Six v. Shaner, 26 Md. 415; Gale v. Morris, 29 N. J. Eq. 224; Marquat v. Marquat, 7 How. Pr. (N. Y.) 417; Bower v. Oyster, 3 P. & W. (Pa.) 239; Boehl v. Wadgymar, 54 Tex. 589; Bailey v. Warner, 28 Vt. 87. But see Sprague v. Cochran, 144 N. Y. 104, 38 N. E. 1000; McCarty v. Brackenridge, 1 Tex. Civ. App. 170.

[35] La Cotts v. La Cotts (Ark.), 159 S. W. 1111; Union Mut. Life Ins. Co. v. Slee, 123 Ill. 57, 12 N. E. 543, 13 N. E. 222; Klock v. Walter, 70 Ill. 416; Beatty v. Brummett, 94 Ind. 76; Byers v. Johnson, 89 Iowa 278, 56 N. W. 449; Stroup v. Haycock, 56 Iowa 729, 10 N. W. 257; Roberts v. McMahan, 4 Greene (Iowa) 34; Nichols v. Marquess, 141 Ky. 642, 133 S. W. 562; Sheffield v. Day, 28 Ky. 754, 90 S. W. 545; Howe v. Courtney, 32 Ky. L. 711, 107 S. W. 206; Guenther v. Wisdom, 27 Ky. L. 230, 84 S. W. 771; Potter v. Kimball, 186 Mass. 120, 71 N. E. 308; Anderson v. Smith, 103 Mich. 446, 61 N. W. 778; Wenzel v. Weigand, 92 Minn. 152, 99 N. W. 633; Phillips v. Jackson, 240 Mo. 310, 144 S. W. 112; English v. Ralnear (N. J. Eq.), 55 Atl. 41; Barkelew v. Taylor, 8 N. J. Eq. 206; Moore v. Nye, 66 Hun 628, 21 N. Y. S. 94; Sahler v. Signer, 37 Barb. (N. Y.) 329; Williams v. Avery, 131 N. Car. 188, 42 S. E. 582; Wilson v. Giddings, 28 Ohio St. 554; Gaines v. Brokerhoff, 136 Pa. St. 175, 19 Atl. 958; Guinn v. Locke, 1 Head (Tenn.) 110; Liskey v. Snyder, 56 W. Va. 610, 49 S. E. 515; Beebe v. Wisconsin Mtg. Loan Co., 117 Wis. 328, 93 N. W. 1103; Phelan v. Fitzpatrick, 84 Wis. 240, 54 N. W. 614; Hoile v. Bailey, 58 Wis. 434, 17 N. W. 322. But see Hibernian Banking Assn. v. Commercial Nat. Bank, 157 Ill. 524, 41 N. E. 919; Price v. Evans, 26 Mo. 30; Merritt v. Brown, 19 N. J. Eq. 286; Jones v. Pierce, 134 Pa. St. 533, 19 Atl. 689. Where the parol evidence was not strong enough to make the transaction a mortgage. An agreement to buy in property and hold it in trust to secure payments, creates an equitable mortgage. Lutz v. Hoyle (N. Car.), 83 S. E. 749.

[36] Lounsbury v. Norton, 59 Conn.

senior lien, agreeing to give plaintiff a certain time to redeem, and there
can be no foreclosure by a private sale.[37]   A conveyance to one who
advances money for the benefit of another under an agreement of
the latter to purchase at a certain price may be regarded as a mortgage to the latter for the amount of the purchase-money which the
purchaser may foreclose.[38]

§ 165. **Agreement entered upon corporate records—Consent judgment—Conditional agreement.**—Upon this principle, the entry of an
agreement by a corporation upon its records, that a certain bond for
title should be pledged to certain of its members as security for liabilities which they were about to incur for the company, was held to
be an equitable mortgage; and although a deed of trust was afterward
made in conformity with the resolution, yet these members, having
acted upon the faith of it before the deed of trust was made, were
held to be entitled to the security as from that time, and the deed of
trust was regarded only as a confirmation of the agreement, and as
having relation to the resolution.[39]

The entry of a consent judgment, declaring that "defendant has
an equity to redeem" land on payment of a certain sum within a

170, 22 Atl. 153; Trogdon v. Trogdon, 164 Ill. 144, 45 N. E. 575; Byers
v. Johnson, 89 Iowa 278, 56 N. W.
449; Barthell v. Syverson, 54 Iowa
160, 6 N. W. 178; Brey v. Barbour,
14 Ky. 655, 20 S. W. 899; Staugh-
ton v. Simpson, 69 Minn. 314, 72 N.
W. 126; Sweetzer's Appeal, 71 Pa.
St. 264; Wilson v. McWilliams, 16 S.
Dak. 96, 91 N. W. 453; Shank v.
Groff, 43 W. Va. 337, 27 S. E. 340.

[37] McLure v. National Bank of
Commerce, 252 Mo. 510, 160 S. W.
1005.

[38] Wright v. Shumway, 1 Biss.
(U. S.) 23, 30 Fed. Cas. No. 18093;
Watts v. Kellar, 56 Fed. 1; Hughes
v. McKenzie, 101 Ala. 415, 13 So.
609; Banks v. Walters, 95 Ark. 501,
130 S. W. 519; Campbell v. Freeman, 99 Cal. 546, 34 Pac. 113; Purdy
v. Bullard, 41 Cal. 444; Hidden v.
Jordan, 21 Cal. 92; Lindsay v. Matthews, 17 Fla. 575; Doris v. Story,
122 Ga. 611, 50 S. E. 348; Fleming
v. Georgia R. Bank, 120 Ga. 1023,
48 S. E. 420; Stewart v. Fellows,
128 Ill. 480, 20 N. E. 657; Smith v.
Cremer, 71 Ill. 185; Smith v. Sackett, 15 Ill. 528; Davis v. Hopkins,

15 Ill. 519; Rogers v. Davis, 91
Iowa 730, 59 N. W. 265; Stratton
v. Rotrock, 84 Kans. 198, 114 Pac.
224; Weekly v. Ellis, 30 Kans. 507,
2 Pac. 96; McKenney v. Page, 146
Ky. 682, 143 S. W. 382; McPherson
v. Hayward, 81 Maine 329, 17 Atl.
164; Stinchfield v. Milliken, 71
Maine 567; Holton v. Meighen, 15
Minn. 69; Malloy v. Malloy, 35
Nebr. 224, 52 N. W. 1097; Leahigh
v. White, 8 Nev. 147; Carr v. Carr,
52 N. Y. 251; Hall v. O'Connell, 52
Ore. 164, 95 Pac. 717, 96 Pac. 1070;
Fessler's Appeal, 75 Pa. St. 483;
Houser v. Lamont, 55 Pa. St. 311,
93 Am. Dec. 755; Hewitt v. Huling,
11 Pa. St. 27; Robinson v. Lin-
coln Sav. Bank, 85 Tenn. 363, 3 S.
W. 656; Lucia v. Adams, 36 Tex.
Civ. App. 454, 82 S. W. 335; Pen-
nington v. Hanby, 4 Munf. (Va.)
140; Beebe v. Wisconsin Mtg. Loan
Co., 117 Wis. 328, 93 N. W. 1103;
Jordain v. Fox, 90 Wis. 99, 62 N.
W. 936; Schriber v. LeClair, 66
Wis. 579, 29 N. W. 570; Holle v.
Bailey, 58 Wis. 434, 17 N. W. 322.

[39] Miller v. Moore, 3 Jones Eq.
(N. Car.) 431.

specified time and that he shall be absolutely debarred on default, establishes an equitable mortgage.[40]

The maker of two notes gave an instrument to his sureties on the notes reciting that they were given for the purchase of land, and providing, "In case I fail to pay said notes, I do bind myself, my heirs, etc., to convey to said sureties the aforesaid land." It was held that, upon the failure of the principal to pay the notes, the sureties were entitled, not to an absolute conveyance, but to a mortgage.[41]

§ 166. **Defective instruments—Conveyances in trust for support and special purposes.**[42]—An instrument which does not transfer the legal estate may yet operate as an equitable transfer of it in the nature of a mortgage.[43] Thus, a mortgage to certain executors from which the word "heirs," creating a fee, was omitted, and the word "successors" used in its stead was held to be an equitable mortgage in fee, and was reformed.[44] Such was held to be the effect of an agreement under seal made by one to whom land was conveyed in consideration that he should support and maintain the grantor, whereby the produce of the land was pledged for that purpose, and if that should prove insufficient the entire fee was appropriated.[45] Such, too, is a similar instrument in which the signer agrees to maintain his father and mother during their natural lives, and as security for the fulfilment of the agreement conveys and grants to them "each and severally a life lien or dower or lien of maintenance for life" in real estate.[46] A written agreement by the owner of land to pay his creditor in possession thereof a certain sum, giving him possession instead of interest, till the land was sold to pay the debt, has been held to constitute an equitable mortgage.[47] The words, "we mortgage the property," ac-

---

[40] Bunn v. Braswell, 139 N. Car. 135, 51 S. E. 927.

[41] Courtney v. Scott, Litt. Sel. Cas. (Ky.) 457; Wayt v. Carwithen, 21 W. Va. 516.

[42] Defective and informal mortgages are specially treated in § 168 post.

[43] Howard v. Iron &c. Co., 62 Minn. 298, 64 N. W. 896; White v. University Land Co., 49 Mo. App. 619; Leiweke v. Jordan, 59 Mo. App. 564; Mennde v. Delaire, 2 Desaus. (S. Car.) 450.

[44] Gale v. Morris, 29 N. J. Eq. 222; First Nat. Bank v. Adam (Ill.), 25 N. E. 576; Brown v. Bank, 44 Ohio St. 269, 6 N. E. 648; New Vien-

na Bank v. Johnson, 47 Ohio St. 306, 24 N. E. 506.

[45] Hiatt v. Parker, 29 Kans. 765; Webster v. Cadwallader, 133 Ky. 500, 118 S. W. 327, 134 Am. St. 470; Price v. Hobbs, 47 Md. 359; Campau v. Chene, 1 Mich. 400; Doescher v. Spratt, 61 Minn. 326, 63 N. W. 736; Chase v. Peck, 21 N. Y. 581; Abbott v. Sanders, 80 Vt. 179, 66 Atl. 1032; Davis v. Davis, 81 Vt. 259, 69 Atl. 876, 130 Am. St. 1035. But see Bethlehem v. Armis, 40 N. H. 34, 77 Am. Dec. 700.

[46] Gilson v. Gilson, 2 Allen (Mass.) 115.

[47] Blackburn v. Tweedie, 60 Mo. 505.

companied by a provision for the sale of it upon nonpayment of money thus secured, have been held sufficient to create a mortgage.[48]

A conveyance by a testator's son of his interest in a remainder, before sale of the realty by the executors under a power of sale, creates an equitable mortgage.[49] And the conclusion was the same in the case of a commissioner's deed executed to the guardian of the heirs of a purchaser at a judicial sale, reserving to the heirs the right to redeem.[50]

An instrument whereby a corporation "pledges the real and personal estate of said company" for the payment of a debt or the fulfilment of a contract may be enforced as a mortgage against the company and all persons claiming under it with notice; and is not rendered invalid for the reason that the property of the company is pledged without specification, or that the amount secured is not stated, or the time of redemption fixed.[51] An instrument which recites that the maker of it had employed certain persons as counsel to prosecute a claim to certain land, and promises the payment of a certain sum "at the end of the litigation out of the land," is a mortgage.[52] It indicates the creation of a lien, and specifies the debt intended to be secured, and the property upon which it is to take effect. And so an agreement in a lease, that the lessor "is to have a lien" upon certain property for the faithful performance of the lessee's obligation to pay rent, is in effect a mortgage.[53]

A covenant by a debtor, to execute to his creditor a mortgage upon the debtor's share under his father's will, whenever a division shall have been made, is a mortgage.[54] So is a provision in a deed that the grantee shall pay certain legacies or certain liens which are a charge upon the property conveyed.[55] So, also, is an agreement not under seal which provides that the purchase-money of land should be secured by the property, if not resold by the purchaser, and if sold, then paid from the proceeds.[56] A seal is not necessary to make an

[48] De Leon v. Higuera, 15 Cal. 483. See also Barroilhet v. Battelle, 7 Cal. 450.

[49] Archer v. Archer, 147 App. Div. 44, 131 N. Y. S. 661.

[50] Green v. Maddox, 97 Ark. 397, 134 S. W. 931.

[51] White Water Val. Canal Co. v. Vallette, 21 How. (U. S.) 414, 16 L. ed. 154; Mobile &c. R. Co. v. Talman, 15 Ala. 472. See also Hamilton Trust Co. v. Clemes, 163 N. Y. 423, 57 N. Y. 614; Husted v. Ingraham, 75 N. Y. 251; Hale v. Bank, 64 N. Y. 550; Bryce v. Massey, 35 S. Car. 127, 14 S. E. 768.

[52] Jackson v. Carswell, 34 Ga. 279.

[53] First Nat. Bank v. Adam (Ill.), 25 N. E. 576; Whiting v. Eichelberger, 16 Iowa 422.

[54] Lynch v. Utica Ins. Co., 18 Wend. (N. Y.) 236.

[55] Mitchell v. Wade, 39 Ark. 377; Howard v. Iron &c. Co., 62 Minn. 298, 64 N. W. 896; Stewart v. Hutchins, 6 Hill (N. Y.) 143.

[56] Racouillat v. Sansevain, 32 Cal. 376.

instrument a good equitable mortgage. An unsealed instrument pledging the real and personal estate of a corporation for the performance of a contract is an equitable mortgage.[58] So is a power of attorney executed by a debtor to his creditor, authorizing the latter to convey the debtor's property unless he should pay the debt within a time named.[59] So an agreement by the legal owner of land, that a mortgage of the land by one who had no title should nevertheless be a valid lien upon it, is a good equitable mortgage.[60]

Land was conveyed to a trustee to hold for the separate use of a married woman, reserving to her the right with her husband to sell all or any part of the same whenever she might elect to do so. She and her husband made a deed of trust of the land, to which the trustee was not a party; but, by a writing under his hand and seal of the same date, he agreed "that the above trust deed may be executed, and, in the event that a sale of the above-named lands shall have to be made, I will unite in the deed conveying, provided the said sale is made according to the terms of this trust deed." It was held that the deed, though not passing the legal title, yet created a lien on the land as an equitable mortgage.[61]

The purchaser of lands of a decedent at a sale by order of the probate court, before payment of the entire purchase-money or the conveyance of the title, may convey his imperfect equitable title by mortgage.[62] A mortgage executed to a partnership in its firm name, to secure a debt to the firm, duly executed and recorded, constitutes a valid lien in favor of the firm as security for such debt.[63]

But a recital in a deed, that it is subject to a prior mortgage de-

[57] Racouillat v. Sansevain, 32 Cal. 376; Portwood v. Outton, 3 B. Mon. (Ky.) 247; Lewis v. Small, 71 Maine 552; Abbott v. Godfroy, 1 Mich. 178; Lebanon Sav. Bank v. Hollenbeck, 29 Minn. 322, 13 N. W. 145; Dunn v. Raley, 58 Mo. 134; Jones v. Brewington, 58 Mo. 210; Harrington v. Fortner, 58 Mo. 468; Watkins v. Vrooman, 51 Hun 175, 5 N. Y. S. 172; Spencer v. Haynes, 12 Phila. (Pa.) 452; Woods v. Wallace, 22 Pa. St. 171; Westerly Sav. Bank v. Stillman Mfg. Co., 16 R. I. 497, 17 Atl. 918; Bullock v. Whipp, 15 R. I. 195, 2 Atl. 309; Bryce v. Massey, 35 S. Car. 127, 14 S. E. 768; Holley v. Curry, 56 W. Va. 70, 51 S. E. 135, 112 Am. St. 944; Atkinson v. Miller, 34 W. Va. 115, 11 S. E. 1007, 9 L. R. A. 544; Knott

v. Shepherdstown Mfg. Co., 30 W. Va. 790, 5 S. E. 266; Wayt v. Carwithen, 21 W. Va. 516.

[58] Donald v. Hewitt, 33 Ala. 534; Coster v. Bank of Georgia, 24 Ala. 37; Kelly v. Payne, 18 Ala. 371; Mobile & C. P. R. Co. v. Talman, 15 Ala. 472; Bank of Kentucky v. Vance, 4 Litt. (Ky.) 169; Abbott v. Godfroy, 1 Mich. 178; Campbell v. Worthington, 6 Vt. 448; Whitworth v. Gaugain, 3 Hare 416.

[59] Pemberton v. Simmons, 100 N. Car. 316, 6 S. E. 122.

[60] Watkins v. Vrooman, 51 Hun 175, 5 N. Y. S. 172.

[61] Bensimer v. Fell, 35 W. Va. 15, 12 S. E. 1078.

[62] Washington v. Bogart, 119 Ala. 377, 24 So. 245.

[63] New Vienna Bank v. Johnson,

scribed, does not make an equitable mortgage of an instrument which does not pass the owner's estate. A married woman owning land joined her husband in a mortgage which she signed only in release of dower. Subsequently she executed in due form a mortgage which recited that the property was subject to that mortgage. It was held that the mortgagee in the former mortgage could not enforce his mortgage against the wife, or against the holder of the second mortgage.[64]

§ 167. **Agreements charging specific lands.**—A written agreement that attempts to appropriate specific property to the payment of a debt, and gives the creditor possession of it to hold till the debtor shall make sale of the land and satisfy the debt from such sale, the occupation of the land and the doing of certain work to offset interest on the debt, constitutes an equitable mortgage binding upon the owner of the land, and upon any one who buys of him with notice of the agreement.[65] An agreement on the back of a note, making it a charge upon particular land, is an equitable mortgage. In this way an agreement intended to operate as a revival of a mortgage note which had been paid may be rendered effectual, although ineffectual to revive the mortgage lien.[66]

So, an equitable mortgage is created by a duly executed and acknowledged agreement, reciting that it shall be a lien upon a certain farm, until compensation for trees planted thereon shall be received;[67] and by an agreement of the equitable owner of land, that the holder of the legal title may hold it as security for the payment of a sum of money borrowed by the former of a third person.[68]

A provision in a lease, giving the lessor a lien for the rent on cer-

47 Ohio St. 306, 24 N. E. 503; Chicago Lumber Co. v. Ashworth, 26 Kans. 212. It has been held that a conveyance to a firm is a conveyance to the members as tenants in common, who hold the title in trust for the firm; Beaman v. Whitney, 20 Maine 413; Jones v. Neale, 2 Pat. & H. (Va.) 339.

That a partnership may acquire an equitable estate in real property is decided in Rammelsberg v. Mitchell, 29 Ohio St. 22, 52.

[64] Franklin Sav. Bank v. Miller, 17 R. I. 272, 21 Atl. 542.

[65] White Water Val. Canal Co. v. Vallette, 21 How. (U. S.) 414, 16 L. ed. 154; Wilson v. Boyce, 92 U.

S. 320, 23 L. ed. 608; Daggett v. Rankin, 31 Cal. 321; Hackett v. Watts, 138 Mo. 502, 40 S. W. 113; Blackburn v. Tweedie, 60 Mo. 505; McQuie v. Peay, 58 Mo. 58; Cummings v. Jackson, 55 N. J. Eq. 805, 38 Atl. 763; Gale v. Morris, 29 N. J. Eq. 224; Dunman v. Coleman, 59 Tex. 199; Wayt v. Carwithen, 21 W. Va. 516; Hoile v. Bailey, 58 Wis. 434, 17 N. W. 322. But see Allen v. Montgomery, 48 Miss. 101.

[66] Bell v. Pelt, 51 Ark. 433, 11 S. W. 684; Peckham v. Haddock, 36 Ill. 38.

[67] Ward v. Stark, 91 Ark. 268, 121 S. W. 382.

[68] Chadwick v. Clapp, 69 Ill. 119.

tain property[69] or on buildings and fixtures to be erected by the lessee,[70] has been held to create an equitable mortgage. Debenture bonds, issued by a corporation, pledging its property for the payment thereof, constitute an equitable mortgage.[71] So, an agreement made by bondholders secured by a mortgage of a railroad, that certain preference bonds secured by a subsequent mortgage should be a lien on the railroad prior to the bonds held by the several signers of the agreement, operates as a pledge or equitable mortgage of the interest of such bondholders under the prior mortgage; but of course such agreement does not in any way affect the interest or the priority of the lien of any bondholders who do not sign the agreement.[72]

A mortgage made by a person individually to himself as guardian to secure moneys belonging to his ward would be regarded in a court of equity as a valid security against the guardian, and would be given effect for the purpose of protecting the interest of the ward. After a sale of the mortgaged premises, a judgment in a foreclosure suit would estop the parties from questioning the mortgage, and a sale would confer a good title upon the purchaser.[73]

It has even been held that if land intended to be included in a mortgage is omitted by mistake, and a judgment is subsequently rendered against the mortgagor, the lien of the judgment creditor is subject to the equity of the mortgage.[74]

§ 168. Defective or informal mortgages.[75]

—Instruments which attempt to create a legal mortgage or trust deed, and fail through some defect in their execution or form, and written contracts intended to operate as mortgages or as charges upon property, which are too informal or defective to operate at law, are generally given effect and enforced as equitable mortgages.[76] A mortgage, or trust deed, which

---

[69] Barroilhet v. Battelle, 7 Cal. 450; Whiting v. Eichelberger, 16 Iowa 422.

[70] First Nat. Bank v. Adam (Ill.), 25 N. E. 576.

[71] Seymour v. Canandaigua &c. R. Co., 25 Barb. (N. Y.) 284; Poland v. Lamoille R. Co., 52 Vt. 171; Duncan v. Manchester &c. Waterworks, 8 Price 697. See also William Firth Co. v. South Carolina Loan &c. Co., 122 Fed. 569, 59 C. C. A. 73; Kirkpatrick v. Eastern Milling &c. Co., 137 Fed. 387, 69 C. C. A. 579.

[72] Poland v. Lamoille Val. R. Co., 52 Vt. 144.

[73] Lyon v. Lyon, 67 N. Y. 250.

[74] Martin v. Nixon, 92 Mo. 26, 4 S. W. 503. Is this decision a safe precedent?

[75] See also ante § 166. Defective mortgages, omission of seal, words creating fee, etc.

[76] Hunt v. Rhodes, 1 Pet. (U. S.) 1; Wood v. Holly Mfg. Co., 100 Ala. 326; O'Neal v. Seixas, 85 Ala. 80; Bell v. Pelt, 51 Ark. 433, 11 S. W. 684, 4 L. R. A. 247, 14 Am. St. 57; Peers v. McLaughlin, 88 Cal. 294, 22 Am. St. 306; Remington v. Higgins, 54 Cal. 624; Love v. Sierra Nevada &c. Co., 32 Cal. 639, 91 Am. Dec. 602; Racouillat v. Sansevain, 32 Cal. 376; Daggett v. Rankin, 31

can not be enforced by a sale under the power or by a judgment of foreclosure, on account of the omission of some formality requisite to a complete mortgage or deed of trust, will nevertheless be regarded as an equitable mortgage, and the lien will be enforced by special proceedings in equity. The attempt to create a security in legal form upon specific property having failed, effect is given to the intention of the parties, and the lien enforced as an equitable mortgage.[77]

Any agreement between the parties in interest that shows an intention to create a lien may be in equity a mortgage.[78] As stated by Judge Story,[79] "If a transaction resolve itself into a security, whatever may be its form, and whatever name the parties may choose to give it, it is in equity a mortgage." Effect has been given in this way

Cal. 321; Margarum v. J. S. Christie Orange Co., 37 Fla. 165, 19 So. 637; Edwards v. Hall, 93 Ill. 326; Peckham v. Haddock, 36 Ill. 38 (defective renewal); Vaniman v. Gardner, 99 Ill. App. 345; Brown v. Brown, 103 Ind. 23, 2 N. E. 233; Millholand v. Tiffany, 64 Md. 455; Sanders v. McDonald, 63 Md. 503; Dyson v. Simmons, 48 Md. 207; Johnson v. Canby, 29 Md. 217; Price v. McDonald, 1 Md. 414, 54 Am. Dec. 657; Tiernan v. Poor, 1 Gill & J. (Md.) 216, 19 Am. Dec. 225; Abbott v. Godfroy, 1 Mich. 178; Lebanon Sav. Bank v. Hollenbeck, 29 Minn. 322; Ross v. Worthington, 11 Minn. 438, 88 Am. Dec. 95; Burnett v. Boyd, 60 Miss. 627; Blackburn v. Tweedie, 60 Mo. 505; McQuie v. Peay, 58 Mo. 58; McClurg v. Phillips, 49 Mo. 315; Davis v. Clay, 2 Mo. 161; Gale v. Morris, 29 N. J. Eq. 222; Sprague v. Cochran, 144 N. Y. 104, 38 N. E. 1000; Smith v. Smith, 125 N. Y. 224, 26 N. E. 259; Perry v. Board of Missions, 102 N. Y. 99, 6 N. E. 116; Coman v. Lackey, 80 N. Y. 350; Husted v. Ingraham, 75 N. Y. 257; Payne v. Wilson, 74 N. Y. 348; Chase v. Peck, 21 N. Y. 583; National Bank v. Lanier, 7 Hun (N. Y.) 623; Launing v. Tompkins, 45 Barb. (N. Y.) 316; Lake v. Dowd, 10 Ohio 415; Muskingum v. Carpenter, 7 Ohio 21, 28 Am. Dec. 616; Brown v. Farmers' Supply Co., 23 Ore. 544; Moore v. Thomas, 1 Ore. 201; Delaire v. Keenan, 3 Desaus. Eq. (S. Car.) 74, 4 Am. Dec. 604; Dulaney v. Willis, 95 Va. 606, 29

S. E. 324, 63 Am. St. 815; Miller v. Rutland &c. R. Co., 36 Vt. 452; Feely v. Bryan, 55 W. Va. 586, 47 S. E. 307; Harrigan v. Gilchrist, 121 Wis. 127, 99 N. W. 909; Frank v. Hicks, 4 Wyo. 502.

[77] Margarum v. Christie Orange Co., 37 Fla. 165, 19 So. 637; Dyson v. Simmons, 48 Md. 220; Tiernan v. Poor, 1 Gill & J. (Md.) 216, 19 Am. Dec. 225; Payne v. Wilson, 74 N. Y. 348; Sprague v. Cochran, 144 N. Y. 104, 38 N. E. 1000, revg. 70 Hun 512; Sullivan v. Corn Exch. Bank, 154 App. Div. 292, 139 N. Y. S. 97; Atkinson v. Miller, 34 W. Va. 115, 11 S. E. 1007 (quoting text); Frank v. Hicks, 4 Wyo. 502, 35 Pac. 475, 1025 (quoting text).

[78] Gest v. Packwood, 39 Fed. 525; Courtner v. Etheredge, 149 Ala. 78, 43 So. 368; Bell v. Pelt, 51 Ark. 433, 11 S. W. 684; Daggett v. Rankin, 31 Cal. 321; Fidelity &c. Co. v. Shenandoah Val. R. Co., 33 W. Va. 761, 11 S. E. 58; Knott v. Manufacturing Co., 30 W. Va. 790, 5 S. E. 266; Wayt v. Carwithen, 21 W. Va. 516. See also cases in preceding note and § 162 note. The intent to create an equitable mortgage must be manifest as distinguished from an intent to apply the proceeds from the sale of the property to the payment of the debt. Smith v. Rainey, 9 Ariz. 362, 83 Pac. 463. See post §§ 264, 265.

[79] Flagg v. Mann, 2 Sum. (U. S.) 486, and see cases cited in Harrigan v. Gilchrist, 121 Wis. 127, 99 N. W. 909, 981 (quoting Judge Story).

to a deed of trust in which the name of the trustee was accidentally omitted;[80] to a mortgage from which the name of the mortgagee was omitted;[81] to a mortgage in which the grantees were insufficiently designated as "Stark Brothers;"[82] to a mortgage from which the name of the grantor's husband was omitted;[83] to one from which a seal was omitted by mistake;[84] to one sealed in fact, but not expressed to be sealed;[85] to one imperfectly acknowledged, or not acknowledged at all;[86] or not witnessed as a deed of real estate is required to be.[87]

It has been held that effect will not be given to a mortgage witnessed, acknowledged, and recorded, but not signed by the mortgagor,[88] but there is authority contra.[89] Although a mortgage signed in blank, and afterward filled in by an agent of the grantor, is not a legally executed deed, it may, however, create an equitable lien which the courts will enforce.[90] An instrument in the form of a chattel mortgage but intended as security on real property will be construed as an equitable mortgage.[91]

§ 169. Corporate mortgages executed in name of agent.—A mortgage defectively executed in the name of an agent, though purporting to be the mortgage of the corporation, is held to be binding in equity if it appear that the officer or agent had authority to bind it, and by accident or mistake executed it in his own name instead of the name of the company.[92] In such a case, before the Supreme Court of Cali-

---

[80] Burnside v. Wayman, 49 Mo. 356; McQuie v. Peay, 58 Mo. 56; Dulaney v. Willis, 95 Va. 606, 29 S. E. 324, 64 Am. St. 815.

[81] Dyson v. Simmons, 48 Md. 207.

[82] Stark v. Kirkley, 129 Mo. App. 353, 108 S. W. 625.

[83] Dietrich v. Deavitt, 81 Vt. 160, 69 Atl. 661.

[84] Gill v. Clark, 54 Mo. 415; Dunn v. Raley, 58 Mo. 134; Harrington v. Fortner, 58 Mo. 468; McClurg v. Phillips, 49 Mo. 315, 57 Mo. 214. See ante § 166 note.

[85] Jones v. Brewington, 58 Mo. 210.

[86] Racouillat v. Sansevain, 32 Cal. 376; Dyson v. Simmons, 48 Md. 214; Price v. McDonald, 1 Md. 403, 54 Am. Dec. 657; Black v. Gregg, 58 Mo. 565; Watkins v. Vrooman, 51 Hun 175, 5 N. Y. S. 172; Moore v. Thomas, 1 Ore. 201; Frank v. Hicks, 4 Wyo. 502, 35 Pac. 475, 1025.

[87] Longdon v. Wakeley, 62 Fla. 530, 56 So. 408; Abbott v. Godfroy, 1 Mich. 178; Watkins v. Vrooman, 51 Hun 175, 5 N. Y. S. 172; White v. Denman, 16 Ohio 59; Lake v. Doud, 10 Ohio 415; Muskingum Bank v. Carpenter, 7 Ohio 21, 28 Am. Dec. 616; Moore v. Thomas, 1 Ore. 201; Stelts v. Martin, 90 S. Car. 14, 72 S. E. 550; Bryce v. Massey, 35 S. Car. 127, 14 S. E. 768; Morrill v. Morrill, 53 Vt. 74, 38 Am. Rep. 659.

[88] Goodman v. Randall, 44 Conn. 321.

[89] Martin v. Nixon, 92 Mo. 26, 4 S. W. 503.

[90] Fox v. Palmer, 25 N. J. Eq. 416.

[91] Standorf v. Shockley, 16 N. Dak. 73, 111 N. W. 622, 11 L. R. A. (N. S.) 869. See ante § 60.

[92] Welsh v. Usher, 2 Hill Ch. (S. Car.) 167, 29 Am. Dec. 63; Miller v. Rutland &c. R. Co., 36 Vt. 452. See ante § 127.

fornia,[93] it was urged that the defective execution of the mortgage was caused by a mistake of law, and that therefore the defective execution could not be aided. In answer to this, Mr. Justice Shaffter, delivering the opinion of the court, replies that, where there is a defective execution of a power, it is a matter of no equitable moment whether the error came of a mistake of law or mistake of fact. It is enough that the power existed, and that there was an attempt to act under it. The relief is not so much by way of reforming the instrument as by aiding its defective execution, which aid is administered through or by the application of well-settled maxims of the law; or, as in the class of cases to which this belongs, the instrument defectively executed as a deed is considered as properly executed as a contract for a deed; and therefore as requiring neither reformation nor aid, but as ripe for enforcement, according to the methods peculiar to courts of equity.

In order that an instrument defectively executed may be declared a mortgage, it must appear that the instrument was attempted to be executed by the mortgagor, in pursuance of an agreement indicating an intent that the property described is to be held or transferred as security for an obligation or debt of the mortgagor. Thus a written instrument reciting that a corporation named has mortgaged certain property, signed by one person as president and by another as secretary and treasurer in their own names, sealed with their seals, and acknowledged by them as their act and deed, will not be held to be an equitable mortgage, in the absence of allegations and proof that it was attempted to be executed by the corporation, or its authorized agents, as security for an obligation of the corporation.[94] No particular form of words is necessary for an agent to bind his principal, provided it appears from the mortgage that he intended it as the act of his principal. Where such intent appeared, it was held that the signature Arthur W. Magill (L. S.), agent for the Middletown Manufacturing Company, was sufficient to bind the corporation.[95]

§ 170. **Mortgage by implied trust.**—If a mortgage be made to two persons conditioned to secure the payment of a debt to one of them only, the legal estate would vest in them as tenants in common; but

---

[93] Love v. Sierra Nevada, L. W. &c. Co., 32 Cal. 639, 91 Am. Dec. 602.

[94] Brown v. Farmers' Supply Depot Co., 23 Ore. 541, 32 Pac. 548.

[95] Magill v. Hinsdale, 6 Conn. 464, 16 Am. Dec. 70.

the one having no claim secured would be a trustee to the extent of his moiety, and hold it in trust to secure the debt due the other.[96]

The fact that a mortgage and the note that it secures are made payable in the alternative to one or the other of two definitely named payees does not render them void; but such note and mortgage are enforcible in the courts and all the parties named as alternating payees should join in the suit to enforce such contracts.[97]

In like manner, where one advances money to pay off a mortgage, which is thereupon assigned for his protection to one of the owners of a part of the property, it is a trust in the hands of the latter, and may be established, as against all parties having notice of these facts, as an equitable lien, although the mortgage has been discharged of record.[98] In a case where the maker of a note purchased incumbered land and caused the conveyance to be made to the payee to secure the note, the payee was declared an equitable mortgagee, who held the legal title subject to a resulting trust in favor of the maker.[99]

A conveyance to a creditor as trustee to sell and apply the proceeds in payment of certain enumerated debts due to him and to others, and then return any balance to the grantor, the creditors assenting in writing to such conveyance, has the effect of a mortgage for their benefit.[1] The owner of land who built a mill for a party who went into possession under an agreement to buy and pay for the premises in a certain time, has an equitable mortgage thereon.[2] A written agreement by a creditor to reconvey property to a debtor, if the indebtedness was discharged within a year, otherwise to sell and apply the proceeds to the debt, constitutes a declaration of trust and an equitable mortgage.[3]

A mortgage may be given to secure the mortgagee and also a third person, and the fact that it was given in part for the benefit of another may be made out wholly by parol proof.[4] And so a mortgage given to the cashier of a bank in his individual name, for a debt due

[96] Root v. Bancroft, 10 Metc. (Mass.) 44.

[97] Seedhouse v. Broward, 34 Fla. 509, 16 So. 425.

[98] King v. McVickar, 3 Sandf. Ch. (N. Y.) 192.

[99] Windt v. Covert, 152 Cal. 350, 93 Pac. 67.

[1] Fox v. Fraser, 92 Ind. 265. See ante § 62.

[2] McCrillis v. Cole, 25 R. I. 156, 55 Atl. 196.

[3] Drovers' Deposit Nat. Bank v. Newgass, 147 N. Y. S. 4. Where plaintiff and defendant purchase land as tenants in common and plaintiff pays the entire purchase-money and cost of improvements, defendant agreeing to repay his share as rapidly as possible from sales and income, the intent to create an equitable mortgage does not appear. Smith v. Rainey, 9 Ariz. 362, 83 Pac. 463.

[4] Price v. Brown, 98 N. Y. 388.

the bank, is a valid security in favor of the bank.[5] The court will in such cases enforce the implied trust.

§ 171. **Assignment of rents and profits.**—An assignment of rents and profits of land as security is an equitable mortgage. Such an assignment, in the words of Lord Thurlow, "is an odd way of conveying; but it amounts to an equitable lien, and would entitle the assignee to come into equity and insist upon a mortgage."[6] But a mere agreement to apply such rents and profits to the payment of a debt has been held insufficient to create an equitable mortgage.[7] And likewise an agreement by a planter to ship his crop to a factor to reimburse him for advances and supplies furnished, does not create an equitable mortgage on the crops produced.[8] A deed providing that it shall become void upon default in payment of purchase-money, after which the grantee should hold as tenant and pay rent, but not providing for any lien on the crops, is not an equitable mortgage.[9]

A formal mortgage of a leasehold estate amounts only to an assignment of the rents and profits for the whole term, in states where foreclosure can not be effected by a sale, but only by a strict foreclosure or a proceeding in that nature.[10] An equitable mortgage may be created on crops to be raised, which will attach as soon as they are in esse.[11]

A stipulation in a lease, that the building erected by the lessee "is mortgaged as security" for rent, is a good mortgage.[12] An assignment of a lease absolutely, accompanied with a bond stating it to have been made to secure the payment of a debt, and providing for a reconveyance upon payment, is a mortgage,[13] in the same way that an absolute conveyance in fee accompanied by such a bond is a mortgage. An assignment of a lease proved by parol to be security for a debt, is a mortgage.[14] An irrevocable power of attorney to collect rents, given

[5] Lawrenceville Cement Co. v. Parker, 60 Hun 586, 15 N. Y. S. 577.

[6] Charter Oak L. Ins. Co. v. Gisborne, 5 Utah 319, 15 Pac. 253; Ex parte Willis, 1 Ves. Jun. 162; Abbott v. Stratten, 3 Jo. & Lat. 603. See also Gest v. Packwood, 39 Fed. 525 (lease with pledge of rents and profits); Providence &c. Steamboat Co. v. Fall River, 187 Mass. 45, 72 N. E. 338; Cradock v. Scottish Provident Inst., 63 L. J. Ch. 15, 69 L. T. 380. But see Alexander v. Berry, 54 Miss. 422.

[7] Alexander v. Berry, 54 Miss. 422.

[8] Allen v. Montgomery, 48 Miss. 101.

[9] Levy v. McDonnell, 92 Ark. 324, 122 S. W. 1002.

[10] Hulett v. Soullard, 26 Vt. 295. See post § 785.

[11] Creech v. Long, 72 S. Car. 25, 51 S. E. 614.

[12] Barroilhet v. Battelle, 7 Cal. 450.

[13] Jackson v. Green, 4 Johns. (N. Y.) 186.

[14] Providence &c. Steamboat Co. v. Fall River, 187 Mass. 45, 72 N. E. 338.

as security, is, as between the parties, an equitable mortgage of the rents.[15]

II. *By Assignments of Contracts of Purchase*

§ 172. Assignment of contract to purchase as security.—An assignment by the vendee of a contract for the purchase of land made as security for a debt or loan, may be regarded as an equitable mortgage.[1] The rules applicable to a mortgage of real property govern it both as to the effect of it and the mode of enforcing it.[2]

Even though the assignee of a land contract should acquire a deed from the vendor, he still holds the land merely as a mortgagee in equity.[3] Irrespective of the form of assignment, and though it be absolute, if intended as a security, it will be construed in equity as a mortgage.[4]

Where one having a contract for the purchase of land agrees with

---

[15] Smith Co. v. McGuinness, 14 R. 1. 59; Abbott v. Stratten, 3 Jo. & Lat. 603, 9 Ir. Eq. 233.

[1] Andrews v. Cone, 124 U. S. 720; Shoecraft v. Bloxham, 124 U. S. 730, 31 L. ed. 574; 8 Sup. Ct. 686; Heard v. Heard (Ala.), 61 So. 343; Hays v. Hall, 4 Port. (Ala.) 374, 30 Am. Dec. 530; Commercial Bank v. Pritchard, 126 Cal. 600, 59 Pac. 130; Fitzhugh v. Smith, 62 Ill. 486; Hunter v. Hatch, 45 Ill. 178; Semour v. Freeman, Smith (Ind.) 25; Laughlin v. Braley, 25 Kans. 147; Sibley v. Ross, 88 Mich. 315, 50 N. W. 379; Niggeler v. Maurin, 34 Minn. 118, 24 N. W. 369; Smith v. Lackor, 23 Minn. 454; Hackett v. Watts, 138 Mo. 502, 40 S. W. 113; Burrows v. Hovland, 40 Nebr. 464, 58 N. W. 947; Scharman v. Scharman, 38 Nebr. 39; Malloy v. Malloy, 35 Nebr. 224; Lipp v. South Omaha &c. Syndicate, 24 Nebr. 692; Stoddard v. Whiting, 46 N. Y. 627; Patrono v. Patrono, 127 App. Div. 29, 111 N. Y. S. 268; Titcomb v. Fonda J. &c. R. Co., 38 Misc. 630, 78 N. Y. S. 226; Brockway v. Wells, 1 Paige (N. Y.) 617; Lovejoy v. Chapman, 23 Ore. 571, 32 Pac. 687; Stephens v. Allen, 11 Ore. 188, 3 Pac. 168; Rhines v. Baird, 41 Pa. St. 256; Russell's Appeal, 15 Pa. St. 319; Gilkerson v. Connor, 24 S. Car. 321; Roddy v. Elam, 12 Rich. Eq. (S. Car.) 343; Morris v. Nyswanger, 5 S. Dak. 307, 58 N. W. 800; Bull v. Sykes, 7 Wis. 449; Brayton v. Jones, 5 Wis. 117.

[2] Brockway v. Wells, 1 Paige (N. Y.) 617.

[3] Purdy v. Bullard, 41 Cal. 444; Smith v. Cremer, 71 Ill. 185; Baker v. Bishop Hill Colony, 45 Ill. 264; Newhouse v. Hill, 7 Blackf. (Ind.) 584; Gamble v. Ross, 88 Mich. 315; Sinclair v. Armitage, 12 N. J. Eq. 174; Fessler's Appeal, 75 Pa. St. 483.

[4] Fitzhugh v. Smith, 62 Ill. 486; Meigs v. McFarlan, 72 Mich. 194; Crawford v. Osmun, 70 Mich. 561; Brockway v. Wells, 1 Paige (N. Y.) 617; Lovejoy v. Chapman, 23 Ore. 571.

another that he shall pay the purchase-money and take a deed of the land for his security until repaid, the arrangement amounts to a mortgage of such equitable title.[5] In like manner, if the owner of land-warrants secures a debt by having them entered in the name of his creditor, such entry is a mortgage.[6]

A mortgage made by one who holds only a bond or contract of purchase passes only the title he has in the premises at the time, subject to be enlarged by the mortgagor's acquiring afterward the legal title. Such mortgagor has a mortgageable interest.[7] The mortgage amounts to a qualified assignment of the bond or contract. If the contract and mortgage be executed formally so that they may be recorded, the record is notice to any subsequent purchaser from the vendor of the mortgagee's right to purchase the property under the contract, if the vendee does not perform the condition of the mortgage.[8] The vendor and vendee can not rescind the contract as against such mortgagee after the vendor has actual notice of the mortgage. If a second mortgagee of such an equitable title be obliged for his own protection to pay the purchase-money remaining due upon the bond, his lien for the money so advanced is superior to that of the first mortgagee of such equitable interest.[9]

Whether such an instrument is a mortgage or a contract of purchase and resale depends upon the inquiry whether any indebtedness existed at the time of the execution of the instrument. To make the instrument a mortgage, there must be a debt which the mortgage secures.[10] Therefore a contract made more than twelve months after the sale of property on a foreclosure, whereby one party agreed to advance money to take up the certificate of sale and hold it for his own benefit unless the other parties, the heirs of the mortgagor, should repay the amount advanced within a certain time, is not a mortgage, but a contract to convey.[11]

---

[5] Banks v. Walters, 95 Ark. 501, 130 S. W. 519; Purdy v. Bullard, 41 Cal. 444; Doris v. Story, 122 Ga. 611, 50 S. E. 348; King v. McVickar, 3 Sandf. Ch. (N. Y.) 192; Fessler's Appeal, 75 Pa. St. 483; McClintock v. McClintock, 3 Brewst. (Pa.) 76; Chadwell v. Wheless, 3 Lea (Tenn.) 312.

An executed contract whereby the first party took title to property and the second had an option to purchase and hold it to secure future advances was held to be an equitable mortgage. Tenvoorde v.

Tenvoorde (Minn.), 150 N. W. 396.

[6] Dwen v. Blake, 44 Ill. 135.

[7] Muehlberger v. Schilling, 3 N. Y. S. 705.

[8] Alden v. Garver, 32 Ill. 32; Steinkemeyer v. Gillespie, 82 Ill. 253.

[9] Steinkemeyer v. Gillespie, 82 Ill. 253.

[10] Burgett v. Osborne, 172 Ill. 227, 50 N. E. 206; Carpenter v. Plagge, 192 Ill. 82, 61 N. E. 530.

[11] Carpenter v. Plagge, 192 Ill. 82, 61 N. E. 530.

§ 172a. **Conveyance conditioned upon payment of purchase-price.**
—A deed to a purchaser, stipulating that the fee title shall not rest
in the grantee until the purchase-money is paid,[12] or that the grantee
shall be seized in fee upon payment of a certain sum,[13] or conditioned
to be void upon default in payments, is an equitable mortgage.[14]

§ 173. **Assignment of bond to convey.**—A bond for a conveyance
may be assigned by way of mortgage. If the assignee subsequently
obtains the legal title to the land by virtue of the bond, and surrenders that, he will hold the land subject to the right of his assignor to
redeem.[15] The assignee under such a bond for conveyance succeeds
to all the rights of the purchaser.[16] Such a bond is itself sometimes
declared to be in equity equivalent to a conveyance of the property,
with a mortgage back; so that the assignment of it is equivalent to
the assignment of a mortgage.[17]

When land is sold on credit, and a bond is given to the purchaser to
make title on payment of the purchase-money, the effect of the contract is to create a mortgage, the same as if the vendor had conveyed
the land by an absolute deed to the purchaser, and taken back a
mortgage to secure the payment of the purchase-money. The lien so
created is an incumbrance on the land, not only against the purchaser
and his heirs, but also against all subsequent purchasers.[18] It is said
that bonds for title came into common use through the inability of
the vendor, under the public land system of the United States, to
make title at the time of the sale.

---

[12] Pugh v. Holt, 27 Miss. 461.
[13] Lucas v. Hendrix, 92 Ind. 54.
[14] Carr v. Holbrook, 1 Mo. 240;
Austin v. Donner, 25 Vt. 558. See
post § 268.
[15] Fenno v. Sayre, 3 Ala. 458;
Lewis v. Boskins, 27 Ark. 61;
Christy v. Dana, 34 Cal. 548;
Steinkemeyer v. Gillespie, 82 Ill.
253; Baker v. Bishop Hill Colony,
45 Ill. 264; Alden v. Garver, 32 Ill.
32; Newhouse v. Hill, 7 Blackf.
(Ind.) 584; Laughlin v. Braley, 25
Kans. 147; Jones v. Lapham, 15
Kans. 540; Alderson v. Ames, 6
Md. 52; Sinclair v. Armitage, 12
N. J. Eq. 174; Neligh v. Michenor,
11 N. J. Eq. 539; Gilkerson v. Con-
nor, 24 S. Car. 321; Bull v. Sykes,
7 Wis. 449; Button v. Schroyer, 5
Wis. 598.
[16] Lewis v. Boskins, 27 Ark. 61;

Alden v. Garver, 32 Ill. 32; Baker
v. Bishop Hill Colony, 45 Ill. 264;
Steinkemeyer v. Gillespie, 82 Ill.
253.
[17] Jones v. Lapham, 15 Kans. 540,
per Brewer, J.; Button v. Schroyer,
5 Wis. 598. See also Sposedo v.
Merriman (Maine), 90 Atl. 387.
But see Sheffield v. Hurst, 31 Ky.
L. 890, 104 S. W. 350.
[18] Pintard v. Goodloe, Hemp. (U.
S.) 502; Thredgill v. Pintard, 12
How. (U. S.) 24; Strauss v. White,
66 Ark. 167, 51 S. W. 64; McConnell v. Beattie, 34 Ark. 113; Holman v. Patterson, 29 Ark. 357;
Lewis v. Boskins, 27 Ark. 61; Shall
v. Biscoe, 18 Ark. 142; Moore v.
Anders, 14 Ark. 628, 60 Am. Dec.
551; Smith v. Robinson, 13 Ark.
533; Tanner v. Hicks, 4 Smed. &
M. (Miss.) 294; Graham v. Mc-

§ 174. Purchaser's interest—Improvements.—Although the contract of sale be conditional, it providing that the purchaser shall do certain things before he shall be entitled to the conveyance of the land, the purchaser has an interest, before the performance of the things to be done on his part, which he may assign by way of security. By complying with all the conditions of the contract he acquires an equitable title, and when he has that he may compel a conveyance of the legal title. He may also sell his interest, and by agreement reserve a lien upon the contract to secure his vendee's note for the purchase-price, and, upon the failure of his vendee to pay as agreed, he may, in an action upon the note and to foreclose his lien upon the contract, have judgment upon the note, and a decree of sale of the interest under the contract to satisfy it. There is a sufficient interest in the land to support the action, although it does not amount to a title or estate.[19]

Where one takes possession of land and expends large sums of money upon it in repairs and improvements on the promise of the owner to convey the property to him, the former has an equitable mortgage on the property to the amount of such expenditure, as against the owner's creditors.[20]

§ 175. Assignment of partial interest.—The assignment of a partial interest in a contract of purchase, as security for the payment of a debt, is an equitable mortgage; and the mortgagee may enforce his rights in equity against the assignor and those claiming under him with notice of his rights. The holder of the legal title may be enjoined from making a transfer to any one else of the property covered by the assignment.[21]

§ 176. Assignment of public land certificates.—The assignment of a certificate of purchase of public lands issued by a state or the United States operates as an equitable mortgage, when intended to secure a debt due from the assignor to the assignee.[22] It may be enforced for

Campbell, Meigs (Tenn.) 52, 33 Am. Dec. 126; Paine v. McDowell, 71 Vt. 28, 41 Atl. 1042.

[19] Curtis v. Buckley, 14 Kans. 449.
[20] King v. Thompson, 9 Pet. (U. S.) 204, 13 Pet. (U. S.) 128.
[21] Northup v. Cross, Seld. Notes (N. Y.) 111.
[22] Hill v. Eldred, 49 Cal. 398; Stewart v. McLaughlin, 11 Colo. 458; Dwen v. Blake, 44 Ill. 135;

Combs v. Nelson, 91 Ind. 123; Crumbaugh v. Smock, 1 Blackf. (Ind.) 305; Gunderman v. Gunnison, 39 Mich. 313; Case v. McCabe, 35 Mich. 100; Burrows v. Hovland, 40 Nebr. 264; Malloy v. Malloy, 35 Nebr. 224; Murray v. Walker, 31 N. Y. 399; Stover v. Bounds, 1 Ohio St. 107; Ross v. Mitchell, 28 Tex. 150; Jarvis v. Dutcher, 16 Wis. 307; Dodge v. Silverthorn, 12 Wis. 644;

the debt, and for money paid by the assignee in order to prevent a forfeiture of the title.[23] A clause in a mortgage of a land certificate, empowering the mortgagee to locate, enter upon, enjoy, and dispose of said land, as if acquired by a good and lawful title, only amplifies the security without rendering the conveyance absolute.[24] The mortgage is of course subject to the payment of the amount due upon the certificate.[25] If the purchaser pay this, the amount so paid becomes a prior lien upon the proceeds of a foreclosure sale of the land.[26]

A mortgage made by assigning a contract of purchase, or a land certificate, may be foreclosed by a bill in equity, in which a decree will be made for the sale of the right under the contract.[27]

An assignment of land certificates, such, for instance, as the school land certificates in some states, which are by their terms transferable by assignment and delivery, amounts to an equitable mortgage.[28] A mortgage by a purchaser of school lands before he has completed his three years' occupancy, required by the laws of Texas, has been held a valid lien against a succeeding purchaser after proof of occupancy.[29]

A settler upon public lands under the homestead act, after making proof of compliance with all the requirements of the law, so as to be entitled to a patent, may make a valid mortgage although the patent has not been issued.[30] But if he sell the land to another who obtains the title from the United States, the mortgagee will lose his title.[31]

§ 176a. **Mortgage of stock in unincorporated companies.**—Certificates of stock in an unincorporated joint stock company, representing an interest in real estate, may be mortgaged in equity. The mortgage in such case is of course subject to the debts of the company, and to existing equities in favor of other stockholders.[32]

§ 177. **Mortgage of public lands.**—A pre-emptor of public land can not mortgage his interest before entry. Before a valid mortgage

---

Mowry v. Wood, 12 Wis. 413. See also Wright v. Shumway, 1 Biss. (U. S.) 23; Hays v. Hall, 4 Port. (Ala.) 374, 30 Am. Dec. 530.

[23] Hill v. Eldred, 49 Cal. 398.

[24] Ross v. Mitchell, 28 Tex. 150.

[25] Dodge v. Silverthorn, 12 Wis. 644.

[26] Dodge v. Silverthorn, 12 Wis. 644.

[27] Crumbaugh v. Smock, 1 Blackf. (Ind.) 305.

[28] Mowry v. Wood, 12 Wis. 413; Jarvis v. Dutcher, 16 Wis. 307.

[29] Harwell v. Harbison, 43 Tex. Civ. App. 343, 95 S. W. 30.

[30] Orr v. Stewart, 67 Cal. 275; Klempp v. Northrop, 137 Cal. 414, 70 Pac. 284; Nycum v. McAllister, 33 Iowa 374; Townsend v. Fenton, 30 Minn. 528; Jones v. Yoakum, 5 Nebr. 265; Orr v. Ulyatt, 23 Nev. 134, 43 Pac. 916.

But one mortgaging such land is estopped by his own act from disputing the validity of the lien so created by him. Kirkaldie v. Larrabee, 31 Cal. 455, 89 Am. Dec. 205.

[31] Bull v. Shaw, 48 Cal. 455.

[32] Durkee v. Stringham, 8 Wis. 1.

can be made of a pre-emption of public land, an entry of it according to law must be made. The statutes of the United States provide that any grant or conveyance made before entry shall be void. Even where a mortgage is regarded as neither a grant nor a conveyance, and therefore not within the letter of the statute, it is construed to include a mortgage within its prohibition. The intention of the act was, that the title should be perfect and unincumbered when it passes from the United States by the entry to the settler.[33]

But, on the other hand, there are numerous decisions to the effect that an ordinary mortgage by a pre-emptor of land, prior to the time of making his final proofs, is not a grant or conveyance within the prohibitory clause of the statute.[34] An assignment of a pre-emptor's

---

[33] Sec. 13 of the Act of Congress, September 4, 1841, Rev. Stat. § 2262, provides that, before an entry shall be allowed, the claimant shall make oath that "he has not directly or indirectly made any agreement or contract, in any manner, with any person or persons, whatsoever, by which the title which he might acquire from the government of the United States should inure in whole or in part to the benefit of any person except himself." And it also provides that "any grant or conveyance which he may have made, except in the hands of a bona fide purchaser for valuable consideration, shall be null and void." See also post § 2296; Warren v. Van Brunt, 19 Wall. (U. S.) 646; Moffat v. Bulson, 96 Cal. 106, 30 Pac. 1022; Bull v. Shaw, 48 Cal. 455; Mellison v. Allen, 30 Kans. 382, 2 Pac. 97; Green v. Houston, 22 Kans. 35; Brewster v. Madden, 15 Kans. 249; Penn v. Ott, 12 La. Ann. 233; Woodbury v. Dorman, 15 Minn. 338; McCue v. Smith, 9 Minn. 252, 86 Am. Dec. 100; Bass v. Buker, 6 Mont. 442, 12 Pac. 922; Craig v. Tappin, 2 Sandf. Ch. (N. Y.) 78. See ante § 136.

[34] Norris v. Heald, 12 Mont. 282, 29 Pac. 1121, is the most recent and important decision to this effect. Blake, C. J., reviews the decisions, and cites several decisions of the secretaries of the Department of the Interior holding that the statute does not prohibit mortgages by pre-emptors made in good faith for borrowed money.

Larson v. Weisbecker, 1 Dec. Dep. Int. 422, April 24, 1882, followed in Ray's App., 6 Dec. Dep. Int. 340, October 11, 1887; and Haling v. Eddy, 9 Dec. Dep. Int. 337, September 7, 1889. In the first of these decisions Mr. Teller, the secretary, said: "I am aware that the former rulings of this department, following the precedent of an early decision, have held that an outstanding mortgage given by a pre-emptor upon the lands embraced in his filing defeats his right of entry, upon the ground that such mortgage is a contract or agreement by which title to the lands might inure to some other person than himself. A careful consideration of this section leads me to a different conclusion, and to the opinion that, unless it shall appear, under the rules of law applicable to the construction of contracts, or otherwise, that the title shall inure to another person, it does not debar the right of entry; and that the mere possibility that the title may so result, as in the case of an ordinary mortgage, is not sufficient to forfeit the claim." Norris v. Heald, 12 Mont. 282, 29 Pac. 1121, overrules the earlier decision of the same court to the contrary. Bass v. Buker, 6 Mont. 442, 12 Pac. 922. The good faith of the mortgagor becomes a material consideration in this view of the statute. This is recognized by Chief Justice Blake, who says: "The purpose for which a sum of money may be borrowed becomes material to show that the mort-

certificate of location, by way of security for a debt, is an equitable mortgage of the assignor's interest.[35] If an occupant having a right of pre-emption mortgages his interest for a valuable consideration, and subsequently commutes the same, proves his occupation, pays the purchase-price, and receives a patent of the land, the mortgage is a valid lien upon the property, and the title thus acquired inures to the benefit of the mortgagee.[36] The purpose of the Act of Congress that no government lands acquired as homesteads shall, in any event, become liable to the satisfaction of any debt or contract prior to the issuance of the patent therefor,[37] is to protect the entryman and to prevent any involuntary appropriation of the land to the satisfaction of debts incurred prior to the issuance of the patent; and therefore a mortgage upon government land which had been entered as a homestead and for which final proof had been made, but for which no patent had been issued, is valid.[38] And such a mortgage is valid although given to secure a debt contracted before such proof was made.[39]

§ 178. **Mortgages under act of legislature.**—A mortgage may be constituted by act of legislature,[40] as where a railroad company accepted certain bonds issued under an act which declared that the bonds should "constitute a first lien and mortgage upon the road and

gagor is acting in good faith, and not in collusion with the mortgagee to convey the title, and evade the provisions of the law. The loan of money to enable the settler to buy seed for planting, or the necessaries of life, is as legitimate as the purchase of land from the government." See also Hubbard v. Mulligan, 13 Colo. App. 116, 57 Pac. 738; Wilcox v. John, 21 Colo. 367, 40 Pac. 880; Fuller v. Hunt, 48 Iowa 163; Nycum v. McAllister, 33 Iowa 374; Jones v. Tainter, 15 Minn. 512; Cheney v. White, 5 Nebr. 261, 25 Am. Rep. 487; Jones v. Yoakum, 5 Nebr. 265; Guaranty Sav. Bank v. Bladow, 6 N. Dak. 108, 69 N. W. 41; Larison v. Wilbur, 1 N. Dak. 284, 47 N. W. 381; Paige v. Peters, 70 Wis. 178, 35 N. W. 328.

[35] Wright v. Shimway, 1 Biss. (U. S.) 23; Christy v. Dana, 34 Cal. 548; Stover v. Bounds, 1 Ohio St. 107; Dodge v. Silverthorn, 12 Wis. 644; Orr v. Stewart, 67 Cal. 275, 7 Pac. 693; Kirkaldie v. Larrabee, 31 Cal. 455, 89 Am. Dec. 205.

[36] Whitney v. Buckman, 13 Cal. 536; Fuller v. Hunt, 48 Iowa 163; Nycum v. McAllister, 33 Iowa 374; Newkirk v. Marshall, 35 Kans. 77, 10 Pac. 571; Lang v. Morey, 40 Minn. 396, 42 N. W. 88; Stark v. Duvall, 7 Okla. 213, 54 Pac. 453; Fariss v. Deeming Inv. Co., 5 Okla. 496, 49 Pac. 926; Spies v. Newberg, 71 Wis. 279, 37 N. W. 417.

[37] Rev. Stat. § 2296.

[38] Smart v. Kennedy, 123 Ala. 627, 26 So. 198; McCollum v. Edmonds, 109 Ala. 322, 324, 19 So. 501; Kirkaldie v. Larrabee, 31 Cal. 455; Nycum v. McAllister, 33 Iowa 374; Moore v. McIntosh, 6 Kans. 39; Lang v. Morey, 40 Minn. 396, 42 N. W. 88; Townsend v. Fenton, 30 Minn. 528, 16 N. W. 421; Cheney v. White, 5 Nebr. 261, 25 Am. Rep. 487; Jones v. Yoakum, 5 Nebr. 265; Logue v. Atkeson, 35 Tex. Civ. App. 303, 80 S. W. 137.

[39] Jones v. Yoakum, 5 Nebr. 265.

[40] See Jones on Corporate Bonds and Mortgages, § 39-44.

property" of the company. The word "property" includes all the lands of the company, and any sale made by it is subject to the mortgage.[41]

To constitute a statutory lien it must clearly appear that it was intended that the statute should have this effect.[42] Such a lien may be released by the authority that created it,[43] or another person may be substituted by agreement of parties in place of the original lienholder.[44]

The bonds of a corporation, pledging its real and personal property for the payment of the debt, are treated in equity as a mortgage.[45]

III. *By Deposit of Title Deeds*

§ 179. Deposit of title deeds—Effect generally in England and America.—An equitable mortgage may at common law be created by deposit of the title deeds of a legal or an equitable estate as security for the payment of money. This method of creating a lien upon land is of frequent use in England,[1] and is sometimes

---

[41] Wilson v. Boyce, 92 U. S. 320, 23 L. ed. 608; Whitehead v. Vineyard, 50 Mo. 30.

[42] Cincinnati v. Morgan, 3 Wall. (U. S.) 275; Brunswick &c. R. Co. v. Hughes, 52 Ga. 557.

[43] Murdock v. Woodson, 2 Dill. (U. S.) 188; Woodson v. Murdock, 22 Wall. (U. S.) 351.

[44] Ketchum v. Pacific Railroad, 4 Dill. (U. S.) 78.

[45] White Water Valley Canal Co. v. Vallette, 21 How. (U. S.) 414; Donald v. Hewitt, 33 Ala. 534; Coster v. Bank of Georgia, 24 Ala. 37; Kelly v. Payne, 18 Ala. 371; Mobile &c. P. R. Co. v. Talman, 15 Ala. 472; Coe v. Johnson, 18 Ind. 218; Bank of Kentucky v. Vance, 4 Litt. (Ky.) 169; Abbott v. Godfroy, 1 Mich. 178; Campbell v. Worthington, 6 Vt. 448; Whitworth v. Gaugain, 3 Hare 416;

London Banking Co. v. Ratcliffe, 6 App. Cas. 722.

[1] Ashworth v. Mounsey, 9 Exch. 175; Baynard v. Woolley, 20 Beav. 586; Darke v. Williamson, 25 Beav. 622; Mellor v. Porter, 25 Ch. Div. 158; Hanke v. Vernon, 2 Cox 12; Burgess v. Moxon, 2 Jur. (N. S.) 1059; Meggison v. Foster, 7 Jur. 546; Nat. Bank v. Cherry, L. R. 3 P. C. C. 299; Astbury v. Astbury, 78 L. T. (N. S.) 494; Meux v. Smith, 2 Mont. D. & D. 789; Pain v. Smith, 2 Myl. & K. 417; Lloyd v. Attwood, 3 De G. & J. 614; Casberd v. Ward, 6 Price 411; Lewthwaite v. Clarkson, 2 Y. & Coll. 370; Bozon v. Williams, 3 Y. & J. 150; Pye v. Daubuz, 2 Dick. 759; Richards v. Barrett, 3 Esp. N. P. 102; Russel v. Russel, 1 Bro. C. C. 269; Matthews v. Goodday, 8 Jur. (N. S.) 90, 31 L. J. Ch. 282, 5 L. T.

adopted in the United States,[2] though generally repudiated here,[3] as contrary to the policy of the registration laws and in violation of the statute of frauds.

In England, in the absence of a general system of recording, the

(N. S.) 572, 10 Wkly. Rep. 148; Shaw v. Foster, L. R. 5 H. L. 321, 42 L. J. Ch. 49, 27 L. T. (N. S.) 281, 20 Wkly. Rep. 907; Unity &c. Banking Assn. v. King, 4 Jur. (N. S.) 470; Watson v. Chapman, 18 L. T. (N. S.) 705; Whitebread v. Jordan, 1 Y. & C. 303; Ex parte Bowdaile, 2 Mont. & A. 398; Ex parte Bulteel, 2 Cox 243; Ex parte Coming, 9 Ves. 117; Ex parte Coombe, 4 Madd. 249; Ex parte Crossfield, 3 Ir. Eq. 67; Ex parte Holthausen, L. R. 9 Ch. App. 728; Ex parte Kensington, 2 Ves. & B. 83; Ex parte Hooper, 1 Mer. 1; Ex parte Langston, 17 Ves. 227, 11 Rev. Rep. 66, 34 Eng. Reprint 88; Ex parte Mountford, 14 Ves. 606; Ex parte Skinner, 1 Dea. & Ch. 403; Ex parte Whitebread, 19 Ves. 929; Zimmerman v. Sproat, 26 Ont. L. R. 448.

[2] Mandeville v. Welch, 5 Wheat. (U. S.) 277, 5 L. ed. 87; First Nat. Bank v. Caldwell, 4 Dill. (U. S.) 314; Higgins v. Manson, 126 Cal. 467, 58 Pac. 907; Hall v. McDuff, 24 Maine 311; Carey v. Rawson, 8 Mass. 159; Bullowa v. Orgo, 57 N. J. Eq. 428, 41 Atl. 494; Gale v. Morris, 29 N. J. Eq. 222; Brewer v. Marshall, 19 N. J. Eq. 542, 97 Am. Dec. 679; Griffin v. Griffin, 18 N. J. Eq. 104; Robinson v. Urquhart, 12 N. J. Eq. 523; Hamilton Trust Co. v. Clemes, 163 N. Y. 423, 57 N. E. 614; Rockwell v. Hobby, 2 Sandf. Ch. (N. Y.) 9; Bloom v. Noggle, 4 Ohio St. 45 (dictum that deposit equivalent to an agreement to execute a mortgage); Hackett v. Reynolds, 4 R. I. 512; Hutzler v. Phillips, 26 S. Car. 137, 4 Am. St. 687 (deposit as a bona fide immediate security); Jarvis v. Dutcher, 16 Wis. 307. See post §§ 186, 187. See also Carpenter v. Black Hawk &c. Min. Co., 65 N. Y. 51; Jackson v. Parkhurst, 4 Wend. (N. Y.) 376; Chase v. Peck, 21 N. Y. 581; Jackson v. Dunlap, 1 Johns. Cas. (N. Y.) 114, 1 Am. Dec. 100; Griffin v. Griffin, 18 N. J. Eq. 104 (announcing the rule in New

York); Boyce v. Shiver, 3 S. Car. 528; Welsh v. Usher, 2 Hill Eq. (S. Car.) 170, 29 Am. Dec. 63; Harper v. Barsh, 10 Rich. Eq. (S. Car.) 154; Mowry v. Wood, 12 Wis. 413; Dodge v. Silverthorn, 12 Wis. 644. In Biebinger v. Continental Bank, 99 U. S. 143, the court held that no mortgage was created as no money was loaned and no debt created, but seemed to recognize the doctrine of an equitable mortgage by deposit of title deeds. Compare Williams v. Hill, 19 How. (U. S.) 246.

[3] The doctrine was rejected in the following cases: Lehman v. Collins, 69 Ala. 127; Pierce v. Parrish, 111 Ga. 725, 37 S. E. 79; Davis v. Davis, 88 Ga. 191, 14 S. E. 194 (statutory provision); English v. McElroy, 62 Ga. 413; Tuller v. Leaveton, 143 Iowa 162, 121 N. W. 515, 136 Am. St. 756; In re Snyder, 138 Iowa 553, 114 N. W. 615; Vanmeter v. McFaddin, 8 B. Mon. (Ky.) 435; Gardner v. McClure, 6 Minn. 250; Gothard v. Flynn, 25 Miss. 58; Hackett v. Watts, 138 Mo. 502, 40 S. W. 113; Bloomfield State Bank v. Miller, 55 Nebr. 243, 75 N. W. 569, 70 Am. St. 381, 44 L. R. A. 387; Probasco v. Johnson, 2 Disn. (Ohio) 96; Edwards v. Trumbull, 50 Pa. St. 509; Bowers v. Oyster, 3 Pa. St. 239; Shitz v. Dieffenbach, 3 Pa. St. 233; Spencer v. Haynes, 12 Phila. (Pa.) 454, 34 Leg. Int. (Pa.) 140; Haselden v. Hamer (S. Car.), 81 S. E. 424; Parker v. Carolina Sav. Bank, 53 S. Car. 583, 31 S. E. 673, 69 Am. St. 888; Meador v. Meador, 3 Heisk. (Tenn.) 562; Bicknell v. Bicknell, 31 Vt. 498. See also Sidney v. Stevenson, 11 Phila. (Pa.) 178, 33 Leg. Int. (Pa.) 42; Hutzler v. Phillips, 26 S. Car. 136, 1 S. E. 502, 4 Am. St. 687; Boyce v. Shiver, 3 S. Car. 515; Williams v. Stratton, 10 Sm. & M. (Miss.) 418; Gebensleben's Estate, 3 Lack. Jur. (Pa.) 19; Rickert v. Madeira, 1 Rawle (Pa.) 325. See cases in favor of the doctrine, §§ 183-185.

possession of the title deeds of an estate is evidence of title. A transfer can not be made without them. No one is supposed to have the right to retain them unless he has a legal or equitable claim to the estate they represent. In all transfers of real estate the original deeds go with the property as evidences of title, and their examination by the solicitor of the parties is a prerequisite to every sale. Except in the counties of Middlesex and York, there are no registries where search can be made to ascertain the titles to lands, with the exception of copyhold titles, which are always to be found recorded in the manor courts. The only security which the purchaser has for the validity of his grantor's title is possession of the deeds which establish it. In the United States, however, the reason for this doctrine does not exist. The registry system dispenses with the necessity of any production of title deeds, and supplies all the evidence to protect both vendor and vendee. It furnishes at once a true statement of the present condition of all legal rights to land; and if an original conveyance is ever lost or destroyed, a copy from the record is received as an equivalent.[4]

§ 180. **Doctrine in England criticized.**—The doctrine in England is well established,[5] although it has been received with considerable disapprobation. "Now, since the case of Russell v. Russell," says Kindersley, V. C.,[6] "this is well settled: that supposing A, owing money to B, deposits the title deeds of his estate with B for the purpose of a security, even without any writing, it is a good equitable mortgage; it gives B a lien; and notwithstanding the expressions of regret of Lord Eldon that the law should be so, even in his time, we find him saying he could not disturb it; since that time it has been acted upon over and over again. That doctrine can not now, then, be disturbed."

§ 181. **Effect of deposit—Future advances.**—The legal effect of the deposit is, that the mortgagor contracts that his interest in the land shall be liable for the debt, and that he will make such a mortgage or conveyance as may be necessary to vest that interest in the mortgagee.[7] It binds whatever interest he has in the whole property described in the title deeds. It does not imply that he will make perfect title to the property, but that he will give effect to the interest he has in it at the time, or may acquire afterward during the deposit,

---

[4] Probasco v. Johnson, 2 Disn. (Ohio) 96, 98.

[5] See cases cited in § 179 ante.

[6] Lacon v. Allen, 3 Drew. 579. See also National Bank v. Cherry, L. R. 3 P. C. C. 299; Ex parte Kensington, 2 V. & B. 79; Ex parte Coombe, 1 Rose 268, 17 Vesey Jr. 369, 34 Eng. Reprint 142.

[7] Pryce v. Bury, 2 Drew. 41, per Kindersley, V. C.

by the discharge of an incumbrance upon it, or the like.[8] As a rule the equitable mortgage created covers the whole property comprised in the deeds,[9] including appurtenances and fixtures.[10] One holding title deeds as indemnity against contingent liabilities is not entitled to a formal mortgage before he has paid anything on account of such liability, but is entitled to a memorandum giving the terms of the deposit.[11]

The deposit may be made to cover subsequent advances by a subsequent parol agreement to that effect between the parties, without a return of the deeds and a new deposit of them.[12]

In this respect an equitable mortgage is a broader security than a legal one; for a legal mortgage can not be enlarged in its effect by a subsequent parol agreement that it shall secure further advances; but although the mortgagee holds the title deeds, he is not entitled to say that he holds them as a deposit,[13] unless the parties make an express agreement that they shall be so held.[14]

There must be clear proof that the further advances were made on the faith of the deposit.[15] Such proof may, however, be by parol, even though the deposit was accompanied by a written memorandum.[16]

---

[8] Ex parte Bisdee, 1 Mont. D. & D. 333; In re Baker, 1 M., D. & De G. 333.

[9] Ashton v. Dalton, 2 Colly. 565; Ex parte Bisdee, 1 Mont. D. & D. 333; Chissum v. Dewes, 5 Russ. 29.

[10] Ex parte Barclay, 5 De G. M. & G. 413; Ex parte Price, 2 Mont. D. & D. 518; Williams v. Evans, 23 Beav. 239; Ex parte Astbury, L. R. 4 Ch. 630; Longbottom v. Berry, L. R. 5 Q. B. 123; Meux v. Jacobs, L. R. 7 H. L. 481; Ex parte Moore &c. Banking Co., 14 Ch. Div. 379; Ex parte Tagart, 1 De Gex 531; Ex parte Broadwood, 1 Mont. D. & D. 631; Ex parte Lloyd, 3 D. & C. 765; Mather v. Fraser, 2 K. & J. 536; Waterfall v. Penistone, 6 El. & Bl. 876, 88 E. C. L. 876; Williams v. Evans, 23 Beav. 239 (fixtures included in mortgage created by deposit of lease); Rutter v. Daniel, 30 W. R. 724 (license necessary to use of public house); In re Brien, 11 L. R. Ir. 213 (license). See post § 437.

[11] Sporle v. Whayman, 20 Beav. 607.

[12] Ex parte Hearn, Buck 165; Ex parte Hooper, 19 Ves. Jr. 477; Ex parte Langston, 17 Ves. 227; Ex

parte Nettleship, 2 Mont. D. & D. 124; Ex parte Whitbread, 19 Ves. Jr. 209; Ede v. Knowles, 2 Y. & Coll. 172; Baynard v. Woolley, 20 Beav. 586; Ex parte Kensington, 2 V. & B. 79, 83.

In the latter case Lord Eldon said: "In the cases alluded to I went the length of stating that, where the deposit originally was for a particular purpose, that purpose may be enlarged by a subsequent parol agreement; and this distinction appeared to me to be too thin, that you should not have the benefit of such an agreement unless you added to the terms of that agreement the fact that the deeds were put back into the hands of the owner, and a redelivery of them required; on which fact there is no doubt that the deposit would amount to an equitable lien, within the principle of these cases."

[13] Ex parte Hooper, 9 Ves. 477, 1 Mer. 7.

[14] In re Henry, Ex parte Crossfield, 3 Ir. Eq. 67.

[15] Ex parte Whitbread, 19 Ves. Jr. 209; Kebell v. Philpott, 2 Jur. 739.

[16] Ex parte Nettleship, 2 Mont. D.

If the deposit is accompanied by any written instrument, the terms of the latter must be referred to, to determine the exact nature and effect of the deposit.[17]

§ 182. **What deeds must be deposited.**—It is not necessary that every material deed relating to the property should be deposited;[18] nor is it necessary that they should show a title in the mortgagor by including the deed by which he acquired title.[19] A deposit of title deeds, omitting the conveyance to the mortgagor, has priority over a subsequent deposit of the latter deed alone.[20] Likewise a deposit of deeds by a joint tenant, after partition, omitting the partition deed, does not invalidate the security.[21] It has even been held that a deposit of one of the title deeds was sufficient, where the others were in the hands of the depositor's solicitors.[22] An equitable mortgage of copyhold estates may be created by a mere deposit of the copy of the court roll.[23]

§ 183. **Deposit for preparation of legal mortgage.**—A deposit of title deeds with a solicitor, agent or attorney, for the purpose of preparing a legal mortgage, and with the intention that they shall operate as an equitable security until a legal mortgage is drawn and executed, creates an equitable mortgage.[24] But where the deeds are

& D. 124; Ex parte Kensington, 2 Ves. & B. 79.

[17] Shaw v. Foster, L. R. 5 H. L. Cas. 321.

[19] Ex parte Wetherell, 11 Ves. Jr. 398, 401, 32 Eng. Reprint 1141; Ex parte Arkwright, 3 Mont. D. & De G. 129; Ex parte Chippendale, 1 Deac. 67, 38 E. C. L. 375; Ex parte Farley, 5 Jur. 512; Ex parte Haigh, 11 Ves. Jr. 403, 8 Rev. Rep. 189, 32 Eng. Reprint 1143; Ex parte Pott, 7 Jur. 159; Dixon v. Muckleston, L. R. 8 Ch. 155, 42 L. J. Ch. 210, 27 L. T. (N. S.) 804, 21 Wkly. Rep. 178; Roberts v. Croft, 24 Beav. 223; Rice v. Rice, 2 Drew. 76; Whitebread v. Jordan, 1 Y. & Coll. 303; Lacon v. Allen, 3 Drew. 582, 26 L. J. Ch. 18, 61 Eng. Reprint 1024. In the latter case, Kindersley, V. C., said: "The question is, is it necessary that every title deed should be deposited? Suppose the owner has lost an important deed, could he not deposit the rest? In each case we must judge whether the instruments deposited are material parts of the title; and if they are, it is not necessary to say there are other deeds material, if there is sufficient evidence to show that the deposit was made for the purpose of creating a mortgage."

[19] Roberts v. Croft, 24 Beav. 223, affg. 2 De G. & J. 1.

[20] Roberts v. Croft, 24 Beav. 223, affg. 2 De G. & J. 1.

[21] Ex parte Farley, 1 Mont. D. & D. 683, 10 L. J. (N. S.) Bky. 55, 5 Jur. 512.

[22] Ex parte Chippendale, 2 Mont. & A. 299.

[23] Whitebread v. Jordan, 1 Y. & Coll. 303; Ex parte Warner, 19 Ves. Jr. 202; Lewis v. John, 9 Sim. 366. It would seem that, under the Torrens system, this rule would prevail, and deposit of the official certificate of title would be sufficient.

[24] Edge v. Worthington, 1 Cox Ch. 211, 1 Rev. Rep. 20, 29 Eng. Reprint 1133; Hockley v. Bantock, 1 Russ. 141, 38 Eng. Reprint 55; Keys v.

delivered merely to have a mortgage prepared, with no intention of creating a present lien on the property, no equitable mortgage arises.[25]

"The principle of an equitable mortgage is," said Lord Eldon,[26] "that the deposit of the deeds is evidence of the agreement; but if they are deposited for the express purpose of preparing the security of a legal mortgage, is not that stronger than an implied intention?" Where no written contract or memorandum accompanies the deposit, the presumption that a mortgage was intended, arising from the possession of the deeds, may be rebutted by parol evidence of the circumstances under which the deeds were left, and of the intention of the parties in the matter.[27] Of course a statement in writing of the purpose for which the deposit was made can not be contradicted.[28]

§ 184. What law governs.—The law of the place of contract governs the validity of a mortgage by the deposit of title deeds. When a citizen of a foreign country, by the law of which a lien can not be created in this way, being in England, there makes a deposit of title deeds as security, his contract is governed by the law of England.[29] The deposit of title deeds to a house in Shanghai by London merchants was held to create an equitable mortgage governed by the law of England, though it was not registered according to the law of Shanghai.[30]

§ 185. Doctrine generally rejected in America.—In America the doctrine of a mortgage by deposit of title deeds has been adopted only to a very limited extent. Generally something more is required than

Williams, 2 Jur. 611, 7 L. J. Exch. 59, 3 Y. & C. Exch. 55; Lloyd v. Attwood, 3 De G. & J. 614, 5 Jur. (N. S.) 1322, 29 L. J. Ch. 97, 60 Eng. Ch. 475, 44 Eng. Reprint 1405; Ex parte Bruce, 1 Rose 374; Ex parte Bulteel, 2 Cox 243; Ex parte Hooper, 1 Mer. 7, 19 Ves. 477; Ex parte Wright, 19 Ves. Jr. 255, 34 Eng. Reprint 513. See also Fenwick v. Potts, 8 De G. M. & G. 506.

[25] Ex parte Bulteel, 2 Cox Ch. 243, 2 Rev. Rep. 39, 30 Eng. Reprint 113; Norris v. Wilkinson, 12 Ves. Jr. 192, 33 Eng. Reprint 73; Hutzler v. Phillips, 26 S. Car. 136, 1 S. E. Rep. 502, 4 Am. St. 687.

[26] Ex parte Bruce, 1 Rose 374. See also Ex parte Wright, 19 Ves. 255, 258.

[27] Ex parte Langston, 17 Ves. 227; Lucas v. Dorrien, 1 Moo. 29, 7 Taunt. 278.

[28] Ex parte Coombe, 17 Ves. 369, 34 Eng. Reprint 142; Baynard v. Woolley, 20 Beav. 583.

[29] Ex parte Holthausen, L. R. 9 Ch. App. 722. In Varden Seth San v. Luckeathy, 9 Moo. Ind. App. 303, it was held that where the contract is not made with reference to any particular law, and the law of the place where the land is situated does not forbid, and the general law of the place is English, an equitable mortgage may be created by deposit of title deeds. See also Ex parte Pollard, Mont. & C. 239; Coote v. Jecks, L. R. 13 Eq. 597.

[30] Ex parte Holthausen, L. R. 9 Ch. App. 722.

a mere verbal agreement or understanding that the creditor is to hold them as security or indemnity. To create a lien upon land in this way would be, it is declared, to repeal judicially the statutes of fraud and perjuries, making void sales not evidenced by writing. The doctrine, moreover, is not compatible with the registry system.

The attempts to apply the doctrine have not been very numerous, it being generally understood that it has no application here. The doctrine, therefore, may be considered as generally rejected, so far as it sustains a mortgage upon a verbal or implied promise in connection with the deposit of the deeds.[31]

Even where the deposit of title deeds does not create an equitable mortgage, a court of equity will not prevent enforcement of the lien by compelling the depositee to surrender the deeds to either the depositor or his heirs, before the debt is paid.[32]

§ 186. **Doctrine applied.**—Yet in several cases mortgages created in this way have been sustained,[33] especially where an equity is shown beyond the mere deposit of title deeds.[34] The deposit of a deed, conveying the legal title to an estate as security for the amount of a

---

[31] Lehman v. Collins, 69 Ala. 127; Pierce v. Parrish, 111 Ga. 725, 37 S. E. 79; Davis v. Davis, 88 Ga. 191, 14 S. E. 194; English v. McElroy, 62 Ga. 413; Tuller v. Leaverton, 143 Iowa 162, 121 N. W. 515, 136 Am. St. 756; In re Snyder, 138 Iowa 553, 114 N. W. 615, 19 L. R. A. (N. S.) 206; Vanmeter v. McFaddin, 8 B. Mon. (Ky.) 435; Gardner v. McClure, 6 Minn. 250; Gothard v. Flynn, 25 Miss. 58; Hackett v. Watts, 138 Mo. 502, 40 S. W. 113; Bloomfield State Bank v. Miller, 55 Nebr. 243, 75 N. W. 569, 70 Am. St. 831, 44 L. R. A. 387; Probasco v. Johnson, 2 Disn. (Ohio) 96; Edwards v. Trumbull, 50 Pa. St. 509; Shitz v. Dieffenbach, 3 Pa. St. 233; Bowers v. Oyster, 3 Pa. St. 239; Spencer v. Haynes, 12 Phila. (Pa.) 452; Haselden v. Hamer (S. Car.), 81 S. E. 424; Parker v. Carolina Sav. Bank, 53 S. Car. 583, 31 S. E. 673, 69 Am. St. 888; Meador v. Meador, 3 Heisk. (Tenn.) 562; Bicknell v. Bicknell, 31 Vt. 498. See also Sidney v. Stevenson, 33 Leg. Int. (Pa.) 42; Hutzler v. Phillips, 26 S. Car. 136, 1 S. E. 502, 4 Am. St. 687; Boyce v. Shiver, 3 S. Car. 515; Williams v. Stratton, 10 Sm. & M. (Miss.) 418; Gebensleben's Estate, 3 Lack. Jur. (Pa.) 19; Rickert v. Madeira, 1 Rawle (Pa.) 325. See cases in favor of the doctrine, ante § 183.

[32] Griffin v. Griffin, 18 N. J. Eq. 104; Sidney v. Stevenson, 11 Phila. (Pa.) 178, 33 Leg. Int. (Pa.) 42.

[33] Mandeville v. Welch, 5 Wheat. (U. S.) 277; Higgins v. Manson, 126 Cal. 467, 58 Pac. 907; Carey v. Rawson, 8 Mass. 159; Bullowa v. Orgo, 57 N. J. Eq. 428, 41 Atl. 494; Martin v. Bowen, 51 N. J. Eq. 452; Gale v. Morris, 29 N. J. Eq. 222; Griffin v. Griffin, 18 N. J. Eq. 104; Hamilton Trust Co. v. Clemens, 163 N. Y. 423, 57 N. E. 614; Carpenter v. Black Hawk &c. Co., 65 N. Y. 43; Jackson v. Parkhurst, 4 Wend. (N. Y.) 369; Rockwell v. Hobby, 2 Sandf. Ch. (N. Y.) 9; Hackett v. Reynolds, 4 R. I. 512; Boyce v. Shiver, 3 S. Car. 528; Jarvis v. Dutcher, 16 Wis. 307. See Hutzler v. Phillips, 26 S. Car. 136, 1 S. E. 502, 4 Am. St. 687. See cases cited in ante § 179.

[34] Woodruff v. Adair, 131 Ala. 530, 32 So. 515; First Nat. Bank v. Caldwell, 4 Dill. (U. S.) 314.

mortgage released by the person receiving the deposit, was held to constitute an equitable mortgage, as between the original parties and those subject to their equities.[35] Likewise it has been held that the deposit of title deeds of an equitable or legal estate creates an equitable mortgage, which must be foreclosed in equity to establish the lien.[36] A court of equity in such case will not compel the holder of the deeds to deliver them up until he has received payment of the debt for which they were pledged.[37] On the contrary, it will establish the lien and enforce a sale of the depositor's interest, and the interest of those subject to this equity.[38] A suit in equity is the proper means to establish the lien, and the decree should be for a sale, if the debt be not paid by a given day.[39]

§ 187. **Written memorandum with deposit.**—A written memorandum makes the deposit a mortgage. Even where a deposit of title deeds upon a verbal agreement that they shall be held as security for a debt does not constitute an equitable mortgage, a written agreement to the same effect accompanying the deeds will make the transaction a mortgage, generally in America.[40] As already noticed, such written agreement alone, without the deposit of title deeds, is regarded as an equitable mortgage.

Parol evidence is inadmissible to contradict the purpose of a deposit accompanied by a written memorandum.[41]

A deposit of title deeds accompanied by an agreement for a loan and an advance of the money is an equitable mortgage, and parties thereafter dealing with the debtor with knowledge of the facts, deal at their peril.[42] An equitable mortgage results from the deposit and

---

[35] Hackett v. Reynolds, 4 R. I. 512; Rockwell v. Hobby, 2 Sandf. Ch. (N. Y.) 9; Jackson v. Dunlap, 1 Johns. Cas. (N. Y.) 114; Chase v. Peck, 21 N. Y. 581. The cases cited in support of the doctrine in America are criticized in Bloomfield State Bank v. Miller, 55 Nebr. 243, 75 N. W. 569.

[36] Jarvis v. Dutcher, 16 Wis. 308; Mowry v. Wood, 12 Wis. 413.

[37] See Griffin v. Griffin, 18 N. J. Eq. 104, decided with reference to New York law.

[38] Hackett v. Reynolds, 4 R. I. 512; Jarvis v. Dutcher, 16 Wis. 308.

[39] Jarvis v. Dutcher, 16 Wis. 307.

[40] Higgins v. Manson, 126 Cal. 467, 58 Pac. 907, 77 Am. St. 192; Webb v. Carter, 62 Ga. 415; In re Snyder,

138 Iowa 553, 114 N. W. 615, 19 L. R. A. (N. S.) 206; Carey v. Rawson, 8 Mass. 159; Hackett v. Watts, 138 Mo. 502, 40 S. W. 113; Martin v. Bowen, 51 N. J. Eq. 452, 26 Atl. 823; Luch's Appeal, 44 Pa. St. 519; Edwards v. Trumbull, 50 Pa. St. 509; Rankin v. Mortimere, 7 Watts (Pa.) 372; Spencer v. Haynes, 12 Phila. (Pa.) 452. See also Mallory v. Mallory, 86 Ill. App. 193; First Nat. Bank v. Caldwell, 4 Dill. (U. S.) 314. Contra: Gardner v. McClure, 6 Minn. 250 (deposit with written instrument creates merely a lien, not an equitable mortgage).

[41] Ex parte Coombe, 17 Ves. Jr. 369.

[42] Carpenter v. Black &c. Min. Co., 65 N. Y. 51; Jackson v. Parkhurst,

assignment of land certificates, absolute in form, but intended as security for debts and advances.[43]

§ 188. Remedy under equitable mortgage by deposit of title deeds.

—The remedy under an equitable mortgage created by a deposit of title deeds or other equitable transfer, to cut off the equity of redemption, is by a bill in equity,[44] for foreclosure.[45] An equitable mortgagee may proceed to foreclose an agreement to give a mortgage or a defectively executed mortgage, without first seeking the specific enforcement of the agreement or the reformation of the defective mortgage.[46] But an equitable mortgage created by the defective execution of a legal mortgage can not be foreclosed by advertisement.[47] When, however, a mortgage is created by a conveyance of an equitable estate legal in form, it may be foreclosed in the ordinary way.

When a mortgage is effected by an assignment of an executory contract of purchase, a foreclosure and sale operate only to transfer the debt to the purchaser, who becomes in equity the assignee of the mortgagor's contract, and entitled to the full benefit of it without redemption. Such a mortgage is ineffectual to transfer the legal title, although the mortgagor may have subsequently acquired that. It can only be enforced as an equitable lien.[48]

When necessary for his protection the equitable mortgagee may obtain a decree enjoining the mortgagor from conveying the land to a bona fide purchaser.[49]

Whether an absolute deed was given as an equitable mortgage or not is a question which must be decided by a court of equity. It can not be determined at law, as, for instance, in a petition for partition.[50]

4 Wend. (N. Y.) 369; Rockwell v. Hobby, 2 Sandf. Ch. (N. Y.) 9; Hammond v. Bush, 8 Abb. Prac. (N. Y.) 167; Mowry v. Wood, 12 Wis. 428.

[43] Case v. McCabe, 35 Mich. 100.

[44] Case v. McCabe, 35 Mich. 100; Mowry v. Wood, 12 Wis. 413; Jarvis v. Dutcher, 16 Wis. 307.

[45] Sappington v. Boly, 12 Mo. 567; Stewart v. Hutchinson, 29 How. Pr. (N. Y.) 181; Perry v. Board of Missions, 102 N. Y. 106; Parker v. Housefield, 2 Myl. & K. 419.

[46] Love v. Sierra Nev. &c. Co., 32 Cal. 639, 91 Am. Dec. 602; Cummings v. Jackson, 55 N. J. Eq. 805; Sprague v. Cochran, 144 N. Y. 104. See also Beatty v. Clark, 20 Cal. 11.

[47] Ross v. Worthington, 11 Minn. 438, 88 Am. Dec. 95.

[48] Stewart v. Hutchinson, 29 How. Pr. (N. Y.) 181.

[49] Northrup v. Cross, Seld. Notes (N. Y.) 111; London &c. Banking Co. v. Lewis, 21 Ch. Div. 490; Spiller v. Spiller, 3 Swanst. 556; Hadley v. London Bank, 3 De G. J. & S. 63.

[50] Bailey v. Knapp, 79 Maine 205, 9 Atl. 356.

CHAPTER VI

VENDOR'S LIEN BY CONTRACT OR RESERVATION

§ 189. **Lien by contract not a vendor's lien.**—A lien by contract is not a vendor's lien. The interest of a vendor who has given an ordinary contract or bond for the sale of land, but retains the title to the land in himself, is often spoken of in the cases as a vendor's lien;[1] but it is conceived that this is a misuse of terms, which should be avoided as leading to confusion. There is a fundamental distinction between a vendor's security in such case and the lien implied by law, and properly known as a vendor's lien.[2] When the legal title remains in the vendor, the vendee has merely an equity of redemption in the land, and no act of his can possibly affect the vendor's title; while, in case of a mere lien in the vendor, the fee is in the purchaser, who may at any time discharge the lien by conveying the land to a bona fide

---

[1] See Neel v. Clay, 48 Ala. 252; Hill v. Grigsby, 32 Cal. 55; Stevens v. Chadwick, 10 Kans. 406, 15 Am. Rep. 348; Smith v. Rowland, 13 Kans. 245.
[2] Lowery v. Peterson, 75 Ala. 109;
Bankhead v. Owen, 60 Ala. 457; Baker v. Compton, 52 Tex. 252. See also Good v. Jarrard, 93 S. Car. 229, 76 S. E. 698, 43 L. R. A. (N. S.) 383.

purchaser for value.[3] In the one case the vendor has a lien without any title, and in the other he has the title without any occasion for a lien. His title, by the terms of the contract, is his security; and he can not in any way be divested of his title, except the vendee fulfils his contract, and by that means becomes entitled to a conveyance. The relation of vendor and· vendee in such case bears a strong similitude to that of mortgagee and mortgagor. The vendor, having the title, has a substantial. security; having no title, he has by implication a lien in name, but it exists only in name until a court of equity has given it force by a decree.[4]

The relation between vendor and vendee is in equity substantially that of equitable mortgagee and mortgagor, the vendee holding an equity which is subject to foreclosure by the vendor.[5]

A lien by contract "has none of the odious characteristics of the vendor's equitable lien."[6]

When the vendor retains the legal title, the interest of the purchaser is insecure, unless the contract of purchase be recorded; for the land

[3] Sykes v. Betts, 87 Ala. 537, 6 So. 428; Driver v. Hudspeth, 16 Ala. 348; Hutton v. Moore, 26 Ark. 382; Sparks v. Hess, 15 Cal. 186, per Ch. J. Field; Reese v. Burts, 39 Ga. 565; Hitt v. Pickett, 91 Ky. 644, 12 Ky. L. 51, 11 S. W. 9; Wells v. Smith, 44 Miss. 296; Pitts v. Parker, 44 Miss. 247; Neil v. Rosenthal, 120 App. Div. 810, 105 N. Y. S. 681; Hines v. Perkins, 2 Heisk. (Tenn.) 395; White v. Blakemore, 8 Lea (Tenn.) 49; Ransom v. Brown, 63 Tex. 188; Hale v. Baker, 60 Tex. 217; Shelton v. Jones, 4 Wash. 692, 30 Pac. 1061; Church v. Smith, 39 Wis. 492, per Lyon, J. A purchaser from a vendee is bound to investigate the vendor's title even though the deed to such vendee has not been recorded. Runge v. Gilbrough (Tex. Civ. App.), 87 S. W. 832.

[4] "It is, in short, a right which has no existence until it is established by the decree of a court in the particular case." Per Story, J., in Gilman v. Brown, 1 Mason (U. S.) 191. "His lien is an individual equity, of no force until declared by a court of equity," quoted in Campbell v. Rankin, 28 Ark. 401; Hutton v. Moore, 26 Ark. 382.

[5] Hardin v. Boyd, 113 U. S. 756, 28 L. ed. 1141; Moses v. Johnson, 88 Ala. 517, 7 So. 146, 16 Am. St. 58; Lowery v. Peterson, 75 Ala. 109; Bankhead v. Owen, 60 Ala. 457; Micou v. Ashurst, 55 Ala. 607; Roper v. Cook, 7 Ala. 322; Chapman v. Chunn, 5 Ala. 397; Haley v. Bennett, 5 Port. (Ala.) 470; Richardson v. Wren, 11 Ariz. 395, 95 Pac. 124; Gessner v. Palmateer, 89 Cal. 89, 24 Pac. 608, 13 L. R. A. 187; Sparks v. Hess, 15 Cal. 186; Merritt v. Judd, 14 Cal. 59; Fostoria Gold Min. Co. v. Hazard, 44 Colo. 495, 99 Pac. 758; Wells v. Francis, 7 Colo. 396, 4 Pac. 49; Hutchinson v. Crane, 100 Ill. 269; Wright v. Troutman, 81 Ill. 374; Green v. Cook, 29 Ill. 186; Robinson v. Appleton, 22 Ill. App. 351; Fitzhugh v. Maxwell, 34 Mich. 138; Strickland v. Kirk, 51 Miss. 795; Gaston v. White, 46 Mo. 486; Johnson v. Cochrane, 84 N. Car. 446; Edward v. Thompson, 71 N. Car. 177; Graham v. McCampbell, Meigs (Tenn.) 52, 33 Am. Dec. 126; Baker v. Compton, 52 Tex. 252; St. Paul &c. Lumber Co. v. Bolton, 5 Wash. 763, 32 Pac. 787; Wood v. Mastick, 2 Wash. Ter. 64, 3 Pac. 612; Schriber v. LeClair, 66 Wis. 579, 29 N. W. 570; Church v. Smith, 39 Wis. 495; Button v. Schroyer, 5 Wis. 598.

[6] Per Chief Justice Watkins, in

is subject to sale by the vendor, and subject to levy upon execution by his creditors.[7]

It is just as proper to call a mortgage given for purchase-money a vendor's lien as to call by that name the lien of one who has given a contract to sell, but retains the legal title, or who has reserved a lien in his deed of conveyance. It is often said that a vendor's lien may arise as well before the conveyance as after it.[8] But the same courts which give this name to the lien retained by a vendor, who holds the legal title as security for the performance of the contract of sale, generally proceed to point out the differences between this lien and that which is implied upon a conveyance; and inasmuch as the only likeness between the two liens is in their both securing the purchase-money, it is proposed, in treating of the subject, to confine the term "vendor's lien" to that lien which is in equity implied to belong to a vendor for the unpaid purchase-price of land sold and conveyed by him.

Under a contract for the sale of land which says nothing about a reservation in the deed of the vendor's lien, or about any security being given for the deferred payments of purchase-money, the vendor has the right to insert in his deed a clause reserving such a lien.[9]

§ 190. Legal effect of title bond.—The legal effect of a title bond or agreement for a deed, is sometimes said to be like a deed by the vendor and a mortgage back by the vendee.[10] There can be no sensible distinction between the case of a legal title conveyed to secure the payment of a debt, and a legal title retained to secure payment.[11] The vendor holds the legal title, and all persons must necessarily take notice of it; and although the vendee enter into possession, his deed will of course convey only his equitable title.[12] Like a mortgagor in possession, he has an equity of redemption; while the vendor holds the

Moore v. Anders, 14 Ark. 628, 60 Am. Dec. 551.

[7] Bell v. McDuffie, 71 Ga. 264; Evans v. Ashe, 50 Tex. Civ. App. 54, 108 S. W. 389, 1190; Lacey v. Smith (Tex. Civ. App.), 111 S. W. 965; Diffie v. Thompson (Tex. Civ. App.), 88 S. W. 381.

[8] English v. Russell, 1 Hempst. (U. S.) 35; Hill v. Grigsby, 32 Cal. 55; Amory v. Reilly, 9 Ind. 490; Servis v. Beatty, 32 Miss. 52; Yancey v. Mauck, 15 Grat. (Va.) 300, distinguished in Wright v. Troutman, 81 Ill. 374.

[9] Hatcher v. Hatcher, 1 Rand. (Va.) 53; Findley v. Armstrong, 23 W. Va. 113; Warren v. Branch, 15 W. Va. 21.

[10] Hardin v. Boyd, 113 U. S. 756, 5 Sup. Ct. 771, 28 L. ed. 1141; Wells v. Francis, 7 Colo. 396, 4 Pac. 49; Willman v. Friedman, 3 Idaho 734, 35 Pac. 37. See also Bigler v. Jack, 114 Iowa 667, 87 N. W. 700.

[11] Lowery v. Peterson, 75 Ala. 109; Bankhead v. Owen, 60 Ala. 457.

[12] New York &c. Co. v. Plumer, 96 Pa. St. 99.

title by reservation rather than by grant, as in the case of an ordinary mortgage. The equitable estate of the vendee may be alienated or devised as real estate, and upon his death it will descend to his heirs; while on the other hand, although the vendor holds the legal title, upon his death the securities he has taken for the purchase-money go to his personal representative.[13] Although the vendor's remedy upon the note or contract or bond taken for the purchase-money be barred by the statute of limitations, or by the discharge in bankruptcy of the vendee, the lien upon the land is not affected. As in respect to mortgages, the vendor's lien will in such case be presumed to have been satisfied after the lapse of twenty years, and the continued possession of the vendee;[14] and on the other hand, if the vendor remain in possession, so long as he recognizes the vendee as the equitable owner the statute does not begin to run; and after it does begin to run, the vendee may at any time within the same period redeem the title.[15]

The position of the vendor being regarded substantially as that of a mortgagee, the possession of the vendee is not adverse to the vendor.[16] When after such a contract the vendor pays delinquent taxes upon the land,[17] or, at the request of the vendee, pays for improvements upon the property, which by the terms of the contract the vendee was himself to make before receiving a conveyance, the amount so

[13] Lewis v. Hawkins, 23 Wall. (U. S.) 119, 23 L. ed. 113; Masterson v. Pullen, 62 Ala. 145; Relfe v. Relfe, 34 Ala. 500, 73 Am. Dec. 467; Martin v. O'Bannon, 35 Ark. 62; McConnell v. Beattie, 34 Ark. 113; Schearff v. Dodge, 33 Ark. 340; Holman v. Patterson, 29 Ark. 357; Lewis v. Boskins, 27 Ark. 61; Purdy v. Bullard, 41 Cal. 444; Merritt v. Judd, 14 Cal. 59; Scroggins v. Hoadley, 56 Ga. 165; Smith v. Price, 42 Ill. 399; Greene v. Cook, 29 Ill. 186; Smith v. Moore, 26 Ill. 392; Dukes v. Turner, 44 Iowa 575; Walkenhorst v. Lewis, 24 Kans. 420; Lingan v. Henderson, 1 Bland Ch. (Md.) 236; Schorn v. McWhirter, 8 Baxt. (Tenn.) 201; Schorn v. McWhirter, 6 Baxt. (Tenn.) 311; Cleveland v. Martin, 2 Head (Tenn.) 128; Irvine v. Muse, 10 Heisk. (Tenn.) 477; White v. Blakemore, 8 Lea (Tenn.) 49; Skaggs v. Kelly (Tenn.), 42 S. W. 275; Richards v. Fisher, 8 W. Va. 55; Button v. Schroyer, 5 Wis. 598. In Nebraska, where a vendor has no implied lien for purchase-money, in all cases where he has contracted to convey, but has made no conveyance, he has an equitable lien, as between him and the vendee, and those claiming under such vendee with notice. Birdsall v. Cropsey, 29 Nebr. 672, 44 N. W. 857, 29 Nebr. 679, 45 N. W. 921; Whitehorn v. Cranz, 20 Nebr. 392, 30 N. W. 406; Rhea v. Reynolds, 12 Nebr. 128, 10 N. W. 549; Dorsey v. Hall, 7 Nebr. 460. If a vendee makes payment of any part of the consideration after receiving notice of an adverse equity, to that extent he is not a bona fide purchaser. Savage v. Hazard, 11 Nebr. 323, 9 N. W. 83; Birdsall v. Cropsey, 29 Nebr. 672, 44 N. W. 857, 29 Nebr. 679, 45 N. W. 921; Earle v. Burch, 21 Nebr. 702, 33 N. W. 254.

[14] Lewis v. Hawkins, 23 Wall. (U. S.) 119, 23 L. ed. 113.

[15] Harris v. King, 16 Ark. 122.

[16] Burnett v. Caldwell, 9 Wall. (U. S.) 290, 19 L. ed. 712.

[17] Lillie v. Case, 54 Iowa 177, 6 N. W. 254.

paid becomes a further lien upon the property, which the vendor may enforce by a sale of the vendee's interest under the contract.[18] If the vendor who retains the title also retains possession of the land as security for the purchase-money, he is not liable to the vendee for the rent of the premises.[19]

§ 191. **Security not impaired by holder of contract.**—The holder of the contract can not impair the security. The legal title of the vendor in such case is not affected by any liens created by the person who holds the contract of purchase, as, for instance, a mechanic's lien for labor and materials furnished him;[20] or a conveyance or mortgage by him;[21] or judgment or attachment against him.[22]

Such claims necessarily arise after the lien created by the contract, and must be subject to that lien. The vendee can not possibly do anything to impair that lien, any more than a mortgagor can, after the execution of his mortgage, do anything with his title to impair that security. But if the vendor, after a lien has attached to the interest of the vendee for materials used in the construction of a house upon the premises, takes a reconveyance of the premises, and as a part of the consideration of the reconveyance assumes the lien debt, the lien may be enforced against the whole land.[23]

The right of dower of the widow of the vendee is subordinate to this lien.[24] No homestead right in the property can be acquired by the purchaser as against the lien.[25]

If the vendee sells the property to another, his lien upon the land for the purchase-money is subordinate to the lien of the original vendor; and a surety upon the purchase-notes given by the first vendee has an equity to have the land sold, for the payment of these notes,

[18] Grove v. Miles, 71 Ill. 376, 58 Ill. 338.

[19] Worrel v. Smith, 6 Colo. 141.

[20] Thorpe v. Durbon, 45 Iowa 192; Seitz v. Union Pac. R. R. Co., 16 Kans. 133; Cochran v. Wimberly, 44 Miss. 503. See also Harville v. Lowe, 47 Ga. 214.

[21] Williams v. Cunningham, 52 Ark. 439, 12 S. W. 1072; Beattie v. Dickinson, 39 Ark. 205; Harvill v. Lowe, 47 Ga. 214; Sitz v. Deihl, 55 Mo. 17; Carter v. Sims, 2 Heisk. (Tenn.) 166; Rogers v. Blum, 56 Tex. 1; Wood v. O'Hanlon, 50 Tex. Civ. App. 642, 111 S. W. 178. See

also Tuck v. Calvert, 33 Md. 209; Hadley v. Nash, 69 N. Car. 162.

[22] Tuck v. Calvert, 33 Md. 209; Hadley v. Nash, 69 N. Car. 162; Roberts v. Francis, 2 Heisk. (Tenn.) 127. See also Wooten v. Ballinger, 17 Fla. 289; Jones v. Sackett, 36 Mich. 192; Paris Exch. Bank v. Beard, 49 Tex. 358; Grubbs v. Wysors, 32 Grat. (Va.) 127; Shipe v. Repass, 28 Grat. (Va.) 716; Davis v. Vass, 47 W. Va. 811, 35 S. E. 826.

[23] Adams v. Russell, 85 Ill. 284.

[24] Zeischang v. Helmke (Tex. Civ. App.), 84 S. W. 436; Roush v. Miller, 39 W. Va. 638.

[25] Berry v. Boggess, 62 Tex. 239.

superior to any equity which any claimant under such vendee can have on the land.[26]

After a title bond or a contract of sale has been given for the conveyance of lands upon the payment of the purchase-money, the lands are not subject to sale under execution at law at the suit of one obtaining judgment afterward against the vendor; the lien of the vendee prevails against the lien of the judgment creditor, which can operate only upon the interest of the vendor at the time of its rendition.[27]

§ 192. **Reservation of lien in deed as creating an equitable mortgage.**—An express reservation in a deed of a lien upon the land conveyed creates an equitable mortgage, and when the deed is recorded every one is bound to take notice of the incumbrance.[28] Thus, where land was sold, and for the purchase-money several promissory notes of the purchaser were taken, and these were described in the deed of conveyance, and expressly made a lien upon the land conveyed, a purchaser on execution obtained only an equity of redemption subject to such lien.[29]

To create such a lien there must be something more than a mere recitation that the purchase-money, to a certain amount, remains unpaid; this amount must be expressly charged upon the land conveyed.[30] The lien must be expressly reserved in order to be enforcible against

[26] Beattie v. Dickinson, 39 Ark. 205.

[27] Shinn v. Taylor, 28 Ark. 523; Taylor v. Eckford, 11 Sm. & M. (Miss.) 21; Money v. Dorsey, 7 Sm. & M. (Miss.) 15.

[28] Putnam v. Summerlin, 168 Ala. 390, 53 So. 101; Eichelberger v. Gitt, 104 Pa. St. 64; Exchange &c. Bank v. Bradley, 15 Lea (Tenn.) 279; Webster v. Mann, 56 Tex. 119, 42 Am. Rep. 688; Ufford v. Wells, 52 Tex. 612; Baker v. Compton, 52 Tex. 252; Coles v. Withers, 33 Grat. (Va.) 186. See also Hall v. Mobile &c. R. Co., 58 Ala. 10; McKeown v. Collins, 38 Fla. 276, 21 So. 103; Atlanta Sand &c. Co. v. Haile, 106 Ga. 498, 32 S. E. 606; Hill v. Cole, 84 Ga. 245, 10 S. E. 739; Gordon v. Johnson, 186 Ill. 18, 57 N. E. 790; Davis v. Hamilton, 50 Miss. 213; Stratton v. Gold, 40 Miss. 778; Talbot v. Roe, 171 Mo. 421, 71 S. W. 682; First Nat. Bank v. Edgar, 65 Nebr. 340, 91 N. W. 404; Honaker v. Jones, 102 Tex. 132, 113 S. W. 748; Ufford v.

Wells, 52 Tex. 612; Caldwell v. Fraim, 32 Tex. 310; Smith v. Pate (Tex. Civ. App.), 43 S. W. 312.

[29] Davis v. Hamilton, 50 Miss. 213; Stratton v. Gold, 40 Miss. 778; Stephens v. Mott, 81 Tex. 115, 16 S. W. 731; Caldwell v. Fraim, 32 Tex. 310. Quoted with approval in Hall v. Mobile &c. R. Co., 58 Ala. 10.

[30] Heist v. Baker, 49 Pa. St. 9. There is a broad distinction between the rights of a vendor under an absolute deed with warranty which recites the existence of unpaid purchase-money notes, but retains no express lien in terms for their payment, and his rights under a deed which declares that a lien is reserved for unpaid purchase-money. Under the former, the vendor has parted with title, and has only an implied vendor's lien for purchase-money; under the latter, the superior title remains with the vendor, and the deed is the evidence of an executory contract. Baker v. Compton, 52 Tex. 252, per

subsequent purchasers without notice.[31] A note or bond given for the purchase-money of land conveyed does not create a lien upon it.[32] It does not, though it recites upon its face that it is given for purchase-money of the land, stick to the land. But a reservation of a purchase-money lien in a note given for the land renders the sale executory in the same manner as if the reservation were contained in the deed itself.[33] But a grant of land, "to have and to hold the same under and subject, nevertheless, to the payment" of a certain sum at the decease of the grantee, constitutes a charge upon the land, in whosesoever hands it may be.[34]

Effect should be given to the intention of the vendor to reserve a lien, where he has not expressly done so, provided such intention may be gathered from the language used.[35]

A deed of land "charged with the payment" of certain specified sums creates a lien in the nature of a mortgage, and not in the nature of a vendor's lien.[36] A lien is effectually reserved in a deed which describes the notes given for the purchase-money, and the habendum is "to have and to hold on the payment of the notes herein above stated."[37] No particular words are essential for creating a lien by express reservation. All that is necessary is, that the words used should distinctly convey the idea that the vendor retains a lien on the land. A stipulation that the "land shall be bound for the notes" given for the purchase-money creates an effectual lien.[38]

A purchaser who buys land sold under a decree of court, which on its face reserves a lien for the purchase-money, buys subject to the lien reserved.[39]

Gould, J.; Proetzel v. Rabel, 21 Tex. Civ. App. 559, 54 S. W. 373; Harris v. Shields, 111 Va. 643, 69 S. E. 933.

[31] Neff v. Elder, 84 Ark. 277, 105 S. W. 260, 120 Am. St. 67.

[32] Smith v. High, 85 N. Car. 93; Hoskins v. Wall, 77 N. Car. 249; Ransom v. Brown, 63 Tex. 188; Baker v. Compton, 52 Tex. 252. See also Proetzel v. Rabel, 21 Tex. Civ. App. 559, 54 S. W. 373. But see Briggs v. Planters' Bank, Freeman's Ch. (Miss.) 574; Broom v. Herring, 45 Tex. Civ. App. 653, 101 S. W. 1023.

[33] Lundy v. Pierson, 67 Tex. 233, 2 S. W. 737; McKelvain v. Allen, 58 Tex. 383; New England Loan &c. Co. v. Willis, 19 Tex. Civ. App. 128, 47 S. W. 389; Miller v. Linguist (Tex. Civ. App.), 141 S. W. 170; Buckley v. Runge (Tex. Civ. App.),

136 S. W. 533. A deed retaining a lien and notes executed at the same time as evidence of the debt reserved must be construed as parts of the same contract. Beckham v. Scott (Tex. Civ. App.), 142 S. W. 80.

[34] Eichelberger v. Gitt, 104 Pa. St. 64; Heist v. Baker, 49 Pa. St. 9.

[35] Lipscomb v. Fuqua, 55 Tex. Civ. App. 535, 121 S. W. 193.

[36] Stanhope v. Dodge, 52 Md. 483.

[37] Blaisdell v. Smith, 3 Bradw. (Ill.) 150.

[38] Moore v. Lackey, 53 Miss. 85; Lipscomb v. Fuqua, 55 Tex. Civ. App. 535, 121 S. W. 193; Miller v. Linguist (Tex. Civ. App.), 141 S. W. 170. See also Pugh v. Holt, 27 Miss. 461; Carr v. Holbrooke, 1 Mo. 240.

[39] Ross v. Swan, 7 Lea (Tenn.) 463.

A stipulation in a deed, that the title shall not vest in the grantee until the purchase-money is paid, amounts in equity to a mortgage.[40] So does a deed providing that it shall be absolute on the payment of certain notes, but in default of payment shall be void.[41]

A lien may be reserved for the security of a note for the purchase-money made payable to a third person.[42]

When a deed is executed in compliance with an ordinary agreement for the sale of land, part of the consideration for which is to be paid at the time and part at a future day, and nothing is said about a lien or other security for the future payments, the vendor has a right to insert in his deed a clause reserving a vendor's lien for the unpaid purchase-money.[43]

If upon an absolute sale the possession be expressly reserved to the grantor for one year, the right of possession will vest in the grantee at the end of the year, in the absence of any provision to the contrary, although a part of the purchase-price remains unpaid.[44]

A reservation may be made of the crops to be raised on the granted land, to secure interest on the purchase-money, and such reservation creates a valid lien which may be foreclosed.[45]

§ 193. **Lien reserved, a lien by contract.**—A lien for the purchase-money expressly reserved by a vendor in his deed of conveyance is a lien created by contract, and not by implication of law. It is a contract that the land shall be burdened with the lien until the note is paid. It is really a mortgage. The lien, then, becomes a matter of record when the deed is recorded.[46] It is not waived by the taking

---

[40] Pugh v. Holt, 27 Miss. 461; Lavigne v. Naramore, 52 Vt. 267.

[41] Carr v. Holbrook, 1 Mo. 240.

[42] Mize v. Barnes, 78 Ky. 506.

[43] Findley v. Armstrong, 23 W. Va. 113.

[44] Evans v. Enloe, 64 Wis. 671, 26 N. W. 170.

[45] Darling v. Robbins, 60 Vt. 347, 15 Atl. 177; Baxter v. Bush, 29 Vt. 465, 70 Am. Dec. 429. The interest on interest and attorney's fees may be included in the reservation. Masterson v. Burnett (Tex. Civ. App.), 37 S. W. 987.

[46] Ober v. Gallagher, 93 U. S. 199, 23 L. ed. 829; Armentrout v. Gibbons, 30 Grat. (Va.) 632.

White v. Downs, 40 Tex. 225, per Gray, J. "The vendor's lien, however, properly understood, is not in all respects the same as the express lien often reserved in deeds of conveyance for payment of purchase-money, nor as strict mortgages or deeds of trust for it, nor yet as the security held by a vendor who has only given a bond for the title. These are often confounded with the vendor's lien, because security of the purchase-money is common to all of them. But the vendor's lien arises wholly from inference or implication, which is invisible, and can not be recorded; the others are from express contract, visible to all, and may be recorded. All of the same consequences do not, therefore, necessarily result, as to assignees or holders of the debt secured by the vendor's lien, nor as to purchasers of the land liable to it, as between the original parties and privies, as do often occur in the cases of ex-

of other security, as is the case with an ordinary vendor's lien.[47] Thus the taking of additional security in the form of a trust deed for other lands does not affect the lien reserved.[48] Nor is it waived or impaired by pursuit of the remedy at law.[49] It is governed by the same rules which govern a mortgage. It passes by an assignment of the note secured by it.[50] It is foreclosed as a mortgage; and there is the same right of redemption for a limited period after a foreclosure sale.[51]

"The reservation of the vendor's lien in the deed of conveyance," says Mr. Justice Bradley, of the Supreme Court of the United States,[52] "is equal to a mortgage taken for the purchase-money contemporaneously with the deed, and nothing more. The purchaser has the equity of redemption precisely as if he had received a deed and given a mortgage for the purchase-money." The legal title passes to the purchaser subject to the lien, and the land is subject to attachment and execution as his property, just as an equity of redemption is subject.[53]

The lien differs also from a vendor's lien in that it may secure the performance of any covenant or undertaking agreed upon, instead of a fixed sum payable in money; as, for instance, it may secure an agreement to pay in specific articles.[54]

Upon the sale of leasehold property with certain personal property

---

press lien by contract." See also Bozeman v. Ivey, 49 Ala. 75; Robinson v. Woodson, 33 Ark. 307; Dingley v. Bank of Ventura, 57 Cal. 467; Carpenter v. Mitchell, 54 Ill. 126; Smith v. Rowland, 13 Kans. 245; Moore v. Lackey, 53 Miss. 85; Stratton v. Gold, 40 Miss. 778; Eichelberger v. Gitt, 104 Pa. St. 64; Daniels v. Moses, 12 S. Car. 130; Webster v. Mann, 52 Tex. 416; Peters v. Clements, 46 Tex. 114.

[47] Carpenter v. Mitchell, 54 Ill. 126; Wilcox v. First Nat. Bank, 93 Tex. 322, 55 S. W. 317. See also Bozeman v. Ivey, 49 Ala. 75; Kent v. Williams, 114 Cal. 537, 46 Pac. 462; McCaslin v. State, 44 Ind. 151; Schwarz v. Stein, 29 Md. 112; Strickland v. Summerville, 55 Mo. 164; Nixon v. Knollenberg, 92 Mo. App. 20; Price v. Laure, 49 Tex. 74; Warren v. Branch, 15 W. Va. 21; Dunlap v. Shanklin, 10 W. Va. 662.

[48] Price v. Lauve, 49 Tex. 74.

[49] Branch v. Taylor, 40 Tex. Civ. App. 248, 89 S. W. 813; Howard v. Herman, 9 Tex. Civ. App. 79, 29 S. W. 542; Fayette Land Co. v. Louisville &c. R. Co., 93 Va. 274, 24 S. E. 1016; Kane v. Mann, 93 Va. 239, 24 S. E. 938.

[50] Markoe v. Andras, 67 Ill. 34; Carpenter v. Mitchell, 54 Ill. 126. See also Gordon v. Johnson, 186 Ill. 18, 57 N. E. 790; Reynolds v. Morse, 52 Iowa 155, 2 N. W. 1070; Kimbrough v. Curtis, 50 Miss. 117; Powell v. Powell, 217 Mo. 571, 117 S. W. 1113; Atteberry v. Burnett, 52 Tex. Civ. App. 617, 114 S. W. 159.

[51] Markoe v. Andras, 67 Ill. 34; quoted with approval in Hall v. Mobile &c. R. Co., 58 Ala. 10; and in Dingley v. Bank of Ventura, 57 Cal. 467; Pullen v. Ward, 60 Ark. 90, 28 S. W. 1084.

[52] King v. Young Men's Assn., 1 Woods (U. S.) 386.

[53] Chitwood v. Trimble, 58 Tenn. 78; Gordon v. Rixey, 76 Va. 694.

[54] Harvey v. Kelly, 41 Miss. 490, 93 Am. Dec. 267.

thereon for a gross sum for both, the reservation of a lien in the instrument of transfer is effectual, and will be enforced by a sale of both the real and personal property.[55]

If upon purchase of land part payment be made in the notes of third persons, and the conveyance expressly stipulates that the vendor in no way waives his lien by reason of taking the personal securities, the reservation creates a contract lien in the nature of an equitable mortgage, which may be enforced upon nonpayment of the note.[56]

§ 194. Reservation of lien in deed as creating mortgage.

—Such a reservation may appropriately be said to amount substantially to a mortgage, where by this term is meant simply a lien. Thus, in a case in the Circuit Court of the United States for Tennessee, the court, having said that the vendee stands (substantially) in the same position as if he had executed a mortgage to the vendor for the purchase-money, explained that, of course, while the court assimilated the lien to that of a mortgage, it did not mean the old common-law mortgage, in its technical sense, but the modern signification of that term, as one applied to any lien created by express contract of the parties as a security for a debt. Such a reservation creates an express lien by contract or agreement of the parties; and that is all that is meant by a mortgage in half or more of the states.[57]

The lien is not an equitable mortgage, but is merely treated in equity as a mortgage, and enforced as such.[58] "If not a mortgage, it approximates one more nearly than an ordinary vendor's lien."[59]

§ 195. Personal liability of purchaser accepting a mortgage deed.

—Ordinarily a purchaser under such a deed would not be personally liable for the purchase-money, unless he had by note or some other writing bound himself for its payment. The general rule is that no personal obligation is implied from the giving of a mortgage deed, unless there is an express stipulation or covenant in the deed to that effect, or there be some separate promise in writing to pay the money.[60]

[55] Ruhl v. Ruhl, 24 W. Va. 279. See post § 1071.

[56] Kyle v. Bellenger, 79 Ala. 516.

[57] Kirk v. Williams, 24 Fed. 437. See also Hall v. Mobile &c. R. Co., 58 Ala. 10; Bingley v. Bank of Ventura, 57 Cal. 467; Atlanta Land &c. Co. v. Haile, 106 Ga. 498, 32 S. E. 606; Davis v. Hamilton, 50 Miss. 213; Talbot v. Roe, 171 Mo. 421, 71 S. W. 682; Honaker v. Jones, 102 Tex. 132, 113 S. W. 748; Webster v. Mann, 52 Tex. 416.

[58] Priddy v. Smith, 106 Ark. 79, 152 S. W. 1028, 44 L. R. A. (N. S.) 285; Harris v. Haynie, 37 Ark. 348.

[59] Carpenter v. Mitchell, 54 Ill. 126, 129, per Walker, J.

[60] Dolinski v. First Nat. Bank (Tex. Civ. App), 139 S. W. 1. Where a vendor takes purchase-money notes and reserves a lien in his

In Tennessee, however, it is held that, in an action against the grantee to recover the purchase-money, the fact that he has accepted a deed in which a lien is reserved, is conclusive proof of a promise on his part to pay the money.[61]

As there exists no promise, either express or implied, to the original vendor on the part of a subsequent purchaser with notice, the courts are uniform in holding that, in a proceeding to foreclose the vendor's lien, no personal judgment can be taken against a subsequent vendee.[62]

§ 196. Title imperfect until the debt is paid.

—The vendee's title is imperfect until the debt is paid. When land has been conveyed by a deed, reserving a lien upon it for the purchase-money, the lien is an incumbrance upon it, and an execution sale of it as the property of the vendee should be made as of incumbered property.[63] It has precedence over a prior judgment against the vendee. It is superior to interests subsequently acquired.[64] Thus if the grantee erects buildings on the land, and mortgages both buildings and land, the grantor has a superior lien, and may enforce it against both land and buildings.[65]

The vendee's title is imperfect until this debt is paid, though the debt for the purchase-money be barred by the statute of limitations.[66] Though the vendor can not enforce his lien by suit to recover the money and foreclose the lien, he can assert his superior title to the land as owner. He can not be evicted after he has regained possession.[67] Every one purchasing his title must have notice of the lien reserved. He has notice only of the debt and simple interest, unless more be reserved.[68] This lien is in fact an equitable mortgage. In the case of an implied lien, the courts have generally been unwilling to extend it beyond the security of the vendor, because it might tend to embarrass the vendee's right of disposing of the property by giving

deed and the vendee conveys to another who expressly agrees to pay such notes and the holder of the lien releases such second vendee the first vendee is also released. Mays v. Sanders (Tex. Civ. App.), 36 S. W. 108. See post §§ 748-770.

[61] Kirk v. Williams, 24 Fed. 437.

[62] Teal v. Lewis, 85 Ala. 218, 4 So. 695; Wilson v. Lyon, 51 Ill. 530; Bates v. Childers, 5 N. Mex. 62, 20 Pac. 164; Spence v. Morris (Tex. Civ. App.), 28 S. W. 405.

[63] Robinson v. Appleton, 124 Ill.

276, 15 N. E. 761; Thompson v. Heffner, 11 Bush (Ky.) 353.

[64] Kalteyer v. Mitchell (Tex. Civ. App.), 110 S. W. 462; Colquitt v. Sturm (Tex. Civ. App.), 91 S. W. 872; Flach v. Zanderson (Tex. Civ. App.), 91 S. W. 348.

[65] Parsons v. Hoyt, 24 Iowa 154; Louisville Bldg. Assn. v. Korb, 79 Ky. 190.

[66] Hale v. Baker, 60 Tex. 217.

[67] Hale v. Baker, 60 Tex. 217.

[68] Stricklin v. Cooper, 55 Miss. 624.

countenance to secret liens upon it; but this reason does not apply when the lien is reserved by express contract in the deed.[69]

The effect of a lien expressly reserved can not be controlled by evidence of a verbal agreement that there should be no lien.[70] In Pennsylvania, however, the law upon this subject is exceptional; for it is held that a charge upon land created by the parties to a conveyance is divested by a subsequent sheriff's sale, unless the charge be in the nature of a testamentary provision for the grantor's wife for children, or incapable of valuation, or is expressly created to run with the land.[71] It is declared that the doctrine of equitable liens was never admitted into the jurisprudence of this state. Moreover, the policy of the law is, that judicial sales shall pass property clear of all liens, and the courts have yielded with reluctance to making the exceptions above named. Accordingly, it is held that a recital in a deed that the purchase-money remains unpaid, and is to be paid annually, does not create a lien which a subsequent judicial sale will not divest.[72] Neither does a recital that the deed is made subject to a mortgage held by a person named for a specified sum create such a lien, when there was in fact no mortgage, but a judgment which subsequently expired. It was urged that the deed created a charge upon the land, and that, as this charge appeared upon the face of the title, a subsequent mortgagee had notice of it, and took subject to it. But it was held, inasmuch as this recital did not amount to a condition, and inasmuch as the charge was not within either of the exceptions named, it was divested and destroyed by a sheriff's sale under a subsequent mortgage. The remedy after such sale, if there be any, is upon the fund created by the sale.[73]

§ 197. Obligation of a married woman.

—A married woman is bound by a contract to purchase,[74] or a contract in the nature of a

[69] Stratton v. Gold, 40 Miss. 778; Masterson v. Cohen, 46 Tex. 520; Peters v. Clements, 46 Texas. 114. When a lien is reserved in the deed, failure to record the deed or the destruction of the deed will not affect the vendor's lien. Texarkana Nat. Bank v. Daniel (Tex. Civ. App.), 31 S. W. 704. See also De Steaguer v. Pittman, 54 Tex. Civ. App. 316, 117 S. W. 481.

[70] Hutchinson v. Patrick, 22 Tex. 318.

[71] Strauss's Appeal, 49 Pa. St. 353; Hiester v. Green, 48 Pa. St. 96, 86 Am. Dec. 569; Stewartson v. Watts, 8 Watts (Pa.) 392; Bear v. Whisler, 7 Watts (Pa.) 144.

[72] Hiester v. Green, 48 Pa. St. 96, 86 Am. Dec. 569.

[73] Pierce v. Gardner, 83 Pa. St. 211.

[74] In North Carolina, when entered into according to requirements of statute. Johnston v. Cochrane, 84 N. Car. 446. See also Sarver v. Clarkson, 156 Ind. 316, 59 N. E. 933; Grimes v. Grimes, 141 Ind. 480, 40 N. E. 912; Whetstone v. Baker, 140 Ind. 213, 39 N. E. 868.

mortgage for purchase-money of land conveyed to her, and created by the vendor's reserving in the deed to her a lien upon the land for the security of her note given for such purchase-money.[75]

The right to subject the lien to the payment of the purchase-money arises not from the note, but from the deed; the reason for the rule being that, having accepted the vendor's title to the land, she is estopped from denying him the right to subject the same to the payment of the purchase-money.[76] Her mortgage for purchase-money, although invalid by reason of her husband not joining in its execution, has been regarded as a declaration preserving a vendor's lien, or as a declaration of a trust in favor of the vendor.[77] Even where the note of a married woman imposes no personal obligation upon her, she can be put to her election under a sale to her by title bond either to pay her note for the purchase-money, or to surrender the land and all claim to it.[78]

§ 198. **Waiver of the lien.**—A lien reserved by contract, or existing in the vendor by reason of his not having parted with the legal title, having given only a bond or contract of sale, is of course not lost nor waived as an implied lien is waived by accepting other securities.[79] Neither does a change of notes, nor the substitution of the

---

[75] Bedford v. Burton, 106 U. S. 338, 1 Sup. Ct. 98, 27 L. ed. 112; Chilton v. Braiden, 2 Blackf. (U. S.) 458, 17 L. ed. 304; Carpenter v. Mitchell, 54 Ill. 126; Weller v. Monroe, 21 Ky. L. 1705, 55 S. W. 1078; Jackson v. Rutledge, 3 Lea (Tenn.) 626, 31 Am. Rep. 655; Weinberg v. Rempe, 15 W. Va. 829; Radford v. Carwile, 13 W. Va. 572.

[76] Chilton v. Lyons, 2 Blackf. (U. S.) 458, 17 L. ed. 304; Perry v. Roberts, 30 Ind. 244, 95 Am. Dec. 689; Bybee v. Smith, 88 Ky. 648, 11 S. W. 722; Weller v. Monroe, 21 Ky. L. 1705, 55 S. W. 1078; Adams v. Feeder, 19 Ky. L. 581, 41 S. W. 275; Johnson v. Jones, 51 Miss. 860; Cashman v. Henry, 75 N. Y. 103, 31 Am. Rep. 437; Kent v. Gerhard, 12 R. I. 92, 34 Am. Rep. 612; Jackson v. Rutledge, 3 Lea (Tenn.) 626, 31 Am. Rep. 655.

[77] Morrison v. Brown, 83 Ill. 562.

[78] Hendrick v. Foote, 57 Miss. 117; Johnson v. Jones, 51 Miss. 860; Willingham v. Leake, 7 Baxt. (Tenn.) 453.

[79] Spears v. Taylor, 149 Ala. 180,

42 So. 1016; Bozeman v. Ivey, 49 Ala. 75; Huffman v. Cauble, 86 Ind. 591; McCaslin v. State, 44 Ind. 151; Bradley v. Curtis, 79 Ky. 327, 2 Ky. L. 329; Lewis v. Pusey, 8 Bush (Ky.) 615; Lusk v. Hopper, 3 Bush (Ky.) 179, 185; Hurley v. Hollyday, 35 Md. 469; Schwarz v. Stein, 29 Md. 112; Magruder v. Peter, 11 Gill & J. (Md.) 217; Strickland v. Summerville, 55 Mo. 164; Adams v. Cowherd, 30 Mo. 458; Whitehurst v. Yandall, 7 Baxt. (Tenn.) 228; Sehorn v. McWhirter, 6 Baxt. (Tenn.) 313; Fogg v. Rogers, 2 Coldw. (Tenn.) 290; Hines v. Perkins, 2 Heisk. (Tenn.) 395; Price v. Lauve, 49 Tex. 74; Knisely v. Williams, 3 Grat. (Va.) 265, 46 Am. Dec. 193; Hatcher v. Hatcher, 1 Rand. (Va.) 53; Dunlap v. Shanklin, 10 W. Va. 662. To the contrary, not good law: Hawkins v. Thurman, 1 Idaho 598. See also Spears v. Taylor, 149 Ala. 180, 42 So. 1016; Acree v. Stone 142 Ala. 156, 37 So. 934; Elswick v. Matney, 132 Ky. 294, 116 S. W. 718, 136 Am. St. 180; Rhodes v. Arthur, 19 Okla. 520, 92 Pac. 244.

notes of another person,[80] as for instance those of a subsequent purchaser, nor the reducing the notes to judgment, affect the lien;[81] nor does the taking of new notes by an assignee in his own name, and extending the time of payment.[82] Where the waiver has been obtained by any kind of fraud its priority may be asserted.[83] It is not waived by taking under duress depreciated currency in payment of the debt.[84] It is not waived by a judgment and sale upon execution of the interest of the vendee in the land.[85] The burden of proof is upon the vendee to show a waiver;[86] and so long as the debt exists the lien will not be presumed to have been waived except upon clear and convincing testimony.[87]

The vendor who has an express lien may by his acts or declarations waive it, as, for instance, by inducing another to buy the property as unincumbered; or by permitting and encouraging the administrator

[80] Hitt v. Pickett, 91 Ky. 644, 12 Ky. L. 51, 11 S. W. 9; Hill v. Downs, 9 Ky. L. 767, 6 S. W. 650. Where a vendor takes the note of a third person for a part of the purchase-price of her land and renews the note and collects the interest thereon for many years, he may thereby waive his vendor's lien. Spence v. Palmer, 115 Mo. App. 76, 90 S. W. 749. See also Spears v. Taylor, 149 Ala. 180, 42 So. 1016; Acree v. Stone, 142 Ala. 156, 37 So. 934; Hood v. Hammond, 128 Ala. 569, 30 So. 540, 86 Am. St. 159; Scott v. Edgar, 159 Ind. 38, 63 N. E. 452.

[81] Woodward v. Echols, 58 Ala. 665; Bozeman v. Ivey, 49 Ala. 75; Bradford v. Harper, 25 Ala. 337; Chitwood v. Trimble, 58 Tenn. 78; Coles v. Withers, 33 Grat. (Va.) 186. See also Branch v. Taylor, 40 Tex. Civ. App. 248, 89 S. W. 813; Howard v. Herman, 9 Tex. Civ. App. 79, 29 S. W. 542; Fayette Land Co. v. Louisville &c. R. Co., 93 Va. 274, 24 S. E. 1016; Kane v. Mann, 93 Va. 239, 24 S. E. 938. Where the grantee assigns notes to the grantor for the land purchased, the lien reserved in the deed only secures the liability of the grantee as assignor of the notes and his release from such liability will release the lien. Pritchett v. Hape, 21 Ky. L. 408, 51 S. W. 608.

[82] Conner v. Banks, 18 Ala. 42, 52 Am. Dec. 209.

[83] Hooper v. Central Trust Co., 81 Md. 559, 32 Atl. 505, 29 L. R. A. 262.

[84] Luddington v. Gabbert, 5 W. Va. 330. The vendor was compelled in this case to receive Confederate treasury notes during the rebellion. Where an express waiver is pleaded to a suit to foreclose a reserved lien, a reply denying an agreed waiver and alleging the taking of security on land purporting to be owned by the defendant as additional security, and averring fraudulent representations to induce the taking of such security, raises the issue of waiver or nonwaiver and is good. Wittliff v. Biscol (Tex. Civ. App.), 128 S. W. 1153. See also Jones v. Byrne, 149 Fed. 457.

[85] Carter County Court v. Butler, 81 Ky. 597, 5 Ky. L. 661; Dickason v. Eby, 73 Mo. 133, per Norton, J.; Lewis v. Chapman, 59 Mo. 371.

[86] Spears v. Taylor, 149 Ala. 180, 42 So. 1016; Tillar v. Clayton, 75 Ark. 446, 88 S. W. 972; Stiekle v. High Standard Steel Co., 78 N. J. Eq. 549, 80 Atl. 500, 78 N. J. Eq. 578, 80 Atl. 503; Sehorn v. McWhirter, 8 Baxt. (Tenn.) 201; Whitehurst v. Yandall, 7 Baxt. (Tenn.) 228; Sehorn v. McWhirter, 6 Baxt. (Tenn.) 311; Springman v. Hawkins, 52 Tex. Civ. App. 249, 113 S. W. 966. See also Dowling v. McCall, 124 Ala. 633, 26 So. 959.

[87] Selna v. Selna, 125 Cal. 357, 58 Pac. 16, 73 Am. St. 47.

of the vendee to sell the property to satisfy the lien, and bidding at the sale. Such bidding at the sale could properly be interpreted by the purchaser as a waiver of the lien, and as an acknowledgment that the vendor was looking solely to the proceeds of the sale, and not to the land itself, for the satisfaction of his claim.[88]

The taking of other security is not a waiver of vendor's lien reserved, as is the case with an implied lien, unless it be shown by direct evidence, or by the circumstances of the case, that the vendor relied wholly on such other security.[89]

The vendor remaining clothed with the legal title, it is presumed that he retained it as an absolute security for the purchase-money, and a waiver or abandonment of the lien can hardly be shown.[90] A bond with personal security, taken for the purchase-money, does not imply a waiver of the lien under a contract for sale which makes no provision about the reservation of a lien. It may be shown, however, by direct evidence, or by the circumstances of the case, that the vendor relied only on the bond and security, and in that case he would be required to execute a deed without reserving a vendor's lien.[91] A lien reserved in the deed of sale is not lost by the recovery of a judgment for the debt, and the issuing of an execution thereon. But a sale under the execution releases the lien.[92] This lien is equivalent to a mortgage, and, as in the case with a mortgage, a judgment does not affect the lien. It is discharged only by payment, or an express release.[93] A sale by the vendee to one who purchases with notice does not affect the vendor's rights.[94] If the lien is reserved in the deed, or the vendor retains the title, the purchaser necessarily has notice.[95]

If a note be taken for the amount of the lien, and remedy upon the

---

[88] Butler v. Williams, 5 Heisk. (Tenn.) 241; Drumm Com. Co. v. Core, 47 Tex. Civ. App. 216, 105 S. W. 843. A vendor who has reserved a lien may release a part of the land from the lien by his express act, but where he does so he has a lien on the remaining land for the whole debt. Smith v. Owen, 49 Tex. Civ. App. 51, 107 S. W. 929.

[89] Daniels v. Moses, 12 S. Car. 130; Byrns v. Woodward, 10 Lea (Tenn.) 444; Hodges v. Roberts, 74 Tex. 517, 12 S. W. 222; Frazier v. Hendren, 80 Va. 265; Warren v. Branch, 15 W. Va. 21.

[90] Robinson v. Appleton, 124 Ill.

276, 15 N. E. 761; Şehorn v. Mc-Whirter, 8 Baxt. (Tenn.) 201; Rogers v. Blum, 56 Tex. 1.

[91] Warren v. Branch, 15 W. Va. 21.

[92] Woods v. Ellis, 85 Va. 471, 7 S. E. 852.

[93] Stephens v. Greene County Iron Co., 11 Heisk. (Tenn.) 71; Mulherin v. Hill, 5 Heisk. (Tenn.) 58; Hines v. Perkins, 2 Heisk. (Tenn.) 395; Exchange &c. Bank v. Bradley, 15 Lea (Tenn.) 279; Byrns v. Woodward, 10 Lea (Tenn.) 444.

[94] Stone Cattle &c. Co. v. Boon, 73 Tex. 548, 11 S. W. 544.

[95] Hitt v. Pickett, 91 Ky. 644, 12 Ky. L. 51, 11 S. W. 9.

note be lost by negligence, the reserved lien may still be enforced as securing the debt represented by the note.[96]

A lien reserved is not waived by subsequently taking a mortgage of the same property; and though the property without the knowledge of the grantor has in the meantime been mortgaged to another person, without anything having been done by the grantor to induce the taking of such mortgage, the grantor may have the property sold to enforce his lien; or, if he has foreclosed his mortgage, he may have the property resold under his lien for the benefit of the purchaser under the foreclosure sale.[97]

§ 199. **Order of liability of parcels sold.**—Purchasers of land, subject to a lien by contract for the payment of purchase-money, have the same equities as between themselves as purchasers subject to a formal mortgage. The rule of contribution in the inverse order of sale applies where the same rule applies in the case of mortgages. Simultaneous purchasers should contribute pro rata.[98] And, as in the case of mortgages, the vendor, in making sale of the land to enforce his lien, should first sell the lot last sold by the vendee, and so on in the inverse order until satisfaction is obtained.[99] While subpurchasers take subject to the lien of the original vendor, they may require him to exhaust the portion remaining in the hands of the vendee.[1]

If the vendee sells a portion of the land to various subpurchasers, and retains a portion himself, this should be first subjected to the lien; and if the vendor releases this portion, and it is of sufficient value to pay the whole amount of the lien, he can not subject any part of the land conveyed to subpurchasers to the lien. The value of the part released is to be estimated as of the date of the release, without regard to the increase of the value of this portion after the purchase, or after the decree of sale to enforce the lien.[2]

[96] Hodges v. Roberts, 74 Tex. 517, 12 S. W. 222.

[97] Bradford v. Howe, 11 Ky. L. 10, 11 S. W. 466. Failure of a vendor to reserve his lien in a mortgage taken by him will not waive the lien. The lien is merely merged in the mortgage. Bradbury v. Donnell, 136 Mo. App. 676, 119 S. W. 21.

[98] Dukes v. Turner, 44 Iowa 575; Wilkes v. Smith, 4 Heisk. (Tenn.) 86.

[99] Alabama v. Stanton, 5 Lea (Tenn.) 423; John M. Bonner Memorial Home v. Collin County Nat. Bank, 57 Tex. Civ. App. 313, 122 S. W. 430; Watson v. Vansickle (Tex. Civ. App.), 114 S. W. 1160; Whitten v. Saunders, 75 Va. 563. See also Diamond Flint Glass Co. v. Boyd, 30 Ind. App. 485, 66 N. E. 479.

[1] Burton v. Henry, 90 Ala. 281, 7 S. E. 925.

[2] Boyce v. Stanton, 15 Lea (Tenn.) 346; Watson v. Vansickle (Tex. Civ. App.), 114 S. W. 1160; modified Vansickle v. Watson, 103 Tex. 37, 123 S. W. 112.

§ 200. **Account of** vendor in possession.—When a vendor, after giving a bond or contract of sale, remains in possession, and there is delay in making the conveyance beyond the time set for it, the vendee should be credited with a share of the rents and profits received from the use and enjoyment of the property, proportioned to the amount he may have paid on his purchase.[3]

As a general rule, where the vendor of land in an executory contract wrongfully keeps the vendee out of possession, the latter is entitled to recover damages for the withholding of the premises from him, or for use and occupation for the time he is so kept out of possession.[4] Such damages will generally be measured by the amount of rents and profits accrued during the time possession is retained by the vendor.[5]

§ 201. **Assignment of purchase-money note or bond.**—An assignee of a note or bond given for purchase-money by one who has taken a contract of sale, or who has taken a conveyance in which a lien upon the land is expressly reserved, like the assignee of a note secured by mortgage, is entitled to the benefit of the security, and may enforce specific performance of the contract of sale, or may enforce the lien reserved.[6]

[3] Grove v. Miles, 71 Ill. 376.
[4] Covell v. Cole, 16 Mich. 223; Abrahamson v. Lamberson, 68 Minn. 454, 71 N. W. 676; Bostwick v. Beach, 103 N. Y. 414, 9 N. E. 41.
[5] Shawhan v. Long, 26 Iowa 488, 96 Am. Dec. 164; Parsons v. Lunsford, 21 Ky. L. 1536, 55 S. W. 885; Gilmore v. Hunt, 66 Pa. St. 321.
[6] Ober v. Gallagher, 93 U. S. 199, 23 L. ed. 829; Lowery v. Peterson, 75 Ala. 103; Wolffe v. Nall, 62 Ala. 24; Hall v. Mobile &c. R. Co., 58 Ala. 10; Roper v. Day, 48 Ala. 509; Wells v. Morrow, 38 Ala. 125; Kelly v. Payne, 18 Ala. 371; Roper v. McCook, 7 Ala. 318; Hall v. Click, 5 Ala. 363, 39 Am. Dec. 327; Talieferro v. Barnett, 37 Ark. 511; McConnell v. Beattie, 34 Ark. 113; overruling Sheppard v. Thomas, 26 Ark. 617; Campbell v. Rankin, 28 Ark. 401; Moore v. Anders, 14 Ark. 628, 60 Am. Dec. 551; Gordon v. Johnson, 186 Ill. 18, 57 N. E. 790; Steinkemeyer v. Gillespie, 82 Ill. 253; Wright v. Troutman, 81 Ill. 374; Markoe v. Andras, 67 Ill. 34; Carpenter v. Mitchell, 54 Ill. 126; Blaisdell v. Smith, 3 Bradw. (Ill.) 150;
Walkenhorst v. Lewis, 24 Kans. 420; Stevens v. Chadwick, 10 Kans. 406, 15 Am. Rep. 348; Bradley v. Curtis, 79 Ky. 327, 2 Ky. L. 329; Duncan v. Louisville, 13 Bush (Ky.) 378, 26 Am. Rep. 201; Forwood v. Dehoney, 5 Bush (Ky.) 174; Lusk v. Hopper, 3 Bush (Ky.) 179; Hobson v. Edwards, 57 Miss. 128; Hendrick v. Foote, 57 Miss. 117; Moore v. Lackey, 53 Miss. 85; Kimbrough v. Curtis, 50 Miss. 117; Robinson v. Harbour, 42 Miss. 795, 97 Am. Dec. 501, 2 Am. Rep. 671; Stratton v. Gold, 40 Miss. 778; Terry v. George, 37 Miss. 539; Tanner v. Hicks, 4 Sm. & M. (Miss.) 294; Dollahite v. Orme, 2 Sm. & M. (Miss.) 590; Carter v. Leonard, 65 Nebr. 670, 91 N. W. 574; Walker v. Kee, 16 S. Car. 76; McClintic v. Wise, 25 Grat. (Va.) 448, 18 Am. Rep. 694. See also Stephens v. Anthony, 37 Ark. 571; Talieferro v. Barnett, 37 Ark. 511; Martin v. O'Bannon, 35 Ark. 62; Richardson v. Hamlett, 33 Ark. 237; Rogers v. James, 33 Ark. 77; Shall v. Biscoe, 18 Ark. 142; Felton v. Smith, 84 Ind. 485; Reynolds v. Morse, 52 Iowa 155, 2 N. W. 1070; Bills v. Mason, 42

The lien is regarded as incident to the debt,[7] and passes to the assignee whether the title has passed or not.[8]

If a vendor who retains the legal title for his security assigns the notes taken for the purchase-money, he then holds the legal title as trustee for the holder of the notes, and he can not properly do anything to defeat the rights of such holder. If, regardless of the trust, he conveys the land to a stranger, who purchases in good faith, the vendor then becomes a trustee of the purchase-money which he has realized, for the benefit of the holder of the notes he assigned.[9] The assignment of a note which upon its face shows that it was given in consideration of the purchase-money of land, or expressly reserves a lien upon it, passes the lien to the assignee, who may enforce it.[10] Though there

---

Iowa 329; Rakestraw v. Hamilton, 14 Iowa 147; Blair v. Marsh, 8 Iowa 144; Powell v. Powell, 217 Mo. 571, 117 S. W. 1113; Adams v. Cowherd, 30 Mo. 458; Hadley v. Nash, 69 N. Car. 162; Burkhart v. Howard, 14 Ore. 39, 12 Pac. 79; Cleveland v. Martin, 2 Head (Tenn.) 128; Tharpe v. Dunlap, 4 Heisk. (Tenn.) 674; Osborne v. Royer, 1 Lea (Tenn.) 217; McCamly v. Waterhouse, 80 Tex. 340, 16 S. W. 19; Atteberry v. Burnett, 52 Tex. Civ. App. 617, 114 S. W. 159; Shelton v. Jones, 4 Wash. 692, 30 Pac. 1061.

The cases seem to be uniform upon this point, with the exception of those in Ohio.

By statute in Arkansas, Dig. of Stats. 1904, § 510, the lien, when reserved in the deed, is made assignable by a transfer of the note or other obligation for the debt, provided the lien is expressed upon the face of the deed of conveyance. See also Campbell v. Rankin, 28 Ark. 401, 407.

In California and Idaho it is provided that where a buyer of real property gives to the seller a written contract for the payment of all or part of the price, an absolute transfer of such contract by the seller waives his lien to the extent of the sum payable under the contract; but a transfer of such contract in trust to pay debts, and return the surplus, is not a waiver of the lien.

Cal. Civ. Code 1906, § 3047; Idaho Rev. Code 1908, § 3442.

[7] Lowery v. Peterson, 75 Ala. 109; State Bank v. Brown, 142 Iowa 190, 119 N. W. 81, 134 Am. St. 412; Chitwood v. Trimble, 2 Baxt. (Tenn.) 78. His lien is prior to a subsequent attachment levied on a judgment against his assignor. Hamilton-Brown Shoe Co. v. Lewis, 7 Tex. Civ. App. 509, 28 S. W. 101.

In Georgia it was held under a former statute, that if a note for the purchase-money be transferred without indorsement or guaranty, the purchaser's equity became complete as against the vendor, and the land was subject to levy and sales as his property. Hunt v. Harbor, 80 Ga. 746, 6 S. E. 596; Carhart v. Reviere, 78 Ga. 173, 1 S. E. 222; Neal v. Murphey, 60 Ga. 388; McGregor v. Matthis, 32 Ga. 417.

[8] State Bank v. Brown, 142 Iowa 190, 119 N. W. 81, 134 Am. St. 412.

[9] Conner v. Banks, 18 Ala. 42, 52 Am. Dec. 209; Cummings v. Oglesby, 50 Miss. 153; Pitts v. Parker, 44 Miss. 247; Skaggs v. Nelson, 25 Miss. 88; Parker v. Kelly, 10 Sm. & M. (Miss.) 184; Atteberry v. Burnett, 52 Tex. Civ. App. 617, 114 S. W. 159. The assignee of notes secured by a reserved lien, may under a plea of not guilty prove that the notes have not been paid and thereby defeat a suit by the original vendee for possession. Polk v. Kyser, 21 Tex. Civ. App. 676, 53 S. W. 87.

[10] Aycock Bros. Lumber Co. v. First Nat. Bank, 54 Fla. 604, 45 So. 501; Bailey v. Smock, 61 Mo. 213; Osborne v. Royer, 1 Lea (Tenn.)

has been a partial failure of the consideration for the assignment, the assignor can not subsequently seek to enforce the lien before such assignment has been declared void.[11]

One who takes title from the vendor, with knowledge of an outstanding note for the purchase-money previously assigned by the vendor, takes subject to the lien of such note,[12] unless the note was transferred after maturity, or in such manner that it is subject in the hands of the holder to all equities the maker may have against it.[13] As against his assignee, the vendor can not be heard to dispute his own title to the land, or to aver that he has not an estate coextensive with that he has contracted to convey.[14]

§ 202. Order of payment of several notes.—Where several notes are given for the purchase-price, the assignment of any number less than the whole carries with it so much of the lien as is necessary for their protection.[15] In case there are several notes or bonds secured in this way, the same equitable rule is applied as to the order of payment of such notes or bonds that is applied when they are secured by a formal mortgage or trust deed; that which was first assigned carries so much of the lien as is necessary to pay it, unless there be an express agreement otherwise,[16] or some equity in favor of the vendor.[17]

Such assignee, moreover, is entitled to all the remedies of the vendor to enforce the lien; and the latter can not, by any act of his, deprive the assignee of these remedies.[18]

217; Murray v. Able, 19 Tex. 213, 70 Am. Dec. 330.

[11] Green v. Betts, 1 McCrary (U. S.) 72, 1 Fed. 289.

[12] Young v. Atkins, 4 Heisk. (Tenn.) 529; Houghton v. Rogan, 17 Tex. Civ. App. 285, 42 S. W. 1018.

[13] Shinn v. Fredericks, 56 Ill. 439.

[14] Lowery v. Peterson, 75 Ala. 109.

[15] Preston v. Ellington, 74 Ala. 133; Grigsby v. Hair, 25 Ala. 327; Summers v. Kilgus, 14 Bush (Ky.) 449; Nashville Trust Co. v. Smythe, 94 Tenn. 513, 29 S. W. 903, 27 L. R. A. 663, 45 Am. St. 748; Menken v. Taylor, 4 Lea (Tenn.) 445; McClintic v. Wise, 25 Grat. (Va.) 448, 18 Am. Rep. 694.

[16] Menken v. Taylor, 4 Lea (Tenn.) 445; Paxton v. Rich, 85 Va. 378, 7 S. E. 531, 1 L. R. A. 639; McClintic v. Wise, 25 Grat. (Va.) 448, 18 Am. Rep. 694. Otherwise in Texas, unless it appears that it was the intention that the assignee should be first paid. Salmon v. Downs, 55 Tex. 243. A later decision in this state places the rule pretty much in accord with the general rule. Whitehead v. Fisher, 64 Tex. 638; Douglass v. Blount, 22 Tex. Civ. App. 493, 55 S. W. 526; Walcott v. Carpenter (Tex. Civ. App.), 132 S. W. 981. See also Preston v. Ellington, 74 Ala. 133; Barkdill v. Herwig, 30 La. Ann. 618.

As to the rule in Mississippi, see Aaron v. Warner, 62 Miss. 370; Christian v. Clark, 10 Lea (Tenn.) 630; Forwood v. Dehoney, 5 Bush (Ky.) 174.

[17] Grubbs v. Wysors, 32 Grat. (Va.) 127.

[18] McClintic v. Wise, 25 Grat. (Va.) 448, 18 Am. Rep. 694.

§ 203. **Notice to purchaser when deed does not refer to a note.**—
If the deed which retains a lien for purchase-money does not refer to
any note or bond for such purchase-money, a subsequent purchaser is
not bound to make inquiry for it, and is not affected by any equity in
favor of the assignee of the note or bond. A vendor who had taken a
negotiable note for the purchase-money of land conveyed by a deed
which reserved a lien for the purchase-money, but did not refer to the
note, afterward indorsed the note to one person, and contracted to sell
the land to another, who paid the purchase-money, and thereupon took
from the first vendee a conveyance of the property. The second vendee
was ignorant of the existence of the outstanding note, and of any claim
by the holder of it to the purchase-money. It was held that the second
vendee took the property unaffected by any lien in favor of the holder
of the note.[19] "Other things being equal, purchasers are favored both
at law and in equity above creditors, and so also the condition of the
defendant is best. The chancellor prefers to allow a loss to rest where
he finds it, rather than to transfer it to another equally entitled to
his consideration; he prefers to allow rather than to inflict injustice,
and to abstain from acting at all when all he can do is to shift a loss
from one innocent person to another."[20]

The assignee of the note in such case does not stand upon the same
ground with the assignee of a mortgage note, where the latter is described in the mortgage. The giving of a note for the purchase-money
secured by a vendor's lien is not so universal a practice as to make it
incumbent upon a subpurchaser, in the absence of any reference to the
note in the deed, to make inquiry for such a note. And so where a note
given in consideration of a contract for the conveyance of land was
transferred to a third person, and the contract was afterward canceled
by the parties to it, and the land conveyed to others, it was held that
the holder of the note had no lien upon the property.[21]

§ 204. **Subrogation to the lien.**—A mere voluntary payment of a
vendor's lien, where payment is unnecessary for the protection of

---

[19] National Val. Bank v. Harman,
75 Va. 604. As to the protection afforded a purchaser against an unrecorded assignment, or a cancelation
of mortgage with notes outstanding,
see Henderson v. Pilgrim, 22 Tex.
464; Smith v. Keohane, 6 Bradw.
(Ill.) 585; Turpin v. Ogle, 4 Bradw.
(Ill.) 611; Walker v. Schreiber, 47
Iowa 529; Bowling v. Cook, 39 Iowa
200; Bank of Indiana v. Anderson,
14 Iowa 544, 83 Am. Dec. 390; Bacon v. Van Schoonhoven, 19 Hun (N.
Y.) 158; Torrey v. Deavitt, 53 Vt.
331.

[20] Summers v. Kilgus, 14 Bush
(Ky.) 449, per Coffer, J.

[21] McMillen v. Rose, 54 Iowa 522,
6 N. W. 728; Proctor v. Hart, 72
Miss. 288, 16 So. 595.

the person making the same, and not required by any contract with the vendor or vendee, does not raise any equitable right of subrogation to the lien of the vendor.[22]

But a surety upon a note given to the vendor for the purchase-money, upon paying the note is subrogated to the vendor's lien for the purchase-money, if no equity in favor of the vendor would thereby be displaced. But a surety upon the first of three notes given for the purchase-money, upon paying such note is not entitled to be subrogated to the vendor's lien in respect to that note, when the result of such subrogation would be to displace the vendor to his prejudice in respect to his lien for the security of the other notes for the purchase-money, as would be the case if the land were an inadequate security for the payment of all notes.[23] However, a surety can have no subrogation until he has paid the entire debt.[24]

As a general rule, persons loaning the vendee money with which to pay the amount of the lien become subrogated to the rights of the vendor thereunder,[25] but only to his rights as a creditor and not to the superior legal title held by him.[26]

Also one who pays off a vendor's lien at the instance of the debtor upon an agreement with him that he shall have a lien for his reimbursement is subrogated to the vendor's lien.[27] And a vendee paying a purchase-money debt of his vendor for which the holder has a vendor's lien is entitled to be subrogated to such lien.[28] One who has advanced money to the purchaser to enable him to pay a note or bond for the purchase-money may be subrogated to the vendor's lien.[29]

[22] Rodman v. Sanders, 44 Ark. 504; Nichol v. Dunn, 25 Ark. 129; Martin v. Martin, 164 Ill. 640, 45 N. E. 1007, 56 Am. St. 219; Greishaber v. Farmer, 19 Ky. L. 1028, 42 S. W. 742.

[23] Grubbs v. Wysors, 32 Grat. (Va.) 127. See also Barnes v. Barnes, 24 Ky. L. 1732, 72 S. W. 282; Riggs v. Chapman, 2 Ky. L. 473, 46 S. W. 692; Nalle v. Farrish, 98 Va. 130, 34 S. E. 985.

[24] McConnell v. Beattie, 34 Ark. 113; Menken v. Taylor, 4 Lea (Tenn.) 445.

[25] Scott v. Land, Mtg., Inv. &c. Co., 127 Ala. 161, 28 So. 709; North American Trust Co. v. Lanier, 78 Miss. 418, 28 So. 804, 84 Am. St. 635; Hatton v. Bodan Lumber Co., 57 Tex. Civ. App. 478, 123 S. W. 163; John M. Bonner Memorial Home v. Collin County Nat. Bank, 57 Tex. Civ. App. 313, 122 S. W. 430. But see Rodman v. Sanders, 44 Ark. 504; Austin v. Underwood, 37 Ill. 439, 87 Am. Dec. 252; Wooldridge v. Scott, 69 Mo. 669.

[26] Hatton v. Bodan Lumber Co., 57 Tex. Civ. App. 478, 123 S. W. 163. But see Bougner v. Laughlin, 23 Ky. L. 1161, 64 S. W. 856.

[27] Bell v. Bell, 174 Ala. 446, 56 So. 926, 37 L. R. A. (N. S.) 1203; Allen v. Caylor, 120 Ala. 251, 24 So. 512, 74 Am. St. 31; Warford v. Hankins, 150 Ind. 489, 50 N. E. 468; Hulings v. Hulings Lumber Co,. 38 W. Va. 351, 18 S. E. 620.

[28] Fulkerson v. Taylor, 100 Va. 426, 41 S. E. 863.

[29] Brown v. Rash, 40 Tex. Civ. App. 203, 89 S. W. 438; Price v. Davis, 88 Va. 939, 14 S. E. 704.

§ **205. Statute of limitations.**—A lien founded upon contract may be enforced although the debt be barred by the statute of limitations.[30] The revival of a debt barred by the statute of limitations revives a vendor's lien incident thereto.[31]

The relation of a purchaser by title bond to his vendor is similar to that of mortgagor to mortgagee, and his possession is in like manner consistent with his obligation to pay the money secured, and does not become adverse except under circumstances which would make a mortgagor's possession adverse.[32] A vendor's lien under an agreement or bond to convey, where the purchaser enters into possession without receiving a conveyance, is not barred by the statute of limitations until the lapse of twenty years without the payment of interest, or other recognition of the indebtedness on the part of the purchaser. Yet payment may be established by circumstances such as would satisfy a jury that the continued existence of the debt was highly improbable.[33]

§ **206. No obligation to exhaust personalty before resorting to realty.**—The obligation first to exhaust the personal remedy, which is a rule of equity adopted by some courts as to liens arising by implication of law, has no application when the lien is created by express contract.[34]

Even in cases of liens arising by implication of law, the better rule seems to be, that the vendor may enforce his lien in equity without first attempting to collect his debt by an action at law.[35] The heir or

---

[30] Bizzell v. Nix, 60 Ala. 281, 31 Am. Rep. 38; Driver v. Hudspeth, 16 Ala. 348; Waddell v. Carlock, 41 Ark. 523; Coldcleugh v. Johnson, 34 Ark. 312; White v. Blakemore, 8 Lea (Tenn.) 49; McPherson v. Johnson, 69 Tex. 484, 6 S. W. 798; Smith v. Owen, 43 Tex. Civ. App. 411, 97 S. W. 521; White v. Cole, 9 Tex. Civ. App. 277, 29 S. W. 1148; Dittman v. Iselt (Tex. Civ. App.), 52 S. W. 96; Barber v. Hoffman (Tex. Civ. App.), 37 S. W. 769; Paxton v. Rich, 85 Va. 378, 7 S. E. 531. See also Hulbert v. Clark, 128 N. Y. 295, 28 N. E. 638, 14 L. R. A. 59.

[31] Windom v. Howard, 86 Tex. 560, 26 S. W. 483.

[32] Lewis v. Hawkins, 23 Wall. (U. S.) 119, 23 L. ed. 113; Butler v. Douglass, 1 McCrary (U. S.) 630, 3 Fed. 612; Adair v. Adair, 78 Mo.

630; Lewis v. McDowell, 88 N. Car. 261; Daniels v. Moses, 12 S. Car. 130; Gudger v. Barnes, 4 Heisk. (Tenn.) 570.

[33] Hardin v. Boyd, 113 U. S. 756, 28 L. ed. 1141, 5 Sup. Ct. 771; Phillips v. Adams, 78 Ala. 225; May v. Wilkinson, 76 Ala. 543.

[34] Sparks v. Hess, 15 Cal. 186; Huffman v. Cauble, 86 Ind. 591; McCaslin v. State, 44 Ind. 151; Smith v. Rowland, 13 Kans. 245. But see Bryant v. Stephens, 58 Ala. 636.

[35] Campbell v. Roach, 45 Ala. 667; Owen v. Moore, 14 Ala. 640; Mayes v. Hendry, 33 Ark. 240; Burgess v. Fairbanks, 83 Cal. 215, 23 Pac. 292, 17 Am. St. 230; Sparks v. Hess, 15 Cal. 186; Richardson v. Baker, 5 J. J. Marsh (Ky.) 323; Pratt v. Clark, 57 Mo. 189; Stewart v. Caldwell, 54 Mo. 536.

devisee of the vendee generally may compel payment of the unpaid purchase-money to be made out of the personal estate.[36]

§ 207. **Proceedings to enforce lien.**—To enforce a lien for the purchase-money reserved by the vendor in his deed, the same proceedings are had as in case of a formal mortgage. The same persons must be made parties.[37]

If the vendee has sold any part or the whole of his interest, his grantee must be made a party;[38] and so must any one who has acquired a lien upon the property through him.[39] But it has been held that persons to whom a grantee in a deed, in which a vendor's lien was reserved, has conveyed the land before suit brought to enforce the lien, are not necessary parties; but a failure to make them parties leaves open their right to redeem.[40]

Where a party in possession and his vendor had merely an equity in the property, and the party in possession acquired his rights with notice by the recitals of the deed, under which he claims that the purchase-

---

[36] Sutherland v. Harrison, 86 Ill. 363; Wright v. Holbrook, 32 N. Y. 587; Livingston v. Newkirk, 3 Johns. Ch. (N. Y.) 312; Lamport v. Beeman, 34 Barb. (N. Y.) 239; O'Conner v. O'Conner, 88 Tenn. 75, 13 S. W. 447, 7 L. R. A. 33.

[37] Wells v. Francis, 7 Colo. 396, 4 Pac. 49. Where the purchaser of land, upon which a lien was reserved, conveys the same to his wife for life and on her remarriage, to any children that might yet be born, the children are not proper or necessary parties to a foreclosure of such lien. Shannon v. Ruttery (Tex. Civ. App.), 140 S. W. 858. See also Boynton v. Salinger, 147 Iowa 537, 126 N. W. 369; Maas v. Morgenthaler, 136 App. Div. 359, 120 N. Y. S. 1004; Atteberry v. Burnett, 52 Tex. Civ. App. 617, 114 S. W. 159.

[38] Ballard v. Carter, 71 Tex. 161, 9 S. W. 92.

[39] King v. Young Men's Assn., 1 Woods (U. S.) 386; Gaston v. White, 46 Mo. 486.

In Iowa it is provided by statute that the vendor of real estate who has given a bond or other writing to convey it, and part or all of the purchase-money remains unpaid after the day fixed for payment, whether the time is or is not of the essence of the contract, may file his petition asking the court to require the purchaser to perform his contract, or to foreclose and sell his interest in the property. The vendee in such cases, for the purpose of the foreclosure is treated as a mortgagor of the property purchased, and his rights may be foreclosed in a similar manner. Code 1897, §§ 4297, 4298; Dukes v. Turner, 44 Iowa 575. In Tennessee it is provided by statute that liens on realty retained in favor of vendors on the face of the deed, also mortgages, deeds of trust, and assignments of realty executed to secure debts, shall be barred and the liens discharged, unless suits to enforce the same be brought within ten years from the maturity of the debt, provided that this statute shall not run against existing liens only from the date of the passage of this act. Acts 1885, ch. 9; Code 1896, § 4465. For cases cited, see Shannon's Supp., §§ 5326–5329. See post § 1541.

[40] Talbot v. Roe, 171 Mo. 421, 71 S. W. 682.

money has not been paid, it is not necessary to make such party in possession a party to the foreclosure proceedings.[41]

"The rights of the vendee," says Mr. Justice Bradley,[42] "being the same as those of a mortgagor, they must be extinguished in the same way. They are vested and well defined in the law. They constitute an estate called, it is true, by the name of an equity of redemption; but still an estate which may be conveyed, incumbered, and laid under other liens. And the heirs and assigns of the vendee, and subsequent holders of liens on the property against him, can not be disregarded or ignored by the original vendor or his assigns, when they desire to extinguish this estate."

As, in the case of a suit to foreclose a mortgage, a person claiming adversely to the mortgage title should not be made a party, so to a bill to enforce a vendor's lien under a title bond a person claiming adversely to the title should not be made a party, because the rights of such a claimant can not be litigated and settled in such proceeding.[43]

§ 208. **Remedies of vendor.**—Moreover, the vendor, like a mortgagee, has several remedies, and may pursue all of them concurrently; he may bring an action at law to recover the debt, an action of trespass or ejectment for the possession of the land, or a suit in equity to enforce the lien.[44]

[41] Robinson v. Black, 56 Tex. 215.

[42] King v. Young Men's Assn., 1 Woods (U. S.) 386.

[43] Wells v. Francis, 7 Colo. 396, 4 Pac. 49; Neeley v. Ruleys, 26 W. Va. 686; Moreland v. Metz, 24 W. Va. 119, 49 Am. Rep. 246; Cunningham v. Hedrick, 23 W. Va. 579; Arnold v. Coburn, 32 W. Va. 272, 9 S. E. 21. In West Virginia it is held that it is not necessary, before entering a decree of sale under a lien, to ascertain the existence and amount of other liens upon the property and their priorities, though subsequent to the vendor's lien, or to make the lienors parties.

[44] Micou v. Ashurst, 55 Ala. 607; McConnell v. Beattie, 34 Ark. 113; Palmer v. Harris, 100 Ill. 276. Where a vendor holds a reserved lien and brings an action to foreclose the same and the foreclosure is void for informalities, he does not lose the lien reserved. Evans v. Bentley, 9 Tex. Civ. App. 112, 29 S. W. 497, 36 S. W. 1070. Where purchasers of land agree to execute security to the vendor and thereby induce him to release his reserved lien and such vendees refuse to carry out their agreement, the vendor may still enforce his lien. Dishman v. Frost (Tex. Civ. App.), 140 S. W. 358. He may sue to recover the land, though the note is barred by the statute of limitations. Johnson v. Lockhart, 16 Tex. Civ. App. 32, 40 S. W. 640. The assignee of notes where a lien is reserved in the deed may in case of default in payment enforce the lien and recover the land even though the notes are barred. White v. Cole, 87 Tex. 500, 29 S. W. 759. See also Pitman v. Robbins (Tex. Civ. App.), 59 S. W. 600. The vendor on the purchaser's default may elect to rescind the contract and recover the real estate or recover judgment for the debt and foreclose his lien. Atteberry v. Burnett, 52 Tex. Civ. App. 617, 114 S. W. 159. See also Fowler v. Coates, 128 App. Div. 381, 112 N. Y. S. 849. He may foreclose his lien on any notes that are due. Pamplin v.

The vendor seeking to enforce the lien should set forth the terms of the agreement, and, if the title is still in him, he should aver his ability and willingness to convey the land according to the terms of sale, if the payment of the purchase-money and the execution of the conveyance are intended by the contract to be concurrent and contemporaneous acts, or the contract makes the purchase-money due and payable only on the tender of a deed of conveyance.[45] But if the purchase-money be made payable on a day certain, the payment of this is not dependent upon the making of title; and in such case it is not necessary for the vendor, in a bill to enforce the lien, to aver an offer on his part to convey, or to aver his readiness to make title.[46] The vendee who has secured possession under his contract, and insists upon maintaining possession, is not permitted to deny his liability on the note, bond, or contract for the purchase-money. If he resists payment of the purchase-money, he must offer to restore the possession of the land to the vendor.[47] An averment also of the amount of purchase-money remaining unpaid is necessary to sustain a judgment for a sale of the land to satisfy the amount due upon the contract.[48] In some states a strict foreclosure of such a lien is allowed.[49] But a strict foreclosure is not generally allowed where such a decree is not made in the foreclosure of mortgages.[50] A decree foreclosing this right of the vendee to purchase should give him a definite time within which to perform his contract.[51] Where a lien is reserved for the security of a bond for purchase-money, the lien may be enforced in equity though the bond be lost.[52] A purchaser under a contract of purchase can not maintain a suit for specific performance after he has assigned to another his right to receive the

Rowe, 100 Ark. 144, 139 S. W. 1105. See also Calvin v. Duncan, 12 Bush (Ky.) 101; Gaston v. White, 46 Mo. 486; Johnston v. Cochrane, 84 N. Car. 446; Clifton v. Charles, 53 Tex. Civ. App. 448, 116 S. W. 120; Atteberry v. Burnett, 52 Tex. Civ. App. 617, 114 S. W. 159; Curtis Land &c. Co. v. Interior Land Co., 137 Wis. 341, 118 N..W. 853, 129 Am. St. 1068.

[45] McKleroy v. Tulane, 34 Ala. 78.

[46] Munford v. Pearce, 70 Ala. 452; Burkett v. Munford, 70 Ala. 423; May v. Lewis, 22 Ala. 646; Reeve v. Downs, 22 Kans. 330.

[47] Reeve v. Downs, 22 Kans. 330; Harvey v. Morris, 63 Mo. 475; Brock v. Hidy, 13 Ohio St. 306; McIndoe v. Morman, 26 Wis. 588, 7 Am. Rep. 96.

[48] Calvin v. Duncan, 12 Bush (Ky.) 101. See also Johnston v. Cochrane, 84 N. Car. 446. Where a vendor sues for the land itself he need not refund that part of the purchase-money paid by the vendee. Branch v. Taylor, 40 Tex. Civ. App. 248, 89 S. W. 813. In every case the vendor may sue to recover the land, where the contract is executory if his right has not been waived. Crain v. National Life Ins. Co., 55 Tex. Civ. App. 406, 120 S. W. 1098.

[49] Vail v. Drexel, 9 Bradw. (Ill.) 439. See post § 1541.

[50] Fitzhugh v. Maxwell, 34 Mich. 138.

[51] Keller v. Lewis, 53 Cal. 113; Vail v. Drexel, 9 Bradw. (Ill.) 439.

[52] Robinson v. Dix, 18 W. Va. 528.

conveyance, for he has then no cause of action unless it be as trustee for his assignee.[53]

§ 209. · **Tender of performance.**—It is no defense to an equitable action to enforce a lien under a contract for unpaid purchase-money, that the vendor did not tender a deed before bringing suit.[54] After the time for the performance of the contract has passed, without any offer by either party to perform on that day, there can be no action at law upon it by either, but either may claim a specific performance in equity, making an offer of performance in the bill.[55] If no tender was made before bringing suit, the complainant must aver a readiness and willingness to execute a deed that will vest the title in the purchaser. In Indiana it is held that the tender must be kept good by bringing the deed into court,[56] but generally an offer to deliver the deed is sufficient. If an action to foreclose the lien be brought, not by the vendor, but by his personal representatives, they should show that they are able and willing to give a deed, or else make the heir or devisee who holds the legal title in trust for the purchaser a party to the suit, so that he will be bound by it.[57]

The vendee under a contract for the sale of lands, having performed his part of the contract, need not tender the vendor's deed for his signature, when the latter has denied the vendee's right to a conveyance under the contract.[58] If the vendee seeks enforcement of the contract and pleads a tender of a sum to pay the balance of the purchase-price, he thereby admits that the vendor is entitled to a decree of foreclosure for the amount tendered.[59]

§ 210. **Temporary eviction of vendee.**—If the vendee has been evicted and kept for a time only out of the possession of the land, and

---

[53] Green v. Betts, 1 McCrary (U. S.) 72.

[54] Munford v. Pearce, 70 Ala. 452; Wakefield v. Johnson, 26 Ark. 506; Evans v. Feeny, 81 Ind. 532; Paschal v. Brandon, 79 N. Car. 504. See also Stokes v. Acklen (Tenn.), 46 S. W. 316.

[55] Freeson v. Bissell, 63 N. Y. 168; Bruce v. Tilson, 25 N. Y. 194; Stevenson v. Maxwell, 2 N. Y. 408. See also Security Sav. &c. Co. v. Mackenzie, 33 Ore. 209, 52 Pac. 1046. But see McKenzie v. Baldridge, 49 Ala. 564; Watson v. Bell, 45 Ala. 452; Turner v. Lassiter, 27 Ark. 662; Newton v. Hull, 90 Cal. 487, 27 Pac. 429; McCaslin v. State, 44 Ind. 151; McWilliam v. Brookens, 39 Wis. 334.

[56] Goodwine v. Morey, 111 Ind. 68, 12 N. E. 82; Overly v. Tipton, 68 Ind. 410; Sowle v. Holdridge, 63 Ind. 213; Melton v. Coffelt, 59 Ind. 310; Smith v. Turner, 50 Ind. 367.

[57] Thomson v. Smith, 63 N. Y. 301. In an action to foreclose a vendor's lien reserved in a sale contract plaintiff must aver his willingness to perform by making a deed as provided in the contract. Powell v. Hunter, 204 Mo. 293, 102 S. W. 1020; Tillar v. Clayton, 76 Ark. 405, 88 S. W. 972.

[58] Davis v. Robert, 89 Ala. 402, 8 So. 114, 18 Am. St. 126.

[59] Portsmouth Sav. Bank v. Yeiser, 81 Nebr. 343, 116 N. W. 38.

then resumed its occupancy and enjoyment, when the defect in his vendor's title has been cured, in a suit by the vendor to enforce his lien the vendee is entitled to recoup the value of the estate for the period of dispossession.[60] But the vendee can not claim, as special damages on account of his temporary eviction, that he has closed out a lucrative business, changed his residence, disposed of property at a sacrifice, and made expenditures looking to the occupation of the land during the season, which resulted in loss, for such damages are speculative and remote.[61]

Where the vendor surrenders possession, and afterward, without the vendee's consent, retakes the possession, he is liable to such vendee for any rents received by him while so in possession.[62]

§ 211. **Lien of vendor exhausted by foreclosure sale.**—If a vendor, who has entered into a contract to convey upon the payment of the purchase-money, elects to foreclose his contract of sale, he can not, after the land has been sold and bid in by him for a part only of the judgment, and then redeemed by the purchaser, still claim to have a vendor's lien upon the land for the balance of the purchase-money.[63] The decree must conform to the pleadings. If the bill asks for a sale of the land under the lien, or for a rescission of the contract of sale, a decree can not be entered for the satisfaction of the purchaser's note for the unpaid purchase-money; that the vendor retain the moneys received by him; that the purchaser retain possession of the land, and that the title be vested in him. The decree should either enforce the vendor's lien or rescind the contract.[64] A vendor who has taken notes for the purchase-money can not enforce his lien by a sale of the land until all the notes are due, in the absence of a stipulation or statute to that effect.[65] The rule is the same as that which governs the fore-

---

[60] See Christy v. Ogle, 33 Ill. 295; Moreland v. Metz, 24 W. Va. 119, 49 Am. Rep. 246. The vendor can not enforce his vendor's lien where his title fails and the vendee is compelled to purchase title from another. Williams v. Finley, 99 Tex. 468, 90 S. W. 1087. A purchaser can not prevent a foreclosure of a vendor's lien because of defects in title of a part of the land where no eviction is shown and where he does not offer to pay the notes justly due. Frantz v. Masterson (Tex. Civ. App.), 133 S. W. 740.

[61] Gunter v. Beard, 93 Ala. 227, 9 So. 389.

[62] Crockett v. Gray, 39 Kans. 659, 18 Pac. 595.

[63] Todd v. Davey, 60 Iowa 532, 15 N. W. 421; Wall v. Club Land &c. Co. (Tex. Civ. App.), 88 S. W. 534.

[64] Baldwin v. Whaley, 78 Mo. 186.

[65] Brame v. Swain, 111 N. Car. 540, 15 S. E. 938. Under Kentucky Civ. Code 1895, § 694, the whole of a tract of land can not be sold to satisfy notes for the purchase-money, unless all of them are due at the date of the judgment for the sale, though all the notes are held by the same person, but only so much of the land may be sold as is sufficient to satisfy the notes that are due;

closure of a mortgage under like circumstances. But a personal judgment against defendant may be had on the notes due at the commencement of the action.

§ 212. **Effect of sale of land to pass growing crops.**—A sale of the land under order of court to satisfy the lien passes the growing crops, unless they are reserved in the order of sale.[66] But the vendor's lien is subordinate to any lawful lien existing upon the crops at the time it is sought to charge them with the vendor's lien.[67] Before the vendor, however, can resort to the rents and profits of the land sold in payment of the debt for purchase-money, he must allege in his bill or prove that the land itself is insufficient to pay the debt, the land being the primary fund for its satisfaction, and the rents and profits only an incidental fund.[68]

A clause in a deed which provides that the grantee may cut and sell the timber on the land, a lien for the purchase-money being reserved, is interpreted as being made for the purpose of enabling the purchaser to pay the purchase-money. If, therefore, the purchaser makes a mortgage of the land to one who advanced him money to make the purchase, and the mortgagee files a bill to foreclose, alleging the superiority of the vendor's lien, and that the timber had been so wasted that the land would not more than satisfy it, a decree directing a sale of the land to pay the vendor's lien, and of the timber to pay the mortgage debt, is erroneous, for there was no intention to sever the title of the timber from that of the land. The mortgage created a lien on the land subordinate to the lien for purchase-money, but it created no lien on the timber separate from the land.[69]

§ 213. **Restraint of purchaser from impairing vendor's lien.**—A purchaser in possession under a contract of sale may be restrained from impairing the vendor's lien by the removal of buildings or otherwise. If the vendee sell the buildings to one who buys with knowledge of a fraudulent intent to impair the vendor's lien, no title passes as against the vendor, who may, under a judgment obtained against

and if the property can not be advantageously divided, none of it can be sold until all the notes fall due. Gentry v. Walker, 93 Ky. 405, 14 Ky. L. 351, 20 S. W. 291; Leopold v. Furber, 84 Ky. 214, 8 Ky. L. 198, 1 S. W. 404; following Faught v. Henry, 13 Bush (Ky.) 471. See post § 1459.
[66] Yates v. Smith, 11 Bradw. (Ill.)

459; Smith v. Hague, 25 Kans. 246; Johnston v. Smith, 70 Ala. 108. See post §§ 658, 676, 699, 780.
[67] Wooten v. Bellinger, 17 Fla. 289.
[68] Moore v. Knight, 6 Lea (Tenn.) 427.
[69] Sikes v. Page, 12 Ky. L. 780, 15 S. W. 248.

the vendee for purchase-money, levy on and sell the house in the hands of the purchaser. But inasmuch as the vendee in possession is the equitable owner, he may properly remove buildings and fences, if this does not impair the vendor's security; thus, he may remove them for the purpose of erecting better ones in the place of those removed. The vendor in such case would have no right to interfere. He could not maintain replevin for the house removed, or for the timbers composing the house.[70]

[70] Weed v. Hall, 101 Pa. St. 592.

CHAPTER VII

I. *When They Constitute a Mortgage in Law*

§ 241. Defeasance an essential requisite of a mortgage—Form—Parties to defeasance.—A defeasance has been defined as a deed or written instrument which defeats the force or operation of some other deed.[1] It is immaterial whether the contract which constitutes the de-

---

[1] Bouvier in his Law Dictionary defines "defeasance" to be an instrument which defeats the force or operation of some other deed or of an estate. That which is in the same deed is called a "condition"; and that which is in another deed is a "defeasance." Simmons v. West Virginia Ins. Co., 8 W. Va. 474. Defeasance "is fetched from the French word defaire, i. e., to defeat or undo; infectum reddere quod factum est." The true meaning of this language is that it is to make void the principal deed. Co. Litt. 237a. "A defeasance is an instrument which avoids or defeats the force and operation of some other deed, and that which in the same deed would be called a 'condition' of it in another deed is a 'defeasance'; but it must contain proper words to defeat or put an end to the deed of which it is intended to be a defeasance, as that it should be void or of no force or effect." Lippincott v. Tilton, 14 N. J. L. 361. See also Flagg v. Mann, 1 Fed. Cas. No. 202.

A defeasance is a collateral deed, made at the same time with a feoffment or other conveyance, containing certain conditions upon the performance of which the estate then

296

feasance be incorporated in the same instrument or in a separate instrument contemporaneously executed.[2] It may exist merely in parol;[3] but it must, nevertheless, exist in some form.[4] The grantor must have a conditional right to have the property restored to him. There must be a valid and binding agreement of some sort on the part of the grantee to yield up the property received by him, when the conditions upon which the conveyance was made have been performed, else there is lacking an element indispensable to a mortgage.

At law the defeasance must be in favor of the grantor himself, and not in favor of any third person. It does not avail anything that the conveyance contains a condition for a reconveyance, if the reconveyance is to be made to some one other than the grantor; whatever else such an instrument may be, it is not a mortgage.[5]

In equity the rule is different, and the transaction is a mortgage, although the defeasance be to some one other than the grantor; thus, for instance, it may be in the form of an agreement by one person to purchase property at a foreclosure sale, or other public sale, and to hold it until the purchase-money be repaid by the party who receives the agreement.[6]

created may be defeated or totally undone. Miller v. Quick, 158 Mo. 495, 59 S. W. 955. See also Shaw v. Erskine, 43 Maine 371; Harrison v. Trustees of Phillips' Academy, 12 Mass. 456.

In the construction of a statute relating to absolute conveyances intended to be defeasible, the word "defeasible" was defined as "capable of being, or liable to be avoided, annulled, or undone." Kinney v. Heatherington, 38 Okla. 74, 131 Pac. 1078; Comp. L. of Okla. 1909, § 1196.

[2] Dubuque Nat. Bank v. Weed, 57 Fed. 513; Rowan v. Sharp's Rifle Mfg. Co., 31 Conn. 1; Lynch v. Jackson, 123 Ill. 360, 14 N. E. 697; Johnson v. Prosperity Loan &c. Assn., 94 Ill. App. 260; Porter v. White, 128 N. Car. 42, 38 S. E. 24; Wilson v. Shoenberger, 31 Pa. St. 295. In New Hampshire the defeasance must be in the conveyance. Gen. Laws, ch. 136, § 2. Somersworth Sav. Bank v. Roberts, 38 N. H. 22; Boody v. Davis, 20 N. H. 140, 51 Am. Dec. 210; Bassett v. Bassett, 10 N. H. 64.

[3] See post ch. VIII., § 282 et seq.

[4] See ante § 69.

[5] Micou v. Ashurst, 55 Ala. 607; Low v. Henry, 9 Cal. 538; Magnusson v. Johnson, 73 Ill. 156; Carr v. Rising, 62 Ill. 14; Stephenson v. Thompson, 13 Ill. 186; Warner v. Jennings, 44 Ind. App. 574, 89 N. E. 908; Warren v. Lovis, 53 Maine 463; Shaw v. Erskine, 43 Maine 371; Treat v. Strickland, 23 Maine 234; Flagg v. Mann, 14 Pick. (Mass.) 467, 479; Bickford v. Daniels, 2 N. H. 71; Pardee v. Treat, 82 N. Y. 385; Hill v. Grant, 46 N. Y. 496; Payne v. Patterson, 77 Pa. St. 134; Penn. Life Ins. Co. v. Austin, 42 Pa. St. 257; Marvin v. Titsworth, 10 Wis. 320. Likewise a separate written defeasance must be made between the same persons who were parties to the first deed, and must be signed and executed by the person whose estate is to be defeated. Miller v. Quick, 158 Mo. 495, 59 S. W. 955. An absolute conveyance to a mortgagee in settlement of foreclosure proceedings, is not rendered a mortgage by an option to purchase, concurrently given to a third person. Braun v. Vollmer, 89 App. Div. 43, 85 N. Y. S. 319.

[6] Martin v. Pond, 30 Fed. 15;

At law, to constitute a mortgage the conveyance must be made by the mortgagor, and the defeasance by the mortgagee. A bond, therefore, made by the grantee to his grantor, in consideration of the conveyance, and conditioned to support his grantor for life, and in case of neglect to reconvey the land, does not constitute a mortgage. If the deed be made by the person by whom the conditions are to be performed, and he takes back a bond for a reconveyance on the performance of the conditions, the transaction may be a mortgage. But in the above case the deed is to the person by whom the conditions are to be performed, and his bond is simply a covenant to reconvey, which may be specifically enforced in equity. There is no conveyance from the supposed mortgagor to the supposed mortgagee. Although such a transaction is not a legal mortgage, the bond may be enforced in equity by a decree for reconveyance.[7] An agreement to reconvey to the husband or wife of the grantor is a valid mortgage.[8] A conveyance by two parties with an agreement to reconvey to one has been held not to constitute a mortgage.[9]

A written contract giving the grantor in an absolute deed time to redeem by paying the amount of the debt will be construed as a mortgage, even though the contract specifically limits the time for redemption.[10] The word "redeem" used in a contract collateral to a deed does not necessarily imply that an indebtedness is secured or that a de-

Lindsay v. Matthews, 17 Fla. 575; First Nat. Bank v. Ashmead, 23 Fla. 379, 2 So. 657; Terwilligar v. Ballard, 64 Fla. 158, 59 So. 244. (Conveyance in trust to secure debt of third person); Reigard v. McNeil, 38 Ill. 400; Bradford v. Helsell, 150 Iowa 732, 130 N. W. 908; Davis v. Clifton, 145 Ky. 173, 140 S. W. 161 (agreement to reconvey to debtor's wife); Sheffield v. Day, 28 Ky. L. 754, 90 S. W. 545; Stinchfield v. Milliken, 71 Maine 567; Jeffery v. Hursh, 58 Mich. 246, 25 N. W. 176, 27 N. W. 7; Ferry v. Miller, 164 Mich. 429, 129 N. W. 721 (agreement to reconvey to husband of grantor); Pardee v. Treat, 82 N. Y. 385; Carr v. Carr, 52 N. Y. 251; Stoddard v. Whiting, 46 N. Y. 627; Ryan v. Dox, 34 N. Y. 307, 90 Am. Dec. 696; Despard v. Walbridge, 15 N. Y. 374; Weed v. Stevenson, Clarke (N. Y.) 166; Umfreville v. Keeler, 1 Thomp. & C. (N. Y.) 486; Barton v. May, 3 Sandf. Ch. (N. Y.) 450; McBurney v. Wellman, 42 Barb. (N. Y.) 390; Sahler v. Signer, 37 Barb. (N. Y.) 329, 44 Barb. (N. Y.) 606; Spicer v. Hunter, 14 Abb. Pr. (N. Y.) 4; Lane v. Shears, 1 Wend. (N. Y.) 433; Peterson v. Clark, 15 Johns. (N. Y.) 205; Muller v. Flavin, 13 S. Dak. 595, 83 N. W. 687. See also Flagg v. Mann, 2 Sumn. (U. S.) 486. See post §§ 268, 331.

[7] Robinson v. Robinson, 9 Gray (Mass.) 447, 69 Am. Dec. 301. But see Davis v. Davis, 81 Vt. 259, 69 Atl. 876, 130 Am. St. 1035; Chase v. Peck, 21 N. Y. 581, where the grantee in such case pledged the land and the produce of it.

[8] Davis v. Clifton, 145 Ky. 173, 140 S. W. 161; Mills v. Darling, 43 Maine 565; Ferry v. Miller, 164 Mich. 429, 129 N. W. 721.

[9] Vance v. Anderson, 113 Cal. 532, 45 Pac. 816.

[10] Smith v. Hoff, 23 N. Dak. 37, 135 N. W. 772, Ann. Cas. 1914C, 1072.

feasance is intended, for it may be used to mean repurchase or regain; and the latter construction will apply if no debt is shown.[11]

§ 242. **Informal defeasance or agreement to reconvey.**—The usual proviso in a legal mortgage is, that upon the payment of the debt, or performance of the duty named, "then this deed shall be void." But any equivalent expression may be used.[12] If it appear from the whole instrument that it was intended to be a security for the payment of a debt or the performance of a duty, it is a mortgage, although there be no express provision that upon the fulfilment of the condition the deed shall be void.[13] The form of the defeasance is immaterial,[14] if the intent to avoid the absolute conveyance clearly appears. The substance and not the form of the expression is chiefly to be regarded; and an enlarged and liberal view is taken to ascertain and carry into effect the intention of the parties.[15]

---

[11] Cold v. Beh, 152 Iowa 368, 132 N. W. 73.

[12] Bernstein v. Humes, 71 Ala. 260; Adams v. Stevens, 49 Maine 362; Cowles v. Marble, 37 Mich. 158; Pearce v. Wilson, 111 Pa. St. 14, 2 Atl. 99, 56 Am. Rep. 243; Wisconsin Cent. R. Co. v. Wisconsin &c. Land Co., 71 Wis. 94, 36 N. W. 837; Hoyt v. Fass, 64 Wis. 273, 25 N. W. 45.

The following clause in a deed, "Nevertheless, this deed of conveyance is null and void and of no effect until all the purchase-money is paid, then of full force and effect," is merely a lien or mortgage to secure the unpaid purchase-money. The deed does not become void absolutely upon a noncompliance with the condition. Miskelly v. Pitts, 9 Baxt. (Tenn.) 193.

A stipulation that the grantee will restore the deed if the money shall be paid within a time named is a sufficient proviso or defeasance. Kramer v. Brown, 114 Ala. 612, 21 So. 817, citing Reeves v. Abercrombie, 108 Ala. 535, 19 So. 41; Daniels v. Lowery, 92 Ala. 519, 8 So. 352; Peagler v. Stabler, 91 Ala. 308, 9 So. 157. See ante § 69.

[13] Snyder v. Bunnell, 64 Ind. 403; Steel v. Steel, 4 Allen (Mass.) 417; Lanfair v. Lanfair, 18 Pick. (Mass.) 299; Austin v. First Nat. Bank, 100 Mich. 613, 59 N. W. 597; Doescher v. Spratt, 61 Minn. 326, 63 N. W.

736; Pearce v. Wilson, 111 Pa. St. 14, 2 Atl. 99, 56 Am. Rep. 243; McCamant v. Roberts, 80 Tex. 316, 15 S. W. 1054 (quoting text).

[14] Adams v. Stevens, 49 Maine 362; Scott v. McFarland, 13 Mass. 309; Taylor v. Weld, 5 Mass. 109; Bayley v. Bailey, 5 Gray (Mass.) 505; Pearce v. Wilson, 111 Pa. St. 14, 2 Atl. 99, 56 Am. Rep. 243; Guthrie v. Kahle, 46 Pa. St. 331; In re Myer's Appeal, 42 Pa. St. 518; Wilson v. Shoenberger, 31 Pa. St. 295; Reitenbaugh v. Ludwick, 31 Pa. St. 131; Kelly v. Thompson, 7 Watts (Pa.) 401; Rankin v. Mortimere, 7 Watts (Pa.) 372; Kerr v. Gilmore, 6 Watts (Pa.) 405; Miskelly v. Pitts, 9 Baxt. (Tenn.) 193; Austin v. Downer, 25 Vt. 558. A defeasance in the form of a pawn ticket, referring to real estate conveyed as security for a loan, is sufficient. Lee v. Wilkinson (Miss.), 62 So. 275. A defeasance inserted in a warranty deed providing that the instrument "shall be void" upon payment, "otherwise of full force," is sufficient. Scott v. Hughes, 124 Ga. 1000, 53 S. E. 453.

[15] Steel v. Steel, 4 Allen (Mass.) 417; Lanfair v. Lanfair, 18 Pick. (Mass.) 299; Burnett v. Wright, 135 N. Y. 543, 21 N. E. 253 (quoting text); Skinner v. Cox, 4 Dev. L. (N. Car.) 99. In determining whether a deed is a mortgage the form is not controlling; it is a

It is well settled that a conveyance with an agreement, condition, or stipulation incorporated therein that the same shall become null and void, or cease and determine, or become of no effect, or that the estate so conveyed shall be reconveyed when the money is paid, or other equivalent expression, is a mortgage, and not an absolute conveyance. The form of the defeasance is immaterial if the intention clearly appears from the language employed. Any stipulation or agreement that plainly indicates an intention to return or reconvey the property, upon payment of the sum named, constitutes a mortgage.[16] If there be in the deed itself, or in any separate deed executed at the same time, and constituting with the conveyance one transaction, a provision that the estate shall be reconveyed upon the payment of the debt, such stipulation constitutes a defeasance as much as if the words "on condition," or "provided, however," were used.[17] Thus, a reservation by a grantor of the privilege of redeeming within a specified time creates a mortgage, if the deed was given to secure a debt.[18]

The condition of defeasance need not necessarily be inserted in the body of the deed. It has the same effect when added underneath in such a way as to be part of the deed, or when executed separately.[19] A condition written upon the back of a mortgage may be held to be a part of the deed, and therefore together with it may constitute a mortgage.[20]

mortgage if executed to secure a debt. Calahan v. Dunker, 51 Ind. App. 436, 99 N. E. 1021. Where the wording and substance of a deed and contemporaneous agreement explaining the transaction exclude the theory that a debt existed or that a mortgage was intended, the deed can not operate as a mortgage. Smith v. Smith, 153 Ala. 504, 45 So. 168. An instrument in the form of a warranty deed, but containing a clause that should the grantor pay to the grantee a certain sum by a given date, "the instrument shall be void; otherwise of full force," is a mortgage, and not a deed. Scott v. Hughes, 124 Ga. 1000, 53 S. E. 453.

[16] Pearce v. Wilson, 111 Pa. St. 14, 2 Atl. 99, 56 Am. Rep. 243.

[17] Ferguson v. Miller, 4 Cal. 97; Whitcomb v. Sutherland, 18 Ill. 578; Oldham v. Halley, 2 J. J. Marsh. (Ky.) 113; Scott v. McFarland, 13 Mass. 309; Taylor v. Weld, 5 Mass. 109; National Bank v. Tennessee Coal &c. R. Co., 62 Ohio St. 564, 57 N. E. 450; McCamant v. Roberts, 80 Tex. 316, 15 S. W. 1054; Austin v. Downer, 25 Vt. 558. But the instrument is not a mortgage at law unless equivalent words are used. Goddard v. Coe, 55 Maine 385. For cases upon separate agreement as defeasance see post § 244 note.

[18] Stryker v. Hershy, 38 Ark. 264; Mellon v. Lemmon, 111 Pa. St. 56, 2 Atl. 56.

[19] Baldwin v. Jenkins, 23 Miss. 206; Kent v. Allbritain, 5 Miss. 317. See also Epperson v. Epperson, 108 Va. 471, 62 S. E. 344; Perkins v. Dibble, 10 Ohio 433, 36 Am. Dec. 97.

[20] Stocking v. Fairchild, 5 Pick. (Mass.) 181; Graham v. Way, 38 Vt. 19; Whitney v. French, 25 Vt. 663 (indorsement of condition sufficient though not signed).

§ 242a. **Lease with agreement to reconvey.**—In accordance with the foregoing rules concerning agreements to reconvey, in deeds and collateral instruments, a lease for years, in which the lessor acknowledges the receipt in advance of a sum in full for the rent of the premises during the term, and in which "the lessee covenants, promises, and agrees to reconvey said premises to the lessor upon the payment of the aforesaid sum and interest thereon," is a mortgage, and the relation of the parties is that of mortgagor and mortgagee.[21] Where a conveyance is made to secure a debt and the grantee executes to his grantor a term lease containing an option to repurchase during the term, the transaction has been held to constitute a mortgage.[22] If the lessee receives rents and profits, before the term expires, to the amount of the sum advanced by him, and interest thereon, his estate for years is thereupon defeated, and the lessor is restored to his old estate. But if no interest on the money advanced was ever demanded or paid, the transaction will be construed as an actual lease and renting and there can be no redemption.[23]

Likewise a lease, absolute in form, for a term of years, conveying to the lessee the timber on a tract of land for a stated amount paid on delivery of the instrument, may be shown to be a mortgage to secure repayment of the original sum.[24] A mortgage deed disguised in the form of a lease, with the purchase-money to be paid as rent, and stipulating that if the annual rent was not paid when due, the lease was to terminate and title and possession to revest in the lessor, is nevertheless a mortgage.[25] But where the assignor of a lease given to secure

[21] Nugent v. Riley, 1 Metc. (Mass.) 117, 35 Am. Dec. 355.

[22] Reitze v. Humphreys, 53 Colo. 177, 125 Pac. 518. But see City Lumber Co. v. Hollands (Mich.), 148 N. W. 361.

[23] Stockton v. Dillon, 66 N. J. Eq. 100, 57 Atl. 487.

[24] Johnson v. Hattaway, 155 Ala. 516, 46 So. 760.

[25] Barnett v. Williams, 31 Ky. L. 255, 101 S. W. 1191. See also De Bartlett v. De Wilson, 52 Fla. 497, 42 So. 189. An absolute deed accompanied by a lease from the grantee to the grantor, with the exclusive option to repurchase, was held a mortgage. Fort v. Colby (Iowa), 144 N. W. 393. But the execution of a lease from the holder of the legal title to one claiming equitable ownership, does not

necessarily disprove such equitable ownership. Jones v. Gillett, 142 Iowa 506, 118 N. W. 314. Where a deed accompanied by a lease to the grantor was not intended as a mortgage, and had not been obtained by fraud or imposition, it will not be declared a mortgage. Strong v. Taylor (Ark.), 158 S. W. 123. Where a person who purchased a lot was unable to pay the balance due on the price, and conveyed to a company which advanced the amount due and erected a house on the lot, giving back a lease to the purchaser for a term of years, providing that if all instalments of rent were promptly paid thereunder with taxes, the property would be reconveyed to such purchaser at the end of the lease, and providing for forfeiture upon nonpayment, the

a debt, subsequently conveys the premises to the assignee for a consideration much larger than the original debt, the transaction is not a mortgage, though there be an agreement to reassign.[26] Where the grantee in a deed executed to the executor of the grantor's husband a ninety-nine-year renewable lease, subject to a ground rent equal to six per cent. on the price, and the lease contained no stipulation for redemption, the facts were held insufficient to constitute a mortgage.[27]

§ 243. **Objections to a separate defeasance.**—It is sometimes for the convenience of the parties to make the defeasance by a separate instrument, so that the grantee, in the absence of a record of this instrument, is apparently the absolute owner. This form of mortgage has been used sometimes to the prejudice of the mortgagor, and the courts have at times discouraged the use of it as much as possible. Thus at an early date Lord Chancellor Talbot observed:[28] "In the northern parts it is the custom in drawing mortgages to make an absolute deed, with the defeasance separate from it; but I think it a wrong way, and to me it will always appear with a face of fraud, for the defeasance may be lost, and then an absolute conveyance is set up. I would discourage the practice as much as possible." In another case Lord Chancellor Hardwicke declared it to be an imposition upon the mortgagor not to insert the provision for reconveyance in the deed itself.[29] Objections to this form of mortgage have been made by other judges; but a deed absolute in form, intended to operate as a security, if given in good faith to secure an actual indebtedness, is not constructively fraudulent as to the grantor's other creditors.[30]

---

facts were held insufficient to have the deed declared a mortgage, upon default. Copenny v. Southern Realty Co., 174 Ala. 378, 56 So. 721.

[26] Morrison v. Jones, 31 Mont. 154, 77 Pac. 507.

[27] Rosenstock v. Keyser, 104 Md. 380, 65 Atl. 37.

[28] Cotterell v. Purchase, Cas. Temp. Talbot 61.

[29] Baker v. Wind, 1 Ves. Sen. 160.

[30] McClure v. Smith, 14 Colo. 297, 23 Pac. 786, and all the cases cited in this chapter. In the case above cited Chief Justice Helm said: "If there be a bona fide debt for which the security is given; if there be no understanding with the mortgagee to hold the overplus, or to hold the property after payment of his debt, secretly, for the benefit of the mortgagor; if there be no collusion on the part of the mortgagee with the mortgagor in keeping the defeasance unrecorded, or in keeping secret the exact nature of the transaction, for the purpose of deceiving creditors; in short, if the mortgagee is simply endeavoring, in good faith, to obtain that precedence on the security of his debt which the law permits—the mere isolated fact that he takes an absolute deed, instead of a mortgage, will not, in and of itself alone, render his lien nugatory. The law prescribes no absolute and inflexible form for mortgages upon realty." Jefferson County Bank v. Hummel, 11 Colo. App. 337, 53 Pac. 286. There are a few early cases in which it was held that such a deed is

§ 244. **Absolute deed and separate defeasance—Effect at law.—** At law an absolute deed and separate absolute defeasance or agreement to reconvey, executed at the same time as security for a debt amount to a mortgage.[31] Such a deed and agreement to reconvey the

constructively fraudulent. Bryant v. Young, 21 Ala. 264; Smyth v. Carlisle, 16 N. H. 464; Friedley v. Hamilton, 17 Serg. & R. (Pa.) 70; Manufacturers' &c. Bank v. Bank of Pennsylvania, 7 Watts & S. (Pa.) 335; North v. Belden, 13 Conn. 376. It is quite certain, however, that none of these decisions would be followed now.

[31] Teal v. Walker, 111 U. S. 242, 28 L. ed. 415, 4 Sup. Ct. 420; Lanahan v. Sears, 102 U. S. 318, 26 L. ed. 180; Dow v. Chamberlin, 5 McLean (U. S.) 281; Alter v. Clark, 193 Fed. 153; Merrihew v. Fort, 98 Fed. 899; Martin v. Pond, 30 Fed. 15; Thomas v. Livingston, 155 Ala. 546, 46 So. 851 (grantor's right to repurchase); Rose v. Gandy, 137 Ala. 329, 34 So. 239 (grantor's right to repurchase); Seawright v. Parmer (Ala.), 7 So. 201; Cosby v. Buchanan, 81 Ala. 574, 1 So. 898; Sims v. Gaines, 64 Ala. 392; Freeman v. Baldwin, 13 Ala. 246; Sherrer v. Harris (Ark.), 13 S. W. 730. See also Adams v. Hopkins, 144 Cal. 19, 77 Pac. 712; Malone v. Roy, 94 Cal. 341, 29 Pac. 712; Rogers v. Jones, 92 Cal. 80, 28 Pac. 97; Smith v. Smith, 80 Cal. 323, 21 Pac. 4, 22 Pac. 186, 549; Booth v. Hoskins, 75 Cal. 271, 17 Pac. 225; McClure v. Smith, 14 Colo. 297, 23 Pac. 786; Walker v. Tiffin Min. Co., 2 Colo. 89; Gunn's Appeal, 55 Conn. 149, 10 Atl. 498; Waters v. Williamson, 21 D. C. 24; Jones v. Wight, 8 Hawaii 614; Kelley v. Leachman, 2 Idaho 1112, 29 Pac. 849; Wilson v. Thompson, 4 Idaho 678, 43 Pac. 557; Pritchard v. Butler, 4 Idaho 518, 43 Pac. 73; Linkemann v. Knepper, 226 Ill. 473, 80 N. E. 1009; In re Bennett's Estate, 168 Ill. 658; Helbreg v. Schumann, 150 Ill. 12, 37 N. E. 99, 41 Am. St. 339; Jackson v. Lynch, 129 Ill. 72, ·22 N. E. 246; Bearss v. Ford, 108 Ill. 16; Ewart v. Walling, 42 Ill. 453; Snyder v. Griswold, 37 Ill. 216; Preschbaker ·. Feaman, 32 Ill. 475; Barlow v. Cooper, 109 Ill. App. 375; Lowe v. Turpie, 147 Ind. 652, 44 N. E. 25, 37 L. R. A. 233; Lentz v. Martin, 75 Ind. 228; Crassen v. Swoveland, 22 Ind. 427; Watkins v. Gregory, 6 Blackf. (Ind.) 113; Harbison v. Lemon, 3 Blackf. (Ind.) 51, 23 Am. Dec. 376; Wysong v. Sells, 44 Ind. App. 238, 88 N. E. 954; Beidelman v. Koch, 42 Ind. App. 423, 85 N. E. 977; White v. Redenbaugh, 41 Ind. App. 580, 82 N. E. 110; Bigler v. Jack, 114 Iowa 667, 87 N. W. 700; Thompson v. People's Bldg. &c. Co., 114 Iowa 481, 87 N. W. 438; Haggerty v. Brower, 105 Iowa 395, 75 N. W. 321; Radford v. Folsom, 58 Iowa 473, 12 N. W. 536; Scott v. Mewhirter, 49 Iowa 487; Chase v. Abbott, 20 Iowa 154; Caruthers v. Hunt, 18 Iowa 576; Vennum v. Babcock, 13 Iowa 194; Calhoun v. Anderson, 78 Kans. 746, 98 Pac. 274; Wiswell v. Simmons, 77 Kans. 622, 95 Pac. 407; Overstreet v. Baxter, 30 Kans. 55, 1 Pac. 825; McKenney v. Page, 146 Ky. 682, 143 S. W. 382; Davis v. Clifton, 145 Ky. 173, 140 S. W. 161; Honore v. Hutchings, 8 Bush (Ky.) 687; Ogden v. Grant, 6 Dana (Ky.) 473; Edrington v. Harper, 3 J. J. Marsh. (Ky.) 353, 20 Am. Dec. 145; Fulwiler v. Roberts, 26 Ky. L. 297, 80 S. W. 1148; Frey v. Campbell, 8 Ky. L. 772, 3 S. W. 368; Snow v. Pressey, 82 Maine 552, 20 Atl. 78, 85 Maine 408, 27 Atl. 272; Bunker v. Barron, 79 Maine 62, 8 Atl. 253, 1 Am. St. 282; Stowe v. Merrill, 77 Maine 550; Clement v. Bennett, 70 Maine 207; Knight v. Dyer, 57 Maine 174; Warren v. Lovis, 53 Maine 463; Brown v. Holyoke, 53 Maine 9; Smith v. Monmouth Mut. Fire Ins. Co., 50 Maine 96; Mills v. Darling, 43 Maine 565; Shaw v. Erskine, 43 Maine 371; Purrington v. Pierce, 38 Maine 447; McLaughlin v. Shepherd, 32 Maine 143, 52 Am. Dec. 646; Blaney v. Bearce, 2 Maine 132; Gaither v. Clarke, 67 Md. 18, 8 Atl. 740; Stanhope v. Dodge, 52 Md. 483; Burns v. Hunnewell (Mass.), 104 N. E. 494; Short v. Caldwell, 155

estate upon payment of a certain sum of money, or upon the performance of some other condition, have always been held to constitute a

Mass. 57, 28 N. E. 1124; Harrison v. Phillips Academy, 12 Mass. 456; Holbrook v. Finney, 4 Mass. 566, 3 Am. Dec. 243; Erskine v. Townsend, 2 Mass. 493, 3 Am. Dec. 71; Murphy v. Calley, 1 Allen (Mass.) 107; Bayley v. Bailey, 5 Gray (Mass.) 505; Judd v. Flint, 4 Gray (Mass.) 557; Waters v. Randall, 6 Metc. (Mass.) 479; Marden v. Babcock, 2 Metc. (Mass.) 99; Nugent v. Riley, 1 Metc. (Mass.) 117, 35 Am. Dec. 355; Flagg v. Mann, 14 Pick. (Mass.) 467; Newhall v. Burt, 7 Pick. (Mass.) 157; Rice v. Rice, 4 Pick. (Mass.) 349; Clark v. Landon, 90 Mich. 83, 51 N. W. 357; Jeffery v. Hursh, 58 Mich. 246, 25 N. W. 176, 27 N. W. 7; Ferris v. Wilcox, 51 Mich. 105, 16 N. W. 252; Enos v. Sutherland, 11 Mich. 538; Batty v. Snook, 5 Mich. 231; Swetland v. Swetland, 3 Mich. 482; Butman v. James, 34 Minn. 547, 27 N. W. 66; Benton v. Nicoll, 24 Minn. 221; Archambau v. Green, 21 Minn. 520; Weide v. Gehl, 21 Minn. 449; Hill v. Edwards, 11 Minn. 22; Sharkey v. Sharkey, 47 Mo. 543; Copeland v. Yoakum, 38 Mo. 349; Grogan v. Valley Trading Co., 30 Mont. 229, 76 Pac. 211; Names v. Names, 48 Nebr. 701, 67 N. W. 751; Riley v. Starr, 48 Nebr. 243, 67 N. W. 187; Nelson v. Atkinson, 37 Nebr. 577, 56 N. W. 313; Connolly v. Giddings, 24 Nebr. 131, 37 N. W. 939; First Nat. Bank v. Kreig, 21 Nev. 404, 32 Pac. 641; Essex County Nat. Bank v. Harrison, 57 N. J. Eq. 91, 40 Atl. 209; Vliet v. Young, 34 N. J. Eq. 15; Merritt v. Brown, 19 N. J. Eq. 286; Van Wagner v. Van Wagner, 7 N. J. Eq. 27; Dickey v. Goertner, 146 N. Y. S. 264; Weed v. Stevenson, Clarke (N. Y.) 166; Clark v. Henry, 2 Cow. (N. Y.) 324; Draper v. Draper, 71 Hun 349, 24 N. Y. S. 1127; Peterson v. Clark, 15 Johns. (N. Y.) 205; Brown v. Bement, 8 Johns. (N. Y.) 96; Henry v. Davis, 7 Johns. Ch. (N. Y.) 40; Dey v. Dunham, 2 Johns. Ch. (N. Y.) 182; Decker v. Leonard, 6 Lans. (N. Y.) 264; Hall v. Van Cleve, 11 N. Y. Leg. Obs. 281; Holmes v. Grant, 8 Paige (N. Y.) 243; Brown v. Dean, 3 Wend. (N. Y.) 208; Lane v. Shears, 1 Wend. (N. Y.) 433; Watkins v. Williams, 123 N. Car. 170, 31 S. E. 388; Poston v. Jones, 122 N. Car. 536, 29 S. E. 951; Robinson v. Willoughby, 65 N. Car. 520; Mason v. Hearne, 1 Busb. Eq. (N. Car.) 88; Smith v. Hoff, 23 N. Dak. 37, 135 N. W. 772, Ann. Cas. 1914C, 1072; Wells v. Geyer, 12 N. Dak. 316, 96 N. W. 289; Sun Fire Ins. Office v. Clark, 53 Ohio St. 414, 42 N. E. 248; Marshall v. Stewart, 17 Ohio 356; Weiseham v. Hocker, 7 Okla. 250, 54 Pac. 464; Raski v. Wise, 56 Ore. 72, 107 Pac. 984; Wellenberg v. Minard, 37 Ore. 621, 62 Pac. 532; Safe Deposit &c. Co. v. Linton, 213 Pa. 105, 62 Atl. 566; Pearce v. Wilson, 111 Pa. St. 14, 2 Atl. 99, 56 Am. Rep. 243; McClurkan v. Thompson, 69 Pa. St. 305; Houser v. Lamont, 55 Pa. St. 311, 93 Am. Dec. 755; Guthrie v. Kahle, 46 Pa. St. 331; Wilson v. Shoenberger, 31 Pa. St. 295; Brown v. Nickle, 6 Pa. St. 390; Friedley v. Hamilton, 17 S. & R. (Pa.) 70, 17 Am. Dec. 638; Johnston v. Gray, 16 S. & R. (Pa.) 361, 16 Am. Dec. 577; Stoever v. Stoever, 9 S. & R. (Pa.) 434; Manufacturers' &c. Bank v. Bank of Pennsylvania, 7 W. & S. (Pa.) 335; Dimond v. Enoch, Add. (Pa.) 356; Gubbings v. Harper, 7 Phila. (Pa.) 276; Kelly v. Thompson, 7 Watts (Pa.) 401; Jaques v. Weeks, 7 Watts (Pa.) 261; Kerr v. Gilmore, 6 Watts (Pa.) 405; Colwell v. Woods, 3 Watts (Pa.) 188, 27 Am. Dec. 345; Knowles v. Knowles, 25 R. I. 464, 56 Atl. 775; Francis v. Francis, 78 S. Car. 178, 58 S. E. 804; Brickle v. Leach, 55 S. Car. 510, 33 S. E. 720; Bowman v. Felts (Tenn.), 42 S. W. 810; Hammonds v. Hopkins, 3 Yerg. (Tenn.) 525; Blizzard v. Craigmiles, 7 Lea (Tenn.) 693; Moores v. Wills, 69 Tex. 109, 5 S. W. 675; Baxter v. Dear, 24 Tex. 17; Williams v. Chambers (Tex. Civ. App.), 26 S. W. 270; Tuggle v. Berkeley, 101 Va. 83, 43 S. E. 199; Reynolds v. Scott, Brayt. (Vt.) 75; Thorne v. Joy, 15 Wash. 83, 45 Pac. 642; Hoffman v. Ryan, 21 W. Va. 415; Davis v. Demming,

legal mortgage, if the instruments are of the same date, or were executed and delivered at the same time and as one transaction.[32] As between the parties themselves, the relation is the same as if the mortgage had been in the ordinary form.[33] It is sufficient that the deed
and defeasance are substantially contemporaneous and were manifestly meant to constitute a mortgage.[34] A defeasance made after the
record of the deed is sufficient where the deed was made without the
knowledge of the grantee, and the obligation to reconvey was made
upon his being informed of it.[35] When the deed and defeasance are
executed at the same time, or are agreed upon at the same time, it is
a conclusion of law that they constitute a legal mortgage.[36] The fact
that possession of the property is given to the grantee by the contract
for reconveyance does not affect the character of the transaction.[37]

A bond for reconveyance by a grantee in a warranty deed, upon payment by the grantor of a debt to the grantee is an instrument of defeas-

---

12 W. Va. 246; Falbe v. Caves, 151
Wis. 54, 138 N. W. 87; Von Oehsen
v. Brown, 148 Wis. 236, 134 N. W.
377; Wolf v. Theresa Village Mut.
Fire Ins. Co., 115 Wis. 402, 91 N.
W. 1014; Brinkman v. Jones, 44
Wis. 498; Plato v. Roe, 14 Wis. 453;
Knowlton v. Walker, 13 Wis. 264;
Second Ward Bank v. Upmann, 12
Wis. 499. See also Ray v. Tatum,
72 Fed. 112. In Georgia a conveyance by deed to secure any debt, the
grantor taking a bond for reconveyance upon the payment of such debt,
upon the payment of the debt passes
the title to the property till the
debt is repaid and is held to be an
absolute conveyance, with the right
reserved by the vendor to have said
property reconveyed to him upon
the payment of the debt or debts
intended to be secured agreeably to
the terms of the contract and not
a mortgage. Code 1895, § 2771. For
construction of this provision, see
also Pirkle v. Equitable Mtg. Co., 99
Ga. 524; Marshall v. Hodgkins, 99
Ga. 592; Broach v. Smith, 75 Ga.
159; McElmurray v. Blodgett, 120
Ga. 9, 47 S. E. 531 (grantor's right
to repurchase); Burckhalter v.
Planters' Loan &c. Bank, 100 Ga.
428. Under this statute a deed giv-
en to secure a debt may be foreclosed by the grantee as a mortgage,

notwithstanding a provision therein
that it is to be construed as a deed
passing title, and not as a mortgage, such provision being for the
benefit of the grantee who may
waive it at his election.
[32] Scott v. McFarland, 13 Mass.
308; Taylor v. Weld, 5 Mass. 109;
Erskine v. Townsend, 2 Mass. 493,
3 Am. Dec. 71; Nugent v. Riley, 1
Metc. (Mass.) 117, 35 Am. Dec. 355;
Lanfair v. Lanfair, 18 Pick. (Mass.)
299; Newhall v. Burt, 7 Pick.
(Mass.) 157; Stocking v. Fairchild,
5 Pick. (Mass.) 181; Eaton v. Whiting, 3 Pick. (Mass.) 484; Clark v.
Landon, 90 Mich. 83, 51 N. W. 357.
[33] Short v. Caldwell, 155 Mass. 57,
28 N. E. 1124; Tilden v. Greenwood,
149 Mass. 567, 22 N. E. 45.
[34] Jeffery v. Hursh, 58 Mich. 246,
25 N. W. 176, 27 N. W. 7. See post
§ 245.
[35] Harrison v. Phillips Academy,
12 Mass. 456.
[36] Clark v. Landon, 90 Mich. 83,
51 N. W. 357; Jeffery v. Hursh, 58
Mich. 246, 25 N. W. 176, 27 N. W.
7; Waters v. Crabtree, 105 N. Car.
394, 11 S. E. 240; Wilson v. Shoenberger, 31 Pa. St. 295; Reitenbaugh
v. Ludwick, 31 Pa. St. 131.
[37] Clark v. Landon, 90 Mich. 83,
51 N. W. 357.

ance and raises a mortgage.[38] A provision or reservation giving the grantor the right to repurchase at a certain price within a specified time may be equivalent to an agreement by the grantee to reconvey, and constitute a mortgage.[39] A contract contemporaneous with a deed, whereby the grantee agrees to sell and the grantor to buy the land for the amount constituting the consideration, renders the transaction presumptively a mortgage.[40] A provision for a forfeiture in a contract to reconvey which was in fact a defeasance, accompanying a deed, amounts only to a mortgage.[41]

The instrument of defeasance must be of as high a nature as is required in the deed or conveyance itself; and consequently in states where seals have not been abolished, a written agreement to reconvey not under seal, though made at the same time with the deed, does not at law constitute a mortgage.[42] If not under seal, the agreement will constitute a mortgage only in equity.[43]

The defeasance must also be absolute. A contract which gives the grantee the option to reconvey, or pay a sum of money, is not a defeasance which, in connection with the deed, will constitute a mort-

---

[38] Watkins v. Gregory, 6 Blackf. (Ind.) 113; Harbison v. Lemon, 3 Blackf. (Ind.) 51, 23 Am. Dec. 376; Wysong v. Sells, 44 Ind. App. 238, 88 N. E. 954; Brown v. Holyoke, 53 Maine 9; Harrison v. Phillips Academy, 12 Mass. 456; Holbrook v. Finney, 4 Mass. 566, 3 Am. Dec. 243; Erskine v. Townsend, 2 Mass. 493, 3 Am. Dec. 71; Waters v. Randall, 6 Metc. (Mass.) 479; Marden v. Babcock, 2 Metc. (Mass.) 99; Clark v. Landon, 90 Mich. 83, 51 N. W. 357; Jeffery v. Hursh, 58 Mich. 246, 25 N. W. 176, 27 N. W. 7; Ferris v. Wilcox, 51 Mich. 105, 16 N. W. 252, 47 Am. Rep. 551; Enos v. Sutherland, 11 Mich. 538; Batty v. Snook, 5 Mich. 231; Swetland v. Swetland, 3 Mich. 482; Butman v. James, 34 Minn. 547, 27 N. W. 66; Archambau v. Green, 21 Minn. 520; Weide v. Gehl, 21 Minn. 449; Hill v. Edwards, 11 Minn. 22; Grogan v. Val. Trading Co., 30 Mont. 229, 76 Pac. 211; Van Wagner v. Van Wagner, 7 N. J. Eq. 27; Holmes v. Grant, 8 Paige (N. Y.) 243; Watkins v. Williams, 123 N. Car. 170, 31 S. E. 388; Friedley v. Hamilton, 17 S. & R. (Pa.) 70, 17 Am. Dec. 638; Kelly v. Thompson, 7 Watts (Pa.) 401; Jaques v. Weeks, 7 Watts (Pa.) 261; Kerr v. Gilmore, 6 Watts (Pa.) 406; Francis v. Francis, 78 S. Car. 178, 58 S. E. 804. See also Reynolds v. Reynolds, 42 Wash. 107, 84 Pac. 579.

[39] Thomas v. Livingston, 155 Ala. 546, 46 So. 851; Rose v. Gandy, 137 Ala. 329, 34 So. 239; McElmurray v. Blodgett, 120 Ga. 9, 47 S. E. 531. See post § 261.

[40] Calhoun v. Anderson, 78 Kans. 746, 98 Pac. 274.

[41] Barlow v. Cooper, 109 Ill. App. 375; Second Ward Bank v. Upmann, 12 Wis. 499.

[42] Flint v. Sheldon, 13 Mass. 443, 7 Am. Dec. 162; Kelleran v. Brown, 4 Mass. 443; Murphy v. Calley, 1 Allen (Mass.) 107; Scituate v. Hanover, 16 Pick. (Mass.) 222; Flagg v. Mann, 14 Pick. (Mass.) 467; Cutler v. Dickinson, 8 Pick. (Mass.) 386; Jewett v. Bailey, 5 Greenl. (Maine) 87; Warren v. Lovis, 53 Maine 463; French v. Sturdivant, 8 Maine 246; Runlet v. Otis, 2 N. H. 167; Lund v. Lund, 1 N. H. 39, 8 Am. Dec. 29. But see Harrison v. Phillips Academy, 12 Mass. 456.

[43] Reading v. Weston, 8 Conn. 117, 20 Am. Dec. 97; Fitch v. Miller, 200 Ill. 170, 179, 65 N. E. 650 (quoting text); Green v. Capps, 142 Ill. 286, 31 N. E. 597; West v. Reed, 55 Ill. 242; Kelleran v. Brown, 4 Mass. 443; Eaton v. Green, 22 Pick. (Mass.)

gage. The fee is absolute in the grantee if he so elect.[44] And likewise an absolute conveyance to a mortgagee in settlement of foreclosure proceedings, is not rendered a mortgage by an option to purchase, concurrently given to a third person.[45] Where there is no obligation[46] or only a conditional obligation[47] to pay the amount for which the reconveyance was to be made, the transaction is usually intended and considered as a conditional sale and not as a mortgage. The rule that when the evidence is doubtful, a deed absolute on its face is deemed a mortgage[48] applies to an agreement to reconvey.[49] It has been held that, when the grantee in an absolute deed agrees to reconvey upon payment of a valid existing debt, the transaction is conclusively presumed to be a mortgage;[50] but the mere agreement of such grantee to reconvey does not necessarily show that the transaction was a mortgage to secure a debt, even though the sum to be paid upon reconveyance is equal to the sum secured by a former mortgage.[51] Not every agreement to reconvey even upon payment of a certain sum within a specified time constitutes a mortgage, but the intention of the parties controls, as shown by all the circumstances, the terms of the instrument and parol agreements not conflicting with such terms.[52]

An absolute deed with a defeasance passes the legal title to the prop-

526; Flagg v. Mann, 14 Pick. (Mass.) 467; Cutler v. Dickinson, 8 Pick. (Mass.) 386; Skinner v. Cox, 4 Dev. L. (N. Car.) 59; Phelan v. Fitzpatrick, 84 Wis. 240, 54 N. W. 614.

[44] Thompson v. People's Bldg. &c. Co., 114 Iowa 481, 87 N. W. 438; Bigler v. Jack, 114 Iowa 667, 87 N. W. 700; Fuller v. Pratt, 10 Maine 197. Conversely the grantor's option to repurchase, with no absolute obligation, will not render the deed a mortgage. Yost v. First Nat. Bank, 66 Kans. 605, 72 Pac. 209; Fabrique v. Cherokee Coal &c. Co., 69 Kans. 733, 77 Pac. 584; Smith v. Hoff, 23 N. Dak. 37, 135 N. W. 772, Ann. Cas. 1914 C, 1072; Smyth v. Reed, 28 Utah 262, 78 Pac. 478; Hinchman v. Cook, 45 Wash. 490, 88 Pac. 931; Hoover v. Bouffleur, 74 Wash. 382, 133 Pac. 602. See also Braun v. Vollmer, 89 App. Div. 43, 85 N. Y. S. 319. See post § 264.

[45] Braun v. Vollmer, 89 App. Div. 43, 85 N. Y. S. 319; Hoover v. Bouffleur, 74 Wash. 382, 133 Pac. 602.

[46] Bell v. Shiver (Ala.), 61 So.

881; White v. Redenbaugh, 41 Ind. App. 580, 82 N. E. 110; Parks v. Sullivan (Tex. Civ. App.), 152 S. W. 704. See post §§ 260, 265, 343.

[47] Mittesteadt v. Johnson, 75 Wash. 550, 135 Pac. 214.

[48] See post §§ 258, 279.

[49] Elliott v. Bozorth, 52 Ore. 391, 97 Pac. 632.

[50] Beidelman v. Koch, 42 Ind. App. 423, 85 N. E. 977.

[51] Miller v. Smith, 20 N. Dak. 96, 126 N. W. 499; Devore v. Woodruff, 1 N. Dak. 143, 45 N. W. 701; Hesser v. Brown, 40 Wash. 688, 82 Pac. 934. See post §§ 261, 267. A conveyance, with the right to repurchase, is not necessarily a mortgage. Conway v. Alexander, 7 Cranch (U. S.) 237; Slowey v. McMurray, 27 Mo. 113, 72 Am. St. 251; Hill v. Grant, 46 N. Y. 496; Glover v. Payn, 19 Wend. (N. Y.) 518.

[52] Keeline v. Clark, 132 Iowa 360, 106 N. W. 257; First Nat. Bank v. Edwards, 84 Kans. 495, 115 Pac. 118; Luesenhop v. Einsfeld, 93 App. Div. 68, 87 N. Y. S. 268.

erty even in states in which it is held that a mortgage in the usual form does not pass the title.[53]

§ 245. Deed and defeasance as part of same transaction.

—At law the deed and defeasance must be part of the same transaction, and must take effect at the same time; for a subsequent defeasance without a new consideration, is a mere nudum pactum, and since no rights arise under it, it can not convert an instrument once a deed into a mortgage.[54] It seems sufficient, however, that the instruments are substantially contemporaneous; and the lapse of an hour or even a day between the execution of a deed and agreement to reconvey has been held insufficient to deprive the transaction of the character of a mortgage.[55] A subsequent defeasance can not be allowed to affect the prior conveyance. The transaction must be a mortgage at its inception, and can not become so afterward. The defeasance must be such that it may be considered as if it were annexed to, or inserted in, the same deed, and construed as containing the condition upon the performance of which the estate may be defeated.[56] The two instruments, if contempo-

[53] Hughes v. Davis, 40 Cal. 117; Jay v. Welchel, 78 Ga. 786, 3 S. E. 906; Thaxton v. Roberts, 66 Ga. 704; McLaren v. Clark, 30 Ga. 423, 7 S. E. 230; First Nat. Bank v. Tighe, 49 Nebr. 299, 68 N. W. 490; Gallagher v. Giddings, 33 Nebr. 222, 49 N. W. 1126; Kemper v. Campbell, 44 Ohio St. 210; Loring v. Melendy, 11 Ohio 355; Baird v. Kirtland, 8 Ohio 21. But see Moisant v. McPhee, 92 Cal. 76, 28 Pac. 46; First Nat. Bank v. Ashmead, 23 Fla. 379, 2 So. 657. See post § 339.

[54] Ingram v. Illges, 98 Ala. 511, 13 So. 548; Bryan v. Cowart, 21 Ala. 92; Freeman v. Baldwin, 13 Ala. 246; Bunker v. Barron, 79 Maine 62, 8 Atl. 253, 1 Am. St. 282; Clement v. Bennett, 70 Maine 207; Warren v. Lovis, 53 Maine 463; Shaw v. Erskine, 43 Maine 371; McLaughlin v. Shepherd, 32 Maine 143, 52 Am. Dec. 646; Bennock v. Whipple, 12 Maine 346, 28 Am. Dec. 186; Trull v. Skinner, 17 Pick. (Mass.) 213; Emerson v. Murray, 4 N. H. 171, 17 Am. Dec. 407; Griswold v. Fowler, 6 Abb. Pr. (N. Y.) 113; Potter v. Langstrath, 151 Pa. St. 216, 25 Atl. 76; Plumer v. Guthrie, 76 Pa. St. 441; Wilson v. Shoenberger, 31 Pa.

St. 295; Murray v. McCarthy, 3 Sad. (Pa.) 383, 6 Atl. 243; Kelly v. Thompson, 7 Watts (Pa.) 401; Waters v. Crabtree, 105 N. Car. 394, 11 S. E. 240. See also Thomas v. Livingston, 155 Ala. 546, 46 So. 851. A bond delivered by the grantee three years after delivery of the absolute deed, conditioned to reconvey to the grantor the same land, does not constitute a defeasance and thereby render the conveyance a mortgage. Stowe v. Merrill, 77 Maine 550, 1 Atl. 684. And so a deed is not proved a mortgage by the grantee's acknowledgment under seal made over a year after the execution of the deed, that he held the land as security for a note. Waters v. Crabtree, 105 N. Car. 394, 11 S. E. 240. But see Scott v. Henry, 13 Ark. 112; Hall v. Arnott, 80 Cal. 348, 22 Pac. 200. See post § 246.

[55] Sebree v. Thompson, 31 Ky. L. 1146, 104 S. W. 781 (an hour); Gubbings v. Harper, 7 Phila. (Pa.) 276 (a day).

[56] Murphy v. Calley, 1 Allen (Mass.) 107, and cases cited. A collateral writing executed an hour after the deed has been held a valid defeasance, although nothing had

raneous, will be construed together as one,[57] and the estate conveyed in the deed may control and explain a defective description of such estate in the defeasance.[58]

If, at the time of executing an absolute deed, the parties verbally agree that a defeasance shall be executed subsequently on request, such defeasance, when executed, will relate back to the deed and make it a mortgage.[59] But, in the absence of such agreement connecting the defeasance with the original transaction, there is not a mortgage even in equity, but only an agreement to reconvey. "Neither courts of law nor courts of equity can make or modify a valid contract. They can only determine what they are, and give them effect. Courts of equity can only give effect to and administer rights created by and growing out of them that courts of law can not, by reason of their peculiar organization and rigorous methods of procedure. Nor has a court of equity authority to change the settled nature of an instrument, and make it different from, and serve a purpose different from, that contemplated by the parties when they made it."[60]

It is not necessary that the deed and bond of defeasance should both bear the same date.[61] If these have once been given, and a reconveyance made in accordance with the terms of the bond, and subsequently the premises are reconveyed to the obligor, under an agreement that the same bond shall continue in force for another reconveyance, this amounts to a redelivery of the bond, and makes the transaction a mortgage.[62] Where the defeasance is of a different date from the deed, parol evidence is admissible to prove that they were delivered at the same time, and are part of the same transaction.[63] It is not necessary

been said about it before that time. Sebree v. Thompson, 31 Ky. L. 1146, 104 S. W. 781. See post § 246.

[57] Adams v. Hopkins, 144 Cal. 19, 77 Pac. 712; In re Bennett's Estate, 168 Ill. App. 658. See also Thomas v. Livingston, 155 Ala. 546, 46 So. 851. See post § 264.

[58] Turner v. Cochran, 30 Tex. Civ. App. 549, 70 S. W. 1024.

[59] Cosby v. Buchanan, 81 Ala. 574; Sears v. Dixon, 33 Cal. 326; Lovering v. Fogg, 18 Pick. (Mass.) 540; Doty v. Norton, 133 App. Div. 106, 117 N. Y. S. 793 (same day); Reitenbaugh v. Ludwick, 31 Pa. St. 131. See also Scott v. Henry, 13 Ark. 112; Waters v. Crabtree, 105 N. Car. 394, 11 S. E. 240. The agreement upon which the two instruments rest must antedate them both, and a

parol agreement at the time the deed is executed, that the grantee will later give a bond for reconveyance to the grantor, will not render the conveyance a mortgage, although the bond is afterward given. Lund v. Lund, 1 N. H. 39, 8 Am. Dec. 29.

[60] Waters v. Crabtree, 105 N. Car. 394, 11 S. E. 240, per Merrimon, C. J.

[61] Harrison v. Phillips Academy, 12 Mass. 456; McIntier v. Shaw, 6 Allen (Mass.) 83; Newhall v. Burt, 7 Pick. (Mass.) 157. See post § 246.

[62] McIntier v. Shaw, 6 Allen (Mass.) 83. See also Judd v. Flint, 4 Gray (Mass.) 557.

[63] Brown v. Holyoke, 53 Maine 9; Waters v. Crabtree, 105 N. Car. 394, 11 S. E. 240.

that the deed and defeasance should in terms refer to each other.[64] Their connection may be established by parol evidence.[65]

§ 246. Contemporaneous execution and delivery—Date.

—Although it is not material that the instruments should bear the same date,[66] it is essential that they should be executed[67] and delivered at the same

[64] A defeasance intended to cover two prior absolute conveyances, has that effect though not referring to the latter conveyance. Turner v. Cochran, 30 Tex. Civ. App. 549, 70 S. W. 1024.

[65] Preschbaker v. Feaman, 32 Ill. 475. See post § 277.

[66] Harrison v. Phillips Academy, 12 Mass. 455; McIntier v. Shaw, 6 Allen (Mass.) 83; Newhall v. Burt, 7 Pick. (Mass.) 157. See also Kraemer v. Adelsberger, 122 N. Y. 467, 25 N. E. 859.

[67] Lanahan v. Sears, 102 U. S. 318, 26 L. ed. 180; Dow v. Chamberlin, 5 McLean (U. S.) 281; Martin v. Pond, 30 Fed. 15; Cosby v. Buchanan, 81 Ala. 574, 1 So. 898; Sims v. Gaines, 64 Ala. 392; Freeman v. Baldwin, 13 Ala. 246; Walker v. Tiffin Gold &c. Min. Co., 2 Colo. 89; In re Gunn's Appeal, 55 Conn. 149, 10 Atl. 498; Rowan v. Sharp's Rifle Mfg. Co., 31 Conn. 1; Morrison v. Markham, 78 Ga. 161, 1 S. E. 425; Clark v. Lyon, 46 Ga. 202; Bearss v. Ford, 108 Ill. 16; Ewart v. Walling, 42 Ill. 453; Preschbaker v. Feaman, 32 Ill. 475; Lentz v. Martin, 75 Ind. 228; Crassen v. Swoveland, 22 Ind. 427; Watkins v. Gregory, 6 Blackf. (Ind.) 113; Harbison v. Lemon, 3 Blackf. (Ind.) 51, 23 Am. Dec. 376; Radford v. Folsom, 58 Iowa 473, 12 N. W. 536; Caruthers v. Hunt, 18 Iowa 576; Overstreet v. Baxter, 30 Kans. 55, 1 Pac. 825; Honore v. Hutchings, 8 Bush (Ky.) 687; Ogden v. Grant, 6 Dana (Ky.) 473; Edrington v. Harper, 3 J. J. Marsh. (Ky.) 353, 20 Am. Dec. 145; Frey v. Campbell, 8 Ky. L. (abst.) 772, 3 S. W. 368; Bunker v. Barron, 79 Maine 62, 1 Am. St. 282; Stowe v. Merrill, 77 Maine 550, 1 Atl. 684; Clement v. Bennett, 70 Maine 207; Warren v. Lovis, 53 Maine 463; Brown v. Holyoke, 53 Maine 9; Mills v. Darling, 43 Maine 565; Shaw v. Erskine, 43 Maine 371; McLaughlin v. Shepard, 32 Maine 143, 52 Am. Dec. 646; Bennock v. Whipple, 12 Maine 346, 28 Am. Dec. 186; Blaney v. Bearce, 2 Maine 132; Gaither v. Clarke, 67 Md. 18; Harrison v. Phillips Academy, 12 Mass. 455; Murphy v. Calley, 1 Allen (Mass.) 107; Woodward v. Pickett, 8 Gray (Mass.) 617; Bayley v. Bailey, 5 Gray (Mass.) 505; Judd v. Flint, 4 Gray (Mass.) 557; Clark v. Landon, 90 Mich. 83, 51 N. W. 357; Jeffery v. Hursh, 58 Mich. 246, 25 N. W. 176, 27 N. W. 7; Ferris v. Wilcox, 51 Mich. 105, 16 N. W. 252, 47 Am. Rep. 551; Enos v. Sutherland, 11 Mich. 538; Batty v. Snook, 5 Mich. 231; Butman v. James, 34 Minn. 547, 27 N. W. 66; Benton v. Nicoll, 24 Minn. 221; Archambau v. Green, 21 Minn. 520; Hill v. Edwards, 11 Minn. 22; Sharkey v. Sharkey, 47 Mo. 543; Copeland v. Yoakum, 38 Mo. 349; Connolly v. Giddings, 24 Nebr. 131, 37 N. W. 939; Vliet v. Young, 34 N. J. Eq. 15; Weed v. Stevenson, Clarke Ch. (N. Y.) 166; Clark v. Henry, 2 Cow. (N. Y.) 324; Peterson v. Clark, 15 Johns. (N. Y.) 205; Henry v. Davis, 7 Johns. Ch. (N. Y.) 40; Decker v. Leonard, 6 Lans. (N. Y.) 264; Hall v. Van Clene, 11 N. Y. Leg. Obs. 281; Brown v. Dean, 3 Wend. (N. Y.) 208; Lane v. Shears, 1 Wend. (N. Y.) 433; Robinson v. Willoughby, 65 N. Car. 520; Mason v. Hearne, 45 N. Car. 88; Marshall v. Stewart, 17 Ohio 356; McClurkan v. Thompson, 69 Pa. St. 305; Houser v. Lamont, 55 Pa. St. 311, 93 Am. Dec. 755; Guthrie v. Kahle, 46 Pa. St. 331; Gubbings v. Harper, 7 Phila. (Pa.) 276; Friedley v. Hamilton, 17 Serg. & R. (Pa.) 70, 17 Am. Dec. 638; Johnston v. Gray, 16 Serg. & R. (Pa.) 361, 16 Am. Dec. 577; Stoever v. Stoever, 9 Serg. & R. (Pa.) 434; Manufacturers' &c. Bank v. State Bank, 7 Watts & S. (Pa.) 335, 42 Am. Dec. 240; Jaques v. Weeks, 7 Watts (Pa.) 261; Kerr v. Gilmore,

time.[68] In equity, however, it is immaterial that the deeds and the agreement to reconvey be executed at different times;[69] and, as will be noticed elsewhere, it is immaterial that there be any bond or agreement to reconvey, parol evidence being sufficient to prove the transaction to be a mortgage.[70] Thus where a deed and defeasance are of different dates, and the latter recites that they were delivered the same day, parol evidence is admissible to explain the discrepancy.[71] A subsequent defeasance must be based on a sufficient consideration, unless it be professedly executed in explanation of the intention of the parties at the time of the conveyance, and of the true character of the instrument. A mere voluntary agreement to reconvey can not be enforced.[72]

§ 247. **Defeasance delivered in escrow.**—A deed deposited in escrow by a mortgagor to be delivered to the mortgagee if the debt is not paid within a given time, is regarded as a defeasance and takes effect

6 Watts (Pa.) 405; Colwell v. Woods, 3 Watts (Pa.) 188, 27 Am. Dec. 345; Blizzard v. Craigmiles, 7 Lea (Tenn.) 693; Hammonds v. Hopkins, 3 Yerg. (Tenn.) 525; Moores v. Wills, 69 Tex. 109, 5 S. W. 675; Baxter v. Dear, 24 Tex. 17, 76 Am. Dec. 89; Reynolds v. Scott, Brayt. (Vt.) 75; Hoffman v. Ryan, 21 W. Va. 415; Brinkman v. Jones, 44 Wis. 498; Plato v. Roe, 14 Wis. 453; Knowlton v. Walker, 13 Wis. 264; Second Ward Bank v. Upmann, 12 Wis. 499.

[68] Teal v. Walker, 111 U. S. 242, 28 L. ed. 415; Freeman v. Baldwin, 13 Ala. 246; Clark v. Lyon, 46 Ga. 202; Ewart v. Walling, 42 Ill. 453; Harbison v. Lemon, 3 Blackf. (Ind.) 51, 23 Am. Dec. 376; Edrington v. Harper, 3 J. J. Marsh. (Ky.) 353, 20 Am. Dec. 145; Frey v. Campbell, 8 Ky. L. (Abst.) 772, 3 S. W. 368; Bunker v. Barron, 79 Maine 62, 8 Atl. 253, 1 Am. St. 282; Cotton v. McKee, 68 Maine 486; Shaw v. Erskine, 43 Maine 371; Blaney v. Bearce, 2 Maine 132; Murphy v. Calley, 1 Allen (Mass.) 107; Judd v. Flint, 4 Gray (Mass.) 557; Lanfair v. Lanfair, 18 Pick. (Mass.) 299; Newhall v. Burt, 7 Pick. (Mass.) 157; Stocking v. Fairchild, 5 Pick. (Mass.) 181; Taylor v. Weld, 5 Mass. 109; Kelleran v. Brown, 4 Mass. 443; Jeffery v. Hursh, 58 Mich. 246, 25 N. W. 176, 27 N. W. 7; Enos v. Sutherland, 11 Mich. 538; Butman

v. James, 34 Minn. 547, 27 N. W. 66; Copeland v. Yoakum, 38 Mo. 349; Kraemer v. Adelsberger, 122 N. Y. 467, 25 N. E. 859; Peterson v. Clark, 15 Johns. (N. Y.) 205; Decker v. Leonard, 6 Lans. (N. Y.) 264; Mason v. Hearne, 45 N. Car. 88; Haines v. Thomson, 70 Pa. St. 434; Kelly v. Thompson, 7 Watts (Pa.) 401; Kerr v. Gilmore, 6 Watts (Pa.) 405; Colwell v. Woods, 3 Watts (Pa.) 188, 27 Am. Dec. 345; Manufacturers' &c. Bank v. State Bank, 7 Watts & S. (Pa.) 335, 42 Am. Dec. 240; Brinkman v. Jones, 44 Wis. 498; Second Ward Bank v. Upmann, 12 Wis. 499.

[69] Williams v. Chadwick, 74 Conn. 252, 50 Atl. 720; Mills v. Mills, 26 Conn. 213; Sebree v. Thompson, 31 Ky. L. 1146, 104 S. W. 781; Taber v. Hamlin, 97 Mass. 489, 93 Am. Dec. 113.

[70] Scott v. Henry, 13 Ark. 112; Walker v. Tiffin Min. Co., 2 Colo. 89; Brinkman v. Jones, 44 Wis. 498. See post §§ 282–395.

[71] Haines v. Thompson, 70 Pa. St. 434.

[72] Ingram v. Illges, 98 Ala. 511, 13 So. 548; Bryan v. Cowart, 21 Ala. 92; Bunker v. Barron, 79 Maine 62, 8 Atl. 253, 1 Am. St. 282; Trull v. Skinner, 17 Pick. (Mass.) 213; Vasser v. Vasser, 23 Miss. 378; Griswold v. Fowler, 6 Abb. Pr. (N. Y.) 113; Waters v. Crabtree, 105 N. Car. 394, 11 S. E. 240.

from the time of deposit.[73] If the agreement to reconvey be delivered as an escrow, to be delivered to the obligee upon the repayment of the money within a certain time, it is not executed and delivered at the same time with the deed, so as to constitute part of the same transaction, and therefore the transaction is not a mortgage.[74]

A conveyance absolute on its face was made to one who advanced money to the grantor, and at the same time executed an agreement to reconvey the land, upon repayment of the money advanced, within thirty days; and both instruments were placed in the hands of a third person, with instructions if repayment was not so made, to deliver both instruments to the grantee. The money not being repaid, both instruments, after the default, were delivered to the grantee, the grantor so directing. It was held that the deed, on its delivery to the grantee, conveyed the land to him absolutely, and was not a mortgage. The maxim, "Once a mortgage, always a mortgage," was declared inapplicable to the case, because the conveyance never was a mortgage. The transaction was to the effect that, if the advance was repaid in thirty days, it should be a loan; but if not repaid in that time, it should be the consideration for an absolute conveyance of the land in question.[75]

Where a debtor who had given a mortgage, at the instance of his creditor executed an absolute deed, and placed it in escrow, to be delivered to the defendant on default to save foreclosure fees, it was held that the deed was in effect a mortgage and the debtor was entitled to redeem.[76]

§ 247a. Extrinsic evidence to connect deed and defeasance—Leading cases.—In order to constitute a mortgage, the deed and written defeasance must correspond in all essential particulars, appearing either on their face or by extrinsic evidence to constitute parts of the 'same transaction.[77] If the deed and defeasance do not on their face

---

[73] Holden Land &c. Stock Co. v. Interstate Trading Co., 87 Kans. 221; 123 Pac. 733; Moorhead v. Ellison, 56 Tex. Civ. App. 444, 120 S. W. 1049; Plummer v. Ilse, 41 Wash. 5, 82 Pac. 1009, 2 L. R. A. (N. S.) 627, 111 Am. St. 997.

[74] Bodwell v. Webster, 13 Pick. (Mass.) 411. The case of Carey v. Rawson, 8 Mass. 159, in apparent conflict with the above, is explained on the ground that the deed in that case was not considered as an escrow, but as a deed taking effect presently, without the performance of the conditions; but in Bodwell v. Webster, 13 Pick. (Mass.) 411, the bond having been delivered in escrow, and the conditions never being performed, it was never delivered to the obligee. See also Exton v. Scott, 6 Sim. 31; Glendenning v. Johnston, 33 Wis. 347.

[75] Glendenning v. Johnston, 33 Wis. 347. See also Leggett v. Edwards, Hopk. Ch. (N. Y.) 530; Henley v. Hotaling, 41 Cal. 22.

[76] Plummer v. Ilse, 41 Wash. 5, 82 Pac. 1009, 2 L. R. A. (N. S.) 627, 111 Am. St. 997.

[77] A trifling discrepancy between the description contained in the

show that the transaction is a security for a debt, the instruments do not, as a matter of law, constitute a mortgage, though they may be proved to be such by extrinsic evidence.[78]

Instructive cases involving this distinction have been decided by the Supreme Court of the United States. In Teale v. Walker[79] the defeasance showed upon its face that the absolute deed was intended to secure a note given by the grantor for money borrowed of the grantee. These instruments, executed at the same time, disclosed a debt and an absolute deed as security, and were accordingly held to constitute by themselves a mortgage.

In Wallace v. Johnstone[80] no debt was disclosed upon the face of the papers, and no fact showing whether the deed was intended as a security or not. Mr. Justice Lamar, delivering the opinion of the court, said: "If this question could be determined by an inspection of the written papers alone, the transaction was clearly not a mortgage, but an absolute sale and deed, accompanied by an independent contract between the vendee and a third person, not a party to the sale, to convey the lands to him upon his payment of a fixed sum within a certain time. Upon their face there are none of the indicia by which courts are led to construe such instruments to be intended as a mortgage or security for a loan; nothing from which there can be inferred the existence of a debt, or the relation of borrower and lender between the parties to the deeds, or between the parties to the contract. * * * A deed of lands absolute in form, with general warranty of title, and an agreement by the vendee to reconvey the property to the vendor or a third person upon his payment of a fixed sum within a specified time, do not of themselves constitute a mortgage, nor will they be held to operate as a mortgage, unless it is clearly shown, either by parol evidence or by the attendant circumstances, such as the condition and relation of the parties, or gross inadequacy of price, to have been intended by the parties as a security for a loan or an existing debt."

In a later case upon this point[81] the grantor conveyed land by an absolute deed, and the grantee executed a contemporaneous agreement to reconvey upon the payment of a specified sum of money on a given

---

deed and defeasance is immaterial. Brown v. Holyoke, 53 Maine 9; Turner v. Cochran, 30 Tex. Civ. App. 549, 70 S. W. 1024.

[78] See ante § 244.

[79] Teal v. Walker, 111 U. S. 242, 28 L. ed. 415, 4 Sup. Ct. 420.

[80] Wallace v. Johnstone, 129 U. S.

58, 32 L. ed. 619, 9 Sup. Ct. 243. See also Carroll v. Tomlinson, 192 Ill. 398, 61 N. E. 484.

[81] Bogk v. Gassert, 149 U. S. 17, 37 L. ed. 631, 13 Sup. Ct. 738, affg. Gassert v. Bogk, 7 Mont. 585, 19 Pac. 281. See post § 304a.

date. Two days thereafter the grantor accepted a lease of the same land from the grantee, upon the expiration of which the latter brought an action for the restitution of the premises. It was held that the instruments did not, as a matter of law, constitute a mortgage, but their effect was a question for the jury, upon all the evidence in the case. In delivering the opinion of the court, Mr. Justice Brown said: "In the case under consideration there is no mention made, in either of the three instruments, of a debt, a loan, a note, or anything from which the relation of borrower and lender can be inferred; and the case in this particular is distinguishable from that of Teale v. Walker, and is more nearly analogous to that of Wallace v. Johnstone. * * * The inadequacy of price was undoubtedly great, but this would not of itself authorize the court to take the question from the jury. * * * The case was evidently a proper one to go to the jury, who were left to determine the question whether the instruments were intended as a mortgage, and were instructed that, if they found them to be such, the plaintiffs could not recover.'

§ 248. Parol evidence to connect the deed and defeasance.—Parol evidence is admissible to connect the deed and defeasance to show that they are parts of the same transaction, and that together they were intended to constitute a mortgage.[82] Thus an instrument bearing a date subsequent to the deed may be shown by parol to have been executed at the same time, or orally agreed upon at the same time and subsequently reduced to writing.[83] If the instruments themselves show their connection, and that the purpose of the transaction was to secure a debt, no parol proof is necessary.[84] Such proof is introduced, not to contradict or vary the writings, but to show that they are really one

[82] Gay v. Hamilton, 33 Cal. 686; First Nat. Bank v. Ashmead, 23 Fla. 379, 2 So. 657; Franklin v. Ayer, 22 Fla. 654; Preschbaker v. Feaman, 32 Ill. 475; Tillson v. Moulton, 23 Ill. 648; Brown v. Holyoke, 53 Maine 9; Smith v. Hoff, 23 N. Dak. 37, 135 N. W. 772, Ann. Cas. 1914 C, 1042; Haines v. Thomson, 70 Pa. St. 434; Reitenbaugh v. Ludwick, 31 Pa. St. 131; Kelly v. Thompson, 7 Watts (Pa.) 401; Turner v. Cochran, 30 Tex. Civ. App. 549, 70 S. W. 1024; Beebe v. Wisconsin Mortgage Loan Co., 117 Wis. 328, 93 N. W. 1103. See also Blackstock v. Robertson, 42 Colo. 472, 94 Pac. 336.

[83] First Nat. Bank v. Ashmead, 23 Fla. 379, 2 So. 657; Nicolls v. McDonald, 101 Pa. St. 514; Umbenhower v. Miller, 101 Pa. St. 71.

[84] First Nat. Bank v. Ashmead, 23 Fla. 379, 2 So. 657. The deed and defeasance may be connected by similar descriptions, though such descriptions are not identical. Turner v. Cochran, 30 Tex. Civ. App. 549, 70 S. W. 1024. A written agreement referring to a deed contemporaneously executed will be construed with the deed as one instrument. Smith v. Smith, 153 Ala. 504, 45 So. 168.

arrangement, and were agreed upon at the same time.[85] It is also admissible to show that the defeasance has been lost or destroyed by fraud or mistake.[86]

The legal effect of the deed and bond to reconvey, when the instruments are not ambiguous, is a matter of law for the court.[87]

When the conveyance and the agreement to reconvey on payment of the purchase-money are on their face of even date, and disclose a debt secured, the transaction is necessarily a mortgage, and parol evidence of a different understanding by the parties will not be received to convert it into a conditional sale.[88] When the two instruments are of different dates, such evidence is admissible. If the agreement recite that the deed was delivered on the same day with the agreement, although the dates are different, prima facie the transaction is a mortgage; but evidence is admissible to account for the discrepancy between the dates and the execution of the paper; and such evidence may show that the deed was executed upon a sale, and not as security.[89] Where the deed and agreement to reconvey are not executed at the same time, the determination of the question whether they constitute a mortgage or not depends entirely upon the intention of the parties as ascertained from the circumstances.[90] When the agreement to reconvey is executed subsequently to the deed the question whether the transaction is a mortgage or a sale is one of fact for the jury.[91] If it be acknowledged or proved that it was in the beginning a sale, the burden of proof is upon the grantor to establish a change in its character.[92]

§ 249. **Illegal condition in defeasance.**—If the defeasance expresses a condition that is illegal, or contrary to public policy, as where the grantee stipulates that, if he should not procure two witnesses to testify to a certain state of facts, the deed should be null and void, the

---

[85] Umbenhower v. Miller, 101 Pa. St. 71; Wilson v. Shoenberger, 31 Pa. St. 295; Reitenbaugh v. Ludwick, 31 Pa. St. 131.

[86] Marks v. Pell, 1 Johns. Ch. (N. Y.) 594.

[87] Keith v. Catchings, 64 Ga. 773

[88] Voss v. Eller, 109 Ind. 260, 10 N. E. 74; Proctor v. Cole, 66 Ind. 576; Gassert v. Bogk, 7 Mont. 585, 19 Pac. 281; Kerr v. Gilmore, 6 Watts (Pa.) 405; Brown v. Nickle, 6 Pa. St. 390. In the latter case it was remarked that Kerr v. Gilmore "pushed the doctrine to its utmost verge." See ante § 244.

[89] Haines v. Thompson, 70 Pa. St. 434. See also Baisch v. Oakeley, 68 Pa. St. 92; Gubbings v. Harper, 7 Phila. (Pa.) 276.

[90] Haines v. Thomson, 70 Pa. St. 434; Baisch v. Oakeley, 68 Pa. St. 92; Wilson v. Shoenberger, 31 Pa. St. 295; Kelly v. Thompson, 7 Watts (Pa.) 401; Kerr v. Gilmore, 6 Watts (Pa.) 405.

[91] Wilson v. Shoenberger, 31 Pa. St. 295.

[92] Haines v. Thomson, 70 Pa. St. 434.

transaction will not be held to constitute a mortgage, because, the legal estate having once vested in the grantee, it can not be divested by his failure to perform the illegal stipulation, but the deed to him becomes and remains absolute.[93] If the condition of defeasance be that the mortgagee shall not oppose his debtor's discharge in insolvency the mortgage is void as against public policy.[94]

A mortgage given in composition of a felony, or upon a promise not to prosecute a crime, or a mortgage executed to procure a nolle prosequi to an indictment pending against the mortgagor, is likewise against public policy and void.[95] Equity will not permit foreclosure of such mortgages.[96] But a mortgage given by an employé for part of a sum embezzled by him, is valid and enforcible where it was not obtained as a consideration for his release from the charge of embezzlement.[97] A mortgage or an absolute deed in the nature of a mortgage given to secure performance of a gambling contract,[98] the illegal maintenance of a saloon,[99] or the enforcement of a champertous agreement,[1] is void. A mortgagor may, however, be permitted to redeem, although the mortgage was given to secure notes founded on a consideration which was illegal or against public policy.[2]

§ 250. The necessary incident of redemption.—When it is once established that the separate instrument is a defeasance, the convey-

[93] Patterson v. Donner, 48 Cal. 369. See post §§ 618–622.

[94] Benicia Agricultural Works v. Estes, 98 Cal. XVII, 32 Pac. 938; Estudillo v. Meyerstein, 72 Cal. 317, 13 Pac. 869; Bell v. Leggett, 7 N. Y. 176; Rice v. Maxwell, 13 Sm. & M. (Pa.) 289, 53 Am. Dec. 85.

[95] Johnson v. Graham Bros. Co., 98 Ark. 274, 135 S. W. 853; Small v. Williams, 87 Ga. 681, 13 S. E. 589; Crowder v. Reed, 80 Ind. 1 (agreement to procure nolle prosequi); Wildey v. Collier, 7 Md. 273, 61 Am. Dec. 346 (agreement to procure nolle prosequi); Atwood v. Fisk, 101 Mass. 363, 100 Am. Dec. 124; Pearce v. Wilson, 111 Pa. St. 14, 2 Atl. 99, 56 Am. Rep. 243; Pierce v. Kibbee, 51 Vt. 559 (renewal of such a mortgage, void); Collins v. Blantern, 2 Wils. 341.

[96] Small v. Williams, 87 Ga. 681, 13 S. E. 589; Bane v. Detrick, 52 Ill. 19; Owens v. Green, 103 Ky. 342, 20 Ky. L. 44, 45 S. W. 84; Maxfield v. Hoecker, 49 Hun (N. Y.) 605, 17 N. Y. St. 344, 2 N. Y. S. 77; Herbst v. Manss, 8 Ohio Dec. 215, 6 Wkly. L. Bul. 336. See also Williams v. Englebrecht, 34 Ohio St. 383.

[97] Hunt v. Hunt (Ore.), 134 Pac. 1180. See also Birmingham Lot Co. v. Taylor (Ala.), 62 So. 521; Schrommer v. Farwell, 56 Ill. 542; Maddox v. Rowe, 154 Ky. 417, 157 S. W. 714; Loud v. Hamilton (Tenn.), 51 S. W. 140, 45 L. R. A. (N. S.) 400.

[98] Chicago International Bank v. Vankirk, 39 Ill. App. 23; Luetchford v. Lord, 132 N. Y. 465, 30 N. E. 859; Krake v. Alexander, 86 Va. 206, 9 S. E. 991; Barnard v. Backhous, 52 Wis. 693, 6 N. W. 252, 9 N. W. 595.

[99] Dierkes v. Wideman, 143 Mich. 181, 106 N. W. 735.

[1] Gilbert v. Holmes, 64 Ill. 548.

[2] Thompson v. Lindsay, 243 Mo. 53, 145 S. W. 472; Cowles v. Raquet, 14 Ohio 38.

ance assumes the character of a mortgage with the inseparable incident of redemption, which no agreement of the parties, that the estate shall be absolute if the money be not paid at the day fixed, can waive.[3] The courts will give no effect to such an agreement; for the parties can not thus avoid the necessity of a foreclosure, or restrict or defeat the debtor's right of redemption.[4] The intent of the parties contrary to the rules of law avails nothing. The right of redemption, therefore, can not be affected by receipts and accounts given by the grantor to the grantee, mentioning the deed as an absolute conveyance.[5] Although it may have been the actual purpose and intention of the parties in making and accepting a deed absolute in form instead of the usual form of a mortgage, to create a security which would cut off the right of redemption and save the expense of foreclosure, yet the courts hold that if it appears to have been intended as a mortgage, the right of redemption can not be thus relinquished, the matter being beyond their control.[6]

In all cases, a condition express or implied, that the deed shall be void if payment be made at the day, is in equity regarded as substantially performed by payment, and thereupon reconveyance may be enforced.[7]

[3] Neikirk v. Boulder Nat. Bank, 53 Colo. 350, 127 Pac. 137 (citing text); Jackson v. Lynch, 129 Ill. 72, 22 N. E. 246; Mooney v. Byrne, 163 N. Y. 86, 57 N. E. 163; Kelton v. Brown (Tenn.), 39 S. W. 541.

[4] Hodgkins v. Wright, 127 Cal. 688, 60 Pac. 431; Jackson v. Lynch, 129 Ill. 72, 21 N. E. 580, 22 N. E. 246; Bearss v. Ford, 108 Ill. 16; Barlow v. Cooper, 109 Ill. App. 375; Johnson v. Prosperity Loan &c. Assn., 94 Ill. App. 260; Reilly v. Cullen, 159 Mo. 322, 60 S. W. 126; First Nat. Bank v. Sargeant, 65 Nebr. 594, 91 N. W. 595, 59 L. R. A. 296; Fahay v. State Bank, 1 Nebr. (Unoff.), 89, 95 N. W. 505; Van Wagner v. Van Wagner, 7 N. J. Eq. 27; Youle v. Richards, 1 N. J. Eq. 534, 23 Am. Dec. 722; Anonymous, 3 N. Car. 26; Halo v. Schick, 57 Pa. St. 319; Johnston v. Gray, 16 Serg. & R. (Pa.) 361, 16 Am. Dec. 577; Ehert v. Chapman, 8 Baxt. (Tenn.) 27; Jefferies v. Hartel (Tex. Civ. App.), 51 S. W. 653. But see Luesenhop v. Einsfeld, 93 App. Div. 68, 87 N. Y. S. 268.

[5] Bayley v. Bailey, 5 Gray (Mass.) 505.

[6] Johnson v. Prosperity Loan &c. Assn., 94 Ill. App. 260.

[7] Anthony v. Anthony, 23 Ark. 479; Sherrer v. Harris (Ark.), 13 S. W. 730; Lindsay v. Matthews, 17 Fla. 575; Endel v. Walls, 16 Fla. 786; Clark v. Lyon, 46 Ga. 202; Clark v. Finlon, 90 Ill. 245; Hunter v. Hatch, 45 Ill. 178; Ewart v. Walling, 42 Ill. 453; Reigard v. McNeil, 38 Ill. 400; Tillson v. Moulton, 23 Ill. 648; Church v. Cole, 36 Ind. 34; Thompson v. People's Bldg. Co., 114 Iowa 481, 87 N. W. 438; Brush v. Peterson, 54 Iowa 243, 6 N. W. 287; Scott v. Mewhirter, 49 Iowa 487; Wilson v. Patrick, 34 Iowa 362; Holliday v. Arthur, 25 Iowa 19; Richardson v. Barrick, 16 Iowa 407; Moore v. Wade, 8 Kans. 380; Howe v. Russell, 36 Maine 115; Baugher v. Merryman, 32 Md. 185; McIntier v. Shaw, 6 Allen (Mass.) 83; Steel v. Steel, 4 Allen (Mass.) 417; Parks v. Hall, 2 Pick. (Mass.) 206; Phœnix v. Gardner, 13 Minn. 430; Vasser v. Vasser, 23 Miss. 378; Wilson v. Drumrite, 21 Mo. 325; Davis v.

Neither can the right of redemption be restricted to the mortgagor personally, as such a restriction is inconsistent with the nature of a mortgage and void.[8]

A deed absolute in form, with an agreement under seal made by the grantee at the same time, promising to reconvey within a specified time upon repayment of the sum paid for the deed, with interest, constitutes a mortgage, although it is stipulated that, if the grantor fails to repay the sum within the time specified, the agreement shall be void and the deed absolute, "with no right of redemption." This latter provision is, in fact, quite decisive of the understanding of the parties that the transaction was a conveyance of the estate, defeasible upon the payment of money.[9]

The right to redeem and the right to foreclose are reciprocal. The mortgagee may demand payment, and may foreclose the mortgage whenever the mortgagor has the right to redeem.[10]

§ 251. Right of redemption indefeasible.—The mortgagor is not allowed to renounce beforehand his privilege of redemption. Generally, every one may renounce any privilege or surrender any right he has; but an exception is made in favor of debtors who have mortgaged their property, for the reason that their necessities often drive them to make ruinous concessions in order to raise money. When one borrows money

---

Clay, 2 Mo. 161; Bingham v. Thompson, 4 Nev. 224; Somersworth Savings Bank v. Roberts, 38 N. H. 22; Judge v. Reese, 24 N. J. Eq. 387; Sweet v. Parker, 22 N. J. Eq. 453; De Camp v. Crane, 19 N. J. Eq. 166; Vanderhaise v. Hugues, 13 N. J. Eq. 244; Mooney v. Byrne, 163 N. Y. 86, 57 N. E. 163; Miller v. McGuckin, 15 Abb. N. Cas. (N. Y.) 204; Simon v. Schmidt, 41 Hun (N. Y.) 318; Poston v. Jones, 122 N. Car. 536, 29 S. E. 951; Cotterell v. Long, 20 Ohio 464; Miami Exporting Co. v. Bank of U. S., Wright (Ohio) 249; in re Danzeisen's Appeal, 73 Pa. St. 65; In re Sweetser's Appeal, 71 Pa. St. 264; Odenbaugh v. Bradford, 67 Pa. St. 96; In re Harper's Appeal, 64 Pa. St. 315; Halo v. Schick, 57 Pa. St. 319; Nichols v. Reynolds, 1 R. I. 30, 36 Am. Dec. 238; Hinson v. Partee, 11 Humph. (Tenn.) 587; Webb v. Patterson, 7 Humph. (Tenn.) 431; Mc-Gan v. Marshall, 7 Humph. (Tenn.) 121; Bennett v. Union Bank, 5 Humph. (Tenn.) 612; Wright v. Bates, 13 Vt. 341; Mott v. Harrington, 12 Vt. 199; Yates v. Yates, 21 Wis. 473; Rogan v. Walker, 1 Wis.

[8] Johnston v. Gray, 16 Serg. & R. (Pa.) 361, 16 Am. Dec. 577. See also McClurkan v. Thompson, 69 Pa. St. 305; Martin v. Allen, 67 Kans. 758, 74 Pac. 249 (time for redemption limited to three years—construed as sale with right to repurchase).

[9] Murphy v. Calley, 1 Allen (Mass.) 107, and cases cited; Mooney v. Byrne, 163 N. Y. 86, 57 N. E. 163. See also Sheffield v. Day, 28 Ky. L. 754, 90 S. W. 545.

[10] Taylor v. McClain, 60 Cal. 651; Sheppard v. Wagner, 240 Mo. 409, 144 S. W. 394 (time for redemption limited to three years—construed as mortgage).

upon the security of his property, he is not allowed by any form of words to preclude himself from redeeming.[11]

A stipulation, that unless the debt is paid within a certain time the deed shall be absolute, will not be given that effect, because the very terms of the agreement show that the instrument is a mortgage, and such agreement of the parties in the mortgage itself or otherwise, made at the time, is without effect.[12] The transaction, being in reality a mortgage, remains a mortgage until the time of redemption is barred by some of the modes acknowledged by law, the agreement of the parties not being one of such modes.[13] The grantor can not agree that upon default his mortgage shall become an absolute conveyance. A subsequent agreement that the equity of redemption should be extinguished, or that what was originally a mortgage shall be regarded as

---

[11] Peugh v. Davis, 96 U. S. 332, 24 L. ed. 775; Nelson v. Kelly, 91 Ala. 569, 8 So. 690; McMillan v. Jewett, 85 Ala. 476, 5 So. 145; Stoutz v. Rouse, 84 Ala. 309, 4 So. 170; Fields v. Helms, 82 Ala. 449, 3 So. 106; Parmer v. Parmer, 74 Ala. 285; Robinson v. Farrelly, 16 Ala. 472; Quartermous v. Kennedy, 29 Ark. 544; Green v. Butler, 26 Cal. 595; Pierce v. Robinson, 13 Cal. 116; Pritchard v. Elton, 38 Conn. 434; Horton v. Murden, 117 Ga. 72, 43 S. E. 786; Jackson v. Lynch, 129 Ill. 72, 21 N. E. 580, 22 N. E. 246; Bearss v. Ford, 108 Ill. 16; Clark v. Finlon, 90 Ill. 245; Tennery v. Nicholson, 87 Ill. 464; Willets v. Burgess, 34 Ill. 494; Wynkoop v. Cowing, 21 Ill. 570; Turpie v. Lowe, 114 Ind. 37, 15 N. W. 834; Brush v. Peterson, 54 Iowa 243, 6 N. W. 287; Reed v. Reed, 75 Maine 264; Baxter v. Child, 39 Maine 110; Bayley v. Bailey, 5 Gray (Mass.) 505; Union Trust Co. v. Charlotte Gen. Elec. Co., 152 Mich. 568, 116 N. W. 379; Batty v. Snook, 5 Mich. 231; Sheppard v. Wagner, 240 Mo. 409, 144 S. W. 394; Griffin v. Cooper, 73 N. J. Eq. 465, 68 Atl. 1095; Clark v. Condit, 18 N. J. Eq. 358; Vanderhaize v. Hugues, 13 N. J. Eq. 244; Youle v. Richards, 1 N. J. Eq. 534, 23 Am. Dec. 722; Clark v. Henry, 3 Cow. (N. Y.) 324; Remsen v. Hay, 2 Edw. Ch. (N. Y.) 535; Simon v. Schmidt, 41 Hun (N. Y.) 318; Henry v. Clark, 7 Johns. Ch. (N. Y.) 40; Wilson v. Fisher, 148 N. Car. 535, 62 S. E. 622; Gillis v. Martin, 17 N. Car. 470, 25 Am. Dec. 729; Stover v. Bounds, 1 Ohio St. 107; Worley v. Carter, 30 Okla. 642, 121 Pac. 669 (quoting text); Rankin v. Mortimere, 7 Watts (Pa.) 372; Johnston v. Gray, 16 Serg. & R. (Pa.) 361, 16 Am. Dec. 577; Cherry v. Bowen, 4 Sneed (Tenn.) 415; Wing v. Cooper, 37 Vt. 169; Baxter v. Willey, 9 Vt. 276, 31 Am. Dec. 623; Plummer v. Ilse, 41 Wash. 5, 82 Pac. 1009, 2 L. R. A. (N. S.) 627, 111 Am. St. 997; Broad v. Self, 9 Jur. (N. S.) 885. See post § 1045.

[12] Halbert v. Turner, 233 Ill. 531, 84 N. E. 704; Jones v. Gillett, 142 Iowa 506, 118 N. W. 314; First Nat. Bank v. Sargent, 65 Nebr. 594, 91 N. W. 595, 59 L. R. A. 296; Riley v. Starr, 48 Nebr. 243, 67 N. W. 187; State Bank v. Mathews, 45 Nebr. 659, 63 N. W. 930, 50 Am. St. 565; Nelson v. Atkinson, 37 Nebr. 577, 56 N. W. 313; Tower v. Fetz, 26 Nebr. 706, 42 N. W. 884, 18 Am. St. 795; Fahay v. State Bank, 1 Nebr. (Unoff.) 89, 95 N. W. 505; Macauley v. Smith, 132 N. Y. 524, 30 N. E. 997; Conover v. Palmer Co., 60 Misc. 241, 111 N. Y. S. 1074; Farrow v. Work, 39 Okla. 734, 136 Pac. 739; Worley v. Carter, 30 Okla. 642, 121 Pac. 669.

[13] Halbert v. Turner, 233 Ill. 531, 84 N. E. 704; Grover v. Hawthorne, 62 Ore. 77, 121 Pac. 808 (equity of redemption extinguished only by regular foreclosure).

an absolute conveyance, is open to the same objection, and will not be sustained unless fairly made upon a new consideration, and no undue advantage is taken by the creditor.[14] The burden is therefore upon the creditor to show that the right of redemption was given up deliberately and for an adequate consideration.[15]

Though a mortgagor may sell all his interest to the mortgagee, for an additional consideration, where the transaction is without fraud or undue influence, to insist on what was really a mortgage as a sale is a fraud in equity.[16] Where a mortgagee purchases the mortgaged premises, and the evidence shows fraud and undue influence, and the transaction is unfair, and an unconscionable advantage has been taken against the mortgagor, equity will declare a deed absolute on its face to be a mortgage.[17] Generally, when the consideration of the conveyance was an existing debt, a provision that, if the amount required for a repurchase be not paid at the time specified, the agreement for repurchase shall be null and void, or that there shall be no redemption afterward, is looked upon as a device to deprive the debtor of his right of redemption, and is therefore disregarded.[18]

§ 252. Cancelation of defeasance—Conversion of mortgage into absolute sale.—An absolute conveyance originally intended as security, and constituting a mortgage in equity, may afterward be converted into an unconditional transfer and absolute sale, by release of the debtor's equity of redemption; but its effect can only be changed

[14] Mills v. Mills, 26 Conn. 213; Hutchinson v. Page, 246 Ill. 71, 92 N. E. 571; Cassem v. Heustis, 201 Ill. 208, 66 N. E. 283, 94 Am. St. 160; Scholl v. Hopper, 134 Ky. 83, 119 S. W. 770; Sears v. Gilman, 199 Mass. 384, 85 N. E. 466; Henry v. Davis, 7 Johns. Ch. (N. Y.) 40; Miller v. Smith, 20 N. Dak. 96, 126 N. W. 499; Ullman v. Devereux, 46 Tex. Civ. App. 459, 102 S. W. 1163; Wright v. Bates, 13 Vt. 341. See also Stratton v. Rotrock, 84 Kans. 198, 114 Pac. 224 (requirement of a subsequent, superceding contract); Miller v. Smith, 20 N. Dak. 96, 126 N. W. 499 (intention to change mortgage into conditional sale with option to repurchase). A deed absolute on its face purporting to convey the equity of redemption to the mortgagee, if intended as a mortgage, will be treated as such. Lynch v. Ryan, 132 Wis. 271, 111 N. W. 707.

[15] Villa v. Rodriguez, 12 Wall. (U. S.) 323, 20 L. ed. 406; Locke v. Palmer, 26 Ala. 312; Bearss v. Ford, 108 Ill. 16; Brown v. Gaffney, 28 Ill. 149; Baugher v. Merryman, 32 Md. 185; Shaw v. Walbridge, 33 Ohio St. 1. A deed made to replace a lost deed which was in fact a mortgage, was also a mortgage, though the grantee in the deed paid an additional sum to procure execution of the duplicate deed. Borders v. Allen, 33 Ky. L. 194, 110 S. W. 240.

[16] Cassem v. Heustis, 201 Ill. 208, 66 N. E. 283, 94 Am. St. 160; Wagg v. Herbert, 19 Okla. 525, 92 Pac. 250.

[17] Wagg v. Herbert, 19 Okla. 525, 92 Pac. 250.

[18] Enos v. Sutherland, 11 Mich. 538; Batty v. Snook, 5 Mich. 231.

by a new contract, founded upon adequate consideration, both fair and reasonable in its terms and free from fraud and undue influence.[19] And so a deed of defeasance, made at the same time with an absolute deed, may afterward, upon sufficient consideration, be canceled, so as to give an absolute title to the mortgagee, if no rights of third parties have intervened;[20] but no agreement can be made at the time of creating the mortgage that will entitle the mortgagee, at his election, to hold the estate free from condition, and not subject to redemption.[21] Thus, if it be agreed that the grantee, whenever he shall be compelled to pay certain liabilities, against which the deed was given as security, may then take immediate possession of the estate, according to certain estimated values, to such an extent as shall be equal to the debt or liability so paid by him, this stipulation does not change the nature of the transaction, which must still be treated as a mortgage.[22] An agreement extinguishing the equity of redemption must be fair.[23]

If the bond of defeasance, which was given at the time of taking the deed, be surrendered and destroyed at the expiration of the time limited, and a new bond be given upon a consideration partly new, by which the grantee agrees to reconvey the premises upon payment, within an additional time, of a larger sum, the grantor thereby surrenders his title as mortgagor, and the grantee becomes the owner in fee of the land.[24] If the original bond be given up and a new bond to

---

[19] McMillan v. Jewett, 85 Ala. 476, 5 So. 145; Cramer v. Wilson, 202 Ill. 83, 66 N. E. 869; Cassem v. Heustis, 201 Ill. 208, 66 N. E. 283, 94 Am. St. 160; Carpenter v. Carpenter, 70 Ill. 457; LeComte v. Pennock, 61 Kans. 330, 59 Pac. 641; Dougherty v. McColgan, 6 Gill & J. (Md.) 275; Fahay v. O'Neill State Bank, 1 Nebr. (Unoff.) 89, 95 N. W. 505 (notwithstanding express agreement); Shaw v. Walbridge, 33 Ohio St. 1; Wilson v. Giddings, 28 Ohio St. 554; Wagg v. Herbert, 19 Okla. 525, 92 Pac. 250; Sadler v. Taylor, 49 W. Va. 104, 38 S. E. 583; Hursey v. Hursey, 56 W. Va. 148, 49 S. E. 367 (without new consideration). Conversion of the mortgage into an absolute sale, if fair may be accomplished by a mere parol agreement. McMillan v. Jewett, 85 Ala. 476, 5 So. 145; Shaw v. Walbridge, 33 Ohio St. 1. See post § 338.

[20] Cramer v. Wilson, 202 Ill. 83, 66 N. E. 869; Haggerty v. Brower, 105 Iowa 395, 75 N. W. 321; Sears v. Gilman, 199 Mass. 384, 85 N. E. 466; Falis v. Conway Mut. Fire Ins. Co,. 7 Allen (Mass.) 46; Waters v. Randall, 6 Metc. (Mass.) 479; Trull v. Skinner, 17 Pick. (Mass.) 213; Youle v. Richards, 1 N. J. Eq. 534, 23 Am. Dec. 722; Seawell v. Hendricks, 4 Okla. 435, 46 Pac. 557. See also Stetson v. Gulliver, 2 Cush. (Mass.) 494; Clark v. Finlon, 90 Ill. 245 (substitution of new defeasance).

[21] Harrison v. Phillips Academy, 12 Mass. 456; Trull v. Skinner, 17 Pick. (Mass.) 213.

[22] Waters v. Randall, 6 Metc. (Mass.) 479.

[23] Miller v. Smith, 20 N. Dak. 96, 126 N. W. 499. See ante § 251.

[24] Carpenter v. Carpenter, 70 Ill. 457; Maxfield v. Patchen, 29 Ill. 39; Falis v. Conway Mut. Fire Ins. Co., 7 Allen (Mass.) 46; Rice v. Rice, 4 Pick. (Mass.) 349.

a third person be executed in place of it, the transaction loses it character of a mortgage. A subsequent cancelation of the evidence of indebtedness, with a parol agreement that the deed, originally intended as a mortgage, shall convey the absolute title, will not convert the mortgage into a deed.[25]

Where the mortgage relation constituted by an absolute deed and a contemporaneous agreement is terminated by a release executed by the mortgagor to the mortgagee a further agreement by the latter giving the former a right to purchase the property within a time expressly limited and made material does not revive the mortgage relation. "Here the transaction was as evidenced by the second deed and agreement, that the mortgage relation was to cease; that the respondent was to become the absolute owner of the property by the voluntary transfer by the complainant of all his remaining right in the property, upon condition that he should have the further right to purchase it within a fixed time. This condition was not fulfilled by the complainant, and he has therefore no right, as mortgagee or otherwise to ask for a further time either to purchase or redeem."[26] When once the defeasance has been delivered up for a valid consideration to be canceled, and the original transaction is thus confirmed as a sale, and is treated as such by the grantor, it can not afterward be treated as a mortgage and foreclosed.[27]

But in states where a mortgage, whatever its form may be, creates merely a lien in the mortgagee while the legal title remains in the mortgagor, the surrender or cancelation of the defeasance is insufficient to restore the title to the mortgagee.[28] If the contract for reconveyance be surrendered upon the express agreement of the grantee to reconvey upon the grantor's paying a certain sum then found to be due, the surrender will not prevent the mortgagor's redeeming upon the terms agreed upon.[29]

§ 253. Record of separate defeasance.—The recording of the defeasance is not necessary in order to give it full effect as between the parties themselves,[30] but only as against other persons; and as against

---

[25] Keller v. Kirby, 34 Tex. Civ. App. 404, 79 S. W. 82. See post § 338.

[26] Tripler v. Campbell, 22 R. I. 262, 47 Atl. 385; per Stiness, C. J., citing Wilson v. Giddings, 28 Ohio St. 554; Falis v. Conway Mut. F. Ins. Co., 7 Allen (Mass.) 46.

[27] Shubert v. Stanley, 52 Ind. 46.

[28] Brinkman v. Jones, 44 Wis. 498.

[29] Clark v. Finlon, 90 Ill. 245.

[30] Bailey v. Myrick, 50 Maine 171; Jackson v. Ford, 40 Maine 381; Harrison v. Morton, 87 Md. 671, 40 Atl. 897; Owens v. Miller, 29 Md. 144; Short v. Caldwell, 155 Mass. 57, 28 N. E. 1124; Bryan v. Insurance Co., 145 Mass. 389, 14 N. E.

them it is not necessary when the conveyance on its face does not purport to be absolute.[31] Under some statutes no benefit is derived from recording an absolute deed intended as a mortgage, unless the defeasance is recorded therewith.[32] The same rule is established by judicial decision in Pennsylvania;[33] and under the Pennsylvania statute a deed will not be construed as a mortgage unless the defeasance or other writing explaining its character is recorded.[34]

In several states it is provided by statute that a bond of defeasance shall not defeat an absolute estate against any one other than the maker, his heirs, devisees, or persons having actual notice thereof, unless it be recorded.[35] If the bond be not recorded, a person having no knowledge of it may, of course, purchase the property, or attach it as belonging absolutely to the grantee; but if he has actual notice of the bond as constituting a part of the transaction of the conveyance, any right he acquires in the property is subject to the mortgage created by the bond.[36] If the defeasance recorded be an instrument not entitled to be recorded, as, for instance, when it has not been acknowledged, the record of it is not constructive notice, and a purchaser from the grantee without notice of the defeasance will acquire a good title notwithstanding such recorded defeasance.[37] Under such statutes it is held that a separate defeasance not recorded can not be introduced in

454; Moors v. Albro, 129 Mass. 9; Bayley v. Bailey, 5 Gray (Mass.) 505; Marston v. Williams, 45 Minn. 116, 47 N. W. 644, 22 Am. St. 719; Butman v. James, 34 Minn. 547, 27 N. W. 66. See also Smith v. Monmouth Mutual Ins. Co., 50 Maine 96; Stetson v. Gulliver, 2 Cush. (Mass.) 494. See post § 513.

[31] Russell v. Waite, Walk. Ch. (Mich.) 31.

[32] There are such statutes in Maryland, Nebraska, New Hampshire, New Jersey, New York, North Dakota and South Dakota. See post § 513 note.

[33] Corpman v. Baccastow, 84 Pa. St. 363; Calder v. Chapman, 52 Pa. St. 359, 91 Am. Dec. 163; Edwards v. Trumbull, 50 Pa. St. 509; Luch's Appeal, 44 Pa. St. 519; In re Hendrickson's Appeal, 24 Pa. St. 363; Jaques v. Weeks, 7 Watts (Pa.) 261. See also Clark v. Condit, 18 N. J. Eq. 358; McAulay v. Porter, 71 N. Y. 173; Gerken v. Sonnabend, 130 N. Y. S. 605.

[34] Safe Deposit &c. Co. v. Linton,

213 Pa. St. 105, 62 Atl. 566; Lohrer v. Russell, 207 Pa. 105, 56 Atl. 333; In re Rockhill's Estate, 29 Pa. Super. Ct. 28; Friedley v. Hamilton, 17 Serg. & R. (Pa.) 70, 17 Am. Dec. 638.

[35] Such statutes exist in Alabama, Alaska, California, Delaware, Indiana, Kansas, Maine, Massachusetts, Michigan, Minnesota, North Dakota, Oregon, Pennsylvania, Rhode Island, Wisconsin and Wyoming. See post § 513 note.

[36] Purrington v. Pierce, 38 Maine 447; Tufts v. Tapley, 129 Mass. 380; Newhall v. Burt, 7 Pick. (Mass.) 157; Newhall v. Pierce, 5 Pick. (Mass.) 450; Butman v. James, 34 Minn. 547, 27 N. W. 66; Corpman v. Baccastow, 84 Pa. St. 363; Friedley v. Hamilton, 17 Serg. & R. (Pa.) 70, 17 Am. Dec. 638; Manufacturers' &c. Bank v. Bank of Pennsylvania, 7 Watts & S. (Pa.) 335, 42 Am. Dec. 240; Catlin v. Bennatt, 47 Tex. 165. See post § 513.

[37] Cogan v. Cook, 22 Minn. 137.

evidence to show that an absolute conveyance is a mortgage, for the court can not assume or know that it ever would be recorded; but it will have that effect if recorded at any time before it is introduced in evidence.[38] Notice of the existence of a bond of defeasance is not to be inferred from the fact alone that the grantor continues in possession after the deed given by him has been recorded.[39] Under the general statute of Texas requiring all conveyances of land and mortgages to be recorded in order to affect creditors and subsequent purchasers, a deed absolute in form, but given to secure a debt, may be shown to be an equitable mortgage, and the record is sufficient as against a creditor of the grantee who attached the land without notice that the conveyance was not absolute.[40] To constitute notice of a legal mortgage as distinguished from one that is equitable merely, a purchaser must have reason to believe that the conveyance and bond were executed and delivered so as to form one transaction.[41]

There is a difference of opinion as to the meaning of the words "actual notice" in these statutes. On the one hand, a strict construction is given them, making actual knowledge of the defeasance necessary to charge third persons with actual notice. Thus, for instance, actual notice is not to be implied from knowledge that the grantor has remained in open and visible possession after his conveyance of the land by absolute deed.[42] But on the other hand it is held that knowledge of such possession on the part of a subsequent purchaser is evidence to be considered upon the question of actual notice of the grantor's rights. "Actual notice" is distinguished from mere "notice" by holding that no constructive knowledge can be imputed to the purchaser as a ground of notice; for example, actual, open, and visible occupation, whether known to the purchaser or not, would not impute actual notice to the purchaser of the rights of the occupant, but would be evidence of such notice if the occupation were known to the purchaser. The rule is stated to be, that notice must be held to be actual when the subsequent purchaser has actual knowledge of such facts as would put a prudent man upon inquiry, which, if prosecuted with or-

[38] Smith v. Monmouth Mut. F. Ins. Co., 50 Maine 96; Tomlinson v. Monmouth Mut. F. Ins. Co., 47 Maine 232.

[39] Newhall v. Pierce, 5 Pick. (Mass.) 450.

[40] Long v. Fields, 31 Tex. Civ. App. 241, 71 S. W. 774.

[41] Newhall v. Burt, 7 Pick. (Mass.) 157.

[42] Crassen v. Swoveland, 22 Ind. 427; Lamb v. Pierce, 113 Mass. 72; White v. Foster, 102 Mass. 375; Story's Eq. Jur. § 399. See post § 543.

dinary diligence, would lead to actual notice of the right or title in conflict with that which he is about to purchase.[43]

These provisions do not require that every conveyance of land accompanied by a conditional agreement shall be recorded as a mortgage, but only when the agreement is analogous to that of the usual condition in a mortgage, as, for instance, an agreement providing that if certain acts are performed, the deed shall not operate, but shall become void.[44]

§ 254. **Circumstances determining effect of record as notice.—** Whether the record furnishes notice of the nature of the transaction depends upon attendant circumstances. Although the instruments may in fact constitute a mortgage as between the parties, yet, if they do not of themselves show that they are parts of one transaction, but were executed on different days, and each is complete in itself and independent of the other, the record of them is not notice to a subsequent purchaser that they constitute a mortgage. He is bound only by what appears of record, and he has a right to assume, from the record in such case, that there was an absolute sale merely, with a subsequent agreement for repurchase.[45] It is usual, however, to make such reference in the bond to the debt secured, or to the deed or conveyance, that it is apparent from the construction of these instruments alone that the transaction was a mortgage, and a purchaser is then bound accordingly.[46]

A purchaser has notice when he has actual knowledge of such circumstances as would put a prudent man upon inquiry, and by prosecuting such inquiry, he may ascertain the actual right or title.[47] But knowledge of the open and visible possession by the grantor after his conveyance by absolute deed is not sufficient to imply actual notice.[48]

In 1736 land was conveyed by an absolute deed, and the grantee, in 1742, conveyed the land by a deed in which it was recited that his grantee had purchased the grantor's right of redemption. This recital,

[43] Brinkman v. Jones, 44 Wis. 498, per Taylor, J. See also Wilson v. Miller, 16 Iowa 111; Porter v. Sevey, 43 Maine 519. See post § 339; Maupin v. Emmons, 47 Mo. 304; Musgrove v. Bonser, 5 Ore. 313, 20 Am. Rep. 737.

[44] Macaulay v. Porter, 71 N. Y. 173.

[45] Weide v. Gehl, 21 Minn. 449; Waters v. Crabtree, 105 N. Car. 394, 11 S. E. 240. See also Patnode v. Deschenes, 15 N. Dak. 100, 106 N. W. 573.

[46] Hill v. Edwards, 11 Minn. 22.

[47] Wilson v. Miller, 16 Iowa 111; Porter v. Sevey, 43 Maine 519; Maupin v. Emmons, 47 Mo. 304; Musgrove v. Bonser, 5 Ore. 313, 20 Am. Rep. 737; Brinkman v. Jones, 44 Wis. 498.

[48] Crassen v. Swoveland, 22 Ind. 427; Lamb v. Pierce, 113 Mass. 72; White v. Foster, 102 Mass. 375.

however, was held to be no ground for presuming that the first deed was a mortgage.[49] Equity will not enforce an agreement to reconvey land on the payment of a certain sum, where the record thereof had been destroyed by fire, and the party relying on the agreement had neglected for twenty years to re-record it, particularly where the relief is sought against a bona fide purchaser, without notice, who has been in possession many years.[50]

§ 255. **Notice by possession.**[51]—When the mortgage is effected by an absolute deed accompanied by a separate defeasance, possession and actual occupation by the mortgagor is sufficient to put a purchaser from the grantee upon inquiry, and to charge him with notice of the mortgagor's rights.[52] It is not to be presumed that a bona fide purchaser will buy land without ascertaining, or making an attempt to ascertain, the claims of the person in open possession.[53] Such open and exclusive possession is notice to all the world of any claim which he who is in possession has upon the land. It is not to be supposed that any man who wishes in good faith to purchase the land will do so without knowing what are the claims of a person who is in open possession. He is chargeable, therefore, with knowledge of such claims.[54]

But possession by a person other than the vendor is not sufficient to charge the purchaser with notice, if the vendor delivers possession to him on demand; and such a purchaser for value from a person holding by a deed absolute on its face obtains a good title against the party seeking to redeem.[55] Nor is continuance in possession by the grantor after the recording of the deed made by him sufficient to impart notice of a bond for reconveyance.[56]

A conveyance of the premises by the mortgagee to a third person amounts to an assignment of the mortgage only if the grantee has notice in any way of the defeasance.[57]

[49] King v. Little, 1 Cush. (Mass.) 436.

[50] Waters v. Crabtree, 105 N. Car. 394, 11 S. E. 240.

[51] See post §§ 586–601.

[52] Daubenspeck v. Platt. 22 Cal. 330; Brighton v. Doyle, 64 Vt. 616, 25 Atl. 694.

[53] Daubenspeck v. Platt, 22 Cal. 330; Pritchard v. Brown, 4 N. H. 397, 17 Am. Dec. 431.

[54] Pritchard v. Brown, 4 N. H. 397, 17 Am. Dec. 431. See also Brown v. Gaffney, 28 Ill. 149; New v. Wheaton, 24 Minn. 406.

[55] Pancake v. Cauffman, 114 Pa. St. 113, 7 Atl. 67.

[56] Newhall v. Pierce, 5 Pick. (Mass.) 450.

[57] Halsey v. Martin, 22 Cal. 645; Berdell v. Berdell, 20 N. Y. Week. Dig. 81.

II. *When They Constitute a Sale or Conditional Sale*

§ **256. Effect of construction—Relative advantages to parties.**—The advantage of considering the transaction a mortgage is not all on the side of the grantor; and as between a mortgage and a conditional sale, the latter may be the more for his benefit. In this way he avoids the continuance, or the incurring, of a debt. If at the close of the time limited for reconveyance he is not in condition to perform the contract, or does not desire to, there is no obligation resting upon him to do so. It is his option to repurchase or not. But if the transaction be a mortgage in the beginning, it is always a mortgage. The grantor is not allowed to speculate upon the chances attending the transaction, and, upon finding that the property is worth the amount of the debt, to call a mortgage a conditional sale; or, on the other hand, when he finds that the property has increased in value, and that there would be an advantage in redeeming, to call what was actually a conditional sale a mortgage. The character of the transaction is fixed at its inception.

§ **257. Construction in equity.**—Cases involving the distinction between mortgages and conditional sales are usually brought before

courts of equity for adjudication.[1] At law, as has already been noticed, an agreement for a reconveyance, to constitute a defeasance and
make the transaction a mortgage, must be executed at the same time
with the conveyance, and as a part of the same transaction, and must
be under seal; while in equity any evidence, whether it be in writing
or merely parol, which clearly shows that the conveyance was in fact
intended only as a security, will make the transaction a mortgage; and
if there be a written agreement for reconveyance, it matters not how
informal it may be, or when it was executed.[2] It follows, therefore,
that a court of equity will often pronounce that to be an equitable
mortgage which at law would be considered a conditional sale. A court
of equity is not concluded by the form of the transaction, whether this
seems to indicate a mortgage or a conditional sale, but will have regard
to the actual facts.[3] "A court of law," says Judge Story,[4] "may be
compelled, in many cases, to say that there is no mortgage," when a
court of equity would not hesitate a moment in pronouncing that there
is an equitable mortgage." But since the doctrine of treating a conditional sale as a mortgage is a creature of equity, it will not be applied where injustice would result or the parties have unreasonably
slept on their rights.[5]

§ 258. Intention the criterion — Attending circumstances. —
Whether a conveyance be a mortgage or a conditional sale must be determined by a consideration of all the surrounding facts and circum-

[1] Smith v. Smith, 153 Ala. 504, 45 So. 168; Fort v. Colby (Iowa), 144 N. W. 393; Mason v. Fichner, 120 Minn. 185, 139 N. W. 485; Duell v. Leslie, 207 Mo. 658, 106 S. W. 489; Jeffreys v. Charlton, 72 N. J. Eq. 340, 65 Atl. 711; Williams v. Mc-Manus, 90 S. Car. 490, 73 S. E. 1038; Yates v. Caswell (Tex. Civ. App.), 126 S. W. 914; Musick v. O'Brien (Tex. Civ. App.), 102 S. W. 458. See post § 282.

[2] Flagg v. Mann, 2 Sumn. (U. S.) 486; Pearson v. Seay, 38 Ala. 643; Williams v. Chadwick, 74 Conn. 252, 50 Atl. 720; Mills v. Mills, 26 Conn. 213; Sebree v. Thompson, 31 Ky. L. 1146, 104 S. W. 781; Dougherty v. McColgan, 6 Gill & J. (Md.) 275; Taber v. Hamlin, 97 Mass. 489, 93 Am. Dec. 113.

[3] McNamara v. Culver, 22 Kans. 661. Form of defeasance immate-rial: Adams v. Stevens, 49 Maine 362; Scott v. McFarland, 13 Mass. 309; Taylor v. Weld, 5 Mass. 109; Bayley v. Bailey, 5 Gray (Mass.) 505; Pearce v. Wilson, 111 Pa. St. 14, 2 Atl. 99, 56 Am. Rep. 243; Guth-rie v. Kahle, 46 Pa. St. 331; In re Myers' Appeal, 42 Pa. St. 518; Wil-son v. Shoenberger, 31 Pa. St. 295; Reitenbaugh v. Ludwick, 31 Pa. St. 131; Kelly v. Thompson, 7 Watts (Pa.) 401; Rankin v. Mortimere, 7 Watts (Pa.) 372; Kerr v. Gilmore, 6 Watts (Pa.) 405; Miskelly v. Pitts, 9 Baxt. (Tenn.) 193; Austin v. Dow-ner, 25 Vt. 558. A defeasance in the form of a pawn ticket, referring to real estate conveyed as security for a loan, is sufficient. Lee v. Wilkin-son (Miss.), 62 So. 275. See ante § 242.

[4] Flagg v. Mann, 2 Sumn. (U. S.) 486.

[5] Sheffield v. Hurst, 31 Ky. L. 890, 104 S. W. 350.

stances of the case,[6] including the conduct and relation of the parties,[7] and their relative knowledge or ignorance of business.[8] "A glance at the numerous adjudications in controversies of this kind will suffice to show that each case must be decided in view of the peculiar circumstances which belong to it and mark its character, and that the only safe criterion is the intention of the parties, to be ascertained by considering their situation and the surrounding facts, as well as the written memorials of the transaction."[9] If both parties to the instrument intend that it shall operate merely as security for a debt, it is a mortgage though in the form of an absolute deed.[10] The intention of the

[6] Horbach v. Hill, 112 U. S. 144, 28 L. ed. 671, 5 Sup. Ct. 81; Nelson v. Wadsworth, 171 Ala. 603, 55 So. 120; Pendergrass v. Burris, 77 Cal. 19, 19 Pac. 187, 11 Am. St. 231; Lynch v. Lynch, 22 Cal. App. 653, 135 Pac. 1101; Elliott v. Connor, 63 Fla. 408, 58 So. 241; Wylly-Gabbett Co. v. Williams, 53 Fla. 872, 42 So. 910; Heath v. Williams, 30 Ind. 495; Davis v. Stonestreet, 4 Ind. 101; Beidelman v. Koch, 42 Ind. App. 423, 85 N. E. 977; Keeline v. Clark, 132 Iowa 360, 106 N. W. 257; Hughes v. Sheaff, 19 Iowa 335; First Nat. Bank v. Edwards, 84 Kans. 495, 115 Pac. 118; Tucker v. Witherbee, 130 Ky. 269, 113 S. W. 123 (quoting text); Edrington v. Harper, 3 J. J. Marsh. (Ky.) 353, 20 Am. Dec. 145; Trimble v. McCormick, 12 Ky. L. 857, 15 S. W. 258; Miller v. Miller, 101 Md. 600, 61 Atl. 210; King v. McCarthy, 50 Minn. 222, 52 N. W. 648; Gassert v. Bogk, 7 Mont. 585, 19 Pac. 281; Sanders v. Ayres, 63 Nebr. 271, 88 N. W. 526; Devore v. Woodruff, 1 N. Dak. 143, 45 N. W. 701; Elliott v. Bozorth, 52 Ore. 391, 97 Pac. 632; Stephens v. Allen, 11 Ore. 188, 3 Pac. 168; Bradley v. Helgerson, 14 S. Dak. 593, 86 N. W. 634 (though the grantee is called a trustee); Harrison v. Hogue (Tex. Civ. App.), 136 S. W. 118; Goodbar v. Bloom, 43 Tex. Civ. App. 434, 96 S. W. 657 (quoting text); Gray v. Shelby, 83 Tex. 405, 18 S. W. 809; Loving v. Milliken, 59 Tex. 423; Gibbs v. Penny, 43 Tex. 560; Stampers v. Johnson, 3 Tex. 1; Duerden v. Solomon, 33 Utah 468, 94 Pac. 978; Batchelder v. Randolph, 112 Va. 296, 71 S. E. 533; Bachrach v. Bachrach, 111 Va. 232, 68 S. E. 985;

Hudkins v. Crim (W. Va.), 78 S. E. 1043; Fridley v. Somerville, 60 W. Va. 272, 54 S. E. 502. See post §§ 278, 326.

[7] Lynch v. Lynch, 22 Cal. App. 653, 135 Pac. 1101; Elliott v. Connor, 63 Fla. 408, 58 So. 241; Connor v. Connor, 59 Fla. 467, 52 So. 727; Hull v. Burr, 58 Fla. 432, 50 So. 754; De Bartlett v. De Wilson, 52 Fla. 497, 42 So. 189; First Nat. Bank v. Edwards, 84 Kans. 495, 115 Pac. 118; Elliott v. Bozorth, 52 Ore. 391, 97 Pac. 632; Bachrach v. Bachrach, 111 Va. 232, 68 S. E. 985; Tuggle v. Berkeley, 101 Va. 83, 43 S. E. 199.

[8] Irwin v. Coleman, 173 Ala. 175, 55 So. 492; Abercrombie v. Carpenter, 150 Ala. 294, 43 So. 746; Rose v. Gandy, 137 Ala. 329, 34 So. 239; Hamilton v. Holmes, 48 Ore. 453, 87 Pac. 154. But see Harrison v. Hogue (Tex. Civ. App.), 136 S. W. 118. See post § 278.

[9] Tucker v. Witherbee, 130 Ky. 269, 113 S. W. 123 (quoting text); Cornell v. Hall, 22 Mich. 377, per Graves, J.; Stephens v. Allen, 11 Ore. 188, 3 Pac. 168.

[10] Hays v. Emerson, 75 Ark. 551, 87 S. W. 1027; Connor v. Connor, 59 Fla. 467, 52 So. 727; Hurd's Illinois Rev. Stat. 1913, p. 1665, § 12; Beidelman v. Koch, 42 Ind. App. 423, 85 N. E. 977; Dusenbery v. Bidwell, 86 Kans. 666, 121 Pac. 1098; Stratton v. Rotrock, 84 Kans. 198, 114 Pac. 224; Vaughn v. Smith, 148 Ky. 531, 146 S. W. 1094; Guenther v. Wisdom, 27 Ky. L. 230, 84 S. W. 771; In re Schmidt, 114 La. 78, 38 So. 26; Powell v. Crow, 204 Mo. 481, 102 S. W. 1024; Jeffreys v. Charlton, 72 N. J. Eq. 340, 65 Atl. 711; Farrow v. Work, 39 Okla. 734, 136 Pac. 739;

parties is the only true and infallible test, and this intention is to be gathered from the circumstances attending the transaction and the conduct of the parties, as well as from the face of the written contract.[11] While in all doubtful cases the courts will construe the contract to be a mortgage rather than a conditional sale,[12] yet, when a

Goodbar v. Bloom, 43 Tex. Civ. App. 434, 96 S. W. 657 (citing text); Fridley v. Somerville, 60 W. Va. 272, 54 S. E. 502. See post § 264.

[11] Smith v. Smith, 153 Ala. 504, 45 So. 168; Rees v. Rhodes, 3 Ariz. 235, 73 Pac. 446; McIver v. Roberts (Ark.), 165 S. W. 273; Henley v. Hotaling, 41 Cal. 22; Elliott v. Connor, 63 Fla. 408, 58 So. 241; Connor v. Connor, 59 Fla. 467, 52 So. 727; Burnside v. Terry, 46 Ga. 621; Calahan v. Dunker, 51 Ind. App. 436, 99 N. E. 1021; Beidelman v. Koch, 42 Ind. App. 423, 85 N. E. 977; Keeline v. Clark, 132 Iowa 360, 106 N. W. 257; Hughes v. Sheaff, 19 Iowa 335; Dusenbery v. Bidwell, 86 Kans. 666, 121 Pac. 1098; First Nat. Bank v. Edwards, 84 Kans. 495. 115 Pac. 118; Stratton v. Rotrock, 84 Kans. 198, 114 Pac. 224; Vaughn v. Smith, 148 Ky. 531, 146 S. W. 1094; Borders v. Allen, 33 Ky. L. 194, 110 S. W. 240; In re Schmidt, 114 La. 78, 38 So. 26; Hurd v. Chase, 100 Maine 561, 62 Atl. 660; Hawes v. Williams, 92 Maine 483, 43 Atl. 101; Miller v. Miller, 101 Md. 600, 61 Atl. 210; Hopper v. Smyser, 90 Md. 363, 45 Atl. 206 (quoting text); Powell v. Crow, 204 Mo. 481, 102 S. W. 1024; Arnold v. Fraser, 43 Mont. 540, 117 Pac. 1064; Jeffreys v. Charlton, 72 N. J. Eq. 340, 65 Atl. 711; Smith v. Jensen, 16 N. Dak. 408, 114 N. W. 306; Farrow v. Work, 39 Okla. 734, 136 Pac. 739; Fawcett v. McGahan-McKee Lumber Co., 39 Okla. 68, 134 Pac. 388; Kinney v. Heatherington, 38 Okla. 74, 131 Pac. 1078; Worley v. Carter, 30 Okla. 642, 121 Pac. 669; Harmon v. Grants Pass Banking &c. Co., 60 Ore. 69, 118 Pac. 188; Walton v. Moore, 58 Ore. 237, 113 Pac. 58; Elliott v. Bozorth, 52 Ore. 391, 97 Pac. 632; Hall v. O'Connell, 52 Ore. 164, 95 Pac. 717; Hume v. Le Compte (Tex. Civ. App.), 142 S. W. 934; Harrison v. Hogue (Tex. Civ. App.), 136 S. W. 118; Elliott v. Morris (Tex. Civ. App.), 121 S. W. 209;

Moorhead v. Ellison, 56 Tex. Civ. App. 444, 120 S. W. 1049; Beverly v. Davis (Wash.), 140 Pac. 696; Hoover v. Bouffleur, 74 Wash. 382, 133 Pac. 602; Johnson v. National Bank, 65 Wash. 261, 118 Pac. 21; Hudkins v. Crim (W. Va.), 78 S. E. 1043; Fridley v. Somerville, 60 W. Va. 272, 54 S. E. 502; Smith v. Crosby, 47 Wis. 160, 2 N. W. 104. See ante §162.

[12] Conway v. Alexander, 7 Cranch (U. S.) 218, 3 L. ed. 321; Morton v. Allen (Ala.), 60 So. 866; Irwin v. Coleman, 173 Ala. 175, 55 So. 492; Nelson v. Wadsworth, 171 Ala. 603, 55 So. 120; Hubert v. Sistrunk (Ala.), 53 So. 819; Glass v. Hieronymus, 125 Ala. 140, 28 So. 71; Reeves v. Abercrombie, 108 Ala. 535, 19 So. 41; Daniels v. Lowery, 92 Ala. 519, 8 So. 352; Peagler v. Stabler, 91 Ala. 308, 9 So. 157; Moseley v. Moseley, 86 Ala. 289, 5 So. 732; Cosby v. Buchanan, 81 Ala. 574, 1 So. 898; Douglass v. Moody, 80 Ala. 61; Mitchell v. Wellman, 80 Ala. 16; Gibson v. Martin, 38 Ark. 207; Sears v. Dixon, 33 Cal. 326; Elliott v. Connor, 63 Fla. 408, 58 So. 241; Rankin v. Rankin, 111 Ill. App. 403; Keithley v. Wood, 47 Ill. App. 102; White v. Redenbaugh, 41 Ind. App. 580, 82 N. E. 110; Fort v. Colby (Iowa), 144 N. W. 393; Jones v. Gillett, 142 Iowa 506, 118 N. W. 314; Vaughn v. Smith, 148 Ky. 531, 146 S. W. 1094; Scholl v. Hopper, 134 Ky. 83, 119 S. W. 770; Tucker v. Witherbee, 130 Ky. 269, 113 S. W. 123; Skinner v. Miller, 5 Litt. (Ky.) 84; Phillips v. Jackson, 240 Mo. 310, 144 S. W. 112; Donovan v. Boeck, 217 Mo. 70, 116 S. W. 543; Mooney v. Byrne, 163 N. Y. 86, 57 N. E. 163; Poindexter v. McCannon, 1 Dev. Eq. (N. Car.) 377, 18 Am. Dec. 591; Smith v. Hoff, 23 N. Dak. 37, 135 N. W. 772, Ann. Cas. 1914 C, 1072; Smith v. Jensen, 16 N. Dak. 408, 114 N. W. 306; Kinney v. Smith, 58 Ore. 158, 113 Pac. 854; Bickel v. Wessinger, 58 Ore.

conditional sale is clearly established, it will be enforced.[13] Courts scrutinize with care all transactions where a sale has been the result of negotiations initiated by an application for a loan. Yet when it clearly appears a sale was intended, it will be upheld.[14]

If the relation of debtor and creditor in any given case existed in the beginning, and the debt still subsists as to the consideration of the conveyance, the transaction will be treated as a mortgage.[15] The test is whether the debt continued or was extinguished.[16] If the debt was extinguished by a fair agreement, and the grantor has the privilege merely of refunding if he pleases, by a given time, and thereby entitle himself to a reconveyance, the transaction is a conditional sale, and the equity of redemption does not continue.[17] The grantor who neglects

98, 113 Pac. 34; Elliott v. Bozorth, 52 Ore. 391, 97 Pac. 632; Stephens v. Allen, 11 Ore. 188, 3 Pac. 168; Walker v. McDonald, 49 Tex. 458; Gray v. Shelby (Tex.), 18 S. W. 809; Hume v. Le Compte (Tex. Civ. App.), 142 S. W. 934; Duerden v. Solomon, 33 Utah, 468, 94 Pac. 978; King v. Newman, 2 Munf. (Va.) 40; Robertson v. Campbell, 2 Call. (Va.) 421; Rogers v. Burrus, 53 Wis. 530, 9 N. W. 786. See post § 279.

[13] Felton v. Grier, 109 Ga. 320, 35 S. E. 175; Bloodgood v. Zeily, 2 Caines Cas. (N. Y.) 124; Pennington v. Hanby, 4 Munf. (Va.) 140; Davis v. Thomas, 1 Russ. & M. 506; Goodman v. Grierson, 2 Ball. & B. 274.

[14] Ahern v. McCarthy, 107 Cal. 382, 40 Pac. 482; Miller v. Green, 138 Ill. 565, 28 N. E. 837; Shays v. Norton, 48 Ill. 100; Flagg v. Mann, 14 Pick. (Mass.) 467; Turner v. Kerr, 44 Mo. 429; Holmes v. Fresh, 9 Mo. 201; McDonald v. McLeod, 1 Ired. Eq. (N. Car.) 221; De France v. De France, 34 Pa. St. 385; Sadler v. Taylor, 49 W. Va. 104, 38 S. E. 583.

[15] Irwin v. Coleman, 173 Ala. 175, 55 So. 492; Rodgers v. Burt, 157 Ala. 91, 47 So. 226; Smith v. Smith, 153 Ala. 504, 45 So. 168; Voss v. Eller, 109 Ind. 260, 10 N. E. 74; Sebree v. Thompson, 31 Ky. L. 1146, 104 S. W. 781; Duell v. Leslie, 207 Mo. 658, 106 S. W. 489; Gibson v. Morris State Bank (Mont.), 140 Pac. 76; Samuelson v. Mickey, 73 Nebr. 852, 103 N. W. 671; Tannyhill v. Pepperl, 70 Nebr. 31, 96 N. W. 1005;

Mitchell v. Morgan (Tex. Civ. App.), 165 S. W. 883; Johnson v. National Bank of Commerce, 65 Wash. 261, 118 Pac. 21. See, with particular reference to subsisting debt, the following cases: Rodgers v. Burt, 157 Ala. 91, 47 So. 226; Thomas v. Livingston, 155 Ala. 546, 46 So. 851; Wynn v. Fitzwater (Ala.), 44 So. 97; Rushton v. McIlvene, 88 Ark. 299, 114 S. W. 709; Holmes v. Warren, 145 Cal. 457, 78 Pac. 954; Scott v. Hughes, 124 Ga. 1000, 53 S. E. 453; Fabrique v. Cherokee Coal &c. Co., 69 Kans. 733, 77 Pac. 584; Phillips v. Jackson, 240 Mo. 310, 144 S. W. 112; Farrow v. Work, 39 Okla. 734, 136 Pac. 739; Harmon v. Grants Pass Banking &c. Co., 60 Ore. 69, 118 Pac. 188; Francis v. Francis, 78 S. Car. 178, 58 S. E. 804; Harrison v. Hogue (Tex. Civ. App.), 136 S. W. 118; Blake v. Lowry, 43 Tex. Civ. App.17, 93 S. W. 521; Mittlesteadt v. Johnson, 75 Wash. 550, 135 Pac. 214; Hursey v. Hursey, 56 W. Va. 148, 49 S. E. 367. See post § 265.

[16] Bickel v. Wessinger, 58 Ore. 98, 113 Pac. 34; Francis v. Francis, 78 S. Car. 178, 58 S. E. 804; Mittlesteadt v. Johnson, 75 Wash. 550, 135 Pac. 214.

[17] Martin v. Martin, 123 Ala. 191, 26 So. 525; Fabrique v. Cherokee Coal &c. Co., 69 Kans. 733, 77 Pac. 584; Hopper v. Smyser, 90 Md. 363, 45 Atl. 206; Blumberg v. Beekman, 121 Mich. 647, 80 N. W. 710; Duell v. Leslie, 207 Mo. 658, 106 S. W. 489; Woodworth v. Morris, 56 Barb. (N. Y.) 97; Brown v. Dewey, 2

to perform the condition on which the privilege of repurchasing depends will not be relieved.[18]

§ 259. **Intention considered in Conway v. Alexander.**—This matter was carefully considered by the Supreme Court of the United States in Conway v. Alexander.[19] Land had been conveyed to a third person in trust, to reconvey to the grantor if he should repay the purchase-money before a day named, and, if not, then to convey to his creditor. The grantor brought a bill to redeem, whereupon the court held that, in the absence of a bond, note, or other evidence of indebtedness, the transaction must be regarded as a conditional sale; and, as the complainant had not tendered the money at the time provided, that the bill should be dismissed. Chief Justice Marshall, delivering the opinion of the court, said: "To deny the power of two individuals, capable of acting for themselves, to make a contract for the purchase and sale of lands defeasible by the payment of money at a future day, or in other words, to make a sale with a reservation to the vendor of a right to repurchase the same land at a fixed price and at a specified time, would be to transfer to the courts of chancery, in a considerable degree, the guardianship of adults as well as infants. Such contracts are certainly not prohibited either by the letter or the policy of the law. But the policy of the law does prohibit the conversion of a real mortgage into a sale; and as lenders of money are less under the pressure

Barb. (N. Y.) 28, 1 Sandf. (N. Y.) 56; Robinson v. Cropsey, 2 Edw. Ch. (N. Y.) 138, 6 Paige (N. Y.) 480; Whitney v. Townsend, 2 Lans. (N. Y.) 249; Holmes v. Grant, 8 Paige (N. Y.) 243; Cockrill v. Whitworth (Tenn.), 52 S. W. 524; Kunert v. Strong, 103 Wis. 70, 79 N. W. 32. See also Osborne v. Morgan, 171 Ill. App. 549. See post § 265.

[18] Hughes v. Sheaff, 19 Iowa 335.

[19] 7 Cranch (U. S.) 218, 3 L. ed. 321. "In this case," said Chief Justice Marshall, "the form of the deed is not in itself conclusive either way. The want of a covenant to repay the money is not complete evidence that a conditional sale was intended, but is a circumstance of no inconsiderable importance. If the vendee must be restrained to his principal and interest, that principal and interest ought to be secure. It is, therefore, a necessary ingredient in a mortgage, that the mortgagee should have a remedy against the person of the debtor. If this remedy really exists, its not being reserved in terms will not affect the case. But it must exist in order to justify a construction which overrules the express words of the instrument. Its existence in this case is certainly not to be collected from the deed. There is no acknowledgment of a pre-existing debt, nor any covenant for repayment. An action at law for the recovery of the money certainly could not have been sustained; and if, to a bill in chancery praying a sale of the premises, and a decree for so much money as might remain due, Robert Alexander had answered that this was a sale and not a mortgage, clear proof to the contrary must have been produced to justify a decree against him." See also Flagg v. Mann, 2 Sumn. (U. S.) 486; Hopper v. Smyser, 90 Md. 363, 382, 45 Atl. 206.

of circumstances which control the perfect and free exercise of the judgment than borrowers, the effort is frequently made by persons of this description to avail themselves of the advantage of this superiority, in order to obtain inequitable advantages. For this reason the leaning of courts has been against them, and doubtful cases have generally been decided to be mortgages. But as a conditional sale, if really intended, is valid, the inquiry in every case must be, whether the contract in the specific case is a security for the repayment of money, or an actual sale."

§ 260. **Evidence of intention—Existence of the debt secured.—** In order to convert what appears to be a conditional sale into a mortgage, the evidence should be so clear as to leave no doubt that the real intention of the parties was to execute a mortgage;[20] otherwise the intention appearing on the face of the deed ought to prevail. There is no absolute rule that the covenant to reconvey shall be regarded either in law or equity as a defeasance.[21] It may well be that a person buys land in satisfaction of a precedent debt, or for a consideration then paid, and at the same time contracts to reconvey the lands upon the payment of a certain sum, and there is no intention on the part of either party that the transaction should be, in effect, a mortgage. The covenant or agreement to reconvey is not necessarily either at law or in equity a defeasance. It is one fact which may, in connection with other facts, go to show that the parties really intended the deed to operate as a mortgage; but standing alone it does not produce that result. Something more is necessary; and an indispensable thing is a debt by the grantor to the grantee for which the conveyance is security.[22] If there exists a debt to be secured its nature and form is

[20] Henley v. Hotaling, 41 Cal. 22; Mulhaupt v. Youree, 35 La. Ann. 1052; Cotton v. McKee, 68 Maine 486; Winters v. Earl, 52 N. J. Eq. 52, 28 Atl. 15; Fullerton v. McCurdy, 55 N. Y. 637.

[21] Henley v. Hotaling, 41 Cal. 22.

[22] Wallace v. Johnstone, 129 U. S. 58, 32 L. ed. 619, 9 Sup. Ct. 243; Horbach v. Hill, 112 U. S. 144, 28 L. ed. 670, 5 Sup. Ct. 81; Stollenwerck v. Marks (Ala.), 65 So. 1024; Bell v. Shiver (Ala.), 61 So. 881; Irwin v. Coleman, 173 Ala. 175, 55 So. 492; Nelson v. Wadsworth, 171 Ala. 603, 55 So. 120; Rodgers v. Burt, 157 Ala. 91, 47 So. 226; Thomas v. Livingston, 155 Ala. 546, 46 So. 851; Smith v. Smith, 153 Ala. 504, 45 So. 168; Wynn v. Fitzwater (Ala.), 44 So. 97; Robinson v. Gassoway (Ala.), 39 So. 1023; Perdue v. Bell, 83 Ala. 396, 3 So. 698; Haynie v. Robertson, 58 Ala. 37; Rushton v. McIllvene, 88 Ark. 299, 114 S. W. 709; Prefumo v. Russell, 148 Cal. 451, 83 Pac. 810; Holmes v. Warren, 145 Cal. 457, 78 Pac. 954; Scott v. Hughes, 124 Ga. 1000, 53 S. E. 453; Caraway v. Sly, 222 Ill. 203, 78 N. E. 588; Bearss v. Ford, 108 Ill. 16; Rue v. Dole, 107 Ill. 275; Rankin v. Rankin, 111 Ill. App. 403; Wolfe v. McMillan, 117 Ind. 587, 592, 20 N. E. 509; Henninger v. McGuire, 146 Iowa 270, 125 N. W. 180; Jones v. Gillett, 142 Iowa 506, 118 N. W. 314; Veeder v. Veeder, 141 Iowa 492, 120

not material.[23] It is sufficient that the debt is recited in the deed, and it is not necessary that it should be evidenced by a separate written instrument.[24] The time for payment of the debt, and the rate of in-

N. W. 61; Farmers' &c. Bank v. Kackley, 88 Kans. 70, 127 Pac. 539; Fabrique v. Cherokee Coal &c. Co., 69 Kans. 733, 77 Pac. 584; Eckert v. McBee, 27 Kans. 232; Fuson v. Chestnut, 33 Ky. L. 249, 109 S. W. 1192; Sebree v. Thompson, 31 Ky. L. 1146, 104 S. W. 781; Edrington v. Harper, 3 J. J. Marsh. (Ky.) 353, 20 Am. Dec. 145; Hopper v. Smyser, 90 Md. 363, 45 Atl. 206; Olney v. Brown, 163 Mich. 125, 128 N. W. 241; Heaton v. Darling, 66 Minn. 262, 68 N. W. 1087; Butman v. James, 34 Minn. 547, 27 N. W. 66; Buse v. Page, 32 Minn. 111, 19 N. W. 736, 20 N. W. 95; Lipscomb v. Talbott, 243 Mo. 1, 147 S. W. 798; Donovan v. Boeck, 217 Mo. 70, 116 S. W. 543; Duell v. Leslie, 207 Mo. 658, 106 S. W. 489; Gibson v. Morris State Bank (Mont.), 140 Pac. 76; Morrison v. Jones, 31 Mont. 154, 77 Pac. 507; Samuelson v. Mickey, 73 Nebr. 852, 103 N. W. 671; Tannyhill v. Pepperl, 70 Nebr. 31, 96 N. W. 1005; Bascombe v. Marshall, 129 App. Div. 516, 113 N. Y. S. 991; Mooney v. Byrne, 163 N. Y. 86, 57 N. E. 163; Miller v. Smith, 20 N. Dak. 96, 126 N. W. 499; McGuin v. Lee, 10 N. Dak. 160, 86 N. W. 714; Farrow v. Work, 39 Okla. 734, 136 Pac. 739; Grover v. Hawthorne, 62 Ore. 77, 121 Pac. 808; Harmon v. Grants Pass Banking &c. Co., 60 Ore. 69, 118 Pac. 188; Bickel v. Wessinger, 58 Ore. 98, 113 Pac. 34; Eldriedge v. Hoefer, 52 Ore. 241, 93 Pac. 246; Callahan's Estate, 13 Phila. (Pa.) 381; Francis v. Francis, 78 S. Car. 178, 58 S. E. 804; Hodge v. Weeks, 31 S. Car. 276, 9 S. E. 953; Jones v. Jones, 20 S. Dak. 632, 108 N. W. 23; Calhoun v. Lumpkin, 60 Tex. 185; Mitchell v. Morgan (Tex. Civ. App.), 165 S. W. 883; Parks v. Sullivan (Tex. Civ. App.), 152 S. W. 704; Harrison v. Hogue (Tex. Civ. App.), 136 S. W. 118; O'Neill v. O'Neill (Tex. Civ. App.), 135 S. W. 729; Hall v. Jennings (Tex. Civ. App.), 104 S. W. 489; Blake v. Lowry (Tex. Civ. App.),

93 S. W. 521; Holladay v. Willis 101 Va. 274, 43 S. E. 616; Mittlesteadt v. Johnson, 75 Wash. 550, 135 Pac. 214; Johnson v. National Bank of Commerce, 65 Wash. 261, 118 Pac. 21; Boyer v. Paine, 60 Wash. 56, 110 Pac. 682; Fridley v. Somerville, 60 W. Va. 272, 54 S. E. 502; Hursey v. Hursey, 56 W. Va. 148, 49 S. E. 367; Kerr v. Hill, 27 W. Va. 576; Polly v. Gumney (Wis.), 147 N. W. 356; McCourt v. Peppard, 126 Wis. 326, 105 N. W. 809; Wolf v. Theresa Village Mut. Fire Ins. Co., 115 Wis. 402, 91 N. W. 1014.

"The owner of the lands may be willing to sell at the price agreed upon, and the purchaser may also be willing to give his vendor the right to repurchase upon specified terms; and if such appears to be the intention of the parties, it is not the duty of the court to attribute to them a different intention. Such a contract is not opposed to public policy, nor is it in any sense illegal; and courts would depart from the line of their duties should they, in disregard of the real intention of the parties, declare it to be a mortgage." Per Chief Justice Rhodes in Henley v. Hotaling, 41 Cal. 22. See post § 335.

[23] Batcheller v. Batcheller, 144 Ill. 471, 33 N. E. 24 (contingent liability insufficient); Bearss v. Ford, 108 Ill. 16 (existing mortgage debt); Clark v. Seagraves, 186 Mass. 430, 71 N. E. 813 (debt due a third person); Bethlehem v. Annis, 40 N. H. 34, 77 Am. Dec. 700 (unliquidated damages insufficient); Meeker v. Warren, 66 N. J. Eq. 146, 57 Atl. 421 (debt due a third person); Stelts v. Martin, 90 S. Car. 14, 72 S. E. 550; Kaphan v. Toney (Tenn.), 58 S. W. 909 (fiduciary obligation for misappropriated funds); Jones v. Cullen, 100 Tenn. 1, 42 S. W. 873 (liability as indorser).

[24] Brant v. Robertson, 16 Mo. 129; Graham v. Stevens, 34 Vt. 166, 80 Am. Dec. 675. See also Overstreet v. Baxter, 30 Kans. 55, 1 Pac. 825.

terest need not appear, but will be implied.[25] Parol evidence is admissible to show the existence of a debt to be secured by the conveyance intended as a mortgage.[26]

§ **261. Stipulations and recitals of intention.**—A contract of repurchase may upon its face show that the parties really intended an absolute sale, with the privilege to the vendor of repurchasing on the terms named. It will be so interpreted when the provisions of the contract are inconsistent with the idea that a mortgage to secure an indebtedness was intended.[27] The agreement upon its face may be either an agreement to reconvey merely, or may amount with the deed to a mortgage,[28] in which case a resort to evidence outside of these instruments may be necessary to determine the character of the transaction.[29]

An agreement to reconvey on payment by the grantor of a valid existing debt is conclusively presumed to be a mortgage, and no stipulation of the parties can make it otherwise.[30] An express provision that the contract for reconveyance should be regarded only as a contract to reconvey and not as evidence that the deed was intended as a mortgage, if consistent with the whole transaction, should be given effect as declaring the intention of the parties that it should not create a mortgage.[31] An agreement between a mortgagor and the holder of a

[25] McMillan v. Bissell, 63 Mich. 66, 29 N. W. 737; Helm v. Boyd, 124 Ill. 370, 16 N. E. 85 (no time for payment specified). See also Wilson v. Kirkland, 172 Ala. 72, 55 S. W. 174.

[26] Locke v. Moulton, 96 Cal. 21, 30 Pac. 957; People v. Irwin, 14 Cal. 428; McNamara v. Culver, 22 Kans. 661. But see Thomas v. McCormack, 9 Dana (Ky.) 108 (parol evidence not admissible to contradict the deed).

[27] Hanford v. Blessing, 80 Ill. 188; Voss v. Eller, 109 Ind. 260, 10 N. E. 74; Hays v. Carr, 83 Ind. 275; Yost v. First Nat. Bank, 66 Kans. 605, 72 Pac. 209; Pumilia v. De George (Tex. Civ. App.), 74 S. W. 813; Smith v. Crosby, 47 Wis. 160, 2 N. W. 104.

[28] Hickox v. Lowe, 10 Cal. 197. In this case a debtor conveyed to his creditor, and took back an agreement to reconvey whenever the grantor should repay the consideration, with a stipulated sum per month for the use of the money, with a provision that, if the net

rents per month should exceed that sum, the grantee should apply them to the payment of the consideration.

[29] Parish v. Gates, 29 Ala. 254; McCarron v. Cassidy, 18 Ark. 34; Snyder v. Griswold, 37 Ill. 216; Bishop v. Williams, 18 Ill. 101; McNamara v. Culver, 22 Kans. 661; Devore v. Woodruff, 1 N. Dak. 143, 45 N. W. 701; Rich v. Doane, 35 Vt. 125.

[30] Beidelman v. Koch, 42 Ind. App. 423, 85 N. E. 977. See also McRobert v. Bridget (Iowa), 149 N. W. 906.

[31] Ford v. Irwin, 18 Cal. 117; Henley v. Hotaling, 41 Cal. 22; Chicago, B. &c. R. Co. v. Watson, 113 Ill. 195; Hays v. Carr, 83 Ind. 275; Donovan v. Boeck, 217 Mo. 70, 116 S. W. 543; McGuin v. Lee, 10 N. Dak. 160, 86 N. W. 714; Jasper v. Hazen, 4 N. Dak. 1, 58 N. W. 454, 23 L. R. A. 58. An express provision that a conveyance is not a mortgage but an absolute conveyance, which is wholly inconsistent with the facts

mortgage, reciting that default had been made in payment of the note secured, that the mortgagor had conveyed the premises by warranty deed in consideration of the cancelation of the debt, and providing that the holder would reconvey upon payment of the debt within a specified time and further reciting that the agreement should not be construed to be a mortgage, was accordingly held to be a conditional sale and not a mortgage.[32] If an instrument declares that it is a conditional deed and not a mortgage, and is to be absolute upon the nonpayment of a sum mentioned at a time specified, it is to be construed as a conditional deed and not a mortgage.[33]

Sometimes the terms of the agreement for reconveyance may not be conclusive that a sale was intended with the privilege of repurchasing, but may be so inconsistent with any other theory that very little further evidence to the same effect will lead to this determination.[34] On the other hand, an absolute deed of land, which contains a recital that it was executed to secure the payment of a loan of money, shows upon its face that it is a mortgage.[35] A debtor conveyed land to his creditor as security, under an agreement that the debtor was to remain in possession for a certain time, during which he might pay the debt and receive a reconveyance. If he should sell the land, he was to pay the debt and keep the excess, and if the creditor should sell it he was to pay the excess to the debtor. It was held that the agreement amounted to a mortgage, and the creditor could not maintain unlawful detainer, after the expiration of the stipulated time within which the debtor might pay the debt and receive a reconveyance.[36] Where an antecedent indebtedness constitutes the consideration for the conveyance, payment whereof was intended to be secured, a recital purporting to cancel an antecedent indebtedness does not preclude the application of the principles by which an absolute deed is declared a mortgage.[37]

§ 262. **Actual sale—Rights of parties.**—A purchaser is entitled to have an actual sale enforced. When there is, in fact, a sale instead of a mortgage, but the grantor subsequently claims the transaction to

---

of the case does not render absolute a conveyance which is shown to have been executed for the purpose and with the intention of securing the payment of money. Connor v. Connor, 59 Fla. 467, 52 So. 727.

[32] Donovan v. Boeck, 217 Mo. 70, 116 S. W. 543.

[33] Burnside v. Terry, 45 Ga. 621. See also Chaires v. Brady, 10 Fla. 133; Rue v. Dole, 107 Ill. 275; Saxton v. Hitchcock, 47 Barb. (N. Y.) 220; Reed v. Parker, 33 Wash. 107, 74 Pac. 61.

[34] Hanford v. Blessing, 80 Ill. 188.

[35] Montgomery v. Chadwick, 7 Iowa 114.

[36] Hunter v. Maanum, 78 Wis. 656, 48 N. W. 51.

[37] Shields v. Simonton, 65 W. Va. 179, 63 S. E. 972.

be a mortgage, the grantee may maintain a bill in equity to have it decreed a sale.[38] A purchaser is as much entitled to have his rights protected as is a mortgagor. A sale in connection with an agreement for repurchase comes very near in form and substance to a mortgage, but the rights of the parties are very different.[39] While a mortgage may be redeemed at any time before the right is cut off by foreclosure, there can be no redemption under a conditional sale after the day appointed. This is the contract of the parties, and either one of them is entitled to have it enforced according to its terms.[40] The option to repurchase may be a personal privilege which can not be enforced in case of the death of the obligee during the continuance of the option.[41] A deed executed at the same time as a mortgage, upon the same consideration, to the same party and covering the same land, is merely additional security, and operates as a mortgage.[42]

If it appears that a mortgage of a large tract of land was made to secure a loan, and at the same time the mortgagor made a conveyance to the mortgagee of four acres of land not included in the mortgage, and that this conveyance was made as a bonus to induce the mortgagee to advance the money, in the absence of any undue advantage taken by the mortgagee, the mortgagor can not have this conveyance declared to be additional security for the loan, and in effect a mortgage.[43]

A mortgagor, upon being notified that the mortgagee would proceed to foreclose the mortgage for nonpayment of interest, which had been due for several years, replied that he preferred to make a deed of the property rather than to have a sale made under the mortgage; and accordingly he executed a deed absolute in form, and took back a con-

---

[38] Kahn v. Weill, 42 Fed. 704; Manasse v. Dinkelspiel, 68 Cal. 404, 9 Pac. 547; Gassert v. Bogk, 7 Mont. 585, 600, 19 Pac. 281; Rich v. Doane. 35 Vt. 125. See also Conway v. Alexander, 7 Cranch (U. S.) 218, 3 L. ed. 321.

[39] Conway v. Alexander, 7 Cranch (U. S.) 218, 3 L. ed. 321; Flagg v. Mann, 14 Pick. (Mass.) 467.

[40] Henley v. Hotaling, 41 Cal. 22; People v. Irwin, 14 Cal. 428, 18 Cal. 117; Phipps v. Munson, 50 Conn. 267; Hanford v. Blessing, 80 Ill. 188; Carr v. Rising, 62 Ill. 14; Shays v. Norton, 48 Ill. 100; Dwen v. Blake, 44 Ill. 135; Pitts v. Cable, 44 Ill. 103; Trucks v. Lindsey, 18 Iowa 504; Cornell v. Hall, 22 Mich. 377; Merritt v. Brown, 19 N. J. Eq. 287; Brown v. Dewey, 2 Barb. (N. Y.) 28; Holmes v. Grant, 8 Paige (N. Y.) 243; Glover v. Payn, 19 Wend. (N. Y.) 518; Haines v. Thomson, 70 Pa. St. 434; Rich v. Doane, 35 Vt. 125; Ransome v. Frayser, 10 Leigh (Va.) 592; Moss v. Green, 10 Leigh (Va.) 251, 34 Am. Dec. 731; Schriber v. Le Clair, 66 Wis. 579, 29 N. W. 570; Joy v. Birch, 4 Cl. & F. 57; Pegg v. Wisden, 16 Beav. 239; Perry v. Meddowcroft, 4 Beav. 197; Barrell v. Sabine, 1 Vern. 268; St. John v. Wareham, cited in Thornborough v. Baker, 3 Swanst. 628; Ensworth v. Griffiths, 1 Bro. P. C. 149.

[41] Newton v. Newton, 11 R. I. 390, 23 Am. Rep. 476.

[42] Belieu v. Card (Nebr.), 145 N. W. 976.

[43] Butts v. Robson, 5 Wash. 268, 31 Pac. 760.

tract for the conveyance of the land to him upon the payment of a sum agreed upon within one year. His notes were surrendered, and he executed no new obligation to pay the mortgage debt. It was held that the transaction was a conditional sale, and not a mortgage.[44]

§ 263. **Character of transaction fixed in inception.**—The character of the transaction is fixed at its inception and is what the intention of the parties makes it.[45] The form of the transaction and the circumstances attending it are the means of finding out the intention.[46] If it was a mortgage in the beginning it remains so,[47] in accordance with the maxim "once a mortgage always a mortgage";[48] and if it was a conditional sale at the start no lapse of time will make a mortgage of it. The recording of the conveyance as a mortgage, if it was intended as a sale with a right of repurchase at the option of the grantor, does not make it a mortgage.[49] If not a security in the beginning, but an absolute sale or a conditional sale, no subsequent event, short of a new agreement between the parties, can convert it into a mortgage.[50] Where an instrument contains the exact terms agreed on by the par-

[44] Rue v. Dole, 107 Ill. 275.

[45] Knowles v. Williams, 58 Kans. 221, 48 Pac. 856; Kleinschmidt v. Kleinschmidt, 9 Mont. 477, 24 Pac. 266; Gassert v. Bogk, 7 Mont. 585, 19 Pac. 281; Macauley v. Smith, 132 N. Y. 524, 30 N. E. 997; Poston v. Jones, 122 N. Car. 536, 29 S. E. 951; Devore v. Woodruff, 1 N. Dak. 143, 45 N. W. 701; Gray v. Shelby, 83 Tex. 405, 18 S. W. 809; Davis v. Brewster, 59 Tex. 93; Goodbar v. Bloom, 42 Tex. Civ. App. 434, 96 S. W. 657 (citing text); Wasatch Min. Co. v. Jennings, 5 Utah 251, 15 Pac. 65; Clambey v. Copeland, 52 Wash. 580, 100 Pac. 1031 (quoting text). See post § 340.

[46] Goodbar v. Bloom, 43 Tex. Civ. App. 434, 96 S. W. 657 (quoting text). See ante § 258 and post § 278.

[47] Elliott v. Connor, 63 Fla. 408, 58 So. 241; Connor v. Connor, 59 Fla. 467, 52 So. 727; Hawes v. Williams, 92 Maine 483, 43 Atl. 101; Poston v. Jones, 122 N. Car. 536, 29 S. E. 951; Goodbar v. Bloom, 43 Tex. Civ. App. 434, 96 S. W. 657 (quoting text); Wasatch Min. Co. v. Jennings, 5 Utah 243, 16 Pac. 399 (quoting text); Clambey v. Copland, 52 Wash. 580, 100 Pac. 1031; Hudkins

v. Crim (W. Va.), 78 S. E. 1043; Hursey v. Hursey, 56 W. Va. 148, 49 S. E. 367.

[48] Rees v. Rhodes, 3 Ariz. 235, 73 Pac. 446; Elliott v. Connor, 63 Fla. 408, 58 So. 241; Connor v. Connor, 59 Fla. 467, 52 So. 727; Doyle v. Ringi (Ind.), 102 N. E. 18; Ferguson v. Boyd (Ind. App.), 79 N. E. 549, 169 Ind. 537, 81 N. E. 71; Loeb v. McAlister, 15 Ind. App. 643, 41 N. E. 1061, 44 N. E. 378; Stratton v. Rotrock, 84 Kans. 198, 114 Pac. 224; McPherson v. Hayward, 81 Maine 329, 17 Atl. 164; Reed v. Reed, 75 Maine 264; Vanderhaize v. Hugues, 13 N. J. Eq. 244; Wilson v. Giddings, 28 Ohio St. 554; Clambey v. Copland, 52 Wash. 580, 100 Pac. 1031; Hudkins v. Crim (W. Va.), 78 S. E. 1043. See post § 340.

[49] Morrison v. Brand, 5 Daly (N. Y.) 40; Jackson v. Richards, 6 Cow. (N. Y.) 617. See post § 276.

[50] Reed v. Reed, 75 Maine 264; Buse v. Page, 32 Minn. 111, 19 N. W. 736, 20 N. W. 95; Finck v. Adams, 36 N. J. Eq. 188; Kearney v. Macomb, 16 N. J. Eq. 189; Clark v. Henry, 2 Cow. (N. Y.) 324; Goodbar v. Bloom, 43 Tex. Civ. App. 434, 96 S. W. 657 (quoting text).

ties, and expresses their intent and meaning, the fact that they thought it a mortgage, while it was in fact a conditional sale, does not change its character or effect.[51]

§ 264. **Intention to secure repayment of money.**—If intended by the parties as a security for money, an absolute conveyance is in equity a mortgage. Of course it is entirely competent for persons capable of acting for themselves to make a sale with a reservation to the vendor of a right to repurchase the same land at a fixed price, and at a specified time; and the inquiry in every case therefore is, whether the contract is a security for the repayment of money, or an actual or conditional sale.[52] The rule at law and in equity is the same in respect

[51] Hershey v. Luce, 56 Ark. 320, 19 S. W. 963; Goodbar v. Bloom, 43 Tex. Civ. App. 434, 96 S. W. 657 (quoting text).

[52] Conway v. Alexander, 7 Cranch (U. S.) 218, 3 L. ed. 321; In re Borg, 184 Fed. 640; Lindbloom v. Kidston, 2 Alaska 292; Hubert v. Sistrunk (Ala.), 53 So. 819; Smith v. Smith, 153 Ala. 504, 45 So. 168; Crismon v. Kingman Plow Co., 106 Ark. 166, 152 S. W. 989; American Mtg. Co. v. Williams, 103 Ark. 484, 145 S. W. 234; Rushton v. McIllvene, 88 Ark. 299, 114 S. W. 709; Land v. May, 73 Ark. 415, 84 S. W. 489; Blakemore v. Byrnside, 7 Ark. 505; Johnson v. Clark, 5 Ark. 321; Porter v. Clements, 3 Ark. 364; Cal. Civ. Code, § 2924; Shirley v. All Night and Day Bank (Cal.), 134 Pac. 1001; Beckman v. Waters, 161 Cal. 581, 119 Pac. 922; Renton v. Gibson, 148 Cal. 650, 84 Pac. 186; Anglo-Californian Bank v. Cerf, 147 Cal. 384, 81 Pac. 1077; Whitehouse v. Whitehouse, 22 Cal. App. 565, 135 Pac. 509; Schumacher v. Langford, 20 Cal. App. 61, 127 Pac. 1057; Elliott v. Connor, 63 Fla. 408, 58 So. 241 (citing text); Berry v. Williams (Ga.), 81 S. E. 881; Fleming v. Georgia R. Bank, 120 Ga. 1023, 48 S. E. 420; Spence v. Steadman, 49 Ga. 133; Clark v. Lyon, 46 Ga. 202; Bergen v. Johnson, 21 Idaho 619, 123 Pac. 484; Hannah v. Vensel, 19 Idaho 796, 116 Pac. 115; Hurd's Illinois Rev. Stat. 1913, p. 1665, § 12; Risser v. Patton, 232 Ill. 353, 83 N. E. 914; Morriss v. Blackman, 179 Ill. 103, 53 N. E. 547; Whittemore v. Fisher, 132 Ill. 243, 24 N. E. 636; Jackson v. Lynch, 129 Ill. 72, 21 N. E. 580; Bearss v. Ford, 108 Ill. 16; Klock v. Walter, 70 Ill. 416; Ewart v. Walling, 42 Ill. 453; Preschbaker v. Feaman, 32 Ill. 475; Tillson v. Moulton, 23 Ill. 648; Wilson v. Rehm, 117 Ill. App. 473; McCorkle v. Richards, 112 Ill. App. 495 (master's deed given as security); Sinclair v. Guzenhauser, 179 Ind. 78, 98 N. E. 37; Ferguson v. Boyd (Ind. App.), 79 N. E. 549, 169 Ind. 537, 81 N. E. 71; Crassen v. Swoveland, 22 Ind. 427; Watkins v. Gregory, 6 Blackf. (Ind.) 113; Harbison v. Lemon, 3 Blackf. (Ind.) 51, 51 Am. Dec. 376; Calahan v. Dunker, 51 Ind. App. 436, 99 N. E. 1021; Beidelman v. Koch, 42 Ind. App. 423, 85 N. E. 977; Fort v. Colby (Iowa), 144 N. W. 393; Baxter v. Pritchard, 122 Iowa 590, 98 N. W. 372, 101 Am. St. 282; Montgomery v. Chadwick, 7 Iowa 114; Wiswell v. Simonds, 77 Kans. 622, 95 Pac. 407; Tucker v. Witherbee, 130 Ky. 269, 113 S. W. 123; Guenther v. Wisdom, 27 Ky. L. 230, 84 S. W. 771; Brey v. Barbour (Ky.), 20 S. W. 899; Hurd v. Chase, 100 Maine 561, 62 Atl. 660; Hawes v. Williams, 92 Maine 483, 43 Atl. 101; Hicks v. Hicks, 5 Gill & J. (Md.) 75; Clark v. Seagraves, 186 Mass. 430, 71 N. E. 813; Campbell v. Dearborn, 109 Mass. 130, 12 Am. Rep. 671; Ehle v. Looker (Mich.), 148 N. W. 378; Olney v. Brown, 163 Mich. 125, 128 N. W. 241; Flynn v. Holmes, 145 Mich. 606, 108 N. W. 685, 11 L. R. A. (N. S.) 209; Weise v. Anderson, 134.

to the obligation as a security. In both courts the intention of the parties, that the conveyance is to stand merely as a security for a debt,

Mich. 502, 96 N. W. 575; Sanborn v. Sanborn, 104 Mich. 180, 62 N. W. 371; Enos v. Sutherland, 11 Mich. 538; Teal v. Scandinavian-American Bank, 114 Minn. 435, 131 N. W. 486; Buse v. Page, 32 Minn. 111, 19 N. W. 736, 20 N. W. 95; Weide v. Gehl, 21 Minn. 449; Holton v. Meighen, 15 Minn. 69; Hill v. Edwards, 11 Minn. 22; Duell v. Leslie, 207 Mo. 658, 106 S. W. 489; Stumpe v. Kopp, 201 Mo. 412, 99 S. W. 1073; O'Neill v. Capelle, 62 Mo. 202; Sharkey v. Sharkey, 47 Mo. 543; Copeland v. Yoakum, 38 Mo. 349; Tibeau v. Tibeau, 22 Mo. 77; Wilson v. Drumrite, 21 Mo. 325; Gassert v. Strong, 38 Mont. 18, 98 Pac. 497; Morrison v. Jones, 31 Mont. 154, 77 Pac. 507; Huston v. Canfield, 57 Nebr. 345, 77 N. W. 763; Lipp v. Syndicate, 24 Nebr. 692, 40 N. W. 129; Leahigh v. White, 8 Nev. 147; Cramer v. Cale, 72 N. J. Eq. 210, 73 Atl. 813; Meeker v. Warren, 66 N. J. Eq. 146, 57 Atl. 421; Montgomery v. Beecher (N. J. Eq.), 31 Atl. 451; Pidcock v. Swift, 51 N. J. Eq. 405, 27 Atl. 470; White v. Megill (N. J. Eq.), 18 Atl. 355; Garland v. Sperling, 6 N. Mex. 623, 30 Pac. 925; Shields v. Russell, 66 Hun (N. Y.) 226; Mooney v. Byrne, 163 N. Y. 86, 57 N. E. 163; Mutual Life Ins. Co. v. Nicholas, 144 App. Div. 95, 128 N. Y. S. 902; Doty v. Norton, 133 App. Div. 106, 117 N. Y. S. 793; White v. Walsh, 62 Misc. 423, 114 N. Y. S. 1015; Conover v. Palmer, 123 App. Div. 817, 108 N. Y. S. 480; Connor v. Atwood, 4 N. Y. S. 561; Norris v. Schuyler, 4 N. Y. S. 558; Robinson v. Willoughby, 65 N. Car. 520; Vallely v. First Nat. Bank, 14 N. Dak. 580, 106 N. W. 127, 5 L. R. A. (N. S.) 387, 116 Am. St. 700; Jasper v. Hazen, 4 N. Dak. 1, 58 N. W. 454, 23 L. R. A. 58; National Bank v. Tennessee &c. R. Co., 62 Ohio St. 564, 57 N. E. 450; Marshall v. Stewart, 17 Ohio 356; Worley v. Carter, 30 Okla. 642, 121 Pac. 669; Wagg v. Herbert, 19 Okla. 525, 92 Pac. 250; Yingling v. Redwine, 12 Okla. 64, 69 Pac. 810; Balduff v. Griswold, 9 Okla. 438, 60 Pac. 223; Weiseham v. Hocker, 7 Okla. 250, 54 Pac. 464;

Houser v. Lamont, 55 Pa. St. 311, 93 Am. St. 755; Guthrie v. Kahle, 46 Pa. St. 331; Cole v. Bolard, 22 Pa. St. 431; Wheeland v. Swartz, 1 Yeates (Pa.) 579; Krug v. Kautz, 21 S. Dak. 461, 113 N. W. 623; Kidd v. Sparks (Tex. Civ. App.), 167 S. W. 799; Yates v. Caswell (Tex. Civ. App.), 126 S. W. 914; Lapowski v. Shith, 1 Tex. Civ. App. 391, 20 S. W. 957; Baxter v. Dear, 24 Tex. 17, 76 Am. Dec. 89; Duerden v. Solomon, 33 Utah 468, 94 Pac. 978; Crahan v. Chittenden, 82 Vt. 410, 74 Atl. 86; Winn v. Cooper, 37 Vt. 169; Hudkins v. Crim (W. Va.), 78 S. E. 1043; Dudley v. Buckley, 68 W. Va. 630, 70 S. E. 376; Shields v. Simonton, 65 W. Va. 179, 63 S. E. 972; Furguson v. Bond, 39 W. Va. 561, 20 S. E. 591; Klinck v. Price, 4 W. Va. 4, 6 Am. Rep. 268; Falbe v. Caves, 151 Wis. 54, 138 N. W. 87; Wells v. Scanlan, 124 Wis. 229, 102 N. W. 571; Schneider v. Reed, 123 Wis. 488, 101 N. W. 682; Schierl v. Newburg, 102 Wis. 552, 78 N. W. 761; Schriber v. Le Clair, 66 Wis. 579, 29 N. W. 570; Hoile v. Bailey, 58 Wis. 434, 448, 17 N. W. 322; Brinkman v. Jones, 44 Wis. 498; Plato v. Roe, 14 Wis. 453; Second Ward Bank v. Upmann, 12 Wis. 499. See also Rev. Code N. Dak. 1905, § 6153; Adams v. McIntyre, 22 N. Dak. 337, 133 N. W. 915. But see Baxter v. Pritchard, 122 Iowa 590, 98 N. W. 372, 101 Am. St. 282. By statute in some states, every transfer of property made as security for another act, other than a trust, is a mortgage. Renton v. Gibson, 148 Cal. 650, 84 Pac. 186; Krug v. Kautz, 21 S. Dak. 461, 113 N. W. 623. In Robinson v. Cropsey, 2 Edw. Ch. (N. Y.) 138, the court say: "If a deed or conveyance be accompanied by a condition or matter of defeasance expressed in the deed, or even contained in a separate instrument, or exist merely in parol, let the consideration for it have been a preexisting debt or a present advance of money to the grantor, the only inquiry necessary to be made is, whether the relation of debtor and creditor remains, and a debt still

stamps it infallibly as a mortgage.[53] The intention may be to secure
other obligations than the payment of money. A deed given to secure
the grantee as surety for the grantor has been held a mortgage.[54] To
determine the intention of the parties instruments executed at the
same time, constituting one transaction, are to be read together.[55] Thus
a deed and a separate instrument contemporaneously executed and giving the grantor the right to repurchase within a specified time will be
construed together to determine whether the contract is a mortgage
or a conditional sale.[56] Of course the mere secret intention of either
party to an absolute conveyance as to the purpose of it is without effect
in determining the character of it.[57]

The rights of the parties to the conveyance must be reciprocal. If
the transaction be in the nature of a mortgage, so that the grantor
may insist upon a reconveyance, the grantee at the same time may
insist upon repayment; but if it be a conditional sale, so that the
grantor need not repurchase except at his option, the grantee can not
insist upon repayment.[58] If both parties to a warranty deed intend
that it shall operate as a conveyance and not as security for a debt,
and redemption by repayment under the bond for reconveyance is entirely optional with the grantor, the transaction is a conditional sale
and not a mortgage.[59]

subsists between the parties; for if
it does, then the conveyance must
be regarded as a security for the
payment, and be treated in all respects as a mortgage. On the other
hand, where the debt forming the
consideration for the conveyance is
extinguished at the time by the express agreement of the parties, or
the money advanced is not paid by
way of loan, so as to constitute a
debt and liability to repay it, but
by the terms of the agreement the
grantor has the privilege of refunding or not at his election, then it
must be purchase-money, and the
transaction will be a sale upon condition, which the grantor can defeat
only by a repurchase, or performance of the condition on his part
within the time limited for the purchase, and in this way entitle himself to a reconveyance of the property." A conveyance by a bankrupt
prior to bankruptcy to his wife not
as a gift but to secure her for
money contributed to the construction of buildings on the realty con-

veyed, was held a mortgage; and
such real estate could not be omitted from the bankrupt's schedule.
In re Borg, 184 Fed. 640.
[53] Tillison v. Moulton, 23 Ill. 648.
[54] Meeker v. Warren (N. J. Eq.),
57 Atl. 421.
[55] Adams v. Hopkins, 144 Cal. 19,
77 Pac. 712; In re Bennett's Estate,
168 Ill. App. 658; Turner v. Cochran, 30 Tex. Civ. App. 549, 70 S. W.
1024. See ante § 245.
[56] Thomas v. Livingston, 155 Ala.
546, 46 So. 851. See also Adams v.
Hopkins, 144 Cal. 19, 77 Pac. 112.
[57] Haney v. Clark, 65 Tex. 93.
[58] Text quoted with approval in
McNamara v. Culver, 22 Kans. 661;
Eckert v. McBee, 27 Kans. 232;
Williams v. Owen, 10 Sim. 386; Davis v. Thomas, 1 Russ. & M. 506;
Shaw v. Jeffery, 13 Moore P. C. 432;
Goodman v. Grierson, 2 Ball & B.
274; Alderson v. White, 2 De G. &
J. 97; Tapply v. Sheather, 8 Jur. (N.
S.) 1163.
[59] Fabrique v. Cherokee Coal &c.
Co., 69 Kans. 733, 77 Pac. 584; Yost

An absolute deed was made, with an agreement by the grantee, executed at the same time, whereby it was stipulated that the grantor might at his election repurchase the lands for a certain sum in three months, and for certain other and greater sums in six and twelve months respectively, provided he would so elect at the expiration of six months from the date of the agreement, which sums were largely in excess of the consideration expressed in the deed, and six per cent. interest thereon. The election to repurchase·not having been made within the time stipulated, the purchaser refused to allow a repurchase, and claimed that the sale and deed were absolute: the evidence showing that the transaction was really a loan, it was held that the grantor might redeem upon the payment of the consideration expressed in the deed, with interest.[60] The reservation of an absolute life estate out of property conveyed as security for performance of a bond to support the grantor operates as a mortgage.[61]

§ **265. Existence of the debt.**—The existence of the debt is the test. If an absolute conveyance be made and accepted in payment of an existing debt, and not merely as security for it, an agreement by the grantee to reconvey the land to the grantor upon receiving a certain sum within a specified time does not create a mortgage, but a conditional sale, and the grantee holds the premises subject only to the right of the grantor to demand a reconveyance according to the terms of the agreement.[62] If the debt is not extinguished by the conveyance,

v. First Nat. Bank, 66 Kans. 605, 72 Pac. 209; Smith v. Hoff, 23 N. Dak. 37, 135 N. W. 772, Ann. Cas. 1914 C, 1072; Smythe v. Reed, 28 Utah 262, 78 Pac. 478; Hoover v. Bouffleur, 74 Wash. 382, 133 Pac. 602; Hinchman v. Cook, 45 Wash. 490, 88 Pac. 931. Conversely the grantee's option to reconvey is a conditional sale. See ante § 244.

[60] Klinck v. Price, 4 W. Va. 4, 6 Am. Rep. 268.

[61] Hurd v. Chase, 100 Maine 561, 62 Atl. 660. See post § 388 et seq.

[62] Villa v. Rodriguez, 12 Wall. (U. S.) 323, 20 L. ed. 406; Stollenwerck v. Marks (Ala.), 65 So. 1024; Bell v. Shiver (Ala.), 61 So. 881; Nelson v. Wadsworth, 171 Ala. 603, 55 So. 120; Rodgers v. Burt, 157 Ala. 91, 47 So. 226; Farrow v. Cotney, 153 Ala. 550, 45 So. 69 (deed given by wife in satisfaction of her husband's debt); Smith v. Smith, 153 Ala. 504, 45 So. 168; Maxwell v. Herzfeld, 149 Ala. 67, 42 So. 987; Robinson v. Gassoway (Ala.), 39 So. 1023; Pearson v. Dancy, 144 Ala. 427, 39 So. 474; Martin v. Martin, 123 Ala. 191, 26 So. 525; Adams v. Pilcher, 92 Ala. 474, 8 So. 757; Vincent v. Walker, 86 Ala. 333, 5 So. 465; McMillan v. Jewett, 85 Ala. 476, 5 So. 145; Perdue v. Bell, 83 Ala. 396, 3 So. 698; Booker v. Waller, 81 Ala. 549, 8 So. 225; Douglass v. Moody, 80 Ala. 61; Turner v. Wilkinson, 72 Ala. 364; Mobile Building &c. Assn. v. Robertson, 65 Ala. 382; Tisdale v. Maxwell, 58 Ala. 42; Haynie v. Robertson, 58 Ala. 37; Peoples v. Stolla, 57 Ala. 53; Wells v. Morrow, 38 Ala. 125 (circumstances rendering the transaction a mortgage); West v. Hendrix, 28 Ala. 226; Robinson v. Farrelly, 16 Ala. 475; Hays v. Emerson, 75 Ark. 551, 87 S. W. 1027; Stryker

but continues as a subsisting obligation, the transaction will be re-

v. Hershy, 38 Ark. 264; Cooley v. Miller, 156 Cal. 510, 105 Pac. 981; Prefumo v. Russell, 148 Cal. 451, 83 Pac. 810; Hillhouse v. Dunning, 7 Conn. 139; Pitts v. Maier, 115 Ga. 281, 41 S. E. 570 (overruling Frost v. Allen, 57 Ga. 326); Pirkle v. Mortgage Co., 99 Ga. 524 (so far as in conflict); Murphy v. Purifoy, 52 Ga. 480; Spence v. Steadman, 49 Ga. 133; Linkemann v. Knepper, 226 Ill. 473, 80 N. E. 1009 (absolute deed given in consideration of the grantee's satisfaction of the grantor's debt); Caraway v. Sly, 222 Ill. 203, 78 N. E. 588; Cassem v. Heustis, 201 Ill. 208, 66 N. E. 283, 94 Am. St. 160; Crane v. Chandler, 190 Ill. 584, 60 N. E. 826; Burgett v. Osborne, 172 Ill. 227, 50 N. E. 206; Kerting v. Hilton, 152 Ill. 658, 38 N. E. 941; Batcheller v. Batcheller, 144 Ill. 471, 33 N. E. 24; Fisher v. Green, 142 Ill. 80, 31 N. E. 172; Freer v. Lake, 115 Ill. 662, 4 N. E. 512; Union Mut. Life Ins. Co. v. Slee, 110 Ill. 35; Rue v. Dole, 107 Ill. 275; Magnusson v. Johnson, 73 Ill. 156; Pitts v. Cable, 44 Ill. 103; Sutphen v. Cushman, 35 Ill. 186; Osborne v. Morgan, 171 Ill. App. 549; Rankin v. Rankin, 111 Ill. App. 403; Rogers v. Beach, 115 Ind. 413, 17 N. E. 609; Voss v. Eller, 109 Ind. 260, 10 N. E. 74; Bigler v. Jack, 114 Iowa 667, 87 N. W. 700; Bridges v. Linder, 60 Iowa 190, 14 N. W. 217 (quoting text); Trucks v. Sheaff, 19 Iowa 343; Hughes v. Sheaff, 19 Iowa 335; Hall v. Savill, 3 Greene (Iowa) 37, 54 Am. Dec. 485; Fabrique v. Cherokee Coal &c. Co., 69 Kans. 733, 77 Pac. 584; Honore v. Hutchings, 8 Bush (Ky.) 687; Hawes v. Williams, 92 Maine 483, 43 Atl. 101; Reed v. Reed, 75 Maine 264; Stinchfield v. Milliken, 71 Maine 567; French v. Sturdivant, 8 Maine 246; Duell v. Leslie, 207 Mo. 658, 106 S. W. 489; Stowe v. Banks, 123 Mo. 672, 27 S. W. 847; O'Neill v. Capelle, 62 Mo. 202; Slowey v. McMurray, 27 Mo. 113, 72 Am. Dec. 251; Brant v. Robertson, 16 Mo. 129; Morrison v. Jones, 31 Mont. 154, 77 Pac. 507; Kleinschmidt v. Kleinschmidt, 9 Mont. 477, 24 Pac. 266; Gassert v. Bogk,

7 Mont. 585, 19 Pac. 281; Harrah v. Smith, 79 Nebr. 51, 112 N. W. 337; Kraemer v. Adelsberger, 122 N. E. 469, 25 N. E. 859; Odell v. Montross, 68 N. Y. 499; Morrison v. Brand, 5 Daly (N. Y.) 40; Glover v. Payn, 19 Wend. (N. Y.) 518; Pemberton v. Simmons, 100 N. Car. 316, 6 S. E. 122; King v. Kincey, 1 Ired. Eq. (N. Car.) 187, 36 Am. Dec. 40; Miller v. Smith, 20 N. Dak. 96, 126 N. W. 499; McGuin v. Lee, 10 N. Dak. 160, 86 N. W. 714; Gray v. Shelby, 83 Tex. 405, 18 S. W. 809; Seeligson v. Singletary, 66 Tex. 271, 17 S. W. 541; Ruffier v. Womack, 30 Tex. 332; Parks v. Sullivan (Tex. Civ. App.), 152 S. W. 704; Stringfellow v. Braselton, 54 Tex. Civ. App. 1, 117 S. W. 204; Rotan Grocery Co. v. Turner, 46 Tex. Civ. App. 534, 102 S. W. 932; Pumilia v. DeGeorge (Tex. Civ. App.), 74 S. W. 813; Wilcox v. Tennant, 13 Tex. Civ. App. 220, 35 S. W. 865; Boyer v. Paine, 60 Wash. 56, 110 Pac. 682; Thacker v. Morris, 52 W. Va. 220, 43 S. E. 141, 94 Am. St. 928; Kerr v. Hill, 27 W. Va. 576; Hoffman v. Ryan, 21 W. Va. 415; Davis v. Demming, 12 W. Va. 246; Hoile v. Bailey, 58 Wis. 434, 17 N. W. 322; Smith v. Crosby, 47 Wis. 160, 2 N. E. 104.

In Adams v. Pilcher, 92 Ala. 474, 8 So. 757, Coleman, J., forcibly stated the law upon this subject, saying: "If the parties intended a sale, whether in payment of an antecedent debt or a present consideration paid, with the right to repurchase within a specified time, and for an agreed price, the purchaser becomes the owner of the property, and the vendor of the right to repurchase, if he sees proper to do so. No obligations rest upon the grantor to do so. It is optional whether he will or not. If he declines to do so, the vendee has no cause of action against him, either by reason of money paid, or for the debt satisfied by the conveyance. If there remain in the vendee a cause of action for the money paid, or, in the other case, for the antecedent debt, this will

garded as a mortgage.[63] A debt either pre-existing or created at the time, or contracted to be created, is an essential requisite of a mortgage.[64] "A mortgage is, in equity, a hypothecation or pledge of property for the security of a debt. There must be a debt, or there can be no security for its payment. Hence it is said, if there is no debt, there

determine the transaction to have been intended as a mortgage, not an absolute conveyance. It is not left optional with the grantor to determine whether he owes a debt to the grantee or not, and, by his election to owe a debt to the grantee, convert a sale with the right of repurchase into a mortgage. His power to elect to repurchase or redeem exists only where there is a sale with the right to repurchase. If a mortgage was intended by the parties, the debt exists, whether he consents or not, and the mortgagee has the same legal authority to enforce the instrument as a mortgage as the grantor to have the instrument declared a mortgage."

An absolute conveyance of property in partial satisfaction of a debt accompanied by an agreement that if the property enhances in value to a certain extent within a specified time, notes given in satisfaction of the remainder of the debt shall be canceled, does not constitute an equitable mortgage. Pearson v. Dancy, 144 Ala. 427, 39 So. 474. See post §§ 267, 325.

[63] Thomas v. Livingston, 155 Ala. 546, 46 So. 851; Wynn v. Fitzwater (Ala.), 44 So. 97; American Mfg. Co. v. Williams, 103 Ark. 484, 145 S. W. 234; Rushton v. McIllvene, 88 Ark. 299, 114 S. W. 709; Holmes v. Warren, 145 Cal. 457, 78 Pac. 954; Scott v. Hughes, 124 Ga. 1000, 53 S. E. 453; Fabrique v. Cherokee Coal &c. Co., 69 Kans. 733, 77 Pac. 584; Duell v. Leslie, 207 Mo. 658, 106 S. W. 489; Samuelson v. Mickey, 73 Nebr. 852, 103 N. W. 671; Tannyhill v. Pepperl, 70 Nebr. 31, 96 N. W. 1005; Farrow v. Work, 39 Okla. 734, 136 Pac. 739; Caro v. Wollenberg (Ore.), 136 Pac. 866; Harmon v. Grant's Pass Banking &c. Co., 60 Ore. 69, 118 Pac. 188; Bickel v. Wessinger, 58 Ore. 98 113 Pac. 34; Francis v. Francis, 78 S. Car. 178,

58 S. E. 804; Harrison v. Hogue (Tex. Civ. App.), 136 S. W. 118; Blake v. Lowry, 43 Tex. Civ. App. 17, 93 S. W. 521; Mittlesteadt v. Johnson, 75 Wash. 550, 135 Pac. 214; Hursey v. Hursey, 56 W. Va. 148, 49 S. E. 367.

[64] Irwin v. Coleman, 173 Ala. 175, 55 So. 492; Hubert v. Sistrunk (Ala.), 53 So. 819; Thomas v. Livingston, 155 Ala. 546, 46 So. 851; Smith v. Smith, 153 Ala. 504, 45 So. 168; Wynn v. Fitzwater (Ala.), 44 So. 97; Lindbloom v. Kidston, 2 Alaska 292; American Mtg. Co. v. Williams, 103 Ark. 484, 145 S. W. 234; Rushton v. McIllvene, 88 Ark. 299, 114 S. W. 709; Land v. May, 73 Ark. 415, 84 S. W. 489; Holmes v. Warren, 145 Cal. 457, 78 Pac. 954; Bergen v. Johnson, 21 Idaho 619, 123 Pac. 484; Hannah v. Vensel, 19 Idaho 796, 116 Pac. 115; Sinclair v. Gunzenhauser, 179 Ind. 78, 98 N. E. 37; Ferguson v. Boyd (Ind. App.), 79 N. E. 549, 169 Ind. 537, 81 N. E. 71; Beidelman v. Koch, 42 Ind. App. 423, 85 N. E. 977; Fort v. Colby (Iowa), 144 N. W. 393; Henninger v. McGuire, 146 Iowa 270, 125 N. W. 180; Jones v. Gillett, 142 Iowa 506, 118 N. W. 314; Veeder v. Veeder, 141 Iowa 492, 120 N. W. 61; Chandler v. Chandler, 76 Iowa 574, 51 N. W. 319; Bridges v. Linder, 60 Iowa 190 (quoting text); Farmers' &c. Bank v. Kackley, 88 Kans. 70, 127 Pac. 539; Eckert v. McBee, 27 Kans. 232; McNamara v. Culver, 22 Kans. 661; Tucker v. Witherbee, 130 Ky. 269, 113 S. W. 123; Fuson v. Chestnut, 33 Ky. L. 249, 109 S. W. 1192; Sebree v. Thompson, 31 Ky. L. 1146, 104 S. W. 781; Olney v. Brown, 163 Mich. 125, 128 N. W. 241; Weise v. Anderson, 134 Mich. 502, 96 N. W. 575; Lipscomb v. Talbott, 243 Mo. 1, 147 S. W. 798; Donovan v. Boeck, 217 Mo. 70, 116 S. W. 543; Duell v. Leslie, 207 Mo. 658, 106 S. W. 489; Gibson v. Morris State Bank (Mont.), 140 Pac.

can be no mortgage. Debt, in this connection, means a duty or obligation to pay, for the enforcement of which an action will lie."[65]

The absolute deed may secure advances to be made, and in that case the mortgage becomes effectual when the advances are made.[66] "Where there is no debt and no loan, it is impossible to say that an agreement to resell will change an absolute deed into a mortgage."[67]

A deed executed to secure the payment of a note, representing an

76; Morrison v. Jones, 31 Mont. 154, 77 Pac. 507; Samuelson v. Mickey, 73 Nebr. 852, 103 N. W. 671; Tannyhill v. Pepperl, 70 Nebr. 31, 96 N. W. 1005; Doty v. Norton, 133 App. Div. 106, 117 N. Y. S. 793; Bascombe v. Marshall, 129 App. Div. 516, 113 N. Y. S. 991; Miller v. Smith, 20 N. Dak. 96, 126 N. W. 499; Vallely v. First Nat. Bank, 14 N. Dak. 580, 106 N. V 127, 5 L. R. A. (N. S.) 387, 116 Am. St. 700; Farrow v. Work, 39 Okla. 734, 136 Pac. 739; Caro v. Wollenberg (Ore.), 136 Pac. 866; Grover v. Hawthorne, 62 Ore. 77, 121 Pac. 808; Harmon v. Grant's Pass Banking &c. Co., 60 Ore. 69, 118 Pac. 188; Bickel v. Wessinger, 58 Ore. 98, 113 Pac. 34; Eldriedge v. Hoefer, 52 Ore. 241, 93 Pac. 246, judgment modified 94 Pac. 563; Francis v. Francis, 78 S. Car. 178, 58 S. E. 804; Jones v. Jones, 20 S. Dak. 632, 108 N. W. 23; Kidd v. Sparks (Tex. Civ. App.), 167 S. W. 799; Mitchell v. Morgan (Tex. Civ. App.), 165 S. W. 883; Harrison v. Hogue (Tex. Civ. App.), 136 S. W. 118; O'Neill v. O'Neill (Tex. Civ. App.), 135 S. W. 729; Yates v. Caswell (Tex. Civ. App.), 126 S. W. 914; Hall v. Jennings (Tex. Civ. App.), 104 S. W. 489; Goodbar v. Bloom, 43 Tex. Civ. App. 434, 96 S. W. 657 (quoting text); Blake v. Lowry (Tex. Civ. App.), 93 S. W. 521; Crahan v. Chittenden, 82 Vt. 410, 74 Atl. 86; Tuggle v. Berkeley, 101 Va. 83, 43 S. E. 199; Mittlesteadt v. Johnson, 75 Wash. 550, 135 Pac. 214; Johnson v. National Bank of Commerce, 65 Wash. 261, 118 Pac. 21; Fridley v. Somerville, 60 W. Va. 272, 54 S. E. 502; Hursey v. Hursey, 56 W. Va. 148, 49 S. E. 367; Polly v. Gumney (Wis.), 147 N. W. 356; McCourt v. Peppard, 126 Wis.

326, 105 N. W. 809; Wolf v. Theresa Village Mut. Fire Ins. Co., 115 Wis. 402, 91 N. W. 1014. Rev. Stat. Wis., 1898, § 2243.

The owner of a house and lot, in possession, not being able to pay an existing mortgage thereon, deeded it to a party who paid the mortgage, the latter giving an option to a relative of the owner to repurchase the property, the owner being advised at the time that her deed divested her of all interest. Subsequently the party holding the option refused to purchase the property, which was then sold to a third party. It was held that since the payment of the mortgage did not constitute a new debt, but a consideration for the deed to the property, no mortgage arose by implication, but the transaction was a conditional sale. Holladay v. Willis, 101 Va. 274, 43 S. E. 616.

[65] Stollenwerck v. Marks (Ala.), 65 So. 1024; Nelson v. Wadsworth, 171 Ala. 603, 55 So. 120; Vincent v. Walker, 86 Ala. 333, 5 So. 465; Douglass v. Moody, 80 Ala. 61. See also Haynie v. Robertson, 58 Ala. 37; McKinstry v. Conly, 12 Ala. 678.

[66] Bull v. Coe, 77 Cal. 54, 18 Pac. 808; Cramer v. Cale, 72 N. J. Eq. 210, 73 Atl. 813.

[67] Per Bronson, J., in Glover v. Payn, 19 Wend. (N. Y.) 518. See also Vincent v. Walker, 86 Ala. 333, 5 So. 465; Rue v. Dole, 107 Ill. 275; Mooney v. Byrne, 163 N. Y. 86, 57 N. E. 163; Macauley v. Smith, 132 N. Y. 524, 30 N. E. 997; Barry v. Hamburg-Bremen F. Ins. Co., 110 N. Y. 1, 17 N. E. 405; Odell v. Montross, 68 N. Y. 499; Meehan v. Forrester, 52 N. Y. 277; McGuin v. Lee, 10 N. Dak. 160, 86 N. W. 714. See post § 266.

indebtedness, is a mortgage.[68] Thus a deed made to secure and indemnify the grantee as the accommodation indorser of notes made by the grantor was held a mortgage.[69]

The debt may not be evidenced by any bond or note, or covenant to pay it; so that the facts and circumstances of the transaction must be inquired into in order to ascertain whether the consideration of the deed was really a debt or loan; if not one or the other, the deed can hardly be a mortgage.[70] It is not material that there should be any note or bond or other written evidence of debt, nor is it material that the indebtedness should have arisen in any particular manner. It is only material that there should be a bona fide debt.[71]

The law on this subject is well stated by Judge Parker in a New York case.[72] He says: "In determining whether a contract is to be treated as a mortgage, or a conditional sale, or a conveyance in fee, courts have commented upon the presence or absence of various particulars which commonly accompany mortgages, but the essential feature necessary to create a mortgage is that it should be a conveyance intended as a security. Such evidently was the purpose of the contract before us, but the plaintiff calls attention to the absence of a covenant to pay the amount of the indebtedness. It was agreed that interest should be paid on the full amount; that, after sales should be made, the proceeds should be applied in reduction of the amount of the then existing obligation; and that the firm would pay the difference, if any should remain. So that, while there was not an agreement in terms to pay the entire indebtedness, such may be said to have been the purpose and effect of the agreement; but in any event, the absence of such a covenant is not conclusive, but is a circumstance to be considered in construing the contract."

An agreement by the grantee in an absolute conveyance, that if the

---

[68] Lindbloom v. Kidston, 2 Alaska 292; Land v. May, 73 Ark. 415, 84 S. W. 489; Doty v. Norton, 133 App. Div. 106, 117 N. Y. S. 793; Crahan v. Chittenden, 82 Vt. 410, 74 Atl. 86.

[69] Dudley v. Buckley, 68 W. Va. 630, 70 S. E. 376.

[70] Conway v. Alexander, 7 Cranch (U. S.) 218, 3 L. ed. 321; Henley v. Hotaling, 41 Cal. 22; Galt v. Jackson, 9 Ga. 151; Reed v. Reed, 75 Maine 264; Flagg v. Mann, 14 Pick. (Mass.) 467; Lund v. Lund, 1 N. H. 39, 8 Am. Dec. 29. The absence of any written evidence of a debt is a circumstance indicating a sale, and not a mere conveyance to secure the payment of a debt. Grubb v. Brendel, 52 Ind. App. 531, 100 N. E. 872. On the other hand, the existence of a written promise to repay money advanced is strong evidence of an existing personal debt and mortgage, though not conclusive. Beverly v. Davis (Wash.), 140 Pac. 696.

[71] Overstreet v. Baxter, 30 Kans. 55, 1 Pac. 825; Graham v. Stevens, 34 Vt. 166, 80 Am. Dec. 675.

[72] Kraemer v. Adelsberger, 122 N. Y. 467, 25 N. E. 859. See also Morris v. Budlong, 78 N. Y. 543; Horn v. Keteltas, 46 N. Y. 605.

grantor should, within a certain time, bring him the amount of the consideration of the deed with interest, he would deliver up the deed, but otherwise the grantor should forfeit all claim to such deed, was held not to be a defeasance of a mortgage, as there was no debt secured, but merely a contract to reconvey on certain terms.[73] But whenever a debt is recognized by the parties or established by evidence, such an agreement serves to make a mortgage of the conveyance,[74] as where a grantee, a year after the making of the deed, gave a bond reciting that there had been a loan, and that the conveyance was made to secure it, the transaction was a mortgage, although the bond contained a condition, that if the money was not paid on a day named, the obligation should be void.[75] And so where a grantee executed a bond to the grantor reciting the deed and the grantor's indebtedness, and providing that if the debt should be paid on or before a certain day the bond should be void, but that the bond should remain in force if the grantee after payment should neglect to reconvey the land, the transaction was a mortgage.[76]

If an absolute deed was intended as security, it is a mortgage, though the bond for reconveyance makes time of the essence of the contract.[77] In a case before the Supreme Court of California,[78] the agreement was that the grantee should execute a bond to reconvey the premises; but the grantor did not agree to repurchase, and the bond was delivered as an escrow, and it remained an escrow until after the time therein mentioned for the execution of the deed, and was then canceled. If the deed was intended as a mortgage, says the court, the mortgagee would have a right of action to foreclose the mortgage; but if he had brought such an action, the answer that there was no promise,

---

[73] Pearson v. Seay, 35 Ala. 612; Reading v. Weston, 7 Conn. 143, 18 Am. Dec. 89; Robertson v. Moline M. Stoddard Co., 106 Iowa 414, 76 N. W. 736; Bridges v. Linder, 60 Iowa 190, 14 N. W. 217.

[74] Voss v. Eller, 109 Ind. 260, 10 N. E. 74; Reed v. Reed, 75 Maine 264; Hart v. Eppstein, 71 Tex. 752, 10 S. W. 85; Alstin v. Cundiff, 52 Tex. 453.

[75] Montgomery v. Chadwick, 7 Iowa 114.

[76] Van Wagner v. Van Wagner, 7 N. J. Eq. 27.

[77] Cassem v. Heustis, 201 Ill. 208, 66 N. E. 283, 94 Am. St. 160; Jackson v. Lynch, 129 Ill. 72, 21 N. E.

589, 22 N. E. 246; Tennery v. Nicholson, 87 Ill. 464.

[78] Henley v. Hotaling, 41 Cal. 22. This case differs from Sears v. Dixon, 33 Cal. 326, in the important particular that in that case the mortgagor covenanted to repay the purchase-money at a fixed time, and, under the name of rent, to pay interest thereon at a stipulated rate; and the court also found that the parties intended to execute a mortgage; but in this case the court found that the parties intended the deed to be in fact, as it was in form, an absolute conveyance. See ante § 247.

either express or implied, on the part of the alleged mortgagor to re-pay the purchase-money would have been a complete bar.

§ 266. **Effect of absolute deed to secure a loan.**—An absolute con-veyance to secure a loan of money is generally held to be a mortgage,[79] and equity will look through the forms in which the lender has en-veloped the transaction.[80]   When an absolute conveyance has been made upon an application for a loan, and an agreement is made to reconvey upon payment of the money advanced, as a general rule the transaction is adjudged to constitute a mortgage.[81]   In each case the purpose of the grantor was in the beginning to borrow money; and unless a change be shown in his intentions it is presumed that any use he may have made of his real estate, in connection with it, was merely as a pledge to secure a loan.[82]

The parties having originally met upon the footing of borrowing and lending, although a different consideration be recited in the deed, it will be considered a mortgage until it be shown that the parties afterward bargained for the property independently of the loan.[83]   But an application for a loan may in any case result in a sale of land ab-solutely or conditionally, and because the transaction began with such an application it is not to be concluded that it necessarily ended in a

[79] Alter v. Clark, 193 Fed. 153; Whitehouse v. Whitehouse, 22 Cal. App. 565, 135 Pac. 509; Schumacher v. Langford, 20 Cal. App. 61, 127 Pac. 1057; Fleming v. Georgia R. Bank, 120 Ga. 1023, 48 S. E. 420; Garvin v. Vincent, 27 Ky. L. 1076, 87 S. W. 804; Ehle v. Looker (Mich.), 148 N. W. 378; Restrick Lumber Co. v. Wyrembolski, 164 Mich. 71, 128 N. W. 1083; Stumpe v. Kopp, 201 Mo. 412, 99 S. W. 1073; Conover v. Palmer, 123 App. Div. 817, 108 N. Y. S. 480; Worley v. Carter, 30 Okla. 642, 121 Pac. 669; Wagg v. Herbert, 19 Okla. 525, 92 Pac. 250; Krug v. Kautz, 21 S. Dak. 461, 113 N. W. 623; Froidevaux v. Jordan, 64 W. Va. 388, 62 S. E. 686; Wells v. Scanlan, 124 Wis. 229, 102 N. W. 571; Schneider v. Reed, 123 Wis. 488, 101 N. W. 682. A deed executed as security for a loan does not become a mortgage until the actual advance of the loan. Schu-macher v. Langford, 20 Cal. App. 61, 127 Pac. 1057.
[80] Garvin v. Vincent, 27 Ky. L.

1076, 87 S. W. 804; Wagg v. Her-bert, 19 Okla. 525, 92 Pac. 250.
[81] Russell v. Southard, 12 How. (U. S.) 139, 13 L. ed. 927; Parme-lee v. Lawrence, 44 Ill. 405; Miller v. Thomas, 14 Ill. 428; Crassen v. Swoveland, 22 Ind. 427; Wheeler v. Ruston, 19 Ind. 334; Cross v. Hep-ner, 7 Ind. 359; Kellum v. Smith, 33 Pa. St. 158; Brown v. Nickle, 6 Pa. St. 390; McSorley v. Hughes, 12 N. Y. S. 179; Holmes v. Grant, 8 Paige (N. Y.) 243; Hart v. Epp-stein, 71 Tex. 752, 10 S. W. 85; Hoffman v. Ryan, 21 W. Va. 415; Davis v. Demming, 12 W. Va. 246.
[82] Mobile Bldg. &c. Assn. v. Rob-ertson, 65 Ala. 382; Crews v. Threadgill, 35 Ala. 334; Greenwood Bldg. Assn. v. Stanton, 28 Ind. App. 548; Anon., 3 Hayw. (N. Car.) 26; Davis v. Hemenway, 27 Vt. 589; Kerr v. Hill, 27 W. Va. 576; Van-gilder v. Hoffman, 22 W. Va. 1.
[83] Morris v. Nixon, 1 How. (U. S.) 118, 11 L. ed. 69; Crews v. Thread-gill, 35 Ala. 334; Smith v. Doyle, 46 Ill. 451. See also Dwen v. Blake,

loan.[84] The language of the courts, in some cases, would seem to imply that a court of equity would always allow redemption in such case; but although such transactions should be carefully scrutinized, when it appears that the negotiations resulted in a sale absolute or conditional this will be supported.[85]

Where a party borrows money from a bank to pay for land, and causes the conveyance to be made to the bank, and gives his note reciting that it is secured by the deed, such conveyance, though absolute on its face, is a deed to secure the payment of the loan.[86] Where the owners of lots conveyed them to secure a loan, and the grantees gave back a land contract showing a balance unpaid, the transaction was held a mortgage.[87] On the other hand, where there was no intimation of a proposition to borrow money or secure a loan by mortgage before or after the execution of an absolute deed, the transaction was construed to be what it appeared on its face.[88]

Evidence that the grantee in a deed refused to take a mortgage upon the property when approached upon the subject, tends to show that an absolute deed to him and his agreement to resell were not intended by him merely as a mortgage.[89]

The terms of a contract, to the effect that the grantee would reconvey upon the payment of a certain sum and interest, less the rents he might receive, tend to show that the debt, whether pre-existing or created at the time, was not extinguished, although it be declared in the contract that it is merely an agreement to reconvey, and not in acknowledgment of a mortgage.[90]

§ 267.   **Conveyance in satisfaction of debt—Agreement to reconvey.** —Where an absolute deed is executed in consideration of a precedent debt, accompanied by an agreement to reconvey to the grantor upon

44 Ill. 135; Richardson v. Barrick, 16 Iowa 407; Leahigh v. White, 8 Nev. 147; Phillips v. Hulsizer, 20 N. J. Eq. 398; Fiedler v. Darrin, 50 N. Y. 437, 59 Barb. (N. Y.) 651; Tibbs v. Morris, 44 Barb. (N. Y.) 138; Marvin v. Prentice, 49 How. (N. Y.) 385; Sweetzer's Appeal, 71 Pa. St. 264; Knowlton v. Walker, 13 Wis. 264.

[84] Bogk v. Gassert, 149 U. S. 17, 37 L. ed. 631, 13 Sup. Ct. 738.

[85] Hanford v. Blessing, 80 Ill. 188; Flagg v. Mann, 14 Pick. (Mass.) 467; Cobb v. Day, 106 Mo. 278, 17 S. W. 323 (quoting text); Turner v. Kerr, 44 Mo. 429; Holmes v.

Fresh, 9 Mo. 201; McDonald v. McLeod, 1 Ired. Eq. (N. Car.) 221.

[86] Fleming v. Georgia R. Bank, 120 Ga. 1023, 48 S. E. 420. See also Whitehouse v. Whitehouse, 22 Cal. App. 565, 135 Pac. 509.

[87] Restrick Lumber Co. v. Wyrembolski, 164 Mich. 71, 128 N. W. 1083.

[88] Conway v. Alexander, 7 Cranch (U. S.) 218, 3 L. ed. 321. See also Hubert v. Sistrunk (Ala.), 53 So. 819.

[89] Bacon v. National German-Am. Bank, 191 Ill. 205, 60 N. E. 846; Conner v. Clapp, 37 Wash. 299, 79 Pac. 929.

[90] People v. Irwin, 14 Cal. 428.

payment of the consideration, a decisive test whether the transaction constitutes a mortgage or a conditional sale is found in the question whether the debt was discharged by the deed or subsisted afterward. An absolute deed delivered in payment of a debt is not converted into a mortgage merely because the grantee therein gives a contemporaneous stipulation binding him to reconvey, on being reimbursed, within an agreed period, an amount equal to the debt and the interest thereon. If the conveyance extinguishes the debt and the parties so intend, so that a plea of payment would bar an action thereon, the transaction will be held an absolute or conditional sale, and not a mortgage.[91]

[91] Farrow v. Cotney, 153 Ala. 550, 45 So. 69; Martin v. Martin, 123 Ala. 191, 26 So. 525; Knaus v. Dreher, 84 Ala. 319, 4 So. 287; Perdue v. Bell, 83 Ala. 396, 3 So. 698; West v. Hendrix, 28 Ala. 226; Rees v. Rhodes, 3 Ariz. 235, 73 Pac. 446; Rushton v. McIlvene, 88 Ark. 299, 114 S. W. 709; Holmes v. Warren, 145 Cal. 457, 78 Pac. 954; Farmer v. Grose, 42 Cal. 169; Page v. Vilhac, 42 Cal. 75; Pendergrass v. Burris (Cal.), 19 Pac. 187; Hickox v. Lowe, 10 Cal. 197; Phipps v. Munson, 50 Conn. 267; Carroll v. Tomlinson, 192 Ill. 398, 61 N. E. 484, 85 Am. St. 344; Freer v. Lake, 115 Ill. 662, 4 N. E. 512; Bearss v. Ford, 108 Ill. 16; Rue v. Dole, 107 Ill. 275 (quoting and approving text); Johnson v. Prosperity Loan &c. Assn., 94 Ill. App. 260; Mann v. Jobusch, 70 Ill. App. 440; Glass v. Doane, 15 Ill. App. 66; Rogers v. Beach, 115 Ind. 413, 17 N. E. 609; Voss v. Eller, 109 Ind. 260, 10 N. E. 74; Hays v. Carr, 83 Ind. 275; Bridges v. Linder, 60 Iowa 190, 14 N. W. 217; Hughes v. Sheaff, 19 Iowa 335; Elston v. Chamberlain, 41 Kans. 354, 21 Pac. 259; Howe v. Austin, 40 La. Ann. 323, 4 So. 315; Baugher v. Merryman, 32 Md. 185; Knight v. Hartman, 93 Mich. 69, 52 N. W. 1044; Shultes v. Stivers, 66 Minn. 517, 69 N. W. 639; Weathersly v. Weathersly, 40 Miss. 462, 90 Am. Dec. 344; Hoopes v. Bailey, 28 Miss. 328; Duell v. Leslie, 207 Mo. 658, 106 S. W. 489; Turner v. Kerr, 44 Mo. 429; Slowey v. McMurray, 27 Mo. 113, 72 Am. Dec. 251; Harrah v. Smith, 79 Nebr. 51, 112 N. W. 337; Samuelson v. Mickey, 73 Nebr. 852, 103 N. W. 671; Tannyhill v. Pepperl, 70 Nebr. 31, 96 N. W. 1005; Doying v. Chesebrough (N. J. Eq.), 36 Atl. 893; Phillips v. Hulsizer, 20 N. J. Eq. 308; Kearney v. Macomb, 16 N. J. Eq. 189; Blazy v. McLean, 129 N. Y. 44, 29 N. E. 6; Randall v. Sanders, 87 N. Y. 578; Morrison v. Brand, 5 Daly (N. Y.) 40; Whitney v. Townsend, 2 Lans. (N. Y.) 249; Coburn v. Anderson, 62 How. Pr. (N. Y.) 268; McGuin v. Lee, 10 N. Dak. 160, 86 N. W. 714; Duclos v. Walton, 21 Ore. 323, 28 Pac. 1; Null v. Fries, 110 Pa. St. 521, 1 Atl. 551; Callahan's Estate, 13 Phila. (Pa.) 381; Tripler v. Campbell, 22 R. I. 262, 47 Atl. 385; Francis v. Francis, 78 S. Car. 178, 58 S. E. 804; Creswell v. Smith, 61 S. Car. 575, 39 S. E. 757; Brown v. Bank of Sumter, 55 S. Car. 51, 32 S. E. 816; Shiver v. Arthur, 54 S. Car. 184, 32 S. E. 310; Miller v. Yturria, 69 Tex. 549, 7 S. W. 206; Calhoun v. Lumpkin, 60 Tex. 185; Stringfellow v. Breselton, 54 Tex. Civ. App. 1, 117 S. W. 204; Goodbar v. Bloom, 43 Tex. Civ. App. 434, 96 S. W. 657 (quoting text); Boyer v. Paine, 60 Wash. 56, 110 Pac. 682; Neeson v. Smith, 47 Wash. 386, 92 Pac. 131; Hesser v. Brown, 40 Wash. 688, 82 Pac. 934; Dabney v. Smith, 38 Wash. 40, 80 Pac. 199; Swarm v. Boggs, 12 Wash. 246, 40 Pac. 941; Hursey v. Hursey, 56 W. Va. 148, 49 S. E. 367; Sadler v. Taylor, 49 W. Va. 104, 38 S. E. 583; Weltner v. Thurmond, 17 Wyo. 268, 98 Pac. 590, 99 Pac. 1128, 129 Am. St. 1113. See ante §§ 244, 265, and post §§ 325, 326.

And so if there was in fact a sale, an agreement by the purchaser to resell the property within a limited time, at the same price, does not convert it into a mortgage.[92] A farmer agreed with another that he might sell the farm and have all he could obtain above $2,000; and, to give effect to this agreement, the farmer conveyed to him the land, and took back a reconveyance, on condition that the reconveyance should be void upon the payment of $2,000. The transaction was of course held to be a conditional sale.[93]

But if the indebtedness be not canceled, equity will regard the conveyance as a mortgage, whether the grantee so regard it or not. He can not at the same time hold the land absolutely and retain the right to enforce payment of the debt on account of which the conveyance was made. The test, therefore, in cases of this sort, by which to determine whether the conveyance is a sale or a mortgage, is to be found in the question whether the debt was discharged or not by the conveyance.[94] If in the subsequent transactions of the parties there is no recognition in any way of the relation of debtor and creditor, and the vendee for a considerable period holds possession without paying interest or rent, these facts go to show that there is only an agreement for repurchase and not a mortgage.[95]

§ 268. **Agreement to reconvey in default of purchase-price—Advances secured by deed or bond to reconvey.**—Where one induces a third person to purchase land from him, and the purchaser agrees to reconvey the land to the grantor if certain payments are made to him within a specified time, in default of payment there is no right of re-

[92] Eckert v. McBee, 27 Kans. 232; Mason v. Moody, 26 Miss. 184; Gassert v. Bogk, 7 Mont. 585, 19 Pac. 281. See also Rogers v. Beach, 115 Ind. 413, 17 N. E. 609. See ante § 244, and post § 271.

[93] Porter v. Nelson, 4 N. H. 130. See post § 270.

[94] Rue v. Dole, 107 Ill. 275; Sutphen v. Cushman, 35 Ill. 186; Voss v. Eller, 109 Ind. 260, 10 N. E. 609; Bigler v. Jack, 114 Iowa 667, 87 N. W. 700; Macauley v. Smith, 132 N. Y. 524, 30 N. E. 997; Wallace v. Smith, 155 Pa. St. 78, 25 Atl. 807 (quoting text); Null v. Fries, 110 Pa. St. 521, 1 Atl. 551; Goodbar v. Bloom, 43 Tex. Civ. App. 434, 96 S. W. 657 (quoting text); Wasatch

Min. Co. v. Jennings, 5 Utah 243, 16 Pac. 399 (quoting text).

[95] Goodbar v. Bloom, 43 Tex. Civ. App. 434, 96 S. W. 657 (quoting text); O'Reilly v. Donoghue, Ir. Rep. 10 Eq. 73. The Master of the Rolls acted upon this principle in a transaction held to be a sale where the agreement for repurchase was founded upon the following letter: "At any time within the next ten years you come forward and pay me £160, provided you want it for yourself or any of your children. * * * I will hand you possession of the same with pleasure, and become your yearly tenant." See also Wolfe v. McMillan, 117 Ind. 587, 20 N. E. 509.

demption afterward.[96] If the relation of debtor and creditor is not created between the parties, the transaction is not a mortgage, but a conditional sale.[97] If, however, the money paid by the purchaser was intended to be in fact a loan, the deed will be regarded as a mortgage rather than an absolute sale.[98] This is the test to be applied in every case. It is a question of fact, for the determination of which equity allows a wide range of inquiry into the relations of the parties and the circumstances of the case; and from the facts the law deduces the inference, either that there was a sale absolutely or upon condition, or else that the transaction was a mortgage.[99]

When a person advances money, and at the same time receives a deed and gives back to the grantor a bond to reconvey, these facts tend to show that the transaction is a loan and a security. But the case is different when the obligation to convey is given to a person other than the grantor.[1] A conveyance in consideration that the grantee and her husband would advance the balance due on the price, and that the grantors might continue to live on the premises during their lives, after which the property should go to the grantee, is not a mortgage.[2]

§ 269. Continuing debt and promise to pay.—That there is no continuing debt is a strong circumstance to show that the transaction is a contract for repurchase.[3] If the proof establishes that the consideration money was a loan, and the party receiving it is personally liable for its payment, that constitutes it a debt; it does not require a writing

---

[90] Stephenson v. Thompson, 13 Ill. 186; Hull v. McCall, 13 Iowa 467; Roberts v. McMahan, 4 Greene (Iowa) 34; Hill v. Grant, 46 N. Y. 496; Becker v. Howard, 75 Wis. 415, 44 N. W. 755. See post § 331.

[97] Galt v. Jackson, 9 Ga. 151; Chapman v. Ogden, 30 Ill. 515; McLaughlin v. Royce, 108 Iowa 254, 78 N. W. 1105; Humphreys v. Snyder, Morris (Iowa) 263. See post § 272.

[98] Harrington v. Foley, 108 Iowa 287, 79 N. W. 64; Jenkins v. Stewart, 13 Ky. L. 112, 16 S. W. 356.

[99] Micou v. Ashurst, 55 Ala. 607; Baker v. Fireman's Fund Ins. Co., 79 Cal. 34, 21 Pac. 357; Stinchfield v. Milliken, 71 Maine 567; Rice v. Rice, 4 Pick. (Mass.) 349; Henry v. Davis, 7 Johns. Ch. (N. Y.) 40; Robinson v. Willoughby, 65 N. Car.

520; Devore v. Woodruff, 1 N. Dak. 143, 45 N. W. 701; Sweetzer's Appeal, 71 Pa. St. 264; Todd v. Campbell, 32 Pa. St. 250; Hiester v. Maderia, 3 Watts & S. (Pa.) 384; McNees v. Swaney, 50 Mo. 388; Turner v. Kerr, 44 Mo. 429; Goulding v. Bunster, 9 Wis. 513.

[1] Carr v. Rising, 62 Ill. 14. See also Smith v. Sackett, 15 Ill. 528; Davis v. Hopkins, 15 Ill. 519, for cases where a third party furnished the money, but was not a party to the transaction. See post § 331.

[2] Gustin v. Crockett, 51 Wash. 67, 97 Pac. 1091;

[3] Duell v. Leslie, 207 Mo. 658, 106 S. W. 489; Parks v. Sullivan (Tex. Civ. App.), 152 S. W. 704. See ante §§ 260, 265.

to make it such,[4] nor is it extinguished by or merged in a mortgage taken for security.[5] Unless the relation of debtor and creditor existed between the parties in the beginning in reference to the consideration of the conveyance, and the relation continues so that the grantee would have the right to call upon the grantor to supply any deficiency that might arise in a case of a foreclosure and sale of the premises, the agreement to reconvey in connection with the deed constitutes a conditional sale.[6] If there was no loan in the beginning, or if a prior debt was extinguished by the conveyance, and the grantor merely has the privilege of repaying if he pleases, by a given time, and of receiving a reconveyance, the transaction is a conditional sale.[7]

A mortgagee commenced proceedings to foreclose his mortgage, believing the security inadequate, but by agreement with the mortgagor the proceedings were dismissed, and the mortgagor executed a deed to the mortgagee, and the mortgagee satisfied the mortgage of record, and the mortgagor was to have the privilege of selling the land within six months, and retaining all moneys which he might receive over and above a specified sum, which he was to pay to the mortgagee. The mortgagor made no promise to pay any sum to the mortgagee, but in case of a resale the latter was to receive several thousand dollars less than the mortgage debt. There was no provision for the payment of interest. The mortgagee at once took possession of the land. The transaction was construed, not to be a mortgage, but a conditional sale, to become absolute on the mortgagor's failure to sell the land within the time specified. In addition to the fact that there was no promise to pay, there were many circumstances which repelled the presumption that either party supposed that the deed was held as security.[8]

There can be no mortgage without a debt. There may be agreements for the performance of obligations other than the payment of money; but leaving these out of view, it is essential that there be an agreement, either express or implied, on the part of the mortgagor, or some one in whose behalf he executes the mortgage, to pay to the

---

[4] See post § 282 et seq.

[5] Porter v. Clements, 3 Ark. 364; Farmer v. Grose, 42 Cal. 169; Phillips v. Hulszier 29 N. J. Eq. 308.

[6] Blakemore v. Brynside, 7 Ark. 505; Johnson v. Clark, 5 Ark. 321; Hoopes v. Bailey, 28 Miss. 328; Duell v. Leslie, 207 Mo. 658, 106 S. W. 489; Slowey v. McMurray, 27 Mo. 113, 72 Am. Dec. 251; Gassert v. Bogk, 7 Mont. 585, 19 Pac. 281; McGuin v. Lee. 10 N. Dak. 160, 86 N. W. 714; Saxton v. Hitchcock, 47 Barb. (N. Y.) 220; Robinson v. Cropsey, 2 Edw. Ch. (N. Y.) 138; De Bruhl v. Maas, 54 Tex. 464.

[7] Bell v. Shiver (Ala.), 61 So. 881; Stahl v. Dehn, 72 Mich. 645, 40 N. W. 922; De Bruhl v. Maas, 54 Tex. 464.

[8] Fletcher v. Northcross (Cal.), 32 Pac. 328.

mortgagee a sum of money either on account of a pre-existing debt or a present loan.[9]

§ 270. **Grantee's option to purchase.**—An agreement that the grantee may buy the property absolutely, after a specified time, is regarded as a circumstance tending to show that the transaction is a conditional sale. Thus where the grantee's covenant, executed at the same time with an absolute conveyance to him, recited that this was made for the purpose of paying a certain sum of money, and stipulated that he would not convey the premises within one year without the consent of the grantor, and, if the grantor within that time should find a purchaser, the grantee would convey the land on receiving the amount with interest for which the land had been conveyed to him; and that in case such sale should not be made within the year, it should then be submitted to certain persons named, to determine what additional sum the grantee should pay for the land, which sum he covenanted to pay, the transaction was held not to be a mortgage, but a conditional sale, giving the grantee the right to recover possession of the land, after the expiration of the year, in ejectment against the grantor.[10]

In like manner an agreement by the grantee, made as a part of the transaction, to account to the grantor for a portion of the profits which may be realized on a resale of the premises if made within a specified time, and to sell if a specified price can be obtained, is not inconsistent with the vesting of the title.[11]

A conveyance made for the purpose of securing future loans, accompanied by an oral agreement to convey on reimbursement, has been held to be a mortgage.[12]

§ 271. **Grantee's option to resell.**—On the other hand, an agreement that the grantee may sell all the property for the best possible price and retain from the proceeds the amount due him, paying the residue to the grantor, shows that the transaction is a mortgage.[13] In

[9] Henley v. Hotaling, 41 Cal. 22, per Rhodes, C. J. See also Voss v. Eller, 109 Ind. 260, 10 N. E. 74; Usher v. Livermore, 2 Iowa 117; Klein v. McNamara, 54 Miss. 90. See post § 272.

[10] Daniels v. Johnson, 24 Mich. 430; Baker v. Thrasher, 4 Denio (N. Y.) 493.

[11] Cadman v. Peter, 12 Fed. 363, affirmed 118 U. S. 73, 30 L. ed. 78, 6 Sup. Ct. 957; Macaulay v. Porter, 71 N. Y. 173. See ante § 267.

[12] Madigan v. Mead, 31 Minn. 94, 16 N. W. 539.

[13] Robinson v. Gassoway (Ala.), 39 So. 1023; Beckman v. Wilson, 61 Cal. 335; Kidd v. Teeple, 22 Cal. 255; Blackstock v. Robertson, 42 Colo. 472, 94 Pac. 336; Crane v. Buchanan, 29 Ind. 570; Truman v. Truman, 79 Iowa 506, 44 N. W. 721; Ogden v. Grant, 6 Dana (Ky.) 473; Hagthorp v. Hook, 1 Gill & J. (Md.) 270; Curtiss v. Sheldon, 47 Mich. 262, 11 N. W. 151; Law-

case the land should sell for a less sum than the debt, the grantee is
entitled to recover the deficiency.[14]

And so a conveyance to a trustee with power to sell the land, pay
the creditor from the proceeds, and deliver the balance to the grantor
on his failure to pay the debt, is a mortgage, and subject to the provisions of a registry law relating to mortgages.[15] A written agreement
by a purchaser of timber land providing for the payment of the proceeds to the mortgagee in payment of the purchase-price was held to
be a mortgage and not a contract of purchase.[16] An agreement between co-owners of land reciting a conveyance by one, of his half interest, to the other for a specified consideration, and providing that if
the grantee disposed of the land, the real consideration should be whatever he realized from the sale, the grantor to have credit upon his debt

---

rence v. Farmers' Loan &c. Co., 13
N. Y. 200; Gillis v. Martin, 2 Dev.
Eq. (N. Car.) 470, 25 Am. Dec. 729;
Stephens v. Allen, 11 Ore. 188, 3
Pac. 168; Ruffners v. Putney, 12
Grat. (Va.) 541; Hoffman v. Ryan,
21 W. Va. 415. See also Duclos v.
Walton, 21 Ore. 323, 28 Pac. 1; Colgan v. Farmers' &c. Bank, 59 Ore.
469, 117 Pac. 807. A deed, accompanied by a contract requiring the
grantee to resell and account for
the excess above the grantor's
debt, and giving the grantor the
right to redeem, is in effect a mortgage. Colgan v. Farmers' &c. Bank
(Ore.), 138 Pac. 1070. The owner
of an·equity of redemption agreed
with one who advanced money to
redeem the land that the latter
should have the right within two
years to sell the land, pay the advancements and interest and account for the proceeds. Thereafter,
without any new consideration, the
owner executed a warranty deed of
the land to the wife of the party
redeeming, subject to the mortgages referred to in the original
agreement. It was held that such
contract and deed should be considered a mortgage and the owner's rights did not lapse by his
failure to pay such advances within two years. Malone v. Danforth,
137 Mich. 227, 100 N. W. 445. But
see Fuson v. Chestnut, 33 Ky. L.
249, 109 S. W. 1192; Duell v. Leslie,
207 Mo. 658, 106 S. W. 489. Such
agreement is not alone sufficient to

convert the deed into a mortgage.
Rogers v. Beach, 115 Ind. 413, 17
N. E. 609. Where there was already a mortgage upon land for
nearly its full value, and, to save
the expense of foreclosure, the
mortgagor conveyed the land to the
mortgagee, the latter agreeing by
writing that, if he should sell the
same for a greater sum than his
debt and expense, he would pay the
former all sums of money in excess of the same, it was held that
the transaction was not a mortgage with a power of sale in the
mortgagee as trustee, but that he
was liable on his promise in an action at law, or for money had and
received, when there was such surplus in his hands arising from the
sale. Eaton v. Whiting, 3 Pick.
(Mass.) 484. See also Trimble v.
McCormick, 12 Ky. L. 857, 15 S.
W. 358; Jones v. Blake, 33 Minn.
362, 23 N. W. 538; Tower v. Fetz,
26 Nebr. 706, 42 N. W. 884, 18 Am.
St. 795; Clark v. Haney, 62 Tex.
511, 50 Am. Rep. 536.

[14] Palmer v. Gurnsey, 7 Wend.
(N. Y.) 248, distinguished and
questioned in Baker v. Thrasher,
4 Denio (N. Y.) 493; Macaulay v.
Porter, 71 N. Y. 173.

[15] Woodruff v. Robb, 19 Ohio 212.
See also Walsh v. Brennan, 52 Ill.
193; Irwin v. Longworth, 20 Ohio
581. But see Alleghany R. &c. Co.
v. Casey, 79 Pa. St. 84.

[16] Hurst v. Winchester Bank, 154
Ky. 358, 157 S. W. 685.

to the grantee for the amount so realized, was held to constitute a mortgage.[17]

But a stipulation that if the grantor can, within a limited time, "dispose of the land conveyed to better advantage," he may do so, pay-. ing to the grantee the "consideration money" mentioned in the deed, does not make the instrument a mortgage.[18] And so a covenant by the grantor, who is a joint tenant, not to make partition without the advice and consent of the grantee, does not turn a conditional sale into a mortgage.[19] A statement by the grantee in an absolute deed that, when he got back out of the real estate conveyed to him the money he had advanced the grantor, he would deed the remainder back to the grantor, will not impress on the deed the characteristics of an equitable mortgage.[20] An agreement by the grantee in an absolute deed that he will not convey the premises within a specified time without consent of the grantor, and that if the grantor within that time should find a purchaser, the grantee would convey on receiving the amount with interest for which the land was conveyed to him, renders the transaction a conditional sale and not a mortgage.[21]

§ 272. **Absence of agreement to pay debt.**—The fact that there is no agreement for the payment of the debt is a circumstance entitled to considerable weight, as tending to show that the conveyance was not intended as a mortgage, and that the relation of debtor and creditor did not exist, but is not conclusive.[22] Nor does the absence of an agreement for repayment show conclusively that the transaction was a conditional sale.[23] "The want of a covenant to repay the money,"

[17] Horn v. Bates (Ky.), 114 S. W. 763.

[18] Stratton v. Sabin, 9 Ohio 28, 34 Am. Dec. 418.

[19] Cotterell v. Purchase, For. 61, Cas. temp. Talb. 61.

[20] Smith v. Smith, 153 Ala. 504, 45 So. 168.

[21] Duell v. Leslie, 207 Mo. 658, 106 S. W. 489.

[22] Locke v. Moulton, 96 Cal. 21, 30 Pac. 957; Jarvis v. Woodruff, 22 Conn. 548; Bacon v. Brown, 19 Conn. 34; White v. Redenbaugh, 41 Ind. App. 580, 82 N. E. 110 (citing text); Flagg v. Mann, 14 Pick. (Mass.) 467; Niggeler v. Maurin, 34 Minn. 118, 24 N. W. 369; Madigan v. Mead, 31 Minn. 94, 16 N. W. 539; Fisk v. Stewart, 24 Minn. 97; Jeffreys v. Charlton, 72 N. J. Eq. 340, 65 Atl. 711; Doying v. Chese-

brough (N. J. Eq.), 36 Atl. 893; Macaulay v. Smith, 132 N. Y. 524, 30 N. E. 997; Morris v. Budlong, 78 N. Y. 543; Matthews v. Sheehan, 69 N. Y. 585; Horn v. Keteltas, 46 N. Y. 605; Brumfield v. Boutall, 24 Hun (N. Y.) 451; Holmes v. Grant, 8 Paige (N. Y.) 243; Brown v. Dewey, 1 Sandf. Ch. (N. Y.) 56; McGuin v. Lee, 10 N. Dak. 160, 86 N. W. 714; McCamant v. Roberts, 80 Tex. 316, 15 S. W. 580; Hubby v. Harris, 68 Tex. 91, 3 S. W. 553; Schriber v. Le Clair, 66 Wis. 579, 29 N. W. 570, 889; Rockwell v. Humphrey, 57 Wis. 410, 15 N. W. 394.

[23] Conway v. Alexander, 7 Cranch (U. S.) 218, 3 L. ed. 321; White v. Redenbaugh, 41 Ind. App. 580, 82 N. E. 110; Davis v. Stonestreet, 4 Ind. 101.

says Chief Justice Marshall,[24] "is not complete evidence that a conditional sale was intended, but is a circumstance of no inconsiderable importance." No conveyance can be a mortgage unless made for the purpose of securing the payment of a debt, or the performance of a duty either existing or created at the time, or else to be created or to arise in the future. But it is not necessary that the debt or duty should be evidenced by any express covenant, or by any separate written security.[25] Although a mortgage can not be a mortgage on one side only, but must be a mortgage with both parties,[26] yet this principle is applicable to the lien upon the land only, and not to the personal obligation.

The fact that there is no collateral undertaking by the grantor for the payment of money, or the performance of any obligation, is by no means conclusive of the nature of the transaction. This is only one circumstance to be regarded in ascertaining whether it is to be treated as a mortgage or a sale with a contract for repurchase.[27] It affects the equitable rights and claims of the parties. If there be no contract for the repayment of the money, the grantee must bear any loss arising from depreciation in value; and it would seem equitable, on the other hand, that he should have the benefit of any advance in the value of the property, if the repurchase be not made within the stipulated period.

A debtor conveyed to his sureties certain land, taking from them a bond providing that the obligors should pay his debt, and stating that "the intent of the deed was to indemnify and save them harmless." The bond also referred to the deed as "indemnity and security in addition to security" of other lands mortgaged to the obligors, and stipulated that the land should not be sold for three years, so that the debtor "may redeem if he chooses to do so." If the obligors were not "reimbursed" within the three years, they were to hold the lands free from all claim on the debtor's part, but they agreed to place no obstacles in the way of his "paying said debts and redeeming the said lands." The transaction was adjudged to be a mortgage, and not a

---

[24] In Conway v. Alexander, 7 Cranch (U. S.) 218, 3 L. ed. 321.

[25] Fisk v. Stewart, 24 Minn. 97; Brant v. Robertson, 16 Mo. 129.

[26] Copleston v. Boxwill, 1 Ch. Ca. 1; White v. Ewer, 2 Vent. 340. See ante § 264.

[27] Flint v. Sheldon, 13 Mass. 443, 448, 7 Am. Dec. 162; Kelly v. Beers, 12 Mass. 387; Murphy v. Calley, 1 Allen (Mass.) 107; Flagg v. Mann, 14 Pick. (Mass.) 467; Bodwell v. Webster, 13 Pick. (Mass.) 411; Rice v. Rice, 4 Pick. (Mass.) 349; Brant v. Robertson, 16 Mo. 129; Brown v. Dewey, 1 Sandf. (N. Y.) 56, 2 Barb. (N. Y.) 28; Stephens v. Allen, 11 Ore. 188, 3 Pac. 168.

conditional sale, although there was no covenant on the part of the grantor to pay the debt.[28]

§ 273. **Interest—Payable in form of rent.**—The fact that interest is payable, by the terms of the contract, upon the money advanced by the person who takes the title to the property, is a circumstance tending to show that the transaction was a loan upon security instead of a conditional sale. Anything tending to show that there was a subsisting debt, or an advance by way of loan, goes to prove the transaction to be a mortgage.[29]

What is in fact a payment of interest is sometimes disguised under the payment of rent by the grantor in possession to the grantee; but although the transaction has the appearance of a conditional sale, the payment of rent in lieu of interest may be a circumstance tending to show that it is in fact a mortgage.[30] If a conveyance of land be made in fee, and the grantee give back a bond to reconvey upon repayment of the consideration money, and to permit the grantor to occupy the premises at a rent equal to the interest on the consideration, these are parts of one and the same transaction, and constitute a mortgage.[31]

The owner of land occupied by him as a homestead executed an absolute conveyance of it in consideration of one thousand dollars, and the grantee at the same time executed with him a joint instrument

---

[28] Wing v. Cooper, 37 Vt. 169.

[29] Farmer v. Grose, 42 Cal. 169; Harbison v. Houghton, 41 Ill. 522; Turpie v. Lowe, 114 Ind. 37, 15 N. E. 834; Murphy v. Calley, 1 Allen (Mass.) 107; Lee v. Wilkinson (Miss.), 62 So. 275; Kraemer v. Adelsberger, 122 N. Y. 467, 25 N. E. 859, per Parker, J.; Wilson v. Fisher, 148 N. Car. 535, 62 S. E. 622; Wells v. Geyer, 12 N. Dak. 316, 96 N. W. 289; Hesser v. Brown, 40 Wash. 688, 82 Pac. 934. See also Honore v. Hutchings, 8 Bush (Ky.) 687.

"Hutchings and Honore, in 1861, jointly purchased thirty acres of land near Chicago, Ill. Hutchings advanced the entire purchase-price, took a conveyance to himself, and executed a writing in which, among other things, 'it is agreed between said parties that, when said land is sold, said Hutchings is to have first his six thousand dollars so advanced, and ten per cent. interest, and the profits over and above said

sum are to be equally divided between said parties. * * * This arrangement is to continue eighteen months, when, if the property has not been sold, said Honore is to pay one-half the sum so advanced, with the accrued interest, or said Hutchings is to be the sole owner of the same.' The land was not sold within the time specified, and Honore failed to pay any part of the sum advanced. In 1869 Hutchings sold the land for $100,000, and refused to pay any part of the profits to Honore. But it was decided that Hutchings held the legal title to one-half the land in trust for Honore, and must account for the proceeds according to the agreement."

[30] Bearss v. Ford, 108 Ill. 16; Ewart v. Walling, 42 Ill. 453; Preschbaker v. Feaman, 32 Ill. 475; Woodward v. Pickett, 8 Gray (Mass.) 617; Wright v. Bates, 13 Vt. 341.

[31] Woodward v. Pickett, 8 Gray (Mass.) 617.

stipulating that the grantor should have the privilege of repurchasing the premises for the same price, at any time within twelve months, and should remain in possession, and pay rent at the rate of forty dollars per month until such repurchase, or the expiration of the twelve months. He remained in possession eleven years, and paid over twelve hundred dollars as rents. The transaction was held to be a mortgage; that the rent was a device to screen usury, and that the debt had been extinguished by the payments made.[32]

The owner of land agreed with a third person to build a mill for him, and to sell him the land and the mill at an agreed price, the third person agreeing to buy the land and mill within a certain number of years, paying a certain sum each year, and interest on the price of the land and money expended in erecting the mill. The third person also agreed to furnish a part of the materials. It was held that in equity the owner of the land stood as a mortgagee to the third person.[33]

§ 274. **Continued possession of grantor.**—The continued possession of the grantor, as is elsewhere noticed with reference to proving by parol that an absolute conveyance is not a sale, is a circumstance tending to show that the agreement for repurchase, in connection with the deed, constitutes a mortgage rather than a conditional sale.[34] But this circumstance is not conclusive, and other considerations may show that an absolute or conditional sale was really intended.[35]

[32] In Boatright v. Peck, 33 Tex. 68.

[33] McCrillis v. Cole, 25 R. I. 156, 55 Atl. 196, 105 Am. St. 875.

[34] Richmond v. Richmond, Fed. Cas. No. 11801; Bentley v. Phelps, Fed. Cas. No. 1331, 2 Woodb. & M. (U. S.) 426; Nelson v. Wadsworth, 171 Ala. 603, 55 So. 120; Parks v. Parks, 66 Ala. 326; Crews v. Threadgill, 35 Ala. 334; Prefumo v. Russell, 148 Cal. 451, 83 Pac. 810; Berry v. Williams (Ga.), 81 S. E. 881; Clark v. Finlon, 90 Ill. 245; Strong v. Shea, 83 Ill. 575; Gibson v. Eller, 13 Ind. 124; Ingalls v. Atwood, 53 Iowa 283, 5 N. W. 160; Eames v. Woodson, 120 La. 1031, 46 So. 13; Rester v. Powell, 120 La. 406, 45 So. 372; Jameson v. Emerson, 82 Maine 359, 19 Atl. 831; Stevens v. Hulin, 53 Mich. 93, 18 N. W. 569; Pidcock v. Swift, 51 N. J. Eq. 405, 27 Atl. 470; Luesenhop v. Einsfield, 93 App. Div. 68, 87 N. Y. S. 268; Robinson v. Willoughby, 65 N. Car. 520; Streator v. Jones, 10 N. Car. 423; McGill v. Thorne, 70 S. Car. 65, 48 S. E. 994; Lewie v. Hallman, 53 S. Car. 18, 30 S. E. 601; Lewis v. Bayless, 90 Tenn. 280, 16 S. W. 376; Gray v. Shelby, 83 Tex. 405, 18 S. W. 809; Azzalia v. Le Claire, 23 Utah 401, 64 Pac. 1106; Wright v. Bates, 13 Vt. 341; Tuggle v. Berkeley, 101 Va. 83, 43 S. E. 199; Ransome v. Frayser, 10 Leigh (Va.) 592; Hursey v. Hursey, 56 W. Va. 148, 49 S. E. 367; Ferguson v. Boyd, 39 W. Va. 561, 20 S. E. 591; Gilchrist v. Beswick, 33 W. Va. 168, 10 S. E. 371; Hoffman v. Ryan, 21 W. Va. 415; Lawrence v. Du Bois, 16 W. Va. 443; Davis v. Demming, 12 W. Va. 246; Ogle v. Adams, 12 W. Va. 213. See post §§ 328, 600, the cases being equally applicable here.

[35] Buffum v. Porter, 70 Mich. 623, 38 N. W. 600; Shiver v. Arthur, 54 S. Car. 184, 32 S. E. 310; Matheney v. Sandford, 26 W. Va. 386.

Retention of possession by the grantor coupled with payment of taxes by him and admissions by the grantee, constitutes sufficient ground for holding an absolute deed a mortgage; although the mere retention of possession might have been otherwise explained.[36]

Where a grantee by absolute deed executed a contract to reconvey on payment of a debt owing by the grantor, the transaction was held a mortgage, notwithstanding that the grantee took possession and refused to accept an ordinary mortgage, on account of the expense of foreclosure.[37]

One holding a mortgage upon a farm after commencing proceedings to foreclose entered into an arrangement with the mortgagor and a third person to whom the mortgagor was indebted whereby the latter bought the property at the foreclosure sale and executed a new mortgage to the former mortgagee. At the same time the debtor entered into a written contract with the third person whereby the latter was to convey to the debtor on repayment of the amount together with the amount which the debtor owed him, etc., the debtor to assume the new mortgage. The debtor was to retain possession of the farm. It was held that the relation between the debtor and the third person was that of mortgagor and mortgagee.[38]

§ 275. **Inadequacy of price.**—Inadequacy of price is one of the circumstances which are considered as of weight, as tending to show that an absolute conveyance accompanied by an agreement to reconvey is a mortgage rather than a conditional sale. This alone will not authorize a court to give the grantor a right to redeem, but in connection with other evidence affords much ground of inference that the transaction was not really what it purports to be.[39]

[36] Hursey v. Hursey, 56 W. Va. 148, 49 S. E. 367.
[37] Wiswell v. Simmons, 77 Kans. 622, 95 Pac. 407.
[38] English v. Rainear (N. J. Eq.), 55 Atl. 41.
[39] Russell v. Southard, 12 How. (U. S.) 139, 13 L. ed. 927; Morris v. Nixon, 1 How. (U. S.) 118, 11 L. ed. 69; Martin v. Martin, 123 Ala. 191, 26 So. 525; Adams v. Pilcher, 92 Ala. 474, 8 So. 757; Peagler v. Stabler, 91 Ala. 308, 9 So. 157; Vincent v. Walker, 86 Ala. 333, 5 So. 465; Perdue v. Bell, 83 Ala. 396, 3 So. 698; Douglass v. Moody, 80 Ala. 61; Rapier v. Gulf City Paper Co., 77 Ala. 126; Pearson v. Seay, 35 Ala. 612; Crews v. Threadgill, 35 Ala. 334; West v. Hendrix, 28 Ala. 226; Lynch v. Lynch, 22 Cal. App. 653, 135 Pac. 1101; Elliott v. Connor, 63 Fla. 408, 58 So. 241; Rue v. Dole, 107 Ill. 275; Carr v. Rising, 62 Ill. 14; Turpie v. Lowe, 114 Ind. 37, 15 N. E. 834; Davis v. Stonestreet, 4 Ind. 101; Calahan v. Dunker, 51 Ind. App. 436, 99 N. E. 1021; White v. Redenbaugh, 41 Ind. App. 580, 82 N. E. 110 (citing text); Bigler v. Jack, 114 Iowa 667, 87 N. W. 700; Bridges v. Linder, 60 Iowa 190, 14 N. W. 217 (quoting text); Oldham v. Halley, 2 J. J. Marsh. (Ky.) 113; Fulwiler v. Roberts, 26 Ky. L. 297, 80 S. W. 1148; Trimble

Inadequacy of price, to be of controlling effect, must be gross.[40] If it be very inadequate, it is a circumstance tending to show a loan and mortgage; but it is not conclusive. Nor would the fact of the adequacy of the price, taken in connection with the absence of any obligation to repay the money, be conclusive that a conditional sale was intended.[41] Nevertheless, the fact that the consideration is fully equal to the value of the land is evidence of some weight that the transaction was a sale and not a mortgage, because men in making a loan do not usually advance the full amount of the land.[42] But it has been held that even where the value of the property was less than the debt secured, the conveyance was nevertheless a mortgage.[43]

If the transaction creates no debt or loan, but only a right to repur-

v. McCormick, 12 Ky. L. 857, 15 S. W. 358; Eames v. Woodson, 120 La. 1031, 46 So. 13; Rester v. Powell, 120 La. 406, 45 So. 372; Bonnette v. Wise, 111 La. 855, 35 So. 953; Reed v. Reed, 75 Maine 264; Thompson v. Banks, 2 Md. Ch. 430; Campbell v. Dearborn, 109 Mass. 130, 12 Am. Rep. 671; Freeman v. Wilson, 51 Miss. 329; Donovan v. Boeck, 217 Mo. 70, 116 S. W. 543; Jeffreys v. Charlton, 72 N. J. Eq. 340, 65 Atl. 711; Mooney v. Byrne, 163 N. Y. 86, 57 N. E. 163; Lawrence v. Farmers' L. &c. Co., 13 N. Y. 200; Brown v. Dewey, 2 Barb. (N. Y.) 28; Robinson v. Cropsey, 6 Paige (N. Y.) 480; Harris v. Hirsch, 121 App. Div. 767, 106 N. Y. S. 631; Steel v. Black, 3 Jones Eq. (N. Car.) 427; Streator v. Jones, 3 Hawks (N. Car.) 423; Kemp v. Earp, 7 Ired. Eq. (N. Car.) 167; Sellers v. Stalcup, 7 Ired. Eq. (N. Car.) 13; Forester v. Van Auken, 12 N. Dak. 175, 96 N. W. 301; Wagg v. Herbert, 19 Okla. 525, 92 Pac. 250; Harmon v. Grants Pass Banking &c. Co., 60 Ore. 69, 118 Pac. 188; Kinney v. Smith, 58 Ore. 158, 113 Pac. 854; Gray v. Shelby, 83 Tex. 405, 18 S. W. 809; Douglass v. Culverwell, 3 Gif. 251; Langton v. Horton, 5 Beav. 9; Thornborough v. Baker, 3 Swanst. 628; Davis v. Thomas, 1 Russ. & M. 506; Williams v. Owen, 5 M. & C. 303. Inadequacy of consideration coupled with a confidential relation between the parties will be considered in an action to declare a deed a mortgage. Lynch v. Lynch, 22 Cal. App.

653, 135 Pac. 1101. The conveyance of a residence and garden lot in consideration of taxes amounting only to the value of the latter constitute a mortgage rather than a conditional sale, the requisites of inadequacy of consideration, retention of possession, and a debt to be secured, concurring. Tuggle v. Berkeley, 101 Va. 83, 43 S. E. 199.

In Wharf v. Howell, 5 Binn. (Pa.) 499, a lot worth eight hundred dollars was conveyed in consideration of two hundred dollars, with an agreement to reconvey upon the payment of this sum within three months. See post § 329.

[40] Elliott v. Maxwell, 7 Ired. Eq. (N. Car.) 246; Forester v. Van Auken, 12 N. Dak. 175, 96 N. W. 301. The fact that land worth seven dollars per acre was sold for five dollars per acre is not alone sufficient to render the deed a mortgage, particularly where the grantors retained a life estate. Lynch v. Lynch, 22 Cal. App. 653, 135 Pac. 1101.

[41] Brown v. Dewey, 2 Barb. (N. Y.) 28, 1 Sandf. Ch. (N. Y.) 56.

[42] Carr v. Rising, 62 Ill. 14, per Walker, J.; Jeffreys v. Charlton, 72 N. J. Eq. 340, 65 Atl. 711; in re Dunbar's Estate, 51 Pa. Super. Ct. 216; Hesser v. Brown, 40 Wash. 688, 82 Pac. 934. See also Dabney v. Smith, 38 Wash. 40, 80 Pac. 199 (property of less value than the debt).

[43] Lipscomb v. Talbott, 243 Mo. 1, 147 S. W. 798.

chase, it is immaterial whether the consideration for the reconveyance is fixed at the same price paid for the conveyance, or at an advanced price.[44]

§ 276. Subsequent acts and admissions as evidence—Record.—In determining whether a deed was intended to operate as a mortgage, verbal admissions are entitled to little weight.[45] The acts or declarations of one party in reference to the transaction afterward will not change its character. The transaction remains what the parties made it in the beginning, until by mutual agreement they change it. It can hardly be said that the treatment of an absolute deed as conditional by the grantee can make it a mortgage. If it was a mortgage in the beginning, his admission of the fact only relieves the mortgagor from proving it. If it was not a mortgage in the beginning, his treating it as such has no effect unless the mortgagor concurs in so treating it, so that in fact, by mutual agreement, the character of the instrument is changed.[46]

But subsequent acts and admissions of the parties have been considered as corroborative of a pre-existing intent concerning the nature of the transaction.[47] Thus an admission by the grantee of a declaration at the time of the conveyance of his willingness to receive back within five years the money advanced, coupled with retention of possession and payment of taxes by the grantor, and the conduct of both parties recognizing an interest of the grantor in the land, was considered sufficient evidence of a mortgage.[48]

When the transaction is otherwise a conditional conveyance and not a mortgage, the latter character is not imparted to it by the mere fact that the instrument is recorded as a mortgage.[49]

§ 277. Parol evidence—Questions for jury.—Parol evidence is admissible in equity to show that a conditional sale, and not a mortgage was intended, in case there is nothing on the face of the papers to de-

[44] West v. Hendrix, 28 Ala. 226; Pitts v. Cable, 44 Ill. 103; French v. Sturdivant, 8 Maine 246; Glover v. Payn, 19 Wend. (N. Y.) 518.

[45] Richardson v. Beaber, 62 Misc. 542, 115 N. Y. S. 821.

[46] See, on this point, but not wholly agreeing with the statement in the text, Holmes v. Fresh, 9 Mo. 201; Thomaston Bank v. Stimpson, 21 Maine 195; Nichols v. Reynolds, 1 R. I. 30, 36 Am. Dec. 238. See also Harris v. Hirsch, 121 App. Div.

767, 106 N. Y. S. 631; Waters v. Crabtree, 105 N. Car. 394, 11 S. E. 240 (subsequent admission by grantee under seal not conclusive).

[47] Elliott v. Bozorth, 52 Ore. 391, 97 Pac. 632; Hoskins v. Hoskins, 27 Ky. L. 980, 87 S. W. 320 (declarations of the grantor's father).

[48] Hursey v. Hursey, 56 W. Va. 148, 49 S. E. 367.

[49] Morrison v. Brand, 5 Daly (N. Y.) 40; Jackson v. Richards, 6 Cow. (N. Y.) 617.

termine whether the transaction was the one or the other.[50] The question is then to be decided by the jury, under instructions, and not by the court.[51] For this purpose evidence of the repeated assertions of the grantee that he had bought the property and owned it, of his repeated denials that the grantor had any interest in it, and of acts of ownership inconsistent with the position of a mere mortgagee may be received.[52]

But if the instrument on its face be a mortgage, or if a deed and bond of defeasance be executed together as part of the same transaction, and therefore constitute a mortgage, parol evidence is not admissible to show that the parties intended that the transaction should operate as a conditional sale.[53] It is then for the court to construe the instruments and determine their legal effect.[54] Parol evidence, if admitted, would contradict the writing; the court must construe the instrument without resort to parol proof.[55] No agreement or intention

---

[50] Bogk v. Gassert, 149 U. S. 17, 37 L. ed. 631, 13 Sup. Ct. 738; Heath v. Williams, 30 Ind. 495; Bigler v. Jack, 114 Iowa 667, 87 N. W. 700; Gassert v. Bogk, 7 Mont. 585, 19 Pac. 281. In Alabama, however, it is declared that parol proof is inadmissible to show that an absolute conveyance was intended to operate as a conditional sale, or a sale with a right to redeem. Peagler v. Stabler, 91 Ala. 308, 9 So. 157, per Coleman, J.: "It is only when the writings, whether executed as a whole or in separate instruments, express what purports to be a conditional sale, are considered with parol evidence that courts incline to construe the instruments to be a mortgage rather than a conditional sale; or if the instruments be absolute in form, and it be admitted there was a contemporaneous agreement, different from that expressed in the writings, such admission may be important, in weighing the parol evidence offered to show that the conveyance, though absolute in form, was intended to operate as a mortgage." See also Daniels v. Lowery, 92 Ala. 519, 8 So. 352. The fact that a party who advanced money refused to make a loan or take a mortgage as security, is evidence that the conveyance made to him did not constitute a mortgage. Conner v. Clapp, 37

Wash. 299, 79 Pac. 929. But see Taber v. Hamlin, 97 Mass. 489, 93 Am. Dec. 113. It has been frequently held in the United States court that evidence, either written or oral, is admissible in an action to declare an absolute deed a mortgage, to show the real character of the transaction. Jackson v. Lawrence, 117 U. S. 679, 29 L. ed. 1024; Brick v. Brick, 98 U. S. 514, 25 L. ed. 256; Peugh v. Davis, 96 U. S. 332, 24 L. ed. 775; Babcock v. Wyman, 19 How. (U. S.) 289, 15 L. ed. 644; Russell v. Southard, 12 How. (U. S.) 139, 13 L. ed. 927.

[51] Bogk v. Gassert, 149 U. S. 17, 37 L. ed. 631, 13 Sup. Ct. 738; Baker v. Fireman's Fund Ins. Co., 79 Cal. 34, 21 Pac. 357; Wolfe v. McMillan, 117 Ind. 587, 20 N. E. 509; Alstin v. Cundiff, 52 Tex. 453.

[52] Hanford v. Blessing, 80 Ill. 188; Langton v. Horton, 5 Beav. 9; Newcomb v. Bonham, 1 Vern. 8, 214, 232. See ante § 246, and post § 282.

[53] Snyder v. Griswold, 37 Ill. 216; Gassert v. Bogk, 7 Mont. 585, 19 Pac. 281.

[54] Voss v. Eller, 109 Ind. 260, 10 N. E. 74; Buse v. Page, 32 Minn. 111, 19 N. W. 736, 20 N. W. 95; Alstin v. Cundiff, 52 Tex. 453.

[55] Reitenbaugh v. Ludwick, 31 Pa. St. 131; Woods v. Wallace, 22 Pa. St. 171; Wharf v. Howell, 5 Binn.

of the parties, whether at the time of the transaction or subsequently, can change the redeemable character of a mortgage.[6]

And, on the other hand, parol evidence is admissible in equity to show that a formal conveyance, with a defeasance executed at the same time or afterward, constituted in fact a mortgage, and not a conditional sale.[58]

But although a formal conveyance can be shown to be a mortgage by extrinsic evidence, a formal mortgage can not be shown to be a conditional sale.[59] The reason of the rule, that a formal conveyance may be shown by parol to be a mortgage, while a formal mortgage can not be shown to be a conditional sale by the same means, is, that "in the one case such proof raises an equity consistent with the writing, while in the other it would contradict the writing."[60] When the transaction is a sale with a right of repurchase, and the grantor claims it to be a mortgage, a bill will lie to have the sale established.[61]

Such evidence is inadmissible at law.[62] It is received only in equity, and when there exist equitable grounds for its admission. It is held, too, that the rule admitting parol evidence in equity for the purposes mentioned does not extend to an official conveyance, such as the deed of a sheriff selling under process.[63] Such officer has no power to make any sale other than an absolute one.

§ 278. **Circumstances evidencing intention—Relation and capacity of parties—Payment of taxes.**—As previously noted, the intent of the parties to an absolute deed that it should operate as a mortgage may be shown by the circumstances surrounding the transaction,[64] includ-

(Pa.) 499; McClintock v. McClintock, 3 Brewst. (Pa.) 76; Kunkle v. Wolfersberger, 6 Watts (Pa.) 126.

[56] Reitenbaugh v. Ludwick, 31 Pa. St. 131; Woods v. Wallace, 22 Pa. St. 171; Wharf v. Howell, 5 Binn. 390; Kunkle v. Wolfersberger, 6 Watts (Pa.) 126; Colwell v. Woods, 3 Watts (Pa.) 188, 27 Am. Dec. 345; Hart v. Eppstein, 71 Tex. 752, 10 S. W. 85; Wing v. Cooper, 37 Vt. 169.

[58] Farmer v. Grose, 42 Cal. 169; Reitenbaugh v. Ludwick, 31 Pa. St. 390. See also Gay v. Hamilton, 33 Cal. 686; Bearss v. Ford, 108 Ill. 16; Tillson v. Moulton, 23 Ill. 648; Heath v. Williams, 30 Ind. 495.

[59] Reitenbaugh v. Ludwick, 31 Pa. St. 131; Wharf v. Howell, 5 Binn.

(Pa.) 499; McClintock v. McClintock, 3 Brews. (Pa.) 76.

[60] Woods v. Wallace, 22 Pa. St. 171; Per Gibson, C. J., in Kunkle v. Wolfersberger, 6 Watts (Pa.) 126.

[61] Rich v. Doane, 35 Vt. 125.

[2] Bragg v. Massie, 38 Ala. 89, 79 Am. Dec. 82; Heath v. Williams, 30 Ind. 495; Belote v. Morrison, 8 Minn. 87; McClane v. White, 5 Minn. 178; Webb v. Rice, 6 Hill (N. Y.) 219. Contra, Tillson v. Moulton, 23 Ill. 648. See post § 282.

[63] Ryan v. Dox, 25 Barb. (N. Y.) 440.

[64] Horbach v. Hill, 112 U. S. 144, 28 L. ed. 670, 5 Sup. Ct. 81; Nelson v. Wadsworth, 171 Ala. 603, 55 So. 120; Pendergrass v. Burris, 77 Cal. 19, 19 Pac. 187, 11 Am. St. 231;

ing the relations between the parties[65] and the grantor's ignorance of business.[66] Financial embarrassment of the grantor is a circumstance which will be considered as tending to show that an absolute deed was intended as a mortgage.[67]

Lynch v. Lynch, 22 Cal. App. 653, 135 Pac. 1101; Elliott v. Connor, 63 Fla. 408, 58 So. 241; Wylly-Gabbett Co. v. Williams, 53 Fla. 872, 42 So. 910; Heath v. Williams, 30 Ind. 495; Davis v. Stonestreet, 4 Ind. 101; Beidelman v. Koch, 42 Ind. App. 423, 85 N. E. 977; Keeline v. Clark, 132 Iowa 360, 106 N. W. 257; Hughes v. Sheaff, 19 Iowa 335; First Nat. Bank v. Edwards, 84 Kans. 495, 115 Pac. 118; Edrington v. Harper, 3 J. J. Marsh. (Ky.) 353, 20 Am. Dec. 145; Trimble v. McCormick, 12 Ky. L. 857, 15 S. W. 358; Miller v. Miller, 101 Md. 600, 61 Atl. 210; King v. McCarthy, 50 Minn. 222, 52 N. W. 648; Gassert v. Bogk, 7 Mont. 585, 19 Pac. 281, 1 L. R. A. 240; Sanders v. Ayres, 63 Nebr. 271, 88 N. W. 526; Devore v. Woodruff, 1 N. Dak. 143, 45 N. W. 701; Elliott v. Bozorth, 52 Ore. 391, 97 Pac. 632; Stephens v. Allen, 11 Ore. 188, 3 Pac. 168; Bradley v. Helgerson, 14 S. Dak. 593, 86 N. W. 634; Harrison v. Hogue (Tex. Civ. App.), 136 S. W. 118; Goodbar Co. v. Bloom, 43 Tex. Civ. App. 434, 96 S. W. 657 (quoting text); Gray v. Shelby, 83 Tex. 405, 18 S. W. 809; Loving v. Milliken, 59 Tex. 423; Gibbs v. Penny, 43 Tex. 560; Stampers v. Johnson, 3 Tex. 1; Duerden v. Solomon, 33 Utah 468, 94 Pac. 978; Batchelder v. Randolph, 112 Va. 296, 71 S. E. 533; Bachrach v. Bachrach, 111 Va. 232, 68 S. E. 985; Hudkins v. Crim (W. Va.), 78 S. E. 1043; Fridley v. Somerville, 60 W. Va. 272, 54 S. E. 502. See ante § 258.

[65] Elliott v. Connor, 63 Fla. 403, 58 So. 241; Connor v. Connor, 59 Fla. 476, 52 So. 727, 28 L. R. A. (N. S.) 102; Hull v. Burr, 58 Fla. 432, 50 So. 754; De Bartlett v. De Wilson, 52 Fla. 497, 42 So. 189; First Nat. Bank v. Edwards, 84 Kans. 495, 115 Pac. 118; Elliott v. Bozorth, 52 Ore. 391, 97 Pac. 632; Bachrach v. Bachrach, 111 Va. 232, 68 S. E. 985; Tuggle v. Berkeley, 101 Va. 83, 43 S. E. 199. See also Lynch v. Lynch, 22 Cal. App. 653, 135 Pac. 1101.

[66] Where a deed was signed by an ignorant person, upon representation that it was a copy of an agreement for a loan to be secured by the property conveyed, it was declared a mortgage, and ordered to be canceled. Irwin v. Coleman, 173 Ala. 175, 55 So. 492.

Where a wife, to relieve her husband from embarrassment, conveys to his creditor her separate property to secure his indebtedness, and the creditor must have known her purpose, the conveyance will be held a mortgage, and the property may be redeemed by the wife. Elliott v. Connor, 63 Fla. 408, 58 So. 241.

A deed executed by an illiterate servant conveying a house and lot to his master to whom he was indebted, reserving the right of possession without paying rent, and the right to repurchase within three years, was considered a mortgage, although no note or bond was given. Rose v. Gandy, 137 Ala. 329, 34 So. 239.

Where an ignorant person being old and unable to read writing, though he could read printing and could sign his name, signed a deed which was not read to him but which he was told was a mortgage, the grantee being intelligent, and the grantor thereafter made improvements and paid taxes on the land, he was entitled to redeem. Abercrombie v. Carpenter, 150 Ala. 294, 43 So. 746.

The mere fact that a grantor misunderstood a transaction to be a mortgage is not sufficient to establish the fact. Harrison v. Hogue (Tex. Civ. App.), 136 S. W. 118. See also Hamilton v. Holmes, 48 Ore. 453, 87 Pac. 154.

[67] Hull v. Burr, 58 Fla. 432, 50 So. 754; Murray v. Butte-Monitor Tunnel Min. Co., 41 Mont. 449, 110 Pac. 497, 112 Pac. 1132; Montgomery v. Beecher (N. J. Eq.), 31 Atl. 451;

Payment of taxes by the grantor after execution of a deed is further evidence that it was not intended as an absolute conveyance, but merely as a mortgage;[68] while payment of taxes by the grantee indicates that he regarded himself as owner, and negatives the idea of a mortgage.[69]

Evidence of attending circumstances and the relations of the parties is admitted not for the purpose of contradicting and varying the deed, but to construe and explain it, and to establish an equity superior to its terms.[70]

§ 278a. **Effect of minor circumstances.**—Very slight circumstances showing that the transfer was not understood at the time to be absolute, but was made to secure the repayment of the sum advanced, may be sufficient to turn the scale, if the evidence be not clear whether the transaction was a sale or only a mortgage.[71] And so, where there is an agreement to reconvey, very slight circumstances will suffice, in relation to such a transaction, to determine its character,—whether it is a mortgage or an absolute conveyance with a stipulation securing the grantor a reconveyance upon certain terms and within a certain time.[72] Thus the circumstance that the reconveyance is to be made upon payment of the precise amount of the consideration, with interest, is taken into consideration as favoring the conclusion that a loan was made.[73] A memorandum extending the time for payment and redemption of the land, in reference to a contract to reconvey, is evidence that the transaction was a mortgage and not a conditional sale.[74] The fact that the grantee undertook to pay only so much money as was required to remove liens on the land conveyed is a circumstance indicating that the transaction was only a mortgage.[75] The fact that the deed contains a covenant by the grantee assuming the payment of a prior mortgage is also a circumstance entitled to consideration in determining

Steel v. Black, 56 N. Car. 427; Blackwell v. Overby, 41 N. Car. 38; Streator v. Jones, 10 N. Car. 423; Gilchrist v. Beswick, 33 W. Va. 168, 10 S. E. 371.

[68] Parks v. Parks, 66 Ala. 326; Boocock v. Phipard, 52 Hun (N. Y.) 614, 5 N. Y. S. 228, 24 N. Y. St. 267, 1 Silv. (N. Y.) 407; O'Toole v. Omlie, 8 N. Dak. 444, 79 N. W. 849.

[69] Hart v. Randolph, 142 Ill. 521, 32 N. E. 517; Petty v. Petty, 52 S. Car. 54, 29 S. E. 406; Slawson v. Denton (Tenn.), 48 S. W. 350. But see Hume v. Le Compte (Tex. Civ. App.), 142 S. W. 934.

[70] Stephens v. Allen, 11 Ore. 188, 3 Pac. 168.

[71] McKinney v. Miller, 19 Mich. 142.

[72] Waite v. Dimick, 10 Allen (Mass.) 364.

[73] Hickox v. Lowe, 10 Cal. 197. See ante § 275.

[74] Scholl v. Hopper, 134 Ky. 83, 119 S. W. 770.

[75] Fort v. Colby (Iowa), 144 N. W. 393.

what was the purpose of the parties in making the contract, but it is not controlling.[76]

§ 279. **Presumptions of construction in doubtful cases.**—When it is doubtful whether the transaction is a mortgage or a conditional sale, it will generally be treated as a mortgage,[77] although it is in some of the cases said that the transaction, appearing upon its face to be a conditional sale, will be held to be such when no circumstances appear showing an intention that it should be considered a mortgage.[78]

Courts of equity will generally seek to avoid the harshness of forfeiture for failure to comply strictly with the terms of a contract of conditional sale and give the benefit of any doubt arising upon the evidence to the grantor's right to redeem; always inclining against a conditional sale, and in favor of a mortgage.[79] "It is unquestionably

[76] Kraemer v. Adelsberger, 122 N. Y. 467, 25 N. E. 859, per Parker, J., in his language.

[77] Flagg v. Mann, 2 Sumn. (U. S.) 486; Russell v. Southard, 12 How. (U. S.) 139, 13 L. ed. 927; Irwin v. Coleman, 173 Ala. 175, 55 So. 492; Nelson v. Wadsworth, 171 Ala. 603, 55 So. 120; Hubert v. Sistrunk (Ala.), 53 So. 819; Vincent v. Walker, 86 Ala. 333, 5 So. 465; Cosby v. Buchanan, 81 Ala. 574, 1 So. 898; Bacon v. Brown, 19 Conn. 34; Elliott v. Connor, 63 Fla. 408, 58 So. 241; Rankin v. Rankin, 111 Ill. App. 403; Wolfe v. McMillan, 117 Ind. 587, 20 N. E. 509; Heath v. Williams, 30 Ind. 495; White v. Redenbaugh, 41 Ind. App. 580, 82 N. E. 110; Fort v. Colby (Iowa), 144 N. W. 393; Trucks v. Lindsey, 18 Iowa 504; Vaughn v. Smith, 148 Ky. 531, 146 S. W. 1094; Baugher v. Merryman, 32 Md. 185; Cornell v. Hall, 22 Mich. 377; Klein v. McNamara, 54 Miss. 90; Phillips v. Jackson, 240 Mo. 310, 144 S. W. 112; Donovan v. Boeck, 217 Mo. 70, 116 S. W. 543; O'Neill v. Capelle, 62 Mo. 202; Turner v. Kerr, 44 Mo. 429; Brant v. Robertson, 16 Mo. 129; Desloge v. Ranger, 7 Mo. 327; McRobert v. Bridget (Iowa), 149 N. W. 906; Smith v. Jensen, 16 N. Dak. 408, 114 N. W. 306; Bickel v. Wessinger, 58 Ore. 98, 113 Pac. 34; Stephens v. Allen, 11 Ore. 188, 3 Pac. 168; Hume v. Le Compte (Tex. Civ. App.), 142 S. W. 934; Moorhead v. Ellison, 56 Tex. Civ. App. 444, 120 S. W. 1049; De Bruhl v. Maas, 54 Tex. 464; Duerden v. Solomon, 33 Utah 468, 94 Pac. 978; Snavely v. Pickle, 29 Grat. (Va.) 27; Gilchrist v. Beswick, 33 W. Va. 168, 10 S. E. 371. See ante § 258, post §§ 335, 336. But see Johnson v. Scrimshire, 42 Tex. Civ. App. 611, 93 S. W. 712; Gasaway v. Ballin, 57 Wash. 355, 106 Pac. 905, and cases cited.

[78] Swetland v. Swetland, 3 Mich. 482; Robinson v. Cropsey, 2 Edw. Ch. (N. Y.) 138.

[79] Morton v. Allen (Ala.), 60 So. 866; Williams v. Reggan, 111 Ala. 621, 20 So. 614; Reeves v. Abercrombie, 108 Ala. 535, 19 So. 41; Daniels v. Lowery, 92 Ala. 519, 8 So. 352; Peagler v. Stabler, 91 Ala. 308, 9 So. 157; Cosby v. Buchanan, 81 Ala. 574, 1 So. 898; Turner v. Wilkinson, 72 Ala. 361; Mobile Building &c. Assn. v. Robertson, 65 Ala. 382; McNeil v. Norsworthy, 39 Ala. 156; Crews v. Threadgill, 35 Ala. 334; Locke v. Palmer, 26 Ala. 312; Turnipseed v. Cunningham, 16 Ala. 501, 1 Am. Dec. 190; Scott v. Henry, 13 Ark. 112; Hickox v. Lowe, 10 Cal. 196; Pensoneau v. Pulliam, 47 Ill. 58; Bishop v. Williams, 18 Ill. 101; Williams v. Bishop, 15 Ill. 553; Miller v. Thomas, 14 Ill. 428; Heath v. Williams, 30 Ind. 496; Jones v. Gillett, 142 Iowa 506, 118 N. W. 314; Baird v. Reininghaus, 87 Iowa 167, 54 N. W. 148; Barthell v. Syverson, 54 Iowa 162, 6 N. W. 178; Scott v. Mewhirter, 49

true that, in cases where upon all the circumstances the mind is uncertain whether a security or a sale was intended, the courts, when
compelled to decide between them, will be somewhat guided by prudential considerations, and will consequently lean to the conclusion
that a security was meant, as more likely than a sale to subserve the
ends of abstract justice and avert injurious consequences. And where
the idea that a security was intended is conveyed with reasonable distinctness by the writings, and no evil practice or mistake appears, the
court will incline to regard the transaction as a security rather than a
sale, because in such a case the general reasons which favor written
evidence concur with the reason just suggested."[80]

Chief Justice Marshall, in setting forth the reason for the rule, says:
"Lenders of money are less under the pressure of circumstances which
control the perfect and free exercise of the judgment than borrowers;
the effort is frequently made by persons of this description to avail
themselves of the advantage of this superiority, in order to obtain inequitable advantages. For this reason the leaning of courts has been
against them, and doubtful cases have generally been decided to be
mortgages. * * * A conditional sale made in such a situation, at
a price bearing no proportion to the value of the property, would bring
suspicion on the whole transaction."[81]

Iowa 487; Hughes v. Sheaff, 19
Iowa 335; Trucks v. Lindsey, 18
Iowa 504; Jenkins v. Stewart
(Ky.) 16 S. W. 356; Reed v. Reed,
75 Maine 264; Baugher v. Merryman,
32 Md. 185; Artz v. Grove, 21 Md.
456; Dougherty v. McColgan, 6 Gill
& J. (Md.) 275; Cornell v. Hall, 22
Mich. 377; McKinney v. Miller, 19
Mich. 142; Holton v. Meighen, 15
Minn. 69; Freeman v. Wilson, 51
Miss. 329; King v. Greves, 42 Mo.
App. 168; Gassert v. Bogk, 7 Mont.
585, 19 Pac. 281; Mooney v. Byrne,
163 N. Y. 86, 57 N. E. 163; Mat-
thews v. Sheehan, 69 N. Y. 585;
Brown v. Dewey, 2 Barb. (N. Y.)
28; Horn v. Keltetas, 42 How. Pr.
(N. Y.) 138; Robinson v. Cropsey,
6 Paige (N. Y.) 480; Glover v.
Payne, 19 Wend. (N. Y.) 518; Poin-
dexter v. McCannon, 1 Dev. Eq. (N.
Car.) 377, 18 Am. Dec. 591; Smith
v. Hoff, 23 N. Dak. 37, 135 N. W.
772, Ann. Cas. 1914C, 1072; Kinney
v. Smith, 58 Ore. 158, 113 Pac. 854

(citing text); Elliott v. Bozorth, 52
Ore. 391, 97 Pac. 632; Stephens v.
Allen, 11 Ore. 188, 3 Pac. 168; Fee
v. Cobine, 11 Ir. Eq. 406; Eglauch
v. Labadie, Rap. Jud. Que. 21 C. S.
481. "A resort, however, to a formal conditional sale, as a device to
defeat the equity of redemption,
will, of course, when shown, be unavailing for that purpose. And the
possibility of such resort, together
with other considerations, has
driven courts of equity to adopt as
a rule that, when it is doubtful
whether the transaction is a conditional sale or a mortgage, it will
be held to be the latter." Trucks v.
Lindsey, 18 Iowa 504, per Cole, J.
See also Reed v. Reed, 75 Maine
264.

[80] Cornell v. Hall, 22 Mich. 377,
per Graves, J. See also Sowles v.
Wilcox, 127 Mich. 77, 86 N. W. 689.

[81] Conway v. Alexander, 7 Cranch
(U. S.) 218, 3 L. ed. 321.

§ 279a. Trend of decisions.—The authorities have not been in full accord upon the question whether, in a doubtful case, the court should presume that the deed was intended to be an absolute conveyance or a mortgage; yet the trend of the decisions seems to be to the effect that the party claiming that a deed was intended as a mortgage should establish that fact by clear and convincing evidence, and slight or indefinite evidence will not be permitted to change the character of the instrument from what it appears on its face to be, into a mortgage. The rule may be stated to be, that the evidence offered to show that a deed was intended as a mortgage should be satisfactory, and sufficient to overcome the strong presumption created by the language of the deed—that it is what it purports to be, an absolute conveyance—and where the evidence is doubtful and unsatisfactory, the deed must be held to be absolute.[82] Some authorities go so far as to say that the proof that a mortgage was intended must leave no room for a reasonable or substantial doubt.[83]

[82] Cadman v. Peter, 118 U. S. 73, 30 L. ed. 78; Coyle v. Davis, 116 U. S. 108, 29 L. ed. 583; Howland v. Blake, 97 U. S. 624, 24 L. ed. 1027; Satterfield v. Malone, 35 Fed. 445, 1 L. R. A. 35; Glass v. Hieronymus, 125 Ala. 140, 28 So. 71, 82 Am. St. 225; Downing v. Woodstock Iron Co., 93 Ala. 262, 9 So. 177; Knaus v. Dreher, 84 Ala. 319, 4 So. 287; Williams v. Cheatham, 19 Ark. 278; Mahoney v. Bostwick, 96 Cal. 53, 30 Pac. 1020, 31 Am. St. 175; Henley v. Hotaling, 41 Cal. 22; Perot v. Cooper, 17 Colo. 80, 28 Pac. 391, 31 Am. St. 258; Armor v. Spalding, 14 Colo. 302, 23 Pac. 789; Adams v. Adams, 51 Conn. 544; Matthews v. Porter, 16 Fla. 466; Heaton v. Gaines, 198 Ill. 479, 64 N. E. 1081; Williams v. Williams, 180 Ill. 361, 54 N. E. 229; Burgett v. Osborne, 172 Ill. 227, 50 N. E. 206; Strong v. Strong, 126 Ill. 301, 18 N. E. 665, affg. 27 Ill. App. 148; Helm v. Boyd, 124 Ill. 370, 16 N. E. 85; Bailey v. Bailey, 115, Ill. 551, 4 N. E. 394; Conwell v. Evill, 4 Blackf. (Ind.) 67; Langer v. Merservey, 80 Iowa 158, 45 N. W. 732; Wright v. Mahaffey, 79 Iowa 96, 40 N. W. 112 Ensminger v. Ensminger, 75 Iowa 89, 39 N. W. 208, 9 Am. St. 462; Allen v. Fogg, 66 Iowa 229, 23 N. W. 643; Knight v. McCord, 63 Iowa 429, 19 N. W. 310 Kibby v. Harsh, 61 Iowa 196, 16 N. W. 85; Hyatt v. Cochran, 37 Iowa 309; Knapp v. Bailey, 79 Maine 195, 9 Atl. 122, 1 Am. St. 295; Faringer v. Ramsey, 2 Md. 365; Tilden v. Streeter, 45 Mich. 533, 8 N. W. 502; Johnson v. Van Velsor, 43 Mich. 208, 5 N. W. 265; Williams v. Stratton, 10 Sm. & M. (Miss.) 418; Cobb v. Day, 106 Mo. 278, 17 S. W. 323 Pierce v. Traver, 13 Nev. 526; Bingham v. Thompson, 4 Nev. 224; Wilson v. Parshall, 129 N. Y. 223, 29 N. E. 297; Erwin v. Curtis, 43 Hun (N. Y.) 292, 6 N. Y. St. 116; Holmes v. Grant, 8 Paige (N. Y.) 243; Hinton v. Pritchard, 107 N. Car. 128, 12 S. E. 242, 10 L. R. A. 401; McNair v. Pope, 100 N. Car. 404, 6 S. E. 234; Moore v. Ivey, 43 N. Car. 192; Albany &c. Canal Co. v. Crawford, 11 Ore. 243, 4 Pac. 113; Pancake v. Cauffman, 114 Pa. St. 113, 7 Atl. 67; in re Lance's Appeal, 112 Pa. St. 456, 4 Atl. 375; Logne's Appeal, 104 Pa. St. 136; in re Hartley's Appeal, 103 Pa. St. 23; Edwards v. Wall, 79 Va. 321; Kerr v. Hill, 27 W. Va. 576; Hunter v. Maanum, 78 Wis. 656, 48 N. W. 51; McCormick v. Herndon, 67 Wis. 648, 31 N. W. 303; Schriber v. Le Clair, 66 Wis. 579, 29 N. W. 570; Butler v. Butler, 46 Wis. 430, 1 N. W. 70.

[83] Townsend v. Peterson, 12 Colo. 491, 21 Pac. 619; A. J. Dwyer Pine

§ 280. **Rule applied to assignments.**—The same considerations as to determining the character of the transaction apply to an assignment of a mortgage, accompanied by an agreement to reassign within a time mentioned. In Henry v. Davis[84] the Chancellor said: "It is clearly established by the answer and proofs that the bond and mortgage were assigned by the plaintiff to the defendant by way of mortgage, to secure the payment of $225 by a given day; and any agreement that the assignment was to be an absolute sale, without redemption upon default of payment on the day, was unconscientious, oppressive, illegal, and void. The equity of redemption still existed in the plaintiff, notwithstanding any such agreement." The same considerations apply also to an assignment of a lease made in connection with an agreement to reassign, and to the determination of the question whether they constitute a mortgage or a conditional sale of the leasehold estate.[85] But an absolute lease is not deemed a mortgage because the rent is to go in satisfaction of a debt.[86]

§ 281. **Mortgage distinguished from a trust.**—A mortgage or a trust deed in the nature of a mortgage differs from a trust, in that in a mortgage or a trust in the nature of a mortgage the property is to revert or be conveyed to the grantor upon the payment of the debt secured.[87] A mortgage is created by an instrument conveying land to a trustee to secure a note executed by the grantor to such trustee, and providing for foreclosure on default.[88]

It is the purport of several Maryland decisions that where a conveyance is made to the grantee as security for a loan to a third party, who is the real purchaser, a resulting trust is established in his favor, and the transaction is substantially a mortgage.[89]

A declaration of trust made by one to whom a conveyance was made,

Land Co. v. Whiteman, 92 Minn. 55, 99 N. W. 362; Gerhardt v. Tucker, 187 Mo. 46, 85 S. W. 552; Farmers' &c. Bank v. Smith, 61 App. Div. 315, 70 N. Y. S. 536; Shattuck v. Bascom, 55 Hun (N. Y.) 14, 9 N. Y. S. 934, 28 N. Y. St. 333; Little v. Braun, 11 N. Dak. 410, 92 N. W. 800; Jasper v. Hazen, 4 N. Dak. 1, 51 N. W. 583; Beebe v. Wisconsin Mtg. Loan Co,. 117 Wis. 328, 93 N. W. 1103; Becker v. Howard, 75 Wis. 415, 44 N. W. 755; McCormick v. Herndon, 67 Wis. 648, 31 N. W. 303.

[84] Henry v. Davis, 7 Johns. Ch.

(N. Y.) 40. See also Warren v. Emerson, 1 Curtis (U. S.) 239.

[85] Polhemus v. Trainer, 30 Cal. 685. See also King v. King, 3 P. Wms. 358; Goodman v. Grierson, 2 Ball & B. 274.

[86] Halo v. Schick, 57 Pa. St. 319.

[87] Neikirk v. Boulder Nat. Bank, 53 Colo. 350, 127 Pac. 137; Hoffman v. Mackall, 5 Ohio St. 124, 64 Am. Dec. 637; In re Lance's Appeal, 112 Pa. St. 456, 4 Atl. 375.

[88] Brown v. Hall, 32 S. Dak. 225, 142 N. W. 854.

[89] Miller v. Miller, 101 Md. 600, 61 Atl. 210; Pickett v. Wadlow, 94

upon his advancing money for the benefit of one having an agreement for the purchase of the land, may be treated, in connection with the conveyance, as a mortgage rather than a trust.[90] A debtor conveyed all his real estate to one of his creditors by an absolute deed, the creditor making a declaration of trust that he would sell the property, pay the debt due himself, and sums to be advanced by him for the payment of other debts of the grantor, and after retaining a certain sum for commissions would reconvey what might remain of the property to the grantor. The transaction was adjudged to be a mortgage, and not an assignment for the benefit of creditors, so that no one but the grantor could call upon the grantee to account.[91] The equity of redemption

Md. 567, 51 Atl. 423; Hopper v. Smyser, 90 Md. 363, 45 Atl. 206; Dryden v. Hanway, 31 Md. 254, 100 Am. Dec. 61; Dougherty v. McColgan, 6 Gill & J. (Md.) 275.

[90] Brumfield v. Boutall, 24 Hun (N. Y.) 451. See also Stewart v. Fellows, 128 Ill. 480, 17 N. E. 476; Stephens v. Allen, 11 Ore. 188, 3 Pac. 168.

[91] Vance v. Lincoln, 38 Cal. 586; Koch v. Briggs, 14 Cal. 256, 73 Am. Dec. 651; Turpie v. Lowe, 114 Ind. 37, 15 N. E. 834; Comstock v. Stewart, Walk. (Mich.) 110; Gothainer v. Grigg, 32 N. J. Eq. 567; Hoffman v. Mackall, 5 Ohio St. 124, 64 Am. Dec. 637; Woodruff v. Robb, 19 Ohio 212; Taylor v. Cornelius, 60 Pa. St. 187; Myer's Appeal, 42 Pa. St. 518; Chambers v. Goldwin, 5 Ves. 834; Bell v. Carter, 17 Beav. 11; Jenkin v. Row, 5 De G. & S. 107. The fact that an instrument contains no provision for restoring the title to the grantor, but provides that the grantee may sell at his discretion, is somewhat inconsistent with the theory of a mortgage; for in mortgages the defeasance ordinarily provides that, upon payment of the debt, title to the premises incumbered shall revert to the mortgagor. Armor v. Spalding, 14 Colo. 302, 23 Pac. 789.

In In re Lance's Appeal, 112 Pa. St. 456, 4 Atl. 375, the court say that a mortgage is distinguishable from a trust in this only, that the property in it is to revert to the mortgagor on the discharge of the obligation for the performance of which it is pledged. In Hoffman v. Mackall, 5 Ohio St. 124, 64 Am. Dec. 637, the court say: "A mortgage is a conveyance of an estate, or pledge of property as security for the payment of money, or the performance of some other act, and conditioned to become void upon such payment or performance. A deed of trust in the nature of a mortgage is a conveyance in trust by way of security, subject to a condition of defeasance or redemption at any time before the sale of the property. A deed conveying land to a trustee as mere collateral security for the payment of a debt, with the condition that it shall become void on the payment of the debt when due, and with power to the trustee to sell the land and pay the debt in case of default on the part of the debtor, is a deed of trust in the nature of a mortgage. By an absolute deed of trust the grantor parts absolutely with the title, which rests in the grantee, unconditionally, for the purpose of the trust. The latter is a conveyance to a trustee for the purpose of raising a fund to pay debts; while the former is a conveyance in trust for the purpose of securing a debt, subject to a condition of defeasance." A deed stated that it was given to indemnify the grantor's sureties on a certain bond, payable at her death, and to save them from pecuniary harm, conveyed "in trust, however, as aforesaid, to the intent" that the beneficiaries "shall have possession, exclusive control and management of the lots, and be entitled to all the profits and rents";

was still subject to attachment by the creditors of the grantor. But a conveyance expressly in trust to pay debts, and after the debts are paid in trust for one of the grantors, was held not to be a mortgage,[92] and, therefore, the creditors could not maintain a suit for foreclosure or sale. In such a conveyance, a covenant on the part of the debtor to pay the debts would, doubtless, make a mortgage of it.[93]

A declaration of trust by a grantee, to the effect that the money to be paid by him belonged to certain creditors of the grantor, is not in the nature of a defeasance, and does not with the deed constitute a mortgage.[94]

and the trustee, at the death of the grantor or thereafter, as the beneficiaries may direct, shall "make and convey such title as is vested in him" to any person or persons whom the beneficiaries may designate. The instrument was held to be in the nature of a mortgage, and not an absolute conveyance. Fontainn v. Schulenburg &c. Lumber Co., 109 Mo. 55, 18 S. W. 1147. See further as to the distinction between a mortgage and a trust. Turpie v. Lowe, 114 Ind. 37, 15 N. E. 834. See also Catlett v. Starr, 70 Tex. 485, 7 S. W. 844.

[92] Charles v. Clagett, 3 Md. 82; McMenomy v. Murray, 3 Johns. Ch. (N. Y.) 435; Ladd v. Johnson, 32 Ore. 195, 49 Pac. 756; Marvin v. Titsworth, 10 Wis. 320. The latter case citing, as to distinction between a trust and a mortgage, Flagg v. Walker, 113 U. S. 659, 28 L. ed. 1072, 5 Sup. Ct. 697. Title Guarantee &c. Co. v. Northern Counties Inv. Trust, 73 Fed. 931; Turner v. Watkins, 31 Ark. 429; Soutter v. Miller, 15 Fla. 625; Newman v. Samuels, 17 Iowa 528; McDonald v. Kellogg, 30 Kans. 170, 2 Pac. 507; Hoffman v. Mackall, 5 Ohio St. 124, 64 Am. Dec. 637; Woodruff v. Robb, 19 Ohio 212; Kinney v. Heatley, 13 Ore. 35, 7 Pac. 359; Catlett v. Starr, 70 Tex. 485, 7 S. W. 844.

[93] Taylor v. Emerson, 4 Dr. & War. 117; Holmes v. Matthews, 3 Eq. 450. See also Pemberton v. Simmons, 100 N. Car. 316, 6 S. E. 122.

[94] Frick's Appeal, 87 Pa. St. 327.

CHAPTER VIII

PAROL EVIDENCE TO PROVE AN ABSOLUTE DEED A MORTGAGE

I. *The Grounds Upon Which it is Admitted,* §§ 282-323

II. *What Facts are Considered,* §§ 323a-342d

I. *The Grounds Upon Which it is Admitted*

§ 282. Grounds for admission in equity—Parol evidence inadmissible at law.—It is a settled rule and practice of courts of equity to set aside a formal deed, and allow the grantor to redeem upon proof, even by parol evidence, that the conveyance was not a sale, but merely a security for a debt, and therefore a mortgage. Except where, as in New Hampshire and Georgia, the exercise of this power is prohibited by statute, there is probably now no dissent anywhere from the doctrine that in equity a deed may be converted into a mortgage whenever there are proper equitable grounds for the exercise of the power. To this extent there is substantial uniformity in the decisions of the courts of the United States and of the several states. But as to the grounds upon which this equitable power is exercised there is much diversity of opinion, and there is also considerable diversity of adjudication in the application of the doctrine. Under what circumstances and upon what evidence this power shall be exercised, it is only reasonable to expect considerable divergence of practice in different courts. The cases in which the courts have been called upon to receive parol evidence to show that a deed absolute in terms is a mortgage are very numerous. For these reasons, and because the subject is of much practical importance, a statement of the various grounds upon which such evidence is admitted in each of the several states is given in the following sections.

At law it is generally agreed that parol evidence to show that a deed absolute on its face was intended only as a mortgage is inadmissible.[1] However, in California,[2] Illinois,[3] Iowa,[4] Pennsylvania, Texas,[5] and Wisconsin[6] such evidence is admissible at law.

Parol evidence is admissible in equity to show that a deed absolute in form is in fact a mortgage, not because the rules of evidence are different in equity from what they are at law, but because the jurisdiction and power of the courts with reference to dealing with the facts presented are different. The rules of evidence are the same in both courts. The question whether an absolute deed was intended to operate as a mortgage is one which belongs exclusively to equity tri-

[1] Bragg v. Massie, 38 Ala. 89, 69 Am. Dec. 82; Benton v. Jones, 8 Conn. 186; Reading v. Weston, 8 Conn. 117; Thompson v. Burns, 15 Idaho 572, 99 Pac. 111 (citing text); Finlon v. Clark, 118 Ill. 32, 7 N. E. 475; Farley v. Goocher, 11 Iowa 570; More v. Wade, 8 Kans. 380; Staton v. Commonwealth, 2 Dana (Ky.) 397; Bailey v. Knapp, 79 Maine 205, 9 Atl. 356; Stinchfield v. Milliken, 71 Maine 567; Bryant v. Crosby, 36 Maine 562, 58 Am. Dec. 767; Thomaston Bank v. Stimpson, 21 Maine 195; Gates v. Sutherland, 76 Mich. 231, 42 N. W. 1112; Jones v. Blake, 33 Minn. 362; Belote v. Morrison, 8 Minn. 87; McClane v. White, 5 Minn. 178; Hogel v. Lindell, 10 Mo. 483; Webb v. Rice, 6 Hill (N. Y.) 219; Taylor v. Baldwin, 10 Barb. (N. Y.) 582; Billings-

ley v. Stutler, 52 W. Va. 92, 43 S. E. 96. See article 13 West Jur. 193, fully examining this subject. See ante § 277. But see Swart v. Service, 21 Wend. (N. Y.) 36, 34 Am. Dec. 211.

[2] Jackson v. Lodge, 36 Cal. 28; Cunningham v. Hawkins, 27 Cal. 603, 85 Am. Dec. 73. See post § 288.

[3] Northern Assur. Co. v. Chicago Mut. Bldg. &c. Assn., 198 Ill. 474, 64 N. E. 979; Tillson v. Moulton, 23 Ill. 648; Miller v. Thomas, 14 Ill. 428; Coates v. Woodworth, 13 Ill. 654.

[4] McAnnulty v. Seick, 59 Iowa 586, 13 N. W. 743.

[5] In Pennsylvania, and Texas, there are no chancery courts, and this evidence is admitted at law. See post §§ 312, 316.

[6] Barchent v. Snyder, 128 Wis. 423, 107 N. W. 329. See post § 320.

bunals, and over which common-law tribunals have no jurisdiction whatever.[7] This distinction is not observed, however, in those courts which exercise both legal and equitable jurisdiction, and in which both legal and equitable defenses may be interposed in the same action.[8]

§ 283. **Equitable grounds—Transfers to defraud creditors.**—To obtain relief the plaintiff must have equitable grounds for it. The grounds on which courts of equity admit oral evidence, to show that a deed absolute in form is in fact a mortgage, are purely equitable, and relief is refused whenever the equitable consideration is wanting.[9] Therefore, when a debtor has made an absolute conveyance of his land to one creditor for the purpose of defrauding his other creditors, he is in no condition to ask a court of equity to interfere actively in his behalf to help him get his land back again, and thus secure to him the fruits of his fraudulent devices.[10] "One who comes for relief into a court whose proceedings are intended to reach the conscience of the parties must first have that standard applied to his own conduct in the transactions out of which his grievance arises. If that condemns himself, he can not insist upon applying it to the other party."[11] An oral agreement between the debtor and the creditor who took the conveyance, whereby the latter agreed to reconvey the land upon payment of the debt due him, is not deemed in such case an equitable ground for relief. The court will interfere only for the benefit of those whom the debtor intended to defraud. It is true that a grantee, whose rights were not infringed, can not set up the grantor's fraud against other creditors in the conveyance, to defeat any legal claim or interest which the fraudulent debtor may seek to enforce. But the difficulty is, that when the debtor has no legal right, but comes into equity seeking relief, he has in such case no equitable standing, and must go out of court.

A fraudulent grantor will not be aided in redeeming his absolute conveyance as being a mortgage only. Thus, if he has executed such conveyance to his creditor to secure a debt to the latter, and at the same time to hinder and delay other creditors, an oral agreement of the grantee to reconvey the land to the grantor on payment of the

[7] Stinchfield v. Milliken, 71 Maine 567; Foley v. Kirk, 33 N. J. Eq. 170; See also Calahan v. Dunker, 51 Ind. App. 436, 99 N. E. 1021.

[8] Wakefield v. Day, 41 Minn. 344, 43 N. W. 71; Despard v. Walbridge, 15 N. Y. 374; Webb v. Rice, 6 Hill (N. Y.) 219.

[9] Fitch v. Miller, 200 Ill. 170, 65 N. E. 650.

[10] Hassam v. Barrett, 115 Mass. 256; Arnold v. Mattison, 3 Rich. Eq. (S. Car.) 153; Webber v. Farmer, 4 Bro. P. C. 170; Baldwin v. Cawthorne, 19 Ves. 166.

[11] Mr. Justice Wells, in Hassam v. Barrett, 115 Mass. 256. See also Ybarra v. Lorenzana, 53 Cal. 197; Parrott v. Baker, 82 Ga. 364, 9 S. E.

debt will not be enforced in equity.[12] The heirs of such grantor stand in no better position than he, with respect to a right to declare an absolute conveyance in form a mortgage in effect.[13]

But the rights of a widow in land conveyed by her husband in fee to a creditor to secure him, and to defraud other creditors, are not affected by such fraudulent intent, unless she was aware of and participated in the same; and, if she be innocent in the premises, the absolute conveyance will, as to her rights, be declared a mortgage.[14]

§ 284. **Grounds for admission of parol evidence under English decisions.**—The English decisions are to the effect that in equity an absolute conveyance may be construed to be a mortgage when the defeasance has been omitted by fraud or accident;[15] when the grantee has made a separate defeasance, although merely verbal;[16] or when by the payment of interest, or other circumstances, it appears that the conveyance was intended to be a mortgage.[17]

§ 285. **Doctrine in the United States Courts.**—The decisions of the Supreme Court of the United States, and the circuit and district courts, are uniform in admitting parol evidence to show that an absolute conveyance is in fact a mortgage.[18] The admission of such evi-

1068; Kitts v. Wilson, 130 Ind. 492, 29 N. E. 401 (quoting text).

[12] Kitts v. Willson, 130 Ind. 492, 29 N. E. 401; Henry v. Stevens, 108 Ind. 281, 9 N. E. 356; Edwards v. Haverstick, 53 Ind. 348; Sweet v. Tinslar, 52 Barb. (N. Y.) 271; Bolt v. Rogers, 3 Paige (N. Y.) 154.

[13] Kitts v. Willson, 130 Ind. 492, 29 N. E. 401; Wilson v. Campbell, 119 Ind. 286, 290, 21 N. E. 893; Springer v. Drosch, 32 Ind. 486; Laney v. Laney, 2 Ind. 196; Moseley v. Moseley, 15 N. Y. 334; Stewart v. Ackley, 52 Barb. (N. Y.) 283; Patnode v. Darveau, 112 Mich. 127, 70 N. W. 439; Gorrell v. Alspaugh, 120 N. Car. 362, 27 S. E. 85; Battle v. Street, 85 Tenn. 282, 2 S. W. 284.

[14] Kitts v. Willson, 130 Ind. 492, 29 N. E. 401.

[15] Maxwell v. Mountacute, Prec. Ch. 526; Card v. Jaffray, 2 Sch. & Lef. 374; England v. Codrington, 1 Eden 169; Dixon v. Parker, 2 Ves. Sen. 219, per Lord Hardwicke; Irnham v. Child, 1 Bro. C. C. 92; Portmore v. Morris, 2 Bro. C. C. 219; Lincoln v. Wright, 4 De G. & J. 16.

[16] Manlove v. Bale, 2 Vern. 84; Lincoln v. Wright, 4 De G. & J. 16; Whitfield v. Parfitt, 15 Jur. 852.

[17] Allenby v. Dalton, 5 L. J. K. B. 312; Cripps v. Jee, 4 Bro. C. C. 472; Sevier v. Greenway, 19 Ves. 413.

[18] Risher v. Smith, 131 U. S. clvi, 24 L. ed. 808; Peugh v. Davis, 96 U. S. 332, 24 L. ed. 775; Amory v. Lawrence, 3 Cliff. (U. S.) 523; Andrews v. Hyde, 3 Cliff. (U. S.) 516; Wyman v. Babcock, 2 Curtis (U. S.) 386; Babcock v. Wyman, 19 How. (U. S.) 289, 15 L. ed. 644; Russell v. Southard, 12 How. (U. S.) 139, 13 L. ed. 627; Morris v. Nixon, 1 How. (U. S.) 118, 11 L. ed. 69; Sprigg v. Bank of Mount Pleasant, 14 Pet. (U. S.) 201, 10 L. ed. 419; Sprigg v. Bank, 1 McLean (U. S.) 384, affd. 14 Pet. 201, 10 L. ed. 419; Eldredge v. Jenkins, 3 Story (U. S.) 181; Flagg v. Mann, 2 Sumn. (U. S.) 486; Taylor v. Luther, 2 Sumn. (U. S.) 228; Hughes v. Edwards, 9 Wheat. (U. S.) 489, 6 L. ed. 142; Bentley v. Phelps, 2 Wood. & M. (U. S.) 426; Nicholson v. Hayes, 174 Fed. 653, 98 C. C. A. 407; Lewis v. Wells, 85 Fed. 896; Villa v. Rodriguez, Fed. Cas. No. 172, revg. 12 Wall. (U. S.) 323. See also Jackson v. Lawrence, 117 U. S. 679, 29 L. ed. 1024, 6 Sup. Ct. 915.

dence is not limited to cases in which express deceit or fraud in taking the conveyance in that form is shown. It is admitted where the instrument of defeasance has been "omitted by design upon mutual confidence between the parties." It is admitted to show the real intention of the parties, and the real nature of the transaction. It is admitted even in cases where the person taking an absolute deed had expressed at the time his unwillingness to accept a mortgage.[19] In Russell v. Southard[19a] the Supreme Court declared that when it is alleged and proved that a loan was really intended, and the grantee sets up the loan as a payment of purchase-money, and the conveyance as a sale, both fraud and a vice in the consideration are sufficiently averred and proved to require a court of equity to hold the transaction to be a mortgage; and that, whenever the transaction is in substance a loan of money upon security of the land conveyed, a court of equity is bound to look through the forms in which the contrivance of the lender has enveloped it, and declare the conveyance to be a mortgage. In the case of Peugh v. Davis[20] the court also declare that as the equity, upon which the court acts in such cases, arises from the real character of the transaction, any evidence, written or oral, tending to show this, is admissible. The evidence must be clear, unequivocal and convincing,[21] and must leave no substantial doubt of the intent to create a mortgage.[22]

§ 286. **Alabama.**—In Alabama a court of equity will not by parol evidence establish a deed absolute on its face as a mortgage "unless the proofs are clear, consistent, and convincing" that it was not intended as an absolute purchase, but was intended as a security for money.[23] Such evidence seems by the earlier cases to have been ad-

---

[19] Williams v. Chadwick, 74 Conn. 252, 50 Atl. 720; Mills v. Mills, 26 Conn. 213; Susman v. Whyard, 149 N. Y. 127, 43 N. E. 413.

[19a] 12 How. (U. S.) 139, 13 L. ed. 627.

[20] Peugh v. Davis, 96 U. S. 332. See also Risher v. Smith, 131 U. S. App. 156; Horbach v. Hill, 112 U. S. 144, 5 Sup. Ct. 81.

[21] Campbell v. Northwest Eckington Imp. Co., 229 U. S. 561, 57 L. ed. 1330, 33 Sup. Ct. 796; Wallace v. Johnstone, 129 U. S. 58, 32 L. ed. 619, 9 Sup. Ct. 243; Coyle v. Davis, 116 U. S. 108, 6 Sup. Ct. 314; Conway v. Alexander, 7 Cranch (U. S.) 218, 3 L. ed. 321; Guarantee Gold Bond Loan &c. Co. v. Edwards, 164 Fed. 809.

[22] Wallace v. Johnstone, 129 U. S. 58, 32 L. ed. 619, 9 Sup. Ct. 243; Conway v. Alexander, 7 Cranch (U. S.) 218, 3 L. ed. 321.

[23] Harrison v. Maury, 157 Ala. 227, 47 So. 724; Thornton v. Pinckard, 157 Ala. 206, 47 So. 289; Rodgers v. Burt, 157 Ala. 91, 47 So. 226; Johnson v. Hattaway, 155 Ala. 516, 46 So. 760; Jones v. Kennedy, 138 Ala. 502, 35 So. 465; Rose v. Gandy, 137 Ala. 329, 34 So. 239; Glass v. Hieronymus, 125 Ala. 140, 28 So. 71, 82 Am. St. 225; Kramer v. Brown, 114 Ala. 612, 21 So. 817; Peagler v. Stabler, 91 Ala. 308, 9 So. 157; Knaus v. Dreher, 84 Ala. 319, 4 So. 287; Cosby v. Buchanan, 81 Ala. 574, 1 So. 898; Turner v. Wilkinson, 72 Ala. 361; Parks v. Parks,

mitted upon the ground of fraud, accident, or mistake,[24] but the later
cases admit parol evidence generally, to show the real character of the
transaction,[25] and that a deed absolute in form was intended to operate
as security for a debt.[26] Thus where an absolute deed of land is given
to enable the grantee to pay off a prior mortgage thereon it must be
clearly shown that the grantee as well as the grantor intended it to
operate as a mortgage.[27] It is in equity and not at law that parol
evidence is admissible in such cases.[28] Where the controversy is
whether the contract was a conditional sale or mortgage, oral testimony
will be resorted to in equity to ascertain what was in fact the contract
made by the parties, and if the court can not, upon a thorough consideration of the testimony say with reasonable satisfaction that the
writings evidence a conditional conveyance of the fee and were not
intended as a mortgage, then the court will lean toward the theory
that the writings were intended as a mortgage. This rule does not seem
to prevail where the controversy is whether the deed was in fact an
unconditional sale or was only intended as a mortgage to secure the
debt.[29]

To authorize the court to declare a deed absolute on its face to be
a mortgage, the evidence must be clear and satisfactory.[30] It is not

66 Ala. 326; Phillips v. Croft, 42 Ala.
477.

[24] Wells v. Morrow, 38 Ala. 125;
Crews v. Threadgill, 35 Ala. 334;
Parish v. Gates, 29 Ala. 254; West
v. Hendrix, 28 Ala. 226; Brantley
v. West, 27 Ala. 542; Locke v. Palmer, 26 Ala. 312; Bryan v. Cowart,
21 Ala. 92; Bishop v. Bishop, 13 Ala.
475; English v. Lane, 1 Port. (Ala.)
328.

[25] Morton v. Allen (Ala.), 60 So.
866; Richter v. Noll, 128 Ala. 198,
30 So. 740; Williams v. Reggan, 111
Ala. 621, 20 So. 614; Reeves v. Abercrombie, 108 Ala. 535, 19 So. 41;
Jordan v. Garner, 101 Ala. 411, 13
So. 678; Ingram v. Illges, 98 Ala.
511, 13 So. 548; Adams v. Pilcher,
92 Ala. 474, 8 So. 757; Vincent v.
Walker, 86 Ala. 333, 5 So. 465; Mc-
Millan v. Jewett, 85 Ala. 476, 5 So.
145; Knaus v. Dreher, 84 Ala. 319,
4 So. 287; Stoutz v. Bouse, 84 Ala.
309; 4 So. 170; Perdue v. Bell, 83
Ala. 396, 3 So. 698; Cosby v. Buchanan, 81 Ala. 574, 1 So. 898; Robinson v. Farrelly, 16 Ala. 472. The
Alabama Code of 1896, § 1041, providing that no parol trusts concern-

ing land can be created except by
implication of law, does not prevent
the introduction of parol evidence
to show that a deed absolute on its
face was intended as a mortgage.
Glass v. Hieronymus, 125 Ala. 140,
28 So. 71, 82 Am. St. 225.

[26] Rodgers v. Burt, 157 Ala. 91, 47
So. 226; Johnson v. Hattaway, 155
Ala. 516, 46 So. 760; Shreve v. Mc-
Gowin, 143 Ala. 665, 42 So. 94.

[27] Thornton v. Pinckard, 157 Ala.
206, 47 So. 289.

[28] Morton v. Allen (Ala.), 60 So.
866; Rodgers v. Burt, 157 Ala. 91,
47 So. 226; Bragg v. Massie, 38 Ala.
89, 106, 79 Am. Dec. 82; Jones v.
Trawick, 31 Ala. 253; Parish v.
Gates, 29 Ala. 254.

[29] Morton v. Allen (Ala.), 60 So.
866. See also Irwin v. Coleman, 173
Ala. 175, 55 So. 492.

[30] Tribble v. Singleton, 158 Ala.
308, 48 So. 481; Harper v. T. N.
Hays Co., 149 Ala. 174, 43 So. 360;
Rose v. Gandy, 137 Ala. 329, 34 So.
239; Glass v. Hieronymus, 125 Ala.
140, 28 So. 71, 82 Am. St. 225; Kramer v. Brown, 114 Ala. 612, 21 So.
817.

sufficient to raise merely a doubt whether the instrument speaks the intention of the parties. The court must be satisfied by at least a clear preponderance of the evidence that a mortgage was intended and clearly understood by the grantee as well as the grantor. This severe rule does not apply in cases where the writings express a conditional sale, or where it is admitted that there was a contemporaneous agreement different from that expressed in the instrument.[31] The law is well settled, that "in a court of equity, the character of the conveyance must be determined by the clear and certain intention of the parties; and if there be an agreement between them that it shall operate as a security for a debt, it can and will operate only as a mortgage. The agreement may be expressed in the deed, or in a separate writing, or it may rest in parol."[32]

§ 286a. **Arizona.**—By statute in Arizona, every transfer of real property, other than a trust, made only as security for the performance of another act, is to be deemed a mortgage, and the fact that a transfer was made subject to defeasance may be proved by parol, except as against a subsequent purchaser or incumbrancer without notice, though the fact does not appear by the terms of the instrument.[33] In admitting parol and extrinsic evidence, the court is not restricted to any particular kind of evidence, but may take into consideration almost any pertinent matters which tend to prove the real intention and understanding of the parties and the true nature of the transaction.[34]

§ 287. **Arkansas.**—In Arkansas parol evidence is admissible to show an absolute deed to be a mortgage.[35] The ground of its admission is stated in some of the cases to be fraud or mistake;[36] but in later cases it seems to be held generally admissible to show the intention of the parties, and the fact that the transaction was really a mortgage, intended as security.[37] Accordingly it is held that where land is conveyed as security, or where land is purchased at judicial sale under an

[31] Morton v. Allen (Ala.), 60 So. 866; Reeves v. Abercrombie, 108 Ala. 535, 19 So. 41.

[32] Harrison v. Maury, 157 Ala. 227, 47 So. 724, quoting Douglass v. Moody, 80 Ala. 61.

[33] Arizona Rev. Stat. 1913, §§ 4095, 4096.

[34] Rees v. Rhodes, 3 Ariz. 235, 73 Pac. 446.

[35] Rushton v. McIllvene, 88 Ark. 299, 114 S. W. 709; Reynolds. v. Blanks, 78 Ark. 527, 94 S. W. 694; Harmon v. May, 40 Ark. 146; Anthony v. Anthony, 23 Ark. 479; McCarron v. Cassidy, 18 Ark. 34; Scott v. Henry, 13 Ark. 112; Blakemore v. Byrnside, 7 Ark. 505; Johnson v. Clark, 5 Ark. 321.

[36] Jordan v. Fenno, 13 Ark. 593; Blakemore v. Byrnside, 7 Ark. 505.

[37] Harman v. May, 40 Ark. 146; Anthony v. Anthony, 23 Ark. 479.

agreement that the purchaser shall hold the title as security for money advanced the owner, the transaction constitutes a mortgage in equity, and the agreement may be proved by parol evidence, since it is not within the statute of frauds.[38]

In a recent case the court adopting the language of Mr. Pomeroy says: "The general doctrine is fully established, and certainly prevails in a great majority of the states, that the grantor and his representatives are always allowed in equity to show, by parol evidence, that a deed absolute on its face was only intended to be a security for the payment of a debt, and thus to be a mortgage, although the parties deliberately and knowingly executed the instrument in its existing form, and without any allegations of fraud, mistake, or accident in its mode of execution. The sure test and the essential requisite are the continued existence of a debt. If there is no indebtedness, the conveyance can not be a mortgage. If there is a debt existing, and the conveyance was intended to secure its payment, equity will regard and treat the absolute deed as a mortgage. The presumption, of course, arises that the instrument is what it purports on its face to be, an absolute conveyance of the land. To overcome this presumption, and to establish its character as a mortgage, the cases all agree that the evidence must be clear, unequivocal, and convincing, for otherwise the natural presumption will prevail."[39]

§ 288. California.—In California, parol evidence is admissible in law[40] as well as in equity[41] to show that a deed absolute upon its face was intended as a mortgage, and such evidence is not restricted to cases of fraud, accident, or mistake. If the evidence shows that the

[38] La Cotts v. La Cotts (Ark.), 159 S. W. 1111.

[39] Rushton v. McIlvene, 88 Ark. 299, 114 S. W. 709, citing Cadman v. Peter, 118 U. S. 73, 30 L. ed. 78, 6 Sup. Ct. 957; Coyle v. Davis, 116 U. S. 108, 29 L. ed. 583, 6 Sup. Ct. 314; Hays v. Emerson, 75 Ark. 551, 87 S. W. 1027; Harman v. May, 40 Ark. 146; Trieber v. Andrews, 31 Ark. 163; Williams v. Cheatham, 19 Ark. 278; 3 Pomeroy's Equity Jurisprudence (3d ed.), § 1196, and cases cited. See also, to the effect that the evidence must be clear, unequivocal and convincing: Ford v. Nunnelley (Ark.), 165 S. W. 291; Grummer v. Price, 101 Ark. 611, 143 S. W. 95; Prickett v. Williams (Ark.), 161 S. W. 1023; La Cotts v. La Cotts (Ark.), 159 S. W. 1111; Gates v. McPeace, 106 Ark. 583, 153 S. W. 797; Grismon v. Kingman Plow Co., 106 Ark. 166, 152 S. W. 989; Edwards'v. Bond, 105 Ark. 314, 151 S. W. 243; Griffin v. Welch, 88 Ark. 336, 114 S. W. 710; Reynolds v. Blanks, 78 Ark. 527, 94 S. W. 694: That the evidence must be clear and decisive, see Harman v. May, 40 Ark. 146; Trieber v. Andrews, 31 Ark. 163; Williams v. Cheatham, 19 Ark. 278.

[40] Vance v. Lincoln, 38 Cal. 586; Jackson v. Lodge, 36 Cal. 28; Cunningham v. Hawkins, 27 Cal. 603.

[41] Todd v. Todd, 164 Cal. 255, 128 Pac. 413; Beckman v. Waters, 161 Cal. 581, 119 Pac. 922; Couts v. Winston, 153 Cal. 686, 96 Pac. 357; An-

deed was intended merely as security for the payment of a debt, it is a mortgage, "no matter how strong the language of the deed or any instrument accompanying it might be."[42] Notwithstanding the code provision that a mortgage can be created only by writing executed with the formalities required in a grant of real property, a deed absolute on its face may in equity be shown by parol evidence to have been intended as a mere mortgage, and the debt intended to be secured thereby, whether present or future, may also be shown by parol evidence, although not specified in the deed or in any contemporaneous writing.[43] Evidence of the circumstances and relations existing between the parties is admitted, not for the purpose of contradicting or varying the deed, but to establish an equity superior to its terms.[44] The deed must speak for itself, but the objects and purposes of the parties in executing the instrument may be inquired into. Fraud in the use of the deed is as much a ground for the interposition of equity as fraud in its creation. In Pierce v. Robinson,[45] Mr. Justice Field forcibly

---

glo-Californian Bank v. Cerf, 147 Cal. 384, 81 Pac. 1077; Holmes v. Warren, 145 Cal. 457, 78 Pac. 954; Woods v. Jensen, 130 Cal. 200, 62 Pac. 473; Ahern v. McCarthy, 107 Cal. 382, 40 Pac. 482; Malone v. Roy, 94 Cal. 341, 29 Pac. 712; Montgomery v. Spect, 55 Cal. 352; Vance v. Lincoln, 38 Cal. 586; Raynor v. Lyons, 37 Cal. 452; Gay v. Hamilton, 33 Cal. 686; Cal. Civ. Code §2924.

[42] Todd v. Todd, 164 Cal. 255, 128 Pac. 413; Woods v. Jensen, 130 Cal. 200, 62 Pac. 473.

[43] Cal. Civ. Code § 2922; Anglo-Californian Bank v. Cerf, 147 Cal. 384, 81 Pac. 1077.

[44] Ahern v. McCarthy, 107 Cal. 382, 40 Pac. 482; Locke v. Moulton, 96 Cal. 21, 30 Pac. 957; Husheon v. Husheon, 71 Cal. 407, 12 Pac. 410; Arnot v. Baird (Cal.), 12 Pac. 386.

[45] Pierce v. Robinson, 13 Cal. 116, overruling the earlier cases of Lee v. Evans, 8 Cal. 424, and Low v. Henry, 9 Cal. 538, restricting such evidence to cases of fraud, accident or mistake. In further illustration of the reason of the rule, the learned judge says: "Unless parol evidence can be admitted, the policy of the law will be constantly evaded. Debtors, under the force of pressing necessities, will submit to almost any exactions for loans of a trifling amount compared with the value of the property, and the equity of redemption will elude the grasp of the court, and rest in a simple good faith of the creditor. A mortgage, as I have observed, is in form a conveyance of the conditional estate, and the assertion of a right to redeem from a forfeiture involves the same departure from the terms of the instrument as in the case of an absolute conveyance executed as security. The conveyance upon condition by its terms purports to vest the entire estate upon the breach of the condition, just as the absolute conveyance does in the first instance. The equity arises and is asserted in both cases upon exactly the same principles, and is enforced without reference to the agreement of the parties, but from the nature of the transaction to which the right attaches, from the policy of the law, as an inseparable incident." See also Garwood v. Wheaton, 128 Cal. 399, 60 Pac. 961; Blair v. Squire, 127 Cal. xviii, 59 Pac. 211; Murdock v. Clarke, 90 Cal. 427, 27 Pac. 275; Butler v. Hyland, 89 Cal. 575, 26 Pac. 1108; Hall v. Arnott, 80 Cal. 348, 22 Pac. 200; Brison v. Brison, 75 Cal. 525, 17 Pac. 689; Booth v. Hoskins, 75 Cal. 271, 17 Pac. 225; Raynor v. Drew, 72 Cal. 307, 13 Pac. 866; Healy v. O'Brien, 66 Cal. 517, 6 Pac. 386;

and clearly declares these to be the true grounds for the admission of parol evidence to show that a deed absolute in its terms is in fact a mortgage. Such a deed being a mortgage does not pass the title to the land.[46]

It is declared by statute that every transfer of an interest in real estate, other than in trust made only as a security for the performance of another act, is to be deemed a mortgage.[47] The fact that the transfer is made subject to defeasance may be proved, though it does not appear by the terms of the instrument. To show that an absolute deed was intended to be a mortgage in the absence of direct evidence, the evidence of intention must be clear and the fact can not be established merely by inferences and arguments.[48] The evidence must be clear, specific and decisive.[49]

Where the evidence is doubtful whether an instrument was intended as a mortgage or not, a subsequent reference to it as a mortgage, by the mortgagees, in a release, will be considered in determining the question.[50] It is also proper to admit in evidence a receipt given by the grantor to the grantee for money for a final payment upon the land, together with a contract between the parties whereby the grantee agreed to sell the land to the grantor for a certain price before a specified date.[51]

§ 288a. Colorado.—It is provided by statute in Colorado that a deed may be proved by oral testimony to be in effect a mortgage.[52] In

Taylor v. McLain, 64 Cal. 513, 2 Pac. 399; Montgomery v. Spect, 55 Cal. 352; Kuhn v. Rumpp, 46 Cal. 299; Farmer v. Grose, 42 Cal. 169; Vance v. Lincoln, 38 Cal. 586; Raynor v. Lyons, 37 Cal. 452; Jackson v. Lodge, 36 Cal. 28; Gay v. Hamilton, 33 Cal. 686; Hopper v. Jones, 29 Cal. 18; Cunningham v. Hawkins, 24 Cal. 403, 85 Am. Dec. 73; Lodge v. Turman, 24 Cal. 385; Johnson v. Sherman, 15 Cal. 287, 76 Am. Dec. 481.

[46] Moisant v. McPhee, 92 Cal. 76, 28 Pac. 46; Fisher v. Witham, 132 Pa. St. 488, 19 Atl. 276.

[47] Cal. Civil Code, §§ 2924, 2925. Under this statute a deed executed as security for a debt, is a mortgage. Shirley v. All Night and Day Bank, 166 Cal. 50, 134 Pac. 1001; Peninsular Trade &c. Co. v. Pacific S. W. Co., 123 Cal. 689, 56 Pac. 604; Husheon v. Husheon, 71 Cal. 407, 12 Pac. 410.

[48] Falk v. Wittram, 120 Cal. 479, 52 Pac. 707, 65 Am. St. 184; Ahern v. McCarthy, 107 Cal. 382, 40 Pac. 482; Ganceart v. Henry, 98 Cal. 281, 33 Pac. 92; Henley v. Hotaling, 41 Cal. 22; Peres v. Crocker (Cal.), 47 Pac. 928; Meeker v. Shuster (Cal.), 47 Pac. 580.

[49] Renton v. Gibson, 148 Cal. 650, 84 Pac. 186; Penney v. Simmons, 99 Cal. 380, 33 Pac. 1121; Couts v. Winston, 153 Cal. 686, 96 Pac. 357 (clear, consistent, and convincing); Emery v. Lowe, 140 Cal. 379, 73 Pac. 981 (clear and satisfactory proof).

[50] Adams v. Hopkins, 144 Cal. 19, 77 Pac. 712.

[51] Holmes v. Warren, 145 Cal. 457, 78 Pac. 954.

[52] Code Civ. Proc. 1908, § 280; Davis v. Pursel (Colo.), 134 Pac. 107; Reitze v. Humphreys, 53 Colo. 177, 125 Pac. 518; Blackstock v. Robertson, 42 Colo. 472, 94 Pac. 336; Hall v. Linn, 8 Colo. 264, 5 Pac. 641; Quinn v. Kellogg, 4 Colo. App. 157,

this state the admission of parol evidence, in a proceeding to have deeds absolute on their face declared mortgages and to enforce an equity of redemption, is not subject to the objection that an interest in real property is sought to be created or established by parol.[53] The authorities generally hold that when the papers fail to recite the existance of a debt to be secured, and on their face purport otherwise, parol evidence may be resorted to, to show the intent of the parties and the true nature of the transaction; and if it appears that there was a loan and a debt resulting therefrom, the transaction will be declared to be a mortgage to secure such debt.[54]

The evidence in cases of this character must be not merely a preponderance in weight, but must be clear, certain and conclusive that the deed was executed, delivered and accepted as a mortgage.[55] Mere preponderance of evidence in favor of a party on whom the burden lies is not sufficient. In the language of the court in a comparatively recent case: "The proof must be clear, certain, satisfactory, unequivocal, trustworthy, and convincing, and some cases say, conclusive. In short, the case must be made out with that fulness and precision which is essential to a conviction in a criminal case—beyond a reasonable doubt."[56]

§ 289. Connecticut.—In Connecticut the court in one case seemed to regard it as an undecided question whether parol evidence is admissible to show that an absolute deed is a mortgage,[57] but in a later case it was held that an absolute deed, if intended as a security for a debt, is to be regarded as a mortgage.[58] In early cases it was held

35 Pac. 49. As to the evidence, see Davis v. Hopkins, 18 Colo. 153, 32 Pac. 70; Perot v. Cooper, 17 Colo. 80, 28 Pac. 391; Jefferson County Bank v. Hummell, 11 Colo. App. 337, 53 Pac. 286. See also Butsch v. Smith, 40 Colo. 64, 90 Pac. 61; Jefferson County Bank v. Hummell, 11 Colo. App. 337, 53 Pac. 286.

[53] Heron v. Weston, 44 Colo. 379, 100 Pac. 1130.

[54] Reitze v. Humphreys, 53 Colo. 177, 125 Pac. 518; Heron v. Weston, 44 Colo. 379, 100 Pac. 1130. Parol proof that the grantor by absolute deed was obliged to borrow the entire consideration for the deed, and obtain a surety to sign a note for the loan was admissible as a circumstance to be considered in determining the issue whether the deed was in fact a mortgage. Butsch v. Smith, 40 Colo. 64, 90 Pac. 61.

[55] Perot v. Cooper, 17 Colo. 80, 28 Pac. 391, 31 Am. St. 258.

[56] Baird v. Baird, 48 Colo. 506, 111 Pac. 79; Butsch v. Smith, 40 Colo. 64, 90 Pac. 61; Davis v. Hopkins, 18 Colo. 153, 32 Pac. 70; Perot v. Cooper, 17 Colo. 80, 28 Pac. 391, 31 Am. St. 258; Armor v. Spalding, 14 Colo. 302, 23 Pac. 789; Townsend v. Petersen, 12 Colo. 491, 21 Pac. 619; Bohm v. Bohm, 9 Colo. 100, 10 Pac. 790; Whitsett v. Kershow, 4 Colo. 419; Fetta v. Vandevier, 3 Colo. App. 419, 34 Pac. 168.

[57] Osgood v. Thompson Bank, 30 Conn. 27.

[58] Williams v. Chadwick, 74 Conn. 252, 50 Atl. 720; French v. Burns, 35 Conn. 359.

that such evidence was inadmissible in courts of law, either as between the parties or between third persons.[59] An absolute deed may be shown to be a mortgage by evidence from any paper signed by the grantee showing that the deed was given as security only.[60] In equity parol evidence seems to have been admitted to show that the defeasance was omitted by fraud or mistake.[61]

§ 290. **Delaware.**—A court of equity will treat a deed absolute in form as a mortgage, or a conveyance in trust for the payment of debts, if the parties in executing it intended it as a security. But where there was no deception, undue influence, or other fraudulent means employed to procure a deed absolute in form, the party relying upon parol evidence to prove that there was an agreement, understanding, or intention that the instrument should be in effect a mortgage or security for the payment of an indebtedness, must adduce clear and convincing proof.[62]

§ 290a. **District of Columbia.**—A deed absolute in form may be shown by parol evidence to have been intended as a security for money and will be so treated in equity as a mortgage.[63] A deed absolute in form will not be construed as a mortgage where the evidence is unsatisfactory and only sufficient to throw doubt on the transaction.[64]

§ 291. **Florida.**—In Florida it is provided by statute that all conveyances made with the intention of securing the payment of money shall be deemed mortgages.[65] Accordingly it has been held that an

---

[59] Benton v. Jones, 8 Conn. 186; Reading v. Weston, 8 Conn. 117, 20 Am. Dec. 97, 7 Conn. 143. See also Butler v. Catling, 1 Root (Conn.) 310. But see Brainerd v. Brainerd, 15 Conn. 575.

[60] Belton v. Avery, 2 Root (Conn.) 279, 1 Am. Dec. 70; French v. Lyon, 2 Root (Conn.) 69.

[61] French v. Burns, 35 Conn. 359; Collins v. Tillou, 26 Conn. 368, 38 Am. Dec. 398; Mills v. Mills, 26 Conn. 213; Jarvis v. Woodruff, 22 Conn. 548; Bacon v. Brown, 19 Conn. 29; Brainerd v. Brainerd, 15 Conn. 575; Washburn v. Merrills, 1 Day (Conn.) 139, 2 Am. Dec. 59; Daniels v. Alvord, 2 Root (Conn.) 196.

[62] Walker v. Farmers' Bank, 8 Houst. (Del.) 258, 14 Atl. 819. per Salisbury, Ch.; Hall v. Livingston, 3 Del. Ch. 348.

[63] Balloch v. Hooper, 6 Mack, (D. C.) 421; Hubbard v. Stetson, 3 MacArthur (D. C.) 113; Peugh v. Davis, 96 U. S. 332, 2 MacAr. (D. C.) 14; Nieman v. Mitchell, 2 App. (D. C.) 195.

[64] Hayward v. Mayse, 1 App. (D. C.) 133; Hubbard v. Stetson, 3 MacArthur (D. C.) 113.

[65] Gen. Stat. 1906, § 2494. Connor v. Connor, 59 Fla. 467, 52 So. 727; DeBartlett v. De Wilson, 52 Fla. 497, 42 So. 189; State First Nat. Bank v. Ashmead, 23 Fla. 379, 2 So. 657. An express agreement that a conveyance is not a mortgage but an absolute conveyance, which is wholly inconsistent with the facts of the case does not render absolute a conveyance which under the statute is shown to have been executed "for the purpose and with the

instrument must be deemed and held a mortgage, whatever may be its form, if, taken alone or in connection with the surrounding facts and attendant circumstances, it appears to have been given for the purpose or with the intention of securing the payment of money, and the mere absence of terms of defeasance can not determine whether it is a mortgage or not.[66] The statute does not change the rule as to the admission of parol evidence to show that a deed absolute on its face was intended as a mortgage; but some ground for equitable interference must be shown, such as fraud, accident, or mistake in the execution of the instrument.[67]

In a late case the court says that parol evidence is admissible in equity to show that an absolute deed was intended as a mortgage; that the court looks beyond the terms of the instrument to the real transaction; that any evidence tending to show this is admissible;[68] and that in case of doubt, the instrument will be held to be a mortgage.[69]

§ 292. **Georgia.**—In Georgia it is provided by statute that a deed absolute on its face, accompanied with possession of the property, shall not be proved, at the instance of the parties, by parol evidence, to be a mortgage only, unless fraud in its procurement is the issue to be

---

intention of securing the payment of money." Connor v. Connor, 59 Fla. 467, 52 So. 727. A deed absolute made with the intention of securing the payment of money is to be deemed merely a mortgage, and according to repeated decisions it may be enforced as a mortgage for the debt it was intended to secure, though no mention of the debt is made in the instrument itself, and the evidence of the debt rests in other writings or in parol only. Equitable Bldg. &c. Assn. v. King, 48 Fla. 252, 37 So. 181.

[66] Connor v. Connor, 59 Fla. 467, 25 So. 727.

[67] Matthews v. Porter, 16 Fla. 466; Chaires v. Brady, 10 Fla. 133; Lindsay v. Matthews, 17 Fla. 577. "This question," says Du Pont, C. J., in the latter case, "has been a fruitful source of litigation in the courts of the country, and there has been great diversity and contradiction in the adjudications of the several states constituting the late Union. In some of them, any evidence going to show the inten-

tion of the parties is admissible to fix the character of the instrument; while in others it is held that such evidence only as tends to show fraud, accident, mistake, or trust will be permitted. We are not aware that there has been any authoritative adjudication of the question in this state, and it is now presented to us as one of first impression. The theory upon which the former class of adjudications proceed is, that the fact of a deed being given as security determines its character, and not the evidence of the fact. Also, that parol evidence that a deed is a mortgage is not heard in contradiction of the deed, but in explanation of the transaction to prevent the perpetration of fraud by the mortgagee." See also Franklin v. Ayer, 22 Fla. 654; Walls v. Endel, 20 Fla. 86; Shear v. Robinson, 18 Fla. 379.

[68] Connor v. Connor, 59 Fla. 467, 52 So. 727; First Nat. Bank v. Ashmead, 23 Fla. 379, 2 So. 657.

[69] Connor v. Connor, 59 Fla. 467, 52 So. 727.

tried.[70] Such a deed passes the legal title, and enables the grantee to recover possession by ejectment, although a formal mortgage does not.[71] It may, nevertheless, be used as security for a debt.[72] "It does not follow, because a mortgage is only security, that every security is only a common mortgage."[73]

While parol evidence is inadmissible to convert an absolute deed into a mortgage, where possession has been surrendered to the grantee, the deed of a grantor remaining in possession may be proved by parol to be a mortgage.[74] A grantor in possession may defend his possession by pleading an equitable plea and doing equity; that is, tendering the debt and interest. When the deed has served its purpose, that is, when the debt is discharged, the facts having been established by competent evidence, the creditor will be compelled to reconvey.[75] He is treated as holding the title in trust for his debtor.[76] Evidence of the value of the property is material upon the issue whether a deed is an absolute conveyance or a mortgage.[77]

It is further provided by statute that an absolute conveyance of real property by deed to secure a debt, where the vendor takes a bond for reconveyance upon payment of such debt, shall pass the title to the vendee till the debt secured has been paid, and shall be held an absolute conveyance with the right reserved to the vendor to have the property reconveyed upon payment of the debt, and shall not operate as a

[70] Georgia Code 1911, § 3258; Hall v. Waller, 66 Ga. 483; Keith v. Catchings, 64 Ga. 773. See also Spence v. Steadman, 49 Ga. 133; New England Mtg. Sec. Co. v. Jarver, 60 Fed. 660, 9 C. C. A. 190, 23 U. S. App. 114. But it may be shown by such evidence to be a mortgage in a contest between general creditors of the mortgagor and his widow claiming dower in the property. Carter v. Hallahan, 61 Ga. 314. See ante §26.

[71] Ashley v. Cook, 109 Ga. 653, 35 S. E. 89; Mitchell v. Fullington, 83 Ga. 301, 9 S. W. 1083; McLaren v. Clark, 80 Ga. 423, 7 S. E. 230; Broach v. Smith, 75 Ga. 159; Thaxton v. Roberts, 66 Ga. 704; Code 1882, § 1969; Code 1895, § 2771.

[72] Jewell v. Walker, 109 Ga. 241, 34 S. E. 337; Carter v. Gunn, 64 Ga. 651; Broach v. Barfield, 57 Ga. 601.

[73] Biggers v. Bird, 55 Ga. 650, 652.

[74] Lowe v. Findley, 141 Ga. 380, 81 S. E. 230; Mercer v. Morgan, 136 Ga. 632, 71 S. E. 1075; Bashinski v. Swint, 133 Ga. 38, 65 S. E. 152; Spencer v. Schuman, 132 Ga. 515, 64 S. E. 466; Askew v. Thompson, 129 Ga. 325, 58 S. E. 854; Georgia Civ. Code 1910, § 3258. Where it was contended that an absolute deed was given to secure a debt, which had been fully paid before suit, evidence is admissible that the grantor had asked the grantee if he was not to make a deed back to the grantor's wife when the money was paid, and that at first the grantee laughed and did not answer, and then said "Yes." Spencer v. Schuman, 132 Ga. 515, 64 S. E. 466.

[75] See Ga. Laws 1889, p. 118; Laws 1893, p. 117.

[76] Biggers v. Bird, 55 Ga. 650; Lackey v. Bostwick, 54 Ga. 45; Hopkins v. Watts, 27 Ga. 490.

[77] Chapman v. Ayer, 95 Ga. 581, 23 S. E. 131; Rodgers v. Moore, 88 Ga. 88, 13 S. E. 962; Pope v. Marshall, 78 Ga. 635, 4 S. E. 116.

mortgage.[78] Where a deed is given to secure an indebtedness not specified therein, and no bond for reconveyance is made, parol evidence is admissible to show that the deed was given to secure an indebtedness already existing to the amount expressed as a consideration, and also to secure future advances.[79] The creditor may sue for the debt secured and may have a special judgment subjecting the property to the payment of the debt.[80]

§ 292a.   Idaho.—The intention of the parties to an absolute deed may be ascertained by parol testimony, and when ascertained will be carried out by the courts.[81] The evidence that the instrument is security for a debt and not a conveyance of title must be clear and satisfactory.[82] Under the statute of Idaho, every transfer of an interest in real property other than in trust, made only as security for the performance of another act, is to be deemed a mortgage, and this is, applicable although the conveyance be a deed absolute on its face without any defeasance or condition expressed therein.[83]

§ 293.   Illinois.—In Illinois it is provided by statute that every deed of real estate intended as security, though absolute in terms, shall be considered as a mortgage.[84] Such intention may be proved by parol[85] in an action at law where the title is not directly in issue.[86]

In order to change an absolute sale into a mortgage, the evidence

---

[78] Civil Code 1910, § 3306.

[79] Hester v. Gairdner, 128 Ga. 531, 58 S. E. 165.

[80] Jewell v. Walker, 109 Ga. 241, 34 S. E. 337.

[81] Thompson v. Burns, 15 Idaho 572, 99 Pac. 111; Felland v. Vollmer Mill &c. Co., 6 Idaho 120, 53 Pac. 268; Winters v. Swift, 2 Idaho 60, 3 Pac. 15.

[82] Bergen v. Johnson, 21 Idaho 619, 123 Pac. 484.

[83] Hannah v. Vensel, 19 Idaho 796, 116 Pac. 115.

[84] Caraway v. Sly, 222 Ill. 203, 78 N. E. 588; Merriman v. Schmitt, 211 Ill. 263, 71 N. E. 986; Union Mutual L. Ins. Co. v. Slee, 123 Ill. 57, 12 N. E. 543, 13 N. E. 222; Hurd's Rev. Stat. 1913, ch. 95, § 12, p. 1665.

[85] Deadman v. Yantis, 230 Ill. 243, 82 N. E. 592, 120 Am. St. 291; Merriman v. Schmitt, 211 Ill. 263, 71 N. E. 986; Moffett v. Hanner, 154 Ill. 649, 39 N. E. 474; Whittemore v. Fisher, 132 Ill. 243, 24 N. E. 636;

Pearson v. Pearson, 131 Ill. 464, 23 N. E. 418; Helm v. Boyd, 124 Ill. 370, 16 N. E. 85; Workman v. Greening, 115 Ill. 477, 4 N. E. 385; Halesy v. Jackson, 66 Ill. 139; Tillson v. Moulton, 23 Ill. 648; Bellinski v. National Brew. Co., 124 Ill. App. 45; Ætna Ins. Co. v. Jacobson, 105 Ill. App. 283. See also Northern Assur. Co. v. Chicago Mut. Bldg. Assn., 198 Ill. 474, 64 N. E. 979; Bartling v. Brasuhn, 102 Ill. 441. But proof that the grantor made the conveyance to secure an indebtedness to the grantee, on an understanding that the grantor might redeem by paying the indebtedness when he became able to do so, is insufficient to render an absolute deed a mortgage. Caraway v. Sly, 222 Ill. 203, 78 N. E. 588.

[86] German Ins. Co. v. Gibe, 162 Ill. 251, 44 N. E. 490, affd. 59 Ill. App. 614; May v. May, 158 Ill. 209, 42 N. W. 56.

must clearly show the intention of parties to make a mortgage,[87] and a mere preponderance of evidence is insufficient.[88] To convert a deed absolute in form into a mortgage the burden of overcoming the presumption of law that the deed is what it purports to be rests upon the party claiming that it is a mortgage.[89]

To overcome the express terms of the deed, a debt must exist, and the liability to pay it. The kind of parol evidence which is properly receivable to show an absolute deed to be a mortgage is that of facts and circumstances of such a nature as, in a court of equity, will control the operation of a deed, and not of loose declarations of parties touching their intentions or understanding. The latter is a dangerous species of evidence upon which to disturb the title to land, being extremely liable to be misunderstood or perverted. If the papers show upon their face a sale and agreement for repurchase, to make the transaction a mortgage the evidence must do more than create a doubt as to the character of the transaction.[90]

[87] Deadman v. Yantis, 230 Ill. 243, 82 N. E. 592, 120 Am. St. 291 (clear and convincing evidence); Gannon v. Moles, 209 Ill. 180, 70 N. E. 689; Heaton v. Gaines, 198 Ill. 479, 64 N. E. 1081; Low v. Graff, 80 Ill. 360; Knockamus v. Shepard, 54 Ill. 500; Babcock v. Babcock, 179 Ill. App. 188 (clear and decisive evidence); Martinet v. Duff, 178 Ill. App. 199 (clear, strong, definite, unequivocal, convincing and satisfactory); Hoglund v. Royal Trust Co., 159 Ill. App. 390; Gray v. Hayhurst, 157 Ill. App. 488 (clear, satisfactory, and convincing); Hill v. Viele, 128 Ill. App. 5 (clear, sufficient and convincing evidence); Rankin v. Rankin, 111 Ill. App. 403 (clear, satisfactory and convincing); May v. May, 55 Ill. App. 488, affd. 158 Ill. 209, 42 N. E. 56.

[88] Martinet v. Duff, 178 Ill. App. 199.

[89] Deadman v. Yantis, 230 Ill. 243, 82 N. E. 592, 120 Am. St. 291; Rankin v. Rankin, 216 Ill. 132, 74 N. E. 763; Gannon v. Moles, 209 Ill. 180, 70 N. E. 689; Heaton v. Gaines, 198 Ill. 479, 64 N. E. 1081, affg. 100 Ill. App. 26; Martinet v. Duff, 178 Ill. App. 199; Bartoletti v. Hoerner, 154 Ill. App. 336; Belinski v. National Brew. Co., 124 Ill. App. 45.

[90] Whittemore v. Fisher, 132 Ill. 243, 24 N. E. 636; Strong v. Strong, 126 Ill. 301, 18 N. E. 665; Darst v. Murphy, 119 Ill 343, 9 N. E. 887; Bailey v. Bailey, 115 Ill. 551, 4 N. E. 394; Bearss v. Ford, 108 Ill. 16; Union Mut. L. Ins. Co. v. White, 106 Ill. 67; Bartling v. Brasuhn, 102 Ill. 441; Clark v. Finlon, 90 Ill. 245; Hancock v. Harper, 86 Ill. 445; Knowles v. Knowles, 86 Ill. 1; Westlake v. Horton, 85 Ill. 228; Sharp v. Smitherman, 85 Ill. 153; Strong v. Shea, 83 Ill. 575; Wilson v. McDowell, 78 Ill. 514; Heald v. Wright, 75 Ill. 17; Magnusson v. Johnson, 73 Ill. 156; Smith v. Cremer, 71 Ill. 185; Klock v. Walter, 70 Ill. 416; Remington v. Campbell, 60 Ill. 516; Alwood v. Mansfield, 59 Ill. 496; Price v. Karnes, 59 Ill. 276; Lindauer v. Cummings, 57 Ill. 195; Shays v. Norton, 48 Ill. 100; Ennor v. Thompson, 46 Ill. 214; Christie v. Hale, 46 Ill. 117; Hunter v. Hatch, 45 Ill. 178; Parmelee v. Lawrence, 44 Ill. 405; Dwen v. Blake, 44 Ill. 135; Pitts v. Cable, 44 Ill. 103; Taintor v. Keys, 43 Ill. 332; Ewart v. Walling, 42 Ill. 453; Reigard v. McNeil, 38 Ill. 400; Snyder v. Griswold, 37 Ill. 216; Silsbee v. Lucas, 36 Ill. 462; Roberts v. Richards, 36 Ill. 339; Sutphen v. Cushman, 35 Ill. 186; Preschbaker v. Feaman, 32 Ill. 475; Maxfield v. Patchen, 29 Ill. 39; Shaver v. Woodward, 28 Ill. 277; Weider v. Clark, 27 Ill. 251;

Evidence of fraud, or undue advantage or oppression, is allowed, as tending to show that an absolute conveyance should be regarded as a mortgage.[91] If the fact be established by parol evidence that there was a loan of money, equity regards the deed as a security for the repayment of the money loaned.[92] To establish this fact, a parol agreement that the land conveyed should be held by the grantee as security for money loaned the grantor, or paid for his benefit, may be proved,[93] or that it should be held to indemnify the grantee for moneys to be paid by him on the debts of the grantor.[94] In short, any evidence is admissible which tends to show the relations between the parties, or to show any other fact or circumstance of a nature to control the deed, and establish such an equity as would give a right of redemption.[95]

De Wolf v. Strader, 26 Ill. 225; Tillson v. Moulton, 23 Ill. 648; Davis v. Hopkins, 15 Ill. 519; Miller v. Thomas, 14 Ill. 428; Coates v. Woodworth, 13 Ill. 654; Bartoletti v. Hoerner, 154 Ill. App. 336; Rankin v. Rankin, 111 Ill. App. 403. See ante §§ 265, 267, concerning existence of the debt.

[91] Brown v. Gaffney, 28 Ill. 149.

[92] Wynkoop v. Cowing, 21 Ill. 570; Williams v. Bishop, 15 Ill. 553, 18 Ill. 101; Smith v. Sackett, 15 Ill. 528; Davis v. Hopkins, 15 Ill. 519.

[93] Scanlan v. Scanlan, 134 Ill. 630, 25 N. E. 652; Reigard v. McNeil, 38 Ill. 400.

[94] Roberts v. Richards, 36 Ill. 339.

[95] In Sutphen v. Cushman, 35 Ill. 186, Mr. Justice Beckwith states very clearly the rule governing the admission of parol evidence in such cases: "In determining whether the transaction consummated by the deed in question was an absolute sale or should be regarded merely as a mortgage, we entirely disregard the testimony of those witnesses introduced for the purpose of establishing their understanding of the nature of the transaction, and who relate conversations of the parties. The conveyance purports to convey an absolute estate to the grantee, and it must be taken as the exponent of the right of the parties, unless some equity is shown, not founded on the mere allegation of a contemporaneous understanding inconsistent with the terms of the deed, but independently both of the deed itself and of the understanding with which it was executed. The right to redeem lands conveyed can not be established by simply proving that such was the understanding on which the deed was executed, because equity as well as the law, will seek for the understanding of the parties in the deed itself. The right must be one paramount to, and independent of, the terms of the deed, as well as of the understanding between the parties at the time it was executed. Parol evidence is admissible so far as it conduces to show the relations between the parties, or to show any other fact or circumstance of a nature to control the deed, and to establish such an equity as would give a right of redemption, and no further. In the application of this rule, parol evidence is received to establish the fact that a debt existed, or money was loaned on account of which the conveyance was made; for such facts will, in a court of equity, control the operation of the deed. So, too, in regard to any other fact or circumstance having the same operation. From some expressions of opinion in cases hitherto decided by this court, it has been supposed that a more enlarged rule has been adopted in this state, but a careful examination of them will show that this court has never departed from the rule we now enunciate."

The ground or principle of the doctrine was also considered in Ruckman v. Alwood, 71 Ill. 155, where, after referring to the earlier

Any circumstance tending to illustrate the purpose and intent of the parties, including their declarations at the time of the execution of the instrument, may be given in evidence.[96] But the testimony of a third person who was present at the execution of a trust deed alleged to have been executed as security for the payment of an annuity, is not admissible concerning a conversation between the alleged annuitant and a justice of the peace who drew the papers; nor is the testimony of a person admissible, who advised the making of the agreement, but who was not present when it was signed, to prove a like conversation.[97]

§ 294. Indiana.—The admission of parol evidence to show that an absolute deed was executed merely as security for the payment of money, or the performance of some act, is a well-settled rule in this state.[98] Formerly the ground on which it was received seemed to be

cases in this state, the court say: "It will be perceived that in none of these cases did the court attempt to range the jurisdiction, to turn an absolute deed into a mortgage by parol evidence, under any specific head of equity, such as fraud, accident, or mistake; but the rule seems to have grown into recognition as an independent head of equity. Still it must have its foundation in this, that, where the transaction is shown to have been meant as a security for a loan, the deed will have the character of a mortgage, without other proof of fraud than is implied in showing that a conveyance, taken for the mutual benefit of both parties, has been appropriated solely to the use of the grantee."

[96] Conant v. Riseborough, 139 Ill. 383, 28 N. E. 789, affg. 30 Ill. App. 498; Helm v. Boyd, 124 Ill. 370, 16 N. E. 85; Darst v. Murphy, 119 Ill. 343, 9 N. E. 887; Workman v. Greening, 115 Ill. 477, 4 N. E. 385; Bentley v. O'Bryan, 111 Ill. 53; Bartling v. Brasuhn, 102 Ill. 441; Belinski v. National Brew. Co., 124 Ill. App. 45; Ætna Ins. Co. v. Jacobson, 105 Ill. App. 283.

[97] Miller v. Mandel, 259 Ill. 314, 102 N. E. 760.

[98] Mott v. Fiske, 155 Ind. 597, 58 N. E. 1053; Brown v. Follette, 155 Ind. 316, 58 N. E. 197; Kitts v. Willson, 130 Ind. 492, 29 N. E. 401; Hamilton v. Byram, 122 Ind. 283, 23 N. E. 795; Pickett v. Green, 120 Ind. 584, 22 N. E. 737; Diven v. Johnson, 117 Ind. 512, 20 N. E. 428, 3 L. R. A. 308; Turpie v. Lowe, 114 Ind. 37, 15 N. E. 834; Voss v. Eller, 109 Ind. 260, 10 N. E. 74; Hanlon v. Doherty, 109 Ind. 37, 9 N. E. 782; Singer Mfg. Co. v. Forsyth, 108 Ind. 334, 9 N. E. 372; Cox v. Ratcliffe, 105 Ind. 374, 5 N. E. 5; Beatty v. Brummett, 94 Ind. 76; Landers v. Beck, 92 Ind. 49; Herron v. Herron, 91 Ind. 278; Parker v. Hubble, 75 Ind. 580; Tuttle v. Churchman, 74 Ind. 311; Cravens v. Kitts, 64 Ind. 581; Caress v. Foster, 62 Ind. 145; Butcher v. Stultz, 60 Ind. 170; Graham v. Graham, 55 Ind. 23; Heath v. Williams, 36 Ind. 495; Crane v. Buchanan, 29 Ind. 570; Smith v. Parks, 22 Ind. 59; Cross v. Hepner, 7 Ind. 359; Davis v. Stonestreet, 4 Ind. 101; Hayworth v. Worthington, 5 Blackf. (Ind.) 361, 35 Am. Dec. 126; Blair v. Bass, 4 Blackf. (Ind.) 539; Conwell v. Evill, 4 Blackf. (Ind.) 67; Harbison v. Lemon, 3 Blackf. (Ind.) 51, 23 Am. Dec. 376; Ward v. Tuttle (Ind. App.), 102 N. E. 405; Beidelman v. Koch, 42 Ind. App. 423, 85 N. E. 977; Greenwood Bldg. &c. Assn. v. Stanton, 28 Ind. App. 548, 63 N. E. 574; Matchett v. Knisely, 27 Ind. App. 664; Kelso v. Kelso, 16 Ind. App. 615, 44 N. E. 1013, 45 N.

fraud or mistake; and the attempt to set up such a deed as an absolute conveyance was regarded in itself as a fraud; but the later decisions hold that, without showing any fraud, accident, or mistake, parol evidence is admissible to prove that an absolute deed was intended as a security.[99] The proof that a mortgage was intended must be clear and decisive.[1]

Although a conveyance absolute on its face, without any accompanying defeasance may be shown in equity to be a mortgage as between the parties and persons with notice, it can not so operate against bona fide purchasers.[2]

The owner of a tract of land executed first, second and third mortgages thereon. Thereafter when the first mortgage became due it was paid by the holder of the second mortgage, to whom a deed of the property was given as security for the amount due on both mortgages, it being agreed as a part of the transaction that the time of payment of the second mortgage should be extended. It was held, that the deed given was in fact a mortgage and was a lien superior to that of the third mortgage.[3]

§ **295. Iowa.**—In Iowa parol evidence is admissible, on the ground that to declare that to be a sale which was really a mortgage would be a fraud.[4] The recent cases admit parol evidence generally, to show that a deed absolute in form was given as security[5] and intended as a mortgage.[6]

E. 1065; Loeb v. McAlister, 15 Ind. App. 643, 41 N. E. 1061, 44 N. E. 378.

[99] Cox v. Ratcliffe, 105 Ind. 374, 5 N. E. 5; Beatty v. Brummett, 94 Ind. 76; Smith v. Brand, 64 Ind. 427.

[1] Rogers v. Beach, 115 Ind. 413, 17 N. E. 609; Voss v. Eller, 109 Ind. 260, 10 N. E. 74; Cox v. Ratcliffe, 105 Ind. 374, 5 N. E. 5; Fox v. Fraser, 92 Ind. 265; Lucas v. Hendrix, 92 Ind. 54; Landers v. Beck, 92 Ind. 49; Herron v. Herron, 91 Ind. 278; Parker v. Hubble, 75 Ind. 580; Conwell v. Evill, 4 Blackf. (Ind.) 67.

[2] Calahan v. Dunker, 51 Ind. App. 436, 99 N. E. 1021.

[3] Matchett v. Knisely, 27 Ind. App. 664.

[4] Beroud v. Lyons, 85 Iowa 482, 52 N. W. 486; Berberick v. Fritz, 39 Iowa 700; Johnson v. Smith, 39 Iowa 549; Roberts v. McMahan, 4 Greene (Iowa) 34.

[5] Lavalleur v. Hahn, 152 Iowa 649, 132 N. W. 877, 39 L. R. A. (N. S.) 24.

[6] Cold v. Beh, 152 Iowa 368, 132 N. W. 73; Mahaffy v. Faris, 144 Iowa 220, 122 N. W. 934, 24 L. R. A. (N. S.) 840; Jones v. Gilbert, 142 Iowa 506, 118 N. W. 314, 121 N. W. 5; Kinkead v. Peet, 137 Iowa 692, 114 N. W. 616. Parol evidence is admissible to show that a sheriff's deed was executed under an agreement that the grantee was to hold the legal title as mortgagee subject to redemption by payment of the debt for which the property was sold. Foster v. Rice, 126 Iowa 190, 101 N. W. 771. And the code provision, § 2918, declaring that express trusts in real estate must be executed as deeds of conveyance, does not exclude parol evidence that the grantee in a sheriff's deed agreed to purchase the land sold on execution, and hold it as security for a

Parol testimony to show that an absolute deed was intended as a mortgage is not excluded by the statute of frauds, or by the code provision requiring declarations of trusts or powers to be executed as deeds of conveyance.[7] Such evidence is not admitted to contradict or vary the written deed, but, as an exception to the rule, to show the intention of the parties. The burden of proving that a mortgage was intended is upon the party seeking to establish it as such, and the proof must be clear, satisfactory, and conclusive,[8] and even then the evidence is received with caution. Inadequacy of the consideration paid is a strong circumstance to support the claim that the conveyance was intended to operate as a mortgage; and the fact that the grantor remains in possession is also to be considered in determining this question.[9] The conduct of the parties, and all the surrounding circumstances, will be weighed. It is not necessary to show that a defeasance has been omitted or destroyed by fraud or mistake.[10]

§ 296. Kansas.—In Kansas it is declared that, although such evidence may not be admissible at law, it is in equity. Although no writ-

debt of the land owner. McElroy v. Allfree, 131 Iowa 112, 108 N. W. 116, 117 Am. St. 412.

[7] Iowa Code, § 2918; Salinger v. McAllister (Iowa), 146 N. W. 8. This rule applies also to one acquiring a legal title from a third person, under an agreement with another, who agrees to pay the purchase-price, and for whom the purchase-money is advanced as a loan. Jones v. Gillett, 142 Iowa 506, 118 N. W. 314.

[8] Cold v. Beh, 152 Iowa 368, 132 N. W. 73; Bradford v. Helsell, 150 Iowa 732, 130 N. W. 908; Jones v. Gillett, 142 Iowa 506, 118 N. W. 314; Krebs v. Lauser, 133 Iowa 241, 110 N. W. 443; Betts v. Betts, 132 Iowa 72, 106 N. W. 928; Wright v. Wright, (Iowa), 98 N. W. 137; McLaughlin v. Royce, 108 Iowa 254, 78 N. W. 1105; Haggerty v. Brower, 105 Iowa 395, 75 N. W. 321; Baird v. Reininghaus, 87 Iowa 167, 54 N. W. 148; Langer v. Meservey, 80 Iowa 158, 45 N. W. 732; Ensminger v. Ensminger, 75 Iowa 89, 39 N. W. 208, 9 Am. St. 462; Corliss v. Conable, 74 Iowa 58, 36 N. W. 891; Knight v. McCord, 63 Iowa 429, 19 N. W. 310; Kibby v. Harsh, 61 Iowa 196, 16 N. W. 85; Woodworth v. Carman, 43 Iowa 504; Crawford v. Taylor, 42 Iowa 260;

Zuver v. Lyons, 40 Iowa 510; Green v. Turner, 38 Iowa 112; Hyatt v. Cochran, 37 Iowa 309; Wilson v. Patrick, 34 Iowa 362; Key v. McCleary, 25 Iowa 191; Holliday v. Arthur, 25 Iowa 19; Childs v. Griswold, 19 Iowa 362; Sunderland v. Sunderland, 19 Iowa 325; Gardner v. Weston, 18 Iowa 33; Cooper v. Skeel, 14 Iowa 578; Atkins v. Faulkner, 11 Iowa 326; Corbit v. Smith, 7 Iowa 60, 71 Am. Dec. 431; Noel v. Noel, 1 Iowa 423; Robertson v. Moline Milburn-Stoddard Co., 106 Iowa 414, 76 N. W. 736. Loose random statements by a grantee to disinterested persons that the land was conveyed to him in trust merely are not admissible to show that a deed was intended as a mortgage. England v. England, 94 Iowa 716, 61 N. W. 920. Where the agreement to reconvey expressly provides that it shall not be considered as a mortgage, very strong evidence is required to prove that a deed with an agreement to reconvey constitutes a mortgage. Irish v. Steeves, 154 Iowa 286, 134 N. W. 634.

[9] Wilson v. Patrick, 34 Iowa 362; Trucks v. Lindsey, 18 Iowa 504.

[10] Bigler v. Jack, 114 Iowa 667, 87 N. W. 700.

ten defeasance was ever executed between the parties, their understanding, intention, or agreement may be shown to create a parol of defeasance. The mortgage results from the facts of the case, and the statute of frauds and the statute relating to trusts, while making void parol agreements respecting land, do not make void an estate which results from, or is created by, operation of law. This evidence is admitted to show the facts of the case which render the deed defeasible.[11] That an instrument purporting to be an absolute deed of conveyance may be shown by parol evidence to have been intended as security for the payment of money or the performance of an act is, in effect, implied by statute,[12] and has been frequently ruled in judicial decision.[13] The deed may be declared a mortgage not only upon the application of the grantor, but also upon application of his creditors who seek to reach his interest by attachment.[14] The evidence must be clear and decisive,[15] leaving no substantial doubt that a mortgage was intended.[16]

§ 297. **Kentucky.**—Until recently parol evidence was admitted in this class of cases only upon the ground of fraud or mistake.[17] Especially if the transaction be infected with usury, it is admissible to show that the real character of the transaction is different from what it purports to be.[18] In some decisions an absolute deed has been held

---

[11] McDonald v. Kellogg, 30 Kans. 170, 2 Pac. 507; Glynn v. Home Bldg Assn., 22 Kans. 746; Moore v. Wade, 8 Kans. 380; Barnes v. Crockett, 4 Kans. App. 777, 46 Pac. 997.

[12] Kans. Gen. Stat. 1909, § 5195; Saylor v. Crooker, 89 Kans. 51, 130 Pac. 689.

[13] Farmers' &c. Bank v. Kackley, 88 Kans. 70, 127 Pac. 539; Hubbard v. Cheney, 76 Kans. 222, 91 Pac. 793, 123 Am. St. 129, note p. 133; Abrams v. Abrams, 74 Kans. 888, 88 Pac. 70; Martin v. Allen, 67 Kans. 758, 74 Pac. 249; Yost v. Bank, 66 Kans. 605, 72 Pac. 209; McNamara v. Culver, 22 Kans. 661. Parol proof may be resorted to to show that a deed to a husband and wife jointly was intended as a mortgage to secure money advanced by her toward the purchase-price. Hubbard v. Cheney, 76 Kans. 222, 91 Pac. 793, 123 Am. St. 129. Where a part of the land covered by a mortgage is released from its operation and other land is deeded by the mortgagor to the mortgagee it may be shown upon foreclosure that such deed was intended as security only. Where the mortgage was given by husband and wife, and upon partial release, other land is deeded by the husband alone to the mortgagee, evidence that the deed was a mortgage is admissible against the wife, as well as the husband, she having joined in the answer. Hilt v. Griffin, 77 Kans. 782, 90 Pac. 808.

[14] Bennett v. Wolverton, 24 Kans. 284.

[15] Winston v. Burnell, 44 Kans. 367, 24 Pac. 477, 21 Am. St. 289.

[16] Elston v. Chamberlin, 41 Kans. 354, 21 Pac. 259.

[17] Munford v. Green, 103 Ky. 140; Crutcher v. Muir, 90 Ky. 142, 13 S. W. 435; Blanchard v. Kenton, 4 Bibb (Ky.) 451; Skinner v. Miller, 5 Litt. (Ky.) 84.

[18] Cook v. Colyer, 2 B. Mon. (Ky.) 71; Stapp v. Phelps, 7 Dana (Ky.) 296; Lindley v. Sharp, 7 Mon. (Ky.)

to be a mortgage, though neither fraud nor mistake was shown in its execution, or the intention of the parties as shown by the attendant circumstances.[19] Parol evidence has been held admissible to show that an assignment by a purchaser at commissioner's sale to a third person who had become surety for the purchase-money, was not an absolute conveyance of the purchaser's right, but was made for the purpose of protecting the surety.[20] The burden of proof to show an absolute deed to be a mortgage is upon the grantor, whose unsupported testimony, when denied by the grantor is insufficient.[21]

Until the most recent decisions the Court of Appeals has adhered to the statement that parol evidence is admissible only in case there is an allegation of fraud or mistake.[22] But parol evidence is now admissible to show an absolute deed a mortgage, though there is no plea of fraud or mistake, or of any over-reaching in a relation of trust or confidence.[23] Such evidence must be clear and satisfactory.[24]

§ 297a.   **Louisiana.**—A conveyance in the form of an absolute sale, but intended and understood by both parties to be a security for a debt, is a mortgage, and does not vest the ownership in the apparent buyer. Parol evidence is admissible to show the real nature of the conveyance.[25] The later authorities construe Civil Code, art. 2236,

---

248; Murphy v. Trigg, 1 Mon. (Ky.) 72.

[19] Seiler v. Northern Bank, 86 Ky. 128, 5 S. W. 536; Davis v. Eastham, 81 Ky. 116; Timmons v. Center (Ky.), 43 S. W. 437; Brey v. Barbour (Ky.), 20 S. W. 899; Gossum v. Gossum (Ky.), 15 S. W. 1057; Green v. Ball, 4 Bush. (Ky.) 586.

[20] Crockett's Guardian v. Waller, 29 Ky. L. 1155, 96 S. W. 860.

[21] Runyon v. Pogue (Ky.), 42 S. W. 910.

[22] Bennett v. Bennett, 137 Ky. 17, 121 S. W. 495, Ann. Cas. 1912 A, 407; Munford v. Green, 103 Ky. 140; Crockett's Guardian v. Waller, 29 Ky. L. 1155, 96 S. W. 860. See also Crutcher v. Muir, 90 Ky. 142, 13 S. W. 435, 29 Am. St. 356. Where tho court say that in Seiler v. Northern Bank, 86 Ky. 128, there was no question involving the right to introduce parol evidence to vary a written instrument.

[23] Smith v. Berry, 155 Ky. 686, 160 S. W. 247; Vaughn v. Smith, 148 Ky. 531, 146 S. W. 1094; Leibel v. Tandy, 146 Ky. 101, 141 S. W. 1183; Brown v. Spradlin, 136 Ky. 703, 125 S. W. 150; Hobbs v. Rowland, 136 Ky. 197, 123 S. W. 1185; overruling Munford v. Green, 103 Ky. 140, 44 S. W. 419; and Holtheide v. Smith, 24 Ky. L. 2535, 74 S. W. 689. See also Graham v. Fischer (Ky.), 110 S. W. 386; Hobbs v. Rowland, 136 Ky. 197, 123 S. W. 1185; Oberdorfer v. White, 25 Ky. L. 1629, 78 S. W. 436.

[24] Stokeley v. Flanders (Ky.), 128 S. W. 608.

[25] Crozier v. Ragan, 38 La. Ann. 154; Parmer v. Mangham, 31 La. Ann. 348. In Mulhaupt v. Youree, 35 La. Ann. 1052, it was held that where, in a sale with an agreement of redemption, possession was given to the purchaser, written evidence alone is admissible to show the sale a mortgage unless fraud or error be charged. See also Eames v. Woodson, 120 La. 1031, 46 So. 13; Franklin v. Sewall, 110 La. 292, 34 So. 448.

to the effect that a sale of lands or immovable property, can not be shown to be an antichresis, as between the parties or their heirs, except by a counter letter or answers to formal interrogatories propounded to the apparent owner, or by proof of fraud or mistake.[26]

§ 298. **Maine.**—In Maine, by statutory definition, mortgages of real estate include those made in the usual form in which the condition is set forth in the deed, and those made by a conveyance appearing on its face to be absolute, with a separate instrument of defeasance executed at the same time, or as part of the same transaction.[27] Parol evidence is not admissible at law to convert an absolute deed into a mortgage.[28] In equity a resulting trust was formerly held to arise in favor of a grantor who had conveyed land by an absolute deed to secure a debt due to the grantee, under which redemption might be had within a reasonable time.[29]

Under the more recent decisions a new rule in equity has been adopted. Where the proof is clear and convincing, a deed absolute on its face may be construed to be an equitable mortgage.[30] In a case upon this subject the court said: "It is a sound policy as well as principle to declare, that to take an absolute conveyance as a mortgage, without any defeasance, is in equity a fraud."[31] The intention of the

[26] Harang v. Ragan, 134 La. 201, 63 So. 875; Breaux v. Royer, 129 La. 894, 57 So. 164 (parol evidence admissible only in case of fraud or error); Maskrey v. Johnson, 122 La. 791, 48 So. 266; Eames v. Woodson, 120 La. 1031, 46 So. 13 (parol evidence admissible in favor of liens of vendor in case of fraud or error). See also Mulhaupt v. Youree, 35 La. Ann. 1052; Janney v. Ober, 28 La. Ann. 281; West v. Hickman, 14 La. Ann. 610; Theurer v. Schmidt, 10 La. Ann. 125; Ranaldson v. Hamilton, 5 La. Ann. 203; Dabadie v. Poydras, 3 La. Ann. 153. But see Ker v. Evershed, 41 La. Ann. 15, 6 So. 566; Crozier v. Ragan, 38 La. Ann. 154; Newman v. Shelly, 36 La. Ann. 100; Testart v. Belot, 31 La. Ann. 795; Frost v. Bebout, 14 La. Ann. 104.

[27] Maine Rev. Stat. 1903, ch. 92, § 1, p. 794.

[28] Bryant v. Crosby, 36 Maine 562, 58 Am. Dec. 767; Ellis v. Higgins, 32 Maine 34; Thomaston Bank v. Stimpson, 21 Maine 195.

[29] Richardson v. Woodbury, 43 Maine 206; Howe v. Russell, 36 Maine 115; Whitney v. Batchelder, 32 Maine 313.

[30] Bradley v. Merrill, 88 Maine 319, 34 Atl. 160; Libby v. Clark, 88 Maine 32, 33 Atl. 657; Jameson v. Emerson, 82 Maine 359, 19 Atl. 831; Reed v. Reed, 75 Maine 264; Stinchfield v. Milliken, 71 Maine 567; Lewis v. Small, 71 Maine 552. This doctrine was first allowed in this state in Rowell v. Jewett, 69 Maine 293; affirmed in Knapp v. Bailey, 79 Maine 195, 9 Atl. 122. Since the statute of 1874, ch. 175, conferring full jurisdiction in equity, the court has complete jurisdiction over equitable mortgages. Reed v. Reed, 75 Maine 264.

The dictum of the court in Richardson v. Woodbury, 43 Maine 206, that a resulting trust arises in such case, is not supported by any reliable authority or well-grounded reason, and it has never been followed. Reed v. Reed, 75 Maine 264, per Virgin J.

[31] Stinchfield v. Milliken, 71 Maine 567.

parties is the criterion, and this may be ascertained from any facts within or without the deed.

§ 299. Maryland.—Parol evidence was formerly admitted only to show that the defeasance was omitted or destroyed by fraud or mistake.[32] Fraud may be inferred from the facts and circumstances of the case, from the character of the contract, or from the situation of the parties.[33] Parol evidence is admitted upon the same principle that it is admitted to establish a resulting trust.[34] It has been said that such evidence is admitted not to contradict or vary the terms of the instrument, but to establish an equity paramount to the mere form of the conveyance.[35]

According to the more recent cases, it is admitted not only to prevent fraud and oppression, but to promote substantial justice between the parties, and to carry out their real intentions.[36] Thus parol evidence is admissible to prove a deed to have been intended as a mortgage,[37] not only between the parties, but as against all deriving title from the grantee, who are not bona fide purchasers.[38] The evidence must be clear and decisive.[39] An oral agreement to permit repurchase, though made for a valuable consideration, raises a mere option, and not a mortgage.[40]

§ 300. Massachusetts.—In Massachusetts parol evidence is admitted in these cases, not to vary, add to, or contradict the deed, but to establish the fact of an inherent fault in the transaction or its consideration, which affords ground for avoiding the effect of the deed by restraining its operation or defeating it altogether.[41] This doctrine

---

[32] Baugher v. Merryman, 32 Md. 185; Artz v Grove, 21 Md. 456, 474; Farrell v. Bean, 10 Md. 217; Bank of Westminster v. Whyte, 1 Md. Ch. 536, 3 Md. Ch. 508; Dougherty v. McColgan, 6 Gill & J. (Md.) 275; Bend v. Susquehanna Bridge &c. Co., 6 Har. & J. (Md.) 128, 14 Am. Dec. 261. See also Price v. Gover, 40 Md. 102.

[33] Thompson v. Banks, 2 Md. Ch. 430, 3 Md. Ch. 138; Watkins v. Stockett, 6 Har. & J. (Md.) 435; Brogden v. Walker, 2 Har & J. (Md.) 285.

[34] Booth v. Robinson, 55 Md. 419; Cochrane v. Price (Md.), 8 Atl. 361.

[35] Pickett v. Wadlow, 94 Md. 564, 51 Atl. 423; Booth v. Robinson, 55 Md. 419.

[36] Gaither v. Clarke, 67 Md. 18, 8 Atl. 740; Booth v. Robinson, 55 Md. 419, 451.

[37] Miller v. Miller, 101 Md. 600, 61 Atl. 210; Funk v. Harshman, 110 Md. 127, 72 Atl. 665.

[38] Funk v. Harshman, 110 Md. 127, 72 Atl. 665.

[39] Funk v. Harshman, 110 Md. 127, 72 Atl. 665; Cochrane v. Price (Md.), 8 Atl. 361; Faringer v. Ramsey, 2 Md. 365.

[40] Riggin v. Robinson, 117 Md. 81, 83 Atl. 143. But see Hopper v. Smyser, 90 Md. 363, 45 Atl. 206.

[41] Campbell v. Dearborn, 109 Mass. 130, 12 Am. Rep. 671; Cullen v. Carey, 146 Mass. 50, 15 N. E. 131; Pond v. Eddy, 113 Mass. 149; McDonough v. O'Neil, 113 Mass. 92;

is regarded as a sound and salutary principle of equity jurisprudence, when properly administered; but it is declared to be a power to be exercised with the utmost caution, and only when the grounds of interference are fully made out, so as to be clear from doubt. "It is not enough," says Mr. Justice Wells, "that the relation of borrower and lender, or debtor and creditor, existed at the time the transaction was entered upon. Negotiations, begun with a view to a loan or security for a debt, may fairly terminate in a sale of the property originally proposed for security. And if, without fraud, oppression, or unfair advantage taken, a sale is the real result, and not a form adopted as a cover or pretext, it should be sustained by the court. It is to the determination of this question that the parol evidence is mainly directed."[42] The late cases admit parol evidence generally to show that a deed absolute on its face is in fact security for a debt, and hold that the introduction of such parol proof of a mortgage is not in conflict

McDonough v. Squire, 111 Mass. 217; Glass v. Hulbert, 102 Mass. 24, 3 Am. Rep. 418; Newton v. Fay, 10 Allen (Mass.) 505. Prior to the Statute of 1855, ch. 194, § 1, Gen. Stat. ch. 113, § 2, conferring upon the Supreme Judicial Court jurisdiction in equity "in all cases of fraud, and of conveyances or transfers of real estate in the nature of mortgages," the jurisdiction of the court in relation to the foreclosure and redemption of mortgages was confined to cases of a defeasance contained in the deed, or in some other instrument under seal. Flint v. Sheldon, 13 Mass. 443, 7 Am. Dec. 162; Boyd v. Stone, 11 Mass. 442; Stackpole v. Arnold, 11 Mass. 27, 6 Am. Dec. 150; Kelleran v. Brown, 4 Mass. 443; Coffin v. Loring, 9 Allen (Mass.) 154; Lincoln v. Parsons, 1 Allen (Mass.) 388; Eaton v. Green, 22 Pick. (Mass.) 526; Flagg v. Mann, 14 Pick. (Mass.) 467; Bodwell v. Webster, 13 Pick. (Mass.) 411. Saunders v. Frost, 5 Pick. (Mass.) 259, 16 Am. Dec. 394. But before that statute parol evidence had been frequently admitted where there was a deed and a provision for a reconveyance, to show the real nature of the transaction; and the instruments had been construed as constituting a mortgage when it was shown that the transaction was really and essentially a loan of money. Flagg v. Mann, 14 Pick. (Mass.) 467; Carey v. Rawson, 8 Mass. 159; Taylor v. Weld, 5 Mass. 109; Kelleran v. Brown, 4 Mass. 443; Erskine v. Townsend, 2 Mass, 493, 3 Am. Dec. 71; Rice v. Rice, 4 Pick. (Mass.) 349; Parks v. Hall, 2 Pick. (Mass.) 206. But the question whether, in the absence of any written defeasance, an absolute deed could be converted into a mortgage, or restricted in its operation so as to allow a redemption, when shown to be in fact merely security for a loan, was not decided until it came before the court in Campbell v. Dearborn, 109 Mass. 130, 12 Am. Rep. 671, though the question had been discussed in Newton v. Fay, 10 Allen (Mass.) 505, and, so far as concerned the statute of frauds, in Glass v. Hulbert, 102 Mass. 24, 3 Am. Rep. 418. The opinion of Mr. Justice Wells, in Campbell v. Dearborn, contains a full and able discussion of the whole subject.

[42] Campbell v. Dearborn, 109 Mass. 130, 143, 12 Am. Rep. 671.

with the statute of frauds.[43] The testimony, however, must establish an equity in the grantor's favor.[44]

There is no presumption of law arising from the fact that one person is indebted to another that a deed of land absolute in form given by the creditor was or was not intended as a mortgage.[45] Dissent is expressed, in the opinion of the court already quoted, from the doctrine advanced in some of the cases, that the subsequent attempt to retain the property, and refusal to permit it to be redeemed, constitute a fraud and breach of trust, which afford ground of jurisdiction and judicial interference. "There can be no fraud, or legal wrong, in the breach of a trust from which the statute withholds the right of judicial recognition. Such conduct may sometimes appear to relate back and give character to the original transaction, by showing in that an express intent to deceive and defraud. But ordinarily it will not be connected with the original transaction otherwise than constructively, or as involved in it as its legitimate consequence and natural fruit."[46] The fault is in the original transaction rather than in the grantee's subsequent conduct in relation to it. As between borrower and lender, or debtor and creditor, an absolute deed given as security, and a renunciation of all legal right of redemption, are regarded as so significant of oppression, and so calculated to invite to or result in wrong and injustice on the part of the stronger toward the weaker party in the transaction, as in themselves to constitute a quasi fraud against which equity ought to relieve—in the same way that it does against the strict letter of an express condition of forfeiture.[47]

§ **301. Michigan.**—Parol evidence is admissible to convert an absolute deed into a mortgage,[48] in favor either of the grantor or his heirs.[49] It is admitted to show the intention of the parties in the

[43] Jennings v. Demmon, 194 Mass. 108, 80 N. E. 471; Alexander v. Grover, 190 Mass. 462, 77 N. E. 487; Clark v. Seagraves, 186 Mass. 430, 71 N. E. 813; Potter v. Kimball, 186 Mass. 120, 71 N. E. 308; Hennessey v. Conner, 139 Mass. 120, 29 N. E. 475.

[44] Sears v. Gilman, 199 Mass. 384, 85 N. E. 466.

[45] Crowell v. Keene, 159 Mass. 353, 34 N. E. 405.

[46] Campbell v. Dearborn, 109 Mass. 130, 12 Am. Rep. 671.

[47] Per Wells, J., in Hassen v. Barrett, 115 Mass. 256.

[48] Olney v. Brown, 163 Mich. 125, 128 N. W. 241; Schmidt v. Barclay, 161 Mich. 1, 125 N. W. 729; Ruch v.

Ruch, 159 Mich. 231, 124 N. W. 52; Carveth v. Winegar, 133 Mich. 34, 94 N. W. 381; Sowles v. Wilcox, 127 Mich. 166, 86 N. W. 689; Abbott v. Gruner, 121 Mich. 140, 79 N. W. 1065; McArthur v. Robinson, 104 Mich. 540, 62 N. W. 713; Reilly v. Brown, 87 Mich. 163, 49 N. W. 557; Hurst v. Beaver, 50 Mich. 612, 16 N. W. 165; Barber v. Miller, 43 Mich. 248, 5 N. W. 92; Johnson v. Van Velsor, 43 Mich. 208, 5 N. W. 265; Emerson v. Atwater, 7 Mich. 12; Swetland v. Swetland, 3 Mich. 482; Wadsworth v. Loranger, Har. (Mich.) 113.

[49] Olney v. Brown, 163 Mich. 125, 128 N. W. 241.

transaction, but whether as an exception under the statute of frauds, or upon the ground of fraud, the court in one case expressly leave undetermined;[50] but in another it is said that neither the statute of frauds nor the statute requiring powers and trusts to be created in writing is encroached upon by a court of equity in exercising its jurisdiction in this class of cases; that a different construction would make them what they were never intended to be—a shield for the protection of oppression and fraud; that the court will interfere between creditor and debtor to prevent oppression; and that to give relief in such cases has ever been the province of courts of equity, whose chief excellence consists in a wise and judicious exercise of this part of their jurisdiction.[51] Evidence of all the circumstances surrounding the transaction, the conversation at the time, and the value of the land is admissible.[52]

The burden of proof is upon the grantor to prove beyond a reasonable doubt that his deed was meant to be in effect a mortgage.[53] While a preponderance of evidence has been held sufficient,[54] it has also been said that the evidence of intention to create a mortgage must be clear and convincing.[55]

§ **302. Minnesota.**—Parol evidence is admissible in equity of the circumstances under which the deed was made, and the relation subsisting between the parties.[56] At first it was held to be admissible

[50] Fuller v. Parrish, 6 Mich. 211.
[51] Emerson v. Atwater, 7 Mich. 12.
[52] Carveth v. Winegar, 133 Mich. 34, 94 N. W. 381.
[53] Kellogg v. Northrup, 115 Mich. 327, 73 N. W. 230; McArthur v. Robinson, 104 Mich. 540, 62 N. W. 713; Etheridge v. Wisner, 86 Mich. 166, 48 N. W. 1087; McMillan v. Bissel, 63 Mich. 66, 29 N. W. 737; Tilden v. Streeter, 45 Mich. 533, 8 N. W. 502; Nickodemus v. Nickodemus, 45 Mich. 385, 8 N. W. 86.
[54] Schmidt v. Barclay, 161 Mich. 1, 125 N. W. 729; Cady v. Burgess, 144 Mich. 523, 108 N. W. 414; Kellogg v. Northrup, 115 Mich. 327, 73 N. W. 230; Sanborn v. Sanborn, 104 Mich. 180, 62 N. W. 371 (preponderance of proof sufficient).
[55] Smith v. Smith, 177 Mich. 268, 143 N. W. 86; Dalton v. Mertz, 173 Mich. 153, 138 N. W. 1055; Rathbone v. Maltz, 155 Mich. 306, 118 N. W. 991.
[56] Grannis v. Hitchcock, 118 Minn. 462, 137 N. W. 186; Stitt v. Rat Portage Lumber Co., 96 Minn. 27,

104 N. W. 561; Philips v. Mo, 91 Minn. 311, 97 N. W. 969; Backus v. Burke, 63 Minn. 272, 65 N. W. 459; Terry v. Wilson, 50 Minn. 570, 52 N. W. 973; Nye v. Swan, 49 Minn. 431, 52 N. W. 39; Marshall v. Thompson, 39 Minn. 137, 39 N. W. 309; Madigan v. Mead, 31 Minn. 94, 16 N. W. 539; Weide v. Gehl, 21 Minn. 449; Phœnix v. Gardner, 13 Minn. 430. See also Webster v. McDowell, 102 Minn. 445, 113 N. W. 1021. The fact that a deed is in fact a mortgage may be established by circumstantial evidence, especially where the grantor is dead. Holien v. Slee, 120 Minn. 261, 139 N. W. 493. Parol proof is admissible to show that the deed was in fact a mortgage to secure future advances and the performance of a contract, though the mortgagor did not yet have title to the land. Stitt v. Rat Portage Lumber Co., 96 Minn. 27, 104 N. W. 561. Minn. Rev. Laws 1905, § 3361, requiring a written defeasance to be recorded where intended to render an absolute deed defeasible does

only upon the ground of fraud, mistake, or surprise in making or executing the instrument; but, subsequently, it was held to be admissible
to show the real character of the transaction. In a court of law, such
evidence can not be received on any ground.[57] Equity will not, upon
mere conjecture or unsubstantial evidence, convert an absolute deed
into a mortgage.[58] The evidence must be clear and positive, and
reasonably conclusive, but need not amount to proof beyond a reasonable doubt.[59]

§ 303. **Mississippi.**—In Mississippi it is well settled that parol evidence will be admitted in equity to show that an absolute deed was
intended to be security for money, and therefore a mortgage.[60] It is
received to explain the true character of the transaction. For this
purpose, the conduct of the parties at the time and subsequently, and
all the attending circumstances, may be looked at; and when it is
shown that the consideration of the conveyance was a loan or a debt,
the courts always incline to regard it as a mortgage.[61] By statute a
conveyance absolute on its face, where the maker parts with the possession, can not be proved by parol evidence to be a mortgage only,
unless fraud in its procurement be the issue to be tried.[62] The statute

not imply that a writing is necessary between the parties, but serves
merely to protect persons dealing in
land on faith of the record title.
Jones v. Bradley Timber &c. Supply Co., 114 Minn. 415, 131 N. W.
494. Evidence that a third person
was present when the deed was delivered, who had agreed to redeem
from the foreclosure sale in settlement of which the deed was given,
and that the grantee knew such
fact, was properly excluded as evidence of a collateral fact not pertinent to the issue. Philips v. Mo,
91 Minn. 311, 97 N. W. 969. An
instrument executed by a grantee
under absolute deed, after death of
the mortgagor for a sale of part of
the property involved to one of the
grantor's heirs, and to accept the
quitclaim deed of the grantor's
widow to another portion of the
property, was admissible to show
conduct of defendant inconsistent
with his claim of absolute ownership. Holien v. Slee, 120 Minn. 261,
139 N W. 493.

[57] Swedish-Am. Nat. Bank v. Germania Bank, 76 Minn. 409, 79 N.

W. 399; Belote v. Morrison, 8 Minn.
87; McClane v. White, 5 Minn. 178,
keeping within the statute of frauds.

[58] Minneapolis Threshing Mach.
Co. v. Jones, 95 Minn. 127, 103 N.
W. 1017.

[59] Baumgartner v. Corliss, 115
Minn. 11, 131 N. W. 638; Stitt v.
Rat Portage Lumber Co., 96 Minn.
27, 104 N. W. 561; A. J. Dwyer Pine
Land Co. v. Whiteman, 92 Minn. 55,
99 N. W. 362.

[60] Fultz v. Peterson, 78 Miss. 128,
28 So. 829; Klein v. McNamara, 54
Miss. 90; Freeman v. Wilson, 51
Miss. 329 and cases cited; Little-
wort v. Davis, 50 Miss. 403 and cases
cited; Weathersly v. Weathersly, 40
Miss. 462, 90 Am. Dec. 344; Anding
v. Davis, 38 Miss. 574, 594; Soggins
v. Heard, 31 Miss. 426; Vasser v.
Vasser, 23 Miss. 378; Prewett v.
Dobbs, 13 Sm. & M. (Miss.) 431;
Watson v. Dickens, 12 Sm. & M.
(Miss.) 608.

[61] Freeman v. Wilson, 51 Miss. 329.

[62] Annot. Code 1892, § 4233. See
also Culp v. Wooten, 79 Miss. 503,
31 So. 1; Schwartz v. Lieber, 79
Miss. 257, 30 So. 649.

applies only where the vendor parts with the possession of the property.[63]

§ 304. **Missouri.**—A conveyance intended as a security at the time of its execution, though absolute in form, is treated as a mortgage. Such intention may be shown by parol evidence, on the ground that the denial of the trust character of the deed by the grantee is a fraud on his part, which gives a court of equity jurisdiction of the case, and thus enables it to hold to the verbal or implied defeasance as effectually as if this had been a formal written one.[64] It is not admissible at law.[65] Concerning the sufficiency of the evidence, it has been held that it must be satisfactory as to its credibility, unequivocal as to its terms and meaning, and clear and convincing beyond a reasonable doubt.[66] Where a quitclaim deed is asserted to be a mortgage parol evidence is admissible that the mortgagors were elderly people in straitened circumstances, and that they conveyed the property to enable the grantee to sell part of the land and discharge an existing mortgage.[67]

§ 304a. **Montana.**—Parol evidence is received to show that an absolute deed was in fact a mortgage. Where there is a deed and a contract to reconvey, they in law constitute a mortgage, if the papers upon their face show a loan. "Parol evidence will be received to show that the transaction was in fact a mortgage; but it seems that where the papers on their face show a mortgage, parol evidence will not be admitted to show that it was in fact a sale. Where the papers do not show that a security was meant, it is incumbent upon the party seeking to establish a mortgage to show that a mortgage was intended.

[63] Heirmann v. Stricklin, 60 Miss. 234.

[64] Brightwell v. McAfee, 249 Mo. 562, 155 S. W. 820; O'Neill v. Capelle, 62 Mo. 202. See also Jones v. Rush, 156 Mo. 364, 57 S. W. 118; Bobb v. Wolff, 148 Mo. 335, 49 S. W. 996; Book v. Beasley, 138 Mo. 455, 40 S. W. 101; Cobb v. Day, 106 Mo. 278, 17 S. W. 323; Schradski v. Albright, 93 Mo. 42, 5 S. W. 807; Zittlosen Tent Co. v. Exchange Bank, 57 Mo. App. 19; Slowey v. McMurray, 27 Mo. 113, 72 Am. Dec. 251; Tibeau v. Tibeau, 22 Mo. 77; Wilson v. Drumrite, 21 Mo. 325; Johnson v. Huston, 17 Mo. 58; Hogel v. Lindell, 10 Mo. 483; Quick v. Turner, 26 Mo. App. 29.

[65] Hogel v. Lindell, 10 Mo. 483. Under the practice act, the rule allowing the admission of parol evidence in such cases seems to be regarded as a rule of evidence which may be invoked even in an action which, under the old system, would be termed an action at law. Quick v. Turner, 26 Mo. App. 29; Wood v. Matthews, 73 Mo. 477.

[66] Rinkel v. Lubke, 246 Mo. 377, 152 S. W. 81; Gerhardt v. Tucker, 187 Mo. 46, 85 S. W. 552. See also Brightwell v. McAfee, 249 Mo. 562, 155 S. W. 820.

[67] Brightwell v. McAfee, 249 Mo. 562, 155 S. W. 820.

Where there is a deed and a contract to reconvey, and oral evidence has been introduced tending to show that the transaction was one of security, and leaving upon the mind a well-founded doubt as to the nature of the transaction, then courts of equity incline to construe the transaction as a mortgage. But where there is a deed alone, and it is sought to show a parol defeasance, then it seems the evidence must be clear and convincing."[68]

§ 305. Nebraska.—In Nebraska a formal conveyance may be shown to be a mortgage by extrinsic evidence. "This rule seems to be founded on the principle that in such case the proof raises an equity which does not contradict the writing or affect its validity, but simply varies its import so far as to show the true intention and object of the parties without a written defeasance, and establish the trust purpose for which the deed was executed. But to thus vary the legal import of such absolute deed, and especially when fraud, accident, mistake, or surprise is not alleged, the evidence in reference to the understanding and intention of the parties, at the time of the execution of the writing, must be clear, certain, and conclusive, before a court of chancery will determine such writing to be a mortgage security only."[69]

The later decisions strongly assert the general doctrine that, when by satisfactory evidence it is established that an absolute deed was executed and intended as a security in the nature of a mortgage, a court of equity will carry out the intention of the parties by declaring it a mortgage.[70]

Where land has been conveyed by absolute deed in satisfaction of a pre-existing mortgage thereon, a subsequent parol promise to recon-

[68] Gassert v. Bogk, 7 Mont. 585, 19 Pac. 281, quoted from the able opinion of Judge Bach, affirmed by the Supreme Court in Bogk v. Gassert (U. S.), 13 Sup. Ct. 738. See also Gibson v. Morris State Bank (Mont.), 140 Pac. 76. See ante § 247a.

[69] O'Hanlon v. Barry, 87 Nebr. 522, 127 N. W. 860; Huston v. Canfield, 57 Nebr. 345, 77 N. W. 763; Stall v. Jones, 47 Nebr. 706, 66 N. W. 653; Kemp v. Small, 32 Nebr. 318, 49 N. W. 169; Tower v. Fetz, 26 Nebr. 706, 42 N. W. 884, 18 Am. St. 795; Eiseman v. Gallagher, 24 Nebr. 79, 37 N. W. 941; Newman v. Edwards, 22 Nebr. 248, 34 N. W. 382; McHugh v. Smiley, 17 Nebr. 626, 24 N. W. 277; Deroin v. Jennings, 4 Nebr. 97; Schade v. Bessinger, 3 Nebr. 140; Wilson v. Richards, 1 Nebr. 342; Fahay v. State Bank, 1 Nebr. (Unoff.) 89, 95 N. W. 505. But where an absolute deed was given as a mortgage, the grantee, in order to defeat the equity of redemption on the ground of a parol settlement or an oral election to regard the conveyance as an absolute deed, must establish such parol agreement by a clear preponderance of the evidence. Sprecher v. Folda, 94 Nebr. 201, 142 N. W. 539.

[70] Wilde v. Homan, 58 Nebr. 634, 79 N. W. 546; Morrow v. Jones, 41 Nebr. 867, 60 N. W. 369; Kemp v. Small, 32 Nebr. 318, 49 N. W. 169; Tower v. Fetz, 26 Nebr. 706, 42 N. W. 884, 18 Am. St. 795.

vey to the grantor, without any new consideration, will not sustain an action to declare the deed a mortgage and redeem from the liens which have been canceled.[71]

Where a party acquires title by purchase at a sheriff's sale under a parol agreement with the judgment debtor to hold the title as security for the loan of the money to satisfy the lien, and to reconvey when the money is refunded, parol evidence is admissible to show the nature of the transaction.[72]

§ 306. **Nevada.**—In Nevada a conveyance absolute upon its face may be shown by parol to be a mortgage. It is not received to contradict the deed, but to prove an equity superior to it.[73] The proof on the part of the plaintiff must be clear, satisfactory and convincing. The presumption is in favor of the natural effect of the instrument. The evidence to overcome such presumption should be so cogent, weighty and convincing as to leave no doubt upon the mind.[74]

§ 307. **New Hampshire.**—In New Hampshire it is provided by statute that every conveyance of lands made for the purpose of securing the payment of money or the performance of any other thing in the condition thereof stated is a mortgage; but that no conveyance in writing of any lands shall be defeated, nor any estate incumbered by any agreement, unless it is inserted in the condition of the conveyance, and made part thereof, stating the sum of money to be secured, or other thing to be performed.[75] But a proviso that if the grantor comply with the conditions of a bond executed by him to the grantee at the same time, the deed shall be void, sufficiently sets forth the thing to be done.[76] And a condition to indemnify the mortgagee against loss, by reason of having indorsed certain notes payable at banks named, is sufficiently certain to warrant the admission of parol evidence to show what notes were intended to be secured.[77] An indemnifying clause in a mortgage, to hold one "harmless from all liabilities where he is bound for me," is sufficient to admit evidence of the iden-

[71] Samuelson v. Mickey, 73 Nebr. 852, 106 N. W. 461.

[72] Dickson v. Stewart, 71 Nebr. 424, 98 N. W. 1085, 115 Am. St. 596.

[73] Cookes v. Culbertson, 9 Nev. 199; Saunders v. Stewart, 7 Nev. 200; Bingham v. Thompson, 4 Nev. 224; Carlyon v. Lannan, 4 Nev. 156.

[74] Pierce v. Traver, 13 Nev. 526; Bingham v. Thompson, 4 Nev. 224.

[75] Stat. July 3, 1829; Pub. Stats. 1901, ch. 139, §§ 1, 2; Knickerbocker Trust Co. v. Penacook Mfg. Co., 100 Fed. 814; Boody v. Davis, 20 N. H. 140, 51 Am. Dec. 210.

[76] New Hampshire v. Willard, 10 N. H. 210; Bassett v. Bassett, 10 N. H. 64.

[77] Benton v. Sumner, 57 N. H. 117.

tity of a note as one for the payment of which the mortgage was intended as security.[78]

Under this statute a parol agreement entered into between the grantor and grantee at the time of the delivery of the deed that the grantee should give a bond to reconvey, even after a bond is subsequently given in pursuance of such agreement, does not make the conveyance a mortgage.[79] Even a bond executed at the same time with the conveyance, providing that the conveyance shall be void upon payment of a certain sum of money, does not constitute a mortgage. The defeasance must be inserted in the deed itself; and a deed without such defeasance confers an absolute title upon the grantee.[80]

§ 308. **New Jersey.**—The efficacy of the parol evidence is not to establish an agreement to reconvey, the specific performance of which a court of equity will enforce, but to establish the true nature and effect of the instrument by showing the object for which it was made. It is well settled that this may be done.[81] The proof by parol evidence that a deed was intended as a mortgage, must be clear and convincing.[82]

The question in every case is, whether the transaction was a sale and conveyance, coupled with an agreement for a reconveyance, or whether it was a security for a loan. "Any means of proof may be used to show it to be the latter: the declaration of the parties; the relations subsisting between them; the possession of the premises retained by the complainant; the value of the property, compared with the money paid; the understanding that the sums advanced should be repaid; and the payment of interest meanwhile on the amount. The distinction between parol evidence to vary a written instrument and parol evidence showing facts which control its operation is employed to reconcile the allowance of such proofs with the statute of frauds and the general rule of common law. Deeds absolute on their face

[78] Barker v. Barker, 62 N. H. 366; Farrington v. Barr, 36 N. H. 86.

[79] Boody v. Davis, 20 N. H. 140, 51 Am. Dec. 210; Clark v. Hobbs, 11 N. H. 122; Porter v. Nelson, 4 N. H. 130; Runlet v. Otis, 2 N. H. 167; Lund v. Lund, 1 N. H. 39, 8 Am. Dec. 29.

[80] Tifft v. Walker, 10 N. H. 150.

[81] Vanderhoven v. Romaine, 56 N. J. Eq. 1, 39 Atl. 129; Winters v. Earl, 52 N. J. Eq. 52, 28 Atl. 15; Frink v. Adams, 36 N. J. Eq. 485; Budd v. Van Orden, 33 N. J. Eq. 143; Sweet v. Parker, 22 N. J. Eq. 453; Crane v. Decamp, 21 N. J. Eq. 414; Condit v. Tichenor, 19 N. J. Eq. 43; Vandegrift v. Herbert, 18 N. J. Eq. 466; Lokerson v. Stillwell, 13 N. J. Eq. 357; Crane v. Bonnell, 2 N. J. Eq. 264; Youle v. Richards, 1 N. J. Eq. 534.

[82] This rule was recognized in Wilson v. Terry, 70 N. J. Eq. 231, 62 Atl. 310.

have been frequently decreed to be mortgages by this court, and the grantors allowed to redeem.'[83]'

A parol agreement is admissible to prove that a mortgage, though absolute in terms, was given as collateral security for the payment of the mortgagor's chattel mortgage; for such evidence does not vary the terms of the instrument.[84]

§ **308a. New Mexico.**—An absolute unconditional deed may be shown to be a mortgage by agreement of the parties, and this agreement may be proved by parol evidence.[85] Only a preponderance of evidence seems to be necessary.[86]

§ **309. New York.**—In New York such evidence was admitted in some of the earlier cases solely upon the ground of fraud or mistake.[87] But Chancellor Kent apparently thought the only fraud necessary to be shown was the fraud on the part of the grantee in attempting to convert a mortgage into an absolute sale;[88] and it is distinctly asserted in other cases that it is not necessary to prove that the deed was given in this form through fraud or mistake.[89] This evidence is admitted in all cases without reference to the reason why a written defeasance was omitted, or why the grantee denies the redeemable character of the

---

[83] Per Vice-Chancellor Dodd, in Sweet v. Parker, 22 N. J. Eq. 453; Hogan v. Jaques, 19 N. J. Eq. 123, 97 Am. Dec. 644. See also Phillips v. Hulsizer, 20 N. J. Eq. 308.

[84] Wilbur v. Jones, 80 N. J. Eq. 520, 86 Atl. 769.

[85] Alexander v. Cleland, 13 N. Mex. 524, 86 Pac. 425; King v. Warrington, 2 N. Mex. 318.

[86] Alexander v. Cleland, 13 N. Mex. 524, 86 Pac. 425.

[87] Taylor v. Baldwin, 10 Barb. (N. Y.) 582; Webb v. Rice, 6 Hill (N. Y.) 219. In the latter case it was held that such evidence is inadmissible at law, and earlier cases at law in which it had been admitted were overruled. Strong v. Stewart, 4 Johns. Ch. (N. Y.) 167; Marks v. Pell, 1 Johns. Ch. (N. Y.) 594; Stevens v. Cooper, 1 Johns. Ch. (N. Y.)

425, 7 Am. Dec. 499; Swart v. Service, 21 Wend. (N. Y.) 36. 35 Am. Dec. 211; Patchin v. Pearce, 12 Wend. (N. Y.) 61.

[88] Strong v. Stewart, 4 Johns. Ch. (N. Y.) 167.

[89] Brown v. Clifford, 7 Lans. (N. Y.) 46, per Mr. Justice Mullin: "I have said that parol evidence was admissible, although no fraud or mistake in making the deed was alleged or proved, and I say this because in nearly all of the cases cited, and in the numerous others upon the same point, no fraud or mistake was either alleged or proved, nor was any suggestion made that any such allegation or proof was necessary to justify the court in admitting the parol evidence."

conveyance. It is admitted to show what the transaction really was,[90] and that it was intended as security for money.[91]

[90] Horn v. Keteltas, 46 N. Y. 605. "It is now too late," says Mr. Justice Allen, delivering the judgment in this case, "to controvert the proposition that a deed, absolute upon its face, may in equity be shown, by parol or other extrinsic evidence, to have been intended as a mortgage; and fraud or mistake in the preparation or as to the form of the instrument is not an essential element in an action for relief, and to give effect to the intention of the parties. The courts of this state are fully committed to the rule. It is not enough to authorize a reconsideration of the questions, that the rule has been authoritatively adjudged otherwise as a rule of evidence in common-law courts, and that eminent judges have contended earnestly against its adoption as a rule in courts of equity. Notwithstanding their protests, the rule has been, upon the fullest consideration, deliberately established, and can not now be lightly departed from."

The learned judge refers to the earlier cases in New York, saying: "The principle was recognized by the Chancellor in Holmes v. Grant, 8 Paige (N. Y.) 243, although it was not applied in that case, and had been before asserted under like circumstances in Robinson v. Cropsey, 2 Edw. (N. Y.) 138. "It was expressly adjudged in Strong v. Stewart, 4 Johns. Ch. (N. Y.) 167, that parol evidence was admissible to show that a mortgage only was intended by an assignment absolute in terms; and to the same effect is Clark v. Henry, 2 Cow. (N. Y.) 324, which was followed by this court in Murray v. Walker, 31 N. Y. 399. In Hodges v. Tennessee Marine &c. Ins. Co., 8 N. Y. 416, the court says that 'from an early day in this state the rule, that parol evidence is admissible for the purpose named, has been established as the law of our courts of equity, and it is not fitting that the question should be re-examined, and the cases in which it has been so adjudged are cited with approval.' In Sturtevant v. Sturtevant, 20 N. Y. 39, 75 Am. Dec. 371, the same judge, pronouncing the opinion as in the case last cited, distinguishes between the case of a mortgage and trust; and it was decided that, while a deed absolute in terms could be shown to be a mortgage, a trust in favor of the grantee could not be established by parol. See also Despard v. Walbridge, 15 N. Y. 374. The rule does not conflict with that other rule which forbids that a deed or other written instrument shall be contradicted or varied by parol evidence. The instrument is equally valid, whether intended as an absolute conveyance or a mortgage. Effect is only given to it according to the intent of the parties, and courts of equity will always look through the forms of a transaction and give effect to it, so as to carry out the substantial intent of the parties." Odell v. Montross, 68 N. Y. 499; Meehan v. Forrester, 52 N. Y. 277; Carr v. Carr, 52 N. Y. 251, 4 Lans. (N. Y.) 314; Fiedler v. Darrin, 50 N. Y. 437; Stoddard v. Whiting, 46 N. Y. 627; Sturtevant v. Sturtevant, 20 N. Y. 39, 75 Am. Dec. 371; Despard v. Walbridge, 15 N. Y. 374; Hodges v. Tennessee Marine &c. Ins. Co., 8 N. Y. 416; Clifford v. Gates, 70 Hun 597, 23 N. Y. S. 1085; Barton v. Lynch, 69 Hun 1, 23 N. Y. S. 217; Erwin v. Curtis, 43 Hun (N. Y.) 292; Simon v. Schmidt, 41 Hun (N. Y.) 318. See also Van Dusen v. Worrell, 4 Abb. App. Dec. (N. Y.) 473; Gilroy v. Everson-Hickok Co., 118 App. Div. 733, 103 N. Y. S. 620; Loomis v. Loomis, 60 Barb. (N. Y.) 22; Clark v. Henry, 2 Cow. (N. Y.) 324; McIntyre v. Humphreys, 1 Hoff. (N. Y.) 31; Marks v. Pell, 1 Johns. Ch. (N. Y.) 594; Moses v. Murgatroyd, 1 Johns. Ch. (N. Y.) 119, 7 Am. Dec. 478; Brown v. Clifford, 7 Lans. (N. Y.) 46; Van Buren v. Olmstead, 5 Paige (N. Y.) 9; Whittick v. Kane, 1 Paige (N. Y.) 202.

[91] Bork v. Martin, 132 N. Y. 280, 30 N. E. 584, 28 Am. St. 570; In re Mechanics' Bank, 156 App. Div. 343, 141 N. Y. S. 473; Richardson v. Beaber, 62 Misc. 542, 115 N. Y. S. 821.

Where it was claimed that a vendor of land held title merely as security, exclusion of parol evidence that the purchase-money under a contract for the purchase of land had been substantially paid was held erroneous.[92] And where an heir conveyed, by an instrument absolute on its face, his interest as devisee under his parent's will, parol evidence was held admissible to show the conveyance was intended as a mortgage.[93]

The evidence that a deed absolute on its face was intended as a mortgage must be clear and satisfactory,[94] and according to recent decisions must be convincing and conclusive beyond a reasonable doubt.[95]

§ 310. North Carolina.—Parol evidence has generally been admitted only upon the usual grounds of equity jurisdiction in cases of fraud, undue advantage, ignorance, accident, and mistake.[96] "In equity plaintiffs are allowed, by making the proper preliminary allegations,— as that a certain clause was intended to be inserted in a written instrument, but was omitted by the ignorance or mistake of the draftsman; or by some fraud or circumvention of the opposite party; or some oppression or advantage taken of the plaintiff's necessities; or when an unlawful trust was designedly omitted to evade the law,— to call for a discovery on the oath of the defendant. If the fact is confessed, the plaintiff can have relief. If it be denied, although it was for a long time questioned, it is now settled that, provided the matter can be established, not merely by the declarations of the parties or the unaided memory of the witnesses, but by facts and circumstances dehors the instrument, such as are more tangible and less liable to be mistaken than mere words, equity will give relief, by considering the clause thus shown to have been omitted as if it had been set out in the instrument."[97] Thus, where there was a preliminary

[92] Brown v. Crossman, 206 N. Y. 471, 100 N. E. 42.

[93] Nevius v. Nevius, 117 App. Div. 236, 101 N. Y. S. 1091.

[94] Reich v. Cochran, 102 N. Y. S. 827, affirmed 139 App. Div. 931, 124 N. Y. S. 1127 (clear and convincing evidence); In re Holmes, 79 App. Div. 264, 79 N. Y. S. 592, affd. 176 N. Y. 603, 68 N. E. 1118.

[95] Richardson v. Beaber, 62 Misc. 542, 115 N. Y. S. 821; Bascombe v. Marshall, 129 App. Div. 516, 113 N. Y. S. 991.

[96] Hall v. Lewis, 118 N. Car. 509, 24 S. E. 209; Sprague v. Bond, 115 N. Car. 530, 20 S. E. 709; Green v. Sherrod, 105 N. Car. 197, 10 S. E. 986; Norris v. McLam, 104 N. Car. 159, 10 S. E. 140; Egerton v. Jones, 102 N. Car. 278, 9 S. E. 2, 12 S. E. 434; Elliott v. Maxwell, 7 Ired. (N. Car.) 246; Sellers v. Stalcup, 7 Ired. Eq. (N. Car.) 13; Kelly v. Bryan, 6 Ired. Eq. (N. Car.) 283; Blackwell v. Overby, 6 Ired. Eq. (N. Car.) 38; M'Laurin v. Wright, 2 Ired. Eq. (N. Car.) 94; McDonald v. McLeod, 1 Ired. Eq. (N. Car.) 221; Steel v. Black, 3 Jones Eq. (N. Car.) 427; Glisson v. Hill, 2 Jones Eq. (N. Car.) 256; Cook v. Gudger, 2 Jones Eq. (N. Car.) 172.

[97] Kelly v. Bryan, 6 Ired. Eq. (N.

allegation of oppression to account for the omission of the defeasance, and it was shown that the plaintiff was hard pressed for money, and was forced to consent to the omission of this clause; and it was further shown that there was great inadequacy of price, and that the plaintiff retained possession and paid interest, he was allowed tô redeem.[98]

The grantor having executed a deed, knowing it to be absolute, must be deemed to have intended it to be so, unless there is strong and clear proof of mistake or imposition.[99] Evidence merely of the declarations of the parties is not sufficient, but there must be evidence of facts and circumstances inconsistent with the idea of an absolute sale.[1] Parol evidence of admissions on the part of the grantee that the deed was intended as a mere security are not alone sufficient. There must also be shown facts or circumstances inconsistent with the idea of an absolute conveyance, and proof of fraud, oppression, ignorance, or mistake, so as to account for the conveyance being absolute on its face, when such was not the intention.[2] The evidence must be clear and convincing.[3]

Recent cases, however, seem to dispense with the proof of fraud, accident or mistake as prerequisite to the introduction of parol evidence that a deed was intended as a mortgage. The court adopting the language of a New York decision says: "It is well established that a deed, absolute on its face, can be shown by parol or other extrinsic evidence to have been intended as a mortgage; and that, the relation of mortgagor and mortgagee being thus established, all the rights and obligations incident to that relation attach to the parties."[4]

However disguised may be the terms, if the real object of the transaction be the taking or holding of land for the security of a loan or debt, it is in equity a mortgage, and if necessary the subsequent con-

---

Car.) 283, per Pearson, J. See also Poston v. Jones, 122 N. Car. 536, 29 S. E. 951; Egerton v. Jones, 107 N. Car. 284, 12 S. E. 434; Hinton v. Pritchard, 107 N. Car. 128, 12 S. E. 242; Norris v. McLam, 104 N. Car. 159, 10 S. E. 140; Egerton v. Jones, 102 N. Car. 278, 9 S. E. 2; Bonham v. Craig, 80 N. Car. 224.

[98] Streator v. Jones, 3 Hawks (N. Car.) 423, 1 Murph. 499. In such case the relation of mortgagor and mortgagee must be alleged and proved. Norris v. McLam, 104 N. Car. 159, 10 S. E. 140.

[99] Elliott v. Maxwell, 7 Ired. Eq. (N. Car.) 246.

[1] Watkins v. Williams, 123 N. Car. 170, 31 S. E. 388.

[2] Green v. Sherrod, 105 N. Car. 197, 10 S. E. 986; Glisson v. Hill, 2 Jones Eq. (N. Car.) 256; Brothers v. Harrill, 2 Jones Eq. (N. Car.) 209; Cook v. Gudger, 2 Jones Eq. (N. Car.) 172. Admissions of parties, in their pleadings, may stand for the writings required by the statute of frauds. Sandling v. Kearney, 154 N. Car. 596, 70 S. E. 942.

[3] Watkins v. Williams, 123 N. Car. 170, 31 S. E. 388.

[4] Sandling v. Kearney, 154 N. Car. 596, 70 S. E. 942, quoting Carr v. Carr, 52 N. Y. 251.

duct of the parties, with reference to the matter, may be examined to ascertain their true intent, as the giving of a note for the money or receiving part payment or interest on the same.[5]

§ 310a. North Dakota.—It is provided that every transfer of an interest in real estate not in trust, made as a security for the performance of another act, is to be deemed a mortgage; and the fact that the transfer was made subject to defeasance may be proved, except as against a subsequent purchaser or incumbrancer for value and without notice, though it does not appear by the terms of the instrument.[6] Thus an instrument in the form of an absolute deed may be proved by parol testimony to be a mortgage, as between the parties and all others with knowledge of its purpose.[7] The declarations of the parties both at the time of execution and subsequently are also admissible to determine their real intention and the nature of the instrument.[8]

A deed absolute in form will not be declared a mortgage unless the evidence is clear, satisfactory and convincing that such was the intent of the parties when the deed was executed.[9] This rule applies only to parol evidence, and where there is a defeasance in a collateral paper or contract for resale, no such rule of strict proof applies.[10]

§ 311. Ohio.—Parol evidence is admitted to show that an absolute deed is a mortgage. If given as a security it is a mortgage, whatever its form; and the fact of its being so given, and not the evidence of the fact, determines its character. In such a case a trust arises in favor of the grantor. Being a tacit trust, it is more difficult to establish than one that is expressed; but when it is ascertained, the same consequences attach to it. The evidence for this purpose must be clear, certain, and conclusive.[11]

[5] Sandling v. Kearney, 154 N. Car. 596, 70 S. E. 942.

[6] Civil Code N. Dak. 1913, §§ 6151, 6153. O'Toole v. Omlie, 8 N. Dak. 444, 79 N. W. 849.

[7] Omlie v. O'Toole, 16 N. Dak. 126, 112 N. W. 677. See also Smith v. Jensen, 16 N. Dak. 408, 114 N. W. 306. The form of the deed is not controlling, parol evidence being admissible to show what the agreement was. Miller v. Smith, 20 N. Dak. 96, 126 N. W. 499.

[8] Miller v. Smith, 20 N. Dak. 96, 126 N. W. 499.

[9] Adams v. McIntyre, 22 N. Dak. 337, 133 N. W. 915; Miller v. Smith, 20 N. Dak. 96, 126 N. W. 499; Smith v. Jensen, 16 N. Dak. 408, 114 N. W. 306; Northwestern Fire &c. Ins. Co. v. Lough, 13 N. Dak. 601, 102 N. W. 160; Wells v. Geyer, 12 N. Dak. 316, 96 N. W. 289; Forester v. Van Auken, 12 N. Dak. 175, 96 N. W. 301; Little v. Brawn, 11 N. Dak. 410, 92 N. W. 800; McGuin v. Lee, 10 N. Dak. 160, 86 N. W. 714; Jasper v. Hazen, 4 N. Dak. 1, 58 N. W. 454, 23 L. R. A. 58; Devore v. Woodruff, 1 N. Dak. 143, 45 N. W. 701.

[10] Smith v. Hoff, 23 N. Dak. 37, 135 N. W. 772, Ann. Cas. 1914 C, 1072.

[11] Kemper v. Campbell, 44 Ohio St. 210, 6 N. E. 566; Shaw v. Walbridge,

§ 311a. Oklahoma.—A deed absolute on its face given as security may be shown by parol evidence to be a mortgage.[12] The holder of such deed can only acquire title by foreclosure. The mortgagor must enforce his rights by redemption.[13] Where a transaction is in substance a loan of money upon security of real estate, equity will look behind the forms in which the contrivance of the lender has enveloped it, and if satisfied by extraneous or parol evidence, will declare the conveyance a mortgage.[14]

§ 311b. Oregon.—Parol evidence is admissible to show that a deed absolute on its face was intended to operate as a mortgage,[15] whether the deed is between the parties to the suit or is procured to be made to the grantee therein by a third person.[16] Such evidence is admitted not to contradict a written instrument of conveyance, but for the purpose of establishing the intent of the parties.[17] The deed must speak for itself and a contradictory provision or condition can not be ingrafted upon a deed absolute in form by parol evidence.[18]

The intention of the parties is the only safe criterion for determining whether the transaction is a mortgage, and for the purpose of showing such intention evidence may be given of the situation of the parties; of the value of the property as compared with the price fixed for it; of the conduct of the parties before and after the transaction; and of all the surrounding facts and circumstances, so far as they serve to explain the real character of the transaction.[19] The evidence must be clear and satisfactory, and sufficient to overcome the presumption that the instrument is what it purports to be.[20]

33 Ohio St. 1; Wilson v. Giddings, 28 Ohio St. 554; Slutz v. Desenberg, 28 Ohio St. 371; Mathews v. Leaman, 24 Ohio St. 615; Cotterell v. Long, 20 Ohio 464; Marshall v. Stewart, 17 Ohio 356; Stall v. Cincinnati, 16 Ohio St. 169; Miller v. Stokely, 5 Ohio St. 194; Miami Exporting Co. v. Bank of United States, Wright (Ohio) 249.

[12] Wagg v. Herbert, 19 Okla. 525, 92 Pac. 250; Weiseham v. Hocker, 7 Okla. 250, 54 Pac. 464; Balduff v. Griswold, 9 Okla. 438, 60 Pac. 223; Comp. Laws Okla. 1909, §§ 1196, 1198; Laws 1897, p. 95, § 12. See also Krauss v. Potts, 38 Okla. 674, 135 Pac. 362.

[13] Weiseham v. Hocker, 7 Okla. 250, 54 Pac. 454.

[14] Wagg v. Herbert, 19 Okla. 525, 92 Pac. 250. See ante § 266.

[15] Grover v. Hawthorne, 62 Ore. 77, 121 Pac. 808; Elliott v. Bozorth, 52 Ore. 391, 97 Pac. 632; Eldriedge v. Hoefer, 52 Ore. 241, 93 Pac. 246, judgment modified 94 Pac. 563; Swegle v. Belle, 20 Ore. 323, 25 Pac. 633; Hurford v. Harned, 6 Ore. 362.

[16] Bickel v. Wessinger, 58 Ore. 98, 113 Pac. 34.

[17] Grover v. Hawthorne, 62 Ore. 77, 121 Pac. 808.

[18] Harmon v. Grants Pass Banking &c. Co., 60 Ore. 69, 118 Pac. 188.

[19] Marshall v. Williams, 21 Ore. 268, 28 Pac. 137; Swegle v. Belle, 20 Ore. 323, 25 Pac. 633; Stephens v. Allen, 11 Ore. 188, 3 Pac. 168.

[20] Beall v. Beall, 67 Ore. 33, 135

The rule that an absolute deed given as security for the repayment of a loan may be shown by parol to be intended as a mortgage, applies where the purchaser of land borrows the purchase-money and causes the title to pass directly from the vendor to the creditor as security for the loan.[21]

§ 312. **Pennsylvania.**—The courts of this state have no general equity jurisdiction. Mortgages are dealt with as matters of strict law; and yet parol evidence, under restrictions as to its sufficiency, was, prior to the statute of 1881, admitted to show that an absolute conveyance is in fact a mortgage.[22] That statute requires a written defeasance to reduce an absolute deed to a mortgage, and therefore the cases relating to the use of parol evidence to convert such a deed into a mortgage are now applicable only to deeds executed before the passage of that statute.[23] "In strict law," said Chief Justice Lowrie, "no mortgage is allowed that is not proved by written evidence, and the judge may not admit any lower evidence on equitable grounds without seeing that justice imperiously demands it. The case of a lost instrument is a useful analogy. If, in such a case, the judge refuses

Pac. 185; Bickel v. Wessinger, 58 Ore. 98, 113 Pac. 34; Osgood v. Osgood, 35 Ore. 1, 56 Pac. 1017; Albany &c. Canal Co. v. Crawford, 11 Ore. 243, 4 Pac. 113. The evidence must be clear, consistent and convincing. Hall v. O'Connell, 52 Ore. 164, 95 Pac. 717, decree modified on rehearing 96 Pac. 1070. Proof of intention to create a mortgage ought clearly to preponderate. Harmon v. Grants Pass Banking &c. Co., 60 Ore. 69, 118 Pac. 188.

[21] Hall v. O'Connell, 52 Ore. 164, 95 Pac. 717, decree modified on rehearing 96 Pac. 1070.

[22] Wallace v. Smith, 155 Pa. St. 78, 25 Atl. 807; Fisher v. Witham, 132 Pa. St. 488, 19 Atl. 276; Pancake v. Cauffman, 114 Pa. St. 113; Hartley's Appeal, 103 Pa. St. 23; Huoncker v. Merkey, 102 Pa. St. 462; Umbenhower v. Miller, 101 Pa. St. 71; Stewart's Appeal, 98 Pa. St. 377; Paige v. Wheeler, 92 Pa. St. 282; Fessler's Appeal, 75 Pa. St. 483; McClurkan v. Thompson, 69 Pa. St. 305; Odenbaugh v. Bradford, 67 Pa. St. 96; Harper's Appeal, 64 Pa. St. 315, 7 Phila. 276; Houser v. Lamont, 55 Pa. St. 311, 93 Am. Dec. 755; Guthrie v. Kahle, 46 Pa. St. 331; Kenton v. Vandergrift, 42 Pa. St. 339; Rhines v. Baird, 41 Pa. St. 256; Kellum v. Smith, 33 Pa. St. 158; Todd v. Campbell, 32 Pa. St. 250; Cole v. Bolard, 22 Pa. St. 431; McLanahan v. McLanahan, 6 Humph. (Pa.) 99; Friedley v. Hamilton, 17 Serg. & R. (Pa.) 70, 71 Am. Dec. 638; Kelly v. Thompson, 7 Watts (Pa.) 401; Jaques v. Weeks, 7 Watts (Pa.) 261; Kerr v. Gilmore, 6 Watts (Pa.) 405; Kunkle v. Wolfersberger, 6 Watts (Pa.) 126; Manufacturers' &c. Bank v. Bank of Pa., 7 Watts & S. (Pa.) 335; Reeder v. Trullinger, 151 Pa. St. 287, 24 Atl. 1104. In this case the deed was before the Act of June 8, 1881.

[23] By statute it is provided that no defeasance should have the effect of reducing an absolute deed to a mortgage unless it be made in writing, signed, sealed, acknowledged, and delivered by the grantee, and recorded within sixty days from the execution of the same. Laws of 1881, p. 84, Purd. Pa. Dig. 1905, p. 1180, § 154, p. 5395, § 22. McHendry v. Shaffer, 242 Pa. 476, 89 Atl. 587. This statute does not impair the obligation of contracts. Felts'

to hear secondary evidence until he is perfectly satisfied that the justice of the case can not be otherwise administered, much more, it would seem, ought this to be so where the evidence, which the law makes not merely primary but essential, never had any existence."[24] Therefore it is held that mere evidence of verbal declarations by the parties, unless corroborated by other facts and circumstances, is not a proper substitute for the written evidence required by law.[25]

The presumption always is that the deed is what it purports to be. To prove it otherwise, the evidence must be clear and convincing. If the intention of the parties be to create a mortgage rather than a conveyance, this must be established, not merely by loose conversations between the parties, or by declarations to third persons, but by facts and circumstances outside the deed, inconsistent with the idea of an absolute purchase.[26] The principle upon which parol evidence is admitted is to show and explain the true intention and purpose of the parties, in order to develop the real character of the transaction.[27] Whether the transaction is to be regarded as an absolute conveyance or a mortgage depends more upon its attendant circumstances than upon any express agreement making it defeasible; and it is doubtful whether parol proof of an agreement to reconvey, standing alone and without fraud, would be permitted to convert it into a mortgage. But

Appeal (Pa.), 17 Atl. 195. But an agreement which does not amount to a defeasance, and is not executed and recorded as provided, may amount to a sale with a declaration of trust. Potter v. Langstrath (Pa.), 25 Atl. 76. Unless a written defeasance is executed, and acknowledged by the grantee, and duly recorded, a grantee can not be declared a trustee, ex maleficio, unless fraud is alleged. O'Donnell v. Vandersaal, 213 Pa. 551, 63 Atl. 60.

[24] An action for damages for the breach of a parol contract to convey land can not be sustained where it appears that such contract was merely a parol defeasance of an absolute deed. Molly v. Ulrich, 133 Pa. St. 41, 19 Atl. 305. "Equitable principles are continually insinnating themselves into the system of the law. Our law abounds with principles that were formerly purely equitable. And the process by which this takes place is perfectly natural; for, in the progress of society, and in the natural changes of its customs, exceptional principles are constantly demanding recognition, and continually enlarging their sphere, until they become general, and thus truly legal. In this way the social system keeps pace with the changes of social purposes and principles, and never requires any violent disruption." De France v. De France, 34 Pa. St. 385, per Lowrie, C. J.

[25] De France v. De France, 34 Pa. St. 385; Todd v. Campbell, 32 Pa. St. 250.

[26] Barber v. Lefavour, 176 Pa. St. 331, 35 Atl. 202; Wallace v. Smith, 155 Pa. St. 78, 25 Atl. 807; Lance's Appeal, 112 Pa. St. 456; Logue's Appeal, 104 Pa. St. 136; Hartley's Appeal, 103 Pa. St. 23; Nicolls v. McDonald, 101 Pa. St. 514; Rowand v. Finney, 96 Pa. St. 192; Todd v. Campbell, 32 Pa. St. 250, per Strong, J.

[27] Kerr v. Gilmore, 6 Watts (Pa.) 405.

facts and circumstances inconsistent with its being an absolute conveyance may be proved; and if they are clear and convincing enough
to authorize a court of equity to infer that the conveyance was intended to secure a loan, under the jurisprudence of this state they
should be submitted to a jury to find whether the transaction was a
mortgage.[28] The proof must establish an agreement for a reconveyance substantially contemporaneous with the execution and delivery
of the deed, and not rest on the subsequent admissions and declarations of the mortgagee only. The agreement need not, however, be
express; it may be inferred from circumstances.[29] The testimony of
the grantor, not supported by other witnesses or circumstances, is insufficient.[30] The evidence must be clear, precise, indubitable, and
sufficient to satisfy the mind of a chancellor; otherwise it is error to
submit it to the jury.[31]

A parol agreement, upon conveyance of land by a debtor to a creditor in satisfaction of a debt, that both parties should attempt to sell
the property and that upon sale any surplus above the debt should be
paid to the debtor, does not render the transaction a mortgage with
an unrecorded defeasance, void under the statute.[32]

After default, a mortgager conveyed the property absolutely to the
mortgagee, and the mortgagee conveyed it to a relative without consideration. Subsequently the mortgagor sought to compel reconveyance under a parol agreement permitting redemption on payment of
principal and interest within a year. It was held that because of the
failure of the grantor to require a written defeasance in accordance
with the statute, no trust or equity of redemption could be enforced.[33]

§ 313. Rhode Island.

§ 313. **Rhode Island.**—Parol evidence is admissible to show that an
absolute deed was intended as a mortgage, and that the defeasance

---

[28] Kinports v. Boynton, 120 Pa. St.
306, 14 Atl. 135; Pearson v. Sharp,
115 Pa. St. 254, 9 Atl. 38; Huoncker
v. Merkey, 102 Pa. St. 462; Nicolls
v. McDonald, 101 Pa. St. 514; Plumer v. Guthrie, 76 Pa. St. 441; Mc-
Clurkan v. Thompson, 69 Pa. St.
305; Baisch v. Oakeley, 68 Pa. St.
92; Rhines v. Baird, 41 Pa. St. 256.

[29] Plumer v. Guthrie, 76 Pa. St.
441. "Less than this would not only
conflict with the rules of evidence
which prescribe the manner in
which a written instrument may be
changed by parol, but also defeat

the wise provision of the statute of
frauds." Per Mercur, J. See also
Moran v. Munhall, 204 Pa. 242, 53
Atl. 1094.

[30] Barber v. Lafavour, 176 Pa. St.
331, 35 Atl. 202.

[31] Pancake v. Cauffman, 114 Pa.
St. 113, 7 Atl. 67; Lance's Appeal,
112 Pa. St. 456, 4 Atl. 375; Munger
v. Casey (Pa. St.), 17 Atl. 36; Porter v. Mayfield, 21 Pa. St. 263.

[32] Moran v. Munhall, 204 Pa. 242,
53 Atl. 1094.

[33] Wingenroth v. Dellenbach, 219
Pa. 536, 69 Atl. 84.

has been omitted or destroyed by fraud or mistake, or omitted by design, upon mutual confidence between the parties.[34]

Where a deed absolute in form was given as security for the grantee's indorsement of the grantor's note, there being a contemporaneous written instrument from the grantee by the terms of which he agreed that if the note was paid to transfer the land on demand, a reconveyance was necessary to revest the title in the grantor.[35]

§ 314. **South Carolina.**—Parol evidence is received to convert an instrument absolute on its face into a defeasible instrument, where the omission to reduce the defeasance to writing was occasioned by fraud or mistake.[36] It appears by recent cases that it may be received to show the intention of the parties to secure a debt and create a mortgage;[37] but the evidence must be very clear and convincing.[38] In the absence of clear, unequivocal, and convincing evidence, the presumption will prevail that a deed of conveyance is what on its face it appears to be.[39] The burden of proof is on the party alleging the absolute deed to be a mortgage.[40]

§ 314a. **South Dakota.**—A deed absolute may by parol evidence be shown to be a mortgage.[41] The statute is similar to that of North Dakota.[42] But it has been held that the code provision that a transfer of property as security for the performance of an act is to be deemed a mortgage, does not authorize parol evidence concerning the intent of the parties in the execution of an absolute deed, without limitations

[34] Taylor v. Luther, 2 Sumn. (U. S.) 228; Nichols v. Reynolds, 1 R. I. 30, 36 Am. Dec. 238.

[35] Knowles v. Knowles, 25 R. I. 464, 56 Atl. 775.

[36] Carter v. Evans, 17 S. Car. 458; Walker v. Walker, 17 S. Car. 329; Arnold v. Mattison, 3 Rich. Eq. (S. Car.) 153.

[37] Leland v. Morrison, 92 S. Car. 501, 75 S. E. 889; Surasky v. Weintraub, 90 S. Car. 522, 73 S. E. 1029; Welborn v. Dixon, 70 S. Car. 108, 49 S. E. 232; Brickle v. Leach, 55 S. Car. 510, 33 S. E. 720; Brown v. Bank, 55 S. Car. 51, 32 S. E. 816; Shiver v. Arthur, 54 S. Car. 184, 32 S. E. 310; Petty v. Petty, 52 S. Car. 54, 29 S. E. 406; Campbell v. Linder, 50 S. Car. 169, 27 S. E. 648; McAteer v. McAteer, 31 S. Car. 313, 9 S. E. 966; Hodge v. Weeks, 31 S. Car. 276, 9 S. E. 953; Brownlee v. Martin, 21 S. Car. 392.

[38] Banks v. Frith, 97 S. Car. 362, 81 S. E. 677; Williams v. McManus, 90 S. Car. 490, 73 S. E. 1038; Hodge v. Weeks, 31 S. Car. 276, 9 S. E. 953; Nesbitt v. Cavender, 27 S. Car. 1, 2 S. E. 702; Arnold v. Mattison, 3 Rich. Eq. (S. Car.) 153.

[39] Creswell v. Smith, 61 S. Car. 575, 39 S. E. 757; Brown v. Bank of Sumter, 55 S. Car. 51, 32 S. E. 816.

[40] Miller v. Price, 66 S. Car. 85, 44 S. E. 584.

[41] Meyer v. Davenport Elevator Co., 12 S. Dak. 172, 80 N. W. 189; Ashton v. Ashton, 11 S. Dak. 610, 79 N. W. 1001.

[42] Rev. Code S. Dak. 1903, §§ 2044, 2046. See ante § 310a.

or qualifications as to the interest intended to be conveyed.[43] And an absolute deed, though intended as a mortgage, has been held under the code to convey the absolute title, as against one claiming under the grantee's assignee for the benefit of creditors, without notice of the parol defeasance.[44]

§ 315. **Tennessee.**—It is well settled that, although a conveyance be absolute in its terms, it may be shown by parol proof to be a mortgage. It seems to be admitted for the purpose of showing the intention of the parties and the real character of the transaction.[45] When a parol defeasance is shown, the effect of it is to reduce the title under an absolute deed to what was intended by the parties, a defeasible estate; a security for a debt, instead of a sale.[46] The evidence, however, must be clear and decisive, as the presumption is in favor of the deed as it appears upon its face.[47]

A decree confirming a partition sale and vesting title in one who has advanced purchase-money for a bidder who was unable to comply with his bid may be held a mortgage where it clearly appears that the title was taken by him as security only for the repayment of the money advanced.[48]

§ 316. **Texas.**—The doctrine that parol evidence is admissible to prove that an absolute deed was intended merely as a security for the payment of a debt, is fully recognized.[49] And conversely, parol testi-

[43] Bernardy v. Colonial &c. Mtg. Co., 20 S. Dak. 193, 105 N. W. 737.
[44] S. Dak. Civ. Code, § 2071; Grigsby v. Verch (S. Dak.), 146 N. W. 1075.
[45] Jones v. Cullen, 100 Tenn. 1, 42 S. W. 873; Bowman v. Felts (Tenn.), 42 S. W. 810; Robinson v. Lincoln Savings Bank, 85 Tenn. 363, 3 S. W. 656; Nichols v. Cabe, 3 Head (Tenn.) 92; Ruggles v. Williams, 1 Head (Tenn.) 141; Guinn v. Locke, 1 Head (Tenn.) 110; Jones v. Jones, 1 Head (Tenn.) 105; Hinson v. Partee, 11 Humph. (Tenn.) 587; Ballard v. Jones, 6 Humph. (Tenn.) 455; Leech v. Hillsman, 8 Lea (Tenn.) 747; Yarborough v. Newell, 10 Yerg. (Tenn.) 376; Lane v. Dickerson, 10 Yerg. (Tenn.) 373; Brown v. Wright, 4 Yerg. (Tenn.) 57.
[46] Ruggles v. Williams, 1 Head (Tenn.) 141.
[47] Sellers v. Sellers (Tenn.), 53 S. W. 316; Slawson v. Denton (Tenn.), 48 S. W. 350; Nickson v. Toney, 3 Head (Tenn.) 655; Haynes v. Swann, 6 Heisk. (Tenn.) 560; Lane v. Dickerson, 10 Yerg. (Tenn.) 373; Hickman v. Quinn, 6 Yerg. (Tenn.) 96; Hammonds v. Hopkins, 3 Yerg. (Tenn.) 525; Overton v. Bigelow, 3 Yerg. (Tenn.) 513.
[48] Spicer v. Johnson (Tenn.), 61 S. W. 1041.
[49] Nagle v. Simmank, 54 Tex. Civ. App. 432, 116 S. W. 862; Stafford v. Stafford, 29 Tex. Civ. App. 73, 71 S. W. 984; Hexter v. Urwitz, 6 Tex. Civ. App. 580, 25 S. W. 1101; White v. Harris, 85 Tex. 42, 19 S. W. 1077; McLean v. Ellis, 79 Tex. 398, 15 S. W. 394; Ullman v. Jasper, 70 Tex. 446, 7 S. W. 763; Hubby v. Harris, 68 Tex. 91, 3 S. W. 558; Calhoun v. Lumpkin, 60 Tex. 185; Loving v. Milliken, 59 Tex. 423; Gibbs v. Penny, 43 Tex. 560; Ruffier v. Womack, 30 Tex. 332; Grooms

mony of the intention of the parties is admissible to rebut the intention that the deed is a mortgage.[50] Where there is an absolute conveyance and an oral or written agreement to reconvey, parol evidence is admissible to show the real situation of the parties, the existence of a debt, the intention to secure its payment, and the actual character of the instruments, as evidence of a mortgage, between the original parties, and as against those claiming under the grantee except bona fide purchasers for value without notice.[51]

Parol evidence is admitted to show that the deed was really executed and delivered upon certain trusts, not reduced to writing, which the grantee promised to perform. These trusts existing in parol are established to prevent the fraudulent use of the deed or written instrument.[52] It is not necessary that there should be any charge of fraud, mistake, or surprise to afford a foundation for the introduction of such evidence.[53] When it is attempted to use the deed for a fraudulent purpose, or one wholly different from that intended by the parties, equity interposes to prevent the fraud and establish the trust. The trust must be shown with "clearness and certainty,"[54] and it has sometimes been said that it must be shown by the testimony of more than one witness, unless that testimony be supported by corroborating circumstances.[55]

A few cases have held it error for the court to instruct the jury

v. Rust, 27 Tex. 231; Mann v. Falcon, 25 Tex. 271; Cuney v. Dupree, 21 Tex. 211; Hannay v. Thompson, 14 Tex. 142; McClenny v. Floyd, 10 Tex. 159; Miller v. Thatcher, 9 Tex. 482, 60 Am. Dec. 172; Mead v. Randolph, 8 Tex. 191; Carter v. Carter, 5 Tex. 93; Stampers v. Johnson, 3 Tex. 1. In an action to declare an absolute deed a mortgage, it may be shown that the grantor, when he made depositions stating that the instrument was intended as a mortgage, was mentally incompetent, though insanity was not pleaded. Kellner v. Randle (Tex. Civ. App.), 165 S. W. 509. Prior to the execution of a deed, it was orally agreed in two separate conversations that the deed to be executed should be security for money loaned. It was held that such parol agreement would control the character of the instrument, and it was error to limit the evidence of such conversations by instruction that it had been admitted for throwing light on the final trade, but that the jury were to determine the cause according to the understanding and agreement of the parties when the trade was finally consummated by delivery of the deed. Grier v. Casares (Tex. Civ. App.), 76 S. W. 451.

[50] Browning v. Currie (Tex. Civ. App.), 140 S. W. 479.

[51] Hall v. Jennings (Tex. Civ. App.), 104 S. W. 489.

[52] Moreland v. Barnhart, 44 Tex. 275; Grooms v. Rust, 27 Tex. 231; Mead v. Randolph, 8 Tex. 191.

[53] Mead v. Randolph, 8 Tex. 191; Carter v. Carter, 5 Tex. 93.

[54] Miller v. Yturria, 69 Tex. 549, 7 S. W. 206; Pierce v. Fort, 60 Tex. 464; Markham v. Carothers, 47 Tex. 21; Hughes v. Delaney, 44 Tex. 529; Moreland v. Barnhart, 44 Tex. 275.

[55] Moreland v. Barnhart, 44 Tex. 275 and cases cited.

that the proof that an absolute deed is a mortgage must be "clear and convincing," as exacting a higher degree of proof than the law requires in cases of this character.[56] But several recent cases state the prevailing rule that one who claims a deed absolute on its face to be a mortgage has the burden of establishing the fact by clear and satisfactory evidence.[57] As in Pennsylvania, there being no court of chancery, such evidence must be passed upon by a jury.[58]

§ 316a. Utah.—An absolute conveyance may be shown to be a mortgage by parol evidence that the consideration of it is a loan, or that the instrument was obtained by fraud, mistake or undue influence.[59] Equity will look beyond the terms of an absolute deed and inquire into the object of the parties and the real nature of the transaction, and when it is shown that the deed is one of security only it will be given effect as such.[60] In determining whether an instrument should be treated as a deed or mortgage the courts will consider all the facts and circumstances of the transaction, the object and purpose for which it was given and received, and whether it was given as security or for a bargain and sale of the land.[61]

§ 317. Vermont.—In Vermont parol testimony is admissible to show that a deed absolute in terms was in fact made as security for money loaned, if the grantor has remained in possession, and the title has continued in the grantee.[62] If he has parted with the title, the grantor loses his right to redeem. The fact that the grantor remains in possession is always regarded as a strong circumstance tending to show that the deed is a mortgage.[63] The absence of any written evi-

---

[56] Wallace v. Berry, 83 Tex. 328, 18 S. W. 595; Miller v. Yturria, 69 Tex. 549, 7 S. W. 206; Prather v. Wilkens, 68 Tex. 187, 4 S. W. 252.

[57] Harrison v. Hogue (Tex. Civ. App.), 136 S. W. 118; Frazer v. Seureau (Tex. Civ. App.), 128 S. W. 649; Stringfellow v. Braselton, 54 Tex. Civ. App. 1, 117 S. W. 204; Rotan Grocery Co. v. Turner, 46 Tex. Civ. App. 534, 102 S. W. 932; Lowry v. Carter, 46 Tex. Civ. App. 488, 102 S. W. 930; Irvin v. Johnson, 44 Tex. Civ. App. 436, 98 S. W. 405; Goodbar v. Bloom, 43 Tex. Civ. App. 434, 96 S. W. 657.

[58] Ullman v. Jasper, 70 Tex. 446, 7 S. W. 663; Miller v. Yturria, 69 Tex. 549, 7 S. W. 206; Moreland v. Barnhart, 44 Tex. 275; Ruffier v.

Womack, 30 Tex. 332; Carter v. Carter, 5 Tex. 93.

[59] Ewing v. Keith, 16 Utah 312, 52 Pac. 4; Wasatch Min. Co. v. Jennings, 5 Utah 243, 385, 16 Pac. 399, 15 Pac. 65.

[60] Duerden v. Solomon, 33 Utah 468, 94 Pac. 978.

[61] Duerden v. Solomon, 33 Utah 468, 94 Pac. 978.

[62] Morgan v. Walbridge, 56 Vt. 405; Crosby v. Leavitt, 50 Vt. 239.

[63] Hills v. Loomis, 42 Vt. 562; Wing v. Cooper, 37 Vt. 169; Rich v. Doane, 35 Vt. 125; Bigelow v. Topliff, 25 Vt. 273, 60 Am. Dec. 264; Hyndman v. Hyndman, 19 Vt. 9, 46 Am. Dec. 171; Wright v. Bates, 13 Vt. 341; Mott v. Harrington, 12 Vt. 199; Baxter v. Willey, 9 Vt. 276, 31

dence of a debt does not make the deed less effectual as a mortgage.[64] The circumstances existing at the time of the execution of the deed determine its character, regardless of the effect resulting from changed conditions of the parties.[65]

The ground upon which parol evidence is admitted was stated in an early case to be that when the instrument is in fact a mortgage, and there is an attempt to set it up as an absolute conveyance, there is a fraudulent application or use made of it which a court in chancery may interfere with to prevent.[66] In later cases, however, parol evidence seems to be admitted on the broad, equitable ground of showing the intention of the parties that the absolute deed should operate as a security for a debt.[67] More than a mere preponderance of evidence is required; it must exclude all reasonable doubt on the question.[68]

§ 318. **Virginia.**—Parol evidence is admitted in equity to determine whether a deed shall be considered a mortgage or an absolute purchase,[69] and the evidence is not restricted to cases of fraud, accident or mistake.[70] The court is governed by the intention of the parties. The question is whether the parties intended to treat of a purchase, or to secure the repayment of money. To determine this, the whole circumstances of the transaction will be examined.[71] The evidence must be clear, unequivocal and convincing.[72]

Am. Dec. 623; Campbell v. Worthington, 6 Vt. 448. In Mussey v. Bates, 60 Vt. 271, 14 Atl. 457, the state of the pleadings made parol evidence inadmissible. In Conner v. Chase, 15 Vt. 764, it was held that such evidence was inadmissible to show that a deed of warranty, followed by possession through several successive grantees by similar deeds, was a mortgage.

[64] Graham v. Stevens, 34 Vt. 166, 80 Am. Dec. 675.

[65] Herrick v. Teachout, 74 Vt. 196, 52 Atl. 432.

[66] Wright v. Bates, 13 Vt. 341.

[67] Hills v. Loomis, 42 Vt. 562; Rich v. Doane, 35 Vt. 125.

[68] Skeels v. Blanchard (Vt.), 81 Atl. 913.

[69] Skeels v. Blanchard (Vt.) 81 Atl. 913.

[70] Batchelder v. Randolph, 112 Va. 296, 71 S. E. 533; Bachrach v. Bachrach, 111 Va. 232, 68 S. E. 985.

[71] Tuggle v. Berkeley, 101 Va. 83, 43 S. E. 199; French v. Williams,

82 Va. 462, 4 S. E. 591; Bruce v. Slemp, 82 Va. 352, 4 S. E. 692; Edwards v. Wall, 79 Va. 321; Robertson v. Campbell, 2 Call (Va.) 421; Chapman v. Turner, 1 Call (Va.) 280, 1 Am. Dec. 514; Summers v. Darne, 31 Grat. (Va.) 791; Snavely v. Pickle, 29 Grat. (Va.) 27; Phelps v. Seely, 22 Grat. (Va.) 573; Dabney v. Green, 4 Hen. & Munf. (Va.) 101, 4 Am. Dec. 503; Bird v. Wilkinson, 4 Leigh (Va.) 266; Crawford v. Jarrett, 2 Leigh (Va.) 630; Pennington v. Hanby, 4 Munf. (Va.) 140; King v. Newman, 2 Munf. (Va.) 40; Breckenridge v. Auld, 1 Rob. (Va.) 148; Thompson v. Davenport, 1 Wash. (Va.) 125; Ross v. Norvell, 1 Wash. (Va.) 14, 1 Am. Dec. 422.

[72] Hill v. Saunders, 115 Va. 50, 78 S. E. 559; Motley v. Carstairs, 114 Va. 429, 76 S. E. 948; Batchelder v. Randolph, 112 Va. 296, 71 S. E. 533; Bachrach v. Bachrach, 111 Va. 232, 68 S. E. 985; Holladay v. Willis, 101 Va. 274, 43 S. E. 616.

§ 318a. **Washington.**—The common-law rule that evidence will not be admitted to show that a deed is in fact a mortgage, and the chancery rule that it will only be received to show fraud and mistake, do not prevail in this state, but the true intent of the parties may be shown by competent testimony.[73]

When it is shown by parol or other extrinsic evidence that the parties intended a mortgage, or security for a debt, a deed absolute on its face will be treated as such.[74] Where there is no written defeasance, strict proof of such intention is required and the evidence must be clear, satisfactory, unequivocal, and convincing in favor of the party seeking to have the instrument declared a mortgage.[75]

§ 319. **West Virginia.**—The rule in relation to the admission of parol evidence, to show that a deed is a mortgage, is the same as that which prevails in Virginia. The real nature of the transaction may be shown by parol evidence of surrounding circumstances.[76]

Parol evidence that a deed absolute on its face is intended as a mortgage is inadmissible in a suit at law.[77] Equity admits such evidence not to vary or contradict the deed, but to establish an independent equity founded upon the intent of the parties.[78] The evidence must be clear and decisive.[79]

§ 320. **Wisconsin.**—In Wisconsin the admissibility of parol proof, to show a deed absolute on its face to be a mortgage, is the settled

[73] Dempsey v. Dempsey, 61 Wash. 632, 112 Pac. 755.
[74] Ross v. Howard, 31 Wash. 393, 72 Pac. 74; Miller v. Ausenig, 2 Wash. T. 22, 3 Pac. 111.
[75] Beverly v. Davis (Wash.), 140 Pac. 696; Hansen v. Abrams, 76 Wash. 457, 136 Pac. 678; Mittlesteadt v. Johnson, 75 Wash. 550, 135 Pac. 214; Hoover v. Bouffleur, 74 Wash. 382, 133 Pac. 602; Kegley v. Skillman, 68 Wash. 637, 123 Pac. 1081; Johnson v. National Bank of Commerce, 65 Wash. 261, 118 Pac. 21; Washington Safe Deposit &c. Co. v. Lietzow, 59 Wash. 281, 109 Pac. 1021; Sahlin v. Gregson, 46 Wash. 452, 90 Pac. 592; Reynolds v. Reynolds, 42 Wash. 107, 84 Pac. 579.
[76] Shank v. Groff, 43 W. Va. 337,

27 S. E. 340; McNeel v. Auldridge, 34 W. Va. 748, 12 S. E. 851; Gilchrist v. Beswick, 33 W. Va. 168, 10 S. E. 371; Kerr v. Hill, 27 W. Va. 576; Matheney v. Sandford, 26 W. Va. 386; Vangilder v. Hoffman, 22 W. Va. 1; Hoffman v. Ryan, 21 W. Va. 415; Lawrence v. DuBois, 16 W. Va. 443; Troll v. Carter, 15 W. Va. 267; Davis v. Demming, 12 W. Va. 246; Klinck v. Price, 4 W. Va. 4, 6 Am. Rep. 268, citing the above cases in Virginia.
[77] Billingsley v. Stutler, 52 W. Va. 92, 43 S. E. 96.
[78] Shields v. Simonton, 65 W. Va. 179, 63 S. E. 972.
[79] Way v. Mayhugh, 57 W. Va. 175, 50 S. E. 724; Vangilder v. Hoffman, 22 W. Va. 1.

law.[80] This is not only the rule in equity,[81] but at law as well. The evidence, however, must be clear and convincing, equal in force to that upon which a deed will be reformed, and leaving no substantial doubt that the real intention of the parties was to execute a mortgage security.[82]

Where a grantor had fraudulently represented himself as owner of the land conveyed, evidence in favor of the grantee, that the deed was given as security and intended as a mortgage is not objectionable on the ground that it altered the terms of the written contract.[83]

As to the grounds upon which the evidence is admitted, it was said in an early case that "it is the fraudulent use of the deed which equity interposes to detect and prevent, and for this purpose parol proof is admissible, not to vary the deed, but to maintain the equity which attaches to the transaction inherently, and which the deed or contract of the parties does not create and can not·destroy. If an equity of redemption really attaches to the transaction itself, any attempt to defeat that equity by setting up the deed as absolute is fraudulent."[84]

But in the later cases, parol evidence seems to have been admitted upon the broad ground of showing that the absolute deed was intended

[80] Lynch v. Ryan, 132 Wis. 271, 112 N. W. 427; Barchent v. Snyder, 128 Wis. 423, 107 N. W. 329; Wilcox v. Bates, 26 Wis. 465. "Notwithstanding what was said in the opinion in Rasdall v. Rasdall, 9 Wis. 379, as to the admissibility of parol evidence to prove an absolute deed a mortgage, upon principle it has since been frequently held by this court that the admissibility of such evidence had been so long established by authority as to have become a rule of property, which ought not to be changed by the judicial department." Per Paine, J. See also Beebe v. Wisconsin Mtg. Loan Co., 117 Wis. 328, 93 N. W. 1103; Schierl v. Newburg, 102 Wis. 552, 78 N. W. 761; McCormick v. Herndon, 67 Wis. 648, 31 N. W. 303; Schriber v. Le Clair, 66 Wis. 579, 29 N. W. 570, 889; Parish v. Reeve, 63 Wis. 315, 23 N. W. 568; Rockwell v. Humphrey, 57 Wis. 410, 15 N. W. 394; Starks v. Redfield, 52 Wis. 349, 9 N. W. 168; Butler v. Butler, 46 Wis. 430, 1 N. W. 70; Spencer v. Fredendall, 15 Wis. 666; Sweet v. Mitchell, 15 Wis. 641; Plato v. Roe, 14 Wis. 453.

[81] Kent v. Agard, 24 Wis. 378; Kent v. Lasley, 24 Wis. 654. "The doctrine that a deed absolute in its terms can be thus transformed into a mortgage, and the title of the holder defeated, is purely an equitable, and not a legal, doctrine. It had its origin in the Court of Chancery, in which court alone the remedy could formerly be administered. The rules and practice of that court were such as to afford many safeguards to the rights of the grantee, and to obviate many evils which must otherwise have grown up out of the doctrine." Per Dixon, C. J.

[82] Becker v. Howard, 75 Wis. 415, 44 N. W. 755; McCormick v. Herndon, 67 Wis. 648, 31 N. W. 303; Sable v. Maloney, 48 Wis. 331, 4 N. W. 479; Smith v. Crosby, 47 Wis. 160, 2 N. W. 104; McClellan v. Sanford, 26 Wis. 595; Harrison v. Juneau Bank, 17 Wis. 340; Fowler v. Adams, 13 Wis. 458; Lake v. Meacham, 13 Wis. 355; Newton v. Holley, 6 Wis. 592.

[83] Hurlbert v. T. D. Kellogg Lumber &c. Co., 115 Wis. 225, 91 N. W. 673.

[84] Rogan v. Walker, 1 Wis. 527.

by the parties to operate as a security for a debt.[85]   Parol evidence is admissible to show that the purpose of several writings, taken together, was to create a mortgage, though they bear on their face no semblance thereof.[86]

§ 321.   **Review of cases.**—A review of the cases, with reference to the grounds upon which parol evidence is admitted to prove that an absolute conveyance is a mortgage in equity, will show that in the earliest cases, both in England and America, it was admitted solely upon the ground of fraud, accident, or mistake, which are ordinary grounds of equity jurisdiction.   In several states this is still declared by the courts or by statute to be the only ground upon which their interference, in such case, can be justified; or, at any rate, there have been no decisions which distinctly place such interference upon any other ground.[87]   Such seems to be the doctrine in Connecticut, Georgia, North Carolina, and Rhode Island.[88]

In a few states, as for instance Missouri and Ohio, the intention of the parties to create a security only seems to be regarded as raising a trust in favor of the grantor which equity will enforce.[89]

In New Hampshire and Pennsylvania, no conveyance is a mortgage unless the condition is inserted in the deed.

But the doctrine in this country, now generally accepted, is that the admission of parol evidence is not confined to cases of distinct fraud on the part of the grantee in obtaining a deed without a defeasance, or mistake on the part of the grantor in giving such a deed.   The doctrine declared by the Supreme Court of the United States in Russell v. Southard,[90] and Peugh v. Davis,[91] and by the Supreme Court of Massachusetts in several cases,[92] is, that the mere fact that an absolute deed was intended merely as security affords ground of jurisdiction to courts of equity to interfere and give relief; that a security in this form is so calculated to be an instrument of oppression and wrong as

---

[85] McFarlane v. Loudon, 99 Wis. 620, 75 N. W. 394, 67 Am. St. 883; Becker v. Howard, 75 Wis. 415, 44 N. W. 755; Schriber v. Le Clair, 66 Wis. 579, 29 N. W. 570, 289; Hoile v. Bailey, 58 Wis. 448, 17 N. W. 322; Starks v. Redfield, 52 Wis. 349, 9 N. W. 168; Howe v. Carpenter, 49 Wis. 697, 6 N. W. 357.

[86] Beebe v. Wisconsin Mtg. Loan Co., 117 Wis. 328, 93 N. W. 1103.

[87] Marshall v. Williams, 21 Ore. 268, 28 Pac. 137 (following text).

[88] See ante §§ 285, 300. See also Maxwell v. Mountacute, Prec. Ch. 526; Walker v. Walker, 2 Atk. 98; Joynes v. Statham, 3 Atk. 388; Pym v. Blackburn, 3 Ves. Jr. 34; Townshend v. Stangroom, 6 Ves. 328.

[89] This was formerly the case in Maine. See ante § 298.

[90] See ante § 285.

[91] 96 U. S. 332.

[92] See ante §300.

in itself to constitute a quasi fraud, which equity should relieve against; that the fraud or fault is inherent in the transaction itself, and does not arise out of the subsequent conduct of the grantee in attempting to retain the property. This doctrine is declared with more or less distinctness in the later decisions of the courts of Alabama, Arkansas, California, Colorado, Delaware, Florida, Illinois, Indiana, Iowa, Kansas, Kentucky, Louisiana, Maryland, Massachusetts, Maine, Michigan, Minnesota, Mississippi, Nebraska, Nevada, New Jersey, New Mexico, New York, North Dakota, South Carolina, South Dakota, Tennessee, Texas, Vermont, Virginia, Washington, West Virginia and Wisconsin.

§ 321a. **Strict construction of rule admitting parol evidence.**— Although parol evidence is now generally admitted to prove the intention of the parties, the courts say that the rule is not to be enlarged in its application, but is to be strictly construed.[93] Consequently, parol evidence is admissible so far as it tends to show the relation between the parties, or any other fact or circumstance to control the nature of the deed and establish an equity of redemption, but no further.[94] And such evidence is admissible only to show the intention of the parties at the time of the execution of the deed.[95] It has also been held that parol evidence is not admissible to show that a conveyance, appearing on its face to be a mortgage, was in fact intended to operate as an absolute or conditional sale.[96]

§ 322. **Statute of frauds—Rule prohibiting contradiction of written instruments.**—The statute of frauds was at first supposed to stand in the way of allowing a g_rant, absolute on its face, to be established by parol evidence as a mortgage. But the courts, after a struggle and much hesitation, established the doctrine, as otherwise it was found that the statute designed to prevent frauds and perjuries would become in this way an effectual instrument of fraud or injustice.[97] It is now well settled that it does not violate the statute of frauds to

[93] Howland v. Blake, 7 Biss. (U. S.) 40, 12 Fed. Cas. No. 6792, affd. 97 U. S. 624, 24 L. ed. 1027.

[94] Sutphen v. Cushman, 35 Ill. 186; Hall v. Jennings (Tex. Civ. App.), 104 S. W. 489.

[95] Barrett v. Carter, 3 Lans. (N. Y.) 68; Hall v. Jennings (Tex. Civ. App.), 104 S. W. 489.

[96] Johnson v. Prosperity Loan &c. Assn., 94 Ill. App. 260; Woods v. Wallace, 22 Pa. St. 171; Brown v. Nickle, 6 Pa. St. 390; Kunkle v. Wolfersberger, 6 Watts (Pa.) 126; Eckford v. Berry, 87 Tex. 415, 28 S. W. 937. See also Wolfe v. McMillan, 117 Ind. 587, 20 N. E. 509.

[97] The doctrine was established only after a struggle. Carr v. Carr, 52 N. Y. 251; Sprague v. Bond, 115 N. Car. 530.

admit parol evidence of the real agreement,[98] as an element in the proof of fraud, or other vice in the transaction, which is relied upon to defeat the written instrument.[99]

Although the admission of such evidence is placed upon different grounds by different courts, there is substantial unanimity in holding that, when once the fact is established that the grant was intended as a mortgage, the conveyance will be so regarded. The statute of frauds does not interpose any insuperable obstacle to granting relief in such a case, because relief, if granted, is obtained by setting aside the deed; and parol evidence is availed of to establish the equitable grounds for impeaching that instrument, and not for the purpose of setting up some other or different contract to be substituted in its place. The equities of the parties are adjusted according to the nature of the transaction and the facts and circumstances of the case, including the real agreement.[1] Lord Hardwicke said that such evidence has nothing to do with the statute of frauds.[2]

Neither does the rule which excludes parol testimony to contradict

---

[98] Wyman v. Babcock, 2 Curt. (U. S.) 386, Fed. Cas. No. 18113; Jenkins v. Eldredge, 3 Story (U. S.) 299, Fed. Cas. No. 7267; Glass v. Hieronymus, 125 Ala. 140, 28 So. 71, 82 Am. St. 225; Sewell v. Price, 32 Ala. 97; La Cotts v. La Cotts (Ark.), 159 S. W. 1111; Byers v. Locke, 93 Cal. 493, 29 Pac. 119, 27 Am. St. 212; Whitsett v. Kershow, 4 Colo. 419; Union Mut. Life Ins. Co. v. White, 106 Ill. 67; Reigard v. McNeil, 38 Ill. 400; Brown v. Follette, 155 Ind. 316, 58 N. E. 197; Landers v. Beck, 92 Ind. 49; Salinger v. McAllister (Iowa), 146 N. W. 8; Jones v. Gillett, 142 Iowa 506, 118 N. W. 314, 121 N. W. 5; McDonald v. Kellogg, 30 Kans. 170, 2 Pac. 507; Glynn v. Home Bldg. Assn., 22 Kans. 746; Moore v. Wade, 8 Kans. 380; Barnes v. Crockett, 4 Kans. App. 777, 5 Kans. App. 48, 46 Pac. 997; Reed v. Reed, 75 Maine 264; Jennings v. Demmon, 194 Mass. 108, 80 N. E. 471; Potter v. Kimball, 186 Mass. 120, 71 N. E. 308; Hennessey v. Conner, 139 Mass. 120, 29 N. E. 475; Campbell v. Dearborn, 109 Mass. 130, 12 Am. Rep. 671; Klein v. McNamara, 54 Miss. 90; Anding v. Davis, 38 Miss. 574, 77 Am. Dec. 658; Chance v. Jennings, 159 Mo. 544, 61 S. W. 177;

Sweet v. Parker, 22 N. J. Eq. 453; Carr v. Carr, 52 N. Y. 251; Sturtevant v. Sturtevant, 20 N. Y. 39, 75 Am. Dec. 371; Streator v. Jones, 10 N. Car. 423; Mathews v. Leaman, 24 Ohio St. 615; Swegle v. Belle, 20 Ore. 323, 25 Pac. 633; Sweetzer's Appeal, 71 Pa. St. 264; Pattison v. Horn, 1 Grant (Pa.) 301; Guinn v. Locke, 1 Head (Tenn.) 110; Wasatch Min. Co. v. Jennings, 5 Utah 385, 16 Pac. 399; Jordan v. Warner, 107 Wis. 539, 83 N. W. 946; Cotterell v. Purchase, Cas. temp. Talbot, 61; Lincoln v. Wright, 4 De G. & J. 16; Walker v. Walker, 2 Atk. 98. See also Phillips v. Hulsizer, 20 N. J. Eq. 308; Sweet v. Mitchell, 15 Wis. 641. But see Emerson v. Atwater, 7 Mich. 12.

[99] Amory v. Lawrence, 3 Cliff. (U. S.) 523; Wyman v. Babcock, 2 Curtis (U. S.) 386; Taylor v. Luther, 2 Sum. (U. S.) 228; Reed v. Reed, 75 Maine 264; Campbell v. Dearborn, 109 Mass. 130, 12 Am. Rep. 671; Glass v. Hulbert, 102 Mass. 24, 3 Am. Rep. 418; Newton v. Fay, 10 Allen (Mass.) 505; Horn v. Keteltas, 46 N. Y. 605.

[1] Campbell v. Dearborn, 109 Mass. 130, 12 Am. Rep. 671, per Wells, J.

[2] Walker v. Walker, 2 Atk. 98.

or vary a written instrument have any application to such a case.[3] This rule has reference to the language used by the parties. That can not be qualified or varied from its natural import, but must speak for itself. The rule does not forbid an inquiry into the object of the parties in executing and receiving the instrument. Thus it may be shown that a deed was made to defraud creditors, or to give a preference, or to secure a loan, or for any other object not apparent on its face. The object of parties in such cases will be considered by a court of equity; it constitutes a ground for the exercise of its jurisdiction, which will always be asserted to prevent fraud or oppression, and to promote justice.[4] The courts have frequently remarked, in admitting parol evidence, that it was not received to contradict or vary the terms of the instrument, but to prove an equity superior to the mere form of the conveyance.[5] The rule excluding parol evidence to contradict or vary a written instrument, is limited in its application to the parties to the instrument and their privies.[6]

Where a creditor, holding an absolute deed as security, has in a fair transaction released to the debtor other security on his parol agreement to release his interest in the land to the creditor, the debtor will not be allowed to invoke the statute of frauds in an action to cancel his absolute conveyance, but the court will leave this absolute deed to carry the estate in fee, as it purports to do.[7]

[3] Florida First Nat. Bank v. Ashmead, 23 Fla. 379, 2 So. 657; Northern Assur. Co. v. Chicago Mut. Bldg. &c. Assn., 198 Ill. 474, 64 N. E. 979; Bearss v. Ford, 108 Ill. 16; Pickett v. Wadlow, 94 Md. 564, 51 Atl. 423; Booth v. Robinson, 55 Md. 419; Grier v. Casares (Tex. Civ. App.), 76 S. W. 451; Shields v. Simonton, 65 W. Va. 179, 63 S. E. 972; Wolf v. Theresa Village Mut. Fire Ins. Co., 115 Wis. 402, 91 N. W. 1014; Hurlbert v. T. D. Kellogg Lbr. &c. Co., 115 Wis. 225, 91 N. W. 673; Butler v. Butler, 46 Wis. 430, 1 N. W. 70. See also Brick v. Brick, 98 U. S. 514, 25 L. ed. 256; Kinkead v. Peet, 137 Iowa 692, 114 N. W. 616.

[4] Peugh v. Davis, 96 U. S. 332, per Field, J.; Brick v. Brick, 98 U. S. 514, 25 L. ed. 256.

[5] Pierce v. Robinson, 13 Cal. 116; Cold v. Beh, 152 Iowa 368, 132 N. W. 73; Bradford v. Helsell, 150 Iowa 732, 130 N. W. 908; Jones v. Gillett, 142 Iowa, 506, 118 N. W.

314; Beroud v. Lyons, 85 Iowa 482, 52 N. W. 486; Pickett v. Wadlow, 94 Md. 564, 51 Atl. 423; Booth v. Robinson, 55 Md. 419; Schade v. Bessinger, 3 Nebr. 140; Cookes v. Culbertson, 9 Nev. 199; Saunders v. Stewart, 7 Nev. 200; Kelly v. Bryan, 41 N. Car. 283; Rogan v. Walker, 1 Wis. 527. In Massachusetts parol evidence is admitted not to vary or contradict the deed, but to establish an inherent fault in the transaction or its consideration. Cullen v. Carey, 146 Mass. 50, 15 N. E. 131; Pond v. Eddy, 113 Mass. 149; McDonough v. O'Niel, 113 Mass. 92; McDonough v. Squire, 111 Mass. 217; Campbell v. Dearborn, 109 Mass. 130, 12 Am. Rep. 671.

[6] Northern Assur. Co. v. Chicago Mut. Bldg. &c. Assn., 198 Ill. 474, 64 N. E. 979; Harts v. Emery, 184 Ill. 560, 56 N. E. 865; Silsbury v. Blumb, 26 Ill. 287.

[7] Bazemore v. Mullins, 52 Ark. 207, 12 S. W. 474.

§ 323. Statute of frauds—Subsequent fraudulent conduct of grantor.—The grantor is not estopped from showing the true character of the transaction by reason that he has sworn, on an application for discharge in bankruptcy, that he had no interest in the land. The original transaction being without fraud, the subsequent improper conduct of the mortgagor, even if he were guilty of perjury, would not affect his right. At any rate the mortgagee can not make the misconduct of the mortgagor, about which he need not concern himself, a ground for the nonperformance of his own contract.[8]

The statute of frauds can not be set up as inconsistent with showing that an absolute deed was intended by the parties merely as a security of the payment of money.[9] On the other hand, parol evidence has been frequently admitted on the ground that it is a fraud for the grantee to declare that to be a sale which was really a mortgage.[10] If the grantee deny the trust raised by a verbal defeasance, on proof of the trust, such denial is regarded in some courts as a fraud, and the grantee is held to be as firmly bound by his verbal agreement as he would be by a written one, "hedged about with all the formal solemnity known to the law."[11]

Apart from the statute of frauds, parol evidence is admissible to show that an absolute deed was intended as a mortgage, not only as between the original parties, but as against third persons, provided they have not been misled by the form of the instrument, or acted in reliance upon it.[12] But such evidence is not admissible as against a subsequent purchaser without notice.[13]

An agreement between the grantee and a third person that the land

---

[8] Smith v. Cremer, 71 Ill. 185.

[9] Russell v. Southard, 12 How. (U. S.) 139, 13 L. ed. 927; Raynor v. Lyons, 37 Cal. 452; Lee v. Evans, 8 Cal. 424; Salinger v. McAllister (Iowa), 146 N. W. 8; Jones v. Gillett, 142 Iowa 506, 118 N. W. 314, 121 N. W. 5; McDonald v. Kellogg, 30 Kans. 170, 2 Pac. 507; Glynn v. Home Bldg. Assn., 22 Kans. 746; Jennings v. Demmon, 194 Mass. 108, 80 N. E. 471; Potter v. Kimball, 186 Mass. 120, 71 N. E. 308; Hennessey v Conner, 139 Mass. 120, 29 N. E. 475; Sweet v. Parker, 22 N. J. Eq. 453; Payne v. Patterson, 77 Pa. St. 134; Maffit v. Rynd, 69 Pa. St. 380, and cases cited; Houser v. Lamont, 55 Pa. St. 311, 93 Am. Dec. 755. See ante § 322.

[10] Russell v. Southard, 12 How. (U. S.) 139, 13 L. ed. 927; Roberts v. McMahan, 4 Greene (Iowa) 34; Brightwell v. McAfee, 249 Mo. 562, 155 S. W. 820; O'Neill v. Capelle, 62 Mo. 202; Strong v. Stewart, 4 Johns. Ch. (N. Y.) 167; Markham v. Carothers, 47 Tex. 21; Hughes v. Delaney, 44 Tex. 529; Moreland v. Barnhart, 44 Tex. 275; Wright v. Bates, 13 Vt. 341; Rogan v. Walker, 1 Wis. 527.

[11] O'Neill v. Capelle, 62 Mo. 202.

[12] Walton v. Cronly, 14 Wend. (N. Y.) 63. See also Carter v. Hallahan, 61 Ga. 314.

[13] Hills v. Loomis, 42 Vt. 562; Conner v. Chase, 15 Vt. 764.

shall be conveyed to him upon the payment by him of the purchase-money and interest, is within the statute of frauds, because such a conveyance and agreement do not constitute a mortgage.[14] To constitute a mortgage, such agreement must be made with the grantor and not with a stranger. A promise by a third person to purchase the property, and convey it to the grantor, is open to the same objection.[15]

One claiming the benefit of such an agreement must show that at that time he had an equitable interest in the property. A mortgagee having foreclosed his mortgage, which was in the form of a trust deed, and purchased the property at the foreclosure sale, the mortgagor claimed there was a verbal agreement with him that the premises should still be held as security for the payment of the mortgage debt, and that when the rents received had been sufficient for that purpose the premises should be reconveyed to the mortgagor; that afterward the mortgagor procured another person to advance the money for the payment of the mortgage debt, and the former mortgagor thereupon conveyed the property to this other person by absolute deed; and that this purchaser made an agreement to the same effect with the former mortgagor. The evidence was not very satisfactory. Mr. Justice Hunt, delivering the opinion of the Supreme Court in this case, declared that, unless the equity of redemption of the mortgagor was kept alive by the alleged agreement with his mortgagee, he had no interest which could sustain a parol agreement by the purchaser from the mortgagee to buy the property for the mortgagor's benefit and to convey to him when required. Such an agreement is one creating by parol a trust or interest in lands, which can not be sustained under the statute of frauds. It is a naked promise by one to buy lands in his own name, pay for them with his own money, and hold them for the benefit of another. It can not be enforced in equity, and is void.[16]

---

[14] Wilson v. McDowell, 78 Ill. 514; Payne v. Patterson, 77 Pa. St. 134. See also Sweet v. Mitchell, 15 Wis. 641.

[15] Wilson v. McDowell, 78 Ill. 514; Perry v. McHenry, 13 Ill. 227; Stephenson v. Thompson, 13 Ill. 186.

[16] Howland v. Blake, 97 U. S. 624, 11 Chicago L. N. 139, 7 Biss. 40. See also Levy v. Brush, 45 N. Y. 589; Digby v. Jones, 67 Mo. 104; Richardson v. Johnson, 41 Wis. 100, 22 Am. Rep. 712. See post §§ 331, 332.

II. *What Facts are Considered*

§ **323a. General considerations.**—The Supreme Court of Iowa, in determining whether an absolute deed is intended as a mortgage, considers the following as the most important questions: First, whether there was a continuing obligation by the grantor to pay a debt which it is claimed the deed was made to secure; second, the value of the land as compared with the debt which was to be secured; third, how have the parties treated the conveyance; fourth, in what form are the written evidences of the transaction; and fifth, what sort of testimony is relied on to show that the deed was accepted as security for a debt?[1] In Ohio, the course of decisions in this class of cases indicates that courts are vigilant to discover whether a condition of defeasance in law or fact attaches to the deed absolute in form. To this end they scrutinize the prior pecuniary relations of the parties, each toward the other, contemporaneous acts bearing on the question, all after acts and admissions of the parties that are competent to be considered as evidence in relation to the transaction, any material inadequacy of consideration, and the terms of any written agreement entered into by the parties.[2] The Supreme Court of Oregon, in recent cases, follows and approves

[1] Ridings v. Marengo Sav. Bank, 147 Iowa 608, 125 N. W. 200.

[2] Slutz v. Desenberg, 28 Ohio St. 371.

this line of Ohio decisions,[3] and in enumerating the tests to determine whether a deed was intended as a mortgage, mentions among other circumstances, the pecuniary relation of the parties, their previous negotiations, their contemporaneous acts and declarations, and subsequent acts and admissions.[4] In a recent Arkansas case the court considered among other circumstances the situation of the parties, the property conveyed, its value, the price paid, defeasances verbal or written, and the acts and declarations of the parties.[5] The courts of Kentucky consider particularly, the relation of debtor and creditor, the inadequacy of price, and imminent danger of loss of the property by the debtor, as facts which will lead the court to declare the instrument a mortgage, rather than a deed.[6]

§ 324. **Intention of the parties—Conduct and declarations.**—In admitting parol and extrinsic evidence, the court is not restricted to any particular kind of evidence, but may take into consideration any pertinent matters which tend to prove the real understanding of the parties, and the true nature of the transaction.[7] The true character of the conveyance will be inquired into, and effect given to the intention of the parties as ascertained by their conduct and declarations at the time and subsequently.[8]

Thus, a statement in a deed or a verbal agreement made at the time

[3] Kramer v. Wilson, 49 Ore. 333, 90 Pac. 183.

[4] Elliott v. Bozorth, 52 Ore. 391, 97 Pac. 632.

[5] McIver v. Roberts (Ark.), 165 S. W. 273.

[6] Smith v. Berry, 155 Ky. 686, 160 S. W. 247.

[7] Rees v. Rhodes, 3 Ariz. 235; 73 Pac. 446; Hurd v. Chase, 100 Maine 561, 62 Atl. 660; Phillips v. Mo, 91 Minn. 311, 97 N. W. 969. See also Blackwell v. Overby, 41 N. Car. 38 (proof of facts and circumstances inconsistent with purchase admitted although direct proof of intention excluded); Bentley v. Phelps, 2 Woodb. & M. (U. S.) 426, 3 Fed. Cas. No. 1331 (proof by admissions of grantee and receipts of money from grantor together with continued possession of grantor).

[8] Russell v. Southard, 12 How. (U. S.) 139, 13 L. ed. 927; Morris v. Nixon, 1 How. (U. S.) 118, 11 L. ed. 69; Sprigg v. Bank of Mt. Pleasant, 14 Pet. (U. S.) 201, 10 L. ed. 419; Hughes v. Edwards, 9 Wheat. (U. S.) 489, 6 L. ed. 142; Reavis v. Reavis, 103 Fed. 813; Harrison v. Maury, 157 Ala. 227, 47 So. 724; Rodgers v. Burt, 157 Ala. 91, 47 So. 226; Rose v. Gandy, 137 Ala. 329, 34 So. 239; Parmer v. Parmer, 88 Ala. 545, 7 So. 657; Vincent v. Walker, 86 Ala. 333, 5 So. 465; Eiland v. Radford, 7 Ala. 724, 42 Am. Dec. 610; McIver v. Roberts (Ark.), 165 S. W. 273; Hodgkins v. Wright, 127 Cal. 688, 60 Pac. 431; Brandt v. Thompson, 91 Cal. 458, 27 Pac. 763; Hall v. Arnot, 80 Cal. 348, 22 Pac. 200; Manasse v. Dinkelspiel, 68 Cal. 404; Montgomery v. Spect, 55 Cal. 352; Lodge v. Turman, 24 Cal. 385; Daubenspeck v. Platt, 22 Cal. 330; Elliott v. Connor, 63 Fla. 408, 58 So. 241; Connor v. Connor, 59 Fla. 467, 52 So. 727; Deadman v. Yantis, 230 Ill. 243, 82 N. E. 592, 120 Am. St. 291; Darst v. Murphy, 119 Ill. 343, 9 N. E. 887; Workman v. Greening, 115 Ill. 477, 4 N. E. 385; Reigard v. McNeil, 38

of the conveyance, that it shall operate as security for a loan of money,

Ill. 400; Whitcomb v. Sutherland, 18 Ill. 578; Williams v. Bishop, 15 Ill. 553; Purviance v. Holt, 8 Ill. 394; Steele v. Steele, 112 Ill. App. 409; Zimmerman v. Marchland, 23 Ind. 474; Calahan v. Dunker, 51 Ind. App. 436, 99 N. E. 1021; Beidelman v. Koch, 42 Ind. App. 423, 85 N. E. 977; Ferguson v. Boyd (Ind. App.), 79 N. E. 549, 81 N. E. 71; Loeb v. McAlister, 15 Ind. App. 643, 41 N. E. 1061, 44 N. E. 378; Keeline v. Clark, 132 Iowa 360, 106 N. W. 257; Laub v. Romans, 131 Iowa 427, 105 N. W. 102; Ingalls v. Atwood, 53 Iowa 283, 5 N. W. 160; Dusenbery v. Bidwell, 86 Kans. 666, 121 Pac. 1098; First Nat. Bank v. Edwards, 84 Kans. 495, 115 Pac. 118; Stratton v. Rotrock, 84 Kans. 198, 114 Pac. 224; Smith v. Berry, 155 Ky. 686, 160 S. W. 247; Vaughn v. Smith, 148 Ky. 531, 146 S. W. 1094; McKibben v. Diltz, 138 Ky. 684, 128 S. W. 1082, 137 Am. St. 408; Brown v. Spradlin, 136 Ky. 703, 125 S. W. 150; Borders v. Allen, 33 Ky. L. 194, 110 S. W. 240; In re Schmidt, 114 La. 78, 38 So. 26; Hurd v. Chase, 100 Maine 561, 62 Atl. 660; Bradley v. Merrill, 88 Maine 319, 34 Atl. 160; Libby v. Clark, 88 Maine 32, 33 Atl. 657; Reed v. Reed, 75 Maine 264; Miller v. Miller, 101 Md. 600, 61 Atl. 210; Ferris v. Wilcox, 51 Mich. 105, 16 N. W. 252; Freeman v. Wilson, 51 Miss. 329; Prewett v. Dobbs, 21 Miss. 431; Sheppard v. Wagner, 240 Mo. 409, 144 S. W. 394, rehearing denied 145 S. W. 420; Gibbs v. Haughowout, 207 Mo. 384, 105 S. W. 1067; Powell v. Crow, 204 Mo. 481, 102 S. W. 1024; Cobb v. Day, 106 Mo. 278, 17 S. W. 323; O'Neill v. Capelle, 62 Mo. 202; Worley v. Dryden, 57 Mo. 226; Tibeau v. Tibeau, 22 Mo. 77; Brant v. Robertson, 16 Mo. 129; Arnold v. Fraser, 43 Mont. 540, 117 Pac. 1064; Sanders v. Ayres, 63 Nebr. 271, 88 N. W. 526; Kemp v. Small, 32 Nebr. 318, 49 N. W. 169; Fahay v. State Bank of O'Neill, 1 Nebr. (Unoff.) 809, 95 N. W. 505; Jeffreys v. Charlton, 72 N. J. Eq. 340, 65 Atl. 711; Crane v. Bonnell, 2 N. J. Eq. 264; Mooney v. Byrne, 163 N. Y. 86, 57 N. E. 163; Lane v. Sears, 1 Wend. (N. Y.) 433; Strong v. Gambier, 155 App. Div. 294, 140 N. Y. S. 410; Conover v. Palmer, 123 App. Div. 817, 108 N. Y. S. 480; Faulkner v. Cody, 45 Misc. 64, 91 N. Y. S. 633; Miller v. Smith, 20 N. Dak. 96, 126 N. W. 499; Smith v. Jensen, 16 N. Dak. 408, 114 N. W. 306; Okla. Comp. Laws 1909 § 1196; Farrow v. Work, 39 Okla. 734, 136 Pac. 739; Fawcett v. McGahan-McKee Lumber Co., 39 Okla. 68, 134 Pac. 388; Kinney v. Heatherington, 38 Okla. 74, 131 Pac. 1078; Worley v. Carter, 30 Okla. 642, 121 Pac. 669; Beall v. Beall (Ore.), 135 Pac. 185; Grover v. Hawthorne, 62 Ore. 77, 121 Pac. 808; Harmon v. Grants Pass Banking &c. Co., 60 Ore. 69, 118 Pac. 188; Walton v. Moore, 58 Ore. 237, 114 Pac. 105; Mansfield v. Hill, 56 Ore. 400, 107 Pac. 471, judgment modified 108 Pac. 1007; Elliott v. Bozorth, 52 Ore. 391, 97 Pac. 632; Hall v. O'Connell, 52 Ore. 164, 95 Pac. 717; Null v. Fries, 110 Pa. St. 52, 1 Atl. 551; Cole v. Bolard, 22 Pa. St. 431; Niles v. Lee, 31 S. Dak. 234, 140 N. W. 259; Overton v. Bigelow, 3 Yerg. (Tenn.) 513; Mitchell v. Morgan (Tex. Civ. App.), 165 S. W. 883; Hume v. Le Compte (Tex. Civ. App.), 142 S. W. 934; Harrison v. Hogue (Tex. Civ. App.), 136 S. W. 118; Yates v. Caswell (Tex. Civ. App.), 126 S. W. 914; Elliott v. Morris (Tex. Civ. App.) 121 S. W. 209; Moorhead v. Ellison, 56 Tex. Civ. App. 444, 120 S. W. 1049; Nagle v. Simmank, 54 Tex. Civ. App. 432, 116 S. W. 862; Moore v. Kirby, 52 Tex. Civ. App. 200, 115 S. W. 632 (declaration that grantor "could have the land" upon payment of a debt, admissible); Middleton v. Johnston (Tex. Civ. App.), 110 S. W. 789; Musick v. O'Brien (Tex. Civ. App.), 102 S. W. 458; Gazley v. Herring (Tex.), 17 S. W. 17; Loving v. Milliken, 59 Tex. 423; Ruffier v. Womack, 30 Tex. 332; Carter v. Carter, 5 Tex. 93; Abbott v. Sanders, 80 Vt. 179, 66 Atl. 1032, 13 L. R. A. (N. S.) 725, 130 Am. St. 974; Beverly v. Davis (Wash.), 140 Pac. 696; Hoover v. Bouffleur, 74 Wash. 382, 133 Pac. 602; Johnson v. Na-

or as indemnity to a surety, if clearly proved, is decisive of the character of the transaction.[9] And so is an agreement that the deed shall stand only as security for a debt, and that in case of a sale by the grantee the excess of the proceeds over the debt shall be paid to the grantor. Such an agreement and deed constitute a mortgage; and therefore the agreement is not void, as an attempt to create a trust by parol.[10] Declarations of a party to the deed and to the action to declare such deed a mortgage, may be received in evidence as against himself.[11] It is proper to admit evidence of the previous negotiations of the parties, their agreements and conversations, and their dealings prior to and leading up to the execution of the deed.[12] The statements and declarations of the parties made pending negotiations, and at the final execution of the deed and contract to reconvey, are admissible to show that the deed was intended as security for a debt.[13] Positive

tional Bank of Commerce, 65 Wash. 261, 118 Pac. 21; Dempsey v. Dempsey, 61 Wash. 632, 112 Pac. 755; Hudkins v. Crim (W. Va.), 78 S. E. 1043; Froidevaux v. Jordan, 64 W. Va. 388, 62 S. E. 686, 131 Am. St. 911; Fridley v. Somerville, 60 W. Va. 272, 54 S. E. 502; Cumps v. Kiyo, 104 Wis. 456, 80 N. W. 937; Rockwell v. Humphrey, 57 Wis. 410, 15 N. W. 394; Smith v. Crosby, 47 Wis. 160, 2 N. W. 104. The intention of the grantee to give the grantor any profit that was realized on a final sale of the property would not justify a finding that the deed was intended as mere security for a loan. Harris v. Hirsch, 121 App. Div. 767, 106 N. Y. S. 631. The intention governing the nature of the conveyance must be that of both parties, and where a homestead is conveyed the intention of the grantor and his wife, regardless of the grantee's intent can not be conclusive. Nagle v. Simmank, 54 Tex. Civ. App. 432, 116 S. W. 862. See ante §§ 162, 168, 258, 321.

[9] Dorthan Guano Co. v. Ward, 132 Ala. 380, 31 So. 748; Anthony v. Anthony, 28 Ark. 479; First Nat. Bank. v. Ashmead, 23 Fla. 379, 2 So. 657; Hibernian Banking Assn. v. Commercial Nat. Bank, 157 Ill. 524, 41 N. E. 919; Ashton v. Shepherd, 120 Ind. 69, 22 N. E. 98; Anding v. Davis, 38 Mich. 574, 77 Am. Dec. 658; Wolf v. Theresa Village

Mut. F. Ins. Co. (Wis.), 91 N. W. 1014. See ante §§ 264, 266.

On the other hand, it has been held that verbal admissions are entitled to little weight. Richardson v. Beaber, 62 Misc. 542, 115 N. Y. S. 821; Everett v. Estes, 66 So. 615.

Where the grantee in a deed admitted that it was intended as a mortgage, evidence that third parties understood the instrument as an absolute conveyance will not overcome the admission of the grantee and intention of the parties. Kellner v. Randle (Tex. Civ. App.), 165 S. W. 509.

[10] Crane v. Buchanan, 29 Ind. 570; Tower v. Fetz, 26 Nebr. 106, 42 N. W. 884, 18 Am. St. 795.

[11] Adams v. Hopkins, 144 Cal. 19, 77 Pac. 712; Ross v. Brusie, 64 Cal. 245, 30 Pac. 811; Hopper v. Smyser, 90 Md. 363, 45 Atl. 206.

[12] Beidelman v. Koch, 42 Ind. App. 423, 85 N. E. 977; Beroud v. Lyons, 85 Iowa 482, 52 N. W. 486; Toledo First Nat. Bank v. Central Chandelier Co., 17 Ohio Cir. Ct. 443, 9 Ohio Cir. Dec. 807; Lewie v. Hallman, 53 S. Car. 18, 30 S. E. 601. See also McRobert v. Bridget (Iowa), 149 N. W. 906; Harris v. Hirsch, 121 App. Div. 767, 106 N. Y. S. 631. See also Norton v. Lea (Tex. Civ. App.), 170 S. W. 267.

[13] Adams v. Hopkins, 144 Cal. 19, 77 Pac. 712; Peugh v. Davis, 2 MacArthur (D. C.) 14; Burnside v.

evidence that the grantee in the deed refused to take a mortgage indicates that the deed to him and his agreement to reconvey were not intended by him as a mortgage.[14]

Vague and uncertain evidence as to admissions of the grantee that the grantor had a right to redeem, when coupled with the grantor's temporary retention of possession and slight inadequacy of price, does not render the deed a mortgage, especially where the grantor was informed that the deed was an actual conveyance.[15] Evidence of the conduct of the parties at the time of the transaction and subsequently, must be clear and convincing, in order to establish that the deed was intended as a mortgage.[16] It is said in some cases that parol evidence of an agreement that a conveyance should operate as security, should be supported by other facts and circumstances which are incompatible with the idea of a purchase, and leave no fair doubt that a security only was intended.[17]

Where a husband and wife made a conveyance absolute in terms of property belonging to the wife, the husband conducting the negotiation with the grantee, the intent of the wife in delivering the deeds governs as to the nature of the transaction. If her understanding was that the deed was only a security for her husband's debt, then the transaction is a mortgage, whatever may have been the intention as between the husband and his creditor before the instrument was delivered.[18]

But on the question whether a deed absolute, executed by a dece-

Terry, 45 Ga. 621; Helbreg v. Schumann, 150 Ill. 12, 37 N. E. 99, 41 Am. St. 339; Darst v. Murphy, 119 Ill. 343, 9 N. E. 887; Bartling v. Brasuhn, 102 Ill. 441; Ruckman v. Alwood, 71 Ill. 155; Reigard v. McNeil, 38 Ill. 400; Whitcomb v. Sutherland, 18 Ill. 578; Williams v. Bishop, 15 Ill. 553; Purviance v. Holt, 3 Gil. (Ill.) 394; McLaughlin v. Royce, 108 Iowa 254, 78 N. W. 1105; Beroud v. Lyons, 85 Iowa 482, 52 N. W. 486; Hoskins v. Hoskins, 27 Ky. L. 980, 87 S. W. 320; Phoenix v. Gardner, 13 Minn. 430; Freeman v. Wilson, 51 Miss. 329; Jones v. Rush, 156 Mo. 364, 57 S. W. 118; Haussknecht v. Smith, 161 N. Y. 663, 57 N. E. 1112; Wollenberg v. Minard, 37 Ore. 621, 62 Pac. 532; Tompkins v. Merriman, 6 Kulp (Pa.) 543; Dupree v. Estelle, 72 Tex. 575, 10 S. W. 666; Sadler v. Taylor, 49 W. Va. 104, 38 S. E. 583.

But see Sowell v. Barrett, 45 N. Car. 50; Allen v. McRae, 39 N. Car. 325.

[14] Bacon v. National &c. Bank, 191 Ill. 205, 60 N. E. 846; Bentley v. O'Bryan, 111 Ill. 53; Flagg v. Mann, 14 Pick. (Mass.) 467; Gazley v. Herring (Tex.), 17 S. W. 17; Conner v. Clapp, 37 Wash. 299, 79 Pac. 929; Becker v. Howard, 75 Wis. 415, 44 N. W. 755. See also Vincent v. Walker, 86 Ala. 333, 5 So. 465.

[15] Edwards v. Wall, 79 Va. 321.

[16] Bartling v. Brasuhn, 102 Ill. 441.

[17] Blackwell v. Overby, 6 Ired. Eq. (N. Car.) 68; Kelly v. Bryan, 6 Ired. Eq. (N. Car.) 283. The intent at the time of delivery of the deed governs. Sanders v. Ayres, 63 Nebr. 271, 88 N. W. 526.

[18] Davis v. Brewster, 59 Tex. 93, revg. 56 Tex. 478.

dent in his lifetime, was intended as a mortgage, evidence of conversations of the grantor with a third person, had after the execution of the deed, tending to show its intent, is not admissible.[19] Under the general rule that a party to a contract will be held to the construction that his own actions have put upon it, a party to an absolute deed, having treated it as a mortgage, is bound by such construction.[20] Thus, where a father conveyed land to his daughter subject to a mortgage, and a subsequent agreement between him and the mortgagee contained a recital that the daughter was the owner of the equity of redemption, such recital showed, in absence of evidence to the contrary, that the deed was intended to be absolute and that the daughter was the actual owner.[21]

§ 325. **Evidence of continuing debt.**—Evidence of the continuance of the debt, such as the payment of interest upon it, or the extension of the time of payment, is generally conclusive of the character of the original transaction as a mortgage.[22] It shows either that the pre-existing debt was not surrendered or canceled at the time of the conveyance, or, in case there was no such debt, it shows that one was then created.[23] If the mortgagee retains the evidence of a pre-existing indebtedness, and receives rent from the mortgagor, this will be regarded as payment of interest and as evidence of a mortgage.[24]

Parol evidence is admissible to show the existence of the debt to be secured by the conveyance alleged to be a mortgage.[25] Although no note or other evidence of indebtedness is given, a loan of a certain sum raises an indebtedness, and a deed executed to secure such a loan, with

---

[19] Jones v. Jones, 17 N. Y. S. 905.
[20] Ferguson v. Boyd (Ind. App.), 79 N. E. 549, 81 N. E. 71 (citing cases).
[21] Braun v. Vollmer, 89 App. Div. 43, 85 N. Y. S. 319.
[22] Reeves v. Abercrombie, 108 Ala. 535, 19 So. 41; Turner v. Wilkinson, 72 Ala. 361; Ahern v. McCarthy, 107 Cal. 382, 40 Pac. 482; Hall v. Arnott, 80 Cal. 348, 22 Pac. 200; Montgomery v. Spect, 55 Cal. 352; Westlake v. Horton, 85 Ill. 228; Eaton v. Green, 22 Pick. (Mass.) 526; Klein v. McNamara, 54 Miss. 90; Riley v. Starr, 48 Nebr. 243, 67 N. W. 187; Budd v. Van Orden, 33 N. J. Eq. 143; Ruffier v. Womack, 30 Tex. 332; Lawrence v. Du Bois, 16 W. Va. 443. See ante § 265. However disguised may be the terms, if the real object of the

transaction be the taking or holding of land for the security of a loan or debt, it is in equity a mortgage, and if necessary the subsequent conduct of the parties, with reference to the matter, may be examined to ascertain their true intent, as the giving of a note for the money or receiving part payment or interest on the same. Sandling v. Kearney, 154 N. Car. 596, 70 S. E. 942; Campbell v. Worthington, 6 Vt. 448.
[23] Farmer v. Grose, 42 Cal. 169; Gilchrist v. Beswick, 33 W. Va. 168, 10 S. E. 371.
[24] Ennor v. Thompson, 46 Ill. 214.
[25] Locke v. Moulton, 96 Cal. 21, 30 Pac. 957; People v. Irwin, 14 Cal. 428; McNamara v. Culver, 22 Kans. 661. But see Thomas v. McCormack, 9 Dana (Ky.) 108.

a privilege of redemption during the grantor's lifetime, will be considered a mortgage.[26] The indebtedness secured by an absolute deed intended as a mortgage, although not specified in the deed or in any contemporaneous writing, and whether a present or future obligation, may be shown by parol evidence.[27] Where there is no bond to reconvey nor any written evidence to fix the amount of an indebtedness secured by an absolute deed it may be shown by parol evidence that the deed was given to secure an indebtedness already existing to the amount expressed as a consideration, and also to secure future advances.[28] The taking of judgment for the consideration money is evidence that an absolute deed was intended to be a mortgage.[29]

Of course, where there is no written acknowledgment of a debt or express promise to pay, the party who attempts to impeach the deed is obliged to make out his proofs by other and less decisive means. The absence of such evidence of debt is far from being conclusive that the transaction was a sale.[30] Formal mortgages are sometimes made without any personal liability on the part of the mortgagor. Moreover, when it is considered that the occasion for any inquiry in such case, as to the nature of the transaction, arises from the adoption of forms and outward appearances supposed to differ from the fact, it is hardly reasonable that the absence of a written contract of debt should be regarded as of more significance than the absence of a formal defea-

---

[26] Halbert v. Turner, 233 Ill. 531, 84 N. E. 704. See also Jones v. Gillett, 142 Iowa 506, 118 N. W. 314, 121 N. W. 5; Brant v. Robertson, 16 Mo. 129; Graham v. Stevens, 34 Vt. 166, 80 Am. Dec. 675.

[27] Anglo-Californian Bank v. Cerf, 147 Cal. 384, 81 Pac. 1077.

[28] Hester v. Gairdner, 128 Ga. 531, 58 S. E. 165. See also Huntington v. Kneeland, 187 N. Y. 563, 80 N. E. 1111. See post §§ 352, 365, 367a, 374.

[29] Hamet v. Dundass, 4 Pa. St. 178. "In all this class of cases," says Chief Justice Poland, in Rich v. Doane, 35 Vt. 125, "one principle has universally been recognized, that, in order to convert a conveyance absolute upon its face into a mortgage, or security merely, there must be a debt to be secured. Some of the cases go so far as to hold that there must be a debt in such form that it can be enforced by action against the debtor, while others have denied it. We have no

occasion now to decide whether the debt must be such that it could be enforced by action against the debtor; the tendency of later cases seems to be against it. But all agree that there must be a debt or loan to be secured, that the relation of debtor and creditor must exist between the grantor and grantee, in order to lay the foundation for converting an absolute deed in form into a mere security. In this case there was no note or bond, or evidence of debt, executed by the defendants; and though this is by no means conclusive, still it is a circumstance favorable to the orator, as, if the parties intended the conveyance merely as a security for a loan or debt, it would have been natural that the ordinary evidence of a debt should have been required and given."

[30] Russell v. Southard, 12 How. (U. S.) 139, 13 L. ed. 927; Robinson v. Farrelly, 16 Ala. 472; Miller v. Green, 37 Ill. App. 631, affd. 138

sance.[31] But the burden of proof is upon the grantor in an action to redeem to show that the relation of debtor and creditor existed between the grantor and grantee after the delivery of the deed.[32]

A mortgage in the form of an absolute conveyance is quite frequently and properly taken when the amount of the debt to be secured is uncertain, and depends wholly or in part upon future advances.[33]

§ 326. Satisfaction or survival of the debt—Burden of proof.[34]— When the transaction is shown to have been based upon a pre-existing debt, the question to be settled is, whether the intention of the parties was to cancel that debt or to secure it. This is a question of fact, for the determination of which not only the negotiations had at the time of the conveyance, but also the subsequent acts of the parties in relation to it, are to be considered. The mere fact that there was a debt at the time is not conclusive that the conveyance was a mortgage for its security. It can hardly be said that it raises a presumption of a mortgage, though the courts have generally manifested a disposition to construe all conveyances coupled with a stipulation for a reconveyance at a future day as mortgages. But whatever presumption of this kind there may be, it is readily repelled by any facts showing that the debt was surrendered and canceled at the time of the conveyance. The burden is then upon the grantor to show that the deed is not to have effect according to its terms.[35] The fact that the grantor's note or other written evidence of an existing debt, was canceled by the grantee or surrendered to the grantor without a written renewal, is strong evidence that the parties regarded the debt as extinguished and the deed as a conditional sale.[36]

Ill. 565, 28 N. E. 837; Flagg v. Mann, 14 Pick. (Mass.) 467; Morris v. Budlong, 78 N. Y. 543; Brown v. Dewy, 1 Sandf. Ch. (N. Y.) 56.

[31] Per Wells, J., in Campbell v. Dearborn, 109 Mass. 130, 12 Am. Rep. 671.

[32] McCormick v. Herndon, 67 Wis. 648, 31 N. W. 303; Helms v. Chadbourne, 45 Wis. 60.

[33] Abbott v. Gregory, 39 Mich. 68.

[34] For full discussion of satisfaction and survival of debt see ante §§ 265, 267, 269.

[35] Manasse v. Dinkelspiel, 68 Cal. 404, 9 Pac. 547; Montgomery v. Spect, 55 Cal. 352; Ford v. Irwin, 18 Cal. 117, 14 Cal. 428; Rice v. Dole, 107 Ill. 275; Dillon v. Dillon, 24 Ky. L. 781, 69 S. W. 1099; Gassert v. Bogk, 7 Mont. 585, 19 Pac. 281; Hogarty v. Lynch, 6 Bosw. (N. Y.) 138; Eckford v. De Kay, 8 Paige (N. Y.) 89; Baisch v. Oakeley, 68 Pa. St. 92; Lewis v. Bayliss, 90 Tenn. 280, 16 S. W. 376; Snavely v. Pickle, 29 Grat. (Va.) 27; Matheney v. Sandford, 26 W. Va. 386. For burden of proof see post § 335.

[36] Kahn v. Weill, 42 Fed. 704; Adams v. Pilcher, 92 Ala. 474, 8 So. 757; Locke v. Palmer, 26 Ala. 312; Waite v. Dimick, 10 Allen (Mass.) 364; Harmon v. Grants Pass Banking &c. Co., 60 Ore. 69, 118 Pac. 188; Ewing v. Keith, 16 Utah 312, 52 Pac. 4. See also Miller v. Green, 37 Ill. App. 631 (cancelation without delivery); Holmes v. Grant, 8 Paige (N. Y.) 243. This

If the transaction was based upon a mortgage previously existing between the parties, and the mortgage notes were given up and no other evidences of debt were taken in their place, and the mortgagor was credited with the amount of the mortgage notes upon his making an absolute conveyance of the mortgaged land to the mortgagee, the presumption is strong, if not conclusive, that such absolute conveyance was not intended to operate as a mortgage.[37]

It is wholly improbable that a creditor, already having a mortgage to secure his demand, should take another mortgage in the form of an absolute conveyance of the same property, for the same debt, without any apparent advantage. Even in case a mortgagor gives an absolute deed of the mortgaged land, under a parol agreement that the mortgagee shall sell the land, deduct from the proceeds the amount of the mortgage debt, and pay the residue to the mortgagor, the deed does not thereby become a mortgage. After making such a conveyance, the mortgagor had no further title to or interest in the land as such, his only interest being in the proceeds to be obtained on a sale of the land by the former mortgagee.[38]

Although the securities are not surrendered, if the debt is absolutely extinguished, a simple right to repurchase does not make the conveyance a mortgage.[39] Whether the transaction is a mortgage or not is determined by the answer to the inquiry, whether it was the intention of the parties to secure the payment of the debt or to extinguish it.[40] If the object of the parties was to satisfy the debt, the conveyance must necessarily vest the estate absolutely in the grantee, and it can not of course take effect as a mortgage,[41] even if the conveyance contains a

circumstance is not conclusive. Conant v. Riseborough, 139 Ill. 383, 28 N. E. 789; Sanders v. Ayres, 63 Nebr. 271, 88 N. W. 526.

[37] Adams v. Pilcher, 92 Ala. 474; 8 So. 757. In Stoutz v. Rouse, 84 Ala. 309, 4 So. 170, it was held that a conveyance of the property to the mortgagee in payment of the mortgage debt, with the right to redeem within two years from the date of the deed, in like manner and upon the same terms and conditions as if the property had been sold under a decree of the chancery court, was a sale with the privilege of repurchase within two years, having the effect to reduce the equity of redemption to a statutory right of redemption; and that mere inadequacy of consideration will not justify the setting aside of such a transaction. See also Goree v. Clements, 94 Ala. 337, 10 So. 906; Peagler v. Stabler, 91 Ala. 308, 9 So. 157.

[38] Wilson v. Parshall, 129 N. Y. 223, 29 N. E. 297, 7 N. Y. S. 479.

[39] Baxter v. Willey, 9 Vt. 276, 31 Am. Dec. 623.

[40] Todd v. Campbell, 32 Pa. St. 250; Bigelow v. Topliff, 25 Vt. 273, 60 Am. Dec. 264; Toler v. Pender, 1 Dev. & B. Eq. 445. See also Hall v. Arnott, 80 Cal. 348, 22 Pac. 200; McDonald v. Kellogg, 30 Kans. 170, 2 Pac. 507; Allegheny R. &c. Co. v. Casey, 79 Pa. St. 84; Loving v. Milliken, 59 Tex. 423. See ante § 265.

[41] Elston v. Chamberlain, 41 Kans. 354, 21 Pac. 259; Carter v. Williams, 23 La. Ann. 281; Hoopes v.

redemption clause.[42] But the fact that the evidence of the indebtedness is retained after the conveyance is strong evidence that the debt was not extinguished and that a mere security was intended.[43]

§ 327. Actual sale after application for loan.—The transaction may have been a sale, although the application of the grantor was in the first place for a loan. Of course, where an absolute conveyance or a deed of trust is executed with the understanding between the parties that the title is to be transferred forever from the grantor to the grantee, his heirs and assigns, the deed is not a mortgage but a sale.[44] In such a case, the person applied to having refused to deal except as a purchaser, and a conveyance having been made to him without his giving any contract to reconvey, the court refused, after a long lapse of time, to convert the transaction into a mortgage, upon evidence of loose conversations to the effect that the grantee would reconvey upon repayment, although coupled with evidence of inadequacy of consideration.[45]

§ 328. Continued possession of grantor.—The continued possession of the grantor is also evidence tending to show that the conveyance was a mortgage.[46] This fact alone is not very important, but adds

Bailey, 28 Miss. 328; Slee v. Manhattan Co., 1 Paige (N. Y.) 48.

[42] West v. Hendrix, 28 Ala. 226.

[43] Ennor v. Thompson, 46 Ill. 214; Wright v. Mahaffey, 76 Iowa 96, 40 N. W. 112; McMillan v. Bissell, 63 Mich. 66, 29 N. W. 737.

[44] McDonald v. Kellogg, 30 Kans. 170, 2 Pac. 507, per Valentine, J.

[45] De France v. De France, 34 Pa. St. 385; Albany &c. Canal Co. v. Crawford, 11 Ore. 243, 4 Pac. 113.

[46] Nelson v. Wadsworth, 171 Ala. 603, 55 So. 120; Parks v. Parks, 66 Ala. 326; Crews v. Threadgill, 35 Ala. 334; Prefumo v. Russell, 148 Cal. 451, 83 Pac. 810; Daubenspeck v. Platt, 22 Cal. 330; Berry v. Williams, 141 Ga. 642, 81 S. E. 881. In Georgia parol evidence is held inadmissible to convert an absolute deed into a mortgage, where possession has been surrendered to the grantee, but under the Civil Code of 1910, § 3258, a deed by a grantor remaining in possession may be proved by parol to be a mortgage. Lowe v. Findley, 141 Ga. 380, 81 S. E. 230; Mercer v. Morgan, 136 Ga. 632, 71 S. E. 1075; Bashinski v. Swint, 133 Ga. 38, 65 S. E. 152; Spencer v. Schuman, 132 Ga. 515, 64 S. E. 466; Askew v. Thompson, 129 Ga. 325, 58 S. E. 854; Clark v. Finlon, 90 Ill. 245; Strong v. Shea, 83 Ill. 575; Gibson v. Eller, 13 Ind. 124; Ingalls v. Atwood, 53 Iowa 283, 5 N. W. 160; Eames v. Woodson, 120 La. 1031, 46 So. 13; Rester v. Powell, 120 La. 406, 45 So. 372; Franklin v. Sewall, 110 La. 292, 34 So. 448; Jameson v. Emerson, 82 Maine 359, 19 Atl. 831; Thompson v. Banks, 2 Md. Ch. 430; Campbell v. Dearborn, 109 Mass. 130, 12 Am. Rep. 671; Stevens v. Hulin, 53 Mich. 93, 18 N. W. 569; Pidcock v. Swift, 51 N. J. Eq. 405, 27 Atl. 470; Luesenhop v. Einsfeld, 93 App. Div. 68, 87 N. Y. S. 268; Robinson v. Willoughby, 65 N. Car. 520; Steator v. Jones, 10 N. Car. 423; Steel v. Black, 3 Jones Eq. (N. Car.) 427; Kemp v. Earp, 7 Ired. Eq. (N. Car.) 167; Sellers v. Stalcup, 7 Ired. Eq. (N. Car.) 13; O'Toole v. Omlie, 8 N. Dak. 444, 79 N. W. 849; McGill v. Thorne, 70 S. Car. 65, 48

weight to other considerations which tend to this conclusion. It is rebutted by proof of an agreement by the grantor to pay rent.[47]

That the grantor continues to pay the taxes on the land conveyed is a fact to be considered in support of his claim that the conveyance was intended as a mortgage only.[48]

On the other hand, the fact that the grantee has entered into possession and made improvements strengthens the presumption that the conveyance is absolute.[49] Thus, where a grantee and his successors, relying upon their absolute ownership of the premises under the original conveyance and a subsequent release by the grantor, incurred additional expense and paid taxes and assessments so that it would be impossible to restore them to their original situation, the grantor could not set up the original conveyance as a mere mortgage.[50]

§ 329. **Inadequacy of price.**—Inadequacy of price is also a circumstance tending to show that the transaction is a mortgage rather than a sale, just as it is when there is a written agreement for a reconveyance,[51] but this fact alone does not authorize a court to declare

S. E. 994; Lewie v. Hallman, 53 S. Car. 18, 30 S. E. 601; Lewis v. Bayless, 90 Tenn. 280, 16 S. W. 376; Ruffier v. Womack, 30 Tex. 332; Azzalia v. Le Claire, 23 Utah 401, 64 Pac. 1106; Wright v. Bates, 13 Vt. 341; Tuggle v. Berkeley, 101 Va. 83, 43 S. E. 199; Edwards v. Hall, 79 Va. 321; Hursey v. Hursey, 56 W. Va. 148, 49 S. E. 367; Furguson v. Bond, 39 W. Va. 561, 20 S. E. 591; Gilchrist v. Beswick, 33 W. Va. 168, 10 S. E. 371; Kerr v. Hill, 27 W. Va. 576; Matheney v. Sandford, 26 W. Va. 386; Vangilder v. Hoffman, 22 W. Va. 1; Hoffman v. Ryan, 21 W. Va. 415; Lawrence v. Du Bois, 16 W. Va. 443; Davis v. Demming, 12 W. Va. 246; Ogle v. Adams, 12 W. Va. 213; Cotterell v. Purchase, Cas. temp. Talbot, 61; Lincoln v. Wright, 4 De Gex & J. 16. See also Nicholson v. Hayes, 174 Fed. 653, 98 C. C. A. 407. See ante §§ 255, 274 and post § 597. In Vermont parol testimony is admissible to show that a deed absolute in terms was in fact made as security for money loaned, if the grantor has remained in possession, and the title has continued in the grantee. Crosby v. Leavitt, 50 Vt. 239. See also Mussey v. Bates, 60

Vt. 271, 14 Atl. 457; Morgan v. Walbridge, 56 Vt. 405; Hills v. Loomis, 42 Vt. 562; Wing v. Cooper, 37 Vt. 169; Rich v. Doane, 35 Vt. 125; Bigelow v. Topliff, 25 Vt. 273, 60 Am. Dec. 264; Hyndman v. Hyndman, 19 Vt. 9, 46 Am. Dec. 171; Conner v. Chase, 15 Vt. 764; Wright v. Bates, 13 Vt. 341; Mott v. Harrington, 12 Vt. 199; Baxter v. Willey, 9 Vt. 276, 31 Am. Dec. 623; Campbell v. Worthington, 6 Vt. 448.

[47] Danner Land Co. v. Insurance Co., 77 Ala. 184.

[48] Bocock v. Phipard, 5 N. Y. S. 228.

[49] Woodworth v. Carman, 43 Iowa 504. See also Blake v. Taylor, 142 Ill. 482, 32 N. E. 401.

[50] Luesenhop v. Einsfeld, 93 App. Div. 68, 87 N. Y. S. 268.

[51] Russell v. Southard, 12 How. (U. S.) 139, 13 L. ed. 927; Conway v. Alexander, 7 Cranch (U. S.) 218, 3 L. ed. 321; Morris v. Nixon, 1 How. (U. S.) 118, 11 L. ed. 69; Nelson v. Wadsworth, 171 Ala. 603, 55 So. 120; Hubert v. Sistrunk (Ala.), 53 So. 819; Rodgers v. Burt, 157 Ala. 91, 47 So. 226; Glass v. Hieronymus, 125 Ala. 140, 28 So. 71, 82 Am. St. 225; Martin v. Martin,

a deed absolute upon its face to be a mortgage,[21] and other circumstances may render this of little or no weight.[53] Inadequacy of price,

123 Ala. 191, 26 So. 525; Williams v. Reggan, 111 Ala. 621, 20 So. 614; Adams v. Pilcher, 92 Ala. 474, 8 So. 757; Peagler v. Stabler, 91 Ala. 308, 9 So. 157; Vincent v. Walker, 86 Ala. 333, 5 So. 465; Perdue v. Bell, 83 Ala. 396, 3 So. 698; Douglass v. Moody, 80 Ala. 61; Rapier v. Gulf City Paper Co., 77 Ala. 126; Turner v. Wilkinson, 72 Ala. 361; Pearson v. Seay, 35 Ala. 612; Crews v. Threadgill, 35 Ala. 334; West v. Hindsey, 28 Ala. 226; Husheon v. Husheon, 71 Cal. 407, 12 Pac. 410; Pierce v. Robinson, 13 Cal. 116; Butsch v. Smith, 40 Colo. 64, 90 Pac. 61; Elliott v. Connor, 63 Fla. 408, 58 So. 241; Matthews v. Porter, 16 Fla. 466; Chapman v. Ayer, 95 Ga. 581, 23 S. E. 131; Rodgers v. Moore, 88 Ga. 88, 13 S. E. 962; Pope v. Marshall, 78 Ga. 635, 4 S. E. 116; Helm v. Boyd, 124 Ill. 370, 16 N. E. 85; Rue v. Dole, 107 Ill. 275; Carr v. Rising, 62 Ill. 14; Turpie v. Lowe, 114 Ind. 37, 15 N. E. 834; Davis v. Stonestreet, 4 Ind. 101; Grubb v. Brendel, 52 Ind. App. 531, 100 N. E. 872; Calahan v. Dunker, 51 Ind. App. 436, 99 N. E. 1021; White v. Redenbaugh, 41 Ind. App. 580, 82 N. E. 110; Fort v. Colby (Iowa), 144 N. W. 393; Bigler v. Jack, 114 Iowa 667, 87 N. W. 700; Conlee v. Heying, 94 Iowa 734, 62 N. W. 678; Caldwell v. Meltveldt, 93 Iowa 730, 61 N. W. 1090; Bridges v. Linder, 60 Iowa 190, 14 N. W. 217; Wilson v. Patrick, 34 Iowa 362; Trucks v. Lindsey, 18 Iowa 504; Gossum v. Gossum (Ky.), 15 S. W. 1057; Oldham v. Halley, 2 J. J. Marsh. (Ky.) 113; Fulwiler v. Roberts, 26 Ky. L. 297, 80 S. W. 1148; Burch v. Nicholas, 26 Ky. L. 264, 80 S. W. 1132; Trimble v. McCormick, 12 Ky. L. 857, 15 S. W. 358; Eames v. Woodson, 120 La. 1031, 46 So. 13; Rester v. Powell, 120 La. 406, 45 So. 372; Bonnette v. Wise, 111 La. 855, 35 So. 953; Reed v. Reed, 75 Maine 264; Thompson v. Banks, 2 Md. Ch. 430; Campbell v. Dearborn, 109 Mass. 130, 12 Am. Rep. 671; Schmidt v. Barclay, 161 Mich. 1, 125 N. W. 729; Carveth v. Winegar, 133 Mich. 34, 94 N. W. 381; Klein v. McNamara, 54 Miss. 90; Freeman v. Wilson, 51 Miss. 329; Brightwell v. McAfee, 249 Mo. 562, 155 S. W. 820; Donovan v. Boeck, 217 Mo. 70, 116 S. W. 543; Mooney v. Byrne, 163 N. Y. 86, 57 N. E. 163; Lawrence v. Farmers' L. &c. Co., 13 N. Y. 200; Brown v. Dewey, 2 Barb. (N. Y.) 28; Robinson v. Cropsey, 6 Paige (N. Y.) 480; Steel v. Black, 56 N. Car. 427; Sellers v. Stalcup, 43 N. Car. 13; Kemp v. Earp, 42 N. Car. 167; Streator v. Jones, 10 N. Car. 423; Forester v. Van Auken, 12 N. Dak. 175, 96 N. W. 301; Wagg v. Herbert, 19 Okla. 525, 92 Pac. 250; Harmon v. Grants Pass Banking &c. Co., 60 Ore. 69, 118 Pac. 188; Kinney v. Smith, 58 Ore. 158, 113 Pac. 854; Overton v. Bigelow, 3 Yerg. (Tenn.) 513; Norton v. Lea (Tex. Civ. App.), 170 S. W. 267; Temple Nat. Bank v. Warner, 92 Tex. 226, 47 S. W. 515; Gray v. Shelby, 83 Tex. 405, 18 S. W. 809; Gibbs v. Penny, 43 Tex. 560; Rich v. Doane, 35 Vt. 125; Tuggle v. Berkeley, 101 Va. 83, 43 S. E. 199; Hesser v. Brown, 40 Wash. 688, 82 Pac. 934; Gilchrist v. Beswick, 33 W. Va. 168, 10 S. E. 371; Kerr v. Hill, 27 W. Va. 576; Vangilder v. Hoffman, 22 W. Va. 1; Lawrence v. Du Bois, 16 W. Va. 443; Davis v. Demming, 12 W. Va. 246. See also Russell v. Southard, 12 How. (U. S.) 139, 13 L. ed. 927; Simpson v. Denver &c. Bank, 93 Fed. 309, 35 C. C. A. 306 (consideration less than half the value of property). See ante § 275.

[52] Lynch v. Lynch, 22 Cal. App. 653, 135 Pac. 1101; Walker v. Farmers' Bank (Del.), 14 Atl. 819; Story v. Springer, 155 Ill. 25, 39 N. E. 570, affg. 43 Ill. App. 495; Pierce v. Traver, 13 Nev. 526; Coles v. Perry, 7 Tex. 109. See also Rodgers v. Burt, 157 Ala. 91, 47 So. 226.

[53] Matheney v. Sandford, 26 W. Va. 386; Lynch v. Lynch, 22 Cal. App. 653, 135 Pac. 1101; Harris v. Hirsch, 121 App. Div. 767, 106 N. Y. S. 631.

to be of controlling effect, must be gross.[54] On the other hand the fact that the amount paid by the vendee was the entire value of the property, is inconsistent with the idea that a mortgage was intended.[55]

§ 330. **Delay in claiming absolute title.**—Delay in asserting an absolute deed to be a mortgage has not the same effect upon the rights of the parties that attends delay in seeking to enforce in equity the performance of an executory contract.[56] Once a mortgage always a mortgage is the maxim of the law, and payment does not stand on the footing of performance in equity. The character of the deed being fixed by the evidence as conditional, the mortgagor has the same time to make payment that any other debtor has. The right to foreclose and the right to redeem are reciprocal, and if one is barred the other is also barred.[57] The only effect that delay can have in such a case is in its bearing on the primary question of mortgage or no mortgage. The poverty of the mortgagor, and many other circumstances, may sufficiently explain this. No lapse of time short of that which is sufficient to bar the action will prevent the introduction of parol evidence to show a deed was "intended as a mortgage."[58]

An absolute deed will be construed as a mortgage where the grantor continued in possession and control of the property, treating it as his own, and the parties continued to deal with each other as though the title had not passed.[59]

But lapse of time, in connection with other evidence, is a circumstance to be considered.[60] When, for more than seven years the mort-

---

[54] Lynch v. Lynch, 22 Cal. App. 653, 135 Pac. 1101; Hemsted v. Hemsted, 150 Iowa 635, 130 N. W. 413; Harris v. Hirsch, 121 App. Div. 767, 106 N. Y. S. 631. Inadequacy though gross, was held not to be conclusive in Donovan v. Boeck, 217 Mo. 70, 116 S. W. 543; Elliott v. Maxwell, 7 Ired. Eq. (N. Car.) 246; Forester v. Van Auken, 12 N. Dak. 175, 96 N. W. 301. See also Sahlin v. Gregson, 46 Wash. 452, 90 Pac. 592.

[55] Gannon v. Moles, 111 Ill. App. 19; Rathbone v. Maltz, 155 Mich. 306, 118 N. W. 991; Powell v. Crow, 204 Mo. 481, 102 S. W. 1024; Jeffreys v. Charlton, 72 N. J. Eq. 340, 65 Atl. 711.

[56] Odenbaugh v. Bradford, 67 Pa. St. 96.

[57] Fitch v. Miller, 200 Ill. 170, 65

N. E. 650; Green v. Capps, 142 Ill. 286, 31 N. E. 597.

[58] Mott v. Fiske, 155 Ind. 597, 58 N. E. 1053; Anding v. Davis, 38 Miss. 574, 77 Am. Dec. 658.

[59] Richmond v. Richmond, Fed. Cas. No. 11801.

[60] Downing v. Woodstock Iron Co., 93 Ala. 262, 9 So. 177; Schradski v. Albright, 93 Mo. 42, 5 S. W. 807; Stevenson v. Saline Co., 65 Mo. 425; Landrum v. Union Bank, 63 Mo. 48; Tull v. Owen, 4 Y. & C. 192. See also Broaddus v. Potts, 140 Ky. 583, 131 S. W. 510 (deed thirty years old); Cobb v. Day, 106 Mo. 278, 17 S. W. 323. In the latter case the plaintiff, after making a deed absolute in form, made no claim that it was a mortgage for six years, during which time he had paid no taxes, and the grantee

gagor had claimed no ownership in the land and had not offered to pay the interest on the note or the annual taxes, such delay was considered in holding a deed to be absolute.[61] When the grantor had conveyed by a warranty deed, and possession followed the deed through several successive grantees, parol evidence that a mortgage was intended has been refused. Length of time short of the period that will bar redemption affords a strong presumption against such a claim.[62] A lapse of fourteen years from the time of the transaction has been considered a material circumstance.[63] And where the bill to redeem was not filed until thirteen years after the conveyance, and it also appeared that more than seven years had elapsed since the grantee distinctly refused to recognize the grantor's claim of an equity of redemption, and there was no sufficient excuse for the delay, the laches was held to be such as to bar any right to relief.[64]

It has been held that if the mortgagee himself could not have pleaded the period of limitations or laches his heirs and devisees could not do so.[65] A bill to declare a deed, executed in 1886, to be a mortgage, alleging that the grantor remained in possession until 1901, brought by the heirs of the grantor who died intestate in 1907, was held not to be demurrable on ground of laches.[66] Delay by the heirs of a grantor for eight years after the youngest heir came of age, to file a bill to remove an equitable mortgage as a cloud, which was seventeen years after the time allowed for redemption under the ancestor's contract, will be held to constitute laches. Laches in filing a bill to enforce a right of redemption can not be excused upon the ground of ignorance of the contract upon which such right was based, where any examination of the records would have led to the discovery of such contract and any rights they might have had thereunder. In determining whether there has been laches in exercising a right of redemption, a court of equity is not necessarily controlled by the period of limitation as fixed in actions at law.[67]

Laches in bringing an action to declare an absolute deed a mortgage is a mixed question of law and fact, and is not generally de-

had made improvements, without any protest on the part of the plaintiff. It was held that a court of equity would not interfere.

[61] Hesser v. Brown, 40 Wash. 688, 82 Pac. 934.

[62] McCoy v. Gentry, 73 Ala. 105; Conner v. Chase, 15 Vt. 764.

[63] Goree v. Clements, 94 Ala. 337, 10 So. 906; Maher v. Farwell, 97 Ill. 56. So a lapse of seven years. De France v. De France, 34 Pa. St. 385.

[64] Maher v. Farwell, 97 Ill. 56.

[65] McKenney v. Page, 146 Ky. 682, 143 S. W. 382.

[66] Nelson v. Wadsworth, 171 Ala. 603, 55 So. 120

[67] Fitch v. Miller, 200 Ill. 170, 65 N. E. 650.

terminable by the court, upon demurrer, unless it is apparent that the delay was without excuse, and was prejudicial to the grantee.[68]

§ 331. **Conveyance by third person—Debtor's right to redeem.**— In equity it is regarded as unnecessary that the conveyance should be made by the debtor. It is sufficient that he has an interest in the property, either legal or equitable. Having such an interest, if he procure a conveyance of the property to one who pays the price of it, or makes an advance upon it, under an arrangement that he shall be allowed to have the property upon repaying the money advanced, he has a right to redeem. The grantee in such case acquires title by his act, and as security for his debt, and therefore holds the title as his mortgagee.[69] Thus, if a person advances for another, at his request, the purchase-money of land which the latter contracts to buy, and the deed be made to the person who advances the money, he is as much a mortgagee as if the land had been conveyed to him directly by the debtor,[70] and parol evidence is admissible to prove the

[68] Salinger v. McAllister (Iowa), 146 N. W. 8. See also Beekman v. Hudson River R. Co., 35 Fed. 3; Bulkley v. Bulkley, 2 Day (Conn.) 363; Gay v. Havermale, 27 Wash. 390, 67 Pac. 804.

[69] Wright v. Shumway, 1 Biss. (U. S.) 23; Martin v. Pond, 30 Fed. 15; Hughes v. McKenzie, 101 Ala. 415, 13 So. 609; Nelson v. Kelly, 91 Ala. 569, 8 So. 690; Parmer v. Parmer, 88 Ala. 545, 7 So. 657; Terwilliger v. Ballard, 64 Fla. 158, 59 So. 244; First Nat. Bank v. Ashmead, 23 Fla. 379, 2 So. 657; Lindsay v. Matthews, 17 Fla. 575; Smith v. Cremer, 71 Ill. 185; Reigard v. McNeil, 38 Ill. 400; Beatty v. Brummett, 94 Ind. 76; Rector v. Shirk, 92 Ind. 31; Stephenson v. Arnold, 89 Ind. 426; Bradford v. Helsell, 150 Iowa 732, 130 N. W. 908; McPherson v. Hayward, 81 Maine 329, 17 Atl. 164; Stinchfield v. Milliken, 71 Maine 567; Union Sav. Bank v. Pool, 143 Mass. 203, 9 N. E. 545; Darling v. Darling, 123 Mich. 307, 82 N. W. 48; Jeffery v. Hursh, 58 Mich. 246, 25 N. W. 176, 27 N. W. 7; Fisk v. Stewart, 24 Minn. 97; Pardee v. Treat, 82 N. Y. 385; Carr v. Carr, 52 N. Y. 251; Stoddard v. Whiting, 46 N. Y. 627; Murray v. Walker, 31 N. Y. 399; McBurney v. Wellman, 42 Barb. (N. Y.) 390;

Balduff v. Griswold, 9 Okla. 438, 60 Pac. 223; Houser v. Lamont, 55 Pa. St. 311, 93 Am. Dec. 755; Tant v. Guess, 35 S. Car. 605, 16 S. E. 472; Muller v. Flavin, 13 S. Dak. 595, 83 N. W. 687; Lewis v. Bayliss, 90 Tenn. 280, 16 S. W. 376; Sweet v. Mitchell, 15 Wis. 641. See also Davis v. Clifton, 145 Ky. 173, 140 S. W. 161 (agreement to reconvey to debtor's wife); Ferry v. Miller, 164 Mich. 429, 129 N. W. 721 (agreement to reconvey to husband of grantor). See ante §§ 241, 268, 323.

[70] Hidden v. Jordan, 21 Cal. 92; Strong v. Shea, 83 Ill. 575; Smith v. Knoebel, 82 Ill. 392; Hardin v. Eames, 5 Bradw. (Ill.) 153; Barnett v. Nelson, 46 Iowa 495; Brumfield v. Boutall, 24 Hun (N. Y.) 541; Hall v. O'Connell, 52 Ore. 164, 95 Pac. 717, decree modified on rehearing 96 Pac. 1070; Lucia v. Adams, 36 Tex. Civ. App. 454, 82 S. W. 335; Borrow v. Borrow, 34 Wash. 684, 76 Pac. 305; Beebe v. Wisconsin Mortgage Loan Co., 117 Wis. 328, 93 N. W. 1103. See also Sterck v. Germantown Homestead Co., 27 Pa. Super. Ct. 336. A delivery of deeds by the owner of property to one who advanced money to keep the land from sale, "to cover the debt" until redemption within a certain

nature of such transaction as a mortgage.[71]

If part only of the purchase-money be advanced by such grantee, he has a lien upon the whole land, and not merely upon an undivided interest in proportion to the amount of his advance.[72] Where a purchaser of land had paid part of the price and a third person advanced the balance as a loan, receiving a conveyance from the vendor as security, under an agreement to convey to the purchaser upon repayment of the loan, the deed was held a mortgage as between the purchaser and the third person.[73]

But where a mortgagor, to prevent foreclosure, conveyed the land by absolute deed to a third person, who agreed to pay the mortgage debt and reconvey the land to the mortgagor upon payment within a specified time, the transaction was held not to be a mortgage, but a sale with privilege of repurchase, especially since the mortgagor did not apply to the third person for a loan, and the third person did not propose to make a loan.[74]

At law, when a trustee, at the request of the husband of the cestui que trust, and acting as her agent in fact, sold certain trust land to one who agreed to convey the land to the husband on his repaying the purchase-money, it was declared that the transaction did not constitute a mortgage, and could not be dealt with as such.[75] In like manner, where one at the request of a debtor, whose land had been sold on execution, purchased the land, agreeing by parol with the debtor that, upon his paying the purchase-money and interest, he would con-

period, or to be sold thereafter, is a mortgage. Horton v. Murden, 117 Ga. 72, 43 S. E. 786. But it has been held that a quitclaim deed from a mortgagor to a mortgagee, given to avoid foreclosure, together with an agreement from the mortgagee to reconvey upon due payment, was not an equitable mortgage, but an absolute conveyance. Bailey v. St. Louis Union Trust Co., 188 Mo. 483, 87 S. W. 1003. Where the original conveyance was made under a parol trust, by which the grantee was to hold the title for the grantor's benefit, subject to his order, and under the direction of the grantor the grantee conveyed the property to one who held a mortgage on the premises, to secure the mortgage indebtedness and save foreclosure, the deed reciting that it passed only such interest as was received in the deed from the grantor, the mortgage creditor was still a mere mortgagee and not the owner of the absolute title. Lynch v. Ryan, 132 Wis. 271, 112 N. W. 427.

[71] Hall v. O'Connell, 52 Ore. 164, 95 Pac. 717, decree modified on re-hearing 96 Pac. 1070; Borrow v. Borrow, 34 Wash. 684, 76 Pac. 305.

[72] Hidden v. Jordan, 21 Cal. 92.

[73] Sandling v. Kearney, 154 N. Car. 596, 70 S. E. 942.

[74] Hubert v. Sistrunk (Ala.), 53 So. 819.

[75] Pennsylvania Life Ins. Co. v. Austin, 42 Pa. St. 257. The transaction was held not to be a mortgage, where a purchaser at a trustee's sale at request of the owners, took title in his own name by deed absolute in form agreeing to convey to them at any time within five years upon payment of the amount due. Lamberson v. Bashore, 167

vey it to him, or, if the land should be sold for more than this, to pay the surplus to the debtor, it was held that this transaction did not constitute a mortgage, because the debtor had no interest in the land at the time of this agreement, and of the purchase made in consequence of it. The purchase was not conditional between such purchaser and his grantor, who alone was interested in the property at that time. There was no agreement that the land was, under any circumstances, to revert to his grantor. But if one holding a bond or agreement for a deed, after paying a portion of the purchase-money, procure a third person to pay the balance, and the land is conveyed to him as security, he agreeing to reconvey within a certain time on payment of his advances, the transaction is a mortgage.[76] Such holder of the agreement for purchase has an interest in the land by reason of the payment made by him.

If the person who procures another to purchase land, upon a verbal understanding that the purchaser will convey it to him upon being reimbursed the amount paid with interest, had no interest in the land either legal or equitable, the transaction is regarded as a mere contract of sale, and not a mortgage.[77]

§ 332. **Purchase at judicial sale for benefit of equitable owner.**—The rule which converts an absolute deed into a mortgage to conform with the intention of the parties to create a security, applies not only to voluntary conveyances by the grantor, but also to deeds received by purchasers at judicial sales, under an agreement with the debtor that the title should be held as security for a debt or loan, and be defeasible by payment of the money due.[78] One who purchases at a foreclosure, execution, or other judicial sale, for the benefit of the equitable owner, and thus acquires the title at a price below the value of the property, may be deemed a trustee of the party for whom he has undertaken the purchase;[79] and parol evidence is admissible to

Cal. 387, 139 Pac. 817. See ante § 323.

[76] McClintock v. McClintock, 3 Brewst. (Pa.) 76.

[77] Caprez v. Trover, 96 Ill. 456.

[78] Sandling v. Kearney, 154 N. Car. 596, 70 S. E. 942. See also San Jose Safe Deposit Sav. Bank v. Madera Bank, 121 Cal. 539, 54 Pac. 83; Reitze v. Humphreys, 53 Colo. 171, 125 Pac. 518; Klock v. Walter, 70 Ill. 416; Smith v. Doyle, 46 Ill. 451; McKibben v. Diltz, 138 Ky. 684, 128 S. W. 1082; Gaines v. Brockerhoff,

136 Pa. St. 175, 19 Atl. 958; Jones v. Pierce, 134 Pa. St. 533, 19 Atl. 689; Thacker v. Morris, 52 W. Va. 220, 43 S. E. 141, 94 Am. St. 928.

[79] Green v. Maddox, 97 Ark. 397, 134 S. W. 931; Sandfoss v. Jones, 35 Cal. 481; Nichols v. Otto, 132 Ill. 91, 23 N. E. 411; Union Mut. L. Ins. Co. v. Slee, 123 Ill. 57, 12 N. E. 543, 13 N. W. 222; McKibben v. Diltz, 138 Ky. 684, 128 S. W. 1082, 137 Am. St. 408; Martin v. Martin, 16 B. Mon. (Ky.) 8; Williams v. Williams, 8 Bush (Ky.) 241; McDon-

prove that the purchaser agreed to take title merely as security, and to reconvey when the money was refunded, creating in effect a mortgage.[80]

Such an agreement, although verbal merely, is not within the statute of frauds. The trust in such case arises or results upon the conveyance. It is a fraud to refuse to execute the agreement, and a court of equity will not permit the grantee to use the statute of frauds as an instrument of fraud. It would seem, however, that there can be no resulting trust unless the person claiming it has some interest in the property. "If A purchases an estate with his own money," says Chancellor Kent, "and takes the deed in the name of B, a trust results to A because he paid the money. The whole foundation of the trust is the payment of the money, and that must be clearly proved. If, therefore, the party who sets up a resulting trust made no payment, he can not be permitted to show by parol proof that the purchase was made for his benefit or on his account. This would be to overturn the statute of frauds."[81]

This distinction is illustrated by a case which was twice before the Supreme Court of Illinois. Land having been advertised for sale under a senior mortgage, the owner and the junior mortgagee arranged with a third person to bid the land off for the amount of both mortgages, and the junior mortgagee furnished the money to pay the amount due on the first mortgage, with the understanding that the owner might have further time in which to sell the land and pay off the amount due on both mortgages, with interest upon them. The transaction was held to amount to a mortgage, and to entitle the

---

ough v. O'Neil, 113 Mass. 92; Reece v. Roush, 2 Mont. 586; Dickson v. Stewart, 71 Nebr. 424, 98 N. W. 1085, 115 Am. St. 596; Snyder v. Greaves (N. J.), 21 Atl. 291; Ryan v. Dox, 34 N. Y. 307, 90 Am. Dec. 696; Brown v. Lynch, 1 Paige (N. Y.) 147; Davis v. Van Wyck, 18 N. Y. S. 885; Sandling v. Kearney, 154 N. Car. 596, 70 S. E. 942; Wilson v. Giddings, 28 Ohio St. 554; Adams v. Cooty, 60 Vt. 395, 15 Atl. 150; Phelan v. Fitzpatrick, 84 Wis. 240, 54 N. W. 614; Swift v. Lumber Co., 71 Wis. 476, 37 N. W. 441; Hoile v. Bailey, 58 Wis. 434, 17 N. W. 322. But see Lamberson v. Bashore, 167 Cal. 387, 139 Pac. 817. The same rule applies in case of a purchase under like circumstances at a tax sale. Nelson v. Kelly, 91 Ala. 569, 8 So. 690. See ante § 323.

[80] La Cotts v. La Cotts (Ark.), 159 S. W. 1111; Nichols v. Otto, 132 Ill. 91, 23 N. E. 411; McKibben v. Diltz, 138 Ky. 684, 128 S. W. 1082, 137 Am. St. 408; Dodge v. Brewer, 31 Mich. 227; Dickson v. Stewart, 71 Nebr. 424, 98 N. W. 1085, 115 Am. St. 596; Brown v. Johnson, 115 Wis. 430, 91 N. W. 1016.

[81] Botsford v. Burr, 2 Johns. Ch. (N. Y.) 405, followed in Magnusson v. Johnson, 73 Ill. 156; Perry v. McHenry, 13 Ill. 227 and cases cited; Ranstead v. Otis, 52 Ill. 30; Holmes v. Holmes, 44 Ill. 186; Stephenson v. Thompson, 13 Ill. 168; Robertson v. Robertson, 9 Watts (Pa.) 32; Haines v. O'Conner, 10 Watts (Pa.) 313, 36 Am. Dec. 180.

owner to a conveyance upon payment according to the understanding.[82] But when the case was first before the court, it did not appear that the owner had paid any portion of the purchase-money at the sale, and therefore the bill to enforce the trust was dismissed.[83]

One who furnishes a purchaser at judicial sale the balance of the purchase-money, and who, upon demanding security, receives a conveyance, directly or through an intermediary, is a mere mortgagee.[84] In like manner it may be shown that one purchasing at a sheriff's sale really purchased for the benefit of the debtor, and upon agreement to convey to him upon a subsequent repayment of the amount paid.[85] And one who, upon request of a debtor, takes an assignment of sheriff's certificates on a foreclosure sale, and gives back an agreement to reconvey for the amount paid for the certificates, which obligates the debtor to purchase and pay such amount, is considered a mortgagee.[86] Where a creditor who is beneficiary under a trust deed be-

---

[82] Klock v. Walter, 70 Ill. 416. See Illinois cases cited on rule that absolute conveyance as a security is a mortgage.

[83] Walter v. Klock, 55 Ill. 362. In Merritt v. Brown, 19 N. J. Eq. 286, where the purchaser at a foreclosure sale agreed to allow the mortgagor to repurchase within a given time, it was held that he was not entitled to relief after that time. He had paid nothing, and no trust resulted in his favor.

[84] Dillon v. Dillon, 24 Ky. L. 781, 69 S. W. 1099.

[85] Smith v. Doyle, 46 Ill. 451; Beatty v. Brummett, 94 Ind. 76; McElroy v. Allfree, 131 Iowa 112, 108 N. W. 116, 117 Am. St. 412; Foster v. Rice, 126 Iowa 190, 101 N. W. 771; Roberts v. McMahan, 4 Greene (Iowa) 34; Price v. Evans, 26 Mo. 30 (where an agreement to reconvey in such case was regarded as a temporary privilege and not a mortgage, in view of the circumstances of the case); Dickson v. Stewart, 71 Nebr. 424, 98 N. W. 1085, 115 Am. St. 596; Barkelew v. Taylor, 8 N. J. Eq. 206; Levy v. Brush, 45 N. Y. 589; Ryan v. Dox, 34 N. Y. 307, 90 Am. Dec. 696; Sahler v. Signer, 37 Barb. (N. Y.) 329; Brownlee v. Martin, 28 S. Car. 364, 6 S. E. 148; Robinson v. Lincoln Sav. Bank, 85 Tenn. 363, 3 S. W. 656; Guinn v. Locke, 1 Head (Tenn.) 110; Schriber v. Le Clair, 66 Wis. 579, 29 N. W. 570, 889; Howe v. Carpenter, 49 Wis. 697, 6 N. W. 357; Saunders v. Gould, 124 Pa. St. 237, 16 Atl. 807; Logne's Appeal, 104 Pa. St. 136; Heath's Appeal, 100 Pa. St. 1; Jackman v. Ringland, 4 Watts & S. (Pa.) 149; Heister v. Mederia, 3 Watts & S. (Pa.) 384; Fox v. Heffner, 1 Watts & S. (Pa.) 372. These Pennsylvania cases are cited and approved in Gaines v. Brockerhoff, 136 Pa. St. 175, 19 Atl. 958, in which case it appeared that a debtor and a creditor, between whom business and friendly relations had existed for a long time, agreed that the creditor, who had obtained a judgment, was to bid in the debtor's land at the sheriff's sale, and that on payment of the judgment the land should be reconveyed to the debtor. The debtor remained in possession of a part of the land without payment of rent, made valuable improvements, and paid off an incumbrance. Other parts of the land were sold by the creditor, on consultation with and at prices fixed by the debtor. The creditor distinctly recognized this agreement by acts, declarations and a course of dealing through a series of years. It was held that the sheriff's deed was a mortgage.

[86] Smith v. Hoff, 23 N. Dak. 37.

comes a purchaser under the form of a sale by the trustee, for a consideration equal to the debt and expenses of the sale, which is far less than the fair value of the land, with an understanding that, if the debtor pays such sum within thirty days, such sale or conveyance is to be void, equity will treat such conveyance as a mere security for the debt, and will allow reasonable additional time to redeem the land, or will subject the land to public sale for payment of the debt, interest and expenses.[87]

The trust may be supported, it would seem, even when the person who claims the benefit of the purchase has not actually paid any money toward the purchase, if under an arrangement with the purchaser he has abstained from bidding himself, so that the purchaser has obtained the property at a price much below its real value. The person for whom the property was bought under such an arrangement is considered as having an interest in it.[88]

A transaction whereby one who is embarrassed conveys land to another, on his promise to obtain a loan for him to pay his debts from a building association, and apply the rents to the repayment of the loan, and to reconvey the land when the building association shall expire, is a mortgage and not a trust.[89] Whenever there is in fact an advance of money, to be returned within a specified time, upon the security of an absolute conveyance, the law converts the transaction into a mortgage, whatever may be the understanding of the parties.[90] It does not matter that they may have called it a trust and accordingly executed a paper which they called a declaration of trust.[91] Even a sheriff's sale will be converted into a mortgage when it is made the means to carry out the agreement of the parties to raise money by way of loan, and the loan is made in consequence of it.[92]

§ 333. **Assignment of a mortgage as collateral.**—The same rules that determine the admissibility of parol evidence to establish an absolute deed as a mortgage are equally applicable to show that an assignment of a mortgage, absolute in form, is in fact not a sale, but

135 N. W. 772, Ann. Cas. 1914C, 1072.

[87] Thacker v. Morris, 52 W. Va. 220, 43 S. E. 141.

[88] Marlatt v. Warwick, 18 N. J. Eq. 108; Barkelew v. Taylor, 8 N. J. Eq. 206.

[89] Danzeisen's Appeal, 73 Pa. St. 65. also Church v. Cole, 36 Ind. See

[90] Harper's Appeal, 64 Pa. St. 315.

See also Sandling v. Kearney, 154 N. Car. 596, 70 S. E. 942; Steinruck's Appeal, 70 Pa. St. 289; Campbell v. Worthington, 6 Vt. 448.

[91] Norris v. Schuyler, 4 N. Y. S. 558; Connor v. Atwood, 4 N. Y. S. 561.

[92] Sweetzer's Appeal, 71 Pa. St. 264.

only collateral security for a loan.[93] Such evidence does not vary or contradict the writing, but establishes a limitation inherent in the transaction, and a court of equity will restrict it accordingly.[94] The chief inquiry always is, whether a debt was created by the transaction and continued afterward. The character of security once having attached to the mortgage, this character continues through whatever changes it may undergo in the hands of the assignee; and attaches to money collected upon the mortgage, and to a title that has become absolute by foreclosure.[95]

§ 334. **Assignment of contract of purchase.**—An assignment of a contract of purchase as security is a mortgage, and when the assignee has completed the payments, and taken a conveyance to himself, the relation of the parties remains the same. Under the principle, once a mortgage always a mortgage, the transaction retains that character until it is either foreclosed or redeemed.[96] Although the assignment be absolute in form, it will be construed in equity as a mortgage,[97] if

---

[93] Pond v. Eddy, 113 Mass. 149; Briggs v. Rice, 130 Mass. 50. So the assignment of a lease for a term of years. Commercial Bank v. Pritchard, 126 Cal. 600, 59 Pac. 130. See ante § 280 and post § 827. If the debt secured be a bond or other non-negotiable instrument, the second assignee would acquire only the interest of the first assignee. Bush v. Lathrop, 22 N. Y. 535. If the mortgage secures a negotiable note, the assignee secured under an absolute assignment, though for only a small part of the amount secured by the mortgage, may himself assign to another; and this second assignee for value before maturity, without notice of the limited interest of the assignor, may enforce it for the full amount. Briggs v. Rice, 130 Mass. 50. United States v. Sturges, 1 Paine (U. S.) 525. See post, § 827.

[94] Pond v. Eddy, 113 Mass. 149.

[95] Pond v. Eddy, 113 Mass. 149.

[96] Hays v. Hall, 4 Port. (Ala.) 374, 30 Am. Dec. 530; Smith v. Cremer, 71 Ill. 185; Gamble v. Ross, 88 Mich. 315, 50 N. W. 379; Meigs v. McFarlan, 72 Mich. 194, 40 N. W. 246; Niggeler v. Maurin, 34 Minn. 118, 24 N. W. 369; Hackett v. Watts, 138 Mo. 502, 40 S. W. 113;

Burrows v. Hoveland, 40 Nebr. 464, 58 N. W. 947; Scharman v. Scharman, 38 Nebr. 39, 56 N. W. 704; Malloy v. Malloy, 35 Nebr. 224, 52 N. E. 1097; Lipp v. South Omaha Land Synd., 24 Nebr. 692, 40 N. W. 129; Russell's Appeal, 15 Pa. St. 319; Fredericks v. Corcoran, 12 Wkly. N. Cas. (Pa.) 60; Tant v. Guess, 35 S. Car. 605, 16 S. E. 472, 476 (quoting text); Roddy v. Elam, 12 Rich. Eq. (S. Car.) 343; Brayton v. Jones, 5 Wis. 117. See also Andrews v. Cone, 124 U. S. 720, 31 L. ed. 564, 8 Sup. Ct. 686; Laub v. Romans, 131 Iowa 427, 105 N. W. 102; Gilkerson v. Connor, 24 S. Car. 321; Washington Safe Deposit &c. Co. v. Lietzow, 59 Wash. 281, 109 Pac. 1021; Cooper v. Strauber, 50 Ore. 556, 89 Pac. 641 (contract transferred absolutely and not as security). The same rule applies to an assignment of a partial interest in such a contract. Northrup v. Cross, Seld. Notes (N. Y.) 111.

[97] Fitzhugh v. Smith, 62 Ill. 486; Meigs v. McFarlan, 72 Mich. 194, 40 N. W. 246; Crawford v. Osmun, 70 Mich. 561, 38 N. W. 573; Brockway v. Wells, 1 Paige (N. Y.) 617; Lovejoy v. Chapman, 23 Ore. 571, 32 Pac. 687.

it was intended as security. The burden of proving that such an assignment was intended as a mortgage is upon the assignor.[98]

Parol evidence is admissible to prove that an assignment of rights under contract for the purchase of land was not an absolute conveyance, but a mere security; and all facts and circumstances evidencing the mutual intention of the parties will be considered, including their declarations concerning repayment, improvement of the property, and disposition of the rents and profits.[99] An informal assignment by a purchaser of land at a judicial sale, to a third person in consideration of the latter having become surety for the payment of the bonds for the purchase-money, may be shown by parol evidence to have been made for the purpose of protecting the surety and not as an absolute conveyance, especially where such assignment did not embrace the entire antecedent parol agreement.[1]

§ 335. **Burden of proof—Strictness of proof.**—The presumption is that an absolute conveyance is what it purports on its face to be,[2] and the burden of proof that the instrument is a mortgage or security for a debt rests upon the grantor or other party who makes that contention.[3] Therefore, he is required to make strict proof of the fact.

[98] Morris v. Nyswanger, 5 S. Dak. 307, 58 N. W. 800.
[99] Laub v. Romans, 131 Iowa 427, 105 N. W. 102 and cases cited.
[1] Crockett's Guardian v. Waller, 29 Ky. L. 1155, 96 S. W. 860.
[2] Rodgers v. Burt, 157 Ala. 91, 47 So. 226; Rushton v. McIllvene, 88 Ark. 299, 114 S. W. 709; Ahern v. McCarthy, 107 Cal. 382, 40 Pac. 482; Heaton v. Gaines, 198 Ill. 479, 64 N. E. 1081; Williams v. Williams, 180 Ill. 361, 54 N. E. 229; Martinet v. Duff, 178 Ill. App. 199; Gray v. Hayhurst, 157 Ill. App. 488; Betts v. Betts, 132 Iowa 72, 106 N. W. 928; Funk v. Harshman, 110 Md. 127, 72 Atl. 665; Crane v. Read, 172 Mich. 642, 138 N. W. 223; Kellogg v. Northrup, 115 Mich. 327, 73 N. W. 230; Harmon v. Grants Pass Banking &c. Co., 60 Ore. 69, 118 Pac. 188; Elliott v. Bozorth, 52 Ore. 391, 97 Pac. 632; Williams v. McManus, 90 S. Car. 490, 73 S. E. 1038; Shiver v. Arthur, 54 S. Car. 184, 32 S. E. 310; McLean v. Ellis, 79 Tex. 398, 15 S. W. 394; Hill v. Saunders, 115 Va. 60, 78 S. E. 559; Batchelder v. Randolph, 112 Va. 296, 71 S. E. 533;

Bachrach v. Bachrach, 111 Va. 232, 68 S. E. 985; Beverly v. Davis (Wash.), 140 Pac. 696; Mittlesteadt v. Johnson, 75 Wash. 550, 135 Pac. 214; Johnson v. National Bank of Commerce, 65 Wash. 261, 118 Pac. 21; Dempsey v. Dempsey, 61 Wash. 632, 112 Pac. 755.
[3] Birmingham Lot Co. v. Taylor (Ala.), 62 So. 521; Jones v. Kennedy, 138 Ala. 470, 35 So. 465; McIver v. Roberts (Ark.), 165 S. W. 273; Strong v. Taylor (Ark.), 153 S. W. 123; Edwards v. Bond, 105 Ark. 314, 151 S. W. 243; Grummer v. Price, 101 Ark. 611, 143 S. W. 95; Hays v. Emerson, 75 Ark. 551, 87 S. W. 1027; Bryant v. Broadwell, 140 Cal. 490, 74 Pac. 33; Black Eagle Oil Co. v. Belcher, 22 Cal. App. 258, 133 Pac. 1153; Butsch v. Smith, 40 Colo. 64, 90 Pac. 61; Davis v. Hopkins, 18 Colo. 153, 32 Pac. 70; Perot v. Cooper, 17 Colo. 80, 28 Pac. 391, 31 Am. St. 258; Armor v. Spaulding, 14 Colo. 302, 23 Pac. 789; Townsend v. Peterson, 12 Colo. 491, 21 Pac. 619; Bohm v. Bohm, 9 Colo. 100, 10 Pac. 790; Whitsett v. Kershow, 4 Colo. 419; Fetta v. Vande-

Having deliberately given the transaction the form of a bargain and sale, slight and indefinite evidence should not be permitted to change its character.[4] The proof must be clear, unequivocal, and convincing.[5]

vier, 3 Colo. App. 419, 34 Pac. 168; Mitchell v. Mason, 65 Fla. 208, 61 So. 579; Elliott v. Connor, 63 Fla. 408, 58 So. 241; Deadman v. Yantis, 230 Ill. 243, 82 N. E. 592, 120 Am. St. 291; Rankin v. Rankin, 216 Ill. 132, 74 N. E. 763; Gannon v. Moles, 209 Ill. 180, 70 N. E. 689; Heaton v. Gaines, 198 Ill. 479, 64 N. E. 1081, affg. 100 Ill. App. 26; Martinet v. Duff, 178 Ill. App. 199; Bartoleth v. Hoerner, 154 Ill. App. 336; Belinski v. National Brew. Co., 124 Ill. App. 45; Grubb v. Brendel, 52 Ind. App. 531, 100 N. E. 872; Fort v. Colby (Iowa), 144 N. W. 393; Ridings v. Marengo Sav. Bank, 147 Iowa 608, 125 N. W. 200; Betts v. Betts, 132 Iowa 72, 106 N. W. 928; Jennings v. Demmon, 194 Mass. 108, 80 N. E. 471; Schmidt v. Barclay, 161 Mich. 1, 125 N. W. 729; Miller v. Peter, 158 Mich. 336, 122 N. W. 780; Kellogg v. Northrup, 115 Mich. 327, 73 N. W. 230; Tilden v. Streeter, 45 Mich. 533, 8 N. W. 502; Brightwell v. McAfee, 249 Mo. 562, 155 S. W. 820; Powell v. Crow, 204 Mo. 481, 102 S. W. 1024; Gibson v. Morris State Bank (Mont.), 140 Pac. 76; Mealey v. Howard, 79 N. J. Eq. 93, 81 Atl. 1108; Lake v. Weaver (N. J.), 70 Atl. 81; Winters v. Earl, 52 N. J. Eq. 52, 28 Atl. 15; Fullerton v. McCurdy, 55 N. Y. 637; Northwestern Fire &c. Ins. Co. v. Lough, 13 N. Dak. 601, 102 N. W. 160; Beall v. Beall (Ore.), 135 Pac. 185; Harmon v. Grants Pass Banking &c. Co., 60 Ore. 69, 118 Pac. 188; Elliott v. Bozorth, 52 Ore. 391, 97 Pac. 632; Haines v. Thomson, 70 Pa. St. 434; Todd v. Campbell, 32 Pa. St. 250; Miller v. Price, 66 S. Car. 85, 44 S. E. 584; Commercial &c. Bank v. Cassem (S. Dak.), 145 N. W. 551; Lowry v. Carter, 46 Tex. Civ. App. 488, 102 S. W. 930; Irvin v. Johnson, 44 Tex. Civ. App. 436, 98 S. W. 405; McLean v. Ellis, 79 Tex. 398, 15 S. W. 394; Miller v. Yturria, 69 Tex. 549, 7 S. W. 206; Motley v. Carstairs, 114 Va. 429, 76 S. E. 948; Holladay v. Willis, 101 Va. 274, 43 S. E. 616; Dempsey v. Dempsey, 61 Wash. 632, 112 Pac. 755; Fridley v. Somerville, 60 W. Va. 272, 54 S. E. 502; Coates v. Marsden, 142 Wis. 106, 124 N. W. 1057. The uncorroborated testimony of the grantor's agent alone held insufficient to prove an agreement that an absolute deed should operate as a trust deed. Gerhardt v. Tucker, 187 Mo. 46, 85 S. W. 552. See ante § 326.

[4] Knowles v. Knowles, 86 Ill. 1; Sharp v. Smitherman, 85 Ill. 153; Magnusson v. Johnson, 73 Ill. 156; Smith v. Cremer, 71 Ill. 185; Price v. Karnes, 59 Ill. 276; Parmelee v. Lawrence, 44 Ill. 405; Dwen v. Blake, 44 Ill. 135; Taintor v. Keyes, 43 Ill. 332; Bass v. Bell, 64 S. Car. 177, 41 S. E. 893 (vague and indefinite conversation concerning agreement to reconvey); Hansen v. Abrams, 76 Wash. 457, 136 Pac. 678; Hudkins v. Crim (W. Va.), 78 S. E. 1043.

[5] Cadman v. Peter, 118 U. S. 73, 30 L. ed. 78, 6 Sup. Ct. 957; Coyle v. Davis, 116 U. S. 108, 29 L. ed. 583, 6 Sup. Ct. 314; Howland v. Blake, 97 U. S. 624, 7 Biss. 40; Peugh v. Davis, 96 U. S. 332, 25 L. ed. 775, 2 MacArth. (D. C.) 14; Bogk v. Gassert, 149 U. S. 17, 37 L. ed. 631, 13 Sup. Ct. 738; Jones v. Brittan, 1 Woods. (U. S.) 667; Satterfield v. Malone, 35 Fed. 445; Tribble v. Singleton, 158 Ala. 308, 48 So. 481; Harrison v. Maury, 157 Ala. 227, 47 So. 724; Thornton v. Pinckard, 157 Ala. 206, 47 So. 289; Rodgers v. Burt, 157 Ala. 91, 47 So. 226; Harper v. T. N. Hays Co., 149 Ala. 174, 43 So. 360; Jones v. Kennedy, 138 Ala. 502, 35 So. 465; Downing v. Woodstock Iron Co., 93 Ala. 262, 9 So. 177; Peagler v. Stabler, 91 Ala. 308, 9 So. 157; Knaus v. Dreher, 84 Ala. 319, 4 So. 287; Cosby v. Buchanan, 81 Ala. 574, 1 So. 898; Mitchell v. Wellman, 80 Ala. 16; Marsh v. Marsh, 74 Ala. 418; Turner v. Wilkinson, 72 Ala. 361; Parks v. Parks, 66 Ala. 326; Phillips v. Croft, 42 Ala. 477; Parish v. Gates, 29 Ala. 254; McIver v. Roberts (Ark.), 165

S. W. 273; Ford v. Nunnelley (Ark.), 165 S. W. 291; Prickett v. Williams (Ark.), 161 S. W. 1023; La Cotts v. La Cotts (Ark.), 159 S. W. 1111; Gates v. McPeace, 106 Ark. 583, 153 S. W. 797; Edwards v. Bond, 105 Ark. 314, 151 S. W. 243; Grummer v. Price, 101 Ark. 611, 143 S. W. 95; Griffin v. Welch, 88 Ark. 336, 114 S. W. 710; Rushton v. McIllvene, 88 Ark. 299, 114 S. W. 709; Reynolds v. Blanks, 78 Ark. 527, 94 S. W. 694; Hays v. Emerson, 75 Ark. 551, 87 S. W. 1027; Harman v. May, 40 Ark. 146; Williams v. Cheatham, 19 Ark. 278; Couts v. Winston, 153 Cal. 686, 96 Pac. 357; Renton v. Gibson, 148 Cal. 650, 84 Pac. 186; Emery v. Lowe, 140 Cal. 379, 73 Pac. 981; Blair v. Squire, 127 Cal. 18, 59 Pac. 211; Falk v. Wittram, 120 Cal. 479, 50 Pac. 707, 65 Am. St. 184; Ahern v. McCarthy, 107 Cal. 382, 40 Pac. 482; Penney v. Simmons, 99 Cal. 380, 33 Pac. 1121; Mahoney v. Bostwick (Cal.), 30 Pac. 1020; Henly v. Hotaling, 41 Cal. 22; Davis v. Pursel (Colo.), 134 Pac. 107; Baird v. Baird, 48 Colo. 506, 111 Pac. 79; Butsch v. Smith, 40 Colo. 64, 90 Pac. 61; Perot v. Cooper, 17 Colo. 80, 28 Pac. 391, 31 Am. St. 258; Armor v. Spaulding, 14 Colo. 302, 23 Pac. 789; Townsend v. Peterson, 12 Colo. 491, 21 Pac. 619; Whitsett v. Kershow, 4 Colo. 419; Persse v. Atlantic-Pacific R. Tunnel Co., 5 Colo. App. 117, 37 Pac. 951; Adams v. Adams, 51 Conn. 544; Walker v. Bank, 8 Houst. (Del.) 258, 14 Atl. 819, 10 Atl. 94; Hall v. Livingston, 3 Del. Ch. 348; Nieman v. Mitchell, 2 App. (D. C.) 195; Hayward v. Mayse, 1 App. (D. C.) 133; Balloch v. Hooper, 6 MacArth. (D. C.) 421; Matthews v. Porter, 16 Fla. 466; Bergen v. Johnson, 21 Idaho 619, 123 Pac. 484; Deadman v. Yantis, 230 Ill. 243, 82 N. E. 592, 120 Am. St. 291 (clear and convincing evidence); Gannon v. Moles, 209 Ill. 180, 70 N. E. 689; Heaton v. Gaines, 198 Ill. 479, 64 N. E. 1081, affg. 100 Ill. App. 26; Williams v. Williams, 180 Ill. 561, 54 N. E. 229; Strong v. Strong, 126 Ill. 301, 27 Ill. App. 148; Helm v. Boyd, 124 Ill. 370, 16 N. E. 85; Darst v. Murphy, 119 Ill. 343, 9 N. E. 887; Bailey v. Bailey, 115 Ill. 551, 4 N. E. 394; Workman v. Greening, 115 Ill. 447; Bartling v. Brasuhn, 102 Ill. 441;

Maher v. Farwell, 97 Ill. 56; Hancock v. Harper, 86 Ill. 445; Low v. Graff, 80 Ill. 360; Price v. Karnes, 59 Ill. 276; Knockamus v. Shepard, 54 Ill. 500; Shays v. Norton, 48 Ill. 100; Martinet v. Duff, 178 Ill. App. 199; Hoglund v. Royal Trust Co., 159 Ill. App. 390; Gray v. Hayhurst, 157 Ill. App. 488; Hill v. Viele, 128 Ill. App. 5; Rankin v. Rankin, 111 Ill. App. 403; May v. May, 55 Ill. App. 488, affg. 158 Ill. 209, 42 N. E. 56; Rogers v. Beach, 115 Ind. 413, 17 N. E. 609; Voss v. Eller, 109 Ind. 260, 10 N. E. 74; Cox v. Ratcliffe, 105 Ind. 374, 5 N. E. 5; Fox v. Fraser, 92 Ind. 265; Lucas v. Hendrix, 92 Ind. 54; Landers v. Beck, 92 Ind. 49; Herron v. Herron, 91 Ind. 278; Parker v. Hubble, 75 Ind. 580; Conwell v. Evill, 4 Blackf. (Ind.) 67; Cold v. Beh, 152 Iowa 368, 132 N. W. 73; Krebs v. Lauser, 133 Iowa 241, 110 N. W. 443; Betts v. Betts, 132 Iowa 72, 106 N. W. 928; Wright v. Wright, 122 Iowa 549, 98 N. W. 472; McLaughlin v. Royce, 108 Iowa 254, 78 N. W. 1105; Haggerty v. Brower, 105 Iowa 395, 75 N. W. 321; England v. England, 94 Iowa 716, 61 N. W. 920; Baird v. Reinghaus, 87 Iowa 167, 54 N. W. 148; Langer v. Merservey, 80 Iowa 159, 45 N. W. 732; Wright v. Mahaffey, 76 Iowa 96; Ensminger v. Ensminger, 75 Iowa 89, 39 N. W. 208, 9 Am. St. 462; Corliss v. Conable, 74 Iowa 58, 36 N. W. 891; Allen v. Fogg, 66 Iowa 229, 23 N. W. 643; Knight v. McCord, 63 Iowa 429, 19 N. W. 310; Kibby v. Harsh, 61 Iowa 196, 16 N. W. 85; Woodworth v. Carman, 43 Iowa 504; Crawford v. Taylor, 42 Iowa 260; Zuver v. Lyons, 40 Iowa 510; Green v. Turner, 38 Iowa 112; Hyatt v. Cochran, 37 Iowa 309; Wilson v. Patrick, 34 Iowa 362; Key v. McCleary, 25 Iowa 191; Holliday v. Arthur, 25 Iowa 19; Childs v. Griswold, 19 Iowa 362; Sunderland v. Sunderland, 19 Iowa 325; Gardner v. Weston, 18 Iowa 533; Cooper v. Skeel, 14 Iowa 578; Atkins v. Faulkner, 11 Iowa 326; Corbit v. Smith, 7 Iowa 60; Noel v. Noel, 1 Iowa 423; Reeder v. Gorsuch, 55 Kans. 553, 40 Pac. 897; Winston v. Burnell, 44 Kans. 367, 24 Pac. 477, 21 Am. St. 289; Stokeley v. Flanders (Ky.), 128 S. W. 608; Runyon v. Pogue (Ky.), 42 S.

W. 910; Bradley v. Merrill, 88 Maine 319, 34 Atl. 160; Libby v. Clark, 88 Maine 32, 33 Atl. 657; Jameson v. Emerson, 82 Maine 359, 19 Atl. 831; Knapp v. Bailey, 79 Maine 195, 9 Atl. 122; Reed v. Reed, 75 Maine 264; Stinchfield v. Milliken, 71 Maine 567; Rowell v. Jewett, 69 Maine 293; Richardson v. Woodbury, 43 Maine 206; Funk v. Harshman, 110 Md. 127, 72 Atl. 665; Cochrane v. Price (Md.), 8 Atl. 361; Farringer v. Ramsay, 2 Md. 365; Commonwealth v. Reading Sav. Bank, 137 Mass. 431; Smith v. Smith, 177 Mich. 268, 143 N. W. 86; Dalton v. Mertz, 173 Mich. 153, 138 N. W. 1055; Rathbone v. Maltz, 155 Mich. 306, 118 N. W. 991; Sowles v. Wilcox, 127 Mich. 166, 86 N. W. 689; Tilden v. Streeter, 45 Mich. 533, 8 N. W. 502; Johnson v. Van Velsor, 43 Mich. 208, 5 N. W. 223; Case v. Peters, 20 Mich. 298; Stitt v. Rat Portage Lumber Co., 96 Minn. 27, 104 N. W. 561; A. J. Dyer Pine Land Co. v. Whiteman, 92 Minn. 55, 99 N. W. 362; Williams v. Stratton, 18 Miss. 418; Brightwell v. McAfee, 249 Mo. 562, 155 S. W. 820; Rinkel v. Lubke, 246 Mo. 377, 152 S. W. 81; Gerhardt v. Tucker, 187 Mo. 46, 85 S. W. 552; Jones v. Rush, 156 Mo. 364, 27 S. W. 118; Cobb v. Day, 106 Mo. 278, 17 S. W. 323; Worley v. Dryden, 57 Mo. 226; Quick v. Turner, 26 Mo. App. 29; Gibson v. Morris State Bank (Mont.), 140 Pac. 76; Gassert v. Bogk, 7 Mont. 585, 19 Pac. 281, 1 L. R. A. 240; O'Hanlon v. Barry, 87 Nebr. 522, 127 N. W. 860; Wilde v. Homan, 58 Nebr. 634, 79 N. W. 546; Huston v. Canfield, 57 Nebr. 345, 77 N. W. 763; Stall v. Jones, 47 Nebr. 706, 66 N. W. 653; Kemp v. Small, 32 Nebr. 318, 49 N. W. 169; Tower v. Fetz, 26 Nebr. 706, 42 N. W. 884, 18 Am. St. 795; Eiseman v. Gallagher, 24 Nebr. 79, 37 N. W. 941; Newman v. Edwards, 22 Nebr. 248, 34 N. W. 382; McHugh v. Smiley, 17 Nebr. 626, 24 N. W. 277; Deroin v. Jennings, 4 Nebr. 97; Schade v. Bessinger, 3 Nebr. 140; Wilson v. Richards, 1 Nebr. 342; Fahay v. State Bank, 1 Nebr. (unoff.) 89, 95 N. W. 505; Pierce v. Traver, 13 Nev. 526; Bingham v. Thompson, 4 Nev. 224; Reich v. Cochran, 102 N. Y. 827. affd. 139 App. Div. 931, 124 N. Y. S. 1127;

Richardson v. Beaber, 62 Misc. 542, 115 N. Y. S. 821; In re Holmes, 79 N. Y. S. 592; Sidway v. Sidway, 7 N. Y. S. 421; Haas v. Nanert, 19 N. Y. St. 472, 2 N. Y. S. 723; Shattuck v. Bascom, 55 Hun (N. Y.) 14; Erwin v. Curtis, 43 Hun (N. Y.) 292; Marks v. Pell, 1 Johns. Ch. (N. Y.) 594; Holmes v. Grant, 8 Paige (N. Y.) 243; Watkins v. Williams, 123 N. Car. 170, 31 S. E. 388; Hinton v. Pritchard, 107 N. Car. 128, 12 S. E. 242; McNair v. Pope, 100 N. Car. 404, 6 S. E. 234; Smiley v. Pearce, 98 N. Car. 185, 3 S. E. 631; Williams v. Hodges, 95 N. Car. 32; Leggett v. Leggett, 88 N. Car. 108; Moore v. Ivey, 8 Ired. Eq. (N. Car.) 192; Brown v. Carson, Busb. Eq. (N. Car.) 272; Clement v. Clement, 1 Jones Eq. (N. Car.) 184; Adams v. McIntyre, 22 N. Dak. 337, 133 N. W. 915; Miller v. Smith, 20 N. Dak. 96, 126 N. W. 499; Smith v. Jensen, 16 N. Dak. 408, 114 N. W. 306; Wells v. Geyer, 12 N. Dak. 316, 96 N. W. 289; Forester v. Van Auken, 12 N. Dak. 175, 96 N. W. 301; Little v. Braun, 11 N. Dak. 410, 92 N. W. 800; McGuin v. Lee, 10 N. Dak. 160, 86 N. W. 714; Jasper v. Hazen, 4 N. Dak. 1, 58 N. W. 454; Devore v. Woodruff, 1 N. Dak. 143, 45 N. W. 701; Kemper v. Campbell, 44 Ohio St. 210, 6 N. E. 566; Shaw v. Walbridge, 33 Ohio St. 1; Wilson v. Giddings, 28 Ohio St. 554; Slutz v. Desenberg, 28 Ohio St. 371; Mathews v. Leaman, 24 Ohio St. 615; Cotterell v. Long, 20 Ohio 464; Marshall v. Stewart, 17 Ohio 356; Stall v. Cincinnati, 16 Ohio St. 169; Miller v. Stokely, 5 Ohio St. 194; Miami Exporting Co. v. Bank of United States, Wright (Ohio) 249; Beall v. Beall, 67 Ore. 33, 135 Pac. 185; Bickel v. Wessinger, 58 Ore. 98, 113 Pac. 34; Hall v. O'Connell, 52 Ore. 164, 95 Pac. 717, decree modified on rehearing 96 Pac. 1070; Osgood v. Osgood, 35 Ore. 1, 56 Pac. 1017; Albany &c. Canal Co. v. Crawford, 11 Ore. 243, 4 Pac. 113; Barber v. Lefavour, 176 Pa. St. 331, 35 Atl. 202; Wallace v. Smith, 155 Pa. St. 78, 25 Atl. 807, 35 Am. St. 868; Pancake v. Cauffman, 114 Pa. St. 113, 7 Atl. 67; Lance's Appeal, 112 Pa. St. 456, 4 Atl. 375; Logne's Appeal, 104 Pa. St. 136; Hartley's Appeal, 103 Pa. St. 23; Nicolls v. McDonald, 101

There must be a clear preponderance of evidence.[6] As a general rule, the uncorroborated testimony of a single witness, whether the

Pa. St. 514; Stewart's Appeal, 98 Pa. St. 377; Rowand v. Finney, 96 Pa. St. 192; Haines v. Thompson, 70 Pa. St. 434; Todd v. Campbell, 32 Pa. St. 250; Porter v. Mayfield, 21 Pa. St. 263; Banks v. Frith, 97 S. Car. 362, 81 S. E. 677; Williams v. McManus, 90 S. Car. 490, 73 S. E. 1038; Miller v. Price, 66 S. Car. 85, 44 S. E. 584; Arnold v. Mattison, 3 Rich. Eq. (S. Car.) 153; Sellers v. Sellers (Tenn.), 53 S. W. 316; Slawson v. Denton (Tenn.), 48 S. W. 350; Nickson v. Toney, 3 Head (Tenn.) 655; Haynes v. Swann, 6 Heisk. (Tenn.) 560; Lane v. Dickerson, 10 Yerg. (Tenn.) 373; Hickman v. Quinn, 6 Yerg. (Tenn.) 96; Hammonds v. Hopkins, 3 Yerg. (Tenn.) 525; Overton v. Bigelow, 3 Yerg. (Tenn.) 513; Harrison v. Hogue (Tex. Civ. App.), 136 S. W. 118; Frazer v. Seureau (Tex. Civ. App.), 128 S. W. 649; Stringfellow v. Braselton, 54 Tex. Civ. App. 1, 117 S. W. 204; Rotan v. Turner, 46 Tex. Civ. App. 534, 102 S. W. 932; Lowry v. Carter, 46 Tex. Civ. App. 488, 102 S. W. 930; Irvin v. Johnson, 44 Tex. Civ. App. 436, 98 S. W. 405; Goodbar v. Bloom, 43 Tex. Civ. App. 434, 96 S. W. 657; Miller v. Yturria, 69 Tex. 549, 7 S. W. 206; Brewster v. Davis, 56 Tex. 478, 59 Tex. 93; Markham v. Carothers, 47 Tex. 21; Hughes v. Delaney, 44 Tex. 529; Gazley v. Herring (Tex.), 17 S. W. 17; Hill v. Saunders, 115 Va. 60, 78 S. E. 559; Motley v. Carstairs, 114 Va. 429, 76 S. E. 948; Batchelder v. Randolph, 112 Va. 296, 71 S. E. 533; Bachrach v. Bachrach, 111 Va. 232, 68 S. E. 985; Holladay v. Willis, 101 Va. 274, 43 S. E. 616; Edwards v. Wall, 79 Va. 321; Beverly v. Davis (Wash.), 140 Pac. 696; Hansen v. Abrams, 76 Wash. 457, 136 Pac. 678; Mittlesteadt v. Johnson, 75 Wash. 550, 135 Pac. 214; Hoover v. Bouffleur, 74 Wash. 382, 133 Pac. 602; Kegley v. Skillman, 68 Wash. 637, 123 Pac. 1081; Johnson v. National Bank, 65 Wash. 261, 118 Pac. 21; Washington Safe Deposit &c. Co. v. Lietzow, 59 Wash. 281, 109 Pac. 1021; Sahlin v. Gregson, 46 Wash. 452, 90 Pac. 592; Reynolds v. Reynolds, 42 Wash. 107,

84 Pac. 579; Way v. Mayhugh, 57 W. Va. 175, 50 S. E. 724; Kerr v. Hill, 27 W. Va. 576; Vangilder v. Hoffman, 22 W. Va. 1; Becker v. Howard, 75 Wis. 415, 44 N. W. 755; McCormick v. Herndon, 67 Wis. 648, 31 N. W. 303; Schriber v. Le Clair, 66 Wis. 579, 29 N. W. 570, 889; Rockwell v. Humphrey, 57 Wis. 410, 15 N. W. 394; Sable v. Maloney, 48 Wis. 331, 4 N. W. 479; Smith v. Crosby, 47 Wis. 160, 2 N. W. 104; Butler v. Butler, 46 Wis. 430, 1 N. W. 70; McClellan v. Sanford, 26 Wis. 595; Kent v. Lasley, 24 Wis. 654; Harrison v. Bank, 17 Wis. 340; Fowler v. Adams, 13 Wis. 458; Lake v. Meacham, 13 Wis. 355; Newton v. Holley, 6 Wis. 592; Hunter v. Maanum, 78 Wis. 656, 48 N. W. 51. The rule stated in these cases is as follows: "To convert a deed absolute into a mortgage, the evidence should be so clear as to leave no substantial doubt that the real intention of the parties was to execute a mortgage." The rule in Texas is an exception to the general rule. It is held to be error to require clear and satisfactory proof. Wallace v. Berry (Tex.), 18 S. W. 595. This rule is applicable only to cases in which it is sought to establish a trust upon the declarations or evidence of the trustee, as in Moreland v. Barnhart, 44 Tex. 275. It is error to instruct a jury that they can not find a deed absolute on its face to be a mortgage, unless the fact that it was so intended should be established by two witnesses, or by one witness and strong corroborating circumstances. Pierce v. Fort, 60 Tex. 464. See ante § 260.

[6] Nelson v. Wadsworth (Ala.), 61 So. 895; Morton v. Allen (Ala.), 60 So. 866; Hopper v. Jones, 29 Cal. 18; Eames v. Hardin, 111 Ill. 634; Miner v. Hess, 47 Ill. 170; Knight v. McCord, 63 Iowa 429, 19 N. W. 310; Gardner v. Weston, 18 Iowa 533; Winston v. Burnell, 44 Kans. 367, 24 Pac. 477, 21 Am. St. 289; Stockbridge Iron Co. v. Hudson Iron Co., 107 Mass. 290; Etheridge v. Wisner, 86 Mich. 166, 48 N. W. 1087; McMillan v. Bissell, 63 Mich. 66, 29 N.

grantor or another, is not sufficient to convert an absolute deed into a mortgage.[7] The unsupported testimony of the plaintiff, contradicted by the defendant, is insufficient to convert an absolute deed into a mortgage.[8] The fact that the grantor understood the transaction to be a mortgage is not alone sufficient to prove it to be so.[9] If the evidence is doubtful and unsatisfactory, if it fails to overcome the strong presumption arising from the terms of the absolute deed by testimony entirely clear and convincing beyond reasonable controversy, the deed must have effect in accordance with its terms.[10] "The security of titles and sound public policy require that a party alleging that a deed, absolute in form, is nevertheless a mortgage, should show it by very satisfactory evidence; and where he attempts to show it by oral evidence, his proof should amount to more than a mere guess or surmise, or even inferences which are just as consistent with one theory of the deed as the other."[11] When there is a substantial conflict in the evidence, a mere preponderance is not sufficient to warrant a change in the character of a deed or other solemn instrument of writing.[12]

One who has assigned a contract for the purchase of real estate, and

---

W. 737; Sloan v. Becker, 34 Minn. 491, 26 N. W. 730; Harmon v. Grants Pass Banking &c. Co., 60 Ore. 69, 118 Pac. 188; McClellan v. Sanford, 26 Wis. 595; Kent v. Lasley, 24 Wis. 654.

[7] Hubbard v. Stetson, 3 MacArthur (D. C.) 113; Blake v. Taylor, 142 Ill. 482, 32 N. E. 401; Arnold v. Mattison, 3 Rich. Eq. (S. Car.) 153; Muckelroy v. House, 21 Tex. Civ. App. 673, 52 S. W. 1038; Hamilton v. Flume, 2 Tex. Unrep. Cas. 694. See also Beckett v. Allison, 188 Pa. St. 279, 314, 41 Atl. 623; Yates v. Caswell (Tex. Civ. App.), 126 S. W. 914; Pierce v. Fort, 60 Tex. 464.

[8] Blake v. Taylor, 142 Ill. 482, 32 N. E. 401.

[9] Andrews v. Hyde, 3 Cliff. (U. S.) 516; Jones v. Brittan, 1 Woods (U. S.) 667; Douglass v. Moody, 80 Ala. 61; Reeder v. Gorsuch, 55 Kans. 553, 40 Pac. 897; Phœnix v. Gardner, 13 Minn. 430; Holmes v. Fresh, 9 Mo. 201; Wilson v. Parshall, 129 N. Y. 223, 29 N. E. 297; Jones v. Jones, 17 N. Y. S. 905.

[10] Howland v. Blake, 97 U. S. 624; Shattuck v. Bascom, 9 N. Y. 934. Per Barker, P. J. "Many of the cases hold that, upon the unsupported evidence of an interested witness, a decree declaring a deed absolute in terms to be only an instrument for the security of a debt can not be sustained. In other cases it is held that, where the evidence of a party rests chiefly in the evidence of one witness, and that is disputed by a witness equally credible, a case for relief is not made out." Thus an absolute deed will not be declared a mortgage on the unsupported testimony of the grantor. Adams v. Pilcher, 92 Ala. 474, 8 So. 757; Wilson v. Parshall, 129 N. Y. 223, 29 N. E. 297, affg. 7 N. Y. S. 479. As stated by Mr. Justice Graves in Tilden v. Streeter, 45 Mich. 540, 8 N. W. 502, "a party seeking to modify the operation of the instrument, and prove himself entitled, against the terms of his own deed, to an equity of redemption, is not only bound to make out that the transaction was, in truth and justice, nothing more than the giving of security, but is required to do so by a force of evidence sufficient to command the unhesitating assent of every reasonable mind."

[11] Wilson v. Parshall, 129 N. Y. 223, 29 N. E. 297, per Earl, J.

[12] Perot v. Cooper, 17 Colo. 80, 28 Pac. 391.

permitted the assignee to take an absolute deed from the owner, can not be allowed to redeem upon an allegation, without proof, that the transaction was in fact a mortgage, and that he assented to it upon the confidence that it would be so treated by his creditor.[13] Testimony of admissions by the grantee, made subsequently to the conveyance, that the conveyance was intended as a mortgage, may, with corroborating circumstances, be sufficient to establish the fact;[14] but alone is not sufficient.[15]

When, however, it is once admitted that the deed was made merely to secure a debt, and the question is, what is the amount of the debt, the burden is upon the grantee to show it.[16]

[13] Hogarty v. Lynch, 6 Bosw. (N. Y.) 138.

[14] Bentley v. Phelps, 2 Woodb. & M. (U. S.) 426; McIntyre v. Humphreys, 1 Hoff. Ch. (N. Y.) 31.

[15] Ross v. Brusie, 64 Cal. 245; Nicolls v. McDonald, 101 Pa. St. 514; Todd v. Campbell, 32 Pa. St. 250.

[16] Freytag v. Hoeland, 23 N. J. Eq. 36. It was admitted that the deed, though absolute on its face, was given as security only, and therefore a mortgage. The plaintiff, who sought to recover the property, claimed that it was security for $700 only; the defendant claimed that it was security not only for that sum, but for previous advances of about $5,300. The plaintiff denied that these advances were made to him or on his credit, and said that the advances were made to his wife and daughter for a different consideration. The circumstances of the case, in the language of the chancellor, are "novel and peculiar." Hoeland was a butcher, and followed his trade at Newark, and afterward in California and Nevada. He also speculated in mining rights in the latter states. He prospered and had money. Freytag was a carpenter; he worked at his trade in Newark, where Hoeland boarded for a time in his family. At this time either Mrs. Freytag proposed to Hoeland, or Hoeland proposed to Mrs. Freytag, to elope together. Each said the offer came from the other, and it was virtuously rejected by the party testifying. The result was that Hoeland changed his boarding place, and Mr. Freytag, in an encounter with him, got a wound over his eye, the scar of which he still bore. But notwithstanding these inharmonious circumstances, Hoeland was again received as a boarder by Mrs. Freytag, with whom he was on very friendly and confidential terms.

Katinka, the daughter of the Freytags, was growing up toward womanhood, and Hoeland took a fancy to her, and proposed to make her his wife when the proper time should arrive. In this he had the support of the mother. Katinka submitted passively, though it did not appear that she ever engaged herself to him. Freytag was an easy-going, submissive man, who did not get on in the world. Katinka had some talent for music, and took lessons to fit her for taking part in concerts and the opera. Hoeland, at the solicitation of the mother and daughter, furnished them with money. In 1868 the Freytags went to Europe; Freytag returned, but the mother and daughter went to Milan, and remained for Katinka's musical education. There Hoeland sent money to them, at the earnest request of the daughter, who in one of her letters almost promised to come back to him at San Francisco. The correspondence and all the arrangements were conducted without consulting Freytag. "It would not be strange," said the chancellor, "if a young woman of promise, however humble her origin, who had taken lessons of masters of music, especially in Italy,

The general rule above stated is not, however, applied with uniform strictness to all cases. Wherever the transaction is between parties whose relations are of a close fiduciary character, the party seeking to have the absolute deed declared to be a mortgage is not held to the same exactitude and strictness of proof, nor is the testimony offered in support of the bill to be viewed with the same scrutiny, as in those cases where the parties deal with each other at arms' length.[17]

Whether the evidence is of such character and strength as to show that the absolute deed was intended as a mortgage is a question for the trial court to determine,[18] but the determination of facts and circumstances as evidence of intention to create a security, has frequently been held a question for the jury, particularly where the evidence is conflicting.[19]

§ 336. **Rights of grantor—Payment prerequisite to redemption.—** When it has been proved that a deed absolute in form was intended as a mortgage, the respective rights of the parties will be determined by the law governing the relations between mortgagor and mort-

where the art has reached its highest cultivation, should show some reluctance to fulfil an engagement made for her in childhood, and marry a practical butcher far older than herself, and live with him in Nevada or California. Some indications of this feeling, or perhaps a conclusion that mother and daughter had been using his attachment and hopes to obtain his money without any regard to fulfilling his expectations, seemed to have aroused Hoeland to his situation, and to have changed his course regarding them."

In the summer of 1869, Hoeland was in Jersey City; Freytag saw him, and, being pressed for money, applied to him for a loan, which was at first refused. Afterward he consented to advance $700, on receiving an absolute conveyance of a house and lot subject to a mortgage of $8,000, but worth twice that sum; and such was the arrangement made. Hoeland claimed that the conveyance secured the advances to the mother and daughter, who were still in Europe. The chancellor held that the burden was upon the grantee to show that more than the $700 was secured; and that

there was no proof that any further sum was secured.

[17] Lindsay v. Lindsay (Colo.), 27 Pac. 877, per Bissell, J.; Bohm v. Bohm, 9 Colo. 100, 10 Pac. 790.

[18] Brison v. Brison, 90 Cal. 323, 27 Pac. 186; Cochrane v. Wilson (Tex.), 160 S. W. 593; Fridley v. Somerville, 60 W. Va. 272, 54 S. E. 502; Mahoney v. Bostwick, 96 Cal. 53, 30 Pac. 1020. In the latter case De Haven, J., said: "That court ought always to be governed, in weighing the evidence and reaching its conclusion as to the facts, by this rule, which requires the plaintiff in an action like this to present a case free from doubt, and, unless the evidence is such as to leave in the mind of the trial judge a clear and satisfactory conviction that the instrument which in form is a deed was intended by all the parties thereto as a mortgage, the finding should be against the plaintiff."

[19] Tappen v. Eshelman, 164 Ind. 338, 73 N. E. 688; Culbreth v. Hall, 159 N. Car. 588, 75 S. E. 1096; Kellner v. Randle (Tex. Civ. App.), 165 S. W. 509; Bradford v. Malone, 33 Tex. Civ. App. 349, 77 S. W. 22. See also Reich v. Dyer, 180 N. Y. 107, 72 N. E. 922; Johnson v. Woodworth,

gagee.[20] The grantor has the right to redeem, by paying the amount secured with interest, and may enforce the right at any time before foreclosure, even after the time stipulated for payment, and although the conveyance provides for forfeiture for nonpayment at such time.[21] The grantor on redeeming or seeking a reconveyance must comply with his agreement, and pay the amount due.[22] On the principle that "he who seeks equity must do equity," a grantor, who seeks to redeem land from a conveyance made to secure the performance of a verbal agreement to pay a certain sum of money in gold coin, should be held to a full compliance with the terms of his agreement, as a condition precedent to a reconveyance.[23]

On this ground it has been held that, although a loan upon land has been put in the form of an absolute deed and an agreement to reconvey, for the purpose of covering up a contract for usurious interest, the mortgagor is not entitled to the statutory penalties or forfeitures for usury, but must pay on redeeming the amount of the original loan, with legal interest.[24]

Equity will not relieve a grantor on his own application from the consequences of an absolute deed made to protect his property from his creditors.[25] The grantor by absolute deed may sell and convey or mortgage his equity of redemption; and subsequent purchasers or incumbrancers may redeem.[26]

In the absence of an express agreement in regard to possession, it

134 App. Div. 715, 119 N. Y. S. 146; Brown v. Crossman, 206 N. Y. 471, 100 N. E. 42.

[20] Sheppard v. Wagner, 240 Mo. 409, 144 S. W. 394, 145 S. W. 420; Carr v. Carr, 52 N. Y. 251; Yingling v. Redwine, 12 Okla. 64, 69 Pac. 810.

[21] Carter v. Gunn, 64 Ga. 651; Allen v. Frost, 62 Ga. 659; Phinizy v. Clark, 62 Ga. 623; West v. Bennett, 59 Ga. 507; Jackson v. Lynch, 129 Ill. 72, 21 N. E. 580, 22 N. E. 246; Roberts v. Richards, 36 Ill. 339; Keithley v. Wood, 47 Ill. App. 102, affd. 151 Ill. 566, 38 N. E. 149, 42 Am. St. 265; Thompson v. Banks, 3 Md. Ch. 138; Doty v. Norton, 133 App. Div. 106, 117 N. Y. S. 793; Balduff v. Griswold, 9 Okla. 438, 60 Pac. 223; England v. Codrington, 1 Eden 169, 28 Eng. Reprint 649. The grantor can require only a reconveyance of the interest originally conveyed by the mortgage. Hall v. Arnott, 80 Cal. 348, 22 Pac. 200.

Upon payment of the debt and satisfaction of conditions, the grantor is entitled to a reconveyance of the property. Farris v. King, 27 Ark. 404.

[22] White v. Lucas, 46 Iowa 319; Westfall v. Westfall, 16 Hun (N. Y.) 541; Kemper v. Campbell, 44 Ohio St. 210, 6 N. E. 566. Payment must include all amounts due the grantee. Saunders v. Savage (Tenn.), 63 S. W. 218.

[23] Cowing v. Rogers, 34 Cal. 648; Jeffery v. Robbins, 167 Ill. 375, 47 N. E. 725.

[24] Heacock v. Swartwout, 28 Ill. 291.

[25] Arnold v. Mattison, 3 Rich. Eq. (S. Car.) 153; Hassam v. Barrett, 115 Mass. 256. See ante § 283.

[26] Hillock v. Frizzle, 10 N. Brunsw. 655; O'Reilly v. Wilkes, 8 Can. L. J. 135. See also Moore v. Universal Elevator Co., 122 Mich. 48, 80 N. W. 1015.

has generally been held that the grantor can not hold possession against the demand of the grantee; since an absolute deed, though given as security, must be regarded as vesting both the legal title and right of possession in the grantee.[27] The grantee, as a mortgagee in possession, must account to the grantor for rents and profits.[28]

§ 337. **Rights of judgment creditors.**—A grantor by absolute deed has no interest in the land, at law; he has only an equity to redeem by performing the agreement of defeasance; and such an equity is not an estate in the land to which a judgment lien can attach, or which can be sold under execution at law.[29] But in equity, a judgment creditor may show the character of his debtor's conveyance for the purpose of rendering the equity of redemption available as assets for satisfaction of his demands.[30]

A judgment creditor having purchased his debtor's land at a sale under execution issued upon his judgment, may show that an absolute conveyance of the land made by his debtor was in fact a mortgage, and he is entitled to a conveyance of it upon paying any balance due upon the mortgage.[31] And without having made a purchase upon execution,

[27] Richards v. Crawford, 50 Iowa 494; Burdick v. Wentworth, 42 Iowa 440; Jeffery v. Hursh, 42 Mich. 563, 4 N. W. 303; Bennett v. Robinson, 27 Mich. 26. But see Le Conte v. Pennock, 61 Kans. 330, 59 Pac. 641; Connolly v. Giddings, 24 Nebr. 131, 37 N. W. 939; Murray v. Walker, 31 N. Y. 399. In Indiana it is held that the grantee under an absolute deed has only a prima facie right to possession, but proof that the deed is a mortgage is a good defense to an action to enforce such right. Cox v. Ratcliffe, 105 Ind. 374, 5 N. E. 5.

[28] Haworth v. Taylor, 108 Ill. 275; Tedens v. Clark, 24 Ill. App. 510; Kinkead v. Peet, 153 Iowa 199, 132 N. W. 1095; Fultz v. Peterson, 78 Miss. 128, 28 So. 829.

[29] Loring v. Melendy, 11 Ohio 355; Baird v. Kirtland, 8 Ohio 21; McCabe v. Thompson, 6 Grant Ch. (U. C.) 175; McDonald v. McDonell, 2 Grant Err. & App. (U. C.) 393. But see Parrott v. Baker, 82 Ga. 364, 9 S. E. 1068.

[30] De Wolf v. Strader, 26 Ill. 225, 79 Am. Dec. 371; Allen v. Kemp, 29 Iowa 452; Macauley v. Smith, 132 N. Y. 524, 30 N. E. 997; Manufacturers' Bank v. Rugee, 59 Wis. 221,

18 N. W. 251. See also Andrus v. Burke, 61 N. J. Eq. 297, 48 Atl. 228. It has been held that the grantee in an absolute deed intended as a mortgage, must carefully and truly disclose the nature of his security, when questioned by a creditor of the mortgagor, and an untruthful, material statement, or unfair concealment will postpone such security to that of a subsequent attaching creditor. Geary v. Porter, 17 Ore. 465, 21 Pac. 442. Such a conveyance may also work a fraud upon other creditors of the grantor, by putting his property out of their reach, or hindering them in enforcing their claims, and thus be voidable as to them. Fuller &c. Co. v. Gaul, 85 Ill. App. 500, affd. 185 Ill. 43, 56 N. Y. 1077. See also Lynch v. Raleigh, 3 Ind. 273. But a deed made to defraud creditors may be avoided only by them, and equity will not aid the grantor himself, but will refuse to declare his deed a mortgage. Kitts v. Willson, 130 Ind. 492, 29 N. E. 401; Patnode v. Darveau, 112 Mich. 127, 70 N. W. 439, 71 N. W. 1095.

[31] Judge v. Reese, 24 N. J. Eq. 387; Vandegrift v. Herbert, 18 N. J. Eq.

a creditor of the grantor may show that such absolute deed is really a mortgage, and may enforce a judgment against the property or the proceeds of it to the extent of the surplus, after satisfying the debt for the security of which it was conveyed.[32] A judgment obtained against the grantor by a creditor, after the making of an absolute deed which is really a mortgage, becomes a lien upon the equity of redemption, just as it would if a formal mortgage had been given.[33]

On the other hand, a creditor of the grantee who levies upon land held by the latter under an absolute deed which is really a mortgage, can obtain no higher or better title than the grantee himself had. The mortgagor is entitled to redeem the land upon payment of the mortgage debt.[34]

§ 338. **Parol waiver of defeasance by mortgagor.**—By an independent parol agreement the mortgagor may waive his rights under a deed which was originally in effect a mortgage, and if this agreement is supported by a consideration, or is partially acted on by the parties or fully performed, the mortgagor is estopped to deny the grantee's absolute title.[35] The grantee has the legal title already, and the grantor may cut off all right to redeem, by a receipt of an adequate consideration therefor and an informal release of all his interest in the property.[36] But the new agreement must not only

466; Clark v. Condit, 18 N. J. Eq. 358; Van Buren v. Olmstead, 5 Paige (N. Y.) 9.

[32] Dwen v. Blake, 44 Ill. 135; De Wolf v. Strader, 26 Ill. 225, 79 Am. Dec. 371; Allen v. Kemp, 29 Iowa 452.

[33] Christie v. Hale, 46 Ill. 117.

[34] Leech v. Hillsman, 8 Lea (Tenn.) 747.

[35] McMillan v. Jewett, 85 Ala. 476, 5 So. 145; Deadman v. Yantis, 230 Ill. 243, 82 N. E. 592; Cramer v. Wilson, 202 Ill. 83, 66 N. E. 869; Haggerty v. Brower, 105 Iowa 395, 75 N. W. 321; Vennum v. Babcock, 13 Iowa 194; Scholl v. Hopper, 134 Ky. 83, 119 S. W. 770; Sears v. Gilman, 199 Mass. 384, 85 N. E. 466; Trull v. Skinner, 17 Pick. (Mass.) 213; Shaw v. Walbridge, 33 Ohio St. 1; Jordan v. Katz, 89 Va. 628, 16 S. E. 866; Phelps v. Seely, 22 Gratt. (Va.) 573. See also Hutchinson v. Page, 246 Ill. 71, 92 N. E. 571. A security contract in the nature of a mortgage may be changed into an absolute conveyance with an option to repurchase. On such issues the intention of the parties and the fairness of the transaction will be considered. The form of conveyance is not controlling, and parol evidence is admissible to show the real agreement. Miller v. Smith, 20 N. Dak. 96, 126 N. W. 499. But see Cramer v. Wilson, 202 Ill. 83; Van Keuren v. McLaughlin, 19 N. J. Eq. 187; Ullman v. Devereux, 46 Tex. Civ. App. 459, 102 S. W. 1163. A deed executed as a mortgage can not pass title to the mortgagee by the party subsequently canceling the evidence of indebtedness, and making a parol agreement that the deed shall convey the absolute title. Keller v. Kirby, 34 Tex. Civ. App. 404, 79 S. W. 82. See ante §§ 251, 252, and post § 711.

[36] Scanlan v. Scanlan, 134 Ill. 630, 25 N. E. 652. "Where a mortgage is in the form of an absolute conveyance, a bona fide agreement between the parties to vest the entire estate

be founded upon adequate consideration, but must be fair and reasonable in its terms and free from fraud and undue influence.[37]

A subsequent parol agreement that the grantor shall not redeem, but that his deed to the grantee shall be indefeasible, must be clearly established by the evidence to cut off the right of redemption. If the evidence of such settlement and agreement is conflicting, with the weight in favor of the grantor, the relief will be granted on payment of the debt and interest in full.[38]

The person having the right to redeem may release his right by abandoning possession and all claim to the property, and his abandonment may be regarded as a foreclosure by the mortgagee in whom is the legal title.[39] An absolute deed which was in effect a mortgage was subject to a prior trust deed which the grantee had not assumed to pay. The grantor afterward informed the grantee that he could not pay this incumbrance, and that he elected to abandon the property, and the grantee thereupon bought in the property at the trustee's sale. He acquired good title thereby, since, after the grantor elected to abandon the property, there was no longer any confidential relation between them.[40]

A mortgagor who abandons his right to redeem from an absolute conveyance, and elects to treat the conveyance as an absolute deed instead of a mortgage, is bound by such election, and can not afterward redeem.[41] He may also verbally waive his right of redemption in favor of another person, and after a long acquiescence in the transaction, the other in the meantime having redeemed the land and improved it, he will not be allowed to redeem from him.[42] When the

---

in the mortgagee will be sustained, and the execution of a formal deed will not be required, provided the transaction is fair, and not attended with oppression or fraud or undue influence and the mortgagee has not availed himself of his position to obtain an advantage over the mortgagor." Per Baker, J. See also Seymour v. Mackay, 126 Ill. 341, 18 N. E. 552; Carpenter v. Carpenter, 70 Ill. 457; West v. Reed, 55 Ill. 242.

[37] McMillan v. Jewett, 85 Ala. 476, 5 So. 145; Cassem v. Heustis, 201 Ill. 208, 66 N. E. 283, 94 Am. St. 160. See also Miller v. Smith, 20 N. Dak. 96, 126 N. W. 499; Wagg v. Herbert, 19 Okla. 525, 92 Pac. 250. See ante §§ 251, 252.

[38] Marshall v. Williams, 21 Ore. 268, 28 Pac. 137

[39] Adams v. Cooty, 60 Vt. 395, 15 Atl. 150.

[40] Turner v. Littlefield, 142 Ill. 630, 32 N. E. 522.

[41] Maxfield v. Patchen, 29 Ill. 39.

[42] Carpenter v. Carpenter, 70 Ill. 457. The plaintiff in this case, having been unsuccessful in a love matter with a girl in the neighborhood, started for California, and when he reached Chicago, on the road, he wrote to his father to redeem the land and it should be his; that he would never return from California until he was able to set his heel up the neck of the Gnil tribe (relatives of the girl). The father redeemed the land, sold it, and invested the proceeds in other land. It was held that the father was not liable to account, especially after

grantee goes into possession and makes valuable improvements, and with the knowledge of the grantor, sells the property, the latter is estopped to claim that his deed was a mortgage.[43] In any event redemption must be made within the time allowed by the statute of limitations.[44]

§ 339. **Grantee's rights against third persons.**—As to third persons the grantee may exercise all the rights of an absolute owner[45] whether the transaction be a mortgage or a conditional sale. A bona fide purchaser takes the land discharged of the grantor's equity of redemption. A creditor of the grantee may levy upon the land as the grantee's property.[46] If the grantee makes a mortgage of such land to one who has no notice that his title is not absolute in fact as well as in form, the grantor is of course estopped to claim title as against such mortgagee. The grantor's right of redemption is subject to such mortgage.[47] In such case the grantee is held out to the world as the owner of the land, and innocent persons are at liberty to deal with him as such owner. The rule in equity that, where one of two innocent persons must suffer by the fraud of a third person, he who trusted the third person and placed the means in his hands to commit the wrong must bear the loss, is applicable. The grantor, in order to maintain an action for rent, can not show that his deed was intended as a mortgage, and that he is entitled to the position and rights of a mortgagor in possession.[48]

A grantee by an absolute deed which shows no defeasance, nor any right to one, is entitled to the possession of the property in law;[49] for the mortgagor at most has only an equity. But if the papers show a

a lapse of eighteen years unexplained.

[43] Woodworth v. Carman, 43 Iowa 504; Pratt v. Jarvis, 8 Utah 5, 28 Pac. 869.

[44] Westfall v. Westfall, 16 Hun (N. Y.) 541.

[45] Wyman v. Babcock, 2 Curtis (U. S.) 386; Turner v. Wilkinson, 72 Ala. 361; Pico v. Gallardo, 52 Cal. 206; McCarthy v. McCarthy, 36 Conn. 177; Jenkins v. Rosenberg, 105 Ill. 157; Weide v. Gehl, 21 Minn. 449; Gentry v. Gamblin, 79 Miss. 437, 28 So. 809; Digby v. Jones, 67 Mo. 104, 18 Am. L. Reg. (N. S.) 132; Gruber v. Baker, 20 Nev. 453, 23 Pac. 858; Brophy Min. Co. v. Brophy &c. Min. Co., 15 Nev. 101; Frink v. Adams, 36 N. J. Eq. 485;

Groton Savings Bank v. Batty, 30 N. J. Eq. 126, 19 Alb. L. J. 340; Meehan v. Forrester, 52 N. Y. 277; Fiedler v. Darrin, 59 Barb. (N. Y.) 651; Westfall v. Westfall, 16 Hun (N. Y.) 541; Kemper v. Campbell, 44 Ohio St. 210, 6 N. E. 566; Pancake v. Cauffman, 114 Pa. St. 113, 7 Atl. 67; Sweetzer v. Atterbury, 100 Pa. St. 18; Hills v. Loomis, 42 Vt. 562.

[46] Parrott v. Baker, 82 Ga. 364, 9 S. E. 1068.

[47] Turman v. Bell, 54 Ark. 273, 15 S. W. 886; Lawrence v. Guaranty Invest. Co., 51 Kans. 222, 32 Pac. 816.

[48] Abbott v. Hanson, 24 N. J. L. 493

[49] Jeffery v. Hursh, 42 Mich. 563,

defeasance, or an arrangement which amounts to a defeasance, and the mortgagor is left in possession, the mortgagee can not, in a state where the mortgagor is entitled to possession until foreclosure, recover possession.[50] A mortgagor who has delivered possession to the grantee can not recover possession from him without paying the debt and redeeming the mortgage. But if the mortgagor has not delivered possession to the grantee, he can recover the land from one who is not the grantee and does not hold under him, without redeeming.[51]

A purchaser who has knowledge that his grantor, though holding the estate by an absolute conveyance, nevertheless is in fact only a mortgagee, acquires a defeasible estate only, and it is defeasible upon the same terms as it was in the hands of the original grantee.[52] Possession by the equitable owner is notice of his rights to a purchaser,[53] and if the holder of the legal title holds it as security for a usurious loan, a purchaser from him acquires no better title than the grantor had.[54] And so a purchaser who has paid no valuable consideration for his conveyance occupies a position no better than his grantor.[55] A mortgage was made of certain mills to secure the sum of four thousand dollars; and the mortgagor also conveyed to the mortgagee other land absolutely, as security for a further sum of six thousand dollars. The mortgagee assigned the mortgage and conveyed the land to a third person, who had notice of the character of the prior conveyance. This assignee foreclosed the mortgage upon the mills, and purchased them upon the sale. He then mortgaged the mills and the other lands to the former mortgagee; and it was held that this mortgage was a lien upon the other lands only to the extent of the original loan upon them of six thousand dollars, upon the payment of which sum the original owner was entitled to redeem.[56]

One who deals with an agent is bound to know his authority, and if he takes a deed executed to him by the principal he is bound to know

4 N. W. 303; Bennett v. Robinson, 27 Mich. 26; Wetherbee v. Green, 22 Mich. 311, 7 Am. Rep. 653.
[50] Ferris v. Wilcox, 51 Mich. 105, 16 N. W. 252, 47 Am. Rep. 551.
[51] Parker v. Hubble, 75 Ind. 580.
[52] Kendall v. Davis, 55 Ark. 318, 18 S. W. 185; Le Comte v. Pennock, 61 Kans. 330, 59 Pac. 641.
[53] See post § 586.
[54] Amory v. Lawrence, 3 Cliff. (U. S.) 523; Kuhn v. Rumpp, 46 Cal. 299; Jenkins v. Rosenberg, 105 Ill. 157; Bartling v. Brasuhn, 102 Ill. 441; Smith v. Knoebel, 82 Ill. 392;

Graham v. Graham, 55 Ind. 23; Radford v. Folsom, 58 Iowa 473, 12 N. W. 536; Eiseman v. Gallagher, 24 Nebr. 79, 37 N. W. 941; Houser v. Lamont, 55 Pa. St. 311, 93 Am. Dec. 755; Tant v. Guess, 35 S. Car. 605, 16 S. E. 472 (quoting text); Zane v. Fink, 18 W. Va. 693; Lawrence v. Du Bois, 16 W. Va. 443. See ante §§ 254, 255.
[55] Lawrence v. Du Bois, 16 W. Va. 443.
[56] Turman v. Bell, 54 Ark. 273, 15 S. W. 886; Williams v. Thorn, 11 Paige (N. Y.) 459.

the conditions imposed upon the agent as to the delivery of the deed. Where a married woman executed a deed absolute in form of her own property, and delivered it to her husband to be delivered as security for a certain amount, and the husband delivered the deed to the grantee in payment for a larger sum he owed the grantee, who was aware of the purpose for which the deed was made, the deed could be held for no other purpose.[57]

§ 340. **Once a mortgage always a mortgage.**—If originally taken as a mortgage, nothing but a subsequent agreement of the parties can change its character, and deprive the mortgagor of his right of redemption; and even such an agreement can not change its character as to intervening interests.[58] This right can not be waived or abandoned by any stipulation of the parties made at the time, even if embodied in the mortgage.[59] Neither the failure of the mortgagor to pay the debt, nor any act or intent of the mortgagee can convert a deed originally intended as a mortgage into an absolute conveyance in the absence of a subsequent superseding contract.[60] If not intended as a security in the beginning, but as an absolute or conditional sale, no subsequent

[57] Gilbert v. Deshon, 107 N. Y. 324, 14 N. E. 318.
[58] Morris v. Nixon, 1 How. (U. S.) 118; Peagler v. Stabler, 91 Ala. 308, 9 So. 157; McKinstry v. Conly, 12 Ala. 678; Elliott v. Connor, 63 Fla. 408, 58 So. 241; Connor v. Connor, 59 Fla. 467, 52 So. 727; Ferguson v. Boyd (Ind. App.), 79 N. E. 549, 169 Ind. 537, 81 N. E. 71; Loeb v. McAlister, 15 Ind. App. 643, 41 N. E. 1061, 44 N. E. 378; Haggerty v. Brower, 105 Iowa 395, 75 N. W. 321; Stratton v. Rotrock, 84 Kans. 198, 114 Pac. 224; Le Comte v. Pennock, 61 Kans. 330, 59 Pac. 641; Hawes v. Williams, 92 Maine 483, 43 Atl. 101; McPherson v. Hayward, 81 Maine 329, 17 Atl. 164; Reed v. Reed, 75 Maine 264; Clark v. Landon, 90 Mich. 83, 51 N. W. 357; Batty v. Snook, 5 Mich. 231; Sheppard v. Wagner, 240 Mo. 409, 144 S. W. 394; Vanderhaize v. Hugues, 13 N. J. Eq. 244; Macauley v. Smith, 132 N. Y. 524, 30 N. E. 997; Carr v. Carr, 52 N. Y. 251; Horn v. Keteltas, 46 N. Y. 605; Murray v. Walker, 31 N. Y. 400; Elliott v. Wood, 53 Barb. (N. Y.) 285; Tibbs v. Morris, 44 Barb. (N. Y.) 138; Parsons v. Mumford, 3 Barb. Ch. (N. Y.) 152; Clark v. Henry, 2 Cow. (N. Y.) 324; Bunacleugh v. Poolman, 3 Daly (N. Y.) 236; Remsen v. Hay, 2 Edw. Ch. (N. Y.) 535; Cooper v. Whitney, 3 Hill (N. Y.) 95; Henry v. Davis, 7 Johns. Ch. (N. Y.) 40; Marks v. Pell, 1 Johns. Ch. (N. Y.) 594; Williams v. Thorn, 11 Paige (N. Y.) 459; Palmer v. Gurnsey, 7 Wend. (N. Y.) 248; Wilson v. Giddings, 28 Ohio St. 554; Poston v. Jones, 122 N. Car. 536, 29 S. E. 951; Tant v. Guess, 35 S. Car. 604, 16 S. E. 472; Brownlee v. Martin, 2 S. Car. 392; Clambey v. Copland, 52 Wash. 580, 100 Pac. 1031; Hudkins v. Crim (W. Va.), 78 S. E. 1043; Hursey v. Hursey, 56 W. Va. 148, 49 S. E. 367. An absolute deed executed in blank, intended to operate as a mortgage is not altered in its character because the grantee holds it in trust for others. Strong v. Gambier, 155 App. Div. 294, 140 N. Y. S. 410. See ante §§ 251, 263.
[59] Peugh v. Davis, 96 U. S. 332, per Field, J.; Turpie v. Lowe, 114 Ind. 37, 15 N. E. 834. See ante § 251 and cases cited.
[60] Stratton v. Rotrock, 84 Kans. 198, 114 Pac. 224.

event, short of a new agreement between the parties, can convert it into a mortgage.[61]

The maxim, "once a mortgage always a mortgage," applies to such a deed; and if a purchaser take a conveyance from the grantee, with a knowledge that the grantor claims an interest in the property, he takes it charged with the same equities with which it was charged in the hands of the mortgagee.[62] But this maxim was never intended, and has never been construed, to prevent a mortgagee, by subsequent contract, from purchasing the equity of redemption, or from obtaining a release of it, for an adequate consideration.[63]

The mortgagor may make a subsequent release of the equity of redemption, but an adequate consideration is necessary to support it. It must be for a consideration that would be deemed reasonable if the transaction were between other parties. The transaction must in all respects be fair, with no unconscientious advantage taken by the mortgagee.[64] Such a release will not be inferred from equivocal circumstances and loose expressions. It must appear by a writing importing in terms a transfer of the mortgagor's interest, or such facts must be shown as will estop him afterward to assert any interest.[65] In determining whether an instrument of uncertain import in itself was intended to operate as a release, the fact that the value of the property was at the time greatly in excess of the amount then paid, and of that originally secured, and the fact that the mortgagor retained possession of the land and cultivated it, are strong evidence tending to show that a release was not intended.[66]

A mere agreement of sale between the parties executed long after

---

[61] Reed v. Reed, 75 Maine 264; Buse v. Page, 32 Minn. 111, 19 N. W. 736, 20 N. W. 95; Finck v. Adams, 36 N. J. Eq. 188; Kearney v. Macomb, 16 N. J. Eq. 189; Clark v. Henry, 2 Cow. (N. Y.) 324; Goodbar v. Bloom, 43 Tex. Civ. App. 434, 96 S. W. 657.

[62] French v. Burns, 35 Conn. 359; Connor v. Connor, 59 Fla. 467, 52 So. 727; Doyle v. Ringo (Ind.), 102 N. E. 18; Ferguson v. Boyd (Ind. App.), 79 N. E. 549, 169 Ind. 537, 81 N. E. 71 (citing text); Greenwood Bldg. Assn. v. Stanton, 28 Ind. App. 548; Loeb v. McAlister, 15 Ind. App. 643, 41 N. E. 1061, 44 N. E. 378; Vanderhaize v. Hugues, 13 N. J. Eq. 244; Wilson v. Giddings, 28 Ohio St. 554; Hudkins v. Crim (W. Va.), 78 S. E. 1043.

[63] Peagler v. Stabler, 91 Ala. 308, 9 So. 157. See also Hutchison v. Page, 246 Ill. 71, 92 N. E. 571; Deadman v. Yantis, 230 Ill. 243, 82 N. E. 592; Cassem v. Heustis, 201 Ill. 208, 66 N. E. 283, 94 Am. St. 160; Scholl v. Hopper, 134 Ky. 83, 119 S. W. 770; Sears v. Gilman, 199 Mass. 384, 85 N. E. 466; Miller v. Smith, 20 N. Dak. 96, 126 N. W. 499; Ullman v. Devereux, 46 Tex. Civ. App. 459, 102 S. W. 1163. See ante § 251.

[64] Linnell v. Lyford, 72 Maine 280; Marshall v. Thompson, 39 Minn. 137, 39 N. W. 309; Niggeler v. Maurin, 34 Minn. 118, 24 N. W. 369; Ford v. Olden, L. R. 3 Eq. Cas. 461.

[65] Peugh v. Davis, 96 U. S. 332.

[66] Peugh v. Davis, 96 U. S. 332; Walker v. Farmers' Bank, 8 Houst. (Del.) 258, 14 Atl. 819.

the deed intended as a mortgage, without any new consideration, does not alter the character of the original transaction.[67] A subsequent agreement which allowed the grantor in an absolute deed intended as a mortgage, to have the use and possession of the land conveyed so long as the grantee and his heirs desired, free from rent, in consideration of paying for repairs and taxes, was held not to alter the original character of the transaction.[68]

§ 341. **Grantee's liability for mortgaged land sold by him.**—Although a grantee in an absolute deed intended as a mortgage has the power to convey it by a good indefeasible title to a purchaser without notice, yet he is liable to the mortgagor for the value of the land so conveyed; and he can not defend an action to recover such value by showing that the mortgagor's title was invalid, and that the legal title has since been bought in by the purchaser. The imperfection of the title did not justify his placing it beyond the reach of the mortgagor. It is the duty of the mortgagee upon receiving payment to restore the land, without regard to the condition of the title, in no worse condition, so far as his own acts could affect it, than it was when he received it. But in estimating the value of the land sold, the sum paid for an outstanding title, although paid by the purchaser and not by the mortgagee, may be deducted from the value of the land.[69]

According to some decisions the measure of damages against the grantee, where he is not chargeable with actual fraud, is the full value of the land at the time he sold it, without regard to the price actually received.[70] Under other authorities, the grantee will be required to account to the owner of the equity of redemption for all that he received above the amount of the debt originally secured by the deed.[71] Under this rule the grantee who has sold the land, is liable for the proceeds of the sale, deducting the amount due him and a reasonable compensation for effecting the sale.[72] He is not allowed to show that

[67] Hursey v. Hursey, 56 W. Va. 148, 49 S. E. 367.

[68] Brown v. Spradlin, 136 Ky. 703, 125 S. W. 150.

[69] Adkins v. Lewis, 5 Ore. 292.

[70] Gibbs v. Meserve, 12 Ill. App. 613; Enos v. Sutherland, 11 Mich. 538; Wilson v. Drumrite, 24 Mo. 304; Hausknecht v. Smith, 11 App. Div. 185, 42 N. Y. S. 611; Bissell v. Bozman, 17 N. Car. 229. See also Van Dusen v. Worrell, 3 Keyes (N. Y.) 311; 4 Abb. Dec. (N. Y.) 473, 5 Abb. Pr. (N. S.) (N. Y.) 286, 36 How. Pr. 463.

[71] Shillaber v. Robinson, 97 U. S. 68, 24 L. ed. 967; Sheldon v. Bradley, 37 Conn. 324; Crassen v. Swoveland, 22 Ind. 427; Linnell v. Lyford, 72 Maine 280; Cornell v. Pierson, 8 N. J. Eq. 478.

[72] Van Dusen v. Worrell, 4 Abb. App. Dec. 473; Boothe v. Fiest, 80 Tex. 141, 15 S. W. 799, value at time

the price received in consequence of liberal terms of payment, or for any other reason, is in excess of the market value of the lands.[73]

If a creditor has taken an absolute title to real estate of his debtor as security which is subject to a mortgage and buys the property at a foreclosure sale under the mortgage, he holds the land subject to the original trust, and if he sells it he is accountable to the debtor for the proceeds less the amount paid by him in acquiring the mortgage title.[74]

When the grantee has wrongfully conveyed the property, the grantor may at his election claim the proceeds of the sale,[75] or the value of the land at the time when the debtor's right to have it restored to him is established.[76] But in a suit for the proceeds it is not necessary for the plaintiff to make a tender, as the grantee by the sale has put it out of his power to convey.[77]

If the grantee in an absolute deed intended as a mortgage exchanges the land with the consent of the mortgagor for other land, the latter is confined to his right of redemption of the property taken on exchange.[78]

If the grantee has mortgaged the land to one having no notice of the grantee's defeasible title, the grantor's rights are postponed to the lien of the mortgage. The grantor's rights are not extinguished, and the mortgagee, after having notice of the grantor's rights, must make the grantor a party to his foreclosure suit, or he will not be bound by the decree. The grantor in such case may redeem from the foreclosure sale by paying the mortgage debt.[79]

The statute of limitations applicable to actions of assumpsit applies to an action for an excess of proceeds of a sale of such land above the mortgage debt. A suit to recover the land or to redeem would not be barred by a lapse of time shorter than that which would bar an action of ejectment at law. But a claim to the proceeds of a sale is not a claim to real property, but only for the recovery of money. The statute of limitations applies to proceedings in equity only by

of trial; Jackson v. Stevens, 108 Mass. 94, in an action for money had and received; Heister v. Maderia, 3 Watts & S. (Pa.) 384; Barkelew v. Taylor, 8 N. J. Eq. 206.

[73] Budd v. Van Orden, 53 N. J. Eq. 143.

[74] Kilgour v. Scott, 101 Fed. 359.

[75] Meehan v. Forrester, 52 N. Y. 277.

[76] Enos v. Sutherland, 11 Mich. 538; Mooney v. Byrne, 163 N. Y. 86, 57 N. E. 163; Hart v. Ten Eyck, 2 Johns. Ch. (N. Y.) 62, 117; Vanderhoven v. Romaine, 56 N. J. Eq. 1, 39 Atl. 129.

[77] Davis v. Van Wyck, 64 Hun (N. Y.) 186, 18 N. Y. S. 885.

[78] Over v. Carolus, 171 Ill. 552, 49 N. E. 514.

[79] Turman v. Bell, 54 Ark. 273, 15 S. W. 886.

analogy; and the analogous case at law is an action of assumpsit, or an action of account, and not an action of ejectment.[80]

The statute of limitations does not run in favor of a grantee in a deed absolute on its face, but intended to be a mortgage. His possession is not adverse.[81] But the grantor may lose his right by laches.[82]

§ 342. Redemption in equity—Grantee's right to relief.

A bill in equity may be maintained to redeem, as from a mortgage, land which the defendant holds by deed from the plaintiff, upon evidence that the deed, though absolute in form, was really taken as security for a loan.[83] Under the rule that "he who seeks equity must do equity," the grantor must fulfil, or offer to fulfil, all the obligations of a mortgagor.[84] The bill must necessarily admit the existence of a debt on the part of the grantor to the grantee. If the bill be for accounting and not one to redeem, it is not bad for failing to allege a tender of the amount due.[85] But it is not generally considered necessary that the grantor should include in his bill a tender or offer to pay the money admitted to be due or to be ascertained upon an accounting.[86] If the amount of the debt is not agreed upon, and is uncertain, the amount should be ascertained by proper proceedings. The decree is for a reconveyance of the land upon the payment, within a time

---

[80] Amory v. Lawrence, 3 Cliff. (U. S.) 523; Hancock v. Harper, 86 Ill. 445; Mills v. Mills, 115 N. Y. 80, 21 N. E. 714, revg. 47 Hun (N. Y.) 631. But see Hunter v. Hunter, 50 Mo. 445.

[81] Wyman v. Babcock, 2 Curtis (U. S.) 386; affd. in Babcock v. Wyman, 19 How. (U. S.) 289; Butler v. Hyland, 89 Cal. 575, 26 Pac. 1108.

[82] Miller v. Smith, 44 Minn. 127, 46 N. W. 324; Becker v. Howard, 75 Wis. 415, 44 N. W. 755.

[83] Collins v. Gregg, 109 Iowa 506, 80 N. W. 562. If the grantee refuses to recognize the instrument as a mortgage, and will not permit redemption by payment, the grantor may bring a bill in equity to declare the deed a mortgage and to compel the grantee to permit redemption and to reconvey to the grantor; but a bill can not be maintained merely to ascertain whether the relation of mortgagor and mortgagee exists. Micou v. Ashurst, 55 Ala. 607. It is

not necessary to ask reformation of the deed before filing a bill to redeem, since a deed given to secure a debt is considered a mortgage. Rogan v. Walker, 1 Wis. 527. Where it is not necessary to reform a deed, the fact that it is a mortgage may be shown at law. Barchent v. Snyder, 128 Wis. 423, 107 N. W. 329.

[84] Cowing v. Rogers, 34 Cal. 648; Heacock v. Swartwout, 28 Ill. 291. For other conditions precedent to relief, see Holden Land &c. Co. v. Interstate Trading Co., 87 Kans. 221, 123 Pac. 733.

[85] Brown v. Follette, 155 Ind. 316, 58 N. E. 197.

[86] Taylor v. Dillenburg, 168 Ill. 235, 48 N. E. 41; Dwen v. Blake, 44 Ill. 135; Barnard v. Cushman, 35 Ill. 451; Brown v. Follette, 155 Ind. 316, 58 N. E. 197; Tucker v. Witherbee, 130 Ky. 269, 113 S. W. 123; Marvin v. Prentice, 49 How. Pr. (N. Y.) 385. See also Bone v. Lansden, 85 Ala. 562, 6 So. 611.

named, of the amount which may be found due the grantee, or upon compliance with such terms as the court may impose, and that in default of such payment the bill be dismissed.[87]

The delivery of a deed absolute in form invests the grantee with the legal title, even though the transaction is converted into an equitable mortgage by the subsequent execution of an unsealed agreement to reconvey; and no affirmative action to divest the mortgagor of his right of redemption is necessary to invest the mortgagee with full legal title.[88]

It is usually the grantor who seeks relief in equity to have an absolute deed declared a mortgage, but the grantee may also have this relief in a proper case.[89] And the grantee may also maintain an action in foreclosure of the deed as a mortgage.[90] Thus, where an absolute conveyance was made by a confidential agent and adviser to his principal, and the latter claimed that the conveyance was taken as security for a loan, though the former claimed that it was a sale, the court declared that the burden of sustaining the validity and good faith of the dealing was upon the agent; and gave relief by decreeing a rescission of the sale, and payment by the agent of the money obtained with interest, upon the principal's tendering to the agent a deed properly executed reconveying the land to him. The court further directed that execution should issue against the agent for the amount of the loan if the money should not be paid.[91]

If the debt for which an absolute conveyance has been made as security be canceled, the grantor may be required to reconvey the land in an action brought for that purpose.[92]

[87] Chicago &c. Rolling Mill Co. v. Scully, 141 Ill. 408, 30 N. E. 1062; Westlake v. Horton, 85 Ill. 228; McDonough v. Squire, 111 Mass. 217; Campbell v. Dearborn, 109 Mass. 130, 12 Am. Rep. 671. In South Carolina it is said that the mortgagor is entitled to a reference to have the amount of the debt ascertained, and to a decree for the sale of the premises for its payment, and for the payment of the surplus, if any, to the mortgagor. Carter v. Evans, 17 S. Car. 458. That the grantor may be required to pay other debts due from him to the holder of the legal title, though not unsecured, see post §§ 360, 1083.

[88] Fitch v. Miller, 200 Ill. 170, 65 N. E. 650.

[89] Bryan v. Cowart, 21 Ala. 92; Kellogg v. Northrup, 115 Mich. 327, 73 N. W. 230; McMillan v. Bissell, 63 Mich. 66, 29 N. W. 737 (bill by grantee's executors).

[90] Bryan v. Cowart, 21 Ala. 92; Reid v. McMillan, 189 Ill. 411, 59 N. E. 948; Herron v. Herron, 91 Ind. 278; Kellogg v. Northrup, 115 Mich. 327, 73 N. W. 230; McMillan v. Bissell, 63 Mich. 66, 29 N. W. 737; Yingling v. Redwine, 12 Okla. 64, 69 Pac. 810; White v. Daniell, 141 Wis. 273, 124 N. W. 405.

[91] Tappan v. Aylsworth, 13 R. I. 582.

[92] Blazy v. McLean, 12 N. Y. S. 672.

But the grantor, while standing in the position of a mortgagor, can not maintain a suit to quiet the title in himself. He can quiet a mortgage upon his property only by paying it. A decree in such a suit, quieting the title to the land in the grantor against a purchaser from the grantee, "except as a mortgagee thereof having a mortgagee's interest therein, to be determined by a proper suit of foreclosure," is erroneous.[93]

§ 342a. **Bona fide purchasers from grantee.**—A purchaser from such grantee is not a bona fide purchaser without notice until he has paid all the purchase-money, and therefore he is not entitled to hold the land for which he has made part payment as against the mortgagor, even though he had no notice that the deed was a mortgage; but he is entitled to be reimbursed the part payment he has actually made before the property can be taken from him.[94]

The grantee who has conveyed the land to a bona fide purchaser so that there can be no redemption of the land is liable to a judgment for redemption in money.[95] An absolute conveyance intended as a mortgage will retain its character in the hands of subsequent purchasers with notice of the rights of the parties; and hence, if a purchaser from the original grantee knew the nature of the transaction, or knew of facts sufficient to put him on inquiry, he can not claim to be the absolute owner, but the mortgagor may redeem from him, as well as from the grantee.[96] But where the third person has purchased in good faith for a valuable consideration, relying on the

[93] Brandt v. Thompson, 91 Cal. 458, 27 Pac. 763. Such a decree first undertakes to quiet the grantor's title, and then disturbs it again by declaring the purchaser's right to foreclose. If the purchaser's debt should become barred by the statute of limitations, then, by this decree, the grantor would have his title quieted without paying the mortgage debt, the very thing which equity says can not be done. The grantor can have no remedy in the premises without paying or tendering the amount due on the mortgage. Per McFarland, J.

[94] Macauley v. Smith, 132 N. Y. 524, 30 N. E. 997, 10 N. Y. S. 578, reversed. In this case it was held that a creditor of this mortgagor might attach the land, and the judgment which followed the attachment became a specific lien

upon the land itself, and the land could be sold upon execution; and also that the judgment creditor might, in aid of his execution, maintain an action to have the absolute deed of his debtor declared to be a mortgage.

[95] See post § 1060a.

[96] Union Mut. Life Ins. Co. v. Slee, 123 Ill. 57, 13 N. E. 222; Smith v. Knoebel, 82 Ill. 392; Shaver v. Woodward, 28 Ill. 277; Brown v. Gaffney, 28 Ill. 149; Howat v. Howat, 101 Ill. App. 158; Hurst v. Beaver, 50 Mich. 612, 16 N. W. 165; Eiseman v. Gallagher, 24 Nebr. 79, 37 N. W. 941; Smith v. Jensen, 16 N. Dak. 408, 114 N. W. 306; Erickson v. Hammond, 135 Wis. 573, 116 N. W. 244. See also Baumgartner v. Corliss, 115 Minn. 11, 131 N. W. 638.

apparent absolute title of the original grantee, without notice of the defeasance agreement, he takes an indefeasible title, and the original grantor has no right of redemption against him.[97]

§ 342b. **Liability of mortgagee under absolute deed on exchange of land.**—If a mortgagee by an absolute deed, the defeasance not being recorded, exchanges the land for other land which is conveyed to him, and he afterward sells the land conveyed to him in exchange, he is chargeable, at the mortgagor's election, with the value of the land taken in exchange instead of the price at which he sold it. If the mortgagee, who is in such case a trustee, has sold the land for less than its value, it is properly his own loss. By choosing to dispose of the land as his own, the mortgagee could not rid himself of responsibility in respect to the price obtained.[98]

§ 342c. **Effect of absolute deed in vesting title and right of possession—Compensation for improvements.**—In some states, though the mortgage is by a deed absolute in form, the grantee acquires no legal title to the land. The deed is a mere security, just as a formal mortgage is in the same states.[99] The grantee can acquire the legal title only by a subsequent conveyance by the grantor, or by purchase upon a foreclosure sale under the mortgage. The mortgagee under such absolute deed has no right of possession except under the conditions which would give a formal mortgagee the right of possession.[1]

---

[97] Jenkins v. Rosenberg, 105 Ill. 157; Maxfield v. Patchen, 29 Ill. 39; Jolivet v. Chaves, 125 La. 923, 52 So. 99; Tufts v. Tapley, 129 Mass. 380; Kemp v. Small, 32 Nebr. 318, 49 N. W. 169; Gruber v. Baker, 20 Nev. 453, 23 Pac. 858, 9 L. R. A. 302; Murphy v. Plankinton Bank, 13 S. Dak. 501, 83 N. W. 575. See post § 1060a. But it has been held that the existence of an innocent purchaser, who has made improvements, will not prevent declaring a warranty deed to be a mortgage, as the purchaser can be allowed for the improvements. Carveth v. Winegar, 133 Mich. 34, 94 N. W. 381.

[98] Darling v. Harmon, 47 Minn. 166, 94 N. W. 686.

[99] Prefumo v. Russell, 148 Cal. 451, 83 Pac. 810; Murdock v. Clarke, 90 Cal. 427, 27 Pac. 275; Hall v. Arnott, 80 Cal. 348, 22 Pac. 200; Smith v. Smith, 80 Cal. 323, 21 Pac. 4, 22 Pac. 186, 549; Booth v. Hoskins, 75 Cal. 271, 17 Pac. 225; Raynor v. Drew, 72 Cal. 307, 13 Pac. 866; Healy v. O'Brien, 66 Cal. 517, 6 Pac. 386; Taylor v. McLain, 64 Cal. 513, 2 Pac. 399. When an absolute deed is declared to be a mortgage, the mortgagor's equity can not be cut off by a decree divesting him of it unless he shall pay the sum found due within a time limited, but the title remains in him until divested by foreclosure and sale. Byrne v. Hudson, 127 Cal. 254, 59 Pac. 597; First Nat. Bank v. Ashmead, 23 Fla. 379, 2 So. 657; First Nat. Bank v. Kreig, 21 Nev. 404, 32 Pac. 641; Odell v. Montross, 68 N. Y. 499; Adair v. Adair, 22 Ore. 115, 29 Pac. 193; Cumps v. Kiyo, 104 Wis. 656, 80 N. W. 937; Howe v. Carpenter, 49 Wis. 697, 6 N. W. 357; Brinkman v. Jones, 44 Wis. 498.

[1] Smith v. Smith, 80 Cal. 323, 21 Pac. 4. A grantee under a conveyance absolute in form has no great-

Moreover, although such grantee, by a defeasance, has agreed to convey the title to the grantor on payment of the debt, a bill for specific performance will not lie, since, by a decree for the grantor therein, he would not obtain the title which the grantee agreed to convey.[2]

But in other states, in which a formal mortgage is held not to pass the legal title, a deed absolute in form, intended to operate as a mortgage, does pass such title.[3] In states where an absolute conveyance intended as security vests the legal title in the grantee, no action is necessary to divest the grantor of his equitable right to redeem.[4]

A grantee in possession under an absolute deed intended as a mortgage, is in the position of a mortgagee in possession, and is not ordinarily entitled to reimbursement for improvements made by him on the land.[5]

---

er rights than an ordinary mortgagee, and therefore is not entitled to possession, if not stipulated for or voluntarily conceded by the grantor. Cox v. Ratcliffe, 105 Ind. 374, 5 N. E. 5; Radford v. Folsom, 58 Iowa 473, 12 N. W. 536; Le Comte v. Pennock, 61 Kans. 330, 59 Pac. 641; Meighen v. King, 31 Minn. 115, 16 N. W. 702; Connolly v. Giddings, 24 Nebr. 131, 37 N. W. 939; Murray v. Walker, 31 N. Y. 399; Van Vleck v. Enos, 88 Hun 348, 68 N. Y. St. 572, 34 N. Y. S. 754. See also Richards v. Crawford, 50 Iowa 494; Burdick v. Wentworth, 42 Iowa 440. But see Locke v. Moulton, 96 Cal. 21, 30 Pac. 957; Pico v. Gallardo, 52 Cal. 206.

[2] Franz v. Orton, 75 Ill. 100; Adair v. Adair, 22 Ore. 115, 29 Pac. 193.

[3] Woodward v. Jewell, 140 U. S. 247, 11 Sup. Ct. 784; McLaren v. Clark, 80 Ga. 423, 7 S. E. 230; Thaxton v. Roberts, 66 Ga. 704; Woodson v. Veal, 60 Ga. 562; Lackey v. Bostwick, 54 Ga. 45. When a deed absolute is declared to be a mortgage, a special judgment may be extended subjecting the property to the payment of the debt. Jewell v. Walker, 109 Ga. 241, 34 S. E. 337. See ante § 26. Haggerty v. Brower, 105 Iowa 395, 400, 75 N. W. 321; Richards v. Crawford, 50 Iowa 494; Bordick v. Wentworth, 42 Iowa 440; Farley v. Goocher, 11 Iowa 570; Jeffery v. Hursh, 42 Mich. 563, 4 N. W. 303; Gallagher v. Giddings, 33

Nebr. 222, 49 N. W. 1126. "The legal title in such an equitable mortgage being in the grantee, where the grantor brings an action to redeem the premises, and his petition is dismissed by reason of his default in making payments by the day set in the decree for redemption, and no privilege is given to bring another action, the grantor's right of redemption is thereby extinguished. It constitutes a complete bar to any further litigation of the same subject between the same parties and privies." Per Norval, J.

[4] Smith v. Murphy, 58 Ala. 630; Fitch v. Miller, 200 Ill. 170, 65 N. E. 650; West v. Frederick, 62 Ill. 191; Brophy Min. Co. v. Brophy &c. Gold Min. Co., 15 Nev. 101. See also Lindberg v. Thomas, 137 Iowa 48, 114 N. W. 562; Bailey v. Frazier, 62 Ore. 142, 124 Pac. 643; Frazer v. Seureau (Tex. Civ. App.), 128 S. W. 649. But see Moisant v. McPhee, 92 Cal. 76, 28 Pac. 46; Smith v. Smith, 80 Cal. 323, 21 Pac. 4, 22 Pac. 186; Jackson v. Lodge, 36 Cal. 28; State First Nat. Bank v. Ashmead, 23 Fla. 379, 2 So. 657.

[5] Malone v. Roy, 107 Cal. 518, 40 Pac. 1040; Mahoney v. Bostwick, 96 Cal. 53, 30 Pac. 1020, 31 Am. St. 175; Halbert v. Turner, 233 Ill. 531, 84 N. E. 704; Miller v. Curry, 124 Ind. 48, 24 N. E. 219. See also Foley v. Foley, 15 App. Div. 276, 44 N. Y. S. 588; Harpers' Appeal, 64 Pa. St. 315. See post § 779.

§ 342d. **Redemption by grantor after conveyance by grantee to a bona fide purchaser.**—The grantor in an absolute deed which is in fact a mortgage may maintain a suit for redemption against the grantee although the latter has conveyed the land to a bona fide purchaser so that it can not be reached, and although an action against the grantee to recover for money had and received would be barred by the statute of limitations; and the court will substitute a judgment for redemption in money to the amount of the actual value of the land, for a judgment of redemption in land. The Court of Appeals of New York, in a decision to this effect, said: "Guided by the cardinal principle that the wrongdoer shall make nothing from his wrong, equity so molds and applies its plastic remedies as to force from him the most complete restitution which his wrongful act will permit.[6] When he can not restore the land it will compel him to restore that which stands in his hands for the land, and will not permit him to assert that it is not land when the assertion would be profitable to himself but unjust to the one whom he wronged. He can not escape by offering to pay what he received on selling the lands, but must pay the value at the time of the trial. * * * It is the wrongful conveyance by the mortgagee in possession, under a deed absolute on its face, that enables a court of equity to hold on to the case after ordinary redemption has been shown to be impossible, and to allow such a redemption against the wrongdoer as will prevent him from gaining by his wrong, and will give the plaintiff her due as nearly as may be."[7] When, however, the grantor and equitable owner of land under a deed intended to operate as a mortgage, knowing the circumstances, permits a bona fide purchaser to deal with the actual mortgagee as owner, the grantor is estopped to claim relief against such purchaser.[8]

[6] Enos v. Sutherland, 11 Mich. 538, citing May v. Le Claire, 11 Wall. (U. S.) 217; Budd v. Van Orden, 33 N. J. Eq. 143; Hart v. Ten Eyck, 2 Johns. Ch. (N. Y.) 62, 108; Miller v. McGuckin, 15 Abb. N. Cas. (N. Y.) 204; Van Dusen v. Worrell, 4 Abb. Ct. App. Dec. 473.

[7] Mooney v. Byrne, 163 N. Y. 86, 57 N. E. 163.

[8] Richardson v. Beaber, 62 Misc. 542, 115 N. Y. S. 821.

CHAPTER IX

DEBT SECURED

I. *Description of the Debt*

§ **343. General description of debt sufficient.**—It is not essential that the mortgage itself should contain a description of the debt intended to be secured. It is not essential that there be a note or bond or other obligation separate from the mortgage.[1] Nor does a failure to state the amount of the debt render the mortgage void.[2]

---

[1] O'Connor v. Nadel, 117 Ala. 595, 23 So. 532; Schierl v. Newberg, 102 Wis. 552, 78 N. W. 761. See also Lee v. Fletcher, 46 Minn. 49, 48 N. W. 456, 12 L. R. A. 171; Nazro v. Ware, 38 Minn. 443, 38 N. W. 359; Spedden v. Sykes, 51 Wash. 267, 98 Pac. 752. See ante § 70.

[2] Robinson v. Williams, 22 N. Y. 380; Spedden v. Sykes, 51 Wash. 267, 98 Pac. 752. See ante § 70 and post § 515.

It is only necessary that there be a debt or a duty to be performed, either present or to arise in the future;[3] and that this be recited in the mortgage. This need not be evidenced by any writing. The nature and amount of the indebtedness secured may be expressed in terms so general that subsequent purchasers and attaching creditors must look beyond the deed to ascertain both the existence and amount of the debt.[4]

Even a deed absolute in form, if in fact intended by the parties as a security for subsequent advances or liabilities to be assumed by the grantee in the grantor's behalf,[5] is a valid security against judgment or execution creditors, or other incumbrancers, although such intention does not appear upon the deed, or by any evidence in writing. Though the amount of the debt be left blank, this may be supplied by parol evidence.[6]

Where a mortgage is given to indemnify one who becomes a surety upon a bond in which the mortgagor is principal, a misdescription of the particular bond may be corrected by parol testimony so as to identify the bond described in the mortgage with the one upon which the mortgagee became surety, and the mere misdescription of the bond will not have the effect to render the mortgage invalid as a lien upon the property described, either as to the mortgagor himself or his vendees.[7]

All the description required to be made of the debt is a general one, which will put those interested upon inquiry.[8] A condition to

---

[3] Knight v. Coleman, 117 Ala. 266, 22 So. 974; Stuyvesant v. Western Mtg. &c. Co., 22 Colo. 28, 43 Pac. 144; Brookings v. White, 49 Maine 476; Gassert v. Bogk, 7 Mont. 585, 19 Pac. 281. See also Carpenter v. Plagge, 192 Ill. 82, 61 N. E. 530; Perkins v. Trinity Realty Co., 69 N. J. Eq. 723, 61 Atl. 167; Huntington v. Kneeland, 102 App. Div. 284, 92 N. Y. S. 944.

[4] Ricketson v. Richardson, 19 Cal. 330; Gardner v. Cohn, 191 Ill. 553, 61 N. E. 492; Burnett v. Wright, 135 N. Y. 543, 32 N. E. 253; Keagy v. Trout, 85 Va. 390, 7 S. E. 329. See ante § 70, and post § 579.

[5] Gibson v. Seymour, 4 Vt. 518; approved in Seymour v. Darrow, 31 Vt. 122. See also Anglo-Californian Bank v. Cerf, 147 Cal. 384, 81 Pac. 1077; Huntington v. Kneeland, 105 App. Div. 629, 93 N. Y. S. 845.

[6] Burnett v. Wright, 135 N. Y. 543, 32 N. E. 253. See also Ladd v. Lookout Mt. Distilling Co., 147 Ala. 173, 40 So. 610; Dunn v. Burke, 139 Ill. App. 12.

[7] Emerson v. Knight, 130 Ga. 100, 60 S. E. 255.

[8] Curtis v. Flinn, 46 Ark. 70; Beach v. Osborne, 74 Conn. 405, 50 Atl. 1019; Bouton v. Doty, 69 Conn. 531, 37 Atl. 1064; Hubbard v. Savage, 8 Conn. 215; Boyd v. Ratcliff, 140 Ind. 393, 39 N. E. 860, 49 Am. St. 203; Winn v. Lippincott Inv. Co., 125 Mo. 528, 28 S. W. 998; Williams v. Moniteau Nat. Bank, 72 Mo. 292; Hogdon v. Shannon, 44 N. H. 572; Hurd v. Robinson, 11 Ohio St. 232; Patterson v. Johnston, 7 Ohio 225; McDaniels v. Colvin, 16 Vt. 300, 42 Am. Dec. 512; Goff v. Price, 42 W. Va. 384, 26 S. E. 287.

pay the mortgagee "what I may owe him on book" may cover not only the present but the future indebtedness of the mortgagor, at least until the mortgagee should receive express notice of subsequent incumbrances or interests, and he is not bound to watch the registry for subsequent conveyances. And so a mortgage to secure the payment of one thousand five hundred dollars, which the mortgagor owed on book account, and by several notes, without specifying the amount or date of any particular note, sufficiently describes the debt.[9] A mortgage to secure a claim on book account for goods sold and delivered, in about the sum of five thousand dollars, is sufficient to secure the mortgagee's actual claim not exceeding that sum.[10] A mortgage conditioned to pay the mortgagee "all the notes and agreements I now owe or have with him," may secure the mortgagee for payments made as an indorser for the mortgagor under an existing agreement.[11] A condition to pay "all sums that the mortgagee may become liable to pay by signing or otherwise" is not too indefinite, and includes any legal liability he may incur for the mortgagor.[12]

A mortgage securing a definite sum and all other claims due to two mortgagees was held to include the debts due to one of them individually as well as the debts due to them jointly, where it appeared that it was the intention of the parties to secure the individual as well as the joint debts.[13] But a mortgage expressly providing that it secures a certain indebtedness can not be made to cover other debts or obligations.[14]

The consideration named in a mortgage does not limit the debt secured when it appears on the face of the mortgage that it was intended to secure several notes together amounting to a much larger sum than that named for the consideration.[15]

A mortgage may be made to secure an annuity; and if no principal sum or obligation other than the annual payment be named, and the power to sell or foreclose is only in the event of default in the pay-

---

[9] Merrills v. Swift, 18 Conn. 257, 46 Am. Dec. 315. See also Shirras v. Caig, 7 Cranch (U. S.) 34, 3 L. ed. 260; Truscott v. King, 6 Barb. (N. Y.) 346; Stuyvesant v. Hall, 2 Barb. Ch. (N. Y.) 151.

[10] Curtis v. Flinn, 46 Ark. 70; Lewis v. De Forest, 20 Conn. 427.

[11] Seymour v. Darrow, 31 Vt. 122.

[12] Soule v. Albee, 31 Vt. 142.

[13] Snow v. Pressey, 85 Maine 408, 27 Atl. 272. "It often happens," say the court, "that the language of a written contract is susceptible of more than one meaning. And in such cases, it is always allowable to take into consideration the situation of the parties and the circumstances under which the writing was made, in order to ascertain its true meaning." See also Boody v. Davis, 20 N. H. 140, 51 Am. Dec. 210.

[14] Briggs v. Steele, 91 Ark. 458, 121 S. W. 754.

[15] Shoemake v. Smith, 80 Iowa 655, 45 N. W. 744.

ment of the annual sums, then the mortgagor is not entitled to redeem or to extinguish the annuity by the payment of a principal sum.[16]

§ 344. **Stating amount of debt** secured.—It is not generally necessary that the amount of the debt be stated in the mortgage, whether the sum to be certain or uncertain.[17] But it is better conveyancing to state the amount of an ascertained debt. When the mortgage is given to secure future advances, it is of course not practicable to state in the mortgage itself anything more than a limit to which such advances may reach; and while such a limit is required by some courts, it is generally held to be sufficient that the mortgage sets forth the foundation of such liability, or such data as will put any one interested upon the track to find out the extent of the liability. Moreover, when the mortgage is given to secure a debt, the amount of which is not ascertained, it is sufficient if the mortgage contains such facts about it as will lead an interested party to ascertain the real state of the incumbrance. But if the mortgage is given to secure an ascertained debt, the amount of that debt ought to be stated; and accordingly it has been held that a mortgage given to secure an existing debt of a fixed amount, which is described in the condition of the mortgage only as a note due from the mortgagor to the mortgagee, of a certain date, payable on demand with interest, without specifying the amount, is not a valid security against subsequent incumbrances.[18] This is

[16] Northern Cent. R. Co. v. Hering, 93 Md. 164, 48 Atl. 461.

[17] Curtis v. Flinn, 46 Ark. 70; Pike v. Collins, 33 Maine 38; Somersworth Sav. Bank v. Roberts, 38 N. H. 22.

[18] Hart v. Chalker, 14 Conn. 77. Chief Justice Williams, delivering the opinion of the court, said: "Whether this omission was owing to design or accident, we are not informed. In either case the effect would be the same; and the public would not have that information which it was intended should be given, and which, if generally neglected, would make our records of little value. Indeed, if such a general description is good, it would seem as if it were enough to say, 'This mortgage is intended to secure any debt due;' for there would be little more danger, in that case, of substituting fictitious debts, than in this where the sum is omitted; for he who would substitute fictitious debts, under that general description, would have very little additional restraint from the fact that the date and time were given. It is said that there is enough to put a person on inquiry, and that is all a court of equity requires. That principle, however, we do not think is applicable to cases of this class, where there is a certain known debt. If it is to be adopted as a general rule, it would overturn all the cases in which this court have held that the description was too indefinite." The cases cited by the Chief Justice in this connection are: St. John v. Camp, 17 Conn. 222; Booth v. Barnum, 9 Conn. 286, 23 Am. Dec. 339; Bolles v. Chauncey, 8 Conn. 390; Crane v. Deming, 7 Conn. 387; Pettibone v. Griswold, 4 Conn. 158, 10 Am. Dec. 106. The rule is the same in Illinois: Metropolitan Bank v. Godfrey, 23 Ill. 579, 604; Battenhausen v. Bullock, 11 Bradw. (Ill.)

required, not by any specific provision of the registry law, but the spirit of the system requires that the record should disclose, with as much certainty as the nature of the case will admit of, the real state of the incumbrance.

A mortgage describing as an absolute indebtedness a note given as security for a contingent liability assumed by the mortgagee, such as that of an indorser, is not good against a bona fide purchaser of the land without notice.[19] A reference to a note without specifying its contents is not sufficient to put subsequent purchasers upon inquiry.[20] But it is held that a recorded mortgage is not deprived of its effect as constructive notice by the fact that the principal of the note is not expressly stated, where such amount can be readily calculated from other data given in the mortgage.[21]

Some of the Connecticut and Illinois cases require a degree of

---

655, affd. Bullock v. Battenhousen, 108 Ill. 28.

A similar decision was made in a Kentucky case. Pearce v. Hall, 12 Bush (Ky.) 209. The condition was for the payment of a note fully described, with the exception that the amount was not set out, nor was there anything in the conveyance from which any inference whatever as to the amount could be drawn. It was held that a subsequent attaching creditor had precedence. Mr. Justice Lindsay said: "We are satisfied that a mortgage, to be good against a purchaser for a valuable consideration, or a creditor, must not only be lodged for record in the proper office, but must, as far as is reasonably practicable, set out the amount of the debt for the payment of which the parties intend it as a security. We do not mean to intimate that an omission to state the date of the note, or the time at which it will fall due, or the precise amount of the debt, even when the amount is ascertained, is essential to make the mortgage valid; but to hold the omission in this case immaterial would be in effect to say that a mortgage need only show that the mortgagor is indebted to the mortgagee, and that purchasers and creditors must, upon that recital, ascertain for themselves, as best they can, the amount of the indebtedness."

In Maryland no mortgage is valid except as between the parties thereto, unless there be indorsed thereon an oath or affirmation of the mortgagee that the consideration in said mortgage is true and bona fide as therein set forth; this affidavit may be made at any time before the mortgage is recorded, and the affidavit must be recorded with the mortgage. The affidavit may be made by one of several mortgagees, or by an agent of the mortgagee; and the agent must, in addition to the affidavit above mentioned, make affidavit that he is agent of the mortgagee. The president or other officer of a corporation, or the executor of the mortgage, may make such affidavit. R. Code Md. 1878, p. 389, §§ 35, 36. The fact that the oath was taken can only be established by a formal indorsement upon the mortgage; it is not the subject of parol proof. The record of the mortgage without the affidavit is not constructive notice. Reiff v. Eshleman, 52 Md. 582. The affidavit need not be in the words prescribed by statute, but it is sufficient that it is of equivalent import and effect. Stanhope v. Dodge, 52 Md. 483.

[19] Stearns v. Porter, 46 Conn. 313.

[20] Harper v. Edwards, 115 N. Car. 246, 20 S. E. 392.

[21] Gardner v. Cohn, 191 Ill. 553, 61 N. E. 492.

strictness in describing the indebtedness not required elsewhere.[22]

It is generally sufficient if it appears that the debt is secured, and that the amount of it may be ascertained by reference to other instruments, or by inquiry otherwise. Accordingly it is held, contrary to the decisions above noticed, that a reference in a mortgage to a note or bond secured by it, without specifying its contents, is sufficient to put subsequent purchasers upon inquiry as to the contents of the note or bond, and to charge them with notice to the same extent as if the amount and terms of the note or bond had been fully set forth.[23] It is not even necessary that the amount of the note should be specified in the mortgage, when it is otherwise fully and accurately described.[24]

The description of the debt must be correct as far as it goes, so as to inform creditors and subsequent purchasers what amount is charged on the land, and must be full enough to direct attention to the sources of correct information, and be such a description of the debt as not to mislead or deceive as to its nature or amount.[25]

A description of a mortgage note which gives its date, the names of the maker and payee, the date of its maturity, and the rate and times of payment of interest, though the amount of the note be not stated, is a sufficient description to identify the note, and the recording of the mortgage gives notice to a subsequent purchaser of the existence of the lien and of the amount of it.[26]

§ 345. **Debt must come fairly within terms used.**—A mortgage to secure all the debts due from the grantor to the grantee, and all lia-

[22] The earlier cases in Connecticut are not supported by the later decisions in that state. Utley v. Smith, 24 Conn. 290, 63 Am. Dec. 163; Hurd v. Robinson, 11 Ohio St. 232. But the requirements as to stating the debt still are that the nature and amount of the indebtedness shall be stated with all reasonable certainty. Subsequent incumbrancers have a right to know, with all the certainty the case admits of, the amount already secured on the property, and the nature of the indebtedness so secured. Hill v. Banks, 61 Conn. 25, 23 Atl. 712.

[23] Pike v. Collins, 33 Maine 38. See also Shirras v. Caig, 7 Cranch (U. S.) 34, 3 L. ed. 260; Merrills v. Swift, 18 Conn. 257, 46 Am. Dec. 315; Barker v. Barker, 62 N. H. 366; Farr v. Doxtater, 29 N. Y. St. 531, 9 N. Y. S. 141; Harper v. Edwards,

115 N. Car. 246, 20 S. E. 392; Seymour v. Darrow, 31 Vt. 122; Vanmeter v. Vanmeter, 3 Grat. (Va.) 148.

[24] Fetes v. O'Laughlin, 62 Iowa 532, 17 N. W. 764; Somersworth Sav. Bank v. Roberts, 38 N. H. 22.

[25] Bowen v. Ratcliff, 140 Ind. 393, 39 N. E. 860, 49 Am. St. 203; Goff v. Price, 42 W. Va. 384, 26 S. E. 287.

[26] Fetes v. O'Laughlin, 62 Iowa 532, 17 N. W. 764. In Battenhausen v. Bullock, 11 Bradw. (Ill.) 665, it was claimed that the record of a mortgage which does not state the amount of the debt secured, though the note given for it is otherwise fully described, is not notice of any incumbrance, and does not put a subsequent purchaser upon inquiry as to the amount of the incumbrance. This case should not be relied upon elsewhere as an authority.

bilities of the latter as surety for the former, is valid without a more particular description.[27] But when it is attempted to describe the debts secured, to entitle a debt to the benefit of the security it must come fairly within the terms used in the mortgage. The debt described in the mortgage is the debt secured.[28]

Usually all that is required is that the debt be sufficiently described and limited in the mortgage, so that it may be recognized and distinguished from other debts or obligations.[29] But a statement in a mortgage of the amount of the debt secured is not conclusive in that regard, and the mortgagor may show that the lien was for a less sum,[30] or even that the mortgage lien was given for a different purpose than that stated therein.[31] A reference to a larger amount in an unexecuted agreement between the parties can not control the description in the mortgage.[32]

A mortgage which correctly described other debts and then mentioned "a note or notes for about three hundred fifty dollars," was held not to include six notes amounting to over one thousand five hundred dollars.[33] In like manner, a mortgage securing "an account for about fifty dollars" does not include accounts exceeding nine hundred dollars.[34] A mortgage to secure a gross sum, which the mortgagee was at liberty to furnish in materials toward the erection of a house

---

[27] Michigan Ins. Co. v. Brown, 11 Mich. 265; Vanmeter v. Vanmeter, 3 Grat. (Va.) 148. See also Machette v. Wanless, 1 Colo. 225; Huntington v. Kneeland, 102 App. Div. 284, 92 N. Y. S. 944; Spedden v. Sykes, 51 Wash. 267, 98 Pac. 755.

[28] Flower v. O'Bannon, 43 La. Ann. 1042, 10 So. 376. See also Mantle v. Dabney, 44 Wash. 193, 87 Pac. 122.

[29] Hughes v. Edwards, 9 Wheat. (U. S.) 489, 6 L. ed. 146; Ray v. Hallenbeck, 42 Fed. 381; Moran v. Gardemeyer, 82 Cal. 96, 23 Pac. 6; King v. Kilbride, 58 Conn. 109, 19 Atl. 519; Hough v. Bailey, 32 Conn. 288; Walker v. Doane, 131 Ill. 27, 22 N. E. 1006; Kellogg v. Frazier, 40 Iowa 502; Partridge v. Swazey, 46 Maine 414; Boyd v. Parker, 43 Md. 182; Warner v. Brooks, 14 Gray (Mass.) 107; Johns v. Church, 12 Pick. (Mass.) 557, 23 Am. Dec. 651; Aull v. Lee, 61 Mo. 160; Gilman v. Moody, 43 N. H. 239; Robertson v. Stark, 15 N. H. 109; Bank of Buffalo v. Thompson, 121 N. Y. 280, 24 N. E. 473; Williams v. Silliman, 74 Tex.

626, 12 S. W. 534; Paine v. Benton, 32 Wis. 491.

[30] Huckaba v. Abbott, 87 Ala. 409, 6 So. 48; Louisville Banking Co. v. Leonard, 90 Ky. 106, 11 Ky. L. 917, 13 S. W. 521; Ruloff v. Hazen, 124 Mich. 570, 83 N. W. 370; Nazro v. Ware, 38 Minn. 443, 38 N. W. 359; Burnett v. Wright, 135 N. Y. 543, 32 N. E. 253; Mackey v. Brownfield, 13 Serg. & R. (Pa.) 239.

[31] Saunders v. Dunn, 175 Mass. 164, 55 N. E. 893; Hannan v. Hannan, 123 Mass. 441, 25 Am. Rep. 121; Wearse v. Peirce, 24 Pick. (Mass.) 141; Holsman v. Boiling Spring Bleaching Co., 14 N. J. Eq. 335; Baird v. Baird, 145 N. Y. 659, 40 N. E. 222, 28 L. R. A. 375; Hill v. Hoole, 116 N. Y. 299, 22 N. E. 547, 5 L. R. A. 620.

[32] Turnbull v. Thomas, 1 Hughes (U. S.) 172.

[33] Storms v. Storms, 3 Bush (Ky.) 67.

[34] Storms v. Storms, 3 Bush (Ky.) 67.

for the mortgagor, does not cover a collateral liability assumed by the mortgagee as surety or guarantor for the mortgagor.[35] A mortgage executed to secure a note for five thousand dollars payable in six months does not secure a note for three thousand dollars payable in thirty days, if the latter note was given in a new and independent transaction upon the failure of negotiations for a loan of the first-mentioned sum.[36]

A mortgage which expressly recites that it is given to secure the prompt payment of rent according to the terms of a certain written lease, and names the amount secured, which amount corresponds with the amount agreed in the lease to be paid as rent, does not secure rents which become due after the expiration of such lease under a tenancy arising by implication of law from holding over after such lease expired.[37]

§ 346. **Particular debts or obligations secured.**—A mortgage to secure an unliquidated debt, as, for instance, an open book account, is good.[38] So is a mortgage to secure an agreement of indemnity or any other agreement.[39] So is a mortgage by a trustee to secure the payment of the moneys in his hands belonging to the trust estate, the amount of which is then unascertained. So is a mortgage to secure the fidelity of an agent or factor;[40] or a mortgage to secure any

[35] Doyle v. White, 26 Maine 341, 45 Am. Dec. 110. A mortgage to secure the payment of dues to a building association does not secure the payment of a sum in addition thereto, there being no express agreement to pay such additional sum. Whipperman v. Smith, 93 Ind. 275.

[36] Walker v. Carleton, 97 Ill. 582. A mortgage conditioned as security, in addition to the principal sum named, "for all further advances to the mortgagor by the mortgagee that may exist, arise, or be contracted before the satisfaction hereof," does not secure a subsequent note, indorsed by the mortgagor, and by him transferred to the mortgagee. The mortgagee could go out and buy up the notes of third parties, upon which the mortgagor was a simple indorser, and hold them as secured by that mortgage. Moran v. Gardemeyer, 82 Cal. 96, 23 Pac. 6. See post § 378.

[37] Fields v. Mott, 9 N. Dak. 621, 84 N. W. 555.

[38] In New Hampshire, where a statute requires that the debt shall be expressed in the mortgage, it can not be made to cover unliquidated damages. Bethlehem v. Annis, 40 N. H. 34, 77 Am. Dec. 700. See also Shirras v. Caig, 7 Cranch (U. S.) 34, 3 L. ed. 260; United States v. Sturges, 1 Paine (U. S.) 525, Fed. Cas. No. 16414; Merrills v. Swift, 18 Conn. 257, 46 Am. Dec. 315; Emery v. Owings, 7 Gill (Md.) 488, 48 Am. Dec. 580; Barker v. Barker, 62 N. H. 366; Farr v. Doxtater, 29 N. Y. St. 531, 9 N. Y. S. 141; De Mott v. Benson, 4 Edw. Ch. (N. Y.) 297; Esterly v. Purdy, 50 How. Pr. (N. Y.) 350; Seymour v. Darrow, 31 Vt. 122; Vanmeter v. Vanmeter, 3 Grat. (Va.) 148; Fisher v. Otis, 3 Pin. (Wis.) 78, 3 Chand. 83.

[39] Cook v. Bartholomew, 60 Conn. 24, 22 Atl. 444. See also Cazort &c. Co. v. Dunbar, 91 Ark. 400, 121 S. W. 270; Emerson v. Knight, 130 Ga. 100, 60 S. E. 255; Fidelity &c. Co. v. Oliver, 57 Wash. 31, 106 Pac. 483.

[40] Stoughton v. Pasco, 5 Conn. 442, 13 Am. Dec. 72.

balance that may remain after application to the debt of moneys that may be collected upon other securities held by the creditor;[41] or a mortgage to secure all the indebtedness of the mortgagor to the mortgagee;[42] or to secure the payment of a debt which existed before the making of a mortgage.[43] But a mortgage to secure a particular debt can not be extended by subsequent parol agreement to secure other debts.[44] The obligation may consist of an implied promise of the mortgagor to pay the money loaned him by the mortgagee.[45] A description of a debt secured by the mortgage as a certain sum, "or thereabout," is sufficient to put a person upon inquiry as to the amount of the incumbrance, and the mortgage is good for a sum not very materially larger than that mentioned.[46]

Although a mortgage be given for a definite sum, it is competent to prove by parol that it was given to secure an open account, the balance of which is continually varying,[47] or to secure payment to be made in materials under a prior agreement between the parties.[48] A mortgage to secure future and contingent debts is good against a prior unregistered mortgage.[49]

If a mortgage be given to secure an unliquidated debt, or an unadjusted account, or balance of account, the burden is upon the holder of it to produce the accounts and prove what is due.[50] A sum to be ascertained by an award may be secured by mortgage. But where it was provided that the referees, taking certain data stated in the mortgage as their rule or guide, should make their award and return it in writing to the parties within thirty days after their appointment, the award having failed by reason of the misconduct of the arbitrators, it was held that the mortgage was security for the amount of an award

[41] Clarke v. Bancroft, 13 Iowa 320.
[42] Hoye v. Burford, 68 Ark. 256, 57 S. W. 795.
[43] Morse v. Godfrey, 3 Story (U. S.) 364, Fed. Cas. No. 9856; Gafford v. Stearns, 51 Ala. 434; Rea v. Wilson, 112 Iowa 517, 84 N. W. 539; Chaffee v. Atlas Lumber Co., 43 Nebr. 224, 61 N. W. 637, 47 Am. St. 753; Mingus v. Condit, 23 N. J. Eq. 313; Delancey v. Stearns, 66 N. Y. 157. See post § 460.
[44] Hester v. Gairdner, 128 Ga. 531, 58 S. E. 165; Leger v. Leger, 118 La. 322, 42 So. 951; Hayhurst v. Morin, 104 Maine 169, 71 Atl. 707. But see

Huntington v. Kneeland, 187 N. Y. 563, 80 N. E. 1111.
[45] Todd v. Todd, 164 Cal. 255, 128 Pac. 413.
[46] Booth v. Barnum, 9 Conn. 286, 23 Am. Dec. 339.
[47] Esterly v. Purdy, 50 How. Pr. (N. Y.) 350; quoted with approval in Moses v. Hatfield, 27 S. Car. 324, 3 S. E. 538.
[48] Rees v. Logsdon, 68 Md. 95, 11 Atl. 708.
[49] Moore v. Ragland, 74 N. Car. 343.
[50] De Mott v. Benson, 4 Edw. Ch. (N. Y.) 297.

to be made in this manner, and that the mortgagees could not have relief in equity upon a bill for a sale of the mortgaged property.[51]

§ 347. **Recital of antecedent debt.**—Whether a mortgage given to secure an antecedent debt entitles the mortgagee to the position of a purchaser for value is a question elsewhere considered,[52] upon which the adjudications are not in harmony. A recital in the mortgage that the mortgagor is indebted to the mortgagee in a certain sum, for which "he has given his checks," does not imply that the mortgage was given for an antecedent debt.[53]

§ 348. **Where mortgage given for greater or less sum than actual debt.**—A mortgage given as security for a part of the indebtedness of the mortgagor to the mortgagee, such as one given to secure the sum of three thousand dollars when the mortgagor was indebted to the mortgagee in the sum of ten thousand dollars and upward, the balance of an account current between them, can not be objected to on the ground that the mortgagee could not, under the recording system, be allowed to take a mortgage to secure a part of the debt, and hold it as a valid security on the property until the whole debt is paid. The objection was not to any uncertainty in the debt intended to be .secured, but rather to the application of subsequent payments made by the debtor, without any specific direction at the time as to their application. But it was held that the payments were properly applicable to the unsecured part of the debt, and that the mortgage remained a valid security for the remainder of the debt.[54] But where a mortgage specifies the amount secured thereby, the presumption is, in the absence of special indemnity covenants, that the mortgage was given only as security for the sum named.[55]

A mortgage given for a greater sum than the amount due, without fraudulent intent, is valid to the extent of the actual debt.[56] In such case the mortgagor may show that the lien was for a less sum than that expressed in the mortgage.[57]

[51] Emery v. Owings, 7 Gill (Md.) 488, 48 Am. Dec. 580.

[52] See post §§ 459, 460.

[53] Winchester v. Baltimore &c. R. Co., 4 Md. 231. See also Tennis Coal Co. v. Asher, 143 Ky. 223, 136 S. W. 197.

[54] Chester v. Wheelwright, 15 Conn. 562.

[55] Bergdoll v. Sopp, 232 Pa. 21, 81 Atl. 62.

[56] Nazro v. Ware, 38 Minn. 443, 38

N. W. 359; Gordon v. Preston, 1 Watts (Pa.) 385, 26 Am. Dec. 75. See also Mutual Loan Assn. v. Tyre (Del.), 81 Atl..48.

[57] Huckaba v. Abbott, 87 Ala. 409, 6 So. 48; Louisville Banking Co. v. Leonard, 90 Ky. 106, 11 Ky. L. 917, 13 S. W. 521; Felder v. Leftwich, 123 La. 931, 49 So. 645; Ruloff v. Hazen, 124 Mich. 570, 83 N. W. 370; Nazro v. Ware, 38 Minn. 443, 38 N. W. 359; Burnett v. Wright, 135 N.

§ 349. Note described in mortgage.—The description of the note secured need not be made with the utmost particularity, but only so that it may be reasonably identified.[58] Thus it is sufficient for the mortgage to recite that it is given to secure ten promissory notes of a specified date, without stating when the notes become due and what amount they call for.[59] A condition to secure "all and any notes the said grantees may hold against me" is sufficient.[60] But a mere reference to a note without specifying its contents is not sufficient to put subsequent purchasers on inquiry.[61] The note may be described according to its tenor and effect.[62]

The omission to state in the mortgage the amount of the note secured is not fatal.[63]

An omission to state the date of a note, or the date of maturity, or the precise amount of the debt when its amount is ascertained will not render the description faulty for uncertainty.[64] The omission in the mortgage of the words "or order," in describing a note payable to the mortgagee or order, is not such a variance as to render the note inadmissible in evidence.[65]

A mortgage conditioned to pay a note in a certain penal sum, when in fact the note was without penalty, is not invalid for want of reasonable certainty. The whole sum of the penalty may be due, and no one could be misled except through his own negligence to make inquiry as to the amount due.[66] A condition that the mortgage shall be void upon the payment of the notes described in another mortgage, referred to by date and record in another county of the state, sufficiently indicates the amount secured, and is valid.[67] A mortgage is sufficient which refers to a note which had been made out but not signed, and which, by mistake or fraud, never was signed, though it was agreed that it should be executed.[68]

Y. 543, 32 N. E. 253; Mackey v. Brownfield, 13 Serg. & R. (Pa.) 239.

[58] Winchell v. Coney, 54 Conn. 24; Webb v. Stone, 24 N. H. 282. See also Bowen v. Ratcliff, 140 Ind. 393, 39 N. E. 860, 49 Am. St. 203. See ante § 71.

[59] Hollenbeck v. Woodford, 13 Ind. App. 113, 41 N. E. 348.

[60] Magirl v. Magirl, 89 Iowa 342, 56 N. W. 510; Page v. Ordway, 40 N. H. 253.

[61] Harper v. Edwards, 115 N. Car. 246, 20 S. E. 392.

[62] Allen v. Lathrop, 46 Ga. 133; Hoskins v. Cole, 34 Ill. App. 541;

Aull v. Lee, 61 Mo. 160; Somersworth Sav. Bank v. Roberts, 38 N. H. 22.

[63] Wilson v. Vaughn, 61 Miss. 472.

[64] In re Farmers' Supply Co., 170 Fed. 502; Utley v. Smith, 24 Conn. 290, 63 Am. Dec. 163; Babcock v. Lisk, 57 Ill. 327; Merrill v. Elliott, 55 Ill. App. 34; Pearce v. Hall, 12 Bush (Ky.) 209.

[65] Hough v. Bailey, 32 Conn. 288.

[66] Frink v. Branch, 16 Conn. 260.

[67] Kellogg v. Frazier, 40 Iowa 502.

[68] Volmer v. Stagerman, 25 Minn. 234.

A mortgage conditioned to pay whatever sum the mortgagor might owe the mortgagee, either as maker or indorser of any notes or bills, bonds, checks, over-drafts, or securities of any kind given by him, according to the conditions of any such writings obligatory, executed by him to the mortgagee as collateral security, secures only such debts as are evidenced by writing.[69]

The recitals in a mortgage are competent evidence against the mortgagor to prove the consideration of the note described in it.[70] It will be presumed that a "note," referred to in a mortgage or deed of trust, is not under seal.[71]

When the validity of the mortgage is attacked by a creditor or a purchaser, parol evidence is admissible to show the real consideration, and what note was actually intended to be described.[72] As the note is the evidence of the debt and the mortgage the security therefor, there is no debt secured by the mortgage where no note is executed as prescribed in the mortgage.[73]

§ 350. **Effect of variance between note and description thereof in mortgage.**—It is not necessary that all the particulars of the note or other obligation secured by a mortgage should be specified in the conditions of it, in order to identify it as the note intended to be secured. If the paper offered in evidence agrees with the description contained in the mortgage so far as that goes, only in that this description is not complete, the possession and production of the instrument are prima facie evidence that it is the same mentioned in the condition. If, however, the description in the condition varies from the paper offered in evidence in certain particulars, then the mere possession of it might not furnish even prima facie evidence that it is the obligation intended to be secured.[74] It is only necessary that the mortgage should state correctly sufficient facts to identify the paper with reasonable certainty; and then, if some particulars of the description do not correspond precisely with the instrument produced, it is not material.[75]

[69] Walker v. Paine, 31 Barb. (N. Y.) 213.

[70] Warner v. Brooks, 14 Gray (Mass.) 107. See post §§ 1223, 1225.

[71] Jackson v. Sackett, 7 Wend. (N. Y.) 94; Walker v. McConnico, 10 Yerg. (Tenn.) 228.

[72] Nazro v. Ware, 38 Minn. 443, 38 N. W. 359.

[73] Leader Pub. Co. v. Grant Trust &c. Co., 174 Ind. 192, 91 N. E. 498.

[74] Robertson v. Stark, 15 N. H. 109. See also Colby v. Everett, 10 N. H. 429; Weber v. Illing, 66 Wis. 79, 27 N. W. 834.

[75] This is illustrated by the case of a mortgage to secure "a certain promissory note made and delivered on or about the eighth day of August, 1867, * * * payable on or about one year from date, to the N. W. U. P. Company," signed by three

While a mortgage may modify the contract, an irreconcilable contradiction by the mortgage of the terms of the notes can not be allowed to affect the contract as shown by the notes. The indebtedness is represented by the notes which constitute the primary contract. To these the mortgage is collateral, and to them it refers only for the purpose of identification of the debt and contract.[76] When a note agrees in some respects with the description, but varies in others, it may be proved by parol to be the one intended in the mortgage.[77] Thus, a variance of the note offered in connection with the mortgage from the description in the condition, in that the note is payable with interest annually, whereas the mortgage describes the note as payable with interest, is not a material one.[78] If, however, the note produced be totally variant from that described in the mortgage, such evidence is inadmissible in an action at law.[79]

It is no objection to the validity of a mortgage that it does not state the names of the holders of the notes secured, when they are otherwise identified; and such a mortgage, when duly recorded, is notice to subsequent purchasers of the property of the existence of the notes intended to be secured, and they are bound by the legal effect of the incumbrance.[80] A mortgage for the payment of a debt, according to the condition of a bond recited in the mortgage, will not be avoided in equity for the reason that the day of payment of the bond has already passed. At law, the condition being impossible, the deed would be regarded as absolute; but in equity it is a security merely like an ordinary mortgage.[81]

Where a mortgage was conditioned for the payment of a sum of

persons, for a sum named. In a foreclosure suit, the note produced was dated August 6, 1867, payable on or before September 1, 1868, to the Northwestern Union Packet Company, at the National Bank of La Crosse, and was for the same sum and signed by the same persons named in the mortgage; but there was a condition inserted that it might be paid by the delivery of a barge in lieu of money. The note was admitted in evidence as sufficiently identified by the description in the mortgage. Paine v. Benton, 32 Wis. 491. Ogborn v. Eliason, 77 Ind. 393. See also Partridge v. Swazey, 46 Maine 414; Williams v. Hilton, 35 Maine 547, 58 Am. Dec. 729; Johns v. Church, 12 Pick. (Mass.) 557, 23 Am. Dec. 651;

Whitney v. Hale, 67 N. H. 385, 30 Atl. 417; Boody v. Davis, 20 N. H. 140, 51 Am. Dec. 210; McKinster v. Babcock, 26 N. Y. 378; Harper v. Edwards, 115 N. Car. 246, 20 So. 392; Hurd v. Robinson, 11 Ohio St. 232.

[76] Ferris v. Johnson, 136 Mich. 227, 98 N. W. 1014.

[77] Williams v. Hinton, 35 Maine 547; Sweetser v. Lowell, 33 Maine 446; Cushman v. Luther, 53 N. H. 562; Melvin v. Fellows, 33 N. H. 401; Stanford v. Andrews, 12 Heisk. (Tenn.) 664.

[78] Webb v. Stone, 24 N. H. 282.

[79] Follett v. Heath, 15 Wis. 601.

[80] Boyd v. Parker, 43 Md. 182.

[81] Hughes v. Edwards, 9 Wheat. (U. S.) 489, 6 L. ed. 142.

money on a day named, the year being left blank, according to the
tenor of a promissory note for that sum, and the note was never
made, and only a small part of the money loaned, for which a receipt
was given, it was considered that the bargain was incomplete, and the
mortgage of no effect. It was regarded as never having been executed
for the purpose of having effect according to its tenor.[82]

The mortgage need not set forth a literal copy of the note secured
by it. If the amount of the note is stated, it does not matter that
other important particulars are omitted.[83] It is sufficient to describe
its legal effect.[84] The condition of a mortgage to secure the payment
"of fifty dollars in sixty days from the date hereof, meaning and intending the legal claims and demands the mortgagee has against me,"
is not void for uncertainty; the true construction of it being that it
secures the payment of the sum due, not exceeding that amount.[85]

§ 351. Note and mortgage construed together.—The note and mortgage are construed together.[86] When there is any uncertainty as to
the amount secured by the mortgage, the notes referred to in it are
competent evidence to explain the language as against the mortgagor,
or one who purchased the equity of redemption with notice of the
notes intended to be secured; as when the mortgage described the debt
as "two promissory notes, bearing even date herewith, for the sum of
five hundred dollars, one payable in 1852, and the other in 1853," and
the notes were for five hundred dollars each. Such evidence is not
contradictory to the language of the mortgage, but explanatory.[87]
Where a mortgage described a bond secured by it as of a certain sum,
a bond for a smaller sum, and dated one day later, may be shown in
evidence to have been substituted for the bond described, and, in an
action to foreclose, judgment may be rendered for the amount of the
latter bond.[88]

[82] Parker v. Parker, 17 Mass. 370.
[83] King v. Kilbride, 58 Conn. 109,
19 Atl. 519.
[84] Aull v. Lee, 61 Mo. 160.
[85] Machette v. Wanless, 1 Colo.
225; Michigan Ins. Co. v. Brown, 11
Mich. 266; North v. Crowell, 11 N.
H. 251.
[86] Lockrow v. Cline, 4 Kans. App.
716, 46 Pac. 720; Kansas Loan &c.
Co. v. Gill, 2 Kans. App. 488, 43 Pac.
991; Cabell v. Knote, 2 Kans. App. 68,
43 Pac. 309. See also Trinity County
Bk. v. Haas, 151 Cal. 553, 91 Pac.
385; Meyer v. Weber, 133 Cal. 681,
65 Pac. 1110; San Gabriel Val. Bank

v. Lake View Town Co. (Cal. App.),
86 Pac. 727; Spesard v. Spesard, 75
Kans. 87, 88 Pac. 576; Kingsley v.
Anderson, 103 Minn. 510, 115 N. W.
642; Bartels v. Davis, 34 Mont. 285,
85 Pac. 1027; Security Trust &c. Co.
v. Ellsworth, 129 Wis. 349, 109 N. W.
125.
[87] McDonald v. Second Nat. Bank,
106 Iowa 517, 76 N. W. 1011; Crafts
v. Crafts, 13 Gray (Mass.) 360;
Moses v. Hatfield, 27 S. Car. 324, 3
S. E. 538.
[88] Baxter v. McIntire, 13 Gray
(Mass.) 168.

The note and mortgage may supplement each other in stating the debt secured;[89] as where the mortgage states the rate of interest, which is omitted from the note,[90] or where the note provides for interest at ten per cent. per annum, and the mortgage provides for the same rate of interest payable annually;[91] and, inasmuch as the mortgage provides for something respecting which the note was silent, the mortgage governs the contract in this respect.[92] But where a mortgage provides for the payment of a certain sum with interest, and recites that upon such payment the deed, as well as a promissory note for the amount stated, with interest, shall be void, but the note makes no mention of interest, parol evidence is admissible to show that the note was the only debt secured by the mortgage.[93] If there is a conflict between the note and the mortgage as to the amount of interest recoverable upon default of payment, the terms of the note control.[94]

The note and mortgage may supplement each other in other ways.[95] Thus, if the mortgage provides that upon any default in the payment of interest the whole mortgage debt shall become due, a note representing the mortgage debt, though it does not contain this provision, becomes due upon such default, and a personal judgment may be rendered against the maker of the note for the deficiency after applying the amount obtained from a sale of the mortgaged property.[96] A like provision in the mortgage note affects the mortgage from which it is omitted.[97]

[89] Wheeler &c. Mfg. Co. v. Howard, 28 Fed. 741; Chambers v. Marks, 93 Ala. 412, 9 So. 74; Hill v. Banks, 61 Conn. 25, 23 Atl. 712; Leedy v. Nash, 67 Ind. 311; Cleavenger v. Beath, 53 Ind. 172; Swearingen v. Labrier, 93 Iowa 147, 61 N. W. 431, 26 L. R. A. 765; Dean v. Ridgway, 82 Iowa 757; Clayton v. Whitaker, 68 Iowa 412, 27 N. W. 296; Stanclift v. Norton, 11 Kans. 218; Stowe v. Merrill, 77 Maine 550, 1 Atl. 684; Lantry v. French, 33 Nebr. 524, 5 N. W. 679; McCaughrin v. Williams, 15 S. Car. 505; Evenson v. Bates, 58 Wis. 24, 15 N. W. 837.

[90] Elliott v. Deason, 64 Ga. 63.

[91] Richards v. Holmes, 18 How. (U. S.) 143, 15 L. ed. 304; Winchell v. Coney, 54 Conn. 24, 5 Atl. 354; Bangs v. Fallon, 179 Mass. 77, 60 N. E. 403; May v. Gates, 137 Mass. 389; Jarvis v. Fox, 90 Mich. 67, 51 N. W. 272.

[92] Dobbins v. Parker, 46 Iowa 357.

See also Mowry v. Sanborn, 68 N. Y. 153.

[93] Hampden Cotton Mills v. Payson, 130 Mass. 88.

[94] New England Mtg. Sec. Co. v. Casebier, 3 Kans. App. 741, 45 Pac. 452.

[95] Wheeler &c. Mfg. Co. v. Howard, 28 Fed. 741; Commercial Exchange Bank v. McLeod, 67 Iowa 718, 25 N. W. 894; Shores v. Doherty, 65 Wis. 153, 26 N. W. 577.

[96] Gregory v. Marks, 8 Biss. (U. S.) 44, Fed. Cas. No. 5802. Opposed to this is the decision in Hutchinson v. Benedict, 49 Kans. 545, 31 Pac. 147, where it was held that the terms of the note must govern in such case, on the ground that the mortgage is but an incident of the debt evidenced by the note. See post § 1179.

[97] Fletcher v. Daugherty, 13 Nebr. 224, 13 N. W. 207.

The negotiable character of a note or bond is not affected by a recital therein that it is according to the conditions of a mortgage, where the terms of the latter instrument, construed with the note or bond, would not affect the essential elements of negotiability.[98]

The debt stated in the note as one sum may be changed by the mortgage into several sums which are charged upon particular lots, so that the mortgagor may pay any one of these sums within the time stated, and become entitled to a discharge of the lot on which such sum was made a charge.[99] The notes secured are prima facie evidence of the amount of the mortgage debt.[1]

Where three papers instead of two are employed to express the mortgage contract these are all to be construed together; as where the three papers were a mortgage, a promissory note payable on demand and an agreement by which payment, so far at least as it related to a foreclosure of the mortgage, was postponed until the decease of the mortgagor, or until he should make default in paying the monthly instalments or keeping the buildings reasonably insured for the mortgagee's benefit. "Construing the note and mortgage as embracing the contemporaneous agreement,[2] the note is payable, with interest monthly, at the rate named on demand after the decease of the mortgagor if the interest is paid when due, and if not, on demand after a default in the payment of interest; and the mortgage secures the payment of the note and the performance of the mortgagor's agreement in respect to insurance. The mortgage could not be foreclosed so long as the mortgagor made payments and kept up the insurance according to his agreement."[3]

Where the note and mortgage are at variance in some particular it has been held that the terms of the note shall govern inasmuch as the note is the principal obligation and the mortgage merely an incident thereto; as where a note drawing interest at seven per cent. provided that upon default in the payment of interest the entire principal shall at the option of the holder become due and twelve per cent. interest

[98] Farmer v. First Nat. Bank, 89 Ark. 132, 115 S. W. 1141, 131 Am. St. 79; Hunter v. Clarke, 184 Ill. 158, 56 N. E. 297, 75 Am. St. 160; Bank of Carroll v. Taylor, 67 Iowa 572, 25 N. W. 810; Brooke v. Struthers, 110 Mich. 562, 68 N. W. 272, 35 L. R. A. 536; Dutton v. Ives, 5 Mich. 515; Blumenthal v. Jassoy, 29 Minn. 177, 12 N. W. 517; Bradbury v. Kinney, 63 Nebr. 754, 89 N. W. 257; Cunningham v. McDonald, 98 Tex. 316, 83 S. W. 372; Thorp v. Mindeman, 123 Wis. 149, 101 N. W. 417, 68 L. R. A. 146, 107 Am. St. 1003.

[99] Barge v. Klausman, 42 Minn. 281, 44 N. W. 69.

[1] Ording v. Burnet, 178 Ill. 28, 52 N. E. 851.

[2] Hill v. Huntress, 43 N. H. 480.

[3] Sanborn v. Ladd, 69 N. H. 222, 223, 39 Atl. 1072, per Chase, J.

shall be paid from that time, but the mortgage provided that on such default interest should be computed at twelve per cent. from the date of the note, it was held that interest should be computed in accordance with the note.[4]

§ 352. Identity of note and amount thereof shown by parol evidence.

—While it is true that a written contract can not be contradicted or varied by parol evidence, yet such evidence is competent to apply a written contract to its proper subject-matter.[5] Thus parol evidence is admissible to identify a note, and show that the note produced is the one referred to in the mortgage.[6] Such evidence has been admitted to show that a mortgage made to Ebenezer Hall 3d, conditioned for the payment of a note of the same date, in fact secured a note to Ebenezer Hall which was dated several months earlier.[7] In the same case, a further discrepancy of one thousand years in the date of the note was considered so palpably a mere clerical mistake that no explanation of it was required. In general it may be said that a mortgage is not invalid, either between the parties, or as to third persons, on account of uncertainty in the description of the debt, when, upon the ordinary principle of allowing extrinsic evidence to apply a written contract to its proper subject-matter, the debt intended to be secured can be shown.[8]

Very considerable latitude has been allowed in admitting evidence to show that securities offered at the trial of an action to foreclose a mortgage are really substitutes for those described in it; and they have been held to be secured by it, although not corresponding in any

---

[4] Keys v. Lardner, 55 Kans. 331, 40 Pac. 644.

[5] Jones v. Guaranty &c. Co., 101 U. S. 622, 25 L. ed. 1030; Emerson v. Knight, 130 Ga. 400, 60 S. E. 255; Moses v. Hatfield, 27 S. Car. 324, 3 S. E. 538. See also in this connection Hester v. Gairdner, 128 Ga. 531, 58 S. E. 165; Bowen v. Ratcliff, 140 Ind. 393, 39 N. E. 860, 49 Am. St. 203; Spedden v. Sykes, 51 Wash. 267, 98 Pac. 752.

[6] Jones v. Guaranty &c. Co., 101 U. S. 622, 25 L. ed. 1030; Duval v. McLoskey, 1 Ala. 708; Stowe v. Merrill, 77 Maine 550, 1 Atl. 684; Hall v. Tay, 131 Mass. 192; Goddard v. Sawyer, 9 Allen (Mass.) 78; Johns v. Church, 12 Pick. (Mass.) 557, 23 Am. Dec. 651; Nazro v. Ware, 38 Minn. 43, 38 N. W. 359; Aull v. Lee,

61 Mo. 160; Bell v. Fleming, 12 N. J. Eq. 13; Jackson v. Bowen, 7 Cow. (N. Y.) 13. See also Shoemaker v. Smith, 80 Iowa 655, 45 N. W. 744; Mossop v. Creditors, 41 La. Ann. 296, 6 So. 134; Blair v. Harris, 75 Mich. 167, 42 N. W. 790; Caldwell v. Sisson, 150 Mo. App. 547, 131 S. W. 140; McAteer v. McAteer, 31 S. Car. 313, 9 S. E. 966. See post §§ 367, 384.

[7] Hall v. Tufts, 18 Pick. (Mass.) 455.

[8] Clark v. Hyman, 55 Iowa 14, 7 N. W. 386, 39 Am. Rep. 160; Gill v. Pinney, 12 Ohio St. 38; Hurd v. Robinson, 11 Ohio St. 232; Tousley v. Tousley, 5 Ohio St. 78. See also In re Farmers' Supply Co., 170 Fed. 502.

particular with those described in the mortgage.[9] But it has been held that where there is a totally false description of the note intended to be secured, parol evidence is inadmissible to identify the note in an action at law.[10]

A mortgage which recited that it was given to secure the payment of a note described, "and also in consideration of the further sum of five hundred dollars," paid to the mortgagor, was held to be security for the sum of five hundred dollars in addition to the note. Parol evidence of this further indebtedness of five hundred dollars was allowed, as not enlarging the terms of the mortgage, but simply showing the true amount. A mortgage conditioned to pay a certain sum, and also to secure a bond, the condition of which covers all liabilities of the debtor to the mortgagee, is construed to cover all indebtedness under the bond, the amount and nature of which may be shown by parol.[11] In some jurisdictions, however, the statute requires that the amount of the debt intended to be secured be specifically stated in the mortgage.[12]

§ 352a.   **Parol proof of debt where mortgage is in form an absolute conveyance.**—In case the mortgage is in the form of an absolute conveyance for a nominal consideration, the debt secured may be shown by any competent written or parol evidence. In the absence of any proof of intention to limit the security, it might be presumed that such a deed is security for all sums due from the grantor to the grantee. In South Carolina the rule has been held to be, that the grantor shall not be permitted to redeem except upon paying whatever he may owe to the person holding the legal title, both the debt which the absolute conveyance was given to secure and all other debts, whether secured or unsecured, which the grantor may owe at the time he seeks to redeem such conveyance to the person who holds the title.[13] But if the

[9] Baxter v. McIntire, 13 Gray (Mass.) 168, per Dewey, J.; Gunn v. Jones, 67 Ga. 398.

[10] Follett v. Heath, 15 Wis. 601.

[11] Babcock v. Lisk, 57 Ill. 327; New Hampshire Bank v. Willard, 10 N. H. 210. See also Felder v. Leftwich, 123 La. 931, 49 So. 645.

[12] Page v. Ordway, 40 N. H. 253. See also Mans v. McKellip, 38 Md. 231.

[13] Walker v. Walker, 17 S. Car. 329, qualified by O'Neill v. Bennett, 33 S. Car. 243, 11 S. E. 727, and Lake v. Shumate, 20 S. Car. 23. "The reason for the distinction is this: When a mortgagee, holding a formal, legal mortgage, undertakes to enforce his rights thereunder, he is proceeding to enforce rights resting in contract, and hence he is confined to the terms of the contract, as agreed upon by the parties at the time the contract was entered into in the solemn form of a mortgage. He can not, therefore, be permitted to show that his mortgage, which was originally intended to secure one debt, has, by a subsequent parol agreement, been so extended as to cover another debt, not contemplated by the parties at the time the

deed is given and accepted as security for a particular debt or loan, the better rule is that it can not be held as security for any other debt, and the restriction of the security to the particular debt may be proved by parol.[14] Where there is nothing in a written contract to reconvey, to show the amount of the debt, parol evidence is admissible to show that the deed was given to secure existing indebtedness of the amount stated as a consideration for the deed and for future advances.[15]

§ 353. **Note or bond not necessary to validity of deed of trust or mortgage.**—A deed of trust or mortgage is valid without any note or bond, although it purports to secure a note or bond, and substantially describes it.[16] It is not necessary that there should be any personal liability on the part of the mortgagor for the debt secured by the mortgage.[17]

An alteration of the note secured not fraudulently made, though it may destroy the written evidence of the debt, does not affect the mortgage.[18] But it has been held that an alteration of the note which

contract which he is seeking to enforce was entered into. But where, as in this case, one who holds the legal title to a tract of land under an absolute conveyance, seeking to enforce his legal rights thereunder, is met by a showing on the part of his grantor that, although he holds the legal title, equity will not permit him to enforce it, because at the time it was executed such paper was not intended to operate as an absolute conveyance, but was intended merely as a security for the payment of a debt, and hence if the paper were allowed the effect of an absolute conveyance it would operate as a fraud, it is not a question of contract, but one of pure equity; and the maxim that he who seeks equity must himself do equity applies." Per McIver, C. J., in Levi v. Blackwell, 35 S. Car. 511, 15 S. E. 243. See post § 1084. See also Jacoby v. Funkhouser, 147 Ala. 254, 40 So. 291.

[14] McKee v. Jordan, 50 N. J. Eq. 306, 24 Atl. 398. In this case the conveyance which was made by a mother to secure a loan to her son and constituted the son's apparent authority, did not bear on its face authority to pledge it for any particular sum, but, at the time of its delivery, the mortgagee had explicit notice that the son's authority was limited, or intended to be limited, to an authority to pledge for $600. Defendant chose, in the face of this notice, to accept and rely upon the son's false statement that his mother had authorized him to pledge it for $850. In so doing, he relied upon the statement of the son, and not on the apparent authority of the possession of the deed. He was not misled by that or any act of the complainant, and can not, therefore, cast upon her his loss. The case is distinguishable from Moore v. Metropolitan Nat. Bank, 55 N. Y. 41, cited and relied upon by the mortgagee.

[15] Hester v. Gairdner, 128 Ga. 531, 58 S. E. 165.

[16] Baldwin v. Raplee, 4 Ben. (U. S.) 433, Fed. Cas. No. 801; Bradley v. Merrill, 88 Maine 319, 34 Atl. 160; Mitchell v. Burnham, 44 Maine 286; Smith v. People's Bank, 24 Maine 185; Goodhue v. Berrien, 2 Sandf. Ch. (N. Y.) 630.

[17] Mills v. Darling, 43 Maine 565; Cook v. Johnson, 165 Mass. 245, 43 N. E. 96, citing Campbell v. Dearborn, 109 Mass. 130, 12 Am. Rep. 671; Rice v. Rice, 4 Pick. (Mass.) 349; Glover v. Payn, 19 Wend. (N. Y.) 518.

[18] Clough v. Seay, 49 Iowa 111; Mersman v. Werges, 112 U. S. 139,

destroys it, whether made fraudulently or not, will defeat an action on the mortgage.[19] The mortgage debt exists independently of the note. The inquiry is, Does the debt exist? If it does, it is not essential that there should be any evidence of it beyond what is furnished by the recitals of the deed.[20] The validity of a mortgage does not depend upon the description of the debt contained in the deed, nor upon the form of the indebtedness, whether it be by note or bond, or otherwise; it depends rather upon the existence of the debt it is given to secure.[21] Since the mortgage secures the debt, and not the evidence thereof, it is unaffected by changes in the form of such evidence.[22] But the mortgage creates no lien unless the note secured evidences a debt.[23]

If a note and mortgage be made and the mortgage recorded, the destruction of the note by agreement pending further negotiations and the making of a new note of the same description do not invalidate the mortgage.[24] Although there be no note or bond, and no time is specified for the payment of the mortgage debt, the mortgage, if given to secure a debt that actually exists, is valid, and may be enforced immediately.[25] A mortgage to secure a note thereto attached is binding though the note attached is not signed. The note may be read in evidence as a part of the mortgage.[26]

Though the note has been given by an executor under authority conferred by a will to mortgage real estate to obtain money for the payment of the testator's debts, and only imports the executor's personal liability, still the mortgage, being a pledge of the property by

28 L. ed. 641, 5 Sup. Ct. 65; Souza v. Lucas (Cal. App.), 100 Pac. 115; Vogle v. Ripper, 34 Ill. 100, 85 Am. Dec. 298; Edington v. McLeod, 87 Kans. 426, 124 Pac. 163, 41 L. R. A.. (N. S.) 230, Ann. Cas. 1913 E, 243; Wilson v. Hayes, 40 Minn. 531, 42 N. W. 467, 4 L. R. A. 196, 12 Am. St. 754; Smith v. Smith, 27 S. Car. 166, 3 S. E. 78, 13 Am. St. 633.

[19] Tate v. Fletcher, 77 Ind. 102; Sherman v. Sherman, 3 Ind. 337.

[20] Eacho v. Cosby, 26 Grat. (Va.) 112. See also Flagg v. Mann, 2 Sumn. (U. S.) 486, Fed. Cas. No. 4847; Goodhue v. Berrien, 2 Sandf. Ch. (N. Y.) 630; Burger v. Hughes, 5 Hun (N. Y.) 180.

[21] Hodgdon v. Shannon, 14 N. H. 572; Farmers' Loan &c. Co. v. Cur-

tis, 7 N. Y. 466; Coutant v. Servoss, 3 Barb. (N. Y.) 128; Griffin v. Cranston, 1 Bosw. (N. Y.) 281; Jackson v. Bowen, 7 Cow. (N. Y.) 13. Quoted with approval in Moses v. Hatfield, 27 S. Car. 324, 3 S. E. 538.

[22] Willette v. Gifford, 46 Ind. App. 185, 92 N. E. 186.

[23] McCourt v. Peppard, 126 Wis. 326, 105 N. W. 809.

[24] Parks v. Frahm, 54 Kans. 676, 39 Pac. 185.

[25] Carnall v. Duval, 22 Ark. 136; Brookings v. White, 49 Maine 479; McCaughrin v. Williams, 15 S. Car. 515, 516 (quoting text). But see Coleman v. Fisher (Ark.), 41 S. W. 49.

[26] McFadden v. State, 82 Ind. 558.

him as executor, and the money having been obtained and used by him for the estate, would be enforcible.[27]

If a mortgage be taken to secure the payment of an account for present and future advances, a note for a part of such advances is entitled to a proportionate part of the mortgage security.[28]

§ 354. **Effect of clerical error in describing debt.**—The lien of a mortgage is not affected by a clerical inaccuracy in the description of the debt; as, for instance, in the date of the note secured, or in time of its payment.[29] A slight mistake in the copy of a note embodied in the mortgage given to secure it is not fatal to the validity of the mortgage, when it is apparent that the debt and note sued on are the debt and note referred to in the mortgage.[30] Defects in the description of mortgage notes which can be readily remedied by parol evidence are immaterial.[31]

The amount of the bond secured by a mortgage having been left blank, and the mortgage having been recorded without the blank being filled, the mortgagor afterward executed a writing under seal, stating that the sum, two thousand dollars, was omitted, and should have been inserted, and this writing was attached to the page on which the registry was made. This was held to be a sufficient record as against a subsequent mortgage.[32] Moreover, if the amount of the mortgage debt be left blank, this may be supplied by parol or other extrinsic evidence.[33] A mistake in describing the mortgage note does not ordinarily invalidate the security.[34] A mortgage which describes the note it secures by giving the date, the amount, the time of payment, and the rate of interest, is sufficient without giving the names of the makers.[35] Parol evidence is admissible to prove that the note produced is the note intended to be described.[36] A mistake in the amount secured by a deed of trust, even to the extent of one-half thereof, does not vitiate the deed if it does not assume to state the amount with accuracy, and the claim is one of that character about which the party might well be mistaken as to what the indebtedness was.[37]

---

[27] Iowa Loan &c. Co. v. Holderbaum, 86 Iowa 1, 52 N. W. 549.

[28] Adger v. Pringle, 11 S. Car. 527.

[29] Tousley v. Tousley, 5 Ohio St. 78. See post § 515.

[30] Moore v. Russell, 133 Cal. 297, 65 Pac. 624, 85 Am. St. 166.

[31] Williams v. Moniteau Nat. Bank, 72 Mo. 292; Aull v. Lee, 61 Mo. 160.

[32] Lambert v. Hall, 7 N. J. Eq. 410, 651.

[33] Burnett v. Wright, 135 N. Y. 543, 32 N. E. 253.

[34] Porter v. Smith, 13 Vt. 492.

[35] Ogborn v. Eliason, 77 Ind. 393.

[36] Williams v. Hilton, 35 Maine 547, 58 Am. Dec. 729; Bourne v. Littlefield, 29 Maine 302; Nazro v. Ware, 38 Minn. 443, 38 N. W. 359.

[37] Bumpas v. Dotson, 7 Humph. (Tenn.) 310, 46 Am. Dec. 81.

A description in a deed of trust or the debt secured, as being a note signed by the maker and indorsed by another, may be corrected in equity so as to cover a bond signed by the principal, and also signed by a surety as such.[38] But ordinarily it is not necessary to first correct the mortgage before introducing parol evidence to show the real consideration.[39]

§ 355.   **Extension of lien by renewal or extension of secured debt.**— The renewal of the original note of the mortgagor does not affect the security,[40] nor does an extension of the time of payment waive other terms and conditions of the mortgage,[41] except by initiating a new period for the statute of limitations.[42] But it is provided by statute in some states that where the debt is renewed the mortgage must also be renewed, and such renewal of the mortgage must be in writing.[43] No change in the form of the debt will release the mortgage lien so long as the identity of the debt can be traced.[44]

A mortgage to secure a note described, "and any renewals thereof," secures such renewals and interest added.[45] But a mortgage given to secure the payment at maturity of the notes of another does not secure renewal notes substituted in place of them. The mortgagor stands in the relation of surety for the debtor, and his obligation can not be continued without his consent.[46]

It is questioned whether a mortgage can be modified by substituting for a part of the bond secured by it a due bill payable at a different time, and to a different person; it certainly can not be so changed

---

[38] In re Clarke, 2 Hughes (U. S.) 405, Fed. Cas. No. 2843.

[39] Nazro v. Ware, 38 Minn. 443, 38 N. W. 359.

[40] Walters v. Walters, 73 Ind. 425; Kidder v. McIlhenny, 81 N. Car. 123; Hyman v. Devereux, 63 N. Car. 624; McCaughrin v. Williams, 15 S. Car. 505; Enston v. Friday, 2 Rich. L. (S. Car.) 427; Bank of South Carolina v. Rose, 1 Strob. Eq. (S. Car.) 257; Lover v. Bessenger, 9 Baxt. (Tenn.) 393; Williams v. Starr, 5 Wis. 534. In California the renewal of the note or other contract for the payment of the mortgage debt does not create a new mortgage after the original mortgage has been barred by the statute of limitations; for the Civil Code, § 2922, provides that a mortgage can be created, renewed, or extended only by writing, executed with the formalities required in the case of a grant of real property. Wells v. Harter, 56 Cal. 342. See post §§ 924–942, 1207.

[41] Brockway v. McClun, 243 Ill. 196, 90 N. E. 374.

[42] Wilcox v. Gregory, 135 Cal. 217, 67 Pac. 139; Newhall v. Hatch, 134 Cal. 269, 66 Pac. 266; Southern Pac. Co. v. Prosser, 122 Cal. 413, 55 Pac. 145; London &c. Bank v. Bandmann, 120 Cal. 220, 52 Pac. 583, 65 Am. St. 179.

[43] Cal. Civ. Code, § 2922; Moore v. Gould, 151 Cal. 723, 91 Pac. 616.

[44] Gribben v. Clement, 141 Iowa 144, 119 N. W. 596, 133 Am. St. 157.

[45] Barbour v. Tompkins, 31 W. Va. 410, 7 S. E. 1.

[46] Ayres v. Wattson, 57 Pa. St. 360.

and the security transferred to the due bill, except upon a clear show-ing that such was the agreement when the exchange was made.[47] If a deed is made to secure a particular debt, it can not be extended by a subsequent parol agreement so as to secure other debts. This may be done by written contract.[48] But a subsisting mortgage may, by agreement of the mortgagor, be made security for a further or other debt than that for which it was originally given.[49]

By a parol agreement, a mortgage can not be so altered in its operation as to stand as security for a new debt, different in character and amount from that mentioned in the instrument, payable at a dif-ferent time and to another person, especially where the conduct of the parties at the time of the transaction evidenced no such understand-ing.[50] An agreement that a promissory note shall be substituted for notes of a larger amount already secured by a mortgage, and if paid at maturity shall be considered a payment and discharge pro tanto of those notes of the mortgage, and that the mortgage shall be held as collateral security for the new note, and not be discharged or can-celed until that is paid, does not create a lien upon the mortgaged property to secure its payment. The note is not given in renewal or consolidation of the mortgage notes, or any of them. The relation of the parties is not changed. No new right in the mortgaged prop-erty is given, and no new lien is created.[51]

§ 356. **Several mortgages for one debt, and one mortgage for sev-eral debts.**—When several mortgages are made of distinct parcels of land to secure one and the same debt, they constitute in effect one mortgage, and their unity is determined by the debt secured.[52] Parol evidence is admissible for this purpose, and, whether the debt be de-scribed in the same way in the different mortgages or not, it may be shown that they are only additional security for the same debt.[53] A mortgage given to secure separate debts to several persons is several

---

[47] Tucker v. Alger, 30 Mich. 67.

[48] Johnson v. Anderson, 30 Ark. 745; Hester v. Gairdner, 128 Ga. 531, 58 S. E. 165; Pierce v. Parrish, 111 Ga. 725, 37 S. E. 79; Wylly v. Screven, 98 Ga. 213, 25 S. E. 435; Huntington v. Kneeland, 102 App. Div. 284, 92 N. Y. S. 944; Stoddard v. Hart, 23 N. Y. 556.

[49] State Mut. Bldg. &c. Assn. v. Millville Imp. Co., 76 N. J. Eq. 336, 70 Atl. 300.

[50] Morris v. Alston, 92 Ala. 502, 9 So. 315.

[51] Howe v. Wilder, 11 Gray (Mass.) 267. This agreement was regarded the same as if the mortgagee had said, "Give me your note for $600; if paid, I will indorse it on the mort-gages; if not, the mortgages are to stand as they are."

[52] Franklin v. Gorham, 2 Day (Conn.) 142, 2 Am. Dec. 86; West-erly Sav. Bank v. Stillman Mfg. Co., 16 R. I. 497, 17 Atl. 918. See ante § 135.

[53] Anderson v. Davies, 6 Munf. (Va.) 484.

in its nature, as much as if several instruments had been simultaneously executed.[54]

But it has been held that where notes due originally to different persons are secured by a single mortgage, no priority of payment out of the mortgage fund is given to the debt first maturing, but the proceeds are to be distributed pro rata.[55] Where a mortgage covering several separate lots is given to secure several separate debts and distinct sums of money, the instrument is in legal effect a separate and distinct mortgage on each lot to secure several separate and distinct sums of money.[56]

§ 357. Effect of enlarging or extending debt or obligation secured. —A mortgage for a specific sum can not be enlarged or extended to cover other debts or further advances,[57] as against others who have acquired rights in the property. Neither can the mortgagor as against them increase the charge upon the land by confessing judgment, and thus compounding the interest,[58] or by making the debt payable in gold coin instead of currency,[59] or by increasing the rate of interest.[60] The mortgage being given to secure a certain debt is valid for that purpose only; but whatever may be the form of the debt, if it can be traced, the security for it remains good.[61] A mortgage securing a note stated to be for a definite sum when in fact the note

[54] Gardner v. Diederichs, 41 Ill. 158; Burnett v. Pratt, 22 Pick. (Mass.) 556; Thayer v. Campbell, 9 Mo. 280; Eccleston v. Clipsham, 1 Saund. 153.

[55] Fielder v. Varner, 45 Ala. 429; Chaplin v. Sullivan, 128 Ind. 50, 27 N. E. 425; Shaw v. Newsom, 78 Ind. 335; Goodall v. Mopley, 45 Ind. 355; Coons v. Clifford, 58 Ohio St. 480, 51 N. E. 39.

[56] Mason v. Goodnow, 41 Minn. 9, 42 N. W. 482; Hull v. King, 38 Minn. 349, 37 N. W. 792.

[57] Large v. Van Doren, 14 N. J. Eq. 208; Stoddard v. Hart, 23 N. Y. 556; Townsend v. Empire Stone Dressing Co., 6 Duer (N. Y.) 208, and cases cited. See also Briggs v. Steel, 91 Ark. 458, 121 S. W. 754; Langerman v. Puritan Dining Room Co., 21 Cal. App. 637, 132 Pac. 617; Provident Mut. Bldg. &c. Assn. v. Shaffer, 2 Cal. App. 216, 83 Pac. 274; Lewter v. Price, 25 Fla. 574, 6 So. 439; Tunno v. Robert, 16 Fla. 738; Perrin v. Kellogg, 38 Mich. 720;

Beekman Fire Ins. Co. v. First M. E. Church, 29 Barb. (N. Y.) 658, 18 How. Pr. 431; Merchants' State Bank v. Tufts, 14 N. Dak. 238, 103 N. W. 760, 116 Am. St. 682; Webb v. Crouch, 70 W. Va. 580, 74 S. E. 730, Ann. Cas. 1914A, 728. See post § 947.

[58] McGready v. McGready, 17 Mo. 597.

[59] Belloc v. Davis, 38 Cal. 242; Taylor v. Atlantic &c. R. Co., 55 How. Pr. (N. Y.) 275. See also Poett v. Stearns, 31 Cal. 78.

[60] Burchard v. Frazer, 23 Mich. 224.

[61] Van Wagner v. Van Wagner, 7 N. J. Eq. 27; Patterson v. Johnston, 7 Ohio 225. See also Wilkerson v. Tillman, 66 Ala. 532; Deuser v. Walkup, 43 Mo. App. 625; Prescott v. Hayes, 43 N. H. 593; Jagger Iron Co. v. Walker, 76 N. Y. 521; Chapman v. Jenkins, 31 Barb. (N. Y.) 164; McCaughrin v. Williams, 15 S. Car. 505. See post §§ 924-942.

given is for a larger sum is a security only for the smaller sum recited in the mortgage.[62]

A mortgage given to secure future advances, not to exceed a certain amount, is valid, and is a lien on the mortgaged property for advances not exceeding the amount specified.[63] But a mortgage reciting that it was given for a note and "such future advances" as may be made during a given year secures the note only.[64]

As against the mortgagor, his agreement that the mortgage shall stand as security to the mortgagee for further advances, although it be oral only, is valid, and after the advances have been made upon the faith of it, a court of equity will not allow the mortgagor to redeem without performing it.[65] It will apply to him the maxim, that he who seeks equity must do equity. It will also apply the same rule to any one claiming under him with notice. Therefore, where the assignees in insolvency of the mortgagor have conveyed the equity of redemption to his wife, without consideration and with notice of such agreement, a court of equity will decline to aid her to redeem the mortgage in violation of this contract.[66] So, in answer to a bill in equity by an assignee in bankruptcy to redeem a mortgage, it is competent for the holder of the mortgage to show that the bankrupt had, for a valuable consideration, orally agreed that a mortgage made by him to another person, and paid in large part, should not be discharged, but should be assigned to the creditor as security for further loans and debts. Such oral agreement could not be set up against a subsequent mortgagee, or against an attaching creditor; nor could it be set up against the mortgagor or his assignee in a suit at law, but it may be in equity.[67]

In Pennsylvania the courts do not tolerate an oral mortgage or secret lien; and therefore a mortgage given by tenants in common to secure a partnership debt can not, after payment, be kept alive as security for an individual debt of one of them.[68]

---

[62] Schroeder v. Bobbitt, 108 Mo. 289, 18 S. W. 1093. See also Abert v. Kornfeld, 128 App. Div. 547, 112 N. Y. S. 884; Bergdoll v. Sopp, 232 Pa. 21, 81 Atl. 62.

[63] Du Bois v. First Nat. Bank, 43 Colo. 400, 96 Pac. 169; Perkins &c. Co. v. Drew (Ky.), 122 S. W. 526.

[64] Benton-Shingler Co. v. Mills, 13 Ga. App. 632, 79 S. E. 755.

[65] Sheats v. Scott, 133 Ala. 642, 32 So. 573; Walker v. Walker, 17 S. Car. 329, 337. This case is referred to and distinguished in O'Neill v. Bennett, 33 'S. Car. 243, 11 S. E. 727. See also Hayhurst v. Morin, 104 Maine 169, 71 Atl. 707. See post § 947.

[66] Stone v. Lane, 10 Allen (Mass.) 74. See also Brooks v. Brooks, 169 Mass. 38, 47 N. E. 448; Joslyn v. Wyman, 5 Allen (Mass.) 62; Crafts v. Crafts, 13 Gray (Mass.) 360.

[67] Upton v. National Bank, 120 Mass. 153.

[68] Thomas' Appeal, 30 Pa. St. 378,

§ 358. Taxes and assessments.[69]—There is an apparent exception to the rule that the mortgage debt can not, as against third persons, be increased after the execution of the mortgage; and that is, that money paid by the mortgagee, to redeem the premises from a tax sale, or from any charge which is a paramount lien upon the property, becomes a part of the mortgage debt, and may be enforced by foreclosure.[70] But a mortgagee, whether in or out of possession, can not acquire a tax title and hold it for the purpose of destroying the title of his mortgagor.[71]

In the absence of a covenant, a mortgagee who has a mere lien is under no duty to pay taxes, and although the mortgage contains a provision authorizing the mortgagee to pay the taxes upon the mortgagor's failure so to do does not obligate him to pay the same.[72] The mortgage is usually so drawn that in terms it includes under the security any payments that may be made by the mortgagee in consequence of any default of the mortgagor. But without any such provision, the payment by the mortgagee of charges which are a prior lien, and the removal of which is essential to his own protection and safety, gives him in equity not only a right to retain the amount paid out of the proceeds of the land when sold upon foreclosure, as against the mortgagor,[73] but also preference by way of subrogation over even prior incumbrancers who have been protected by such payment.[74]

Prior to the sale for taxes the mortgagee of the premises may pay the taxes and thereby acquire by a species of subrogation a lien for the

reversing 3 Phila. (Pa.) 62, under name Pechin v. Brown, dissenting opinion, p. 99; and to same effect see O'Neill v. Capelle, 62 Mo. 202.

[69] See ante § 77, and post § 1134.

[70] Windett v. Union Mut. Ins. Co., 144 U. S. 581, 36 L. ed. 551, 12 Sup. Ct. 751; Hill v. Eldred, 49 Cal. 398; Mix v. Hotchkiss, 14 Conn. 32; Robinson v. Sulter, 85 Ga. 875, 11 S. E. 887; Parsons v. Gas Light Co., 108 Ill. 380; Hall v. Gould, 79 Ill. 16; Wright v. Langley, 36 Ill. 381; Robinson v. Ryan, 25 N. Y. 320; Kortright v. Cady, 23 Barb. (N. Y.) 490, 5 Abb. Pr. (N. Y.) 358; Faure v. Winans, Hopk. (N. Y.) 283, 14 Am. Dec. 545; Burr v. Veeder, 3 Wend. (N. Y.) 412; Worcester v. Boston, 179 Mass. 41, 60 N. E. 410; Skilton v. Roberts, 129 Mass. 306. An agreement to pay taxes before they become delinquent is not fulfilled by paying the taxes on the day they become delinquent. National Life Ins. Co. v. Butler, 61 Nebr. 449, 85 N. W. 437.

[71] Shepard v. Vincent, 38 Wash. 493, 80 Pac. 777. But see Jones v. Black, 18 Okla. 344, 88 Pac. 1052.

[72] Jones v. Black, 18 Okla. 344, 88 Pac. 1052.

[73] Dale v. McEvers, 2 Cow. (N. Y.) 118; Rapelye v. Prince, 4 Hill (N. Y.) 119, 40 Am. Dec. 267; Silver Lake Bank v. North, 4 Johns. Ch. (N. Y.) 370. Contra, Savage v. Scott, 45 Iowa 130. But a later case in that state. Barthell v. Syverson, 54 Iowa 160, 6 N. W. 178. See also Sanborn Co. v. Alston, 153 Mich. 463, 117 N. W. 625; Sands v. Kaukauna Water Power Co., 115 Wis. 229, 91 N. W. 679.

[74] Cook v. Kraft, 3 Lans. (N. Y.) 512. See post § 1080. But see Manning v. Tuthill, 30 N. J. Eq. 29.

amount so paid which in respect to priority occupies the same position as the tax lien.[75] But in Connecticut it is held that a mortgagee in a mortgage containing no condition as to the payment of taxes and assessments, who, on account of his mortgagor's failure to pay taxes, pays the same in order to protect his security, is not thereby subrogated to the state's rights or remedies for the enforcement of such taxes, so as to be entitled to a foreclosure of the title to the premises under the tax lien.[76]

Even after a foreclosure sale the mortgagee may pay outstanding taxes upon the property, or may redeem it from tax sales in order to give a clear title to the purchaser, and his right to take such payments out of the proceeds of the sale is the same that it would have been had he made the payments before the sale.[77]

In Vermont, however, it is held that mortgagees who have obtained a decree of foreclosure are not justified in paying taxes assessed on the mortgaged premises before the equity of redemption expires, and after redemption by the mortgagor can not recover from him the amount so paid.[78]

If, however, the mortgage contains no covenant for the payment of taxes, and the mortgagor conveys the equity of redemption, the grantee assuming the mortgage, and afterward the property becomes incumbered by taxes which the mortgagee is forced to pay, upon a foreclosure of the mortgage, in determining the deficiency for which the mortgagor is liable, the amount paid by the mortgagee for taxes can not be deducted from the proceeds of the sale, because the mortgagor is not bound to pay the taxes after his conveyance.[79] Taxes and assessments upon mortgaged lands, whether ordinary taxes, or assessment for sewers or the like, and water rates, are preferred debts under the bankrupt and insolvent laws. If, therefore, such taxes and assessments be laid upon mortgaged land before the bankruptcy of the owner, they should be paid by the assignee in full out of the estate in his hands in exoneration of the mortgage.[80] If the mortgaged premises be foreclosed and purchased by the mortgagee, he is

[75] Farmer v. Ward, 75 N. J. Eq. 33, 71 Atl. 401; Dunsmuir v. Port Angeles Gas &c. Co., 30 Wash. 586, 71 Pac. 9.

[76] Sperry v. Butler, 75 Conn. 369, 53 Atl. 899.

[77] Gormley v. Bunyan, 138 U. S. 623, 34 L. ed. 1086, 11 Sup. Ct. 453.

[78] Fulton v. Aldrich, 76 Vt. 310, 57 Atl. 108.

[79] Marshall v. Davies, 16 Hun (N. Y.) 606. The term "assessments" includes assessments for sewers, paving and all betterments in general which may be lawfully made a tax upon the property of abutting owners. National Life Ins. Co. v. Butler, 61 Nebr. 449, 85 N. W. 437.

[80] In re Moller, 8 Ben. (U. S.) 526, Fed. Cas. No. 9699.

still entitled, upon application to the bankruptcy court, to have an order directing the assignee to pay the taxes in full out of the bankrupt's estate. Although the law makes the taxes a lien upon the premises in respect of which they are levied and made, yet they are personal debts of the owner of the premises, and can be collected from his personal property. If the taxes be not paid, and the land be sold to pay them, the sale would be a sale to satisfy a liability of the bankrupt. No formal proof of the debt is necessary before granting such application.

If the remedy upon the mortgage is barred by the statute of limitations, a claim of the mortgagee for taxes paid on the mortgaged land can not be enforced against it. The claim for taxes, which is merely incidental to the mortgage, falls with the mortgage.[81]

A water tax which becomes due upon the mortgaged premises after an adjudication of bankruptcy should be paid by the assignee as a part of the proper expenses of his administration.[82]

§ 359. Solicitor's fee.—In addition to the mortgage debt, the mortgage may be made to secure the payment of a reasonable fee of a solicitor in case of a foreclosure of the mortgage.[83] Such a fee is intended as an indemnity to the mortgagee for expenditures necessarily made to protect his interests.[84] The amount of such fee may be specified in the mortgage or left to the discretion of the court.[85] Such fees become part of the mortgage debt,[86] and the stipulation becomes binding as soon as the mortgage is placed in an attorney's hands, though he has done nothing toward collecting the debt secured.

Where the mortgage provides for the recovery of a certain per cent. of the amount due as attorney's fees it is the duty of the court to make the allowance accordingly.[87] Where the note secured by the

[81] Hill v. Townly, 45 Minn. 167, 47 N. W. 653; Spencer v. Devering, 8 Minn. 461.

[82] In re Moller, 8 Ben. (U. S.) 526, Fed. Cas. No. 9699.

[83] Bronson v. La Crosse &c. R. Co., 2 Wall. (U. S.) 283, 17 L. ed. 725; Hewitt v. Dean, 91 Cal. 5, 27 Pac. 423; Hitchcock v. Merrick, 15 Wis. 522; Rice v. Cribb, 12 Wis. 179. See also Wells v. American Mtg. Co., 109 Ala. 430, 20 So. 136; Huber v. Brown, 243 Ill. 274, 90 N. E. 748; Scott v. Carl, 24 Pa. Super. Ct. 460. See post §§ 635, 1606. But see Sage v. Riggs, 12 Mich. 313.

[84] Huber v. Brown, 243 Ill. 274, 90 N. E. 748, Wilson v. Ott, 173 Pa. St. 253, 34 Atl. 23, 51 Am. St. 767.

[85] By some courts it is held to be in the discretion of the court to make a reasonable and just allowance, without regard to the amount specified in the mortgage. Moran v. Gardemeyer, 82 Cal. 96, 23 Pac. 6. See also Peachy v. Witter, 131 Cal. 316, 63 Pac. 468; Avery v. Maude, 112 Cal. 565, 44 Pac. 1020.

[86] Hayward v. Hayward, 114 La. 476, 38 So. 424.

[87] Cooper v. Bank of Indian Territory, 4 Okla. 632, 46 Pac. 475 Haywood v. Miller, 14 Wash. 660, 45 Pac. 307.

mortgage in express terms contracts to pay a stipulated and definite sum as attorney's fees for the foreclosure of such mortgage, it is proper for the court to decree such stipulated sum as an attorney's fee, without proofs as to its reasonableness.[88] The stipulation may be enforced as well against subsequent purchasers and incumbrancers as against the mortgagor himself.[89] Such fee is presumed to be in addition to the taxable costs allowed by law.[90] Such a stipulation, if not unreasonable in amount, has been regarded as imposing a penalty, rather than as giving compensation to the mortgagee for expenses incurred in consequence of the mortgagor's default.[91]

Equity will not relieve against such a contract fairly entered into, unless, under the color of a provision for the costs and expenses of enforcing the mortgage lien, an unreasonable and oppressive exaction be made of the debtor, so that the stipulation amounts in fact to a penalty which he incurs by his default. In such case equity will interpose her shield to protect the debtor.[92] If, however, the provision be a reasonable compensation to the mortgagee for expenses that may be incurred by the default of the mortgagor, it is a proper addition to the mortgage debt, and it is not collected as costs, but is a part of the judgment to which the mortgagee is entitled.[93] The lien of the mortgage covers such a provision as much as the debt itself; and it also attaches to the costs of suit, and to expenses necessarily incurred in enforcing the mortgage, although not specially provided for.[94]

§ 360. **Lien limited to debt secured.**—The mortgagee can not tack to his mortgage any debt not secured thereby, and require its payment by the mortgagor as a condition to his right to redeem.[95] It is presumed that the consideration recited in the mortgage is the amount of

---

[88] Carhart v. Allen, 56 Fla. 763, 48 So. 47.

[89] Pierce v. Kneeland, 16 Wis. 672, 84 Am. Dec. 726.

[90] Easton v. Woodbury, 71 S. Car. 250, 50 S. E. 790; Hitchcock v. Merrick, 15 Wis. 522.

[91] Daly v. Maitland, 88 Pa. St. 384, 13 West. Jur. 204, 32 Am. Rep. 457, overruling Robinson v. Loomis, 51 Pa. St. 78, which declared the stipulation not to be a penalty. See also Renshaw v. Richards, 30 La. Ann. 398. The stipulation in these latter cases was five per cent. But in Daly v. Maitland, 88 Pa. St. 384, where the mortgage was for $14,000,

the court declared five per cent. to be unreasonable, and suggested that two per cent. would be ample.

[92] Daly v. Maitland, 88 Pa. St. 384. See also Scott v. Carl, 24 Pa. Super. Ct. 460.

[93] Daly v. Maitland, 88 Pa. St. 384. But see Alexandrie v. Saloy, 14 La. Ann. 327.

[94] Hurd v. Coleman, 42 Maine 182.

[95] Edwards v. Dwight, 68 Ala. 389; Schiffer v. Feagin, 51 Ala. 335; Barthell v. Syverson, 54 Iowa 160, 6 N. W. 178; Bacon v. Cottrell, 13 Minn. 194. See also Briggs v. Steele, 91 Ark. 458, 121 S. W. 754. See post § 1081.

the debt.[96] A mortgage executed to secure the payment of notes of a definite amount can not, after the payment of the notes, be made available to secure further advances, unless it is so provided in the mortgage, or by a legal contract between the parties.[97] Where a mortgage is given by a husband and wife to secure a certain note signed by the husband and such note is paid in full, the husband may not without the consent of his wife agree that the mortgage shall stand security for another debt.[98] Where the mortgage is given as security for a certain debt, the parties may subsequently agree that it shall stand as security for other debts.[99] A verbal agreement is generally held insufficient for that purpose.[1] But when such was the purpose of the mortgage in the beginning, there is no objection that it secures an existing demand and also future advances.[2]

A penalty of twenty per cent. imposed by statute for omitting prompt payment of school money loaned upon mortgage is not a lien under the mortgage, but is imposed upon the borrower only.[3] Under a mortgage to a building association, expressly securing only monthly payments, the payment of fines and other dues to the association is not secured.[4]

§ 361. **Increasing the rate of interest.**—The parties to a mortgage can not, as against subsequent purchasers or incumbrancers, stipulate by an unrecorded agreement for a higher rate of interest than that provided in the mortgage as recorded, nor can they by such means incorporate into the mortgage any additional indebtedness.[5] The interest can not be changed from currency to gold, which is then at a premium.[6] A subsequent mortgagee or purchaser has the right to redeem by paying the amount due according to its terms.[7] But the owner of the equity of redemption may bind himself and charge the

---

[96] Cady v. Burgess, 144 Mich. 523, 108 N. W. 414.

[97] Johnson v. Anderson, 30 Ark. 745; Brooks v. Brooks, 169 Mass. 38, 47 N. E. 448. See also Ladd v. Lookout Mt. Distilling Co., 147 Ala. 173, 40 So. 610.

[98] Mantle v. Dabney, 44 Wash. 193, 87 Pac. 122.

[99] Huntington v. Kneeland, 102 App. Div. 284, 92 N. Y. S. 944, 16 Ann. Cas. (N. Y.) 13.

[1] Levi v. Blackwell, 35 S. Car. 511, 15 S. E. 243; O'Neill v. Bennett, 33 S. Car. 243, 11 S. E. 727; Lindsay v. Garvin, 31 S. Car. 259, 9 S. E. 862.

[2] Carpenter v. Plagge, 192 Ill. 82,

61 N. E. 530; North v. Crowell, 11 N. H. 251. See post § 1078.

[3] Bradley v. Snyder, 14 Ill. 262, 58 Am. Dec. 564.

[4] Hamilton Bldg. Assn. v. Reynolds, 5 Duer. (N. Y.) 671.

[5] Bunker v. Barron, 79 Maine 62. See also Havens v. Jones, 45 Mich. 253, 7 N. W. 818; Smith v. Graham, 34 Mich. 302; Spear v. Hadden, 31 Mich. 265 Burchard v. Frazer, 23 Mich. 224; Bassett v. McDonel, 13 Wis. 444.

[6] Taylor v. Atlantic &c. R. Co. 55 How. Pr. (N. Y.) 275.

[7] Gardner v. Emerson, 40 Ill. 296.

land for the payment of an increased rate of interest by an agreement in writing.[8] There must be, however, a consideration to support his agreement. Future indulgence of the debtor for an indefinite period, his debt being already due, is consideration enough.[9] A stipulation in a mortgage that interest at a higher rate than that reserved upon making the loan shall be paid after a default in payment of the principal or interest is binding and may be enforced.[10]

§ 362. **Redelivery for a new obligation.**—A mortgage which has been satisfied and delivered up to the mortgagor, without being canceled, may be again delivered by him as a valid security for another debt, by agreement of the parties, if there are no intervening rights. The delivery of the security gave it efficacy in the beginning; and if, after having used it for one purpose, the mortgagor redelivers it for another purpose, the redelivery gives it vitality again, except as against intervening interests.[11] The mortgage may not be assigned, however, to a third person as security for a new loan to the mortgagor as against a subsequent mortgagee having no notice of the agreement.[12] Also where a note secured by a mortgage has been paid in full and delivered with the mortgage to the mortgagor it operates as a full satisfaction of the mortgage, and an assignment and delivery of the note and mortgage by the original mortgagee to another creditor of the mortgagor, as a security for debt, under a parol arrangement between all the parties, does not revive the original mortgage or create any valid lien.[13]

§ 363. **How recorded mortgage may be made to secure further sum.**—A mortgage already recorded may be made to secure a further sum, by an indorsement upon the mortgage executed and acknowledged with the usual formalities of a deed, and recorded with a proper reference to the record of the mortgage. This has been done where the mortgage was given to secure an acceptor of drafts, and by such an indorsement it was made to apply in all of its provisions and terms as security for other drafts. The record of the indorsement made a

---

[8] Smith v. Graham, 34 Mich. 302.
[9] Taylor v. Thomas, 61 Ga. 472.
[10] Pawtucket Ins. Co. v. Landers, 5 Kans. App. 623, 47 Pac. 621; Sheldon v. Pruessnor, 52 Kans. 579, 35 Pac. 201. But in Nebraska such a provision is regarded as being in the nature of a penalty and will not be enforced; Connecticut Mut. Ins. Co. v. Westentroff, 58 Nebr. 379, 78 N. W. 724. See post § 1141.

[11] Underhill v. Atwater, 22 N. J. Eq. 16, per Zabriskie Ch. See ante § 338 and post §§ 947, 948, where the subject is more fully considered.
[12] Bogert v. Striker, 148 N. Y. 194, 42 N. E. 582, 51 Am. St. 684.
[13] Bailey v. Rockafellow, 57 Ark. 216, 21 S. W. 227; Thompson v. George, 86 Ky. 311, 9 Ky. L. 588, 5 S. W. 760.

valid extension of the condition of the mortgage as first made and recorded to the further liability incurred by the mortgagee.[14] And it has been held that an oral agreement between the mortgagor and the mortgagee to allow the mortgage to stand as security for an additional sum advanced by the mortgagee to the mortgagor will be enforced in equity where there are no intervening rights of third persons.[15]

II. *Future Advances*

§ **364. In general.**—There has been much diversity of opinion among courts and law-writers on the question of the validity of mortgages to secure future advances, and as to the rights of mortgagees under such mortgages against subsequent purchasers and incumbrancers. Formerly such mortgages were regarded with jealousy, but their validity is now fully recognized and established.[1] And so a deed of trust in the nature of a mortgage may be a valid security for future debts.[2]

Although the record must show the existence of the mortgage in order to avail anything as a notice, yet it is generally conceded that it need not show the exact amount of the incumbrance. But while according to some authorities the limit of these advances should be named, so that an inquirer may know that the incumbrance can not

---

[14] Choteau v. Thompson, 2 Ohio St. 114. See also Sheats v. Scott, 133 Ala. 642, 32 So. 573.

[15] Langerman v. Puritan Dining Room Co., 21 Cal. App. 637, 132 Pac. 617.

[1] Ackerman v. Hunsicker, 85 N. Y. 43, 39 Am. Rep. 641, per An-

drews, J. See also Straeffer v. Rodman, 146 Ky. 1, 141 S. W. 742, Ann. Cas. 1913C, 549; Heal v. Evans Creek Coal &c. Co., 71 Wash. 225, 128 Pac. 211.

[2] Diggs v. Fidelity &c. Co., 112 Md. 50, 75 Atl. 517.

exceed a certain amount,[3] according to others there is no necessity for limiting the amount of the intended advances in any way, if the mortgage shows that future advances are covered by it,[4] and this is true as between the original parties even though the making of such advances is left to the option or discretion of the mortgagee.[5] Generally the amount intended to be advanced need not be stated, provided it can be otherwise ascertained by the description.[6]

But even where a limitation is necessary in order to constitute a continuing security which will not be affected by subsequent conveyances, a recorded mortgage for an unlimited sum is notice to a subsequent incumbrancer as to all sums advanced upon the mortgage before the subsequent lien attaches.[7] Moreover, the record of the subsequent mortgage is no notice to such prior mortgagee that any subsequent lien has attached.[8] The subsequent mortgagee can limit the credit that may be safely given under the mortgage for future advances only by giving the holder of it express notice of his lien, and a notice also that he must make no further advances on the credit of that mortgage.[9] The mortgage will then stand as security for the real equitable claims of the mortgagee, whether they existed at the date of the mortgage or arose afterward, but prior to the receipt of such notice.[10] If such mortgagee is not under any obligation to make advances, and after notice of a subsequent mortgage does make further advances, to the extent of such advances the subsequent mortgagee has the right of precedence.[11] But if such mortgagee is under obligation to make the

---

[3] In re Young's Estate, 3 Md. Ch. 461; Bell v. Fleming, 12 N. J. Eq. 13, 490; Beekman v. Frost, 18 Johns. (N. Y.) 544, 9 Am. Dec. 246. See also Du Bois v. First Nat. Bank, 43 Colo. 400, 96 Pac. 169; Benton-Shingler Co. v. Mills, 13 Ga. App. 632, 79 S. E. 755; Perkins &c. Co. v. Drew (Ky.), 122 S. W. 526.

[4] Lovelace v. Webb, 62 Ala. 271; Tapia v. Demartini, 77 Cal. 383, 19 Pac. 641; Witczinski v. Everman, 51 Miss. 841; Ackerman v. Hunsicker, 85 N. Y. 43, 39 Am. Rep. 641. See also Cazort &c. Co. v. Dunbar, 91 Ark. 400, 121 S. W. 270; Langerman v. Puritan Dining Room Co., 21 Cal. App. 637, 132 Pac. 617; Huntington v. Kneeland, 187 N. Y. 563, 80 N. E. 1111.

[5] Langerman v. Puritan Dining Room Co., 21 Cal. App. 637, 132 Pac. 617.

[6] United States v. Hooe, 3 Cranch (U. S.) 73, 2 L. ed. 370; Crane v. Deming, 7 Conn. 387; Allen v. Lathrop, 46 Ga. 133; Farr v. Doxtater, 29 N. Y. St. 531, 9 N. Y. S. 141.

[7] Freiberg v. Magale, 70 Tex. 116, 7 S. W. 684.

[8] Schmidt v. Zahrndt, 148 Ind. 447, 47 N. E. 335; Robinson v. Williams, 22 N. Y. 380. See post § 371.

[9] Ward v. Cooke, 17 N. J. Eq. 93; McDaniels v. Colvin, 16 Vt. 300, 42 Am. Dec. 512. See post § 371.

[10] Ripley v. Harris, 3 Biss. (U. S.) 199; Buchanan v. International Bank, 78 Ill. 500; Nelson v. Boyce, 7 J. J. Marsh. (Ky.), 401, 23 Am. Dec. 411; Farnum v. Burnett, 21 N. J. Eq. 87; Speer v. Whitfield, 10 N .J. Eq. 107.

[11] Frye v. Bank of Illinois, 11 Ill. 367; Spader v. Lawler, 17 Ohio 371, 49 Am. Dec. 461. This decision was

advances, he is entitled to the security, whatever may be the incumbrances subsequently made upon the property, and whether he has notice of them or not.[12]

§ 365. English and American doctrine compared.—Mortgages to secure future advances have always been sanctioned by the common law. An early case is thus stated in Viner's Abridgement: A mortgages to B for a term of years to secure a certain sum of money already lent to the mortgagor, as also such other sums as should thereafter be lent or advanced to him. Afterward A makes a second mortgage to C for a certain sum, with notice of the first mortgage, and then the first mortgagee, having notice of the second mortgage, lends a further sum. The question was, upon what terms the second mortgagee should be allowed to redeem the first; and Cowper, the Lord Chancellor, held that he should not redeem without paying all that was due, as well the money lent after as that lent before the second mortgage was made; "for it was the folly of the second mortgagee, with notice, to take such a security."[13] This case, however, was critically examined by Lord Chancellor Campbell, before the House of Lords, in the case of Hopkinson v. Rolt,[14] and he declared the representation made by the reporters, that the first mortgagee had notice of the second mortgage, to be without foundation. The doctrine supposed to have been laid down in Gordon v. Graham is declared unsound, and is overruled; and the doctrine in England is therefore settled, that a first mortgagee can not claim the benefit of the security for optional advances made by him after notice of a second mortgage upon the property.[15] This question is examined elsewhere;[16] and these two cases are referred to in this connection as the leading cases in England upon the subject, and as showing that future advances may be secured if the mortgage be properly made for that purpose.[17]

In this country, mortgages made in good faith for the purpose of securing future debts have generally been sustained, both in the early

---

based somewhat upon the effect of the statute of that state relating to mortgages. Ladue v. Detroit &c. R. Co., 13 Mich. 380, 87 Am. Dec. 759.

[12] See post § 372.

[13] Gordon v. Graham, 7 Vin. Abr. 52, pl. 3, 2 Eq. Cas. Abr. 598.

[14] 9 H. L. Cas. 514, 7 Jur. (N. S.) 1209. The English cases are carefully reviewed in Rolt v. Hopkinson, 25 Beav. 461.

[15] The opinion of the court was delivered to this effect by Lords Campbell and Chelmsford; but Lord Cranworth gave a dissenting opinion, to the effect that the law was recently laid down by Lord Cowper, as reported.

[16] See post §§ 368-374.

[17] Burgess v. Eve, L. R. 13 Eq. 450; Daun v. London Brewery Co., L. R. 8 Eq. 155; Menzies v. Lightfoot, L. R. 11 Eq. 459.

and in the recent cases.[18] Such a mortgage is valid even as against · creditors and subsequent purchasers.[19] It does not matter that the

[18] National Bank v. Whitney, 103 U. S. 99, 26 L. ed. 443; Jones v. Guaranty &c. Co., 101 U. S. 622, 25 L. ed. 1030, 2 Fed. 747; Schulze v. Bolting, 8 Biss. (U. S.) 174; Ripley v. Harris, 3 Biss. (U. S.) 199; Shirras v. Caig, 7 Cranch (U. S.) 34, 3 L. ed. 260; United States v. Hooe, 3 Cranch (U. S.) 73, 2 L. ed. 370; Lawrence v. Tucker, 23 How. (U. S.) 14, 16 L. ed. 474; Schuelenburg v. Martin, 1 McCrary (U. S.) 348; Leeds v. Cameron, 3 Sum. (U. S.) 488; London &c. Bank v. Bandmann, 120 Cal. 220, 52 Pac. 583, 65 Am. St. 179, construing Civ. Code, § 2922. Hendon v. Morris, 110 Ala. 106, 20 So. 27; Forsyth v. Preer, 62 Ala. 443; Moore v. Terry, 66 Ark. 393. Where the mortgage was to secure the sum of $100, due at a time fixed "and all other indebtedness which may then be due." Brewster v. Clamfit, 33 Ark. 72; Du Bois v. First Nat. Bank, 43 Colo. 400, 96 Pac. 169; Hubbard v. Savage, 8 Conn. 215; Collins v. Carlile, 13 Ill. 254; Louisville Banking Co. v. Leonard, 90 Ky. 106, 13 S. W. 521; New Orleans Nat. Bkg. Assn. v. Le Breton, 120 U. S. 765, 30 L. ed. 821, 7 Sup. Ct. 772. The La. Civil Code, art. 3292, provides that a mortgage may be given for an obligation which has not yet risen into existence, as when a man grants a mortgage by other way of security for indorsement which another promises to make for him. Bunker v. Barron, 93 Maine 87, 44 Atl. 372; Doyle v. White, 26 Maine 341, 45 Am. Dec. 110; Diggs v. Fidelity &c. Co., 112 Md. 50, 75 Atl. 517; Brooks v. Lester, 36 Md. 65; Taft v. Stoddard, 142 Mass. 545, 8 N. E. 586; Hall v. Tay, 131 Mass. 192; Goddard v. Sawyer, 9 Allen (Mass.) 78; Commercial Bank v. Cunningham, 24 Pick. (Mass.) 270, 35 Am. Dec. 322; Citizens' Sav. Bank v. Kock, 117 Mich. 225, 75 N. W. 458; Drummer v. Smedley, 110 Mich. 466, 68 N. W. 260; Newkirk v. Newkirk, 56 Mich. 525, 23 N. W. 206; Brackett v. Sears, 15 Mich. 244; Madigan v. Mead, 31 Minn. 94, 16 N. W. 539; Foster v. Reynolds, 38· Mo. 553; Reeves v. Evans (N. J. Eq.), 34 Atl. 477; Griffin v. New Jersey Oil Co., 11 N. J. Eq. 49; Ackerman v. Hunsicker, 85 N. Y. 43, 39 Am. Rep. 641; Fassett v. Smith, 23 N. Y. 252; Truscott v. King, 6 N. Y. 147; James v. Morey, 2 Cow. (N. Y.) 246, 292, 14 Am. Dec. 475; Brinckerhoff v. Lansing, 4 Johns. Ch. (N. Y.) 65, 8 Am. Dec. 538; Union Nat. Bank v. Moline, 7 N. Dak. 201, 73 N. W. 527; Hendrix v. Gore, 8 Ore. 406; Farrabee v. McKerrihan, 172 Pa. St. 234, 33 Atl. 583, 51 Am. St. 374; Garber v. Henry, 6 Watts (Pa.) 57; Seaman v. Fleming, 7 Rich. Eq. (S. Car.) 283; Klein v. Glass, 53 Tex. 37; Keyes v. Bump, 59 Vt. 391, 69 Atl. 598; McDaniels v. Colvin, 16 Vt. 300, 42 Am. Dec. 512; Heal v. Evans Creek Coal &c. Co., 71 Wash. 225, 128 Pac. 211; McCarty v. Chalfant, 14 W. Va. 531. See also Straeffer v. Rodman, 146 Ky. 1, 141 S. W. 742, Ann. Cas. 1913C; 549; Perkins &c. Co. v. Drew (Ky.), 122 S. W. 526; Lamm v. Armstrong, 95 Minn. 434, 104 N. W. 304, 111 Am. St. 479; Huntington v. Kneeland, 187 N. Y. 563, 80 N. E. 1111; Merchants' State Bank v. Tufts, 14 N. Dak. 238, 103 N. W. 760, 116 Am. St. 682; Tinkham v. Wright (Tex. Civ. App.), 163 S. W. 615; Openshaw v. Dean (Tex. Civ. App.), 125 S. W. 989; Jones on Chattel Mortgages, §§ 94-98.

[19] Jones v. Guaranty &c. Co., 101 U. S. 622, 25 L. ed. 1030; Shirras v. Caig, 7 Cranch (U. S.) 34, 3 L. ed. 260; United States v. Hooe, 3 Cranch (U. S.) 73, 2 L. ed. 370; Tully v. Harloe, 35 Cal. 302, 95 Am. Dec. 102; Boswell v. Goodwin, 31 Conn. 74, 81 Am. Dec. 169; Collins v. Carlisle, 13 Ill. 254; Commercial Bank v. Cunningham, 24 Pick. (Mass.) 270, 35 Am. Dec. 322; Summers v. Roos, 42 Miss. 749, 2 Am. Rep. 653; Robinson v. Williams, 22 N. Y. 380; Kramer v. Farmers' &c. Bank, 15 Ohio 253; Nicklin v. Betts Spring Co., 11 Ore. 406, 5 Pac. 51, 50 Am. Rep. 477; McDaniels v. Colvin, 16 Vt. 300, 42 Am. Dec. 512.

future advances are to be made to a third person, or for his benefit at the request of the mortgagor.[20] Neither is the validity of a mortgage to secure future advances affected by the fact that the advances are to be made in materials for building instead of money.[21] A mortgage is not fraudulent because it is given for a larger amount than the actual loan made at the time, with a view to its covering future loans up to the amount of the mortgage.[22]

§ 366. **Statutory requirements.**—In some states there are statutory provisions, requiring the debt secured to be described in the mortgage, which restrict the right to make mortgages for future advances. Thus, in Maryland it is provided by statute that no mortgage or deed in the nature of a mortgage, shall be a lien or charge on any estate or property for any other or different principal sum or sums of money than appear on the face of the mortgage, and are specified and recited in it, and particularly mentioned and expressed to be secured thereby at the time of executing it; and further, that no mortgage, or deed in the nature of a mortgage, shall be a lien or charge for any sum or sums of money to be loaned or advanced after the same is executed, except from the time said loan or advance is actually made; and that no mortgage to secure such future loans or advances shall be valid unless the amount or amounts of the same, and the times when they are to be made, shall be specifically stated in said mortgages.[23] A mortgage to secure future advances not to exceed a limited amount may be enforced to the amount of the advances made upon it within that limit, although such advances were made after the mortgagee had received notice of a junior incumbrance.[24] The statute requiring the amount to be stated is a modification of the common law, under which the mortgage would be equally valid without such limitation.

In New Hampshire it is provided that no conveyance in writing of

---

[20] Maffitt v. Rynd, 69 Pa. St. 380, and cases cited.

[21] Tapia v. Demartini, 77 Cal. 383, 19 Pac. 641; Doyle v. White, 26 Maine 341, 45 Am. Dec. 110; Brooks v. Lester, 36 Md. 65. See also Miller v. Ward (Maine), 88 Atl. 400.

[22] Allen v. Fuget, 42 Kans. 672, 22 Pac. 725.

[23] Ann. Code 1911, art. 66, § 2, p. 1518. This restriction does not apply to mortgages to indemnify the mortgagee against loss from being indorser or security, nor to any mortgage given by brewers to malt-sters to secure the payment to the latter of debts contracted by the former for malt and other material used in the making of malt liquors.

This amendment and addition to the Code does not apply to Anne Arundel, Baltimore, St. Mary's and Prince George's counties.

See also Baltimore High Grade Brick Co. v. Amos, 95 Md. 571, 52 Atl. 582, 53 Atl. 148, for an extended discussion of this statement. And see Maus v. McKellip, 38 Md. 231.

[24] Wilson v. Russell, 13 Md. 494, 71 Am. Dec. 645.

any lands shall be defeated, or any estate incumbered by any agreement, unless it is inserted in the condition of the conveyance and made a part thereof, stating the sum of money to be secured, or other thing to be performed.[25]   And it is also provided that no estate conveyed in mortgage shall be holden by the mortgagee for the payment of any sum of money, or the performance of any other thing, the obligation or liability to the payment or performance of which arises, is made, or contracted after the execution and delivery of such mortgage.[26] It is held, however, that a mortgage executed in good faith, conditioned to secure a definite sum, part of the consideration of which is the agreement of the mortgagee to pay certain sums to and for the use of the mortgagor, and to perform certain labor for the mortgagor, is neither prohibited nor fraudulent as against the creditors of the mortgagor.[27] But the court did not wish to be understood as holding that a mortgage given to secure an absolute note, intended as a security for advances thereafter to be made, would be valid if at the time of the execution of the mortgage the amount of the advances was not agreed upon, or the mortgagee was under no obligation to make them. Under this statute the mortgage may be void as to the part of the consideration which is altogether future, but valid for the part which was a debt at the time the mortgage was executed.[28]

In Georgia a mortgage may be made to secure future advances not limited in amount,[29] although the statute of the state provides that

[25] A mortgage to secure the mortgagee from loss on account of an indorsement of the mortgagor's note is not invalid because made to secure a debt "contracted after the execution and delivery of the mortgage." Pub. Stats. of New Hampshire, 1901, ch. 138, § 3. A mortgage executed as security for an indorsement which was not made till the following day is not given to secure future advances. It also secures renewals of the paper originally indorsed. Stavers v. Philbrick, 68 N. H. 379, 36 Atl. 16. See also Fessenden v. Taft, 65 N. H. 39, 17 Atl. 713; Weed v. Barker, 35 N. H. 386.

[26] A mortgage made in part to secure a fixed sum of money agreed to be paid by the mortgagee on the happening of a definite contingency is not within this prohibition. Fessenden v. Taft, 65 N. H. 39, 17 Atl. 713. The assignment of a mortgage given for an existing debt, as security for future advances, is not within the prohibition of the statute. Lime Rock Nat. Bank v. Mowry, 68 N. H. 598, 22 Atl. 555. Gen. Stat. ch. 122, §§ 2, 3; Gen. Laws 1878, ch. 136, §§ 2, 3; Pub. Stats. 1901, ch. 139, §§ 2, 3.

[27] Stearns v. Bennett, 48 N. H. 400. A mortgage conditioned to secure a note the consideration of a part of which is a credit of an agreed sum by the mortgagee, on his books, to the mortgagor, is not prohibited. Abbot v. Thompson, 58 N. H. 255.

[28] Leeds v. Cameron, 3 Sumn. (U. S.) 488; Johnson v. Richardson, 38 N. H. 353; New Hampshire Bank v. Willard, 10 N. H. 210.

[29] Allen v. Lathrop, 46 Ga. 133. The debt was described as advances in supplies and money for the purpose of carrying on the farm for the year 1870.

a mortgage shall "specify the debt to secure which it is given."[30] So long as the means for determining the amount of the debt are pointed out, it is immaterial that the amount is not stated, or is from its very nature indefinite.[31] But it has been held that a mortgage reciting that it was given for a note and "such future advances" as may be made during a given year is valid only as security for the note.[32]

In construing the California Civil Code, section 2922, providing that "a mortgage can be created, renewed or extended only by writing executed with the formalities required in the case of a grant to real property" the court held that the term "extended" refers to the broadening of the security to cover additional advances, and does not apply to a mortgage securing a present debt and advances for which new notes afterward were given.[33]

§ 367. **Degree of certainty requisite in describing future liabilities.** —Future liabilities intended to be secured should be described with reasonable certainty. If the nature and amount of the incumbrance is so described that it may be ascertained by the exercise of ordinary discretion and diligence, this is all that is required.[34] On this principle a mortgage for the payment of such sums of money as the mortgagee might advance, in pursuance of an agreement mentioned in the condition of a certain bond given by the mortgagee to the mortgagor of even date, contains reasonable notice of the incumbrance.[35]

A mortgage securing future advances, although its purpose does not appear upon its face, is good if the amount of the advances is within the sum named as the amount secured.[36] A mortgage for two hundred dollars was executed as a basis of credit to that extent for goods which

[30] Civ. Code 1910, § 3257.

[31] Allen v. Lathrop, 46 Ga. 133.

[32] Benton-Shingler Co. v. Mills, 13 Ga. App. 632, 79 S. E. 755.

[33] London &c. Bank v. Bandmann, 120 Cal. 220, 52 Pac. 583, 65 Am. St. 179.

[34] Shirras v. Caig, 7 Cranch (U. S.) 34, 3 L. ed. 260; United States v. Hooe, 3 Cranch (U. S.) 73, 2 L. ed. 370; United States v. Sturges, 1 Paine (U. S.) 525; Beach v. Osborne, 74 Conn. 405, 50 Atl. 1019, 1118; Bouton v. Doty, 69 Conn. 531, 37 Atl. 1064; Hubbard v. Savage, 8 Conn. 215. This case did away with the doubt with which such mortgages were spoken of in the earlier cases of Pettibone v. Griswold, 4 Conn. 158, 10 Am. Dec. 106; Shepard v. Shepard, 7 Conn. 387; Stoughton v. Pasco, 5 Conn. 442. See also Collier v. Faulk, 69 Ala. 58; Brewster v. Clamfit, 33 Ark. 72; Crane v. Deming, 7 Conn. 387; First Nat. Bank v. Morsell, 1 MacArth. (D. C.) 155; Allen v. Lathrop, 46 Ga. 133; Louisville Banking Co. v. Leonard, 90 Ky. 106, 13 S. W. 521; Farr v. Doxtater, 29 N. Y. St. 531, 9 N. Y. S. 141.

[35] Crane v. Deming, 7 Conn. 38.

[36] Du Bois v. First Nat. Bank, 43 Colo. 400, 96 Pac. 169; Dummer v. Smedley, 110 Mich. 466, 68 N. W. 260, 38 L. R. A. 490; Reeves v. Evans (N. J. Eq.), 34 Atl. 477.

the mortgagee might sell to the mortgagor, with the understanding that the mortgagor should make such payments that the balance against him should at no time exceed that amount. An account was opened and continued for some years. It was held that the condition of the mortgage was not exceptionable as not disclosing with sufficient certainty the nature and extent of the incumbrance.[37] Where the condition of a deed was, that "in case the grantor pays to the grantee the sum of one thousand six hundred dollars, with interest, on or before the first of January, 1843, then this deed shall be void and of no effect, otherwise to remain in full force," and the grantor then owed the grantee about one thousand one hundred dollars, and it was agreed that the grantee should advance him a further sum to make up the

[37] Mix v. Cowles, 20 Conn. 420. The Supreme Court of the United States in Townsend v. Todd, 91 U. S. 452, 23 L. ed. 413, in a case arising in Connecticut, followed the decisions of that state upon this point. After referring to the earlier decisions of that state, the court said: "In Mix v. Cowles, 20 Conn. 420, and Potter v. Holden, 31 Conn. 385, the Supreme Court of that state held to its principles in words, but in effect considerably relaxed the rule. If those cases stood alone, or if there was no later case, there would be some room for doubt what the rule should be. The somewhat recent case, however, of Bramhall v. Flood, 41 Conn. 72, fully and distinctly reasserts the rule laid down in the earlier cases. It is there held that the mortgage must truly describe the debt intended to be secured, and that it is not sufficient that the debt be of such a character that it might have been secured by the mortgage had it been truly described.. In most of the states a mortgage like the one before us, reciting a specific indebtedness, but given in fact to secure advances or indorsements thereafter to be made, is a valid security, and would be good to secure the $6,000 actually advanced before other incumbrances were placed upon the property."

Where the mortgagor, being insolvent, made a mortgage to secure a note of $2,600 to a creditor to whom he was indebted in the sum of $1,500, and who was surety for him in the sum of $1,100 more, the mortgage was held a valid security for the $1,500, but, as against the mortgagor's creditors, not for the part which was intended to indemnify the mortgagee against his liabilities as surety, because that is a claim not described in the mortgage; and the real nature of the transaction should appear in the condition of the mortgage. Sanford v. Wheeler, 13 Conn. 165, 33 Am. Dec. 389.

On this principle the same court held, in North v. Belden, 13 Conn. 376, 35 Am. Dec. 83, that a mortgage to secure a note of $500, when in fact the mortgage was intended as security for such indorsements as the mortgagee might make for the mortgagor to that amount, and which were actually made and the notes paid by the mortgagee, was not valid against subsequent incumbrances. And so a condition to pay all notes which the mortgagee might indorse or give for the mortgagor, and all receipts which the mortgagee might hold against the mortgagor, was held to be too indefinite and uncertain to make the mortgage valid against subsequent parties in interest.

There is nothing to limit the liability, or to give others the means of finding out the extent of it. Pettibone v. Griswold, 4 Conn. 158, 10 Am. Dec. 106.

These Connecticut cases, however, are without general support elsewhere.

full amount of the mortgage, it was held that the condition sufficiently described the nature and character of the indebtedness to be secured to constitute a valid security against subsequent incumbrances.[38]

A mortgage conditioned for the payment of all sums due and to become due is sufficiently certain.[39] And this is true although the description given for the main indebtedness be insufficient.[40] A mortgage to "secure all past indebtedness due and owing" from the mortgagor to the mortgagee is sufficiently certain.[41] A mortgage conditioned to pay the mortgagee "what I may owe him on book" was construed to refer to future accruing accounts, upon its appearing that there was no account subsisting between the parties when the mortgage was given.[42] Upon its appearing that the mortgage was given in part to cover future advances, the burden is upon the mortgagee to show what advances have been made.[43]

But it is not to be inferred that it is generally essential that the amount of the intended advances should be stated, or in any way limited. On the contrary, by the weight of authority, mortgages to secure indefinite future advances are valid.[44] It is necessary, however, that the debt reasonably conform to the particulars of the description, in order to be covered by the mortgage.[45]

A mortgage for future advances may be made a continuing security for advances made at any time, so that when advances have been made to the amount limited by the mortgage, and these are paid either wholly or in part, the mortgage will continue as a security for new advances within the limit named.[46] A mortgage given to secure pay-

---

[38] Bacon v. Brown, 19 Conn. 29.

[39] Steckel v. Standley, 107 Iowa 694, 77 N. W. 489; Michigan Insurance Co. v. Brown, 11 Mich. 266. See also Bowen v. Ratcliff, 140 Ind. 393, 39 N. E. 860, 49 Am. St. 203.

[40] Bowen v. Ratcliff, 140 Ind. 393, 39 N. E. 860, 49 Am. St. 203.

[41] Machette v. Wanless, 1 Colo. 225. See also Farabee v. McKerrihan, 172 Pa. St. 234, 33 Atl. 583, 51 Am. St. 734.

[42] McDaniels v. Colvin, 16 Vt. 300, 42 Am. Dec. 512.

[43] Fisher v. Otis, 3 Pin. (Wis.) 78, 3 Chand. 83.

[44] Brewster v. Clamfit, 33 Ark. 72; Jarratt v. McDaniel, 32 Ark. 598. See also Merrills v. Swift, 18 Conn. 257, 46 Am. Dec. 315; Citizens' Sav. Bank v. Kock, 117 Mich. 118, 75 N. W. 444; Barker v. Barker, 62 N. H. 366; Farr v. Doxtater, 29 N. Y.

St. 531, 9 N. Y. S. 141; Keyes v. Bump, 59 Vt. 391, 9 Atl. 598. See also Seymour v. Darrow, 31 Vt. 122. See post §§ 373–375.

[45] Moran v. Gardemeyer, 82 Cal. 96, 23 Pac. 6; Walker v. Rand, 131 Ill. 27, 22 N. E. 1006; Babcock v. Lisk, 57 Ill. 327; Storms v. Storms, 3 Bush (Ky.) 77; Doyle v. White, 26 Maine 341, 45 Am. Dec. 110; Hall v. Tufts, 18 Pick. (Mass.) 455; Bank of Buffalo v. Thompson, 121 N. Y. 280, 24 N. E. 473; Walker v. Paine, 31 Barb. (N. Y.) 213.

[46] Douglass v. Reynolds, 7 Pet. (U. S.) 113, 8 L. ed. 626; Shirras v. Caig, 7 Cranch (U. S.) 34, 3 L. ed. 260; United States v. Hooe, 3 Cranch (U. S.) 73, 2 L. ed. 370; Lawrence v. Tucker, 23 How. (U. S.) 14, 16 L. ed. 474; Courier-Journal Job Printing Co. v. Schaeffer-Meyer Brew. Co., 101 Fed. 699;

ment for goods, which the mortgagee might thereafter sell to the mortgagor, gives the mortgagee an implied authority to continue to sell goods to the mortgagor under the security of the mortgage, as in the case of a continuing guaranty; but the authority is revoked by the death of the mortgagor.[47] A mortgage to secure future advances is valid for advances not exceeding the sum specified, though by mistake the mortgage recites that it is for a debt already accrued.[48]

§ 367a. **Parol evidence to identify future advances.**—Parol evidence is admissible to identify the future advances intended to be secured by a mortgage. Though the mortgage on its face is for the payment of a specific sum of money, parol evidence is admissible to show that it was really intended to secure future advances to be made from time to time.[49] Where the description is not sufficiently particular to make the identification of the advances sure, parol evidence is admissible to connect such advances with the mortgage, and supply the deficiencies of the description. The amount as well as the purpose of the security may be thus established.[50]

A mortgage made by a married woman as security for sales of goods to be made by the mortgagee to her husband may be shown by parol evidence to have been intended to secure sales made to the husband by a firm of which the mortgagee was a member.[51]

§ 368. **Advances made after notice of subsequent liens.**—The early English decisions, and some authorities in this country, hold that a mortgage for future advances is a first lien on the property as to all advances secured by the mortgage, no matter when made, and this without reference to the question whether the mortgagee was obligated by contract to make further advances or whether he knew of the in-

Brown v. Kiefer, 71 N. Y. 610; Robinson v. Williams, 22 N. Y. 380; Kramer v. Trustees, 15 Ohio 253; Shores v. Doherty, 65 Wis. 153, 26 N. W. 577; Jones on Chattel Mortgages, § 94.

[47] Hyland v. Habich, 150 Mass. 112, 22 N. E. 765, 15 Am. St. 174.

[48] Perkins &c. Co. v. Drew (Ky.), 122 S. W. 526.

[49] Shirras v. Caig, 7 Cranch (U. S.) 34, 3 L. ed. 260; Wilkerson v. Tillman, 66 Ala. 532; Louisville Banking Co. v. Leonard, 90 Ky. 106, 13 S. W. 521; McKinster v. Babcock, 26 N. Y. 378. See also Barnhart v. Edwards, 115 Cal. xvii, 47 Pac. 251; Du Bois v. First Nat. Bank, 43 Colo. 400, 96 Pac. 169. See ante § 352.

[50] Du Bois v. First Nat. Bank, 43 Colo. 400, 96 Pac. 169; Hester v. Gairdner, 128 Ga. 531, 58 S. E. 165; Ackerman v. Hunsicker, 85 N. Y. 43, 39 Am. Rep. 621; Bank of Utica v. Finch, 3 Barb. Ch. (N. Y.) 293, 49 Am. Dec. 175; Craig v. Tappin, 2 Sandf. Ch. (N. Y.) 78.

[51] Hall v. Tay, 131 Mass. 192, Endicott, J., said: "We can see no reason why, in the absence of any specific statement in the mortgage as to the character of the advances, parol evidence may not be intro-

ferior lien.[52] But the later English decisions and a majority of the cases in this country adhere to the rule that a subsequent lien will take precedence over the mortgage as to all advances made after the mortgagee had notice of the prior incumbrance.[53] As will be presently noticed, this general proposition is subject to qualifications; but whenever a subsequent mortgage has precedence, as a general rule a subsequent judgment has precedence under like circumstances;[54] but a mortgage for future unlimited advances is good against all advances made before recovery of the judgment.[55]

A mortgage given to secure advances has priority over a subsequent judgment against the mortgagor as to all advances made before the mortgagee has notice of the judgment and as to subsequent renewal notes given for such advances. In such a case verbal notice of the existence of the judgment is sufficient.[56]

Advances covered by a mortgage have preference over the claims of junior incumbrancers, who have become such with notice of an agreement under the mortgage for the advances.[57] Mortgages to secure future advances or liabilities are valid and fixed securities against subsequent purchasers, or attaching creditors of the mortgagor, although the advances are made or the liabilities assumed after the record of such later deeds or attachments; and although it is optional with the

---

duced to identify and prove what advances were in fact intended by the parties. It is competent for the purpose of showing the actual consideration. There certainly would be no objection to it if the mortgage had been made in the same terms to the firm by name. And if made to one of the firm for the benefit of the firm, and in consequence thereof the advances were made by the firm, evidence of the actual advances made by the firm would be competent."

[52] Rowan v. Sharp's Rifle Mfg. Co., 29 Conn. 282; Brinkmeyer v. Helbling, 57 Ind. 435; Brinkmeyer v. Browneller, 55 Ind. 487; Wilson v. Russell, 13 Md. 494, 71 Am. Dec. 645; Witczinski v. Everman, 51 Miss. 841; Gordon v. Graham, 7 Vin. Abr. 52, 2 Eq. Cas. Abr. 598.

[53] Frye v. Bank of Illinois, 11 Ill. 367; Hughes v. Worley, 1 Bibb (Ky.) 200; Bell v. Fleming, 12 N. J. Eq. 13, 490; Hall v. Crouse, 13 Hun. (N. Y.) 557; Todd v. Outlaw, 79 N. Car. 235; Spader v. Lawler,

17 Ohio 371, 49 Am. Dec. 461. See also Tapia v. Demartini, 77 Cal. 383, 11 Am. St. 288, 19 Pac. 641; Boswell v. Goodwin, 31 Conn. 74; Central Trust Co. v. Continental Iron Works, 51 N. J. Eq. 605, 28 Atl. 595, 40 Am. St. 539; Griffin v. New Jersey Oil Co., 11 N. J. Eq. 49; Ackerman v. Hunsicker, 85 N. Y. 43, 39 Am. Rep. 621; Reynolds v. Webster, 71 Hun 378, 55 N. Y. St. 6, 24 N. Y. S. 1133; Wisconsin Planing Mill Co. v. Schuda, 72 Wis. 277, 39 N. W. 558.

[54] Brinkerhoff v. Marvin, 5 Johns. Ch. (N. Y.) 320; Goodhue v. Berrien, 2 Sandf. Ch. (N. Y.) 630; Yelverton v. Shelden, 2 Sandf. Ch. (N. Y.) 481; Craig v. Tappin, 2 Sandf. Ch. (N. Y.) 78.

[55] Robinson v. Williams, 22 N. Y. 380.

[56] Schmidt v. Hedden (N. J. Eq.), 38 Atl. 843.

[57] Truscott v. King, 6 N. Y. 147; Kramer v. Farmers' &c. Bank, 15 Ohio 253.

mortgagee whether he will make such advancements or assume such liabilities or not, if they are made or assumed in good faith, and without notice of any subsequent intervening incumbrance.[58]

§ 369. **Theory where mortgagee is not bound to make advancements.**—But where the mortgagee is not bound to make the advances or assume the liabilities, and he has actual notice of a later incumbrance upon the property for an existing debt or liability, such later incumbrance will take precedence of the mortgage as to all advances made after such notice.[59] Whether constructive notice by the record of the later incumbrance should have the same effect as actual notice, and whether the option of the mortgagee to make the advances should operate to give the mortgage effect as to subsequent incumbrances only from the time the advances are in fact made, are questions upon which the cases are not agreed.[60] There are cases which hold that a mortgagee is not affected with knowledge of a subsequent mortgage or other incumbrance, within the rule, by the recording of such mortgage, but that he may with safety make advances until he has actual knowledge of such subsequent incumbrance.[61] And there are other decisions to the effect that, even though advances are made with knowledge of an incumbrance accruing since the date of the mortgage in favor of third persons, they take precedence thereof, provided the mak-

[58] Shirras v. Caig, 7 Cranch (U. S.) 34, 3 L. ed. 260; Conard v. Atlantic Ins. Co., 1 Peters (U. S.) 386, 7 L. ed. 189; Crane v. Deming, 7 Conn. 387; Schmidt v. Zahrndt, 148 Ind. 447, 47 N. E. 335; Anderson v. Liston, 69 Minn. 82, 72 N. W. 52; Williams v. Gilbert, 37 N. J. Eq. 84; Sayre v. Hewes, 32 N. J. Eq. 652; Ward v. Cook, 17 N. J. Eq. 99; Truscott v. King, 6 Barb. (N. Y.) 346; Union Nat. Bank v. Milburn &c. Co., 7 N. Dak. 201, 73 N. W. 527; McDaniels v. Colvin, 16 Vt. 300, 42 Am. Dec. 512.

[59] Ripley v. Harris, 3 Biss. (U. S.) 199; Tapia v. Demartini, 77 Cal. 383, 19 Pac. 641, 11 Am. St. 288; Boswell v. Goodwin, 31 Conn. 74, 81 Am. Dec. 169; Schmidt v. Zahrndt, 148 Ind. 447, 47 N. E. 335; Brinkmeyer v. Browneller, 55 Ind. 487, 4 Cent. L. J. 370; Ladue v. Detroit &c. R. Co., 13 Mich. 380 and cases cited; Schmidt v. Hedden (N. J. Eq.), 38 Atl. 843; Omaha Coal C. &c.

Co. v. Suess, 54 Nebr. 379, 74 N. W. 620; Williams v. Gilbert, 37 N. J. Eq. 86; Sayre v. Hewes, 32 N. J. Eq. 652; Ackerman v. Hunsicker, 85 N. Y. 43, 39 Am. Rep. 621; Union Nat. Bank v. Milburn &c. Co., 7 N. Dak. 201, 73 N. W. 527; National Bank v. Gunhouse, 17 S. Car. 489; Seaman v. Fleming, 7 Rich. Eq. (S. Car.) 283; McDaniels v. Colvin, 16 Vt. 300, 42 Am. Dec. 512; Home Sav. &c. Assn. v. Burton, 20 Wash. 688, 56 Pac. 940.

[60] See post § 372.

[61] Savings &c. Soc. v. Burnett, 106 Cal. 514, 39 Pac. 922; Frye v. Bank of Illinois, 11 Ill. 367; Nelson v. Boyce, 7 J. J. Marsh. (Ky.) 401, 23 Am. Dec. 411; Ward v. Cooke, 17 N. J. Eq. 93; Ackerman v. Hunsicker, 85 N. Y. 43, 39 Am. Rep. 621; Union Nat. Bank v. Milburn &c. Co., 7 N. Dak. 201, 73 N. W. 527; McDaniels v. Colvin, 16 Vt. 300, 42 Am. Dec. 512.

ing of such advances was not optional with the mortgagee, but he was bound by contract to make them.[62]

Where, however, by the terms of the mortgage the advances are to be made within a limited time, it is a valid security for only those liabilities which arise within that time.[63] A mortgage was made to secure the mortgagee for his liability as indorser of such notes as the mortgagor might desire him to indorse within a certain time and amount, and at his option to do so. A second mortgage in similar terms was made to another indorser. It was held that the first mortgagee, for such indorsements as he made after actual notice of the incumbrance of the second mortgage, and of the indorsements made under the security of it, should be postponed to such claims under the second mortgage.[64] The principle of the decision is, that the mortgagee not being bound by his contract to make the indorsements or future advances, the equity of a junior incumbrancer for an existing debt, or of an attaching creditor, will intervene and take precedence of any advances made or liabilities incurred after actual notice of the subsequent lien. Such junior incumbrancer or creditor acquires a lien upon the property as it then is, and as it is optional with the prior mortgagee whether he will advance or indorse any further, he is not allowed knowingly to prejudice the rights of subsequent incumbrancers, or destroy their lien, by adding voluntarily to his own incumbrance. They have an equity superior to his right to make further advances.

§ 370. **Mortgage for obligatory advances.**—A mortgage for obligatory advances is a lien from its execution. If by the terms of the mortgage an obligation is imposed upon the mortgagee to make the advances, the mortgage will remain security for all the advances he is required to make, although other incumbrances may be put upon the property before they are made, and he has knowledge of such incumbrances.[65] Thus, where a railroad company made a mortgage to a trus-

---

[62] Ripley v. Harris, 3 Biss. (U. S.) 199, Fed. Cas. No. 11853; Boswell v. Goodwin, 31 Conn. 74; Brinkmeyer v. Browneller, 55 Ind. 487; Heintze v. Bentley, 34 N. J. Eq. 562.

[63] Miller v. Whittier, 36 Maine 577; Burt v. Gamble, 98 Mich. 402, 57 N. W. 261. Compare Bryce v. Massey, 35 S. Car. 127, 14 S. E. 768.

[64] Boswell v. Goodwin, 31 Conn. 74.

[65] Lovelace v. Webb, 62 Ala. 271;

Boswell v. Goodwin, 31 Conn. 74, 81 Am. Dec. 169; Rowan v. Sharp's Rifle Mfg. Co., 29 Conn. 282; Crane v. Deming, 7 Conn. 387; Richards v. Waldron, 20 D. C. 585; Schmidt v. Zahrndt, 148 Ind. 447, 47 N. E. 335; Brinkmeyer v. Helbling, 57 Ind. 435; Brinkmeyer v. Browneller, 55 Ind. 487; Wilson v. Russell, 13 Md. 494, 71 Am. Dec. 645; Commercial Bank v. Cunningham, 24 Pick. (Mass.) 270, 35 Am. Dec. 322; Griffin v. Burtnett, 4 Edw. Ch. (N. Y.) 673; Ackerman v. Hunsicker,

tee upon all its property then owned, or afterward to be acquired, to secure bonds which the company had agreed to issue to a contractor
in part payment for the building of its road, it was held that the
mortgage took precedence of a lien for material afterward furnished
the company and used upon the road, although the advances were made
after notice of the materialman's claim of a lien.[66] In such case the
mortgagee's lien as to all the advances made by him will be superior
to subsequent liens, whether the subsequent liens may have attached
either before or after such advances were made, and without regard
to whether the mortgagee had notice or not of the existence of such
subsequent incumbrances, either before or after making future advances.

Upon a first mortgage to secure a building loan of twenty thousand
dollars a bank advanced fifteen thousand dollars and retained five
thousand dollars, under an agreement with the mortgagor that the
latter sum should not be paid "until the said building shall be in such
progress to completion that the mortgagee shall deem it safe to advance said balance." A second mortgagee acquired the equity in the
property by foreclosure, and brought a bill to redeem from the first
mortgage. The bank had paid out the whole of the five thousand dollars retained by it upon orders from the mortgagor, leaving the
amount of four hundred and fifty dollars due to it for interest. It
was contended by the second mortgagee that the bank ought to have
applied the amount of four hundred and fifty dollars to the payment
of this interest from the five thousand dollars retained by it, and could
not require that sum to be paid by the second mortgagee in redeeming
from the bank's mortgage. It was held that the bank could not be
compelled to make such set-off.[67]

Where a mortgage was made to secure advances for improving the

21 Hun (N. Y.) 56, 85 N. Y. 43, 39
Am. Rep. 621; Moroney's Appeal,
24 Pa. St. 372; Lyle v. Ducomb, 5
Binn. (Pa.) 585; Nelson v. Iowa
Eastern R. Co., 8 Am. Railroad Rep.
82. See also Witczinski v. Everman, 51 Miss. 841.

[66] Nelson v. Iowa Eastern R. Co.,
8 Am. Railroad Rep. 82.

[67] Tillinghast v. North End Savings Bank, 178 Mass. 458, 459, 59
N. E. 1016. Mr. Justice Morton
said: "The case is not, therefore,
a case for the application of the
rule that a prior incumbrancer having two or more securities for his
debt will be compelled to resort
first to that on which the subsequent incumbrancer has no lien.
The case relates rather to the application of the proceeds of the
mortgage loan itself. What the effect, if any, would have been if the
second mortgagee upon taking their
mortgage had notified the bank of
that fact, and had notified it not
to pay over to the mortgagor the
$5,000 or any part thereof, or if
they had given such notice to the
bank immediately upon the foreclosure, we need not consider, as
no such notice was given. No doubt

premises, an advancement made after a sale of the property under execution was held superior to the purchaser's title.[68]

§ 371. **Hopkinson v. Rolt.**[69]—The question in this case was accurately and tersely stated by Lord Chancellor Chelmsford in the judgment appealed from: "A prior mortgage for present and future advances; a subsequent mortgage of the same description; each mortgagee has notice of the other's deeds; advances are made by the prior mortgagee after the date of the subsequent mortgage, and with full knowledge of it: is the prior mortgagee entitled to priority for these advances over the antecedent advance made by the subsequent mortgagee?" In Gordon v. Graham[70] this question was answered affirmatively; but the House of Lords overruled this case, and answered the question in the negative. Lord Chancellor Campbell forcibly presents the argument for this view of the question.[71] Some American authori-

---

the bank could have offset the $450 against the interest due it if the mortgagor had agreed that it might. Whether it could have done so if they did not agree, it is not necessary to decide."

[68] Rowan v. Sharp's Rifle Mfg. Co., 29 Conn. 282; Gerrity v. Wareham Sav. Bank, 202 Mass. 214, 88 N. E. 1084.

[69] 9 H. L. C. 514.

[70] This decision had previously been questioned by Mr. Coventry, in a note to Powell on Mtg. 534, note (e), and by Lord St. Leonards, 2 Dru. & War. 431, 6 H. L. C. 589. See ante § 365.

[71] Hopkinson v. Rolt, 9 H. L. C. 514. "The first mortgagee is secure as to past advances, and he is not under any obligation to make any further advances. He has only to hold his hand when asked for a further loan. Knowing the extent of the second mortgage, he may calculate that the hereditaments mortgaged are an ample security to the mortgagees; and if he doubts this, he closes his account with the mortgagor, and looks out for a better security. The benefit of the first mortgage is only lessened by the amount of any interest which the mortgagor afterwards conveys to another, consistent with the rights of the first mortgagee. Thus far the mortgagor is entitled to do what he pleases with his own. The consequence certainly is, that after executing such a mortgage as we are considering, the mortgagor, by executing another such mortgage, and giving notice of it to the first mortgagee, may at any time give a preference to the second mortgagee as to subsequent advances, and, as to such advances, reduce the first mortgagee to the rank of puisne incumbrancer. But the first mortgagee will have no reason to complain, knowing that this is his true position, if he chooses voluntarily to make further advances to the mortgagor. The second mortgagee can not be charged with any fraud upon the first mortgagee, in making the advances, with notice of the first mortgage; for, by the hypothesis, each has notice of the security of the other, and the first mortgagee is left in full possession of his option to make or refuse further advances, as he may deem it prudent. The hardship upon bankers from this view of the subject at once vanishes when we consider that the security of the first mortgage is not impaired without notice of a second, and that, when this notice comes, the bankers have only to consider, as they do, as often as they discount a bill of exchange, what is the credit of their customer, and whether the proposed transaction is likely to lead to profit or to loss."

ties, however, lean toward the rule laid down in the case of Gordon v. Graham.[72]

§ 372. Notice of subsequent liens depending on the registry acts only.—A prior mortgagee is affected only by actual notice of a subsequent mortgage, and not by constructive notice from the recording of the second mortgage, and for all advances made by such mortgagee before receiving such notice of a subsequent incumbrance his mortgage is a valid security. Such, it is conceived, is the rule supported by reason and the weight of authority.[73] These authorities seem to proceed upon the theory that the mortgage as against subsequent incumbrances becomes a lien for the whole sum advanced from the time of its execution and record, and not from each separate amount advanced from the time of such advancement.

Where a person having mortgaged land to secure a present loan, and also future advances, afterward declared a homestead upon it, and subsequently obtained further advances without disclosing the fact that he had declared a homestead, the mortgagee was protected as to such advances made on the faith of the security.[74] The recording of the declaration is not notice to the prior mortgagee. Nothing short of actual notice to the mortgagee of such declaration would affect him. It is elsewhere observed that the recording acts give notice to subsequent purchasers and incumbrancers, and do not affect those whose rights are already fixed by the previous record of their own deeds.[75]

---

[72] 7 Vin. Abr. 52, pl. 3, 2 Eq Cas. Abr. 598; Brinkmeyer v. Helbling, 57 Ind. 435; Brinkmeyer v. Browneller, 55 Ind. 487; Wilson v. Russell, 13 Md. 494, 71 Am. Dec. 640; Witcziniski v. Everman, 51 Miss. 841.

[73] Tapia v. Demartini, 77 Cal. 383, 19 Pac. 641, 11 Am. St. 288; Rowan v. Sharp's Rifle Mfg. Co., 29 Conn. 282 (in the latter case, however, the advances were obligatory); Schmidt v. Zahrndt, 148 Ind. 447, 47 N. E. 335; Brinkmeyer v. Browneller, 55 Ind. 487; Nelson v. Boyce, 7 J. J. Marsh. (Ky.) 401, 23 Am. Dec. 411; Bunker v. Barron, 93 Maine 87, 44 Atl. 372; Wilson v. Russell, 13 Md. 494, 71 Am. Dec. 645; Central Trust Co. v. Continental Iron Works, 51 N. J. Eq. 605, 28 Atl. 595; Ward v. Cooke, 17 N. J. Eq. 93; Ackerman v. Hunsicker, 85 N. Y. 44, 39 Am. Rep. 621; Robinson v. Williams, 22 N. Y. 380; Truscott v. King, 6 Barb. (N. Y.) 147, 346, 6 N. Y. 166; Livingston v. McInlay, 16 Johns. (N. Y.) 165; Union Nat. Bank v. Moline, 7 N. Dak. 201, 73 N. W. 527 (where this matter is fully and ably discussed); McDaniels v. Colvin, 16 Vt. 300, 42 Am. Dec. 512; McCarty v. Chalfant, 15 W. Va. 514, 548, per Haymond, J., but point not decided. See also Shirras v. Caig, 7 Cranch (U. S.) 34, 3 L. ed. 260; Savings &c. Soc. v. Burnett, 106 Cal. 514, 39 Pac. 922; Crane v. Deming, 7 Conn. 387; Frye v. Bank of Illinois, 11 Ill. 367; Burdett v. Clay, 8 B. Mon. (Ky.) 287; Williams v. Gilbert, 37 N. J. Eq. 84; Griffin v. New Jersey Oil Co., 11 N. J. Eq. 49; Reynolds v. Webster, 71 Hun 378, 55 N. Y. St. 6, 24 N. Y. S. 1133; Pennock v. Copeland, 1 Phila. (Pa.) 29.

[74] In re Haake, 7 N. Bank. R. 61, 2 Sawyer, 231.

[75] See article on this subject, 11 Am. Law Reg. (N. S.) 273, by Judge

Whether the mortgage intended to secure future advances discloses the nature of the transaction or not, there is no good reason why it should not remain a valid security for all advances that may be made until the mortgagee receives actual notice of subsequent claims upon the property. The burden of ascertaining the amount of an existing incumbrance should rest upon him who takes a conveyance of the property subject to the mortgage. He has notice by the record of the existence of a mortgage for the full amount of the intended advances; and if he wishes to stop the advances where they are at the time of recording his subsequent deed, it is only reasonable to require him to give actual notice of his claim upon the property; otherwise he should not be heard to complain that the prior incumbrance amounts at any future time to the full sum for which it appeared of record to be an incumbrance.[76] Nevertheless, there are some authorities to the effect that the first mortgagee has constructive notice of the second mortgage from the record of it.[77] These decisions are based upon the theory that a mortgage is only security for the payment of money, and when there was no money due there could be no mortgage, and hence a mortgage could have no effect as to third parties unless the record disclosed what amount is actually secured. This position is supported by Mr. Justice Christiancy, of Michigan, in an elaborate opinion, in which a mortgage for future optional advances is treated as effectual only from the time the advances are actually made.[78]

Mitchell, the learned editor, who in conclusion remarks: "So far as we may venture a personal opinion, therefore, we think the rule, that the recording of the second mortgage is not notice to the first mortgagor, is supported by the better reasons, and that the weight of authority is still in its favor, though we are bound to concede that of late there is an apparent tendency to the opposite rule." See post § 562.

[76] Lovelace v. Webb, 62 Ala. 271, an important case. A mortgage which expressly provides that it shall secure any future indebtedness of the mortgagor to the mortgagee on account of sales of goods, or that may arise in any other manner, will secure the payment of debts of the mortgagor of a different nature from the debts which the mortgage was primarily given to secure. Freiberg v. Magale, 70 Tex. 116, 7 S. W. 684.

[77] Spader v. Lawler, 17 Ohio 371, 49 Am. Dec. 461, by a divided court; Frye v. Bank of Illinois, 11 Ill. 367; Stone v. Welling, 14 Mich. 514; Griffin v. New Jersey Oil Co., 11 N. J. Eq. 49; Ketcham v. Wood, 22 Hun (N. Y.) 64; Bank of Montgomery County's Appeal, 36 Pa. St. 170, sub nominee Parker v. Jacoby, 3 Grant's Cas. (Pa.) 300; Ter-Hoven v. Kerns, 2 Pa. St. 96. See also Collins v. Carlile, 13 Ill. 254; Ladue v. Detroit &c. R. Co., 13 Mich. 380, 87 Am. Dec. 759; Nicklin v. Betts Spring Co., 11 Ore. 406, 5 Pac. 1, 50 Am. Rep. 477. This question was discussed but not decided in Boswell v. Goodwin, 31 Conn. 74, 81 Am. Dec. 169, 12 Am. Law Reg. 79, note by Judge Redfield. See also 11 Am. Law Reg. 1

[78] Ladue v. Detroit &c. R. Co., 13 Mich. 380, 87 Am. Dec. 759. In this case Judge Christiancy says: "The instrument can only take effect as a mortgage or incum-

When there is no obligation upon the mortgagee to make the advances, and the amount of them and the times when they are to be made are not agreed upon, some authorities hold that the mortgage is a lien, as against intervening incumbrances, only from the time the advances upon it are made, and not from the time of the execution of the mortgage.[79] This was the decision with reference to a mortgage given to secure the payment of notes and bills to be discounted for the mortgagor, and for all liabilities of every kind he might be under to the mortgagee.[80] When a mortgage is given to secure future accommodation indorsements, the amount of which is wholly undefined, a subsequent mortgage or deed taken in good faith is held to have precedence over the prior mortgage as to any indorsements made afterward.[81]

But the better authorities are against that view. A mortgage to secure future advances is a conveyance within the recording acts, and

brance from the time when some debt or liability shall be created, cr some binding contract is made, which is to be secured by it. Until this takes place, neither the land, nor the parties, nor third persons, are bound by it. It constitutes, of itself, no binding contract. Either party may disregard or repudiate it at his pleasure. It is but a part of an arrangement merely contemplated as probable, and which can only be rendered effectual by the future consent and further acts of the parties. It is but a kind of conditional proposition, neither binding nor intended to bind either of the parties, till subsequently assented to or adopted by both."

As to the inconvenience which is supposed to result to the first mortgagee by requiring him to examine the record every time he makes advances upon such a mortgage, the learned judge says: "It is, at most, but the same inconvenience to which all other parties are compelled to submit when they lend money on the security of real estate—the trouble of looking to the value of the security. But, in truth, the inconvenience is very slight. Under any rule of decision, they would be compelled to look to the record title when the mortgage is originally taken. At the next advance they have only to look back

to this period; and for any future advance, only back to the last, which would generally be but the work of a few minutes, and much less inconvenience than they have to submit to in their ordinary daily business in making inquiries as to the responsibility, the signatures, and identity of the parties to commercial paper. But if there be any hardship, it is one which they can readily overcome by agreeing to make the advances; in other words, by entering into some contract for the performance of which, by the other party, the mortgage may operate as a security. They can hardly be heard to complain of it as a hardship, that the courts refuse to give them the benefits of a contract which, from prudential or other considerations, they were unwilling to make, and did not make until after the rights of other parties have intervened. Courts can give effect only to the contracts the parties have made, and from the time they took effect." Gillam v. Barnes, 123 Mich. 119, 82 N. W. 38.

[79] Nicklin v. Betts Spring Co., 11 Ore. 406, 5 Pac. 1, 50 Am. Rep. 477.

[80] McClure v. Roman, 52 Pa. St. 458; Bank of Montgomery County's Appeal, 36 Pa. St. 170; Parker v. Jacoby, 3 Grant's Cas. (Pa.) 300.

[81] Babcock v. Bridge, 29 Barb. (N. Y.) 427.

the record is notice to subsequent purchasers and incumbrancers, who are thereby put upon inquiry as to the extent of the advance made and to be made. The mortgage is a potential lien for the full amount of the advances contemplated, and through the record subsequent purchasers and incumbrancers have notice of the extent and purpose of the mortgage.[82]

§ 373. **Priority of recorded mortgage expressed to cover future advances.**—The rule that a recorded mortgage expressed to cover future advances has priority in all cases over subsequent conveyances and incumbrances, has full support in recent discussions, and must now be regarded as a settled rule of law. Notwithstanding all the distinctions and refinements which have been introduced into the law on this subject by the many conflicting adjudications upon it, there is strong reason and authority for the rule that a mortgage to secure future advances, which on its face gives information enough as to the extent and purpose of the contract, so that any one interested may by ordinary diligence ascertain the extent of the incumbrance, whether the extent of the contemplated advances be limited or not, and whether the mortgagee be bound to make the advances or not, will prevail over the supervening claims of purchasers or creditors, as to all advances made within the terms of such mortgage, whether made before or after the claims of such purchasers or creditors arose, or before or after the mortgagee had notice of them. If the mortgage contains enough to show a contract between the parties, that it is to stand as a security to the mortgagee for such indebtedness as may arise from the future dealings between the parties, it is sufficient to put a purchaser or incumbrancer on inquiry, and if he fails to make it he is not entitled to

---

[82] Ackerman v. Hunsicker, 85 N. Y. 43, 39 Am. Rep. 621. Per Andrews, J.: "It is claimed, however, that the mortgage did not become an actual lien or incumbrance until the advances were made, and that as to each advance it became in effect a new mortgage as of the time when such advance was made, and that as to indorsements made subsequent to the docketing of the judgments, the mortgage must be deemed a subsequent lien. It is manifestly true that the mortgage did not become enforceable by the plaintiff until he had incurred liability as an indorser. But the plaintiff's mortgage was an instrument capable of being recorded under the statute before any liability had been incurred. It is the general practice to record mortgages and docket judgments taken to secure future advances and contemplated liabilities before an actual indebtedness arises. On being recorded, the record is notice to subsequent purchasers and incumbrancers, and they are put upon inquiry, and have the means of ascertaining to what extent advances have been made, and by notice to prevent further advances to their prejudice."

protection as a bona fide purchaser.[83] Such a mortgage is considered as good against subsequent incumbrances to the full amount of the advances provided for, or even verbally agreed for, and the mortgagee is held to have a right to rely upon it, and to make such advances without regard to what other incumbrances may afterward have been put upon the property.[84] This view of the doctrine of mortgages to secure future advances is strongly expressed by Mr. Justice Campbell in a comparatively recent case in Mississippi.[85]

[83] Tapia v. Demartini, 77 Cal. 383, 19 Pac. 641, 11 Am. St. 288; Ackerman v. Hunsicker, 85 N. Y. 43, 39 Am. Rep. 621. See also Staniels v. Whitcher, 72 N. H. 451, 57 Atl. 678.

[84] Tapia v. Demartini, 77 Cal. 383, 19 Pac. 641, 11 Am. St. 288; Lewis v. Hartford Silk Mfg. Co., 56 Conn. 25, 12 Atl. 637; Louisville Banking Co. v. Leonard, 90 Ky. 106, 13 S. W. 521; Ackerman v. Hunsicker, 85 N. Y. 43, 39 Am. Rep. 621; Freiberg v. Magale, 70 Tex. 116, 7 S. W. 684; Keyes v. Bump, 59 Vt. 391, 9 Atl. 598.

[85] Witczinski v. Everman, 51 Miss. 841. The court say: "There has been much diversity of views between courts and law-writers on the question of the validity of mortgages for future advances, and the rights of mortgagees in such mortgages as against purchasers and junior incumbrancers of the mortgaged property. Some have held that a mortgage which does not specify that for which it is given so distinctly as to give definite information on the face of the mortgage of what it secures, so as to render it unnecessary for the inquirer to look beyond the mortgage and seek information aliunde, is void as against creditors and purchasers. Others have held that a mortgage for future advances is valid as to all advances made under it before notice by the mortgagee of the supervening rights of purchasers or incumbrancers. Others have announced that a mortgage for future advances to be made, or liability to be incurred, when duly recorded, is valid as a security for indebtedness incurred under it, in accordance with its terms.

"There have been suggested modifications of these views, and a distinction has been drawn between mortgages in which the mortgagee is obligated to advance a given sum and those in which he is not so bound. We decline to follow the devious ways to which we are pointed by conflicting adjudications and suggestions, and prefer to pursue the plain path in which principle directs us, and will declare the rule to be observed in the courts of this state on the subject under consideration, which, strangely enough, has not been heretofore decided in this state. A mortgage to secure future advances, which on its face gives information as to the extent and purpose of the contract, so that a purchaser or junior creditor may, by an inspection of the record, and by ordinary diligence and common prudence, ascertain the extent of the incumbrance, will prevail over the supervening claim of such purchaser or creditor as to all advances made by the mortgagee within the terms of such mortgage, whether made before or after the claim of such purchaser or creditor arose. It is not necessary for a mortgage for future advances to specify any particular or definite sum which it is to secure. It is not necessary for it to be so completely certain as to preclude the necessity of all extraneous inquiry. If it contains enough to show a contract that it is to stand as a security to the mortgagee for such indebtedness as may arise from future dealings between the parties, it is sufficient to put a purchaser or incumbrancer on inquiry, and, if he fails to make it in the proper quarter, he can not claim protection as a bona fide purchaser. The law requires mortgages

Even though no specific sum be named in the mortgage as to what future advances it was intended to secure, if the instrument on its face gives information as to the extent and purpose of the contract between the parties, that it is to stand as security for future advances, it will be sufficient to put a subsequent incumbrancer on notice of probable future dealings between the parties affecting the mortgaged property, and the duty of investigating the extent of liability that may attach to the property by reason of the mortgage devolves upon such incumbrancer.[86]

§ 374. **Necessity for specifying that future debts are to be secured.** —It is not necessary that the mortgage should express on its face that it is given to secure future advances. It may be given for a specific sum, and it will then be security for a debt to that amount.[87] This

to be recorded for the protection of creditors and purchasers. When recorded, a mortgage is notice of its contents. If it gives information that it is to stand as security for all future indebtedness to accrue from the mortgagor to the mortgagee, a person examining the record is put upon inquiry as to the state of dealing between the parties, and the amount of indebtedness covered by the mortgage, and is duly advised of the rights of the mortgagee, by the terms of the mortgage, to hold the mortgaged property as security to him for such indebtedness as may accrue to him. Thus informed, it is the folly of any one to buy the mortgaged property, or take a mortgage on it, or give credit on it; and if he does so, his claim must be subordinated to the paramount right of the senior mortgagee, who, in thus securing himself by mortgage, and filing it for record as required by law, has advertised the world of his paramount claim on the property covered by his mortgage, and is entitled to advance money and extend credit according to the terms of his contract thus made with the mortgagor, who can not complain, for such is his contract; and third persons afterward dealing with him can not be heard to complain, for they are affected with full notice, by the record, of what has been agreed on by the mortgagor and mort-

gagee." Followed in Gray v. Helm, 60 Miss. 131. Quoted and followed in Lovelace v. Webb, 62 Ala. 271.

[86] Savings &c. Soc. v. Burnett, 106 Cal. 514, 39 Pac. 922; Tapia v. Demartini, 77 Cal. 383, 19 Pac. 641, 11 Am. St. 288.

[87] Huckaba v. Abbott, 87 Ala. 409, 6 So. 48; Forsyth v. Preer, 62 Ala. 443; Tapia v. Demartini, 77 Cal. 383, 19 Pac. 641, 11 Am. St. 288; Tully v. Harloe, 35 Cal. 302, 95 Am. Dec. 102; Richards v. Waldron, 20 D. C. 545; Yock Kee v. Hilo Mercantile Co., 13 Hawaii 426; Darst v. Gale, 83 Ill. 136; Collins v. Carlisle, 13 Ill. 254; Louisville Banking Co. v. Leonard, 90 Ky. 105, 13 S. W. 521; Morris v. Cain, 39 La. Ann. 712, 1 So. 797, 2 So. 418; Pickersgill v. Brown, 7 La. Ann. 297; Witczinski v. Everman, 51 Miss. 841; Foster v. Reynolds, 38 Mo. 553; Griffin v. New Jersey Oil Co., 11 N. J. Eq. 49; Murray v. Barney, 34 Barb. (N. Y.) 336; Bank of Utica v. Finch, 3 Barb. Ch. (N. Y.) 293, 49 Am. Dec. 175; Townsend v. Empire Stone Dressing Co., 6 Duer (N. Y.) 208; Wescott v. Gunn, 4 Duer (N. Y.) 107; Walker v. Snediker, Hoff. (N. Y.) 145; Craig v. Tappin, 2 Sandf. Ch. (N. Y.) 78; Hendrix v. Gore, 8 Ore. 406; Moroney's Appeal, 24 Pa. St. 372; Moses v. Hatfield, 27 S. Car. 324, 3 S. E. 538 (quoting text); McCarty v. Chalfant, 14 W. Va. 531.

definite sum will then limit the extent of the lien. There must be some limit to the amount which the mortgage is to secure, either by express limitation or by stating generally the object of the security.

If the limit be not defined in any way, it can be good only for the advances made at the time, and such others as may afterward be made before any other incumbrances are made upon the property mortgaged.[88] A mortgage which merely declares that it is to secure such advances as shall thereafter be made by the mortgagee to the mortgagor, or such indebtedness as shall thereafter arise between them, should, it would seem, be held invalid either as against the policy of the law or as constituting evidence of fraud.[89]

The sum expressed by the mortgage may cover a present indebtedness as well as future advances, and it is not necessary that the one should be separated from the other on the face of the mortgage.[90] The sum or amount named as the consideration of the mortgage is of no moment, as the mortgage stands as security for the amount of liability or indebtedness incurred under the contract for advances set forth in the condition of the mortgage. It is not essential even that any sum be named in the consideration clause.[91]

The consideration named in the mortgage does not limit the amount for which it may be security, if from the whole instrument it appears that it was intended to secure a future indebtedness beyond this amount.[92]

A mortgage which in terms secures a promissory note for a specified amount may actually be intended to secure future advances to that amount.[93] If in such case the mortgagee assigns the note before it is due to one taking it in good faith, and without notice that the note was given for future advances, the assignee takes it subject to no equities in favor of the mortgagor; but the latter must pay the full amount of the note upon redemption or foreclosure.[94] The fact that the mortgagee in assigning the note and mortgage assigns his "inter-

---

[88] Fassett v. Smith, 23 N. Y. 252; Robinson v. Williams, 22 N. Y. 380.

[89] Tully v. Harloe, 35 Cal. 302, 95 Am. Dec. 102; Pettibone v. Griswold, 4 Conn. 158, 10 Am. Dec. 106; Garber v. Henry, 6 Watts (Pa.) 57. But see Jarratt v. McDaniel, 32 Ark. 598; Allen v. Lathrop, 46 Ga. 133; Michigan Ins. Co. v. Brown, 11 Mich. 265; Witczinski v. Everman, 51 Miss. 841; Robinson v. Williams, 22 N. Y. 380.

[90] Tully v. Harloe, 35 Cal. 302, 95 Am. Dec. 102; Summers v. Roos, 42 Miss. 749, 2 Am. Rep. 653; Hendrix v. Gore, 8 Ore. 406; Evenson v. Bates, 58 Wis. 94, 15 N. W. 837.

[91] Keyes v. Bump, 59 Vt. 391, 9 Atl. 598.

[92] Citizens Sav. Bank v. Kock, 117 Mich. 225, 75 N. W. 458.

[93] Bassett v. Daniels, 136 Mass. 547.

[94] Bassett v. Daniels, 136 Mass. 547.

est" in them, is not notice to the assignee that the mortgage was given to secure future advances.[95]

An absolute conveyance may be used to secure future advances, or to secure an existing debt and also future advances. The agreement to reconvey when the advances are repaid is sufficient, although it exists in parol only.[96] If the mortgage specifies the amount intended to be secured thereby, parol evidence is generally admissible to identify the debts, and such evidence, if satisfactory, may extend the protection of the mortgage over indebtedness created after its execution, but intended by the parties thereto to be secured thereby.[97]

§ 375. Form of agreement for advances.—According to the weight of authority, a mortgage to secure future advances may, without impairing its validity, be in the same form as if it were to secure pre-existing indebtedness. The agreement under which advances to a certain amount are to be made need not be in writing, to be binding and effectual against subsequent liens, when it has been acted upon.[98] Thus, if a mortgage is made to secure future advances to be used in the construction of a building on the mortgaged land, and a mortgage for the contemplated amount is made and recorded, it has priority against a mechanic's lien for materials furnished in the construction of such building to the full amount of the mortgage, if the advances are actually made to that amount, although the agreement under which they are made is verbal only.[99]

[95] Bassett v. Daniels, 136 Mass. 547.

[96] Fessler's Appeal, 75 Pa. St. 483; Harper's Appeal, 64 Pa. St. 315, 7 Phila. 276; Myers's Appeal, 42 Pa. St. 518; Rhines v. Baird, 41 Pa. St. 256; Kellum v. Smith, 33 Pa. St. 158. But see Metropolitan Bank v. Godfrey, 23 Ill. 579.

[97] Kirby v. Raynes, 138 Ala. 194, 35 So. 118, 100 Am. St. 39; Lovelace v. Webb, 62 Ala. 271; Tapia v. Demartini, 77 Cal. 383, 19 Pac. 641, 11 Am. St. 288; Tully v. Harloe, 35 Cal. 302, 95 Am. Dec. 102; Bacon v. Brown, 19 Conn. 29; Foster v. Reynolds, 38 Mo. 553.

[98] Hendon v. Morris, 110 Ala. 106, 20 So. 27; Wilkerson v. Tillman, 66 Ala. 532; Forsyth v. Preer, 62 Ala. 443; Tison v. People's Sav. Loan Assn., 57 Ala. 323; Tapia v. Demartini, 77 Cal. 383, 386, 19 Pac. 641, 11 Am. St. 288. But it has been held that, as against the wife's right of homestead, a mortgage ex-ecuted by her with her husband to secure an existing debt, and future advances to the husband orally agreed for, is not valid to cover such future advances. The incumbrance for future advances, being a mere oral agreement, constitutes a power in another to incumber the homestead at will, and is not a conveyance executed and acknowledged by husband and wife, as required by statute, and is not enforcible. Merced Bank v. Rosenthal, 99 Cal. 39, 31 Pac. 849. See also Langerman v. Puritan Dining Room Co., 21 Cal. App. 637, 132 Pac. 617; Du Bois v. First Nat. Bank, 43 Colo. 400, 96 Pac. 169; Reed v. Rochford, 62 N. J. Eq. 186, 50 Atl. 70.

[99] Platt v. Griffith, 27 N. J. Eq. 207. The court, citing Moroney's Appeal, 24 Pa. St. 372. Macintosh v. Thurston, 25 N. J. Eq. 242 (written agreement of the mortgagee to

If such agreement be in writing, it is not necessary that it should appear of record.[1] But a parol agreement that a mortgage shall cover any indebtedness of the mortgagor to the mortgagee for goods after-ward to be purchased will not cover an indebtedness for goods pur-chased of the mortgagee by a partnership subsequently entered into by the mortgagor; for an indebtedness of the partnership is not within the terms of the original agreement.[2]

The agreement for the advances must be contemporaneous. A mort-gage can not be made available to secure future advances by any subse-quent parol agreement, in preference to the lien of a junior incum-brance.[3] But where the agreement is oral, it seems to be in effect abrogated by the creation of subsequent incumbrances without the knowledge of it, and after the mortgagor has executed subsequent con-veyances and incumbrances, the mortgagee seems to be no longer at lib-erty to make advances or permit the incurring of indebtedness upon the parol agreement.[4]

§ 376. **Necessity for stating amount and time for making advance-ments.**—The omission to state on the face of the mortgage the time when the first advances are to be made is not material. It is sufficient that they are to be made from time to time, as the mortgagor may de-sire, during a specified period.[5] The amounts of the several advances, and the times when they were actually made, and the object of the mortgage, may be shown by extrinsic proof, for in such case the proof does not contradict the mortgage, or alter its legal operation and effect in any way.[6] Although the deed purports to be in consideration of a definite sum in hand paid at the time, it may be shown by parol evi-dence that the deed was made to secure advances made and to be made to that extent.[7]

furnish the money considered im-material in these cases); Taylor v. La Bar, 25 N. J. Eq. 222. Fully sus-tained in Lovelace v. Webb, 62 Ala. 271.

[1] Taylor v. Cornelius, 60 Pa. St. 187; Moroney's Appeal, 24 Pa. St. 372; Thomas v. Davis, 3 Phila. (Pa.) 171.

[2] Parkes v. Parker, 57 Mich. 57, 23 N. W. 458.

[3] Truscott v. King, 6 N. Y. 147, 161, per Jewett, J.; Walker v. Sned-iker, Hoff. (N. Y.) 145; Hall v. Crouse, 13 Hun (N. Y.) 557.

[4] Tapia v. Demartini, 77 Cal. 383, 19 Pac. 641, 11 Am. St. 288; Wag-

ner v. Breed, 29 Nebr. 720, 46 N. W. 286; Central Trust Co. v. Conti-nental I. W., 51 N. J. Eq. 605, 28 Atl. 595, 40 Am. St. 539; Merchants' State Bank v. Tufts, 14 N. Dak. 238, 103 N. W. 760, 116 Am. St. 682.

[5] Wilson v. Russell, 13 Md. 494, 71 Am. Dec. 645. See also Ahern v. White, 39 Md. 409.

[6] Hall v. Crouse, 13 Hun (N. Y.) 557.

[7] Huckaba v. Abbott, 87 Ala. 409, 6 So. 48; Tapia v. Demartini, 77 Cal. 383, 19 Pac. 641; Cole v. Albers, 1 Gill (Md.) 412; Foster v. Rey-nolds, 38 Mo. 553; Moses v. Hat-

Parol evidence is also admissible to show that the mortgage was given to secure advances to be made by a party not named in the mortgage.[8]

When a mortgage has been given in terms to secure future advances and acceptances, and the mortgagee, in a suit to enforce the mortgage, produces drafts of the mortgagor upon him, there is no presumption that the drafts were drawn against funds of the drawer, but the burden is upon the mortgagor to show this if he makes the claim.[9]

Parties to a mortgage can not extend it to cover advances made after its execution, by a parol agreement made a few days after the making of the advances, based on no new or valuable consideration, and which was not made in pursuance of any understanding between the parties before the making of advances.[10]

§ 377. **Limitations of security must be observed.**—All limitations of the security must be observed. Although, as already seen, a mortgage made in good faith to secure future debts expected to be contracted, or advances to be made in the course of dealing between the parties, is a good and valid security,[11] yet if limited by the terms of the mortgage, either as to amount or the time within which the advances are to be made, or the nature of them, the limitation must be strictly observed; thus a mortgage to secure credits, indorsements or advances to be made within a limited time secures none made afterward.[12]

As a general rule, advances in excess of the amount of a mortgage are not secured by it.[13] Thus where at the same time with the making of a mortgage of land conditioned for the payment of two thou-

field, 27 S. Car. 324, 3 S. E. 538, 540. See also Du Bois v. First Nat. Bank, 43 Colo. 400, 96 Pac. 169; Perkins &c. Co. v. Drew (Ky.), 122 S. W. 526; Reed v. Rochford, 62 N. J. Eq. 186, 50 Atl. 70.

[8] Hall v. Crouse, 13 Hun (N. Y.) 557. See also Craig v. Tappin, 2 Sandf. Ch. (N. Y.) 78; Blackmar v. Sharp, 23 R. I. 412, 50 Atl. 852.

[9] Lewis v. Wayne, 25 Ga. 167.

[10] Hayhurst v. Morin, 104 Maine 169, 71 Atl. 707.

[11] Shirras v. Caig, 7 Cranch (U. S.) 34, 3 L. ed. 260; United States v. Hooe, 3 Cranch (U. S.) 73, 2 L. ed. 370; Commercial Bank v. Cunningham, 24 Pick. (Mass.) 270, 35 Am. Dec. 322; Bank of Utica v. Finch, 3 Barb. Ch. (N. Y.) 293, 49

Am. Dec. 175; James v. Morey, 2 Cow. (N. Y.) 246, 292, 6 Johns. Ch. 417, 14 Am. Dec. 475; Walker v. Snediker, Hoff. (N. Y.) 145; Brinckerhoff v. Lansing, 4 Johns. Ch. (N. Y.) 65, 8 Am. Dec. 538; Yelverton v. Shelden, 2 Sandf. Ch. (N. Y.) 481. See also Straeffer v. Rodman, 146 Ky. 1, 141 S. W. 742; Tinkham v. Wright (Tex. Civ. App.), 163 S. W. 615; Heal v. Evans Creek Coal &c. Co., 71 Wash. 225, 128 Pac. 211.

[12] Miller v. Whittier, 36 Maine 577; Burt v. Gamble, 98 Mich. 402, 57 N. W. 261.

[13] McComb v. Barcelona Apartment Assn., 10 N. Y. St. 552, 56 Hun 644, 10 N. Y. S. 546. See also Perkins &c. Co. v. Drew (Ky.), 122 S. W. 526.

sand two hundred dollars and interest, an agreement under seal was executed by the mortgagor and mortgagee, by which, after referring to the mortgage, the mortgagor agreed to finish a house on the mortgaged land, the mortgagee agreeing to furnish the material, and the mortgagor covenanted to pay the cost of the material and one thousand dollars for the land; it was then provided that the cost of the land and the cost of the material, "whether more or less than said two thousand two hundred dollars, shall be received in payment of said note and in discharge of said mortgage." It was held that the mortgagor was entitled to redeem the premises from the mortgage on paying the sum mentioned therein, although the sum due under the agreement was much larger.[14]

Where a building loan mortgage provided that the mortgagee should retain from the mortgagor the sum secured and apply same to the payment of liens created in the erection of a building, it was held that the mortgagee was not entitled to apply the money so retained to a purpose other than that specified in the mortgage.[15] Where a mortgage was given to secure a note and further advances by the mortgagee and all other indebtedness of the mortgagor to the mortgagee, and authorized the mortgagee to pay incumbrances on the premises, it was held that the mortgagee could not buy up obligations of the mortgagor disconnected from the mortgage or the premises, and hold the same as secured by such mortgage.[16]

A limitation in terms of the amount of the advances to be made may be controlled by other expressions in the mortgage as to the purpose of the advances; thus, where the controlling purpose was to secure advances sufficient to enable the mortgagor to raise a crop of cotton, advances beyond the sum specified were protected.[17]

If limited in amount and time, and the full amount be once advanced and repaid, and further loans are made within the time limited, these are covered by the mortgage as against subsequent purchasers.[18]

§ 378. **Where part only of advances have been made.**—Where the mortgagee is under obligation to make future advances and fails to

[14] Ford v. Davis, 168 Mass. 116, 46 N. E. 435.

[15] Tice v. Moore, 82 Conn. 244, 73 Atl. 133; Equitable Sav. &c. Assn. v. Hewitt, 67 Ore. 280, 135 Pac. 864; Brunswick Realty Co. v. University Inv. Co. (Utah), 134 Pac. 608.

[16] Provident Mut. Bldg. &c. Assn.

v. Shaffer, 2 Cal. App. 216, 83 Pac. 274; Moran v. Gardemeyer, 82 Cal. 96, 23 Pac. 6.

[17] Bell v. Radcliff, 32 Ark. 645. See also Du Bois v. First Nat. Bank, 43 Colo. 400, 96 Pac. 169.

[18] Wilson v. Russell, 13 Md. 494, 71 Am. Dec. 645.

do so, if no other debt is secured by the instrument the mortgage is without consideration and can not be enforced for another purpose,[19] and if the mortgagee advance only a part of the sum contemplated in the mortgage, it is a valid security for so much as he does advance,[20] and for so much only. For the advances actually made, the mortgage is good against the mortgagor's assignee in bankruptcy.[21] Likewise if a mortgage be given for a loan and for the price of lands to be conveyed, and the mortgagee wrongfully refuses to convey the land, the mortgage can be enforced only for the money advanced.[22]

A mortgage was taken upon a building partly completed, the mortgagee advancing a part of the money under an agreement to pay the balance of the loan thirty-five days after the completion of the building, which was to be finished before a certain date, the agreement also providing that if the building should not be completed by the time agreed, the mortgagee might take charge of and complete the work, and the sums so expended should be considered a part of the balance to be advanced. The mortgagor by his own fault did not complete the building within the required time, and the mortgagee did not take charge of nor complete the work, and was not asked to, and did not offer to advance the balance of the mortgage, though he was always ready and able to advance the balance upon the completion of the building according to the agreement. It was held that the mortgagee was not entitled to interest on the money not advanced.[23]

If the mortgagee fails or refuses to make any advances according to his agreement, and retains possession of the lands under an absolute deed intended as a mortgage, the mortgagor can not recover the amount of the promised advances. He can recover such special damages as

---

[19] Mizner v. Kussell, 29 Mich. 229.

[20] Forsyth v. Preer, 62 Ala. 443; Morris v. Cain, 39 La. Ann. 712, 1 So. 797, 2 So. 418; Watts v. Bonner, 66 Miss. 629, 6 So. 187; Coleman v. Galbreath, 53 Miss. 303; Freeman v. Auld, 44 Barb. (N. Y.) 14; Dart v. McAdam, 27 Barb. (N. Y.) 187. See, in this connection, the case of Walker v. Carleton, 97 Ill. 582, where a loan for $5,000 had been agreed upon, and a note and trust deed for that sum executed, and the deed recorded, when the lender was able to furnish only $3,000 of the amount, for which sum he took a separate note payable in a short time. A majority of the court held that the trust deed did not secure the smaller note.

This decision seems to be erroneous. Craig, Scott and Sheldon, JJ., dissenting, take the correct view of the case when they say: "Equity regards substance, not form. The substance of the transaction was that there was but $3,000 furnished, instead of $5,000, and the former was accepted in lieu of the latter; and the trust deed to the extent of $3,000 was valid and enforcible."

[21] Schulze v. Bolting, 8 Biss. (U. S.) 174.

[22] Robinson v. Cromelein, 15 Mich. 316.

[23] Lewin v. Folsom, 171 Mass. 188. 50 N. E. 523.

have resulted from the mortgagee's refusal to make the advances; but in case no special damages are shown, the mortgagor can recover only nominal damages.[24] Of course he can have the mortgage or conveyance released.

When a mortgage is an open one, as, for instance, one made by an absolute conveyance, or to secure undefined future advances, the mortgagee is entitled to recover under it only so much as he shows affirmatively to be due. Any doubt and uncertainty, it is said, should operate against the mortgagee and not in his favor.[25]

III. *Mortgage of Indemnity*

§ 379. **Description of the indemnity.**—Very much of what has already been stated, in regard to present and future debts secured by mortgages, is applicable to mortgages made to indemnify a mortgagee against liabilities incurred or to be incurred by him in behalf of the mortgagor.[1] Mortgages of indemnity are perhaps most often given as security for liabilities to be incurred in the future, so that they are to this extent mortgages to secure future advances. Such mortgages generally declare the purpose for which they are given, and set out particularly the liabilities incurred or to be incurred by the mortgagee. But this is not essential. A mortgage given for a definite sum, without specifying the liabilities secured, may be shown by parol evidence to have been given to indemnify the mortgagee against his liability as an indorser or surety for the mortgagor.[2] Thus, where a mortgage recited that the mortgagor was indebted to the mortgagee in a certain sum, "being for money advanced," and that the mortgage was made to secure the payment of such debt, the mortgagee was not precluded

---

[24] Turpie v. Lowe, 114 Ind. 37, 15 N. E. 834; Watts v. Bonner, 66 Miss. 629, 6 So. 187.

[25] Kline v. McGuckin, 25 N. J. Eq. 433.

[1] Whitney v. Hale, 67 N. H. 385, 30 Atl. 417.

[2] Shirras v. Caig, 7 Cranch (U. S.) 34, 3 L. ed. 260; Lawrence v. Tucker, 23 How. (U. S.) 14, 16 L. ed. 474; Hubbard v. Savage, 8 Conn. 215; Simpson v. Robert, 35 Ga. 180; McKinster v. Babcock, 26 N. Y. 378; Bank of Utica v. Finch, 3 Barb. Ch. (N. Y.) 293, 49 Am. Dec. 175.

from showing that the real consideration of the mortgage was the indorsement by him of the mortgagor's note for that sum. "The question of consideration was raised by the defendant's proving, by the mortgagee, that no money was advanced to him upon the mortgage. It thus became proper, if not necessary, to show what the real consideration was, and this was all that was done. The plaintiff had a valid mortgage, as to the mortgagor." He would not be permitted to impeach it by showing that the consideration was not money advanced to him, and shut out evidence of the true consideration.[3]

If the mortgage contains a general description sufficient to embrace the liability intended by the parties to be secured, and to put a person examining the records upon inquiry, and direct him to the proper source for more minute and particular information of the amount of the incumbrance, it is all that fair dealing demands.[4] "There can not be a more fair, bona fide, and valuable consideration than the drawing or indorsing of notes at a future period, for the benefit and at the request of the mortgagor; and nothing is more reasonable than the providing a sufficient indemnity beforehand."[5] It is undoubtedly desirable that the true consideration be fully stated, and when this is not done the instrument may be open to the suspicion that it was made to deceive the mortgagor's creditors; but the true consideration may in all cases be explained,[6] and parol evidence is admissible to show it.[7] Where a mortgage is given to indemnify one who becomes a surety upon a bond in which the mortgagor is principal, a misdescription of the particular bond will not render the mortgage invalid, either as to the mortgagor or his vendee, but the description may be corrected by parol testimony so as to identify the bond described in the mortgage with the one upon which the mortgagee became surety.[8]

§ 380. **What description of liability sufficient.**—An indemnity mortgage is sufficient as such if the debt or obligation against which

---

[3] Per Marvin, J., in McKinster v. Babcock, 26 N. Y. 378.

[4] Cazort &c. Co. v. Dunbar, 91 Ark. 400, 121 S. W. 270; Hoye v. Burford, 68 Ark. 256, 57 S. W. 795; Curtis v. Flinn, 46 Ark. 70.

[5] Per Tilghman, C. J., in Lyle v. Ducomb, 5 Binn. (Pa.) 585. See also Duncan v. Miller, 64 Iowa 223, 20 N. W. 161; Adams v. Niemann, 46 Mich. 135, 18 N. W. 719; Forbes v. McCoy, 15 Nebr. 632, 20 N. W. 17; Williams v. Silliman, 74 Tex. 626, 12 S. W. 534.

[6] Commercial Bank v. Cunningham, 24 Pick. (Mass.) 270, 35 Am. Dec. 322; Gardner v. Webber, 17 Pick. (Mass.) 407; McKinster v. Babcock, 26 N. Y. 378.

[7] Cutler v. Steele, 93 Mich. 204, 53 N. W. 521. See also Emerson v. Knight, 130 Ga. 100, 60 S. E. 255; Hester v. Gairdner, 128 Ga. 531, 58 S. E. 165; Bowen v. Ratcliff, 140 Ind. 393, 39 N. E. 860, 49 Am. St. 203.

[8] Jones v. Guaranty &c. Co., 101 U. S. 622, 25 L. ed. 1030; Emerson v. Knight, 130 Ga. 100, 60 S. E. 255;

the mortgagee is intended to be protected is described with reasonable certainty.[9] A general description of the liability is sufficient. A mortgage to indemnify an indorser for liability on notes to be indorsed within two years from the date of the mortgage, to an amount not exceeding sixteen thousand dollars at any one time, and a renewal of such notes, was sustained as against a purchaser from the mortgagee.[10] A mortgage to indemnify one for indorsing "a note of two thousand dollars, made payable to the order of the grantor, and by him signed and indorsed," is not void for uncertainty. The note intended may be identified by parol evidence.[11] In like manner, as under a mortgage conditioned to indemnify the mortgagee for indorsements of certain notes payable at two banks specified, parol evidence is admissible to show what notes had been indorsed by the mortgagee and were intended to be secured.[12]

A mortgage reciting that it was to secure the payment of a certain bond and collateral for a certain other mortgage, and that payments on the latter mortgage and all interest paid thereon should be credited to such former mortgage, also that on payment by the mortgagor of a certain sum, less than the mortgage debt, with interest, the holder of such former mortgage would discharge it, was not security for the entire debt, but only for the amount required to be paid for its discharge.[13]

A condition to indemnify the mortgagee against liability as surety for the mortgagor, a certain sum being mentioned, be the debts more or less, covers all debts for which the mortgagee is surety, be they more or less.[14] A mortgage conditioned to save the mortgagee harmless for indorsing notes for the mortgagor, when thereafter requested, to the amount of seven thousand dollars, and also renewal notes, is

---

Harlan County v. Whitney, 65 Nebr. 105, 90 N. W. 993, 101 Am. St. 610.

[9] Cazort &c. Co. v. Dunbar, 91 Ark. 400, 121 S. W. 270; Utley v. Smith, 24 Conn. 290, 63 Am. Dec. 163; Ketchum v. Jauncey, 23 Conn. 123; Lewis v. De Forest, 20 Conn. 427; Burdett v. Clay, 8 B. Mon. (Ky.) 287; Goddard v. Sawyer, 9 Allen (Mass.) 78; Benton v. Sumner, 57 N. H. 117; Gilman v. Moody, 43 N. H. 239; First Nat. Bank v. Byard, 26 N. J. Eq. 255.

[10] Utley v. Smith, 24 Conn. 290, 63 Am. Dec. 163. The court, Ellsworth, J., said: "Were this an original question, it would be difficult, we think, to sustain the deeds against

this objection, but it is not; and although our early decisions would hold them void for vagueness, our decisions for the last ten or fifteen years have gone further, and established the law to be liberal enough to sustain mortgages quite as indefinite and vague as the present."

[11] Goddard v. Sawyer, 9 Allen (Mass.) 78.

[12] Barker v. Barker, 62 N. H. 366; Benton v. Sumner, 57 N. H. 117; Melvin v. Fellows, 33 N. H. 401.

[13] Abert v. Kornfeld, 128 App. Div. 547, 112 N. Y. S. 884.

[14] Orr v. Hancock, 1 Root (Conn.) 265.

not invalid for uncertainty as against subsequent incumbrances.[15] Nor is a mortgage invalid which is given to secure an "accommodation indorser and signer on sundry notes, drafts, and bills of exchange, now maturing in sundry banks, and in the hands of sundry individuals, to the amount of fifty thousand dollars, a particular description of which we are not able to give, or in whose hands they are."[16] A recital in a mortgage that the mortgagee had indorsed two bills of exchange, when in fact he had indorsed only one, and had paid the other for the honor of the drawer, does not invalidate the security.[17] A mortgage for a definite sum, but expressed to be "given to secure whatever indebtedness may at any time exist from the mortgagor to the mortgagee," does not restrict the indebtedness secured to such debts as may be contracted directly from the mortgagor to the mortgagee, but includes also any obligations the mortgagor may incur by indorsing the notes of another party. The terms of the mortgage are broad enough to cover any kind of indebtedness.[18]

A mortgage made to indemnify one against loss by reason of his becoming a surety for the mortgagor, which provides that the property shall be liable for "no more than five thousand dollars," is a limitation upon any increase of the debt secured above that amount, yet interest is recoverable as an incident to the debt.[19]

A mortgage made to secure indorsers upon a note contemplated to be discounted at a particular bank, and so expressed in the deed, is valid, although the note be discounted in a bank other than that named, and is subsequently transferred to a third bank. A subsequent incumbrancer can not invalidate the mortgage for this reason, unless he can show that he was misled by this description, and advanced money upon the land, or acquired an interest in it after inquiry, and in the confidence that no such lien existed.[20]

A mortgage indemnifying a purchaser of land from loss by reason of a failure of title to a portion of it, covers the actual loss sustained by the purchaser from his eviction from such land.[21]

But it has been held that in order for an indemnity mortgage to be valid against creditors, the affidavit must show that the mortgage was

---

[15] Ketchum v. Jauncey, 23 Conn. 123. See also Brander v. Bowmar, 16 La. 370; Linton v. Purdon, 9 Rob. (La.) 482; Kramer v. Bank, 15 Ohio 253.

[16] Lewis v. De Forest, 20 Conn. 427.

[17] Fetter v. Cirode, 4 B. Mon. (Ky.) 482.

[18] First Nat. Bank v. Byard, 26 N. J. Eq. 255.

[19] Stafford v. Jones, 91 N. Car. 189.

[20] Patterson v. Johnston, 7 Ohio 225.

[21] Ralston v. Effinger, 86 Va. 1008, 11 S. E. 975.

taken in good faith to indemnify against any loss resulting from the liability stated in the mortgage. A mere statement that the claim on which the mortgagee is surety is just and unpaid was held not sufficient.[22]

§ 381. **Obligation covered by an indemnity mortgage.**—All limitations of the security must be observed. But if the sum for which the mortgage of indemnity is given be limited, the security can not be extended beyond that amount. But on the other hand a mortgage conditioned to be void upon the payment of a certain sum upon a note of another for a much larger amount does not entitle the mortgagor to the benefit of payments upon the note by the promisor.[23] In order to create a liability upon a mortgage made to guarantee a contemplated loan to another, the loan must correspond with the recital of it in the mortgage.[24]

A mortgage made to secure one from all liability, which he may incur by reason of his becoming surety or indorser on the notes of the mortgagor, does not secure notes given to the mortgagee for money loaned by him, and as evidence of such loan;[25] and a mortgage conditioned for the payment of all sums of money owing by the mortgagor to the mortgagee as maker or indorser of any notes, bills of exchange, bonds, checks, or securities of any kind given by him, does not secure a debt not evidenced by an instrument in writing.[26] A mortgage conditioned to secure a bank for all notes, bills, or checks which have been or shall be made, drawn, indorsed, or accepted by the mortgagor, or discounted by said bank for his benefit, and to pay all balances of account, and all sums of money due or owing by him to said bank on any account whatever, does not cover the indebtedness of a firm of which the mortgagor subsequently became a member.[27]

§ 382. **A continuing security.**—A mortgage given to indemnify an indorser or surety on a note is a continuing security for all renewals of such note until it is finally paid.[28] So long as the liability con-

---

[22] Blandy v. Benedict, 42 Ohio St. 295; Nesbit v. Worts, 37 Ohio St. 378.

[23] Popple v. Day, 123 Mass. 520.

[24] Thomas v. Olney, 16 Ill. 53. See also In re Griffiths, 1 Lowell (U. S.) 431; Ryan v. Shawneetown, 14 Ill. 20; Townsend v. Empire Stone Dressing Co., 6 Duer (N. Y.) 208.

[25] Clark v. Oman, 15 Gray (Mass.) 521.

[26] Walker v. Paine, 31 Barb. (N. Y.) 213. See also Lauderdale v. Hallock, 15 Miss. 622.

[27] Bank of Buffalo v. Thompson, 121 N. Y. 280, 24 N. E. 473.

[28] Chapman v. Jenkins, 31 Barb. (N. Y.) 164; Babcock v. Morse, 19 Barb. (N. Y.) 140; Brinckerhoff v. Lansing, 4 Johns. Ch. (N. Y.) 65, 8 Am. Dec. 538. The protection of a mortgage given to a mortgagee as surety on the mortgagor's note extends to a liability incurred by the

tinnes, the security continues also.[29] Thus a bond and mortgage given to indemnify a surety will remain valid and enforcible, although by its terms the bond expires before the expiration of the contract on which the surety is bound.[30] Although 'made for a definite sum to a bank to secure the liabilities of a firm for the payment of certain notes, the bank stipulating to discharge the mortgage when the mortgagors should cease to be under any liabilities to the bank, it is a valid security for new notes given to the bank in renewal of the original notes, and subsequent purchasers can not object to it because the agreement of the bank was not recorded, or that the new notes were made or indorsed by a new firm, formed by taking in another partner.[31] When a particular liability for which an indemnity mortgage is given is paid off wholly or in part by the mortgagee, if so intended the mortgage will continue as a security for new liabilities arising within the limit fixed.[32] Under a mortgage given to secure the maker of accommodation notes, and renewals of them from time to time, it is not necessary in order to constitute the new notes renewals, that they should be given for the same amounts and at the same periods as the original notes, or that each should be applied to discharge its immediate predecessor.[33]

But if the surety loans to the principal debtor the money to pay the original debt, and takes the debtor's own note, or that of his firm, for the amount, this is not a renewal of the original debt, but a new debt, to which a mortgage taken by the surety for his indemnity does not attach.[34]

A mortgage to two persons, who were in fact copartners, though not so described in the mortgage, intended "as a continuing security and indemnity" for indorsements in any form incurred and to be incurred for the mortgagors, includes not merely such liabilities as were incurred by the mortgagees jointly as copartners, but such as were incurred by either of them, separately and individually.[35] A mortgage to secure a partnership against liability for indorsements embraces

mortgagee jointly with the mortgagor for money borrowed to pay the original note. Nesbit v. Worts, 37 Ohio St. 378.

[29] Hawkins v. May, 12 Ala. 673; Mayer v. Grottendick, 68 Ind. 1 (quoting text). See also Courier-Journal Job Printing Co. v. Schaeffer-Meyer Brew. Co., 101 Fed. 699; Hyland v. Habich, 150 Mass. 112, 22 N. E. 765, 15 Am. St. 174.

[30] Springs v. Brown, 97 Fed. 405.

[31] Commercial Bank v. Cunningham, 24 Pick. (Mass.) 270, 35 Am. Dec. 322. The mortgage may properly provide in terms that it shall be a continuing security. Fassett v. Smith, 23 N. Y. 252.

[32] Courier-Journal Job Printing Co. v. Schaefer-Meyer Brew Co., 101 Fed. 699, 41 C. C. A. 614.

[33] Gault v. McGrath, 32 Pa. St. 392.

[34] Burson v. Andes, 83 Va. 445, 8 S. E. 249.

[35] National Bank v. Bigler, 83 N. Y. 51.

such a liability for indorsements made in the name of the firm after the secret withdrawal of one of its members.[36]

An assignment of a mortgage of indemnity carries only the right to recover the amount for which the mortgagee could then enforce it. The assignment is a limitation of the security to the amount then actually paid, and a reassignment of the mortgage does not restore the security for more than the amount for which it was a security before the assignment.[37]

A mortgage to indemnify a surety upon a guardian's bond extends to a renewal of the bond.[38]

§ 383. **When indemnity mortgage becomes a lien.**—A mortgage of indemnity to a surety is a lien from the time of its execution and delivery, and not merely from the time when the mortgagee pays the debt on which he is surety,[39] and therefore it takes precedence of a conveyance made by the mortgagor, or of a judgment rendered against him, after the execution of the mortgage and before the mortgagee has paid the debt so as to become entitled to enforce the security.[40] It is sometimes said that a mortgage given to secure one who is expected to make, indorse, or accept negotiable paper for the accommodation of another, is a lien from the time such liability is incurred;[41] but whenever there is a legal obligation to incur the liability the mortgage is a lien from the time of its delivery.[42] When there is no obligation to incur such future liabilities, the mortgage constitutes a lien from the time the liability is incurred, and is preferable to a judgment rendered afterward,[43] but not to incumbrances made before advances, of which the mortgagee had notice at the time of the advances.

An executor gave to his sureties a mortgage to indemnify them against "all loss, cost, damage, and expense which they could or might be put to by reason of their being sureties on his bond." The executor filed his account showing a certain balance in his hands. The court

[36] Buffalo City Bank v. Howard, 35 N. Y. 500.

[37] O'Hara v. Baum, 88 Pa. St. 114.

[38] Bobbitt v. Flowers, 1 Swan (Tenn.) 511.

[39] Krutsinger v. Brown, 72 Ind. 466. This case further holds that, of two indemnifying mortgages, that which is first executed and duly recorded is the prior lien.

[40] Burdett v. Clay, 8 B. Mon. (Ky.) 287; State v. Hemingway, 69 Miss.

491, 10 So. 575; Watson v. Dickens, 20 Miss. 608.

[41] Choteau v. Thompson, 2 Ohio St. 114; Bank of Commerce Appeal, 44 Pa. St. 423; Bank of Montgomery County's Appeal, 36 Pa. St. 170.

[42] Taylor v. Cornelius, 60 Pa. St. 187; Lyle v. Ducomb, 5 Binn. (Pa.) 585.

[43] Kramer v. Farmers' &c. Bank, 15 Ohio 253; Hartley v. Kirlin, 45 Pa. St. 49.

approved the account, and ordered the fund to be distributed. The executor was at this time insolvent, and one of the sureties advanced the money to pay the legacies. These payments were made before suit was brought, and before any demand was made upon the sureties by the legatees. It was held that the surety was entitled to all the benefit of the mortgage as against an intervening judgment creditor who obtained judgment shortly after the mortgage was executed.[44]

Where a mortgage is given to indemnify the mortgagee against loss on account of his becoming a surety of the mortgagor, and the contemplated contract of suretyship is never entered into, the mortgage fails for want of consideration, although the object of the proposed surety contract was to enable the mortgagor to secure funds with which to discharge a debt owed by him to the mortgagee.[45]

§ 384. **How character and purpose of indemnity mortgage may be shown.**—Parol evidence is admissible to show the true character of a mortgage, and for what purpose and what consideration it was given. Although it is for a definite sum, and secures the payment of notes for definite amounts, it may be shown that it is simply one of indemnity,[46] or for future advances.[47] When the object is simply to indemnify the mortgagee for a liability he has incurred or may incur, the amount of the mortgage, or of the mortgage notes, serves merely to limit the extent of the security. Upon the foreclosure of such a mortgage, the amount for which judgment is to be rendered is the amount the mortgagee has been compelled to pay under the liability

[44] Smith v. Harry, 91 Pa. St. 119. See ante §§ 352, 367a.

[45] Stone v. Palmer, 166 Ill. 463, 46 N. E. 1080.

[46] Jones v. Guaranty &c. Co., 101 U. S. 622, 25 L. ed. 1030; United States v. Sturges, 1 Paine (U. S.) 525; Stearns v. Porter, 46 Conn. 313; Bishop v. Warner, 19 Conn. 460; Simmons Hdw. Co. v. Thomas, 147 Ind. 313, 46 N. E. 645; Mayer v. Grottendick, 68 Ind. 1 (quoting text); Price v. Gover, 40 Md. 102; Simons v. Bank, 93 N. Y. 269; Merchants' Nat. Bank v. Hall, 83 N. Y. 338; Agawam Bank v. Strever, 18 N. Y. 502; Moses v. Hatfield, 27 S. Car. 324, 3 S. E. 538 (quoting text). See also Johnson v. Calnan, 19 Colo. 168, 34 Pac. 905, 41 Am. St. 224; Douglas v. Chatham, 41 Conn. 211; Cutler v. Steele, 93 Mich. 204, 53 N.

W. 521; Harlan v. Whitney, 65 Nebr. 105, 90 N. W. 993, 101 Am. St. 610; Bartlett v. Remington, 59 N. H. 364; Bayles v. Crossman, 5 Ohio Dec. 354; Cole v. Satsop R. Co., 9 Wash. 487, 37 Pac. 700, 43 Am. St. 858; Paine v. Benton, 32 Wis. 491. A mortgage reciting that it is given as "security for the payment of any and all notes, checks, and drafts indorsed by [the mortgagee] for the benefit or accommodation of the mortgagor, or of any firm in which he is interested, or in any way connected," will be held to secure not only past but all future indorsements, when it appears that, at the time it was executed, there was but one indorsement outstanding, and that on a note of the mortgagor's firm. Farr v. Doxtater, 9 N. Y. S. 141.

[47] McAteer v. McAteer, 31 S. Car.

for which he was secured, with interest from the date of the payment. The amount and date of the mortgage note are wholly disregarded in ascertaining this sum.[48]

A distinction is taken between a mortgage conditioned to secure against a specific thing, and one of indemnity against damage by reason of the nonperformance of the thing specified. Where the indemnity provided is against a "charge" or "fixed legal liability," the obligee is to be saved from the thing specified, and the right of action becomes complete on the defendant's failure to do the particular thing he agreed to perform; while, on the other hand, where the covenant is for indemnity only, and against resultant damages, these must be actually suffered before an action can be maintained.[49]

A mortgage given as a continuing security and indemnity for and against all liabilities the mortgagees had incurred or might thereafter incur for the mortgagor as indorsers, is not a mortgage of indemnity merely, but one of security as well, and therefore it is not essential to a recovery to show that damages have been sustained; but the right of the mortgagees to resort to the security arises when their liability is fixed.[49a]

If a mortgage given to secure the mortgagee from loss by reason of his having become a surety upon a note executed by one of the mortgagors stipulates that the mortgagors "will pay the sum of money above secured," a cause of action accrues to the mortgagee upon failure of the maker of the note to pay the note when it becomes due, without the mortgagee's first paying the note.[50]

§ 385. **Respective rights of principal creditor and surety.**—The principal creditor is entitled to the benefit of a mortgage given for the indemnity of a surety.[51] Three joint indorsers of the paper of a manufacturing company executed separate mortgages to a trustee under an agreement that, if either should pay more than his equal proportion of the notes indorsed, he should recover from each of the others the shares they ought respectively to contribute. It was held that the

313, 9 S. E. 966; Kaphan v. Ryan, 16 S. Car. 352.

[48] Vogan v. Caminetti, 65 Cal. 438; Athol Savings Bank v. Pomroy, 115 Mass. 573. See ante § 64.

[49] Gilbert v. Wiman, 1 N. Y. 550, 49 Am. Dec. 359, as stated by Finch, J., in National Bank v. Bigler, 83 N. Y. 51.

[49a] Goff v. Hedgcock, 144 Ind. 415, 43 N. E. 644; Shaw v. Loud, 12 Mass. 447.

[50] Gunel v. Cue, 72 Ind. 34; Gilbert v. Wiman, 1 N. Y. 550, 49 Am. Dec. 359; Thomas v. Allen, 1 Hill (N. Y.) 145; Wilson v. Stilwell, 9 Ohio St. 467, 75 Am. Dec. 477; Loosemore v. Radford, 9 M. & W. 657.

[51] Jones on Pledges, §§ 523-533.

agreement and mortgages secured not merely equality of payment between the sureties, but also secured the payment of the indorsed notes to the holders who might join with the trustee in enforcing the mortgages.[52]

The principal creditor is not entitled to the benefit of a mortgage given to a surety until the liability of the latter is fixed.[53] If the indorser is discharged by the laches of the creditor, he can not claim the benefit of the mortgage.[54] The condition of such a mortgage is broken when the mortgagor fails to pay the debt at the time stipulated, so that the mortgagee is exposed to a suit.[55] He may then at once proceed to foreclose the mortgage without notice or further action on his part.[56] When the condition is to indemnify the mortgagee against the support of a third person, it is a sufficient breach that the mortgagee is compelled to pay for such support for a part of the time.[57]

If the mortgage to the surety include a debt due to himself, as well as the debt for which he is liable as surety, as between himself and the principal creditor the latter is entitled to be first paid out of the proceeds of the mortgage, on the ground that such mortgagee is a quasi trustee for the creditor in respect of the indemnity thus obtained.[58] It is not a valid objection to an indemnifying mortgage that it includes security for debts due to the sureties themselves. The only difference this makes is that the debts for which the sureties are liable, and for which the mortgage was given by way of indemnity, must first be paid.[59]

§ 386. **Release of security by indemnity mortgagee.**—Under what circumstances one who has taken a mortgage solely for his own indemnity may release the security does not seem to be determined. As against the principal creditor, who is entitled to the benefit of the securities held by the surety, it would seem at any rate that after a default on the part of the principal debtor, and the liability of the surety had thus become fixed, he could not release the securities held by him. As against his own creditors, after he has become insolvent, it would also seem that he could not release a mortgage or other security held by him as indemnity.[60] If the mortgage held by him be anything

[52] Seward v. Huntington, 26 Hun (N. Y.) 217.
[53] Tilford v. James, 7 B. Mon. (Ky.) 336.
[54] Tilford v. James, 7 B. Mon. (Ky.) 336.
[55] Shaw v. Loud, 12 Mass. 447.
[56] Butler v. Ladue, 12 Mich. 173.

[57] Whitton v. Whitton, 38 N. H. 127, 75 Am. Dec. 163.
[58] Ten Eyck v. Holmes, 3 Sandf. Ch. (N. Y.) 428.
[59] Simmons Hdw. Co. v. Thomas, 147 Ind. 313, 46 N. E. 645.
[60] Woodville v. Reed, 26 Md. 179.

more than one of indemnity, if, for instance, it in terms secures the original debt, he has no right to discharge it.

An indorser of certain notes took from the maker of them a mortgage as security from any loss the indorser might sustain from the nonpayment of the notes. The proviso was that the mortgagor should pay the notes at their maturity "to the holders of them," or to the indorser, should the latter be compelled to take them up; the mortgagee subsequently released the mortgage before the notes were paid, and the mortgagor conveyed the premises to a purchaser. The holder of the mortgage notes then filed a bill to foreclose the mortgage; and it was held that the mortgage was a security for the payment of the notes, as well as an indemnity to the indorser; that it inured to the benefit of any one in whose hands the notes might be, provided he is a bona fide holder of them; and that consequently the mortgagee had no power to release the mortgage, so as to deprive the holder of the notes of the benefit of this security.[61] Where the surety himself has received such securities from the principal debtor on account of an obligation assumed, equity creates a quasi trust in relation thereto in favor of the creditor and cosureties until the debt is discharged. The surety has no right to discharge or defeat such trust.[62]

§ 387. **Not after liability is fixed.**—A mortgage given to indemnify a surety or indorser does not, in the first instance, attach to the debt; and whatever equity may arise in favor of the creditor with regard to the security arises afterward, and in consequence of the insolvency of the parties primarily holders for the debt. Until this equity arises, the surety has a right in equity as well as at law to release the security. Even after such insolvency the mortgagee may surrender the security, if he does it in good faith, and before any claim is made upon him for it. The application of it for the benefit of third persons can only be accomplished by the interposition of a court of equity, and in case the mortgagee still retains the security.[63]

The general rule with respect to indemnity mortgages is that, where the instrument contains a promise to pay the obligations for which the mortgagee is liable as surety, the mortgage creates a trust, and an equitable lien for the full benefit of the principal creditor; and it makes no difference that such principal creditor did not act upon the

---

[61] Boyd v. Parker, 43 Md. 182.
[62] Albion State Bank v. Knickerbocker, 125 Mich. 311, 84 N. W. 311; Union Nat. Bank v. Rich, 106 Mich. 319, 64 N. W. 339.

[63] Jones v. Quinnipiack Bank, 29 Conn. 25; Post v. Tradesmen's Bank, 28 Conn. 420; Thrall v. Spencer, 16 Conn. 139; Homer v. Savings Bank, 7 Conn. 478; Simmons Hardware Co.

credit of such security in the first instance, or even know of its existence.[64]

There seems to be a distinction between those conveyances made by a principal to a surety both for the purpose of protecting him and to secure the payment of the debt and those executed merely to indemnify the sureties against liability. If the conveyances are made to the surety for the purpose of securing the payment of the debt, the creditor has an interest therein which the surety can not destroy. But if the conveyance to the surety is only to indemnify him, then such security does not, in the first instance, attach to the debt, and whatever equity may arise in favor of the creditor with regard to the security arises afterward, and in consequence of the insolvency of the parties principally liable for the debt. Until this equity arises the surety has a right in equity as well as at law to release the security. Even after such insolvency the mortgagee may surrender the security if he does it in good faith and before any claim is made upon him for it. The application of it for the benefit of third persons can only be accomplished by the interposition of a court of equity, and in case the mortgagee still claims security, or when he has conveyed it under circumstances tending to show bad faith or collusion between him and the mortgagor.[65]

But after the principal debtor has become insolvent, the surety can not make a valid agreement with the holder, or any party interested in one of the notes on which he is indemnified by the mortgage, that the security shall be first applied to such note; the holders of all such notes are entitled in equity to share in the property in proportion to their respective claims.[66]

When a mortgage is given to indemnify an indorser, the creditor has an equitable claim to the security, and after the liability is fixed is entitled to have the mortgage assigned to him. This is the rule not only where the condition is that the mortgagor shall pay the debt, but also where it merely stipulates that he shall indemnify the surety.[67]

v. Thomas, 149 Ind. 313, 46 N. E. 645.

[64] Griffis v. First Nat. Bank. 168 Ind. 546, 81 N. E. 490; Plaut v. Storey, 131 Ind. 46, 30 N. E. 886; Durham v. Craig, 79 Ind. 117.

[65] Daniel v. Hunt, 77 Ala. 567; Dyer v. Jacoway, 76 Ark. 171, 88 S. W. 901; Steward v. Welch, 84 Maine 308, 24 Atl. 860; Pool v. Doster, 59 Miss. 258; Fertig v. Henne, 197 Pa. St. 560, 47 Atl. 840.

[66] Lewis v. De Forest, 20 Conn. 427.

[67] New Bedford Inst. for Savings v. Fairhaven Bank, 9 Allen (Mass.) 175; Riddle v. Bowman, 27 N. H. 236; Phillips v. Thompson, 2 Johns. Ch. (N. Y.) 418, 7 Am. Dec. 535; Thornton v. Nat. Exchange Bank, 71 Mo. 221; Aldrich v. Martin, 4 R. I. 520; Saylors v. Saylors, 3 Heisk. (Tenn.) 525.

Thus, a mortgage by the principal maker of a promissory note to his surety, conditioned that the principal will pay the note and save the surety harmless, creates a trust and an equitable lien for the holder of the note; and even after the surety's liability to the holder of the note is barred by the statute of limitations, he holds the property subject to such trust and lien.[68] If he has foreclosed the mortgage, and obtained an absolute title to the property, the same trust still attaches to it.[69] This equitable lien binds the property, after a transfer of it by the mortgagee to one who has notice of the trust. The mortgage is treated as a mere security for the debt; and when the debt is assigned by the mortgagee, it carries with it in equity, as an incident, a right to have the estate appropriated for the payment of the debt in the hands of the assignee. To carry out and enforce this equity, the mortgagee is regarded as the trustee of those to whom he has assigned the debt secured by the mortgage, and can be compelled to appropriate it for their benefit.[70]

IV. *Mortgages for Support*

§ 388. Whether strictly mortgages.—It has sometimes been questioned whether a deed conditioned for the support and maintenance of a person, or for the performance of any other duty, the damages for a breach of which are unliquidated, can be regarded as strictly a mortgage. Early definitions of mortgages are found by which no conditional conveyances are mortgages except such as are made for the security of a loan of money; others include all conveyances made as security for any debt; while the later doctrine generally is, that a conveyance conditioned for the performance of any contract is a mortgage.[1] But in some of the cases it is said that many contracts,

[68] Steward v. Welch, 84 Maine 308, 24 Atl. 860; Eastman v. Foster, 8 Metc. (Mass.) 19.
[69] Eastman v. Foster, 8 Metc. (Mass.) 19.
[70] Steward v. Welch, 84 Maine 308, 24 Atl. 860; Rice v. Dewey, 13 Gray (Mass.) 47.
[1] Per Bell, C. J., in Bethlehem v. Annis, 40 N. H. 34, 77 Am. Dec. 700;

Cook v. Bartholomew, 60 Conn. 24, 22 Atl. 444. See also Powers v. Patten, 71 Maine 583; Gilson v. Gilson, 2 Allen (Mass.) 115; Hawkins v. Clermont, 15 Mich. 511; Day v. Towns, 76 N. H. 200, 81 Atl. 405; Chase v. Peck, 21 N. Y. 581; Coleman v. Whitney, 62 Vt. 123, 20 Atl. 322, 9 L. R. A. 517.

the performance of which may be secured by conveyances of land, have such peculiarities that the rules of law relating to mortgages can have but a very partial if any application to them.[2]

Where a warranty deed contained an agreement on the part of the grantee that, in consideration of the conveyance that he would pay a certain yearly amount to the grantors, and support and care for them during their lives, it was held that the deed did not become absolute until performance of the agreement, and that the grantors retained a lien or charge upon the land to secure such performance.[3] Where the grantee accepts the deed and enters into possession of the premises he becomes bound by the agreement, and the provision for support is equivalent to a life annuity.[4]

In New Hampshire, although it is provided by statute[5] that "every conveyance of lands made for the purpose of securing the payment of money, or the performance of any other thing in the condition thereof stated, is a mortgage," it is held that a deed conditioned for support, and implying the personal services of the mortgagor, is not a mortgage. Neither the grantor nor the grantee, under such a deed, can assign his interest. The contract is for services to be rendered by the one person to the other in person. The former, having assumed a personal trust, can not substitute another person in his place to fulfil it.[6] Upon his death, a sale of the estate by his administrator under license of court, subject to this duty, passes no title, and the purchaser can not maintain a bill to redeem.[7] But it has occasionally been held that, in case of nonperformance of the stipulation for support, the right of redemption by payment of adequate damages will be recognized.[8] One who takes a mortgage for the support of himself and his wife is a trustee for his wife, and on his death and a breach of the condition of the mortgage the court will appoint a trustee to appropriate the land for the purposes of the trust.[9] And on the other

---

[2] Bethlehem v. Annis, 40 N. H. 34, 77 Am. Dec. 700, per Bell, C. J. See also Soper v. Guernsey, 71 Pa. St. 219.

[3] Childs v. Rue, 84 Minn. 323, 87 N. W. 918; Doesche v. Spratt, 61 Minn. 326, 63 N. W. 736.

[4] Hutchinson v. Hutchinson, 46 Maine 154; Exum v. Canty, 34 Miss. 533; Spalding v. Hallenbeck, 30 Barb. (N. Y.) 292; Shontz v. Brown, 27 Pa. St. 123.

[5] Gen. Stat, 1867, 253, ch. 122, § 1; Gen. Laws 1878, ch. 136, § 1; Pub. Stats. 1901, ch. 139, § 1.

[6] Flanders v. Lamphear, 9 N. H. 201. See also Bethlehem v. Annis, 40 N. H. 34, 77 Am. Dec. 700; Eastman v. Batchelder, 36 N. H. 141, 72 Am. Dec. 295. But see Bodwell Granite Co. v. Lane, 83 Maine 168, 21 Atl. 829; Bryant v. Erskine, 55 Maine 153; Austin v. Austin, 9 Vt. 420.

[7] Eastman v. Batchelder, 36 N. H. 141, 72 Am. Dec. 295.

[8] Bethlehem v. Annis, 40 N. H. 34, 77 Am. Dec. 700; Henry v. Tupper, 29 Vt. 358.

[9] Perkins v. Perkins. 60 N. H. 373.

hand, it is held that the person who is to receive the personal service can not assign the obligation and security to another, so as to enable such other person to enforce it, unless, perhaps, where there has been an actual breach and an entry for condition broken before the assignment.[10]

In Pennsylvania, upon somewhat different grounds, it is said that when a father conveys land to his son, and takes a reconveyance, conditioned for the faithful performance of covenants to support, although such reconveyance may be termed a mortgage, it is something more than a mortgage; for in an ordinary mortgage, when the object of security is accomplished, the conveyance becomes void; but if there be a breach of the condition to support, and the father in consequence takes possession, the son can not claim upon his father's death that the title should vest in him, notwithstanding he has failed to perform his covenants. That would be no security that the son would perform his covenants, but an inducement for him to break them. It would enable him to throw off all the trouble and responsibility of his contract, and, simply by waiting a few years without doing anything, get the property for nothing. Nothing can give effectual security for the performance of such covenants but the right to revest the entire estate upon a breach. The son, having broken his covenants to support his father during life, has no possible equity on his death to demand a reconveyance. A recovery in ejectment by the father after breach as effectually revests the title in him as would a re-entry for condition broken.[11] But the courts generally treat as mortgages conveyances conditioned for the support and maintenance of the mortgagees. They are generally in such terms that the court can by an award of damages compensate the mortgagees for a nonperformance

[10] Bryant v. Erskine, 55 Maine 153; Bethlehem v. Annis, 40 N. H. 34, 77 Am. Dec. 700. In this case Chief Justice Bell said: "Wherever the condition, when broken, gives rise to no claim for damages whatever, or to a claim for unliquidated damages, the deed is not to be regarded as a mortgage in equity, but as a conditional deed at common law. It has the incidents of a mortgage only to a limited extent, and the party, if relieved by a court of equity from a forfeiture resulting from the nonperformance of the condition, will not be relieved as in cases of a mortgage. It is not, however, intended to say that the same principle of justice, which has led courts of equity to establish the system of relief from forfeitures in the case of mortgages, will not entitle a party to analogous relief in cases where the design of the parties is to make a conveyance by way of security."

[11] Soper v. Guernsey, 71 Pa. St. 219. The defeasance in this case was: "Provided always, nevertheless, that if the said party of the first part shall and does well, truly, and faithfully perform all and singular the aforesaid covenants, promises, and agreements unto the said party of the second part, according to the true intent and meaning

of the personal services;[12] but it rests in the sound discretion of the court whether a forfeiture shall be relieved in this way.[13] Such a mortgage is not void for uncertainty in not defining the support to be furnished; for this will be construed to be such support as is proper and suitable for the person to be supported according to his station in life; and the amount required for such support can be ascertained with reasonable certainty.[14]

§ 389. **Mortgagor's right of possession implied.**—Generally, when land has been conveyed to the mortgagor by the mortgagee, who has taken a mortgage of the same, conditioned for his support, there is a necessary implication, nothing appearing to the contrary, that the mortgagee is not to enter until there is a breach of the condition.[15] A conveyance made on condition of support may, upon proof of condition broken, be rescinded by a court of equity.[16] The possession of the property is generally essential to the mortgagor to enable him to perform the condition. The mortgagee can not then maintain an action for possession until there has been a breach of condition.

If a mortgage for the support of a person for life be followed by a lease of the same premises for life given by the mortgagor to the mortgagee, the lease is regarded as merely giving the mortgagee the possession and use of the premises. The lease does not extinguish the mortgage, but is merely ancillary to it, and its enjoyment may pro tanto operate as a satisfaction of the covenants of the bond or agreement for support.[17]

Where a father conveyed a farm to his son in consideration that he should support his father and mother during their lives, and the son, fearing that the farm would be seized for a debt he owed, conveyed it to his mother on her express oral promise to reconvey it to him so soon as the debt should be settled, and the debt was afterward

---

thereof, without fraud or delay, then this indenture and the estate hereby granted shall become void."
[12] 2 Greenl. Cruise 80, n; Hoyt v. Bradley, 27 Maine 242; Borst v. Crommie, 19 Hun (N. Y.) 209; Austin v. Austin, 9 Vt. 420; Simpson v. Edmiston, 23 W. Va. 675. Chancellor Phelps, in this case, said: "There is certainly no difficulty in making compensation for past maintenance, any more than in any case of a contract to perform services." Hiatt v. Parker, 29 Kans. 765.
[13] Henry v. Tupper, 29 Vt. 258.

[14] Simpson v. Edmiston, 23 W. Va. 675.
[15] Bryant v. Erskine, 55 Maine 153; Brown v. Leach, 35 Maine 39; Abele v. McGuigan, 78 Mich. 415, 44 N. W. 398; Rhoades v. Parker, 10 N. H. 83; Flanders v. Lamphear, 9 N. H. 201; Dearborn v. Dearborn, 9 N. H. 117. See ante § 80 and post §§ 668, 702.
[16] De Long v. De Long, 56 Wis. 514, 14 N. W. 591; Blake v. Blake, 56 Wis. 392, 14 N. W. 173.
[17] Lashley v. Souder (N. J. Eq.), 24 Atl. 919.

secured by the mother and finally paid, it was held that the conveyance to the mother was in effect a mortgage to protect her interest, and therefore was not fraudulent as to the son's creditors.[18]

§ 390. Alternative condition.—When a mortgage is conditioned to pay a certain sum or to support the mortgagee, the mortgagor has his election which alternative he will take, and, if he elect to furnish support, he is entitled to possession of the premises in order to be enabled to comply with the condition he has chosen to perform. But having once made the election he can not revoke it. His election is also conclusive upon the mortgagee, who can not have the election in the beginning, and much less can he have part performance of one of the alternatives, and then claim the entire performance of the other.[19] The election having been made, the mortgage becomes security for the performance of the condition chosen as effectually as if that alone had been set forth.[20] But a mortgage to secure the payment of five hundred dollars in five years, "to be paid in furnishing the mortgagee," during that period, "a good and sufficient home and support," does not give the mortgagor his election to pay the money.[21]

Under a mortgage for support with an alternative condition to pay the mortgagee a sum of money if he should choose to leave the mortgagor and be supported elsewhere, a person who supported the mortgagee elsewhere during an illness while upon a visit, is not entitled to recover the money from the mortgagor, and the mortgaged property is not chargeable for the support of the mortgagee elsewhere, unless he was justified in leaving the mortgagor.[22] Where the mortgagee is the person designated in the mortgage to whom the support is to be furnished, he can not transfer his interest in the mortgage so as to give another the right to such support.[23]

§ 391. Where the support is to be furnished.—When no place is stipulated where the mortgagee is to receive support, he has a right to be supported wherever he may choose to live, provided he does not

---

[18] Powers v. Patten, 71 Maine 583; Abele v. McGuigan, 78 Mich. 415, 44 N. W. 393.

[19] Bryant v. Erskine, 55 Maine 153. "It is laid down as a general rule that, in case an election is given of two several things, he who is the first agent, and ought to do the first act, shall have the decision; as if a man grants a rent of 20s. or a robe to one and his heirs, the grantor shall have the election, for he is the first agent, by payment of one or the delivery of the other." 3 Bac. Abr. Election, B, p. 309.

[20] Furbish v. Sears, 2 Cliff. (U. S.) 454; Lindsey v. Bradley, 53 Vt. 682.

[21] Hawkins v. Clermont, 15 Mich. 511. See also Evans v. Norris, 6 Mich. 369.

[22] Lindsey v. Bradley, 53 Vt. 682.

[23] Bryant v. Erskine, 55 Maine 153;

create any needless expense to the mortgagor.[24] When it is provided that the support is to be furnished on the granted premises, but that the mortgagor, with his family, may also reside there, the latter has no right to insist that the mortgagee shall become a part of his family or receive support at his table, and in the apartments occupied by him. A refusal to furnish such support in a separate room is a breach of the condition.[25] If the place where support is to be furnished is left ambiguous in the mortgage, parol evidence is admissible to explain the ambiguity, and show the intention of the parties.[26]

The condition of such a mortgage is broken by the mortgagor's declining to pay for the board of the mortgagee at a suitable place, although he make no special demand upon the mortgagor for such support.[27]

A mortgage conditioned to provide a home in the house on the premises obliges the mortgagor, notwithstanding his removal from the premises, and the house becoming, by natural decay, and without his fault, much dilapidated and not worth repairing, to provide a home there, or to furnish an equivalent elsewhere, but does not oblige him to supply food, clothing, or fuel. The fact that the mortgagor actually furnished such supplies for some time after making the mortgage does not affect this construction.[28]

It is not sufficient proof of a breach of contract to support a person during life, to show that he left the house of the obligor and resided elsewhere for several years, but without at any time requesting him to fulfil his agreement, or in any way manifesting to him an intention or desire to hold him to the performance of the obligation.[29]

Where a mortgage by a son to his mother was conditioned "to provide a horse for said Margery to ride to meeting and elsewhere, when necessary; find her firewood for one fire, to be drawn and cut at the door, fit for use; give her a good cow, and keep said cow for her dur-

---

Bethlehem v. Annis, 40 N. H. 34, 77 Am. Dec. 700.

[24] Rowell v. Jewett, 69 Maine 293; Wilder v. Whittemore, 15 Mass. 262; Thayer v. Richards, 19 Pick. (Mass.) 398; Flanders v. Lamphear, 9 N. H. 201; Borst v. Crommie, 19 Hun (N. Y.) 209; Young v. Young, 59 Vt. 342, 10 Atl. 528.

[25] Hubbard v. Hubbard, 12 Allen (Mass.) 586. See also Thayer v. Richards, 19 Pick. (Mass.) 398; Powers v. Mastin, 62 Vt. 433, 20 Atl. 105.

[26] Young v. Young, 59 Vt. 342, 10 Atl. 528. For a provision which leaves it optional with the mortgagee to reside with the mortgagor or to be supported in some other place, see Dickinson v. Dickinson, 59 Vt. 678, 10 Atl. 821.

[27] Pettee v. Case, 2 Allen (Mass.) 546.

[28] Gibson v. Taylor, 6 Gray (Mass.) 310.

[29] Jenkins v. Stetson, 9 Allen (Mass.) 128; Thayer v. Richards, 19 Pick. (Mass.) 398; Rhoades v. Parker, 10 N. H. 83.

ing the natural life of her the said Margery," it was held that the destruction of the house in which the mother lived with her son did not exempt him from the performance of the condition, and that he was bound to furnish the wood at such place as she should make her home, within a reasonable and convenient distance; that if the mortgagee was obliged to sell the cow in consequence of its not being properly kept, it was not necessary, in order to charge him with the cost of keeping a cow for the time subsequent to the sale, that the mortgagee should purchase a cow and tender her to the mortgagor to be kept.[30]

§ 392. **Persons who are to perform condition for support.**—As already stated, a mortgage for support is in its nature a contract for personal services, and, especially when by its terms the condition is to be performed by the mortgagor, his heirs, executors, or administrators, the duty can not be transferred to a third person. Upon the death of the mortgagor, the condition must be kept by his heirs, executors, or administrators, and the mortgaged property subject to this duty can not be disposed of by the administrator for the payment of the mortgagor's debts;[31] and a creditor of the mortgagor can not levy upon the land and eject the mortgagor because he can not perform the condition.[32] Of course, the contract itself may determine the question whether the support must be furnished by the mortgagor personally or not. It would seem that, if the contract does not expressly or impliedly provide that it shall be fulfilled by the mortgagor himself, it may be performed by any one else. But aside from the terms of the contract, there seems to be some divergence of opinion as to the personal character of the obligation to support. Some courts allow compensation in damages for a breach of this condition.[33]

The mortgagor's interest in land mortgaged to secure the mortgagee's support may be sold upon execution against the mortgagor, for he has an actual interest in the land so mortgaged. He owns it, subject to the mortgage. "If he could not assign or convey any right to perform the condition in the mortgage, he could divest

[30] Fiske v. Fiske, 20 Pick. (Mass.) 499.

[31] Ridley v. Ridley, 87 Maine 445, 32 Atl. 1005; Bryant v. Erskine, 55 Maine 153; Bethlehem v. Annis, 40 N. H. 34, 77 Am. Dec. 700; Eastman v. Batchelder, 36 N. H. 141, 72 Am. Dec. 295. See also Cross v. Carson, 8 Blatchf. (Ind.) 138, 44 Am. Dec. 742; Thomas v. Record, 47 Maine 500, 74 Am. Dec. 500; Flanders v.

Lamphear, 9 N. H. 201; White v. Bailey, 65 W. Va. 573, 64 S. E. 1019, 23 L. R. A. (N. S.) 232; Fluharty v. Fluharty, 54 W. Va. 407, 46 S. E. 199.

[32] Ridley v. Ridley, 87 Maine 445, 32 Atl. 1005; Greenleaf v. Grounder, 86 Maine 298, 29 Atl. 1082.

[33] Joslyn v. Parlin, 54 Vt. 670; Henry v. Tupper, 29 Vt. 358; Austin v. Austin, 9 Vt. 420.

himself of all his interest in the land. That interest was his own, to be disposed of as he saw fit. His grantee might not have acquired the right to perform the condition, but he acquired the land subject to the condition. If the condition should never be performed by the mortgagor, his grantee might lose the land. If the condition should be performed, the grantee of the mortgagor would hold the land free of the condition."[34]

§ 393. **Foreclosure.**—A mortgage for the support of the grantee and his wife during their lives may be foreclosed by the administrator of the grantee, for a breach of condition occurring both before and after the grantee's death, although his widow does not join in the suit.[35] But where a mortgage was conditioned to support the mortgagee during her lifetime, and there was no evidence of a breach of the condition, or of any demand for support other than what was furnished, it was held that the administrator of the mortgagee could not foreclose the mortgage for the benefit of persons who had boarded the mortgagee at the mortgagor's request. The mortgage was regarded as for the benefit of the mortgagee, and not for the benefit of those who might furnish her with support. Whatever claim they severally had for boarding and taking care of her at the mortgagor's request was against him personally, and not against her or her estate.[36]

Where, upon the separation of husband and wife, the wife's brother, in consideration of a sum paid by the husband, agreed to support the wife without cost or expense to the husband, and to save him harmless from all charge for her support, and secured the agreement by a mortgage, the wife, though not a party to the agreement, was allowed to enforce it, since it was made for her benefit.[37]

Where the consideration of a deed is the grantee's mortgage on the premises conditioned that he will support the grantors, during life, no place being specified where such support shall be furnished them, they are not obliged to receive such support at the mortgagor's house, but are entitled to have it at such reasonable place as they may select; and when, with knowledge of such selection, the mortgagor fails to furnish such support required by his contract, and declares his intention not to do so, or pay for any support which may be furnished by others, the condition of the mortgage is broken, and an action of fore-

[34] Bodwell Granite Co. v. Lane, 83 Maine 168, 21 Atl. 829.

[35] Marsh v. Austin, 1 Allen (Mass.) 235. See also French v. Case, 77 Mich. 64, 43 N. W. 1056.

[36] Daniels v. Eisenlord, 10 Mich. 454.

[37] Coleman v. Whitney, 62 Vt. 123, 20 Atl. 322.

closure may be maintained for the reasonable value of the support provided by others, though it was provided without the request of the mortgagor or demand upon him to furnish the support required.[38]

Where a mortgage from a son to his parents, for their support, provides also for the use of a horse and buggy when they, or either of them, may desire it, there is a breach of the condition upon a failure to furnish it on a reasonable demand by either of them alone, and either of them may have a separate action for damages. The provision is not joint, but several. The damages allowed should cover the actual damage sustained. No decree can be made for future violations of this provision. It is impossible to determine in advance what damages may result from a failure to perform the condition.[39]

An instrument under seal but not acknowledged, in which the maker agrees to support his father and mother during their natural lives, and as security for the fulfilment of the agreement conveys and grants to them, "each and severally, a life lien or dower, or lien of maintenance for life," in real estate, is a mortgage; and upon a breach of the agreement, an action for possession of the premises may be sustained by the father alone.[40]

If the mortgagor give a bond in a fixed sum conditioned for the maintenance and support of the mortgagee, such sum will be regarded as a penalty, and the mortgage can not be treated as one to secure the payment of that sum absolutely, unless there be a stipulation that this sum shall be regarded as liquidated damages for any default.[41]

Instead of a judgment of foreclosure and sale, in some states a judgment of strict foreclosure, or for rescinding of the conveyance, will be entered.[42]

Where one of the conditions of a mortgage is that the mortgagor should remain in possession and support the mortgagee, the burden is upon the mortgagee to show a breach of the condition.[43]

§ 394. **Agreement for arbitration.**—Under a mortgage to secure the performance of a bond or contract conditioned to support the mortgagee, a stipulation "that, should either party be dissatisfied with the fulfilling of the above bond, it shall be submitted" to three per-

---

[38] Tuttle v. Burgett, 53 Ohio St. 498, 42 N. E. 427, 30 L. R. A. 214, 53 Am. St. 649.

[39] Tucker v. Tucker, 24 Mich. 426, 35 Mich. 365.

[40] Gilson v. Gilson, 2 Allen (Mass.) 115. See also Lanfair v. Lanfair, 18 Pick. (Mass.) 299. The judgment may be in the nature of a strict foreclosure. See post § 1556.

[41] Wright v. Wright, 49 Mich. 624, 14 N. W. 571; Bresnahan v. Bresnahan, 46 Wis. 385, 14 N. W. 571.

[42] Bresnahan v. Bresnahan, 46 Wis. 385, 14 N. W. 571; Bogie v. Bogie, 41 Wis. 209.

[43] Davis v. Poland, 99 Maine 345, 59 Atl. 520.

sons named, "and their decision shall be final," does not prevent an action for breach of condition by the mortgagee. This comes within the general principle that an agreement for arbitration shall not deprive one of his legal remedies.[44] If an award is made under such a stipulation, it is a debt subject to attachment by trustee process or garnishment by the creditors of the mortgagee.[45]

§ 395. **Redemption.**—Such a mortgage may be redeemed after breach.[46] It has been held, however, that no such right exists; that where the condition calls for the support of the mortgagee or some other person, the land can not be redeemed by the payment of a sum of money.[47] A court of equity may grant relief from the forfeiture of a condition for the maintenance of the mortgagee when the forfeiture has been accidental or unintentional, and not attended with irreparable injury. But the granting of relief in such a case rests in the sound discretion of the court.[48]

[44] Hill v. More, 40 Maine 515. See also Dickinson v. Dickinson, 59 Vt. 678, 10 Atl. 821.

[45] Dickinson v. Dickinson, 59 Vt. 678, 10 Atl. 821.

[46] Rowell v. Jewett, 69 Maine 293; Bryant v. Erskine, 55 Maine 153; Bethlehem v. Annis, 40 N. H. 34, 77 Am. Dec. 700. See also Hoyt v. Bradley, 27 Maine 242; Fiske v. Fiske, 20 Pick. (Mass.) 499; Wilder v. Whittemore, 15 Mass. 262; Austin v. Austin, 9 Vt. 420.

[47] Hawkins v. Clermont, 15 Mich. 511; Evans v. Norris, 6 Mich. 369; Soper v. Guernsey, 71 Pa. St. 219.

[48] Henry v. Tupper, 29 Vt. 358, 375. Redfield, C. J., said: "We must all feel that cases of the character before the court should be received with something more of distrust, and relief afforded with more reserve and circumspection, than in ordinary cases of collateral duties. And although we are not prepared to say that it must appear that in all cases the failure arises from surprise, or accident, or mistake, we certainly should not grant relief when the omission was wilful and wanton, or attended with suffering or serious inconvenience to the grantee, or there was any good ground to apprehend a recurrence of the failure to perform. * * * The case might occur where the refusal to afford daily support would be wanton or wicked; indeed, where it might proceed from murderous intentions even; and it is even supposable that the treatment of those who were the objects of the services should be such as to subject the grantor to indictment for manslaughter, or murder even, and possibly to ignominious punishment and to death. To afford relief in such a case, for the benefit of the heirs, would be to make the court almost partakers in the offense. And the case, upon the other hand, is entirely supposable, and not of infrequent occurrence, where, through mere inadvertence, a technical breach may have occurred in the nonperformance of some unimportant particular, in kind or degree, where, through perhaps mere difference in construction, or error in judgment, one may have suffered a forfeiture of an estate at law of thousands of dollars in value, where the collateral service was not of a dollar's value, and attended with no serious inconvenience to the grantee. Not to afford relief in such case would be a discredit to the enlightened jurisprudence of the English nation, and those American states which have attempted to follow the same model." See also Soper v. Guernsey, 71 Pa. St. 219; Dunklee v. Adams, 20 Vt. 415, 1 Am. Dec. 44. See ante § 388.

CHAPTER X

INSURANCE

I. *Insurable Interests of Mortgagor and Mortgagee, §§ 396–399*

II. *Insurance by the Mortgagor for the Benefit of the Mortgagee, §§ 400–417*

III. *Insurance by the Mortgagee, §§ 418–421*

IV. *A Mortgage is not an Alienation, §§ 422–427*

I. *Insurable Interests of Mortgagor and Mortgagee*

§ 396. Nature of fire insurance contract.—The fundamental principle at the base of every contract of insurance affecting an interest in property is that of indemnity.[1] Thus insurance against fire is a contract of indemnity with the assured against any loss he may sustain by the burning of the buildings. He must have some interest in the property insured, as owner, mortgagee, or otherwise, to make the contract effectual. If he never had any interest, or if at the time of the loss he had ceased to have any interest, he can not claim anything under the contract; for he has suffered no loss. He may upon transferring his interest in the estate at the same time transfer the policy of insurance, and such transfer, being assented to by the underwriter, constitutes a new and original promise to the assignee to indemnify him. "But such undertaking," said Shaw, C. J., "will be binding, not because the policy is in any way incident to the estate or runs with the land, but in consequence of the new contract."[2]

---

[1] McDonald v. Black, 20 Ohio 185, 55 Am. Dec. 448; Castellain v. Preston, L. R. 11 Q. B. D. 380.

[2] Donnell v. Donnell, 86 Maine 518, 30 Atl. 67; Macomber v. Cambridge Mut. F. Ins. Co., 8 Cush. (Mass.) 133; Wilson v. Hill, 3 Metc. (Mass.) 66; Murdock v. Chenango County Mut. Ins. Co., 2 N. Y. 210; Johannes v. Phœnix Ins. Co., 66 Wis. 50, 27 N. W. 414, 57 Am. Rep. 249. See also Palatine Ins. Co. v. O'Brien, 107 Md. 341, 68 Atl. 484, 16 L. R. A. (N. S.) 1055n; Morrison v. Tennessee M. &c. Ins. Co., 18 Mo. 262, 59 Am. Dec. 299n; Rogers v. Shawnee Fire

§ 397. Insurable interests.—The mortgagor may insure the full value of the property, and recover the full amount insured, if at the time of the loss he had the right of redemption;[3] and it matters not that the mortgagee has taken possession of the premises.[4] Neither does it matter that his right in equity has been seized and sold on execution; his insurable interest continues so long as he has the right to redeem from such sale, and he may upon a loss recover the whole amount insured.[5]

The mortgagee and the mortgagor may both insure their separate interests at the same time.[6] Such insurance is not liable to the objection of a double insurance, because to constitute this the two policies must be not only upon the same property, but also for the benefit of the same person, and for the same entire risk.[7] So where the mortgagor and mortgagee insure their respective interests in property in different companies, each company is liable in case of loss according to the insurable interest of the insured in the property.[8]

A trustee in a deed of trust in the nature of a mortgage in like manner has an insurable interest distinct from that of the grantor.[9]

A conveyance of the mortgaged property by the mortgagor in no way affects the mortgagee's right to insure his interest.[10]

Ins. Co., 132 Mo. App. 275, 111 S. W. 592; Cummings v. Cheshire County Mut. F. Ins. Co., 55 N. H. 457; Cross v. National F. Ins. Co., 132 N. Y. 133, 30 N. E. 390; Farmers' Ins. Co. v. Butler, 38 Ohio St. 128; Chrisman v. State Ins. Co., 16 Ore. 283, 18 Pac. 466; Steinmeyer v. Steinmeyer, 64 S. Car. 413, 42 S. E. 184, 59 L. R. A. 319, 92 Am. St. 809.

[3] Insurance Co. v. Stinson, 103 U. S. 25, 26 L. ed. 473; Carpenter v. Providence &c. Ins. Co., 16 Pet. (U. S.) 495, 10 L. ed. 1044. See also McDonald v. Black, 20 Ohio 185, 55 Am. Dec. 448.

[4] Illinois F. Ins. Co. v. Stanton, 57 Ill. 354; Stephens v. Illinois Mut. Fire Ins. Co., 43 Ill. 327.

[5] Strong v. Manufacturers' Ins. Co., 10 Pick. (Mass.) 40, 20 Am. Dec. 507.

[6] Manson v. Phœnix Ins. Co., 64 Wis. 26, 24 N. W. 407, 54 Am. Rep. 573. See also Carpenter v. Providence Washington Ins. Co., 16 Pet. (U. S.) 495, 10 L. ed. 1044; Mahoney v. State Ins. Co. , 133 Iowa 570, 110 N. W. 1041, 9 L. R. A. (N. S.) 490; King v. State &c. Ins. Co., 7 Cush.

(Mass.) 1, 54 Am. Dec. 683; Key v. Continental Ins. Co., 101 Mo. App. 344, 74 S. W. 162; Hanover Fire Ins. Co. v. Bohn, 48 Nebr. 743, 67 N. W. 774, 58 Am. St. 719; Traders' Ins. Co. v. Robert, 9 Wend. (N. Y.) 404; Jones on Chattel Mortgages, § 100.

[7] Westchester F. Ins. Co. v. Foster, 90 Ill. 121; Dick v. Franklin F. Ins. Co., 10 Mo. App. 376, 81 Mo. 103; Ætna Ins. Co. v. Tyler, 16 Wend. (N. Y.) 385, 30 Am. Dec. 90.

[8] Hardy v. Lancashire Ins. Co., 166 Mass. 210, 44 N. E. 209, 33 L. R. A. 241, 55 Am. St. 395; Tuck v. Hartford F. Ins. Co,. 56 N. H. 326.

[9] Carpenter v. Providence, &c. Ins. Co., 16 Pet. (U. S.) 495, 10 L. ed. 1044; Honore v. Insurance Co., 51 Ill. 409; Suffolk Ins. Co. v. Boyden, 9 Allen (Mass.) 123; Dick v. Franklin F. Ins. Co., 10 Mo. App. 376; Foster v. Van Reed, 70 N. Y. 19, 26 Am. Rep. 544. A policy insuring the "estate of A B, deceased," is valid. Magoun v. Fireman's Fund Ins. Co., 86 Minn. 486, 91 N. W. 5.

[10] Dick v. Franklin F. Ins. Co., 10 Mo. App. 376.

The owner of an equity of redemption obtained a policy of insurance which contained a provision that he should not be entitled to recover any greater proportion of the loss than the amount insured might bear to the whole sum insured on the same property, without reference to the solvency or liability of other insurers. The owner had at the time of the loss another policy on his interest in another company; and the mortgagee had a policy on his interest in a third company. The jury were properly directed to apportion the loss between the companies having insurance upon the mortgagor's interest, without taking into account the value of the interest of the mortgagee insured by him; that is to say, in apportioning the loss, the value of the equity of redemption was taken as a basis, and not the value of the entire property.[11]

The insurable interest of the holder of the mortgage is measured by the value of his lien, if this does not exceed the value of the property.[12] He may recover according to his interest at the time of the loss. It does not matter that the mortgage is not valid at law, so long as it is valid in equity, as in the case of a mortgage by a husband to his wife, made for a just and valuable consideration.[13]

The mortgagee may insure as general owner without disclosing his interest unless this is inquired about, or he may insure his interest as mortgagee.[14] When an inquiry is made respecting his interest, or when he undertakes to make a disclosure of his interest, his representations must be substantially correct or the policy will be void. But the mere fact of not disclosing his interest will not have that effect.

A mortgagee, who upon assigning the mortgage has indorsed the note, has an insurable interest in the mortgaged property. And that interest is sufficiently described by calling him "mortgagee," though the policy provides that the interest of the assured, whether as owner, trustee, mortgagee, lessee, or otherwise, shall be truly stated.[15]

[11] Tuck v. Hartford F. Ins. Co., 56 N. H. 326.

[12] Sussex County Mut. Ins. Co. v. Woodruff, 26 N. J. L. 541; Tillou v. Kingston Mut. Ins. Co., 7 Barb. (N. Y.) 570; Slocovich v. Oriental Mut. Ins. Co., 13 Daly (N. Y.) 264; Kernochan v. New York Bowery F. Ins. Co., 5 Duer (N. Y.) 1, 17 N. Y. 428; Excelsior Fire Ins. Co. v. Royal Ins. Co., 7 Lans. 138, 55 N. Y. 343, 14 Am. Rep. 271.

[13] Mix v. Andes Ins. Co,. 9 Hun (N. Y.) 397.

[14] Buck v. Phœnix Ins. Co,. 76 Maine 586; Sussex County Mut. Ins. Co. v. Woodruff, 26 N. J. L. 541; Titus v. Glens Falls Ins. Co., 81 N. Y. 410; Norwich Fire Ins. Co. v. Boomer, 52 Ill. 442, 4 Am. Rep. 618, per Mr. Justice Walker: "Neither reason, authority, nor the contract of assurance, so far as we can see, required the mortgagee, unless interrogated, to state the nature of his interest in the property."

[15] Williams v. Roger Williams Ins. Co., 107 Mass. 377, 9 Am. Rep. 41.

Upon payment of the mortgage debt the mortgagee's insurable interest ceases; and upon part payment his insurable interest is the amount of the debt remaining unpaid.[16]

When a purchaser at foreclosure sale, subject to redemption, procures and pays for insurance on the property to which he holds a certificate of purchase, the contract of indemnity so procured is a personal contract between the purchaser and the insurance company, which does not inure to the benefit of the person entitled to redeem.[17] If the insured, at the time of the issuance of the policy, had lost the property through foreclosure of a mortgage upon it, and the time for redemption has expired, he has no insurable interest.[18]

§ 398. **How long mortgagor's interest remains insurable.**—The mortgagor's interest remains insurable so long as he has a right to redeem the land. It continues after a sale of his equity of redemption on execution until his right to redeem from such sale is barred; and he may recover the insurance notwithstanding the sale.[19] What the value of his redeemable interest may be is immaterial; the whole sum insured may be recovered, if this does not exceed the value of the property.[20] In like manner the mortgagor's insurable interest continues after a foreclosure sale when a right to redeem exists after such a sale, so long as this right exists; and when there is no right of redemption after such sale, it would seem that he retains an insurable interest until the deed is delivered in pursuance of the sale. The purchaser has no right to the possession of the property until he receives the deed, and in the meantime the mortgagor has at least the right to occupy or to collect the rents; and until then the sale is not complete, nor is the right to redeem conclusively barred.[21]

[16] Sussex County Mut. Ins. Co. v. Woodruff, 26 N. J. L. 541. See also Carpenter v. Providence Washington Ins. Co., 16 Pet. (U. S.) 495, 10 L. ed. 1044.

[17] Deming Inv. Co. v. Dickerman, 63 Kans. 728, 66 Pac. 1029. Per Pollock, J.: "The purchaser, having collected that which he has purchased and for which he has paid, is under no obligation to account for it, either by reduction in the amount necessary to redeem or to the redemptioner." Citing McIntire v. Plaisted, 68 Maine 363; Cushing v. Thompson, 34 Maine 496; King v. State Mutual Fire Insurance Co., 7 Cush. (Mass.) 1, 54 Am. Dec. 683.

[18] Pope v. Glens Falls Ins. Co., 136 Ala. 670, 34 So. 29.

[19] Strong v. Manufacturers' Ins. Co., 10 Pick. (Mass.) 40, 20 Am. Dec. 507. See also Rawson v. Bethesda Baptist Church, 221 Ill. 216, 77 N. E. 560, 6 L. R. A. (N. S.) 448n; Stephens v. Illinois Mut. F. Ins. Co., 43 Ill. 327; Richland County Mut. Ins. Co. v. Sampson, 38 Ohio St. 672.

[20] Strong v. Manufacturers' Ins. Co., 10 Pick. (Mass.) 40, 20 Am. Dec. 507.

[21] Gordon v. Massachusetts F. &c. Ins. Co., 2 Pick. (Mass.) 249; Buffalo Steam-Engine Works v. Sun Mut. Ins. Co., 17 N. Y. 401; Insurance Co. v. Sampson, 38 Ohio St.

Even after a mortgagor has conveyed his equity of redemption subject to the mortgage, or his grantee has assumed the payment of it, he retains an insurable interest, because he is liable upon the mortgage note to the holder of the mortgage, and is therefore interested in the preservation of the property charged with the payment of it.[22] Where an owner of real estate gave two mortgages thereon, and then conveyed his equity of redemption, taking back an obligation to support himself and wife, secured by a third mortgage, he has an insurable interest in the property, not only because he holds the third mortgage, but also because he is the maker of the notes secured by the first two and is personally bound for their payment.[23] And even after an absolute conveyance, intended, however, as a security merely, and therefore in equity a mortgage, the mortgagor retains an insurable interest.[24]

§ 399. When application should state incumbrance.—The existence of a mortgage upon a building, for the insurance of which application is made, is a material fact, if inquired about, and any misrepresentation in regard to the existence of the incumbrance or the amount of it will render void the policy.[25] Although the original

672. In McLaren v. Hartford F. Ins. Co., 5 N. Y. 151, it was held that the mortgagor could not recover for a loss happening after a sale under a decree of foreclosure, and before the delivery of the deed, having then no insurable interest; but this ruling is doubted in Cheney v. Woodruff, 45 N. Y. 98. See also Brown v. Frost, Hoff. Ch. (N. Y.) 41.

[22] Buck v. Phœnix Ins. Co., 76 Maine 586; Strong v. Manufacturers' Ins. Co., 10 Pick. (Mass.) 40, 20 Am. Dec. 507; Waring v. Loder, 53 N. Y. 581; Herkimer v. Rice, 27 N. Y. 163. See also Hanover Fire Ins. Co. v. Bohn, 48 Nebr. 743, 67 N. W. 774, 58 Am. St. 719.

[23] Buck v. Phœnix Ins. Co., 76 Maine 586.

[24] Walsh v. Philadelphia F. Assn., 127 Mass. 383; Hodges v. Tennessee Marine &c. Ins. Co., 8 N. Y. 416.

[25] Davenport v. North Eastern Mut. F. Ins. Co., 6 Cush. (Mass.) 340; Van Buren v. St. Joseph County Village F. Ins. Co., 28 Mich. 398. Stating the mortgage to be about $3,000, when it was in fact $4,000, has that effect. Hayward v. North Eastern Mut. F. Ins. Co., 10 Cush. (Mass.) 444. And to like effect, Brown v. People's Mut. Ins. Co., 11 Cush. (Mass.) 280. Void also when subject to a pre-existing mortgage not recorded. Packard v. Agawam Mut. F. Ins. Co., 2 Gray (Mass.) 334. Misrepresentation as to the existence of mortgage: Ætna Ins. Co. v. Resh, 40 Mich. 241; Murphy v. People's Eq. Mut. F. Ins. Co., 7 Allen (Mass.) 239; Towne v. Fitchburg Mut. F. Ins. Co., 7 Allen (Mass.) 51; Falis v. Conway Mut. F. Ins. Co., 7 Allen (Mass.) 46; Draper v. Charter Oak F. Ins. Co., 2 Allen (Mass.) 569; Bowditch Mut. F. Ins. Co. v. Winslow, 8 Gray (Mass.) 38, 3 Gray 415; Titus v. Glens Falls Ins. Co., 81 N. Y. 410; Woodward v. Republic F. Ins. Co., 32 Hun (N. Y.) 365; Byers v. Farmers' Ins. Co., 35 Ohio St. 606, 35 Am. Rep. 623; Smith v. Columbia Ins. Co., 17 Pa. St. 253, 55 Am. Dec. 546. Whether a deed of trust is compatible with an entire, unconditional, and sole ownership of the property by the assured, see Manhattan F. Ins. Co. v. Weill, 28 Grat. (Va.) 389, 26 Am. Rep. 364.

amount of the mortgage be correctly stated, a failure to disclose the existence of accumulated interest to a large amount has been held to invalidate the policy.[26] But if the principal of the mortgage be correctly stated, the omission to include interest upon it then accruing, but not then due, does not make the representation of the amount of the incumbrance untrue, nor render the policy void.[27] The failure of an applicant for insurance to disclose the existence of a mortgage which has been paid, or one which is invalid by reason of its having been obtained by fraud, does not render the policy void.[28]

Where the application is oral and no inquiry is made as to the character and condition of the title, a failure to disclose the existence of incumbrances will not, in the absence of fraud, avoid the policy.[29] And where there is a written application containing answers to specific questions, an innocent failure by an applicant to communicate facts about which he is not asked, will not avoid the policy.[30] Where an application was made upon a printed form furnished by the company, and which contained a paragraph reading, "The aforesaid premises are not incumbered by mortgage or otherwise to exceed the sum of $——," was not completed by the applicant filling out the blank, and it was held neither an assent nor dissent to the fact of the existence of a mortgage.[31]

Knowledge on the part of the insurer of the existence of a mortgage may be inferred from the circumstances of the case, though not actually disclosed by the insured;[32] thus where the insurers of property, upon which there was at the time an undisclosed mortgage, afterward insured the interest of the mortgagee and later still renewed the first policy, the circumstances warranted a finding that the insurers knew of the mortgage when they renewed the policy to the mortgagor.[33] Knowledge on the part of an agent of the insurers of an incumbrance

[26] Jacobs v. Eagle Mut. F. Ins. Co., 7 Allen (Mass.) 132.

[27] Titus v. Glens Falls Ins. Co., 81 N. Y. 410.

[28] Lycoming Fire Ins. Co. v. Jackson, 83 Ill. 302, 25 Am. Rep. 386.

[29] Seal v. Farmers' &c. Ins. Co,. 59 Nebr. 253, 80 N. W. 807; Arthur v. Palatine Ins. Co., 35 Ore. 27, 57 Pac. 62, 76 Am. St. 450.

[30] Hosford v. Germania F. Ins. Co., 127 U. S. 399, 32 L. ed. 196, 8 Sup. Ct. 1199; Washington Mills Emery Mfg. Co. v. Weymouth &c. Mut. F. Ins. Co., 135 Mass. 503; Sibley v. Prescott Ins. Co., 57 Mich. 14, 23 N. W. 473; Boggs v. America Ins. Co., 30 Mo. 63; Carson v. Jersey City Ins. Co., 43 N. J. L. 300, 39 Am. Rep. 584, affd. 44 N. J. L. 210; Browning v. Home Ins. Co., 71 N. Y. 508, 27 Am. Rep. 86; Campbell v. American Fire Ins. Co., 73 Wis. 100, 40 N. W. 661.

[31] Parker v. Otsego &c. Ins. Co., 47 App. Div. 204, 62 N. Y. S. 199, affd. 168 N. Y. 655; 61 N. E. 1132.

[32] Woodward v. Republic F. Ins. Co., 32 Hun (N. Y.) 365.

[33] State Ins. Co. v. Todd, 83 Pa. St. 272.

will be imputed to the insurers themselves.[34] Knowledge of the existence of an incumbrance on the part of the agent authorized to solicit the insurance will bind the company, although the application filled up by him stated that there was no incumbrance.[35]

Although the policy be taken upon the interest of a mortgagee, a concealment of the existence of prior mortgages held by him·when their disclosure was called for avoids the policy.[36]

When incumbrances are not made material by an inquiry in relation to them, the applicant is not bound to disclose them. It is only necessary that he should have an insurable interest.[37]

II. *Insurance by the Mortgagor for the Benefit of the Mortgagee*

§ 400. Effect of provision in mortgage for insurance in favor of mortgagee.

—When the mortgage provides that the mortgagor shall keep the premises insured for the benefit of the mortgagee, and in fulfilment of this covenant he takes out a policy of insurance in his own name, which is not assigned to the mortgagee or made payable to him

---

[34] Holmes v. Drew, 16 Hun (N. Y.) 491.

[35] Boetcher v. Hawkeye Ins. Co,. 47 Iowa 253; Woodward v. Republic F. Ins. Co., 32 Hun (N. Y.) 365.

[36] Smith v. Columbia Ins. Co., 17 Pa. St. 253, 55 Am. Dec. 546.

[37] Lycoming F. Ins. Co. v. Jackson, 83 Ill. 302, 25 Am. Rep. 386; Norwich Fire Ins. Co. v. Boomer, 52 Ill. 442, 4 Am. Rep. 618.

in any way, the mortgagee is regarded as having an equitable lien upon the proceeds of the policy;[1] and if his mortgage is duly recorded, the covenant for insurance is regarded by some authorities as running with the land, and as giving notice of the right to others, so that no subsequent assignment of the policy would affect his rights.[2] It is immaterial in this respect whether the policy existed at the time of the mortgage, or was afterward taken out by the mortgagor.[3] After the insurance company having the risk has been notified of such equitable lien in favor of the mortgagee, it can not pay the loss to the mortgagor, except at its peril, until the rights of the mortgagee shall have been adjusted.[4] The mortgagee in such case stands in the position of an assignee of a chose in action; he must enforce his rights in the name of the mortgagor, but his interest is sufficient to enable him to hold the proceeds against an attaching creditor or any subsequent assignee. But these cases which support the claim of the mortgagee to insurance obtained by the mortgagor in his own name are regarded as resting upon special facts which justify the inference that the insurance in question was obtained by the mortgagor with the intent to

[1] Wheeler v. Insurance Co., 101 U. S. 439, 25 L. ed. 1055; In re Sands Ale Brew. Co., 3 Biss. (U. S.) 175; Eastern Milling &c. Co. v. Eastern Milling &c. Co., 125 Fed. 143; Norwich F. Ins. Co. v. Boomer, 52 Ill. 442, 4 Am. Rep. 618; Chipman v. Carroll, 53 Kans. 163, 35 Pac. 1109; Thomas v. Vonkapff, 6 Gill & J. (Md.) 372; Providence County Bank v. Benson, 24 Pick. (Mass.) 204; Miller v. Aldrich, 31 Mich. 408; Ames v. Richardson, 29 Minn. 330; Hyde v. Hartford Fire Ins. Co., 70 Nebr. 503, 97 N. W. 629, 113 Am. St. 796; Cromwell v. Brooklyn F. Ins. Co., 44 N. Y. 42, 4 Am. Rep. 641, per Earl, C.; Dunlop v. Avery, 24 Hun (N. Y.) 509; Carter v. Rockett, 8 Paige (N. Y.) 437; Vernon v. Smith, 5 Barn. & Ald. 1.

A provision that the mortgagor shall keep the building insured for the benefit of the mortgagee "to the amount of —— thousand dollars" is incomplete and does not bind the mortgagor to insure for any amount. The blank not being filled the mortgage contains no agreement requiring the mortgagee to insure for any amount. McCaslin v. Advance Mfg. Co., 155 Ind. 298, 58 N. E. 67,

citing Palmer v. Poor, 121 Ind. 135, 6 L. R. A. 469, 22 N. E. 984; Wieltfong v. Schafer, 121 Ind. 264, 23 N. E. 91. See also American Ice Co. v. Eastern Trust &c. Co., 188 U. S. 626, 47 L. ed. 623, 23 Sup. Ct. 432; Eastern Milling &c. Co. v. Eastern Milling &c. Co., 125 Fed. 143; Hyde v. Hartford Fire Ins. Co., 70 Nebr. 503, 97 N. W. 629, 113 Am. St. 796; Ætna Ins. Co. v. Thompson, 68 N. H. 20, 40 Atl. 396, 73 Am. St. 552; Doughty v. Van Horn, 29 N. J. Eq. 90; Wattengel v. Schultz, 11 Misc. 165, 65 N. Y. St. 148, 32 N. Y. S. 91; Nichols v. Baxter, 5 R. I. 491.

[2] In re Sands Ale Brew. Co., 3 Biss. (U. S.) 175.

[3] Nichols v. Baxter, 5 R. I. 491. The policy in this case was in existence when the mortgage was made, and conformed in amount to the required insurance; and the court found as a fact that the intention of the parties was that this particular policy should be assigned to the mortgagee. See also Chipman v. Carroll, 53 Kans. 163, 35 Pac. 1109; Ames v. Richardson, 29 Minn. 330.

[4] Grange Mill Co. v. Western Assur. Co., 118 Ill. 396, 9 N. E. 274.

perform his agreement to insure for the benefit of the mortgagee, or that the agreement had reference to the insurance already obtained. Accordingly, where there was no ground for such inference, and the insurance company paid the amount of loss to the mortgagor, the Supreme Court of Massachusetts held that the mortgagee had no equitable lien upon the policy, and could not recover in the name of the mortgagor.[5]

When the mortgagor, in a mortgage containing such a covenant, has procured a policy in his own name, and after a loss has delivered the policy to a third person in trust, to collect the insurance money, and pay from it the mortgage debt, the mortgagee thereupon has an equitable lien upon the policy which he may enforce, although the mortgagor afterward obtains possession of the policy and fraudulently seeks to avail himself of it for his sole benefit.[6] The mortgagee is entitled to an equitable lien on the proceeds of a second policy taken out by the mortgagor in his own name, and assigned to others for prior debts, and payable to them as their interests might appear, where the mortgage provides that the mortgagor will not impair the lien, and the second policy causes a scaling of the first.[7] A mortgagee is entitled to the benefit of a policy upon the mortgaged property under a covenant for insurance where the mortgagor represented that the property was covered by this particular policy which he agreed to transfer as collateral security, but in fact transferred a policy upon a building which had been removed from the mortgaged premises, and retained the policy he agreed to assign. It was fraud in him to assign a worthless policy, and retain the policy expressly stipulated for the mortgagee's security.[8]

When a lessee has effected insurance under a provision in his lease that a policy shall be taken by him, and the money payable under it shall be applied in restoring the premises, the benefit of the insurance passes by a mortgage of his term without special mention of it.[9]

In general, however, it may be said that a covenant to insure for the benefit of the mortgagee is not a covenant running with the land, but is entirely personal in its character; and therefore the holder of a mortgage can not claim the benefit of an insurance procured by a

[5] Stearns v. Quincy Mut. F. Ins. Co., 124 Mass. 61, 26 Am. Rep. 647. See also Farmers' Loan &c. Co. v. Penn Plate Glass Co., 103 Fed. 132.

[6] Hazard v. Draper, 7 Allen (Mass.) 267. See also Providence County Bank v. Benson, 24 Pick. (Mass.) 204.

[7] Wilson v. Hakes, 36 Ill. App. 539.

[8] Doughty v. Van Horn, 29 N. J. Eq. 90.

[9] Garden v. Ingram, 23 L. J. Ch. 478.

purchaser of the equity of redemption from the mortgagor.[10] But if the purchaser or his agent has an indorsement made upon the policy, making the loss payable to the mortgagee, the latter is entitled to the insurance, and his right to receive it can not be revoked by a cancelation of the indorsement made without his knowledge or assent.[11] But where the mortgagor after failing to insure in accordance with such a covenant transfers the property to a voluntary assignee for the benefit of creditors, insurance taken out by such assignee who stands in the shoes of the assignor, must be assumed to be taken out in fulfilment of the mortgagor's covenant, and in the event of loss the amount collected under the policies inures to the benefit of the mortgagee, and can not be retained by the assignee as representing his interest, or that of general unsecured creditors, in the equity of the property.[12]

The purchaser of an equity of redemption subject to a mortgage which requires the mortgagor to insure for the benefit of the mortgagee is not bound by such covenant.[13]

Where the agreement to keep insurance for the benefit of the mortgagee was merely verbal, but the mortgagor had acted upon it by obtaining such insurance, and his grantee having knowledge of the agreement subsequently surrendered this policy and took another, which was not payable to the mortgagee, it was held that he was nevertheless entitled in equity to have the insurance money applied in payment of the mortgage debt.[14]

§ 401. **Where no covenant or agreement to insure.**—But the mortgagee, merely as such, has no interest either in law or equity, in a policy of insurance taken out by the mortgagor upon the mortgaged premises for his own benefit, in the absence of any covenant or agreement requiring mortgagor to insure for the benefit of the mortgagee.[15] So if there is no covenant or agreement in the mortgage that the premises shall be insured for the benefit of the mortgagee, the mere

[10] Farmers' Loan &c. Co. v. Penn Plate Glass Co., 186 U. S. 434, 46 L. ed. 1234, 103 Fed. 132. Citing In re Norwich, 118 U. S. 468, 30 L. ed. 134; Columbia Ins. Co. v. Lawrence, 10 Pet. (U. S.) 507, 9 L. ed. 512; In re Sands Ale Brew. Co., 3 Biss. (U. S.) 175; Thomas v. Vonkapff, 6 Gill & J. (Md.) 372; Miller v. Aldrich, 31 Mich. 408; Ellis v. Kreutzinger, 27 Mo. 311; Reid v. McCrum, 91 N. Y. 412; Dunlop v. Avery, 89 N. Y. 592; Masury v. Southworth, 9 Ohio St. 340; Nichols v. Baxter, 5 R. I. 491; Vernon v. Smith, 5 Barn. & Ald. 1.

[11] Reid v. McCrum, 91 N. Y. 412.

[12] American Ice Co. v. Eastern Trust &c. Co., 188 U. S. 626, 47 L. ed. 623.

[13] Farmers' Loan &c. Co. v. Penn Plate Glass Co., 103 Fed. 132.

[14] Miller v. Aldrich, 31 Mich. 408.

[15] Nordyke &c. Co. v. Gery, 112 Ind. 535, 13 N. E. 683, 2 Am. St. 219; Ryan v. Adamson, 57 Iowa 30, 10 N. W. 287; Nichols v. Baxter, 5 R. I. 491.

fact that his mortgage covers the property insured and the insured is personally liable for the debt gives the mortgagee no corresponding claim upon the policy or the proceeds of it.[16] Where a mortgagee has no interest in a policy of insurance effected by the mortgagor upon the mortgaged premises for his own benefit, such mortgagee can not, upon foreclosure, and his security proving inadequate by reason of the destruction of the house, be subrogated to the rights of the mortgagor against the insurance company for money due on the policy.[17] His claim is then no better than that of any creditor of the mortgagor. The policy is strictly a personal contract. It does not attach to the mortgage or to the realty. It has even been held that a mere covenant by the mortgagor to effect insurance, without any stipulation that it is for the benefit of the mortgagee, or that the loss shall be paid to him, does not imply that the mortgagor shall apply the insurance money either in discharge of the mortgage debt or in restoration of the property.[18]

§ 402. **Equitable lien in favor of mortgagee.**—The mortgagee may have an equitable lien upon a policy taken by the mortgagor, although the mortgage provides that the mortgagee himself may insure. While a mortgagee, merely as such, has no interest in or claim to a policy of insurance effected by the mortgagor upon the property mortgaged for his benefit, and each has an insurable interest, and may effect separate insurance, yet one insurance for the benefit of both is generally provided for by a covenant or condition that the mortgagor shall keep the premises insured for the benefit of the mortgagee, and the policy should then be taken out by the mortgagor, payable to the mortgagee in case of loss, or the policy should be assigned to him. But if the mortgagor afterward takes out a policy in his own name and fails to

[16] Carpenter v. Providence Washington Ins. Co., 16 Pet. (U. S.) 495, 10 L. ed. 1044; Columbia Ins. Co. v. Lawrence, 10 Pet. (U. S.) 507, 9 L. ed. 512; Hancox v. Fishing Ins. Co., 3 Sum. (U. S.) 132, Fed. Cas. No. 6013; Vandegraaff v. Medlock, 3 Port. (Ala.) 389, 29 Am. Dec. 256; Ryan v. Adamson, 57 Iowa 30, 10 N. W. 287; Chipman v. Carroll, 53 Kans. 163, 35 Pac. 1109; Wilson v. Hill, 3 Metc. (Mass.) 66; Ames v. Richardson, 29 Minn. 330, 13 N. W. 137; Carter v. Rockett, 8 Paige (N. Y.) 437; McDonald v. Black, 20 Ohio 185, 55 Am. Dec. 448; Nichols v. Baxter, 5 R. I. 491; Plimpton v. Insurance Co., 43 Vt. 497, 5 Am. Rep. 297; Lynch v. Dalzell, 4 Bro. Parl. Cases 431; Neale v. Reid, 3 Dow. & Ry. 156; Lees v. Whiteley, L. R. 2 Eq. 143; Powles v. Innes, 11 M. & W. 10. See also Ridley v. Ennis, 70 Ala. 463; Commercial Union Assur. Co. v. Scammon, 126 Ill. 355, 18 N. E. 562, 9 Am. St. 607; Lindley v. Orr, 83 Ill. App. 70.

[17] Ryan v. Adamson, 57 Iowa 30, 10 N. W. 287.

[18] Lees v. Whiteley, L. R. 2 Eq. 143.

assign it, or to make it payable to the mortgagee, such a contract in the mortgage creates an equitable lien in favor of the mortgagee, upon the money due, for a loss under such a policy, to the extent of his interest, although the mortgage contained a provision that the mortgagee, in default of the mortgagor's insuring, might take out a policy at the expense of the mortgagor, and under the security of the mortgage, for the premiums. The insurance company, and an assignee of the policy on notice of the rights of the mortgagee prior to the assignment, are subject to the equity.[19]

A mortgagee can not assert an equitable lien on the proceeds of an insurance policy taken out in the name of the mortgagor long after the execution of the mortgage, where the evidence fails clearly to establish a valid agreement on the part of the mortgagor to insure for the benefit of the mortgagee.[20] Nor can a mortgagee who has purchased the mortgaged premises at his own foreclosure sale for the amount of his debt, recover on a policy procured by the mortgagor as further security for him and made payable to him, where the loss occurred after his purchase of the premises and during the period of redemption.[21]

§ 403. **Rights of subsequent assignee of policy affected by mortgagee's lien.**—How far this equitable lien can affect another person who has subsequently acquired a specific assignment of the policy is a question not very definitely settled by the authorities.[22] In the case cited, there was no occasion for the court to go further than to hold that this equitable lien was binding upon the mortgagor, and after his decease upon his legal representatives. Mr. Justice Archer, however, in delivering the opinion of the court, expressed the view that if the

---

[19] Wheeler v. Insurance Co., 101 U. S. 439, 25 L. ed. 1055; Nichols v. Baxter, 5 R. I. 491. See also Miller v. Aldrich, 31 Mich. 408.

[20] Swearingen v. Hartford Ins. Co., 52 S. Car. 309, 29 S. E. 722.

[21] Reynolds v. London &c. F. Ins. Co., 128 Cal. 16, 60 Pac. 467, 79 Am. St. 17.

[22] Thomas v. Vonkapff, 6 Gill & J. (Md.) 372. Archer, J., said: "But here the administrators have a mere naked legal right, subject to the mortgagee's equity. That the administrators represent the creditors can not change the character of this equity of the mortgagee, or weaken its efficacy. The particular creditor and the general creditor stand in different attitudes. The former never trusted to the personal credit of the mortgagor, but trusted and looked to this particular fund, to satisfy his debt or give him security for it. The general creditors trusted to a personal credit alone. What has produced this fund? The advance of money upon its faith. * * * But again: the covenant is expressly for the benefit of the particular creditor, not for the benefit of the general creditors; and if they participate in it, they get that which they never could have looked to, and the extent to which they derive advantage from it, to the same extent do they

insurance policy or fund had been passed over by the mortgagor, for a valuable consideration without notice, to a third person, the right of such third person would prevail, because he would have an equity also; and, having the possession, he would be protected, on the principle that the title of one who has both a fair possession and an equitable title shall be preferred to that of a mere equitable interest.

In another aspect of the case, the learned judge expressed views which go far toward sustaining the position that the lien created in favor of the mortgagee by the covenant for insurance is good against one who might afterward take an assignment of the policy. "That this is a covenant running with the land can, we think, scarcely be doubted. The covenants to repair and rebuild are admittedly so. And what is this but in effect a modified covenant to repair and build? The insurance is to be kept up, so that in case of loss by fire the sum insured shall be immediately applied to rebuilding the property on the premises. Being of this character, it would run with the land, just as would an ordinary and absolute covenant to repair or rebuild; and, running with the land, the record of the mortgage would be notice to all the general creditors, and they would, therefore, have no just pretensions to participate in the fund, to the prejudice of the particular creditor."

Insurance upon the mortgaged premises taken out by the mortgagor in his own name, who has agreed to insure the same for the benefit of the mortgagee, will be presumed to have been taken for the mortgagee's benefit, and the latter may enforce an equitable lien on the proceeds arising therefrom; but he can not enforce such lien against a good faith assignee of the policy to whom it was transferred after loss, for value, and to whom the insurer has paid the proceeds of the policy.[23]

§ 404. **Mortgagee's lien valid as against mortgagor's assignee.**— That the lien created by such a covenant is valid as against the mortgagor's assignee in bankruptcy was decided in a comparatively recent case in the District Court of the United States for the Northern District of Illinois,[24] and there was an intimation by the court that a

take from that creditor who looked exclusively to it." See also Giddings v. Seevers, 24 Md. 363.

[23] Swearingen v. Hartford F. Ins. Co., 56 S. Car. 355, 34 S. E. 449.

[24] In re Sands Ale Brew. Co., 3 Biss. (U. S.) 175. Mr. Justice Blodgett said: "My conclusion then is, that the covenant by the bankrupt to insure operated to assign in equity to the petitioner the benefit of any insurance effected by the mortgaged property. It is no answer to say that the mortgagee might have insured in default of insurance by the mort-

specific assignment to a particular creditor would not have avoided the effect of the covenant.

§ 405. Maine statute construed.—In Maine it is provided by statute[25] that a mortgagee of any real estate shall have a lien upon any policy of insurance against loss by fire procured thereon by the mortgagor, to take effect from the time he files with the secretary of the company a written notice briefly describing the mortgage, the estate conveyed, and the sum remaining unpaid thereon. If the mortgagor consents in writing filed with the secretary that the whole or a part of the sum secured by the policy shall be applied to the payment of the mortgage, the mortgagee's receipt shall be a sufficient discharge. If the mortgagor does not so consent, the mortgagee may, at any time within sixty days after a loss, enforce his lien by a suit against the mortgagor, and the company as his trustee, in which judgment may be rendered for what is found due upon the policy, notwithstanding the time of payment of the whole sum secured by the mortgage has not arrived.[26]

In order to preserve and enforce his lien the mortgagee must file with the secretary of the insurance company a written notice, briefly describing his mortgage, the estate conveyed thereby, the sum remaining unpaid thereon, and must, within sixty days after the loss, begin suit against the company as trustee of the mortgagor.[27]

The amount recovered is first applied to the payment of the costs

---

gagor, because the mortgagor had insured, and his insurance inured at once to the benefit of the mortgagee. It is urged by way of argument in behalf of one creditor—the Union National Bank—that if all or part of these policies had been assigned to that creditor, they could have been held then as against the petitioner, and that the assignee, holding for the benefit of all creditors, occupies the same position; but this argument is fallacious, because it overlooks or ignores the fact that all creditors had notice of the petitioner's equitable right to this insurance money, and could acquire no valid interest therein as against him. Equity made this assignment the moment the insurance was effected, if the mortgagor did not do it. * * * The lien is neither doubtful nor general, but is clear and specific. It is but carry-ing out the intent of the parties, and giving the mortgagee the security he had bargained for, and which he had given the whole world notice he was entitled to."

[25] Rev. Stat. 1871, ch. 49, §§ 32-36; Rev. Stat. 1903, ch. 49, §§ 54-58. The statute annuls all provisions of a policy at variance with it. Emery v. Piscataqua F. &c. Ins. Co., 52 Maine 322.

[26] A mortgagee has no lien upon a policy procured by the mortgagor which the insurers have in good faith settled before the expiration of sixty days after loss, and before any notice of the loss has been filed with the secretary, although such notice be afterward filed within the sixty days. Burns v. Collins, 64 Maine 215.

[27] Knowlton v. Black, 102 Maine 503, 67 Atl. 563.

of suit, and then to the payment of the mortgage debt; and the balance, if any, is retained by the company and paid to the mortgagor. When two or more mortgagees claim the benefit of this lien, their rights are determined according to the priority of their claims and mortgages by the principles of law. When a mortgagee claims the benefit of this lien, any policy of insurance previously or subsequently procured by him on his interest as mortgagee is void, unless it is consented to by the company insuring the mortgagor's interest.

§ 406. **Loss payable to the mortgagee.**—When a policy is taken in the name of the mortgagor, but the insurance is made payable to the mortgagee in case of loss, the contract is with the mortgagor, and is for the insurance of his interest, and the mortgagee can recover only in case the mortgagor could have done so, unless the policy contains special provisions in favor of the mortgagee.[28] The making of the policy payable to the mortgagee is regarded as an appointment to receive any money which might become due from the insurers by reason of any loss which the mortgagor might sustain. It is still a contract to indemnify the mortgagor against a loss, and not a contract to indemnify the mortgagee.[29]

Such a provision in the policy does not constitute an assignment thereof in the mortgagee's favor, but is simply an order on the insurance company to pay to the mortgagee in case of loss, an amount equal

---

[28] Brunswick Sav. Inst. v. Commercial Union Ins. Co., 68 Maine 313, 28 Am. Rep. 56; Fitchburg Savings Bank v. Amazon Ins. Co., 125 Mass. 431; Smith v. Union Ins. Co., 120 Mass. 90; Franklin Savings Institution v. Central Mut. F. Ins. Co., 119 Mass. 240; Turner v. Quincy Mut. F. Ins. Co., 109 Mass. 568; Fogg v. Middlesex Mut. F. Ins. Co., 10 Cush. (Mass.) 337; Loring v. Manufacturers' Ins. Co., 8 Gray (Mass.) 28; Hale v. Mechanics' Mut. Fire Ins. Co., 6 Gray (Mass.) 169, 66 Am. Dec. 410; Moore v. Hanover F. Ins. Co., 141 N. Y. 219, 36 N. E. 191; Weed v. London &c. F. Ins. Co., 116 N. Y. 106, 22 N. E. 229; Perry v. Lorillard F. Ins. Co., 61 N. Y. 214; Bidwell v. Northwestern Ins. Co., 19 N. Y. 179; Grosvenor v. Atlantic F. Ins. Co., 17 N. Y. 391; Merwin v. Star F. Ins. Co., 7 Hun (N. Y.) 659. The fact that the policy is payable to the mortgagee is not inconsistent with an allegation, in a criminal prosecution of the mortgagor for burning a building with intent to defraud the insurers, that the building was insured to the accused. State v. Byrne, 45 Conn. 273. See also Monroe Bldg. &c. Assn. v. Liverpool &c. Ins. Co., 50 La. Ann. 1243, 24 So. 238; Post Printing &c. Co. v. Insurance Co., 189 Pa. St. 300, 42 Atl. 192, 44 L. R. A. 272; Swearingen v. Hartford Ins. Co., 52 S. Car. 309, 29 S. E. 722; Boyd v. Thuringia Ins. Co., 25 Wash. 447; Staats v. Georgia Home Ins. Co., 57 W. Va. 571, 50 S. E. 815; Keith v. Royal Ins. Co., 117 Wis. 531, 94 N. W. 295.

[29] Continental Insurance Co. v. Hulman, 92 Ill. 145, 34 Am. Rep. 122; Jones v. Haines, 117 Iowa 77; Dodge v. Hamburg-Bremen F. Ins. Co., 4 Kans. App. 415, 46 Pac. 125; Milliken v. Woodward (N. J.), 45 Atl. 796; Grosvenor v. Insurance Co., 17 N. Y. 391; Williamson v. Insur-

to his interest.[30] Thus, when a mortgagor has procured a policy "as his interest might appear," the loss, if any, payable to the mortgagee as collateral security for the mortgage debt, the mortgagee has no authority to consent to the cancelation of the policy; and if he does so, and takes out a new policy in his own name, he will have only the same rights under it that he had under the old policy. Therefore, if a loss occurs, and the mortgagor restores the building to the same condition it was in before, the insurance is payable to the mortgagor and not to the mortgagee, the latter having sustained no loss or damage.[31]

In a case before the Court of Appeals of New York[32] Mr. Justice Harris described the rights of the parties in such a case as follows: "The undertaking to pay the plaintiff was an undertaking collateral to and dependent upon the principal undertaking to insure the mortgagor. The effect of it was, that the defendants agreed that, whenever any money should become due to the mortgagor upon the contract of insurance, they would, instead of paying it to the mortgagor himself, pay it to the plaintiff. The mortgagor must sustain a loss for which the insurers were liable, before the party appointed to receive the money would have a right to claim it. It is the damage sustained by the party insured, and not by the party appointed to receive payment, that is recoverable from the insurers." It was accordingly held in this case, that, the mortgagor having parted with his interest in the property before the loss, the mortgagee, to whom the loss was payable, could not recover. Such a result is generally prevented by a provision in favor of the mortgagee, that no alienation by the mortgagor shall affect the mortgagee's right to recover;[33] and frequently protection is extended to the mortgagee so far as to prevent the invalidating of the policy by any act of the mortgagor or owner of the property insured.[34] Without some such provision a stipulation in a policy making the loss payable to the mortgagee does not interfere with a forfeiture of the policy by the acts or omissions of the assured.[35]

ance Co., 86 Wis. 393, 57 N. W. 46. But see Burrows v. McCalley, 17 Wash. 269, 49 Pac. 508.

[30] Carpenter v. Providence Washington Ins. Co., 16 Pet. (U. S.) 495, 10 L. ed. 1044; Connecticut Mut. L. Ins. Co. v. Scammon, 4 Fed. 263; Brunswick Sav. Inst. v. Commercial Union Ins. Co., 68 Maine 313, 28 Am. Rep. 56; Gillett v. Liverpool &c. Ins. Co., 73 Wis. 203, 41 N. W. 78, 9 Am. St. 784.

[31] In re Moore, 6 Daly (N. Y.) 541.

[32] Grosvenor v. Atlantic Fire Ins.

Co., 17 N. Y. 391. Contra that the mortgagee may recover, see East v. New Orleans Ins. Co., 76 Miss. 697, 26 So. 691; Oakland Home Ins. Co. v. Bank of Commerce, 47 Nebr. 717, 66 N. W. 646, 58 Am. St. 633.

[33] Macomber v. Cambridge Mut. F. Ins. Co., 8 Cush. (Mass.) 133.

[34] Springfield F. &c. Ins. Co. v. Allen, 43 N. Y. 389, 3 Am. Rep. 711. See also Hanover F. Ins. Co. v. Bohn, 48 Nebr. 743, 67 N. W. 774, 58 Am. St. 719.

[35] Jones v. Haines, 117 Iowa 77.

§ 406a. Effect of saving provision in favor of mortgagee.—A stipulation that no sale or transfer of the property shall vitiate the right of the mortgagee to recover in case of loss, or that no act or default of any person other than such mortgagee or his agents shall affect his right to recover, prevents a forfeiture of the policy as to his interest, after a sale of the property, in consequence of the breach of a condition of the policy, such as a condition making the policy void if further insurance be obtained without the consent of the insurers.[36] Where there is attached to the policy a mortgage clause making the loss payable to the mortgagee therein named as his interest may appear, and providing that the insurance shall not be invalidated by acts or negligence of the mortgagor, it is held that such mortgage clause constitutes an independent contract of insurance between the company and the mortgagee which can not be invalidated by the acts or omissions of the mortgagor, whether they occurred at the time of the issuance of the policy or prior or subsequent thereto.[37] A necessary consequence of a sale is that the purchaser has a right to insure his interest. The object of the stipulation is to secure the insurance of the mortgagee's interest, and to avoid the defeat of this security by any sale or transfer of the property; and by a fair interpretation of the contract it means that the mortgagee's right to recover shall not be vitiated by any of the natural consequences or incidents of sale.[38]

A policy issued to a mortgagor, payable to the mortgagee, as his interest may appear, and containing a provision making it void in case of any change in title or possession, has been held avoided by foreclosure, whereby the property vested in the mortgagee.[39] But it has

See also Davis v. German American Ins. Co., 135 Mass. 251; Grosvenor v. Atlantic F. Ins. Co., 17 N. Y. 391; Hocking v. Virginia &c. Ins. Co., 99 Tenn. 729, 42 S. W. 451, 39 L. R. A. 148, 63 Am. St. 862; Boyd v. Thuringia Ins. Co., 25 Wash. 447, 65 Pac. 785, 55 L. R. A. 165; Gillett v. Liverpool &c. Ins. Co., 73 Wis. 203, 41 N. W. 78, 9 Am. St. 784.

[36] Eliot Five Cents Savings Bank v. Commercial Union Assn. Co., 142 Mass. 142, 7 N. E. 550. See also Franklin Ins. Co. v. Wolff, 23 Ind. App. 549, 54 N. E. 772; Monroe Bldg. &c. Assn. v. Liverpool &c. Ins. Co., 50 La. Ann. 1243, 24 So. 238; Lewis v. Guardian F. &c. Assur. Co., 93 App. Div. 157, 87 N. Y. S. 525, affd.

181 N. Y. 392, 74 N. E. 224, 106 Am. St. 557.

[37] Hanover F. Ins. Co. v. Bohn, 48 Nebr. 473, 67 N. W. 774, 58 Am. St. 719.

[38] City Five Cents Sav. Bank v. Penn F. Ins. Co., 122 Mass. 165. See also Scania Ins. Co. v. Johnson, 22 Colo. 476, 45 Pac. 431; Adams v. Rockingham Mut. F. Ins. Co., 29 Maine 292; Rosenstein v. Traders' Ins. Co., 79 App. Div. 481, 79 N. Y. S. 736.

[39] McKinney v. Western Assur. Co., 97 Ky. 474, 17 Ky. L. 325, 30 S. W. 1004; Brunswick Sav. Inst. v. Commercial Union Ins. Co., 68 Maine 313, 28 Am. Rep. 56; Hagaman v. Allemania F. Ins. Co., 38 Leg. Inst.

been held that a transfer of possession and control of the insured property to the mortgagee is not a breach of a policy issued to the mortgagor, and assigned, with the insurer's consent, to the mortgagee, though the policy contained a provision that it should become void if the property was sold or conveyed.[40]

If a policy, though containing a mortgage clause protecting the mortgagee from the consequences of the acts and omissions of the mortgagor, provides that the mortgagee shall notify the insurer of any increased hazard which shall come to his knowledge, the policy is rendered void by the failure of the mortgagee to comply with this provision.[41]

Aside from any saving provision in favor of the mortgagee, any act of the mortgagor, either in procuring the policy or in dealing with the property afterward, which would avoid the policy as to him, will avoid it equally as to the mortgagee; as by a misrepresentation as to the use made of the property,[42] or a violation of one of the provisions of the policy in procuring over-insurance.[43] But no admissions or declarations by the owner after a loss are admissible to defeat a recovery by the mortgagee upon the policy.[44]

§ **406b.** **Interest of mortgagee is that existing at date of policy.**— Where a policy taken by a mortgagor is made payable to a mortgagee "as his interest shall appear," the interest of the mortgagee covered by the policy is that existing at its date and not an interest under subsequent mortgages in force at the date of the loss. "Whether the clause is to be considered as an assignment by the mortgagor of an insurance

---

(Pa.) 375; Hoxsie v. Providence Mut. F. Ins. Co., 6 R. I. 517. But see Continental Ins. Co. v. Ward, 50 Kans. 346, 31 Pac. 1079.

[40] Washington Ins. Co. v. Hayes, 17 Ohio St. 432, 93 Am. Dec. 628.

[41] Cole v. Germania F. Ins. Co., 99 N. Y. 36; Graham v. Fireman's Insurance Co., 87 N. Y. 69, 41 Am. Rep. 348.

[42] Merwin v. Star Fire Ins. Co., 7 Hun (N. Y.) 659.

[43] Buffalo Steam Engine Works v. Sun Mut. Ins. Co., 17 N. Y. 401.

In California it is provided that where a mortgagor of property effects insurance in his own name, providing that the loss shall be payable to the mortgagee, or assigns a policy of insurance to the mortgagee, the insurance is deemed to be upon the interest of the mortgagor, who does not cease to be a party to the original contract, and any act of his which would otherwise avoid the insurance will have the same effect, although the property is in the hands of the mortgagee.

If an insurer assents to the transfer of an insurance from a mortgagor to a mortgagee, and at the time of his assent imposes further obligations on the assignee, making a new contract with him, the acts of the mortgagor can not affect his rights. Civil Code, §§ 2541, 2542; Codes & Stats. 1877, §§ 7541, 7542.

[44] Browning v. Home Ins. Co., 71 N. Y. 508, 27 Am. Rep. 86.

upon his interest, or as a contract made with the insured by which, in a certain contingency, it promises to pay to the mortgagee an amount to be determined, it seems to us clear that the nature of the interest and the extent of the risk must be made known at the time when the contract is made, in order that the premium may be measured thereby. While the insurance company can not be compelled to pay more than the face of the policy, yet to obtain the advantages of subrogation, if the plaintiff's contention is correct, it may be compelled to pay several times that amount. The clause in regard to subrogation is inserted as of value to the company, and must be taken into consideration in measuring the risk assumed and the consideration paid therefor; but if this amount can not be determined when the contract is made, and may be so great as to make the subrogation clause worthless, it ceases to be one of the elements of the contract."[45] But where by the terms of a policy any loss is payable to the mortgagee, he is prima facie entitled to payment thereunder to the extent of his secured debt, though the mortgage be renewed to him after the issuance of the policy, the amount of the debt not being increased.[46]

§ 407. **Equivalent to assignment.**—In general, the provision of a policy that the loss, if any, shall be paid to the mortgagee, operates to give the mortgagee precisely the same rights and interest in the policy which he would have if, without such words, the mortgagor had assigned the policy to him as collateral security to the mortgage debt.[47]

If a mortgagor, after assigning a policy of insurance to the mortgagee as collateral security for the mortgage debt, satisfies the mortgage, he becomes subrogated to the rights of the mortgagee in the policy, and may maintain an action thereon for a loss.[48]

The insured can, of course, no more adjust a loss payable to the mortgagee than he could release it.[49] He can not enter into an accord

---

[45] Attleborough Savings Bank v. Security Ins. Co., 168 Mass. 147, 46 N. E. 390, per Lathrop, J.

[46] Continental Ins. Co. v. Thomasson, 27 Ky. L. 158, 84 S. W. 546.

[47] Magoun v. Fireman's Fund Ins. Co., 86 Minn. 486, 91 N. W. 5; Ennis v. Harmony F. Ins. Co., 2 Bosw. (N. Y.) 516; Grosvenor v. Atlantic F. Ins. Co., 5 Duer (N. Y.) 517, 17 N. Y. 391; Luckey v. Gannon, 37 How. Pr. (N. Y.) 134. Such mortgagee is the "assured," within the meaning of a clause in the policy requiring the "assured" to deliver the preliminary loss statement;

Armstrong v. Agricultural Ins. Co., 31 N. Y. St. 201, 9 N. Y. S. 873. Quoted with approval, Connecticut Mut. L. Ins. Co. v. Scammon, 4 Fed. 263, 117 U. S. 634, 29 L. ed. 1007, 6 Sup. Ct. 889. See also Brown v. Roger Williams Ins. Co., 5 R. I. 394.

[48] Billings v. German Ins. Co., 34 Nebr. 502, 52 N. W. 397. See also 18 Am. Law. Reg. (N. S.) 737.

[49] Harrington v. Fitchburg Mut. F. Ins. Co., 124 Mass. 126. See also Hall v. Philadelphia F. Assn., 64 N. H. 405, 13 Atl. 648.

and satisfaction, nor submit the adjustment of loss to arbitration without the mortgagee's knowledge and consent.[50] But the mortgagor has a right to enter into an appraisement of the loss according to the terms of the policy, without notice to the mortgagee and without his approval.[51] The insurer can not terminate the contract before the date fixed by the policy, without notice to the mortgagee.[52] He can not revoke the direction to pay the mortgagee as his interest may appear, or cancel the indorsement without the knowledge and consent of the mortgagee.[53]

In Massachusetts it is provided that in case of loss upon property hereafter insured within the terms of the fire insurance policies thereon, all such insurers thereof, upon the proper presentation of proofs by the claimants in accordance with the provisions of the policy, together with an authentic statement of the title showing the rights and interests of all parties therein, shall pay all mortgages expressly protected by any policies taken out in the name of the mortgagor, in the order of their priority, to the extent of their respective policies or interests in their respective mortgage claims, before the owner of the equity of redemption in said property shall receive anything; but this provision does not enlarge the amount which any insurance company would otherwise pay on account of any loss; and any payment so made by any such company under its policy in accordance with the provisions of this act, whether to the person named in the policy or not, shall be deemed and taken to be in payment and satisfaction of the liability of such company under its policy to the full extent of such payment.[54]

§ 408. Who may bring suit.—When the policy is taken out by the mortgagor in his name, payable in case of loss to the mortgagee, the mortgagor should, with the assent of the mortgagee, sue on the policy in his own name. The mortgagor in such case is the party for whose benefit the insurance really operates, whether payment be made to himself or to the mortgagee.[55] The assent of the mortgagee, to

---

[50] Hathaway v. Orient Ins. Co., 134 N. Y. 409, 32 N. E. 40, 17 L. R. A. 514; Brown v. Roger Williams Ins. Co., 5 R. I. 394. But see Collinsville Sav. Soc. v. Boston Ins. Co., 77 Conn. 676, 60 Atl. 647, 69 L. R. A. 924.

[51] Chandos v. American F. Ins. Co., 84 Wis. 184, 54 N. W. 390, 19 L. R. A. 321.

[52] Magoun v. Fireman's Fund Assn., 86 Minn. 486, 91 N. W. 5;

Lattan v. Royal Ins. Co., 45 N. J. L. 453.

[53] Miller v. Aldrich, 31 Mich. 408; Reid v. McCrum, 91 N. Y. 412; Security Co. v. Panhandle Nat. Bank, 93 Tex. 575, 57 S. W. 22.

[54] Acts 1878, ch. 132, § 2; Rev. L. 1902, ch. 118, § 58.

[55] Meriden Sav. Bank v. Home Ins. Co., 50 Conn. 396; Continental Ins. Co. v. Hulman, 92 Ill. 145, 34 Am. Rep. 122; Patterson v. Triumph Ins.

whom a policy is payable as his interest may appear, to the prosecution of an action thereon by the mortgagor is sufficient to entitle the latter to maintain it.[56] The contract of insurance in such case is with the mortgagor, notwithstanding the loss is payable to the mortgagee. This direction in the policy is not an assignment of it, and, although it is assented to by the insurer, the contract with the mortgagor is not thereby merged or extinguished.[57] In an action on such a policy by the mortgagor, the insurer may plead payment to the mortgagee as performance. The rights of the mortgagee, and of the insurers as well, may be protected in all cases by a payment of the money into court.[58]

There is some confusion and contradiction in the cases in regard to the right of action upon a policy procured by a mortgagor payable in case of loss to the mortgagee. The principle underlying the subject is, that the real party to the contract, in whom the entire interest in it is vested, is the proper party to enforce it. If a policy be taken by a mortgagee in this way, he alone dealing with the company and paying the premiums, he is the real party to the contract and the proper party to sue,[59] if the policy covers only the mortgaged property and does not in amount exceed the mortgagee's interest.[60] In like manner, if the entire interest in the policy has been vested in the mortgagee, or assigned to him, or if the whole amount of the policy is made payable

Co., 64 Maine 500; Turner v. Quincy Mut. F. Ins. Co., 109 Mass. 568; Jackson v. Farmers' Mut. F. Ins. Co., 5 Gray (Mass.) 52; Farrow v. Commonwealth Ins. Co., 18 Pick. (Mass.) 53, 29 Am. Dec. 564. See also Fire Ins. Co. v. Felrath, 77 Ala. 194, 54 Am. Rep. 58.

[56] Green v. Star Fire Ins. Co., 190 Mass. 586, 77 N. E. 649.

[57] Friemansdorf v. Watertown Ins. Co., 9 Biss. (U. S.) 167; Bates v. Equitable Ins. Co., 10 Wall. (U. S.) 33, 19 L. ed. 882; Illinois Mut. F. Ins. Co. v. Fix, 53 Ill. 151, 5 Am. Rep. 38; Brunswick Sav. Inst. v. Commercial Union Ins. Co., 68 Maine 313, 28 Am. Rep. 56; Minnock v. Eureka F. &c. Ins. Co., 90 Mich. 236, 51 N. W. 367; Hartford F. Ins. Co. v. Davenport, 37 Mich. 609; Clay F. &c. Ins. Co. v. Huron S. &c. Mfg. Co., 31 Mich. 346; Van Buren v. St. Joseph County Village F. Ins. Co., 28 Mich. 398; Martin v. Frank-

lin F. Ins. Co., 38 N. J. L. 140, 20 Am. Rep. 372; Grosvenor v. Atlantic F. Ins. Co., 17 N. Y. 391.

[58] Martin v. Franklin F. Ins. Co., 38 N. J. L. 140, 20 Am. Rep. 372.

[59] Westchester F. Ins. Co. v. Foster, 90 Ill. 121; Chamberlain v. New Hampshire F. Ins. Co., 55 N. H. 249.

[60] Hopkins Mfg. Co. v. Aurora F. &c. Ins. Co., 48 Mich. 148, 11 N. W. 846; Hartford F. Ins. Co. v. Davenport, 37 Mich. 609; Magoun v. Fireman's Fund Ins. Co., 86 Minn. 486, 91 N. W. 5, 91 Am. St. 370; Bacot v. Phœnix Ins. Co., 96 Miss. 223, 50 So. 729, 25 L. R. A. (N. S.) 1226, Ann. Cas. 1912B, 262; Oakland Home Ins. Co. v. Bank of Commerce, 47 Nebr. 717, 66 N. W. 646, 36 L. R. A. 673, 58 Am. St. 663; Phenix Ins. Co. v. Omaha L. &c. Co., 41 Nebr. 834, 60 N. W. 133, 25 L. R. A. 679.

to the mortgagee, without qualification express or implied, or it be less in amount than the debt, he may enforce it by suit.[61]

Ordinarily, however, there remains by the very terms of a policy insuring the mortgagor, but payable to the mortgagee in case of loss, or by necessary implication from such a policy, an equitable interest in the mortgagor. A debt to the mortgagee is implied, and the making of the policy payable to him implies that his interest is limited to the amount of this debt. Therefore, in the ordinary case of a policy made in this way, there is a divided interest; partly in the mortgagor and partly in the mortgagee. The direction that payment in case of loss be made to the mortgagee is a contingent order or stipulation.[62] Making a policy payable to a mortgagee in case of loss is a mere appointment of the insurance to the extent of the mortgagee's interest; it does not constitute an assignment of the policy, so as to authorize the mortgagee to sue in his own name.[63]

Under the codes of practice of some states, as in New York and other states which have adopted the same practice, the mortgagee may maintain such suit in his own name, by virtue of a provision that suits shall be maintained in the name of the real party in interest. Sometimes the mortgagee is by statute, or by stipulation in the policy or charter of the company, given the right to enforce such a policy. But aside from authority so conferred, the mortgagor as a general rule, so long as he retains an insurable interest, may bring the suit. There can be no division of causes of action on a single insurance policy. Whoever sues must be able to enforce the whole liability.[64] Therefore, when a partial interest in the policy remains in the mortgagor, the mortgagee can not sue as the party to whom the loss is payable. And for the same reason, if the policy cover property in part not subject to the mortgage, the mortgagee can not sue upon it, either in his own name

[61] Berthold v. Clay F. Ins. Co., 2 Mo. App. 311; Hadley v. New Hampshire Fire Ins. Co., 55 N. H. 110. Under the Code practice in New York, so long as the mortgage debt remains unpaid, the action should be brought by the mortgagee in his own name, or he should be joined as a party. Ennis v. Harmony F. Ins. Co., 3 Bosw. (N. Y.) 516; Frink v. Hampden Ins. Co., 45 Barb. (N. Y.) 384, 31 How. Pr. 30; Roussel v. St. Nicholas Ins. Co., 9 J. & S. (N. Y.) 279. See also Trust Co. of Georgia v. Scottish Union &c. Ins. Co., 119 Ga. 672, 46 S. E. 855.

[62] Brunswick Savings Inst. v.

Commercial Union Ins. Co., 68 Maine 313, 28 Am. Rep. 56.

[63] Fire Ins. Co. v. Felrath, 77 Ala. 194, 54 Am. Rep. 58. See also Continental Ins. Co. v. Hulman, 92 Ill. 145, 34 Am. Rep. 122; Smith v. Union Ins. Co., 120 Mass. 90; Griswold v. American Cent. Ins. Co., 1 Mo. App. 97; Baldwin v. Phoenix Ins. Co., 60 N. H. 164.

[64] Hartford F. Ins. Co. v. Davenport, 37 Mich. 609. If the policy is issued payable to the mortgagee "as his interest may appear," balance to the mortgagor, the latter may after the insurer has paid the sum due on the mortgage debt, main-

or that of the mortgagor.[65] For if the suit be in his own name, with reference to his own interest, the insurers would be liable to another suit by the mortgagor upon the same policy; and if the mortgagee be allowed, against the consent of the mortgagor, to prosecute a suit in his name, the insurers would be required to pay one loss by instalments to different persons. Under the codes in force in some of the states, persons having several interests in such a contract may join in enforcing it.[66] If the mortgagee's interest exceeds the amount of the insurance, the whole interest being in the mortgagee, he may sue upon the policy alone.[67]

The burden is upon the mortgagee to prove that the amount due under the mortgage equals or exceeds the amount payable under the policy.[68] If the indebtedness is less than the amount of loss under the policy, the mortgagor and mortgagee may each recover his share.[69] Where the insurance exceeds the interest of a mortgagee under a loss payable clause, and the mortgagee refuses to sue, the insured may sue and make the mortgagee a party defendant where it appears that he is entitled to the excess.[70]

§ 408a. When mortgagee may maintain action in his own name.—

If, however, the mortgage clause in a policy be in legal effect an agreement to pay the insurance or any part of it directly to the mortgagee, recognizing him as a distinct party in interest, and not a mere appointment to pay the loss to him, he may maintain the action in his own name.[71]

When a mortgagor effects an insurance, payable in case of loss to the mortgagee, the former holds the legal title, and may maintain

tain an action at law on the policy in his own name for the balance. Scottish Union Ins. Co. v. Enslie, 78 Miss. 157, 28 So. 822.

[65] Stearns v. Quincy Mut. F. Ins. Co,. 124 Mass. 61, 26 Am. Rep. 647.

[66] As in Wisconsin: Strohn v. Hartford F. Ins. Co., 33 Wis. 648, 37 Wis. 625, 19 Am. Rep. 777.

[67] Maxey v. New Hampshire F. Ins. Co., 54 Minn. 272, 55 N. W. 1130; Lowry v. Insurance Co., 75 Miss. 43, 21 So. 664; Traveler's Ins. Co. v. California Ins. Co., 1 N. Dak. 151, 45 N. W. 703; Hammel v. Queen Ins. Co., 50 Wis. 240, 6 N. W. 805, 41 Am. Rep. 1. See also Roussel v. St. Nicholas Ins. Co., 52 How. Pr. (N. Y.) 495, 41 N. Y. Super. Ct. 279. Otherwise where Code prac-

tice does not prevail. Fire Ins. Co. v. Felrath, 77 Ala. 194, 54 Am. Rep. 58.

[68] Capital City Ins. Co. v. Jones, 128 Ala. 361, 30 So. 674.

[69] Capital City Ins. Co. v. Jones, 128 Ala. 361, overruling Fire Ins. Co. v. Felrath, 77 Ala. 194, 54 Am. Rep. 58.

[70] Ampersand Hotel Co. v. Home Ins. Co., 62 Misc. 116, 115 N. Y. S. 1108.

[71] Meriden Sav. Bank v. Home Ins. Co., 50 Conn. 396; Hartford F. Ins. Co. v. Olcott, 97 Ill. 439; Westchester F. Ins. Co. v. Foster, 90 Ill. 121; Richelieu &c. Nav. Co. v. Thames &c. Ins. Co., 58 Mich. 132, 24 N. W. 547; Hastings v. Westchester F. Ins. Co., 73 N. Y. 141. See

an action on the policy for the use of the mortgagee.[72] The subsequent payment of the mortgage debt does not prevent a recovery against the insurance company; but the mortgagor may still recover in the name of the mortgagee, if necessary, or in his own name.[73] A mortgagor, after making a policy payable to his mortgagee, can no more bind the mortgagee by an adjustment of the amount of the loss than he can bind him by a release of it.[74]

On the other hand, if a mortgagee as such take out a policy upon his interest for the benefit of the mortgagor with the agreement that any sum that might be received for a loss should be credited upon the mortgage debt, the mortgagor is the proper party to maintain a suit.[75]

The mortgagor may in his own name enforce specific performance of a provision in the policy giving the insurers the election to rebuild, after they have made such election and neglected to perform the contract. The action is upon the contract to rebuild and not strictly upon the policy, and the cause of action is in the insured and not in the mortgagee.[6]

At common law the assignee of a policy of insurance can not maintain an action upon it in his own name; and unless authorized so to do by general law, or by the act incorporating the insurance company, the suit must be in the name of the insured for the use of the assignee.[77]

A mortgagee is entitled to maintain an action in his own name on a policy issued to the mortgagor and made payable in case of loss to the mortgagee "as his interest may appear."[78] Especially is this true where the mortgage debt exceeds the value of the insurance and the

also Ebensburg Bldg. &c. Assn. v. Westchester Fire Ins. Co., 28 Pa. Super. Ct. 341; German Ins. Co. v. Gibbs, 42 Tex. Civ. App. 407, 92 S. W. 1068. See post § 413.

[72] Illinois Fire Ins. Co. v. Stanton, 57 Ill. 354.

[73] Norwich Fire Ins. Co. v. Boomer, 52 Ill. 442, 4 Am. Rep. 618; Concord Union Mut. F. Ins. Co. v. Woodbury, 45 Maine 447.

[74] Harrington v. Fitchburg Mut. F. Ins. Co., 124 Mass. 126.

[75] Ætna Ins. Co. v. Baker, 71 Ind. 102.

[76] Heilmann v. Westchester F. Ins. Co., 75 N. Y. 7.

[77] Illinois F. Ins. Co. v. Stanton, 57 Ill. 354; New England F. Ins. Co. v. Wetmore, 32 Ill. 221.

[78] Palmer Sav. Bank v. Insurance Co., 166 Mass. 189, 44 N. E. 211. Field, C. J., said: "It is the practice of the courts of the states of this country generally, although not universally, in such a case as the present to permit the mortgagee to sue in his own name. In some states, it is true, a person for whose benefit a simple contract is made, although not a party to it, is permitted to sue upon it. In some a joint action by the mortgagor and mortgagee is permitted, where the mortgage debt does not exhaust the insurance; in some a distinction is taken between a policy where the loss is payable to a mortgagee without any limitation, and one where the loss is payable to a mortgagee according to his interest; and in some the mortgagor and mortgagee

mortgage embraces all the insured property.[79] Under a policy making "the loss, if any, payable to the mortgagee as his interest should appear," the mortgagee has been allowed to recover the insurance, although the ownership of the property had changed without the consent of the insurer contrary to one of the conditions of the policy.[80] In Massachusetts, under a policy issued to a mortgagor and made payable in case of loss to the mortgagee "as his interest may appear," the practice is for the mortgagee to maintain an action in his own name.[81] It has also been held that the mortgagor can sue in his own name, with the assent of the mortgagee.[82] Chief Justice Field, in the principal case cited, said: "The effect of such a policy is the same as if the mortgagor had taken out the insurance in his own name, and then assigned it to the mortgagee to the extent of his interest, and the insurance company had assented to the assignment and had promised the mortgagee that no act or default of the mortgagor should defeat the right of the mortgagee to recover to the extent of his interest."[83]

each can sue according to his interest." See also Union Inst. &c. v. Phœnix Ins. Co., 196 Mass. 230, 81 N. E. 994, 14 L. R. A. (N. S.) 459.

[79] Trust Co. v. Scottish Union &c. Ins. Co., 119 Ga. 672, 46 S. E. 855; Franklin Ins. Co. v. Wolff, 23 Ind. App. 549, 54 N. E. 772; Lowry v. Insurance Co., 75 Miss. 43, 21 So. 664, 37 L. R. A. 779, 65 Am. St. 587.

[80] Welch v. British Am. Assur. Co., 148 Cal. 223, 82 Pac. 964, 113 Am. St. 223.

[81] Palmer Savings Bank v. Insurance Co., 166 Mass. 189, 44 N. E. 211, citing Eliot Five Cents Savings Bank v. Commercial Union Assur. Co., 142 Mass. 142, 7 N. E. 550; Wheeler v. Watertown Ins. Co., 131 Mass. 1; Fitchburg Savings Bank v. Amazon Ins. Co., 125 Mass. 431; Smith v. Union Ins. Co., 120 Mass. 90; Foote v. Hartford Ins. Co., 119 Mass. 259; Franklin Savings Institution v. Central Ins. Co., 119 Mass. 240; Fogg v. Middlesex Ins. Co., 10 Cush. (Mass.) 337; Macomber v. Cambridge Ins. Co., 8 Cush. (Mass.) 133; Barrett v. Union Ins. Co., 7 Cush. (Mass.) 175; Loring v. Manufacturers' Ins. Co., 8 Gray (Mass.) 28; Hale v. Mechanics' Ins. Co., 6 Gray (Mass.) 169.

[82] Palmer Savings Bank v. Insurance Co., 166 Mass. 189, 44 N. E. 211, per Field, C. J., citing Kyte v. Commercial Union Assur. Co., 144 Mass. 43, 10 N. E. 518; Turner v. Quincy Ins. Co., 109 Mass. 568; Jackson v. Farmers' Ins. Co., 5 Gray (Mass.) 52.

[83] Palmer Savings Bank v. Insurance Co., 166 Mass. 189, 44 N. E. 211, per Field, C. J., citing Fire Ins. Co. v. Felrath, 77 Ala. 194; Meriden Savings Bank. v. Home Ins. Co., 50 Conn. 396; Bartlett v. Iowa State Ins. Co., 77 Iowa 86, 41 N. W. 579; Westchester Fire Ins. Co. v. Coverdale, 48 Kans. 446, 29 Pac. 682; Motley v. Manufacturers' Ins. Co., 29 Maine 337; Coates v. Pennsylvania Ins. Co., 58 Md. 172; Minnock v. Eureka F. &c. Ins. Co., 90 Mich. 236, 51 N. W. 367; Hartford Ins. Co. v. Davenport, 37 Mich. 609; Ermentrout v. American Ins. Co., 60 Minn. 418, 62 N. W. 543; Maxcy v. New Hampshire Ins. Co., 54 Minn. 272, 55 N. W. 1130; Graves v. American Live Stock Ins. Co., 46 Minn. 130, 48 N. W. 684; Chamberlain v. New Hampshire Ins. Co., 55 N. H. 249; State Ins. Co. v. Maackens, 38 N. J. L. 564; Martin v. Franklin Fire Ins. Co., 38 N. J. L. 140; Winne v. Niagara Ins. Co., 91 N. Y. 185; Cone v. Niagara Ins. Co., 60 N. Y. 619; Travellers' Ins. Co. v. California Ins. Co., 1 N. Dak. 151, 45 N. W. 703; Tilley v. Connecticut Ins. Co., 86 Va. 811, 11 S.

§ 409. Application of insurance to mortgage debt.—The mortgagee is bound to receive the whole insurance, and apply it to the debt. Where a policy of insurance is taken out by the mortgagor, payable to the mortgagee in case of loss, the insurer is bound to pay the whole loss to the mortgagee, who is holden to apply the amount received, so far as is necessary to discharge the mortgage; and in case the mortgage debt has been previously paid, the mortgagee would receive the sum paid for the use of the mortgagor. In such case, the continued existence of the mortgage debt is not essential to a recovery for the benefit of the mortgagor, because the policy is his, and is upon his interest, which is in no way diminished by the discharge of the mortgage.[84] If the policy contain a provision that "No sale of the property shall affect the right of the mortgagee to recover in case of loss under this policy," and a sale be made and the policy forfeited before a loss occurs, the mortgagee is still bound to recover the amount from the insurers, and to apply the avails first to the discharge of the mortgage debt, and the surplus to the benefit of the mortgagor; and the insurers, if they have taken a transfer of the mortgage upon paying the loss, stand in no better position than the mortgagee, as they have full knowledge of the existence of the policy and of its provisions; and the purchaser of the equity of redemption is entitled to the benefit of the money paid on the loss, and may redeem upon paying the balance due upon the mortgage after deducting the amount payable for the loss.[85]

If, however, the policy further provides that when a loss after a forfeiture is paid to the mortgagee, the insurer shall be subrogated to the mortgagee's rights under the mortgage to the extent of such payment, and may pay the full amount of the debt to the mortgagee, and shall thereupon receive an assignment of the mortgage, and a loss occurs after a forfeiture of the policy, and the mortgagee, upon receiving the amount due on the mortgage, assigns the mortgage to the insurer, the owner of the equity can not redeem without paying to the insurer the full amount of such mortgage debt.[86]   •

E. 120; Williamson v. Michigan Ins. Co., 86 Wis. 393, 57 N. W. 46; Hammel v. Queen Ins. Co., 50 Wis. 240, 6 N. W. 805; Mitchell v. London Assur. Co., 15 Ont. App. 262.

[84] Concord Union Mut. Fire Ins. Co. v. Woodbury, 45 Maine 447; Clark v. Wilson, 103 Mass. 219, 4 Am. Rep. 532; Suffolk F. Ins. Co. v. Boyden, 9 Allen (Mass.) 123; King v. State Mutual Fire Ins. Co., 7 Cush. (Mass.) 1, 54 Am. Dec. 683, per Shaw, C. J.; Waring v. Loder, 53 N. Y. 581. See also Smith v. Packard, 19 N. H. 575.

[85] Graves v. Hampden Fire Ins. Co., 10 Allen (Mass.) 281. The mortgagor merely lost the surplus over the debt by his alienation.

[86] Allen v. Watertown Ins. Co., 132 Mass. 480. See post § 412.

If the policy stipulates that the mortgagee shall, in case of loss, assign his mortgage to the insurer to the amount of the loss paid, the mortgagee can not recover for a loss until he has complied with such stipulation.[87]

Where the insurance was taken out by the mortgagor, with loss payable to the mortgagee, and the policy, as to the mortgagor, has, by its terms, become forfeited, the mortgagor has no longer a beneficial interest in the policy, and can not compel the application on the mortgage debt of the amount due to, or received by, the mortgagee upon a loss.[88] If it be provided in the mortgage that the mortgagor shall insure in a certain sum for the benefit of the mortgagee, or that the mortgagee may cause the property to be insured at the expense of the mortgagor, and that the premium shall be covered by the mortgage security, then in effect the policy is furnished by the mortgagor, and any money recovered under it inures to him in going toward paying his debt to the mortgagee.[89] The mortgagee receives the proceeds to apply in the first place to the payment of the mortgage debt, and then he is trustee for the mortgagor for any balance left in his hands.[90] If in such case the mortgagee pays the premium, he may charge the amount in his account against the mortgagor. But in the absence of any such contract the mortgagee could not charge to the mortgagor a premium paid by him for insurance. Any insurance obtained by him on his own interest is for his own benefit. The fiduciary relation existing between the mortgagee and mortgagor, in some limited matters, does not extend to such an insurance of the mortgagee's interest. Before entry for condition broken, that relation is a matter of contract.[91]

If the holder of the mortgage receives the insurance money after the mortgage debt is due, and afterward, without indorsing the amount received upon the mortgage note, assigns the note and mortgage, the mortgagor can not maintain a bill to have this amount indorsed upon the note. His remedy is to redeem.[92]

If the mortgagee effects an insurance at the request, and cost, and

[87] Dick v. Franklin F. Ins. Co., 10 Mo. App. 376; Foster v. Van Reed, 70 N. Y. 19, revg. 5 Hun. (N. Y.) 321, 26 Am. Rep. 544.

[88] Insurance Co. v. Martin, 151 Ind. 209, 51 N. E. 361; Allen v. Watertown F. Ins. Co., 132 Mass. 480; Haley v. Manufacturers' F. &c. Ins. Co., 120 Mass. 292; Sterling F. Ins. Co. v. Beffrey, 48 Minn. 9, 50 N. W. 922; Hastings v. Westchester F. Ins. Co., 73 N. Y. 141.

[89] Wilcox v. Allen, 36 Mich. 160.

[90] Mix v. Hotchkiss, 14 Conn. 32; Fowley v. Palmer, 5 Gray (Mass.) 549.

[91] King v. State Mutual Fire Ins. Co., 7 Cush. (Mass.) 1, 54 Am. Dec. 683; Dobson v. Land, 8 Hare 216, 4 De G. & S. 575; Bellamy v. Brickenden, 2 Jo. & Hem. 137.

[92] Stevens v. Hayden, 129 Mass. 328.

for the benefit of the mortgagor, as well as his own, the latter has a right, in case of loss, to have the insurance money applied to the mortgage debt.[93] But in case the mortgagee, at his own expense and without any agreement with the mortgagor, obtains insurance upon his interest in the mortgaged property, and collects the proceeds of the policy from the insurer after loss, the mortgagor has no interest in such proceeds, and can not make the mortgagee account therefor.[94]

§ 409a. **Where real estate mortgagee holds chattel mortgage upon personalty on premises.**—When a mortgagee of real estate also holds a chattel mortgage upon personal property on the premises, with insurance upon both, and the insurance upon the personal property is payable to the mortgagee as his interest may appear, money received by him from this insurance is applicable in the first instance to the chattel mortgage debt, and not to the real estate mortgage indebtedness. Where the chattel mortgage was given to secure the mortgagee against liability as surety for the mortgagor, it inures to the benefit of a cosurety; and the proceeds of insurance upon the personal property mortgaged can not, without the consent of a cosurety, be diverted from the object of the chattel mortgage and applied upon the debt secured by the real estate mortgage, to which the chattel mortgage was not collateral and for which the mortgagee's cosurety was not liable.[95]

§ 410. **When debt not due.**—When the mortgaged property is insured for the benefit of the mortgagee, such insurance is collateral to the debt, and money recovered from the insurance is still collateral, and can not be applied by the mortgagee to payment of the mortgage debt without the consent of the mortgagor if the debt be not due, and the mortgagee has no right to demand payment, or upon default to convert the securities.[96]

---

[93] Honore v. Lamar F. Ins. Co., 51 Ill. 409; Stinchfield v. Milliken, 71 Maine 567; Concord Union Mut. F. Ins. Co. v. Woodbury, 45 Maine 447; Callahan v. Linthicum, 43 Md. 97, 20 Am. Rep. 106; Pendleton v. Elliott, 67 Mich. 496, 35 N. W. 97; Imperial F. Ins. Co. v. Bull, 18 Can. S. C. 697.

[94] Concord Union Mut. F. Ins. Co. v. Woodbury, 45 Maine 447; Burlingame v. Goodspeed, 153 Mass. 24, 26 N. E. 232, 10 L. R. A. 495; White v. Brown, 2 Cush. (Mass.) 412; Young v. Craig, 4 Am. L. Reg. (O. S.) (Pa.) 384; Cranes v. Farmers' F. Ins. Co., 20 Pa. Super. Ct. 634; Dunbrack v. Neall, 55 W. Va. 565, 47 S. E. 303.

[95] Sherman v. Foster, 158 N. Y. 587, 53 N. E. 504; Crisfield v. Murdock, 127 N. Y. 315, 27 N. E. 1046.

[96] Fergus v. Wilmarth, 117 Ill. 542. See also Gordon v. Ware Sav. Bank, 115 Mass. 588; Quarles v. Clayton, 87 Tenn. 308, 10 S. W. 505, 3 L. R. A. 170; Naquin v. Texas Sav. &c. Assn., 95 Tex. 313, 67 S. W. 85, 58 L. R. A. 711, 93 Am. St. 855; Early v. Flannery, 47 Vt. 253.

The insurance money received by the mortgagee takes the place of the mortgaged property, and the mortgagee would receive it, if the debt was due and unpaid, as he would receive the mortgaged property which it represented, to reasonably account for its use; but if no part of the debt was due he would hold it in the same manner, unless he or the mortgagor saw fit to use it to restore the property burned.[97] If under such circumstances the money received from the insurance be paid by the mortgagee to the mortgagor, for restoring the premises so as to make them as valuable as before the fire, a second mortgagee has no equity to have the amount so received applied for his benefit in reduction of the debt secured by the first mortgage.[98]

But there may be circumstances which will make it incumbent upon a mortgagee who allows the mortgagor to apply the proceeds of an insurance to the restoration of the property to see that the mortgagor actually uses the money for this purpose. Other parties in interest may have an equity requiring the application of the insurance by the mortgagee to be either in payment of the debt due him, or in making the security to this extent more valuable.[99]

§ 411. Payment of loss under policy payable to mortgagee.—The insurers upon paying a loss upon a policy payable to the mortgagee have no claim to be subrogated to the rights of the mortgagee.[1] But there are cases which hold that the insurance company will be subrogated to the rights of the mortgagee under the mortgage in the proportion that the insurance paid bears to the mortgage debt.[2] Where the

[97] Williams v. Lilley, 67 Conn. 50, 34 Atl. 765, 37 L. R. A. 150; Fergus v. Wilmarth, 117 Ill. 542, 7 N. Y. 508; Gordon v. Ware Sav. Bank, 115 Mass. 588; Naquin v. Texas Sav. &c. Assn., 95 Tex. 313, 67 S. W. 85, 58 L. R. A. 711, 93 Am. St. 855; Union Sav. Bank &c. Co. v. Bedell, 74 Vt. 108, 52 Atl. 270; Powers v. New England F. Ins. Co., 69 Vt. 494, 38 Atl. 148.

[98] Gordon v. Ware Savings Bank, 115 Mass. 588.

[99] Connecticut Mut. L. Ins. Co. v. Scammon, 4 Fed. 263, modified 117 U. S. 634, 29 L. ed. 1007, 6 Sup. Ct. 889.

[1] Home Ins. Co. v. Marshall, 48 Kans. 235, 29 Pac. 161; German Ins. Co. v. Smelker, 38 Kans. 285, 16 Pac. 735; Pendleton v. Elliott, 67 Mich. 496, 35 N. W. 97; Cone v. Insurance Co., 60 N. Y. 619; Mercantile Mut. Ins. Co. v. Calebs, 20 N. Y. 173; Kernochan v. New York Bowery Fire Ins. Co., 17 N. Y. 428, 5 Duer (N. Y.) 1. See also Washington Fire Ins. Co. v. Kelly, 32 Md. 421, 3 Am. Rep. 149, as to right of subrogation upon loss pending contract of sale.

[2] Norwich F. Ins. Co. v. Boomer, 52 Ill. 442, 4 Am. Rep. 618; Honore v. Lamar Ins. Co., 51 Ill. 409; Concord Ins. Co. v. Woodbury, 45 Maine 447; Callahan v. Linthicum, 43 Md. 97, 20 Am. Rep. 106; Sussex County Mut. Ins. Co. v. Woodruff, 26 N. J. L. 541; Ulster County Sav. Inst. v. Leake, 73 N. Y. 161, 29 Am. Rep. 115; Excelsior F. Ins. Co. v. Royal Ins. Co., 55 N. Y. 343, 14 Am. Rep. 271; Ætna F. Ins. Co. v. Tyler, 16 Wend. (N. Y.) 385, 30 Am. Dec. 90.

policy is made payable to the mortgagee, the insurer can not avoid the liability for a loss by purchasing the mortgage.[3] If after such a loss the mortgagee brings suit in the name of the assured upon the policies and obtains judgment, but, instead of enforcing the judgment, enforces payment of the mortgage by foreclosure, the assured is entitled to the benefit of the judgment against the insurers, who have no claim to be relieved from the judgment.[4]

§ 412. **Agreement to assign to insurers.**—The effect of an insurance procured in this way is not qualified by a clause in the policy, that in case of loss the assured shall assign to the insurers an interest in the mortgage equal to the amount of the loss paid; or by an assignment made in pursuance of such a provision, or of any subsequent agreement between the parties. Under such an assignment the amount of the loss must be applied in reduction of the mortgage debt, and the insurers can hold the mortgage only for the balance of the debt remaining after such payment.[5]

Policies of insurance now generally provide that, in case of the payment of any loss to a mortgagee whose interest is insured, the insurers shall be subrogated to that extent to his rights under the mortgage.[6]

A stipulation in a policy payable in case of loss to a mortgagee, that in case the policy becomes void as to the mortgagor the insurers may pay the debt to the mortgagee and take an assignment of the mortgage is binding not only upon the mortgagor, but upon an assignee of the policy. The debt is not paid by such assignment of the mortgage, and the mortgagor or a purchaser from him of the mortgaged property can not redeem the mortgage without paying the full amount due upon the mortgage.[7] Where the mortgagor has forfeited his rights under the policy, it may still be kept alive for the benefit of the mortgagee on condition that the insurer shall be subrogated.[8]

[3] Phœnix Ins. Co. v. Dolan, 50 Kans. 725, 32 Pac. 390; Home Insurance Co. v. Marshall, 48 Kans. 235, 29 Pac. 161.

[4] Robert v. Traders' Ins. Co., 17 Wend. (N. Y.) 631, revg. 9 Wend. 404.

[5] Davis v. Quincy Mut. F. Ins. Co., 10 Allen (Mass.) 113; Waring v. Loder, 53 N. Y. 581; Foster v. Van Reed, 5 Hun (N. Y.) 321, 70 N. Y. 19, 26 Am. Rep. 544; Thornton v. Enterprise Ins. Co., 71 Pa. St. 234.

[6] Springfield F. &c. Ins. Co. v. Allen, 43 N. Y. 389, 3 Am. Rep. 711. See also New Hampshire F. Ins. Co. v. National L. Ins. Co., 112 Fed. 199; Dick v. Franklin F. Ins. Co., 10 Mo. App. 376; Foster v. Van Reed, 70 N. Y. 19, 26 Am. Rep. 544; Alamo F. Ins. Co. v. Davis, 25 Tex. Civ. App. 342, 60 S. W. 802. See ante § 409.

[7] Badger v. Platts, 68 N. H. 222, 44 Atl. 296.

[8] Hare v. Headley, 54 N. J. Eq. 545, 35 Atl. 445; Ulster County Sav. Inst. v. Leake, 73 N. Y. 161, 29 Am.

§ 413. Effect of provision for subrogation.—When a policy provides for the subrogation of the insurers to the rights of the mortgagee, in case of payment to the mortgagee for a loss under the policy which the insurers would not have been liable to pay to the owner, the contract, from being primarily one insuring the mortgagor, and making the mortgagee an equitable assignee, is by these special provisions, upon the happening of certain events, regarded as resolved in effect into an insurance of the interest of the mortgagee as such, and into a personal contract with the mortgagee, in which the mortgagor has no interest.[9]

To entitle the insurer to subrogation under the terms of the clause, the facts must be such that as against the mortgagor there would be by the terms of the policy an actual exemption from liability.[10] A provision in a policy taken out by the mortgagee that, if the company pays the mortgagee, and shall claim as to the mortgagor that no liability existed, it shall be subrogated to all the rights of the mortgagee, who shall transfer to it the notes and mortgage, in order to be valid, must be construed as requiring proof that the policy is void as to the

Rep. 115; Springfield F. &c. Ins. Co. v. Allen, 43 N. Y. 389, 3 Am. Rep. 711; Utter v. Lewis, 10 Pa. Dist. 50. Compare Allen v. Watertown F. Ins. Co., 132 Mass. 480.

[9] Stinchfield v. Milliken, 71 Maine 567; Allen v. Watertown F. Ins. Co., 132 Mass. 480; Sterling F. Ins. Co. v. Beffrey, 48 Minn. 9, 50 N. W. 922; Badger v. Platts, 68 N. H. 222, 44 Atl. 296; Hastings v. Westchester F. Ins. Co., 73 N. Y. 141; Ulster County Sav. Inst. v. Leake, 73 N. Y. 161, revg. 11 Hun (N. Y.) 515, 29 Am. Rep. 115. There is a Massachusetts decision relating to a subsequent agreement for subrogation. A mortgagee, to whom a policy of insurance had been made payable in case of loss, entered for a breach of condition, so that the policy by its terms became void. Subsequently the insurance company, at the request of the mortgagee, without receiving any new consideration, made an indorsement on the policy which recited that the mortgagee had entered for breach of condition, and provided that the policy should attach and cover his interest as such; that the insurance as to the interest of the mortgagee should not be invalidated by any act or neglect of the mortgagor; and that whenever the insurer should pay the mortgagee any sum for loss under the policy, and should claim that as to the mortgagor or owner no liability existed, the insurer should be subrogated to the legal rights of the mortgagee under all securities held as collateral to the mortgage debt. A loss having occurred after the indorsement was made, it was held that the mortgagee could not maintain an action for it. Davis v. German-American Ins. Co., 135 Mass. 251.

In Hastings v. Winchester Ins. Co., 73 N. Y. 141, it was suggested that the stipulation for subrogation to the legal rights of the mortgagee, upon payment to him, to the extent of such payment is a consideration; but the learned judge who delivered the opinion in the Massachusetts case objects to this view. It must be confessed, however, that the New York decision seems to present the broader and better view of the question.

[10] Traders' Ins. Co. v. Race, 142 Ill. 338, 31 N. E. 392.

mortgagor.[11] The insurance money, when paid under such a policy to the mortgagee, is not a payment to that extent of the mortgage debt, but is in effect a payment by the insurers toward the purchase of the mortgage. The mortgagor or his successor has no beneficial interest in the policy, and can not compel an application on the debt of the amount due upon a loss. The insurers in such case may recover on the note and mortgage assigned to them by the mortgagee.[12]

Another view, differing a little from the above, is taken by the courts of Connecticut. Instead of holding such an arrangement with the mortgagee to be a distinct and independent contract of insurance, they regard it rather as an agreement relating to an existing policy, by which certain conditions are dispensed with and certain privileges are secured to the insurers which they would not otherwise have, and the mortgagee is made a party to the contract of insurance.[13]

Any limitations or conditions annexed to this right of subrogation must be observed. Thus, under a policy of insurance which provides that, if the insurers should pay the amount of the insurance to the mortgagee, claiming that, as to the mortgagor, no liability exists, they should, to the extent of such payment, be subrogated to the rights of the mortgagee, the insurers, on payment to the mortgagee, do not become subrogated to his rights unless they are in fact not liable on the policy as against the mortgagor. The right of the insurers to be subrogated as claimed depends upon whether the policies had been legally forfeited under the conditions therein contained.[14]

§ 413a. Stipulations for protection of mortgagee against acts of owner.—When the policy is made payable to a mortgagee, he is generally protected against the acts of the owner of the property by a provision of the policy that it shall not be forfeited by any alienation or other act on his part. If a policy so providing also contains a further

[11] Traders' Ins. Co. v. Race, 142 Ill. 338, 31 N. E. 392; Loewenstein v. Queen Ins. Co., 227 Mo. 100, 127 S. W. 72.

[12] Insurance Co. v. Martin, 151 Ind. 209, 51 N. E. 361.

[13] Meriden Sav. Bank v. Home Ins. Co., 50 Conn. 396.

[14] Traders' Ins. Co. v. Race (Ill.), 29 N. E. 846, affd. 142 Ill. 338, 31 N. E. 392. When the case was last before the court, it said: "The right to subrogate, however, can not be said to depend upon the naked claim of appellants that there is no liability on the policies to appellee, but the facts must warrant such claim. The claim to entitle them to an assignment and subrogation must be made in good faith, and be based upon a state of facts which, under the contract of insurance, would entitle them to exemption from liability. The rights of a party insured can not be made to depend upon the arbitrary claim of the insurer." Citing Davenport v. Ledger, 80 Ill. 574; Furlong v. Cox, 77 Ill. 293; Van Arman v. Byington, 38 Ill. 443.

provision that in case of a payment of the loss to the mortgagee the insurer shall be entitled to an assignment of the mortgage, upon the happening of a loss and the assignment of the policy to the insurers, it will be a valid security in their hands if the mortgagor or owner of the property, to whom the policy was issued, has alienated the property prior to the loss, so that the policy has become void as to him, though saved from forfeiture as against the mortgagee. The principal party insured then has no right to claim the sum paid upon the loss as a payment on the mortgage debt.[15]

A provision in a policy obtained by the mortgagor and payable to a mortgagee, that "no sale or transfer of the property insured shall vitiate the right of the mortgagee to recover in case of loss," as a necessary consequence, protects the mortgagee from the acts of any subsequent purchaser or mortgagee, although those acts be in violation of provisions of the policy; as, for instance, a provision making the policy void if the assured should obtain further insurance without giving written notice to the insurance company and obtaining its consent. A necessary consequence of a sale of the property is, that the purchaser has a right to insure his interest; and the object of the stipulation being to avoid the defeat of the policy by any sale or transfer of the property, the fair interpretation of the stipulation is, that the mortgagee's right to recover shall not be vitiated by any of the natural consequences or incidents of a sale.[16]

Of course if a mortgagee, by an indorsement upon the policy, stands merely in the position of one to whom the policy is made payable, without any stipulation for his protection against the acts of the assured, his right to recover may be vitiated by the violation of any of the provisions of the policy by any owner or occupant of the premises.[17] The mortgagee does not in such case become an assignee of the policy, and can recover only what the assured could recover. If a policy be assigned to a mortgagee, and he gives a deposit note and becomes liable to assessments, a new contract of insurance is created, which is in effect an insurance of the mortgagee's interest, and in that case he is not affected by the subsequent acts of the party originally insured.[18]

[15] Springfield F. &c. Ins. Co. v. Allen, 43 N. Y. 389, 3 Am. Rep. 711.

[16] City Five Cents Savings Bank v. Pennsylvania F. Ins. Co., 122 Mass. 165.

[17] Franklin Savings Institution v. Central Mut. F. Ins. Co., 119 Mass. 240; Fogg v. Middlesex Mut. F. Ins. Co., 10 Cush. (Mass.) 337; Loring v. Manufacturers' Ins. Co., 8 Gray (Mass.) 28; Hale v. Mechanics' Mut. F. Ins. Co., 6 Gray (Mass.) 169, 66 Am. Dec. 410; Van Buren v. St. Joseph County Village Ins. Co., 28 Mich. 398.

[18] Foster v. Equitable Mut. F. Ins. Co., 2 Gray (Mass.) 216.

By a provision known as the "union mortgage clause" a stipulation is usually made that in case of loss the policy is made payable to the mortgagee, and that his interest as payee shall not be invalidated or affected by any act or omission of the mortgagor.[19] Such clause in a policy operates as an independent insurance upon the mortgagee's interest, and gives him the same protection as if he had taken out a separate policy, free from the conditions imposed upon the owner.[20]

§ 413b. Condition against procuring other insurance.—A policy taken by a mortgagor for the benefit of the mortgagee provided that it should become void if the assured should, without the written consent of the insurers, obtain other insurance upon the property. The mortgagee, without the knowledge of the mortgagor and before default, procured other insurance payable to himself as mortgagee. The insurers contended that the mortgagor's policy was rendered void by a breach of this condition; but it was held that there was no breach of the condition, although the policy contained a clause that the mortgagor should keep the mortgaged buildings insured for the benefit of the mortgagee, who was authorized, in case of default, to procure insurance; for inasmuch as the mortgagor was not in default, the mortgageee, in procuring insurance, acted for himself, and not as the mortgagor's agent.[21] Where the policy is in the name of the mortgagor, and is made payable to the mortgagee as his interest may appear, a subsequent policy obtained by the mortgagor is in violation of the condition against procuring other insurance.[22]

A mortgagee to whom loss in a policy is made payable, and who accepts and retains a policy which shows on its face that the mortgagor

---

[19] Lancashire Ins. Co. v. Boardman, 58 Kans. 339, 49 Pac. 92, 62 Am. St. 621; Eliot Five Cents Sav. Bank v. Commercial Union Assur. Co., 142 Mass. 142, 7 N. E. 550; Ulster County Sav. Inst. v. Leake, 73 N. Y. 161, 29 Am. Rep. 115; Springfield F. &c. Ins. Co. v. Allen, 43 N. Y. 389, 3 Am. Rep. 711.

[20] Syndicate Ins. Co. v. Bohn, 65 Fed. 165, 12 C. C. A. 531, 27 L. R. A. 614; Collinsville Sav. Soc. v. Boston Ins. Co., 77 Conn. 676, 60 Atl. 647, 69 L. R. A. 924. Compare Glens Falls Ins. Co. v. Porter, 44 Fla. 568, 33 So. 473; Hartford F. Ins. Co. v. Olcott, 97 Ill. 439; Queen Ins. Co. v. Dearborn Sav. &c. Assn., 75 Ill. App. 371, affd. 175 Ill. 115, 51

N. E. 717; Magoun v. Fireman's Fund Ins. Co., 86 Minn. 486, 91 N. W. 5, 91 Am. St. 370; Burnham v. Royal Ins. Co., 75 Mo. App. 394; Phenix Ins. Co. v. Omaha Trust Co., 41 Nebr. 834, 60 N. W. 133, 25 L. R. A. 679; Eddy v. London Assur. Corp., 143 N. Y. 311, 38 N. E. 307, 25 L. R. A. 686; Smith v. Union Ins. Co., 25 R. I. 260, 55 Atl. 715, 105 Am. St. 882; Ormsby v. Phenix Ins. Co., 5 S. Dak. 72, 58 N. W. 301.

[21] Titus v. Glens Falls Ins. Co., 81 N. Y. 410.

[22] Sias v. Roger Williams ins. Co., 8 Fed. 187; Gillett v. Liverpool &c. Ins. Co., 73 Wis. 203, 41 N. W. 78, 9 Am. St. 784.

is insured, can not say that he is not affected by the imputed knowledge of the mortgagor as to the issuance of a policy, for the purpose of avoiding the effect of other insurance procured by the latter.[23] But invalid insurance taken by the owner of the property in violation of this provision can not be considered in determining the right of the mortgagee when the policy provides that his interest shall not be invalidated by any act of the owner.[24]

§ 414. **When mortgagee may charge for insurance.**—As between mortgagor and mortgagee, the duty to pay premiums rests primarily on the former,[25] and the mere retention of policies by the latter will not render him liable unless he requested the issuance of the policies or receives the benefit thereof under circumstances raising an implied promise to pay.[26] But insurance effected by a mortgagee upon the mortgaged estate, without any provision authorizing him or obligating the mortgagor to do so, can not be charged to the mortgagor.[27] Premiums paid by a mortgagee for insurance on the mortgaged property can not be recovered by him upon foreclosure, in the absence of a stipulation in the mortgage giving him this right.[28]

If the mortgage contains a condition that the mortgagor shall "keep the buildings standing on the land aforesaid insured against fire in a sum not less than two thousand five hundred dollars, for the benefit of the said mortgagee," and the mortgagor fails to insure, the mortgagee may effect insurance, and is entitled to credit for the premiums paid by him.[29] For a still stronger reason is this the case when the mortgage provides that upon the failure of the mortgagor to keep this condition, the mortgagee may insure.[30] The mortgagor, having failed to comply with his contract, can not take advantage of his own wrong

[23] Holbrook v. Baloise F. Ins. Co., 117 Cal. 561, 49 Pac. 555.

[24] Eddy v. London Assur. Corp., 143 N. Y. 311, 38 N. E. 307, 25 L. R. A. 686.

[25] Reid v. State Bank, 119 N. Y. S. 242; Muddle v. Van Slyke, 63 Misc. 229, 118 N. Y. S. 473.

[26] Reid v. State Bank, 119 N. Y. S. 242.

[27] Nordyke v. Gery, 112 Ind. 535, 13 N. E. 683; Saunders v. Frost, 5 Pick. (Mass.) 259, 16 Am. Dec. 394; Faure v. Winans, Hopk. Ch. (N. Y.) 283, 14 Am. Dec. 545; Dobson v. Land, 8 Hare 216, 4 De G. & S. 575.

[28] Miller v. Hunt, 6 Idaho 523, 57 Pac. 315; Culver v. Brinkerhoff, 180 Ill. 548, 54 N. E. 585.

[29] Baker v. Jacobson, 183 Ill. 171, 55 N. E. 724; Fowley v. Palmer, 5 Gray (Mass.) 549. The insurance in this case was payable to the mortgagee "for whom it may concern." Barthell v. Syverson, 54 Iowa 160, 6 N. W. 178. See also Harper v. Ely, 70 Ill. 581; Stinchfield v. Milliken, 71 Maine 567; Leland v. Collver, 34 Mich. 418; McLean v. Burr, 16 Mo. App. 240; Ferguson v. Dickinson (Tex. Civ. App.), 138 S. W. 221.

[30] Overby v. Fayetteville Bldg. &c. Assn., 81 N. Car. 56. See also Neale v. Albertson, 39 N. J. Eq. 382.

and decline to pay the premium. The condition that the mortgagor should insure distinguishes the case from that class of cases where the mortgagee insures his own interest in the mortgaged premises; such insurance he must effect at his own expense. Then he is not holden to account for the proceeds. But when the mortgage gives the mortgagee the right to insure at the expense of the mortgagor, and he does so, and charges the premium to the mortgagor, the amount received from the insurance must be accounted for toward the payment of the mortgage debt.[31] Although it may be difficult to prove that the mortgagee in any particular case effected the insurance under the provision of the mortgage and at the expense of the mortgagor, so that he is accountable for the proceeds, the difficulty is one brought upon the mortgagor by his own failure to perform his contract;[32] and if he has no such proof he must take the mortgagee's word for it. But he can not charge for premiums paid for insurance to a larger amount than is stipulated for in the mortgage.[33]

The mortgagee will not be allowed for insurance effected by himself, in the absence of any stipulation in the mortgage that the mortgagor shall keep the property insured for the mortgagee's benefit or that premiums of insurance paid by the mortgagee shall be a charge upon the property.[34] But if the mortgagee, at the request of the mortgagor, takes out insurance on the mortgaged premises, and pays the premium, the amount of the premium so paid is a charge on the premises.[35]

§ 415. **Rule where condition not in form of direct covenant.**—The rule is the same where the condition to keep insurance is not in the form of a direct covenant, as where the condition was,[36] that if the grantor shall repay the loan, "and, until such payment, keep the buildings standing on the land aforesaid insured against fire, in a sum not less than $250, for the benefit of the mortgagee, and payable to him in case of loss, at some insurance office approved by him; or, in default thereof, shall, on demand, pay to said mortgagee all such sums of

---

[31] Pendleton v. Elliott, 67 Mich. 235, 35 N. W. 97.

[32] Per Chief Justice Shaw, in Fowley v. Palmer, 5 Gray (Mass.) 549.

[33] Conover v. Grover, 31 N. J. Eq. 539.

[34] Pierce v. Faunce, 53 Maine 351; Saunders v. Frost, 5 Pick. (Mass.) 259, 16 Am. Dec. 394; Clark v.

Smith, 1 N. J. Eq. 121; Faure v. Winans, Hopk. Ch. (N. Y.) 283, 14 Am. Dec. 545.

[35] Mix v. Hotchkiss, 14 Conn. 32.

[36] Nichols v. Baxter, 5 R. I. 491. The form of mortgage in this case is the ordinary form used in Massachusetts. See also Barthell v. Syverson, 54 Iowa 160, 6 N. W. 178.

money as the said mortgagee shall reasonably pay for such insurance, with interest," then the deed should be void.

In Connecticut it is provided by statute that premiums paid by the mortgagee of any property, for insuring his interest therein against loss by fire, shall be deemed to be a part of the mortgage debt, and shall be refunded to him before he can be required to release his title.[37]

§ 416. Nature of liability of mortgagee charging for insurance.—

A mortgagee charging for insurance is liable as an insurer. If he charges the mortgagor with the premiums for an insurance for a certain time as part of the loan, and undertakes to procure the insurance, he is bound to keep the policies alive during that period, and he is himself liable as an insurer if, in consequence of his neglect to pay the premiums, the policies expire.[38] The extent of the liability is the same as an insurance company's would have been had the policies been continued by the payment of the premiums.

§ 417. Return premium.—

A return premium upon a policy procured by the mortgagor and assigned to the holder of a mortgage, which is subsequently paid by a purchaser of the equity of redemption, in accordance with his agreement with the mortgagor to assume and pay it, belongs to the mortgagor, and he may recover the amount of it from any one else who collects it.[39]

But where a mortgagee took out a policy in which the mortgagor was named as the assured, but it was made payable in case of loss to the mortgagee, and it was stipulated that the assured might terminate the policy at any time, in which case the insurance company could retain a proportionate part of the premium, and shortly afterward the mortgagee sold the land under a power of sale, and the policy was canceled and a new one issued to the purchaser, without any rebate being paid to the mortgagee, it was held that the mortgagor could not recover the rebate of premium from the mortgagee. The mortgagor should either have surrendered the policy immediately before the sale with the mortgagee's consent, or should have sold the policy to the

---

[37] Gen. Stat. 1875, p. 358. See English statute providing for adding to the principal sum secured premiums paid by the mortgagee for insurance, which, by the terms of the deed, should be obtained by the mortgagor, 23 & 24 Vict. ch. 145, §§ 11, 12.

[38] Soule v. Union Bank, 45 Barb. (N. Y.) 111, 30 How. Pr. 105.

[39] Merrifield v. Baker, 9 Allen (Mass.) 29; Felton v. Brooks, 4 Cush. (Mass.) 203; Rafsnyder's Appeal, 88 Pa. St. 436.

purchaser and obtained the consent of the insurance company thereto.[40]

Upon a foreclosure sale a mortgagee to whom a policy has been transferred as collateral security for the mortgage debt is entitled to the deposit premium, when by the terms of the policy the insurable interest of both the mortgagee and mortgagor is divested, and the proceeds of the sale are insufficient to pay the mortgage debt.[41]

III. Insurance by the Mortgagee

§ 418. **General considerations.**—Insurance obtained by the mortgagee when the mortgage contains the usual covenant for insurance on the part of the mortgagor, and an agreement that, in case of his failure to do so, the mortgagee or his representatives may make such insurance, and the mortgage shall secure the repayment of the premiums, is not necessarily presumed to be under this authority, especially if it be taken "on his interest as mortgagee."[1] A mortgagee may insure his interest as mortgagee, and he may make such terms with the insurer as they may agree upon. When, therefore, the mortgagee procures a policy with a provision that in case of loss the assured shall assign to the insurer an interest in the mortgage equal to the amount of loss paid, this provision is paramount to the contract between the mortgagor and mortgagee, and the insurer is entitled, upon payment of a loss under the policy, to an assignment of the mortgage; and in an action to foreclose the mortgage the mortgagor can not claim an application of the amount of the insurance as payment upon the mortgage.[2] Such a case is distinguished from cases where there was no agreement in the policy obtained by the mortgagee as to subrogation. If there be nothing in the policy inconsistent with the contract between the mortgagor and mortgage, this contract may be regarded as an explanation of the policy obtained by the mortgagee; and the policy will be regarded as having been obtained under the provisions of the mortgage and for the benefit of the mortgagor. Thus, in a case

[40] Parker v. Smith Charities, 127 Mass. 499.

[41] Rafsnyder's Appeal, 88 Pa. St. 436.

[1] Foster v. Van Reed, 70 N. Y. 19, revg. 5 Hun (N. Y.) 321, 26 Am. Rep. 544.

[2] Foster v. Van Reed, 70 N. Y. 19, 26 Am. Rep. 544.

before the Court of Appeals in New York,[3] upon a policy effected under such a provision in the mortgage, Mr. Justice Andrews said: "The authority given in the mortgage was an authority to the mortgagee to procure an insurance for the benefit of both parties. This is the fair interpretation. It was immaterial to the mortgagor whether the insurance was in his name or in the name of the mortgagee, if the avails of it in case of loss should apply in reduction of the debt. The mortgagee had no interest to procure an insurance limited to his own protection merely, where the expense was to be paid by the other party and was secured on the land." There is an implied obligation arising from the procuring of the insurance upon the request of the mortgagor, or at his expense, that the insurance money when paid shall be applied to the mortgage debt.[4]

In construing a clause attached to an insurance policy which provided that in case of loss under the policy, it should be paid to the mortgagee and if the insurer should claim that no liability existed as to the mortgagor, it should, upon such payment, be subrogated to the rights of the mortgagee under the mortgage to the extent of such payment, and should receive an assignment pro tanto of the mortgage security, it is held that in order for the insurer to avail itself of the right to be subrogated to the rights of the mortgagee, instead of applying the payment of the loss toward the satisfaction of the mortgage, it is not sufficient for it merely to claim that no liability existed on the policy as to the mortgagor, but it must allege and prove a state of facts which, under the contract of insurance, would entitle it to exemption from liability to the mortgagor.[5]

Whenever the insurance has been effected at the request or by the authority of the mortgagor, or at his expense, or under circumstances that would make him chargeable with the premium, he is entitled to have the money paid on the policy applied to the extinguishment of his debt.[6] The insurance having been paid for by the mortgagor, though taken in the name of the mortgagee as if absolute owner, the fact that the mortgagor has paid the debt secured by the mortgage

[3] Waring v. Loder, 53 N. Y. 581.
[4] Holbrook v. American Ins. Co., 1 Curtis (U. S.) 193; Clinton v. Hope Ins. Co., 45 N. Y. 454; Buffalo Steam Engine Works v. Sun Mut. Ins. Co., 17 N. Y. 401.
[5] Sun Ins. Office v. Heiderer, 44 Colo. 293, 99 Pac. 39; Traders' Ins. Co. v. Race, 142 Ill. 338, 31 N. E. 392; Home Ins. Co. v. Marshall, 48 Kans. 235, 29 Pac. 161; Hare v. Headley, 54 N. J. Eq. 545, 35 Atl. 445.
[6] Honore v. Lamar F. Ins. Co., 51 Ill. 409; Stinchfield v. Milliken, 71 Maine 567; Pendleton v. Elliott, 67 Mich. 496, 35 N. W. 97; Nelson v. Insurance Co., 43 N. J. Eq. 256, 11 Atl. 681.

does not prevent a recovery for a loss against the insurers. The mortgagor in such case is the beneficial party, and has the right to recover in the name of the mortgagee.[7]

Where a mortgagee holding a mortgage containing the usual insurance clause obtained, at the expense of the mortgagor, a policy insuring him as mortgagee, and afterward, upon taking an additional mortgage upon the same property, also containing the insurance clause, applied for a new policy to cover both amounts, and a policy was issued which contained an additional clause providing that the insurance company should only be liable for any deficiency that might remain after the mortgagee had exhausted his primary security, and this clause was not noticed till after a loss occurred, it was held that the insertion of this clause was a fraud upon the mortgagee, and that the policy should be reformed by striking out this clause.[8]

Where a mortgage provides that the mortgagee may insure the property and charge the premium paid for insurance in case the mortgagor fails to insure, the mortgagee is not chargeable with want of ordinary care in the selection of an insurance company; and in case the property is burned and the insurance company proves insolvent the mortgagee is not chargeable with negligence. Such facts constitute no defense to the enforcement of the mortgage debt, the provision of the mortgage not being a covenant to insure on the part of the mortgagee which the mortgagors could bring into force by their own default, but merely an option, in the exercise of which the mortgagee acted as agent for the mortgagors, and its action was ratified by the repayment of the premium without objection to the company selected, of which the mortgagors were chargeable with notice if they failed to make inquiry.[9]

§ 419. **Effect of insurance of mortgagee's interest.**—A mortgagee of real estate has an insurable interest therein, which he may insure on his own account; and when he does so he insures, not the real estate, but his interest therein arising from his lien. He can only insure to the amount of his mortgage debt.[10] But an insurance of a mortgagee's

[7] Norwich F. Ins. Co. v. Boomer, 52 Ill. 442, 4 Am. Rep. 618.

[8] Hay v. Star F. Ins. Co., 13 Hun (N. Y.) 496.

[9] Southern Build. &c. Assn. v. Miller, 110 Fed. 35.

[10] Carpenter v. Providence Washington Ins. Co., 16 Pet. (U. S.) 495, 10 L. ed. 1044; Hanover F. Ins. Co. v. Bohn, 48 Nebr. 743, 67 N. W. 774, 58 Am. St. 719; Hadley v. New Hampshire Ins. Co., 55 N. H. 110; Excelsior Fire Ins. Co. v. Royal Ins. Co., 55 N. Y. 343, 14 Am. Rep. 271; McDonald v. Black, 20 Ohio 185, 55 Am. Dec. 448; Smith v. Columbia Ins. Co., 17 Pa. St. 253, 55 Am. Dec. 546.

interest is not an insurance of the mortgage debt, as has been said in some cases, nor is it an indemnity against the loss of that debt by a loss or damage to the property mortgaged, so that, if the mortgaged property after the loss is still enough in value to pay the debt, there has been in effect no loss.[11] This subject was fully explained by Mr. Justice Folger, in a case before the Court of Appeals in New York,[12] and he clearly shows that the insurance of a mortgage inter-

[11] Carpenter v. Providence Washington Ins. Co., 16 Pet. (U. S.) 495, 10 L. ed. 1044, per Story, J.; Kernochan v. New York Bowery Fire Ins. Co., 17 N. Y. 428, per Strong, J.; Ætna F. Ins. Co. v. Tyler, 16 Wend. (N. Y.) 385, 30 Am. Dec. 90, per Chancellor Walworth; Smith v. Columbia Ins. Co., 17 Pa. St. 253, 55 Am. Dec. 546; Mathewson v. Western Assur. Co., 4 L. Can. Jur. 57. See also Sussex County Mut. Ins. Co. v. Woodruff, 26 N. J. L. 541.

[12] Excelsior Fire Ins. Co. v. Royal Ins. Co., 55 N. Y. 343, 14 Am. Rep. 271, per Folger, J. "Fire underwriters in these days, in this state, are the creatures of statute, and have no rights, save such as the state gives to them. They may agree that they will pay such loss or damage as happens by fire to property. They are limited to this. It was not readily that it was first held that they could agree with a mortgagor or lienor of property, to reimburse to him the loss caused to him by fire. He is not the owner of it; how, then, can he insure it, was the query. And the effort was not to enlarge the power of the insurer so that it might insure a debt, but to bring the lienor within the scope of that power, so that the property might be insured for his benefit. And it was done by holding that, as his security did depend upon the safety of the property, he had an interest in its preservation, and so had such interest as that he might take out a policy upon it against loss by fire, without meeting the objection that it was a wagering policy. The policy did not, therefore, become one upon the debt, and for indemnification against its loss; but still remained one upon the prop-

erty, and against loss or damage to it. It is doubtless true, as is said by Gibson, J., in 17 Pa. St. 253, that in effect it is the debt which is insured. It is only as an effect, however; an effect resulting from the primary act of insurance of the property which is the security for the debt. It is the interest in the property which gives the right to obtain insurance, and the ownership of the debt, a lien upon the property, creates that interest. The agreement is usually, as it is in fact in this case, for insuring, from loss or damage by fire, the property. The interest of the mortgagor is in the whole property, just as it exists undamaged by fire, at the date of the policy. If that property is consumed in part, though what there be left of it is equal in value to the amount of the mortgage debt, the mortgage interest is affected. It is not so great, or so safe, or so valuable, as it was before. It was for indemnity against this very detriment, this very decrease in value, that the mortgagee sought insurance and paid his premium.

"To say that it is the debt which is insured against loss, is to give to most, if not all, fire insurance companies a power to do a kind of business which the law and their charters do not confer. They are privileged to insure property against loss or damage by fire. They are not privileged to guarantee the collection of debts. If they are they may insure against the insolvency of the debtor. No one will contend this; and it will be said, it is not by a guaranty of the debt, but an indemnity is given against the loss of the debt by an insurance against perils to the property by fire. This is but coming to our position: that it is the

est is not an insurance of the debt, but of the interest of the mortgagee in the property upon the safety of which depends his security,
and that upon the happening of a loss the insurer is bound to make
good the loss without regard to the value of the property remaining.
The mortgagee's rights to the proceeds of the insurance taken out by
him is not affected by the fact that the property is still, even after the
loss insured against, sufficient security for the amount of the mortgage.[13]

§ 420. **Insurer subrogated to rights of mortgagee.**—It being settled that an insurance made by a mortgagee of his own interest, at his
own expense, and upon his own motion, is an insurance of his interest
in the property, and not of the debt secured, and that the insurers are
liable to pay him the whole amount of the damage to the property,
it remains to be considered whether either the mortgagor can claim
that the payment shall be applied in discharge of his debt, or the
insurers can claim the mortgage security by assignment or subrogation.

In the first place, it is the undisputed doctrine of all the cases that
the mortgagor himself can claim no benefit from such insurance.[14] He
has no claim, in case of loss, to have the proceeds of the insurance
applied on the mortgage debt.[15] The question in dispute is, whether,

---

property which is insured against
the loss by fire, and the protection
to the debt is the sequence thereof.
As the property it is which is insured against loss, it is the loss
which occurs to it which the insurer contracts to pay, and for such
loss he is to pay within the
limit of his liability, irrespective
of the value of the property unde-
stroyed. So as to the remark, that
it is the capacity of the property
to pay the debt which is insured.
This is true in a certain sense; but
it is as a result and not as a primary undertaking. The undertaking is that the property shall not
suffer loss by fire; that is, in
effect, that its capacity to pay the
mortgage debt shall not be diminished. When an appreciable loss
has occurred to the property from
fire, its capacity to pay the mortgage debt has been affected; it is
not so well able to pay the debt
which is upon it. The mortgage interest, the insurable interest, is

lessened in value, and the mortgagee, the insuree, is affected, and
may call upon the insurer to make
him as good again as he was when
he effected his insurance."

[13] Ætna Ins. Co. v. Baker, 71 Ind.
102; Foster v. Equitable Mut. F.
Ins. Co., 2 Gray (Mass.) 216; Ex-
celsior Fire Ins. Co. v. Royal Ins.
Co., 55 N. Y. 343, 14 Am. Rep. 271;
Smith v. Columbia Ins. Co., 17 Pa.
St. 253, 55 Am. Dec. 546;

[14] Russell v. Southard, 12 How.
(U. S.) 139, 13 L. ed. 927; Ely v.
Ely, 80 Ill. 532; Stinchfield v. Milli-
ken, 71 Maine 567; Clark v. Wilson,
103 Mass. 219, 4 Am. Rep. 532; Suf-
folk Ins. Co. v. Boydon, 9 Allen
(Mass.) 123; White v. Brown, 2
Cush. (Mass.) 412; Fowler v.
Palmer, 5 Gray (Mass.) 549; Foster
v. Van Reed, 70 N. Y. 19, 26 Am.
Rep. 544; Dobson v. Land, 8 Hare
216, 4 De G. & Sm. 575; Bellamy v.
Brickenden, 2 Johns. & Hem. 137.

[15] Russell v. Southard, 12 How.
(U. S.) 139, 13 L. ed. 927; Honore

upon payment of the loss under such a policy, the insurer shall be
subrogated to the security held by the mortgagee, or whether he may,
after having collected the insurance money, proceed to collect the
mortgage debt from the mortgagor, and the property mortgaged.

The general rule and the weight of authority is, that the insurer is
thereupon subrogated to the rights of the mortgagee under the mortgage. This is put upon the analogy of the situation of the insurer to
that of a surety.[16] In Massachusetts, however, the insurer is not
entitled to be subrogated to the rights of the mortgagee, and the
latter may recover both the proceeds of the insurance and the full
amount of the mortgage.[17] The mortgagor and mortgagee have each
an insurable interest. If the mortgagee obtains insurance on his own
account, and the premium is not paid by or charged to the mortgagor,
the latter can not claim the benefit of a payment of the policy;[18] but
the insurer is entitled to be subrogated to the claim of the mortgagee,
and may recover upon the note.[19] If, however, the insurer receives
the premium knowing that the mortgagor has paid or agreed to pay it,
he is not entitled to be subrogated to the rights of the mortgagee, as a
mere matter of equity, in the absence of a stipulation therefor in the
policy.[20]

v. Lamar F. Ins. Co., 51 Ill. 409;
Stinchfield v. Milliken, 71 Maine
567; McIntire v. Plaisted, 68 Maine
363; White v. Brown, 2 Cush.
(Mass.) 412; Excelsior F. Ins. Co.
v. Royal Ins. Co., 55 N. Y. 343, 14
Am. Rep. 271.

[16] Norwich Fire Ins. Co. v. Boomer,
52 Ill. 442, 4 Am. Rep. 618; Honore
v. Lamar F. Ins. Co., 51 Ill. 409;
Dick v. Franklin F. Ins. Co., 10 Mo.
App. 376, affd. 81 Mo. 103; Bound
Brook Mut. F. Ins. Assn. v. Nelson,
41 N. J. Eq. 485; Sussex County
Mut. Ins. Co. v. Woodruff, 26 N. J.
L. 541. See also Honore v. Lamar
F. Ins. Co., 51 Ill. 409; Ulster County
Sav. Inst. v. Leake, 73 N. Y. 161,
29 Am. Rep. 115; Excelsior F. Ins.
Co. v. Royal Ins. Co., 55 N. Y. 343,
14 Am. Rep. 271; Springfield F. &c.
Ins. Co. v. Allen, 43 N. Y. 389, 3
Am. Rep. 711; Kernochan v. New
York Bowery F. Ins. Co., 5 Duer.
(N. Y.) 1; Baker v. Monumental
Sav. &c. Assn., 58 W. Va. 408, 52
S. E. 403, 3 L. R. A. (N. S.) 79,
12 Am. St. 996.

[17] King v. State Mut. F. Ins. Co.,
7 Cush. (Mass.) 1, 54 Am. Dec. 683;

Suffolk Fire Ins. Co. v. Boyden, 9
Allen (Mass.) 123.

[18] Stinchfield v. Milliken, 71 Maine
567; Insurance Co. v. Woodbury, 45
Maine 447; White v. Brown, 2 Cush.
(Mass.) 412.

[19] Concord Union Mut. F. Ins. Co.
v. Woodbury, 45 Maine 447; Calla-
han v. Linthicum, 43 Md. 97, 20 Am.
Rep. 106; Sussex County Mut. Ins.
Co. v. Woodruff, 26 N. J. L. 541;
Foster v. Van Reed, 70 N. Y. 19,
26 Am. Rep. 544; Cone v. Niagara
F. Ins. Co., 60 N. Y. 619; Excelsior
Fire Ins. Co. v. Royal Ins. Co., 55
N. Y. 343, 14 Am. Rep. 271; Kerno-
chan v. N. Y. Bowery F. Ins. Co.,
17 N. Y. 428; De Wolf v. Capital
City Ins. Co., 16 Hun (N. Y.) 116;
Ætna Ins. Co. v. Tyler, 16 Wend.
(N. Y.) 385, 30 Am. Dec. 90.

[20] Dick v. Franklin F. Ins. Co.,
10 Mo. App. 376, per Thompson, J.,
affd. 81 Mo. 103; Cone v. Niagara
F. Ins. Co., 60 N. Y. 619; Kernochan
v. Insurance Co., 17 N. Y. 428, 441.
See also Phœnix Ins. Co. v. Chadbourne, 31 Fed. 300; Baker v. Fireman's Fund Ins. Co., 79 Cal. 34,
21 Pac. 357; Ætna Ins. Co. v. Baker,

Upon this principle it has been held that, upon payment of the mortgage debt, the equitable liability of the mortgagee to the mortgagor for the money received from the insurers is a sufficient consideration to support a promise by the mortgagee to allow the amount secured by him upon the mortgage debt, and that an action may be maintained on such promise.[21] If insurance be effected upon the interest of the assured as mortgagee, at his own expense, the insurers, upon payment of a loss and tender of the balance due on the mortgage, have in some courts been held not entitled to have the mortgage assigned to them, or to be subrogated to the rights of the assured under the mortgage, either in law or in equity. The mortgagee's insurance is not an insurance of the debt, although the amount of that is the measure of his insurable interest in the property.[22]

71 Ind. 102; Home Ins. Co. v. Marshall, 48 Kans. 235, 29 Pac. 161; Pendlton v. Elliott, 67 Mich. 496, 35 N. W. 97; Havens v. Germania Ins. Co., 135 Mo. 649, 37 S. W. 497; Hare v. Headley, 54 N. J. Eq. 545, 35 Atl. 445:

[21] Callahan v. Linthicum, 43 Md. 97, 20 Am. Rep. 106, Alvey and Grason, JJ., dissenting.

[22] King v. State Mutual Fire Ins. Co., 7 Cush. (Mass.) 1, 54 Am. Dec. 683. In this case Chief Justice Shaw said: "The case supposed is this: A man makes a loan of money, and takes a bond and mortgage for security. Say the loan is for ten years. He gets insurance on his own interest as mortgagee. At the expiration of seven years the buildings are burnt down; he claims and recovers a loss to the amount insured, being equal to the greater part of the debt. He afterward secures the amount of his debt from the mortgagor, and discharges his mortgage. Has he received a double satisfaction for one and the same debt?

"He surely may recover of the mortgagor, because he is his debtor, and on good consideration has contracted to pay. The money received from the underwriters was not a payment of his debt; there was no privity between the mortgagor and the underwriters; he had not contracted with them to pay it for him, on any contingency; he had paid them nothing for so doing. They did not pay because the mortgagor owed it, but because they had bound themselves, in the event which has happened, to pay a certain sum to the mortgagee.

"But the mortgagee, when he claims of the underwriters, does not claim the same debt. He claims a sum of money due to him upon a distinct and independent contract, upon a consideration, paid by himself, that upon a certain event, to wit, the burning of a particular house, they will pay him a sum of money expressed. Taking the risk or remoteness of the contingency into consideration, in other words the computed chances of loss, the premium paid and the sum to be received are intended to be, and in theory of law are, precisely equivalent. * * * Suppose—for, in order to test a principle, we may put a strong case—suppose the debt has been running twenty years, and the premium is at five per cent., the creditor may pay a sum equal to the whole debt in premiums, and yet never receive a dollar of it from either of the other parties. Not from the underwriters, for the contingency has not happened, and there has been no loss by fire; nor from the debtor, because, not having authorized the insurance at his expense, he is not liable for the premium paid.

"What, then, is there inequitable, on the part of the mortgagee, toward either party, in holding both

§ 421. King v. State Mutual Fire Insurance Co.—The insurer has no interest in the mortgage debt; and there is no privity between him and the mortgagor. Neither can the mortgagor claim any part of the money so recovered as a payment of the mortgage debt, in whole or in part; but he must still pay the whole mortgage debt to the mortgagee.[23] If, however, the mortgage debt was paid, and the mortgage discharged before the loss occurred, the mortgagee's insurable interest having terminated, he has no claim to recover.[24]

IV. *A Mortgage is not an Alienation*

§ 422. General rule.—With reference to the usual provision in the policy of insurance, that it shall become void upon an alienation of the property insured, or upon any transfer or change of title, the general rule is that a mortgage, whether executed before or after the policy is issued, is not an alienation or change of title until foreclosure is complete, or the mortgagor's title is otherwise wholly divested in consequence of the mortgage.[1] But a mortgage is a breach of a condition against "all alienations and alterations in the ownership, situation, or state of the property insured by this company, in any

sums? They are both due upon valid contracts with him, made upon adequate considerations paid by himself. There is nothing inequitable to the debtor, for he pays no more than he originally received in money loaned; nor to the underwriter, for he has only paid upon a risk voluntarily taken, for which he was paid by the mortgagee a full and satisfactory equivalent."

See also Concord Union Mut. Fire Ins. Co. v. Woodbury, 45 Maine 447; Cushing v. Thompson, 34 Maine 496; Clark v. Wilson, 103 Mass. 219, 4 Am. Rep. 532; Suffolk Fire Ins. Co. v. Boyden, 9 Allen (Mass.) 123; Foster v. Equitable Mut. F. Ins. Co., 2 Gray (Mass.) 216.

[23] King v. State Mutual- Fire Ins. Co., 7 Cush. (Mass.) 1, 54 Am. Dec. 683; White v. Brown, 2 Cush. (Mass.) 412; McIntire v. Plaisted, 68 Maine 363; Bean v. Atlantic &c. R. Co., 58 Maine 82; Concord Union Mut. F. Ins. Co. v. Woodbury, 45 Maine 447; Cushing v. Thompson, 34 Maine 496.

[24] Graves v. Hampden Ins. Co., 10 Allen (Mass.) 281; Sussex County Mut. Ins. Co. v. Woodruff, 26 N. J. L. 541.

[1] Friezen v. Allemania F. Ins. Co., 30 Fed. 352; Aurora F. Ins. Co. v. Eddy, 55 Ill. 213; Hartford Ins. Co. v. Walsh, 54 Ill. 164; Commercial Ins. Co. v. Spankneble, 52 Ill. 53, 4 Am. Rep. 582; Hanover F. Ins. Co.

material particular."[2] So also where the condition was against alienation "by sale, mortgage, assignment, or otherwise."[3] In North Carolina the giving of a mortgage effects such a change of title and interest of the assured as avoids the policy, when not assented to by
the insurer in the manner prescribed by the policy.[4] So long as the
period of redemption has not expired, a foreclosure sale is not an
alienation.[5]

Even a sale under a power contained in the mortgage does not
amount to an alienation, when the mortgagee himself becomes the
purchaser through a third party, and the sale is repudiated by the
mortgagor, and is subsequently set aside by a decree of court.[6] But

v. Connor, 20 Ill. App. 297; Indiana
Mut. Fire Ins. Co. v. Coquillard, 2
Ind. 645. But see M'Culloch v. In-
diana Mut. Fire Ins. Co., 8 Blackf.
(Ind.) 50; Lancashire Ins. Co. v.
Monroe, 101 Ky. 12, 39 S. W. 434;
Smith v. Monmouth Mut. Fire Ins.
Co., 50 Maine 96; Pollard v. Somer-
set Mut. Fire Ins. Co., 42 Maine 221;
Bryan v. Traders' Ins. Co., 145 Mass.
389, 14 N. E. 454; Powers v. Guard-
ian Ins. Co., 136 Mass. 108, 49 Am.
Rep. 20; Judge v. Conn. Ins. Co.,
132 Mass. 521; Rice v. Tower, 1 Gray
(Mass.) 426; Jackson v. Mass. Mut.
Fire Ins. Co., 23 Pick. (Mass.) 418,
34 Am. Dec. 69; Guest v. New Hamp-
shire F. Ins. Co., 66 Mich. 98, 33
N. W. 31; Loy v. Home Ins. Co.,
24 Minn. 315, 31 Am. Rep. 346;
Jecko v. Insurance Co., 7 Mo. App.
308; Shepherd v. Union Mut. Fire
Ins. Co., 38 N. H. 232; Dutton v.
North Eastern Mut. Fire Ins. Co.,
29 N. H. 153; Rollins v. Columbian
Mut. Fire Ins. Co., 25 N. H. 200;
Folsom v. Belknap County Mut. Fire
Ins. Co., 1 N. H. 231; Barry v. Ham-
burg-Bremen F. Ins. Co., 110 N. Y.
1, 17 N. E. 405; Conover v. Mutual
Ins. Co., 3 Denio (N. Y.) 254, 1
Comst. 290; Van Duesen v. Charter
Oak Ins. Co., 1 Rob. (N. Y.) 55;
Byers v. Insurance Co., 35 Ohio St.
606; Kronk v. Birmingham Ins. Co.,
91 Pa. St. 300; Howard F. Ins. Co.
v. Bruner, 23 Pa. St. 50. See also
Bushnell v. Farmers' Mut. Ins. Co.,
110 Mo. App. 223, 85 S. W. 103;
Koshland v. Hartford Fire Ins. Co.,
31 Ore. 402, 49 Pac. 866; Peck v.
Girard Fire &c. Ins. Co., 16 Utah

121, 51 Pac. 255, 67 Am. St. 600;
Wolf v. Theresa Village Mut. Fire
Ins. Co., 115 Wis. 402, 91 N. W.
1014.

[2] Edmands v. Mutual Safety Fire
Ins. Co., 1 Allen (Mass.) 311, 79
Am. Dec. 746.

[3] Edes v. Hamilton Mut. Ins. Co.,
3 Allen (Mass.) 362.

[4] Modlin v. Atlantic Fire Ins. Co.,
151 N. Car. 35, 65 S. E. 605.

[5] United States Insurance Co. v.
Stinson, 103 U. S. 25, 26 L. ed. 473;
Columbian Ins. Co. v. Lawrence, 2
Peters (U. S.) 25, 7 L. ed. 335; Es-
sex Sav. Bank v. Meriden F. Ins.
Co., 57 Conn. 335, 17 Atl. 930; Hop-
kins Mfg. Co. v. Aurora F. &c. Ins.
Co., 48 Mich. 148, 11 N. W. 846. See
also Stephens v. Illinois Mut. Fire
Ins. Co., 43 Ill. 327; Campbell v.
Hamilton Mut. Ins. Co., 51 Maine
69; Stuart v. Reliance Ins. Co., 179
Mass. 434, 60 N. E. 929; Strong v.
Manufacturers' Ins. Co., 10 Pick.
(Mass.) 40, 20 Am. Dec. 507; Loy
v. Home Ins. Co., 24 Minn. 315, 31
Am. Rep. 346; Bragg v. New Eng-
land Mut. Fire Ins. Co., 25 N. H.
289; Marts v. Cumberland Mut. Fire
Ins. Co., 44 N. J. L. 478; Haight v.
Continental Ins. Co., 92 N. Y. 51;
Mt. Vernon Mfg. Co. v. Summit
County Mut. Fire Ins. Co., 10 Ohio
St. 347; Farmers' Mut. Ins. Co. v.
Graybill, 74 Pa. St. 17; Hammel v.
Queen's Ins. Co., 54 Wis. 72, 11 N.
W. 349, 41 Am. Rep. 1.

[6] Scammon v. Commercial Union
Ins. Co., 20 Ill. App. 500; Insurance
Co. v. Sampson, 38 Ohio St. 672.

it has been held that a mortgagee's purchase at a foreclosure of property insured, under a power of sale in the mortgage, is a breach of a condition against a sale without insurer's consent, contained in a policy payable to the mortgagee as his interest might appear.[7]

The policy may, however, provide that it shall be void in case of an incumbrance on the property at the time the policy is issued, or an incumbrance thereupon be afterward created, and then of course a mortgage or other incumbrance will render the policy void.[8] This provision is waived if the insurer knew when the policy was issued that it was subject to a mortgage and made no objection.[9]

In general a mortgage is not an alienation until foreclosure is complete; and a foreclosure is not complete until a transfer of title under a foreclosure sale. Thus where, previous to the loss, a decree of sale on foreclosure had been entered, and the property had been put up for sale and bid off by the mortgagee, but no deed had been delivered, and because of the fire the mortgagee refused to accept a deed, it was held that the policy had not become void by sale or alienation, and that the original owner had an insurable interest at the time of the fire.[10]

§ 423. Effect of mortgage in form an absolute deed.

—If, however, the mortgage is by a deed absolute in form, this operates as a transfer or change of title, and puts an end to an insurance conditioned to be void in that event,[11] although there be a defeasance exe-

---

[7] Boston Co-Operative Bank v. American Central Ins. Co., 201 Mass. 350, 87 N. E. 594, 23 L. R. A. (N. S.) 1147.

[8] Hicks v. Farmers' Ins. Co., 71 Iowa 119, 32 N. W. 201, 60 Am. Rep. 781; Ellis v. State Ins. Co., 68 Iowa 578, 27 N. W. 762, 61 Iowa 577, 16 N. W. 744; 56 Am. Rep. 863; Mallory v. Farmers Ins. Co., 65 Iowa 450, 21 N. W. 756; Schumitsch v. American Ins. Co., 48 Wis. 26, 3 N. W. 595. Not by mortgage on adjoining parcel. Eddy v. Hawkeye Ins. Co., 70 Iowa 472, 30 N. W. 808, 59 Am. Rep. 444. As to effect of a change of incumbrances, see Russell v. Cedar Rapids Ins. Co., 71 Iowa 69, 32 N. W. 95; Hankins v. Rockford Ins. Co., 70 Wis. 1, 35 N. W. 34; Kansas Farmers' F. Ins. Co. v. Saindon, 53 Kans. 623, 36 Pac. 983. Increasing an existing incumbrance contrary to the terms of the policy avoids it. Bowlus v. Phenix Ins. Co., 133 Ind. 106, 32 N. E. 319; Kansas Farmers' Fire Ins. Co. v. Saindon, 53 Kans. 623, 36 Pac. 983.

[9] Georgia Home Ins. Co. v. Stein, 72 Miss. 943, 18 So. 414.

[10] Marts v. Cumberland Ins. Co., 44 N. J. L. 478.

[11] Western Mass. Ins. Co. v. Riker, 10 Mich. 279. "There may be a transfer or change of title without a sale. Should A convey a piece of property to B to hold in secret trust for him, there would be a transfer or change of title from A to B, but there would be no sale of the property or an actual parting with it to B for a valuable consideration, although the conveyance on its face would import a sale from A to B. And if the trust, instead of being secret, appeared on the face of the conveyance, there would still be a change of title. The title would no

cuted at the same time, if this be not recorded in accordance with a statute providing that an absolute conveyance shall not be defeated or affected by an unrecorded defeasance, as against any person other than the maker of the defeasance or his heirs or devisees, or persons having actual notice thereof.[12]

Some courts, however, hold that a conveyance which equity will treat as a mortgage does not terminate the interest of the assured, or make void the policy under the alienation clause.[13] If there be a written defeasance which is seasonably recorded, the two instruments constitute a mortgage as effectually as if the defeasance was contained in the deed, and there can be no pretense that there is an absolute conveyance.[14] Even if the defeasance be not recorded, the deed is not an alienation which will avoid the policy.[15] But it has been held that where the defeasance was not under seal and the transaction appeared to be a transfer in payment of a pre-existing debt with an option of repurchase, there is a breach of the condition against alienation.[16] A conveyance of real estate by a debtor to a creditor under the provisions of the Georgia code is not an alienation of the property within the prohibition against a change of title.[17]

§ 424. Entry to foreclose.—Where a policy provided that "the entry of a foreclosure of a mortgage" should be deemed an alienation of the property, and the company should not be holden for any loss occurring afterward, it was held that this did not mean an actual and complete foreclosure, but had reference to an entry by the mortgagee

longer be in A but in B, his grantee. We think such a conveyance would clearly come within the condition of the policy and put an end to the insurance."

See also Phœnix Ins. Co. v. Asberry, 95 Ga. 792, 22 S. E. 717; Bennett v. Mutual F. Ins. Co., 100 Md. 337, 60 Atl. 99; Farmers' &c. Ins. Co. v. Hahn, 1 Nebr. (nnoff.) 510, 96 N. W. 255.

[12] Tomlinson v. Monmouth Mut. F. Ins. Co., 47 Maine 232; Foote v. Hartford Ins. Co., 119 Mass. 259. See also Bryan v. Traders' Ins. Co., 145 Mass. 389, 14 N. E. 454; Dailey v. Westchester F. Ins. Co., 131 Mass. 173.

[13] Holbrook v. American Ins. Co., 1 Curtis (U. S.) 193; Hodges v. Tennessee Marine &c. Ins. Co., 8 N. Y. 416. See also Nussbaum v. Northern Ins. Co,. 37 Fed. 524, 1 L. R. A. 704; Commercial Ins. Co. v. Spankneble, 52 Ill. 53, 4 Am. Rep. 582; Ætna Ins. Co. v. Jacobson, 105 Ill. App. 283; Trumbull v. Portage County Mut. Ins. Co., 12 Ohio 305; Burkhart v. Farmers' Union Assn. &c. Co., 11 Pa. Sup. Ct. 280; Tittemore v. Vermont Mut. Fire Ins. Co., 20 Vt. 546.

[14] Smith v. Monmouth Mut. F. Ins. Co., 50 Maine 96.

[15] Bryan v. Traders' Ins. Co., 145 Mass. 389, 14 N. E. 454. See also Aurora F. Ins. Co. v. Eddy, 55 Ill. 213.

[16] Adams v. Rockingham Mut. F. Ins. Co., 29 Maine 292. Compare Foote v. Hartford F. Ins. Co., 119 Mass. 259.

[17] Phœnix Ins. Co. v. Asberry, 95 Ga. 792, 22 S. E. 717.

upon a breach of condition for the purpose of foreclosure. Under the system of foreclosure in use in Massachusetts, such entry duly recorded, and followed by possession for three years, accomplishes a foreclosure.[18] Where the condition was against the "passing or entry of a decree of foreclosure, it has been held to refer only to a decree of strict foreclosure, not to a decree for sale.[19]

§ 424a. Condition against commencement of foreclosure proceedings.—Where an insurance policy contains a condition against the commencement of foreclosure proceedings, the institution of such proceedings will avoid the policy.[20] Such a condition is not inconsistent with a clause making the policy payable to the mortgagee in case of loss.[21] Such a condition is valid; and it is held that the service of a petition of foreclosure on the insured is a commencement of the proceedings.[22] In regard to such a policy it was contended in behalf of the mortgagee that the insurers having issued such a policy, with notice of the interest of the mortgagee in the property, and with an agreement to pay him the loss, if any, they could not afterward call in question the natural result and incident of such a mortgage title, namely, the foreclosure thereof, but must be held to have agreed to it in advance. But it was held otherwise.[23] The clause, "commencement

---

[18] McIntire v. Norwich Fire Ins. Co., 102 Mass. 230, 3 Am. Rep. 458. The court says: "The first step toward foreclosure is the manifestation of the intent to foreclose, which is to be indicated in such manner as the law points out, accompanied with a formal registration in the public records. It is very manifest, as we think, that the words 'the entry of a foreclosure,' as used in the policy, are not to be interpreted as meaning exactly the same thing as a consummated and finished foreclosure. The policy provides not merely for the transfer but the change of title, and the insurer may very naturally have considered an entry for foreclosure as a material change in the title of the assured, and in his relation to the property. The parties in their contract have taken pains to avoid saying simply that 'the foreclosure of a mortgage' shall be deemed an alienation. There would be no occasion for them to say that, inasmuch as the law would plainly have said it for them."

[19] Minnock v. Eureka F. &c. Ins. Co., 90 Mich. 236, 51 N. W. 367; Pearman v. Gould, 42 N. J. Eq. 4, 5 Atl. 811.
[20] Quinlan v. Providence Washington Ins. Co., 133 N. Y. 356, 31 N. E. 31, 28 Am. St. 645; Hayes v. United States Fire Ins. Co., 132 N. Car. 702, 44 S. E. 404; Norris v. Hartford F. Ins. Co., 55 S. Car. 450, 74 Am. St. 765. Contra Butz v. Ohio Farmers' Ins. Co., 76 Mich. 263, 42 N. W. 1119, 15 Am. St. 316.
[21] Meadows v. Hawkeye Ins. Co., 62 Iowa 387, 17 N. W. 600.
[22] Findlay v. Union Mut. F. Ins. Co., 74 Vt. 211, 52 Atl. 429, 93 Am. St. 885. Compare Sharp v. Scottish Union &c. Ins. Co., 136 Cal. 542, 69 Pac. 253.
[23] Moore v. Hanover F. Ins. Co., 141 N. Y. 219, 36 N. E. 191; Titus v. Glens Falls Ins. Co., 81 N. Y. 410. The court, in reply to this argument, says: "This reasoning does not carry conviction to our minds. A provision that a policy shall be void in the case of foreclosure proceedings is common in

of foreclosure proceedings," has been held to mean the institution of judicial proceedings for the enforcement of the mortgage; and waivers of legal delays, and other waivers of a nature to facilitate and expedite the judicial proceedings, if ever begun, do not constitute of themselves the commencement of foreclosure proceedings.[24]

A condition that, if the mortgage be foreclosed without the consent of the insurers, the policy shall be void, is broken by a foreclosure without such consent. But if the insurers are notified of the pendency of the foreclosure suit, and their consent to the same is asked, and no reply is made to the request, the insurers are liable for a loss occurring eight days after such notice and six days after the entry of the decree of foreclosure. There was either a waiver of the condition, or a neglect to refuse the consent as promptly as the occasion required, whereby the mortgagee was deprived of all power to protect himself by new insurance in case of a refusal.[25]

insurance policies, and we must assume that experience has shown to underwriters that such proceedings increase the risk to the insurer. The insurance company might have been willing, for the premium charged, to insure this barn with the mortgage upon it, and yet not willing to insure it in case of proceedings to foreclose the mortgage. It did assent to mortgage, and agree that the loss, if any, be paid to the mortgagee, but it did not assent to continue the insurance in case the risk was increased by proceedings to foreclose the mortgage. Before commencing the foreclosure the plaintiff should have obtained the assent of the insurance company. It might have examined the circumstances and granted such assent without any conditions, or it might have required an additional premium for the increased risk. It might have refused altogether, and in that case the plaintiff could have delayed his foreclosure until the end of the year, or surrendered the policy and procured insurance elsewhere. Even if the provision were found to be very inconvenient and embarrassing, there is no help for it. There it is, and we can not take it out of the policy by construction.

There are two provisions: one, that liens, without the assent of the company, shall avoid the policy; and another, that foreclosure proceedings shall avoid it; and effect must be given to both. According to the construction contended for on the part of the plaintiff, the latter provision would be wholly useless or nullified in every case, because all liens avoid the policy unless assented to; and according to that construction, when assented to, foreclosure proceedings may be instituted without avoiding the policy. If such proceedings may be instituted as incident to the mortgage, then they may be carried to their conclusion by a sale and conveyance, and thus, by assenting to a mortgage, a company may be held to have assented to a change of title of the insured property. Such a construction is unreasonable and unwarranted." But in this case it was held that the insurance company had by its acts waived the forfeiture.

[24] Stenzel v. Pennsylvania F. Ins. Co., 110 La. 1019, 35 So. 271, 98 Am. St. 481.

[25] Armstrong v. Agricultural Ins. Co., 56 Hun (N. Y.) 399, 31 N. Y. St. 201, 9 N. Y. S. 873.

§ 425. Where title becomes absolute by strict foreclosure.—But when the title becomes absolute in the mortgagee by a strict foreclosure, or by a foreclosure effected by entry and possession, or when the title passes to another by a sale under a power contained in the mortgage, or by a sale under a decree of court in a foreclosure suit, the transfer is then complete, and the change of title is an alienation within the terms of the policy of insurance.[26] In order to avoid the insurance, the foreclosure must not only be complete, but valid also.[27] When, however, there is a right of redemption after sale, and there is no change of possession until the period for redemption has expired, the foreclosure does not operate as "a sale, transfer, or change in title," within the meaning of a policy, so as to defeat a recovery for a loss accruing after the sale, and before the expiration of the time of redemption.[28] But a verbal promise by the mortgagee to sell the land to the mortgagor, made after the expiration of the period for redemption, without consideration of any kind, will not so continue the mortgagor's interest as to keep the policy in force.[29] In case, however, the foreclosure is effected by the mortgagor for the benefit of the mortgagee, who signs the premium note and pays the assessments, foreclosure is not an alienation, if the mortgagee thereby obtains absolute title to the property, as he is already the person liable under the contract of insurance.[30]

§ 426. Alteration of ownership.—But a mortgage is a violation of a condition against an "alteration of ownership,"[31] or change of "interest" of the assured,[32] as also of a condition against a sale or alienation "in whole or in part."[33] A breach of such or other like condition avoids the policy; and the breach is sufficiently established, in the

[26] Essex Sav. Bank v. Meriden F. Ins. Co., 57 Conn. 335, 17 Atl. 930; McKissick v. Mill Owners' Mut. F. Ins. Co., 50 Iowa 116; Brunswick Sav. Inst. v. Commercial Union Ins. Co., 68 Maine 313, 26 Am. Rep. 56; Campbell v. Hamilton Mut. Ins. Co., 51 Maine 69; Abbott v. Hampden Mut. F. Ins. Co., 30 Maine 414; Macomber v. Cambridge Mut. F. Ins. Co., 8 Cush. (Mass.) 133; McLaren v. Hartford Fire Ins. Co., 5 N. Y. 151; Mt. Vernon Mfg. Co. v. Summit County Mut. Fire Ins. Co., 10 Ohio St. 347; Georgia Home Ins. Co. v. Kinnier, 28 Grat. (Va.) 88.

[27] Niagara F. Ins. Co. v. Scammon,

144 Ill. 490, 28 N. E. 919, 19 L. R. A. 114; Richland County Mut. Ins. Co. v. Sampson, 38 Ohio St. 672.

[28] Loy v. Home Ins. Co., 24 Minn. 315, 31 Am. Rep. 346.

[29] Essex Sav. Bank v. Meriden F. Ins. Co., 57 Conn. 335, 17 Atl. 930.

[30] Esch v. Home Ins. Co., 78 Iowa 334, 43 N. W. 229; Bragg v. North Eastern Mut. Fire Ins. Co., 25 N. H. 289.

[31] Edmands v. Mutual Safety Fire Ins. Co., 1 Allen (Mass.) 311, 79 Am. Dec. 746.

[32] East Texas F. Ins. Co. v. Clarke, 79 Tex. 23, 15 S. W. 166.

[33] Abbott v. Hampden Mut. Fire

absence of any evidence to the contrary, by putting in evidence a certified copy of the record of the mortgage.[34]

A conveyance and mortgage back to secure the purchase-money is such an alienation as will avoid a policy upon the property, although it is provided that the mortgagee shall retain possession until the purchase-money is paid.[35] But a conveyance by the insured, with a simultaneous reconveyance in trust for the first grantor, is held not to be such an alienation or transfer.[36] And so if the sale and reconveyance constitute merely a conditional sale, they are regarded as parts of one entire contract, and are held not to be such an alienation as will avoid the policy.[37]

A foreclosure of a mortgage is such a transfer of the property as will terminate an insurance conditioned to be void "if any change shall take place in the title or possession of the property," or "if the property is disposed of, so that all interest on the part of the assured has ceased."[38]

§ 426a. Change of title, interest or possession.—The weight of authority supports the view that the execution of a mortgage on the insured premises is not a breach of the condition against a change of title, interest or possession.[39] Nor is this provision violated by the existence of a mortgage on the property at the time the policy was issued, as the condition refers only to subsequent changes.[40] Policies sometimes contain conditions requiring the disclosure of existing incumbrances, and render the policy void if this is not done; but no such provision appears in the standard forms that are now required by

Ins. Co., 30 Maine 414; Bates v. Com. Ins. Co., 13 Ohio Dec. 851.

[34] Gould v. Holland Purchase Ins. Co., 16 Hun (N. Y.) 538.

[35] German-American Bank v. Agricultural Ins. Co., 8 Mo. App. 401; Moulthrop v. Farmers' Mut. F. Ins. Co., 52 Vt. 123; Tittemore v. Vermont Mut. Fire Ins. Co., 20 Vt. 546.

[36] Morrison v. Tennessee Mar. &c. Ins. Co., 18 Mo. 262, 59 Am. Dec. 299.

[37] Tittemore v. Vermont Mut. Fire Ins. Co., 20 Vt. 546.

[38] Bishop v. Clay F. &c. Ins. Co., 45 Conn. 430.

[39] Commercial Ins. Co. v. Spankneble, 52 Ill. 53, 4 Am. Rep. 582; Forehand v. Niagara Ins. Co., 58 Ill. App. 161; Germania F. Ins. Co. v. Stewart, 13 Ind. App. 627, 42 N. E. 286; Taylor v. Merchants' &c. Ins.

Co., 83 Iowa 402, 49 N. W. 994; Smith v. Monmouth &c. Ins. Co., 50 Maine 96; Judge v. Connecticut F. Ins. Co., 132 Mass. 521; Rice v. Tower, 67 Mass. 426; Loy v. Home Ins. Co., 24 Minn. 315, 31 Am. Rep. 346; Barry v. Hamburg &c. Ins. Co., 110 N. Y. 1, 17 N. E. 405; Conover v. Mutual Ins. Co., 1 N. Y. 290, 4 How. Pr. 365; Sun Fire Office v. Clark, 53 Ohio St. 414, 42 N. E. 248, 38 L. R. A. 562; Byers v. Farmers' Ins. Co., 35 Ohio St. 606, 35 Am. Rep. 623; Peck v. Girard &c. Ins. Co., 16 Utah 121, 51 Pac. 255, 67 Am. St. 600; Hartford &c. Ins. Co. v. Lasher Stocking Co., 66 Vt. 439, 29 Atl. 629, 44 Am. St. 859.

[40] Morotock Ins. Co. v. Rodefer, 92 Va. 747, 24 S. E. 393, 53 Am. St. 846.

statute in many states. Of course the execution of a mortgage for the purpose of paying off a mortgage which was in existence at the time the policy was executed is not a breach of this provision against the creation of a future incumbrance.[41] A mortgage on the insured property by a person who holds the legal title will not avoid a policy under a prohibition against changes in the title without the consent of the company indorsed upon the policy, if such mortgage is merely the obligation of the mortgagor and not of the insured.[42] Where the policy contains a condition that it shall be void if there is any change in the title, or the creation of an incumbrance, and to which is attached a mortgage slip protecting the rights of a mortgagee against a breach of condition by the mortgagor, the rights of such mortgagee are not affected by a transfer of the title or the creation of an incumbrance by the mortgagor.[43]

§ 427. **Effect of conveyance subsequent to assignment of policy to mortgagee.**—If the mortgagor has already assigned the policy to the mortgagee with the consent of the insurers, his subsequent transfer of the equity of redemption is no breach of the stipulation in the policy against alienation, so far as the assignee is concerned.[44]

This view has been criticized in some courts as contrary to the principle of public policy, that no man shall be allowed to bargain for an advantage to arise from the destruction of property.[45]

Where a mortgagor sells the mortgaged property and indorses an assignment of the policy of insurance to the purchaser, who agrees to pay the debt, and assigns to him the policy properly indorsed thereon, and both grantor and grantee request the mortgagee, who is in possession and control of the policy, to secure the consent of the insurance company to such assignment, and the mortgagee neglects so to do, by reason whereof the insurance company is relieved from all liability to such grantee, and the mortgaged property is afterward wholly or partially destroyed by fire, the grantee may set up a counterclaim for damages in an action brought by the mortgagee to foreclose the mort-

[41] Aurora F. Ins. Co. v. Eddy, 55 Ill. 213; McKibban v. Des Moines &c. Ins. Co., 114 Iowa 41, 86 N. W. 38; Koshland v. Home Mut. Ins. Co, 31 Ore. 321, 49 Pac. 864, 50 Pac. 567.

[42] Hoose v. Prescott Ins. Co., 84 Mich. 309, 47 N. W. 587, 11 L. R. A. 340.

[43] Phœnix Ins. Co. v. Omaha Loan &c. Co., 41 Nebr. 834, 60 N. W. 133, 25 L. R. A. 679; Boyd v. Thuringia

Ins. Co., 25 Wash. 447, 65 Pac. 785, 55 L. R. A. 165.

[44] Fogg v. Middlesex Mut. Fire Ins. Co,. 10 Cush. (Mass.) 337; Foster v. Equitable Mut. Fire Ins. Co., 2 Gray (Mass.) 216; Bragg v. North Eastern Mut. Fire Ins. Co., 25 N. H. 289; Boynton v. Clinton &c. Mut. Ins. Co., 16 Barb. (N. Y.) 254.

[45] Kernochan v. New York Bowery F. Ins. Co., 17 N. Y. 428.

gage. This rule is equally applicable to an action to foreclose a mortgage by one holding it, by assignment, in trust for certain outstanding obligations of the mortgagee, where the policy has been left in the hands of the mortgagee to be cared for and renewed, if necessary.[46]

Where a policy of insurance payable to the mortgagee provided that an unauthorized change in the title should vitiate the policy, in an action on the policy by the mortgagee it was held that evidence of a conveyance of the property to an officer of the mortgage company made to avoid a foreclosure was not objectionable as varying conveyance by parol.[47]

It is held that the mortgage clause attached to the policy is a separate contract between the insurer and the mortgagee, and an alienation by the mortgagor or a failure of the mortgagee to give notice of the change of ownership, as required by a condition in the policy, will not avoid the insurance.[48] And where the policy contains such clause, an alienation by the mortgagor does not affect the rights of the mortgagee's assignee.[49]

[46] First National Bank v. Renn, 63 Kans. 334, 65 Pac. 698.

[47] Northern Assur. Co. v. Chicago Mut. Bldg. Assn., 198 Ill. 474, 64 N. E. 979.

[48] City Five Cents Sav. Bank v. Pennsylvania F. Ins. Co., 122 Mass. 165; Pioneer Sav. &c. Co. v. St. Paul F. &c. Ins. Co., 68 Minn. 170, 70 N. W. 979; Washburn Mill Co. v. Fire Assn. Philadelphia, 60 Minn. 68, 61 N. W. 828, 51 Am. St. 500; Kabrich v. State Ins. Co., 48 Mo. App. 393; Phœnix Ins. Co. v. Omaha L. &c. Co., 41 Nebr. 834, 60 N. W. 133, 25 L. R. A. 679; Southern Bldg &c. Assn. v. Pennsylvania F. Ins. Co., 23 Pa. Super. Ct. 88.

[49] Whiting v. Burkhardt, 178 Mass. 535, 60 N. E. 1, 52 L. R. A. 788, 86 Am. St. 503.

CHAPTER XI

I. *Rules for Determining What Fixtures a Mortgage Covers*

§ 428. In general.[1]—A mortgage of real property, as a general rule, carries as part of the security all fixtures belonging to the realty, without any special mention of them being made in the conveyance. In determining what chattels when annexed to the land become fixtures, and therefore bound by a mortgage, very much the same rules

[1] See further on this subject, Jones on Chattel Mortgages, §§ 123-137; Jones on Liens, §§ 1384-1388; and Jones on Corporate Bonds and Mortgages, §§ 70-79, 136-144, and Jones on Real Property, §§ 1665-1769.

apply as between a grantor and his grantee in case of an absolute con- veyance,[2] but although in the case of a deed the construction is gen- erally favorable to holding that things attached to the land are part and parcel of the realty rather than personalty, yet in the construction of a mortgage even greater favor in the same way seems to be shown the mortgagee. The reason seems not to be far away. When the ques- tion arises under a mortgage, the mortgagor always has the right to redeem, and in this way to gain the benefit of any addition made to the realty; and any one claiming under him has only his rights, and acquires these with full knowledge of the incumbrance and of the con- dition of the property.

All buildings and other fixtures annexed to the freehold become part of it, and inure to the benefit of those who are entitled to it; both to the mortgagee as an increased security for his debt, and to the mortgagor to the same extent as enhancing the value of his equity of redemption.[3] The latter can obtain the full benefit of all improve- ments he has made by paying his debt and regaining his estate by re- demption. This rule, and the exceptions to it as well, are applicable to deeds of trust equally with mortgages.[4]

A building erected upon the mortgaged land without the consent of the mortgagee may be sold by him as a part of the mortgaged prop- erty, and his right is not affected by the fact that the building was erected under an agreement with the mortgagor that it should be and remain the personal property of the party erecting it.[5]

The mortgagor, for most purposes, is regarded as the owner of the

---

[2] McFadden v. Allen, 134 N. Y. 489, 32 N. E. 21; Snedeker v. War- ring, 12 N. Y. 170; Laflin v. Griffiths, 35 Barb. (N. Y.) 58; Gardner v. Finley, 19 Barb. (N. Y.) 317; Main v. Schwarzwaelder, 4 E. D. Smith (N. Y.) 273; Robinson v. Preswick, 3 Edw. Ch. (N. Y.) 246; Foote v. Gooch, 96 N. Car. 265, 60 Am. Rep. 411; Longstaff v. Meagoe, 2 Adol. & El. 167. See also Williams v. Chi- cago Exhibition Co., 188 Ill. 19, 58 N. E. 611; Pfluger v. Carmichael, 54 App. Div. 153, 66 N. Y. S. 417; Kin- near v. Scenic R. Co., 223 Pa. 390, 72 Atl. 808; McCrillis v. Cole, 25 R. I. 156, 55 Atl. 196, 105 Am. St. 875; Gunderson v. Swarthout, 104 Wis. 186, 80 N. W. 465, 76 Am. St. 860.

[3] Williams v. Chicago Exhibition Co., 188 Ill. 19, 58 N. E. 611; Baird v. Jackson, 98 Ill. 78; Wood v. Whe- len, 93 Ill. 153; Peoria Stone &c. Works v. Sinclair, 146 Iowa 56, 124 N. W. 772; Coltharp v. West, 127 La. 430, 53 So. 675; Butler v. Page, 7 Metc. (Mass.) 40; Hunt v. Hunt, 14 Pick. (Mass.) 374, 25 Am. Dec. 400; Graeme v. Cullen, 23 Grat. (Va.) 266.

[4] Moore v. Valentine, 77 N. Car. 188; Graeme v. Cullen, 23 Grat. (Va.) 266. See also Hill v. Farmers' &c. Nat. Bank, 97 U. S. 450, 24 L. ed. 1051.

[5] Meagher v. Hayes, 152 Mass. 228, 25 N. E. 105, 23 Am. St. 819; Guern- sey v. Wilson, 134 Mass. 482; Cole v. Stewart, 11 Cush. (Mass.) 181; Butler v. Page, 7 Metc. (Mass.) 40. See also Ekstrom v. Hall, 90 Maine 186, 38 Atl. 106.

estate; indeed, he is so regarded for all purposes, except so far as it is necessary to recognize the mortgagee as legal owner for the purposes of his security. The improvements, therefore, which the mortgagor, remaining in possession and enjoyment of the mortgaged premises, makes upon them, in contemplation of law he makes for himself, and to enhance the general value of the estate, and not for its temporary enjoyment.[6]

Where a mortgagee is entitled to fixtures attached to the mortgaged premises, a purchaser at a foreclosure sale under such mortgage will also be entitled to the fixtures, though he knew that the vendor of the property attached attempted to reserve title to same.[7]

§ 429. **Intention—Adaptation to use.**—The intention with which an article of personal property is attached to the realty, whether for temporary use or for permanent improvement, has within certain limits quite as much to do with the determination of the question whether it has thereby become a permanent fixture, as has the way and manner in which it is attached.[8] In the more recent cases the intention with which a chattel is attached to the realty has become more and more

[6] Winslow v. Merchants' Ins. Co., 4 Metc. (Mass.) 306, 38 Am. Dec. 368; Gaffield v. Hapgood, 17 Pick. (Mass.) 192, 28 Am. Dec. 290; Hunt v. Hunt, 14 Pick. (Mass.) 374, 25 Am. Dec. 400.

[7] Crocker-Wheeler Co. v. Genessee Recreation Co., 134 N. Y. S. 61.

[8] Holly Mfg. Co. v. New Chester Water Co., 48 Fed. 879; Rogers v. Prattville Mfg. Co., 81 Ala. 483, 1 So. 643, 60 Am. Rep. 171; Tillman v. Lacy, 80 Ala. 103; Lavenson v. Standard Soap Co., 80 Cal. 245, 22 Pac. 184; Fratt v. Whittier, 58 Cal. 126; Seedhouse v. Broward, 34 Fla. 509, 16 So. 425; Williams v. Chicago Exhibition Co., 188 Ill. 19, 58 N. E. 611; Arnold v. Crowder, 81 Ill. 56, 25 Am. Rep. 260; Kelly v. Austin, 46 Ill. 156, 92 Am. Dec. 242; Jones v. Ramsey, 3 Bradw. (Ill.) 303; Johnson v. Mosher, 82 Iowa 29, 47 N. W. 996; Ottumwa Woolen Mill Co. v. Hawley, 44 Iowa 57, 24 Am. Rep. 719; Smith Paper Co. v. Servin, 130 Mass. 511; Studley v. Ann Arbor Sav. Bank, 112 Mich. 181, 70 N. W. 426; Manwaring v. Jenison, 61 Mich. 117, 27 N. W. 899; Robertson v. Corsett, 39 Mich. 777; Wolford v. Baxter, 33 Minn. 12, 53 Am. Rep. 1; Perkins v. Swank, 43 Miss. 349; Rogers v. Brokaw, 25 N. J. Eq. 496; Quinby v. Manhattan Cloth &c. Co., 24 N. J. Eq. 260; McRea v. Central Nat. Bank, 66 N. Y. 489; Voorhees v. McGinnis, 48 N. Y. 278; Potter v. Cromwell, 40 N. Y. 287, 100 Am. Dec. 485; Bishop v. Bishop, 11 N. Y. 123, 62 Am. Dec. 68 (hop poles); Hart v. Sheldon, 34 Hun (N. Y.) 38; Sullivan v. Toole, 26 Hun (N. Y.) 203; Foote v. Gooch, 96 N. Car. 265, 1 S. E. 525, 60 Am. Rep. 411; Harmony Bldg. Assn. v. Berger, 99 Pa. St. 320; Morris' Appeal, 88 Pa. St. 368; Kisterbock v. Lanning, 19 Wkly. N. Cas. (Pa.) 54, 7 Atl. 596; Padgett v. Cleveland, 33 S. Car. 339, 11 S. E. 1069; Sweetzer v. Jones, 35 Vt. 317, 82 Am. Dec. 639; Hill v. Wentworth, 28 Vt. 428, per Bennett, J.; Taylor v. Collins, 51 Wis. 123, 8 N. W. 22.

the decisive test whether or not the chattel has become a part of the realty.[9] Such intention may be inferred from circumstances.[10]

If the article is something necessary for the proper enjoyment of the estate, it may be presumed that it was annexed for its permanent improvement, and therefore that it goes to the benefit of the mortgagee. The fixtures may be so adapted to the building in which they are placed, and to the purposes for which the building is to be used, as to show clearly that they were designed to be permanent.[11] Such, for instance, are the fixtures in a manufactory necessary for furnishing the motive power, or for the proper carrying on of the business.[12] A mortgage of a machine-shop includes a lathe and other fixtures necessary for the prosecution of the business of the shop.[13] A mortgage of a building erected for a steam saw-mill, and which would be of little use for any other purpose, embraces also the boilers, engines, saws, gearing and machinery necessary for the working of the mill, and without which it would be incomplete.[14] Boilers, engines, shaft-

---

[9] Hill v. Farmers' &c. Nat. Bank, 97 U. S. 450, 24 L. ed. 1051; New York Life Ins. Co. v. Allison, 107 Fed. 179, 46 C. C. A. 229; Choate v. Kimball, 56 Ark. 55, 19 S. W. 108; Mill Co. v. Hawley, 44 Iowa 57; Readfield Telephone &c. Co. v. Cyr, 95 Maine 287, 49 Atl. 1047; Smith v. Bay State Sav. Bank, 202 Mass. 482, 88 N. E. 1086; Maguire v. Park, 140 Mass. 21, 1 N. E. 750; Hubbell v. East Cambridge &c. Sav. Bank, 132 Mass. 447, 42 Am. Rep. 446; Smith Paper Co. v. Servin, 130 Mass. 511; Allen v. Mooney, 130 Mass. 155; Southbridge Sav. Bank v. Exeter Mach. Works, 127 Mass. 542; Turner v. Wentworth, 119 Mass. 459; Cosgrove v. Troescher, 62 App. Div. 123, 70 N. Y. S. 764; McRea v. Central Nat. Bank, 66 N. Y. 489; Cooper v. Harvey, 16 N. Y. S. 660; Alberson v. Elk Creek Gold-Min. Co., 39 Ore. 552, 65 Pac. 978; Shelton v. Piner (Tex. Civ. App.), 126 S. W. 65; Hopewell Mills v. Taunton Sav. Bank, 150 Mass. 519, 23 N. E. 327. Knowlton, J., referring to some of these cases, says: "These cases seem to recognize the true principle on which the decisions should rest, only it should be noted that the intention to be sought is not the undisclosed purpose of the actor, but the intention implied and manifested by his act. It is an intention which settles, not merely his own rights, but the rights of others who have or who may acquire interests in the property. They can not know his secret purpose; and their rights depend, not upon that, but upon the inferences to be drawn from what is external and visible. In cases of this kind, every fact and circumstance should be considered which tends to show what intention, in reference to the relation of the machine to the real estate, is properly imputable to him who put it in position."

[10] Equitable Guarantee &c. Co. v. Knowles, 8 Del. Ch. 106, 67 Atl. 961; Young v. Chandler, 102 Maine 251, 66 Atl. 539.

[11] Equitable Trust Co. v. Christ, 2 Flip. (U. S.) 699.

[12] William Firth Co. v. South Carolina Loan &c. Co., 122 Fed. 569; Tillman v. DeLacy, 80 Ala. 103; Millikin v. Armstrong, 17 Ind. 456; Feeder v. Van Winkle, 53 N. J. Eq. 370, 33 Atl. 399; Keve v. Paxton, 26 N. J. Eq. 107; Crane v. Brigham, 11 N. J. Eq. 29.

[13] Hoskin v. Woodward, 45 Pa. St. 42. See also Triumph Elec. Co. v. Patterson, 211 Fed. 244.

[14] Quinby v. Manhattan Cloth &c. Co., 24 N. J. Eq. 260; Brennan v.

ing and steam-pipes for heating a large building are covered by a mortgage of the realty.[15]

The principles by which to determine whether a personal article after being attached to the realty still remains a chattel are two: first, the mode and degree of the annexation; and, second, the purpose of it.[16] The first can not of course be defined with any exactness. The modes of annexation may be almost as numerous as the instances that occur. The degrees of physical force with which the chattels are annexed may be as many as the modes of annexation. The degree may be very slight, and yet be sufficient to make the article a fixture and part of the realty. As the result of the numerous cases, it is safe to say that this is the less important part of the criterion. If the intent is manifest that the chattel is attached to the estate for its permanent improvement, the mode and degree in which it is attached are of little importance. In a case before the English Court of Queen's Bench,[17] in regard to a hydraulic press placed in a factory, but not essential to its work, Mr. Justice Mellor said: "If we could see, as in the gasworks case,[18] an intention that the chattel should remain fixed to the factory so long as the factory remained a factory, then we might think the press to be sufficiently fixed to become a part of the freehold; but we see no such intention."

While it is true, as a general proposition, that the intention of the parties is to be determined by a construction of the language used in the conveyance, it is also undoubtedly true that collateral agreements extrinsic to the conveyance may control the question as to what articles pass as a part of the realty conveyed.[19] It has been held that this question may also be controlled by evidence of other transactions

Whitaker, 15 Ohio St. 446. See also Humes v. Higman, 145 Ala. 215, 40 So. 128.

[15] Ex parte Montgomery, 4 Irish Ch. 520. In this case the Lord Chancellor said: "I find that all the cases come around to the same question, namely, what are fixtures? Now, it appears to me that this does not at all depend upon the power of removal; the owner in fee has the right to remove all fixtures; the tenant has a right to remove fixtures erected for trade purposes; but until they are severed they are still fixtures, and as between mort-gagor and mortgagee they are not removable, though the mortgagor remain in possession. I therefore think that the possibility of removal is not so much the test as the nature of the article." See also Young v. Hatch, 99 Maine 465, 59 Atl. 950.

[16] Hellawell v. Eastwood, 6 Exch. 295; Clarke v. Crownshaw, 3 B. & Ad. 804.

[17] Parsons v. Hind, 14 W. R. 860.

[18] Regina v. Lee, L. R. 1 Q. B. 241, 14 W. R. 311.

[19] Foster v. Prentiss, 75 Maine 279; Elliott v. Wright, 30 Mo. App. 217.

which show that the intention of the parties to the conveyance was that particular fixtures should be treated as personalty.[20]

§ 429a. **Criterion for determining character of fixture.**—The criterion adopted by several courts for determining whether property ordinarily regarded as personal becomes a part of the realty is the united application of the following requisites: first, actual annexation to the realty, or something appurtenant thereto; second, appropriateness to the use or purpose of that part of the realty with which it is connected; third, the intention of the party making the annexation to make the article a permanent accession to the freehold,—this intention being inferred from the nature of the article affixed, the relation and situation of the party making the annexation, the structure and mode of annexation, and the purpose or use for which the annexation has been made.[21]

It is in the application of the criterion that the courts chiefly differ. While some look to physical attachment to the realty as the chief requisite of a fixture, others regard chiefly the intention of the party making the annexation, and hence arises an irreconcilable conflict of authorities. The mode and degree of annexation may determine the intention. Especially is this the case when an article is attached so as to be an inseparable and permanent part of the realty. When the annexation is less complete, it may still afford convincing evidence of the intention; as, for instance, where the building is constructed expressly to receive the machine or other article, and this could not be removed without material injury to the building, or where the article would be of no value for use in that particular building, or could not

[20] Zeller v. Adam, 30 N. J. Eq. 421; Fortman v. Goepper, 14 Ohio St. 558.

[21] So stated in Teaff v. Hewitt, 1 Ohio St. 511, 59 Am. Dec. 634, and expressly adopted in Potter v. Cromwell, 40 N. Y. 287, 100 Am. Dec. 485; Rogers v. Prattville Mfg. Co., 81 Ala. 483, 1 So. 643, 60 Am. Rep. 171; Tillman v. De Lacy, 80 Ala. 103; Choate v. Kimball, 56 Ark. 55, 19 S. W. 108; Capen v. Peckham, 35 Conn. 88; Sword v. Low, 122 Ill. 487, 13 N. E. 826; Binkley v. Forkner, 117 Ind. 176, 19 N. E. 753; Dudley v. Hurst, 67 Md. 44, 8 Atl. 901; Thomas v. Davis, 76 Mo. 72, 43 Am. Rep. 756; State Savings Bank v. Kercheval, 65 Mo. 682, 27 Am. Dec. 310; Doughty v. Owen (N. J.), 19 Atl. 540; Speiden v. Parker, 46 N. J. Eq. 292, 19 Atl. 21; McMillan v. New York Water Proof Paper Co., 29 N. J. Eq. 610; Williamson v. New Jersey Southern R. Co., 29 N. J. Eq. 311; Blancke v. Rogers, 26 N. J. Eq. 563; Quinby v. Manhattan Cloth &c. Co., 24 N. J. Eq. 260; McRea v. Central Nat. Bank, 66 N. Y. 489; Cooper v. Harvey, 16 N. Y. S. 660; Brennan v. Whitaker, 15 Ohio St. 446. See also William Firth Co. v. South Carolina Loan &c. Co., 122 Fed. 569, 59 C. C. A. 73; In re Goldville Mfg. Co., 118 Fed. 892; State Security Bank v. Hoskins, 130 Iowa 339, 106 N. W. 764, 8 L. R. A. (N. S.) 376; Atlantic Safe Deposit &c. Co. v. Atlantic City

be removed without being destroyed or greatly damaged.[22] The question thus becomes usually a question of mixed law and fact.[23] If the description of the property expressly includes buildings and engines, boilers, and fixed machinery appurtenant to the same, effect must be given to such description of the fixtures, for it is obvious that by their use property was intended and included which was no part of the realty, and which would not pass by a mortgage upon it alone.[24]

A custom which is general in the place where the land lies, to treat certain articles as removable chattels, when they are attached to land merely for temporary use, may serve to determine the intention of the parties in any particular case, for the reason that it must be presumed that they contracted with reference to such custom. Thus, where, after the execution of a mortgage, the mortgagor placed on the premises a boiler, saw-rig, shingle-mill, and planer, which could be removed without injury to the freehold, though he did not disclose to the mortgagee his intention that they should not become a permanent accession to the freehold, yet it was held, as it was shown to be customary to put such articles on land and remove them at will, that they were not fixtures, but chattels which the mortgagor or those claiming under him might remove.[25]

It has been held that a custom to put certain articles upon premises for temporary use and to remove them when desirable, prevented their becoming fixtures when placed on the premises by a mortgagor after the making of the mortgage, since there was an absence of the intention requisite to make them part of the realty.[26] So a gas stove and window shades running on rollers, placed by a mortgagor in an ordinary dwelling-house for a single family, not shown to have been intended to be occupied or used differently from common dwelling-

Laundry Co., 64 N. J. Eq. 140, 53 Atl. 212; Filley v. Christopher, 39 Wash. 22, 80 Pac. 834, 109 Am. St. 853.

[22] Equitable Trust Co. v. Christ, 2 Flip. (U. S.) 599; Western Union Tel. Co. v. Burlington &c. R. Co., 11 Fed. 1; Tillman v. De Lacy, 80 Ala. 103; Sword v. Low, 122 Ill. 487, 13 N. E. 826; Campbell v. Roddy, 44 N. J. Eq. 244, 14 Atl. 279, 6 Am. St. 889; McRea v. Central Nat. Bank, 66 N. Y. 489; Ford v. Cobb, 20 N. Y. 344; Henkel v. Dillon, 15 Ore. 610, 17 Pac. 148.

[23] Hopewell Mills v. Taunton Sav.

Bank, 150 Mass. 519, 23 N. E. 327, 15 Am. St. 235; Southbridge Savings Bank v. Mason, 147 Mass. 500, 18 N. E. 406; Carpenter v. Walker, 140 Mass. 416, 5 N. E. 160; Maguire v. Park, 140 Mass. 21, 1 N. E. 750; Allen v. Mooney, 130 Mass. 155; Turner v. Wentworth, 119 Mass. 459.

[24] Beaupre v. Dwyer, 43 Minn. 485, 45 N. W. 1094.

[25] Choate v. Kimball, 56 Ark. 55, 19 S. W. 108.

[26] Bemis v. First Nat. Bank, 63 Ark. 625, 40 S. W. 127; Choate v. Kimball, 56 Ark. 55, 19 S. W. 108.

houses, are personal property, there being nothing to show that he intended to annex them as a permanent addition to the real estate.[27]

§ 430. **Effect of enumerating fixtures in mortgage.**—The fact that a mortgage enumerates some fixtures, but does not enumerate others, which afterward become the subject of dispute, affords reason to suppose that these were intentionally omitted in the mortgage deed, and did not pass by it;[28] upon the principle, "Expressio unius est exclusio alterius."

This principle is illustrated in a case where it became necessary to construe a deed which conveyed two dwelling-houses and a foundry, and it was held that if the granting part of the deed had mentioned only the dwelling-houses and the foundry, the fixtures in each would have passed; but as the deed went on to say "together with all grates, boilers, bells and other fixtures in and about the said two dwelling-houses," while no mention was made of fixtures in the foundry, those of the latter did not pass.[29]

§ 431. **Effect of mortgage of chattels or agreement for removal.**—The fact that a chattel has been mortgaged before, or at the time, it was attached to the realty, has weight as an implied agreement between the parties in leading to the determination that such mortgage carries the fixture as against a mortgage of the realty already existing but is not by any means conclusive;[30] and an agreement made by the mortgagor with a third person to whom the chattels belonged, that they should remain his after they are affixed to the realty until paid for, or that they should be subject until paid for to his right to remove them, has been held to have the same effect. In a case before the Court

---

[27] Hook v. Bolton, 199 Mass. 244, 85 N. E. 175, 17 L. R. A. (N. S.) 699, 127 Am. St. 487; Hall v. Law Guarantee &c. Soc., 22 Wash. 305, 60 Pac. 643, 79 Am. St. 935.

[28] Trappes v. Harter, 2 C. & M. 153.

[29] Hare v. Horton, 5 B. & Ad. 715, 27 E. C. L. 160. But see Leonard v. Stickney, 131 Mass. 541.

[30] United States v. New Orleans Railroad, 12 Wall. (U. S.) 362, 20 L. ed. 434; Tibbetts v. Moore, 23 Cal. 208; Sword v. Low, 122 Ill. 487, 13 N. E. 826; Binkley v. Forkner, 117 Ind. 176, 19 N. E. 753; Miller v. Wilson, 71 Iowa 610, 33 N. W. 128; First Nat. Bank v. Elmore, 52 Iowa 541, 3 N. W. 547; Eaves v. Estes, 10 Kans. 314, 15 Am. Rep. 345; Carpenter v. Allen, 150 Mass. 281, 22 N. E. 900; Carpenter v. Walker, 140 Mass. 416, 5 N. E. 160; Burrill v. Wilcox Lumber Co., 65 Mich. 571, 32 N. W. 824; Edwards &c. Lumber Co. v. Rank, 57 Nebr. 323, 77 N. W. 765, 73 Am. St. 514; Arlington Mill &c. Co. v. Yates, 57 Nebr. 286, 77 N. W. 677; Sheldon v. Edwards, 35 N. Y. 279; Ford v. Cobb, 20 N. Y. 344; Henry v. Von Brandenstein, 12 Daly (N. Y.) 480; Hart v. Sheldon, 34 Hun (N. Y.) 38; Case Mfg. Co. v. Garver, 45 Ohio St. 289, 13 N. E. 493. See also Bass Foundry v. Gallentine, 99 Ind. 525, where it was held a mortgage of the realty attaches to machinery attached to it under an agreement

of Appeals of New York,[31] it was held that such an agreement preserved the character of the chattels as personal property when they would otherwise have become fixtures so as to pass by a mortgage of the realty. But it was said that, while there was no doubt that the owner of the land intended that the articles, which were an engine and boilers, should ultimately become a part of the realty, and be permanently affixed to it, yet this intention was subordinate to the prior intention expressed by the agreement, that the act of annexing them should not change their character as chattels until the price should be fully paid.

If a person who takes a mortgage upon real property has actual notice of a mortgage upon chattels which are afterward annexed to the mortgaged realty, he can not hold such annexed chattels under his mortgage as against the holder of the chattel mortgage.[32]

The execution of a chattel mortgage by the owner of the land, upon machinery which he afterward places in a building thereon, is regarded as an unequivocal declaration of his intention that the act of annexation shall not change or take away the character of the machinery as personalty until the debt secured by the mortgage has been fully paid.[33] The mortgagee of the chattels has priority, so far as that can

that the title to the machinery should not pass until it was paid for; Folsom v. Moore, 19 Maine 252; Zeller v. Adam, 30 N. J. Eq. 421; Fortman v. Goepper, 14 Ohio St. 558; Alberson v. Elk Creek Gold Min. Co., 30 Ore. 552, 65 Pac. 978; Jones on Chattel Mortgages, §§ 124-137. See post § 445.

[31] Tifft v. Horton, 53 N. Y. 377, 13 Am. Rep. 537. This case is not entirely in accord with the case of Voorhees v. McGinnis, 48 N. Y. 278, which related to an engine and boilers which were covered by a chattel mortgage. It seems, however, that part of the articles had been attached to the realty before the execution of the chattel mortgage.

[32] Rowland v. West, 17 N. Y. S. 330. "On the question of notice, it is undoubtedly true that, so far as the plaintiff was dealing with real estate in taking her mortgage, she was not affected with notice by the filing of the chattel mortgage. As the court said at the circuit, as the purchaser of real estate she need only to inquire at the county clerk's office for liens on real estate, and was not required to extend her inquiry to the town clerk's office in search of chattel mortgages. * * * Upon the facts in this case the filing of the defendant's chattel mortgage was notice to the plaintiff that the lien existed."

[33] Holly Mfg. Co. v. New Chester Water Co., 48 Fed. 879; Wood v. Holly Mfg. Co., 100 Ala. 326, 46 Am. St. 56, 13 So. 948; Ware v. Hamilton Brown Shoe Co,. 92 Ala. 151, 9 So. 136; Vann v. Lumsford, 91 Ala. 576, 8 So. 719; Tillman v. De Lacy, 80 Ala. 103; Harris v. Powers, 57 Ala. 139; Sword v. Low, 122 Ill. 487, 13 N. E. 826; Binkley v. Forkner, 117 Ind. 176, 19 N. E. 753, 3 L. R. A. 33; Campbell v. Roddy, 44 N. J. Eq. 244, 14 Atl. 279, 6 Am. St. 889; Tifft v. Horton, 53 N. Y. 377, 13 Am. Rep. 537; Monarch Laundry v. Westbrook, 109 Va. 382, 63 S. E. 1070; Tunis Lumber Co. v. R. G. Dennis Lumber Co., 97 Va. 682, 34 S. E. 613.

be given him without impairing the security previously given to the mortgagee of the land.[34]

If the real estate is subject to a mortgage when chattels are annexed to it, which are not at the time subject to any personal mortgage, or to any equitable agreement for their subsequent removal, the chattels, if of the nature to become fixtures, become so immediately upon being attached to the land; and any chattel mortgage, or agreement that the articles should be considered personal property, will have no effect.[35] The chattels once having been annexed to the realty and become bound by a mortgage of the realty can not be dissevered, except with the consent of the mortgagee.

In a case where machinery for a saw-mill was sold to the owner under a condition that it should remain the property of the vendor until paid for, and after a part of it had been set up in the mill a mortgage was made of the mill premises, the mortgagee having no notice of this agreement, it was held that the part of the machinery which had been put up in the mill passed by the mortgage; but that as to such of the machinery as was then lying in the mill yard the mortgagee gained no title as against the unpaid vendor.[36]

The giving of a bill of sale or chattel mortgage on articles attached to the realty at the same time as the giving of a deed or real estate mortgage may have been done for the purpose of guarding against a mistake as to the character of the property.[37]

It has been held that a purchase-money mortgage given on the sale of a large manufacturing plant, and which expressly includes fixtures, covered all articles necessary or convenient for the transaction of the business, although the mortgagee had conveyed part of the machinery to the purchaser by a bill of sale.[38]

It has been said that whether a chattel mortgage given to secure the purchase-price of property annexed to real estate shall be postponed to a prior mortgage on the realty "must depend upon the inquiry whether

[34] Fosdick v. Schall, 99 U. S. 235, 25 L. ed. 339; Meagher v. Hayes, 152 Mass. 228, 25 N. E. 105, 23 Am. St. 819; McFadden v. Allen, 134 N. Y. 489, 32 N. E. 21, 19 L. R. A. 446.

[35] United States v. New Orleans R., 12 Wall. (U. S.) 362, 20 L. ed. 434; Vanderpoel v. Van Allen, 10 Barb. (N. Y.) 157.

[36] Miller v. Wilson, 71 Iowa 610, 33 N. W. 128; Davenport v. Shants, 43 Vt. 546.

[37] Studley v. Ann Arbor Sav. Bank, 112 Mich. 181, 70 N. W. 426; Miles v. McNaughton, 111 Mich. 350, 69 N. W. 481; McRea v. Central Nat. Bank, 66 N. Y. 489; Trowbridge v. Hayes, 21 Misc. 234, 45 N. Y. S. 635; Homestead Land Co. v. Becker, 96 Wis. 206, 71 N. W. 117; Stevens v. Barfoot, 13 Ont. App. 366.

[38] Cooper v. Harvey, 62 Hun 618, 41 N. Y. St. 594, 16 N. Y. S. 660; Morris' Appeal, 88 Pa. St. 368.

or not the preservation of the rights of the holder of the chattel mortgage will impair or diminish the security of the real estate mortgagee as it was when he took it. If it will not, then it would be inequitable that the latter should defeat or destroy the security of the former. If it will, then it was the folly or misfortune of the holder of the chattel mortgage that he permitted the property to be annexed to a freehold from which it can not be removed without diminishing or impairing an existing mortgage thereon."[39]

§ 431a. **Character of personalty reimpressed upon chattels after annexation.**—By agreement of the persons interested, the character of personalty may be reimpressed upon chattels after this has been lost by annexation to the land so that the chattels have become fixtures, but have not been so incorporated with the realty as to lose their identity, provided the reconversion of the fixtures into personalty does not interfere with the rights of creditors or of third persons. Thus the owner of land upon which were the plant and machinery of a marine railway had contracted to sell the property, and a third person advanced the money to the purchaser to enable him to make the cash payment required, under an oral agreement between the lender, the vendor, and the vendee that the lender should advance the money and take title to the plant and machinery as security, and that he could remove the same at any time. The owner conveyed the land, and took back a mortgage to secure the remainder of the purchase-money. In an action to foreclose the mortgage it was held that the agreement was valid, and thereby the fixtures became personalty and were not covered by the mortgages, though the mortgages except for the agreement would cover the fixtures. The oral agreement is not within the rule that forbids parol evidence to contradict a written instrument, because the lender upon the security of the chattels was not a party to the written instrument, namely, the mortgage.[40]

The parties to a mortgage may by agreement at the time of the execution of a mortgage determine that certain articles upon the mortgaged land shall not be covered by the mortgage as fixtures, and the agreement will control, even if, as a matter of law, such articles would generally pass with the land as fixtures.[41] In such case the fixture

[39] Binkley v. Forkner, 117 Ind. 176, 19 N. E. 753, 3 L. R. A. 33.
[40] Tyson v. Post, 108 N. Y. 217, 15 N. E. 316. See also Foster v. Mabe, 3 Ala. 402, 37 Am. Dec. 749; Bostwick v. Leach, 3 Day (Conn.) 476; Strong v. Doyle, 110 Mass. 92; Moody v. Aiken, 50 Tex. 65. Contra, Meyers v. Schemp, 67 Ill. 469.
[41] Richards v. Gilbert, 116 Ga. 382; Foster v. Prentiss, 75 Maine 279; Elliott v. Wright, 30 Mo. App. 217.

will be removable, notwithstanding the annexation was permanent in character, provided, always, that the removal can be made without any permanent material damage to the estate.[42]

When the parties immediately concerned, by an agreement between themselves, manifest their purpose that the property, although it is annexed to the soil, shall retain its character as personalty, then, except as against persons who occupy the relation of innocent purchasers without notice, the intention of the parties will prevail, unless the property be of such nature that it necessarily becomes incorporated into and a part of the realty by the act and manner of annexation.[43]

The intention of the parties as to fixtures may also be shown by evidence of other transactions between the parties.[44] As such an agreement does not relate to an interest in the land it may be by parol.[45] But after the fixture has once been attached to the realty its personal character can not be established by parol evidence as against a mortgagee of the land.[46]

§ 432. **Hired fixtures.**—It has been held that boilers put into a steam-mill, after the execution of a mortgage upon the mill, under an agreement with the mortgagor that he should have the use of them at a certain rental, and that they should remain the property of the person who put them in, and who should have the privilege of removing them at his pleasure, were not subject to the mortgage.[47]

In like manner machinery put into a mill subject to a mortgage, merely to exhibit it to the public by one not a party to the mortgage, is not covered by the mortgage.[48] Although such machinery be afterward bought by one of the mortgagors, if this be not done with the intent to use it in connection with the business carried on upon the

[42] De Lacy v. Tillman, 83 Ala. 155, 3 So. 294; Foster v. Prentiss, 75 Maine 279; Carpenter v. Allen, 150 Mass. 281, 22 N. E. 900; Manwaring v. Jenison, 61 Mich. 117, 27 N. W. 899; John Van Range Co. v. Allen (Miss.), 7 So. 499; Elliott v. Wright, 30 Mo. App. 217; Voorhees v. McGinnis, 48 N. Y. 278; Hart v. Sheldon, 34 Hun (N. Y.) 38; Vail v. Weaver, 132 Pa. St. 363, 19 Atl. 138, 19 Am. St. 598; Benedict v. Marsh, 127 Pa. St. 309, 18 Atl. 26; Harkey v. Cain, 69 Tex. 146, 6 S. W. 637; Buzzell v. Cummings, 61 Vt. 213, 18 Atl. 93.

[43] Binkley v. Forkner, 117 Ind. 176, 19 N. E. 753, 3 L. R. A. 33; Taylor v. Watkins, 62 Ind. 511.

[44] Zeller v. Adam, 30 N. J. Eq. 421; Fortman v. Goepper, 14 Ohio St. 558.

[45] Broaddus v. Smith, 121 Ala. 335, 26 So. 34, 77 Am. St. 61; Tyson v. Post, 108 N. Y. 217, 15 N. E. 316, 2 Am. St. 409; Dubois v. Kelly, 10 Barb. (N. Y.) 496; Weston &c. R. Co. v. Deel, 90 N. Car. 110.

[46] Gibbs v. Estey, 15 Gray (Mass.) 587; Noble v. Boswith, 19 Pick. (Mass.) 314.

[47] Hill v. Sewald, 53 Pa. St. 271, 91 Am. Dec. 209.

[48] Stell v. Paschal, 41 Tex. 640.

premises, it does not then come within the operation of the mortgage.[49]

§ 433. Buildings erected on mortgaged premises.—Buildings

erected on the mortgaged premises by the mortgagor are annexed to the freehold and can not be removed by him, or by any one under his authority, or without his authority, while the debt remains unpaid.[50] Thus, where, without the consent of the mortgagee, a building is erected upon mortgaged land under an agreement with the mortgagor that it shall remain personal property, it becomes part of the realty and passes by a foreclosure sale of the premises.[51]

But buildings erected on mortgaged lands by a third person under an agreement with the mortgagor who was in possession, by which agreement the right of removal was reserved, with knowledge of and without objection from the mortgagee, may be removed by the person erecting them where such removal in no way impairs the mortgagee's original security.[52] And when a building is erected merely for temporary use, and it is apparent that there was an intention that it should not become attached to the land even so slightly as by the sinking into the soil of the blocks upon which it rested, the mortgagee of the land will acquire no interest in it, although placed there by the mortgagor. If erected by a firm of which the mortgagor is a member for purposes of trade, it is all the more clear that it was not intended as a permanent improvement, or to become a part of the realty.[53]

But a building erected by the side of a mill for use as an office in connection with the mill was held to be a part of the realty, although intended to be temporary only, and to be ultimately removed, and not attached to the mill nor fixed to the ground, but resting upon wooden blocks upon the surface of the earth. The use for which the building was erected was regarded as determining its character as part of the realty.[54] The mortgagor can not convert a permanent structure erected thereon into personalty merely by executing a chattel mort-

---

[49] Stell v. Paschal, 41 Tex. 640.

[50] Baird v. Jackson, 98 Ill. 78; Wood v. Whelen, 93 Ill. 153; Dorr v. Dudderar, 88 Ill. 107; Matzon v. Griffin, 78 Ill. 477; New Orleans Nat. Bank v. Raymond, 29 La. Ann. 355, 29 Am. Rep. 335; Tarbell v. Page, 155 Mass. 256, 29 N. E. 585; Guernsey v. Wilson, 134 Mass. 482; Cole v. Stewart, 11 Cush. (Mass.) 181; Butler v. Page, 7 Metc. (Mass.) 40; Winslow v. Merchants' Ins. Co., 4 Metc. (Mass.) 306, 38 Am. Dec. 368; Burnside v. Twitchell, 43 N. H. 390; Sweetzer v. Jones, 35 Vt. 317, 82 Am. Dec. 639, per Kellogg, J.; Frankland v. Moulton, 5 Wis. 1. See also Ekstrom v. Hall, 90 Maine 186, 38 Atl. 106.

[51] Meagher v. Hayes, 152 Mass. 228, 25 N. E. 105, 23 Am. St. 819.

[52] Paine v. McDowell, 71 Vt. 28, 41 Atl. 1042.

[53] Kelly v. Austin, 46 Ill. 156, 92 Am. Dec. 243.

[54] Wight v. Gray, 73 Maine 297;

gage, and thus defeat the real estate mortgage in so far as it applies to such structure.[55]

The fact that a house erected on mortgaged land rests on posts, instead of masonry, does not give the builder a right, as against the mortgagee, to remove such house, on the failure of the owner of the premises to pay for the labor and material used, unless, at the time of its erection, there was an agreement to that effect between the parties.[56]

The owner of a lot of land, having by parol license allowed a third person to erect a building upon it, afterward made a mortgage of it to one who had no notice of such license. It was held that the mortgagee was entitled to the building, and having entered into possession might maintain trespass against one removing it; and it was held, too, that the mere fact that the person who erected the building occupied it was no notice of his claim to it.[57]

§ 433a. Fixtures in and about a house.—A mortgage of a house passes the presses, cupboards, glazed doors, movable partitions, grates, ranges, and other like fixtures contained in it.[58] But it has been held that doors, mantels, casings, etc., ordered for the purpose of being used in a house but never attached to the building, are not fixtures, and so did not pass to the mortgagee.[59]

The mortgage also passes the windows and blinds, though temporarily separated from the house; the door-keys;[60] a sun dial erected on a permanent foundation;[61] a furnace so placed in a house that it can not be removed without disturbing the brick-work of the house, and causing a portion of the ceiling to fall.[62] Without regard to the

State Savings Bank v. Kercheval, 65 Mo. 682, 27 Am. Rep. 310.

[55] Peoria Stone &c. Works v. Sinclair, 146 Iowa 56, 124 N. W. 772.

[56] Rowland v. Sworts, 17 N. Y. S. 399.

[57] Prince v. Case, 10 Conn. 375; Powers v. Dennison, 30 Vt. 752.

[58] Andrews v. Powers, 66 App. Div. 216, 72 N. Y. S. 597; Longstaff v. Meagoe, 2 Ad. & El. 167; Colegrave v. Dias Santos, 2 Barn. & Cress. 76; Monti v. Barnes, 70 Law J. K. B. 225, 1 K. B. 205, 83 Law T. 619, 49 Wkly. Rep. 147. But see Central Union Gas Co. v. Browning, 210 N. Y. 10, 103 N. E. 822.

[59] Blue v. Gunn, 114 Tenn. 414, 87 S. W. 408, 69 L. R. A. 892, 108 Am. St. 912.

[60] Liford's case, 11 Coke 50.

[61] Snedeker v. Warring, 12 N. Y. 170.

[62] Stockwell v. Campbell, 39 Conn. 362, 12 Am. Rep. 393; Young v. Hatch, 99 Maine 465, 59 Atl. 950; Maguire v. Park, 140 Mass. 21, 1 N. E. 750; Towne v. Fiske, 127 Mass. 125, 34 Am. Rep. 353; Turner v. Wentworth, 119 Mass. 459; Tyler v. White, 68 Mo. App. 607; Rahway Sav. Inst. v. Irving St. Baptist Church, 36 N. J. Eq. 61; Duffus v. Howard Furnace Co., 8 App. Div. 567, 40 N. Y. S. 925; Pratt v. Baker, 92 Hun 331, 36 N. Y. S. 928; Maine v. Schwarzwaelder, 4 E. D. Smith (N. Y.) 273; Filley v. Christopher, 39 Wash. 22, 80 Pac. 834. Whether a portable furnace set in brick is a

matter of injury by the removal of the furnace, some courts regard a furnace as necessarily a fixture, because it is adapted to the use of the realty, and was annexed as a permanent improvement.[63] But a portable iron furnace for heating a house, standing on the cellar floor, and held in position merely by its own weight, and capable of being removed without injury to the building, is not a fixture covered by a mortgage of the realty.[64] Articles of furniture are not fixtures, though attached to the building. On this principle gas fixtures adjusted to the gas pipes do not pass with the realty.[65] Mantel mirrors hung upon hooks driven into the walls, and pier mirrors, though made to order for the house, and having cornices of the same design as those of the room and connected with them, but so attached that they can be removed and put into another house, are not covered by a mortgage of the realty.[66] But mirrors set into the walls, so as to be a part of them at the time of the erection of a house, are a part of the realty.[67] A show-case with drawers and sash, though fastened in place by nails, does not become part of the realty.[68] But it is held that a "bar" fastened by nails and screws to the walls and floor of a building used by the mortgagor as a saloon, was a part of the realty and passed by a mortgage.[69] Shelving and counters in a store, though nailed to the building, and necessary for its use as a store, and so used for many years, are not a part of the realty.[70] Radiators in a house or other

part in realty, is a question of fact, or of mixed law and fact. Allen v. Mooney, 130 Mass. 155.

[63] Fuller-Warren Co. v. Harter, 110 Wis. 80, 85 N. W. 698, 84 Am. St. 867.

[64] Rahway Sav. Inst. v. Irving St. Baptist Church, 36 N. J. Eq. 61. "It can not be held that the mere fact that a chattel is placed in a part of a house which has been adapted to receive it, will make it a fixture; for example, a bedstead in a house obviously would not be made a fixture by the mere fact that it was placed in an alcove made to receive a bedstead." Per Runyon, Ch.

[65] Towne v. Fiske, 127 Mass. 125, 34 Am. Rep. 353; Guthrie v. Jones, 108 Mass. 191; Wall v. Hinds, 4 Gray (Mass.) 256, 64 Am. Dec. 64; McKeage v. Hanover F. Ins. Co., 81 N. Y. 38, 37 Am. Rep. 471, affd., 16 Hun 239; Shaw v. Lenke, 1 Daly (N. Y.) 487; Lawrence v. Kemp, 1 Duer (N. Y.) 363; Condit v. Good-win, 108 App. Div. 360, 95 N. Y. S. 1122; Vaughen v. Haldeman, 33 Pa. St. 522, 75 Am. Dec. 622; Montague v. Dent, 10 Rich. (S. Car.) 135, 67 Am. Dec. 572; Hall v. Law Guarantee &c. Soc., 22 Wash. 305, 60 Pac. 643, 79 Am. St. 935. See also Capehart v. Foster, 61 Minn. 132, 63 N. W. 257, 52 Am. St. 582; Hall v. Law Guarantee &c. Soc., 22 Wash. 305, 60 Pac. 643, 79 Am. St. 935.

[66] McKeage v. Hanover F. Ins. Co., 81 N. Y. 38, 37 Am. Rep. 471, affg. 16 Hun. 239.

[67] Ward v. Kilpatrick, 85 N. Y. 413, 39 Am. Rep. 674.

[68] Cross v. Marston, 17 Vt. 533, 44 Am. Dec. 353.

[69] Woodham v. First Nat. Bank, 48 Minn. 67, 50 N. W. 1015, 31 Am. St. 622.

[70] Johnson v. Mosher, 82 Iowa 29, 47 N. W. 996. But see Woodham v. First Nat. Bank, 48 Minn. 67, 50 N. W. 1015, where the counter was a bar in a saloon fastened to the floor by nails and screws.

building are regarded as a part of the heating plant and as intended to be permanently annexed to the realty.[71]

Where premises mortgaged contain a hot water heating apparatus consisting of a heater set on the cellar bottom connected by pipes running through the walls with radiators, the radiators not being fastened to the floors, such fixtures form part of the realty and are covered by the mortgage.[72] Even electric light fixtures have been regarded as part of the realty as between mortgagors and mortgagees.[73]

A mortgage of a plantation will not cover the wagons and tools used upon it, or the stock and cattle, unless such property be expressly included in the mortgage.[74] A mortgage of a tract of land does not include as a fixture a portable steam saw-mill, boiler, and engine which are not attached to the soil, but may be moved from place to place.[75]

Manure made in the ordinary course of husbandry upon a farm in possession of the mortgagor is so attached to the realty that, in the absence of any express stipulation to the contrary, it is considered a part of the realty, either as appurtenant to the freehold or as being in the nature of a fixture. The title to it is vested in the mortgagee, and the mortgagor has no right to remove it, and can give no title to it by sale.[76]

§ 434. **Nursery stock.**—Trees and shrubs planted in a nursery garden, for the temporary purpose of cultivation and growth until they are fit for market, and then to be taken up and sold, pass by a mort-

[71] Capehart v. Foster, 61 Minn. 132, 63 N. W. 257, 52 Am. St. 582. But see National Bank v. North, 160 Pa. St. 303, 28 Atl. 694.

[72] Young v. Hatch, 99 Maine 465, 59 Atl. 950.

[73] Canning v. Owen, 22 R. I. 624, 48 Atl. 1033. The court says: "We can see no reason whatever why such fixtures are not as much a part of the realty as radiators, water-faucets, set-tubs, bath-tubs, and bowls, portable furnaces connected with hot-air pipes for heating the building, storm-doors and storm-windows, window-blinds, whether inside or outside, fire-grates, pumps, mantels, and such other things as are annexed to the freehold with a view to the improvement thereof." As to kitchen ranges see Jennings v.

Vahey, 183 Mass. 47. But see Hall v. Law Guarantee &c. Soc., 22 Wash. 305, 60 Pac. 643, 79 Am. St. 935.

[74] Vason v. Ball, 56 Ga. 268.

[75] Taylor v. Watkins, 62 Ind. 511.

[76] Chase v. Wingate, 68 Maine 204, 28 Am. Rep. 36. See also Norton v. Craig, 68 Maine 275; Fay v. Muzzey, 13 Gray (Mass.) 53, 74 Am. Dec. 619; Kittredge v. Woods, 3 N. H. 503, 14 Am. Dec. 393. This rule does not apply as to manure made in livery stables. Daniels v. Pond, 21 Pick. (Mass.) 367, 32 Am. Dec. 269; Parsons v. Camp, 11 Conn. 525; nor to manure hauled from the barnyard and piled on a small lot which is sold. Collier v. Jenks, 19 R. I. 137, 32 Atl. 208, 61 Am. St. 741.

gage of the land, so that neither the mortgagor nor his assignee or creditors can remove them as personal property.[77]

One claiming that trees and shrubs, whether growing naturally or planted and cultivated for any purpose, are not part of the realty, must show special circumstances which take the particular case out of the general rule; he must show that the parties intended that they should be regarded as personal chattels. The mere fact that the trees and shrubs were the stock in trade of the mortgagor in his business as a nursery gardener is insufficient for this purpose. They are prima facie parcel of the land itself, and would pass to a vendee upon a sale of the land unless specially excepted, and in the same way, unless excepted, pass to a mortgagee.[78] Although planted by the mortgagor after the execution of the mortgage, they become a part of the realty and part of the mortgage security.[79]

A mortgagee who acquired title to the mortgaged premises by sheriff's deed under foreclosure after giving assurance to the mortgagor that he claimed no interest in nursery stock of great value placed by the mortgagor on the mortgaged land, and that he would not claim the trees when he got his deed, is estopped thereafter to deny the mortgagor's title and right of possession of the nursery stock, and the mortgagor may maintain an action to recover the possession thereof.[80]

Where one having a stock of nursery trees growing on land in which he has no interest joins the owner of the land in a mortgage thereon, and at the time calls attention to the nursery stock as enhancing the value of the land as security, such stock will be regarded as part of the realty; and the mortgagee removing or injuring such stock while his interest is merely that of a mortgagee is liable, as for injury to the land.[81]

As between landlord and tenant, the general rule is that the latter may remove nursery trees. As between mortgagor and mortgagee, or vendor and vendee, however, the rule is different, and nursery trees planted by the owner of real estate become a part of the realty, and pass, as such, under a mortgage, although so long as the mortgagor has the right to redeem he would have the right, in the ordinary course of trade, to sell such of the stock as was suitable for transplanting.[82]

[77] Maples v. Millon, 31 Conn. 598; Adams v. Beadle, 47 Iowa 439, 29 Am. Rep. 487. See also DuBois v. Bowles, 30 Colo. 44, 69 Pac. 1067; King v. Wilcomb, 7 Barb. (N. Y.) 263; Bank of Lansingburgh v. Crary, 1 Barb. (N. Y.) 542.

[78] Per Hinman, C. J., in Maples v. Millon, 31 Conn. 598.

[79] Price v. Brayton, 19 Iowa 309.

[80] Wallace v. Dodd, 136 Cal. 210, 68 Pac. 693.

[81] DuBois v. Bowles, 30 Colo. 44, 69 Pac. 1067.

[82] DuBois v. Bowles, 30 Colo. 44, 69 Pac. 1067; Maples v. Millon, 31 Conn. 598; Adams v. Beadle, 47 Conn. 598.

§ **435. Fixtures annexed before execution of mortgage.**—A fixture annexed to land before the execution of the mortgage will pass by the mortgage without any special mention of the fixture, and even without any general description of it, or evidence of intention to include it, such as might be afforded as to machinery or other articles employed for manufacturing purposes by a special mention of a mill aside from the description of the land.[83] This was the decision in an early case in Massachusetts,[84] in which it was held that a kettle in a fulling-mill set in brick-work, and used for dyeing cloth, passed by a mortgage of the land upon which the mill stood. The grounds of the decision were, that this fixture could not be removed without actual injury to the mill; that it was essential to the use of the mill; and that, being attached to it at the time of making the mortgage, it passed by it as part of the security.

As a general rule, a mortgage of land passes the fixtures already upon it without any special mention being made of them. They pass with the estate and as a part of it. In a mortgage deed the premises were described as certain land "with the paper-mill, etc., thereon, and water privilege, appurtenances, etc., together with all its privileges and appurtenances." The machinery in controversy was fastened to the floor of the mill by means of iron bolts with nuts upon the ends of them. The machinery, however, could be removed without injury to the building, and might be used in other paper-mills. The machinery was subsequently attached by a creditor of the mortgagor, but it was held that it passed by the mortgage of the land and mill as a part of the realty.[85]

Iowa 439, 29 Am. Rep. 487; Price v. Brayton, 19 Iowa 309.

[83] Clore v. Lambert, 78 Ky. 224. See also William Firth Co. v. South Carolina L. &c. Co., 122 Fed. 569; Solomon v. Staiger, 65 N. J. L. 617, 48 Atl. 996; McCrillis v. Cole, 25 R. I. 156, 55 Atl. 196, 105 Am. St. 875; Canning v. Owen, 22 R. I. 624, 84 Atl. 1033, 84 Am. St. 858.

[84] Union Bank v. Emerson, 15 Mass. 159. See also Hamilton v. Huntley, 78 Ind. 521, 41 Am. Rep. 593; Southbridge Sav. Bank v. Stevens Tool Co., 130 Mass. 547. In Hunt v. Mullanphy, 1 Mo. 508, 14 Am. Dec. 300, a kettle annexed in like manner to the freehold was held not to be covered by the mortgage, on the ground that it was not permanently annexed.

[85] Burnside v. Twitchell, 43 N. H. 390; Lathrop v. Blake, 23 N. H. 46. In Gale v. Ward, 14 Mass. 352, 7 Am. Dec. 223, the fact that certain carding machines could be removed from the mill without injury to it, and might be used in any other building erected for a similar purpose, was a reason for considering them personal property, and not covered by a mortgage of the realty. A like view was taken in Fullam v. Stearns, 30 Vt. 443, in respect to a planing machine, a circular saw

The mortgagee is entitled to have his lien respected as to all that was realty when he accepted the security.[85a] The mortgage of a factory by a general name, or terms of description commonly understood to embrace all its essential parts, covers the machinery belonging thereto.[86]

The intention of the parties to a purchase-money mortgage, as regards fixtures, may be gathered from their intention in the other part of the transaction, namely, the sale of the property by the mortgagee to the mortgagor. Thus the owner of a twine factory, the land upon which it was situated, and the machinery in the mill, contracted to sell the whole for a gross sum, and executed a conveyance describing the land only, and took back a mortgage with the same description. This was held to cover the machinery of the mill, on the ground that the parties manifestly intended the mortgage to cover the same property that passed by the deed.[87]

But where, upon the sale of a brewery, a deed was given of the real estate and a separate bill of sale of the fixtures, and the vendor took a mortgage for a part of the purchase-money, containing a description of the land alone, and the purchaser afterward gave a mortgage of the fixtures mentioned in the bill of sale, it was held that the fixtures were not included in the mortgage of the land.[88] But if it appears that a manufacturing establishment was sold as a whole for a gross sum, the mere fact that a bill of sale was made of part of the fixtures does not change their character; but a mortgage of the land and improvements for the purchase-money will cover whatever was a fixture to the realty.[89]

And so if it appears that mill property containing machinery is conveyed and a purchase-money mortgage given, the vendor at the same time giving a bill of sale of the machinery and taking back a chattel mortgage thereon, the machinery will pass as realty by the conveyance.[90]

A mortgage of a mill passes the stones, tackling and implements

and frame and a boring machine, and in Kendall v. Hathaway, 67 Vt. 122, 30 Atl. 859, in respect to a cider mill and a shingle mill. See, on meaning of "appurtenances" in a chattel mortgage of a building, Frey v. Drahos, 6 Nebr. 1, 39 Am. Rep. 353.

[85a] McFadden v. Allen, 134 N. Y. 489, 32 N. E. 21, 19 L. R. A. 446.

[86] Delaware &c. R. Co. v. Oxford Iron Co., 36 N. J. Eq. 452; Hoskin v. Woodward, 45 Pa. St. 42. But see McCosh v. Barton, 2 Ont. L. Rep. 77.

[87] McRea v. Central Nat. Bank, 66 N. Y. 489.

[88] Zeller v. Adam, 30 N. J. Eq. 421; Fortman v. Goepper, 14 Ohio St. 558.

[89] Morris' Appeal, 88 Pa. St. 368.

[90] Cooper v. Harvey, 62 Hun (N. Y.) 618, 41 N. Y. St. 594, 16 N. Y. S. 660.

necessary for working it.[91] A mortgage of a sugar-house carries with it an engine and machinery attached to it.[92]

Machinery set in bricks and run by steam power, for the purpose of manufacturing cottonseed oil, constitutes a part of the realty, and part of the security under a mortgage of the realty.[93] A cotton-gin and press are fixtures and a part of the freehold, and are carried by a mortgage of it, whether erected before or after the mortgage.[94] Hoppoles upon a farm are covered by a mortgage of the land.[95] Platform scales fastened to sills laid upon a brick wall set in the ground, intended for permanent use, are fixtures.[96] Of course, whenever it appears from the instrument itself that the parties did not intend that the machinery in the mill should be covered by the mortgage, it will not constitute a part of the mortgagee's security.[97]

A mortgage of a mill which in terms includes "all the machinery now or hereafter to be placed" in the mill, covers machinery subsequently acquired by the mortgagor by purchase, and not by bailment, and placed on the premises, as against a lease subsequently executed by the mortgagor to the seller for the purpose of revesting title in the latter until payment of the price.[98]

§ 436. Chattels annexed after execution of mortgage.—Chattels attached to the realty after the execution of a mortgage of it become a part of the mortgage security, if they are attached for the permanent improvement of the estate and not for a temporary purpose and are adapted to the use to which the realty is devoted,[99] or if they are such

[91] Place v. Fagg, 4 Man. & R. 277.

[92] Citizens' Bank v. Knapp, 22 La. Ann. 117. See also Hutchins v. Masterson, 46 Tex. 551, 26 Am. Rep. 286.

[93] Theurer v. Nautre, 23 La. Ann. 749. See also William Firth Co. v. South Carolina L. &c. Co., 122 Fed. 569; Tate v. Blackburne, 48 Miss. 1; Bond v. Coke, 71 N. Car. 97; Jones v. Bull, 85 Tex. 136, 19 S. W. 1031.

[94] Bond v. Coke, 71 N. Car. 97; Latham v. Blakely, 70 N. Car. 368; Fairis v. Walker, 1 Bailey (S. Car.) 540. See also Degraffenreid v. Scruggs, 4 Humph. (Tenn.) 451, 40 Am. Dec. 658. Contra Hancock v. Jordan, 7 Ala. 448, 42 Am. Dec. 600; Cole v. Roach, 37 Tex. 413.

[95] The lien of the mortgagee upon them is superior to the title acquired by one who, with knowledge of such mortgage, takes a chattel mortgage upon the poles immediately after their removal from the farm, to secure an antecedent debt. Sullivan v. Toole, 26 Hun (N. Y.) 203.

[96] Arnold v. Crowder, 81 Ill. 56, 25 Am. Rep. 260; Bliss v. Whitney, 9 Allen (Mass.) 114, 85 Am. Dec. 745.

[97] Waterfall v. Penistone, 6 El. & Bl. 876. See also Begbie v. Fenwick, L. R. 8 Ch. App. 1075, 19 W. R. 402; Brown on Fixtures (3d ed), pp. 148, 149.

[98] Knowles Loom Works v. Ryle, 97 Fed. 730.

[99] Hill v. Farmers' &c. Nat. Bank, 97 U. S. 450, 24 L. ed. 1051; Tibbetts v. Moore, 23 Cal. 208; Seedhouse v. Broward, 34 Fla. 509, 16 So. 425; Cunningham v. Cureton, 96 Ga. 489, 23 S. E. 420; Williams v. Chicago Exhibition Co., 188 Ill.

as are regarded as permanent in their nature,[1] or if they are so fastened or attached to the realty that the removal of them would be an injury to it.[2] A mortgagor left in possession, who improves the premises by the erection of new works, or by the introduction of new machinery intended to be permanent, is not at liberty to impair the increased security by removing them.[3] Nor can a mortgagor in possession, without the consent of the mortgagee, authorize another to erect buildings on the mortgaged land and remove them.[4]

The same rule applies to articles annexed to the premises by a sub-

19, 58 N. E. 611; Wood v. Whelen, 93 Ill. 153; Ward v. Yarnelle, 173 Ind. 535, 91 N. E. 7; Bowen v. Wood, 35 Ind. 268; Ottumwa Woolen Mill Co. v. Hawley, 44 Iowa 57, 24 Am. Rep. 719; Mutual Ben. Life Ins. Co. v. Huntington, 57 Kans. 744, 48 Pac. 19. In some cases considerable stress has been placed upon the fact that the personal chattels had already been mortgaged as personalty before they were attached to the realty. Eaves v. Estes, 10 Kans. 314, 15 Am. Rep. 345; Bank of Louisville v. Baumiester, 87 Ky. 6, 7 S. W. 170; Weil v. Lapeyre, 38 La. Ann. 303; Ekstrom v. Hall, 90 Maine 186, 38 Atl. 106; Wight v. Gray, 73 Maine 297; Parsons v. Copeland, 38 Maine 537; Corliss v. McLagin, 29 Maine 115; McKim v. Mason, 3 Md. Ch. 186; Hopewell Mills v. Taunton Sav. Bank, 150 Mass. 519, 23 N. E. 327, 6 L. R. A. 249, 15 Am. St. 235; Southbridge Sav. Bank v. Mason, 147 Mass. 500, 18 N. E. 406, 1 L. R. A. 350; Thompson v. Vinton, 121 Mass. 139; Pierce v. George, 108 Mass. 78, 11 Am. Rep. 310; Cole v. Stewart, 11 Cush. (Mass.) 181; Butler v. Page, 7 Metc. (Mass.) 40, 39 Am. Dec. 757; Winslow v. Merchants' Ins. Co., 4 Metc. (Mass.) 306, 38 Am. Dec. 368; Curry v. Schmidt, 54 Mo. 5l5; Dutro v. Kennedy, 9 Mont. 101, 22 Pac. 763; Langdon v.. Buchanan, 62 N. H. 657; Burnside v. Twitchell, 43 N. H. 390; Pettengill v. Evans, 5 N. H. 54; Roddy v. Brick, 42 N. J. Eq. 218, 6 Atl. 806 Delaware &c. R. Co. v. Oxford Iron Co., 36 N. J. Eq. 452; Doughty v. Owen (N. J. Eq.), 19 Atl. 540; McFadden v. Allen, 134 N. Y. 489, 32 N. E. 21, affg. 3

N. Y. S. 356; Davidson v. Westchester Gas Light Co., 99 N. Y. 558, 2 N. E. 892; McRea v. Central Nat. Bank, 66 N. Y. 489; Snedeker v. Warring, 12 N. Y. 170; McMillan v. Leaman, 101 App. Div. 436, 91 N. Y. S. 1055; Rice v. Dewey, 54 Barb. (N. Y.) 455; Gardner v. Finley, 19 Barb. (N. Y.) 317; Sullivan v. Toole, 26 Hun (N. Y.) 203; Berliner v. Piqua Club Assn., 32 Misc. 470, 66 N. Y. S. 791; Phœnix Mills v. Miller, 4 N. Y. St. 787; Cooper v. Harvey, 16 N. Y. S. 660; Foote v. Gooch, 96 N. Car. 265, 1 S. E. 525, 60 Am. Rep. 411; Bond v. Coke, 71 N. Car. 97; Roberts v. Dauphin Deposit Bank, 19 Pa. St. 71; Harlan v. Harlan, 15 Pa. St. 507, 53 Am. Dec. 612; Davenport v. Shants, 43 Vt. 546. Ex parte Belcher, 4 Dea. & Chit. 703; Hubbard v. Bagshaw, 4 Sim. 326; Ex parte Reynal, 2 Mont. D. & De G. 443; Walmsley v. Milne, 7 C. B. (N. S.) 115, 97 E. C. L. 115, 29 L. J. C. P. 97, 6 Jur. (N. S.) 125, 1 L. T. (N. S.) 62, 8 W. R. 138; Meux v. Jacobs, L. R. 7, H. L. 493; Longbottom v. Berry, L. R. 5 Q. B. Div. 123; Rogers v. Ontario Bank, 21 Ont. Rep. 416; London &c. Loan Co. v. Pulford, 8 Ont. Rep. 150; Paterson v. Pyper, 20 U. C. C. P. 278. See post § 436b.

[1] Coleman v. Stearns Mfg. Co., 38 Mich. 30. See also Mutual Benefit Life Ins. Co. v. Huntington, 57 Kans. 744, 48 Pac. 19.

[2] Clore v. Lambert, 78 Ky. 224.

[3] Foote v. Gooch, 96 N. Car. 265, 1 S. E. 525, 60 Am. Rep. 411.

[4] Ekstrom v. Hall, 90 Maine 186, 38 Atl. 106.

sequent grantee or vendee in possession under an executory contract to purchase.[5]

The question whether fixtures annexed to the realty after a mortgage of it has already been executed become a part of it, and thus become also subject to the mortgage, is a different one in some respects from that which arises when the same fixtures are already attached to the realty when the mortgage is made. As to those articles which in their nature are such as to render it doubtful whether they should be properly classed as fixtures or not, the tendency of the decisions seems to be to require stronger evidence of intention that things annexed to the realty after the making of the mortgage are actually fixtures, and therefore form with the land one security, than is required when they are affixed before the making of the mortgage.[6]

The reason of this apparently is, that, when the personal articles are already attached to the realty when the mortgage is taken, it is more likely that they entered into the consideration of the parties, in estimating the value of the security, than it is when they are not attached to the realty and may never be.[7]

It is true that there may be, in the taking of a mortgage before the fixtures are annexed, an expectation of an increased value to arise from their being subsequently attached to the realty, as when a building has been erected for a certain purpose, and it is contemplated that the machinery or other articles adapted to be used in it will be placed in it; but it is evident that less reliance would be placed upon this expectation than upon the actual fact of the existence of the things upon the mortgaged estate. It does not follow, however, from the fact that the fixtures constituted no part of the mortgage security when it was taken, that they may therefore be removed without any wrong to the mortgagee. He is entitled to the benefit of any improvement of the

---

[5] Ogden v. Stock, 34 Ill. 522; Poor v. Oakman, 104 Mass. 309; Lynde v. Rowe, 12 Allen (Mass.) 100; Cooper v. Adams, 6 Cush. (Mass.) 87; Eastman v. Foster, 8 Metc. (Mass.) 19; Glidden v. Bennett, 43 N. H. 306; McFadden v. Allen, 134 N. Y. 489, 32 N. E. 21, affg. 3 N. Y. S. 356. See also Sieberling v. Miller, 207 Ill. 443, 69 N. E. 800; Gunderson v. Kennedy, 104 Ill. App. 117; Lapham v. Norton, 71 Maine 83; Hinkley &c. Iron Co. v. Black, 70 Maine 473, 35 Am. Rep. 346; Cutter v. Wait, 131 Mich. 508, 91 N. W. 753, 100 Am. St. 619; Morley v. Quimby, 131 Mich. 140, 92 N. W. 943; Andrews v. Powers, 66 App. Div. 216, 72 N. Y. S. 597; Chandler v. Hamell, 57 App. Div. 305, 67 N. Y. S. 1068; Moore v. Vallentine, 77 N. Car. 188.

[6] Tillman v. De Lacy, 80 Ala. 103; Gardner v. Finley, 19 Barb. (N. Y.) 317; Kendall v. Hathaway, 67 Vt. 122, 30 Atl. 859; Buzzell v. Cummings, 61 Vt. 213, 18 Atl. 93. But see Muehling v. Muehling, 181 Pa. St. 483, 37 Atl. 527, 59 Am. St. 674.

[7] Clore v. Lambert, 78 Ky. 224 (approving text).

property from whatever cause it may arise, just as he may suffer from a depreciation of it arising from accident or neglect, or from fluctuations in value due to general causes.[8]

The track of a railroad laid upon mortgaged lands under an arrangement with the mortgagor, without condemnation under the right of eminent domain, is subject to the mortgage lien, and may be sold with the land under foreclosure proceedings.[9] Rails necessarily become an actual part of the permanent structure of a railroad, and are inseparable from it without destruction to the road. In that respect they are like the stones and brick of a house. The same rule applies to other permanent structures of a railroad, such as bridges.[10]

A mortgage by a gas company of its real estate with all the appurtenances thereto, its gas mains, sewer pipes, and meters, covers an enlargement of its works, and an extension of its mains and pipes.[11] A mortgage by such company of its office furniture and fixtures covers additions made thereto from time to time as the necessities of the works required.[12]

Detachable and removable machinery is susceptible of ownership distinct from the land and buildings, and may be the subject of particular and separate liens.[13] Such machinery, when affixed to the realty, does not become subject to an existing mortgage of the realty unless it is affixed by the owner of the chattel or with his assent. Thus, if machinery belonging to a third person be put into a mill upon a written agreement that it is to remain subject to the order of such third person until it be paid for in full, the act of the millowner in affixing the machinery to the mill is not sufficient to subject it to the operation of an existing mortgage.[14] The owner of the machinery is not put upon inquiry as to the state of the title to the mill so as to be charged with constructive notice of the mortgage, and he does not assent to the affixing of the machinery to the realty absolutely, but only in a qualified way.[15]

---

[8] Roberts v. Dauphin Deposit Bank, 19 Pa. St. 71.

[9] Meriam v. Brown, 128 Mass. 391; Hunt v. Bay State Iron Co., 97 Mass. 279; Price v. Weehawken Ferry Co., 31 N. J. Eq. 31.

[10] Porter v. Pittsburg &c. Steel Co., 122 U. S. 267, 30 L. ed. 1210, 7 Sup. Ct. 1206.

[11] Wood v. Whelen, 93 Ill. 153.

[12] Wood v. Whelen, 93 Ill. 153.

[13] Holly Mfg. Co. v. New Chester Water Co., 48 Fed. 879; Vail v. Weaver, 132 Pa. St. 363, 19 Atl. 138; Benedict v. Marsh, 127 Pa. St. 309, 18 Atl. 26; Harlan v. Harlan, 20 Pa. St. 303.

[14] Northwestern Mut. L. Ins. Co. v. George, 77 Minn. 319, 79 N. W. 1028, 1064.

[15] Cochran v. Flint, 57 N. H. 514; Page v. Edwards, 64 Vt. 124, 23 Atl. 917; Buzzell v. Cummings, 61 Vt. 213, 18 Atl. 93; Davenport v. Shants, 43 Vt. 546. In Vail v. Weaver, 132 Pa. St. 363, 19 Atl. 138, it was held

In England, while it is held that fixtures can not be removed without the assent of the mortgagee, it is held that such assent may be found in the mere fact that the mortgagor has been allowed to remain in possession and deal with the property.[16]

A mortgagee in possession, who has erected buildings and other fixtures, may lawfully take them down and remove them, if they are not so connected with the soil that they can not be removed without prejudice to it. So long as he is in possession he may exercise the right of removal, and need not resort to a proceeding in equity for the purpose of declaring and enforcing such right.[17]

§ 436a. **Agreement that chattels may retain character as personalty.**—By agreement chattels may retain their character as personalty after their annexation to the land, though in the absence of such agreement they would become fixtures to the land and subject to an existing mortgage.[18] Such an agreement binds the holder of an existing mortgage of the realty if he is a party to it. If he is not a party to it, ordinary chattels annexed to the realty for the permanent repair or improvement of it become a part of the realty and subject to the existing mortgage. But the chattels may be of such a character, and their annexation to the realty such, that they will not lose their character as personalty if they are annexed with the intention of the owner of the equity and of the person interested in the chattels that they should retain their original character. Thus, telegraph or telephone wires strung upon poles may by such agreement remain personalty.[19]

If the landowner, after placing a mortgage upon chattels for the purchase-price or otherwise, or incumbers the chattels in any other

---

that the engine, machinery, and appliances of an electric light plant erected upon and firmly attached to real estate do not pass to a purchaser of the real estate at a sale upon a mortgage of the realty, made and recorded before the plant was placed by the mortgagor on the mortgaged premises, unless it was the intention to make the plant a part of the realty when it was erected. To like effect see Holly Mfg. Co. v. New Chester Water Co., 48 Fed. 879. This rule in Vermont "is put upon the ground that the mortgagee has parted with nothing on the faith of the annexations being a part of the realty, and there-

fore has no reason to complain." Paine v. McDowell, 71 Vt. 28, 41 Atl. 1042.

[16] Gough v. Wood (1894), 1 Q. B. 713, 724; Cumberland Union Banking Co. v. Maryport Hematite Iron &c. Co. (1892), 1 Ch. 415; Sanders v. Davis, 15 Q. B. Div. 218.

[17] Cooke v. Cooper, 18 Ore. 142, 22 Pac. 945.

[18] Oil City Boiler Works v. New Jersey Water &c. Co., 81 N. J. L. 491, 79 Atl. 451; Tyson v. Post, 108 N. Y. 217, 15 N. E. 316; Sisson v. Hibbard, 75 N. Y. 542; Ford v. Cobb, 20 N. Y. 344.

[19] Union Safe Deposit &c. Co. v. Telegraph Co., 36 Fed. 288.

way, as by purchasing them with a reservation of title in the vendor, should annex such chattels to his land, there must be implied from the existence of the chattel mortgage or other incumbrance an intention on his part that the chattels are not to be annexed permanently, to the detriment of the mortgagee or lienor.[20]

Machinery, buildings and in fact almost anything may be made to retain its character of personalty by agreement, if it is not so incorporated in the realty as to become so much a part of it that it can not be removed without materially injuring or destroying the realty. Thus an agreement that a building of a temporary nature should remain personalty has been held binding as against parties to an existing mortgage.[21] But it has been held that an agreement that ranges placed in a tenement house should remain personalty does not bind the mortgagee of the real estate.[22]

§ 436b. **Rights of vendor or mortgagee of chattels as against existing mortgage of realty.**—There are two well defined and contrary views as to the effect of a chattel mortgage upon personal articles which are attached to mortgaged realty. Although a chattel mortgage of things about to be annexed to the realty is a contract, express or implied, between the owner of the chattels and the owner of the realty that these things shall retain their chattel character after their annexation to the realty and may be removed if necessary to enforce the chattel mortgage, yet according to one line of authorities, such things even if they can be removed, without injury to the realty, are a part of the security of the mortgagee of the realty, and can not be removed without his consent. This is sometimes called the Massachusetts doctrine because it was first established in that state. In one case in that state Mr. Justice Hoar said:[23] "We think it is not in the power of the mortgagor, by any agreement made with a third person after the execution of the mortgage, to give to such person the right to hold any-

---

[20] Binkley v. Forkner, 117 Ind. 176, 19 N. E. 753, 3 L. R. A. 33; Carpenter v. Allen, 150 Mass. 281, 22 N. E. 900; Hunt v. Bay State Iron Co., 97 Mass. 279; Jenks v. Colwell, 66 Mich. 420, 33 N. W. 528, 11 Am. St. 502; Tibbetts v. Horne, 65 N. H. 242, 23 Atl. 145, 15 L. R. A. 56, 23 Am. St. 31; Campbell v. Roddy, 44 N. J. Eq. 244, 14 Atl. 279, 6 Am. St. 889; Davenport v. Shants, 43 Vt. 546.

[21] Shelton v. Piner (Tex. Civ. App.), 126 S. W. 65. See also Central Union Gas Co. v. Browning, 146 App. Div. 783, 131 N. Y. S. 464; Bullock Electric Mfg. Co. v. Lehigh Val. Trac. Co., 231 Pa. St. 129, 80 Atl. 568.

[22] Mechanics' &c. Bank v. Bergen Heights Realty Corp., 137 App. Div. 45, 122 N. Y. S. 33.

[23] Clary v. Owen, 15 Gray (Mass.) 522, citing Winslow v. Merchants' Ins. Co., 4 Metc. (Mass.) 306.

thing to be attached to the freehold, which as between mortgagor and mortgagee would become a part of the realty."

In the same court it was held that a building removed upon mortgaged land without the mortgagee's consent, became a part of the realty, subject to the mortgage, although the mortgagor agreed with the owner of the building that it should remain personal property with the right of such owner to remove it; and that the purchaser of the land at a foreclosure sale under the mortgage became the owner of the building though he was notified at the sale of such agreement.[24]

Even under this rule if the chattels are generally deemed movables, such as curtain poles, gas fixtures in a house or machines which are only attached to a building sufficiently to keep them steady or in place, they do not inure to the benefit of the mortgagee of the land.[25]

Under this view of the law a chattel mortgage of fixtures to be annexed to mortgaged land, or an agreement that such fixtures shall retain their chattel character, is not binding upon such prior mortgagee of the land without notice to him and his consent.[26]

A chattel mortgage of fixtures given concurrently with a real estate mortgage covering the same property does not conclusively fix their

[24] Meagher v. Hayes, 152 Mass. 228, 25 N. E. 105, 23 Am. St. 819; Hunt v. Bay State Iron Co., 97 Mass. 279. For other Massachusetts authorities, see Pierce v. George, 108 Mass. 78, 11 Am. Rep. 310; Meagher v. Hayes, 152 Mass. 228, 25 N. E. 105; Southbridge Sav. Bank. v. Mason, 147 Mass. 500, 18 N. E. 406; Smith Paper Co. v. Servin, 130 Mass. 511; McConnell v. Blood, 123 Mass. 47. Followed also in Frankland v. Moulton, 5 Wis. 1; Fuller-Warren Co. v. Harter, 110 Wis. 80, 85 N. W. 698, 84 Am. St. 867, and a learned and full note in the latter report; Gunderson v. Swarthout, 104 Wis. 186, 80 N. W. 465, 76 Am. St. 860; Homestead Land Co. v. Becker, 96 Wis. 206, 71 N. W. 117; Kendall Mfg. Co. v. Rundle, 78 Wis. 150, 47 N. W. 364; Taylor v. Collins, 51 Wis. 123, 8 N. W. 22; Smith v. Waggoner, 50 Wis. 155, 6 N. W. 568; Porter v. Pittsburg Bessemer Steel Co,. 120 U. S. 649, 30 L. ed. 830, 7 Sup. Ct. 741, 122 U. S. 267, 30 L. ed. 1210, 7 Sup. Ct. 1206; Evans v. Kister, 92 Fed. 828; Phœnix Iron Works Co. v. New York Security &c. Co., 83 Fed. 757; Watertown S. E. Co. v. Davis, 5 Houst. (Del.) 192; Beeler v. C. C. Mercantile Co., 81 Idaho 644, 70 Pac. 943, 60 L. R. A. 283; Fifield v. Farmers' Nat. Bank, 148 Ill. 163, 35 N. E. 802, 39 Am. St. 166; Brass Foundry Works v. Gallentine, 99 Ind. 525; Hamilton v. Hunkle, 78 Ind. 521, 41 Am. Rep. 593; Miller v. Walson, 71 Iowa 610, 33 N. W. 128; Stillman v. Flenniken, 58 Iowa 450, 10 N. W. 842; Ekstrom, v. Hall, 90 Maine 186, 38 Atl. 106; Hawkins v. Hersey, 86 Maine 394, 30 Atl. 14; Wight v. Gray, 73 Maine 297; McFadden v. Allen, 134 N. Y. 489, 32 N. E. 21, limiting or overruling some earlier cases.

[25] Jennings v. Vahey, 183 Mass. 47; Carpenter v. Walker, 140 Mass. 416, 5 N. E. 160; Maguire v. Park, 140 Mass. 21, 1 N. E. 750; Manning v. Ogden, 70 Hun (N. Y.) 399, 24 N. Y. S. 70.

[26] Hawkins v. Hersey, 86 Maine 394, 30 Atl. 14; Bartholomew v. Hamilton, 105 Mass. 239. See also Hershberger v. Johnson, 37 Ore. 109, 60 Pac. 838.

character as personal property as against the real estate mortgagee.[27] Where the chattels have been so annexed as to become an integral part of the realty, the retention of title thereto or the reservation of a lien thereon has been held to be ineffectual to preserve the rights of the seller, as against a prior mortgage of the realty.[28] Moreover under this rule the fact that the chattel may be removed from the mortgaged realty without injury thereto is immaterial.[29]

The contrary doctrine that chattels permanently annexed to mortgaged realty can by agreement with the mortgagor or by the implied agreement arising from a chattel mortgage be made to preserve their character as personalty, as against the mortgagee of the realty, is firmly maintained in several states.[30]

To preserve the personal character of fixtures as against an existing mortgage of the realty a chattel or agreement that the fixtures

[27] Studley v. Ann Arbor Sav. Bank, 112 Mich. 181, 70 N. W. 426.

[28] Porter v. Pittsburg Bessemer Steel Co., 122 U. S. 267, 30 L. ed. 1210, 7 Sup. Ct. 1206; United States v. New Orleans R., 12 Wall. (U. S.) 362, 20 L. ed. 434; Guaranty Trust Co. v. Galveston City R. Co., 107 Fed. 311, 46 C. C. A. 305; Evans v. Kister, 92 Fed. 828, 35 C. C. A. 28; Phœnix Iron Works Co. v. New York Security &c. Co., 83 Fed. 757, 28 C. C. A. 76; Westinghouse Electric Mfg. Co. v. Citizens' Street R. Co., 24 Ky. L. 334, 68 S. W. 463; New Jersey v. Cruse (N. J. Eq.), 90 Atl. 673; Great Western Mfg. Co. v. Bathgate, 15 Okla. 87, 79 Pac. 903; Bullock Electric Mfg. Co. v. Lehigh Valley Traction Co., 231 Pa. 129, 80 Atl. 568.

[29] Fuller-Warren Co. v. Harter, 110 Wis. 80, 85 N. W. 698.

[30] Broaddus v. Smith, 121 Ala. 335, 26 So. 34, 77 Am. St. 61; Warren v. Liddell, 110 Ala. 232, 20 So. 89 (conditional sale); Miller v. Griffin, 102 Ala. 610, 15 So. 238; Wood v. Holly Mfg. Co., 100 Ala. 326, 13 So. 948, 46 Am. St. 56; Anderson v. Creamery Package Mfg. Co., 8 Idaho 200, 67 Pac. 493, 56 L. R. A. 554, 101 Am. St. 188; Schumacker v. Edward P. Allis Co., 70 Ill. App. 556; Binkley v. Forkner, 117 Ind. 176, 19 N. E. 753; Eaves v. Estes, 10 Kans. 314, 15 Am. Rep. 345; Baldwin v. Young, 47 La. Ann. 1466, 17 So. 883; Jenks v. Colwell, 66 Mich. 420, 33 N. W.

528, 11 Am. St. 502 (conditional sale); Burrill v. Wilcox Lumber Co., 65 Mich. 571, 32 N. W. 824; Crippen v. Morrison, 13 Mich. 23; Northwestern Mut. Life Ins. Co. v. George, 77 Minn. 319, 79 N. W. 1028, 1064; Merchants' Nat. Bank v. Stanton, 55 Minn. 211, 56 N. W. 821, 43 Am. St. 491; Warner v. Kenning, 25 Minn. 173; American Laundry Machinery Co. v. Citizens' Nat. Life Ins. Co. (Miss.), 65 So. 113; Edwards &c. Lumber Co. v. Rank, 57 Nebr. 323, 77 N. W. 765, 73 Am. St. 514; Arlington Mill &c. Co. v. Yates, 57 Nebr. 286, 77 N. W. 677; Tibbetts v. Horne, 65 N. H. 242, 23 Atl. 145, 23 Am. St. 31; General Electric Co. v. Transit Equip. Co., 57 N. J. Eq. 460, 42 Atl. 101; Campbell v. Roddy, 44 N. J. Eq. 244, 14 Atl. 279, 6 Am. St. 889; Rogers v. Brokaw, 25 N. J. Eq. 496; Cox v. New Bern Lighting &c. Co., 151 N. Car. 62, 65 S. E. 648, 134 Am. St. 966; Belvin v. Raleigh Paper Co., 123 N. Car. 138, 31 S. E. 655; Blanchard v. Eureka Planing Mill Co., 58 Ore. 37, 113 Pac. 55, 37 L. R. A. (N. S.) 133; Henkle v. Dillon, 15 Ore. 610, 17 Pac. 148; Paine v. McDowell, 71 Vt. 28, 41 Atl. 1042; Buzzell v. Cummings, 61 Vt. 213, 18 Atl. 93; Barnes v. Barnes, 6 Vt. 388; German Sav. &c. Soc. v. Weber, 16 Wash. 95, 47 Pac. 224; Hurxthal v. Hurxthal, 45 W. Va. 584, 32 S. E. 237. But see Brass Foundry Works v. Gallentine, 99 Ind. 525; Hamilton

may be removed should be made prior to their annexation to the realty.[31]

Where this view of the law prevails, if machinery under mortgage is placed in a mill already mortgaged, it becomes subject to the realty mortgage, to the extent that is necessary to keep the security thereof unimpaired. So far as the personalty mortgage is concerned, if such machinery is mortgaged to its full value and it will not damage the mill property by its removal, the mortgagee or purchaser may remove the same, otherwise he must make good the damage caused by such removal. When such mortgaged personal property is attached to the mortgaged realty, the mortgagor has only an equity of redemption therein, to which the mortgage on the realty at once attaches.[32]

§ 436c. **Rights of mortgagee of realty as to chattels annexed prior to mortgage.**—When a mortgage of real estate is made after chattels are annexed thereto under a chattel mortgage, or under an agreement that they shall retain their personal character, such mortgagee of the realty having no notice of such chattel mortgage or agreement is not bound thereby.[33]

---

v. Huntley, 78 Ind. 521, 41 Am. Rep. 593.

[31] Miller v. Walson, 71 Iowa 610, 33 N. W. 128; First Nat. Bank v. Elmore, 52 Iowa 541, 3 N. W. 547; Sowden v. Craig, 26 Iowa 156, 96 Am. Dec. 125; Davenport v. Shants, 43 Vt. 546.

[32] Hurxthal v. Hurxthal, 45 W. Va. 584, 32 S. E. 237. Citing Sword v. Low, 122 Ill. 487, 13 N. E. 826; Eaves v. Estes, 10 Kans. 314; Campbell v. Roddy, 44 N. J. Eq. 244, 14 Atl. 279; Sisson v. Hibbard, 75 N. Y. 542; Tifft v. Horton, 53 N. Y. 377; Ford v. Cobb, 20 N. Y. 344.

[33] Seedhouse v. Broward, 34 Fla. 509, 16 So. 425; Cunningham v. Cureton, 96 Ga. 489, 23 S. E. 420; Baird v. Jackson, 98 Ill. 78; Wood v. Whelen, 93 Ill. 153; Matzon v. Griffin, 78 Ill. 477; New Orleans Nat. Bank v. Raymond, 29 La. Ann. 355, 29 Am. Rep. 335; Wight v. Gray, 73 Maine 297; Hawkins v. Hersey, 46 Maine 394, 30 Atl. 14; Hopewell Mills v. Taunton Sav. Bank, 150 Mass. 519, 23 N. E. 327; Carpenter v. Allen, 150 Mass. 281, 22 N. E. 900; Carpenter v. Walker, 140 Mass. 416, 5 N. E. 160; Southbridge Sav.

Bank v. Stevens Tool Co., 130 Mass. 547; Southbridge Sav. Bank v. Exeter Works, 127 Mass. 542; Thompson v. Vinton, 121 Mass. 139; Hunt v. Bay State Iron Co., 97 Mass. 279; Watson v. Alberts, 120 Mich. 508, 79 N. W. 1048; Wickes v. Hill, 115 Mich. 333, 73 N. W. 375; Dutro v. Kennedy, 9 Mont. 101, 22 Pac. 763; Tibbetts v. Horne, 65 N. H. 242, 23 Atl. 145, 23 Am. St. 31; Burnside v. Twitchell, 43 N. H. 390; Foote v. Gooch, 96 N. Car. 265, 1 S. E. 525, 60 Am. Rep. 411; Bond v. Coke, 71 N. Car. 97; Brennan v. Whitaker, 15 Ohio St. 446; Davenport v. Shants, 43 Vt. 546; Sweetzer v. Jones, 35 Vt. 317; Wade v. Donau Brewing Co., 10 Wash. 284, 38 Pac. 1009. There are some decisions, however, which hold in such case that the chattel character of fixtures may be retained even against a subsequent mortgagee of the realty without notice. Case v. L'Oebel, 84 Fed. 582; Adams Machine Co. v. Interstate Bldg. Assn., 119 Ala. 97, 24 So. 857; Warren v. Liddell, 110 Ala. 232, 20 So. 89; Richardson v. Copeland, 6 Gray (Mass.) 536, 66 Am. Dec. 424; Deane v. Hutchinson, 40

A mortgagee of land is not bound to examine the records for chattel mortgages covering fixtures which have been so attached as to become an integral part of the real estate.[34] But where buildings and machinery have been openly impressed with the character of personalty prior to the giving of a real estate mortgage, they will retain that character as against the mortgagee with notice, in the absence of other controlling circumstances.[35] The chattel mortgage is not of itself notice to such subsequent mortgagee of the realty.

A subsequent purchaser or mortgagee of the realty knowing at the time of his purchase or mortgage of the existence of a chattel mortgage upon the fixtures, or of an agreement by the owner that the fixtures might be removed, may be regarded as having taken his deed or mortgage subject to such chattel mortgage or agreement.[36]

In those jurisdictions where a bona fide purchaser of land is held to take it subject to rights of third persons in fixtures, the same rule would doubtless be applied to subsequent mortgagees without notice.

436d. Effect of after-acquired property clause.—A clause in a prior mortgage of real estate to the effect that the mortgage shall cover after-acquired property does not give the mortgagee a superior claim to chattels annexed thereto, as against the vendor by a conditional sale contract, since such clause in a mortgage attaches only to such interest as the mortgagor has when the mortgage is executed.[37]

N. J. Eq. 83, 2 Atl. 292; Hirsch v. Graves Elev. Co., 53 N. Y. S. 664; Case Mfg. Co. v. Garven, 45 Ohio St. 289; Brennan v. Whitaker, 15 Ohio St. 446. Contra, see First Nat. Bank v. Adam, 138 Ill. 483, 28 N. E. 955; Sword v. Low, 122 Ill. 487, 13 N. E. 826; Peoria Stone &c. Works v. Sinclair, 146 Iowa 56, 124 N. W. 772; Sowden v. Craig, 26 Iowa 156, 96 Am. Dec. 125; Reyman v. Henderson Nat. Bank, 98 Ky. 748, 34 S. W. 697; Patton v. Phœnix Brick Co., 167 Mo. App. 8, 150 S. W. 1116; Atlantic Safe Deposit & Trust Co. v. Atlantic City Laundry Co., 64 N. J. Eq. 140, 53 Atl. 212; Lindsay v. Kinback, 4 Lack. Leg. N. (Pa.) 256.

[34] Elliott v. Hudson, 18 Cal. App. 642, 124 Pac. 108.

[35] Horn v. Indianapolis Nat. Bank, 125 Ind. 381, 25 N. E. 558, 9 L. R. A. 676, 21 Am. St. 231.

[36] Greither v. Alexander, 15 Iowa 470; Warner v. Kenning, 25 Minn. 173; Fryatt v. Sullivan Co., 5 Hill

(N. Y.) 116; Waller v. Bowling, 108 N. Car. 289, 12 S. E. 990; Rowland v. West, 62 Hun (N. Y.) 583; Simons v. Pierce, 16 Ohio St. 215; San Antonio Brewing Assn., v. Arctic Ice Mach. Mfg. Co., 81 Tex. 99, 16 S. W. 797.

[37] Wood v. Holly Mfg. Co., 100 Ala. 326, 13 So. 948, 46 Am. St. 56; J. L. Mott Iron Works v. Middle States Loan &c. Co., 17 App. D. C. 584; Cox v. New Bern Lighting &c. Co., 151 N. Car. 62, 65 S. E. 648, 134 Am. St. 966, 18 Am. & Eng. Ann. Cas. 936; Detroit Steel Cooperage Co. v. Sistersville Brew. Co., 195 Fed. 447; In re Sunflower State Refining Co,. 195 Fed. 180; In re Williamsburg Knitting Mill, 190 Fed. 871; Tippett v. Barham, 180 Fed. 76, 103 C. C. A. 430, 37 L. R. A. (N. S.) 119; Holt v. Henley, 232 U. S. 637, 34 Sup. Ct. 459. But see Union Trust Co. v. Southern Sawmills &c. Co., 166 Fed. 193, 92 C. C. A. 101;

Whether the vendor's right to the chattels is inferior to that of a prior mortgagee under an after-acquired property clause would seem to depend upon whether the chattels have been so attached as to have become a part of the realty.[38]

Where title to a machine was retained as security for the payment of the purchase-price, it was held that the lien of a deed of trust which, by its terms, covered any machinery, tools, and fixtures which might thereafter be acquired by the grantor therein, did not attach to the machine, because the title to it never vested in the purchaser.[39]

Under an after-acquired property clause contained in a mortgage, any property acquired by the mortgagor subsequent to the date of the execution and delivery of the mortgage, and which is within the general description contained therein, will become as fully subject to the lien of the mortgage in equity as if such property had been owned by the mortgagor at the date of the execution and delivery of the mortgage.[40]

§ 436e. **Where new fixtures replace old.**—There seems to be a difference of opinion with reference to the effect upon the rights of the parties of the circumstance that the fixtures to which the vendor reserves title take the place of old and worn-out fixtures removed from the premises. In one case the court said: "The old machinery was subject to the mortgage; the mortgagor could not substitute new for old, and compel the mortgagee purchasing at the foreclosure sale to take the mill in a dismantled condition, because of a contract made by the mortgagor with some third person, to which the mortgagee was not a party, to which he never consented, and of which he had no notice."[41]

On the other hand it has been held that machinery sold under a contract of conditional sale will retain the character of personalty against the holder of an existing mortgage on the realty, notwithstanding that machinery in place when the realty mortgage was given has been removed to make room for the new machinery.[42] Boilers

---

[38] In re Sunflower State Refining Co., 195 Fed. 180.

[39] Defiance Mach. Works v. Trisler, 21 Mo. App. 69.

[40] Thompson v. White Water Valley R. Co., 132 U. S. 68, 33 L. ed. 256, 10 Sup. Ct. 29; Branch v. Jesup, 106 U. S. 468, 27 L. ed. 279, 1 Sup. Ct. 495; Galveston, H. &c. R. Co. v. Cowdrey, 11 Wall. (U. S.) 459, 20 L. ed. 199; Pennock v. Coe, 23

How. (U. S.) 117, 16 L. ed. 436; Tippett v. Barham, 180 Fed. 76, 103 C. C. A. 430, 37 L. R. A. (N. S.) 119.

[41] Bass Foundry &c. Works, v. Gallentine, 99 Ind. 525. See also National Bank v. Levanseler, 115 Mich. 372, 73 N. W. 399; Smith v. Blake, 96 Mich. 542, 55 N. W. 978.

[42] Page v. Edwards, 64 Vt. 124, 23 Atl. 917; Buzzell v. Cummings, 61

hired for use in a mill, which could be removed without other injury than taking down the boiler wall, has been held not subject to an existing mortgage on the realty, though they replaced others which had become worn out.[43]

§ 437. **Rights of equitable mortgagee to hold fixtures.**—An equitable mortgagee has the same right to hold fixtures as part of his security that a legal mortgagee has.[44] A woolen manufacturer mortgaged, by deposit of the title-deeds, a piece of land, with a building upon it, and then built a mill upon the land and fitted it with a steam-engine and machinery necessary for his trade. Subsequently he assigned to another all the machinery and fixtures in the mill, and after this executed to the equitable mortgagee a legal mortgage of the estate. The Court of Queen's Bench held that all the machines which were fixed in a quasi permanent manner to the floor, roof, or side-walls passed to the equitable mortgagee, but that those which were merely removable articles passed to the assignee under the bill of sale.[45]

Where an equitable mortgage was created by the deposit of a lease, unaccompanied by any agreement, it was held that the tenant's fixtures were included in the mortgage.[46]

§ 438. **Waiver of claim to fixtures by mortgagee of realty.**—If the mortgagee assent to an arrangement between the mortgagor and a mechanic, whereby the latter builds and sets up a machine upon the mortgaged premises, under a contract that the machine shall remain his property until paid for, or if the mortgagee, being in possession, treats it as personal property and consents to its removal, a subsequent assignee of the mortgage can not insist that under it he became the owner of the machine, as property annexed to the realty by the mortgagor. Such an agreement supersedes the general law as to fixtures between the mortgagor and mortgagee.[47]

Vt. 213, 18 Atl. 93; Davenport v. Shants, 43 Vt. 546.

[43] Hill v. Sewald, 53 Pa. St. 271, 91 Am. Dec. 209.

[44] Meux v. Jacobs, L. R. 7 H. L. 481; Williams v. Evans, 23 Beav. 239; Ex parte Astbury, L. R. 4 Ch. App. 630. See also Ex parte Barclay, 5 De G. M. & G. 413; Ex parte Price, 2 Mont. D. & D. 518; Ex parte Moore &c. Banking Co., 14 Ch. Div. 379; Ex parte Tagart, 1 De Gex 531; Ex parte Broadwood, 1 Mont. D. & D. 631; Ex parte Lloyd, 3 D. & C. 765; Mather v. Fraser, 2 K. & J. 536; Waterfall v. Penistone, 6 El. & Bl. 876, 88 E. C. L. 876.

[45] Longbottom v. Berry, L. R. 5 Q. B. Div. 123, 39 L. J. (N. S.) Q. B. Div. 87. See also Tebb v. Hodge, 39 L. J. (N. S.) C. P. 56.

[46] Williams v. Evans, 23 Beav. 239.

[47] Frederick v. Devol, 15 Ind. 357; Bartholomew v. Hamilton, 105 Mass. 239. See also Wight v. Gray, 73 Maine 297.

Where the consent of .the mortgagee of the realty to the arrangement is obtained, the rights of the chattel mortgagee or seller retaining title to the fixture, until payment of the purchase-price, may be enforced.[48]   And such is the case, also, where a person sets up a steam-engine and boiler upon land owned by another, under an agreement that he may remove them at any time, and afterward takes a mortgage of the land from the owner of it. The engine and boiler never become the property of the mortgagor, or fixtures to the land, and therefore are not included in the mortgage.[49]

It is also held that where it was expressly agreed that a steam-engine and its appurtenances should continue to be the property of the seller until he should receive a chattel mortgage thereon and a mortgage upon the land, an assignee of a prior mortgage on the land, with notice of the chattel mortgage on the engine, took subject thereto.[50]

A mortgagee waives his claim that certain machinery and tools in a mill are covered by his mortgage by requesting the mortgagor, after he had removed such machinery and tools, to repay to him the amount he had paid upon them as taxes, and by accepting and retaining the money so demanded, with full knowledge of the facts and situation of the property.[51]

§ 439.   **Rights of mortgagee of realty to fixtures annexed by lessee after mortgage.**—If fixtures be added to the property by a tenant at will of the mortgagor after the mortgage, the right to remove them is determined by the rule which prevails as between mortgagor and mortgagee, and not that which prevails as between landlord and tenant; and they can not be removed without the consent of the mortgagee.[52]

[48] Hawkins v. Hersey, 86 Maine 394, 30 Atl. 14; Bartholomew v. Hamilton, 105 Mass. 239; Pierce v. Emery, 32 N. H. 484; Fuller-Warren Co. v. Harter, 110 Wis. 80, 85 N. W. 698, 53 L. R. A. 603, 84 Am. St. 867.

[49] Taft v. Stetson, 117 Mass. 471. An assignee of a mortgage is protected against payments made to the mortgagee by a purchaser of the property who has assumed the payment of the incumbrance, the purchaser believing that the mortgagee still owned the mortgage and the debt secured, notwithstanding the assignee has not recorded the assignment or given notice thereof

to any one. The equities of the purchaser in such case must be regarded as latent equities of third persons. Schultz v. Sroelowitz, 191 Ill. 249, 61 N. E. 92.

[50] Crippen v. Morrison, 13 Mich. 23.

[51] Foster v. Prentiss, 75 Maine 279.

[52] Tarbell v. Page, 155 Mass. 256, 29 N. E. 585; Meagher v. Hayes, 152 Mass. 228, 25 N. E. 105, 23 Am. St. 819; Hunt v. Bay State Iron Co., 97 Mass. 279; Lynde v. Rowe, 12 Allen (Mass.) 100; Clary v. Owen, 15 Gray (Mass.) 522; Merchants' Nat. Bank v. Stanton, 55 Minn. 211, 56 N. W. 821, 43 Am. St. 491; Perkins v. Swank, 43 Miss. 349; Andrews v. Day Button Co., 132 N. Y.

This seems to be a logical consequence of the rule that a mortgagor can not by agreement confer rights of removal not possessed by himself.[53]

It does not avail the tenant that he annexed the fixtures under a special contract with the mortgagor,[54] or that the holder of the mortgage, who seeks to enforce his claim to the fixtures, took the assignment of the mortgage with notice of the tenant's claim.[55]

But it has been held that an agreement between landlord and tenant giving the latter the right to remove articles annexed by him, may be enforced against one claiming under a prior mortgage of the realty provided the security of the mortgage is not affected by a removal of the articles,[56] and this is true even though the agreement was not made until after foreclosure, if made during the period of redemption.[57]

If a lease containing a stipulation giving the lessee the right to remove fixtures is made before the mortgage, the mortgagee takes the mortgage subject to the stipulations for removal, and also subject to the recognized right of the lessee to annex and remove at pleasure certain classes of articles.[58] Where the lease was made after the mortgage, and the mortgage, in the particular jurisdiction, is re-

---

348, 30 N. E. 831; Day v. Perkins, 2 Sandf. Ch. (N. Y.) 359; Belvin v. Raleigh Paper Co., 123 N. Car. 138, 31 S. E. 655; Hey v. Bruner, 61 Pa. St. 87.

[53] Seedhouse v. Broward, 34 Fla. 509, 16 So. 425; Cunningham v. Cureton, 96 Ga. 489, 23 S. E. 420; Bowen v. Wood, 35 Ind. 268; Ottumwa Woolen Mill Co. v. Hawley, 44 Iowa 57, 24 Am. Rep. 719; Mutual Ben. Life Ins. Co. v. Huntington, 57 Kans. 744, 48 Pac. 19; Dutro v. Kennedy, 9 Mont. 101, 22 Pac. 763.

[54] Clary v. Owen, 15 Gray (Mass.) 552. The mortgage will even attach to machinery put into a mill by the maker for trial, and to be purchased upon its proving satisfactory. Hamilton v. Huntley, 68 Ind. 521, 41 Am. Rep. 593. In this case the person who ordered the machinery was not the owner, but a tenant of the mill. The machinery was attached to the mill only in a temporary manner, so that it could be removed without injury to the mill. It was to become the property of the tenant of the mill upon his giving his notes for the price of the machinery after sixty days' trial of it. The tenant

refused to accept the machinery and give his notes as agreed, and he subsequently quit possession of the mill, leaving the machinery in it, and another tenant took possession of it. It was held that, as between the makers of the machinery and the mortgagee, the machinery was part of the realty. See also Bass Foundry v. Gallentine, 99 Ind. 525. There is a tendency in some cases to hold that where the fixtures are erected by a tenant of the mortgagor, under an agreement that they shall remain the property of the tenant, the mortgagee can not interpose, before taking possession of the premises, to prevent the carrying out of such agreement. Tifft v. Horton, 53 N. Y. 377, 380, 13 Am. Rep. 537.

[55] Clary v. Owen, 15 Gray (Mass.) 552.

[56] Broaddus v. Smith, 121 Ala. 335, 26 So. 34, 77 Am. St. 61; Paine v. McDowell, 71 Vt. 28, 41 Atl. 1042.

[57] Pioneer Sav. &c. Co. v. Fuller, 57 Minn. 60, 58 N. W. 831.

[58] Union Terminal Co. v. Wilmar &c. R. Co., 116 Iowa 392, 90 N. W. 92.

garded merely as a lien, the mortgagor, retaining the legal title, has the right to make a lease, which is valid as against the mortgagee, in so far as it does not affect his security, and the lessee would have the same right to annex and remove fixtures as if no mortgage had been given, provided their removal does not render the premises less valuable as a security than they were at the date of the mortgage.[59]

Where, during the pendency of a suit to foreclose a mortgage, a stranger, by permission of the mortgagor, erected a barn on the mortgaged premises, it was held that as against the mortgagee he had no right to remove it.[60]

A lessee who has erected a building upon mortgaged land, under an arrangement with the mortgagor, by leasing the building to the mortgagee after the latter has purchased the mortgaged premises upon foreclosure sale, is estopped from setting up title thereto in himself.[61]

When permanent structures are erected by a lessee upon the mortgaged estate under an agreement with the mortgagor, the mortgagee's consent is necessary for their removal;[62] but if they are erected for a temporary purpose, and with the intention of removing them, the lessee may remove them at any time during his term.

A tenant's fixtures are not brought within a subsequent mortgage of the premises by his neglect to remove them on a renewal of his lease by a new landlord.[63] Where one who has leased land to a firm buys out the right of one of the partners and afterward gives a mortgage on the premises, the possession of the new firm is notice to the mortgagee that erections put up by the former firm are not covered by the mortgage, because the other partner's rights can not be taken away.[64]

If a lessee subsequently purchases the reversion of the premises,

[59] Pioneer Sav. &c. Co. v. Fuller, 57 Minn. 60, 58 N. W. 831; Bernheimer v. Adams, 70 App. Div. 114, 75 N. Y. S. 93; Sprague Nat. Bank v. Erie R. Co., 22 App. Div. 526, 48 N. Y. S. 65. But see McFadden v. Allen, 134 N. Y. 489, 32 N. E. 21, 19 L. R. A. 446.

[60] Preston v. Briggs, 16 Vt. 124.

[61] Betts v. Wurth, 32 N. J. Eq. 82.

[62] Wiggins Ferry Co. v. Ohio &c. R. Co., 142 U. S. 396, 35 L. ed. 1055, 12 Sup Ct. 188; Kelly v. Austin, 46 Ill. 156, 92 Am. Dec. 243; Hewitt v. Watertown Steam Engine Co., 65 Ill. App. 153; Cooper v. Johnson, 143 Mass. 108, 9 N. E. 33; Holbrook v. Chamberlin, 116 Mass. 155, 17 Am. Rep. 146; Lake Superior Ship Canal Co. v. McCann, 86 Mich. 106, 48 N. W. 692; Early v. Burtis, 40 N. J. Eq. 501; Hughes v. Shingle Co., 51 S. Car. 1, 28 S. E. 2; Tunis Lumber Co. v. R. G. Dennis Lumber Co., 97 Va. 682, 34 S. E. 613.

[63] Kerr v. Kingsbury, 39 Mich. 150, 33 Am. Rep. 362.

[64] Kerr v. Kingsbury, 39 Mich. 150, 33 Am. Rep. 362.

machinery and other fixtures set up by him become subject to an existing mortgage of the realty.[65]

If a lessee mortgages his leasehold estate, the same rules in relation to fixtures upon the estate apply as between him and his mortgagee that would apply if he owned the estate in fee.[66]

Trade fixtures set up by a partnership upon land owned by the individual partners, which the partnership has no interest in beyond the use, do not become part of the realty, and may be removed by the partnership when its occupation of the premises ceases.[67]

§ 440. **Right of mortgagee of tenant's fixtures to remove same after surrender of lease.**—If a lessee mortgages tenant's fixtures, and afterward surrenders his lease, the mortgagee has a right to enter and sever them. The surrender of the term does not operate to extinguish the right or interest already granted, but is subject to that interest, for the support of which the original term still continues. The mortgagee's right to sever the fixtures from the freehold is an interest of a peculiar nature, in many respects rather partaking of the character of a chattel than of an interest in real estate. "But we think," said Mr. Justice Williams, in a case before the English Court of Common Pleas,[68] "that it is so far connected with the land that it may be considered a right or interest in it, which, if the tenant grants away, he shall not be allowed to defeat his grant by a subsequent voluntary act of surrender."[69]

§ 441. **Removal of trade or manufacturing fixtures by tenant.**—It is a settled rule of law that fixtures annexed to the freehold by a tenant for the purposes of trade or manufacture may be removed by him at the expiration of his term, whenever the removal of them is not contrary to any prevailing practice, and the articles can be removed without causing material injury to the freehold.[70] The pur-

---

[65] Jones v. Detroit Chair Co., 38 Mich. 92, 31 Am. Rep. 314.

[66] Shuart v. Taylor, 7 How. Pr. (N. Y.) 251; Ex parte Bentley, 2 M. D. & De G. 591; Ex parte Wilson, 4 Dea. & Chittenden 143, 2 Mont. & Ayr. 61.

[67] Robertson v. Corsett, 39 Mich. 777.

[68] London &c. Loan &c. Co. v. Drake, 6 C. B. (N. S.) 798.

[69] Saint v. Pilley, L. R. 10 Exch. 137; Adams v. Goddard, 48 Maine 212; Dobscheutz v. Holliday, 82 Ill.

371; Free v. Stuart, 39 Nebr. 220; 57 N. W. 991.

[70] McConnell v. Blood, 123 Mass. 47, 25 Am. Rep. 12; Holbrook v. Chamberlin, 116 Mass. 155, 17 Am. Rep. 146; Guthrie v. Jones, 108 Mass. 191; Polle v. Rouse, 73 Miss. 713, 19 So. 481; Coombs v. Beaumont, 5 B. & Ad. 72; Trappes v. Harter, 3 Tyrw. 603; Tyler on Fixtures, p. 267. See also Royce v. Latshaw, 15 Colo. App. 420, 62 Pac. 627; Updegraff v. Lesem, 15 Colo. App. 297, 62 Pac. 342; Dreiske v.

pose of this rule is to encourage the putting up of works beneficial to the public by persons whose tenure of the property is so short or so uncertain that they would not make the improvements or put in the machinery necessary for the profitable pursuit of their business, unless they had the right of removing these things at the termination of their tenancy. The reason of this rule does not apply when the fixtures are annexed by one who has, instead of the limited interest of a tenant, an unlimited ownership in fee; or an ownership which is qualified only by the condition of a mortgage upon the land which it is presumed he intends to fulfil, and which at any rate he would be estopped to say he did not intend to meet, and thus to keep the ownership of the land. Even after a forfeiture of the condition, he is allowed a considerable time within which to redeem, or else obtain the full value of the land and of all the personal articles he has affixed to it by a sale of the whole interest upon foreclosure. In a case before the Court of Exchequer,[71] the question of the application of this rule to the removal of a steam-engine and boiler, used in a saw-mill upon the mortgaged premises before the execution of the mortgage, was fully discussed. It was found by the jury that these things were put up by the mortgagor, not to improve the inheritance, but for the better use of the property, and that they could be removed without any appreciable damage to the freehold; but the court held that these findings were immaterial, because the right of the mortgagee attached by reason of the annexation to the land, and therefore that the intention of the mortgagor in respect of them could not prevail against the legal effect of the deed.

People's Lumber Co., 107 Ill. App. 285; Baker v. McClurg, 96 Ill. App. 165; Ward v. Earl. 86 Ill. App. 635; Gordon v. Miller, 28 Ind. App. 612, 63 N. E. 774; Union Terminal Co. v. Wilmer &c. R. Co., 116 Iowa 392, 90 N. W. 92; L. A. Thompson Scenic R. Co. v. Young, 90 Md. 278, 44 Atl. 1024; Winner v. Williams, 82 Miss. 669, 35 So. 308; Cohen v. Wittemann, 100 App. Div. 338, 91 N. Y. S. 493; Couch v. Welsh, 24 Utah 36, 66 Pac. 600; Tunis Lumber Co. v. R. G. Dennis Lumber Co., 97 Va. 682, 34 S. E. 613.

[71] Climie v. Wood, L. R. 3 Exch. 257. Kelly, C. B., delivering the judgment of the court, said: "It is a case between mortgagor and mortgagee, and no authority has been cited to show that a mortgagor is entitled to remove such trade fixtures. There have been several cases where the courts have decided that, upon the true construction of the mortgage deeds, trade fixtures were removable by the mortgagor, but not one to show that such right exists without a special provision. A mortgage is a security or pledge for a debt, and it is not unreasonable, if a fixture be annexed to land at the time of the mortgage, or if the mortgagor in possession afterward annexes a fixture to it, that the fixtures shall be deemed an additional security for the debt, whether it be a trade fixture or a fixture of any other kind. It has already been observed that no authority has been cited to show that trade fixtures may be re-

This case was carried by appeal to the Exchequer Chamber,[72] where the judgment of the court below and the law there declared were affirmed. Mr. Justice Willes, speaking of the reason why the engine and boiler, though they might have been removed by a tenant at the expiration of his term, yet could not be removed by a mortgagor, said: "And we are of opinion that the decisions which establish a tenant's right to remove trade fixtures do not apply as between mortgagor and mortgagee any more than between heir at law and executor. The irrelevancy of these decisions to cases where the conflicting parties are mortgagor and mortgagee was pointed out in Walmsley v. Milne,[73] and we concur with the observations made in that case by the Court of Common Pleas." As illustrating this distinction and the reason of it, the learned judge quotes the language of Lord Cottenham, in a case before the House of Lords, where it was sought to extend the rule in regard to trade fixtures to a case arising between an heir at law and executor.[74]

If the premises are mortgaged by the lessor during the existence of a tenancy, the mortgagee, or any one deriving title to the premises under the mortgage, occupies the position of the lessor toward

moved by the mortgagor, but there are several to the contrary; and unless we are prepared to overrule them, our judgment must be adverse to the plaintiff." To like effect see Cullwick v. Swindell, L. R. 3 Eq. Cas. 249, per Lord Romilly; Ex parte Cotton, 2 Mont. D. & De G. 725; Hawtry v. Butlin, L. R. 8 Q. B. Div. 290, 21 W. R. 633; Maples v. Millon, 31 Conn. 598; Day v. Perkins, 2 Sandf. Ch. (N. Y.) 359.

[72] Climie v. Wood, L. R. 4 Exch. 328.

[73] 7 C. B. (N. S.) 115.

[74] Fisher v. Dixon, 12 Cl. & F. 312. "The principle upon which a departure has been made from the old rule of law in favor of trade appears to me to have no application to the present case. The individual who erected the machinery was the owner of the land, and of the personal property which he erected and employed in carrying on the works: he might have done what he liked with it; he might have disposed of the land; he might have disposed of the machinery; he might have separated them again. It was therefore not at all necessary, in order to encourage him to erect those new works which are supposed to be beneficial to the public, that any rule of that kind should be established, because he was master of his own land. It was quite unnecessary, therefore, to seek to establish any such rule in favor of trade as applicable here, the whole being entirely under the control of the person who erected this machinery." To like effect Chief Justice Shaw, in a case before the Supreme Court of Massachusetts, Winslow v. Merchants' Insurance Co., 4 Metc. (Mass.) 306, 38 Am. Dec. 368, said: "The mortgagor, to most purposes, is regarded as the owner of the estate; indeed, he is so regarded to all purposes, except so far as it is necessary to recognize the mortgagee as legal owner for the purposes of his security. The improvements, therefore, which the mortgagor, remaining in the possession and enjoyment of the mortgaged premises, makes upon them, in contemplation of law he makes for himself, and to enhance the general value of the estate, and not for its temporary enjoyment."

the lessee; and the latter may remove in that case fixtures erected by him whenever he could do so as against his lessor.[75]

It has been said that it is immaterial whether the mortgagee of the land had notice that the articles were trade fixtures, since he could not acquire any interest other than what the mortgagor had, and besides the very character of the structure, and of the business carried on therein, were sufficient to put him on inquiry.[76] A receiver who rebuilt a trade fixture with the proceeds of insurance, after loss by fire, was held to have the right to remove same as against one claiming under a mortgage subsequent to the lease.[77]

§ 442. **Vermont rule.**—In Vermont the rule as to fixtures seems to be exceptionally strict in requiring that they shall in all cases be substantially attached to the freehold, and in holding that it is not sufficient to make personal chattels a part of the freehold that they are attached to the building in which they are used in a manner adapted to keep them steady, or that they are essential to the occupation of the building for the business carried on in it. "The rule requiring actual annexation," says Mr. Justice Bennett,[78] "is not affected by those cases where a constructive annexation has been held sufficient. These cases may be regarded as exceptions to the general rule, or else as cases where the things were mere incidents to the freehold, and became a part of it, and passed with it, upon a principle different from that of its being a fixture." It was, moreover, said that reference must be had not only to the annexation, but also to the object and purpose of it; and that to change the nature and legal qualities of a chattel into a fixture requires not only a positive act on the part of the person making the annexation, but also that his intention to make this change should particularly appear; and that, if this intention be left in doubt, the article should still be regarded as personal property. It was accordingly held in this case that, in a mortgage of a mill for manufacturing paper, the iron shafting used to communicate the motive power to the machinery, and fastened to the building by means of bolts, should be regarded as a constituent part of the mill, and therefore as included in a mortgage of that; but that a large iron boiler supported by brick-work, laid on a stone foundation placed on the ground near the center of the building, and also the machines

[75] Globe Marble Mills Co. v. Quinn, 76 N. Y. 23, 32 Am. Rep. 259.
[76] Royce v. Latshaw, 15 Colo. App. 420, 62 Pac. 627.

[77] Union Terminal Co. v. Wilmar &c. A. R. Co., 116 Iowa 392, 90 N. W. 92.
[78] Hill v. Wentworth, 28 Vt. 429.

for grinding rags into pulp, the paper-presses, and other machinery, were no part of the real estate, as between the mortgagor and mortgagee.

This decision was followed by another to like effect in the same court, holding that, while the steam-engine and boilers used in a marble mill were fixtures as between mortgagor and mortgagee, yet the saw-frames, though fastened to the building by bolts, were not such fixtures. The manner in which they were attached to the building was not considered to be such as to operate to change their character as chattels.[79]

§ 443. **Statutory provisions.**—In Vermont it is provided by statute that machinery attached to or used in any shop, mill, printing-office, or factory may be mortgaged by deed, executed, acknowledged, and recorded as deeds of real estate. Such mortgages may be assigned, discharged, or foreclosed like mortgages of real estate.[80] The statute does not apply to a case where machinery was set up subsequent to and not mentioned in a mortgage of the realty whereto it is attached, but the rights of the parties are to be determined by the law established by the decisions of the court prior to the statute.[81]

In Connecticut it is provided that the fixtures of a manufacturing or mechanical establishment, or of a printing or publishing house, the furniture of a dwelling-house, and the hay in a barn, and other things enumerated, may be mortgaged with the realty when the mortgage contains a particular description of the machinery, furniture, or other property, to the same effect as if the same were a part of the real estate. The same may be mortgaged separate from the realty, if particularly described, and the deed be executed, acknowledged, and recorded in all respects as a mortgage of land.[82]

In Rhode Island it is provided that the water-wheels, steam-engines, boilers, main belts which first give motion to the shafting, all shafting, whether upright or horizontal, and hangers for the same, except such as are used to drive a special machine, all drums, pulleys, wheels, gearing, steam-pipes, gas-pipes and gas fixtures, water-pipes and fixtures, kettles and vats set and used in any mechanical or manufacturing

[79] Sweetzer v. Jones, 35 Vt. 317, 82 Am. Dec. 639. See also Kendall v. Hathaway, 67 Vt. 122, 30 Atl. 859; Hackett v. Amsden, 57 Vt. 432; Newhall v. Kinney, 56 Vt. 591; Davenport v. Shants, 43 Vt. 546; Harris v. Haynes, 34 Vt. 220; Bartlett v. Wood, 32 Vt. 372; Fullam v. Stearns, 30 Vt. 443; Sturgis v. Warren, 11 Vt. 433; Tobias v. Francis, 3 Vt. 425, 23 Am. Rep. 217.

[80] Rev. Stat. 1894, § 2269.

[81] Kendall v. Hathaway, 67 Vt. 122, 30 Atl. 859.

[82] Gen. Stat. 1902, § 4132.

establishment, shall be regarded as real estate, whenever the same belong to the owner of the real estate to which they are attached. All other machinery, tools, and apparatus of every description, used and employed in any manufacturing establishment, are declared to be personal estate.[83]

II. *Machinery in Mills*

§ 444. **Intention with reference to machinery in mills.**—A distinction is properly made between such fixtures in a mill as are indispensable to its use as a mill, and the movable machines used in it, which may be dispensed with upon a change in business to which the mill may be readily adapted.[1] Of the former class are such as are used for furnishing the motive power; and if the mill is adapted to one business only, the machinery necessary for that business may be included in the same class.[2] To this class also belongs machinery

---

[83] 1 Stim. Am. St. Law. §§ 2100–2102.

[1] Tillman v. De Lacy, 80 Ala. 103; Smith Paper Co. v. Servin, 130 Mass. 511; McConnell v. Blood, 123 Mass. 47, 25 Am. Rep. 12; Farrar v. Chauffetete, 5 Denio (N. Y.) 527; Morris' Appeal, 88 Pa. St. 368; Price v. Jenks, 14 Phila. (Pa.) 228. See also Shepard v. Blossom, 66 Minn. 421, 69 N. W. 221, 61 Am. St. 431.

[2] Harkness v. Sears, 26 Ala. 493, 62 Am. Dec. 742; Sands v. Pfeiffer, 10 Cal. 258; Kloess v. Katt, 40 Ill. App. 99; Otis v. May, 30 Ill. App. 581; Jenney v. Jackson, 6 Ill. App. 32; Sparks v. State Bank, 7 Blackf. (Ind.) 469; Ottumwa Woolen Mill Co. v. Hawley, 44 Iowa 57, 24 Am. Rep. 719; New Orleans Canal &c. Co. v. Leeds, 49 La. Ann. 123, 21 So. 168; McKim v. Mason, 3 Md. Ch. 186; Southbridge Sav. Bank v. Exeter Mach. Works, 127 Mass. 542; McConnell v. Blood, 123 Mass. 47, 25 Am. Rep. 12; Winslow v. Merchants' Ins. Co., 4 Metc. (Mass.) 306, 38 Am. Dec. 368; Coleman v. Stearns Mfg. Co., 38 Mich. 30; Dutro v. Kennedy, 9 Mont. 101, 22 Pac. 763; Despatch Line of Packets v. Bellamy Mfg. Co., 12 N. H. 205, 37 Am. Dec. 203; Lee v. Hubschmidt Bldg. &c. Co., 55 N. J. Eq. 623, 37 Atl. 769; Speiden v. Parker, 46 N. J. Eq. 292, 19 Atl. 21; Scheifele v. Schmitz, 42 N. J. Eq. 700, 1 Atl. 698; Delaware, L. &c. R. Co. v. Oxford Iron Co., 36 N. J. Eq. 452; Keeler v. Keeler, 31 N. J. Eq. 181; McMillan v. Fish, 29 N. J. Eq. 610; Potts v. New Jersey Arms Co., 17 N. J. Eq. 395; Crane v. Brigham, 11 N. J. Eq. 29; Doughty v. Owen (N. J. Eq.), 19 Atl. 540; Berliner v. Piqua Club Assn., 32 Misc. 470, 66 N. Y. S. 791; Bigler v. Nat. Bank, 26 Hun (N. Y.) 520; Phœnix Mills v. Miller, 4 N. Y. St. 787, 17 N. Y. S. 158; Cooper v. Harvey, 16 N. Y. S. 660; Horne v. Smith, 105 N. Car. 322, 11 S. E. 373, 18 Am. St. 903; Case Manufacturing Co. v. Garver, 45 Ohio St. 289, 13 N. E. 493; Brennan v. Whitaker, 15 Ohio St. 446; Teaff v. Hewitt, 1 Ohio St. 511, 59 Am. Dec. 634; Barker v. Cincinnati Pressed Brick Co., 4 Ohio Dec. 270; Helm v. Gilroy, 20

specially adapted to carry out the purpose for which the mill was erected, and presumably to increase its value, although it may be removed without injury to the building.[3]

Of the other class are movable machines used in a mill adapted to various kinds of business, which may be wholly set aside, and still the value and usefulness of the mill property would not be materially

Ore. 517, 26 Pac. 851; Vail v. Weaver, 132 Pa. St. 363, 19 Atl. 138, 19 Am. St. 598; Roberts v. Dauphin Deposit Bank, 19 Pa. St. 71; Jones v. Bull, 85 Tex. 136, 19 S. W. 1031; Phelan v. Boyd (Tex.), 14 S. W. 290; Sweetzer v. Jones, 35 Vt. 317, 82 Am. Dec. 639; Harris v. Haynes, 34 Vt. 220; Hill v. Wentworth, 28 Vt. 428; Frankland v. Moulton, 5 Wis. 1; Walmsley v. Milne, 7 C. B. (N. S.) 115, 97 E. C. L. 115; Longbottom v. Berry, L. R. 5 Q. B. Div. 123; Climie v. Wood, L. R. 3 Exch. 257, L. R. 4 Exch. 329; Hobson v. Gorringe, 1 Ch. 182; Cross v. Barnes, 46 L. J. Q. B. Div. 479, 36 L. T. (N. S.) 693; Schrieber v. Malcolm, 8 Grant's Ch. (U. C.) 433; Minhinnick v. Jolly, 29 Ont. Rep. 238; Don v. Warner, 28 Nova Scotia 202; Oates v. Cameron, 7 U. C. Q. B. Div. 228; Dickson v. Hunter, 29 Grant's Ch. (U. C.) 73.

[3] Southbridge Sav. Bank v. Mason, 147 Mass. 500, 18 N. E. 406; Pierce v. George, 108 Mass. 78; Hopewell Mills v. Taunton Sav. Bank, 150 Mass. 519, 23 N. E. 327, 15 Am. St. 235. In the latter case Knowlton, J., said: "We are of opinion that this rule is applicable to the case at bar. The building mortgaged was a cotton-mill; and the machinery in controversy was all procured for use in the manufacture of cotton cloth. Most of it was heavy; and there is much to indicate that, while there were changes in the kinds of goods manufactured, the machines were not of a kind intended to be moved from place to place, but to be put in position and there used with the building until they should be worn out, or until, for some unforeseen cause, the real estate should be changed, and put to a different use. Of most of them, it is said in the agreed statement that they were fastened to the floor for the purpose of steadying them when in use; but it is also said that this is not a statement of the only purpose for which they were fastened. They seem to have been attached to the building, and connected with the motive power, with a view to permanence." See also Hill v. Farmers' &c. Nat. Bank, 97 U. S. 450, 24 L. ed. 1051; William Firth Co. v. South Carolina L. &c. Co., 122 Fed. 569, 59 C. C. A. 73; Fisk v. People's Nat. Bank, 14 Colo. App. 21, 59 Pac. 63; Cunningham v. Cureton, 96 Ga. 489, 23 S. E. 420; Calumet Iron &c. Co. v. Lathrop, 36 Ill. App. 249; Stillman v. Flenniken, 58 Iowa 450, 10 N. W. 842, 43 Am. Rep. 120; Ottumwa Woollen Mill Co. v. Hawley, 44 Iowa 57, 24 Am. Rep. 719; Swoop v. St. Martin, 110 La. 237, 34 So. 426; Parsons v. Copeland, 38 Maine 537; Lord v. Detroit Sav. Bank, 132 Mich. 510, 93 N. W. 1063; Lyle v. Palmer, 42 Mich. 314, 3 N. W. 921; Farmers' Loan &c. Co. v. Minneapolis Engine Works, 35 Minn. 543, 29 N. W. 349; Langdon v. Buchanan, 62 N. H. 657; Knickerbocker Trust Co. v. Penn Cordage Co., 66 N. J. Eq. 305, 58 Atl. 409, 105 Am. St. 640; Atlantic Safe Deposit &c. Co. v. Atlantic City Laundry Co., 64 N. J. Eq. 140, 53 Atl. 212; Roddy v. Brick, 42 N. J. Eq. 218, 6 Atl. 806; Delaware &c. R. Co. v. Oxford Iron Co., 36 N. J. Eq. 452; McRea v. Bank, 66 N. Y. 489; Cooper v. Harvey, 16 N. Y. S. 660; Morris' Appeal, 88 Pa. St. 368; Harlan v. Harlan, 15 Pa. St. 507; McFadden v. Crawford, 36 W. Va. 671, 15 S. E. 408, 32 Am. St. 894; Patton v. Moore, 16 W. Va. 428, 37 Am. Rep. 789; Taylor v. Collins, 51 Wis. 123, 8 N. W. 22; Longbottom v. Berry, L. R. 5 Q. B. Div. 123; Holland v. Hodgson, L. R. 7 C. P. 328.

impaired. Such machinery, not being indispensable to the enjoyment of the realty, is generally considered not to be a part of it, and not to pass by a mortgage of it.[4]

The courts of different states are not agreed as to the legal status of articles of machinery; for, while the policy of some seems to be to treat them as chattels wherever the intention of the parties will permit, other courts are disposed to regard them as fixtures to the realty.

A mortgage was made of certain land, and the mills thereon.[5] In the mills were various articles of machinery for carding, spinning, and preparing cotton yarn and cotton twine. These were subsequently seized upon an execution against the mortgagor, and were claimed as well by the mortgagee. It appeared that the machines might be easily removed without injury to them or to the building, and might be used for the same purpose in any other building.[6] The court held that they were not properly fixtures, and therefore not subject to the mortgage. Under quite similar circumstances a mortgage of a woolen factory was held not to pass the looms used in it for the manufacture of broadcloth, and merely fastened to the floor by screws to keep them in their places.[7] In these cases the intention was held to govern the character of the articles under consideration. It is to be observed, however, that other courts have decided cases quite similar, if not altogether like these cited from the

---

[4] Carpenter v. Walker, 140 Mass. 416, 5 N. E. 160; Maguire v. Park, 140 Mass. 21, 1 N. E. 750; Hubbell v. Savings Bank, 132 Mass. 447, 42 Am. Rep. 446; South Bridge Sav. Bank v. Exeter Machine Works, 127 Mass. 542, 25 Am. Rep. 47; McConnell v. Blood, 123 Mass. 47, 25 Am. Dec. 12; Winslow v. Merchants' Ins. Co., 4 Metc. (Mass.) 306, 38 Am. Dec. 368; Robertson v. Corsett, 39 Mich. 777; Wolford v. Baxter, 33 Minn. 12, 21 N. W. 744, 53 Am. Rep. 1; Scheifele v. Schmitz, 42 N. J. Eq. 700, 11 Atl. 257; Pennsylvania Mut. Ins. Co. v. Semple, 38 N. J. Eq. 575; Rogers v. Brokaw, 25 N. J. Eq. 496; Gale v. Ward, 14 Mass. 352, 7 Am. Dec. 233. In the latter case, Mr. Chief Justice Parker said the articles in controversy "must be considered as personal property, because, although in some sense attached to the freehold, yet they could be easily disconnected, and were capable of being used in any other building erected for similar purposes."

[5] Vanderpoel v. Van Allen, 10 Barb. (N. Y.) 157. See also Potter v. Cromwell, 40 N. Y. 287, 100 Am. Dec. 485; Cresson v. Stout, 17 Johns. (N. Y.) 116, 8 Am. Dec. 373.

[6] The highest authorities agree in holding that these facts alone should have little weight in deciding the question. See cases cited in this section, and Walmsley v. Milne, 7 C. B. (N. S.) 115.

[7] Murdock v. Gifford, 18 N. Y. 28. In the Supreme Court it was held that the mortgage carried the looms, on the ground that they were intended to be a permanent and essential part of the woolen factory. Murdock v. Harris, 20 Barb. (N. Y.) 407. See McRea v. Central Nat. Bank, 66 N. Y. 489, for a review of the cases in New York. See also Blancke v. Rogers, 26 N. J. Eq. 563; Rogers v. Brokaw, 25 N. J. Eq. 496.

New York reports, directly contrary to the decisions in these;[8] and it is to be further observed that the policy of the decisions in New York, Vermont, and Ohio seems to be to favor treating machinery and like articles fixed to the realty as chattels.[9] Other courts, for good reasons, hold such machinery to be fixtures, and to be covered by a mortgage of the realty without particular mention. Thus, in a case decided in Iowa,[10] the mortgage, after describing the land, upon which was situated a woolen manufactory filled with machinery for making cloth from wool, granted "all and singular the tenements, hereditaments, and appurtenances thereto belonging or in any wise appertaining." Other mortgages were subsequently made which in terms covered the machinery, and upon a foreclosure of the former mortgage a contention arose in regard to the machinery of the mill. The court, after critically reviewing the cases, say: "It being conceded by all the cases that the engine, boiler, and attachments, being the motive power, are fixtures, and that the stones or burrs of a grist-mill, with the attachments, are likewise fixtures, it is not easy to understand why any dividing line should be made at the point where the belting attaches to the other machinery. Is there anything in the whole record of this case tending to show that the machinery in question was intended to be any less permanent than the engine, shafting, or belt? The fair presumption is, that the whole machinery, including that now in question, was placed in the building with the intention that it should remain there as part of the machinery until worn out or displaced by other. This assumption is as strong and controlling as to the carding-machines, spinning-jacks, etc., as it is as to the engine, shafting, and belts." Therefore the court conclude that all of the machinery which was propelled by the engine was part of the real estate, and passed by the foreclosure sale.[11]

There is no certain criterion by which to determine in all cases what belongs to the one class and what to the other. Different courts decide differently in regard to the same articles; and even the decisions of the same court do not always seem to be perfectly consistent. The varying circumstances of the cases seem sometimes to have

---

[8] Ottumwa Woolen Mill Co. v. Hawley, 44 Iowa 57, 24 Am. Rep. 719.

[9] Teaff v. Hewitt, 1 Ohio St. 511, 59 Am. Dec. 634. See ante § 442.

[10] Ottumwa Woolen Mill Co. v. Hawley, 44 Iowa 57, 24 Am. Rep. 719.

[11] To like effect see Parsons v. Copeland, 38 Maine 537; Teaff v. Hewitt, 1 Ohio St. 511, 59 Am. Dec. 634; Harlan v. Harlan, 15 Pa. St. 507, 53 Am. Dec. 612.

an immediate influence upon the determination of the courts, greater than the statement of them in the reports would seem to warrant. But in doubtful cases, where the mode and extent of the annexation of the chattels to the realty do not determine their character as fixtures, the intention with which they were put upon the estate, whether for permanent use or for a temporary purpose, comes in with a controlling influence to settle the doubt.[12] This intention is to be gathered, not merely or chiefly from the manner in which the chattels are annexed to the realty, but from the character of the improvement, whether it is essential to the proper use of the realty.[13]

It is held that the mere placing of machinery in position in a building with intent to make it a permanent part of a manufacturing plant, does not make it part of the real estate unless it is actually or constructively attached to the building or to the land. It may be sufficient if the machines be secured or bolted to the floor, or the ponderous machines weighing from three to four tons resting upon the floor, by their own weight, may under certain circumstances be treated as part of the realty.[14]

Some courts are inclined to regard all things used in a factory, which are a part of the machinery necessary in the process of manufacture, as fixtures and covered by a mortgage of the factory;[15] while other courts are inclined to regard all movable machinery, not indispensable to carrying on the work of the factory, as personalty.[16]

A mortgage of a manufacturing plant which covers machinery,

---

[12] Tolles v. Winton, 63 Conn. 440, 28 Atl. 542; Stockwell v. Campbell, 39 Conn. 362, 12 Am. Rep. 393; Capen v. Peckham, 35 Conn. 88; Kelly v. Austin, 46 Ill. 156, 92 Am. Dec. 243, per Walker, J.; Ottumwa Woolen Mill Co. v. Hawley, 44 Iowa 57, 24 Am. Rep. 719; Smith Paper Co. v. Servin, 130 Mass. 511; Ferris v. Quimby, 41 Mich. 202, 2 N. W. 9; Keeler v. Keeler, 31 N. J. Eq. 181; McRea v. Central Nat. Bank, 66 N. Y. 489; Morris' Appeal, 88 Pa. St. 368; Shelton v. Ficklin, 32 Grat. (Va.) 727.

[13] Rogers v. Prattville Mfg. Co., 81 Ala. 483, 1 So. 643, 60 Am. Rep. 171; Tillman v. De Lacy, 80 Ala. 103; Lavenson v. Standard Soap Co., 80 Cal. 245, 22 Pac. 184; Carpenter v. Walker, 140 Mass. 416, 5 N. E. 160; Maguire v. Park, 140 Mass. 21, 1 N.

E. 750; Shelton v. Ficklin, 32 Grat. (Va.) 727; Green v. Phillips, 26 Grat. (Va.) 752, 21 Am. Rep. 323.

[14] Shepard v. Blossom, 66 Minn. 421, 69 N. W. 221, 61 Am. St. 431; Washington Nat. Bank v. Smith, 15 Wash. 160, 45 Pac. 736.

[15] Johnson v. Wiseman, 4 Metc. (Ky.) 357, 83 Am. Dec. 475; Huston v. Clark, 162 Pa. St. 435, 29 Atl. 866.

[16] Maguire v. Park, 140 Mass. 21, 1 N. E. 750; Farmers' Loan &c. Co. v. Minneapolis Eng. &c. Works, 35 Minn. 543, 29 N. W. 349; Wolford v. Baxter, 33 Minn. 12, 21 N. W. 744, 53 Am. Rep. 1; Keeler v. Keeler, 31 N. J. Eq. 181; Rogers v. Brokaw, 25 N. J. Eq. 496; Chase v. Tacoma Box Co., 11 Wash. 377, 39 Pac. 639; Cherry v. Arthur, 5 Wash. 787, 32 Pac. 744.

covers machinery subsequently put in to replace machinery that is old, worn out, or not well adapted to the purposes of the business.[17]

§ 445. Effect of subsequent chattel mortgage of machinery.—An existing mortgage of the realty may have priority of a chattel mortgage of machinery subsequently annexed, although the chattel mortgage be made at the time the articles were attached.[19]

If the mortgagee of the chattels has actual knowledge of the mortgage of the realty, or constructive knowledge of it by record, his mortgage of chattels annexed or about to be annexed to the realty is subject to the legal consequences of the annexing of such chattels to the mortgaged realty. In a Massachusetts case, the right to certain machinery in a building used as a machine-shop was contested between a mortgagee of the real estate and a mortgagee of the machinery described as personal property.[20] Before either of the mortgages was made, the mortgagor owned the machine-shop, and also the machinery, and used both for manufacturing purposes. It was held that such machines and their appurtenances as were specially adapted to be used in the shop and were annexed to it passed by the mortgage of the real estate. In this class were included punches, polishing frames, vibrators, a polisher and fan-blower, the pulleys, shafting, and hangers. These were bolted or screwed to the floors or timbers of the building, although it appeared that they could be removed without substantial injury to it. The wheels belonging to the polishing machines were placed in the same class, although they could be detached and removed without injury. But other articles not appearing to be essential parts of the shop, and not attached to it, were held not to pass by the mortgage of the real property, but by the mortgage of the personalty. Of these articles not considered fixtures in any sense of the word were

---

[17] Sturgis Nat. Bank v. Levanseler, 115 Mich. 372, 73 N. W. 399.

[19] Roddy v. Brick, 42 N. J. Eq. 218. See also Fisk v. People's Nat. Bank, 14 Colo. App. 21, 59 Pac. 63; Bass Foundry v. Gallentine, 99 Ind. 525; Pierce v. George, 108 Mass. 78, 11 Am. Rep. 310; Tibbetts v. Horne, 65 N. H. 242, 23 Atl. 145; Voorhees v. McGinnis, 48 N. Y. 278; Henry v. Von Brandenstein, 12 Daly (N. Y.) 480; Cooper v. Harvey, 16 N. Y. S. 660; Buzzell v. Cummings, 61 Vt. 213, 18 Atl. 93; Smith v. Waggoner, 50 Wis, 155, 6 N. W. 568. See contra Padgett v. Cleveland, 33 S.

Car. 339, 11 S. E. 1069; Jones on Chattel Mortgages, §§ 123–135. See ante §§ 436b, 436c.

[20] Pierce v. George, 108 Mass. 78, 11 Am. Rep. 310. See also Millikin v. Armstrong, 17 Ind. 456; First Nat. Bank v. Elmore, 52 Iowa 541, 3 N. W. 547; Parsons v. Copeland, 38 Maine 537; Allen v. Woodard, 125 Mass. 400, 28 Am. Rep. 250; McConnell v. Blood, 123 Mass. 47, 25 Am. Rep. 12; Winslow v. Merchants' Ins. Co., 4 Metc. (Mass.) 306, 38 Am. Dec. 368; Richardson v. Copeland, 6 Gray (Mass.) 536, 66 Am. Dec. 424.

the lathes fastened to a bench by screws, and operated by a foot movement; grindstones resting upon frames standing upon the floor; a rattler and frame, tack machines, the slitter, the anvils, the vises, the lathes, and a portable forge.

In a case in Ohio a similar question arose between the holder of a chattel mortgage of the fixtures and a mortgagee of the realty in respect to the boilers, engines, saws, and gearing of a steam saw-mill.[21] The chattel mortgage was made before the articles were annexed to the property, but it recited that they were designed to be used in the mortgagor's saw-mill, and power was given the mortgagees to take possession of them upon default, whether they should be attached to the freehold and in law become a part of the realty or not. The mortgage of the real estate was afterward taken without notice of this agreement. The record of the chattel mortgage was constructive notice only of an incumbrance upon chattels; but when the mortgage of the real estate was made, these things were not chattels, but real estate, and the record of the mortgage as a chattel mortgage was no notice to the mortgagee of the realty. The court declared that it devolved upon the mortgagee of the chattels, who sought to change the legal character of the property after it was annexed to the realty and to create incumbrances upon it, either to pursue the mode prescribed by law for incumbering the kind of estate to which it appeared to the world to belong, and for giving notice of such incumbrance; or, otherwise, take the risk of its loss in case it should be sold and conveyed

---

[21] Brennan v. Whitaker, 15 Ohio St. 446. For a similar case with like decision, see Frankland v. Moulton, 5 Wis. 1. See also Fortman v. Goepper, 14 Ohio St. 558. In Voorhees v. McGinnis, 48 N. Y. 278, the owner of a saw and grist mill erected a substantial building, and placed therein a steam-engine, boiler, shafting, and gearing, which were constructed with special reference to the place in which they were to be used, but without any intent on the part of the person making the improvement either of making them a part of the freehold, or of removing them in the future, and gave a real estate mortgage upon the property. Subsequently the boiler and machinery were removed for the purpose of having them replaced by a new boiler and new machinery, and, while the new boiler and machinery were at the shop for repair, the owner of the mill gave a chattel mortgage upon them; and after the repairs were completed, and the mill was in running order, he gave another mortgage upon them and other machinery. After the repairs and before the last chattel mortgage, he gave a second real estate mortgage on the premises, and the plaintiff acquired title under the foreclosure and sale on the two real estate mortgages. The holders of the chattel mortgages removed the machinery covered by these mortgages. It was held that, although the mortgagor had no special intent upon the subject, the facts disclosed that the boiler, engine, shafting, and gearing were permanent accessions to the freehold.

as part of the real estate of a purchaser without notice.[22] As against a mortgagee of the realty, to sustain a claim to the fixtures, there must be either an actual severance of them previously made, or actual notice of the agreement by the mortgagor that they should be severed.

If machinery, already subject to a chattel mortgage, be affixed to the realty, with the assent of the mortgagee, it becomes a question whether the chattel mortgage lien is lost as against an existing mortgagee of the realty, or as against subsequent purchasers and mortgagees of the realty, or creditors who subsequently obtain liens upon it. The intention and agreement of the parties has much to do with the determination of the question whether the chattels annexed to the realty retain their character as personal property.[23]

An engine and boiler mortgaged to the maker were set up on a foundation, and an engine-house was built over them. The land was already subject to a mortgage. It was held that the mortgagee of the land acquired no title to the engine and boiler as against the mortgagee of these chattels, although it appeared that they could not be removed without some injury to the walls built up about them; for the chattels could be removed without taking away or destroying that which was essential to the support of the main building, or other part of the real estate to which they were attached, and without destroying or of necessity injuring the chattels themselves.[24]

A water-wheel and necessary shafting and gearing put into a sawmill, under an agreement which amounted to a conditional sale, retain their identity and character as chattels as against a mortgagee whose mortgage covered the mill when these things were attached.[25] But machinery permanently attached to land and belonging to the

[22] Per White, J., in Brennan v. Whitaker, 15 Ohio St. 446. He dissents from the ruling in Ford v. Cobb, 20 N. Y. 344, where it was held that an agreement evidenced by a chattel mortgage was effectual against a subsequent purchaser of the land without notice; and cites to the contrary Richardson v. Copeland, 6 Gray (Mass.) 536, and other cases.

[23] Manwaring v. Jenison, 61 Mich. 117, 27 N. W. 899; Campbell v. Roddy, 44 N. J. Eq. 244, 14 Atl. 279, 6 Am. St. 889; Tifft v. Horton, 53 N. Y. 377, 13 Am. Rep. 537; Potter v. Cromwell, 40 N. Y. 287, 100 Am. Dec. 485; Sheldon v. Edwards, 35 N Y. 279; Rowland v. West, 62 Hun 583, 43 N. Y. St. 698, 17 N. Y. S. 330.

[24] Tifft v. Horton, 53 N. Y. 377, 13 Am. Rep. 537. See also Miller v. Griffin, 102 Ala. 610, 15 So. 238; Tibbetts v. Moore, 23 Cal. 208; Anderson v. Creamery Package Mfg. Co., 8 Idaho 200, 67 Pac. 493, 56 L. R. A. 554, 101 Am. St. 188; Long v. Cockern, 128 Ill. 29, 21 N. E. 201, affg. 29 Ill. App. 304; First Nat. Bank v. Elmore, 52 Iowa 541, 3 N. W. 547; Eaves v. Estes, 10 Kans. 314, 15 Am. Rep. 345. But see Voorhees v. McGinnis, 48 N. Y. 278; Frankland v. Moulton, 5 Wis. 1.

[25] Page v. Edwards, 64 Vt. 124, 23 Atl. 917; Buzzell v. Cummings, 61 Vt. 213, 18 Atl. 93; Davenport v.

owner thereof, which was used in a manufactory, will be treated as a fixture and pass by a real estate mortgage given by him, although a chattel mortgage was given at the same time upon the machinery for the purpose of insuring against a possible mistake as to its character.[26]

§ 446. **Machinery furnishing motive power.**—A steam-engine and boiler, with the appurtenances belonging to them, permanently affixed, and used for furnishing the motive power of a mill, together with the shafts and pulleys connected with the engine, are fixtures, and pass to a mortgagee of the realty.[27] The machinery of the motive power, whether a steam-engine or a water-wheel, and all the shafting and other means of communicating this power, are as a general rule fixtures.[28] A steam-engine and boilers fixed in a mill by the mortgagor after the execution of the mortgage become subject to it.[29] It is not

Shants, 43 Vt. 546. See in connection Tibbetts v. Horne, 65 N. H. 242, 23 Atl. 145, 15 L. R. A. 56, 23 Am. St. 31; Cochran v. Flint, 57 N. H. 514.

[26] Studley v. Ann Arbor Sav. Bank, 112 Mich. 181, 70 N. W. 426; Homestead Land Co. v. Becker, 96 Wis. 206, 71 N. W. 117.

[27] Tillman v. De Lacy, 80 Ala. 103; Lavenson v. Standard Soap Co., 80 Cal. 245, 22 Pac. 184, 13 Am. St. 147; Ottumwa Woolen Mill Co. v. Hawley, 44 Iowa 57, 24 Am. Rep. 719; Southbridge Sav. Bank v. Exeter Machine Works, 127 Mass. 542; Coleman v. Stearns Mfg. Co., 38 Mich. 30; Scheifele v. Schmitz, 42 N. J. Eq. 700, 11 Atl. 257; Roddy v. Brick, 42 N. J. Eq. 218, 6 Atl. 806; Keeler v. Keeler, 31 N. J. Eq. 181; Watson v. Watson Mfg. Co., 30 N. J. Eq. 483; Quinby v. Manhattan Cloth &c. Co., 24 N. J. Eq. 260; Doughty v. Owen (N. J. Eq.), 19 Atl. 540; Sweetzer v. Jones, 35 Vt. 317, 82 Am. Dec. 639; Harris v. Haynes, 34 Vt. 220; Taylor v. Collins, 51 Wis. 123, 8 N. W. 22; Hubbard v. Bagshaw, 4 Sim. 326; In re McKibben, 4 Ir. Ch. (N. S.) 520. See also Larue v. American Diesel Engine Co., 176 Ind. 609, 96 N. E. 772; Prudential Ins. Co. v. Guild (N. J. Eq.), 64 Atl. 694; Berliner v. Piqua Club Assn., 32 Misc. 470, 66 N. Y. S. 791; Albert v. Uhrich, 180 Pa. St. 283, 36 Atl. 745; McCrillis v. Cole, 25 R. I. 156, 55 Atl. 196, 105 Am. St. 875; Zim-

mermann v. Bosse, 60 Wash. 556, 111 Pac. 796; Gunderson v. Swarthout, 104 Wis. 186, 80 N. W. 465, 76 Am. St. 860. But see Padgett v. Cleveland, 33 S. Car. 339, 11 S. E. 1069.

[28] Powell v. Monson &c. Mfg. Co., 3 Mason (U. S.) 459, Fed. Cas. No. 11357; McConnell v. Blood, 123 Mass. 47, 25 Am. Rep. 121; Keeler v. Keeler, 31 N. J. Eq. 181; Keve v. Paxton, 26 N. J. Eq. 107; Hill v. Wentworth, 28 Vt. 428. In Rhode Island, by statute, the water-wheels, steam-engines, boilers, main belts, which first give motion to the shafting, all shafting, whether upright or horizontal, and hangers for the same, except such as are used to drive a special machine, all drums, pulleys, wheels, gearing, steam pipes, gas-pipes and gas-fixtures, water-pipes and fixtures, kettles and vats set and used in any mechanical or manufacturing establishment, are declared to be real estate, whenever the same belong to the owner of the real estate to which they are attached. All other machinery, tools, and apparatus of every description, used and employed in any manufacturing establishment, are declared to be personal estate, and as such shall be considered, in assignments of dower, in attachments, and in all cases whatsoever, except in the assessment and payment of taxes. P. S. 1882, ch. 171, §§ 1, 2.

[29] Cope v. Romeyne, 4 McLean (U. S.) 384, Fed. Cas. No. 3207; Rice

material that they are the property of another, as, for instance, that they were leased to the mortgagor, if he annexes them to the freehold with the consent of the owner.[30]

But if the land and the engine are held by different titles, the latter does not necessarily become part of the realty when set up and used by one who does not own the land.[31] Even if they were subject at the time to a chattel mortgage, this would not hold against the mortgage of the realty after they are attached to it.[32] Nor does it make any difference that, although erected in a permanent manner, they can be removed without injury to the building in which they are placed or with which they are connected.[33] A mortgage of a factory by a lessee passes to the mortgagee a steam engine used in it, although the lessor could not claim it.[34]

Machinery furnishing motive power has occasionally been held to be personalty in view of the intention with which it was annexed,[35] or the mode of annexation.[36]

§ 447. Various articles of machinery.

A shingle-machine put into a mill by a mortgagor becomes a part of the mortgage security.[37] Mill-saws attached to a saw-mill and used in it become a part of the realty, and subject to a mortgage of the mill previously made.[38] Heavy

v. Adams, 4 Harr. (Del.) 332; Dudley v. Hurst, 67 Md. 44, 8 Atl. 901; McKim v. Mason, 3 Md. Ch. Dec. 186; Winslow v. Merchants' Ins. Co., 4 Metc. (Mass.) 306, 38 Am. Dec. 368; Randolph v. Gwynne, 7 N. J. Eq. 88, 51 Am. Dec. 265.

[30] Fryatt v. Sullivan Co., 5 Hill (N. Y.) 116. See also Roberts v. Dauphin Deposit Bank, 19 Pa. St. 71.

[31] Robertson v. Corsett, 39 Mich. 777.

[32] Voorhees v. McGinnis, 48 N. Y. 278; Frankland v. Moulton, 5 Wis. 1. But see Padgett v. Cleveland, 33 S. Car. 339, 11 S. E. 1069.

[33] Sparks v. State Bank, 7 Blackf. (Ind.) 469; Voorhees v. McGinnis, 48 N. Y. 278.

[34] Day v. Perkins, 2 Sandf. Ch. (N. Y.) 359.

[35] Tillman v. De Lacy, 80 Ala. 103; Crane v. Brigham, 11 N. J. Eq. 29; Randolph v. Gwynne, 7 N. J. Eq. 88, 51 Am. Dec. 265; Vail v. Weaver, 132 Pa. St. 363, 19 Atl. 138, 19 Am. St. 598; Padgett v. Cleveland, 33 S. Car. 339, 11 S. E. 1069.

[36] Carpenter v. Walker, 140 Mass.

416, 5 N. E. 160; Early v. Burtis, 40 N. J. Eq. 501, 4 Atl. 765. See also Long v. Cockern, 128 Ill. 29, 21 N. E. 201; McLaughlin v. Nash, 14 Allen (Mass.) 136, 92 Am. Dec. 741.

[37] Corliss v. McLagin, 29 Maine 115. In Trull v. Fuller, 28 Maine 545, the owner of a saw-mill made a mortgage of a clapboard-machine and shingle-machine set up in the saw-mill and used there, which was recorded as a personal mortgage. Subsequently a creditor of the mortgagor levied an execution upon the land and mill, and it was held that these machines passed to a purchaser of real estate under the execution as parcel of the realty. But in Wells v. Maples, 15 Hun (N. Y.) 90, a shingle-machine not fastened to the building, except so far as necessary to keep it in place, was held not to be covered by a mortgage of the realty. A similar decision was made in Choate v. Kimball, 56 Ark. 55, 19 S. W. 108.

[38] Robertson v. Corsett, 39 Mich. 777; Coleman v. Stearns Mfg. Co., 38 Mich. 30; Johnston v. Morrow, 60

machinery for making paper, fastened to a building or to its foundations, is regarded as a fixture.[30] So machinery in a fruit-canning factory.[40] So machinery for manufacturing soap.[41] So a vacuum pan in a milk condensing plant.[42] So machinery in a brewery.[43] So machinery in a nail factory.[44] So machinery in a cotton mill.[45] So machinery in a laundry plant.[46] So machinery in a cordage factory.[47] So pieces of machinery in a sugar mill, which if removed would be only scrap iron.[48] So heavy machinery in brick works.[49] So a cupola and crane bricked into a factory.[50] So an elevator and its appurtenances.[51] So a machine for turning kegs, a machine for joining staves, and a machine for cutting staves, were held to pass by a mortgage of a keg factory in which they were used, and to which they were attached.[52]

But, on the other hand, a planing and matching machine, and a machine for making moldings, used in a sash and blind factory, were held not to pass by a mortgage of the realty.[53] And so machinery in a saw-mill, attached by screws and bolts, but removable without in-

Mo. 339; Burnside v. Twitchell, 43 N. H. 390. See also Humes v. Higman, 145 Ala. 215, 40 So. 128; Helm v. Gilroy, 20 Ore. 517, 26 Pac. 851.

[39] Hill v. Farmers' &c. Nat. Bank, 97 U. S. 450, 24 L. ed. 1051; Fish v. New York Water Proof Paper Co., 29 N. J. Eq. 16; Quinby v. Manhattan Cloth &c. Co., 24 N. J. Eq. 260. See also First Nat. Bank v. Adam, 138 Ill. 483, 28 N. E. 955; Bowen v. Wood, 35 Ind. 268; Lathrop v. Blake, 23 N. H. 46; Walrath v. Henderson, 6 Wkly. Dig. (N. Y.) 293.

[40] Dudley v. Hurst, 67 Md. 44, 8 Atl. 901.

[41] Lavenson v. Standard Soap Co., 80 Cal. 245, 22 Pac. 184.

[42] State Bank v. Fish, 120 N. Y. S. 365.

[43] Scheifele v. Schmitz, 42 N. J. Eq. 700, 1 Atl. 698; Neilson v. Williams, 42 N. J. Eq. 291, 11 Atl. 257. See also Equitable Trust Co. v. Christ, 47 Fed. 756; Farmers' &c. Bank v. Cover, 1 Hayw. & H. (D. C.) 177, Fed. Cas. No. 4653. But see Dehring v. Beck, 146 Mich. 706, 110 N. W. 56; Wolford v. Baxter, 33 Minn. 12, 53 Am. Rep. 1; Fitzgerald v. Atlanta Home Ins. Co., 61 App. Div. 350, 70 N. Y. S. 552, holding casks, bottles, and packing cases to

be personalty; Meyer v. Orynski (Tex. Civ. App.), 25 S. W. 655.

[44] Delaware, L. &c. R. Co. v. Oxford Iron Co., 36 N. J. Eq. 452.

[45] William Firth Co. v. South Carolina L. &c. Co., 122 Fed. 569, 59 C. C. A. 73.

[46] Atlantic Safe Deposit &c. Co. v. Atlantic City Laundry Co., 64 N. J. Eq. 140, 53 Atl. 212.

[47] Knickerbocker Trust Co. v. Penn Cordage Co., 66 N. J. Eq. 305, 58 Atl. 409, 105 Am. St. 640; McRea v. Central Nat. Bank, 66 N. Y. 489.

[48] Folse v. Triche, 113 La. 915, 37 So. 875; Swoop v. St. Martin, 110 La. 237, 34 So. 426.

[49] Fisk v. People's Nat. Bank, 14 Colo. App. 21, 59 Pac. 63; Simpson Brick-Press Co. v. Wormley, 61 Ill. App. 460. But see C. W. Raymond Co. v. Ball, 210 Fed. 217.

[50] Lord v. Detroit Sav. Bank, 132 Mich. 510, 93 N. W. 1063.

[51] Condit v. Goodwin, 44 Misc. 312, 89 N. Y. S. 827.

[52] Laflin v. Griffiths, 35 Barb. (N. Y.) 58. See also Snedeker v. Warring, 12 N. Y. 170; Walker v. Sherman, 20 Wend. (N. Y.) 636.

[53] Rogers v. Brokaw, 25 N. J. Eq. 496. See also Wells v. Maples, 15 Hun (N. Y.) 90.

jury to the building, do not constitute a part of the realty.[54] And so machines used in a shoe-shop, although attached to the building by nails and bolts, are not covered by a mortgage of the realty.[55]

To constitute such machines fixtures, they must be actually annexed to the freehold in such a way as to evince an intention of making them a permanent accession to the freehold.[56]

Where, in the case of machinery, the principal part is a fixture by actual annexation to the soil, parts not physically annexed, but which, if removed, would leave the principal thing unfit for use, and would not of themselves, and standing alone, be well adapted for general use elsewhere, are considered constructively annexed.[57]

The wires of an electric light company, engaged in lighting a city, are an integral part of the company's lot of land, and machinery situated upon the lot for producing the light, and they pass as fixtures under a mortgage of the lot with all machinery and appurtenances.[58]

§ 448.　**Looms in a mill.**—In the English courts there have been several cases involving the determination of the question whether looms in a mill pass by mortgage of it in which they are not particularly named.[59] A mortgage was made of a mill "with the ware-house, counting-house, engine-house, boiler-house, weaving-shed, wash-house, gas-works, and reservoirs belonging, adjoining, or near thereto, and also the steam-engine, shafting, going-gear, machinery, and all other fixtures whatever," affixed to the land and premises. The assignees

---

[54] Neufelder v. Third St. &c. R. Co., 23 Wash. 470, 63 Pac. 197, 53 L. R. A. 600, 83 Am. St. 831.

[55] McConnell v. Blood, 123 Mass. 47, 25 Am. Rep. 12; Padgett v. Cleveland, 33 S. Car. 339, 11 S. E. 1069. But see Fifield v. Farmers' Nat. Bank, 148 Ill. 163, 35 N. E. 802, 39 Am. St. 166; Helm v. Gilroy, 20 Ore. 517, 26 Pac. 851.

[56] In re Eagle Horseshoe Co., 163 Fed. 699; Roddy v. Brick, 42 N. J. Eq. 218; Blancke v. Rogers, 26 N. J. Eq. 563; Kendall v. Hathaway, 67 Vt. 122, 30 Atl. 859.

[57] Dudley v. Hurst, 67 Md. 44, 8 Atl. 901. "Thus the key of a lock, the sail of a windmill, the leather belting of a saw-mill, although actually severed from the principal thing and stored elsewhere, pass by constructive annexation. They must be such as to go to complete the machinery which is affixed to the

land, and which, if removed, would leave the principal thing incomplete and unfit for use." Per Stone, J. In this case the entire machinery of a fruit-canning factory was held to pass under a mortgage, though some articles, such as crates, capping-machines, and work-tables, were not actually annexed to the soil; but being essentially necessary to the working of the principal machinery, they were regarded as constructively annexed.

[58] Fechet v. Drake, 2 Ariz. 239, 12 Pac. 694; Régina v. North Staffordshire R. Co., 3 El. & El. 392. See also New York Security &c. Co. v. Saratoga Gas &c. Co., 157 N. Y. 689, 51 N. E. 1092; Vail v. Weaver, 132 Pa. St. 363, 19 Atl. 138, 19 Am. St. 598.

[59] Holland v. Hodgson, L. R. 7 C. P. 328, 41 L. J. C. P. (N. S.) 146, 20 W. R. 990.

in bankruptcy of the mortgagor took possession of and sold, among other things, a large number of looms that were in the mill. Each loom rested upon four feet, and was attached to the floor by means of a wooden plug driven through each foot. The mortgagee claimed the looms as part of his security, and the Court of Common Pleas gave judgment in his favor, and this was affirmed by the Court of Exchequer Chamber.[60]

The American cases are to like effect; and it is not essential that the machinery is attached to the building otherwise than by its own

[60] In the latter court Mr. Justice Blackburn said: "Since the decision of this court in Climie v. Wood, L. R. 3 Exch. 257, and on appeal, L. R. 4 Exch. 328, it must be considered as settled law (except perhaps in the House of Lords), that what are commonly known as trade or tenant's fixtures form part of the land, and pass by a conveyance of it; and that though, if the person who erected those fixtures was a tenant with a limited interest in the land, he has a right as against the freeholder to sever the fixtures from the land, yet, if he be a mortgagor in fee he has no right as against his mortgage. * * * It was admitted, and we think properly admitted, that where there is a conveyance of the land the fixtures are transferred, not as fixtures, but as a part of the land, and the deed of transfer does not require registration as a bill of sale."

The learned judge further says that it has been contended, and justly, that Hellawell v. Eastwood, 6 Exch. 295, is very like the present case, with this exception: that there the tenant had a limited interest only, whereas here he has the fee; and if that case should apply to this case, it would follow (but for that exception, perhaps) that the looms which were in question remained chattels. But that case was decided in 1851. In 1853, the Court of Queen's Bench had, in Wiltshear v. Cottrell, 1 E. & B. 674, to consider what articles passed by the conveyance in fee of a farm; and there the court decided that a certain threshing-machine inside a barn, fixed by screws and bolts to four posts which were let into the earth, passed by the conveyance. It seems difficult to point out how the threshing-machine in that case was more for the improvement of the inheritance of the farm than the looms in the present case were for the improvement of the manufactory. Then there was the case of Mather v. Fraser, 2 Kay & J. 536, in 1856, and that of Walmsley v. Milne, 7 C. B. (N. S.) 115, in 1859, in which similar decisions to that in Wiltshear v. Cottrell were given. These cases "seem authorities for this principle,—that when an article is affixed by the owner of the fee, though only affixed by bolts and screws, it is to be considered as part of the land, at all events where the object of setting up the article is to enhance the value of the premises to which it is annexed, for the purposes to which those premises are applied. The threshing-machine in Wiltshear v. Cottrell was affixed by the owner of the fee to the barn as an adjunct to the barn, and to improve its usefulness as a barn, in much the same way as the hay-cutter in Walmsley v. Milne was affixed to the stable as an adjunct to it, and to improve its usefulness as a stable. And it seems difficult to say that the machinery in Mather v. Fraser was not as much affixed to the mill as an adjunct to it, and to improve the usefulness of the mill as such, as either the threshing-machine or the hay-cutter." In conclusion, he says, it is of great importance that the law as to what is the security of a mortgage should be settled, and that these decisions should not be reversed unless clearly wrong.

weight.[61] But a mortgage of a woolen factory has been held not to pass the looms used in it for the manufacture of broadcloth, the looms being merely fastened to the floor by screws to keep them in their places.[62]

§ 449. Cotton looms.—Under a mortgage of a mill for the manufacture of cotton cloth, with the appurtenances, "together with the steam-engines, boilers, shafting, piping, mill-gearing, gasometers, gas-pipes, drums, wheels, and all and singular other the machines, fixtures, and effects fixed up in or attached or belonging to the said mill or factory, buildings, or premises," the question arose, upon a subsequent sale of the estate under a power of sale contained in the mortgage, whether a large number of looms for weaving cotton yarn into cloth, and which were set into the floors without any fastening, passed by mortgage, and by the subsequent sale. Lord Romilly, giving the decision of the Court of Chancery,[63] said: "My opinion is that those words mean that the mill and everything that properly belongs to the mill is the thing that is mortgaged. I do not think that the furniture of the mill does properly belong to the mill; it is liable to be changed from time to time. * * * I do not doubt that looms are machinery in one sense, but the question is, are they properly speaking machinery belonging to the mill? In one sense, no doubt, they belong to the mill, because they are put into the mill, but I read those words as 'belonging essentially to the mill,' and forming necessarily a part of it, whatever may be the purpose to which the mill may be applied. To whatever purpose the mill may be applied, the steam-power, the gas-lighting, and the like, do form a part of it; the others are merely accidental, and no more form a part of the mill than a carpet forms part of a house. If a house and all the things belonging to the house were assigned, that would not necessarily include the furniture unless it was so specified. * * * I am clear the looms are not fixtures in any proper sense of the term."[64]

In like manner, in a comparatively recent case in New Jersey, it was held that spinning-frames, twisting-frames, and like machinery,

[61] Equitable Guarantee &c. Co. v. Knowles, 8 Del. Ch. 106, 67 Atl. 961; Lyle v. Palmer, 42 Mich. 314, 3 N. W. 921; Cavis v. Beckford, 62 N. H. 229, 13 Am. St. 554. See ante § 444.

[62] Murdock v. Gifford, 18 N. Y. 28. See also McRea v. Central Nat. Bank, 66 N. Y. 498.

[63] Hutchinson v. Kay, 23 Beav. 413. See also McKim v. Mason, 3 Md. Ch. Dec. 186, relating to machinery for the manufacture of cotton goods. See ante § 444.

[64] Not in accord with ante §§ 444, 448 and post § 450.

though fastened to the floors by nails or screws, or held in position by cleats, are personal property, and pass under a chattel mortgage as against a mortgage of the realty subsequently given; but that the steam-engine, boilers, shafting, belting, couplings and pulleys used to communicate the power, the water-wheels and water-wheel governors, the gas-generator and gas-pump connected with it, the gas-pipes and burners, and the steam-heating pipes, whether laid on hooks along the walls or resting on the floor, are parts of the mill and pass by the mortgage of the realty as against a prior chattel mortgage.[65]

Hardly in accord with these cases is a decision in Massachusetts. The mortgage of a cotton mill covered also "all machinery, tools, and fixtures therewith appertaining." The mill was built for, and had always been used for, the manufacture of cotton cloth. The question arose whether the mortgage covered certain looms subsequently put into the mill. These looms were not specially built for use in this particular mill, and could equally well be used for the same purpose in any other cotton-mill, with the ordinary room to hold them, and power to operate them. Said loooms were each about seven feet long, three feet wide, two and one-half feet high, and of six hundred pounds weight, screwed down to the flooring of the weaving-room in order to steady them when in use, and connected by pulleys, belts, and shafting with the power operating the factory. They did not replace machines like them, and were used for the manufacture of a kind of cloth different from that made in the mill when it was mortgaged. It was held that the machinery became a part of the realty and was subject to the mortgage.[66]

§ 450. Machinery of a silk-mill.—A silk manufacturer mortgaged certain land, "also all that silk-mill there erected or in the course of erection, and all other buildings then or thereafter to be erected thereon; and also all those the steam-engine or steam-engines, boilers, steam-pipes, main shafting, mill gearing, mill-wright's work, and all other machinery and fixtures whatsoever there erected or set up, or to be thereafter, etc., upon the said plat of land, mill, and premises, with the appurtenances."[67] A second mortgage was made more comprehensive in terms; and the first mortgagee having sold the property under an order of court, the question arose upon a claim by the second

[65] Keeler v. Keeler, 31 N. J. Eq. 181.

[66] Hopewell Mills v. Taunton Sav. Bank, 150 Mass. 519, 23 N. E. 327, 15 Am. St. Rep. 235. The opinion by Mr. Justice Knowlton deserves careful study.

[67] Haley v. Hammersley, 3 De Gex, F. & J. 587, 9 W. R. 562.

mortgagee whether the spinning-mills and other machinery passed under the first mortgage. The Master of the Rolls held that only such machinery passed by the mortgage under the words "other machinery" as was of the same nature with the articles specified in the enumeration previously made, and that therefore only the machinery used for the purpose of giving power to the mill was included in the mortgage. On appeal, however, it was decided that all the machinery placed in the mill, whether for creating power or for being moved, was included in the mortgage. "It seems rather improbable," said Lord Chancellor Campbell, "that the parties should have contemplated such a damaging disruption of the machinery as must take place if the mortgagees, in seeking to make good their security, must tear in pieces the machinery in the mill, removing and selling one-half of it, which would be comparatively of little value without the other half." He concurs with the Vice-Chancellor Page Wood, in his general view of the law upon this subject in Mather v. Fraser,[68] and is of opinion that, according to the true construction of the mortgage deed, all the disputed articles are included in the mortgage to the defendants.

§ **451. Machinery in iron rolling-mill.**—A mortgage of an iron rolling-mill was held to pass the entire set of rolls used in the mill, whether in place and fixed for use or temporarily detached.[69] The rolls, being adapted to the manufacture of bars of different shapes and sizes, can not all be used at once; but they are equally a part of the mill when unfixed to give place to others. "Duplicates necessary and proper for an emergency," said Chief Justice Gibson, "consequently follow the realty, on the principle by which duplicate keys of a banking-house or the toll-dishes of a mill follow it." A similar decision was made in a comparatively recent case in England.[70]

[68] 2 K. & J. 536.

[69] Voorhis v. Freeman, 2 Watts & S. (Pa.) 116, 37 Am. Dec. 490. See also McFadden v. Crawford, 36 W. Va. 671, 15 S. E. 408, 32 Am. St. 894.

[70] Ex parte Astbury, L. R. 4 Ch. App. 630. Mr. Justice Giffard, giving the opinion, said: "There appear to be connected with rolling machines parts which, beyond all doubt, are not fixed, in the strict sense of the term; but it is in evidence that if a machine is ordered it is sent with one set of rolls, and it is quite manifest that without rolls the machine could not do any part of the work for which it is made. One set of rolls clearly passes. But we have here duplicate rolls, and with reference to them—I am not now speaking of rolls which can be considered as in any sense unfinished, but of duplicate rolls which have been actually fitted to the machine—I can not see why, if one set of rolls passes, the duplicate rolls should not pass also. It comes, in fact, to this, that the machine with one set of rolls is a perfect

In the same case it was held that the straightening plates embedded in the floor were also fixtures, but that the weighing machines were not.

III. *Rolling Stock of Railways*

§ 452. Rolling stock and fixtures generally.—Whether the rolling stock and fixtures of a railroad are personal property, or are in some sense fixtures, and therefore pass by a mortgage of the realty, is a question that has been much discussed, and the decisions are conflicting. On the one hand it is said that railway cars are a necessary part of the entire establishment; that their wheels are fitted to the rails; that they are peculiarly adapted to the use of the railway, and can not be used for any other purpose; and that they are necessary incidents of the real estate in a mortgage of it. In an early case before the Supreme Court of New York, it was decided that rolling stock was to be deemed fixtures.[1] But the Court of Appeals several

machine, but the machine with a duplicate set is a more perfect machine. * * * The fact is that, whether there is one set of rolls or a duplicate set, they are each part and parcel of the machine, and come within the term 'belonging to the machine as a part of it.' Dictum, of Lord Cottenham in Fisher v. Dixon, 12 Cl. & F. 312. Then comes the case as to the different sizes of rolls. But if the duplicates of the same size pass, it follows that the rolls of different sizes pass, if they render the machine still more perfect than if the rolls were all of the same size. * * * But I can not hold that the rolls which have never been fitted to the machine, and have never been used in the machine, and which require something more to be done to them before they are fitted to the machine, belong to the machine, or that they are essential parts of it."

[1] Farmers' Loan &c. Co. v. Hendrickson, 25 Barb. (N. Y.) 484. Mr. Justice Strong, delivering the opinion of the court, said: "The property of a railway company consists mainly of the road-bed, the rails upon it, the depot erections, and the rolling stock, and the franchises to hold and use them. The road-bed, the rails fastened to it, and the buildings at the depots, are clearly real property. That the locomotives and passenger, baggage, and freight cars are a part, and a necessary part, of the entire establishment, there can be no doubt. Are they so permanently and inseparably connected with the more substantial realty as to become constructively fixtures? * * * It may be that if an appeal should be made to the common sense of the community, it would be determined that the term 'fixtures' could not well be applied to such movable carriages as railway cars. But such cars move no more rapidly than do pigeons from a dovecote or fish in a pond, both of which are annexed to the realty."

This decision was followed in Stevens v. Buffalo &c. R. Co., 31 Barb. (N. Y.) 590, and Beardsley v. Ontario Bank, 31 Barb. (N. Y.) 619, holding that rolling stock is personalty, and a mortgage of it subject to the Chattel Mortgage Act. A few years later the same court held that a mortgage of a railroad need not be recorded as a chattel mortgage in

years afterward established the doctrine in this state to be that rolling stock is personal in its character, and that a mortgage of it must be recorded as a chattel mortgage.[2]

The federal courts have held that all property essential to the operation of a railroad, including the right of way, road-bed, ties, rails, side-tracks, switches, depots, station-houses, water tanks, and other fixtures, together with the rolling stock and other necessary movable appliances, are real estate.[3]

The same ruling is made by the courts of many states,[4] in some of which, however, the character of rolling stock as property is fixed by statute.[5] In those states in which the subject is uncontrolled by statute, the preponderance of authority is to the effect that only the land owned by the railroad company, together with the ties, rails and other structures permanently affixed thereto, is realty; and that engines, cars, and other movable appliances are to be regarded for most purposes as personalty.[6]

As a summary of the adjudications upon this subject, it may be said that, while there are many and strong arguments for holding that rolling stock is part of the realty of a railroad,[7] and this view seems

order to bind the rolling stock. Bement v. Plattsburgh &c. R. Co., 47 Barb. (N. Y.) 104, 51 Barb. 45.

[2] Hoyle v. Plattsburgh &c. R. Co., 54 N. Y. 314, 13 Am. Rep. 595; Randall v. Elwell, 52 N. Y. 521, 11 Am. Rep. 747.

[3] Gloucester Ferry Co. v. Pennsylvania, 114 U. S. 196, 29 L. ed. 158, 5 Sup. Ct. 826; Minnesota Co. v. St. Paul Co., 2 Wall. (U. S.) 609, 17 L. ed. 886; Pennock v. Coe, 23 How. (U. S.) 117, 16 L. ed. 436; Farmers' Loan &c. Co. v. St. Joseph &c. R. Co., 3 Dill (U. S.) 412, Fed. Cas. No. 4669; Union Loan &c. Co. v. Southern Cal. Motor Rd. Co., 51 Fed. 840.

[4] Palmer v. Forbes, 23 Ill. 301; Louisville &c. R. Co. v. State, 25 Ind. 177, 87 Am. Dec. 358; Farmers' Loan &c. Co. v. Hendrickson, 25 Barb. (N. Y.) 484; Youngman v. Elmira &c. R. Co., 65 Pa. St. 278; Webster Lumber Co. v. Keystone L. &c. Co., 51 W. Va. 545, 42 S. E. 632, 66 L. R. A. 33.

[5] 1 Stimson's Am. St. Law. § 468. See also Phillips v. Winslow, 18 B. Mon. (Ky.) 431, 68 Am. Dec. 729;

Miller v. Rutland &c. R. Co., 36 Vt. 452.

[6] Neilson v. Iowa Eastern R. Co., 51 Iowa 184, 1 N. W. 434, 33 Am. Rep. 124; Boston &c. R. Co. v. Gilmore, 37 N. H. 410, 72 Am. Dec. 336; Williamson v. New Jersey S. R. Co., 29 N. J. Eq. 311; Hoyle v. Plattsburgh &c. R. Co., 54 N. Y. 314, 13 Am. Rep. 595; Randall v. Elwell, 52 N. Y. 521, 11 Am. Rep. 747; Coe v. Columbus &c. R. Co., 10 Ohio St. 372, 75 Am. Dec. 518; Chicago &c. R. Co. v. Ft. Howard, 21 Wis. 44, 91 Am. Dec. 458.

[7] Meyer v. Johnston, 53 Ala. 237, 332; Titus v. Mabee, 25 Ill. 257; Hunt v. Bullock, 23 Ill. 320; Palmer v. Forbes, 23 Ill. 301; Phillips v. Winslow, 18 B. Mon. (Ky.) 431, 68 Am. Dec. 729; Douglass v. Cline, 12 Bush (Ky.) 608; Morrill v. Noyes, 56 Maine 458, 96 Am. Dec. 486; State v. Northern Cent. R. Co., 18 Md. 193; Pierce v. Emery, 32 N. H. 484; Youngman v. Elmira &c. R. Co., 65 Pa. St. 278; Covey v. Pittsburgh, Fort Wayne &c. R. Co., 3 Phila. (Pa.) 173.

to have the support of the United States courts,[7a]—the weight of authority in the state courts seems to be against that position.[7b]

The question of what is permanently affixed to a railroad right of way is one partly of law and partly of fact, mainly dependent on the purpose of the builders, whether, for example, it be to construct a main line or side branches for temporary use.[8]

§ 452a. What fixtures included under railroad mortgage.—The extent of property covered by a railroad mortgage is a matter of interpretation under the rules applicable to the interpretation of mortgages by individuals, reference, however, being had to the authorizing statute.[9]

Fixtures, whether acquired before or after the execution of such mortgage, are subject to its lien.[10]

On the principle that fixtures, though subsequently severed, are subject to the lien of a mortgage of the freehold, worn-out rails replaced by new ones have been held to be included in a railroad mortgage; and so of new rails not yet laid.[11] A track laid merely for a temporary use has been held not to come under the lien as part of the realty;[12] so have repair tools,[13] fuel[14] and furniture.[15]

A mortgage of a railroad, if its terms cover such future acquisitions,

[7a] Pennock v. Coe, 23 How. (U. S.) 117; Galveston R. Co. v. Cowdrey, 11 Wall. (U. S.) 459; Dunham v. Cincinnati &c. R. Co., 1 Wall. (U. S.) 254; Minnesota Co. v. St. Paul Co., 2 Wall. (U. S.) 609; Farmers' Loan &c. Co. v. St. Joseph &c. R. Co., 3 Dill. 412; Clinton v. Springfield R. Co., 6 Biss. 529; Pullam v. Cincinnati &c. R. Co., 4 Biss. 35.

[7b] Williamson v. New Jersey Southern R. Co., 29 N. J. Eq. 311; Coe v. Columbus &c. R. Co., 10 Ohio St. 372, 75 Am. Dec. 518; Boston &c. R. Co. v. Gilmore, 37 N. H. 410, 22 Am. Dec. 336. See also Jones on Corporate Bonds and Mortgages, §§ 136-144.

[8] Van Keuren v. Central R. Co., 38 N. J. L. 165.

[9] Wilson v. Gaines, 103 U. S. 417, 26 L. ed. 401; Coe v. New Jersey Midland &c. R. Co., 31 N. J. Eq. 105.

[10] Porter v. Pittsburg &c. Steel Co., 122 U. S. 267, 30 L. ed. 1210, 7 Sup. Ct. 1206; Wood v. Whelen, 93 Ill. 153.

[11] Palmer v. Forbes, 23 Ill. 301; Brainerd v. Peck, 34 Vt. 496; First Nat. Bank v. Anderson, 75 Va. 250; Farmers' Loan &c. Co. v. Commercial Bank, 11 Wis. 207, 15 Wis. 424, 82 Am. Dec. 689.

[12] Van Keuren v. Central R. Co., 38 N. J. L. 165.

[13] Lehigh &c. Co. v. Central R. Co., 35 N. J. Eq. 379; Williamson v. New Jersey &c. R. Co., 29 N. J. Eq. 311, revg. 28 N. J. Eq. 277; Brainerd v. Peck, 34 Vt. 496. But see Delaware, L. &c. R. Co. v. Oxford Iron Co., 36 N. J. Eq. 452.

[14] Hunt v. Bullock, 23 Ill. 320. But see Coe v. McBrown, 22 Ind. 252; Phillips v. Winslow, 18 B. Mon. (Ky.) 431, 68 Am. Dec. 729.

[15] Raymond v. Clark, 46 Conn. 129; Titus v. Mabee, 25 Ill. 257; Hunt v. Bullock, 23 Ill. 320; Lehigh &c. Co. v. Central R. Co., 35 N. J. Eq. 379; Southbridge Savings Bank v. Mason, 147 Mass. 500, 18 N. E. 406, 1 L. R. A. 350. But see Wood v. Whelen, 93 Ill. 153.

will, however, be held in equity to apply to after-acquired rolling stock,[16] even if not specially mentioned; although it has been held that loose rolling stock, such as engines and cars, is, in such a case, subject to the lien on it[17] when it comes into the mortgagor's hands.[18]

IV. *Remedies for Removal of Fixtures*

§ **453. Remedies of mortgagee in general—Replevin.**—The mortgagee may follow and take fixtures covered by a mortgage of the realty, and improperly removed, wherever he can find them.[1] The mortgagor himself can of course gain no right to hold them as against the mortgagee. A purchaser from the mortgagor has no such right, because he is affected with knowledge of the existing lien, and as against the mortgagee his purchase is therefore fraudulent and void. "Even without knowledge of the mortgage," says Chief Justice Lowrie, of Pennsylvania,[2] "it is hard to see how a purchaser could be relieved from this responsibility; for all purchasers, hirers, and renters are bound to ascertain, or take the risk of assuming, the title of their vendors and lessors. But may not a mortgagor sell in the usual way the lumber, firewood, coal, ore, or grain found growing on the land, without violating the rights of the mortgagee? Yes, he may, until the mortgagee stops him by ejectment or estrepement, for those things are usually intended for consumption and sale, and the sale of them is the usual way of raising the money to pay the mortgage. But in the case of a factory or other building it is from the use of it as it is, and not by its consumption or its sale by piecemeal, that all its profits are to be derived."

[16] Galveston, H. &c. R. Co. v. Cowdrey, 11 Wall (U. S.) 459, 20 L. ed. 199; Pennock v. Coe, 23 How. (U. S.) 117, 16 L. ed. 436; Scott v. Clinton &c. R. Co., 6 Biss. (U. S.) 529, Fed. Cas. No. 12527; Meyer v. Johnston, 53 Ala. 237, 64 Ala. 603; Phillips v. Winslow, 18 B. Mon. (Ky.) 431, 68 Am. Dec. 729; Hamlin v. Jerrard, 72 Maine 62; Morrill v. Noyes, 56 Maine 458, 96 Am. Dec. 486; Nichols v. Mase, 94 N. Y. 160.

[17] Meyer v. Johnston, 53 Ala. 237, 64 Ala. 603; Maryland v. Northern Central R. Co., 18 Md. 193. But see Miller v. Rutland &c. R. Co., 36 Vt. 452.

[18] United States v. New Orleans R. Co., 12 Wall (U. S.) 362, 20 L. ed. 434; Contracting &c. Co. v. Continental Trust Co., 108 Fed. 1; Boston Safe Deposit &c. Co. v. Bankers' &c. Tel. Co., 36 Fed. 288.

[1] See post §§ 687, 688.

[2] Hoskin v. Woodward, 45 Pa. St. 42.

The mortgagee's right of action is based upon his general legal ownership under his mortgage, or upon his actual or constructive possession at the time of severance.[3] The mortgagee, having the legal title to the property, may maintain replevin for fixtures removed from the realty.[4]

Articles retaining their character as personalty by virtue of an express or implied agreement, and which have been wrongfully severed from the realty, may be recovered by the mortgagee in an action in replevin.[5] If after the foreclosure of a mortgage the mortgagor wrongfully removes a house from the land, the purchaser having the legal title may maintain replevin for it.[6]

It is held, however, under a different view of the nature of a mortgage, that when a fixture, as, for instance, a house, annexed to the real estate by the mortgagor, is afterward, before the foreclosure of the mortgage, by him removed from the premises and sold, although it was part of the mortgaged premises, the mortgagee can not recover it from the purchaser; that by the removal he has lost his right to the property, though he might still have a cause of action for the waste.[7] But justice would seem to demand, and authority supports this position, that one purchasing what he either actually or constructively knows to be mortgaged to another shall not be allowed to shelter himself behind his wrongful act, and say that thereby the nature of the property was changed. The remedy of the mortgagee, in states where a mortgage is regarded as merely a lien for security, is not at law but in equity; not replevin to recover the property severed, but generally injunction to restrain the commission of waste.[8]

Even in New Jersey, where the mortgagee is regarded as having the legal title for the purpose of asserting and maintaining his pos-

---

[3] Gooding v. Shea, 103 Mass. 360; Verner v. Betz, 46 N. J. Eq. 256, 19 Atl. 206. See ante § 144 and post § 688.

[4] Dutro v. Kennedy, 9 Mont. 101, 22 Pac. 763. See this case, also, on the question of damages in such suit for the removal of the fixtures.

[5] Ott v. Specht, 8 Houst. (Del.) 61, 12 Atl. 721; Adams v. Tully, 164 Ind. 292, 73 N. E. 595; Hartwell v. Kelly, 117 Mass. 235; Gill v. De Armant, 90 Mich. 425, 51 N. W. 527; Weathersby v. Sleeper, 42 Miss. 732; Hines v. Ament, 43 Mo. 298; Page v. Urick, 31 Wash. 601, 72 Pac. 454, 96 Am. St. 924.

[6] Matzon v. Griffin, 78 Ill. 477. See post § 688.

[7] Clark v. Reyburn, 1 Kans. 281; Harris v. Bannon, 78 Ky. 568. To like effect see Citizens' Bank v. Knapp, 22 La. Ann. 117; Buckout v. Swift, 27 Cal. 433, 87 Am. Dec. 90; Woehler v. Endter, 46 Wis. 301, 50 N. W. 1099.

[8] Williams v. Chicago Exhibition Co., 188 Ill. 19, 58 N. E. 611; Vanderslice v. Knapp, 20 Kans. 647; Dudley v. Hurst, 67 Md. 44, 8 Atl. 901; State Sav. Bank v. Kercheval, 65 Mo. 682; Verner v. Betz, 46 N. J. Eq. 256, 19 Atl. 206; Taylor v. Collins, 51 Wis. 123, 8 N. W. 22.

session, he is not allowed to maintain replevin for fixtures wrongfully removed;[9] but he may maintain an action on the case for the injury to the security.[10] Where a mortgagor in possession removed a building to another lot of land, to make room for part of a larger building and improvements, and sold the lot, and building affixed to it, to a bona fide purchaser, it was held, on a bill for foreclosure of the mortgage, that the building could not be returned to the mortgaged land, and the remedy of the mortgagee was at law for the removal of the building.[11]

If the owner of the equity of redemption moves a house from the mortgaged premises to another tract of land not covered by the mortgage, the lien on the house is not thereby impaired. The court may decree a sale of the house in its new situs, under the mortgage, with leave to the purchaser to remove or roll the building off again.[12] Where a house was wrongfully removed from mortgaged premises and permanently attached to other real estate, it was held that replevin was not the proper remedy, but the mortgagee might recover damages for its removal.[13]

The mortgage lien may be enforced as against one who has purchased the house without knowledge that it had been removed from the mortgaged land.[14]

§ 454. Mortgagee's remedy against mortgagor for removal of fixtures.—The mortgagee, by virtue of his interest in the property, may maintain an action against the mortgagor for removing fixtures, and thereby causing substantial and permanent injury and depreciation to the mortgaged estate. The owner of the equity has no more right than a stranger to impair the security of the mortgage. The damages are measured by the extent of the injury, and not by the insufficiency of the remaining security. The mortgagee is not obliged to apply in the first place the property that remains at any valuation whatever. "He is entitled to the full benefit of the entire mortgaged estate for the full payment of his entire debt."[15]

[9] Kircher v. Schalk, 39 N. J. L. 335. See post § 688.

[10] Verner v. Betz, 46 N. J. Eq. 256, 19 Atl. 206; Jackson v. Turrell, 39 N. J. L. 329.

[11] Verner v. Betz, 46 N. J. Eq. 256, 19 Atl. 206.

[12] Turner v. Mebane, 110 N. Car. 413, 14 S. E. 974.

[13] Dorr v. Dudderar, 88 Ill. 107. See also Ricketts v. Dorrell, 55 Ind. 470.

[14] Partridge v. Hemenway, 89 Mich. 454, 50 N. W. 1084.

[15] Byrom v. Chapin, 113 Mass. 308. Otherwise, where a mortgage is regarded as a mere lien and not a title to the land. There the insufficiency of the security must be shown. Gardner v. Heartt, 3 Denio (N. Y.) 232; Lane v. Hitchcock, 14 Johns. (N. Y.) 213.

But a different rule of damages prevails in states where a mortgage is regarded as merely an equitable conveyance to secure the debt. In those states it necessarily follows that an action by a mortgagee for any injury to the premises must be based, not upon the injury to the premises, in which he has only an equitable interest, but upon the loss occasioned to him by impairing his security. The measure of his damages is therefore limited to the loss he may sustain upon his security.[16] Under this rule the action must rest upon proof that, before the alleged injury, the mortgaged premises were of sufficient value to pay the plaintiff's mortgage, or a part of it, and that, by reason of such injury, they became inadequate for that purpose.[17] This is the rule in New York and New Jersey.[18]

[16] Schalk v. Kingsley, 42 N. J. L. 32; Van Pelt v. McGraw, 4 N. Y. 110. In the New York case the court said: "This action is not based upon the assumption that the plaintiff's land has been injured, but that his mortgage as a security has been impaired. His damages, therefore, would be limited to the amount of injury to the mortgage, however great the injury to the land might be."

[17] Schalk v. Kingsley, 42 N. J. L. 32, per Van Syckel, J.

[18] In Schalk v. Kingsley, 42 N. J. L. 32, the Supreme Court, discussing these different rules of damages, their adaptation to the nature of the mortgagee's estate, and the practical results produced by each, says: "There is much force in the Massachusetts view, that the mortgagee is entitled to be protected in the enjoyment of the security for which he contracted, however ample it may be, and the wrongdoer himself ought not to complain if he is compelled to restore what he unlawfully removed. Especially would this be so in the case of a mortgage maturing at a remote future period, when the real value of the premises would depend upon contingencies which might not be foreseen. But while injustice may in some cases be done by rejecting this rule, it is not in harmony with the nature of the mortgagee's estate, and its adoption in practice would lead to many difficulties. In Massachusetts, by force and effect of the mortgage, and as between the parties to the mortgage, the right of possession also passes immediately to the mortgagee, and carries with it the incidents of a right to sue in trespass for any injury to the freehold. There it may be a necessary logical sequence that in an action at law, the damages, which represent the injury to the premises, must go to the owner of the legal estate.

"The objections to the Massachusetts rule are obvious, and are not met, in my judgment, by the court in Gooding v. Shea, before cited. Such litigation would frequently result to the benefit of the mortgagor, by whose consent the wrong was committed, by operating as a satisfaction of the mortgage when the premises were still ample to satisfy the mortgage debt. A more serious objection would exist in the fact that the action would be maintainable for every slight injury to the freehold. The person who purchased and removed a stick of timber or a cord of wood, or the mechanic who tore down an old building preparatory to the erection of a new one, or who made any alteration in the structures upon the premises which might be deemed in any degree detrimental to their value, would be amenable to suit. But admitting that the third mortgagee may sue and recover for the entire injury to the premises, how shall the damages be appropriated, and how would the wrongdoer be shielded from further recovery by the first and second

When such injury has been done, there can be but one recovery for it, and a reasonable satisfaction made in good faith to a prior mortgagee bars an action by a subsequent mortgagee. If after the removal of the fixtures, and before the mortgagee brings an action of trespass to recover their value, he sells the mortgaged premises under a power of sale, and receives therefrom more than enough to pay his claim and all prior incumbrances, this fact may be shown in mitigation of his claim for damages.[19] But upon the question whether the injury had been settled and satisfied by payment to the first mortgagee, evidence is admissible to show that the articles removed were of greater value than the sum so paid, and that the damage done to the premises by their removal was greater than the value of the articles so removed.[20] In Wisconsin it is held the mortgagee after a decree of foreclosure may maintain an action for an injury done the mortgaged premises, either by the mortgagor or by a stranger, provided the security be thereby impaired and the mortgagor be insolvent.[21]

A mortgagee may recover the value of fixtures wrongfully removed

mortgagees? The prior mortgagees could not be made parties to such suit, and they would not be bound by the verdict as to the amount of damages found in favor of the third mortgagee; and, in our practice, there is no method in which the injury to each mortgagee could be ascertained, and the distribution properly made. In fact, the rule repels the idea of distribution, for it is based upon the notion that the mortgagee plaintiff is entitled to the entire damage done to the lands. A rule which would subject a defendant to pay to each of several mortgagees the full amount of damage which he had committed upon the premises would unhesitatingly be condemned.

"It is therefore suggested, in the Massachusetts cases, that but one recovery would be allowed, and that would afterward be appropriated under the direction of the court. Aside from the entire absence of any recognized procedure in our courts of law by which the several parties in interest could be bound by the verdict, and by which an appropriation could be made, such a course would manifestly be mere circumlocution, leading to the practical adoption of the other rule; for, in the end, the distribution would necessarily be made upon the basis of the actual loss to each mortgagee.

"All these difficulties would be obviated by adopting the injury to the security as the basis of damages. Under that rule, no suit can be maintained unless the plaintiff sustains a substantial injury; and each mortgagee in turn may, without reference to the other, recover such damage as he can show he has sustained on his part.

"The action must rest upon proof that, before the alleged injury, the mortgaged premises were of sufficient value to pay the plaintiff's mortgage, or a part of it, and that, by reason of such injury, they became inadequate for that purpose. In that view the extent of the loss can be approximately computed. This, in my opinion, is the better rule, and one which, in its practical application, will not be attended with any serious difficulty."

[19] King v. Bangs, 120 Mass. 514.
[20] Byrom v. Chapin, 113 Mass. 308.
[21] Jones v. Costigan, 12 Wis. 677, 78 Am. Dec. 771.

from the mortgaged premises, although since such removal of them the property has been sold under a power in his mortgage, and he has himself purchased it at a price sufficient to satisfy his claim. His title is sufficient to sustain a cause of action.[22]

§ 455. **Remedy of mortgagee out of possession.**—A mortgagee not having possession, or the right of possession, can not maintain an action of tort in the nature of trespass quare clausum fregit against a stranger for breaking and entering the mortgaged premises and removing fixtures. But the right to recover damages for the value of the fixtures is separable from that to recover for "breach to the close."[23]

The right of present possession only affects the form of action. The right to recover depends upon the title, and not upon possession or the right of possession. In an action of tort for forcibly entering the house and removing fixtures, the mortgagee, even before condition broken, may recover the full amount of damage done to the estate by the removal, without regard to the sufficiency of his security. Until the whole debt be paid, he can not be deprived of any substantial part of his entire security without full redress therefor. "As the injury affects the estate, it may be sued for directly by any one in whom the legal interest is vested. A second or third mortgagee, though not in possession, has a sufficient interest in the estate to maintain an action for such an injury. Although it is true that a stranger may thus be liable to either of the several mortgagees, as well as to the mortgagor, it does not follow that he is liable to all successively. The superior right is in the party having superiority of title. But the defendant can resist neither by merely showing that another may also sue or has sued. If he would defeat the claim of either, he must show that another having a superior right has appropriated the avails of the claim to himself. The demand is not personal to either mortgagee, but arises out of and pertains to the estate; and, when recovered, applies in payment, pro tanto, of the mortgage debt, and thus ultimately for the benefit of the mortgagor, if he redeems."[24]

The mortgagee, even before entering into possession, can maintain an action against the mortgagor or any other person who severs and

[22] Laflin v. Griffiths, 35 Barb. (N. Y.) 58.

[23] Gooding v. Shea, 103 Mass. 360, 4 Am. Rep. 563; Woodman v. Francis, 14 Allen (Mass.) 198; Page v. Robinson, 10 Cush. (Mass.) 99.

[24] Per Wells, J., in Gooding v. Shea, 103 Mass. 360, 4 Am. Rep. 563. In New Jersey the action is upon the case. Jackson v. Turrell, 39 N. J. L. 329.

removes from the mortgaged estate any articles which have been annexed to and made part of it. It makes no difference as against the mortgagee that the fixtures are severed by accident. Therefore, if a building be partly destroyed by fire, the mortgagor has no right to sell such parts of it as are saved; and he can not maintain an action for the price of such articles if the value of the land is less than the amount of the mortgage debt, and the mortgagee has entered for breach of the condition and forbidden the payment to the mortgagor.[25]

When the mortgagee has no right to enter and the mortgagor can be deprived of possession only by a foreclosure and sale, he may retain possession after the sale until the delivery of the deed to the purchaser; but if he removes fixtures in the meantime, the purchaser may recover them by an action of replevin. The purchaser's deed takes effect by relation at the date of the mortgage, and passes fixtures subsequently annexed by the mortgagor.[26]

A mortgagee not in actual possession and who has not entered to foreclose can not maintain trespass against the owner of the equity of redemption for cutting grass on the land, as the owner has a right to take every annual crop.[27] But if the property detached from the realty be fixtures subject as part of the realty to a mortgage, the mortgagee, whether in possession of the premises or not, may sue for the recovery of the things themselves in an action of replevin;[28] or may sue in trespass for damage done the freehold; or he may, in an action of trover, recover their value.[29] A tort-feasor has no right to complain of the form of the remedy.

---

[25] Wilmarth v. Bancroft, 10 Allen (Mass.) 348.

[26] Sands v. Pfeiffer, 10 Cal. 258. But see Alexander v. Shonyo, 20 Kans. 705; Vanderslice v. Knapp, 20 Kans. 647. See ante § 453 and post § 684.

[27] Woodward v. Pickett, 8 Gray (Mass.) 617.

[28] Laflin v. Griffiths, 35 Barb. (N. Y.) 58.

[29] Hitchman v. Walton, 4 M. & W. 409; Holland v. Hodgson, L. R. 7 C. P. 328.

CHAPTER XII

RECORDING AS AFFECTING PRIORITY[1]

I. *Nature and Application of Registry Acts,* §§ 456–487a
II. *Requisites as to Execution and Acknowledgment,* §§ 488–503
III. *Requisites as to the Time and Manner of Recording,* §§ 504–514a
IV. *Errors in the Record,* §§ 515–522
V. *The Effect of a Record Duly Made,* §§ 523–537
VI. *Torrens System of Registration,* §§ 537a–537g

I. *Nature and Application of Registry Acts*

[1] See in general on this subject Jones on Real Property, ch. xxxi, §§ 1386–1498.

671

§ 456. **Statutory provisions in general.**—In most of the states mortgages are required by statute to be recorded in the same manner as other conveyances of real property, in order to charge third persons acquiring interests in the property, such as subsequent purchasers, mortgagees, and judgment creditors.[2] In general, the statutes pro-

---

[2] Alabama: Code 1907, §§ 3383, 3384.

Alaska: Civ. Code 1900, § 98; Nestor v. Holt, 1 Alaska 567.

Arizona: Civ. Code 1901, par. 749, Rev. Stat. 1913, § 2080.

Arkansas: Dig. of Stat. 1904, § 763; Dodd v. Parker, 40 Ark. 536; Fry v. Martin, 33 Ark. 203.

California: Civ. Code 1906, §§ 1169–1171, 1214, 2950, 2952.

Colorado: Ann. Stats. 1891, § 446; Mills Ann. Stat. 1912, § 836, p. 390.

Connecticut: Gen. Stat. 1902, § 4036.

Delaware: Rev. Code 1874, p. 503, §§ 14–17.

District of Columbia: Rev. Stat. 1874, §§ 446, 447, as amended Apr. 29, 1878, 20 Stats. at Large, ch. 69; Code of Law 1911, §§ 521, 523.

Florida: Gen. Stat. 1906, § 2480.

Georgia: Code 1910, §§ 3259, 3260, 4198.

Idaho: Rev. Code 1908, §§ 3405, 3408.

Illinois: Hurds Rev. Stat. 1913, ch. 30, p. 534, §§ 28, 31, ch. 95, p. 1663, § 4.

Indiana Burns' Ann. Stat. 1914, §§ 3957, 3962.

Iowa: Code 1897, § 2925.

Kansas: Gen. Stat. 1889, §§ 1128–1130, 3885; Gen. Stat. 1909, §§ 1670, 1671.

Kentucky: Stat. 1909, §§ 494–498a; Russell's Stat. § 2062. See Tennis Coal Co. v. Asher, 143 Ky. 223, 136 S. W. 197.

Louisiana: Rev. Code 1889, §§ 2264–2266; Civ. Code 1912, §§ 3329, 3342–3348, 3370. In this state the registry preserves the evidence of mortgages during ten years reckoning from the day of its date; its effect ceases, even against the contracting parties, if the inscriptions have not been renewed, before the expiration of this time, in the manner in which they were first made. As to necessity of reinscription, see Batey v. Woolfolk, 20 La. Ann. 385; Kohn v. McHatton, 20 La. Ann. 223; Levy v. Mentz, 23 La. Ann. 261; Adams v. Daunis, 29 La. Ann. 315; Watson v. Bondurant, 30 La. Ann. 1; Succession of Gayle, 30 La. Ann. 351; Patterson v. De la Ronde, 8 Wall. (U. S.) 292, 19 L. ed. 415; Bondurant v. Watson, 103 U. S. 281, 26 L. ed. 447. Neither inscription nor reinscription necessary as against the parties or their heirs. Cucullu v. Hernandez, 103 U. S. 105, 26 L. ed. 322. Omission to reinscribe does not destroy the lien. Its rank only is affected. Norres v. Hays, 44 La. Ann. 907, 11 So. 462; Shepherd v. Orleans Cotton Press Co., 2 La. Ann. 100. A new act of mortgage does away with the necessity of a reinscription. Hart v. Caffrey, 30 La. Ann. 894, 2 So. 788. Notice is not

vide that such conveyances shall not be valid as against persons other than the grantor, his heirs and devisees, and persons having notice thereof, unless they are recorded in the registry of deeds for the county in which the land is situated.

equivalent to registry. Boyer v. Joffrion, 40 La. Ann. 657, 4 So. 872. The pendency of a suit to foreclose the mortgage does not supply the omission to reinscribe. Pickett v. Foster, 149 U. S. 505, 37 L. ed. 829, 13 Sup Ct. 998. The object of the reinscription is to obviate the necessity of searching for mortgages more than ten years back. To effect it, a new description of the property is necessary; and a mere reference to the previous mortgage is not sufficient. Shepherd v. Orleans Cotton Press Co., 2 La. Ann. 100; Hyde v. Bennett, 2 La. Ann. 799; Poutz v. Reggio, 25 La. Ann. 637.

Maine: Rev. Stat. 1883, ch. 73, §§ 8, 9.

Maryland: Rev. Code 1888, art. 24, §§ 13-16; Ann. Code 1911, art. 21, §§ 31, 32, p. 502; also art. 21, § 19, p. 497.

Massachusetts: Pub. Stat. 1882, ch. 120, § 14; Rev. Laws 1902, ch. 127, p. 1222, §§ 4, 7, 14.

Michigan: Ann. Stats. 1882, §§ 5683-5689; Ann. Stat. 1913, §§ 10843, 10850. The statute applies to mortgages as well as deeds. Jackson City Bank v. Campbell, 172 Mich. 541, 138 N. W. 254.

Minnesota: Gen. Stat. 1913, § 6844.

Mississippi: Code 1906, §§ 2784, 2787, 2788; Mississippi Valley Co. v. Chicago, St. L. &c. R. Co., 58 Miss. 846, 38 Am. Rep. 348.

Missouri: Rev. Stat. 1909, §§ 2809, 2811.

Montana: Rev. Code 1907, §§ 4648, 5751-5754. A mortgage is a conveyance within the code relative to the recording of conveyances. Cornish v. Woolverton, 32 Mont. 456, 81 Pac. 4.

Nebraska: Comp. Stat. 1885, ch. 73, §§ 1618; Ann. Stat. 1911, §§ 10816-10818.

Nevada: Rev. Laws 1912, §§ 1038-1040; Grellet v. Heilshorn, 4 Nev. 526.

New Hampshire: P. Stat. 1891,

ch. 136, § 4; P. Stat. 1901, ch. 137, § 4.

New Jersey: Rev. 1877, pp. 155, 705, 706; Supp. 1886, pp. 133, 135; Comp. Laws 1911, p. 1541, § 21, p. 1552, § 53. See also Den v. Wade, 20 N. J. L. 291. The Mortgage Registry Act does not apply to mortgages of leasehold estates. Hutchinson v. Bramhall, 42 N. J. Eq. 372, 7 Atl. 873, reversing Deane v. Hutchinson, 40 N. J. Eq. 83, 2 Atl. 292. Subsequently a statute was enacted requiring mortgages or leasehold estates to be recorded, and making the recording acts applicable thereto. Laws 1887, ch. 161. The registry act applies as against the state. Clement v. Bartlett, 33 N. J. Eq. 43.

New Mexico: Comp. Laws 1884, §§ 429, 2761-2762; Comp. Laws 1897, §§ 3953-3955.

New York: Birdseye's Consol. Laws 1909, p. 5090, § 291. A mortgage is a conveyance, under the statute. Sullivan v. Corn Exch. Bank, 154 App. Div. 292, 139 N. Y. S. 97.

North Carolina: Pell's Revisal 1908, ch. 18, § 982. Witherell v. Murphy, 154 N. Car. 82, 69 S. E. 748.

North Dakota: Rev. Code 1905, §§ 5038, 5039, 5042; Comp. Laws 1913, ch. 49, §§ 5550, 5594-5598. An unrecorded executory contract for a deed to a purchaser in possession, is a mortgage and a "conveyance," entitled to record under the statute. Simonson v. Wenzel, 27 N. Dak. 638, 147 N. W. 804.

Ohio: 1 Rev. Stat. 1892, §§ 1143, 4132-4135; Gen. Code 1910, § 8542.

Oklahoma: Comp. Laws 1909, §§ 1195-1199.

Oregon: Lord's Oregon Laws 1910, § 7129.

Pennsylvania: Purdon's Dig. 1905, §§ 154-166.

Rhode Island: Pub. Stat. 1882, ch. 173, §§ 3, 4; Gen. Laws 1909, ch. 253, p. 875, § 6. But this statute does not make an unacknowledged

In somewhat different terms, but with like effect, the statutes of some states provide that conveyances shall be void as to subsequent purchasers and creditors in good faith and for a valuable consideration without notice, until and except they are recorded or left for record in the proper registry of deeds. Everywhere a record properly made is constructive and absolute notice of the conveyance as recorded.[3]

The order of priority between persons claiming liens on the same property, by mortgage or otherwise, is fixed by the order in which they are filed for record. In other words, priority of record gives

deed void as to others having actual notice of its existence. Westerly Sav. Bank v. Stillman Mfg. Co., 16 R. I. 497, 17 Atl. 918.

South Carolina: Code 1912, § 3542.

South Dakota: Rev. Code 1903, C. C. p. 734, § 986, p. 829, § 2065.

Tennessee: Code 1884, §§ 2811, 2837, 2843, 2887-2890; Code 1896, §§ 3697, 3705, 3712.

Texas: 2 Rev. Civ. Stats. 1889, arts. 4332-4334; Sayles' Civ. Stat. 1914, art. 1104.

Utah: Comp. Laws 1888, §§ 2610-2613; Comp. Laws 1907, § 1975; Neslin v. Wells, 104 U. S. 428, 26 L. ed. 802.

Vermont: Constitution, ch. 2, § 35; Rev. Laws 1880, ch. 97, §§ 1927-1935; Pub. Stat. 1906, §§ 2579-2581.

Virginia: Code 1904, ch. 109, §§ 2465-2467; McCormack v. James, 36 Fed. 14; Hunton v. Wood, 101 Va. 54, 43 S. E. 186.

Washington: Code and Stat. 1910, §§ 8781-8787.

West Virginia: Code 1887, ch. 74, §§ 4-8; Code 1913, §§ 3805, 3834-3836.

Wisconsin: Stat. 1913, §§ 2241-2244.

Wyoming: Rev. Stat. 1887, §§ 15-25; Comp. Stat. 1910, §§ 3646, 3653-3656.

See the following decisions in the United States courts upon the necessity of recording: Pickett v. Foster, 149 U. S. 505, 37 L. ed. 829, 13 Sup. Ct. 998; Lovell v. Cragin, 136 U. S. 130, 34 L. ed. 372, 10 Sup. Ct. 1024; Bacon v. Northwestern Mut. L. Ins. Co., 131 U. S. 258, 33 L. ed. 128, 9 Sup. Ct. 787; Ridings v. Johnson, 128 U. S. 212, 32 L. ed.

401, 9 Sup. Ct. 72; Stevenson v. Texas &c. R. Co., 105 U. S. 703, 26 L. ed. 1215; Patterson v. De la Ronde, 8 Wall (U. S.) 292, 19 L. ed. 415; Beals v. Hale, 4 How. (U. S.) 37, 11 L. ed. 865; Anthony v. Butler, 13 Pet. (U. S.) 423, 10 L. ed. 229; Bank of Alexandria v. Herbert, 8 Cranch (U. S.) 36, 3 L. ed. 479; Brudenell v. Vaux, 2 Dall. (U. S.) 302, Fed. Cas. No. 2049; Sturgess v. Cleveland Bank, 3 McLean (U. S.) 140, Fed. Cas. No. 13571; Hunt v. Innis, 2 Woods (U. S.) 103, Fed. Cas. No. 6892; Truman v. Weed, 67 Fed. 645, 14 C. C. A. 595; Wright v. Buckman, 39 Fed. 243; Metropolitan Trust Co. v. Pennsylvania &c. R. Co., 25 Fed. 760. See also to the effect that a mortgage of land is a "conveyance" within the meaning of the recording acts; Stewart v. Powers, 98 Cal. 514, 33 Pac. 486; Tolman v. Smith, 74 Cal. 345, 16 Pac. 189; Hassey v. Wilke, 55 Cal. 525; Odd Fellows' Sav. Bank v. Banton, 46 Cal. 603; Hull v. Diehl, 21 Mont. 71, 52 Pac. 782; Sullivan v. Corn Exch. Bank, 154 App. Div. 292, 139 N. Y. S. 97; Larned v. Donovan, 84 Hun 533, 65 N. Y. St. 852, 32 N. Y. S. 731; Ward v. Isbill, 73 Hun 550, 56 N. Y. St. 185, 26 N. Y. S. 141; Fries v. Null, 154 Pa. St. 373, 26 Atl. 554; Rowell v. Williams, 54 Wis. 636, 12 N. W. 86. For effect of record generally, and failure to record, see post §§ 523, 527.

[3] See the statutes cited above for such provision in the following states: Alabama, Arizona, Colorado, Georgia, Idaho, Kentucky, Missouri, Nebraska, New Mexico, North Dakota, Oregon, South Caro-

priority of title, as a general rule;[4] and this priority dates from the time the instrument is delivered to the recorder for record. A mortgage is a conveyance with a condition; and the mortgagee is a purchaser; and in most of the states there are no special provisions in relation to recording mortgages, but the general provisions as to record apply as well to mortgages.

§ 457. **Books of record.**—In most of the states, all instruments relating to the title to real estate are recorded in the same books of record, but in several states it is provided by statute that all mortgages shall be recorded in separate books kept for this purpose only.[5] A record not made in the proper book does not operate as constructive notice.[6] A deed absolute in form intended as a mortgage should be

lina, South Dakota, Wisconsin, Wyoming.

[4] Bennett Lumber Co. v. Martin, 132 Ga. 491, 64 S. E. 484; Huebsch v. Scheel, 81 Ill. 281; Jones v. Jones, 16 Ill. 117; Givanovitch v. Baton Rouge Hebrew Cong., 36 La. Ann. 272; Ogle v. King, 22 La. Ann. 391; Dunwell v. Bidwell, 8 Minn. 34; Rumery v. Loy, 61 Nebr. 755, 86 N. W. 478; Burrows v. Hovland, 40 Nebr. 464, 58 N. W. 947; Allen v. Bolen, 114 N. Car. 560, 18 S. E. 964; Quinnerly v. Quinnerly, 114 N. Car. 145, 19 S. E. 99; Bloom v. Noggle, 4 Ohio St. 45; Day v. Clark, 25 Vt. 397; Morris v. Bentley, 2 N. W. Ter. (Can.) 253. See also Cope v. Crichton, 30 Ont. 603; Burns' Rev. Stat. Indiana 1914, § 3962; Rev. Code Louisiana 1913, § 3329; Purdon's Pennsylvania Digest 1905, p. 1181, § 158.

[5] California: Civ. Code 1906, § 1171.

Florida: Rev. Stat. 1892, § 1391; Gen. Stat. 1906, §§ 2480, 2481. See Ivey v. Dawley, 50 Fla. 537, 39 So. 498.

Idaho: Rev. Stat. 1887, § 2999; Code 1911, § 3158.

Louisiana: Rev. Code 1913, § 2252.

Michigan: Ann. Stat. 1882, § 567; Ann. Stat. 1913, §§ 10841, 10842. See as to what instrument should be recorded as a mortgage, Balen v. Mercier, 75 Mich. 42, 42 N. W. 666.

Nebraska: Ann. Stat. 1911, § 9604.

New Mexico: Comp. Laws 1897, § 3957.

New York: Birdseye's Consol. Laws 1909, Real Property Law § 315.

North Dakota: Comp. Laws 1913, § 5560.

Ohio: Gen. Code 1910, § 2757.

Oregon: Laws 1910, § 7126.

South Dakota: Civ. Code 1903, § 967, p. 731.

Texas: Sayles' Civ. Stat. 1914, art. 6796; Cavanaugh v. Peterson, 47 Tex. 197. This provision is held to be directory. Lignoski v. Crooker, 86 Tex. 324, 24 S. W. 278; Kennard v. Mabry, 78 Tex. 151, 14 S. W. 272. But a mechanic's lien need not be recorded. Quinn v. Logan, 67 Tex. 600, 4 S. W. 247.

Mortgages of personal property are generally recorded separately from mortgages and other instruments relating to real property. In some states separate books are required for releases of mortgages and other liens, for mechanics' liens, for marriage contracts, and in a few states separate books are required for each class of instruments relating to real property. See post § 511.

[6] Kent v. Williams, 146 Cal. 3, 79 Pac. 527; Cady v. Purser, 131 Cal. 552, 63 Pac. 844, 82 Am. St. 391; Baker v. Lee, 49 La. Ann. 874, 21 So. 588; Cordeviolle v. Dawson, 26 La. Ann. 534; Colomer v. Morgan, 13 La. Ann. 202; Deane v. Hutchinson, 40 N. J. Eq. 83, 2 Atl. 292; Parsons v. Lent, 34 N. J. Eq. 67; Wil-

recorded in the book of mortgages, and has been held void as to subsequent bona fide purchasers and mortgagees, when recorded only in the book of deeds. But the weight of authority seems to be that the recording of such instruments in the book of deeds is sufficient.[7]

Usage may determine the validity of a record. Thus, where mortgages of real and personal property are required to be recorded in separate books, and a mortgage embracing both real and personal property is recorded only in the book of real estate mortgages, it is held to be sufficiently recorded to make it constructive notice of the lien upon the personal property, it appearing that it is the custom to record such mortgages in this manner without making a double record.[8]

§ 458. Time allowed for record—Effect of record in general.—The recording acts of several states provide that mortgages shall be recorded within a specified time after execution.[9] The effect of this pro-

liamson v. New Jersey So. R. Co., 29 N. J. Eq. 311; Purdy v. Huntington, 42 N. Y. 334, 1 Am. Rep. 532; Gillig v. Maass, 28 N. Y. 191; Stoddard v. Rotton, 5 Bosw. (N. Y.) 378; James v. Morey, 2 Cow. (N. Y.) 246, 6 Johns. Ch. 417, 14 Am. Dec. 475; Bank for Savings v. Frank, 56 How. Pr. (N. Y.) 403, 45 Super. Ct. 404; Clute v. Robinson, 3 Johns. (N. Y.) 595; Dey v. Dunham, 2 Johns. Ch. (N. Y.) 182, 15 Johns. 555; Grimstone v. Carter, 3 Paige (N. Y.) 421, 24 Am. Dec. 230; White v. Moore, 1 Paige (N. Y.) 551; Warner v. Winslow, 1 Sandf. Ch. (N. Y.) 430; Brown v. Dean, 3 Wend. (N. Y.) 208; Howells v. Hettrick, 13 App. Div. 366, 43 N. Y. S. 183; Van Thorniley v. Peters, 26 Ohio St. 471; Calder v. Chapman, 52 Pa. St. 359, 91 Am. Dec. 163; Luch's Appeal, 44 Pa. St. 519; Knowlton v. Walker, 13 Wis. 264; Reed v. Wilson, 23 Ont. 552. See also Ivey v. Dawley, 50 Fla. 537, 39 So. 498 (record in Miscellaneous Book sufficient prior to statute of 1892); Grand Rapids Nat. Bank v. Ford, 143 Mich. 402, 107 S. W. 76, 114 Am. St. 668 (absolute deed intended as a mortgage); Gordon v. Constantine Hydraulic Co., 117 Mich. 620, 76 N. W. 142 (lease containing mortgage clause). See post § 511.

[7] See post § 511.

[8] Anthony v. Butler, 13 Pet. (U.

S.) 423, 10 L. ed. 229; Boyle Ice Machine Co. v. Gould, 73 Cal. 153, 14 Pac. 609; Harriman v. Woburn Elec. Light Co., 163 Mass. 85, 39 N. E. 1004. See post § 511.

[9] Alabama: Under the Code of 1896, §§ 1005. 1006, the time for record was limited to thirty days. Miller v. Griffin, 102 Ala. 610, 15 So. 238; Cook v. Parham, 63 Ala. 456; De Vendal v. Malone, 25 Ala. 272; Coster v. Bank of Georgia, 24 Ala. 37. But this section has been rewritten, and under the Code of 1907, § 3383, mortgages to secure debts, created at the date thereof, are made void as to purchasers, mortgagees, and judgment creditors, without notice, unless recorded before the accrual of the right of such purchasers, mortgagees or judgment creditors.

Delaware: A mortgage for purchase-money recorded within thirty days after its execution has precedence of any judgment or other lien of prior date. Other deeds and mortgages must be recorded within three months after delivery in order to avail against a subsequent fair creditor, mortgagee, or purchaser for a valuable consideration without notice. Rev. Code 1874, pp. 504, 505, § 21; Laws 1881, ch. 520; Laws 1883, p. 509.

Georgia: Deeds must be recorded within one year and mortgages

vision is not to invalidate the mortgage as between the parties, if not recorded within the time specified. It is admissible in evidence, and

within thirty days from date, or they will be postponed to other liens or purchases made prior to the record without notice of the un-recorded conveyance. The record of mortgage not made within the time prescribed is notice from the time of record. Code 1882, §§ 1959, 1960, 2705; Civ. Code 1910, § 3260; North v. Goebel, 138 Ga. 739, 76 S. E. 46; Maddox v. Wilson, 91 Ga. 39, 16 S. E. 213; Myers v. Picquet, 61 Ga. 260; Adair v. Davis, 71 Ga. 769. Under the code mortgages not re-corded within the time required re-main valid as against the mort-gagor. North v. Goebel, 138 Ga. 739, 76 S. E. 46.

Indiana: Under the Act of 1875, in force till January 1, 1914, deeds and mortgages not recorded within forty-five days from their execution are fraudulent and void as against subsequent purchasers, or mort-gagees in good faith and for a val-uable consideration. Rev. Stat. 1888, §§ 2931, 2932. Schmidt v. Zahronlt, 148 Ind. 447, 47 N. E. 335. But valid as to existing creditors. American T. &c. Bank v. McGetti-gan, 152 Ind. 582, 52 N. E. 793. As to proof of recording, see Moore v. Glover, 115 Ind. 367, 16 N. E. 163; Carson v. Eickhoff, 148 Ind. 596, 47 N. E. 1067 (second mortgage duly recorded preferred to first mort-gage not recorded in forty-five days). Under Burns' Ann. Stat. 1914, § 3962, deeds and mortgages take priority according to the time of filing for record, and are fraudu-lent and void as to a subsequent purchaser or mortgagee in good faith for a valuable consideration, having his deed or mortgage first recorded.

Kentucky: Deeds other than deeds of trust and mortgages, by residents of the state, sixty days from date; by persons residing out of the state in the United States, four months; by persons out of the United States, twelve months. Gen. Stat. 1888, p. 315, § 14. But see Statutes 1909, §§ 496, 497.

Maryland: Deeds and mortgages, within six months from date. Ann. Code 1911, art. 21, §§ 13-15. When so recorded they take effect as be-tween the parties from their date; otherwise they are not valid for the purpose of passing the title. A mortgage not recorded within six months has priority over general creditors at its date, but not over subsequent creditors. Sixth Ward Bldg. Assn. v. Willson, 41 Md. 506; Pfeaff v. Jones, 50 Md. 263; Dyson v. Simmons, 48 Md. 207; Hearn v. Purnell, 110 Md. 458, 72 Atl. 906; Hoffman v. Gosnell, 75 Md. 577, 24 Atl. 28.

Oregon: Deeds and mortgages must be recorded within five days after execution. Laws 1910, § 7129.

Pennsylvania: Deeds and mort-gages must be recorded within six months after execution. Purdon's Dig. 1905, p. 1181, § 155. This pro-vision was first enacted in 1715, for the protection of subsequent mort-gagees and others from loss by se-cret pledges of property. The six months allowed are calendar months. Brudenell v. Vaux, 2 Dall. (Pa.) 302. By recent statute, ap-plicable to Philadelphia alone, deeds and other conveyances are valid as against subsequent pur-chasers only from the date of rec-ord. Purdon's Ann. Dig., p. 2110, § 5.

The statute of 1893, p. 109, re-quires all deeds affecting lands in this state to be recorded within ninety days from the date of execu-tion; and unless so recorded they shall be adjudged fraudulent and void against any subsequent mort-gagee for a valid consideration or any creditor. See also Davey v. Ruffell, 162 Pa. St. 143, 29 Atl. 894.

A mortgage recorded before a deed of the same land is recorded has priority over the deed, though the deed was recorded within six months from its execution and the mortgage was not. Fries v. Null, 154 Pa. St. 573, 26 Atl. 554.

A mortgage for purchase-money, if recorded within sixty days from its execution, has priority. Bright-ly's Purdon's Dig., p. 588; Bratton's

is an equitable lien, although not so recorded.[10] The failure to comply with this requirement only goes to the effect of the mortgage as to subsequent purchasers. As to purchasers whose conveyances are registered before a mortgage recorded after the expiration of the limited time, the mortgage is ineffectual.[11] If not recorded within the limited time, a subsequent recordation is ineffectual,[12] at least against third persons whose rights have intervened.[13] Thus, a mortgage recorded

Appeal, 8 Pa. St. 164; Parke v. Neeley, 90 Pa. St. 52. Of two mortgages for purchase-money recorded within the sixty days, that which is first recorded has priority. Dungan v. American L. Ins. &c. Co., 52 Pa. St. 253. With the exception of mortgages for purchase-money, no mortgage is a lien until left for record; but when recorded, the priority of lien is according to the priority of record. Brooke's Appeal, 64 Pa. St. 127; Foster's Appeal, 3 Pa. St. 79; Brightly's Dig. 1872, p. 478. If two or more deeds are left on the same day, they take priority according to the time they were left at the office for record. Brooke's Appeal, 64 Pa. St. 127. If the mortgage remains unrecorded at the time of the death of the mortgagor, though good against him while he lived, it is not good against his creditors after his decease, but must then come in with his general debts. Brightly's Purdon's Dig., p. 588; Nice's Appeal, 54 Pa. St. 200; Adams' Appeal, 1 Pa. St. 447.

South Carolina: Deeds, deeds of trust and mortgages, and statutory liens are valid, so as to affect subsequent creditors or purchasers for valuable consideration without notice, only when recorded within forty days from the time of execution. Summers v. Brice, 36 S. Car. 204, 15 S. E. 374. Pub. Stat. 1882, § 1776. The Civil Code 1893, § 1968, as amended in 1898 and embodied in Civil Code 1902, § 2456, provides that all mortgages and instruments in the nature of mortgages shall be valid against subsequent creditors only when recorded within forty days after execution. See Miller v. Wroton, 82 S. Car. 97, 63 S. E. 62, affd. 63 S. Y. 449. But after the record of a mortgage, although not made within the forty days, no superior lien can be ac-

quired by judgment or otherwise. Brown v. Sartor, 87 S. Car. 116, 69 S. E. 88. See also Code of 1912, § 3542, limiting the time for record to ten days.

Virginia: Any conveyance recorded within ten days from the day of its acknowledgment shall, unless it be a mortgage, or a deed of trust not in consideration of marriage, be as valid as to creditors and subsequent purchasers as if recorded on the day of acknowledgment. Code 1904, § 2467.

In several states, provisions allowing time for recording instruments have been repealed, as in California, District of Columbia, Indiana, Mississippi, New Jersey, North Carolina and Ohio, and it is not probable that like provisions now remaining upon the statute books will remain many years longer.

[10] Charter v. Graham, 56 Ill. 19; Sixth Ward Bldg. Assn. v. Willson, 41 Md. 506; Plume v. Bone, 13 N. J. L. 63; Den v. Watkins, 6 N. J. L. 445; Penman v. Hart, 2 Bay (S. Car.) 251; Ashe v. Livingston, 2 Bay (S. Car.) 80; Ash v. Ash, 1 Bay (S. Car.) 304; Rootes v. Holliday, 6 Munf. (Va.) 251.

[11] Cowan v. Green, 2 Hawks (N. Car.) 384.

[12] Alexandria Bank v. Herbert, 8 Cranch. (U. S.) 36, 3 L. ed. 479; Steiner v. Clisby, 95 Ala. 91, 10 So. 240, 11 So. 294; Harding v. Allen, 70 Md. 395, 17 Atl. 377; Sixth Ward Bldg. Assn. v. Willson, 41 Md. 506; Ridley v. McGehee, 13 N. Car. 40; Woodrow v. Blythe, 2 Del. Co. (Pa.) 18; Mowry v. Crocker, 33 S. Car. 436, 12 S. E. 3; Bloom v. Simms, 27 S. Car. 90, 3 S. E. 45; Williams v. Beard, 1 S. Car. 309. See also Jumonville v. Sharp, 27 La. Ann. 461.

[13] Wyman v. Russell, 4 Biss. (U.

several months after the period for recording had elapsed and after rights to liens in favor of mechanics and materialmen had arisen, is inferior to the statutory liens, though notice of them was not filed till after the recording of the mortgage.[14] Of two mortgages of equal equity, recorded within the time limited after execution, that which is first recorded has priority.[15] Mere delay and failure to record a mortgage within the prescribed time, does not render the mortgage fraudulent as to existing or subsequent creditors, especially if induced by the mortgagor's promise to pay within such time.[16]

The effect of these provisions is that the record, when made within the prescribed time, relates back to the date of delivery of the instrument, and gives it priority over an instrument of subsequent date or delivery, although this has already been recorded.[17] A record made after the prescribed time operates as notice only from the time of delivery of the instrument for record.[18] As between conveyances neither of which is recorded within the prescribed time, the ordinary rule of priority of record prevails, and preference is given to the instrument first recorded.[19] The terms of the statute may determine the question of priority between instruments not recorded within the prescribed time.

S.) 307, Fed. Cas. No. 18115; Miller v. Griffin, 102 Ala. 610, 15 So. 238; Tolle v. Alley, 15 Ky. L. 529, 24 S. W. 113; Porche v. Le Blanc, 12 La. Ann. 778; Stanhope v. Dodge, 52 Md. 483; Pfeaff v. Jones, 50 Md. 263; Plume v. Bone, 13 N. J. L. 63; Fries v. Null, 158 Pa. St. 15, 27 Atl. 867; South Carolina L. &c. Co. v. McPherson, 26 S. Car. 431, 2 S. E. 267.

[14] Jenckes v. Jenckes, 145 Ind. 624, 44 N. E. 632; Rev. Stat. 1894, § 3350.

[15] Wood v. Lordier, 115 Ind. 519, 18 N. E. 34; Gibson v. Keyes, 112 Ind. 568, 14 N. E. 591, modifying or reversing Cain v. Hanna, 63 Ind. 408; Den v. Roberts, 4 N. J. L. 315; Dungan v. American Life Ins. &c. Co., 52 Pa. St. 253.

[16] National State Bank v. Sanford Fork &c. Co., 157 Ind. 10, 60 N. E. 699.

[17] Clarke v. White, 12 Pet. (U. S.) 178, 9 L. ed. 1046; Betz v. Mulin, 62 Ala. 365; Nichols v. Hampton, 46 Ga. 253; Anderson v. Dugas, 29 Ga. 440; Breckenridge v. Todd, 3 T. B.

Mon. (Ky.) 52, 16 Am. Dec. 83; Claiborne v. Holmes, 51 Miss. 146; Northrup v. Brehmer, 8 Ohio 392.

[18] Delane v. Moore, 14 How. (U. S.) 253, 14 L. ed. 409; Wyman v. Russell, 4 Biss. (U. S.) 307; Mallory v. Stodder, 6 Ala. 801; Hockenhull v. Oliver, 80 Ga. 89, 4 S. E. 328; Adair v. Davis, 71 Ga. 769; McGuire v. Barker, 61 Ga. 339; Anderson v. Dugas, 29 Ga. 440; Gilchrist v. Gough, 63 Ind. 576, 30 Am. Rep. 250; Meni v. Rathbone, 21 Ind. 454; Harding v. Allen, 70 Md. 395, 17 Atl. 377; Claiborne v. Holmes, 51 Miss. 146; Sanborn v. Adair, 29 N. J. Eq. 338; South Carolina Loan Co. v. McPherson, 26 S. Car. 431, 2 S. E. 267; King v. Fraser, 23 S. Car. 543; McNamee v. Huckabee, 20 S. Car. 190; Steele v. Mansell, 6 Rich. L. (S. Car.) 614. In South Carolina, prior to January 1, 1877, a valid record could not be made after the time limited. Bloom v. Simms, 27 S. Car. 90, 3 S. E. 45.

[19] Adair v. Davis, 71 Ga. 769; Reasoner v. Edmundson, 5 Ind. 393; Northrup v. Brehmer, 8 Ohio 392;

If the second deed is executed after the first deed has been recorded, though not within the time limited, the first deed has priority.[20] If the second deed be made before the first deed is recorded, and the second deed be recorded within the time limited, but the first deed be not so recorded, though recorded before the second deed, the second deed has priority by virtue of relation back to the time of its execution.[21]

Such a provision is a pernicious one, and is the source of much more inconvenience and fraud than it can possibly prevent. It practically amounts to a withdrawal of the protection of the registry law for the period allowed for registration. A purchaser is never sure of his own priority until he has waited for the prescribed time to elapse after the recording of the deed to himself.

§ 459. **Mortgagees as bona fide purchasers—Consideration.**—A mortgagee of real estate for a valuable consideration is a purchaser within the meaning of the recording laws. This is declared by statute in some states, and in others it is a rule of judicial construction.[22] A valid consideration, in some form, either a contemporaneous loan, or agreement for future advances, or some surrender of value, is necessary to entitle a mortgagee to the protection given a bona fide purchaser.[23] If the mortgage is given and accepted in good faith, with-

---

Fleschner v. Sumpter, 12 Ore. 161, 6 Pac. 506; McNamee V. Huckabee, 20 S. Car. 190.

[20] Adair v. Davis, 71 Ga. 769; Steele v. Mansell, 6 Rich. L. (S. Car.) 437.

[21] Leger v. Doyle, 11 Rich. L. (S. Car.) 109, 70 Am. Dec. 240, per Wardlaw, J.; McNamee v. Huckabee, 20 S. Car. 190, per McGowan, J.; Carson v. Eickhoff, 148 Ind. 596, 47 N. E. 1067.

[22] Carpenter v. Longan, 16 Wall. (U. S.) 271, 21 L. ed. 313; Whelan v. McCreary, 64 Ala. 319; Fargason v. Edrington, 49 Ark. 207, 4 S. W. 763; Warner v. Watson, 35 Fla. 402, 17 So. 654; Broward v. Hoeg, 15 Fla. 370; Walden v. A. P. Brantley Co., 116 Ga. 298, 42 S. E. 503; Parker v. Barnesville Sav. Bank, 107 Ga. 650, 34 S. E. 365; Herff v. Griggs, 121 Ind. 471, 23 N. E. 279; Patton v. Eberhart, 52 Iowa 67, 2 N. W. 954; Jordan v. McNeil, 25 Kans. 459; Chapman v. Miller, 130 Mass. 289; McDowell v. Lockhart, 93 N. Car. 191; Flechner v. Sump-

ter, 12 Ore. 161; Haynsworth v. Bischoff, 6 S. Car. 159; Moore v. Walker, 3 Lea (Tenn.) 656; Bass v. Wheless, 2 Tenn. Ch. 531; Weinberg v. Rempe, 15 W. Va. 829; Rowell v. Williams, 54 Wis. 636; 12 N. W. 86. See post § 710.

[23] Craft v. Russell, 67 Ala. 9; Whelan v. McCreary, 64 Ala. 319; Watts v. Burnett, 56 Ala. 340; Coleman v. Smith, 55 Ala. 368; Short v. Battle, 52 Ala. 456; Doe v. Reeves, 10 Ala. 137; General Ins. Co. v. United States Ins. Co., 10 Md. 517, 69 Am. Dec. 174; Brooks v. Owen, 112 Mo. 251, 19 S. W. 723, 20 S. W. 492; Wheeler v. Kirtland, 24 N. J. Eq. 552; Simons v. First Nat. Bank, 93 N. Y. 269 (agreement for future advances); First Nat. Bank v. Robinson, 105 App. Div. 193, 94 N. Y. S. 767; Outterson v. Dilts, 66 Hun 629, 49 N. Y. St. 277, 21 N. Y. S. 163 (surrender of title to personalty as a consideration); Halbert v. Paddleford (Tex. Civ. App.), 33 S. W. 592.

out fraud, and is supported by an actual present consideration, the mortgagee is a bona fide purchaser for value, and is protected against adverse claims of which he has no notice,[24] including prior conveyances,[25] and other existing liens and claims.[26] "When I speak of a purchaser for a valuable consideration," says Lord Hardwicke, "I include a mortgagee, for he is a purchaser pro tanto."[27] A mortgagee is a purchaser for value under a mortgage given to indemnify a surety against a contemporaneous liability, and he is protected against latent equities of which he had no notice.[28]

[24] Kisner v. Trigg, 98 U. S. 50, 25 L. ed. 83; Woodruff v. Adair, 131 Ala. 530, 32 So. 515; Rogers v. Adams, 66 Ala. 600; Wells v. Morrow, 38 Ala. 125; Turman v. Bell, 54 Ark. 273, 15 S. W. 886, 26 Am. St. 35; Bush v. Golden, 17 Conn. 594; Scott v. Atlas Sav. &c. Assn., 114 Ga. 134, 39 S. E. 942; Lane v. Partee, 41 Ga. 202; Erwin v. Hall, 18 Ill. App. 315; Lehman v. Hawks, 121 Ind. 541, 23 N. E. 670; Herff v. Griggs, 121 Ind. 471, 23 N. E. 279; Koon v. Tramel, 71 Iowa 132, 32 N. W. 243; Hewitt v. Rankin, 41 Iowa 35; Straeffer v. Rodman, 146 Ky. 1, 141 S. W. 742, Ann. Cas. 1913C, 549; Thompson v. Whitbeck, 47 La. Ann. 49, 16 So. 570; Pierce v. Faunce, 47 Maine 507; Dana v. Newhill, 13 Mass. 498; Shepard v. Shepard, 36 Mich. 173; Masterson v. West End &c. R. Co., 72 Mo. 342; Fair v. Howard, 6 Nev. 304; Sternberg v. Sternberg (N. J. Eq.), 69 Atl. 492; Werner v. Franklin Nat. Bank, 166 N. Y. 619, 59 N. E. 1132; Drake v. Paige, 127 N. Y. 562, 28 N. E. 407; La Farge Fire Ins. Co. v. Bell, 22 Barb. (N. Y.) 54; Maas v. Dunmyer, 21 Okla. 434, 96 Pac. 591; Kieffer v. Victor Land Co., 53 Ore. 174, 90 Pac. 582, 98 Pac. 877; Landigan v. Mayer, 32 Ore. 245, 51 Pac. 649, 67 Am. St. 521; Lancaster v. Dolan, 1 Rawle (Pa.) 231, 18 Am. Dec. 625; Haynsworth v. Bischoff, 6 S. Car. 159; Brigham v. Thompson, 12 Tex. Civ. App. 562, 34 S. W. 358; Wallwyn v. Lee, 9 Ves. Jr. 24, 7 Rev. 142, 32 Eng. Reprint 509. See also Williams v. Lewis, 158 N. Car. 571, 74 S. E. 17 (second mortgagee not a bona fide purchaser); Scott v. Farnam, 55 Wash. 336, 104 Pac. 639; Shoufe v. Griffiths, 4 Wash. 161, 30 Pac. 93, 31 Am. St. 910 (doctrine of bona fide purchasers not applied to mortgage of equitable estate).

[25] Kindred v. New England Mtg. Sec. Co., 116 Ala. 192, 23 So. 56; Harding v. Tate, 23 Ky. L. 1918, 68 S. W. 17; Keith &c. Coal Co. v. Bingham, 97 Mo. 196, 10 S. W. 32; Farmer v. Fisher, 197 Pa. St. 114, 46 Atl. 892; Summers v. Brice, 36 S. Car. 204, 15 S. E. 374; Parrish v. Mahany, 10 S. Dak. 276, 73 N. W. 97, 66 Am. St. 715; McKeen v. Sultenfuss, 61 Tex. 325; Hays v. Tilson (Tex.), 35 S. W. 515. See also Ross v. Sweeney, 12 Ky. L. 861, 15 S. W. 357; Valentine v. Lunt, 115 N. Y. 496, 22 N. E. 209 (bona fide purchaser of subsequent mortgagee protected though conveyance is void for duress); Charlestown v. Page, 1 Speer's Eq. (S. Car.), 159 (rights of purchaser from mortgagee, without notice).

[26] Gerson v. Pool, 31 Ark. 85; Austin v. Pulschen, 112 Cal. 528, 44 Pac. 788; Salter v. Baker, 54 Cal. 140; Edwards v. Thom, 25 Fla. 222, 5 So. 707; Robbins v. Moore, 129 Ill. 30, 21 N. E. 934; Clark v. Hunt, 3 J. J. Marsh. (Ky.) 553; Mairs v. Bank of Oxford, 58 Miss. 919; Cornet v. Bertelsmann, 61 Mo. 118; Drake v. Paige, 52 Hun 292, 24 N. Y. St. 131, 5 N. Y. S. 466; Patterson v. Johnson, 7 Ohio 225; Moran v. Wheeler, 87 Tex. 179, 27 S. W. 54; Shurtz v. Johnson, 28 Grat. (Va.) 657.

[27] Willoughby v. Willoughby, 1 T. R. 763. See also Salter v. Baker, 54 Cal. 140; Seevers v. Delashmutt, 11 Iowa 174; Porter v. Green, 4 Iowa 571; Singer Mfg. Co. v. Chalmers, 2 Utah 542.

[28] Bartlett v. Varner, 56 Ala. 580.

A trustee in a deed of trust is also a purchaser for value. He occupies the same ground with respect to notice, either actual or constructive, of any outstanding equities, that a mortgagee does.[29] A deed of trust, given as security for bonds to be issued later, is inoperative as a security, unless the bonds are actually issued to bona fide creditors, before liens of other creditors attach to the property conveyed.[30]

A voluntary mortgage may not be regarded as a purchase for value. Thus, a deed made by a father to his daughter of a very valuable farm by way of settlement upon himself for life and for his wife and daughter after his death does not make the daughter a purchaser for value so as to entitle her to prevail over a prior unrecorded conveyance by the father.[31] The rule would be similar in case of a mortgage made for a like consideration. Although a mortgagee does not record his mortgage, he does not lose his lien as against a subsequent grantee without notice, who pays no consideration.[32] But a party holding under an unrecorded mortgage or trust deed can not prevail over a subsequent grantee without notice who has paid any valuable consideration.[33]

Although a part of the consideration for a mortgage may fail, as based upon a pre-existing debt, or otherwise insufficient to render the mortgagee a bona fide purchaser, the mortgage may be a valid and preferred security as to the remainder.[34]

§ 460. **Pre-existing debt as consideration.**—A mortgage given to secure a pre-existing debt is by some courts distinguished from one upon which the consideration is paid at the time of its execution; and the same rule is applied in case of a purchase in consideration of the grantee's canceling an existing debt of the grantor. The mortgage or deed made to secure a pre-existing debt does not constitute the grantee a purchaser for value in good faith. The former, although given upon a valid consideration as between the parties, is not regarded as a purchase for a valuable consideration which will entitle the mortgagee to protection against prior equities, although he had no notice of them

[29] Kesner v. Trigg, 98 U. S. 50, 25 L. ed. 83; New Orleans Canal &c. Co. v. Montgomery, 95 U. S. 16, 24 L. ed. 346; Gilbert v. Lawrence, 56 W. Va. 281, 49 S. E. 155.

[30] Allen v. Montgomery R. Co., 11 Ala. 437.

[31] Ten Eyck v. Witbeck, 135 N. Y. 40, 31 N. E. 994, 31 Am. St. 809.

[32] Roberts v. W. H. Hughes Co., 86 Vt. 76, 83 Atl. 807.

[33] Openshaw v. Dean (Tex. Civ. App.), 125 S. W. 989.

[34] Wells v. Morrow, 38 Ala. 125; Klaes v. Klaes, 103 Iowa 689, 72 N. W. 777; Gibson v. Wheless, 2 Tenn. Ch. 531.

when he took the mortgage.[85] He must have parted with some value or some right upon the faith of the mortgage and at the time of it, to entitle him to protection as a purchaser. He must have received some new consideration, or must have relinquished some security for

[85] People's Sav. Bank v. Bates, 120 U. S. 556, 30 L. ed. 754, 7 Sup. Ct. 679; Bybee v. Hawkett, 8 Sawy. (U. S.) 176, 12 Fed. 649; Morse v. Godfrey, 3 Story (U. S.) 364; Hill v. Hite, 79 Fed. 826; Gewin v. Shields, 167 Ala. 593, 52 So. 887; Anniston Carriage Works v. Ward, 101 Ala. 670, 14 So. 417; Anthe v. Heide, 85 Ala. 236, 4 So. 380; Banks v. Long, 79 Ala. 319; Jones v. Robinson, 77 Ala. 499; Craft v. Russell, 67 Ala. 9; Cook v. Parham, 63 Ala. 456; Thurman v. Stoddard, 63 Ala. 336; Alexander v. Caldwell, 55 Ala. 517; Coleman v. Smith, 55 Ala. 368; Short v. Battle, 52 Ala. 456; Gafford v. Stearns, 51 Ala. 434; Wells v. Morrow, 38 Ala. 125; Miller v. Mattison, 105 Ark. 201, 150 S. W. 710; Haldiman v. Taft, 102 Ark. 45, 143 S. W. 112; Fargason v. Edrington, 49 Ark. 207; Withers v. Little, 56 Cal. 370; Salisbury Sav. Soc. v. Cutting, 50 Conn. 113; Harris v. Evans, 134 Ga. 161, 67 S. E. 880; Collins v. Moore, 115 Ga. 327, 41 S. E. 609; Chance v. McWhorter, 26 Ga. 315; Warford v. Hankins, 150 Ind. 489, 50 N. E. 468; Adams v. Vanderbeck, 148 Ind. 92, 45 N. E. 645, 47 N. E. 24, 62 Am. St. 497; Citizens Nat. Bank v. Judy, 146 Ind. 322, 43 N. E. 259; First Nat. Bank v. Connecticut Mut. Life Ins. Co., 129 Ind. 241, 28 N. E. 695; Durham v. Craig, 79 Ind. 117; Gilchrist v. Gough, 63 Ind. 576, 30 Am. Rep. 250; Senneff v. Brackey (Iowa), 146 N. W. 24; Rea v. Wilson, 112 Iowa 517, 84 N. W. 539; Smith v. Moore, 112 Iowa 60, 83 N. W. 813; Koon v. Tramel, 71 Iowa 132, 32 N. W. 243; Phelps v. Fockler, 61 Iowa 340, 14 N. W. 729, 16 N. W. 210; Port v. Embree, 54 Iowa 14, 6 N. W. 83; Holmes v. Stix, 104 Ky. 351, 20 Ky. L. 593, 47 S. W. 243; Buffington v. Gerrish, 15 Mass. 156, 8 Am. Dec. 97; Clark v. Flint, 22 Pick. (Mass.) 231, 33 Am. Dec. 733; Maynard v. Davis, 127 Mich. 571, 86 N. W. 1051; Edwards v. McKernan, 55 Mich. 520, 22 N. W. 20; Boxheimer v. Gunn, 24 Mich. 372; Whittacre v. Fuller, 5 Minn. 503; Schumpert v. Dillard, 55 Miss. 348; Hinds v. Pugh, 48 Miss. 268; Perkins v. Swank, 43 Miss. 349; McLeod v. First Nat. Bank, 42 Miss. 99; Reeves v. Evans (N. J. Eq.), 34 Atl. 477; Martin v. Bowen, 51 N. J. Eq. 452, 26 Atl. 823; Lamb v. Lamb (N. J. Eq.), 23 Atl. 1009; Pancoast v. Duval, 26 N. J. Eq. 445; Wheeler v. Kirtland, 24 N. J. Eq. 552; Mingus v. Condit, 23 N. J. Eq. 313; Breed v. National Bank, 171 N. Y. 648, 63 N. E. 1115; Constant v. Rochester University, 111 N. Y. 604, 19 N. E. 631, 2 L. R. A. 734, 7 Am. St. 769; Young v. Guy, 87 N. Y. 467; Union Dime Savings Inst. v. Duryea, 67 N. Y. 84; De Lancey v. Stearns, 66 N. Y. 157; Weaver v. Barden, 49 N. Y. 286; Hiscock v. Phelps, 49 N. Y. 97; Van Heusen v. Radcliff, 17 N. Y. 580, 72 Am. Dec. 480; O'Brien v. Fleckenstein, 86 App. Div. 140, 83 N. Y. S. 499; Stalker v. McDonald, 6 Hill (N. Y.) 93, 40 Am. Dec. 389; Coddington v. Bay, 20 Johns. (N. Y.) 637, 11 Am. Dec. 342; Constant v. Am. Bap. Soc., 21 J. & S. (N. Y.) 170; Bank of Savings v. Frank, 13 J. & S. (N. Y.) 404; Cary v. White, 7 Lans. (N. Y.) 1, 52 N. Y. 138; Padgett v. Lawrence, 10 Paige (N. Y.) 170, 40 Am. Dec. 232; Manhattan Co. v. Evertson, 6 Paige (N. Y.) 457; Dickerson v. Tillinghast, 4 Paige (N. Y.) 215, 25 Am. Dec. 528; Westervelt v. Haff, 2 Sandf. Ch. (N. Y.) 98; Small v. Small, 74 N. Car. 16; Donaldson v. State Bank, 16 N. Car. 103, 18 Am. Dec. 577; Lewis v. Anderson, 20 Ohio St. 281; Ashton's Appeal, 73 Pa. St. 153; Marsh v. Ramsey, 57 S. Car. 121, 35 S. E. 433; Summers v. Brice, 36 S. Car. 204, 15 S. E. 374; Zorn v. Savannah &c. R. Co., 5 S. Car. 90; Brown v. Vanlier, 7 Humph. (Tenn.) 239; Moody v. Martin (Tex. Civ. App.), 117 S. W. 1015; Stacey v. Henke, 32 Tex. Civ. App. 462, 74 S. W. 925; Spurlock v. Sullivan, 36 Tex.

a pre-existing debt due him.[36] But if the mortgagee at the time of taking the mortgage released other security and extended the time of payment the mortgage will be sustained.[37]

If the mortgagee upon taking the mortgage has surrendered any valuable right, such as a prior mortgage upon the property, the new mortgage is based upon a valuable consideration as much as if he had paid money for it.[38] Thus the surrender of a vendor's lien, a mechanic's lien, or a note indorsed by a surety, or any other security already held for a pre-existing debt, if given contemporaneously and if so intended, will be a sufficient new consideration to constitute the mortgagee a purchaser for value.[39] If an antecedent debt is accom-

---

511; McDonald v. Johns, 62 Wash. 521, 114 Pac. 175, 33 L. R. A. (N. S.) 57; Funk v. Paul, 64 Wis. 35, 24 N. W. 419. See also Steffian v. Milmo Nat. Bank, 69 Tex. 513, 6 S. W. 823; McKamey v. Thorp, 61 Tex. 648; Ayres v. Duprey, 27 Tex. 593, 86 Am. Dec. 657. The same rule was laid down in Illinois in the case of Metropolitan Bank v. Godfrey, 23 Ill. 579. In later cases, however, it has been held, so far as negotiable paper is concerned, that an indorsee taking it before maturity as payment or security for a pre-existing debt is a holder for value, and takes it free from latent defenses on the part of the maker. Doolittle v. Cook, 75 Ill. 354; Manning v. McClure, 36 Ill. 490. In the latter case Mr. Justice Lawrence, referring to Metropolitan Bank v. Godfrey, 23 Ill. 579, said: "We do not desire to be understood as overruling that position; but if that question comes again before us, it will be open to argument whether a different principle should be applied to conveyances of real estate from that which all the members of the court agree should be applied to the indorsement of a promissory note."

One who takes a trust deed to secure a note given as additional security for a pre-existing debt, and credits the discounted amount of the note on the debt, is not a bona fide purchaser. Moody v. Martin (Tex. Civ. App.), 117 S. W. 1015. A creditor who takes from his debtor a deed to land to secure a pre-existing debt, without any change of condition, or present payment, or other new consideration, will not be considered a bona fide purchaser, protected against an easement of which he has no notice. Harris v. Evans, 134 Ga. 161, 67 S. E. 880. Under the law merchant, one taking negotiable paper before maturity in payment of or as security for an antecedent debt becomes a bona fide holder, but that rule does not extend to one taking a mortgage merely as security for an antecedent debt without advancing a new consideration. Haldiman v. Taft, 102 Ark. 45, 143 S. W. 112. A new mortgage given to replace one lost or omitted in process of registration, is not an ordinary mortgage given to secure an antecedent debt, and is entitled to greater consideration in equity than a mortgage given to secure an antecedent debt. Brace v. Superior Land Co., 65 Wash. 681, 118 Pac. 910.

[36] Wilson v. Knight, 59 Ala. 172; Bartlett v. Varner, 56 Ala. 580; Withers v. Little, 56 Cal. 370; Schumpert v. Dillard, 55 Miss. 348; Hinds v. Pugh, 48 Miss. 268; Perkins v. Swank, 43 Miss. 349; Lawrence v. Clark, 36 N. Y. 128; Webster v. Van Steenbergh, 46 Barb. (N. Y.) 211; Pickett v. Barron, 29 Barb. (N. Y.) 505; Spurlock v. Sullivan, 36 Tex. 511.

[37] Alston v. Marshall, 112 Ala. 638, 20 So. 850. See also Hunt v. Hunt, 67 Ore. 178, 134 Pac. 1180.

[38] Constant v. University of Rochester, 111 N. Y. 604, 19 N. E. 631, 7 Am. St. 769, 2 L. R. A. 734.

[39] Wilson v. Knight, 59 Ala. 172; Constant v. Rochester University,

panied by any new or contemporaneous consideration, even such as an extension of time, the creditor is protected as a bona fide purchaser.[40]

A definite extension of the time for payment of a pre-existing debt is considered a new consideration, which will make the mortgagee a purchaser for value.[41] If, however, a mortgage is given to secure the mortgagee against a liability already incurred by him as surety for the mortgagor, it stands in the same position as a mortgage for a pre-existing debt.[42]

A mortgage to secure future indebtedness constitutes the mortgagee a purchaser from the time that advances are made by the mortgagee under the mortgage without actual notice of a subsequent mortgage.[43]

But a mortgage to secure an antecedent debt is perfectly valid as between the parties, and as against all others who had at the time no equitable interest in the property; whatever may be its effect as to purchasers or incumbrances.[44] Moreover, such a mortgage, if taken without notice of one given to secure a future indebtedness, has precedence of it, if it be first recorded.[45]

The mortgagee for an antecedent debt acquires a lien upon the property to the extent only of the mortgagor's equitable interest at the time. Thus, if the mortgagor has then contracted to sell the land, and the vendee has paid a portion of the purchase-money, the mortgage is a lien only to the extent of the unpaid purchase-money upon such contract. But after the vendee has received notice of the mort-

111 N. Y. 604, 19 N. E. 631, 2 L. R. A. 734, 7 Am. St. 769; Norwalk Nat. Bank v. Lanier, 7 Hun (N. Y.) 623; Lane v. Logue, 12 Lea (Tenn.) 681 (surrender of vendor's lien).

[40] Whitfield v. Riddle, 78 Ala. 99; Cook v. Parham, 63 Ala. 456. See also Douglas v. Miller, 102 App. Div. 94, 92 N. Y. S. 514; Branch v. Griffin, 99 N. Car. 173, 5 S. E. 393. See post § 461.

[41] See post § 461.

[42] Southerland v. Fremont, 107 N. Car. 565, 12 S. E. 237. See also Uhler v. Semple, 20 N. J. Eq. 288. See post § 461.

[43] Simons v. First Nat. Bank, 93 N. Y. 269.

[44] Turner v. McFee, 61 Ala. 468; Steiner v. McCall, 61 Ala. 406; Machette v. Wanless, 1 Colo. 225; Usina v. Wilder, 58 Ga. 178; Kranert v. Simon, 65 Ill. 344; McLeish v. Hanson, 157 Ill. App. 605; Rea

v. Wilson, 112 Iowa 517, 84 N. W. 539; Johnston v. Robuck, 104 Iowa 523, 73 N. W. 1062; Chadwick v. Devore, 69 Iowa 637, 29 N. W. 757; Meyer v. Evans, 66 Iowa 179, 23 N. W. 386; Duncan v. Miller, 64 Iowa 223, 20 N. W. 161; Laylin v. Knox, 41 Mich. 40, 1 N. W. 913; Laubenheimer v. McDermott, 5 Mont. 512, 6 Pac. 344; Brooks v. Owen (Mo.), 20 S. W. 492; Longfellow v. Barnard, 58 Nebr. 612, 617, 79 N. W. 255, 76 Am. St. 117; Chaffee v. Atlas Lumber Co., 43 Nebr. 224, 61 N. W. 637; Henry v. Vliet, 36 Nebr. 138, 54 N. W. 122; Turner v. Killian, 12 Nebr. 380, 12 N. W. 101; Perkins v. Trinity Realty Co., 69 N. J. Eq. 723, 61 Atl. 167; Sargent v. Cooley, 12 N. Dak. 1, 94 N. W. 576; Smith v. Worman, 19 Ohio St. 145; Moore v. Fuller, 6 Ore. 272, 25 Am. Rep. 524; Paine v. Benton, 32 Wis. 491.

[45] National Bank v. Whitney, 103 U. S. 99, 26 L. ed. 443.

gage, he can not make a valid payment of the remainder of the purchase-money.[46]

This rule requiring the payment of an actual consideration at the
time of the transaction to constitute a bona fide purchaser, within the
meaning of the recording acts, does not apply to any one but the original mortgagee. He being protected by the recording acts from a prior
unrecorded conveyance, any one who takes an assignment from him
is entitled to the same protection, although the assignee parts with no
valuable consideration for the assignment, and even though he has
actual notice of the prior unrecorded conveyance.[47]

If the sole consideration of a conveyance be the love and affection
of the grantor, it will not hold against a prior unrecorded mortgage
of the same property, or against a mortgage imperfectly recorded.[48]

But numerous authorities hold that a mortgagee who has taken
his mortgage in good faith to secure a pre-existing debt, or a purchaser who has received a conveyance in consideration of his canceling a pre-existing debt, is entitled to be regarded as a purchaser, and
to be protected as such.[49] The weight of authority, however, seems to
be against this position.

[46] Young v. Guy, 87 N. Y. 457, affg.
23 Hun 1.

[47] Wood v. Chapin, 13 N. Y. 509,
67 Am. Dec. 62; Webster v. Van
Steenbergh, 46 Barb. (N. Y.) 211.

[48] Toole v. Toole, 107 Ga. 472, 33
S. E. 686; Bishop v. Schneider, 46
Mo. 472, 2 Am. Rep. 533; Aubuchon
v. Bender, 44 Mo. 560; Parrish v.
Mahany, 12 S. Dak. 278, 81 N. W.
295, 76 Am. St. 604. See also Cotton v. Graham, 84 Ky. 672, 8 Ky.
L. 658, 2 S. W. 647. But see Ray
v. Hollenbeck, 42 Fed. 381.

[49] Gassen v. Hendrick, 74 Cal. 444,
16 Pac. 242; Schluter v. Harvey, 65
Cal. 158, 3 Pac. 659; Frey v. Clif-
ford, 44 Cal. 335; Robinson v. Smith,
14 Cal. 94. See also Partridge v.
Smith, 2 Biss. (U. S.) 183; Withers
v. Little, 56 Cal. 370; Citizens' Nat.
Bank v. Judy, 146 Ind. 322, 43 N.
E. 259; Wert v. Naylor, 93 Ind. 431;
Hewitt v. Powers, 84 Ind. 295;
Evans v. Pence, 78 Ind. 439; Mc-
Laughlin v. Ward, 77 Ind. 383; Gil-
christ v. Gough, 63 Ind. 576, 30 Am.
Rep. 250; Babcock v. Jordan, 24
Ind. 14. The doctrine is modified to
the extent that such a mortgage
does not cut off prior secret equi-
ties. Busenbarke v. Ramey, 53 Ind.

499; Hayner v. Eberhardt, 37 Kans.
308, 15 Pac. 168; Jackson v. Reid,
30 Kans. 10, 1 Pac. 308; Soule v.
Shotwell, 52 Miss. 236.

In State Bank v. Frame, 112
Mo. 502, 20 S. W. 620. Mac-
farlane, J., says: "Whether the
satisfaction of a pre-existing debt
is a consideration sufficient to
protect a purchaser of real estate
against a prior unrecorded deed, of
which he has no notice, has never
been definitely and directly passed
upon by this court, so far as we
are advised." After reviewing the
Missouri cases, the most important
of which are Crawford v. Spencer,
92 Mo. 498, 4 S. W. 713; Fitzgerald
v. Barker, 96 Mo. 661, 10 S. W. 45;
Redpath v. Lawrence, 42 Mo. App.
101; Lawrence v. Owens, 39 Mo.
App. 318; Feder v. Abrahams, 28
Mo. App. 454; Hess v. Clark, 11
Mo. App. 492, he continues: "We
think the rule deducible from these
authorities is, that a deed made in
consideration of the absolute discharge of a pre-existing debt of the
grantor, or an adequate portion of
it, will constitute the grantee a
purchaser for value, so as to protect him against a previous unre-

§ 461. Extension of debt as consideration.

§ **461.** **Extension of debt as consideration.**—A definite extension of time for the payment of an existing debt, by a valid agreement, for any period however short, though it be for a day only, is a valuable consideration, and is sufficient to support a mortgage, or a conveyance, as a purchase for a valuable consideration.[50] But the mere taking of collateral security on time is not by itself, and in the absence of any agreement beyond it, an extension of the time of payment of the original debt; and therefore a mortgage taken as security in such way is not a purchase for value.[51]

The extension of time must be given at the time and in consider-

corded deed of the same grantor. By the satisfaction of the debt the creditor divests himself of the right of an action, or of securing the original liability and places himself in a worse condition than he would have done by a definite forbearance of the debt." Herbage v. Moodie, 51 Nebr. 837, 71 N. W. 778; Dorr v. Meyer, 51 Nebr. 94, 70 N. W. 543; Fair v. Howard, 6 Nev. 304; Branch v. Griffin, 99 N. Car. 173, 5 S. E. 393; Bank v. Bridgers, 98 N. Car. 67, 3 S. E. 826, 2 Am. St. 378; Brem v. Lockhart, 93 N. Car. 191; Potts v. Blackwell, 4 Jones Eq. (N. Car.) 58; Cammack v. Soran, 30 Grat. (Va.) 292; Gilbert v. Lawrence, 56 W. Va. 281, 49 S. E. 155. But a conveyance in consideration of the extinguishment of a precedent debt makes the grantee a bona fide purchaser for value. Adams v. Vanderbeck, 148 Ind. 92, 45 N. E. 645, 47 N. E. 24; Wert v. Naylor, 93 Ind. 431.

[50] Randolph v. Webb, 116 Ala. 135, 22 So. 550; Alston v. Marshall, 112 Ala. 638, 20 So. 850; Whitfield v. Riddle, 78 Ala. 99; Jones v. Robinson, 77 Ala. 499; Downing v. Blair, 75 Ala. 216; Craft v. Russell, 67 Ala. 9; Thames v. Rembert, 63 Ala. 561; Cook v. Parham, 63 Ala. 456; Fargason v. Edrington, 49 Ark. 207, 4 S. W. 763; Gilchrist v. Gough, 63 Ind. 576, 30 Am. Rep. 250; Davis v. Lutkiewiez, 72 Iowa 254, 33 N. W. 670; Koon v. Tramel, 71 Iowa 132, 32 N. W. 243; Phelps v. Fockler, 61 Iowa 340, 14 N. W. 729, 16 N. W. 210; Sullivan Sav. Inst. v. Young, 55 Iowa 132, 7 N. W. 480; Port v. Embree, 54 Iowa 14, 6 N.

W. 83; De Mey v. Defer, 103 Mich. 239, 61 N. W. 524; Schumpert v. Dillard, 55 Miss. 348; Morrill v. Skinner, 57 Nebr. 164, 77 N. W. 375; O'Brien v. Fleckenstein, 86 App. Div. 140, 83 N. Y. S. 499, affd. 180 N. Y. 350, 73 N. E. 30, 105 Am. St. 768; Cary v. White, 52 N. Y. 138; Hale v. Omaha Nat. Bank, 1 J. & S. (N. Y.) 40; First Nat. Bank v. Lamont, 5 N. Dak. 393, 67 N. W. 145; Farmers' &c. Nat. Bank v. Wallace, 45 Ohio St. 152, 12 N. E. 439; Farmers' &c. Bank v. Citizens' Bank, 25 S. Dak. 91, 125 N. W. 642; Farmers' Nat. Bank v. James, 13 Tex. Civ. App. 550, 36 S. W. 288; Watts v. Corner, 8 Tex. Civ. App. 588, 27 S. W. 1087. See also Missouri Broom Mfg. Co. v. Guymon, 115 Fed. 112, 53 C. C. A. 16. An employer who accepted a mortgage for money embezzled, extending the time for repayment of the amount, was held a bona fide purchaser for value as against the employe's wife, who was induced to sign the mortgage by her husband's false representation. Hunt v. Hunt, 67 Ore. 178, 134 Pac. 1180. Under the Civil Code of South Dakota §§ 986, 987, making a "conveyance" void as against subsequent bona fide purchasers and incumbrancers of record, a mortgage though given to secure a pre-existing debt is supported by a sufficient consideration, where a definite extension of the time of payment is granted. Farmers' &c. Bank v. Citizens' Nat. Bank, 25 S. Dak. 91, 125 N. W. 642. See post §§ 532, 610.

[51] Cary v. White, 52 N. Y. 138, revg. 7 Lans. 1; Wood v. Robinson,

ation of the mortgage. A mortgagee is not considered a purchaser for value, merely because the result of the mortgage may be to extend the time of payment.[52] Where a mortgage is made in terms to secure an existing note, and the mortgage declares that "the same shall be paid in the manner following," giving future days of payment beyond the time of payment mentioned in the note, the mortgage extends the time of payment of the note. The mortgage in such case, by reason of the extension of the time of payment, is founded upon a valuable consideration. The date of payment in the note and the date of payment in the mortgage being inconsistent, the latter should prevail.[53]

A mortgage made to secure a loan made at the time, as well as a pre-existing debt, is based upon a valid consideration.[54]

§ 462. **Judgment creditors as purchasers—Priority of mortgages over judgments and attachments.**—A judgment creditor is not a purchaser within the recording acts, unless he is made so by statute.[55] He was not regarded as a purchaser at common law. In a case in Peere Williams, "it was granted," said the reporter, "that if Lord Winchelsea, the covenantor, had made a mortgage of the premises for a valuable consideration and without notice, such mortgagee, in regard that he might have pleaded his mortgage, and would have been as a purchaser without notice, should have held place against the intended purchaser, for then the money would have been lent on the title and credit of the land, and would have attached on the land; which would not be so in the case of a judgment creditor, who, for aught that appears, might have taken out execution against the person or goods of the party that gave the judgment; and a judgment is a general security, not a specific lien on the land."[56] And in another case given by the same reporter it was said, that "one can not call a

---

22 N. Y. 564. The dictum in the case of Pratt v. Coman, 37 N. Y. 440, to the contrary, is denied in Cary v. White, 52 N. Y. 138. The courts have been disposed to limit the authority of Cary v. White to the facts of that case. Hubbard v. Gurney, 64 N. Y. 467; Durkee v. Nat. Bank, 36 Hun (N. Y.) 565; Grocers' Bank v. Penfield, 7 Hun (N. Y.) 279.

[52] Ingenhuett v. Hunt, 15 Tex. Civ. App. 248, 39 S. W. 310.

[53] Durkee v. National Bank, 36 Hun (N. Y.) 565.

[54] Branch v. Griffin, 99 N. Car. 173, 5 S. E. 398; Bank v. Bridgers, 98 N. Car. 67, 3 S. E. 826.

[55] Hacker v. White, 22 Wash. 415, 60 Pac. 1114, 79 Am. St. 945; Dawson v. McCarty, 21 Wash. 314, 57 Pac. 816, 75 Am. St. 841; Kargar v. Steele-Wedeles Co,. 103 Wis. 286, 79 N. W. 216. See also Foster v. Hobson, 131 Iowa 58, 107 N. W. 1101; Swarts v. Stees, 2 Kans. 236, 85 Am. Dec. 588; Gaston v. Merriam, 33 Minn. 271, 22 N. W. 614.

[56] Finch v. Winchelsea, 1 P. Wms. 277.

judgment creditor a purchaser, nor has such creditor any right to the land; he has neither jus in re nor ad rem."[57]

The recording acts do not change the common law in this respect, unless they in terms interpose to protect a judgment lien; and where they do not it stands, as at common law, subject to the prior conveyance, though this be not recorded.[58] If there be an existing mortgage at the time the judgment is rendered, the judgment will bind only the equity of redemption, whether the mortgage be recorded or not, or whether the judgment creditor had or had not actual notice of the mortgage when he obtained the judgment.[59] In such case a purchaser at the execution sale under the judgment will take subject to the mortgage.[60] But a sale under a senior execution will defeat the lien of a junior mortgage, although the mortgagee may have the liens marshaled in equity to secure satisfaction out of the personalty.[61]

A recorded mortgage is superior to a subsequent attachment.[62] An attachment of land upon the debt of one holding the record title does not avail at all against the equitable owner of the estate, or against one claiming under a mortgage or deed not recorded.[63] There is no ·appreciable distinction between an attachment and a levy of an execution or a judgment lien, except that which results from the amount of expense incurred in the latter proceedings, and such expense can not be regarded as placing the creditor in the situation of a bona fide purchaser.[64] Whether the lien be by attachment or by judgment, it is

---

[57] Brace v. Marlborough, 2 P. Wms. 491.

[58] Knell v. Green St. Bldg. Assn., 34 Md. 67. See post § 465.

[59] Hackett v. Callender, 32 Vt. 97. Contra see Persons v. Van Tassel, 15 S. Dak. 362, 89 N. W. 861.

[60] Johnston v. Crawley, 22 Ga. 348; McIntire v. Garmany, 8 Ga. App. 802, 70 S. E. 198; Knapp v. Jones, 143 Ill. 375, 32 N. E. 382; Meacham v. Steele, 93 Ill. 135; Morton v. White, 2 Ind. 663; De Blanc v. Dumartrait, 3 La. Ann. 542; Nulsen v. Wishon, 68 Mo. 383; Minor Lumber Co. v. Thompson, 91 Nebr. 93, 135 N. W. 429; Lovejoy v. Lovejoy, 31 N. J. Eq. 55.

[61] Gadberry v. McClure, 4 Strob. Eq. (S. Car.) 175.

[62] Beamer v. Freeman, 84 Cal. 554, 24 Pac. 169; First Nat. Bank v. Hayzlett, 40 Iowa 659; Iowa Loan &c. Co. v. Mowery, 67 Iowa 113, 24 N. W. 747; Western Union Tel. Co.

v. Caldwell, 141 Mass. 489, 6 N. E. 737; Longstreet v. Shipman, 5 N. J. Eq. 43. See also Claflin v. South Carolina R. Co,. 8 Fed. 118, 4 Hughes 12 (mortgage defectively recorded); Newton First Nat. Bank v. Jasper County Bank, 71 Iowa 486, 32 N. W. 400; Northwestern Forwarding Co. v. Mahaffey, 36 Kans. 152, 12 Pac. 705; Campion v. Kille, 14 N. J. Eq. 229; Temple v. Hooker, 6 Vt. 240. A defect in the mortgage, or conduct of the mortgagee creating an estoppel may defeat his priority. Scrivener v. Dietz, 68 Cal. 1, 8 Pac. 609.

[63] Le Clert v. Oullahan, 52 Cal. 252; Hart v. Farmers' &c. Bank, 33 Vt. 252.

[64] Cover v. Black, 1 Pa. St. 493, per Chief Justice Gibson; Shryock v. Waggoner, 28 Pa. St. 430; Heister v. Fortner, 2 Binn. (Pa.) 40, 4 Am. Dec. 417; Rodgers v. Gibson, 4 Yeates (Pa.) 111.

a lien only upon the real estate, or the interest in it owned by the debtor, not upon that owned by another, as is the case when the debtor has conveyed it or mortgaged it, although the deed be unrecorded. The creditor is entitled to the same rights as the debtor had, and to no more.[65]

§ 463. Unrecorded mortgage preferred to judgment.—The priority of mortgage and judgment liens is determined at common law by the date of their acquisition, the first in time being the first in right.[66]

[65] Tarver v. Ellison, 57 Ga. 54; Scott v. McMurran, 7 Blackf. (Ind.) 284; Goodenough v. McCoid, 44 Iowa 659; Dunwell v. Bidwell, 8 Minn. 34; Lambertville Nat. Bank v. Boss (N. J.) 13 Atl. 18; Jackson v. Dubois, 4 Johns. (N. Y.) 216; Wertz's Appeal, 65 Pa. St. 306.

[66] Bronson v. La Crosse &c. R. Co., 2 Wall. (U. S.) 283, 17 L. ed. 725; First Nat. Bank v. Caldwell, 4 Dill. (U. S.) 314, Fed. Cas. No. 4798; McArthur v. Caldwell, 31 Fed. 521; Trapnall v. Richardson, 13 Ark. 543, 58 Am. Dec. 338; Cambridge Tile Co. v. W. B. Scaife &c. Co., 137 Ga. 281, 73 S. E. 492; Marshall v. Hodgkins, 99 Ga. 592, 27 S. E. 748; Horne v. Seisel, 92 Ga. 683, 19 S. E. 709; Osborne v. Hill, 91 Ga. 137, 16 S. E. 965; McAlpin v. Bailey, 76 Ga. 687; Hughes v. Mt. Vernon Bank, 4 Ga. App. 23, 60 S. E. 809; Tyrrell v. Ward, 102 Ill. 29; Spalding v. Heideman, 96 Ill. App. 405; Paxton v. Sterne, 127 Ind. 289, 26 N. E. 557; Morton v. White, 2 Ind. 663; Curie v. Wright, 140 Iowa 651, 119 N. W. 74; Weare v. Williams, 85 Iowa 253, 52 N. W. 328; Markson v. Buchan, 33 Kans. 739, 7 Pac. 578; Portwood v. Outton, 3 B. Mon. (Ky.) 247; Reigle v. Leiter, 8 Md. 405; Chandler v. Parsons, 100 Mich. 313, 58 N. W. 1011; Talbot v. Barager, 37 Minn. 208, 34 N. W. 23; Marlow v. Johnson, 31 Miss. 128; Sayre v. Coyne (N. J. Eq.), 33 Atl. 300; Tichenor v. Tichenor, 45 N. J. Eq. 664, 18 Atl. 301; Lambertville Nat. Bank v. Boss (N. J. Eq.), 13 Atl. 18; Westervelt v. Voorhis, 42 N. J. Eq. 179, 6 Atl. 665; People v. Bacon, 99 N. Y. 275, 2 N. E. 4; Stevens v. Watson, 45 How. Pr. (N. Y.) 104; McKenzie v. Bismarck Water Co., 6 N. Dak. 361, 71 N. W. 608; Porter v. Barclay, 18 Ohio St. 546; Kramer v. Farmers' &c. Bank, 15 Ohio 253; Fleek v. Zillhaver, 117 Pa. St. 213, 12 Atl. 420; Kelso v. Kelly, 14 Pa. St. 204; Lynch v. Dearth, 2 Pen. & W. (Pa.) 101; Moore's Appeal, 7 Watts & S. (Pa.) 298; Febeiger v. Craighead, 2 Yeates (Pa.) 42, 1 L. ed. 778; Drewery v. Columbia Amusement Co., 87 S. Car. 445, 69 S. E. 879, 1094; Coleman v. Hamburg Bank, 2 Strob. Eq. (S. Car.) 285, 49 Am. Dec. 671; Blose v. Bear, 87 Va. 177, 12 S. E. 294, 11 L. R. A. 705; Nutt v. Summers, 78 Va. 164; American Sav. &c. Bank v. Helgesen, 64 Wash. 54, 116 Pac. 837, Ann. Cas. 1913 A, 390; Badeley v. Consolidated Bank, 38 Ch. Div. 238, 57 L. J. Ch. 468, 59 L. T. (N. S.) 419. See also Penn Mutual Life Ins. Co. v. Heiss, 141 Ill. 35, 31 N. E. 138, 33 Am. St. 273 (judgments against railroad by abutting owners preferred to mortgage bonds); Bell v. Cassem, 158 Ill. 45, 41 N. E. 1089, 29 L. R. A. 571 (prior mortgage preferred to subsequent judgment under Illinois Dram-Shop Act.); Seeberger v. Campbell, 88 Iowa 63, 55 N. W. 20 (judgments against legal owner, who is a mere trustee, postponed to mortgages given by the equitable owner). This rule of priority applies to an equitable mortgage, Cayce v. Stovall, 50 Miss. 396; and to an absolute deed intended as a mortgage, Edler v. Clark, 51 Fed. 117; and to a mortgage covering after-acquired property, Rice v. Kelso, 57 Iowa 115, 7 N. W. 3, 10 N. W. 335; People's Trust Co. v. Brooklyn &c. R. Co., 121 App. Div. 604, 106 N. Y. S. 782; and to a junior mortgage securing a debt to the

A mortgage recorded prior to an entry of judgment which is a lien upon the property takes precedence of the judgment lien,[67] and a foreclosure of the mortgage, or a sale of the property under a power in the mortgage, defeats the judgment lien;[68] and a mortgage recorded prior to an attachment is superior to the attachment lien, although the order for attachment be in the sheriff's hands at the time, but the attachment has not been actually made.[69]

If the judgment becomes a lien only from the date of its record, then as against a deed priority depends upon the priority of record. An attachment which takes effect from the time of delivering the order to the officer takes precedence of the lien of a mortgage executed before the order of attachment comes to the hands of the officer, but not recorded till afterward.[70] And so a judgment which is a lien from the time it is docketed takes precedence of a mortgage executed and recorded after the docketing of the judgment.[71] If the judgment becomes a lien upon the real estate of the debtor from the date of entry or docketing, the order of priority between a judgment lien and a mortgage lien depends upon the order in which they are respectively entered and recorded;[72] at least where there are no intervening equities, arising from actual notice.[73]

A creditor having actual notice of a prior unrecorded mortgage at the time of obtaining his judgment lien,[74] or before the debt was con-

United States, Hoppock v. Shober, 69 N. Car. 153.

[67] Horne v. Seisel, 92 Ga. 683, 19 S. E. 709; Kennard v. Mabry, 78 Tex. 151, 14 S. W. 272.

[68] Gray v. Patton, 13 Bush (Ky.) 625; McKenzie v. Bismarck Water Co., 6 N. Dak. 361, 71 N. W. 608.

[69] Coles v. Berryhill, 37 Minn. 56, 33 N. W. 213; Belbaze v. Ratto, 69 Tex. 636, 7 S. W. 501. See also Rice-Stix Dry Goods Co. v. Saunders, 128 La. 82, 54 So. 479.

[70] Cross v. Fombey, 54 Ark. 179, 15 S. W. 461.

[71] Gulley v. Thurston, 112 N. Car. 192, 17 S. E. 13.

[72] Ludlow v. Clinton Line R. Co., 1 Flip. (U. S.) 25, Fed. Cas. No. 8600; Martinez v. Lindsey, 91 Ala. 334, 8 So. 787; Snell v. Cummins, 67 Ark. 261, 54 S. W. 342; Cabot v. Armstrong, 100 Ga. 438, 28 S. E. 123; Bell v. Cassem, 158 Ill. 45, 41 N. E. 1089, 29 L. R. A. 571; Warner v. Helm, 6 Ill. 220; Wood v. Young, 38 Iowa 102; Vanstory v. Thornton,

112 N. Car. 196, 17 S. E. 566, 34 Am. St. 483; Laurent v. Lanning, 32 Ore. 11, 51 Pac. 80; Britton v. Bean, 4 Phila. (Pa.) 289; Miller v. Wroton, 82 S. Car. 97, 63 S. E. 62, 449; Carraway v. Carraway, 27 S. Car. 576, 5 S. E. 157; Hill v. Rixey, 26 Grat. (Va.) 72.

[73] Hutchinson v. Bramhall, 42 N. J. Eq. 372, 7 Atl. 873.

[74] Williams v. Tatnall, 29 Ill. 553; Thomas v. Vanlieu, 28 Cal. 616; Mead v. New York, H. &c. R. Co., 45 Conn. 199. See also Cheesebrough v. Millard, 1 Johns. Ch. (N. Y.) 409, 7 Am. Dec. 494. It is immaterial how the knowledge was acquired. A judgment creditor who was joined in foreclosure of a mortgage on the property, can not deny actual notice of the mortgage. Newhall v. Hatch, 134 Cal. 269, 66 Pac. 266, 55 L. R. A. 673. Notice of a prior incumbrance which is void in law does not affect the right of a creditor. Hubbard v. Savage, 8 Conn. 215.

tracted,[75] will hold his lien subject to such mortgage. A deed or mortgage executed and recorded after a judgment has been entered against the mortgagor is of course subject to the judgment lien,[76] unless the mortgagor holds the land in trust, such as a resulting trust in favor of his wife.[77] As between a mortgage and a judgment rendered in a county different from that in which the land is, priority is determined by priority of registration in the county where the land is situate.[78]

The rules for determining priority between a judgment docketed on the same day on which a mortgage is recorded, vary in the different states. In Delaware, a judgment is a lien during the entire day of its entry, and has priority over a mortgage recorded at any hour the same day.[79] In Pennsylvania there is no priority as between a mortgage and a judgment entered of record on the same day, and the record not showing which was first recorded, they are payable pro rata as equal liens.[80] This rule seems to prevail in South Carolina and Tennessee, the judgment and mortgage being of equal rank, in the absence of proof of actual priority.[81] In Ohio the lien of a judgment relates back to the day and hour fixed by statute for the opening of the term of court, at which the judgment was rendered.[82]

Under a statute which provides that a mortgage recorded within a certain time after its date shall take effect as between the parties from its date, a judgment recovered subsequently to the date of a mortgage, and before the recording of it, binds only the equity of redemption, and is subject to the mortgage without regard to the question of actual notice, if the mortgage is subsequently recorded within the time prescribed by law.[83] A deed or mortgage recorded after the time prescribed takes priority over the claims of all creditors who have not previously established a lien.[84]

[75] Lahr's Appeal, 90 Pa. St. 507; Britton's Appeal, 45 Pa. St. 172.

[76] Tarver v. Ellison, 57 Ga. 54; Lambertville Nat. Bank v. Boss (N. J.), 13 Atl. 18; Vanstory v. Thornton, 112 N. Car. 196, 17 S. E. 566.

[77] Seeberger v. Campbell, 88 Iowa 63, 55 N. W. 20.

[78] Firebaugh v. Ward, 51 Tex. 409.

[79] Hollingsworth v. Thompson, 5 Har. (Del.) 432.

[80] Hendrickson's Appeal, 24 Pa. St. 363; Claason's Appeal, 22 Pa. St. 359; Clawson v. Eichbaum, 2 Grant Cas. (Pa.) 130; Maze v. Burke, 12 Phila. (Pa.) 335; Doolittle v. Barry,

2 Phila. (Pa.) 354. But see Magaw v. Garrett, 25 Pa. St. 319.

[81] Ex parte Stagg, 1 Nott & McC. (S. Car.) 405; Murfree v. Carmack, 4 Yerg. (Tenn.) 270, 26 Am. Dec. 232.

[82] Hemminway v. Davis, 24 Ohio St. 150; Davis v. Messenger, 17 Ohio St. 231. See also Follett v. Hall, 16 Ohio 111, 47 Am. Dec. 365.

[83] Knell v. Green St. Building Assn., 34 Md. 67. See ante § 458 and post § 544.

[84] South Carolina Loan &c. Co. v. McPherson, 26 S. Car. 431, 2 S. E. 267.

§ 464. Priority of unrecorded mortgage over subsequent judgment.

—In most of the states, a judgment obtained by a creditor and duly entered and docketed, without notice of an unrecorded mortgage previously given by his debtor on the same land, will have priority over the mortgage, and the mortgage will not be enforcible against the land, until the creditor is satisfied.[85] But in several states an unrecorded deed or mortgage is preferred to a subsequent judgment. A judgment or attaching creditor is not considered a purchaser within the recording acts of these states, for a judgment lien or attachment is not protected by them; and a deed or mortgage being valid without being recorded, for all purposes except that of preserving its lien against bona fide purchasers and mortgagees, is valid against a subsequent judgment lien.[86] In such case it makes no difference that the

---

[85] Lash v. Hardick, 5 Dill. (U. S.) 505, Fed. Cas. No. 8097; Chadwick v. Carson, 78 Ala. 116; Barker v. Bell, 37 Ala. 354; De Vendell v. Hamilton, 27 Ala. 156; Cleveland v. Shannon (Ark.), 12 S. W. 497; Hawkins v. Files, 51 Ark. 417, 11 S. W. 681; New England Mtg. &c. Co. v. Ober, 84 Ga. 294, 10 S. E. 625; Holst v. Burrus, 79 Ga. 111, 4 S. E. 108; Richards v. Myers, 63 Ga. 762; Shepherd v. Burkhalter, 13 Ga. 443, 58 Am. Dec. 523; Tarboro v. Micks, 118 N. Car. 162, 24 S. E. 729; Bostic v. Young, 116 N. Car. 766, 21 S. E. 552; Building &c. Assn. v. Clark, 43 Ohio St. 427, 2 N. E. 846; Tousley v. Tousley, 5 Ohio St. 78; White v. Denman, 1 Ohio St. 110; Jackson v. Luce, 14 Ohio 514; Mayham v. Coombs, 14 Ohio 428; Acklin v. Waltermier, 19 Ohio Cir. Ct. 372, 10 Ohio Cir. Dec. 629; Lahr's Appeal, 90 Pa. St. 507; Jaques v. Weeks, 7 Watts (Pa.) 261; Barnett v. Squyres, 93 Tex. 193, 54 S. W. 241, 77 Am. St. 854; Hunton v. Wood, 101 Va. 54, 43 S. E. 186; Heermans v. Montague (Va.), 20 S. E. 899; McCance v. Taylor, 10 Grat. (Va.) 580; McCullough v. Sommerville, 8 Leigh (Va.) 415. See also Dutton v. McReynolds, 31 Minn. 66, 16 N. W. 468; Golcher v. Brisbin, 20 Minn. 453; Sipley v. Wass, 49 N. J. Eq. 463, 24 Atl. 233; Voorhis v. Westervelt, 43 N. J. Eq. 642, 12 Atl. 533, 3 Am. St. 315; Thomas v. Kelsey, 30 Barb. (N. Y.) 268; Schmidt v. Hoyt, 1 Edw. (N. Y.) 652; Jackson v. Dubois, 4 Johns. (N. Y.) 216; Meier v. Kelly, 22 Ore. 136, 29 Pac. 265.

[86] Withnell v. Courtland Wagon Co., 25 Fed. 372; Ukiah Bank v. Petaluma Sav. Bank, 100 Cal. 590, 35 Pac. 170; Hoag v. Howard, 55 Cal. 564; Plant v. Smythe, 45 Cal. 161; Pixley v. Huggins, 15 Cal. 127; Shirk v. Thomas, 121 Ind. 147, 22 N. E. 976, 16 Am. St. 381; Heberd v. Wines, 105 Ind. 237; Wright v. Jones, 105 Ind. 17; Foltz v. Wert, 103 Ind. 404; Hays v. Reger, 102 Ind. 524; Boyd v. Anderson, 102 Ind. 217; Orth v. Jennings, 8 Blackf. (Ind.) 420; Albia State Bank v. Smith, 141 Iowa 255, 119 N. W. 608; Curie v. Wright, 140 Iowa 651, 119 N. W. 74; Rea v. Wilson, 112 Iowa 517, 84 N. W. 539; Sigworth v. Meriam, 66 Iowa 474, 24 N. W. 4; Duncan v. Miller, 64 Iowa 223, 20 N. W. 161; Phelps v. Fockler, 61 Iowa 340, 14 N. W. 729, 16 N. W. 210; First Nat. Bank v. Hayzlett, 40 Iowa 659; Hoy v. Allen, 27 Iowa 208; Churchill v. Morse, 23 Iowa 229, 92 Am. Dec. 422; Evans v. McGlasson, 18 Iowa 150; Hays v. Thode, 18 Iowa 51; Welton v. Tizzard, 15 Iowa 495; Patterson v. Linder, 14 Iowa 414; Seevers v. Delashmutt, 11 Iowa 174, 77 Am. Dec. 139; Bell v. Evans, 10 Iowa 353; Norton v. Williams, 9 Iowa 528; Wallace v. Mahaffey, 36 Kans. 152, 12 Pac. 705; Plumb v. Bay, 18 Kans. 415; Holden v. Garrett, 23 Kans. 98, where the subject is quite fully considered; Swarts v. Stees, 2 Kans. 236,

mortgage was given to secure future advances, which had not been made when the judgment was rendered.[87] It has even been held that lands omitted from a deed or mortgage by mistake may be regarded as conveyed by an unrecorded deed or mortgage so far as a subsequent judg-. ment is concerned; and the lien of the judgment will be subject to the equity of such deed or mortgage. This decision is based upon a statute which is held to accord priority only to a lien evidenced by some instrument "required to be recorded."[88]

A judgment lien is subject to every possible description of equity in favor of a third person against the debtor at the time the judgment lien attached, "and it is immaterial whether the rights of such third party consist of an equitable estate or interest in the judgment debtor's land, an equitable lien on his land, or a mere equity against a debtor which attaches to or affects his land."[89]

85 Am. Dec. 588; Clift v. Williams, 105 Ky. 559, 49 S. W. 328, 51 S. W. 821; Commonwealth v. Robinson, 96 Ky. 553; Forepaugh v. Appold, 17 B. Mon. (Ky.) 625; Righter v. Forrester, 11 Bush (Ky.) 278; Morton v. Robards, 4 Dana (Ky.) 258; Knell v. Green St. Bldg. Assn., 34 Md. 67. Since Gen. Stat. 1878, ch. 40, § 21, a judgment takes precedence of an unrecorded deed. Dutton v. M'Reynolds, 31 Minn. 66; Welles v. Baldwin, 28 Minn. 408; Greenleaf v. Edes, 2 Minn. 264; Kelly v. Mills, 41 Miss. 267; Martin v. Nixon, 92 Mo. 26, 4 S. W. 503; Fox v. Hall, 74 Mo. 315; Black v. Long, 60 Mo. 181; Sappington v. Oeschli, 49 Mo. 244; Reed v. Ownby, 44 Mo. 204; Potter v. McDowell, 43 Mo. 93; Stilwell v. McDonald, 39 Mo. 282; Draper v. Bryson, 26 Mo. 108, 69 Am. Dec. 483; Davis v. Ownsby, 14 Mo. 170, 55 Am. Dec. 105; Vaughn v. Schmalsle, 10 Mont. 186, 25 Pac. 102, 10 L. R. A. 411; A. J. Minor Lumber Co. v. Thompson, 91 Nebr. 93, 135 N. W. 429; Hubbart v. Walker, 19 Nebr. 94, 26 N. W. 713; Mansfield v. Gregory, 11 Nebr. 297, 9 N. W. 87; Harral v. Gray, 10 Nebr. 186, 4 N. W. 1040; Galway v. Malchow, 7 Nebr. 285; Sullivan v. Corn Exchange Bank, 154 App. Div. 292, 139 N. Y. S. 97 (decided under New York Real Property Law, § 291); Lamont v. Cheshire, 65 N. Y. 30; Thomas v. Kelsey, 30 Barb. (N. Y.) 268; Buchan v. Sumner, 2 Barb. Ch. (N. Y.) 165, 47 Am. Dec. 305; Stevens v. Watson, 4 Abbott Dec. (N. Y.) 302; Schmidt v. Hoyt, 1 Edw. (N. Y.) 652; Wilder v. Butterfield, 50 How. Pr. (N. Y.) 385; Jackson v. Dubois, 4 Johns. (N. Y.) 216; Shryock v. Waggoner, 28 Pa. St. 430; Cover v. Black, 1 Pa. St. 493; Carraway v. Carraway, 27 S. Car. 576, 5 S. E. 157; Coleman v. Hamburg Bank, 2 Strob. Eq. (S. Car.) 285, 49 Am. Dec. 671; Kohn v. Lapman, 13 S. Dak. 78, 82 N. W. 408; Roblin v. Palmer, 9 S. Dak. 36, 67 N. W. 949; Bateman v. Backus, 4 Dak. 433, 34 N. W. 66; Cowardin v. Anderson, 78 Va. 88; Floyd v. Harding, 28 Grat. (Va.) 401; Dawson v. McCarty, 21 Wash. 314; Karger v. Steele-Wedeles Co., 103 Wis. 286, 79 N. W. 216; Burgh v. Francis, 1 Eq. Cas. Abr. 320, pl. 1; Burn v. Burn, 3 Ves. 582; Finch v. Winchelsea, 1 P. Wms. 277.

Otherwise in Ohio, where a mortgage takes effect only from the time it is recorded. See post § 467.

[87] Thomas v. Kelsey, 30 Barb. (N. Y.) 268.

[88] Galway v. Malchow, 7 Nebr. 285.

[89] Baker v. Morton, 12 Wall. (U. S.) 150, 20 L. ed. 262; Peck v. Williams, 113 Ind. 256, 15 N. E. 270; Churchill v. Morse, 23 Iowa 229; Bush v. Bush, 33 Kans. 556, 6 Pac. 794; Sweet v. Jacocks, 6 Paige (N. Y.) 355; Meier v. Kelly, 22 Ore. 136,

The lien of a mortgage unrecorded at the date of a judgment, but recorded before the sale upon an execution thereon, is prior to the lien of the judgment, and the purchaser buys with constructive notice of the mortgage.[90] And likewise a prior unrecorded mortgage takes precedence over a sale under attachment or execution, if recorded before the sheriff's deed based upon such sale.[91]

But where a statute provides that a mortgage shall not be a lien upon the property until it shall have been recorded, then the doctrine of notice, it has been held, does not apply to the creditor, but to purchasers only.[92] And a statute providing that a mortgage shall not be valid against creditors until recorded, has been held to apply only to subsequent creditors without notice, who by their own activity have acquired a lien upon the property before the mortgage is recorded.[93] A statute postponing an unrecorded mortgage to all other liens obtained prior to its record, refers only to liens obtained during the lifetime of the grantor.[94]

An unrecorded mortgage given by an ancestor retains its priority over a judgment recorded against an heir at law during the lifetime of the ancestors, although the judgment creditor had no notice of the mortgage when he recovered his judgment.[95]

A statute conferring authority to mortgage leasehold estates, being in derogation of common law, must be strictly construed, and a provision therein for recording must be strictly complied with. Hence the recording of a leasehold mortgage and any extension thereof is absolutely necessary to give validity to the lien as against creditors of the mortgagor.[96]

29 Pac. 265; Snyder v. Martin, 17 W. Va. 276. See also Long v. Fields, 31 Tex. Civ. App. 241, 71 S. W. 774.

[90] Holden v. Garrett, 23 Kans. 98, which see for a full discussion of the subject; followed in Wallace v. Mahaffey, 36 Kans. 152, 12 Pac. 705. A confession of judgment and a mortgage, acknowledged and delivered on the same day, without intention as to preference will be considered equal liens, although the confession of judgment was docketed before the mortgage was recorded. Adirondack Hdw. Co. v. Walsh, 74 Misc. 594, 134 N. Y. S. 562.

[91] A. J. Minor Lumber Co. v. Thompson, 91 Nebr. 93, 135 N. W. 429.

[92] Holden v. Garrett, 23 Kans. 98; Davis v. Ownsby, 14 Mo. 170, 55 Am. Dec. 105; Hulings v. Guthrie, 4 Pa. St. 123; Jaques v. Weeks, 7 Watts (Pa.) 261. These cases seem to be overruled in Solms v. McCulloch, 5 Pa. St. 473; but the authority of the latter case is questioned in Uhler v. Hutchinson, 23 Pa. St. 110.

[93] In re Watson, 201 Fed. 962 (construing Kentucky Statute 1903, § 496).

[94] Civ. Code Georgia 1895, § 2727; Hawes v. Glover, 126 Ga. 305, 55 S. E. 62.

[95] Voorhis v. Westervelt, 43 N. J. Eq. 642, 12 Atl. 533. See also Vreeland v. Claflin, 24 N. J. Eq. 313.

[96] Stock v. German Catholic Press Co., 230 Pa. 127, 79 Atl. 414; Febei-

§ 465. Priority of judgment liens and attachments under registry laws.

—But, on the other hand, under the registry laws of many states it is held that the lien of a judgment or attachment is superior to an unrecorded mortgage, or to a recorded mortgage which is defectively executed, in the absence of actual notice of the mortgage on the part of the judgment or attaching creditor, or of the execution purchaser.[97]

ger v. Craighead, 4 Dall. (Pa.) 151, 1 L. ed. 778; Bennett v. Calhoun Loan &c. Assn., 9 Rich. Eq. (S. Car.) 163; Willis v. Heath (Tex.), 18 S. W. 801; Jewett v. Brock, 32 Vt. 65; Benton v. McFarland, 26 Vt. 610. See also Lane v. Lloyd, 33 Ky. 570, 110 S. W. 401. See also, concerning priority of mortgage given between the issuance of the first execution and an alias, Gamble v. Fowler, 58 Ala. 576; Bates v. Bailey, 57 Ala. 73.

[97] Taylor v. Miller, 13 How. (U. S.) 287, 14 L. ed. 149; Hitz v. National Metropolitan Bank, 111 U. S. 722, 28 L. ed. 577, 4 Sup. Ct. 613; Stevenson v. Texas R. Co., 105 U. S. 703, 26 L. ed. 1215; Benton v. Woolsey, 12 Pet. (U. S.) 27, 9 L. ed. 987; Lash v. Hardick, 5 Dill. (U. S.) 505, Fed. Cas. No. 8097; Ludlow v. Clinton Line R. Co., 1 Flipp. (U. S.) 25, Fed. Cas. No. 8600; United States v. Griswold, 7 Saw. (U. S.) 311, 332; United States v. Devereux, 90 Fed. 182, 32 C. C. A. 564; Compton v. Sharpe, 174 Ala. 149, 56 So. 967; King v. Paulk, 85 Ala. 186, 4 So. 825; Barker v. Bell, 37 Ala. 354; De Vendell v. Hamilton, 27 Ala. 156; Cleveland v. Shannon (Ark.), 12 S. W. 497; Hawkins v. Files, 51 Ark. 417, 11 S. W. 681; Main v. Alexander, 9 Ark. 112, 47 Am. Dec. 732; Moor v. Watson, 1 Root (Conn.) 388; Andrews v. Mathews, 59 Ga. 466 (provided the judgment debt was antecedent to the date of the mortgage); Richards v. Myers, 63 Ga. 762; Georgia Civil Code 1895, § 2727; Georgia Civil Code 1910, § 3260 (postponing an unrecorded mortgage to other liens obtained prior to its record); Cambridge Tile Co. v. W. B. Scaife &c. Co., 137 Ga. 281, 73 S. E. 492; Illinois Rev. Stat. 1891, ch. 30, § 30; Reichert v. McClure, 23 Ill. 516; Massey v. Westcott, 40 Ill. 160; McFadden v. Worthington, 45 Ill. 362; Guiteau v. Wisely, 47 Ill. 433; Columbus Buggy Co. v. Graves, 108 Ill. 459; Roane v. Baker, 120 Ill. 308, 11 N. E. 246; Munford v. McIntyre, 16 Ill. App. 316; Wicks v. McConnell, 102 Ky. 434, 20 Ky. L. 84, 43 S. W. 205; Gallagher v. Galletley, 128 Mass. 367; Coffin v. Ray, 1 Metc. (Mass.) 212; Berryhill v. Smith, 59 Minn. 285, 61 N. W. 144; Dutton v. McReynolds, 31 Minn. 66, 16 N. W. 468; Lamberton v. Merchants' Bank, 24 Minn. 281; Mississippi Valley Co. v. Chicago, St. L. & New Orleans R. Co., 58 Miss. 846; Humphreys v. Merrill, 52 Miss. 92. Walton v. Hargroves, 42 Miss. 18, 97 Am. Dec. 429; Westervelt v. Voorhis, 42 N. J. Eq. 179, 6 Atl. 665; Hoag v. Sayre, 33 N. J. Eq. 552; Sharp v. Shea, 32 N. J. Eq. 65; Roll v. Rea, 57 N. J. L. 647, 32 Atl. 214; Howell v. Brewer (N. J.), 5 Atl. 137; Moore v. Davey, 1 N. Mex. 303; Tarboro v. Micks, 118 N. Car. 162, 24 S. E. 729; King v. Portis, 77 N. Car. 25; Van Thorniley v. Peters, 26 Ohio St. 471; Tousley v. Tousley, 5 Ohio St. 78; Fosdick v. Barr, 3 Ohio St. 471; White v. Denman, 1 Ohio St. 110, 16 Ohio 59; Holliday v. Franklin Bank, 16 Ohio 533; Paine v. Mooreland, 15 Ohio 435, 45 Am. Dec. 585; Mayham v. Coombs, 14 Ohio 428; Dickey v. Henarie, 15 Ore. 351, 15 Pac. 464; Baker v. Woodward, 12 Ore. 3, 6 Pac. 173; Carpman v. Baccastow, 84 Pa. St. 363; Uhler v. Hutchinson, 23 Pa. St. 110; Hulings v. Guthrie, 4 Pa. St. 123; Hibberd v. Bovier, 1 Grant Cas. (Pa.) 266; Butler v. Maury, 10 Humph. (Tenn.) 420; McKeen v. Sultenfuss, 61 Tex. 325; Arledge v. Hail, 54 Tex. 398; Mainwaring v. Templeman, 51 Tex. 205; Grimes v. Hobson, 46 Tex. 416; Ayres v. Du-

The statutes of these states in terms provide that unrecorded conveyances shall be void as to creditors, or subsequent incumbrancers. In several states the statutes refer to "creditors" generally, without restriction to judgment creditors.[98] But the statutes of Alabama, Arkansas, Colorado, Minnesota and New Jersey refer to "judgment creditors," and simple contract creditors are not protected.[99] An unrecorded mortgage or conveyance is not valid against "subsequent creditors," under the statutes of Delaware, Maryland, Oklahoma, and under the wording of the earlier statutes of South Carolina and Texas.[1] In Indiana, Kansas, New Hampshire and Rhode Island, the

prey, 27 Tex. 593; Ranney v. Hogan, 1 Tex. Unrep. Cas. 253; Campbell v. Nonpareil Fire-Brick &c. Co., 75 Va. 291; Hill v. Rixey, 26 Grat. (Va.) 72; McCance v. Taylor, 10 Grat. (Va.) 580; McCullough v. Sommerville, 8 Leigh (Va.) 415; Parkersburg Nat. Bank v. Neal, 28 W. Va. 744; Anderson v. Nagle, 12 W. Va. 98. See also Shepherd v. Burkhalter, 13 Ga. 443, 58 Am. Dec. 523; Orth v. Jennings, 8 Blackf. (Ind.) 420; Albia State Bank v. Smith, 141 Iowa 255, 119 N. W. 608 (judgment creditor purchasing at execution sale protected); Baker v. Atkins, 107 La. 490, 32 So. 69; Golcher v. Brisbin, 20 Minn. 453. Where, however, the outstanding equity of a third person is one that arises by operation of law, and is incapable of being made a matter of record, the registry laws have no application, and the judgment creditor remains, as at common law, a mere volunteer. Kelly v. Mills, 41 Miss. 267.

[98] Void as against "creditors": Arizona: Rev. Stat. 1913, § 2080; Reid v. Kleyenstauber, 7 Ariz. 58, 60 Pac. 879. See also National Cash Register Co. v. Bradbury, 12 Ariz. 99, 95 Pac. 180.

District of Columbia: Code 1911, § 521.

Florida: Gen. Stat. 1906, § 2480.

Idaho: Rev. Code 1908, § 3408. See Lewiston Nat. Bank v. Martin, 2 Idaho 734, 23 Pac. 920.

Illinois: Rev. Stat. 1913, ch. 30, § 31, p. 534.

Kentucky: Stat. 1909, § 494.

Louisiana: Merrick's Rev. Code 1912, § 3329. See Pickersgill v. Brown, 7 La. Ann. 297.

Mississippi: Code 1906, § 2784.

Nebraska: Ann. Stat. 1911, § 10816.

North Carolina: Pell's Revisal 1908, ch. 18, § 982.

Tennessee: Ann. Code 1896, § 3749.

Texas: Sayles' Civ. Stat. 1914, § 1104.

Virginia: Code 1904, § 2465.

West Virginia: Code 1913, §§ 3834, 3835.

[99] Void as against "judgment creditors": Alabama: Code 1907, § 3383; McGhee v. Importer's Bank, 93 Ala. 192, 9 So. 734.

Arkansas: Stat. 1904, § 763.

Colorado: Mill's Ann. Stat. 1912, § 836; Emery v. Yount, 7 Colo. 107, 1 Pac. 686.

Minnesota: Gen. Stat. 1913, § 6844.

New Jersey: Comp. Stat. 1910, p. 1552, § 53.

[1] Not valid as against "subsequent creditors": Delaware: Rev. Code 1874, p. 504.

Maryland: Ann. Code 1911, art. 21, § 32, p. 502.

Oklahoma: Comp. Laws 1909, § 1195.

South Carolina: Gen. Stat. 1882, § 1776. Under this statute a judgment obtained after the execution of a mortgage, upon a debt contracted before its execution, can not be considered a subsequent debt. Carraway v. Carraway, 27 S. Car. 576, 5 S. E. 157. See Code 1912, § 3542.

Texas: Rev. Civ. Stats. 1889,

statutes make unrecorded conveyances void except as between the parties.[2] Connecticut, Maine, Massachusetts, Vermont, Louisiana, Missouri, Nevada and New Mexico, have similar statutes declaring that an unrecorded mortgage is void against other persons than the grantors, their heirs and devisees, and persons having actual notice.[3] In New York, Ohio, Pennsylvania, Michigan, and many of the western states, creditors are not mentioned in the statutes requiring record.[4]

A purchaser under execution sale following such judgment or attachment is, of course, in like manner protected against a prior unrecorded deed of which he had no notice.[4a] But a judgment creditor who purchases at his own execution sale is presumed to know of the

§ 4332. See also Sayles Civ. Stat. 1914, § 1104.

[2] Indiana: Burns' Rev. Stat. 1914, § 3957. See State Bank v. Backus, 160 Ind. 682, 69 N. E. 512; Hutchinson v. First Nat. Bank, 133 Ind. 271, 30 N. E. 952, 36 Am. St. 537.

Kansas: Gen. Stat. 1909, §§ 1671, 1672.

New Hampshire: Gen. Stat. 1891, ch. 136, § 4.

Oregon: Laws 1910, § 7129 (void as to third persons if not duly recorded).

Rhode Island: Pub. Stat. 1882, ch. 173, § 4; Gen. Laws 1909, ch. 253, §§ 7, 11.

[3] Connecticut: Gen. Stat. 1902, § 4036.

Louisiana: Rev. Code 1889, §2266. See Merrick's Rev. Code 1912, §§ 3329, 2251, 2262, 2264.

Maine: Rev. Stat. 1883, ch. 73, § 8. Under Laws 1895, p. 37, any one interested in real estate of which another holds an unrecorded deed may compel the latter to record his deed.

Massachusetts: Rev. Laws 1902, ch. 127, § 4, p. 1222.

Missouri: 1 Rev. Stat. 1889, §2420. See Rev. Stat. 1909, §§ 2810, 2811.

Nevada: Rev. Laws 1912, § 1038.

New Mexico: Comp. Laws 1897, § 3960.

Vermont: Pub. Stat. 1906, § 2581.

[4] Creditors not mentioned in these states: California: Civ. Code 1906, § 1214.

Georgia: Code 1911, § 3260 (unrecorded mortgage postponed to all other liens or purchases prior to

the record). See Rea v. Wilson, 112 Iowa 517, 84 N. W. 539.

Iowa: Code 1897, § 2925; but it is held that an unrecorded mortgage is not void as against creditors who have not acquired a lien. In re Lement v. McKibben, 91 Iowa 345, 59 N. W. 207.

Michigan: Ann. Stat. 1882, § 5683; Howell's Stat. 1913, § 10850. See Cutler v. Steele, 93 Mich. 204, 53 N. W. 521.

Montana: Rev. Code 1907, § 4683.

Nevada: Gen. Stat. 1885, § 2594.

New Mexico: Laws 1887, ch. 10. See Comp. Laws 1897, § 3960.

New York: Birdseye's Consol. Laws 1909, Real Property Law, § 291.

North Dakota: Comp. Laws 1913, § 5594.

Ohio: Gen. Code 1910, § 8543.

Oregon: Laws 1910, § 7129.

Pennsylvania: Purd. Dig. 1905, p. 1181, § 158.

South Dakota: Rev. Code 1903, § 2069. See Murphy v. Plankinton Bank, 13 S. Dak. 501, 83 N. W. 575; Kohn v. Lapham, 13 S. Dak. 78, 82 N. W. 408.

Utah: Comp. Laws 1907, § 1975.

Washington: Code 1910, § 8781.

Wisconsin: Stat. 1913, § 2241.

Wyoming: Comp. Stat. 1910, §§ 3653-3656.

[4a] Andrews v. Mathews, 59 Ga. 466; McFadden v. Worthington, 45 Ill. 362; Garwood v. Garwood, 9 N. J. L. 193; Jackson v. Chamberlin, 8 Wend. (N. Y.) 620; Paine v. Mooreland, 15 Ohio 435, 45 Am. Dec. 585; Morrison v. Funk, 23 Pa. St. 421; Ehle v. Brown, 31 Wis. 405.

existence of prior mortgages.[5] It does not matter that the judgment was for a pre-existing debt,[6] or that the subsequently recorded mortgage was given to secure purchase-money.[7] In Ohio, inasmuch as the statute declares that mortgages shall take effect only from the time they are left for record, a judgment recovered after the date of a mortgage, and before it is recorded, takes precedence of it.[8] Yet, in this state, a judgment creditor is not a purchaser, nor is he in any way entitled to the privileges of that position.[9]

A receiver appointed for and in the interest of general creditors is entitled to the debtor's real estate in preference to a mortgagee whose mortgage, though executed before the receiver's appointment, was not delivered till afterward.[10]

A mortgage which is not recorded in the county where the land conveyed lies, is not effective against creditors or purchasers. If a mortgage of land lying in two counties be recorded in but one, a foreclosure sale passes the land in both, as against a purchaser under a judgment docketed in the county where the mortgage was not recorded subsequently to the foreclosure proceedings. The want of registration does not disable the debtor from disposing of the property by a valid conveyance before the judgment lien attaches; nor does it prevent the court, in a proceeding to which the debtor is a party, from transferring it by a judicial sale.[11]

§ 466. Knowledge of unrecorded conveyance by judgment or attachment creditor.—Generally, knowledge on the part of a judgment or attaching creditor of an unrecorded conveyance of the debtor's property affects him as it would a purchaser; that is, the notice is equivalent to a record of the deed.[12] But although the creditor has notice

Otherwise in Mississippi: Kelly v. Mills, 41 Miss. 267.

[5] Throckmorton v. O'Reilly (N. J. Eq.), 55 Atl. 56.

[6] Uhler v. Semple, 20 N. J. Eq. 288.

[7] Roane v. Baker, 120 Ill. 308, 11 N. E. 246.

[8] National Bank v. Tennessee &c. Co., 62 Ohio St. 564, 57 N. E. 450. Mayham v. Coombs, 14 Ohio 428.

Under a statute of the state of Kansas, quite similar in effect, the Supreme Court of the latter state took a different view. Holden v. Garrett, 23 Kans. 98.

[9] Tousley v. Tousley, 5 Ohio St. 78.

[10] Cheney v. Maumee Cycle Co., 64 Ohio St. 205, 60 N. E. 207.

[11] King v. Portis, 77 N. Car. 25, 81 N. Car. 382.

[12] Wyatt v. Stewart, 34 Ala. 716; De Vendell v. Doe, 27 Ala. 156; Mead v. New York &c. R. Co., 45 Conn. 199; Goodard v. Prentice, 17 Conn. 546; Doyle v. Wade, 23 Fla. 90, 1 So. 516; Columbus Buggy Co. v. Graves, 108 Ill. 459; Sinking Fund Comrs. v. Wilson, 1 Ind. 356; Swan v. Moore, 14 La. Ann. 833; Priest v. Rice, 1 Pick. (Mass.) 164, 11 Am. Dec. 156; Lamberton v. Merchants' Nat. Bank, 24 Minn. 281; Loughridge v. Bowland, 52 Miss. 546; Humphreys v. Merrill, 52 Miss. 92;

of an unrecorded conveyance, a purchaser at the sale upon execution is not affected by it, and, being without notice himself, he acquires a title superior to the unrecorded mortgage.[13] And, on the other hand, a judgment creditor having gained priority over an unrecorded mortgage, a purchaser at the execution sale obtains the same priority, notwithstanding he has notice of the mortgage.[14] But knowledge acquired by an attaching or judgment creditor after his lien has attached does not displace or affect it.[15]

If a creditor's attorney have actual notice of a conveyance of his debtor's land, he is as much debarred from claiming relief, as a bona fide creditor without notice thereof, as if he had had such actual notice himself, although the creditor denies notice in his answer under oath.[16]

An illegal or unsuccessful attempt to record a mortgage is not notice to a subsequent judgment creditor; and a mortgage improperly recorded for want of probate is postponed to a judgment founded on an antecedent debt, so that a purchaser under execution will acquire a good title against the mortgagee.[17]

Bass v. Estill, 50 Miss. 300; Henderson v. Downing, 24 Miss. 106; Merchants' Bldg. &c. Assn. v. Barber (N. J. Eq.), 30 Atl. 865; Hutchinson v. Bramhall, 42 N. J. Eq. 372, 7 Atl. 873; Britton's Appeal, 45 Pa. St. 172; Uhler v. Hutchinson, 23 Pa. St. 110; Stroud v. Lockart, 4 Dall. (Pa.) 153; Barnett v. Squyres, 93 Tex. 193, 54 S. W. 241, 77 Am. St. 854; Hart v. Farmers' &c. Bank, 33 Vt. 252; Young v. Devries, 31 Grat. (Va.) 304; Floyd v. Harding, 28 Grat. (Va.) 401. See post § 538. In Tennessee it is held that notice, while effectual as against subsequent purchasers, does not avail as against creditors. Coward v. Culver, 12 Heisk. (Tenn.) 540; Lookout Bank v. Noe, 86 Tenn. 21, 5 S. W. 433. A judgment creditor who has joined in foreclosure proceedings can not deny actual notice of the mortgage. Newhall v. Hatch, 134 Cal. 269, 66 Pac. 266, 55 L. R. A. 673. A mere statement of a debtor to his creditor who is inquiring after the debtor's property and assets, that his property is mortgaged for all it is worth, is not notice of any particular mortgage, so as to give an unrecorded mortgage preference over a subsequent judgment. Condit v. Wilson, 36 N. J. Eq. 370. A judgment creditor who relases his judgment debtor to borrow money on a mortgage, is chargeable with notice of such mortgage, and he can not set up a judgment recovered after delivery of the mortgage, though it is not recorded before entry of the judgment. Hutchinson v. Bramhall, 42 N. J. Eq. 372, 7 Atl. 873.

[13] Miles v. King, 5 S. Car. 146.

[14] Smith v. Jordan, 25 Ga. 687; Wait v. Savage (N. J. Eq.), 15 Atl. 225.

[15] Loughridge v. Bowland, 52 Miss. 546; Humphreys v. Merrill, 52 Miss. 92; Hulings v. Guthrie, 4 Pa. St. 123.

[16] Dickerson v. Bowers, 42 N. J. Eq. 295, 11 Atl. 142.

[17] Andrews v. Mathews, 59 Ga. 466. See also Carper v. McDowell, 5 Grat. (Va.) 212; Manufacturers' &c. Bank v. Pennsylvania Bank, 7 Watts & S. (Pa.) 335, 42 Am. Dec. 240.

§ 467. Purchaser at execution sale—Notice and possession as affecting priority.—In most states, a purchaser of mortgaged property at execution sale under judgment against the mortgagor, takes subject to the paramount lien of the mortgage, and such purchaser can not recover possession until the mortgage debt is paid.[18] An execution under a judgment junior to a mortgage, binds only the debtor's equity of redemption, and the purchaser at the execution sale takes subject to the mortgage.[19] But in states requiring mortgages to be recorded, if a mortgage is not recorded within the time prescribed by statute,

[18] Rust v. Electric Lighting Co., 124 Ala. 202, 27 So. 263; Lovelace v. Webb, 62 Ala. 271; McDonald v. Foster, 5 Ala. 664; Whitmore v. Tatum, 54 Ark. 457, 16 S. W. 198, 26 Am. St. 56; Allen v. Phelps, 4 Cal. 256; Chester v. Wheelwright, 15 Conn. 562; Hitch v. Bailey, 115 Ga. 891, 42 S. E. 252; Tarver v. Ellison, 57 Ga. 54; Johnston v. Crawley, 25 Ga. 316, 71 Am. Dec. 173; Funk v. McReynold, 33 Ill. 481; Merritt v. Niles, 25 Ill. 282; Rahm v. Butterfield, 82 Ind. 163; Sinking Fund Comrs. v. Wilson, Smith (Ind.) 221; Hendryx v. Evans, 120 Iowa 310, 94 N. W. 853; Bush v. Herring, 113 Iowa 158, 84 N. W. 1036; Thomas v. McKay, 5 Bush (Ky.) 475; Dougherty v. Linthicum, 8 Dana (Ky.) 194; Forrest v. Phillips, 2 Metc. (Ky.) 194; Worsham v. Lancaster, 20 Ky. L. 701, 47 S. W. 448; Hubbard v. Ratcliffe, 13 Ky. L. 640; Terrio v. Guidry, 5 La. Ann. 589; Montgomery v. McGimpsey, 7 Sm. & M. (Miss.) 557; Meade v. Thompson, Walk. (Miss.) 450; Hubble v. Vaughan, 42 Mo. 138; State v. Cryts, 87 Mo. App. 440; Orr v. Broad, 52 Nebr. 490, 72 N. W. 850; Porter v. Parmley, 52 N. Y. 185, 14 Abb. Pr. (N. S.) (N. Y.) 16; Lansingburgh Bank v. Crary, 1 Barb. (N. Y.) 542; Weaver v. Toogood, 1 Barb. (N. Y.) 238; Jackson v. Hull, 10 Johns. (N. Y.) 216; Snyder v. Stafford, 11 Paige (N. Y.) 71; Cole v. White, 26 Wend. (N. Y.) 511; Halyburton v. Greenlee, 72 N. Car. 316; Anderson v. Holloman, 46 N. Car. 169; Ormond v. Faircloth, 5 N. Car. 35; State v. Laval, 4 McCord (S. Car.) 336; Erwin v. Blanks, 60 Tex. 583; Wilkins v. Bryarly (Tex.), 46 S. W. 266; Murrell v. Kelly &c. Shoe Co., 18 Tex. Civ. App. 114, 44 S. W. 27; Jones v. Herrick, 35 Wash. 434, 77 Pac. 798; Hamilton v. Carter, 12 Wash. 510, 41 Pac. 911. In Pennsylvania the mortgage must be a prior lien to all others, except other mortgages, ground-rents and purchase-money due the state, in order to continue a subsisting lien on the property after sale under a junior execution. Meigs v. Bunting, 141 Pa. St. 233, 21 Atl. 588, 23 Am. St. 273; Hohman's Appeal, 127 Pa. St. 209, 17 Atl. 902; Saunders v. Gould, 124 Pa. St. 237, 16 Atl. 807; Commonwealth v. Susquehanna &c. R. Co., 122 Pa. St. 306, 15 Atl. 448, 1 L. R. A. 225; Rheim Bldg. Assn. v. Lea, 100 Pa. St. 210; Zeigler's Appeal, 26 Pa. St. 465; Shryock v. Jones, 22 Pa. St. 303; Carpenter v. Koons, 20 Pa. St. 222; Glover v. Patterson, 104 Ga. 17, 30 S. E. 414. See also Ragan v. Coley, 4 Ga. App. 421, 61 S. E. 862; Gouwens v. Gouwens, 237 Ill. 506, 86 N. E. 1067, 127 Am. St. 338.

[19] Newberry v. Bulkey, 5 Day (Conn.) 384; McIntire v. Garmany, 8 Ga. App. 802, 70 S. E. 198; Johnston v. Crawley, 22 Ga. 348; Knapp v. Jones, 143 Ill. 375, 32 N. E. 382; Meacham v. Steele, 93 Ill. 135; Morton v. White, 2 Ind. 663; De Blanc v. Dumartrait, 3 La. Ann. 542; Nulsen v. Wishon, 68 Mo. 383; A. J. Minor Lumber Co. v. Thompson, 91 Nebr. 93, 135 N. W. 429; Lovejoy v. Lovejoy, 31 N. J. Eq. 55; Febeiger v. Craighead, 4 Dall. (Pa.) 151, 1 L. ed. 778; Bennett v. Calhoun Loan &c. Assn., 9 Rich. Eq. (S. Car.) 163; Willis v. Heath (Tex.), 18 S. W. 801; Jewett v. Brock, 32 Vt. 65; Benton v. McFarland, 26 Vt. 610.

a judgment against the mortgagor obtained before foreclosure, by a creditor without notice of the mortgage, takes priority over the mortgage, and an execution sale under the judgment extinguishes the lien of the mortgage.[20]

A purchaser at an execution sale without notice, either actual or constructive, of any interest or equity of a third person, is a purchaser for a valuable consideration, and is entitled to the protection of the registry acts, though the judgment did not make the judgment creditor a bona fide purchaser entitled to such protection.[21] But if the purchaser at the execution sale had at the time actual or constructive notice of the rights or equities of third persons in the land, he acquires a title subject to such rights and equities.[22] Possession operates as notice to the judgment creditor, and to the purchaser at the execution sale, of the purchaser's rights, just as it does to a subsequent purchaser.[23]

If the judgment creditor himself becomes the purchaser at the execution sale, he is not, according to the weight of authority, entitled to the position of a bona fide purchaser for value as against unrecorded conveyances.[24] Yet there are numerous authorities which hold that the judgment creditor so purchasing is a purchaser for value within the

---

[20] Taylor v. Miller, 14 How. (U. S.) 287, 14 L. ed. 149; Jordan v. Mead, 12 Ala. 247; Smith v. Jordan, 25 Ga. 687; Shepherd v. Burkhalter, 13 Ga. 443, 58 Am. Dec. 523; Hendryx v. Evans, 120 Iowa 310, 94 N. W. 853; Godchaux v. Dicharry, 34 La. Ann. 579; Hargreaves v. Merken, 45 Nebr. 668, 63 N. W. 951; Bennet v. Fooks, 1 Nebr. 465; McKnight v. Gordon, 13 Rich. Eq. (S. Car.) 222, 94 Am. Dec. 164. See also Mansfield v. Johnson, 51 Fla. 239, 40 So. 196, 120 Am. St. 159.

[21] McNitt v. Turner, 16 Wall. (U. S.) 352, 21 L. ed. 341; Thomas v. Vanlieu, 28 Cal. 616; Lee v. Bermingham, 30 Kans. 312; Den v. Richman, 13 N. J. L. 43; Jackson v. Chamberlain, 8 Wend. (N. Y.) 620; Holmes v. Buckner, 67 Tex. 107; Ayres v. Duprey, 27 Tex. 593, 86 Am. Dec. 657; Ehle v. Brown, 31 Wis. 405. But see Parker v. Prescott, 87 Maine 444, 32 Atl. 1001; Nugent v. Priebatsch, 61 Miss. 402.

[22] Apperson v. Burgett, 33 Ark. 328; Patterson v. Esterling, 27 Ga. 205; Curtis v. Root, 28 Ill. 367; Hoy v. Allen, 27 Iowa 208; Righter v. Forrester, 1 Bush (Ky.) 278; Perry v. Trimble, 25 Ky. L. 725, 76 S. W. 343; Priest v. Rice, 1 Pick. (Mass.) 164, 11 Am. Dec. 156; Ismon v. Loder, 135 Mich. 345, 97 N. W. 769; Fox v. Hall, 74 Mo. 315, 41 Am. Rep. 316; Black v. Long, 60 Mo. 181; Sappington v. Oeschli, 49 Mo. 244; Potter v. McDowell, 43 Mo. 93; Davis v. Ownsby, 14 Mo. 170, 55 Am. Dec. 105; Schroeder v. Gurney, 73 N. Y. 430; Hackett v. Callender, 32 Vt. 97.

[23] Weld v. Madden, 2 Cliff. (U. S.) 584; King v. Paulk, 85 Ala. 186, 4 So. 825; Glendenning v. Bell, 70 Tex. 632, 8 S. W. 324; Woodson v. Collins, 56 Tex. 168.

[24] O'Rourke v. O'Connor, 39 Cal. 442; Kelly v. Mills, 41 Miss. 267; McAdow v. Black, 6 Mont. 601, 13 Pac. 377; Wright v. Douglass, 10 Barb. (N. Y.) 97; Rutherford v. Green, 2 Ired. Eq. (N. Car.) 121; Orme v. Roberts, 33 Tex. 768.

recording acts, although the entire purchase-price is applied in payment of the debt.[25]

§ 468. Purchase-money mortgages—Priority—Joinder of wife.—

A mortgage given at the time of the purchase of real estate, to secure the payment of purchase-money, or the balance thereof, has preference over all judgments, mortgages, liens and other debts of the mortgagor, to the extent of the land purchased. It is so provided by statute in several states.[26] In other states the same precedence is given to purchase-money mortgages without the aid of any statute.[27] It has been

[25] Fash v. Ravesies, 32 Ala. 451; Hunter v. Watson, 12 Cal. 363, 73 Am. Dec. 543; Courson v. Walker, 94 Ga. 175, 21 S. E. 287; Rasin v. Swann, 79 Ga. 703, 4 S. E. 882; Smith v. Jordan, 25 Ga. 687; Frazier v. Crafts, 40 Iowa 110; Gower v. Doheney, 33 Iowa 36; Condit v. Wilson, 36 N. J. Eq. 370; Sharp v. Shea, 32 N. J. Eq. 65; Wood v. Chapin, 13 N. Y. 509, 27 Am. Dec. 62. But see Stevenson v. Texas R. Co., 105 U. S. 703, 26 L. ed. 1215; Wright v. Douglas, 10 Barb. (N. Y.) 97; Wallace v. Campbell, 54 Tex. 87; Grace v. Wade, 45 Tex. 522.

[26] Delaware: Rev. Code 1874, p. 504, Amended Code 1893, p. 630, § 21.

Georgia: Act of 1875. Prior to that act dower had preference to such a mortgage. See Georgia Code 1911, § 5248, also § 4048. Wilson v. Peebles, 61 Ga. 218; Carter v. Hallahan, 61 Ga. 314.

Indiana: 1 Rev. Stat. 1888, § 1089, 2 Rev. Stat. 1876, p. 334, Burns' Ann. Stat. 1914, § 1136.

Kansas: 1 Gen. Stat. 1889, § 3888, Gen. Stat. 1909, § 5198.

Maryland: 2 Pub. Gen. Laws 1888, art. 66, § 4, 2 Ann. Code 1911, art. 66, § 4, p. 1519; Glenn v. Clark, 53 Md. 608; Heuisler v. Nickum, 38 Md. 275; Ahern v. White, 39 Md. 409.

Mississippi: Code 1906, § 2780.

New Jersey: Rev. Stat. 1877, p. 167, § 77; Comp. Stat. 1910, p. 1535, § 4, p. 3301, § 10; Daly v. New York &c. R. Co,. 55 N. J. Eq. 595, 38 Atl. 202; Protection Bldg. &c. Assn. v. Knowles, 54 N. J. Eq. 519, 34 Atl. 1083; Hopler v. Cutler (N. J. Eq.), 34 Atl. 746; Bradley v. Bryan, 43 N. J. Eq. 396 13 Atl. 806.

New York: 4 Rev. Stat. (8th ed.) 1889, p. 2454.

North Carolina: 1 Code 1883, § 1272.

West Virginia: Roush v. Miller, 39 W. Va. 638, 20 S. E. 662. Under the recording acts of Washington, the question of priority between one holding a purchase-money mortgage and another can not be raised unless the mortgages concur in time or the priorities are controlled by some contract or equities arising between the several mortgagees. Wakefield v. Fish, 62 Wash. 564, 114 Pac. 180.

[27] Threefoot v. Hillman, 130 Ala. 244, 30 So. 513, 89 Am. St. 39; Cochran v. Adler, 121 Ala. 442, 25 So. 761; Campbell v. Anderson, 107 Ala. 656, 18 So. 218; McRae v. Newman, 58 Ala. 529; Tolman v. Smith, 85 Cal. 280, 24 Pac. 743; Guy v. Carriere, 5 Cal. 511. See also Wiser v. Clinton, 82 Conn. 148, 72 Atl. 928; Courson v. Walker, 94 Ga. 175, 21 S. E. 287; Rasin v. Swann, 79 Ga. 703, 4 S. E. 882; Scott v. Warren, 21 Ga. 408; Kneen v. Halin, 6 Idaho 621, 59 Pac. 14; Wehrheim v. Smith, 226 Ill. 346, 80 N. E. 908; Roane v. Baker, 120 Ill. 308, 11 N. E. 246; Elder v. Derby, 99 Ill. 228; Wright v. Troutman, 81 Ill. 374; Christie v. Hale, 46 Ill. 117; Fitts v. Davis, 42 Ill. 391; Austin v. Underwood, 37 Ill. 438, 87 Am. Dec. 254; Curtis v. Root, 20 Ill. 54; Spitzer v. Williams, 98 Ill. App. 146; Fletcher v. Holmes, 32 Ind. 497; Laidley v. Aikin, 80 Iowa 112, 45 N. W. 384; Koon v. Tramel, 71 Iowa 132, 32 N. W. 243; Phelps v. Fockler, 61 Iowa 340, 14 N. W. 729, 16 N. W. 210; Parsons v. Hoyt, 24 Iowa 154; Grant v.

said that the lien of a purchase-money mortgage is entitled to the
highest consideration in a court of equity.[28] Thus a purchase-money
mortgage takes precedence of a prior mortgage covering after-acquired
property, given by the same mortgagor before he took title.[29] If a
mortgage is in fact given for purchase-money, the fact need not be
recited or appear on its face, to give it priority.[30] But the contrary
fact may be proved against it, as well as fraud, which would postpone
it to other liens.[31]

The purchase-money mortgage executed and recorded contemporaneously with a title deed, has preference over a prior mortgage given
by the purchaser to a creditor and recorded before the title deed, since
the purchaser had no title when he executed the first mortgage. The

Dodge, 43 Maine 489; Hooper v. Cen-
tral Trust Co., 81 Md. 559, 32 Atl.
505, 29 L. R. A. 262; Ahern v.
White, 39 Md. 409; Clark v. Monroe,
14 Mass. 351; Marin v. Knox, 117
Minn. 428, 136 N. W. 15, 40 L. R.
A. (N. S.) 272; Peaslee v. Hart, 71
Minn. 319, 73 N. W. 976; Moody v.
Tschabold, 52 Minn. 51, 53 N. W.
1023; Schoch v. Birdsall, 48 Minn.
441, 51 N. W. 382 (quoting text);
Jacoby v. Crowe, 36 Minn. 93, 30 N.
W. 441; Stewart v. Smith, 36 Minn.
82, 30 N. W. 430; Bolles v. Carli, 12
Minn. 113; Banning v. Edes, 6 Minn.
402; Bainbridge v. Woodburn, 52
Miss. 95; Rogers v. Tucker, 94 Mo.
346, 7 S. W. 414; Morris v. Pate, 31
Mo. 315; Henry McShane Mfg. Co.
v. Kolb, 59 N. J. Eq. 146, 45 Atl.
553; Bradley v. Bryan, 43 N. J. Eq.
396, 13 Atl. 806; Clark v. Butler, 32
N. J. Eq. 664; Boies v. Benham, 127
N. Y. 620, 28 N. E. 657, 14 L. R. A.
55; Pope v. Mead, 99 N. Y. 201, 1 N.
E. 671; Wilson v. Smith, 52 Hun
171, 22 N. Y. St. 367, 4 N. Y. S. 915;
Bunting v. Jones, 78 N. Car 242;
Martin v. Vandeveer, 41 Ohio St.
437; Jarvis v. Hannan, 40 Ohio St.
334; Ward v. Carey, 39 Ohio St. 361;
Stephenson v. Haines, 16 Ohio St.
478; Commonwealth Title Ins. &c.
Co. v. Ellis, 192 Pa. St. 321, 43 Atl.
1034, 73 Am. St. 816; Coleman v.
Reynolds, 181 Pa. St. 317, 37 Atl.
543; City Nat. Bank's Appeal, 91
Pa. St. 163; Glaze v. Watson, 55 Tex.
563; Straus v. Bodeker, 86 Va. 543,
10 S. E. 570; Cowardin v. Anderson,
78 Va. 88; Brace v. Superior Land

Co., 65 Wash. 681, 118 Pac. 910;
Bisbee v. Carey, 17 Wash. 224, 49
Pac. 220. A purchase-money mortgage containing a provision that certain judgments against the mortgagor shall have priority over the
lien of the mortgage, is by such recitals rendered subject to the lien of
the judgments. Stover v. Hellyer
(N. J.), 62 Atl. 698. The fact that
mortgages were not executed until
the delivery of the deed, six years
after the contract of sale of land,
was held not to affect their character as purchase-money mortgages,
or their priority over a judgment
against the vendee rendered before
their execution. Marin v. Knox, 117
Minn. 428, 136 N. W. 15, 40 L. R. A.
(N. S.) 272. See post § 470.
[28] Brace v. Superior Land Co., 65
Wash. 681, 118 Pac. 910.
[29] Farmers' Loan &c. Co. v. Denver &c. R. Co., 126 Fed. 46, 60 C. C.
A. 588; Tolman v. Smith, 85 Cal.
280, 24 Pac. 743; Wendler v. Lambeth, 163 Mo. 428, 63 S. W. 684;
Hinton v. Hicks, 156 N. Car. 24, 71
S. E. 1086. But see Houston v.
Houston, 67 Ind. 276.
[30] Commonwealth Title Ins. &c.
Co. v. Ellis, 192 Pa. St. 321, 43 Atl.
1034, 73 Am. St. 816. See also
Boies v. Benham, 127 N. Y. 620, 28
N. E. 857, 14 L. R. A. 55 (recital
effective between two mortgages re-
corded same day).
[31] Preston v. Wolfshafer, 30 Pittsb.
L. J. (N. S.) (Pa.) 103; Thomas v.
Davis, 3 Phila. (Pa.) 171.

delivery of the deed and execution of the purchase-money mortgage being concurrent, the title did not rest in the purchaser for any appreciable time, but revested immediately under the purchase-money mortgage; for concurrent acts are in law but one act.[32]

A purchase-money mortgage is good and effectual against the wife of the mortgagor, without her joining in the execution of it. The seisin of the husband is instantaneous only; and it is a well-settled rule that in such case no estate or interest can intervene.[33] On the other hand, a mortgage made by a married woman for the purchase-money of the mortgaged land, the mortgagee supposing that she was unmarried, though invalid because of the wife's incapacity to make a separate grant, is a good equitable mortgage; for the deed and mortgage are evidence of an agreement for reconveyance. The wife is affected with a trust for a reconveyance, and a subsequent purchaser with notice would take the title in trust for the payment of the purchase-money.[34] The rules giving preference to a purchase-money mortgage and holding it effectual against the wife of the mortgagor, apply even where the mortgage is made to a third person,[35] who as part of the same transaction advances the purchase-money; but one advancing money is not entitled to be subrogated to the rights of the vendor, where this would result in defeating the vendor's lien or mortgage for the unpaid pur-

[32] Hinton v. Hicks, 156 N. Car. 24, 71 S. E. 1086.

[33] Jones v. Davis, 121 Ala. 348, 25 So. 789; Birnie v. Main, 29 Ark. 591; Frederick v. Emig, 186 Ill. 319, 57 N. E. 883; Walters v. Walters, 73 Ind. 425; Thomas v. Hanson, 44 Iowa 651; Hinds v. Ballou, 44 N. H. 619; Mills v. Van Voorhies, 20 N. Y. 412; Stow v. Tifft, 15 Johns. (N. Y.) 458, 8 Am. Dec. 266; Roush v. Miller, 39 W. Va. 638, 20 S. E. 663; Thompson v. Lyman, 28 Wis. 266. A purchase-money mortgage is good against the wife's dower. See post § 470 and cases cited.

[34] Ogle v. Ogle, 41 Ohio St. 359.

[35] Protestant Episcopal Church v. E. E. Lowe Co., 131 Ga. 666, 63 S. E. 136, 127 Am. St. 243; Achey v. Coleman, 92 Ga. 745, 19 S. E. 710; Curtis v. Root, 20 Ill. 54; Butler v. Thornburg, 131 Ind. 237, 30 N. E. 1073 (good against wife not joining); Brower v. Witmeyer, 121 Ind. 83, 22 N. E. 975; Dwenger v. Branigan, 95 Ind. 221; Laidley v. Aitkin, 80 Iowa 112, 45 N. W. 384, 20 Am. St. 408; Kaiser v. Lembeck, 55 Iowa 244, 7 N. W. 519; Mize v. Barnes, 78 Ky. 506; Price v. Davis (Ky.), 22 S. W. 316; Clark v. Monroe, 14 Mass. 351 (good against wife); Amphlett v. Hibbard, 29 Mich. 298 (mortgage for purchase-money valid against homestead though wife of mortgagor did not join); Marin v. Knox, 117 Minn. 428, 136 N. W. 15, 40 L. R. A. (N. S.) 272; Stewart v. Smith, 36 Minn. 82, 30 N. W. 430; Jones v. Tainter, 15 Minn. 512; Billingsley v. Niblett, 56 Miss. 537 (trust deed for purchase-money on homestead good without wife joining); Demeter v. Wilcox, 115 Mo. 634, 22 S. W. 613, 37 Am. St. 422; Rogers v. Tucker, 94 Mo. 346, 7 S. W. 414; Pearl v. Hervey, 70 Mo. 160; Adams v. Hill, 29 N. H. 202; New Jersey Bldg. &c. Co. v. Batchelor, 54 N. J. Eq. 600, 35 Atl. 745; Hopler v. Cutler (N. J. Eq.), 34 Atl. 746; Bradley v. Bryan, 43 N. J. Eq. 396, 13 Atl. 806; McGowan v. Smith, 44 Barb. (N. Y.)

chase-money.[36] But a mortgage executed by a purchaser to a third person before he has received his deed to secure a loan of money to make the cash payment on his purchase is not prior to a mortgage given by the purchaser to secure the balance of the purchase-money, at the time he receives his deed.[37] A mortgage executed to a third person a month after the conveyance, to secure purchase-money advanced by him, has no priority, where the advance was in fact a loan, there being no obligation upon the mortgagee to pay the debt, and no agreement that he should be subrogated to the vendor's rights.[38] Dower attaches as against every one but the mortgagee and his assigns.[39] A homestead exemption can not be set up against a mortgage for the purchase-money,[40] or even against a mortgage to secure money borrowed with which to pay the purchase-price when such mortgage is executed simultaneously with the deed of purchase.[41]

A deed made in consideration that the grantee shall pay to the grantor a specified life annuity, which consideration is expressed in the deed, creates a lien for the performance of the agreement similar in nature to the purchase-money mortgage.[42]

§ 469. **Contemporaneous execution of purchase-money mortgage— Vendor as mortgagee.**—A mortgage for purchase-money, to be entitled to preference, must be executed simultaneously with the deed of conveyance from the vendor. If an interval of time is left between the

232; Haywood v. Nooney, 3 Barb. (N. Y.) 643; Jackson v. Austin, 15 Johns. (N. Y.) 477; Kittle v. Van Dyck, 1 Sandf. Ch. (N. Y.) 76; Moring v. Dickerson, 85 N. Car. 466; Cowardin v. Anderson, 78 Va. 88; Carey v. Boyle, 53 Wis. 574, 11 N. W. 47; Jones v. Parker, 51 Wis. 218, 8 N. W. 124. See also Strong v. Ehle, 86 Mich. 42, 48 N. W. 868. But see Heuisler v. Nickum, 38 Ind. 270; Stansell v. Roberts, 13 Ohio 148, 42 Am. Dec. 193. A mortgage given by the grantee of land to a third person, contemporaneously with the delivery of the deed, has priority over a mechanic's lien for work done and material furnished the grantee under a contract partly performed before the title passed, only to the extent that it secures the purchase-money. New Jersey Bldg. &c. Co. v. Bachelor, 54 N. J. Eq. 600, 35 Atl. 745. See post § 472.

[36] Brower v. Witmeyer, 121 Ind. 83, 22 N. E. 975. See also Nichol-son v. Aney, 127 Iowa 278, 103 N. W. 201. See post § 472.

[37] Protection Bldg. &c. Assn. v. Know, 54 N. J. Eq. 519, 34 Atl. 1083. See also Farmers' Loan &c. Co. v. Denver, L. &c. R. Co., 126 Fed. 46, 60 C. C. A. 588. See post §§ 470, 472.

[38] Cohn v. Hoffman, 50 Ark. 108, 6 S. W. 511.

[39] Young v. Tarbell, 37 Maine 509.

[40] Stanley v. Johnson, 113 Ala. 344, 21 So. 823; Farnsworth v. Hoover, 66 Ark. 367, 50 S. W. 865; Kimble v. Esworthy, 6 Bradw. (Ill.) 517; Roby v. Bismarck Nat. Bank, 4 N. Dak. 156, 59 N. W. 719; Guinn v. Spurgin, 1 Lea (Tenn.) 228. See also Billingsley v. Niblett, 56 Miss. 537. See post § 470, and cases cited.

[41] Guinn v. Spurgin, 1 Lea (Tenn.) 228; Middlebrooks v. Warren, 59 Ga. 230. But see ante § 465.

[42] Doescher v. Spratt, 61 Minn. 326, 63 N. W. 736.

two transactions, during which the interest of the purchaser is liable to be seized on execution upon the judgment, this preference is lost, . and the judgment is entitled to priority.[43] It is not necessary, however, that the deed and mortgage should be executed at the same hour, or even on the same day, provided the execution of the two instruments constituted part of one continuous transaction, and were so intended.[44] But where the mortgage is not executed until a considerable time after the deed, they can not be construed as simultaneous and the mortgage will be postponed to the intervening valid liens.[45]

If the instruments are delivered at the same time, it does not matter that they were executed on different days, because they take effect only from the delivery.[46] And the fact that the mortgage was not executed until the delivery of the deed, six years after the contract for sale, has been held not to affect its priority as a purchase-money mortgage.[47] The provision that a mortgage from a purchaser to a vendor, delivered simultaneously with the deed, to secure the purchase-money, shall be preferred to a previous judgment against the vendee, does not imply that in every other case such judgment shall have preference. A mortgage from a lessee to his lessor, delivered at the same time with the lease, to secure future advances, is within this provision.[48]

If the vendor neglects to take a mortgage for purchase-money until after the execution of a mortgage to a third person for value and without notice, the mortgage for purchase-money is subject to the prior mortgage.[49]

In some states a provision of statute, that a mortgage for purchase-

---

[43] Gould v. Adams, 108 Cal. 365, 41 Pac. 408; Gould v. Wise, 97 Cal. 532, 32 Pac. 576, 33 Pac. 323; Ahern v. White, 39 Md. 409; Heuisler v. Nickum, 38 Md. 270; Foster's Appeal, 3 Pa. St. 79; Trigg v. Vermillion, 113 Mo. 230, 20 S. W. 1047. A purchase-money mortgage must be simultaneous with the deed to have preference over a mechanic's lien. Libbey v. Tidden, 192 Mass. 175, 78 N. E. 313.

[44] Pascault v. Cochran, 34 Fed. 358; Marin v. Knox, 117 Minn. 428, 136 N. W. 15, 40 L. R. A. (N. S.) 272; Stewart v. Smith, 36 Minn. 82, 30 N. W. 430, 1 Am. St. 651; Banning v. Edes, 6 Minn. 402; Demeter v. Wilcox, 115 Mo. 634, 22

S. W. 613, 37 Am. St. 422; Spring v. Short, 90 N. Y. 538.

[45] Cohn v. Hoffman, 50 Ark. 108, 6 S. W. 511; Roane v. Baker, 120 Ill. 308, 11 N. E. 246; Ansley v. Pasahro, 22 Nebr. 662, 35 N. W. 885.

[46] Maybury v. Brien, 15 Pet. (U. S.) 21, 10 L. ed. 11; Pascault v. Cochran, 34 Fed. 358; Banning v. Edes, 6 Minn. 402; Cake's Appeal, 23 Pa. St. 186, 62 Am. Dec. 328; Lafayette Bldg. &c. Assn. v. Erb (Pa.), 8 Atl. 62; Summers v. Darne, 31 Grat. (Va.) 791.

[47] Marin v. Knox, 117 Minn. 428, 136 N. W. 15, 40 L. R. A. (N. S.) 272.

[48] Ahern v. White, 39 Md. 409.

[49] Houston v. Houston, 67 Ind. 276.

money shall be preferred to any previous judgment which may have been obtained against the purchaser, applies only to a mortgage made by the purchaser to the vendor, and not to a mortgage made to a third person to secure the payment of money which was applied by the purchaser to the payment of the purchase-money for the land. The term "purchase-money" does not include money that may be borrowed to complete a purchase, but that which is stipulated to be paid by the purchaser to the vendor. It is only between them that it is purchase-money. As between the purchaser and a third party, it is simply borrowed money. To give this provision any other construction would be to assign and enlarge the vendor's lien without limit.[50]

A husband, on whose property there was a valid mortgage in favor of the wife, having borrowed money from a third person to purchase land from the government, after making the entry, executed a mortgage on the same day to secure the amount loaned, registering the mortgage a few days later. It was held that the latter mortgage for the loan was inferior to the wife's which existed before and attached to the land immediately when it was purchased.[51]

The effect of a mortgage to secure purchase-money, executed simultaneously with the deed to the vendee, is, that the vendee has only an instantaneous seisin, and the legal title remains with the vendor, who becomes the mortgagee of the land.[52]

A reservation in a conveyance of an annual rent, with a condition that the grantor may enter and take possession in case of nonpayment, is in effect a conveyance and mortgage back for the purchase-money, and is superior to any other incumbrance which the grantee can create.[53]

§ 470. Dower, homestead, and judgment liens ineffective against purchase-money mortgages.—A purchase-money mortgage, executed simultaneously with the deed of purchase, excludes any claim or lien arising through the mortgagor, such as a right of dower,[54] or home-

[50] Heuisler v. Nickum, 38 Md. 270; Anderson v. Ames, 6 Md. 52; Stansel v. Roberts, 13 Ohio 148, 4 2 Am. Dec. 193; Calmes v. McCracken, 8 S. Car. 87. See also Fontenot v. Soileau, 2 La. Ann. 774. See post § 472. In Claybaugh v. Byerly, 7 Gill (Md.) 354, 48 Am. Dec. 575, it was decided that a junior mortgage was entitled to no preference over a prior one by showing that the money received upon it was applied in payment of judgments which had priority. But see ante § 464, and

Flanagan v. Cushman, 48 Tex. 241, that a homestead right does not intervene in such case. The better and more general rule is stated in post § 472.

[51] Fontenot v. Soileau, 2 La. Ann. 774.

[52] Baker v. Clepper, 26 Tex. 629, 84 Am. Dec. 591.

[53] Stephenson v. Haines, 16 Ohio St. 478.

[54] Mayburry v. Brien, 15 Pet. (U. S.) 21, 10 L. ed. 646; Eslava v. Lepretre, 21 Ala. 504, 56 Am. Dec.

stead,[55] or a judgment[56] or another mortgage,[57] and no statute is neces-

266; Brigham v. Brigham, 113 Ga. 810, 39 S. E. 309; Harrow v. Grogan, 219 Ill. 288, 76 N. E. 350; Gibson v. Brown, 214 Ill. 330, 73 N. E. 578; Lohmeyer v. Durbin, 206 Ill. 574, 69 N. E. 523; Nottingham v. Colvert, 1 Ind. 527; Thomas v. Hanson, 44 Iowa 651; Gully v. Ray, 18 B. Mon. (Ky.) 107; Garton v. Bates, 4 B. Mon. (Ky.) 366; Moore v. Rollins, 45 Maine 493; Grant v. Dodge, 43 Maine 489; Smith v. Stanley, 37 Maine 11, 58 Am. Dec. 771; Gammon v. Freeman, 31 Maine 243; Hobbs v. Harvey, 16 Maine 80; Stanwood v. Dunning, 14 Maine 290; Glenn v. Clark, 53 Md. 580; McCauley v. Grimes, 2 Gill & J. (Md.) 318, 20 Am. Dec. 434; Purdy v. Purdy, 3 Md. Ch. 547; Smith v. McCarty, 119 Mass. 519; King v. Stetson, 11 Allen (Mass.) 407; Pendleton v. Pomeroy, 4 Allen (Mass.) 510; Webster v. Campbell, 1 Allen (Mass.) 313; Clark v. Munroe, 14 Mass. 351; Holbrook v. Finney, 4 Mass. 566, 3 Am. Dec. 243; Whitehead v. Middleton, 2 How. (Miss.) 692; Hinds v. Ballou, 44 N. H. 619; Adams v. Hill, 29 N. H. 202; Bullard v. Bowers, 10 N. H. 500; Griggs v. Smith, 12 N. J. L. 22; Mills v. Van Voorhies, 20 N. Y. 412, 10 Abb. Pr. (N. Y.) 152; Cunningham v. Knight, 1 Barb. (N. Y.) 399; Jackson v. Dewitt, 6 Cow. (N. Y.) 316; Coats v. Cheever, 1 Cow. (N. Y.) 460; Sherwood v. Vandenburgh, 2 Hill (N. Y.) 303; Stow v. Tifft, 15 Johns. (N. Y.) 458, 8 Am. Dec. 266; Bell v. New York, 10 Paige (N. Y.) 49; Kittle v. Van Dyck, 1 Sandf. Ch. (N. Y.) 76; Culver v. Harper, 27 Ohio St. 464; Welch v. Buckins, 9 Ohio St. 331; Rands v. Kendall, 15 Ohio 671; Reed v. Morrison, 12 Serg. & R. (Pa.) 18; Bogie v. Rutledge, 1 Bay (S. Car.) 312; Frazier v. Center, 1 McCord Eq. (S. Car.) 270; Henagan v. Harllee, 10 Rich. Eq. (S. Car.) 285; Pledger v. Ellerbe, 6 Rich. L. (S. Car.) 266, 60 Am. Dec. 123; Wheatley v. Calhoun, 12 Leigh (Va.) 264, 37 Am. Dec. 654; Seekright v. Moore, 4 Leigh (Va.) 30, 24 Am. Dec. 704; George v. Cooper, 15 W. Va. 666; 4 Kent Com. 39.

[55] Stanley v. Johnson, 113 Ala. 344, 21 So. 823; Moses v. Home Bldg. &c. Assn., 100 Ala. 465, 14 So. 412; Farnsworth v. Hoover, 66 Ark. 367, 50 S. W. 865; McHendry v. Reilly, 13 Cal. 75; Montgomery v. Tutt, 11 Cal. 190; Lassen v. Vance, 8 Cal. 271, 68 Am. Dec. 322; Dillon v. Byrne, 5 Cal. 455; Kimble v. Esworthy, 6 Bradw. (Ill.) 517; Andrews v. Alcorn, 13 Kans. 351; Cohen v. Ripy, 17 Ky. L. 1078, 33 S. W. 625; Williston v. Schmidt, 28 La. Ann. 416; Fournier v. Chisholm, 45 Mich. 417, 8 N. W. 100; Amphlett v. Hibbard, 29 Mich. 298; Jones v. Tainter, 15 Minn. 512; Peterson v. Fisher, 85 Nebr. 745, 124 N. W. 145, 133 Am. St. 688; Irwin v. Gay, 3 Nebr. (Unoff.) 153, 91 N. W. 197; Hopper v. Parkinson, 5 Nev. 233; Roby v. Bismarck Nat. Bank, 4 N. Dak. 156, 59 N. W. 719, 50 Am. St. 633; Starkey v. Wainwright, 6 Ohio N. P. 32; Boles v. Walton, 32 Tex. Civ. App. 595, 74 S. W. 81; McNeil v. Moore, 7 Tex. Civ. App. 536, 27 S. W. 163; Cornish v. Frees, 74 Wis. 490, 43 N. W. 507.

[56] Protestant Episcopal Church v. E. E. Lowe Co., 131 Ga. 666, 63 S. E. 136, 127 Am. St. 243 (citing text); Courson v. Walker, 94 Ga. 175, 21 S. E. 287; Scott v. Warren, 21 Ga. 408; Wehrheim v. Smith, 226 Ill. 346, 80 N. E. 908; Roane v. Baker, 120 Ill. 308, 11 N. E. 246; Gorham v. Farson, 119 Ill. 425, 10 N. E. 1; Fitts v. Davis, 42 Ill. 391; Curtis v. Root, 20 Ill. 53; Parsons v. Hoyt, 24 Iowa 154; Rochereau v. Colomb, 27 La. Ann. 337; Clark v. Munroe, 14 Mass. 351; Banning v. Edes, 6 Minn. 402; Clark v. Butler, 32 N. J. Eq. 664; Frelinghuysen v. Colden, 4 Paige (N. Y.) 204; Cake's Appeal, 23 Pa. St. 186, 62 Am. Dec. 328; Foster's Appeal, 3 Pa. St. 79; Masterson v. Burnett, 27 Tex. Civ. App. 370, 66 S. W. 90; Straus v. Bodeker, 86 Va. 543, 10 S. E. 570; Cowardin v. Anderson, 78 Va. 88; Summers v. Darne, 31 Grat. (Va.) 791; Bisbee v. Carey, 17 Wash. 224, 49 Pac. 220.

[57] Ely v. Pingry, 56 Kans. 17, 42 Pac. 330; Moring v. Dickinson, 85 N. Car. 466; Coleman v. Reynolds,

sary to effect this. "It is a principle of law," says Chief Justice Caton, of Illinois,[58] "too familiar to justify a reference to the authorities, that a mortgage given for the purchase-money of land, and executed at the same time the deed is executed to the mortgagor, takes precedence of a judgment against the mortgagor. The execution of the deed and of the mortgage being simultaneous acts, the title to the land does not for a single moment rest in the purchaser, but merely passes through his hands and vests in the mortgagee, without stopping at all in the purchaser, and during this instantaneous passage the judgment lien can not attach to the title. This is the reason assigned by the books why the mortgage takes precedence of the judgment, rather than any supposed equity which the vendor might be supposed to have for the purchase-money." Where a purchaser receiving a deed to land, simultaneously conveys it to another as security for a loan used in discharging the purchase-price, and the two conveyances are part of the same transaction, the title passes through the borrower unaffected, by the lien of a judgment against the borrower, which would have attached, had the title remained in him. This principle applies equally, where only part of the purchase-money is paid, and the security deed is given to secure the balance, as where the security deed is given for the whole purchase-price.[59] A purchase-money mortgage, like any other, must be recorded and due diligence is required of the mortgagee in so doing. Accordingly it has been held that a purchase-money mortgage loses its priority if a later mortgage is first recorded;[60] or if a mortgagee has no notice of the purchase-money mortgage, or a mortgagee with such notice assigns to one who purchases for

181 Pa. St. 317, 37 Atl. 543; City Nat. Bank Appeal, 91 Pa. St. 163. See also Bolles v. Carli, 12 Minn. 113; Howell v. Howell, 29 N. Car. (7 Ired.) 491, 47 Am. Dec. 335. Thus a purchase-money mortgage has priority over an earlier mortgage covering after-acquired property, given before the mortgagor acquired title. Farmers' Loan &c. Co. v. Denver &c. R. Co., 126 Fed. 46, 60 C. C. A. 588; Tolman v. Smith, 85 Cal. 280, 24 Pac. 743; Wendler v. Lambeth, 163 Mo. 428, 63 S. W. 684. But see Houston v. Houston, 67 Ind. 276. See post § 471.

[58] Curtis v. Root, 20 Ill. 54. See also Blatchford v. Boyden, 122 Ill. 657, 13 N. E. 801.

[59] Protestant Episcopal Church v.

E. E. Lowe Co., 131 Ga. 666, 63 S. E. 136, 127 Am. St. 243.

[60] Jackson v. Reid, 30 Kans. 10, 1 Pac. 308; Pyles v. Brown, 189 Pa. St. 164, 42 Atl. 11, 69 Am. St. 794; In North Carolina, a purchase-money mortgage is not entitled to priority over a subsequent mortgage which is first recorded though the last mortgagee has notice of the prior unrecorded mortgage. Quinnerly v. Quinnerly, 114 N. Car. 145, 19 S. E. 99. In Pennsylvania a purchase-money mortgage, to be entitled to priority over other liens, is required, by statute, to be recorded within sixty days after its execution. Allen v. Oxnard, 152 Pa. St. 621, 25 Atl. 568.

full value and without notice of the purchase-money mortgage; but if the assignment is not made until after the purchase-money mortgage is recorded, the assignee obtains no priority.[61] But it has also been frequently held that the priority of a purchase-money mortgage is not lost by the mere fact that the holder allows a junior mortgage to be first recorded, in the absence of other circumstances indicating his assent to the postponement of his security.[62] A mortgage given to secure money advanced to purchase an outstanding tax title to the mortgaged property, is entitled to priority over liens existing at the time of the sale for taxes.[63] A change in the form of the security for the purchase-money, as from a mortgage to a deed of trust, will not change the character of the debt. The consideration continues to be purchase-money.[64]

§ 471. **Mortgage recorded before acquisition of title postponed to purchase-money mortgage.**—The record of a mortgage made and recorded before the execution of the conveyance to the mortgagor, is not notice to the vendor, and is not as to him a purchase-money mortgage. The lien of the true purchase-money mortgage to the vendor attaches eo instanti upon the execution of the vendor's deed, as a part of an indivisible transaction.[65] Therefore a mortgage for purchase-money, executed and recorded contemporaneously with the deed of purchase, has priority of a mortgage executed by the purchaser before he concluded the purchase, though this was made to secure a loan with which to make the cash payment, and this mortgage was recorded before the

[61] Brower v. Witmeyer, 121 Ind. 83, 22 N. E. 975. A recital in a deed was held insufficient notice of an unrecorded purchase-money mortgage, to affect a purchaser from the grantee. See Volk v. Eaton, 219 Pa. 649, 69 Atl. 91.

[62] Continental Investment &c. Soc. v. Wood, 168 Ill. 421, 48 N. E. 221; Roane v. Baker, 120 Ill. 308, 11 N. E. 246; Brainard v. Hudson, 103 Ill. 218; Elder v. Derby, 98 Ill. 228; Moshier v. Knox College, 32 Ill. 155; Phelps v. Fockler, 61 Iowa 340, 14 N. W. 729, 16 N. W. 210; McKenzie v. Hoskins, 23 Maine 230; Heffron v. Flanigan, 37 Mich. 274; Jacoby v. Crowe, 36 Minn. 93, 30 N. W. 441; Oliver v. Davy, 34 Minn. 292, 25 N. W. 629.

[63] Kaiser v. Lembech, 55 Iowa 244, 7 N. W. 519.

[64] Austin v. Underwood, 37 Ill. 438,

87 Am. Dec. 254; Curtis v. Root, 20 Ill. 53; Kimble v. Esworthy, 6 Ill. App. 517; Kaiser v. Lembeck, 55 Iowa 244, 7 N. W. 519; Clark v. Munroe, 14 Mass. 351; Adams v. Hill, 29 N. H. 202; Haywood v. Nooney, 3 Barb. (N. Y.) 643; Jackson v. Austin, 15 Johns. (N. Y.) 477; Summers v. Darne, 31 Grat. (Va.) 791.

[65] Tolman v. Smith, 85 Cal. 280, 24 Pac. 743; Faircloth v. Jordan, 18 Ga. 350; Continental Ins. &c. Soc. v. Wood, 168 Ill. 421, 48 N. E. 221; Schoch v. Birdsall, 48 Minn. 441, 51 N. W. 382; Oliver v. Davy, 34 Minn. 292, 25 N. W. 629; Daly v. New York &c. R. Co., 55 N. J. Eq. 595, 38 Atl. 202; Protection Bldg. &c. Assn. v. Knowles, 54 N. J. Eq. 519, 34 Atl. 1083, affd. 55 N. J. Eq. 822, 41 Atl. 1116; Boyd v. Mundorf, 30 N. J. Eq. 545; Page v. Waring, 76

mortgage to the vendor.[66] And such purchase-money mortgage has been given priority over one previously made to secure a loan to make cash payment, and assigned to a purchaser for value after the purchase-money mortgage had been recorded.[67] The purchase-money mortgage is particularly entitled to priority where the vendor receiving it has no knowledge of the previous mortgage.[68] The purchase-money mortgage might become a second lien by the acquiescence of the vendor in the claim of priority for the other mortgage.[69]

Where, however, a purchaser of land executed a mortgage to a loan company for a part of the purchase-price and also a mortgage to the vendor and the deed and mortgages were filed for record on the same day, first the mortgage to the loan company, next the deed and last the mortgage to the vendor, the mortgage to the loan company was held to be entitled to priority, as the vendor was chargeable with all the knowledge the record imparted.[70]

Where an owner of land, subject to a life estate, gave a mortgage thereon covering any after-acquired title and interest, and the life estate was later conveyed to the mortgagor, a trust deed to secure the purchase-price thereof was held superior to the mortgage given before the mortgagor acquired title to the life estate.[71]

A judgment obtained against the mortgagor before the purchase

N. Y. 463; Dusenbury v. Hulbert, 59 N. Y. 541; Trust Co. v. Maltby, 8 Paige (N. Y.) 361; Hinton v. Hicks, 156 N. Car. 24, 71 S. E. 1086; Calder v. Chapman, 52 Pa. St. 359. See also Gould v. Adams, 108 Cal. 365, 41 Pac. 408; Ely v. Pingry, 56 Kans. 17, 42 Pac. 330; Hinton v. Hicks, 156 N. Car. 24, 71 S. E. 1086. See post § 541.

[66] Gould v. Wise, 97 Cal. 532, 32 Pac. 576; Brower v. Witmeyer, 121 Ind. 83, 22 N. E. 975; Koevening v. Schmitz, 71 Iowa 175, 32 N. W. 320; Ely v. Pingry, 56 Kans. 17, 42 Pac. 330; Heffron v. Flanigan, 37 Mich. 274; Schoch v. Birdsall, 48 Minn. 441, 51 N. W. 382; Truesdale v. Brennan, 153 Mo. 600, 55 S. W. 147; Ford v. Unity Church, 120 Mo. 498, 25 S. W. 394; Rogers v. Tucker, 94 Mo. 346, 7 S. W. 414; Turk v. Funk, 68 Mo. 18, 30 Am. Rep. 771; Protection Bldg. &c. Assn. v. Chickering, 55 N. J. Eq. 822, 41 Atl. 1116; Protection Bldg. &c. Assn. v. Knowles, 54 N. J. Eq. 519, 34 Atl. 1083; Brasted v. Sutton, 29 N. J.

Eq. 513; City Nat. Bank Appeal, 91 Pa. St. 163; Frazier v. Center, 1 McCord Eq. (S. Car.) 270; Cox v. Carson, 3 Head (Tenn.) 607.

[67] Bradford v. Russell, 79 Ind. 64.

[68] Schoch v. Birdsall, 48 Minn. 441, 51 N. W. 382.

[69] Mutual Loan Assn. v. Elwell, 38 N. J. Eq. 18.

[70] Roane v. Baker, 120 Ill. 308, 11 N. E. 246; Curtis v. Root, 20 Ill. 518; Dusenbury v. Hulbert, 59 N. Y. 541; Ward v. Carey, 39 Ohio St. 361.

[71] Wendler v. Lambeth, 163 Mo. 428, 63 S. W. 684. A vendee's mortgage for purchase-money, executed upon receipt of a deed, takes priority over liens created by the vendee prior to his acquisition of title, or before he had paid the purchase-money. Rogers v. Tucker, 94 Mo. 346, 7 S. W. 414. Citing Curtis v. Root, 20 Ill. 53; Winner v. Investment Co., 125 Mo. 528, 28 S. W. 998; Turk v. Funk, 68 Mo. 18, 30 Am. Rep. 771; Pomeroy's Equity Jurisprudence, Vol. 2, (2d ed.) § 725.

does not take priority over the lien of the purchase-money mortgage, though this be not acknowledged and recorded for a long period after the recording of the deed.[72]

§ 472. **Priority of purchase-money mortgage made to third person.** —A purchase-money mortgage may be made to a third person who advances the purchase-money at the time the purchaser receives his conveyance, and such mortgage is entitled to the same preference over a prior judgment as it would have had if it had been executed to the vendor himself.[73] It is not essential that there should be a prior agreement between the parties to give the mortgages priority. No such condition is necessary. When all the acts of the parties appear to be parts of one transaction, "in its legal effect it is the same as though the purchaser had executed a mortgage to the vendor for the purchase-money, and he had assigned it to the party advancing the money."[74]

A mortgage given for a loan to satisfy a purchase-money mortgage and to procure additional material after the property was acquired, can not itself be considered a purchase-money mortgage; and the prior mortgage having been extinguished by payment, the subsequent mortgagee was not entitled to be subrogated to the rights of the prior mortgagee.[75]

Where the contract of sale provides that the purchase-money mortgage to be given shall be a lien subsequent to the mortgage which the grantee is to negotiate on the premises, a person taking up the latter

[72] Higgins v. Dennis, 104 Iowa 605, 74 N. W. 9.

[73] Protestant Episcopal Church v. E. E. Lowe Co., 131 Ga. 666, 63 S. E. 136, 127 Am. St. 243 (citing text); Achey v. Coleman, 92 Ga. 745, 19 S. E. 710 (citing text); Curtis v. Root, 20 Ill. 54; Butler v. Thornburg, 131 Ind. 237, 40 N. E. 514; Brower v. Witmeyer, 121 Ind. 83, 22 N. E. 975; Dwenger v. Branigan, 96 Ind. 221; Laidley v. Aikin, 80 Iowa 112, 45 N. W. 384; Kaiser v. Lembeck, 55 Iowa 244, 7 N. W. 244; Parsons v. Hoyt, 24 Iowa 154; Mize v. Barnes, 78 Ky. 506; Price v. Davis (Ky.), 22 S. W. 316; Clark v. Munroe, 14 Mass. 351; Marin v. Knox, 117 Minn. 428, 136 N. W. 15, 40 L. R. A. (N. S.) 272; Stewart v. Smith, 36 Minn. 82, 30 N. W. 430, 1 Am. St. 651; Jones v. Tainter, 15 Minn. 512; Demeter v. Wilcox, 115 Mo. 634, 22 S. W. 613, 37 Am. St. 422; Pearl v. Hervey, 70 Mo. 160; Adams v. Hill, 29 N. H. 202; Haywood v. Nooney, 3 Barb. (N. Y.) 643; Jackson v. Austin, 15 Johns. (N. Y.) 477; Moring v. Dickerson, 85 N. Car. 466; Cowardin v. Anderson, 78 Va. 88; Carey v. Boyle, 53 Wis. 574, 11 N. W. 47; Jones v. Parker, 51 Wis. 218, 8 N. W. 124. See also Cohn v. Hoffman, 50 Ark. 108, 6 S. W. 511; Hill v. Cole, 84 Ga. 245, 10 S. E. 739. See ante § 468. Otherwise in Ohio and Maryland, by reason of the terms of the statute. Stansell v. Roberts, 13 Ohio 148; Heuisler v. Nickum, 38 Md. 270.

[74] Haywood v. Nooney, 3 Barb. (N. Y.) 643. See also Protestant Episcopal Church v. E. E. Lowe Co., 131 Ga. 666, 63 S. E. 136, 127 Am. St. 243 (citing text).

[75] Nicholson v. Aney, 127 Iowa 278, 103 N. W. 201.

mortgage acquires a lien on the premises prior to that of the purchase-money mortgage.[76]

§ 473. Deed and purchase-money mortgage as one transaction— Priority over homestead, dower, and mechanics' liens.—It must appear, however, that the deed and mortgage constituted but one transaction.[77] The seisin of the purchaser being merely a transitory one, no lien can intervene, and therefore the same rule applies to the exclusion of any intervening lien, as, for instance, a lien for labor and materials furnished the purchaser, who has entered before the execution of the deed and mortgage, which are afterward delivered simultaneously;[78] or an agreement made in relation to the premises by the purchaser before the purchase;[79] or right of homestead;[80] or right of dower.[81] If there be an interval of time between the purchase and the making of a mortgage to secure the purchase-money, the wife is not barred of her right of dower by reason of any recitals made by the husband in the mortgage deed in which the wife does not join.[82] In

---

[76] Peters v. Eden, 72 App. Div. 585, 73 N. Y. S. 936, 36 Misc. 490.

[77] Van Loben Sels v. Bunnell, 120 Cal. 680, 53 Pac. 266; Grant v. Dodge, 43 Maine 489; Wheadon v. Mead, 72 Minn. 372, 75 N. W. 598; Stewart v. Smith, 36 Minn. 82, 30 N. W. 430; Banning v. Edes, 6 Minn. 402; Demeter v. Wilcox, 115 Mo. 634, 22 S. W. 613, 37 Am. St. 422; Spring v. Short, 90 N. Y. 538. See Hurlbert v. Weaver, 24 Minn. 30, for peculiar circumstances under which a deed and mortgage executed at different times were regarded as constituting one transaction.

[78] Guy v. Carriere, 5 Cal. 511; Clark v. Butler, 32 N. J. Eq. 664; Macintosh v. Thurston, 25 N. J. Eq. 242; Strong v. Van Deursen, 23 N. J. Eq. 369; Lamb v. Cannon, 38 N. J. L. 362. See also Osborne v. Barnes, 179 Mass. 597, 61 N. E. 276; Saunders v. Bennett, 160 Mass. 48, 35 N. E. 111, 39 Am. St. 456; Ansley v. Pasahro, 22 Nebr. 662, 35 N. W. 885. Otherwise in Georgia by statute. Code 1882, § 1979; Code 1911, § 3352; Tanner v. Bell, 61 Ga. 584. A mechanic's lien may intervene where the deed and mortgage were not really part of the same transaction, though recorded simultaneously. Libbey v. Tidden, 192 Mass. 175, 78 N. E. 313.

[79] Bolles v. Carli, 12 Minn. 113; Morris v. Pate, 31 Mo. 315.

[80] Peterson v. Hornblower, 33 Cal. 266; Carr v. Caldwell, 10 Cal. 380, 70 Am. Dec. 740; Lane v. Collier, 46 Ga. 580; Allen v. Hawley, 66 Ill. 164; Magee v. Magee, 51 Ill. 500, 99 Am. Dec. 571; Austin v. Underwood, 37 Ill. 438, 87 Am. Dec. 254; Nichols v. Overacker, 16 Kans. 54; New England Jewelry Co. v. Merriam, 2 Allen (Mass.) 390; Amphlett v. Hibbard, 29 Mich. 298; Hopper v. Parkinson, 5 Nev. 233; Hand v. Savannah &c. R. Co., 12 S. Car. 314; Jones v. Parker, 51 Wis. 218. See Pratt v. Topeka Bank, 12 Kans. 570, for a case where a mortgage given upon a homestead by husband and wife was partly paid, and a new mortgage for the balance given by the husband alone, explained in Greeno v. Barnard, 18 Kans. 518. See ante § 464.

[81] Grant v. Dodge, 43 Maine 489; Bunting v. Jones, 78 N. Car. 242; George v. Cooper, 15 W. Va. 666; Jones v. Parker, 51 Wis. 218.

[82] Tibbetts v. Langley Mfg. Co., 12 S. Car. 465.

such case, also, a judgment rendered against the grantee prior to the purchase takes precedencê of the mortgage.[83]

Where a vendee executes a mortgage to secure a loan of money with which to pay the purchase-price of realty, after the purchase and receipt of a deed therefor, the mortgagee does not become entitled to a vendor's lien, and his equity is not superior to that of judgment creditors, whose judgments antedate the deed.[84]

A suit to foreclose a mortgage, given to secure the purchase-money of land, is not a suit for the enforcement of a vendor's lien. A mortgage for purchase-money has priority over a mechanic's lien for a building erected by the purchaser before he received a deed, and while he held a bond for a deed, and although the lien was filed before the making of the deed.[85]

§ 473a. Priority of purchase-money mortgage over mechanics' liens.—A purchase-money mortgage given before the attachment of a mechanic's lien, of course, takes priority thereof.[86] But a purchase-money mortgage may take priority though subsequent in time to a mechanic's lien. Thus, where a person in possession of property under a contract of sale, or otherwise than as owner, makes improvements thereon, and subsequently delivers a purchase-money mortgage, upon receiving a deed to the property, such mortgage has priority over mechanics' liens arising out of the improvements.[87] This rule

[83] Cohn v. Hoffman, 50 Ark. 108, 6 S. W. 511.

[84] Gilman v. Dingeman, 49 Iowa 308, distinguishing Parsons v. Hoyt, 24 Iowa 154.

[85] Virgin v. Brubaker, 4 Nev. 31. But to have such priority the purchase-money mortgage must be simultaneous with the deed, so that seisin in the vendee is only instantaneous, excluding the mechanic's lien. Libbey v. Tidden, 192 Mass. 175, 78 N. E. 313; Brown v. Haddock, 199 Mass. 480, 85 N. E. 573.

[86] Hill v. Aldrick, 48 Minn. 73, 50 N. W. 1020; Hoagland v. Lowe, 39 Nebr. 397, 58 N. W. 197; Kelly's Appeal, 1 Sad. (Pa.) 280, 2 Atl. 868; McCree v. Campion, 5 Phila. (Pa.) 9. See also Haupt Lumber Co. v. Westman, 49 Minn. 397, 52 N. W. 33; Fanning v. Belle Terre Estates, 152 App. Div. 718, 137 N. Y. S. 595. By statute in Georgia a materialman or laborer has a lien

superior to a prior purchase-money mortgage, unless he has actual notice of such mortgage; even though the mortgage was first foreclosed. Georgia Civ. Code 1895, §§ 2792, 2793, 2804; Baisden v. Holmes-Hartsfield Co., 4 Ga. App. 122, 60 S. E. 1031.

[87] Erwin v. Acker, 126 Ind. 133, 25 N. E. 888; Thorpe v. Durbon, 45 Iowa 192; Missouri &c. Lumber Co. v. Reid, 4 Kan. App. 4, 45 Pac. 722; Rochford v. Rochford, 188 Mass. 108, 74 N. E. 299, 108 Am. St. 465; Saunders v. Bennett, 160 Mass. 48, 35 N. E. 111, 39 Am. St. 456; Perkins v. Davis, 120 Mass. 408; Moody v. Tschabold, 52 Minn. 51, 53 N. W. 1023; Oliver v. Davy, 34 Minn. 292, 25 N. W. 629; Wilson v. Lubke, 176 Mo. 210, 75 S. W. 602, 98 Am. St. 503; Russell v. Grant, 122 Mo. 161, 26 S. W. 958, 43 Am. St. 563; Virgin v. Brubaker, 4 Nev. 31; Lamb v. Cannon, 38 N. J. L. 362; Gibbs v.

applies only to a contemporaneous purchase-money mortgage, given as part of the transaction by which the property is conveyed to the purchaser; and if the mortgagor had more than a mere transitory seisin, the mechanics' liens have priority over the mortgage given after acquiring title,[88] although such mortgage was given to secure unpaid purchase-money.[89] A mortgage given by a purchaser to a third person to secure a loan to pay the purchase-money, as part of the transaction by which the purchaser obtains his deed, has priority over mechanics' liens arising out of improvements on the property commenced before the purchaser acquired title.[90]

§ 474. **Necessity of record and acknowledgment between parties and their privies.**—The statutes do not make the recording of a mortgage essential to its validity between the parties. Consequently, the recording of a mortgage is not necessary as against the mortgagor;[91]

Grant, 29 N. J. Eq. 419; Paul v. Hoept, 28 N. J. Eq. 11; Mac Intosh v. Thurston, 25 N. J. Eq. 242; Strong v. Van Deursen, 23 N. J. Eq. 369; Rees v. Ludington, 13 Wis. 276, 80 Am. Dec. 741. See also Hillhouse v. Pratt, 74 Conn. 113, 49 Atl. 905 (contract of sale prohibiting acts creating liens). But see Avery v. Clark, 87 Cal. 619, 25 Pac. 919, 22 Am. St. 272.

[88] Osborne v. Barnes, 179 Mass. 597, 61 N. E. 276; Saunders v. Bennett, 160 Mass. 48, 35 N. E. 111, 39 Am. St. 456. See also McCausland v. West Duluth Land Co., 51 Minn. 246, 53 N. W. 464 (purchase-money mortgage given after mechanic's liens accrued).

[89] Ansley v. Pasahro, 22 Nebr. 662, 35 N. W. 885.

[90] Birmingham Bldg. &c. Assn. v. Boggs, 116 Ala. 587, 22 So. 852, 67 Am. St. 147; Middletown Sav. Bank v. Fellowes, 42 Conn. 36; Thaxter v. Williams, 14 Pick. (Mass.) 49; New Jersey Bldg. &c. Co. v. Bachelor, 54 N. J. Eq. 600, 35 Atl. 745; Campbell's Appeal, 36 Pa. St. 247, 78 Am. Dec. 375; Weldon v. Gibbon, 2 Phila. (Pa.) 176. If mechanics' liens have attached to the vendor's interest in the property they take priority over a mortgage to a third person advancing the purchase-money, for he can stand in no better position than the vendor. Fin-

layson v. Crooks, 47 Minn. 74, 49 N. W. 398.

[91] Shields v. Shiff, 124 U. S. 351, 31 L. ed. 445, 8 Sup. Ct. 510; Delane v. Moore, 14 How. (U. S.) 253, 14 L. ed. 163; Levinz v. Will, 1 Dall. (U. S.) 430; Rogers v. Page, 140 Fed. 596, 72 C. C. A. 164; Ward v. Ward, 131 Fed. 946; Smith v. Branch Bank, 21 Ala. 125; Andrews v. Burns, 11 Ala. 691; Larkin v. Hagan, 14 Ariz. 63, 126 Pac. 268; National Cash Register Co. v. Bradbury, 12 Ariz. 99, 95 Pac. 180; Reid v. Kleyenstauber, 7 Ariz. 58, 60 Pac. 879; Western Tie &c. Co. v. Campbell (Ark.), 169 S. W. 253; Rhea v. Planters' Mut. Ins. Assn., 77 Ark. 57, 90 S. W. 850; Downing v. Le Du, 82 Cal. 471, 23 Pac. 202; Christy v. Burch, 25 Fla. 942, 2 So. 258; Snow v. Lake, 20 Fla. 656, 51 Am. Rep. 625; Stewart v. Mathews, 19 Fla. 752; Cooper v. Bacon (Ga.), 84 S. E. 123; North v. Goebel, 138 Ga. 739, 76 S. E. 46; Hawes v. Glover, 126 Ga. 305, 55 S. E. 62; Janes v. Penny, 76 Ga. 796; Gardner v. Moore, 51 Ga. 268; Georgia Civ. Code 1910, § 3260; Roane v. Baker, 120 Ill. 308, 11 N. E. 246; Seaver v. Spink, 65 Ill. 441; Alvis v. Morrison, 63 Ill. 181, 14 Am. Rep. 117; Semple v. Miles, 3 Ill. 315; Kirkpatrick v. Caldwell, 32 Ind. 299; Perdue v. Aldridge, 19 Ind. 290; Davis v. Lutkiewiz, 72 Iowa 254, 33 N. W. 670;

or against his heirs on whom the law casts the property, and who are

Duncan v. Miller, 64 Iowa 223, 20 N. W. 161; First National Bank v. Hayzlett, 40 Iowa 659; Clark v. Connor, 28 Iowa 311; Carleton v. Byington, 18 Iowa 482; Horseman v. Todhunter, 12 Iowa 230; Northwestern Forwarding Co. v. Mahaffey, 36 Kans. 152, 12 Pac. 705; Taylor v. McDonald, 2 Bibb (Ky.) 420; Robertson v. Sebastian, 30 Ky. L. 883, 99 S. W. 933; Mills v. East Feliciana, 25 La. Ann. 142; Boissac v. Downs, 16 La. Ann. 187; Haines v. Verrett, 11 La. Ann. 122; Howard Mut. Loan &c. Assn. v. McIntyre, 3 Allen (Mass.) 571; Trigg v. Vermillion, 113 Mo. 230, 20 S. W. 1047; Stevens v. Hampton, 46 Mo. 404; McKenzie v. Beaumont, 70 Nebr. 179, 97 N. W. 225; Blair State Bank v. Stewart, 57 Nebr. 58, 77 N. W. 370; Stevens v. Morse, 47 N. H. 532; Ames v. Robert, 17 N. Mex. 609, 131 Pac. 994; Moore v. Davey, 1 N. Mex. 303; Wood v. Chapin, 13 N. Y. 509, 67 Am. Dec. 62; Jackson v. Colden, 4 Cow. (N. Y.) 266; Forrester v. Parker, 14 Daly (N. Y.) 208; Pancoast v. American Heating &c. Co., 66 How. Pr. (N. Y.) 49; St. Marks F. Ins. Co. v. Harris, 13 How. Pr. (N. Y.) 95; Jackson v. West, 10 Johns. (N. Y.) 466; Clute v. Robinson, 2 Johns. (N. Y.) 595; McBrayer v. Harrill, 152 N. Car. 712, 68 S. E. 204; Smith v. Fuller, 152 N. Car. 7, 67 S. E. 48; Williams v. Jones, 95 N. Car. 504; Brem v. Lockhart, 93 N. Car. 191; Leggett v. Bullock, Busb. L. (N. Car.) 283; Stewart v. Hopkins, 30 Ohio St. 502; Sidle v. Maxwell, 4 Ohio St. 236; Bloom v. Noggle, 4 Ohio St. 45; Fosdick v. Barr, 3 Ohio St. 471; Snyder v. Betz, 2 Ohio C. Ct. 485, 1 Ohio Cir. Dec. 602; Moore v. Thomas, 1 Ore. 201; Girard Trust Co. v. Baird, 212 Pa. 41, 61 Atl. 507, 1 L. R. A. (N. S.) 405; Levinz v. Will, 1 Dall. (Pa.) 430, 1 L. ed. 209; Betts v. Letcher, 1 S. Dak. 182, 46 N. W. 193; Literer v. Huddleston (Tenn.), 52 S. W. 1003; Herman v. Clark (Tenn.), 39 S. W. 873; Cavanaugh v. Peterson, 47 Tex. 197; Gregg v. Gregg, 33 Tex. 462; Utah Comp. Laws 1907, § 1975;

Wilder v. Wilder, 82 Vt. 123, 72 Atl. 203; Claridge v. Evans, 137 Wis. 218, 118 N. W. 198, 25 L. R. A. (N. S.) 144. The rule is the same in Maryland, even under a statute that "no deed shall be valid for the purpose of passing title unless acknowledged and recorded." See also Snowden v. Pitcher, 45 Md. 260; Talcott v. Crippen, 52 Mich. 633, 18 N. W. 392. An unrecorded mortgage is not only valid between the parties, but constitutes a valid lien against all except subsequent purchasers or lienors. Rhea v. Planters' Mut. Ins. Co., 77 Ark. 57, 90 S. W. 850. Since an unrecorded mortgage is valid between the parties and their privies, the holder may foreclose without proving that the mortgage has been recorded. McKenzie v. Beaumont, 70 Nebr. 179, 97 N. W. 225. An unrecorded deed being valid between the parties, divests the title of the grantor so that it does not pass to a subsequent mortgagee, who takes only the estate belonging to the grantor at the time of the grant. Ames v. Robert, 17 N. Mex. 609, 131 Pac. 994. Under a statute requiring record of conveyances for validity against subsequent bona fide purchasers, an unrecorded mortgage to secure future advances gives the mortgagee a valid lien as between the parties and as to all the world, except subsequent purchasers or mortgagees in good faith and for value; Wis. Stat. 1898, §§ 2203, 2209, and 2241. Claridge v. Evans, 137 Wis. 218, 118 N. W. 198, 25 L. R. A. (N. S.) 144. See also McDuffie v. Walker, 125 La. 152, 51 So. 100; Putnam v. White, 76 Maine 551; Moore v. Davey, 1 N. Mex. 303 (under Spanish and Mexican law, record essential between parties). But see Berwin v. Weiss, 28 La. Ann. 363; Gravier v. Hodge, 14 La. 101; Roche v. Groysilliere, 13 La. 238. Under the Louisiana Civil Code, art. 3369, an unrecorded mortgage ceases to have effect after ten years, even between the parties. Tilden v. Morrison, 33 La. Ann. 1067.

mere volunteers in accepting it;[92] or against his personal representatives,[93] or as against creditors other than judgment creditors;[94] or against a subsequent declaration of homestead by his wife who had joined in the mortgage.[95] And even in those states where it is provided by statute that a mortgage shall be recorded within a stipulated time, it is still valid between the parties without registration. The mortgagee by an unrecorded mortgage will be protected by a court of equity, so far as this can be done without infringing upon the rights of subsequent purchasers, or third persons who have in the meantime acquired liens of record upon the property.[96] It is for their protection, however, that a record is provided for. As between the parties themselves, there is no occasion for a public record to give notice. Although it has sometimes been said that the delivery of a mortgage for record is a part of the execution of the instrument, this is not true except so far as the expression has reference to its effect upon those who are not parties to it.[97] An unrecorded mortgage is good against any one claiming under the mortgagor, with notice.[98] Even the destruction of the mortgage before the recording of it, whether by accident or by the wrongful act of a third person, does not annihilate the lien as between the parties and all others claiming with notice.[99] The legal title passes as between the parties, and the interest of the grantee may be levied upon and sold under execution.[1]

[92] Hoes v. Boyer, 108 Ind. 494, 9 N. E. 427; Westervelt v. Voorhis, 42 N. J. Eq. 179, 6 Atl. 665; Building Assn. v. Clark, 43 Ohio St. 427, 2 N. E. 846; Gill v. Pinney, 12 Ohio St. 38; McLaughlin v. Ihmsen, 85 Pa. St. 364; Tryon v. Munson, 77 Pa. St. 250; Wilder v. Wilder, 82 Vt. 123, 72 Atl. 203. A creditor of an heir stands in no better position than the heir himself. Literer v. Huddleston (Tenn.), 52 S. W. 1003.

[93] McBrayer v. Harrill, 152 N. Car. 712, 68 S. E. 204; Wilder v. Wilder, 82 Vt. 123, 72 Atl. 203. Not necessary as against his administrator. Sanders v. Barlow, 21 Fed. 836; Andrews v. Burns, 11 Ala. 691.

[94] Sanders v. Barlow, 21 Fed. 836; Center v. P. &c. Bank, 22 Ala. 743; Daniel v. Sorrells, 9 Ala. 436; Ohio Life Ins. &c. Co. v. Ledyard, 8 Ala. 866.

[95] Kleinsorge v. Kleinsorge, 133 Cal. 412, 65 Pac. 876.

[96] Kirkpatrick v. Caldwell, 32 Ind. 299; Wynn v. Carter, 20 Wis. 107.

[97] Sidle v. Maxwell, 4 Ohio St. 236, limiting Holliday v. Franklin Bank, 16 Ohio 533.

[98] Girard Trust Co. v. Baird, 212 Pa. 41, 61 Atl. 507.

[99] Sloan v. Holcomb, 29 Mich. 153; Lampe v. Kennedy, 56 Wis. 249, 14 N. W. 43. The rule is otherwise in North Carolina, because there registration is necessary to pass a complete legal title. The surrender or destruction of an unregistered deed, therefore, restores the title. Fortune v. Watkins, 94 N. Car. 304.

[1] Newsom v. Kurtz, 86 Ky. 277, 5 S. W. 575. On the other hand, it has been provided by statute in Minnesota that an unrecorded conveyance shall be void as to a judgment against the person in whose name the title appears of record in the registry of the county in which the land is situated. Minnesota

If the grantor makes another deed of the same land to another person whose deed is first recorded, the latter becomes vested with the legal title, and, in a contest between him and a claimant under the destroyed deed, the burden is upon such claimant to show that the subsequent purchaser had notice of the prior conveyance, or did not pay a valuable consideration for the land.[2]

An acknowledgment is not generally essential to the validity of a deed as between the parties, but only requisite to the recording of the instrument so it may become valid as against third parties. The statutes of several states expressly require proper acknowledgment, as a prerequisite to a valid record, which will operate as notice to third persons and subsequent purchasers; although acknowledgment is not prerequisite under the statutes of other states.[3] There may be a valid delivery without an acknowledgment.[4] A mortgage without acknowledgment or record is good against the mortgagor, and his heirs or devisees, and against others who have actual notice of its existence before they acquired title.[5]

If the title is not dependent upon the time of recording, and the record is merely to authorize its introduction as evidence, it may be recorded after action brought to enforce it, and at any time before trial. This rule is equally applicable to the case of an assignment of a mortgage, which may be recorded after the assignee has brought an action to foreclose, and at any time before trial and judgment.[6]

Only subsequent purchasers for value without notice can take advantage of the fact that a prior mortgage is unrecorded.[7]

Where, however, recording is made essential to the validity of the deed of a married woman, no title passes by her conveyance until the instrument is recorded.[8]

§ 475. Assignees and administrators of bankrupt and insolvent mortgagor's estates.

—The assignee of a bankrupt acquires only the

Gen. Stat. 1878, ch. 40, § 21; Gen. Stat. 1913, § 6844; Lebanon Sav. Bank v. Hollenbeck, 29 Minn. 322, 13 N. W. 145; Coles v. Berryhill, 37 Minn. 56, 33 N. W. 213.

[2] Lampe v. Kennedy, 56 Wis. 249.

[3] See post § 495.

[4] Roane v. Baker, 120 Ill. 308; 11 N. E. 246; Darst v. Bates, 51 Ill. 439.

[5] Kennedy v. Northrup, 15 Ill. 148; Semple v. Miles, 3 Ill. 315; Johnston v. Canby, 29 Md. 211; Earle v. Fiske, 103 Mass. 491; Marshall v. Fisk, 6 Mass. 24, 4 Am. Dec. 76; Dole v. Thurlow, 12 Metc. (Mass.) 157; Welch v. Ketcham, 48 Minn. 241, 51 N. W. 113; Youngblood v. Vastine, 46 Mo. 239. See post § 495.

[6] Wolcott v. Winchester, 15 Gray (Mass.) 461.

[7] Merriman v. Hyde, 9 Nebr. 113, 2 N. W. 218.

[8] Sewall v. Haymaker, 127 U. S. 719, 32 L. ed. 299, 8 Sup. Ct. 1348; Rorer v. Roanoke Nat. Bank, 83 Va. 589, 4 S. E. 820.

rights and title of the assignor.[9] In the absence of a statute, the assignment does not pass to the assignee property previously transferred by the assignor by a conveyance good between the parties.[10] The assignee takes the bankrupt's estate subject to any conveyances he has made, although they remain unrecorded. But one who purchases of the assignee, without notice of an unrecorded mortgage, takes the property unincumbered by it.[11] So if an administrator of an insolvent estate, having no knowledge of an unrecorded mortgage on certain real estate of the deceased, sells it under order of court to a purchaser who was also ignorant of the mortgage, and therefore acquired a title unaffected by it, the mortgagee is entitled to be reimbursed from the proceeds of the land in preference to the general creditors.[12] In Ohio, however, it is held that a mortgage of real property, which has not been deposited for record with the recorder of the proper county, before an assignment of the property by the mortgagor for the benefit of his creditors takes effect, is not a valid lien upon the property as against the assignee or the creditors; nor does it become so by being subsequently recorded.[13]

The failure to record a mortgage before insolvency proceedings against the mortgagor will generally defeat the lien of the mortgagee, and his claim is reduced to that of an unsecured creditor.[14] By statute in some states, an assignee or trustee of the insolvent may avoid a mortgage not recorded a certain period prior to the insolvency proceedings.[15] A mortgage given by an insolvent, and withheld from

[9] Campbell Printing Press &c. Co. v. Walker, 22 Fla. 412, 1 So. 59; Haug v. Third Nat. Bank, 95 Mich. 249, 54 N. W. 888; Cutler v. Steele, 93 Mich. 204, 53 N. W. 521; Ætna Ins. Co. v. Thompson, 68 N. H. 20, 40 Atl. 396, 73 Am. St. 552; Griffin v. Marquardt, 17 N. Y. 28; Grube v. Lilienthal, 51 S. Car. 442, 29 S. E. 230.

[10] Drew v. Drum, 44 Mo. App. 25; Muir v. Schenck, 3 Hill (N. Y.) 228, 38 Am. Dec. 633; Thigpen v. Horne, 36 N. Car. 20; Williams v. Bristol Rolling Mill Co., 174 Pa. St. 299, 34 Atl. 442.

[11] Hodgen v. Guttery, 58 Ill. 431.

[12] Kirkpatrick v. Caldwell, 32 Ind. 299. See also Kellogg v. Kelley, 69 Minn. 124, 71 N. W. 924.

[13] Betz v. Snyder, 48 Ohio Ohio St. 492, 28 N. E. 234, 13 L. R. A. 235; Kemper v. Campbell, 44 Ohio St. 210, 6 N. E. 566.

[14] Newtown Sav. Bank v. Lawrence, 71 Conn. 358, 41 Atl. 1054; Bingham v. Jordan, 1 Allen (Mass.) 373, 79 Am. Dec. 748; Briggs v. Parkman, 2 Metc. (Mass.) 258, 37 Am. Dec. 89; Perkins v. Hanson, 71 Minn. 487, 74 N. W. 135; Shay v. Security Bank, 67 Minn. 287, 69 N. W. 920; Wimpfheimer v. Perrine. 65 N. J. Eq. 770, 67 N. J. Eq. 597, 50 Atl. 356; Desany v. Thorp, 70 Vt. 31, 39 Atl. 309. See also Boyd v. Partridge, 94 Maine 440, 47 Atl. 911 (unrecorded deed of insolvent void in hands of bona fide purchaser). But see Thompson-Hiles Co. v. Dodd, 95 Ga. 754, 22 S. E. 673. The failure to record by one not contemplating insolvency is immaterial. Union Trust &c. Co. v. Taylor, 139 Ky. 283, 129 S. W. 828.

[15] Farmers' Exch. Bank v. Purdy, 130 Cal. 455, 62 Pac. 738; Bloom-

record at his request, until after his death, was held invalid against his administrator and the creditors of the estate.[16]

§ 476. **Equitable mortgages included under recording acts.**—Equitable mortgages are generally held to be within the recording acts as much as are legal mortgages.[17] At first a different interpretation was put upon the acts, and a mortgage of an equity or of an equitable estate was not constructive notice when registered.[18] But at an early day in this country it was established, either judicially or by statute, that all rights, incumbrances, or conveyances touching or in any way concerning land, should appear upon the public records, and that conveyances of equitable interests as well as legal were within the registry acts. A mortgage, therefore, of such an interest, if first recorded, is preferred to a mortgage of the legal estate.[19]

field Woolen Mills v. Allender, 101 Iowa 181, 70 N. W. 115; Renouf v. Yates, 94 Maine 77, 46 Atl. 784; Baker v. Kunkel, 70 Md. 392, 17 Atl. 383; Pratt v. Mackey, 172 Mass. 384, 52 N. E. 534; Copeland v. Barnes, 147 Mass. 388, 18 N. E. 65; Grant v. Minneapolis Brew. Co., 68 Minn. 86, 70 N. W. 868.

[16] Sanford v. Deforest, 85 Conn. 694, 84 Atl. 111, overruling Haskell v. Bissell, 11 Conn. 174.

[17] O'Neal v. Seixas, 85 Ala. 80, 4 So. 745, overruling dictum in Bailey v. Timberlake, 74 Ala. 221; Pierce v. Jackson, 56 Ala. 599; Putnam v. White, 76 Maine 551; General Ins. Co. v. United States Ins. Co., 10 Md. 517, 69 Am. Dec. 174; Alderson v. Ames, 6 Md. 52; Edwards v. McKernan, 55 Mich. 520; Carter v. Holman, 60 Mo. 498; Clamorgan v. Lane, 9 Mo. 446; Tarbell v. West, 86 N. Y. 280; Stoddard v. Whiting, 46 N. Y. 627; Hunt v. Johnson, 19 N. Y. 279; Matthews v. Damainville, 43 Misc. 546, 89 N. Y. S. 493; Tefft v. Munson, 63 Barb. (N. Y.) 31, 57 N. Y. 97; Crane v. Turner, 7 Hun (N. Y.) 357; Parkist v. Alexander, 1 Johns. Ch. (N. Y.) 394; Withrell v. Murphy, 154 N. Car. 82, 69 S. E. 748; Todd v. Outlaw, 79 N. Car. 235; Russell's Appeal, 15 Pa. St. 319; Boyce v. Shiver, 3 S. Car. 515; Butler v. Maury, 10 Humph. (Tenn.) 420; Smith v. Neilson, 13 Lea (Tenn.) 461; Atkinson v. Miller, 34 W. Va.

115, 11 S. E. 1007, 9 L. R. A. 544; Jarvis v. Dutcher, 16 Wis. 307. See also Miller v. Wroton, 82 S. Car. 97, 63 S. E. 62. Under Sayles' Annotated Civ. Stat. of Texas, art. 4640, providing that all conveyances and mortgages of land shall be void as to subsequent purchasers for value without notice unless recorded, a grantor may show that an absolute deed given to secure a debt and duly recorded, is an equitable mortgage merely, as against a creditor of the grantee who attached the land without notice that the conveyance was not absolute, and thereby defeat the attachment lien. Long v. Fields, 31 Tex. Civ. App. 241, 71 S. W. 774. Under the Compiled Laws of Oklahoma 1909, § 1198, a bona fide purchaser from the grantee in a recorded deed absolute, given as security, will be protected to the extent of his payment with interest, against all persons except those in possession at the time of such purchase, but any other conveyance by such grantee will be treated as an assignment of the mortgage and indebtedness. Krauss v. Potts, 38 Okla. 674, 135 Pac. 362.

[18] Doswell v. Buchanan, 3 Leigh (Va.) 365, 23 Am. Dec. 280.

[19] United States Ins. Co. v. Shriver, 3 Md. Ch. 381. See also White & Tudor's Lead. Cas. in Eq. (4th Am. ed.), vol. 2, part 1, p. 204, where the cases are collected.

An agreement in the nature of a mortgage or promise to execute a mortgage must be recorded.[20] A deed of trust must be recorded to give it validity against creditors of, or purchasers from the grantor.[21] Thus a conveyance to a trustee with power to sell the land and pay debts, must be recorded.[22] A mortgage upon an equitable estate in land is within the recording acts.[23] A mortgage of an equitable interest under a contract of purchase, although no legal estate passes by it, is within the operation of the registration acts, and should be recorded to entitle it to priority over a subsequent mortgage of the same interest; and an assignment of such a contract as a security for a debt is regarded as a mortgage.[24]

Generally the record of an agreement constituting an equitable mortgage is notice to a subsequent purchaser of the legal estate from the same grantor.[25] One in possession of lands under a parol contract to purchase them may mortgage his interest in them, and the record of the mortgage will be notice to subsequent purchasers and incumbrancers.[26] A declaration of trust, given to secure the repayment of money advanced for the purchase of land, constitutes an equitable mortgage which takes priority over a judgment rendered subsequent to its execution but before its record.[27]

The registry of a conveyance of an equitable title is notice to a subsequent purchaser of the same interest or title from the same grantor; but it is not notice to a purchaser of the legal title from a person who appears by the record to be the real owner. Thus a mortgage by a member of a partnership of his interest in the real estate of the firm,

[20] Cantrell v. Ford (Tenn.), 46 S. W. 581. But see Fash v. Ravesies, 32 Ala. 451.

[21] Withrell v. Murphy, 154 N. Car. 82, 69 S. E. 748.

[22] Woodruff v. Robb, 19 Ohio 212. But see McMenomy v. Murray, 3 Johns. Ch. (N. Y.) 435.

[23] Clark v. Lyster, 155 Fed. 513, 84 C. C. A. 27; O'Neal v. Seixas, 85 Ala. 80, 4 So. 745; General Ins. Co. v. United States Ins. Co., 10 Md. 517, 69 Am. Dec. 174; Balen v. Mercier, 75 Mich. 42, 42 N. W. 666; Crane v. Turner, 67 N. Y. 437, 7 Hun (N. Y.) 357; Parkist v. Alexander, 1 Johns. Ch. (N. Y.) 394; Boyce v. Shiver, 3 S. Car. 515; Jarvis v. Dutcher, 16 Wis. 307.

[24] Bank v. Clapp, 76 N. Car. 482; Simonson v. Wenzel, 27 N. Dak. 638, 147 N. W. 804. A recorded mortgage of an equitable title under a bond for a deed which is not recorded, is not notice to a subsequent purchaser of the legal title from one in possession of the land, as such purchaser's title is not derived through the title of the mortgagor, and he will not take subject to the mortgage, though it is recorded. Irish v. Sharp, 89 Ill. 261.

[25] Putnam v. White, 76 Maine 551; General Ins. Co. v. United States Ins. Co., 10 Md. 517, 69 Am. Dec. 174; Edwards v. McKernan, 55 Mich. 520, 524, 22 N. W. 20; Hunt v. Johnson, 19 N. Y. 279; Parkist v. Alexander, 1 Johns. Ch. (N. Y.) 394; Jarvis v. Dutcher, 16 Wis. 307.

[26] Crane v. Turner, 7 Hun (N. Y.) 357.

[27] German Nat. Bank v. Queen, 159 App. Div. 236, 144 N. Y. S. 195.

the title to which stands in the name of another member of the firm, is properly admitted of record; but it is not notice to a subsequent purchaser or mortgagee of the legal title from such other partner. The two titles have apparently no connection.[28] The record of a mortgage, or other conveyance which is entitled to be recorded, operates as constructive notice to subsequent purchasers claiming under the same grantor, or through one who is the common source of title.[29] The mortgage of an equitable title, such as that constituted by a bond for a deed, is not constructive notice to purchasers of the land from a holder of the legal title in possession of the land, inasmuch as the purchaser's title is not derived through the title of the mortgagor, and he will not take subject to the mortgage of the equitable title, though this be recorded.[30]

§ 477. **Equitable mortgage for precedent debt or present consideration.**—An equitable mortgagee for a precedent debt has no equity superior to that of a creditor having a valid subsequent judgment at law. Between such contestants the first perfected legal title should prevail. The rule is otherwise with regard to bona fide purchasers or equitable mortgagees, where the consideration of the mortgage is paid at the time it is given. Equity in the latter case regards the equitable mortgagee as a bona fide purchaser.[31] "Where a conveyance is made or security taken the consideration of which was an antecedent debt, the grantee or party taking the security is not looked upon as a bona fide purchaser. The expression in the statute is borrowed from the language of courts of equity, and must be interpreted in the sense in which it is there understood; and it is well settled that a grantee or incumbrancer who does not advance anything at the time, takes the interest conveyed, subject to any prior equity attaching to the subject."[32]

§ 478. **Leasehold estates included under recording acts.**—The recording acts apply with like effect to leasehold estates and to mortgages

---

[28] Tarbell v. West, 86 N. Y. 280.
[29] Edwards v. McKernan, 55 Mich. 520, 22 N. W. 20.
[30] Irish v. Sharp, 89 Ill. 261; Halstead v. Bank, 4 J. J. Marsh. (Ky.) 554.
[31] Wheeler v. Kirtland, 24 N. J. Eq. 552.
[32] Wood v. Robinson, 22 N. Y. 564, per Denio, J. See also in support of this view, Jones v. Robinson, 77 Ala. 499; Sweeney v. Bixler, 69 Ala. 539; Craft v. Russell, 67 Ala. 9; Metropolitan Bank v. Godfrey, 23 Ill. 579; Phelps v. Fockler, 61 Iowa 340, 14 N. W. 729, 16 N. W. 210; Halstead v. Bank of Kentucky, 4 J. J. Marsh. (Ky.) 554; Edwards v. McKernan, 55 Mich. 520, 22 N. W. 20; Pancoast v. Duval, 26 N. J. Eq. 445; Mingus v. Condit, 23 N. J. Eq. 313; Cary v. White, 52 N. Y. 138; Ashton's Appeal, 73 Pa. St. 153; Spurlock v. Sullivan, 36 Tex. 511; Swenson v. Seale (Tex.), 28 S. W. 143.

of leasehold estates, of such duration of term as to come within the recording acts of the several states.[33] Such mortgages are not only, as a general rule, within the terms of these acts, but likewise within the reason and spirit of them, inasmuch as they are equally within the mischief for which they provide a remedy; and they do not come under the provisions relating to the recording of mortgages of personal property, as these have reference only to chattels personal.[34]

Under a statute requiring mortgages of leasehold estates to be recorded, it was held that all such mortgages must be recorded together with the lease, and the two deeds showing the actual extent and nature of the mortgagee's interest must be filed for record.[35]

A mortgage of an oil lease has been held to be a conveyance of an interest in land which must be recorded in the same manner as a mortgage of real estate, to affect third persons, although valid as against the mortgagor without being recorded.[36]

A grain elevator of permanent structure, built by a lessee on ground held under a lease which provides that the lessor may terminate the lease on sixty days' notice, and that the lessee may remove his buildings at any time before expiration of the lease, is, together with the leasehold estate, to be classed as real estate, so that the holder of a recorded mortgage thereon has priority over a subsequent execution creditor, even though the mortgagee has not taken possession within two years after the date of the mortgage, as is necessary in case of chattel mortgages.[37]

An option of purchasing the leasehold estate at a fixed price within a limited time does not pass by a mortgage of such leasehold estate. "The person holding the right of option is not a purchaser. He be-

---

[33] Spielmann v. Kliest, 36 N. J. Eq. 199; Decker v. Clarke, 26 N. J. Eq. 163; Breese v. Bange, 2 E. D. Smith (N. Y.) 474; Berry v. Mutual Ins. Co., 2 Johns. Ch. (N. Y.) 603; Johnson v. Stagg, 2 Johns. (N. Y.) 510; Paine v. Mason, 7 Ohio St. 198. The earlier New Jersey cases were in effect overruled by the decision in Hutchinson v. Bramhall, 42 N. J. Eq. 272, 7 Atl. 873; reversing sub. nom. Deane v. Hutchinson, 2 Atl. 292, and holding that the recording act does not apply to leases for years.

In Pennsylvania a leasehold mortgage is required by statute to be recorded with the lease; the mortgage must refer to the record of the lease, or, if it is not recorded, it must be recorded with the mortgage. Hilton's Appeal, 116 Pa. St. 351, 9 Atl. 342. See also First Nat. Bank v. Sheafer (Pa.), 24 Atl. 221; Williams v. Downing, 18 Pa. St. 60; Speer's Assignment, 10 Pa. Super. Ct. 518.

[34] Decker v. Clarke, 26 N. J. Eq. 552.

[35] Downing v. Glen Rock Oil Co., 207 Pa. St. 455, 56 Atl. 995; Sturtevant's Appeal, 34 Pa. St. 149.

[36] Acklin v. Waltermier, 10 Ohio Cir. Dec. 629, 19 Ohio Cir. Ct. 372.

[37] Knapp v. Jones, 143 Ill. 375, 32 N. E. 382, affg. 38 Ill. App. 439, 28 N. E. 820.

comes such only by exercising his right of option, and not until he becomes a purchaser does he acquire anything which a court of law or equity can recognize."[38]

§ 479. **Record of assignments of mortgages.**—The registration laws and the doctrines of priority by record generally extend to assignments of mortgages as well, either by express provision of statute or by judicial construction.[39] Where the statutes themselves do not in terms di-

[38] Conn v. Tonner, 86 Iowa 577, 53 N. W. 320; Sweezy v. Jones, 65 Iowa 273, 21 N. W. 603.

[39] Alaska: Codes 1900, p. 372, § 373.

California: An assignment of a mortgage is not a grant of an estate. Adler v. Sargent, 109 Cal. 42, 21 Pac. 799.

Idaho: Rev. Code 1908, § 3396; Smith v. Keohane, 6 Bradw. (Ill.) 585; Turpin v. Ogle, 4 Bradw. (Ill.) 611.

Indiana: Burns' Ann. Stat. 1914, §§ 1145, 1149. Under the latter section an assignment of a mortgage must be recorded by the assignee under penalty of a loss of ten per cent. of the mortgage debt. See Citizens' State Bank v. Julian, 153 Ind. 655, 55 N. E. 1107; Artz v. Yeager, 30 Ind. App. 677, 66 N. E. 917; Perry v. Fisher, 30 Ind. App. 261, 65 N. E. 935; Tulley v. Citizens' Bank, 18 Ind. App. 240, 47 N. E. 850.

Iowa: Bowling v. Cook, 39 Iowa 200; Cornog v. Fuller, 30 Iowa 212; McClure v. Burris, 16 Iowa 591; Bank v. Anderson, 14 Iowa 544, 83 Am. Dec. 390.

Kansas: Laws 1897, ch. 160, repealed. See Statutes 1901, §§ 4234-4239. Meyers v. Wheelock, 60 Kans. 747, 57 Pac. 956.

Maryland: Morrow v. Stanley, 119 Md. 590, 87 Atl. 484.

Michigan: Burns v. Berry, 42 Mich. 176, 3 N. W. 924.

Minnesota: Foss v. Dullam, 111 Minn. 220, 126 N. W. 820; Huitink v. Thompson, 95 Minn. 392, 104 N. W. 237, 111 Am. St. 476; Robbins v. Larson, 69 Minn. 436, 72 N. W. 456, 65 Am. St. 572; Casserly v. Morrow, 101 Minn. 16, 111 N. W. 654.

Missouri: Rev. Code 1907, §§ 5744, 5745.

Nebraska: Gillian v. McDowall, 66 Nebr. 814, 92 N. W. 991; Ames v. Miller, 65 Nebr. 204, 91 N. W. 250; Rumery v. Loy, 61 Nebr. 755, 86 N. W. 478; Bullock v. Pock, 57 Nebr. 781, 78 N. W. 261; Herbage v. Moodie, 51 Nebr. 837, 71 N. W. 778; Porter v. Ourada, 51 Nebr. 510, 71 N. W. 52; Eggert v. Beyer, 43 Nebr. 711, 62 N. W. 57.

New Jersey: Mott v. German Hospital, 55 N. J. Eq. 722, 37 Atl. 757; Tradesmen's Building Assn. v. Thompson, 31 N. J. Eq. 536; Stein v. Sullivan, 31 N. J. Eq. 409. The New Jersey Conveyance Act of 1898 (2 Comp. Stat. 1910, p. 1553, § 54) concerning the effect of failure to record instruments was held inapplicable to assignments of mortgages. Leonard v. Leonia Heights Land Co., 81 N. J. Eq. 489, 87 Atl. 645.

New York: Birdseye's Consol. Laws 1909, Real Property Law §§ 240, 290, 291, 418; Weideman v. Zielinska, 102 App. Div. 163, 92 N. Y. S. 493 (construing the statute §§ 240, 241, to include assignments); Gibson v. Thomas, 180 N. Y. 483, 78 N. E. 484, 70 L. R. A. 768; Bacon v. Van Schoonhoven, 87 N. Y. 446; Decker v. Boice, 83 N. Y. 215; Westbrook v. Gleason, 79 N. Y. 23; Belden v. Meeker, 47 N. Y. 307, 2 Lans. (N. Y.) 470, overruling Hoyt v. Hoyt, 8 Bosw. (N. Y.) 511; Campbell v. Vedder, 1 Abb. App. Dec: (N. Y.) 295; Purdy v. Huntington, 46 Barb. (N. Y.) 389, 42 N. Y. 334; James v. Morey, 2 Cow. (N. Y.) 246, 14 Am. Dec. 475; Fort v. Burch, 5 Denio (N. Y.) 187; James v. Johnson, 6 Johns. Ch. (N. Y.) 417; Vanderkemp v. Shelton, 11 Paige (N. Y.) 28, Clarke, 321; St. John v. Spaulding, 1 Thomp. & C. (N. Y.) 483.

rectly apply to assignments of mortgages, the courts have generally

Ohio: Strait v. Ady, 6 Ohio Dec. 263.

`Oregon: Lord's Ore. Laws 1910, § 7135.

South Dakota: Pickford v. Peebles, 7 S. Dak. 166, 63 N. W. 779; Merrill v. Hurley, 6 S. Dak. 592, 62 N. W. 958; Merrill v. Luce, 6 S. Dak. 354, 61 N. W. 43, 55 Am. St. 844; Kenny v. McKenzie, 23 S. Dak. 111, 120 N. W. 781, 49 L. R. A. (N. S.) 775 (Laws of South Dakota 1903, p. 1, ch. 1, relative to recording as constructive notice, not retroactive as to assignments).

Utah: Comp. Laws 1888, §§ 2613, 2645; Comp. Laws 1907, §§ 1975, 2000, 2202; Donaldson v. Grant, 15 Utah 231, 49 Pac. 779.

Vermont: Passumpsic Sav. Bank v. Buck, 71 Vt. 190, 44 Atl. 93.

Washington: Gen. Stat. § 1422, does not include assignments of mortgages. Howard v. Shaw, 10 Wash, 151, 38 Pac. 746. But see Remington's Stat. 1910, § 8800.

Wisconsin: Girardin v. Lampe, 58 Wis. 267, 16 N. W. 614; Fallass v. Pierce, 30 Wis. 443. See Wisconsin Statutes 1913, § 2244 (record of assignment not notice to mortgagor or his heirs).

Wyoming: Frank v. Snow, 6 Wyo. 42, 42 Pac. 484, 43 Pac. 78. See also In re Buchner, 202 Fed. 979 (District of Columbia).

In Delaware an assignment of a mortgage attested by one credible witness is valid. Laws 1893, ch. 213, p. 633.

In Indiana before the statute providing for the record of assignments, the record of them was not notice. Hasselman v. McKernan, 50 Ind. 441; Dixon v. Hunter, 57 Ind. 278; Reeves v. Hayes, 95 Ind. 521. Now, by statute, any mortgage of record, or any part thereof, may be assigned, either by an assignment entered on the margin of such record, signed by the person making the assignment and attested by the recorder, or by a separate instrument executed and acknowledged before any person authorized to take acknowledgments, and recorded on such margin, or in the mortgage records of the county. Burns'

Stat. 1894, §§ 1107, 1108; Burns' Ann. Stat. 1914, §§ 1145-1149.

Under the last section of this act, which provides that in a suit to foreclose a mortgage it is sufficient to make the mortgagee or assignee of record parties, an assignee who has not recorded his assignment may lose his mortgage, unless he can prove that the purchaser at the foreclosure sale had notice or knowledge of the assignment at the time of his purchase. Citizens' State Bank v. Julian, 153 Ind. 655, 55 N. E. 1007.

In Kansas a statute was enacted in 1897 with a view to compelling the recording of assignments and prescribing as a penalty for failure to record, that no assignment of a mortgage shall be received against the mortgagor, his heirs, personal representatives or assigns, in any court unless the same shall have been acknowledged and recorded. The statute does not annul the mortgage but prevents the use of the assignment as evidence to establish the ownership of the mortgage. Myers v. Wheelock, 60 Kans. 747, 57 Pac. 956.

In Maryland provision was made for recording assignments at the foot of the mortgage, by Act 1868, ch. 373; Code 1911, art. 21, § 34, p. 504; but this does not affect an equitable assignment. Byles v. Tome, 39 Md. 461.

In Pennsylvania the record of an assignment of a mortgage is notice to subsequent assignees of the mortgage. Neide v. Pennypacker, 9 Phila. (Pa.) 86. And to subsequent purchasers and mortgagees as well. Leech v. Bonsall, 9 Phila. (Pa.) 204. These decisions are based on the act of April 9, 1849, § 14. So far as the general recording Act of 1715 is concerned, "though there has been no express decision that under it an assignment of a mortgage may be recorded, so as to be notice to subsequent purchasers, yet, taking the latest expression of the Supreme Court on the subject, we might so decide without disregarding any binding authority, or any clearly

drawn an inference of intended application.[40] But this liberal construction to include assignments of mortgages has not been invariably adopted by the courts; and many decisions hold that assignments are not within the operation of the recording acts unless they are expressly made so, or the language of the statute is sufficiently comprehensive to fairly include them.[41] An assignment of a recorded mortgage need not be recorded to protect the assignee against a subsequent purchaser of the mortgaged premises, but the assignment must be recorded to protect him against a subsequent assignment from the same assignor, for value and without notice.[42]

The mere assignment of a note, which as an incident carries with it the mortgage securing it, is not an assignment of the mortgage,

indicated opinion of that court." Per Mr. Justice Mitchell in Neide v. Pennypacker, 9 Phila. (Pa.) 86, citing Phillips v. Bank, 18 Pa. St. 394. In the later case of Pepper's Appeal, 77 Pa. St. 373, it was distinctly held that the recording of an assignment is notice to a subsequent assignee under the above statute. Mr. Justice Mercur, delivering the opinion of the court, said it was alleged in the argument that it is not customary in Philadelphia to search the records for assignments of mortgages. Be that as it may, if any custom exists not in harmony with the act, it must give way. Malas usus abolendus est. See also Purdon's Dig. 1905, p. 1181, § 158.

In Virginia the assignee of a mortgage is not regarded as a purchaser, and the record of the assignment is not notice to third persons. Gordon v. Rixey, 76 Va. 694, 701. An assignment to an administrator of a mortgage upon his intestate's land is valid though not recorded, where the contest is between the assignee and the heirs of the mortgagor. Morton v. Blades Lumber Co., 144 N. Car. 31, 56 S. E. 551. See post § 820.

[40] Reeves v. Hayes, 95 Ind. 521, where the subject is ably considered by Chief Justice Elliott; Bowling v. Cook, 39 Iowa 200; Summers v. Kilgus, 14 Bush (Ky.) 449; and by Justices Niblack and Zollars in dissenting opinions. Detwilder v. Heckenlaible, 63 Kans. 627, 66 Pac. 653.

[41] Oregon &c. Trust &c. Co. v. Shaw, 5 Sawy. (U. S.) 336, Fed. Cas. No. 10556; Garrett v. Fernauld, 63 Fla. 434, 57 So. 671 (assignment of a mortgage not a "conveyance or transfer of an interest in land" required to be recorded under § 2480 Gen. Stat. 1906); Reeves v. Hayes, 95 Ind. 521 (before the Indiana Statute requiring record of assignments); Dixon v. Hunter, 57 Ind. 278; Hasselman v. McKernan, 50 Ind. 441; Hull v. Diehl, 21 Mont. 71, 52 Pac. 782; Leonard v. Leonia Heights Land Co., 81 N. J. Eq. 489, 87 Atl. 645 (construing the New Jersey Conveyance Act of 1898, 2 Compt. Stat. 1910, p. 1553, § 54, as inapplicable to the record of assignments of mortgages); James v. Morey, 2 Cow. (N. Y.) 246, 14 Am. Dec. 475; Williams v. Queen City Homestead Co., 31 Ohio Cir. Ct. 438 (construing Ohio Rev. Stat. § 4135); First Nat. Bank v. National Live Stock Bank, 13 Okla. 719, 76 Pac. 130; Watson v. Dundee Mtg. &c. Co., 12 Ore. 474, 8 Pac. 548; Singleton v. Singleton, 60 S. Car. 216, 38 S. E. 462; Williams v. Paysinger, 15 S. Car. 171; Gordon v. Rixey, 76 Va. 694; Fischer v. Woodruff, 25 Wash. 67, 64 Pac. 923, 87 Am. St. 742; Howard v. Shaw, 10 Wash. 151, 38 Pac. 746. An assignment of a mortgage is not within a statute requiring grants of real estate to be recorded. Adler v. Sargent, 109 Cal. 42, 41 Pac. 799.

[42] People's Trust Co. v. Tonkonogy, 144 App. Div. 333, 128 N. Y. S. 1055.

such as is required to be recorded or noted in the margin of the original record of the mortgage.[43] But a mortgage passing as collateral to a negotiable note before maturity must be assigned of record, where required by the registration laws, to give it priority over subsequent mortgages.[44]

An acknowledgment is, of course, essential to a valid record of an assignment.[45] And likewise proper attestation is essential, and the record of an assignment of a mortgage executed by a corporation without the attestation of its secretary as required by statute, is not constructive notice.[46]

The assignment is invalid against subsequent purchasers without notice unless it is recorded. Consequently, if a mortgagee transfers the note secured by the mortgage, or makes a formal assignment of the mortgage which is not recorded, and afterward enters a satisfaction of the mortgage upon the record, or if the mortgagee takes a conveyance of the equity of redemption, and then with an apparent ample title conveys the property to another, the mortgage ceases to be a lien as against one who purchases the property in good faith and without notice.[47] In like manner an assignee of the mortgage is not bound by an unrecorded agreement executed between the parties to the mort-

[43] Perry v. Fisher, 30 Ind. App. 261, 65 N. Y. 935; Burns' Rev. Stat. 1901, § 1107a; Burns' Ann. Stat. 1914, § 1145.

[44] Newman v. Fidelity Saving &c. Assn., 14 Ariz. 354, 128 Pac. 53.

[45] Wright v. Shimek, 8 Kans. App. 353, 55 Pac. 464.

[46] Randall Co. v. Glendenning, 19 Okla. 475, 92 Pac. 158.

[47] Commercial Bank v. King, 107 Ala. 484, 18 So. 243; Beuhler v. McCormick, 169 Ill. 269, 48 N. E. 287; McAuliffe v. Renter, 166 Ill. 491, 46 N. E. 1087; Smith v. Keohane, 6 Bradw. (Ill.) 585; Turpin v. Ogle, 4 Bradw. (Ill.) 611; Connecticut Mut. L. Ins. Co. v. Talbot, 113 Ind. 373, 14 N. E. 586, 3 Am. St. 655; Jenks v. Shaw, 99 Iowa 604, 68 N. W. 900; Bowling v. Cook, 39 Iowa 200; Lewis v. Kirk, 28 Kans. 497, 42 Am. Rep. 173; Swasey v. Emerson, 168 Mass. 118, 46 N. E. 426, 60 Am. St. 368; Commonwealth v. Globe Ins. Co., 168 Mass. 80, 46 N. E. 410; Ferguson v. Glassford, 68 Mich. 36, 35 N. W. 820; Sheldon v. Holmes, 58 Mich. 138, 24 N. W.

795; Porter v. Ourada, 51 Nebr. 510, 71 N. W. 52; Clark v. Mackin, 95 N. Y. 346; Bacon v. Van Schoonhoven, 87 N. Y. 446, 19 Hun (N. Y.) 158; Van Keuren v. Corkins, 66 N. Y. 77; Morris v. Beecher, 1 N. Dak. 130, 45 N. W. 696; Henderson v. Pilgrim, 22 Tex. 464; Girardin v. Lampe, 58 Wis. 267, 16 N. W. 614. Otherwise in Oregon; and California. Watson v. Dundee M. &c. Co., 12 Ore. 474, 8 Pac. 548; Woodward v. Brown, 119 Cal. 283, 51 Pac. 2, 63 Am. St. 108.

In New York the record of an assignment of a recorded mortgage is not necessary as against the subsequent purchaser of the mortgaged land, but only against a subsequent purchaser of the mortgage. Curtis v. Moore, 152 N. Y. 159, 46 N. E. 168.

An unrecorded assignment of a mortgage is good against one who is not a subsequent purchaser or incumbrancer in good faith. State v. Coughran, 19 S. Dak. 271, 103 N. W. 31.

gage, whereby the mortgagee was bound to release a portion of the premises upon receiving a certain sum in payment.[48] An assignee of the mortgage whose assignment is not recorded is barred by a decree foreclosing a prior lien in a suit against his assignor, who appeared of record as owner of the incumbrance, unless his assignment is recorded prior to the deed of sale under such decree.[49] A provision in a mortgage that it shall be nonnegotiable and uncollectible in the hands of any other person than the original mortgagee is not operative against an assignment by process of law or through an order of court.[50] The doctrine, that the assignee of a mortgage takes it subject to all equities existing between the mortgagor or his grantees and the mortgagee, can not be applied to those instruments which are properly designated in the recording acts as conveyances, which both a release of a mortgage and an agreement for such release would be, without nullifying the acts to that extent, and withholding the protection they were designed to confer upon purchasers.[51]

But the record of an assignment of a mortgage is not constructive notice of it to the mortgagor so as to make invalid a payment made by him to the mortgagee.[52] It is desirable, for this reason, that personal notice should be given him of the assignment, though the assignee's title is complete without notice to the owner of the equity of redemption.[53]

A purchaser of the equity of redemption is charged with notice of an assignment of the mortgage which has been recorded prior to the purchase.[54] The record of the assignment is a part of the record title of which he must take notice at the time of his purchase. It has been held that a power of attorney to assign a mortgage,[55] or one to collect

---

[48] Warner v. Winslow, 1 Sandf. Ch. (N. Y.) 430; St. John v. Spalding, 1 Thomp. & C. (N. Y.) 483.

[49] Jones v. Fisher, 88 Nebr. 627, 130 N. W. 269.

[50] Scaife v. Scammon Inv. &c. Assn., 71 Kans. 402, 80 Pac. 957.

[51] St. John v. Spalding, 1 Thomp. & C. (N. Y.) 483.

[52] Hubbard v. Turner, 2 McLean (U. S.) 519; Lockrow v. Cline, 4 Kans. App. 716; Williams v. Keyes, 90 Mich. 290, 51 N. W. 520, 30 Am. St. 438; Gen. Stat. Minn. 1913, § 6843; Robbins v. Larson, 69 Minn. 436, 72 N. W. 456, 65 Am. St. 572; Olson v. Northwestern Guar. Loan Co., 65 Minn. 475, 68 N. W. 100. The statute does not apply to a purchaser from the mortgagor nor to mortgages securing negotiable notes. Stark v. Olsen, 44 Nebr. 646, 63 N. W. 37; Eggert v. Beyer, 43 Nebr. 711, 62 N. W. 57; New York Life Ins. &c. Co. v. Smith, 2 Barb. Ch. (N. Y.) 82; Ely v. Scofield, 35 Barb. (N. Y.) 330. See post § 480 and note.

[53] Jones v. Gibbons, 9 Ves. 407; Ex parte Barnett, 1 De G. 194. See also Barnes v. Long Island Real Est. &c. Co., 88 App. Div. 83, 84 N. Y. S. 951.

[54] Brewster v. Carnes, 103 N. Y. 556, 9 N. E. 323.

[55] Williams v. Birbeck, Hoffm. (N. Y.) 359; Morrison v. Mendenhall, 18 Minn. 232. See also Atkinson v. Patterson, 46 Vt. 750.

a mortgage and discharge it,[56] is not within the recording acts, and therefore a record of them is not notice.

Although the assignment of a debt is not recorded, it carries with it the mortgage securing the same,[57] leaving the original mortgagee without any interest.[58]

§ 480. Record of assignment as notice to mortgagor.—It is provided by statute in several states that the recording of an assignment of a mortgage shall not in itself be deemed notice of such assignment to the mortgagor, his heirs, or personal representatives, so as to invalidate any payment made by them to the person holding the bond or note.[59] But such statutes are not enlarged by construction and apply only to the persons and in the cases specified.[60] Such statutes do not apply to a purchaser of the equity of redemption, or to a subsequent mortgagee, or an assignee of his mortgage, unless it is in terms made applicable to him.[61]

Apart from the statutes, it has been frequently held that the recording of an assignment of a mortgage, will not give constructive notice thereof to the mortgagor, so as to invalidate subsequent payments on the mortgage debt made by him to the mortgagee, and

[56] Jackson v. Richards, 6 Cow. (N. Y.) 617.

[57] Fish v. First Nat. Bank, 150 Fed, 524, 80 C. C. A. 266; Smith v. Godwin, 145 N. Car. 242, 58 S. E. 1089; Morton v. Blades Lumber Co., 144 N. Car. 31, 56 S. E. 551 (assignee asserting rights against heirs of mortgagor); Emmons v. Hawk, 62 W. Va. 526, 59 S. E. 519; Milwaukee Trust Co. v. Van Valkenburgh, 132 Wis. 638, 112 N. W. 1083 (indorsement of note expressly including mortgage security).

[58] Turpin v. Derickson, 105 Md. 620, 66 Atl. 276.

[59] California: Civ. Code 1906, § 2935; Acts 1874, p. 261; Codes & Statutes 1876, § 7935. See Rogers v. Peckham, 120 Cal. 238, 52 Pac. 483.

Kansas: See Statutes 1901, §§ 4234-4239.

Michigan: Howell's Stats. 1913, § 10854; Goodale v. Patterson, 51 Mich. 532, 16 N. W. 890. See also Brooke v. Struthers, 110 Mich. 562, 68 N. W. 272, 35 L. R. A. 536; Williams v. Keyes, 90 Mich. 290, 51 N. W. 520, 30 Am. St. 438; Ingalls v. Bond, 66 Mich. 338, 33 N. W. 404.

Minnesota: Gen. Stat. 1913, § 6843; Robbins v. Larson, 69 Minn. 436, 72 N. W. 456, 65 Am. St. 572; Hostetter v. Alexander, 22 Minn. 559; Johnson v. Carpenter, 7 Minn. 176.

Nebraska: Ann. Stat. 1911, § 10840.

New York: 1 Rev. Stat. (7th ed.), p. 763, § 41; Larned v. Donovan, 155 N. Y. 341, 49 N. E. 942.

Oregon: Lord's Ore. Laws 1910, § 7136.

Utah: Comp. Laws 1907, § 2002.

Wisconsin: Statutes 1913, § 2244.

Wyoming: Comp. Stat. 1910, § 3656. See ante § 479.

[60] Blumenthal v. Jassoy, 29 Minn. 177, 12 N. W. 517; Bull v. Mitchell, 47 Nebr. 647, 66 N. W. 632; Eggert v. Beyer, 43 Nebr. 711, 62 N. W. 57 (not applied to negotiable paper secured by a mortgage); Brewster v. Carnes, 103 N. Y. 556, 9 N. E. 323; Larned v. Donovan, 84 Hun (N. Y.) 533, 65 N. Y. St. 852, 32 N. Y. S. 731.

[61] Robbins v. Larson, 69 Minn. 436, 72 N. W. 456; Viele v. Judson, 82 N. Y. 32. See also Assets Realization Co. v. Clark, 205 N. Y. 105,

actual notice of the assignment is necessary to charge the mortgagor,[62] except where the mortgage is security for a negotiable note.[63] A purchaser of land already subject to a mortgage is chargeable with notice of an assignment of the mortgage which has been recorded prior to his purchase.[64]

On the other hand, in two or three states the record of an assignment is notice to the owner of the equity of redemption, as well as to subsequent purchasers.[65]

The object of the statutory provision that the record of an assignment shall not be deemed in itself notice to the mortgagor, his heirs, or personal representatives, of such assignment, so as to invalidate any payment made by him or them to the mortgagee, is to save the necessity of examining the record every time a payment is made. It is argued, therefore, that for all other purposes the record of the assignment is notice even to the mortgagor. Accordingly under such a provision it has been held that the record of an assignment of a mortgage is constructive notice as against a grantee of the mortgagor that the mortgagee can no longer deal with the mortgage title, and that a subsequent discharge or release of the mortgage executed by the mortgagee is invalid.[66] If the release is obtained by the mortgagor

98 N. E. 457, 41 L. R. A. (N. S.) 462. The rule requiring the assignee to give notice to the mortgagor does not extend to third persons unknown to the assignee. Schumacher v. Wolf, 125 Ill. App. 81.

[62] Murphy v. Barnard, 162 Mass. 72, 38 N. E. 29, 44 Am. St. 340; New York Life Ins. &c. Co. v. Smith, 2 Barb. Ch. (N. Y.). 82; Wolcott v. Sullivan, 1 Edw. Ch. (N. Y.) 399; Pettus v. McGowan, 37 Hun (N. Y.) 409; James v. Johnson, 6 Johns. Ch. (N. Y.) 417; Reed v. Marble, 10 Paige (N. Y.) 409; Foster v. Carson, 147 Pa. St. 157, 23 Atl. 342, 159 Pa. St. 477, 28 Atl. 356, 39 Am. St. 696; Lawton v. Howe, N. Bruns. Eq. Cas. 191.

[63] Merriam v. Bacon, 5 Metc. (Mass.) 95; Jones v. Smith, 22 Mich. 360; Blumenthal v. Jassoy, 29 Minn. 177, 12 N. W. 517. See also Stark v. Olsen, 44 Nebr. 646, 63 N. W. 37. See post § 481.

[64] Brewster v. Carnes, 103 N. Y. 556, 9 N. E. 323.

[65] Indiana: Burns. Ann. Stat. 1914, § 1145 et seq. Connecticut Mut. L. Ins. Co. v. Talbot, 113 Ind. 373, 14 N. E. 586, 3 Am. St. 655. Prior to this statute the record of an assignment was not notice. Reeves v. Hayes, 95 Ind. 521.

New Jersey: Comp. Stat. 1910, p. 3418, §§ 32, 34. If an assignment be not recorded, payment to the mortgagee without knowledge of the assignment and a release by him are binding upon the assignee. Shotwell v. Matthews (N. J. Eq.), 21 Atl. .1067; Weinberger v. Brumberg, 69 N. J. Eq. 669, 61 Atl. 732; Mott v. Newark German Hospital, 55 N. J. Eq. 722, 37 Atl. 757; Fritz v. Simpson, 34 N. J. Eq. 436. See also Devlin v. Collier, 53 N. J. L. 422, 22 Atl. 201.

North Dakota and South Dakota: Civ. Code, § 1629. See Comp Laws N. Dak. 1913, §§ 6742, 6743; Rev. Code S. Dak. 1903, §§ 2056, 2057. Pickford v. Peebles, 7 S. Dak. 166, 63 N. W. 779.

[66] Viele v. Judson, 82 N. Y. 32; Belden v. Meeker, 47 N. Y. 307, 2 Lans. 470.

himself without the payment of any sum of money upon the mortgage debt, the statute does not protect him against the effect of an assignment already recorded.[67]

§ 481. **Effect of recording assignment—Subsequent purchasers— Actual and constructive notice.**—The effect of recording an assignment is not only to protect the assignee against a subsequent sale of the mortgage by the apparent holder of it, but also to prevent a wrongful discharge of it by the mortgagee.[68] It is true that as against subsequent purchasers of the premises, or the holders of subsequent mortgages upon them, and attaching and judgment creditors, the record of a prior mortgage is sufficient notice of its existence without the record of an assignment of the mortgage to one who has purchased it. The failure to record the assignment does not blot out the record of the mortgage itself.[69] And accordingly, several cases hold that a subsequent purchaser or mortgagee can not avoid a prior recorded mortgage on the ground that an assignment of such mortgage was not recorded.[70]

But the assignment of a mortgage is more generally treated as a conveyance, and if not recorded is considered void as against subsequent purchasers of the mortgaged premises affected by the assignment, whereas if the assignment is recorded, it imparts constructive notice of the assignee's rights to such subsequent purchasers.[71]   Of

[67] Belden v. Meeker, 47 N. Y. 307, 2 Lans. 470.

[68] Parmenter v. Oakley, 69 Iowa 388, 28 N. W. 653; Larned v. Donovan, 155 N. Y. 341, affg. 84 Hun 533; Brewster v. Carnes, 103 N. Y. 556, 9 N. E. 323; Viele v. Judson, 82 N. Y. 32; Crane v. Turner, 67 N. Y. 437; Van Keuren v. Corkins, 66 N. Y. 77; Pennsylvania Salt Co. v. Neel, 54 Pa. St. 9; Henderson v. Pilgrim, 22 Tex. 464; Passumpsic Sav. Bank v. Buck, 71 Vt. 190, 44 Atl. 93; Ladd v. Campbell, 56 Vt. 529; Torrey v. Deavitt, 53 Vt. 331. See post §§ 566, 872, 956.

[69] Enos v. Cook, 65 Cal. 175, 3 Pac. 632; Burt v. Moore, 62 Kans. 536, 64 Pac. 57; Fisher v. Cowles, 41 Kans. 418, 21 Pac. 228; Bridges v. Bidwell, 20 Nebr. 185, 29 N. W. 302; Quimby v. Williams, 67 N. H. 489, 41 Atl. 862; Viele v. Judson, 82 N. Y. 32; Campbell v. Vedder, 3 Keyes (N. Y.) 174, 1 Abb. App. Dec. (N. Y.) 295; Sprague v. Rockwell, 51

Vt. 401. It is a too narrow view of the authorities to say that the record of the assignment protects merely against a subsequent assignment by the mortgagee.

[70] Quimby v. Williams, 67 N. H. 489, 41 Atl. 862, 68 Am. St. 685; Wilson v. Kimball, 27 N. H. 300; Bamberger v. Geiser, 24 Ore. 203, 33 Pac. 609; Watson v. Dundee Mtg. &c. Co., 12 Ore. 474, 8 Pac. 548; Smith v. Smith, 23 Tex. Civ. App. 304, 55 S. W. 541.

[71] Foss v. Dullam, 111 Minn. 220, 126 N. W. 820; Gillian v. McDowall, 66 Nebr. 814, 92 N. W. 991; Ames v. Miller, 65 Nebr. 204, 91 N. W. 250; Bacon v. Van Schoonhoven, 87 N. Y. 446; Purdy v. Huntington, 42 N. Y. 334, 1 Am. Rep. 532; Smyth v. Knickerbocker Life Ins. Co., 21 Hun (N. Y.) 241, affd. 84 N. Y. 589; Heilbrun v. Hammond, 13 Hun (N. Y.) 474; Mills v. Comstock, 5 Johns. Ch. (N. Y.) 214; Vanderkemp v. Shelton, 11 Paige (N. Y.)

course the failure to record an assignment is immaterial where the subsequent purchaser had actual knowledge of it.[2]

If the premises are conveyed to the mortgagee after he has assigned the mortgage, there is no merger of the mortgage title.[73] It makes no difference that the assignment is not recorded. If the mortgagee, in this condition of the title, then conveys the estate to one who purchases without knowledge of the assignment of the mortgage, the question arises whether the assignee, having omitted to record his assignment, thus leaving, so far as the record shows, a complete title in the mortgagee, can be protected in his title as against the purchaser from the mortgagee.[74]

Of course such purchaser is charged with constructive notice of the existence of a mortgage, and of the continuance of its lien, by its record. Having this information he is chargeable in law with the further notice that the mortgage is a lien in the hands of any person to whom it may have been legally transferred, and that the record of such transfer is not necessary to its validity, nor as a protection against a purchaser of the property mortgaged, or any other person than a subsequent purchaser in good faith of the mortgage itself, or the bond or debt secured by it; but rather that one purchasing the premises from the mortgagee would take them subject to the lien of the mortgage irrespective of the ownership of it, unless the mortgagee was the owner. That knowledge and notice make it his duty, in the exercise of proper diligence, to inquire whether his vendor, the mortgagee, is still the owner of the mortgage, and his omission to make that inquiry deprives him of the protection of a bona fide purchaser.[75]

28; Clark v. Ulrich, 14 N. Y. St. 4; Brownback v. Ozias, 117 Pa. St. 87, 11 Atl. 301; Neide v. Pennypacker, 9 Phila. (Pa.) 86; Pickford v. Peebles, 7 S. Dak. 166, 63 N. W. 779; Merrill v. Luce, 6 S. Dak. 354, 61 N. W. 43, 55 Am. St. 844; Fallass v. Pierce, 30 Wis. 443; Frank v. Snow, 6 Wyo. 42, 42 Pac. 484, 43 Pac. 78. See also James v. Newman, 147 Iowa 574, 126 N. W. 781; Bridges v. Bidwell, 20 Nebr. 185, 29 N. W. 302. But see Curtis v. Moore, 162 N. Y. 159, 46 N. E. 168, 57 Am. St. 506; Campbell v. Vedder, 1 Abb. Dec. (N. Y.) 295, 3 Keyes 174; Miller v. Lindsley, 19 Hun. (N. Y.) 207; McCurdy v. Leslie, 2 Wkly N. Cas. (Pa.) 273.

[72] Miller v. Larned, 103 Ill. 562;

Artz v. Yeager, 30 Ind. App. 677, 66 N. E. 917.

[73] Purdy v. Huntington, 42 N. Y. 334, 1 Am. Rep. 532; Campbell v. Vedder, 3 Keyes (N. Y.) 174; 1 Abb. App. Dec. 295.

[74] This, then, is the case: "A sells and conveys land to B. B gives back a bond and mortgage for the purchase-money. A sells and assigns the bond and mortgage to C, and afterward receives a conveyance of the equity of redemption from B, and then by a full covenant deed conveys the land, and all his estate and interest in the land to D."

[75] Oregon Trust Co. v. Shaw, 5 Sawy. (U. S.) 336 (quoting and approving the text); Burhans v.

A mortgage covered separate tracts, and after its assignment and before it was recorded the original mortgagees executed a release of part of the property, acknowledging therein a payment of part of the secured debt; which release was recorded; and thereafter and before the assignment was recorded, a third person took a second mortgage upon the property remaining subject to the first mortgage. It was held, that the second mortgagee had the right to rely upon the record, and as against her the payment recited in the release must be considered as having been properly made and the amount secured by the first mortgage reduced to that extent.[76] Where a mortgagee assigned the mortgage as collateral security, and afterward received payment of the debt, but failed to turn it over to the assignee, the landowner who made the payment with constructive notice of the assignment can not defeat foreclosure on the ground that the assignee is estopped to deny mortgagee's agency for the purpose of collecting the debt, without proving the agency or facts constituting an estoppel.[77]

§ 481a. **Recording assignment—Payment of paper before maturity without its production.**—By the weight of authority, a mortgage securing negotiable paper is a mere incident thereto and partakes in its negotiability. Hence the law of negotiable instruments governs the rights of the parties as well as third persons, concerning payment; and payment before maturity to any one other than the holder of the negotiable instrument is at the risk of the payer, and is binding upon the holder of the paper only where express or implied authority to receive such payment existed. Consequently payment of a negotiable note secured by a mortgage, by the mortgagor or his grantee, when made to the mortgagee not in possession of the note and mortgage, is not binding upon an assignee thereof before maturity, who had possession of the papers at the time of payment, unless he had expressly or impliedly authorized such payment.[78] In a recent New York

Hutcheson, 25 Kans. 625, 37 Am. Rep. 274; Purdy v. Huntington, 42 N. Y. 334, overruling 46 Barb. (N. Y.) 389, 1 Am. Rep. 532. See also Van Keuren v. Corkins, 6 Thomp. & C. (N. Y.) 355, 4 Hun 129, 66 N. Y. 77; Gillig v. Maass, 28 N. Y. 191; Warner v. Winslow, 1 Sandf. Ch. (N. Y.) 430. See post § 804.

[76] Frank v. Snow, 6 Wyo. 42, 42 Pac. 484, 43 Pac. 78.

[77] Bettle v. Tiedgen, 85 Nebr. 276, 122 N. W. 890, 77 Nebr. 799, 116 N. W. 959.

[78] New Orleans Canal &c. Co. v. Montgomery, 95 U. S. 16, 24 L. ed. 346; Sawyer v. Prickett, 19 Wall. (U. S.) 146, 22 L. ed. 105; Kennicott v. Wayne County, 16 Wall. (U. S.) 452, 21 L. ed. 319; Carpenter v. Longan, 16 Wall. (U. S.) 271, 21 L. ed. 313; Windle v. Bonebrake, 23 Fed. 165; Baumgartner v. Peterson, 93 Iowa 572, 62 N. W. 27; Brayley v. Ellis, 71 Iowa 155, 32 N. W. 254; Burhans v. Hutcheson, 25 Kans. 625, 37 Am. Rep. 274; Hoffacker v. Manufacturers' Nat. Bank

case, reviewing the decisions upon this subject, it was held that it is the duty of a person paying a note or bond secured by a mortgage to require the production and cancelation of the instrument; and that a payment of the balance due on a mortgage by a purchaser of the equity of redemption, made to the mortgagee to discharge the mortgage, without taking any satisfaction, or requiring production of the securities for cancelation, was of no avail as against the holder of an unrecorded assignment.[79]

A recent Wisconsin decision holds that the indorsee of a note secured by a mortgage having possession of the instruments need not record his assignment, to be protected against payments by the debtor to the original mortgagee.[80] In another Wisconsin decision, the court said that a mortgagor in a mortgage securing a negotiable note, or his subsequent grantee, is not warranted in paying the mortgage indebtedness to the record owner thereof or his agent, relying solely upon the record, where the securities are not in possession of such owner or the person acting as his agent.[81]

The rule that a mortgagor is entitled to deal with the mortgagee as the holder of the mortgage, until he has actual notice of an assign-

(Md.), 23 Atl. 579; Murphy v. Barnard, 162 Mass. 72, 38 N. E. 29, 44 Am. St. 340; Biggerstaff v. Marston, 161 Mass. 101, 36 N. E. 785; Brooke v. Struthers, 110 Mich. 563, 68 N. W. 272, 35 L. R. A. 536; Markey v. Corey, 108 Mich. 184, 66 N. W. 493, 36 L. R. A. 117, 62 Am. St. 698; Williams v. Keyes, 90 Mich. 290, 51 N. W. 520, 30 Am. St. 438; Morrison v. Roehl, 215 Mo. 545, 114 S. W. 981; Borgess Invest. Co. v. Vette, 142 Mo. 560, 44 S. W. 754, 64 Am. St. 567; Dodge v. Birkenfeld, 20 Mont. 115, 49 Pac. 590; Snell v. Margritz, 64 Nebr. 6, 91 N. W. 274; Herbage v. Moodie, 51 Nebr. 837, 71 N. W. 778; Porter v. Ourada, 51 Nebr. 510, 71 N. W. 52; Stark v. Olsen, 44 Nebr. 646, 63 N. W. 37; Eggert v. Beyer, 43 Nebr. 711, 62 N. W. 57; Webb v. Hoselton, 4 Nebr. 308, 19 Am. Rep. 638; Bautz v. Adams, 131 Wis. 152, 111 N. W. 69, 120 Am. St. 1030. The reason advanced in support of this doctrine is that a mortgagor executing a mortgage as security for a negotiable note payable to order, is charged with knowledge that the note is negotiable, and therefore he makes payments to the original mortgagee without production of the note at his peril, as such payments have no effect as against an indorsee thereof who has possession at the time the payments are made. Baumgartner v. Peterson, 93 Iowa 572, 62 N. W. 27.

[79] Assets Realization Co. v. Clark, 205 N. Y. 105, 98 N. E. 457, 41 L. R. A. (N. S.) 462. See also Notes in 21 L. R. A. (N. S.) 52 and 29 L. R. A. (N. S.) 576; Koen v. Miller, 105 Ark. 152, 150 S. W. 411; Exchange Nat. Bank v. Ross, 17 Cal. App. 235, 119 Pac. 398; Scott v. Taylor, 63 Fla. 612, 58 So. 30; Garrett v. Fernauld, 63 Fla. 434, 57 So. 671; Aycock Bros. Lbr. Co. v. First Nat. Bank, 54 Fla. 604, 45 So. 501.

[80] Marling v. Jones, 138 Wis. 82, 119 N. W. 931, 131 Am. St. 996.

[81] Beautz v. Adams, 131 Wis. 152, 111 N. W. 69, 120 Am. St. 1030. See also Bartel v. Brown, 104 Wis. 493, 80 N. W. 801 (emphasizing the importance of protecting holders of commercial paper, and proof of their authority to receive payment by production of the written securities).

ment, has no application when the mortgage is given to secure a negotiable note, and this is transferred before it is due.[82] A different rule prevails in Massachusetts.[83] There the estate of a mortgagee of land is a legal estate, which passes by the same instruments of conveyance as other legal estates. It is declared to be as important to be able to ascertain from the registry the existence or continuance of a mortgage as of any other legal title. "Not unfrequently the whole or part of an estate held in mortgage is released or conveyed when the debt is not paid; and in the absence of fraud, a conveyance by the party who appears on the record to be the owner of the mortgage should be sufficient to protect a purchaser who has no actual or constructive notice of title in any other."[84] Therefore, as held in a later case, "one who takes a conveyance of a mortgage, either by a formal assignment or a quitclaim deed, from a person who appears of record to be the owner of it, will acquire a good title as mortgagee, unless he has actual notice or information of a defect in the title."[85]

§ 482. **Assignee as bona fide purchaser—Notice—Rights and priorities.**—An assignee of a mortgage is a purchaser, and is entitled to the protection of the recording acts as much as a purchaser of the equity of redemption.[86] If he purchases in good faith, and for a valuable consideration, he is not chargeable with any notice his assignor had of prior incumbrances upon the property, provided he records his assignment before such prior mortgage or other deed is recorded.[87] He is then chargeable only with constructive notice, such as is afforded by record, or by open and adverse possession of the premises by another.[88] The assignee gains priority in such case, not by the prior re-

---

[82] Jones v. Smith, 22 Mich. 360.

[83] Blunt v. Norris, 123 Mass. 55, 25 Am. Rep. 14; Welch v. Priest, 8 Allen (Mass.) 165; Wolcott v. Winchester, 15 Gray (Mass.) 461, stated in post § 804.

So by statute in Maryland: Act 1868, ch. 373; Code 1911, art. 21, § 34, p. 504. The act does not affect equitable assignments. Byles v. Tome, 39 Md. 461; Western Maryland &c. Co. v. Goodwin, 77 Md. 271, 26 Atl. 319; Hewell v. Coulbourn, 54 Md. 59.

So in Vermont: Ladd v. Campbell, 56 Vt. 529.

[84] Welch v. Priest, 8 Allen (Mass.) 165.

[85] Stark v. Boynton, 167 Mass. 443, citing Gallagher v. Galletley, 128 Mass. 367; Morse v. Curtis, 140 Mass. 112.

[86] Smyth v. Knickerbocker L. Ins. Co., 84 N. Y. 589; Decker v. Boice, 83 N. Y. 215; Westbrook v. Gleason, 79 N. Y. 23; Butler v. Mazeppa Bank, 94 Wis. 351, 68 N. W. 998.

[87] Decker v. Boice, 83 N. Y. 215.

[88] Jackson v. Reid, 30 Kans. 10, 1 Pac. 308; Bush v. Lathrop, 22 N. Y. 535; Union College v. Wheeler, 59 Barb. (N. Y.) 585; Jackson v. Van Valkenburgh, 8 Cow. (N. Y.) 260; Jackson v. Given, 8 Johns. (N. Y.) 137, 5 Am. Dec. 328; Varick v. Briggs, 6 Paige (N. Y.) 323.

cording of the assigned mortgage, but by the prior recording of his own assignment.[89]

A bona fide assignee of a note and mortgage which is duly recorded, has priority over an elder but unrecorded mortgage of which he had no notice, even though his assignor had notice thereof.[90] Such assignee, however, must first record his title, in states where the recording of assignments is required or permitted, and an assignment recorded after an elder mortgage, will be postponed to it.[91] If the assignee omits to record his assignment, and an elder mortgage of which he had no notice, but of which his assignor had notice, is first recorded, he will hold subject to such elder mortgage; and he would also hold subject to it if such elder mortgage had been recorded before he took the assignment, but after the recording of the mortgage assigned.[92] A formal and valid assignment of a mortgage and the debt secured invests the assignee with all the rights, powers and equities of the mortgagee.[93]

The assignee of a mortgage takes all the rights of his assignor, and if, in the hands of the assignor, it was entitled to priority over another mortgage under the statute because of its priority of record, and of the fact that it was taken by the assignor for a full consideration, and without notice that the other mortgage had in fact been previously executed, it has the same priority in the hands of the assignee, although he may have taken it with knowledge of the facts.[94] An assignment of a mortgage, though not recorded until after the death of the assignor, is superior to the rights of the heirs of the assignor, who are not treated as bona fide purchasers within the recording act.[95]

[89] Decker v. Boice, 83 N. Y. 215. The contrary rule declared in Jackson v. Van Valkenburgh, 8 Cow. (N. Y.) 260, is no longer in force. Bank for Savings v. Frank, 13 J. & S. (N. Y.) 404.

[90] Coonrod v. Kelly, 119 Fed. 841, 56 C. C. A. 353; Harrison v. Yerby (Ala.), 14 So. 321; Dulin v. Hunter, 98 Ala. 539, 13 So. 301; Clasey v. Sigg, 51 Iowa 371, 1 N. W. 590; Paul v. Paul, 23 N. Y. St. 370, 5 N. Y. S. 743; Morris v. Beecher, 1 N. Dak. 130, 45 N. W. 696; Building Assn. v. Clark, 43 Ohio St. 427, 2 N. E. 846. See also Decker v. Boice, 83 N. Y. 215; David Stevenson Brew. Co. v. Iba, 12 Misc. 329, 65 N. Y. St. 784, 33 N. Y. S. 642, 1 Ann. Cas. 356.

[91] English v. Waples, 13 Iowa 57; Rumery v. Loy, 61 Nebr. 755, 86 N. W. 478; Westbrook v. Gleason, 79 N. Y. 23.

[92] Brower v. Witmeyer, 121 Ind. 83, 22 N. E. 975; De Lancey v. Stearns, 66 N. Y. 157; Fort v. Burch, 5 Denio (N. Y.) 187.

[93] Bulkley v. Chapman, 9 Conn. 5; Beatty v. Clement, 12 La. Ann. 82; Holmes v. Holmes, 129 Mich. 412, 89 N. W. 47, 95 Am. St. 444; Smith v. Godwin, 145 N. Car. 242, 58 S. E. 1089.

[94] Coonrod v. Kelly, 119 Fed. 841.

[95] Wellendorf v. Wellendorf, 120 Minn. 435, 139 N. W. 812, 43 L. R. A. (N. S.) 1144.

If a mortgage be assigned, but the assignment is not recorded until after the mortgagor makes a conveyance of the mortgaged premises to the mortgagee, and the latter executes another mortgage of the same, which deed and subsequent mortgage are first recorded, the last mortgage will take precedence of the first; but another mortgage after the recording of the assignment of the first mortgage will be subject thereto.[96]

A second mortgagee assigned his mortgage and part of the debt, but the assignment was not recorded. Subsequently the mortgagor conveyed the land to the second mortgagee. The first mortgagee then released his mortgage, and took a third mortgage on the land for the unpaid principal and interest, without actual knowledge of the assignment, and on the faith of the record and of the second mortgagee's representation that his mortgage had been extinguished by merger. It was held that he was entitled to priority over the assignee claiming under the unrecorded assignment of the second mortgage, though such mortgage was never actually discharged of record.[97]

And so, where there were two successive mortgages of the same land, and the mortgagor in the first mortgage was the mortgagee in the second, and the second mortgage was first recorded and was then assigned to a bona fide purchaser for value before the first mortgage was recorded, but the assignment was not recorded until after the recording of the first mortgage, the mortgagee in the second mortgage could not claim priority, because when he recorded his mortgage he had notice of the prior mortgage which he had himself executed. It was held, in a controversy between assignees of the respective mortgages, that the assignee of the second mortgage could derive no benefit from the prior record of his mortgage, as he stood as to that in the shoes of his assignor; and that he was not entitled to priority by the record of his assignment, because the first mortgage was recorded before the recording of his assignment. But it was conceded that if he had recorded his assignment before the first mortgage was recorded he would have gained a preference.[98]

An assignee of a note and mortgage, who does not receive the instruments, and knows that they are in the possession of a third person,

[96] McCormick v. Bauer, 122 Ill. 573, 13 N. E. 852; Jenks v. Shaw, 99 Iowa 604, 68 N. W. 900, 61 Am. St. 256; Brewster v. Carnes, 103 N. Y. 556, 9 N. E. 323; Butler v. Bank of Mazeppa, 94 Wis. 351, 68 N. W. 998.

[97] Pritchard v. Kalamazoo College, 82 Mich. 587, 47 N. W. 31.

[98] Westbrook v. Gleason, 79 N. Y. 23, reversing same case 14 Hun (N. Y.) 245. This case is stated and approved by Andrews, J., in Decker v. Boice, 83 N. Y. 215.

the note being indorsed in blank, can not be considered a bona fide purchaser without notice.[99] If a mortgagee assigns one of the notes secured by a mortgage, and afterward assigns another note secured by it, together with the mortgage, to another person, the latter assignee is not protected against the assignee of the note as an innocent purchaser, because the mortgage itself is notice to him of the existence of such note.[1]

§ 483. **Priority under different assignments of same mortgage.**— If priority between the different assignments of the same mortgage is not fixed by record, it will generally be determined by the relative equities of the parties, and an assignee who is a purchaser in good faith will be preferred to one who is not.[2] The fact that a later assignee knew of an earlier assignment will postpone him.[3] And so the failure of one assignee to require the production and delivery of the instruments in the hands of a third person, will likewise postpone him.[4]

It is not often that the question of priority of rights under different assignments of the same mortgage can arise, because an assignment is generally accompanied by a delivery of the note or bond secured by the mortgage and of the mortgage itself; and except under peculiar circumstances a person acting in good faith would not take a mere written transfer of the mortgage title without a delivery of these.[5] The fact that the assignor did not have these papers to deliver would be enough ordinarily to put the purchaser on his guard, even if it did not amount to notice to him of a prior assignment. At any rate, the absence of these papers would be enough to put in doubt his good

---

[99] Bunker v. International Harvester Co., 148 Iowa 708, 127 N. W. 1016.

[1] Wilson v. Eigenbrodt, 30 Minn. 4, 13 N. W. 907.

[2] Batchellor v. Richardson, 17 Ore. 334, 21 Pac. 392; Potter v. Stransky, 48 Wis. 235, 4 N. W. 95. See also Chew v. Brumagin, 21 N. J. Eq. 520 (absolute assignment and assignment as collateral); Hoyt v. Thompson, 19 N. Y. 207.

[3] Van Vleet v. Blackwood, 33 Mich. 334; Ubansky v. Shirmer, 111 App. Div. 50, 97 N. Y. S. 577. An assignee's knowledge that the assignor intended to assign the mortgage to another is not sufficient to postpone him. Warden v. Adams, 15 Mass. 233. See also Bunker v. International Harvester Co., 148 Iowa 708, 127 N. W. 1016.

[4] Porter v. King, 1 Fed. 755; Harding v. Durand, 36 Ill. App. 238; Murphy v. Barnard, 162 Mass. 72, 38 N. E. 29, 44 Am. St. 340; Blunt v. Norris, 123 Mass. 55, 25 Am. Rep. 14; Kitchin's Appeal, 196 Pa. St. 321, 46 Atl. 418. See also Buehler v. McCormick, 169 Ill. 269, 48 N. E. 287. But see Richards Trust Co. v. Rhomberg, 19 S. Dak. 595, 104 N. W. 268.

[5] Porter v. King, 1 Fed. 755 (quoting text with approval).

faith in taking the assignment; and would make him chargeable with notice of any defect there may be in the assignor's title.[6]

But if two assignments of the same mortgage by any means are made and taken by different persons in good faith, of course the assignee who first records his assignment would gain the better title to the mortgage, if he has paid full value for it at the time of taking it. If he paid only part of the consideration, then he would have priority only to the extent of the payment made by him; for he is then a purchaser, and entitled to protection only to that extent.[7] In the absence of special equities in either assignee, the general rule prevails that he who is first in time, is first in right.[8]

§ 484. Manner of recording an assignment—Identification of mortgage—Marginal record.—A separate assignment of a mortgage is generally recorded in the same manner as the mortgage itself or any other instrument affecting lands.[9] When an assignment of a mortgage is indorsed upon the mortgage deed, which is referred to as "the within described mortgage," it is sufficient to record the assignment without recording the mortgage with it anew, and identification by cross-references to the respective pages on which instruments are recorded is sufficient.[10] Such reference is usually made by the register from the record of one instrument to the other; but unless required by law, this is not essential. A recital of the names of the parties to the mortgage, and its date, is a sufficient identification of it; although it is usual in addition to this description, when the assignment is not indorsed upon the mortgage, to refer, in the description of it, to the book and page of the record. But neither a reference to the record of the mortgage nor a description of the mortgaged lands is necessary. An assignment is sufficient which so identifies the mortgage that by examining the records the one referred to can be ascertained.[11]

It is usual for the register to note an assignment upon the margin of the record of a mortgage; and in many states it is made by statute his duty to do so. But in the absence of such a statute the

[6] Kellogg v. Smith, 26 N. Y. 18; Brown v. Blydenburgh, 7 N. Y. 141, 57 Am. Dec. 506.

[7] Oregon Trust Co. v. Shaw, 5 Sawyer (U. S.) 336; Wiley v. Williamson, 68 Maine 71; Bush v. Lathrop, 22 N. Y. 535; Purdy v. Huntington, 46 Barb. (N. Y.) 389, 42 N. Y. 334, 1 Am. Rep. 532; Pickett v. Barron, 29 Barb. (N. Y.) 505; Campbell v. Vedder, 3 Keyes (N. Y.) 174; Potter v. Stransky, 48 Wis. 235, 4 N. W. 95. See post § 566.

[8] Conover v. Grover, 31 N. J. Eq. 539.

[9] Merrill v. Luce, 6 S. Dak. 354, 61 N. W. 43, 55 Am. St. 844; Henderson v. Pilgrim, 22 Tex. 464.

[10] Sonie v. Corbley, 65 Mich. 109, 31 N. W. 785; Carli v. Taylor, 15 Minn. 171; Viele v. Judson, 82 N. Y. 32.

[11] Viele v. Judson, 82 N. Y. 32.

omission of the register to do so does not affect the right of the assignee.[12]

A statute requiring assignments of mortgages to be recorded or entered on the margin of the mortgage record, does not extend to the mere assignment of a note which carries the mortgage securing it, as an incident.[13]

Under a statute requiring mortgages to be recorded in separate books, an assignment of a mortgage should be recorded in a book for mortgages, and the record of it in the book for deeds is held to be of no avail.[14]

The certificate of the registry of a mortgage, required by statute to be indorsed thereon, is prima facie evidence of its record.[15]

§ 485. Record of collateral agreement affecting mortgage, or partial release.—The same principles apply equally to the record of any agreement affecting a mortgage. If not executed with the formalities entitling it to be recorded, the record affords no constructive notice of its contents. If, for instance, land subject to a mortgage is sold, and mortgaged back for the purchase-price, the vendor agreeing to pay off the elder mortgage, or in default of so doing to allow the purchaser to pay it, and have the amount of it deducted from the mortgage given for the price of the land, and this agreement, without being entitled to be recorded, is nevertheless put upon record, and the purchaser subsequently pays the elder mortgage as contemplated by the agreement, an assignee of the mortgage for the purchase-money having no actual notice of this agreement, is not concluded by it, but may hold his mortgage for the original amount of it.[16]

A release of a mortgage is a conveyance, required to be recorded, to affect subsequent purchasers and incumbrancers without notice.[17] A release of a part of the mortgaged premises is a conveyance by which the title to real estate may be affected, and, unless it be recorded, it is void against a subsequent assignee of the mortgage for value and

[12] Viele v. Judson, 82 N. Y. 32, overruling Moore v. Sloan, 50 Barb. (N. Y.) 442.

[13] Perry v. Fisher, 30 Ind. App. 261, 65 N. E. 935; construing Burns' Ann. Stat. Indiana 1914, §§ 1145-1149 (Burns' Stat. 1901, § 1107a).

[14] Purdy v. Huntington, 42 N. Y. 334, 1 Am. Rep. 532. See also Gillig v. Maass, 28 N. Y. 191.

[15] Jakway v. Jenison, 46 Mich. 521, 9 N. W. 836.

[16] Dutton v. Ives, 5 Mich. 515.

[17] Palmer v. Bates, 22 Minn. 532; Baker v. Thomas, 61 Hun 17, 39 N. Y. St. 816, 15 N. Y. S. 359; Mutual Life Ins. Co. v. Wilcox, 55 How. Pr. (N. Y.) 43. See also Gibson v. Thomas, 85 App. Div. 243, 83 N. Y. S. 552 (insufficient deposit of release). But see Blume v. Lundry, 130 N. Y. S. 636.

without notice.[18] An unrecorded agreement to release is in like manner void against an assignee of the mortgage in good faith.[19]

Any collateral or subsequent written agreement by the parties to a mortgage, which materially affects or alters the terms or conditions of the original mortgage, should be recorded. Thus an agreement made at the time of executing a deed of trust, whereby the beneficiaries promise the grantor not to sell, until they have sustained loss as sureties on the grantor's bond, is a part of the deed, and is an instrument affecting real estate.[20] And likewise, the written appointment of a substitute trustee, is an instrument in writing affecting lands, within the recording act.[21]

§ 486. **Crops and trees included as part of realty.**—The registry laws apply to sales and mortgages of growing crops and trees, or to an agreement constituting a lien upon them, so long as they are a part of the realty. A verbal agreement, or an agreement in writing not recorded, whereby the crop is pledged by a tenant of land to the owner as security for advances, is of no validity as against a mortgage of it afterward made and duly recorded.[22]

Growing trees are generally considered part of the realty and are embraced in a mortgage of the land,[23] unless expressly excepted.[24] And since a mortgage of standing timber is considered a conveyance of an interest in land, it must be recorded as such; and if filed as a chattel

---

[18] Mutual Life Ins. Co. v. Wilcox, 55 How. Pr. (N. Y.) 43. A registrar is bound to register a partial release. In re Ridout, 2 U. C. C. P. 477. The mortgagor's possession is not notice to a purchaser under foreclosure, of the the rights of the mortgagor under an unrecorded partial release of the premises. Palmer v. Bates, 22 Minn. 532.

[19] St. John v. Spaulding, 1 T. & C. (N. Y.) 483.

[20] Munson v. Ensor, 94 Mo. 504, 7 S. W. 108.

[21] Gooch v. Addison, 13 Tex. Civ. App. 76, 35 S. W. 83.

[22] Jones v. Chamberlin, 5 Heisk. (Tenn.) 210. This case is distinguished from Tedford v. Wilson, 3 Head (Tenn.) 311, where it was agreed that the proceeds of a farm should be liable for the wages of a person who entered into possession of it and carried it on for the owner. Being in possession, he was held to be entitled to apply the crops to

the satisfaction of his claim for wages as against a creditor of the owner, and that the registration act did not apply. As to mortgages of crops, see Jones on Chattel Mortgages, §§ 142-146.

[23] Hutchins v. King, 1 Wall. (U. S.) 53, 17 L. ed. 544; In re Bruce, 9 Ben. (U. S.) 236, Fed. Cas. No. 2045; Adams v. Beadle, 47 Iowa 439, 29 Am. Rep. 487. See also Maples v. Millon, 31 Conn. 598 (trees and shrubs in nursery included); Mann v. English, 38 U. C. Q. B. 240.

[24] Mercantile Trust Co. v. Southern &c. Land Co., 86 Fed. 711, 30 C. C. A. 349; Moisant v. McPhee, 92 Cal. 76, 28 Pac. 46. See also In re Holmes Lumber Co., 189 Fed. 178 (recital of mortgagee's right of access to cut timber); American Nat. Bank v. First Nat. Bank, 52 Tex. Civ. App. 519, 114 S. W. 176 (implied reservation of right to cut timber).

mortgage it will not constitute notice to a subsequent purchaser.[25] But the record of a timber deed in a special book kept for such exceptional instruments was held proper.[16]

A parol contract for the sale of growing trees to be cut and removed from the land is ordinarily a contract for the sale of a chattel interest, though the trees are a part of the realty so long as they remain standing. Therefore, to insure protection against a sale or mortgage of the land before the trees are severed, it is desirable that the sale be recorded. If the owner of land which is mortgaged sells growing trees, and the purchaser cuts and removes the trees without knowledge of the mortgage, which is not recorded, the mortgagee has no title to the timber as against such purchaser, and can not maintain replevin for it.[27]

§ 487. **Mechanics' lien laws affecting priority of mortgages.**—The statutes providing for mechanics' liens qualify and affect and sometimes destroy the priority of conveyances as established by the registry laws; and it is therefore important that these statutes should be considered in connection with the registry laws. Such liens may be given priority of mortgages executed and recorded subsequently to the date of the contract under which the lien is claimed, as is the case in Massachusetts and Maine,[28] but more frequently mechanics' liens are given precedence of mortgages upon the property recorded after the commencement of the work or improvement for which the lien is claimed.[29] The argument in favor of such a provision is, that one who

[25] Williams v. Hyde, 98 Mich. 152, 57 N. W. 98.

[26] Mee v. Benedict, 98 Mich. 260, 57 N. W. 175, 22 L. R. A. 641, 39 Am. St. 543.

[27] Banton v. Shorey, 77 Maine 48.

[28] Saucier v. Maine Supply &c. Co., 109 Maine 342, 84 Atl. 461; Farnham v. Richardson, 91 Maine 559, 40 Atl. 553; Morse v. Dole, 73 Maine 351; Shaughnessy v. Isenberg, 213 Mass. 159, 99 N. E. 975; McDowell v. Rockwood, 182 Mass. 150, 65 N. E. 65; Taylor v. Springfield Lbr. Co., 180 Mass. 3, 61 N. E. 217; Sprague v. McDougall, 172 Mass. 553, 52 N. E. 1077; Carew v. Stubbs, 155 Mass. 549, 30 N. E. 219; Batchelder v. Rand, 117 Mass. 176; Dunklee v. Crane, 103 Mass. 470. See also Monticello Bank v. Sweet, 64 Ark. 502, 43 S. W. 500; Interstate Bldg. &c. Assn. v. Ayers, 177 Ill. 9, 52 N. E. 342; Paddock v. Stout, 121 Ill. 571, 13 N. E. 182. Under the Massachusetts statute, the claim of a third person for labor performed upon a building has been held superior to a purchase-money mortgage to the owner, who had impliedly authorized a contractor to employ the necessary workmen to erect the building. McCormack v. Butland, 191 Mass. 421, 77 N. E. 761. See post § 609 and ante §§468, 473a, concerning priority of purchase-money mortgages and mechanic's liens.

For lien laws affecting the priority of railroad mortgages, see Jones on Liens, §§ 1618-1675.

For a statement of the law as to priority between mechanic's liens and mortgages, see Jones on Liens, §§ 1457-1486.

As to priority of statutory liens for water rates, see Jones on Liens, § 102.

[29] See post § 609.

takes a mortgage upon a building in process of erection, or upon land upon which improvements for which a lien is given are being made, is bound to know that there may be a lien upon the property for the work already done, and to assume that the work is to go forward, and that there may be a further lien for completing the work. It is not desirable, either, that the execution of a mortgage upon the land should be permitted to arrest the work and prevent its completion as would most likely happen if the making of the mortgage had the effect of postponing any lien afterward filed. It is regarded also as just that the mechanic should have the benefit of the labor and materials that go into the property and give it value, rather than the mortgagee, who has taken his mortgage during the progress of the work.[10]

Under such statutes, a mortgage made in good faith to secure future advances on a building, if recorded before the commencement of the building, is entitled to priority over liens for labor or materials, although the advances are not made till after the commencement of the building.[31] A mortgage made to secure future advances will thus have priority over subsequently attaching mechanics' liens, to the extent of the amount advanced, including advances made after accrual of the mechanics' liens,[32] provided such advances were definitely contracted for and were obligatory upon the mortgagee,[33] but voluntary

[10] Davis v. Bilsland, 18 Wall. (U. S.) 659, 21 L. ed. 969; Equitable Life Ins. Co. v. Slye, 45 Iowa 615; Neilson v. Iowa Eastern R. Co., 44 Iowa 71. See also Riverside Lumber Co. v. Schafer, 251 Mo. 539, 158 S. W. 340.

[31] Keystone Iron Works Co. v. Douglass Sugar Co., 55 Kans. 195, 40 Pac. 273; Flint &c. Mfg. Co. v. Douglass Sugar Co., 54 Kans. 455, 38 Pac. 566; Heal v. Evans Creek Coal &c. Co., 71 Wash. 225, 128 Pac. 211; Wisconsin Planing Mill Co. v. Schuda, 72 Wis. 277, 39 N. W. 558. See post § 609. See also McAdams v. Piedmont Trust Co. (N. Car.), 83 S. E. 623.

[32] Anglo-American Sav. &c. Assn. v. Campbell, 13 App. D. C. 581, 43 L. R. A 622; Richards v. Waldron, 20 D. C. 585; Kiene v. Hodge, 90 Iowa 212, 57 N. W. 717; Brooks v. Lester, 36 Md. 65 (advances of materials); Hill v. Aldrich, 48 Minn. 73, 50 N. W. 1020; Central Trust Co. v. Continental Iron Works, 51 N. J. Eq. 605, 28 Atl. 595, 40 Am. St. 539; Jacobus v. Mutual Ben. L. Ins. Co., 27 N. J. Eq. 604; Platt v. Griffith, 27 N. J. Eq. 207; Barnett v. Griffith, 27 N. J. Eq. 201; Taylor v. La Bar, 25 N. J. Eq. 222; Central Trust Co. v. Bartlett, 57 N. J. L. 206, 30 Atl. 583 (mortgage to secure bonds to be issued subsequently); Lipman v. Jackson Architectural Iron Works, 128 N. Y. 58, 27 N. E. 975; Moroney's Appeal, 24 Pa. St. 372; Lyle v. Ducomb, 5 Binn. (Pa.) 585; Blackmar v. Sharp, 23 R. I. 412, 50 Atl. 852; Wroten v. Armat, 31 Grat. (Va.) 228; Home Sav. &c. Assn. v. Burton, 20 Wash. 688, 56 Pac. 940; Wisconsin Planing-Mill Co. v. Schuda, 72 Wis. 277, 39 N. W. 558. See also Martsolf v. Barnwell, 15 Kans. 612; Reed v. Rochford, 62 N. J. Eq. 186, 50 Atl. 70; Page v. Carr, 232 Pa. 371, 81 Atl. 430. But see Allen Co. v. Emerton, 108 Maine 221, 79 Atl. 905; Culmer Paint &c. Co. v. Gleason (Utah), 130 Pac. 66.

[33] Anglo-American Sav. &c. Assn. v. Campbell, 13 App D. C. 581, 43 L. R. A. 622; Whelan v. Exchange

and optional advances by the mortgagee with notice of intervening, liens are postponed thereto.[34] The lien of a holder of corporate bonds and a mortgage, given to secure prior advances to the corporation, after the attachment of a mechanic's lien, and accepted with knowledge thereof, is inferior to the mechanic's lien. Future advances upon such a mortgage can have priority only to the extent of the money actually advanced by the mortgagee and applied to the erection of a new building on the premises, and money expended for furniture in the building is not embraced in such a prior claim.[35]

Under still other statutes, a bona fide mortgagee is regarded as a purchaser who is not affected by a mechanic's lien unless he has received actual or constructive notice of it in a manner prescribed; and the fact that the mechanic is at work upon the building at the time of the mortgage is not actual notice of his lien.[36]

There are statutes, however, which give a mechanic's lien precedence over a mortgage which was a lien on the land before the building was commenced.[37] This lien is waived by taking a mortgage[38] or other security for the amount for which a lien might be claimed.

The commencement of a building, within the meaning of these statutes, is the first labor done on the ground which is made the foundation of the building, and forms part of the work suitable and necessary for its construction.[39] It is some work or labor on the ground,

---

Trust Co., 214 Mass. 121, 100 N. E. 1095; Barnett v. Griffith, 27 N. J. Eq. 201; Taylor v. Le Bar, 25 N. J. Eq. 222; Lipman v. Jackson Architectural Iron Works, 128 N. Y. 58, 27 N. E. 975; Moroney's Appeal, 24 Pa. St. 372; Blackmar v. Sharp, 23 R. I. 412, 50 Atl. 852. See also Bankers' Trust Co. v. Gillespie, 181 Fed. 448, 104 C. C. A. 196; Valley Lbr. Co. v. Wright (Cal. App.), 84 Pac. 58; Weisman v. Volino, 84 Conn. 326, 80 Atl. 81; Platt v. Griffith, 27 N. J. Eq. 207.

[34] Whelan v. Exchange Trust Co., 214 Mass. 121, 100 N. E. 1095; Gray v. McClellan, 214 Mass. 92, 100 N. E. 1093; Finlayson v. Crooks, 47 Minn. 74, 49 N. W. 398, 645. See also Blackmar v. Sharp, 23 R. I. 412, 50 Atl. 852.

[35] Porch v. Agnew Co., 70 N. J. Eq. 328, 61 Atl. 721.

[36] Foushee v. Grigsby, 12 Bush (Ky.) 75; Gere v. Cushing, 5 Bush (Ky.) 304.

[37] As in Oregon: Hill's Ann. Laws, § 3671; Lord's Ore. Laws, 1910, § 7418; Cooper Mfg. Co. v. Delahunt, 36 Ore. 402, 51 Pac. 649, 60 Pac. 1. Although a lien for mining supplies was not filed until after suit to foreclose a mortgage on the mining property, the lien was held prior to the mortgage, the supplies having been furnished in part before the execution of the mortgage. Grants Pass Banking &c. Co. v. Enterprise Min. Co., 58 Ore. 174, 113 Pac. 859, 34 L. R. A. (N. S.) 395.

[38] Trullinger v. Kofoed, 7 Ore. 228, 33 Am. Rep. 708.

[39] Conrad v. Starr, 50 Iowa 470; Kansas Mtg. Co. v. Weyerhaeuser, 48 Kans. 335, 29 Pac. 153; National Mtg. &c. Co. v. Hutchinson Mfg. Co., 6 Kans. App. 673, 50 Pac. 100; Kelly v. Rosenstock, 45 Md. 389; Brooks v. Lester, 36 Md. 65; Pennock v. Hoover, 5 Rawle (Pa.) 291. See also Riverside Lumber Co. v. Schafer, 251 Mo. 539, 158 S. W. 340. But merely clearing, leveling, or fencing the property is not a commence-

such as beginning to dig the foundation, which every one can see and recognize as the commencement of a building; and the work moreover must be done with the intention thus formed of continuing it to completion.[40]

When a building is changed or enlarged, the lien attaches from the commencement of the alteration on the ground, and is subject to liens that had previously attached.[41] As against a mortgage the lien of which attached after such commencement of a building or of alterations and additions to it,[42] a lien can be supported for machinery and fixtures afterward furnished, although not upon the ground at the time, and the work was not done there, but at a distance in shops. When additions to an old building are in their extent and value significant enough to give notice to purchasers and creditors of the change in the character of the property, the additions so made, the work and materials furnished therefor, and the machinery placed therein, are subjects of mechanics' liens as new buildings.[48]

A mechanic's lien for repairing or enlarging a building is not paramount to an existing mortgage upon it, even where such lien relates back to the commencement of the work upon a building, so that, when a mortgage covers a building partially erected, a lien for work done or materials furnished in completing the building would relate back to the time of the commencement of the building, and would take precedence of the mortgage.[44] This rule prevails although the building be changed so that very little of the original structure remains; as, for instance, where there was a mortgage upon a paper-mill which was out of repair and was almost wholly removed, and a new one was erected in its place, and this was supplied with new machinery.[45] A trust deed, duly recorded, has priority over a mechanic's lien, under

---

ment of the building. Central Trust Co. v. Cameron Iron &c. Co., 47 Fed. 136; George M. Newhall Eng. Co. v. Egolf, 185 Fed. 481, 107 C. C. A. 581; Middletown Sav. Bank v. Fellowes, 42 Conn. 36 (fencing); Kiene v. Hodge, 90 Iowa 212, 57 N. W. 717 (filling); Kelly v. Rosenstock, 45 Md. 389; Kansas Mtg. Co. v. Weyerhaeuser, 48 Kans. 335, 29 Pac. 153; Nixon v. Cydon Lodge, 56 Kans. 298, 43 Pac. 236 (excavation for cellar).

[40] Jean v. Wilson, 38 Md. 288; Brooks v. Lester, 36 Md. 65; Mutual Benefit Life Ins. Co. v. Rowand, 26 N. J. Eq. 389. See also Pusey v. Pennsylvania &c. Mills, 173 Fed. 629.

[41] Norris' Appeal, 30 Pa. St. 122.

[42] Parrish and Hazard's Appeal, 83 Pa. St. 111.

[43] Parrish and Hazard's Appeal, 83 Pa. St. 111. A hot water system installed as an integral part of a building to replace a hot air furnace, does not constitute a separate structure or addition, nor take priority over a deed of trust, although the system was removable without material injury to the building. Elliott &c Engineering Co. v. Baker, 134 Mo. App. 95, 114 S. W. 71.

[44] Neilson v. Iowa Eastern R. Co., 44 Iowa 71; Getchell v. Allen, 34 Iowa 559.

[45] Equitable Life Ins. Co. v. Slye, 45 Iowa 615.

a subsequent contract for materials used in an addition to the building of the owner; and one who acquires title through such trust deed, acquires rights superior to the mechanic's lien, without reference to notice or want of notice of the lien.[46]

Mechanics and laborers asserting a lien upon real property for their work, and claiming priority over mortgagees and others who have acquired interest in the property, must make strict proof of all that is essential to the creation of the lien; such, for instance, as proof of the commencement of the work, of its character, and of its completion. The commencement of the work must be shown, for from that date the lien attaches, if at all. The character of the work must be shown, for it is not for all kinds of work that a lien is allowed. The completion of the work must be shown, for notice of claiming a lien must be filed.[47] Whether the work relied on as having been done prior to the mortgage is to be regarded as a commencement of the building is a question of fact, to be determined by the evidence.[48]

In order to have priority the mortgage must be recorded before the building is commenced or the mechanic's lien accrues.[49]

Under several statutes, as, for instance, that existing prior to 1876 in Iowa, the only manner of establishing the priority of a mechanic's lien upon a building, over a pre-existing incumbrance upon the land, was by a sale and removal of the building; and when the nature of the improvement was such that it could not be removed, the lien was

[46] Kircher v. M. Keating &c. Co., 145 Ill. App. 1; W. T. Joyce Co. v. Carroll, Light, Heat &c. Co., 153 Iowa 372, 133 N. W. 785.

[47] Davis v. Alvord, 94 U. S. 545, 24 L. ed. 283; Sunset Lumber Co. v. Bachelder (Cal.), 140 Pac. 35; Trust Co. v. Casey, 131 Ky. 771, 115 S. W. 780. See also Chicago Lbr. Co. v. Des Moines Driving Park, 97 Iowa 25, 65 N. W. 1017 (lien postponed by defective statement though subsequent mortgagee knew of claim); Security Bldg. &c. Union v. Colvin, 27 Pa. Super. Ct. 594 (lien postponed to mortgage because of defective description). Strict compliance with the statute in making and filing such statement can not be waived. Adams v. Central City Granite Brick & Block Co., 154 Mich. 448, 117 N. W. 932.

[48] Kelly v. Rosenstock, 45 Md. 389.

[49] Meyer v. Construction Co., 100 U. S. 457, 25 L. ed. 593; Small v. Foley, 8 Colo. App. 435, 47 Pac. 64; Thielman v. Carr, 75 Ill. 385; Dersch v. Miller, 137 Ky. 89, 122 S. W. 177, 124 S. W. 362; Brooks v. Lester, 36 Md. 65; Ortonville v. Geer, 93 Minn. 501, 101 N. W. 963, 106 Am. St. 445; Stuyvesant v. Browning, 33 N. Y. Sup. Ct. 203; Bell v. Groves, 20 Wash. 602, 56 Pac. 401. But the rule is otherwise in some states. Root v. Bryant, 57 Cal. 48; Rose v. Munie, 4 Cal. 173; Fletcher v. Kelly, 88 Iowa 475, 55 N. W. 474, 21 L. R. A. 347; Mathwig v. Mann, 96 Wis. 213, 71 N. W. 105, 65 Am. St. 47. A lien for material delivered before the record of a mortgage takes priority over such mortgage. J. S. Gabel Lumber Co. v. West, 95 Nebr. 394, 145 N. W. 849; H. F. Cady Lumber Co. v. Miles (Nebr.), 147 N. W. 210. A trust deed given a year after the commencement of the building improvements is inferior to a mechanic's

necessarily postponed to the prior incumbrance upon the land.[50] The lien of the mechanic can not exceed the right of the owner who contracted for the improvements upon the land; and therefore where the owner's interest was an estate in fee of one undivided third part of the property, and a life estate in the remaining two-thirds, the lien of the mechanic was limited to the same interests. The owner of such a part interest in the land would not have the power to remove a building erected by him upon it, and a purchaser under a mechanic's lien would acquire no greater right to remove it.[51] If the owner's interest in the building were such that he might remove it, the right of removal would pass by sale under the mechanic's lien; subject however, to the qualification that the right of removal depends upon the fact whether the building upon which the materials were furnished and the work done is so far an independent structure as to be capable of being removed without material injury to that which would remain.[52] If the building can not be removed without materially injuring or altogether destroying its value,—if it be, for instance, a building of brick, three stories high, with a stone foundation; or if the interest of the owner be such that he had no right of removal as against others,—the lien of a mechanic can not be enforced through a removal of the building.[53]

§ 487a.   **Expenses of administration upon estate of deceased mortgagor.**—The expenses of administration of the estate of a deceased mortgagor are not a lien prior to an existing mortgage on his land, though the other property of the deceased is insufficient to pay such expenses. The lien of the mortgagor being prior in time it must prevail as against such expenses.[54] The mortgagee is entitled to the amount of his mortgage out of the proceeds of the mortgaged property against general creditors of the estate, even where such estate is insolvent.[55] And where the administrator is ordered to sell the mortgaged premises free of liens, the mortgagee is entitled to have the

lien for work and materials. Farnham v. California Safe Deposit &c. Co., 8 Cal. App. 266, 96 Pac. 788.

[50] Conrad v. Starr, 50 Iowa 470.

[51] Conrad v. Starr, 50 Iowa 470; Jessup v. Stone, 13 Wis. 466.

[52] O'Brien v. Pettis, 42 Iowa 293.

[53] Conrad v. Starr, 50 Iowa 470. Where materials furnished for a theater building, under a contract retaining title with the right of removal, had so far become a part of the building that removal would in-jure the building permanently, such right could not be exercised as against a mortgage lien which had attached during construction of the building. Ward v. Yarnelle, 173 Ind. 535, 91 N. E. 7.

[54] Murray's Estate, 18 Cal. 686; Ryker v. Vawter, 117 Ind. 425, 20 N. E. 294; Shepard v. Saltzman, 34 Ore. 40, 54 Pac. 882.

[55] Kirkpatrick v. Caldwell, 32 Ind. 279; Perry v. Borton, 25 Ind. 274.

entire proceeds of the sale applied to the payment of his mortgage debt, even to the exclusion of claims for costs of administration, funeral expenses and expenses of last sickness.[56]

II. *Requisites as to Execution and Acknowledgment*

§ **488. Generally.**—The first requisite to the valid record of any deed is that it shall be executed according to law. Constructive notice and priority by registration can only arise from the record of a valid instrument.[1] If defectively executed, it is not generally entitled to be recorded; but even if it is recorded it is not constructive notice, so as to vest in the grantee or mortgagee any interest in the premises as against subsequent purchasers in good faith without notice.[2]

---

[56] Mayer v. Myers, 129 Ind. 366, 27 N. E. 740; Ryker v. Vawter, 117 Ind. 425, 20 N. E. 294.

[1] Loomis v. Brush, 36 Mich. 40; New England Nat. Bank v. Northwestern Nat. Bank, 171 Mo. 307, 71 S. W. 191, 60 L. R. A. 256; Southern Bldg. &c. Assn. v. Rodgers, 104 Tenn. 437, 58 S. W. 234; Texas Moline Plow Co. v. Klapproth (Tex. Civ. App.), 164 S. W. 399; Stiles v. Japhet, 84 Tex. 91, 19 S. W. 450; Wright v. Lancaster, 48 Tex. 250; Terry v. Cutler, 14 Tex. Civ. App. 520, 39 S. W. 152; Hunt v. Allen, 73 Vt. 322, 50 Atl. 1103; Isham v. Bennington Iron Co., 19 Vt. 230; Wood v. Meyer 36 Wis. 308. See also Colvin v. Warford, 20 Md. 357.

[2] Lynch v. Murphy, 161 U. S. 247, 40 L. ed. 688, 16 Sup. Ct. 523; Strong v. Smith, 3 McLean (U. S.) 362; Lewis v. Baird, 3 McLean (U. S.) 56; Schults v. Moore, 1 McLean (U. S.) 520; Cumberland Bldg. &c. Assn. v. Sparks, 106 Fed. 101; Central Trust Co. v. Georgia Pac. R. Co., 83 Fed. 386 (record of a copy of a railroad mortgage insufficient); Sheridan v. Schimpf, 120 Ala. 475, 24 So. 940; Main v. Alexander, 9 Ark. 112, 47 Am. Dec. 732; McMinn v. O'Connor, 27 Cal. 238; Mesick v. Sunderland, 6 Cal. 297; Kenney v. Jefferson County Bank, 12 Colo. App. 24, 54 Pac. 404; Sumner v. Rhodes, 14 Conn. 135; Carter v. Champion, 8 Conn. 547, 21 Am. Dec. 695; Stallings v. Newton, 110 Ga. 875, 36 S. E. 227; Herndon v. Kimball, 7 Ga. 432, 50 Am. Dec. 406; Mack v. McIntosh, 181 Ill. 633, 54 N. E. 1019; Choteau v. Jones, 11 Ill. 300, 50 Am. Dec. 460; Reeves v. Hayes, 95 Ind. 521; Woodbury v. Fisher, 20 Ind. 387, 83 Am. Dec. 325; Reed v. Coale, 4 Ind.

As said by Pomeroy in his work on Equity Jurisprudence: "The record does not operate as constructive notice, unless the instrument is duly executed, and properly acknowledged or proved, so as to entitle it to be recorded. The statutes generally require, as a condition to registration, that the instrument should be legally executed, and that it should be formally acknowledged or proved, and a certificate thereof annexed. If a writing should be placed upon the records with any of these preliminaries entirely omitted or defectively performed, such a record would be a mere voluntary act, and would have no effect upon the rights of subsequent purchasers or incumbrancers."[3] Story states

283; Brown v. Budd, 2 Ind. 442; Barney v. Little, 15 Iowa 527; Reynolds v. Kingsbury, 15 Iowa 238; Brown v. Lunt, 37 Maine 423; Dewitt v. Moulton, 17 Maine 418; Pfeaff v. Jones, 50 Md. 263; Cockey v. Milne, 16 Md. 200; Johns v. Reardon, 3 Md. Ch. 57; Blood v. Blood, 23 Pick. (Mass.) 80; Sigourney v. Larned, 10 Pick. (Mass.) 72; Woods v. Love, 27 Mich, 308; Buell v. Irwin, 24 Mich. 145; Hall v. Redson, 10 Mich. 21; Galpin v. Abbott, 6 Mich. 17; Dutton v. Ives, 5 Mich. 515; Lowry v. Harris, 12 Minn. 255; Parret v. Shaubhut, 5 Minn. 323, 80 Am. Dec. 424; Marx v. Jordan, 84 Miss. 334, 105 Am. St. 457; Bass v. Estill, 50 Miss. 300; Work v. Harper, 24 Miss. 517; Bishop v. Schneider, 46 Mo. 472, 2 Am. Rep. 533; Stevens v. Hampton, 46 Mo. 404; Salvage v. Haydock, 68 N. H. 484, 44 Atl. 696; Fryer v. Rockefeller, 63 N. Y. 268; James v. Morey, 2 Cow. (N. Y.) 246, 14 Am. Dec. 475; Frost v. Beekman, 1 Johns Ch. (N. Y.) 288; McAllister v. Purcell, 124 N. Car. 262, 32 S. E. 715; Todd v. Outlaw, 79 N. Car. 235; Blake v. Graham, 6 Ohio St. 580, 67 Am. Dec. 360; White v. Denman, 1 Ohio St. 110; McKean v. Mitchell, 35 Pa. St. 269, 78 Am. Dec. 335; Green v. Drinker, 7 Watts & S. (Pa.) 440; Arthur v. Screven, 39 S. Car. 77, 17 S. E. 640; Williams & Co. v. Paysinger, 15 S. Car. 171; Lynch v. Hancock, 14 S. Car. 66; Southern Building &c. Assn. v. Rodgers, 104 Tenn. 437, 58 S. W. 234; Johnson v. Walton, 1 Sneed (Tenn.) 258; Stiles v. Japhet, 84 Tex. 91, 19 S. W. 450; Holliday v. Cromwell, 26 Tex. 188; Hunt v. Allen, 73 Vt. 322, 50 Atl.

1103; Pope v. Henry, 24 Vt. 560; Isham v. Bennington Iron Co., 19 Vt. 230; Stevens v. Brown, 3 Vt. 420, 23 Am. Dec. 215 (copy of deed not entitled to record, and not notice if recorded); Hunton v. Wood, 101 Va. 54, 43 S. E. 186; Pringle v. Dunn, 37 Wis. 449, 19 Am. Rep. 772; Ely v. Wilcox, 20 Wis. 523, 91 Am. Dec. 436.

The decisions of a state court that a mortgage shall be a lien from the time it is filed in the recorder's office, which shall be notice to all persons of the mortgage, and that a mortgage not properly acknowledged constitutes no lien against third persons, though recorded to their knowledge, establish a rule of property, Main v. Alexander, 9 Ark. 112; Ford v. Burks, 37 Ark. 94; Cross v. Fombey, 54 Ark. 179, 15 S. W. 461; Milling Co. v. Mikles, 61 Ark. 123, 32 S. W. 493, and will be followed by the Federal courts.

Thus, in Louisiana, to create a conventional mortgage, two things are essential, namely, there must be an intention by the parties to create a mortgage; and to give effect to that intention it must be expressed with sufficient clearness to serve as notice to third persons when the instrument is recorded. Benjamin's Succession, 39 La. Ann. 612, 2 So. 187. See also Howe v. Powell, 40 La. Ann. 307, 4 So. 450; Pomeroy's Equity Jurisprudence, § 652; Story's Equity Jurisprudence (13th ed.), § 404.

[3] Pomeroy Eq. Jur., § 652; Lynch v. Murphy, 161 U. S. 247, 40 L. ed. 688, 16 Sup. Ct. 523.

the doctrine thus: "The doctrine as to the registration of deeds being constructive notice as to all subsequent purchasers, is not to be understood of all deeds and conveyances which may be de facto registered, but of such only as are authorized and required by law to be registered, and are duly registered in compliance with law. If they are not authorized or required to be registered, or the registry itself is not in compliance with the law, the act of registration is treated as a mere nullity; and then the subsequent purchaser is affected only by such actual notice as would amount to a fraud."[4]

The record of a deed, which appears on its face to have been properly executed and acknowledged, is evidence that the deed was in fact so executed, though the deed, by reason of extrinsic facts, may be void or voidable.[5] As already noticed, equity will give the instrument effect between the parties, according to their intention.[6] Where a recorded mortgage contains a provision not entitled to record, the constructive notice arising from such record will be confined to such portions as are embraced within the recording acts.[7] If a conveyance defectively executed be afterward reformed, it will not affect the interest of one who has in the meantime purchased in good faith, and, according to some authorities, will not affect a lien obtained in the meantime by an attachment, or judgment, or a levy of execution. If for any reason a deed be not executed, acknowledged, or recorded according to the statutory requirements, yet, if it be shown that a subsequent purchaser or creditor had actual notice of the deed, or must be presumed to have had such notice of it, from the defective record, he is chargeable with notice, as in other cases.[8]

Inasmuch as the registration of a deed or mortgage is solely for the benefit and protection of the grantee, and rests wholly in his election, he can not, in the absence of an agreement express or implied to the contrary, hold the grantor liable for the registration fees.[9]

---

[4] Story Eq. Jur. (13th ed.), § 404; Lynch v. Murphy, 161 U. S. 247, 40 L. ed. 688, 16 Sup. Ct. 523.

[5] Choteau v. Jones, 11 Ill. 300, 50 Am. Rep. 460; Clague v. Washburn, 42 Minn. 371, 44 N. W. 130. See also Stevens v. Hampton, 46 Mo. 404; Stevens v. Morse, 47 N. H. 532.

[6] See ante § 474.

[7] Monroe v. Hamilton, 60 Ala. 226 (provision in a mortgage restraining the power of the mortgagor as a partner).

[8] Hastings v. Cutler, 24 N. H. 481; Kerns v. Swope, 2 Watts (Pa.) 75, dictum of C. J. Gibson. But it would seem that actual knowledge of the deed must be proved, and not merely presumed.

The recording of a mortgage defectively executed, and not entitled to record does not give it priority over a subsequent judgment; and reformation will not give it effect as against a judgment rendered before the decree of reformation. Van Thorniley v. Peters, 26 Ohio St. 471.

[9] Simon v. Sewell, 64 Ala. 241.

§ 489. Description of the property—Notice of defective description.—The description of the property conveyed or incumbered by mortgage must be such as reasonably to enable subsequent purchasers to identify the land; otherwise the record of the conveyance is not constructive notice.[10] A conveyance of lands without description of boundary or location, but merely as "all other lands owned by the vendor" in a state named, is inoperative as notice to the public of any particular tract conveyed, if not void for want of description.[11] On the other hand, a mortgage describing the lands as all the lands of the mortgagor in a named county has been held sufficient to pass title to all land owned by him in such county.[12] And in like manner a mortgage of all the lots the mortgagor then owned in a certain town was deemed sufficiently definite, as between the parties.[13]

The record of a trust deed intended to incumber the east one-half of the northeast quarter of a certain section, but written and transcribed as "the one-half of the northeast quarter," does not operate as constructive notice to a purchaser, or put him on inquiry.[14] And likewise the record of a trust deed describing a tract as containing one hundred acres, but designating a smaller tract by boundaries and dis-

[10] Ripley v. Harris, 3 Biss. (U. S.) 199; Bright v. Buckman, 39 Fed. 243; Edwards v. Bender, 121 Ala. 77, 25 So. 1010; Adams v. Edgerton, 48 Ark. 419, 3 S. W. 628; Davis v. Ward, 109 Cal. 186, 41 Pac. 1010, 50 Am. St. 29; Chamberlain v. Bell, 7 Cal. 292, 68 Am. Dec. 260; Slocum v. O'Day, 174 Ill. 215, 51 N. E. 243; Rich v. Trustees of Schools, 158 Ill. 242, 41 N. E. 924; Citizens' Nat. Bank v. Dayton, 116 Ill. 257, 4 N. E. 492; Rodgers v. Kavanaugh, 24 Ill. 533; Rinehardt v. Reifers, 158 Ind. 675, 64 N. E. 459; Murphy v. Hendricks, 57 Ind. 593; Porter v. Bryne, 10 Ind. 146, 71 Am. Dec. 305; Peters v. Ham, 62 Iowa 656, 18 N. W. 296; Port v. Embree, 54 Iowa 14, 6 N. W. 83; Nelson v. Wade, 21 Iowa 49; Halloway v. Platner, 20 Iowa 121, 89 Am. Dec. 517; Stewart v. Huff, 19 Iowa 557; Green v. Witherspoon, 37 La. Ann. 751; Brydon v. Campbell, 40 Md. 331; Stead v. Grosfield, 67 Mich. 289, 34 N. W. 871; Barrows v. Baughman, 9 Mich. 213; Bailey v. Galpin, 40 Minn. 319, 41 N. W. 1054; Thorp v. Merrill, 21 Minn. 336; Simmons v. Fuller, 17 Minn.

485; Goodbar v. Dunn, 61 Miss. 618; Eggleston v. Watson, 53 Miss. 339; Ozark Land &c. Co. v. Franks, 156 Mo. 673, 57 S. W. 540; Cass County v. Oldham, 75 Mo. 50; Baker v. Bartlett, 18 Mont. 446, 45 Pac. 1084; Rutgers v. Kingsland, 7 N. J. Eq. 178; Banks v. Ammon, 27 Pa. St. 172; Lally v. Holland, 1 Swan (Tenn.) 396; Carter v. Hawkins, 62 Tex. 393; Waters v. Spofford, 58 Tex. 115; Florence v. Morien (Va.), 34 S. E. 890; Mundy v. Vawter, 3 Grat. (Va.) 518; Warren v. Syme, 7 W. Va. 474. See ante §§ 65, 66.

[11] Herman v. Deming, 44 Conn. 124; Green v. Witherspoon, 37 La. Ann. 751; Mundy v. Vawter, 3 Grat. (Va.) 518.

[12] Vanmeter v. Vanmeter, 3 Grat. (Va.) 148. See ante § 65.

[13] Starling v. Blair, 4 Bibb. (Ky.) 288. See also Easter v. Severin, 64 Ind. 375; City Nat. Bank v. Barrow, 21 La. Ann. 396; Strouse v. Cohen, 113 N. Car. 349, 18 S. E. 323. See ante §65.

[14] Simmons v. Hutchinson, 81 Miss. 351, 33 So. 21.

tances, operates as notice only in respect to the latter tract, and not to other land necessary to complete the one hundred acres. If all of the boundaries are specified except one, and that may be ascertained from the requirements of the deed, the description is sufficiently definite to render the recorded deed notice of the rights of the parties in the land intended to be covered thereby.[15] Although the opening clause in the description of land in a recorded mortgage is indefinite as to the starting point, where the clause following designates a definite point of commencement the description is sufficient to put creditors of the mortgagor on inquiry.[16]

If a subsequent mortgagee or purchaser has notice of a mistake in the description of a prior conveyance, as, for instance, that the lot was described as number "eighteen" instead of "eight," the correct number, such mortgagee or purchaser will take subject to the prior conveyance, in the same way that he would had the description been correctly given;[17] and the subsequent mortgagee has constructive notice of the mortgage as it was intended to be given, when the premises are well defined and well-known to the parties, and a notice on the margin of a prior defective mortgage referred to a prior deed in which the land was correctly described.[18] The mortgagee can not enforce his mortgage upon the land actually described when he knows that by mistake this particular land was described in place of another lot intended to be described.[19] But when the grantee has no notice of any mistake, and there is no uncertainty on the face of the deed, though in fact the land described is, through mistake, not the land intended to be con-

---

[15] Reid v. Rhodes, 106 Va. 701, 56 S. E. 722. The record of a trust deed describing the property as 160 acres known as the J. B. H. homestead survey is sufficient, at least as against one who is not a bona fide purchaser. Rushing v. Citizens' Nat. Bank of Plainview (Tex. Civ. App.), 162 S. W. 460.

[16] Albia State Bank v. Smith, 141 Iowa 255, 119 N. W. 608.

[17] Hoopeston Building Assn. v. Green, 16 Ill. App. 204; Duncan v. Miller, 64 Iowa 223, 20 N. W. 161; Peters v. Ham, 62 Iowa 656, 18 N. W. 296; Warburton v. Lauman, 2 Greene (Iowa) 420; Cox v. Esteb, 81 Mo. 393.

[18] Bent v. Coleman, 89 Ill. 364. See also Wallace v. Furber, 62 Ind. 103; Newman v. Tymeson, 13 Wis. 172, 80 Am. Dec. 735.

[19] Northrup v. Hottenstein, 38 Kans. 263, 16 Pac. 445.

The clause creating the lien prevails as to the interest conveyed. Thus a mortgage of an undivided fourth part of certain lands is not enlarged by a recital in the description as being one undivided half part.

On the other hand, the interest conveyed by a mortgage is not diminished by an incidental recital as to the source of title. Thus a mortgage of "a certain tract of land, being the same premises conveyed to me by a deed referred to," the mortgagor then owning the entire tract, though only an undivided half of it was conveyed by the deed referred to, is a mortgage of the whole land, and not merely of an undivided half of it, in the

veyed, the record is notice of a conveyance of the land actually described, not of that intended to be described.[20]

A mortgage described certain lots by a town plat which was not recorded, but a plat was subsequently recorded upon which the same lots were described by different numbers. It was held that the record was not enough to put a subsequent purchaser upon inquiry, and that he was not affected with constructive notice of the mortgage.[21] So a mortgage which erroneously described certain lots in University Park, second addition, to west La Fayette, as in "University Park addition to West La Fayette," was held not to be entitled to priority by virtue of recording, against one who took without actual notice.[22]

But the record of a mortgage was held sufficient notice to a subsequent judgment creditor of the mortgagor, where the mortgage correctly described the property, except as situate in a township of which it was once a part, but then included in a new township.[23] A mortgage executed to the state of Indiana for a loan of school funds and describing the premises mortgaged by township and range, without naming the county and state in which they were located, is void for uncertainty in the description.[24] And so, a mortgage describing land as parts of certain sections, without stating the township or range is void for uncertainty.[25]

§ 490. **Apparent error in description.**—When a description in a deed or mortgage is erroneous, and it is apparent what the error is, the record is constructive notice of the deed or mortgage of the lot intended to be described.[26] And so the record of a deed, describing the premises by an impossible sectional number, is sufficient to put a purchaser from the same grantor upon inquiry, and may charge him with notice of the grant actually made or intended to be made.[27] Parol evidence is admissible to identify the land intended when there is an ambiguity or uncertainty in the description.[28]

absence of evidence of any intention to limit the conveyance in this way. Morse v. Morse, 58 N. H. 391.

[20] Wait v. Smith, 92 Ill. 385; Sanger v. Craigue, 10 Vt. 555.

[21] Stewart v. Huff, 19 Iowa 557.

[22] Rinehardt v. Reifers, 158 Ind. 675, 64 N. E. 459.

[23] Mohr v. Scherer, 30 Pa. Super. Ct. 509.

[24] Murphy v. Hendricks, 57 Ind. 593. See also Barron v. Barron, 122 Ala. 194, 25 So. 55; Cochran v. Utt,

42 Ind. 267. See ante §§ 65-66a.

[25] Boyd v. Ellis, 11 Iowa 97; Wilson v. Calder, 8 Kans. App. 856, 55 Pac. 552; Martin v. Kitchen, 195 Mo. 477, 93 S. W. 780. See ante § 66.

[26] Anderson v. Baughman, 7 Mich. 69, 74 Am. Dec. 699; Wolfe v. Dyer, 95 Mo. 545, 8 S. W. 551; People v. Storms, 97 N. Y. 364; Tousley v. Tousley, 5 Ohio St. 78.

[27] Merrick v. Wallace, 19 Ill. 486; Carter v. Hawkins, 62 Tex. 393.

[28] Tranum v. Wilkinson, 81 Ala.

A purchaser who is able from his knowledge of the property to interpret an erroneous description, and give it the meaning intended, is charged with notice from the record of it.[29]

But although a mistake in description be such that the conveyance would be invalidated as against a subsequent purchaser, yet it has been held that a subsequent judgment lien will not for this reason become a paramount lien upon the land intended to be described.[30] Even where a parcel of land which the parties intended to include in the conveyance was wholly omitted in the description, the deed may be reformed in chancery, and the omitted tract included in the conveyance free from any judgment lien which has in the meantime attached to the debtor's real estate.[31]

If the description is such as reasonably to put one upon inquiry as to the property intended to be conveyed, and to lead him to ascertain what that property is, the record will afford constructive notice of a conveyance of that property.[32]

§ 491. **Signature.**—The record of a deed without the signature of the grantor is not constructive notice; and this is so though the instrument was in fact signed, but the signature was omitted by mistake from the record.[33] A signature is binding if made at the proper time and duly acknowledged, whether signed by the person owning the name, or by some one else with his consent.[34]

If the name of the mortgagee be by mistake written in the blank for the mortgagor, and the name of the mortgagor in that left for the mortgagee, but is signed by the right party and purports to secure a

408, 1 So. 201; Salisbury v. Andrews, 19 Pick. (Mass.) 250.

[29] Bright v. Buckman, 39 Fed. 243; Erickson v. Rafferty, 79 Ill. 209; Carter v. Hawkins, 62 Tex. 393.

[30] Yarnell v. Brown, 170 Ill. 362, 48 N. E. 909; White v. Wilson, 6 Blackf. (Ind.) 448, 39 Am. Dec. 437; Welton v. Tizzard, 15 Iowa 495; Swarts v. Stees, 2 Kans. 236, 85 Am. Dec. 588; Gillespie v. Moon, 2 Johns. Ch. (N. Y.) 584, 7 Am. Dec. 559.

[31] White v. Wilson, 6 Blackf. (Ind.) 448. See ante § 99.

[32] Partridge v. Smith, 2 Biss. (U. S.) 183; Vercruysse v. Williams, 112 Fed. 206, 50 C. C. A. 486; Tranum v. Wilkinson, 81 Ala. 408, 1 So. 201; Lewis v. Hinman, 56 Conn. 55, 13 Atl. 143; Citizens' Nat. Bank v. Dayton, 116 Ill. 257; Bent v. Coleman,

89 Ill. 364, 7 Am. Rep. 366; Erickson v. Rafferty, 79 Ill. 209; Merrick v. Wallace, 19 Ill. 486; Myers v. Perry, 72 Ill. App. 450; Dargin v. Beeker, 10 Iowa 571; Roberts v. Bauer, 35 La. Ann. 453; Anderson v. Baughman, 7 Mich. 69, 74 Am. Dec. 699; Cable v. Minneapolis Stock Yards &c. Co., 47 Minn. 417, 50 N. W. 528; Coney v. Laird, 153 Mo. 408, 55 S. W. 96; Gouverneur v. Titus, 6 Paige (N. Y.) 347; Tousley v. Tousley, 5 Ohio St. 78; Rankin v. McCarthy (Tex.), 37 S. W. 979; Nye v. Moody, 70 Tex. 434; Carter v. Hawkins, 62 Tex. 393; Sengfelder v. Hill, 21 Wash. 371, 58 Pac. 250.

[33] Shepherd v. Burkhalter, 13 Ga. 443, 58 Am. Dec. 523. See ante § 81a.

[34] Johnson v. Van Velsor, 43 Mich. 208, 5 N. W. 265.

debt from the party signing to the other, and is acknowledged by the party signing, the mistake in the transposition of the names of the parties being palpable, its record will be notice to subsequent purchasers from the mortgagor of the mistake.[35]

A deed signed by one not described therein as grantor is wholly inoperative either as a conveyance or as notice if recorded.[36] Thus if the name of one person is inserted in a deed as the grantor, but it is signed, acknowledged and delivered by another person not mentioned in the body of the deed, the record thereof can not operate as constructive notice to a subsequent purchaser.[37] A deed signed in a wrong name, or a name by which the grantor is not customarily known, imparts no notice. Such is the case, if a married woman executes a deed under the name she bore prior to her marriage, without mention of her married name.[38]

§ 491a. Omission of mortgagee's name.—A mortgage executed and recorded with the name of the mortgagee omitted does not impart constructive notice of the existence of such mortgage to a subsequent purchaser. With reference to this defect, it has been said: "The mortgage, when executed, was and now is blank as to the name of the mortgagee. The question in this case is not as to whether there might be an implied authority between the mortgagor and the mortgagee to fill up the blank and make the instrument complete. The question is as to the effect of the record of the instrument, in its imperfect condition, as constructive notice to a subsequent purchaser of the property. It has been frequently held that slight omissions in the acknowledgment of a deed destroy the effect of the record as constructive notice. A fortiori, it seems to us, should so important and vital omission as that of the name of the grantee have that effect. The case of Chauncey v. Arnold, 24 N. Y. 330, is in point. In that case it was held that an instrument in the form of a mortgage, but containing the name of no mortgagee, did not become effectual by delivery to one who advanced money upon it, the blank not having been filled at the

[35] Beaver v. Slanker, 94 Ill. 175.

[36] Marx v. Jordan, 84 Miss. 334, 36 So. 386, 105 Am. St. 457; Stone v. Sledge, 87 Tex. 49, 26 S. W. 1068, 47 Am. St. 65. See also Agurs v. Belcher, 111 La. 378, 35 So. 607, 100 Am. St. 485 (signature by mark sufficient though name signed by notary is erroneous); Payne v. Parker, 10 Maine 178, 25 Am. Dec. 226.

[37] Marx v. Jordan, 84 Miss. 334, 36 So. 386, 105 Am. St. 457 (signature of David Bowie to deed reciting Frank Bowie and Frances Bowie as grantors).

[38] Draude v. Rohrer Mfg. Co., 9 Mo. App. 249.

time of suit. * * * The defect in the description of the deed is also, we think, fatal to the effect of the record as constructive notice."[39]

§ 492. Requirement of seal.—Where seals are still in use, conveyances must be executed under seal to entitle them to be recorded.[40] In most states the use of a seal has been wholly dispensed with by statute. In others a scroll is given the same effect as a seal.[41] But where the use of a seal or its equivalent is required, an instrument purporting to be a mortgage, but not executed under seal, is not entitled to be recorded; and if it be copied into the records, it does not impart notice to subsequent purchasers or incumbrancers.[42]

A mortgage without a seal, however, though void as a conveyance of the legal title, will operate as an equitable mortgage, and if recorded, will prevail against a subsequent agreement to give a mortgage,[43] or against a subsequent purchaser with notice of the existence of the unsealed mortgage.[44] Thus an instrument intended as a deed of trust conveying land to secure a debt without a seal, though not effectual as a deed of trust at law, is an equitable mortgage, entitled to record, and when recorded constitutes a valid lien against subsequent purchasers and creditors.[45]

If by accident the seal was omitted a court of equity may grant relief by requiring a seal to be affixed; and the court may grant such relief even after an attempt to foreclose the mortgage.[46]

---

[39] Disque v. Wright, 49 Iowa 538. See ante § 90. The omission of the mortgagee's name is not a defect which can be availed of by a judgment creditor of the mortgagor before levy and sale, as against one who agreed to furnish the payment of the mortgage debt in consideration of subrogation to the rights of the mortgagee. Watson v. Bowman, 142 Iowa 528, 119 N. W. 623.

[40] In re St. Helen Mill Co. 3 Saw. (U. S.) 88; Hebron v. Centre Harbor, 11 N. H. 571; Bowers v. Oyster, 3 Pa. St. 239. See also Moore v. Madden, 7 Ark. 530, 46 Am. Dec. 298; Hughes v. Tong, 1 Mo. 389; Woods v. Wallace, 22 Pa. St. 171. See ante § 81.

[41] See ante § 81, and see Jones' Legal Forms, pp. 1-84.

[42] Racouillat v. Rene, 32 Cal. 450; Racouillat v. Sansevain, 32 Cal. 376; Jones v. Berkshire, 15 Iowa 248, 83 Am. Dec. 412; Arthur v. Screven (S.

Car.), 17 S. E. 640. The recording statute of Missouri embraces all instruments affecting the legal or equitable title to land, and the record of a mortgage imparts notice although no seal or scrawl is attached. McClurg v. Phillips, 57 Mo. 214.

[43] Portwood v. Outton, 3 B. Mon. (Ky.) 247; Harrington v. Fortner, 58 Mo. 468; McClurg v. Phillips, 57 Mo. 214. See also Brydon v. Campbell, 40 Md. 331; Todd v. Eighmie, 4 App. Div. (N. Y.) 9.

[44] Harrington v. Fortner, 58 Mo. 468; McClurg v. Phillips, 57 Mo. 214; Westerly Sav. Bank v. Stillman Mfg. Co., 16 R. I. 497, 17 Atl. 918.

[45] Atkinson v. Miller, 34 W. Va. 115, 11 S. E. 1007, 9 L. R. A. 544, disapproving Pratt v. Clemens, 4 W. Va. 443, and Shattuck v. Knight, 25 W. Va. 590.

[46] Gaylord v. Pelland, 169 Mass. 356, 47 N. E. 1019.

If the instrument was sealed at the time of its execution, the sub-sequent detachment of the seal does not invalidate it, unless it be proved that the seal was detached before the instrument reached the clerk's office for record; and the burden of such proof is upon the party who attacks the validity of the instrument.[47]

§ 493. **Manner of recording seal.**—A seal need not be copied into the record. All that is necessary is, that the record should afford some indication that the instrument was under seal.[48] The fact that the deed purports to be signed and sealed affords a presumption that it was sealed when recorded.[49] Thus a seal may be presumed from the attestation clause.[50] But if the record does not show a copy of the seal, or anything to indicate that there was a seal upon the original deed, the presumption is that there was no seal to the deed when it was executed.[51] The same rule applies to copying the official seal to the certificate of acknowledgment. All that is necessary is, that the record should show in some manner that such a seal was attached to the certificate.[52] A statement in the body of the certificate that the

[47] Van Riswick v. Goodhue, 50 Md. 57.

[48] Jones v. Martin, 16 Cal. 166; Smith v. Dall, 13 Cal. 510; Gale v. Shillock (Dak.), 29 N. W. 661; Summer v. Mitchell, 29 Fla. 179, 10 So. 562, 14 L. R. A. 815, 30 Am. St. 106; Cox v. Stern, 170 Ill. 442, 48 N. E. 906, 62 Am. St. 385; Bucklen v. Hasterlik, 155 Ill. 423, 40 N. E. 561; Switzer v. Knapps, 10 Iowa 72, 74 Am. Dec. 375; Hedden v. Overton, 4 Bibb. (Ky.) 406; Growning v. Behn, 10 B. Mon. (Ky.) 383; Sneed v. Ward, 5 Dana (Ky.) 187; Beardsley v. Day, 52 Minn. 451, 55 N. W. 46; Griffin v. Sheffield, 38 Miss. 359; Hammond v. Gordon, 93 Mo. 223, 6 S. W. 93; Geary v. Kansas City, 61 Mo. 378; Dale v. Wright, 57 Mo. 110; Heath v. Big Falls Cotton Mills, 115 N. Car. 202, 20 S. E. 369; Aycock v. Raleigh &c. R. Co., 89 N. Car. 321; Carpenter v. Frazer, 102 Tenn. 462, 52 S. W. 858; Witt v. Harlan, 66 Tex. 690, 2 S. W. 41; Coffey v. Hendricks, 66 Tex. 676, 2 S. W. 47; Putney v. Cutler, 54 Wis. 66, 11 N. W. 437; Huey v. Van Wie, 23 Wis. 613. See also Racouillat v. Sansevain, 32 Cal. 376; Racouillat v. Rene, 32 Cal. 450; Hadden v. Larned, 87 Ga. 634,

13 S. E. 806; Van Riswick v. Goodhue, 50 Md. 57.

[49] Smith v. Dall, 13 Cal. 510; Growning v. Behn, 10 B. Mon. (Ky.) 383; Heath v. Big Falls Cotton Mills, 115 N. Car. 202, 20 S. E. 369.

[50] Reusens v. Staples, 52 Fed. 91; Carrington v. Potter, 37 Fed. 767; Ellison v. Branstrator, 153 Ind. 146, 54 N. E. 433; Macey v. Stark, 116 Mo. 481, 21 S. W. 1088; McCoy v. Cassidy, 96 Mo. 429, 9 S. W. 926; Todd v. Union Dime Sav. Bank, 118 N. Y. 337, 23 N. E. 299.

[51] Switzer v. Knapps, 10 Iowa 72, 74 Am. Dec. 375; Hiles v. Atlee, 90 Wis. 72, 62 N. W. 940.

[52] Jones v. Martin, 16 Cal. 165; Smith v. Dall, 13 Cal. 510; Gale v. Shillock, 4 Dak. 182, 29 N. W. 661; Sumner v. Mitchell, 29 Fla. 179, 10 So. 562, 14 L. R. A. 815, 30 Am. St. 106; Hadden v. Larned, 87 Ga. 634, 13 S. E. 806; Sneed v. Ward, 5 Dana (Ky.) 187; Griffin v. Sheffield, 38 Miss. 359, 77 Am. Dec. 646; Hammond v. Gordon, 93 Mo. 223, 6 S. W. 93; Addis v. Graham, 88 Mo. 197; Geary v. Kansas City, 61 Mo. 378; Thorn v. Mayer, 12 Misc. 487, 67 N. Y. St. 389, 33 N. Y. S. 664; Coffey v. Hendricks, 66 Tex. 676, 2 S. W. 47;

officer had affixed his seal of office raises a presumption that such was the fact.[53]

§ 494. Requirement of witnesses.

—The record of a deed not executed in compliance with a statute requiring that it shall be attested by two witnesses is not constructive notice,[54] though the defect be not apparent on the face of the instrument, one of the witnesses being the grantor's wife.[55] Thus, where a deed appeared duly attested, but the witnesses thereto neither saw the grantor's sign, nor heard him acknowledge the instrument, the deed was improperly recorded, and the record gave no notice.[56]

But a mortgage attested by one witness under such a statute is good in equity between the parties,[57] and as against all others, whether purchasers or creditors, who had actual notice of the existence of the mortgage.[58]

When a statute provides that a deed, to be recordable, shall be at-

Witt v. Harlan, 66 Tex. 660, 2 S. W. 41; Ballard v. Perry, 28 Tex. 347. See also Emmal v. Webb, 36 Cal. 197; Hadden v. Larned, 87 Ga. 634, 13 S. E. 806; Perry v. Bragg, 111 N. Car. 159, 16 S. E. 10.

[55] Griffin v. Sheffield, 38 Miss. 359, 77 Am. Dec. 646; Addis v. Graham, 88 Mo. 197; Norfleet v. Russell, 64 Mo 176; Geary v. Kansas City, 61 Mo. 378.

[54] Hodgson v. Butts, 3 Cranch (U. S.) 140, 2 L. ed. 391; Carter v. Champion, 8 Conn. 549, 21 Am. Dec. 695; Donalson v. Thomason, 137 Ga. 848, 74 S. E. 762; Baxley v. Baxley, 117 Ga. 60, 43 S. E. 436; White v. Magarahan, 87 Ga. 217, 13 S. E. 509; Gardner v. Moore, 51 Ga. 268; Frostburg Mut. Building Assn. v. Brace, 51 Md. 508; Van Riswick v. Goodhue, 50 Md. 57; Galpin v. Abbott, 6 Mich. 17; Ross v. Worthington, 11 Minn. 438, 88 Am. Dec. 95; Thompson v. Morgan, 6 Minn. 292; Parret v. Shaubhut, 5 Minn. 323, 80 Am. Dec. 424; Hastings v. Cutler, 24 N. H. 481; Schultz v. Tonty Lumber Co., 36 Tex. Civ. App. 448, 82 S. W. 363; New York Life Ins. &c. Co. v. Staats, 21 Barb. (N. Y.) 570; Van Thorniley v. Peters, 26 Ohio St. 471; White v. Denman, 16 Ohio 59, 1 Ohio St. 110; Harper v. Barsh, 10 Rich. Eq. (S. Car.) 149; Batte v. Stone, 4 Yerg. (Tenn.) 168; Riviere v. Wilkens, 31 Tex. Civ. App. 454, 72 S. W.

608; Morrill v. Morrill, 53 Vt. 74, 38 Am. Rep. 659; Potter v. Stransky, 48 Wis. 235, 4 N. W. 95; Pringle v. Dunn, 37 Wis. 449, 19 Am. Rep. 772. See also Johnson v. Sandhoff, 30 Minn. 197, 14 N. W. 889; Clark v. Strong, 105 App. Div. 179, 93 N. Y. S. 514; Simpson v. Simpson, 107 N. Car. 552, 12 S. E. 447; State v. Cowhick, 9 Wyo. 93, 60 Pac. 265. A mortgage attested by one witness who is not an officer authorized by law to attest a mortgage, is not entitled to record, and consequently its record is not notice. Donalson v. Thomason, 137 Ga. 848, 74 S. E. 762. It has been held that, under a statute which does not actually declare a deed without attestation invalid, a deed not properly attested, when actually acknowledged and recorded, affords constructive notice of the actual contents of the record; but not of the deed as actually written, when there was a mistake in recording it. Bryden v. Campbell, 40 Md. 331. See ante § 82.

[55] Carter v. Champion, 8 Conn. 549, 21 Am. Dec. 695.

[56] Baxley v. Baxley, 117 Ga. 60, 43 S. E. 436.

[57] Hastings v. Cutler, 24 N. H. 481; Moore v. Thomas, 1 Ore. 201.

[58] Sanborn v. Robinson, 54 N. H. 239; Hastings v. Cutler, 24 N. H. 481; Morrill v. Morrill, 54 Vt. 74.

tested by two witnesses, and a mortgage so witnessed was by mistake recorded without any copy of the attestation, it was held that the registry was not constructive notice. The recording of the instrument not being in compliance with the law, the registration is a mere nullity; and a subsequent purchaser is affected only by such actual notice as would amount to a fraud.[59]

§ 495. **Acknowledgment or proof.**—The recording acts generally prescribe certain formalities in the execution of a deed which must be complied with to entitle it to be recorded. An acknowledgment or proof of the deed before some officer is in most of the states an essential prerequisite. Without an acknowledgment, or with one that is defective, the record of the deed is unauthorized and is not constructive notice.[60] The statutes of several states expressly require

---

[59] Pringle v. Dunn, 37 Wis. 449, 19 Am. Dec. 772.

[60] Dufphey v. Frenaye, 5 Stew. & P. (Ala.) 215; Larkin v. Hagan (Ariz.), 126 Pac. 268; Reid v. Kleyensteuber, 7 Ariz. 58, 60 Pac. 879; Challis v. German Nat. Bank, 56 Ark. 88, 19 S. W. 115; Conner v. Abbott, 35 Ark. 365; Martin v. O' Bannon, 35 Ark. 62; Haskill v. Sevier, 25 Ark. 152; Jacoway v. Gault, 20 Ark. 190, 73 Am. Dec. 494; Main v. Alexander, 9 Ark. 112, 47 Am. Dec. 732; Wolf v. Fogarty, 6 Cal. 224, 65 Am. Dec. 509; McKeown v. Collins, 38 Fla. 276, 21 So. 103; Edwards v. Thom, 25 Fla. 222, 5 So. 707; New England Mtg. Sec. Co. v. Ober, 84 Ga. 294, 10 S. E. 625; MacKenzie v. Jackson, 82 Ga. 80, 8 S. E. 77; Shepherd v. Burkhalter, 13 Ga. 443, 58 Am. Dec. 523; Willard v. Cramer, 36 Iowa 22; Deming v. State, 23 Ind. 416; Reed v. Coale, 4 Ind. 283; Carleton v. Byington, 18 Iowa 482; Jones v. Berkshire, 15 Iowa 248, 83 Am. Dec. 412; Fisher v. Cowles, 41 Kans. 418, 21 Pac. 228; Meskimen v. Day, 35 Kans. 46, 10 Pac. 14. Though under a former Kansas statute, acknowledgment was not a prerequisite to registration. Brown v. Simpson, 4 Kans. 76; Simpson v. Mundee, 3 Kans. 172; Herd v. Cist (Ky.), 12 S. W. 466; Blight v. Banks, 6 T. B. Mon. (Ky.) 192, 17 Am. Dec. 136; Sitler v. McComas, 66 Md. 135, 6 Atl. 527; Dyson v. Simmons, 48 Md. 207; Johns v. Scott, 5 Md. 81; Price v. McDonald, 1 Md. 403, 54 Am. Dec. 657; Johns v. Reardon, 3 Md. Ch. 57; Blood v. Blood, 23 Pick. (Mass.) 80; Dohm v. Haskin, 88 Mich. 144, 50 N. W. 108; Cogan v. Cook, 22 Minn. 137; Baze v. Asper, 6 Minn. 220; Parret v. Shaubhut, 5 Minn. 323, 80 Am. Dec. 424; Bass v. Estill, 50 Miss. 300; Work v. Harper, 24 Miss. 517; German-American Bank v. Carondelet Real Estate Co., 150 Mo. 570, 51 S. W. 691; Brim v. Fleming, 135 Mo. 597, 37 S. W. 501; Bishop v. Schneider, 46 Mo. 472, 2 Am. Rep. 533; Stevens v. Hampton, 46 Mo. 404; Irwin v. Welch, 10 Nebr. 479; Brinton v. Scull, 55 N. J. Eq. 747, 35 Atl. 843; Frost v. Beekman, 1 Johns Ch. (N. Y.) 288; Stoddard v. Rotton, 18 N. Y. Super. Ct. 378; Armstrong v. Combs, 1 App. Div. 246, 44 N. Y. S. 171; Withrell v. Murphy, 154 N. Car. 82, 69 S. E. 748; Quinnerly v. Quinnerly, 114 N. Car. 145, 19 S. E. 99; White v. Connelly, 105 N. Car. 65, 11 S. E. 177; Todd v. Outlaw, 79 N. Car. 235; Amick v. Woodworth, 58 Ohio St. 86, 50 N. E. 437; White v. Denman, 1 Ohio St. 110; Fleschner v. Sumpter, 12 Ore. 161, 6 Pac. 506; Heister v. Fortner, 2 Binn. (Pa.) 40, 44, 4 Am. Dec. 417; Kerns v. Swope, 2 Watts (Pa.) 75; Barney v. Button, 2 Watts (Pa.) 31; Armstrong v. Austin 45 S. Car. 69, 22 S. E. 763, 29 L. R. A. 772; Woolfolk v. Graniteville Mfg. Co., 22 S. Car. 332; McGuire v. Gal-

proper acknowledgment as prerequisite to a valid record, operative as notice to third persons and subsequent purchasers,[61] whereas acknowledgment is not a prerequisite to record under the statutes of other states.[62]

It has been held, however, that where an acknowledgment is in due form, the only defect in it being a latent one, as, for instance, being taken by the officer out of his jurisdiction, the record of the mortgage is notice to subsequent purchasers in favor of one holding an assignment of the mortgage duly recorded.[63]

The purpose of this requirement is to insure the authenticity of the instrument before admitting it of record. The certificate must be made and attested substantially in the form given by statute; or, where no special form is prescribed, then in accordance substantially with the provisions of the statute respecting it; but it need not be in

---

lagher, 95 Tenn. 349, 32 S. W. 209; Wood v. Cochrane, 39 Vt. 544; Pope v. Henry, 24 Vt. 560; Hunton v. Wood, 101 Va. 54, 43 S. E. 186; Nicholson v. Gloucester Charity School, 93 Va. 101, 24 S. E. 899; Raines v. Walker, 77 Va. 92; Carper v. McDowell, 5 Grat. (Va.) 212; Abney v. Ohio Lumber &c. Co., 45 W. Va. 446, 32 S. E. 256; Cox v. Wayt, 26 W. Va. 807; Girardin v. Lampe, 58 Wis. 267, 16 N. W. 614; Prindle v. Dunn, 37 Wis. 449, 19 Am. Rep. 772; Renwick v. Berryman, 3 Manitoba 387. In Arkansas a defectively acknowledged mortgage has been held void as to all persons except the original parties, even though such persons had actual notice of its existence. Wright v. Graham, 42 Ark. 140; Ford v. Burks, 37 Ark. 91; Conner v. Abbott, 35 Ark. 365.

[61] Arkansas: Stat. 1904, § 763.
Florida: Gen. Stat. 1906, § 2481.
Massachusetts: Rev. Laws 1902, ch. 127, p. 1222, §§ 7, 14.
Mississippi: Code 1906, §·2793.
Nebraska: Code 1911, § 10817.
New Jersey: Comp. Laws 1911, p. 1152, § 52.
Pennsylvania: See Purdon's Pa. Dig. 1905, p. 1181, § 155.
Tennessee: Code 1896, § 3712.
West Virginia: Code 1913, § 3805.
Wyoming: Comp. Stat. 1910, § 3651; State v. Cowhick, 9 Wyo. 95, 60 Pac. 265.

[62] In the following states acknowledgment is not a prerequisite to registration:
Alabama: Code 1907, § 3373.
Colorado: Mills' Ann. Stat. 1912, § 838.
Connecticut: Gen. Stat. 1912, § 4039.
Illinois: A record of a conveyance, though not proven or acknowledged, operates as constructive notice to subsequent purchasers and creditors. Hurds' Rev. Stat. 1913, p. 534, § 31; Morrison v. Brown, 83 Ill. 562; Reed v. Kemp, 16 Ill. 445; Choteau v. Jones, 11 Ill. 300, 50 Am. Dec. 460; Stebbins v. Duncan, 108 U. S. 32, 27 L. ed. 641, 2 Sup. Ct. 313.
Michigan: 2 Ann. Stats. 1882, § 5727. See Howell's Stat. 1913, §§ 10824, 10840.
Washington: Remington's Code 1910, §§ 8781, 8784. See also Nevada Comp. Laws 1900, § 2718. See ante § 83.
[63] Heilbrun v. Hammond, 13 Hun (N. Y.) 474; Angier v. Schieffelin, 72 Pa. St. 106, 13 Am. Rep. 659. See also Ogden Building &c. Assn. v. Mensch, 196 Ill. 554, 63 N. E. 1049, 89 Am. St. 330; Stevens v. Hampton, 46 Mo. 404; Morrow v. Cole, 58 N. J. Eq. 203, 42 Atl. 673; Corey v. Moore, 86 Va. 721, 11 S. E. 114. But see Sitler v. McComas, 66 Md. 135, 6 Atl. 527.

the exact words of the form or of the statute.[64] In aid of the certificate reference may be had[65] to the instrument itself, or to the certificate of the recorder, as, for instance, to fix the date of acknowledgment, in compliance with a statute providing that the certificate of acknowledgment shall contain the time when it is taken.[66]

The record of a mortgage acknowledged before one justice of the peace, when a statute required it to be made before two justices, does not operate as notice.[67]

When a statute requires the acknowledgment of a married woman to be taken separate and apart from her husband, the record is no notice of a lien on her estate unless the acknowledgment is so taken.[68] Where a married woman joined in the granting clause of a mortgage, releasing all her estate in the lands mortgaged, and the certificate recited her execution of the deed and relinquishment of dower and homestead, the execution and acknowledgment was held sufficient to convey her separate estate.[69]

If the acknowledgment be by an agent, the certificate should show with reasonable clearness that the acknowledgment was made on behalf of the constituent, or as being his deed.[70]

A mortgage recorded without having been acknowledged creates no valid lien as against creditors and subsequent purchasers, whether they have actual notice of the mortgage or not; but it is good as between the parties, and on breach of the condition of payment may be enforced against the mortgagor, and on his death against his administrator, in preference to his general creditors.[71]

§ 496. Competency of officer taking acknowledgment.

The officer must be duly appointed and qualified. The registration of a mortgage, acknowledged or proved before an officer who has not been duly appointed or qualified, has no effect in rendering it operative against subsequent purchasers.[72]

[64] Alvis v. Morrison, 63 Ill. 181, 14 Am. Rep. 117; Allen v. Lenoir, 53 Miss. 321; Merriam v. Harsen, 2 Barb. Ch. (N. Y.) 232; Duval v. Covenhoven, 4 Wend. (N. Y.) 561.

[65] Carpenter v. Dexter, 8 Wall. (U. S.) 513, 19 L. ed. 426.

[66] Kelly v Rosenstock, 45 Md. 389.

[67] Dufphey v. Frenaye, 5 Stew. & P. (Ala.) 215. See also Munn v. Lewis, 2 Port. (Ala.) 24.

[68] Muir v. Gallaway, 61 Cal. 498; Coleman v. Billings, 89 Ill. 183; Allen v. Lenoir, 53 Miss. 321; Arm-strong v. Ross, 20 N. J. Eq. 109; Grove v. Zumbro, 14 Grat. (Va.) 501.

[69] Cazort &c. Co. v. Dunbar, 91 Ark. 400, 121 S. W. 270.

[70] McAdow v. Black, 6 Mont. 601, 13 Pac. 377; McDaniels v. Flower Brook Mfg. Co., 22 Vt. 274.

[71] Haskill v. Sevier, 25 Ark. 152; Main v. Alexander, 9 Ark. 112, 47 Am. Dec. 732; Straeffer v. Rodman, 146 Ky. 1, 141 S. W. 742.

[72] Worsham v. Freeman, 34 Ark. 55; Suddereth v. Smyth, 13 Ired. L. (N. Car.) 452.

An acknowledgment of a mortgage taken by a de facto officer is valid.[73] But an officer de facto must act under color of authority and where a mortgage was acknowledged before one who acted as a notary public but whose commission had expired nearly two years before, it was held that such person could not be considered a notary de facto, though he assumed to act as such after his commission expired, until the proof of the mortgage.[74]

It is equally necessary that the officer should act within the limits of his jurisdiction.[75] Some statutes confine the officer's power to take acknowledgments to instruments affecting land within his county or district, in which case an acknowledgment of a mortgage of land lying in another county or district has no effect.[76] But generally a mortgage or other conveyance of land lying in any part of the state may be acknowledged before an officer of any county.[77] A judge, or commissioner, or other officer empowered to take an acknowledgment, can not act out of the state for which he was appointed.[78]

When, however, acknowledgments made before an officer not authorized to act are by statute declared to be good and effectual, in the same way that they would have been had they been taken and certified by an officer properly qualified, one purchasing after such statute has gone into effect is bound to take notice of the conveyance, though until that time the record would be notice to no one.[79]

[73] Crutchfield v. Hewett, 2 App. D. C. 373; Sharp v. Thompson, 100 Ill. 447; 39 Am. Rep. 61; Wilson v. Kimmel, 109 Mo. 260, 19 S. W. 24; Prescott v. Hayes, 42 N. H. 56, 43 N. H. 593. See also Davidson v. State, 135 Ind. 254, 34 N. E. 972.

[74] Hughes v. Long, 119 N. Car. 52, 25 S. E. 743.

[75] Jackson v. Colden, 4 Cow. (N. Y.) 266.

[77] Middlecoff v. Hemstreet, 135 Cal. 173, 67 Pac. 768; Bishop v. Schneider, 46 Mo. 472, 2 Am. Rep. 533. See also Musick v. Barney, 49 Mo. 458 (deed); Hughes v. Wilkinson, 37 Miss. 482; People v. Mutual Life Ins. Co., 65 How. Pr. (N. Y.) 239.

[77] Johns v. Reardon, 3 Md. Ch. 57 (mortgage); Johnson v. McGehee, 1 Ala. 186; Colton v. Seavey, 22 Cal. 496; Doe v. Vandewater, 7 Blackf. (Ind.) 6; Schoolcraft v. Campbell, 6 Blackf. (Ind.) 481; Ford v. Gregory, 10 B. Mon. (Ky.) 175; Gray v. Patton, 2 B. Mon. (Ky.) 12; Moore v. Farrow, 3 A. K. Marsh. (Ky.) 41;

Stansberry v. Pope, 4 Bibb (Ky.) 492; Love v. Taylor, 26 Miss. 567; Dennistoun v. Potts, 26 Miss. 13; Duly v. Brooks, 30 Mo. 515; Van Cortlandt v. Tozer, 17 Wend. (N. Y.) 338; McFerran v. Powers, 1 Serg. & R. (Pa.) 102; Davey y. Ruffel, 14 Pa. Co. Ct. 272; Campbell v. Moon, 16 S. Car. 107.

[76] Jackson v. Humphrey, 1 Johns. (N. Y.) 498; Harris v. Burton, 4 Har. (Del.) 66 (notary); Cowan v. Beall, 1 McAr. D. C. 270 (justice of the peace). A certificate of acknowledgment in which the officer describes himself as "a justice of the peace within and for said county," no county being named, except that in the body of the deed, where both the grantor and grantee resided, is not necessarily invalid. Beckel v. Petticrew, 6 Ohio St. 247; Fuhrman v Loudon, 13 Serg. & R. (Pa.) 386, 15 Am. Dec. 608.

[79] Journeay v. Gibson, 56 Pa. St. 57.

§ 497. Disqualification of officer by interest or relationship.—The taking of an acknowledgment is a ministerial act; therefore it may be done by one who is so related to the parties as to be disqualified as a judge or juror.[80] On grounds of public policy the grantee in an instrument is disqualified from acting as a notary or other official in taking and certifying the acknowledgment of the grantor, and this principle applies to a mortgagee.[81] And likewise a trustee in a deed of trust can not take a valid acknowledgment of it.[82]

An acknowledgment of a mortgage to one of two coexecutors taken before a master who was the coexecutor was held valid, where the face of the mortgage did not disclose his interest therein, the taking of the acknowledgment being considered a ministerial act.[83]

The owner of a note representing an indebtedness secured by a mortgage, being the real party in interest, is disqualified from taking the acknowledgment of such mortgage, and could not qualify himself for this purpose by resorting to the subterfuge of inserting his wife's name in the note as payee.[84] Where a mortgage is made to the payee

---

[80] Lynch v. Livingston, 6 N. Y. 422; Williamson v. Carskadden, 36 Ohio St. 664; Truman v. Lore, 14 Ohio St. 144. In other cases it is declared that the officer act judicially. Homœpathic Mut. L. Ins. Co. v. Marshall, 32 N. J. Eq. 103; Heeter v. Glasgow, 79 Pa. St. 79, 21 Am. Rep. 46; Williams v. Baker, 71 Pa. St. 476; Jones on Real Prop., § 1127.

[81] Green v. Abraham, 43 Ark. 420; Lee v. Murphy, 119 Cal. 364, 51 Pac. 549; Hammers v. Dole, 61 Ill. 307; Hubble v. Wright, 23 Ind. 322 (acknowledgment taken by one of the mortgagees void); Farmers' &c. Bank v. Stockdale, 121 Iowa 748, 96 N. W. 732 (chattel mortgage); City Bank v. Radtke, 87 Iowa 363, 54 N. W. 435; LaPrad v. Sherwood, 79 Mich. 520, 44 N. W. 943; Turner v. Connelly, 105 N. Car. 72, 11 S. E. 179; White v. Connelly, 105 N. Car. 65, 11 S. E. 177; Amick v. Woodworth, 58 Ohio St. 86, 50 N. E. 437. A party to a mortgage can not act as an officer taking the acknowledgment thereto. Meckel Bros. Co. v. DeWitt, 23 Ohio Cir. Ct. 174.

[82] Muense v. Harper, 70 Ark. 309, 67 S. W. 869; Darst v. Gale, 83 Ill. 136; Russell v. Bosworth, 106 Ill. App. 314; Holden v. Brimage, 72 Miss. 228, 18 So. 383; Wasson v.

Connor, 54 Miss. 351; Bennett v. Shipley, 82 Mo. 448; Black v. Gregg, 58 Mo. 565; Dail v. Moore, 51 Mo. 589; Stevens v. Hampton, 46 Mo. 404; Lance v. Tainter, 137 N. Car. 249, 49 S. E. 211; Rothschild v. Daugher, 85 Tex. 332, 20 S. W. 142, 16 L. R. A. 719, 34 Am. St. 811; Brown v. Moore, 38 Tex. 645; Nicholson v. Gloucester Charity School, 93 Va. 101, 24 S. E. 899; Clinch River Veneer Co. v. Kurth, 90 Va. 737, 19 S. E. 878; Jones on Real Prop., § 1125; Tavenner v. Barrett, 21 W. Va. 656 (acknowledgment before one of the trustees as a notary). The fact that the acknowledgment of a trust deed by a married woman was taken by the trustee therein was not alone considered sufficient ground for annulling it at her instance. Weidman v. Templeton (Tenn.), 61 S. W. 102.

[83] Morrow v. Cole, 58 N. J. Eq. 203, 42 Atl. 673.

[84] Hedbloom v. Pierson, 2 Nebr. (Unoff.) 799, 90 N. W. 218. The court, in discussing the question as to what interest will disqualify an officer from taking an acknowledgment says: "Whether such disqualification exists in any case must be determined from the particular facts and circumstances of

of a note to protect a surety thereon, the surety has such an interest in the mortgage as to render its acknowledgment before him void, and the record of the mortgage without effect.[85] An acknowledgment taken before the cashier of a bank of which the mortgagee was president is sufficient, and a mortgage so acknowledged and duly recorded constitutes notice.[86]

The acknowledgment of a mortgage to a corporation, by a notary who is a stockholder and officer of the corporation, is not invalid.[87] And the fact that a mortgage was acknowledged before an officer of a corporation which was agent for a firm of which the mortgagee was a member, does not render the acknowledgment invalid.[88] But a general counsel and stockholder of a mortgagee corporation has been held incompetent to act as a notary to take an acknowledgment of a mortgage, though he may have been a proper witness.[89] The record of a deed of trust given to secure the debt of a charitable corporation is not invalid because the officer who took the acknowledgment was one of the incorporators, and as such entitled to a small fee for attending meetings of the board.[90]

An absolute deed acknowledged before the husband of the grantee therein and given in satisfaction of a debt secured by a trust deed in which the husband was the beneficiary has been held void.[91] It has been held that a married woman may acknowledge a mortgage of her separate estate before her husband, he being a justice of the peace.[92] And a husband's acknowledgment to a mortgage and a privy examination of his wife were not considered invalid because taken by an officer who was related to them.[93]

---

that case. No statute exists in this state which prescribes what relationship or interest of an officer shall disqualify him from taking an acknowledgment in any given case; but it would seem that, on the ground of public policy, an officer should be disqualified from taking an acknowledgment whose direct and beneficial interest would be subserved in having the conveyance made which he acknowledged; and perhaps it may be said, as a very general proposition, that an officer who is a party to a conveyance, or interested therein, is disqualified from taking the acknowledgment of the grantor." The court approves the case of Horbach v. Tyrrell, 48 Nebr. 514, 67 N. W. 485, 37 L. R. A. 434.

[85] Leonhard v. Flood, 68 Ark. 162, 56 S. W. 781.
[86] Kee v. Ewing, 17 Okla. 410, 87 Pac. 297.
[87] Horton v. Columbian Bldg. &c. Soc., 8 Ohio Dec. 169, 6 Wkly. L. Bul. (Ohio) 141. See also Florida Savings Bank &c. Exchange v. Rivers, 36 Fla. 575, 18 So. 850; Horbach v. Tyrrell, 48 Nebr. 514, 67 N. W. 485, 37 L. R. A. 434.
[88] Gilbert v. Garber, 69 Nebr. 419, 95 N. W. 1030.
[89] Maddox v. Wood, 151 Ala. 157, 43 So. 968.
[90] Nicholson v. Gloucester Charity School, 93 Va. 101, 24 S. E. 899.
[91] Jones v. Porter, 59 Miss. 628.
[92] Kimball v. Johnson, 14 Wis. 674.
[93] McAllister v. Pursell, 124 N. Car. 262, 32 S. E. 715.

§ 498. Certificate of official character of officer taking acknowledgment.—The statement or recital of the officer's official character, in the certificate of acknowledgment, is generally considered prima facie evidence of the fact.[94] When a statute requires that a certificate of the official character of the officer before whom the acknowledgment was made shall accompany the certificate of acknowledgment, the filing of the mortgage for record without the latter certificate does not constitute a record of it. If, however, this certificate is subsequently obtained and recorded in the registry where the deed is recorded, the mortgage will be treated as recorded from the date of the filing of this certificate.[95] Although the certificate of official character must show on its face all the material matters required by statute,[96] only a substantial compliance with the statute is required, and technical or unsubstantial objections will not defeat it, or the record of the mortgage which it authenticates.[97]

§ 499. Officer's certification of personal acquaintance with party making acknowledgment.—Upon the same principle, also, when a statute requires that the officer shall certify that he is personally acquainted with the party making the acknowledgment, the omission so to do renders null the acknowledgment and the record.[98] The require-

---

[94] Williams v. Kerr, 113 N. Car. 306, 18 S. E. 501. See also Deery v. Cray, 5 Wall. (U. S.) 795, 18 L. ed. 653; Mott v. Smith, 16 Cal. 533; Thompson v. Morgan, 6 Minn. 292.

[95] Reasoner v. Edmundson, 5 Ind. 393; Ely v. Wilcox, 20 Wis. 523, 91 Am. Dec. 436.

[96] People v. Register of New York, 6 Abb. Prac. (N. Y.) 180.

[97] Wells v. Atkinson, 24 Minn. 161. See also Harding v. Curtis, 45 Ill. 252; Winston v. Gwathmey, 8 B. Mon. (Ky.) 19; Morse v. Hewett, 28 Mich. 481; Harrington v. Fish, 10 Mich. 415.

[98] Davidson v. Alabama Iron &c. Co., 109 Ala. 383, 19 So. 390; Fogarty v. Finlay, 10 Cal. 239, 70 Am. Dec. 714; Kelsey v. Dunlap, 7 Cal. 160; Wolf v. Fogarty, 6 Cal. 224, 65 Am. Dec. 509; Fryer v. Rockefeller, 63 N. Y. 268. See also Rogers v. Adams, 66 Ala. 600; Conner v. Abbott, 35 Ark. 365; Kimball v. Semple, 25 Cal. 400; Gage v. Wheeler, 129 Ill. 197, 21 N. E. 1075; Becker v. Quigg, 54 Ill. 390; Tully v. Davis, 30 Ill. 103, 83 Am. Dec. 179; Short v. Conlee, 28 Ill. 219; Shephard v. Carriel, 19 Ill. 313 (recital "I am satisfied" of grantor's identity not sufficient); Livingston v. Kettelle, 6 Ill. 116, 41 Am. Dec. 166; Brinton v. Seevers, 12 Iowa 389; Gould v. Woodward, 4 G. Greene (Iowa), 82; Pinckney v. Burrage, 31 N. J. L. 21 (certificate that officer is "satisfied" of identity sufficient under New Jersey statute); Thurman v. Cameron, 24 Wend. (N. Y.) 87; Paolillo v. Faber, 56 App. Div. 241, 69 N. Y. S. 638, 9 Ann. Cas. (N. Y.) 32; Cannon v. Deming, 3 S. Dak. 421, 53 N. W. 863; Bone v. Greenlee, 1 Cold. (Tenn.) 29; Johnson v. Walton, 1 Sneed (Tenn.) 258; Frost v. Erath Cattle Co., 81 Tex. 505, 17 S. W. 52, 26 Am. St. 831; Salmon v. Huff, 80 Tex. 133, 15 S. W. 1047; McKie v. Anderson, 78 Tex. 207, 14 S. W. 576; Smith v. Garden, 28 Wis. 685; Peyton v. Peacock, 1 Humph. (Tenn.) 135. In this case, although the improper registration was not insisted upon by the answer, the court upon the exhibition of the deed took notice of the defect.

ment must be substantially complied with.[99] But a literal compliance with the statute is not essential and the certificate is sufficient if it states that the party is "known" to the officer omitting the word "personally."[1] The fact of acknowledgment and the identity of the party executing and acknowledging are the essential facts to be stated in the certificate, and the objection that "personally" was omitted in a certificate that the parties acknowledging a mortgage "were known" to the magistrate, is frivolous.[2] In Connecticut and the earlier New York cases, the officer was presumed to have performed his duty, and to have had personal knowledge or satisfactory proof of the party's identity; so that proof by his certificate was not required.[3]

If the officer taking the acknowledgment certifies that he knows the parties by whom the instrument purports to be executed, when in fact he did not, his certificate, though prima facie valid, upon proof of this fact, is a nullity, both as entitling the paper to be recorded and as affording any proof of its execution, though in fact the instrument was acknowledged by the persons who executed it.[4] But it seems that the length of acquaintance between the officer and the party making the acknowledgment is immaterial, and a mere introduction at the time of the acknowledgment is enough if it satisfies the officer's conscience.[5] As between the parties themselves the mortgage would, of course, be valid upon proof of its execution and delivery.

[99] Ritter v. Worth, 58 N. Y. 627; West Point Iron Co. v. Reymert, 45 N. Y. 703; Troup v. Haight, Hopk. (N. Y.) 239. And see cases cited supra.

[1] Henderson v. Grewell, 8 Cal. 581; Hopkins v. Delaney, 8 Cal. 85; Welch v. Sullivan, 8 Cal. 511; Tully v. Davis, 30 Ill. 103, 83 Am. Dec. 189; Delaunay v. Burnett, 4 Gilm. (Ill.) 454 ("well acquainted" equivalent to personally known); Rosenthal v. Griffin, 23 Iowa 263; Todd v. Jones, 22 Iowa 146 (personal knowledge implied in such certificate); Bell v. Evans, 10 Iowa 353 ("well known" equivalent to personally known); Warner v. Hardy, 6 Md. 525; Brown v. McCormick, 28 Mich. 215; Robson v. Thomas, 55 Mo. 581; Alexander v. Merry, 9 Mo. 514; Sheldon v. Stryker, 42 Barb. (N. Y.) 284, 27 How. Pr. 387; Davis v. Bogie, 11 Heisk. (Tenn.) 315. The expression "personally known" is sufficient where the statute uses the words "personally acquainted." Kelly v. Calhoun, 95 U. S. 710, 24 L. ed. 544.

[2] Henderson v. Grewell, 8 Cal. 581. See also Bryan v. Ramirez, 8 Cal. 461, 48 Am. Dec. 340.

[3] Sandford v. Bulkley, 30 Conn. 344; Northrop v. Wright, 7 Hill (N. Y.) 476; Crowder v. Hopkins, 10 Paige (N. Y.) 183.

[4] Watson v. Campbell, 28 Barb. (N. Y.) 421. "This case," says Mr. Justice Ingraham, "shows the impropriety of a commissioner of deeds, in such an acknowledgment, certifying that he knows the parties, without any other knowledge than a mere introduction, or seeing the signature written. He thereby endangers the security, and exposes himself to liability for damages arising therefrom."

[5] Nippel v. Hammond, 4 Colo. 211; Wood v. Bach, 54 Barb. (N. Y.) 134. But see Jones v. Bach, 48 Barb. (N. Y.) 568.

A certificate of acknowledgment which simply describes the persons acknowledging as "grantors of the within indenture," without stating that they were known to the officer to be the same persons who are described in and who executed it, as prescribed by the statute, is insufficient to entitle the deed to be recorded.[6] Omission of the words "described in and who executed" is immaterial where the certificate recites that the party is known to be the identical person whose name is subscribed to the deed, or who "executed" it.[7] Under a statute requiring the officer to certify that a party was "personally known or proved" to him to be the same person, a certificate identifying the grantor as the party "who by good authority to me given is the identical person," who appeared and acknowledged the deed, was held insufficient;[8] and likewise a certificate which states that the deed was acknowledged by the "above-named persons who executed the foregoing instrument," was held fatally defective.[9] A certificate of acknowledgment to a mortgage, stating that the "above-named mortgagor" personally appeared before a justice, and that he was personally known to him as the identical person who executed the mortgage, was held equivalent to the statement that the individual acknowledging was personally known to the justice to be the person whose name was subscribed to the mortgage. In this case the court said: "The evident object of the legislature, in these directions in relation to the acknowledgment of deeds, is to prevent one individual from personating another. That object we think has been fully accomplished in the present case. The term, 'the above-named mortgagor,' must be understood to mean the real party who was to execute the mortgage."[10]

A notary omitting to state in his certificate that the party acknowledging the mortgage was known to him or identified, is guilty of gross and culpable negligence, and is liable on his official bond for damages resulting therefrom, by postponement of such defective and improp-

[6] Fryer v. Rockefeller, 63 N. Y. 268.
[7] Henderson v. Grewell, 8 Cal. 581; Thurman v. Cameron, 24 Wend. (N. Y.) 87. See also Tiffany v. Glover, 3 G. Greene (Iowa) 387 ("who signed and sealed" equivalent to "whose name is subscribed as a party"); Hunt v. Johnson, 19 N. Y. 279.
[8] Becker v. Quigg, 54 Ill. 390 (deed of married woman).
[9] Brinton v. Seevers, 12 Iowa 389;

Fryer v. Rockefeller, 63 N. Y. 268 (parties described as the "grantors of the within indenture"). See also Miller v. Link, 2 Thomp. & C. (N. Y.) 86 ("personally appeared before me ———, signer and sealer of the foregoing instrument" insufficient).
[10] Livingston v. Kettelle, 1 Gilm. (Ill.) 116, 41 Am. Dec. 166, approving McConnel v. Reed, 2 Scam. (Ill.) 371.

erly recorded mortgage to a later mortgage which exhausted the entire property. By accepting office a notary holds himself out to the world as a person competent to perform the duties of his office. He contracts with those who employ him to perform his duties with integrity, diligence and skill. His neglect is not excused by the fact that the certificate had been partly filled by the attorney for the grantee. A mortgagee is not charged with knowledge of a defect in the certificate by receiving and retaining possession of the instrument. The measure of damages against the notary for such omission is the amount of the debt and interest intended to be secured by the mortgage.[11]

§ 500. **Presumption of regularity from certificate of acknowledgment—Impeachment for fraud.**—The certificate of acknowledgment is not conclusive; but when it is correct in form, and is apparently executed by one authorized to act in the matter, and within his jurisdiction, it is sufficient to admit the deed to record, and is prima facie good.[12] It may be shown that the officer who made the certificate was not in fact authorized to act, or had become incompetent, or that he acted outside his jurisdiction.[13] It may be shown that the deed was never in fact executed or delivered;[14] or that the deed was void when acknowledged by reason of its containing material blanks.[15]

Where a certificate of acknowledgment appears regular upon its face, a strong presumption exists in favor of its truth;[16] and this presumption of regularity must be first overcome by competent evidence;[17] the burden of proof resting upon the party impeaching it.[18]

[11] Fogarty v. Finlay, 10 Cal. 239, 70 Am. Dec. 714.

[12] Holbrook v. Worcester Bank, 2 Curtis (U. S.) 244, Fed. Cas. No. 6597; People v. Snyder, 41 N. Y. 397; Morris v. Keyes, 1 Hill (N. Y.) 540; Jackson v. Schoonmaker, 4 Johns. (N. Y.) 161; Blewett v. Bash, 22 Wash. 536, 61 Pac. 770.

[13] German-American Bank v. Carondelet Real Estate Co., 150 Mo. 570, 51 S. W. 691; Lynch v. Livingston, 6 N. Y. 422. See ante § 496.

[14] Howell v. McCrie, 36 Kans. 636, 14 Pac. 257, 59 Am. Rep. 584; Jackson v. Perkins, 2 Wend. (N. Y.) 308.

[15] Drury v. Foster, 1 Dill. (U. S.) 460.

[16] Goulet v. Dubreuille, 84 Minn. 72, 86 N. W. 779; Albright v. Stevenson, 227 Mo. 333, 126 S. W. 1027; Patnode v. Deschenes, 15 N. Dak. 100, 106 N. W. 573; Ward v. Baker (Tex. Civ. App.), 135 S. W. 620; Adams v. Smith, 11 Wyo. 200, 70 Pac. 1043. The rule is the same with deeds. Barnett v. Proskauer, 62 Ala. 486; Baldwin v. Bornheimer, 48 Cal. 433; Hourtienne v. Schnoor, 33 Mich. 274; Addis v. Graham, 88 Mo. 197; Hultz v. Ackley, 63 Pa. St. 142.

[17] Cameron v. Culkins, 44 Mich. 531, 7 N. W. 157; Johnson v. Van Velsor, 43 Mich. 208, 5 N. W. 265; Hourtienne v. Schnoor, 33 Mich. 274.

[18] Linton v. National Life Insurance Co., 104 Fed. 584, 44 C. C. A. 54; Barnett v. Proskauer, 62 Ala. 486; Bell v. Castleberry, 96 Ark. 564, 132 S. W. 649; Meyer v. Gossett, 38

The officer is prima facie such as he is described to be, de facto and de jure. He is like an officer authorized to take testimony under a special commission. His return must stand until it is impeached by collateral proof. Until this is done his return is proof in itself of his official character, of his signature, and of his acting within his jurisdiction.[19] The fact that he does not recollect the transaction does not affect his certificate.[20]

A mistake in the certificate of acknowledgment, whereby the grantee instead of the grantor appeared to be the person who made the acknowledgment, can not be corrected in a court of equity, so as to give the record of the deed legal effect from the beginning, because it can not be determined from the face of the instrument whether the error consisted in inserting the wrong name, or in taking the acknowledgment of the wrong man.[21]

A mistake in the date of an acknowledgment may be shown and the true date established by parol.[22] The certificate of acknowledgment will not be invalidated by a mistake in the date,[23] nor it would seem even by the absence of a date.[24] A mistake arising from a technical omission in the certificate may be corrected.[25]

As to the statements of fact contained in a certificate of acknowledgment which is regular in form, such, for instance, as the fact that the grantor appeared and acknowledged the execution of the instrument, they can only be impeached for fraud. The certificate is con-

Ark. 377; Langenbeck v. Louis, 140 Cal. 406, 73 Pac. 1086; O'Donnell v. Kelliher, 62 Ill. App. 641; Morris v. Sargent, 18 Iowa 90; Gabbey v. Forgeus, 38 Kans. 62, 15 Pac. 866; Oriol v. Creditors, 22 La. Ann. 32; Hourtienne v. Schnoor, 33 Mich. 274; Ray v. Crouch, 10 Mo. App. 321; Bohan v. Casey, 5 Mo. App. 101; Boyd v. Boyd, 21 App. Div. 361, 47 N. Y. S. 522; Davis v. Davis, 146 N. Car. 163, 59 S. E. 659; Ford v. Osborne, 45 Ohio St. 1, 12 N. E. 526; Swiger v. Swiger, 58 W. Va. 119, 52 S. E. 23; Adams v. Smith, 11 Wyo. 200, 70 Pac. 1043. The fact that a notary who signed a certificate of acknowledgment to a mortgage, was also attorney for the party relying upon the mortgage, does not alter the presumption in favor of the certificate, and the burden of proof is still on the one impeaching it where the notary and other witnesses testify that latter acknowledged the mortgage. Dikeman v. Arnold, 78 Mich. 455, 44 N. W. 407.

[19] Canandarqua Academy v. McKechnie, 19 Hun (N. Y.) 62; Thurman v. Cameron, 24 Wend. (N. Y.) 87, and cases cited.

[20] Tooker v. Sloan, 30 N. J. Eq. 394.

[21] Wood v. Cochrane, 39 Vt. 544.

[22] Hoit v. Russell, 56 N. H. 559; Gest v. Flock, 2 N. J. Eq. 108. But see Greene v. Godfrey, 44 Maine 25. The fact that an acknowledgment in a deed is dated before its execution does not invalidate the deed. Fisher v. Butcher, 19 Ohio 406, 53 Am. Dec. 436.

[23] Mosier v. Momsen, 13 Okla. 41, 74 Pac. 905; Yorty v. Paine, 62 Wis. 154, 22 N. W. 137.

[24] Irving v. Brownell, 11 Ill. 402; Webb v. Huff, 61 Tex. 677.

[25] Edmunds v. Leavell (Ky.), 3 S. W. 134.

clusive of all the facts required by law to be certified therein, and evidence which is merely in contradiction of the facts certified to will not be received.[26] In a few states, including Minnesota and Missouri, a certificate of acknowledgment regular on its face is regarded as prima facie evidence only of the facts recited therein, and may be rebutted by proof that such recitals are not true in fact, without showing fraud or imposition.[27]

As between the parties to a deed or mortgage, evidence is admissible to impeach the certificate for fraud, duress, or imposition in which the grantee participated or of which he had notice before parting with the consideration.[28] As against innocent parties who, in reliance upon the certificate of acknowledgment, have in good faith parted with an adequate consideration, without knowledge or constructive notice that

[26] Paxton v. Marshall, 18 Fed. 361; Hayes v. Southern Home Bldg. Assn., 124 Ala. 663, 26 So. 527, 82 Am. St. 216; American Freehold Land Mtg. Co. v. Thornton, 108 Ala. 258, 19 So. 529, 54 Am. St. 148; Read v. Rowan, 107 Ala. 366, 18 So. 211; American Freehold Land Mtg. Co. v. James, 105 Ala. 347, 16 So. 887; Grider v. American Freehold Land Mtg. Co., 99 Ala. 281, 12 So. 775, 42 Am. St. 58; Shelton v. Aultman &c. Co., 82 Ala. 315, 8 So. 232; Downing v. Blair, 75 Ala. 216; Petty v. Grisard, 45 Ark. 117; Holland v. Webster, 43 Fla. 85, 29 So. 625; Strauch v. Hathaway, 101 Ill. 11, 40 Am. Rep. 193; Russell v. Theological Union, 73 Ill. 337; Graham v. Anderson, 42 Ill. 514, 92 Am. Dec. 89; Johnston v. Wallace, 53 Miss. 331, 24 Am. Rep. 699; Morris v. Linton, 31 Nebr. 537, 85 N. W. 565; Council Bluffs Sav. Bank v. Smith, 59 Nebr. 90, 80 N. W. 270 (quoting text); Barker v. Avery, 36 Nebr. 599, 54 N. W. 989; Phillips v. Bishop, 35 Nebr. 487, 53 N. W. 375; Pereau v. Frederick, 17 Nebr. 117, 22 N. W. 235; Williamson v. Carskadden, 36 Ohio St. 664; Baldwin v. Snowden, 11 Ohio St. 203, 78 Am. Dec. 303; Wester v. Hurt, 123 Tenn. 508, 130 S. W. 842, 30 L. R. A. (N. S.) 358, Ann. Cas. 1912 C, 329; Kennedy v. Security Bldg. &c. Assn. (Tenn.), 57 S. W. 388; Henke v. Stacy, 25 Tex. Civ. App. 272, 61 S. W. 509.

[27] Dodge v. Hollinshead, 6 Minn. 25, 80 Am. Dec. 433; Comings v. Leedy, 114 Mo. 454, 21 S. W. 804; Barrett v. Davis, 104 Mo. 549, 16 S. W. 377; Mays v. Pryce, 95 Mo. 603, 8 S. W. 731; Steffin v. Bauer, 70 Mo. 399; Wannell v. Kem, 57 Mo. 478. See also Moore v. Hopkins, 83 Cal. 270, 23 Pac. 318, 17 Am. St. 248; Pierce v. Georger, 103 Mo. 540, 15 S. W. 848; Young v. Engdahl, 18 N. Dak. 166, 119 N. W. 169. But see Springfield Engine &c. Co. v. Donovan, 147 Mo. 622, 49 S. W. 500. But the proof, to have this effect, must be clear, cogent, and convincing. Bohan v. Casey, 5 Mo. App. 101; Young v. Duvall, 109 U. S. 573, 27 L. ed. 1036, 3 Sup. Ct. 414; Insurance Co. v. Nelson, 103 U. S. 544, 26 L. ed. 436; Mather v. Jarel, 33 Fed. 366.

[28] Grider v. American Freehold Land Mtg. Co., 99 Ala. 281, 12 So. 775, 42 Am. St. 58; Smith v. McGuire, 67 Ala. 34; Holt v. Moore, 37 Ark. 145; Chivington v. Colorado Springs Co., 9 Colo. 597, 14 Pac. 212; Fitzgerald v. Fitzgerald, 100 Ill. 385; Kerr v. Russell, 69 Ill. 666, 18 Am. Rep. 634; Eyster v. Hatheway, 50 Ill. 521, 99 Am. Dec. 537; Long v. Branham, 30 Ky. L. 552, 99 S. W. 271; Davis v. Hamblin, 51 Md. 525; Central Bank v. Copeland, 18 Md. 305, 81 Am. Dec. 597; O'Neil v. Webster, 150 Mass. 572, 23 N. E. 235; Worcester v. Eaton, 13 Mass. 371, 7 Am. Dec. 155; Allen v. Lenoir, 53 Miss. 321; Williamson v. Carskadden, 36 Ohio St. 664; Cover

such certificate is false, parol evidence is not admissible even to show fraud or imposition in procurement of the acknowledgment.[29]

Under the statutes of some states for the special protection of the homestead right, it is required that the wife should acknowledge before the officer that she had released the homestead right.[30] If, for instance, the certificate shows that a married woman was examined separate and apart from her husband, and voluntarily relinquished her rights of dower and homestead in the lands, it can not be impeached by evidence that there was no private examination; that she did not acknowledge the deed as her act and deed; that the contents of the deed were not made known to her; or that she did not release her homestead right. There must first be some allegation and proof of fraud or imposition practiced upon her; or some fraudulent combination between the parties interested and the officer taking the acknowl-

v. Manaway, 115 Pa. St. 338, 8 Atl. 393, 2 Am. St. 552; Darlington's Appeal, 86 Pa. St. 512, 27 Am. Rep. 726; Heeter v. Glasgow, 79 Pa. St. 79, 21 Am. Rep. 46; Hall v. Patterson, 51 Pa. St. 289; Louden v. Blythe, 16 Pa. St. 532, 55 Am. Dec. 527, 27 Pa. St. 22, 67 Am. Dec. 442; Kennedy v. Security Bldg. &c. Assn. (Tenn.), 57 S. W. 388; Pierce v. Fort, 60 Tex. 464; Westbrooks v. Jeffers, 33 Tex. 86; Wiley v. Prince, 21 Tex. 637; Rollins v. Menager, 22 W. Va. 461. See also Breitling v. Chester, 88 Tex. 586, 32 S. W. 527. If the mortgagee has knowledge of circumstances which would put an honest man on inquiry concerning the procurement of the acknowledgment, and wilfully neglects to investigate the fraud, he will be charged with notice of such fraud as if a party thereto. Louden v. Blythe, 27 Pa. St. 22, 67 Am. Dec. 442, 16 Pa. St. 532, 55 Am. Dec. 527.

[29] Linton v. National L. Ins. Co., 104 Fed. 584, 44 C. C. A. 54; Giddens v. Bolling, 99 Ala. 319, 13 So. 511; Moses v. Dade, 58 Ala. 211; Holt v. Moore, 37 Ark. 145; De Arnaz v. Escandon, 59 Cal. 486; Ladew v. Paine, 82 Ill. 221; Marston v. Brittenham, 76 Ill. 611; Kerr v. Russell, 69 Ill. 666, 18 Am. Rep. 634; McHenry v. Day, 13 Iowa 445, 81 Am. Dec. 438; Godsey v. Virginia Iron &c. Co., 26 Ky. L. 657, 82 S. W. 386; Pribble v. Hall, 13 Bush

(Ky.) 61; Kenneday v. Price, 57 Miss. 771; Johnston v. Wallace, 53 Miss. 331, 24 Am. Rep. 699; Springfield Engine &c. Co. v. Donovan, 147 Mo. 622, 49 S. W. 500; Baldwin v. Snowden, 11 Ohio St. 203, 78 Am. Dec. 303; Moore v. Fuller, 6 Ore. 272, 25 Am. Rep. 524; Singer Mfg. Co. v. Rook, 84 Pa. St. 442, 24 Am. Rep. 204; Heeter v. Glasgow, 79 Pa. St. 79, 21 Am. Rep. 46; Williams v. Baker, 71 Pa. St. 476; Hall v. Patterson, 51 Pa. St. 289; Louden v. Blythe, 27 Pa. St. 22, 67 Am. Dec. 442; Shell v. Holston Nat. Bldg. &c. Assn. (Tenn.), 52 S. W. 909; Shields v. Netherland, 5 Lea (Tenn.) 193; Finnegan v. Finnegan, 3 Tenn. Ch. 510; Webb v. Burney, 70 Tex. 322, 7 S. W. 841; Miller v. Yturria, 69 Tex. 549, 7 S. W. 206; Henderson v. Terry, 62 Tex. 281; Pierce v. Fort, 60 Tex. 464; Davis v. Kennedy, 58 Tex. 516; Waltee v. Weaver, 57 Tex. 569; Kocourek v. Marak, 54 Tex. 201, 33 Am. Rep. 623; Pool v. Chase, 46 Tex. 207; Forbes v. Thomas (Tex.), 51 S. W. 1097; Summers v. Sheern (Tex.), 37 S. W. 246; McDannell v. Horrell, 1 Tex. Unrep. Cas. 521.

[30] As in Illinois, both under Act of 1857 and that of 1869. See Hurd's Rev. Stat. 1912, ch. 52, p. 1166, § 4; Warner v. Crosby, 89 Ill. 320. In Indiana, under Acts 1879, p. 129. See also Burns' Ann. Stat. 1914, §§ 3971, 3972.

edgment.[31] There would be no certainty in titles if the officer's certificate could be contradicted by any other evidence. The law directs
him to make his certificate in writing, and when he has made it the
world is to look to that and to nothing else.[32] Parol evidence can only
be admitted to show fraud or duress connected with the acknowledgment, not to contradict the officer's certificate.[33]

But it is held that the certificate of a magistrate to the deed of a
married woman that she was of full age is not conclusive, and that
she can not ratify it after coming of age except by acknowledgment
separate and apart from her husband.[34]

The exception, that the magistrate's certificate is not conclusive of
the facts stated in it when fraud is shown, does not, however, extend
to the case of one who has in good faith purchased without notice of
the fraud; he is protected by the record, notwithstanding the fraud.[35]

---

[31] Insurance Co. v. Nelson, 103 U.
S. 544, 26 L. ed. 436; Hayes v. Southern Home Bldg. &c. Assn., 124 Ala.
663, 26 So. 527, 82 Am. St. 216;
American Freehold Land Mtg. Co.
v. Thornton, 108 Ala. 258, 19 So.
529, 54 Am. St. 148; Coleman v.
Smith, 55 Ala. 368; Miller v. Marx,
55 Ala. 322; Holland v. Webster, 43
Fla. 85, 29 So. 625; Blackman v.
Hawks, 89 Ill. 512; McPherson v.
Sanborn, 88 Ill. 150; Crane v. Crane,
81 Ill. 165; Lowell v. Wren, 80 Ill.
238; Russell v. Baptist Theological
Union, 73 Ill. 337; Kerr v. Russell,
69 Ill. 666, 18 Am. Dec. 634; Monroe v. Poorman, 62 Ill. 523; Graham
v. Anderson, 42 Ill. 514, 92 Am. Dec.
89; M'Neely v. Rucker, 6 Blackf.
(Ind.) 391; Ridgely v. Howard, 3
Har. & McH. (Md.) 321; Bissett v.
Bissett, 1 Har. & McH. (Md.) 211;
Johnson v. Van Velsor, 43 Mich. 208,
5 N. W. 265; Johnston v. Wallace,
53 Miss. 331, 24 Am. Rep. 699; Baldwin v. Snowden, 11 Ohio St. 203,
78 Am. Dec. 303; Moore v. Fuller,
6 Ore. 272, 25 Am. Rep. 524; Lewars
v. Weaver, 121 Pa. St. 268, 15 Atl.
514; Oppenheimer v. Wright, 106
Pa. St. 569; Singer Mfg. Co. v. Rook,
84 Pa. St. 442, 24 Am. Rep. 204;
Heeter v. Glasgow, 79 Pa. St. 79, 21
Am. Rep. 46; Jamison v. Jamison,
3 Whart. (Pa.) 457, 31 Am. Dec.
536; Wester v. Hurt, 103 Tenn. 508,
130 S. W. 842; Williams v. Pouns,
48 Tex. 141; Hartley v. Frosh, 6

Tex. 208, 55 Am. Dec. 772; Lefebvre
v. Dutruit, 51 Wis. 426, 8 N. W. 149,
37 Am. Rep. 833. See also Hitz v.
Jenks, 123 U. S. 297, 31 L. ed. 156,
8 Sup. Ct. 143 (deed); Godsey v.
Virginia Iron &c. Co., 26 Ky. L. 657,
82 S. W. 386. If the certificate is
not in statutory form, she is not
estopped to deny its sufficiency unless guilty of some positive fraud.
Kopke v. Votaw (Tex.), 95 S. W.
15.

[32] Per Tilghman, C. J., in Jourdan
v. Jourdan, 9 Serg. & R. (Pa.) 268,
11 Am. Dec. 724. See also Graham
v. Anderson, 42 Ill. 514, 92 Am. Dec.
89.

[33] Moore v. Fuller, 6 Ore. 272, 25
Am. Rep. 524; Heeter v. Glasgow,
79 Pa. St. 79, 21 Am. Rep. 46; Jamison v. Jamison, 3 Whart. (Pa.) 457,
31 Am. Dec. 536; Homeopathic Mut.
L. Ins. Co. v. Marshall, 32 N. J. Eq.
103. In a note to this case by the
reporter the decisions of the various states upon the question,
whether the officer's certificate is
conclusively or only prima facie
correct, are fully cited. See also
Dowell v. Mitchell, 82 Ky. 47, 5 Ky.
L. 746; Dolph v. Barney, 5 Ore. 191.
[34] Williams v. Baker, 71 Pa. St.
476; Ledger Building Assn. v. Cook,
7 Reporter 409, 19 Alb. L. J. 281.
[35] Heeter v. Glasgow, 79 Pa. St. 79,
21 Am. Rep. 46; Hall v. Patterson,
51 Pa. St. 289.

If he has actual knowledge of fraud or duress in obtaining a wife's acknowledgment to a deed, or knowledge of such circumstances as would naturally lead him to inquiry, he is deprived of the protection accorded to an innocent and bona fide holder. Even less than actual duress will avoid a wife's acknowledgment of a mortgage in the hands of an assignee who ought to have inquired for defenses and did not. It is enough if it be shown that she did it under moral constraint, as, for instance, by threats, persecution, and harshness on the part of her husband. These facts being known to the mortgagee, his assignee is affected by them in case he is not entitled to the protection accorded to one who takes negotiable paper for value before maturity. He should inquire of the mortgagors whether the mortgage is open to any defense.[36]

A substantial compliance with the requirements of such a statute is sufficient.[37]

§ 501. Delivery prerequisite to effective record—Delivery through agents.

—Delivery is another incident necessary to giving effect to the conveyance even as between the parties to it.[38] Although the deed be

[36] Twitchell v. McMurtrie, 77 Pa. St. 383; McCandless v. Engle, 51 Pa. St. 309; Michener v. Cavender, 38 Pa. St. 334, 80 Am. Dec. 486.

[37] Hornbeck v. Mutual Building Assn., 88 Pa. St. 64. See also Hayes v. Southern Home Bldg. &c. Assn., 124 Ala. 663, 26 So. 527, 82 Am. St. 216.

[38] Brumby v. Jones, 141 Fed. 318, 72 C. C. A. 466; Freeman v. Peay, 23 Ark. 439; Humiston v. Preston, 66 Conn. 579, 34 Atl. 544; Edwards v. Thom, 25 Fla. 222, 5 So. 707; Fitch v. Miller, 200 Ill. 170, 65 N. E. 650; Lanphier v. Desmond, 187 Ill. 370, 58 N. E. 343; Hawes v. Hawes, 177 Ill. 409, 53 N. E. 78; Baker v. Updike, 155 Ill. 54, 39 N. E. 587; Johnson v. Prosperity Loan &c. Assn., 94 Ill. App. 260; Honfes v. Schultze, 2 Bradw. (Ill.) 196; Fitzgerald v. Goff, 99 Ind. 28; Henry v. Carson, 96 Ind. 412; Goodwin v. Owen, 55 Ind. 243; Hoadley v. Hadley, 48 Ind. 452; Woodbury v. Fisher, 20 Ind. 387, 83 Am. Dec. 325; Foley v. Howard, 8 Iowa 56; Maynard v. Maynard, 10 Mass. 456, 6 Am. Dec. 146; Parker v. Hill, 8 Meto. (Mass.) 447; Samson v. Thornton, 3 Metc. (Mass.) 275, 37 Am. Dec. 135; Cressinger v. Dessenburg, 42 Mich. 580, 4 N. W. 269; Nazro v. Ware, 38 Minn. 443, 38 N. W. 359; Gadsden v. Thrush, 56 Nebr. 565, 76 N. W. 1060, 45 L. R. A. 654; Hoagland v. Green, 54 Nebr. 164, 74 N. W. 424 (delivery insufficient though mortgagee had manual possession); Yeomans v. Petty, 40 N. J. Eq. 495, 4 Atl. 631; Rapps v. Gottlieb, 142 N. Y. 164, 36 N. E. 1052, affg. 67 Hun 115; Durfee v. Knowles, 50 Hun 601, 18 N. Y. St. 583, 2 N. Y. S. 466; Munoz v. Wilson, 6 N. Y. St. 66; Shirley v. Burch, 16 Ore. 83, 18 Pac. 351, 8 Am. St. 273; Gorham v. Meacham, 63 Vt. 231, 22 Atl. 572, 13 L. R. A. 676; Ault v. Blackman, 8 Wash. 624, 36 Pac. 694; Garmer v. Martin (W. Va.), 80 S. E. 495; Harmon v. Myer, 55 Wis. 85, 12 N. W. 435; Croft v. Bunster, 9 Wis. 503. The execution of a mortgage includes delivery as an essential element. Van Valkenburgh v. Oldham, 12 Cal. App. 572, 108 Pac. 42; John Shillito Co. v. McConnell, 130 Ind. 41, 26 N. E. 95 Nebr. 394, 145 N. W. 849. See ante § 84.

recorded, if it has not been delivered, or the delivery was unauthorized, a subsequent conveyance by the grantor, or a subsequent judgment against him, will take precedence.[39] Delivery becomes effectual when the mortgagor surrenders dominion of a completed mortgage with intent thereby to make it operative.[40] A mortgage must not only be delivered to, but must be accepted by the mortgagee; otherwise the title does not pass. To be delivered, it would seem that the deed must pass under the power of the grantee or some person for his use, with the consent of the grantor.[41]

The fact of the acknowledgment of the deed at a certain date is not by itself evidence that it was delivered at that time, or was ever delivered,[42] though this has been said to be presumptive evidence.[43] The record of the deed is said to be evidence of delivery in a greater degree, but it is not conclusive, of a delivery. It has sometimes been spoken of as a prima facie evidence of delivery.[44] It may be evidence for the jury to consider.[45]

But the registration itself does not operate as a delivery; nor does it supersede the necessity of proof of a delivery.[46] Under the doctrine generally prevailing, the act of the mortgagor in filing the mortgage for record or causing it to be recorded, constitutes only prima facie evidence of a delivery to the mortgagee.[47] Under certain circum-

---

[39] Lanphier v. Desmond, 187 Ill. 370, 378, 58 N. E. 343 (quoting text); Woodbury v. Fisher, 20 Ind. 387, 83 Am. Dec. 325; Goodsell v. Stinson, 7 Blackf. (Ind.) 437; Woolson v. Kelley, 73 Minn. 513, 76 N. W. 258.

[40] Merritt v. Temple, 155 Ind. 497, 58 N. E. 699; Osborne v. Eslinger, 155 Ind. 351, 58 N. E. 439; Anderson v. Anderson, 126 Ind. 62, 24 N. E. 1036; Stokes v. Anderson, 118 Ind. 533, 21 N. E. 331, 4 L. R. A. 313. Delivery may be inferred from circumstances which indicate that the grantor intended to part with dominion of the instrument. In re Goldville Mfg. Co., 118 Fed. 892.

[41] Woodbury v. Fisher, 20 Ind. 387, 83 Am. Dec. 325; Dearmond v. Dearmond, 10 Ind. 191. See ante § 84.

[42] Freeman v. Schroeder, 43 Barb. (N. Y.) 618, 29 How. Pr. (N. Y.) 263; Jackson v. Richards, 6 Cow. (N. Y.) 617.

[43] Pereau v. Frederick, 17 Nebr. 117, 22 N. W. 235; Wyckoff v. Remsen, 11 Paige (N. Y.) 564; Portz v.

Schantz, 70 Wis. 497, 36 N. W. 249.

[44] Moody v. Dryden, 72 Iowa 461, 34 N. W. 210; Sessions v. Sherwood, 78 Mich. 234, 44 N. W. 263; Knolls v. Barnhart, 71 N. Y. 474; Jackson v. Perkins, 2 Wend. (N. Y.) 308; Preston v. Albee, 120 App. Div. 89, 105 N. Y. S. 33 (record presumptive evidence of delivery); Kille v. Ege, 79 Pa. St. 15; Peterson v. Kilgore, 58 Tex. 88.

[45] Jordan v. Farnsworth, 15 Gray (Mass.) 517.

[46] Weber v. Christen, 121 Ill. 91, 11 N. E. 893; Houfes v. Schultze, 2 Bradw. (Ill.) 196, 96 Ill. 335; Skinner v. Baker, 79 Ill. 496; Stiles v. Probst, 69 Ill. 382; Kingsbury v. Burnside, 58 Ill. 310, 11 Am. Rep. 67; National Bank v. Morse, 73 Iowa 174, 34 N. W. 803, 5 Am. St. 670; Foley v. Howard, 8 Iowa 56; Hawkes v. Pike, 105 Mass. 560, 7 Am. Rep. 554; Parker v. Hill, 8 Metc. (Mass.) 447.

[47] Walton v. Burton, 107 Ill. 54; Connard v. Colgan, 55 Iowa 538, 8 N. W. 351; Cobb v. Chase, 54 Iowa

stances, however, the recording of a mortgage at the instance of the mortgagor has been held to amount to a delivery of the instrument to the mortgagee.[48] Thus a delivery to the register for record may be an effectual delivery to the grantee, where such delivery is made at the request of the grantee,[49] or where the register had authority from him to receive it and keep it, or it is so delivered pursuant to a previous agreement between the parties.[50] And so where a mortgagor delivered the mortgage to the recorder for registration, intending it as a complete delivery, and the mortgagee being notified of the transaction, approved it, thereafter receiving interest on the loan, the delivery was deemed sufficient.[51]

A mortgage by a corporation to secure a bond, duly signed, sealed and attested, was taken by the attorney of the corporation and delivered to the trustee therein, who executed its acceptance in the presence of two witnesses, after which it was redelivered to the attorney to be recorded, but was subsequently lost or mislaid, and was not returned to the trustee. It was held that there was a sufficient delivery to render the mortgage valid. The court said: "Delivery is indispensable to the completion of a deed, but this may be done either formally, or delivery may be inferred from circumstances which indicate that the grantor intended to part with the dominion of the instrument and put it into the possession of the trustee."[52]

253, 6 N. W. 300; Foley v. Howard, 8 Iowa 56; Foster v. Beardsley Scythe Co., 47 Barb. (N. Y.) 505; Ford v. McCarthy, 77 Hun 612, 61 N. Y. St. 363, 29 N. Y. S. 786; Geissmann v. Wolf, 46 Hun (N. Y.) 289, 11 N. Y. St. 306; Clymer v. Groff, 220 Pa. 580, 69 Atl. 1119.

[48] Elsberry v. Boykin, 65 Ala. 336; Carnall v. Duval, 22 Ark. 136; Doerner v. Nieberding, 3 Ohio Dec. 519.

[49] Thayer v. Stark, 6 Cush. (Mass.) 11; Dusenbury v. Hulbert, 2 Thomp. & C. (N. Y.) 177.

[50] Ward v. Ward, 144 Fed. 308; Capital City Bank v. Hodgin, 24 Fed. 1; Lawrence v. Lawrence, 181 Ill. 248, 54 N. E. 918; Brunson v. Henry, 140 Ind. 455, 39 N. E. 256; Reid v. Abernethy, 77 Iowa 438, 42 N. W. 364; Hoffman v. Mackall, 5 Ohio St. 124, 64 Am. Dec. 637.

[51] Renken v. Bellmer, 55 Cal. 466.

[52] In re Goldville Mfg. Co., 118 Fed. 892; William Firth Co. v. South Carolina Loan &c. Co., 122 Fed. 569, 59 C. C. A. 73. In Withers v. Jenkins, 6 S. Car. 122, the court says: "It is not necessary to the valid execution of a deed that there should be actual delivery either to the grantee in person, or to some one expressly authorized to accept it on his behalf. Much less is such a requisition essential where the instrument gives a trust conferring on the trustee a mere naked title, coupled with no interest, that he holds for the mere purpose of protecting and preserving the trust for the beneficiaries who may be entitled to these enjoyments. If the grantor, in the absence of the grantee, and without his knowledge, has actually consummated the delivery in accordance with the purpose declared on the face of the instrument, the object to be effected by it is as fully accomplished as if there had been an actual transfer of the paper from the hands of the grantor to those of the grantee."

Delivery to a grantee who is called by a wrong name in the deed identifies the grantee, and vests the title in him.[53]

A deed may be delivered by the grantor's agent. Thus a notary, with whom a note and mortgage are left by the mortgagor, after acknowledging the mortgage before him, will be presumed to have authority to deliver them, in the absence of instructions to the contrary; and a delivery by him to the mortgagee is a sufficient delivery.[54]

Of course a delivery to an agent of the grantee is a delivery to the grantee himself; as, for instance, a delivery to the secretary of a railroad company is sufficient.[55] A delivery of a trust deed to a vice-president of a bank was held a delivery to the bank, notwithstanding his agreement to retain the instrument in his custody and to use it only to satisfy directors who had demanded security.[56] An officer employed by the mortgagee to obtain the execution and acknowledgment of a mortgage is the mortgagee's agent to accept delivery of the instrument.[57] A delivery of a mortgage made by a partner upon the dissolution of the firm to secure a note of the firm, which he has assumed, to the other partner, who is indemnified by the mortgage, is sufficient.[58]

A deed of trust delivered to a third person with directions to deliver it to the mortgagee was held to be constructively delivered to the mortgagee, giving it priority over a judgment lien where the mortgagee told such person to retain it for safekeeping, though the mortgagor, with consent of the mortgagee, took the papers away temporarily to cancel some of the interest notes.[59]

§ 502. **Delivery after recording.**—Where the delivery of a deed or mortgage is essential to its validity, it is a prerequisite to valid registration.[61] And, since there can be no complete delivery without acceptance, the record of an instrument made without the knowledge or assent of the grantee is of no effect until it has been accepted.[62] But

---

[53] Fisher v. Milmine, 94 Ill. 328; Beaver v. Slanker, 94 Ill. 175.

[54] Adams v. Adams, 70 Iowa 253, 30 N. W. 795. The unconditional delivery of a mortgage by a husband, as agent for his wife, though unauthorized, is binding upon her. Alexander v. Welcker, 141 Cal. 302, 74 Pac. 845.

[55] Truman v. McCollum, 20 Wis. 360; Patterson v. Ball, 19 Wis. 243. See ante § 84.

[56] Rushing v. Citizens' Nat. Bank (Tex. Civ. App.), 162 S. W. 460.

[57] Greene v. Conant, 151 Mass. 223, 24 N. E. 44.

[58] Conwell v. McCowan, 81 Ill. 285.

[60] Stahlhuth v. Nagle, 229 Mo. 570, 129 S. W. 687.

[61] Edwards v. Thom, 25 Fla. 222, 5 So. 707; Fitzgerald v. Goff, 99 Ind. 28; Hogadone v. Grange Mut. Fire Ins. Co., 133 Mich. 339, 94 N. W. 1045; Van Auken v. Mizner, 2 Nebr. (Unoff.) 899, 90 N. W. 637; Houston Land &c. Co. v. Hubbard, 37 Tex. Civ. App. 546, 85 S. W. 474.

[62] Parmelee v. Simpson. 5 Wall.

a subsequent acceptance by the grantee or mortgagee of a conveyance delivered to the recording officer will render the record effective against third persons from the time of such acceptance.[63]

A mortgagee taking a mortgage which has been recorded without a delivery takes it subject to a conveyance by the mortgagor made to another person after such record but before the mortgage was delivered.[64] Although a deed is generally considered of no effect until there has been a delivery of it to the grantee, yet a subsequent acceptance by the grantee of a deed filed for record without delivery, has been held to ratify the making and recording of it, and to give it legal effect from the time of filing, as against intermediate incumbrances.[65] When, for instance, one in debt to a bank executed a mortgage to it, and without delivering it sent it to the record office to be recorded, and then sent word to the officers of the bank of the execution of the mortgage, and that they could get it of the recorder, and they replied that "they were glad it was done," this was held a sufficient delivery of the deed to the bank to pass the title as against one to whom the mortgagor made and delivered another mortgage of the same property two days afterward, but after such notification to the bank and reply.[66]

There are cases which hold that a delivery may be made to a stranger in behalf of the mortgagee, and without his authority, and upon his subsequent acceptance of the mortgage the title is regarded as having vested in him from the time of such delivery. Such was held to be the case where one in failing circumstances made a mortgage to a creditor who resided out of the state, without the knowledge of his creditor, and delivered it to his own attorney for the benefit of the creditor, with the request that the attorney should cause it to be

(U. S.) 81, 18 L. ed. 542; Weber v. Christen, 121 Ill. 91, 11 N. E. 893, 2 Am. St. 68; Union Mut. Life Ins. Co. v. Campbell, 95 Ill. 267, 35 Am. Rep. 166; Herbert v. Herbert, 1 Ill. 354, 12 Am. St. 192; Woodbury v. Fisher, 20 Ind. 387, 83 Am. Dec. 325; Parker v. Hill, 8 Metc. (Mass.) 447; Samson v. Thornton, 3 Metc. (Mass.) 275, 37 Am. Dec. 135; Foster v. Beardsley Scythe Co., 47 Barb. (N. Y.) 505; Jackson v. Phipps, 12 Johns. (N. Y.) 418; Cook v. Cook (R. I.), 43 Atl. 537; McCutchin v. Platt, 22 Wis. 561; Miller v. Blinebury, 21 Wis. 676. See ante § 84.
[63] Gould v. Day, 94 U. S. 405, 24 L. ed. 232; Parmelee v. Simpson, 5 Wall. (U. S.) 81, 18 L. ed. 542; Clark v. National Bank, 66 Fed. 404, 13 C. C. A. 545; Parker v. Hill, 8 Metc. (Mass.) 447; Mutual &c. Ins. Co. v. Rowand, 26 N. J. Eq. 389; Wilcox v. Drought, 71 App. Div. (N. Y.) 402, 75 N. Y. S. 960; Farmers' &c. Bank v. Drury, 38 Vt. 426. See ante § 85.

[64] Lanphier v. Desmond, 187 Ill. 370, 58 N. E. 343, affg. 86 Ill. App. 101.

[65] Carnall v. Duval, 22 Ark. 136. See ante § 85.

[66] Farmers' &c. Bank v. Drury, 38 Vt. 426.

recorded and handed to the creditor. The mortgage was accordingly recorded, and afterward received and accepted by the mortgagee; but after the delivery of it to the attorney and the recording of it, and before the attorney had delivered it to the mortgagee, the property was attached by another creditor of the mortgagor's. It was held that the mortgaged estate immediately vested in the mortgagee, whose title was therefore superior to that of the attaching creditor.[67]

It has been held, moreover, that it may be presumed that a mortgagee, in whose favor a mortgage has been executed and placed on record, will assent to it on being notified of its existence; and therefore, although it be made and recorded without his knowledge, and the land is afterward attached by creditors of the mortgagor before the mortgagee has notice of the mortgage, which he afterward assents to and ratifies, he may hold the mortgage lien against such attachments.[68] Thus, an absent mortgagee in whose favor a mortgage has been executed and recorded by the mortgagor is presumed to have accepted the mortgage;[69] and especially where such mortgage is permitted to remain of record, and is recognized by all the parties in interest, the recording is presumed a delivery, and want of manual delivery is immaterial.[70]

There may be some slight presumption of delivery arising from the record of a deed; but when this is overcome, the burden is upon the party claiming title under it to show on actual delivery before a levy upon the land by attachment or execution.[71]

§ 503. When a subsequent delivery becomes operative.—Although a deed be inoperative at the time it is recorded, as when it is recorded before delivery, or is recorded as a deed when intended as a mortgage, and the statutes of the state where it is executed require that it shall be recorded in such case in separate mortgage books, upon a subsequent delivery in the one case, and in the other upon a purchase of the equity of redemption by the mortgagee, the record then becomes

[67] Merrills v. Swift, 18 Conn. 257, 46 Am. Dec. 315, and cases cited. This is doubtful law. See also Johnson v. Farley, 45 N. H. 505. The execution and recording of a deed is valid as against an attaching creditor, whose attachment is levied before actual delivery to the grantee. Hedge v. Drew, 12 Pick. (Mass.) 141, 22 Am. Dec. 416. But see Bell v. Farmers' Bank, 11 Bush (Ky.) 34, 21 Am. Rep. 205; see

Jones on Chattel Mortgages, §§ 104–113.

[68] Ensworth v. King, 50 Mo. 477. This case should not be relied upon in any other state.

[69] In re Immanuel Presbyterian Church, 112 La. 348, 36 So. 408.

[70] Sessions v. Sherwood, 78 Mich. 234, 44 N. W. 263.

[71] Harmon v. Myer, 55 Wis. 85, 12 N. W. 435.

fully operative.[72] The delivery of the deed, or the purchase of the equity of redemption, is equivalent to a delivery of the deed for record at that time, in the same way as when a deed is recorded in anticipation of the completion of a sale. The mortgage is effectual only from the time of such delivery, and any one who has in the meantime before the delivery obtained a lien upon the property has a preference over such mortgagee. His assent to the mortgage makes the mortgage valid, and the record of it notice only from that time.[73] Where, for instance, a mortgage was recorded on the thirteenth day of a certain month, and was held by the mortgagor ready for delivery when he should obtain a loan, and was not delivered until the seventh day of the following month, the latter date was held to be the date of its registry, as against one who in the meantime had acquired a mechanic's lien upon the property.

But if the mortgage be executed and acknowledged, and put upon record by the mortgagor, in pursuance of a prior contract for a loan upon it, which is afterward made in pursuance of the contract, and the mortgage is then delivered upon the payment of the money, it has priority in equity over liens of mechanics and materialmen for work and materials furnished, after the mortgage is recorded, for a building which the mortgagor commenced to erect upon the premises after the recording of the mortgage and before its delivery, the mortgagee having no knowledge of this fact. In such case the mortgage upon delivery has relation to the agreement for the loan, and the registry takes effect and becomes operative as constructive notice before the delivery, and from the time the mortgage was left for record.[74]

The recording of a mortgage is evidence of delivery and acceptance only so far as relates to the validity of the conveyance; and the rule does not apply to a provision in a mortgage which imposes an obligation on the mortgagee to assume the payment of a pre-existing incumbrance on the property.[75]

[72] Warner v. Winslow, 1 Sandf. Ch. (N. Y.) 430. See ante §§ 85-87.
[73] Houfes v. Schultze, 2 Bradw. (Ill.) 196; Mutual Ben. Life Ins. Co. v. Rowand, 26 N. J. Eq. 389; Foster v. Beardsley Scythe Co., 47 Barb. (N. Y.) 505; Jackson v. Richards, 6 Cow. (N. Y.) 617; Hood v. Brown, 2 Ohio 266.
[74] Jacobus v. Mutual Benefit Life Ins. Co., 27 N. J. Eq. 604. The doctrine of relation is fully considered in this case. See also contra, Honfes v. Schultze, 2 Bradw. (Ill.) 196; Pratt v. Potter, 21 Barb. (N. Y.) 589; Judd v. Seekins, 62 N. Y. 266, 3 Thomp. & C. 266.
[75] Swisher v. Palmer, 106 Ill. App. 432,

III. *Requisites as to the Time and Manner of Recording*

§ **504. When record becomes operative as notice.**—In the usual course of recording, each instrument deposited with the recording officer is immediately indorsed with an official time stamp or other memorandum of the fact and time of filing, and placed among the accessible files of newly deposited and untranscribed instruments until it can be copied in the records at length. In due order and course of time, sometimes specified by statute, the recorder enrols it in the record books. This official transcript then becomes the true and only record, since the owner of the instrument usually removes the original from the recorder's office after the enrolment has been made.[1] Since the original instrument is subject to public inspection in the recorder's office between the date of filing and that of transcribing, the completed record is with good reason declared to relate back to the exact time of filing the instrument, and to give constructive notice from that time. Accordingly the record is considered notice from the time of filing and entry of the deed for record. It is sometimes provided by statute that a deed shall be deemed to be recorded when it is filed for record, or noted in an entry book by the recorder as received. But aside from any statutory provision, the judicial interpretation of the effect of the filing is the same.[2]

---

[1] Donald v. Beals, 57 Cal. 399; Hatch v. Haskins, 17 Maine 391; Potter v. Dooley, 55 Vt. 512.

[2] Alabama: Leslie v. Hinson, 83 Ala. 266, 3 So. 443; Mallory v. Stodder, 6 Ala. 801.

Arizona: Rev. Stat. 1913, § 2067.

Arkansas: Dig. of Stats. 1904, § 762; Oates v. Walls, 28 Ark. 244.

California: Civ. Code 1906, § 1170; Cady v. Purser, 131 Cal. 552, 63 Pac. 844; Edwards v. Grand, 121 Cal. 254, 53 Pac. 796.

Colorado: Ann. Stats. 1891, ch. 29, § 446; Shepard v. Murphy, 26 Colo. 350, 58 Pac. 588.

Connecticut: G. S. 1902, § 4036; Lewis v. Hinman, 56 Conn. 55; Franklin v. Cannon, 1 Root (Conn.) 500.

District of Columbia: Code 1911, § 499; Sis v. Boarman, 11 App. D. C. 116.

Florida: Gen. Stat. 1906, § 2488.

Illinois: Hurd's Rev. Stat. 1913, ch. 30, § 30, p. 534; Haworth v. Taylor, 108 Ill. 275; Kiser v. Heuston, 38 Ill. 252; Madlener v. Ruesch, 91

The record as notice dates from the moment the deed was left for record, and was indorsed by the recorder and entered upon the index

Ill. App. 391; Jummel v. Mann, 80 Ill. App. 288.

Indiana: Nichol v. Henry, 89 Ind. 54; Gilchrist v. Gough, 63 Ind. 576, 30 Am. Rep. 250; Kessler v. State, 24 Ind. 313.

Kansas: Gen. Stat. 1909, § 2182; Lee v. Birmingham, 30 Kans. 312, 1 Pac. 73; Poplin v. Mundell, 27 Kans. 138.

Kentucky: Webb v. Austin, 22 Ky. L. 764, 58 S. W. 808; Bank v. Haggin, 1 A. K. Marsh. (Ky.) 306.

Louisiana: Merrick's Code 1913, §§ 2262, 2264. The law governing the recording of mortgages is different from that governing the registry of conveyances, in that a mortgage is not recorded until actually inscribed in the book of mortgages. Schneidau v. New Orleans Land Co., 132 La. 264, 61 So. 225.

Massachusetts: Gillespie v. Rogers, 146 Mass. 610, 16 N. E. 711; Jacobs v. Denison, 141 Mass. 117, 5 N. E. 526.

Michigan: Sinclair v. Slawson, 44 Mich. 123, 38 Am. Rep. 235; People v. Bristol, 35 Mich. 28.

Minnesota: A mortgage is presumed to have been recorded the day it was filed. Stat. 1913, § 6844 et seq.

Mississippi: Code 1906, § 2788. Mangold v. Barlow, 61 Miss. 593, 48 Am. Rep. 84.

Missouri: Bishop v. Schneider, 46 Mo. 472, 2 Am. Rep. 533; Harrold v. Simonds, 9 Mo. 323.

Montana: Civ. Code 1895, § 1591; Donald v. Beals, 57 Cal. 399.

Nebraska: Comp. Stats. 1885, ch. 73, § 15; Ann. Stat. 1911, § 10815; Deming v. Miles, 35 Nebr. 739, 53 N. W. 665, 37 Am. St. 464; Perkins v. Strong, 22 Nebr. 725, 36 N. W. 292.

Nevada: Comp Laws 1900, § 2664.

New Mexico: Comp. Laws 1897, § 3954.

New York: Birdseye's Consol. Laws 1910, Real Property Law, § 317; Mutual L. Ins. Co. v. Dake, 87 N. Y. 257; Bedford v. Tupper, 30 Hun (N. Y.) 174; Simonson v. Falihee, 25 Hun (N. Y.) 570.

North Carolina: Bostic v. Young, 116 N. Car. 766, 21 S. E. 552; Davis v. Whitaker, 114 N. Car. 279, 19 S. E. 699, 41 Am. St. 793; Parker v. Scott, 64 N. Car. 118; Metts v. Bright, 4 Dev. & B. (N. Car.) 173, 32 Am. Dec. 683.

Ohio: Bercaw v. Cockerill, 20 Ohio St. 163; Hoffman v. Mackall, 5 Ohio St. 124, 64 Am. Dec. 637; Tousley v. Tousley, 5 Ohio St. 78; Bloom v. Noggle, 4 Ohio St. 45; Fosdick v. Barr, 3 Ohio St. 471; Brown v. Kirkman, 1 Ohio St. 116; Mayhem v. Coombs, 14 Ohio 428; Magee v. Beatty, 8 Ohio 396.

Oregon: Laws 1910, § 7127.

Pennsylvania: Farabee v. McKerrihan, 172 Pa. St. 234, 33 Atl. 583, 51 Am. St. 734; Clader v. Thomas, 89 Pa. St. 343; Glading v. Frick, 88 Pa. St. 460; Brooke's Appeal, 64 Pa. St. 127.

Rhode Island: Nichols v. Reynolds, 1 R. I. 30, 36 Am. Dec. 238.

South Dakota: Parrish v. Mahany, 10 S. Dak. 276, 73 N. W. 97, 66 Am. St. 715.

Tennessee: Code 1896, § 3749; Woodward v. Boro, 16 Lea (Tenn.) 678.

Texas: Rev. Stat. 1879, § 4334; Sayles' Stat. 1914, § 6828; Harrison v. McMurry, 71 Tex. 122, 8 S. W. 612; Belbaze v. Ratto, 69 Tex. 636, 7 S. W. 501; Copelin v. Shuler (Tex.), 6 S. W. 668; Hudson v. Randolph, 66 Fed. 216, 13 C. C. A. 402.

Vermont: Bigelow v. Topliff, 25 Vt. 273, 60 Am. Dec. 264.

Virginia: Horsley v. Garth, 2 Grat. (Va.) 471, 44 Am. Dec. 393.

Washington: Remington's Code 1910, § 8781.

Wisconsin: St. Croix Land &c. Co. v. Ritchie, 73 Wis. 409, 41 N. W. 345; Pringle v. Dunn, 37 Wis. 449, 19 Am. Rep. 772; Shove v. Larsen, 22 Wis. 142. But in this state the mere filing of the deed, without entering it in the index or reception book, is not a record; International Life Ins. Co. v. Scales, 27 Wis. 640; though the deed be transcribed at length upon the record, Lombard

or entry book, although it was not actually spread upon the record for months, or for any length of time afterward,[3] or was lost and not recorded at all.[4] The entry in the entry book is constructive notice until the deed is spread in full upon the record.[5] It may be kept in the office and referred to until it is transcribed, and the original deed so filed is notice to all the world.[6] When it is spread upon the record, however, it is notice of only what appears upon the record.[7] A presumption in favor of the record will prevail against the testimony of a subsequent purchaser or mortgagee that, at the time of filing his deed for record, no incumbrance upon the property appeared of record.[8]

The record is not defective for the reason that a portion of it was printed instead of being written with pen and ink.[9]

§ 505. **Sufficiency of deposit for registration.**—To constitute a valid filing for record a mortgage or other instrument must be delivered at the recording office, and delivery elsewhere will not render the

v. Culberston, 59 Wis. 433, 18 N. W. 399.

Contrary to the general rule see Iowa: Nickson v. Blair, 59 Iowa 531, 13 N. W. 641; Yerger v. Barz, 56 Iowa 77, 8 N. W. 769.

Wyoming: Comp. Stat. 1910, § 3653. See post §§ 550, 551.

[3] Franklin v. Cannon, 1 Root (Conn.) 500; Benson v. Callaway, 80 Ga. 230, 4 S. E. 851; Kiser v. Heuston, 38 Ill. 252; Bank v. Haggin, 1 A. K. Marsh. (Ky.) 306; Sinclair v. Slawson, 44 Mich. 123, 38 Am. Rep. 235; Wood's Appeal, 82 Pa. St. 116; Brooke's Appeal, 64 Pa. St. 127; Musser v. Hyde, 2 Watts & S. (Pa.) 314; Crews v. Taylor, 56 Tex. 461; Throckmorton v. Price, 28 Tex. 605, 91 Am. Dec. 334; Lane v. Duchac, 73 Wis. 646, 41 N. W. 962.

In Georgia, under the Code, §§ 267, 1957, a mortgage is not recorded until it is actually spread upon the record.

In Texas the cases of Taylor v. Harrison, 47 Tex. 454, 26 Am. Rep. 304, and Woodson v. Allen, 54 Tex. 551, are not consistent with the decisions in the same state cited above. It has been suggested that the apparent conflict in these decisions may have arisen from the fact that, in the cases first cited, the

deeds remained in the recorder's hands, but in the last named cases may have been taken away by the grantees.

In Wisconsin the record of a deed or mortgage becomes effective only when the index entries prescribed by statute have been made. When properly indexed the record relates back to the time of filing. Pringle v. Dunn, 37 Wis. 449, 19 Am. Rep. 772; International Life Ins. Co. v. Scales, 27 Wis. 640; Webb on Record of Title, § 16.

[4] Lee v. Bermingham, 30 Kans. 312, 1 Pac. 73; Perkins v. Strong, 22 Nebr. 725, 36 N. W. 292; Marlet v. Hinman, 77 Wis. 136, 45 N. W. 953, 20 Am. St. 102.

[5] Sinclair v. Slawson, 44 Mich. 123, 6 N. W. 207, 38 Am. Rep. 235.

[6] Nichols v. Reynolds, 1 R. I. 30, 36 Am. Dec. 238; Bigelow v. Topliff, 25 Vt. 273, 60 Am. Dec. 264.

[7] Donald v. Beals, 57 Cal. 399; Hatch v. Haskins, 17 Maine 391; Potter v. Dooley, 55 Vt. 512. See post §§ 549, 550.

[8] Vandercook v. Baker, 48 Iowa 199.

[9] Maxwell v. Hartmann, 50 Wis. 660, 8 N. W. 103. See also Caldwell v. Center, 30 Cal. 539, 89 Am. Dec. 131 (record in pencil insufficient).

record operative, although the officer indorse it as filed.[10] But a delivery at the proper office to a person in charge, is good although made after the usual office hours.[11] A deed is sufficiently recorded by depositing it with the person in charge of the registration office, though such person be neither the official recorder nor a deputy of his, for the recorder is responsible for the acts of the person whom he has placed in charge of the office, and the acts of such person in custody of the records are the acts of the recorder.[12]

The registration of a conveyance being purely a ministerial act, the recorder is not disqualified from acting by reason of his being a party to the deed.[13] The recorder is usually required by statute to attest the record by his signature, but in the absence of such requirement a copy of the record is admissible in evidence though this has not been signed by the officer.[14]

A mortgage or other instrument must be filed with the intention that it should be recorded; and if filed with instructions to the officer not to record it until further notice, it will not be considered recorded until such direction is given,[15] even though the recorder may have in-

---

[10] Edwards v. Grand, 121 Cal. 254, 53 Pac. 796. See also Withrow v. Citizens' Bank, 55 Kans. 378, 40 Pac. 639; Kalb v. Wise, 5 Ohio 533, 5 Ohio N. P. 5; Matter of Jones, 2 Ohio Dec. 409, 7 Ohio N. P. 225; Horsley v. Garth, 2 Grat. (Va.) 471, 44 Am. Dec. 393.

[11] Edwards v. Grand, 121 Cal. 254, 53 Pac. 796.

[12] Cook v. Hall, 6 Ill. 575; Orne v. Barstow, 175 Mass. 193, 55 N. E. 896; Deming v. Miles, 35 Nebr. 739, 53 N. W. 665, 37 Am. St. 464; Deane v. Hutchinson, 40 N. J. Eq. 83, 2 Atl. 292; Stewart v. Beale, 68 N. Y. 629, aff'g. 7 Hun 405; Dodge v. Potter, 18 Barb. (N. Y.) 193; Bishop v. Cook, 13 Barb. (N. Y.) 326; Maley v. Tipton, 2 Head (Tenn.) 403; Fairbanks v. Davis, 50 Vt. 251; Houghton v. Burnham, 22 Wis. 301. But see in regard to entry made by an unauthorized person, Pearson v. Powell, 100 N. Car. 86, 6 S. E. 188. The instrument should be delivered to the official recorder or his deputy. Wilson v. Eifler, 11 Heisk. (Tenn.) 179; Conant's Estate, 43 Ore. 530, 73 Pac. 1018. In Vermont an assistant clerk can act only when the clerk is absent or disabled, and can not receive an instrument for record when the clerk is present. Blair v. Ritchie, 72 Vt. 311, 47 Atl. 1074. Where no one is in charge of the office, it is not sufficient to leave the instrument there with the recording fee; and if it is not recorded until several days later, the record will take effect only from the actual recording. Crouse v. Johnson, 65 Hun 337, 47 N. Y. St. 559, 20 N. Y. S. 177.

[13] Tessier v. Hall, 7 Mart. (O. S.) (La.) 411; Brockenborough v. Melton, 55 Tex. 493. For the same reason the recorder may appoint a deputy to act in his stead. Dodge v. Potter, 18 Barb. (N. Y.) 193.

[14] Wilt v. Cutler, 38 Mich. 189.

[15] Bowen v. Fassett, 37 Ark. 507; Haworth v. Taylor, 108 Ill. 275; Town v. Griffith, 17 N. H. 165; Gibson v. Thomas, 85 App. Div. 243, 83 N. Y. S. 552, affd. 180 N. Y. 483, 73 N. E. 484, 70 L. R. A. 768; Conant's Estate, 43 Ore. 530, 73 Pac. 1018; Turberville v. Fowler, 101 Tenn. 88, 46 S. W. 577; Hunt v. Allen, 73 Vt. 322, 50 Atl. 1103; Blair v. Ritchie, 72 Vt. 311, 47 Atl. 1074. See also Dedman v. Earle, 52 Ark. 164, 12 S. W. 330 (chattel mortgage).

dorsed the time of receiving it.[16] If the officer records it without further directions the record will not constitute notice;[17] but it may become effective by a subsequent ratification.[18]

If a grantee withdraws an instrument from the recorder's office, after it has been filed for record, but before it has been copied into the record books, the operation of the record is suspended until its return,[19] and the purpose or reason for such withdrawal is immaterial.[20] But the record again becomes effective when the instrument is returned to the office.[21]

§ 506.   **Payment of recording fees as prerequisite to valid record.**— The payment of the recording fees is not a prerequisite to a valid record of a deed, if the recorder receives it for record. If he waives his right to a prepayment of such fees, he is bound to make a proper record of the deed,[22] and the record will be valid.[23] Under a statutory provision that no deed shall be admitted to record until the fee for recording is paid, the recording officer is not bound to receive a deed for record until the fee has been paid.[24] Even such a provision is regarded merely as directory, and the record is valid. The recorder in such case assumes the fee or tax,[25] and may obtain reimbursement from the person depositing the instrument for record.[26]

[16] Town v. Griffith, 17 N. H. 165.

[17] Haworth v. Taylor, 108 Ill. 275; Brigham v. Brown, 44 Mich. 59, 6 N. W. 97; Blair v. Ritchie, 72 Vt. 311, 47 Atl. 1074. But see Mercantile Co-Operative Bank v. Brown, 96 Va. 614, 32 S. E. 64.

[18] Blair v. Ritchie, 72 Vt. 311, 47 S. E. 1074.

[19] Lawton v. Gordon, 37 Cal. 202; Kiser v. Heuston, 38 Ill. 252; Yerger v. Barz, 56 Iowa 77, 8 N. W. 769; Webb v. Austin, 22 Ky. L. 764, 58 S. W. 808; Jones v. Parker, 73 Maine 248; Clamorgan v. Lane, 9 Mo. 446; Ward v. Watson, 24 Nebr. 592, 39 N. W. 615; Hickman v. Perrin, 6 Coldw. (Tenn.) 135; Johnson v. Burden, 40 Vt. 567, 94 Am. Dec. 436. See also Murray v. Zeller (N. J.), 59 Atl. 261. An unauthorized removal of the instrument by, a third person without the knowledge of the grantee will not prejudice the record. Parrish v. Mahany, 10 S. Dak. 276, 73 N. W. 97, 66 Am. St. 715; Parker v. Panhandle Nat. Bank, 11 Tex. Civ. App. 702, 34 S. W. 196. See also Marlet v. Hinman, 77 Wis. 136, 45 N. W. 953, 20

Am. St. 102 (record of instrument lost through officer's fault not prejudiced).

[20] Worcester Nat. Bank v. Cheeney, 87 Ill. 602. But see Wilson v. Leslie, 20 Ohio 161.

[21] Woodruff v. Phillips, 10 Mich. 500.

[22] Bussing v. Crain, 8 B. Mon. (Ky.) 593; People v. Bristol, 35 Mich. 28; Ridley v. McGehee, 2 Dev. (N. Car.) 40; Parrish v. Mahany, 10 S. Dak. 276, 73 N. W. 97, 66 Am. St. 715.

[23] Hoffman v. Mackall, 5 Ohio St. 124, 64 Am. Dec. 637; Parrish v. Mahany, 10 S. Dak. 276, 73 N. W. 97, 66 Am. St. 715; Lucas v. Claflin, 76 Va. 269. But see Phillips v. Clark, 4 Metc. (Ky.) 348, 83 Am. Dec. 471 (subsequent purchasers not charged with notice).

[24] Cunninggim v. Peterson, 109 N. Car. 33, 13 S. E. 714.

[25] Hoffman v. Mackall, 5 Ohio St. 124, 64 Am. Dec. 637; Lucas v. Claflin, 76 Va. 269.

[26] Bussing v. Crain, 8 B. Mon. (Ky.) 593.

But where a deed is sent to a recorder by mail or otherwise to be recorded, without the fee for recording, and the recorder in consequence of not receiving the fee "pigeon-holed" it, the deed is not lodged for record so as to be notice to a subsequent bona fide creditor of the vendor.[27] If, however, the recorder receives the deed without the fees being paid, and enters it as a deed received, or indorses such entry upon the deed, and he allows the entry to stand, he can not be heard to contradict such entry upon finding that his fees are not in fact paid.[28]

In the absence of a special agreement, the mortgagor is not liable for the payment of the recording fee, since the registration of the mortgage is solely for the benefit of the mortgagee.[29]

A statute requiring the prepayment of taxes on land and proof thereof by a certificate from the county treasurer as prerequisite to the registration of a deed, has been held unconstitutional, as depriving a person of property without due process of law.[30]

§ 507.   Record of schedule, memorandum, or map annexed to deed. —A schedule, memorandum, or map referred to in a deed, and annexed to it, is a part of the deed, and must be recorded as a part of it.[31] If such schedule, memorandum, or map, be not annexed, indorsed, or otherwise made a part of the deed, it need not be recorded although referred to in the deed.[32] On the other hand, a schedule, memorandum, or map annexed to or indorsed upon a deed is not ordinarily the deed or part of it unless it is referred to in the deed.[33] Where a deed refers to a certain recorded map for description of premises conveyed, a map drawn in pencil and merely pasted between the leaves of the recorder's book, is not duly recorded, and is insufficient

[27] Dickerson v. Bowers, 42 N. J. Eq. 295, 11 Am. St. 142.

[28] Ridley v. McGehee, 2 Dev. (N. Car.) 40.

[29] The record being for the protection of the grantee, it is for him to see that the record is made, and the recording fees paid. Even in case of a mortgage, though it may be customary for a borrower to pay all the expenses attending the loan, including the fees for registering the mortgage securing the loan, the mortgagee can not hold the mortgagor liable for such fees in the absence of an agreement to pay them. Simon v. Sewell, 64 Ala. 241. A stipulation in the mortgage, that the mortgagor shall pay such fees, creates a valid lien for them. Boutwell v. Steiner, 84 Ala. 307, 4 So. 184, 5 Am. St. 375.

[30] State v. Moore, 7 Wash. 173, 34 Pac. 461.

[31] Sawyer v. Pennell, 19 Maine 167.

[32] Shirras v. Caig, 7 Cranch (U. S.) 34, 3 L. ed. 260; Chapin v. Cram, 40 Maine 561. See also Deppen v. Bogar, 7 Pa. Super. Ct. 434; Oppermann v. McGown (Tex.), 50 S. W. 1078; Glenn v. Seeley, 25 Tex. Civ. App. 523, 61 S. W. 959.

[33] McKean &c. Land Imp. Co. v. Mitchell, 35 Pa. St. 269, 78 Am. Dec. 335.

to identify the land. Since the object of the recording acts is a preservation of accurate and durable copies of instruments, a copy made in pencil is not sufficient.[34]

Where a statute provides that the parties offering a plat or map for record shall first acknowledge it, a plat of mortgaged land executed by three persons but properly acknowledged by only two, and not assented to by the mortgagee, is of no effect, where subsequent to the filing of the plat, the title to the mortgaged land passes to the mortgagee by foreclosure and he does nothing to affirm or recognize the plat.[35]

If an additional provision or agreement be indorsed upon a deed or mortgage after its execution, or be embraced in a separate paper, this should be acknowledged as a separate deed; and it is not necessary to record the deed or mortgage again in order to connect it with such additional provision, if this duly refers to the original deed or mortgage which it affects or qualifies.[36]

§ 508. Time of recording—Indorsement—Priority between mortgages recorded same day.—It is not essential to the validity of a registration, that the time of delivery to the register should be entered or indorsed on the deed or mortgage.[37] If such indorsement is made, it constitutes at least prima facie evidence of the fact and time of filing,[38] but, according to the apparent weight of authority, it is not conclusive and may be contradicted by parol evidence.[39] Numerous cases hold, however, that the certificate of the register is conclusive

---

[34] Caldwell v. Center, 30 Cal. 539, 89 Am. Dec. 131.

[35] Alton v. Fischback, 181 Ill. 396, 55 N. E. 150.

[36] Munson v. Ensor, 94 Mo. 504, 7 S. W. 108; Choteau v. Thompson, 2 Ohio St. 114.

[37] Edwards v. Grand, 121 Cal. 254, 53 Pac. 796; Metts v. Bright, 4 Dev. & B. L. (N. Car.) 173, 32 Am. Dec. 683. See also Eufaula Nat. Bank v. Pruett, 128 Ala. 470, 30 So. 731; Cook v. Hall, 1 Gil. (Ill.) 575; Thorn v. Mayer, 12 Misc. 487, 67 N. Y. St. 389, 33 N. Y. S. 664; Bishop v. Cook, 13 Barb. (N. Y.) 326; Cunninggim v. Peterson, 109 N. Car. 33, 13 S. E. 714. The rule is the same concerning chattel mortgages: Gorham v. Summers, 25 Minn. 81; Day &c. Lumber Co. v. Mack, 24 Ky. L. 640, 69 S. W. 712; Bailey v. Costello, 94 Wis. 87, 68 N. W. 663.

[38] Webb v. Austin, 22 Ky. L. 764, 58 S. W. 808. See also Merrick v. Wallace, 19 Ill. 486; Day &c. Lumber Co. v. Mack, 24 Ky. 640, 69 S. W. 712; Head v. Goodwin, 37 Maine 181; Thomas v. Hanson, 59 Minn. 274, 61 N. W. 135; Jackson v. Phillips, 9 Cow. (N. Y.) 94.

[39] Worcester Nat. Bank v. Cheeney, 87 Ill. 602; Budd v. Brooke, 3 Gill (Md.) 198, 43 Am. Dec. 321 (time of filing a question for the jury when controverted); Town v. Griffith, 17 N. H. 165; Cunninggim v. Peterson, 109 N. Car. 33, 13 S. E. 714; Kalb v. Wise, 5 Ohio Dec. 533, 5 Ohio N. P. 5; Blair v. Ritchie, 72 Vt. 311, 47 Atl. 1074; Bartlett v. Boyd, 34 Vt. 256; Horsley v. Garth, 2 Grat. (Va.) 471, 44 Am. Dec. 393. See also Edwards v. Grand, 121 Cal. 254, 53 Pac. 796.

as to the time when a mortgage deed was left for record, as between the mortgagee and a subsequent purchaser or creditor who has attached the mortgaged land subsequently to the time stated in the certificate.[40]

If the recording officer has failed to note the time of receiving a deed for record, the time may be shown by parol evidence.[41] If the mortgage be left at the registry in the absence of the recorder, and it is received and filed by a clerk in charge of the office, the filing is sufficient, though the clerk has no authority to perform the duties of the register. It is the duty of the recording officer to enter and number the mortgage, and the rights of the mortgagee can not be impaired by his omission to do so.[42] The certificate is not, however, conclusive of anything beyond the time of the receipt of the instrument for record, as, for instance, it is not conclusive that it is duly recorded.[43]

If a mortgage be left with a register with no directions to record it,[44] or with directions that it shall not be placed on record until further directions should be given, and it is recorded without such directions ever having been given, there is no effectual recording of it.[45] In such case, if directions should be subsequently received to record the mortgage, the record should be made as of the time when such instructions are received, and not as of the time when the deed was left, nor of the time when it was recorded without authority.[46]

When the time of receiving a mortgage for record as entered in the index book shows upon its face that it was not made at the time

[40] Webb v. Austin, 22 Ky. L. 764, 58 S. W. 808; Hatch v. Haskins, 17 Maine 391; Adams v. Pratt, 109 Mass. 59; Fuller v. Cunningham, 105 Mass. 442; Ames v. Phelps, 18 Pick. (Mass.) 314; Tracy v. Jenks, 15 Pick. (Mass.) 465; Bullock v. Wallingford, 55 N. H. 619; Edwards v. Barwise, 69 Tex. 84.

[41] Metts v. Bright, 4 Dev. & B. (N. Car.) 173, 32 Am. Dec. 683; Boyce v. Stanton, 15 Lea (Tenn.) 346.

[42] Dodge v. Potter, 18 Barb. (N. Y.) 193; Metts v. Bright, 4 Dev. & B. (N. Car.) 173, 32 Am. Dec. 683; Houghton v. Burnham, 22 Wis. 301. See ante §§ 504, 505.

[43] Bubose v. Young, 10 Ala. 365; Worcester Nat. Bank v. Cheeney, 87 Ill. 602; Thorp v. Merrill, 21 Minn. 336; Town v. Griffith, 17 N. H. 165; New York Life Ins. Co. v. White, 17 N. Y. 469; Jackson v. Phillips, 9 Cow. (N. Y.) 94; Cunninggim v. Peterson, 109 N. Car. 33, 13 S. E. 714; Blair v. Ritchie, 72 Vt. 311, 47 Atl. 1074; Wing v. Hall, 47 Vt. 182. See also Budd v. Brooke, 3 Gill (Md.) 198, 43 Am. Dec. 321; Bartlett v. Boyd, 34 Vt. 256; Horsley v. Garth, 2 Grat. (Va.) 471, 44 Am. Dec. 393.

[44] Horsley v. Garth, 2 Grat. (Va.) 471, 44 Am. Dec. 393.

[45] Bowen v. Fassett, 37 Ark. 507; Haworth v. Taylor, 108 Ill. 275; Gibson v. Thomas, 85 App. Div. 243, 83 N. Y. S. 552, affd. 180 N. Y. 483, 73 N. E. 484, 70 L. R. A. 768; Hunt v. Allen, 73 Vt. 322, 50 Atl. 1103.

[46] Bowen v. Fassett, 37 Ark. 507; Yerger v. Barz, 56 Iowa 77, 8 N. W. 769; Brigham v. Brown, 44 Mich. 59, 6 N. W. 97; Town v. Griffith, 17 N. H. 165.

of such reception, the presumption of the correctness of the register's entry is lost,[47] and parol evidence is admissible to show when the deed was actually received for record. The filing of a mortgage for record affords no notice if the deed be withdrawn before it is recorded.[48]

As between two mortgagees, whose mortgages are executed and recorded on the same day, that which was first delivered for record has priority,[49] and parol evidence is admissible to show which was first deposited for record.[50] To ascertain which is prior, the fractional parts of a day are considered, and the legal fiction that there are no fractions of a day does not preclude such determination of priority.[51] The indorsements on different trust deeds, by the recording officer, of their numbers and time of filing for record, is to be regarded as indicating their priority, since each instrument takes effect from the time of filing it for record.[52] To avoid the effect of the recording act, which gives priority among mortgages executed by the same party at the same time, according to their order of record, it must clearly appear that all the mortgages were in fact executed at the same time, and that it was agreed by the parties taking the mortgages that they should be equal liens.[53] In case no entry is made upon the record of the time of the recording of the mortgage, when the law of a state required no such entry, and it appears from the record to have been recorded at an early day, it will be presumed that the record was made within the time required by law after the execution of it.[54]

As between two mortgages acknowledged the same day and recorded the same day and hour, mortgaging the same premises to secure two notes made payable to the same nominal payee, for convenience in negotiating them, that one is entitled to priority which is first entered

---

[47] Metts v. Bright, 4 Dev. & B. (N. Car.) 173, 32 Am. Dec. 683; Hay v. Hill, 24 Wis. 235.

[48] Worcester Nat. Bank v. Cheeney, 87 Ill. 602; Clamorgan v. Lane, 9 Mo. 442; Hickman v. Perrin, 6 Cold. (Tenn.) 135; Lawton v. Gordon, 37 Cal. 202. Under the California statute, Civil Code, §§ 1170, 1213, notice is not imparted until the instrument is spread upon the record in the proper book, but when this is done it relates back to the time of deposit for record. Watkins v. Wilhoit (Cal.), 35 Pac. 646.

[49] Brookfield v. Goodrich, 32 Ill. 363; Boone v. Telles, 2 Ill. App.

539; Spaulding v. Scanland, 6 B. Mon. (Ky.) 353.

[50] Boone v. Telles, 2 Bradw. (Ill.) 539; Spaulding v. Scanland, 6 B. Mon. (Ky.) 353.

[51] New England Mtg. Sec. Co. v. Fry, 143 Ala. 637, 42 So. 57, 111 Am. St. 62; Lemon v. Staats, 1 Cow. (N. Y.) 592. See also Wood v. Lordier, 115 Ind. 519, 18 N. E. 34; Gibson v. Keyes, 112 Ind. 568, 14 N. E. 591.

[52] Madlener v. Ruesch, 91 Ill. App. 391.

[53] White v. Leslie, 54 How. Pr. (N. Y.) 394.

[54] Hall v. Tunnell, 1 Houst. (Del.) 320.

and numbered by the recorder for record and which secures the note bearing the earlier date, if such mortgage is the first one transferred for value.[55]

§ 509. Time of recording—After death of mortgagor.

—Generally, a mortgage may be recorded at any time after its execution, and the record will be effective against all subsequent claims,[56] unless there has been unreasonable delay or laches.[57] A mortgage may be recorded after the death of the mortgagor, if he has in his lifetime made delivery of it. His general creditors can not for that reason claim that the mortgage was inoperative as against them.[58] The recording of a deed is no part of its execution. Neither does a lien attach to the real estate of a debtor in favor of his general creditors immediately upon his death, as against the specific lien of the mortgage which was good against the mortgagor. His heirs take the estate upon his decease subject to the incumbrance; and the lien of the general creditors, which is merely a right to have the real estate in the hands of the heirs applied for their benefit upon a deficiency of the personal assets, attaches to it in the same condition.[59]

In like manner a mortgage executed and delivered before a general assignment of the mortgagor for the benefit of his creditors, or before his bankruptcy, if valid in other respects, is valid against the assignment or the bankruptcy, though not recorded until afterward.[60]

A mortgagor, having borrowed money upon his business property, continued in business deriving credit from the ownership of the property which was apparently unincumbered. Upon his death several years after, the mortgagee discovered that the mortgage, which he had

---

[55] Fischer v. Tuchy, 186 Ill. 143, 57 N. E. 801, affg. 87 Ill. App. 574.

[56] Finley v. Spratt, 14 Bush (Ky.) 225; Citizens' Bank v. Ferry, 32 La. Ann. 310; Herman v. Clark (Tenn.), 39 S. W. 873. See also for application of the rule to chattel mortgages: Hope v. Johnston, 28 Fla. 55, 9 So. 830; Reese v. Taylor, 25 Fla. 283, 5 So. 821; Roe v. Meding, 53 N. J. Eq. 350, 33 Atl. 394. The rule applies even where the statute requires recording "forthwith" or "immediately." Gibson v. Warden, 14 Wall. (U. S.) 244, 20 L. ed. 797; McVay v. English, 30 Kans. 368, 1 Pac. 795; Roe v. Meding, 53 N. J. Eq. 350, 33 Atl. 394; Wilson v. Leslie, 20 Ohio 161; Maverick v. Bohemian Club (Tex.), 36 S. W. 147;

Moore v. Masterson, 19 Tex. Civ. App. 308, 46 S. W. 855; Vickers v. Carnohan, 4 Tex. Civ. App. 305, 23 S. W. 338.

[57] Kappes v. Rutherford Park Assn., 60 N. J. Eq. 129, 46 Atl. 218. See also Longworth v. Close, 1 McLean (U. S.) 282, Fed. Cas. No. 8489; Reese v. Taylor, 25 Fla. 283, 5 So. 821.

[58] Haskell v. Bissell, 11 Conn. 174; Gill v. Pinney, 12 Ohio St. 38; Herman v. Clark (Tenn.), 39 S. W. 873; McCandlish v. Keen, 13 Grat. (Va.) 615. See also Terry v. Briggs, 12 Metc. (Mass.) 17.

[59] Gill v. Pinney, 12 Ohio St. 38.

[60] Mellon's Appeal, 32 Pa. St. 121; Wyckoff v. Remsen, 11 Paige (N. Y.) 564.

instructed the mortgagor to record, had not been recorded, and recorded it prior to any contemplation of insolvency of the mortgagor's estate. It was held that the mortgage constituted a valid lien which was prior to that of the mortgagor's creditors.[61]

§ 510. **Place of record.**—The registration must be made in the registry district within which the land lies, which is generally a county, but in Connecticut and Vermont is a town. In some of the new states and territories in which there is territory which is not yet organized into counties, special provision is made for the recording of deeds of lands lying within such unorganized territory, as by providing that the record shall be made in the county to which such unorganized territory is attached for judicial purposes. And it has been accordingly decided by a federal court that land lying in an unorganized county is to be regarded for all purposes, including registry, as being within the territorial limits of a county to which it is attached for judicial purposes.[62]

After the organization of a new county, a deed or mortgage properly recorded under the law as it existed at the time of the record need not be recorded anew;[63] but a deed that had been executed but not recorded, at the time of the organization of a new county, should be recorded in that county.[64] Where a county is divided into two districts, each district stands as a separate county for purposes of registration; and a mortgage recorded in one district on property situated in the other is not effective against a subsequent mortgage properly recorded in the district where the property is located.[65]

If the land embraced in a deed is situated in more than one county, the deed should be recorded in each county in which any part of the land is situated; otherwise the grantee will not be protected as to that

---

[61] Herman v. Clark (Tenn.), 39 S. W. 873.

[62] Thayer v. Herrick, Fed. Cas. No. 13868.

[63] Chambers v. Haney, 45 La. Ann. 447, 12 So. 621; Parish Board v. Edrington, 40 La. Ann. 633, 4 So. 574; Ellison v. Iler, 22 La. Ann. 470; Hayden v. Nutt, 4 La. Ann. 65; Thomas v. Hanson, 59 Minn. 274, 61 N. W. 135; Koerper v. St. Paul &c. R. Co., 40 Minn. 132, 41 N. E. 656; Bivings v. Gosnell, 133 N. Car. 574, 45 S. E. 942; Hill v. Grant (Tex.), 44 S. W. 1016; Trimble v. Edwards, 84 Tex. 497, 19 S. W. 772; Jones v. Powers, 65 Tex. 207; McKissick v.

Colquhoun, 18 Tex. 148; Williamson v. Work, 33 Tex. Civ. App. 369, 77 S. W. 266. See also Stebbins v. Duncan, 108 U. S. 32, 27 L. ed. 641, 2 Sup. Ct. 313; Lumpkin v. Muncey, 66 Tex. 311, 17 S. W. 732.

[64] Astor v. Wells, 4 Wheat. (U. S.) 466, 4 L. ed. 616; Beaver v. Frick County, 53 Ark. 18, 13 S. W. 134; Green v. Green, 103 Cal. 108, 37 Pac. 188; Garrison v. Haydon, 1 J. J. Marsh. (Ky.) 222, 19 Am. Dec. 70; Geer v. Missouri Lumber &c. Co., 134 Mo. 85, 34 S. W. 1099, 56 Am. St. 489.

[65] Beaver v. Frick County, 53 Ark. 18, 13 S. W. 134.

part of the land lying in the county where the instrument is not recorded.[66] But where a statute only requires a deed to be recorded in the county where a body of land or part thereof lies, registration in either county is sufficient.[67]

It is intended that the registry laws shall enable a person interested in the title to land to ascertain from the records of the county, or other registry district within which the land is situate, what conveyances there are affecting that land. The recording of a deed in a county other than that in which the land is situated does not operate as constructive notice.[68] Thus, where a new county had been created, and a grantee, not being advised of the change, recorded his deed in the old county, instead of the new, the registration was declared worthless as notice.[69]

A subsequent change of the county boundaries by which the land becomes a part of another county does not impose upon the grantee the duty of recording his deed again in such other county.[70] A subsequent discovery made in running a boundary line between two counties or parishes, that mortgaged lands in fact lie beyond the true boundary of the county or parish in which they were supposed to be situated and where the mortgage was recorded, does not affect the

[66] Ludlow v. Clinton Line R. Co., 1 Flip. (U. S.) 25, Fed. Cas. No. 8600; Van Meter v. Knight, 32 Minn. 205, 20 N. W. 142; Harper v. Tapley, 35 Miss. 506; Wells v. Wells, 47 Barb. (N. Y.) 416; Oberholtzer's Appeal, 124 Pa. St. 583, 17 Atl. 143.

[67] Clayton v. Exchange Bank, 121 Fed. 630, 57 C. C. A. 656; Conn v. Manifee, 2 A. K. Marsh. (Ky.) 396, 12 Am. Dec. 417; Day &c. Lumber Co. v. Mack, 24 Ky. L. 640, 69 S. W. 712; Shiveley v. Gilpin, 23 Ky. L. 2090, 66 S. W. 763; Rice v. Sally, 176 Mo. 107, 75 S. W. 398; Perry v. Clift (Tenn.), 54 S. W. 121; Hancock v. Tram Lumber Co., 65 Tex. 225; Mattfeld v. Huntington, 17 Tex. Civ. App. 716, 43 S. W. 53; Brown v. Lazarus, 5 Tex. Civ. App. 81, 25 S. W. 71.

[68] Lewis v. Baird, 3 McLean (U. S.) 56; Beaver v. Frick County, 53 Ark. 18, 13 S. W. 134; St. John v. Conger, 40 Ill. 535; Harang v. Plattsmier, 21 La. Ann. 426; Harper v. Tapley, 35 Miss. 506; Moore v. Davey, 1 N. Mex. 303; King v.

Portis, 77 N. Car. 25; Oberholtzer's Appeal, 124 Pa. St. 583, 17 Atl. 143; Cole v. Ward, 79 S. Car. 573, 61 S. E. 108; Adams v. Hayden, 60 Tex. 223; Hawley v. Bullock, 29 Tex. 216; Perrin v. Reed, 35 Vt. 2; Blackford v. Hurst, 26 Grat. (Va.) 203; Horsley v. Garth, 2 Grat. (Va.) 471, 44 Am. Dec. 393; Pollard v. Lively, 2 Grat. (Va.) 216; Stewart v. McSweeney, 14 Wis. 468. See also Clayton v. Exchange Bank, 121 Fed. 630, 57 C. C. A. 656; Taylor v. McDonald, 2 Bibb (Ky.) 420; Coney v. Laird, 153 Mo. 408, 55 S. W. 96 (erroneous transcription of name of county in a trust deed recorded in proper county, immaterial); Hunt v. Swayze, 55 N. J. L. 33, 25 Atl. 850; Brown v. Edson, 23 Vt. 435.

[69] Astor v. Wells, 4 Wheat. (U. S.) 466, 4 L. ed. 616.

[70] Garrison v. Haydon, 1 J. J. Marsh. (Ky.) 222, 19 Am. Dec. 70; Koerper v. St. Paul &c. R. Co., 40 Minn. 132, 41 N. W. 656; Jones v. Powers, 65 Tex. 207; Melton v. Turner, 38 Tex. 81.

validity of such mortgage.[71] But if the county lines have never been established, the grantee must at his peril ascertain in what county the land is situated.[72]

When a deed already recorded is recorded in another county, the certificate of the recorder of the prior record is not a part of the deed, and need not be copied in the second record.[73]

§ 511. Special books for record of mortgages.

—When it is provided that mortgages shall be recorded in books kept for that purpose separate from other instruments, a mortgage recorded as a deed is not effectual as against subsequent bona fide purchasers or mortgagees; even if the mortgage be in form an absolute deed, but intended as security for a loan of money.[74] If a mortgage is not recorded in the mortgage books, it can not be found by means of the index to those books, and therefore is not regarded as properly recorded.[75] Such a deed is of course valid as between the parties,[76] and, though the record is a nullity, it becomes operative in case the mortgagee afterward acquires the equity of redemption.[77]

---

[71] Stewart v. Walsh, 23 La. Ann. 560; Cumming v. Blossatt, 2 La. Ann. 794.

[72] Jones v. Powers, 65 Tex. 207.

[73] Stinnett v. House, 1 Tex. Unrep. Cas. 484.

[74] Kent v. Williams, 146 Cal. 3, 79 Pac. 527; Cady v. Purser, 131 Cal. 552, 63 Pac. 844, 82 Am. St. 391; Baker v. Lee, 49 La. Ann. 874, 21 So. 588; Cordeviolle v. Dawson, 26 La. Ann. 534; Colomer v. Morgan, 13 La. Ann. 202; Grand Rapids Nat. Bank v. Ford, 143 Mich. 402, 107 S. W. 76, 114 Am. St. 668 (absolute deed intended as a mortgage); Gordon v. Constantine Hydraulic Co., 117 Mich. 620, 76 N. W. 142 (lease containing mortgage clause); Deane v. Hutchinson, 40 N. J. Eq. 83, 2 Atl. 292; Parsons v. Lent, 34 N. J. Eq. 67; Williamson v. New Jersey Southern R. Co., 29 N. J. Eq. 311; Purdy v. Huntington, 42 N. Y. 334, 1 Am. Rep. 532; Gillig v. Maass, 28 N. Y. 191; Stoddard v. Rotton, 5 Bosw. (N. Y.) 378; James v. Morey, 2 Cow. (N. Y.) 246, 6 Johns. Ch. (N. Y.) 417, 14 Am. Dec. 475; Bank for Savings v. Frank, 54 How. Pr. (N. Y.) 403, 45 Sup. Ct. 404; Clute v. Robison, 2 Johns. (N. Y.) 595; Dey v. Dunham, 2 Johns, Ch. (N. Y.) 182, 15 Johns. 555; Grimstone v. Carter, 3 Paige (N. Y.) 421, 24 Am. Dec. 230; White v. Moore, 1 Paige (N. Y.) 551; Warner v. Winslow, 1 Sandf. Ch. (N. Y.) 430; Brown v. Dean, 3 Wend. (N. Y.) 208; Howells v. Hettrick, 13 App. Div. 366, 43 N. Y. S. 183; Van Thorniley v. Peters, 26 Ohio St. 471; Calder v. Chapman, 52 Pa. St. 359, 91 Am. Dec. 163; Luch's Appeal, 44 Pa. St. 519; Drake v. Reggel, 10 Utah 376, 37 Pac. 583; Knowlton v. Walker, 13 Wis. 264. See also Neslin v. Wells, 104 U. S. 428, 26 L. ed. 802; Ivey v. Dawley, 50 Fla. 537, 39 So. 498. The New York statute providing for the recording of mortgages in separate books expressly includes, also, conveyances absolute in terms, but intended as mortgages. Birdseye's Consol. Laws 1910, Real Property Law, § 315, p. 5106. See ante § 457 for statutes.

[75] Luch's Appeal, 44 Pa. St. 519.

[76] James v. Morey, 6 Johns. Ch. (N. Y.) 417, 2 Cow. 246, 14 Am. Dec. 475; Swepson v. Bank, 9 Lea (Tenn.) 713.

[77] Warner v. Winslow, 1 Sandf. Ch. (N. Y.) 430; Grellet v. Heilshorn, 4 Nev. 526; Parsons v. Lunt, 34 N. J. Eq. 67.

A subsequent purchaser or mortgagee, who has actual notice of a mortgage which is improperly recorded as an absolute conveyance, of course takes a title subject to such mortgage, just as he would if the mortgage were not recorded at all. A statute which is merely directory to the recorder in this respect would not invalidate a record of the mortgage not made in the record books specially used for mortgages.[78]

A deed which is in fact a mortgage is entitled to be recorded according to its real rather than its apparent character,[79] and accordingly the courts of several states have held that an absolute deed intended as a mortgage must be recorded in the book of mortgages in order for the record to be effective.[80] But the weight of authority seems to be that the recording of such instrument in the book of deeds is sufficient, although the defeasance rests in parol or in a separate agreement not recorded.[81] Various reasons have been assigned in sup-

[78] Smith v. Smith, 13 Ohio St. 532. See also Haseltine v. Espey, 13 Ore. 301, 10 Pac. 423; Clader v. Thomas, 89 Pa. St. 343; Glading v. Frick, 88 Pa. St. 460; Downing v. Glen Rock Oil Co., 207 Pa. St. 455, 56 Atl. 995.

[79] Shaw v. Wilshire, 65 Maine 485; Nicklin v. Betts Spring Co., 11 Ore. 406, 5 Pac. 51, 50 Am. Rep. 477.

[80] Ives v. Stone, 51 Conn. 446; Stearns v. Porter, 46 Conn. 313; Hart v. Chalker, 14 Conn. 77; North v. Belden, 13 Conn. 376, 35 Am. Dec. 83; Cordeviolle v. Dawson, 26 La. Ann. 534; Purdy v. Huntington, 42 N. Y. 343, 1 Am. Rep. 532; Gillig v. Maass, 28 N. Y. 191; Jackson v. Van Valkenburgh, 8 Cow. (N. Y.) 260; James v. Morey, 2 Cow. (N. Y.) 246, 14 Am. Dec. 475; Dey v. Dunham, 2 Johns. Ch. (N. Y.) 182; Grimstone v. Carter, 3 Paige (N. Y.) 421, 24 Am. Dec. 230; White v. Moore, 1 Paige (N. Y.) 551; Warner v. Winslow, 1 Sandf. Ch. (N. Y.) 430; Brown v. Dean, 3 Wend. (N. Y.) 208; Gregory v. Perkins, 15 N. Car. 50; Williams v. Purcell (Okla.), 145 Pac. 1151; Calder v. Chapman, 52 Pa. St. 359, 91 Am. Dec. 163; Edwards v. Trumbull, 50 Pa. St. 509; In re Luch's Appeal, 44 Pa. St. 519; Hendrickson's Appeal, 24 Pa. St. 363; Friedley v. Hamilton, 17 Serg. & R. (Pa.) 70, 17 Am. Dec. 638; Manufacturers' &c. Bank v. Bank of Pennsylvania, 7 Watts & S.

(Pa.) 335, 42 Am. Dec. 240; McLanahan v. Reeside, 9 Watts (Pa.) 508, 36 Am. Dec. 136. See also Gulley v. Macy, 84 N. Car. 434; Halcombe v. Ray, 1 Ired. L. (N. Car.) 340; Dukes v. Jones, 6 Jones L. (N. Car.) 14; Thompson v. Mack, Harr. (Mich.) 150 (under early statutes). Under Compiled Laws of Michigan, § 8981, providing for different sets of books for the recording of deeds and mortgages, and § 8988, rendering void all conveyances improperly recorded, as against subsequent purchasers; a deed absolute in form but intended as a mortgage is void against a subsequent purchaser if recorded in the book for the record of deeds instead of the record for mortgages; especially since § 8980 requires all absolute deeds not intended as mortgages to be entered in the book of deeds. Grand Rapids Nat. Bank v. Ford, 143 Mich. 402, 107 S. W. 76, 114 Am. St. 668 (quoting text).

[81] Kent v. Williams, 146 Cal. 3, 79 Pac. 527; Gibson v. Hough, 60 Ga. 588; DeWolf v. Strader, 26 Ill. 225, 79 Am. Dec. 371; Clemons v. Elder, 9 Iowa 272; Young v. Thompson, 2 Kans. 83; Ing v. Brown, 3 Md. Ch. 521; Harrison v. Phillips' Academy, 12 Mass. 456; Marston v. Williams, 45 Minn. 116, 47 N. W. 644, 22 Am. St. 719; Benton v. Nicoll, 24 Minn. 221; Bank of Mobile v. Tishomingo Sav. Inst., 62 Miss. 250; Grellet v.

port of such a record, the statutes being construed as merely directory to the recording,[82] or as designating the record books by the form rather than the substance of the instrument,[83] the argument also being advanced that an absolute deed intended as a mortgage passes title, and is at law a deed, though in equity a mortgage.[84]

Except in states whose statutes require a different construction, the record of a conveyance in the form of an absolute deed, in a book kept for the recording of deeds, ought to be held to impart effectual notice of the rights or interests conveyed, although a statute requires mortgages to be recorded in separate books.[85]

Where separate books are designated for recording mortgages of land and chattels, a mortgage including both realty and personality should be recorded in both books.[86] The recording of a mortgage upon

Heilshorn, 4 Nev. 526; Merchants' State Bank v. Tufts, 14 N. Dak. 238, 103 N. W. 760, 116 Am. St. 682; Kemper v. Campbell, 44 Ohio St. 210, 6 N. E. 566; Haseltine v. Espey, 13 Ore. 301, 10 Pac. 423; Ruggles v. Williams, 1 Head (Tenn.) 141; Kennard v. Mabry, 78 Tex. 151, 14 S. W. 272; Seymour v. Darrow, 31 Vt. 122; Gibson v. Seymour, 4 Vt. 518; Knowlton v. Walker, 13 Wis. 264. See also Kent v. Williams, 146 Cal. 3, 79 Pac. 537.

[82] Robertson v. Brown, 5 La. Ann. 154; Gillespie v. Cammack, 3 La. Ann. 248; Smith v. Smith, 13 Ohio St. 532; Kennard v. Mabry, 78 Tex. 151, 14 S. W. 272.

[83] Merchants State Bank v. Tufts, 14 N. Dak. 238, 103 N. W. 760, 116 Am. St. 682.

[84] Benton v. Nicoll, 24 Minn. 221; Kemper v. Campbell, 44 Ohio St. 210, 6 N. E. 566; Haseltine v. Espey, 13 Ore. 301, 10 Pac. 423.

[85] Kennard v. Mabry, 78 Tex. 151, 14 S. W. 272. Chief Justice Stayton said: "Every person is presumed to know that a deed absolute on its face may have been intended by the parties to it only as a mortgage, and that the courts will so hold it to be, if executed only for the purpose of securing a debt. So knowing, every person ought to be held to be affected with notice of every right, less than absolute ownership, the person holding under a deed so recorded has. If the record shows an absolute conveyance, it gives notice of the fact that the vendor has parted with all interest he had in the land, and such notice ought to be binding on a subsequent purchaser or mortgagee, who must know that, as between the parties, on proof of the fact that it was executed to secure a debt, the courts will hold it to be only a mortgage. The decisions which take this view of the question we think the better. Clemons v. Elder, 9 Iowa 272; Young v. Thompson, 2 Kans. 83; Grellet v. Heilshorn, 4 Nev. 526; Haseltine v. Espey, 13 Ore. 301, 10 Pac. 423; Nicklin v. Betts Spring Co., 11 Ore. 406, 5 Pac. 51; Ruggles v. Williams, 1 Head (Tenn.) 141."

[86] Deane v. Hutchinson, 40 N. J. Eq. 83, 2 Atl. 292; Stewart v. Beale, 7 Hun (N. Y.) 405, affd. 68 N. Y. 629; Hunt v. Allen, 73 Vt. 322, 50 Atl. 1103. See also Ward v. Ward, 131 Fed. 946; Ramsdell v. Citizens' Electric &c. Light Co., 103 Mich. 89, 61 N. W. 275; Merrill v. Ressler, 37 Minn. 82, 33 N. W. 117, 5 Am. St. 822; Hardin v. Dolge, 46 App. Div. 416, 61 N. Y. S. 753. But the record of a mortgage of both land and chattels in the book of real estate mortgages has been held sufficient. Anthony v. Butler, 13 Pet. (U. S.) 423, 10 L. ed. 229; Boyle Ice Machine Co. v. Gould, 73 Cal. 153, 14 Pac. 609. Proper entry in a series of books kept for recording instruments affecting real estate imparts constructive notice that both interests in realty and personality are con-

a building and machinery, forming part of the realty, as a chattel mortgage, does not give notice to a subsequent mortgagee of the realty.[87]

§ 512. **Powers of attorney.**—It is sometimes provided by statute that a power of attorney, under which a mortgage is executed, shall be recorded with the deed, which owes its existence to the power, and when this is the case the record of the deed without the power has no legal effect.[88] But, aside from this requirement, it is not necessary that a power should be recorded with the mortgage, or that it should be recorded at all, in order that the mortgage deed when recorded should be notice to all the world.[89]

The record of a power of attorney, when the law does not require it to be recorded, does not amount to constructive notice.[90] And so the record of a deed of trust which is defective because of an insufficient acknowledgment and an unauthorized power of attorney, does

veyed. Long v. Gorman, 100 Mo. App. 45, 79 S. W. 180. Record of a timber deed in a special book kept for such exceptional instruments, was held proper. Mee v. Benedict, 98 Mich. 260, 57 N. W. 175, 22 L. R. A. 641, 39 Am. St. 543. But a mortgage of standing timber has been held to be a mortgage of an interest in land, and the filing thereof as a chattel mortgage was not constructive notice to a subsequent purchaser from the mortgagor. Williams v. Hyde, 98 Mich. 152, 57 N. W. 98. The custom or usage of the recording officer to record mortgages of both real and personal property in the book of real estate mortgages only, was held to support the record of a mixed mortgage so entered. Anthony v. Butler, 13 Pet. (U. S.) 423, 10 L. ed. 229; Harriman v. Woburn Elec. Light Co., 163 Mass. 85, 39 N. E. 1004. See ante § 457.

[87] Peoria Stone &c. Works v. Sinclair, 146 Iowa 56, 124 N. W. 772.

[88] Carnall v. Duval, 22 Ark. 136; Stewart v. Hall, 3 B. Mon. (Ky.) 218. Powers of attorney to convey by deed generally are likewise required to be recorded. Flannery v. O'Brien, 6 Ky. L. (Abst.) 667; Taylor v. McDonald, 2 Bibb (5 Ky.) 420; Moore v. Farrow, 3 A. K. Marsh. (Ky.) 41; Graves v. Ward, 2 Duv. (Ky.) 301; Citizens' Fire

Ins. &c. Co. v. Doll, 35 Md. 89, 6 Am. Rep. 360; Oatman v. Fowler, 43 Vt. 462. See also Voorhies v. Gore, 3 B. Mon. (Ky.) 529. Under a statute providing that a power of attorney to convey land shall be recorded with the deed, the power may be recorded before the deed. Rosenthal v. Ruffin, 60 Md. 324. A copy of a power of attorney to convey land is not entitled to record and if recorded is ineffective; the power must accompany the deed upon the record. Montgomery v. Dorion, 6 N. H. 250; Oatman v. Fowler, 43 Vt. 462.

[89] Wilson v. Troup, 2 Cow. (N. Y.) 195, 14 Am. Dec. 458. The rule applies to deeds generally, and powers of attorney to convey land need not be recorded, apart from statute. Roper v. McFadden, 48 Cal. 346; Anderson v. Dugas, 29 Ga. 440 (record permitted but not required); Moore v. Pendleton, 16 Ind. 481; Rownd v. Davidson, 113 La. 1047, 37 So. 965; Valentine v. Piper, 39 Mass. 85, 33 Am. Dec. 715; Morse v. Hewett, 28 Mich. 481 (record permitted though not expressly provided for); Montgomery v. Dorion, 6 N. H. 250; Tyrrell v. O'Connor, 56 N. J. Eq. 448, 41 Atl. 674; Johnson v. Bush, 3 Barb. Ch. (N. Y.) 207; Diehl v. Stine, 1 Ohio Cir. Ct. 515.

[90] Williams v. Birbeck, Hoff. Ch. (N. Y.) 359.

not operate as constructive notice.[91] The law does not intend that to be known for the existence of which there is no legal necessity.[92]

§ 513. **Record of separate defeasance.**—When an absolute deed is given in the way of security, with a written defeasance back, the rights of the mortgagee are in general fully protected without any record of the defeasance. The recorded deed is sufficient notice of his interest.[93] In fact it is notice of a greater interest than he actually has. In some states, however, the recording of the defeasance with the deed is expressly required as a condition upon which the mortgagee shall derive any benefit from the record of the deed.[94] When the defeasance

---

[91] Lynch v. Murphy, 161 U. S. 247, 40 L. ed. 688, 16 Sup. Ct. 523.

[92] James v. Morey, 2 Cow. (N. Y.) 246, 296, 6 Johns. Ch. 417, 14 Am. Dec. 475.

[93] Ives v. Stone, 51 Conn. 446; Newberry v. Bulkley, 5 Day (Conn.) 384; McClure v. Smith, 115 Ga. 709, 42 S. E. 53; Gibson v. Hough, 60 Ga. 588; Christie v. Hale, 46 Ill. 117; Clemons v. Elder, 9 Iowa 272; Young v. Thompson, 2 Kans. 83; Bailey v. Myrick, 50 Maine 171; Jackson v. Ford, 40 Maine 381; Harrison v. Morton, 87 Md. 671, 40 Atl. 897; Ing v. Brown, 3 Md. Ch. 521; Bayley v. Bailey, 5 Gray (Mass.) 505; Marston v. Williams, 45 Minn. 116, 47 N. W. 644, 22 Am. St. 719; Butman v. James, 34 Minn. 547, 27 N. W. 66; Benton v. Nicoll, 24 Minn. 221; Bank of Mobile v. Tishomingo Sav. Inst., 62 Miss. 250; Livesey v. Brown, 35 Nebr. 111, 52 N. W. 838; Grellet v. Heilshorn, 4 Nev. 526; Kemper v. Campbell, 44 Ohio St. 210, 6 N. E. 566; Security Sav. &c. Co. v. Loewenberg, 38 Ore. 159, 62 Pac. 647; Haseltine v. Espey, 13 Ore. 301, 10 Pac. 423; Ruggles v. Williams, 1 Head (Tenn.) 141; Gibson v. Seymour, 4 Vt. 518; Knowlton v. Walker, 13 Wis. 264. See ante § 253.

[94] There are such statutes in the following named states:

Maryland: Ann. Civil Code Md. 1911, art. 66, § 1, p. 1518. The deed is not made void by neglect to record the defeasance, but the grantee derives no benefit from the record as against subsequent purchasers. Owens v. Miller, 29 Md. 144. See also Harrison v. Morton, 87 Md. 671, 40 Atl. 897; Hoffman v. Gosnell, 75 Md. 577, 24 Atl. 28; Waters v. Riggin, 19 Md. 536; Ing v. Brown, 3 Md. Ch. 521.

Nebraska: Comp. Stats. 1885, ch. 73, § 25, Stat. 1911, § 10825; Livesey v. Brown, 35 Nebr. 111, 52 N. W. 838.

New Hampshire: The defeasance must be embodied in the conveyance itself. Pub. Stat. 1901, ch. 139, § 2, p. 442.

New Jersey: Rev. Stat. 1877, p. 706, § 21, Comp. Stat. 1910, p. 3414, § 21; Essex County Nat. Bank v. Harrison, 57 N. J. Eq. 91, 40 Atl. 209; Clark v. Condit, 18 N. J. Eq. 358.

New York: Birdseye's Consol. Laws 1910, § 320; Mutual Life Ins. Co. v. Nicholas, 144 App. Div. 95, 128 N. Y. S. 902; Hoschke v. Hoschke, 42 Misc. 125, 85 N. Y. S. 1006; McAulay v. Porter, 71 N. Y. 173. See also Leavitt v. Waldemar Co., 151 N. Y. S. 832.

North Dakota: Comp. Laws 1913, §§ 6754, 6755. The same rule is judicially established in Pennsylvania. Calder v. Chapman, 52 Pa. St. 359; Corpman v. Baccastow, 84 Pa. St. 363; Edwards v. Trumbull, 50 Pa. St. 509; Luch's Appeal, 44 Pa. St. 519; Friedley v. Hamilton, 17 Serg. & R. (Pa.) 70; Jacques v. Weeks, 7 Watts (Pa.) 261; Rathfon v. Specht, 18 Pa. Co. Ct. 19. "A mortgage," says Mr. Justice Black, in Hendrick's Appeal, 24 Pa. St. 363, "when in the shape of an absolute conveyance with a separate defeasance, the former being recorded, the latter not, gives the holder no rights against a subsequent incumbrancer. It is good for nothing as a convey-

is not recorded, the obvious effect of the record of the deed alone is to make the grantee the apparent absolute owner of the estate, and the person who holds the defeasance may be barred of all right of redemption by a sale by the mortgagee to one who buys in good faith and without notice of such defeasance.

A judgment creditor of the grantor in such case can not claim that the conveyance is of the character of an unrecorded mortgage, so as to render the property subject to his judgment.[95]

Such absolute deed is in law regarded as merely a deed, and it is only in equity that effect is given to the intention of the parties that it shall operate as a security only. But judgments against such grantor or mortgagor are liens upon his equity of redemption in the premises, and an equitable action to have them so declared may be maintained against a subsequent purchaser having knowledge of the facts, and

ance, because it is in fact not a conveyance; and it is equally worthless as a mortgage, because it does not appear by the record to be a mortgage." Under the Pennsylvania statute a deed will not be construed as a mortgage unless the defeasance or other writing explaining its character is recorded. Purdon's Dig. 1905, p. 1180, § 154. Safe Deposit &c. Co. v. Linton, 213 Pa. St. 105, 62 Atl. 566; Lohrer v. Russell, 207 Pa. 105, 56 Atl. 333; Moran v. Munhall, 204 Pa. St. 242, 53 Atl. 1094; Crotzer v. Bittenbender, 199 Pa. St. 504, 49 Atl. 266; McKibbin v. Peters, 185 Pa. St. 518, 40 Atl. 288; Friedley v. Hamilton, 17 Serg. & R. (Pa.) 70, 17 Am. Dec. 638; In re Rockhill's Estate, 29 Pa. Super. Ct. 28.

South Dakota: Comp. Laws 1887, § 4371; Rev. Code 1903, §§ 2070, 2071, p. 829; Murphy v. Plankinton Bank, 13 S. Dak. 501, 83 N. W. 575. See also Gerken v. Sonnabend, 130 N. Y. S. 605 (mortgage tax law strictly construed and inapplicable to a deed with a defeasance). Although the recording of a deed, without the defeasance gives the mortgage no benefit of the recording act, the record is effective against subsequent judgment creditors of the mortgagor. Mutual Life Ins. Co. v. Nicholas, 144 App. Div. 95, 128 N. Y. S. 902.

[95] Bank of Mobile v. Tishomingo Sav. Inst., 62 Miss. 250. In Connecticut, also, unless the defeasance is recorded with the deed, the instruments being intended to operate as a mortgage, a creditor of the grantor may attach the property as his, for the transaction is regarded as invalid as against the grantor's creditors. Ives v. Stone, 51 Conn. 446. Carpenter, J., delivering the opinion of the court, after reviewing the Connecticut decisions which require the debt secured to be fully and accurately described, said: "This transaction, the defeasance being unrecorded, is contrary to the spirit of all decisions. The record, so far from disclosing the true state of the title, shows it to be an absolute deed instead of a mortgage; it represents the grantee as the owner of the property, whereas the grantor owns it subject to the grantee's debt, and the equity of redemption is concealed and placed apparently beyond the reach of creditors, while a secret trust exists in favor of the grantor. So far from describing the debt with reasonable certainty, the record is entirely silent on the subject, and places it within the power of the parties by collusion, if they are disposed, to set up any claim, and for any amount, as a substitute for the one really intended to be secured. If this transaction can be sustained as a valid mortgage

holding the land under a deed direct from the grantee or mortgagee.[96]

As to third persons, the absolute conveyance is not defeated or affected unless the defeasance is also recorded; and an express declaration to this effect has been made by statute in several states.[97] The object of such statutes is to protect innocent purchasers from the mortgagee, who has apparently an indefeasible title; while the provision whereby the record of the defeasance is enforced, in the states before named, is made for the protection of the mortgagor.

These requirements of statute have no application when the conveyance to which the defeasance relates does not purport upon its face to be absolute and unconditional.[98] While a purchaser in good faith, and without notice from a mortgagee, by an absolute conveyance obtains a title not subject to redemption, yet if the purchaser has notice of the original transaction, he takes only the mortgagee's title; and if there are successive mutations, but always coupled with such notice,

against creditors, it will not only destroy all the benefits of the recording system as respects mortgages, but will enable the parties, by a change in the form of the mortgage, to convert the system itself into an instrument of fraud." See also Stearns v. Porter, 46 Conn. 313; Hart v. Chalker, 14 Conn. 77. The same rule is adopted in North Carolina. Gulley v. Macy, 84 N. Car. 434; Dukes v. Jones, 6 Jones L. (N. Car.) 14; Gregory v. Perkins, 4 Dev. (N. Car.) 50.

[96] Marston v. Williams, 45 Minn. 116, 47 N. W. 644.

[97] Alabama: Code 1907, § 3384.

Alaska: Codes 1900, p. 373, § 100.

California: Civ. Code 1906, § 2950; Payne v. Morey, 144 Cal. 130, 77 Pac. 831.

Delaware: Within sixty days. Code 1893, ch. 520, § 18, p. 629.

Dakota: Comp. Laws 1887, § 4371.

Indiana: Within ninety days from date of deed. Burns' Ann. Stat. 1914, § 3964.

Kansas: Gen. Stat. 1909, § 5195; Holmes v. Newman, 68 Kans. 418, 75 Pac. 501.

Maine: Rev. Stat. 1903, p. 658, § 12; Smith v. Monmouth Mut. Fire Ins. Co., 50 Maine 96.

Massachusetts: Pub. Stat. 1882, Ch. 120 § 23; Moors v. Albro, 129 Mass. 9; Harrison v. Phillips' Academy, 12 Mass. 456; Kelleran v.

Brown, 4 Mass. 443; Newhall v. Burt, 7 Pick. (Mass.) 157; Newhall v. Pierce, 5 Pick. (Mass.) 450.

Michigan: Howell's Stat. 1913, § 10853; Columbia Bank v. Jacobs, 10 Mich. 349, 81 Am. Dec. 792; Russell v. Waite, Walk. Ch. (Mich.) 31.

Minnesota: Gen. Stat. 1913, § 6851; Cogan v. Cook, 22 Minn. 137.

Missouri: Rev. Code 1907, § 5750.

Oklahoma: Comp. Laws 1909, § 1197.

Oregon: Lord's Ore. Laws 1910, § 7133.

Pennsylvania: Within sixty days. Laws 1881, p. 84; Purdon's Pa. Dig. 1905, p. 1181, § 155; Safe Deposit &c. Co. v. Linton, 213 Pa. 105, 62 Atl. 566; Lohrer v. Russell, 207 Pa. 105, 56 Atl. 333; Moran v. Munhall, 204 Pa. 242, 53 Atl. 1094; Crotzer v. Bittenbender, 199 Pa. 504, 49 Atl. 266; Sankey v. Hawley, 118 Pa. St. 30, 13 Atl. 208; In re Rockhill's Estate, 29 Pa. Super. Ct. 28.

Rhode Island: Gen. Laws 1909, p. 898, § 1.

Wisconsin: Stat. 1913, § 2243.

Wyoming: Comp. Stat. 1910, § 3655. See also Lobban v. Garnett, 9 Dana (Ky.) 389; Wolf v. Theresa Village Mut. Fire Ins. Co., 115 Wis. 402, 91 N. W. 1014.

[98] Noyes v. Sturdivant, 18 Maine 104; Russell v. Waite, Walk. (Mich.) 31.

the original conveyance continues as a mortgage.[99] The fact that the grantor remains in possession of the property has been held sufficient to charge the purchaser with such notice.[1] Accordingly, a purchaser in good faith without notice from the grantee in a recorded deed absolute given as security, was held to be protected to the extent of his payment, with interest, against all persons, except those in actual possession at the time of such purchase.[2]

It has been held that the recording of a bond for a deed does not impart notice to a purchaser of the land that the obligee in the bond is in fact a mortgagor, though that was the intent of the parties.[3] And again it has been held that a bond for a deed is not an instrument of defeasance which is required to be recorded.[4] An instrument of defeasance has full effect between the parties without being recorded.[5]

§ 514. **Apparent record title.**—A purchaser may rely upon the legal title as it appears of record. These provisions of statute are only the enactment of a principle that is necessarily deduced from the general provisions of the registry system, and which had already been established by judicial construction.[6] "It is regarded," says Chief Justice Redfield, "as more in conformity to just principles of equity and fair dealing, that the estate of the cestui que trust should be extinguished by the deed of the trustee, than that the equal equity of the purchaser should be defeated, and thus the free and fair transmission of estates be embarrassed and placed under a cloud of suspicion and doubt. The equities of the parties being equal, the legal estate is allowed to prevail, and a rule of policy is at the same time subserved by leaving the transmission of titles unembarrassed as far as practica-

[99] Shaver v. Woodward, 28 Ill. 277; Brown v. Gaffney, 28 Ill. 149; Hall v. Savill, 3 Greene (Iowa) 37, 54 Am. Dec. 485; Williams v. Thorn, 11 Paige (N. Y.) 459.

[1] Mann v. Falcon, 25 Tex. 271.

[2] Kraus v. Potts, 38 Okla. 674, 135 Pac. 362 (under Okla. Comp. Laws 1909, § 1198).

[3] Holmes v. Newman, 68 Kans. 418, 75 Pac. 501.

[4] Holmes v. Newman, 68 Kans. 418, 75 Pac. 501.

[5] Bailey v. Myrick, 50 Maine 171; Jackson v. Ford, 40 Maine 381; Harrison v. Morton, 87 Md. 671, 40 Atl. 897; Owens v. Miller, 29 Md. 144; Short v. Caldwell, 155 Mass. 57, 28 N. E. 1124; Bryan v. Traders' Ins.

Co., 146 Mass. 389, 14 N. E. 454; Moors v. Albro, 129 Mass. 9; Bayley v. Bailey, 5 Gray (Mass.) 505; Marston v. Williams, 45 Minn. 116, 47 N. W. 644, 22 Am. St. 719; Butman v. James, 34 Minn. 547, 27 N. W. 66. See also Stetson v. Gulliver, 2 Cush. (Mass.) 494; Russell v. Waite, Walk. (Mich.) 31.

[6] Harrison v. Phillips Academy, 12 Mass. 456; Newhall v. Burt, 7 Pick. (Mass.) 157; Newhall v. Pierce, 5 Pick. (Mass.) 450; Columbia Bank v. Jacobs, 10 Mich. 849, 81 Am. Dec. 792; Stoddard v. Rotton, 5 Bosw. (N. Y.) 378; Mills v. Comstock, 5 Johns. Ch. (N. Y.) 214; Whittick v. Kane, 1 Paige (N. Y.) 202. See ante, § 339.

ble, thus inspiring confidence, rather than distrust, in the transmission of titles to real estate."[7]

When the mortgage is by a deed absolute in form, and the defeasance is not recorded, the grantee can of course convey a good title to a bona fide purchaser.[8] Thus a bona fide purchaser from the grantee, without notice, actual or constructive, of the defeasible nature of the original conveyance, takes an indefeasible title, and as against him the grantor has no right of redemption.[9] The position of the parties is quite the same when the holder of a mortgage duly recorded has taken a conveyance of the equity of redemption, and has then assigned the mortgage to one who does not record the assignment, and has then conveyed the fee to another. Apparently the mortgagee, at the time of his conveyance in fee, had the complete title by merger of the mortgage in the fee, just as the mortgagee by an absolute deed has it; and the prior assignment of the mortgage by an assignment not recorded amounts to the defeasance not being recorded.[10]

As elsewhere noticed, in some states neither an attaching creditor nor a judgment creditor is regarded as a purchaser, and therefore he acquires by his attachment or judgment no lien upon the land in the hands of the mortgagee holding the title absolutely, as against the equitable cestui que trust, or grantor equitably entitled to the equity of redemption.[11]

§ 514a. Reinscription, in Louisiana and Mississippi.—No renewal of the record of real estate mortgages is required in most states. But under the Louisiana statute, a mortgage on land must be reinscribed within ten years from the original inscription; otherwise it loses priority as a lien against intervening rights of third persons, even though they have actual notice; and a subsequent reinscription is effective

---

[7] Hart v. Farmers' &c. Bank, 33 Vt. 252.

[8] Turman v. Bell, 54 Ark. 273, 15 S. W. 886; Pico v. Gallardo, 52 Cal. 206; Bailey v. Myrick, 50 Maine 171; Tufts v. Tapley, 129 Mass. 380. See ante § 253.

[9] Nelson v. Wadsworth (Ala.), 61 So. 895; Jenkins v. Rosenberg, 105 Ill. 157; Maxfield v. Patchen, 29 Ill. 39; Jolivet v. Chaves, 125 La. 923, 52 So. 99, 32 L. R. A. (N. S.) 1046; Tufts v. Tapley, 129 Mass. 380; Kemp v. Small, 32 Nebr. 318, 49 N. W. 169; Gruber v. Baker, 20 Nev. 453, 23 Pac. 858, 9 L. R. A. 302;

Murphy v. Plankinton Bank, 13 S. Dak. 501, 83 N. W. 575. See also Miller v. Thomas, 14 Ill. 428; Jameson v. Emerson, 82 Maine 359, 19 Atl. 831. But see Carveth v. Winegar, 133 Mich. 34, 94 N. W. 381.

[10] Mills v. Comstock, 5 Johns. Ch. (N. Y.) 214. See also Purdy v. Huntington, 42 N. Y. 334, 1 Am. Rep. 532, revg. 46 Barb. 389.

[11] Hart v. Farmers' &c. Bank, 33 Vt. 252. See also Loring v. Melendy, 11 Ohio 355; Baird v. Kirtland, 8 Ohio 21. But see Parrott v. Baker, 82 Ga. 364, 9 S. E. 1068.

only from the time thereof.[12] Strict compliance with the requirement of reinscription is necessary.[13] Circumstances which would ordinarily stop the running of a statute of limitations do not dispense
with reinscription;[14] and even the pendency of foreclosure proceedings is not equivalent notice.[15]

But the Louisiana statute, like other recording acts, relates only
to the effect of the inscription and reinscription, and not to the validity of the mortgage; and although failure to reinscribe causes loss of
priority and effect against third parties, the mortgage remains a valid
obligation against the mortgagor and his heirs.[16] Thus failure to reinscribe does not discharge the mortgage between the original parties
or affect persons who have not acquired intervening adverse rights,[17]
nor can a purchaser from the mortgagor take advantage of such failure, if he has assumed payment of the mortgage debt.[18]

[12] Louisiana: Rev. Code, art. 3369;
Lovell v. Cragin, 136 U. S. 130, 34 L.
ed. 372, 10 Sup. Ct. 1024; Lemelle v.
Thompson, 34 La. Ann. 1041 (mortgage by minor); Fillastre v. St.
Amand, 32 La. Ann. 352; De St.
Romes v. Blanc, 31 La. Ann. 48;
Byrne v. Citizens' Bank, 23 La. Ann.
275; Levy v. Mentz, 23 La. Ann.
261; Johnson v. Lowry, 22 La. Ann.
205; Kohn v. McHatton, 20 La. Ann.
223; Robinson v. Haynes, 19 La.
Ann. 132. See also Gagneux's Succession, 40 La. Ann. 701, 4 So. 869
(death of mortgagor); Morrison v.
Citizens' Bank, 27 La. Ann. 401;
Liddell v. Rucker, 13 La. Ann. 569
(fraudulent procurement of second
mortgage); Ynogoso's Succession, 13
La. Ann. 559; Roche v. Groysilliere,
13 La. 238 (statute retroactive).
[13] Batey v. Woolfolk, 20 La. Ann.
385; Gremillon's Succession, 4 La.
Ann. 411. See also Hart v. Caffery,
39 La. Ann. 894, 2 So. 788.
[14] Johnson v. Lowry, 22 La. Ann.
205 (record office closed for over
two years); Kohn v. McHatton, 20
La. Ann. 223 (suspension during
Civil War). See also New Orleans
Ins. Assn. v. Labranche, 31 La. Ann.
839.
[15] Pickett v. Foster, 149 U. S. 505,
37 L. ed. 829, 13 Sup. Ct. 998; Watson v. Bondurant, 30 La. Ann. 1;
Barelli v. Delassus, 16 La. Ann. 280;
Young v. New Orleans City Bank,
9 La. Ann. 193; Hyatt v. Gallier, 6
La. Ann. 321.

[16] Pickett v. Foster, 149 U. S. 505,
37 L. ed. 829, 13 Sup. Ct. 998;
Shields v. Shiff, 124 U. S. 351, 31 L.
ed. 445, 8 Sup. Ct. 510; Bondurant
v. Watson, 103 U. S. 281, 26 L. ed.
447; Cucullu v. Hernandez, 103 U.
S. 105, 26 L. ed. 322; Patterson v.
De la Ronde, 8 Wall. (U. S.) 292, 19
L. ed. 415; Pickett v. Foster, 36
Fed. 514; Norres v. Hays, 44 La.
Ann. 907, 11 So. 462; In re Myrick's
Succession, 43 La. Ann. 884, 9 So.
498; In re Gagneux's Succession, 40
La. Ann. 701, 4 So. 869; Factors' &c.
Ins. Co. v. Warren, 37 La. Ann. 85;
Adams v. Daunis, 29 La. Ann. 315;
Villavaso v. Walker, 28 La. Ann.
775; Thompson v. Simmons, 22 La.
Ann. 450; Liddell v. Rucker, 13 La.
Ann. 569; Letaste v. Beraud, 2 La.
Ann. 768; Bethany v. Creditors, 7
Rob. (La.) 61; Lejeune v. Hebert, 6
Rob. (La.) 419; Minor v. Alexander,
6 Rob. (La.) 166. See also Milten-
berger v. Dubroca, 34 La. Ann. 313;
Gegan v. Bowman, 22 La. Ann. 336;
In re Flower's Succession, 12 La.
Ann. 216.
[17] Cucullu v. Hernandez, 103 U. S.
105, 26 L. ed. 322; Norres v. Hays,
44 La. Ann. 907, 11 So. 462; In re
Myrick's Succession, 43 La. Ann.
884, 9 So. 498. See also Roche v.
Groysilliere, 13 La. 238.
[18] Cucullu v. Hernandez, 103 U.
S. 105, 26 L. ed. 322; McDaniel v.
Guillory, 23 La. Ann. 544; Batey v.
Woolfolk, 20 La. Ann. 385; Dupuy
v. Dashiell, 17 La. 60.

The Mississippi statute provides that a trust deed shall cease to be a lien upon property, as to subsequent purchasers, unless a renewal thereof is entered on the record within six months after the remedy to enforce it appears by the record to be barred by the statute of limitations.[19]

IV. *Errors in the Record*

§ 515. Defective record as notice of contents—Clerical errors.—If the record of a deed be defective for any cause, it is constructive notice of only what the record contains, in case the record is not an accurate transcript of the instrument. Persons interested in a title have a right to resort to the records to find out the contents of a deed, and can be considered as having notice of it only as it appears of record. The rule that the deed is notice from the time it is left for record is subject to the qualification that it is correctly transcribed. When the record itself is defective, it is notice of only what appears upon it.[1]

[19] Klaus v. Moore, 77 Miss. 701, 27 So. 612 (construing the Code 1892, § 2462; Code 1906, § 2796).

[1] Davis v. Ward, 109 Cal. 186, 41 Pac. 1010; Page v. Rogers, 31 Cal. 293; Chamberlain v. Bell, 7 Cal. 292, 68 Am. Dec. 260; Shepherd v. Buckhalter, 13 Ga. 443, 58 Am. Dec. 523; Baugher v. Woollen, 147 Ind. 308, 45 N. E. 94; Smith v. Lowry, 113 Ind. 37, 15 N. E. 17; State v. Davis, 96 Ind. 539; Gilchrist v. Gough, 63 Ind. 576, 30 Am. Rep. 250; Disque v. Wright, 49 Iowa 538; Howe v. Thayer, 49 Iowa 154; Miller v. Ware, 31 Iowa 524; Miller v. Bradford, 12 Iowa 14; Taylor v. Hotchkiss, 2 La. Ann. 917; Hill v. McNichol, 76 Maine 314; Stedman v. Perkins, 42 Maine 130; McLarren v. Thompson, 40 Maine 284; Brydon v. Campbell, 40 Md. 331; Johns v. Scott, 5 Md. 81; Barnard v. Campau, 29 Mich. 162; Thompson v. Morgan, 6 Minn. 292; Parrot v. Shaubhut, 5 Minn. 323; Bishop v. Schneider, 46 Mo. 472, 2 Am. Rep. 533; Terrell v. Andrew, 44 Mo. 309; Crosby v. Vleet, 3 N. J. L. 86; Mutual Life Ins. Co. v. Dake, 87 N. Y. 257; Gillig v. Maass, 28 N. Y. 191; New York Life Ins. Co. v. White, 17 N. Y. 469; Peck v. Mallams, 10 N. Y. 509; Bedford v. Tupper, 30 Hun (N. Y.) 174; Simonson v. Falihee, 25 Hun (N. Y.) 570; Frost v. Beekman, 1 Johns. Ch. (N. Y.) 288, 18 Johns. 544; Ford v. James, 4 Keyes (N. Y.) 300; White v. McGarry, 2 Flipp. (U. S.) 572; Jennings v. Wood, 20 Ohio 261; Schell v. Stein, 76 Pa. St. 398, 18 Am. Rep. 416; Heister v. Fortner, 2 Binn. (Pa.) 40, 4 Am. Dec. 417; Potter v. Dooley, 55 Vt. 512; Sanger v. Craigue, 10 Vt. 555; Sanger v. Adams, 8 Vt. 172, 30 Am. Dec. 459; Thomas v. Stuart, 91 Va. 694, 22 S. E. 511; Pringle v. Dunn, 37 Wis. 449, 19 Am. Rep. 772. See also People v. Bristol, 35 Mich. 28; 2 Pom-

This is the view sustained by the greater number of decisions and by the greater weight of reason, as distinguished from the view that the filing of the deed operates as a record of it, and that it is constructive notice from such time of the actual contents of the deed.[2] These different views depend somewhat upon the different terms used by the statutes in regard to the effect of filing or recording of deeds as constructive notice; though it is true that there is a conflict of decisions under statutes substantially the same.

Of course, a record is not invalidated by a mere clerical error in transcribing the instrument not affecting the sense or obscuring its meaning.[3]

Every requirement of statute in relation to the execution and acknowledgment or proof of a deed or mortgage must be complied with in order to gain priority by the record of it.[4] Moreover, the deed as it stands must be spread upon the record correctly, and appear thereon as a valid instrument, showing the prerequisites to a valid registration.[5]

If the record of a mortgage fails to state the amount secured thereby, it will not give constructive notice of such amount.[6] An erroneous

eroy's Eq. Jur., §§ 653, 654. But see Gorham v. Summers, 25 Minn. 81; Bradford v. Tupper, 30 Hun (N. Y.) 174; Simonson v. Falihee, 25 Hun (N. Y.) 570; Bigelow v. Topliff, 25 Vt. 273, 60 Am. Dec. 264; Curtis v. Lyman, 24 Vt. 338, 58 Am. Dec. 174; Ferris v. Smith, 24 Vt. 27; Pringle v. Dunn, 37 Wis. 449, 19 Am. Rep. 772. Where a mortgage is altered after acknowledgment, the defect in recording and constructive notice extends only to elimination of the clause inserted. Johnson v. Northern Minnesota Land &c. Co. (Iowa), 150 N. W. 596. See post §§ 516, 517.

[2] See post § 517.

[3] Turman v. Bell, 54 Ark. 273, 15 S. W. 886, 26 Am. St. 35; Meherin v. Oaks, 67 Cal. 57, 7 Pac. 47; Ogden v. Ogden, 79 Ill. App. 488; Hoopeston Bldg. Assn. v. Green, 16 Ill. App. 204; Poutz v. Reggio, 25 La. Ann. 637; Muehlberger v. Schilling, 19 N. Y. St. 1, 3 N. Y. S. 705; Tousley v. Tousley, 5 Ohio St. 78; Citizens' Bank v. Shaw, 14 S. Dak. 197, 84 N. W. 779; Hart v. Patterson, 17 Tex. Civ. App. 591, 43 S. W. 545; St. Croix Land &c. Co. v.

Ritchie, 73 Wis. 409, 41 N. W. 409. See also Robertson v. Downing Co., 120 Ga. 833, 48 S. E. 429, 102 Am. St. 128; Central Nat. Bank v. Brecheisen, 65 Kans. 807, 70 Pac. 895; Gillespie v. Brown, 16 Nebr. 457, 20 N. W. 632; Hughes v. Debnam, 53 N. Car. 127.

[4] Weed v. Lyon, Harr. (Mich.) 363; Thompson v. Mack, Harr. (Mich.) 150. Only reasonable and practical compliance with the statute is necessary, for example, in indexing, or cross-references by book and page. Downing v. Glen Rock Oil Co., 207 Pa. 455, 56 Atl. 995.

[5] Dean v. Gibson, 34 Tex. Civ. App. 508, 79 S. W. 363; Lander v. Bromley, 79 Wis. 372, 48 N. W. 594; Wood v. Meyer, 36 Wis. 308. See also Du Bose v. Kell, 90 S. Car. 196, 71 S. E. 371.

[6] Bullock v. Battenhousen, 108 Ill. 28; Battenhousen v. Bullock, 11 Ill. App. 665; Bergman v. Bogda, 46 Ill. App. 351; Lacour v. Carrie, 2 La. Ann. 790; Whittacre v. Fuller, 5 Minn. 508; Du Bose v. Kell, 90 S. Car. 196, 71 S. E. 371. See also Bouton v. Doty, 69 Conn. 531, 37 Atl. 1064; Pearce v. Hall, 12 Bush (Ky.)

entry of an amount less than that recited in the mortgage has been held not to be notice of the full amount, but only of the sum appearing on the record. If, for instance, a mortgage for three thousand dollars be, by mistake of the recorder, registered as for three hundred dollars, or a mortgage for four hundred dollars be registered as two hundred dollars, it is notice to subsequent bona fide purchasers of a lien of only that amount.[7] And so if a mortgage for five thousand dollars be recorded as for five hundred dollars, although indexed as a mortgage for five thousand dollars, it is a lien as against a bona fide subsequent mortgagee only for the smaller amount; and the knowledge of such subsequent mortgagee that the mortgage was indexed as a mortgage for the larger amount is not sufficient to charge him with knowledge of the true amount.[8]

Although the record must correctly show the identity of the parties to the mortgage or other instrument,[9] slight errors in this regard will not vitiate the record, especially where no one has been actually misled thereby.[10] The record of a mortgage to partners, in the firm name

209. The record is sufficient if the purchaser is put upon inquiry as to the debt secured. Booth v. Barnum, 9 Conn. 286, 23 Am. Dec. 339; Equitable Building &c. Assn. v. King, 48 Fla. 252, 37 So. 181. Although one of several notes secured by a mortgage was omitted from the description, the record was held to give sufficient notice to a subsequent purchaser where the aggregate amount of the notes was correctly given. Dargin v. Beeker, 10 Iowa 571. Although the record of a mortgage failed to state the amount of the note secured by it, but referred to the note by its date, the names of the maker and payee, the date of its maturity, the rate of interest provided for, and the time of payment, it was held that the record was sufficient. Fetes v. O'Laughlin, 62 Iowa 532, 17 N. W. 764.

[7] Frost v. Beekman, 1 Johns. Ch. (N. Y.) 288 ($3,000 recorded $300); Beekman v. Frost, 18 Johns. (N. Y.) 544, 9 Am. Dec. 246; Peck v. Mallams, 10 N. Y. 509 (actual notice of amount); Terrell v. Andrew, 44 Mo. 309; Hill v. McNichol, 76 Maine 314; Stevens v. Bachelder, 28 Maine 218; Gilchrist v. Gough, 63 Ind. 576, 30 Am. Rep. 250 (mortgage for $5,000 recorded as $500). Where a mortgage was assigned for $2,250, and the records then showed that the mortgage was recorded with the date blank, and that a mortgage for $2,500 had been executed on the same land to the same mortgagee, and that a conveyance had been made to the mortgagee, who assumed the latter mortgage as part of the price, it was constructive notice that the $2,500 mortgage was a substitution for the $2,250 mortgage, and the assignee is not a purchaser without notice. Taylor v. American Nat. Bank, 64 Fla. 525, 60 So. 783.

[8] Gilchrist v. Gough, 63 Ind. 576, 30 Am. Rep. 250.

[9] Johnson v. Wilson, 137 Ala. 468, 34 So. 392, 97 Am. St. 52; Baugher v. Woollen, 147 Ind. 308, 45 N. E. 94; Disque v. Wright, 49 Iowa 538; Jennings v. Wood, 20 Ohio 261 (mistake in grantor's name); In re Sturtevant's Appeal, 34 Pa. St. 149.

[10] Fincher v. Hanegan, 59 Ark. 151, 26 S. W. 821, 24 L. R. A. 543 ("Henry N. Ward" instead of Henry M. Ward); Muehlberger v. Schilling, 19 N. Y. St. 1, 3 N. Y. S. 705 ("Shelleng" instead of "Schilling"); Royster v. Lane, 118 N. Car. 156, 24 S. E. 796. See also Loser v. Plainfield Savings Bank, 149 Iowa 672, 128 N.

containing their surnames only, was held sufficient, notwithstanding a statute requiring the clerk to enter the Christian names and surnames of parties to deeds.[11] Where the name of the mortgagee was omitted by mistake in transcribing the instrument, but appeared in the entry book, the record was held sufficient to impart constructive notice.[12] The record of a mortgage professing on its face to relate exclusively to a married woman's property, but including in the description land of the husband who joined therein, does not operate against third persons as a mortgage of his land.[13]

The description of the mortgaged property must identify it with reasonable certainty, or at least be sufficient to put a subsequent purchaser upon inquiry; otherwise the record thereof will not be constructive notice.[14] And if a material part of the description be omitted from the record, the record is constructive notice of only what appears upon it.[15] But a defect in the record of a mortgage as to the description of the property has been held not to invalidate the lien, where the original instrument was correct.[16] Thus a misdescription in the record of the "northwest quarter" of a certain section as the "southwest quarter" was held not to be prejudicial,[17] and a description of mortgaged land as "thirty acres in" a certain quarter section, which could be identified as the only thirty acres owned by the mortgagor therein and bounded by a certain creek, was held sufficient to charge judgment creditors of the mortgagor with notice.[18]

It is not generally held, however, that it is part of the purchaser's duty to search the original papers to find out whether the recorder has correctly spread their contents upon the record. The obligation of giving notice rests upon the party holding the title. If the recorder occasions a loss to the owner by incorrectly transcribing the deed, he may recover damages of the recorder for such loss.[19]

W. 1101, 31 L. R. A. (N. S.) 1112. But see Johnson v. Wilson, 137 Ala. 468, 34 So. 392, 97 Am. St. 52 (record of mortgage as executed by A. W. Dixon, not notice to purchasers that J. W. Dixon executed it).

[11] Bernstein v. Hobelman, 70 Md. 29, 16 Atl. 374.

[12] Sinclair v. Slawson, 44 Mich. 123, 6 N. W. 207, 38 Am. Rep. 235.

[13] W. F. Taylor Co. v. Sample, 122 La. 1016, 48 So. 439.

[14] See ante § 489.

[15] Disque v. Wright, 49 Iowa 538; Simmons v. Hutchinson, 81 Miss. 351, 33 So. 21; Reid v. Rhodes, 106 Va. 701, 56 S. E. 722. See also Talmadge v. Interstate Bldg. &c. Assn., 105 Ga. 550, 31 S. E. 618; Mettart v. Allen, 139 Ind. 644, 39 N. E. 239. See ante §§ 489, 65 et seq.

[16] Ward v. Stark, 91 Ark. 268, 121 S. W. 382.

[17] Covington v. Fisher, 22 Okla. 207, 97 Pac. 615.

[18] Van Valkenberg v. American &c. Mtg. Co., 87 Fed. 617, 31 C. C. A. 145.

[19] Terrell v. Andrew, 44 Mo. 309. See also Taylor v. Hotchkiss, 2 La. Ann. 917; Ritchie v. Griffiths, 1 Wash. 429, 25 Pac. 341, 12 L. R. A. 384, 22 Am. St. 155.

§ 516. **Error chargeable to grantee and not to third person.**—In accord with the theory that the record of a deed is notice only of what appears of record, there is an important line of cases holding that the registration of a mortgage or other instrument is the duty of the grantee therein, that the recording officer is his agent, and that the grantee must suffer the loss resulting from the failure to record, rather than a third person or subsequent purchaser who has examined the records and acted in ignorance of the omission or mistake.[20] According to these cases third persons are not required to go beyond the registry to ascertain whether the title is good. If there is any error or omission in the registry of a deed or mortgage, the grantee must suffer for it rather than others who afterward consult the records. He may in some cases have recourse against the recorder for damages occasioned by his errors or omissions in recording; but otherwise the loss so occasioned must fall upon him.[21]

In discussing the necessity of an actual, complete and correct record of a deed, including proper indexing and transcription, the Supreme Court of Washington says: "The very object in having it recorded is to give constructive notice to innocent purchasers, and to protect the grantee's title against said purchasers. The law imposes upon him the duty of having his deed recorded. It is not the attempt to record a deed that the law requires; but it is the recording of the deed. It would be an empty benefit, indeed, that would accrue to the buying public if the attempt to record were held to take the place of the record. The obligation rests upon the grantee to give the notice required by the law. He controls the deed. He can put it on record or not, as he pleases. He has the right and the opportunity to see that

---

[20] Cady v. Purser, 131 Cal. 552, 63 Pac. 844, 82 Am. St. 391; Watkins v. Wilhoit, 104 Cal. 395, 38 Pac. 53; Donald v. Beals, 57 Cal. 399; Chamberlain v. Bell, 7 Cal. 292, 68 Am. Dec. 260; Benson v. Green, 80 Ga. 230, 4 S. E. 851; Shepherd v. Buckhalter, 13 Ga. 443, 58 Am. Dec. 523; Gilchrist v. Gough, 63 Ind. 576, 30 Am. Rep. 250; Barney v. McCarty, 15 Iowa 510, 83 Am. Dec. 427; Noyes v. Horr, 13 Iowa 570; Miller v. Bradford, 12 Iowa 14; Taylor v. Hotchkiss, 2 La. Ann. 917; Hill v. McNichol, 76 Maine 314; Brydon v. Campbell, 40 Md. 331; Thompson v. Morgan, 6 Minn. 292; Parret v. Shaubhut, 5 Minn. 323, 80 Am. Dec. 424; Terrell v. Andrew, 44 Mo. 309; Mutual Life Ins. Co. v. Dake, 87 N. Y. 257; Gillig v. Maass, 28 N. Y. 191; Peck v. Mallams, 10 N. Y. 509, Seld. Notes (N. Y.) 199; Bedford v. Tupper, 30 Hun (N. Y.) 174; Simonson v. Falihee, 25 Hun (N. Y.) 570; Beekman v. Frost, 18 Johns. (N. Y.) 544, 9 Am. Dec. 246; Frost v. Beekman, 1 Johns. Ch. (N. Y.) 288; Jennings v. Wood, 20 Ohio 261; Potter v. Dooley, 55 Vt. 512; Sawyer v. Adams, 8 Vt. 172, 30 Am. Dec. 459. See also Baugher v. Woollen, 147 Ind. 308, 45 N. E. 94; Smith v. Lowry, 113 Ind. 37, 15 N. E. 17; State v. Davis, 96 Ind. 539. See ante § 515.

[21] Taylor v. Hotchkiss, 2 La. Ann. 917.

the work is done as he directs it to be done, in legal manner. No one else has this opportunity, and if, from any cause, he fails to give the notice required by law, the consequences must fall upon him. It may be a hardship; but, where one of two innocent persons must suffer, the rule is that the misfortune must rest on the person in whose business, and under whose control, it happened, and who had it in his power to avert it."[22]

§ 517. **Error chargeable to third persons under statutes making mortgage operative upon filing.**—The other view prevails under statutes which make the deed operative as a record from the time it is filed for record, and the apparent weight of authority is that any error in transcribing the deed, as, for instance, in the date of the deed or of the acknowledgment,[23] or in the sum secured by a mortgage, does not prejudice the grantee or mortgagee.[24] The mortgagee is regarded as having discharged his entire duty when he has delivered his mortgage, properly executed and acknowledged, to the recording officer, and as being in the same attitude as if the deed were at that moment correctly spread upon the record book; so that no error in transcription can deprive the deed of its operation as a recorded instrument, and subsequent purchasers are charged with constructive notice, notwithstanding the officer does not properly record the instrument.[25]

[22] Ritchie v. Griffiths, 1 Wash. 429, 25 Pac. 341, 12 L. R. A. 384, 22 Am. St. 155. See also Terrell v. Andrew, 44 Mo. 309.

[23] Grove v. Great Northern Loan Co., 17 N. Dak. 352, 116 N. W. 345, 138 Am. St. 707 (date of mortgage omitted in record); In re Wood's Appeal, 82 Pa. St. 116; In re Brooke's Appeal, 64 Pa. St. 127; Musser v. Hyde, 2 Watts & S. (Pa.) 314. See also Parke v. Neeley, 90 Pa. St. 52; Thomas v. Stuart, 91 Va. 694, 22 S. E. 511 (omission of certain words from acknowledgment of deed). See ante § 89, concerning error in date.

[24] Mims v. Mims, 35 Ala. 23; Dubose v. Young, 10 Ala. 365; Taylor v. American Nat. Bank, 64 Fla. 525, 60 So. 783; Bedford v. Tupper, 30 Hun (N. Y.) 174; Simonson v. Falihee, 25 Hun (N. Y.) 570. A similar view was taken under a statute of Illinois, providing that deeds "shall take effect and be in force from and after the time of filing the same for record." Merrick v. Wallace, 19 Ill.

486; Riggs v. Boylan, 4 Biss. (U. S.) 445; Polk v. Cosgrove, 4 Biss. (U. S.) 437.

So also in Ohio, where the statute provides that a deed "shall take effect and have preference from the time the same is delivered to the recorder." Tousley v. Tousley, 5 Ohio. St. 78.

So in Michigan: Sinclair v. Slawson, 44 Mich. 123, 6 N. W. 207, 38 Am. Rep. 235. See ante § 515.

[25] Riggs v. Boylan, 4 Biss. (U. S.) 445; Polk v. Cosgrove, 4 Biss. (U. S.) 437; Hudson v. Randolph, 66 Fed. 216, 13 C. C. A. 402; Fouche v. Swan, 80 Ala. 151; Mims v. Mims, 35 Ala. 23; Case v. Hargadine, 43 Ark. 144; Oats v. Walls, 28 Ark. 244; Lewis v. Hinman, 56 Conn. 55, 13 Atl. 143; Hine v. Robbins, 8 Conn. 342; Judd v. Woodruff, 2 Root (Conn.) 298; Franklin v. Cannon, 1 Root (Conn.) 500; Hartmyer v. Gates, 1 Root (Conn.) 61; Greenfield v. Stout, 122 Ga. 303, 50 S. E. 111; Chatham v. Bradford, 50 Ga. 327, 15 Am. Rep. 692; Kiser v. Heu-

The omission of the name of the mortgagee from the record, after it had been properly entered in the entry book, does not defeat the mortgage as to subsequent purchasers.[26]

A mistake of the officer in transcribing a mortgage, by which it is made to appear to be a security for a smaller amount than is actually provided for by it, does not impair the mortgage as a security for the amount for which it was actually given, although subsequent purchasers and creditors relying upon the record have taken the incumbrance to be only the amount there disclosed. The lien of a deed or mortgage begins when it is left for record and entered in a proper entry book, required to be kept for the purpose of showing what deeds or mortgages are left for record. The grantee is under no obligation

ston, 38 Ill. 252; Merrick v. Wallace, 19 Ill. 486; Lee v. Bermingham, 30 Kans. 312, 1 Pac. 73; Poplin v. Mundell, 27 Kans. 138; Zear v. Deposit &c. Co., 2 Kans. App. 505, 43 Pac. 977; State Bank v. Haggin, 1 A. K. Marsh. (Ky.) 306; Buckner v. Davis, 19 Ky. L. 1349, 43 S. W. 445 (mortgage recorded several years after delivery to recorder); Swan v. Vogle, 31 La. Ann. 38; Payne v. Pavey, 29 La. Ann. 116; Taylor v. Hotchkiss, 2 La. Ann. 917; Falconer's Succession, 4 Rob. (La.) 5; Hayden v. Peirce, 165 Mass. 359, 43 N. E. 119; Gillespie v. Rodgers, 146 Mass. 610; Getchell v. Moran, 124 Mass. 404; Sykes v. Keating, 118 Mass. 517; Wood v. Simons, 110 Mass. 116; Fuller v. Cunningham, 105 Mass. 442; Jordan v. Farnsworth, 15 Gray (Mass.) 517; Ames v. Phelps, 18 Pick. (Mass.) 314; Tracy v. Jenks, 15 Pick. (Mass.) 465; Sinclair v. Slawson, 44 Mich. 123. 6 N. W. 207, 38 Am. Rep. 235; Mangold v. Barlow, 61 Miss. 593, 48 Am. Rep. 84; Deming v. Miles, 35 Nebr. 739, 53 N. W. 665, 37 Am. St. 464; Perkins v. Strong, 22 Nebr. 725, 36 N. W. 292; Converse v. Porter, 45 N. H. 385; Mutual Ins. Co. v. Dake, 87 N. Y. 257; Bedford v. Tupper, 30 Hun (N. Y.) 174; Simonson v. Falihee, 25 Hun (N. Y. 570. (Otherwise, it seems, in the earlier cases in New York, Frost v. Beekman, 1 Johns. Ch. (N. Y.) 288, 18 Johns. 544; Peck v. Mallams, 10 N. Y. 509); Green v. Garrington, 16 Ohio St. 548; Tousley v. Tousley,

5 Ohio St. 78; Brown v. Kirkman, 1 Ohio St. 116; Covington v. Fisher, 22 Okla. 207, 97 Pac. 615; Board of Comrs. v. Babcock, 5 Ore. 472; Clader v. Thomas, 89 Pa. St. 343; Glading v. Frick, 88 Pa. St. 460; In re Wood's Appeal, 82 Pa. St. 116; Schell v. Stein, 76 Pa. St. 398, 18 Am. Rep. 416; Brooke's Appeal, 64 Pa. St. 127; Prouty v. Marshall, 36 Pa. Sup. Ct. 527; Musser v. Hyde, 2 Watts & S. (Pa.) 314; Nichols v. McReynolds, 1 R. I. 30, 36 Am. Dec. 238; Armstrong v. Austin, 45 S. Car. 69, 22 S. E. 763, 29 L. R. A. 772; Woodward v. Boro, 16 Lea (Tenn.) 678; Swepson v. Exchange &c. Bank, 9 Lea (Tenn.) 713; Flowers v. Wilkens, 1 Swan (Tenn.) 408; Willis v. Thompson, 85 Tex. 301, 20 S. W. 155; Freiberg v. Magale, 70 Tex. 116, 7 S. W. 684; Woodson v. Allen, 54 Tex. 551; Throckmorton v. Price, 28 Tex. 606, 91 Am. Dec. 334; Mercantile &c. Bank v. Brown, 96 Va. 614, 32 S. E. 64; Thomas v. Stuart, 91 Va. 694, 22 S. E. 511; Beverly v. Ellis, 1 Rand. (Va.) 102; Shove v. Larsen, 22 Wis. 142. See also The W. B. Cole, 59 Fed. 182, 8 C. C. A. 78; McGregor v. Hall, 3 Stew. & P. (Ala.) 397; Durrence v. Northern Nat. Bank, 117 Ga. 385, 43 S. E. 726; Cook v. Hall, 6 Ill. 575; Jennings v. Wood, 20 Ohio 261. But see Shepard v. Burkhalter, 13 Ga. 443, 58 Am. Dec. 523; Lally v. Holland, 1 Swan (Tenn.) 396; McLouth v. Hurt, 51 Tex. 115.

[26] Sinclair v. Slawson, 44 Mich. 123, 6 N. W. 207, 38 Am. Rep. 235.

to supervise the work of the recorder, and see that he spreads the deed upon record, or that he puts it upon the index.[27]

If, however, the record is such that it suggests a probable mistake in recording, it puts purchasers upon inquiry and charges them with notice of what the deed contains.[28] In discussing a case where a purchaser was put upon inquiry by examination of a defective record showing his source of title, which disclosed intervening equities, the United States Court of Appeals, per Judge Taft, said: "The proper construction of the recording acts charges every person taking title with all conveyances or mortgages made by any one in the chain of title while he holds title, whether the recording of such conveyances occur then or not. If, upon the record, a prior conveyance seems to be defeated by a subsequent one through delay in recording, then the person taking title must inquire as to the facts which might defeat the statutory effect of such prior record. * * * A purchaser is charged with notice of his chain of title, whether the grantees therein are bona fide purchasers or not."[29]

Moreover, if the grantee is himself guilty of any negligence or irregularity with reference to the recording of his deed, whereby his deed does not appear of record, he can not claim priority as against a subsequent bona fide purchaser. Thus, where a grantee took his deed out of the recorder's office before it was recorded, without noticing that it did not contain the recorder's certificate of recording required by law, the loss was held to fall on him whose want of care and caution made it possible.[30]

§ 518. **Index not essential to record.**—The index is no part of the record, and a mistake in it does not invalidate the notice afforded by

---

[27] In re Wood's Appeal, 82 Pa. St. 116; Payne v. Pavey, 29 La. Ann. 116. See ante § 515.

[28] Lewis v. Hinman, 56 Conn. 55, 13 Atl. 143. See ante § 490.

[29] The W. B. Cole, 59 Fed. 182, 8 C. C. A. 78.

[30] Turman v. Bell, 54 Ark. 273, 15 S. W. 886. Hemingway, J,. said: "If the grantee remove his deed before it is recorded, he places it in the power of the grantor to exhibit a clear title, and thus to mislead and deceive subsequent purchasers. By the exercise of slight care and caution he could have averted such a possibility, but, if he fails to do it, persons ignorant of the deed, who have examined the records, may be induced to purchase, when they have exhausted all usual means of inquiry and information. If they do thus purchase, a loss must be borne. Where should it fall? Upon him whose care and caution did not prevent it, or upon him whose slight care and caution would have prevented it? The question implies its own answer." Oats v. Walls, 28 Ark. 244, holding that, when the deed is once placed in the hands of the recorder, the grantee has no further responsibility, is referred to at length and disposed of as follows: "In so far as that case holds that a deed is notice of its provi-

a record otherwise properly made.[31] Although a deed be omitted from the index, there is constructive notice of it which affects all subsequent purchasers from the time it was left for record.[32] The general policy of the recording acts is to make the filing of a deed, duly executed and acknowledged, with the proper recording officer, constructive notice from that time; and although it be provided that the register shall make an index for the purpose of affording a correct and easy reference to the books of record in his office, the index is designed, not for the protection of the party recording his conveyance, but for the convenience of those searching the records; and instead of being a part of the record, it only shows the way to the record. It is in no way necessary that a conveyance shall be indexed, as well as recorded, in

sions from the time it is filed for record, and that the effect of such notice can not be impaired by the misconduct of the officer, it is approved; but in so far as it holds that the notice continues as against those who in good faith and for value acquire adverse interests after the deed, unrecorded, and, without a certificate of record, is withdrawn from the files, it is overruled."

[31] Amos v. Givens (Ala.), 60 So. 829; Chatham v. Bradford, 50 Ga. 327, 15 Am. Rep. 692; Nichol v. Henry, 89 Ind. 54; Gilchrist v. Gough, 63 Ind. 576, 30 Am. Rep. 250; Agurs v. Belcher, 111 La. 378, 35 So. 607, 100 Am. St. 485; Swan v. Vogel, 31 La. Ann. 38; Bishop v. Schneider, 46 Mo. 472, 2 Am. Rep. 533; Lincoln Bldg. &c. Assn. v. Hass, 10 Nebr. 581, 7 N. W. 327; Semon v. Terhune, 40 N. J. Eq. 364, 2 Atl. 18; Mutual L. Ins. Co. v. Dake, 87 N. Y. 257; Bedford v. Tupper, 30 Hun (N. Y.) 174; Green v. Garrington, 16 Ohio St. 548, 91 Am. Dec. 103; Polk v. Babcock, 5 Ore. 472; Musgrove v. Bonser, 5 Ore. 313; Stockwell v. McHenry, 107 Pa. St. 237, 52 Am. Rep. 475; Greenwood Loan &c. Assn. v. Childs, 67 S. Car. 251, 45 S. E. 167; Armstrong v. Austin, 45 S. Car. 69, 22 S. E. 763, 29 L. R. A. 772; Barrett v. Prentiss, 57 Vt. 297; Curtis v. Lyman, 24 Vt. 338; Oconto v. Jerrard, 46 Wis. 317, 50 N. W. 591; Fallass v. Pierce, 30 Wis. 443; Ely v. Wilcox, 20 Wis. 523, 91 Am. Dec. 436. See also Travelers' Ins. Co. v. Patten, 98 Ind. 209. A mortgage duly deposited in the recorder's office, but actually recorded in the deed-book and indexed in the index of the deeds, is sufficiently recorded to constitute notice from the time it was left for record. A statute requiring recorders to keep two indexes of mortgages separate from the indexes of deeds, but containing no repeal of prior legislation upon the recording of deeds and mortgages, can create no new rule of constructive notice. Farabee v. McKerrihan, 172 Pa. St. 234, 33 Atl. 583, 51 Am. St. 734.

[32] Hampton Lbr. Co. v. Ward, 95 Fed. 3; Amos v. Givens (Ala.), 60 So. 829; Chatham v. Bradford, 50 Ga. 327, 15 Am. Rep. 692; Herndon v. Ogg, 119 Ky. 814, 27 Ky. L. 268, 84 S. W. 754; Bishop v. Schneider, 46 Mo. 472, 2 Am. Rep. 533; Ryan v. Carr, 46 Mo. 483; Perkins v. Strong, 22 Nebr. 725, 36 N. W. 292; Eureka Lumber Co. v. Satchwell, 148 N. Car. 316, 62 S. E. 310; Davis v. Whitaker, 114 N. Car. 279, 19 S. E. 699; Yarrington v. Green, 2 Ohio Dec. 721; Polk v. Babcock, 5 Ore. 472; Stockwell v. McHenry, 107 Pa. St. 237, 52 Am. Rep. 475; Schell v. Stein, 76 Pa. St. 398, 18 Am. Rep. 416; Speer v. Evans, 47 Pa. St. 141; Throckmorton v. Price, 28 Tex. 605, 91 Am. Dec. 334; Curtis v. Lyman, 24 Vt. 338, 58 Am. Dec. 174; Sawyer v. Adams, 8 Vt. 172, 30 Am. Dec. 459; Virginia Bldg. &c. Co. v. Glenn, 99 Va. 460, 39 S. E. 136. See also The W. B. Cole, 59 Fed. 182, 8 C. C. A. 78.

order to make it a valid notice.[33] "Ordinarily the recording of an instrument means the copying of it into the public records kept for the purpose, by or under the direction or authority of the proper public officer. In this sense the index forms no part of the record. The record is complete without it. An index to the record of an instrument is the means provided for pointing out or indicating where the record may be found. It may in many cases be indispensable in order to secure the full benefit of the record to the public. But its office is to facilitate the researches of those having occasion to examine the records; and strictly it can not be said to form part of the record."[34]

When a grantee has delivered his deed to the recorder, notice of its contents is imparted from that time, if it is correctly spread upon the record. He has done all the law requires of him for his protection. The purpose of the index is only to point to the record, but constitutes no

---

[33] Davis v. Whitaker, 114 N. Car. 279, 41 Am. St. 793 (quoting text); Mutual Life Ins. Co. v. Dake, 1 Abb. N. Cas. (N. Y.) 381. Mr. Justice Smith, delivering the opinion of the Supreme Court, said: "It is not a little surprising to find that a question so likely to come up frequently has not arisen in any reported case in this state. I suppose the usual practice in searching the records in the clerk's office is to consult the index, and to rely upon it. That is obviously the most convenient way; and if the index is full and accurate, it saves the necessity of going through the records themselves. But if the index is imperfect and misleads the searcher, as appears to have been the case here, who is to suffer—the party who duly transcribed his mortgage in the record book, or the party who, relying on the index, omitted to look at the record? The question is to be answered by determining whether the index is an essential part of the record—that is to say, whether it is necessary to the completeness and efficiency of the record as a notice to after purchasers." After examining the statutes, and reaching the conclusion that the index is no part of the record, he continues: "In reaching this conclusion, I have not overlooked the practical inconveniences that may result from it in searching records. But the duty of the court is only to declare the law as the legislature has laid it down. Arguments ab inconvenienti may sometimes throw light upon the construction of ambiguous or doubtful words; but where, as here, the language of the law makes it plain, they are out of place. Inconveniences in practice will result whichever way the question shall be decided. The power to remedy them is in the legislature, and not in the courts. Even as the law now stands, the party injured by the omission of the clerk is not without remedy, for he has his action against the clerk." Affirmed by the Court of Appeals, 87 N. Y. 257, and the first part of this section quoted with approval. See this case commented upon and approved, 4 Cent. L. J. 340. See also Bishop v. Schneider, 46 Mo. 472, 2 Am. Rep. 533. The same rule was applied under analogous statutes in New York relating to the filing of chattel mortgages. Dodge v. Potter, 18 Barb. (N. Y.) 193; Dikeman v. Puckhafer, 1 Abb. Pr. (N. S.) (N. Y.) 32. These cases hold that the mortgagee, by filing and depositing his mortgage with the clerk, did all that he could do, and all that he was required to do, in order to perfect his claim, and that the omission of the mortgage from the index, being without his fault or knowledge, did not prejudice him.

[34] Green v. Garrington, 16 Ohio St. 458, 91 Am. Dec. 103.

part of it.[35] In the absence of proof to the contrary, it is presumed that the entry in the general index and the actual recording of a mortgage were simultaneous; and the fact that entries in the record are not made in consecutive order, either according to number or date of receipt, does not affect the validity of the record.[36] Statutory provisions requiring entry books to be kept have been construed similarly to those requiring indexes, and are declared not to make the entry book an essential part of the record.[37]

The neglect of a register of deeds, after a mortgage entitled to be recorded has been left with him for record, to make a note of reference from the record of the certificate of entry by the mortgage for breach of condition to the record of the mortgage, and vice versa, as directed by statute, can not affect the rights of the parties to the mortgage or those claiming under them.[38]

In Pennsylvania, however, under statutes not materially different from those in New York, Chief Justice Woodward reasoned that the mortgage not duly indexed was not constructive notice to third persons; that, as a guide to inquirers, the index is an indispensable part of the recording; and that without it the record affects no party with notice.[39] In this case the purchaser had actual notice of the existence of the mortgage, and therefore could not complain of the want of record; and in that view what was said by the court as to the sufficiency of the record was not material to the result.

It has been held that an index or entry book may be resorted to, to supply omissions or correct errors in the record, and it will constitute notice of a recorded instrument if enough is disclosed to put a prudent examiner upon inquiry.[40] But the correct indexing of a

---

[35] Bishop v. Schneider, 46 Mo. 472, 2 Am. Rep. 533. As to errors of index as to names, see Pinney v. Russell, 52 Minn. 443, 54 N. W. 484; Fincher v. Hanegan, 59 Ark. 151, 26 S. W. 821; Phillips v. McKaig, 36 Nebr. 853, 55 N. W. 259; Oppenheimer v. Robinson, 87 Tex. 174, 27 S. W. 95.

[36] Lane v. Duchac, 73 Wis. 646, 41 N. W. 962.

[37] Nichol v. Henry, 89 Ind. 54. See also Gilchrist v. Gough, 63 Ind. 576, 30 Am. Rep. 250. But see Sinclair v. Slawson, 44 Mich. 123, 6 N. W. 207, 38 Am. Rep. 235.

[38] Hayden v. Peirce, 165 Mass. 359, 43 N. E. 119.

[39] Speer v. Evans, 47 Pa. St. 141. See also Schell v. Stein, 76 Pa. St. 398, 18 Am. Rep. 416.

[40] Disque v. Wright, 49 Iowa 538; Jones v. Berkshire, 15 Iowa 248, 83 Am. Dec. 412; Loser v. Plainfield Sav. Bank, 149 Iowa 672, 128 N. W. 1101; Swan v. Vogel, 31 La. Ann. 38; Sinclair v. Slawson, 44 Mich. 123, 6 N. W. 207, 38 Am. Rep. 235; Piper v. Hilliard, 58 N. H. 198; Pringle v. Dunn, 37 Wis. 449, 19 Am. Rep. 772. See also American Emigrant Co. v. Call, 22 Fed. 765.

mortgage will not validate a defective transcription, entirely omitting the witnesses,[41] or misstating the amount secured.[42]

A mere clerical error in the index will not invalidate the constructive notice of the record, where it would not mislead a careful person in examination of the records.[43]

§ 519. Recorder's liability for errors.—The recording officer is liable in damages for errors and omissions made in recording or indexing a deed; but whether his liability is to the grantee in the deed, or to any third person who is injured by the error or omission, is a question that has given rise to some discussion. In those states in which the rule is adopted that a deed is constructive notice from the time it is left for record, whether it is in fact recorded or not, and is notice of the contents of the deed itself, the grantee could not ordinarily be injured by the omission or error, and consequently the liability of the recorder would be to the subsequent purchaser, who has purchased relying upon the correctness of the record. But without reference to this rule, the recorder should be liable to any third person injured by his negligence.[44]

The recorder is not liable for recording a forged deed unless he

[41] Pringle v. Dunn, 37 Wis. 449, 19 Am. Rep. 772.

[42] Gilchrist v. Gough, 63 Ind. 576, 30 Am. Rep. 250.

[43] Paige v. Lindsey, 69 Iowa 593, 29 N. W. 615; Barney v. Little, 15 Iowa 527; Jones v. Berkshire, 15 Iowa 248, 83 Am. Dec. 412; Agurs v. Belcher, 111 La. 378, 35 So. 607, 100 Am. St. 485. See also Bardon v. Land &c. Imp. Co., 157 U. S. 327, 39 L. ed. 719, 15 Sup. Ct. 650; Hodgson v. Lovell, 25 Iowa 97, 95 Am. Dec. 775.

[44] Hampton Lumber Co. v. Ward, 95 Fed. 3; Stephenson v. Mfg. Co., 84 Fed. 114; Norton v. Kumpe, 121 Ala. 446, 25 So. 841; Reeder v. State, 98 Ind. 114; State v. Davis, 96 Ind. 539; Gilchrist v. Gough, 63 Ind. 576; First Nat. Bank v. Clements, 87 Iowa 542, 54 N. W. 197 (delay in indexing a mortgage); Lee v. Bermingham, 30 Kans. 312; Poplin v. Mundell, 27 Kans. 138; Gordon v. Stanley, 108 La. 182, 32 So. 531; Fox v. Thibault, 33 La. Ann. 32; Commissioners v. Duckett, 20 Md. 468, 83 Am. Dec. 557; Mangold v. Barlow, 61 Miss. 593, 48 Am. Rep. 84; Bishop v. Schneider, 46 Mo. 472, 2 Am. Rep. 533; State v. Green, 24 Mo. App. 80, 100 S. W. 1115 (record of trust deed falsely marked satisfied); Mutual Life Ins. Co. v. Dake, 87 N. Y. 257, affg. 1 Abb. N. Cas. (N. Y.) 381; Clark v. Miller, 54 N. Y. 528; Van Schaick v. Sigel, 58 How. Pr. (N. Y.) 211; State v. Grizzard, 117 N. Car. 105, 23 S. E. 93; Green v. Garrington, 16 Ohio St. 548, 91 Am. Dec. 103; Polk v. Babcock, 5 Ore. 472; Peabody Bldg. &c. Assn. v. Houseman, 89 Pa. St. 261, 33 Am. Rep. 757, 7 Wkly. N. Cas. 193; Houseman v. Girard Mut. Bldg. &c. Assn., 81 Pa. St. 256; Schell v. Stein, 76 Pa. St. 398, 18 Am. Rep. 416; Armstrong v. Austin, 45 S. Car. 69, 22 S. E. 763, 29 L. R. A. 772; Maxwell v. Stuart, 99 Tenn. 409, 42 S. W. 34; Crews v. Taylor, 56 Tex. 461; Curtis v. Lyman, 24 Vt. 338, 58 Am. Dec. 174; Hunter v. Windsor, 24 Vt. 327; Mercantile Co-operative Bank v. Brown, 96 Va. 614, 32 S. E. 64; Johnson v. Brice, 102 Wis. 575, 78 N. W. 1086. See also Spencer v. Registrar, A. C. 503, 75 L. J. P. C. 100, 95 L. T. (N. S.) 316; Har-

knew it was forged.[45] It is not required of the recorder that he shall determine the genuineness or validity of an instrument before recording it.[46]

One who in good faith has taken a subsequent deed or mortgage of the property, on the faith of finding no incumbrance upon the index, has a remedy for damages against the register, whose duty it was under the law to make the index.[47] Where payment was indorsed on the back of a mortgage of certain lands and the register erroneously entered payment upon the margin of the record of a different mortgage between the same parties upon other lands, the register was held liable to a third person who made a loan to the mortgagee, and took a mortgage on the land erroneously released, and suffered loss in consequence.[48]

In Missouri a statute provides that a recorder who neglects or refuses to keep an index to the books of record shall pay to the party aggrieved double the damages which may be occasioned thereby; but the court has suggested that before a purchaser can recover for the failure of the recorder to index a prior mortgage upon the property, he must show that the damage arose from the recorder's neglect, and not from other causes; as, for instance, his own reliance upon false outside representations as to the title without an examination of the index, or from his mistaken reliance upon the covenants of the grantor.[49] In California a similar statute provides for treble damages against a recorder for negligence in recording conveyances, but the court, in a case where the record was made in the wrong book, refused to extend such relief to third persons, holding that the parties aggrieved within the meaning of the act referred only to the parties to the conveyance.[50]

§ 520. Index essential under some statutes.—In a few states, including Iowa and Washington, the index is an essential part of the

rison v. Brega, 20 U. C. Q. B. 324. A recorder is liable for loss arising from his failure to record in the book of mortgages and privileges an act of sale, giving rise to the vendor's privilege, and reserving a mortgage for the unpaid portion of the price. Baker v. Lee, 49 La. Ann. 874, 21 So. 588.

[45] Ramsey v. Riley, 13 Ohio St. 157.

[46] Sacerdotte v. Duralde, 1 La. 482.

[47] Mutual Life Ins. Co. v. Dake, 87 N. Y. 257, affg. 1 Abb. N. Cas. (N. Y.) 381, per Smith, J. See also Gordon v. Stanley, 108 La. 182, 32 So. 531; Van Schaick v. Siegel, 58 How. Pr. (N. Y.) 211.

[48] Mechanics' Bldg. Assn. v. Whitacre, 92 Ind. 547. See also State v. Green, 112 Mo. App. 108, 90 S. W. 403.

[49] Bishop v. Schneider, 46 Mo. 472, 2 Am. Rep. 533.

[50] Watkins v. Wilhoit (Cal.), 35 Pac. 646.

record, and a deed filed but not indexed,[51] or even copied into the record but not indexed,[52] does not impart constructive notice. The laws require a descriptive index to be kept, and prescribe the requisites of the index, and the index is regarded as an integral part of a complete and valid registration.[53]

In discussing the necessity of compliance with the Washington statute, requiring the correct entry of deeds in an index book, showing the time of filing, the names of the parties, the description of the property and the book and page of record, the court says: "The requirements specified above are for the direct and only purpose of giving notice to the public. They are vital provisions, essential to constitute constructive notice. * * * The Iowa statute was substantially as ours, except that the recorder was required to keep a 'fair book,' in which he entered every deed, giving date, parties, and description of land, in addition to the index with about the same requirements as ours. So that there was really more chance for an innocent purchaser to be put on his guard, under their registration laws, in the absence of the index, than under ours; and yet the Supreme Court of that state has uniformly held that the index was necessary to give constructive notice. * * * The law was, no doubt, suggested by the necessity of some such provisions as the records accumulated, and, at the present day, considering the accumulations of deeds, mortgages, and liens of all kinds, affecting real estate, and the rapidity with which such titles are changing every day, if we give the effect of constructive notice to the record at all, the only practical way by which the public can obtain the benefit of that notice is through the medium of the index."[54]

In Wisconsin, the rule has been applied to the record of tax deeds,[55] though not unqualifiedly to mortgages; and the omission of the description in such index is regarded as cured by the recording of the deed at length in the proper record.[56]

---

[51] Whalley v. Small, 25 Iowa 184; Congregational Church Bldg. Soc. v. Scandinavian Free Church, 24 Wash. 433, 64 Pac. 750 (mortgagor's name improperly indexed); Malbon v. Grow, 15 Wash. 301, 46 Pac. 330 (description in index ambiguous but sufficient); Ritchie v. Griffiths, 1 Wash. 429, 25 Pac. 341, 12 L. R. A. 384, 22 Am. St. 155 (fully discussing this view).

[52] Barney v. McCarty, 15 Iowa 510, 83 Am. Dec. 427; Peters v. Ham, 62 Iowa 656, 18 N. W. 296.

[53] Greenwood v. Jenswold, 69 Iowa 53, 28 N. W. 433; Barney v. McCarty, 15 Iowa 510, 83 Am. Dec. 427.

[54] Ritchie v. Griffiths, 1 Wash. 429, 25 Pac. 341, 12 L. R. A. 384, 22 Am. St. 155.

[55] Hiles v. Atlee, 80 Wis. 219, 49 N. W. 816, 27 Am. St. 32; Ramsay v. Hommel, 68 Wis. 12, 31 N. W. 271; Lombard v. Culbertson, 59 Wis. 433, 18 N. W. 399; Potts v. Cooley, 51 Wis. 353, 8 N. W. 153; International Life Ins. Co. v. Scales, 27 Wis. 640.

[56] Lane v. Duchac, 73 Wis. 646, 41

A recital in a mortgage for purchase-money, that the premises are the same conveyed to the mortgagor by the mortgagee by deed of even date, is generally sufficient notice of the mortgage when recorded, although by mistake the lot described is an entirely different lot. Yet in Iowa this recital is held to be an insufficient notice of the conveyance of the lot referred to in the recital, inasmuch as the lot described would appear in the index, and not the lot referred to in the recital.[57] If, however, a deed recites the existence of a prior mortgage of the same land, the grantee is charged with constructive notice of such prior mortgage, though it is not indexed on the records.[58] It is not necessary, however, that the descriptive part of the index should contain more than a reference to the record; and where a description by plan or survey is impracticable, a reference to "certain lots of land,"[59] or "see record,"[60] has been held sufficient; but where the mortgage covered two lots of land, but the description of one of them only was entered in the descriptive column of the index, it was held that the record did not impart constructive notice of the lot not described, and that the consequences of the recorder's error should fall upon the mortgagee, rather than upon subsequent purchasers.[61] The record, though complete in every other respect except that it is not properly indexed, does not operate as constructive notice.[62]

Yet, while an index is insufficient if it would mislead an inquirer by giving a totally wrong description, a mistake in the index reference to the page of the book where the instrument is recorded, the names of the grantor and the grantee being correctly given, does not prevent its operating as constructive notice of the acts which would be disclosed by an examination of the record. The record book and the index book are not considered detached and independent books, but are related and connected, and a party is affected with notice of the contents of the record when an ordinarily diligent search will bring him to a knowledge of such contents. To a competent examiner of the records, finding the name of one entered upon the index as having made a mortgage, it would occur that it was much more likely that

N. W. 962; Pringle v. Dunn, 37 Wis. 449, 19 Am. Rep. 772 (mortgage). See also St. Croix Land &c. Co. v. Ritchie, 73 Wis. 409, 41 N. W. 345 (tax deed); Oconto v. Jerrard, 46 Wis. 317, 50 N. W. 591 (tax deed).
[57] Whalley v. Small, 25 Iowa 184; Breed v. Conley, 14 Iowa 269, 81 Am. Dec. 485; Scoles v. Wilsey, 11 Iowa 261; Calvin v. Bowman, 10 Iowa 529.

[58] Ætna L. Ins. Co. v. Bishop, 69 Iowa 645, 29 N. W. 761.
[59] American Emigrant Co. v. Call, 22 Fed. 765; Bostwick v. Powers, 12 Iowa 456.
[60] White v. Hampton, 13 Iowa 259.
[61] Noyes v. Horr, 13 Iowa 570.
[62] Peters v. Ham, 62 Iowa 656, 18 N. W. 296; Howe v. Thayer, 49 Iowa 154; Gwynn v. Turner, 18 Iowa 1.

the recorder should make an error in entering the page of the record than that he should mistake the name of the mortgagor, or should enter his name at all if he had not recorded the deed.[63]

§ **521. Correction of errors in record.**—A register may correct an error in the record at any time subsequent to the registration. If he has omitted to indicate the seal or scroll opposite the grantor's signature, he may afterward supply the omission, or may record the deed anew.[64] And likewise he may supply the omission of an index entry, and the record will be good from the time of such correction without the necessity of re-recording.[65] Where the doctrine prevails that the record is notice of only what appears of record, though this be defecttive, a correction of a mistake in the record made by the register can not affect the rights of a purchaser without notice of the mistake who has become such after the record was made, but before the making of the correction.[66]

The record of a mortgage, duly transcribed, can not be altered by the recorder, even with the consent of the parties. The proper method to correct a material mistake in a recorded mortgage is to execute and record a new mortgage, reciting that it is given to correct the former mortgage.[67]

§ **521a. Curative statutes.**—In some states curative statutes have been enacted for the purpose of validating records of conveyances which are defective because of omissions or errors in the prescribed formalities, such as the certificate of acknowledgment,[68] the requisite

---

[63] Barney v. Little, 15 Iowa 527. See comments upon this and other Iowa cases, 4 Cent. L. J. 387.

[64] Sellers v. Sellers, 98 N. Car. 13, 3 S. E. 917.

[65] Bardon v. Land &c. Imp. Co., 157 U. S. 327, 39 L. ed. 719, 15 Sup. Ct. 650; Agurs v. Belcher, 111 La. 378, 35 So. 607, 100 Am. St. 485; Hotson v. Wetherby, 88 Wis. 324, 60 N. W. 423.

[66] Chamberlain v. Bell, 7 Cal. 292, 68 Am. Dec. 260; Harrison v. Wade, 3 Cold. (Tenn.) 505; Baldwin v. Marshall, 2 Humph. (Tenn.) 116. See also Jay v. Carthage, 48 Maine 353.

[67] Youtz v. Julliard, 10 Ohio Dec. 298, 20 Wkly. L. Bul. 26. The recorder has no authority to interpolate anything into the original record of an instrument. Burton v.

Martz, 38 Mich. 761; Sellers v. Sellers, 98 N. Car. 13, 3 S. E. 917. A second mortgage covering the same realty and securing the same debt, between the same parties, reciting that it is given to correct a former mortgage, supersedes the first, and the two constitute one mortgage, nothing having intervened to affect the mortgagee's security. Rossbach v. Micks, 89 Nebr. 821, 132 N. W. 526.

[68] Defective acknowledgments of mortgages and deeds have frequently been cured by statute. Raverty v. Fridge, 3 McLean (U. S.) 230, Fed. Cas. No. 11586; Elliott v. Pearce, 20 Ark. 508; Landers v. Bolton, 26 Cal. 393; Logan v. Williams, 76 Ill. 175; Deininger v. McConnel, 41 Ill. 227; Cole v. Wright, 70 Ind. 179; Steeple v. Downing, 60

number of witnesses, or the notarial seal.[69] Although retrospective in their operation,[70] such statutes have generally been held constitutional and valid.[71] They can not, however, impair the rights of third persons which have vested in the meantime;[72] and some curative acts have been applied only to deeds recorded after their passage.[73]

Ind. 478; Jones v. Berkshire, 15 Iowa 248, 83 Am. Dec. 412; Dulany v. Tilghman, 6 Gill & J. (Md.) 461; Hollingsworth v. McDonald, 2 Har. & J. (Md.) 230, 3 Am. Dec. 545; Lariverre v. Rains, 112 Mich. 276, 70 N. W. 583; Brooks v. Fairchild, 36 Mich. 231; Brown v. McCormick, 28 Mich. 215; Brown v. Cady, 11 Mich. 535; Williams v. Butterfield, 182 Mo. 181, 81 S. W. 615; German-American Bank v. Carondelet Real Estate Co., 150 Mo. 570, 51 S. W. 691; Bishop v. Schneider, 46 Mo. 472, 2 Am. Rep. 533; Stevens v. Hampton, 46 Mo. 404; Allen v. Moss, 27 Mo. 354; Tatom v. White, 95 N. Car. 453; Barton v. Morris, 15 Ohio 408; Cable v. Cable, 146 Pa. St. 451, 23 Atl. 223; Journeay v. Gibson, 56 Pa. St. 57; Rigler v. Cloud, 14 Pa. St. 361; Jaques v. Weeks, 7 Watts (Pa.) 261; Green v. Goodall, 1 Coldw. (Tenn.) 404; Rainey v. Gordon, 6 Humph. (Tenn.) 345; Montgomery v. Hobson, Meigs (Tenn.) 437; Baker v. Westcott, 73 Tex. 129, 11 S. W. 157; Butler v. Dunagan, 19 Tex. 559; McCelvey v. Cryer, 8 Tex. Civ. App. 437, 28 S. W. 691; Skellinger v. Smith, 1 Wash. Ter. 369; Williams v. Milwaukee Industrial Exposition Assn., 79 Wis. 524, 48 N. W. 665. See also Smith v. Gale, 144 U. S. 509, 36 L. ed. 521, 12 Sup. Ct. 674 (construing the statute of Dakota Ter.); Farrel Foundry v. Dart, 26 Conn. 376. A subsequent purchaser must take notice of a mortgage defectively acknowledged but validated by statute. Journeay v. Gibson, 56 Pa. St. 57.

[69] Certificate void for want of seal may be validated by statute. Cole v. Wright, 70 Ind. 179; Tidd v. Rines, 26 Minn. 201, 2 N. W. 497; Barton v. Morris, 15 Ohio 408; Jaques v. Weeks, 7 Watts (Pa.) 261; Williams v. Milwaukee Industrial Exposition Assn., 79 Wis. 524, 48 N. W. 665. See also Detroit v. Detroit

&c. R. Co., 23 Mich. 173. If the absence of a seal is fatal to the validity of the certificate, the defect may be cured by statute. Maxey v. Wise, 25 Ind. 1; Kenyon v. Knipe, 2 Wash. Ter. 422, 7 Pac. 854.

[70] Curative acts relating to the acknowledgment of conveyances, have been held to operate retrospectively only, in the following cases: Logan v. Williams, 76 Ill. 175 (under Illinois act of 1829); Jones v. Berkshire, 15 Iowa 248, 83 Am. Dec. 412 (under act of 1858); Reynolds v. Kingsbury, 15 Iowa 238; Stevens v. Hampton, 46 Mo. 404 (act of 1855); Mercer v. Watson, 1 Watts (Pa.) 330, affd. in Watson v, Mercer, 8 Pet. (U. S.) 88, 8 L. ed. 876; Spinning v. Home Bldg. &c. Assn., 26 Ohio St. 483.

[71] Logan v. Williams, 76 Ill. 175; Bishop v. Schneider, 46 Mo. 472, 2 Am. Rep. 533; Stevens v. Hampton, 46 Mo. 404. See also McFaddin v. Evans-Snider-Duel Co., 185 U. S. 505, 46 L. ed. 1012, 22 Sup. Ct. 758; Gillespie v. Reed, 3 McLean (U. S.) 377, Fed. Cas. No. 5436; Wallace v. Moody, 26 Cal. 387; Reed v. Kemp, 16 Ill. 445; Buckley v. Early, 72 Iowa 289, 33 N. W. 769; Brown v. Simpson, 4 Kans. 76; German-American Bank v. White, 38 Minn. 471, 38 N. W. 361; Allen v. Moss, 27 Mo. 354; Barnet v. Barnet, 15 Serg. & R. (Pa.) 72, 16 Am. Dec. 516; Maley v. Tipton, 2 Head (Tenn.) 403.

[72] Logan v. Williams, 76 Ill. 175. See also Carson v. Thompson, 10 Wash. 295, 38 Pac. 1116.

[73] The Illinois Act of 1837, relating to defectively acknowledged instruments, is not retrospective, but intended only to give effect to records made after its enactment. Deininger v. McConnell, 41 Ill. 227. The Ohio Act of 1858, validating acts of notaries public after the expiration of their terms of office, is not retroactive and will not operate to cure an acknowledgment taken

§ 522. Unrecorded or defectively recorded mortgage as an equitable lien.—A deed or mortgage defectively recorded, or not recorded at all, is in some states a good equitable lien, so that, while it has no effect as against subsequent purchasers in good faith, yet it is superior to the claims of creditors under subsequent judgments;[74] and in a few states such lien has been held superior to the claims of general creditors who were such at the date of the mortgage;[75] and it is superior to a subsequent voluntary assignment by the mortgagor for the benefit of creditors.[76] In like manner a mortgage defectively executed, as, for instance, attested by only one witness when two are required, is a good equitable mortgage.[77]

According to the authorities in some states, however, a mortgage defectively recorded, or not recorded at all, is subject to the lien of a judgment or attaching creditor.[78] As against third parties having notice, such mortgage is also a good specific lien which will be enforced in equity.[79] The burden of proving actual notice is upon the

---

before the act was passed. Bernier v. Becker, 37 Ohio St. 72.

[74] See ante § 464.

[75] Lake v. Doud, 10 Ohio 415; Bank of Muskingum v. Carpenter, 7 Ohio 21, 28 Am. Rep. 616; otherwise, however, under later cases in Ohio: White v. Denman, 1 Ohio St. 110; Bloom v. Noggle, 4 Ohio St. 45; Sixth Ward Bldg. Assn. v. Willson, 41 Md. 506. See also Bibb v. Baker, 17 B. Mon. (Ky.) 292; Phillips v. Pearson, 27 Md. 242; Price v. McDonald, 1 Md. 403, 54 Am. Dec. 657; Armstrong v. Carwille, 56 S. Car. 463, 35 S. E. 196. It has been held in Georgia that a mortgage takes precedence over debts due general creditors, whether created before or subsequent to the mortgage. Seaboard Air Line R. Co. v. Knickerbocker Trust Co., 125 Ga. 463, 54 S. E. 138. In Missouri a mortgage unrecorded before a judgment is good against the judgment if recorded before the execution sale under the judgment. Shaw v. Padley, 64 Mo. 519; Valentine v. Havener, 20 Mo. 133. General creditors are not within the protection of the recording laws of North Dakota relating to real estate. Vallely v. First Nat. Bank, 14 N. Dak. 580, 106 N. W. 127, 5 L. R. A. (N. S.) 387, 116 Am. St. 700. The Indiana statute, providing that every

conveyance or mortgage of lands not recorded within forty-five days shall be void as against any subsequent purchaser, lessee, or mortgagee in good faith, does not protect general creditors against unrecorded conveyances. State Bank v. Backus, 160 Ind. 682, 66 N. E. 475, 67 N. E. 512, construing Burns' Ann. Stat. 1901, § 3350. See also Burns' Ann. Stat. 1914, § 3962.

[76] Nice's Appeal, 54 Pa. St. 200.

[77] Abbott v. Godfroy, 1 Mich. 178. See ante §§ 166, 168.

[78] Henderson v. McGhee, 6 Heisk. (Tenn.) 55.

[79] Coonrod v. Kelly, 113 Fed. 378, 119 Fed. 841; Wyatt v. Stewart, 34 Ala. 716; Dearing v. Watkins, 16 Ala. 20; Carpenter v. Lewis, 119 Cal. 18, 50 Pac. 925; Racouillat v. Sansevain, 32 Cal. 376; Gardner v. Moore, 51 Ga. 268; Columbus Buggy Co. v. Graves, 108 Ill. 459; Maxwell v. Brooks, 54 Ind. 98; Blackman v. Henderson, 116 Iowa 578, 87 N. W. 655, 56 L. R. A. 902; Flowers v. Moorman, 27 Ky. L. 728, 86 S. W. 545; Verges v. Prejean, 24 La. Ann. 78; Russum v. Wanser, 53 Md. 92; Dyson v. Simmons, 48 Md. 207; Whitney v. Browne, 180 Mass. 597, 62 N. E. 979; Lamberton v. Merchants' Nat. Bank, 24 Minn. 281; Harrington v. Allen, 48 Miss. 492;

party seeking to establish title by the unrecorded mortgage.[80]

Such an equitable mortgage has been held to be superior to the claims of the mortgagor's general creditors. This was the rule in South Carolina before the Act of 1843, later embodied in the Revised Statutes of that state. A legal mortgage not recorded, or an equitable mortgage incapable of record, was preferred to a subsequent creditor without notice. The consequence of imparting validity to unrecorded mortgages is said to have wrought much injury by impairing confidence in titles, and thereby depreciating the value of real estate. The act above referred to placed subsequent creditors and purchasers upon the same footing.[81]

V. The Effect of a Record Duly Made

§ 523. Record as constructive notice.—The record of a deed or mortgage is constructive notice to all subsequent purchasers and mortgagees in the line of title.[1] As to them the instrument takes effect, not because of its prior execution, but by reason of its prior record. Sub-

---

Finley v. Babb, 173 Mo. 257, 73 S. W. 180; Trigg v. Vermillion, 113 Mo. 230, 20 S. W. 1047; Enyart v. Moran, 64 Nebr. 401, 89 N. W. 1045; Kline v. Grannis, 61 N. J. Eq. 397, 48 Atl. 566; Matthews v. Everitt, 23 N. J. Eq. 473; Harrison v. New Jersey R. &c. Co., 19 N. J. Eq. 488; Moore v. Davey, 1 N. Mex. 303; Westbrook v. Gleason, 79 N. Y. 23; People v. Woodruff, 75 App. Div. (N. Y.) 90, 77 N. Y. S. 722; Nice's Appeal, 54 Pa. St. 200; King v. Fraser, 23 S. Car. 543. See also English v. Lindley, 194 Ill. 181, 62 N. E. 522. But see Wood v. Tinsley, 138 N. Car. 507, 51 S E. 59.

[80] Schoonover v. Foley (Iowa), 94 N. W. 492; Sidelinger v. Bliss, 95 Maine 316, 49 Atl. 1094. But see Sanely v. Crapenhoft, 1 Nebr. (Unoff.) 8, 95 N. W. 352.

[81] Boyce v. Shiver, 3 S. Car. 515. "There is not a single modern writer, whose opinion carries weight, who does not regret that the courts ever favored the introduction of secret liens."

[1] In re The Vigilancia, 68 Fed. 781, 73 Fed. 452, 19 C. C. A. 528; McCormack v. James, 36 Fed. 14; Kent v. Williams, 146 Cal. 3, 79 Pac. 527; Hager v. Spect, 52 Cal. 579; McCabe v. Grey, 20 Cal. 509;

sequent purchasers are bound conclusively by the record of a deed, or other conveyance in the line of their title, as much as the mortgagor himself.[2] It is notice only to subsequent purchasers and incumbran-

Dennis v. Burritt, 6 Cal. 670; Mesick v. Sunderland, 6 Cal. 298; Smith v. Russell, 20 Colo. 554, 80 Pac. 474; Beach v. Osborne, 74 Conn. 405; Ensign v. Batterson, 68 Conn. 298; Hamilton v. Nutt, 34 Conn. 501; Bush v. Golden, 17 Conn. 594; Orvis v. Newell, 17 Conn. 97; Sumner v. Rhodes, 14 Conn. 135; Osborn v. Carr, 12 Conn. 195; Bolles v. Chauncey, 8 Conn. 389; Peters v. Goodrich, 3 Conn. 146; Armstrong v. Ashley, 22 App. D. C. 368; Havighorst v. Bowen, 214 Ill. 90, 73 N. E. 402; Buchanan v. International Bank, 78 Ill. 500; Schmidt v. Zahrndt, 148 Ind. 447, 47 N. E. 335; Begein v. Brehm, 123 Ind. 160, 23 N. E. 496; Blair v. Whittaker, 31 Ind. App. 664, 69 N. E. 182; Wilson v. Godfrey, 145 Iowa 696, 124 N. W. 875; Stastny v. Pease, 124 Iowa 587, 100 N. W. 482; Crooks v. Jenkins, 124 Iowa 317, 100 N. W. 82, 104 Am. St. 326; Thomas v. Kennedy, 24 Iowa 397, 95 Am. Dec. 740; Ogden v. Walters, 12 Kans. 282; Banton v. Shorey, 77 Maine 48; Humphreys v. Newman, 51 Maine 40; Cushing v. Ayer, 25 Maine 383; Hall v. McDuff, 24 Maine 311; Clabaugh v. Byerly, 7 Gill (Md.) 354, 48 Am. Dec. 575; Shaw v. Poor, 6 Pick. (Mass.) 86, 17 Am. Dec. 347; McMechan v. Griffing, 3 Pick. (Mass.) 149, 15 Am. Dec. 198; Campbell v. Keys, 130 Mich. 127, 89 N. W. 720; Mee v. Benedict, 98 Mich. 260, 57 N. W. 175, 22 L. R. A. 641, 39 Am. St. 543; Edwards v. McKernan, 55 Mich. 520, 22 N. W. 20; Doyle v. Stevens, 4 Mich. 87; Robley v. Withers, 95 Miss. 318, 51 So. 719; Tripe v. Marcy, 39 N. H. 439; Locker v. Riley, 30 N. J. Eq. 104; Hoy v. Bramhall, 19 N. J. Eq. 563, 97 Am. Dec. 687; Mitchell v. D'Olier, 68 N. J. L. 375, 53 Atl. 467, 59 L. R. A. 949; Wallace v. Silsby, 42 N. J. L. 1; McPherson v. Rollins, 107 N. Y. 316, 14 N. E. 411, 1 Am. St. 826; Youngs v. Wilson, 27 N. Y. 351; Matthews v. Damainville, 43 Misc. 546, 89 N. Y. S. 493; Schutt v. Large, 6 Barb. (N. Y.) 373; James v. Morey, 2 Cow. (N. Y.) 246, 14 Am. Dec. 475; Wendell v. Wadsworth, 20 Johns. (N. Y.) 659; Brinckerhoff v. Lansing, 4 Johns. Ch. (N. Y.) 65, 8 Am. Dec. 538; Berry v. Mutual Ins. Co., 2 Johns. Ch. (N. Y.) 603; Johnson v. Stagg, 2 Johns. (N. Y.) 510; Parkist v. Alexander, 1 Johns. Ch. (N. Y.) 394; Grandin v. Anderson, 15 Ohio St. 286; Irvin v. Smith, 17 Ohio 226; Souder v. Morrow, 33 Pa. St. 83; Hetherington v. Clark, 30 Pa. St. 393; Barbour v. Nichols, 3 R. I. 187; Annely v. De Saussure, 12 S. Car. 488; Martin v. Sale, Bailey Eq. (S. Car.) 1; Edwards v. Barwise, 69 Tex. 84, 6 S. W. 677; Wells v. Smith, 2 Utah 39; Clason v. Shepherd, 6 Wis. 369. A duly recorded mortgage has priority over an unrecorded vendor's lien. National Bank v. Spot Cash Coal Co., 98 Ark. 597, 136 S. W. 953. The recording of a mortgage is notice to an assignee of a subsequent mortgage, who is considered a purchaser. Elgin City Banking Co. v. Center, 83 Ill. App. 405, affd. 185 Ill. 534, 57 N. E. 439. A subsequent mortgagee without notice of a prior mortgage or deed obtains a superior lien by recording his mortgage first. Brown v. Sartor, 87 S. Car. 116, 69 S. E. 88. See also Gay v. Hudson River Electric Power Co., 190 Fed. 773; Bennett v. United States Land &c. Co. (Ariz.), 141 Pac. 717 (record as notice to subsequent lessee of mortgaged premises); Hunter v. State Bank, 65 Fla. 202, 61 So. 497; Anderson v. Casey-Swasey Co. (Tex. Civ. App.), 120 S. W. 918; Coolidge v. Schering, 32 Wash. 557, 73 Pac. 682; Keene Guaranty Sav. Bank v. Lawrence, 32 Wash. 572, 73 Pac. 680.

[2] North v. Knowlton, 23 Fed. 163; Tripe v. Marcy, 39 N. H. 439; Grandin v. Anderson, 15 Ohio St. 286. See also Leiby v. Wolf, 10 Ohio 83. A recital in a recorded mortgage indicating the mortgagor's source of title, and possession of the premises by a tenant claiming under the same title, con-

cers under the same grantor, or through one who is the common source of title in the line of title to which the recorded deed belongs.[3] Of course, the record of a mortgage operates as notice to persons subsequently acquiring title to the mortgaged premises from the mortgagor,[4] and, so long as the mortgage remains undischarged, the record protects not only the rights of the mortgagee, but those of an assignee of the mortgage as well.[5]

Record of an equitable title is not notice to a purchaser of the legal title from one who appears to be the record owner.[6] And likewise the record of an executory agreement to give a mortgage on the happening of a future event, is not notice to a subsequent purchaser or mortgagee.[7] A mortgage by a stranger to the record title is not construcive notice to an intending purchaser of a prior unrecorded deed to the mortgagor; nor is the fact that the property is assessed to another than the record owner such notice.[8] It is not notice to those who have

stitute notice to subsequent purchasers and mortgagees, putting them upon inquiry, and depriving them of the character of bona fide purchasers. Prest v. Black, 63 Kans. 682, 66 Pac. 1017; Hubbard v. Knight, 52 Nebr. 400, 72 N. W. 473.

[3] Hager v. Spect, 52 Cal. 579; Long v. Dollarhide, 24 Cal. 218; McCabe v. Grey, 20 Cal. 509; Dennis v. Burritt, 6 Cal. 670; Whittington v. Wright, 9 Ga. 23; Kerfoot v. Cronin, 105 Ill. 609; Doolittle v. Cook, 75 Ill. 354; Iglehart v. Crane, 42 Ill. 261; Tilton v. Hunter, 24 Maine 29; Roberts v. Boune, 23 Maine 165, 39 Am. Dec. 614; George v. Wood, 9 Allen (Mass.) 80, 85 Am. Dec. 741; Bates v. Norcross, 14 Pick. (Mass.) 224; Cooper v. Bigly, 13 Mich. 463; James v. Brown, 11 Mich. 25; Baker v. Griffin, 50 Miss. 158; Harper v. Hopkins, 34 Miss. 472; Odle v. Odle, 73 Mo. 289; Draude v. Rohrer Mfg. Co., 9 Mo. App. 249; Traphagen v. Irwin, 18 Nebr. 195; Ross v. Leavitt, 70 N. H. 602, 50 Atl. 110; Hill v. McCarter, 27 N. J. Eq. 41; Ward v. Hague, 25 N. J. Eq. 397; Hoy v. Bramhall, 19 N. J. Eq. 563, 97 Am. Dec. 687; Vanorden v. Johnson, 14 N. J. Eq. 376; Losey v. Simpson, 11 N. J. Eq. 246; Blair v. Ward. 10 N. J. Eq. 119; Tarbell v. West, 86 N. Y. 280; Page v. Waring, 76 N. Y. 463; How-

ard Ins. Co. v. Halsey, 8 N. Y. 271, 59 Am. Dec. 478; Stuyvesant v. Hall, 2 Barb. Ch. (N. Y.) 251; Wheelwright v. De Peyster, 4 Edw. Ch. (N. Y.) 232, 3 Am. Dec. 345; Kyle v. Thompson, 11 Ohio St. 616; Blake v. Graham, 6 Ohio St. 580, 67 Am. Dec. 360; Leiby v. Wolf, 10 Ohio 83; Collins v. Aaron, 162 Pa. St. 539, 29 Atl. 724; Maul v. Rider, 59 Pa. St. 167; Calder v. Chapman, 52 Pa. St. 359; King v. McCarthy, 38 Pa. St. 76; Taylor v. Maris, 5 Rawle (Pa.) 51; Keller v. Nutz, 5 Serg. & R. (Pa.) 246; Woods v. Farmere, 7 Watts (Pa.) 382; Simpkinson v. McGee, 4 Lea (Tenn.) 432; Helms v. Chadbourne, 45 Wis. 60.

[4] Commercial Bank v. Pritchard, 126 Cal. 600, 59 Pac. 130; Thompson v. Flathers, 45 La. Ann. 120, 12 So. 245. A subsequent purchaser with actual or constructive notice acquires the legal title conveyed him, subject to the lien of the mortgage. Davis v. Lanier, 94 Tex. 455, 61 S. W. 385.

[5] Curtis v. Moore, 152 N. Y. 159, 46 N. E. 168, 57 Am. St. 506. See also Babcock v. Young, 117 Mich. 155, 75 N. W. 302.

[6] Tarbell v. West, 86 N. Y. 280; Odle v. Odle, 73 Mo. 289.

[7] Matthews v. Damainville, 100 App. Div. 311, 91 N. Y. S. 524, 15 Ann. Cas. 436.

[8] Advance Thresher Co. v. Esteb,

prior rights of record, or even to those whose rights are contemporaneous with those of the grantor, as, for instance, to his cotenants; therefore, a mortgage by one tenant in common, though duly recorded, is no notice to his cotenant of its existence, or of the claim of the mortgagor to the exclusive ownership of the land.[9]

When a mortgage is recorded prior to another conveyance from the mortgagor, it does not matter that this conveyance was made in pursuance of a contract entered into after the execution of the mortgage, and before the record of it, if nothing had been done toward carrying the contract into execution at the time of the filing of the mortgage for record.[10] From that time it is constructive notice to all who may afterward acquire any interest in the same property. The constructive notice resulting from the record of a mortgage does not deprive a purchaser of the right to rely upon the vendor's positive statements, fraudulently made, that the property was unincumbered, nor does it prevent him from suing for false representation; for such statements if true would have rendered a search of the records unnecessary.[11] But, on the other hand, it has been held that a purchaser of land, incumbered by a duly recorded and unsatisfied mortgage, can not rely upon the assurance of the mortgagor that it has been paid, without making further inquiries, and that he is not protected against a prior unrecorded assignment of the mortgage by procuring a discharge from the mortgagee and recording it.[12]

§ 524. Record as notice of the contents of a mortgage.—A mortgage duly recorded is notice not only of the existence of the mortgage, but of all its contents, so far as these fall within the line of the chain

41 Ore. 469, 69 Pac. 447. Sternberger v. Ragland, 57 Ohio St. 148, 48 N. E. 811. In this case Mr. Justice Williams said: "When a prospective purchaser finds a complete record title in the proposed seller, he is not bound to examine for mortgages made to the latter after he became the owner. Such a mortgage is not in the chain of his title, and is not, therefore, constructive notice to a subsequent purchaser of a prior unrecorded deed made by him to the mortgagor." See also Truitt v. Grandy, 115 N. Car. 54,

20 S. E. 293; Maddox v. Arp, 114 N. Car. 585, 19 S. E. 665; Lumpkin v. Adams, 74 Tex. 96, 11 S. W. 1070; Williams v. Slaughter (Tex. Civ. App.), 42 S. W. 327; Peterson v. McCauley (Tex.), 25 S. W. 826; Sayward v. Thompson, 11 Wash. 706, 40 Pac. 379.

[9] Leach v. Beattie, 33 Vt. 195.
[10] Kyle v. Thompson, 11 Ohio St. 616.
[11] Weber v. Weber, 47 Mich. 569, 11 N. W. 389.
[12] Babcock v. Young, 117 Mich. 155, 75 N. W. 302.

of title.[13] It is notice, too, of the covenants contained in it.[14] It is notice of the debt which the mortgage secured.[15] It is notice of any easements or privileges created by the deed, or referred to in it.[16] It is notice that trustees in a trust deed should have an estate in fee simple in order to execute its provisions, and therefore that an estate in fee passes although words of inheritance have been inadvertently omitted.[17]

Although the debt or the property be not fully described, the record is notice of all that is said about it, and a purchaser is bound by the statements made, and by the information he is put upon the inquiry to find out.[18] It is notice of the statements in it regarding the debt, whether the description be fully set out, or consists of references to other instruments.[19] It is notice of a prior unrecorded mortgage referred to in the covenant against incumbrances.[20] It is notice not only to purchasers, but to the subsequent creditors as well. They can not complain that the transaction is fraudulent, unless they can show that the object of the conveyance was to avoid subsequent indebtedness.[21]

The record imparts notice of all the facts which could have been ascertained by an actual examination thereof, including not only those recited in the record,[22] but also material matters suggested thereby,

[13] Beach v. Osborne, 74 Conn. 405, 50 Atl. 1019; Matt v. Matt, 156 Iowa 503, 137 N. W. 489; Sowden v. Craig, 26 Iowa 156, 96 Am. Dec. 125; Bancroft v. Cousen, 13 Allen (Mass.) 50; George v. Kent, 7 Allen (Mass.) 16; Roussain v. Norton, 53 Minn. 560, 55 N. W. 747; Harrison v. Cachelin, 23 Mo. 117; Stark v. Kirkley, 129 Mo. App. 353, 108 S. W. 625; McPherson v. Rollins, 107 N. Y. 316, 14 N. E. 411, 1 Am. St. 826; Thomson v. Wilcox, 7 Lans. (N. Y.) 376; Grandin v. Anderson, 15 Ohio St. 286; Kyle v. Thompson, 11 Ohio St. 616; Leiby v. Wolf, 10 Ohio 83; Gulf C. &c. R. Co. v. Gill, 86 Tex. 284, 24 S. W. 502.

[14] Morris v. Wadsworth, 17 Wend. (N. Y.) 103.

[15] Dean v. De Lezardi, 24 Miss. 424; Whitney v. Lowe, 59 Nebr. 87, 80 N. W. 266; Youngs v. Wilson, 27 N. Y. 351. See post § 531.

[16] Bellas v. Lloyd, 2 Watts (Pa.) 401.

[17] Randolph v. New Jersey West Line R. Co., 28 N. J. Eq. 49. See also McPherson v. Rollins, 107 N.

Y. 316, 14 N. E. 411, 1 Am. St. 826; Weldon v. Tollman, 67 Fed. 986, 15 C. C. A. 138; citing Williams v. Jackson, 107 U. S. 478, 27 L. ed. 529, 2 Sup. Ct. 814; Livermore v. Maxwell, 87 Iowa 705, 55 N. W. 37.

[18] Bright v. Buckman, 39 Fed. 243; Young v. Wilson, 27 N. Y. 351, revg. 24 Barb. 510. See also Livingstone v. Murphy, 187 Mass. 315, 72 N. E. 1012, 105 Am. St. 400 (insufficient recital in mortgage to put purchaser upon inquiry concerning obligees on the note secured).

[19] Dimon v. Dunn, 15 N. Y. 498.

[20] Taylor v. Mitchell, 58 Kans. 194, 48 Pac. 859.

[21] Hickman v. Perrin, 6 Coldw. (Tenn.) 135.

[22] Weldon v. Tollman, 67 Fed. 986, 15 C. C. A. 138; The W. B. Cole, 59 Fed. 182, 8 C. C. A. 78; Mettart v. Allen, 139 Ind. 644, 39 N. E. 239; Taylor v. Mitchell, 58 Kans. 194, 48 Pac. 859; Livingstone v. Murphy, 187 Mass. 315, 72 N. E. 1012, 105 Am. St. 400; Pleasants v. Blodgett, 39 Nebr. 741, 58 N. W. 423, 42 Am. St. 624; Mitchell v. D'Olier, 68 N. J. L. 375, 53 Atl. 467, 59 L. R. A.

which might be disclosed by reasonable inquiry.[23] But constructive notice from the record of a mortgage can not be more extensive than the facts stated therein, and only embraces information which could have been obtained from an actual inspection of the record.[24]

949; Coon v. Bosque Bonita Land &c. Co., 8 N. Mex. 123, 42 Pac. 77; McPherson v. Rollins, 107 N. Y. 316, 14 N. E. 411, 1 Am. St. 826; Ford v. Green, 121 N. Car. 70, 28 S. E. 132 (record of mortgage as notice of default); Hall v. Donagan, 186 Pa. St. 300, 40 Atl. 493; Waggoner v. Dodson, 96 Tex. 415, 73 S. W. 517; Fulkerson v. Taylor, 102 Va. 314, 46 S. E. 309; Hancock v. McAvoy, 151 Pa. St. 439, 25 Atl. 48; Garrett v. Parker (Tex.), 39 S. W. 147; Powers v. Smith (Tex.), 29 S. W. 416.

[23] Mattlage v. Mulherin, 106 Ga. 834, 32 S. E. 940; Talmadge v. Interstate Bldg. &c. Assn., 105 Ga. 550, 31 S. E. 618; Mettart v. Allen, 139 Ind. 644, 39 N. E. 239; Loser v. Plainfield Sav. Bank, 149 Iowa 672, 128 N. W. 1101; Layman v. Vicknair, 47 La. Ann. 679, 17 So. 265; Carter v. Leonard, 65 Nebr. 670, 91 N. W. 574; McPherson v. Rollins, 107 N. Y. 316, 14 N. E. 411, 1 Am. St. 826; Collins v. Davis, 132 N. Car. 106, 43 S. E. 579; Livingstone v. Murphy, 187 Mass. 315, 72 N. E. 1012, 105 Am. St. 400; Coleman v. Reynolds, 181 Pa. St. 317, 37 Atl. 543; Jenkins v. Adams, 71 Tex. 1, 8 S. W. 603; Taylor v. Harrison, 47 Tex. 454, 26 Am. Rep. 304. See also Northwestern Nat. Bank v. Freeman, 171 U. S. 620, 43 L. ed. 307, 19 Sup. Ct. 36; Mitchell v. D'Olier, 68 N. J. L. 375, 53 Atl. 467, 59 L. R. A. 949. The record showing a deed of property worth $575, for an expressed consideration of $125, with a land contract at the same time, reciting a like amount as the purchase-price, is sufficient notice that the transaction is a mortgage to put one upon inquiry. Cumps v. Kiyo, 104 Wis. 656, 80 N. W. 937. A recorded mortgage by the wife of the owner of property, in which the husband joined only in release of dower, is not constructive notice to persons claiming under the husband, nor sufficient to

put them on inquiry, though the note secured was actually signed by both. In any event, a mortgage which has been satisfied, does not amount to notice of recitals therein. Livingstone v. Murphy, 187 Mass. 315, 72 N. E. 1012, 105 Am. St. 400.

[24] Mims v. Mims, 35 Ala. 23; Johnson v. Wheelock, 63 Ga. 623; Shepherd v. Burkhalter, 13 Ga. 443, 58 Am. Dec. 523; Metropolitan Bank v. Godfrey, 23 Ill. 579; Smith v. Lowry, 113 Ind. 37, 15 N. E. 17; Singer v. Scheible, 109 Ind. 575, 10 N. E. 616; Gilchrist v. Gough, 63 Ind. 576, 30 Am. Rep. 250; Glassburn v. Wireman, 126 Iowa 478, 12 N. W. 421; Fetes v. O'Laughlin, 62 Iowa 532, 17 N. W. 764; Disque v. Wright, 49 Iowa 538; Barney v. McCarty, 15 Iowa 510, 83 Am. Dec. 427; Haynes v. Seachrest, 13 Iowa 455; Hill v. McNichol, 76 Maine 314; Norman v. Towne, 130 Mass. 52; Hinchman v. Town, 10 Mich. 508; Barrows v. Baughman, 9 Mich. 213; Lash v. Edgerton, 13 Minn. 210; Whittacre v. Fuller, 5 Minn. 508; Parret v. Shaubhut, 5 Minn. 323, 80 Am. Dec. 424; Hart v. Gardner, 81 Miss. 650, 33 So. 442; Bishop v. Schneider, 46 Mo. 472, 2 Am. Rep. 533; Stevens v. Hampton, 46 Mo. 404; Westervelt v. Wyckoff, 32 N. J. Eq. 188; Bunker v. Anderson, 32 N. J. Eq. 35; Gale v. Morris, 29 N. J. Eq. 222; Peck v. Mallams, 10 N. Y. 509, Seld. Notes 199; Beekman v. Frost, 18 Johns. (N. Y.) 544, 9 Am. Dec. 246; Branch v. Griffin, 99 N. Car. 173, 5 S. E. 393; Ijames v. Gaither, 93 N. Car. 358; Brown v. Kirkman, 1 Ohio St. 116; Jennings v. Wood, 20 Ohio 261; Schell v. Stein, 76 Pa. St. 398, 18 Am. Rep. 416; Speer v. Evans, 47 Pa. St. 141; In re Luch's Appeal, 44 Pa. St. 519; McLouth v. Hurt, 51 Tex. 115; Sawyer v. Adams, 8 Vt. 172, 30 Am. Dec. 459; Colquhoun v. Atkinson, 6 Munf. (Va.) 550; Davison v. Waite, 2 Munf. (Va.) 527; George v. Butler,

Subsequent purchasers are entitled to rely upon the record, and can not be charged with notice of latent equities or facts not disclosed or suggested by the record itself.[25] Thus, where a mortgage appears satisfied of record by one having apparent authority to discharge it, a subsequent purchaser from the mortgagor, relying upon the record, will be protected although such discharge of record was fraudulently made.[26]

The record of a mortgage on land is constructive notice to a purchaser that the mortgagor claims some interest in the mortgaged land necessitating inquiry,[27] and that the mortgagee has a right therein as the owner of an existing incumbrance; but it is not notice of an assignment or the rights of an assignee.[28]

The record of a mortgage containing a power of sale puts subsequent purchasers upon inquiry whether any proceedings have been had thereunder; so that if there has been a sale under the power, although the deed has not been recorded, a subsequent purchaser from the mortgagor, instead of acquiring an equity of redemption, may find that this has been cut off by sale under the power.[29] The deed executing the power of sale relates back to the execution of the mortgage; and when the mortgage is recorded, it is not necessary to record the deed under the power in order to protect the grantee against attaching creditors of the mortgagor.[30] A recorded mortgage providing that no action can be brought by bondholders upon the bonds secured, until

26 Wash. 456, 67 Pac. 263, 57 L. R. A. 396, 90 Ann. St. 756; State v. Titus, 17 Wis. 241.

[25] Johnson v. Wilson, 137 Ala. 468, 34 So. 392, 97 Am. St. 52; Peck v. Dyer, 147 Ill. 592, 35 N. E. 479; Glassburn v. Wireman, 126 Iowa 478, 102 N. W. 421; Bordelon v. Gumbel, 118 La. 645, 43 So. 264; Lawson v. Conolly, 51 La. Ann. 1753, 26 So. 612; Lacassagne v. Abraham, 48 La. Ann. 1160, 20 So. 672; McCusker v. Goode, 185 Mass. 607, 71 N. E. 76; Hooper v. De Vries, 115 Mich. 231, 73 N. W. 132; Wallach v. Schulze, 22 App. Div. 57, 47 N. Y. S. 936; Thompson v. Rust, 32 Tex. Civ. App. 441, 74 S. W. 924; Fullenwider v. Ferguson, 30 Tex. Civ. App. 156, 70 S. W. 222; Attebery v. O'Neil, 42 Wash. 487, 85 Pac. 270; Sengfelder v. Hill, 21 Wash. 371, 58 Pac. 250. See also

Boynton v. Haggart, 120 Fed. 819, 57 C. C. A. 301; Forrest Milling Co. v. Cedar Falls Mill Co., 103 Iowa 619, 72 N. W. 1076.

[26] Slaughter v. State, 132 Ind. 465, 31 N. E. 1112; Day v. Brenton, 102 Iowa 482, 71 N. W. 538, 63 Ann. St. 460; Cornog v. Fuller, 30 Iowa 212; Lowry v. Bennett, 119 Mich. 301, 77 N. W. 935; Lindauer v. Younglove, 47 Minn. 62, 49 N. W. 384; Evans v. Roanoke Sav. Bank, 95 Va. 294, 28 S. E. 323.

[27] Pleasants v. Blodgett, 39 Nebr. 741, 58 N. W. 423, 42 Am. St. 624.

[28] Friend v. Yahr, 126 Wis. 291, 104 N. W. 997, 1 L. R. A. (N. S.) 891, 110 Am. St. 924.

[29] Heaton v. Prather, 84 Ill. 330; Dixie Grain Co. v. Quinn (Ala.), 61 So. 886.

[30] Farrar v. Payne, 73 Ill. 82.

the trustee is notified of default, constitutes constructive notice of such provision to purchasers of the bonds.[31]

The record of a chattel mortgage of something attached to the realty, such as standing timber, is not notice to a subsequent purchaser or mortgagee of the land.[32] Where mortgages and deeds are recorded in different books, it has been held that a deed recorded in the mortgage record or a mortgage recorded in the deed record is not constructive notice.[33]

§ 525. Priority fixed by original record.

—Priority once gained can not be lost. The registry of a deed or mortgage is equivalent to a notice of it to all persons who may subsequently become interested in the property, and fully protects the grantee's rights. A mortgage having once obtained priority by record does not lose its place by being held by any one under an unrecorded assignment.[34] And although the mortgagee had notice of a prior unrecorded mortgage, or there are equities such that his own mortgage is in his hands subject to them, yet if he assigns his mortgage for a valuable consideration to one who has no notice of the earlier mortgage or of such equities, the assignee is entitled to hold the mortgage as a prior lien upon the land, solely upon the ground that it was first recorded.[35]

Having recorded his mortgage, the mortgagee is not bound to give personal notice of his mortgage to one who purchases of the mortgagor; and a delay of ten years, or for any other period less than the statute period of limitation, to make any claim of the purchaser under the mortgage, does not impair his rights under the mortgage either at law or in equity; and the fact that the mortgagor has in the meantime become insolvent does not prejudice his claim upon the property.[36]

[31] Belleville Sav. Bank v. Southern Coal &c. Co., 173 Ill. App. 250.

[32] Williams v. Hyde, 98 Mich. 152, 57 N. W. 98. See also Alliance Trust Co. v. Nettleton Hardwood Co., 74 Miss. 584, 21 So. 396, 36 L. R. A. 155, 60 Am. St. 531.

[33] Neslin v. Wells, 104 U. S. 428, 26 L. ed. 802; In re Luch's Appeal, 44 Pa. St. 519; Drake v. Reggel, 10 Utah 376, 37 Pac. 583. See ante §§ 457, 511.

[34] Zehner v. Johnston, 22 Ind. App. 452, 53 N. E. 1080; Neosho Valley Inv. Co. v. Sharpless, 63 Kans. 885, 65 Pac. 667; Jackson v. Dubois, 4 Johns. (N. Y.) 216; Brinckerhoff v. Lansing, 4 Johns. Ch. (N. Y.) 65, 8 Am. Dec. 538; Parkist v. Alexander, 1 Johns. Ch. (N. Y.) 394; Campbell v. Vedder, 3 Keyes (N. Y.) 174, 1 Abb. Dec. 295. See also People's Trust Co. v. Tonkonogy, 144 App. Div. 333, 128 N. Y. S. 1055; Douglass v. Peele, Clarke (N. Y.) 563; Johnson v. Stagg, 2 Johns. (N. Y.) 510; Williams v. Brown, 127 N. Car. 51, 37 S. E. 86; Bacon v. Wood, 22 R. I. 255, 47 Atl. 388; King v. Harrington, 2 Aik. (Vt.) 33, 16 Am. Dec. 675.

[35] Corning v. Murray, 3 Barb. (N. Y.) 652.

[36] Dick v. Balch, 8 Pet. (U. S.)

A mortgage being duly recorded, the subsequent dealings of the mortgagor and others claiming under him have no effect whatever upon it. If, for instance, the mortgagor subsequently sells the land and reserves a right of way, this right remains subject to the title of the mortgagee, and a sale under a mortgage destroys this, as well as the title to the remainder of the land.[37]

In accordance with these principles, it follows that a junior deed or mortgage duly recorded, without notice of a prior unrecorded deed or mortgage, has precedence of it.[38] And, as between a mortgage and a deed of the same land, the instrument first recorded takes priority, notwithstanding its subsequent execution.[39] In other words, deeds and mortgages take precedence in the order of the record. This precedence follows them through any subsequent transfer, or through any proceedings to enforce the liens. When the mortgage first recorded is foreclosed, a purchaser at the foreclosure sale obtains a complete and absolute title. But a purchaser at a foreclosure sale, under the mortgage recorded next in order of time, obtains only an equity of redemption of the prior mortgage.[40]

30, 8 L. ed. 856; Mason v. Philbrook, 69 Maine 57; Rice v. Dewey, 54 Barb. (N. Y.) 455.

[37] King v. McCully, 38 Pa. St. 76.

[38] Routh v. Spencer, 38 Ind. 393; Cook v. Stone, 63 Iowa 352, 19 N. W. 280; Harang v. Plattsmier, 21 La. Ann. 426; Peychaud v. Citizens' Bank, 21 La. Ann. 262; Burns v. Berry, 42 Mich. 176, 3 N. W. 924; Harrington v. Allen, 48 Miss. 492; Pomet v. Scranton, 1 Walk. (Miss.) 406; Taylor v. Thomas, 5 N. J. Eq. 331; Grant v. Bissett, 1 Caines Cas. (N. Y.) 112; Ramsey v. Jones, 41 Ohio St. 685.

[39] Ferry v. Burnell, 5 McCrary (U. S.) 1, 14 Fed. 807; Gay v. Hudson River &c. Power Co., 190 Fed. 773; North v. Knowlton, 23 Fed. 163; Hibernia Sav. &c. Soc. v. Farnham, 153 Cal. 578, 86 Pac. 9, 126 Am. St. 129; Emeric v. Alvarado, 90 Cal. 444, 27 Pac. 356; Miller v. Shaw, 103 Ill. 277; Reasoner v. Edmundson, 5 Ind. 393; Ogden v. Walters, 12 Kans. 282; Boyer v. Joffrion, 40 La. Ann. 657, 4 So. 872; Somes v. Skinner, 3 Pick. (Mass.) 52; Harrington v. Allen, 48 Miss. 492; Westbrook v. Gleason, 89 N. Y. 641, 79 N. Y. 23; Frost v. Peacock, 4 Edw. (N. Y.) 678; Cowan v. Green, 9 N. Car. 384;

Hulett v. Mutual Life Ins. Co., 114 Pa. St. 142, 6 Atl. 554; Whiteside v. Watkins (Tenn.), 58 S. W. 1107; Anderson v. Casey-Swasey Co. (Tex. Civ. App.), 120 S. W. 918; Hays v. Tilson, 18 Tex. Civ. App. 610, 45 S. W. 479; Stuart v. Ferguson, Hayes 452; Lee v. Clutton, 46 L. J. Ch. 48, 35 L. T. (N. S.) 84, 24 Wkly. Rep. 942; Bay v. Kearns, 4 Brit. Col. 536; Renwick v. Berryman, 3 Manitoba 387; Scrafton v. Quincey, 2 Ves. 413, 28 Eng. Reprint 264. See also Robley v. Withers, 95 Miss. 318, 51 So. 719; Farmers' &c. Bank v. Citizens' Nat. Bank, 25 S. Dak. 91, 125 N. W. 642. A mortgage actually recorded but defectively acknowledged does not attain priority. Evans v. Etheridge, 99 N. Car. 43, 5 S. E. 386. A power of sale contained in a mortgage, is a part of the security, and protected by the statute against a prior unrecorded deed. Bell v. Twilight, 22 N. H. 500.

[40] Buchanan v. International Bank, 78 Ill. 500; Mathews v. Aikin, 1 N. Y. 595; Gilbert v. Averill, 15 Barb. (N. Y.) 20; Tice v. Annin, 2 Johns. Ch. (N. Y.) 125; Vanderkemp v. Shelton, 11 Paige (N. Y.) 28.

§ 526. Effect of destruction of record.—The destruction of the record in no manner affects the constructive notice afforded by the recording of the deed.[41] And likewise a subsequent mutilation of the record does not affect the rights of persons holding under a recorded instrument, who had nothing to do with the making of the alteration.[42] If the deed itself has been preserved, the recorder's certificate of its having been duly recorded is of the highest class of evidence,[43] and has even been held conclusive.[44] So, also, the index book in which the deed is described, and its record certified in the proper book, are good evidence of the fact that the deed was recorded.[45]

Other secondary evidence may show that the deed was filed for record;[46] and when this is the case, the testimony of an attorney of a purchaser, that he examined an abstract of the title to the property, which purported to be a full and complete abstract, and did not find a prior deed of trust upon the premises, is not sufficient to show that there was no record of it, as it does not follow that the abstract was what it purported to be.[47]

It has been held that the partial or total destruction of a record book containing a deed duly recorded does not impair the lien thereof, or affect the record as legal notice;[48] but the record of a deed partially destroyed, so as not to show that the deed was properly acknowledged for registration, was held not to charge subsequent purchasers with constructive notice.[49]

[41] Paxson v. Brown, 61 Fed. 874, 10 C. C. A. 135; Franklin Sav. Bank v. Taylor, 53 Fed. 854, 4 C. C. A. 55; Ashburn v. Spivey, 112 Ga. 474, 37 S. E. 703; Sharp v. American Freehold L. Mtg. Co., 95 Ga. 415, 22 S. E. 633; Quinn v. Perkins, 159 Ill. 572, 43 N. E. 759; Tucker v. Shaw, 158 Ill. 326, 41 N. E. 914; Franklin Sav. Bank v. Taylor, 131 Ill. 376, 23 N. E. 397; Hall v. Shannon, 85 Ill. 473; Curyea v. Berry, 84 Ill. 600; Heaton v. Prather, 84 Ill. 330; Steele v. Boone, 75 Ill. 457; Gammon v. Hodges, 73 Ill. 140; Shannon v. Hall, 72 Ill. 354; Alvis v. Morrison, 63 Ill. 181; Hyatt v. Cochran, 69 Ind. 436; Thomas v. Hanson, 59 Minn. 274, 61 N. W. 135; Myers v. Buchanan, 46 Miss. 397; Geer v. Missouri Lumber &c. Co., 134 Mo. 85, 34 S. W. 1099, 56 Am. St. 489; Crane v. Dameron, 98 Mo. 567, 12 S. W. 251; Addis v. Graham, 88 Mo. 197; Deming v. Miles, 35 Nebr. 739, 53 N. W. 665, 37 Am. St. 464; Reck v.

Clapp, 98 Pa. St. 581; Mattfeld v. Huntington, 17 Tex. Civ. App. 716, 43 S. W. 53; Fitch v. Boyer, 51 Tex. 336; Armentrout v. Gibbons, 30 Grat. (Va.) 632.

[42] Dodd v. Doty, 98 Ill. 393; Merrick v. Wallace, 19 Ill. 486; Reck v. Clapp, 98 Pa. St. 581.

[43] Paxson v. Brown, 61 Fed. 874, 10 C. C. A. 135; Alvis v. Morrison, 63 Ill. 181, 14 Am. Rep. 117.

[44] Webb v. Austin, 22 Ky. L. 764, 58 S. W. 808.

[45] Alvis v. Morrison, 63 Ill. 181, 14 Am. Rep. 117; Smith v. Lindsey, 89 Mo. 76, 1 S. W. 88.

[46] Stebbins v. Duncan, 108 U. S. 32, 27 L. ed. 641, 2 Sup. Ct. 313; Smith v. Lindsey, 89 Mo. 76, 1 S. W. 88; Cowles v. Hardin, 91 N. Car. 231.

[47] Steele v. Boone, 75 Ill. 457.

[48] Myers v. Buchanan, 46 Miss. 397.

[49] Weber v. Moss, 3 Tex. Civ. App. 13, 21 S. W. 609.

Where the registry office and its records have been destroyed by fire, evidence of the execution of a mortgage and of its loss, with slight circumstances in regard to the recording of it, have been held enough to sustain a presumption that it was recorded, as against a prior mortgagee who claims priority on the ground that such mortgage was never recorded.[50]

A landowner, in order to protect his rights, need not, unless he choose, incur the trouble and expense of restoring the record under an act providing for the restoration of burnt records.[51] A mortgagee may foreclose his mortgage, although in the meantime the mortgagor has sold and conveyed the mortgaged premises to one who had no knowledge of the existence of the mortgage, and who took possession and retained it several years with the knowledge of the mortgagee, who did not file his bill to foreclose his mortgage for six years afterward.[52] A restoration of the record may be had, if desired, upon proof of proceedings for foreclosure of a mortgage in a court of general jurisdiction, a decree of sale, a sale under it, and its approval by the court, and the delivery of a certificate of purchase; and the court will thereupon order the execution of a deed to the purchaser, and a surrender of possession to him.[53]

§ 526a. **Destroyed records—Procedure for establishing title.**—In a few states, including Illinois and California, there are statutes, sometimes known as Burnt Records acts, providing special procedure in equity for establishing title to property evidenced by public records which have been lost or destroyed.[54] Under the Illinois statute, an

---

[50] Hunt v. Innis, 2 Woods (U. S.) 103; Heacock v. Lubuke, 107 Ill. 396; Alston v. Alston, 4 S. Car. 116; Harrison v. McMurray, 71 Tex. 122, 8 S. W. 612.

[51] Ashburn v. Spivey, 112 Ga. 474, 37 S. E. 703; Gammon v. Hodges, 73 Ill. 140; Hyatt v. Cochran, 69 Ind. 436; Evans v. Templeton, 69 Tex. 375, 6 S. W. 843. But see Greer v. Willis (Tex.), 81 S. W. 1185; Weber v. Moss, 3 Tex. Civ. App. 13, 21 S. W. 609 (under statutory provision requiring re-recording within four years after destruction). A burnt record will not be restored on the petition of one whose title would not be aided by such restoration, and when the title of another would be clouded. Beattie v. Whipple, 154 Ill. 273, 40 N. E. 340.

[52] Hall v. Shannon, 85 Ill. 473; Shannon v. Hall, 72 Ill. 354, 22 Am. Rep. 146.

[53] Curyea v. Berry, 84 Ill. 600. See as to effect of decree re-establishing a record under a statute, Hunt v. Innis, 2 Woods (U. S.) 103.

[54] American Land Co. v. Zeiss, 219 U. S. 47, 55 L. ed. 82, 31 Sup. Ct. 200 (California statute construed); Gormley v. Clark, 134 U. S. 338, 33 L. ed. 909, 10 Sup. Ct. 554; Lofstad v. Murasky, 152 Cal. 64, 91 Pac. 1008; Title &c. Restoration Co. v. Kerrigan, 150 Cal. 289, 88 Pac. 356, 8 L. R. A. (N. S.) 682; Seaboard Nat. Bank v. Ackerman, 16 Cal. App. 55, 116 Pac. 91; Harding v. Fuller, 141 Ill. 308, 30 N. E. 1053. See also Arnett v. Birmingham Coal &c. Co., 173 Ala. 532, 55 So. 831.

action to establish title may be maintained by a party out of possession against another in possession of land,[55] but the California statute
expressly requires actual possession as a prerequisite to maintenance
of the action.[56] The right to maintain such an action is not affected
by the fact that there are adverse claimants,[57] or that other questions
relating to the title are involved,[58] or that the claimant's title rests
upon the statute of limitations.[59]

§ 527. **Bona fide purchasers without notice of unrecorded mortgage.**—Any one purchasing land in good faith, without notice of an
unrecorded mortgage, takes it discharged of the lien;[60] and he can

[55] Harding v. Fuller, 141 Ill. 308,
30 N. E. 1053.

[56] American Land Co. v. Zeiss, 191
Fed. 125, 111 C. C. A. 605; Lofstad
v. Murasky, 152 Cal. 64, 91 Pac. 1008
(constructive possession insufficient).

[57] Harding v. Fuller, 141 Ill. 308,
30 N. E. 1053; Gage v. Caraher, 125
Ill. 447, 17 N. E. 777. See also Mc-
Campbell v. Mason, 151 Ill. 500, 38
N. E. 672.

[58] Gage v. Thompson, 161 Ill. 403,
43 N. E. 1062; Harding v. Fuller,
141 Ill. 308, 30 N. E. 1053; Gage v.
Du Puy, 134 Ill. 132, 24 N. E. 866;
Gage v. Caraher, 125 Ill. 447, 17 N.
E. 777.

[59] Miller v. Stalker, 158 Ill. 514,
42 N. E. 79.

[60] Neslin v. Wells, 104 U. S. 428,
26 L. ed. 802; Steiner v. Clisby, 95
Ala. 91, 10 So. 240; Wood v. Lake,
62 Ala. 489; De Vendal v. Malone,
25 Ala. 272; Ohio Life Ins. &c. Co. v.
Ledyard, 8 Ala. 866; Nestor v. Holt,
1 Alaska 567; Brown v. Nelms, 86
Ark. 368, 112 S. W. 373; Fry v. Martin, 33 Ark. 203; Jacoway v. Gault,
20 Ark. 190, 73 Am. Dec. 494; Beach
v. Osborne, 74 Conn. 405; McRaney
v. Perry, 9 Ga. App. 738, 72 S. E.
188; English v. Lindley, 194 Ill. 181,
62 N. E. 522; Huebsch v. Scheel, 81
Ill. 281; Hodgen v. Guttery, 58 Ill.
431; Holbrook v. Dickenson, 56 Ill.
497; Brazleton v. Brazleton, 16 Iowa
417; Louisville Bldg. &c. Assn. v.
Greene, 22 Ky. L. 959, 59 S. W. 508;
White v. Union Bank, 6 La. Ann.
162; Belding Sav. Bank v. Moore,
118 Mich. 150, 76 N. W. 368; Burns
v. Berry, 42 Mich. 176, 3 N. W. 924;
Pancoast v. Duval, 26 N. J. Eq. 445;
Westbrook v. Gleason, 89 N. Y. 641;
Jackson v. McChesney, 7 Cow. (N.
Y.) 360, 17 Am. Dec. 521; Ward v.
Isbill, 73 Hun 550, 56 N. Y. St. 185,
26 N. Y. S. 141; Riley v. Hoyt, 29
Hun (N. Y.) 114; Jackson v. Camp-
bell, 19 Johns. (N. Y.) 281; Gouver-
neur v. Lynch, 2 Paige (N. Y.) 300;
Burke v. Allen, 3 Yeates (Pa.) 351;
Williams v. Beard, 1 S. Car. 309;
Barnwell v. Porteus, 2 Hill Eq. (S.
Car.) 219; Burke v. Allen, 3 Yeates
(Pa.) 351; Openshaw v. Dean
(Tex. Civ. App.), 125 S. W. 989;
Garner v. Boyle (Tex.), 79 S. W.
1066; Roberts v. W. H. Hughes Co.,
86 Vt. 76, 83 Atl. 807; Hunton v.
Wood, 101 Va. 54, 43 S. E. 186;
Preston v. Nash, 76 Va. 1; Coolidge
v. Schering, 32 Wash. 557, 73 Pac.
682; Cox v. Wayt, 26 W. Va. 807;
Allison v. Manzke, 118 Wis. 11, 94
N. W. 659; Battison v. Hobson, 2
Ch. 403, 65 L. J. Ch. 695, 74 L. T.
(N. S.) 689, 44 Wkly. Rep. 615;
Credland v. Potter, L. R. 10 Ch. 8,
44 L. J. Ch. 169, 31 L. T. (N. S.)
522, 23 Wkly. Rep. 36; In re Wight,
L. R. 16 Eq. 41, 43 L. J. Ch. 66, 28
L. T. (N. S.) 491, 21 Wkly. Rep.
667; Vansickler v. Pettit, 5 Can.
L. J. 41. See also Tennis Coal Co.
v. Asher, 143 Ky. 223, 136 S. W. 197;
King v. Huni, 25 Ky. L. 2266, 81 S.
W. 254. A bona fide purchaser has
also been held to be protected
against a prior unrecorded mortgage, although the mortgage was
subsequently registered before the
purchaser's deed. Hawley v. Bennett, 5 Paige (N. Y.) 104. See also
McGuire v. Barker, 61 Ga. 339.

convey a good title to it, although the mortgage is recorded before he conveys and his vendee has notice of it.[61] In order to take title free from the lien of an unrecorded mortgage, a subsequent purchaser must be a bona fide purchaser in the full sense; he must have taken without actual notice of the unrecorded mortgage,[62] for valuable consideration,[63] under some form of conveyance purporting to grant him a title, lien or other interest in the property.[64]

A purchaser of land without notice of a prior unrecorded mortgage is not charged with notice because his vendor was a purchaser with notice.[65] An unrecorded mortgage is void as against a purchaser without notice, at a sale under execution against the mortgagor;[66] but a mortgage recorded before the sale was held valid although unrecorded when the writ issued.[67]

A purchaser having no actual notice of the mortgage, is not bound to look beyond the line of title in his grantor, and, finding that he acquired a good title, he is not bound to look further; he acquires all the right and title that his grantor acquired. His grantor being entitled to protection against a prior unrecorded mortgage, he is entitled to the same protection, notwithstanding the notice he himself has of such mortgage, and although he is not a purchaser for a valuable consideration.[68]

[61] Losey v. Simpson, 11 N. J. Eq. 246; Tarbell v. West, 86 N. Y. 280; Bush v. Lathrop, 22 N. Y. 535; Cook v. Travis, 20 N. Y. 400; Jackson v. Van Valkenburgh, 8 Cow. (N. Y.) 260; Jackson v. McChesney, 7 Cow. (N. Y.) 360, 17 Am. Dec. 521; Jackson v. Given, 8 Johns. (N. Y.) 137, 5 Am. Dec. 328.

[62] Johnston v. Shortridge, 93 Mo. 227, 6 S. W. 64. See also Varick v. Briggs, 6 Paige (N. Y.) 323.

[63] Schultze v. Houfes, 96 Ill. 335; Freeburg v. Eksell, 123 Iowa 464, 99 N. W. 118; Merriman v. Hyde, 9 Nebr. 113, 2 N. W. 218; Roberts v. W. H. Hughes Co., 86 Vt. 76, 83 Atl. 807. A purchaser of land receiving notice of a prior unrecorded mortgage thereon, after he has paid part of the purchase-money is not entitled to the protection of a purchaser without notice, as to the unpaid balance. Warner v. Whittaker, 6 Mich. 133, 72 Am. Dec. 65; Thomas v. Stone, Walk. Ch. (Mich.) 117. The payment and satisfaction in whole or in part of a pre-existing debt is sufficient to make the creditor a bona fide purchaser for a valuable consideration. Sipley v. Wass, 49 N. J. Eq. 463, 24 Atl. 233. But merely giving credit for the amount of the purchase-money, on claims held by the purchaser against the vendor, was held not a sufficient consideration to accord the protection of a bona fide purchaser. Zorn v. Savannah &c. R. Co., 5 S. Car. 90.

[64] An assignee for the benefit of creditors is not a bona fide purchaser within the meaning of these rules. In re Mellon's Appeal, 32 Pa. St. 121. See also Garner v. Boyle, 97 Tex. 460, 79 S. W. 1066.

[65] Varick v. Briggs, 6 Paige (N. Y.) 323. See also Ward v. Isbill, 73 Hun 550, 56 N. Y. St. 185, 26 N. Y. S. 141.

[66] Barker v. Bell, 37 Ala. 354.

[67] Sappington v. Oeschli, 49 Mo. 244.

[68] Wood v. Chapin, 13 N. Y. 509, 67 Am. Dec. 62; Webster v. Van Steen-

Not only is a purchaser without notice of a prior unrecorded mortgage, or of other equitable claim to the property, entitled to protection, even though he takes the title from one who had actual notice of such claim, but also a purchaser with notice from one who was entitled to protection as a bona fide purchaser without notice is himself entitled to protection against the previous equitable claim upon the estate; for otherwise a bona fide purchaser might be deprived of the power of selling his property for its full value. This protection extends to all persons claiming through the mortgage, whether they had notice at the time of the purchase or not.[69] Although an unrecorded mortgage may be defeated by a subsequent conveyance to a purchaser for value without notice; a mortgagee under an unrecorded mortgage who participated with the mortgagor in organizing a corporation and conveying the mortgaged property to it, is not defeated in asserting his lien against the mortgagor and the corporation which had paid no value for the conveyance.[70] Where an owner of land failed to record his deed, and gave a trust deed thereon which was not recorded, a purchaser without notice from him, or from a commissioner authorized to sell his estate, acquired his title free from such incumbrance.[71]

§ 528.   **Estoppel of mortgagor subsequently acquiring title.**—If one having no title to land conveys it by a duly recorded mortgage with covenants of warranty, and afterward the mortgagor acquires title to the land, the estoppel by which he is bound under the covenants is turned into a good estate in the mortgagee, so that by operation of law the title is considered as vested in him in the same manner as if it had been conveyed to the mortgagor before he executed the mortgage. The mortgagor is estopped to say he was not then seised. Then, if the mortgagor executes another mortgage, and this and the deed by which the mortgagor acquired his title are both recorded together, which mortgagee has the better title? The estoppel binds not only the mortgagor and his heirs, but his assigns as well. A second mortgagee is therefore estopped to aver that the grantor was not seised at the time of his making the first mortgage, and that mortgage being first recorded must have priority.[72]

bergh, 46 Barb. (N. Y.) 211; Clark v. Mackin, 30 Hun (N. Y.) 411; Crane v. Turner, 7 Hun (N. Y.) 357.

[69] Cook v. Travis, 22 Barb. 338, 20 N. Y. 400; Varick v. Briggs, 6 Paige (N. Y.) 323.

[70] Roberts v. W. H. Hughes Co., 86 Vt. 76, 83 Atl. 807.

[71] Hunton v. Wood, 101 Va. 54, 43 S. E. 186.

[72] Christy v. Dana, 34 Cal. 548, 42 Cal. 174; Kirkaldie v. Larrabee, 31

But if a mortgagor has title at the time of executing two mortgages, the fact that one contains covenants of warranty does not give it priority over the other which contains no such covenants, if the latter be first filed for record.[73]

Where the mortgagor was part owner of the mortgaged premises, at the time of giving the mortgage, it was held that the mortgage, though containing a general warranty, conveyed only the interest which the mortgagor had in the land at the time of the execution of the mortgage, and did not pass an interest subsequently acquired by will.[74]

Where the mortgagor was in possession at the date of the mortgage, under a parol contract of sale, the record of the mortgage was held effective though the mortgagor had not yet acquired title, and the holder of a subsequent mortgage was bound thereby.[75] And, where a homestead entrywoman mortgaged her property before obtaining her patent, the recording of the mortgage prior to final proof was held constructive notice, the same as though the mortgage had been executed and recorded after patent.[76]

A quitclaim deed or other deed without warranty does not have the effect of estopping the grantor from setting up a superior right and

Cal. 455, 89 Am. Dec. 205; Salisbury Sav. Soc. v. Cutting, 50 Conn. 113; Yerkes v. Hadley, 5 Dak. 324, 40 N. W. 340, 2 L. R. A. 363; Boone v. Armstrong, 87 Ind. 168; Warburton v. Mattox, Morris (Iowa) 367; Newell v. Burnside Banking Co. (Ky.), 118 S. W. 267; Perkins v. Coleman, 90 Ky. 611, 12 Ky. L. 501, 14 S. W. 640; Pike v. Galvin, 29 Maine 183; White v. Patten, 24 Pick. (Mass.) 324; Somes v. Skinner, 3 Pick. (Mass.) 52; Gotham v. Gotham, 55 N. H. 440; Ward v. Willard, 13 N. H. 389; Kimball v. Blaisdell, 5 N. H. 533, 22 Am. Dec. 476; Semon v. Terhune, 40 N. J. Eq. 364, 2 Atl. Rep. 18; Cooke v. Watson, 30 N. J. Eq. 345; Crane v. Turner, 67 N. Y. 43; Tefft v. Munson, 57 N. Y. 97; Doyle v. Peerless Petroleum Co., 44 Barb. (N. Y.) 239; Farmers' Loan &c. Co. v. Maltby, 8 Paige (N. Y.) 361; Philly v. Sanders, 11 Ohio St. 490, 78 Am. Dec. 316; Jarvis v. Aikens, 25 Vt. 635; Doswell v. Buchanan, 3 Leigh (Va.) 365, 23 Am. Dec. 280. But see White & Tudor's Lead. Cases in Eq. (4th Am. ed.), vol. 2,

pt. 1, p. 212. Under a covenant of warranty, a title subsequently acquired by the mortgagor will inure to the benefit of the mortgagee. Hoyt v. Dimon, 5 Day (Conn.) 479; Yerkes v. Hadley, 5 Dak. 324, 40 N. W. 340, 2 L. R. A. 363; Holbrook v. Debo, 99 Ill. 372; Elder v. Derby, 98 Ill. 228; Pratt v. Pratt, 98 Ill. 184; Gibbons v. Hoag, 95 Ill. 45; Gochenour v. Mowry, 33 Ill. 331; Wells v. Somers, 4 Ill. App. 297; Iowa L. &c. Co. v. King, 58 Iowa 598, 12 N. W. 595; Doswell v. Buchanan, 3 Leigh (Va.) 365, 23 Am. Dec. 280; Trust &c. Co. v. Covert, 32 U. C. Q. B. 222; See ante § 472, and post §§ 529, 679, 782, 825, 1483, 1656, 1671.

[73] Vandercook v. Baker, 48 Iowa 199.

[74] Newell v. Burnside Banking Co. (Ky.), 118 S. W. 267.

[75] Crane v. Turner, 7 Hun (N. Y.) 357, affd. 67 N. Y. 437.

[76] Adam v. McClintock, 21 N. Dak. 483, 131 N. W. 394. See also Bernardy v. Colonial & United States Mortg. Co., 17 S. Dak. 637, 98 N. W. 166, 106 Am. St. 791.

title subsequently acquired from another source.[77] A grantee under a quitclaim deed is not a bona fide purchaser under the recording acts, and his rights are subordinate to a prior unrecorded mortgage.[78]

§ 529. **Mortgage recorded before grantor acquires title.**—To sustain a deed made before the grantor acquires title is certainly a violation of the spirit of the registry system, under which a record is notice only to subsequent purchasers and incumbrancers, in the line of the title to which the recorded deed belongs. It has been insisted therefore, with much force, that a second grantee, under a deed made after the grantor had acquired title and recorded his deed to himself, should be preferred to the first grantee, whose deed the second grantee, in following the title back to the time his grantor acquired title, would not find of record. There are some decisions to the effect that a subsequent purchaser or creditor is not bound to take notice of a conveyance not lying in the line of the title, though actually recorded; and that he is not bound to search for conveyances as against his grantor previous to the time when the grantor obtained his title to the land.[79]

But notwithstanding the objections, the title by estoppel in such cases is generally sustained; and if a purchaser fails to examine the record, to ascertain whether the grantor had made a conveyance prior to the time of receiving and recording the conveyance to himself, he runs the risk of acquiring an imperfect title.[80]

Where a mortgage of certain land is made and recorded before the mortgagor himself acquires title, in order to raise part of the purchase-money, the record thereof is not, under the recording act, notice to the vendor of the land, who subsequently conveys to the mortgagor and takes back a purchase-money mortgage.[81]

Where a mortgagor incumbered land to which he had no title, but subsequently became the mortgagee of the property by a mortgage from the true owner, the record of the first mortgage did not operate

---

[77] Doswell v. Buchanan, 3 Leigh (Tenn.) 365, 23 Am. Dec. 280; Smith v. Pollard, 19 Vt. 272.

[78] Snow v. Lake, 20 Fla. 656, 51 Am. Rep. 625. See post § 582.

[79] Salisbury Sav. Soc. v. Cutting, 50 Conn. 113; Prince v. Case, 10 Conn. 375, 27 Am. Dec. 675; Way v. Arnold, 18 Ga. 181; Bingham v. Kirkland, 34 N. J. Eq. 229; Farmers' Loan &c. Co. v. Maltby, 8 Paige (N. Y.) 361; Calder v. Chapman, 52 Pa. St. 359, 91 Am. Dec. 163; McLana-han v. Reeside, 9 Watts (Pa.) 508, 36 Am. Dec. 136; Woods v. Farmere, 7 Watts (Pa.) 382. See also Crosby v. Ridout, 27 App. D. C. 481; Mc-Cusker v. McEvey, 9 R. I. 528, 10 R. I. 606; Rawle on Covenants (4th ed.), 428; Bigelow on Estoppel, 331.

[80] Digman v. McCollum, 47 Mo. 372; Buckingham v. Hanna, 2 Ohio St. 551, and cases cited in post § 561.

[81] Schoch v. Birdsall, 48 Minn. 441, 51 N. W. 382.

as notice to the owner of the property, as he was not holding the premises under the first mortgagor, and hence a satisfaction of the second mortgage defeated whatever interest passed to the first mortgagee. This decision was rendered under a statute prescribing that if any one makes a conveyance of real estate, not having the legal title, but afterward acquires the same, such after-acquired estate, legal or equitable, shall immediately pass to the grantee.[82]

§ 530. **Record of subsequent deeds by the mortgagor.**—After the mortgage is made and recorded, the record of any deeds subsequently made by the mortgagor is not notice to the mortgagee;[83] and if he has no actual knowledge of any such subsequent deed, he may, without receiving anything upon the mortgage debt, release any portion of the mortgaged property to the mortgagor without impairing his security upon the remainder for the whole mortgage debt; although, if he had notice of a sale of any part of the remaining land, he might be obliged to abate a proportionate part of the mortgage debt in order to protect the purchaser.[84] The equity which entitles a subsequent mortgage incumbrancer to the benefit of such release arises only when the first mortgagee gives it with knowledge at the time of the existence of the subsequent incumbrance. If the subsequent incumbrance be a mechanic's lien, the mere fact that the building was commenced after the

---

[82] Turman v. Sanford, 69 Ark. 95, 61 S. W. 167.

[83] McLean v. Lafayette Bank, 4 McLean (U. S.) 30; Bright v. Buckman, 39 Fed. 243; Birnie v. Main, 29 Ark. 591; Small v. Stagg, 95 Ill. 39; Meacham v. Steele, 93 Ill. 135; Heaton v. Prather, 84 Ill. 330; Doolittle v. Cook, 75 Ill. 354; Iglehart v. Crane, 42 Ill. 261; Burnham v. Citizens' Bank, 55 Kans. 545, 40 Pac. 912; Halstead v. Bank of Kentucky, 4 J. J. Marsh. (Ky.) 554; Clarke v. Cowan, 206 Mass. 252, 92 N. E. 474; George v. Wood, 9 Allen (Mass.) 80, 85 Am. Dec. 316; Dewey v. Ingersoll, 42 Mich. 17, 3 N. W. 235; Cooper v. Bigly, 13 Mich. 463; James v. Brown, 11 Mich. 25; Brown v. Simons, 44 N. H. 475; Cogswell v. Stout, 32 N. J. Eq. 240; Kipp v. Merselis, 30 N. J. Eq. 99; Hill v. McCarter, 27 N. J. Eq. 41; Hoy v. Bramhall, 19 N. J. Eq. 563, 97 Am. Dec. 687; Vanorden v. Johnson, 14 N. J. Eq. 376, 82 Am. Dec. 254; Blair v. Ward, 10 N. J. Eq. 119; Howard Ins. Co. v. Halsey, 8 N. Y. 271, 59 Am. Dec. 478; Truscott v. King, 6 Barb. (N. Y.) 346; Stuyvesant v. Hall, 2 Barb. Ch. (N. Y.) 151; Talmadge v. Wilgers, 4 Edw. Ch. (N. Y.) 239; Wheelwright v. De Peyster, 4 Edw. Ch. (N. Y.) 232, 3 Am. Dec. 232; Raynor v. Wilson, 6 Hill (N. Y.) 469; Westbrook v. Gleason, 14 Hun (N. Y.) 245; King v. McVickar, 3 Sandf. Ch. (N. Y.) 192; Stuyvesant v. Hone, 1 Sandf. Ch. (N. Y.) 419; Union Nat. Bank v. Moline, 7 N. Dak. 201, 73 N. W. 527; Sarles v. McGee, 1 N. Dak. 365, 48 N. W. 231; Ranney v. Hardy, 43 Ohio St. 157; Leiby v. Wolf, 10 Ohio 83; Taylor v. Maris, 5 Rawle (Pa.) 51; Lake v. Shumate, 20 S. Car. 23; Howard v. Clark, 71 Vt. 424, 45 Atl. 1042; Johnson v. Valido Marble Co., 64 Vt. 337, 25 Atl. 441; Hall v. Williamson Grocery Co., 69 W. Va. 671, 72 S. E. 780. See post § 723.

[84] Hall v. Edwards, 43 Mich. 473, 5 N. W. 652; Cogswell v. Stone, 32 N. J. Eq. 240.

mortgage was given, and that the mortgagee knew this, is not sufficient to charge him with knowledge of the lien.[85]

The holder of a duly recorded deed of trust, given to secure future advances, is affected only by actual notice of a lien subsequently acquired on the property, and his deed of trust is a valid and prior security for all advances made before actual notice of a subsequent lien.[86]

An agreement between a prior mortgagee and the mortgagor, by which insurance money received by the former was used by the latter in rebuilding, does not affect the priority of his lien as against a subsequent mortgage of which he had no actual knowledge.[87]

Whatever may be the equities of the subsequent mortgagee, a prior mortgagee is not bound by them unless he has actual notice, or such notice as should put him upon inquiry.[88] There can be no retrospective effect to the record. A mortgagee, having recorded his deed, secures the protection of the registry laws, and he is not required to search the record from time to time to see whether other conveyances have been put upon the record. While the law requires every man to deal with his own so as not to injure another, it imposes a greater obligation on the second mortgagee to take care of his own interests than upon the first mortgagee to take care of them for him. To make it the duty of the first mortgagee to inquire before he acts, lest he may injure some one, would be to reverse this rule, and make it his duty to do for the second mortgagee what the latter should do for himself.[89]

In like manner, the recording of a mortgage affords no notice whatever to a prior purchaser of the land, who is in possession under a bond for a deed, so that the mortgagee had constructive notice of his rights, and without actual notice he may lawfully complete his payments to his vendor without becoming liable to such mortgagee.[90]

[85] Ward v. Hague, 25 N. J. Eq. 397; McIlvain v. Mutual Assn. Co., 93 Pa. St. 30.

[85] Babcock v. Lisk, 57 Ill. 327; Dean v. De Lezardi, 24 Miss. 424; Whitney v. Lowe, 59 Nebr. 87, 80 N. W. 266; Youngs v. Wilson, 27 N. Y. 351; Cumps v. Kiyo, 104 Wis. 656, 80 N. W. 937. A recorded mortgage for an unlimited amount is notice of all sums advanced upon it before the subsequent lien attached. Robinson v. Williams, 22 N. Y. 380. See also Bell v. Fleming, 12 N. J. Eq. 13 (record of mortgage securing future advances).

[87] Johnson v. Valido Marble Co., 64 Vt. 337, 25 Atl. 441.

[88] Dewey v. Ingersoll, 42 Mich. 17, 3 N. W. 235; Straight v. Harris, 14 Wis. 509; Duester v. McCamus, 14 Wis. 307.

[89] Birnie v. Main, 29 Ark. 591; James v. Brown, 11 Mich. 25. See ante § 372.

[90] Doolittle v. Cook, 75 Ill. 354.

§ 531. **Extent of the lien.**—The record of the mortgage is notice of an incumbrance for the amount specified in it, or so referred to as to put subsequent purchasers upon inquiry as to the extent of the lien.[91] If it specifies the sum secured, it is notice only to the extent and amount of the debt stated, and can not be enlarged to include any other debts and claims not specified.[92] It is not notice of any claim which is not so specified or referred to.[93] If the record of a mortgage does not disclose the nature and amount of the debt secured, it is not notice to subsequent purchasers or incumbrancers.[94] The record itself must be examined, and it has been held that a record in the index specifying the amount, is not notice of the consideration of a mortgage.[95]

Subsequent purchasers are bound by nothing more than is disclosed by record, unless express notice is proved.[96] As against them, if the mortgage debt is not payable with interest, they can not be prejudiced by any change of interest, although, in case there be other security for the debt, they can not object to the application of that to the payment of interest in the first place.[97] But actual notice of the amount secured by a mortgage is binding upon a subsequent purchaser, although there be a mistake in the record.[98]

§ 532. **Extension of mortgage.**—An agreement for further time, and a higher rate of interest, is not binding upon the property, or upon subsequent purchasers, unless duly executed and recorded. It is merely a personal obligation between the parties, and the increased indebtedness can not operate as a lien upon the land.[99] Where a definite extension of the time of payment is granted, a mortgage for an

[91] Hall v. Williamson Grocery Co., 69 W. Va. 671, 72 S. E. 780; Straight v. Harris, 14 Wis. 509. See post § 723.

[92] Bacon v. Brown, 19 Conn. 29; Walden v. Grant, 8 Mart. (N. S.) (La.) 565; Hinchman v. Town, 10 Mich. 508; Mills v. Kellogg, 7 Minn. 469; Whittacre v. Fuller, 5 Minn. 508; Ketcham v. Wood, 22 Hun (N. Y.) 64; Beekman v. Frost, 18 Johns. (N. Y.) 544, 9 Am. Dec. 246. See also Babcock v. Bridge, 29 Barb. (N. Y.) 427; Hall v. Read, 28 Tex. Civ. App. 18, 66 S. W. 809. But see Keyes v. Bump, 59 Vt. 391, 9 Atl. 598 (recital of consideration immaterial). See ante §§ 515, 524.

[93] Hinchman v. Town, 10 Mich. 508.

[94] Bullock v. Battenhousen, 108 Ill. 28; Battenhousen v. Bullock, 11 Ill. App. 665; Bergman v. Bogda, 46 Ill. App. 351; Lacour v. Carrie, 2 La. Ann. 790; Whittacre v. Fuller, 5 Minn. 508; Du Bose v. Kell, 90 S. Car. 196, 71 S. E. 371. See ante § 515.

[95] Gilchrist v. Gough, 63 Ind. 576, 30 Am. Rep. 250.

[96] See ante § 524.

[97] Lash v. Edgerton, 13 Minn. 210. See post § 533.

[98] Frost v. Beekman, 1 Johns. Ch. (N. Y.) 288.

[99] Gardner v. Emerson, 40 Ill. 296; Davis v. Jewett, 3 Greene (Iowa) 226. See ante § 361.

antecedent debt is supported by a sufficient consideration to constitute the mortgagee a purchaser for value within the protection of the recording act.[1] An agreement for extension duly recorded, but which does not identify the mortgage by any sufficient reference, has no greater effect by reason of the record.[2]

§ 533. Rate of interest.—The mortgage is a lien only for the rate of interest specified in it, or for the rate established by law when it is simply made payable with interest.[3] If the parties to the mortgage subsequently agree upon an advanced rate, this agreement is not binding upon subsequent purchasers, unless it is executed with the formalities which entitle it to be recorded, and it is in fact duly recorded before others acquire any interest in the property.

In like manner, where a mortgage was given without interest, but with a verbal agreement that the mortgagee should receive certain rents in lieu of interest, he can not, as against a subsequent mortgagee who had no notice of this agreement, enlarge his demand beyond what appeared of record, and claim a lien upon the property for the payment of interest as well as principal.[4]

After the making of a mortgage, the parties to it can not make an agreement for the payment of a higher rate of interest than that stipulated for in the mortgage, that will be a lien upon the premises as against a purchaser of the property before such agreement was made, or after it was made but without notice of it.[5] Such an agreement can not operate to the prejudice of the intervening rights of third persons, such as junior mortgagees, redeeming from the prior mortgage by paying the debt secured.[6]

---

[1] Farmers' &c. Bank v. Citizens' Nat. Bank, 25 S. Dak. 91, 125 N. W. 642. See ante § 461.

[2] Bassett v. Hathaway, 9 Mich. 28.

[3] Where neither the mortgage nor its record disclosed the rate of interest, although the note secured drew two and one-half per cent. per month, the lien operated as notice only of the principal and seven per cent. per annum, against subsequent purchasers and incumbrancers. Whittacre v. Fuller, 5 Minn. 508. Where the record of a mortgage showed that the mortgagor agreed to pay a greater than the legal rate of interest after maturity, subsequent incumbrancers can not object to such payments and application

of interest. Mills v. Kellogg, 7 Minn. 469. See also Taylor v. Atlantic &c. R. Co., 55 How. Pr. (N. Y.) 275. See ante § 361.

[4] St. Andrews Church v. Tompkins, 7 Johns. Ch. (N. Y.) 14.

[5] Davis v. Jewett, 3 G. Greene (Iowa) 226; Bunker v. Barron, 79 Maine 62, 8 Atl. 253, 1 Am. St. 282; McGregor v. Mueller, 1 Cin. Super. Ct. 486, 13 Ohio Dec. 676; Bassett v. McDonel, 13 Wis. 444; Matson v. Swift, 5 Jur. 645; In re Houston, 2 Ont. 84; Totten v. Watson, 17 Grant Ch. (U. C.) 233; Murchie v. Theriault, 1 N. Brunsw. Eq. 588.

[6] Gardner v. Emerson, 40 Ill. 296; Smith v. Graham, 34 Mich. 302.

But in case of a mortgage for the purchase-money, the wife having no right of dower except in the surplus above the mortgage, an agreement to pay a higher rate of interest in consideration of an extension of time may be enforced against the property, so far as the wife's dower is concerned.[7]

§ 534. **Mortgages executed and recorded simultaneously.**—The recording acts have no application to mortgages executed and recorded simultaneously.[8] When two mortgages on the same property, given to different mortgagees are recorded at the same time there is no priority between them, but they are equal liens.[9] Neither have the recording acts any application to mortgages executed at the same time and held by the same person, for he has, of necessity, notice of both.[10] The record of one before the other is in such case without effect.[11] Mortgages executed and recorded simultaneously are concurrent liens, whether in the hands of the mortgagee or in the hands of assignees. Nor have the acts any application when the mortgages expressly declare that neither is to have precedence of the other, but are to be alike security for the several debts.[12] Nor have they any application as between two mortgages given for purchase-money at the same time; and when this fact appears upon the face of the deeds, the prior record of one gives it no priority over the other.[13]

The rights of the parties in such cases may sometimes be controlled by other considerations; and if there be any priority of one over the other, that priority is determined by considerations of equity.[14] Equitable rights and agreements as to priority are recognized and enforced only in courts of equity.[15] Priority may be given to one mortgage

---

[7] Thompson v. Lyman, 28 Wis. 266.

[8] Stafford v. Van Rensselaer, 9 Cow. (N. Y.) 316, affg. Hopk. 569; Douglass v. Peele, Clarke (N. Y.) 563.

[9] Koevenig v. Schmitz, 71 Iowa 175, 32 N. W. 320; Terry v. Moran, 75 Minn. 249, 77 N. W. 777; Jones v. Phelps, 2 Barb. Ch. (N. Y.) 440; Bonstein v. Schweyer, 212 Pa. 19, 61 Atl. 447 (no priority between mortgages filed at the same moment). See also Mason v. Daily (N. J. Eq.), 44 Atl. 839. A sale under one of two mortgages simultaneously recorded discharges the other. Bonstein v. Schweyer, 212 Pa. 19, 61 Atl. 447.

[10] Vredenburgh v. Burnet, 31 N. J. Eq. 229; Gansen v. Tomlinson, 23 N. J. Eq. 405.

[11] The mere fact that one mortgage was handed to the recorder an instant before the other does not give it priority. Koevenig v. Schmitz, 71 Iowa 175, 32 N. W. 320.

[12] Howard v. Chase, 104 Mass. 249.

[13] Greene v. Deal, 4 Hun 703.

[14] Schaeppi v. Glade, 195 Ill. 62, 62 N. E. 874; Fischer v. Tuohy, 186 Ill. 143, 57 N. E. 801; Stafford v. Van Rensselaer, 9 Cow. (N. Y.) 316; Wilcox v. Drought, 36 Misc. 351, 73 N. Y. S. 587.

[15] Jones v. Phelps, 2 Barb. Ch. (N. Y.) 440.

over another by agreement of the parties, even though there was no actual difference in the time of recording.[16]

As between two mortgages acknowledged the same day and recorded simultaneously, mortgaging the same premises to secure two notes made payable to the same nominal payee, for convenience in negotiating them, that one is entitled to priority which is first entered and numbered by the recorder for record and which secures the note bearing the earlier date, if such mortgage is the first one transferred for value.[17]

When two mortgages executed at different dates are recorded on the same day, and there is nothing to show which was in fact first recorded, the presumption of law is that the recording of them was concurrent, and each party stands charged with notice of the equities of the other on that day, at the same moment; though in such case the mortgage which is prior in execution is regarded as having the superior equity.[18] When two mortgages are filed on the same day, they take priority according to the hour and minute when filed.[19] The mere order in which two mortgages are inscribed in the record is not evidence to prove that one was filed before the other.[20]

[16] Corbin v. Kincaid, 33 Kans. 649, 7 Pac. 145; Gilman v. Moody, 43 N. H. 239. See also Naylor v. Throckmorton, 7 Leigh (Va.) 98, 30 Am. Dec. 492. See post § 607a.

[17] Fischer v. Tuohy, 186 Ill. 143, 57 N. E. 801, affg. 87 Ill. App. 574.

[18] Houfes v. Schultze, 2 Bradw. (Ill.) 196; Deininger v. McConnel, 41 Ill. 227; Hatch v. Haskins, 17 Maine 391. In Alabama, however, the junior mortgage is given priority. This result is based upon the provision of the Code, § 1811, declaring all mortgages to be void as to purchasers for a valuable consideration and mortgages without notice, unless recorded before the accrual of the rights of such purchasers or mortgagees. In the case of mortgages simultaneously recorded, though the execution of one was prior to the execution of the other, it is said that, at the time of the accrual of the right of the junior mortgagee, the prior mortgage was inoperative and void as to him, unless he had notice of it. Wood v. Lake, 62 Ala. 489. "The fact that both mortgages were filed for record at the same time does not change the effect of the statute of registration. It does not require the second mortgage to be recorded before the first is recorded in order to preserve its preference. It simply declares the unrecorded prior mortgage inoperative and void as against the subsequent mortgagees, when their mortgage is executed and received without notice of the first." Steiner v. Clisby, 95 Ala. 91, 10 So. 240, 11 So. 294; Coster v. Bank, 24 Ala. 37. In Minnesota under Gen. Stat. 1894, § 767, Gen. Stat. 1913, §§ 904, 905, providing that priority of registration shall prima facie depend upon the number of the instrument where several mortgages are executed and recorded at the same hour the document numbers given to the instruments in the register's office prima facie determine the priority in the order in which the instruments are numbered. Connecticut Mut. L. Ins. Co. v. King, 72 Minn. 287, 75 N. W. 376.

[19] Fischer v. Tuohy, 87 Ill. App. 574; Bonstein v. Schweyer, 212 Pa. 19, 61 Atl. 447. See also Lemon v. Staats, 1 Cow. (N. Y.) 592.

[20] Hatch v. Haskins, 17 Maine 391. See also Bonstein v. Schweyer, 212 Pa. 19, 61 Atl. 447.

In some states the order in which they are numbered by the recorder, upon being filed or in the record book, is prima facie evidence of the order in which they were received for record, the one bearing the lower number being presumed the first lien;[21] but where instruments are handed to the recorder at the same time, he can not fix their priority by the mere order in which he numbers them, either accidentally or by design.[22]

The chief effect of recording an assignment of a mortgage is to protect the assignee from a subsequent sale of the mortgage.[23] The assignment when not recorded is void as against a subsequent purchaser of the mortgage. Therefore, when two simultaneous mortgages of the same land are made under an agreement that they shall be equal liens, the prior record of one gives it no preference over the other. Such a mortgage is not within the terms of a statute declaring an unrecorded conveyance void against a subsequent conveyance first recorded. A simultaneous conveyance is not a subsequent conveyance. An assignment is a conveyance of a mortgage, and if it be not recorded it is void against a subsequent purchaser of the mortgage.[24] There is a further use in recording an assignment in the indirect protection that the record affords the holder of the mortgage as against innocent subsequent purchasers of the mortgaged land; for there may be grounds for the purchaser's believing that the mortgage had been paid, and, the assignment not being recorded, the purchaser would be prevented from making inquiries of the real owner of the mortgage.[25] Accordingly, an unrecorded assignment is generally held invalid as against subsequent purchasers and lienors in good faith without actual notice.[26]

[21] Madlener v. Ruesch, 91 Ill. App. 391; Connecticut Mut. Life Ins. Co. v. King, 72 Minn. 287, 75 N. W. 376; Neve v. Pennell, 2 Hem. & M. 170, 33 L. J. Ch. 19, 9 L. T. Rep. (N. S.) 285, 11 Wkly. Rep. 986, 71 Eng. Reprint 427.

[22] Schaeppi v. Glade, 195 Ill. 62, 62 N. E. 874.

[23] See ante § 474.

[24] Greene v. Warnick, 64 N. Y. 220.

[25] Brownback v. Ozias, 117 Pa. St. 87, 11 Atl. 301.

[26] Citizens' State Bank v. Julian, 153 Ind. 655, 55 N. E. 1007; Jenks v. Shaw, 99 Iowa 604, 68 N. W. 900, 61 Am. St. 256; Pritchard v. Kalamazoo College, 82 Mich. 587, 47 N. W. 31; Cannon v. Wright, 49 N. J. Eq. 17, 23 Atl. 285; Breed v. Auburn Nat. Bank, 171 N. Y. 648, 63 N. E. 1115; Spicer v. First Nat. Bank, 170 N. Y. 562, 62 N. E. 1100; Crane v. Turner, 67 N. Y. 437; Henniges v. Paschke, 9 N. Dak. 489, 84 N. W. 350, 81 Am. St. 588; State v. Coughran, 19 S. Dak. 271, 103 N. W. 31; Seattle Nat. Bank v. Ally, 66 Wash. 610, 120 Pac. 94. The assignee is thus left at the mercy of the assignor in respect to payment and discharge of the mortgage. Connecticut Mut. Life Co. v. Talbot, 113 Ind. 373, 14 N. E. 586, 3 Am. St. 655; Peaks v. Dexter, 82 Maine 85, 19 Atl. 100; Lea v. Welsh, 12 Ohio Cir. Ct. 670, 4 Ohio Cir. Dec. 190; Strait v. Ady, 6 Ohio S.

If an assignee of one of two simultaneous mortgages be regarded as a subsequent purchaser of some interest in the real estate, then he is affected by the record of the other mortgage, as well as that of which he has taken an assignment; and if either or both contain a recital showing that they are simultaneous, or that both were given for the purchase-money of the same land, then the prior record of one can give it no preference over the other.[27]

If one of two simultaneous mortgages made to the same person be assigned with the representation that it is a first lien upon the premises, this representation will make it so as against the assignor. But as against a subsequent assignee of the other, without notice, such representation is a secret equity by which he is not bound.[28]

§ 535. **Simultaneous mortgages for purchase-money.**—Where two or more mortgages are made simultaneously to different persons, and are so connected with each other that they may be regarded as one transaction, each mortgagee having notice of the other mortgage, they will be held to take effect in such order of priority or succession as shall best carry into effect the intention and best secure the rights of all the parties.[29] When the equities of the two mortgages are equal in point of merit, the oldest in point of time will prevail.[30] If there be no intention to give any preference to either, no preference as between the mortgagees can be obtained by priority of record.[31] And a mere undisclosed desire or intention of a mortgagor to give priority to one mortgage over the other will not accomplish such purpose.[32] The recording acts in such case have no application. But if one of such mortgages be assigned to a purchaser in good faith without notice of any superior equity in the holder of the other mortgage, such assignee is entitled to the priority gained by an earlier record of his

& C. Pl. Dec. 273, 4 Ohio N. P. 86; In re Mortgage, 5 Ohio S. & C. Pl. Dec. 556, 7 Ohio N. P. 534; Passumpsic Sav. Bank v. Buck, 71 Vt. 190, 44 Atl. 92.

[27] Van Aken v. Gleason, 34 Mich. 477; Greene v. Warnick, 64 N. Y. 220.

[28] Vredenburgh v. Burnet, 31 N. J. Eq. 229. In Lane v. Nickerson, 17 Hun (N. Y.) 148, it was held such representation would give priority even as against the purchaser of the other mortgage.

[29] Pomeroy v. Latting, 15 Gray (Mass.) 435; Gilman v. Moody, 43 N. H. 239; Jones v. Phelps, 2 Barb. Ch. (N. Y.) 440; Douglass v. Peele, Clarke (N. Y.) 563. See also Mutual Loan &c. Assn. v. Elwell, 38 N. J. Eq. 18; Crombie v. Rosentock, 19 Abb. N. Cas. (N. Y.) 312; Herron v. Herron, 19 Ohio Cir. Ct. 160, 10 Ohio Cir. Dec. 525.

[30] Houfes v. Schultze, 2 Bradw. (Ill.) 196; Naylor v. Throckmorton, 7 Leigh (Va.) 98, 30 Am. Dec. 492.

[31] Sparks v. State Bank, 7 Blackf. (Ind.) 469; Koevenig v. Schmitz, 71 Iowa 175, 32 N. W. 320; Van Aken v. Gleason, 34 Mich. 477; Rhoades v. Canfield, 8 Paige (N. Y.) 545.

[32] Koevenig v. Schmitz, 71 Iowa 175, 32 N. W. 320.

mortgage, even if the other mortgage was superior in equity.[33] Upon a foreclosure sale under such mortgage the purchaser would be entitled to the same priority which the assignee would have.[34]

If two mortgages be made to the same person to secure purchase-money, though in the mortgagee's hands one has no priority over the other, he may assign one in such a way as to give it priority over the other subsequently assigned by him.

A foreclosure, under a power of sale, of one of two mortgages designed to be simultaneous, is not effectual to settle the relative rights of the purchaser and the holder of the other mortgage, a bill in equity being necessary to determine them and to marshal the assets. To effect this a sale is necessary, unless one of the parties take up the other's mortgage.[35]

§ 536. **Simultaneous mortgages of which one is for purchase-money.**—If a purchaser of land, at the instant of receiving his deed, executes and delivers two mortgages of it, one to his grantor to secure a payment of a part of the purchase-money, and the other to a third person, and all the deeds are entered for record at the same moment, the mortgage to his grantor takes precedence. The deed and the mortgage for the purchase-money are parts of one transaction, and give the purchaser only an instantaneous seisin. Moreover, the deed and mortgages being all delivered at the same time, the several grantees must be considered as knowing all that took place concerning them, and the third person, therefore, as knowing of the mortgage for the purchase-money, to which his own became subject as effectually, by his knowledge of its existence, as it would have been if it had been posterior in time of entry for record.[36]

A vendor of real estate who records his mortgage at the same instant that the deed from him is recorded has no occasion to examine the records for incumbrances created by his vendee upon the property prior to the recording of his deed. If there be delay in recording such deed and mortgage, and the vendee executes another mortgage of the same property to a stranger, and this is recorded before the deed to the vendee and his mortgage for the purchase-money are recorded, the

---

[33] Westbrook v. Gleason, 79 N. Y. 23; Corning v. Murray, 3 Barb. (N. Y.) 652; Decker v. Boice, 19 Hun (N. Y.) 152, 83 N. Y. 215.

[34] Decker v. Boice, 19 Hun (N. Y.) 152, 83 N. Y. 215.

[35] Van Aken v. Gleason, 34 Mich. 477.

[36] Clark v. Brown, 3 Allen (Mass.) 509; Heffron v. Flanigan, 37 Mich. 274; Brasted v. Sutton, 29 N. J. Eq. 513; City Nat. Bank Appeal, 91 Pa. St. 163. See also Hassell v. Hassell, 129 Ala. 326, 29 So. 695; Ivy v. Yancey, 129 Mo. 501, 31 S. W. 937.

recording of the mortgage to such third person is not notice to the vendor, because at that time the deed to the vendee had not been recorded.[37]

For the same reason, a purchase-money mortgage has precedence of mechanics' liens placed upon a building between the execution of the contract of purchase and the conveyance, although the conveyance and mortgage are made when the building is almost finished.[38]

But if a purchase-money mortgage and another mortgage be executed and delivered at the same time, so that they take effect upon the estate at the same instant, and the recording of the purchase-money mortgage is delayed and the other is first recorded, the latter will, in the absence of any notice of the purchase-money mortgage, be held to be superior in right.[39]

Where three mortgages are filed for record simultaneously, the question of priority may be determined by parol evidence that the money secured by two of them was to be advanced certainly without conditions, for erection of buildings at all events, while the third was not to become effective unless it became necessary to draw the money upon it to pay interest on the other two, and that the money was not so drawn until after the money had been advanced on the two mortgages.[40]

§ 537. **English doctrine of tacking.**—The English doctrine of tacking incumbrances, or adding to the mortgage debt, arose under a system of titles where there was no registration.[41] It has no application to registered mortgages in this country, and a mortgage given as security for a particular debt can not be enlarged to cover any ad- ·

---

[37] Boyd v. Mundorf, 30 N. J. Eq. 545; Losey v. Simpson, 11 N. J. Eq. 246; Continental L. Soc. v. Wood, 168 Ill. 421, 48 N. E. 221 (quoting text).

[38] Gibbs v. Grant, 29 N. J. Eq. 419; Paul v. Hoeft, 28 N. J. Eq. 11; MacIntosh v. Thurston, 25 N. J. Eq. 242; Strong v. Van Deursen, 23 N. J. Eq. 369; Lamb v. Cannon, 38 N. J. L. 382. See also Van Loben Sels v. Bunnell, 120 Cal. 680, 53 Pac. 266; Hillhouse v. Pratt, 74 Conn. 113, 49 Atl. 905; Anglo-American &c. Bldg. Assn. v. Campbell, 13 App. D. C. 581, 43 L. R. A. 622; Wilson v. Lubke, 176 Mo. 210, 75 S. W. 602, 98 Am. St. 503; New Jersey Bldg. &c. Assn. v. Bachelor, 45 N. J. Eq. 600, 35 Atl. 745; Mutual Aid Bldg.

&c. Co. v. Gashe, 56 Ohio St. 273, 46 N. E. 985.

[39] Houston v. Houston, 67 Ind. 276; Dusenbury v. Hulbert, 2 Thomp. & C. (N. Y.) 177.

[40] Schaeppi v. Glade, 195 Ill. 62, 62 N. E. 874.

[41] Tacking in England was abolished by the Vendor and Purchaser Act of 1874. The dimensions to which the learning on this subject had grown may be gathered from the fact that in Mr. Coventry's edition of Powell on Mortgages, published in 1822, it occupies one hundred and twenty-five pages. See Lloyd v. Attwood, 3 De G. & J. 614, 5 Jur. (N. S.) 1322, 29 L. J. Ch. 97, 60 Eng. Ch. 614, 44 Eng. Reprint 1405; Ex parte Berridge, 7 Jur.

ditional claim, either in respect to redemption or foreclosure.[42] Registered mortgages are payable according to the priority of their record.[43] It is well settled here that a mortgage given as security for a particular debt, whether present or prospective, can not be enforced for another and different debt.[44] Even apart from the question of notice, the doctrine could have no application in states where a mortgage is a mere equitable lien and does not convey a legal title. Another kind of tacking arises when the mortgagee attaches to the mortgage lien other debts not included in the mortgage. This he may do, so far as the mortgagor is concerned, when an express or implied agreement exists allowing him to do so; but he can not tack other debts to his mortgage as against intervening mortgagees and judgment creditors.[45]

1141, 3 Mont. D. & De G. 464. See also Frere v. Moore, 8 Price 475, 22 Rev. Rep. 759. Even under the English doctrine the first mortgagee must have no notice of the second lien. Toulmin v. Steere, 3 Meriv. 210, 17 Rev. Rep. 67, 36 Eng. Reprint 81.

[42] Parmer v. Parmer, 74 Ala. 285; Cohn v. Hoffman, 56 Ark. 119, 19 S. W. 233; Chase v. McDonald, 7 Harr. & J. (Md.) 160; Wing v. McDowell, Walk. (Mich.) 175; Bacon v. Cottrell, 13 Minn. 194; White v. Rovall, 121 App. Div. 12, 105 N. Y. S. 624; James v. Morey, 2 Cow. (N. Y.) 246, 14 Am. Dec. 475; Burnet v. Denniston, 5 Johns. Ch. (N. Y.) 35; Dorrow v. Kelly, 1 Dall. (Pa.) 142, 1 L. ed. 73; Siter v. McClanachan, 2 Grat. (Va.) 280. See ante § 360.

[43] Farrell v. Lewis, 56 Conn. 280, 14 Atl. 931; Osborn v. Carr, 12 Conn. 195; Averill v. Guthrie, 8 Dana (Ky.) 82; Equitable Securities Co. v. Talbert, 49 La. Ann. 1393, 22 So. 762; Loring v. Cooke, 3 Pick. (Mass.) 48; Wing v. McDowell, Walk. (Mich.) 175; Grant v. United States Bank, 1 Caines' Cas. (N. Y.) 112; Brazee v. Lancaster Bank, 14 Ohio 318; Anderson v. Neff, 11 Serg. & R. (Pa.) 208; Chandler v. Dyer, 37 Vt. 345; Siter v. McClanachan, 2 Grat. (Va.) 280. It is prohibited by statute in Georgia. Code 1911, § 3265. See ante §§ 357, 360, and post § 1082.

[44] In re Shevill, 11 Fed. 858; Baldwin v. Raplee, 2 Fed. Cas. No. 801, 4 Ben. 433; Morris v. Alston, 92 Ala. 502, 9 So. 315; Ross v. Hodges, 108 Ark 270, 157 S. W. 391; Butler v. Adler-Goldman Commission Co., 62 Ark. 445, 35 S. W. 1110; Neumann v. Moretti, 146 Cal. 25, 79 Pac. 510; Lewter v. Price, 25 Fla. 574, 6 So. 439; Fleming v. Georgia Railroad Bank, 120 Ga. 1023, 48 S. E. 420; Stone v. Palmer, 68 Ill. App. 338; Des Moines Sav. Bank v. Kennedy, 142 Iowa 272, 120 N. W. 742; Schadel v. St. Martin, 11 La. Ann. 175; Heyhurst v. Morin, 105 Maine 169, 71 Atl. 707; Harris v. Hooper, 50 Md. 537; Woodin v. Sparta Furniture Co., 59 Mich. 58, 26 N. W. 504; Parkes v. Parker, 57 Mich. 57, 23 N. W. 458; Lambertville Nat. Bank v. McCready Bag &c. Co. (N. J. Eq.), 15 Atl. 388, 1 L. R. A. 334; White v. Rovall, 121 App. Div. 12, 105 N. Y. S. 624; Powell v. Harrison, 88 App. Div. 228, 85 N. Y. S. 452; Norris v. W. C. Belcher Land Mtg. Co., 98 Tex. 176, 82 S. W. 500, 83 S. W. 799; Beardsley v. Tuttle, 11 Wis. 74.

[45] Orvis v. Newell, 17 Conn. 97; Hughes v. Worley, 1 Bibb. (Ky.) 200; Averill v. Guthrie, 8 Dana (Ky.) 82; Chase v. M'Donald, 7 Har. & J. (Md.) 160; Towner v. Wells, 8 Ohio 136; Siter v. McClanachan, 2 Grat. (Va.) 280; Colquhoun v. Atkinsons, 6 Munf. (Va.) 550.

§ 537a. Origin and adoption of Torrens System.—In several states, including California, Colorado, Illinois, Massachusetts, Minnesota, New York, Oregon and Washington, there now exist statutory provisions for a system of judicial registration of land titles commonly known as the Torrens system.[1] The system was formulated by Sir Robert Torrens, an Irish emigrant to Australia, where the system was first adopted in 1857. The same general plan of registration has been in use in parts of Europe for centuries, and there is nothing new about the fundamental principles involved;[2] but the statutes have been discussed as most radical in their operation, and frequently attacked as unconstitutional.[3] The effect of such registration is to make a certificate of title, issued by the official designated in the statute, conclusive as to the character of the title of the person to whom it is issued, and as to all the rights, liens and incumbrances of other persons,

[1] California (adopted 1897), Robinson v. Kerrigan, 151 Cal. 40, 90 Pac. 129, 121 Am. St. 90. Colorado (adopted 1903), People v. Crissman, 41 Colo. 450, 92 Pac. 949. Illinois (enacted in 1895 and 1897), People v. Simon, 176 Ill. 165, 52 N. E. 910, 44 L. R. A. 801, 68 Am. St. 175. See also Peters v. Dicus, 254 Ill. 379, 98 N. E. 560. Massachusetts (adopted 1898), McQuesten v. Commonwealth, 198 Mass. 172, 83 N. E. 1037; Tyler v. Judges of Court of Registration, 175 Mass. 71, 55 N. E. 812, 51 L. R. A. 433; Battelle v. New York, N. H. &c. R. Co., 211 Mass. 442, 97 N. E. 1004; Baxter v. Bickford, 201 Mass. 495, 88 N. E. 7. Minnesota (adopted 1901), Baart v. Martin, 99 Minn. 197, 108 N. W. 945, 116 Am. St. 394; Peters v. Duluth, 119 Minn. 96, 137 N. W. 390; Kuby v. Ryder, 114 Minn. 217, 130 N. W. 1100; Hendricks v. Hess, 112 Minn. 252, 127 N. W. 995; Doyle v. Wagner, 108 Minn. 443, 122 N. W. 316; State v. Westfall, 85 Minn. 437, 89 N. W. 175, 57 L. R. A. 297, 89 Am. St. 571. The New York statute, adopted in 1908, embodies the essential features of the other Torrens laws, but contains certain provisions peculiar to itself. See 8 Columbia L. Rev. 438, article by Alfred Reeves. Oregon (adopted 1901). See Lewis v. Chamberlain, 61 Ore. 150, 121 Pac. 430. Washington (adopted 1907). See Remington's Code 1910, §§ 8806–8905. The system was adopted in Hawaii and the Philippines in 1903. See 41 American Law Review 751, report of attorney-general concerning court of land registration. See also In re Building &c. Assn., 13 Philippine 575; De Aldecoa v. Government, 13 Philippine 159. See generally Brewster on Conveyancing, ch. xxix, § 432, et seq.; 14 Bench & Bar 1, editorial; Niblack on the Torrens System.

[2] Land Transfer by Registration of Title in Germany and Austria-Hungary, Am. Law Rev., Vol. 31, p. 827.

[3] See post § 537b.

in connection with the title.[4] Considering the objections to the proposed system, the chief justice of South Australia demurred to it as "both unwise and impracticable," but in 1857 it was adopted in that colony and has since been adopted throughout Australia, where its popularity has brought most of the land of Australia under the law. New Zealand and several Canadian provinces then adopted the system, and England finally followed the colonies.[5]

§ 537b. **Constitutionality of statutes.**—In the United States, the original Illinois statute of 1895 was declared unconstitutional, on the ground that it conferred judicial powers upon registrars and examiners of title;[6] but the subsequent Illinois statute of 1897 was upheld as constitutional.[7] The Ohio statute of 1896 was declared unconstitutional and repealed;[8] but the statutes in other jurisdictions have generally been sustained by the courts.[9]

The constitutional objections most generally urged, but usually without success, against the statutes have been that they deprive persons of their property without due process of law,[10] that they deny equal protection of the laws,[11] that they confuse judi-

---

[4] See post § 537c.

[5] Similar acts were adopted in 1861 by Queensland; in 1862 by New South Wales, Victoria and Tasmania; in 1870 by New Zealand; in 1874 by Western Australia; and in 1876 by Fiji. 8 Columbia L. Rev. 438. The Canadian Act is discussed in 29 Can. L. T. 695, article by A. McLeod. McKillop v. Alexander, 45 Can. Sup. Ct. 551, 4 Sask. L. R. 111; 38 and 39 Vict., ch. 87, 1875; 60 and 61 Vict., ch. 65, 1897.

[6] People v. Chase, 165 Ill. 527, 46 N. E. 454, 36 L. R. A. 105.

[7] People v. Simon, 176 Ill. 165, 52 N. E. 910, 68 Am. St. 175, 44 L. R. A. 801.

[8] State v. Guilbert, 56 Ohio St. 575, 47 N. E. 551, 38 L. R. A. 519, 60 Am. St. 756; 65 Cent. L. J. 449, article by W. F. Meier; 8 Columbia L. Rev. 438.

[9] Robinson v. Kerrigan, 151 Cal. 40, 90 Pac. 129, 121 Am. St. 90; People v. Crissman, 41 Colo. 450, 92 Pac. 949. In 1898 the system was adopted in Massachusetts and upheld by a divided court. Tyler v. Judges of Court of Registration. 175 Mass. 71, 55 N. E. 812, 51 L. R. A. 433. See also Tyler v. Judges of

Court of Registration, 179 U. S. 405, 45 L. ed. 252, 21 Sup. Ct. 206; Lancy v. Snow, 180 Mass. 411, 62 N. E. 735; In re Welsh, 175 Mass. 68, 55 N. E. 1043. The Minnesota act of 1901 was also declared constitutional. State v. Westfall, 85 Minn. 437, 89 N. W. 175, 57 L. R. A. 297, 89 Am. St. 571; Dewey v. Kimball, 89 Minn. 454, 95 N. W. 317, 895, 96 N. W. 704; Reed v. Carlson, 89 Minn. 417, 95 N. W. 303.

[10] Robinson v. Kerrigan, 151 Cal. 40, 90 Pac. 129, 121 Am. St. 90; People v. Crissman, 41 Colo. 450, 92 Pac. 949; People v. Simon, 176 Ill. 165, 52 N. E. 910, 44 L. R. A. 801, 68 Am. St. 175; Tyler v. Judges of Court of Registration, 175 Mass. 71, 55 N. E. 812, 51 L. R. A. 433; State v. Westfall, 85 Minn. 437, 89 N. W. 175, 89 Am. St. 571, 57 L. R. A. 297.

[11] Robinson v. Kerrigan, 151 Cal. 40, 90 Pac. 129, 121 Am. St. 90; People v. Crissman, 41 Colo. 450, 92 Pac. 949. See also Jackson v. Glos, 249 Ill. 388, 94 N. E. 502; Culver v. Walters, 248 Ill. 163, 93 N. E. 747. The provision for receiving in evidence abstracts made in the ordinary course of business has recently been held constitutional.

cial and administrative and executive functions, and delegate judicial powers to ministerial officers such as registrars, recorders, and examiners of title,[12] that they are special legislation,[13] that they provide for new county officers not chosen by election or appointment under the constitution,[14] and that their enactment under vote by counties is a delegation of legislative power.[15] Further objections have been urged that the statutes make no provision for notice before registration of transfers after the initial registration,[16] and that no action to recover the land can be maintained after sixty days.[17] The objection to the provision for an indemnity fund was sustained among other objections rendering the Ohio statute unconstitutional.[18] Under our constitution, too, close adherence to the foreign statutes seems detrimental, and both the Ohio and Illinois acts were declared unconstitutional because the Australian model was followed too closely.[19] Many of the constitutional objections have been met in framing the later statutes and others have been surmounted by the courts in sustaining them.

§ 537c.   General principles of registration.—The details of American statutes vary, but the underlying principles are the same. The distinguishing feature of the Torrens system is the registration of the title itself, instead of the evidence of title.[20] It provides not merely

Brooke v. Glos, 243 Ill. 392, 90 N. E. 751, 134 Am. St. 374, construing Hurd's Rev. Stat. 1908, ch. 30, § 61.

[12] Robinson v. Kerrigan, 151 Cal. 40, 90 Pac. 129, 121 Am. St. 90; People v. Crissman, 41 Colo. 450, 92 Pac. 949; People v. Simon, 176 Ill. 165, 52 N. E. 910, 44 L. R. A. 801, 68 Am. St. 175; Tyler v. Judges of Court of Registration, 175 Mass. 71, 55 N. E. 812, 51 L. R. A. 433; State v. Westfall, 85 Minn. 437, 89 N. W. 175, 57 L. R. A. 297, 89 Am. St. 571.

[13] Robinson v. Kerrigan, 151 Cal. 40, 90 Pac. 129, 121 Am. St. 90; Milhalik v. Glos, 247 Ill. 597, 93 N. E. 372; People v. Simon, 176 Ill. 165, 52 N. E. 910, 44 L. R. A. 801, 68 Am. St. 175; National Bond &c. Co. v. Hopkins, 96 Minn. 119, 104 N. W. 678, 816. See also State v. Westfall, 85 Minn. 437, 89 N. W. 175, 57 L. R. A. 297, 89 Am. St. 571.

[14] People v. Crissman, 41 Colo. 450, 92 Pac. 949. The objection has also

been urged that examiners were to be appointed instead of elected, and that such appointment was by the court. State v. Westfall, 85 Minn. 437, 89 N. W. 175, 57 L. R. A. 297, 89 Am. St. 571.

[15] People v. Simon, 176 Ill. 165, 52 N. E. 910, 44 L. R. A. 801, 68 Am. St. 175.

[16] Tyler v. Judges of Court of Registration, 175 Mass. 71, 55 N. E. 812, 51 L. R. A. 433.

[17] State v. Westfall, 85 Minn. 437, 89 N. W. 175, 57 L. R. A. 297, 89 Am. St. 571.

[18] State v. Guilbert, 56 Ohio St. 575, 47 N. E. 551, 38 L. R. A. 519, 60 Am. St. 756.

[19] People v. Chase, 165 Ill. 527, 46 N. E. 454, 36 L. R. A. 105; State v. Guilbert, 56 Ohio St. 575, 47 N. E. 551, 38 L. R. A. 519, 60 Am. St. 756.

[20] State v. Westfall, 85 Minn. 437, 89 N. W. 175, 57 L. R. A. 297, 89 Am. St. 571.

for the recording of deeds or instruments affecting the title; but for an official registration, under which the title to the land passes by entry of the transfer, and not by the execution and delivery of the deed. It is intended that the register shall show the exact condition of the title to real property upon a single page or folio, and all dealings with the land must be entered thereon.

The objects of the system are the creation of an indefeasible title in the registered owner, simplification in the transfer of land, certainty and facility in the proof of title by reference to a certificate issued by a government official, made conclusive by law, and finally the saving to the community of the cost of a new examination of title in connection with each transfer or transaction affecting the land.

Registration under the Torrens system is a purely voluntary act on the part of the applicant,[21] and he may withdraw his application at any time before the final decree.[22] A formal document called a certificate of title, is issued after a judicial proceeding in the nature of a suit to quiet title and all subsequent transactions affecting the title are noted on this certificate, or on a new one substituted therefor.

§ 537d. Procedure for registration.—In order to meet the constitutional requirement of due process of law and to establish a starting point binding upon all the world, the initial registration of title, upon which the certificate is issued, must be the result of judicial proceedings.[23] There must be notice to all having interests adverse to those of the applicant for registration; and only judicial officers may exercise judicial functions, whether as to the initial registration or subsequent transactions concerning the title. The statutes usually provide all details of procedure for registration.[24]

Ordinarily the first step under the acts is a written application for

[21] Tyler v. Judges of Court of Registration, 175 Mass. 71, 55 N. E. 812, 51 L. R. A. 433.

[22] Foss v. Atkins, 204 Mass. 337, 90 N. E. 578; McQuesten v. Commonwealth, 198 Mass. 172, 83 N. E. 1037.

[23] State v. Westfall, 85 Minn. 437, 89 N. W. 175, 57 L. R. A. 297, 89 Am. St. 571. But see Loewenstein v. Page, 16 Philippine 84.

[24] Robinson v. Kerrigan, 151 Cal. 40, 90 Pac. 129, 121 Am. St. 90; People v. Crissman, 41 Colo. 450, 92 Pac. 949; People v. Simon, 176 Ill. 165, 52 N. E. 910, 44 L. R. A. 801, 68 Am. St. 175; McQuesten v. Commonwealth, 198 Mass. 172, 83 N. E. 1037; Tyler v. Judges of Court of Registration, 175 Mass. 71, 55 N. E. 812, 51 L. R. A. 433; Kuby v. Ryder, 114 Minn. 217, 130 N. W. 1100; State v. Westfall, 85 Minn. 437, 89 N. W. 175, 57 L. R. A. 297, 89 Am. St. 571. See Smith v. Martin, 69 Misc. 108, 124 N. Y. S. 1064; Flores v. Director, 17 Philippine 512; Aguillon v. Director, 17 Philippine 506. See also Beers Torrens System, §§ 52-63; 65 Cent. L. J. 449, article by W. F. Neier; 8 Columbia L. Rev. 438; 14 Bench & Bar 1.

registration by the person claiming ownership of the land in fee simple, fully describing the land and showing the source of title and the existence of adverse claims, liens and incumbrances.[25] The application is signed and sworn to by the applicant and addressed to the court having jurisdiction under the statute.

Upon the filing of the application it is referred to the official examiners of title who make a thorough examination and report to the court.[26] Under the Massachusetts statute the examiner deals with the application, merely as a conveyancer at common law examining a title;[27] but under the Illinois statute the examiner is analogous to a master in chancery.[28] The ordinary rules of evidence and objection thereto, apply.[29] Ex parte examinations of abstracts are improper.[30] Objections to the report of the examiner, in the nature of a special demurrer may be filed, and should specify the grounds therefor with clearness and certainty.[31] The court, however, may require further proof to determine the rights of the parties, and is not bound by the opinion of the examiner.[32]

[25] Robinson v. Kerrigan, 151 Cal. 40, 90 Pac. 129, 121 Am. St. 90; People v. Crissman, 41 Colo. 450, 92 Pac. 949; Tyler v. Judges of Court of Registration, 175 Mass. 71, 55 N. E. 812, 51 L. R. A. 433; Baart v. Martin, 99 Minn. 197, 108 N. W. 945, 116 Am. St. 394; State v. Westfall, 85 Minn. 437, 89 N. W. 175, 57 L. R. A. 297, 89 Am. St. 571; Lachman v. People, 127 N. Y. S. 912; Duffy v. Shirden, 139 App. Div. 755, 124 N. Y. S. 529. Several lots of land included in one application must be contiguous or be related by chain of title. Culver v. Waters, 248 Ill. 163, 93 N. E. 747. See Beers Torrens System, §§ 41-50. In Illinois the application is addressed to the judges of the circuit court for the county in chancery. In Massachusetts it is addressed to the judge of the court of land registration, a court specially constituted by the registration act with exclusive original jurisdiction of such applications. In Colorado and Minnesota it is made to the district court of the county in which the land is situated.

[26] People v. Crissman, 41 Colo. 450, 92 Pac. 949; Glos v. Holberg,

220 Ill. 167, 77 N. E. 80; McQuesten v. Commonwealth, 198 Mass. 172, 83 N. E. 1037; Tyler v. Judges of Court of Registration, 175 Mass. 71, 55 N. E. 812, 51 L. R. A. 433; Dewey v. Kimball, 89 Minn. 454, 95 N. W. 317, 895, 96 N. W. 704; State v. Westfall, 85 Minn. 437, 89 N. W. 175, 57 L. R. A. 297, 89 Am. St. 571. See Mundt v. Glos, 246 Ill. 636, 93 N. E. 49; Lachman v. People, 127 N. Y. S. 912. See also McMahon v. Rowley, 238 Ill. 31, 87 N. E. 66; Torrens System § 23.

[27] McQuesten v. Commonwealth, 198 Mass. 172, 82 N. E. 1037.

[28] Glos v. Holberg, 220 Ill. 167, 77 N. E. 80; Gage v. Consumers' Electric Light Co., 194 Ill. 30, 64 N. E. 653.

[29] Glos v. Grant Bldg. &c. Assn., 229 Ill. 387, 82 N. E. 304; Glos v. Holberg, 220 Ill. 167, 77 N. E. 80; Glos v. Cessna, 207 Ill. 69, 69 N. E. 634.

[30] Glos v. Grant Bldg. &c. Assn., 229 Ill. 387, 82 N. E. 304; Glos v. Holberg, 220 Ill. 167, 77 N. E. 80.

[31] Glos v. Hoban, 212 Ill. 222, 72 N. E. 1.

[32] People v. Crissman, 41 Colo. 450, 92 Pac. 949; Duffy v. Shirden, 139

§ **537e. Notice and hearing—Incumbrances on title.**—The next step is the service of personal process, or notice by publication, upon all parties interested in the property,[33] and any one claiming an interest in or lien upon the property may appear and answer,[34] whether named in the summons or not.[35] All persons known to claim an interest or lien upon the property must be made defendants,[36] but persons unknown who have such interest may be included under a general designation.[37]

After due notice to all parties, the court orders and determines all transfers in regard to the property,[38] and the existence and validity of all claims, liens and mortgages.[39] The court may determine the existence and priority of conflicting liens, but a lien can not be foreclosed in a proceeding to register title.[40]

§ **537f. Decree and certificate of title and incumbrances.**—If the applicant for registration establishes a title entitled to registration, a decree is entered to that effect and the claims of defendants are set aside as mere clouds upon his title.[41] If the applicant fails to prove

App. Div. 755, 124 N. Y. S. 529. See also Lachman v. People, 127 N. Y. S. 912.

[33] Robinson v. Kerrigan, 151 Cal. 40, 90 Pac. 129, 121 Am. St. 90; People v. Crissman, 41 Colo. 450, 92 Pac. 949; Tyler v. Judges of Court of Registration, 175 Mass. 71, 55 N. E. 812, 51 L. R. A. 433; Baart v. Martin, 99 Minn. 197, 108 N. W. 945, 116 Am. St. 394; Dewey v. Kimball, 89 Minn. 454, 95 N. W. 317, 895, 96 N. W. 704; Reed v. Siddall, 89 Minn. 417, 95 N. W. 303; State v. Westfall, 85 Minn. 437, 89 N. W. 175, 57 L. R. A. 297, 89 Am. St. 571; Lachman v. People, 127 N. Y. S. 912. See also Alba v. De la Cruz, 17 Philippine 49; Escueta v. Director, 16 Philippine 482.

[34] People v. Crissman, 41 Colo. 450, 92 Pac. 949; State v. Westfall, 85 Minn. 437, 89 N. W. 175, 57 L. R. A. 297, 89 Am. St. 571; Sundermann v. People, 148 App. Div. 124, 132 N. Y. S. 68; Hawes v. United States Trust Co., 142 App. Div. 789, 127 N. Y. S. 632. See Smith v. Martin, 142 App. Div. 60, 126 N. Y. S. 877.

[35] People v. Crissman, 41 Colo. 450, 92 Pac. 949; Sunderman v. People, 130 N. Y. S. 453; Hawes v. United States Trust Co., 142 App.

Div. 789, 127 N. Y. S. 632.

[36] Baart v. Martin, 99 Minn. 197, 108 N. W. 945, 116 Am. St. 394; Dewey v. Kimball, 89 Minn. 454, 95 N. W. 317, 895, 96 N. W. 704; Sunderman v. People, 148 App. Div. 124, 132 N. Y. S. 68; Hawes v. United States Trust Co., 142 App. Div. 789, 127 N. Y. S. 632; Duffy v. Shirden, 139 App. Div. 755, 124 N. Y. S. 529.

[37] People v. Crissman, 41 Colo. 450, 92 Pac. 949; People v. Simon, 176 Ill. 165, 52 N. E. 910, 44 L. R. A. 801, 68 Am. St. 175; State v. Westfall, 85 Minn. 437, 89 N. W. 175, 57 L. R. A. 297, 89 Am. St. 571.

[38] Reed v. Siddall, 94 Minn. 216, 102 N. W. 453; Barkenthien v. People, 136 N. Y. S. 178; Crabbe v. Hardy, 77 Misc. 1, 135 N. Y. S. 119. See also Peters v. Dicus, 254 Ill. 379, 98 N. E. 560; Woodvine v. Dean, 194 Mass. 40, 79 N. E. 882.

[39] First Nat. Bank v. Woburn, 192 Mass. 220, 78 N. E. 307; Reed v. Siddall, 94 Minn. 216, 102 N. W. 453.

[40] Reed v. Siddall, 94 Minn. 216, 102 N. W. 453.

[41] See Glos v. Kingman, 207 Ill. 26, 69 N. E. 632; Smith v. Martin, 142 App. Div. 60, 126 N. Y. S. 877.

a title, entitled to registration, the proceedings are dismissed and no decree is entered against the adverse claimants.[42]

The statutes usually provide for an appeal from the decree, as in other civil actions,[43] and only questions raised by objection or exception before the examiner or the lower court can be urged on appeal.[44] In Massachusetts the appeal is taken from the land court to the superior court with the right to claim a jury, or to the supreme judicial court upon questions of law.[45]

When the decree for registration has been entered and the record duly made, the certificate is issued, completing the registry,[46] and although the original registration was voluntary, the proceedings for registration constitute an agreement running with the land that it shall remain registered land subject to the provisions of the statute.[47]

The certificate of title is conclusive that no outstanding interests or incumbrances exist in other persons, with certain exceptions specified in the statute, such as liens for taxes, short term leases and certain easements, ascertainable by inspection of the premises.[48] All other existing liens and incumbrances, equitable or statutory, are

[42] Glos v. Cessna, 207 Ill. 69, 69 N. E. 634; Glos v. Kingman, 207 Ill. 26, 69 N. E. 632; Magsocay v. Fernando, 17 Philippine 120.

[43] Robinson v. Kerrigan, 151 Cal. 40, 90 Pac. 129, 121 Am. St. 90; Luce v. Parsons, 192 Mass. 8, 77 N. E. 1032; Peters v. Duluth, 119 Minn. 96, 137 N. W. 390; Baart v. Martin, 99 Minn. 197, 108 N. W. 945, 116 Am. St. 394; State v. Westfall, 85 Minn. 437, 89 N. W. 175, 57 L. R. A. 297, 89 Am. St. 571; People v. O'Loughlin, 136 N. Y. S. 339; Lewis v. Chamberlain, 61 Ore. 150, 121 Pac. 430 (prayer for appeal must be at time of decree). See also Glos v. Hoban, 212 Ill. 222, 72 N. E. 1; Foss v. Atkins, 201 Mass. 158, 87 N. E. 189, 204 Mass. 337, 90 N. E. 578; Kurby v. Ryder, 114 Minn. 217, 130 N. W. 1100; Lachmann v. Brookfield, 135 N. Y. S. 261; Beers Torrens System, § 65; 14 Bench & Bar 1, editorial.

[44] McMahon v. Rowley, 238 Ill. 31, 87 N. E. 66; Cregar v. Spitzer, 244 Ill. 208, 91 N. E. 418; Gage v. Consumers' Electric Light Co., 194 Ill. 30, 64 N. E. 653. See also Glos v. Hoban, 212 Ill. 222, 72 N. E. 1.

[45] Weeks v. Brooks, 205 Mass. 458, 92 N. E. 45 (denial of jury by land court); McQuesten v. Commonwealth, 198 Mass. 172, 83 N. E. 1037; Luce v. Parsons, 192 Mass. 8, 77 N. E. 1032; Tyler v. Judges of Court of Registration, 175 Mass. 71, 55 N. E. 812, 51 L. R. A. 433. See also Blake v. Rogers, 210 Mass. 588, 97 N. E. 68; Bigelow Carpet Co. v. Wiggin, 209 Mass. 542, 95 N. E. 938; Bishop v. Burke, 207 Mass. 133, 93 N. E. 254; Old Colony St. R. Co. v. Thomas, 205 Mass. 529, 91 N. E. 1006; Cohasset v. Moors, 204 Mass. 173, 90 N. E. 978; Welsh v. Briggs, 204 Mass. 540, 90 N. E. 1146; Woodbine v. Dean, 194 Mass. 40, 79 N. E. 882; Foss v. Atkins, 193 Mass. 486, 79 N. E. 763; First Nat. Bank v. Woburn, 192 Mass. 220, 78 N. E. 307; McQuesten v. Attorney-General, 187 Mass. 185, 72 N. E. 965.

[46] Robinson v. Kerrigan, 151 Cal. 40, 90 Pac. 129, 121 Am. St. 90. See Cusar v. Government, 13 Philippine 319.

[47] Tyler v. Judges of Court of Registration, 175 Mass. 71, 55 N. E. 812, 51 L. R. A. 433.

[48] Baart v. Martin, 99 Minn. 197,

noted upon the record and the certificate, and the holder thereof acquires an indefeasible title to the property,[49] free from all incumbrances except those so noted.[50]

Where a mortgage for purchase-money was lost by a failure of the court, in registering land under the Torrens act, to note it in the decree, and a new mortgage was duly executed and registered upon discovery of the mistake, the new mortgage was held to be a prior lien to that of an unregistered mortgage executed prior to the renewal mortgage, but subsequent to the original purchase-money mortgage. In such case the new mortgage was not considered an ordinary mortgage given to secure an antecedent debt, but was entitled to greater consideration in equity, as relating back to the original mortgage.[51]

The statutes usually provide a short period within which persons having an adverse claim or lien upon the property, who were not served with process, may come in and assert their claims,[52] and contain special exceptions in regard to fraud.[53] An assignment or discharge of the mortgage is also noted in the certificate and registration book.

Subsequent mortgages are also required to be noted upon the certificate and record, generally by filing with the registrar a copy of the proceedings or instrument upon which the lien is based.[54] In case of a subsequent mortgage on the land, the statutes sometimes provide for a duplicate certificate of title to be issued to the mortgagee, a memorandum thereof being noted on the original certificate in the registration book; while some times the mortgage itself is given to the mortgagee, a duplicate being held by the registrar for notation in the registration book.

In a case where the duplicate certificate of registration was wrong-

108 N. W. 945, 116 Am. St. 394; Beers Torrens System, §§ 27, 28. See also 8 Columbia L. Rev. 438.

[49] Robinson v. Kerrigan, 151 Cal. 40, 90 Pac. 129, 121 Am. St. 90; State v. Westfall, 85 Minn. 437, 89 N. W. 175, 57 L. R. A. 297, 89 Am. St. 571. See Hawes v. Clark, 136 N. Y. S. 188.

[50] Robinson v. Kerrigan, 151 Cal. 40, 90 Pac. 129, 121 Am. St. 90; State v. Westfall, 85 Minn. 437, 89 N. W. 175, 57 L. R. A. 297, 89 Am. St. 571. See also Doyle v. Wagner, 108 Minn. 443, 122 N. W. 316; 65 Cent. L. J. 449, article by W. F. Neier.

[51] Brace v. Superior Land Co., 65 Wash. 681, 118 Pac. 910.

[52] Robinson v. Kerrigan, 151 Cal. 40, 90 Pac. 129, 121 Am. St. 90; Baart v. Martin, 99 Minn. 197, 108 N. W. 945, 116 Am. St. 394; Reed v. Siddall, 89 Minn. 417, 95 N. W. 303. See also Doyle v. Wagner, 108 Minn. 443, 122 N. W. 316; Beers Torrens System, § 65; 65 Cent. L. J. 449.

[53] Baart v. Martin, 99 Minn. 197, 108 N. W. 945, 116 Am. St. 394 (exception in case of fraud implied in equity); 8 Columbia L. Rev. 438.

[54] Buzon v. Licauco, 13 Philippine 354; 8 Columbia L. Rev. 438.

fully obtained by the owner of the land from the holder of an unregistered mortgage, and used in procuring registration of a later mortgage, it was held that it did not affect the rights of the mortgagee under the later mortgage, where the latter had no knowledge of the fact or of any claim in the certificate by the holder of the unregistered mortgage.[55]

Where a conveyance is executed, a new certificate is generally issued to the grantee,[56] the deed being considered merely as a contract between the parties·conferring authority for the transfer of the registered title to the grantee.[57]

An indemnity fund provided by the statutes is raised by a fee for registration based upon the assessed value of the property,[58] and set aside for compensation of parties having an interest or lien against the property, whose rights have been cut off by the decree without their fault.[59]

[55] Brace v. Superior Land Co., 65 Wash. 681, 118 Pac. 910.

[56] Robinson v. Kerrigan, 151 Cal. 40, 90 Pac. 129, 121 Am. St. 90; State v. Westfall, 85 Minn. 437, 89 N. W. 175, 57 L. R. A. 297, 89 Am. St. 571; 65 Cent. L. J. 449. See Buzon v. Licauco, 13 Philippine 354.

[57] 65 Cent. L. J. 449. See Buzon v. Licauco, 13 Philippine 354.

[58] State v. Westfall, 85 Minn. 437, 89 N. W. 175, 57 L. R. A. 297, 89 Am. St. 571; Beers Torrens System, § 89.

[59] People v. Simon, 176 Ill. 165, 52 N. E. 910, 44 L. R. A. 801, 68 Am. St. 175; State v. Westfall, 85 Minn. 437, 89 N. W. 175, 57 L. R. A. 297, 89 Am. St. 571; 43 Am. L. Rev. 97, article by Richard W. Hale; 14 Bench & Bar 1, editorial; 65 Cent. L. J. 449; 8 Columbia L. Rev. 438; Beers Torrens System, §§ 8, 9, 89-93.

CHAPTER XIII

I. *Notice as Affecting Priority under the Registry Acts*

§ 538. **General doctrine of notice in United States.**—The doctrine of notice as affecting priority is generally adopted in this country. Subsequent purchasers, who have notice of a prior unrecorded mortgage, are affected by their knowledge of it in the same way that the prior record of the mortgage would affect them.[1] A mortgagee who has

---

[1] Lord v. Doyle, 15 Fed. Cas. No. 8505, 1 Cliff. (U. S.) 453; Wyatt v. Stewart, 34 Ala. 716; Dearing v. Watkins, 16 Ala. 20; San Luis Obispo County Bank v. Fox, 119 Cal. 61, 51 Pac. 11; May v. Borel, 12 Cal. 91; Hartford &c. Transp. Co. v. First Nat. Bank, 46 Conn. 569; Mead v. New York &c. R. Co., 45 Conn. 199; Hamilton v. Nutt, 34 Conn. 501; Thompson v. Maxwell, 16 Fla. 773; English v. Lindley, 194 Ill. 181, 62 N. E. 522 (burden of proving notice); Interstate Bldg. &c. Assn. v. Ayres, 177 Ill. 9, 52 N. E. 342; Ætna L. Ins. Co. v. Ford, 89 Ill. 252; Erickson v. Rafferty, 79 Ill. 209; Willis v. Henderson, 5 Ill. 13, 38 Am. Dec. 120; Aurora Nat. Loan Assn. v. Spencer, 81 Ill. App. 622; Mann v. State, 116 Ind. 383, 19 N. E. 181; Jones v. Bamford, 21 Iowa 217; Bell v. Thomas, 2 Iowa 384; Foster Lumber Co. v. Harlan County Bank, 71 Kans. 158, 80 Pac. 49, 114 Am. St. 470; Short v. Fogle, 42 Kans. 349, 22 Pac. 323; King v. Huni, 118 Ky. 450, 81 S. W. 254, 25 Ky. L. 2266, 85 S. W. 723; Flowers v. Moorman, 27 Ky. L. 728, 86 S. W.

actual knowledge or legal notice of a prior conveyance, mortgage, or other lien on the premises, takes subject thereto, and is not protected as a bona fide purchaser.[2] Thus a subsequent mortgagee, who has

545; Copeland v. Copeland, 28 Maine 525; Ohio L. Ins. &c. Co. v. Ross, 2 Md. Ch. 25; Livingstone v. Murphy, 187 Mass. 315, 72 N. E. 1012, 105 Am. St. 400; Boxheimer v. Gunn, 24 Mich. 372; Fitzhugh v. Barnard, 12 Mich. 104; Seiberling v. Tipton, 113 Mo. 373, 21 S. W. 4; Knox County v. Brown, 103 Mo. 223, 15 S. W. 382; Whitman v. Taylor, 60 Mo. 127; Beatie v. Butler, 21 Mo. 313, 64 Am. Dec. 234; Chancellor v. Bell, 45 N. J. Eq. 538, 17 Atl. 684; Conover v. Von Mater, 18 N. J. Eq. 481; Smallwood v. Lewin, 15 N. J. Eq. 60; Hendrickson v. Woolley, 39 N. J. L. 307; McPherson v. Rollins, 107 N. Y. 316, 14 N. E. 411, 1 Am. St. 826; Farmers' L. &c. Co. v. Walworth, 1 N. Y. 433; Butler v. Viele, 44 Barb. (N. Y.) 166; Stoddard v. Rotton, 5 Bosw. (N. Y.) 378; Jackson v. Van Valkenburgh, 8 Cow. (N. Y.) 260; Fort v. Burch, 5 Den. (N. Y.) 187; Frost v. Beekman, 1 Johns. Ch. (N. Y.) 288; Dunham v. Dey, 15 Johns. (N. Y.) 556, 8 Am. Dec. 282; Wiggins v. Campbell, 4 Ohio Dec. (Reprint) 410, 2 Cleve. Law J. 122; Hall v. Donagan, 186 Pa. St. 300, 30 Atl. 493; Solms v. McCulloch, 5 Pa. St. 473; Stroud v. Lockart, 4 Dall. (Pa.) 153, 1 L. ed. 779; Hibberd v. Bovier, 1 Grant (Pa.) 266; Barr v. Kinard, 3 Strob. (S. Car.) 73; Martin v. Sale, Bailey Eq. (S. Car.) 1; Parker v. Randolph, 5 S. Dak. 549, 59 N. W. 722, 29 L. R. A. 33; Grotenkemper v. Carver, 9 Lea (Tenn.) 280; Kirkpatrick v. Ward, 5 Lea (Tenn.) 434; Hoffman v. Blume, 64 Tex. 334; Griffin v. Stone River Nat. Bank (Tex. Civ. App.), 80 S. W. 254; Hicks v. Hicks (Tex. Civ. App.), 26 S. W. 227; Buzzell v. Still, 63 Vt. 490, 22 Atl. 619, 25 Am. St. 777; Morrill v. Morrill, 53 Vt. 74, 38 Am. Rep. 659; Rootes v. Holliday, 6 Munf. (Va.) 251; Reichert v. Neuser, 93 Wis. 513, 67 N. W. 939; Rowell v. Williams, 54 Wis. 636, 12 N. W. 86; Mueller v. Brigham, 53 Wis. 173, 10 N. W. 366; Carter v. Carter, 4 Jur. (N. S.) 63, 3 Kay & J. 617, 27

L. J. Ch. 74, 69 Eng. Reprint 1256; Carlisle City &c. Banking Co. v. Thompson, 33 Wkly. Rep. 199; Hiern v. Mill, 13 Ves. Jr. 114, 9 Rev. Rep. 149, 33 Eng. Reprint 1256 (equitable mortgage by deposit of title deeds preferred to subsequent purchase with notice); Greaves v. Tofield, 14 Ch. D. 563, 50 L. J. Ch. 118, 43 L. T. Rep. (N. S.) 100, 28 Wkly. Rep. 840; Lee v. Clutton, 46 L. J. Ch. 48, 35 L. T. Rep. (N. S.) 84, 24 Wkly. Rep. 942; Wormald v. Maitland, 35 L. J. Ch. 69, 12 L. T. Rep. (N. S.) 535, 6 New Rep. 218, 13 Wkly. Rep. 832. See also Pancake v. Cauffman, 114 Pa. St. 113, 7 Atl. 67; Jones v. Hudson, 23 S. Car. 494; Conner v. Chase, 15 Vt. 764; Bank v. Doherty, 42 Wash. 317, 84 Pac. 872, 4 L. R. A. (N. S.) 1191, 114 Am. St. 123. But see Butler v. Wheeler, 82 Ky. 475, 6 Ky. L. Rep. 477; Building Assn. v. Clark, 43 Ohio St. 427, 2 N. E. 846. In Arkansas, Louisiana, North Carolina and Ohio the rule does not apply, and actual notice in lieu of recording is not sufficient to charge subsequent purchasers and mortgagees. See post § 539.

[2] German Sav. &c. Soc. v. Tull, 136 Fed. 1, 69 C. C. A. 1; Camp v. Peacock &c. Co., 129 Fed. 1005, 64 C. C. A. 490; Kent v. Williams, 146 Cal. 3, 79 Pac. 527; De Leonis v. Hammel, 1 Cal. App. 390, 82 Pac. 349; Patterson v. De Long, 11 Colo. App. 103, 52 Pac. 687; Norton v. Birge, 35 Conn. 250; Slater v. Hamacher, 15 App. Cas. (D. C.) 558; Goodwynne v. Bellerby, 116 Ga. 901, 43 S. E. 275; Interstate Bldg. &c. Assn. v. Ayres, 177 Ill. 9, 52 N. E. 342; Boyd v. Boyd, 128 Iowa 699, 104 N. W. 798, 111 Am. St. 215; Glassburn v. Wireman, 126 Iowa 478, 102 N. W. 421; Heively v. Matteson, 54 Iowa 505, 6 N. W. 732; Strong v. Centers (Ky.), 128 S. W. 69 (evidence sufficient as notice); Averill v. Guthrie, 8 Dana (Ky.), 82; Bates v. Frazier, 27 Ky. L. 576, 85 S. W. 757; Gore v. Condon, 82 Md. 649, 33 Atl. 261; McMechen v.

actual or constructive notice of a prior mortgage, will take subject to it.[3]

A judgment creditor with actual knowledge or notice, takes subject to a prior unrecorded deed or mortgage;[4] and whatever is sufficient

Maggs, 4 Harr. & J. (Md.) 132; Arnold v. Whitcomb, 83 Mich. 19, 46 N. W. 1029; Jackson &c. R. Co. v. Davison, 65 Mich. 437, 37 N. W. 537; Gothainer v. Grigg, 32 N. J. Eq. 567; Olyphant v. Phyfe, 166 N. Y. 630, 60 N. E. 1117; Newton v. McLean, 41 Barb. (N. Y.) 285; King v. Wilcomb, 7 Barb. (N. Y.) 263; Spears v. New York, 10 Hun (N. Y.) 160; Martin v. Eagle Creek Development Co., 41 Ore. 448, 69 Pac. 216; Babcock v. Wells, 25 R. I. 23, 54 Atl. 596, 105 Am. St. 848; Kuker v. Jarrott, 61 S. Car. 265, 39 S. E. 530; Messervey v. Barelli, 2 Hill Eq. (S. Car.) 567; Hanrick v. Gurley, 93 Tex. 458, 54 S. W. 347; Spurlock v. Sullivan, 36 Tex. 511; Wells v. Houston, 23 Tex. Civ. App. 629, 57 S. W. 584; Smith v. Smith, 23 Tex. Civ. App. 304, 55 S. W. 541; Hampshire v. Greeves (Tex. Civ. App.), 130 S. W. 665; Rogers v. Tompkins (Tex. Civ. App.), 87 S. W. 379; Patterson v. Tuttle (Tex. Civ. App.), 27 S. W. 758; Bank v. Doherty, 42 Wash. 317, 84 Pac. 872, 4 L. R. A. (N. S.) 1191; Scott v. Isaacsen, 56 W. Va. 314, 49 S. E. 254; Lowrey v. Finkleston, 149 Wis. 222, 134 N. W. 344; Gall v. Gall, 126 Wis. 390, 105 N. W. 953, 5 L. R. A. (N. S.) 603; John v. Larson, 28 Wis. 604; Eyre v. Dolphin; 2 Ball & B. 290, 12 Rev. Rep. 94; Hennessey v. Bray, 33 Beav. 96, 55 Eng. Reprint 302; De Witte v. Addison, 80 L. T. Rep. (N. S.) 207.

[3] Nelson v. Dunn, 15 Ala. 501; Ennesser v. Hudek, 169 Ill. 494, 48 N. E. 673; Council Bluffs Lodge v. Billups, 67 Iowa 674, 25 N. W. 846; Bell v. Thomas, 2 Iowa 384; Mutual Benefit Life Ins. Co. v. Huntington, 57 Kans. 744, 48 Pac. 19; Flowers v. Moorman, 27 Ky. L. 728, 86 S. W. 545; Underwood v. Ogden, 6 B. Mon. (Ky.) 606; Wattles v. Slater, 154 Mich. 666, 118 N. W. 486; Morris v. White, 36 N. J. Eq. 324; Conover v. Van Mater, 18 N. J. Eq. 481; Willink v. Morris Canal Co., 4 N. J. Eq. 377; La Farge

Fire Ins. Co. v. Bell, 22 Barb. (N. Y.) 54; Fort v. Burch, 6 Barb. (N. Y.) 60; Jackson v. Van Valkenburgh, 8 Cow. (N. Y.) 260; Kirkpatrick v. Ward, 5 Lea (Tenn.) 434; National Mut. Bldg. &c. Assn. v. Blair, 98 Va. 490, 36 S. E. 513; Beverley v. Brooke, 2 Leigh (Va.) 425; Power v. Standish, 8 Ir. Eq. 526; Rolland v. Hart, L. R. 6 Ch. 678, 40 L. J. Ch. 701, 25 L. T. Rep. (N. S.) 191, 19 Wkly. Rep. 962; Bradley v. Riches, 9 Ch. Div. 189, 47 L. J. Ch. 811, 38 L. T. Rep. (N. S.) 810, 26 Wkly. Rep. 910; Punchard v. Tomkins, 31 Wkly. Rep. 286; Evans v. Bicknell, 6 Ves. Jr. 174, 5 Rev. Rep. 245, 31 Eng. Reprint 998. But see McAllister v. Purcell, 124 N. Car. 262, 32 S. E. 715.

[4] Jordan v. Mead, 12 Ala. 247; Wallis v. Rhea, 10 Ala. 451, 12 Ala. 646; Larkin v. Hagan, 14 Ariz. 63, 126 Pac. 268; Byers v. Engles, 16 Ark. 543; Newhall v. Hatch, 134 Cal. 269, 66 Pac. 266, 55 L. R. A. 673; Columbus Buggy Co. v. Graves, 108 Ill. 459; Williams v. Tatnall, 29 Ill. 553; Sinking Fund Comrs. v. Wilson, 1 Ind. 356; Fords v. Vance, 17 Iowa 94; Bunker v. Gordon, 81 Maine 66, 16 Atl. 341; Lamberton v. Merchants' Nat. Bank, 24 Minn. 281; Bass v. Estill, 50 Miss. 300; Walker v. Gilbert, Freem. Ch. (Miss.) 85; Hutchinson v. Bramhall, 42 N. J. Eq. 372, 7 Atl. 873; Britton's Appeal, 45 Pa. St. 172; Barnett v. Squyres (Tex. Civ. App.), 52 S. W. 612; Stovall v. Odell, 10 Tex. Civ. App. 169, 30 S. W. 66. See also Duke v. Clark, 59 Miss. 465 (bona fide assignee of judgment not chargeable with assignor's knowledge); Hulings v Guthrie, 4 Pa. St. 123; Hibberd v. Bovier, 1 Grant (Pa.) 266. But see Winston v. Hodges, 102 Ala. 304, 15 So. 528; Coward v. Culver, 12 Heisk. (Tenn.) 540; Lillard v. Rucker, 9 Yerg. (Tenn.) 64; March v. Chambers, 30 Grat. (Va.) 299; Eidson v. Huff, 29 Grat. (Va.) 338. See ante § 466. Creditors whose judgments are re-

to charge a purchaser with notice will charge a judgment creditor.[5] According to some authorities, notice to the creditor must be given before judgment, and notice after judgment before levy of execution is insufficient.[6]

The doctrine of notice is the same under statutes which declare without qualification that an unacknowledged or unrecorded deed shall be void as against purchasers, or as against all persons who are not parties to the conveyance.[7] The record is constructive notice only; but it is notice to all the world that comes after; and it is conclusively presumed that every person interested has knowledge not only of the deed, but of its precise language.[8] Any other notice must in the nature of things be limited in its extent, but, so far as it goes, its effect is equitably not any less, certainly, than that of the record. Having notice of a mortgage defectively executed or recorded, or not recorded at all, a subsequent purchaser can not claim priority for his own deed.[9] As between him and the mortgagee, it is the same as if the prior mortgage had been duly recorded.[10] Therefore priority among mortgagees and grantees depends not only upon the date of their deeds and the date of their record, but also upon the knowledge they have of the true state of the facts as to the title, and of the rights and

covered after notice of a recorded deed, which had a parol defeasance, take subject to such mortgage and are not bona fide purchasers. Miller v. Wroton, 82 S. Car. 97, 63 S. E. 62, affd. 63 S. E. 449.

[5] H. C. Tack Co. v. Ayers, 56 N. J. Eq. 56, 38 Atl. 194. See also Clark v. Greene, 73 Minn. 467, 76 N. W. 263 (inclosure and sign insufficient notice); Condit v. Wilson, 36 N. J. Eq. 370 (debtor's statement insufficient).

[6] Columbus Buggy Co. v. Graves, 108 Ill. 459; Uhler v. Hutchinson, 23 Pa. 110. See also Davidson v. Cowan, 16 N. Car. 470.

[7] Westerly Sav. Bank v. Stillman Mfg. Co., 16 R. I. 497, 17 Atl. 918; Bullock v. Whipp, 15 R. I. 195, 2 Atl. 309; Rowell v. Williams, 54 Wis. 636, 12 N. W. 86; Mueller v. Brigham, 53 Wis. 173, 10 N. W. 366. See ante § 456.

[8] Beach v. Osborne, 74 Conn. 405, 50 Atl. 1019, 1118; Ensign v. Batterson, 68 Conn. 298, 36 Atl. 51; Hamilton v. Nutt, 34 Conn. 501; Hunt v. Mansfield, 31 Conn. 488; Sumner v. Rhodes, 14 Conn. 135;

Stark v. Kirkley, 129 Mo. App. 353, 108 S. W. 625. See ante § 524.

[9] Gardner v. Moore, 51 Ga. 268 (defective attestation); Coe v. Winters, 15 Iowa 481 (defective record); Forepaugh v. Appold, 17 B. Mon. (Ky.) 625; Russum v. Wanser, 53 Md. 92 (notice of mortgage without affidavit of consideration sufficient); Johnston v. Canby, 29 Md. 211 (defective acknowledgment, indorsement of consideration, or defective record immaterial in case of actual notice); Work v. Harper, 24 Miss. 517 (actual notice of a mortgage, defectively acknowledged and recorded, insufficient, after levy).

[10] Smith v. Nettles, 13 La. Ann. 241; Hill v. McNichol, 76 Maine 314; Copeland v. Copeland, 28 Maine 525; Ohio Life Ins. &c. Co. v. Ross, 2 Md. Ch. Dec. 25; Smallwood v. Lewin, 15 N. J. Eq. 60; Jackson v. Van Valkenburgh, 8 Cow. (N. Y.) 260; Pike v. Armstead, 1 Dev. Eq. (N. Car.) 110; Solms v. McCulloch, 5 Pa. St. 473.

equities of those who have not fixed their priority by duly recording their deeds.[11] And if a mortgagee once had knowledge of facts regarding a prior incumbrance or claim, it is immaterial that he failed to recall them when he accepted the mortgage,[12] or misapprehended their legal effect.[13] But a lien which has once attached can not be divested by the mortgagee's subsequent discovery of facts which would have affected its priority.[14]

Notice of an invalid deed or mortgage does not affect a purchaser.[15] Thus, under the statutes of New York, a deed in fee of a freehold estate not duly acknowledged or attested does not take effect as against a subsequent purchaser; and consequently a purchaser with notice of a prior deed which is void under this statute may treat such prior deed as void.[16] But a purchaser may have actual notice of a valid deed from a record of it which does not operate as constructive notice by reason of its not having been executed according to the statute.[17]

There is a presumption that the first recorded mortgage has priority; and the burden of proving that the mortgagee in such mortgage had knowledge of the existence of a mortgage or prior execution rests upon the party who makes this claim.[18] Any material evidence, including parol testimony, is admissible to prove whether the mortgagee in fact had actual notice of prior liens or claims.[19]

The notice, however, may lose its effect through the agreement of

[11] Coonrod v. Kelly, 113 Fed. 378; Continental Inv. &c. Soc. v. Wood, 168 Ill. 421, 48 N. E. 221; Inter-State Build. &c. Assn. v. Ayers, 117 Ill. 9, 52 N. E. 342 (quoting text); Lemon v. Terhune, 40 N. J. Eq. 364, 2 Atl. 18; Vredenburgh v. Burnet, 31 N. J. Eq. 229; La Farge Fire Ins. Co. v. Bell, 22 Barb. (N. Y.) 54; Merchants' Bank v. Ballou, 98 Va. 112, 32 S. E. 481.

[12] Hunt v. Clark, 6 Dana (Ky.) 56.

[13] Willis v. Vallette, 4 Metc. (Ky.) 186; Ledos v. Kupfrian, 28 N. J. Eq. 161.

[14] Davis v. Greve, 32 La. Ann. 420; Barrett v. Eastham (Tex. Civ. App.), 86 S. W. 1057.

[15] Erwin v. Shuey, 8 Ohio St. 509. See also Fisk v. Osgood, 58 Nebr. 486, 78 N. W. 924 (deed without consideration). A creditor is not affected by notice of a void incumbrance. Hubbard v. Savage, 8 Conn. 215.

[16] Nellis v. Munson, 108 N. Y. 453, 15 N. E. 739; Chamberlain v. Spargur, 86 N. Y. 603.

[17] Hastings v. Cutler, 24 N. H. 48; Musgrove v. Bonser, 5 Ore. 313, 20 Am. Rep. 737. But see Cumberland Bldg. &c. Assn. v. Sparks, 111 Fed. 647, 49 C. C. A. 510 (under Arkansas statute).

[18] Sheffey v. Bank of Lewisburg, 33 Fed. 315; Pollak v. Davidson, 87 Ala. 551, 6 So. 312; Bush v. Golden, 17 Conn. 594; Ryder v. Rush, 102 Ill. 338; Citizens' State Bank v. Julian, 153 Ind. 655, 55 N. E. 1007; Peoria Stone &c. Works v. Sinclair, 146 Iowa 56, 124 N. W. 772 (chattel mortgage); Spofford v. Weston, 29 Maine 140; Pomroy v. Stevens, 11 Metc. (Mass.) 244; Hendrickson v. Woolley, 39 N. J. Eq. 307; Barnett v. Squyres, 93 Tex. 193, 54 S. W. 241, 77 Am. St. 654.

[19] Hodges v. Winston, 94 Ala. 576, 10 So. 535; Wittenbrock v. Cass, 110 Cal. 1, 42 Pac. 300.

the mortgagee of the unrecorded mortgage. Thus where a mortgagee agreed to keep his mortgage off the record in order to enable the mortgagor to borrow money on the property by giving a first mortgage, and such agreement was made known to the mortgagee taking the mortgage second in date, at or before its execution, and his mortgage was first recorded, such notice will not give the unrecorded mortgage priority.[20]

Undoubtedly it was the purpose of the laws providing for the registry of conveyances of land to enable every one by this means to determine fully the title to the land, without depending upon the possession of the title deeds, or upon inquiry or notice outside of the registry. The symmetry of the registry system has been disturbed and broken in upon by judicial construction, in order to prevent a fraudulent use of the statute, which it is to be presumed the statute did not intend. To allow one who has actual or implied notice of a prior unrecorded deed of the same property, or such notice of equitable rights of other persons in the property, to obtain priority by recording his own deed, would be to enable him to take advantage of the registry laws to obtain an unfair or fraudulent advantage by means of them. Exceptions to the literal application of the law have therefore been engrafted upon it to meet the equitable consequences of such notice.[21]

The general principle that actual notice is equivalent to recording, applies only where there is nothing in the statute to indicate a contrary intention. Where recording is expressly made necessary to the validity of the instrument, it is held that actual notice will not operate as an equivalent.[22]

§ 539. **Contrary doctrine in Arkansas, Louisiana, North Carolina and Ohio.**—As already noticed, it has been questioned whether the courts ought ever to have suffered the question of actual notice to be agitated against one whose conveyance is duly registered.[23] The basis of the doctrine of notice is, that it is unconscientious and fraudulent

---

[20] Hendrickson v. Woolley, 39 N. J. Eq. 307.

[21] See Hart v. Farmers' &c. Bank, 33 Vt. 252, per Chief Justice Redfield.

[22] Ross v. Menefee, 125 Ind. 432, 25 N. E. 545; Lockwood v. Slevin, 26 Ind. 124; Chenyworth v. Daily, 7 Ind. 284; Travis v. Bishop, 13 Metc. (Mass.) 304.

[23] Per Colcock, J., in Price v. White, Bailey Eq. (S. Car.) 240; per Sir Williom Grant, in Wyatt v. Barwell, 19 Ves. 435; Benham v. Keane, 1 Johns. & Hem. 685; Ford v. White, 16 Beav. 120; Donahue v. Mills, 41 Ark. 421; Canal Co. v. Russell, 68 Ill. 426; Allen v. Cadwell, 55 Mich. 8, 20 N. W. 692; Moore v. Thomas, 1 Ore. 201.

to permit a junior purchaser to defeat a prior conveyance or incumbrance of which he has knowledge.[24] But it has been doubted whether this doctrine does not give occasion to more fraud than it prevents; and whether vigilance in recording a mortgage should not be rewarded as much as vigilance in obtaining it.[25] Accordingly, as regards mortgages, the statutes of a few states make the recording of them essential to their validity as against third persons. Thus in Arkansas it is provided that a mortgage shall be a lien from the time the same is filed in the recording office, and not before; and actual notice does not avail to give it validity as against third persons.[26] And since, under the statute of Arkansas, an improperly recorded mortgage does not create a valid lien as against subsequent purchasers, the federal court has held that a mortgagee can not impute fraud to the purchaser of the mortgaged property although he bought with actual knowledge of the mortgage, and with the intention of defeating it.[27]

Under a similar statute in Louisiana, an unrecorded mortgage is invalid against third persons, though they have full knowledge of it.[28]

Under the registration law in North Carolina it is held that no notice, however full and formal, will supply the place of registration of a deed of trust or mortgage; the statute declaring that they shall not be valid at law to pass any property as against creditors or purchasers for a valuable consideration but from their registration.[29] Con-

[24] Harrington v. Allen, 48 Miss. 492. The object of the doctrine of notice is to prevent a person from doing an act which will do an injury to another. Spencer v. Spencer, 3 Jones Eq. (N. Car.) 404. See post § 572.

[25] Per Hitchcock, J., in Mayham v. Coombs, 14 Ohio 428.

[26] Dig. of Stats. 1904, § 5396; Cumberland Bldg. &c. Assn. v. Sparks, 111 Fed. 647, 49 C. C. A. 510; Dodd v. Parker, 40 Ark. 536; Fry v. Martin, 33 Ark. 203; Jacoway v. Gault, 20 Ark. 190, 73 Am. Dec. 494. But see Rubel v. Parker, 107 Ark. 314, 155 S. W. 114; American Bldg. &c. Assn. v. Warren, 101 Ark. 163, 141 S. W. 765 (notice by possession).

[27] Cumberland Bldg. &c. Assn. v. Sparks, 111 Fed. 647, 49 C. C. A. 510.

[28] Ridings v. Johnson, 128 U. S. 212, 32 L. ed. 401, 9 Sup. Ct. 72 (under act of 1855, Rev. Stat. 1870, p. 617); Adams v. Daunis, 29 La.

Ann. 315. See Merrick's Rev. Civ. Code 1912, § 3329 et seq. Under the early Louisiana cases actual notice was equivalent to record. Planters' Bank of Georgia v. Allard, 8 Mart. (N. S.) (La.) 136; Rachal v. Normand, 6 Rob. (La.) 88; Smith v. Nettles, 13 La. Ann. 241. See also Noble v. Cooper, 7 Rob. (La.) 44; Parker v. Walden, 6 Mart. (N. S.) (La.) 713.

[29] McAllister v. Purcell, 124 N. Car. 262, 32 S. E. 715; Blalock v. Strain, 122 N. Car. 283, 29 S. E. 408; Hooker v. Nichols, 116 N. Car. 157, 21 S. E. 207; Quinnerly v. Quinnerly, 114 N. Car. 145, 19 S. E. 99; Killebrew v. Hines, 104 N. Car. 182, 10 S. E. 159, 17 Am. St. 672; Hinton v. Leigh, 102 N. Car. 28, 8 S. E. 890; Traders' Nat. Bank v. Woodlawn Mfg. Co., 100 N. Car. 345, 5 S. E. 81; Traders' Nat. Bank v. Lawrence Mfg. Co., 96 N. Car. 298, 3 S. E. 363; Todd v. Outlaw, 79 N. Car. 235; King v. Portis, 77 N. Car. 25; Deal v. Palmer, 72 N. Car. 582;

sequently, a second mortgagee will have priority over an unregistered mortgage, though he took with actual notice of the first mortgage.[30]

But if a mortgage states that the land conveyed had previously been conveyed in trust to secure the payment of a certain debt, although such first mortgage was not recorded till after the second mortgage was recorded, and therefore was inoperative as to the second mortgage, yet the holder of the first mortgage is entitled to satisfaction out of the land in preference to the holder of the second mortgage; for the latter mortgage is regarded as creating a trust for the payment of the prior mortgage in preference to the second mortgage.[31] However, it has been held that recitals in a deed that the purchase-price has been paid will not protect a subsequent mortgagee of the land conveyed, who has been told otherwise before making the loan.[32]

Under the recording acts of Ohio, the doctrine of notice has no place, inasmuch as all mortgages take effect from the time they are delivered to the recorder.[33] A judgment recovered after the date of the mortgage, and before it is recorded, takes precedence of it.[34] The admission of evidence of actual notice of a prior unrecorded deed, as affecting a mortgagee's right of priority, is attended with all the danger and uncertainty incident to parol evidence, when used for the purpose of affecting written instruments and disturbing titles, and for this reason the policy has been adopted in this state of allowing the whole question of priority to be settled by the simple fact of prior registry. This furnishes a clear and certain standard of decision incapable of variation, and thus avoids a very fruitful source of litigation.[35]

§ 540. **Record of subsequent conveyances with notice.**—The right of the first purchaser or mortgagee to preserve his title by recording

Robinson v. Willoughby, 70 N. Car. 358; Leggett v. Bullock, Busb. L. (N. Car.) 283; Fleming v. Burgin, 2 Ired. Eq. (N. Car.) 584. See also for rule under earlier statutes, Davidson v. Cowan, 16 N. Car. 470; Pike v. Armstead, 16 N. Car. 110. Code 1883, § 1254; Pell's Revisal 1908, § 982.

[30] McAllister v. Purcell, 124 N. Car. 262, 32 S. E. 715.

[31] Hinton v. Leigh, 102 N. Car. 28, 8 S. E. 890.

[32] Wilson v. Shocklee, 94 Ark. 301, 126 S. W. 832.

[33] Ohio Rev. Stat. 1890, § 4133; Gen. Code 1910, § 8542; Home Build-

ing Assn. v. Clark, 43 Ohio St. 427, 2 N. E. 846; Bercaw v. Cockerill, 20 Ohio St. 163, and cases there cited; Erwin v. Shuey, 8 Ohio St. 509; Bloom v. Noggle, 4 Ohio St. 45; Boos v. Ewing, 17 Ohio 500, 49 Am. Dec. 478; Holliday v. Franklin Bank, 16 Ohio 533; White v. Denman, 16 Ohio 59; Mayham v. Coombs, 14 Ohio 428; Stansell v. Roberts, 13 Ohio 148, 42 Am. Dec. 193. See also Astor v. Wells, 4 Wheat. (U. S.) 466.

[34] Holliday v. Franklin Bank, 16 Ohio 533; Mayham v. Coombs, 14 Ohio 428.

[35] Per Ranney, J., in Bloom v.

his deed continues after any number of subsequent conveyances in the chain of title derived from the second grantee of the original grantor, although the deeds in this chain of title have all been duly recorded, provided that such subsequent purchasers, one and all, have bought either with knowledge of the prior unrecorded deed or without paying valuable consideration. So long as this state of things continues, the prior title will hold, and may be perfected by record. But so soon as any one in the chain of title under the second conveyance purchases in good faith for a valuable consideration, and places his deed on record, the title under the first unrecorded deed is gone forever,[36] unless it be conveyed to a former owner who was charged with notice of the prior equity.

Noggle, 4 Ohio St. 45; Kemper v. Campbell, 44 Ohio St. 210, 6 N. E. 566; Building Assn. v. Clark, 43 Ohio St. 427, 2 N. E. 846.

[36] This point is fully illustrated in the case of Fallass v. Pierce, 30 Wis. 443, which was several times argued before the court, and was finally decided in a well-considered opinion by Chief Justice Dixon. Using the same illustration given above, he says: "If, for example, in the case supposed, C took his deed with knowledge of the prior conveyance to B, and had then conveyed to D, who had like knowledge, and D should convey to E, and so on, conveyances should be executed to the end of the alphabet, each subsequent grantee having knowledge of B's prior right, and all of their conveyances being recorded, yet then, if B should record his deed before the last grantee with knowledge, and Z should make conveyance, the purchaser from Z would be bound to take notice of B's rights, and of the relations existing between them, and all the subsequent purchasers from C to Z inclusive. And in the same case, if Z should sell to a purchaser in good faith for value from him, yet if B should get his conveyance recorded before that of such purchaser, his title would be preferred because of such first record. And it is manifest that the same result would follow if in the case supposed none of the subsequent grantees, from C to Z inclusive, paid any valuable consideration for the land; or if, in the case of such successive grantee, his title was defective and invalid as against B, either by reason of his knowledge of B's title, or because he was a mere volunteer, paying no consideration whatever for the conveyance." The case of Ely v. Wilcox, 20 Wis. 523, 91 Am. Dec. 436, is overruled. Fallass v. Pierce, 30 Wis. 443, is followed in Girardin v. Lampe, 58 Wis. 267, 16 N. W. 614; Erwin v. Lewis, 32 Wis. 276; and discussed in Marling v. Milwaukee Realty Co., 127 Wis. 363, 106 N. W. 844, 5 L. R. A. (N. S.) 412, 115 Am. St. 1017. See White and Tudor's Lead. Cas. in Eq. (4th Am. ed.), vol. 2, pt. 1, p. 212, for a dissent to this line of decisions, because they make it requisite to search for conveyances from two persons during the same period. The authorities cited in support of this view are the earlier cases in Massachusetts and Wisconsin.

In Day v. Clark, 25 Vt. 397, the rule is laid down that the record of the prior deed after the second is notice to a purchaser from the vendee in the second that there is such a prior deed; but the record of it is no notice that the vendee in the second deed, at the time he secured it, had notice of the first deed, and without such notice the title of the purchaser from the vendee in the second but first recorded deed would not be affected by the fraud or knowledge of his vendor. The doctrine of the text is also supported by Mahoney v. Middleton, 41 Cal. 41; Bayles v. Young, 51 Ill.

This class of cases very frequently presents questions of the greatest difficulty; and the language of Lord Chancellor Northington is generally applicable to any one of them: "This is one of those cases which are always very honorably labored by the counsel at the bar, and determined with great anxiety by the court, as some of the parties must be shipwrecked in the event."[37]

§ 541. **Examination of records for incumbrances against prior unrecorded conveyances.**—As a general rule a purchaser is not bound to search the records for incumbrances as against a title that does not appear of record.[38] Generally, therefore, the record of any mortgage prior to the conveyance by which the mortgagor took his title is no notice of the incumbrance to a subsequent purchaser.[39] The record of a conveyance by a grantor who appears to be a stranger to the record title, is not notice to one subsequently dealing in good faith with the person holding the record title.[40] Otherwise a subsequent purchaser would have to examine the records indefinitely to protect himself, and the practical advantages of the recording system would be nullified.[41]

127; Sims v. Hammond, 33 Iowa 368; English v. Waples, 13 Iowa 57; Hill v. McNichol; 76 Maine 314. See Woods v. Garnett, 72 Miss. 78, 16 So. 390, 4 Ballard R. P. § 715, and cases cited and criticised. See post § 559.

[37] See Stanhope v. Verney, 2 Eden 81.

[38] Stockwell v. State, 101 Ind. 1; Stead v. Grosfield, 67 Mich. 289, 34 N. W. 871; Schoch v. Birdsall, 48 Minn. 441, 51 N. W. 382 (citing text); Losey v. Simpson, 11 N. J. Eq. 3, 246; Oliphant v. Burns, 146 N. Y. 218, 40 N. E. 980; Cook v. Travis, 20 N. Y. 400; Clark v. Mackin, 30 Hun (N. Y.) 411.

[39] Tolman v. Smith, 85 Cal. 280, 24 Pac. 743; Montgomery v. Keppel, 75 Cal. 128, 19 Pac. 178; Faircloth v. Jordan, 18 Ga. 350; Continental Ins. &c. Soc. v. Wood, 168 Ill. 421, 48 N. E. 221; Elder v. Derby, 98 Ill. 228; Ely v. Pingry, 56 Kans. 17, 42 Pac. 330; Wing v. McDowell, Walk. (Mich.) 175; Schoch v. Birdsall, 48 Minn. 441, 51 N. W. 382 (citing text); Daly v. New York &c. R. Co., 55 N. J. Eq. 595, 38 Atl. 202; Protection Bldg. &c. Assn. v. Knowles, 54 N. J. Eq. 519, 34 Atl. 1083; Bing-

ham v. Kirkland, 34 N. J. Eq. 229; Boyd v. Mundorf, 30 N. J. Eq. 545; Tarbell v. West, 86 N. Y. 280; Page v. Waring, 76 N. Y. 463; Farmers' Loan &c. Co. v. Maltby, 8 Paige (N. Y.) 361 Calder v. Chapman, 52 Pa. St. 359, 91 Am. Dec. 163; Sayward v. Thompson, 11 Wash. 706, 40 Pac. 379. See also Hinton v. Hicks, 156 N. Car. 24, 71 S. E. 1086. But see Tefft v. Munson, 57 N. Y. 97. See ante §§ 471, 523.

[40] Texas Lumber Mfg. Co. v. Branch, 60 Fed. 201, 8 C. C. A. 562; Tennessee Coal &c. R. Co. v. Gardner, 131 Ala. 599, 32 So. 622; Pearce v Smith, 126 Ala. 116, 28 So. 37; Bates v. Norcross, 14 Pick. (Mass.) 224; Robertson v. Rentz, 71 Minn. 489, 74 N. W. 133; Hart v. Gardner, 81 Miss. 650, 33 So. 442, 497; Ford v. Unity Church Soc., 120 Mo. 498, 25 S. W. 394, 23 L. R. A. 561, 41 Am. St. 711; Shackleton v. Allen Chapel African M. E. Church, 25 Mont. 421, 65 Pac. 428; Oliphant v. Burns, 146 N. Y. 218, 40 N. E. 980; Advance Thresher Co. v. Esteb, 41 Ore. 469, 69 Pac. 447. But see Balch v. Arnold, 9 Wyo. 17, 59 Pac. 434.

[41] Hetzel v. Barber, 69 N. Y. 1; Buckingham v. Hanna, 2 Ohio St.

The whole object of the registry acts is to protect subsequent purchasers and incumbrancers against previous conveyances which are not recorded, and to deprive the holder of previous unregistered conveyances of his right of priority which he would have at the common law. The title upon record is the purchaser's protection. The registry of a deed is notice only to those who claim through or under the grantor by whom the deed was executed.[42] When one link in the chain of title is wanting, there is no clue to guide the purchaser in his search to the next succeeding link by which the chain is continued. When the purchaser has traced the title down to an individual, out of whom the record does not carry it, the registry acts make that title the purchaser's protection.[43]

There is, however, a well recognized exception to the rule that the record is notice only to persons claiming under it. Where the subsequent purchaser, first recording his instrument, is chargeable with actual notice of a prior conveyance, a purchaser from him after record of the prior conveyance, is chargeable with constructive notice from such record, and is put on inquiry as to whether his grantor took a good title.[44] Thus the circumstances may be such that a purchaser

551; Sands v. Beardsley, 32 W. Va. 594, 9 S. E. 925. See also Salisbury Sav. Soc. v. Cutting, 50 Conn. 113, and note. But see Edwards v. McKernan, 55 Mich. 520, 22 N. W. 20; Digman v. McCollum, 47 Mo. 372; Van Diviere v. Mitchell, 45 S. Car. 127, 22 S. E. 759.

[42] Tennessee Coal &c. R. Co. v. Gardner, 131 Ala. 599, 32 So. 622; Turman v. Sanford, 69 Ark. 95, 61 S. W. 167; Goodkind v. Bartlett, 153 Ill. 419, 38 N. E. 1045; Grundies v. Reid, 107 Ill. 304; Miller v. Larned, 103 Ill. 562; Irish v. Sharp, 89 Ill. 261; Manly v. Pettee, 38 Ill. 128; Roberts v. Richards, 84 Maine 1, 24 Atl. 425; Spofford v. Weston, 29 Maine 140; Hart v. Gardner, 81 Miss. 650, 33 So. 442, 497; Harper v. Bibb, 34 Miss. 472, 69 Am. Dec. 397; Becker v. Stroeher, 167 Mo. 306, 66 S. W. 1083; Odle v. Odle, 73 Mo. 289; Digman v. McCollum, 47 Mo. 372; Crockett v. Maguire, 10 Mo. 34; Chowen v. Phelps, 26 Mont. 524, 69 Pac. 54; Sharon v. Minnock, 6 Nev. 377; Cook v. Travis, 20 N. Y. 400; Todd v. Eighmie, 4 App. Div. 9, 38 N. Y. S. 304, 73 N. Y. St. 671; Abraham v. Mayer, 7 Misc. 250, 58 N. Y. St. 29, 27 N. Y. S. 264; Doran v. Dazey, 5 N. Dak. 167, 64 N. W. 1023, 57 Am. St. 550; Sternberger v. Ragland, 57 Ohio St. 148, 48 N. E. 811; Blake v. Graham, 6 Ohio St. 580, 67 Am. Dec. 360; Leiby v. Wolf, 10 Ohio 83; Collins v. Aaron, 162 Pa. St. 539, 29 Atl. 724; Maul v. Rider, 59 Pa. St. 167; Woods v. Farmere, 7 Watts (Pa.) 382, 32 Am. Dec. 772; Kansas City Land Co. v. Hill, 87 Tenn. 589, 11 S. W. 797, 5 L. R. A. 45; Parker v. Meredith (Tenn.), 59 S. W. 167; Runge v. Gilbough (Tex. Civ. App.), 87 S. W. 832; Williams v. Slaughter (Tex. Civ. App.), 42 S. W. 327; Jenkins v. Adams, 71 Tex. 1, 8 S. W. 603; Holmes v. Buckner, 67 Tex. 107, 2 S. W. 452; Drake v. Reggel, 10 Utah 376, 37 Pac. 583; Claiborne v. Holland, 88 Va. 1046, 14 S. E. 915. See also Lewis v. Jackson, 165 Mass. 481, 43 N. E. 206.

[43] Per Chancellor Williamson, in Losey v. Simpson, 11 N. J. Eq. 246; Roll v. Rea, 50 N. J. L. 264, 12 Atl. 905. See also Cook v. Travis, 20 N. Y. 400; Parkist v. Alexander, 1 Johns. Ch. (N. Y.) 394.

[44] North v. Knowlton, 23 Fed. 163; County Bank v. Fox, 119 Cal. 61, 51 Pac. 11; Mahoney v. Middleton,

will be bound to search the records for incumbrances as against a title which does not appear upon the records; as, for instance, when he has actual notice of the existence of a mortgageable estate in another prior to the date of the conveyance to himself. One holding an executory contract of purchase, or one in possession of land under a contract of sale, though the contract be by parol, has a mortgageable interest, and a mortgage of it may be legally and properly recorded, so as to take precedence of a subsequent conveyance of the property if the sub-sequent purchaser had actual notice of the existence of the mortgageable estate in the mortgagor prior to his receiving his own deed.[45]

A recital in a deed that the grantee had been in possession of the granted farm since a given date, several months prior to the deed, under a contract for the purchase of it, is actual notice to one claiming under the title of such deed that the grantee had been in possession before he received a deed of the land; and the law charges him with notice that such grantee had, during such possession, a mortgageable interest in the land; and he is bound to search the records for incumbrances against the title from the time the grantee entered into possession under the contract, and he is bound by a mortgage made by such grantee while in possession under the contract of sale and before receiving a deed.[46]

§ 542. **Notice of a secret trust.**—It is frequently the case that an estate which appears by the record to be absolutely the property of the grantee is in fact held by him in trust for another person. In such

41 Cal. 41; Morrison v. Kelly, 22 Ill. 609, 74 Am. Dec. 169; English v. Waples, 13 Iowa 57; Van Aken v. Gleason, 34 Mich. 477; Woods v. Garnett, 72 Miss. 78, 16 So. 390; Schutt v. Large, 6 Barb. (N. Y.) 373; Jackson v. Post, 9 Cow. (N. Y.) 120, 15 Wend. 588; Goelet v. McManus, 1 Hun (N. Y.) 306; Ring v. Steele, 3 Keyes (N. Y.) 450; Van Rensselaer v. Clark, 17 Wend. (N. Y.) 25, 31 Am. Dec. 280; Parrish v. Mahany, 10 S. Dak. 276, 73 N. W. 97, 66 Am. St. 715; Butler v. Mazeppa Bank, 94 Wis. 351, 68 N. W. 998; Fallass v. Pierce, 30 Wis. 443 disapproving the authority of Ely v. Wilcox, 20 Wis. 523, 91 Am. Dec. 436 to the contrary; Erwin v. Lewis, 32 Wis. 276. But see Morse v. Curtis, 140 Mass. 112, 54 Am. Rep. 456.

45 Crane v. Turner, 7 Hun (N. Y.) 357. See ante § 469.

46 Crane v. Turner, 7 Hun (N. Y.) 357. Mr. Justice Follett, by way of illustration, said: "If, January first, a grantee receives a deed and enters into possession, but neglects to record the deed, or it is destroyed, and subsequently he receives a new deed bearing a later date, and reciting that it is confirmatory of a deed dated January first, under which he has been in possession since that date, and which deed has been lost, it would not be held that a search back to the date of the confirmatory deed was due diligence in a person who had actual notice of the recital, even though accompanied by the inquiry of the grantee, and if he should take a mortgage, and record it, it would not have precedence over a duly recorded mortgage given between the dates of the first and second deeds."

case, any one who deals with him in respect to this estate, with knowledge of the trust, takes it subject to the trust, and will be required to perform it and discharge the lien.[47] If the conveyance, though absolute in form, be in fact a mortgage, a purchaser with knowledge of this fact takes the estate subject to the mortgage. "Though a purchaser may buy in an incumbrance, or lay hold on any plank to protect himself, yet he shall not protect himself by the taking a conveyance from a trustee after he had notice of the trust, for, by taking a conveyance with notice of the trust, he himself becomes the trustee, and must not, to get a plank to save himself, be guilty of a breach of trust."[48]

If a trustee conveys land to one who has notice of the trust, the grantee is put upon inquiry as to the terms of the trust.[49] Since a trustee is not presumed to have authority to mortgage the trust property, a person taking such a mortgage is bound to use due diligence to ascertain whether the act of the trustee is in violation of the trust;[50] and if such mortgagee or one holding under him has actual or constructive notice of a breach of trust, his rights are subordinate to those of the cestui que trust, and he holds the mortgage as trustee.[51] Where an instrument limiting the trustee's authority to mortgage the

[47] Wormley v. Wormley, 8 Wheat. (U. S.) 421, 5 L. ed. 651; Boone v. Chiles, 10 Pet. (U. S.) 177, 9 L. ed. 388; Caldwell v. Carrington, 9 Pet. (U. S.) 86, 9 L. ed. 60; Oliver v. Piatt, 3 How. (U. S.) 333, 11 L. ed. 622; Jones v. Shaddock, 41 Ala. 262; Learned v. Tritch, 6 Colo. 432; Jackson v. Blackwood, 4 McAr. (D. C.) 188, 1 Ky. L. 71; Harris v. Brown, 124 Ga. 310, 52 S. E. 610, 2 L. R. A. (N. S.) 828; Butler v. Butler, 164 Ill. 171, 45 N. E. 426; West v. Fitz, 109 Ill. 425; Graham v. Graham, 85 Ill. App. 460; Lyons v. Bodenhamer, 7 Kans. 455; Harwood v. Pearson, 122 Mass. 425; Wright v. Dame, 22 Pick. (Mass.) 55; Smith v. Walser, 49 Mo. 250; McWaid v. Blair State Bank, 58 Nebr. 618, 79 N. W. 620; Dillaye v. Commercial Bank, 51 N. Y. 345; Smith v. Bowen, 35 N. Y. 83; Murray v. Ballou, 1 Johns. Ch. (N. Y.) 566; James v. Cowing, 17 Hun (N. Y.) 256; Dixon v. Caldwell, 15 Ohio St. 412, 86 Am. Dec. 487; Sadler's Appeal, 87 Pa. St. 154; Sergeant v. Ingersoll, 7 Pa. St. 340; Luscombe v. Grigsby, 11 S. Dak. 408, 78 N. W. 357; Wethered

v. Boon, 17 Tex. 143; Mansfield v. Wardlow (Tex. Civ. App.), 91 S. W. 859; Schenck v. Wicks, 23 Utah 576, 65 Pac. 732; Haslam v. Haslam, 19 Utah 1, 56 Pac. 243; Anon. 2 Freem. 137, pl. vii; Cory v. Eyre, 1 De G. J. & S. 149; Ferrars v. Cherry, 2 Vern. 384.

[48] Saunders v. Dehew, 2 Vern. 271. See also Hall v. Savill, 3 G. Greene (Iowa) 37, 54 Am. Dec. 485.

[49] Mayfield v. Turner, 180 Ill. 332, 54 N. E. 418.

[50] Sternfels v. Watson, 139 Fed. 505; Snyder v. Collier, 85 Nebr. 552, 123 N. W. 1023, 133 Am. St. 682; Kenworthy v. Levi, 214 Pa. 235, 63 Atl. 690; Sweeny v. Montreal Bank, 12 Can. Sup. Ct. 661.

[51] Griffin v. Blanchar, 17 Cal. 70; Dotterer v. Pike, 60 Ga. 29; Union Mut. L. Ins. Co. v. Spaids, 99 Ill. 249; Bomar v. Gist, 25 S. Car. 340; Mathews v. Heyward, 2 S. Car. 239; Mansfield v. Wardlow (Tex. Civ. App.), 91 S. W. 859; Fitch v. Currie, 19 Nova Scotia 522; Birkbeck Loan Co. v. Johnston, 3 Ont. L. Rep. 497, 1 Ont. Wkly. Rep. 163. See also De Leonis v. Hammel, 1 Cal.

property is on record, it is notice of such limitation on the trustee's authority.[52]

One who acquires the legal title to land with notice of an equitable mortgage in another will be decreed to hold the legal title for the benefit of the equitable mortgagee.[53] An equitable mortgage in favor of a third party advancing money to a vendee to purchase land, under an agreement to execute a mortgage to secure such advance, will be given priority over a mortgage on the land taken by a party who has notice of the rights of the equitable mortgagee.[54]

II. *Actual Notice*

§ 543. Forms of notice.—There are three kinds of notice, actual, implied, and constructive. Since the doctrine of notice as affecting the priority of incumbrances arises from the equitable view that it is fraud in one, who has notice of an adverse claim in another, to attempt to acquire a title to the prejudice of the interest of which he has been made aware, it is obvious that the actual culpability involved by the notice must depend altogether upon the kind and degree of notice received. Yet the legal consequences are the same, whatever the kind

---

App. 390, 82 Pac. 349; Boyer v. Libey, 88 Ind. 235.

[52] Marx v. Clisby, 126 Ala. 107, 28 So. 388. But it has been held that where the record of a trust deed expressly prohibiting the creation of incumbrances has been destroyed by fire and re-established by decree of court without such prohibition, it is no longer notice of the trustee's want of authority. Franklin Sav. Bank v. Taylor, 53 Fed. 854, 4 C. C. A. 55.

[53] Lounsbury v. Norton, 59 Conn. 170, 22 Atl. 153; Gale v. Morris, 29 N. J. Eq. 222.

[54] Foster Lumber Co. v. Harlan Co. Bank, 71 Kans. 158, 80 Pac. 49, 114 Am. St. 470.

and degree of the notice may be, provided the notice is imputed at all. Notice, however, is not necessarily or commonly knowledge, though in legal effect it may be equivalent to knowledge. In its broad legal sense, notice has been defined as positive information, concerning a fact, actually communicated to a party by an authorized person, or actually derived by him from a proper source, or else presumed by law to have been acquired by him, which information is regarded as equivalent, in its legal effects, to full knowledge of the fact, and to which the law attributes the same consequences as would be imputed to knowledge.[1]

§ **544. Actual notice defined.**—Actual notice literally means direct personal knowledge.[2] Yet the term is often used in a broader sense as including notice implied from indirect or circumstantial evidence.[3] Actual notice is not limited to express knowledge directly communicated, for it is seldom that ultimate facts can be communicated in a manner so direct and unequivocal as to exclude all doubt as to their existence and authenticity. Actual notice includes knowledge of facts and circumstances so pertinent in character as to enable reasonably cautious and prudent persons to investigate and ascertain the ulti-

---

[1] Cleveland Woolen Mills v. Sibert, 81 Ala. 140, 1 So. 773, 2 Pom. Eq. Jur, § 594.

[2] Story's Eq. Jur. § 399; Crassen v. Swoveland, 22 Ind. 427; Spofford v. Weston, 29 Maine 140; Baltimore v. Williams, 6 Md. 235; Keith v. Wheeler, 159 Mass. 161, 34 N. E. 174; Lamb v. Pierce, 113 Mass. 72; Abbe v. Justus, 60 Mo. App. 300, 1 Mo. App. 144; Casey v. Steinmeyer, 7 Mo. App. 556; Rogers v. Jones, 8 N. H. 264; Williamson v. Brown, 15 N. Y. 354. See also Jordan v. Pollock, 14 Ga. 145 (notice directly and personally given); Kirkham v. Moore, 30 Ind. App. 549, 65 N. E. 1042 (actual knowledge not equivalent to actual notice); Jackson v. Waldstein (Tex. Civ. App.), 27 S. W. 26 (express information of a fact). It is immaterial how actual knowledge is obtained, and a verbal communication is sufficient notice. Schmidt v. Hedden (N. J. Eq.), 38 Atl. 843. And it has been held immaterial from whom the information comes. Willcox v. Hill, 11 Mich. 256; Jaeger v. Hardy, 48 Ohio St. 335, 27 N. E. 863.

The statutes of Massachusetts provide that no unrecorded deed shall be valid save as against the grantors and persons having "actual notice thereof." By actual notice is not meant necessarily that a person must actually have seen or been told of the deed by the grantor, but it means any intelligible information of it, either verbal or in writing, coming from a source which a party ought to give heed to. Curtis v. Mundy, 3 Metc. (Mass.) 405; George v. Kent, 7 Allen (Mass.) 16. This provision was first adopted in the Rev. Stat. of 1836, before which time implied or constructive notice was held to be sufficient, but now has no effect. Parker v. Osgood, 3 Allen (Mass.) 487. See also Lawrence v. Stratton, 6 Cush. (Mass.) 163; Pomroy v. Stevens, 11 Metc. (Mass.) 244; Sibley v. Leffingwell, 8 Allen (Mass.) 584; Dooley v. Wolcott, 4 Allen (Mass.) 406.

[3] Pope v. Nichols, 61 Kans. 230, 59 Pac. 257; Knapp v. Bailey, 79 Maine 195, 9 Atl. 122.

mate facts.[4] Whether it exists in any particular case, and whether it is sufficient to charge the party whom it is sought to affect by it, is a question of fact to be considered and determined upon the evidence in each particular case. It is deemed effectual and sufficient when the evidence shows that the matters relating to the prior claim or interest of another, constituting notice of it, are brought distinctly to the knowledge and attention of the person it is sought to affect.[5]

Whether "actual notice" means actual knowledge or includes constructive knowledge, in statutes requiring actual notice to affect a purchaser, is a question upon which the decisions are not in harmony. In Massachusetts it is held that, although a purchaser has knowledge that the lands had been sold and purchased by another person, yet if no deed had been recorded, and the purchaser had no knowledge that a deed had been made, he is not chargeable with actual notice.[6] Therefore proof of open and notorious occupation and improvement, or of other facts which would reasonably put a purchaser upon inquiry, is not sufficient;[7] but one claiming under an unrecorded deed must prove that the subsequent purchaser had actual knowledge of some claim or right of the person holding possession, or actual knowledge or notice of the unrecorded deed. It is competent, however, to present to the jury evidence of implied or constructive notice to the purchaser of an unrecorded deed in connection with direct evidence that he had actual notice of such deed.[8] Moreover, actual knowledge of an unrecorded deed does not mean that the purchaser shall have positive and certain knowledge of its existence, or such knowledge as he would acquire by seeing the deed, or being told of it by the grantor. It is such knowledge as men usually act upon in their ordinary affairs.[9] This con-

[4] Pope v. Nichols, 61 Kans. 230, 59 Pac. 257. See also White v. Fisher, 77 Ind. 65, 40 Am. Rep. 287.

[5] Jackson L. &c. R. Co. v. Davison, 65 Mich. 437, 37 N. W. 537; Michigan Mut. L. Ins. Co. v. Conant, 40 Mich. 530; Vest v. Michie, 31 Grat. (Va.) 149.

[6] Lamb v. Pierce, 113 Mass. 72, 6 Gray's Cas. 462; Pomroy v. Stevens, 11 Metc. (Mass.) 244, 6 Gray's Cas. 446.

[7] White v. Foster, 102 Mass. 375; Sibley v. Leffingwell, 8 Allen (Mass.) 584; Parker v. Osgood, 3 Allen (Mass.) 487; Mara v. Pierce, 9 Gray (Mass.) 306; Pomroy v. Stevens, 11 Metc. (Mass.) 244. See also Crassen v. Swoveland, 22 Ind.

427. But see White v. Fisher, 77 Ind. 65, 40 Am. Rep. 287. In Missouri, possession under the mortgagee will not charge the purchaser with notice, but may be considered with other evidence in proof of actual notice. Whitman v. Taylor, 60 Mo. 127. In Maine, an entry under an unrecorded deed, followed by continuous, visible occupancy, is only implied notice of a change of title; and is not equivalent to the registry of the deed. Hewes v. Wiswell, 8 Greenl. (Maine) 94.

[8] Sibley v. Leffingwell, 8 Allen (Mass.) 584.

[9] In Curtis v. Mundy, 3 Metc. (Mass.) 405, Putnam, J., said: "We think the notice should be so ex-

struction of the requirement of actual notice to affect a subsequent purchaser gives full effect to the words, and is in accordance with the definition of them given by the best writers. This construction, moreover, gives full effect to the registry laws, and enables purchasers to rely upon them fully and implicitly without searching the outside world to ascertain the true state of the title. It simply requires of all persons who hold or claim any interest in real estate, that they shall use due care and diligence in placing their rights beyond all danger by obtaining and putting upon record proper deeds.

It is true, however, that in most other states in which there are statutes requiring "actual notice" or "knowledge" to affect a purchaser, a less strict interpretation of the word is adopted, and actual notice does not imply actual knowledge. While actual notice of an unrecorded deed is distinguished from mere notice such as would be imputed from actual, open, and visible occupation, whether known to the purchaser or not, yet the words are held to include constructive knowledge, imputed from actual, open, and visible occupation, where such occupation is in fact known to the purchaser,[10] or from other facts which constructively charge him with notice. Notice is regarded as actual when the purchaser either knows of the existence of the ad-

---

press and satisfactory to the party as that it would be a fraud in him subsequently to purchase, attach, or levy upon the land, to the prejudice of the first grantee."

[10] Vattier v. Hinde, 7 Pet. (U. S.) 252, 8 L. ed. 675; Hunt v. Dunn, 74 Ga. 120; Crooks v. Jenkins, 124 Iowa 317, 100 N. W. 82, 104 Am. St. 326; Allen v. McCalla, 25 Iowa 464, 96 Am. Dec. 56; Wilson v. Miller, 16 Iowa 111; Pope v. Nichols, 61 Kans. 230, 59 Pac. 257; Greer v. Higgins, 20 Kans. 420; Johnson v. Clark, 18 Kans. 157; Knapp v. Bailey, 79 Maine 195, 9 Atl. 122; Porter v. Sevey, 43 Maine 519; Webster v. Maddox, 6 Maine 256; Ringgold v. Bryan, 3 Md. Ch. 488; Price v. McDonald, 1 Md. 403, 54 Am. Dec. 567; Teal v. Scandinavian-American &c. Bank, 114 Minn. 435, 131 N. W. 486; Niles v. Cooper, 98 Minn. 39, 107 N. W. 744; State Bank v. Frame, 112 Mo. 502, 20 S. W. 620; Maupin v. Emmons, 47 Mo. 304; Speck v. Riggin, 40 Mo. 405; Vaughn v. Tracy, 22 Mo. 415, 25 Mo. 318, 69 Am. Dec. 471; McKinzie v. Perrill,

15 Ohio St. 162; Kelley v. Stanbery, 13 Ohio 408; Manaudas v. Mann, 14 Ore. 450, 13 Pac. 449; Musgrove v. Bonser, 5 Ore. 313, 26 Am. Rep. 737; Bohlman v. Coffin, 4 Ore. 313; Toland v. Corey, 6 Utah 392, 24 Pac. 190; Gall v. Gall, 126 Wis. 390, 105 N. W. 953, 5 L. R. A. (N. S.) 603; Brinkman v. Jones, 44 Wis. 498. The court says: "We recognize the obligation to give some effect to the term 'actual notice,' as distinguished from mere 'notice,' and must therefore hold that no constructive knowledge shall be imputed to the purchaser as a ground of notice. For example, this court has held that actual, open, and visible occupation, whether known to the purchaser or not, shall be deemed sufficient notice to the purchaser of the rights and equities of such occupant. This rule could not be applied to a case like the one at bar, unless such actual occupation was known to the purchaser." See also Cunningham v. Brown, 44 Wis. 72. See ante § 253.

verse claim of title, or is conscious of having the means of such knowledge.[11]

In other states, under statutes that speak of "notice" instead of "actual notice," for stronger reasons, actual knowledge or actual notice is not meant, but such notice only as might be charged upon a purchaser if he had used the means of knowledge he actually possessed.[12]

The South Carolina statute, expressly providing that possession of real property shall not operate as notice of an instrument required to be recorded, and that actual notice shall be deemed sufficient to supply the place of registration only when such notice is of the instrument or its nature or purport, has been held not to affect the rule that possession by a grantor in a deed which was in fact a mortgage is notice to a subsequent purchaser of the rights of such grantor.[13]

§ 545. **Actual notice implied from circumstances.**—Notice implied from circumstances has been called actual notice in the second degree.[14] Most of the courts have construed the statutes requiring actual notice or knowledge so as to include this species of actual notice as well as notice by direct evidence. Actual notice under this broader use of the term includes all instances of actual notice established by circumstantial evidence. "If a party has knowledge of such facts as would lead a fair and prudent man, using ordinary caution, to make further inquiries, and he avoids the inquiry, he is chargeable with notice of the facts which by ordinary diligence he would have ascertained. He has no right to shut his eyes against the light before him. He does a wrong not to heed the 'signs and signals' seen by him. It may be well concluded that he is avoiding notice of that which he in realty believes or knows. Actual notice of facts which, to the mind of a pru-

---

[11] Gaines v. Summers, 50 Ark. 322, 7 S. W. 301; Erickson v. Rafferty, 79 Ill. 209; White v. Fisher, 77 Ind. 65, 40 Am. Rep. 287; Clark v. Holland. 72 Iowa 34, 33 N. W. 350, 2 Am. St. 230; Michigan Mut. L. Ins. Co. v. Conant, 40 Mich. 530; Drey v. Doyle, 99 Mo. 459, 12 S. W. 287; Speck v. Riggin, 40 Mo. 405; Williamson v. Brown, 15 N. Y. 354, 6 Gray's Cas. 449.

[12] Protection Bldg. &c. Assn. v. Knowles, 54 N. J. Eq. 519, 34 Atl. 1083; Traylor v. Townsend, 61 Tex. 144.

[13] Manigault v. Lofton, 78 S. Car.

499, 59 S. E. 534, construing S. Car. Code 1902, § 2457; Johnson v. Badger M. &c. Co., 13 Nev. 351. See also Larkin v. Hagan, 14 Ariz. 63, 126 Pac. 268 (actual notice to creditors, of mortgage defectively acknowledged by corporation).

[14] Wilson v. Miller, 16 Iowa 111; Knapp v. Bailey, 79 Maine 195; Maupin v. Emmons, 47 Mo. 304; Speck v. Riggin, 40 Mo. 405. Notice may be inferred from circumstances as well as proved by direct evidence. Fisher v. Borden, 111 Va. 535, 69 S. E. 636.

dent man, indicate notice, is proof of notice."[15] In the words of Mr. Justice Strong, "Means of knowledge, with the duty of using them, are in equity equivalent to knowledge itself."[16] Notice of a prior deed or mortgage thus imputable from an opportunity to acquire knowledge, coupled with the duty to seek it, whether termed actual or constructive notice, has the effect of postponing the subsequent grantee or mortgagee charged therewith.[17]

§ 546. **Degrees of actual notice—Rumors, and sources of information.**—The degrees and kinds of actual notice are of course without number, ranging from a formal written statement of the lien, giving all its details, to a mere verbal declaration of the fact of its existence; it may be one given expressly as a notice, or it may have come in an accidental way. But neither the manner of the notice nor the purpose of it is material,[18] even a verbal communication being sufficient.[19] The degree of the notice, however, is material. "Flying reports are many times fables and not truth."[20] The information must be sufficient to furnish a basis of investigation, and a mere rumor or suspicion that some other person claims an interest in the property will not affect a person with notice of such interest.[21]

---

[15] Knapp v. Bailey, 79 Maine 195, per Peters, C. J., denying the views expressed in Spofford v. Weston, 29 Maine 140.

[16] Cordova v. Hood, 17 Wall. (U. S.) 1, 21 L. ed. 587.

[17] Montgomery v. Keppel, 75 Cal. 128, 19 Pac. 178, 7 Am. St. 125; Russell v. Ranson, 76 Ill. 167; Duncan v. Miller, 64 Iowa 223, 20 N. W. 161; Livingstone v. Murphy, 187 Mass. 315, 72 N. E. 1012, 105 Am. St. 400; Quimby v. Williams, 67 N. H. 489, 41 Atl. 862, 68 Am. St. 685. See also Beeman v. Cooper, 64 Vt. 305, 23 Atl. 794; Fidelity Ins. &c. Co. v. Shenandoah Valley R. Co., 32 W. Va. 244, 9 S. E. 180. See post §§ 547, 571, 579.

[18] Wailes v. Cooper, 24 Miss. 208; Smith v. Smith, 2 Compt. & M. 231; North British Ins. Co. v. Hallett, 7 Jur. (N. S.) 1263.

[19] Schmidt v. Hedden (N. J. Eq.), 38 Atl. 843; Jackson v. Condict, 57 N. J. Eq. 522, 41 Atl. 374; Wattles v. Slater, 154 Mich. 666, 118 N. W. 486.

[20] Wildgoose v. Wayland, Gouldsb. 147, pl. 67, per Lord Keeper Eger-ton. See also Doyle v. Teas, 5 Ill. 202; Butler v. Stevens, 26 Maine 484; Buttrick v. Holden, 13 Metc. (Mass.) 355; Wilson v. McCullough, 23 Pa. St. 440.

[21] Hardy v. Harbin, 1 Sawyer (U. S.) 194; Flagg v. Mann, 2 Sumn. (U. S.) 486; Satterfield v. Malone, 35 Fed. 445; Parkhurst v. Hosford, 21 Fed. 827; Tompkins v. Henderson, 83 Ala. 391, 3 So. 774; Lambert v. Newman, 56 Ala. 623; Smith v. Yule, 31 Cal. 180, 89 Am. Dec. 167; Hall v. Livingston, 3 Del. Ch. 348; Ratteree v. Conley, 74 Ga. 153; Otis v. Spencer, 102 Ill. 622, 40 Am. Rep. 617; Slattery v. Rafferty, 93 Ill. 277; Chicago v. Witt, 75 Ill. 211; Pittman v. Sofley, 64 Ill. 155; First Nat. Bank v. Farmers' &c. Nat. Bank, 171 Ind. 323, 82 N. E. 1013, 86 N. E. 417 (equivocal circumstances); Foust v. Moorman, 2 Ind. 17; Weare v. Williams, 85 Iowa 253, 52 N. W. 328; Wilson v. Miller, 16 Iowa 111; Butler v. Stevens, 26 Maine 484; Buttrick v. Holden, 13 Metc. (Mass.) 355; Shepard v. Shepard, 36 Mich. 173; Loughridge v. Bowland, 52 Miss. 546; Brick v. Paine,

Formerly the rule was, that such notice, to be binding, must proceed from some person interested in the property.[22] But this limitation is too restricted to be accurate, and a better statement of the rule is that information coming from a stranger, in order to charge a purchaser with notice, must be more specific and direct than that coming from a party in interest.[23] Under some of the later cases, casual or accidental information seems to be insufficient, and the knowledge constituting notice must be acquired by the purchaser while making inquiries for the protection of his own interests, or in dealing in some way with the property or the title to it, in his own interest and behalf.[24] Thus, where an attorney at law had drawn a mortgage and attested and acknowledged it, and the mortgage remained unrecorded for nine years, when he himself took a mortgage upon the same property from the same grantor, it was held that he would not be presumed to still have knowledge of the prior mortgage; since mere casual knowledge, without his interests being affected, imposed on him no duty to remember.[25] It has been held that knowledge that a mortgagor was a married man at the time he acquired title to the premises, did

50 Miss. 648; Wailes v. Cooper, 24 Miss. 208; Protection Bldg. &c. Assn. v. Knowles, 54 N. J. Eq. 519, 34 Atl. 1083; Green v. Morgan (N. J. Eq.), 21 Atl. 857; Condit v. Wilson, 36 N. J. Eq. 370; Fort v. Burch, 6 Barb. (N. Y.) 60; Jackson v. Van Valkenburgh, 8 Cow. (N. Y.) 260; Allen v. Allen, 121 N. Car. 328, 28 S. E. 513; Fleming v. Burgin, 37 N. Car. 584; Jaeger v. Hardy, 48 Ohio St. 335, 27 N. E. 863, per Williams, C. J.; Woodworth v. Paige, 5 Ohio St. 70; Raymond v. Flavel, 27 Ore. 219, 40 Pac. 158; Bugbee's Appeal, 110 Pa. St. 331, 1 Atl. 273; Hottenstein v. Lerch, 104 Pa. St. 454; Maul v. Rider, 59 Pa. St. 167; Churcher v. Guernsey, 39 Pa. St. 84; Wilson v. McCullough, 23 Pa. St. 440, 62 Am. Dec. 347; Jaques v. Weeks, 7 Watts (Pa.) 261; Kerns v. Swope, 2 Watts (Pa.) 75; Rutherford v. Jenkins (Tenn.), 54 S. W. 1007; Hawley v. Bullock, 29 Tex. 216; Martel v. Somers, 26 Tex. 551; Bacon v. O'Connor, 25 Tex. 213; Wethered v. Boon, 17 Tex. 143; College &c. Line v. Ide, 15 Tex. Civ. App. 273, 40 S. W. 64; French v. Loyal Co., 5 Leigh (Va.) 627; Connell v. Connell, 32 W. Va. 319, 9 S. E. 252; Lamont v. Stimson, 5 Wis. 443; Parker v. Kane, 4 Wis. 1, 65 Am. Dec. 283; Jolland v. Stainbridge, 3 Ves. Jr. 478. See post § 548.

[22] Rogers v. Hoskins, 14 Ga. 166; Van Duyne v. Vreeland, 12 N. J. Eq. 142; Woodworth v. Paige, 5 Ohio St. 70; Peebles v. Reading, 8 Serg. & R. (Pa.) 484; Ripple v. Ripple, 1 Rawle (Pa.) 386; Lamont v. Stimson, 5 Wis. 443, 62 Am. Dec. 696; Natal Land Co. v. Good, 2 L. R. P. C. 121; Barnhart v. Greenshields, 9 Moore P. C. 18, 36. See also Parkhurst v. Hosford, 21 Fed. 827.

[23] Wilcox v. Hill, 11 Mich. 256. See also Butcher v. Yocum, 61 Pa. St. 168, 100 Am. Dec. 625; Martel v. Somers, 26 Tex. 551; McNames v. Phillips, 9 Grant Ch. (U. C.) 314. The extent to which a purchaser is charged with notice of a claim and its character may be determined by the interest of the person making the communication. Wahl v. Stoy, 72 N. J. Eq. 607, 66 Atl. 176.

[24] Arden v. Arden, 29 Ch. D. 702, 54 L. J. Ch. 655, 52 L. T. Rep. (N. S.) 610, 33 Wkly. Rep. 593. See also Smith v. Wofford (Tex. Civ. App.), 97 S. W. 143.

[25] Goodwin v. Dean, 50 Conn. 517.

not charge one who accepted a mortgage from him, four years later, with knowledge that the marriage relation continued to exist.[26]

Of course, formal and technical notice can be given only by the person directly interested; but a stranger can give information which will affect a purchaser by putting him upon inquiry as to the fact. Information from a person directly interested in the property is entitled to more weight than the statements of a stranger are entitled to; but it may be stated as a general proposition that, if the information be derived from any other source entitled to credit, and it be definite, it will be equally binding as if it came from the party himself.[27] Information sufficient to put one upon inquiry may consist of statements made by the claimant of an adverse right,[28] or by his friend or relative or any disinterested third person in a position to know and impart the facts with reasonable certainty.[29] And it has been held that the knowledge of one of two parties jointly interested may be imputed to the other.[30] Thus, if one about to purchase land is informed by the recorder that the vendor had already given a deed of the same property to another person who had deposited his deed for record, but had withdrawn it before it was recorded, this information, being from a trustworthy source, and being definite as regards the existence of the prior deed, and affording the means of pursuing the inquiry, operates as notice to the purchaser of such prior unrecorded deed.[31]

§ 547. **Facts and circumstances putting purchaser upon inquiry.**— It is a well-settled principle in equity, that information sufficient to put one on inquiry in regard to an adverse right is prima facie sufficient to charge him with notice of such right. But what is sufficient to put a purchaser upon inquiry, and affect him with the facts which

[26] Webb v. John Hancock Mut. Life Ins. Co., 162 Ind. 616, 69 N. E. 1006, 66 L. R. A. 632.

[27] Lawton v. Gordon, 37 Cal. 202; Curtis v. Mundy, 3 Metc. (Mass.) 405; Willcox v. Hill, 11 Mich. 256; Bartlett v. Glasscock, 4 Mo. 62; Jackson v. Van Valkenburgh, 8 Cow. (N. Y.) 260; Jaeger v. Hardy, 48 Ohio St. 335, 27 N. E. 863; Tucker v. Constable, 16 Ore. 407, 19 Pac. 13; Mulliken v. Graham, 72 Pa. St. 484; Butcher v. Yocum, 61 Pa. St. 168, 100 Am. Rep. 625; Philips v. Bank of Lewiston, 18 Pa. St. 394; Martel v. Somers, 26 Tex. 551.

[28] Davis v. Kennedy, 105 Ill. 300; Nelson v. Sims, 23 Miss. 383, 57 Am. Dec. 144; Epley v. Witherow, 7 Watts (Pa.) 163.

[29] Lawton v. Gordan, 37 Cal. 202; Cox v. Milner, 23 Ill. 476; Curtis v. Mundy, 3 Metc. (Mass.) 405; Jackson, L. & S. R. Co. v. Davison, 65 Mich. 416, 32 N. W. 726; Jaeger v. Hardy, 48 Ohio St. 335, 27 N. E. 863; Butcher v. Yocum, 61 Pa. St. 168, 100 Am. Dec. 625.

[30] Haven v. Emery, 33 N. H. 66 (notice to bondholders through trustee); Freeman v. Laing (1899), 2 Ch. 355, 68 L. J. Ch. 586, 81 L. T. Rep. (N. S.) 167, 48 Wkly. Rep. 9 (joint tenants).

[31] Lawton v. Gordon, 37 Cal. 202.

the inquiry might lead to, is determined by equitable considerations, and is difficult to state in the form of a rule universally applicable. In each case it must be determined whether the facts and circumstances disclosed are such as to charge the conscience of the purchaser with the duty of following up the inquiry.[32] In general, a notice of a claim, right, or interest affecting a title is sufficient if it is such a notice as a man of ordinary intelligence would act upon if it affected his ordinary business affairs.[33] It has been said that any form of notice sufficient to excite attention, and put a party upon his guard or call for inquiry, is notice of everything to which such inquiry would have led; every unusual circumstance being a ground of suspicion and demanding investigation.[34]

A very brief and general statement by an adverse claimant is sufficient to charge a purchaser with the duty of further investigation.[35]

[32] Chicago v. Witt, 75 Ill. 211; Wilson v. Hunter, 30 Ind. 466; Deason v. Taylor, 53 Miss. 697; Barrett v. Baker, 136 Mo. 512, 37 S. W. 130; Arlington State Bank v. Paulsen, 57 Nebr. 717, 78 N. W. 303; Baker v. Bliss, 39 N. Y. 70; Fassett v. Smith, 23 N. Y. 252; Williamson v. Brown, 15 N. Y. 354; In re Tabor Street, 26 Pa. Sup. Ct. 167; Harrison v. Boring, 44 Tex. 255; Passumpic Sav. Bank v. First Nat. Bank, 53 Vt. 82.

[33] Ringgold v. Waggoner, 14 Ark. 69; Prouty v. Devin, 118 Cal. 258, 50 Pac. 380; Booth v. Barnum, 9 Conn. 286, 23 Am. Dec. 339; O'Connor v. Mahoney, 159 Ill. 69, 142 N. E. 378; Mason v. Mullahy, 145 Ill. 383, 34 N. E. 36; Frick v. Godare, 144 Ind. 170, 42 N. E. 1015; France v. Holmes, 84 Iowa 319, 51 N. W. 152; Shoemaker v. Smith, 80 Iowa 655, 45 N. W. 744; Millar &c. Co. v. Olney, 69 Mich. 560, 37 N. W. 558; Willcox v. Hill, 11 Mich. 256; Barrett v. Baker, 136 Mo. 512, 37 S. W. 130; Hedrick v. Atchison, T. &c. R. Co., 120 Mo. 516, 25 S. W. 759; State Bank v. Frame, 112 Mo. 502, 20 S. W. 620; Barrett v. Davis, 104 Mo. 549, 16 S. W. 377; Drey v. Doyle, 99 Mo. 467, 12 S. W. 287; Meier v. Blume, 80 Mo. 179; Musgrove v. Bonser, 5 Ore. 313, 20 Am. Rep. 737; Bohlman v. Coffin, 4 Ore. 313; Bradlee v. Whitney, 108 Pa. St. 362; Barnes v. M'Clinton, 3 Pa. St. 67; Harrison v. Boring, 44 Tex. 255; Helms v. Chadbourne, 45 Wis. 60; Lloyd v. Banks, L. R. Ch. 488, 37 L. J. Ch. 881, 16 Wkly. Rep. 988. In Curtis v. Mundy, 3 Metc. (Mass.) 405, Putnam, J., said: "Information of the giving of a deed brought home to a party with as much authority as the fact of the marriage or death of a friend in the newspaper would be, as we think, actual notice within the statute. And if such actual notice or information should prove to be true, the party receiving it would be affected by it as much as if he had seen the transaction, and so had actual knowledge of the fact; as if, for example, after he had witnessed the conveyance he had gone with great haste and put an attachment upon the estate before the grantee, with ordinary diligence, had time to put his deed upon record. The statute, which is declaratory of the principles of common law, considers such conduct to be fraudulent and will protect the party, who was thus intended to be deprived of his estate, as completely as if his deed had been recorded before the attachment." See post § 548.

[34] Russell v. Ranson, 76 Ill. 167; Webb v. John Hancock Mut. Life Ins. Co., 162 Ind. 616, 69 N. E. 1006, 66 L. R. A. 632.

[35] Russell v. Petree, 10 B. Mon. (Ky.) 184.

Notice may be inferred from slight circumstances when it is shown that the purchaser and the vendor, who has made a prior conveyance or incumbrance of the same property, are intimately associated in business, or intimately related by blood or connected by marriage.[36] Thus, also where an entry of a satisfaction of a mortgage is made by one who occupies a double position of owner and trustee under a mortgage of the land, it has been held, that the purchaser is put on inquiry as to his authority to discharge it.[37] And where the records show that an administrator, in violation of law, was indirectly the purchaser of property at his own sale, the facts are sufficient to put an ordinarily prudent man on inquiry, and a subsequent mortgagee or grantee of the property is not a bona fide purchaser.[38] A trustee can not lawfully release a trust deed for the benefit of his wife, without payment of the note or debt secured; and the fact that the payee has possession of the uncanceled note before maturity is sufficient to put the mortgage creditor on inquiry whether the note has been paid in fact.[39]

But in general it may be said that a mere want of caution does not charge a purchaser with notice.[40] It is not enough that he might entertain a mere suspicion of an unknown equity or interest. It is not enough that an over-prudent and cautious man, if his attention had been called to the suspicious circumstance, would have been likely to seek an explanation of it. There must be some clear neglect to inquire, after having some notice of some definite equity or interest in another.

The mere fact that a purchaser knows of the existence of a debt for unpaid purchase-money does not make him chargeable with notice of an unrecorded mortgage securing such purchase-money.[41] The fact that a mortgage was given to release an attachment does not charge another mortgagee of the same premises, whose mortgage was first

---

[36] Trefts v. King, 18 Pa. St. 157.
[37] Kirsch v. Tozier, 143 N. Y. 390, 38 N. E. 375.
[38] Veeder v. McKinley-Lanning Loan &c. Co., 61 Nebr. 892, 86 N. W. 982.
[39] Lang v. Metzger, 86 Ill. App. 117.
[40] Dudley v. Witter, 46 Ala. 664; Hall v. Livingston, 3 Del. Ch. 348; Reynolds v. Carlisle, 99 Ga. 730, 27 S. E. 169; Grundies v. Reid, 107 Ill. 304; Cavin v. Middleton, 63 Iowa 618, 19 N. W. 805; Wilson v. Miller, 16 Iowa 111; Willis v. Valette, 4 Metc. (Ky.) 186; Briggs v. Rice, 130 Mass. 50; Buttrick v. Holden, 13 Metc. (Mass.) 355; Woodworth v. Paige, 5 Ohio St. 70; Raymond v. Flavel, 27 Ore. 219, 40 Pac. 158; Ware v. Egmont, 4 De G., M. & G. 460; Parker v. Conner, 93 N. Y. 118, 45 Am. Rep. 178. Some of these cases probably go too far in stating that the purchaser's negligence must go to the extent of being gross or culpable in order to affect him with notice. See post § 572.

[41] Pollak v. Davidson, 87 Ala. 551, 6 So. 312; Bell v. Tyson, 74 Ala. 353.

recorded, with constructive notice of the first named mortgage.[42] A mortgagee's knowledge of the existence of bonds issued by the mortgagor does not charge him with knowledge of a mortgage made to secure them.[43] But such knowledge may be notice of a vendor's lien.[44]

But a purchaser of land with notice that his vendor holds under a bond for title, and that one of the purchase-notes mentioned in the bond is not paid, is not a bona fide purchaser for value as against the assignee of such note by assignment previously made.[45] And so a mortgagee of land who took with knowledge that the purchase-price therefor had not been paid, took subject to the vendor's lien.[46] And, likewise, a mortgagee of land who has notice that the mortgagor has not made full payment for the property and that his title deed is still in escrow, is chargeable with notice of facts which he could have acquired in the exercise of ordinary diligence and prudence, including the fact that a purchase-money mortgage was deposited with the deed.[47]

Where a judgment upon a note exists against a mortgagor, though apparently satisfied of record, and there is a recital on the docket of a subsequent assignment of the judgment in trust to the indorsers of the note, who were in fact mere sureties, such recital was sufficient to put subsequent mortgagees of land belonging to the makers of the note on inquiry as to the rights of such indorsers; and neglecting such inquiry, they took subject to such rights.[48]

The mere fact that one who was a witness to an unrecorded mortgage afterward became the purchaser of the land from the mortgagor is not sufficient to affect him with notice of the mortgage.[49] But it was held that one who took an acknowledgment of a deed and delivered it

[42] Beeman v. Cooper, 64 Vt. 305, 23 Atl. 794.

[43] Johnson v. Valido Marble Co., 64 Vt. 337, 25 Atl. 441. Where a mortgagor had assumed a prior mortgage recited in his title deed, the mortgagee was chargeable with notice of the fact, which could have been ascertained by inquiry, that the former mortgage was given to secure coupon bonds still outstanding in a third person; and therefore the bondholders will have priority over the subsequent mortgagee. Farmers' and Drovers' Bank v. German Ins. Bank, 23 Ky. L. 2008, 66 S. W. 280.

[44] Overall v. Taylor, 99 Ala. 12, 11 So. 738; Koch v. Roth, 150 Ill. 212, 37 N. E. 317.

[45] Dishmore v. Jones, 1 Coldw. (Tenn.) 555; Payne v. Abercrombie, 10 Heisk. (Tenn.) 161; Lytle v. Turner, 12 Lea (Tenn.) 641.

[46] Harter v. Capital City Brew. Co., 66 N. J. Eq. 432, 57 Atl. 1132, affg. 64 N. J. Eq. 155, 53 Atl. 560.

[47] Balfour v. Parkinson, 84 Fed. 855, affd. Balfour v. Hopkins, 93 Fed. 564, 35 C. C. A. 445.

[48] Patton v. Cooper, 132 N. Car. 791, 44 S. E. 676.

[49] Goodwin v. Dean, 50 Conn. 517; Vest v. Michie, 31 Grat. (Va.) 149, 31 Am. Rep. 722.

to the grantee is chargeable with notice of the grantee's title.[50] An attorney who has drafted a mortgage for a client upon certain land and afterward accepts from the mortgagor a deed of the same land, takes with notice of the mortgage.[51]

If an assignee of a mortgage has notice that it was made to his assignor without consideration for the purpose of raising money by its sale, he is put upon inquiry whether any liens intervened between its date and his purchase of it; and the fact that the mortgagor offers it for sale is a circumstance to put the purchaser upon inquiry.[52]

A purchaser may be charged with notice by the fact that he is paying a very inadequate price for the property.[53] The fact that the value of the mortgaged premises is not sufficient to secure two loans is evidence, though not conclusive, that a second mortgagee had no notice of a prior incumbrance.[54]

A purchaser may also be charged with notice from any suspicious circumstances affecting the transaction.[55] Thus, where a debtor, under circumstances showing great embarrassment, and otherwise suspicious, gave to a creditor an assignment of a mortgage covering the amount of the debt, it was held that there was enough in the circumstances of the transaction to put the creditor upon inquiry as to a prior assignment by the same debtor to another person, and he was therefore charged with notice thereof.[56]

The mere possession and control of a mortgage by the mortgagor raises no presumption that it has been paid, and the production of the mortgage with the seals torn off has been held not alone sufficient to relieve a subsequent purchaser from the duty to make inquiry as to cancelation.[57]

§ 548. **Sufficiency of notice or ground of inquiry.**—Notice, to supply the place of registry, must be sufficient to make inquiry upon; it must be more than what is barely sufficient to put the party upon in-

---

[50] Greenlee v. Smith, 4 Kans. App. 733, 46 Pac. 543.

[51] Wittkowsky v. Gidney, 124 N. Car. 437, 32 S. E. 731. But see Goodwin v. Dean, 50 Conn. 517 (where nine years intervened).

[52] Mullison's Estate, 68 Pa. St. 212.

[53] Lounsbury v. Norton, 59 Conn. 170, 22 Atl. 153, per Andrews, C. J.; Hume v. Franzen, 73 Iowa 25, 34 N. W. 490; Runkle v. Gaylord, 1 Nev. 123; Durant v. Crowell, 97 N.

Car. 367; Hoppin v. Doty, 25 Wis. 573.

[54] Matteson v. Blackmer, 46 Mich. 393, 9 N. W. 445.

[55] Eck v. Hatcher, 58 Mo. 235; Tillinghast v. Champlin, 4 R. I. 173, 67 Am. Dec. 510.

[56] Hoyt v. Hoyt, 8 Bosw. (N. Y.) 511.

[57] Harrison v. Johnson, 18 N. J. Eq. 420, revd. 19 N. J. Eq. 488.

quiry.[58] In some cases it is even said that, to break in upon the registry acts, the notice must be such as will, with the attending circumstances, affect the party with fraud.[59]

Circumstances which are merely equivocal will not charge a subsequent purchaser or incumbrancer with the duty of making inquiry.[60] The notice must be clear and undoubted;[61] and when that is the case it is regarded as per se evidence of fraud for one to attempt to defeat a prior incumbrance by setting up a subsequent deed.[62]

A grantee or mortgagee of realty is chargeable with notice of a prior mortgage or deed, if he is acquainted with facts which would raise a doubt in the mind of an ordinarily prudent man, and demand investigation, which if diligently and properly pursued would lead to the discovery of the prior conveyance. In general it may be said that the facts disclosed amount to notice when they are such as render it incumbent on the purchaser or mortgagee to inquire, and at the same time enable him to prosecute the inquiry successfully.[63] If in such case

[58] Tompkins v. Henderson, 83 Ala. 391, 3 So. 774; Reed v. Gannon, 50 N. Y. 345; Williamson v. Brown, 15 N. Y. 354; Webster v. Van Steenbergh, 46 Barb. (N. Y.) 211; Fort v. Burch, 6 Barb. (N. Y.) 60; Jackson v. Van Valkenburgh, 8 Cow. (N. Y.) 260; Dey v. Dunham, 2 Johns. Ch. (N. Y.) 182; College &c. Line v. Ide, 15 Tex. Civ. App. 273, 40 S. W. 64.

[59] Goodwin v. Dean, 50 Conn. 517; Hall v. Livingston, 3 Del. Ch. 348; Pittman v. Sofley, 64 Ill. 155; Holmes v. Stout, 10 N. J. Eq. 419; Dey v. Dunham, 2 Johns. Ch. (N. Y.) 182; Woodworth v. Paige, 5 Ohio St. 70; Vest v. Michie, 31 Grat. (Va.) 149, 31 Am. Rep. 722; Munday v. Vawter, 3 Grat. (Va.) 518; Jones v. Smith, 1 Hare 43. See ante § 546.

[60] Arnold v. Barnett, 90 Ga. 334, 17 S. E. 91; Slattery v. Rafferty, 93 Ill. 277; First Nat. Bank v. Farmers' &c. Nat. Bank, 171 Ind. 323, 82 N. E. 1013, 84 N. E. 1077, 86 N. E. 417; Sheldon v. Holmes, 58 Mich. 138, 24 N. W. 795; Protection Bldg. &c. Assn. v. Knowles, 54 N. J. Eq. 519, 34 Atl. 1083. See ante § 546.

[61] Smith v. Yule, 31 Cal. 180, 89 Am. Dec. 167; Rogers v. Wiley, 14 Ill. 65, 56 Am. Dec. 491; Condit v. Wilson, 36 N. J. Eq. 370; Riley v. Hoyt, 29 Hun (N. Y.) 114; Wilson v. McCullough, 23 Pa. St. 440, 62 Am. Dec. 347; West v. Reid, 2 Hare 249; Hine v. Dodd, 2 Atk. 275.

[62] Pittman v. Sofley, 64 Ill. 155; Loughridge v. Bowland, 52 Miss. 546; Morris v. White, 36 N. J. Eq. 324; Cambridge Valley Bank v. Delano, 48 N. Y. 326; Acer v. Wescott, 46 N. Y. 384, 7 Am. Rep. 255; Dunham v. Dey, 15 Johns. (N. Y.) 554, 8 Am. Dec. 282.

[63] Balfour v. Parkinson, 84 Fed. 855; Tompkins v. Henderson, 83 Ala. 391, 3 So. 774; Webb v. Robbins, 77 Ala. 176; Prouty v. Devin, 118 Cal. 258, 50 Pac. 380; Stockton Bldg. &c. Assn. v. Chalmers, 65 Cal. 93, 3 Pac. 101; Thompson v. Pioche, 44 Cal. 508; Galland v. Jackman, 26 Cal. 80, 85 Am. Dec. 172; Boswell v. Goodwin, 31 Conn. 74, 81 Am. Dec. 169; Booth v. Barnum, 9 Conn. 286, 23 Am. Dec. 339; Goodwynne v. Bellerby, 116 Ga. 901, 43 S. E. 275; Simms v. Freiherr, 100 Ga. 607, 28 S. E. 288; Hunt v. Dunn, 74 Ga. 120; Stokes v. Riley, 121 Ill. 166, 11 N. E. 877; Hunter v. Stoneburner, 92 Ill. 75; Heaton v. Prather, 84 Ill. 330; Chicago v. Witt, 75 Ill. 211; Hankinson v. Barbour, 29 Ill. 80; Rupert v. Mark, 15 Ill. 540; Garrett v. Simpson, 115 Ill. App. 62; Clark v. Plumstead, 11 Ill. App. 57; Slocum v. Slocum, 9 Ill. App. 142; Webb v. John Hancock Mut. Life

he wilfully closes his eyes and remains ignorant of facts he would ascertain by a reasonable inquiry, he is affected with notice of them just as much as he would be had he made the inquiry.[64]

Ins. Co., 162 Ind. 616, 69 N. E. 1006, 66 L. R. A. 632; Indiana B. &c. R. Co. v. McBroom, 114 Ind. 198, 15 N. E. 831; Wilson v. Godfrey, 145 Iowa 696, 124 N. W. 875; Shoemaker v. Smith, 80 Iowa 655, 45 N. W. 744; Leas v. Garverich, 77 Iowa 275, 42 N. W. 194; Wilson v. Miller, 16 Iowa 111; Hull v. Noble, 40 Maine 459; Spofford v. Weston, 29 Maine 140; Border State Sav. Inst. v. Wilcox, 63 Md. 525; Stockett v. Taylor, 3 Md. Ch. 537; Allen v. Cadwell, 55 Mich. 8, 20 N. W. 692; Michigan Mut. L. Ins. Co. v. Conant, 40 Mich. 530; Converse v. Blumrach, 14 Mich. 109, 90 Am. Dec. 230; Lindauer v. Younglove, 47 Minn. 62, 49 N. W. 384; Plant v. Shryock, 62 Miss. 821; Loughridge v. Bowland, 52 Miss. 546; Buck v. Paine, 50 Miss. 648; McLeod v. First Nat. Bank, 42 Miss. 99; Conn. Mut. Life Ins. Co. v. Smith, 117 Mo. 261, 22 S. W. 623, 38 Am. St. 656; Seiberling v. Tipton, 113 Mo. 373, 21 S. W. 4; Loring v. Groomer, 110 Mo. 632, 19 S. W. 950; Taafee v. Kelley, 110 Mo. 127, 19 S. W. 539; Meier v. Blume, 80 Mo. 179; Maupin v. Emmons, 47 Mo. 304; Bartlett v. Glasscock, 4 Mo. 62; McWaid v. Blair State Bank, 58 Nebr. 618, 79 N. W. 620; Arlington State Bank v. Paulsen, 57 Nebr. 717, 78 N. W. 303; Eiseman v. Gallagher, 24 Nebr. 79; Janvrin v. Janvrin, 60 N. H. 169; Nute v. Nute, 41 N. H. 60; Rogers v. Jones, 8 N. H. 264; Kellogg v. Randolph, 71 N. J. Eq. 127, 63 Atl. 753; Parker v. Parker (N. J.), 56 Atl. 1094; Kline v. Grannis, 61 N. J. Eq. 397, 48 Atl. 566; Jackson v. Condict, 57 N. J. Eq. 522, 41 Atl. 374; Ledos v. Kupfrian, 28 N. J. Eq. 161; Hoy v. Bramhall, 19 N. J. Eq. 563, 97 Am. Dec. 687; Willink v. Morris Canal &c. Co., 4 N. J. Eq. 377; Ellis v. Horrman, 90 N. Y. 466; Hoyt v. Hoyt, 85 N. Y. 142, 17 Hun 192; Cambridge Bank v. Delano, 48 N. Y. 326; Acer v. Westcott, 46 N. Y. 384, 7 Am. Rep. 355; Baker v. Bliss, 39 N. Y. 70; Williamson v. Brown, 15 N. Y. 554; Howard Ins. Co. v. Halsey, 4 Sandf. (N. Y.) 565;

Williams v. Lewis, 158 N. Car. 571, 74 S. E. 17; Patton v. Cooper, 132 N. Car. 791, 44 S. E. 676; Branch v. Griffin, 99 N. Car. 173, 5 S. E. 393; Blackwood v. Jones, 4 Jones Eq. (N. Car.) 54; Hibbs v. Union Cent. Life Ins. Co., 40 Ohio St. 543; Scott v. Lewis, 40 Ore. 37, 66 Pac. 299; Exon v. Dancke, 24 Ore. 110, 32 Pac. 1045; Carter v. Portland, 4 Ore. 339; Flitcraft v. Commonwealth Title &c. Trust Co., 11 Pa. 114, 60 Atl. 557; Bradlee v. Whitney, 108 Pa. St. 362; Mulliken v. Graham, 72 Pa. St. 484; Maul v. Rider, 59 Pa. St. 167; Wilson v. McCullough, 23 Pa. St. 440, 62 Am. Dec. 347; Dunning v. Reese, 7 Kulp (Pa.) 201; Wolfe v. Citizens' Bank (Tenn.), 42 S. W. 39; Paine v. Abercrombie, 10 Heisk. (Tenn.) 161; Ramirez v. Smith, 94 Tex. 184, 59 S. W. 258; Traylor v. Townsend, 61 Tex. 144; Powell v. Haley, 28 Tex. 52; Wells v. Houston, 23 Tex. Civ. App. 629, 57 S. W. 584; Smith v. Smith, 23 Tex. Civ. App. 304, 55 S. W. 541; Moody v. Martin (Tex. Civ. App.), 117 S. W. 1015; Keyser v. Clifton (Tex. Civ. App.), 50 S. W. 957; Brown v. Wilson (Tex. Civ. App.), 29 S. W. 530; Adams v. Soule, 33 Vt. 538; Stevens v. Goodenough, 26 Vt. 676; Blaisdell v. Stevens, 16 Vt. 179; Fisher v. Borden, 111 Va. 535, 543, 69 S. E. 636; Hall v. Caldwell, 97 Va. 311, 33 S. E. 596; Robinson v. Crenshaw, 84 Va. 348, 5 S. E. 222; Effinger v. Hall, 81 Va. 94; Wood v. Krebbs, 30 Grat. (Va.) 708; Long v. Weller, 29 Grat. (Va.) 347; Crumlish v. Railroad Co., 32 W. Va. 244; Cain v. Cox, 23 W. Va. 594; Helms v. Chadbourne, 45 Wis. 60; Parker v. Kane, 4 Wis. 1, 65 Am. Dec. 283; Pilcher v. Rawlings, L. R. 11 Eq. 53, 40 L. J. Ch. 105, 23 L. T. Rep. (N. S.) 756, 19 Wkly. Rep. 217; Birch v. Ellames, Anstr. 427, 3 Rev. Rep. 601; Montefiore v. Browne, 7 H. L. Cas. 241, 4 Jur. (N. S.) 1201, 11 Eng. Reprint 96. See also First Nat. Bank v. Farmers &c. Nat. Bank, 171 Ind. 373, 86 N. E. 417.

[64] Kyle v. Ward, 81 Ala. 120, 1 So. 468; Montgomery v. Keppel, 75 Cal.

A second mortgagee is chargeable with notice of facts which he might have learned by inquiry of the first mortgagee, where he was told by the mortgagor of the existence of an unrecorded first mortgage; and an examination of the records by the second mortgagee and a search by an abstracter at his instance did not constitute proper or sufficient inquiry.[65]

§ 549. Notice of owner's intention to execute mortgage.—Knowledge of the actual existence of a prior conveyance or incumbrance is essential to actual notice; and information of the grantor's intention or agreement to execute it is insufficient.[66] Notice of an intention on the part of the owner of property to execute a lien upon it does not prevent the person having such notice from taking a valid incumbrance upon it. But where a prior mortgage, which was intended to be a conveyance in fee, was by mistake, as executed, only a conveyance for life, and a second mortgagee had such actual notice of it as induced him to believe that the mortgage was in fee, it was, as against him, held to be a mortgage in fee.[67]

Moreover, notice of an intention to execute a deed is not notice of the contents of the deed as executed.[68] A creditor may by his vigilance secure his demand, if possible, by taking a mortgage from his debtor, just as he might by an attachment, although he knew that another creditor intended to make an attachment in the one case, or to take a mortgage in the other, and had taken steps for effecting this.[69] Notice

128, 19 Pac. 178; Hankinson v. Barber, 29 Ill. 80; Allen v. McCalla, 25 Iowa 464, 96 Am. Dec. 56; Bliss, 39 N. Y. 70; Williamson v. Brown, 15 N. Y. 554; Burnham v. Brennan, 10 J. & S. (N. Y.) 49; Bunting v. Ricks, 2 Dev. & Bat. Eq. (N. Car.) 130; Musgrove v. Bonser, 5 Ore. 313, 20 Am. Rep. 737; Bonner v. Stephens, 60 Tex. 616; Blaisdell v. Stephens, 16 Vt. 179; Brinkman v. Jones, 44 Wis. 498; White & Tudor's Lead. Cas., 4th Am. ed., vol ii, part 1, pp. 152-155.

[65] Wattles v. Slater, 154 Mich. 666, 118 N. W. 486; Munroe v. Eastman, 31 Mich. 283; Shotwell v. Harrison, 30 Mich. 179. See also Blatchley v. Osborn, 33 Conn. 226.

[66] Ponder v. Scott, 44 Ala. 241; Koon v. Tramel, 71 Iowa 132, 32 N. W. 243; Butler v. Stevens, 26 Maine 484; Cushing v. Hurd, 4 Pick. (Mass.) 253, 16 Am. Dec. 335; Brewster v. Clough, 4 Ohio Dec. (reprint) 25; Clark v. Paquette, 66 Vt. 386, 29 Atl. 370. But see Dye v. Forbes, 34 Minn. 13, 24 N. W. 309. Knowledge by one secured under a trust deed for future advances, that his debtor intends to give a second trust deed does not affect his security. Hall v. Williamson Grocery Co., 69 W. Va. 671, 72 S. E. 780. A purchaser with notice of an agreement between the vendor and another, amounting to an equitable mortgage on the land, takes subject to the rights of the equitable mortgagee. Blackburn v. Tweedie, 60 Mo. 505; Foster Lumber Co. v. Harlan County Bank, 71 Kans. 158, 80 Pac. 49, 114 Am. St. 470. See post § 550.

[67] Gale v. Morris, 30 N. J. Eq. 285.
[68] Ponder v. Scott, 44 Ala. 241.
[69] Warden v. Adams, 15 Mass. 233; Cushing v. Hurd, 4 Pick. (Mass.) 253, 16 Am. Dec. 335.

of an unrecorded mortgage will defeat an attachment levied upon the land as property of the grantor, but mere knowledge of his intention to mortgage will not have that effect.[70]

§ 550. **Inquiry concerning deeds not in the chain of title.**—A purchaser is not put upon inquiry by notice of a deed not in the line of title under which he claims.[71] He is not put upon inquiry by notice of a deed which does not necessarily affect the property in question, especially if he is at the same time told that in fact it does not affect it, but relates to other property.[72] But if the notice be of an instrument that actually does affect the land, though there may be some doubt on the information obtained whether the land is included or not, the purchaser will be charged with full notice of the instrument if he fails to make suitable inquiry.[73]

An equitable mortgage in favor of one advancing money to a vendee to purchase land, under an oral agreement to execute a mortgage to secure the loan, will be given priority over a mortgage on the land to a party who has notice of the rights of the equitable mortgagee.[74]

If a purchaser buys either the legal estate or an equitable interest in land, having knowledge of an outstanding equitable interest, he is chargeable with notice of any record of a conveyance or incumbrance of that interest. Knowledge of an equitable interest carries with it notice of the condition of such interest as it appears upon the public records.[75] But it is held that a purchaser of the legal title is not bound to take notice of a registered lien or incumbrance against the former owner of the equitable title, through whom the purchaser does not deraign title, and whose name does not appear in the chain of title.[76]

§ 551. **Inquiry of reliable and disinterested parties.**—The inquiry should be prosecuted by recourse to reliable and disinterested sources

---

[70] Cushing v. Hurd, 4 Pick. (Mass.) 253, 16 Am. Dec. 335.

[71] Satterfield v. Malone, 35 Fed. 445; Continental Inv. &c. Soc. v. Wood, 168 Ill. 421, 48 N. E. 221; St. John v. Conger, 40 Ill. 535; Ely v. Pingry, 56 Kans. 17, 42 Pac. 330; Schoch v. Birdsall, 48 Minn. 441, 51 N. W. 382; Hetherington v. Clark, 30 Pa. St. 393; Woods v. Farmere, 7 Watts (Pa.) 382, 32 Am. Dec. 772; Ely v. Wilcox, 20 Wis. 523. See ante § 541.

[72] Jones v. Smith, 1 Phillips 244, 1 Hare 43.

[73] Price v. McDonald, 1 Md. 403, 54 Am. Dec. 657; Doran v. Dazey, 5 N. Dak. 167, 64 N. W. 1023, 57 Am. St. 550; Hudson v. Warner, 2 H. & G. 415.

[74] Foster Lumber Co. v. Harlan County Bank, 71 Kans. 158, 80 Pac. 49, 114 Am. St. 470; Blackburn v. Tweedie, 60 Mo. 505.

[75] Jones v. Lapham, 15 Kans. 540.

[76] Harper v. Bibb, 34 Miss. 472, 69 Am. Dec. 397; Baker v. Griffin, 50 Miss. 158.

of information. It is not safe to rely upon the statements of the vendor, or of one who has a motive for misleading the inquirer,[77] but all other reasonable and available sources of information must be exhausted.[78] Thus where a mortgagee knows that at least part of the purchase-price remains unpaid by his mortgagor, an inquiry of the mortgagor and a denial by him of the existence of any lien on the land is not sufficient to entitle the mortgagee to protection as a bona fide purchaser, since it was his duty to inquire directly from the original vendor; the mortgagor being interested adversely to the vendor's lien.[79]

If the claimant of an adverse interest be questioned by a purchaser regarding such interest, and he refuses to answer or is unable to do so, he should not be allowed to allege that the purchaser was put upon inquiry and is chargeable with notice.[80] The purchaser in such case can hardly be charged with bad faith in not prosecuting the inquiry, and not obtaining information which was peculiarly within the knowledge of such adverse claimant. On the contrary, the adverse claimant might, under some circumstances, be chargeable with bad faith in attempting to mislead the purchaser.[81] And so, if a person in possession of land misleads the purchaser making inquiry, by misrepresentation or suppression of material facts, he is thereby estopped from afterward asserting against the purchaser, the claim or equity he ought to have disclosed.[82]

By merely examining the records, a purchaser put upon inquiry as to a prior unrecorded deed does not discharge his duty in following up

---

[77] Singer v. Jacobs, 11 Fed. 559; Overall v. Taylor, 99 Ala. 12, 11 So. 738; Blatchley v. Osborn, 33 Conn. 226; Russell v. Petree, 10 B. Mon. (Ky.) 184; Price v. McDonald, 1 Md. 403, 54 Am. Dec. 657; Littleton v. Giddings, 47 Tex. 109; Moody v. Martin (Tex. Civ. App.), 117 S. W. 1015. The fact that a purchaser has been misled by false statements of his vendor is not sufficient to protect him. Skeel v. Spraker, 8 Paige (N. Y.) 182.

[78] Dudley v. Witter, 46 Ala. 664; Skeel v. Spraker, 8 Paige (N. Y.) 182; Littleton v. Giddings, 47 Tex. 109.

[79] Overall v. Taylor, 99 Ala. 12, 11 So. 738. See also Foster v. Stall-worth, 62 Ala. 547; Moody v. Martin (Tex. Civ. App.), 117 S. W. 1015.

[80] McGehee v. Gindrat, 20 Ala. 95; Kelly v. Fairmount Land Co., 97 Va. 227, 33 S. E. 598.

[81] Broome v. Beers, 6 Conn. 198; Platt v. Squire, 12 Metc. (Mass.) 494; Fay v. Valentine, 12 Pick. (Mass.) 40, 22 Am. Dec. 397; Lesley v. Johnson, 41 Barb. (N. Y.) 359; Brinckerhoff v. Lansing, 4 Johns. Ch. (N. Y.) 65, 8 Am. Dec. 528; Carr v. Wallace, 7 Watts (Pa.) 394; Epley v. Witherow, 7 Watts (Pa.) 163; Miller v. Bingham, 29 Vt. 82; Stafford v. Ballou, 17 Vt. 329.

[82] Yates v. Hurd, 8 Colo. 343, 8 Pac. 575; Losey v. Simpson, 11 N. J. Eq. 246.

the inquiry, for the records can give him no information respecting an unrecorded deed.[83]

§ 552. Diligence in prosecuting inquiry—Erroneous descriptions.—

If a purchaser put upon inquiry fails to prosecute it with due diligence, he is conclusively presumed to have notice of the facts that a due inquiry would have disclosed.[84] When it is shown that a purchaser had knowledge of facts sufficient to put him on inquiry as to the existence of some right or title in conflict with the title or interest he is about to purchase, he is presumed to have made the inquiry, and ascertained the extent of such prior right, or to have been guilty of a degree of negligence equally fatal to his claim to be considered a bona fide purchaser.[85] He is chargeable with notice of all facts that he might have learned by the exercise of reasonable diligence, prosecuting

[83] Blatchley v. Osborn, 33 Conn. 226; Wattles v. Slater, 154 Mich. 666, 118 N. W. 486; Munroe v. Eastman, 31 Mich. 283; Shotwell v. Harrison, 30 Mich. 179; Reck v. Clapp, 98 Pa. St. 581.

[84] Rankin Mfg. Co. v. Bishop, 137 Ala. 271, 34 So. 991; Foster v. Stallworth, 62 Ala. 547; Kenniff v. Caulfield, 140 Cal. 34, 73 Pac. 803; Bryan v. Tormey, 84 Cal. 126, 21 Pac. 725, 24 Pac. 319; Montgomery v. Keppel, 75 Cal. 128, 19 Pac. 178; Filmore v. Reithman, 6 Colo. 120; Walker v. Neil, 117 Ga. 733, 45 S. E. 387; Hunt v. Dunn, 74 Ga. 120; Stokes v. Riley, 121 Ill. 166, 11 N. E. 877; Chicago, R. I. &c. R. Co. v. Kennedy, 70 Ill. 350; Hankinson v. Barbour, 29 Ill. 80; Doyle v. Teas, 5 Ill. 202; Webb v. John Hancock Mut. L. Ins. Co., 162 Ind. 616, 69 N. E. 1006, 66 L. R. A. 632; Blair v. Whitaker, 31 Ind. App. 664, 69 N. E. 182; Wilson v. Miller, 16 Iowa 111; Russell v. Petree, 10 B. Mon. (Ky.) 184; Mayor v. Williams, 6 Md. 235; Price v. McDonald, 1 Md. 403, 54 Am. Dec. 657; Schweiss v. Woodruff, 73 Mich. 473, 41 N. W. 511; Oliver v. Sanborn, 60 Mich. 346, 27 N. W. 527; Converse v. Blumrich, 14 Mich. 109, 90 Am. Dec. 230; Loughridge v. Bowland, 52 Miss. 546; Buck v. Paine, 50 Miss. 648; McLeod v. First Nat. Bank, 42 Miss. 99; Bradford v. Anderson, 60 Nebr. 368, 83 N. W. 173; Eiseman v. Gallagher, 24 Nebr. 79,

37 N. W. 941; Nute v. Nute, 41 N. H. 60; Warren v. Swett, 31 N. H. 332; Sweet v. Henry, 175 N. Y. 268, 67 N. E. 574; Parker v. Conner, 93 N. Y. 118, 45 Am. Rep. 178; Cambridge Valley Bank v. Delano, 48 N. Y. 326; Howard Ins. Co. v. Halsey, 4 Sandf. (N. Y.) 577, 8 N. Y. 271, 59 Am. Dec. 478; Patton v. Cooper, 132 N. Car. 791, 44 S. E. 676; Collins v. Davis, 132 N. Car. 106, 43 S. E. 579; Wittkowsky v. Gidney, 124 N. Car. 437, 32 S. E. 731; Maul v. Rider, 59 Pa. St. 167; Jaques v. Weeks, 7 Watts (Pa.) 61; Maybin v. Kirby, 4 Rich. Eq. (S. Car.) 105; Traylor v. Townsend, 61 Tex. 144; Bacon v. O'Connor, 25 Tex. 213; Blaisdell v. Stevens, 16 Vt. 179; Effinger v. Hall, 81 Va. 94; Bigelow v. Brewer, 29 Wash 670, 70 Pac. 129; Clark v. Sayres, 55 W. Va. 512, 47 S. E. 312; Ward v. Russell, 121 Wis. 77, 98 N. W. 939; Beebe v. Wisconsin Mortg. Loan Co., 117 Wis. 328, 93 N. W. 1103; Helms v. Chadbourne, 45 Wis. 60; Brinkman v. Jones, 44 Wis. 498; Pringle v. Dunn, 37 Wis. 449, 19 Am. Rep. 772; Whitbread v. Boulnois, 1 Young & Coll. Ex. 303; Kennedy v. Green, 3 Myl. & Keene 699; Hanbury v. Litchfield, 2 Myl. & Keene 629; Maxfield v. Burton, 17 L. R. Eq. 15; Hoxie v. Carr, 1 Sumn. 173.

[85] Williamson v. Brown, 15 N. Y. 354, per Selden, J.; Maul v. Rider, 59 Pa. St. 167.

the inquiry in the right direction.[86] Having notice of the existence of an unrecorded deed, he has notice of all its contents.[87]

A description of land which is ambiguous or inconsistent may be sufficient to put the purchaser upon inquiry as to the land intended to be conveyed.[88] The purchaser is certainly chargeable with notice if he knows that the description is erroneous, and from his knowledge of the property is able to interpret the deed as it was intended to be made.[89] And a mortgage containing an incomplete or erroneous description of the property conveyed, is a valid lien against a subsequent purchaser or mortgagee with notice of the mortgage and of the mistake in it, so that it retains priority upon reformation in equity.[90] The peculiar coincidence of the identity of description by metes and bounds in three mortgages executed by the same mortgagor to the same mortgagee, was held sufficient to put a subsequent mortgagee upon inquiry, and charge him with knowledge of the existence of all three mortgages, which were explainable only on the theory of a mistake in the description.[91]

§ 553. Effect of due inquiry—Evidence.

A purchaser put upon inquiry may rebut the presumption of notice by showing that he made due investigation without discovering the prior right or title he was bound to investigate.[92] The question whether he has made due inquiry

[86] Passumpsic Sav. Bank v. First Nat. Bank, 53 Vt. 82; Fisher v. Borden, 111 Va. 535, 69 S. E. 636; Seymour v. Darrow, 31 Vt. 122.

[87] Martin v. Cauble, 72 Ind. 67; George v. Kent, 7 Allen (Mass.) 16; Willink v. Morris Canal &c. Co., 4 N. J. Eq. 377; Steere v. Childs, 15 Hun (N. Y.) 511; Wells v. Houston, 23 Tex. Civ. App. 629, 57 S. W. 584; Hill v. Murray, 56 Vt. 177; Jones v. Williams, 24 Beav. 47. Knowledge of the existence of an incumbrance is constructive notice of its extent. Willink v. Morris Canal &c. Co., 4 N. J. Eq. 377; Skeel v. Spraker, 8 Paige (N. Y.) 182.

[88] Shoemaker v. Smith, 80 Iowa 655, 45 N. W. 744; Kellogg v. Randolph, 71 N. J. Eq. 127, 63 Atl. 753; Carter v. Hawkins, 62 Tex. 393. See also Michigan Mut. Life Ins. Co. v. Conant, 40 Mich. 530.

[89] Carter v. Hawkins, 62 Tex. 393.

[90] Woodworth v. Guzman, 1 Cal. 203; Yarnell v. Brown, 170 Ill. 362, 48 N. E. 909, 62 Am. St. 380; Mil-mine v. Burnham, 76 Ill. 362; Shoemaker v. Smith, 80 Iowa 655, 45 N. W. 744; Peters v. Ham, 62 Iowa 656, 18 N. W. 296; Warburton v. Lauman, 2 Greene (Iowa) 420; Kimble v. Harrington, 91 Mich. 281, 51 N. W. 936; Hunt v. Hunt, 38 Mich. 161; Brown v. Morrill, 45 Minn. 483, 48 N. W. 328; Cox v. Esteb, 81 Mo. 393; Young v. Cason, 48 Mo. 259; Kellogg v. Randolph, 71 N. J. Eq. 127, 63 Atl. 753; Ilse v. Seinsheimer, 76 Tex. 459, 13 S. W. 329; McLaughlin v. Job, 41 Wis. 465; Lumber Co. v. Rennie, 21 Can. S. Ct. 218. See also Stewart v. Huff, 19 Iowa 557 (total misdescription of mortgaged premises, not notice).

[91] Kellogg v. Randolph, 71 N. J. Eq. 127, 63 Atl. 753.

[92] McGehee v. Gindrat, 20 Ala. 95; Thompson v. Pioche, 44 Cal. 508; Gregory v. Savage, 32 Conn. 250; Bell v. Davis, 75 Ind. 314; Schweiss v. Woodruff, 73 Mich. 473, 41 N. W. 511; Barnard v. Campau, 29 Mich. 162, 165; Rhodes v. Outcalt, 48 Mo.

is one of fact, to be investigated by the jury;[93] and consequently the results of the inquiry, including the statements made in reply to the inquiry, may be given in evidence, though such evidence is not competent upon the question of the evidence of the prior right or title in regard to which the inquiry was made.[94]

If a purchaser put upon inquiry as to some claim or title affecting the validity of the title to the land he is about to purchase, makes proper inquiry in regard to the matter of the persons having or claiming an adverse interest in the property, and they conceal or withhold the information sought, such persons can not afterward charge him with notice of the right or claim not disclosed.[95]

The person put upon inquiry is in the first instance only bound to apply to the party in interest for information, and is not obliged to press his inquiries further unless the answer he receives corroborates the prior statements, or reveals the existence of other sources of information. When he has followed the best sources of information to ascertain the truth of the rumors or statements which have put him upon inquiry, and has been misled, he ought not to be chargeable with notice of statements which he has endeavored in vain to verify, es-

---

367; Rogers v. Jones, 8 N. H. 264; Parker v. Conner, 93 N. Y. 118, 45 Am. Rep. 178; Cambridge Valley Bank v. Delano, 48 N. Y. 326; Acer v. Westcott, 46 N. Y. 384, 7 Am. Rep. 355; Williamson v. Brown, 15 N. Y. 354; Hoyt v. Shelden, 3 Bosw. (N. Y.) 267; Brownback v. Ozias, 117 Pa. St. 87, 11 Atl. 301; Wilson v. Williams, 25 Tex. 54.

[93] Doyle v. Teas, 5 Ill. 202; Wilson v. Miller, 16 Iowa 111; Knapp v. Bailey, 79 Maine 195, 9 Atl. 122, 1 Am. St. 295; Vaughn v. Tracy, 22 Mo. 415; Nute v. Nute, 41 N. H. 60; Griffith v. Griffith, 1 Hoffm. Ch. (N. Y.) 153, reversed 9 Paige 315; Trefts v. King, 18 Pa. St. 157; College Park Electric Belt Line v. Ide, 15 Tex. Civ. App. 273, 40 S. W. 64; French v. Loyal Co., 5 Leigh (Va.) 627; Hiern v. Mill, 13 Ves. Jr. 120. See also Williamson v. Brown, 15 N. Y. 354; Whitebread v. Jordan, 1 Y. & C. Exch. 303; Jones v. Smith, 1 Hare 43. The sufficiency of the evidence is for the jury, but its competency is for the court. Pollak v. Davidson, 87 Ala. 551, 6 So. 312; Vaughn v. Tracy, 22 Mo. 415; Nute

v. Nute, 41 N. H. 60; Morris v. Daniels, 35 Ohio St. 406. It has been held that actual notice is to be proved by direct evidence, and not implied from circumstances. Peeples v. Reading, 8 Serg. & R. (Pa.) 484. *See also Keith v. Wheeler, 159 Mass. 161, 34 N. E. 174. Where actual notice has been divided into express and implied notice, it has been said that express notice is to be proved by direct evidence, but that implied notice may be established by proof of circumstances from which it is inferable as a fact. Williamson v. Brown, 15 N. Y. 354. See also Knapp v. Bailey, 79 Maine 195, 9 Atl. 122, 1 Am. St. 295; Rhodes v. Outcalt, 48 Mo. 367.

[94] Rogers v. Wiley, 14 Ill. 65, 56 Am. Dec. 491; Chiles v. Conley, 2 Dana (Ky.) 21; McMechan v. Griffing, 3 Pick. (Mass.) 149, 15 Am. Dec. 198; Nute v. Nute, 41 N. H. 60; Parker v. Conner, 93 N. Y. 118, 45 Am. Rep. 178; Schutt v. Large, 6 Barb. (N. Y.) 373.

[95] Kelly v. Fairmount Land Co., 97 Va. 227, 33 S. E. 598. See also McGehee v. Gindrat, 20 Ala. 95.

pecially in favor of the party misleading him. The equitable doctrine of constructive notice can not be invoked to relieve a party from responsibility for his own misstatements.[96]

The omission to make inquiry is immaterial where such inquiry would not have led to a knowledge of material facts constituting notice. If the conduct of the party sought to be charged would have been the same whether or not he had made the inquiry, his omission can not be ground for charging him with notice.[97]

§ 554. **Burden of proof.**—The burden of proof is upon the person who claims priority, and charges another with notice, to make out affirmatively that the other has such notice.[98] But in case fraud has been proved, the party claiming through the fraudulent transaction has the burden of proving his own good faith and want of notice.[99] Even where no fraud is shown, it is held in some cases that the burden of proof is upon the party claiming under the second deed that he is a purchaser in good faith and for a valuable consideration without notice.[1] It has been held to be prima facie proof of lack of notice to

[96] Converse v. Blumrich, 14 Mich. 109, 90 Am. Dec. 230.

[97] Cambridge Valley Bank v. Delano, 48 N. Y. 326; Birdsall v. Russell, 29 N. Y. 220; King v. Travis, 4 Hayw. (Tenn.) 280; Meux v. Bell, 1 Hare 86.

[98] Pollak v. Davidson, 87 Ala. 551, 6 So. 312; Lambert v. Newman, 56 Ala. 623; Bartlett v. Varner, 56 Ala. 580; Center v. Planters' &c. Bank, 22 Ala. 743; Gerson v. Pool, 31 Ark. 85; Ryder v. Rush, 102 Ill. 338; Brown v. Welch, 18 Ill. 343, 68 Am. Dec. 549; Rogers v. Wiley, 14 Ill. 65, 56 Am. Dec. 491; Boyd v. Boyd, 128 Iowa 699, 104 N. W. 798, 111 Am. St. 215; McCormick v. Leonard, 38 Iowa 272; Miles v. Blanton, 3 Dana (Ky.) 525; Marshall v. Dunham, 66 Maine 539; Butler v. Stevens, 26 Maine 484; Livingstone v. Murphy, 187 Mass. 315, 72 N. E. 1012, 105 Am. St. 400; Sheldon v. Holmes, 58 Mich. 138, 24 N. W. 795; Sheldon v. Powell, 31 Mont. 249, 78 Pac. 491, 107 Am. St. 429; Atlantic City v. New Auditorium Pier Co., 67 N. J. Eq. 610, 59 Atl. 158; Van Wagenen v. Hopper, 8 N. J. Eq. 684; Newton v. McLean, 41 Barb. (N. Y.) 285; Fort v. Burch, 6 Barb. (N. Y.) 60; Giles v. Hunter, 103 N. Car. 194,

9 S. E. 549; Lane v. De Bode, 29 Tex. Civ. App. 602, 69 S. W. 437; Vest v. Michie, 31 Grat. (Va.) 149, 31 Am. Rep. 722. See also Barnett v. Squyres, 93 Tex. 193, 54 S. W. 241, 77 Am. St. 854; Turner v. Cochran (Tex. Civ. App.), 63 S. W. 151. A purchaser from a grantee with notice must prove lack of notice on his own part. Gallatian v. Cunningham, 8 Cow. (N. Y.) 361.

[99] Whelan v. McCreary, 64 Ala. 319; Davis v. Nolan, 49 Iowa 683; Letson v. Reed, 45 Mich. 27, 7 N. W. 231; Berry v. Whitney, 40 Mich. 65; McLeod v. Lloyd, 43 Ore. 260, 71 Pac. 795, 74 Pac. 491.

[1] Yeend v. Weeks, 104 Ala. 331, 16 So. 165; Bell v. Pleasant, 145 Cal. 410, 78 Pac. 957, 104 Am. St. 61; Kenniff v. Caulfield, 140 Cal. 34, 73 Pac. 803; Beattie v. Crewdson; 124 Cal. 577, 57 Pac. 463; Bassick Min. Co. v. Davis, 11 Colo. 130, 17 Pac. 294; Rush v. Mitchell, 71 Iowa 333, 32 N. W. 367; Sillyman v. King, 36 Iowa 207; Arlington State Bank v. Paulsen, 57 Nebr. 717, 78 N. W. 303; American Exch. Bank. v. Fockler, 49 Nebr. 713, 68 N. W. 1039; Bowman v. Griffith, 35 Nebr. 361, 53 N. W. 140; Ferry v. Laible, 31 N. J. Eq. 566; Weber v. Rothchild, 15 Ore.

show that the prior instrument was not recorded.[2] It has also been held that want of notice may be inferred from proof that the junior claimant took for value and in due course of business.[3]

Under the Texas decisions, it seems that the burden is on a junior purchaser to show that he purchased for value and without notice; but in the case of a lien creditor the burden is placed on the prior purchaser to show that the creditor had notice before his lien attached.[4] A recital in the purchaser's deed that he had paid the purchase-money is not sufficient evidence to establish that fact so as to constitute him an innocent purchaser for value.[5]

§ 555. **Notice before payment of consideration.**—Notice has effect if received at any time before the trade is completed by the payment of the consideration. A subsequent purchaser is bound by notice of a prior unrecorded conveyance, or of any other right or title to the property, although not received till after he has agreed upon the terms of the trade, if it be received before he has actually paid the consideration, or in any way put himself to disadvantage by a partial completion of the transaction.[6] The reason assigned in support of this rule is

385, 15 Pac. 650; Richards v. Snyder, 11 Ore. 501, 6 Pac. 186; Lupo v. True, 16 S. Car. 579; Green v. Robertson, 30 Tex. Civ. App. 236, 70 S. W. 345.

[2] Lake v. Hancock, 38 Fla. 53, 20 So. 811, 56 Am. St. 159.

[3] Wright v. Larson, 51 Minn. 321, 53 N. W. 712, 38 Am. St. 504; Newton v. Newton, 46 Minn. 33, 48 N. W. 450.

[4] Turner v. Cochran, 94 Tex. 480, 61 S. W. 923. See also Barnett v. Squyres, 93 Tex. 193, 54 S. W. 241, 77 Am. St. 854; Green v. Robertson, 30 Tex. Civ. App. 236, 70 S. W. 345.

[5] Bremer v. Case, 60 Tex. 151; Watkins v. Edwards, 23 Tex. 443.

[6] Wormley v. Wormley, 8 Wheat (U. S.) 421, 5 L. ed. 651; Flagg v. Mann, 2 Sumn. (U. S.) 486; Wood v. Mann, 1 Sumn. (U. S.) 506; Hoxie v. Carr, 1 Sumn. (U. S.) 173; Bank of United States v. Lee, 5 Cranch (U. S.) 319, Fed. Cas. No. 922; Trice v. Comstock, 121 Fed. 620, 57 C. C. A. 646, 61 L. R. A. 176; Balfour v. Parkinson, 84 Fed. 855; Wells v. Morrow, 38 Ala. 125; Nelson v. Dunn, 15 Ala. 501; Moore v. Clay, 7 Ala. 742; Cooper v. Ryan, 73 Ark.

37, 83 S. W. 328; Duncan v. Johnson, 13 Ark. 190; Mackey v. Bowles, 98 Ga. 730, 25 S. E. 834; Schultze v. Houfes, 96 Ill. 335; Baldwin v. Sager, 70 Ill. 503; Keys v. Test, 33 Ill. 316; Moshier v. Knox College, 32 Ill. 155; Brown v. Welch, 18 Ill. 343, 68 Am. Dec. 549; Anderson v. Hubble, 93 Ind. 570, 47 Am. Rep. 394; Heck v. Fink, 85 Ind. 6; Rhodes v. Green, 36 Ind. 7; Wilson v. Hunter, 30 Ind. 466; Walker v. Cox, 25 Ind. 271; Lewis v. Phillips, 17 Ind. 108, 79 Am. Dec. 457; Dugan v. Battier, 3 Blackf. (Ind.) 245, 25 Am. Dec. 105; Gallion v. McCaslin, 1 Blackf. (Ind.) 91, 12 Am. Rep. 208; Kitteridge v. Chapman, 36 Iowa 348; Barney v. McCarty, 15 Iowa 510, 83 Am. Dec. 427; English v. Waples, 13 Iowa 57; Blight v. Banks, 6 T. B. Mon. (Ky.) 191, 17 Am. Dec. 136; Nantz v. McPherson, 7 T. B. Mon. (Ky.) 597, 18 Am. Dec. 216; Halstead v. Bank of Kentucky, 4 J. J. Marsh. (Ky.) 554; Palmer v. Williams, 24 Mich. 328; Blanchard v. Tyler, 12 Mich. 329, 86 Am. Dec. 57; Warner v. Whittaker, 6 Mich. 133, 72 Am. Dec. 65; Dixon v. Hill, 5 Mich. 404; Thomas v. Stone, Walk. Ch. (Mich.)

that the completion of the purchase, after notice of the prior equity, is a fraud upon the prior claimant.[7]

There is some conflict of authority in the application of the rule, and considerations of natural justice and equity are frequently allowed to modify its rigor, to suit the exigencies of the particular facts. As a general rule, the purchaser is not entitled to protection if he receives notice before he acquires title by deed,[8] even though he has paid the entire purchase-price before notice;[9] and the same principle has been applied to cases of part payment.[10]

Under the general rule prevailing in the United States, if the purchaser has not obtained the legal title before notice of the prior equity, even though he may have an equitable title by contract and payment without notice, he can not defeat or postpone the prior equity by acquiring the legal estate after notice, unless his own equity is of superior merit; for in order to obtain priority as a bona fide purchaser

117; Minor v. Willoughby, 3 Minn. 239; Parker v. Foy, 43 Miss. 260, 5 Am. Rep. 484; Kilcrease v. Lum, 36 Miss. 569; Bishop v. Schneider, 46 Mo. 472, 2 Am. Rep. 533; Aubuchon v. Bender, 44 Mo. 560; Paul v. Fulton, 25 Mo. 156; Halsa v. Halsa, 8 Mo. 303; Patten v. Moore, 32 N. H. 382; Brinton v. Scull, 55 N. J. Eq. 747, 35 Atl. 843; Dean v. Anderson, 34 N. J. Eq. 496; Haughwort v. Murphy, 21 N. J. Eq. 118; Losey v. Simpson, 11 N. J. Eq. 246; Weaver v. Barden, 49 N. Y. 286; Penfield v. Dunbar, 64 Barb. (N. Y.) 239; Jewett v. Palmer, 7 Johns. Ch. (N. Y.) 65, 11 Am. Dec. 401; Heatley v. Finster, 2 Johns. Ch. (N. Y.) 159; Murray v. Ballou, 1 Johns. Ch. (N. Y.) 566; Frost v. Beekman, 1 Johns. Ch. (N. Y.) 288, reversed 18 Johns. 544, 9 Am. Dec. 246; Farmers' Loan Co. v. Maltby, 8 Paige (N. Y.) 361; Howlett v. Thompson, 1 Ired. Eq. (N. Car.) 369; Morris v. Daniels, 35 Ohio. St. 406; Wood v. Rayburn, 18 Ore. 3, 22 Pac. 521; Musgrove v. Bonser, 5 Ore. 313, 20 Am. Rep. 737; Henry v. Raiman, 25 Pa. St. 354, 64 Am. Dec. 703; Hoffman v. Strohecker, 7 Watts. (Pa.) 86, 32 Am. Dec. 740; Bush v. Bush, 3 Strob. Eq. (S. Car.) 131, 51 Am. Dec. 675; Peay v. Seigler, 48 S. Car. 496, 26 S. E. 885, 59 Am. St. 731; Lynch v. Hancock, 14 S. Car. 66; Otis v.

Payne, 86 Tenn. 663, 8 S. W. 848; Pillow v. Shannon, 3 Yerg. (Tenn.) 508; Bonner v. Stephens, 60 Tex. 616; Fraim v. Frederick, 32 Tex. 294; Wilcox v. Calloway, 1 Wash. (Va.) 38; Tibbs v. Zirkle, 55 W. Va. 49, 46 S. E. 701, 104 Am. St. 977; Everts v. Agnes, 4 Wis. 343, 65 Am. Dec. 314; Beckett v. Cordley, 1 Bro. C. C. 353.

[7] Gallion v. McCaslin, 1 Blackf. (Ind.) 91, 12 Am. Dec. 208; Fraim v. Frederick, 32 Tex. 294; Curtis v. Lunn, 6 Munf. (Va.) 42.

[8] Mackey v. Bowles, 98 Ga. 730, 25 S. E. 834; Hoover v. Donally, 3 Hen. & M. (Va.) 316; Blair v. Owles, 1 Munf. (Va.) 38; Clark v. Sayres, 55 W. Va. 512, 47 S. E. 312; More v. Mayhow, Ch. Cas. (pt. 1) 34, Freem. Ch. 175, 18 Vin. Abr. 115. See also Frost v. Beekman, 1 Johns. Ch. (N. Y.) 288, 9 Am. Dec. 246.

[9] Fash v. Ravesies, 32 Ala. 451; Gallion v. McCaslin, 1 Blackf. (Ind.) 91, 12 Am. Dec. 208; Corn v. Sims, 3 Metc. (Ky.) 391; Peabody v. Fenton, 3 Barb. Ch. (N. Y.) 451; Wigg v. Wigg, 1 Atk. 384. See also Halley v. Oldham, 5 B. Mon. (Ky.) 233, 41 Am. Dec. 262; Bush v. Bush, 3 Strob. Eq. (S. Car.) 131, 51 Am. Dec. 675.

[10] Mackey v. Bowles, 98 Ga. 730 (recovery of partial payment); Harrison v. Boring, 44 Tex. 255.

without notice, he must acquire not only the equitable, but the legal title without notice.[11]

In England, however, and some of the states, a purchaser who without notice and for value has acquired an equitable title may thereafter, even with notice of the prior equity, acquire the legal estate and become entitled to full protection as a bona fide purchaser;[12] provided he acquires such interest without breach of trust.[13]

If a mortgagee has notice of a prior unrecorded mortgage before paying over the money secured by his mortgage, he takes subject to the unrecorded mortgage, though his own mortgage has already been recorded.[14] But after the sale is completed by the payment of the consideration, notice of a prior mortgage is without effect.[15]

§ 556. Part payment before notice—Payment by notes.—A purchaser who has paid a part of the purchase-money before receiving notice of prior equities or rights is protected to the extent of such payment, but no further.[16] He is entitled to invoke the aid of the equita-

[11] Fash v. Ravesies, 32 Ala. 451; Dodd v. Doty, 98 Ill. 393 (burden upon holder of prior equity); Corn v. Sims, 3 Metc. (Ky.) 391; Wing v. McDowell, Walk. Ch. (Mich.) 175; Nulsen v. Wishon, 68 Mo. 383; Boskowitz v. Davis, 12 Nev. 446; Grimstone v. Carter, 3 Paige (N. Y.) 421, 24 Am. Dec. 230; Goldsborough v. Turner, 67 N. Car. 403; Craig v. Leiper, 2 Yerg. (Tenn.) 193, 24 Am. Dec. 479; Lewis v. Madisons, 1 Munf. (Va.) 303. See also Mackey v. Bowles, 98 Ga. 730, 25 S. E. 834; Halley v. Oldham, 5 B. Mon. (Ky.) 233, 41 Am. Dec. 262; Bush v. Bush, 3 Strob. Eq. (S. Car.) 131, 51 Am. Dec. 675. But see Carroll v. Johnston, 2 Jones Eq. (55 N. Car.) 120; Jones v. Zollicoffer, 4 N. Car. 645, 7 Am. Dec. 708.

[12] Campbell v. Brackenridge, 8 Blackf. (Ind.) 471; Weston v. Dunlap, 50 Iowa 183; Gjerness v. Mathews, 27 Minn. 320, 7 N. W. 355; Zellman v. Moore, 21 Grat. (Va.) 313; Lewis v. Madisons, 1 Munf. (Va.) 303; Sanders v. Deligne, 2 Freem. Ch. 124; Huntington v. Greenville, 1 Vern. 52; Bassett v. Nosworthy, Finch 102; Goleborn v. Alcock, 2 Sim. 552; Stanhope v. Verney, 2 Eden 85; Bailey v. Barnes, 1 Ch. 25; Blackwood v. London

Chartered Bank, L. R. 5 P. C. 92; Carter v. Carter, 3 Kay & J. 636, criticising Sherley v. Fagg, Ch. Cas. (pt. 1) 68, and Turner v. Buck, 22 Vin. Abr. 21. See also Phelps v. Morrison, 24 N. J. Eq. 195; Gibler v. Trimble, 14 Ohio 323. But see Gallion v. McCaslin, 1 Blackf. (Ind.) 91, 12 Am. Dec. 208; Curtis v. Lunn, 6 Munf. (Va.) 42.

[13] Saunders v. Dehew, 2 Vern 271; Allen v. Knight, 5 Hare 272, 11 Jur. 527; Baillie v. McKewan, 35 Beav. 177; Munford v. Stohwasser, L. R. 18 Eq. 556; Carter v. Carter, 3 Kay & J. 617.

[14] Schultze v. Houfes, 96 Ill. 335; Otis v. Payne, 86 Tenn. 663, 8 S. W. 848.

[15] Redden v. Miller, 95 Ill. 336; Syer v. Bundy, 9 La. Ann. 540; Watkins v. Reynolds, 123 N. Y. 211, 25 N. E. 322; Lynch v. Hancock, 14 S. Car. 66; Jamison v. Gjemenson, 10 Wis. 411.

[16] Flagg v. Mann, 2 Sumn. (U. S.) 547; Craft v. Russell, 67 Ala. 9; Florence S. M. Co. v. Zeigler, 58 Ala. 221; Wells v. Morrow, 38 Ala. 125; Dufphey v. Frenaye, 5 Stew. & P. (Ala.) 215; Marchbanks v. Banks, 44 Ark. 48; Combination Land Co. v. Morgan, 95 Cal. 548, 30 Pac. 1102; Redden v. Miller, 95 Ill. 336; Slat-

ble principle, that he who asks equity must do equity, and therefore the adverse claimant should reimburse the amount actually paid by the purchaser before receiving notice of the claim.[17] In accord with this view it is held that where the purchaser has paid part of the price before notice, and taken possession under contract, he may complete his purchase by paying the balance and taking a conveyance; and can only be deprived of the estate so acquired on condition of being reimbursed for the sums paid before notice.[18] Although a purchaser has obtained a conveyance of the legal title before notice, if he receives notice before paying any part of the purchase-money, he is not protected as a bona fide purchaser. In such case, notice before payment is equivalent to notice before the contract, for he could still protect himself by withholding payment.[19] But he is not protected in any pay-

tery v. Rafferty, 93 Ill. 277; Baldwin v. Sager, 70 Ill. 503; Moshier v. Knox College, 32 Ill. 155; Lewis v. Phillips, 17 Ind. 108, 79 Am. Dec. 457; Kitteridge v. Chapman, 36 Iowa 348; Hardin v. Harrington, 11 Bush (Ky.) 367; Eubank v. Poston, 5 T. B. Mon. (Ky.) 285; Lain v. Morton, 23 Ky. L. 438, 63 S. W. 286; Sheldon v. Holmes, 58 Mich. 138, 24 N. W. 795; Warner v. Whittaker, 6 Mich. 133, 72 Am. Dec. 65; Dixon v. Hill, 5 Mich. 404; Thomas v. Stone, Walk. Ch. (Mich.) 117; Parker v .Foy, 43 Miss. 260, 5 Am. Rep. 484; Servis v. Beatty, 32 Miss. 52. See also Digby v. Jones, 67 Mo. 104; Paul v. Fulton, 25 Mo. 156; Brinton v. Scull, 55 N. J. Eq. 747, 35 Atl. 843; Haughwout v. Murphy, 22 N. J. Eq. 531; Losey v. Simpson, 11 N. J. Eq. 246; Macauley v. Smith, 132 N. Y. 524, 30 N. E. 997, 10 N. Y. S. 578; Pickett v. Barron, 29 Barb. (N. Y.) 505; Stalker v. McDonald, 6 Hill (N. Y.) 93, 40 Am. Dec. 389; Farmers' L. &c. Co. v. Maltby, 8 Paige (N. Y.) 361; Tufts v. Tufts, 18 Wend. (N. Y.) 621; Fessler's Appeal, 75 Pa. St. 483; Juvenal v. Jackson, 14 Pa. St. 519; Beck v. Uhrich, 13 Pa. St. 636, 53 Am. Dec. 507, 16 Pa. St. 499; Uhrich v. Beck, 13 Pa. St. 639; Lewis v. Bradford, 10 Watts (Pa.) 82; Kunkle v. Wolfersberger, 6 Watts (Pa.) 126; Evans v. Templeton, 69 Tex. 375, 6 S. W. 843, 5 Am. St. 71; Fraim v. Frederick, 32 Tex. 294; Duval v. Bibb, 4 Hen. & M. (Va.) 113, 4 Am.

Dec. 506; Webb v. Bailey, 41 W. Va. 463, 23 S. E. 644; Mitchell v. Dawson, 23 W. Va. 86; Everts v. Agnes, 4 Wis. 343, 65 Am. Dec. 314. See also Wood v. Mann, 1 Sumn. (U. S.) 512; Cox v. Romine, 9 Grat. (Va.) 27. But see Doswell v. Buchanan, 3 Leigh (Va.) 365, 23 Am. Dec. 280.

[17] Kiteridge v. Chapman, 36 Iowa 348; Youst v. Martin, 3 Serg. & R. (Pa.) 423; Bellas v. McCarty, 10 Watts (Pa.) 13.

[18] Youst v. Martin, 3 Serg. & R. (Pa.) 423. See also Phelps v. Morrison, 24 N. J. Eq. 195; Union Canal Co. v. Young, 1 Whart. (Pa.) 410, 30 Am. Dec. 212.

[19] Wormley v Wormley, 8 Wheat. (U. S.) 421, 5 L. ed. 651; Garnett v. Macon, 2 Brock. (U. S.) 185, Fed. Cas. No. 5245, 6 Call 308; Trice v. Comstock, 57 C. C. A. 646, 121 Fed. 620, 61 L. R. A. 176; Kenniff v. Caulfield, 140 Cal. 34, 73 Pac. 803; Beattie v. Crewdson, 124 Cal. 577, 57 Pac. 463; Combination Land Co. v. Morgan, 95 Cal. 548, 30 Pac. 1102; Eversdon v. Mayhew, 65 Cal. 163, 3 Pac. 641; Redden v. Miller, 95 Ill. 336; Citizens' State Bank v. Julian, 153 Ind. 655, 55 N. E. 1007; Smith v. Schweigerer, 129 Ind. 363, 28 N. E. 696; Anderson v. Hubble, 93 Ind. 570, 47 Am. Rep. 394; Holcroft v. Hunter, 3 Blackf. (Ind.) 147; Kitteridge v. Chapman, 36 Iowa 348; Sillyman v. King, 36 Iowa 207; Halstead v. Bank of Kentucky, 4 J. J. Marsh. (Ky.) 554; Price v. Mc-

ment made by him after receiving notice of any prior right or equity in another.[20] A payment by giving a mortgage for a part of the purchase-money, after the purchaser had received notice of a prior unrecorded conveyance, does not protect the purchaser, and any payment made by him upon such mortgage is made in his own wrong.[21]

While the weight of authority supports the rule that a purchaser having made part payment before notice will be protected pro tanto, yet in some jurisdictions, including Indiana, partial payment does not seem to alter the rule, and a purchaser is entitled to no protection unless he has taken a conveyance and paid the purchase-money in full before notice.[22]

Donald, 1 Md. 403, 54 Am. Dec. 657; Matson v. Melchor, 42 Mich. 477, 4 N. W. 200; Palmer v. Williams, 24 Mich. 328; Blanchard v. Tyler, 12 Mich. 339, 86 Am. Dec. 57; Minor v. Willoughby, 3 Minn. 225; Cassady v. Wallace, 102 Mo. 575, 15 S. W. 138; Bishop v. Schneider, 46 Mo. 472, 2 Am. Rep. 533; Paul v. Fulton, 25 Mo. 156; Greenlee v. Marquis, 49 Mo. App. 290; Veith v. McMurtry, 26 Nebr. 341, 42 N. W. 6; Keyser v. Angle, 40 N. J. Eq. 481, 4 Atl. 641; Dean v. Anderson, 34 N. J. Eq. 496; Harris v. Norton, 16 Barb. (N. Y.) 264; Jewett v. Palmer, 7 Johns. Ch. (N. Y.) 65, 11 Am. Dec. 401; Murray v. Finster, 2 Johns. Ch. (N. Y.) 155; Howlett v. Thompson, 1 Ired. Eq. (N. Car.) 369; Halloran v. Holmes, 13 N. Dak. 411, 101 N. W. 310; Wood v. Rayburn, 18 Ore. 3, 22 Pac. 521; Juvenal v. Jackson, 14 Pa. St. 519; Ellis v. Young, 31 S. Car. 322, 9 S. E. 955; Hutchins v. Chapman, 37 Tex. 612; Fraim v. Frederick, 32 Tex. 294; Hardingham v. Nicholls, 3 Atk. 304; Tildesley v. Lodge, 3 Smale & G. 543. See also Wells v. Morrow, 38 Ala. 125; Hayden v. Charter Oak Driving Park, 63 Conn. 142, 27 Atl. 232; Walton v. Hargroves, 42 Miss. 18, 97 Am. Dec. 429; Corrigan v. Schmidt, 126 Mo. 304, 28 S. W. 874; Arnholt v. Hartwig, 73 Mo. 485; Wallace v. Wilson, 30 Mo. 335; Cheek v. Waldron, 39 Mo. App. 21; McNichols v. Richter, 13 Mo. App. 515; Frost v. Beekman, 1 Johns. Ch. (N. Y.) 288, reversed 18 Johns. 544, 9 Am. Dec. 246; Bush v. Bush, 3 Strob. Eq. (S.

Car.) 131, 51 Am. Dec. 675; Williams v. Hollingsworth, 1 Strob. Eq. (S. Car.) 103, 47 Am. Dec. 527; Barstow, v. Beckett, 122 Fed. 140, reversed in 148 Fed. 562, 78 C. C. A. 248, on the ground that purchaser relied on an attorney employed by her to pass upon the title, and she was not chargeable with his fraud in the matter affecting the title.

[20] Wells v. Morrow, 38 Ala. 125; Redden v. Miller, 95 Ill. 336; Slattery v. Rafferty, 93 Ill. 277; Blanchard v. Tyler, 12 Mich. 339, 86 Am. Dec. 57; Warner v. Whittaker, 6 Mich. 133, 72 Am. Dec. 65; Edwards v. Missouri &c. R. Co., 82 Mo. App. 96; Frost v. Beekman, 1 Johns. Ch. (N. Y.) 288; Fraim v. Frederick, 32 Tex. 294; Bullock v. Sprowls (Tex. Civ. App.), 54 S. W. 657; Tate v. Kramer, 1 Tex. Civ. App. 427, 23 S. W. 255; Duval v. Bibb, 4 Hen. & M. (Va.) 113, 4 Am. Dec. 506; Hamlin v. Wright, 26 Wis. 50. See also Palmer v. Williams, 24 Mich. 328; Garmire v. Willy, 36 Nebr. 340, 54 N. W. 562; Murray v. Finster, 2 Johns. Ch. (N. Y.) 155; Curtis v. Hitchcock, 10 Paige (N. Y.) 399.

[21] Marchbanks v. Banks, 44 Ark. 48; Quirk v. Thomas, 6 Mich. 76; Losey v. Simpson, 11 N. J. Eq. 246; Jewett v. Palmer, 7 Johns. Ch. (N. Y.) 65, 11 Am. Dec. 401.

[22] Heck v. Fink, 85 Ind. 6; Dugan v. Vattier, 3 Blackf. (Ind.) 245, 25 Am. Dec. 105; Gallion v. McCaslin, 1 Blackf. (Ind.) 91, 12 Am. Dec. 208; Tourville v. Naish, 3 P. Wms. 306; Henderson v. Graves, 2 U. C. Err. & App. 21. See also Anderson

Even if the purchaser has given a mortgage, receiving a bond or a note not negotiable, before receiving notice of a prior unrecorded deed, but receives such notice afterward, before making payment of the note and mortgage, he is not entitled to claim the protection of a bona fide purchaser, and a subsequent payment of the note is in his own wrong.[23] This is upon the ground that it is in the power of the purchaser to resist the payment of his mortgage, in whosesoever hands it may be. But if the purchaser has given a negotiable note secured by mortgage for a part of the purchase-money, the assignee of such mortgage takes it free from all prior equities, and it is not in the power of the mortgagor to resist the payment; and therefore the giving of such a mortgage for a part of the purchase-money is a payment which protects the purchaser against any equities of which he had no notice before the giving of the mortgage, though he may have received notice while the mortgage is still outstanding.[24]

When the purchase has been completed by payment of the purchase-money and conveyance of the legal title, before actual or constructive notice to the purchaser, notice reaching him thereafter is ineffectual against the estate he has acquired and his rights as a bona fide purchaser.[25]

§ **557. Purchaser with notice from one without notice.**—A purchaser with notice may acquire a good title from one who was a purchaser for value without notice. The rule that a purchaser of property, with notice of some prior adverse claim to or interest in such property, takes subject to such interest, is subject to the limitation that, if a person with such notice acquires a legal title to the property from one who is without such notice, he is entitled to the same protection as his vendor, as otherwise it would very much clog the sale of estates.[26] A pur-

v. Hubble, 93 Ind. 570, 47 Am. Rep. 394; Lewis v. Phillips, 17 Ind. 108, 79 Am. Dec. 457.

[23] Rhodes v. Green, 36 Ind. 7; Lewis v. Phillips, 17 Ind. 108, 79 Am. Dec. 457; Green v. Green, 41 Kans. 472, 21 Pac. 586; Blanchard v. Tyler, 12 Mich. 339, 86 Am. Dec. 57; Haughwout v. Murphy, 21 N. J. Eq. 118.

[24] Hall v. Hall, 38 Ala. 131; Digby v. Jones, 67 Mo. 104.

[25] Mundine v. Pitts, 14 Ala. 84; English v. Lindley, 194 Ill. 181, 62 N. E. 522; Baldwin v. Sager, 70 Ill. 503; Owings v. Jouit, 2 A. K. Marsh. (Ky.) 380; Syer v. Bundy, 9 La.

Ann. 540; Gouverneur v. Lynch, 2 Paige (N. Y.) 300; Newlin v. Osborne, 6 Jones L. (51 N. Car.) 128, 72 Am. Dec. 566; Juvenal v. Jackson, 14 Pa. St. 519; Hoult v. Donahue, 21 W. Va. 294. See also Chew v. Barnet, 11 Serg. & R. (Pa.) 389.

[26] Piatt v. Vattier, 1 McLean (U. S.) 146; Bean v. Smith, 2 Mason (U. S.) 252; Wood v. Mann, 1 Sumn. (U. S.) 506; Boone v. Chiles, 10 Pet. (U. S.) 177, 9 L. ed. 388; Mead v. Gallatin, 151 Fed. 1006, 81 C. C. A. 192; Reed v. Munn, 148 Fed. 737, 80 C. C. A. 215; Ryan v. Staples, 78 Fed. 563, 23 C. C. A. 551; Whitfield v. Riddle, 78 Ala. 99; Bartlett v.

chaser without notice would otherwise be deprived of the full measure of protection to which he is entitled, that is, a free right of disposal,—

Varner, 56 Ala. 580; Cahalan v. Monroe, 56 Ala. 303; White v. Moffett, 108 Ark. 490, 158 S. W. 505; Fargason v. Edrington, 49 Ark. 207, 4 S. W. 763; Abadie v. Lobero, 36 Cal. 390; Moore v. Allen, 26 Colo. 197, 57 Pac. 698, 77 Am. St. 255; Blatchley v. Osborn, 33 Conn. 226; Doyle v. Wade, 23 Fla. 90, 1 So. 516; Eldridge v. Post, 20 Fla. 579; Mays v. Redman, .134 Ga. 870, 68 S. E. 738; Peavy v. Dure, 131 Ga. 104, 62 S. E. 47; Lee v. Cato, 27 Ga. 637, 73 Am. Dec. 746; Colquitt v. Thomas, 8 Ga. 258; English v. Lindley, 194 Ill. 181, 62 N. E. 522; Peck v. Arehart, 95 Ill. 113; St. Joseph Manuf. Co. v. Daggett, 84 Ill. 556; Shinn v. Shinn, 15 Bradw. (Ill.) 141; Buck v. Foster, 147 Ind. 530, 46 N. E. 920, 62 Am. St. 427; Klinger v. Lemler, 135 Ind. 77, 34 N. E. 698; Old Nat. Bank v. Findley, 131 Ind. 225, 31 N. E. 62; Trentman v. Eldridge, 98 Ind. 525; Arnold v. Smith, 80 Ind. 417; Studabaker v. Langard, 79 Ind. 320; Sharpe v. Davis, 76 Ind. 17; Evans v. Nealis, 69 Ind. 148; McShirley v. Birt, 44 Ind. 382; East v. Pugh, 71 Iowa 162, 32 N. W. 309; Hurley v. Osler, 44 Iowa 642; Ashcraft v. De Armond, 44 Iowa 229; Chambers v. Hubbard, 40 Iowa 432; Varney v. Deskins, 146 Ky. 27, 141 S. W. 411; Lindsey v. Rankin, 4 Bibb (Ky.) 482; Hill v. McNichol, 76 Maine 314; Brackett v. Ridlon, 54 Maine 426; Pierce v. Faunce, 47 Maine 507; Livingstone v. Murphy, 187 Mass. 315, 72 N. E. 1012, 105 Am. St. 400; Trull v. Bigelow, 16 Mass. 406, 8 Am. Dec. 444; Dana v. Newhall, 13 Mass. 498; Glidden v. Hunt, 24 Pick. (Mass.) 221; Boynton v. Rees, 8 Pick. (Mass.) 329, 19 Am. Dec. 326; Shotwell v. Harrison, 22 Mich. 410; Godfroy v. Disbrow, Walk. Ch. (Mich.) 260; Equitable Securities Co. v. Sheppard, 78 Miss. 217, 28 So. 842; Fulton v. Woodman, 54 Miss. 158; Price v. Martin, 46 Miss. 489; Lusk v. McNamer, 24 Miss. 58; Hendricks v. Calloway, 211 Mo. 536, 111 S. W. 60; Van Syckel v. Beam, 110 Mo. 589, 19 S. W. 946; Drey v. Doyle, 99 Mo. 459, 12 S. W. 287; Craig v. Zimmerman, 87 Mo. 475, 56 Am. Rep. 466; Funkhouser v. Lay, 78 Mo. 458; Ford v. Axelson, 74 Nebr. 92, 103 N. W. 1039; Bell v. Twilight, 18 N. H. 159, 45 Am. Dec. 367; Holmes v. Stout, 10 N. J. Eq. 410; Paul v. Kerswell, 60 N. J. L. 273, 37 Atl. 1102; Roll v. Rea, 50 N. J. L. 264, 12 Atl. 905; Jospe v. Danis, 138 App. Div. 544, 123 N. Y. S. 360; Lacustrine Fer. Co. v. Lake Guano &c. Co., 82 N. Y. 476; Wood v. Chapin, 13 N. Y. 509, 67 Am. Dec. 62; Webster v. Van Steenbergh, 46 Barb. (N. Y.) 211; Cook v. Travis, 22 Barb. (N. Y.) 338, affd. 20 N. Y. 400; Demarest v. Wynkoop, 3 Johns. Ch. (N. Y.) 147, 8 Am. Dec. 467; Bumpus v. Platner, 1 Johns. Ch. (N. Y.) 213; Varick v. Briggs, 6 Paige (N. Y.) 323; Allison v. Hagan, 12 Nev. 38; Phillips v. Buchanan Lumber Co., 151 N. Car. 519, 66 S. E. 603; Taylor v. Kelly, 3 Jones Eq. (N. Car.) 240; Card v. Patterson, 5 Ohio St. 319; Ashton's Appeal, 73 Pa. St. 153; Church v. Ruland, 64 Pa. 432; Filby v. Miller, 25 Pa. St. 264; Bracken v. Miller, 4 Watts & S. (Pa.) 102; Hood v. Fahnestock, 8 Watts (Pa.) 489, 34 Am. Dec. 489; Southern R. Co. v. Carroll, 86 S. Car. 56, 67 S. E. 4, 138 Am. St. 1017; Perkins v. Hays, Cooke (Tenn.) 189, 5 Am. Dec. 680; Long v. Shelton (Tex. Civ. App.), 155 S. W. 945; Masterson v. Crosby (Tex. Civ. App.), 152 S. W. 173; Phillips v. Campbell (Tex. Civ. App.), 146 S. W. 319; Thomason v. Berwick, 52 Tex. Civ. App. 153, 113 S. W. 567; Laffare v. Knight (Tex. Civ. App.), 101 S. W. 1034; Allen v. Anderson (Tex. Civ. App.), 96 S. W. 54; Garner v. Boyle, 34 Tex. Civ. App. 42, 77 S. W. 987; Long v Fields, 31 Tex. Civ. App. 241, 71 S. W. 774; Hickman v. Hoffman, 11 Tex. Civ. App. 605, 33 S. W. 257; Goddard v. Reagan, 8 Tex. Civ. App. 272, 28 S. W. 352; Barber v. Richardson, 57 Vt. 408; Day v. Clark, 25 Vt. 397; Rorer Iron Co. v. Trout, 83 Va. 397, 2 S. E. 713; Bernard v. Benson, 58 Wash. 191, 108 Pac. 439, 137 Am. St. 1051; Hawkes v. Hoffman, 56 Wash. 120,

the right to sell and transfer a perfect title to any purchaser. The rule is obviously necessary to secure a purchaser, without notice, the full benefit of his purchase.[27]

Therefore, if a person takes a mortgage or other conveyance with notice of a prior incumbrance, but takes it from one who purchased for value without such notice, and therefore acquired a title good against such incumbrance, such subsequent purchaser with notice may shelter himself under the protection which the law affords his grantor; he takes the latter's rights.[28] Thus a person charged with notice may take a valid conveyance from a purchaser of realty for value without notice of a prior unrecorded conveyance,[29] or incumbrance.[30] The grantor must, however, have been a purchaser for value, and not merely a volunteer who took a title subject to equities, as in such case the purchaser from him would take subject to the same equities.[31]

Furthermore the grantor must have purchased the legal title, and if he held the equitable title only, the rule does not apply.[32] When the party without notice is only a nominal party, and the real party in interest has notice, neither can be considered a purchaser without notice.[33] And the fact that the trustee in a trust deed has no notice of an existing incumbrance will not protect the beneficiary, purchasing with notice at a sale by the trustee under a power in the deed.[34]

One who takes a mortgage, with notice of a prior unrecorded mortgage, is not the less a purchaser with notice, and subject to such mortgage, because he is at the same time informed that the debt secured by such mortgage is usurious.[35]

By the weight of authority a judgment creditor who has notice of

105 Pac. 156, 24 L. R. A. (N. S.) 1038; Pringle v. Dunn, 37 Wis. 449, 467, 19 Am. Rep. 772; Lowther v. Carlton, 2 Atk. 242; Brandlyn v. Ord, 1 Atk. 571; Harrison v. Forth, Prec. Ch. 51; Sweet v. Southcote, 2 Bro. Ch. 66, 1 Bro. C. C. 353. See also Houston Oil Co. v. Bayne (Tex. Civ. App.), 141 S. W. 544.

[27] Lee v. Cato, 27 Ga. 637, 73 Am. Dec. 746; Truluck v. Peeples, 3 Ga. 446; Studabaker v. Langard, 79 Ind. 320; Johns v. Sewell, 33 Ind. 1; Holmes v. Stout, 10 N. J. Eq. 419.

[28] Chance v. McWhirter, 26 Ga. 315; Harrington v. Allen, 48 Miss. 492.

[29] Chandler v. Tardy, 58 Ala. 150; Mallory v. Stodder, 6 Ala. 801; English v. Lindley, 194 Ill. 181, 62 N. E.

522; Shotwell v. Harrison, 22 Mich. 410; Bell v. Twilight, 18 N. H. 159, 45 Am. Dec. 367; Holmes v. Stout, 10 N. J. Eq. 419; Roll v. Rea, 50 N. J. L. 264, 12 Atl. 905; Webster v. Van Steenbergh, 46 Barb. (N. Y.) 211; Foster v. Bailey, 82 S. Car. 378, 64 S. E. 423.

[30] Ashmore v. Whatley, 99 Ga. 150, 24 S. E. 941.

[31] Johns v. Sewell, 33 Ind. 1.

[32] Boone v. Chiles, 10 Pet. (U. S.) 177, 9 L. ed. 388.

[33] Runkle v. Gaylord, 1 Nev. 123; Murphy v. Nathans, 46 Pa. St. 508. See also Chance v. McWhorter, 26 Ga. 315.

[34] Gerson v. Pool, 31 Ark. 85.

[35] Beverley v. Brooke, 2 Leigh (Va.) 425.

an unrecorded mortgage at the time of docketing or entering the judgment, holds his lien subject to the mortgage.[36] In several states, however, actual notice is not sufficient, where the conveyance is not recorded.[37]

It is no defense to one who takes a deed of land, with actual knowledge on his part of a previous mortgage upon it, that the parties to the mortgage agreed that it should not be recorded, and the mortgagee received a written guaranty "to hold him harmless from any loss by reason of not recording the deeds."[38]

§ 558. Repurchase by grantee with notice—Revival of existing equities.—But the title of a purchaser without notice can not be transferred free from equities back to a prior grantor who was charged with notice at the time he acquired his former title, for a purchaser can not be allowed to clear off the existing equities, of which he had notice, by transferring the title to an innocent purchaser, and then repurchasing the property. The existing equities of which he had knowledge revive and attach to the property to the same extent that they formerly attached to it in his hands.[39] Thus, a second mortgage, which in the hands of the mortgagee is subject to a prior subsisting mortgage by reason of his notice thereof, it not being a lien of record,

[36] United States v. Griswold, 8 Fed. 556, 7 Sawy. (U. S.) 311; Byers v. Engles, 16 Ark. 543; Thomas v. Vanlieu, 28 Cal. 616; Columbus Buggy Co. v. Graves, 108 Ill. 459; Williams v. Tatnall, 29 Ill. 553; Sinking Fund Comrs. v. Wilson, 1 Ind. 356; Fords v. Vance, 17 Iowa 94; Lamberton v. Merchants' Nat. Bank, 24 Minn. 281; Bass v. Estill, 50 Miss. 300; Walker v. Gilbert, Freem. Ch. (Miss.) 85; Hutchinson v. Bramhall, 42 N. J. Eq. 372, 7 Atl. 873; Britton's Appeal, 45 Pa. St. 172; Barnett v. Squyres (Tex. Civ. App.), 52 S. W. 612; Stovall v. Odell, 10 Tex. Civ. App. 169, 30 S. W. 66. See also Clark v. Greene, 73 Minn. 467, 76 N. W. 263 (insufficient notice by posting signs); H. C. Tack Co. v. Ayers, 56 N. J. Eq. 56, 38 Atl. 194; Condit v. Wilson, 36 N. J. Eq. 370 (insufficient statement by debtor); Hulings v. Guthrie, 4 Pa. St. 123; Hibberd v. Bovier, 1 Grant Cas. (Pa.) 266. See ante § 461.

[37] Winston v. Hodges, 102 Ala. 304, 15 So. 528; Smith v. Jordan, 25 Ga. 687; Coward v. Culver, 12 Heisk. (Tenn.) 540; Lillard v. Rucker, 9 Yerg. (Tenn.) 64; March v. Chambers, 30 Grat. (Va.) 299; Eidson v. Huff, 29 Grat. (Va.) 338.

[38] Lord v. Doyle, 1 Cliff. (U. S.) 453.

[39] Bourquin v. Bourquin, 120 Ga. 115, 47 S. E. 639; Johnson v. Gibson, 116 Ill. 294, 6 N. E. 205; Trentman v. Eldridge, 98 Ind. 525; Durham v. Craig, 79 Ind. 117; Mitchell v. Aten, 37 Kans. 33, 14 Pac. 497; Brophy Min. Co. v. Brophy &c. Gold &c. Min. Co., 15 Nev. 101; Allison v. Hagan, 12 Nev. 38; Clark v. McNeal, 114 N. Y. 287, 21 N. E. 405; Schutt v. Large, 6 Barb. (N. Y.) 373; Bumpus v. Platner, 1 Johns. Ch. (N. Y.) 213; Church v. Ruland, 64 Pa. St. 432; Church v. Church, 25 Pa. St. 278; Ely v. Wilcox, 26 Wis. 91; Troy City Bank v. Wilcox, 24 Wis. 671; In re Stapleford Colliery Co., 14 Ch. D. 445, 49 L. J. Ch. 498, 42 L. T. Rep. (N. S.) 891; Bovey v. Smith, 1 Vern. Ch. 60, 23 Eng. Reprint 310.

becomes, in the hands of an assignee for value and without notice, free of such prior equitable lien. But the priority of the second mortgage is lost if it be again assigned to the former owner, who had notice of the prior equity of the first mortgage; and it is also lost, and the equity of the first mortgage reattaches, in case there is a foreclosure sale under the second mortgage, and the second mortgagee, who had notice of the prior equity of the first mortgage, becomes the purchaser at such foreclosure sale.[40]

Where land included in a trust deed had previously been conveyed to a third person and reconveyed to the grantor, and the third person, while holding title, had informed the grantee in the trust deed of a fraud of the grantor, it was held that such previous wrongful conduct of the grantor in his dealings with such third person was not sufficient to require the grantee to make inquiries as to the reconveyance executed by the third person, and did not prevent the grantee from being a bona fide purchaser.[41]

Where a grantee of certain land gave a mortgage thereon to secure joint notes of the grantor and grantee, and reconveyed the property to the grantor before the mortgage was recorded, the mortgage being recorded before the deed of reconveyance, it was held that the mortgage was entitled to priority, and was a valid lien on the property, since it was given with the approval and for the benefit of the grantee.[42]

§ 559. Purchaser without notice from one with notice of prior equity.—A person without notice may in good faith acquire a legal title from one who has notice of a prior equitable right or outstanding unrecorded title.[43] In Massachusetts this is declared to be a rule of

[40] Clark v. McNeal, 114 N. Y. 287, 21 N. E. 405.

[41] Smith v. Wofford (Tex. Civ. App.), 97 S. W. 143.

[42] Kehl v. Burgener, 106 Ill. App. 336.

[43] Bean v. Smith, 2 Mason (U. S.) 252; Mallory v. Stodder, 6 Ala. 801; Sears v. Douthitt, 18 Cal. App. 774, 124 Pac. 453; Lee v. Cato, 27 Ga. 637, 73 Am. Dec. 746; Truluck v. Peeples, 3 Ga. 446; Paris v. Lewis, 85 Ill. 597; Dawkins v. Kions, 53 Ind. 164; Brown v. Budd, 2 Ind. 442; Arnett's Committee v. Owens, 23 Ky. L. 1409, 65 S. W. 151; Hardin v. Harrington, 11 Bush (Ky.) 367; Willis v. Valette, 4 Metc. (Ky.) 186; Colgin v. Courrege, 106 La. 684, 31 So. 144; Hill v. McNichol, 76 Maine 314; Brackett v. Ridlon, 54 Maine 426; Pierce v. Faunce, 47 Maine 507; Knox v. Silloway, 10 Maine 201; Morse v. Curtis, 140 Mass. 112, 2 N. E. 929, 54 Am. Rep. 456; Trull v. Bigelow, 16 Mass. 406; Connecticut v. Bradish, 14 Mass. 296; Glidden v. Hunt, 24 Pick. (Mass.) 221; Somes v. Brewer, 2 Pick. (Mass.) 184, 13 Am. Dec. 406; Price v. Martin, 46 Miss. 489; Mullins v. Butte Hdw. Co., 25 Mont. 525, 65 Pac. 1004, 87 Am. St. 430; Hoit v. Russell, 56 N. H. 559; Bell v. Twilight, 18 N. H. 159, 45 Am. Dec. 367; Smith v. Vreeland, 16 N. J. Eq. 198; Dan-

property established by the early decisions cited, which ought not to be departed from. The owner of land mortgaged it to A, and then mortgaged it to B, who had notice of the earlier mortgage, and who recorded his mortgage before the mortgage to A was recorded. After both mortgages were recorded, B assigned his mortgage to C, who had no actual notice of the mortgage to A. It was held, on a writ of entry by A against C, that C had the better title to the land.[44] The last purchaser's "own bona fides is a good defense, and the mala fides of his vendor ought not to invalidate it." Therefore, although one who has notice of a prior unrecorded mortgage can not himself purchase the land, or take a mortgage upon it, without its being subject to such unrecorded mortgage, yet if he sells the land or the mortgage to a purchaser in good faith, before the recording of the prior mortgage, the purchaser from him will acquire a title superior to the unrecorded mortgage; but should such purchaser omit to record his deed or assignment until the mortgage is recorded, he would stand in no better position than his assignor.[45]

In like manner an attaching creditor without notice of an unrecorded deed will hold the estate, although the debtor had notice of it.[46] And in accord with the general rule, a bona fide purchaser without

bury v. Robinson, 14 N. J. Eq. 213, 82 Am. Dec. 244; Slattery v. Schwannecke, 118 N. Y. 543, 23 N. E. 922; Wood v. Chapin, 13 N. Y. 509, 67 Am. Dec. 62; Jackson v. Van Valkenburgh, 8 Cow. (N. Y.) 260; Demarest v. Wynkoop, 3 Johns. Ch. (N. Y.) 129, 8 Am. Dec. 467; Varick v. Briggs, 6 Paige (N. Y.) 323; Phillips v. Stroup, 1 Monag. (Pa.) 517, 17 Atl. 220; Jones v. Hudson, 23 S. Car. 494; Moore v. Curry, 36 Tex. 668; Pringle v. Dunn, 37 Wis. 449, 19 Am. Rep. 772; Mertins v. Joliffe, Amb. 311, 313; Attorney-General v. Wilkins, 17 Beav. 285; Harrison v. Forth, Prec. Ch. 51; M'Queen v. Farquhar, 11 Ves. 467. See also Robertson v. United States Live Stock Co. (Iowa), 145 N. W. 535.

[44] Morse v. Curtis, 140 Mass. 112. The court refers to Flynt v. Arnold, 2 Metc. (Mass.) 619, where Shaw, C. J., expresses his individual opinion against the earlier decisions; but the judgment of the court was put upon another ground, and his remarks are to be considered in the

light of dicta, and not as overruling the earlier adjudications. "The better rule, and the one the least likely to create confusion of titles, seems to us to be, that, if a purchaser, upon examining the registry, finds a conveyance from the owner of the land to his grantor, which gives him a perfect record title completed by what the law, at the time it is recorded, regards as equivalent to a livery of seisin, he is entitled to rely upon such record title, and is not obliged to search the records afterward, in order to see if there has been any prior unrecorded deed of the original owner."

[45] Harrington v. Allen, 48 Miss. 492; Westbrook v. Gleason, 79 N. Y. 23, revg. 14 Hun 245; Fort v. Burch, 5 Denio (N. Y.) 187; Jackson v. Van Valkenburgh, 8 Cow. (N. Y.) 260; Doherty v. Stimmel, 40 Ohio St. 294; Stroud v. Lockhart, 4 Dall. (Pa.) 153, 1 L. ed. 779; Claiborne v. Holland, 88 Va. 1047, 14 S. E. 915. See ante § 475.

[46] Coffin v. Ray, 1 Metc. (Mass.) 212.

notice, from a fraudulent grantee, will be protected in his purchase.[47] And where a purchaser at sheriff's sale, by fraudulent representations, purchases land at a mere nominal price, a bona fide purchaser from him without notice of the fraud, will be protected in his purchase.[48]

And so, where one obtains a deed of land without consideration, by fraud and imposition upon the grantor, and has it duly recorded, a bona fide purchaser from him without notice of the fraud, paying a valuable consideration, will take a valid title against the first grantor.[49] Likewise, where one, who has made a voluntary conveyance, subsequently conveys the land for a valuable consideration to one who knows of the voluntary conveyance, and the grantee in the latter deed conveys the land to another who has no notice, the last grantee will be protected against the voluntary deed.[50]

III. *Implied Notice*

§ 560. Notice to agents, attorneys, and trustees.—Implied notice arises out of the legal relation of a person who has no notice with another who has notice. Thus notice to the principal is implied from notice to his agent. When an agent acquires a knowledge of any matters or instruments affecting the title of any lands, about the purchase or mortgage of which he is employed, and this knowledge is such that it is his duty to communicate it to his principal, the law imputes this knowledge to the principal; or, in other words, notice to the principal

---

[47] Lee v. Cato, 27 Ga. 637, 73 Am. Dec. 746; Herndon v. Kimball, 7 Ga. 432, 50 Am. Dec. 406; Colgin v. Courrege, 106 La. 684, 31 So. 144; Hoffman v. Noble, 47 Mass. 68, 39 Am. Dec. 711; Phillips v. Buchanan Lumber Co., 151 N. Car. 519, 66 S. E. 603.

[48] Herndon v. Kimball, 7 Ga. 432, 50 Am. Dec. 406.

[49] Somes v. Brewer, 19 Mass. 184, 13 Am. Dec. 406. Green v. Tanner, 49 Mass. (8 Metc.) 411; Hoffman v. Noble, 47 Mass. 68, 39 Am. Dec. 711; See also Rowley v. Bigelow, 29 Mass. 307, 23 Am. Dec. 607; Anderson v. Blood, 152 N. Y. 285, 46 N. E. 493, 57 Am. St. 515; Whitehorn v. Hines, 1 Munf. (Va.) 557.

[50] West v. Wright, 121 Ga. 470, 49 S. E. 285.

of such matters or instruments is implied.[1] Such notice is sometimes called constructive, but it is really implied from the identity of principal and agent, and not imputed by virtue of a construction placed upon their conduct or relation.

Notice to an agent, to bind the principal, must be brought home to the agent while engaged in the business and negotiation of the principal, and when it would be a breach of trust in the former not to communicate the knowledge to the latter.[2] The actual relation of

[1] Smith v. Ayer, 101 U. S. 320, 25 L. ed. 955; May v. Le Claire, 11 Wall. (U. S.) 217, 20 L. ed. 50; Dennis v. Atlanta Nat. Bldg. &c. Assn., 136 Fed. 539, 69 C. C. A. 315; Chapman v. Hughes, 134 Cal. 641, 58 Pac. 298, affd. 66 Pac. 982; Donald v. Beals, 57 Cal. 399; Bauer v. Pierson, 46 Cal. 293; Clark v. Fuller, 39 Conn. 238; First Nat. Bank v. New Milford, 36 Conn. 93; Bouton v. Cameron, 205 Ill. 50, 68 N. E. 800; Fischer v. Tuohy, 186 Ill. 143, 57 N. E. 801; Inter-State Bldg. &c. Assn. v. Ayers, 177 Ill. 9, 52 N. E. 342; Miller v. Whelan, 158 Ill. 544; 42 N. E. 59; Haas v. Sternbach, 156 Ill. 44, 41 N. E. 51; Whitney v. Burr, 115 Ill. 289, 3 N. E. 434; Blair v. Whitaker, 31 Ind. App. 664, 69 N. E. 182; Sowler v. Day, 58 Iowa 252, 12 N. W. 297; Yerger v. Barz, 56 Iowa 77, 8 N. W. 769; Walker v. Schreiber, 47 Iowa 529; Smith v. Dunton, 42 Iowa 48; Greer v. Higgins, 8 Kans. 519; Willis v. Vallette, 4 Metc. (Ky.) 186; Sponable v. Hanson, 87 Mich. 204, 49 N. W. 644; Taylor v. Young, 56 Mich. 285, 22 N. W. 799; Allen v. Poole, 54 Miss. 323; Johnston v. Shortridge, 93 Mo. 227, 6 S. W. 64 (notice to president and secretary of corporation); Meier v. Blume, 80 Mo. 179; Coggswell v. Griffith, 23 Nebr. 334, 36 N. W. 538; Hovey v. Blanchard, 13 N. H. 145; Losey v. Simpson, 11 N. J. Eq. 246; Stanley v. Chamberlin, 39 N. J. L. 565; Benedict v. Arnoux, 154 N. Y. 715, 49 N. E. 326; Constant v. University of Rochester, 111 N. Y. 604, 19 N. E. 631, 2 L. R. A. 734, 7 Am. St. 769; Dusenbury v. Hulbert, 59 N. Y. 541; Williamson v. Brown, 15 N. Y. 354; Jackson v. Van Valkenburgh, 8 Cow. (N. Y.) 260; Bank of U. S. v. Davis, 2 Hill. (N. Y.) 451; Josephthal v. Heyman, 2 Abb. N. Cas. (N. Y.) 22; Josephthal v. Steffen, 8 N. Y. Wkly. Dig. 61; Bigley v. Jones, 114 Pa. St. 510, 7 Atl. 54; Farrington v. Woodward, 82 Pa. St. 259; Myers v. Ross, 3 Head. (Tenn.) 59; Tagg v. Tenn. Nat. Bank, 9 Heisk. (Tenn.) 479; Hampshire v. Greeves (Tex. Civ. App.), 130 S. W. 665 (notice of prior unrecorded mortgage to president of bank taking subsequent mortgage); Schreckhise v. Wiseman, 102 Va. 9, 45 S. E. 745; Fuller v. Bennett, 2 Hare 394; Nixon v. Hamilton, 2 Dr. & Wal. 364, 1 Ir. Eq. 46. See also Lindley v. Martindale, 78 Iowa 379, 43 N. W. 233; Russell v. Sweezey, 22 Mich. 235; Hickman v. Green, 123 Mo. 165, 22 S. W. 455, 27 S. W. 440, 29 L. R. A. 39; Cowan v. Withrow, 111 N. Car. 306, 16 S. E. 397.

[2] Satterfield v. Malone, 35 Fed. 445; Farmer v. American Mtg. Co., 116 Ala. 410, 22 So. 426; Pepper v. George, 51 Ala. 190; May v. Borel, 12 Cal. 91; Clark v. Fuller, 39 Conn. 238; Fry v. Shehee, 55 Ga. 208; Roderick v. McMeekin, 204 Ill. 625, 68 N. E. 473; Yerger v. Barz, 56 Iowa 77, 8 N. W. 769; Smith v. Dunton, 42 Iowa 48; Ely v. Pingry, 56 Kans. 17, 42 Pac. 330; Mitchell v. Aten, 37 Kans. 33, 14 Pac. 497; Greer v. Higgins, 20 Kans. 420; School District v. Taylor, 19 Kans. 287; Willis v. Vallette, 4 Metc. (Ky.) 186; Russell v. Sweezey, 22 Mich. 235; Tucker v. Tilton, 55 N. H. 223; Constant v. University of Rochester, 111 N. Y. 604, 19 N. E. 631, 2 L. R. A. 734, 7 Am. St. 769; Weisser v. Denison, 10 N. Y. 68, 61 Am. Dec. 731; Hodgkins v. Montgomery County Ins. Co., 34 Barb. (N. Y.) 213; New York Cent. Ins. Co. v. National Protection Ins. Co., 20 Barb. (N. Y.) 468; Haywood v.

agency must also be established;[3] and a mortgagor, merely intrusted with a mortgage for record, does not become the agent of the mortgagee in such sense that his knowledge of a prior incumbrance will be imputed to the mortgagee.[4]

Notice to an attorney not retained in the matter in regard to which notice to the attorney is shown is not notice to the principal.[5] Thus, where a mortgagee's attorney had acquired knowledge of a prior unrecorded deed against the mortgaged premises, through inquiry of the grantee's husband concerning an abstract, it was held that the attorney's knowledge could not be imputed to the mortgagee, since it was not acquired in foreclosing the mortgage or transacting business for the mortgagee.[6] The knowledge or notice of facts acquired by an attorney, while engaged in the business of his client, is knowledge or notice of them by the client himself,[7] unless he is party to a fraud or his adverse interest is such as to induce him to conceal the infor-

Shaw, 16 How Pr. (N. Y.) 119; Barbour v. Wiehel, 116 Pa. St. 308, 9 Atl. 520; Houseman v. Girard Loan Assn., 81 Pa. St. 256; Caughman v. Smith, 28 S. Car. 605, 5 S. E. 362; Schreckhise v. Wiseman, 102 Va. 9, 45 S. E. 745; Morrison v. Bausemer, 32 Grat. (Va.) 225; Pacific Mfg. Co. v. Brown, 8 Wash. 347, 36 Pac. 273; Connell v. Connell, 32 W. Va. 319, 9 S. E. 252; Pringle v. Dunn, 37 Wis. 449, 19 Am. Rep. 772; Hoppock v. Johnson, 14 Wis. 303; Lloyd v. Attwood, 3 De G. & J. 614, 5 Jur. (N. S.) 1322, 29 L. J. Ch. 97, 60 Eng. Ch. 475, 44 Eng. R. 1405.

[3] Farmer v. American Mtg. Co., 116 Ala. 410, 22 So. 426; Ely v. Pingry, 56 Kans. 17, 42 Pac. 330; Caughman v. Smith, 28 S. Car. 605, 5 S. E. 362. See also Wyllie v. Pollen, 32 L. J. (N. S.) Ch. 782 (acting in ministerial capacity insufficient). A purchaser of land, taking a deed in his own name, does not by selling it to another, erasing his own name from the deed, and inserting the name of the other, thereby become the agent of the other so as to charge him with notice which he had. Kenney v. Jaynes, 26 Colo. 154, 56 Pac. 562.

[4] Anketel v. Converse, 17 Ohio St. 11, 91 Am. Dec. 115; Hoppock v. Johnson, 14 Wis. 303.

[5] Mack v. McIntosh, 181 Ill. 633, 54 N. E. 1019; Geyer v. Geyer, 75 N. J. Eq. 124, 78 Atl. 449; Slattery v. Schwannecke, 118 N. Y. 543, 23 N. E. 922; Arrington v. Arrington, 114 N. Car. 151, 19 S. E. 351; Steinmeyer v. Steinmeyer, 55 S. Car. 9, 33 S. E. 15; Melms v. Pabst Brewing Co., 93 Wis. 153, 66 N. W. 518, 57 Am. St. 899.

[6] Slattery v. Schwannecke, 118 N. Y. 543, 23 N. E. 922.

[7] Smith v. Ayer, 101 U. S. 320, 25 L. ed. 955; McNitt v. Turner, 16 Wall. (U. S.) 352, 21 L. ed. 341; May v. Le Claire, 11 Wall. (U. S.) 217, 20 L. ed. 50; Polk v. Cosgrove, 4 Biss. (U. S.) 437, Fed. Cas. No. 11248; Jennings v. Carter, 53 Ark. 242, 13 S. W. 800; Thomas v. Van lieu, 28 Cal. 616; Stokes v. Riley, 121 Ill. 166, 11 N. E. 877; Senneff v. Brackey (Iowa), 146 N. W. 24; Foy v. Armstrong, 113 Iowa 629, 85 N. W. 753; Shoemake v. Smith, 80 Iowa 655, 45 N. W. 744; Sowler v. Day, 58 Iowa 252, 12 N. W. 297; Jones v. Bamford, 21 Iowa 217; Lee v. Bermingham, 30 Kans. 312; Bunker v. Gordon, 81 Maine 66, 16 Atl. 341; Low v. Low, 177 Mass. 306, 59 N. E. 57; Den v. Richman, 13 N. J. L. 43; Josephthal v. Heyman, 2 Abb. N. Cas. (N. Y.) 22; Jackson v. Van Valkenburgh, 8 Cow. (N. Y.) 260; Griffith v. Griffith, 9 Paige (N. Y.) 315; Westervelt v. Haff, 2 Sandf. Ch. (N. Y.) 98; Jackson v. Chamberlain, 8 Wend. (N. Y.) 620; Holmes v. Buckner, 67 Tex. 107, 2 S. W.

mation.[8] It has been held that a mortgagee is charged with knowledge of a prior incumbrance, acquired by his attorney, though the latter was the only attorney employed in the transaction and acted for both parties.[9]

Notice imparted to the proper agent or officer of a mortgagee corporation will be imputed to the corporation.[10] Notice to one interested in the purchase of land, though his name does not appear in the conveyance, this being made to another, is notice to the latter.[11] Notice to a trustee is generally notice to the cestui que trust.[12] Notice to one of several trustees jointly holding title is notice to all.[13]

The general rule of partnership that notice to an active partner concerning partnership affairs operates as notice to the firm is applied to a partner purchasing with notice of the condition of a title in relation to incumbrances.[14] Thus where a mortgage is executed to a firm, knowledge by one of its members that the mortgagor had not paid the purchase-money for the land mortgaged, whereby his vendor had a lien thereon for the purchase-money, will affect all the members of the firm with notice of such fact, so that the lien is superior to the mortgage.[15]

452; Sickles v. White, 66 Tex. 178, 17 S. W. 543; Ayres v. Duprey, 27 Tex. 593, 86 Am. Dec. 657; Fordtran v. Cunningham (Tex. Civ. App.), 141 S. W. 562; Ehle v. Brown, 31 Wis. 405; Maxfield v. Burton, 17 L. R. Eq. 15; Berwick v. Price (1905), 1 Ch. 632, 74 L. J. Ch. 249, 92 L. T. Rep. (N. S.) 110 Tweedale v. Tweedale, 23 Beav. 341, 53 Eng. Reprint 134. See also Berwick v. Price, 74 Law J. Ch. 249, (1905) 1 Ch. 632, 92 Law T. 110. See ante § 466.

[8] Cave v. Cave, 15 Ch. Div. 639, 49 L. J. Ch. 505, 42 L. T. (N. S.) 730, 28 Wkly. Rep. 793.

[9] Atterbury v. Wallis, 8 De G. M. & G. 454, 2 Jur. (N. S.) 117, 25 L. J. Ch. 792, 4 Wkly. Rep. 734, 57 Eng. Ch. 353, 44 Eng. Reprint 465. The mortgagor's attorney who prepares the papers and is the only attorney employed, will not be considered the attorney for the mortgagee without the latter's consent to such relation. Espin v. Pemberton, 2 De G. & J. 547, 5 Jur. (N. S.) 157, 28 L. J. Ch. 311, 7 Wkly. Rep. 221, 60 Eng. Ch. 425, 44 Eng. Reprint 1380.

[10] Wilson v. McCullough, 23 Pa. St. 440, 62 Am. Dec. 347; Kirklin v. Atlas Savings &c. Assn. (Tenn.), 60 S. W. 149. See post § 570.

[11] Stanley v. Green, 12 Cal. 148; Wise v. Tripp, 13 Maine 9; Littleton v. Giddings, 47 Tex. 109.

[12] Pope v. Pope, 40 Miss. 516; Schoolfield v. Cogdell, 120 Tenn. 618, 113 S. W. 375 (notice to a trustee of a prior unrecorded mortgage sufficient). See also Willis v. Vallette, 4 Metc. (Ky.), 186 (remote notice to trustee taking subsequent mortgage insufficient); Allen v. Stewart, 214 Mass. 109, 100 N. E. 1092. But see Gritchell v. Kreidler, 12 Mo. App. 497; Morrison v. Bausemer, 32 Grat. (Va.) 225.

[13] Chapman v. Chapman, 91 Va. 367, 21 S. E. 813, 50 Am. St. 846; Meux v. Bell, 1 Hare 73; Smith v. Smith, 2 Cromp. & M. 231 (notice to one of several trustees sufficient, though he was not then acting). See also Browne v. Savage, 4 Drew 635, 5 Jur. (N. S.) 1020, 7 W. R. 571.

[14] Renfro v. Adams, 62 Ala. 302; Watson v. Wells, 5 Conn. 468; Loeb v. Stern, 198 Ill. 371, 64 N. E. 1043.

[15] Overall v. Taylor, 99 Ala. 12, 11 So. 738.

But it seems that in the absence of agency, partnership or some trust or fiduciary relationship, raising a mutual obligation to impart knowledge, a contrary doctrine obtains, and consequently notice of a prior incumbrance or conveyance to one of several joint owners or tenants in common, will not operate as notice to the others by mere force of the relationship.[16] It has been held that one taking mortgaged lands by descent is chargeable with knowledge of the terms and conditions of the mortgage.[17]

Where a solicitor induced a client to take a mortgage upon the lands of a third person situate in the county of Middlesex, in England, and soon afterward induced a second client to advance money on a mortgage of the same lands, without informing him of the existence of the first mortgage, and the second mortgage was registered before the first mortgage was registered, it was held that the holder of the second mortgage must be taken to have had, through the solicitor, notice of the first mortgage, and could not by the prior registration obtain priority.[18] Lord Chancellor Hatherley said: "It has been held over and over again that notice to a solicitor of a transaction, and about a matter as to which it is part of his duty to inform himself, is actual notice to the client. Mankind would not be safe if it were held that, under such circumstances, a man has not notice of that which his agent has actual notice of. The purchaser of an estate has, in ordinary cases, no personal knowledge of the title, but employs a solicitor, and can never be allowed to say that he knew nothing of some prior incumbrance because he was not told of it by his solicitor."

Notice to an agent of facts rendering a note and mortgage purchased by him for his principal a second lien, is notice to the principal, where the latter is informed that the agent is exercising his own discretion as to the investment and accepts his action without objection, receiving the note and mortgage from him and afterward receiving four semi-annual instalments of interest.[19]

---

[16] Wait v. Smith, 92 Ill. 385; Burt v. Batavia Paper Mfg. Co., 86 Ill. 66 (knowledge of one of several corporators of an incumbrance on property purchased by corporation, not chargeable to his association); Snyder v. Sponable, 1 Hill (N. Y.) 567, affd. 7 Hill 427 (notice of prior unrecorded mortgage imparted to husband, not chargeable to wife as joint tenant); Wiswall v. McGowan, 1 Hoff. Ch. (N. Y.) 125 (modified 2 Barb. 270); Rippetoe v. Dwyer, 65 Tex. 703 (notice of prior incumbrance to one purchaser not chargeable to his joint purchaser). See also Parker v. Kane, 4 Wis. 1, 65 Am. Dec. 283.

[17] Fleming v. Hager, 121 Iowa 205, 96 N. W. 752.

[18] Rolland v. Hart, L. R. 6 Ch. App. 678.

[19] Fischer v. Tuohy, 186 Ill. 143, 57 N. E. 801, affg. 87 Ill. App. 574.

§ 561. Principle underlying doctrine.—"It is a moot question upon what principle this doctrine rests," says Vice Chancellor Kindersley,[20] "it has been held by some that it rests on this: that the probability is so strong that the solicitor would tell his client what he knows himself, that it amounts to an irresistible presumption that he did tell him; and so you must presume actual notice on the part of the client. I confess my own impression is, that the principle on which the doctrine rests is this: that my solicitor is alter ego,—he is myself; I stand in precisely the same position as he does in the transaction, and therefore his knowledge is my knowledge; and it would be a monstrous injustice that I should have the advantage of what he knows without the disadvantage. But whatever be the principle upon which the doctrine rests, the doctrine itself is unquestionable."

"In such a case," said Lord Chancellor Brougham,[21] "it would be most iniquitous and most dangerous, and give shelter and encouragement to all kinds of fraud, were the law not to consider the knowledge of one as common to both, whether it be so in fact or not."

It is an elementary principle of the law of agency, applying also to attorneys, that loyalty to the principal's interests requires an agent to disclose every material fact concerning the subject-matter of the agency that comes within his knowledge and memory, in the course of his agency. The law, following the inference of fact, conclusively presumes the agent to have performed this duty of informing his principal, and the latter is therefore affected with knowledge of all the material facts of which the agent receives notice or acquires knowledge while acting in the course of his employment and within the scope of his authority. These principles of agency have been repeatedly applied to purchasers of realty, affected by notice to their agents and attorneys.[22]

[20] Boursot v. Savage, L. R. 2 Eq. 134.
[21] Kennedy v. Green, 3 Myl. & K. 699. See also Bradley v. Riches, L. R. 9 Ch. D. 189.
[22] Harris v. American Bldg. &c. Assn., 122 Ala. 545, 25 So. 200; Farmer v. American Mortgage Co., 116 Ala. 410, 22 So. 426; Continental Bldg. &c. Assn. v. Boggess, 158 Cal. 469, 111 Pac. 357; Chapman v. Hughes, 134 Cal. 641, 58 Pac. 298, 60 Pac. 974, 66 Pac. 982; Northern Assur. Co. v. Stout, 16 Cal. App. 548, 117 Pac. 617; New York, N. H. &c. R. Co. v. Russel, 83 Conn. 581, 78 Atl. 324; Bryant v. Booze, 55 Ga. 438; Bouton v. Cameron, 205 Ill. 50, 68 N. E. 800; Roderick v. McMeekin, 204 Ill. 625, 68 N. E. 473; Fischer v. Tuohy, 186 Ill. 143, 57 N. E. 801; Field v. Campbell, 164 Ind. 389, 72 N. E. 260, 108 Am. St. 301; Condon v. Barnum (Iowa), 106 N. W. 514; Gardner v. Early, 72 Iowa 518, 34 N. W. 311; Geel v. Goulden, 168 Mich. 413, 134 N. W. 484; Hickman v. Green, 123 Mo. 165, 22 S. W. 455, 27 S. W. 440, 29 L. R. A. 39; Brown v. Columbus (N. J. Eq.), 75 Atl. 917; Fordtran v. Cunningham (Tex. Civ. App.), 141 S. W. 562.

§ 562. Notice acquired in same transaction.—The notice must be in the same transaction. Notice to the agent binds the principal only when it is given to or acquired by him in the transaction in which the principal employs him.[23] The reason for this limitation has been stated to be, that an agent can not stand in the place of the principal until the relation is constituted; and that, as to all the information which he has previously acquired, the principal is a mere stranger.[24] Another explanation commonly made of the rule is, that the agent may have forgotten the former transaction. Under this latter view of the doctrine, the criticism of Lord Eldon[25] might well be regarded as shaking it; but it is suggested in later cases that it was not the purpose of his dictum to question the general doctrine itself. At any rate this has been insisted upon ever since his time, and may be regarded as settled.[26]

Upon such considerations, the rule imputing notice to a purchaser

[23] Warrick v. Warrick, 3 Atk. 291, per Lord Hardwicke; Fitzgerald v. Fauconberge, Fitz. G. 207; 2 White & Tudor's Lead. Cas. in Eq. (4th Am. ed.), pt. 1, pp. 170, 173; Rolland v. Hart, L. R. 6 Ch. App. 678; Fuller v. Benett, 2 Hare 394; Pepper v. George, 51 Ala. 190; Lewis v. Equitable Mtg. Co., 94 Ga. 572, 21 S. E. 224; Boardman v. Taylor, 66 Ga. 638; Roderick v. McMeekin, 204 Ill. 625, 68 N. E. 473; McCormick v. Wheeler, 36 Ill. 114; Farmers' Bank v. Butterfield, 100 Ind. 229; Foulks v. Reed, 89 Ind. 370; Yerger v. Barz, 56 Iowa 77, 8 N. W. 769; Roach v. Karr, 18 Kans. 529, 26 Am. Rep. 788; Willis v. Vallette, 4 Metc. (Ky.) 186; Weisser v. Denison, 10 N. Y. 68, 61 Am. Dec. 731; Howard Ins. Co. v. Halsey, 8 N. Y. 271, 59 Am. Dec. 478; New York Central Ins. Co. v. National Ins. Co., 20 Barb. (N. Y.) 468; Houseman v. Girard Mut. B. &c. Assn., 81 Pa. St. 256; Barnes v. McClinton, 3 Pa. St. 67, 23 Am. Dec. 62; Hood v. Fahnestock, 8 Watts (Pa.) 489, 34 Am. Dec. 489; Boggs v. Varner, 6 Watts & S. (Pa.) 469; Bracken v. Miller, 4 Watts & S. (Pa.) 102; Caughman v. Smith, 28 S. Car. 605, 5 S. E. 362; Blumenthal v. Brainerd, 38 Vt. 402, 91 Am. Dec. 350. It was said in substance by Lord Hardwicke, in Warrick v. Warrick, 3 Atk. 291, 26 Eng. Reprint 970, that notice to the agent or counsel, who was employed in the business by another person, or in another business, and at another time, is no notice to his client who employs him afterward. It would be very mischievous if it was so; for the man of most practice and greatest eminence would then be the most dangerous to employ. See ante § 560.

[24] Mountford v. Scott, 3 Madd. 40. See also Morrison v. Bausemer, 32 Grat. (Va.) 225; Fuller v. Benett, 2 Hare 394, per Sir J. Wigram. But see Sowler v. Day, 58 Iowa 252, 12 N. W. 297.

[25] When the case of Mountford v. Scott was on appeal before Lord Eldon, L. C. (Turn. & R. 274), he remarked that "it might fail to be considered whether one transaction might not follow so close upon the other as to render it impossible to give a man credit for having forgotten it. I should be unwilling to go so far as to say that, if an attorney has notice of a transaction in the morning, he shall be held in a court of equity to have forgotten it in the evening." See also Constant v. American Bap. Soc., 21 J. & S. (N. Y.) 170; Brotherton v. Hatt, 2 Vern. 574; Hargreaves v. Rothwell, 1 Keen 154.

[26] Fuller v. Benett, 2 Hare 394.

from knowledge of his agent has sometimes been qualified with the provision that the knowledge must have been present in the agent's mind at the time of the purchase.[27] But it has been held that notice to an agent is notice to his principal, even where the latter interferes before the agent has concluded the negotiations and completes the transaction in person, the agent not participating in the final stages of the transaction.[28]

When the agent or attorney is employed by a person in several mortgage transactions, and he acts for the mortgagees also in all of them, although the transactions are distinct, the later mortgagees are said to be affected with notice of the earlier mortgages, on the ground that the transactions follow each other so closely that they amount to a continuous dealing with the same title.[29] This exception would remain good only when the mortgagor was the same in all the transactions, and the same attorney is employed in all.

§ 563. **Duty to impart notice material to transaction.**—The notice must be of some matter material to the transaction; of some thing which it is the duty of the agent to make known to the principal.[30] Thus the principal is not charged with notice of his agent's secret information, acquired confidentially as attorney for a former client, and which he was bound by professional confidence to withhold.[31] Where an attorney acting in his individual capacity, sells land to a layman who employs no attorney, the former sustains no relation of trust or confidence, and owes no duty to impart his professional knowledge concerning the title.[32]

If the agent acts merely in a ministerial capacity, as, for instance, in obtaining the execution of a deed, the principal is not affected with the agent's knowledge.[33] In like manner, a mortgagor to whom a

---

[27] Satterfield v. Malone, 35 Fed. 445, 1 L. R. A. 35; Armstrong v. Abbott, 11 Colo. 220, 17 Pac. 517; Mack v. McIntosh, 181 Ill. 633, 54 N. E. 1019; Constant v. Rochester University, 111 N. Y. 604, 19 N. E. 631, 2 L. R. A. 734, 7 Am. St. 769.

[28] Bryant v. Booze, 55 Ga. 438.

[29] Brotherton v. Hatt, 2 Vern. 574; Hargreaves v. Rothwell, 1 Keen 154; Winter v. Anson, 1 Sim. & St. 434, 3 Russ. 488. See also Distilled Spirits, 11 Wall. (U. S.) 356, 20 L. ed. 167.

[30] Wyllie v. Pollen, 32 L. J. (N. S.) Ch. 782; Mack v. McIntosh, 181 Ill. 633, 54 N. E. 1019; Wood v. Ray-

burn, 18 Ore. 3, 22 Pac. 521. See also Day v. Wamsley, 33 Ind. 145; Fairfield Sav. Bank v. Chase, 72 Maine 226, 39 Am. Rep. 319; Trentor v. Pothen, 46 Minn. 298, 49 N. W. 129, 24 Am. St. 225. See ante § 560.

[31] Hunter v. Watson, 12 Cal. 363, 73 Am. Dec. 543; Mack v. McIntosh, 181 Ill. 633, 54 N. E. 1019; Driffill v. Goodwin, 23 Grant Ch. (U. C.) 431.

[32] Rykert v. Miller, 14 Grant Ch. (U. C.) 25. See post § 565.

[33] Wyllie v. Pollen, 32 L. J. (N. S.) Ch. 782 (obtaining execution).

mortgage is intrusted for record is not such an agent of the mortgagee that notice to him of an incumbrance, or his knowledge of it, is constructive notice to the mortgagee.[34] As pointed out by Lord Westbury,[35] a solicitor whose notice affects his client must be a solicitor "for the confidential purpose of advising;" otherwise there is no duty on his part to communicate the knowledge to the client, and the doctrine of implied notice has no application.

Notice of the existence of an unrecorded mortgage upon the property to an officer employed to make an attachment is notice to the plaintiff, and is equivalent to a record in protecting it against the attachment.[36] But such knowledge on the part of an attorney who makes the writ, but has no agency in procuring the attachment, has been held not to affect the plaintiff.[37] The mere relation of mortgagor and mortgagee is not sufficient to charge the latter with notice of facts known to the former.[38]

§ 564. **Rule when agent or attorney acts for both parties.**—When the same agent or attorney is employed by both parties in the same transaction, his knowledge is then the knowledge of both the vendor and vendee, of both the mortgagor and mortgagee.[39] A principal who knows that his agent is also acting as agent for the party adversely interested in a transaction with him, and yet consents that he may act as his agent, is estopped from denying the notice and knowledge which the agent has during the negotiation.[40] Since the interest of vendor and purchaser are diametrically opposed, such knowledge and consent to the dual agency is essential to effectual notice through the agent. To permit the seller or his agent to act as the agent of the buyer inaugurates so dangerous a conflict between self-interest and

---

[34] Anketel v. Converse, 17 Ohio St. 11, 91 Am. Dec. 115; Hoppock v. Johnson, 14 Wis. 303.
[35] In Wyllie v. Pollen, 32 L. J. (N. S.) Ch. 782.
[36] Tucker v. Tilton, 55 N. H. 223.
[37] Tucker v. Tilton, 55 N. H. 223.
[38] Tritch v. Norton, 10 Colo. 337, 15 Pac. 680.
[39] Pine Mountain Iron &c. Co. v. Bailey, 94 Fed. 258, 36 C. C. A. 229; Griffin v. Franklin, 224 Mo. 667, 123 S. W. 1092 (grantor's attorney also agent for purchaser); Smith v. Farrell, 66 Mo. App. 8; Losey v. Simpson, 11 N. J. Eq. 246; Holley v. Still, 91 S. Car. 487, 74 S. E. 1065; Baldwin v. Root, 90 Tex.

546, 40 S. W. 3; Sheldon v. Cox, Amb. 624. See also Astor v. Wells, 4 Wheat. (U. S.) 466, 4 L. ed. 616; Constant v. Am. Bap. Soc., 21 J. & S. (N. Y.) 170; Fischer v. Tuohy, 186 Ill. 143, 57 N. E. 801, where the agent making a loan was an investment company.
[40] Astor v. Wells, 4 Wheat. (U. S.) 466, 4 L. ed. 616; Pine Mountain Iron &c. Co. v. Bailey, 94 Fed. 258, 36 C. C. A. 229; Fitzsimmons v. Southern Express Co., 40 Ga. 330; Alexander v. Northwestern Christian University, 57 Ind. 466; Leekins v. Nordyke &c. Co., 66 Iowa 471, 24 N. W. 1; Adams Mining Co. v. Senter, 26 Mich. 73.

duty that the law has wisely removed the temptation by forbidding the relation. No one can be a vendor or the agent of a vendor and the purchaser or the agent of the purchaser at the same time, unless he first obtains the consent of the party with whom he deals, after a complete disclosure of all the facts which condition his relation. The law absolutely prohibits the vendor from being at the same time the agent of a purchaser, unless the latter consents to the relation after he knows that his agent is the seller.[41]

In such cases of dual agency it seems that the rule that the agent's notice must be in the same transaction is less strictly adhered to.[42] Thus, where a person made two successive mortgages of the same property, and then gave a further charge to the first mortgagee, and the same solicitor was employed in all three transactions, it was held that the first mortgagee had implied notice of the second mortgagee's incumbrance, and that the latter was entitled to priority over the further charge to the first mortgagee.[43] A mortgagee is not chargeable with notice of facts within the knowledge of the borrower's agents who negotiated the loan for the borrower, and are not the agents of the mortgagee in any way.[44]

Where a solicitor is employed and acts for both mortgagor and mortgagee notice of a prior incumbrance held by such solicitor is imputable to the mortgagee.[45] But where the mortgagor's solicitor is the only solicitor employed in the transaction, he will not be considered the attorney for the mortgagee unless there is some consent on the part of the latter to constitute the relation.[46]

§ 565. **Rule when attorney is the mortgagor.**—When the attorney himself is the mortgagor, the rule, that the knowledge of the attorney is the knowledge of the client, does not apply; it does not follow in such case that the mortgagee has constructive notice of facts connected with the title which are known to the mortgagor.[47] Therefore,

[41] Pine Mountain Iron &c. Co. v. Bailey, 94 Fed. 258, 36 C. C. A. 229; McKinley v. Williams, 74 Fed. 94, 20 C. C. A. 312; Warren v. Burt, 58 Fed. 101, 7 C. C. A. 105; Bunton v. Palm (Tex.), 9 S. W. 182. See also Thomson-Houston Elec. Co. v. Capital Elec. Co., 56 Fed. 849; Frenkel v. Hudson, 82 Ala. 158, 2 So. 758, 60 Am. Rep. 736; DeKay v. Hackensack Water Co., 38 N. J. Eq. 158; Voltz v. Blackmar, 64 N. Y. 440.
[42] Fuller v. Benett, 2 Hare 403; Brotherton v. Hatt, 2 Vern. 574.

[43] Hargreaves v. Rothwell, 1 Keen 154. See also Jamison v. Gjemenson, 10 Wis. 411.
[44] Allen v. McCullough, 99 Ala. 612, 12 So. 810.
[45] Atterbury v. Wallis, 8 De G. M. & G. 454, 2 Jur. (N. S.) 117, 2 L. J. Ch. 792, 4 Wkly. Rep. 734, 57 Eng. Ch. 353, 44 Eng. Reprint 465.
[46] Espin v. Pemberton, 2 De G. & J. 547, 5 Jur. (N. S.) 158, 28 L. J. Ch. 311.
[47] Bang v. Brett, 62 Minn. 4, 63 N. W. 1067; Hope F. Ins. Co. v. Cam-

where one was attorney for two persons, and executed to one of them a mortgage, which was not recorded, and afterward executed another mortgage of the same premises to the other, and this mortgage was recorded, it was held that the priority of the latter mortgage was not affected by the attorney's knowledge of the mortgage first executed.[48] Whenever the agent is "the contriver, the actor, and the gainer of the transaction," the reason for charging the principal with notice of the facts no longer exists.[49] And as a general rule, knowledge of an agent in relation to the matter in which he is acting will not be imputed to his principal, when his interests are adverse to those of the principal.[50]

§ 566. **Fraudulent concealment from principal.**—In like manner, when the agent is guilty of any fraud, for the carrying out of which it is necessary that he should conceal it from his principal, notice of it can not be imputed to the latter.[51] Thus, where an agent fraudulently and collusively with a borrower, loaned his principal's money upon security of a mortgage of homestead lands, contrary to his instructions, the agent's knowledge that the premises were a homestead will not be imputed to the principal.[52] And generally where a land

brelling, 1 Hun (N. Y.) 493; Hewitt v. Loosemore, 9 Hare 449; Espin v. Pemberton, 3 De G. & J. 547. But Sheldon v. Cox, Amb. 624, is regarded as an authority to the contrary, followed in Majoribanks v. Hovenden, 6 Ir. Eq. 238; Rorke v. Lloyd, 13 Ir. Ch. 273; Tucker v. Henzill, 4 Ir. Ch. 513.

[48] Hope F. Ins. Co. v. Cambrelling, 1 Hun (N. Y.) 493. See also McCormick v. Wheeler, 36 Ill. 114, 85 Am. Dec. 388; Winchester v. Baltimore & S. R. Co., 4 Md. 231; Rolland v. Hart, 6 Ch. App. 678, per Lord Hatherley; Kennedy v. Green, 3 Myl. & K. 699.

[49] Kennedy v. Green, 3 Myl. & K. 699.

[50] Frenkel v. Hudson, 82 Ala. 158, 2 So. 758, 60 Am. Rep. 736; Booker v. Booker, 208 Ill. 529, 70 N. E. 709, 100 Am. St. 250; Jummel v. Mann, 80 Ill. App. 288, affd. 183 Ill. 523, 56 N. E. 161; Smith v. Boyd, 162 Mo. 146, 62 S. W. 439; Bunton v. Palm (Tex.), 9 S. W. 182. See also Central Coal &c. Co. v. Good, 120 Fed. 793, 57 C. C. A. 161; Bank of Overton v. Thompson, 118 Fed. 798, 56 C. C. A. 554; Brown v. Harris, 139 Mich. 372, 102 N. W. 960; Luton v.

Sharp, 94 Mich. 202, 53 N. W. 1054; Traber v. Hicks, 131 Mo. 180, 32 S. W. 1145; Ætna Indemnity Co. v. Schroeder, 12 N. Dak. 110, 95 N. W. 436.

[51] Western Mtg. &c. Co. v. Ganzer, 63 Fed. 647, 11 C. C. A. 371; Cowan v. Curran, 216 Ill. 598, 75 N. E. 322; Dillaway v. Butler, 135 Mass. 479; Traber v. Hicks, 131 Mo. 180, 32 S. W. 1145; Benedict v. Arnoux, 154 N. Y. 715, 49 N. E. 326; Fulton Bank v. New York &c. Canal Co., 4 Paige (N. Y.) 127; Musser v. Hyde, 2 Watts & S. (Pa.) 314; Allen v. Garrison, 92 Tex. 546, 50 S. W. 335; Cooper v. Ford, 29 Tex. Civ. App. 253, 69 S. W. 487; Scripture v. Scottish-American Mtg. Co., 20 Tex. Civ. App. 153, 49 S. W. 644; Kennedy v. Green, 3 Myl. & K. 699; In re European Bank, 5 Ch. App. 358. See also Thomson-Houston Electric Co. v. Capitol Electric Co., 65 Fed. 341, 12 C. C. A. 643; Geyer v. Geyer, 75 N. J. Eq. 124, 78 Atl. 449.

[52] Scripture v. Scottish-American Mtg. Co., 20 Tex. Civ. App. 153, 49 S. W. 644. See also Western Mfg. Co. v. Ganzer, 63 Fed. 647, 11 C. C. A. 371; Cooper v. Ford, 29 Tex. Civ. App. 253, 69 S. W. 487.

agent professes to act for both the seller and the buyer, the law exacts from him the most perfect good faith, fairness and honesty, when it is sought to enforce the contract, or to impute to the principal knowledge of the agent.[53]

The fraud must exist independently of the question whether the act was communicated to the principal of not.[54] "It must be made out that distinct fraud was intended in the very transaction, so as to make it necessary for the solicitor to conceal the facts from his client, in order to defraud him."[55] The High Court of Justice of England, applying these principles in a case where a trustee who was a solicitor used trust funds in purchasing an estate which was conveyed to his brother, and afterward acted as solicitor for the mortgagee in raising money on the estate, held that the fraud of the solicitor ran through the whole transaction, and prevented the imputation of notice.[56]

In other words, if the act done by the agent is such as can not be said to be done by him in the character of agent, but is done by him in the character of a party to an independent fraud on his principal, it is not to be imputed to the principal as an act done by his agent.[57] Or, to state the matter somewhat differently, notice is imputed to the principal by reason of the agent's knowledge, unless there are such circumstances in the case, independent of the fact under inquiry, as to raise an inevitable conclusion that the notice had not been communicated.[58] "As soon as the agent forms the purpose of dealing with his principal's property for his own benefit and advantage, or for the benefit and advantage of other persons who are opposed in interest, he ceases, in fact, to be an agent acting in good faith for the interest of his principal, and his action thereafter based upon such purpose is deemed to be in fraud of the rights of his principal, and the presumption that he has disclosed all the facts that have come to his knowledge no longer prevails."[59]

§ 567. **Relationship of husband and wife.**—Notice is not necessarily implied out of the relationship of husband and wife. A mar-

[53] Cowan v. Curran, 216 Ill. 598, 75 N. E. 322.
[54] Atterbury v. Wallis, 8 De G., M. & G. 454; Sharpe v. Foy, 4 Ch. App. 35; Hewitt v. Loosemore, 9 Hare, 499.
[55] Rolland v. Hart, 6 Ch. App. 678.
[56] Cave v. Cave, 15 Ch. D. 639.
[57] Cave v. Cave, 15 Ch. D. 639, per Fry, J.; Espin v. Pemberton, 3 De . G. & J. 547.
[58] Thompson v. Cartwright, 33 Beav. 178.
[59] Benedict v. Arnoux, 154 N. Y. 715, 49 N. E. 326, per Haight, J., citing Innerarity v. Merchants' Nat. Bank, 139 Mass. 332, 1 N. E. 282, 52 Am. Rep. 710; Hudson v. Randolph, 66 Fed. 216; Weissar v. Denison, 10 N. Y. 68; Frenkel v. Hudson, 82 Ala. 158, 2 So. 758; Kettle-

ried woman is not chargeable with knowledge of facts affecting the title to real estate purchased by her, because her husband has knowledge of such facts, in case the purchase is not made through his agency, and he takes no part in the negotiations.[60] But the wife purchasing land through her husband acting as her agent, takes subject to the incumbrances or other defects of which he had knowledge.[61] Thus the wife is chargeable with notice, in purchasing land through her husband, who has knowledge that the transfer is made in fraud of the grantor's wife.[62] Where a loan agent, negotiating a loan for a married woman, agreed to investigate the title offered her as security, the fact that her husband verified such examination was held insufficient to constitute him her agent in the transaction so as to charge her with his knowledge of facts affecting the title.[63]

§ 568. Notice of joint owner's or copartner's interest.—A purchaser from one of two joint owners is chargeable with notice of the interest of the other, when this interest is shown by the conveyance to which he must look for his vendor's title.[64] Thus, if the deed to his grantor shows that the land was bought with partnership funds or for partnership purposes, the purchaser from one of the joint owners is chargeable with notice of the partnership equities.[65] The purchaser is not chargeable with notice that the land is partnership property merely from knowledge that the owners are partners, and that they use the lands for partnership purposes, in case there is nothing in the purchase-deeds of such owners to indicate that it was bought for part-

well v. Watson, 21 Ch. D. 685, 707; Cave v. Cave, 15 Ch. D. 639.

[60] Satterfield v. Malone, 35 Fed. 445; Leowen v. Forsee, 137 Mo. 29, 38 S. W. 712; Snyder v. Sponable, 1 Hill (N. Y.) 567, 7 Hill 427; Smith v. Miller, 66 Tex. 74, 17 S. W. 399; Pringle v. Dunn, 37 Wis. 449, 19 Am. Rep. 772. See also Weightman v. Washington Critic Co., 4 App. D. C. 136; Graham Paper Co. v. St. Joseph &c. Pub. Co., 79 Mo. App. 504.

[61] Miller v. Whelan, 158 Ill. 544, 42 N. E. 59; Forsythe v. Brandenburg, 154 Ind. 588, 57 N. E. 247; Retherford v. Wright, 41 Ind. App. 163, 83 N. E. 520; Gardner v. Early, 72 Iowa 518, 34 N. W. 311; Tate v. Tate, 10 Ohio C. D. 321, 19 Ohio C. C. 532. See also Satterfield v. Malone, 35 Fed. 445, 1 L. R. A. 35; Parker v. Meredith (Tenn.), 59 S.

W. 167 (presumption of notice from husband to wife rebutted by their direct testimony); Allen v. Garrison, 92 Tex. 546, 50 S. W. 335; Smith v. Miller, 66 Tex. 74, 17 S. W. 399.

[62] Tate v. Tate, 10 Ohio C. D. 321, 19 Ohio C. C. 532.

[63] Francis v. Reeves, 137 N. Car. 269, 49 S. E. 213.

[64] Campbell v. Roach, 45 Ala. 667. See also Patrick v. Chenault, 6 B. Mon. (Ky.) 315; Gibson v. Winslow, 46 Pa. St. 380, 84 Am. Dec. 552. A mortgage of joint property is not binding on co-tenants who do not join in its execution, unless they are estopped to deny it by knowledge or acquiescence. South Carolina State Bank v. Campbell, 2 Rich. Eq. (S. Car.) 179.

[65] Brewer v. Browne, 68 Ala. 210. See also United States v. Groome,

nership purposes.[66] And a bona fide purchaser of a partner's legal title in partnership realty, having no notice of equitable rights of the copartners or their creditors, will be protected both in law and equity.[67]

§ 569. **Notice of partnership equities.**—But if a purchaser has knowledge that the land is partnership property, and he attempts to purchase the individual interest of one partner, he buys subject to the equitable rights of the other partners. The purchaser is put upon inquiry by such knowledge as to the equitable rights of the other partners, and takes subject to such rights.[68] The purchaser with such knowledge is also bound by the equities of the partnership creditors. Thus, where one purchased of a surviving partner the undivided half of a parcel of land upon which there was a planing mill, knowing that the land was purchased and the mill built with partnership funds, and had always been applied to partnership uses, that the firm was largely indebted, if not insolvent, and that none of its debts had been paid by the surviving partner, who conducted the sale secretly, and absconded with the proceeds of the sale immediately upon its completion, the purchaser was held to be affected by his knowledge, and by the circumstances of the transaction, so that he took the title subject to the trust with which it was affected in the hands of his vendor.[69]

13 App. D. C. 460; Williams v. Love, 39 Tenn. 80, 73 Am. Dec. 191; Mansfield v. Neese, 21 Tex. Civ. App. 584, 54 S. W. 370.

[66] Brewer v. Browne, 68 Ala. 210; Kepler v. Erie Dime Sav. &c. Co., 101 Pa. St. 602; Lefevre's Appeal, 69 Pa. St. 122, 8 Am. Rep. 229; Tillinghast v. Champlin, 4 R. I. 173, 67 Am. Dec. 510; Reynolds v. Buckman, 35 Mich. 80, Cooley, C. J., said: "Real estate held by partners may or may not be partnership property, but usually it is not so unless partnership assets have been used to purchase it, unless it was put in originally as a part of the joint estate. But generally the fact that two or more persons make use of property, in which their interests are apparently several for partnership purposes, is very far from indicating an understanding that it is partnership estate, much less any such conclusive understanding that others would be

bound to take notice." But see Bergeron v. Richardott, 55 Wis. 129, 12 N. W. 384.

[67] Robinson Bank v. Miller, 153 Ill. 244, 38 N. E. 1078, 27 L. R. A. 449, 46 Am. St. 883; Rivarde v. Rousseau, 7 La. Ann. 3; Tillinghast v. Champlin, 4 R. I. 173, 67 Am. Dec. 510. See also Bond Realty Co. v. Pounds, 128 App. Div. 91, 112 N. Y. S. 433.

[68] Hoxie v. Carr, 1 Sumn. (U. S.) 173; Sigourney v. Munn. 7 Conn. 324; Dyer v. Clark, 5 Metc. (Mass.) 562; Tillinghast v. Champlin, 4 R. I. 173, 67 Am. Dec. 510.

[69] Tillinghast v. Champlin, 4 R. I. 173, 67 Am. Dec. 510. The circumstance that a mortgage was executed to three persons does not create a mutual agency, so that notice to one will affect the others. Snyder v. Sponable, 1 Hill (N. Y.) 567; Steiner v. Clisby, 95 Ala. 91, 10 So. 240, 11 So. 294.

Where the record title of property appears in two persons, and the purchaser is informed before completion of the purchase that a claim to the whole of the land is made by one of such persons or his grantee, the title is taken subject to this claim, and may be defeated by evidence that the land was acquired by the owners of record as partners and had been awarded to one of them upon a settlement of partnership affairs.[70] "Real estate held by partners may or may not be partnership property, but usually it is not so unless partnership assets have been used to purchase it, or unless it was put in originally as a part of the joint estate. But generally the fact that two or more persons make use of property in which their interests are apparently several, for partnership purposes, is very far from indicating an understanding that others would be found to take notice. The several interests still remain several, and each may deal with his own as he will, and any private arrangement that would change this could not bind third parties who had acted in ignorance of it."[71]

§ 570. Notice to corporations through officers and agents.—Notice, to affect a corporation, must be brought home to the president and directors, or to some officer to whom the matter to which the notice relates has been specially given in charge.[72] Thus, to affect a bank, which is about to take a mortgage, with notice of a prior unrecorded deed, it is not sufficient to show that the cashier had such notice.[73] Especially where there are several agents or officers acting for the same principal or corporation, it seems that notice of prior rights to an agent or officer entirely unconcerned in the subsequent transaction will not charge his principal. And it has been held that a bank or other corporation may sustain its position as a bona fide purchaser of a mortgage by proof that its officers, through whom the business was actually transacted, had no knowledge of the mortgagor's fraud upon his vendor, and it is not necessary for the bank to disprove notice to every officer or agent through whom notice might have been com-

[70] Murrell v. Mandelbaum, 85 Tex. 22, 19 S. W. 880, 34 Am. St. 777.

[71] Reynolds v. Ruckman, 35 Mich. 80.

[72] Robertson v. United States Live Stock Co. (Iowa), 145 N. W. 535; Wilson v. McCullough, 23 Pa. St. 440, 62 Am. Dec. 347; Kirklin v. Atlas Savings &c. Assn. (Tenn.), 60 S. W. 149. See also In re Buchner, 202 Fed. 979; Hampshire v. Greeves (Tex. Civ. App.), 130 S. W.

665 (notice to president sufficient).

[73] Wilson v. McCullough, 23 Pa St. 440, 60 Am. Dec. 347. But see Johnston v. Shortridge, 93 Mo. 227, 6 S. W. 64 (cashier and manager). Notice concerning the fraudulent release of a mortgage can not be imputed to a bank from knowledge of the agents of another bank, in an antagonistic relation to it. In re Buchner, 205 Fed. 454, 123 C. C. A. 522.

municated.[74] Even notice to an individual director, who has no duty to perform in relation to such notice or the matter to which the notice relates, can not be considered notice to the corporation.[75]

A corporation purchasing real estate is not chargeable with knowledge of outstanding equities therein, although its managing officer had such knowledge, when it was obtained years before the organization of the corporation, unless such knowledge is shown to be present in the mind of the officer at the time of the transaction.[76] Notice to an agent of a corporation has the same effect as notice to an agent of an individual. The agent is not affected by notice except while he is acting in the matter to which the notice relates. Notice to an individual director is not notice to the corporation, unless the director at the time is officially engaged in the business of the corporation.[77] Notice to a director, while he is acting solely for himself and not for the corporation, is not notice to the corporation, and can not affect its rights.[78] When, however, the director has official duties to perform in respect to the matter, and the faithful performance of these duties renders it incumbent upon him to communicate the information to the other officers of the corporation, then the corporation stands affected with the director's knowledge in the same manner as if he had acquired it while in the discharge of his official duties.[79] A corporation is chargeable with the knowledge of its general manager that a mortgage assigned to it was in fraud of creditors.[80] A corporation taking a mortgage of land is not chargeable with constructive notice of a prior conveyance of it by the mortgagor, because the latter was, at the date of the deed and of the mortgage, a director of the company, for in such a transaction the mortgagor deals with the company as a third party on his own behalf acting for himself. with and against the company, and not for it.[81]

[74] Robertson v. United States Live Stock Co. (Iowa), 145 N. W. 535.
[75] Fulton Bank v. New York &c. Canal Co., 4 Paige (N. Y.) 127.
[76] Red River Valley Land &c. Co. v. Smith, 7 N. Dak. 236, 74 N. W. 194.
[77] Bank of United States v. Davis, 2 Hill (N. Y.) 451.
[78] Winchester v. Baltimore &c. R. Co., 4 Md. 231; Barnes v. Trenton Gas Light Co., 27 N. J. Eq. 33; La Farge F. Ins. Co. v. Bell, 22 Barb. (N. Y.) 54.
[79] Fulton Bank v. New York &c. Canal Co., 4 Paige (N. Y.) 127.

[80] In re Sweet, 20 R. I. 557, 40 Atl. 502.
[81] La Farge F. Ins. Co. v. Bell, 22 Barb. (N. Y.) 54. "If his position as a director," says Mr. Justice Emott, "could make him the agent, or rather identify him entirely with the plaintiffs in such sort as to charge them with constructive notice of all the facts with which he was personally acquainted as to the title to lands in which they had any interest, in any case, it could not be so when he did not become concerned as their especial agent, or transact business in their be-

Notice to the president of a corporation can not be considered notice to the corporation where the president is acting in his own interests or for interests adverse to the corporation. Hence, if he is a member of a real estate firm through which a loan is negotiated with the corporation for a third person, in the interest of the firm, the corporation is not chargeable with the knowledge of its president, which he does not communicate, concerning payment of prior incumbrances out of the money loaned.[52]

IV. Constructive Notice

§ 571. General principles of constructive notice.—Constructive notice is that which is imputed to a person upon strictly legal inference of matters which he necessarily ought to know, or which, by the exercise of ordinary diligence, he might know.[1] Constructive notice

half. Most clearly it can not be the case where the facts concerned his private affairs, and the transaction was one in which he was dealing with the company as a third party on his own behalf, and acting for himself with and against them."
[52] Leaverns v. Presbyterian Hospital, 173 Ill. 414, 50 N. E. 1079, 64 Am. St. 125. See also Central Nat. Bank v. Pipkin, 66 Mo. App. 592.
[1] Townsend v. Little, 109 U. S. 504, 27 L. ed. 1012, 3 Sup. Ct. 357; Griffith v. Griffith, Hoff. (U. S.) 153; Mettart v. Allen, 139 Ind. 644, 39 N. E. 239; Knapp v. Bailey, 79 Maine 195, 9 Atl. 122; Rice v. Winters, 45 Nebr. 517, 63 N. W. 830; Rogers v. Jones, 8 N. H. 264; Weildier v. Farmers' Bank, 11 Serg. & R. (Pa.) 134; Kennedy v. Green, 3 Myl. & K. 699; Hewitt v. Loosemore, 9 Hare 449; Espin v. Pemberton, 3 De G. & J. 547; Hiern v. Mill, 13 Ves. 121. See article on Constructive Notice by William L. Scott, 17 Am. Law Rev. 849. As to the term ordinary diligence, see Pasumpsic Sav. Bank v. Nat. Bank, 53 Vt. 82. Constructive notice has been defined as evidence of notice, the presumption of which is so violent that the court will not even allow of its being controverted. Townsend v. Little, 109 U. S. 504, 27 L. ed. 1012, 3 Sup. Ct. 357; White v. Fisher, 77 Ind. 65, 40 Am. Rep. 287; Fuller v. McMahon (Iowa), 94 N. W. 205; Baltimore v. Whittington, 78 Md. 231, 27 Atl. 984; Schweiss v. Woodruff, 73 Mich. 473, 41 N. W. 511; Francis v. Kansas City &c. R. Co., 110 Mo. 387, 19 S. W. 935; Rogers v. Jones, 8 N. H. 264; Van Doren v. Robinson, 16 N. J. Eq. 256; Cambridge Valley Bank v. Delano, 48 N. Y. 326; Kirklin v. Atlas Savings &c. Assn. (Tenn.), 60 S. W. 149; Hewitt v. Loosemore, 9

of a prior deed or mortgage, arising out of an opportunity to acquire knowledge, coupled with a duty to seek it, has the same effect as actual notice in postponing the rights of a subsequent grantee or mortgagee, taking with such notice.[2] In its broad sense, constructive notice thus borders upon actual notice, and includes facts and circumstances demanding inquiry; but inferences of fact are more properly classified under actual notice, where this subject is more fully treated.[3]

The most familiar instance of constructive notice is that which under the registry laws is afforded by the record of a deed. Every subsequent inquirer is bound to know the existence and contents of such deed, and it is not admissible for him to show that his attorney examined the records and failed to find the deed of record.[4]

But there are various other kinds of constructive notice, and a purchaser or mortgagee is as much bound by the knowledge thus imputed to him, of matters and instruments affecting the title to property, as he would be if he were informed of them by a deed properly recorded. Whether the person charged with such notice actually had knowledge of the facts affecting the property in question, or might have learned them by inquiry, or whether he studiously abstained from inquiry for the very purpose of avoiding notice, he is alike presumed to have had notice.[5]

§ 572. Constructive notice based upon fraud or negligence.—Constructive notice is imputed either upon the ground of fraud or of negligence. It does not exist without one or the other. "If, in short, there is not actual notice that the property is in some way affected," says Vice Chancellor Wigram,[6] "and no fraudulent turning away from a knowledge of facts which the res gestæ would suggest to a prudent

---

Hare 450; Plumb v. Fluitt, 2 Anst. 432, per Eyre, C. B.

[2] Montgomery v. Keppel, 75 Cal. 128, 19 Pac. 178, 7 Am. St. 125; Russell v. Ranson, 76 Ill. 167; Duncan v. Miller, 64 Iowa 223, 20 N. W. 161; Livingstone v. Murphy, 187 Mass. 315, 72 N. E. 1012, 105 Am. St. 400; Quimby v. Williams, 67 N. H. 489, 41 Atl. 862, 68 Am. St. 685; Fidelity Ins. &c. Co. v. Shenandoah Valley R. Co., 32 W. Va. 244, 9 S. E. 180. See also Beeman v. Cooper, 64 Vt. 305, 23 Atl. 794. Constructive notice arises from a party's knowledge of facts which ought to have put him on further inquiry, or from his wilfully abstaining

from inquiry to avoid notice. Espin v. Pemberton, 3 De G. & J. 547; Gress v. Evans, 1 Dak. 387, 46 N. W. 1132.

[3] See ante §§ 545, 547, 548.

[4] Edwards v. Barwise, 69 Tex. 84, 6 S. W. 677. See ante §§ 523, 524, 546.

[5] Whitbread v. Jordan, 1 Y. & C. Exch. 303; Bisco v. Banbury, 1 Ch. Cas. 287; Jones v. Smith, 1 Hare 43; Ware v. Egmont, 4 De G., M. & G. 460. See also cases collected in 2 White & Tudor's Lead. Cas. 4th Am. ed., p. 121; Jackson v. Blackwood, 4 McAr. (U. S.) 188.

[6] Jones v. Smith, 1 Hare 43, affd. 1 Ph. 244.

mind; if mere want of caution, as distinguished from fraudulent and wilful blindness, is all that can be imputed to a purchaser,—there the doctrine of constructive notice will not apply; there the purchaser will in equity be considered, as in fact he is, a bona fide purchaser without notice." In another case Vice Chancellor Turner said: "When this court is called upon to postpone a legal mortgage, its powers are invoked to take away a legal right, and I see no ground which can justify it in doing so, except fraud, or gross and wilful negligence, which in the eye of this court amounts to fraud."[7]

Following the English doctrine, there is a line of American decisions restricting constructive notice to cases of gross negligence or fraud in the conduct of the purchaser; and holding that he is only chargeable where he purposely avoided knowledge or knowingly and designedly abstained from making inquiry: in other words, that wilful and fraudulent blindness, as distinct from mere want of caution is essential to constructive notice.[8]

§ 573. **Notice of adverse interest without particulars.**—Notice of the existence of an adverse right, title, or lien, without the particulars of it, is sufficient to charge a purchaser, if the nature of it could have been ascertained by inquiry;[9] and knowledge of the existence of an instrument such as a contract or conveyance will charge a purchaser

---

[7] Hewitt v. Loosemore, 9 Hare 449.

[8] Simmons Creek Coal Co. v. Doran, 142 U. S. 417, 35 L. ed. 1063, 12 Sup. Ct. 239; Dudley v. Witter, 46 Ala. 664; Hall v. Livingston, 3 Del. Ch. 348; Reynolds v. Carlisle, 99 Ga. 730, 27 S. E. 169; Anthony v. Wheeler, 130 Ill. 128, 22 N. E. 494, 17 Am. St. 281; Grundies v. Reid, 107 Ill. 304; Calvin v. Middleton, 63 Iowa 618, 19 N. W. 805; Wilson v. Miller, 16 Iowa 111; Willis v. Vallette, 4 Metc. (Ky.) 186; Briggs v. Rice, 130 Mass. 50; Buttrick v. Holden, 13 Metc. (Mass.) 355; Millar v. Olney, 69 Mich. 560, 37 N. W. 558; Larzelere v. Starkweather, 38 Mich. 96; Loughridge v. Bowland, 52 Miss. 546; Parker v. Conner, 93 N. Y. 118, 45 Am. Rep. 178; Dutchess County Mut. Ins. Co. v. Hachfield, 73 N. Y. 226; Acer v. Westcott, 46 N. Y. 384, 7 Am. Rep. 355; Woodworth v. Paige, 5 Ohio St. 70; Crossen v. Oliver, 37 Ore. 514, 61 Pac. 885; Raymond v. Flavel, 27 Ore. 219, 40 Pac. 158; Peebles v. Reading, 8 Serg. & R. (Pa.) 484; Lodge v. Simonton, 2 P. & Watts (Pa.) 446, 23 Am. Dec. 36; Vest v. Michie, 31 Grat. (Va.) 149, 31 Am. Rep. 722; Le Neve v. Le Neve, 3 Atk. 646, 26 Eng. Reprint 1172; Ware v. Egmont, 4 De G., M. & G. 460. See also Trinidad v. Milwaukee &c. Smelting &c. Co., 63 Fed. 883, 11 C. C. A. 479; McClanachan v. Siter, 2 Grat. (Va.) 280; Hewitt v. Loosemore, 9 Hare 449. Mere negligent omission to make inquiry is not alone sufficient. Reynolds v. Carlisle, 99 Ga. 730, 27 S. E. 169. The fact that the purchaser required security in addition to the covenants of warranty is not alone sufficient proof that he had notice of outstanding equities. Lamont v. Stimson, 5 Wis. 443.

[9] Poulet v. Johnson, 25 Ga. 403; Martin v. Cauble, 72 Ind. 67; Ridgeway v. Holliday, 59 Mo. 444; Werner v. Litzsinger, 45 Mo. App. 106; Pearson v. Daniel, 22 N. Car. 360. Notice of a claim is insufficient, if the nature of it could not be ascer-

with notice of its terms.[10] If a purchaser of land has notice of any lien or incumbrance, he is chargeable with notice of the extent thereof,[11] although misstated to him by the vendor,[12] and he is bound by any information he might have obtained by inquiry of the lienor or incumbrancer.[13] "The rules in respect to notice to purchasers, of adverse titles or claims, other than such as is imparted by the records, are not founded upon any arbitrary provisions of law, but have their origin in the considerations of prudence and honesty which guide men in their ordinary business transactions. No man, on being told by the recorder that a certain deed had been filed in his office, and that it had been withdrawn, would doubt that the deed existed; and if he was intending to purchase the property, common prudence would dictate to him the necessity of making inquiry of the grantee for the deed, unless he was incorrectly advised that deeds took precedence solely from priority of record."[14]

One who has knowledge of a prior unrecorded mortgage upon some portion of the premises of which he is about to purchase a part is bound by such knowledge to ascertain the extent of that mortgage, and whether it covers the portion of the property he is about to acquire an interest in, and he will be postponed to such prior mortgage, even if this proves to be an incumbrance upon the whole property.[15] Having notice of its existence, he is chargeable with constructive notice of all its contents.[16] One having notice of the existence of a mortgage can only acquire an interest subordinate to it, though the mort-

---

tained. Massie v. Greenhow, 2 Patt. & H. (Va.) 255.

[10] Mayfield v. Turner, 180 Ill. 332, 54 N. E. 418 (instrument creating a trust); Kidder v. Flanders, 73 N. H. 345, 61 Atl. 675 (contract); Wahl v. Stoy, 72 N. J. Eq. 607, 66 Atl. 176; Hill v. Murray, 56 Vt. 177 (conveyance); Hamilton v. Royse, 2 Sch. & Lef. 315.

[11] Foster v. Stallworth, 62 Ala. 547; Martin v. Cauble, 72 Ind. 67; Skeel v. Spraker, 8 Paige (N. Y.) 182; Fidelity Ins. Co. v. Shenandoah Valley Co., 32 W. Va. 244, 9 S. E. 180; Farrow v. Rees, 4 Beav. 18, 4 Jur. 1028, 49 Eng. Reprint 243.

[12] Foster v. Stallworth, 62 Ala. 547; Skeel v. Spraker, 8 Paige (N. Y.) 182; Beauce v. Muter, 5 Moore P. C. 69, 13 Eng. Reprint 416; Taylor v. Baker, 5 Price 306, 19 Rev. Rep. 625.

[13] Foster v. Stallworth, 62 Ala.

547; Martin v. Cauble, 72 Ind. 67; Ormes v. Weller, 21 Ky. L. 763, 52 S. W. 937.

[14] Lawton v. Gordon, 37 Cal. 202. [15] 2 White & Tudor's Lead. Cas. in Eq. (4th ed.), pt. 1, 190; Willink v. Morris C. &c. Co., 4 N. J. Eq. 377; Guion v. Knapp, 6 Paige (N. Y.) 35, 27 Am. Dec. 741; Jones v. Williams, 24 Beav. 47; Hall v. Smith, 14 Ves. 426.

[16] Webb v. Robbins, 77 Ala. 176 Martin v. Cauble, 72 Ind. 67; Pike v. Goodnow, 12 Allen (Mass.) 472; George v. Kent, 7 Allen (Mass.) 16; Willink v. Morris Canal &c. Co., 4 N. J. Eq. 377; Skeel v. Spraker, 8 Paige (N. Y.) 182; Ijames v. Gaither, 93 N. Car. 358; Barr v. Kinard, 3 Strobh. (S. Car.) 73; Fidelity Ins. &c. Co. v. Shenandoah Valley Co., 32 W. Va. 244, 9 S. E. 180. See ante § 524.

gage fails to recite the amount of the note which it was given to secure,[17] or it recites that it was given to secure "any indebtedness" of
the mortgagor to the mortgagee, and these words referred only to a
future indebtedness.[18] A purchaser of real estate, having notice that
his vendor still owes part of the purchase-money is put upon inquiry
as to the amount unpaid.[19]

One having notice that an estate is incumbered is not justified in
assuming that the incumbrance is one already known to him; he is
bound to inquire into the nature and extent of the charge referred
to.[20] A mortgagee having notice that his mortgagor had only an estate on condition subsequent is postponed to the grantor's equity, although he did not know the condition had been broken.[21] A notice of
a lease is notice of all the covenants and provisions contained in it.[22]

§ 574. **Notice from recitals in deeds.**—When a person claims under
a deed which by its recitals leads him to other facts affecting the title
to the property, he is presumed to know such facts; for it would be
gross negligence in him not to make inquiry as to the facts he is thus
put in the way of ascertaining.[23] A recital or description in a deed,

[17] Wilson v. Vaughan, 61 Miss. 472.
[18] Morris v. Murray, 82 Ky. 36; Simons v. First Nat. Bank, 93 N. Y. 269. See ante § 344.
[19] Wilson v. Hunter, 30 Ind. 466.
[20] Jones v. Williams, 24 Beav. 47.
[21] Gall v. Gall, 126 Wis. 390, 105 N. W. 953, 5 L. R. A. (N. S.) 603.
[22] Taylor v. Stibbert, 2 Ves. Jr. 437; Hall v. Smith, 14 Ves. Jr. 426, 9 Rev. Rep. 313, 33 Eng. Reprint 584; Brydges v. Chandos, 2 Ves. Jr. 417, 30 Eng. Reprint 702.
[23] Cordova v. Hood, 17 Wall. (U. S.) 1, 21 L. ed. 587; Oliver v. Piatt, 3 How. (U. S.) 333, 11 L. ed. 622; Rafferty v. Mallory, 3 Biss. (U. S.) 362; Lipse v. Spear, 4 Hughes (U. S.) 535; Reeves v. Vinacke, 1 Mc-Crary (U. S.) 213; Central Trust Co. v. Wabash, St. L. &c. R. Co., 29 Fed. 546; Tennessee &c. R. Co. v. East Alabama R. Co., 73 Ala. 426; Corbitt v. Clenny, 52 Ala. 480; Burch v. Carter, 44 Ala. 115; Costello v. Graham, 9 Ariz. 257, 80 Pac. 336; White v. Moffett, 108 Ark. 490, 158 S. W. 505; Thompson v. Bowen, 87 Ark. 490, 113 S. W. 26; Hardy v. Heard, 15 Ark. 184; Rea v. Haffenden, 116 Cal. 596, 48 Pac. 716; Hassey v. Wilke, 55 Cal. 525; Ham-

ilton v. Nutt, 34 Conn. 501; Sigourney v. Munn, 7 Conn. 324; Shoemaker v. Chappell, 4 Mack. (D. C.) 413; Simms v. Freiherr, 100 Ga. 607, 28 S. E. 288; Rosser v. Cheney, 61 Ga. 468; Stager v. Crabtree, 177 Ill. 59, 52 N. E. 378; Lagger v. Mutual Union Loan &c. Assn., 146 Ill. 283, 33 N. E. 946; Dean v. Long, 122 Ill. 447, 14 N. E. 34; United States Mortgage Co. v. Gross, 93. Ill. 483; Russell v. Ranson, 76 Ill. 167; Chicago, R. I. &c. R. Co. v. Kennedy, 70 Ill. 350; Ætna Life Ins. Co. v. Ford, 39 Ill. 252; Morris v. Hoyle, 37 Ill. 150, 87 Am. Dec. 243; Clark v. Plumstead, 11 Ill. App. 57; Foster v. Strong, 5 Bradw. (Ill.) 223; Smith v. Lowry, 113 Ind. 37, 15 N. E. 17; State v. Davis, 96 Ind. 539; Hazlett v. Sinclair, 76 Ind. 488, 40 Am. Rep. 254; Wiseman v. Hutchinson, 20 Ind. 40; Larrance v. Lewis, 51 Ind. App. 1, 98 N. E. 892; Gregory v. Arms, 48 Ind. App. 562, 96 N. E. 196; Shoemake v. Smith, 80 Iowa 655, 45 N. W. 744; Clark v. Holland, 72 Iowa 34, 33 N. W. 350, 2 Am. St. Rep. 230; Huber v. Bossart, 70 Iowa 718, 29 N. W. 608; Ætna Life Ins. Co. v. Bishop, 69 Iowa 645, 29 N. W. 761; Clark v.

to have this effect, must be in the course of the title under which the

Bullard, 66 Iowa 746, 24 N. W. 561; Fetes v. O'Laughlin, 62 Iowa 532, 17 N. W. 764; State v. Shaw, 28 Iowa 67; Crossdale v. Hill, 78 Kans. 140, 96 Pac. 37; Prest v. Black, 63 Kans. 682, 66 Pac. 1017; Knowles v. Williams, 58 Kans. 221, 48 Pac. 856; Taylor v. Mitchell, 58 Kans. 194, 48 Pac. 859; Dotson v. Merritt, 141 Ky. 155, 132 S. W. 181; Louisville H. &c. R. Co. v. Baskett (Ky.) 121 S. W. 957; Deskins v. Big Sandy Co., 121 Ky. 601, 28 Ky. L. 565, 89 S. W. 695; Bailey v. Southern R. Co., 112 Ky. 424, 22 Ky. L. 1397, 60 S. W. 631, 61 S. W. 31; Anderson v. Layton, 3 Bush (Ky.) 87; Bakewell v. Ogden, 2 Bush (Ky.) 265; Pike v. Collins, 33 Maine 38; Green v. Early, 39 Md. 223; Bryan v. Harvey, 18 Md. 113; Sargent v. Hubbard, 102 Mass. 380; George v. Kent, 7 Allen (Mass.) 16; Wait v. Baldwin, 60 Mich. 622, 27 N. W. 697; Baker v. Mather, 25 Mich. 51; Fitzhugh v. Barnard, 12 Mich. 104; Mason v. Payne, Walk. Ch. (Mich.) 459; Bergstrom v. Johnson, 111 Minn. 247, 126 N. W. 899; Ross v. Worthington, 11 Minn. 438, 88 Am. Dec. 95; Daughaday v. Paine, 6 Minn. 443 (Gil. 304); Baldwin v. Anderson, 103 Miss. 462, 60 So. 578; Spellman v. McKeen, 96 Miss. 693, 51 So. 914; Binder v. Weinberg, 94 Miss. 817, 48 So. 1013; Stovall v. Judah, 74 Miss. 747, 21 So. 614; Deason v. Taylor, 53 Miss. 697; Gulf Coast Canning Co. v. Foster (Miss.), 17 So. 683; Wailes v. Cooper, 24 Miss. 208; Case v. Goodman, 250 Mo. 112, 156 S. W. 698; Marshall v. Hill, 246 Mo. 1, 151 S. W. 131; Adams v. Gossom, 228 Mo. 566, 129 S. W. 16; Gross v. Watts, 206 Mo. 373, 104 S. W. 30, 121 Am. St. 662; Freeman v. Moffitt, 119 Mo. 280, 25 S. W. 87; Mason v. Black, 87 Mo. 329; Bronson v. Wanzer, 86 Mo. 408; Tydings v. Pitcher, 82 Mo. 379; Poage v. Wabash R. Co. 24 Mo. App. 199; Lyon v. Gombert, 63 Nebr. 630, 88 N. W. 774; Buchanan v. Balkum, 60 N. H. 406; Brown v. Eastman, 16 N. H. 588; Jennings v. Dixey, 36 N. J. Eq. 490; Sea Grove Build. Assn. v. Parsons (N. J. Eq.), 17 Atl. 834; Van Doren v. Robinson, 16 N. J. Eq. 256; Mitchell v. D'Olier, 68 N. J. L. 375, 53 Atl. 467, 59 L. R. A. 949; Roll v. Rea, 50 N. J. L. 264, 12 Atl. 905; Sweet v. Henry, 175 N. Y. 268, 67 N. E. 574; Reed v. Gannon, 50 N. Y. 345; Cambridge Valley Bank v. Delano, 48 N. Y. 326; Acer v. Westcott, 46 N. Y. 384, 7 Am. Rep. 355; Howard Ins. Co. v. Halsey, 8 N. Y. 271, 59 Am. Dec. 478; Gibert v. Peteler, 38 Barb. (N. Y.) 488; Dunham v. Dey, 15 Johns. (N. Y.) 554, 8 Am. Dec. 282; Whistler v. Cole, 81 Misc. 519, 143 N. Y. S. 478; Holmes v. Holmes, 86 N. Car. 205; Christmas v. Mitchell, 38 N. Car. 535; O'Toole v. Omlie, 8 N. Dak. 444, 79 N. W. 849; Bonner v. Ware, 10 Ohio 465; Reeder v. Bar, 4 Ohio 446, 22 Am. Dec. 762; Martin v. Eagle Development Co., 41 Ore. 448, 69 Pac. 216; In re Mulholland's Estate, 224 Pa. St. 536, 73 Atl. 932, 132 Am. St. 791; Pyles v. Brown, 189 Pa. St. 164, 42 Atl. 11, 69 Am. St. 794; Parke v. Neeley, 90 Pa. St. 52; Ogden v. Porterfield, 34 Pa. St. 191; Kerr v. Kitchen, 17 Pa. St. 433; Knouff v. Thompson, 16 Pa. St. 357; Bellas v. Lloyd, 2 Watts (Pa.) 401; Teague v. Sowder, 121 Tenn. 132, 114 S. W. 484; Kansas City Land Co. v. Hill, 87 Tenn. 589, 11 S. W. 797; Pulliam v. Wilkerson, 7 Baxt. (Tenn.) 611; McGavrock v. Deery, 1 Coldw. (Tenn.) 265; Payne v. Abercrombie, 10 Heisk. (Tenn.) 161; Waggoner v. Dodson, 96 Tex. 415, 73 S. W. 517; Kirby v. Estill, 75 Tex. 484, 12 S. W. 807; Polk v. Chaison, 72 Tex. 500, 10 S. W. 581; Renick v. Frazier, 55 Tex. 102; Peters v. Clements, 46 Tex. 114; McRimmon v. Martin, 14 Tex. 318; Loomis v. Cobb (Tex. Civ. App.), 159 S. W. 305; Freund v. Sabin (Tex. Civ. App.), 159 S. W. 168; Carver v. Ledbetter (Tex. Civ. App.), 147 S. W. 348; Hawkins v. Potter (Tex. Civ. App.), 130 S. W. 643; Davidson v. Ryle, 103 Tex. 209, 124 S. W. 616, 125 S. W. 881; Carlisle v. King (Tex. Civ. App.), 122 S. W. 581, affd. 103 Tex. 620, 133 S. W. 241; Nelson v. Brown (Tex. Civ. App.), 111 S. W. 1106; Houston Ice &c. Co. v. Henson (Tex.), 93 S. W. 713; San Augustine County v. Mad-

purchaser claims.[24] A purchaser is affected with notice of recitals in conveyances forming his chain of title and material thereto, whether recorded or not;[25] and a purchaser under a conveyance referring to an unrecorded deed is chargeable with notice of its contents.[26] But recitals in collateral and immaterial deeds incidentally referred to,

den, 39 Tex. Civ. App. 257, 87 S. W. 1056; King v. Summerville (Tex.), 80 S. W. 1050, affd. 98 Tex. 332, 83 S. W. 680; O'Mahoney v. Flannagan, 34 Tex. Civ. App. 244, 78 S. W. 245; Robinson v. Crenshaw, 84 Va. 348, 5 S. E. 222; Argenbright v. Campbell, 3 Hen. & M. (Va.) 144; Pocahontas Tanning Co. v. St. Lawrence Boom &c. Co., 63 W. Va. 685, 60 S. E. 890; Reichert v. Neuser, 93 Wis. 513, 67 N. W. 939; Bennett v. Keehn, 67 Wis. 154, 29 N. W. 207, 30 N. W. 12; Dailey v. Kastell, 56 Wis. 444, 14 N. W. 635; Wier v. Simmons, 55 Wis. 637, 13 N. W. 873; Pringle v. Dunn, 37 Wis. 449, 19 Am. Rep. 772; Bacon v. Bacon, Tothill 133; Moore v. Bennett, 2 Ch. Cas. 246; Pilcher v. Rawlins, L. R. 11 Eq. 53. It is a familiar and thoroughly well-settled principle of realty law that a purchaser has constructive notice of every matter connected with or affecting his estate which appears by recital, reference, or otherwise, upon the face of any deed which forms an essential link in the chain of instruments through which he deraigns his title. The rationale of the rule is that any description, recital of fact, or reference to other documents puts the purchaser upon inquiry, and he is bound to follow up this inquiry, step by step, from one discovery to another and from one instrument to another, until the whole series of title deeds is exhausted and a complete knowledge of all the matters referred to and affecting the estate is obtained. Being thus put upon inquiry, the purchaser is presumed to have prosecuted it until its final result and with ultimate success. Loomis v. Cobb (Tex. Civ. App.), 159 S. W. 305. See ante § 524.

[24] Polk v. Cosgrove, 4 Biss. (U. S.) 437, 19 Fed. Cas. 11248; Burch v. Carter, 44 Ala. 115; Hazlett v. Sinclair, 77 Ind. 488, 40 Am. Rep. 254; Corbin v. Sullivan, 47 Ind. 356; Sullivan v. Mefford, 143 Iowa 210, 121 N. W. 569; Mueller v. Engeln, 12 Bush (Ky.) 441; Burke v. Beveridge, 15 Minn. 205; Knox Co. v. Brown, 103 Mo. 223, 15 S. W. 382; Mason v. Black, 87 Mo. 329; Tydings v. Pitcher, 82 Mo. 379; Dingman v. McCollum, 47 Mo. 372; Chandler v. Robinson (N. J. Eq.), 75 Atl. 180; McCrea v. Newman, 46 N. J. Eq. 473, 19 Atl. 198; Coleman v. Barklew, 27 N. J. L. 357; Treadwell v. Inslee, 120 N. Y. 458, 24 N. E. 651; Boggs v. Varner, 6 Watts & S. (Pa.) 469; Bellas v. Lloyd, 2 Watts (Pa.) 401; Ramiriz v. Smith, 94 Tex. 184, 59 S. W. 258; Brokel v. McKechnie, 69 Tex. 32, 6 S. W. 623.

[25] Abbott v. Parker, 103 Ark. 425, 147 S. W. 70; Stidham v. Matthews, 29 Ark. 650; Bailey v. Southern R. Co., 112 Ky. 424, 22 Ky. L. 1397, 60 S. W. 631, 61 S. W. 31; White v. Foster, 102 Mass. 375; Daughaday v. Paine, 6 Minn. 443; Buchanan v. Balkum, 60 N. H. 406; Sweet v. Henry, 175 N. Y. 268, 67 N. E. 574; Hancock v. McAvoy, 151 Pa. St. 439, 25 Atl. 48; Woodward v. Ross (Tex. Civ. App.), 153 S. W. 158; Runge v. Gilbough (Tex.), 87 S. W. 832; Davis v. Tebbs, 81 Va. 600. See also Haas v. Fontenot, 132 La. 812, 61 So. 831.

[26] Stanley v. Schwalby, 162 U. S. 255, 40 L. ed. 960, 16 Sup. Ct. 754; Cincinnati, I. &c. R. Co. v. Smith, 127 Ind. 461, 26 N. E. 1009; White v. Foster, 102 Mass. 375; Cook v. Farrington, 10 Gray (Mass.) 70; Henderson v. Cameron, 73 Miss. 843, 20 So. 2; Paul v. Kerswell, 60 N. J. L. 273, 37 Atl. 1102; Hancock v. McAvoy, 151 Pa. St. 439, 25 Atl. 48; Graham v. Hawkins, 1 Tex. Unrep. Cas. 514.

not as relating in any way to the title of the property, or to the consideration paid for it, do not affect the purchasers.[27]

The recitals must be sufficiently clear to put the purchaser upon inquiry, and to lead him to the requisite information.[28] If the recital does not explain itself, it must refer to some deed or fact which will explain it, to make it constructive notice.[29] Notice flowing from matters of record can never be more extensive than the facts stated or referred to.[30] A purchaser put upon inquiry by recitals, is not entitled to rely upon his vendor's representations contradicting such recitals.[31]

The description of a grantee as trustee in a recorded deed is notice of a trust of some description and puts a subsequent purchaser or mortgagee upon inquiry as to the existence or nature of such trust.[32] If a deed shows that it was made under a decree of court, the purchaser is bound to take notice of the facts disclosed by the record of the proceedings in which the decree was rendered.[33]

[27] Kansas City Land Co. v. Hill, 87 Tenn. 589, 11 S. W. 797; Burch v. Carter, 44 Ala. 115; Mendelsohn v. Armstrong, 52 La. Ann. 1300, 27 So. 735.

[28] Racouillat v. Rene, 32 Cal. 450; Russell v. Ranson, 76 Ill. 167; Briggs v. Rice, 130 Mass. 50; Spellman v. McKeen, 96 Miss. 693, 51 So. 914; Bell v. Twilight, 22 N. H. 500; Acer v. Westcott, 46 N. Y. 384, 7 Am. Rep. 355; McDaniel v. Harley (Tex.), 42 S. W. 323; McBride v. Moore (Tex.), 37 S. W. 450; Durst v. Daugherty, 81 Tex. 650, 17 S. W. 388. Vague and indefinite recitals do not amount to notice. Pyles v. Brown, 186 Pa. St. 164, 42 Atl. 11, 69 Am. St. 794. See post § 576.

[29] Morris v. Murray, 82 Ky. 36; Van Slyck v. Skinner, 41 Mich. 186; Bell v. Twilight, 22 N. H. 500, 45 Am. Dec. 367; Cambridge Valley Bank v. Delano, 48 N. Y. 326; White v. Carpenter, 2 Paige (N. Y.) 217; Kaine v. Denniston, 22 Pa. St. 202; French v. Loyal Land Co., 5 Leigh (Va.) 627. In Sanborn v. Robinson, 54 N. H. 239, at the close of the description in a mortgage, the following words were inclosed in parenthses:
(Of six hundred dollars said premises are subject to a former) It was held that this was notice of a prior mortgage of that amount.

[30] Norman v. Towne, 130 Mass. 52; Briggs v. Rice, 130 Mass. 50; Gale v. Morris, 29 N. J. Eq. 222; Branch v. Griffin, 99 N. Car. 173, 5 S. E. 393. See ante § 524.

[31] Bergstrom v. Johnson, 111 Minn. 247, 126 N. W. 899; Waggoner v. Dodson, 96 Tex. 415, 73 S. W. 517; Patman v. Harland, 17 Ch. D. 353, 50 L. J. Ch. 642, 44 L. T. (N. S.) 728, 29 Wkly. Rep. 707. On the other hand it has been held that recitals in a deed that the purchase-price had been paid will not protect a subsequent mortgagee who had been told otherwise before making the loan. Wilson v. Shocklee, 94 Ark. 301, 126 S. W. 832.

[32] Mercantile Nat. Bank v. Parsons, 54 Minn. 56, 55 N. W. 825, 40 Am. St. 299; Case v. Goodman, 250 Mo. 112, 156 S. W. 698; Snyder v. Collier, 85 Nebr. 552, 123 N. W. 1023, 133 Am. St. 682; Studebaker Bros. Mfg. Co. v. Hunt (Tex.), 38 S. W. 1134. See also Knowles v. Williams, 58 Kans. 221, 48 Pac. 856; Marbury v. Ehlen, 72 Md. 206, 19 Atl. 648, 20 Am. St. 467; Turner v. Edmonston, 210 Mo. 411, 109 S. W. 33, 124 Am. St. 739; Tradesmen's Nat. Bank v. Looney, 99 Tenn. 278, 42 S. W. 149, 38 L. R. A. 837, 63 Am. St. 830.

[33] Gulf Coast Canning Co. v. Foster (Miss.), 17 So. 683. See as to bond not referred to in court record

A recital of a mortgage which defectively describes the land in a deed under which a purchaser from the mortgagor claims title charges him with notice of it.[34]

A purchaser by a deed which refers to a recorded mortgage of the same land by his grantor has notice of a statement in such mortgage that the grantor reserved the trees growing on the land, the same having been sold to a third person.[35]

A description of a portion of the land described in a deed as "land, the title to which is in A, given as collateral security to pay certain notes," is sufficient notice to the purchaser of an unrecorded mortgage to A to preserve the priority of the mortgage.[36] But a purchaser from one who has covenanted to pay all legal mortgages and incumbrances of whatever nature and description on the premises is not put upon inquiry as to any incumbrance not of record, when there is a mortgage of record to which the covenant could properly refer. Neither could he be charged with constructive notice of a mortgage improperly recorded, as, for instance, one without seal.[37]

A note secured by a mortgage or deed of trust, and referring to such mortgage or deed by a statement that the note is secured by a mortgage or deed of trust, as the case may be, gives notice of the terms of the mortgage or deed of trust, so far as these terms in any way qualify the terms of the note, and the holder of the note is bound by such provisions of the mortgage;[38] thus, he is bound by a provision in the mortgage that the nonpayment of interest on the note shall have the effect of making the note due and payable at once.[39]

§ 575. Recital of existing mortgage.—One who purchases land by a deed, which expressly recites that the premises are subject to a mortgage, has notice of the mortgage from the recital, and can not claim against it, although it be not recorded.[40] And a purchaser or mort-

for payment of attorney fees, Interstate Bldg. &c. Assn. v. McCartha, 43 S. Car. 72, 20 S. E. 807.

[34] Knox Co. v. Brown, 103 Mo. 223.

[35] White v. Faster, 102 Mass. 375.

[36] Dunham v. Dey, 15 Johns. (N. Y.) 555, 8 Am. Dec. 282.

[37] Racouillat v. Rene, 32 Cal. 450.

[38] Orrick v. Durham, 79 Mo. 174.

[39] Clark v. Bullard, 66 Iowa 747, 24 N. W. 561; Noell v. Gaines, 68 Mo. 649.

[40] Reeves v. Vinacke, 1 McCrary (U. S.) 213; Hull v. Sullivan, 63 Ga. 126; Walls v. State, 140 Ind. 16,

38 N. E. 177; Garrett v. Puckett, 15 Ind. 485; Ætna L. Ins. Co. v. Bishop, 69 Iowa 645, 29 N. W. 761; Taylor v. Mitchell, 58 Kans. 194, 48 Pac. 859; Howard v. Chase, 104 Mass. 249; George v. Kent, 7 Allen (Mass.) 16; Kitchell v. Mudgett. 37 Mich. 81; Baker v. Mather, 25 Mich. 51; Carter v. Leonard, 65 Nebr. 670, 91 N. W. 574; Westervelt v. Wyckoff, 32 N. J. Eq. 188; Lafayette Bldg. &c. Assn. v. Erb, 5 Sad. (Pa.) 40, 8 Atl. 62; Reichert v. Neuser, 93 Wis. 513, 67 N. W. 939. See post §§ 736, 744.

gagee is likewise chargeable with knowledge of a mortgage or other incumbrance which is recited or distinctly referred to in any deed in the chain of title under which he claims.[41] "The principle of equity is well established that a purchaser of land is chargeable with notice, by implication, of every fact affecting the title which would be discovered by an examination of the deeds, or other muniments of title of his vendor, and of every fact as to which the purchaser, with reasonable prudence or diligence, ought to become acquainted. If there is sufficient contained in any deed or record, which a prudent purchaser ought to examine, to induce an inquiry in the mind of an intelligent person, he is chargeable with knowledge or notice of the facts so contained."[42]

A grantee who knowingly accepts a conveyance containing a clause assuming the payment of an existing mortgage becomes personally liable therefor.[43] The grantee must, however, have knowledge that the

[41] Talmadge v. Interstate Bldg. &c. Assn., 105 Ga. 550, 31 S. E. 618; Ætna L. Ins. Co. v. Ford, 89 Ill. 252; Rose v. Provident Sav. &c. Assn., 28 Ind. App. 25, 62 N. E. 293; Ætna L. Ins. Co. v. Bishop, 69 Iowa 645, 29 N. W. 761; Clark v. Bullard, 66 Iowa 747, 24 N. W. 561; Prest v. Black, 63 Kans. 682; 66 Pac. 1017; Hall v. Wright, 137 Ky. 39, 127 S. W. 516; Farmers' &c. Bank v. German Ins. Bank, 23 Ky. L. 2008, 66 S. W. 280; Mounot v. Williamson, 7 Mart. (N. S.) (La.) 381; Michigan Mut. L. Ins. Co. v. Conant, 40 Mich. 530; Baker v. Mather, 25 Mich. 51; Knox v. Brown, 103 Mo. 223, 15 S. W. 382; Hubbard v. Knight, 52 Nebr. 400, 72 N. W. 473; Westervelt v. Wyckoff, 32 N. J. Eq. 188; Bentley v. Gardner, 45 App. Div. 216, 60 N. Y. S. 1056; Newton v. Manwarring, 56 Hun 645, 32 N. Y. St. 389, 10 N. Y. S. 347; Hinton v. Leigh, 102 N. Car. 28, 8 S. E. 890; LaFayette Bldg. &c. Assn. v. Erb, 5 Sad. (Pa.) 40, 8 Atl. 62; Arlington Heights Realty Co. v. Citizens' R. &c. Co. (Tex. Civ. App.), 160 S. W. 1109; Hiser v. Hiser, 13 Montg. Co. Rep. 49; Greenwood v. Churchill, 6 Beav. 314, 12 L. J. Ch. 400, 49 Eng. Reprint 846; Farrow v. Rees, 4 Beav. 18, 4 Jur. 1028, 49 Eng. Reprint 243 (general recital of existence of mortgage sufficient without specification). See also Bragg v. Lamport, 96 Fed. 630, 38 C. C. A. 467; Foster v. Jett, 74 Fed. 678, 20 C. C. A. 670; Central Trust Co. v. Wabash &c. R. Co., 29 Fed. 546; Foster v. Bowles, 138 Cal. 346, 71 Pac. 494, 649; Patton v. Eberhart, 52 Iowa 67, 2 N. W. 954; Fullerton v. McBride, 90 Miss. 420, 43 So. 684; Frye v. Hubbell, 74 N. H. 358, 68 Atl. 325, 17 L. R. A. (N. S.) 1197; Peck v. Mallams, 10 N. Y. 509; Crofut v. Wood, 3 Hun (N. Y.) 571, 6 Thomps. & C. 314. A mortgagee who accepts a mortgage note, expressly reciting that the mortgage is a second mortgage, is estopped to deny the validity and priority of the first mortgage. Setze v. First Nat. Bank, 140 Ga. 603, 79 S. E. 540. A mortgagee is chargeable with knowledge disclosed by an abstract showing that the mortgaged land was community property. Tomlinson v. Drought (Tex. Civ. App.), 127 S. W. 262. A recital of incumbrances in a real estate mortgage does not give the mortgagee notice of a chattel mortgage upon a building and machinery forming a part of the realty. Peoria Stone &c. Works v. Sinclair, 146 Iowa 56, 124 N. W. 772.

[42] Cambridge Valley Bank v. Delano, 48 N. Y. 329.

[43] Foster v. Atwater, 42 Conn. 244; Hadley v. Clark, 8 Idaho 497, 69 Pac. 319; Thomas v. Home Mut.

deed contains the assumption clause;[44] and if he accepts the conveyance in ignorance thereof he may repudiate the transaction upon discovery of the facts,[45] provided he acts promptly before exercising acts
of ownership.[46] In like manner, and for stronger reasons, one who has
purchased land subject to a mortgage, which he agrees to pay, takes
a title subject to the mortgage, although it be not recorded, or be recorded in such a way that it is not notice.[47] Where a mortgagor's title
deed recites his assumption of a prior mortgage, a subsequent mortgagee is charged with notice thereof, and of the rights of bondholders
secured thereunder.[48]

Many authorities lay down the rule that a grantee is estopped to
deny the validity of any mortgage to which his deed recites that the
conveyance to him is subject.[49] But some authorities hold that such

Bldg. & Loan Assn., 243 Ill. 550, 90
N. E. 1081; Bay v. Williams, 112
Ill. 91, 1 N. E. 340, 54 Am. Rep. 209;
Dean v. Walker, 107 Ill. 540, 47 Am.
Rep. 467; Blakeslee v. Hoit, 116 Ill.
App. 83; Martindale v. Parsons, 98
Ind. 174; Beeson v. Green, 103 Iowa
406, 72 N. W. 555; Hendricks v.
Brooks, 80 Kans. 1, 101 Pac. 622,
132 Am. St. 186; Neiswanger v. Mc-
Clellan, 45 Kans. 599, 26 Pac. 18;
Williams v. Fowle, 132 Mass. 385;
Reed v. Paul, 131 Mass. 129; Locke
v. Homer, 131 Mass. 93, 41 Am. Rep.
199; Furnas v. Durgin, 119 Mass.
500, 20 Am. Rep. 341; Kollen v.
Sooy, 172 Mich. 214, 137 N. W. 808;
Unger v. Smith, 44 Mich. 22, 5 N.
W. 1069; Crawford v. Edwards, 33
Mich. 354; Smith v. Davis, 90 Mo.
App. 533; MacAdaras v. King, 10 Mo.
App. 578; Huyler v. Atwood, 26 N.
J. Eq. 504; Sparkman v. Gove, 44
N. J. L. 252; Bowen v. Beck, 94 N.
Y. 86, 46 Am. Rep. 124; Campbell
v. Smith, 71 N. Y. 26, 27 Am. Rep.
5; Ranney v. McMullen, 5 Abb. N.
Cas. (N. Y.) 246; Windle v. Hughes,
40 Ore. 1, 65 Pac. 1058; Connor v.
Jones (S. Dak.), 72 N. W. 463;
Davis v. Hulett, 58 Vt. 90, 4 Atl. 139;
Ludington v. Harris, 21 Wis. 239.
See also Merriman v. Schmitt, 211
Ill. 263, 71 N. E. 986; Swisher v.
Palmer, 106 Ill. App. 432; Elser v.
Williams, 104 Ill. App. 238; Boisot
v. Chandler, 82 Ill. App. 261; Baer
v. Knewitz, 39 Ill. App. 470; Mun-
sell v. Beals, 5 Kans. App. 736, 46
Pac. 984; Rutland Sav. Bank v.

White, 4 Kans. App. 435, 46 Pac.
29; Heffernan v. Weir, 99 Mo. App.
301, 72 S. W. 1085. Effect of recital
as estoppel against grantee, see
Lynch v. Moser, 72 Conn. 714, 46
Atl. 153; Cram v. Ingalls, 18 N. H.
613; Moulton v. Haskell, 50 Minn.
367, 52 N. W. 960.
[44] Keller v. Ashford, 3 Mackey (D.
C.) 444; Merriman v. Schmitt, 211
Ill. 263, 71 N. E. 986; Adams v.
Wheeler, 122 Ind. 251, 23 N. E. 760;
Kelly v. Geer, 101 N. Y. 664, 5 N. E.
332.
[45] Metzger v. Huntington, 139 Ind.
501, 37 N. E. 1084, 39 N. E. 235;
Green v. Stone (N. J.), 32 Atl. 706;
Cordts v. Hargrave, 29 N. J. Eq. 446.
[46] Keller v. Ashford, 133 U. S. 610,
33 L. ed. 667, 10 Sup. Ct. 494; Ver
Planck v. Lee, 19 Wash. 492, 53 Pac.
724.
[47] Ross v. Worthington, 11 Minn.
438, 88 Am. Dec. 95. See also Smith
v. Lowry, 113 Ind. 37, 15 N. E. 17;
Higgins v. Dennis, 104 Iowa 605, 74
N. W. 9; Fitzgerald v. Barker, 85
Mo. 13; Carter v. Leonard, 65 Nebr.
670, 91 N. W. 574. A covenant to
pay a prior mortgage to which a
later one is made subject, may be
implied from the exception of the
covenant against incumbrances. Ja-
maica Sav. Bank v. Butler, 79 Vt.
372, 65 Atl. 92.
[48] Farmers' &c. Bank v. German
Ins. Bank, 29 Ky. L. 2008, 66 S. W.
280.
[49] American Water Works Co. v.
Farmers' L. &c. Co., 73 Fed. 956, 20

a recital does not estop the grantee where the incumbrance recited is not expressly assumed by the grantee or made a part of the consideration.[50] A mortgagee, whose mortgage recites that another mortgage is a first lien upon the property, can not claim that his mortgage takes precedence of a new mortgage afterward executed and recorded, to correct a mistake in the description of the property in the first mortgage.[51] Furthermore, the recitals in a deed under which a mortgagor holds title are constructive notice to a mortgagee.[52]

Where two mortgages made by the same person upon the same land, as parts of one transaction, though dated on different days, refer to each other, the question of priority depends upon the intention of the parties as determined by the terms in which the references are made.[53]

Where a mortgage takes effect only from its delivery for record, and its priority is not affected by notice of a prior unrecorded mortgage, of course the mere mention of a prior mortgage in the deed, as, for instance, excepting it from the covenants of warranty,[54] does not affect the priority given by the record; yet, if the mortgage be expressly made subject to another, priority of record will avail nothing.[55] Moreover, one taking a mortgage made expressly subject to a prior mortgage can not avoid it and acquire a larger lien than contracted

C. C. A. 133; Garrett v. Puckett, 15 Ind. 485; Foy v. Armstrong, 113 Iowa 629, 85 N. W. 753; Fuller v. Hunt, 48 Iowa 163; Taylor v. Riggs, 8 Kans. App. 323, 57 Pac. 44; Citizens' Bank v. Webre, 44 La. Ann. 334, 10 So. 728; Johnson v. Thompson, 129 Mass. 398; Howard v. Chase, 104 Mass. 249; Tuite v. Stevens, 98 Mass. 305; Moulton v. Haskell, 50 Minn. 367, 52 N. W. 960; Alt v. Banholzer, 36 Minn. 57, 29 N. W. 674; Hopkins v. Wolley, 81 N. Y. 77; Freeman v. Auld, 44 N. Y. 50; Styles v. Price, 64 How. Pr. (N. Y.) 227; Pittman v. Hall, 5 N. Y. St. 853; Riley v. Rice, 40 Ohio St. 441; Mott v. Maris (Tex.), 29 S. W. 825; Walsh v. Ford, 27 Tex. Civ. App. 573, 66 S. W. 854. See also Stein v. Indianapolis Bldg., L. &c. Assn., 18 Ind. 237, 81 Am. Dec. 353; Hopkins v. Wolley, 81 N. Y. 77; Russell v. Kinney, 1 Sandf. Ch. (N. Y.) 34; Hartley v. Tatham, 24 How. Pr. (N. Y.) 505, 23 N. Y. Super. Ct. 273. But see Purdy v. Coar, 109 N. Y. 448, 17 N. E. 352, 4 Am. St. 491.

[50] Brooks v. Owen, 112 Mo. 251, 19

S. W. 723, 20 S. W. 492; Briggs v. Seymour, 17 Wis. 255; Farmers' L. &c. Co. v. Commercial Bank, 15 Wis. 424, 82 Am. Dec. 689. See also Robinson Bank v. Miller, 153 Ill. 244, 38 N. E. 1078, 27 L. R. A. 449, 46 Am. St. 883; Hasenritter v. Kirchhoffer, 79 Mo. 239. Estoppel to set up usury where incumbrance is part of consideration. Stiger v. Bent, 111 Ill. 328; Trusdell v. Dowden, 47 N. J. Eq. 396, 20 Atl. 972; Pinnell v. Boyd, 33 N. J. Eq. 190; Conover v. Hobert, 24 N. J. Eq. 120; Dolman v. Cook, 14 N. J. Eq. 56.

[51] Council Bluffs Lodge v. Billups, 67 Iowa 674, 25 N. W. 846.

[52] Steere v. Childs, 15 Hun (N. Y.) 511; Wells v. Houston, 23 Tex. Civ. App. 629, 57 S. W. 584.

[53] Iowa College v. Fenno, 67 Iowa 244, 25 N. W. 152. See also Coleman v. Carhart, 74 Ga. 392; Pomeroy v. Latting, 15 Gray (Mass.) 435; Jones v. Phelps, 2 Barb. Ch. (N. Y.) 440.

[54] Bercaw v. Cockerill, 20 Ohio St. 163.

[55] Coe v. Columbus, P. &c. R. Co., 10 Ohio St. 372, 75 Am. Dec. 518.

for, although that mortgage be invalid as against the mortgagor.[56] When a mortgage is expressly excepted from a covenant of warranty in a deed, this exception charges the purchaser with notice of the mortgage, although the mortgage be not recorded.[57]

§ 576. Recital of credit in prior deed.—Where there is a recital in a prior deed that the sale was made upon credit, a subsequent purchaser is bound to inquire whether the purchase-money has been paid, or whether the vendor has a lien for it;[58] and the mere fact that the time of payment of the purchase-money, as recited in the deed, has elapsed does not authorize him to presume that it was paid.[59] Only the lapse of the period of limitations will excuse failure to make such inquiry.[60] Recitals relied upon as constructive notice must be so clear and distinct as to put an ordinarily prudent purchaser upon inquiry, and must be so far correct and intelligible that upon proper inquiry they would lead the purchaser to knowledge of the incumbrance or defect in title with which he is sought to be charged.[61] It has been said that the purchaser must have been guilty of gross negligence in not properly investigating the title in question.[62] No more than ordi-

[56] Freeman v. Auld, 44 N. Y. 50, revg. 44 Barb. 14, 37 Barb. 587; Hardin v. Hyde, 40 Barb. (N. Y.) 435.

[57] Morrison v. Morrison, 38 Iowa 73.

[58] Cordova v. Hood, 17 Wall. (U. S.) 1, 21 L. ed. 587; Whitfield v. Riddle, 78 Ala. 99; Atlanta Land &c. Co. v. Haile, 106 Ga. 498, 32 S. E. 606; Croskey v. Chapman, 26 Ind. 333; Wiseman v. Hutchinson, 20 Ind. 40; Johnston v. Gwathney, 4 Litt. (Ky.) 317, 14 Am. Dec. 135; Woodward v. Woodward, 7 B. Mon. (Ky.) 116; Thornton v. Knox, 6 B. Mon. (Ky.) 74; Honore v. Bakewell, 6 B. Mon. (Ky.) 67, 43 Am. Dec. 147; Deason v. Taylor, 53 Miss. 697; Hoggatt v. Wade, 10 Smed. & M. (Miss.) 143; Tydings v. Pitcher, 82 Mo. 379; Orrick v. Durham, 79 Mo. 174; Major v. Bukley, 51 Mo. 227; Scott v. McCullock, 13 Mo. 13; Lytle v. Turner, 12 Lea (Tenn.) 641; Simmons v. Redmond (Tenn.), 62 S. W. 366; Willis v. Gay, 48 Tex. 463, 26 Am. Rep. 328; Moore v. Scott (Tex.), 38 S. W. 394; Bergman v. Blackwell (Tex. Civ. App.), 23 S. W. 243; Atterberry v. Burnett (Tex. Civ.

App.), 130 S. W. 1028. See also Warford v. Hankins, 150 Ind. 489, 50 N. E. 468; Shuttleworth v. Kentucky Coal &c. Co., 22 Ky. L. 1806, 61 S. W. 1013. But see Robinson v. Owens, 103 Tenn. 91, 52 S. W. 870.

[59] Deason v. Taylor, 53 Miss. 697. But see Robinson v. Owens, 103 Tenn. 91, 52 S. W. 870.

[60] Allen v. Poole, 54 Miss. 323.

[61] Wood v. Pitman Coal Co., 90 Ky. 588, 12 Ky. L. 499, 14 S. W. 588; Mendelsohn v. Armstrong, 52 La. Ann. 1300, 27 So. 735; Jennings v. Dockham, 99 Mich. 253, 58 N. W. 66; Spellman v. McKeen, 96 Miss. 693, 51 So. 914; Bell v. Twilight, 22 N. H. 500; McDaniel v. Harley (Tex.), 42 S. W. 323; Lewis v. Madisons, 1 Munf. (Va.) 303. See also Harrison v. Johnson, 18 N. J. Eq. 420; Acer v. Westcott, 46 N. Y. 384, 7 Am. Rep. 355; McBride v. Moore (Tex.), 37 S. W. 450; Durst v. Daugherty, 81 Tex. 650, 17 S. W. 388. See ante § 574.

[62] Acer v. Westcott, 46 N. Y. 384, 7 Am. Rep. 355; Moore v. Kane, 24 Ont. 541.

nary prudence and diligence is required, however, on the part of a purchaser, and therefore, if the reference be to an incumbrance which has been discharged of record, it does not charge him with notice of the existence of another and entirely different incumbrance.[63]

The reservation by deed of a vendor's lien is a substantial charge upon the land and affects all subsequent purchasers;[64] and a reservation of such a lien in a final decree of a court of record has the same effect.[65]

Where a deed of trust recites that it is made to secure promissory notes, and the laws of the state recognize notes under seal which are barred in ten years and notes not under seal which are barred in five years, and it is not specified whether the notes secured are under seal or not, one who accepts a subsequent mortgage on the same property, more than five, but less than ten years from the making of the first mortgage, is bound to inquire whether the notes secured by the first incumbrance were executed under seal, and having failed to do so the first incumbrancer is not estopped from showing that the notes held by him were sealed instruments.[66]

§ 577. **Effect of notice upon mortgaged premises sold in parcels.**— As elsewhere shown, where the mortgaged premises have been sold in parcels to different persons at different times, in the absence of any intervening equities, the several parcels are subject to the mortgage, and are to be resorted to in the inverse order of alienation.[67] This rule applies where the successive purchasers have actual or constructive notice of the prior sales.[68] But the parcel last sold can not be applied in satisfaction of the mortgage, in exoneration of the parcels first sold, unless the last purchaser had notice of the earlier sales.[69]

When, however, the first purchaser expressly takes subject to the mortgage, he has, of course, no equity as against the mortgagor that

[63] Cambridge Valley Bank v. Delano, 48 N. Y. 326.

[64] Lincoln v. Purcell, 2 Head (Tenn.) 142, 73 Am. Dec. 196.

[65] Martin v. Neblett, 86 Tenn. 383, 7 S. W. 123.

[66] Foster v. Jett, 74 Fed. 678, 20 C. C. A. 670.

[67] Iglehart v. Crane, 42 Ill. 261; McKinney v. Miller, 19 Mich. 142; First Nat. Bank v. Cox (Tex. Civ. App.), 139 S. W. 1; Hawkins v. Potter (Tex. Civ. App.), 130 S. W. 643. See post § 1620.

[68] Sanford v. Hill, 46 Conn. 42; Lock v. Fulford, 52 Ill. 166; Iglehart v. Crane, 42 Ill. 261; Miami Exporting Co. v. United States Bank, Wright (Ohio) 249; Root v. Collins, 34 Vt. 173; Lyman v. Lyman, 32 Vt. 79, 76 Am. Dec. 151; State v. Titus, 17 Wis. 241. See also Sternberger v. Hanna, 42 Ohio St. 305 (possession as notice).

[69] Ricker v. Greenbaum, 13 Fed. 363; Brown v. Simons, 44 N. H. 475; Hill v. Howell, 36 N. J. Eq. 25; Sanborn v. Adair, 27 N. J. Eq. 425; Ellison v. Pecare, 29 Barb. (N. Y.) 333; Stanly v. Stocks, 16 N. Car. 314; Warwick Inst. for Savings v. Providence, 12 R. I. 144.

the portion still held by the latter shall be first applied to the payment of the incumbrance; and having no equity against him, he has none against his grantee. By taking such a deed he consents that the land shall remain subject to its pro rata share of the debt.[70]

§ 578. Notice of prior incumbrances recited in mortgage.—A purchaser having actual notice of a mortgage is affected with any other incumbrances which are referred to in that mortgage, or in other deeds to which the deeds first referred to may in turn refer.[71] Where a mortgage contains a recital of a former mortgage, the subsequent mortgagee is not a bona fide purchaser.[72] And a recital in a mortgage that it is second to one previously executed to a third party is binding upon the mortgagee accepting it.[73] Having notice of the mortgage the purchaser is bound to know the contents of it, and that would lead him to other deeds, in which, pursued from one to another, the whole case would be discovered to him.[74] Though the contents of a deed be stated to a purchaser, and he relies upon such statement, and the statement be erroneous, he is bound by its real contents;[75] and, in like manner, if he has knowledge of an unrecorded mortgage, and rests upon the vendor's assurance that the debt secured by it has been satisfied, he does so at his peril.[76]

§ 579. Inquiry concerning debt secured.—A general description of the debt is sufficient to put all parties interested upon inquiry, and to charge them with notice of all facts that could be obtained by the exercise of ordinary diligence and the prosecution of the inquiry in

[70] Briscoe v. Power, 47 Ill. 447.
[71] Howard Ins. Co. v. Halsey, 8 N. Y. 271, 59 Am. Dec. 475; Green v. Slayter, 4 Johns. Ch. (N. Y.) 38; Bisco v. Banbury, 1 Ch. Cas. 287; Coppin v. Fernyhough, 2 Bro. C. C. 291; Hope v. Liddell, 21 Beav. 183. See also Bent v. Coleman, 89 Ill. 364; Cambridge Valley Bank v. Delano, 48 N. Y. 326; Fidelity Ins. Co. v. Shenandoah Val. R. Co., 32 W. Va. 244, 9 S. E. 180.
[72] Rose v. Provident Sav. &c. Assn., 28 Ind. App. 25, 62 N. E. 293.
[73] Herring v. Fitts, 43 Fla. 54, 30 So. 804, 99 Am. St. 108.
[74] Bisco v. Banbury, 1 Ch. Cas. 287, per Lord Chancellor. See also Willink v. Morris Canal &c. Co., 4 N. J. Eq. 377; Skeel v. Spraker, 8 Paige (N. Y.) 182.

[75] Jones v. Smith, 1 Hare 43, on appeal affirmed, 1 Ph. 244 and cases cited. But see Drysdale v. Mace, 2 Sm. & G. 225, 5 De G. M. & G. 103. Where recitals put a purchaser upon inquiry, he is not entitled to rely upon the vendor's contradictory statements. Bergstrom v. Johnson, 111 Minn. 247, 126 N. W. 899; Waggoner v. Dodson, 96 Tex. 415, 73 S. W. 517; Patman v. Harland, 17 Ch. D. 353, 50 L. J. Ch. 642, 44 L. T. Rep. (N. S.) 728, 29 Wkly. Rep. 707.
[76] Overall v. Taylor, 99 Ala. 12, 11 So. 738; Price v. McDonald, 1 Md. 403, 54 Am. Dec. 657; Hudson v. Warner, 2 Harris & G. (Md.) 415; Moody v. Martin (Tex. Civ. App.), 117 S. W. 1015. See ante § 551.

the right direction.[77] A party wilfully closing his eyes against the lights to which his attention has been directed, and which, if followed, would lead to a knowledge of all the facts, is chargeable with notice of every fact that he could have obtained by the exercise of reasonable diligence.[78] While literal exactness in describing the mortgage liability is not essential, so as to preclude the necessity of extraneous inquiry, yet the description of the debt secured must be sufficiently definite to enable subsequent purchasers and mortgagees or creditors to discover the amount or extent of the incumbrance by the exercise of common prudence and ordinary diligence.[79] In other words, to render a mortgage valid as against strangers, it must give reasonable notice of the liability secured.[80]

A few of the earlier cases, under certain codes, have held that where the mortgage is given to secure an ascertained debt, the amount of that debt must be stated or specified, but even these cases can not be considered authority that the sum secured must be recited in the mortgage.[81] It is sufficient notice of an incumbrance to put a purchaser upon inquiry, that the mortgage, duly recorded, names a sum of $500 in addition to a note secured.[82]

In like manner, where a mortgage secured several notes, but in the record the description of one of them was omitted, though the aggregate amount of the notes was given correctly, it was held that the mortgage was notice to a purchaser for the full amount of the mort-

---

[77] Curtis v. Flinn, 46 Ark. 70; Ricketson v. Richardson, 19 Cal. 330; Stoughton v. Pasco, 5 Conn. 442, 13 Am. Dec. 72; Gardner v. Cohn, 191 Ill. 553, 61 N. E. 492; Pearce v. Hall, 75 Ky. 209; Morris v. Murray, 5 Ky. L. (abstract) 774; Williams v. Moniteau Nat. Bank, 72 Mo. 292; Burnett v. Wright, 135 N. Y. 543, 32 N. E. 253; Passumpsic Sav. Bank v. First Nat. Bank, 53 Vt. 82; Seymour v. Darrow, 31 Vt. 122. But see Bullock v. Battenhousen, 108 Ill. 28; Morris v. Murray, 82 Ky. 36; McCrea v. Newman, 46 N. J. Eq. 473, 19 Atl. 198. See ante §§ 343, 471.

[78] Jackson, L. &c. R. Co. v. Davison, 65 Mich. 416, 37 N. W. 537; Converse v. Blumrich, 14 Mich. 109.

[79] Ricketson v. Richardson, 19 Cal. 330; Hart v. Chalker, 14 Conn. 77; Booth v. Barnum, 9 Conn. 286, 23 Am. Dec. 339; Stoughton v. Pasco, 5 Conn. 442, 13 Am. Dec. 72; Morris v. Murray, 5 Ky. L. (abstract)

774. A mortgage to be valid must in some way describe and identify the indebtedness intended to be secured. Bowen v. Ratcliff, 140 Ind. 393, 39 N. E. 860, 49 Am. St. 203.

[80] Shepard v. Shepard, 6 Conn. 37; Stoughton v. Pasco, 5 Conn. 442, 13 Am. Dec. 72; Pettibone v. Griswold, 4 Conn. 158, 10 Am. Dec. 106.

[81] Hart v. Chalker, 14 Conn. 77; Gibson v. Hough, 60 Ga. 588; Thomas v. Olney, 16 Ill. 53.

[82] Passumpsic Sav. Bank v. First Nat. Bank, 53 Vt. 82 (quoting text); Babcock v. Lisk, 57 Ill. 327; Heaton v. Prather, 84 Ill. 330; Vredenburgh v. Burnet, 31 N. J. Eq. 229. But where a mortgage recites a specified indebtedness, less a certain credit due the mortgagor for material furnished, the description of the mortgage debt was held too indefinite to operate as notice against a subsequent mortgagee. Morris v. Murray, 82 Ky. 36, 5 Ky. L. 821. See ante § 343.

gage notes.[83] Where a deed was made subject to "two mortgages for two thousand dollars," with warranty against all claims, "except said mortgages," and there were two prior mortgages, one for one thousand five hundred dollars, which was recorded, and of which the purchaser had actual knowledge, and one of two thousand dollars, which was not recorded, and of which he had no notice except such as was given by the deed, it was held that the recitals in the deed were sufficient to put him upon inquiry, and to charge him with actual knowledge of the unrecorded mortgage.[84]

§ 580. **Reasonable diligence in inquiry.**—The limit of inquiry necessary in any case is that required by the use of reasonable diligence. What is reasonable diligence can not be determined by any general rule, but must vary with the circumstances of each case.[85] Thus where a mortgage was given to a retiring partner, to secure him against the liabilities of the partnership, and also for the "balance which should be due him on the purchase of such property," and notes were given for such purchase-money, but no mention of them was made in the mortgage, it was held that a second mortgagee, who had taken his mortgage after inquiring of both the mortgagor and the mortgagee whether anything was due for purchase-money, and received the answer from both that it was all paid, was entitled to priority over the prior mortgagee, and even as against the assignee of one of the notes given for purchase-money.[86]

Where a subsequent purchaser or mortgagee knows that some paper has been executed which may or may not affect the title to the prop-

---

[83] Dargin v. Beeker, 10 Iowa 571. See also Merrills v. Swift, 18 Conn. 257, 46 Am. Dec. 315.

[84] Hamilton v. Nutt, 34 Conn. 501. But see McCrea v. Newman, 46 N. J. Eq. 473, 19 Atl. 198.

[85] See ante § 552.

[86] Passumpsic Sav. Bank v. National Bank, 53 Vt. 82. Veazey, J., delivering the opinion of the court, said: "Where the form or specification of the obligation intended to be secured is described or referred to, or where the description indicates that the debt is specified in some written form, or is of such a character that it is practicable to be pursued by inquiry beyond the parties to the mortgage, and the facts as to its payment determined, the authorities indicate that a purchaser or subsequent incumbrancer proceeds at his peril. The parties to the mortgage have furnished him the means of finding out the facts; therefore he must find them out. But such is not this case. Here the parties gave no clue to any discovery attainable beyond themselves. Under such circumstances, it seems to us that inquiry of those persons is the use of that degree of diligence which the law requires; and that, in view of the facts alluded to, the defendant's mortgage should prevail." See also Blatchley v. Osborn, 33 Conn. 226; Leiman's Estate, 32 Md. 225; Lindauer v. Younglove, 47 Minn. 62, 49 N. W. 384; Maupin v. Emmons, 47 Mo. 304; Cambridge Valley Bank v. Delano, 48 N. Y. 326.

erty, it is his duty to ascertain its exact nature and effect;[87] and likewise, if he knows there are liens on the property, he must ascertain their particulars.[88]

The record of a foreclosure suit may affect one who derives title under a foreclosure sale with knowledge of another unsatisfied mortgage upon the premises, and of the equity of the holder of that mortgage as against the purchaser at that sale.[89]

§ 581. **Conveyance of equity of redemption to mortgagee as notice of assignment of mortgage.**—A conveyance of land to the mortgagee subject to a mortgage may or may not imply that he has assigned the mortgage. It has already been noticed that a deed conveying land subject to a certain mortgage, or warranting it against all incumbrances except the mortgage, is notice to all persons claiming under such deed of the existence of the mortgage. If such a deed of the equity of redemption be made to the mortgagee himself, it is a question of fact for a jury whether such recital or warranty implies that the mortgage is not then held by the mortgagee, or is notice to his attaching creditors that the mortgage has been assigned to another.[90]

A conveyance of the equity of redemption by the mortgagor to the mortgagee after the latter has assigned the mortgage in good faith to a third person, does not effect a merger or extinguish the lien of the mortgage.[91]

The record of a purchase-money mortgage is not notice of the conveyance for which such mortgage was given, so as to invalidate the title of one who subsequently purchases of the vendor before the first deed given by him is recorded.[92]

§ 582. **Release or quitclaim of mortgagor's interest.**—One who merely takes a release of all the interest of the mortgagor, while an

[87] In re Rixstine's Estate, 3 Pa. Dist. 227. See also In re Burns, 171 Fed. 1008; W. C. Belcher Land Mortgage Co. v. Norris, 29 Tex. Civ. App. 361, 68 S. W. 548.

[88] Jones v. Williams, 24 Beav. 47, 3 Jur. (N. S.) 1066, 5 Wkly. Rep. 775, 53 Eng. Reprint 274.

[89] Locker v. Riley, 30 N. J. Eq. 104.

[90] Clark v. Jenkins, 5 Pick. (Mass.) 280.

[91] Case v. Fant, 53 Fed. 41, 3 C. C. A. 418; Oregon &c. Trust Inv. Co. v. Shaw, Fed. Cas. No. 10557, 6 Sawy. (U. S.) 52; Chicago International Bank v. Wilkshire, 108 Ill. 143; Buchanan v. International Bank, 78

Ill. 500; Edgerton v. Young, 43 Ill. 464; Cole v. Beale, 89 Ill. App. 426; Durham v. Craig, 79 Ind. 117; White v. Hampton, 13 Iowa 259; Felgner v. Slingluff, 109 Md. 474, 71 Atl. 978; Lime Rock Nat. Bank v. Mowry, 66 N. H. 598, 22 Atl. 555, 13 L. R. A. 294; Curtis v. Moore, 152 N. Y. 159, 46 N. E. 168, 57 Am. St. 506; Purdy v. Huntington, 42 N. Y. 334, 1 Am. Rep. 532.

[92] Pierce v. Taylor, 23 Maine 246; Losey v. Simpson, 11 N. J. Eq. 246 (and it is not notice to one claiming under the mortgagee); Center v. Planters' &c. Bank, 22 Ala. 743.

unrecorded mortgage made by him is outstanding, obtains only the mortgagor's equity of redemption subject to such mortgage.[93]

By the weight of authority a grantee in a quitclaim deed can not be accorded the protection of a purchaser for value without notice, since such instrument purports to convey only such interest as the grantor may then have in the property, thus putting the purchaser upon inquiry as to any defects in the title by way of outstanding incumbrances or otherwise.[94] In some jurisdictions the rule has been altered by the recording acts; and it is held that a grantee by quitclaim deed may obtain, as against a prior unrecorded mortgage or conveyance, the protection accorded a bona fide purchaser.[95] In other jurisdictions, under statutes making a quitclaim deed equivalent to a deed

[93] Smith v. Branch Bank, 21 Ala. 125.

[94] Villa v. Rodriguez, 12 Wall. (U. S.) 323, 20 L. ed. 406; Gest v. Packwood, 34 Fed. 368, 13 Sawy. (U. S.) 202; Dodge v. Briggs, 27 Fed. 160; Runyon v. Smith, 18 Fed. 579; Clemmons v. Cox, 114 Ala. 350, 21 So. 426; Wood v. Holly Mfg. Co., 100 Ala. 326, 13 So. 948, 46 Am. St. 56; Morris v. Wheat, 8 App. Cas. (D. C.) 379; Fries v. Griffin, 35 Fla. 212, 17 So. 66; Leland v. Isenbeck, 1 Idaho 469; O'Neill v. Wilcox, 115 Iowa 15, 87 N. W. 742; Young v. Charnquist, 114 Iowa 116, 86 N. W. 205; Hannan v. Seidentopf, 113 Iowa 658, 86 N. W. 44; Davis v. Nolan, 49 Iowa 683; Springer v. Bartle, 46 Iowa 688; Smith v. Rudd, 48 Kans. 296, 29 Pac. 310; Goddard v. Donaha, 42 Kans. 754, 22 Pac. 708; Kelly v. McBlaine, 6 Kans. App. 523, 50 Pac. 963; Peters v. Cartier, 80 Mich. 124, 45 N. W. 73, 20 Am. St. 508; Condit v. Maxwell, 142 Mo. 266, 44 S. W. 467; Eoff v. Irvine, 108 Mo. 378, 18 S. W. 907, 32 Am. St. 609; Mason v. Black, 87 Mo. 329; Mann v. Best, 62 Mo. 491; Stoffel v. Schroeder, 62 Mo. 147; Ridgeway v. Holliday, 59 Mo. 444; McAdow v. Black, 6 Mont. 601, 13 Pac. 377; Bowman v. Griffith, 35 Nebr. 361, 53 N. W. 140; Pleasants v. Blodgett, 32 Nebr. 427, 49 N. W. 453, 39 Nebr. 741, 58 N. W. 423, 42 Am. St. 624; Hoyt v. Schuyler, 19 Nebr. 652, 28 N. W. 306; Low v. Shaffer, 24 Ore. 239, 33 Pac. 678; American Mortgage Co. v. Hutchinson, 19 Ore. 334, 24 Pac. 515; Baker v. Woodward, 12 Ore. 3, 6

Pac. 173; Fowler v. Will, 19 S. Dak. 131, 102 N. W. 598, 117 Am. St. 938; Parker v. Randolph, 5 S. Dak. 549, 59 N. W. 722, 29 L. R. A. 33; Hows v. Butterworth (Tenn.), 62 S. W. 1114; Huff v. Crawford, 89 Tex. 214, 34 S. W. 606; Threadgill v. Bickerstaff, 87 Tex. 520, 29 S. W. 757; Harrison v. Boring, 44 Tex. 255; Hamman v. Keigwin, 39 Tex. 34; Rodgers v. Burchard, 34 Tex. 441, 7 Am. Rep. 283; Dupree v. Frank (Tex.), 39 S. W. 988; Clark v. Sayers, 55 W. Va. 512, 47 S. E. 312. See also Steele v. Sioux Valley Bank, 79 Iowa 339, 44 N. W. 564, 7 L. R. A. 524, 18 Am. St. 370; Marshall v. Roberts, 18 Minn. 405, 10 Am. Rep. 201; Prentice v. Duluth Storage &c. Co., 58 Fed. 437, 7 C. C. A. 293 (construing the Minnesota statute); Virginia &c. Coal Co. v. Fields, 94 Va. 102, 26 S. E. 426.

[95] White v. McGarry, 47 Fed. 420 (construing the Michigan statute); Boynton v. Haggart, 120 Fed. 819, 57 C. C. A. 301 (quitclaim in chain of title); Nidever v. Ayers, 83 Cal. 39, 23 Pac. 192; Graff v. Middleton, 43 Cal. 341; Smith v. McClain, 146 Ind. 77, 45 N. E. 41; Elliott v. Buffington, 149 Mo. 663, 51 S. W. 408; Hope v. Blair, 105 Mo. 85, 16 S. W. 595, 24 Am. St. 366; Ebersole v. Rankin, 102 Mo. 488, 15 S. W. 422; Munson v. Ensor, 94 Mo. 504, 7 S. W. 108; Campbell v. Laclede Gas Light Co., 84 Mo. 352; Willingham v. Hardin, 75 Mo. 429; Boogher v. Neece, 75 Mo. 383; Fox v. Hall, 74 Mo. 315, 41 Am. Rep. 316.

of bargain and sale, it has been held that a grantee by a quitclaim is protected as a purchaser for value without notice.[96]

V. *Lis Pendens*

SECTION	SECTION
583. Doctrine of lis pendens.	585. Lis pendens as affected by actual notice.
584. Service of writ is notice.	

§ 583. Doctrine of lis pendens.—The force and effect of the recording of a deed or mortgage are limited not only by the actual notice which the grantee may have of prior unrecorded conveyances, but also by constructive notice of rights and claims of other parties, furnished by the pendency of an action in relation to the title of the property, notice of the pendency of which has been filed according to law.[1] Al-

[96] Bradbury v. Davis, 5 Colo. 265; Morgan v. Clayton, 61 Ill. 35; Smith v. McClain, 146 Ind. 77, 45 N. E. 41. See also Brady v. Spurck, 27 Ill. 478; Butterfield v. Smith, 11 Ill. 485; McConnel v. Reed, 4 Scam. (5 Ill.) 117, 38 Am. Dec. 124; Citizens' Bank v. Shaw, 14 S. Dak. 197, 84 N. W. 779.

[1] Lacassagne v. Chapuis, 144 U. S. 119, 36 L. ed. 368, 12 Sup. Ct. 659; Whiteside v. Haselton, 110 U. S. 296, 28 L. ed. 152, 4 Sup. Ct. 1; Tilton v. Cofield, 93 U. S. 163, 23 L. ed. 858; Hargrove v. Cherokee Nation, 129 Fed. 186, 63 C. C. A. 276, affg. 4 Ind. Ter. 129, 69 S. W. 823; Pitt v. Rodgers, 104 Fed. 387, 43 C. C. A. 600; Center v. P. &c. Bank, 22 Ala. 743. The suit is notice from the time when service is perfected. Hoole v. Attorney-General, 22 Ala. 190; Galbreath v. Estes, 38 Ark. 599; Holman v. Patterson, 29 Ark. 357; Ashley v. Cunningham, 16 Ark. 168; Di Nola v. Allison, 143 Cal. 106, 76 Pac. 976, 65 L. R. A. 419, 101 Am. St. 84; Partridge v. Shepard, 71 Cal. 470, 12 Pac. 480; Sharp v. Lumley, 34 Cal. 611; Long v. Neville, 29 Cal. 132; Wattson v. Dowling, 26 Cal. 124; Montgomery v. Byers, 21 Cal. 107; Cheever v. Minton, 12 Colo. 557, 21 Pac. 710, 13 Am. St. 258; Powell v. National Bank of Commerce, 19 Colo. App. 57, 74 Pac. 536; Norton v. Birge, 35 Conn. 250; King v. Bill, 28 Conn. 593; Elizabethport Cordage Co. v. Whitlock, 37 Fla. 190, 20 So. 255; Swift v. Dederick, 106 Ga. 35, 31 S. E. 788; Seabrook v. Brady, 47 Ga. 650; Rubel v. Title Guarantee &c. Co., 101 Ill. App. 439, affd. 199 Ill. 110, 64 N. E. 1033; Williams v. Chicago Exhibition Co., 188 Ill. 19, 58 N. E. 611; Harms v. Jacobs, 160 Ill. 589, 43 N. E. 745; Walker v. Douglas, 89 Ill. 425; Roberts v. Fleming, 53 Ill. 196; Jackson v. Warren, 32 Ill. 331; Loomis v. Riley, 24 Ill. 307; Buser v. Shepard, 107 Ind. 417, 8 N. E. 280; Wilson v. Hefflin, 81 Ind. 35; Truitt v. Truitt, 38 Ind. 16; Kern v. Hazelrigg, 11 Ind. 443, 71 Am. Dec. 360; Jackson v. Centerville &c. R. Co., 64 Iowa 292, 20 N. W. 442; Tredway v. McDonald, 51 Iowa 663, 2 N. W. 567; Blanchard v. Ware, 37 Iowa 305, 43 Iowa 530; McGregor v. McGregor, 21 Iowa 441; Wilkinson v. Elliott, 43 Kans. 590, 23 Pac. 614, 19 Am. St. 158; Boyd v. Emmons, 103 Ky. 393, 45 S. W. 364, 20 Ky. L. 107; Wallace v. Marquett, 88 Ky. 130, 10 S. W. 374, 10 Ky. L. 750; Gossom v. Donaldson, 18 B. Mon. (Ky.) 230, 68 Am. Dec. 723; Middleton v. Davis-Rankin Bldg. &c. Co., 20 Ky. L. 263, 45 S. W. 896; Bell v. Chicago &c. R. Co., 34 La. Ann. 785; Smith v. Hodsdon, 78 Maine 180, 3 Atl. 276; Snowman v. Harford, 62 Maine 434; Berry v. Whittaker, 58 Maine 422; Snowman v. Harford, 57 Maine 397; Sinclair v. Auxiliary Realty Co., 99 Md. 223, 57 Atl. 664; Boulden v. Lanahan, 29 Md. 200; Schaferman v. O'Brien, 28 Md. 565, 92 Am. Dec. 708; Inloe v. Harvey, 11 Md. 519; Tongue v. Morton, 6 Har. & J. (Md.)

though lis pendens has the effect of constructive notice, it has frequently been held that the doctrine is not founded upon notice, but upon reasons of public policy and necessity.[2] The doctrine of lis pendens is founded upon the consideration that no suit could be successfully terminated if, during its pendency, the property could be trans-

21; Haven v. Adams, 8 Allen (Mass.) 363; Barrowscale v. Tuttle, 5 Allen (Mass.) 377; Steele v. Taylor, 1 Minn. 274; Osborne v. Crump, 57 Miss. 622; Allen v. Poole, 54 Miss. 323; Bailey v. Winn, 113 Mo. 155, 20 S. W. 21; Real Est. Sav. Inst. v. Collonious, 63 Mo. 290; Turner v. Babb, 60 Mo. 342; Martin v. Abbott, 72 Nebr. 89, 100 N. W. 142; Scudder v. Sargent, 15 Nebr. 102, 17 N. W. 369; McPherson v. Housel, 13 N. J. Eq. 299; Allen v. Morris, 34 N. J. L. 159; Ladd v. Stevenson, 112 N. Y. 325, 19 N. E. 842, 8 Am. St. 748; Ayrault v. Murphy, 54 N. Y. 203; Mitchell v. Smith, 53 N. Y. 413; Harrington v. Slade, 19 Barb. (N. Y.) 162; Young v. Guy, 23 Hun (N. Y.) 1, affd. 87 N. Y. 457; Lawrence v. Conklin, 17 Hun (N. Y.) 228; Murray v. Ballou, 1 Johns. Ch. (N. Y.) 566; Salsbury v. Benton, 7 Lans. (N. Y.) 352; Dancy v. Duncan, 96 N. Car. 111, 1 S. E. 455; Stewart v. Wheeling &c. R. Co., 53 Ohio St. 151, 41 N. E. 247, 29 L. R. A. 438; Brundage v. Biggs, 25 Ohio St. 652; Ludlow v. Kidd, 2 Ohio 541; Bergman v. Inman, 43 Ore. 456, 72 Pac. 1086, 73 Pac. 341, 99 Am. St. 771; Youngman v. Elmira R. Co., 65 Pa. St. 278; Hersey v. Turbett, 27 Pa. St. 418; Martin v. Neblett, 86 Tenn. 383, 7 S. W. 123; American Exchange Bank v. Andrews, 12 Heisk. (Tenn.) 306; Tharpe v. Dunlap, 4 Heisk. (Tenn.) 674; Wortham v. Boyd, 66 Tex. 401, 1 S. W. 109; Lee v. Salines, 15 Tex. 495; Hicks v. Porter, 38 Tex. Civ. App. 334, 85 S. W. 437; Virginia Iron &c. Co. v. Roberts, 103 Va. 661, 49 S. E. 984; Wood v. Krebbs, 30 Grat. (Va.) 708; Stout v. Philippi Mfg. &c. Co., 41 W. Va. 339, 23 S. E. 571, 56 Am. St. 843; Wilfong v. Johnson, 41 W. Va. 283, 23 S. E. 730; Brown v. Cohn, 95 Wis. 90, 69 N. W. 71, 60 Am. St. 83;

Helms v. Chadbourne, 45 Wis. 60; In Louisiana, a purchaser is not chargeable with notice of judicial proceedings in which the title of the property is involved, unless he is a party to such proceedings. Notice in this state is not as a rule equivalent to registry. Boyer v. Joffrion, 40 La. Ann. 657, 4 So. 872; Tyler v. Thomas, 25 Beav. 47; Worsley v. Scarborough, 3 Atk. 392; Bellamy v. Sabine, 1 De G. & J. 566, 2 White & Tudor's Lead. Cas. in Eq. (4th Am. ed.), pt. 1, pp. 192 et seq. See post § 1411.

[2] Greenwood v. Warren, 120 Ala. 71, 23 So. 686; Durand v. Lord, 115 Ill. 610, 4 N. E. 483; First Nat. Bank v. Farmers' &c. Bank, 171 Ind. 323, 86 N. E. 417; Smith v. Kimball, 36 Kans. 474, 13 Pac. 801; Watson v. Wilson, 2 Dana (Ky.) 406, 26 Am. Dec. 459; Turner v. Babb, 60 Mo. 342; O'Reilly v. Nicholson, 45 Mo. 160; Dodd v. Lee, 57 Mo. App. 167; Carr v. Lewis Coal Co., 15 Mo. App. 551, affd. 96 Mo. 149, 8 S. W. 907, 9 Am. St. 328; Geishaker v. Pancoast, 57 N. J. Eq. 60, 40 Atl. 200; Haughwout v. Murphy, 22 N. J. Eq. 531; Lamont v. Cheshire, 65 N. Y. 30; Arrington v. Arrington, 114 N. Car. 151, 19 S. E. 351; Houston v. Timmerman, 17 Ore. 499, 21 Pac. 1037, 4 L. R. A. 716, 11 Am. St. 848; Dovey's Appeal, 97 Pa. St. 153; Bowen v. Kirkland, 17 Tex. Civ. App. 346, 44 S. W. 189; Newman v. Chapman, 2 Rand. (Va.) 93, 14 Am. Dec. 766; Cresap v. Brown, 69 W. Va. 658, 72 S. E. 751; Kellogg v. Fancher, 23 Wis. 21, 99 Am. Dec. 96. It is immaterial for practical purposes, whether the doctrine of lis pendens is considered as based on constructive notice or on public policy. Norris v. Ile, 152 Ill. 190, 38 N. E. 762, 43 Am. St. 233.

ferred so that it would not be bound by the decree or judgment in the hands of the assignee.[3]

The doctrine of lis pendens is applied to mortgagees[4] and incumbrancers pendente lite,[5] as well as purchasers in general.[6] A party, taking a trust deed of land pending a suit against the grantor, is charged with notice of the title asserted, and the particular relief demanded in such suit.[7] This doctrine of lis pendens, however, is not carried to the extent of making it constructive notice of a prior unregistered deed;[8] as, for instance, proceedings to foreclose an unre-

[3] Allen v. Poole, 54 Miss. 323; Hiern v. Mill, 13 Ves. 114.

[4] Stout v. Lye, 103 U. S. 66, 26 L. ed. 428; Laporte v. Northern Trust Co., 187 Fed. 20, 109 C. C. A. 74; Owen v. Kilpatrick, 96 Ala. 421, 11 So. 476; Burleson v. McDermott, 57 Ark. 229, 21 S. W. 222; Brown v. Bocquin, 57 Ark. 97, 20 S. W. 813; Whitney v. Higgins, 10 Cal. 547, 70 Am. Dec. 748; Elizabethport Cordage Co. v. Whitlock, 37 Fla. 190, 20 So. 255; Magnusson v. Charlson, 32 Ill. App. 580; Warford v. Sullivan, 147 Ind. 14, 46 N. E. 27; Fee v. Moore, 74 Ind. 319; Harlock v. Barnhizer, 30 Ind. 370; Cooley v. Brayton, 16 Iowa 10; Taylor v. United States Building &c. Assn., 110 Ky. 84, 22 Ky. L. 1560, 60 S. W. 927; Middleton v. Davis-Rankin Bldg. &c. Co., 20 Ky. L. 263, 45 S. W. 896; Hart v. Hayden, 79 Ky. 346, 2 Ky. L. (abstract) 219, 2 Ky. L. 359; Watson v. Wilson, 2 Dana (Ky.) 406, 26 Am. Dec. 459; Lacassagne v. Abraham, 48 La. Ann. 1160, 20 So. 672; Masson v. Saloy, 12 La. Ann. 776; Gillespie v. Cammack, 3 La. Ann. 248; Campbell's Case, 2 Bland. (Md.) 209, 20 Am. Dec. 360; Becker v. Stroeher, 167 Mo. 306, 66 S. W. 1083; Parrotte v. Dryden, 73 Nebr. 291, 102 N. W. 610; Turner v. Houpt, 53 N. J. Eq. 526, 33 Atl. 28; Cook v. Mancius, 5 Johns. Ch. (N. Y.) 89; Hovey v. Hill, 3 Lans. (N. Y.) 167; Sears v. Hyer, 1 Paige (N. Y.) 483; Youngman v. Elmira &c. R. Co., 65 Pa. St. 278; Portland &c. R. Co. v. Ladd, 47 Wash. 88, 91 Pac. 573.

[5] Masson v. Saloy, 12 La. Ann. 776; Steele v. Taylor, 1 Minn. 274. The assignee of a mortgage is an incumbrancer. Hovey v. Hill, 3 Lans. (N. Y.) 167. And an assignee of a mortgage pending an action to fore-

close, set aside, or enjoin enforcement thereof, takes subject to the decree. Case v. Bartholow, 21 Kans. 300; Craig v. Ward, 1 Abb. Dec. (N. Y.) 454, 3 Keyes 387, 3 Abb. Pr. (N. S.) 235; Zeiter v. Bowman, 6 Barb. (N. Y.) 133.

[6] Lewers v. Atcherly, 222 U. S. 285, 56 L. ed. 202, 32 Sup. Ct. 94; Rexford v. Brunswick-Balke-Collender Co., 181 Fed. 462, 104 C. C. A. 210; Boynton v. Chicago Mill &c. Co., 84 Ark. 203, 105 S. W. 77; Abbott v. Land &c. Co., 161 Cal. 42, 118 Pac. 425; Roach v. Riverside Water Co., 74 Cal. 263, 15 Pac. 776; Nemo v. Farrington, 7 Cal. App. 443, 94 Pac. 874; Buckhorn Plaster Co. v. Consolidated Plaster Co., 47 Colo. 516, 108 Pac. 27; Schmuck v. Missouri &c. R. Co., 87 Kans. 152, 123 Pac. 887; Bell v. Diesem, 86 Kans. 364, 121 Pac. 335; Kitchener v. Jehlik, 85 Kans. 684, 118 Pac. 1058; Parker v. Vaughn, 85 Kans. 324, 116 Pac. 882; Missouri, K. &c. R. Co. v. Murphy, 75 Kans. 707, 90 Pac. 290; Sherburne v. Strawn, 52 Kans. 39, 34 Pac. 405; Fletcher v. Wireman, 152 Ky. 565, 153 S. W. 982; Smith v. Munger, 93 Miss. 627, 47 So. 676; Leerburger v. Hennessey Realty Co., 154 App. Div. 158, 138 N. Y. S. 921; Gilman v. Carpenter, 22 S. Dak. 123, 115 N. W. 659; Hosack v. Darman, 44 Tex. 154; Lyne v. Wilson, 1 Rand. (Va.) 114; Portland &c. R. Co. v. Ladd, 47 Wash. 88, 91 Pac. 573; Goff v. McLain, 48 W. Va. 445, 37 S. E. 566, 86 Am. St. 64; McCord v. Akeley, 132 Wis. 195, 111 N. W. 1100, 122 Am. St. 956. But see Gardner v. Peckham, 13 R. I. 102.

[7] New England L. &c. Co. v. Miller (Tex.), 40 S. W. 646.

[8] Douglass v. McCrackin, 52 Ga. 596; Newman v. Chapman, 2 Rand.

corded mortgage do not constitute such a lis pendens as would be notice to a purchaser of the mortgaged property.

Only those persons are charged with notice, or are affected by a lis pendens, who pending the suit purchase from a party to the suit,[9] or derive title from one so purchasing.[10] A third person acquiring rights before the action is pending, or before the filing of notice thereof as required, is not bound by the judgment or decree.[11]

It is now generally provided by statute that notice of lis pendens, in order to affect subsequent purchasers, shall be filed in the registry of deeds where the land is situated.[12]

§ 584. **Service of writ is notice.**—Notice from a lis pendens arises from the time of the service of the writ, and not from the time of the issuance of it, or the time of filing the bill.[13] The lis pendens is notice

(Va.) 93, 14 Am. Dec. 766; 1 Story's Eq. Jur., § 406. See also Page v. Street, Speers Eq. (S. Car.) 159; Wyatt v. Barwell, 19 Ves. Jr. 435, 13 Rev. Rep. 236, 34 Eng. Reprint 578. But see Bolling v. Carter, 9 Ala. 921; Mayne v. Jones, 34 Cal. 483; Dickson v. Todd, 43 Ill. 504; National Bank of Metropolis v. Sprague, 21 N. J. Eq. 530.

[9] Bright v. Buckman, 39 Fed. 243; Scarlett v. Gorham, 28 Ill. 319; Parsons v. Hoyt, 24 Iowa 154; Herrington v. Herrington, 27 Mo. 560; Allen v. Morris, 34 N. J. L. 159; Stuyvesant v. Hone, 1 Sandf. Ch. (N. Y.) 419; Parks v. Jackson, 11 Wend. (N. Y.) 442, 25 Am. Dec. 656; Green v. Rick, 124 Pa. St. 130, 15 Atl. 497; French v. Loyal Co., 5 Leigh (Va.) 627.

[10] Norton v. Birge, 35 Conn. 250.

[11] Farmers' Loan &c. Co. v. Meridian Waterworks Co., 139 Fed. 661; Dalander v. Howell (Colo. App.), 124 Pac. 744; Kennedy v. Afdal, 229 Ill. 295, 82 N. E. 291; Noyes v. Crawford, 118 Iowa 15, 91 N. W. 799, 96 Am. St. 363; Farmers' Nat. Bank v. Fletcher, 44 Iowa 252; Thomas v. Smith, 8 Kans. App. 855, 54 Pac. 695; Parks v. Smoot, 105 Ky. 63, 48 S. W. 146, 20 Ky. L. 1043; Lacassagne v. Abraham, 48 La. Ann. 1160, 20 So. 672; Bennett v. Hotchkiss, 20 Minn. 165; Snowden v. Tyler, 21 Nebr. 199, 31 N. W. 661; Hunt v. Haven, 52 N. H. 162; Haughwout v. Murphy, 22 N. J. Eq. 531; People

v. Connolly, 8 Abb. Pr. (N. Y.) 128; Hopkins v. McLaren, 4 Cow. (N. Y.) 667; Murray v. Lyeburn, 2 Johns. Ch. (N. Y.) 441; Buxton v. Sargent, 7 N. Dak. 503, 75 N. W. 811; Trimble v. Boothby, 14 Ohio 109, 45 Am. Dec. 526; Appleby v. Mullaney, 9 Ohio S. & C. P. Dec. 765, 7 Ohio N. P. 120; Walker v. Goldsmith, 14 Ore. 125, 12 Pac. 537; Rodgers v. Dibrell, 6 Lea (Tenn.) 69; Curtis v. Lunn, 6 Munf. (Va.) 42.

[12] Richardson v. White, 18 Cal. 102; Snow v. Russell, 94 Maine 322, 47 Atl. 536; Jorgenson v. Minneapolis &c. R. Co., 25 Minn. 206.

[13] Wheeler v. Walton &c. Co., 65 Fed. 720; Watford v. Oates, 57 Ala. 290; Center v. Planters' &c. Bank, 22 Ala. 743; Majors v. Cowell, 51 Cal. 478; Figge v. Rowlen, 84 Ill. App. 238, affd. 185 Ill. 234, 57 N. E. 195; Farmers' Nat. Bank v. Fletcher, 44 Iowa 252; Straeffer v. Rodman, 146 Ky. 1, 141 S. W. 742, Ann. Cas. 1913 C, 549; Sanders v. McDonald, 63 Md. 503; Spencer Co. v. Koell, 91 Minn. 226, 97 N. W. 974; Allen v. Poole, 54 Miss. 323; Allen v. Mandeville, 26 Miss. 397; Bailey v. McGinnis, 57 Mo. 362; O'Neill v. Clark, 33 N. J. Eq. 444; Haughwout v. Murphy, 22 N. J. Eq. 545; Fuller v. Hilton, 76 N. Y. 190; Leitch v. Wells, 48 N. Y. 585; Murray v. Ballou, 1 Johns. Ch. (N. Y.) 566; Hayden v. Bucklin, 9 Paige (N. Y.) 512; Jackson v. Roberts, 1 Wend. (N. Y.) 478; Bennet v. Williams, 5 Ohio St.

of every fact in the pleadings pertinent to the matter in issue or the relief sought,[14] and of the contents of the exhibits filed and proved.[15] If the facts suggest further inquiry, the lis pendens is notice of any other facts which could have been ascertained in the pursuit of such inquiry with ordinary prudence and diligence.[16] But a purchaser or mortgagee acquiring interest pendente lite is not affected with notice of facts not alleged in the pleadings or put in issue.[17] Notice by lis pendens that a party to an action is the real owner of land, or of the equity of redemption therein, is equivalent to actual notice of such party's claim thereto.[18]

In order that the notice may attach, the property involved in the suit must be so pointed out in the proceedings that it may be identified by those interested in it.[19] Since questions of title and boundary are not put in issue or determined in an action to enforce a lien for the purchase-money of land, such matters are not lis pendens.[20]

461; Staples v. White, 88 Tenn. 30, 12 S. W. 339; Humphrey v. Beaumont Irr. Co., 41 Tex. Civ. App. 308, 93 S. W. 180. See also United States v. Cooper, 196 Fed. 584; Armstrong Cork Co. v. Merchants' Refrigerator Co., 184 Fed. 199, 107 C. C. A. 93.

[14] Center v. Planters' &c. Bank, 22 Ala. 743; Davis v. Miller Signal Co., 105 Ill. App. 657; Ray v. Roe, 2 Blackf. (Ind.) 258, 18 Am. Dec. 159; Smith v. Kimball, 36 Kans. 474, 13 Pac. 801; Jones v. McNarrin, 68 Maine 334, 28 Am. Rep. 66; Allen v. Poole, 54 Miss. 323; Bryant Timber Co. v. Wilson, 151 N. Car. 154, 65 S. E. 932, 134 Am. St. 982; Davis v. Christian, 15 Grat. (Va.) 11; Stout v. Philippi Mfg. &c. Co., 41 W. Va. 339, 23 S. E. 571, 56 Am. St. 843. See also Fash v. Ravesies, 32 Ala. 451; Cossett v. O'Riley, 160 Mich. 101, 125 N. W. 39.

[15] Center v. Planters' &c. Bank, 22 Ala. 743; Davis v. Miller Signal Co., 105 Ill. App. 657; Allen v. Poole, 54 Miss. 323.

[16] Laporte v. Northern Trust Co., 187 Fed. 20, 109 C. C. A. 74; Seibert v. Louisville, 125 Ky. 292, 30 Ky. L. 1317, 101 S. W. 325; Jones v. McNarrin, 68 Maine 334, 28 Am. Rep. 66; Bryant Timber Co. v. Wilson, 151 N. Car. 154, 65 S. E. 932, 134 Am. St. 982.

[17] Alexander v. Pendleton, 8 Cranch (U. S.) 462, 3 L. ed. 624; Weller v. Dreyfus, 26 Fed. 824; Sanford v. Hill, 46 Conn. 42; Ray v. Roe, 2 Blackf. (Ind.) 258, 18 Am. Dec. 159; St. John v. Strauss, 60 Kans. 136, 55 Pac. 845; Morton v. Jones, 136 Ky. 797, 125 S. W. 247; Griffith v. Griffith, Hoffm. Ch. (N. Y.) 153, revd. 9 Paige 315; Walker v. Goldsmith, 14 Ore. 125, 12 Pac. 537; Cowie v. Harker, 32 S. Dak. 516, 143 N. W. 895; New England L. &c. Co. v. Miller (Tex.), 40 S. W. 646; Davis v. Christian, 15 Grat. (Va.) 11. See also Leavell v. Poore, 91 Ky. 321, 15 S. W. 858, 13 Ky. L. 51; Green v. Slayter, 4 Johns. Ch. (N. Y.) 38.

[18] Wilson v. Hefflin, 81 Ind. 35; Ætna L. Ins. Co. v. Stryker, 42 Ind. App. 57, 83 N. E. 647.

[19] Miller v. Sperry, 2 Wall. (U. S.) 237, 17 L. ed. 827; Low v. Pratt, 53 Ill. 438; Allen v. Poole, 54 Miss. 323; Drake v. Crowell, 40 N. J. L. 58; Green v. Slayter, 4 Johns. Ch. (N. Y.) 38; Potter v. Rowland, 8 N. Y. 448; Todd v. Outlaw, 79 N. Car. 235. See also Jaffray v. Brown, 17 Hun (N. Y.) 575 (all the real property in a specified county too indefinite); McLean v. Baldwin, 136 Cal. 565, 69 Pac. 259 (erroneous description in addition to boundaries rejected as surplusage); Watson v. Wilcox, 39 Wis. 643, 20 Am. Rep. 63.

[20] Beal v. Arnold, 1 Ky. L. (abstract) 403.

The mention, in a creditor's bill against the debtor's interest as a devisee, concerning an existing mortgage on that interest, and including the mortgagee as a defendant, without putting in issue the validity of the mortgage, or asking any relief in regard to it, does not create such lis pendens as to affect the validity of a sale under the mortgage.[21]

The law of lis pendens does not apply to a suit for divorce and alimony,[22] unless the petition is that the alimony be assigned out of a particular parcel of land.[23] Neither does it apply to a common lawsuit brought to obtain a money judgment for a debt.[24] Consequently, where the holder of a vendor's lien sues the vendee to recover the amount of the lien, but does not attempt to enforce the lien itself, the suit is not constructive notice to a purchaser from the defendant, while the suit is pending.[25]

§ 585. **Lis pendens as affected by actual notice.**—If the plaintiff in a suit, before filing the statutory notice of lis pendens, had knowledge that the defendant had conveyed his land by a valid deed, but that the purchaser had not recorded it, he can not by a levy upon the land of an execution obtained in such writ acquire any lien upon such land as against the purchaser.[26] On the other hand, one who pur-

---

[21] Cockrill v. Maney, 2 Tenn. Ch. 49.

[22] McClelland v. Phillips, 6 Colo. App. 47, 39 Pac. 893; Ulrich v. Ulrich, 3 Mackey (D. C.) 290; Frakes v. Brown, 2 Blackf. (Ind.) 295; Scott v. Rogers, 77 Iowa 483, 42 N. W. 377; Feigley v. Feigley, 7 Md. 537, 61 Am. Dec. 375; Daniel v. Hodges, 87 N. Car. 95; Gilmore v. Gilmore, 58 N. Car. 284; Hamlin v. Bevans, 7 Ohio 161, 28 Am. Dec. 625; Brightman v. Brightman, 1 R. I. 112; Almond v. Almond, 4 Rand. (Va.) 662, 15 Am. Dec. 781.

[23] Ulrich v. Ulrich, 3 Mackey (D. C.) 290; Wilkinson v. Elliott, 43 Kans. 590, 23 Pac. 614, 19 Am. St. 158; Garver v. Graham, 6 Kans. App. 344, 51 Pac. 812; Powell v. Campbell, 20 Nev. 232, 20 Pac. 156, 2 L. R. A. 615, 19 Am. St. 350; Daniel v. Hodges, 87 N. Car. 95; Tolerton v. Williard, 30 Ohio St. 579; Spencer v. Spencer, 9 R. I. 150; Brightman v. Brightman, 1 R. I. 112. But see Houston v. Timmerman, 17 Ore. 499, 21 Pac. 1037, 4 L. R. A. 716, 11 Am. St. 848.

[24] Carson v. Fears, 91 Ga. 482, 17 S. E. 342; St. Joseph Mfg. Co. v. Daggett, 84 Ill. 556; Gales v. Christy, 4 La. Ann. 293; Armstrong v. Carwile, 56 S. Car. 463, 35 S. E. 196; Shearon v. Henderson, 38 Tex. 245; White v. Perry, 14 W. Va. 66; Fulton Bldg. Assn. v. Hooker, 6 Ohio Dec. (reprint) 1123, 10 Am. L. Rec. 559, 7 Wkly. L. Bul. 48.

[25] Briscoe v. Bronaugh, 1 Tex. 326, 48 Am. Dec. 108.

[26] Lamont v. Cheshire, 65 N. Y. 30; Welsh v. Schoen, 59 Hun (N. Y.) 356, 36 N. Y. St. 538, 13 N. Y. S. 71; Powell v. Jenkins, 14 Misc. 83, 69 N. Y. St. 582, 35 N. Y. S. 265; Coe v. Manseau, 62 Wis. 81, 22 N. W. 155. See also Hibernia Sav. &c. Soc. v. Cochran, 141 Cal. 653, 75 Pac. 315; Kursheedt v. Union Dime Sav. Inst., 118 N. Y. 358, 23 N. E. 473, 7 L. R. A. 229; Bell v. Gittere, 14 N. Y. St. 61; Slattery v. Schwannecke, 44 Hun 75, 7 N. Y. St. 430, affd. 118 N. Y. 543, 23 N. E. 922; Payson v. Jacobs, 38 Wash. 203, 80 Pac. 429; Eldridge v. Stenger, 19 Wash. 697, 54 Pac. 541. But see Collingwood

chases with actual notice of the pendency of a suit affecting the land takes subject to the decree, and can not object that statutory notice of the pendency of the suit was not filed.[27]

Notice by lis pendens is notice only of pending proceedings. It is not notice to a purchaser whose conveyance was made before the commencement of the action.[28] The lis pendens continues until the fruits of the litigation are secured, or until terminated by a judgment or decree against the party entitled to the benefit of the lis pendens. When the litigation is ended, and the rights of all parties have been determined, the notice ceases.[29]

Under many of the recording acts, a suit will not be constructive notice after the rendition of a judgment, decree, or order affecting real estate, unless such judgment is duly registered or recorded against the property, like a deed or other conveyance.[30] Some statutes expressly provide for the cancelation or discharge of the notice upon the record, after final disposition of the cause;[31] and others empower

v. Brown, 106 N. Car. 362, 10 S. E. 868.

[27] King v. Davis, 137 Fed. 222; Phelps v. Elliott, 35 Fed. 455; Daggs v. Wilson, 6 Ariz. 388, 59 Pac. 150; Jennings v. Bouldin, 98 Ark. 105, 134 S. W. 948; Hibernia Sav. &c. Soc. v. Lewis, 117 Cal. 577, 47 Pac. 602, 49 Pac. 714; Wise v. Griffith, 78 Cal. 152, 20 Pac. 675; Powell v. National Bank of Commerce, 19 Colo. App. 57, 74 Pac. 536; Ray v. Hocker, 65 Fla. 265, 61 So. 500; Richards v. Cline, 176 Ill. 431, 52 N. E. 907; McCauley v. Rogers, 104 Ill. 578; Rowell v. Klein, 44 Ind. 290, 15 Am. Rep. 235; Baker v. Pierson, 5 Mich. 456 (filing of statutory notice immaterial); Dorr v. Steichen, 18 Minn. 26; Parrotte v. Dryden, 73 Nebr. 291, 102 N. W. 610; Varnum v. Bolton Shoe Co., 171 N. Y. 658, 63 N. E. 1123; Uhl v. Irwin, 3 Okla. 388, 41 Pac. 376; Pacific Mfg. Co. v. Brown, 8 Wash. 347, 36 Pac. 273. See also Shumaker v. Davidson, 116 Iowa 569, 87 N. W. 441; Bruff v. Thompson, 31 W. Va. 16, 6 S. E. 352.

[28] Coulter v. Lumpkin, 94 Ga. 225, 21 S. E. 461; Farmers' Nat. Bank v. Fletcher, 44 Iowa 252.

[29] Grattan v. Wiggins, 23 Cal. 16; Empire Land &c. Co. v. Engley, 18 Colo. 388, 33 Pac. 153; Cheever v. Minton, 12 Colo. 557, 21 Pac. 710, 13 Am. St. 258; Page v. Waring, 76 N. Y. 463; Sheridan v. Andrews, 49 N. Y. 478; Arrington v. Arrington, 114 N. Car. 151, 19 S. E. 351. See also Breen v. Lennon, 10 App. Div. (N. Y.) 36; St. Regis Paper Co. v. Santa Clara Lbr. Co., 34 Misc. 428, 69 N. Y. S. 904, affd. 62 App. Div. 538, 71 N. Y. S. 82. But see Carpenter v. Lewis, 119 Cal. 18, 50 Pac. 925; Moreland v. Strong, 115 Mich. 211, 73 N. W. 140, 69 Am. St. 553; Bennett v. Hotchkiss, 20 Minn. 165; Shaw v. Barksdale, 25 S. Car. 204; Frank v. Jenkins, 11 Wash. 611, 40 Pac. 220.

[30] Dudley v. Witter, 46 Ala. 664; Boyer v. Joffrion, 40 La. Ann. 657, 4 So. 872; Hall v. Sauntry, 72 Minn. 420, 75 N. W. 720, 71 Am. St. 497; Berryhill v. Smith, 59 Minn. 285, 61 N. W. 144; Frank v. Jenkins, 11 Wash. 611, 40 Pac. 220; Prickett v. Muck, 74 Wis. 199, 42 N. W. 256; Cutler v. James, 64 Wis. 173, 24 N. W. 874, 54 Am. Rep. 603; Helms v. Chadbourne, 45 Wis. 60; Hoyt v. Jones, 31 Wis. 389. See also Laws Maine 1893, ch. 301, § 3; Gen. Laws R. I. 1896, ch. 246, § 13; and statutes of the various states.

[31] Arrington v. Arrington, 114 N. Car. 151, 19 S. E. 351; Washington Dredging &c. Co. v. Kinnear, 24 Wash. 405, 64 Pac. 522 (notice as cloud upon title); King v. Branscheid, 32 Wash. 634, 73 Pac. 668.

the court to order cancelation of the notice upon other grounds, such as failure to make a bona fide and full prosecution.[32] The cancelation of the notice of lis pendens terminates its effect as against those subsequently dealing with the title.[33] If the plaintiff does not diligently prosecute the action, the effect of lis pendens ceases, and a person acquiring rights pending the litigation is not affected thereby.[34]

VI. *Possession as Notice*

§ 586. **Possession by tenant, purchaser, or other occupant, as notice.**—Possession by one who is not the owner of record is a fact which should induce one proposing to purchase to inquire whether the possession is founded on any right or title. It is notice of the rights of the occupant, whatever they may be; and if he claim by deed his possession is regarded by most authorities as equivalent to the

---

[32] Pooley v. Bosanquet, 7 Ch. Div. 541; Baxter v. Middleton, 1 Ch. 313 (1898); Jervis v. Berridge, 44 L. J. Ch. 164, 31 L. T. (N. S.) 426, 23 Wkly. Rep. 43. See also concerning discontinuance or unreasonable neglect to proceed in the action: Cohen v. Ratkowsky, 43 App. Div. 196, 59 N. Y. S. 344; Jarvis v. American &c. Mfg. Co., 93 App. Div. 234, 87 N. Y. S. 742; Shandley v. Levine, 44 Misc. 23, 89 N. Y. S. 717; Wagner v. Perry, 51 Hun 199, 21 N. Y. St. 386, 3 N. Y. S. 880; McKean v. National Life Assn., 24 Misc. 511, 53 N. Y. S. 980, 28 Civ. Proc. 146, 6 N. Y. Ann. Cas. 179; Parks v. Murray, 40 Hun 640, 2 N. Y. St. 135. A long delay in prosecution, pending a continuance was held insufficient as a ground for cancelation, under a statute which did not specify the grounds for cancelation of notice. Herring v. Bender, 48 W. Va. 498, 37 S. E. 568.

[33] Valentine v. Austin, 58 Hun 398, 34 N. Y. St. 638, 12 N. Y. S. 196; McVay v. Tousley, 20 S. Dak. 258, 105 N. W. 932. See also Mitchell v. Smith, 53 N. Y. 413.

[34] Johnston v. Standard Min. Co., 148 U. S. 360, 37 L. ed. 480, 13 Sup. Ct. 585; Bridger v. Exchange Bank, 126 Ga. 821, 56 S. E. 97, 8 L. R. A. (N. S.) 463, 115 Am. St. 118; Tinsley v. Rice, 105 Ga. 285, 31 S. E. 174; Davis v. Bonar, 15 Iowa 171; Roberts v. Cardwell, 154 Ky. 483,

recording of such deed.[1] Thus, possession by a person other than the mortgagor, at the time of the execution of a mortgage, is sufficient to

157 S. W. 711; Woodward v. Johnson, 122 Ky. 160, 28 Ky. L. 1091, 90 S. W. 1076; Kelley v. Culver, 116 Ky. 241, 25 Ky. L. 443, 75 S. W. 272; Taylor v. Carroll, 89 Md. 32, 42 Atl. 920, 44 L. R. A. 379; Hammond v. Paxton, 58 Mich. 393, 25 N. W. 321; Boice v. Conover, 69 N. J. Eq. 530, 61 Atl. 159; Bybee v. Summers, 4 Ore. 354; Preston v. Tubbin, 1 Vern. Ch. 286, 23 Eng. Reprint 474. See also Johnson v. Gartman, 173 Ala. 290, 55 So. 906.

[1] Kirby v. Tallmadge, 160 U. S. 379, 40 L. ed. 463, 16 Sup. Ct. 349; Horbach v. Porter, 154 U. S. 549, 18 L. ed. 30, 14 Sup. Ct. 1160; Noyes v. Hall, 97 U. S. 34, 24 L. ed. 909; Lea v. Polk Co. Copper Co., 21 How. (U. S.) 493, 16 L. ed. 203; Landes v. Brant, 10 How. (U. S.) 348, 13 L. ed. 449; Weld v. Madden, 2 Cliff. (U. S.) 584; Johnson v. Glancy, 4 Blatchf. (U. S.) 94, 28 Am. Dec. 45; Gamble v. Black Warrior Coal Co., 172 Ala. 669, 55 So. 190; Lester v. Walker, 172 Ala. 104, 55 So. 619; Rankin Mfg. Co. v. Bishop, 137 Ala. 271, 34 So. 991; Kent v. Dean, 128 Ala. 600, 30 So. 543; Scheuer v. Kelly, 121 Ala. 323, 26 So. 4; Reynolds v. Kirk, 105 Ala. 446, 17 So. 95; Price v. Bell, 91 Ala. 180, 8 So. 565; Anthe v. Heide, 85 Ala. 236, 4 So. 380; Headley v. Bell, 84 Ala. 346, 4 So. 391; Tutwiler v. Montgomery, 73 Ala. 263; Bernstein v. Humes, 71 Ala. 260; Sawyers v. Baker, 66 Ala. 292; Phillips v. Costley, 40 Ala. 486; Garrett v. Lyle, 27 Ala. 586; Burt v. Cassety, 12 Ala. 734; Campbell v. Southwestern Tel. &c. Co., 108 Ark. 569, 158 S. W. 1035; Rubel v. Parker, 107 Ark. 314, 155 S. W. 114; Barrett v. Durbin, 106 Ark. 332, 153 S. W. 265; Sproull v. Miles, 82 Ark. 455, 102 S. W. 204; Kendall v. Davis, 55 Ark. 318, 18 S. W. 185; Turman v. Bell, 54 Ark. 273, 15 S. W. 886; Gill v. Hardin, 48 Ark. 409; Byers v. Engles, 16 Ark. 543; Beattie v. Crewdson, 124 Cal. 577, 57 Pac. 463; Stonesifer v. Kilburn, 122 Cal. 659, 55 Pac. 587; Austin v. Pulschen, 112 Cal. 528, 44 Pac. 788; Peasley v. McFadden, 68 Cal. 611, 10 Pac. 179; Jones v. Marks, 47 Cal. 242; Thompson v. Pioche, 44 Cal. 508; Moss v. Atkinson, 44 Cal. 3; Smith v. Yule, 31 Cal. 180, 89 Am. Dec. 167; Fair v. Stevenot, 29 Cal. 486; Davis v. Pursel, 55 Colo. 287, 134 Pac. 107; Runyan v. Snyder, 45 Colo. 156, 100 Pac. 420; Allen v. Moore, 30 Colo. 307, 70 Pac. 682; Harral v. Leverty, 50 Conn. 46, 47 Am. Rep. 608; Tate v. Pensacola &c. Land &c. Co., 37 Fla. 439, 20 So. 542, 53 Am. St. 251; Massey v. Hubbard, 18 Fla. 688; McRae v. McMinn, 17 Fla. 876; Terrell v. McLean, 130 Ga. 633, 61 S. E. 485; Garbutt v. Mayo, 128 Ga. 269, 57 S. E. 495, 13 L. R. A. (N. S.) 58; Bridger v. Exchange Bank, 126 Ga. 821, 56 S. E. 97, 8 L. R. A. (N. S.) 463, 115 Am. St. 118; Austin v. Southern Home Bldg. &c. Assn., 122 Ga. 439, 50 S. E. 382; Baldwin v. Sherwood, 117 Ga. 827, 45 S. E. 216; Collins v. Moore, 115 Ga. 327, 41 S. E. 609; Cox v. Jones, 76 Ga. 296; Finch v. Beal, 68 Ga. 594; Jewell v. Holland, 61 Ga. 608; Feirbough v. Masterson, 1 Idaho 135; Merchants' &c. State Bank v. Dawdy, 230 Ill. 199, 82 N. E. 606; Heppe v. Szozepanski, 209 Ill. 88, 70 N. E. 737, 101 Am. St. 221; Prouty v. Tilden, 164 Ill. 163, 45 N. E. 445; Parker v. Shannon, 137 Ill. 376, 27 N. E. 525; Jaques v. Lester, 118 Ill. 246, 8 N. E. 795; Tillotson v. Mitchell, 111 Ill. 518; Clevinger v. Ross, 109 Ill. 349; White v. White, 105 Ill. 313; Brainard v. Hudson, 103 Ill. 218; Cowen v. Loomis, 91 Ill. 132; Strong v. Shea, 83 Ill. 575; Doolittle v. Cook, 75 Ill. 354; Cabeen v. Breckenridge, 48 Ill. 91; Truesdale v. Ford, 37 Ill. 210; Keys v. Test, 33 Ill. 316; Brown v. Gaffney, 28 Ill. 149; Morrison v. Kelly, 22 Ill. 609; Santee v. Day, 111 Ill. App. 495; Helm v. Kaddatz, 107 Ill. App. 413; Stagg v. Small, 4 Bradw. (Ill.) 192; Adams v. Betz, 167 Ind. 161, 78 N. E. 649; Barnes v. Union School Township, 91 Ind. 301; Sutton v. Jervis, 31 Ind. 265, 99 Am. Dec. 631; Rothschild v. Leonhard, 33 Ind. App. 452, 71 N. E. 673; Elsbury v. Shull, 32 Ind. App. 556, 70 N. E. 287; Blair v. Whittaker, 31 Ind. App. 664, 69 N. E. 182; Kirkhan v. Moore, 30 Ind. App. 549, 65 N. E.

put the mortgagee upon inquiry as to the rights of the person in pos-

1042; Sanders v. Sutlive (Iowa), 143 N. W. 492; John v. Penegar, 158 Iowa 366, 139 N. W. 915; Seberg v. Iowa Trust &c. Bank, 141 Iowa 99, 119 N. W. 378; Crooks v. Jenkins, 124 Iowa 317, 100 N. E. 82, 104 Am. St. 326; Truth Lodge No. 213 v. Barton, 119 Iowa 230, 93 N. W. 106, 97 Am. St. 303; Zuber v. Johnson, 108 Iowa 273, 79 N. W. 76; Kruger v. Walker, 94 Iowa 506, 63 N. W. 320; Leebrick v. Stahle, 68 Iowa 515, 27 N. W. 490; Moore v. Pierson, 6 Iowa 279, 71 Am. Dec. 409; Penrose v. Cooper, 86 Kans. 597, 121 Pac. 1103; Gray v. Zellmer, 66 Kans. 514, 72 Pac. 228; Deetgen v. Richter, 33 Kans. 410, 6 Pac. 595; Greer v. Higgins, 20 Kans. 420; School District v. Taylor, 19 Kans. 287; Johnson v. Clark, 18 Kans. 157; Lyons v. Bodenhamer, 7 Kans. 455; Bryant v. Main, 25 Ky. L. 1242, 77 S. W. 680; Goins v. Allen, 4 Bush (Ky.) 608; Hackwith v. Damron, 1 Mon. (Ky.) 235; Duval v. Wilmer, 88 Md. 66, 41 Atl. 122; Border State Sav. Inst. v. Wilcox, 63 Md. 525; Bryan v. Harvey, 18 Md. 113; Ringgold v. Bryan, 3 Md. Ch. 488; Toupin v. Peabody, 162 Mass. 473, 39 N. E. 280; Cunningham v. Pattee, 99 Mass. 248; Holden v. Butler, 173 Mich. 116, 138 N. W. 1071; Delosh v. Delosh, 171 Mich. 175, 137 N. W. 81; Brady v. Sloman, 156 Mich. 423, 120 N. W. 795; Howatt v. Green, 139 Mich. 289, 102 N. W. 734; Banks v. Allen, 127 Mich. 80, 86 N. W. 383; Holmes v. Deppert, 122 Mich. 275, 80 N. W. 1094; Oconto v. Lundquist, 119 Mich. 264, 77 N. W. 950; Miner v. Wilson, 107 Mich. 57, 64 N. W. 874; Corey v. Smalley, 106 Mich. 257, 64 N. W. 13; Weisberger v. Wisner, 55 Mich. 246, 21 N. W. 331; Allen v. Cadwell, 55 Mich. 8, 20 N. W. 692; Parsell v. Thayer, 39 Mich. 467; Russell v. Sweezey, 22 Mich. 235; Doyle v. Stevens, 4 Mich. 87; Niles v. Cooper, 98 Minn. 39, 107 N. W. 744, 13 L. R. A. (N. S.) 49; Thompson v. Borg, 90 Minn. 209, 95 N. W. 896; New v. Wheaton, 24 Minn. 406; Groff v. Ramsey, 19 Minn. 43; Morrison v. March, 4 Minn. 325; Bolton v. Roebuck, 77 Miss. 710, 27 So. 630; Hiller v. Jones, 66 Miss. 636, 6 So. 465;

Taylor v. Mosely, 57 Miss. 544; Strickland v. Kirk, 51 Miss. 795; Squires v. Kimball, 208 Mo. 110, 106 S. W. 502; Shaffer v. Detie, 191 Mo. 377, 90 S. W. 131; Davis v. Wood, 161 Mo. 17, 61 S. W. 695; Wiggenhorn v. Daniels, 149 Mo. 160, 50 S. W. 807; Pike v. Robertson, 79 Mo. 615; Roberts v. Moseley, 64 Mo. 507; Vaughn v. Tracy, 22 Mo. 415, 25 Mo. 318, 69 Am. Dec. 471; Bartlett v. Glasscock, 4 Mo. 62; McParland v. Peters, 87 Nebr. 829, 128 N. W. 523; Fall v. Fall, 75 Nebr. 104, 106 N. W. 412, 113 N. W. 175, 121 Am. St. 767; Oberlender v. Butcher, 67 Nebr. 410, 93 N. W. 764; Lipp v. Land Syndicate, 24 Nebr. 692, 40 N. W. 129; Conlee v. McDowell, 15 Nebr. 184; Brophy Min. Co. v. Brophy &c. Gold Min. Co., 15 Nev. 101; Stillings v Stillings, 67 N. H. 584, 42 Atl. 271; Janvrin v. Janvrin, 60 N. H. 169; Forest v. Jackson, 56 N. H. 357; Patten v. Moore, 32 N. H. 382; Emmons v. Murray, 16 N. H. 385; Rogers v. Jones, 8 N. H. 264; Wood v. Price, 79 N. J. Eq. 620, 81 Atl. 983, 38 L. R. A. (N. S.) 772, Ann. Cas. 1913A, 1210; Schwoebel v. Storrie, 76 N. J. Eq. 466, 74 Atl. 969; Brown v. Columbus (N. J. Eq.), 75 Atl. 917; English v. Rainear (N. J.), 55 Atl. 41; Hodge v. Amerman, 40 N. J. Eq. 99, 2 Atl. 257; Losey v. Simpson, 11 N. J. Eq. 246; Holmes v. Stout, 10 N. J. Eq. 419; Cox v. Devinney, 65 N. J. L. 389, 47 Atl. 569; Roll v. Rea, 50 N. J. L. 264, 12 Atl. 905; Van Keuren v. Central R. Co., 38 N. J. L. 165; Carthage Tissue Paper Mills v. Carthage, 200 N. Y. 1, 93 N. E. 60; Gibson v. Thomas, 180 N. Y. 483, 73 N. E. 484, 70 L. R. A. 768; Sanders v. Riedinger, 164 N. Y. 564, 58 N. E. 1092, affg. 30 App. Div. 277, 51 N. Y. S. 937; Hallinan v. Murphy, 159 N. Y. 554, 54 N. E. 1092, affg. 88 Hun 72, 68 N. Y. St. 674, 34 N. Y. S. 618; Ward v. Metropolitan El. R. Co., 152 N. Y. 39, 46 N. E. 319, affg. 82 Hun 545, 31 N. Y. S. 527; Phelan v. Brady, 119 N. Y. 587, 23 N. E. 1109, 8 L. R. A. 211; Seymour v. McKinstry, 106 N. Y. 230, 12 N. E. 348, 14 N. E. 94; Westbrook v. Gleason, 79 N. Y. 23; Union College Trustees v. Wheeler, 61 N.

Y. 88; Cavalli v. Allen, 57 N. Y. 508; Moyer v. Hinman, 13 N. Y. 186; Caccioppoli v. Lemmo, 152 App. Div. 650, 137 N. Y. S. 643; Webster v. Van Steenbergh, 46 Barb. (N. Y.) 211; Orleans Bank v. Flagg, 3 Barb. Ch. (N. Y.) 318; Chesterman v. Gardner, 5 Johns. Ch. (N. Y.) 29; Bank v. Rubenstein, 78 Misc. 465, 138 N. Y. S. 647; Farmers Loan &c. Co. v. Maltby, 8 Paige (N. Y.) 361; Grimstone v. Carter, 3 Paige Ch. (N. Y.) 421; Gouverneur v. Lynch, 2 Paige (N. Y.) 300; Tuttle v. Jackson, 6 Wend. (N. Y.) 213; Lee v. Giles, 161 N. Car. 541, 77 S. E. 852; Falls of Neuse Mfg. Co. v. Hendricks, 106 N. Car. 485, 11 S. E. 568; Mayo v. Leggett, 96 N. Car. 237, 1 S. E. 622; Staton v. Davenport, 95 N. Car. 11; Tankard v. Tankard, 79 N. Car. 54; Edwards v. Thompson, 71 N. Car. 177; Laws of North Carolina 1885, ch. 147, § 1, Pell's Revisal 1908, § 980; O'Toole v. Omlie, 8 N. Dak. 444, 79 N. W. 849; Ranney v. Hardy, 43 Ohio St. 157, 1 N. E. 523; McKinzie v. Perrill, 15 Ohio St. 162; Kelley v. Stanberry, 13 Ohio St. 408; Williams v. Sprigg, 6 Ohio St. 585; Brown v. Trent, 36 Okla. 239, 128 Pac. 895; Randall v. Lingwall, 43 Ore. 383, 73 Pac. 1; Scott v. Lewis, 40 Ore. 37, 66 Pac. 299; Manaudas v. Mann, 14 Ore. 450, 13 Pac. 449; Wertheimer v. Thomas, 168 Pa. St. 168, 31 Atl. 1096; Bidwell v. Evans, 156 Pa. St. 30, 26 Atl. 817; Anderson v. Brinser, 129 Pa. St. 376, 11 Atl. 809, 18 Atl. 520, 6 L. R. A. 205; Bugbee's Appeal, 110 Pa. St. 331, 1 Atl. 273; Rowe v. Ream, 105 Pa. St. 543; Kerr v. Day, 14 Pa. St. 112, 53 Am. Dec. 526; Randall v. Silverthorn, 4 Pa. St. 173; Lightner v. Mooney, 10 Watts (Pa.) 407; Woods v. Farmere, 7 Watts (Pa.) 372, 52 Am. Dec. 772; Harris v. Arnold, 1 R. I. 125; Folk v. Brooks, 91 S. Car. 7, 74 S. E. 46; Daniel v. Hester, 29 S. Car. 147, 7 S. E. 65; Sweatman v. Edmunds, 28 S. Car. 58, 5 S. E. 165; Graham v. Nesmith, 24 S. Car. 285; Biemann v. White, 23 S. Car. 490; Sheorn v. Robinson, 22 S. Car. 32; Phillis v. Gross, 32 S. Dak. 438, 143 N. W. 373; Johnson v. Olberg, 32 S. Dak. 346, 143 N. W. 292; Huffman v. Cooley, 28 S. Dak. 475, 134 N. W. 49; Kuteman v. Carroll (Tex.), 80 S. W. 842; Jinks v. Mop-

pin (Tex.), 80 S. W. 390; Glendenning v. Bell, 70 Tex. 632, 8 S. W. 324; Cameron v. Romele, 53 Tex. 238; Mullins v. Wimberly, 50 Tex. 457; Hawley v. Bullock, 29 Tex. 216; Watkins v. Edwards, 23 Tex. 443; Tolar v. Dev. Co. (Tex. Civ. App.), 153 S. W. 911; Hudson v. Jones (Tex. Civ. App.), 143 S. W. 197; Parrish v. Williams (Tex. Civ. App.), 79 S. W. 1097; Smith v. James, 22 Tex. Civ. App. 154, 54 S. W. 41; Brown v. Wilson (Tex. Civ. App.), 29 S. W. 530; Stahn v. Hall, 10 Utah 400, 37 Pac. 585; Sowles v. Butler, 71 Vt. 271, 44 Atl. 355; Orr v. Clark, 62 Vt. 136, 19 Atl. 929; Canfield v. Hard, 58 Vt. 217, 2 Atl. 136; Perkins v. West, 55 Vt. 265; Rublee v. Mead, 2 Vt. 544; Ely v. Johnson, 114 Va. 31, 75 S. E. 748; Chapman v. Chapman, 91 Va. 397, 21 S. E. 813, 50 Am. St. 846; Rorer Iron Co. v. Trout, 83 Va. 397, 2 S. E. 713, 5 Am. St. 285; Effinger v. Hall, 81 Va. 94; Preston v. Nash, 76 Va. 1; Bendon v. Parfit, 74 Wash. 645, 134 Pac. 185; Turner v. Creech, 58 Wash. 439, 108 Pac. 1084; Peterson v. Philadelphia Mtg. &c. Co., 33 Wash. 464, 74 Pac. 585; Lowther Oil Co. v. Miller-Sibley Oil Co., 53 W. Va. 501, 44 S. E. 433, 97 Am. St. 1027; Western Min. &c. Co. v. Peytona Cannel Coal Co., 8 W. Va. 406; Keilly v. Severson, 149 Wis. 251, 135 N. W. 875; Roberts v. Decker, 120 Wis. 102, 97 N. W. 519; Prickett v. Muck, 74 Wis. 199, 42 N. W. 256; Lamoreaux v. Huntley, 68 Wis. 24, 31 N. W. 331; Meade v. Gilfoyle, 64 Wis. 18, 24 N. W. 413; Coe v. Manseau, 62 Wis. 81, 22 N. W. 155; Brinkman v. Jones, 44 Wis. 498; Cunningham v. Brown, 44 Wis. 72; Ehle v. Brown, 31 Wis. 405; Wicke v. Lake, 21 Wis. 410, 94 Am. Dec. 552, 25 Wis. 71; Fery v. Pfeiffer, 18 Wis. 510; James v. Lichfield, L. R. 9 Eq. 51; Taylor v. Stibbert, 2 Ves. Jr. 437; Daniels v. Davidson, 16 Ves. 240; Holmes v. Powell, 8 De G. M. & G. 572; Bailey v. Richardson, 9 Hare 734; Moreland v. Richardson, 24 Beav. 33; Wilson v. Hart, L. R. 1 Ch. App. 463; Butcher v. Stapely, 1 Vern Ch. 363, 23 Eng. Reprint 524. In Maine the rule prevailed prior to Rev. Stat. of 1841; Beal v. Gordon, 55 Maine 482; Clark v. Bosworth, 51 Maine 528; Hull v. Noble, 40 Maine 459;

session, and he takes the mortgage subject to such rights.[2] Thus also
the possession of a tenant is notice of his interest in the land, whatever that interest may be, and, perhaps, notice also of his landlord's
title;[3] and so, the possession of a cestui que trust is notice of his
beneficial interest in the property.[4]

Possession by a vendee under a contract of purchase, whether it be

Hanly v. Morse, 32 Maine 287; Matthews v. Demerritt, 22 Maine 312;
Webster v. Maddox, 6 Maine 256.
See also Lyon v. Moore, 259 Ill. 23,
102 N. E. 179. But see Norfolk &c.
Tract. Co. v. White, 113 Va. 102, 73
S. E. 467. The mere fact that a person other than the vendor is in possession of property is not sufficient
to charge a purchaser with notice,
where possession is delivered to the
purchaser upon demand. Pancake
v. Cauffman, 114 Pa. St. 113, 7 Atl.
67.

[3] Dennis v. Atlanta Nat. Bldg. &c.
Assn., 136 Fed. 539, 69 C. C. A. 315;
Bright v. Buckman, 39 Fed. 243;
Ferguson v. Dent, 24 Fed. 412; Kent
v. Bean, 128 Ala. 600, 30 So. 543;
Reynolds v. Kirk, 105 Ala. 446, 17
So. 95; Anthe v. Heide, 85 Ala. 236,
4 So. 380; American Building &c.
Assn. v. Warren, 101 Ark. 163, 141
S. W. 765; Jowers v. Phelps, 33 Ark.
465; Waters v. Williamson, 21 D. C.
24; Linder v. Whitehead, 116 Ga.
206, 42 S. E. 358; Sanford v. Davis,
181 Ill. 570, 54 N. E. 977; Joiner v.
Duncan, 174 Ill. 252, 51 N. E. 323;
Brainard v. Hudson, 103 Ill. 218;
Weber v. Shelby, 116 Ill. App. 31;
Griffin v. Haskins, 22 Ill. App. 264;
Crooks v. Jenkins, 124 Iowa 317,
100 N. W. 82, 104 Am. St. 326; Scha-
fer v. Wilson, 113 Iowa 475, 85 N.
W. 789; Humphrey v. Moore, 17
Iowa 193; International Harvester
Co. v. Myers, 86 Kans. 497, 121 Pac.
500, 39 L. R. A. (N. S.) 528; Martin
v. Hall, 30 Ky. L. 1110, 100 S. W.
343; Boggs v. Anderson, 50 Maine
161; McLaughlin v. Shepherd, 32
Maine 143, 52 Am. Dec. 646; Van
Baalen v. Cotney, 113 Mich. 202, 71
N. W. 491; Hubbard v. Smith, 2
Mich. 207; Teal v. Scandinavian-
American Bank, 114 Minn. 435, 131
N. W. 486; Jellison v. Halloran, 44
Minn. 199, 46 N. W. 332; New v.
Wheaton, 24 Minn. 406; Abbey v.

Taber, 134 N. Y. 615, 32 N. E. 649;
Schneider v. Mahl, 84 App. Div. 1,
82 N. Y. S. 27; Bassett v. Wood, 55
Hun 587, 29 N. Y. St. 901, 9 N. Y. S.
79; Swanstrom v. Day, 46 Misc. 311,
93 N. Y. S. 192; Braman v. Wilkinson, 3 Barb. (N. Y.) 151; Lawrence
v. Conklin, 17 Hun (N. Y.) 228;
Union College v. Wheeler, 5 Lans.
(N. Y.) 160; New York L. Ins. &c.
Co. v. Cutler, 3 Sand. Ch. (N. Y.)
176; Ranney v. Hardy, 43 Ohio St.
157, 1 N. E. 523; Edwards v. Montgomery, 26 Okla. 862, 110 Pac. 779;
Sweatman v. Edmunds, 28 S. Car.
58, 5 S. E. 165; Ramirez v. Smith, 94
Tex. 184, 59 S. W. 258; Pride v. Whitfield (Tex.), 51 S. W. 1100; Compton
v. Seley (Tex.), 27 S. W. 1077; Gall
v. Gall, 126 Wis. 390, 105 N. W. 953,
5 L. R. A. (N. S.) 603; Matesky v.
Feldman, 75 Wis. 103, 43 N. W. 733.
See also La Forest v. Downer, 63
Ore. 176, 126 Pac. 995; McIntosh v.
Bowers, 143 Wis. 74, 126 N. W. 548.
A mortgagee may rely upon a statement of one in possession that he is
tenant of the mortgagor. Bush v.
Roberts, 57 Ore. 169, 110 Pac. 790.

[3] See post § 589.

[4] McVey v. McQuality, 97 Ill. 93;
McDaniel v. Peabody, 54 Iowa 305,
6 N. W. 538; Rogers v. Scarff, 3 Gill
(Md.) 127; Oberlender v. Butcher,
67 Nebr. 410, 93 N. W. 764; Jones v.
Johnston Harvester Co., 8 Nebr. 446,
1 N. W. 443; Ferrin v. Errol, 59 N.
H. 234; Pritchard v. Brown, 4 N. H.
397, 17 Am. Dec. 431; Flaherty v.
Cramer, 62 N. J. Eq. 758, 48 Atl.
565; Ross v. Hendrix, 110 N. Car.
403, 15 N. E. 4; Petrain v. Kiernan,
23 Ore. 455, 32 Pac. 158; Hawley v.
Geer (Tex.), 17 S. W. 914; Klender
v. Fenske, 53 Wis. 118, 10 N. W. 370.
But see Scott v. Gallagher, 14 Serg.
& R. (Pa.) 333, 16 Am. Dec. 508;
Yocom v. Morris, 3 Phila. (Pa.)
414 (direct and express notice necessary).

per$onal or by a tenant, is constructive notice of his equitable rights as purchaser, and any one taking a mortgage under such circumstances from his vendor takes subject to his rights.[5] The mortgage lien in such case covers the property only to the extent of the unpaid purchase-money.[6]

The rule that possession is equivalent to notice prevails generally in the United States. In a few states, however, "actual notice" is essential in order to dispense with registration, and consequently possession does not amount to notice, and does not have the effect of putting a purchaser upon inquiry, though proof of possession may be made in connection with evidence of actual notice.[7] But in these states knowledge of adverse possession, though it be open and notorious, does not of itself amount to notice of the occupant's title or right.

§ 587.   Inquiry by purchaser concerning adverse possession.—The prevailing rule, however, is that possession is notice although it be not actually known to the purchaser.[8] It is a fact which the purchaser

[5] Reynolds v. Kirk, 105 Ala. 446, 17 So. 95; Sawyers v. Baker, 66 Ala. 292; American Bldg. &c. Assn. v. Warren, 101 Ark. 163, 141 S. W. 765; Collins v. Moore, 115 Ga. 327, 41 S. E. 609; Tillotson v. Mitchell, 111 Ill. 518; Doolittle v. Cook, 75 Ill. 354; Van Baalen v. Cotney, 113 Mich. 202, 71 N. W. 491; Kirby v. Bank of Carrollton, 102 Miss. 190, 59 So. 10; Braman v. Wilkinson, 3 Barb. (N. Y.) 151; Orleans Bank v. Flagg, 3 Barb. Ch. (N. Y.) 316; Ranney v. Hardy, 43 Ohio St. 157, 1 N. E. 523; McIntosh v. Bowers, 143 Wis. 74, 126 N. W. 548; First Nat. Bank v. Chafee, 98 Wis. 42, 73 N. W. 318; Cunningham v. Brown, 44 Wis. 72. See also Francis v. Jefferson County Sav. Bank, 167 Ala. 548, 52 So. 906. But see Gray v. Harvey, 17 N. Dak. 1, 113 N. W. 1034 (possession of tenant). Possession of land by a purchaser under a parol contract of purchase is sufficient to charge a subsequent purchaser or mortgagee with notice of the purchaser's rights. Mowrey v. Davis, 12 Ind. App. 681, 40 N. E. 1108; Duval v. Wilmer, 88 Md. 66, 41 Atl. 122; Whitsett v. Miller, 1 Tex. Unreported Cas. 203; Cunningham v. Brown, 44 Wis. 72.

[6] Westbrook v. Gleason, 14 Hun (N. Y.) 245, 79 N. Y. 23; Young v. Guy, 12 Hun (N. Y.) 325, 23 Hun 1, affd. 87 N. Y. 457; Houzik v. Delaglise, 65 Wis. 494, 27 N. W. 171.

[7] Harrall v. Leaverty, 50 Conn. 46; Moore v. Jourdan, 14 La. Ann. 414; Poydras v. Laurens, 6 La. Ann. 772; In Maine, since Rev. Stat. of 1841, Boggs v. Anderson, 50 Maine 161; Beal v. Gordon, 55 Maine 482; Clarke v. Bosworth, 51 Maine 528; Goodwin v. Cloudman, 43 Maine 577. See also Knapp v. Bailey, 79 Maine 195; Lamb v. Pierce, 113 Mass. 72; Sibley v. Leffingwell, 8 Allen (Mass.) 584; Dooley v. Walcott, 4 Allen (Mass.) 406; Parker v. Osgood, 3 Allen (Mass.) 487; Mara v. Pierce, 9 Gray (Mass.) 306; Pomroy v. Stevens, 11 Metc. (Mass.) 224; Boynton v. Rees, 8 Pick. (Mass.) 329, 19 Am. Dec. 326; McMechan v. Griffing, 3 Pick. (Mass.) 149, 15 Am. Dec. 198.

[8] Scroggins v. McDougal, 8 Ala. 382; Scheerer v. Cuddy, 85 Cal. 270, 24 Pac. 713; Tate v. Pensacola &c. Land Co., 37 Fla. 439, 20 So. 542, 53 Am. St. 251; Smith v. Jackson, 76 Ill. 254; Moreland v. Lemasters, 4 Blackf. (Ind.) 383; Wolf v. Zabel, 44 Minn. 90, 46 N. W. 81; Hodge v. Amerman, 40 N. J. Eq. 99, 2 Atl. 257; McCall v. Yard, 11 N. J. Eq. 58; Royce v. Flint, 1 Alb. L. J. (N. Y.) 238; Ranney v. Hardy, 43 Ohio

should know, and he is thereby put upon inquiry as to the possessor's rights.[9] Possession does not amount to constructive notice of the nature and extent of the rights of the person in possession; but it puts the purchaser upon inquiry as to such rights. He is bound to pursue the inquiry with diligence, and to ascertain what those rights are.[10] Inquiries should be made, in the first instance, of the person in actual possession; and the mortgagee is chargeable with notice of all the facts affecting the validity of the mortgage, which he could have ascertained by proper inquiry of such person.[11] A purchaser who negligently or intentionally fails to inquire as to the fact of possession, or as to the title or interests of the person in possession, is affected with notice of such title or interest as the possessor actually has. Such a purchaser can not claim the position of a purchaser in good faith without notice. But a subsequent purchaser or mortgagee can disprove his knowledge of the claims of a person in possession by showing that he made every proper inquiry concerning the rights of the occupant and failed to obtain information.[12] A purchaser's knowledge

St. 157, 1 N. E. 523; Sheorn v. Robinson, 22 S. Car. 32; Huffman v. Cooley, 28 S. Dak. 475, 134 N. W. 49; Betts v. Letcher, 1 S. Dak. 182, 46 N. W. 193; Brinkman v. Jones, 44 Wis. 498. The rule is particularly applicable where the purchaser could have easily acquired knowledge of the fact, but neglected to visit the premises. Smith v. Jackson, 76 Ill. 254. But it has been held that possession charges the purchaser with notice, although he lives in another state. Edwards v. Thompson, 71 N. Car. 177.

In Missouri it seems that knowledge of adverse possession is essential to charge the purchaser. Masterson v. West End &c. R. Co., 5 Mo. App. 64, affd. 72 Mo. 342; Casey v. Steinmeyer, 7 Mo. App. 556.

[9] Pique v. Arendale, 71 Ala. 91; American Bldg. &c. Assn. v. Warren, 101 Ark. 163, 141 S. W. 765 (citing text); Hughes Bros. v. Redus, 90 Ark. 149, 118 S. W. 414; Dutton v. Warschauer, 21 Cal. 609, 82 Am. Dec. 765; International Harvester Co. v. Myers, 86 Kans. 497, 121 Pac. 500, 39 L. R. A. (N. S.) 528; Loughridge v. Bowland, 52 Miss. 546; Schwoebel v. Storrie, 76 N. J. Eq. 466, 74 Atl. 969; Hodge v.

Amerman, 40 N. J. Eq. 99, 2 Atl. 257; Losey v. Simpson, 11 N. J. Eq. 246; Smith v. Fuller, 152 N. Car. 7, 67 S. E. 48; Edwards v. Thompson, 71 N. Car. 177; Ranney v. Hardy, 43 Ohio St. 157, 1 N. E. 523; Randall v. Lingwall, 43 Ore. 383, 73 Pac. 1; Hottenstein v. Lerch, 104 Pa. St. 454; Kerr v. Day, 14 Pa. St. 112, 53 Am. Dec. 526; Bilman v. White, 23 S. Car. 490; Sheorn v. Robinson, 22 S. Car. 32; Chapman v. Chapman, 91 Va. 397, 21 S. E. 813, 50 Am. St. 846. See also Kirby v. Tallmadge, 160 U. S. 379, 40 L. ed. 463, 16 Sup. Ct. 349.

[10] Flagg v. Mann, 2 Sumn. (U. S.) 486; Thompson v. Pioche, 44 Cal. 508; International Harvester Co. v. Myers, 86 Kans. 497, 121 Pac. 500, 39 L. R. A. (N. S.) 528; Rogers v. Jones, 8 N. H. 264; Williamson v. Brown, 15 N. Y. 354; Grimstone v. Carter, 3 Paige (N. Y.) 421, 24 Am. Dec. 230; Kerr v. Day, 14 Pa. St. 112, 53 Am. Dec. 526; Hoppin v. Doty, 25 Wis. 573; Daniels v. Davison, 16 Ves. 249.

[11] Collins v. Moore, 115 Ga. 327, 41 S. E. 609. See also Austin v. Southern Home Bldg. Assn. 122 Ga. 439, 50 S. E. 382.

[12] Hellman v. Levy, 55 Cal. 117.

of the condition of the land, as by the presence of structures thereon, may be sufficient to put him on inquiry concerning the existence of some adverse right or easement.[13]

§ 588. **Nature of adverse claim.**—Possession is not necessarily evidence of any particular title; it is evidence of some title, and puts the purchaser upon inquiry as to the title or interest the occupant holds or claims.[14] Possession under an apparent claim of ownership has been held to constitute notice to purchasers of whatever interest the person actually in possession has in the fee,[15] whether the interest be either legal or equitable.[16] If the person in possession has no title or right of possession whatever, but is a mere intruder, his possession is not notice and does not put a purchaser on inquiry.[17]

Although the principle of constructive notice may be applied to protect an occupant with equitable rights, it may not be invoked to protect one who has no equity, and an occupant without any just claim will not be protected as against a purchaser for value,[18] especially where the occupant seeks the aid of the doctrine to cover his own fraud or misrepresentation.[19] If the purchaser makes due inquiry,

[13] Webb v. Robbins, 77 Ala. 176; Blatchley v. Osborn, 33 Conn. 226; Paul v. Connersville &c. R. Co., 51 Ind. 527; Randall v. Silverthorn, 4 Pa. St. 173. See post § 592.

[14] Kent v. Dean, 128 Ala. 600, 3 So. 543; Munn v. Burges, 70 Ill. 604; Leach v. Ansbacher, 55 Pa. St. 85; Jaques v. Weeks, 7 Watts (Pa.) 261; Harris v. Arnold, 1 R. I. 126; Smith v. Miller, 63 Tex. 72. A purchaser of land in the possession of another should inquire by what tenure possession is then held, and not merely the character in which the possession was originally obtained. Williams v. Brown, 14 Ill. 200. See ante § 587.

[15] Kirby v. Tallmadge, 160 U. S. 379, 40 L. ed. 463, 16 Sup. Ct. 349; Walker v. Neil, 117 Ga. 733, 45 S. E. 387; Carr v. Brennan, 166 Ill. 108, 47 N. E. 721, 57 Am. St. 119; Rock Island &c. R. Co. v. Dimick, 144 Ill. 628, 32 N. E. 291, 19 L. R. A. 105; Morrison v. Morrison, 140 Ill. 560, 30 N. E. 768; Farmers' Nat. Bank v. Sperling, 113 Ill. 273; Haworth v. Taylor, 108 Ill. 275; Sanford v. Weeks, 38 Kans. 319, 16 Pac. 465, 5 Am. St. 748; Dengler v. Fowler, 94 Nebr. 621, 143 N. W. 944;

Losey v. Simpson, 11 N. J. Eq. 246; Cornell v. Maltby, 165 N. Y. 557, 59 N. E. 291; Phelan v. Brady, 119 N. Y. 587, 23 N. E. 1109, 8 L. R. A. 211; Betts v. Letcher, 1 S. Dak. 182, 46 N. W. 193; Chapman v. Chapman, 91 Va. 397, 21 S. E. 813, 50 Am. St. 846.

[16] Kirby v. Tallmadge 160 U. S. 379, 40 L. ed. 463, 16 Sup. Ct. 349; Houston Oil Co. v. Green, 202 Fed. 874, 121 C. C. A. 232; Brunson v. Brooks, 68 Ala. 248; Rock Island &c. R. Co. v. Dimick, 144 Ill. 628, 32 N. E. 291, 19 L. R. A. 105; Sanford v. Weeks, 38 Kans. 319, 16 Pac. 465, 5 Am. St. 748; Dengler v. Fowler, 94 Nebr. 621, 143 N. W. 944.

[17] Wright v. Wood, 23 Pa. St. 120; Western Mining &c. Co. v. Coal Co., 8 W. Va. 406.

[18] Gill v. Hardin, 48 Ark. 409, 3 S. W. 519; Minton v. New York El. R. Co., 130 N. Y. 332, 29 N. E. 319.

[19] Yates v. Hurd, 8 Colo. 343, 8 Pac. 575; Groton Sav. Bank v. Batty, 30 N. J. Eq. 126; Losey v. Simpson, 11 N. J. Eq. 246. See also Broussard v. Broussard, 45 La. Ann. 1035, 13 So. 699; Converse v. Blumrich, 14 Mich. 109, 90 Am. Dec. 230.

and such inquiry fails to disclose any title or interest in the person in possession, the presumptive notice from possession is rebutted.[20] A mortgagee who, in reliance upon the record title, takes a mortgage upon property from one to whom it has been transferred by a fraudulent grantee, is not chargeable with constructive notice of the fraud, although the person defrauded occupies the property, where at the time such person was ignorant of the fraud perpetrated and could not have disclosed the fact to the mortgagee had he made inquiry.[21]

§ 589. Possession of tenant as notice.—A purchaser of land in the possession of a tenant of the vendor has notice of the actual interest of the tenant and of the whole extent of that interest, and is bound to admit the tenant's claim so far as it could be enforced against the vendor.[22] And likewise, a subsequent mortgagee is charged with constructive notice of the legal and equitable rights of a tenant in posses-

[20] Flagg v. Mann, 2 Sumn. (U. S.) 486; Thompson v. Pioche, 44 Cal. 508; Pell v. McElroy, 36 Cal. 268; Fair v. Stevinot, 29 Cal. 486; Austin v. Southern Home Bldg. &c. Assn., 122 Ga. 439, 50 S. E. 382; Riley v. Quigley, 50 Ill. 304, 99 Am. Dec. 516; Brown v. Anderson, 1 T. B. Mon. (Ky.) 198; M'Mechan v. Griffing, 3 Pick. (Mass.) 149, 15 Am. Dec. 198; Brophy Min. Co. v. Brophy &c. Gold &c. Min. Co., 15 Nev. 101; Nutting v. Herbert, 37 N. H. 346; Rogers v. Jones, 8 N. H. 264; Fassett v. Smith, 23 N. Y. 252; Williamson v. Brown, 15 N. Y. 354; Lower v. Wightman, 5 Leg. Gaz. (Pa.) 45; Harris v. Arnold, 1 R. I. 126; Huffman v. Cooley, 28 S. Dak. 475, 134 N. W. 49; Betts v. Letcher, 1 S. Dak. 182, 46 N. W. 193; Hewitt v. Loosemore, 9 Hare 449; Jones v. Smith, 1 Hare 43.

[21] Cornell v. Maltby, 165 N. Y. 557, 59 N. E. 291.

[22] Flagg v. Mann, 2 Sumn. (U. S.) 486, 1 Fed. Cas. No. 4847; Scheerer v. Cuddy, 85 Cal. 270, 24 Pac. 713; Dreyfus v. Hirt, 82 Cal. 621, 23 Pac. 193; Peasley v. McFadden, 68 Cal. 611, 10 Pac. 179; McRae v. McMinn, 17 Fla. 876; Parker v. Gortatowsky, 127 Ga. 560, 56 S. E. 846; Clarke v. Beck, 72 Ga. 127; Coari v. Olsen, 91 Ill. 273; Williams v. Brown, 14 Ill. 200; Joseph v. Wild, 146 Ind. 249, 45 N. E. 467; Leebrick v. Stahle, 68 Iowa 515, 27 N. W. 490; Russell v. Moore, 3 Metc. (Ky.) 436; Hull v.

Noble, 40 Maine 459; Toupin v. Peabody, 162 Mass. 473, 39 N. E. 280; Cunningham v. Pattee, 99 Mass. 248; Brady v. Sloman, 156 Mich. 423, 120 N. W. 795; Trumpower v. Marcey, 92 Mich. 529, 52 N. W. 999; Lambert v. Weber, 83 Mich. 395, 47 N. W. 251; Starkey v. Horton, 65 Mich. 96, 31 N. W. 626; McKee v. Wilcox, 11 Mich. 358, 83 Am. Dec. 743; Ogden v. Garrison, 82 Nebr. 302, 117 N. W. 714, 17 L. R. A. (N. S.) 1135; Friedlander v. Rider, 30 Nebr. 783, 47 N. W. 83, 9 L. R. A. 700; Smith v. Gibson, 25 Nebr. 511, 41 N. W. 360; Havens v. Bliss, 26 N. J. Eq. 363; McCall v. Yard, 11 N. J. Eq. 58; Seymour v. McKinstry, 106 N. Y. 230, 12 N. E. 348, 14 N. E. 94; Page v. Waring, 76 N. Y. 463; Trustees Union College v. Wheeler, 61 N. Y. 88; De Ruyter v. Trustees, 2 Barb. Ch. (N. Y.) 555; Chesterman v. Gardner, 5 Johns. Ch. (N. Y.) 29, 9 Am. Dec. 265; Spofford v. Manning, 6 Paige (N. Y.) 383; Bassett v. Wood, 9 N. Y. S. 79; Whitham v. Lehmer, 22 Okla. 627, 98 Pac. 351; Hottenstein v. Lerch, 104 Pa. St. 454; Marsh v. Nelson, 101 Pa. St. 57; Evans v. Bidwell, 76 Pa. St. 497; Kerr v. Day, 14 Pa. St. 112, 53 Am. Dec. 526; Hood v. Fahnestock, 1 Pa. St. 470, 44 Am. Dec. 147; Glendenning v. Bell, 70 Tex. 632, 8 S. W. 324; Mullins v. Wimberly, 50 Tex. 457; Howell v. Denton (Tex.), 68 S. W. 1002; Ehle v. Brown, 21 Wis. 405;

sion under a lease;[23] as well as the claims of a third person through such tenant.[24]

Although the rule is otherwise in England,[25] it is now well settled in the United States that a tenant's possession of real estate is constructive notice of his landlord's title;[26] for such possession imposes upon the purchaser the obligation of inquiring by what right the tenant holds. In order that a tenant's possession may be notice of his landlord's title, the tenancy must have begun after the lessor acquired his title.[27]

By the weight of authority, where an owner conveys land in posses-

Fery v. Pfeiffer, 18 Wis. 510; Daniels v. Davison, 16 Ves. 249.

[25] Kerr v. Kingsbury, 39 Mich. 150, 33 Am. Rep. 362; Toland v. Corey, 6 Utah 392, 24 Pac. 190; Allen v. Gates, 73 Vt. 222, 50 Atl. 1092. See also Bell v. Twilight, 18 N. H. 159, 45 Am. Dec. 367; Staples v. Fenton, 5 Hun (N. Y.) 172.

[24] Collins v. Moore, 115 Ga. 327, 41 S. E. 609; Wrede v. Cloud, 52 Iowa 371, 3 N. W. 400; Morrison v. March, 4 Minn. 422; Baldwin v. Johnson, 1 N. J. Eq. 441; Welsh v. Schoen, 59 Hun 356, 36 N. Y. St. 538, 13 N. Y. S. 71; Martin v. Jackson, 27 Pa. St. 504, 67 Am. Dec. 489.

[25] Hunt v. Luck, 1 Ch. 428, 71 L. J. Ch. 239, 86 L. T. (N. S.) 68, 18 T. L. R. 265, 50 Wkly. Rep. 291; Barnhart v. Greenshields, 9 Moore P. C. 18, 14 Eng. Reprint 204; Hanbury v. Litchfield, 2 Mylne & K. 629.

[26] United States v. Sliney, 21 Fed. 894; Price v. Bell, 91 Ala. 180, 8 So. 565; Brunson v. Brooks, 68 Ala. 248; Storthz v. Chapline, 71 Ark. 31, 70 S. W. 465; Peasley v. McFadden, 68 Cal. 611, 10 Pac. 179; Thompson v. Pioche, 44 Cal. 508; O'Rourke v. O'Connor, 39 Cal. 442; Landers v. Bolton, 26 Cal. 393; Dutton v. Warschauer, 21 Cal. 609, 82 Am. Dec. 765; Clarke v. Beck, 72 Ga. 127; Peck v. Bartelme, 220 Ill. 199, 77 N. E. 216; Mallett v. Kaehler, 141 Ill. 70, 30 N. E. 549; Thomas v. Burnett, 128 Ill. 37, 21 N. E. 352, 4 L. R. A. 222; Crawford v. Chicago &c. R. Co., 112 Ill. 314; Haworth v. Taylor, 108 Ill. 275; Whitaker v. Miller, 83 Ill. 381; Smith v. Jackson, 76 Ill. 254; Frary v. Orton, 75 Ill. 100; Townsend v. Blanchard,

117 Iowa 36, 90 N. W. 519; O'Neill v. Wilcox, 115 Iowa 15, 87 N. W. 742; Rogers v. Turpin, 105 Iowa 183, 74 N. W. 925; Dickey v. Lyon, 19 Iowa 544; Penrose v. Cooper, 86 Kans. 597, 121 Pac. 1103; Deetjen v. Richter, 33 Kans. 410, 414, 6 Pac. 595; Hanly v. Morse, 32 Maine 287; Thompson v. Borg, 90 Minn. 209, 95 N. W. 896; New v. Wheaton, 24 Minn. 406; Morrison v. March, 4 Minn. 325; Levy v. Holberg, 67 Miss. 526, 7 So. 431; Conlee v. McDowell, 15 Nebr. 184, 18 N. W. 60; Wood v. Price, 79 N. J. Eq. 620, 81 Atl. 983, 38 L. R. A. (N. S.) 772, Ann. Cas. 1913 A, 1210; Purcell v. Enright, 31 N. J. Eq. 74; Wanner v. Sisson, 29 N. J. Eq. 141; Bank v. Flagg, 3 Barb. Ch. (N. Y.) 316; Edwards v. Thompson, 71 N. Car. 177; Randall v. Lingwall, 43 Ore. 383, 73 Pac. 1; Duff v. McDonough, 155 Pa. St. 10, 25 Atl. 608; Hottenstein v. Lerch, 104 Pa. St. 454; Kerr v. Day, 14 Pa. St. 112, 53 Am. Dec. 526; Hood v. Fahnestock, 1 Pa. St. 470, 44 Am. Dec. 147; Collum v. Sanger, 98 Tex. 162, 82 S. W. 459, 83 S. W. 184; McCamant v. Roberts, 80 Tex. 316, 15 S. W. 580, 1054; Glendenning v. Bell, 70 Tex. 632, 8 S. W. 324; Woodson v. Collins, 56 Tex. 168; Mainwarring v. Templeman, 51 Tex. 205; Huntington v. Mattfield (Tex.), 55 S. W. 361; Mattfield v. Huntington, 17 Tex. Civ. App. 716, 43 S. W. 53. But see Flagg v. Mann, 2 Sumn. (U. S.) 486; Beattie v. Butler, 21 Mo. 313, 64 Am. Dec. 234.

[27] Conlee v. McDowell, 15 Nebr. 184, 18 N. W. 60; Burt v. Baldwin, 8 Nebr. 487, 1 N. W. 457.

sion of his tenant, and the tenant merely attorns to the grantee without any visible change of possession, the tenant's continued possession is not of itself constructive notice of the grantee's title, to a subsequent purchaser from the grantor.[28] But in a few states the contrary doctrine prevails, and the tenant's possession upon attornment is considered sufficient to excite inquiry on the part of the subsequent purchaser, and charge him with constructive notice of the prior grantee's title.[29]

If the tenant changes his character by taking an agreement to purchase, or he has this right under his lease and exercises his option to purchase, his possession amounts to notice of his equitable title as purchaser.[30]

The fact that one had been a tenant of a portion of a building, and continued to be a tenant until he took possession under his contract of purchase, does not impair the notice imparted by such possession.[31]

§ 590. Possession notice during continuance.—Possession is notice only during its continuance.[32] In order to operate as notice, or to suggest inquiry to a purchaser, the adverse possession must have existed at the time of the purchase.[33] A former possession which has ceased is not sufficient, although there is still evidence of it on the land.[34] A purchaser is not bound to take notice of an antecedent pos-

---

[28] Griffin v. Hall, 111 Ala. 601, 20 So. 485; Bynum v. Gold, 106 Ala. 427, 17 So. 667; Troy v. Walter, 87 Ala. 233, 6 So. 54; Fitzgerald v. Williamson, 85 Ala. 585, 5 So. 309; King v. Paulk, 85 Ala. 186, 4 So. 825; Feinberg v. Stearns, 56 Fla. 279, 47 So. 797, 131 Am. St. 119; Stockton v. Jacksonville Nat. Bank, 45 Fla. 590, 34 So. 897; Veazie v. Parker, 23 Maine 170; Roberts v. Grace, 16 Minn. 126; Loughridge v. Bowland, 52 Miss. 546; Burt v. Baldwin, 8 Nebr. 487, 1 N. W. 457. But see Tutwiler v. Montgomery, 73 Ala. 263; Brunson v. Brooks, 68 Ala. 248.

[29] Mallett v. Kaehler, 141 Ill. 70, 30 N. E. 549; Haworth v. Taylor, 108 Ill. 275; Hannan v. Seidentopf, 113 Iowa 658, 86 N. W. 44; Duff v. McDonough, 155 Pa. St. 10, 25 Atl. 608; Mainwarring v. Templeman, 51 Tex. 205; Duncan v. Matula (Tex.), 26 S. W. 638; Mattfeld v. Huntington, 17 Tex. Civ. App. 716, 43 S. W. 53. See also Smith v. James, 22 Tex. Civ. App. 154, 54 S. W. 41.

[30] Coari v. Olsen, 91 Ill. 273; Russell v. Moore, 3 Metc. (Ky.) 436; Smith v. Gibson, 25 Nebr. 511, 41 N. W. 360; Chesterman v. Gardner, 5 Johns. Ch. (N. Y.) 32, 9 Am. Dec. 265; Kerr v. Day, 14 Pa. St. 112; Knight v. Bowyer, 23 Beav. 609; Taylor v. Stibbert, 2 Ves. Jr. 437.

[31] Phelan v. Brady, 119 N. Y. 587, 23 N. E. 1109.

[32] Masterson v. West-End Narrow-Gauge R. Co., 5 Mo. App. 64, affd. in 72 Mo. 342; Coleman v. Barklew, 27 N. J. L. 357; Meehan v. Williams, 48 Pa. St. 238; Ely v. Wilcox, 20 Wis. 523, 91 Am. Dec. 436.

[33] Christopher v. Curtis-Attalla Lumber Co., 175 Ala. 484, 57 So. 837; Hunter v. Watson, 12 Cal. 363, 73 Am. Dec. 543; Roussain v. Norton, 53 Minn. 560, 55 N. W. 747; Bingham v. Kirkland, 34 N. J. Eq. 229; Bost v. Setzer, 87 N. Car. 187.

[34] Aden v. Vallejo, 139 Cal. 165, 72 Pac. 905; Hayward v. Mayse, 1 App. Cas. (D. C.) 133; Sanford v. Weeks, 38 Kans. 319, 16 Pac. 465, 5 Am.

session which has ceased prior to his negotiations to purchase, and he need not inquire as to the title or right of the former occupant.[35] However, if the possession existed at the time of the purchase, the fact that the conveyance was executed after possession had ceased, is immaterial.[36] An occupant's rights are not altered or prejudiced by a compulsory surrender of possession to a subsequent purchaser with notice of the contract and claim of ownership.[37]

§ 591. **Open notorious and exclusive possession.**—Possession, to operate as implied notice, must be visible and open, notorious and exclusive, and not merely a constructive possession.[38] Possession is in-

St. 748; Roussain v. Norton, 53 Minn. 560, 55 N. W. 747; Hiller v. Jones, 66 Miss. 636, 6 So. 465; Bost v. Setzer, 87 N. Car. 187; Wright v. Wood, 23 Pa. St. 120. See also Christopher v. Curtis-Attalla Lumber Co., 175 Ala. 484, 57 So. 837.

[35] Campbell v. Brackenridge, 8 Blackf. (Ind.) 471; Hewes v. Wiswell, 8 Maine 94; Meehan v. Williams, 48 Pa. St. 238; Ehle v. Brown, 31 Wis. 405.

[36] Bergeron v. Richardott, 55 Wis. 129, 12 N. W. 384.

[37] Van Epps v. Clock, 53 Hun 638, 25 N. Y. St. 896, 7 N. Y. S. 21.

[38] Kirby v. Tallmadge, 160 U. S. 379, 40 L. ed. 463, 16 Sup. Ct. 349; Townsend v. Little, 109 U. S. 504, 27 L. ed. 1012; Noyes v. Hall, 97 U. S. 34, 24 L. ed. 909; Gum v. Equitable Trust Co., 1 McCrary (U. S.) 51; Adams-Booth Co. v. Reid, 112 Fed. 106; Bright v. Buckman, 39 Fed. 243; Sloss &c. Steel &c. Co. v. Taff, 178 Ala. 382, 59 So. 658; Christopher v. Curtis-Attalla Lumber Co., 175 Ala. 484, 57 So. 837; O'Neal v. Prestwood, 153 Ala. 443, 45 So. 251; Wells v. American Mtg. Co., 109 Ala. 430, 20 So. 136; Bernstein v. Humes, 71 Ala. 260; Schumacher v. Truman, 134 Cal. 430, 66 Pac. 591; Hellman v. Levy, 55 Cal. 117; Smith v. Yule, 31 Cal. 180, 89 Am. Dec. 167; Fair v. Stevenot, 29 Cal. 486; Dutton v. Warschauer, 21 Cal. 609, 82 Am. Dec. 765; Jerome v. Carbonate Nat. Bank, 22 Colo. 37, 43 Pac. 215; Tate v. Pensacola &c. Co., 37 Fla. 439, 20 So. 542, 53 Am. Rep. 251; Sanford v. Davis, 181 Ill. 570, 54 N. E. 977; Adam v. Tolman, 180 Ill. 61, 54 N. E. 174; Robertson v. Wheeler, 162 Ill. 566, 44 N. E. 870; Thomas v. Burnett, 128 Ill. 37, 21 N. E. 352; Irwin v. Dyke, 114 Ill. 302, 1 N. E. 913; Smith v. Jackson, 76 Ill. 254; Bogue v. Williams, 48 Ill. 371; Morrison v. Kelly, 22 Ill. 610, 14 Am. Dec. 169; Foulks v. Reed, 89 Ind. 370; Jefferson, M. &c. R. Co. v. Oyler, 82 Ind. 394; Lindley v. Martindale, 78 Iowa 379, 43 N. W. 233; Gray v. Zelmer, 66 Kans. 514, 72 Pac. 228; Beaubien v. Hindman, 38 Kans. 471, 16 Pac. 796; Trezize v. Lacy, 22 Kans. 742; Butler v. Stevens, 26 Maine 484; Hawes v. Wiswell, 8 Maine 94; Kendall v. Lawrence, 22 Pick. (Mass.) 540; M'Mechan v. Griffing, 3 Pick. (Mass.) 149, 15 Am. Dec. 198; Smith v. Greenop, 60 Mich. 361, 26 N. W. 832; McKee v. Wilcox, 11 Mich. 358, 83 Am. Dec. 743; Norton v. Metropolitan Life Ins. Co., 74 Minn. 484, 77 N. W. 298, 539; Stovall v. Judah, 74 Miss. 747, 21 So. 614; Brophy Mining Co. v. Brophy &c. M. Co., 15 Nev. 101; Patten v. Moore, 32 N. H. 382; Bell v. Twilight, 22 N. H. 500, 50 Am. Dec. 367; Schwoebel v. Storrie, 76 N. J. Eq. 466, 74 Atl. 969; Rankin v. Coar, 46 N. J. Eq. 566, 22 Atl. 177, 11 L. R. A. 661; Hodge v. Amerman, 40 N. J. Eq. 99, 2 Atl. 257; McCall v. Yard, 11 N. J. Eq. 58; Holmes v. Stout, 10 N. J. Eq. 419; Cox v. Devinney, 65 N. J. L. 389, 47 Atl. 569; Coleman v. Barklew, 27 N. J. L. 357; Holland v. Brown, 140 N. Y. 344, 35 N. E. 577; Pope v. Allen, 90 N. Y. 298; Page v. Waring, 76 N. Y. 463; Brown v. Volkening, 64 N. Y. 76; Webster v. Van Steenbergh, 46 Barb. (N. Y.) 211; Merritt v. Northern R. Co., 12 Barb. (N. Y.)

sufficient if merely equivocal,[39] temporary, or occasional.[40] It must be unambiguous and not liable to be misconstrued.[41]

Actual residence upon the land is not necessary to constructive notice of title; actual possession and continuous acts of ownership being sufficient.[42] But the erection of permanent improvements is generally held sufficient to constitute notice.[43] Possession of land by one who has built a house upon it and is living in it, or by one who has built fences around his lot, is sufficiently open and patent to put parties in interest upon inquiry, and to charge them with notice of all they might learn by such inquiry.[44] Possession of a city lot was held suffi-

605 (constructive possession by survey insufficient); Tuttle v. Jackson, 6 Wend. (N. Y.) 213, 21 Am. Dec. 306; Bost v. Setzer, 87 N. Car. 187; Tankard v. Tankard, 79 N. Car. 54; Webber v. Taylor, 2 Jones Eq. (N. Car.) 91; Ranney v. Hardy, 43 Ohio St. 157; Williams v. Sprigg, 6 Ohio St. 585; Railroad Employes Bldg. &c. Assn. v. Dawson, 5 Ohio S. & C. Pl. Dec. 583, 7 Ohio N. P. 601; Scott v. Lewis, 40 Ore. 37, 66 Pac. 299; Meehan v. Williams, 48 Pa. St. 238; Martin v. Jackson, 27 Pa. St. 504, 67 Am. Dec. 489; Ellis v. Young, 31 S. Car. 322, 9 S. E. 955; Curry v. Williams (Tenn.), 38 S. W. 278; Satterwhite v. Rosser, 61 Tex. 166; Blankenship v. Douglas, 26 Tex. 225, 82 Am. Dec. 608; Canfield v. Hard, 58 Vt. 217, 2 Atl. 136; Peery v. Elliott, 101 Va. 709, 44 S. E. 919; Peterson v. Philadelphia Mtg. &c. Co., 33 Wash. 464, 74 Pac. 585; Wickes v. Lake, 25 Wis. 71; Ely v. Wilcox, 20 Wis. 523, 91 Am. Dec. 436.

[39] Townsend v. Little, 109 U. S. 504, 27 L. ed. 1012, 3 Sup. Ct. 357; Sloss &c. Steel &c. Co. v. Taff, 178 Ala. 382, 59 So. 658; Morrison v. Kelly, 22 Ill. 609, 74 Am. Dec. 169; Rankin v. Coar, 46 N. J. Eq. 566, 22 Atl. 177, 11 L. R. A. 661; Holland v. Brown, 140 N. Y. 344, 35 N. E. 577; Pope v. Allen, 90 N. Y. 298; Brown v. Volkening, 64 N. Y. 76; Billington v. Welsh, 5 Binn. (Pa.) 129, 6 Am. Dec. 406.

[40] Kendrick v. Colyar, 143 Ala. 597, 42 So. 110; Jerome v. Carbonate Nat. Bank, 22 Colo. 37, 43 Pac. 215; Masterson v. West-End Narrow-Gauge R. Co., 5 Mo. App. 64, affd. 72 Mo. 342; Coleman v. Barklew, 27 N. J. L. 357; Holland v. Brown, 140 N. Y.

344, 35 N. E. 577; Brown v. Volkening, 64 N. Y. 76; Williams v. Sprigg, 6 Ohio St. 585; Meehan v. Williams, 48 Pa. St. 238.

[41] Sloss &c. Steel &c. Co. v. Taff, 178 Ala. 382, 59 So. 658; Rankin Mfg. Co. v. Bishop, 137 Ala. 271, 34 So. 991; Wells v. American Mtg. Co., 109 Ala. 430, 20 So. 136; Lindley v. Martindale, 78 Iowa 379, 43 N. W. 233; Brown v. Volkening, 64 N. Y. 76; Wickes v. Lake, 25 Wis. 71.

[42] Jerome v. Carbonate Nat. Bank, 22 Colo. 37, 43 Pac. 215; Thomas v. Burnett, 128 Ill. 37, 21 N. E. 352, 4 L. R. A. 222; Morrison v. Kelly, 22 Ill. 609, 74 Am. Dec. 169; Hodge v. Amerman, 40 N. J. Eq. 99, 2 Atl. 257. See also Coleman v. Barklew, 27 N. J. L. 357; Phelan v. Brady, 19 Abb. N. Cas. (N. Y.) 289, affd. 49 Hun 607, 16 N. Y. St. 942, 1 N. Y. S. 626, 21 Abb. N. Cas. 286; Wickes v. Lake, 25 Wis. 71.

[43] Stagg v. Small, 4 Ill. App. 192; Barnes v. Union School, 91 Ind. 301; Crapo v. Cameron, 61 Iowa 447, 16 N. W. 523 (permanent brick building upon city lot); Carthage Tissue Paper Mills v. Carthage, 200 N. Y. 1, 93 N. E. 60; Congdon v. Morgan, 14 S. Car. 587; Harold v. Sumner, 78 Tex. 581, 14 S. W. 995; Smith v. Profitt, 82 Va. 832, 1 S. E. 67; Kuhl v. Lightle, 29 Wash. 137, 69 Pac. 630.

[44] Bright v. Buckman, 39 Fed. 243; Pride v. Whitfield (Tex.), 51 S. W. 1100. See also Williams v. Dongan, 20 Mo. 186 (building a dwelling, residence, and cultivation); Parrish v. Williams (Tex.), 79 S. W. 1097 (occupying a house and partly fencing).

ciently open and notorious where the purchaser fenced three sides of it, the fourth being inaccessible, cleared it of brush and timber, and planted shrubbery thereon.[45] Possession by the purchaser of a tenement house, who had formerly been a tenant of a part of the house, and who, on purchase, removed to the rooms before occupied by the housekeeper of the vendor, and was known as owner, and collected the rent from all the tenants, is sufficiently open and visible to be notice of his ownership, so as to defeat a mortgage taken before his deed is recorded, and without knowledge of it.[46]

The cutting of wood or timber continued year after year or continuously is an act showing possession, and indicating a right or title.[47] So does openly ploughing or cultivating a field,[48] or fastening the doors and nailing up the windows of a house in which there is furniture,[49] or any acts which clearly show such an appropriation of the property as one would exercise over his own property and not over property which he did not claim to own.[50] The occasional cutting of wood upon the land under such circumstances that these acts might be regarded as acts of trespass rather than acts of ownership is not evidence of actual possession such as constitute notice.[51]

A notice posted on a board set up on the land that it is for sale, by an agent whose name and address is given, is notice of the owner's rights sufficient to put a purchaser upon inquiry.[52]

Where a purchaser under an unrecorded contract was present from time to time with the record owner, during the construction of a building on the premises, his possession was not exclusive, in merely superintending the construction of the cellar, setting out shrubbery

[45] Flint v. Long, 12 Wash. 342, 41 Pac. 49.

[46] Phelan v. Brady, 119 N. Y. 587, 23 N. E. 1109. See also Gall v. Gall, 126 Wis. 390, 105 N. W. 953, 5 L. R. A. (N. S.) 603.

[47] Nolan v. Grant, 51 Iowa 519, 1 N. W. 709; Krider v. Lafferty, 1 Whart. (Pa.) 303.

[48] Lyman v. Russell, 45 Ill. 281; Wickes v. Lake, 25 Wis. 71. See also International Harvester Co. v. Myers, 86 Kans. 497, 121 Pac. 500, 39 L. R. A. (N. S.) 528; Richards v. Snyder, 11 Ore. 501, 6 Pac. 186; Biemann v. White, 23 S. Car. 490. But see Sanford v. Weeks, 38 Kans. 319, 16 Pac. 465. Possession of lands by a contract purchaser who resided thereon, cut timber, and cultivated the land, charged subsequent pur-chasers and mortgagees with notice of his rights. Gainer v. Jones, 176 Ala. 408, 58 So. 288.

[49] Wrede v. Cloud, 52 Iowa 371, 3 N. W. 400.

[50] Jerome v. Carbonate Nat. Bank, 22 Colo. 37, 43 Pac. 215, citing Ewing v. Burnet, 11 Pet. (U. S.) 41, 9 L. ed. 624; Simmons Creek Coal Co. v. Doran, 142 U. S. 417, 35 L. ed 1063, 12 Sup. Ct. 239; Mason v. Mullahy, 145 Ill. 383, 34 N. E. 36; Hatch v. Bigelow, 39 Ill. 546; Brown v. Volkening, 64 N. Y. 76.

[51] Holmes v. Stout, 10 N J. Eq. 419. See also Brown v. Volkening, 64 N. Y. 76.

[52] Hatch v. Bigelow, 39 Ill. 546. But see Clark v. Green, 73 Minn. 467, 76 N. W. 263; Lynde v. Williams, 68 Mo. 360.

and cleaning windows, and was therefore not notice to a subsequent mortgagee of the record owner.[53]

The possession must be exclusive, and therefore possession by a purchaser under an unrecorded conveyance is no notice of title as against a subsequent incumbrancer, where the grantor also lived on the premises as a member of the grantee's family.[54] Thus it has been held that possession by a son under a voluntary oral agreement and an undelivered deed from his father, was not sufficient to put a subsequent mortgagee of his father upon inquiry as to the extent of the son's claim, since he possessed no equitable right to the land as against his father, in whom the legal title remained.[55]

§ 592. **Occupation of an easement—Railways and crossings.**—The use or occupation of an easement in land by a third party is notice to purchasers or mortgagees of whatever right the user of the easement may have to maintain it.[56] The occupation by a grantor of an easement in adjoining land which he has conveyed without a reservation of the easement, being inconsistent with the grant, is notice, to a purchaser from the grantee, of a parol reservation of the easement.[57] The easement may be patent, as in the case of a footpath; or there may be such occupation of it as to put a purchaser upon inquiry. The owner of a house sold to his adjoining neighbor the right of using two chimneys in the partition wall and received the consideration, but never made any grant of the easement. He afterward sold the house without saying anything about his neighbor's right to use two of the chimneys. But as there were fourteen chimney-pots on the wall, and

[53] Roderick v. McMeekin, 204 Ill. 625, 68 N. E. 473.

[54] Jerome v. Carbonate Nat. Bank, 22 Colo. 37, 43 Pac. 215; Geyer v. Geyer, 75 N. J. Eq. 124, 78 Atl. 449; Puckett v. Reed, 3 Tex. Civ. App. 350, 22 S. W. 515; Derrett v. Britton, 35 Tex. Civ. App. 485, 80 S. W. 562. See also Rubel v. Parker (Ark.), 155 S. W. 114. Where three brothers had equal interests in farm land, the elder holding the legal title, it was held that occupancy by the two minor brothers in the usual manner of farming and stock raising, though without residence, was sufficiently open, notorious and exclusive to put a mortgagee of the elder brother upon inquiry, and

since the inquiry was not pursued with due diligence the rights of the minor brothers were unaffected by the mortgage. International Harvester Co. v. Myers, 86 Kans. 497, 121 Pac. 500, 39 L. R. A. (N. S.) 528.

[55] Huntley v. San Francisco Sav. Union, 130 Cal. 46, 62 Pac. 255.

[56] Smith v. Smith, 21 Cal. App. 378, 131 Pac. 890; Ashelford v. Willis, 194 Ill. 492, 62 N. E. 817; Joseph v. Wild, 146 Ind. 249, 45 N. E. 467 (stairway over adjoining vacant lot); Kamer v. Bryant, 103 Ky. 723, 46 S. W. 14, 20 Ky. L. 340; Randall v. Silverthorn, 4 Pa. St. 173.

[57] Randall v. Silverthorn, 4 Pa. St. 173.

only twelve flues in the house, the court held that the purchaser was put on inquiry and had constructive notice of the neighbor's right.[58]

Where the owner of certain lots and a narrow strip of land adjoining them, erected a building on the property so that the wall extended upon the strip, and then mortgaged the three lots and the building, it was held that the mortgagee purchasing at foreclosure sale was entitled to an easement upon the strip of land, necessary to the enjoyment of the building, as against one holding under a subsequent trust deed from the mortgagor.[59]

The existence of a railroad over a tract of land, with its embankments, excavations, and tracks, is notice to a purchaser of such land of an outstanding right or easement inconsistent with an absolute and exclusive title in the grantor. It is the duty of the purchaser to inquire by what right the railroad is built over the land, and he has notice of such rights as the owners of the railroad may have acquired.[60] The possession is not restricted to the land actually fenced in.[61] But mere possession and use of a railroad track in a street abutting property is not notice to a purchaser of an unrecorded deed from his grantor, executed to the company several months previously and granting permission to lay additional tracks.[62] The existence of an open way for cattle, under a railroad, is notice of an easement for that purpose to subsequent purchasers and mortgagees of the railroad sufficient to put them upon inquiry.[63] Where a railroad with the power of eminent domain lays tracks with the consent of the landowner, a mortgage subsequently executed by him does not cover the tracks in

---

[58] Hervey v. Smith, 22 Beav. 299, 302. The Master of the Rolls said: "Here the defendant buys the house and finds twelve flues in it, but fourteen chimneys in the wall. The question is, was he not bound to see that he alone had twelve out of the fourteen, and does it not follow that two must have been used by the adjoining neighbor? He might not have thought fit to count them or look at them, but I think he was put on inquiry, and that he can not now say that he had no notice of the agreement by which Felton sold the right to Cubitt."

[59] Carrigg v. Mechanics' Sav. Bank, 136 Iowa 261, 111 N. W. 329.

[60] Kindred v. Union Pac. R. Co., 56 L. ed. 1216, 225 U. S. 582, 32 Sup. Ct. 780; Chicago &c. R. Co. v. Wright, 153 Ill. 307, 38 N. E. 1062; Indiana, B. &c. R. Co. v. McBroom, 114 Ind. 198, 15 N. E. 831; Campbell v. Indianapolis &c. R. Co., 110 Ind. 490, 11 N. E. 482; Jeffersonville, M. &c. R. Co. v. Oyler, 60 Ind. 383; Paul v. Connersville &c. R. Co., 51 Ind. 527; Kamer v. Bryant, 103 Ky. 723, 20 Ky. L. 340, 46 S. W. 14; Edwards v. Missouri &c. R. Co., 82 Mo. App. 96; Donovan v. Erie R. Co., 77 Misc. 548, 137 N. Y. S. 113; Day v. Atlantic &c. R. Co., 41 Ohio St. 392.

[61] Warner v. Fountain, 28 Wis. 405.

[62] Varwig v. Cleveland &c. R. Co., 54 Ohio St. 455, 44 N. E. 92.

[63] Rock Island & P. R. Co. v. Dimick, 144 Ill. 628, 32 N. E. 291, 19 L. R. A. 105.

the roadbed, though the land was not condemned and no compensation was paid.[64]

The use of a ditch or mill-race through the land conveyed has been held sufficient notice of an easement to subsequent purchasers.[65] And likewise, a right outstanding in a third person to overflow the land conveyed by the erection of a mill-dam, or the flooding of land by a prior grantee, has been held notice to a subsequent purchaser.[66]

§ 593. Equivocal or temporary possession.—An equivocal, occasional, or temporary possession will not take the case out of the operation of the registry laws.[67] The protection furnished by these laws can not be taken away except upon clear proof of a want of good faith in the party claiming their protection, and a clear right in him who seeks to establish notice by means of possession.[68] To have that effect the adverse possession must be unequivocally hostile to the mortgagor.[69]

The circumstances must be such that a prudent man would be put upon inquiry, and would be chargeable with bad faith if he did not inquire. "We would observe," said Chief Justice Parsons, in an early case in Massachusetts,[70] "that the statute requiring the registry of conveyances being so very beneficial, and it being so easy to conform to it, when a prior conveyance not recorded until after one of a subsequent date is attempted to be supported on the ground of fraud in the second purchaser, the fraud must be very clearly proved." The using of lands for pasturing, or for cutting timber, is not such an occupancy as will charge a purchaser with notice. The possession must be accompanied by improvement of the property to constitute notice.[71] But the cutting of timber coupled with clearing and cultiva-

---

[64] Nittany Valley R. Co. v. Empire Steel Co., 218 Pa. 224, 67 Atl. 349.

[65] Franklin v. Pollard Mill Co., 88 Ala. 318, 6 So. 685; Randall v. Silverthorn, 4 Pa. St. 173.

[66] Snowden v. Wilas, 19 Ind. 10, 81 Am. Dec. 370; How v. Chesapeake &c. Canal Co., 5 Harr. (Del.) 245.

[67] Boynton v. Rees, 8 Pick. (Mass.) 329, 19 Am. Dec. 326; Masterson v. West End & R. Co., 72 Mo. 342; Williams v. Sprigg, 6 Ohio St. 585.

[68] Bogue v. Williams, 48 Ill. 371; Sanford v. Weeks, 38 Kans. 319, 16 Pac. 465; Butler v. Stevens, 26 Maine 484; Coleman v. Barklew, 27 N. J. L. 337; Union College v. Wheeler, 59 Barb. (N. Y.) 585; Merritt v. Northern R. Co., 12 Barb. (N. Y.) 605; Brown v. Volkening, N. Y. Ct. of Appeals, 2 N. Y. W. Dig. 86.

[69] Francis v. Jefferson County Sav. Bank, 167 Ala. 548, 52 So. 906; Hammond v. Paxton, 58 Mich. 393, 25 N. W. 321; Phillips v. Owen, 99 App. Div. 18, 90 N. Y. S. 947, 15 Ann. Cas. 361.

[70] Norcross v. Widgery, 2 Mass. 506.

[71] McMechan v. Griffing, 3 Pick. (Mass.) 149, and cases cited, 15 Am. Dec. 198; Holmes v. Stout, 10 N. J. Eq. 419; Union College v. Wheeler, 59 Barb. (N. Y.) 585, and cases cited. See also Bright v. Buckman,

tion of land, lying in a densely timbered and thinly populated country, may be such acts of possession as to charge a subsequent mortgagee with notice.[72] And the inclosure of an eighty-acre tract with other land by a wire fence, and using the land for pasturing cattle, constitutes notice.[73]

One purchasing or taking a mortgage of premises in the possession of a tenant is bound to inquire into the nature and extent of the tenant's interest, and is affected with notice of that interest whatever it may be.[74] Such possession is also held to be notice of a collateral agreement held by the tenant for the purchase of the property.[75]

Generally, a mortgagee is not chargeable with notice arising from a mixed possession or joint occupancy shared by the mortgagor and relatives, as where husband and wife, parent and child, or brother and sister, live together on the same premises; although the person sharing such tenancy with the mortgagor may have actual claims upon the estate originating prior to the mortgage.[76] A husband and wife, who had long occupied a farm, conveyed it to their son, and took back a mortgage conditioned for their support, but omitted to record it. They continued upon the farm, they and their son constituting one family, and all contributing to its support. Some years afterward the son made a second mortgage, which was duly recorded; but the second mortgagee was regarded as having had notice of the legal title of the first mortgagees.[77] A joint residence of husband and wife does not give notice of any claim of interest in the land by the wife.[78] The occupation of land by minor children with their father is not notice of a claim on the part of the children as heirs of their deceased mother; and a bona fide purchaser at foreclosure sale under a mort-

39 Fed. 243 (fencing, cultivation and improvement).

[72] Wickes v. Lake, 25 Wis. 71.

[73] Millard v. Wegner, 68 Nebr. 574, 94 N. W. 802.

[74] Cunningham v. Pattee, 99 Mass. 248.

[75] Kerr v. Day, 14 Pa. St. 112, 53 Am. Dec. 526; Knight v. Bowyer, 23 Beav. 609, 641; Taylor v. Stibbert, 2 Ves. Jr. 437.

[76] Atlanta Nat. Bldg. &c. Assn. v. Gilmer, 128 Fed. 293; Paulus v. Latta, 93 Ind. 34; Elliott v. Lane, 82 Iowa 484, 48 N. W. 720, 31 Am. St. 504; Iowa L. &c. Co. v. King, 58 Iowa 598, 12 N. W. 595; Bell v. Twilight, 22 N. H. 500; Geyer v. Geyer,

75 N. J. Eq. 124, 78 Atl. 449; Rankin v. Coar, 46 N. J. Eq. 566, 22 Atl. 177, 11 L. R. A. 661; Swanstrom v. Day, 46 Misc. 311, 93 N. Y. S. 192; Cary v. White, 7 Lans. (N. Y.) 1; Patterson v. Mills, 121 N. Car. 258, 28 S. E. 368; Attebery v. O'Neil, 42 Wash. 487, 85 Pac. 270. See also Allen v. Cadwell, 55 Mich. 8, 20 N. W. 692. But see Loan Co. v. Garrison, 16 Ont. 81.

[77] Boggs v. Anderson, 50 Maine 161. See also Harrison v. New Jersey R. &c. Co., 19 N. J. Eq. 488.

[78] Neal v. Perkerson, 61 Ga. 345. See also Paulus v. Latta, 93 Ind. 34; Iowa L. &c. Co. v. King, 58 Iowa 598, 12 N. W. 595.

gage executed by the father upon the premises is free from any claim by the children.[79]

If the owner of land conveys only a partial interest in it, as, for instance, the wood and timber growing upon it, and takes back a mortgage which is not recorded, his continued possession is not notice of his claim to the wood and timber, as against one who has purchased upon the faith of his bill of sale.[80]

Actual possession of land, by one who holds an unrecorded contract of purchase, or a bond for a deed, is notice of his rights to one who takes a mortgage on the land from the vendor, and the mortgagee will take a lien only on the vendor's right.[81] Such vendee in possession is not bound to examine the records for subsequent incumbrances of the land by his vendor, nor is the record notice thereof to him.[82] Though the vendor executes a mortgage while the vendee is in possession under his contract, until actual notice of the mortgage the purchaser may safely continue to make payments of the purchase-money to his vendor.

But a mortgage made by the vendor, while such vendee is in possession, creates a valid lien on the interest remaining in the vendor at the time of its execution, which, before conveyance, is the legal title, and a beneficial estate in the lands to the extent of the unpaid purchase-money; and payments made on the purchase-money to the vendor by the purchaser, after he has knowledge of the mortgage, will be unavailing as against the mortgagee.[83] But the possession of a mortgagee whose mortgage is recorded is not notice of his claim under an agreement to purchase the premises, although a rumor of his purchase was current in the neighborhood;[84] for in such case his pos-

---

[79] Attebery v. O'Neil, 42 Wash. 487, 85 Pac. 270.

[80] Patten v. Moore, 32 N. H. 382.

[81] Bright v. Buckman, 39 Fed. 243; Doolittle v. Cook, 75 Ill. 354; Moyer v. Hinman, 13 N. Y. 180; Gouverneur v. Lynch, 2 Paige (N. Y.) 300; Jaeger v. Hardy, 48 Ohio St. 335, 27 N. E. 863.

[82] Jaeger v. Hardy, 48 Ohio St. 335, 27 N. E. 863.

[83] Young v. Guy, 87 N. Y. 457; Ten Eick v. Simpson, 1 Sandf. Ch. (N. Y.) 244; Jaeger v. Hardy, 48 Ohio St. 335, 27 N. E. 863; Lefferson v. Dallas, 20 Ohio St. 68; Fasholt v. Reed, 16 Serg. & R. (Pa.) 266.

In Jaeger v. Hardy, 48 Ohio St. 335, 27 N. E. 863, Chief Justice Williams on this point further said: "If it be conceded, as some authorities maintain, that, as the vendor is a mere trustee of the lands for the vendee, and that the latter is the trustee of the purchase-money for the former, the lien of a mortgage executed by the vendor, after the contract of sale, does not attach to the lands, but only to his claim against his vendee for whatever may then remain unpaid on the purchase, still the mortgage would, at least, be operative to transfer to the mortgagee, for his security, the mortgagor's claim against the purchaser."

[84] Plumer v. Robertson, 6 Serg. & R. (Pa.) 179.

session is consistent with the record title, and it may well be taken for granted that he holds under the recorded title. Possession is notice only of the legal or equitable interest in the land of the person in possession. It vests the purchaser with notice of every fact and circumstance which he might have learned by making inquiry of the occupant, but it does not impose upon him the duty of searching the record in the name of such occupant to ascertain what title he has parted with.[85]

§ 594.   **Possession inconsistent with purchaser's title.**—Possession, to operate as notice, should be inconsistent with the title upon which the purchaser relies.[86] If the possession is consistent with the record title, the purchaser is not bound to make any inquiry concerning the title as indicated by the possession. No inquiry is suggested by the possession.[87] If a person in possession holds under a deed upon record, apparently sufficient to explain his possession, a subsequent purchaser is not affected with notice of any other undisclosed title or interest which the occupant may have.[88]

A deed to one in his own right, when recorded, becomes notice to

[85] Losey v. Simpson, 11 N. J. Eq. 246; Bassett v. Wood, 9 N. Y. S. 79 (quoting text).
[86] McNeil v. Polk, 57 Cal. 323; Smith v. Yule, 31 Cal. 180, 89 Am. Dec. 167; Staples v. Fenton, 5 Hun (N. Y.) 172. "The rule is universal that, if the possession be consistent with the recorded title, it is no notice of an unrecorded title." Kirby v. Tallmadge, 160 U. S. 379, 40 L. ed. 463, 16 Sup. Ct. 349. Schumacher v. Truman, 134 Cal. 430, 66 Pac. 591 (husband's possession as cotenant of wife).
[87] Plumer v. Robertson, 6 Serg. & R. (Pa.) 179.
[88] Kirby v. Tallmadge, 160 U. S. 379, 40 L. ed. 463, 16 Sup. Ct. 349; Townsend v. Little, 109 U. S. 504, 27 L. ed. 1012, 3 Sup. Ct. 357; Storthz v. Chapline, 71 Ark. 31, 70 S. W. 465; Fargason v. Edrington, 49 Ark. 207, 4 S. W. 763; Schumacher v. Truman, 134 Cal. 430, 66 Pac. 591; Smith v. Yule, 31 Cal. 180, 89 Am. Dec. 167; Sanguinetti v. Rossen, 12 Cal. App. 623, 107 Pac. 560; Wrede v. Cloud, 52 Iowa 371, 3 N. W. 400; Rogers v. Hussey, 36 Iowa 664; Behrens v. Crawford, 32 Ky. L. 1281, 108 S. W. 288; Dutton v. McReynolds, 31 Minn. 66, 16 N. W. 468. See also May v. Sturdivant, 75 Iowa 116, 39 N. W. 221, 9 Am. Rep. 463; Hafter v. Strange, 65 Miss. 323, 3 So. 190, 7 Am. St. 659; Hurley v. O'Neill, 26 Mont. 269, 67 Pac. 626; Mullins v. Butte Hardware Co., 25 Mont. 525, 65 Pac. 1004, 87 Am. St. 430; Dengler v. Fowler, 94 Nebr. 621, 143 N. W. 944; Great Falls Co. v. Worster, 15 N. H. 412; Red River Valley Land &c. Co. v. Smith, 7 N. Dak. 236, 74 N. W. 194; Farmers' &c. Nat. Bank v. Wallace, 45 Ohio St. 152, 12 N. E. 439; Woods v. Farmere, 7 Watts (Pa.) 382, 32 Am. Dec. 772; Stewart v. Crosby (Tex.), 26 S. W. 138; Kilgore v. Graves, 2 Tex. Civ. Cas. § 409. The rule does not apply where the title by deed has been apparently extinguished by an execution sale and sheriff's deed, and the occupant can not be presumed to be holding under his recorded deed. Wrede v. Cloud, 52 Iowa 371, 3 N. W. 400. Nor does the rule apply where it appears by the record that the occupant holds under a deed from a stranger to the title. Bank of Mendocino v. Baker, 82 Cal. 114, 22 Pac. 1037, 6 L. R. A. 833.

all persons that his possession under the deed is in his own right, and a purchaser from him is not required to make further inquiry as to the right by which he holds possession.[89] His possession is not notice of any title or claim beyond that which he holds under his recorded deed.[90] Thus where a widow held possession of a homestead as guardian of a minor child and also as a parol licensee of her adult children, it was held that the latter possession was not so distinctive as to put a subsequent purchaser or mortgagee upon inquiry, or to operate as notice of secret equities.[91] The owner and occupant of a house conveyed it in fee to a son, and, taking back a lease for life, remained in possession. The son, before the lease was recorded, gave a mortgage on the property to one who made reasonable inquiries as to liens. It was held that the possession of the former owner under the lease was not such as to give the mortgagee notice of any rights in the premises.[92]

§ 595. **Possession of part of the premises described in a conveyance.** —Possession of a part of the premises described in a deed or mortgage may be notice to a purchaser or mortgagee of the condition of the title of the entire tract, if the purchaser or mortgagee has actual notice of the possession; for, having such notice, he is bound to follow up the inquiry, and, if that would necessarily lead to the knowledge of the possession of the other part by another person under the same title, he is affected with notice of possession of such other part.[93] But if his notice of the possession of a part be constructive only, its effect can not be extended to lands outside the limits of the possession.[94] In such cases the possession of the occupant is deemed coextensive with the boundaries described in the deed.[95] The rule that possession

[89] Fargason v. Edrington, 49 Ark. 207, 4 S. W. 763.

[90] Dutton v. McReynolds, 31 Minn. 66, 16 N. W. 468; Great Falls Co. v. Worster, 15 N. H. 412.

[91] Sanguinetti v. Rossen, 12 Cal. App. 623, 107 Pac. 560.

[92] Staples v. Fenton, 5 Hun (N. Y.) 172. A like discussion on similar facts was made in Bell v. Twilight, 18 N. H. 159, 45 Am. Dec. 367; but the same reasons were not assigned. The same view was taken in a case where the grantors conveyed a farm to their son, and took back a mortgage conditioned for their support. Boggs v. Anderson, 50 Maine 161.

[93] Watson v. Mancill, 76 Ala. 600;

Terrell v. McLean, 130 Ga. 633, 61 S. E. 485; Feirbaugh v. Masterson, 1 Idaho 135; Boyer v. Chandler, 160 Ill. 394, 43 N. E. 803, 32 L. R. A. 113; Morrison v. Morrison, 140 Ill. 560, 30 N. E. 768; Jeffersonville &c. R. Co. v. Oyler, 82 Ind. 394; Watters v. Connelly, 59 Iowa 217, 13 N. W. 82; Nolan v. Grant, 51 Iowa 519, 1 N. W. 709; Holland v. Brown, 140 N. Y. 344, 35 N. E. 577; Watkins v. Edwards, 23 Tex. 443. But see Hodges v. Winston, 94 Ala. 576, 10 So. 535.

[94] Daggs v. Ewell, 3 Woods (U. S.) 344; Jeffersonville, M. &c. R. Co. v. Oyler, 82 Ind. 394.

[95] Watson v. Mancill, 76 Ala. 600; Roberts v. Unger, 30 Cal. 676; Gale

of part of a tract under color of title is notice of the occupant's claim to the whole only applies where there is no other person in possession claiming adversely to him.[96] And where the vendor retains possession of part of the land sold, the purchaser's possession of the remainder is not constructive notice as to the part in the possession of the vendor.[97] But if a grantor sells ·a part of his land, and the grantee enters into possession of this part, his possession is notice of his title though it rests in parol or the deed has not been recorded.[8]

§ 596. **Possession as notice of homestead rights.**—Possession may be notice of the homestead rights of the possessor. Thus in Texas, the Constitution of which state provides that no mortgage of the homestead shall be valid except for purchase-money, or for improvements thereon,[99] the fact that certain land is occupied and used by the owner as a homestead is to be determined by the visible facts of use and enjoyment, though the husband and wife, in order to obtain a mortgage loan, have falsely declared under oath that the lands mortgaged are not their homestead. Their representations do not estop them from claiming their homestead exemption under the statute, such representations being contrary to the visible and actual facts. The court in this case says: "The fact of actual possession and use as the home of the family was one against which the lender could not shut its eyes. Every person dealing with land must take notice of an actual, open, and exclusive possession; and where this, concurring with interest in the possessor, makes it a homestead, the lender stands charged with notice of that fact, it matters not what declarations to the contrary the borrower may make."[1]

The rule also applies to purchasers of vendor's lien notes with knowledge that the security upon which they are based is a homestead held in visible and open possession.[2] After refusing to make a loan upon certain homestead land, known to be in the possession of a husband and wife, a lender's agent agreed that if the land was sold and

v. Shillock, 4 Dak. 182, 29 N. W. 661; Fletcher v. Ellison, 1 Tex. Unrep. Cas. 661.

[96] Watson v. Mancill, 76 Ala. 600; Jeffersonville &c. R. Co. v. Oyler, 82 Ind. 394; Fletcher v. Ellison, 1 Tex. Unrep. Cas. 661.

[97] Jeffersonville &c. R. Co. v. Oyler, 82 Ind. 394; Wade v. Hiatt, 32 N. Car. 302. See also Cincinnati &c. R. Co. v. Smith, 127 Ind. 461, 26 N. E. 1009.

[98] Patton v. Hollidaysburg, 40 Pa. St. 206.

[99] Art. xvi, § 50:

[1] Texas L. &c. Co. v. Blalock, 76 Tex. 85, 13 S. W. 12, per Chief Justice Stayton; Equitable Mortgage Co. v. Lowry, 55 Fed. 165.

[2] Felsher v. Halenza (Tex.), 68 S. W. 638; Harbers v. Levy, 33 Tex. Civ. App. 480, 77 S. W. 261.

a vendor's lien reserved thereon, he would purchase the lien note. A simulated sale was made to the brother of the owner, and such note executed and sold to the agent of the lender, though the conveyance was not recorded, and the husband and wife retained possession of the homestead. The facts were held sufficient to charge the agent with knowledge of the fraud, which would preclude recovery on the note by his principal.[3] A party having knowledge of the occupancy of land as a homestead for many years, and knowing all the parties, made a loan upon collateral security of certain vendor's lien notes, which were in fact fraudulently executed under a simulated conveyance. Although having no direct knowledge of the fraud, the lender knew of the transaction under cover of which the notes were given by the owner of the homestead. It was held that he was not a bona fide purchaser being charged with notice by the mortgagor's possession of the homestead, and reasonable inquiry would have elicited the facts and uncovered the fraud in the execution of the notes.[4]

§ 597. **Continued possession of grantor as notice of rights reserved.** —Possession by a grantor, after a full recorded conveyance, is not constructive notice to subsequent purchasers of any right reserved in the land or claimed by the grantor.[5] "It is the obvious design of our

---

[3] Felsher v. Halenza (Tex.), 68 S. W. 838.

[4] Harbers v. Levy, 33 Tex. Civ. App. 480, 77 S. W. 261.

[5] Gill v. Hardin, 48 Ark. 409, 3 S. W. 519, per Hemingway, J.; in Turman v. Bell, 54 Ark. 273, 15 S. W. 886. "On the other side it is said that the execution of a warranty deed without reservation is a most solemn declaration by the grantor that he has parted with all his rights in the property, and directly negatives the reservation of any right; that those who see the deed are warranted in relying upon such declaration as much as if it had been made to them orally upon an inquiry, and that, if they acquire interests in faith of such reliance, the grantor in possession will be estopped to assert any rights secretly reserved from the grant; that, as the grantor has declared that he parted with his entire estate, strangers about to deal with the property would reasonably refer his continuous possession to the sufferance of his grantee, and would

not reasonably think to refer it to a reserved right." Morgan v. Mc. Cuin, 96 Ark. 512, 132 S. W. 459; Malette v. Wright, 120 Ga. 735, 48 S. E. 229 Quick v. Milligan, 108 Ind. 419, 9 N. E. 392, 58 Am. Rep. 49; Jeffersonville &c. R. Co. v. Oyler, 82 Ind. 394; Tuttle v. Churchman, 74 Ind. 311; Crossen v. Swordland, 22 Ind. 427; Work v. Brayton, 5 Ind. 396; Dodge v. Davis, 85 Iowa 77, 52 N. W. 2; McCleery v. Wakefield, 76 Iowa 529; 41 N. W. 210, 2 L. R. A. 529; May v. Sturdivant, 75 Iowa 116, 39 N. W. 221, 9 Am. St. 463; Sprague v. White, 73 Iowa 670, 35 N. W. 751; Koon v. Tramel, 71 Iowa 132, 32 N. W. 243; Hockman v. Thuma, 68 Kans. 519, 75 Pac. 486; McNeil v. Jordan, 28 Kans. 7; Hoffman v. Gosnell, 75 Md. 577, 24 Atl. 28; Hennessey v. Andrews, 60 Mass. (6 Cush.) 170; Newhall v. Pierce, 5 Pick. (Mass.) 450; McEwen v. Keary, 178 Mich. 6, 144 N. W. 524; Abbott v. Gregory, 39 Mich. 68; Humphrey v. Hurd, 29 Mich. 44; Bennett v. Robinson, 27 Mich. 26; Dawson v. Dan-

recording laws to protect purchasers from latent legal or equitable titles. Hence, its operation in such cases in giving notice to the world protects all persons against fraud by the grantors wrongfully selling lands a second time. And, as a general rule, when the same person has executed two deeds for the same land, the first deed recorded will hold the title, unless the junior grantee has purchased with notice, in which case a prior recording of his deed would not avail against the prior deed of which he had notice. The statute has only given the priority to the junior deed first recorded, when the grantee has acted in good faith. If, at the time he makes the purchase, he has notice of an elder unrecorded deed, he must be regarded as acting in bad faith, and neither principles of justice nor the policy of the law will permit him to avail of the priority of the record. It then follows that actual, visible, open possession being regarded as notice equal to the recording of the deed under which the grantee is in possession, the person holding the first conveyance, and being in open, visible possession before the junior deed is recorded, must be held to be the owner of the title, as against the grantee in the junior deed."[6]

Where a grantor took a mortgage while in possession from his grantee after the latter had given a mortgage to another, the last named mortgage, being first recorded, was held to have priority.[7] The reason for this exception to the general rule is in some cases said to be, that a subsequent purchaser is entitled to rely upon the presump-

bury Bank, 15 Mich. 489; Bloomer v. Henderson, 8 Mich. 295, 77 Am. Dec. 453; Burt v. Baldwin, 8 Nebr. 487; Brophy Min. Co. v. Brophy &c. Min. Co., 15 Nev. 101; Bell v. Twilight, 18 N. H. 159; Bingham v. Kirkland, 34 N. J. Eq. 229; Groton Sav. Bank v. Batty, 30 N. J. Eq. 133; Van Keuren v. Central R. Co., 38 N. J. L. 165; Seymour v. McKinstrey, 106 N. Y. 230, 12 N. E. 348, 14 N. E. 94; Staples v. Fenton, 5 Hun (N. Y.) 172; New York L. Ins. Co. v. Cutler, 3 Sandf. Ch. (N. Y.) 176; Red River Valley Land &c. Co. v. Smith, 7 N. Dak. 236, 74 N. W. 194; Lowe v. Wheeling &c. R. Co., 12 Ohio Cir. Ct. 743, 4 Ohio Cir. Dec. 85; Forsha v. Longworth, 1 Ohio Cir. Ct. 271, 1 Ohio Cir. Dec. 149, affd. in 22 Wkly. L. Bul. 354; La Forest v. Downer, 63 Ore. 176, 126 Pac. 995; Randall v. Lingwall, 43 Ore. 383, 73 Pac. 1; Exon v. Dancke, 24 Ore. 110, 32 Pac. 1045; Eastham v. Hunter, 98 Tex. 560, 86 S. W. 323; Hoffman v. Blume, 64 Tex. 334; Hurt v. Cooper, 63 Tex. 362; Eylay v. Eylay, 60 Tex. 315; Summers v. Sheern (Tex.), 37 S. W. 246; Hickman v. Hoffman, 11 Tex. Civ. App. 605, 33 S. W. 257; Murry v. Carlton, 65 Wash. 364, 118 Pac. 332, 44 L. R. A. (N. S.) 314; Mateskey v. Feldman, 75 Wis. 103, 43 N. W. 733; Schwallback v. Milwaukee &c. R. Co., 69 Wis. 292, 34 N. W. 128, 2 Am. St. 740; Denton v. White, 26 Wis. 679. See also Scott v. Gallagher, 14 Serg. & R. (Pa.) 333, 16 Am. Dec. 508; Jinks v. Moppin (Tex.), 80 S. W. 390.

[6] Cabeen v. Breckenridge, 48 Ill. 91, per Walker, J.

[7] Koon v. Tramel, 71 Iowa 132, 32 N. W. 243. See also Murray v. Carlton, 65 Wash. 364, 118 Pac. 332, 44 L. R. A. (N. S.) 314.

tion that possession retained after a conveyance may be presumed to be a mere holding over at will, until it becomes convenient for the grantor to remove from the land. Moreover, a party ought not to be allowed to contradict the force and effect of a full conveyance by the mere fact of possession after his deed has been recorded.[8] He is estopped from setting up any claim or title founded upon possession against the terms of his own deed.[9]

When, however, the grantor's right or title under which he holds possession was acquired after the making of his deed, he is entitled to the same protection as a third person, and his possession is notice of his rights to the same extent that the possession of a third person is notice of his rights. Some courts, however, hold that the grantor's possession after a conveyance by him, especially if long continued, is notice of some interest or title in him not disclosed in his deed. Possession by the grantor is not regarded as substantially different from possession by a third person.[10] This view has frequently been recog-

[8] Koon v. Tramel, 71 Iowa 132, 32 N. W. 243; Bloomer v. Henderson, 8 Mich. 395, 77 Am. Dec. 453; Hafter v. Strange, 65 Miss. 323, 3 So. 190; Eylay v. Eylay, 60 Tex. 315; Mateskey v. Feldman, 75 Wis. 103, 43 N. W. 733.

[9] Van Keuren v. Central R. Co., 38 N. J. L. 165.

[10] Turman v. Bell, 54 Ark. 273, 15 S. W. 886, Hemingway, J., delivering the opinion, said: "Those that sustain the application of this rule say that by the terms of the deed the grantor has not the right of possession, and that his continuing possession gives notice that he has rights reserved not expressed in the deed; that, inasmuch as the records disclose no right of possession, it is but reasonable to conclude that the continuing possession rests upon some right not disclosed by the records, and that the reasonableness of such conclusion imposes upon persons about to deal with the land the duty to make inquiry." Shiff v. Andress, 147 Ala. 690, 40 So. 824; Pell v. McElroy, 36 Cal. 268; Daubenspeck v. Platt, 22 Cal. 330; Ronan v. Bluhm, 173 Ill. 277, 50 N. E. 694; Rock Island &c. R. Co. v. Dimick, 144 Ill. 628, 32 N. E. 291, 19 L. R. A. 105; Ford v. Marcall, 107 Ill. 136; White v. White, 89 Ill. 460; Illinois Cent. R. Co. v. McCullough, 59 Ill. 166; Metropolitan Bank v. Godfrey, 23 Ill. 579; Hopkins v. Garrard, 7 B. Mon. (Ky.) 312; Lytle v. Fitzpatrick, 24 Ky. L. 93, 67 S. W. 988; Boggs v. Anderson, 50 Maine 161; McLaughlin v. Shepherd, 32 Maine 143, 52 Am. Dec. 646; McKechnie v. Hoskins, 23 Maine 230; Webster v. Maddox, 6 Maine 256; New v. Wheaton, 24 Minn. 406; Groff v. Ramsey, 19 Minn. 44; Morrison v. March, 4 Minn. 325; Smith v. Myers, 56 Nebr. 503, 76 N. W. 1084; Kahre v. Rundle, 38 Nebr. 315, 56 N. W. 888; Hansen v. Berthelsen, 19 Nebr. 433, 27 N. W. 423; Seymour v. McKinstry, 106 N. Y. 230, 12 N. E. 348, 14 N. E. 94; Smith v. Phillips, 9 Okla. 297, 60 Pac. 117; Wright v. Bates, 13 Vt. 341; Lamoreux v. Huntley, 68 Wis. 24, 31 N. W. 331; Hoppin v. Doty, 25 Wis. 573. See also Stevenson v. Campbell, 185 Ill. 527, 57 N. E. 414; Broussard v. Broussard, 45 La. Ann. 1085, 13 So. 699 (purchase with knowledge and approval of vendor); Palmer v. Bates, 22 Minn. 532; Cornell v. Maltby, 165 N. Y. 557, 59 N. E. 291, affg. 35 App. Div. 630, 56 N. Y. S. 1111. But see Cook v. Travis, 20 N. Y. 400, affg. 22 Barb. 338.

nized in cases where a grantor has given an absolute deed, which was intended to operate merely as a mortgage, there being no defeasance, or the defeasance given not being recorded.[11]

Where through fraud or mistake the grantor's deed includes land other than that intended to be conveyed, his continued possession is constructive notice to a subsequent purchaser from the grantee.[12]

§ 598. Long continued possession of grantor.—When the grantor's possession has continued for a long period, the presumption of a claim of right hostile to the title granted arises in every case where such possession is inconsistent with the rights of the grantee; and in such case a court or jury might find the possession adverse from the nature of the possession, without proof of an express declaration on the part of the occupant that he claimed to hold in hostility to his grant.[13] If, on the other hand, the possession has continued after the making of the deed but a short time, it might be reasonably referred to the sufferance of the grantee.[14] Thus possession of grantors, continuing eight days after their deed was given and recorded, was not notice to a mortgagee, then making a loan to the grantee on security of the premises, of any rights of the grantors inconsistent with their deed.[15]

If the grantor's possession is consistent with the rights of his grantee, notice may be imparted by it.[16] No notice is imparted by the joint possession of the grantor and grantee.[17]

The possession of a cestui que trust, exercising all the rights of ownership, does not impart notice to a purchaser of the legal title from

---

[11] Hulin v. Stevens, 53 Mich. 93, 18 N. W. 569; Bennett v. Robinson, 27 Mich. 26. This case is distinguished from Bloomer v. Henderson, 8 Mich. 395, above cited, for the reason that the possession in that case was comparatively recent, while the possession in Bennett v. Robinson had continued for nearly three years. See post § 600.

[12] Holland v. Brown, 140 N. Y. 344, 35 N. E. 577; Mullins v. Wimberly, 50 Tex. 457; Bumpas v. Zachary (Tex.), 34 S. W. 672.

[13] American Bldg. &c. Assn. v. Warren, 101 Ark. 163, 141 S. W. 765; Turman v. Bell, 54 Ark. 273, 15 S. W. 886; Stevens v. Castel, 63 Mich. 11, 29 N. W. 828; Bennett v. Robinson, 27 Mich. 26; Emmons v. Murray, 16 N. H. 385; Brinkman v. Jones, 44 Wis. 498, per Taylor, J. See also Morgan v. McCuin, 96 Ark. 512, 132 S. W. 459.

[14] American Bldg. &c. Assn. v. Warren, 101 Ark. 163, 141 S. W. 765 (citing text); Turman v. Bell, 54 Ark. 273, 15 S. W. 886; Kelly v. Palmer, 91 Minn. 133, 97 N. W. 578; Bloomer v. Henderson, 8 Mich. 395, 77 Am. Dec. 453; Horbach v. Boyd, 64 Nebr. 129, 89 N. W. 644.

[15] McEwen v. Keary, 178 Mich. 6, 144 N. W. 524 (eight days).

[16] Chalfin v. Malone, 9 B. Mon. (Ky.) 496, 50 Am. Dec. 525; Cramer v. Benton, 4 Lans. (N. Y.) 291; Butler v. Phelps, 17 Wend. (N. Y.) 642; Brinkman v. Jones, 44 Wis. 498.

[17] McCarthy v. Nicrosi, 72 Ala. 332, 47 Am. Rep. 418; Foulks v. Reed, 89 Ind. 370; Jeffersonville, M. &c. R. Co. v. Oyler, 82 Ind. 394; Butler v. Stevens, 26 Maine 484; Bell v. Twilight, 18 N. H. 159, 45 Am. Dec. 367; Billington v. Welsh, 5 Binn. (Pa.) 129, 6 Am. Dec. 406; Cameron v. Romele, 53 Tex. 238.

the trustee. His possession does not become adverse until the legal title is conveyed in violation of the trust.[18]

§ 599. Possession of mortgagor after foreclosure.—The continued possession of the mortgagor after the premises have been sold under a foreclosure against him is not deemed constructive notice of any subsequent title or interest he may have acquired which does not appear of record.[19] Due diligence on the part of the mortgagee in obtaining information, after having been put upon inquiry, is a test of good faith.[20] Where the owner of mortgaged premises remained in actual possession after a void foreclosure sale and execution of the sheriff's deed, it was held that parties accepting mortgages on such premises from the purchasers at the sheriff's sale, took the mortgages with full knowledge of the rights of the owner in possession, and were not innocent mortgagees, entitled to liens on the premises under their mortgages.[21] A judgment debtor, continuing in possession of land which has been sold under execution against him, may be presumed to hold under the title of the purchaser. The debtor's possession suggests no further inquiry.[22]

§ 600. Continued possession of mortgagor under unrecorded defeasance.—If the mortgage be by an absolute deed, the defeasance of which is not recorded, the mortgagor's continued possession and occupation of the premises, within the knowledge of grantees of the mortgagee, is held by some courts to be sufficient notice of the mortgagor's title;[23] but by others his possession is not regarded as notice of the defeasance,[24] for the principle that possession is notice of the possessor's title is intended to protect only equitable rights, and not

---

[18] Scott v. Gallagher, 14 Serg. & R. (Pa.) 333, 16 Am. Dec. 508. This doctrine is, however, repudiated in Pell v. McElroy, 36 Cal. 268.

[19] Dawson v. Danbury Bank, 15 Mich. 489. See also Cook v. Travis, 20 N. Y. 400.

[20] Reed v. Gannon, 50 N. Y. 345.

[21] Hedlin v. Lee, 21 N. Dak. 495, 131 N. W. 390.

[22] Cook v. Travis, 20 N. Y. 400.

[23] Pell v. McElroy, 36 Cal. 268; Daubenspeck v. Platt, 22 Cal. 330; Hulin v. Stevens, 53 Mich. 93, 18 N. W. 569; Teal v. Scandinavian-American Bank, 114 Minn. 435, 131 N. W. 486; New v. Wheaton, 24 Minn. 406, 2 N. W. 203. One who accepts mortgages from the grantee in a deed absolute in form intended as a mortgage, with knowledge of such grantor's actual possession, and who fails to make inquiry concerning his rights, is not a mortgagee in good faith. Teal v. Scandinavian-American Bank, 114 Minn. 435, 131 N. W. 486.

[24] Wooldridge v. Miss. Valley Bank, 36 Fed. 97; Asher v. Mitchell, 9 Bradw. (Ill.) 335; Crassen v. Swoveland, 22 Ind. 427; Farnsworth v. Childs, 4 Mass. 637, 3 Am. Dec. 249; Hennessey v. Andrews, 6 Cush. (Mass.) 170; Newhall v. Burt, 7 Pick. (Mass.) 157; Newhall v.

to cover the possessor's fraud, or to protect him when he has no equity.[25]

In accord with this view, it has been held that the grantor's continued possession, after conveyance subject to an oral agreement that the grantee would hold the title in trust for the grantor, was not such constructive notice to the grantee's mortgagee as to put the latter upon inquiry concerning the grantor's rights.[26] It seems immaterial that the absolute deed itself is unrecorded, and it has been held that continued possession by the grantor whose absolute deed remained unrecorded did not operate as notice of a vendor's lien, to a subsequent purchaser from the grantee who exhibited his absolute deed upon the sale.[27]

The fact that a grantor after an absolute conveyance remains in possession has frequently been regarded as a circumstance tending to show that the transaction was a mortgage, and sufficient to put others upon inquiry as to the fact.[28] In like manner it has been held that where land is conveyed, and at the same time mortgaged back for the security of the purchase-money, and the grantor becoming the mortgagee continues in actual possession and occupation of the land, but neither the deed nor the mortgage is recorded, and the mortgagor in the meantime makes another mortgage of it to a third person. the mortgage for the purchase-money is entitled to priority.[29]

§ 601. Estoppel of occupant to rely upon possession as notice.—
An occupant of land may be estopped by his acts from claiming that his possession imparts notice.[30] Thus, as against an innocent

Pierce, 5 Pick. (Mass.) 450; Brophy Mining Co. v. Brophy &c. Min. Co., 15 Nev. 101; Patten v. Moore, 32 N. H. 382; Groton Savings Bank v. Batty, 30 N. J. Eq. 126; La Forest v. Downer, 63 Ore. 176, 126 Pac. 995; Bryant v. Grand Lodge (Tex. Civ. App.), 152 S. W. 714; Brinkman v. Jones, 44 Wis. 498.

[25] Stafford Nat. Bank v. Sprague, 17 Fed. 784; Sawyers v. Baker, 66 Ala. 292; Gill v. Hardin, 48 Ark. 409, 3 S. W. 519; Yates v. Hurd, 8 Colo. 343, 8 Pac. 575; Atkins v. Paul, 67 Ga. 97; Groton Sav. Bank v. Batty, 30 N. J. Eq. 126; Losey v. Simpson, 11 N. J. Eq. 246; Minton v. New York &c. R. Co., 130 N. Y. 332, 29 N. E. 319; Berryhill v. Kirchner, 96 Pa. St. 489.

[26] La Forest v. Downer, 63 Ore. 176, 126 Pac. 995.

[27] Bryant v. Grand Lodge (Tex. Civ. App.), 152 S. W. 714.

[28] Mercer v. Morgan, 136 Ga. 632, 71 S. E. 1075; Campbell v. Dearborn, 109 Mass. 130, 12 Am. Rep. 671; Lawrence v. Du Bois, 16 W. Va. 443; Lincoln v. Wright, 4 De G. & J. 16. See also McLean v. Clapp, 141 U. S. 429, 35 L. ed. 804, 12 Sup. Ct. 29. See ante §§ 274, 328.

[29] McKechnie v. Hoskins, 23 Maine 230; Parsell v. Thayer, 39 Mich. 467; But see Koon v. Tramel, 71 Iowa 132, 32 N. W. 243. See ante § 468 et seq.

[30] Groton Sav. Bank v. Batty, 30 N. J. Eq. 126; Minton v. New York Elev. R. Co., 130 N. Y. 332, 29 N. E. 319; Gill v. Hardin, 48 Ark. 409, 3 S. W. 519.

mortgagee, notice from possession can not be set up by an occupant who, for the purpose of concealing his interest from creditors, placed the title in the name of another, and, after the latter had given a mortgage upon the land, kept silent and permitted the mortgagor to borrow more money of the mortgagee on a second mortgage; when, if such occupant had notified the mortgagee of his claim upon his first being made aware of the existence of the earlier mortgage, the mortgagee might have collected the mortgage debt, and would not have made the second loan on the security of the land.[81]

"The object of the law in holding such possession constructive notice, where it has been so held, is to protect the possessor from the acts of others who do not derive their title from him; not to protect him against his own acts, and especially against his own deed. If a party executes and delivers to another a solemn deed of conveyance of the land itself, and suffers that deed to go upon record, he says to all the world, 'Whatever right I have, or may have claimed to have in this land, I have conveyed to my grantee; and though I am yet in possession, it is for a temporary purpose, without claim of right, and merely as a tenant at sufferance to my grantee.' This is the natural inference to be drawn from the recorded deed, and in the minds of all men, would be calculated to dispense with the necessity of further inquiry upon the point. All presumption of right or claim of right is rebutted by his own act or deed. One of the main objects of the registry law would be defeated by any other rule."[32]

The owner of land conveyed it by absolute deed intended as a mortgage, and the grantee independently executed mortgages thereon to a third person, while the owner was still in actual possession and occupancy of the property. The mortgagee was expressly informed before the mortgages were executed that the owner was so in possession, and the owner promptly notified the mortgagee, that the mortgagor had no interest in the land and had no right to mortgage it, and demanded the release and discharge thereof. It was held that the owner in possession was not estopped to question the validity of the mortgages.[33]

[81] Groton Sav. Bank v. Batty, 30 N. J. Eq. 126.

[32] Bloomer v. Henderson, 8 Mich. 395, 405, 77 Am. Dec. 453, and cases cited.

[33] Teal v. Scandinavian-American Bank, 114 Minn. 435, 131 N. W. 486.

VII. *Fraud as Affecting Priority*

§ 602. Fraudulent concealment of incumbrance.—Another instance of constructive fraud arises when a person having a mortgage upon an estate conceals or denies its existence, or so acts in relation to it as to induce another to purchase the estate, or to loan additional money upon it, in the belief that it is free from incumbrance. Such fraudulent concealment will estop the first mortgagee from asserting his lien.[1] What circumstances will amount to a fraudulent concealment or misrepresentation may depend in some measure upon the inquiry whether the prior mortgage is recorded or not; and, moreover, different considerations will control in cases of this sort, where a registry system is in full operation, as it is in this country, from those that prevail in England, where the possession of the title deeds for the most part stands in place of registration. But whatever the circumstances may be, "the rule of law is clear that, where one by his words or conduct wilfully causes another to believe the existence of a certain state of things, and induces him to act on that belief so as to alter his own previous position, the former is concluded from averring against the latter a different state of things as existing at the same time."[2]

§ 603. Estoppel of mortgagee by fraudulent concealment or misrepresentation.—A mortgagee allowing or inducing another to purchase the property as unincumbered, without disclosing his mortgage, may be precluded from setting it up against such purchaser;[3] such, for instance, is the case of an attorney who acts for the mortgagor in drawing a deed for the conveyance of land from the mortgagor to a purchaser, but does not disclose a mortgage he himself holds upon the

---

[1] Chapman v. Hamilton, 19 Ala. 121; Webb v. Austin, 22 Ky. L. 764, 58 S. W. 808; Short v. Currier, 153 Mass. 182, 26 N. E. 444; Tucker v. Jackson, 60 N. H. 214; Chester v. Greer, 5 Humph. (Tenn.) 26; Green v. Price, 1 Munf. (Va.) 449; Ibbottson v. Rhodes, 2 Vern. Ch. 554, 23 Eng. Reprint 958; Pickard v. Sears, 6 Ad. & El. 469. See also Lorch v. Aultman, 75 Ind. 162; Geary v. Porter, 17 Ore. 465, 21 Pac. 442.

[2] Per Lord Denman, C. J., in Pickard v. Sears, 6 Ad. & El. 469. See also Carpenter v. Wright, 52 Kans. 221, 34 Pac. 798; Matlack v. Shaffer, 51 Kans. 208, 32 Pac. 890; Curtis v. Stilson, 38 Kans. 302, 16 Pac. 678; Peter v. Russell, 1 Eq. Cas. Abr. 322; Savage v. Foster, 9 Mod. 35; Sharpe v. Foy, L. R. 4 Ch. App. 35; Berrisford v. Milward, 2 Atk. 49.

[3] See ante § 602.

property, though he knows that the purchaser is buying it for its value in ignorance of the mortgage.[4]

A mortgagee, however, whose mortgage is recorded, will not be so postponed merely because he knew that the mortgagor was making a subsequent conveyance of the premises, and did not make known his title:[5] to have this effect, there must be actual and intentional fraud on his part;[6] or he must have done some act, or made some representation to influence the conduct of another by inducing a belief of a given state of facts, when such party, having acted upon such belief, would be injured by showing a different state of facts. An estoppel in pais then arises against him. But he loses no right by neglecting to give a personal notice of his mortgage to one who is purchasing. The purchaser is presumed to know of the mortgage which has been duly recorded. He is bound at his peril to investigate the title.[7]

So, also, if a first mortgagee, having notice of a second mortgage, does anything to the prejudice of the latter,—as for instance, if he releases any part of the mortgaged premises without receiving payment of any part of his mortgage debt,—he is, to the extent of injury done, postponed to the second mortgage.[8] A mortgagee may not assert his lien against a subsequent purchaser or mortgagee to whom he made misleading statements or false representations in regard to payment of the debt secured by his mortgage, or the amount remaining due upon it, or the property covered by the mortgage, or his priority relative to other liens, or other material particulars.[9]

[4] L'Amoureux v. Vanderburgh, 7 Paige (N. Y.) 316. See also Lee v. Munroe, 7 Cranch (U. S.) 366; Lindley v. Martindale, 78 Iowa 379, 43 N. W. 233.

[5] Carter v. Champion, 8 Conn. 549, 21 Am. Dec. 695; Clabaugh v. Byerly, 7 Gill (Md.) 354, 48 Am. Dec. 575; Collier v. Miller, 137 N. Y. 332, 33 N. E. 374; Brinckerhoff v. Lansing, 4 Johns. Ch. (N. Y.) 65, 8 Am. Dec. 538; Paine v. French, 4 Ohio 318; Lipscomb v. Goode, 57 S. Car. 182, 35 S. E. 493; Palmer v. Palmer, 48 Vt. 69.

[6] Brinckerhoff v. Lansing, 4 Johns. Ch. (N. Y.) 65, 8 Am. Dec. 538; Paine v. French, 4 Ohio 318; Palmer v. Palmer, 48 Vt. 69. See also Marston v. Brackett, 9 N. H. 336; Story Eq. Juris. § 391.

[7] Reynolds v. Kirk, 105 Ala. 446, 17 So. 95; Steele v. Adams, 21 Ala. 534; Rector v. Board of Improvement, 50 Ark. 116, 6 S. W. 519; Bramble v. Kingsbury, 39 Ark. 131; Clabaugh v. Byerly, 7 Gill (Md.) 354, 48 Am. Dec. 575; Rice v. Dewey, 54 Barb. (N. Y.) 455; Brinckerhoff v. Lansing, 4 Johns. Ch. (N. Y.) 65, 8 Am. Dec. 538.

[8] Bailey v. Gould, Walk. (Mich.) 478. See post §§ 604a, 605.

[9] Freeman v. Brown, 96 Ala. 301, 11 So. 249; Hendricks v. Kelly, 64 Ala. 388; Broome v. Beers, 6 Conn. 198; Lasselle v. Barnett, 1 Blackf. (Ind.) 150, 12 Am. Dec. 217; Pickersgill v. Brown, 7 La. Ann. 297; Platt v. Squire, 12 Metc. (Mass.) 494; Newman v. Mueller, 16 Nebr. 523, 20 N. W. 843; Bissell v. Reiss, 3 Alb. L. J. (N. Y.) 302. See also Wells v. Pierce, 42 N. Y. 102, 4 Abb. Dec. (N. Y.) 559.

If a mortgagee represents to another person that the debt secured by the mortgage has been paid or satisfied, and that nothing is due on it, and thereby induces him to release other security and take a mortgage of the same land, the last mortgage, as between the two mortgagees, will take priority of the first, although the first was on record when such representation was made, as the person making the representation is estopped from disputing the truth of it with respect to the other, who was thereby induced to alter his condition.[10] And so if the first mortgagee in any way combines with the mortgagor to induce another to loan money upon the estate in ignorance of the first mortgage, this fraud will, without doubt, postpone his own mortgage.[11] And so if a second mortgagee stands by and sees the mortgagor induce the first mortgagee to release his mortgage, and take an assignment of another mortgage which he supposes to be next in priority to his own, but which is in fact subsequent to the second mortgage, as against the second mortgagee, this subsequent mortgage will be preferred to his own.[12] When the holder of one of two mortgage deeds, executed on the same day, has represented to a person about to take an assignment of the other mortgage that the deeds were delivered at the same time, and that there was no priority in his deed, he is precluded from claiming a priority against such person.[13]

On the other hand, if third persons having an interest, whether as owners, lienholders, or creditors, practice fraud upon the mortgagee, in order to invalidate his security or postpone it to their own claims, they will be estopped to contest the validity and priority of his mortgage.[14]

---

[10] Freeman v. Brown, 96 Ala. 301, 11 So. 249; Lasselle v. Barnett, 1 Blackf. (Ind.) 150, 12 Am. Dec. 217; Platt v. Squire, 12 Metc. (Mass.) 494; Fay v. Valentine, 12 Pick. (Mass.) 40, 22 Am. Dec. 391; Chester v. Greer, 5 Humph. (Tenn.) 26; Miller v. Bingham, 29 Vt. 82; Heane v. Rogers, 9 Barn. & Cres. 577. The release of a trust deed can not be relied upon by one chargeable with notice that the same is fraudulent. Abraham Lincoln Bldg. &c. Assn. v. Zuelk, 124 Ill. App. 109. Although the release of a trust deed by the trustees before payment of the debt secured is a breach of trust, such release will protect a subsequent innocent mortgagee for value without notice of nonpayment. Martin v. Poole, 36 App. D. C. 281.

[11] Dennis v. Burritt, 6 Cal. 670; Wight v. Prescott, 2 Barb. (N. Y.) 196; Peter v. Russell, 1 Eq. Cas. Abr. 322; Northern Counties &c. Ins. Co. v. Whipp, 26 Ch. Div. 482, 53 L. J. Ch. 629, 51 L. T. R. (N. S.) 806, 32 Wkly. Rep. 626. See also Thomas v. Kelsey, 30 Barb. (N. Y.) 268.

[12] Stafford v. Ballou, 17 Vt. 329.

[13] Broome v. Beers, 6 Conn. 198.

[14] Grimes v. Kimball, 8 Allen (Mass.) 153; Corey v. Alderman, 46 Mich. 540, 9 N. W. 844; Waldo v. Richmond, 40 Mich. 380; Buswell v. Davis, 10 N. H. 413; Neligh v. Michenor, 11 N. J. Eq. 539; Schurtz v. Colvin, 55 Ohio St. 274, 45 N. E. 527; Woodbury v. Bruce,

If the holder of a conveyance absolute in form but in fact intended as a mortgage, sets it up as a purchase, he can not be considered a bona fide mortgagee.[15] One who takes a mortgage in the form of an absolute deed is bound, when questioned by a creditor of the mortgagor or other party in interest, to fully and truly disclose the nature of his security; and a false statement of a material fact in relation to such security, or a failure to give the information required, will postpone his mortgage.[16]

Where a mortgage and a deed were executed by the same grantor upon the same property to different persons without any reference in either deed to the other, and the agent of the mortgagee was guilty of negligence or bad faith in not recording the mortgage until after the deed was filed for record, the agent can not afterward purchase the land from the grantee of the deed and hold the title as against the mortgagee, for the priority of the deed is founded upon his own negligence, and he must hold subject to the rights of the mortgagee for whom he acted as agent.[17]

Where a mortgagee's agent had refused a loan because the property offered as security had been attached as equitably belonging to the mortgagor's grantor, and the loan was finally induced by such grantor's written statement that the mortgagor held the absolute title, the grantor may not assert want of good faith on the part of the mortgagee's agent in failing to make further inquiry.[18]

The presence of an agent of a mortgagee at a receiver's sale of mortgaged property and his attestation of such sale without disclosing the mortgagee's title, and without objection, does not estop the mortgagee from objecting to the sale, where he was not a party to the proceeding and the agent was not authorized to waive his principal's rights.[19]

59 Vt. 624, 11 Atl. 52; London Freehold &c. Property Co. v. Suffield, 2 Ch. 608, 66 L. J. Ch. 790, 77 L. T. Rep. (N. S.) 445, 46 Wkly. Rep. 102. See also Jones v. Levering, 116 Mo. App. 377, 91 S. W. 980.
[15] Metropolitan Bank v. Godfrey, 23 Ill. 579.

[16] Geary v. Porter, 17 Ore. 465, 21 Pac. 442.
[17] Mitchell v. Aten, 37 Kans. 33, 14 Pac. 497.
[18] La Forest v. Downer, 63 Ore. 176, 126 Pac. 995.
[19] Lorch v. Aultman, 75 Ind. 162.

VIII. *Negligence and Miscellaneous Matters Affecting Priority*

§ **604. Negligence as evidence of fraud.**—Negligence is not fraud, though it may be evidence of it.[1] When a person having a mortgage upon an estate, or other interest in it, negligently puts it in the power of another to sell or mortgage the property to a third person who is ignorant of such mortgage or interest, he can not afterward assert his own title in priority to the title of the party whom he has suffered to be deceived.[2] By negligence is meant the want of that reasonable degree of diligence and care which a man of ordinary prudence and capacity would be expected to exercise in the same circumstances.

A person taking a mortgage or other conveyance of real estate is chargeable with notice of such facts as are indicated upon the face of the deeds, whether they indicate anything to him or not; for if he does not use the precaution, which common prudence requires, to employ a solicitor, he is in the same situation, with respect to constructive notice, as he would have been had he employed a solicitor.[3]

A mortgagee is likewise estopped to assert his priority where he has previously neglected to insist upon it, under circumstances which imposed upon him such a duty toward third persons,[4] or where he has

---

[1] Jones v. Smith, 1 Hare 43; Worthington v. Morgan, 16 Sim. 457.

[2] Briggs v. Jones, L. R. 10 Eq. 92; Rice v. Rice, 2 Drew 73; Robinson's Law of Priority, 54; 1 Fisher on Mtg. (3d ed.) 550. In Briggs v. Jones, L. R. 10 Eq. 92, Lord Romilly thus stated the principle of this rule: "A person who puts it in the power of another to deceive and raise money must take the consequences. He can not afterward rely on a particular or a different equity." Most of the English cases upon this point relate to the matter of the delivery of title-deeds, and therefore are for the most part of use in this country only as illustrating the general principles of the law of notice. See also Thorpe

v. Hodsworth, L. R. 7 Eq. 139; Layard v. Maud, L. R. 4 Eq. 397; Northern Counties &c. Ins. Co. v. Whipp, 26 Ch. Div. 482, 53 L. J. Ch. 629, 51 L. T. R. (N. S.) 806, 32 Wkly. Rep. 626; Union College v. Wheeler, 61 N. Y. 88; Stafford v. Ballou, 17 Vt. 329.

[3] Kennedy v. Green, 3 Myl. & K. 699. The Master of the Rolls referring to this case in Greensdale v. Dare, 20 Beav. 284, said that the doctrine of this case requires to be administered with the greatest care and delicacy, and that probably each case must stand upon the peculiar facts belonging to it.

[4] Sullivan v. Corn Exch. Bank, 154 App. Div. 292, 139 N. Y. S. 97; Ducros v. Fortin, 8 Rob. (La.) 165

already received satisfaction of his debt by judgment and sale on execution.[5] However, it has been held that mere carelessness or want of prudence in guarding his own interests will not postpone the first mortgagee, when not accompanied by fraud or breach of good faith toward others.[6]

Where owners of land failed to exercise ordinary business precaution, and were induced by fraud to convey their land to a corporation, a mortgagee who took the usual precautions before lending money to the corporation and accepted a mortgage on the land as security, acquired a valid mortgage.[7]

Where the beneficiary of a trust deed loaned money in good faith and in reliance upon the record title, without any negligence or knowledge of fraud by the borrower in making the trust deed a first lien on the land tendered as security, it was held that the beneficiary could not be prejudiced by such fraud.[8]

§ 604a.   Renewal or substitution of mortgages.—Whether a second mortgage between the same parties and upon the same lands given upon the release or cancelation of the first is taken merely as a renewal or in payment and satisfaction of the first mortgage depends largely upon the intention of the parties. Where the intention of the parties is simply to make a renewal and extension of the old debt, and the satisfaction of the old mortgage and the taking of a new one are practically simultaneous acts or parts of the same transaction, the taking of the second mortgage is not considered an extinguishment of the first, but a renewal thereof, and does not give priority to intervening judgment or mortgage creditors of the mortgagor,[9] especially,

(estoppel by acquiescence through failure to answer citation). See also Dugan v. Lyman (N. J. Eq.), 23 Atl. 657 (acquiescence of a mere volunteer, acting for mortgagee, insufficient); Blair v. St. Louis &c. R. Co., 22 Fed. 471 (neglect to foreclose upon default); Mayo v. Cartwright, 30 Ark. 407 (no presumption of acquiescence when mortgage is recorded); Boyles v. Knight, 123 Ala. 289, 26 So. 939.

[5] Delaware &c. Canal Co. v. Bonnell, 46 Conn. 9; Exline v. Lowery, 46 Iowa 556.

[6] Northern Counties of England F. Ins. Co. v. Whipp, 26 Ch. D. 482, 53 L. J. Ch. 629, 51 L. T. Rep. (N. S.) 806, 32 Wkly. Rep. 626. See also Martin v. Central L. &c. Co., 78 Iowa 504, 43 N. W. 301; Teal v. Scandinavian &c. Bank, 114 Minn. 435, 131 N. W. 486. The mere fact that a mortgagee left the title deeds with the mortgagor is not alone sufficient to postpone the first mortgage to a second, taking without notice. There must be fraud or gross negligence. Berry v. Mutual Ins. Co., 2 Johns. Ch. (N. Y.) 603.

[7] Trammell v. Mower (Ala.), 62 So. 528.

[8] Zimmer v. Farr, 225 Ill. 457, 80 N. E. 261.

[9] Griffin v. International Trust Co., 161 Fed. 48, 88 C. C. A. 212; Swift v. Kortrecht, 112 Fed. 709, 50 C. C. A. 429; Higman v. Humes, 127 Ala. 404, 30 So. 733; Dillon v. Byrne, 5 Cal. 455; Roberts v. Doan, 180

where the renewal or substitution is made in good faith, without notice of the intervening lien, and without any intention to release the original lien.[10] The rule, however, does not apply where there is evidence of an intention to waive the lien of the prior mortgage or to effect a payment thereof;[11] neither is the rule applicable where the new mortgage is given to a different person, from whom the debtor bor-

Ill. 187, 54 N. E. 207; Campbell v. Trotter, 100 Ill. 281; Shaver y. Williams, 87 Ill. 469; Christie v. Hale, 46 Ill. 117; McChesney v. Ernst, 89 Ill. App. 164, affd. in 186 Ill. 617, 58 N. E. 399; Pouder v. Ritzinger, 119 Ind. 597, 20 N. E. 654; Calvert v. Landgraf, 34 Ind. 388; Matchett v. Knisely, 27 Ind. App. 664, 62 N. E. 87; Watson v. Bowman, 142 Iowa 528, 119 N. W. 623; St. Croix Lumber Co. v. Davis, 105 Iowa 27, 74 N. W. 756; Young v. Shaner, 73 Iowa 555, 35 N. W. 629, 5 Am. St. 701; French v. Poole, 83 Kans. 281, 111 Pac. 488; Rowe v. Simmons, 14 Ky. L. 780, 21 S. W. 872; Eggeman v. Eggeman, 37 Mich. 436; Drane v. Newsom, 73 Miss. 422, 19 So. 200; Bramlett v. Watlin, 71 Miss. 902, 15 So. 934; Sledge v. Obenchain, 58 Miss. 670; Van Duyne v. Shann, 41 N. J. Eq. 311, 7 Atl. 429; Northeastern Permanent Sav. &c. Assn. v. Barker, 66 Hun 635, 50 N. Y. St. 543, 21 N. Y. S. 832; Flagler v. Malloy, 56 Hun 643, 30 N. Y. St. 612, 9 N. Y. S. 573; Benson v. Maxwell, 10 Sad. (Pa.) 380, 14 Atl. 161; Parker v. Parker, 52 S. Car. 382, 29 S. E. 805; Maas v. Tacquard, 33 Tex. Civ. App. 40, 75 S. W. 350. See also Watson v. Bowman, 142 Iowa 528, 119 N. W. 623; Washington v. Slaughter, 54 Iowa 265, 6 N. W. 291; Fish v. Anstey Constr. Co., 71 Misc. 2, 130 N. Y. S. 927; Paris v. Lawyers' Title Ins. &c. Co., 141 App. Div. 866, 126 N. Y. S. 753; Lowenfeld v. Empire City Woodworking Co., 249 App. Div. 617, 124 N. Y. S. 178; United States v. Crookshank, 1 Edw. (N. Y.) 233. But see Stearns v. Godfrey, 16 Maine 158; Woollen v. Hillen, 9 Gill (Md.) 185, 52 Am. Dec. 690; Traders' Nat. Bank v. Woodlawn Mfg. Co., 100 N. Car. 345, 5 S. E. 81; Traders' Nat. Bank v. Lawrence Mfg. Co., 96 N. Car. 298, 3 S.

E. 363; Union &c. Bank v. Smith, 107 Tenn. 476, 64 S. W. 756; Atkinson v. Plum, 50 W. Va. 104, 40 S. E. 587, 58 L. R. A. 788; First Nat. Bank v. Citizens' State Bank, 11 Wyo. 32, 70 Pac. 726, 100 Am. St. 925. See also McIntire v. Garmany, 8 Ga. App. 802, 70 S. E. 198; Lowenfeld v. Wimpie, 203 N. Y. 646, 97 N. E. 1108.

[10] Griffin v. International Trust Co., 161 Fed. 48, 88 C. C. A. 212; Wooster v. Cavender, 54 Ark. 153, 15 S. W. 192, 26 Am. St. 31; Sidener v. Pavey, 77 Ind. 241; Drury v. Briscoe, 42 Md. 154; Laconia Sav. Bank v. Vittum, 71 N. H. 465, 52 Atl. 848, 93 Am. St. 561; Institute Building &c. Assn. v. Edwards, 81 N. J. Eq. 359, 86 Atl. 962; Hutchinson v. Swartsveller, 31 N. J. Eq. 205; Barnes v. Camack, 1 Barb. (N. Y.) 392; Turner Bau Verein No. 3 v. Dalheimer, 1 Ohio S. & C. Pl. Dec. 237, 2 Ohio N. P. 248; Pearce v. Buell, 22 Ore. 29, 29 Pac. 78; Upton v. Hugos, 7 S. Dak. 476, 64 N. W. 523; Workingman's Bldg. &c. Assn. v. Williams (Tenn.), 37 S. W. 1019.

[11] Brown v. Dunckel, 46 Mich. 29, 8 N. W. 537; St. Albans Trust Co. v. Farrar, 53 Vt. 542. The mortgagee may lose his priority upon substitution of mortgages by conduct toward the junior incumbrancer operating as an equitable estoppel. McLeod v. Wadland, 25 Ont. 118. It has been held that the renewal is effective where the junior mortgagee or creditor has not acted to his prejudice in reliance on the cancellation or discharge of the first mortgage. International Trust Co. v. Davis &c. Mfg. Co., 70 N. H. 118, 46 Atl. 1054. See also Geib v. Reynolds, 35 Minn. 331, 28 N. W. 923; Kidder v. Barnes, 18 N. Dak. 276, 122 N. W. 378.

rowed the money to pay off the old mortgage,[12] nor where the new mortgage secures a distinct debt from the old, or an additional debt;[13] the satisfaction in such cases operating as a complete discharge of the first mortgage.

To properly effect a renewal of the first mortgage without loss of priority, it is necessary that the release or cancelation of the old mortgage and the giving of the new should be parts of the same transaction, or so nearly simultaneous as to clearly evidence the intention of the parties to make the latter a mere continuation or renewal of the former. If a considerable interval of time elapses, the priority of lien is lost.[14] A recital in the new mortgage that it is given in renewal of the old is perhaps the best evidence of such intention, to preserve its priority; but the absence of such recital will not necessarily affect the right of priority, especially where the junior mortgagee knew of the transaction.[15] It has been held that an extension or renewal agreement need not be recorded to operate against subsequent incumbrancers or purchasers.[16]

§ 605. Loss of priority by release or satisfaction.—It sometimes happens that a mortgagee may lose his position of priority, and, without intending to impair his own security, find himself in the place of a subsequent mortgagee, through want of care in dealing with the mortgaged property. Thus, if a mortgagee knowingly and understandingly cancels his mortgage when there is a second mortgage upon the property, and in lieu of the mortgage takes an absolute conveyance of the property, or a new mortgage, in the absence of any fraud on the part of the holder of the second mortgage, the lien of the first mortgage will not be revived, nor the second mortgagee prevented from reaping the benefit of the priority of his mortgage upon the records.[17]

---

[12] Holt v. Baker, 58 N. H. 276; Banta v. Garmo, 1 Sandf. Ch. (N. Y.) 383. But see Elliott v. Tainter, 88 Minn. 377, 93 N. W. 124; Chetwynd v. Allen, 1 Ch. 353, 68 L. J. Ch. 160, 80 L. T. Rep. (N. S.) 110, 47 Wkly. Rep. 200.

[13] Edwards v. Thom, 25 Fla. 222, 5 So. 707; Brown v. Dunckel, 46 Mich. 29, 8 N. W. 537; McKeen v. Haseltine, 46 Minn. 426, 49 N. W. 195; Smith v. Bynum, 92 N. Car. 108. See also Gerrity v. Wareham Sav. Bank, 202 Mass. 214, 88 N. E. 1084; Buzzell v. Still, 63 Vt. 490, 22 Atl. 619, 25 Am. St. 777. But see

McIntire v. Garmany, 8 Ga. App. 802, 70 S. E. 198.

[14] Lester v. Richardson, 69 Ark. 198, 62 S. W. 62; Elizabethport v. Whitlock, 37 Fla. 190, 20 So. 255.

[15] Roberts v. McNeal, 80 Ill. App. 536.

[16] Kraft v. Holzman, 206 Ill. 548, 69 N. E. 574. See also Whittacre v. Fuller, 5 Minn. 508.

[17] Frazee v. Inslee, 2 N. J. Eq. 239. The chancellor said that to revive the mortgage in such case would be giving encouragement to negligence, and would destroy the value of a public record. Keohane v.

As a general rule the entry upon the record of a formal release or satisfaction of a mortgage, whatever may be its effect upon the rights or equities of the original parties, will operate in favor of a junior lienor without notice of such equities, thus giving his lien priority;[18] unless the release or satisfaction was made for a special purpose, such as a renewal, without any intention to displace the lien of the mortgage, and the junior lienor had notice thereof.[19]

If the first mortgagee has knowledge of subsequent liens, he has no right to release his mortgage to the prejudice of such liens;[20] and if he would thus impair the security of a junior mortgagee by releasing the mortgagor from personal liability, the' first mortgagee thereby postpones his own lien to that of the second mortgagee.[21]

Smith, 97 Ill. 156; Skeele v. Stocker. 11 Bradw. (Ill.) 143; Daws v. Craig, 62 Iowa 515, 17 N. W. 778; Holt v. Baker, 58 N. H. 276; Hutchinson v. Bramhall, 42 N. J. Eq. 372, 7 Atl. 873; Smith v. Brackett, 36 Barb. (N. Y.) 571; Banta v. Garmo, 1 Sandf. Ch. (N. Y.) 383. A partial release of the first mortgage inures pro tanto to the benefit of the second mortgage. Warner v. Blakeman, 36 Barb. (N. Y.) 501. See also Emery v. Vaughan, 18 Ky. L. 281, 36 S. W. 9. See rule of pro rata division, post §§ 822, 874c, 966-971, 1701.

[18] Persons v. Shaeffer, 65 Cal. 79, 3 Pac. 94; Havighorst v. Bowen, 214 Ill. 90, 73 N. E. 402; Oliver v. Gill, 48 Ill. App. 424; Smith v. Lowry, 113 Ind. 37, 15 N. E. 17; Valley Nat. Bank v. Des Moines Nat. Bank, 116 Iowa 541, 90 N. W. 342; Stanbrough v. Daniels, 88 Iowa 314, 55 N. W. 466; Bank of Indiana v. Anderson, 14 Iowa 544, 83 Am. Dec. 390; Marple v. Marple, 63 Kans. 426, 65 Pac. 645; Golding v. Golding, 43 La. Ann. 555, 9 So. 638; Moran v. Roberge, 84 Mich. 600, 48 N. W. 164; Ferguson v. Glassford, 68 Mich. 36, 35 N. W. 820; Harrison v. Johnson, 18 N. J. Eq. 420; New York Co-Operative Bldg. &c. Assn. v. Brennan, 62 App. Div. 610, 70 N. Y. S. 916; Traders' Nat. Bank v. Woodlawn Mfg. Co., 100 N. Car. 345, 5 S. E. 81; Morris v. Beecher, 1 N. Dak. 130, 45 N. W. 696; Steele v. Walter, 204 Pa. St. 257, 53 Atl. 1097; Quattlebaum v. Black, 24 S. Car. 48; Evans v. Roan-

oke Sav. Bank, 95 Va. 294, 28 S. E. 323; Conner v. Welch, 51 Wis. 431, 8 N. W. 260. See also Tolman v. Smith, 85 Cal. 280, 24 Pac. 743; McCarthy v. Miller, 122 Ill. App. 299; Barnes v. Mott, 64 N. Y. 397, 21 Am. Rep. 625; Warner v. Blakeman, 36 Barb. (N. Y.) 501; Jamison v. Gjemenson, 10 Wis. 411; Engine Wks. Co. v. Livingstone, 7 Ont. L. R. 740, 3 Ont. W. R. 670.

[19] Edwards v. Weil, 99 Fed. 822, 40 C. C. A. 105; Farmers' Bank v. Butterfield, 100 Ind. 229.

[20] McLean v. Lafayette Bank, 3 McLean (U. S.) 587, Fed. Cas. No. 8888. See also Nelson v. McKee (Ind. App.), 99 N. E. 447; Turner v. Parker, 10 Rob. (La.) 154; Schaad v. Robinson, 50 Wash. 283, 97 Pac. 104.

[21] Sexton v. Pickett, 24 Wis. 346. The junior mortgagee may insist upon payment or acts of satisfaction of the senior lien, in order to secure for himself the priority to which he has become entitled and to prevent reinstatement of the senior mortgage, to his prejudice. Cowley v. Shelby, 71 Ala. 122; Fox v. Blossom, 17 Blatchf. (U. S.) 352, Fed. Cas. No. 5008; Redin v. Branham, 43 Minn. 283, 45 N. W. 445; Conlon v. Minor, 94 App. Div. 458, 88 N. Y. S. 224; Angel v. Boner, 38 Barb. (N. Y.) 425; Sawyer v. Senn, 27 S. Car. 251, 3 S. E. 298. See also Webster v. Ypsilanti Canning Co., 149 Mich. 489, 113 N. W. 7.

In case the entry of the satisfaction of a mortgage is procured by fraud or deception, or is made without the proper authority, the lien of the mortgagee is not thereby postponed to a junior incumbrancer, but may be restored or the satisfaction canceled,[22] especially where the junior incumbrancer had actual or constructive notice of the continuing rights of the senior mortgagee.[23] Where, however, the fraudulent or unauthorized entry of satisfaction was due to the mortgagee's own negligence or laches, the satisfaction must stand and his priority is lost.[24] The same principles apply to the fraudulent release of a trust deed by the trustee, without receiving satisfaction.[25]

Where a senior mortgage is released without being paid, and at the same time a new mortgage is taken for the same sum, the question arises whether the junior mortgage is thereby let into the position of priority. Although the transaction be a simultaneous one, and is not intended to impair the lien of the first mortgage, it is held that the

[22] Appelman v. Gara, 22 Colo. 397, 45 Pac. 366; Stanley v. Valentine, 79 Ill. 544; McConnell v. American Nat. Bank (Ind. App.), 103 N. E. 809; Foster v. Paine, 63 Iowa 85, 18 N. W. 699, 56 Iowa 622, 10 N. W. 214; Bruse v. Nelson, 35 Iowa 157; Wiscomb v. Cubberly, 51 Kans. 580, 33 Pac. 330; Horton v. Cutler, 28 La. Ann. 331; De St. Romes v. Blanc, 20 La. Ann. 424, 96 Am. Dec. 415; Robinson v. Sampson, 23 Maine 388; Sheldon v. Holmes, 58 Mich. 138, 24 N. W. 795; Keeler v. Hannah, 52 Mich. 535, 18 N. W. 346; Whipple v. Fowler, 41 Nebr. 675, 60 N. W. 15; Collignon v. Collignon, 52 N. J. Eq. 516, 28 Atl. 794; Heyder v. Excelsior Bldg. &c. Assn., 42 N. J. Eq. 403, 8 Atl. 310, 59 Am. Rep. 49; Lockard v. Joines (N. J.), 23 Atl. 1075; Young v. Hill, 31 N. J. Eq. 429; Harris v. Cook, 28 N. J. Eq. 345; Harrison v. New Jersey R. &c. Co., 19 N. J. Eq. 488; Waterman v. Webster, 108 N. Y. 157, 15 N. E. 380; Fassett v. Smith, 23 N. Y. 252; Weaver v. Edwards, 39 Hun (N. Y.) 233, affd. 121 N. Y. 653, 24 N. E. 1092; King v. McVickar, 3 Sandf. Ch. (N. Y.) 192; 'Lambert v. Leland, 32 N. Y. Super. Ct. 218; Kern v. A. P. Hotaling Co., 27 Ore. 205, 40 Pac. 168, 50 Am. St. 710; Independent Bldg. &c. Assn. v. Real Estate Title Ins. &c. Co., 156 Pa. St. 181, 27 Atl. 62; Brown v. Henry, 106 Pa. St. 262; Wilton v. Mayberry, 75 Wis. 191, 43 N. W. 901, 6 L. R. A. 61, 17 Am. St. 193.

[23] Connecticut Gen. L. Ins. Co. v. Burnstine, 131 U. S. cliii, 24 L. ed. 706; Eldridge v. Connecticut Gen. L. Ins. Co., 3 MacArthur (D. C.) 301; Etzler v. Evans, 61 Ind. 56; Howe v. White (Ind. App.), 67 N. E. 203; Ferguson v. Glassford, 68 Mich. 36, 35 N. W. 820; Pierie v. Metz, 9 Pa. Dist. 341.

[24] Wittenbrock v. Parker, 102 Cal. 93, 36 Pac. 374, 24 L. R. A. 197, 41 Am. St. 172; Robbins v. Todman, 28 Kans. 491; Heyder v. Excelsior Bldg. &c. Assn., 42 N. J. Eq. 403, 8 Atl. 310, 59 Am. Rep. 49; Harris v. Cook, 28 N. J. Eq. 345; Charleston v. Ryan, 22 S. Car. 339, 53 Am. Rep. 713.

[25] Connecticut Gen. L. Ins. Co. v. Eldredge, 102 U. S. 545, 26 L. ed. 245; Jackson v. Blackwood, 4 MacArthur & M. (D. C.) 188; Chicago &c. R. Land Co. v. Peck, 112 Ill. 408; Barbour v. Scottish-American Mtg. Co., 102 Ill. 121; Southerland v. Fremont, 107 N. Car. 565, 12 S. E. 237; Evans v. Roanoke Sav. Bank, 95 Va. 294, 28 S. E. 323. See also Havighorst v. Bowen, 214 Ill. 90, 73 N. E. 402.

release, if it be absolute in terms, will discharge the lien, and the new mortgage will be only a subordinate lien.[26]

But when a creditor to whom land has been conveyed in trust, to secure a debt, by a deed absolute in form reconveys it to his grantor, and simultaneously takes back a mortgage to secure the same debt, he does not lose his lien in equity as against a judgment rendered against the debtor subsequent to the original conveyance.[27]

§ 606. **Priority between notes secured by same mortgage.**—Priority of lien between the holders of several notes secured by a mortgage is, by some authorities, determined according to the order of their maturity.[28] If judgment is obtained on one of the notes, that takes

[26] Woollen v. Hillen, 9 Gill (Md.) 185. To the same effect, see also Neidig v. Whiteford, 29 Md. 178; Lester v. Richardson, 69 Ark. 198, 62 S. W. 62.

[27] Christie v. Hale, 46 Ill. 117; International Trust Co. v. Davis &c. Mfg. Co., 70 N. H. 118, 46 Atl. 1054; Holt v. Baker, 58 N. H. 276. See post §§ 927a and 971.

[28] McVay v. Bloodgood, 9 Port. (Ala.) 547; Wilson v. Hayward, 6 Fla. 171; Schultz v. Plankinton Bank, 141 Ill. 116, 30 N. E. 346, 33 Am. St. 290; Koester v. Burke, 81 Ill. 436; Herrington v. McCollum, 73 Ill. 476; Gardner v. Diederichs, 41 Ill. 158; Funk v. McReynolds, 33 Ill. 481; Vansant v. Allmon, 23 Ill. 30; Sargent v. Howe, 21 Ill. 148; Chandler v. O'Neil, 62 Ill. App. 418; Horn v. Bennett, 135 Ind. 158, 34 N. E. 321, 24 L. R. A. 800; Parkhurst v. Watertown Steam Engine Co., 107 Ind. 594, 8 N. E. 634; Gerber v. Sharp, 72 Ind. 553; Doss v. Ditmars, 70 Ind. 451; People's Sav. Bank v. Finney, 63 Ind. 460; Minor v Hill, 58 Ind. 176, 26 Am. Rep. 71; Davis v. Langsdale, 41 Ind. 399; Crouse v. Holman, 19 Ind. 30; Murdock v. Ford, 17 Ind. 52; Harris v. Harlan, 14 Ind. 439; Hough v. Osborne, 7 Ind. 140; Stanley v. Beatty, 4 Ind. 134; State Bank v. Tweedy, 8 Blackf. (Ind.) 447, 46 Am. Dec. 486; Gilman v. Heitman, 137 Iowa 336, 113 N. W. 932; Leavitt v. Reynolds, 79 Iowa 348, 44 N. W. 567, 7 L. R. A. 365; Walker v. Scheiber, 47 Iowa 529; Massie v. Sharpe, 13 Iowa 542; Sangster v. Love, 11 Iowa 580; Hinds v. Mooers, 11 Iowa 211; Robinson v. Waddell, 53 Kans. 402, 36 Pac. 730; Aultman-Taylor Co. v. McGeorge, 31 Kans. 329, 2 Pac. 778; Richardson v. McKim, 20 Kans. 346; Wilson v. Eigenbrodt, 30 Minn. 4, 13 N. W. 907; Huffard v. Gottberg, 54 Mo. 271; Thompson v. Field, 38 Mo. 320; Mitchell v. Ladew, 36 Mo. 526, 88 Am. Dec. 156; Hunt v. Stiles, 10 N. H. 466; Speer v. Whitfield, 10 N. J. Eq. 107; Bridenbecker v. Lowell, 32 Barb. (N. Y.) 9; Anderson v. Sharp, 44 Ohio St. 260, 6 N. E. 900; Winters v. Franklin Bank, 33 Ohio St. 250; Kyle v. Thompson, 11 Ohio St. 616; Wohlgemuth v. Standard Drug Co., 8 Ohio Cir. Dec. 9, 14 Ohio Cir. Ct. Rep. 316; Belding v. Manly, 21 Vt. 550; Gwathmeys v. Ragland, 1 Rand. (Va.) 466; McClintic v. Wise, 25 Grat. (Va.) 448, 18 Am. Rep. 694; American Sav. Bank &c. Co. v. Helgesen, 64 Wash. 54, 116 Pac. 837, Ann. Cas. 1913A, 390;. Norris v. Beaty, 6 W. Va. 477; Pierce v. Shaw, 51 Wis. 316, 8 N. W. 209; Lyman v. Smith, 21 Wis. 674; Marine Bank v. International Bank, 9 Wis. 57; Wood v. Trask, 7 Wis. 566, 76 Am. Dec. 230. See also Shaw v. Crandon State Bank, 145 Wis. 639, 129 N. W. 794. The rule applies only where the holders of the respective notes stand equally in equity as to each other, and as to the acquisition of their security. Shaw v. Crandon State Bank, 145 Wis. 639, 129 N. W. 794. See post §§ 1699-1702, 1939.

the place of the note on which it was rendered.[29] The holder of the note first maturing may, upon default, or at any time afterward, foreclose and sell the premises in satisfaction of his debt.[30] His delay to enforce his rights does not impair his prior right.[31]

But the mortgagee may, by agreement at the time of assigning a portion of the debt or one or more of the notes or bonds secured by his mortgage, give to the assignee priority to the extent of the amount assigned him, irrespective of the time of maturity.[32] And therefore, one who takes an assignment of a part of the notes secured by a mortgage should inquire of the maker and of the payee whether the others have been sold with a preferred lien upon the security. It is negligence on his part not to make such inquiry; and if the preferred lien has been given, it will be valid against such assignee.[33] And where the parties to a mortgage, securing several debts or notes, agree upon the order in which they shall be paid, by recital in the mortgage, such a stipulation is binding upon them and their assignees with notice.[34] One holding a mortgage securing several promissory notes may assign part of the notes, and a corresponding interest in the mortgage, giving priority to the assignee, or a pro rata interest in the security, according to the terms of the assignment.[35]

But the rule having the greater weight of authority is a pro rata application of the security whereby the several holders of the notes secured by a mortgage though they mature at different times are en-

---

[29] Funk v. McReynolds, 33 Ill. 481.

[30] Lyman v. Smith, 21 Wis. 674; Marine Bank v. International Bank, 9 Wis. 57; Wood v. Trask, 7 Wis. 566, 76 Am. Dec. 230. Upon default in payment of one note, the mortgagee may take up that and the other notes not due. and hold the mortgage as security therefor, as against a subsequent mortgagor. Mead v. Hammond, 107 App. Div. 575, 95 N. Y. S. 241.

[31] Lyman v. Smith, 21 Wis. 674.

[32] Grattan v. Wiggins, 23 Cal. 16; Walker v. Dement, 42 Ill. 272; Morgan v. Kline, 77 Iowa 681, 42 N. W. 558; Cooper v. Ulmann, Walk. Ch. (Mich.) 251; Solberg v. Wright, 33 Minn. 224, 22 N. W. 381; Thayer's Appeal, 6 Sad. (Pa.) 392, 9 Atl. 498. See also Earle v. Sunnyside Land Co., 150 Cal. 214, 88 Pac. 920;

Jennings v. Moore, 83 Mich. 231, 47 N. W. 127, 21 Am. St. 601.

[33] Walker v. Dement, 42 Ill. 272.

[34] Richards v. Holmes, 18 How. (U. S.) 143, 15 L. ed. 304; Walters v. Ward, 153 Ind. 578, 55 N. E. 735; Dunham v. W. Steele Packing &c. Co., 100 Mich. 75, 58 N. W. 627; Ellis v. Lamme, 42 Mo. 153; West End Trust Co. v. Wetherill, 77 N. J. Eq. 590, 78 Atl. 756 (priority of interest over principal); Coon v. Bosque Bonita Land &c. Co., 8 N. Mex. 123, 42 Pac. 77; Wohlgemuth v. Standard Drug Co., 14 Ohio Cir. Ct. 316, 8 Ohio Cir. Dec. 9 (stipulation binding only upon assignees with notice).

[35] Romberg v. McCormick, 194 Ill. 205, 62 N. E. 537; Howard v. Schmidt, 29 La. Ann. 129; Lane v. Davis, 14 Allen (Mass.) 225.

titled in the absence of any express agreement to share pro rata the proceeds of a sale of the mortgaged property.[36]

A mortgage executed by one partner in the partnership name of real estate belonging to the firm, to secure a partnership debt, conveys the legal interest of such partner and the equitable interest of the copartner; as where A executed a mortgage in the firm name of A & Bro., and himself acknowledged it. But a person taking a subsequent mortgage, properly executed by both partners, has priority as to the interest of the partner who did not execute the first mortgage.[37] A mortgage by one tenant in common of his interest in partnership real estate, made for a valid consideration to one who has no notice of the partnership, is not subject to any equities arising out of the partnership relation of the grantor.[38]

§ 607. Priority between unrecorded mortgages.—As between several unrecorded mortgages or other conveyances, that of prior execution takes precedence,[39] and, in determining such priority, fractions

[36] Penzel v. Brookmire, 51 Ark. 105, 10 S. W. 15, 14 Am. St. 23; Grattan v. Wiggins, 23 Cal. 16; Hall v. McCormick, 31 Minn. 280, 17 N. W. 620; Wilson v. Eigenbrodt, 30 Minn. 4, 13 N. W. 907; Henderson v. Herrod, 10 Smed. & M. (Miss.) 631, 49 Am. Dec. 41; Studebaker Bros. Mfg. Co. v. McCurgur, 20 Nebr. 500, 30 N. W. 686; Commercial Bank v. Jackson, 7 S. Dak. 135, 63 N. W. 548; Keyes v. Wood, 21 Vt. 331. See post §§ 822, 1699–1702.

[37] Haynes v. Seachrest, 13 Iowa 455; Chavener v. Wood, 2 Ore. 182. See also Brazleton v. Brazleton, 16 Iowa 417.

[38] McDermot v. Laurence, 7 Serg. & R. (Pa.) 438, 10 Am. Dec. 468. See also Frink v. Branch, 16 Conn. 260; Frothingham v. Shephard, 1 Aik. (Vt.) 65. See ante §§ 119, 120.

[39] Bragg v. Lamport, 96 Fed. 630, 38 C. C. A. 467; Schimberg v. Waite, 93 Ill. App. 130; Houfes v. Schultze, 2 Ill. App. 196; Reagan v. First Nat. Bank, 157 Ind. 623, 61 N. E. 575, 62 N. E. 701; Union Mut. L. Ins. Co. v. Abbott, 95 Ind. 238; McFadden v. Hopkins, 81 Ind. 459; Krutsinger v. Brown, 72 Ind. 466; Hoadley v. Hadley, 48 Ind. 452; Growning v. Behn, 10 B. Mon. (Ky.) 383; Spaulding v. Scanland, 6 B.

Mon. (Ky.) 353; Ker v. Ker, 42 La. Ann. 870, 8 So. 595; Wing v. McDowell, Walk. Ch. (Mich.) 175; Westervelt v. Voorhis, 42 N. J. Eq. 179, 6 Atl. 665; Ely v. Scofield, 35 Barb. (N. Y.) 330; Berry v. Mutual Ins. Co., 2 Johns. Ch. (N. Y.) 603; Marbury v. Jones, 112 Va. 389, 71 S. E. 1124; Naylor v. Throckmorton, 7 Leigh (Va.) 98, 30 Am. Dec. 492; Kelso v. Russell, 33 Wash. 474, 74 Pac. 561. See also Bragg v. Lamport, 96 Fed. 630, 38 C. C. A. 467; Louisville Bldg. Assn. v. Korb, 79 Ky. 190, 2 Ky. L. (abst.) 71. The rule applies as between successive mortgages of after-acquired property; the mortgage first in point of time being the senior lien. Boston Safe Deposit &c. Co. v. Bankers' &c. Tel. Co., 36 Fed. 288. Execution determining the priority of mortgages includes delivery, and it is the date of delivery rather than that of the written execution which determines priority. Koesenig v. Schmitz, 71 Iowa 175, 32 N. W. 320. Where acknowledgment is part of the execution, priority of proper acknowledgment may determine priority of right. Fugman v. Jiri Washington Bldg. &c. Assn., 209 Ill. 176, 70 N. E. 644. A mortgage purporting to secure a note of even

of a day will be considered.[40] Generally successive mortgages upon the same property are entitled to priority of payment out of its proceeds in the order in which they have attached as liens upon it,[41] though exceptional circumstances or special equities may entitle a junior lien to preference.[42]

Where one of two equitable mortgages is first in time, it is first in right.[43] Also, when both of the mortgages are purely legal, and both are taken for value, the first in time is the first in right. But one who pays value without notice takes precedence of a prior taker without value.[44] The holder of a legal mortgage usually prevails in a contention against the holder of an equitable mortgage where neither is recorded, unless the former acquired his lien after the equitable mortgage was taken, and either without value or with notice of the prior mortgage.[45]

Of two mortgages executed at the same time, to secure debts which mature at different times, if there be no other ground of priority, according to the authorities in some states that is the prior lien which secures the payment of the note which first falls due. The rule is the same as it is when one mortgage secures debts maturing at different times; they are to be paid in the order of their maturity.[46] It makes

---

date which is in fact not executed until six years later and is then dated back to the date of the mortgage, will be postponed to a second mortgage executed after the making of the first mortgage but before the signing of the note. Ogden v. Ogden, 180 Ill. 543, 54 N. Y. 750.

[40] Wood v. Lordier, 115 Ind. 519, 18 N. E. 34; Gibson v. Keyes, 112 Ind. 568, 14 N. E. 591. See also Jones v. Phelps, 2 Barb. Ch. (N. Y.) 440. But see Coleman v. Carhart, 74 Ga. 392.

[41] Goodbar v. Dunn, 61 Miss. 618; Ayers v. Staley (N. J. Eq.), 18 Atl. 1046; Lavalette v. Thompson, 13 N. J. Eq. 274; Central Trust Co. v. West India Imp. Co., 169 N. Y. 314, 62 N. E. 387, revg. 48 App. Div. 147, 63 N. Y. S. 853; Bank of Florence v. Gregg, 46 S. Car. 169, 24 S. E. 64.

[42] Brown v. Baker, 22 Nebr. 708, 36 N. W. 273; McConnell v. Muldoon, 24 N. Y. S. 902, 30 Abb. N. Cas. 352; Bank of Ireland v. Cogry Spinning Co. (1900), 1 Ir. 219. The fact that a mortgage is given to secure pre-existing debts will not give it preference over prior equities.

Warford v. Hankins, 150 Ind. 489, 50 N. E. 468. But see Kaehler v. Dibblee, 32 Wis. 19.

[43] Spring v. Short, 90 N. Y. 538; Phillips v. Phillips, 4 De G., F. & J. 218.

[44] McCracken v. Flanagan, 141 N. Y. 174, 36 N. E. 10; Ten Eyck v. Witbeck, 135 N. Y. 40, 31 N. E. 994, 31 Am. St. 809.

[45] Jones v. Van Doren, 130 U. S. 684, 32 L. ed. 1072; First Nat. Bank v. Connecticut M. Life Ins. Co., 129 Ind. 241, 28 N. E. 695; Warnock v. Harlow, 96 Cal. 298, 31 Pac. 166, 31 Am. St. 209; Fahn v. Bleckley, 55 Ga. 81; Martin v. Bower, 51 N. J. Eq. 452, 26 Atl. 823; Drake v. Paige, 127 N. Y. 562, 28 N. E. 407; Anderson v. Blood, 152 N. Y. 285, 46 N. E. 493, 57 Am. St. 515; Stephens v. Weldon, 151 Pa. St. 520, 25 Atl. 28.

[46] Roberts v. Mansfield, 32 Ga. 228; Gardner v. Diederichs, 41 Ill. 158; Murdock v. Ford, 17 Ind. 52; Harris v. Harlan, 14 Ind. 439; Isett v. Lucas, 17 Iowa 503; Bank of U. S. v. Covert, 13 Ohio 240; Marine Bank v. International Bank, 9 Wis. 57. According to other authorities this

no difference in the order of payment that, after the assignment of the note first maturing to one person, the note next maturing is assigned to another with the mortgage or trust deed. The holding of the mortgage security gives no preference in order of payment.[47] In other states such mortgages confer equal rights; and the fact that one becomes due before the other gives no priority.[48]

Mere recitals in a subsequent mortgage can not prejudice the rights of a prior mortgagee, acquired before its execution.[49]

A prior mortgage barred by the statute of limitations will be postponed to a junior lien.[50]

§ 607a. Priority between simultaneous mortgages.—Where several mortgages are executed and recorded at the same time, whether the parties intended that one of them should have priority is a matter of fact for the jury to determine from the evidence of such intention.[51] For the purpose of carrying such intention into effect the law will presume that the mortgage which was intended to be preferred was first delivered.[52] Where mortgages on the same property are executed and delivered simultaneously to parties having knowledge of each other's rights, to secure debts of equal standing, and there is no evidence of intention to prefer one mortgage to the other, they are considered equal and concurrent liens, although not recorded simultaneously.[53]

Though the mortgagor intended that one should have priority, and first delivered that one to the recorder, yet if the recorder's certificate

circumstance is no evidence to determine the fact of priority. Gilman v. Moody, 43 N. H. 239; Granger v. Crouch, 86 N. Y. 494. See post § 1699.

[47] Gwathmeys v. Ragland, 1 Rand. (Va.) 466.

[48] Shaw v. Newsom, 78 Ind. 335; Riddle v. George, 58 N. H. 25; Collera v. Huson, 34 N. J. Eq. 38. Post §§ 1699-1707.

[49] Clabaugh v. Byerly, 7 Gill (Md.) 354, 48 Am. Dec. 575.

[50] A revival indorsed upon the first mortgage note, after execution of the second mortgage, will not restore the first mortgage to priority. Lord v. Morris, 18 Cal. 482. Priority is not restored by a subsequent renewal. Moore v. Porter (Tex. Civ. App.), 138 S. W. 426. But it has been held that a second mortgage, executed after suit upon the note secured by the first mortgage

has been barred, but before foreclosure of the first mortgage is barred, is not entitled to precedence over the first mortgage. Mackie v. Lansing, 2 Nev. 202.

[51] Rose v. Provident Sav. &c. Assn., 28 Ind. App. 25, 62 N. E. 293; Utley v. Dunkelberger, 86 Iowa 469, 53 N. W. 408; Gilman v. Moody, 43 N. H. 239; Butler v. Bank of Mazeppa, 94 Wis. 351, 68 N. W. 998; Jones v. Parker, 51 Wis. 218, 8 N. W. 124. See ante § 534.

[52] Jones v. Phelps, 2 Barb. Ch. (N. Y.) 440; Trompczynski v. Struck, 105 Wis. 437; Butler v. Mazeppa Bank, 94 Wis. 351.

[53] Walker v. Buffandeau, 63 Cal. 312; Daggett v. Rankin, 31 Cal. 321; Lampkin v. First Nat. Bank, 96 Ga. 487, 23 S. E. 390; Cain v. Hanna, 63 Ind. 408; Rhoades v. Canfield, 8 Paige (N. Y.) 545.

showed that they were filed for record simultaneously, neither has priority of record over the other.[54] The fact that one instrument was handed to the recorder an instant before the other is immaterial. Neither is the intention with which the act was done important.[55] And where mortgages are handed to the recorder at the same time, he can not fix their priority by the mere order in which he numbers them.[56] But it is said by the Supreme Court of Minnesota that, "when two mortgages on the same land, executed by a mortgagor to two different mortgagees, and filed for record at the same time by the common agent of the mortgagees, and no instructions are given, the priority of the liens is determined presumptively by the order in which the instruments are numbered by the register of deeds."[57]

§ 608. **Agreements fixing priority.**—The parties may, as between themselves, make a valid agreement, though it be verbal only, that one of two mortgages shall be prior to the other, and the order of record is then immaterial unless they are subsequently assigned to other persons who have no notice of the agreement;[58] although, ac-

[54] Lampkin v. First Nat. Bank, 96 Ga. 487, 23 S. E. 390; Terry v. Moran, 75 Minn. 249, 77 N. W. 777. Priority may be indicated by the numbering; Connecticut Mut. L. Ins. Co. v. King, 72 Minn. 287, 75 N. W. 376.

[55] Koevenig v. Schmitz, 71 Iowa 175, 32 N. W. 320.

[56] Schaeppi v. Glade, 195 Ill. 62, 62 N. E. 874.

[57] Edmonston v. Wilbur, 99 Minn. 495, 110 N. W. 3.

[58] Wallace v. McKenzie, 104 Cal. 130, 37 Pac. 859; Beasley v. Henry, 6 Bradw. (Ill.) 485; McCaslin v. Advance Mfg. Co., 155 Ind. 298, 58 N. E. 67; Wayne &c. Loan Assn. v. Moats, 149 Ind. 123, 48 N. E. 793; Sparks v. State Bank, 7 Blackf. (Ind.) 469; Corbin v. Kincaid, 33 Kans. 649, 7 Pac. 145; New England Loan &c. Co. v. Wood, 2 Kans. App. 624, 42 Pac. 940; Fudickar v. Monroe Athletic Club, 49 La. Ann. 1457, 22 So. 381; Lehman v. Godberry, 40 La. Ann. 219, 4 So. 316; Grunert v. Becker, 100 Mich. 50, 58 N. W. 608; Dye v. Forbes, 34 Minn. 13, 24 N. W. 309; Chadbourn v. Rahilly, 28 Minn. 394, 10 N. W. 420; Union Mortgage &c. Co. v. Peters, 72 Miss. 1058, 18 So. 497, 30 L. R. A. 829;

Loewen v. Forsee, 137 Mo. 29, 38 S. W. 712, 59 Am. St. 489; Hasenritter v. Kirchhoffer, 79 Mo. 239; Ryan v. West, 63 Nebr. 894, 89 N. W. 416; Rogers v. Central L. &c. Co., 49 Nebr. 676, 68 N. W. 1048; Shaw v. Abbott, 61 N. H. 254; New Jersey Bldg. &c. Ins. Co. v. Bachelor, 54 N. J. Eq. 600, 35 Atl. 745; New York Chemical Mfg. Co. v. Peck, 6 N. J. Eq. 37; Lovett v. Demarest, 5 N. J. Eq. 113; Abert v. Kornfeld, 128 App. Div. 547, 112 N. Y. S. 884; Taylor v. Wing, 84 N. Y. 471; Freeman v. Schroeder, 43 Barb. (N. Y.) 618, 29 How. Pr. 263; Jones v. Phelps, 2 Barb. Ch. (N. Y.) 440; Decker v. Boice, 19 Hun (N. Y.) 152; Rhoades v. Canfield, 8 Paige (N. Y.) 545; Raleigh Nat. Bank v. Moore, 94 N. Car. 734; Rigler v Light, 90 Pa. St. 235; Maze v. Burke, 12 Phila. (Pa.) 335; Parker v. Parker, 52 S. Car. 382, 29 S. E. 805; Bank v. Campbell, 2 Rich. Eq. (S. Car.) 179; Poland v. Lamoille Valley R. Co., 52 Vt. 144; Trompczynski v. Struck, 105 Wis. 437, 81 N. W. 650. See also Mississippi Val. Trust Co. v. Washington Northern R. Co., 212 Fed. 776; Newby v. Fox, 90 Kans. 317, 133 Pac. 890, 47 L. R. A. (N. S.) 302; Londner v. Perlman, 129 App.

cording to some authorities, the want of notice on the part of the assignee makes no difference, but the mortgage continues subject to the equity of this arrangement.[59] But such an agreement itself, when in writing, is not entitled to record, and therefore, if recorded, is not notice to subsequent purchasers;[60] and in that case the record of it would not be constructive notice to an assignee of the deferred mortgage. But if such assignee had knowledge of the agreement, he would take subject to the equities thereby conferred.[61]

An agreement between parties to a mortgage to continue its lien after payment in full is valid as between them; and if future advances are made thereon, subsequent creditors or lienors with notice of the agreement are bound thereby.[62] And parties interested in property may agree, on sufficient consideration that a foreclosure sale under a prior mortgage should be subject to a junior lien, and that the latter should remain a lien on the property after a sale under the former.[63]

A mortgagee has an unquestionable right to waive his priority in favor of a subsequent mortgagee.[64] If a prior mortgagee releases his mortgage in order to enable the mortgagor to raise money upon the same property, with which to make improvements thereon, such mortgagee can not afterward be heard to object that the money was raised by the second mortgagee upon discount of other paper of the mortgagor, or that the mortgagor failed to expend the money as he had agreed.[65]

If the holder of a first mortgage knowing of the existence of a second mortgage releases his mortgage and takes a new one in its place, the second mortgage becomes the prior lien, although the first mort-

Div. 93, 113 N. Y. S. 420; Matthews v. Damainville, 43 Misc. 546, 89 N. Y. S. 493. See also Horner v. Scott (Pa.), 89 Atl. 555. A parol agreement by a debtor to substitute a party advancing money to pay liens on premises can not avail against execution creditors whose liens are otherwise superior. Lane v. Lloyd, 33 Ky. L. 570, 110 S. W. 401.

[59] Cable v. Ellis, 86 Ill. 525; Walters v. Ward, 153 Ind. 578, 55 N. E. 735; Rose v. Provident Sav. &c. Assn., 28 Ind. App. 25; Hendrickson v. Woolley, 39 N. J. Eq. 307; Conover v. Van Mater, 18 N. J. 481; Freeman v. Schroeder, 43 Barb. (N. Y.) 618, 29 How. Pr. 263.

[60] Gillig v. Maass, 28 N. Y. 191.

[61] Bank v. Frank, 13 J. & S. (N. Y.) 404.

[62] Girard Trust Co. v. Baird, 212 Pa. 41, 61 Atl. 507.

[63] Brown v. Barber, 244 Mo. 138, 148 S. W. 892.

[64] Wayne &c. Loan Assn. v. Moats, 149 Ind. 123, 48 N. E. 793; Fudicker v. Monroe Athletic Club, 49 La. Ann. 1457, 22 So. 381; Mutual Life Ins. Co. v. Sturges, 33 N. J. Eq. 328; Taylor v. Wing, 84 N. Y. 471, 23 Hun 233; Frost v. Yonkers Sav. Bk., 70 N. Y. 553, 26 Am. Rep. 627; Raleigh Nat. Bank v. Moore, 94 N. Car. 734; Poland v. Lamoille Valley R. Co., 52 Vt. 144; Clason v. Shepherd, 6 Wis. 369.

[65] Darst v. Bates, 95 Ill. 493. See also Hendrickson v. Woolley, 39 N. J. Eq. 307.

gage was a release with an understanding with the mortgagor that he would arrange with the second mortgagee so as to give the new mortgage the same priority that the discharged mortgage originally held.[66]

A mere admission by one of two mortgagees, whose mortgages were executed, delivered, and recorded on the same day, that there is no priority of one mortgage over the other, although made by a writing signed by him, does not preclude his afterward claiming a priority in time for his own mortgage, because such admission is, like a parol declaration, subject to be explained or contradicted.[67] But such writing would be admissible in evidence to show that the deeds took effect simultaneously.[68] But an agreement as to priority may be proved by parol.[69]

Without any agreement, there may be facts and circumstances which will entitle one of two mortgages recorded at the same time to an equitable priority over the other;[70] and on the other hand, although one mortgage may have been recorded before another, there may be facts which will entitle the two mortgages to stand upon an equality. An instance of the latter kind occurs when a trustee, having two funds, loans them to the same person, upon two distinct mortgages, without the intention of giving one priority to the other.[71] Moreover, the mortgage first recorded, and therefore prima facie the prior lien, may be shown to have been conditionally recorded; and a second mortgage, recorded before the condition was complied with, may be entitled to precedence.[72]

The party benefited by an agreement to subordinate need not be directly a party to such agreement. Thus the advancement of money by the makers of building loans is sufficient acceptance of the vendor's agreement to subordinate purchase-money mortgages to building loans on the same property, without such makers joining in the agreement.[73] A second mortgage executed to obtain money to redeem land from an execution sale against the mortgagor, under an express agreement that it should be a prior lien, is superior to the rights of the first mortgagee, benefited by the redemption.[74] And so the maker of

[66] Workingman's Bldg. &c. Assn. v. Williams (Tenn.), 37 S. W. 1019.

[67] Beers v. Broome, 4 Conn. 247. See also Maze v. Burke (Pa.), 12 Phila. 335.

[68] Beers v. Hawley, 2 Conn. 467.

[69] Maze v. Burke, 12 Phila. (Pa.) 335.

[70] Stafford v. Van Rensselaer, 9 Cow. (N. Y.) 316.

[71] Rhoades v. Canfield, 8 Paige (N. Y.) 545.

[72] Freeman v. Schroeder, 43 Barb. (N. Y.) 618.

[73] Londner v. Perlman, 129 App. Div. 93, 113 N. Y. S. 420.

[74] New England Mtg. Sec. Co. v. Fry, 143 Ala. 637, 42 So. 57, 111 Am. St. 62.

notes secured by a trust deed need not be a consenting party to the postponement of the lien to a subsequent one, by the holders of the notes.[75]

It is no ground for giving priority to a junior mortgage that the money received upon it was used in conserving the mortgaged property, or in improving it in any way. Although a portion of a line of railway subject to a mortgage be wholly constructed by money raised on a second mortgage, yet this fact gives the latter no priority over the former. The prior mortgage, although given before the road is built, attaches as fast as it is built, and to all property covered by the terms of the mortgage, as fast as it comes into existence.[76] Where the first mortgagee formally waives his lien, in favor of the second mortgagee, and the second mortgagee agrees that the money he loans shall be applied to the improvement of the property, but allows mechanics' liens to accumulate against the property, he will be obliged to satisfy the mechanics' liens out of his prior lien, so as to protect the first mortgagee therefrom.[77] And where the owner of land already incumbered obtains loans secured by trust deeds, under an agreement that the proceeds should be applied in satisfaction of the first incumbrance and in the erection of a building, the lenders are entitled to priority only in so far as the proceeds of the loan are actually applied in reduction of the first incumbrance and improvement of the property.[78]

[75] Jackson v. Grosser, 121 Ill. App. 363, affd. 218 Ill. 494, 75 N. E. 1032.

[76] Galveston Railroad Co. v. Cowdrey, 11 Wall. (U. S.) 459, 20 L. ed. 199. "Had the first mortgage," says Mr. Justice Bradley, "been given before a shovel had been put into the ground toward constructing the railroad, yet if it assumed to convey and mortgage the railroad, which the company was authorized by law to build, together with its superstructure, appurtenances, fixtures and rolling stock, these several items of property, as they came into existence, would become instantly attached to and covered by the deed, and would have fed the estoppel created thereby. No other rational or equitable rule can be adopted for such cases. To hold otherwise would render it necessary for a railroad company to borrow in small parcels as sections of the road were completed and trust deeds could be safely given thereon. The practice of the country and its necessities are coincident with the rule." See also Willink v. Morris Canal &c. Co., 4 N. J. Eq. 377; Clarke v. Calvert, 72 App. Div. 630, 78 N. Y. S. 17.

[77] Wayne &c. Loan Assn. v. Moats, 149 Ind. 123, 48 N. E. 793.

[78] Joralmon v. McPhee, 31 Colo. 26, 71 Pac. 419. Where a loan company failed to include in its building loan agreement a provision that the mortgage should be a first lien, and used part of the loan to pay off the first mortgage, it was held, under a statute preferring a materialman filing a lien under such circumstances, that the loan company had thereby subjected its interest in the property to the lien of the materialman, relying on the agreement that the entire building loan should be devoted to the building under construction. Pennsylvania Steel Co. v. Title Guaranty &c. Co., 50 Misc. 51, 100 N. Y. S. 299, affd. 120 App. Div. 879, 105 N. Y. S. 1135.

§ 609. Priority between mortgages and mechanics' liens.—A mortgage executed before the commencement of a building erected on the land is paramount to a mechanic's lien for work and materials furnished for the building by one having actual or constructive notice of such mortgage.[79] A mortgage existing at the time of the accrual of a mechanic's lien retains its priority notwithstanding the fact that the value of the mortgage security is increased by the labor and material

[79] Folsom v. Cragen, 11 Colo. 205, 17 Pac. 515; Stone v. Tyler, 173 Ill. 147, 50 N. E. 688; Green v. Sprague, 120 Ill. 416, 11 N. E. 859; Ward v. Yarnelle, 173 Ind. 535, 548, 91 N. E. 7; Zehner v. Johnston, 22 Ind. App. 452, 53 N. E. 1080; Bartlett v. Bilger, 92 Iowa 732, 61 N. W. 233; Ryder v. Cobb, 68 Iowa 235, 26 N. W. 91; Hershee v. Hershey, 15 Iowa 185; Nixon v. Cydon Lodge, 56 Kans. 298, 143 Pac. 236; Jean v. Wilson, 38 Md. 288; Davidson v. Stewart, 200 Mass. 393, 86 N. E. 779; Hoover v. Wheeler, 23 Miss. 314; Elliott & Barry Engineering Co. v. Baker, 134 Mo. App. 95, 114 S. W. 71; Bradford v. Anderson, 60 Nebr. 368, 83 N. W. 173; Grand Island Banking Co. v. Koehler, 57 Nebr. 649, 78 N. W. 265; Eckels v. Stuart, 212 Pa. 161, 61 Atl. 820; Lyle v. Ducomb, 5 Binn. (Pa.) 585; Jessup v. Stone, 13 Wis. 466. See also Allis-Chalmers Co. v. Central Trust Co., 190 Fed. 700, 111 C. C. A. 428, 39 L. R. A. (N. S.) 84; Wimberly v. Mayberry, 94 Ala. 240, 10 So. 157, 14 L. R. A. 305; McClain v. Hutton, 131 Cal. 132, 61 Pac. 273, 63 Pac. 182, 622; Seely v. Neill, 37 Colo. 198, 86 Pac. 334; Pacific States Sav., Loan &c. Co. v. Dubois, 11 Idaho 319, 83 Pac. 513; Davidson v. Stewart, 200 Mass. 393, 86 N. E. 779; Boggs v. McEwen, 69 Nebr. 705, 96 N. W. 666; Henry &c. Co. v. Halter, 58 Nebr. 685, 79 N. W. 616. In Tritch v. Norton, 10 Colo. 337, 15 Pac. 680, there was a new commencement under a new contract after an intervening mortgage. See also 2 Jones on Liens, §§ 1457, 1492. Knowledge of the mortgagee's officers, when making the loan, that a building was being constructed on the premises under contract will postpone their mortgage, although negotia-tions for the mortgage preceded the contract. Saucier v. Maine Supply &c. Co., 109 Maine 342, 84 Atl. 461. A mortgage placed on land after work on an unfinished building thereon had ceased, has priority over the lien of a contractor who subsequently finished the building, and such priority applies to both the land and the building. May v. Mode, 142 Mo. App. 656, 123 S. W. 523. A mortgage executed while a building is in process of construction and near completion, which recites that it is executed to enable the mortgagor to raise funds to complete the building and to pay outstanding obligations, is not inferior to lien claims arising after the execution of the mortgage, but the mortgage and the lien claims are equal, and neither have priority over the other. Such a mortgage amounts to an agreement that the proceeds shall be applied on the construction account, and materialmen and laborers may have it so applied. Ward v. Yarnelle, 173 Ind. 535, 91 N. E. 7. Where the filing of notice of mechanics' liens is required by statute, the mere fact that the mortgagee had knowledge that work was being performed on the mortgaged premises and that materials were being furnished, did not constitute actual notice of the existence of a mechanic's lien for such labor and material; and although such performance of work might be considered constructive notice, putting the purchaser upon inquiry, it was not the constructive notice required by the statute. Scheas v. Boston, 31 Ky. L. 157, 101 S. W. 942; citing Foushee v. Grigsby, 12 Bush (Ky.) 75. See ante § 487.

upon which the lien is based,[80] or that the building is so altered or enlarged that little of the original structure remains.[81]

The fact that the mortgagor contemplated the improvements for which the lien is claimed, does not give the lien priority where the mortgage was executed before the contract for the improvements;[82] nor does the knowledge of the mortgagee that the mortgagor intends to build upon the property give the mechanic's lien priority.[83] And generally the mere fact that the mortgagee knew of the work and did not object thereto does not affect its priority;[84] though under some statutes the mortgagee's consent to the improvement or failure to object upon notice, may have this effect.[85] If a mortgagee encourages the improvement of the property by an agreement to subordinate his lien to the cost thereof, his mortgage is of course postponed to the liens for labor and material.[86]

If a mortgagee, while in possession, erects a house on the premises, a mechanic's lien for this work is subject to the mortgage.[87] A mortgagee out of possession is not an owner within the meaning of a statute giving a lien for labor and materials furnished under a contract with or by consent of the owner, nor can such mortgagee be held to have consented to the displacement of his own lien merely because he had knowledge of the improvements.[88]

In accordance with the general rule, a mortgage for purchase-money, given prior to the accrual of a mechanic's lien, will take priority thereof.[89] Even a subsequent purchase-money mortgage may have priority. Thus where a purchaser in possession of property under contract of sale or otherwise, makes improvements thereon, and executes and de-

[80] Thorpe Block Sav. &c. Assn v. James, 13 Ind. App. 522, 41 N. E. 978. See also Toledo &c. R. Co. v. Hamilton, 134 U. S. 296, 33 L. ed. 905, 10 Sup. Ct. 546; Soule v. Borelli, 80 Conn. 392, 68 Atl. 979. But see Climax Lumber Co. v. Bay City Mach. Works, 163 Ala. 654, 50 So. 935.

[81] Equitable L. Ins. Co. v. Slye, 45 Iowa 615. See ante § 487.

[82] Sullivan v. Texas Briquette &c. Co., 94 Tex. 541, 63 S. W. 307.

[83] Holmes v. Hutchins, 38 Nebr. 601, 57 N. W. 514.

[84] Allis-Chalmers Co. v. Central Trust Co., 190 Fed. 700, 111 C. C. A. 428, 39 L. R. A. (N. S.) 84; Pride v. Viles, 3 Sneed (Tenn.) 125; Security Mortgage &c. Co. v. Caruthers, 11 Tex. Civ. App. 430, 32 S. W.

837. See also Williams v. Santa Clara Min. Assn., 66 Cal. 193, 5 Pac. 85; Capital Lumbering Co. v. Ryan, 34 Ore. 73, 54 Pac. 1093.

[85] Bristol-Goodson Electric Light &c. Co. v. Bristol Gas &c. Co., 99 Tenn. 371, 42 S. W. 19. See also Seely v. Neill, 37 Colo. 198, 86 Pac. 334.

[86] Cummings v. Emslie, 49 Nebr. 485, 68 N. W. 621, and cases cited.

[87] Ferguson v. Miller, 6 Cal. 402.

[88] Central Trust Co. v. Bodwell Water Power Co., 181 Fed. 735.

[89] Hill v. Aldrich, 48 Minn. 73, 50 N. W. 1020; Hoagland v. Lowe, 39 Nebr. 397, 58 N. W. 197; Clark v. Butler, 32 N. J. Eq. 664; Campbell's Appeal, 36 Pa. St. 247; Kelly's Appeal, 1 Sad. (Pa.) 280, 2 Atl. 868. See ante §§ 463, 473, 473a.

livers to the vendor a purchase-money mortgage, upon receiving a deed to the property, such mortgage is prior to mechanics' liens arising out of the improvements.[90]

As a general rule, a mechanic's lien has priority over a mortgage executed after lien accrued,[91] on commencement of the building,[92] or

[90] Erwin v. Acker, 126 Ind. 133, 25 N. E. 888; Thorpe v. Durbon, 45 Iowa 192; Missouri Valley Lumber Co. v. Reid, 4 Kans. App. 4, 45 Pac. 722; Rochford v. Rochford, 188 Mass. 108, 74 N. E. 299, 108 Am. St. 465; Saunders v. Bennett, 160 Mass. 48, 35 N. E. 111, 39 Am. St. 456; Perkins v. Davis, 120 Mass. 408; Moody v. Tschabold, 52 Minn. 51, 53 N. W. 1023; Oliver v. Davy, 34 Minn. 292, 25 N. W. 629; Wilson v. Lubke, 176 Mo. 210, 75 S. W. 602, 98 Am. St. 503; Russell v. Grant, 122 Mo. 161, 26 S. W. 958, 43 Am. St. 563; Virgin v. Brubaker, 4 Nev. 31; Gibbs v. Grant, 29 N. J. Eq. 419; Paul v. Hoeft, 28 N. J. Eq. 11; Macintosh v. Thurston, 25 N. J. Eq. 242; Strong v. Van Deursen, 23 N. J. Eq. 369; Lamb v. Cannon, 38 N. J. L. 362; Rees v. Ludington, 13 Wis. 276, 80 Am. Dec. 741.

[91] Atkins v. Volmer, 21 Fed. 697; Spence v. Etter, 8 Ark. 69; Soule v. Hurlbut, 58 Conn. 511, 20 Atl. 610; Dunham v. Woodworth, 158 Ill. App. 486; Interstate Bldg. &c. Assn. v. Ayers, 71 Ill. App. 529; Carriger v. Mackey, 15 Ind. App. 392, 44 N. E. 266; Lamb v. Hanneman, 40 Iowa 41; Thomas v. Hoge, 58 Kans. 166, 48 Pac. 844; First Nat. Bank v. Chowning Electric Co., 142 Ky. 624, 134 S. W. 1156; Lenel's Succession, 34 La. Ann. 868; Shaughnessy v. Isenberg, 213 Mass. 159, 99 N. E. 975; Brown v. Haddock, 199 Mass. 480, 85 N. E. 573; Osborne v. Barnes, 179 Mass. 597, 61 N. E. 276; Batchelder v. Hutchinson, 161 Mass. 462, 37 N. E. 452; Carew v. Stubbs, 155 Mass. 549, 30 N. E. 219; Buntyn v. Shippers' Compress Co., 63 Miss. 94; Goodwin v. Cunningham, 54 Nebr. 11, 74 N. W. 315; Ansley v. Pasahro, 22 Nebr. 662, 35 N. W. 885; Graton &c. Mfg. Co. v. Woodworth-Mason Co., 69 N. H. 177, 38 Atl. 790; Currier v. Cummings, 40 N. J. Eq. 145, 3 Atl. 174; Gordon v. Torrey, 15 N. J. Eq. 112,

82 Am. Dec. 273; Morris County Bank v. Rockaway Mfg. Co., 14 N. J. Eq. 189; Cheesborough v. Asheville Sanatorium, 134 N. Car. 245, 46 S. E. 494; Turner v. St. John, 8 N. Dak. 245, 78 N. W. 340; Blanshard v. Schwartz, 7 Okla. 23, 54 Pac. 303; Drewery v. Columbia Amusement Co., 87 S. Car. 445, 69 S. E. 879, 1094; Gillespie v. Bradford, 7 Yerg. (Tenn.) 168, 27 Am. Dec. 494; Fields v. Daisy Gold Min. Co., 25 Utah 76, 69 Pac. 528; Powell v. Nolan, 27 Wash. 318, 67 Pac. 712, 68 Pac. 389; H. C. Houston Lumber Co. v. Wetzel & T. R. Co., 69 W. Va. 682, 72 S. E. 786.

[92] Davis v. Bilsland, 18 Wall. (U. S.) 659, 21 L. ed. 969; In re Matthews, 109 Fed. 603; Joralman v. McPhee, 31 Colo. 26, 71 Pac. 419; Nixon v. Cydon Lodge, 56 Kans. 298, 43 Pac. 236; Rosenthal v. Maryland Brick Co., 61 Md. 590; Kay v. Towsley, 113 Mich. 281, 71 N. W. 490; Ortonville v. Geer, 93 Minn. 501, 101 N. W. 963, 106 Am. St. 445; Miller v. Stoddard, 54 Minn. 486, 56 N. W. 131; Hewson-Herzog Sup. Co. v. Cook, 52 Minn. 534, 54 N. W. 751; Gardner v. Leck, 52 Minn. 522, 54 N. W. 746; Malmgren v. Phinney, 50 Minn. 457, 52 N. W. 915, 18 L. R. A. 753; Glass v. Freeberg, 50 Minn. 386, 52 N. W. 900, 16 L. R. A. 335; Landau v. Cottrill, 159 Mo. 308, 60 S. W. 64; Nold v. Ozenberger, 152 Mo. App. 439, 133 S. W. 349; Schulenburg v. Hayden, 146 Mo. 583, 48 S. W. 472; DuBois v. Wilson, 21 Mo. 213; Hydraulic Press Brick Co. v. Bormans, 19 Mo. App. 664; Murray v. Swanson, 18 Mont. 533, 46 Pac. 441; Hahn v. Bonacum, 76 Nebr. 837, 107 N. W. 1001; Chapman v. Brewer, 43 Nebr. 890, 62 N. W. 320, 47 Am. St. 779; Cheshire Provident Inst. v. Stone, 52 N. H. 365; Federal Trust Co. v. Guigues, 76 N. J. Eq. 495, 74 Atl. 652; Gordon v. Torrey, 15 N. J. Eq.

of the work, or the furnishing of materials;[93] and the fact that the purchase-price of the land was paid out of the mortgage loan does not give the mortgage priority.[94] And so the fact that the mortgagor concealed the existence of mechanics' liens from the mortgagee in obtaining the loan or himself procured the filing of such liens, will not defeat their priority over the mortgage.[95] A mere preference agreement by the mortgagor with the mortgagee to keep the premises

112, 82 Am. Dec. 273; Morris County Bank v. Rockaway Mfg. Co., 14 N. J. Eq. 189; Robertson Lumber Co. v. Clarke, 24 N. Dak. 134, 138 N. W. 984; Bastien v. Barras, 10 N. Dak. 29, 84 N. W. 559; Haxtun &c. Co. v. Gordan, 2 N. Dak. 246, 50 N. W. 708, 32 Am. St. 776; Harrisburg Lbr. Co. v. Washburn, 29 Ore. 150, 44 Pac. 390; Reynolds v. Miller, 177 Pa. St. 168, 35 Atl. 702; Hahn's Appeal, 39 Pa. St. 409; Bassett v. Swarts, 17 R. I. 215, 21 Atl. 352; H. C. Behrens Lumber Co. v. Lager, 26 S. Dak. 160, 128 N. W. 698, Ann. Cas. 1913A, 1128; Farmers' &c. Nat. Bank v. Taylor, 91 Tex. 78, 40 S. W. 876; Oriental Hotel Co. v. Griffiths, 88 Tex. 574, 33 S. W. 652, 30 L. R. A. 765, 53 Am. St. 790; Alfree Mfg. Co. v. Henry, 96 Wis. 327, 71 N. W. 370; H. C. Houston Lbr. Co. v. Wetzel, 69 W. Va. 682, 72 S. E. 786; Mathwig v. Mann, 96 Wis. 213, 71 N. W. 105; Lampson v. Bowen, 41 Wis. 484. Under the Kentucky statute of 1909, § 2463, a mechanic's lien takes effect from the commencement of the labor and furnishing of material, provided the lienor files his statement before record of the mortgage. Trust Co. of America v. Casey, 131 Ky. 771, 115 S. W. 780; Scheas v. Boston, 31 Ky. L. 157, 101 S. W. 942. See also Reinhart v. Shutt, 15 Ont. 325.

[93] Courtney v. Insurance Co., 49 Fed. 309, 1 C. C. A. 249; In re Hoyt, Fed. Cas. No. 6805, 3 Biss. (U. S.) 436 (Wisconsin statute); Pacific Mut. L. Ins. Co. v. Fisher, 106 Cal. 224, 39 Pac. 758; Crowell v. Gilmore, 18 Cal. 370, 17 Cal. 194, 13 Cal. 54; Tritch v. Norton, 10 Colo. 337, 15 Pac. 680; Pacific States Sav., Loan &c. Co. v.

Dubois, 11 Idaho 319, 83 Pac. 513; Sioux City Elec. Supply Co. v. Sioux City &c. Elec. R. Co., 106 Iowa 573, 76 N. W. 838; Iowa Mortg. Co. v. Shanquest, 70 Iowa 124, 29 N. W. 820; Humboldt Bldg. Assn. v. Volmering, 20 Ky. L. 899, 47 S. W. 1084 (actual notice to mortgagee); Milner v. Norris, 13 Minn. 455 (Gil. 424); General Fire Extinguisher Co. v. Schwartz Bros. Commission Co., 165 Mo. 171, 65 S. W. 318; Reilly v. Hudson, 62 Mo. 383; Viti v. Dixon, 12 Mo. 479; Keller v. Carterville Bldg. &c. Assn., 71 Mo. App. 465; Western Iron Works v. Montana Pulp &c. Co., 30 Mont. 550, 77 Pac. 413; Johnson v. Puritan Min. &c. Co., 19 Mont. 30, 47 Pac. 337; Murray v. Swanson, 18 Mont. 533, 46 Pac. 441; H. F. Cady Lumber Co. v. Miles (Nebr.), 147 N. W. 210; Chapman v. Brewer, 43 Nebr. 890, 62 N. W. 320, 47 Am. St. 779; Henry &c. Co. v. Fisherdick, 37 Nebr. 207, 55 N. W. 643; Cahn v. Romandorf, 4 Nebr. (Unoff.) 84, 93 N. W. 411; Morris County Bank v. Rockaway Mfg. Co., 14 N. J. Eq. 189; Dunavant v. Caldwell &c. R. Co., 122 N. Car. 999, 29 S. E. 837; Lookout Lumber Co. v. Mansion Hotel &c. R. Co., 109 N. Car. 658, 14 S. E. 35; Woodman v. Richardson, 1 Ohio Cir. Ct. 191, 1 Ohio Cir. Dec. 104; McDonald v. Kelly, 14 R. I. 335; Electric Light &c. Co. v. Bristol Gas &c. Co., 99 Tenn. 371, 42 S. W. 19; Schultze v. Alamo Ice &c. Co., 2 Tex. Civ. App. 236, 21 S. W. 160; Cushwa v. Improvement Loan &c. Assn., 45 W. Va. 490, 32 S. E. 259.

[94] Wetmore v. Marsh, 81 Iowa 677, 47 N. W. 1021; Thomas v. Hoge, 58 Kans. 166, 48 Pac. 844.

[95] Gordon v. Torrey, 15 N. J. 112, 82 Am. Dec. 273.

free from other incumbrances can not affect the priority of mechanics' liens.[96]

Where by statute, a mechanic's lien attaches at the time when the building contract is made, a mortgage given thereafter is subject to the mechanic's lien,[97] although the mortgage is executed and recorded before work is performed or materials delivered.[98] But, to entitle the lien claimant to priority there must have been a contract for the improvement, in existence at the time of the mortgage, and the mortgagee must have had actual or constructive notice thereof.[99]

Lien laws in force at the time of the execution of a mortgage enter into and become a part of the contract; and if these laws provide that certain liens shall be paramount over all other incumbrances, whether prior or subsequent, a mortgagee takes his mortgage subject to such liens as may afterward be acquired under the statute.[1] But laws enacted after the execution of a mortgage can not have the effect of creating a lien superior to such existing mortgage, for such laws

---

[96] Oriental Hotel Co. v. Griffiths, 88 Tex. 574, 33 S. W. 652, 30 L. R. A. 765, 53 Am. St. 790. Where a trust deed in the nature of a mortgage provided that the mortgagor should pay all liens on the property, or that the trustee therein should be reimbursed for such payment, it was held that such provision did not in equity inure to the benefit of mechanic lienors. Cummings v. Consolidated Mineral Water Co., 27 R. I. 195, 61 Atl. 353. Where a written contract for a building loan, duly filed, provided that the mortgage securing the building loan should be a first mortgage, and that an existing mortgage should be satisfied, an oral agreement that the existing mortgage should be paid out of the building loan was not a modification of the written contract, which would subject the mortgage securing the loan to the mechanic's lien. Pennsylvania Steel Co. v. Title Guarantee &c. Co., 193 N. Y. 37, 85 N. E. 820. A claim of a lumber company for lumber used in constructing a house on mortgaged premises can not of itself be deemed an incumbrance within the meaning of a clause in the mortgage authorizing the mortgagee to pay off incumbrances, especially where the lumber company has taken no steps to assert a lien. Provident Mut. Bldg. Loan Assn. v. Shaffer, 2 Cal. App. 216, 83 Pac. 274.

[97] Continental and Commercial Trust and Savings Bank v. Corey Bros. Const. Co., 208 Fed. 976; Interstate Bldg. &c. Assn. v. Ayers, 177 Ill. 9, 52 N. E. 342; Paddock v. Stout, 121 Ill. 571, 13 N. E. 182; Saucier v. Maine Supply &c. Co., 109 Maine 342, 84 Atl. 461; Farnham v. Richardson, 91 Maine 559, 40 Atl. 553; Morse v. Dole, 73 Maine 351; McDowell v. Rockwood, 182 Mass. 150, 65 N. E. 65; Taylor v. Springfield Lumber Co., 3, 61 N. E. 217; Sprague v. McDougall, 172 Mass. 553, 52 N. E. 1077; Carew v. Stubbs, 155 Mass. 549, 30 N. E. 219; Bachelder v. Rand, 117 Mass. 176; Dunklee v. Crane, 103 Mass. 470. See also Phoenix Mut. L. Ins. Co. v. Batchen, 6 Ill. App. 621.

[98] Morse v. Dole, 73 Maine 351; Carew v. Stubbs, 155 Mass. 549, 30 N. E. 219.

[99] Sly v. Pattee, 58 N. H. 102.

[1] Warren v. Sohn, 112 Ind. 213, 13 N. E. 863.

are repugnant to the provisions of the Federal Constitution forbidding the impairment by any state of the obligations of a contract.[2]

Municipal assessments for improvements, which are declared by statute to be a lien, may be paramount to a mortgage of the premises, whether the mortgage be prior or subsequent to the assessment.[3] The lien of a drainage assessment, in Indiana, is subordinate to the lien of a pre-existing mortgage.[4] It is subordinate to a mortgage executed prior to the filing of a petition to enforce such lien.[5]

A mortgage lien will not be postponed in favor of a subsequent lien, on the ground that the judgment was obtained for material and work furnished in making improvements on the mortgaged premises, on the faith and reliance of a verbal agreement made by the mortgagee with the mortgagor to loan him money to make and pay for such improvements.[6]

[2] Yeatman v. King, 2 N. Dak. 421, 51 N. W. 721.

[3] Hand v. Startup, 38 N. J. Eq. 115; Murphy v. Beard, 138 Ind. 560, 38 N. E. 33. The legislature may give an assessment for the construction of drains priority over pre-existing mortgages. Baldwin v. Moroney, 173 Ind. 574, 91 N. E. 3, 30 L. R. A. (N. S.) 761.

[4] Chaney v. State, 118 Ind. 494, 21 N. E. 45; State v. Insurance Co., 117 Ind. 251, 20 N. E. 144; Cook v. State, 101 Ind. 446; Deisner v. Simpson, 72 Ind. 435; Murphy v. Beard, 138 Ind. 560, 38 N. E. 33. The fact that the prior mortgagee had notice of the construction of the ditch and of the pendency of the drainage proceedings is of no importance. Killian v. Andrews, 130 Ind. 579, 30 N. E. 700.

[5] State v. Loveless, 133 Ind. 600, 33 N. E. 622; Pierce v. Ætna L. Insurance Co., 131 Ind. 284, 31 N. E. 68.

[6] Montrose Hardware Co. v. Montrose Inv. Co., 10 Colo. App. 161, 50 Pac. 204.

CHAPTER XIV

VOID AND USURIOUS MORTGAGES

I. *Void Mortgages,* §§ 609a–632
II. *Usury,* §§ 633–663

I. *Void Mortgages*

§ 609a. **Introductory.**—In this chapter it is proposed to treat briefly of some of the circumstances under which a mortgage duly executed and recorded may be declared defective or void. These circumstances are inherent in the transaction itself, and in some form vitiate the consideration of the mortgage. For the most part, they are the same vices which invalidate any contract. Want or failure of consideration, and fraud or usury in it, are not matters peculiar to mortgages; and it is, of course, impossible to treat at length of these matters, which are themselves the subjects of general treatises under the titles of Contracts, Frauds, and Usury. Only adjudications relating especially to mortgages are presented, and these not fully on those points

998

which are common to all contracts. The subject, however, opens one inquiry not presented in other contracts, and that is, whether the law of the place where the mortgaged land is situated, when the contract has been executed in another state or country, should govern as to the law of usury applicable to it; or should govern, too, as to other statutes which may invalidate the contract; and therefore this part of the subject has been examined more fully than its importance would seem to justify, except upon the principle that the importance of questions treated of should be determined by the relative difficulty or uncertainty attending them.

§ 610. **Consideration.**—In general the same defenses may be made to an action on a mortgage, the statute of limitations excepted, that may be made to an action on the debt,—as that it was given for an illegal consideration, or was obtained by duress and fraud.[1] But there are cases which hold that a mortgage shares the same immunity from defenses as the note it secures, where the note has been assigned to a bona fide purchaser for value before maturity.[2] And it has been held that failure or want of consideration as between the parties to a mortgage, can not be set up as a defense by a purchaser of the lands subject to the mortgage, which is in fact part of the consideration, whether he has expressly assumed the mortgage as part of the purchase-money or not.[3]

A mortgage, like every other contract, must be founded on a valuable consideration. The consideration need not be one moving directly from the mortgagee to the mortgagor; but any benefit to the mortgagor or to a stranger, or damage or loss to the mortgagee, rendered or sustained at the request of the mortgagor, is sufficient.[4] An agree-

---

[1] Atwood v. Fisk, 101 Mass. 363, 100 Am. Dec. 124, per Ames, J.; Vinton v. King, 4 Allen (Mass.) 562; Bush v. Cooper, 26 Miss. 599, 59 Am. Dec. 270. See also Jones v. Dannenberg Co., 112 Ga. 426, 37 S. E. 729, 52 L. R. A. 271; Hodson v. Eugene Glass Co., 156 Ill. 397, 40 N. E. 971; Shippen v. Whittier, 117 Ill. 282, 7 N. E. 642; Manley v. Felty, 146 Ind. 194, 45 N. E. 74; Walker v. Thompson, 108 Mich. 686, 66 N. W. 584. See ante §§ 64, 70, and post chapters xxxii, division 3, xxix, division 5.

[2] Carpenter v. Longan, 16 Wall. (U. S.) 271, 21 L. ed. 313; First Nat. Bank v. Flath, 10 N. Dak. 281, 86 N. W. 867; American Sav. Bank &c. Co. v. Helgesen, 67 Wash. 572, 122 Pac. 26, 64 Wash. 54, 116 Pac. 837.

[3] Patten v. Pepper Hotel Co., 153 Cal. 460, 96 Pac. 296.

[4] Rockafellow v. Peay, 40 Ark. 69; Sykes v. Lafferty, 27 Ark. 407; Magruder v. State Bank, 18 Ark. 9; Parsons v. Clark, 132 Mass. 569; Popple v. Day, 123 Mass. 520; Harlan v. Harlan, 20 Pa. St. 303. See also Richardson v. Wren, 11 Ariz. 395, 95 Pac. 124, 16 L. R. A. (N. S.) 190; Thackaberry v. Johnson, 228 Ill. 149, 81 N. E. 828; First Nat. Bank v. Keller, 127 App. Div. 435, 111 N. Y. S. 729; Heilig v. Heilig, 28 Pa. Super. Ct. 396; 1 Selwyn's N. P. 43. See post § 1490.

ment to extend the time of payment of a debt is a sufficient consideration.[5]

In a mortgage of indemnity the liability of the mortgagee to loss
or damage is a sufficient consideration for the mortgage.[6] A liability
to loss on the part of the mortgagee is a consideration for a mortgage
given to secure him against it, as much as is a direct benefit to the
mortgagor, of whatever nature it may be.[7] The real consideration
may always be shown if it becomes material.[8]

It is not necessary that there should be a money consideration.[9] Nor
is it essential that the consideration be valuable, otherwise the absolute control of the owner over his property would be taken away.[10]

A mortgage without a valuable consideration is good as against all
persons except creditors whose claims existed at the time the mortgage
was executed.[11]

Any valuable consideration sufficient to uphold a conveyance is a
sufficient consideration to support a mortgage. The relationship of
blood between a father and child is sufficient. Thus, a mortgage by a
daughter to her father as security for the debts of her deceased husband, though they could not be enforced against her, will be upheld.[12]
But if a father furnishes money to his son for the purchase of land
which is conveyed to the son, without any understanding concerning
the repayment of the purchase-money, the presumption is that the
money was an advancement, and the son did not become his father's
debtor therefor. A mortgage afterward given by the son to the father

[5] Hill v. Yarborough, 62 Ark. 320,
35 S. W. 433; Maclaren v. Percival,
102 N. Y. 675, 6 N. E. 582; Pennsyl-
vania Coal Co. v. Blake, 85 N. Y.
226; Forrester v. Parker, 14 Daly
(N. Y.) 208. See also Franklin
Sav. Bank v. Taylor, 53 Fed. 854,
4 C. C. A. 55; First Nat. Bank v.
Davis, 146 Ill. App. 462; Huffman v.
Darling, 153 Ind. 22, 53 N. E. 939;
Port v. Embree, 54 Iowa 14, 6 N.
W. 83; Morrill v. Skinner, 57 Nebr.
164, 77 N. W. 375; O'Brien v. Fleck-
enstein, 180 N. Y. 350, 73 N. E. 30,
105 Am. St. 768; Dempsey v. Mc-
Kenna, 18 App. Div. 200, 45 N. Y.
S. 973; Farmers' Nat. Bank v.
James, 13 Tex. Civ. App. 550, 36 S.
W. 288. See ante § 461.

[6] Simpson v. Robert, 35 Ga. 180.
See also Griffis v. First Nat. Bank
(Ind. App.), 79 N. E. 230; Kramer
v. Farmers' &c. Bank, 15 Ohio 253;
Lyle v. Ducomb, 5 Binn. (Pa.) 585.

[7] Haden v. Buddensick, 4 Hun (N.
Y.) 649, 49 How. Pr. 241.

[8] Flynn v. Flynn, 68 Mich. 20, 35
N. W. 817. See also In re Farmers'
Supply Co., 170 Fed. 502; Perkins
&c. Co. v. Drew (Ky.), 122 S. W. 526.

[9] De Celis v. Porter, 65 Cal. 3, 2
Pac. 257, 3 Pac. 120.

[10] Campbell v. Tompkins, 32 N. J.
Eq. 170; Farnum v. Burnett, 21 N.
J. Eq. 87; Hill v. Gettys, 135 N.
Car. 373, 47 S. E. 449.

[11] Brooks v. Dalrymple, 12 Allen
(Mass.) 102; Brigham v. Brown, 44
Mich. 59, 6 N. W. 97; Campbell v.
Tompkins, 32 N. J. Eq. 170; Buck-
lin v. Bucklin, 40 N. Y. 141, 1 Abb.
App. Dec. 242.

[12] Ray v. Hallenbeck, 42 Fed. 381.
See also Cates v. Seagraves (Ind.
App.), 105 N. E. 594. But see Welch
v. Graham, 124 N. Y. S. 945.

to secure the repayment of such money is without consideration, and may be void as to his creditors.[13]

If the consideration is valuable it need not be adequate. If there be no fraud or imposition, a mortgage deliberately made for the least consideration, with full knowledge by the mortgagor of all the circumstances, is valid. A recital in the mortgage of a consideration of one dollar, the receipt of which is acknowledged by the mortgagor, prima facie shows a valuable and real consideration, and its actual payment; and, in the absence of opposing proof, such a consideration is sufficient to support the mortgage.[14]

In Maryland, under a provision of statute that no mortgage shall be valid except as between the parties, unless there be indorsed thereon an oath or affirmation of the mortgagee that the consideration in said mortgage is true and bona fide as therein set forth,[15] the want of such affidavit is fatal to the validity of the mortgage when it is assailed by a creditor, or by a subsequent bona fide purchaser.[16] One claiming under the mortgagor with notice stands in no better position in this respect than the mortgagor himself.[17]

As already noticed, a pre-existing debt is a sufficient consideration to support a mortgage as between the parties,[18] though it is not in

---

[13] Higham v. Vanosdol, 125 Ind. 74, 25 N. E. 140.

[14] Lawrence v. McCalmont, 2 How. (U. S.) 426, 11 L. ed. 326; Grimball v. Mastin, 77 Ala. 553; Bolling v. Munchus, 65 Ala. 558. See also First Nat. Bank v. Bennett, 215 Ill. 398, 74 N. E. 405; Nelson v. Hall, 60 N. H. 274; Todd v. Outlaw, 79 N. Car. 235.

[15] Code Pub. Civ. Laws (1912), art. 21, §§ 32, 33. This affidavit may be made at any time before the mortgage is recorded, before any one authorized to take the acknowledgment of a mortgage, and the affidavit shall be recorded with the mortgage.

The affidavit may be made by one of several mortgagees, or by an agent of a mortgagee, who shall, in addition to the above affidavit, make affidavit, to be indorsed on the mortgage, that he is such agent, which affidavit is proof of such agency; and the president or other officer of a corporation, or the executor of the mortgage, may make

such affidavit. Code 1860, art. 20, § 30, p. 137. If the certificate does not show that the agent made oath that he was the agent of the mortgagee, the declaration of the justice of the peace that the affiant appeared before him as the agent of the mortgagee can not be construed as meaning that he made oath that he was the agent. Such a mortgage does not comply with the statute and is fatally defective. Milholland v. Tiffany, 64 Md. 455, 2 Atl. 831. See also Cahoon v. Miers, 67 Md. 573, 11 Atl. 278; Brown v. Stewart, 56 Md. 421. See ante § 366.

[16] Cockey v. Milne, 16 Md. 200.

[17] Phillips v. Pearson, 27 Md. 242.

[18] Evans v. Pence, 78 Ind. 439. See also McLeish v. Hanson, 157 Ill. App. 605; First Nat. Bank v. Davis, 146 Ill. App. 462; Lehrenkrauss v. Bonnell, 199 N. Y. 240, 92 N. E. 637; Hunt v. Hunt, 67 Ore. 178, 134 Pac. 1180; Reed v. Rochford, 62 N. J. Eq. 186, 50 Atl. 70; Sargent v. Cooley, 12 N. Dak. 1, 94 N. W. 576. See ante § 460.

some states sufficient to make the mortgagee a purchaser for value so as to protect him against the rights of third persons.[19]

It has been held that a moral obligation to pay a pre-existing debt is a sufficient consideration to support a mortgage.[20]

§ 611. **Consideration prior or subsequent to the mortgage.**—It is not necessary that any consideration should pass at the time of the execution of the mortgage. That may be either a prior or a subsequent matter. Mortgages are very frequently given to secure existing debts, in which case, though the consideration is generally altogether a past one, the mortgages are valid.[21] A mortgage given to indemnify a surety against loss is founded upon a sufficient consideration, although it is given after the surety has incurred the obligation.[22]

Moreover, the renewal of a note, or extension of the time of payment of a debt, is a sufficient consideration for a mortgage by a third person to secure such debt.[23]

Sometimes, however, a mortgage is made for the purpose of raising money by a subsequent negotiation of the mortgage, or of bonds secured by it, in which case the consideration is subsequent, and the mortgage has no validity until it is transferred to some one for value, or the bonds are negotiated, and it is then subject to any incumbrance intervening before the record of it;[24] but upon the negotiation of the mortgage, or of the bonds secured by it, the mortgage takes effect in

[19] See ante § 460. See also Collins v. Moore, 115 Ga. 327, 41 S. E. 609; Schumpert v. Dillard, 55 Miss. 348; Empire State Trust Co. v. Fisher, 67 N. J. Eq. 602, 60 Atl. 940; Reeves v. Evans (N. J.), 34 Atl. 477; Martin v. Bowen, 51 N. J. Eq. 452, 26 Atl. 823; O'Brien v. Fleckenstein, 86 App. Div. 140, 83 N. Y. S. 499, affirmed 180 N. Y. 350, 73 N. E. 30, 105 Am. St. 768; Wilcox v. Drought, 36 Misc. 351, 73 N. Y. S. 587; Lewis v. Anderson, 20 Ohio St. 281.

[20] Fourth Nat. Bank v. Craig, 1 Nebr. (Unoff.) 849, 96 N. W. 185.

[21] Wright v. Shumway, 1 Biss. (U. S.) 23; Magruder v. State Bank, 18 Ark. 9; Usina v. Wilder, 58 Ga. 178; Evans v. Pence, 78 Ind. 439; Wright v. Bundy, 11 Ind. 398; Adams v. Adams, 70 Iowa 253, 30 N. W. 795; Duncan v. Miller, 64 Iowa 223, 20 N. W. 161 (quoting text); Cooley v.

Hobart, 8 Iowa 358; Moore v. Fuller, 6 Ore. 272, 25 Am. Rep. 524. See also Vaughan v. Marable, 64 Ala. 60; Wright v. Towle, 67 Mich. 255, 34 N. W. 578; Egan v. Fuller, 35 Minn. 515, 29 N. W. 313; Longfellow v. Barnard, 58 Nebr. 612, 79 N. W. 255, 76 Am. St. 117; Reed v. Rochford, 62 N. J. Eq. 186, 50 Atl. 70; Sargent v. Cooley, 12 N. Dak. 1, 94 N. W. 576.

[22] Williams v. Silliman, 74 Tex. 601, 12 S. W. 534. See also Stocking v. Sage, 1 Conn. 519; Doty v. Wilson, 14 Johns. (N. Y.) 378.

[23] Magruder v. State Bank, 18 Ark. 9; Bank of Muskingum v. Carpenter, Wright (Ohio) 729.

[24] De Lancey v. Stearns, 66 N. Y. 157; Schafer v. Reilly, 50 N. Y. 61; Cady v. Jennings, 17 Hun (N. Y.) 213; Johnson v. McCurdy, 83 Pa. St. 282; Mullison's Estate, 68 Pa. St. 212. See ante § 86.

favor of the holder of it or of the bonds.[25] A mortgage for a larger amount than the loan at the time, but so made with a view of covering future loans up to the amount of the mortgage, is not conclusive of fraud, but is open to explanation to show the good faith of the parties to the transaction.[26]

A mortgage given to secure a pre-existing debt of another is invalid unless supported by a new consideration,[27] but if the mortgagee increases his risk in some manner, this will render the mortgagee a purchaser for value.[28]

§ 612. Want or failure of consideration—To and against whom available.

—Want of consideration, or the failure of it, is a good defense for the mortgagor or his grantee in good faith to an action upon the mortgage.[29] But this defense can not be made against an assignee of a note and mortgage who has taken title thereto in good faith before the maturity of the note.[30]

A grantee of land, who, as a part of the consideration for the conveyance to him, has assumed and agreed to pay a mortgage debt on the land so purchased, can not avoid liability on the ground that there was no consideration for the mortgage debt.[31]

A mortgage for a fixed sum, founded on no consideration except an undertaking to furnish goods which were never furnished, can not be enforced, except in the hands of a bona fide assignee for value.[32]

Where a mortgage and accompanying bond are given on no other

---

[25] Roberts v. Bauer, 35 La. Ann. 453; Wood v. Condit, 34 N. J. Eq. 434; Thompson v. Humboldt Safe Deposit &c. Co. (Pa.), 9 Atl. 511.

[26] Allen v. Fuget, 42 Kans. 672, 22 Pac. 725.

[27] Richardson v. Wren, 11 Ariz. 395, 95 Pac. 124, 16 L. R. A. (N. S.) 190; Bell v. Bell, 133 Mo. App. 570, 113 S. W. 667.

[28] Richardson v. Wren, 11 Ariz. 395, 95 Pac. 124, 16 L. R. A. (N. S.) 190.

[29] Brown v. Witts, 57 Cal. 304; Scott v. Magloughlin, 133 Ill. 33, 24 N. E. 1030; Smith v. Newton, 38 Ill. 230; Kramer v. Williamson, 135 Ind. 655, 35 N. E. 388; Conwell v. Clifford, 45 Ind. 392; Cotton v. Graham, 84 Ky. 672, 2 S. W. 674; Hannan v. Hannan, 123 Mass. 441, 25 Am. Rep. 121; Wearse v. Peirce, 24

Pick. (Mass.) 141; Anderson v. Lee, 73 Minn. 397, 76 N. W. 24; Devlin v. Quigg, 44 Minn. 534, 47 N. W. 258; Briggs v. Langford, 107 N. Y. 680, 14 N. E. 502, revg. 35 Hun 667. See also Morris v. Mix, 4 Kans. App. 654, 46 Pac. 58; Bigelow v. Bigelow, 93 Maine 439, 45 Atl. 513; Saunders v. Dunn, 175 Mass. 164, 55 N. E. 893; Anderson v. Lee, 73 Minn. 397, 76 N. W. 24; Eakin v. Shultz, 61 N. J. Eq. 156, 47 Atl. 274; Cassada v. Stabel, 98 App. Div. 600, 90 N. Y. S. 533; Roscoe v. Safford, 61 App. Div. 289, 70 N. Y. S. 309. See post § 1297.

[30] Campbell v. O'Connor, 55 Nebr. 638, 76 N. W. 167.

[31] Stuyvesant v. Western Mtg. &c. Co., 22 Colo. 28, 43 Pac. 144; Lang v. Dietz, 191 Ill. 161, 60 N. E. 841.

[32] Fisher v. Meister, 24 Mich. 447.

consideration than promises of the mortgagee, none of which he fulfils, there is a failure of consideration.[33]

A mortgage given for future credit, if no advances are made upon it and no further credit is given, is without consideration. If taken for that purpose it can not be enforced for a different purpose.[34] The sum named in the deed as the consideration is of no importance when in terms the mortgage secures future advances.[35] It is security to the extent of the amount named in the mortgage, although it purports on its face to be given to secure an amount advanced at the time.[36] It is security for the advances actually made upon it, and for nothing further. When given to secure future advances, or the value of goods to be purchased, it is valid to the extent of the goods sold or the advances made on account of the mortgage, although the mortgagor be in fact insolvent at the time, and becomes bankrupt shortly afterward.[37]

Where a deed of trust secures a sum of money, with interest, "together with the additional sum of ten thousand dollars, which the party of the first part hereby agrees to pay to the party of the second part without interest," and the promise to pay this additional sum, though not void for usury, is a mere bonus for the loan of the money, such promise is without consideration, and can not be enforced.[38]

Under laws which require every agreement or undertaking upon consideration of marriage, except mutual promises to marry, to be in writing, a mortgage made by a wife to secure the performance of her verbal agreement before marriage to pay her husband a certain sum of money, as an equivalent for any right of dower she might have in his property, is without consideration and void, because her agreement is void.[39]

A note and mortgage given in settlement of a claim for damages made by the payee on account of the adultery of the maker with the former's wife, and executed after the cause of action for the tort was barred by the statute, are without consideration and void.[40]

Whatever may be the recitals or statements in a mortgage as to the

[33] Newman v. Overbaugh, 116 N. Y. S. 369.

[34] Mitzner v. Kussel, 29 Mich. 229; Fisher v. Meister, 24 Mich. 447; McDowell v. Fisher, 25 N. J. Eq. 93.

[35] Miller v. Lockwood, 32 N. Y. 293.

[36] Perkins &c. Co. v. Drew (Ky.), 122 S. W. 526.

[37] Marvin v. Chambers, 12 Blatchf.

(Ind.) 495; In re Johnson, Petitioner, 20 R. I. 108, 37 Atl. 531. See also Du Bois v. First Nat. Bank, 43 Colo. 400, 96 Pac. 169.

[38] More v. Calkins, 95 Cal. 435, 30 Pac. 583.

[39] Ennis v. Ennis, 48 Hun (N. Y.) 11.

[40] Peterson v. Breitag, 88 Iowa 418, 55 N. W. 86.

consideration, either party to it may show the truth in regard to it,[41] and a third person having an interest may question the consideration.[42]

§ 612a. **Acts of agents invalidating mortgage.**—When a mortgage has been intrusted to an agent for the purpose of raising money, and the agent uses it for another purpose, either wholly or in part, as, for instance, to secure a judgment against other persons, such use is a misappropriation of it, such as will invalidate the security,[43] unless the assignee be entitled to the protection accorded to a bona fide holder of negotiable paper. If an agent who is authorized only to receive a conveyance of lands to his principal takes a conveyance to himself, and makes a mortgage to one having notice of the fact, it is void as against the principal.[44]

An officer or agent, who takes a mortgage to himself to secure the payment of a debt to his principal, holds it by implication of law as trustee for the principal.[45]

Where a mortgage is made for the purpose of paying existing incumbrances, and the mortgagee intrusts an agent, through whom the application for the loan was made, with a draft for payment of such incumbrances, and the agent absconds with the proceeds of the draft, the mortgage is without consideration and void, though the draft was made payable to the mortgagor, and he indorsed it at the request of the agent. The agent in such case is the mortgagee's agent, and not the agent of the mortgagor.[46]

A landowner applied to an agent, who had previously obtained a loan for him, for a new loan, with which to take up the first mortgage. The agent had at that time collected money for a person for whom he acted in making loans, and converted it to his own use. He sent the application for the loan to this person, who instructed him to make the loan out of the money collected. A note and mortgage were executed by the landowner, and delivered to the agent, who promised to pay the first mortgage. The agent sent the second mortgage to his

[41] Murdock v. Cox, 118 Ind. 266, 20 N. E. 786; Colt v. McConnell, 116 Ind. 249, 19 N. E. 106; Flynn v. Flynn, 68 Mich. 20, 35 N. W. 817; Wimberly v. Wortham (Miss.), 3 So. 459; McAteer v. McAteer, 31 S. Car. 313, 9 S. E. 966.

[42] Mossop v. Creditors, 41 La. Ann. 296, 6 So. 134; Smith v. Conrad, 15 La. Ann. 579.

[43] Craver v. Wilson, 14 Abb. Pr. (N. S.) (N. Y.) 374; Davis v. Bechstein, 69 N. Y. 440, 25 Am. Rep. 218.

[44] Wisconsin Bank v. Morley, 19 Wis. 62.

[45] Rood v. Winlow, Walk. (Mich.) 340. In this case the mortgage was to a county commissioner, the debt being due to the county.

[46] Figley v. Bradshaw, 35 Nebr. 337, 53 N. W. 148.

principal, and soon afterward absconded, leaving the first mortgage unpaid. The second mortgage was held to be without consideration.[47]

Where it appeared that the mortgagor never received any consideration for his mortgage, but that the mortgagee paid the money to a conveyancer a fortnight and more before the mortgage was executed, relying upon the supposed honesty of the conveyancer, and without any evidence that he was authorized to receive it, the conveyancer having run away with the money, the mortgage was held to be invalid.[48]

Where the consideration is paid to one designated in the application as the mortgagor's agent, and such agent never delivers same to his principal, but appropriates it to his own use, the mortgage may nevertheless be enforced.[49]

§ 613. Mortgage under seal importing consideration.—A mortgage under seal implies consideration at common law, and none need be proved, and it is good if it is shown that none was given. Neither courts of law nor equity will allow the consideration to be inquired into for the sake of declaring the instrument void for want of consideration, but they will for the purpose of ascertaining what is due upon it.[50] Also a trust deed under seal imports a consideration without proof.[51]

In New Jersey it is provided by statute that the defense of fraud in the consideration of a deed may be made as fully as if the instrument were not under seal;[52] and in New York a seal affords only presumptive evidence of a sufficient consideration; and this presumption may be rebutted in the same manner and to the same extent as if the instrument were not under seal.[53]

A mortgage imports a consideration, so that the burden is upon the party who sets up the want of consideration to prove that it was

[47] Security Co. v. Kent, 83 Iowa 30, 48 N. W. 1047.

[48] Sergeant v. Martin, 133 Pa. St. 122, 19 Atl. 568.

[49] American Mtg. Co. v. King, 105 Ala. 358, 16 So. 889.

[50] Farnum v. Burnett, 21 N. J. Eq. 87; Calkins v. Long, 22 Barb. (N. Y.) 97; Parker v. Parmele, 20 Johns. (N. Y.) 130, 11 Am. Dec. 632; Maxwell v. Hartmann, 50 Wis. 660, 8 N. W. 103. See also Ambrose v. Drew, 139 Cal. 665, 73 Pac. 543; Cotton v. Graham, 84 Ky. 672, 8 Ky. L. 658, 2 S. W. 647; Forbes v. Mc-Coy, 15 Nebr. 632, 20 N. W. 17; Campbell v. Tompkins, 32 N. J. Eq. 170.

[51] Thackaberry v. Johnson, 228 Ill. 149, 81 N. E. 828.

[52] New Jersey: Compiled Stat. 1907-1910, Vol. 2, p. 2622. See also Feldman v. Gamble, 26 N. J. Eq. 494.

[53] New York: Code Civ. Pro. 1909, § 840. Best v. Thiel, 79 N. Y. 15; Torry v. Black, 58 N. Y. 185; Gray v. Barton, 55 N. Y. 68, 14 Am. Rep. 181; Craver v. Wilson, 47 N. Y. 673, 14 Abb. Pr. (N. S.) 374. See also

made without consideration or was procured by fraud.[54] There is also a presumption that the consideration stated in the mortgage is correctly stated, and very convincing proof is required to rebut this presumption.[55] This presumption is conclusive in favor of a bona fide purchaser of the mortgage.[56]

§ 614. **When mortgage may be made by way of a gift.**—A mortgage may be made by way of gift, when the rights of creditors are not thereby interfered with.[57] When executed and delivered it is as valid as if it were based upon a full consideration. It is not open to the objection that it is a voluntary executory agreement, but may be enforced according to its terms as an executed conveyance.[58]

But the fact that a mortgage is given without consideration may have an important bearing on any disputed question concerning the delivery or recording of it.[59]

A mortgage made by a husband to his wife through a third person to secure her for money which he has obtained from her, and which he is in equity liable to her for, is founded upon a sufficient consideration. Although the husband might have contested the wife's claim, by proof that she had given the money to her husband, so that no liability to account for it arose, yet in the absence of such proof the wife is not required to show that the transaction was not a gift, or to establish the continuance of her husband's equitable liability to her.[60]

The consideration for a mortgage and bond secured thereby is insufficient, where the transaction was intended merely as a gift by a father to his daughter, who is of age, married, and living apart from

Quackenbush v. Mapes, 123 App. Div. 242, 107 N. Y. S. 1047; Hall v. Thomas, 111 N. Y. S. 979.

[54] Commercial Exchange Bank v. McLeod, 67 Iowa 718, 25 N. W. 894, 54 Am. Rep. 36. See also Feldman v. Gamble, 26 N. J. Eq. 494; Best v. Thiel, 79 N. Y. 15.

[55] Wiswall v. Ayres, 51 Mich. 324, 16 N. W. 667. See also Schuster v. Sherman, 37 Nebr. 842, 56 N. W. 707; Burnett v. Wright, 135 N. Y. 543, 32 N. E. 253; Corbett v. Clute, 137 N. Car. 546.

[56] Maxwell v. Hartmann, 50 Wis. 660.

[57] Gale v. Gould, 40 Mich. 515.

[58] Peabody v. Peabody, 59 Ind. 556; Brooks v. Dalrymple, 12 Allen (Mass.) 102; Campbell v. Tompkins, 32 N. J. Eq. 170; Bucklin v. Bucklin, 1 Abb. App. Dec. (N. Y.) 242.

[59] Brigham v. Brown, 44 Mich. 59, 6 N. W. 97.

[60] Cole v. Lee, 45 N. J. Eq. 779, 18 Atl. 854. Per Magie, J.: "It is well settled that, on proof that a husband has received his wife's money, a court of equity will compel him and his representatives to account to her at least for the principal received, and they can only discharge themselves by showing that the husband disposed of the money according to the wife's directions, or that it was a gift to him," citing Jones v. Davenport, 44 N. J. Eq. 33, 13 Atl. 652; Greiner v. Greiner, 35 N. J. Eq. 140; Clawson v. Riley, 34 N. J. Eq. 348; Black v. Black, 30 N. J. Eq. 215; Vreeland v. Schoonmaker, 16 N. J. Eq. 512; Rusling v. Rusling, 47 N. J. L. 1; Horner v. Webster, 33 N. J. L. 387.

him with her husband, and it was not intended he should be called upon to pay it or any interest during his life.[61]

§ 615. Mortgage made for accommodation of another.

—To support a mortgage made for the accommodation of another, there must be a consideration; but it is sufficient that this consideration arises upon the subsequent negotiation of the mortgage by the mortgagee. In states where a pre-existing debt is not regarded as a valid consideration, if the debt of a third person, which is secured by assigning the mortgage, be already incurred, there must be a new and distinct consideration for the obligation incurred by the mortgagor as surety or guarantor of that debt. But if the debt secured be incurred at the same time that the mortgage is given, and this collateral undertaking enters into the inducement to the creditor for giving the credit, then the consideration for such contract is regarded as consideration also for the collateral undertaking by way of mortgage.[62]

A mortgage made for the accommodation of another, upon the understanding that the money should be realized in a particular manner, is not fraudulently misappropriated though the money be obtained in a way different from that which was intended, provided it be negotiated so that the substantial purpose for which it was designed is attained. It is not material that it be negotiated in the precise manner contemplated, unless the interest of the party making it be prejudiced by the manner in which it is used.[63]

It is sufficient consideration for a mortgage to secure the debt or obligation of a third person that the mortgagee agrees to refrain from bringing threatened proceedings to set aside a conveyance of property from the debtor to the mortgagee.[64] So the release of a mortgage has been held to be a valid consideration for the execution of another mortgage by a third person upon a different piece of land.[65]

Where a debt was past due and the creditor demanded payment or security, the tender by the debtor and the acceptance by the creditor of the mortgage of a third person is sufficient consideration for such mortgage, even though there is no release of the debtor or express extension of time of payment.[66]

---

[61] Welch v. Graham, 124 N. Y. S. 945.

[62] Davidson v. King, 51 Ind. 224. See ante § 458.

[63] Wood v. Condit, 34 N. J. Eq. 434; Jacobsen v. Dodd, 32 N. J. Eq. 403; Duncan v. Gilbert, 29 N. J. L. 521.

[64] First Nat. Bank v. Keller, 127 App. Div. 435, 111 N. Y. S. 729.

[65] Englert v. Dale, 25 N. Dak. 587, 142 N. W. 169.

[66] Perkins v. Trinity Realty Co., 69 N. J. Eq. 723, 61 Atl. 167.

§ 616. Estoppel to deny consideration.—A mortgagor may be estopped to deny a consideration for his mortgage. He is not, however, estopped from showing a failure or want of consideration for the note secured by the mortgage as against the mortgagee, except by his own representations, or those made by others with his knowledge and consent.[67] Thus it is good defense to foreclosure that the mortgagee had no title to another tract than that mortgaged, but which he conveyed to the mortgagor with a warranty and for the purchase-price of which the mortgage was given.[68] But this defense can not be taken against an assignee for value before maturity.[69]

It is held that the assignee of a mortgage or other security collateral to negotiable paper takes the collateral subject to defenses in a court of equity, although the paper secured is not subject to defenses at law.[70]

Such mortgage, though void between the original parties, is valid in the hands of a bona fide assignee without notice of the illegal consideration for which it was given.[71]

It is held in Illinois that a grantor in a trust deed may make any defense against foreclosure by an assignee of the note and trust deed, although assignment was made before maturity of the note, that he can make to a foreclosure proceeding instituted by the original owner of the note and trust deed.[72]

[67] Jones v. Jones, 20 Iowa 388; Wearse v. Peirce, 24 Pick. (Mass.) 141. See also Nelson v. McPike, 24 Ind. 60.

[68] Smith v. Newton, 38 Ill. 230.

[69] Stilwell v. Kellogg, 14 Wis. 461; Cornell v. Hichens, 11 Wis. 353. See also Carpenter v. Longan, 16 Wall. (U. S.) 271, 21 L. ed. 313; Campbell v. O'Connor, 55 Nebr. 638, 76 N. W. 167; First Nat. Bank v. Flath, 10 N. Dak. 281, 86 N. W. 867; Wright v. Pipe Line Co., 101 Pa. St. 204, 47 Am. Rep. 701. But see Walker v. Thompson, 108 Mich. 686, 66 N. W. 584, where the note was nonnegotiable.

[70] Towner v. McClelland, 110 Ill. 542; Miller v. Larned, 103 Ill. 562; Equitable Securities Co. v. Talbert, 49 La. Ann. 1393, 22 So. 762; Butler v. Slocomb, 33 La. Ann. 170, 39 Am. Rep. 265; Bacon v. Abbott, 137 Mass. 397; Baily v. Smith, 14 Ohio St. 396, 84 Am. Dec. 385; Dearman v. Trimmier, 26 S. Car. 506, 2 S. E. 501.

[71] Taylor v. Page, 6 Allen (Mass.) 86; Brigham v. Potter, 14 Gray (Mass.) 522; Cazet v. Field, 9 Gray (Mass.) 329; Earl v. Clute, 2 Abb. App. Dec. (N. Y.) 1, and cases cited.

In North Carolina: It is provided by statute that no conveyance or mortgage, made to secure the payment of a debt, shall be void in the hands of a purchaser for value without notice, for the reason that consideration of the debt was forbidden by law. Pell's Revisal of 1908, Vol. 1, § 965. This statute applies to usurious mortgages. Coor v. Spicer, 65 N. Car. 401. See also Cattle v. Cleaves, 70 Maine 256; Doe v. Burnham, 31 N. H. 426; Norris v. Langley, 19 N. H. 423; Cowing v. Altman, 71 N. Y. 435, 27 Am. Rep. 70; Campbell v. Jones, 2 Tex. Civ. App. 263, 21 S. W. 723.

[72] Lauf v. Cahill, 231 Ill. 220, 83 N. E. 155.

Sometimes the mortgagee may, in effect, give a better title than he himself holds. "In the case of a conveyance of real estate to defraud creditors, the grantee can not hold, but one who takes it from him without notice may. But the law goes further in favor of commerce, and gives a high degree of character and honor to bills of exchange and promissory notes in the hands of an indorsee without actual or constructive notice of anything affecting their validity or credit."[73] But this rule does not apply to notes which are by statute made absolutely null and void, as notes made in violation of statutes against usury and gaming sometimes are.[74]

A certificate made by a mortgagor at the time of giving the mortgage, that there is no defense to it, estops him as against a purchaser of the mortgage from setting up fraud or want of consideration.[75] A married woman is estopped by such certificate equally with any other mortgagor.[76] Admissions which estop the husband also estop his wife who has joined in the mortgage to release her dower and homestead rights.[77]

A mortgagor may be estopped from denying the validity of his mortgage by reason of representations made with his knowledge and assent representing its validity, or based upon the assumption of its validity. Thus, where a trustee of a savings bank, to make up a deficiency in its assets caused by a loss for which the trustees were supposed to be personally liable, executed a mortgage which was assigned to the bank, he was not allowed to set up the defense of want of consideration, inasmuch as the mortgage was with his knowledge and assent reported to the banking department, and represented to the depositors of the bank as a portion of its assets, and the bank was upon the strength thereof, and of other similar securities, permitted to continue business.[78]

A note and mortgage deposited in escrow, and afterward fraudulently taken and put in circulation, without the terms and conditions of the deposit having been complied with, are doubtless void in the

[73] Per Shaw, C. J., in Cazet v. Field, 9 Gray (Mass.) 329.

[74] Kendall v. Robertson, 12 Cush. (Mass.) 156; Bowyer v. Bampton, 2 Stra. 1155. See also Bozeman v. Allen, 48 Ala. 512; Shank v. Washington Exch. Bank, 124 Ga. 508, 52 S. E. 621; Glenn v. Farmers' Bank, 70 N. Car. 191; Brisbane v. Lestarjette, 1 Bay (S. Car.) 113.

[75] Schenck v. O'Neill, 23 Hun (N. Y.) 209; Hutchison v. Gill, 91 Pa.

St. 253. The court in the latter case remark that it is unnecessary to say what would be the effect of actual fraud in procuring the "no defense" paper. See also Silver v. Kent, 105 Fed. 840.

[76] Payne v. Burnham, 62 N. Y. 69; Smyth v. Munroe, 19 Hun (N. Y.) 550.

[77] Casler v. Byers, 129 Ill. 657, 22 N. E. 507.

[78] Best v. Theil, 79 N. Y. 15.

hands of a purchaser or assignee for value without notice. In such case the mortgage never has a legal existence, and the rules of commercial paper have no application to the note accompanying it, although it be negotiable in form.[9']

§ 617. **Effect of illegality of consideration.**—Illegality of consideration avoids a mortgage, whether it consist in a violation of the common law or of a statute.[1] But knowledge on the part of the mortgagee that the mortgage-money is to be used for an illegal purpose is no defense to foreclosure proceedings.[2]

The consideration of a note may be so far illegal as to invalidate it, even in the hands of a bona fide holder, where such note is given in violation of the express terms of a statute.[3]

A mortgage given to secure a debt made illegal by statute, as, for instance, a debt incurred for intoxicating liquors illegally sold to the mortgagor, can not be enforced; and such a mortgage is invalid although not given to the seller of the liquors, but at his request to a creditor of his, who knew that the consideration was illegal.[4] But if the mortgage be given for an illegal consideration, and the consideration not being performed the mortgagee enters to foreclose, and keeps possession till foreclosure is complete, he then has an absolute title, and the value of the land is applied by operation of law to the payment of the debt secured by the mortgage. The land is then irretrievably gone, unless the law be such that the illegal consideration, when paid, can be recovered back, not merely in money but in land. It has been held that a payment in land for intoxicating liquors illegally sold could not be recovered back, and therefore that, upon the foreclosure of a mortgage for such a debt, the land can not be recovered by the mortgagor.[5]

---

[70] Cressinger v. Dessenburg, 42 Mich. 580, 4 N. W. 269; Powell v. Conant, 33 Mich. 396; Burson v. Huntington, 21 Mich. 415, 4 Am. Rep. 497; Chipman v. Tucker, 38 Wis. 43, 20 Am. Rep. 1; Andrews v. Thayer, 30 Wis. 228; Tisher v. Beckwith, 30 Wis. 55, 11 Am. Rep. 546; Walker v. Ebert, 29 Wis. 194. See ante § 87.

[1] Gibert v. Holmes, 64 Ill. 548. See also Dixon v. Cuyler, 27 Ga. 248; Henry v. State Bank, 131 Iowa 97, 107 N. W. 1034; Sheldon v. Pruessner, 52 Kans. 579, 35 Pac. 201, 22 L. R. A. 709; Brigham v. Potter, 14 Gray (Mass.) 522; Dier-

kes v. Wideman, 143 Mich. 181, 106 N. W. 735; Corbett v. Clute, 137 N. Car. 546, 50 S. E. 216; Pierson v. Green, 69 S. Car. 559, 48 S. E. 624.

[2] Hines v. Union Savings Bank &c. Co., 120 Ga. 711, 48 S. E. 120.

[3] Kuhl v. M. Gally Univ. Press Co., 123 Ala. 452, 26 So. 535, 82 Am. St. 135; Wyatt v. Wallace, 67 Ark. 575, 55 S. W. 1105; Irwin v. Marquett, 26 Ind. App. 383, 59 N. E. 38, 84 Am. St. 297.

[4] Baker v. Collins, 9 Allen (Mass.) 253. See also Brigham v. Potter, 14 Gray (Mass.) 522.

[5] McLaughlin v. Cosgrove, 99 Mass. 4.

A mortgage and note given to secure wagering contracts, such as the purchase of stocks on margins without any intention to complete the purchase by an actual delivery and receipt of the stocks and the payment of the price therefore, are illegal and void, and a bill in equity will lie to restrain a foreclosure of the mortgage and compel the surrender and cancelation of the note.[6]

A mortgage by a citizen of Tennessee, executed to a citizen of Kentucky after the proclamation of the President declaring the state of Tennessee to be in a state of insurrection, and forbidding all intercourse with its inhabitants, was held void, although the land was situate in the state of Kentucky.[7] A mortgage given in Tennessee during the Civil War, in consideration of a loan in Confederate treasury notes, was after the war held void, on the ground that the consideration of the contract was illegal, being notes issued by an unlawful confederation of states. Such contracts are against public policy, and the courts will not lend their aid to enforce them.[8]

But on the contrary such a mortgage was sustained in Alabama, on the ground that it was valid under the de facto government existing when it was executed.[9]

The fact that a note and mortgage given to secure it were executed in consideration of the mortgagee settling a criminal prosecution against the mortgagor's husband may be shown as a defense to the foreclosure of the mortgage so given, even in the hands of a bona fide holder of such note for value, before due, and without notice.[10]

Where a note secured by a mortgage has been transferred for the sole purpose of evading the payment of taxes, such facts may be pleaded as a defense in a suit to foreclose the mortgage.[11] But an answer alleging that the note and mortgage were taken in the name of the plaintiff in order to enable the real owner to evade taxation, presents no issue and should be stricken out.[12] A party is not precluded from availing himself of a defense of this character by the fact that the paper in controversy is under seal.[13] Where the consideration is

[6] Rice v. Winslow, 182 Mass. 273, citing Lyons v. Coe, 177 Mass. 382, 59 N. E. 59; Harvey v. Merrill, 150 Mass. 1, 22 N. E. 49; Sampson v. Shaw, 101 Mass. 145. See also Dixon v. Cuyler, 27 Ga. 248; Thompson v. Brady, 182 Mass. 321, 65 N. E. 419.

[7] Hyatt v. James, 2 Bush (Ky.) 463, 92 Am. Dec. 505.

[8] Stillman v. Looney, 3 Cold. (Tenn.) 20.

[9] Micou v. Ashurst, 55 Ala. 607; Scheible v. Bacho, 41 Ala. 423.

[10] Jones v. Dannenberg, 112 Ga. 426, 37 S. E. 729, 52 L. R. A. 271.

[11] Sheldon v. Pruessner, 52 Kans. 579, 35 Pac. 201, 22 L. R. A. 709.

[12] Crowns v. Forest Land Co., 99 Wis. 103, 74 N. W. 546.

[13] Calfee v. Burgess, 3 W. Va. 274.

partly legal and partly illegal, the mortgage will be sustained to the extent of the legal consideration if it is separable from the illegal.[14]

§ **618. Contrary to public policy.**—If land be conveyed to one absolutely as security for a sum of money to be due him upon his doing an unlawful act, as, for instance, procuring witnesses to testify to a certain state of facts in behalf of the grantor, the transaction is not a mortgage. The title is not divested upon the grantor's failure to perform the illegal stipulation, but is absolute in him, and the grantor can not recover it either in law or in equity.[15]

A mortgage and note given in consideration that the mortgagee shall not oppose his debtor's discharge in insolvency, and for an assignment of the creditor's claim against the insolvent, which was of the same amount as the note, the estimated value of which was only one-sixth of its face, are void as against public policy.[16]

A mortgage executed in consideration that the mortgagee would use his efforts to obtain a nolle prosequi to an indictment pending against the mortgagor, is against public policy and void.[17] So is one given in composition of a felony, or of a promise not to prosecute for a crime of lower degree than a felony.[18]

Where a wife executes a mortgage to raise money with which to compromise a criminal prosecution against her husband, the amount so paid is not recoverable at a foreclosure sale when the mortgagee knew the object for which the money was raised and assisted in such compromise.[19] But it is no defense to a mortgage that it was given to stop a threatened criminal prosecution, unless an agreement not to prosecute if the mortgage was given is shown.[20]

A note and mortgage given in lieu or in renewal of a note and mortgage, void for this reason are equally void, even in the hands of an assignee for value but with notice of the illegality of the consideration.[21] A mortgage given by a cashier of a bank to a surety on his

---

[14] Lepper v. Conradt, 15 Wyo. 394, 89 Pac. 575.

[15] Patterson v. Donner, 48 Cal. 369.

[16] Benicia Agricultural Works v. Estes (Cal.), 32 Pac. 938; Estudillo v. Meyerstein, 72 Cal. 317, 13 Pac. 869; Rice v. Maxwell, 13 Sm. & M. (Miss.) 289, 53 Am. Dec. 85; Bell v. Leggett, 7 N. Y. 176.

[17] Crowder v. Reed, 80 Ind. 1; Wildey v. Collier, 7 Md. 273, 61 Am. Dec. 346.

[18] Small v. Williams, 87 Ga. 681, 13 S. E. 589; Atwood v. Fisk, 101 Mass. 363, 100 Am. Dec. 124; Pearce v. Wilson, 111 Pa. St. 14, 2 Atl. 99, 56 Am. Rep. 243; Collins v. Blantern, 2 Wils. 341.

[19] Pierson v. Green, 69 S. Car. 559, 48 S. E. 624.

[20] Moyer v. Dodson, 212 Pa. 344, 61 Atl. 937.

[21] Pierce v. Kibbee, 51 Vt. 559.

bond for the amount paid by the surety in settlement of a civil liability growing out of the cashier's defalcations, there being no agreement not to prosecute the cashier criminally, does not contravene public policy.[22]

A mortgage or a deed in the nature of a mortgage, given to secure the performance of a contract contrary to the policy of the law, will not be enforced by a court of equity; such, for instance, as a gambling contract,[23] or a contract which is subject to the objection of champerty.[24] If the mortgagee had no knowledge of the illegal transaction, and no connection with it except to loan money to a surety on the illegal contract to pay a judgment obtained against him, the mortgage is not invalid.[25]

A mortgage given upon lands held by a settler under the pre-emption act, before he has entered the lands at the landoffice, is void under the Act of Congress forbidding any conveyance before such entry.[26] A mortgage executed to secure a loan and duly recorded is not void on the ground of public policy because it was taken in the name of the lender's agent, and by him assigned to the lender, the assignment being withheld from record in order that the lender might thereby escape taxation thereon.[27]

§ 619. Who may take advantage of the illegality.—As a general rule contracts prohibited by statute are void, and courts will neither enforce them nor aid in the recovery of money paid in pursuance of them. "The meaning of the familiar maxim, In pari delicto potior est conditio defendentis, is simply that the law leaves the parties exactly where they stand; not that it prefers the defendant to the plaintiff, but that it will not recognize a right of action, founded on the illegal contract, in favor of either party against the other. They must settle their own questions in such cases without the aid of the courts."[28] The principle in such cases is the same in equity as at law; while the courts will not aid the mortgagee to enforce payment of an illegal mortgage, they will not aid the mortgagor to obtain a cancelation of the incum-

---

[22] Moog v. Strang, 69 Ala. 98.

[23] Krake v. Alexander, 86 Va. 206, 9 S. E. 991. See also Dixon v. Cuyler, 27 Ga. 248.

[24] Gilbert v. Holmes, 64 Ill. 548. See also Muir v. Hamilton, 152 Cal. 634, 93 Pac. 857.

[25] Krake v. Alexander, 86 Va. 206, 9 S. E. 991.

[26] Brewster v. Madden, 15 Kans. 249. As to mortgage of cemetery lot, Lautz v. Buckingham, 4 Lans. (N. Y.) 484. See ante § 176.

[27] Callicott v. Allen, 31 Ind. App. 561, 67 N. E. 196; Thorp v. Smith, 65 N. J. Eq. 400, 54 Atl. 412.

[28] Atwood v. Fisk, 101 Mass. 363, 100 Am. Dec. 124, per Mr. Justice Ames.

brance. Both parties are left without remedy when the contract is one that is prohibited as immoral or against public policy.[29]

But there are cases which hold that in the interest of the public a defendant may set up the defense of illegality to an action on an illegal contract, although such defense amounts to an allegation of his own turpitude.[30]

When the illegal consideration has been paid to one of two persons interested in it, the court will not aid the other to recover his share of it; it does not enforce the sentiment of "honor among thieves."[31]

In a case in Nevada this principle was carried to the extent of declaring void a mortgage given for a full, adequate, and legal consideration, merely because the mortgagee had the mortgage given to a nonresident of the state for the purpose of enabling him to escape taxation upon the amount of the loan. Although the revenue laws of the state contained no prohibition of such a contract, the mortgage was nevertheless declared illegal, as against the policy of the law, and the court refused, for that reason only, to enforce it against the mortgagor.[32] And it was held, moreover, that it was immaterial that the mortgagee afterward paid the full amount of taxes upon the money loaned. The fraud, it was said, consisted in the turpitude of the motive which influenced the mortgagee at the time of the execution of the mortgage.[33]

---

[29] Snyder v. Snyder, 51 Md. 77; James v. Roberts, 18 Ohio 548. But see Sackner v. Sackner, 39 Mich. 39. In Cox v. Wightman, 4 Hun (N. Y.) 799, the principle was applied to a case where a mortgage had been assigned for the purpose of escaping taxation. The assignor, or his administrator, was not allowed to get back the mortgage and bond, though transferred without consideration.

[30] See also McMullen v. Hoffman, 174 U. S. 639, 43 L. ed. 1117, 19 Sup. Ct. 839; William Wilcox Mfg. Co. v. Brazos, 74 Conn. 208, 50 Atl. 722; Jones v. Dannenberg, 112 Ga. 426, 37 S. E. 729, 52 L. R. A. 271; Fields v. Brown, 188 Ill. 111, 58 N. E. 977; Pinney v. First Nat. Bank, 68 Kans. 223, 75 Pac. 119; Hardie v. Scheen, 110 La. 612, 34 So. 707; Somers v. Johnson, 70 N. J. L. 695, 59 Atl. 224; Culp v. Love, 127 N. Car. 457, 37 S. E. 476; Burck v. Abbott, 22 Tex. Civ. App. 216, 54 S. W. 314;

Haddock v. Salt Lake City, 23 Utah 521, 65 Pac. 491.

[31] Woodworth v. Bennett, 43 N. Y. 273, 3 Am. Rep. 706. In the language of Lord Chief Justice Wilmot: "You shall not stipulate for iniquity; all writers upon our law agree in this, no polluted hand shall touch the pure foundations of justice; whoever is a party to an unlawful contract, if he hath once paid the money stipulated to be paid in pursuance thereof, he shall not have the help of a court to fetch it back again; you shall not have a right of action when you come into a court of justice in this unclean manner to recover it back. Procul O! procul este profani." Collins v. Blantern, 2 Wils. 341.

[32] Drexler v. Tyrrell, 15 Nev. 114.

[33] But the cases cited in support of the decision are cases in which the consideration of the contract, as between the parties themselves, was either illegal or contravened

Gaming contracts,[34] contracts made on Sunday, contracts of champerty and maintenance, contracts made in composition of felony, and many others of like nature, might be mentioned as examples. But sometimes contracts are prohibited for the mere protection of one of the parties against an undue advantage which the other party is supposed to possess over him. In such cases the parties are not regarded as being equally guilty, and so the rule is not deemed applicable, though both have violated the law.[35] As an example of this kind, a usurious contract is mentioned, which may be void as to the mortgagee while valid as to the mortgagor.

In accordance with this distinction, a law providing that school funds shall be loaned only upon unincumbered real estate does not render void a mortgage taken in violation of this statute by the officer charged with making the loan. The mortgagor can not claim that such a mortgage is illegal and unenforcible against him.[36]

And so under the national banking law a mortgage for a loan upon real estate security, though impliedly prohibited, is valid between the parties.[37]

A statute providing that a trustee, before entering upon the discharge of his duties, shall give a bond for the faithful discharge of his duties, does not prevent the legal estate vesting in him under a mortgage or deed of trust regularly executed.[38]

---

the policy of the law. In the case before the court, however, there was nothing illegal in the contract as between the parties. It was a contract they were not prohibited from making, and there was a full and complete consideration for it. The only taint in the transaction was the intended fraud upon the revenue laws of the state. For this intended fraud the court upheld the mortgagor in refusing payment of the mortgage; they upheld him in a monstrous injustice, when the revenue laws of the state provided proper and ample punishment for an evasion of them by criminal prosecution. The decision is regarded as wrong in principle. This decision is also regarded as incorrect by Learned, J., in Nichols v. Weed Sewing Machine Co., 27 Hun (N. Y.) 200, affd. 97 N. Y. 650.

[34] As to the effect of a mortgage to secure such contracts under the statutes of New York, see Luetch-

ford v. Lord, 57 Hun (N. Y.) 572, 11 N. Y. S. 597.

[35] Deming v. State, 23 Ind. 416. Cowles v. Raguet, 14 Ohio 38. See also Raguet v. Roll, 7 Ohio 77, 4 Ohio 419; McQuade v. Rosecrans, 36 Ohio St. 442. An important element in this case was, that Raguet not only agreed not to prosecute, but agreed to use his influence to prevent a prosecution. The Ohio cases go further than this general rule would warrant because they hold that, in an action by a mortgagee against the mortgagor to recover possession of the mortgaged lands, the fact that such mortgage was given to compound a felony is no defense. Williams v. Englebrecht, 37 Ohio St. 383.

[36] Deming v. State, 23 Ind. 416. See also Mann v. Best, 62 Mo. 491.

[37] National Bank v. Matthews, 98 U. S. 621, 25 L. ed. 188.

[38] Gardner v. Brown, 21 Wall. (U. S.) 36, 22 L. ed. 527.

§ 620. Where part of consideration legal and part illegal.—The mortgage may be upheld for such part of the consideration as was free from the taint of illegality, when the consideration of a mortgage is made up of several distinct transactions, some of which are legal and others are not, and the one can be separated with certainty from the other.[39] Thus a mortgage undertaking to secure two or more notes has been upheld as security for a legal note, though invalid as to an illegal note.[40]

In equity a mortgage securing a debt usurious in part, but valid in part, may be upheld for the latter, although in terms the statute of usury makes the obligation void altogether. Thus, where the maker of such a mortgage comes into equity, and asks that such a mortgage be surrendered, as a cloud on the title to his lands, and that the court will so direct, although it can not require him to pay the usurious debt, or any part of it, it may require him to pay the other part of it which at law and in equity he owes. The court will require him to do equity before it will administer the relief asked for.[41] A mortgage fraudulently made to include a sum not due or which had been paid, the consideration being entire, and the purpose of the transaction being to defraud creditors, is absolutely void.[42] If the sum secured be made up in part of a sum inadvertently included and without fraudulent intent, then the mortgage may be valid for the actual debt secured, and void as to the rest.[43] But in case the legal and the illegal parts of the consideration are inseparable, the illegal part taints the whole.[44] So, where the note secured by the mortgage is based partly on a legal and partly on an illegal consideration, it would seem to be void as a whole.[45]

---

[39] Corbett v. Woodward, 5 Sawyer (U. S.) 403; Warren v. Chapman, 105 Mass. 87; Carradine v. Wilson, 61 Miss. 573; Carleton v. Woods, 28 N. H. 290; Feldman v. Gamble, 26 N. J. Eq. 494; Williams v. Fitzhugh, 37 N. Y. 444 (applied to usury); Cook v. Barnes, 36 N. Y. 520; McCraney v. Alden, 46 Barb. (N. Y.) 272; Yundt v. Roberts, 5 Serg. & R. (Pa.) 139; Shaw v. Carpenter, 54 Vt. 155, 41 Am. Rep. 837; Robinson v. Bland, 2 Burr. 1077. See also In re Stowe, 6 Nat. Bankr. Reg. 431, Fed. Cas. No. 13513; Loud v. Hamilton (Tenn. Ch.), 51 S. W. 140, 48 L. R. A. 400; Pierson v. Green, 69 S. Car. 559, 48 S. E. 624; Lepper v. Conradt, 15 Wyo. 394, 89 Pac. 575. Contra, Denny v. Dana,

2 Cush. (Mass.) 160, 48 Am. Dec. 655.

[40] Morris v. Way, 16 Ohio 469.

[41] Williams v. Fitzhugh, 37 N. Y. 444.

[42] McQuade v. Rosecrans, 36 Ohio St. 442.

[43] Weeden v. Hawes, 10 Conn. 50.

[44] Reagan v. First Nat. Bank, 157 Ind. 623, 61 N. E. 575, 62 N. E. 701; Crowder v. Reed, 80 Ind. 1.

[45] Brigham v. Potter, 14 Gray (Mass.) 522; Bick v. Seal, 45 Mo. App. 475; McQuade v. Rosecrans, 36 Ohio St. 442. But see Shaw v. Carpenter, 54 Vt. 155, 41 Am. Rep. 837, holding that the mortgage is valid to the extent to which the consideration for the note was legal.

When part of the consideration of a note and mortgage is the suppression of a criminal prosecution against the mortgagor, he can avail himself of this fact as a defense to a suit to enforce either of them; although the prosecution is for an embezzlement of funds, by which the mortgagor not only committed a crime but incurred a debt. The effect upon the mortgage in such case is the same as if the whole consideration had been illegal. The illegal part can not be separated from the legal.[46]

§ 621. **Mortgage valid in part and void in part.**—A mortgage may be valid in part and void in part.[47]

A mortgage of land and slaves, executed while slavery was recognized, was vitiated by the abolition of slavery only as to the lien upon the slaves.[48]

Where a bond of defeasance was assigned by a debtor to a creditor, who paid the debt to secure which the conveyance was made, whereupon the land was conveyed to him, and he gave the debtor a new bond conditioned for the reconveyance of the land upon the payment of the amount of both debts, the transaction, so far as the debt of the second creditor was secured, was void under the insolvent laws; but the conveyance being a valid security for the first debt, the land was a valid security in the hands of the second creditor for the amount paid by him to the first creditor.[49]

A mortgage given by a third person at the solicitation of another to secure his debts for a specific purpose, as, for instance, the purchase-price of certain goods about to be sold him, if fraudulently made to cover in part an existing indebtedness, is void as to such part of it, though valid as to the part used for the purpose intended. Although the mortgagee has taken such mortgage in good faith, if he has not put himself in any worse position in regard to the old indebtedness, and if he had not done anything or parted with anything in reliance upon the mortgage, he can not claim that the surety should suffer for the fraud by reason of negligence in executing the mortgage which rendered the fraud possible.[50]

A mortgage made without fraudulent intent for a larger amount

[46] Atwood v. Fisk, 101 Mass. 363, 100 Am. Dec. 124, per Ames, J.

[47] Leeds v. Cameron, 3 Sum. (U. S.) 488; McMurray v. Connor, 2 Allen (Mass.) 205; Rood v. Winslow, 2 Dougl. (Mich.) 68, Walk. (Mich.) 340; Johnson v. Richardson, 38 N. H. 353.

[48] Lavillebeuvre v. Frederic, 20 La. Ann. 374.

[49] Judd v. Flint, 4 Gray (Mass.) 557.

[50] Smith v. Osborn, 33 Mich. 410.

than the mortgagor's actual indebtedness is not fraudulent, but may be enforced to the extent of such actual debt.[51]

§ 622. **Evidence—Burden of proof.**—The burden of proof is upon the party who sets up the defense of want of consideration or illegality of it, to make it out by clear and strong proof.[52] A mortgage in due form and duly executed implies a valid consideration. But when the consideration of a mortgage is questioned by a creditor of the mortgagor having an interest, as voluntary and fraudulent as to him, the burden of proving a valuable consideration rests upon the mortgagee. When the consideration is admitted or established by proof, the burden of proving that the mortgage is fraudulent in fact is upon the creditor who assails it.[53]

Evidence of the payment of interest upon a mortgage is admissible to show its validity when this is disputed.[54]

The burden of proof as to the consideration may be cast upon the complainant by the answer.[55] Thus where the mortgagor alleges in a verified answer that there was a total want of consideration for the note secured, the burden of proving consideration is on the plaintiff.[56] But the burden is shifted where the mortgage notes import a consideration on their face.[57]

§ 622a. **Construction of statute declaring a mortgage void.**—Under a statute which declares a mortgage void if executed upon land situated in more than one county, its invalidity can not be cured by subsequent legislation repealing this provision, or consolidating the counties in such a way as to bring the mortgaged lands within one county. The word void used in the statute does not mean voidable.[58]

§ 623. **Mortgage for debt contracted on Sunday.**—The statutes forbidding the transaction of business on Sunday have the effect to render void all contracts executed upon that day.[1] But a mortgage

---

[51] Adams v. Niemann, 46 Mich. 135, 8 N. W. 719.
[52] Stuart v. Phelps, 39 Iowa 14; Brigham v. Potter, 14 Gray (Mass.) 522; Feldman v. Gamble, 26 N. J. Eq. 494. See also Langley v. Fitzgerald, 43 Colo. 301, 95 Pac. 923; Waymire v. Shipley, 52 Ore. 464, 97 Pac. 807.
[53] First Nat. Bank v. Bennett, 215 Ill. 398, 74 N. E. 405, revg. Bennett v. First Nat. Bank, 117 Ill. App. 382; Cohn v. Ward, 32 W. Va. 34, 9 S. E. 41.

[54] Floyd v. Morrison, 40 Iowa 188.
[55] Otis v. McCaskill, 51 Fla. 516, 41 So. 458; Mayo v. Hughes, 51 Fla. 495, 40 So. 499.
[56] Chesser v. Chesser (Fla.), 64 So. 357.
[57] Chambers v. Powell (Ala.), 39 So. 919.
[58] Denny v. McCown, 34 Ore. 47, 54 Pac. 952.
[1] Under the Massachusetts statute of 1791, prohibiting the doing of any manner of labor, business, or work between the midnight pre-

executed on Sunday is not void either at common law or under a statutory prohibition of the exercise on that day of acts in the "ordinary calling" of citizens.[2] And under a statute simply prohibiting the performance of work and labor on Sunday, a deed of trust or mortgage executed on that day is not void.[3]

It has sometimes been said that such contracts, being immoral and illegal only as to the time they are entered into, may be affirmed upon a subsequent day, and thus made valid.[4] But it seems incorrect to say that a mere ratification can impart legal efficacy to a contract which has no legal existence.[5] So it has been held that payment on a secular day of interest on a note, void because made on Sunday, does not in itself amount to a new promise to pay the money due.[6]

The logical theory would seem to be, that nothing but an express promise subsequently made, founded upon the consideration emanating from the illegal contract, will avail to support an action having that consideration for its basis. Upon this theory it was held that, although a promissory note made and delivered on Sunday for a loan of money made at the time is illegal and can not be enforced, yet the obligation to return the money is a sufficient consideration to support a mortgage subsequently given to secure it. The mortgage constitutes a new promise founded on such obligation, and having no taint of illegality, such as the note had, it may be enforced.[7]

But a mortgage executed on Sunday without the knowledge of the

---

ceding and the sunset of the Lord's day, and declaring void the execution of any civil process from the midnight preceding to the midnight following that day, it was held that a mortgage executed, acknowledged and· recorded after sunset on Sunday evening was not void. Meader v. White, 66 Maine 90, 22 Am. Rep. 551; Tracy v. Jenks, 15 Pick. (Mass.) 465. A parol agreement entered into on Sunday, extending the time of payment of a mortgage, is void. Rush v. Rush (N. J. Eq.), 18 Atl. 221.

[2] Hellams v. Abercrombie, 15 S. Car. 110, 40 Am. Rep. 684.

[3] Moore v. Murdock, 26 Cal. 514; Johnson v. Brown, 13 Kans. 529; Roberts v. Barnes, 127 Mo. 405, 30 S. W. 113, 48 Am. St. 640; Horacek v. Keibler, 5 Nebr. 355; Boynton v. Page, 13 Wend. (N. Y.) 425; Bloom v. Richards, 2 Ohio St. 387;

Hellams v. Abercrombie, 15 S. Car. 110, 40 Am. Rep. 684.

[4] Adams v. Gay, 19 Vt. 358, per Redfield, J. See Tucker v. West, 29 Ark. 386, for a review of Sunday laws of many of the states.

[5] "The parties can not legalize that which the law has declared illegal. It is competent to them to impart new efficacy to a voidable act, but they have no power to give life to an act which, from reasons of public policy, has been ordained by the legislative authority to be absolutely void." Per Chief Justice Beasley, in Reeves v. Butcher, 31 N. J. L. 224.

[6] Reeves v. Butcher, 31 N. J. L. 224.

[7] Gwinn v. Simes, 61 Mo. 335. In Harrison v. Colton, 31 Iowa 16, it is held that a contract made on Sunday may be afterward ratified. See also Heller v. Crawford, 37 Ind. 279.

mortgagee, and dated, acknowledged, and delivered on the following day, is not void. The mortgagor is estopped from showing that the instrument was executed on a day other than that of which it bears date.[8]

Where a deed of land was executed and delivered on Sunday, to indemnify the mortgagee, and under an oral agreement that he should hold the land in trust for the mortgagor after satisfying his claim, in accordance with which agreement a declaration of trust was afterward executed, it was held that the fact that the deed was executed and delivered on Sunday did not entitle the grantee to hold the land discharged of the trust.[9] The rule, that no action based on a contract made on Sunday can be maintained to enforce its obligations in favor of either party, can not be so applied as to enlarge the interest conveyed by the grantor, or to defeat his equitable title.

§ 624. **Cancelation of mortgage on ground of fraud.**—A mortgage obtained by fraud is void, and a discharge of it may be decreed in equity.[1]

A court of equity will not cancel a mortgage simply because it is made without consideration; nor because the mortgagee fails or refuses to perform or discharge some promise or agreement made at the time of its execution. But it would seem that where the execution of the mortgage has been procured by the false and fraudulent representation that the mortgagee will discharge the obligation assumed, there is no good reason why a court of equity should not grant relief.[2]

[8] Wilson v. Winter, 6 Fed. 16.

[9] Faxon v. Folvey, 110 Mass. 392. "The apparent title conveyed," says Mr. Justice Colt, "was qualified by the trust imposed upon it, as effectually as if the terms of the trust were contained in the deed itself. Neither party to the transaction, nor those claiming under them, can be permitted to take advantage of the alleged illegal act. The title, such as it was, passed to the grantee, and was held, as we have found, in trust. The purpose of the trust declared was neither immoral, contrary to the statutes, nor contrary to public policy; the only illegality charged is in the time when, by the conveyance and agreement, the trust was created. Under such circumstances the law does not interfere to undo what the parties have done, by setting aside their deeds. Neither party can now assert rights inconsistent with the conveyances." See Hall v. Corcoran, 107 Mass. 251, 9 Am. Rep. 30, and cases cited; Myers v. Meinrath, 101 Mass. 366, 3 Am. Rep. 368.

[1] Shirk v. Williamson, 50 Ark. 562, 9 S. W. 307; Mason v. Daly, 117 Mass. 403; Wartemberg v. Spiegel, 31 Mich. 400. See also Richardson v. Barrick, 16 Iowa 407; Terry v. Tuttle, 24 Mich. 206; Hill v. Gettys, 135 N. Car. 373, 47 S. E. 449; Silver Val. Min. Co. v. Baltimore, G. &c. Co., 99 N. Car. 445, 6 S. E. 735; Garretson v. Witherspoon, 15 Okla. 473, 83 Pac. 415; Wright v. Morgan, 4 Bax. (Tenn.) 385.

[2] Hill v. Gettys, 135 N. Car. 373, 47 S. E. 449.

When a deed of land has been procured by fraud, and the grantee has conveyed it to a purchaser in good faith, so that the land itself is beyond the reach of the grantor,[3] yet if such purchaser has given a mortgage for a portion of the purchase-money to the party who fraudulently obtained the deed, he may in equity be compelled to transfer the mortgage to the party defrauded. It is an established doctrine, that when the legal estate has been acquired by fraud, the taker may in equity be regarded as trustee of the party defrauded, who may recover the estate or its avails when these can be distinctly identified.[4] A bill to set aside a mortgage procured by fraud may be filed by one of several mortgagors who have secured the several notes of each by a joint mortgage of one tract of land;[5] or several mortgagors may join as plaintiffs in a bill to obtain a cancelation of a note and mortgage, though the note secured was executed by only one of them.[6] It has been held to be fraud in a creditor to induce his debtor to secure an old debt by mortgage upon the condition of advancing a further sum, and when he has obtained the security to refuse to make the advance, and a court of equity will annul the conveyance. In such case the mortgagee can not claim that there is no loss, and that therefore the mortgage is damnum absque injuria. The mere existence of the mortgage is itself an injury, and an action to enforce it a greater.[7] But the better view is that such a transaction does not afford ground for canceling the mortgage in equity, though it might support an action at law for the injury sustained by reason of the breach of agreement.[8] However, the question whether a mortgage obtained by a creditor as security for a pre-existing debt, under a promise to make further advances, when the creditor had no intention of keeping his promise, is fraudulent, is a question upon which the cases are in conflict;[9] but if the creditor intended to make the advances, and refused to do so on some reasonable ground, the mortgage can not be avoided on the ground of fraud.[10]

A mortgage is void when made by one who has obtained title to the property by fraud or undue influence, the mortgagee having full knowledge of the acts leading up to the execution of the deed to the

[3] Jordan v. McNeil, 25 Kans. 459.
[4] Cheney v. Gleason, 117 Mass. 557.
[5] Moulton v. Lowe, 32 Maine 466.
[6] Bowman v. Gormy, 23 Kans. 306.
[7] Watts v. Bonner, 66 Miss. 629, 6 So. 187; Gross v. McKee, 53 Miss. 536.

[8] Johnson v. Murphy, 60 Ala. 288.
[9] Gross v. McKee, 53 Miss. 536; Johnson v. Murphy, 60 Ala. 288, the latter case holding that such breach of promise is no ground for declaring the mortgage void.
[10] Petty v. Grisard, 45 Ark. 117.

mortgagor and of the fraudulent means by which the mortgagor obtained title.[11]

An administrator who brings an action for the benefit of creditors of the estate to set aside a conveyance made by the decedent in fraud of his creditors, one parcel of which had been previously mortgaged by the decedent to a third person, is only entitled to subject to the claims of such creditors the land fraudulently conveyed in the condition in which it was at the date of the fraudulent deed, and is not entitled to the benefit of the mortgage. The fraudulent grantee, who had raised money and paid off the mortgage made by the decedent is entitled to be subrogated to the rights of the original mortgagee.[12]

The fact that the mortgagor is in possession, and can maintain his possession against the mortgagee at law, does not prevent his maintaining a bill to set aside a fraudulent mortgage.[13]

A party seeking to avoid his contract upon the ground of fraud can do so only by making prompt complaint.[14]

A mortgage given to secure a forged note is void. Thus a mortgage given by a wife upon her separate property for the accommodation of her husband's firm is rendered void by the forgery of her name, as a joint maker with her husband of the note intended to be secured, even in the hands of an innocent assignee.[15]

Where the mortgagee conveys land to the mortgagor, taking a mortgage back for part of the purchase-price, and has falsely represented that the tract contained sixty acres more than it actually did, the mortgagor is entitled to abatement for the shortage upon foreclosure of the mortgage.[16]

A mortgagor seeking cancelation of the mortgage must restore to the mortgagee the amount due under the mortgage, with lawful interest.[17] But this rule does not apply where the mortgage was given to secure a pre-existing indebtedness.[18]

[11] Brummond v. Krause, 8 N. Dak. 573, 80 N. W. 686.

[12] Ackerman v. Merle, 137 Cal. 169, 69 Pac. 983.

[13] Marston v. Brackett, 9 N. H. 336.

[14] Wright v. Peet, 36 Mich. 213.

[15] Morsman v. Werges, 3 Fed. 378.

[16] Harsey v. Busby, 69 S. Car. 261, 48 S. E. 50.

[17] George v. New England Mtg. Security Co., 109 Ala. 548, 20 So. 331; More v. Calkins, 85 Cal. 177, 24 Pac. 729; Pershing v. Wolfe, 6 Colo. App. 410, 40 Pac. 856; Dotterer v. Freeman, 88 Ga. 479, 14 S. E. 863; Hormann v. Hartmetz, 128 Ind. 353, 27 N. E. 731; Burlington v. Cross, 15 Kans. 74; Brill v. Rack, 15 Ky. L. 383, 23 S. W. 511; Pugh v. Cantey, 33 La. Ann. 786; Hanold v. Bacon, 36 Mich. 1; Pounds v. Clarke, 70 Miss. 263, 14 So. 22; Miller v. Gunderson, 48 Nebr. 715, 67 N. W. 769; Bissell v. Kellogg, 65 N. Y. 432; Foltz v. Ferguson, 77 Tex. 301, 13 S. W. 1037; Kelly v. Kershaw, 5 Utah 295, 14 Pac. 804.

[18] Shook v. Southern Bldg. &c. Assn., 140 Ala. 575, 37 So. 409; Jen-

§ 625. Fraudulent intent—How shown.—A fraudulent intent on the part of the mortgagee in obtaining the mortgage must be shown to render it void.[19] To have this effect, it is necessary that there should be something more than mere folly on the part of the mortgagor. A mortgagee may meet an allegation, that a mortgage was obtained through his false and fraudulent representations, by evidence that the mortgagor executed the mortgage without his solicitation. The weight to be given to the evidence is a question for the jury.[20]

Fraud must be proved as an affirmative fact, but it may be discovered and established through circumstances.[21]

Mortgages and deeds of trust duly executed will not be canceled for fraud except on the most clear and convincing proof of their fraudulent character.[22] If the proof is doubtful and unsatisfactory, the writing will be held to correctly express the intention of the parties.[23]

The admitted fact that the books containing the account to secure which deeds of trust were executed had been tampered with, furnishes no reason for holding that the deeds of trust were procured by fraud or misrepresentation.[24]

A fraudulent misrepresentation as to the value of property sold by the mortgagee, in payment of which he has taken a mortgage, does not avoid the mortgage if there was any value at all in the property sold. The property which was the subject of the sale and mortgage must first be restored to the vendor, or a reconveyance tendered, before the mortgage can be rescinded.[25] A defense of fraud as to the value of the property can not be sustained where the mortgagor acted upon his own investigation and judgment in buying the property.[26]

---

kins v. Jonas Schwab Co., 138 Ala. 664, 35 So. 649.

[19] Mills v. Keep, 197 Fed. 360; Mohr v. Griffin, 137 Ala. 456, 34 So. 378; Clarke v. Forbes, 9 Nebr. 476, 4 N. W. 58; Murphy v. Moore, 23 Hun (N. Y.) 95; Johnston v. Derr, 110 N. Car. 1, 14 S. E. 641. See post §§ 1299, 1492.

[20] Blackwell v. Cummings, 68 N. Car. 121. See also Juzan v. Toulmin, 9 Ala. 662, 44 Am. Dec. 448; Vaill v. McPhail, 35 R. I. 412, 87 Atl. 188.

[21] Black v. Epstein, 221 Mo. 286, 120 S. W. 754; Merchants' Nat. Bank v. Greenhood, 16 Mont. 395, 41 Pac. 250.

[22] Langley v. Fitzgerald, 43 Colo. 301, 95 Pac. 923; Ferber v. State

Bank of Pine Island, 116 Minn. 261, 133 N. W. 611; Christian v. Green (Miss.), 45 So. 425; Fitzgibbon v. Parker, 143 App. Div. 463, 128 N. Y. S. 539; Crowe v. Melba Land Co., 76 Misc. 676, 135 N. Y. S. 454; Englert v. Dale, 25 N. Dak. 587, 142 N. W. 169.

[23] Insurance Co. v. Nelson, 103 U. S. 544, 26 L. ed. 436; Howland v. Blake, 97 U. S. 624, 24 L. ed. 1027; Skajewski v. Skaya, 103 Minn. 27, 114 N. W. 247; Goulet v. Dubreuille, 84 Minn. 72, 86 N. W. 779.

[24] Christian v. Green (Miss.), 45 So. 425.

[25] Sanborn v. Osgood, 16 N. H. 112.

[26] San Jose Ranch Co. v. San Jose L. &c. Co., 132 Cal. 582, 64 Pac. 1097.

Fraudulent intent on the part of one of two mortgagees will invalidate the mortgage, although the mortgage secured separate debts, and the other mortgagee did not share in or know of such fraudulent intent.[27]

A mortgage obtained by the fraud or forgery of the mortgagee's agent is void. The mortgagee in such case can not be a purchaser for value.[28]

The representation of a mortgagee that he would not enforce the mortgage is no defense to it, because such a parol promise can not be offered in evidence.[29]

The mere fact that a mortgagor was unable to read, and that the mortgage was not read to him, does not enable him, in the absence of proof of fraud on the part of the mortgagee, to object that the instrument contains an unauthorized stipulation, especially when it was drawn by his own agent.[30]

The question of the sufficiency of a mortgagee's misrepresentations as a ground for cancelation as to the mortgagor may be determined in a suit by his assignee to foreclose, on an application for the surplus money, if any be raised by a sale of the land or by other appropriate action.[31]

§ 626. Mortgage obtained by duress or undue influence.—A mortgage obtained by duress is voidable or void according to the nature of the duress.[32] But a bill to set such mortgage aside must be filed before the maturity thereof.[33] The duress must be something more than the exercise of undue influence.[34]

The insistence upon one's legal rights does not constitute undue influence.[35]

[27] Adams v. Niemann, 46 Mich. 135, 8 N. W. 719.

[28] Laprad v. Sherwood, 79 Mich. 520, 44 N. W. 943.

[29] Catlin v. Fletcher, 9 Minn. 85.

[30] Wilson v. Winter, 6 Fed. 16; Stewart v. Whitlock, 58 Cal. 2; Leslie v. Merrick, 99 Ind. 180; McAlarney v. Paine (Pa.), 10 Atl. 20; Montgomery v. Scott, 9 S. Car. 20, 30 Am. Rep. 1.

[31] Nixon v. Haslett, 74 N. J. Eq. 789, 70 Atl. 987, affd. 75 N. J. Eq. 302, 78 Atl. 1134.

[32] Van Valkenburgh v. Oldham, 12 Cal. App. 572, 108 Pac. 42; Bogue v. Franks, 199 Ill. 411, 65 N. E. 346; 1 Jones on Real Property, § 93.

[33] Kingsley v. Kingsley, 130 Ill. App. 53.

[34] Walker v. Nicrosi, 135 Ala. 353, 33 So. 161; Moog v. Strang, 69 Ala. 98; Gabbey v. Forgeus, 32 Kans. 62, 15 Pac. 866. As to evidence, see Edwards v. Bowden, 103 N. Car. 50, 9 S. E. 194, 6 Am. St. 487; Post v. First Nat. Bank, 138 Ill. 559, 28 N. E. 978; Winfield Nat. Bank v. Croco, 46 Kans. 620, 26 Pac. 939; Benedict v. Roome, 106 Mich. 378' 64 N. W. 193; Weber v. Barrett, 125 N. Y. 18, 25 N. E. 1068; Loud v. Hamilton (Tenn.), 51 S. W. 140, 45 L. R. A. 400; Galusha v. Sherman, 105 Wis. 263, 81 N. W. 495.

[35] Van Valkenburgh v. Oldham, 12 Cal. App. 572, 108 Pac. 42.

Under a statute providing that the consent of the parties to a contract must be free, mutual, and communicated by each to the other, if the consent of a party to a note and mortgage are not freely or voluntarily given, they may be held void even though signed by the party.[36]

A mortgage obtained through threats of prosecution, whether groundless or not, is voidable,[37] and a court of chancery will restrain its collection,[38] or will order it to be canceled, as a cloud on the title.[39] But a mortgage obtained by threat of a lawful arrest for a crime actually committed can not be avoided on the ground of duress.[40]

Relief may be granted against a mortgage extorted by a son from his parents by oppressive means, and for an inadequate consideration, while he practically occupied the position of guardian over them and their property.[41] A mortgage executed by a wife on her separate property, to secure a debt of her husband, under his threat to abandon her if she refused, may be avoided by her if the mortgagee was aware of such threat at the time the mortgage was executed.[42] But where a father procures his adult daughter to make a mortgage to a third party for the father's benefit, the mortgagee, though without actual knowledge of undue influence or duress, is chargeable with the duty of investigating the daughter's freedom of will in making the mortgage.[43] It is even held that a mortgage obtained from a married woman by duress on the part of the husband is void, although the mort-

[36] Van Valkenburgh v. Oldham, 12 Cal. App. 572, 108 Pac. 42.

[37] Johnson v. Graham Bros. Co., 98 Ark. 274, 135 S. W. 853; Smith v. Steely, 80 Iowa 738, 45 N. W. 912; Smith v. Bank of Hamlin, 90 Kans. 299, 133 Pac. 428; Williamson-Halsell, Frazier Co. v. Ackerman, 77 Kans. 502, 94 Pac. 807, 20 L. R. A. (N. S.) 484; Lee v. Ryder, 1 Kans. App. 293; Hoellworth v. McCarthy, 93 Nebr. 246, 140 N. W. 141, 43 L. R. A. (N. S.) 1005; Nebraska Central Building &c. Assn. v. McCandless, 83 Nebr. 536, 120 N. W. 134; Hargreaves v. Korcek, 44 Nebr. 660, 62 N. W. 1086.

[38] Eyster v. Hatheway, 50 Ill. 521, 99 Am. Dec. 537; James v. Roberts, 18 Ohio 548. See also Lightfoot v. Wallis, 12 Bush (Ky.) 498.

[39] Small v. Williams, 87 Ga. 681, 13 S. E. 589; Meech v. Lee, 82 Mich. 274, 46 N. W. 383; Schoener v. Lessauer, 107 N. Y. 111, 13 N. E. 741, revg. 36 Hun 100. A mortgage executed by a wife upon her property to secure a debt of the husband, under the inducement of false and fraudulent charges of embezzlement against the husband, and threats to institute criminal proceedings against him, is void. Singer Mfg. Co. v. Rawson, 50 Iowa 634. It is immaterial that the property was purchased by the husband with money of the party making the threats, and fraudulently conveyed to the wife.

[40] Englert v. Dale, 25 N. Dak. 587, 142 N. W. 169; Hunt v. Hunt (Ore.), 134 Pac. 1180.

[41] Bowe v. Bowe, 42 Mich. 195, 3 N. E. 843.

[42] Line v. Blizzard, 70 Ind. 23; Wallach v. Hoexter, 17 Abb. N. Cas. (N. Y.) 267. As to what threats and commands on the part of the husband amount to duress, see Gabbey v. Forgeus, 32 Kans. 62, 15 Pac. 866.

[43] Lane v. Reserve Trust Co., 30 Ohio Cir. Ct. 367.

gagee took no part in procuring it, on the ground that he allowed the husband to act as his agent, and is bound by his acts.[44] But a married woman can not set up the invalidity of her signature to a mortgage of her homestead on the ground that, not being able to read, she relied on the representations of her husband that the instrument was a note and was of no consequence;[45] for it was gross negligence in her not to require the instrument to be read to her.[46] Nor can a person who is able to read, but through inexcusable neglect signs a mortgage without reading it, complain of false statements made as to its contents.[47]

But where one having the confidence of an illiterate person by fraudulent representations procured the latter to sign a note and mortgage other than the one he supposed he was signing, the fact that he did not require the instrument to be read to him does not preclude him from controverting their execution.[48] A mortgage duly executed by husband and wife, releasing her homestead right can not be avoided, though she did not wish to sign the mortgage, but was induced by her husband to do so, where she understood the transaction.[49] A married woman as well as any one else may be estopped by her deliberate conduct.[50]

The fraud or duress of a husband in procuring his wife's release of homestead does not invalidate the mortgage unless the mortgagee had knowledge of or shared in the wrongful acts of the husband.[51] But where her separate acknowledgment is made essential to a conveyance of her separate estate, if she executes a mortgage during her minority she can not ratify it by paying interest or doing any like act after coming of age. She can only ratify it in the way she could originally execute it, that is, by making a separate acknowledgment of the deed as required by statute. Doubtless she would be estopped in case she

[44] Central Bank v. Copeland, 18 Md. 305, 81 Am. Dec. 597.
[45] Aetna Life Ins. Co. v. Franks, 53 Iowa 618, 6 N. W. 9; Butner v. Blevins, 125 N. Car. 585, 34 S. E. 629; Shell v. Holston Nat. Bldg. &c. Assn. (Tenn.), 52 S. W. 909. See also Knowlson v. Bruist, 86 Mich. 588, 49 N. W. 585.
[46] Roach v. Karr, 18 Kans. 529, 26 Am. Rep. 788; Frickee v. Donner, 35 Mich. 151. But see Colorado Inv. Loan Co. v. Beuchat (Colo.), 111 Pac. 61.
[47] Tracy v. Harris, 5 Ga. App. 392, 63 S. E. 233.
[48] Ray v. Baker, 165 Ind. 74, 74 N. E. 619.

[49] Tackitt v. Tackitt (Ky.), 127 S. W. 987.
[50] Van Sickles v. Town, 53 Iowa 259, 5 N. W. 148; Edgell v. Hagens, 53 Iowa 223, 5 N. W. 136; Norton v. Nichols, 35 Mich. 148; Lefebvre v. Dutruit, 51 Wis. 326, 8 N. W. 149, 37 Am. Rep. 833.
[51] Walker v. Nicrosi, 135 Ala. 353, 33 So. 161; Moog v. Strang, 69 Ala. 98; Aetna Life Ins. Co. v. Franks, 53 Iowa 618, 6 N. W. 9; Edgell v. Hagens, 53 Iowa 223, 5 N. W. 136; J. M. Robinson, Norton & Co. v. Randall, 147 Ky. 45, 143 S. W. 769; Bode v. Jussen, 93 Nebr. 482, 140 N. W. 768.

had deliberately deceived the mortgagee by falsehood; but otherwise her deed would be voidable, and could be confirmed only in the manner indicated.[52] A mortgage given under threats by the creditor of a criminal prosecution for a felony unless the debt be secured, is not void if the debt was actually due, and the debtor was in duty bound to pay or secure it. The giving of the mortgage in such case is not the compounding of a felony.[53] But if a mortgage be given without consideration, under threats of a groundless prosecution, a court of equity will grant relief and restrain the collection of it.[54]

Although the general rule is, that one person can not avoid an obligation by reason of duress of another, there are exceptions to this in case the duress be of the husband or wife, or of parent or child. Thus a parent may avoid a mortgage which he or she has been induced to sign by threats of the prosecution and imprisonment of a son;[55] or a wife may avoid a mortgage of her property which she has executed under threats of the arrest of her husband for embezzlement.[56]

To avoid a mortgage on account of duress by imprisonment, it must appear that the imprisonment was unlawful, and that the mortgage was executed to obtain a release from it. "If I be arrested upon good cause, and, being in prison or under arrest, I make an obligation, feoffment, or any other deed to him at whose suit I am arrested, for my enlargement and to make him satisfaction, this shall not be said to be by duress, but is good and shall bind me."[57] A mortgage given

---

[52] Williams v. Baker, 71 Pa. St. 476; Ledger Building Assn. v. Cook, 34 Leg. Int. (Pa.) 5, 12 Phila. (Pa.) 434. Contra First Nat. Bank v. Bryan, 62 Iowa 42, 17 N. W. 165; Berry v. Berry, 57 Kans. 691, 47 Pac. 837.

[53] Plant v. Gunn, 2 Woods (U. S.) 372; Maddox v. Rowe, 154 Ky. 417, 157 S. W. 714.

[54] James v. Roberts, 18 Ohio 548. See also Cowles v. Raguet, 14 Ohio 38; Raguet v. Roll, 7 Ohio 76.

[55] Brooks v. Berryhill, 20 Ind. 97; Russell v. Durham, 17 Ky. L. 35, 303, 29 S. W. 635; Benedict v. Roome, 106 Mich. 378, 64 N. W. 193; Meech v. Lee, 82 Mich. 274, 46 N. W. 383; Hargreaves v. Korcek, 44 Nebr. 660, 62 N. W. 1086; Beindorff v. Kaufman, 41 Nebr. 824, 60 N. W. 101; Fisher v. Bishop, 108 N. Y. 25, 15 N. E. 331; Dodd v. Averill, 7 App. Div. (N. Y.) 290; Strang v. Peterson, 56 Hun (N. Y.) 418; Foley v. Greene, 14 R. I. 618; Coffman v. Bank, 5 Lea (Tenn.) 232; Bayley v. Williams, 4 Giff. 638; Williams v. Bayley, L. R. 1 H. L. 200; Harris v. Carmody, 131 Mass. 51, 41 Am. Rep. 188. In the case last cited Mr. Justice Morton said: "No more powerful and constraining force can be brought to bear upon a man to overcome his will, and extort from him an obligation, than threats of great injury to his child. Both upon reason and upon the weight of the authorities, we are of opinion that a parent may void his obligation by duress to his child."

[56] Mack v. Prang, 104 Wis. 1, 79 N. W. 770, 45 L. R. A. 407, 76 Am. St. 848.

[57] 1 Shep. Touch. 62. See also Plant v. Gunn, 2 Woods (U. S.) 372; Watkins v. Baird, 6 Mass. 506, 4 Am. Dec. 170; Smillie v. Titus, 32 N. J. Eq. 51. In the reporter's note to this case many authorities are cited.

to a county to secure the payment of a sum of money, as the condition of a pardon, is not void as being given under duress.[58] And so a mortgage given by a defaulting county treasurer, to secure the amount of his debt to the county, is a voluntary obligation and valid.[59]

A mortgage by husband and wife upon their homestead can not be said to have been obtained by duress, even though the deplorable condition of the husband's business affairs and the danger of his being arrested for embezzlement may have aided to influence the wife to sign the mortgage, where, although the mortgagee was one of the victims of the husband's dishonesty, he was in no way connected with the proceedings for the arrest and did not seek to influence the wife's action.[60]

A mortgage given for a legal debt, but with the motive not to incur the risk of offending a wealthy and influential friend, who might prove highly serviceable to the mortgagor and his family, is not given under duress.[61] A mortgage given in consequence of threats made by the creditor to resort to legal proceedings to collect a valid debt is not given under duress.[62]

Whether the use of a criminal prosecution to obtain securities renders them absolutely void and incapable of being enforced, or voidable only so that they may be confirmed by subsequent acts of ratification, depends upon the circumstances of the case, and particularly upon the question whether the prosecution was instituted for the sole purpose of extorting the securities, or was justifiable in itself and not necessarily instituted for that purpose, or conducted in an oppressive manner, and there was just consideration for the securities if properly obtained. Thus a wife, having left her husband on the ground of his adultery, with the purpose of remaining away from him and of filing a bill for separate maintenance, made a criminal complaint and procured his arrest for the crime. The guilt of the husband was unquestionable, and he settled the prosecution by giving to a trustee a mortgage for the benefit of the complainant conditioned for the payment of a certain sum semi-annually during her life. The wife afterward filed a bill for divorce without making claim to any allowance and obtained a decree. The husband made the semi-annual payment for about two years, but then refused to make further payments, and a

[58] Rood v. Winslow, 2 Doug. (Mich.) 68.

[59] State Bank v. Chapelle, 40 Mich. 447; Oconto v. Hall, 42 Wis. 59.

[60] Bogue v. Franks, 199 Ill. 411, 65 N. E. 346.

[61] Dolman v. Cook, 14 N. J. Eq. 56.

[62] Snyder v. Braden, 58 Ind. 143. See also Detroit Nat. Bank v. Blodgett, 115 Mich. 160, 73 N. W. 120, 885.

bill was filed to foreclose the mortgage. Upon the question whether the mortgage was void, or voidable only, and so confirmed by the payments, the Supreme Court of Michigan was evenly divided, the disagreement turning largely upon the motives of the criminal prosecution.[63]

§ 627. Mortgage made to hinder, delay, or defraud creditors.

—Except under bankrupt and insolvent laws, a mortgage made with the intent to prefer one creditor to another is valid;[64] although a mortgage made with the intent upon the part of the mortgagor to hinder, delay, and defraud his creditors is void at common law and by statute generally, except in case the mortgagee did not participate in or have knowledge of such intent.[65] Such mortgage can be declared void as to him only upon proof of his knowledge of the fraudulent intent.[66] A mortgage made with the intent to defraud the mortgagor's creditors, even though it is founded on a perfect consideration, if taken by the mortgagee with knowledge of the fraudulent purpose, and with the view of aiding the execution of it, is void as to creditors.[67] But a mortgage for money loaned, made with the intent on the part of the mortgagee to aid the mortgagor in an attempt to defeat a prior mortgage which was made without consideration with the intent to defraud

---

[63] Lyon v. Waldo, 36 Mich. 345; Graves and Campbell, JJ., holding the mortgage void, and Cooley, C. J., and Marston, J., holding it voidable only, and cured by ratification, able opinions being delivered on each side.

[64] Estes v. Gunter, 122 U. S. 450, 30 L. ed. 1228, 7 Sup. Ct. 1275; Hollingsworth v. Johns, 92 Ga. 428, 17 S. E. 621; Manton v. Seiberling, 107 Iowa 534, 78 N. W. 194; Groetzinger v. Wyman, 105 Iowa 574, 75 N. W. 512; Southern White Lead Co. v. Haas, 73 Iowa 399, 33 N. W. 657; Aulman v. Aulman, 71 Iowa 124, 32 N. W. 240, 60 Am. Rep. 783; Gage v. Parry, 69 Iowa 609, 29 N. W. 822; Perry v. Vezina, 63 Iowa 25, 18 N. W. 657; Giddings v. Sears, 115 Mass. 505; Benson v. Maxwell, 105 Pa. St. 274, 14 Atl. 161, 21 Wkly. N. Cas. 446; Coates v. Wilson, 20 R. I. 106, 37 Atl. 537; Colt v. Sears Commercial Co., 20 R. I. 64, 37 Atl. 311; Perkins v. Hutchinson, 17 R. I. 450, 22 Atl. 1111; Austin v. Sprague Mfg. Co., 14 R. I. 464; Magovern v. Richard, 27 S. Car. 272, 3 S. E. 340; Mona-

ghan Bay Co. v. Dickson, 39 S. Car. 146, 17 S. E. 696, 39 Am. St. 704; Bannister v. Phelps, 81 Wis. 256, 51 N. W. 417; Stevens v. Breen, 75 Wis. 595, 44 N. W. 645; Anstedt v. Bentley, 61 Wis. 629, 21 N. W. 807; Mehlhop v. Pettibone, 54 Wis. 656, 11 N. W. 553, 12 N. W. 443. See Jones on Chattel Mortgages, §§ 333-551.

[65] Price v. Masterson, 35 Ala. 483; Preusser v. Henshaw, 49 Iowa 41; McMaster v. Campbell, 41 Mich. 513, 2 N. W. 836; State v. Nauert, 2 Mo. App. 295; Thorpe v. Thorpe, 12 S. Car. 154. See also Shive v. Merritt, 31 Ky. L. 978, 104 S. W. 368.

[66] Hall v. Heydon, 41 Ala. 242; Wiley v. Knight, 27 Ala. 336; Tickner v. Wiswall, 9 Ala. 305; Shideler v. Fisher, 13 Colo. App. 106, 57 Pac. 864; Farrand v. Caton, 69 Mich. 235, 37 N. W. 199; Lewis v. Dudley, 70 N. H. 594, 49 Atl. 572.

[67] Jones v. Light, 86 Maine 437, 30 Atl. 71; Wyman v. Brown, 50 Maine 139; Moore v. Williamson, 44 N. J. Eq. 496, 15 Atl. 587; Green v. Tantum, 19 N. J. Eq. 105, 21 N. J. Eq. 364.

the mortgagor's creditors, has priority of such prior mortgage, the second mortgagee being to the extent of his loan a bona fide purchaser entitled to avoid the prior fraudulent mortgage, though the mortgagor himself could not avoid it.[68]

A mortgage given in good faith to secure an actual bona fide indebtedness due from the mortgagor to the mortgagee, is not rendered fraudulent per se as to other creditors of the mortgagor because there is included in the mortgage debts due or alleged to be due others; the mortgagee agreeing to pay such debts from the proceeds of the mortgaged property.[69]

A mortgage executed by one pending an action against him is superior to a lien of a subsequent judgment obtained by the plaintiff in the action unless it be shown that the mortgage was taken to defraud such plaintiff.[70] A mortgage given by a debtor to one of his creditors, to secure a debt due the latter, is not rendered fraudulent by an agreement by the creditor thus preferred to give indulgence to the debtor either in the time or manner of payment.[71]

It is incumbent upon the mortgagee to show that the mortgage was made for a valuable and adequate consideration; and when that appears, the burden of proving a fraudulent intent on his part rests with the creditors who assail the transaction.[72] Proof of the embarrassed condition of the mortgagor at the time, and of the mortgagee's relationship to him, is insufficient to establish a fraudulent intent;[73] as is also the fact that the mortgagor immediately afterward executed a general assignment in favor of his creditors.[74]

When the object of a mortgage is solely to secure a debt to the mortgagee, it is not fraudulent at common law, although both the debtor

[68] Hill v. Ahern, 135 Mass. 158. But see dissenting opinion by Devens, J.

[69] Randolph v. Allen, 73 Fed. 23, 19 C. C. A. 353; Chipman v. Stern, 89 Ala. 207, 7 So. 409; Adams v. Ryan, 61 Iowa 733, 17 N. W. 159; Berry v. Berk, 62 Nebr. 535, 87 N. W. 309; Hine v. Bowe, 114 N. Y. 350, 21 N. E. 733; Carpenter v. Muren, 42 Barb. (N. Y.) 300.

[70] Curie v. Wright, 140 Iowa 651, 119 N. W. 74.

[71] United States Nat. Bank v. Westervelt, 55 Nebr. 424, 75 N. W. 857; Harshaw v. Woodfin, 64 N. Car. 568;

Sanders v. Main, 12 Wash. 665, 42 Pac. 122.

[72] Mobile Sav. Bank v. McDonnell, 87 Ala. 736, 6 So. 703, 18 Am. St. 137; Harrington v. Upton, 78 Mich. 28, 43 N. W. 1089; Lewis v. Dudley, 70 N. H. 594, 49 Atl. 572; Bannister v. Phelps, 81 Wis. 256, 51 N. W. 417; Erdall v. Atwood, 79 Wis. 1, 47 N. W. 1124.

[73] Crawford v. Kirksey, 55 Ala. 282, 28 Am. Rep. 704; Troy v. Smith, 33 Ala. 469; Bamfield v. Whipple, 14 Allen (Mass.) 13; Thorpe v. Thorpe, 12 S. Car. 154.

[74] Lyon v. McIlvaine, 24 Iowa 9; Lampson v. Arnold, 19 Iowa 479.

and creditor knew that the effect of it would be to put the property out of the reach of other creditors.[75]

A mortgage given by a husband to secure a bona fide debt to his wife's separate estate is not fraudulent as to other creditors, though he was in failing circumstances when he gave it, provided there is no intent to hinder, delay or defraud other creditors.[76]

An insolvent corporation may mortgage its property for the payment of its debts the same as an individual where it is done in good faith and not for a fraudulent purpose. The facts that the mortgagee had been prior to the time of the mortgage a stockholder and director of the company, and at the time, the principal stockholders of the corporation were a daughter and son-in-law of the mortgagee, are not sufficient to taint the mortgage with fraud.[77]

A mortgage is not rendered fraudulent as to creditors by a stipulation that the mortgagor shall have the privilege, upon regular payment of the interest, of postponing the date of payment of the debt from year to year, in all not to exceed five years, and that upon these terms he may remain in possession of the property.[78] Fraud is not a necessary inference from a provision in a deed of trust postponing a sale for a reasonable length of time, and reserving the use of the property to the grantor in the meantime.[79]

If one of the purposes of making a mortgage was to put the property out of the reach of the mortgagor's creditors, although the principal purpose of the parties was to secure a bona fide debt of the mortgagor, it is nevertheless void as to his creditors.[80] But such a mortgage becomes a valid security purged of fraud when it is assigned to a bona fide purchaser, or to a bona fide creditor of the fraudulent mortgagor without notice of the fraudulent purpose.[81]

The fact that a mortgagee takes possession of the mortgaged prop-

---

[75] Murphy v. Murphy, 74 Conn. 198; Giddings v. Sears, 115 Mass. 505; Oak Creek Valley Bank v. Helmer, 59 Nebr. 176, 80 N. W. 891; Omaha Coal &c. Co. v. Suess, 54 Nebr. 379, 74 N. W. 620.

[76] Reel v. Livingston, 34 Fla. 377, 16 So. 284; Southern White Lead Co. v. Haas, 73 Iowa 399, 33 N. W. 657; Benson v. Maxwell, 10 Sad. (Pa.) 380, 14 Atl. 161; Gerald v. Gerald, 31 S. Car. 171, 6 S. E. 290.

[77] Burchinell v. Bennett, 10 Colo. App. 502, 52 Pac. 51.

[78] Keagy v. Trout, 85 Va. 390, 7 S. E. 329.

[79] Norris v. Lake, 89 Va. 513, 16 S. E. 663.

[80] Farguson v. Johnston, 36 Fed. 134; Crowninshield v. Kittridge, 7 Metc. (Mass.) 520; Heintze v. Bentley, 34 N. J. Eq. 562; Holt v. Creamer, 34 N. J. Eq. 181; Schmidt v. Opie, 33 N. J. Eq. 138; White v. Megill (N. J. Eq.), 18 Atl. 355; Robinson v. Stewart, 10 N. Y. 189; Perry v. Hardison, 99 N. Car. 21, 5 S. E. 230; Cannon v. Young, 89 N. Car. 264.

[81] Longfellow v. Barnard, 58 Nebr. 612, 79 N. W. 255. See post § 827a.

erty, and allows the mortgagor to remain upon the premises and receive the income, is not such evidence of fraud as will postpone the mortgage to debts subsequently incurred by the mortgagor. The extent of the mortgagee's liability to creditors is to account for the proceeds of the property as a credit upon the mortgage debt.[82]

The circumstance that a mortgage is made in the form of an absolute conveyance by a debtor in failing circumstances to a creditor is no evidence of an intention to defraud other creditors.[83] But inasmuch as a mortgage in this form tends to cover up and keep concealed the real nature of the transaction between the parties, it will be closely scrutinized.[84]

But in Alabama such a conveyance is fraudulent and void as against existing creditors, although there may have been no actual intent to defraud. An equity of redemption is property which is capable of being subjected to the payment of debts, in courts of law and of equity; and a transaction, whereby an embarrassed debtor conceals its existence from his creditors, must hinder and delay them.[85]

Neither is a mortgage fraudulent as to creditors because it is given for a greater sum than is due, but in fact to cover in part future advances, although it does not express upon its face that the excess is for future advances.[86] It would be fraudulent, however, if not given in good faith, and the securing of future advances be only a pretense,[87] or if given for a very large sum upon a large amount of property, when in fact the debt was very small.[88]

A mortgage executed by a debtor in failing circumstances, setting out a present indebtedness, may be set aside for fraud upon proof that the recited indebtedness is a pretense,[89] and that the real debt was wages for services largely to be performed in the future.[90]

If given to secure existing liabilities, a mortgage is not void as to creditors because it does not specify the amount secured;[91] nor be-

[82] Decker v. Wilson, 45 N. J. Eq. 772, 18 Atl. 843.

[83] Doswell v. Adler, 28 Ark. 82, and cases cited. But the mortgagee must use good faith and disclose the facts to other creditors making inquiry. Geary v. Porter, 17 Ore. 465, 21 Pac. 442.

[84] Geary v. Porter, 17 Ore. 465, 21 Pac. 442.

[85] Campbell v. Davis, 85 Ala. 56, 4 So. 140; Sims v. Gaines, 64 Ala. 392. See also Moog v. Barrow, 101 Ala. 209, 13 So. 665.

[86] Tully v. Harloe, 35 Cal. 302, 95

Am. Dec. 102; Goff v. Rogers, 71 Ind. 459; Hughes v. Shull, 33 Kans. 127, 5 Pac. 414. See Jones on Chattel Mortgages, § 339.

[87] Farguson v. Johnston, 36 Fed. 134; Tully v. Harloe, 35 Cal. 302, 95 Am. Dec. 102.

[88] Hubbard v. Turner, 2 McLean (U. S.) 519; Liver v. Thielke, 115 Wis. 389.

[89] Stephens v. Stephens, 66 Ark. 356, 50 S. W. 874.

[90] Perry v. Hardison, 99 N. Car. 21, 5 S. E. 230.

[91] Youngs v. Wilson, 27 N. Y. 351,

cause the sum secured was made up in part by an allowance of interest not recoverable at law upon the debt,[92] or that it includes debts due to other persons which the mortgagee has verbally promised to pay.[93]

A mortgage given for the amount of an existing mortgage and an additional sum is not rendered fraudulent because the first mortgage is left uncanceled of record for further security, in the absence of fraudulent intent shown.[94]

The fact that a mortgage given to secure certain creditors of a firm is withheld from record for two years does not of itself make it fraudulent as to other creditors of the firm, but is merely a circumstance to be considered as bearing upon the question of fraud.[95]

§ 628. Mortgage fraudulent with reference to particular persons.—

A mortgage may be fraudulent with reference to a particular creditor of the mortgagor, as, for instance, a mechanic who was induced to delay the signing of a contract for the building of certain houses until the landowner had executed and recorded a mortgage without consideration to a third person, with the intention that the mortgagee should enter under it and defeat the mechanic's lien. The mechanic, in such case, is entitled to maintain a bill to restrain an assignment of the mortgage, and to compel its cancelation, even before the houses are completed and the money under the contract has become due. The

revg. 24 Barb. (N. Y.) 510; Norris v. Lake, 89 Va. 513, 16 S. E. 663.

[92] Spencer v. Ayrault, 10 N. Y. 202.

[93] Carpenter v. Muren, 42 Barb. (N. Y.) 300.

[94] Westerly Sav. Bank v. Stillman Mfg. Co., 16 R. I. 497, 17 Atl. 918. In this case a mortgage was given and recorded, and was partly paid when a further loan was made, and a new mortgage for the new loan and the balance of the old loan, conveying the same property, was given and recorded. The first mortgage was left uncanceled for further security, and the record did not show that it included the debt secured by the first. Durfree, C. J., said: "The objection is, not that the second mortgage was given for more than the mortgagor owed, but that it was given in part for indebtedness already secured by the prior mortgage left uncanceled without disclosing the fact. This is not prohibited by our registry laws, or, in the absence of any fraudulent purpose, by our statutes of fraudulent conveyances, either directly or by clear implication, and therefore, while we are not disposed to approve the transaction, we are nevertheless not prepared to declare it void on the ground that it was against public policy. It is desirable that the records should at all times disclose the true state of the titles there registered, but it is notorious that they do not do so. Mortgages which have been paid are left uncanceled. Mortgages which have been partly paid do not show that they have been partly paid, and have never been supposed to be vitiated thereby. Mortgages on several pieces of property, each given for the same debt, without making reference to the other, have been enforced against junior mortgages and attaching creditors."

[95] Day v. Goodbar, 69 Miss. 687, 12 So. 30.

priority of lien to which the mechanic is entitled may be secured to him beforehand, for his security is impaired by the fraudulent mortgage, and he is exposed to the chance that the mortgage may pass into the hands of a bona fide assignee for value.[96]

A conveyance by a married woman of her entire property to her husband's assignee for the benefit of his creditors was adjudged fraudulent as to an equitable mortgagee of her property. She was not liable for her husband's debts, but was liable for a debt of her own, and had no right to divert her property from her own creditor for the benefit of her husband's creditors.[97]

A trust deed made by a husband without consideration, for the purpose of defrauding the maker's wife of her claim for alimony, is fraudulent as against the wife, and the want of consideration is a sufficient defense to a suit to foreclose the trust deed.[98]

When an existing mortgage is exchanged under a false pretense that the title is to be cleared, and before giving the new mortgage in exchange the mortgagor makes another mortgage with the purpose of giving it priority, even if this be an honest mortgage, but given to secure an old debt, the mortgagee in this is in no position to object to the restoration of the old mortgage in behalf of the original mortgagee.[99]

§ 629. **Fraudulent preferences.**—A mortgage given to secure a debt to a creditor who has, with others, executed a composition with a debtor to accept a portion of their claims in satisfaction, under a secret arrangement whereby the debt of such creditor is to be paid in full, is a fraud upon the other creditors, and is void.[1] But a mortgage

---

[96] Hulsman v. Whitman, 109 Mass. 411. Mortgage by husband to defeat collection of judgment for alimony. Dugan v. Trisler, 69 Ind. 553.
[97] Washburn v. Hammond, 151 Mass. 132, 24 N. E. 33.
[98] Scott v. Magloughlin, 133 Ill. 33, 24 N. E. 1030; Westphal v. Westphal, 81 Minn. 242, 83 N. W. 988.
[99] Eggeman v. Harrow, 37 Mich. 436. See post § 967.
[1] Feldman v. Gamble, 26 N. J. Eq. 494, and cases cited; Lawrence v. Clark, 36 N. Y. 128. See Jones on Chattel Mortgages, §§ 356-366. In Kentucky it is provided by statute that every mortgage made by a debtor in contemplation of insolvency, and with the design to prefer one creditor over another, shall operate as a transfer of the property for the benefit of creditors generally. Gen. Stat. ch. 44, art. 2, § 1. This statute does not prohibit the executing of a mortgage to secure a debt created simultaneously by one in failing circumstances. But a mortgage given by one knowing that he is insolvent, in order to prefer a creditor, to secure an existing debt, together with a debt incurred simultaneously to a creditor who knows the debtor's condition and aids in carrying out the arrangement, is a conveyance for the benefit of creditors generally under the statute. McCann v. Hill, 85 Ky. 574, 4 S. W. 337.

made with the intent to give the mortgagee an unlawful preference is not affected by that fact if such intent was not carried out.[2]

A mortgage made with the intent to prefer contrary to law has been held void against the assignee in bankruptcy of the mortgagor, although the property was a homestead and exempt from execution.[3]

This proposition may well be doubted, however, because the creditors have nothing to do with their debtor's homestead, if it is wholly exempt, and, if the debtor chooses to waive his right of homestead in favor of a mortgagee, the waiver is in his favor only; and consequently it could not be subjected for the benefit of other creditors, nor even to pay the debt of the mortgagor, if there was enough of the mortgaged property to satisfy his debt without resorting to the homestead.[4]

To render a mortgage made by an insolvent debtor void as a preference under the bankrupt law,[5] it was necessary for the assignee to show affirmatively that the mortgagee had reasonable cause to believe that the mortgagor was insolvent at the time he executed the mortgage,[6] and that it was made with intent to defeat the bankrupt law.[7] A similar rule generally prevails under the state insolvent laws.[8] Such intent is always a question of fact, and must be proved to have actually existed.[9] A mortgage made by an insolvent debtor upon his property has been held to constitute an unlawful preference, though made pursuant to an agreement to do so entered into before the insolvency as consideration for a loan; as the mortgage must be contemporaneous with the loan to escape condemnation as a preference.[10]

A creditor may lawfully accept security from an insolvent debtor, but he can not do so for the purpose and with the intention of defrauding other creditors.[11]

The giving of a new mortgage and note to the assignee of a mort-

[2] Corbett v. Woodward, 5 Sawyer (U. S.) 403.

[3] Beals v. Clark, 13 Gray (Mass.) 18.

[4] Levis v. Zinn, 93 Ky. 628, 14 Ky. L. 867, 20 S. W. 1099.

[5] Bankrupt Act of March 2, 1867, § 35; 14 Stat. at Large 534. See Jones on Chattel Mortgages, § 360.

[6] As to "reasonable cause," see Wager v. Hall, 16 Wall. (U. S.) 584, 21 L. ed. 504; Bridges v. Miles, 152 Mass. 249, 25 N. E. 463.

[7] Barbour v. Priest, 103 U. S. 293, 26 L. ed. 478.

[8] Roden v. Ellis, 113 Ala. 652, 21 So. 71; Chapoton v. Creditors, 44 La. Ann. 350, 12 So. 495; Whipple v. Bond, 164 Mass. 182, 41 N. E. 203.

[9] Union Nat. Bank v. State Nat. Bank, 168 Ill. 256, 48 N. E. 169, affg. 68 Ill. App. 43; Whipple v. Bond, 164 Mass. 182, 41 N. E. 203; Bridges v. Miles, 152 Mass. 249, 25 N. E. 461; Cook v. Holbrook, 146 Mass. 66, 14 N. E. 943; Sartwell v. North, 144 Mass. 188, 10 N. E. 824; Ogden State Bank v. Barker, 12 Utah 27, 40 Pac. 769.

[10] Feely v. Bryan, 55 W. Va. 586, 47 S. E. 307.

[11] Ellis v. Musselman, 61 Nebr. 262, 85 N. W. 75.

gage, in consideration of the release of the old mortgage, is valid when given in good faith and without any purpose of preference, though the proceedings in insolvency are begun against the mortgagor shortly afterward.[12]

Under a statute forbidding an insolvent corporation to prefer creditors, a mortgage executed by a corporation will not be held invalid where it does not appear that the corporation was insolvent. A corporation, like an individual, can appropriate its means to the payment of debts in such order and in such amounts and proportions as the directors please.[13]

But a mortgage by a debtor corporation to certain creditors, executed pending a suit to wind up the corporation as an insolvent debtor, or pending a voluntary assignment for the benefit of creditors,[14] is clearly void as being an unlawful attempt to prefer certain creditors. That is was executed in violation of a temporary injunction, in a suit wherein a receiver was asked for, is a further reason why the mortgage is a nullity.[15]

Though a corporation be insolvent but is in possession of its property and in the active prosecution of its business, and intends to continue therein, unless prevented by other creditors, its mortgage to secure a pre-existing debt is not necessarily invalid if the object of the mortgage is, on its part, not to give a preference to one creditor over another, but simply to obtain an extension of credit.[16]

A mortgage executed by an insolvent debtor to secure one of his creditors, delivered only a few moments before the execution of a deed of assignment by such debtor for the benefit of all his creditors, is void; for both instruments in such case should be construed together, and so construed, the mortgage gives a preference in a voluntary assignment to a creditor.[17]

A mortgage executed in good faith by a person about to file a voluntary petition in bankruptcy or insolvency to secure his attorney for

[12] Porter v. Welton (Conn.), 23 Atl. 868.

[13] Atlas Tack Co. v. Exchange Bank, 111 Ga. 703, 36 S. E. 939; Lowry Banking Co. v. Empire Lumber Co., 91 Ga. 623, 17 S. E. 968; Brouwer v. Harbeck, 9 N. Y. 589; Everson v. Eddy, 12 N. Y. S. 872.

[14] Reagan v. First Nat. Bank, 157 Ind. 623, 61 N. E. 575, 62 N. E. 701. See also Swift v. Dyes-Veatch Co., 28 Ind. App. 1.

[15] Bissell v. Besson, 47 N. J. Eq. 580, 22 Atl. 1077.

[16] Damarin v. Huron Iron Co., 47 Ohio St. 581, 26 N. E. 37.

[17] Goldthwaite v. Ellison, 99 Ala. 497, 12 So. 812; Peed v. Elliott, 134 Ind. 536, 34 N. E. 319; John Shillito Co. v. McConnell, 130 Ind. 41, 26 N. E. 832.

advances to be made and services to be rendered in instituting the proceedings and procuring the debtor's discharge is valid.[18]

§ 630. **Who may take advantage of the fraud.**—Though a mortgage be fraudulent and void as to a creditor, the mortgagor can not avoid it.[19] Such a mortgage conveys the property, and is binding between the parties.[20] Although the mortgagee has participated in the fraudulent intent, it is voidable only at the election of the creditors. If they do not intervene, the conveyance stands.[21] The mortgagor will not be heard to allege his own fraud.[22]

A mortgagor who has made a mortgage in fraud of his creditors may redeem without showing that the transaction has been purged of the fraud, because the mortgage is voidable only by the creditors, and is valid as between the parties.[23]

A creditor of the mortgagor, after levying execution on the equity of redemption and purchasing it at the sheriff's sale, may prove that a second mortgage, or a release of the equity to the second mortgagee by the mortgagor, is fraudulent and void by reason of fraud practiced on the mortgagor, although the mortgagor himself has made no. attempt to avoid it.[24] So may a purchaser of the equity of redemption, upon execution sale, maintain an action to set aside a deed on account of fraud.[25] A subsequent judgment creditor may show that a prior mortgage was executed fraudulently and without consideration, in an action by the mortgagee against the owner and such judgment creditor to foreclose the mortgage; and the mortgage may in such suit be subjected to the priority of the judgment.[26]

The right to impeach a mortgage as fraudulent and void as to creditors of the mortgagor does not pass to his assignee by a voluntary general assignment in trust for the benefit of his creditors subse-

---

[18] In re Parsons, 150 Mass. 343, 23 N. E. 50; Citizens' Sav. Bank &c. Co. v. Graham, 68 Vt. 306, 35 Atl. 318.

[19] Stores v. Snow, 1 Root (Conn.) 181. See also Abbe v. Newton, 19 Conn. 20; Salmon v. Bennett, 1 Conn. 525, 7 Am. Dec. 237; Risley v. Parker (N. J. Eq.), 23 Atl. 424; Bonesteel v. Sullivan, 104 Pa. St. 9; Gill v. Henry, 95 Pa. St. 388; Barwick v. Moyse, 74 Miss. 415, 21 So. 238. See ante § 626.

[20] Parkhurst v. McGraw, 24 Miss. 134. See also Kingman Plow Co. v. Knowlton, 143 Iowa 25, 119 N. W. 754.

[21] Upton v. Craig, 57 Ill. 257; Harvey v. Varney, 98 Mass. 118, and cases cited; Colt v. Sears Commercial Co., 20 R. I. 64, 37 Atl. 311.

[22] Per Shaw, C. J., in Dyer v. Homer, 22 Pick. (Mass.) 253.

[23] Stratton v. Edwards, 174 Mass. 374, 378, 54 N. E. 886; Pierce v. Le Monier, 172 Mass. 508, 53 N. E. 125; Stillings v. Turner, 153 Mass. 534, 27 N. E. 671; Harvey v. Varney, 98 Mass. 118.

[24] Ashby v. Ashby, 39 La. Ann. 105, 1 So. 282; Van Deusen v. Frink, 15 Pick. (Mass.) 449.

[25] Matson v. Capelle, 62 Mo. 235.

[26] Kelly v. Lenihan, 50 Ind. 448.

quently executed, and unaffected by any statute in force at the time, for the assignee's relations to the creditors are solely those created by the instrument of assignment.[27]

A subsequent incumbrancer can not set up in defense to a foreclosure suit that the mortgage was intended to hinder, delay, and defraud the mortgagor's creditors. It is only his creditors who have a right to claim that the mortgage is fraudulent for this reason.[28]

Neither can such subsequent incumbrancer set up the defense that the mortgage is void as against public policy, on the ground that it was made in an attempt to escape taxation. Even if the mortgagor could avail himself of these defenses, a subsequent incumbrancer has no right to insist upon them for his own benefit.[29]

An assignee in insolvency or bankruptcy who, with full knowledge of the transaction, treats a mortgage as valid by selling the property subject to the mortgage, can not afterward proceed to set the mortgage aside as an unlawful preference.[30]

Regarding the right of a judgment creditor to sell the land of his debtor upon which there is a mortgage, and after getting a deed, supposing he is purchaser, to set aside the mortgage as fraudulent, whether there are other creditors or not, there is a conflict in the cases.[31] But it would seem that where the debtor holds the title, and that title is sold under execution, neither the creditor under whose judgment the property is sold, nor the purchaser at the sale, can, after deed is obtained, bring action to cancel a prior mortgage on the ground of fraud, without showing that the mortgage was such that, had he brought a creditor's bill before selling to subject the property, he would have been entitled to the relief demanded.[32]

[27] Flower v. Cornish, 25 Minn. 473; otherwise in Colorado, Laws 1885, pp. 27, 318; Mills' Ann. Stat. 1912, § 247; Bailey v. American Nat. Bank, 12 Colo. App. 66, 54 Pac. 912.

[28] Hendon v. Morris, 110 Ala. 106, 20 So. 27; Over v. Carolus, 171 Ill. 552, 49 N. E. 514; Nichols v. Weed Sewing Machine Co., 27 Hun (N. Y.) 200, affd. 97 N. Y. 650; Colt v. Sears Commercial Co., 20 R. I. 64, 37 Atl. 311; Perkins v. Hutchinson, 17 R. I. 450, 22 Atl. 1111.

[29] Nichols v. Weed Sewing Machine Co., 27 Hun (N. Y.) 200, affd. 97 N. Y. 650.

[30] Freeland v. Freeland, 102 Mass. 475; Tuite v. Stevens, 98 Mass. 305; Snow v. Lang, 2 Allen (Mass.) 18;

Colt v. Sears Commercial Co., 20 R. I. 64, 37 Atl. 311.

[31] Teague v. Martin, 87 Ala. 500, 6 So. 362, 13 Am. St. 63; Kingman Plow Co. v. Knowlton, 143 Iowa 25, 119 N. W. 754; Wagner v. Law, 3 Wash. 500, 28 Pac. 1109, 29 Pac. 927, 15 L. R. A. 784, 28 Am. St. 56.

[32] Apperson v. Burgett, 33 Ark. 328; Kingman Plow Co. v. Knowlton, 143 Iowa 25, 119 N. W. 754; Payne v. Burks, 4 B. Mon. (Ky.) 492; White v. Cates, 7 Dana (Ky.) 357; Marshall v. Blass, 82 Mich. 518, 46 N. W. 947, 47 N. W. 516; Messmore v. Huggard, 46 Mich. 558, 9 N. W. 853; Cleveland v. Taylor, 3 Mich. 203; Knoop v. Kelsey, 121 Mo. 642, 26 S. W. 683; Woodward v. Mastin, 106 Mo. 324, 17 S. W. 308;

§ 630a. Effect of conveyance to a trustee to pay debts.—A conveyance by a debtor to a trustee to sell the property and pay his debts to his creditors named, or to all his creditors, with a reservation of the surplus to himself, is in effect a mortgage.[33] The debtor's reservation of the surplus does not make the mortgage fraudulent; but if the assignment is an absolute transfer of all the property of the debtor, the transaction amounts to an assignment for the benefit of creditors, and its validity then depends upon the conformity of the conveyance with the statutes regulating such assignments.[34] But where a mortgagor, being unable to pay his debt, executes an absolute deed of the property to the mortgagee, who received the deed in payment of the debt and agreed that, in case the property should sell for more than enough to satisfy the mortgage debt, he would account to the mortgagor for the surplus, such conveyance can not be treated as a mortgage in equity.[35]

The chief distinction between an assignment for the benefit of creditors and an assignment in trust in the nature of a mortgage is, that in the former case the assignment is an absolute transfer of all the debtor's property for the benefit of all his creditors; while, in the latter case, the assignment is for the security of the creditors, the debtor retaining an equitable title or equity of redemption.[36] Where the instrument is in form a mortgage, and not an assignment for the benefit of creditors, the presumption, until overcome by proof, is that the parties intended it to have effect as a mortgage. The fact that it provides that the mortgagor should surrender immediate possession to the mortgage trustee does not convert it into an assignment. To accomplish that result it must be shown that it was the intention that the debtor should be divested, not only of his control over his property, but also of his title.[37] A mortgage is not rendered fraudulent by a provision, added to a power of sale conferred upon the mortgagee, that he is to hold the residue of the proceeds subject to the order of the mortgagor.[38]

De Grauw v. Mechan, 48 N. J. Eq. 219, 21 Atl. 193; Thigpen v. Pitt, 54 N. Car. 49.

[33] Stafford Nat. Bank v. Sprague, 17 Fed. 784; De Wolf v. Sprague Mfg. Co., 49 Conn. 282; Chafee v. Fourth Nat. Bank, 71 Maine 514, 36 Am. Rep. 345; Austin v. Sprague Mfg. Co., 14 R. I. 464; Union Co. v. Sprague, 14 R. I. 452; Monaghan Bay Co. v. Dickson, 39 S. Car. 146, 17 S. E. 696; Verner v. McGhee, 26 S. Car. 248, 2 S. E. 113; Jones on Chattel Mortgages, §§ 352-355.

[34] Jones on Chattel Mortgages, § 352a.

[35] Weltner v. Thurmond, 17 Wyo. 268, 98 Pac. 590, 99 Pac. 1128.

[36] Hargadine v. Henderson, 97 Mo. 375, 11 S. W. 218.

[37] Smith v. Empire Lumber Co., 57 Ark. 222, 21 S. W. 225; Robson v. Tomlinson, 54 Ark. 229, 15 S. W. 456. substantially in the language of the court.

[38] Coulter v. Lumpkin, 88 Ga. 277, 14 S. E. 614; Calloway v. People's Bank, 54 Ga. 441; Lay v. Seago, 47

§ 631. Estoppel to deny validity.—A mortgagor is not estopped from setting up the invalidity of his mortgage, unless there has been some fraud, misrepresentation, or concealment on his part.[39] But he is estopped from setting up any defense which is inconsistent with representations made by him in obtaining the loan which the mortgage was given to secure, when the lender has relied upon these representations in making the loan and taking the mortgage.[40] Thus, if a mortgagor induce a person to purchase the mortgage by a statement or certificate that a certain sum is due upon it, and that there is no offset or defense to it, the borrower is precluded from claiming that this sum is not the true amount due, or that the mortgage is void, either wholly or in part, for usury.[41] But if the purchaser of the security did not believe the existence of the facts in reference to which the estoppel is sought to be interposed, and did not act upon any such belief, the mortgagor is not estopped to show the real facts of the case.[42]

To create a valid estoppel, the holder of the mortgage must have purchased in reliance upon the truth of the representations. Therefore, where a mortgage and a certificate accompanying it that the mortgage was given "for a good and valid consideration to the full amount thereof, and that the same is subject to no offset or defense whatever," were both procured by fraud, and the purchaser did not rely upon the truth of the certificate, but upon the effect of it, as a matter of law, to protect him, it was held that the mortgagor could still set up the fraud in defense to the mortgage.[43]

A mortgage made to aid an officer in the settlement of his official accounts by making up a deficiency, and used for that purpose, can not

Ga. 82; Rowland v. Coleman, 45 Ga. 204; Banks v. Clapp, 12 Ga. 514; Carey v. Giles, 10 Ga. 9.

[39] Brewster v. Madden, 15 Kans. 249. See also Wilson v. Watts, 9 Md. 356; Radican v. Radican, 22 R. I. 405, 48 Atl. 143; Tucker v. Tucker, 72 S. Car. 295, 51 S. E. 876.

[40] Rogers v. Union Cent. L. Ins. Co., 111 Ind. 343, 12 N. E. 495; Kelley v. Fisk, 110 Ind. 552, 11 N. E. 453.

[41] Smyth v. Munroe, 84 N. Y. 354; Lesley v. Johnson, 41 Barb. (N. Y.) 359; Eitel v. Bracken, 6 J. & S. (N. Y.) 7. "It is a wise and just restriction that, if a mortgagor makes a false statement, orally or in writing, to influence the purchase of the security, he can not take ad-vantage of it as against an innocent purchaser. The law adjudges him to be estopped from profiting by his own fraud." Per Curtis, J.

[42] Wilcox v. Howell, 44 N. Y. 398; Eitel v. Bracken, 6 J. & S. (N. Y.) 7; Van Sickle v. Palmer, 2 Thomp. & C. (N. Y.) 612.

[43] Eitel v. Bracken, 6 J. & S. (N. Y.) 7, per Curtis, J. "It is contrary to good morals that a certificate containing an unadulterated falsehood, and known to both the maker and recipient to be simply such, should be sustained as sufficient to protect the latter in the purchase of a mortgage, because he believed it would so protect him as a matter of law, and would not have bought the mortgage without it."

afterward be repudiated by the maker as invalid. He can not complain that, after having accomplished its purpose by being used as evidence of a loan with his consent, it is held to be a valid obligation.[44] He is estopped, too, from denying the official character of the grantee, as a commissioner of the school fund, although the office had been abolished. The mortgage being intended as a security for the school fund, it will be given the effect intended by the parties, and the maker will not be allowed to deny its recitals.[45]

Payment by a landowner of interest on a mortgage to which his signature was forged, estops him from contesting the validity of the instrument.[46]

§ 632. When mortgage in fraud of creditors may not be invalidated.—A mortgagor is not allowed to invalidate his own deed by showing that it was executed by him for the purpose of defrauding his creditors. A court of equity will not lend its aid to relieve the mortgagor from the consequences of his own fraudulent act, nor will it aid the mortgagee in securing him in the enjoyment of the property, where its interposition is necessary for that purpose. The mortgagee is left to his legal remedies, which will enable him, when invested with the legal title, to recover the possession of the mortgaged property. So far as the contract is executory, he is without remedy, either legal or equitable.[47]

Where the mortgagee can show a prima facie right to recover on the face of the instrument without revealing any fraud in the transaction, the mortgagor will not be permitted to plead as a defense that the mortgage was executed for the purpose of defrauding his creditors of which purpose the mortgagee was aware.[48]

A defense to the enforcement of a mortgage for the want of consideration can not be met by evidence that the mortgage was given with a view to defraud the creditors of the mortgagor.[49] "The general rule of policy is, In pari delicto potior est conditio defendentis. If there was an intent to defraud creditors, it was an intent common to both parties, affecting as well the plaintiff's intestate as the defendant.

[44] Floyd v. Morrison, 40 Iowa 188.
[45] Floyd v. Morrison, 40 Iowa 188.
[46] Rothschild v. Title Guarantee &c. Co., 204 N. Y. 458, 97 N. E. 879, 41 L. R. A. (N. S.) 740; Vohmann v. Michel, 185 N. Y. 420, 78 N. E. 156, 113 Am. St. 921.
[47] Brookover v. Hurst, 1 Metc. (Ky.) 665; United States Mtg. Co. v. Marquam, 41 Ore. 391, 69 Pac. 37.
[48] Pitzele v. Cohn, 217 Ill. 30, 75 N. E. 392; Harvey v. Varney, 98 Mass. 118; Barwick v. Moyse, 74 Miss. 415, 21 So. 238, 60 Am. St. 512; Walker v. Brungard, 13 Smedes & M. (Miss.) 723; Bonesteel v. Sullivan, 104 Pa. St. 9; Williams v. Williams, 34 Pa. St. 312.
[49] Williams v. Clink, 90 Mich. 297, 51 N. W. 453; Judge v. Vogel, 38 Mich. 569.

It is the plaintiff who is the actor, and is seeking to enforce the payment of these notes. It may be held that the defendant would not be permitted to show that the notes were made to delay and defeat creditors as a substantive ground of defense, on the well-known maxim, Nemo allegans suam turpitudinem audiendus sit; and therefore, if a legal consideration were shown, such a defense could not avail. But independently of this ground, he shows want of consideration, and it is the demandant who seeks to rebut that defense by showing that the notes were given as well to defeat creditors as without consideration."[50]

II. *Usury*

---

[50] Wearse v. Pierce, 24 Pick. (Mass.) 141, per Shaw, C. J.; Briggs v. Langford, 107 N. Y. 680, 14 N. E. 502.

§ 633. **Usury laws in general.**—Usury laws apply to mortgages in the same manner that they apply to contracts in general, and the same principles of law are applicable to the inquiry whether they are usurious or not. The subject of usury is of less importance now than it was formerly, for the reason that within a few years usury laws have been repealed in several states, and in others they have been greatly modified, so that only in a few states does usury now invalidate a contract. A brief statement of the laws of the several states with reference to interest and usury is given in a note; but it is to be borne in mind that these laws are at present subject to frequent changes.[1]

[1] Alabama: Eight per cent. Usury forfeits interest, but not principal. The defendant recovers full costs. Code 1907, §§ 4619-4625.

Alaska: Eight per cent. but parties may contract for any rate not exceeding twelve per cent. Ann. Codes 1900, pt. v, §§ 255-258. Forfeiture for usury double the interest collected.

Arizona: Six per cent. when there is no express agreement, but the parties may contract in writing for any rate not in excess of ten per cent. Rev. Stat. 1913, p. 1219.

Arkansas: Six per cent, but parties may contract for any rate not exceeding ten per cent. Usury renders the contract void, both as to principal and interest. Kirb. Dig. 1911, ch. 113.

California: Seven per cent. but the parties may contract for any rate, simple or compound. Civ. Code 1903, §§ 1917-1920.

Colorado: Eight per cent. but parties may stipulate in writing for a higher rate. Mills' Ann. Stats., Revised Edition, 1912, ch. 85.

Connecticut: Six per cent. Payments in excess of that rate can not be set off or recovered back. Gen. Stat. 1888, §§ 2941-2943; Gen. Stat. 1902, §§ 4598, 4599.

Delaware: Six per cent. Usury forfeits a sum of money equal to the whole loan. Rev. Code 1874, ch. 63, § 1.

District of Columbia: Six per cent. Any interest contracted for in excess of six per cent. shall be forfeited. Code 1911, §§ 1178-1186.

Florida: Eight per cent., but any rate may be agreed upon. Contracts for more than ten per cent. interest are void. Double the amount paid over that rate may be recovered. Rev. Stat. 1892, § 2320, Appendix, ch. 4022.

Georgia: Seven per cent., but parties may contract in writing for any rate not exceeding eight per cent. Interest in excess is forfeited. Code 1882, §§ 2050, 2051, 2057; Code 1895, §§ 2876, 2888. Titles made as part of a usurious contract are void; Code 1882, § 2057f. But a mortgage passes no title, and is not void for usury; Holliday v. Lowry Banking Co., 92 Ga. 675, 19 S. E. 28; Hodge v. Brown, 81 Ga. 276, 7 S. E. 282; Frost v. Allen, 57 Ga. 326.

Hawaiian Islands: Legal rate eight per cent.; by written contract, twelve per cent.

Idaho: Seven per cent. Parties may by writing agree to pay a higher rate, not to exceed twelve per cent. per annum. Revised Codes 1908, Vol. I, p. 683.

Illinois: Five per cent., but parties may contract in writing for any rate not exceeding seven per cent. Usury forfeits the entire interest. Corporations can not interpose this defense. Hurd's Rev. Stat. 1912, ch. 74, § 2. See also Fowler v. Equitable Trust Co., 141 U. S. 384, 35 L. ed. 786, 12 Sup. Ct. 1.

Indiana: Six per cent., but parties may contract in writing for any rate not exceeding eight. Usury forfeits the excess. Rev. Stat. 1888.

§§ 5198, 5201. Revision 1901, §§ 7043, 7046; Burns' Rev. 1914, § 7950.

Iowa: Six per cent., but parties may agree in writing for a rate not exceeding eight. Usury forfeits eight per cent. on the contract to the school fund, and only the principal can be recovered. Code 1873, and Rev. Code 1880, §§ 2077, 2080; Code 1897, §§ 3038, 3041; Code, Title 15, ch. 2.

Kansas: Six per cent., but parties may contract in writing for not exceeding ten per cent. Payments in excess are accounted as payments on the principal, and a sum equal to twice the excess over ten per cent. is forfeited. Gen. Stat. 1899, §§ 3482, 3483; Gen. Stat. 1909, §§ 4344-4346.

Kentucky: Six per cent. Usury forfeits the excess above that rate. Stat. 1909, § 2218; Gen. Laws 1899, §§ 2218, 2219.

Louisiana: Five per cent. Eight per cent. may be stipulated. Usury forfeits the entire interest. Civ. Code 1912, art. 2924.

Maine: Six per cent., but the parties may agree in writing for any other rate, but not in excess of fifteen per cent. on loans of less than $200 on personal property. Rev. Stat. ch. 45. See also Lindsay v. Hill, 66 Maine 212.

Maryland: Six per cent. Usury forfeits the interest. Code 1910, art. 49. Acts 1912, ch. 835.

Massachusetts: Six per cent., but parties may contract in writing for any rate. Pub. Stat. 1882, ch. 77, § 3; Rev. Laws 1902, ch. 73, § 3.

Michigan: Five per cent., but parties may contract in writing for not exceeding seven per cent. Usury forfeits the interest, but it can not be recovered after a voluntary payment. A purchaser in good faith of negotiable paper is not affected by the usury. Howell's Ann. Stats., Sec. Ed., 1913, Vol. II, §§ 2869, 2870.

Minnesota: Six per cent. Parties may agree in writing upon any rate not exceeding ten per cent. A contract for more is usurious, and makes void all instruments except negotiable paper in the hands of bona fide purchasers. Interest in excess may be recovered. Laws 1899, ch. 122; Gen. Stat. 1894, §§ 2212, 2213; Gen. Stat. 1913, §§ 5805-5809; Scott v. Austin, 36 Minn. 460, 32 N. W. 89, 864; Jordan v. Humphrey, 31 Minn. 495, 18 N. W. 450; Beal v. White, 28 Minn. 6, 8 N. W. 829. This exception is not applicable to mortgages securing such paper.

Mississippi: Six per cent. is legal rate, but eight per cent. may be provided for in writing. More than eight per cent. is usurious and forfeits all interest. Code 1906, § 2678. Purvis v. Woodward, 78 Miss. 922, 29 So. 917.

Missouri: Six per cent., but parties may contract in writing for any rate not exceeding eight. Usurious interest is credited on the debt. Rev. Stat. 1889, ch. 90; Rev. Stat. 1899, §§ 3705, 3709; Rev. Stat. 1909, § 3782.

Montana: Eight per cent., but parties may stipulate for any rate. Comp. Stats. 1887, ch. 73.

Nebraska: Seven per cent., but parties may contract for a rate not exceeding ten, and this may be taken in advance. Usury forfeits all interest. Comp. Stats. 1885, and 1899, ch. 44; Rev. Stat. 1913, §§ 3346-3351.

Nevada: Seven per cent., but parties may contract in writing for any other rate not exceeding twelve per cent. Rev. Laws 1912, §§ 2499, 2500.

New Hampshire: Six per cent. Usury forfeits three times the excess. Principal and legal interest may be recovered. Gen. Stat. 1867, ch. 213; Acts 1872, ch. 12, § 3; Gen. Laws 1878, ch. 232, §§ 3, 4; Pub. Stat. 1901, ch. 203, § 2.

New Jersey: Six per cent. Usury forfeits all interest. Comp. Stat. 1909-1910, p. 5704; Supp. to Rev. 1886, p. 398.

New Mexico: Six per cent., but by written agreement a rate not exceeding twelve may be agreed for. Taking more than twelve per cent. is a misdemeanor. Usury forfeits double the interest collected. Comp. Laws 1897, §§ 2552, 2553.

New York: Six per cent. Usury makes void the contract, but no corporation can plead the defense. It is also a misdemeanor. Banks are exempt from these penalties. Usury forfeits principal and interest. 3

The National Banking Act[2] provides that banks organized under it may take interest at the rate allowed by the laws of the state where

Rev. Stat. (7th ed.), pp. 2253-2256, 1419; Gen. Bus. Law, §§ 370, 371, 373.

North Carolina: Six per cent. Usury forfeits the entire interest, and twice the amount of interest paid may be recovered. Pell's Revisal of 1908, §§ 1950, 1951; Moore v. Beaman, 111 N. Car. 328, 16 S. E. 177; Gore v. Lewis, 109 N. Car. 539, 13 S. E. 909; Kidder v. McIlhenny, 81 N. Car. 123.

North Dakota: Seven per cent., but parties may contract for a higher rate not exceeding twelve per cent. Usury forfeits all interest. Comp. Laws 1913, §§ 6072, 6076.

Ohio: Six per cent. Parties may contract in writing for not more than eight per cent. Usury forfeits excess of interest. Judgments bear interest at rate of the contract. Gen. Code 1910, §§ 8303, 8305.

Oklahoma: Six per cent., but parties may contract for ten per cent. per annum. Persons contracting for, receiving or retaining a greater rate forfeit all such interest so received, retained or taken. Ind. T. Ann. Stat. 1899, § 3073.

Oregon: Six per cent., but parties may contract for ten per cent. Usury forfeits the interest absolutely. Ann. Laws 1887, §§ 3587-3594.

Pennsylvania: Six per cent. Usurious interest can not be collected, and, if paid, may be recovered by suit brought within six months. Negotiable paper, taken in good faith, is not affected by the discount. Obligations of railroad and canal companies not within the law. Brightly's Purdon's Dig. 1883, pp. 926-928.

Rhode Island: Six per cent., but parties may agree on rate up to thirty per cent. per annum on amounts exceeding fifty dollars, and on rate up to five per cent. per month for not more than three months on amounts not exceeding fifty dollars. Pub. Laws 1909, ch. 434.

South Carolina: Seven per cent., or eight by express contract. Usury forfeits all interest, and makes the lender liable for double the amount received. Gen. Stat. 1882, § 1288; Code 1902, §§ 1662, 1663.

South Dakota: Seven per cent., but parties may contract for not exceeding twelve per cent. Usury forfeits all interest. Rev. Codes 1903, §§ 1417, 1419.

Tennessee: Six per cent. Interest above six per cent. can not be recovered, or, if paid, may be recovered back. Code 1884, §§ 2699-2712.

Texas: Six per cent. By contract ten per cent. may be reserved. The excess is void. Double the amount of usurious interest may be recovered. Act of April 11, 1892; Rev. Stat. 1895, §§ 3097, 3106.

Utah: Eight per cent. is legal rate. Contract agreement or loans for more than twelve per cent. interest is void. Comp. Laws 1907, §§ 124, 1241x.

Vermont: Six per cent. Excess can not be recovered, or, if paid, may be recovered back. Rev. Laws 1880, §§ 1996-2000; Rev. Stat. 1894, § 2301; Pub. Stat. 1906, Title 15, ch. 125.

Virginia: Six per cent. Usury forfeits all interest, corporations excepted. Code 1887, ch. 130; Code 1904, § 2817.

Washington: Six per cent., but twelve per cent. may be agreed upon. Usury forfeits double the interest. Rem. & Bal. Code, § 6251; Reed v. Miller, 4 Wash. St. 426, 25 Pac. 334.

West Virginia: Six per cent. The excess can not be recovered. Corporations can not plead usury. Code 1887, ch. 96; Code 1899, ch. 96.

Wisconsin: Six per cent., but parties may contract for payment and receipt of a rate not exceeding ten per cent per annum. Stat. 1898, § 1691.

Wyoming: Eight per cent., but any rate not exceeding twelve per cent. may be agreed upon. Rev. Stat. 1887, §§ 1310-1316; Comp. Stat. 1910, §§ 3355, 3356.

[2] See ante U. S. Rev. Stats. § 5198.

the banks are located, and no more, except that where by such laws a different rate is limited for banks of issue organized under state laws, the same rate shall be allowed the national banks. When no rate is fixed by state or territorial laws national banks may take not exceeding seven per cent. The penalty for taking a greater rate of interest is a forfeiture of the entire interest reserved; and in case a greater interest has been paid, the debtor may recover twice the amount of the interest thus paid. This statute is exclusive of state legislation for taking usury.[3]

A debt can not be avoided by reason of usury charged by a national bank;[4] nor can a bank, by offering to remit the excess, evade the statute as to forfeiture of the entire interest.[5]

§ 634. **Intent to take usury.**—There is some conflict as to whether an unlawful intent is essential to constitute usury, it being held in some states that an intent to take unlawful interest is an essential element of usury,[6] while in other states a more or less contrary doctrine obtains,[7] but it is settled that the court will look to the real character of the transaction regardless of its form.[8]

To constitute usury there must either be an agreement between the parties by which the borrower promises to pay, and the lender knowingly receives, a higher rate of interest than the statute allows for the loan or forbearance of money, or such greater rate of interest must

---

[3] Oates v. National Bank, 100 U. S. 239, 25 L. ed. 580; Barnet v. National Bank, 98 U. S. 555, 25 L. ed. 212; Farmers' &c. Nat. Bank v. Dearing, 91 U. S. 29, 23 L. ed. 196; De Wolf v. Johnson, 10 Wheat. (U. S.) 367, 6 L. ed. 343; Slaughter v. First Nat. Bank, 109 Ala. 157, 19 So. 430; Florence R. &c. Co. v. Chase Nat. Bank, 106 Ala. 364, 17 So. 720; Rockwell v. Farmers' Nat. Bank, 4 Colo. App. 562, 36 Pac. 905; First Nat. Bank v. McEntire, 112 Ga. 232, 37 S. E. 381; Wiley v. Starbuck, 44 Ind. 298; First Nat. Bank v. Childs, 133 Mass. 248; Davis v. Randall, 115 Mass. 547; Central Nat. Bank v. Pratt, 115 Mass. 539; Norfolk Nat. Bank v. Schwenk, 46 Nebr. 381, 64 N. W. 1073; Barker v. Bank, 59 N. H. 310; Importers' &c. Nat. Bank v. Littell, 46 N. J. L. 506; Oldham v. First Nat. Bank, 85 N. Car. 240; Merchants' &c. Nat. Bank v. Myers, 74 N. Car. 514; Higley v. Bank, 26 Ohio St. 75; Bank

v. Brown, 72 Pa. St. 209; Purdon's Dig., vol. 2, p. 1987; Hill v. Bank, 56 Vt. 582.

[4] Stephens v. Monongahela Bank, 111 U. S. 197, 28 L. ed. 399, 4 Sup. Ct. 337; Cox v. Beck, 83 Fed. 269; Chase Nat. Bank v. Faurot, 149 N. Y. 532, 44 N. E. 164, 35 L. R. A. 605.

[5] Citizens' Nat. Bank v. Donnell, 195 U. S. 369, 49 L. ed. 238, 25 Sup. Ct. 49.

[6] Furr v. Keesler, 3 Ga. App. 188, 59 S. E. 596; Clemens v. Crane, 234 Ill. 215, 84 N. E. 884; Ætna Bldg. &c. Assn. v. Randall, 23 Okla. 45, 99 Pac. 655; Covington v. Fisher, 22 Okla. 207, 97 Pac. 615.

[7] State v. Haney, 130 Mo. App. 95, 108 S. W. 1080.

[8] Klein v. Title Guaranty &c. Co., 166 Fed. 365; Widell v. Citizens' Nat. Bank, 104 Minn. 510, 116 N. W. 919; Knoup v. Carver, 74 N. J. Eq. 449, 70 Atl. 660; Dale v. Duryea, 49 Wash. 644, 96 Pac. 223.

be knowingly and intentionally reserved, taken, or secured for such loan or forbearance.[9]

A mortgage given to secure a just debt is neither invalid as against the mortgagor, nor fraudulent as against his creditors, because interest has been calculated upon the debt and included in the mortgage in excess of the strict legal right, or because interest was charged when no interest at all was collectible at law, if the allowance was just and equitable;[10] or because an item which was subject to objection for usury was inadvertently included in the mortgage loan when the parties had agreed that all the items which might render the loan usurious should be eliminated.[11]

But if a mortgage be given to secure a pre-existing debt, which was tainted with usury, the mortgage will be vitiated by usury of the original indebtedness.[12] A mortgage given in renewal of one that is tainted with usury is itself affected with the same taint.[13] And the consequences of the usury will attend the new security, even when this is given by a third person, if there be no other consideration than the original usurious debt.[14] But if the usurious mortgage be transferred to an innocent holder, and he receives directly from the mortgagor a new one in its stead, the latter can not be impeached on account of the usury in the original mortgage.[15] There is no rule of law which makes it unlawful or usurious in one to loan money, to be used by the borrower in paying a usurious debt to another, if this loan be itself free from usury.[16]

Where one owing a debt induced his creditor to procure a loan upon a mortgage of the debtor's land to a third person, which though executed to the creditor was with the mortgagor's knowledge taken for the benefit of the person who loaned the money, and was immediately transferred to him, usury in the original debt of which the mortgagor is not shown to have had any knowledge, does not affect him.[17]

---

[9] Briggs v. Steele, 91 Ark. 458, 121 S. W. 754.

[10] Spencer v. Ayrault, 10 N. Y. 202.

[11] Jarvis v. Southern Grocery Co., 63 Ark. 225, 38 S. W. 148.

[12] Vickery v. Dickson, 35 Barb. (N. Y.) 96; Thompson v. Berry, 3 Johns. Ch. (N. Y.) 395, 17 Johns. 436; Bell v. Lent, 24 Wend. (N. Y.) 230.

[13] McCraney v. Alden, 46 Barb. (N. Y.) 272; Cope v. Wheeler, 41 N. Y. 303. See also Hoyt v. Bridge-water Copper Mining Co., 6 N. J. Eq. 253, 625.

[14] Exley v. Berryhill, 37 Minn. 182, 33 N. W. 567.

[15] Kilner v. O'Brien, 14 Hun (N. Y.) 414; Sherwood v. Archer, 10 Hun (N. Y.) 73; Sweeney v. Peaslee, 17 N. Y. S. 225. See also Jenkins v. Levis, 25 Kans. 479.

[16] Wilson v. Harvey, 4 Lans. (N. Y.) 507.

[17] May v. Folsom, 113 Ala. 198, 20 So. 984.

Usury to affect a mortgage must relate directly to the mortgage debt. A valid mortgage is not affected by a subsequent usurious agreement, such,[18] for instance, as an agreement by the mortgagor to pay usurious interest to the assignee of the mortgage,[19] or the payment of usurious interest for a renewal.[20] If a mortgage not affected by usury be assigned as collateral security for a debt of the mortgagee, usury taken by the assignee on the latter debt can not be set up as a defense to the mortgage.[21]

But a provision in a mortgage for the payment of a higher rate of interest after maturity of the mortgage debt is by some courts regarded as a penalty which will not be enforced, but the contract rate before maturity will continue afterward.[22]

There must be an intention knowingly to contract for and to take usurious interest, for, if neither party intends it, the law will not infer a corrupt agreement.[23]

Inasmuch as usury depends upon the intent with which it is taken, the court will look into the whole transaction to determine what the intent was, not only into the acts of the parties at the time of the transaction, but subsequently.[24]

A stipulation for the payment of interest at the highest rate allowed by law, at periods shorter than a year, whether semiannually or quarterly, does not make the loan usurious.[25] Nor does an agreement to pay compound interest render the contract usurious.[26] Neither is the

[18] Richardson v. Campbell, 34 Nebr. 181, 51 N. W. 753; Allison v. Schmitz, 31 Hun (N. Y.) 106.

[19] Hann v. Dekater (N. J. Eq.), 20 Atl. 657; Conover v. Hobart, 24 N. J. Eq. 120; Smith v. Hollister, 14 N. J. Eq. 153; Donnington v. Meeker, 11 N. J. Eq. 362.

[20] Dotterer v. Freeman, 88 Ga. 479, 14 S. E. 863.

[21] Stevens v. Reeves, 33 N. J. Eq. 427.

[22] Conrad v. Gibbon, 29 Iowa 120; Richardson v. Campbell, 34 Nebr. 181, 51 N. W. 753; Weyrich v. Hobleman, 14 Nebr. 432, 16 N. W. 436.

[23] Bank of United States v. Waggener, 34 U. S. 378, 9 L. ed. 163; Jordan v. Mitchell, 25 Ark. 258; Moody v. Hawkins, 25 Ark. 197.

[24] Lurton v. Jacksonville Loan &c. Assn., 187 Ill. 141, 58 N. E. 218, affg. 87 Ill. App. 395; Stelle v. Andrews, 19 N. J. Eq. 409; Bardwell v. Howe, Clarke (N. Y.) 281. See also White v. Lucas, 46 Iowa 319;

Guggenheimer v. Geiszler, 81 N. Y. 293; Knickerbocker L. Ins. Co. v. Nelson, 78 N. Y. 137; Fox v. Lipe, 24 Wend. (N. Y.) 164; Dozier v. Mitchell, 65 Ala. 511. Where loan was made through an agent. Robinson v. Blaker, 85 Minn. 242, 88 N. W. 845.

[25] Fowler v. Equitable Trust Co., 141 U. S. 384, 35 L. ed. 786, 12 Sup. Ct. 1; Meyer v. Muscatine, 1 Wall. (U. S.) 384, 17 L. ed. 564; Telford v. Garrels, 132 Ill. 550, 24 N. E. 573; Brown v. Mortgage Co., 110 Ill. 235; Goodrich v. Reynolds, 31 Ill. 490; Mowry v. Bishop, 5 Paige (N. Y.) 98. See also Willett v. Maxwell, 169 Ill. 540, 48 N. E. 473; Swanson v. Realization &c. Corp., 70 Minn. 380, 73 N. W. 165.

[26] Graham v. Fitts, 53 Fla. 1046, 43 So. 512; Abbott v. Stone, 172 Ill. 634, 50 N. E. 328, 64 Am. St. 60; Otis v. Lindsey, 10 Maine 315; Sanford v. Lundquist, 80 Nebr. 414, 118 N. W. 129, 18 L. R. A. (N. S.) 633;

taking of interest at the highest rate allowed by law, in advance for a whole year, usurious.[27] Nor is the taking of a portion of such interest in advance for the whole term of the mortgage usurious.[28]

A loan upon a second mortgage at the highest interest allowed by law is not made usurious by a contract made by the mortgagee with the mortgagor that he will pay off a first mortgage, a smaller amount, upon the same property, having several years to run, and bearing a much lower rate of interest.[29]

A verbal agreement for an additional advantage or compensation to the lender, in addition to interest reserved at the highest legal rate, renders the mortgage usurious.[30]

Equity will interfere, upon a proper application, to prevent the collection of usurious interest by the enforcement of a mortgage, when the debtor has paid or tendered all that either law or equity can require him to pay.[31]

A mortgage loan may be usurious in part and valid in part; as, for instance, when the mortgage covers several distinct loans, one of which was usurious in consequence of the payment of a bonus, but

---

Steen v. Stretch, 50 Nebr. 572, 70 N. W. 48; Rose v. Munford, 36 Nebr. 148, 54 N. W. 129; Kellogg v. Hickok, 1 Wend. (N. Y.) 521; Fobes v. Cantfield, 3 Ohio 17; Goodale v. Wallace, 19 S. Dak. 405, 103 N. W. 651, 117 Am. St. 962; Hale v. Hale, 1 Coldw. (Tenn.) 233, 78 Am. Dec. 490.

[27] Tholen v. Duffy, 7 Kans. 405, and cases cited. See also National Life Ins. Co. v. Donovan, 238 Ill. 283, 87 N. E. 356; Steen v. Stretch, 50 Nebr. 572, 70 N. W. 48.

[28] Fowler v. Equitable Trust Co., 141 U. S. 384, 35 L. ed. 786, 12 Sup. Ct. 1. In this case the term of the mortgage was five years, and three per cent. of the ten per cent. interest was taken out in advance, seven per cent. of the interest being evidenced by coupons attached to the bonds. Mr. Justice Harlan, delivering judgment, said: "Whether that doctrine would apply where the loan was for such period that the exaction by the lender of interest in advance would, at the outset, absorb so much of the principal as to leave the borrower very little of the amount agreed to be loaned to him,

we need not say. The present case does not require any expression of opinion upon such a point, for the interest reserved in advance on the loan to Fowler was only three per cent. out of ten per cent.; and a reservation to that extent, it would seem, is protected by the decisions of the state court. The defense of usury, so far as it rests upon the fact that three per cent. of the stipulated interest was taken in advance by the lender, must, therefore, be overruled." It is to be observed that the decision had reference to the law of the state of Illinois.

[29] Hodgdon v. Davis, 6 Dak. 21, 50 N. W. 478.

[30] Vilas v. McBride, 17 N. Y. S. 171. In this case, as a condition of loaning money on a mortgage on hotel property at the highest legal rate, it was agreed to give the lender the manure made on the property, estimated as worth $100 per year, and the manure was for several years claimed and taken by the lender. Such agreement rendered the mortgage usurious.

[31] Waite v. Ballou, 19 Kans. 601.

the other loans were not usurious. The forfeiture or penalty in such case will be confined to the usurious part only.[32]

The fact that there was included in the loan a commission to the lender for storing, weighing and selling cotton belonging to the borrower, which he had agreed to pay, does not render the loan usurious if the commission is reasonable.[33]

Where a borrower executes a mortgage negotiated by his broker in which, in compliance with the conditions imposed by the lender, the broker's commissions are included, and the lender accepts the security and makes the loan, the broker does not thereby become the agent of the lender, and the loan is not rendered usurious by the commissions included in the mortgage.[34]

Nor is a loan rendered usurious by the fact that the agent of the lender, without the knowledge or consent of the latter, exacts from the borrower a bonus for his service in addition to the highest legal rate of interest, which the contract reserves for the benefit of the lender.[35] But a charge of twenty per cent. of the loan as commission made against the borrower by the lender's agent, knowledge of which is imputed to the lender, makes the transaction usurious, where such commission and the interest added exceed the lawful rate of interest.[36]

Where the total amount of interest charged and the commissions received for making a loan do not exceed the legal rate of interest for the length of time for which the loan was made, the loan is not usurious.[37]

§ 635. **Effect of provision for attorney's fees and damages.**[38]—A stipulation in a mortgage to secure a loan, to pay a reasonable attorney's fee in case of foreclosure, does not render the contract usurious.[39]

---

[32] Mahn v. Hussey, 28 N. J. Eq. 546.

[33] Jarvis v. Southern Grocery Co., 63 Ark. 225, 38 S. W. 148. See also Harmon v. Lehman, 85 Ala. 379, 5 So. 197.

[34] George v. New England Mtg. Sec. Co., 109 Ala. 548, 20 So. 331; Land Mortgage Inv. &c. Co. v. Vinson, 105 Ala. 389, 17 So. 23; American Mtg. Co. v. King, 105 Ala. 358, 16 So. 889; Edinburg Am. Land Mtg. Co. v. Peoples, 102 Ala. 241, 14 So. 656; American Freehold Land Mtg. Co. v. Sewell, 92 Ala. 163, 9 So. 143; Ginn v. New England Mtg. Sec. Co., 92 Ala. 135, 8 So. 388. See also Secor v. Patterson, 114 Mich. 37, 72 N. W. 9.

[35] Vahlberg v. Keaton, 51 Ark. 534, 11 S. W. 878, 4 L. R. A. 462, 14 Am. St. 73; Cox v. Massachusetts Mut. L. Ins. Co., 113 Ill. 382; Ammerman v. Ross, 84 Iowa 359, 51 N. W. 6; Van Wyck v. Watters, 81 N. Y. 352; Barger v. Taylor, 30 Ore. 228, 47 Pac. 618; Franzen v. Hammond, 136 Wis. 239, 116 N. W. 169, 19 L. R. A. (N. S.) 399, 128 Am. St. 1079.

[36] American Mortgage Co. v. Woodward, 83 S. Car. 521, 65 S. E. 739.

[37] National Life Ins. Co. v. Donovan, 238 Ill. 283, 87 N. E. 356.

[38] See post § 1606.

[39] Fowler v. Equitable Trust Co., 141 U. S. 411, 35 L. ed. 794, 12 Sup. Ct. 8; Barton v. Farmers' &c. Nat.

If the contract is lawful in other respects, the conditional stipulation to pay the usual attorney's fee, in the event suit has to be instituted to enforce it, will be legal and founded upon a valuable consideration. Such fee, though not an element of damages, in an ordinary suit for the collection of money, can be made such by an express contract.[40]

The fact that the borrower, in addition to the maximum legal rate of interest reserved on the loan, also paid the attorney of the lender a fee for examining the title to the land mortgaged to secure the debt, did not render the transaction usurious as to the lender, especially when the latter neither authorized the charge nor shared in the fee.[41]

Where a loan is made at the full legal rate of interest, a deduction from the amount loaned, of attorney's fees for examining the title to the land mortgaged, is held not to be usurious.[42] But there are a number of cases which hold that a stipulation to pay a reasonable attorney's fee for instituting and prosecuting a suit to collect the debt is for a penalty or forfeiture, and tends to the oppression of the debtor, is a cover for usury, is without consideration, and contrary to public policy.[43]

A provision for the payment of damages to the amount of five or ten per cent. of the loan, in case of a sale for a breach of the condition, may not be usurious,[44] although on a mortgage for a large amount such a percentage would be unreasonable,[45] and the court would allow only

Bank, 122 Ill. 352, 13 N. E. 503.

[40] Miner v. Paris Exchange Bank, 53 Tex. 559; Roberts v. Palmore, 41 Tex. 617.

[41] Gannon v. Scottish-American Mtg. Co., 106 Ga. 510, 32 S. E. 591.

[42] Cobe v. Guyer, 237 Ill. 516, 86 N. E. 1071.

[43] Dodge v. Tulleys, 144 U. S. 451, 36 L. ed. 501, 12 Sup. Ct. 728; Bendey v. Townsend, 109 U. S. 665, 27 L. ed. 1065, 3 Sup. Ct. 482; Gray v. Havemeyer, 53 Fed. 174, 3 C. C. A. 497; Merchants' Nat. Bank v. Sevier, 14 Fed. 662; Boozer v. Anderson, 42 Ark. 167; Security Co. v. Eyer, 36 Nebr. 507, 54 N. W. 838, 38 Am. St. 735; Dow v. Updike, 11 Nebr. 95, 7 N. W. 857; Tinsley v. Hoskins, 111 N. Car. 340, 16 S. E. 325, 32 Am. St. 801; Shelton v. Gill,

11 Ohio 417; State v. Taylor, 10 Ohio 378; Rixey v. Pearre, 89 Va. 113, 15 S. E. 498; Toole v. Stephen, 4 Leigh (Va.) 581.

[44] Fowler v. Equitable Trust Co., 141 U. S. 384, 35 L. ed. 786, 12 Sup. Ct. 1; Munter v. Linn, 61 Ala. 492; Billingsley v. Dean, 11 Ind. 331; Gambril v. Doe, 8 Blackf. (Ind.) 140, 44 Am. Dec. 760; Siegel v. Drumm, 21 La. Ann. 8; Huling v. Drexell, 7 Watts (Pa.) 126. See ante § 359.

[45] Daly v. Maitland, 88 Pa. St. 384, 32 Am. Rep. 457. In Fowler v. Equitable Trust Co., 141 U. S. 411, 35 L. ed. 794, 12 Sup. Ct. 8, where the stipulation in a trust deed to secure a loan of $10,000 was for a reasonable attorney's fee not ex-

a reasonable sum to be collected.[46] It is in effect only a stipulation to allow compensation for extra and incidental trouble and expense in consequence of the sale; and a provision for the payment of the expenses of foreclosure, and a reasonable attorney's fee, is generally held valid and not obnoxious to the usury laws.[47] Whenever the stipulation is for the payment of something which the court can see is a valid and legitimate charge or expense, it will be upheld; but if the stipulation be so indefinite that the court can not tell whether the payment was intended to be for something legal or illegal, it will not be upheld. Accordingly it has been held that a stipulation for the payment, in case of foreclosure, of the costs "and fifty dollars as liquidated damages for the foreclosure of the mortgage,' is invalid.[48] If this phrase was designed to cover attorney fees, if it was only designed to cover a legitimate charge or expense, why did the parties not say so? If the damages were for usurious interest, of course they could not be allowed.[49]

An agreement, by the borrower of money on the security of a mortgage, to pay a reasonable and proper charge for service to be rendered in examining his title and drafting his securities, would not probably be regarded by any court as constituting usury.[50]

§ 636. **Effect of agreement to pay taxes or insurance.**—An agreement to pay the taxes on the mortgaged property,[51] or on the mortgage

ceeding five per cent. in case of foreclosure, Mr. Justice Harlan said: "The only question of any difficulty is whether the fee stipulated was not excessive. But as the character and extent of the services performed by the plaintiff's attorney were best known to the court below, and in the absence of any evidence as to whether the fee was reasonable, considering the amount involved and the nature of the services rendered, we are not prepared to reverse the decree because of the allowance to the plaintiff of an attorney's fee which does not exceed the highest sum fixed in the deed of trust."

[46] Munter v. Linn, 61 Ala. 492.

[47] Shelton v. Aultman &c. Co., 82 Ala. 315, 8 So. 232; Clawson v. Munson, 55 Ill. 394; Weatherby v. Smith, 30 Iowa 131, 6 Am. Rep. 663; Parham v. Pulliam, 5 Cold. (Tenn.)

497. In Kentucky, however, it is held that a provision for the payment of an attorney's fee upon foreclosure is against public policy, and also usurious in its nature, and can not be enforced. Thomasson v. Townsend, 10 Bush (Ky.) 114; Rilling v. Thompson, 12 Bush (Ky.) 310.

[48] Foote v. Sprague, 13 Kans. 155; Tholan v. Duffy, 7 Kans. 405.

[49] Foote v. Sprague, 13 Kans. 155, per Valentine, J. See also Tholan v. Duffy, 7 Kans. 405; Kurtz v. Sponable, 6 Kans. 395.

[50] See Ellenbogen v. Griffey, 55 Ark. 268, 18 S. W. 126.

[51] Dutton v. Aurora, 114 Ill. 138. See also Kidder v. Vandersloot, 114 Ill. 133, 28 N. E. 460; First Nat. Bank v. Glenn, 10 Idaho 224, 77 Pac. 623, 109 Am. St. 204; Sloane v. Lucas, 37 Wash. 348, 79 Pac. 949.

debt,[52] or the insurance premiums on the mortgaged property,[53] in addition to interest, is held not to be usurious. But where the maximum lawful rate of interest has been charged, an agreement by the mortgagor to pay a "personal property" tax assessed against the mortgagee on account of the debt has been held usurious.[54]

The fact that a mortgage provides for the payment of usurious interest upon money advanced by the mortgagee to pay taxes or insurance does not prevent a recovery upon the principal obligation.[55]

It is not usurious to contract for or to require payment by the mortgagor of a mortgage registry tax upon the mortgage given to secure the loan in addition to the payment of interest at the maximum lawful rate.[56]

§ 637. **Exchange and premiums.**—When no place of payment is named in the mortgage, the debt is generally payable to the mortgagee wherever he may be found. If made payable at the place of residence of the mortgagor, for his accommodation, it is not usurious for him to allow the mortgagee the difference of exchange between the two places; unless it appear that this allowance was a mere device on the part of the mortgagee to evade the usury laws, and to obtain more than legal interest for the use of his money.[57]

A mortgage given in the United States at a time when gold was

---

[52] Banks v. McClellan, 24 Md. 62, 87 Am. Dec. 594; Rauch v. Seip, 112 Mich. 612, 71 N. W. 144; Detroit v. Board of Assessors, 91 Mich. 78, 51 N. W. 787. In California such an agreement is by the Constitution, art. 13, § 5, made null and void. But a contract on the part of the mortgagee to credit the mortgagor with a certain per cent. of the interest if he should produce each year "the proper official receipts showing the payment of all taxes against the property," is not within this provision. The California Pol. Code, § 3627, which gives the owner of the property the privilege of deducting the amount of the taxes paid by him from the mortgage debt, is permissive, and not mandatory, and does not prohibit an action to recover the same from the mortgage. San Gabriel Valley Land Water Co. v. Witmer Bros. Co., 96 Cal. 623, 29 Pac. 500.

[53] New England Mtg. Sec. Co. v. Gay, 33 Fed. 636.

[54] Union Trust Co. v. Radford, 176 Mich. 50, 141 N. W. 1091; Stack v. Detour Lumber &c. Co., 151 Mich. 21, 114 N. W. 876, 16 L. R. A. (N. S.) 616; Green v. Grant, 134 Mich. 462, 96 N. W. 583; Meem v. Dulaney, 88 Va. 674, 14 S. E. 363.

[55] Hughes Bros. Mfg. Co. v. Conyers, 97 Tenn. 274, 36 S. W. 1093.

[56] Lassman v. Jacobson, 125 Minn. 218, 146 N. W. 350, 51 L. R. A. (N. S.) 465; Moore v. Lindsay, 61 Misc. 176, 114 N. Y. S. 684; Gault v. Thurmond, 39 Okla. 673, 136 Pac. 742; American Mtg. Co. v. Woodward, 83 S. Car. 521, 65 S. E. 739. But see Vandervelde v. Wilson, 176 Mich. 185, 142 N. W. 553; Green v. Grant, 134 Mich. 462, 96 N. W. 583; Norris v. W. C. Belcher Land Mtg. Co., 98 Tex. 176, 82 S. W. 500, 83 S. W. 799.

[57] Riley v. Olin, 82 Ga. 312, 9 S. E. 1095; Hughes v. Griswold, 82 Ga. 299, 9 S. E. 1092; Williams v. Hance, 7 Paige (N. Y.) 581.

at a premium, in settlement of a debt due and payable in a foreign country where gold was the basis of the currency, is not usurious by reason of including the current premium on gold.[58]

A mortgage calling for payment in gold coin of the United States of the then standard weight and fineness is valid, and may be enforced in the courts without violating any principle of law or public policy, although legal tender notes and silver may be in circulation.[59] A state can not by statute prohibit a stipulation for the payment of the mortgage debt in gold coin of the United States, and provide that any debt may be paid in any kind of lawful money.[60]

§ 638. Mortgage to building and loan association.—A mortgage to a building and loan association is not usurious when, under the articles of association, in addition to monthly payments of interest, the mortgagor is bound, both by the mortgage and as a member of the association, to pay certain fines and impositions.[61]

A number of cases have adopted the view that the relation between the association and the borrowing member consists in two separate contracts,—the contract of membership and the contract of loan, and in applying this view they hold that stock dues are not to be considered as paid on account of the loan, and are not to be added in determining whether a usurious rate of interest has been charged.[62]

[58] Oliver v. Shoemaker, 35 Mich. 464.

[59] Gregory v. Morris, 96 U. S. 619, 24 L. ed. 740; Bronson v. Rodes, 7 Wall. (U. S.) 229, 19 L. ed. 141; Dorr v. Hunter, 183 Ill. 432, 56 N. E. 159; Belford v. Woodward, 158 Ill. 122; McGoon v. Shirk, 54 Ill. 408.

[60] Dennis v. Moses, 18 Wash. 537, 52 Pac. 333, 40 L. R. A. 302.

[61] Ocmulgee Building &c. Assn. v. Thomson, 52 Ga. 427; Hekelnkaemper v. German Building Assn., 22 Kans. 549; Massey v. Citizens' Building Assn., 22 Kans. 624; Shannon v. Dunn, 43 N. H. 194; Red Bank Mut. Bldg. &c. Assn. v. Patterson, 27 N. J. Eq. 223; Building Loan &c. Assn. v. Vandervere, 11 N. J. Eq. 382 (where reasons are stated); Citizens' Mut. Loan Assn. v. Webster, 25 Barb. (N. Y.) 263; Hagerman v. Ohio Building Assn., 25 Ohio St. 186; Reeve v. Ladies' Bldg. Assn., 56 Ark. 335, 19 S. W. 917; Taylor v. Van Buren Building &c. Assn., 56 Ark. 340, 19 S. W. 918;

Borrowers' &c. Bldg. Assn. v. Eklund, 190 Ill. 257, 60 N. E. 521; Silver v. Barnes, 6 Bing. N. Cas. 180. Contra Citizens' Security &c. Co. v. Uhler, 48 Md. 455; Hensel v. International &c. Loan Assn., 85 Tex. 215, 20 S. W. 116. In Pennsylvania a building association can recover on its mortgage only the money actually advanced to its stockholder, with legal interest. Link v. Germantown Building Assn., 89 Pa. St. 15. As to statement of account between the association and mortgagor, see Peter's Bldg. Assn. v. Jaecksch, 51 Md. 198; McCahan v. Columbian Bldg. Assn., 40 Md. 226.

[62] Bell v. Southern Home Bldg. &c. Assn., 140 Ala. 371, 37 So. 237, 103 Am. St. 41; Farmers' Sav. &c. Assn. v. Kent, 131 Ala. 246, 30 So. 874; Interstate Bldg. &c. Assn. v. Brown, 128 Ala. 462, 29 So. 656; Farmers' Sav. &c. Assn. v. Ferguson, 69 Ark. 352, 63 S. W. 797; Reeve v. Ladies' Bldg. Assn., 56 Ark. 335, 19 S. W. 917, 18 L. R. A. 129; Bank of Loudon v. Armor, 90

There are cases which hold that the loan contract is in the nature of a sale of the member's stock to the association, or, more strictly, an advancement by the association in anticipation of the maturity of the stock.[63] The rate of interest to be paid under such mortgages is necessarily uncertain, and the usury laws are not applicable to such loans. Whenever special privileges as regards the taking of usury are conferred upon such an association, a loan will not be held to be within its operation unless it strictly conforms with the terms of the law.[64] A member of the association, who has given to it a mortgage to secure a loan made to a fellow member, is liable to the same extent as he would be if the loan had been made to himself, and can not plead usury to an action upon the mortgage.[65] In some jurisdictions, however, the courts hold that the contract of a building and loan association is purely one of loan, and that if the premiums and other charges, in connection with the interest charged, exceed the legal rate, the contract is usurious;[66] and a loan by such an association to a person not a member of the association is not exempt from the provisions of the interest laws of the state where the contract is to be performed. If the borrower from such an association has signed no written articles of membership, and there are no recitals of membership in the note or mortgage, he is not estopped to deny such membership, and whether he is a member or not is a question to be determined like any other issue of fact.[67]

A purchaser of land subject to a building association mortgage who

Miss. 709, 44 So. 66; People's Bldg. &c. Assn. v. McPhilamy, 81 Miss. 61, 32 So. 1001, 59 L. R. A. 743, 95 Am. St. 454; Fidelity Sav. Assn. v. Bank of Commerce, 12 Wyo. 315, 75 Pac. 448.

[63] Winget v. Quincy Bldg. &c. Assn., 128 Ill. 67, 21 N. E. 12; Freeman v. Ottawa Bldg. &c. Assn., 114 Ill. 182, 28 N. E. 611; Holmes v. Smythe, 100 Ill. 413.

[64] Williar v. Balt. Butchers' Loan &c. Assn., 45 Md. 546; Birmingham v. Maryland Land &c. Permanent Homestead Assn., 45 Md. 541.

[65] Johnston v. Elizabeth &c. Assn., 104 Pa. St. 394.

[66] Stevens v. Home Sav. &c. Assn., 5 Idaho 741, 51 Pac. 779, 986; Kleimeir v. Covington Perpetual Bldg. &c. Assn., 119 Ky. 724, 24 Ky. L. 735, 70 S. W. 41; Watts v. National Bldg. &c. Assn., 102 Ky. 29, 19 Ky. L. 1007, 42 S. W. 839; Henderson Bldg. &c. Assn. v. Johnson, 88 Ky. 191, 10 Ky. L. 830, 10 S. W. 787, 3 L. R. A. 289; Rowland v. Old Dominion Bldg. &c. Assn., 116 N. Car. 877, 22 S. E. 8; Hanner v. Greensboro Bldg. &c. Assn., 78 N. Car. 188; Buist v. Bryan, 44 S. Car. 121, 21 S. E. 537, 29 L. R. A. 127, 51 Am. St. 787; Crabtree v. Old Dominion Bldg. &c. Assn., 95 Va. 670, 29 S. E. 741, 64 Am. St. 818.

[67] Building Association v. Thompson, 19 Kans. 321. See also Lincoln Building &c. Assn. v. Graham, 7 Nebr. 173; Juniata Building &c. Assn. v. Mixell, 84 Pa. St. 313; Wolbach v. Lehigh Building Assn., 84 Pa. St. 211.

has not specifically assumed the mortgage may set up the defense of usury against the association.[68]

The appointment of a receiver of such an association being equivalent to a dissolution of the corporation, the weekly dues or instalments which a mortgagor has contracted to pay should be computed only down to the time of the appointment.[69]

§ 639. **Validity of contract to resell at an advance property purchased.**—When there has been an absolute conveyance of land, with an agreement to repurchase within a fixed time, at a price exceeding that paid for it, and interest, the transaction may be a conditional sale, in which case it is not affected with usury.[70] If, however, the transaction be a mortgage, it is usurious. If the agreement be that the grantee will reconvey upon the payment of a sum named, which is in fact the debt secured, together with a certain additional sum annually as rent, it may be shown that this annual payment is for interest and taxes, and that, deducting the estimated amount of taxes, the annual payment does not exceed the lawful interest.[71]

It is legally possible for one person to buy property from another and agree to resell it to the vendor at a higher price payable in the future. If such be the actual transaction the law will enforce it. The difficulty frequently arising is to determine whether in a given instance the parties intended a sale or a mortgage.[72] But if the transaction is in fact a loan of a sum of money by the grantee to the grantor at a usurious rate of interest, it is illegal, and the title so obtained is tainted with usury. The transaction, being on its face apparently lawful, might, nevertheless, be shown to be a device for concealing usury.[73]

As already noticed, such a transaction is closely scrutinized by the courts in order to prevent the creditor from depriving the debtor of the right of redemption, which should attach to it as a mortgage. The transaction is, moreover, suspicious, for the reason that it easily affords a ready cloak for usury. It will not be sustained as a conditional sale,

[68] Washington Nat. Building &c. Assn. v. Andrews, 95 Md. 696, 53 Atl. 573.

[69] Peter's Bldg. Assn. v. Jaecksch, 51 Md. 198; Low Street Building Assn. v. Zucker, 48 Md. 449.

[70] McElmurray v. Blodgett, 120 Ga. 90, 47 S. E. 531.

[71] Kidder v. Vandersloop, 114 Ill. 133, 28 N. E. 460.

[72] Rogers v. Bluenstein, 124 Ga. 501, 52 S. E. 617, 3 L. R. A. (N. S.) 213; Felton v. Grier, 109 Ga. 320, 35 S. E. 175; Monroe v. Foster, 49 Ga. 514; Spence v. Steadman, 49 Ga. 133.

[73] Rogers v. Bluenstein, 124 Ga. 501, 52 S. E. 617, 3 L. R. A. (N. S.) 213; Wilkins v. Gibson, 113 Ga. 31, 38 S. E. 374, 84 Am. St. 204; Morrison v. Markham, 78 Ga. 161, 1 S. E. 425.

unless it clearly appears that it was in good faith intended as such, and not as a contrivance to cover usury.[74]

But if the deed was made, not as a security but as a sale in payment of a debt, and the grantee subsequently by virtue of a new agreement reconveyed the land to the grantor for the amount originally paid for it with usurious interest thereon, it is held that the usury in such case does not avoid the deed because it was not a part of the original transaction.[75]

In a mortgage any agreement to pay more than the sum loaned and lawful interest is usury; and usury is constituted not only by the payment of money, but by any arrangement whereby the lender derives a profit or advantage beyond the interest allowed by law.[76] Where the laws make usurious contracts void, any transaction which is in effect a mortgage, though called a sale by the parties, and is usurious in effect, is rendered invalid.[77] The intent is deduced from the fact. If the mortgagee knowingly and voluntarily takes or reserves a greater interest than is allowed by law, his security is thereby rendered void, though it is not if taken by mistake or accident. But aside from mistake or accident, evidence will not be allowed to show that the mortgagee did not intend to violate the statute.[78]

If a sale of land or of goods be made as a mere device to cover a loan and exact excessive interest, the false cover given the transaction will not be allowed to defeat the statute.[79] But a transaction whereby a purchaser of personal property gives a mortgage on land to secure the price, payable in one year, with the maximum rate of interest, and agrees to pay fees for examining the title and for preparing and recording the mortgage, will be adjudged a bona fide sale, and not a cloak for a usurious loan, when it does not appear that the parties considered it a loan, or that the purchaser ever applied for a loan.[80]

---

[74] McLaren v. Clark, 80 Ga. 423, 7 S. E. 230; Pope v. Marshall, 78 Ga. 635, 4 S. E. 116; Morrison v. Markham, 78 Ga. 161, 1 S. E. 425; Gleason v. Burke, 20 N. J. Eq. 300.

[75] Barfield v. Jefferson, 78 Ga. 220, 2 S. E. 554.

[76] Gleason v. Burke, 20 N. J. Eq. 300.

[77] Pope v. Marshall, 78 Ga. 635, 4 S. E. 116.

[78] Fiedler v. Darrin, 50 N. Y. 437. "The plaintiff doubtless hoped and intended to cover up his tracks, to conceal his loan and the reservation of usurious interest, under the weak guise of a purchase and resale, and could well have sworn that he did not intend to bring himself within the condemnation of the law. But he did in fact loan his money at an illegal interest, and has failed in his attempt to evade the consequences." Per Allen, J.

[79] Struthers v. Drexel, 122 U. S. 487, 30 L. ed. 1216, 7 Sup. Ct. 1293; Tillar v. Cleveland, 47 Ark. 287, 1 S. W. 516; Grider v. Driver, 46 Ark. 50; Ford v. Hancock, 36 Ark. 248.

[80] Ellenbogen v. Griffey, 55 Ark. 268, 18 S. W. 126. This was not in form a loan of money, and there

In whatever way the transaction may be disguised, if it be in fact a loan at a usurious rate of interest, the security taken will be declared illegal.[81] The attempt is sometimes made to conceal usury under the guise of rent; as where a mortgage was given to secure a loan of three thousand dollars, without any agreement about interest, but the mortgagee leased the mortgaged premises to the mortgagor at an annual rent of two hundred and seventy dollars, which was held to be an agreement for usurious interest.[82]

§ 640. No forfeiture though transaction usurious.—The grantor is not entitled to any of the penalties or forfeitures given by the statute for usury, even when it is shown that this form of the transaction was used for the purpose of covering up a usurious rate of interest agreed upon between the parties, although a court of equity will allow a debtor to redeem, when, to secure a loan of money, he has made an absolute conveyance of land, and taken an agreement to repurchase. The debtor is entitled to a conveyance upon the payment of the original loan with legal interest; but, having put the transaction into such a form that he is obliged to ask a court of equity for relief from the letter of the contract, which he could not obtain at law, the court will impose terms upon him to do equity.[83]

Where a deed was made, not as security, but as an absolute sale in payment of a debt, and the grantee subsequently agreed that he would reconvey the land to the grantor upon payment of a certain amount equal to the consideration for the deed, together with usurious interest thereon, such transaction does not avoid the deed.[84]

§ 641. Sale of mortgage.—Although a valid mortgage once issued may be sold at a discount without involving the purchaser in any of the consequences of taking usurious interest,[85] yet, if the mortgage

is nothing to show that it was intended as a loan, or that it was such in fact. It was therefore, in substance and in law, a sale. As there was no loan, there could be no agreement to pay excessive interest for a loan.

[81] Andrews v. Poe, 30 Md. 486; Birdsall v. Patterson, 51 N. Y. 43; Fitzsimons v. Baum, 44 Pa. St. 32.

[82] Gordon v. Hobart, 2 Story (U. S.) 243; Morrison v. Markham, 78 Ga. 161, 1 S. E. 425. See also Gaither v. Clark, 67 Md. 18, 8 Atl. 740; Grand Order of O. F. Assn. v. Merklin, 65 Md. 579, 5 Atl. 544. See

also Tillar v. Cleveland, 47 Ark. 287, 1 S. W. 516; Phelps v. Bellows, 53 Vt. 539.

[83] Heacock v. Swartwout, 28 Ill. 291.

[84] Barfield v. Jefferson, 78 Ga. 220, 2 S. E. 554.

[85] Mix v. Madison Ins. Co., 11 Ind. 117; Dunham v. Cudlipp, 94 N. Y. 129; Smith v. Cross, 90 N. Y. 549; Sickles v. Flanagan, 79 N. Y. 224; Dowe v. Schutt, 2 Denio (N. Y.) 621; Lovett v. Dimond, 4 Edw. (N. Y.) 22; Wyeth v. Branif, 14 Hun (N. Y.) 537, revd. 84 N. Y. 627; White v. Turner, 1 Hun (N. Y.)

be made without consideration and for the purpose of being sold, inasmuch as the subsequent sale gives it vitality, and is really the issuing of it, a sale at a discount has the same effect in rendering it void as has the taking of a bonus by the mortgagee.[86] It would seem, however, that one purchasing a mortgage at a discount from the mortgagor's agent, in whose name the mortgage stood, without knowledge of the agency, would not incur any liability for usury.

A purchase of an existing mortgage by a third person at the request of the mortgagor, at a discount from the face of the mortgage, and an agreement by the mortgagor to pay the full amount of the mortgage, the purchaser agreeing to extend the time of payment of the mortgage, do not make the mortgage usurious. A new bond and mortgage for the amount of the original mortgage are not rendered usurious by such purchase at a discount.[87]

Where the mortgagee's agent withheld payment of the money loaned for three or four months, and then paid only a part, but afterward collected interest on the full amount of the mortgage, and it appeared that the acts of the agent were the acts of the mortgagee, it was held that the penalty of usury had been incurred.[88]

Where a vendor of land agreed to take a mortgage for a part of the purchase-money, and in anticipation of the trade arranged to sell the mortgage at a discount, and merely to save the trouble of a transfer had the mortgage made directly to the purchaser of the mortgage, it was held the transaction was not usurious, the evidence showing that it was not a contrivance to evade the usury laws.[89]

A sale of mortgage bonds, issued by a corporation authorized to borrow money on such terms as its directors may determine, for less than their face value, does not render the bonds or mortgage void for usury.[90]

On the other hand, a sale of mortgage securities at a premium by the mortgagee does not subject him to an action for the recovery of the premium on the ground of usury.[91]

623; Sweny v. Peaslee, 17 N. Y. S. 225. See post § 832.

[86] Vickery v. Dickson, 62 Barb. (N. Y.) 272. See also Walter v. Lind, 16 N. J. Eq. 445; Sickles v. Flanagan, 79 N. Y. 224; Brooks v. Avery, 4 N. Y. 225; Culver v. Bigelow, 43 Vt. 249.

[87] Sullivan Savings Inst. v. Copeland, 71 Iowa 67, 32 N. W. 95;

Crane v. Price, 35 N. Y. 494; Sweny v. Peaslee, 17 N. Y. S. 225.

[88] Barr v. African &c. Church (N. J.), 10 Atl. 287.

[89] Armstrong v. Freeman, 9 Nebr. 11, 2 N. W. 353.

[90] Traders' Nat. Bank v. Lawrence Mfg. Co., 100 N. Car. 345, 3 S. E. 363.

[91] Culver v. Bigelow, 43 Vt. 249.

§ 642. Bonus or commission of broker or agent.—If the agent of the mortgagee, in making the loan, exacts a payment to himself by way of commission for making the loan, the agent having special and limited authority, and having no regular and established connection with the lender, the loan is not necessarily nor usually rendered usurious.[92] Thus if a person intrusts another with money to loan and such other loans the same, charging and receiving from the borrower a sum of money in addition to legal interest as compensation for his services, but without any direction by or knowledge of the lender, the transaction is not usurious.[93] The brokerage in excess of legal interest can not affect the principal, when it is paid without his knowledge and he derives no benefit from it.[94] It has been attempted, however, to establish the rule that such brokerage makes the mortgage usurious, unless it be taken by virtue of an independent agreement between the borrower and the broker. If, for instance, the borrower pays to the broker a premium in excess of legal interest, though the latter had been instructed by his principal to loan at lawful interest, and no part of the premium was received by the lender, but the borrower has no knowledge that it is all retained by the agent, the loan is considered usurious.[95] But the later and better considered decisions affirm the rule as first stated.[96] These decisions are based upon the principle

---

[92] Fowler v. Equitable Trust Co., 141 U. S. 384, 35 L. ed. 786, 12 Sup. Ct. 1, per Harlan, J.; Eslava v. Crampton, 61 Ala. 507; Rogers v. Buckingham, 33 Conn. 81; Phillips v. Roberts, 90 Ill. 952; Jennings v. Hunt, 6 Bradw. (Ill.) 523; Landis v. Saxton, 89 Mo. 375, 1 S. W. 359; Van Wyck v. Watters, 81 N. Y. 352, 16 Hun 209; Guggenheimer v. Griszler, 81 N. Y. 293; Mutual L. Ins. Co. v. Kashaw, 66 N. Y. 544; Bell v. Day, 32 N. Y. 165; Condit v. Baldwin, 21 N. Y. 219, 78 Am. Dec. 137; Wyeth v. Branif, 14 Hun (N. Y.) 537, reversed 84 N. Y. 627. See also Sherwood v. Swift, 64 Ark. 662, 43 S. W. 507.

[93] Condit v. Baldwin, 21 N. Y. 219, 78 Am. Dec. 137; Franzen v. Hammond, 136 Wis. 239, 116 N. W. 169, 19 L. R. A. (N. S.) 399, 128 Am. St. 1079.

[94] Fowler v. Equitable Trust Co., 141 U. S. 384, 35 L. ed. 786, 12 Sup. Ct. 1; New England Mtg. Security Co. v. Gay, 33 Fed. 636; American Freehold Mtg. Co. v. Sewall, 92 Ala.

163, 9 So. 143; Ginn v. New England Sec. Co., 92 Ala. 135, 8 So. 388; May v. Flint, 54 Ark. 573, 16 S. W. 575; Hughes v. Griswold, 82 Ga. 299, 9 S. E. 1092; Merck v. American &c. Mortgage Co., 79 Ga. 213, 7 S. E. 265; Ryan v. Sanford, 133 Ill. 291, 24 N. E. 428; Sanford v. Kane, 133 Ill. 199, 205, 24 N. E. 414, 23 Am. St. 603; Telford v. Garrels, 132 Ill. 550, 24 N. E. 573; Hoyt v. Institution, 110 Ill. 390; Pass v. New England Mtg. Sec. Co., 66 Miss. 365, 6 So. 239; Gray v. Van Blarcom, 29 N. J. Eq. 454; Manning v. Young, 28 N. J. Eq. 568; Spring v. Reed, 28 N. J. Eq. 345; Conover v. Van Meter, 18 N. J. Eq. 481; Muir v. Newark Savings Inst., 16 N. J. Eq. 537.

[95] Tiedemann v. Ackerman, 16 Hun (N. Y.) 307; Estevez v. Purdy, 6 Hun (N. Y.) 46. See also Algur v. Gardner, 54 N. Y. 360. The doctrine of these cases is criticized in Gray v. Van Blarcom, 29 N. J. Eq. 454.

[96] Jordan v. Humphrey, 31 Minn.

that the lender did not, either expressly or impliedly, authorize the agent to do an illegal act; and therefore the wrongful act of the agent in extorting a bonus for himself does not affect the lender so long as he does not participate in the extortion or in the results of it, but seeks to enforce the security for the precise amount he loaned with lawful interest.

Upon the same principle a bonus received by one trustee in making a loan upon a mortgage for a trust estate does not avoid the mortgage if it appears that the bonus was taken without the authority or knowledge of the other trustees.[97]

If an attorney take a mortgage in his own name for a client, and receive from the mortgagor a sum of money as compensation for examining the title to the premises, the transaction is not thereby made usurious.[98]

The declarations of an agent of the mortgagor, to whom a mortgage has been made for the purpose of enabling him to borrow money for the mortgagor, that he owned the mortgage, and that it was given upon a previously existing indebtedness to him, if false and unauthorized, are not binding upon the mortgagor, and do not estop him to deny them and set up the defense of usury.[99]

§ 642a. Where agent is general agent of lender.—When the agent is the lender's general agent, having authority to loan his money in such sums and at such times as he pleases, and is only restricted to obtain not less than a stipulated rate of interest, if the agent exacts usury upon his loans, the principal is presumed to have knowledge of such exaction and to have authorized it; and in such case, unless this presumption is rebutted, the transaction will be held usurious.[1] And where the lender thus places his business under the exclusive and unlimited control of a general agent, if the agent exacts usury, the case stands precisely as if it had been done by the principal personally, and such an agent has no right to exact from the borrower, either for alleged services or otherwise, anything which the principal might not

495, 18 N. W. 450; Estevez v. Purdy, 66 N. Y. 446.

[97] Van Wyck v. Watters, 16 Hun (N. Y.) 209; Stout v. Rider, 12 Hun (N. Y.) 574.

[98] Dayton v. Moore, 30 N. J. Eq. 543.

[99] New York Life Ins. &c. Co. v. Beebe, 7 N. Y. 364. But see Ahern v. Goodspeed, 72 N. Y. 108; Platt v. Newcomb, 27 Hun (N. Y.) 186.

[1] Stevens v. Meers, 11 Ill. App. 138. See also American Mtg. Co. v. Woodward, 83 S. Car. 521, 65 S. E. 739; Austin v. Harrington, 28 Vt. 130.

have lawfully exacted had he transacted the business in person.[2] But there are cases holding that the making of usurious loans is not within the apparent scope of a general agency to loan money.[3]

The fact that a loan agent, who is in the habit of sending applications to an insurance company, is the agent of such company for the purpose of procuring insurance, does not constitute him the general agent of the company, so as to render it liable for usury by reason of commissions exacted by him.[4]

Even if the agent has not full authority to make loans for his principal, but only to examine applications and securities and to recommend loans, if his agency is regularly established and continuous, he is in some states regarded so far the agent of the lender that commissions exacted from the borrower, beyond the highest rate of interest allowed by law, render his loans usurious. Thus, where a trust company appointed an agent to procure and forward applications for loans, with the understanding that he should receive no compensation from the company, but is to obtain his remuneration from borrowers, and he thereafter, in communications to the company and others, styles himself as its agent, he must be so considered; and under the law in Illinois a payment to him of a commission by the borrower, for securing a loan from the company at the highest legal rate, makes the transaction usurious.[5]

[2] Fowler v. Equitable Trust Co., 141 U. S. 384, 35 L. ed. 786, 12 Sup. Ct. 1; Banks v. Flint, 54 Ark. 40, 14 S. W. 769, 16 S. W. 477, 10 L. R. A. 459; Rogers v. Buckingham, 33 Conn. 81; Payne v. Newcomb, 100 Ill. 611, 39 Am. Rep. 69; France v. Munro, 138 Iowa 1, 115 N. W. 577, 19 L. R. A. (N. S.) 391; Gokey v. Knapp, 44 Iowa 32; Horkan v. Nesbitt, 58 Minn. 487, 60 N. W. 132; Hall v. Maudlin, 58 Minn. 137, 59 N. W. 985, 49 Am. St. 492; Stein v. Swensen, 46 Minn. 360, 49 N. W. 55, 24 Am. St. 234; Kemmitt v. Adamson, 44 Minn. 121, 46 N. W. 327; Olmsted v. New England Mtg. Secur. Co., 11 Nebr. 487, 9 S. W. 650; Cheney v. White, 5 Nebr. 261, 25 Am. Rep. 487; Pfenning v. Scholer, 43 N. J. Eq. 15, 10 Atl. 833; Dayton v. Dearholt, 85 Wis. 151, 55 N. W. 147.

[3] Manning v. Young, 28 N. J. Eq. 568; Conover v. Van Mater, 18 N. J. Eq. 481; Muir v. Newark Sav. Inst., 16 N. J. Eq. 537; Baldwin v.

Doying, 114 N. Y. 452, 21 N. E. 1007; Stillman v. Northrup, 109 N. Y. 473, 17 N. E. 379; Estevez v. Purdy, 66 N. Y. 446; Condit v. Baldwin, 21 N. Y. 219, 78 Am. Dec. 137.

[4] Massachusetts Mut. L. Ins. Co. v. Boggs, 121 Ill. 119, 13 N. E. 550; Cox v. Massachusetts Mut. L. Ins. Co., 113 Ill. 382.

[5] Fowler v. Equitable Trust Co., 141 U. S. 384, 35 L. ed. 786, 12 Sup. Ct. 1, following Payne v. Newcomb, 100 Ill. 611. See also Insurance Co. v. Boggs, 121 Ill. 119, 13 N. E. 550; Ammondson v. Ryan, 111 Ill. 506; Hoyt v. Institution, 110 Ill. 390; Meers v. Stevens, 106 Ill. 549; Kihlholz v. Wolf, 103 Ill. 362, 366; Phillips v. Roberts, 90 Ill. 492; Boylston v. Bain, 90 Ill. 283; Ballinger v. Bourland, 87 Ill. 513. Mr. Justice Harlan, delivering the opinion in Fowler v. Equitable Trust Co., 141 U. S. 384, 35 L. ed. 786, 12 Sup. Ct. 1, after examining the Illinois cases just cited, said: "In view of the decisions of the Supreme Court of

But if the interest reserved, together with the commission paid to the lender's agent, does not exceed the highest rate of interest allowed by law, the transaction is not usurious.[6]

§ 642b. **Where broker not the agent of lender.**—If the broker or intermediary between the borrower and lender is not the agent of the lender, the latter is not affected by payments made by the borrower to the broker. The rule is well stated by Chief Justice Bleckley in a comparatively recent case in Georgia:[7] "Where the lender of money neither takes nor contracts to take anything beyond lawful interest, the loan is not rendered usurious by what the borrower does in procuring the loan and using its proceeds. Thus, that the borrower contracts with one engaged in the intermediary business of procuring loans, to pay him out of the loan for his services, and does so pay him, such payment will not infect the loan, the lender having no interest in such intermediary business or its proceeds."[8] So it has been held that where the lender, at the request of the borrower, disburses out of the money loaned certain commissions and other expenses of third per-

Illinois, and the manifest policy of the law of that state relating to usury, we can not adjudge that a loan, under a fixed arrangement between the lender and an individual that the latter will act as the agent of the former at a particular place, and obtain compensation for his services by way of commissions exacted from the borrower, is to be governed by the same principles that apply in the case of one holding no relations of agency with the lender, but is a mere broker, who gets his commission from the borrower, without the knowledge, authority, or assent of the lender. It is not consistent with the law of Illinois, as declared by its highest court, that the lender, when taking the highest rate of interest, shall impose upon borrowers the expense of maintaining agencies in different parts of the state through which loans may be obtained. We therefore hold that the exaction by the trust company's agent, pursuant to his general arrangement with it, of commissions over and above the 10 per cent. interest stipulated to be paid by the borrower, rendered this loan usurious."

[6] Fowler v. Equitable Trust Co.,

141 U. S. 411, 35 L. ed. 786, 12 Sup. Ct. 1; Barton v. Farmers' &c. Nat. Bank, 122 Ill. 352, 13 N. E. 503; McGovern v. Union Mut. L. Ins. Co., 109 Ill. 151.

[7] Merck v. American Mortgage Co., 79 Ga. 213, 7 S. E. 265. See also Brown v. Brown, 38 S. Car. 173, 17 S. E. 452, where McIver, C. J., in a dissenting opinion, says: "The fact that the borrower has paid or contracted to pay some one else an amount — however exorbitant — not for the 'hiring, lending, or use of money,' but for the services of such person in negotiating the loan, can not possibly affect the question, for that does not come within the terms of the statute."

[8] Brown v. Brown, 38 S. Car. 173, 17 S. E. 452, McIver, C. J., dissenting; Call v. Palmer, 116 U. S. 98, 29 L. ed. 559, 6 Sup. Ct. 301; Sherwood v. Roundtree, 32 Fed. 113; Payne v. Newcomb, 100 Ill. 611; Brigham v. Myers, 51 Iowa 397, 1 N. W. 613; Nichols v. Osborn, 41 N. J. Eq. 92, 3 Atl. 155; Demarest v. Van Denberg, 41 N. J. Eq. 63, 3 Atl. 69, and cases cited; Bonus v. Trefz, 40 N. J. Eq. 502, 2 Atl. 369; Boyd v. Engelbrecht, 36 N. J. Eq. 612.

sons, as the agent of the borrower in procuring the loan, the transaction is not usurious, since the payment is of no benefit to the lender.[9]

There are, however, numerous decisions to the effect that, if the mortgagee knew when he accepted the loan that the broker was exacting payment beyond a reasonable sum for commissions and expenses, the loan will be held to be usurious, though the broker was not acting as the special agent of the mortgagee, even if the latter did not share in the usurious exaction.

§ 643. Evidence—Burden of proof—Pleading defense.—The burden of proof that the mortgage is usurious is usually upon the mortgagor. He is impeaching his own obligation formally executed under seal, and must establish the facts to constitute usury beyond a reasonable doubt. An even balance of testimony is not sufficient; there must be a clear preponderance.[10]

Usury can not be proved by suspicious circumstances, but must be established by clear and indubitable proof.[11]

When the contract is upon its face for legal interest only, usury can be established only by proof of a corrupt agreement. It is a defense not favored in equity; and, especially when the consequence is to forfeit the whole debt, the defense is considered unconscientious.[12]

---

[9] Kihlholz v. Wolf, 103 Ill. 362.

[10] Hotel Co. v. Wade, 97 U. S. 13, 24 L. ed. 917; New England Mtg. Security Co. v. Gay, 33 Fed. 636. The defense of usury, involving a crime, can not be established by surmise and conjecture, or by inference entirely uncertain. Baldwin v. Doying, 114 N. Y. 452, 21 N. E. 1007; Stillman v. Northrup, 109 N. Y. 473, 17 N. E. 379; Culver v. Pullman, 12 N. Y. S. 663; Sweny v. Peaslee, 17 N. Y. S. 225. If, upon the whole case, the evidence is as consistent with the absence as with the presence of usury, the party alleging the usury must fail. Borden v. School-Dist. No. 38, 47 N. J. Eq. 8, 21 Atl. 40; Gillette v. Ballard, 25 N. J. Eq. 491; Insurance Co. v. Crane, 25 N. J. Eq. 422; Smith v. Marvin, 27 N. Y. 137; Booth v. Sweezy, 8 N. Y. 276; Sweny v. Peaslee, 17 N. Y. S. 225; Morrison v. Verdenal, 5 N. Y. S. 606. In Brolasky v. Miller, 8 N. J. Eq. 790, Mr. Justice Potts said: "Usury must be strictly proved. It is not sufficient for the party who sets it up to make out a probable case. * * * It is not enough that the circumstances proved render it highly probable that there was a corrupt bargain. Such a bargain must be proved, and not left to conjecture." Citing Rowland v. Rowland, 40 N. J. Eq. 281; Morris v. Taylor, 22 N. J. Eq. 438, 22 N. J. Eq. 609; Conover v. Van Mater, 18 N. J. Eq. 481; Barcalow v. Sanderson, 17 N. J. Eq. 460; Tanning Co. v. Turner, 14 N. J. Eq. 326; Brolasky v. Miller, 8 N. J. Eq. 790. See also Houghton v. Burden, 228 U. S. 161, 33 Sup. Ct. 491; In re Fishel, 192 Fed. 412; Klein v. Title Guaranty &c. Co., 166 Fed. 365; Pusser v. Thompson, 132 Ga. 280, 64 S. E. 75, 22 L. R. A. (N. S.) 571; Cobe v. Guyer, 237 Ill. 516, 86 N. E. 1071; Home Bldg. &c. Assn. v. McKay, 217 Ill. 551, 75 N. E. 569, 108 Am. St. 263; Widell v. National Citizens' Bank, 104 Minn. 510, 116 N. W. 919; Ferguson v. Bien, 47 Misc. 418, 94 N. Y. S. 459; Casner v. Hoskins, 64 Ore. 254, 130 Pac. 55, affg. 128 Pac. 841; Curtze v. Iron Dyke Copper Min. Co., 46 Ore. 601, 81 Pac. 815.

[11] Short v. Post, 58 N. J. Eq. 130, 42 Atl. 569.

[12] Conover v. Van Mater, 18 N. J. Eq. 481.

The wrongful act of usury will never be imputed to the parties, and it will not be inferred when the opposite conclusion can be reasonably and fairly reached.[13]

When the penalty is a forfeiture of the illegal interest, or of all interest, even although the defense is not considered unconscientious, the rule of evidence, that the defense must be clearly made out, is applied both at law and in equity.[14]

There is a distinction between the rights of a mortgagor when defending on the ground of usury and his rights when he applies to a court of equity for relief against a usurious contract; for while in the former case he may avail himself fully of the statute, in the latter case he must do equity before he can obtain equity, and must pay the debt with legal interest.[15]

In a mortgage for purchase-money, the fact that the sum secured is greater than that named in the consideration of the conveyance to the mortgagor, with interest, is no evidence that the difference is usury.[16]

When, at the time of an agreement for a mortgage loan, nothing is said as to the rate of interest, the law implies it to be that limited by statute, and to increase or alter it a special agreement is necessary; and if the defense of usury is interposed, the burden of showing that such an agreement was made is upon the mortgagor. Therefore where a mortgagor by the terms of his agreement was to pay the attorney's fees, and one item of the attorney's bill was a commission for obtaining the loan, and there was no foundation for the charge, which was intended for the benefit of the mortgagee, and was in fact retained by him against the objection of the mortgagor, it was held that these facts did not sustain a defense of usury, as there was no agreement or intent on the part of the mortgagor to pay usury, and he was, in fact, entitled to recover the amount retained by the mortgagee.[17]

Usury must be specially and particularly pleaded, or it will not be considered as a defense.[18]

The pleading must set up the usurious contract, specifying its terms

[13] Briggs v. Steele, 91 Ark. 458, 121 S. W. 754.

[14] Conover v. Van Mater, 18 N. J. Eq. 481.

[15] Clark v. Finlon, 90 Ill. 245; Tooke v. Newman, 75 Ill. 215; Gore v. Lewis, 109 N. Car. 539, 13 S. E. 909.

[16] Vesey v. Ocklngton, 16 N. H. 479.

[17] Guggenheimer v. Geiszler, 81 N. Y. 293.

[18] Paddock v. Fish, 10 Fed. 125; Kilpatrick v. Henson, 81 Ala. 464, 1 So. 188; Whately v. Barker, 79 Ga. 790, 4 S. E. 387. See also National Life Ins. Co. v. Donovan, 238 Ill. 283, 87 N. E. 356; Garlick v. Mutual Loan &c. Assn., 116 Ill. App. 311; Ætna Bldg. &c. Assn. v. Randall, 23 Okla. 45, 99 Pac. 655; Fenby v. Hunt, 53 Wash. 127, 101 Pac. 492. See post § 1300.

and the particular facts relied upon to bring it within the prohibition of the usury statute.[19]

Where usury renders the contract void, a sale under a power contained in a usurious mortgage may be enjoined,[20] and an injunction against foreclosure by suit may be granted and continued until a trial of the issue of usury.[21]

§ 644. **Who may interpose defense of usury.**—It has sometimes been held that the defense of usury is so exclusively personal that it can not be made by any one but the mortgagor or his privies in blood, estate, or contract; and that a subsequent incumbrancer or purchaser can not set it up,[22] nor a surety avail himself of usury paid by his

[19] King v. Curtin, 31 App. D. C. 23; Arison Realty Co. v. Bernstein, 111 N. Y. S. 538.

[20] See post § 1808.

[21] Ehrgott v. Forgotston, 17 N. Y. S. 381.

[22] Butts v. Broughton, 72 Ala. 294; McGuire v. Van Pelt, 55 Ala. 344; Baskins v. Calhoun, 45 Ala. 582; Fenno v. Sayre, 3 Ala. 458; Mason v. Pierce, 142 Ill. 331, 31 N. E. 503; Union Nat. Bank v. International Bank, 123 Ill. 510, 14 N. E. 859; Darst v. Bates, 95 Ill. 493; Safford v. Vail, 22 Ill. 327; Sellers v. Botsford, 11 Mich. 59; Cheney v. Dunlap, 27 Nebr. 401, 43 N. W. 178; Holladay v. Holladay, 13 Ore. 523, 11 Pac. 260, 12 Pac. 821; Lamoille Co. Nat. Bank v. Bingham, 50 Vt. 105, 28 Am. Rep. 490; Barbour v. Tompkins, 31 W. Va. 410, 416, 7 S. E. 1; Ready v. Huebner, 46 Wis. 692, 1 N. W. 344, 32 Am. Rep. 749; Bensley v. Homier, 42 Wis. 631; Moses v. Home Bldg. &c. Assn., 100 Ala. 465, 14 So. 412. Nor by mortgagor's wife claiming under a subsequent voluntary conveyance. Cain v. Gimon, 36 Ala. 168. Nor by a terre-tenant of the mortgaged premises. In Hunt v. Acre, 28 Ala. 580, it was assumed that the defense of usury might be set up by the heirs of the mortgagor. In Ready v. Huebner, 46 Wis. 692, 1 N. W. 344, 32 Am. Rep. 749, Cole, J., says: "It is true there is a class of cases which hold that the purchaser generally—not of the mere equity of redemption—of property charged with an usurious lien or claim can allege the usury and defeat the claim, when the conveyance shows that the vendor conveyed the property discharged of such lien. Ludington v. Harris, 21 Wis. 240; Newman v. Kershaw, 10 Wis. 333; Williams v. Tilt, 36 N. Y. 319. The reason given in some of these cases for such a ruling is, that the purchaser, under such circumstances, succeeds to all the relations of his vendor in respect to the property, and therefore necessarily acquires the right to question the validity of the usurious security in protection of his title." Chamberlain v. Dempsey, 36 N. Y. 144; Bullard v. Raynor, 30 N. Y. 197; Hartley v. Harrison, 24 N. Y. 170. In Union Nat. Bank v. International Bank, 123 Ill. 510, 14 N. E. 859, in which it was held that a junior mortgagee not in possession could not set up this defense, Judge Schofield reviewed the earlier cases in Illinois, and showed that the question had never before been adjudicated in that state, though remarks had been made upon it which were unnecessary to the decision of the cases in which they were made. He said: "There can be no ground for pretending that there is privity between the mortgagor and the usurious mortgage and the mortgagee of a subsequent and junior mortgage, other than by contract or in estate; and we think it quite clear that there is no privity in either of these respects. It is enough to say, on the question of privity by contract that the junior mortgagee was neither directly nor indirectly a party

principal.[23] Nor can a junior mortgagee, in case of insolvency of the debtor, plead usury against a prior incumbrance.

But the doctrine more generally adopted is that not only the mortgagor, but any person who is seised of his estate and vested with his rights, unless he has assumed the payment of the mortgage, may interpose this defense, although a mere stranger can not.[24] Thus, a voluntary assignee of the mortgagor for the payment of his debts may set up usury in the mortgage.[25] So may a judgment or execution creditor of the mortgagor;[26] or a purchaser of the equity of redemption,[27] un-

to the usurious contract, and he derives and makes claim to no right through or resulting from it. * * * But it would seem to be self-evident that the same right to elect to plead usury to a mortgage, or to waive the usury and affirm the entire validity of the mortgage, can not be in different and distinct parties in interest at the same time; for, if this were not so, one party might elect to do one thing, and the other party might elect to do directly the opposite, and thus one election would nullify the other. The equity of redemption of the mortgagor is the right to redeem from the first and senior mortgage, either by paying the amount of the principal debt only, or by paying that amount and the amount of interest usuriously contracted to be paid, as he shall elect. The junior mortgage, conveying a lien only on that right, does not cut it off, but leaves it still to be exercised by the mortgagor until he shall terminate it by grant, or it shall be terminated by foreclosure. The junior mortgagee does not, therefore, occupy the same relation toward the property that the mortgagor did before he executed that mortgage; and, since the mortgagor has not parted with his right of election to plead or to waive the defense of usury, it is impossible that the junior mortgagee can have acquired it." See also Hiner v. Whitlow, 66 Ark. 121, 49 S. W. 353, 74 Am. St. 74; Miller v. Parker, 133 Ga. 187, 65 S. E. 410; Jones v. Bryan, 53 Ind. App. 550, 102 N. E. 153; Thomas v. Kentucky Trust &c. Co., 156 Ky. 260, 160 S. W. 1037; Marcum v. Marcum, 154 Ky. 401, 157 S. W. 1101; Schmidt v. Gaukler, 156

Mich. 243, 120 N. W. 746; Osborne v. Fridrich, 134 Mo. App. 449, 114 S. W. 1045; Cable v. Duke, 132 Mo. App. 334, 111 S. W. 909; Building &c. Assn. v. Walker, 59 Nebr. 456, 81 N. W. 308; Terminal Bank v. Dubroff, 66 Misc. 100, 120 N. Y. S. 609; Bruck v. Lambeck, 63 Misc. 117, 118 N. Y. S. 494; Trabue v. Cook (Tex. Civ. App.), 124 S. W. 455; Dickerson v. Bankers' Loan &c. Co., 93 Va. 498, 25 S. E. 548; Fenby v. Hunt, 53 Wash. 127, 101 Pac. 492; Smith v. McMillan, 46 W. Va. 577, 33 S. E. 283.

[23] Lamoille Co. Nat. Bank v. Bingham, 50 Vt. 105, 28 Am. Rep. 490. But see Osborne v. Fridrick, 134 Mo. App. 449, 114 S. W. 1045.

[24] Butts v. Broughton, 72 Ala. 294; Crawford v. Nimmons, 180 Ill. 143, 54 N. E. 209; Mason v. Pierce, 142 Ill. 331, 31 N. E. 503; Union Nat. Bank v. International Bank, 123 Ill. 510, 14 N. E. 859; Maher v. Lanfrom, 86 Ill. 513; Westerfield v. Bried, 26 N. J. Eq. 357; Brolasky v. Miller, 9 N. J. Eq. 807; Mason v. Lord, 40 N. Y. 476; Williams v. Tilt, 36 N. Y. 319; Devlin v. Shannon, 65 How. Pr. (N. Y.) 148; Johnson v. Lasker Real Estate Assn. (Tex.), 21 S. W. 961 (quoting text).

[25] Pearsall v. Kingsland, 3 Edw. Ch. (N. Y.) 195. But a purchaser at a sale by an assignee in bankruptcy can not set up usury in a mortgage. Nance v. Gregory, 6 Lea (Tenn.) 343, 40 Am. Rep. 41.

[26] Thompson v. Van Vechten, 27 N. Y. 568; Carow v. Kelly, 59 Barb. (N. Y.) 239; Dix v. Van Wyck, 2 Hill (N. Y.) 522. Contra Mason v. Pierce, 142 Ill. 331, 31 N. E. 503.

[27] Maher v. Lanfrom, 86 Ill. 513; Banks v. McClellan, 24 Md. 62, 87

less he has assumed the payment of the mortgage, or bought subject to it;[28] or a junior mortgagee.[29]

A mortgagor's grantee of mortgaged premises is not precluded from setting up a plea of usury against the mortgagee by a recital in his deed that it is "subject to a certain mortgage indebtedness of two thousand dollars, and interest thereon."[30]

Any one in legal privity with the mortgagor, unless he has debarred himself of the right to dispute the mortgage, may set up this defense; otherwise the property would be practically inalienable in the hands of the mortgagor, unless he should be willing to affirm the usurious mortgage by selling the property subject to it. But the owner of the property has, of course, the right to sell the property as though such void mortgage did not exist; and the purchaser necessarily acquires all the rights of his vendor to question the validity of the usurious incumbrance.[31]

A mortgagor may waive the usury, and then those holding can not avail themselves of this defense. Moreover, any one claiming under the mortgagor and in privity with him may remove the taint of usury as to both himself and those deriving title from him.[32] A conveyance by the mortgagor subject to an existing mortgage imports a waiver, and his grantee can not set up usury.[33] But a sheriff selling the mortgaged land on execution, or on foreclosure, does not, by conveying subject to a prior mortgage, deprive the purchaser of the right to set up the defense, for he has no power to waive the usury.[34] A voluntary

Am. Dec. 594; Doub v. Barnes, 1 Md. Ch. 127; Bridge v. Hubbard, 15 Mass. 96, 8 Am. Dec. 86; Green v. Kemp, 13 Mass. 515, 7 Am. Dec. 169; Chaffe v. Wilson, 59 Miss. 42; M'Alister v. Jerman, 32 Miss. 142; Gunnison v. Gregg, 20 N. H. 100; Berdan v. Sedgwick, 44 N. Y. 626; Bullard v. Raynor, 30 N. Y. 197; Brooks v. Avery, 4 N. Y. 225; Shufelt v. Shufelt, 9 Paige (N. Y.) 137, 37 Am. Dec. 381; Union Bank v. Bell, 14 Ohio St. 200; Spengler v. Snapp, 5 Leigh (Va.) 478. See post § 746.

[28] Valentine v. Fish, 45 Ill. 462, per Breese, J.; Cleaver v. Burcky, 17 Ill. App. 92; Wright v. Bundy, 11 Ind. 398; Stephens v. Muir, 8 Ind. 352, 65 Am. Dec. 764; Sands v. Church, 6 N. Y. 347; Ferris v. Crawford, 2 Denio (N. Y.) 595. But see Parker v. Sulouff, 94 Pa. St. 527. See post §§ 744, 745, 1494.

[29] Waterman v. Curtis, 26 Conn. 241; Cole v. Bansemer, 26 Ind. 94; Greene v. Tyler, 39 Pa. St. 361; Maloney v. Eaheart, 81 Tex. 281, 16 S. W. 1030; Johnston v. Lasker Real Estate Assn., 2 Tex. Civ. App. 494, 21 S. W. 961. Contra Powell v. Hunt, 11 Iowa 430; Gaither v. Clark, 67 Md. 18, 8 Atl. 740; Union Dime Sav. Inst. v. Clark, 59 How. Pr. (N. Y.) 342. A junior mortgagee may contest the validity of the prior mortgage without offering to redeem and making a tender. Gaither v. Clark, 67 Md. 18, 8 Atl. 740.

[30] Crawford v. Nimmons, 180 Ill. 143, 54 N. E. 209.

[31] Reeder v. Martin, 58 Md. 215; Shufelt v. Shufelt, 9 Paige (N. Y.) 137, 37 Am. Dec. 381.

[32] Warwick v. Dawes, 26 N. J. Eq. 548.

[33] See post § 745.

[34] Pinnell v. Boyd, 33 N. J. Eq. 600.

payment by the mortgagor of the entire mortgage debt destroys all claim of usury, and his conveyance of the mortgaged land to the mortgagee, in consideration of his release from personal liability on the debt, precludes his afterward attacking the mortgage on the ground of usury.[35]

A part payment of the mortgage debt under an agreement with the mortgagee, whereby part of the mortgaged land is released, is not a waiver of usury in the mortgage.[36]

§ 645. **Estoppel to set up usury.**—A mortgagor may be estopped from setting up usury by reason of having executed, after the making of the mortgage, a covenant or certificate under seal that the mortgage was a valid and subsisting lien upon the premises described, especially if an innocent third party is thereby induced to buy the mortgage relying upon the statement. As against the mortgagee himself, or any assignee who knew the fact of usury, it is without effect.

If a purchaser has notice of the usurious character of the instrument, he is not protected by such a certificate, although he relied upon it as a protection in law.[37]

The plea of estoppel can not be invoked to defeat the plea of usury, when interposed by any person otherwise legally entitled to interpose such plea.[38]

The mortgagor may introduce evidence to show that the purchaser never believed, nor acted upon, the statements as true. He may show that the mortgagee shared in a very large fee paid his attorneys in the matter of the loan, and that it was really a cover for usury.[39]

A mortgagor is also estopped from setting up usury in a mortgage as against one whom he has induced to purchase it.[40]

But the mere silence of the mortgagor, without any evidence of circumstances evidencing a fraudulent purpose on his part, does not have the effect of raising an estoppel. It is an essential element of an

[35] Mason v. Pierce, 142 Ill. 331, 31 N. E. 503.

[36] Latrobe v. Hulbert, 6 Fed. 209.

[37] Wilcox v. Howell, 44 N. Y. 398; Eitel v. Bracken, 6 J. & Sp. (N. Y.) 7. In the former case the court, per Earl, C., said that the doctrine of equitable estoppel, being founded upon principles of equity and justice, is only applied to conclude a party by his acts and admissions, when in good conscience he ought not to be permitted to gainsay them; and that it would be preposterous to hold that a party is estopped from claiming that the very instrument supposed to estop him was obtained by fraud.

[38] Ford v. Washington Nat. Bldg. &c. Inv. Assn., 10 Idano 30, 76 Pac. 1010, 109 Am. St. 192.

[39] Van Sickle v. Palmer, 2 Thomp. & C. (N. Y.) 612.

[40] Perdue v. Brooks, 85 Ala. 459, 5 So. 126; Barnett v. Zacharias, 24 Hun (N. Y.) 304. See ante § 642.

estoppel that the party invoking it must have been induced to act upon the representation or concealment of the party against whom it is invoked. Thus the mere presence of the mortgagor, when a mortgage was transferred by the mortgagee without informing the assignee of the usurious transactions on which the mortgage was based, does not estop the mortgagor from setting up usury against the assignee, where it is not shown that the mortgagor was informed of the character of the transfer, and where it does appear that the assignee relied exclusively on the mortgagee's assurances as to the validity and sufficiency of the mortgage.[41]

Payment by a grantee of land of interest on a usurious mortgage given by the grantor will not estop him from showing the fact of usury.[42]

In a suit to declare a deed to be a mortgage, the plaintiff is estopped to complain that the transaction was void for usury.[43]

§ 646. **Usury set up after a foreclosure and sale.**—Under usury laws which make void securities affected with usury, the question arises, What limit is there to the effect of the statute? Does a foreclosure of the mortgage and a sale of the mortgaged property to a third person terminate the right of the mortgagor to avail himself of the usury, or do the consequences of it still attend the property so that the purchaser's title may be rendered void? If the effect of the usury survives the original transaction, in the words of Lord Kenyon,[44] "it might affect the most of the securities in the kingdom; for if, in tracing a mortgage for a century past, it could be discovered that usury had been committed in any part of the transaction, though between other parties, the consequence would be that the whole would be void. It would be a most alarming proposition to the holders of all securities." This question was also answered by an early case in New York, in which Chief Justice Kent, delivering the opinion of the court, said: "The principles of public policy and the security of titles are deeply concerned in the protection of such a purchaser. If the purchase was to be defeated by the usury in the original contract, it would be difficult to set bounds to the mischief of the precedent, or to say in what sequel of transactions, or through what course of successive alienations, and for what time short of that in the statute of lim-

---

[41] Morris v. Alston, 92 Ala. 502, 9 So. 315.

[42] Vilas v. McBride, 62 Hun (N. Y.) 324.

[43] Malone v. Danforth, 137 Mich. 227, 100 N. W. 445.

[44] Cuthbert v. Haley, 8 T. R. 390.

itations, the antecedent defect was to be deemed cured or overlooked, so as to give quiet to the title of the bona fide purchaser. The inconvenience to title would be alarming and enormous. The law has always had a regard to derivative titles when fairly procured; and though it may be true, as an abstract principle, that a derivative title can not be better than that from which it was derived, yet there are many necessary exceptions to the operation of this principle."[45]

A judgment of foreclosure, whether rendered upon confession or upon a regular hearing or trial, can not afterward be questioned on the ground that the debt for which it was rendered was void for usury.[46]

In a suit to recover land, which the plaintiff alleges title to under foreclosure proceedings, the defendant can not attack the validity of such foreclosure on the ground of usury.[47]

After a foreclosure, a mortgage contract is regarded as executed. So long as the contract remains executory, the mortgagor can avail himself of the usury; but when it is executed, and others have in good faith acquired interests in the property, the objection can no longer be raised.[48] But if the mortgagee himself buy the property directly or through an agent at the foreclosure sale, it is held that his title may still be impeached for usury in the mortgage. Being a party to the usurious contract, his situation is no better after the foreclosure than it was before.[49]

[45] Tyler v. Massachusetts Mut. Ins. Co., 108 Ill. 58; Carter v. Moses, 39 Ill. 539; Perkins v. Conant, 29 Ill. 184, 81 Am. Dec. 305; Mumford v. Am. Life Ins. Co., 4 N. Y. 463; Elliott v. Wood, 53 Barb. (N. Y.) 285; Jackson v. Henry, 10 Johns. (N. Y.) 185, 6 Am. Dec. 328.

[46] Bell v. Fergus, 55 Ark. 536, 18 S. W. 931.

[47] Northwestern Mortgage Trust Co. v. Bradley, 9 S. Dak. 495, 70 N. W. 648.

[48] Ferguson v. Soden, 111 Mo. 208, 19 S. W. 727 (quoting text).

[49] Welsh v. Coley, 82 Ala. 363, 2 So. 733; McLaughlin v. Cosgrove, 99 Mass. 4. So with any purchaser who has notice of the usury at the time of sale. Jackson v. Dominick, 14 Johns. (N. Y.) 435; Bissell v. Kellogg, 60 Barb. (N. Y.) 617, 65 N. Y. 432. So with a mortgagee of chattels who has seized the property. Wetherell v. Stewart, 35 Minn. 496, 29 N. W. 196. But in New Jersey it is held that a subsequent mortgagee may set up usury under his petition for the surplus money remaining in court after satisfying prior mortgages. Hutchinson v. Abbott, 33 N. J. Eq. 379. In Minnesota the foreclosure of the usurious mortgage, and sale under the power to one not a bona fide purchaser, does not prevent the granting of relief. Jordan v. Humphrey, 31 Minn. 495, 18 N. W. 450; Exley v. Berryhill, 37 Minn. 182, 33 N. W. 567; Scott v. Austin, 36 Minn. 460, 32 N. W. 864. Only a bona fide purchaser for value without notice is protected under such a sale. Jordan v. Humphrey, 31 Minn. 495, 18 N. W. 450.

Voluntary payments of usury, made with full knowledge of all the facts, can not be recovered back, unless by force of an express statute.[50]

§ 647. Effect of usurious transactions subsequent to execution of mortgage.—A bonus paid to secure the extension of the time of payment of an existing mortgage does not invalidate the mortgage as a security for the original debt.[51]

Where the original transaction is not usurious, a subsequent agreement to pay a usurious rate of interest in consideration of forbearance, does not impart to the contract the taint of usury.[52]

When a mortgage is free from usury in its inception, no subsequent usurious contract in relation to it can affect the mortgage itself. It is only the subsequent contract that is affected by the usury. The mortgage, not being usurious in its origin, is not made so retrospectively by the receipt of usurious interest under an agreement to forbear demand of payment, though the penalty of the statute may be incurred.[53] But if the usury goes back to the original transaction, the mortgage is rendered void by the usury.[54] A provision of the lex loci contractus, rendering void the original contract when extra interest is taken for the forbearance of the payment of money when due, will not be enforced in a foreign state, because the forfeiture is in the nature of a remedy. The lex fori determines the remedy, the lex loci contractus, the validity and construction.[55]

An agreement after maturity of the mortgage debt to pay a rate of interest higher than is allowed by law, as an indemnity to the mortgagee for interest paid by him on money borrowed in another state at such higher rate, will not for that reason be upheld.[56]

---

[50] Riddle v. Rosenfield, 103 Ill. 600; Fessenden v. Taft, 65 N. H. 39, 17 Atl. 713.

[51] Mahoney v. Mackubin, 54 Md. 268; Terhune v. Taylor, 27 N. J. Eq. 80; Trusdell v. Jones, 23 N. J. Eq. 121, 554; Donnington v. Meeker, 11 N. J. Eq. 362; Langdon v. Gray, 52 How. Pr. (N. Y.) 387; Abrahams v. Claussen, 52 How. Pr. (N. Y.) 241; Real Estate Trust Co. v. Keech, 7 Hun (N. Y.) 253, 25 Am. Rep. 181, and cases cited; Sweny v. Peaslee, 17 N. Y. S. 225. See also McEwin v. Humphrey, 1 Ind. Ter. 550, 45 S. W. 114; Morse v. Wellcome, 68 Minn. 210, 70 N. E. 978, 64 Am. St. 471;

Rosenbaum v. Silverman, 22 Misc. 589, 50 N. Y. S. 860.

[52] Nance v. Gray, 143 Ala. 234, 38 So. 916.

[53] Hawhe v. Snydaker, 86 Ill. 197; Lindsay v. Hill, 66 Maine 212, 22 Am. Rep. 564; Thompson v. Woodbridge, 8 Mass. 256. See also Cain v. Bonner (Tex. Civ. App.), 149 S. W. 702.

[54] Smith v. Hathorn, 88 N. Y. 211, reversing 25 Hun 159.

[55] Lindsay v. Hill, 66 Maine 212, 22 Am. Rep. 564.

[56] Eslava v. Lepretre, 21 Ala. 504, 56 Am. Dec. 266.

§ 648. When bonus for extension a proper credit on mortgage debt.

—If a payment made by a mortgagor as a premium for an extension of the time of payment of the principal debt is void for the purpose for which it was made, it should be credited as a payment upon the mortgage debt as of the time when it was made.[57]

Where the person paying a bonus for an extension of payment is not the original mortgage debtor, but one who has purchased the premises subject to the mortgage without assuming the payment of it, such payment is as much usury as if the sum of money secured by the mortgage had been loaned upon a contract to pay more than legal interest, and renders the contract for extension void, and the sum paid for such extension should be applied as a payment upon the mortgage.[58]

Where transactions, although made in the form of payment of one loan and the creation of another, amount in reality to the monthly renewal of an original loan at a usurious rate of interest, all payments in excess of legal interest are to be applied on the principal.[59]

§ 649. When agreement for extension void under usury laws.

—Under some usury laws an agreement to extend the time of payment of a mortgage is void if made in consideration of a usurious payment or contract.[60] But while the cases are in harmony upon this point, they are not agreed whether it is the privilege of the borrower alone to take advantage of the usurious taint of the contract; or whether, for instance, the lender may disregard the contract and proceed before the expiration of such extension to enforce payment or foreclose the mortgage. On the one hand, it is held that the lender can not wilfuly violate the statute against usury, and then take advantage of his own wrong by repudiating the contract; that the borrower or his surety, or personal representative, can alone set up the usury; in other words, that the victim of the usury, and not the usurer, can take advantage of the statute.[61] But even if an extension made upon a usurious payment be binding at the election of the mortgagor, if upon a foreclosure suit he requires that the premium paid shall be credited

[57] Patterson v. Clark, 28 Ga. 526; Nightingale v. Meginnis, 34 N. J. L. 461; Laing v. Martin, 26 N. J. Eq. 93; Trusdell v. Jones, 23 N. J. Eq. 121, 554. See also Church v. Maloy, 70 N. Y. 63; Nunn v. Bird, 36 Ore. 515, 59 Pac. 808.

[58] Ganz v. Lancaster, 169 N. Y. 357, 62 N. E. 413, revg. 50 App. Div. 204.

[59] Mylott v. Skinner, 12 Pa. Super. Ct. 137.

[60] Church v. Maloy, 70 N. Y. 63. See also Milholen v. Meyer, 161 Mo. App. 491, 143 S. W. 540.

[61] Billington v. Wagoner, 33 N. Y. 31; La Farge v. Herter, 9 N. Y. 241. But see Church v. Maloy, 70 N. Y. 63.

he disaffirms the contract for extension.[62] He is entitled to the credit; but, having received that, he is not entitled to the extension, so as to prevent the whole principal from being regarded as due.

A distinction has been taken between a contract for extension founded upon a consideration of an actual payment of money made at the time of the contract, and one made upon an executory contract to pay usury; and it is held that, while the contract is binding upon the creditor in the former case, it is not binding in the latter, as, for instance, when the consideration for the extension is a promissory note of the debtor.[63]

Extension of the time of payment is a sufficient consideration for an agreement to increase the rate of interest upon the debt, and when the arrangement has once been entered upon, without a definite limitation of its continuance being agreed upon, it will be presumed that the increased rate of interest continues as long as the forbearance is granted.[64]

But, on the other hand, the rule has sometimes been declared to be, that the court will not help either party to enforce a usurious contract while it remains executory.[65] A promise to extend the time of payment of a mortgage made in consideration of a note for a usurious premium is void; and the mortgagee may foreclose it before the expiration of the extended time upon his giving up the usurious note. The usurious contract in such case remains executory. It is not the privilege of the borrower alone to take advantage of the usurious taint. The statute makes the contract void.[66]

Where money is owing upon a contract for the payment of a loan, and forbearance is given for such debt upon the condition of receiving more than the legal rate of interest, such forbearance is as much usury as if the sum of money had been absolutely loaned upon a contract to pay more than legal interest.[67]

§ 650. **Validity of agreement to pay compound interest, made before interest due.**—As to compound interest the general rule is, that

---

[62] Kommer v. Harrington, 83 Minn. 114, 85 N. W. 939; Church v. Maloy, 70 N. Y. 63.

[63] Jones v. Trusdell, 23 N. J. Eq. 121, per Chief Justice Beasley; Billington v. Wagoner, 33 N. Y. 31. But see Church v. Maloy, 70 N. Y. 63.

[64] Haggerty v. Allaire Works, 5 Sandf. (N. Y.) 230.

[65] Jones v. Trusdell, 23 N. J. Eq. 121, 554.

[66] Jones v. Trusdell, 23 N. J. Eq. 121.

[67] Ganz v. Lancaster, 169 N. Y. 357, 62 N. E. 413, 58 L. R. A. 151; Perkins v. Hall, 105 N. Y. 539, 12 N. E. 48; Baldwin v. Moffett, 94 N. Y. 82; Wyeth v. Braniff, 84 N. Y. 627.

an executory contract for it can not be enforced; but that the payment of such interest by the debtor, understandingly and under no peculiar circumstances of oppression, does not constitute usury.[1]

There is a decided lack of uniformity of opinion in the decisions bearing on the question of the validity of agreements, made before interest becomes due, to pay interest on interest. Many courts condemn such agreements without making any distinction between agreements simply to pay interest on overdue interest, and agreements for the compounding of interest at regular intervals. An agreement made contemporaneously with the loan contract, providing that the interest shall, if unpaid, itself bear interest, does not obligate the borrower to pay compound interest, except in the event of his failure to pay the interest at maturity. If he fulfil his contract, it is impossible for the lender to collect more than the legal contractual rate of interest. Certainly no one would doubt the right of the parties, after the interest becomes due and unpaid, to include the amount of such interest as the principal of a second note, itself bearing the lawful rate of interest. Conceding this, we see no good reason why parties may not provide in the same instrument for the compounding of interest, when the stipulations of the contract are not such as require a compounding of the interest as a part of the contract, not leaving any option or right in the borrower to avoid paying compound interest. Such a contract is a mere matter of convenience to the parties, and places nothing in the contract they could not lawfully do as an independent transaction.[2]

It is admitted that there is no law prohibiting such a contract, but the courts have adopted the rule from notions of policy;[3] holding that although it may be demanded and recovered as it becomes due, an agreement to pay interest on the interest after it becomes due can not be enforced.[4] Lord Thurlow said:[5] "My opinion is in favor of interest

[1] Culver v. Bigelow, 43 Vt. 249.
[2] Ellard v. Scottish-American Mtg. Co., 97 Ga. 329, 22 S. E. 893; Merck v. American Freehold Land Mtg. Co:, 79 Ga. 213, 7 S. E. 265; Scott v. Saffold, 37 Ga. 384; Burke v. Trabue, 137 Ky. 580, 126 S. W. 125; Palm v. Fancher, 93 Miss. 785, 48 So. 818, 33 L. R. A. (N. S.) 295; Bura v. Thompson, 2 Clark (Pa.) 143; Yaws v. Jones (Tex.), 19 S. W. 443; Lewis v. Paschal, 37 Tex. 315.
[3] For numerous authorities in support of the rule that interest shall not bear interest, except by virtue of an agreement made after the in

terest has become due, see Force v. Elizabeth, 28 N. J. Eq. 403.
[4] Stewart v. Petree, 55 N. Y. 621, 14 Am. Rep. 352; Van Benschooten v. Lawson, 6 Johns. Ch. (N. Y.) 313, 10 Am. Dec. 333; Connecticut v. Jackson, 1 Johns. Ch. (N. Y.) 13, 7 Am. Dec. 471; article in 16 Alb. L. J. 252. See also Eslava v. Lepretre, 21 Ala. 504, 56 Am. Dec. 266; Hochmark v. Richler, 16 Colo. 263, 26 Pac. 818; Bowman v. Neely, 137 Ill. 443, 27 N. E. 758; Drury v. Wolfe, 134 Ill. 294, 25 N. E. 626.
[5] Waring v. Cunliffe, 1 Ves. Jr. 99.

upon interest; because I do not see any reason, if a man does not pay interest when he ought, why he should not pay interest for that also. But I have found the court in a constant habit of thinking the contrary, and I must overturn all the proceedings of the court if I give it." Lord Eldon also said that a bargain for interest on interest was neither unfair nor illegal, but that it could not be allowed because it tended to usury, although it was not usury.[6]

In several states it is now provided by statute that interest upon interest may be contracted for;[7] and it would seem that inasmuch as the

[6] Chambers v. Goldwin, 9 Ves. 254. See also Blackburn v. Warick, 2 Y. & C. 92, per Alderson, B.; Barnard v. Young, 17 Ves. 44; Leith v. Irvine, 1 Myl. & K. 277; Thornhill v. Evans, 2 Atk. 330.

[7] In Michigan it is provided that when any instalment of interest upon any note, bond, mortgage, or other written contract shall have become due, and the same shall remain unpaid, interest may be computed and collected on any such instalment so due and unpaid, from the time at which it became due, at the same rate as specified in any such note, bond, mortgage, or other written contract, not exceeding ten per cent.; and if no rate of interest be specified in such instrument, then at the rate of seven per centum per annum. How. Mich. Stat. 1913, § 2875. But interest can not be computed on interest accruing after the principal is due. McVicar v. Denison, 81 Mich. 348, 45 N. W. 659. Minnesota: Interest can not be compounded; but a contract to pay interest not usurious upon interest overdue is not construed to be usury. G. S. 1891, & 2089. In Missouri parties may contract in writing for the payment of interest upon interest, but the interest shall not be computed oftener than once a year. Where a different rate is not expressed, interest upon interest is at the same rate as interest on the principal debt. R. S. 1889, § 5977; Waples v. Jones, 62 Mo. 440. In California the parties may contract in writing, and agree that if the interest is not punctually paid it shall become part of the principal and bear interest at the same rate. Civil Code, §§ 1917, 1919, 1920.

In view of this statute it is held that a stipulation that the deferred instalments of interest shall bear interest at a higher rate than that borne by the principal is wholly illegal and void. Yndart v. Den, 116 Cal. 533, 58 Am. St. 200, 48 Pac. 618. In Wisconsin it is provided that interest shall not be compounded, or bear interest upon interest, unless there be an agreement to that effect, expressed in writing, and signed by the party to be charged therewith. R. S. 1878, § 1689. On the other hand, express provisions against compound interest have been made in a few states. Arkansas: In no case where a payment shall fall short of paying the interest due at the time of making such payment shall the balance of such interest be added to the principal. Dig. of Stats. 1884, § 4738. At one time the law of Louisiana provided that no stipulation in the original contract to pay interest upon interest should be valid. See Lee v. Goodrich, 21 La. Ann. 278. But a provision in the contract that notes given for interest after maturity has been held not usurious. Scottish-American Mtg. Co. v. Ogden, 49 La. Ann. 8, 21 So. 116. In Idaho compound interest is not allowed, but a debtor may agree in writing to pay interest upon interest overdue at the date of such agreement. R. S., § 1266. In view of this statute, coupon notes given for the interest of the principal debt, which, by their terms, draw interest after maturity, are usurious, although the compound interest provided for in the coupon notes, when added to the simple interest, falls below the legal contractual rates fixed by law. Vermont

objection to such contracts has been that they savored of usury, and inasmuch as it has always been held that the parties may, by a new agreement after the interest has accrued, turn it into principal, in those states where the laws against usury have been abolished there can be no reason why an agreement for turning interest into principal is not valid.[8] But in Nevada, although it is provided by statute that parties may agree in writing for the payment of any rate of interest, it is held in equity that a contract for compound interest can not be enforced.[9] The court say that, "when the Nevada Statute was passed, it was the settled rule of courts of equity to refuse to allow compound interest when their aid was invoked to collect a debt. In courts of law the rule was not so well settled, but we think a majority of the states of this Union, and the English courts of law, had refused to enforce that portion of contracts which provided for the collection of compound interest. None of these rulings were founded on the statutes against usury, but on the general principles of the common law as it existed, without reference to the usury law."

In states where all usury laws have been abolished it would seem that a stipulation for the payment of compound interest is valid and may be enforced.[10] And so, where parties may contract for interest not exceeding a certain rate, a contract may be made for compound interest, provided the interest on the principal debt, together with the interest on the interest coupons, does not exceed at the maturity of the debt the limited rate of interest.[11]

It is generally held that a stipulation to pay interest above the legal rate in case of default in the payment of principal or interest in accordance with the contract imposes a penalty to enforce prompt payment only, and is not usurious.[12]

§ 651. **Validity of agreement to pay interest on interest, made after interest has become due.**—So long as the agreement for compound

Loan &c. Co. v. Hoffman, 5 Idaho 376, 49 Pac. 314, 36 L. R. A. 509, 95 Am. St. 186.

[8] Bradley v. Merrill, 91 Maine 340, 40 Atl. 132; Farwell v. Sturdivant, 37 Maine 308.

[9] Cox v. Smith, 1 Nev. 161, 90 Am. Dec. 476. Questionable.

[10] Clarkson v. Henderson, L. R. 14 Ch. D. 348.

[11] Richardson v. Campbell, 34 Nebr. 181, 51 N. W. 753; Murtagh v. Thompson, 28 Nebr. 358, 44 N.

W. 451; Mathews v. Toogood, 23 Nebr. 536, 37 N. W. 265, 8 Am. St. 131; Reed v. Miller, 1 Wash. St. 426, 25 Pac. 334.

[12] Union Mortgage Banking &c. Co. v. Hagood, 97 Fed. 360; Green v. Brown, 22 Misc. 279, 49 N. Y. S. 163; Law Guarantee &c. Soc. v. Hogue, 37 Ore. 544, 62 Pac. 380, 63 Pac. 690; Parks v. Lubbock (Tex.), 50 S. W. 466; Sloane v. Lucas, 37 Wash. 348, 79 Pac. 949.

interest is executory merely, the courts will not lend their aid to enforce it; but when the contract has been acted upon by the parties, and such interest has been paid, the courts will not require a repayment, nor will they hold the transaction to be in any degree tainted with usury by reason of such payment. Such an agreement does not render a mortgage usurious, but the contract, so far as it provided for usurious interest, is void; but it may be enforced for the debt and interest, even where usury makes void the contract.[13] An agreement to pay interest on interest, made after the interest has accrued, is valid and may be enforced.[14] By such agreement the parties turn the interest into principal. Interest on interest is not recoverable simply on the strength of a demand.[15]

Some recent decisions do away with this distinction, and hold that there is no objection to a contract for interest upon interest.[16]

Some courts hold that a retroactive agreement, made after interest has become due, that it shall bear interest from a time past, is unsupported by any consideration other than the moral consideration resulting from the fact that the interest is in arrear and unpaid.[17]

In Ohio and Iowa it is the settled rule that when interest is payable by the terms of a mortgage at stated periods, without any special agreement to that effect, it becomes principal from the time of payment, and may be recovered as such, with interest from the time it became due. Upon a note which simply provides for the payment of interest

---

[13] Mowry v. Bishop, 5 Paige (N. Y.) 98.

[14] Stickney v. Moore, 108 Ala. 590, 19 So. 76; Ginn v. New England Mtg. &c. Co., 92 Ala. 135, 8 So. 388; Paulling v. Creagh, 54 Ala. 646; Drury v. Wolfe, 134 Ill. 294, 25 N. E. 626; Gilmore v. Bissell, 124 Ill. 488, 16 N. E. 925; Thayer v. Star Mining Co., 105 Ill. 541; Force v. Elizabeth, 28 N. J. Eq. 403; Tylee v. Yates, 3 Barb. (N. Y.) 222; Fobes v. Cantfield, 3 Ohio 17. See also Porter v. Price, 80 Fed. 655, 26 C. C. A. 70; Hochmark v. Richler, 16 Colo. 263, 26 Pac. 818; Meeker v. Hill, 23 Conn. 574; Rose v. Bridgeport, 17 Conn. 243; Camp v. Bates, 11 Conn. 487; Grimes v. Blake, 16 Ind. 160; Niles v. Sinking Fund Comrs., 8 Blackf. (Ind.) 158; Otis v. Lindsey, 10 Maine 315; Banks v. McClellan, 24 Md. 62, 87 Am. Dec. 594; Wilcox v. Howland, 23 Pick. (Mass.) 167; Gay v. Berkey, 137 Mich. 658, 100 N. W. 920; Hoyle v. Page, 41 Mich. 533, 2 N. W. 665; Mason v. Callender, 2 Minn. 350, 72 Am. Dec. 102; Perkins v. Coleman, 51 Miss. 298; Young v. Hill, 67 N. Y. 162, 23 Am. Rep. 99; Hathaway v. Meads, 11 Ore. 66, 4 Pac. 519; Stokely v. Thompson, 34 Pa. St. 210; Stansbury v. Stansbury, 24 W. Va. 634; Craig v. McCulloch, 20 W. Va. 148; Genin v. Ingersoll, 11 W. Va. 549.

[15] Whitcomb v. Harris, 90 Maine 206, 38 Atl. 138; Bannister v. Roberts, 35 Maine 75; Lewin v. Folsom, 171 Mass. 188, 50 N. E. 523.

[16] Hollingsworth v. Detroit, 3 McLean (U. S.) 472; Scott v. Saffold, 37 Ga. 384.

[17] Young v. Hill, 67 N. Y. 162, 23 Am. Rep. 99; Van Benschooten v. Lawson, 6 Johns. Ch. (N. Y.) 313, 10 Am. Dec. 333; Childers v. Deane, 4 Rand. (Va.) 406.

annually, the interest on the interest will be computed at the legal rate provided for cases where the parties do not agree upon a higher rate; and although the interest upon the note be fixed at a higher rate, in the absence of any agreement as to the rate of interest upon accrued interest that rate will not govern.[18] Where interest upon a mortgage note was payable annually, interest upon the delinquent interest was allowed, although the note was made in New York and was payable there, where the rule was otherwise.[19] But when interest on interest is stipulated for, the rate reserved by mortgage, if within the limits allowed by law, will control.[20]

§ 652. Accrued interest forming principal of further mortgage— Tacking to first mortgage.

—Accrued interest is a debt, and even where an agreement made at the time of the loan for converting interest into principal, from time to time as it shall become due, is not allowed because it is regarded as offensive and usurious, yet when it has become due there is no objection to the parties converting such interest into principal, and securing it by a further mortgage. It is regarded as in the nature of a further advance, and not only may it form the consideration of a second or further mortgage, but as between the parties it may be tacked to the first mortgage.[21]

While parties may not prospectively agree that interest may bear interest; but, after interest has accrued and is due, it may be agreed that such interest may bear interest.[22]

If interest be demanded when due, it legally bears interest from that time; or if no demand be proved, then from the commencement of suit.[23]

When a mortgage is given to secure the payment of money in in-

---

[18] Mann v. Cross, 9 Iowa 327; Cramer v. Lepper, 26 Ohio St. 59, 20 Am. Rep. 756.

[19] Burrows v. Stryker, 47 Iowa 477; Preston v. Walker, 26 Iowa 205, 96 Am. Dec. 140.

[20] Watkinson v. Root, 4 Ohio 373; Dunlap v. Wiseman, 2 Disney (Ohio) 398.

[21] Eslava v. Lepretre, 21 Ala. 504, 56 Am. Dec. 266; Pinckard v. Ponder, 6 Ga. 253; Banks v. McClellan, 24 Md. 62, 87 Am. Dec. 594; Fitzhugh v. McPherson 3 Gill (Md.) 408; Quimby v. Cook, 10 Allen (Mass.) 32; Wilcox v. Howland, 23 Pick. (Mass.) 167; Townsend v. Corning, 1 Barb. (N. Y.) 627; Williams v. Hance, 7 Paige (N. Y.) 581; Parham v. Pulliam, 5 Coldw. (Tenn.) 497; Hale v. Hale, 1 Coldw. (Tenn.) 233, 78 Am. Dec. 490; Barbour v. Tompkins, 31 W. Va. 410, 7 S. E. 1 (quoting text). See also Gilmore v. Bissell, 124 Ill. 488, 16 N. E. 925.

[22] Gunn v. Head, 21 Mo. 432; Sanford v. Lundquist, 80 Nebr. 414, 118 N. W. 129, 18 L. R. A. (N. S.) 633; Craig v. McCulloch, 20 W. Va. 148.

[23] Stewart v. Petree, 55 N. Y. 621, 14 Am. Rep. 352; Howard v. Farley, 19 Abb. Pr. (N. Y.) 126; Force v. Elizabeth, 28 N. J. Eq. 403, where authorities are collected in note; Meyer v. Graeber, 19 Kans. 165; article in 16 Alb. L. J. 252.

stalments, to commence at a future day, "with interest semiannually," interest begins to run from the making of the contract. The holder may sue for each half year's interest as it becomes due, although the principal is not due.[24]

§ 652a. Taking interest upon a loan in advance.—Taking interest upon a loan in advance for the ordinary term of commercial paper, or even for a year, or annually in advance, is not usury, though the result in such case is to enable the creditor to make interest upon interest.[25]

As a general rule the taking as discount on a note of interest in advance is not usury whether it is done by a bank or by a corporation or other persons having no banking powers.[26] But if a debtor gives his creditor a new note and mortgage for the amount of the debt, to which is added interest for a year, and also interest on such interest for that period, the transaction may be regarded as usurious.[27]

Also a reservation of interest in advance on a loan for five years is usurious, where the amount reserved and the amount contracted to be paid aggregate a sum in excess of the highest legal rate for the term of the loan.[28]

§ 653. Interest coupons.—Coupon notes have always been treated as an illogical exception to the rule prohibiting the making of an agreement in a single instrument, obligating the promisor to pay interest after due upon interest then unmatured.[29]

It is the general practice for corporations, in making mortgages

[24] Conners v. Holland, 113 Mass. 50; Hastings v. Wiswall, 8 Mass. 455.

[25] Telford v. Garrels, 132 Ill. 550, 24 N. E. 573; Hoyt v. Institution for Savings, 110 Ill. 390; Mitchell v. Lyman, 77 Ill. 525; Goodrich v. Reynolds, 31 Ill. 490; McGill v. Ware, 5 Ill. 21; Rose v. Munford, 36 Nebr. 148, 54 N. W. 122; Leonard v. Cox, 10 Nebr. 541, 7 N. W. 289; Bloomer v. McInerney, 30 Hun 201; Manhattan Co. v. Osgood, 15 Johns. (N. Y.) 162. See also First Nat. Bank v. Waddell, 74 Ark. 241, 85 S. W. 417; Bank of Newport v. Cook, 60 Ark. 288, 30 S. W. 35, 29 L. R. A. 761, 46 Am. St. 171; Hogan v. Hensley, 22 Ark. 413; English v. Smock, 34 Ind. 115, 7 Am. Rep. 215; Cole v. Lockhart, 2 Ind. 631; Willett v. Maxwell, 169 Ill. 540, 48 N. E. 473; Brown v. Cass County Bank, 86 Iowa 527, 53 N. W. 410; Tholen v. Duffy, 7 Kans. 405. But see Ellis v. Terrell, 109 Ark. 69, 158 S. W. 957, holding that the deduction of interest at the highest rate permitted by law on a loan for a longer period than twelve months at the time the loan is made renders the contract usurious.

[26] Vahlberg v. Keaton, 51 Ark. 534, 11 S. W. 878, 4 L. R. A. 462, 14 Am. St. 73; Cole v. Lockhart, 2 Ind. 631; International Bank v. Bradley, 19 N. Y. 245; New York Firemen Ins. Co. v. Sturges, 2 Cow. (N. Y.) 664.

[27] First Nat. Bank v. Davis, 108 Ill. 633.

[28] McCall v. Herring, 116 Ga. 235, 42 S. E. 468; Miller v. Fergerson, 20 Ky. L. 801, 47 S. W. 1081.

[29] Lee v. Melby, 93 Minn. 4, 100 N. W. 379.

upon their property, to attach to the mortgage bonds coupons representing the interest payable at the several times when the interest falls due;[30] and this practice has been adopted in several states quite extensively by individuals, in making ordinary mortgages or trust deeds upon their private property.[31] Such coupons for the payment of definite sums of money at specified times are in effect promissory notes, and are held to draw interest after maturity.[32] Such interest is computed at the legal rate when the rate, as is usual, is not expressed in the coupon itself. The rate of interest provided for in the bonds does not control.[33] But if the interest coupons are not independent obligations nor strictly commercial securities, upon which the mortgagor is liable, the rule that interest coupons bear interest after maturity is not applicable. Thus, if the mortgage is made by a guardian, and it is recited in the bonds and mortgage that he and his estate are exempt from all liability for the moneys borrowed, and the ward is not personally liable, the bonds as well as the coupons are in effect payable out of particular funds, and are not in any sense commercial paper. In such case the coupons do not bear interest after maturity.[34]

As a general rule, there is no sound reason why the parties may not provide that after maturity the coupons shall bear any rate of interest allowed by law.[35]

[30] Gelpecke v. Dubuque, 1 Wall. (U. S.) 175, 17 L. ed. 520; Hollingsworth v. Detroit, 3 McLean (U. S.) 472; Columbia v. King, 13 Fla. 451; Harper v. Ely, 70 Ill. 581; Dunlap v. Wiseman, 2 Disney (Ohio) 398.

[31] Whitney v. Lowe, 59 Nebr. 87, 80 N. W. 266.

[32] Jones on Corp. Bonds and Mortgages, § 256, and numerous cases cited; United States Mtg. Co. v. Sperry, 138 U. S. 313, 34 L. ed. 969, 11 Sup. Ct. 321; Stickney v. Moore, 108 Ala. 590, 19 So. 76; Ginn v. New Eng. Mtg. S. Co., 92 Ala. 135, 8 So. 388; Caldwell v. Dunklin, 65 Ala. 461; Abbott v. Stone, 172 Ill. 634, 50 N. E. 328; Benneson v. Savage, 130 Ill. 352, 22 N. E. 838; Humphreys v. Morton, 100 Ill. 592; Harper v. Ely, 70 Ill. 581. See also Abbott v. Stone, 172 Ill. 634, 50 N. E. 328, 64 Am. St. 60; Hoyle v. Page, 41 Mich. 533, 2 N. W. 665; Martin v. Land Mtg. Bank, 5 Tex. Civ. App. 167, 23 S. W. 1032.

[33] Jones on Corp. Bonds and Mortgages, § 256; Abbott v. Stone, 172 Ill. 634, 50 N. E. 328 (quoting text).

[34] United States Mtg. Co. v. Sperry, 138 U. S. 313, 34 L. ed. 969, 11 Sup. Ct. 321.

[35] In Nebraska it is the law that when a party loans money at the highest legal rate, and coupon notes are taken for the interest, which stipulate that interest shall be allowed thereon after maturity at the maximum rate, the contract may be enforced in strict accord with its terms. But a provision that upon a default in payment of interest the whole debt shall bear interest at a higher rate than it would otherwise bear, is in the nature of a penalty and will not be enforced. Connecticut Mut. L. Ins. Co. v. Westerhoff, 58 Nebr. 379, 78 N. W. 724, 79 N. W. 731; Crapo v. Hefner, 53 Nebr. 251, 73 N. W. 702; overruling Mathews v. Toogood, 23 Nebr. 536, 37 N. W. 265, 8 Am. St. 131, and 25 Nebr. 99, 41 N. W. 130; Omaha Home F. Ins. Co. v. Fitch, 52 Nebr. 88, 71 N. W. 940; Havemeyer v. Paul, 45 Nebr. 373, 63 N. W. 932; Rose v. Mun-

Interest coupons, although detached from the bond, are still covered by the lien of the mortgage given to secure the bond.[36] Such coupons are usually payable to bearer, and may be transferred and presented by any holder.[37]

§ 654. **When mortgagee may enforce payment of interest.**—A provision for the payment of interest annually, and that if not so paid it shall be compounded, is no waiver of the right to enforce payment when due; and if the deed further provides that, upon a failure to pay the debt or interest as it matures, the whole shall become due and payable, upon a failure to pay the interest annually the whole debt or the interest only may be enforced, at the creditor's election.[38] The owner of a mortgage debt may foreclose a mortgage for the unpaid interest coupon subject to the unmatured principal of the debt.[39]

§ 655. **Computation of interest.**—When no payments have been made upon the mortgage, the interest should be computed from the date of the note until the rendition of the decree. It is erroneous to compute the interest to the time of maturity, and, adding it to the principal, then to compute it upon the gross amount to the time of rendering the decree.[40]

The rule for computing interest when a partial payment has been made is to apply the payment in the first place to the interest then due. This is sometimes called the Massachusetts or the United States rule, and was laid down by Chancellor Kent as follows: "When partial payments have been made, apply the payment, in the first place, to the discharging of the interest then due. If the payment exceeds the interest, the surplus goes toward discharging the principal, and the subsequent interest is to be computed on the balance of the principal remaining due. If the payment be less than the interest, the surplus of interest must not be taken to augment the principal, but the interest continues on the former principal until the period when the

ford, 36 Nebr. 148, 54 N. W. 129; Richardson v. Campbell, 27 Nebr. 644, 43 N. W. 405. In Idaho coupon notes given for the interest of the principal debt, which, by their terms, draw interest after maturity, are in contravention of Rev. Stat. 1887, § 1266, Code 1908' § 1540, forbidding compound interest, and are usurious; Vermont Loan &c. Co. v. Hoffman, 5 Idaho 376, 49 Pac. 314, 37 L. R. A. 509, 95 Am. St. 186.

[36] Miller v. Rutland &c. R. Co., 40 Vt. 399, 94 Am. Dec. 414.

[37] Sewall v. Brainerd, 38 Vt. 364. See also Bowman v. Neely, 137 Ill. 443, 27 N. E. 758; Hoyle v. Page, 41 Mich. 533, 2 N. W. 665.

[38] Waples v. Jones, 62 Mo. 440.

[39] Omaha Loan &c. Co. v. Kitton, 58 Nebr. 113, 78 N. W. 374.

[40] Barker v. International Bank, 80 Ill. 96. See also Leonard v. Villars, 23 Ill. 377.

payments, taken together, exceed the interest due, and then the surplus is to be applied toward discharging the principal, and interest is to be computed on the balance as aforesaid." This is the rule generally adopted in this country.[41] What is known as the Connecticut rule is adopted in some states. By this rule, interest is reckoned upon the principal up to the liquidation of the indebtedness, and then the interest on payments up to the same time, and this amount is deducted from the principal and interest.

In computing interest upon a note with interest payable annually, intermediate payments made on account of the interest accruing, but not yet due, should be deducted at the end of the year, without any allowance of interest upon them; but rests should not be made at the time of such intermediate payments, as that would result in giving compound interest upon the loan.[42] It is held that a mortgage should not be declared void as usurious where one method of computing interest showed usury and another method did not.[43] Thus the taking of interest for a portion of a year, on the principle that a year consists of three hundred and sixty days, or twelve months of thirty days each, is not usurious if resorted to in good faith as furnishing an easy method of computation.[44]

§ 656. **General rule and exceptions as to construction and validity of contract.**—The general rule undoubtedly is, that the law of the place where the contract is executed governs as to the construction and validity of it; but there is this well-recognized exception to the rule, or qualification of it, that, where the contract is to be performed in another place, then the law of the place of performance will govern.[1]

When the mortgage debt is by its terms made payable in the state where the land is situated, though the mortgage was executed in another state, the contract, so far as it is personal, is to be interpreted by the laws of the place of performance.[2] But the place where the mortgage is made payable may be different from the place where the land is situated; and the mortgage may have been executed in still a

---

[41] McQueen v. Whetstone, 127 Ala. 417, 433, 30 So. 548; Blum v. Mitchell, 59 Ala. 535; Wallace v. Glaser, 82 Mich. 190, 46 N. W. 227; Payne v. Avery, 21 Mich. 524.

[42] Townsend v. Riley, 46 N. H. 300.

[43] Culmer Paint &c. Co. v. Gleason (Utah), 130 Pac. 66.

[44] Patton v. Bank of La Fayette, 124 Ga. 965, 53 S. E. 664, 5 L. R. A. (N. S.) 592.

[1] Junction R. Co. v. Bank of Ashland, 12 Wall. (U. S.) 226, 20 L. ed. 385; Morgan v. New Orleans, Mobile &c. R. Co., 2 Woods (U. S.) 244; Lindsay v. Hill, 66 Maine 212, 22 Am. Rep. 564; Little v. Riley, 43 N. H. 109; Parham v. Pulliam, 5 Coldw. (Tenn.) 497.

[2] Duncan v. Helm, 22 La. Ann. 418.

third place, and the question arises, By what law is the mortgage then to be governed? "Obligations, in respect to the mode of their solemnization," says Mr. Wharton,[3] "are subject to the rule locus regit actum; in respect to their interpretation, to the lex loci contractus; in respect to the mode of performance, to the law of the place of performance. But the lex fori determines when and how such laws, when foreign, are to be adopted, and, in all cases not specified above, supplies the applicatory law." Mr. Justice Hunt, in a comparatively recent case before the Supreme Court of the United States, after quoting the rule as above laid down, himself states it as follows:[4] "Matters bearing upon the execution, the interpretation, and the validity of a contract are determined by the law of the place where the contract is made.[5] Matters connected with its performance are regulated by the law prevailing at the place of performance. Matters respecting the remedy, such as the bringing of suits, admissibility of evidence, statutes of limitation, depend upon the law of the place where the suit is brought."[6]

§ 657. **What law governs.**—The law of the state governing the contract itself will determine the validity of a contract, secured by a mortgage made in one state upon lands in another state, so far as the usury laws affect it. If the loan is to be repaid in the state where it is made, the contract will be governed by the laws of that state, even when secured by a mortgage of land situate in another state.[7]

If nothing be said about the place of payment, the contract is presumably payable where the parties reside and the contract is made, although the land be situated in another state; and the validity of the contract would be determined by the laws of the place of contract.[8] Thus where a mortgage on land in Wyoming was executed in California to secure a note executed there, and the parties all resided there,

---

[3] Conflict of Laws, § 401.

[4] Scudder v. Union Nat. Bank, 91 U. S. 406, 23 L. ed. 245.

[5] Gault v. Equitable Trust Co., 100 Ky. 578, 38 S. W. 1065. See also Bank v. Doherty, 42 Wash. 317, 84 Pac. 872, 4 L. R. A. (N. S.) 1191.

[6] LaSelle v. Woolery, 14 Wash. 70, 53 Am. St. 855, 44 Pac. 115.

[7] Commercial Bank v. Auze, 74 Miss. 609, 21 So. 754; Brown v. Freeland, 34 Miss. 181; Cope v. Wheeler, 41 N. Y. 303, 53 Barb. 350, 46 Barb. 272; Mills v. Wilson, 88 Pa. St. 118; Kennedy v. Knight, 21 Wis. 340; Newman v. Kershaw, 10 Wis. 333;

3 Kent Com. 460; Story's Conflict of Laws, §§ 287, 292, 293. See also Bank v. Doherty, 42 Wash. 317, 84 Pac. 872, 4 L. R. A. (N. S.) 1191.

[8] Cope v. Alden, 53 Barb. 350, affd. 41 N. Y. 303 (the action was for surplus money). See also Reimsdyk v. Kane, 1 Gall. (U. S.) 371; Fitch v. Remer, 1 Flipp. (U. S.) 15; Cubbeage v. Napier, 62 Ala. 518; Dobbin v. Hewett, 19 La. Ann. 513; Blydenburgh v. Cotheal, 5 N. J. Eq. 631; Williams v. Fitzhugh, 37 N. Y. 444; Williams v. Ayrault, 31 Barb (N. Y.) 364.

and no place of payment was designated either in the note or mortgage, it was held in a suit to foreclose brought in Wyoming that the law of California governed in determining the legality of consideration.[9]

If no place of payment be named, and the mortgagee reside in the state in which the land lies, and the mortgage is there delivered and the loan received by an agent of the mortgagor who resides in another state, the contract will be governed by the law of the former state.[10] But the parties may contract with reference to the law of a state other than that where the land is situated, and, if the note or mortgage be made payable in that state, the law of that state will govern in the construction and legal effect of the contract.[11] The parties may stipulate for interest with reference to the laws of either the place of contract or the place of payment, so long as the provision be made in good faith, and not as a cover for usury.[12]

A corporation chartered in the state of New York was authorized to lend money on bond and mortgage of real estate situated within the United States, at a rate of interest not exceeding the legal rate. This corporation loaned money upon mortgages of land situate in the state of Illinois at nine per cent. per annum, which the law of that state permitted, although the highest rate of interest permitted by the laws of New York was seven per cent. It was held that the mortgage was not usurious, the rate of interest being governed by the law of the state of Illinois. Mr. Justice Harlan, delivering the judgment of the Supreme Court of the United States, said:[13] "The general statute of New York had for its object to regulate the rate of interest upon loans there made, and not the rate upon loans made elsewhere. That state did not assume to fix the maximum of compensation to be paid to the lender for the use of money in other states. * * * The legal rate referred to in the corporation's charter is the rate established by the law of the place where the contract of loan is made. This view is sup-

[9] Conradt v. Lepper, 13 Wyo. 473, 81 Pac. 307.

[10] Mills v. Wilson, 88 Pa. St. 118;

[11] Slacum v. Pomeroy, 6 Cranch (U. S.) 221, 3 L. ed. 205; Fitch v. Remer, 1 Flipp. (U. S.) 15; Nichols v. Cosset, 1 Root (Conn.) 294; Duncan v. Helm, 22 La. Ann. 418; Robinson v. Bland, 2 Burr. 1077. See also Oregon &c. Trust Co. v. Rathbun, 5 Sawyer (U. S.) 32; Buchanan v. Drovers' Nat. Bank, 55 Fed. 223.

[12] Gault v. Equitable Trust Co., 100

Ky. 578, 36 S. W. 1065; Townsend v. Riley, 46 N. H. 300; Peck v. Mayo, 14 Vt. 33, 39 Am. Dec. 205.

[13] United States Mortgage Co. v. Sperry, 138 U. S. 313, 34 L. ed. 969, 11 Sup. Ct. 321, citing Sheldon v. Haxtun, 91 N. Y. 124; Wayne County Savings Bank v. Low, 81 N. Y. 566; Pratt v. Adams, 7 Paige (N. Y.) 615. See also Tilden v. Blair, 21 Wall. (U. S.) 241, 22 L. ed. 632; Scudder v. Union Nat. Bank, 91 U. S. 406, 23 L. ed. 245.

ported by those decisions in New York which hold, in respect to loans made in other states, that the rate of interest allowed by the state where the contract of loan is made will be respected by the courts of New York, although such rate is in excess of that fixed by its own laws, and although, in some of the cases, one of the parties to the contract, the lender, was a resident of that state."

When a contract is made payable in another state for the purpose of evading the usury laws of the state where the contract is executed, the question is not which law shall govern in executing the contract, but which shall decide the fate of the security. Unquestionably it is the law of the place of contract.[14]

By statute in Michigan the interest on mortgages may be made payable out of the state at such place as the parties may agree upon, although the rate of interest in such place may be less than in this state; and the rate of interest reserved is not affected by the laws of the place where payment is to be made.[15]

§ 658. **Mortgage debt payable in state other than where land situated.**—But the laws of another state can not be imported into a contract by a mere mental operation or understanding of the parties, for the purpose of making the character of the loan different from what it is under the law of the place of contract. A mortgage was made in New York, where both of the parties to it resided, of land situate in Wisconsin, and interest was reserved at the rate of twelve per cent., which was legal in the latter, but not in the former state. The only pretext that the loan was made with reference to the law of Wisconsin was that the mortgagor had money due to her there at twelve per cent. interest, which the borrower there desired to retain, and therefore he was willing and agreed to pay that rate for money borrowed in New York to relieve temporary wants. But the loan being made in New York, where it was also to be repaid, and the use of the money being unrestricted, the reason why the borrower was willing to pay more than lawful interest was immaterial. The trans-

[14] Andrews v. Pond, 13 Pet. (U. S.) 65, 10 L. ed. 61; Mix v. Madison Ins. Co., 11 Ind. 117; Meroney v. Atlanta Nat. B. &c. Assn., 112 N. Car. 842, 17 S. E. 637.

[15] Compiled Laws of Mich. 1871, pp. 541, 542; Howell's Stat. 1913, ch. 37, §§ 2878, 2879. A similar statute in Illinois. Act Ill. Feb. 12, 1857, and Feb. 14, 1857, § 14. See also Fowler v. Equitable Trust Co., 141

U. S. 384, 35 L. ed. 786, 12 Sup. Ct. 1. In South Carolina a statute provides that the rate of interest upon mortgages of land within the state shall be governed by the laws of that state without regard to the laws of the state in which the debt is made payable. Laws 1898, p. 747, § 1; Mutual Aid L. Ins. Co. v. Logan, 55 S. Car. 395, 33 S. E. 372.

action was, therefore, governed by the laws of New York, under which the mortgage was usurious.[16] The same decision was reached in a case where the facts were substantially the same, except that the mortgagor resided in Ohio, where the mortgaged lands were situated. The mortgage was executed in New York, and was made payable there; and the contract was therefore governed by the laws of that state.[17] A like decision was made in Ohio with reference to a loan negotiated in the state of New York, where the money was advanced, and a note and mortgage payable there taken as security; although the mortgage covered lands in Ohio, it was held that the laws of the state of New York relating to usury were applicable to the transaction.[18]

There are numerous cases holding that the lex loci contractus governs when the contract is not payable elsewhere.[19] This rule governs in respect to usury, unless the parties, by the express terms of their contract, have in view a different place.[20]

§ 659. Contract valid where made but invalid in place of performance.

—A contract made in a state where it is valid, to be performed in another where it would be invalid, may after all be held valid by referring it to the law of the state where it was made.[21] The question which law shall govern depends upon the law applicable to the con-

[16] Coe v. Wheeler, 41 N. Y. 303, 53 Barb. 350, 46 Barb. 272. A mortgage was made in Tennessee, by residents of that state, of land situate in Mississippi, to secure a loan made by a corporation in New York, in which state the notes were made payable. The notes were usurious, both in Tennessee and in New York. There was a recital in the deed of trust that it, and the notes secured thereby, were made in Mississippi, where they were not usurious, and should be construed according to the laws of that state. It was held that such recital was void, since the laws of a state, and access to its courts, are not the subject of contract. American Mtg. Co. v. Jefferson, 69 Miss. 770, 12 So. 464.

[17] Williams v. Fitzhugh, 37 N. Y. 444.

[18] Lockwood v. Mitchell, 7 Ohio St. 387, 70 Am. Dec. 78.

[19] United States Mtg. Co. v. Sperry, 138 U. S. 313, 34 L. ed. 969, 11 Sup. Ct. 321; Kuhn v. Morrison, 75 Fed. 81; Moore v. Davidson, 18 Ala. 209;

Bigelow v. Burnham, 83 Iowa 120, 49 N. W. 104, 32 Am. St. 294; Hart v. Wills, 52 Iowa 56, 2 N. W. 619, 35 Am. Rep. 255; Templeton v. Sharp, 10 Ky. L. 499, 9 S. W. 507; New York Security &c. Co. v. Davis, 96 Md. 81, 53 Atl. 669; Jones v. Rider, 60 N. H. 452; Watson v. Lane, 52 N. J. L. 550, 20 Atl. 894, 10 L. R. A. 784; Curtis v. Leavitt, 15 N. Y. 9; Grand Rapids School Furniture Co. v. Hammerstein, 45 N. Y. St. 863. 18 N. Y. S. 766; Mills v. Wilson, 88 Pa. St. 118; Clark v. Searight, 135 Pa. St. 173, 19 Atl. 941, 20 Am. St. 868.

[20] Glover v. Equitable Mtg. Co., 87 Fed. 518, 31 C. C. A. 105; Ashurst v. Ashurst, 119 Ala. 219, 24 So. 760; Lanier v. Union Mtg. Bkg. &c. Co., 64 Ark. 39, 40 S. W. 466; Smith v. Parsons, 55 Minn. 520, 57 N. W. 311.

[21] Depau v. Humphreys, 20 Mart. (La.) 1; Pratt v. Adams, 7 Paige (N. Y.) 615; Chapman v. Robertson, 6 Paige (N. Y.) 627; Fisher v. Otis, 3 Chand. (Pa.) 83, 3 Pinn. 78; Peck v. Mayo, 14 Vt. 33, 39 Am. Dec. 205.

tract itself, and not upon the fact that the mortgage, considered alone, would be valid by the law of the state where the lands lie. "The place of payment may, in the absence of any more controlling circumstances, be sufficient to show that the parties intended to refer their contract to the law of that place. But if the loan was actually made in another state, the money to be used there, the parties residing there, the security given there, and if by that law the contract would be valid, and it would be invalid by the law of the place of payment, these facts may well be held to have a stronger influence in showing the intention than the mere place of payment, and, the rule itself resting upon that intention, where the intention is rebutted the rule should cease."[22]

As a general rule the law of the place of payment governs in respect to usury if the interest reserved is not usurious by that law, but is by the law of the place where the contract was made and there are no circumstances sufficient to rebut the presumption that the parties intended to contract with reference to the former law or to show that the place of payment was designated as a mere cover for usury.[23]

Where a mortgage of land in Michigan was executed there, but made payable in New York, where the mortgagee then resided, and the rate of interest was ten per cent., which was usurious in the latter state but was valid in the former, it was held that the mortgagee might elect to proceed to enforce the mortgage in Michigan; for it was to be presumed that the contract was made with reference to the in-

---

[22] Newman v. Kershaw, 10 Wis. 333, per Paine, J. See also Vaccaro v. Asher (Miss.), 11 So. 531. A debtor living in New York was indebted to a resident of Washington for money loaned, as evidenced by a note payable in the latter city. The parties afterward met in Washington, and arranged for a renewal of the note by giving a new note, bearing the same rate of interest as the first note, though it was made payable at a bank in New York. The new note was signed by the debtor and indorsed by a surety in the state of New York, and forwarded to the creditor in Washington, and the old note was thereupon surrendered. It was held that the question of usury was to be determined by the law in Washington, where the note was not usurious, and not by the law of New York. Staples v. Nott, 128 N. Y. 403, 28 N. E. 515, Gray, J., delivering the opinion, said: "For the court to hold, because the note was not actually signed and indorsed in the District of Columbia, where the agreement it evidenced was made, or because it was made payable in another state, that the contract was void as contravening the usury laws of the place of signature and of payment, would be intolerable and against decisions of this court. Western Transp. Co. v. Kilderhouse, 87 N. Y. 430; Wayne Co. Sav. Bank v. Low, 81 N. Y. 566; Sheldon v. Haxtun, 91 N. Y. 124. I think the plaintiff was entitled to recover as upon a contract made under the government of the laws of the District of Columbia, and therefore valid and enforcible in any state."

[23] Junction R. Co. v. Bank of Ashland, 12 Wall. (U. S.) 226, 20 L. ed. 385; Peyton v. Heinekin, 131 U. S. ci, Appx., 20 L. ed. 679; Hamilton v. Fowler, 99 Fed. 18, 40 C. C. A.

terest laws of that state.[24] In like manner, where an application for a loan from a foreign corporation was made to its agents in Alabama, and the corporation paid the money to bankers in New York, who sent it to the agent, who delivered it to the borrower on the execution by him of a mortgage on land in Alabama, the mortgage being made and acknowledged in Alabama, but the mortgage notes being payable in New York, it was held that the contract was governed by the laws of Alabama.[25]

§ 659a. Validity of contract made in one state and payable in another bearing highest rate payable in either.—A contract made in one state to be performed in another may bear the highest rate of interest payable in either, provided the parties contract in good faith, and not for the purpose of evading the laws of the state where such interest is not lawful.[26]

If the interest allowed by the laws of the place of performance is higher than that permitted at the place of the delivery of the contract, the parties may stipulate for the higher interest without incurring the penalties of usury.[27] A note made in Wyoming to a resident of that state by a corporation of that state having most of its property and transacting the greater part of its business in Nebraska, secured by a mortgage of land in the latter state, may lawfully bear a rate of interest allowed by the laws of Wyoming, but usurious in Nebraska, it appearing that the loan was made in good faith, and not as a device for securing interest in excess of that allowed by the laws of Nebraska.[28]

§ 660. The lex rei sitae does not control.—The authorities generally do not regard the circumstance that the loan is secured by mortgage in determining whether it be usurious.[29] Thus a loan made in

---

47; Wittkowski v. Harris, 64 Fed. 712.

[24] Fitch v. Remer, 1 Flipp. (U. S.) 15. See full examination of the question by McLean, J., in this case.

[25] American Mtg. Co. v. Sewell, 92 Ala. 163, 9 So. 143. The facts in the case of Farrior v. Security Co., 88 Ala. 277, 7 So. 200, were almost identical.

[26] Miller v. Tiffany, 1 Wall. (U. S.) 298, 17 L. ed. 540; Brown v. Finance Co., 31 Fed. 516; Townsend v. Riley, 46 N. H. 300; Kilgore v. Dempsey, 25 Ohio St. 413. See also Smith v. Muncie Nat. Bank, 29 Ind. 158.

[27] Ames v. Benjamin, 74 Minn. 335, 77 N. W. 230; Long v. Long, 141 Mo. 352, 44 S. W. 341; Central Nat. Bank v. Cooper, 85 Mo. App. 383.

[28] Coad v. Home Cattle Co., 32 Nebr. 761, 49 N. W. 757.

[29] In Connor v. Bellamont, 2 Ark. 382, Lord Hardwicke allowed Irish interest upon a debt contracted in England, but secured by a bond and mortgage executed in Ireland. In Stapleton v. Conway, 3 Atk. 727, the same eminent judge said that, if a contract is made in England for a mortgage of a plantation in the West Indies, no more than legal in-

New Hampshire, upon land situated there, may be made payable in New York, and may provide for the payment of interest at the rate of seven per cent., being the rate allowed there, though this be a higher rate than that allowed by the laws of New Hampshire, if this arrangement be made in good faith, and not for the purpose of evading the laws of New Hampshire; and such mortgage, with interest at the rate so provided, will be enforced by foreclosure of the mortgage in New Hampshire.[30] Although the mortgage be by express terms payable in New Hampshire, the parties may after its maturity agree that the interest shall be paid "as by law established in New York," where the mortgagor then resided; and such agreement made in good faith will be enforced in New Hampshire. "It is true," said Mr. Justice Bellows, "that in many cases interest may properly be regarded as a mere incident of the debt, and so payable only where the principal is payable; but this is by no means always the case, for by express stipulation the interest may become payable by itself, and a suit maintained for it before the principal becomes due, as in the case of a contract to pay interest annually; so in the case of bonds with coupons attached; and we see no objection to the parties being allowed to fix the amount of interest, and the time and place of payment of it, as they may all other particulars of the contract, provided it be done in good faith, and with no design to evade the usury laws."[31]

A mortgage made in Ohio upon land in that state, but made payable in New York with interest at the rate of ten per cent., which is a legal rate in the former state but not in the latter, was treated as a contract made in Ohio with reference to the laws of that state, although the mortgagee resided in Connecticut, and the loan was made by means of a draft paid in New York.[32]

A like decision was also made in Wisconsin, in a suit to foreclose a mortgage of lands situate in that state, made in New York, where the parties resided, and where the loan was made payable; therefore the laws of that state were held to govern the contract as to its validity and effect;[33] but the decision would have been otherwise in case the

terest shall be paid upon such mortgage; and a covenant in it to pay eight per cent. interest is within the statute of usury, notwithstanding that was the rate of interest where the land lies. See also De Wolf v. Johnson, 10 Wheat. (U. S.) 367, 6 L. ed. 343; McIlwaine v. Ellington, 111 Fed. 578, 49 C. C. A. 446, 55 L. R. A. 933.

[30] Townsend v. Riley, 46 N. H. 300.

[31] In Townsend v. Riley, 46 N. H. 300.

[32] Roelofson v. Atwater, 1 Disney (Ohio) 346.

[33] Newman v. Kershaw, 10 Wis. 333.

mortgage had been made payable in Wisconsin, or perhaps had been made there.[34]

But the courts of New York refused to declare void a mortgage made in Minnesota upon land in that state, with interest at the rate of twenty-five per cent. per annum, although the mortgage debt was made payable in New York; for the rate of interest was considered as fixed with reference to the place of contract.[35]

The law of the place of contract, or of the place of performance, determines the question whether the mortgage be valid or usurious, irrespective of the place where the land which is the subject of the mortgage is situated.[36] The location of the land mortgaged may perhaps in some cases be considered in connection with the place of contract, or the place of performance, in determining whether the parties contracted with reference to the law of the one place or of the other; but on the authorities this seems to be all the consideration that can be given to this circumstance.[37]

It is to be noted in this connection, however, that the fact that a note is secured by a mortgage on land is oftentimes of importance in determining the proper law governing the personal obligation, and therefore the mortgage itself. Thus in many cases involving the contracts of foreign building and loan associations, the fact that the loan was secured by a mortgage on land situate in the state of the forum has been held, in connection with other circumstances, sufficient to show that the parties, in making the loan payable at the domicil of the association, and in some instances in expressly stipulating that it was made with reference to the law of the domicil, acted in bad faith and for the purpose of evading the local law.[38]

§ 661. What law governs as to title and enforcement of lien.—
The lex rei sitae governs as to proceedings to foreclose a mortgage, the

[34] Kennedy v. Knight, 21 Wis. 340, 94 Am. Dec. 543.

[35] Balme v. Wombough, 38 Barb. (N. Y.) 352.

[36] De Wolf v. Johnson, 10 Wheat. (U. S.) 367, 7 L. ed. 343; Andrews v. Torrey, 14 N. J. Eq. 355; Campion v. Kille, 14 N. J. Eq. 229; Dolman v. Cook, 14 N. J. Eq. 56; Cotheal v. Blydenburgh, 5 N. J. Eq. 17, 631; Varick v. Crane, 4 N. J. Eq. 128; Stapleton v. Conway, 3 Atk.

727; Connor v. Bellamont, 2 Atk. 382.

[37] See Kennedy v. Knight, 21 Wis. 340, 94 Am. Dec. 543; Newman v. Kershaw, 10 Wis. 333.

[38] Falls v. United States Sav. &c. Co., 97 Ala. 417, 13 So. 25, 24 L. R. A. 174, 38 Am. St. 194; National Mut. Bldg. &c. Assn. v. Burch, 124 Mich. 57, 82 N. W. 837, 83 Am. St. 311; National Mut. Bldg. &c. Assn. v. Brahan, 80 Miss. 407, 31 So. 840, 57 L. R. A. 793.

manner and terms of sale thereunder, the terms of redemption of the land from the sale, and similar matters.[39]

A loan by a corporation domiciled in one state, to a citizen of another state, and secured by a mortgage on land in the latter state, has been governed in the settlement of interest on foreclosure by the law of such latter state, although the contract of loan and mortgage stipulates that it is solvable by the laws of the state of the domicil of the corporation, and is made with reference to its laws.[40]

The remedy against the mortgagor personally may be pursued wherever the debtor may be, and therefore suit may be brought against him in a state other than that in which the mortgaged premises are; but the lien upon the land can be enforced only in the state where the land is situated. It is a well-settled principle that title to real property must be acquired agreeably to the law of the place where it is situated. This principle applies to mortgages as well as to absolute conveyances;[41] and of course the remedy to enforce the lien must be sought where the property is. The validity of a mortgage must therefore be determined by the law of the state where the mortgaged land is, wherever the deed may have been executed or the mortgage debt made payable.[42]

[39] Connecticut Mut. Ins. Co. v. Cushman, 108 U. S. 51, 27 L. ed. 648, 2 Sup. Ct. 236; Brine v. Hartford F. Ins. Co., 96 U. S. 627, 24 L. ed. 858; McIlwaine v. Ellington, 111 Fed. 578, 49 C. C. A. 446, 55 L. R. A. 933.

[40] Binghampton Trust Co. v. Auten, 68 Ark. 299, 57 S. W. 1105, 82 Am. St. 295; National Loan &c. Assn. v. Burch, 124 Mich. 57, 82 N. W. 837, 83 Am. St. 311; Meroney v. Atlanta &c. Loan Assn., 116 N. Car. 882, 21 S. E. 924, 47 Am. St. 841; Hale v. Cairnes, 8 N. Dak. 145, 77 N. W. 1010, 44 L. R. A. 261, 73 Am. St. 746; People's Bldg. &c. Assn. v. Berlin, 201 Pa. St. 1, 50 Atl. 308, 88 Am. St. 764.

[41] Oregon & Washington T. &c. Co. v. Rathbun, 5 Sawyer (U. S.) 32; Hosford v. Nichols, 1 Paige (N. Y.) 220, per Walworth, Chancellor. See also Van Schaick v. Edwards, 2 Johns. Cas. (N. Y.) 355; Boehme v. Rall (N. J.), 26 Atl. 832, per Green, V. C.; Bentley v. Whittemore, 18 N. J. Eq. 366. In the latter case an assignment for the benefit of creditors was made in New York, where the parties resided, of land situated in New Jersey. The assignment was good under the laws of New York, but was contrary to the law of New Jersey, which prohibited preferences, and, so far as it affected lands there, was held to be void. Chancellor Zabriskie says: "It is well settled in England and the states where the common law is in force that the transfer and descent of real property is governed by the law of the state in which it lies. This rule is without exception, and I am not aware of any case or any authority in which it is questioned."

[42] In support of this position are cited the cases in the last note and the following: Goddard v. Sawyer, 9 Allen (Mass.) 78; cited and approved in Sedgwick v. Laflin, 10 Allen (Mass.) 430, per Gray, J.; Lyon v. McIlvaine, 24 Iowa 9. In Goddard v. Sawyer, 9 Allen (Mass.) 78, a mortgage was made in New Hampshire, where both parties resided, of land in Massachusetts, to indemnify the mortgagee against a liability to arise subsequently.

In regard to these cases it is to be observed that Hosford v. Nichols was decided upon the ground that the contract was in fact executed in New York, where the land was situated, and therefore is no authority for the position that the law of the place where the land is situated, rather than the law of the place of contract, governs as to usury. The later case of Chapman v. Robertson[43] has often been criticized, and, so far as it holds that the lex rei sitae governs as to usury, it has been repeatedly overruled by the later cases in New York. That case was as follows: A person residing in New York, being in England, there negotiated a loan upon the security of a bond and mortgage upon lands in New York, at the legal rate of interest in that state. It was arranged that upon the return of the borrower to New York he should execute and record the mortgage, and that upon the receipt of it in England the mortgagee should deposit the money with the mortgagor's bankers in London for his use. This was done accordingly. The mortgage was usurious under the laws of England; but it was held, in a suit to foreclose the mortgage, that the usury laws of England could not be set up in defense. Chancellor Walworth said: "Upon a full examination of all the cases to be found upon the subject, either in this country or in England, none of which, however, appear to have decided the precise question which arises in this cause, I have arrived at the conclusion that the mortgage executed here, and upon property in this state, being valid by the lex situs, which is also the law of the domicil of the mortgagor, it is the duty of this court to give full effect to the security, without reference to the usury laws of England, which neither party intended to evade or violate by the execution of a mortgage upon lands here."[44]

Such a mortgage being invalid under the laws of New Hampshire, this invalidity was set up to an action in Massachusetts to foreclose the mortgage. The court—Metcalf, J., delivering the opinion — say: "The question as to the validity of the mortgage in this case is to be decided by the law of this state, within which the mortgaged premises are situate, and not by the law of New Hampshire, where it was executed, and where the parties thereto resided." In Sell v. Miller, 11 Ohio St. 331, a mortgage on land in Ohio, executed by a nonresident married woman over eighteen years of age, but under twenty-one, was held good under a statute of Ohio which declares that a married woman over eighteen years of age may make a valid contract, although the married woman in this case, by the law of her domicil, was incapable of contracting.

[43] 6 Paige (N. Y.) 627, 31 Am. Dec. 264.

[44] Chapman v. Robertson, 6 Paige 627, 31 Am. Dec. 264. See also New Eng. Mtg. Co. v. McLaughlin, 87 Ga. 1, 13 S. E. 81; Dugan v. Lewis, 79 Tex. 246, 14 S. W. 1024, 23 Am. St. 332; American Mortg. Co. v. Sewell, 92 Ala. 163, 9 So. 143. In the latter case Coleman, J., delivering the opinion, said: "We are aware that the soundness of the reasoning in the decision in 6 Paige (N. Y.) 627,

Then as to the case of Goddard v. Sawyer, in Massachusetts, that does not relate to the contract, but rather to the form and validity of the instrument itself. The learned judge who gives the opinion refers to a case before the Supreme Court of the United States, holding that title to land by devise can be acquired only under a will duly approved and recorded according to the law of the state in which the lands lie, and in which Mr. Justice Washington says: "It is an acknowledged principle of law that the title and disposition of real property is exclusively subject to the laws of the country where it is situated, which can alone prescribe the mode by which a title to it can pass from one person to another." Another reference in the Massachusetts case is to an earlier case in that state, the principal bearing of which upon the case before the court is in the statement of the principle that "the title to and disposition of real estate must be exclusively regulated by the law of the place in which it is situated." The conclusion therefore is, that, although there are some statements which would seem to support the position that the question of usury in a mortgage executed and made payable in a state other than that where the land is

31 Am. Dec. 264, has been questioned, and Jones in his work on Mortgages (volume 1, §§ 660, 661), says it has been overruled. Most of the authorities which criticise the principle of law laid down generally concede the correctness of the conclusion of the learned chancellor who rendered the decision in the case of Chapman .v. Robertson, Judge Story (Confl. Law), in his criticism (§ 293c), referring to the case of Chapman v. Robertson, says: "The decision itself seems well supported in point of principle; for the parties intended that the whole transaction should be in fact, as it was in form, a New York contract, governed by the laws thereof, *and the repayment of the debt there to be made.*' The italics are ours. There are no facts in the case, except those which arise from the making of the note and mortgage in New York, which authorize the assumption that the money was to be repaid in New York. The two differ as to the place of payment, Story holding it to be a New York contract, and consequently the place of payment presumptively was in New York; the former holding that, as no place of payment was fixed, the law fixed it in England, but further held that although, as a mere personal contract, it would be wholly inoperative until it was received by the lender in England, where the money was then to be deposited with the borrower's banker for his use, yet, on account of the character of the property, being real or heritable property, and the further fact that the mortgage was executed in New York upon property in that state, and being valid by the lex situs, which was also the law of the domicil of the mortgagor, it was the duty of the court to give full effect to the security, without reference to the usury laws of England, which neither party intended to evade, by the execution of the mortgage upon the lands in New York." The case of Dugan v. Lewis was very similar to the Alabama case above considered. The Texas case regarded New York as the locus contractus and locus solutionis, and followed Chapman v. Robertson, 6 Paige (N. Y.) 627, 31 Am. Dec. 264, citing other authorities sustaining it. Judge Henry says there is no reason why the making of the contract in one state instead of in the other, nor

situated is to be determined by the laws of the state where the land is situate, there is really no authority for this position.[45]

§ 662. What laws govern as to form and validity of mortgage deed—As to parties.

But as to the form and validity of the mortgage deed as a conveyance, the law of the place where the land is situated must always govern, though the mortgage was executed in another state.[46] Thus, if the laws of the state where the lands are situate recognize the validity of a mortgage by the deposit of the title deeds by a debtor with his creditor, then the laws of that state govern as to the lien, although the transaction be had in another state.[47] But if such a mortgage be not recognized in the state where the lands are, the fact that a deposit is made in a state or country where a mortgage in this form is recognized will not enable the creditor to enforce it against the lands. And so, if the laws of a state prohibit the making of a mortgage to secure future advances or liabilities, a mortgage in this form of land in that state would not be recognized there, although made in a state where such a mortgage would be valid; and, on the other hand, such a mortgage made in the former state, where it would not be valid, but covering lands in a state where such a mortgage is valid, would be enforced in the latter state, because it is a valid conveyance there.[48]

The capacity of the parties to make a mortgage must be governed by the laws of the state where it is executed. A mortgage executed in the state of Indiana by a married woman domiciled in that state, on real estate situate in Ohio, to secure an obligation as surety to be

why the making it payable in one instead of in the other, should have a controlling influence over the question. Doing either will, in the absence of other evidence, serve to show their purpose and control the result. But not so when they otherwise distinctly provide, or when, from other facts, their intention can be more satisfactorily ascertained.

[45] The only other case referred to is Hosford v. Nichols, 1 Paige (N. Y.) 220. See ante § 657.

[46] Post v. First Nat. Bank, 138 Ill. 559, 28 N. E. 978; Dawson v. Hayden, 67 Ill. 52; Ricks v. Goodrich, 3 La. Ann. 212; Holt v. Knowlton, 86 Maine 456, 29 Atl. 1113; Fessenden v. Taft, 65 N. H. 39, 17 Atl. 713; Boehme v. Rall (N. J.), 26 Atl. 832 (quoting text); Nathan v. Lee, 152 Ind. 232, 52 N. E. 987. In this case a manufacturing corporation, chartered under the laws of New York, removed to New Jersey and executed a chattel and real estate mortgage on property within the latter state to resident creditors, to secure the payment of debts contracted and payable in that state. The mortgage was held valid in New Jersey, although it would be invalid in New York, because the execution of it was contrary to a general statute of that state prohibiting such corporation from transferring its property to creditors in contemplation of insolvency. "The law of its charter having given the company the general power of mortgage, the exercise of that power is subject to the laws and policy of the state in which it lawfully holds the mortgaged real estate." Per Green, V. C.

[47] Griffin v. Griffin, 18 N. J. Eq. 104.

[48] Goddard v. Sawyer, 9 Allen (Mass.) 78.

performed in the state of Indiana, where she is without capacity to make such a contract, is void in Ohio, as well as in Indiana.[49]

§ 663. **Pleading and proof of usury laws of foreign state.**—To avail of the usury laws of another state as a ground for defense, they must be distinctly set up in the answer, and at the hearing must be proved as matters of fact.[50] Under an answer setting up usury without any more specific allegation, and without any averment showing that the contract is governed in this respect by the laws of another state, the defense is limited to the statutes against usury of the state where the action is pending.[51]

It is held that where a defendant in a suit on notes has had no opportunity to plead a statute relative to usury, he is entitled to offer in evidence the appropriate statute without having pleaded it.[52] Until otherwise proved, the laws of another state in regard to usury will be presumed to be the same as those of the lex fori.[53]

When in the course of the pleadings it is discretionary with the court to allow the defense of usury to be set up, the court may refuse to allow the statute of another state whose laws govern the contract to be pleaded, when that statute makes the mortgage wholly void, such a defense being regarded as unconscientious.[54]

The law in force at the time of the delivery of a mortgage governs its validity or construction, so far as these are effected by statute.[55]

A mortgage made in Alabama during the Civil War was enforced in the courts of that state, acting under the Constitution and laws of the United States, after the close of the war, although the consideration of it was a loan of Confederate treasury notes,[56] on the ground that it was valid under the government de facto which then existed.

A stay law, making void and of no effect all mortgages and deeds of trust for the benefit of creditors thereafter executed, whether regis-

---

[49] Evans v. Beaver, 50 Ohio St. 190, 33 N. E. 643, 40 Am. St. 666; Lockwood v. Mitchell, 7 Ohio St. 388; Story Confl. Laws, §§ 65, 66, 66a, 242, 243.

[50] Andrews v. Torrey, 14 N. J. Eq. 355; Campion v. Kille, 14 N. J. Eq. 229; Dolman v. Cook, 14 N. J. Eq. 56; Hosford v. Nichols, 1 Paige (N. Y.) 220; Millard v. Truax, 73 Mich. 381, 41 N. W. 328, 22 Am. St. 705; Klinck v. Price, 4 W. Va. 4, 6 Am. Rep. 268.

[51] Campion v. Kille, 14 N. J. Eq. 229.

[52] Casner v. Hoskins, 64 Ore. 254, 130 Pac. 55.

[53] Van Auken v. Dunning, 81 Pa. St. 464.

[54] Corning v. Ludlum, 28 N. J. Eq. 398.

[55] Smith v. Green, 41 Fed. 455; Latrobe v. Hulbert, 6 Fed. 209; Olson v. Nelson, 3 Minn. 53.

[56] Scheible v. Bacho, 41 Ala. 423, and cases cited. See to the contrary, however, Stillman v. Looney, 3 Coldw. (Tenn.) 20. See ante, § 617.

tered or not, does not apply to a mortgage executed prior to the passage of the act, but registered after its passage.[57] Being valid when made, it is not competent for the legislature afterward to make it invalid.[58] A mortgage made at a time when there is no statute limiting the rate of interest is a valid security, although the rate of interest be extortionate; and its validity is not affected by a subsequent statute or change in the Constitution of the state limiting the rate of interest.[59]

Although the law of the place of contract governs as to the question of usury, yet a law of the place of contract relating to the manner of enforcing the remedy is not binding upon the courts of another state. Thus a statute of the state of New York authorizing a borrower to obtain a cancelation of securities without payment, upon the ground of usury, will not be enforced in Massachusetts.[60]

[57] Harrison v. Styres, 74 N. Car. 290.

[58] Harrison v. Styres, 74 N. Car. 290.

[59] Newton v. Wilson, 31 Ark. 484; Jacoway v. Denton, 25 Ark. 625.

[60] Matthews v. Warner, 112 U. S. 600, 28 L. ed. 851, 5 Sup. Ct. 312. That statute is so strictly construed in New York that it is held not to apply to an assignee in bankruptcy of the borrower: Wheelock v. Lee, 15 Abb. Pr. (N. S.) (N. Y.) 24, revg. 64 N. Y. 242; nor to a purchaser of the equity of redemption. Bissell v. Kellogg, 65 N. Y. 432.

Lightning Source UK Ltd.
Milton Keynes UK
UKHW010914060219
336748UK00007B/193/P